AILA's Asylum Primer

Seventh Edition

AILA Publications

AILA's Occupational Guidebooks

Immigration Options for Artists and Entertainers

Immigration Options for Physicians

Immigration Options for Nurses & Allied Health Care Professionals

Immigration Options for Religious Workers

Immigration Options for Academics and Researchers

Immigration Options for Investors and Entrepreneurs

Statutes, Regulations, Agency Materials & Case Law

Code of Federal Regulations

Immigration & Nationality Act

Core Curriculum

Navigating the Fundamentals of Immigration Law

AILA's Guide to Immigration Law for Paralegals

Toolbox Series

AILA's Immigration Practice Toolbox

AILA's Litigation Toolbox

AILA's Immigration Forms Toolbox

AILA's Focus Series

EB-2 & EB-3 Degree Equivalency
by Ronald Wada

Waivers Under the INA
by Julie Ferguson

Private Bills & Pardons in Immigration
by Anna Gallagher

The Child Status Protection Act
by Charles Wheeler

Immigration Practice Under AC21
by A. James Vazquez-Azpiri & Eleanor Pelta

Online Research Tools

AILALink

Treatises & Primers

Kurzban's Immigration Law Sourcebook
by Ira J. Kurzban

Business Immigration: Law & Practice
by Daryl Buffenstein and Bo Cooper

AILA's Asylum Primer
by Dree K. Collopy

Immigration Consequences of Criminal Activity
by Mary E. Kramer

Representing Clients in Immigration Court
by CLINIC

Provisional Waivers: A Practitioner's Guide
by CLINIC

Essentials of Immigration Law
by Richard A. Boswell

Litigating Immigration Cases in Federal Court
by Robert Pauw

Immigration Law & the Family
by Charles Wheeler

Immigration Law & the Transgender Client
by Transgender Law Center
& Immigration Equality

Immigration Law & the Military
by Margaret D. Stock

Specific Topics

The Waivers Book: Advanced Issues in Immigration Practice

AILA's Guide to U.S. Citizenship & Naturalization Law

The Entrepreneurial Lawyer: How to Run a Successful Immigration Practice

The Diplomatic Visas Handbook

Immigration Practice Pointers

The International Adoption Sourcebook

Periodicals

Inside Immigration: Monograph Series

Seventh Edition

AILA'S ASYLUM PRIMER

A Practical Guide to U.S. Asylum Law and Procedure

DREE K. COLLOPY

AMERICAN IMMIGRATION LAWYERS ASSOCIATION

Website for Corrections and Updates

Corrections and other updates to AILA publications can be found online at: ***www.aila.org/BookUpdates.***

If you have any corrections or updates to the information in this book, please let us know by sending a note to the address below, or e-mail us at ***books@aila.org***.

This publication is designed to provide accurate and authoritative information in regard to the subject matter covered. It is distributed with the understanding that the publisher is not engaged in rendering legal, accounting, or other professional service. If legal advice or other expert assistance is required, the services of a competent professional should be sought.

—from a Declaration of Principles jointly adopted by a Committee of the American Bar Association and a Committee of Publishers

Printed in the United States of America

ISBN 978-1-57370-376-5
Stock No. 53-76

This book is dedicated to the women and children refugees who have languished and continue to languish in prolonged, politically motivated, and unnecessary detention at the facilities in Artesia, NM, Berks County, PA, Dilley, TX, and Karnes City, TX. These women and children have come to the United States seeking protection from the horrific violence they have suffered—beatings, rape, human trafficking, torture—all at the hands of actors that their governments fail and refuse to control. They have come here trying to survive and they have come here to save their children's lives. Yet, they have arrived here in the United States and have been thrown in jail, where they have been kept for months in inhumane conditions and where they are refused meaningful access to counsel and interpreters, witnesses and evidence, family and emotional support, mental health care, and other tools that are essential to seeking protection in any meaningful way. Not a day goes by that I don't think of you, admire your strength, courage, and selflessness, and yearn for the day that you are all treated with the dignity and respect that you deserve as human beings.

I also dedicate this book to the hundreds of volunteers who have stepped away from their practices, families, and lives to donate their time representing the women and children detained in Artesia, Berks, Dilley, and Karnes. As lawyers, they have witnessed nightmarish scenes they never expected to see in the United States of America—dehydrated, listless, and malnourished children clinging to their mothers, while their mothers' pleas for medical care are met with degrading and abusive treatment; indigenous women and children denied access to interpreters and unable to explain why they made such a treacherous journey to seek protection; women recounting the beatings, rape, systematic abuse, and threats they have suffered, while their children sit next to them, quietly coloring; the compounding effect of detention on the trauma that these victims already have suffered; deliberate interferences with access to counsel; and the willful disregard of due process by our own government officials. Yet, these volunteers do not bow, they do not break, they do not quit. They will not be silenced. Not a day goes by that I don't think of you, appreciate your passion and dedication, and stand with you in your daily demand for justice.

PREFACE

At the beginning of 2013, some 35.8 million people worldwide had been forcibly displaced due to conflict and persecution.[1] Unable to turn to their own governments for protection, refugees depend on the compassion and humanity of foreign governments in seeking safety and freedom. It is this core humanitarian principle that underlies U.S. asylum law and its purpose of offering meaningful protection to bona fide refugees. Although protecting refugees may seem like an obvious concept, the human rights considerations involved in refugee and asylum law often collide with national self-interests, the challenges involved in maintaining the integrity of the application process, and the economic and political realities of the sheer scale of the world refugee crisis.[2] This collision has generated one of the most compelling, but also one of the most complex, areas of immigration law—U.S. asylum law. This book is meant to be a comprehensive guide for practitioners, advocates, asylum adjudicators, and students, as they navigate the substantive and procedural labyrinths of this incredibly complicated and constantly evolving area of the law.

Dree K. Collopy
June 2015

---

[1] This figure included about 10.5 million refugees, 23.8 million internally displaced and stateless persons, and 928,230 individuals with pending asylum applications. *See* United Nations High Comm'r for Refugees, UNHCR Global Appeal 2014–15, at 5, *available at www.unhcr.org/528a0a0fe.html* (last visited Oct. 12, 2014).

[2] *See generally*, STEPHEN H. LEGOMSKY, IMMIGRATION AND REFUGEE LAW AND POLICY, at Ch. 11 (Foundation Press ed., 4th ed. 2005).

SUMMARY TABLE OF CONTENTS

AILA'S ASYLUM PRIMER, SEVENTH ED.

APPENDICES

ACKNOWLEDGMENTS

As the previous author of this book, Regina Germain, once said, "No one can write or update a book like this alone." And Gina was most certainly right. I have been incredibly lucky to have so much support from so many amazing people throughout my process of reimagining, updating, and writing the seventh edition of the *Asylum Primer*. First, I want to thank Gina for her hard work in updating the *Primer* through several editions. I was honored to be chosen to carry on her legacy and to continue to improve this gift that she gave to our field.

My heartfelt thanks go out to Danielle Polen and Tatia L. Gordon-Troy, my publishers and editors at AILA, who believed in me, encouraged me, and supervised the editing and publication of this book. I also want to thank Mary Johnson, Associate Director of Marketing & Business Development, for her artistic talents and creative marketing, as well as the staff at AILA National, including Grace Woods, Robert Deasy, and Crystal Williams, who deeply believe in educating and supporting our current and future AILA members and demonstrate their commitment to these values through their publication of tools like the *Primer*.

Given the complexities of U.S. asylum law and procedure, I placed great importance on identifying other experienced practitioners in the field who could review and contribute to my work. There is no doubt in my mind that the *Primer* is a better tool and a more comprehensive guide because of the following experts, of whom I am also fortunate to call my friends: Vanessa Allyn, Cheri Attix, Vikram Badrinath, Mark Barr, Andres Benach, Benjamin Casper, Jennifer Cook, Pamela Goldberg, Lisa Green, Sandra Grossman, Lindsay Harris, Brittney Nystrom, Thomas Ragland, Ben Winograd, and Michelle Mendez, who is my compassionate and intrepid co-professor in the Catholic University of America Columbus School of Law's Immigration Litigation Clinic. These talented and tireless advocates donated their time to contribute their big brains, huge hearts, and many years of experience to each chapter of the *Primer*.

This book could not have been completed without the invaluable assistance of Tarunpal Dhillon and Malissa Tucker, enthusiastic and hard-working law students who will soon be incredible lawyers. Tarun and Malissa applied their thirst for knowledge, strong work ethic, and ability to juggle numerous tasks to the *Primer*, spending countless hours cite-checking and researching complex legal issues. Both Tarun and Malissa will soon be assets to whichever organizations or legal practices they choose to join.

I could not have taken on this massive project without the backing of my partners and the dedicated staff of Benach Ragland LLP. My partners, Andres Benach, Thomas Ragland, and Jennifer Cook, encouraged me throughout this process as I juggled my busy practice with my writing. My staff, Adilene Nuñez, Satsita Muradova, Liana Montecinos, Sandra Arboleda, and Mariela Sanchez, provided me with incredible support, and they continue to ensure that each and every one of my clients receives the impeccable service that each deserves.

I also would like to thank the late, great Michael Maggio, who despite his busy immigration practice, always found time to contribute to our field as a policy and media advocate, a pro bono champion, and a mentor. I have strived to use Michael's well-rounded approach to our work as a model for making my own contributions to our field, and followed this approach in my vision for the *Primer*.

Last, but certainly not least, I would like to thank my family for their lifetime of encouragement, constancy, and love: my dad, Dean, who taught me that everyone, no matter their background, deserves the chance to pursue their dreams; my mom, Deb, the most selfless person I know, who makes this world a better place through her daily acts of kindness; my stepdad, Dave, who demonstrates that with hard work and determination, you can accomplish anything; my sister, Kacy, who never fails to bring me to a place of laughter, joy, and peace; and my wonderful husband, Justin, whose constant love, patience, and support sustains me and makes my work possible.

Dree K. Collopy

June 2015

Detailed Table of Contents

AILA's Asylum Primer, Seventh Ed.

APPENDICES

ABOUT AILA

The American Immigration Lawyers Association (AILA) is a national bar association of more than 14,000 attorneys who practice immigration law and/or work as teaching professionals. AILA member attorneys represent tens of thousands of U.S. families who have applied for permanent residence for their spouses, children, and other close relatives for lawful entry and residence in the United States. AILA members also represent thousands of U.S. businesses and industries who sponsor highly skilled foreign workers seeking to enter the United States on a temporary or permanent basis. In addition, AILA members represent foreign students, entertainers, athletes, and asylum-seekers, often on a pro bono basis. Founded in 1946, AILA is a nonpartisan, not-for-profit organization that provides its members with continuing legal education, publications, information, professional services, and expertise through its 39 chapters and over 50 national committees. AILA is an affiliated organization of the American Bar Association and is represented in the ABA House of Delegates.

American Immigration Lawyers Association
www.aila.org

INTRODUCTION

Before World War I, the United States did not distinguish between refugees and immigrants, processing newcomers through centers like Ellis Island in New York and Angel Island in San Francisco. [1] This generous, open-door immigration policy characterized the first 100 years of the United States of America's existence, as the nation was founded and built by individuals seeking refuge and a better life for their families. Indeed, even before the United States was a country, it offered sanctuary to individuals persecuted for religious and other reasons. One community in the early years of our nation that exemplifies this generous policy was a French refugee settlement called Asylum (or Azilum), settled in 1793 in northeastern Pennsylvania by refugees from the French Revolution.[2]

Even in the 19th century, in the beginning of federal immigration regulation, the United States offered protection to those fleeing persecution. [3] Of course, as one commentator has noted, this tradition of welcoming the persecuted was easier to honor when global population was low, travel was expensive and hazardous, and there were no immigration quotas.[4] However, American symbols have continued to serve as a beacon of hope for the oppressed. As inscribed on the Statue of Liberty, the icon of freedom in the United States:

Give me your tired, your poor,

Your huddled masses yearning to breathe free,

The wretched refuse of your teeming shore,

Send these, the homeless, tempest-tossed to me,

I lift my lamp beside the golden door![5]

This spirit of offering protection to individuals fleeing persecution is the core concept and the origin of U.S. asylum law, which has evolved significantly since the dedication of the Statue of Liberty in 1886.

The evolution of U.S. asylum law began with a period of restriction fueled by prejudice against people of color and non-Protestant Christians, as well as fear of communism and poverty. In 1917, 1921, and 1924, the United States enacted a series of laws that restricted immigration through the use of quotas and ceilings on the

---

[1] *Well-Founded Fear* (Shari Robertson and Michael Camerini 2000).

[2] *See* Elsie Murray, AZILUM: FRENCH REFUGEE COLONY (Tioga Point Museum, 1st ed. 1940).

[3] *See* David A. Martin, ASYLUM CASE LAW SOURCEBOOK: MASTER INDEX AND CASE ABSTRACTS FOR U.S. COURT DECISIONS, at xvii (Thomson West, 2d ed. 1998).

[4] *See* David A. Martin, ASYLUM CASE LAW SOURCEBOOK, *id.*

[5] Emma Lazarus, THE NEW COLOSSUS (1883), *available at www.libertystatepark.com/emma.htm* (last visited Oct. 12, 2014).

number of immigrants allowed from certain parts of the world.[6] During World War II, restriction continued to dominate U.S. immigration policy, including toward refugees, as the United States made little effort to resettle those targeted and threatened by Nazi Germany.[7]

For example, in 1939, while war waged in Europe, the United States refused entry to the *St. Louis*, a ship carrying Jewish refugees. After Cuba reneged on its commitment to let the ship dock in Havana while the United States processed the passengers' paperwork, the *St. Louis* had no choice but to travel on toward U.S. shores. In the United States, the relevant immigrant quotas established in 1924 already had been filled that year, and there was a waiting list of several years. Allowing the passengers of the *St. Louis* to enter with visas would have permitted them to skip the waiting line, and although many were sympathetic to the plight of refugees and critical of Hitler's policies, public opinion in the United States continued to favor immigration restrictions.[8] The Great Depression had fueled sentiments of xenophobia, nativism, and isolationism, with 83 percent of Americans opposed to relaxing restrictions on immigration.[9] Instead of President Franklin Delano Roosevelt issuing an executive order to admit the refugees from the *St. Louis*, the vessel was turned back to Europe, where 254 of its passengers were murdered in concentration camps.[10]

The plight of refugees during World War II, like those passengers of the *St. Louis*, had a profound impact on United Nations and U.S. asylum policies. In 1948, the United Nations declared that "everyone has the right to seek and to enjoy in other countries asylum from persecution,"[11] while the United States passed the Displaced Persons Act of 1948. The Act allowed for a limited period of time certain eligible people who were displaced by the war to enter as permanent residents, and adopted a legal provision to allow people at risk of persecution to remain in the United States.[12] These efforts to alleviate the plight of refugees and find lasting solutions for their safe

---

[6] *Well-Founded Fear* (Shari Robertson and Michael Camerini 2000).

[7] *Id.*

[8] *Voyage of the St. Louis*, U.S. HOLOCAUST MEM'L MUSEUM, *www.ushmm.org/wlc/en/article.php?ModuleId=10005267* (last updated June 20, 2014).

[9] *Id.*

[10] *War Time Fate of the Passengers of the St. Louis*, U.S. HOLOCAUST MEM'L MUSEUM, *www.ushmm.org/wlc/en/article.php?ModuleId=10005431* (last updated June 20, 2014); *Refugees*, U.S. HOLOCAUST MEM'L MUSEUM, *www.ushmm.org/wlc/en/article.php?ModuleId=1005139* (last updated June 20, 2014) (acknowledging the number of Holocaust victims from the *St. Louis*).

[11] Universal Declaration of Human Rights, art. 14(1), G.A. Res. 217, U.N. GAOR, 3d Sess., U.N. Doc. 1/777 (1948).

[12] The Displaced Persons Act of 1948, Pub. L. No. 80-774, §3(a), 62 Stat. 1009, 1010, amended by Act of June 16, 1950, Pub. L. No. 81-555, 64 Stat. 219 (listing the number of visas); *Id.* §7, 62 Stat. 1009, 1012 (giving priority of issuance of a visa to displaced persons fearing persecution). This number was later amended to 400,000. *See* Office of Refugee Resettlement, *History*, DEP'T OF HEALTH AND HUMAN SERVS., *www.acf.hhs.gov/programs/orr/about/history* (last visited Sept. 30, 2014).

and voluntary repatriation, local integration, or resettlement continued throughout the aftermath of World War II and culminated in 1951 at the proceedings of the U.N. Convention Relating to the Status of Refugees (Refugee Convention).[13] The Refugee Convention defined "refugee" as someone who is "unable or … unwilling" to avail him or herself of the protection of his or her country because of a "well-founded fear of being persecuted for reasons of race, religion, nationality, membership [in] a particular social group or political opinion."[14] It limited protection to refugees fearing persecution as a result of events occurring in Europe before January 1, 1951.[15] With this definition, the Refugee Convention set forth the legal foundation for refugee law and policy.

The Immigration and Nationality Act of 1952 (INA),[16] which is the foundation of U.S. immigration law today, allowed the admission of those fleeing persecution, even those who arrived in the United States outside of the formal refugee resettlement program. The INA also included a seventh preference category, INA §203(a)(7), which allowed refugees who were fleeing persecution from communist or communist-dominated countries or from the Middle East to be admitted to the United States.[17]

Although the United States continued with its national origins quota system throughout the 1950s, the 1953 U.S. Refugee Relief Act, and others, overrode national origin quotas for refugees fleeing communist countries and admitted about 340,000 Cubans and 90,000 Soviet Jews.[18] This open policy toward those defecting from communist nations continued until the end of the Cold War. National origin quotas for immigrants and refugees were replaced with ceilings for the Eastern and Western hemispheres in 1965, with priority given to individuals with special skills or family already in the United States.[19]

In response to an outpouring of additional refugees following several historical conflicts, such as the decolonization of Africa in the 1960s and the Cold War, as well as the increasing shift from international war to civil war and internal strife, the United Nations removed the Refugee Convention's temporal and geographic limitations on the protections of refugees in its 1967 U.N. Protocol Relating to the

---

[13] *See* Convention Relating to the Status of Refugees, July 28, 1951, 19 U.S.T. 6259, 189 U.N.T.S. 150 (entered into force Apr. 22, 1954) [hereinafter Refugee Convention].

[14] Convention Relating to the Status of Refugees, at art. 1A.

[15] *Id.*

[16] Immigration and Nationality Act of 1952 (INA), Pub. L. No. 82-414, 66 Stat. 163 (codified as amended at 8 U.S. Code (USC) §1101 *et seq.*).

[17] 8 USC §1153(a)(7) (repealed 1980).

[18] *See* David M. Donahue and Nancy Flowers, THE UPROOTED: REFUGEES AND THE UNITED STATES (Hunter House 1995).

[19] *See* Immigration and Nationality Act of 1965 (Hart-Cellar Act), Pub. L. No. 89-236, 79 Stat. 911, 916-17. The Act was amended in 1978 to provide a single worldwide ceiling for immigrants. *See also* Pub. L. No. 95-417, 92 Stat. 917 (1978).

Status of Refugees (Protocol), which incorporated Articles 2 through 34 of the Refugee Convention.[20] Although it had not signed the Refugee Convention of 1951, the United States acceded to the Protocol in 1968 and became obliged to abide by its provisions, including the definition of "refugee" and the principle of *non-refoulement*.[21] It was not until 1980, however, that Congress passed the Refugee Act[22] in an effort to bring U.S. law into conformity with its international obligations under the Protocol.[23]

The United States has continued to develop its laws and procedures relating to refugees and asylum-seekers. In 1990, the United States created a special corps of asylum officers trained to review asylum applications.[24] In 1996, the United States clarified that refugee status may be based on either past persecution or a well-founded fear of persecution and that individuals fleeing coercive population control methods could seek asylum on account of political opinion. At the same time, however, the United States expanded and added more stringent bars to asylum eligibility and permitted the expedited removal of asylum-seekers who failed to establish a "credible fear" of persecution.[25]

In 1998, Congress passed the Foreign Affairs Reform and Restructuring Act,[26] which prohibits the United States from returning an individual to a country where he or she would be subjected to torture.[27]

In 2001, however, the United States again **expanded** the bars to asylum protection and allowed for the detention of "suspected terrorists" even if they have been granted asylum, in its Uniting and Strengthening America by Providing Appropriate Tools Required to Intercept and Obstruct Terrorism (USA PATRIOT) Act.[28] The United States' REAL ID Act of 2005 made significant changes regarding credibility determinations and corroboration in asylum claims, increasing the evidentiary burden

---

[20] Protocol Relating to the Status of Refugees, Jan. 31, 1967, 19 U.S.T. 6223, 606 U.N.T.S. 267 (entered into force Oct. 4, 1967).

[21] See Part I.B. of chapter 1 for a detailed discussion of the refugee definition and the principle of *nonrefoulement*.

[22] Refugee Act of 1980, Pub. L. No. 96-212, 94 Stat. 102.

[23] See Part II.A.1. of chapter 1 for a detailed discussion of the Refugee Act of 1980.

[24] *See* Immigration Act of 1990, Pub. L. No. 101-649, 104 Stat. 4978, 5030–38; *see also* 55 Fed. Reg. 30, 674 (creating a specially trained corps of Asylum Officers).

[25] Illegal Immigration Reform and Immigrant Responsibility Act of 1996 (IIRAIRA), Pub. L. No. 104-208, div. C, 110 Stat. 3009-546, 689 (defining refugee); *see id.* §203(b)(1)(B)(i)–(ii), 110 Stat. 3009–581 (discussing expedited removal for asylum-seekers who fail to establish a credible fear).

[26] Foreign Affairs Reform and Restructuring Act of 1998, Pub. L. No. 105-277, div. G, §2242(b), 112 Stat. 2681, 2681–822 (codified at 8 USC §1231).

[27] See chapter 4 for a detailed discussion of protection under the Convention Against Torture.

[28] Uniting and Strengthening America by Providing Appropriate Tools Required to Intercept and Obstruct Terrorism (USA PATRIOT ACT) Act of 2001, Pub. L. No. 107-56, 115 Stat. 272 (codified as amended in scattered titles of U.S.C.).

on asylum-seekers.[29] In 2008, the Trafficking Victims Protection Reauthorization Act (TVPRA) specifically addressed the situation of unaccompanied children in removal proceedings, allowing them to apply for asylum initially in a non-adversarial proceeding before U.S. Citizenship and Immigration Services (USCIS). The TVPRA also required that unaccompanied children from "contiguous countries" be screened for potential trafficking and other protection needs prior to returning them to their country of nationality or last habitual residence.[30]

Asylum law in the United States continues to evolve as Congress, often at a stalemate, considers both comprehensive and piecemeal legislation; government agencies issue asylum-related regulations, policy memoranda, and manuals; the Executive Office for Immigration Review and federal courts interpret current asylum laws and policies; and asylum applicants and their representatives strive for fairer and more generous applications of the current law in their individual cases.

[29] REAL ID Act of 2005, Pub. L. No. 109-13, div. B, 119 Stat. 231, 302–23].

[30] Trafficking Victims Protection Reauthorization Act of 2008 (TVPRA), Pub. L. No. 110-457, 122 Stat. 5044.

CHAPTER ONE

SOURCES OF ASYLUM LAW*

This chapter provides an overview of the sources of U.S. asylum law, which are an essential tool for understanding this complex field. It also suggests some resources that may be useful in preparing asylum, withholding of removal, and Convention Against Torture (CAT)[1] claims. These primary sources of U.S. asylum law should be consulted on a continuing basis—after the initial client interview; throughout development of the case theory; during the evidence-gathering process; while drafting affidavits, briefs, and motions; and while planning litigation strategies and oral arguments. Understanding the roots of U.S. asylum law, and the main principles and concepts from which this complicated legal field has developed, will enable practitioners to be more creative and zealous advocates on their clients' behalves as their clients seek protection, safety, and freedom in the United States.

I. International Law

International human rights law has played an important role in the development and implementation of U.S. asylum law. In fact, U.S. asylum law is derived directly from international law; thus, the U.S. court system, the Executive Office for Immigration Review (EOIR), and U.S. Citizenship and Immigration Services (USCIS) all have recognized that it may be appropriate to consider and reference international law when adjudicating applications for asylum, withholding of removal, and protection under the CAT.

---

* The author would like to thank Pamela Goldberg of the United Nations High Commissioner for Refugees for her invaluable input in reviewing chapter 1.

[1] Convention Against Torture and Other Cruel, Inhuman or Degrading Treatment or Punishment, Dec. 10, 1984, art. 3, 1465 U.N.T.S. 85 (entered into force June 26, 1987), 1988 U.S.T. 202, 1465 U.N.T.S. 85 (enacted into U.S. law on October 21, 1998, by Fiscal Year 1999 Omnibus Consolidated and Emergency Supplemental Appropriations Act, Pub. L. No. 104-277, Div. G, Sub. B, Title XXI §2242 of the Foreign Affairs Reform and Restructuring Act of 1998, Pub. L. No. 105-277, 112 Stat. 2681-822 (1998)).

A. Overview of Treaty Law

U.S. asylum law was born out of treaties, which are agreements made between countries. Treaties may be multilateral (between several nations) or bilateral (between two nations). Once entered into, a treaty may become binding on the parties and must be enforced in good faith.

Before a treaty can become a lawfully binding instrument, it must first receive a number of State signatures.[2] Signatures alone, however, do not create a binding legal obligation. Rather, by signing the treaty, a State only provides a preliminary endorsement of the instrument and demonstrates its intent to examine the treaty domestically and consider becoming bound by it. Once the requisite number of States has signed the proposed treaty, those States may ratify it, thereby becoming legally bound by its terms. A State that signs a treaty is not obligated to subsequently ratify it, but Article 18 of the Vienna Convention on the Law of Treaties specifies that any State that signs a treaty "is obliged to refrain from acts which would defeat the object and purpose of a treaty when … [i]t has signed the treaty … until it shall have made its intention clear not to become a party to the treaty."[3] A State that does not sign a treaty but later wishes to be bound by it can do so by acceding to it.

Treaties ratified by the United States are the "supreme law" of the United States under Article IV, Section 2 of the U.S. Constitution. In general, however, the United States does not consider treaties it has acceded to or ratified to be self-executing, which means that the obligations under the instrument will become judicially enforceable only through the passing of national legislation.[4] In the absence of legislation, it falls upon the courts to determine whether a treaty is self-executing.[5] A determination that a treaty is not self-executing means that there is no mechanism under which the court can enforce U.S. international obligations under that treaty.[6] Although such treaties may not be enforceable without legislation, they are useful for other purposes, such as providing guidance for evaluating legal concepts, *e.g.*, whether an act amounts to persecution, whether punishment for a particular crime

---

[2] The number of State signatures required is usually specified in the proposed treaty.

[3] United Nations, *Vienna Convention on the Law of Treaties*, 23 May 1969, at Art. 18(a), United Nations, Treaty Series, vol. 1155, p. 331, *available at www.refworld.org/docid/3ae6b3a10.html* (last visited Mar. 18, 2015).

[4] A key exception to this is the Convention Against Torture (CAT), which the United States made judicially enforceable for individuals seeking protection from return to torture by promulgating regulations, rather than enacting laws, as it has done for its other treaty obligations. As noted by the Board of Immigration Appeals (BIA), the U.S. Senate had declared that Article 3 of the CAT was not self-executing. *See Matter of H–M–V–*, 22 I&N Dec. 256 (BIA 1998). Shortly after that decision, President Bill Clinton enacted a law requiring agencies to issue regulations implementing Article 3 of the CAT. *See* Foreign Affairs Reform and Restructuring Act of 1998, Pub. L. No. 105-277, div. G, §2242(b), 112 Stat. 2681, 2681–822.

[5] *See, e.g., Foster v. Neilson*, 27 U.S. (2 Pet.) 253, 314 (1829), *overruled on other grounds, U.S. v. Percheman*, 32 U.S. (7 Pet.) 51 (1833).

[6] *Foster v. Neilson*, 27 U.S. (2 Pet.) 253, 314 (1829).

constitutes legitimate prosecution or persecution, and whether a crime is considered political.[7]

In contrast, the United States has taken the position that no legislation is necessary to comply with its obligations under certain human rights–related treaties, such as the U.N. Convention Against Transnational Organized Crime, which the United States ratified in 2005.[8] This international agreement requires its signatories to "take appropriate measures within its means to provide effective protection from potential retaliation or intimidation for witnesses in criminal proceedings who give testimony concerning offences covered by this Convention."[9]

With regard to treaties that have been signed by the United States, but not ratified, such as the Convention on the Rights of the Child, USCIS has taken the position—consistent with Article 18 of the Vienna Convention on the Law of Treaties—that the United States must refrain from acts that would defeat the object and purpose of the treaty.[10] Thus, even treaties the United States has signed but not ratified may lend valuable support.

> ➢ **Practice Pointer**: When relying upon and citing to a treaty to which the United States is a signatory, it is important to know if the treaty is self-executing and whether it has been ratified.

B. The 1951 United Nations Convention and the 1967 United Nations Protocol Relating to the Status of Refugees

One of the international treaties having the most significant impact on the development of U.S. asylum law is the United Nations Convention Relating to the Status of Refugees (Refugee Convention)[11] and the 1967 United Nations Protocol Relating to the Status of Refugees (Protocol), which reaffirmed Articles 2–34 of the Refugee Convention and incorporated them by reference.[12] In the wake of World War II, there was massive displacement of people around the world. In response, the United Nations, through its member states, created the Office of the United Nations

---

[7] *See, e.g.*, International Covenant on Civil and Political Rights, Dec. 16, 1966, 999 U.N.T.S. 171 (entered into force Mar. 23, 1976), art. 6 (the right not to be arbitrarily deprived of life), art. 18 (the right to freedom of thought and conscience), art. 14 (the right to a fair trial), art. 22 (freedom of association).

[8] *Rranci v. Mukasey*, 540 F.3d 165, 177–78 (3d Cir. 2008).

[9] United Nations Convention Against Transnational Organized Crime, Nov. 15, 2000, T.I.A.S. 13127, 2225 U.N.T.S. 209, art. 24, para. l.

[10] INS Memorandum, "Guidelines for Children's Asylum Claims" (Dec. 10, 1998), *published on* AILA InfoNet at Doc. No. 99012590 (*posted* Jan. 25, 1999), *reproduced in* 76 INTERPRETER RELEASES 5, 6 n.2 (Jan. 4, 1999), and *available at www.asylumlaw.org/docs/united_states/guidelines/children.pdf.*

[11] *See* Convention Relating to the Status of Refugees, July 28, 1951, 19 U.S.T. 6259, 189 U.N.T.S. 150 (entered into force Apr. 22, 1954) art. I, para. 1.

[12] Protocol Relating to the Status of Refugees, Jan. 31, 1967, 19 U.S.T. 6223, 606 U.N.T.S. 267 (entered into force Oct. 4, 1967) at art. 1, para. 1 [hereinafter Protocol].

High Commissioner for Refugees (UNHCR) on December 14, 1950, to help the approximately one million Europeans who were displaced by the war. Part of UNHCR's mandate was to provide international protection to refugees and seek permanent solutions to their problems; to coordinate international action to protect refugees and safeguard their rights; and to address various related social and humanitarian concerns.[13] Originally, UNHCR was meant to complete its work and disband within three years; however, in 1951, the Refugee Convention[14] was adopted, setting forth the legal foundation for refugee law and policy. The United Nations adopted its 1967 Protocol after several historical conflicts led to an outpouring of additional refugees,[15] reiterating the importance of the legal foundation that UNHCR had created for their protection.[16]

The United States acceded to the Protocol in 1968, and the Refugee Convention and Protocol have been the principal international instruments governing U.S. obligations toward refugees ever since. In fact, many of the Refugee Convention and Protocol's provisions have been incorporated into domestic law, most significantly the definition of "refugee" (Article 1)[17] and the principle of *nonrefoulement* (Article 33).[18] Article 31 prohibits countries from imposing penalties on refugees for their illegal entry or presence. Also included in the Refugee Convention and Protocol are various rights that countries should accord to refugees, such as education (Article 22), travel (Article 28), employment (Articles 17 and 18), housing (Article 21), and social security rights (Article 24). To date, more than 147 countries are parties to the Refugee Convention, the Protocol, or both.[19] These international instruments, along with customary international law and other treaties that the United States has ratified, lay the foundation of U.S. asylum law, in particular the definition of refugee and the principle of *nonrefoulement*.

- **Practice Pointer**: If pursuing a novel claim or one that may have been rejected by one or more courts or administrative tribunals, it may be helpful for practitioners to look to the Refugee Convention and

---

[13] Statute of the Office of the United Nations High Comm'r for Refugees, G.A. Res. 428(V), U.N. Doc A/1775 (Dec. 14, 1950), *available at www.unhcr.org/4d944e589.pdf* (last visited Oct. 11, 2014).

[14] *See* Convention Relating to the Status of Refugees, *supra* note 11.

[15] Some of these historical conflicts the decolonization of Africa in the 1960s, the Cold War, and related regional and internal conflicts around the world. *See* History of UNHCR, UNITED NATIONS HIGH COMM'R FOR REFUGEES, *www.unhcr.org/pages/49c3646cbc.html* (last visited Oct. 12, 2014).

[16] Protocol Relating to the Status of Refugees, *supra* note 12.

[17] INA §101(a)(42); *See* Convention Relating to the Status of Refugees, *supra* note 11, *incorporated by reference*, Protocol Relating to the Status of Refugees, *supra* note 12, at art. I, para. 2.

[18] INA §§101(a)(42), 208, 241(b)(3). *See* Convention Relating to the Status of Refugees, *supra* note 11.

[19] States Parties to the 1951 Convention relating to the Status of Refugees and the 1967 Protocol, UNITED NATIONS HIGH COMM'R FOR REFUGEES, *www.unhcr.org/pages/3b73b0d63.html* (last visited Sept. 30, 2014). The total number of States that are parties to the Refugee Convention are 144 and the total number of States that are parties to the Protocol are 145; 142 States are parties to both instruments.

Protocol, as well as UNHCR's guidance for interpreting and applying the terms contained in the refugee definition, which are discussed below.[20] Under U.S. law, courts are required, whenever possible, to construe domestic laws in a way that is consistent with international obligations. [21] Even USCIS has recognized the importance of international human rights to asylum adjudications, requiring its asylum officers to receive specialized training in international human rights law.[22]

1. The Definition of Refugee

Under the Refugee Convention, as amended by the Protocol, a "refugee" is a person who:

> [O]wing to a well-founded fear of being persecuted for reasons of race, religion, nationality, membership of a particular social group or political opinion, is outside the country of his [or her] nationality and is unable or, owing to such fear, is unwilling to avail himself [or herself] of the protection of that country; or who not having a nationality and being outside the country of his [or her] former habitual residence … is unable or, owing to such fear, is unwilling to return to it.[23]

A person is a refugee as soon as he or she fulfills the criteria contained in the definition and not when he or she is declared or determined to be a refugee by a particular country. In other words, a person does not become a refugee when he or she is recognized, but is recognized because he or she is a refugee.[24]

The Refugee Act of 1980 incorporated the Protocol definition into the United States' Immigration and Nationality Act (INA) using virtually identical language.[25] Congress was keenly aware of the United States' international treaty obligations when it drafted the Refugee Act of 1980. As the U.S. Supreme Court noted:

---

[20] *See infra* Part I.C. of this chapter for a detailed discussion of UNHCR interpretations and guidance.

[21] *Weinberger v. Rossi*, 456 U.S. 25, 32 (1982); *Murray v. Schooner Charming Betsy*, 6 U.S. (2 Cranch) 64, 118 (1804); *Ali v. Ashcroft*, 346 F.3d 873, 885 (9th Cir. 2003).

[22] 8 CFR §§208.1(b), 1208.1(b).

[23] Protocol Relating to the Status of Refugees, *supra* note 12, at art. I, para. 2, *incorporating by reference* art. 1, para. (A)(2) of the Refugee Convention. The Protocol universalized the refugee definition by removing all references to World War II.

[24] *See* Office of the United Nations High Comm'r for Refugees, HANDBOOK AND GUIDELINES ON PROCEDURES AND CRITERIA FOR DETERMINING REFUGEE STATUS UNDER THE 1951 CONVENTION AND THE 1967 PROTOCOL RELATING TO THE STATUS OF REFUGEES (Handbook), ¶28, U.N. Doc. HCR/PRO/4 (updated 2011), *available at www.refworld.org/docid/4f33c8d92.html* (last visited Oct. 12, 2014)

[25] INA §§101(a)(42), 208, 241(b)(3). *See* Convention Relating to the Status of Refugees, *supra* note 11 (added by the Refugee Act of 1980, Pub. L. No. 96-212, 94 Stat. 102, and codified as amended at 8 USC §1101 *et seq.*).

> If one thing is clear from the legislative history of the new definition of 'refugee,' and indeed the entire 1980 Act, it is that one of Congress' primary purposes was to bring United States refugee law into conformance with the [Protocol], to which the United States acceded in 1968.[26]

The U.S. definition of refugee does differ in some ways from the definition found in the Refugee Convention and Protocol, however. Specifically, the 1980 Refugee Act and the Illegal Immigration Reform and Immigrant Responsibility Act (IIRAIRA), which took effect in 1997, clarified in the definition of refugee that refugee status may be based on either past persecution or a well-founded fear of persecution. The 1951 Refugee Convention did not specifically provide that there might be circumstances where an individual no longer fears future persecution but should still be given protection due to previous persecution.[27] The U.S. definition of refugee also specifies that the serious harm a person has suffered or fears due to coercive population control procedures is "on account of political opinion."[28] Finally, the U.S. definition of refugee explicitly excludes from the definition "any person who ordered, incited, assisted, or otherwise participated in the persecution of any person on account of race, religion, nationality, membership in a particular social group, or political opinion."[29] These two provisions are not in the Refugee Convention's definition of refugee.

2. The Principle of Non-Refoulement

The fundamental protection provided by the Refugee Convention and Protocol is the prohibition on returning refugees to countries where they would face persecution. Article 33 of the Refugee Convention sets forth this principle of *nonrefoulement*, or non-return, as follows:

> No Contracting State shall expel or return (*refouler*) a refugee in any manner whatsoever to the frontiers of territories where his [or her] life or freedom would be threatened on account of his [or her] race, religion, nationality, membership of a particular social group or political opinion.[30]

---

[26] *INS v. Cardoza-Fonseca*, 480 U.S. 421, 436–37 (1987) (citations omitted). *See Negusie v. Holder*, 555 U.S. 511, 520 (2009) (citing with approval this quote from *Cardoza-Fonseca*). *See also* H.R. Rep. No. 96-781, at 19 (1980) (Conf. Rep.), *reprinted in* 1980 U.S.C.C.A.N. 160, 161; H.R. Rep. No. 96-608, at 9 (1979); S. Rep. No. 96-256, at 4 (1979).

[27] *Compare* INA §101(a)(42) *with* Convention Relating to the Status of Refugees, *supra* note 11, at art. 1, paras. (C)(5) and C(6). UNHCR, however, has long held the view that past persecution alone can serve as a basis for asylum protection.

[28] INA §101(a)(42).

[29] *Id. See also* chapter 2 for a detailed discussion of the persecutor bar to asylum.

[30] Convention Relating to the Status of Refugees, *supra* note 11, at art. 33, incorporated by reference in art. I, para. 1 of the Protocol.

This principle also has a counterpart in U.S. law, embodied in the withholding of removal provisions of the INA.[31]

C. UNHCR Interpretations and Guidance

The United Nations General Assembly established the UNHCR on December 14, 1950, to provide international protection to refugees and to seek permanent solutions to their problems.[32] With the main principles of U.S. asylum law derived from the Refugee Convention and Protocol, and in view of UNHCR's mandate to oversee the protection of refugees worldwide and its status as a leading international authority on issues relating to refugees, UNHCR's guidance on the interpretation and application of the refugee definition are essential references and sources for understanding U.S. asylum law.[33]

1. UNHCR Handbook and Guidelines on Procedures and Criteria for Determining Refugee Status under the 1951 Convention and the 1967 Protocol relating to the Status of Refugees

A primary resource for ascertaining the views of UNHCR in interpreting and applying the definition of refugee is the *UNHCR Handbook and Guidelines on Procedures and Criteria for Determining Refugee Status under the 1951 Convention and the 1967 Protocol relating to the Status of Refugees* (Handbook), which was first published in 1979 at the request of State parties to the Convention, including the United States.[34] The Handbook is a widely recognized resource for governments and others, and it has become an important source of interpretation and authority in U.S. refugee and asylum law. Although it lacks the "force of law," the U.S. Supreme Court has held that it provides "significant guidance" in construing U.S. obligations under the Protocol.[35] Immigration judges (IJs), the Board of Immigration Appeals (BIA), and federal courts frequently cite the Handbook in decisions interpreting the refugee definition and construing U.S. obligations under international law.[36] Although it is a

---

[31] INA §241(b)(3).

[32] History of UNHCR, UNITED NATIONS HIGH COMM'R FOR REFUGEES, *www.unhcr.org/pages/49c3646cbc.html* (last visited Sept. 30, 2014).

[33] UNHCR currently works in 126 countries, including the United States. Its staff is based in 135 regional and branch offices and 279 remote sub-offices and field offices. History of UNHCR, UNITED NATIONS HIGH COMM'R FOR REFUGEES, *www.unhcr.org/pages/49c3646cbc.html* (last visited Oct. 12, 2014).

[34] The Handbook was most recently reissued in 2011, and now includes all of the *Guidelines on International Protection* issued by UNHCR through the end of 2011. *See* Handbook, *supra* note 24.

[35] *INS v. Cardoza-Fonseca*, 480 U.S. 421, 439 n.22 (1987) (citations omitted); *INS v. Aguirre-Aguirre*, 526 U.S. 415, 427 (1999) (finding that the Handbook provides "some guidance" in construing the refugee provisions of the INA); *Negusie v. Holder*, 555 U.S. 511, 536–37 (2009) (noting that the U.S. Supreme Court in the past has looked to the Handbook for "guidance").

[36] *See Poradisova v. Gonzales*, 420 F.3d 70, 79-81 (2d Cir. 2005); *Chang v. INS*, 119 F.3d 1055, 1061–62 (3d Cir. 1997); *Rodriguez-Roman v. INS*, 98 F.3d 416, 425–26 (9th Cir. 1996); *Matter of S–M–J–*, 21 I&N Dec. 722, 724–25, 729 (BIA 1997); *Matter of Acosta*, 19 I&N Dec. 211, 221 (BIA 1985) (stating that the Handbook is a "useful tool" even though it is not controlling authority).

small, pocket-sized book composed of just 223 paragraphs, the Handbook provides invaluable insight on topics ranging from the meaning of persecution and "serious" crime to the standard for assessing the availability of an internal flight alternative and procedures for adjudicating claims of unaccompanied minors. It also contains the Refugee Convention and Protocol.

As a complement to the Handbook, UNHCR has issued a number of *Guidelines on International Protection* (Guidelines), beginning in 2002. The Guidelines are meant to be read in conjunction with the Handbook and provide interpretive guidance that reflects the evolving nature of protection claims. UNHCR deems the Guidelines to have the same weight of authority as the original Handbook. To date, 10 Guidelines have been issued, including:

- Guidelines on International Protection No. 10: Claims to Refugee Status Related to Military Service (UNHCR, Dec. 3, 2013);
- Guidelines on International Protection No. 9: Claims to Refugee Status Based on Sexual Orientation and/or Gender Identity (UNHCR, Oct. 23, 2012);
- Guidelines on International Protection No. 8: Child Asylum Claims (UNHCR, Dec. 22, 2009);
- Guidelines on International Protection No.7: Victims of Trafficking and Persons at Risk of Being Trafficked (UNHCR, Apr. 7, 2006);
- Guidelines on International Protection No. 6: Religion-Based Refugee Claims (UNHCR, Apr. 28, 2004);
- Guidelines on International Protection No. 5: Application of the Exclusion Clauses (UNHCR, Sept. 4, 2003);
- Guidelines on International Protection No. 4: Internal Flight or Relocation Alternative (UNHCR, July 23, 2003);
- Guidelines on International Protection No. 3: Cessation of Refugee Status (UNHCR, Feb. 10, 2003);
- Guidelines on International Protection No. 2: Membership of a Particular Social Group (UNHCR, May 7, 2002); and
- Guidelines on International Protection No. 1: Gender-Related Persecution (UNHCR, May 7, 2002).[37]

---

[37] All these publications are available on UNHCR's website, at *www.unhcr.org/cgi-bin/texis/vtx/search?page=&comid=4a291c7c6&cid=49aea93ae2&scid=49aea93a6d* (last visited Sept. 30, 2014). In addition to the *Guidelines*, UNHCR has issued two "guidance notes," the *Guidance Note on Refugee Claims relating to Female Genital Mutilation*, available at *www.unhcr.org/refworld/docid/4a0c28492.html* and the *Guidance Note on Refugee Claims relating to Victims of Organized Gangs*, available at *www.unhcr.org/refworld/docid/4bb21fa02.html*.

➢ **Practice Pointer**: The Handbook and Guidelines are "musts" for every asylum practitioner's law library.[38]

2. UNHCR Executive Committee Conclusions

Another source for interpreting the Refugee Convention and Protocol is UNHCR's Executive Committee Conclusions. The Executive Committee consists of more than 70 member states—including the United States, which has been a member since the inception of the Executive Committee in 1959—that meet on an annual basis and reach conclusions by consensus on a variety of refugee issues. Although these conclusions are not formally binding, they represent the views of the international community. Past Executive Committee Conclusions have addressed international protection issues,[39] the protection of children at risk,[40] women and girls at risk,[41] refugees and persons with disabilities,[42] protracted refugee situations,[43] protection measures for intercepted asylum-seekers,[44] the principle of *nonrefoulement*,[45] procedures for determining refugee status,[46] and the detention of refugees and asylum-seekers.[47] These Conclusions typically reflect expressions of concern on particular issues and set out guiding principles for States to consider in addressing those concerns.[48]

3. Other UNHCR Publications

In addition to the Handbook, *Guidelines on International Protection*, and Executive Committee Conclusions, UNHCR issues many other publications that may be useful resources for understanding asylum claims in the United States. For example, UNHCR issues statistics at least twice a year and for a number of specific situations, such as the outpouring of refugees from Syria.[49] Other important UNHCR

---

[38] The Handbook and Guidelines are available at *www.refworld.org/docid/4f33c8d92.html* and *www.unhcr.org/cgi-bin/texis/vtx/search?page=&comid=4a27bad46&cid=49aea93ae2&keywords=RSDguidelines* (last visited Oct. 11, 2014).

[39] DIV. OF INT'L PROT., OFFICE OF THE UNITED NATIONS HIGH COMM'R FOR REFUGEES, A THEMATIC COMPILATION OF EXECUTIVE COMMITTEE CONCLUSIONS NO. 108 (7th ed. 2014), *available at* *www.unhcr.org/53b26db69.html* (last visited Oct. 12, 2014).

[40] *Id.* at No. 107.

[41] *Id.* at No. 105.

[42] *Id.* at No. 110.

[43] *Id.* at No. 109.

[44] *Id.* at No. 97.

[45] *Id.* at No. 6.

[46] *Id.* at No. 8.

[47] *Id.* at No. 44.

[48] These Executive Committee Conclusions are available on UNHCR's website at *www.unhcr.org/pages/49e6e6dd6.html* (last visited Oct. 12, 2014).

[49] UNHCR Statistics and Operational Data, UNITED NATIONS HIGH COMM'R FOR REFUGEES, *www.unhcr.org/pages/49c3646c4d6.html* (last visited Oct. 11, 2014). *See also* Syria Regional Refugee

Continued

publications include eligibility guidelines for assessing the international protection needs of asylum-seekers from specific countries, such as Afghanistan,[50] and guidance notes on particular types of refugee claims, such as female genital mutilation[51] and victims of organized gangs.[52] Finally, UNHCR periodically issues country-specific reports on refugee issues to raise "awareness about refugees and other people of concern and to report on the agency's operations on a global and local level."[53]

In addition to those previously discussed in this chapter, publications from UNHCR that may be useful in preparing or presenting an asylum claim include:

- Beyond Detention: A Global Strategy to Support Governments to End the Detention of Asylum-Seekers and Refugees (UNHCR, June 25, 2014);
- Children on the Run: Unaccompanied Children Leaving Central America and Mexico and the Need for International Protection (UNHCR 2013);
- Women and Girls Fleeing Conflict: Gender and the Interpretation and Application of the 1951 Refugee Convention (UNHCR, Sept. 10, 2012);
- Detention Guidelines: Guidelines on the Applicable Criteria and Standards Relating to the Detention of Asylum-Seekers and Alternatives to Detention (UNHCR, Sept. 2012);
- A Framework for the Protection of Children (UNHCR 2012);
- The Ground with the Least Clarity: A Comparative Study of Jurisprudential Developments relating to "Membership in a Particular Social Group" (UNHCR, Apr. 2012);
- Living in a World of Violence: An Introduction to the Gang Phenomenon (UNHCR, July 1, 2011);
- Guidance Note on Refugee Claims Relating to Victims of Organized Gangs (UNHCR, Mar. 31, 2010);
- Guidance Note on Refugee Claims Relating to Female Genital Mutilation (UNHCR, May 2009); and

---

Response, UNITED NATIONS HIGH COMM'R FOR REFUGEES, *http://data.unhcr.org/syrianrefugees/regional.php* (last visited Oct. 11, 2014).

[50] *See, e.g.*, UNHCR Eligibility Guidelines for Assessing the International Protection Needs of Asylum-Seekers from Afghanistan (Aug. 6, 2013), *available at www.refworld.org/docid/51ffdca34.html* (last visited Oct. 11, 2014).

[51] UNHCR Guidance Note on Refugee Claims relating to Female Genital Mutilation (May 2009), *available at www.refworld.org/docid/4a0c28492.html* (last visited Oct. 11, 2014).

[52] UNHCR Guidance Note on Refugee Claims relating to Victims of Organized Gangs (Mar. 31, 2010), *available at www.refworld.org/docid/4bb21fa02.html* (last visited Oct. 11, 2014).

[53] All UNHCR publications are available at *www.unhcr.org/pages/49c3646c4b8.html* (last visited Sept. 19, 2014).

- Procedural Standards for Refugee Status Determination under UNHCR's Mandate (UNHCR, September 1, 2005).[54]

D. Convention Against Torture and Other Cruel, Inhuman or Degrading Treatment or Punishment

The United States is a signatory to the U.N. Convention Against Torture and Other Cruel, Inhuman or Degrading Treatment or Punishment (CAT), which was codified into U.S. law in 1998.[55] Although the Senate adopted its resolution of advice and consent on October 27, 1990, the CAT did not become effective in the United States until November 20, 1994.[56] Article 3 of the CAT, the *nonrefoulement* provision, is unqualified in providing:

> No State Party shall expel, return (*refouler*) or extradite a person to another State where there are substantial grounds for believing that he [or she] would be in danger of being subjected to torture.
>
> For the purpose of determining whether there are such grounds, the competent authorities shall take into account all relevant considerations including, where applicable, the existence in the State concerned of a consistent pattern of gross, flagrant or mass violations of human rights.[57]

Unlike the Refugee Convention and Protocol, the CAT does not exclude certain classes of individuals deemed to be undeserving of protection (such as individuals convicted of serious crimes), nor does it require a showing that the torture feared be motivated by the victim's race, religion, nationality, membership in a particular social group, or political opinion.[58]

On October 21, 1998, President Bill Clinton signed legislation requiring the legacy Immigration and Naturalization Service (INS) and other government agencies to issue regulations implementing Article 3 of the CAT.[59] Legacy INS and the

---

[54] Each of these publications, along with other UNHCR publications, may be found on the UNHCR website at *www.unhcr.org/pages/49c3646c4b8.html* (last visited Mar. 18, 2015).

[55] Convention Against Torture and Other Cruel, Inhuman or Degrading Treatment or Punishment (CAT), Dec. 10, 1984, 1988 U.S.T. 202, 1465 U.N.T.S. 85 (enacted into U.S. law on October 21, 1998 by Fiscal Year 1999 Omnibus Consolidated and Emergency Supplemental Appropriations Act, Pub. L. No. 104-277, Div. G, Sub. B, Title XXI §2242 of the Foreign Affairs Reform and Restructuring Act of 1998, Pub. L. No. 105-277, 112 Stat. 2681-822 (1998)).

[56] *See* Multilateral Treaties Deposited with the Secretary-General, UNITED NATIONS HIGH COMM'R FOR REFUGEES, U.N. Doc. No. 571 Leg/SER. E/13, IV.9 (1995).

[57] Convention Against Torture and Other Cruel, Inhuman or Degrading Treatment or Punishment (CAT), Dec. 10, 1984, 1988 U.S.T. 202, 1465 U.N.T.S. 85 (enacted into U.S. law on October 21, 1998 by Fiscal Year 1999 Omnibus Consolidated and Emergency Supplemental Appropriations Act, Pub. L. No. 104-277, Div. G, Sub. B, Title XXI §2242 of the Foreign Affairs Reform and Restructuring Act of 1998, Pub. L. No. 105-277, 112 Stat. 2681-822 (1998)), at art. 3.

[58] See chapter 4 for a detailed discussion of the legal standards for relief under the CAT.

[59] *See* Foreign Affairs Reform and Restructuring Act of 1998, Pub. L. No. 105-277, div. G, §2242(b), 112 Stat. 2681, 2681-822.

Executive Office for Immigration Review (EOIR) issued an interim rule on February 19, 1999, which became effective March 22, 1999, setting forth procedures for applying for relief under the CAT. Additional changes were made and issued on December 6, 2000.[60] The regulations effectuating the CAT may be found at 8 CFR §§208.16–.18, 1208.16–.18.

- **Practice Pointer**: It may be useful in asylum cases to consult sources of international humanitarian law, otherwise referred to as the law of armed conflict—the law of war. The most important conventions governing wartime conduct are the four Geneva Conventions, to which the United States is a party.[61] The four Geneva Conventions may provide useful support to an asylum claim in a number of ways. If the asylum applicant is from a country engaged in international or civil war or conflict, some issues to consider are: the treatment of noncombatants, the conduct of combatants, and whether the harm experienced or inflicted amounts to persecution. International humanitarian law may provide guidance in determining whether an act is a legitimate act of war or persecution. An excellent source for information about these and other human rights treaties is the Office of U.N. High Commissioner for Human Rights website at *www.ohchr.org*.[62]

E. Customary International Law

The prohibition against torture is one of the most widely recognized obligations under customary international law. Customary international law encompasses general practices that countries follow from a sense of binding norms that are widely accepted as law, regardless of whether they are obligated to do so by a treaty or domestic law.[63] Customary international law, in the absence of conflicting domestic law, is binding on the United States.[64]

---

[60] See chapter 4 for a detailed discussion of the legislation, case law, regulations, and policy memoranda related to seeking protection under the Convention Against Torture.

[61] The four Geneva Conventions are the Geneva Convention for the Amelioration of the Condition of the Wounded and Sick in Armed Forces in the Field; the Geneva Convention for the Amelioration of the conditions of the Wounded, Sick, and Shipwrecked Members of the Armed Forces at Sea; the Geneva Convention Relative to the Treatment of Prisoners of War; and the Geneva Convention Relative to the Protection of Civilian Persons in Time of War. The United States has not, however, signed, ratified, or acceded to the two additional protocols to the Geneva Conventions – Protocol Additional to the Geneva Conventions of August 2, 1949, and relating to the Protection of Victims of International Armed Conflict (Protocol I), and Protocol Additional to the Geneva Conventions of August 2, 1949, and relating to the Protection of Victims of Non-International armed Conflict (Protocol II).

[62] (Last visited Sept. 30, 2014).

[63] *See generally* T. Buergenthal *et. al.*, INTERNATIONAL HUMAN RIGHTS (3rd ed. 2002).

[64] *The Paquete Habana*, 175 U.S. 677, 700 (1900).

Courts have sometimes looked to customary international law when adjudicating claims of individuals fleeing persecution.[65] The Supreme Court has long recognized that:

> International law is part of our law, and must be ascertained and administered by the courts of justice of appropriate jurisdiction, as often as questions of right depending upon it are duly presented for their determination. For this purpose, where there is no treaty and no controlling executive or legislative act or judicial decision, resort must be had to the customs and usages of civilized nations, and, as evidence of these, to the works of jurists and commentators who by years of labor, research and experience have made themselves peculiarly well acquainted with the subjects of which they treat.[66]

Courts have held, however, that customary international law is not controlling where Congress has specifically enacted a law on the issue.[67] Additionally, the BIA has held that customary international law does not create a remedy from deportation or an independent basis for granting protection to persons who are not refugees.[68]

Customary international law is derived from the following sources:

- The customs and practices that nations actually observe, to the extent that these practices flow from a sense of international legal obligation;

---

[65] *See, e.g.*, *Matter of Abu*, A29 499 143 (IJ Feb. 19, 1997) (Phoenix, AZ) (Richardson, IJ) (holding that return to torture violates customary international law); *Matter of Santos*, A29 564 781 (IJ Aug. 24, 1990) (Arlington, VA) (Nejelski, IJ) (recognizing right of safe haven under customary international law), *reported in* 67 INTERPRETER RELEASES 982 (Aug. 31, 1990)); *Beharry v. Reno*, 183 F. Supp. 2d 584 (E.D.N.Y 2002), *reversed on other grounds*, 329 F.3d 51 (2d Cir. 2003) (ordering a hearing incorporating the customary international law principle of "best interests of the child" in determining whether the father of a U.S. citizen child should be deported). For an in-depth discussion of the customary international law principle prohibiting the removal of a person to a country where he or she faces torture, *see* Kristen B. Rosati, *The United Nations Convention Against Torture: A Detailed Examination of the Convention as an Alternative for Asylum Seekers*, 97-12 IMMIGR. BRIEFINGS 1 (Dec. 1997).

[66] *The Paquete Habana*, *supra* note 64, at 700; *see Filartiga v. Pena-Irala*, 630 F.2d 876, 884 (2d Cir. 1980) (finding that official torture violates customary international law based on the court's examination of "the usage of nations, judicial opinions and the works of jurists").

[67] *See, e.g.*, *Galo-Garcia v. INS*, 86 F.3d 916, 918 (9th Cir. 1996) (stating that because Congress enacted legislation for the admission of refugees, customary international law cannot serve as a separate basis for immigration court jurisdiction); *Echeverria-Hernandez v. INS*, 923 F.2d 688, 694 (9th Cir. 1991), *vacated on other grounds*, 946 F.2d 1481 (1991) (holding that the customary norm of safe haven in times of civil war and conflict was preempted by the enactment of the Refugee Act of 1980 and the executive act of extended voluntary departure).

[68] *Matter of A–E–M–*, 21 I&N Dec. 1157, 1162 (BIA 1998); *Matter of Medina*, 19 I&N Dec. 734, 746 (BIA 1988). *Medina* was distinguished in *Matter of Abu*, A29 499 143 (IJ Feb. 19, 1996) (Phoenix, AZ) (Richardson, IJ), in which the immigration judge noted that he was not "granting relief" under customary international law, but that he was prohibited from entering an order of deportation against a person who would face torture upon return to his country of nationality.

- General principles widely recognized as law by civilized nations, even if these principles are not always observed in practice;
- Decisions of national and international courts in cases involving international legal issues; and
- The writings of scholars and other "most highly qualified publicists."[69]

Although States do not always agree whether a particular principle or obligation has risen to the level of customary international law, it may be useful to consult these sources of customary international law in developing novel legal arguments in asylum, withholding of removal, and CAT claims. U.S. courts are bound to construe U.S. statutes as consistent with the U.S. international obligations, whenever possible.[70]

II. Domestic Law

U.S. asylum law has continued to build on this international law foundation through domestic laws contained within, and amending, the INA,[71] beginning with the Refugee Act of 1980, which brought the United States into compliance with its international obligations under the 1967 Protocol.[72] Another important source of domestic asylum law is the regulations issued by federal agencies, boards, or commissions to explain how the federal agencies intend to carry out the laws related to asylum.[73] Administrative interpretation of the statute and regulations through administrative decisions, policy directives, memoranda and statements, training manuals, and field manuals provides another important layer of domestic asylum

---

[69] *The Paquete Habana*, *supra* note 64, at 700 ("Resort must be had to the customs and usages of civilized nations, and, as evidence of these, to the works of jurists and commentators who by years of labor, research, and experience have made themselves peculiarly well acquainted with the subjects of which they treat."); *Matter of Medina*, *supra* note 68, at 744; U.S. CITIZENSHIP AND IMMIGRATION SERVS., *Asylum Officer Basic Training Course Lesson Plan on International Human Rights Law* (Mar. 1, 2005) at 5–6, available at *www.uscis.gov/sites/default/files/USCIS/Humanitarian/Refugees%20%26%20Asylum/Asylum/AOBTC%20Lesson%20Plans/International-Human-Rights-Law-31aug10.pdf* (last visited Oct. 24, 2014).

[70] *Murray v. Schooner Charming Betsy*, 6 U.S. (2 Cranch) 64, 118 (1804).

[71] The most significant of these Acts include the Refugee Act of 1980, Pub. L. No. 96-212, 94 Stat. 102 (1980); Illegal Immigration Reform and Immigrant Responsibility Act of 1996, Pub. L. No. 104-208, div. C, 110 Stat. 3009-546 (1996); Uniting and Strengthening America by Providing Appropriate Tools Required to Intercept and Obstruct Terrorism Act of 2001, Pub. L. No. 107-56, 115 Stat. 272 (2001); REAL ID Act of 2005, Pub. L. No. 109-13, div. B, 119 Stat. 231, 302-23 (2005); Trafficking Victims Protection Reauthorization Act, Pub. L. No. 110-457, 122 Stat. 5044 (2008).

[72] *See infra* Part II.A.1. for a detailed discussion of the Refugee Act of 1980 and other U.S. statutes.

[73] *See infra* Part II.B. for a detailed discussion of federal regulations.

law.[74] Finally, the federal courts interpret the statutes and regulations as they are applied to individual cases.[75]

A. U.S. Statutes

Since 1952, the provisions of U.S. immigration law have been organized and contained within the INA, the basic body of U.S. immigration law, which is divided into titles, chapters, and sections. The INA makes up Title 8 of the U.S. Code (USC) on "Aliens and Nationality." Thus, there are two ways to cite to statutory provisions of U.S. asylum law—by the INA section or by the USC title and section numbers. For example, the section of the INA that addresses asylum may be referred to as INA §208 or as 8 USC §1158. Though both are correct, the INA citation is most commonly used before the U.S. asylum offices, the U.S. immigration courts, and the BIA. The USC citation, on the other hand, is most commonly used before the U.S. circuit courts of appeals and other federal courts. The INA has been amended many times since its creation in 1952, and the major amendments relating to refugees and asylum-seekers are discussed below.

1. Refugee Act of 1980

Twelve years after the United States acceded to the Protocol, the Refugee Act of 1980 significantly revised U.S. law in an effort to bring the United States into compliance with its legal obligations under the Protocol.[76] The Refugee Act of 1980 created a legal framework for refugees to apply from abroad and for asylum-seekers to apply from within the United States. It adopted a definition of "refugee" that is virtually identical to the Protocol definition, and made revisions to the INA's withholding of removal section—the *nonrefoulement* provision—to make it mandatory and to include exceptions or exclusion clauses found in the Refugee Convention and Protocol.

The principal provisions of the Refugee Act of 1980 that concern asylum applicants in the United States are found in INA §101(a)(42), the definition of refugee; INA §208, asylum eligibility; and former INA §243(h), the *nonrefoulement* provision.[77] Under the Refugee Act of 1980, a "refugee" is defined as:

> [A]ny person who is outside any country of such person's nationality or, in the case of a person having no nationality, is outside any country in which such person last habitually resided, and who is unable or unwilling to return to, and

---

[74] *See infra* Parts II.C–G. for a detailed discussion of sources of administrative interpretations.

[75] *See infra* Part II.H. for a detailed discussion of federal court decisions.

[76] Refugee Act of 1980, *supra* note 71.

[77] INA §§101(a)(42), 208, and former §243(h), now found at §241(b)(3). The Illegal Immigration Reform and Immigrant Responsibility Act of 1996 (IIRAIRA) modified these provisions of the Refugee Act of 1980 and moved some of them to new sections of the INA. *See* IIRAIRA, *supra* note 71, discussed *infra* Part II.A.2. of this chapter. In 2005, the REAL ID Act added new provisions to INA §208 regarding credibility determinations, corroboration, the burden of proof, and judicial review. *See* REAL ID Act, *supra* note 71, discussed *infra* Part II.A.4. of this chapter.

> is unable or unwilling to avail himself or herself of the protection of, that country because of persecution or a well-founded fear of persecution on account of race, religion, nationality, membership in a particular social group, or political opinion.[78]

The refugee definition explicitly excludes, "[A]ny person who ordered, incited, assisted, or otherwise participated in the persecution of any person on account of race, religion, nationality, membership in a particular social group, or political opinion."[79]

Pursuant to the Refugee Act of 1980, INA §208 authorized the granting of asylum to individuals who are physically present or arriving in the United States, regardless of their status, and who meet the definition of refugee.[80] This section has since been substantially revised.[81]

The *nonrefoulement* provision of the Refugee Act of 1980, previously known as withholding of deportation and now known as withholding of removal,[82] provides protection to individuals whose lives or freedom would be threatened on account of race, religion, nationality, membership in a particular social group, or political opinion if returned to their home countries.[83]

2. Illegal Immigration Reform and Immigrant Responsibility Act

The asylum amendments under the Illegal Immigration Reform and Immigrant Responsibility Act of 1996 (IIRAIRA) have been described as the most significant revision to U.S. asylum law since the adoption of the Refugee Act of 1980.[84] The new provisions included a revised definition of refugee, a revised *nonrefoulement* provision, new bars to asylum eligibility, and a new expedited removal process. Highlights of the most significant changes under IIRAIRA, which took effect on April 1, 1997, are discussed below.

Under IIRAIRA, the term "refugee" was amended to include that:

> [A] person who has been forced to abort a pregnancy or to undergo involuntary sterilization, or who has been persecuted for failure or refusal to undergo such a procedure or for other resistance to a coercive population control program, shall be deemed to have been persecuted on account of political opinion, and a

---

[78] INA §101(a)(42)(A). IIRAIRA amended this definition by adding a sentence regarding persons fleeing coercive population control programs to clarify that such claims are based on political opinion. *See* IIRAIRA, *supra* note 71, discussed *infra* Part II.A.2. of this chapter.

[79] INA §101(a)(42)(B).

[80] INA §208(a)(1), (B)(1)(A). IIRAIRA and the REAL ID Act substantially revised this section.

[81] See *infra* Parts II.A.2. and II.A.4. of this chapter.

[82] See chapter 2 for a detailed discussion of withholding of removal under INA §241(b)(3).

[83] INA §243(h) (revised and moved to INA §241(b)(3) by IIRAIRA).

[84] *See* Daniel C. Horne and L. Ari Weitzhandler, *Asylum Law after the Illegal Immigration Reform and Immigrant Responsibility Act*, 97-4 IMMIGR. BRIEFINGS 1 (Apr. 1997).

person who has a well-founded fear that he or she will be forced to undergo such a procedure or subject to persecution for such failure, refusal, or resistance shall be deemed to have a well-founded fear of persecution on account of political opinion.[85]

The purpose of this amendment was to ensure that asylum claims brought on the basis of coercive population control programs were recognized as being based on political opinion, rather than the other protected grounds. The number of individuals who could be admitted to the United States as refugees or granted asylum under this new provision was limited to 1,000 per year at that time.[86]

IIRAIRA also included provisions stating that an individual who "has been convicted of an aggravated felony (or felonies) for which [he or she] has been sentenced to an aggregate term of imprisonment of at least 5 years shall be considered to have committed a particularly serious crime," making him or her ineligible for withholding of removal.[87] Individuals barred from such relief may only pursue a claim for relief under the CAT.[88]

For a few months prior to the enactment of IIRAIRA, the Antiterrorism and Effective Death Penalty Act permitted the U.S. attorney general (AG) to grant withholding of removal "to ensure compliance" with the 1967 Protocol, "notwithstanding any other provision of law."[89] Nevertheless, in *Matter of Q–T–M–T–*, 21 I&N Dec. 639, 655 (BIA 1996), the BIA construed the aggravated felony bar to be in compliance with the Protocol, thereby barring individuals from *nonrefoulement* protection even though the crime would not be particularly serious under international law standards.[90]

IIRAIRA also added several bars to asylum eligibility; for the first time, U.S. law imposed a deadline for filing an asylum application. Applicants must file within one year after their arrival in the United States, unless they are able to establish extraordinary circumstances for the delay or the existence of changed circumstances that materially affect their eligibility for asylum. Under INA §208(a), an individual is ineligible to apply for asylum in the United States if he or she: (1) may be removed to

---

[85] IIRAIRA, *supra* note 71, at §601(a)(1), 110 Stat. 3009-689; *see* INA §101(a)(42)(B).

[86] INA §207(a)(5), *repealed by* the REAL ID Act, *supra* note 71. The REAL ID Act of 2005 later removed this numerical limitation. *See infra* Part II.A.4. of this chapter for a detailed discussion of the REAL ID Act.

[87] IIRAIRA, *supra* note 71, at §305(a), 110 Stat. 3009-602 (effective Apr. 1, 1997); *see* INA §241(b)(3)(B) (making an applicant ineligible for withholding of removal if the applicant has committed a particularly serious crime).

[88] See chapter 3 for a detailed discussion of relief under the Convention Against Torture.

[89] Antiterrorism and Effective Death Penalty Act of 1996, Pub. L. No. 104-132, 110 Stat. 1214 (1996).

[90] See chapter 2 for a detailed discussion of the aggravated felony bar.

a safe third country; (2) did not file within one year after his or her arrival in the United States; or (3) was previously denied asylum.[91]

Moreover, under INA §208(b), asylum may not be granted if the applicant has committed a particularly serious crime or a serious nonpolitical crime, is found to be a danger to the security of the United States, has engaged in terrorist activities, is affiliated with a terrorist organization, or is found to be firmly resettled in a third country. After the terrorist attacks on September 11, 2001, Congress added additional bars to asylum for individuals associated with terrorist activities.[92]

One of the most controversial provisions in IIRAIRA is the section on expedited removal at INA §235. Under this process, sometimes referred to as summary exclusion, a noncitizen who arrives at a port of entry with purportedly false documents or no documents will be removed from the United States without further hearing or review, unless the individual indicates a fear of persecution or a desire to apply for asylum, or alleges that he or she was previously granted permanent residency or refugee/asylee status.[93] These provisions have been expanded in recent years to include individuals apprehended in the interior of the United States.[94]

3. USA PATRIOT Act

Just six weeks after the September 11, 2001, terrorist attacks, Congress enacted sweeping changes to the INA with the passage of the Uniting and Strengthening America by Providing Appropriate Tools Required to Intercept and Obstruct Terrorism Act (USA PATRIOT Act).[95] The USA PATRIOT Act added to the already extensive list of bars to asylum and withholding of removal.[96] Now, any individual who "used [his or her] position of prominence within any country to endorse or espouse terrorist activity, or to persuade others to support terrorist activity" is barred if the Secretary of State determines that such actions undermine U.S. efforts to reduce or eliminate terrorist activities.[97]

The USA PATRIOT Act also expands the definition of terrorist activity to include the use of "[any] weapon or dangerous device," in addition to those previously listed, which included chemical, biological, and nuclear weapons, as well as explosives and firearms.[98] This bar only applies if the weapon is used "other than for mere personal

[91] See chapter 2 for a detailed discussion of the exceptions to these provisions.

[92] See *infra* Part II.A.3. of this chapter and chapter 2 for a detailed discussion of these statutory bars.

[93] See chapter 6 for a detailed discussion of the expedited removal and reinstatement of removal procedures.

[94] See chapter 6 for a detailed discussion of the expansion of expedited removal.

[95] Uniting and Strengthening America by Providing Appropriate Tools Required to Intercept and Obstruct Terrorism Act (USA PATRIOT Act), Pub. L. No. 107-56, 115 Stat. 272 (Oct. 26, 2001).

[96] *See* Regina Germain, *Rushing to Judgment: The Unintended Consequences of the USA PATRIOT Act for Bona Fide Refugees*, 16 GEO. IMMIGR. L.J. 505, 509 (2002).

[97] USA PATRIOT ACT, *supra* note 95, at § 411, 115 Stat. 272, 346; *see* INA §212(a)(3)(B)(i)(VII).

[98] USA PATRIOT ACT, *supra* note 95, at § 411, 115 Stat. 272, 346; *see* INA §212(a)(3)(B)(iii)(V).

monetary gain" and "with the intent to endanger, directly or indirectly, the safety of one or more individuals or to cause substantial damage to property."[99]

Perhaps the most controversial provision of the act is the mandatory detention section that allows the AG to certify and detain, possibly indefinitely, noncitizens deemed to be a threat to national security.[100] Such noncitizens may be held in custody irrespective of any relief from removal for which they may be eligible or have been granted, including asylum.[101]

4. The REAL ID Act

On May 11, 2005, the REAL ID Act brought even more changes to U.S. asylum law, as well as sweeping repercussions in other areas of immigration and national security law. The new provisions that impacted asylum-seekers included a statutory description of the burden of proof for asylum, which clarified that the burden of proof is on the applicant to establish that he or she is a refugee within the meaning of the statutory definition and that a protected ground must be "at least one central reason" why he or she was persecuted or fears persecution.[102]

In meeting this burden of proof, the REAL ID Act increased the evidentiary burden on asylum applicants significantly, articulating clear requirements for credibility determinations and the near-necessity of providing corroborating evidence in support of testimony.[103] Prior to the REAL ID Act, an applicant's testimony alone could be sufficient to sustain his or her burden of proof. However, under the REAL ID Act, testimony alone, without corroboration, may only be sufficient if the testimony "is credible, is persuasive, and refers to specific facts."[104] In determining whether testimony is credible, the trier of fact may consider the applicant's or witness's:

> [D]emeanor, candor … responsiveness … the inherent plausibility of the applicant's or witness's account, the consistency between the applicant's or witness's written and oral statements, … the internal consistency of each such statement, the consistency of such statements with other evidence of record, … and any inaccuracies or falsehoods in such statements, without regard to whether an inconsistency, inaccuracy, or falsehood goes to the heart of the applicant's claim, or any other relevant factor.[105]

---

[99] INA §212(a)(3)(B)(iii)(V)(b).

[100] USA PATRIOT ACT, *supra* note 95, at §412(a), 115 Stat. 272, 351; *see* INA §236A.

[101] *See generally* INA §§236A(a)(2)–(3).

[102] REAL ID Act, *supra* note 71, at §101(a)(3)(B), 119 Stat. 231, 302–03 (codified as INA §208(b)(1)(B)). *See* INA §208(b)(1)(B)(i). *See infra* chapter 4 for a detailed discussion of burdens of proof.

[103] *See* INA §208(b)(1)(B)(ii)–(iii).

[104] INA §208(b)(1)(B)(ii).

[105] INA §208(b)(1)(B)(iii).

Most significantly, under the REAL ID Act, "Where the trier of fact determines that the applicant should provide evidence that corroborates otherwise credible testimony, such evidence must be provided unless the applicant does not have the evidence and cannot reasonably obtain the evidence."[106]

In addition to the increased evidentiary burden on asylum applicants, the REAL ID Act eliminated the cap on the number of coercive population control asylum cases that could be granted each year (previously 1,000).[107] The REAL ID Act also made several changes to provisions related to inadmissibility for terrorism-related activities.[108] For example, it changed the definition of "terrorist activity" to cover various actions including hijacking, kidnapping, assassination, use of nuclear, biological, or chemical agents, use of explosives, firearms, or other dangerous devices, and other activities.[109] Additionally, the REAL ID Act expanded the definition of "engage in terrorist activity" to include committing a terrorist activity, preparing or planning a terrorist activity, gathering information on potential targets for terrorist activities, soliciting funds for terrorist activities or organizations, soliciting individuals to engage in such conduct or to become a member of a terrorist organization, and providing material support for terrorist activities, individuals, or organizations.[110] The REAL ID Act did, however, provide a waiver for the bar against asylum eligibility for providing material support to a terrorist organization if the applicant did not know or should not reasonably have known that his or her act would provide such material support.[111]

Finally, the REAL ID Act clarified that the provisions of the INA limiting or eliminating judicial review do not preclude the review of constitutional claims or questions of law raised in a petition for review filed before the U.S. circuit courts of appeals.[112] Some provisions of the REAL ID Act were effective immediately; others applied only to asylum applications filed on or after May 11, 2005.[113]

---

[106] INA §208(b)(1)(B)(ii). See chapter 4 for a detailed discussion of credibility, corroboration, and the evidentiary burden on asylum-seekers.

[107] REAL ID Act, *supra* note 71, at §101(g)(2), 119 Stat. 231, 305 (codified by removing INA §207(a)(5)).

[108] See chapter 2 for a detailed discussion of the terrorism-related grounds of inadmissibility and how they affect asylum and withholding of removal claims.

[109] REAL ID Act at §103(a)(i), 119 Stat. 231, 306–07 (codified at INA §212(a)(3)(B)(i)).

[110] *Id.* at §103(b), 119 Stat. 231, 307 (codified at INA §212(a)(3)(B)(iv)).

[111] *Id.* at §103(b)(iv)(VI), 119 Stat. 231, 307–08 (codified at INA §212(a)(3)(B)(iv)(VI)).

[112] *Id.* at §106, 119 Stat. 231, 310 (codified at INA §242(a)(2)(D)). See chapters 11 and 12 for detailed discussions of administrative and judicial review.

[113] *See, e.g.*, *Matter of S–B–*, 24 I&N Dec. 42, 43 (BIA 2006) (holding that the provisions regarding credibility determinations only apply to asylum applications filed on or after May 11, 2005). See chapter 4 for a detailed discussion of credibility, corroboration, and other evidentiary requirements in meeting the burden of proof.

5. *The Trafficking Victims Protection Reauthorization Act of 2008*

On December 23, 2008, President George W. Bush signed into law the Trafficking Victims Protection Reauthorization Act (TVPRA).[114] The TVPRA, which took effect on March 23, 2009, provides several additional protections to unaccompanied children seeking asylum, including:

- The requirement that unaccompanied children from contiguous countries be screened for international protection needs;
- The ability of unaccompanied children to seek asylum initially in a non-adversarial proceeding before the USCIS Asylum Division, instead of removal proceedings;
- The inapplicability of the one-year filing deadline and safe third country agreement to unaccompanied children;
- The assurance by the Department of Health and Human Services (HHS) to provide pro bono counsel, to the greatest extent practicable and consistent with INA §292, to those unaccompanied children who are or have been in Department of Homeland Security (DHS) custody; and
- The authorization of DHS to appoint independent child advocates for child trafficking victims and other vulnerable unaccompanied children.

The TVPRA was reauthorized on March 7, 2013, as Title XII of the Violence Against Women Reauthorization Act of 2013.[115] Its reauthorization provided updated procedures for determining initial jurisdiction over asylum applications filed by unaccompanied minor children, required that DHS consider using alternatives to detention programs in placing unaccompanied minors transferred from HHS to DHS custody upon reaching age 18, and expanded the child advocate program for vulnerable and trafficked unaccompanied minors.[116]

B. Regulations

Since 2000, final regulations regarding procedures, definitions, and the burden of proof in asylum, withholding of removal, and CAT claims have been issued.[117] These regulations have been amended over time to ensure their consistency with the various statutory changes.

> ➢ **Practice Pointer**: In preparing an asylum case, it is important for practitioners to review carefully the applicable regulations. The regulations often set forth definitions and additional procedural

---

[114] Trafficking Victims Protection Reauthorization Act (TVPRA), Pub. L. No. 110-457, 122 Stat. 5044–5091.

[115] Violence Against Women Reauthorization Act of 2013, Pub. L. No. 113-4, §§1201–64, 127 Stat. 54, 136-60 (containing the 2013 amendments to the TVPRA).

[116] *See id.*; *infra* chapter 10 for a detailed discussion of asylum law and procedure for children.

[117] *See, e.g.*, 65 Fed. Reg. 76121–38 (Dec. 6, 2000).

requirements that will assist in preparing the claim. As immigration regulations change frequently, it is important that practitioners never rely on outdated sources.

Regulations that do not fall within the scope of a statutory delegation of authority are *ultra vires* and may be challenged in court. Even a long-standing agency regulation is not entitled to deference if it conflicts with the plain language of the statute.[118] Additionally, if DHS violates a regulatory requirement, IJs and the BIA are permitted to exclude evidence or invalidate the proceedings if the purpose of the regulation is to benefit the individual and the violation prejudiced his or her interests.[119]

C. Board of Immigration Appeals Decisions

BIA decisions are another important source of authority governing U.S. asylum claims. The BIA is the administrative reviewing body charged with reviewing decisions by IJs and interpreting immigration statutes and regulations. The BIA does not, however, have authority to review credible or reasonable fear determinations made by asylum officers and IJs in the expedited removal process under INA §235(b)(1)(C).

BIA decisions are binding on all officers and employees of DHS and all IJs, except in circuits where the federal courts have struck down those decisions.[120] The AG, however, has the authority to review decisions made by the BIA.[121] For example, the AG exercised this authority in in *Matter of R–A–*, vacating the BIA's reversal of a grant of asylum based on domestic violence.[122] The AG also vacated the BIA's bond determination in *Matter of D–J–*,[123] and the BIA's denial of withholding of removal based on past female genital mutilation in *Matter of A–T–*.[124]

The BIA designates select decisions as precedent decisions.[125] These precedent decisions are first designated as interim decisions and later published in *Administrative Decisions Under Immigration & Nationality Laws of the United States*

---

[118] *See Brown v. Gardner*, 513 U.S. 115, 120–21 (1994) ("legislative silence as to [an agency's] practice over the last 60 years" is trumped by the plain language of the statute); *Demarest v. Manspeaker*, 498 U.S. 184, 190 (1991) (a long-standing agency interpretation of a statute is not entitled to deference, and even subsequent reenactment of the statute does not constitute an adoption of a previous administrative construction where the law is plain) (citation omitted).

[119] *Matter of Garcia-Flores*, 17 I&N Dec. 325 (BIA 1980).

[120] 8 CFR §1003.1(g). See chapters 11 and 12 for detailed discussions of administrative and judicial review.

[121] 8 CFR §1003.1(h); *Matter of Leon-Orosco and Rodriguez-Colas*, 19 I&N Dec. 136 (A.G. 1984), *reversed on other grounds*, *Fernandez-Roque v. Smith,* 599 F. Supp. 1103 (N.D. Ga. 1984).

[122] *Matter of R–A–*, 22 I&N Dec. 906 (AG 2001).

[123] *Matter of D–J–*, 23 I&N Dec. 572 (AG 2003) (holding that a Haitian asylum-seeker's release on bond was unwarranted due to national security concerns).

[124] *Matter of A–T–*, 24 I&N Dec. 617 (AG 2008).

[125] 8 CFR §1003.1(g).

(abbreviated as I&N Dec.).[126] The BIA also has published cumulative indexes to its decisions, which are available online.[127] Sometimes BIA precedent decisions are cited by their interim decision number.[128] Nonprecedential BIA decisions also may be useful sources of interpretation and support for various asylum claims. Although unpublished BIA decisions are not binding on the BIA, IJs, or asylum officers, some courts have recognized the BIA's nonprecedent decisions as an expression of the BIA's position on a particular issue and have given those unpublished decisions deference.[129] Courts also have held that the BIA abuses its discretion if it inexplicably departs from prior precedent.[130]

➢ **Practice Pointer**: A few significant but nonprecedential "Indexed Decisions" are posted in the EOIR Virtual Law Library available at *www.justice.gov/eoir/vll/intdec/lib_indecitnet.html.*[131] Another useful resource for unpublished BIA decisions is the Index of Unpublished BIA Decisions published by the Immigrant & Refugee Appellate Center. The Index contains links and summaries to hundreds of unpublished decisions selected for their potential to assist respondents in removal proceedings. It is organized by subject matter and is updated on a monthly basis. More information on this resource is available at *www.irac.net/unpublished/.*[132] Unpublished BIA decisions are searchable on LEXIS-NEXIS (IMMIG; BIA-AAU database) and Westlaw (FIM-BIA database).

Although the BIA lacks jurisdiction to rule on the constitutionality of the INA and the regulations,[133] where possible, it must construe statutes to achieve results that are

---

[126] These decisions are available online at *www.justice.gov/eoir/vll/intdec/lib_indecitnet.html.*

[127] *See, e.g.*, Index to Interim Decisions 2526–3765 at *www.usdoj.gov/eoir/vll/intdec/Index_2526 to3633.pdf.*

[128] *See, e.g.*, *Matter of Acosta*, 19 I&N Dec. 211 (BIA 1985), *overruled in part on other grounds, Matter of Mogharrabi,* 19 I&N Dec. 439 (BIA 1987) (numbering the interim decision as 2986).

[129] *Miranda-Alvarado v. Gonzales*, 449 F.3d 915, 920–24 (9th Cir. 2006) (holding that a BIA case is not entitled to *Chevron* deference on judicial review when the BIA summarily affirms an IJ's decision) (as amended); *Lagandaon v. Ashcroft*, 383 F.3d 983, 987 (9th Cir. 2004) (citing *Hernandez v. Ashcroft*, 345 F.3d 824, 839 n. 13 (9th Cir. 2003)); *Davila-Bardales v. INS*, 27 F.3d 1, 5–6 (1st Cir. 1994) ("[W]e see no earthly reason why the mere fact of nonpublication should permit an agency to take a view of law that is flatly contrary to the view it set out in earlier cases … without explaining why it is doing so.").

[130] *See, e.g.*, *Margalli-Olvera v. INS*, 43 F.3d 345, 357 (8th Cir. 1994) (citation omitted); *Yepes-Prado v. INS*, 10 F.3d 1363, 1372 (9th Cir. 1993).

[131] *www.justice.gov/eoir/vll/intdec/lib_indecitnet.html* (last visited Mar. 18, 2015).

[132] *www.irac.net/unpublished/* (last visited Mar. 18, 2015).

[133] *See, e.g.*, *Matter of L–S–J–*, 21 I&N Dec. 973 (BIA 1997).

consistent—rather than in conflict—with constitutional protections. The BIA also lacks the authority to ignore or disregard regulations promulgated by the AG.[134]

> ➢ **Practice Pointer**: Even though the BIA lacks jurisdiction to rule on constitutionality, constitutional issues should always be raised in appeals to the BIA because doing so maintains these important issues for any future appeals to the U.S. circuit courts of appeals.[135]

D. Attorney General Opinions

Under the Judiciary Act of 1789, the AG has authority to render opinions on questions of law when requested by the President and heads of Executive Branch departments.[136] The AG has delegated responsibility for preparing the formal opinions of the AG to the Office of Legal Counsel.[137] Thus, on occasion, the AG has directed the Office of Legal Counsel at the Department of Justice to prepare formal opinions related to U.S. asylum law for issuance to federal agencies, including DHS and legacy INS.[138]

E. Field Manuals and Internal Agency Guidelines

Legacy INS had its own internal guidelines, called Operations Instructions (OIs). The sections relevant to asylum procedures included §§209 (adjustment) and 223a (travel documents). OI §208 was out of date and was removed from the OIs in 1997. OIs did not have the force of law, but provided general guidance for legacy INS employees. While federal courts have jurisdiction to review the validity of agency practices and internal procedures,[139] they did not have the authority to enforce OIs.[140]

---

[134] *Matter of Anselmo*, 20 I&N Dec. 25, 30 (BIA 1989).

[135] See chapters 11 and 12 for detailed discussions of administrative and judicial review.

[136] 28 USC §§511–13 (2014).

[137] 28 USC §510 (2014).

[138] *See, e.g.*, Office of Legal Counsel, Dep't of Justice, *Legal Obligations of the United States under Article 33 of the Refugee Convention*, 15 Op. O.L.C. 86 (Dec. 12, 1991), *available at www.justice.gov/sites/default/files/olc/opinions/1991/12/31/op-olc-v015-p0086.pdf* (last visited Oct. 1, 2014); Office of Legal Counsel, Dep't of Justice, *Deportation Proceedings of Joseph Patrick Thomas Doherty*, 12 Op. O.L.C. 1 (June 9, 1988), *available at www.justice.gov/sites/default/files/olc/opinions/1988/06/31/op-olc-v012-p0001.pdf* (last visited Oct. 1, 2014).

[139] *McNary v. Haitian Refugee Ctr, Inc.*, 498 U.S. 479, 491–94 (1991).

[140] *Fano v. O'Neill*, 806 F.2d 1262, 1263–64 (5th Cir. 1987) (holding that OIs are only internal guidelines that do not confer substantive rights nor establish procedures on which a petitioner for immigration benefits may rely); *Pasquini v. Morris*, 700 F.2d 658, 661–62 (11th Cir. 1983) (holding that OIs are for the administrative convenience of the INS and do not confer substantive rights).

DHS now has issued a series of field manuals to replace the OIs:[141]

- *U.S. Customs and Border Protection (CBP) Inspector's Field Manual*:[142] The first such DHS field manual to be issued (first published March 13, 1998), it deals with issues arising at ports of entry. Some of the sections relevant to asylum claims are §16.3 (asylees and asylum applicants), §17.11 (asylum claims), and §23.18 (asylum claims by stowaways);
- *Adjudicator's Field Manual*[143] (updated March 31, 2014), which contains chapter 21.10 on Refugee/Asylee Relative Petitions, chapter 23.6 on Refugee and Asylee Adjustment, and chapter 53 on Refugee Travel Documents;
- *USCIS Policy Manual*[144] (first issued on January 22, 2013)—which will ultimately replace the *Adjudicator's Field Manual*—currently contains Volume 7: Parts L and M on Adjustment of Status for refugees and asylees; and the *Detention and Removal Operations Policy and Procedure Manual*[145] (March 27, 2006), which contains chapter 11.19 on Refugees, Asylum and Withholding of Removal, chapter 20.3 on Asylum, and chapter 20.4 on Withholding or Deferral of Removal.
- *Performance Based National Detention Standards* [146] (2011), which includes information on grievance procedures, group rights presentations, and access to legal materials.[147]

---

[141] *See* INS Memorandum from INS Deputy Comm'r Chris Sale, IIRAIRA Wire #25 (Mar. 31, 1997), *published on* AILA InfoNet at Doc. No. 97033192 (*posted* Mar. 31, 1997).

[142] AILA offers the most complete (least nonredacted) version of the *Inspector's Field Manual* to its members at *http://agora.aila.org*.

[143] ADJUDICATOR'S FIELD MANUAL—*Redacted Public Version*, U.S. CITIZENSHIP & IMMIGRATION SERVS., *available at www.uscis.gov/iframe/ilink/docView/AFM/HTML/AFM/0-0-0-1.html* (last visited Oct. 2, 2014). Note that chapters 71–76 and Appendices 71-1 to 75-7 have been superseded by the *USCIS Policy Manual, Volume 12: Citizenship and Naturalization* as of January 22, 2013. *See Citizenship & Naturalization, in USCIS Policy Manual,* U.S. CITIZENSHIP AND IMMIGRATION SERVS., *available at www.uscis.gov/policymanual/HTML/PolicyManual.html* (last visited Oct. 2, 2014).

[144] USCIS POLICY MANUAL, *supra* note 143. The manual was first issued on January 22, 2013, and USCIS issued a memorandum explaining the planned shift from the *Adjudicator's Field Manual* to the *USCIS Policy Manual. See* Press Release, U.S. Citizenship & Immigration Servs., USCIS Begin Transition to Centralized Policy Manual (Jan. 7, 2013), *available at www.uscis.gov/news/uscis-begins-transition-centralized-policy-manual* (last updated Jan. 7, 2013).

[145] The *Detention and Removal Operations Policy and Procedure Manual* was previously called the *Detention and Deportation Officer's Field Manual. See* memorandum from John P. Torres, Acting Dir. Office of Detention and Removal Operation, U.S. Immigration and Customs Enforcement, to Field Office Dirs., *Detention and Deportation Officer's Field Manual* (Mar. 27, 2006), *published on* AILA InfoNet at Doc. No. 09100571 (*posted* Mar. 27, 2006) (last visited Oct. 2, 2014).

[146] The ICE DETENTION OPERATIONS MANUAL was issued in September of 2000 and provided standards to facilitate consistent conditions of confinement, access to legal representation, and safe and secure operations across the immigration detention system. In September of 2008, the standards were redrafted and released as the *2008 Performance Based National Detention Standards*. *See Detention Operations*, U.S. Immigration and Customs Enforcement, *www.ice.gov/detention-standards/2000/ and www.ice.gov/detention-standards/2008/* (last visited Oct. 2, 2014). ICE again revised its detention

Continued

- *Affirmative Asylum Procedures Manual*[148] (last updated November 2013), which is a USCIS comprehensive manual with information ranging from scheduling interviews to motions to reopen.
- The *Immigration Court and Board of Immigration Appeals Practice Manuals*,[149] as well as the *Immigration Judge Benchbook*,[150] also provide helpful guidance on asylum-related procedures before the immigration courts and appeals before the BIA.

Like the old OIs, these manuals do not have the force of law. For example, to emphasize this point, the first page of the *Inspector's Field Manual* specifically states:

> "Nothing in this manual shall be construed to create any substantive or procedural right or benefit that is legally enforceable by any party against the United States or its agencies or officers or any other person."[151]

Although these manuals do not have the force of law, they are useful tools for understanding and predicting agency interpretations of, and positions on, U.S. asylum law and procedure.

---

standards in 2011, issuing the *Performance Based National Detention Standards 2011*, the text of which ICE corrected and clarified in February of 2013. *See Detention Operations*, U.S. Immigration and Customs Enforcement, *www.ice.gov/doclib/detention-standards/2011/pbnds2011.pdf* and *www.ice.gov/doclib/detention-standards/2011/pbnds2011amend-feb2013.pdf* (last visited Oct. 7, 2014).

[147] Unfortunately, these national detention standards are not complied with and DHS does not insist on compliance. Many contracts with private detention companies are renewed, extended, or left intact despite reports of egregious violations of the national detention standards.

[148] ASYLUM DIV., U.S. CITIZENSHIP & IMMIGRATION SERVS., AFFIRMATIVE ASYLUM PROCEDURES MANUAL (Nov. 2013), *available at www.uscis.gov/files/nativedocuments/AffrmAsyManFNL.pdf*. A hard copy is available from AILA: *see http://agora.aila.org*.

[149] OFFICE OF THE CHIEF IMMIGRATION JUDGE, IMMIGRATION COURT PRACTICE MANUAL (2009), *available at www.justice.gov/eoir/vll/OCIJPracManual/ocij_page1.htm*; BOARD OF IMMIGRATION APPEALS, BOARD OF IMMIGRATION APPEALS PRACTICE MANUAL (Aug. 2014), *available at www.justice.gov/eoir/vll/qapracmanual/apptmtn4.htm*.

[150] EXECUTIVE OFFICE FOR IMMIGRATION REVIEW, U.S. DEP'T OF JUSTICE, IMMIGRATION JUDGE BENCHBOOK, *available at www.justice.gov/eoir/vll/benchbook/* (last updated Aug. 2014).

[151] U.S. CUSTOMS AND BORDER PROTECTION, INSPECTOR'S FIELD MANUAL 1. AILA offers the most complete (least nonredacted) version of the *Inspector's Field Manual* to its members at *http://agora.aila.org*. *See also* USCIS POLICY MANUAL, *supra* note 143 ("The Policy Manual does not create any substantive or procedural right or benefit that is legally enforceable by any party against the United States or its agencies or officers or any other person."); DETENTION AND DEPORTATION OFFICERS' FIELD MANUAL, *supra* note 143 ("Nothing in this manual may be construed to create any substantive or procedural right or benefit that is legally enforceable by any party against the United States, its agencies or officers, or any other person.").

F. Legacy INS's *Basic Law Manual* and the Asylum Officer Basic Training Course Lesson Modules

In the past, a useful tool in preparing asylum claims was the *Basic Law Manual: U.S. Law and INS Refugee/Asylum Adjudications* (1994) (*Basic Law Manual*), which was prepared by the Asylum Division and Office of the General Counsel of legacy INS as a training manual for its asylum officers. USCIS has expanded on the *Basic Law Manual* in its Asylum Officer Basic Training Course (AOBTC), the lesson plans for which are available on the USCIS website.[152] The AOBTC includes lesson plans on credible and reasonable fear determinations, the definition of refugee; the definition of persecution; past persecution and well-founded fear; nexus and the five protected grounds; burdens and standards of proof; bars to asylum; discretion; interviewing; and decision-writing among other topics.[153]

Although neither the *Basic Law Manual* nor the AOBTC have the force and effect of law, they set forth, in detail, the position of USCIS on a wide range of legal issues. Previously, the *Basic Law Manual* had been cited with approval by the BIA for recognizing the need for an asylum adjudicator to acquire general country condition information.[154]

Similarly, in *Matter of H–*,[155] the BIA noted that the *Basic Law Manual* acknowledges that a Somali clan may constitute a "particular social group," and that clan membership is a highly recognizable, immutable characteristic that is acquired at birth and is inextricably linked to family ties. In addition to asylum officers, the IJs, the BIA, and the federal courts are likely to look to the AOBTC for guidance, as they did with the *Basic Law Manual*.[156]

G. Legacy INS, DHS, and EOIR Policy Directives, Memoranda, and Statements

From time to time, DHS and EOIR (composed of the BIA and the immigration courts) issue policy directives in the form of memoranda or guidelines to their employees. These directives have addressed both procedural and substantive topics.

---

[152] *Asylum Division Training Programs*, U.S. CITIZENSHIP & IMMIGRATION SERVS., *available at www.uscis.gov/humanitarian/refugees-asylum/asylum/asylum-division-training-programs* (last updated Mar. 5, 2012).

[153] *See id.*

[154] *Matter of S–M–J–*, 21 I&N Dec. 722, 729 (BIA 1997) (quoting from the *Basic Law Manual* that "[t]he asylum officer should be fully familiar with the reports and country profiles developed by the INS Resource Information Center, with the Department of State's Country Reports of Human Rights Practices for the country being considered, and with reports from Amnesty International and other reputable organizations, including academic institutions.") (citations omitted).

[155] *Matter of H–*, 21 I&N Dec. 337 (BIA 1996).

[156] *See, e.g., Martins v. USCIS*, No. C 13-00591 LB (N.D. Cal. July 3, 2013) (citing the note-taking training given to asylum officers through the AOBTC, which instructs asylum officers on how to "take objective notes and omit subjective opinions, suppositions, or inferences"), *available at www.courthousenews.com/2013/07/10/asylum.pdf*.

While not legally binding on DHS or EOIR, they do provide insight into the views of these agencies on particular topics that may be at issue in an asylum-related case.

In May 1995, for example, legacy INS issued guidelines to all asylum officers for adjudicating women's asylum claims.[157] Among their many important provisions, these guidelines state:

> [R]ape …, sexual abuse and domestic violence, infanticide and genital mutilation are forms of mistreatment primarily directed at girls and women and they may serve as evidence of past persecution on account of one or more of the five grounds.[158]

Another example is the legacy INS general counsel's memorandum concerning human immunodeficiency virus (HIV) infection and relief from deportation issued in February 1996. In that memorandum, legacy INS general counsel adopted recommendations made by the Presidential Advisory Council on acquired immune deficiency syndrome (AIDS) in 1995. The Presidential Advisory Council suggested that legacy INS's efforts against AIDS-related discrimination should include the granting of asylum based on the social group category of HIV-positive individuals.[159]

In response to asylum reform measures implemented in 1995, the Chief IJ issued Operating Policies and Procedures Memorandum No. 96-1, Asylum Request Processing (March 15, 1996), which set forth procedures for various stages of an asylum claim including filing applications, scheduling hearings, filing change of venue motions, and obtaining comments from the Department of State.[160]

After the passage of IIRAIRA, legacy INS issued a detailed memorandum on the implementation of the expedited removal process and how officers should handle persons asserting a fear of persecution or intent to apply for asylum.[161]

With regard to the CAT,[162] both legacy INS and EOIR issued memoranda regarding the implementation of Article 3 relief under the Convention.[163]

---

[157] *See* INS Memorandum from Office of Int'l Affairs, Phyllis Coven, Considerations for Asylum Officers Adjudicating Claims from Women (May 25, 1995), *published on* AILA InfoNet at Doc. No. 95053180 (*posted* May 31, 1995), and *reproduced in* 72 INTERPRETER RELEASES 771 (June 5, 1995).

[158] *Id.* at 4.

[159] *See* INS Memorandum from the General Counsel, David A. Martin, Seropositivity for HIV and Relief From Deportation (Feb. 16, 1996), *reproduced in* 73 INTERPRETER RELEASES 901, 909 (July 8, 1996).

[160] This memorandum is reproduced in 73 INTERPRETER RELEASES 479 (Apr. 12, 1996).

[161] Sale Memorandum, *supra* note 141.

[162] See chapter 4 for a detailed discussion of relief under the Convention Against Torture.

[163] INS Memorandum from Acting Dir., Asylum Div., Joseph E. Langlois, Implementation of Amendments to Asylum and Withholding of Removal Regulations, effective March 22, 1999 (Mar. 18, 1999); EOIR Memorandum from Chief Immigr. Judge, Office of the Chief Immigr. Judge, Michael J. Creppy, Operating Policies and Procedures Memorandum No. 99-5: Implementation of Article 3 of the

Continued

Some more recent examples of memoranda include:

- USCIS Memorandum, "Release of Updated Asylum Division Officer Training Course Lesson Plan, Credible Fear of Persecution and Torture Determinations," (Feb. 28, 2014), *published on* AILA InfoNet at Doc. No.14041845 (*posted* Apr. 18, 2014).
- USCIS Memorandum, "Changes to Case Categories Requiring Asylum Headquarters Review," (Jan. 27, 2014), *published on* AILA InfoNet at Doc. No. 14013044 (*posted* Jan. 30, 2014).[164]
- EOIR, "Operating Policies and Procedures Memorandum 13-02: The Asylum Clock," (Dec. 2, 2013), *published on* AILA InfoNet at Doc. No. 13121063 (*posted* Dec. 10, 2013).[165]
- USCIS Memorandum, "Revised Procedures Regarding Trafficking Victims for the Affirmative Asylum Procedures Manual," (Nov. 26, 2013), *published on* AILA InfoNet at Doc. No. 14013055 (*posted* Jan. 30, 2014).[166]
- USCIS Memorandum, "Asylum Division National Customer Access Standards," (Sept. 28, 2012), *published on* AILA InfoNet at Doc. No. 12122643 (*posted* Dec. 26, 2012).[167]
- ICE Memorandum, "Parole of Aliens Found to Have a Credible Fear of Persecution or Torture," (Dec. 8, 2009), *published on* AILA InfoNet at Doc. No. 11060959 (*posted* June 9, 2011). [168]
- USCIS Update, "USCIS Now Responsible for Initial Adjudication of Asylum Applications from Unaccompanied Minors," (Mar. 25, 2009), *published on* AILA InfoNet at Doc. No. 09032567 (*posted* Mar. 25, 2009).
- EOIR Memorandum, T. Snow, "Classified Information in Immigration Court Proceedings" (Feb 5, 2009), *published on* AILA InfoNet at Doc. No. 09021271 (*posted* Feb. 12, 2009).
- EOIR Memorandum, D. Neal, "EOIR Offers Guidance for Judges on Attorney Telephonic Appearances" (July 30, 2008), *published on* AILA InfoNet at Doc. No. 08080760 (*posted* Aug. 7, 2008); and

---

U.N. Convention Against Torture (May 14, 1999), *available at www.usdoj.gov/eoir/efoia/ocij/oppm99/99_5.pdf.*

[164] Also available at *www.uscis.gov/sites/default/files/USCIS/Outreach/Notes%20from%20Previous%20Engagements/Asy-Changes-CaseCategories-AsyHQ-Review.pdf* (last visited June 7, 2014).

[165] Also available at *www.justice.gov/eoir/efoia/ocij/oppm13/13-02.pdf* (last visited June 7, 2014).

[166] Also available at *www.uscis.gov/sites/default/files/USCIS/Outreach/Notes%20from%20Previous%20Engagements/Asy-Issuance-Rev-Procedures-Trafficking-Victims-Proc-Manual.pdf* (last visited June 7, 2014).

[167] Also available at *www.uscis.gov/sites/default/files/USCIS/Laws/Memoranda/2012/September%202012/ASM-National-Customer-Access-Standards-28sep12.pdf* (last visited June 7, 2014).

[168] Also available at *www.ice.gov/doclib/dro/pdf/11002.1-hd-parole_of_arriving_aliens_found_credible_fear.pdf* (last visited June 7, 2014).

- USCIS Fact Sheet, "Traveling Outside the United States as an Asylum Applicant, Asylee, or a Lawful Permanent Resident Who Obtained Such Status Based on Asylum Status" (Jan. 4, 2007 (revised)).[169]

Other sources of useful information are public statements and press releases issued by USCIS, ICE, CBP, and EOIR public affairs offices, often in question-and-answer format.[170]

> **Practice Pointer**: The American Immigration Lawyers Association (AILA) has liaisons to the various government agencies. These individuals attend regular meetings with leaders of these government agencies to ask policy questions, clarify agency interpretations and procedures, and raise problems and concerns with the agencies. Notes from these meetings are posted on AILA InfoNet and may be searched for at *www.aila.org/research-library*.[171]

H. Federal Court Decisions

Federal courts often are the final arbiters in asylum cases. Decisions by U.S. district courts, U.S. circuit courts of appeals, and the U.S. Supreme Court have interpreted key provisions in the Refugee Act and asylum regulations, and have ruled on constitutional issues raised by asylum-seekers. DHS and the BIA lack the authority to make decisions on constitutional issues and claims that question the validity of their own regulations or statutes. Such claims, as well as non-constitutional challenges to the federal government's treatment of individuals seeking protection from persecution and torture, are often brought through litigation in the federal courts under the Administrative Procedures Act or the INA. Moreover, the INA provides direct appellate review of BIA decisions.[172]

While decisions of the Supreme Court are binding throughout the United States, decisions of the U.S. circuit courts of appeals are binding only in their own circuits. The BIA has historically followed a circuit court's precedent in cases arising within the jurisdiction of that circuit.[173] When the BIA disagrees with a circuit court's position on a given issue, it has declined to follow it outside the circuit court's jurisdiction. The BIA has held, however, that it is not bound to follow the published decisions of U.S. district courts in cases arising within the same district.[174]

Changes under IIRAIRA and the USA PATRIOT Act have limited federal court review for asylum applicants in several areas. For example, amendments to INA §208 bar judicial review of:

---

[169] Available at *www.uscis.gov/files/pressrelease/AsylumTravel122706FS.pdf.*

[170] *See, e.g.*, INS Public Statement, *The 208 Final Rule: Questions and Answers* (Dec. 6, 2000).

[171] *www.aila.org/research-library* (last visited Mar. 18, 2015).

[172] *See* INA §242(a)(1). See chapter 12 for a detailed discussion of judicial review.

[173] *Matter of Anselmo*, 20 I&N Dec. 25, 31–32 (BIA 1989).

[174] *Matter of K–S–*, 20 I&N Dec. 715, 718–20 (BIA 1993).

(1) determinations regarding the availability of a safe third country;

(2) whether the applicant filed within one year of entry;

(3) the applicability of exceptions to the one-year filing deadline; and

(4) the bar for previously denied claims.[175]

Section 208 also bars judicial review of the determination that an individual is ineligible for asylum based on terrorist-related grounds.[176] Moreover, INA §242(b)(4)(D), added by IIRAIRA, provides that the discretionary judgment whether to grant asylum under §208(a) is conclusive unless "manifestly contrary to the law and an abuse of discretion."[177]

The REAL ID Act gave back some limited jurisdiction to the federal courts, allowing the courts to review constitutional claims and questions of law on issues previously barred from judicial review, such as the one-year filing deadline.[178] Under the USA PATRIOT Act, the determination that an individual is subject to detention as a suspected terrorist is reviewable only in habeas corpus proceedings and appeals may only be made to the U.S. Court of Appeals for the D.C. Circuit or the U.S. Supreme Court.[179]

Judicial review of the expedited removal process is even more limited.[180] In most cases, federal courts are barred by statute from reviewing the individual credible fear determinations of asylum officers or IJs. INA §242(e) provides for very limited judicial review of final removal orders entered under the expedited removal process. Judicial review of an individual expedited removal order is only available through habeas corpus and is limited to whether: the petitioner is an alien, was ordered removed under the expedited removal process, and can prove by a preponderance of the evidence that he or she is a lawful permanent resident, or has been admitted as a refugee or granted asylum.[181] Judicial review of the implementation of the expedited removal process is only available in the U.S. District Court for the District of Columbia and must be filed within 60 days after the date that a challenged section, regulation, directive, guideline, or procedure is first implemented.[182]

Despite limits on judicial review under IIRAIRA and the USA PATRIOT Act, the role of the federal courts should not be underestimated. Federal courts have, in the past, played an important role in defining the rights of noncitizens subject to

---

[175] INA §208(a)(3). See chapter 12 for a detailed discussion of judicial review.

[176] INA §208(b)(2)(D).

[177] INA §242(b)(4)(D).

[178] INA §242(a)(2)(D), *modified by* REAL ID Act, *supra* note 71, at §106(a)(2)(D), 119 Stat. 231, 310. See chapter 12 for a detailed discussion of judicial review and the one-year filing deadline.

[179] INA §236A(b); *see* USA PATRIOT ACT, *supra* note 71, at §412, 115 Stat. 272, 350–51.

[180] *See* INA §242(a)(2).

[181] INA §242(e)(2).

[182] INA §§242(e)(3)(A)–(B).

deportation, even before U.S. Congress created a statutory right to judicial review. The right to judicial review, as noted by one commentator, is grounded in the long-standing recognition that a noncitizen facing deportation is threatened with loss of a fundamental liberty interest protected by the U.S. Constitution.[183]

III. Laws of Other Countries

Increasingly, foreign law is at issue in determining eligibility for asylum, withholding of removal, and CAT protection. If a claim involves a nationality or statelessness question,[184] a prosecution vs. persecution question,[185] a firm resettlement question,[186] or a safe third country question,[187] it is essential to consult the case law and statutes of other countries. For example, an applicant may have had a legal immigration status in a third country prior to arriving in the United States and may have to prove she was not "firmly resettled." She may have dual citizenship and may therefore have a safe third country to which she may return. She may be fleeing what at first glance looks like prosecution, but on closer examination of the law and how it was enforced, rises to the level of persecution. She may be stateless because the country in which she was born does not confer citizenship by virtue of being born in its territory. These and other scenarios will require reference to foreign law, specifically other countries' asylum, residency, and citizenship laws.

The BIA has held that foreign law is a matter to be proven by the party seeking to rely on it. In *Matter of Soleimani*,[188] the BIA found that legacy INS had produced no evidence of record to establish that the applicant had been "offered" permanent resettlement under Israel's Law of Return.[189] Absent any such documentation, the BIA held that it could not find that the applicant had been offered permanent resettlement in Israel within the meaning of the firm resettlement concept. In *Abdille v. Ashcroft*, the Third Circuit U.S. Court of Appeals held that legacy INS, as the party seeking to rely on foreign law for firm resettlement purposes, carries the initial burden of proof.[190] Once the trial attorney submits evidence of foreign law sufficient

---

[183] *See* Lucas Guttentag, *The 1996 Immigration Act: Federal Court Jurisdiction—Statutory Restrictions and Constitutional Rights*, 74 INTERPRETER RELEASES 245 (1997). *See also Padilla v. Kentucky*, 130 S. Ct. 1473, 1481, 1486 (2010); *Harisiades v. Shaughnessy*, 342 U.S. 580, 587–88 (1952); *Fong Faw Tan v. Phelan*, 333 U.S. 6, 10 (1948); *Delgadillo v. Carmichael*, 332 U.S. 388, 391 (1947).

[184] *See infra* chapter 2 for a detailed discussion of nationality and statelessness.

[185] *See infra* chapter 2 for a detailed discussion of prosecution versus persecution.

[186] *See infra* chapter 2 for a detailed discussion of firm resettlement.

[187] *See infra* chapter 2 for a detailed discussion of safe third countries.

[188] *Matter of Soleimani*, 20 I&N Dec. 99, 106 (BIA 1989).

[189] *Id.*

[190] *Abdille v. Ashcroft*, 242 F.3d 477, 490–91 (3d Cir. 2001).

to indicate that the firm resettlement bar will apply, the burden shifts to the applicant.[191]

In addition to these issues specific to eligibility for asylum, withholding of removal, and protection under the CAT, it may be advantageous to consult the case law and statutes of other countries for claims involving novel or evolving issues. It is not uncommon for courts to look to the law of other countries, particularly when interpreting a treaty. The Supreme Court has held that in construing a treaty, it is necessary to "look beyond the written words to … the practical construction adopted by the parties."[192] As one commentator stated, "The examination of foreign jurisprudence by courts interpreting common terms under the 1951 Refugee Convention and 1967 Protocol should be a standard exercise, and not an occasional occurrence."[193]

---

[191] *Abdille v. Ashcroft*, at 491 (citing 8 CFR §208.13(c)(2)(ii)); *see also Matter of Annang*, 14 I&N Dec. 502, 502–03 (BIA 1973).

[192] *Air France v. Saks*, 470 U.S. 392, 396 (1985) (citation omitted).

[193] Arthur Helton, *The Use of Comparative Law and Practice under the International Refugee Treaties*, ASYLUM LAW AND PRACTICE IN EUROPE AND NORTH AMERICA: A COMPARATIVE ANALYSIS (G. Koll & J. Bhabha Eds., 1992).

CHAPTER TWO

ASYLUM AND WITHHOLDING OF REMOVAL*

During 2013, 25,199 people were granted asylum in the United States, a decrease of 14 percent from 2012.[1] As policymakers and the federal agencies continue to heighten both the legal and evidentiary standards required to make a successful claim for asylum in the United States, it is increasingly important for advocates and adjudicators to cultivate a deep and thorough understanding of this complex area of immigration law. Such an understanding will assist in better serving bona fide refugees seeking protection and abiding by the United States' own legal obligations.

This chapter provides a brief overview of the U.S. protection system and details the legal standards for demonstrating eligibility for asylum under §208(a) of the Immigration and Nationality Act (INA) and withholding of removal under INA §241(b)(3) while present in the United States. It also discusses the statutes, regulations, case law, and agency policies defining the various concepts involved in those legal standards.[2]

I. The Two Theaters of U.S. Refugee Protection

In U.S. asylum law, the search for protection occurs in two different theaters—outside U.S. territory and within the United States. In order to gain access to the refugee program from outside U.S. territory, refugees must be identified by the United Nations High Commissioner for Refugees (UNHCR), a U.S. embassy, or a designated nongovernmental organization, and then be referred to the U.S. Refugee

* The author would like to thank Vanessa Allyn of Human Rights First, Cheri Attix of the Law Office of Cheri Attix, and Thomas K. Ragland of Benach Ragland LLP for their invaluable input in reviewing this chapter.

[1] Department of Homeland Security, Office of Immigration Statistics, *Annual Flow Report: Refugees and Asylees: 2013* (August 2014).

[2] The legal standards for protection under the Convention Against Torture (CAT) are addressed in ch. 3.

Admissions Program.[3] Once a referral is made, a Resettlement Support Center under contract with the Department of State's Bureau of Population, Refugees, and Migration prepares the case file for presentation to the Department of Homeland Security (DHS) by taking photos, checking the facts in the files, and collecting information for the security clearance process. These centers then coordinate interviews for the applicants before U.S. Citizenship and Immigration Services (USCIS) refugee corps officers, who adjudicate their requests for protection.[4] Overseas refugees must demonstrate that they meet the definition of "refugee" under the INA,[5] and that they are otherwise admissible to the United States.

The President of the United States, in consultation with the U.S. Congress, designates the number of refugees that may be admitted from each region of the world, as well as which individuals will be considered for refugee status on the basis of their group classification or their family relationship to those previously granted asylum or refugee status in the United States.[6] Refugees are categorized into three "priorities."[7] Priority One consists of persons who have individual claims to refugee status.[8] These applicants gain access to the U.S. refugee program through a referral from UNHCR, a U.S. embassy, or a designated nongovernmental organization, as described above.[9] Once their cases are referred, USCIS refugee corps officers interview the applicants to determine whether they meet the refugee definition and are otherwise admissible to the United States.

Priority Two consists of pre-determined groups of people who already have been determined to meet the refugee definition on the basis of their group membership.[10] Some recent Priority Two groups have consisted of religious minorities from Iran and Somali Bantus. These persons are interviewed, but only have to establish their

---

[3] *See* U.S. Citizenship & Immigration Servs., *The U.S. Refugee Admissions Program (USRAP) Consultation & Worldwide Processing Priorities*, *available at www.uscis.gov/humanitarian/refugees-asylum/refugees/united-states-refugee-admissions-program-usrap-consultation-worldwide-processing-priorities* (last updated Apr. 8, 2013).

[4] Andorra Bruno, *Refugee Admissions and Resettlement Policy*, Congr. Research Serv. (Mar. 6, 2014), *available at http://fas.org/sgp/crs/misc/RL31269.pdf.*

[5] *See* Immigration and Nationality Act (INA) §207(a) (providing for the admission of refugees who apply for admission from outside the United States); *See also* INA §101(a)(42)(A) (delineating the contours of refugee classification).

[6] *See, e.g.*, U.S. Dep't of State *et al.*, *Proposed Refugee Admissions for Fiscal Year 2015* (Sept. 18, 2014), *available at www.state.gov/j/prm/releases/docsforcongress/231817.htm.*

[7] U.S. Citizenship & Immigration Servs., *The U.S. Refugee Admissions Program (USRAP) Consultation & Worldwide Processing Priorities*, *available at www.uscis.gov/humanitarian/refugees-asylum/refugees/united-states-refugee-admissions-program-usrap-consultation-worldwide-processing-priorities* (last updated Apr. 8, 2013).

[8] *See, e.g.*, U.S. Dep't of State *et al.*, *Proposed Refugee Admissions for Fiscal Year 2015* (Sept. 18, 2014), *available at www.state.gov/j/prm/releases/docsforcongress/231817.htm.*

[9] *Id.*

[10] *Id.*

membership in the pre-determined group and demonstrate that they are otherwise admissible in order to qualify for refugee status.[11]

Priority Three, or the "family reunification" category, currently consists of the spouses, parents, and unmarried children under the age of 21 of refugees or asylees over the age of 18, who have been in the United States in refugee or asylee status for no more than five years.[12] The refugee or asylee in the United States may initiate the refugee process for his or her family members abroad by completing an Affidavit of Relationship and submitting it to the Department of State through a resettlement-agency affiliate in the refugee or asylee's geographic area.[13] Refugee corps officers then interview the overseas relatives to determine whether they are indeed the spouses, children, or parents of the individual(s) in the United States and to determine whether they are otherwise admissible.[14] DNA testing is frequently used to verify the claimed relationships.[15] Priority Three refugees do not have to establish that they meet the definition of refugee on an individual basis.[16] Additionally, Priority Three is not available to all nationalities, only to those designated by the President of the United States through the Department of State's (DOS) Bureau of Population, Refugees, and Migration in consultation with DHS at the beginning of each fiscal year.[17]

➢ **Practice Pointer**: A refugee who has arrived in the United States, as well as a person granted asylum in the United States, also can file a Form I-730 for his or her spouse and unmarried children under the age of 21. There are no restrictions on nationalities that can file this petition, but it must be filed with USCIS within two years of arrival in the United States as a refugee or the granting of asylee status.[18]

Once a refugee has been legally designated as such and accepted for resettlement in the United States, he or she will be admitted to the United States as a refugee under INA §207. The refugee will then be assigned to a refugee assistance agency under the auspices of the U.S. Department of Health and Human Services' Office of Refugee Resettlement (ORR) for guidance and help in the resettlement process.

---

[11] *Id.*

[12] *Id.*

[13] *Id.*

[14] *Id.*

[15] *Id.*

[16] Occasionally, there will be a household member who is not a parent, spouse, or child of the relative in the United States, but who can establish compelling reasons to be allowed to come to the United States with the other family members. This household member may be granted refugee status, but only if he or she can individually establish that he or she meets the definition of refugee. *See id.*

[17] *Id.*

[18] See chapter 13 for a detailed discussion of I-730 petitions for relatives of asylees.

On the domestic side, individuals with protection needs who already are physically present within the United States seek admission or permission to remain in the United States based on a fear of return to their home countries. These individuals are often referred to as "asylum-seekers" or "asylum applicants," as they seek refugee protection in the form of "asylum" under INA §208. In order to be granted asylum in the United States, asylum-seekers must individually demonstrate that they meet the definition of "refugee" under the INA, among other requirements.[19] There are two main processes for claiming asylum in the United States:[20] affirmatively, by coming forward and submitting an application to DHS, USCIS, or defensively, by submitting or renewing an application before the U.S. Department of Justice (DOJ), Executive Office for Immigration Review (EOIR), while subject to removal proceedings in immigration court.[21] The process by which an asylum applicant has his or her asylum application adjudicated—affirmatively or defensively—will depend on the procedural posture of the case at the time of filing the asylum application.[22]

Accordingly, while overseas refugees and asylum-seekers must meet very similar legal requirements derived from the same sources of law, different procedures are required. This book focuses on the domestic side of asylum law involving asylum-seekers, or individuals who are seeking protection from persecution while already physically present in the United States. This chapter discusses the legal standards for demonstrating asylum eligibility, as well as the statutory bars and other grounds of ineligibility for asylum,[23] whereas the various procedures for seeking asylum in the United States are discussed in chapters 6 through 12. This chapter also discusses the legal standards for demonstrating eligibility for withholding of removal under INA §241(b)(3), a similar form of relief to asylum, as well as the statutory bars and other grounds of ineligibility for withholding of removal.[24]

---

[19] INA §101(a)(42)(A). See *infra* pt. II for a detailed discussion of the legal standards for demonstrating eligibility for asylum under INA §208.

[20] There are different procedures for individuals who seek asylum and withholding of removal upon apprehension at the border or a port of entry after being subject to expedited removal or reinstatement of removal. These individuals may complete credible fear interviews by asylum officers in order to avoid expedited removal from the United States and reasonable fear interviews by asylum officers in order to avoid removal after reinstatement of a prior removal order. If the asylum officer finds that these individuals have a credible or reasonable fear, they are permitted to present their claims in asylum or withholding-only proceedings before an immigration judge. See chapter 6 for a detailed discussion of the legal standards and procedures for seeking protection while subject to expedited removal or reinstatement of removal proceedings.

[21] See chapters 7 and 8 for discussions of the affirmative and defensive asylum procedures.

[22] *See id.*

[23] *See infra* pts. II and IV.

[24] *See infra* pts. III and IV.

II. Legal Standards for Demonstrating Asylum Eligibility

Under INA §208(b), the Attorney General (AG) may, in his or her discretion, grant asylum to an individual who is eligible to apply for asylum and who qualifies as a "refugee" within the meaning of INA §101(a)(42). Under the Homeland Security Act of 2002, this discretion to grant asylum extends to the DHS Secretary and other DHS officials.[25]

The burden of proof is on the applicant to establish that he or she: (1) is eligible to apply for asylum;[26] (2) is a refugee under INA §101(a)(42)(A); and (3) merits a favorable exercise of discretion.[27]

An asylee is an individual who meets the definition of refugee, who was physically present in the United States at the time he or she sought protection.[28] Under the INA, "refugee" is defined as:

> [A]ny person who is outside any country of such person's nationality or, in the case of a person having no nationality, is outside any country in which such person last habitually resided, and who is unable or unwilling to return to, and is unable or unwilling to avail himself or herself of the protection of, that country because of persecution or a well-founded fear of persecution on account of race, religion, nationality, membership in a particular social group, or political opinion.[29]

The definition of refugee was amended in 1996 to clarify that asylum claims for applicants who have fled or who fear coercive population control practices are based on political opinion.[30] Additionally, the refugee definition specifically excludes any individual "who ordered, incited, assisted, or otherwise participated in the persecution

---

[25] *See* Homeland Security Act of 2002, Pub. L. No. 107-296, §§456, 1512, 1517, 116 Stat. 2135, 2200, 2310, & 2311 (codified as amended in scattered sections of 6 USC).

[26] See *infra* pt. IV for a detailed discussion of ineligibility grounds and statutory bars to asylum eligibility.

[27] See chapter 4 for a detailed discussion of the shifting burdens of proof throughout the asylum application process.

[28] INA §208(a).

[29] INA §101(a)(42)(A); 8 USC §1101(a)(42)(A) (2012).

[30] INA §101(a)(42) (establishing that "For purposes of determinations under this Act, a person who has been forced to abort a pregnancy or to undergo involuntary sterilization, or who has been persecuted for failure or refusal to undergo such a procedure or for other resistance to a coercive population control program, shall be deemed to have been persecuted on account of political opinion, and a person who has a well-founded fear that he or she will be forced to undergo such a procedure or subject to persecution for such failure, refusal, or resistance shall be deemed to have a well-founded fear of persecution on account of political opinion."). See *infra* pt. II.E.2.v.b. for a detailed discussion of this amendment and its application to asylum-seekers.

of any person on account of race, religion, nationality, and membership in a particular social group or political opinion."[31]

This definition of refugee that is found in U.S. domestic law was derived from the refugee definition provided in the 1951 Convention Relating to the Status of Refugees, as amended in the 1967 Protocol Relating to the Status of Refugees (Refugee Protocol).[32] The interpretation and application of the refugee definition in U.S. law has evolved over time to conform to changes in the law, agency and court interpretations, guidance from international organizations like UNHCR, and changes in the causes of and responses to refugee crises throughout the world. This section breaks down and analyzes, in order, the various legal concepts that make up the definition of refugee and how those concepts have been interpreted and applied in the domestic setting.

A. Country of Nationality and Statelessness

Since an applicant must first show that he or she is outside his or her country of nationality and that his or her claim of persecution originates in that country,[33] a threshold question in determining eligibility for asylum is the applicant's nationality, or if the individual is stateless, the individual's country of last habitual residence.[34] Generally, "nationality" refers to the individual's citizenship or state of permanent allegiance,[35] while "last habitual residence" is defined as a "place of general abode" or the individual's "principal, actual dwelling place in fact, without regard to intent."[36] The failure of the Immigration Judge (IJ) or the Board of Immigration Appeals (BIA) to address nationality may be grounds for remand.[37]

---

[31] INA §101(a)(42)(B); 8 USC §1101(a)(42)(B) (2012); See *infra* pt. IV.B.1. for a detailed discussion of this bar to asylum and withholding of removal eligibility.

[32] Protocol Relating to the Status of Refugees (Refugee Protocol), *done* Jan. 31, 1967, 606 U.N.T.S. 267 (entered into force Oct. 4, 1967), *available at www.refworld.org/docid/3ae6b3ae4.html*. See chapter 1.

[33] U.N. High Comm'r for Refugees, *Handbook on Procedures and Criteria for Determining Refugee Status* (UNHCR Handbook), ¶ 90 HCR/1P/4/enG/Rev. 3 (2011) *available at www.refworld.org/docid/4f33c8d92.html*.

[34] *Wangchuck v. DHS*, 448 F.3d 524, 528 (2d Cir. 2006) (where the applicant was born in India to Tibetan refugee parents); *Dhoumo v. BIA*, 416 F.3d 172, 173 (2d Cir. 2005) (where the applicant was also born in India of Tibetan parents in a refugee camp); *See also* U.S. Citizenship & Immigration Servs., *Lesson: Asylum Eligibility Part I* at 13, in Asylum Officer Basic Training Course Participant Workbook (AOBTC Workbook) (Mar. 6, 2009), pt. I, *available at www.uscis.gov/USCIS/Humanitarian/Refugees%20&%20Asylum/Asylum/AOBTC%20Lesson%20Plans/Definition-Refugee-Persecution-Eligiblity-31aug10.pdf*.

[35] INA §101(a)(22).

[36] INA §101(a)(33).

[37] *See, e.g., Matter of K–R–Y– and K–C–S–*, 24 I&N Dec. 133 (BIA 2007).

1. Nationality

There are two references to the term "nationality" in the refugee definition. The first—"any person who is outside any country of such person's nationality"[38]—refers to the person's citizenship or state of permanent allegiance.[39] In interpreting what it means for an applicant to be outside his or her country of nationality, the BIA has looked to the definition of "national" found within the INA, which defines "national" as a person owing permanent allegiance to a state.[40] For example, in *Matter of Fatoumata Toure*,[41] the BIA concluded that an applicant who was a citizen of Guinea and feared persecution there was eligible for asylum despite the fact that she possessed a passport from the Ivory Coast. The BIA looked to the INA definition of "national," UNHCR's *Handbook and Guidelines on Procedures and Criteria for Determining Refugee Status under the 1951 Convention and the 1967 Protocol relating to the Status of Refugees* (UNHCR Handbook),[42] and the refugee definition and found that a contrary result would require the deportation of the asylum applicant to a country where she has little or no connection.[43] Thus, the applicant was deemed to be outside her country of nationality, Guinea, and not the Ivory Coast.

In determining the applicant's country of nationality, practitioners should look to the status conferred on the applicant by a state and how the state views the applicant.[44] Possession of a passport creates a presumption that the asylum applicant is a national of that country, unless the passport states otherwise.[45] However, relevant evidence of nationality may also include the asylum applicant's testimony that a passport was issued only for travel purposes or based on misrepresentations or

---

[38] INA §101(a)(42)(A).

[39] *See* INA §§101(a)(21)–(22); *See* UNHCR Handbook, *supra* note 33, ¶ 87. In contrast, when interpreting nationality for purposes of determining the motivation of the persecutor, *i.e.*, persecution on account of "nationality," the term has been defined more broadly to include ethnicity and linguistic groups. *See also* U.S. Citizenship & Immigration Servs., *Lesson: Asylum Eligibility Part I* at 13, in Asylum Officer Basic Training Course Participant Workbook (Mar. 6, 2009), pt. I, pt. 1, at 8 *available at www.uscis.gov/USCIS/Humanitarian/Refugees%20&%20Asylum/Asylum/AOBTC%20Lesson%20 Plans/Definition-Refugee-Persecution-Eligiblity-31aug10.pdf.*; *see also* UNHCR Handbook, *supra* note 33, ¶ 74. (demonstrating that UNHCR shares this interpretation of "nationality" when referring to the motivation of the persecutor to include ethnic and linguistic groups).

[40] INA §101(a)(22).

[41] *Matter of Fatoumata Toure*, No. A24 876 244, 1990 IMMIG. RPTR. LEXIS 1435 (BIA June 26, 1990).

[42] *See* UNHCR Handbook, *supra* note 33, ¶ 90.

[43] *Matter of Fatoumata Toure*, No. A24 876 244, 1990 IMMIG. RPTR. LEXIS 1435 (BIA June 26, 1990).

[44] *See Dhoumo v. BIA*, 416 F.3d 172, 173 (2d Cir. 2005) (stating that "Nationality is a status conferred by a state, and will generally be recognized by other states provided it is supported by a 'genuine link' between the individual and the conferring state.").

[45] *See* UNHCR Handbook, *supra* note 33, ¶ 93.

bribes.[46] Other relevant evidence may include foreign laws regarding issuance of passports and country conditions evidence regarding trends for passport issuance.[47] An applicant's unsupported assertion that a passport was issued only for travel purposes generally is insufficient to rebut the presumption of nationality. However, if that assertion is accompanied by evidence demonstrating that the country in question often issues passports to non-nationals for travel purposes, for example, that evidence may be sufficient to overcome the presumption of nationality.[48] The adjudicator must consider all available evidence as a whole and base his or her conclusion on the nationality that has been established by a preponderance of the evidence.[49] If no nationality is established, the applicant is treated as stateless.

If an applicant is a dual citizen or national, he or she must establish that he or she is unable or unwilling to return to both countries of nationality because of persecution or a well-founded fear of persecution in both countries.[50] Even if the applicant has never resided in or never established any personal ties to one of the countries, the applicant still must demonstrate that he or she is unable or unwilling to return to that country because of persecution or a well-founded fear of persecution in that country.[51]

---

[46] *See Palavra v. INS,* 287 F.3d 690, 694 (8th Cir. 2002) (finding that the BIA failed to perform its fact-finding function when it ignored testimony by the applicant in an affidavit claiming that a passport was issued as a humanitarian accommodation).

[47] *Id.*

[48] *See* UNHCR Handbook, *supra* note 33, ¶ 93.

[49] *See* AOBTC Workbook, pt. I, *supra* note 34, at 10.

[50] *See* INA §101(a)(42)(A) (referring to "any country of such person's nationality" in the definition of refugee); Convention Relating to the Status of Refugees (Refugee Convention), *done* July 28, 19, 189 U.N.T.S. 137, art. 1A(2) ¶ 2 (entered into force Apr. 22, 1954), *available at https://treaties.un.org/pages/ViewDetailsII.aspx?&src=UNTSONLINE&mtdsg_no=V~2&chapter=5&Temp=mtdsg2&lang=en*; *See* UNHCR Handbook, *supra* note 33, ¶ 106; *Matter of B–R–*, 26 I&N Dec. 119 (BIA 2013).

[51] *See* UNHCR Handbook, *supra* note 33, ¶ 106. Congress has carved out an exception to this concept of dual nationality for certain citizens of North Korea. In enacting the North Korean Human Rights Act, Congress clarified that asylum applicants from North Korea are not ineligible for asylum based on "any legal right to citizenship they may enjoy" in South Korea. *See* North Korean Human Rights Act of 2004, Pub. L. No. 108-333, §302(a), 118 Stat. 1287. *But see Matter of K–R–Y– and K–C–S–*, 24 I&N Dec. 133 (BIA 2007) (finding that natives of North Korea, who became citizens of South Korea, were precluded from establishing eligibility for asylum based on their firm resettlement in South Korea). In other words, a citizen of North Korea should not also be treated as a national of South Korea. However, under the exception established in *Matter of K–R–Y– and K–C–S–*, if the citizen of North Korea availed him or herself of the rights of citizenship in South Korea or firmly resettled there, they may be ineligible for asylum. *See also* Joseph E. Langlois, Memorandum to Asylum Office Directors, *North Korean Human Rights Act of 2004*, Washington, D.C. (Oct. 22, 2004); *See* AOBTC Workbook, pt. I, *supra* note 34, at 11.

- **Practice Pointer**: Note that there is a distinction between the issue of multiple nationality and firm resettlement, as discussed in this chapter, *infra* Part IV.B.6. An applicant's residence in a third country does not necessarily mean that he or she was a national of that country, and thus, he or she would not be required to demonstrate inability or unwillingness to return to that country due to persecution or a well-founded fear of persecution. However, that residence would be relevant to determining whether the applicant had firmly resettled in that country for purposes of the firm resettlement bar to asylum eligibility.[52]
- **Practice Pointer**: The law library at the Library of Congress is a useful resource in answering questions regarding nationality. To seek guidance from the Library of Congress, go to *www.loc.gov/rr/askalib/ask-law.html.*[53]

If an applicant is not able to establish nationality, it does not make him or her ineligible for asylum.[54] Rather, the applicant will be considered stateless and his or her asylum eligibility will be determined based on the country of last habitual residence.[55]

2. *Statelessness*

The second reference to the term "nationality" in the refugee definition specifically allows for protection of an individual who has no nationality or who is stateless.[56] The United Nations defines "stateless person" as "a person who is not considered a national by any State under the operation of its law."[57] Thus, it is often essential to review other countries' nationality laws in preparing an asylum claim.

When nationality cannot be established, the applicant is considered "stateless," and the applicant must demonstrate that he or she is "outside any country in which such person last habitually resided."[58] The applicant must also establish persecution or a well-founded fear of persecution in such country of last habitual residence.[59] Being stateless in and of itself does not establish eligibility for asylum.[60]

---

[52] *See* 8 CFR §208.15 (2014); *see also infra* pt. IV.B.6. for a detailed discussion of the firm resettlement bar.

[53] (last visited Mar. 25, 2015).

[54] *See, e.g., Dulane v. INS*, 46 F.3d 988, 997 (10th Cir. 1995).

[55] *See* UNHCR Handbook, *supra* note 33, ¶ 89; *See also, e.g., Dulane*, 46 F.3d at 997.

[56] *See* INA §101(a)(42); 8 USC §1101(a)(42); *See also* UNHCR Handbook, *supra* note 33, ¶¶101–05.

[57] *See* Convention Relating to the Status of Stateless Persons, *done* Sep. 28, 1954 360 U.N.T.S. 117, art. I (1), (entered into force Jun. 6, 1960) [hereinafter Convention regarding Stateless Persons], *available at* www.refworld.org/docid/3ae6b3840.html.

[58] *See* INA §101(a)(42); 8 USC §1101(a)(42) (2012); *see also* UNHCR Handbook, *supra* note 33, ¶¶101–05.

[59] *See* UNHCR Handbook, *supra* note 33, ¶¶ 89, 102; *See also Ahmed v. Keisler*, 504 F.3d 1183, 1191 n.5 (9th Cir. 2007); *see also Faddoul v. INS*, 37 F.3d 185, 190 (5th Cir. 1994). Nationality must be

Continued

Based on the INA definition of residence, the definition of "last habitual residence" has been adopted as "a place of general abode" or the applicant's "principal, actual dwelling place in fact, without regard to intent."[61] This definition was accorded *Chevron*[62] deference by the U.S. Court of Appeals for the Third Circuit in *Paripovic v. Gonzales*, [63] which held that a stateless Croatian last habitually resided in Serbia, where he had lived for two years, even though the stateless applicant did not intend to reside there. The Third Circuit also found the amount of time the applicant resided in Serbia to be relevant to determining whether his residence there was "habitual."[64] There is no bright-line rule for the length of time an applicant must reside somewhere before it is considered "habitual," but rather, the facts must be considered on a case-by-case basis.

The Asylum Officer Basic Training Course (AOBTC) notes that even though an applicant may have resided in more than one country and fear persecution in more than one country, his or her claim "should be analyzed based on the country of *last* habitual residence only."[65] The AOBTC also cautions that "last habitual residence" is distinct from, and should not be confused with, firm resettlement. An applicant may have last habitually resided in a country, even if he or she has not been firmly resettled there.[66] Nevertheless, at least two circuit courts have held that the BIA's determination that a person was firmly resettled in a country is an implicit finding that the person last habitually resided there.[67]

The break-up of the Soviet Union and unresolved land and nationality issues in the Middle East and other regions of the world have contributed to a rising number of stateless persons across the globe. Such persons are afforded protection under U.S. asylum law if they are able to establish past persecution or a well-founded fear of persecution in their country of last habitual residence. For example, Palestinians who resided in Saudi Arabia, Qatar, and the United Arab Emirates—and who, following the Persian Gulf War, were expelled, denied re-entry, and/or had their property

---

established by a preponderance of the evidence; otherwise, the applicant is considered stateless. *See* AOBTC Workbook, pt. I, *supra* note 34, at 10.

[60] *See* UNHCR Handbook, *supra* note 33, ¶ 102; *see also Ahmed*, 504 F.3d at 1191; *Faddoul*, 37 F.3d at 190.

[61] INA §101(a)(33); 8 USC §1101(a)(33) (2012). *See also* 8 CFR §214.7(a)(4)(i) (2014) (defining "habitual residence" as the "place of general abode or a principle, actual dwelling place of a continuing or lasting nature").

[62] *Chevron U.S.A., Inc. v. Natural Resources Defense Council, Inc.*, 467 U.S. 837 (1984).

[63] *Paripovic v. Gonzales*, 418 F.3d 240, 244 (3d Cir. 2005).

[64] *Id.*

[65] AOBTC Workbook, pt. I, *supra* note 34, at 13; *see also* UNHCR Handbook, *supra* note 33, ¶ 104.

[66] AOBTC Workbook, pt. I, *supra* note 34, at 13; *See infra* pt. IV.B.6. for a detailed discussion of firm resettlement.

[67] *Tesfamichael v. Gonzales*, 469 F.3d 109, 115 (5th Cir. 2006); *Al Najjar v. Ashcroft*, 257 F.3d 1262, 1294 (11th Cir. 2001).

confiscated—may be eligible for asylum in the United States.[68] The mere fact that a stateless applicant's country of last habitual residence refuses to allow the applicant to return does not negate an asylum claim from that country.[69] Overall, the country of last habitual residence must be determined on a case-by-case basis.

B. Unable or Unwilling to Return or Avail Oneself of Protection

Once the country of nationality or last habitual residence is established, the asylum applicant must demonstrate that he or she is unable or unwilling to return to, and unable or unwilling to avail him or herself of, the protection of that country because of persecution or a well-founded fear of persecution.[70]

1. Unable or Unwilling to Return

An applicant's fear of return and refusal of their own government's protection is what makes him or her "unwilling" to return to the country in question. As UNHCR's Handbook provides:

> [A]n applicant's well-founded fear of persecution must be in relation to the country of his nationality. As long as he has no fear in relation to the country of his nationality, he can be expected to avail himself of that country's protection. He is not in need of international protection and is therefore not a refugee.[71]

The term "unwilling," therefore, relates to the applicant's fears and refers to individuals who refuse to accept the protection of their home countries.[72]

In contrast, circumstances beyond the will of the applicant or a refusal of protection by the government in question are what make him or her "unable" to avail him or herself of the protection of that country.[73] The UNHCR Handbook recognizes that when a country is in a state of war, including civil war or other grave disturbance, it may either be prevented from extending protection or such protection may be ineffective.[74] Moreover, in cases in which protection by the country of nationality may be purposefully denied to the applicant, such denial of protection may confirm the applicant's fear of persecution and may even be an element of the

---

[68] *See* Immigration and Naturalization Servs., Legal Opinion: Palestinian Asylum Applicants, Genco Op. No. 95-14 (1995 WL 1796321), *reprinted in* 72 INTERPRETER RELEASES 1553 (Nov. 13, 1995); *see also Ouda v. INS*, 324 F.3d 445 (6th Cir. 2003) (granting asylum to a Palestinian forced to leave Kuwait).

[69] *Ouda*, 324 F.3d at 452–53 (6th Cir. 2003) (noting that refusal to accept the applicant could be further evidence of persecution).

[70] INA §101(a)(42); 8 USC §1101(a)(42) (2012). *See also Matter of D–V–*, 21 I&N Dec. 77, 78 (BIA 1993).

[71] UNHCR Handbook, *supra* note 33, ¶ 90.

[72] *Id.* ¶ 100.

[73] UNHCR Handbook, *supra* note 33, ¶ 98-100.

[74] *Id.* ¶ 98.

persecution.[75] Therefore, a denial of services, such as a refusal of a national passport or extension of its validity or denial of admittance to the home territory, may constitute a refusal of protection within the refugee definition.[76]

If an asylum applicant has returned to his or her country of past or feared persecution, such a return may indicate that he or she is willing and able to return. However, returning to the country of past or feared persecution does not in and of itself preclude eligibility for asylum. An applicant may be unwilling and unable to return to the country of past or feared persecution, but circumstances may have compelled his or her return.[77] For example, an applicant may be compelled to return to the country of past or feared persecution to assist family members in fleeing or to tend to sick or dying relatives.[78]

Relevant considerations beyond the reasons the applicant returned to the country of feared persecution include how long the applicant visited the country of past or feared persecution, the circumstances surrounding the visit, and any problems that the applicant faced upon return.[79] For example, an applicant may have been willing and able to return to the country of past or feared persecution, but upon experiencing harm or threats while visiting, the applicant may no longer be willing and able to return. On the other hand, if the applicant was living openly and safely while in the country of past or feared persecution, that may be relevant to whether the applicant's fear of future persecution is well-founded.[80]

Asylum applicants who return to the country of past or feared persecution after filing their applications, absent "compelling reasons," are considered to have

---

[75] *Id.*

[76] *Id.* ¶ 99.

[77] *See De Santamaria v. Att'y Gen.*, 525 F.3d 999 (11th Cir. 2008) (rejecting the argument "that a voluntary return to one's home country always and inherently negates completely a fear of persecution" where the applicant had returned to Colombia to be with her family and to continue to work against her persecutors).

[78] *Cooke v. Mukasey*, 538 F.3d 899, 904-05 (8th Cir. 2008) (finding that a Liberian applicant's failure to seek asylum on an earlier trip did not make his claim less significant and his reason for not seeking asylum was reasonable where he returned home after being persecuted to assist his three minor children in escaping); *Smolniakova v. Gonzales*, 399 F.3d 1037, 1050 (9th Cir. 2005) (reversing the IJ's determination that the respondent would not face persecution because she traveled to Russia on three occasions to tend to her dying mother); *Karouni v. Gonzales*, 399 F.3d 1163, 1175-76 (9th Cir. 2005) (stating that returning to Lebanon for two months and then one month because parents were dying does not constitute substantial evidence that the applicant's fear was not well-founded).

[79] Problems faced upon return, or a lack thereof, may also be relevant to whether the applicant's fear of persecution is well-founded. *See infra* pt. II.D.2. for a detailed discussion of the well-founded fear standards.

[80] See *infra* pt. II.D.2. for a detailed discussion of well-founded fear and return to the country of past or feared persecution.

abandoned their asylum applications unless a preponderance of the evidence indicates that the application has not been abandoned.[81]

- **Practice Pointer**: Practitioners should strongly caution their clients against traveling outside of the United States while their applications are pending, especially to the country of feared persecution. However, if travel is necessary, advance parole must first be obtained.[82]

2. *Unable or Unwilling to Avail Oneself of Protection*

In addition to being unwilling or unable to return to the country of past or feared persecution, the applicant must also demonstrate that he or she is unwilling or unable to avail him or herself of the protection of that country.[83] Even if it might be possible for an applicant to seek protection in his or her country of past or feared persecution, he or she may still be unwilling to do so. The fact that an individual has applied for asylum in the United States should be sufficient proof that he or she is unwilling to seek protection in the country he or she fled.[84] Since the refugee definition permits being either unwilling or unable to avail oneself of protection, if the applicant is able to demonstrate he or she is unwilling to avail him or herself of that protection, he or she does not need to establish an inability to do so.[85] Thus, the filing of an asylum application demonstrates an unwillingness to avail oneself of the country of past or feared persecution and is generally sufficient to satisfy this legal element of asylum eligibility.

C. Definition of Persecution

The applicant's inability or refusal to return to and avail him or herself of the country of nationality or habitual residence must stem from past persecution or a well-founded fear of persecution.[86] To meet the requirements of this standard, the applicant must first show that the harm experienced or feared is sufficiently serious to amount to "persecution."[87] Persecution is a broad term that is not defined in the INA, nor has the BIA specifically defined it.[88] As UNHCR acknowledges in its Handbook, "persecution" is difficult to define:

---

[81] 8 CFR §208.8(b) (2014).

[82] See chapter 13 for a detailed discussion of advance parole and travel while an asylum application is pending.

[83] INA §101(a)(42)(A).

[84] AOBTC Workbook, pt. I, *supra* note 34, at 13.

[85] *See* INA §101(a)(42)(A).

[86] INA §101(a)(42)(A).

[87] AOBTC Workbook, pt. I, *supra* note 34, at 16.

[88] *Stanojkova v. Holder*, 645 F.3d 943, 948–49 (7th Cir. 2011) (explaining that the BIA's regulations and decisions do not provide a useful definition of persecution and criticizing the BIA for abandoning this difficult responsibility to the courts); *Gomes v. Gonzales*, 473 F.3d 746, 753–54 (7th Cir. 2007); *Sahi v. Gonzales*, 416 F.3d 587, 588–89 (7th Cir. 2005) (criticizing the BIA for failing to discharge its

Continued

There is no universally accepted definition of "persecution," and various attempts to formulate such a definition have met with little success … [I]t may be inferred that a threat to life or freedom on account of race, religion, nationality, political opinion or membership of a particular social group is always persecution. Other serious violations of human rights — for the same reasons — would also constitute persecution.[89]

Thus, the job of defining what harm rises to the level of persecution largely has been left to the courts.

In general, case law has defined persecution as "a threat to the life or freedom of, or the infliction of suffering or harm upon, those who differ in a way regarded as offensive,"[90] or to overcome a characteristic of the victim.[91] According to UNHCR, persecution may include a threat to life or freedom, or other serious violations of human rights on account of a protected ground.[92] Customary international law is generally considered to forbid the following human rights violations, even in the absence of a treaty:

- Genocide;
- Slavery;
- Torture, and other cruel, inhuman, or degrading treatment;
- Prolonged detention without notice of and an opportunity to contest the grounds for detention;
- Rape and other severe forms of sexual violence;

---

duty as an agency to define "persecution" and adding, "[W]e haven't a clue as to what it thinks religious persecution is.").

[89] UNHCR Handbook, *supra* note 33, ¶ 51. *See also Chen v. INS*, 359 F.3d 121, 128 (2d Cir. 2004) (non-life threatening violence and physical abuse also constitute torture).

[90] *Matter of Acosta*, 19 I&N Dec. 211, 222 (BIA 1985) (defining persecution as harm or suffering inflicted upon an individual in order to punish the individual for possessing a belief or characteristic the persecutor seeks to overcome). *See also Li v. Att'y Gen.*, 400 F.3d 157, 164-68 (3d Cir. 2005); *Matter of Kasinga*, 21 I&N Dec. 357, 365 (BIA 1996) (holding that persecution is the infliction of harm or suffering by a government, or by persons a government is unwilling and unable to control, to overcome a characteristic of the victim).

[91] *See Matter of Kasinga*, 21 I&N Dec. at 365 (finding that female genital mutilation is a form of persecution). The U.S. Court of Appeals for the First Circuit has noted that persecution is a "protean word, capable of many meanings." *See Kadri v. Mukasey*, 543 F.3d 16, 21 (1st Cir. 2008) (finding that mistreatment can constitute persecution even though it does not embody a direct or unremitting threat to life or freedom). The U.S. Court of Appeals for the Seventh Circuit defines persecution as "punishment or the infliction of harm for political, religious or other reasons that this country does not recognize as legitimate." *See Bace v. Ashcroft*, 352 F.3d 1133, 1137 (7th Cir. 2003) (noting that the actions must rise above the level of mere harassment). The U.S. Court of Appeals for the Eighth Circuit's definition is "the infliction or threat of death, torture, or injury to one's person or freedom…"); *see Ngure v. Ashcroft*, 367 F.3d 975, 989-90 (8th Cir. 2004).

[92] UNHCR Handbook, *supra* note 33, ¶¶ 51–55.

- Violation of the right to recognition as a person in the law; and
- Violation of the right to freedom of thought, conscience, and religion or belief.[93]

However, UNHCR also confirms in its Handbook that less serious harm also may rise to the level of persecution, depending on the circumstances.[94] Other examples of persecution may include:

- Threats to life, confinement, and torture;[95]
- Rape, sexual assault, or other sexual abuse;[96]
- Female genital mutilation;[97]
- Coercive population control, including forced abortion, forced sterilization, harm for failure or refusal to undergo these procedures, and harm for resisting coercive population control programs;[98]

---

[93] AOBTC Workbook, pt. 1, *supra* note 34, at 22-23.

[94] UNHCR Handbook, *supra* note 33, ¶¶ 51-55.

[95] *Chang v. INS*, 119 F.3d 1055, 1066 (3d Cir. 1997).

[96] *Shoafera v. INS*, 228 F.3d 1070, 1074 (9th Cir. 2000). *See also Zubeda v. Ashcroft,* 333 F.3d 463, 472 (3d Cir. 2003) (discussing rape as form of torture); *Hernandez-Montiel v. INS,* 225 F.3d 1084, 1097-98 (9th Cir. 2000) (finding that an applicant who was sodomized and forced to perform oral sex suffered harm rising to the level of persecution); *Angoucheva v. INS*, 106 F.3d 781 (7th Cir. 1997) (per curiam) (remanding to the BIA for consideration of whether a sexual assault that could have led to rape amounted to persecution on account of the applicant's political opinion); *Lopez-Galarza v. INS,* 99 F.3d 954, 959 (9th Cir. 1996) (discussing the physical and psychological harm caused by rape); *Matter of D–V–*, 21 I&N Dec. 77, 79–80 (BIA 1993) (finding pro-Aristide activist who was gang-raped and beaten because of her political views and religion suffered grievous harm and had a well-founded fear of persecution). Some relevant factors to consider in determining whether less severe sexual harm or harassment amounts to persecution include: any resulting psychological harm, the social or cultural perceptions of victims of sexual harm; and other effects on the applicant resulting from the harm. *See, e.g., Angoucheva v. INS*, 106 F.3d 781 (7th Cir. 1997) (per curiam) (remanding for consideration of whether a sexual assault that could have led to rape amounted to persecution).

[97] *Bah v. Mukasey,* 529 F.3d 99 (2d Cir. 2008); *see also Niang v. Gonzales,* 492 F.3d 505 (4th Cir. 2007); *Agbor v. Gonzales,* 487 F.3d 499 (7th Cir. 2007); *Hassan v. Gonzales,* 484 F.3d 513 (8th Cir. 2007); *Barry v. Gonzales*, 445 F.3d 741, 745 (4th Cir. 2006); *Mohammed v. Gonzales*, 400 F.3d 785, 796 (9th Cir. 2005); *Toure v. Ashcroft,* 400 F.3d 44 (1st Cir. 2005); *Niang v. Gonzales,* 422 F.3d 1187 (10th Cir. 2005); *Abay v. Ashcroft*, 368 F.3d 634, 638 (6th Cir. 2004) (threat of female genital mutilation to daughter amounts to a well-founded fear for daughter *and* mother); *Nwaokolo v. INS,* 314 F.3d 303, 308 (7th Cir. 2002); *Abankwah v. INS*, 185 F.3d 18, 23 (2d Cir. 1999); *Matter of S-A-K- & H-A-H-,* 24 I&N Dec. 464 (BIA 2008); *Matter of Kasinga*, 21 I&N Dec. at 365 (finding that female genital mutilation is a form of persecution). An important consideration regarding whether FGM rises to the level of persecution is whether the applicant herself experienced or would experience the procedure as serious harm versus whether the applicant welcomed or would welcome the procedure as a cultural right.

[98] *See* INA §101(a)(42), *as amended by* Illegal Immigration Reform and Immigrant Responsibility Act of 1996, Pub. L. No. 104-208, §601, 101 Stat. 3009-546 [hereinafter IIRAIRA]; *Nai Yuan Jiang v. Holder*, 611 F.3d 1086, 1095-97 (9th Cir. 2011) (finding past persecution under the totality of the circumstances approach, where a man's partner was subjected to forced abortion and he was subjected to detention, fines, prohibition on his marriage to her, and punishment for cohabitation with her);

Continued

- Beatings causing loss of consciousness and/or broken bones;[99]
- Threats and attacks, even if the applicant has not been beaten or physically harmed;[100]
- Illegal arrest, death threats by the military, and being searched for by the government;[101]
- Ethnic cleansing;[102]
- Detention in a concentration camp that includes detention in an underground cell, forced labor, and lack of access to family and friends for a period of several years;[103]

Yuqing Zhu v. Gonzales, 493 F.3d 588 (5th Cir. 2007) (reversing the finding that the abortion was not forced where the applicant underwent an abortion before the authorities discovered she was pregnant, and reasoning that the applicant underwent the abortion because she believed the law required it and she feared severe consequences for her and her child if she did not undergo the abortion); *Wang v. Ashcroft*, 341 F.3d 1015, 1020 (9th Cir. 2003); *Matter of J–S–*, 24 I&N Dec 520 (AG 2008) (vacating *Matter of C–Y–Z–*, 21 I&N Dec. 915 (BIA 1997), & holding that there is no per se eligibility for asylum for spouses of those who are forced to undergo coercive population control methods); *Matter of Y–T–L–*, 23 I&N Dec. 601, 607 (BIA 2003) (holding that "[c]oerced sterilization is better viewed as a permanent and continuing act of persecution that has deprived a couple of the natural fruits of conjugal life, and the society and comfort of the child or children that might eventually have been born to them"); *Matter of X–P–T–*, 21 I&N Dec 634 (BIA 1996) (granting asylum to an applicant who was forcibly sterilized). *See generally,* U.N. High Comm'r for Refugees, *UNHCR Note on Refugee Claims Based on Coercive Family Planning Laws or Policies* (Aug. 2005), *available at* www.refworld.org/docid/4301a9184.html; David A. Martin, Office of General Counsel, *Asylum Based on Coercive Family Planning Policies – Section 601 of the Illegal Immigration Reform and Immigrant Responsibility Act of 1996*, Memorandum to Management Team (Oct. 21, 1996). *See infra* pt. II.E.2.v.b. for a detailed discussion on coercive population control practices as a basis for asylum protection.

[99] *Irasoc v. Mukasey*, 522 F.3d 727, 730 (7th Cir. 2008) (genital beatings by Romanian police officers that caused the applicant to lose consciousness constitute persecution); *Voci v. Gonzales*, 409 F.3d 607, 609 (3d Cir. 2005) (finding multiple beating by the Albanian police, including one in which the applicant suffered a broken knee, amounted to persecution).

[100] *Madrigal v. Holder,* 716 F.3d 499, 504 (9th Cir. 2013) (finding past persecution where members of Los Zetas attempted to find a former member of the Mexican military and sent him a threatening note, coupled with a drive-by-shooting); *Baballah v. Ashcroft*, 367 F.3d 1067, 1074 (9th Cir. 2004); *Jahed v. INS*, 356 F.3d 991, 999 (9th Cir. 2004) (threats of exposing the applicant's past participation in the Mojahedin and extortion amount to persecution); *Rios v. Ashcroft*, 287 F.3d 895, 900 (9th Cir. 2002) (death threats by anonymous callers is sufficient basis to find persecution).

[101] *Bellido v. Ashcroft,* 367 F.3d 840, 845 (8th Cir. 2004) (an illegal arrest, a death threat from the military, and the government's search for the applicant amount to persecution).

[102] *Knezevic v. Ashcroft*, 367 F.3d 1206, 1212 (9th Cir. 2004) (ethnic Serb applicants suffered past persecution by Croats engaged in a campaign of ethnic cleansing).

[103] *Phommasoukha v. Gonzales*, 408 F.3d 1011, 1015 (8th Cir. 2005) (finding that the IJ's determination that imprisonment in a concentration camp does not constitute past persecution was not supported by substantial evidence).

- Detention at a psychiatric institution or forced "treatments";[104]
- Inability to earn a livelihood, travel safely within a country, and forced expulsion from the country;[105]
- A country's program of denaturalization and deportation;[106]
- Forbidding one from practicing his or her religion;[107]
- Repeated beatings and threats;[108]
- Kidnapping, coupled with beatings and/or threats, cumulatively;[109]
- Expulsion from a country, denial of re-entry, and the uncompensated confiscation of property;[110]
- Severe, targeted deprivations on account of a protected ground;[111]
- Recruitment attempts coupled with death threats;[112]

---

[104] *Kojevnikova v. Reno*, No. 97-4214, 1999 U.S. App. LEXIS 6368, at *4–5 (2d Cir. Apr. 6, 1999) (determining that detention for some months at a "psychiatric" institution amounts to past persecution); *Pitcherskaia v. INS*, 118 F.3d 641, 647–48 (9th Cir 1997) (finding that forced institutionalization, electroshock treatments, and drug injections to "treat" the applicant's homosexuality constitute persecution, thereby rejecting the BIA's requirement that the applicant demonstrate that her persecutors intended to harm her).

[105] *Un v. Gonzales*, 415 F.3d 205, 210 (1st Cir. 2005) (finding that verbal death threats may amount to persecution); *Ouda v. INS*, 324 F.3d 445, 454 (6th Cir. 2003).

[106] *Giday v. Gonzales*, 434 F.3d 543, 553–56 (7th Cir. 2006).

[107] *See, e.g.*, *Bucur v. INS*, 109 F.3d 399, 405 (7th Cir. 1997).

[108] *Duarte de Guinac v. INS*, 179 F.3d 1156, 1162 (9th Cir. 1999) (positing that repeated beatings coupled with explicit expressions of ethnic hatred and death threats amounts to persecution); *Borja v. INS*, 175 F.3d 732, 738 (9th Cir. 1999) (finding that beatings and assaults for the purpose of financial extortion constitute persecution).

[109] *Camara v. Att'y Gen.*, 527 F.3d 196, 204–05 (3d Cir. 2009) (finding persecution where a father was kidnapped in front of the applicant and the applicant and her family members were then threatened by an identifiable group in Ivory Coast); *Martinez-Ruiz v. Gonzales*, 479 F.3d 762, 766 n.2 (11th Cir. 2007); *Tarubac v. INS*, 182 F.3d 1114, 1118 (9th Cir. 1999) (finding applicant who was kidnapped, beaten, held without food, and repeatedly threatened was subjected to persecution); *Matter of V–T–S–*, 21 I&N Dec. 792, 798–99 (BIA 1997) (finding that kidnapping is a serious offense that may constitute persecution, but it must be on account of one of the five enumerated grounds).

[110] *See also* Immigration and Naturalization Servs., Legal Opinion: Palestinian Asylum Applicants, Genco Op. No. 95-14 (1995 WL 1796321), *reprinted in* 72 *Interpreter Releases* 1553 (Nov. 13, 1995) (noting that expulsion from a country, denial of re-entry, and the uncompensated confiscation of property may be violations of basic human rights amounting to persecution).

[111] *Begzatowski v. INS*, 278 F.3d 665, 669–70 (7th Cir. 2002) (finding that ethnic Albanian who was physically abused, deprived of bathing facilities, forced into battle without ammunition, and deprived of basic survival tools suffered persecution by the Yugoslavian army).

[112] *Garrovillas v. INS*, 156 F.3d 1010, 1016 (9th Cir. 1998) (finding that recruitment attempts and death threats are sufficient to show persecution).

- Repeated physical assaults, imposed isolation, and deprivation of education;[113]
- Confiscation of property, attempted bomb attack, continuous threats, and a physical assault;[114]
- Detention coupled with threats;[115]
- Detention coupled with physical abuse, cumulatively;[116] and
- Compelling an individual to engage in conduct that is abhorrent to his or her deepest beliefs.[117]

Thus, as this list demonstrates, "persecution" may encompass harm other than threats to life or freedom[118] and other than serious human rights violations. It may include certain physical harm that is not life-threatening, threats, cumulative harm, psychological harm, harm to family members or other third parties, severe economic disadvantage or deprivation of life essentials, confinement and detention, harassment and discrimination, and malignant prosecutions. However, the term "persecution" does not encompass all harm or treatment that society regards as unfair, unjust, or

---

[113] *Matter of S–A–*, 22 I&N Dec. 1328, 1335 (BIA 2000) (finding that repeated physical assaults, imposed isolation, and deprivation of an education amounted to persecution).

[114] *Karki v. Holder*, 715 F.3d 792, 800–06 (10th Cir. 2013) (reversing an asylum denial where the BIA found no past persecution where the Nepalese applicant's property had been confiscated, he was the subject of a missed bomb attack, he was continually threatened by Maoists, and physically assaulted by them resulting in his being treated at a hospital).

[115] *Javhlan v. Holder*, 626 F.3d 1119 (9th Cir. 2010) (finding past persecution where a Mongolian who refused to join the Community Party was briefly held for four to five hours but received many threats to her life, resulting in mental anguish, a nervous breakdown, and a partial stroke); *Diallo v. Att'y Gen..*, 596 F.3d 1329, 1333–34 (11th Cir. 2010) (reversing an asylum denial where a Guinean member of the RPG party was taken into custody after armed soldiers killed his brother and told him he would be executed the next day); *Matter of Toboso-Alfonso,* 20 I&N Dec. 819 (BIA 1990) (detention and threat of imprisonment is persecution).

[116] *Shi v. Att'y Gen.*, 707 F.3d 1231 (11th Cir. 2013) (finding that past persecution was cumulatively established where church services were broken up and the family's Bible confiscated, the applicant was detained for several days, slapped, thrown to the floor, and handcuffed to an iron bar overnight outside in the rain); *Haider v. Holder*, 595 F.3d 276, 286–88 (6th Cir. 2010) (finding cumulative persecution where Algerian police repeatedly stopped and searched the applicant, threatened the applicant repeatedly, sexually humiliated him, punched, and detained him);

[117] *Fatin v. INS*, 12 F.3d 1233, 1242 (3d Cir. 1993) (stating that being forced to renounce one's religious beliefs or to desecrate an object of religious importance might be persecution if the applicant holds strong religious beliefs). *See also* U.N. High Comm'r for Refugees, *UNHCR Guidelines on International Protection: Religion-Based Refugee Claims under Article 1A(2) of the 1951 Convention and/or the 1967 Protocol Relating to the Status of Refugees*, U.N. Doc. HCR/GIP/04/06 (Apr. 28, 2004) [hereinafter UNHCR Guidelines in Religion-Based Refugee Claims], *available at www.unhcr.org/40d8427a4.html* (indicating that forced compliance might rise to the level of persecution if "it becomes an intolerable interference with the individual's own religious belief, identity, or way of life and/or if noncompliance would result in disproportionate punishment").

[118] *INS v. Stevic*, 467 U.S. 407 (1984).

even unlawful or unconstitutional.[119] Nor does the term embrace harm solely arising out of civil strife or anarchy,[120] nor generalized conditions of hardship that affect entire populations.[121] As one commentator has observed:

There being no limits to the perverse side of human imagination, little purpose is served by attempting to list all known measures of persecution. Assessments must be made from case to case by taking account, on the one hand, of the notions of individual integrity and human dignity and, on the other hand, of the manner and degree to which they stand to be injured.[122]

The BIA has clarified that "punitive" or "malignant" intent is not required for harm to constitute persecution.[123] What matters is whether the individual experienced the treatment as harm, not whether the perpetrator intended the treatment as harm.[124] For example, in determining whether female genital mutilation rises to the level of persecution, it is relevant whether the applicant herself experienced or would experience the procedure as serious harm versus whether she welcomed or would welcome the procedure as a cultural right. Therefore, the victim's characteristics, such as his or her age, feelings, opinions, and physical and psychological characteristics, must be considered in determining whether harm rises to the level of persecution.[125] Harm that is not sufficiently serious to amount to persecution for an

---

[119] *See, e.g., Ahmed v. Gonzales*, 467 F.3d 669, 673 (7th Cir. 2006) (finding that general conditions of hardship that affect entire populations are not persecution); *Mikhael v. INS*, 115 F.3d 299, 304 (5th Cir. 1997) (finding no past persecution where applicant was briefly detained twice, his home was bombed, his father was kidnapped and held for three days, and a brother was kidnapped and tortured); *Fatin v. INS*, 12 F.3d 1233, 1240 (3d Cir. 1993) (finding that the applicant failed to establish that the treatment she would face upon return to Iran amounts to persecution); *Prasad v. INS*, 47 F.3d 336 (9th Cir. 1995) (no past persecution where applicant was interrogated, beaten, and kicked while detained for six hours); *Matter of V–T–S–*, 21 I&N Dec. 792, 798 (BIA 1997) (holding that kidnapping was not persecution where the sole motivation was to make money).

[120] *See Matter of Acosta*, 19 I&N Dec. at 222, *modified on other grounds by Matter of Mogharrabi*, 19 I&N Dec. 439 (BIA 1987).

[121] *Capric v. Ashcroft*, 355 F.3d 1075, 1084 (7th Cir. 2004). *But see Popova v. INS*, 273 F.3d 1251 (9th Cir. 2001) (repeated harassment by the police and hospital co-workers, arrests, detentions, and disconnection of telephone amount to persecution); *Matter of O–Z– & I–Z–*, 22 I&N Dec. 23, 25–27 (BIA 1998).

[122] Guy S. Goodwin-Gill & Jane McAdams, THE REFUGEE IN INTERNATIONAL LAW 69 (2d ed. 1996).

[123] *See Matter of Kasinga*, 21 I&N Dec. at 357; Asylum and Withholding Definitions, 65 Fed. Reg. 76588, 76590 (Dec. 7, 2000) (to be codified at 8 CFR pt. 208).

[124] *See* Asylum and Withholding Definitions, 65 Fed. Reg. at 76590 (wherein legacy INS published proposed regulations that define persecution as "the infliction of objectively serious harm or suffering that is subjectively experienced as serious harm or suffering by the applicant…" but where the proposed regulations did not contain an effective date and it is not known when, or if, final regulations will be issued). *See also* AOBTC Workbook, pt. I, *supra* note 34, at 17.

[125] UNHCR Handbook, *supra* note 33, ¶ 52. *See Jorge-Tzoc v. Gonzales,* 435 F.3d 146, 150 (2d Cir. 2006) (finding that the IJ erred in failing to view the harm suffered by the applicant from the perspective of a child of seven years old, which was the age of the child at the time the harm was

Continued

adult, for example, may be sufficiently serious to amount to persecution for a child, especially if the persecutor was aware of the individual circumstances and exploited those circumstances in harming the applicant.[126]

What harm rises to the level of persecution, therefore, has been determined by the courts, and may vary widely between — and even within — circuits. Some of the more debated types of harm are discussed below.

- **Practice Pointer**: Practitioners should conduct thorough legal research in the circuit where their client's application will be presented. Practitioners should highlight their client's facts that are similar to helpful cases, while attempting to distinguish the facts of any potentially harmful cases.

1. Physical Harm

The United States Supreme Court has agreed that persecution may encompass more than threats to life or freedom.[127] In determining whether harm rises to the level of persecution, physical harm is a relevant consideration.[128] It may include violence and physical abuse that is not life-threatening.[129] There is no requirement that the individual have suffered serious injuries,[130] and there is no minimum number of incidents of physical harm required.[131]

---

experienced); *Liu v. Ashcroft,* 380 F.3d 307, 314 (7th Cir. 2004) (considering the applicant's age, 16 years old, in making a determination that the harm she suffered did not rise to the level of persecution).

[126] *See* AOBTC Workbook, pt. I, *supra* note 34, at 17. *See also* U.S. Citizenship & Immigration Servs., *Lesson: Guidelines for Children's Asylum Claims*, in Asylum Officer Basic Training Course Participant Workbook (Sept. 1, 2009) [hereinafter AOBTC Workbook, Guidelines for Children's Asylum], *available at www.uscis.gov/sites/default/files/USCIS/Humanitarian/Refugees%20%26%20 Asylum/Asylum/AOBTC%20Lesson%20Plans/Guidelines-for-Childrens-Asylum-Claims-31aug10. pdf.* See *infra* chapter 10 for a detailed discussion of special asylum standards and procedures for children.

[127] *INS v. Stevic*, 467 U.S. at 407.

[128] *See Ruiz v. Mukasey*, 526 F.3d 31, 37 (1st Cir. 2008) (stating that the BIA can properly consider the absence of physical harm as a factor in deciding whether the level of harm the applicant suffered was serious); *Sanchez-Jimenez, Att'y Gen.*, 492 F.3d 1223 (11th Cir. 2007) (finding that the applicant fortuitously escaping injury did not undermine the fact that being shot at while driving is sufficiently extreme to constitute persecution); *Mihalev v. Ashcroft*, 388 F.3d 722, 730 9th Cir. 2004) (holding that 10-day detention with daily beatings and hard labor constituted past persecution, even though no serious bodily injury); *Asani v. INS*, 154 F.3d 719, 723 (7th Cir. 1998) (remanding for a determination whether having two teeth knocked out and two-week detention with insufficient food and water constituted persecution).

[129] *See Vladimirova v. Ashcroft*, 377 F.3d 690, 696 (7th Cir. 2004) (finding that the IJ's statement that the conduct must involve a "threat to the life or freedom of the victim" is "simply wrong;" and that the beating that the applicant suffered, which resulted in a miscarriage, amounted to persecution); *Chen v. INS*, 359 F.3d 121, 128 (2d Cir. 2004).

[130] *See Asani*, 154 F.3d at 723 (remanding for a determination whether having two teeth knocked out and two-week detention with insufficient food and water constituted persecution); *Mihalev v. Ashcroft*, 388 F.3d 722, 730 9th Cir. 2004) (holding that 10-day detention with daily beatings and hard labor

Continued

Whether physical abuse rises to the level of persecution may depend on "whether [the] harm is systematic rather than reflective of a series of isolated incidents."[132] Courts have found that a series of isolated incidents that are not "systematic," even those including physical harm, may not be sufficient to compel a finding of persecution.[133] Courts often look to the severity, duration, and frequency of physical abuse in order to determine whether the harm amounts to persecution.[134]

---

constituted past persecution, even though no serious bodily injury); *Sanchez-Jimenez,* 492 F.3d at 1223 (finding that the applicant fortuitously escaping injury did not undermine the fact that being shot at while driving is sufficiently extreme to constitute persecution); *Ruiz v. Mukasey*, 526 F.3d 31, 37 (1st Cir. 2008) (stating that the BIA can properly consider the absence of physical harm as a factor in deciding whether the level of harm the applicant suffered was serious).

[131] *See, e.g., Vaduva v. INS,* 131 F.3d 689, 690 (7th Cir. 1997) (finding a single serious beating to constitute persecution). *See also Lumaj v. Gonzales,* 462 F.3d 574, 577 (6th Cir. 2006) (holding that while an isolated incident of persecution can give rise to a finding of past persecution, the single attack must be of "sufficient severity" to rise to the level of persecution).

[132] *Barsoum v. Holder*, 617 F.3d 73, 79 (1st Cir. 2010) ("The severity, duration, and frequency of physical abuse are factors relevant to this determination, as is whether harm is systematic rather than reflective of a series of isolated incidents.") (citations omitted) (internal quotation marks omitted).

[133] *See Kuruca v. Att'y Gen.*, 547 Fed.App. 126 (3d Cir. 2013) (holding that the harm the applicant suffered in Turkey did not rise to the level of persecution because he only suffered one attack resulting in a broken finger and abrasions, and reasoning that the attack was an isolated incident that did not result in serious injury); *Robenko v. Holder*, 693 F.3d 87 (1st Cir. 2012) (finding that the mistreatment the Ukrainian applicant described – detention and physical assault, threatening phone calls, being beaten and having a knife held to her throat – was not "systematic" but rather was "reflective of a series of isolated incidents" over the course of a particularly unpleasant year); *Jian Li Zheng v. Att'y Gen.*, 418 F. App'x 128 (3d Cir. 2011) (holding that the harm suffered by the applicant in China when he was beaten on the head, shoulders, and chest by police in attempting to keep them from taking his wife did not rise to the level of persecution when he was never arrested or otherwise punished for resisting the family planning authorities); *Barsoum v. Holder*, 617 F.3d 73, 79 (1st Cir. 2010) ("The severity, duration, and frequency of physical abuse are factors relevant to this determination, as is whether harm is systematic rather than reflective of a series of isolated incidents.") (citations omitted) (internal quotation marks omitted); *Chadha v. Att'y Gen.*, 386 F. App'x 319 (3d Cir. 2010) (holding that the Indian applicants were not subjected to past persecution on account of their involvement in the women's rights movement because the only act of physical harm was against the husband, and being slapped in the face and beaten on the legs by police did not require professional medical attention and did not amount to persecution); *Aquino-Rovas v. Att'y Gen.*, 431 F. App'x 200 (3d Cir. 2011) (holding that the actions of the MS-13 gang in El Salvador against the applicant – repeated demands for money, repeated attempts to recruit the applicant, and the shooting of the applicant's cousin – did not rise to the level of persecution against the applicant, because he was not threatened or personally harmed by the gang members); *Tasya v. Holder*, 574 F.3d 1 (1st Cir. 2009) (finding that the harm did not rise to the level of persecution for a husband and wife who were mugged and physically assaulted by a group of Muslims while the couple were returning home from church, after the wife had suffered various incidents of verbal abuse and harassment as a child in school and other members of the community's homes and shops had been burned); *Decky v. Holder,* 587 F.3d 104 (1st Cir. 2009) (holding that there was no past persecution where the applicant's injuries from a beating did not require him to go to the hospital, there was no evidence of comparable systematic mistreatment, and the beating was an "isolated event"); *Baharon v. Holder*, 588 F.3d at 228 (stating that a key difference between persecution and less severe mistreatment is that the former is "systematic" while the latter consists of isolated incidents, and finding that the applicant was persecuted in Yemen on account of his ethnicity

Continued

- **Practice Pointer**: In an asylum claim involving physical harm, it is important to document scars and other physical evidence of harm with photographs, affidavits from doctors and other medical professionals, and doctor and hospital records from the applicant's home country if treatment was sought there.
- **Practice Pointer**: Remember that persecution does not even have to be physical, as long as the harm suffered or feared rises to the level of persecution.[135] For example, even the violation of an applicant's fundamental beliefs may constitute persecution.[136]

2. *Threats*

Similarly, in some circumstances, serious threats made against the applicant may constitute persecution.[137] While threats alone may amount to persecution, in order to

---

and work for Sons of Hadramut when he was violently interrogated, detained for three days, beaten causing him "excruciating" pain, and threatened that he would "disappear"); *Traore v. Holder*, 358 F. App'x 677 (6th Cir. 2009) (holding that a single beating of the applicant, a citizen of Cote d'Ivoire, by the military in his home because of his support of the RDR party did not establish past persecution).

[134] *Thapaliya v. Holder*, 750 F.3d 56 (1st Cir. 2014) (holding that the severe beating of the applicant, a native of Nepal, on account of his membership in the anti-Maoist movement was an isolated event insufficient to establish past persecution); *Liu v. Holder*, 632 F.3d 820 (2d Cir. 2011) (finding that being punched repeatedly in the face, chest, and back did not amount to persecution, and noting that Mr. Liu suffered only minor bruising, which required no formal medical attention and had no lasting effect, and that the beating did not occur while he was detained); *Barsoum v. Holder*, 617 F.3d at 79; *Kazemzadeh v. Att'y Gen.*, 577 F.3d 1341, 1353 (11th Cir. 2009) (finding the harm did not rise to the level of persecution where the applicant was arrested, interrogated, beaten for five hours, detained for four days, monitored, and summoned to appear before a court); *Eusebio v. Ashcroft*, 361 F.3d 1088, 1091 (8th Cir. 2004) ("It is a well-established principle that minor beatings and brief detentions, even detentions lasting two or three days, do not amount to political persecution, even if government officials were motivated by political animus."). *But see Sirbu v. Holder*, 718 F.3d 655 (7th Cir. 2013) (finding that being beaten repeatedly on the head to the point of losing consciousness and suffering a concussion while in police custody was "more than sufficient to support a finding of past persecution"); *Shi*, 707 F.3d at 1231 (finding persecution where the applicant was detained for seven days, interrogated twice, slapped in the face, had his chair kicked out from underneath him, was threatened with being beaten by a baton, and was handcuffed to an iron bar outside in the rain overnight, requiring medical attention).

[135] *See Matter of T–Z–*, 24 I&N Dec. 163, 169–71 (BIA 2007). *See also Singh v. INS*, 134 F.3d 962, 967 (9th Cir. 1998); *Borca v. INS*, 77 F.3d 210, 215–17 (7th Cir. 1996).

[136] *Fatin v. INS*, 12 F.3d 1233, 1242 (3d Cir. 1993) (assuming "that the concept of persecution is broad enough to include governmental measures that compel an individual to engage in conduct that is not physically painful or harmful but is abhorrent to that individual's deepest beliefs").

[137] *Crespin-Valladares v. Holder*, 632 F.3d 117 (4th Cir. 2011) (finding that the threats against the applicant and his wife by the MS-13 gang in El Salvador on account of their agreeing to be prosecutorial witnesses rose to the level of persecution because country conditions showed significant gang violence in El Salvador, including vengeance against cooperating witnesses); *Diallo*, 596 F.3d at 1329 (finding past persecution where the applicant received a death threat from a soldier who had already killed the applicant's brother, because a credible threat by a person who has the immediate ability to act on it constitutes persecution regardless of whether the threat is successfully carried out); *Salazar-Paucar v. INS*, 281 F.3d 1069, 1074 (9th Cir. 2002), *amended by* 290 F.3d 264 (9th Cir. 2002).

do so, they must be "highly imminent and menacing in nature."[138] The following factors should be considered in determining whether threats rise to the level of persecution:

(1) whether the persecutor has attempted to act on the threats;

(2) whether the nature of the threat itself is indicative of its seriousness;

(3) whether the persecutor harmed or attempted to harm the applicant in other ways;

(4) whether the persecutor attacked, harassed, or threatened the applicant's family;

(5) whether the persecutor made such threats to others similarly situated to the applicant; and

(6) whether the applicant experienced emotional or psychological harm as a result of the threats.[139]

---

[138] *Chavarria v. Gonzales*, 446 F.3d 508, 518 (3d Cir. 2006) (holding that threats that are not imminent or concrete or did not result in physical violence or harm to the applicant do not constitute past persecution, but finding that the second threat the applicant received because of his imputed political opinion was highly imminent, concrete, and menacing). *See also Li v. Att'y Gen.*, 400 F.3d at 163–65, 165 n.3 (3d Cir. 2005) (finding that threats of sterilization and physical violence did not constitute past persecution because they were neither imminent nor concrete and neither the applicant nor his family were imprisoned, sterilized, or physically harmed, but noting that unfulfilled threats should be considered by the court in its determination of whether the applicant has a well-founded fear of future persecution); *Lim v. INS*, 224 F.3d 929, 936 (9th Cir. 2000) (finding that repeated death threats did not amount to *past* persecution where neither the applicant nor his family were ever "touched, robbed, imprisoned, forcibly recruited, detained, interrogated, trespassed upon, or even closely confronted" during a period of six years and holding that mere threats only amount to past persecution where they "are so menacing as to cause significant actual 'suffering or harm'"); *Boykov v. INS*, 109 F.3d 413, 416–17 (7th Cir. 1997) (holding that an applicant who criticized the communist government, had a friend disappear and later turn up murdered after a confrontation with government police, and who subsequently was threatened that he would "lose his job and his apartment, 'and something even worse could happen'" did not endure conduct that could be categorized as past persecution).

[139] AOBTC Workbook, pt. 1, *supra* note 34, at 18–20. *See also Mejia v. Att'y Gen,* 498 F.3d 1253, 1257–58 (11th Cir. 2007) (finding past persecution where, in addition to receiving death threats – including a condolence letter about his own death – the applicant was beaten with the butt of a rifle and a large rock was thrown at him); *Sanchez Jimenez v. Att'y Gen.,* 492 F.3d 1223, 1233 (11th Cir. 2007) (finding past persecution where, in addition to receiving personal death threats, the Colombian applicant's family members were also threatened with death and his daughter kidnapped to force him to abandon his anti-FARC political activities); *Salazar-Paucar*, 281 F.3d at 1074 (holding that multiple death threats, harm to family, and murders of counterparts constituted past persecution), *amended by* 290 F.3d 964 (9th Cir. 2002); *Navas v. INS,* 217 F.3d 646 (9th Cir. 2000) (finding that an applicant suffered past persecution when military officers, who had just killed the applicant's aunt, chased and shot at him, and when the applicant and his mother were threatened with death when the officers, not finding the applicant at home, beat the applicant's mother); *Garrovillas v. INS,* 156 F.3d 1010 (9th Cir. 1998) (finding that the receipt of three letters in three months containing black ribbons was a threat sufficiently serious to constitute persecution when many other people in the same area had been killed after receiving such letters); *Gonzales-Neyra v. INS,* 122 F.3d 1293, 1295–96 (9th Cir. 1997), *amended by* 133 F.3d 726 (9th Cir. 1998) (finding that the applicant suffered persecution when members of Sendero Luminso threatened him with death, repeatedly came to his house to find him, loitered in front

Continued

In evaluating claims of past persecution, the U.S. Court of Appeals for the Third Circuit limits the type of threats sufficient to show past persecution to those "that are so menacing as to cause significant actual 'suffering or harm.'"[140] The Third Circuit also requires that threats include only those that are "highly imminent and menacing in nature," holding that those that are not imminent or concrete or did not result in physical violence or harm to the applicant do not constitute past persecution.[141] Under this guidance, the court found that a death threat combined with a robbery at gunpoint that mimicked attacks of other members of the targeted group constituted past persecution because it was highly imminent and concrete and the applicant suffered harm from it.[142] By contrast, in *Li v. Att'y Gen.*, the Third Circuit did not characterize threats of sterilization and physical violence as past persecution because they were neither imminent nor concrete, and neither the applicant nor his family were imprisoned, sterilized, or physically harmed.[143] Similarly, the Third Circuit found that the harm did not rise to the level of persecution when gang members threw the applicant and his brother against a wall, pointed a gun in their faces, and threatened to kill them because their father was a police officer who investigated gang violence.[144] The court agreed with the BIA that this was a "one-time occurrence" and the applicant himself had not been harmed, so it was not so extreme as to rise to the level of persecution.[145] However, the court did note that unfulfilled threats should be considered by the court in its determination of whether the applicant has a well-founded fear of future persecution.[146]

The U.S. Court of Appeals for the Seventh Circuit has a similar requirement that threats be of a highly imminent and menacing nature in order to constitute past persecution. The Seventh Circuit also has pointed out that even if threats themselves do not rise to the level of past persecution, unfulfilled threats may indicate danger of future persecution that would make a fear well-founded.[147] Accordingly, the Seventh Circuit held that an applicant who criticized the communist government, had a friend disappear and later turn up murdered after a confrontation with government police,

---

of the family home, and forced the applicant's brother into hiding after threats that the brother would be harmed for not disclosing the applicant's whereabouts); *Sangha v. INS,* 103 F.3d 1482, 1487 (9th Cir. 1997) (finding that applicant suffered persecution when militants beat his father in his presence when demanding that the applicant be turned over to them).

[140] *Chavarria*, 446 F.3d at 518 (quoting *Li v. Att'y Gen.*, 400 F.3d at 159.

[141] *Id.*

[142] *Id.* at 520.

[143] *See Li v. Att'y Gen.*, 400 F.3d at 157.

[144] *Arriza-Escobar v. Att'y Gen.*, 382 F. App'x190 (3d Cir. 2010).

[145] *Id.* (citing *Gomez-Zuluaga v. Att'y Gen.*, 527 F.3d 330, 341 (3d Cir. 2008) ("'[W]e have limited the types of threats constituting persecution to only a small category of cases, and only when the threats are so menacing as to cause significant actual suffering or harm.'").

[146] *Li v. Att'y Gen.*, 400 F.3d at 163–65.

[147] *Boykov v. INS*, 109 F.3d 413, 416–17 (7th Cir. 1997).

and who subsequently was threatened that he would "lose his job and his apartment, 'and something even worse could happen,'" did not endure conduct that could be categorized as past persecution.[148]

The U.S. Court of Appeals for the Ninth Circuit also has held that mere threats only amount to past persecution where they "are so menacing as to cause significant actual 'suffering or harm.'"[149] The Ninth Circuit stated that "repeated and especially menacing death threats can constitute a primary part of a past persecution claim, particularly where those threats are combined with confrontation or other mistreatment."[150] For example, where the applicant's life and business had been threatened by a rebel group because of the applicant's political opinion, the Ninth Circuit found that the person had suffered past persecution.[151]

- **Practice Pointer**: Generally, isolated threats will not rise to the level of persecution.[152] However, even if a threat does not meet the various

---

[148] *Id.*

[149] *Lim*, 224 F.3d at 936.

[150] *Id.* (citing cases finding past persecution with a combination of repeated bribe attempts, personal confrontations and death threats; murder of family members, recruitment attempts, and death threats; and attack on family, personal confrontation, and death threats).

[151] *Gonzales-Neyra v. INS*, 122 F.3d 1293, 1296 (9th Cir. 1997), amended by 133 F.3d 726 (9th Cir. 1998). *C.f. Ventura v. INS*, 264 F.3d 1150, 1154 (9th Cir. 2001) (threats spray-painted on walls of applicant's house by guerrillas amount to well-founded fear of persecution); *Garrovillas v. INS*, 156 F.3d 1010, 1016 (9th Cir. 1998) (three death threats in four months sufficient to establish persecution); *Sangha v. INS*, 103 F.3d 1482, 1487 (9th Cir. 1997) (threats of death and violence from a terrorist group sufficient to establish persecution). *But see Matter of A–E–M–*, 21 I&N Dec. 1159 (BIA 1998) (painted threat on house does not rise to the level of persecution).

[152] *See Gharti-Magar v. Holder*, 551 F. App'x 197 (5th Cir. 2014) (holding that unfulfilled threats that the applicant received from Maoists in Nepal if he did not support them and turn over the money that he earned while working for the United Nations did not rise to the level of past persecution); *Badache v. Holder*, 492 F. App'x 124 (1st Cir. 2012) (finding that a single threat against the applicant by an Islamic militant terrorist group did not amount to past persecution and noting that while threats alone may amount to persecution if they are severe enough to "add up to more than ordinary harassment, mistreatment, or suffering," vague verbal threats "unaccompanied by any significant physical abuse and any government involvement do not amount to persecution"); *Arce v. Holder*, 449 F. App'x 404 (5th Cir. 2011) (holding that verbal threats against the Colombian applicant from unidentified FARC members did not constitute persecution, reasoning that the threats were unaccompanied by any physical harm or other significant deprivation); *Kukalo v. Holder*, 418 F. App'x 450 (6th Cir. 2011) (holding that the Ukrainian applicants failed to produce any evidence of past persecution because persecution "requires more than a few isolated incidents of verbal harassment or intimidation, unaccompanied by any physical punishment, infliction of harm, or significant deprivation of liberty."); *Montes v. Holder*, 394 F. App'x 95 (5th Cir. 2010) (finding that a woman in Guatemala whose family had been threatened on several occasions by a notorious criminal family over a business dispute had not suffered harm amounting to persecution, and emphasizing that persecution "requires more than a few isolated incidents of verbal harassment or intimidation, unaccompanied by any physical punishment, infliction of harm or significant deprivation of liberty"); *Ratnasingam v. Holder*, 556 F.3d 10 (1st Cir. 2009) (holding that the applicant was not subjected to past persecution when he was threatened in person and by phone in Sri Lanka on account of his membership in the Tamil Tigers party, because experiences that do not "rise above unpleasantness, harassment, and even basic suffering" are not persecution);

Continued

thresholds that the courts have established for showing that threats of harm rise to the level of persecution themselves, unfulfilled, specific threats of harm against an applicant on account of one of the five protected grounds may be sufficient to demonstrate a well-founded fear of future persecution.[153]

3. *Cumulative Harm*

No set number of incidents is required; one single incident of harm may be of sufficient severity to rise to the level of persecution, or several incidents considered together may constitute persecution.[154] Overall, harm must be considered "in the aggregate,"[155] and it is error to address incidents of harm in isolation.[156] Thus, even if a particular act does not amount to persecution on its own, it may still rise to the level of persecution when considered cumulatively with other adverse treatment.

As stated in the UNHCR Handbook, "various measures not in themselves amounting to persecution (*e.g.*, discrimination in different forms), in some cases combined with other adverse factors, such as a general atmosphere of insecurity in the country of origin, may amount to persecution on 'cumulative grounds.'"[157] For

---

Ravix v. Mukasey, 552 F.3d 42 (1st Cir. 2009) (finding that a series of isolated threats against a Haitian couple on account of the husband's involvement in an opposition political party amounted to harassment and not persecution, but acknowledging that in certain circumstances, imminent threats alone may be enough to constitute persecution); *Garcia Del Valle v. Holder*, 343 F. App'x 45 (6th Cir. 2009) (finding that the guerrillas' death threats against the applicant and his family if they did not join the rebel cause in Guatemala were insufficient to establish persecution); *Moran-Quinteros v. Holder*, 352 F. App'x 974 (6th Cir. 2009) (holding that the Guatemalan applicant failed to establish past persecution at the hands of the guerrillas, where he identified only one death threat against his family and recounted no incidents of physical harm).

[153] *Lim*, 224 F.3d at 935–36. See *infra* Part II.D.2. for a detailed discussion on establishing well-founded fear of future persecution.

[154] *Compare, e.g., Lumaj v. Gonzales*, 462 F.3d 574, 577 (6th Cir. 2006) (finding that a single incident in which the applicant was beaten at a political rally from which she suffered minor injuries but escaped being arrested by police officers did not rise to the level of persecution), *with Vaduva v. INS*, 131 F.3d 689, 690 (7th Cir. 1997) (finding a single serious beating to rise to the level of persecution).

[155] *Matter of O–Z– & I–Z–*, 22 I&N Dec. 23, 26 (BIA 1998).

[156] *See, e.g., Shi.*, 707 F.3d at 1231; *Ngengwe v. Mukasey*, 543 F.3d 1029, 1037 (8th Cir. 2008).

[157] UNHCR Handbook, *supra* note 33, at ¶ 53; *see also J.P.S. v. Att'y Gen.*, 384 F. App'x 185 (3d Cir. 2010) (holding that the FARC's verbal harassment, constant threats, murder of the applicant's brothers, and repeated physical attacks on the applicant on account of his sexual orientation, even if they did not result in life-threatening injuries to the applicant, may rise to the level of persecution); *Krotova v. Gonzales*, 416 F.3d 1080, 1084 (9th Cir. 2005) (the combination of sustained economic pressure, physical violence and threats against the applicant and her close associates, and the restrictions on her ability to practice her religion cumulatively amount to persecution); *Chand v. INS*, 222 F.3d 1066, 1074 n.15 (9th Cir. 2000) (finding the BIA erred by considering each incident of harm "in isolation, without analyzing the cumulative harm Chand suffered"); *Korablina v. INS*, 158 F.3d 1038, 1045 (9th Cir. 1998) (finding that, cumulatively, the experiences suffered by the petitioner compel the conclusion that she suffered persecution where, in conjunction with the political and social turmoil in her country, she received many threats against her life); *Matter of [name not provided]*, (IJ Dec. 20, 2000) (Baltimore,

Continued

example, cumulative instances of harassment or discrimination considered in totality may amount to persecution if each instance of harm was inflicted on account of a protected ground.[158]

> **Practice Pointer**: Demonstrating many instances of harm in the aggregate may require a practitioner to spend a significant amount of time with his or her client in order to gain the client's trust, build a clear understanding of each instance of harm, and obtain details about each incident. This can be particularly challenging with a traumatized client, who may struggle with recall or may not be forthcoming with details of harm suffered. Often, obtaining a psychological evaluation or recommending that the client see a mental health professional for therapy or counseling can assist in capturing the details about each event.

4. Psychological Harm

Non-physical harm that amounts to persecution may also include psychological harm.[159] In making a claim based on emotional or psychological harm, the applicant's own symptoms, evidence of any treatment needed, the events that caused the psychological harm, and the applicant's individual characteristics, such as age or trauma suffered due to past harm, are relevant considerations.[160]

MD) (Gossart, IJ), *reported in* 78 INTERPRETER RELEASES 233 (Jan. 15, 2001) (finding that refusal to render medical aid, firing or refusing to hire a person, and forcing someone to leave their community or state, due to their HIV status, when viewed cumulatively, amounts to persecution).

[158] *Precetaj v. Holder*, 649 F.3d 72 (1st Cir. 2011) (reversing the BIA and IJ's findings of no past persecution of an Albanian couple on account of their political involvement in the democratic party, where the incidents of threats and violence directed against the applicants were substantial and continued over almost a decade, and where the abuse against the applicant's children was systematic, serious, and designed to send a message to the applicants); *Tomas v. Holder*, 316 F. App'x 510 (7th Cir. 2009) (finding that the applicant's experiences in Bosnia-Herzegovina may have risen to the level of persecution cumulatively, where he suffered a campaign of intimidation and terror that intensified over a nine-month period until he so feared for his life and the safety of his pregnant wife that he abandoned his business and fled); *Mihalev v. Ashcroft,* 388 F.3d 722, 728 (9th Cir. 2004) (finding that an applicant who had established that only one of three incidents occurred on account of his nationality had to base his claim of past persecution on that one incident); *Chand*, 222 F.3d at 1073; *Korablina v. INS*, 158 F.3d 1038, 1045 (9th Cir. 1998); *Singh v. INS*, 94 F.3d 1353, 1360 (9th Cir. 1996); *Matter of O–Z– & I–Z–*, 22 I&N Dec. 23 (BIA 1998).

[159] *Matter of A–K–*, 24 I&N Dec. 275 (BIA 2007). *See also Mashiri v. Ashcroft*, 383 F.3d 1112 (9th Cir. 2004); *Khup v. Ashcroft*, 376 F.3d 898, 904 (9th Cir. 2004). *But see Shoaira v. Ashcroft*, 377 F.3d 837, 844 (8th Cir. 2004).

[160] *See Matter of A–K–,* 24 I&N Dec. at 275 (recognizing that an emotional persecution case could be recognized "where a person persecutes someone close to an applicant, such as a spouse, parent, child or other relative, with the intended purpose of causing emotional harm to the applicant, but does not directly harm the applicant himself"). *See also Mashiri*, 383 F.3d at 1112; *Khup*, 376 F.3d at 904. *But see Niang v. Gonzales,* 492 F.3d 505, 512 (4th Cir. 2007) (holding that parent's psychological suffering based on daughter's feared subjection to FGM upon removal was insufficient to establish persecution); *Shoaira*, 377 F.3d at 844.

Under certain circumstances, severe mental suffering may constitute torture under the Convention Against Torture and would amount to persecution. Examples of psychological torture may include mental harm caused by the intentional infliction or threatened infliction of severe physical pain, administration or threatened administration of mind-altering substances, other procedures calculated to profoundly disrupt the senses or the personality, threat of imminent death, or threat that another person will imminently be tortured or killed.[161]

However, severe mental suffering that does not constitute torture may still be sufficiently serious to rise to the level of persecution. Some examples of psychological harm that amounts to persecution include the applicant living in a state of constant fear due to threats over a prolonged period of time, being forced to witness others being harmed,[162] threats to family members, and being forced to comply with religious laws or practices that are abhorrent to the applicant's own beliefs.[163]

- **Practice Pointer**: A psychological evaluation by a mental health professional can be very effective evidence in documenting psychological harm rising to the level of persecution.

5. Harm to Family Members or Third Parties

Harm to family members or other third parties also may rise to the level of persecution.[164] In making a claim of persecution based on harm to family members or to third parties, the applicant must generally demonstrate that the harm to the third party actually amounted to persecution and caused the applicant's own persecution,

---

[161] *See* 8 CFR §208.18 (2014); *See generally infra* ch. 3 for a detailed discussion of what harm rises to the level of torture.

[162] *See Mashiri,* 383 F.3d at 1112 (finding that the emotional trauma suffered by a native of Afghanistan living in Germany was sufficiently severe to amount to persecution due to all of the experiences she suffered in the aggregate, including witnessing the harm of others who were similarly situated); *see also Khup,* 376 F.3d at 904 (finding that a Burmese Christian preacher suffered past persecution based on death threats and anguish caused when a similarly situated fellow minister was tortured, killed, and dragged through the streets of the town). *But see Shoaira,* 377 F.3d at 844 (holding that psychological trauma that resulted from applicant's witnessing three of her father's four arrests did not amount to past persecution, even where applicant exhibited symptoms of post-traumatic stress disorder).

[163] *See, e.g., Fatin v. INS,* 12 F.3d 1233, 1242 (3d Cir. 1993).

[164] *Matter of A–K–,* 24 I&N Dec. at 278 (recognizing that harm to a third party may constitute persecution of the applicant where the harm is serious enough to amount to persecution and the persecutor's motive in harming the third party was to cause harm to the applicant). *See also Navas v. INS*, 217 F.3d 646, 658 (9th Cir. 2000) (persecution of applicant included murder of two family members and beating of mother); Memorandum from Joseph Langlois on Persecution of an Asylum Applicant's Family Members, Immigration & Naturalization Servs. (June 30, 1997), *published on* AILA InfoNet at Doc. No. 97063090 (*posted* June 30, 1997) (on file with the author), *available at www.aila.org/content/default.aspx?docid=20274* (last visited Mar. 24, 2015).

whether physical or psychological.[165] If the persecutor's motive in harming the third party was actually to punish or harm the applicant him or herself, it is even more likely that the harm may rise to the level of persecution.[166] For example, the USCIS Asylum Division takes the position that forced abortion or forced sterilization of an asylum applicant's *spouse* or severe psychological harm suffered by an applicant from mere knowledge of or actually witnessing harm to another person could be considered persecution of the applicant.[167] On the other hand, harm targeted at family members or third parties that does not harm the applicant him or herself and that was not intended to harm the applicant, usually will not rise to the level of persecution.[168]

---

[165] *Kone v. Holder*, 620 F.3d 760 (7th Cir. 2010) holding that the threat of FGM to the applicants' U.S. citizen daughter could constitute direct persecution of the applicants, because unlike other "derivative harm" FGM cases, both parents were in removal proceedings and could not remain in the U.S. with their daughter, making the likelihood of FGM significantly higher); *Abay v. Ashcroft*, 368 F.3d 634, 641–42 (6th Cir. 2004) (threat of FGM to daughter amounts to a well-founded fear for daughter *and* mother); *See also Baballah v. Ashcroft*, 367 F.3d 1067, 1074–75 (9th Cir. 2004) ("[V]iolence directed against an applicant's family members provides support for a claim of persecution … ."). *But see Matter of A–K–*, 24 I&N Dec. at 275 (an applicant may not establish eligibility for asylum based solely on the fear that his or her daughter will be subjected to FGM); *See also Rodriguez v. Holder*, 366 F. App'x 555 (5th Cir. 2010) (finding that the applicant cannot rely solely on the persecution of his father to qualify for asylum, where his father was targeted and assaulted by FARC members in Colombia because of his political activities); *Olowo v. Ashcroft*, 368 F.3d 692 (7th Cir. 2004) (holding that a parent cannot obtain relief for herself based on potential FGM to her daughter); *Oforji v. Ashcroft*, 354 F.3d 609 (7th Cir. 2003) (holding that a parent cannot obtain relief for herself based on potential FGM to her daughter).

[166] *See Matter of A–K–,* 24 I&N Dec. at 278 (BIA 2007) (recognizing that eligibility can be established based on emotional persecution "where a person persecutes someone close to an applicant, such as a spouse, parent, child or other relative, with the intended purpose of causing emotional harm to the applicant, but does not directly harm the applicant himself"). *See also* Memorandum from Joseph Langlois, *supra* note 163; *See also Chouchkov v. INS*, 220 F.3d 1077 (9th Cir. 2000) (harm to father and mother-in-law and threats against wife amount to persecution of the applicant).

[167] *See* AOBTC Workbook, pt. 1, *supra* note 34, at 26 (emphasis added). *But see Peng Fei Ye v. Holder*, 542 F. App'x 247 (4th Cir. 2013) (holding that the applicant did not suffer past persecution when his wife became pregnant with a second child in China and was forced to terminate her pregnancy, because the petitioner himself was never arrested, detained, sterilized, or physically mistreated by the family planning authorities); *Jiannong Jiang v. Holder*, 400 F. App'x 859 (5th Cir. 2010) (noting that the Court's standard for asylum claims based on forced abortion is high and stating, "With regard to asylum claims based on the coerced abortion or sterilization of one's spouse, to prove persecution this court generally requires some showing of a higher degree of actual harm to the applicant himself or herself than Jiang has shown here"); *Fangwen Yang v. Holder*, 405 F. App'x 825 (5th Cir. 2010) (holding that the applicant did not establish past persecution in China on account of his refusal to abide by the family planning policy, because an applicant's wife's forced abortion does not make the applicant presumptively eligible for asylum or withholding of removal).

[168] *See Perlera-Sola v. Holder*, 699 F.3d 572 (1st Cir. 2012) (stating that persecution on account of kinship applies only where the motivation for persecution is kinship, and not because multiple family members happen to be persecuted for a common reason but the animus is not kinship); *Ashqar v. Holder*, 355 F. App'x 705 (4th Cir. 2009) (finding that the applicant, a citizen of Palestine, had not been persecuted herself, when her husband was arrested, beaten, tortured, and held in jail for sixteen days by the Israeli military for having participated in a demonstration protesting the creation of the State of Israel).

6. *Severe Economic Disadvantage or Deprivation of Life Essentials*

Persecution also may encompass "the deliberate imposition of severe economic disadvantage or the deprivation of liberty, food, housing, employment or other essentials of life."[169] In making a claim that economic deprivation rises to the level of persecution, the applicant must offer some proof he or she suffered a "deliberate imposition of substantial economic disadvantage."[170] Thus, the harm must be both severe and deliberately imposed.[171] According to the BIA, severe economic harm

---

[169] *Matter of Laipenieks*, 18 I&N Dec. 433, 456–57 (BIA 1983), *rev'd on other grounds*, 750 F.2d 1427 (9th Cir. 1985). *See also Matter of T–Z–*, 24 I&N Dec. 163 (BIA 2007) (finding that the deliberate imposition of severe economic disadvantage or the deprivation of liberty, food, housing, employment, or other essentials of life may amount to persecution); *Vicente-Elias v. Mukasey*, 532 F.3d 1086, 1091 (10th Cir. 2008) (upholding the IJ's determination that the poverty and discrimination suffered by the applicant because of his Mayan ancestry does not rise to the level of persecution); *Beck v. Mukasey,* 527 F.3d 737, 741 (8th Cir. 2008) (finding unfair prejudice and discrimination against Romani family in Hungary); *Kadri v. Mukasey*, 543 F.3d 16, 22 (1st Cir. 2008) (remanding applicant's claim that he could not earn a living as a medical doctor in Indonesia due to his sexual orientation); *Yun Jian Zhang v. Gonzales,* 495 F.3d 773 (7th Cir. 2007); *Li v. Gonzales*, 405 F.3d 171, 177 (4th Cir. 2005) (finding that deliberate imposition of severe economic disadvantage may rise to the level of persecution); *Zhen Hua Li v. Att'y Gen.,* 400 F.3d 157, 166 69 (3d Cir. 2005); *Baballah v. Ashcroft*, 367 F.3d 1067, 1075 (9th Cir. 2004) (noting that the IJ erred as a matter of law by requiring the applicant to show an absolute inability to support his family); *Gormley v. Ashcroft,* 364 F.3d 1172 (9th Cir. 2004); *Himri v. Ashcroft,* 378 F.3d 932, 937 (9th Cir. 2004) (finding that a Palestinian applicant's inability to avoid Kuwaiti state-sponsored economic discrimination, which may include denial of the rights to work, attend school, and to obtain drinking water, would amount to persecution), *as amended by* 2004 WL 1879255 (9th Cir. 2004); *Liao v. INS,* 293 F.3d 61, 69–70 (2d Cir. 2002); *Ambati v. Reno,* 233 F.3d 1054, 1060 (7th Cir. 2000); *Minwalla v. INS*, 706 F.2d 831, 835 (8th Cir. 1983); *Berdo v. INS*, 432 F.2d 824, 847 (6th Cir. 1970); *Kovac v. INS*, 407 F.2d 102, 107 (9th Cir. 1969); *Dunat v. Henry*, 297 F.2d 744, 746 (3d Cir. 1961); *Matter of Salama*, 11 I&N Dec. 536 (BIA 1966). *But see Damko v. INS*, 430 F.3d 626, 628 (2d Cir. 2005) (finding that economic restrictions must be so severe that they constitute a threat to life or freedom in order to amount to economic persecution); *Sharif v. INS*, 87 F.3d 932, 934–35 (7th Cir. 1996) (finding that inability to attend college and losing job but finding another does not amount to economic persecution); *see also Mirzoyan v. Gonzales*, 457 F.3d 217, 221–22 (2d Cir. 2006) (criticizing the BIA for not applying a consistent standard for economic persecution claims).

[170] *See Uchida v. Att'y Gen.*, 435 F. App'x 110 (3d Cir. 2011) (finding that the record contains no indication that the fine paid by the applicant to the Chinese government for violations of China's family planning polices was a severe hardship for the applicant, that he paid the fine the day after it was imposed, and that it did not rise to the level of persecution); *Shan Liao v. U.S. Dep't of Justice*, 293 F.3d 61, 70 (2d Cir. 2002) (finding applicant should have submitted proof of income in China, net worth, and other personal financial information).

[171] *Matter of T–Z–*, 24 I&N Dec. at 173. *See Xing Qiang Zhuo v. Att'y Gen..*, 502 F. App'x 176 (3d Cir. 2012) (holding that the imposition of a monetary fine in the amount of 42% of the Chinese applicant's annual earnings, after his wife became pregnant with another child in violation of China's coercive family planning policies, did not rise to the level of past persecution); *Pang v. Holder*, 665 F.3d 1226 (10th Cir. 2012) (finding that the economic penalties imposed on the applicant as a result of his resistance to Chinese population control policies did not rise to the level of past persecution); *Chen v. Att'y Gen.*, 676 F.3d 112 (3d Cir. 2011) (finding that the applicants did not demonstrate a well-founded fear of persecution based on the birth of their two U.S. citizen children and that the fines they would be subjected to would not rise to the level of persecution); *Bao Hui Chen v. Att'y Gen.,,* 438 F. App'x 125 (3d Cir. 2011) (finding that the fines the applicant was required to pay in China because of his refusal to

Continued

means harm that is "above and beyond [the economic difficulties] generally shared by others in the country of origin and involves more than the mere loss of social advantages or physical comforts."[172] However, "a total deprivation of livelihood or a total withdrawal of all economic opportunity" is not required to demonstrate economic deprivation that amounts to persecution.[173]

Courts have found the following forms of economic deprivation to amount to persecution under the facts and evidence presented:

- A fine worth twenty months' salary, combined with being blacklisted from future employment, loss of health benefits, school tuition, and food rations, and the confiscation of the applicant's household furniture and appliances;[174]
- Being reduced to an "impoverished existence," even if the victim is able to "survive;"[175] and
- State-sponsored economic discrimination against a disfavored group within society that could lead to extreme economic harm.[176]

---

abide by China's family planning policies did not amount to "severe" economic deprivation because the applicant and his family continued to receive shelter, food, health care, education, and other basic necessities); *Aquino-Rovas v. Att'y Gen..*, 431 F. App'x 200 (3d Cir. 2011) (finding that the MS-13 gang members' request for money from the applicant in El Salvador did not amount to persecution because there was no indication that the requests for money constituted severe economic restrictions); *Jiang v. Holder*, 436 F. App'x 315 (5th Cir. 2011) (holding that the imposition of economic sanctions against the applicant because of his acts of resistance to the family planning policies in China did not amount to persecution, because the applicant failed to establish that if he and his wife had lost their jobs and their home, they would have been unable to find employment or housing elsewhere); *Mirisawo v. Holder*, 599 F.3d 391 (4th Cir. 2010) (holding that the applicant did not suffer economic persecution in Zimbabwe because at the time of the government's destruction of her house, the applicant had never lived in the house and was living and working in the United States as a live-in housekeeper; therefore, the destruction of her house in Zimbabwe in no way interfered with her ability to provide housing for herself and she was not deprived of a basic necessity that threatened her life or freedom); *Japarkulova v. Holder*, 615 F.3d 696 (6th Cir. 2010) (holding that a series of job losses a citizen of the Kyrgyz Republic incurred due to her opposition to corruption did not constitute past persecution because, although the applicant was fired from a series of jobs, on each occasion she moved quickly to another high-level position in the Kyrgyz economy).

[172] *Matter of T–Z–,* 24 I&N Dec. at 173.

[173] *Id. See also Stserba v. Holder*, 646 F.3d 964 (6th Cir. 2011) (disagreeing with the IJ's determination that the invalidation of the Estonian applicant's medical degree was not persecution because "a sweeping limitation of opportunities to continue to work in an established profession or business may amount to persecution even though the applicant could otherwise survive"); *Borca v. INS,* 77 F.3d 210 (7th Cir. 1996) (noting that total economic deprivation is not required in order to establish persecution).

[174] *Zhen Hua Li v. Att'y Gen.*, 400 F.3d 157, 166–69 (3d Cir. 2005).

[175] *Matter of T–Z–*, 24 I&N Dec. at 174.

[176] *Himri v. Ashcroft*, 378 F.3d 932, 937 (9th Cir. 2004) (finding that the Kuwaiti state-sponsored economic discrimination against a Palestinian applicant, which may include denial of the right to work, attend school, and obtain drinking water, would amount to persecution), as amended by 2004 WL 1879255 (9th Cir. 2004).

On the other hand, under the facts and evidence presented, courts have found the following forms of economic deprivation insufficient to amount to persecution:

- Being relegated to low-level jobs despite advanced schooling;[177]
- Partial destruction of the applicant's home;[178] and
- Loss of employment as a result of a government program, where the government provided unemployment compensation and other similarly situated individuals were able to maintain or regain employment.[179]

In determining whether economic harm constitutes persecution, the following factors should be considered:

(1) the applicant's and his or her family members' earnings;

(2) any sources of income or housing available to the applicant upon loss of employment or housing;

(3) whether the applicant is able to secure other employment or an education;

(4) whether the economic disadvantage the applicant suffered or would suffer differs from that of others in the country of origin and how they differ; and

(5) the specific losses the applicant would suffer, including health benefits, school tuition, food rations, and household furniture and appliances.[180]

> ➢ **Practice Pointer**: Evidence of the applicant's income, property, and relative wealth compared to other households in the area may assist in demonstrating severe economic harm amounting to persecution.

7. *Arrests and Detention*

In general, short periods of detention during which little or no harm to the applicant occurred will not rise to the level of persecution,[181] especially if they are for

---

[177] *Beck v. Mukasey*, 527 F.3d 737, 741 (8th Cir. 2008) (finding unfair prejudice and discrimination against a Romani family in Hungary).

[178] *Yun Jian Zhang v. Gonzales*, 495 F.3d 773 (7th Cir. 2007) (reasoning that the damage could be repaired, the applicant worked in construction, the applicant continued to be gainfully employed, the family was able to find shelter, and the harm did not continue).

[179] *Gormley v. Ashcroft*, 364 F.3d 1172 (9th Cir. 2004).

[180] *Matter of T–Z–*, 24 I&N Dec. at 173.

[181] *See Hong Chen v. Holder*, 2014 WL 983309 (1st Cir. Mar. 14, 2014) (relying on the lack of severe injuries in holding that the applicant's three-day detention by Chinese authorities for participating in the services of an underground church, during which time she was beaten about the head with binders in a manner that resulted in bruising and swelling, did not rise to the level of past persecution); *Mendoza v. Holder*, 553 F. App'x 507 (6th Cir. 2014) (holding that the applicant, a citizen of Guatemala who had been detained by the Guatemalan military for 15 days with his hands tied, questioned eight to 10 times about the guerillas, made to watch beatings of other detainees, and forced to join the civil patrol, did not compel a finding of persecution); *En Hua Zhu v. Holder*, 528 F. App'x 544 (6th Cir. 2013) (finding that the beating with a baton, interrogation, and month-long detention of a Chinese applicant on account of his Christian faith did not rise to the level of persecution because the applicant did not require any medical attention following the beating); *Shi Jin Ou v. Att'y Gen.*, 456 F. App'x 175 (3d Cir. 2012)

Continued

legitimate law enforcement reasons and without mistreatment.[182] However, prolonged detention coupled with significant physical harm and a lack of due process rights may constitute persecution.[183] The following factors should be considered in determining whether detention or confinement rise to the level of persecution:

(1) the length of detention;

(2) the legitimacy of the government action;

(3) any mistreatment of the applicant during detention; and

(holding that the mistreatment the applicant suffered because of his refusal to abide by China's family planning policy – two days' detention during which he was subjected to three beatings that left him sore, but not injured enough to require medical treatment or prevent the petitioner from returning to work the day after his release – did not rise to the level of persecution); *Ly v. Holder*, 421 F. App'x 575 (6th Cir. 2011) (holding that the applicant from Mauritania failed to establish past persecution when he was detained for one month in a small cell with ten other prisoners because isolated periods of imprisonment – even those accompanied by allegations of threats and physical abuse – do not compel a finding of persecution); *Xia Chen v. Att'y Gen.*, 392 F. App'x 962 (3d Cir. 2010) (holding that the applicant's three-day detention in China on account of her Christianity did not rise to the level of persecution because it was relatively brief and, although she was slapped in the face by a police officer, she did not require medical treatment); *Luxun Chen v. Att'y Gen.*, 393 F. App'x 959 (3d Cir. 2010) (holding that the applicant's arrest, physical abuse, and three-day detention in China on the grounds of his family's church did not rise to the level of past persecution); *Lopez de Hincapie v. Gonzales*, 494 F.3d 213, 217 (1st Cir. 2007) (stating that a noncitizen must have experienced something more than "ordinary harassment, mistreatment, or suffering" to demonstrate persecution); *Xiaoguang Gu v. Gonzalez*, 454 F.3d 1014 (9th Cir. 2006) (finding that a Chinese man who had been detained at a police station for three days, interrogated for two hours, and hit on the back with a rod ten times did not suffer past persecution because he did not require any medical treatment); *Prela v. Ashcroft*, 394 F.3d 515 (7th Cir. 2005) (finding that a Kosovar Albanian who was interrogated on three occasions by Serbian police, one time during a detention of 24 hours, and suffered an injury to his hands did not suffer past persecution); *Mei Dan Liu v. Ashcroft*, 380 F.3d 307 (7th Cir. 2004) (finding that a 16-year-old Chinese girl who had been detained for two days by the police, during which she was pushed and her hair was pulled, who had been expelled from school, and whose home had been ransacked by the police did not suffer past persecution).

[182] *See, e.g., Zalega v. INS*, 916 F.2d 1257 (7th Cir. 1990). Short periods of detention during which little or no harm to the applicant occurred, however, may be important events to highlight in demonstrating cumulative harm rising to the level of persecution.

[183] *See Ivanov v. Holder*, 736 F.3d 5 (1st Cir. 2013) (finding that the applicant's three-day detention in a basement by four young skinheads on account of his Pentecostal faith, during which he was "chained and beaten with full plastic water bottles," handcuffed, shocked in the hand, burned with cigarettes on the other hand, and refused food and water amounted to persecution); *Vladimirova v. Ashcroft*, 377 F.3d 690 (7th Cir. 2004) (finding that a Bulgarian Christian who had been detained by the police twice, each time for two days, and who was beaten by police in her home, resulting in a miscarriage had suffered past persecution); *Mihalev v. Ashcroft*, 388 F.3d 722 (9th Cir. 2004) (finding that a Bulgarian of Roma descent who had been detained by police for ten days, during which time he was beaten daily with sandbags and forced to perform heavy labor, had suffered past persecution); *Asani v. INS*, 154 F.3d 719 (7th Cir. 1998) (remanding for a determination whether having two teeth knocked out and being detained for two weeks with insufficient food and water constituted persecution).

(4) whether the applicant was ever accorded any due process rights, such as access to counsel, a trial before a judge, or others.[184]

8. Harassment and Discrimination

In general, the harm suffered must be more than mere harassment or discrimination in order to amount to persecution.[185] Less preferential treatment, for

---

[184] *See* AOBTC Workbook, pt. I, *supra* note 34, at 26–27. *See also, e.g., Zalega,* 916 F.2d at 1257 (holding that short detentions without mistreatment did not amount to persecution).

[185] *Matter of V–F–D–*, 23 I&N Dec. 859 (BIA 2006) (finding that harassment and discrimination based on religion did not amount to persecution); *Matter of A–E–M–*, 21 I&N Dec. 1157, 1159 (BIA 1998) (finding that the single instance of a threat being painted on a house did not rise to the level of persecution). *See also Bera v. Att'y Gen..*, 555 F. App'x 129 (3d Cir. 2014) (finding that the frequent harassment of and discrimination against a Polish citizen because of her conversion to Judaism did not rise to the level of persecution); *Maknojiya v. Holder*, 524 F. App'x 956 (5th Cir. 2013) (holding that the applicant, a Muslim, had not experienced religious-based persecution in India where he was verbally harassed and thrown to the ground by Hindi extremists who also burned two of his cars and some of his grain and feed, and threatened to kill him and harm his family if he did not move to Pakistan); *Nadeak v. Att'y Gen.*, 460 F. App'x 170 (3d Cir. 2012) (holding that isolated attacks that do not require medical care, unfulfilled threats, and general harassment and discrimination at work in Indonesia because of the applicant's Christianity did not rise to the level of persecution); *Hussain v. Holder*, 390 F. App'x 445 (6th Cir. 2010) (holding that the Pakistani applicants were not subjected to persecution when they were harassed at school, including separation from their classmates, threatening insults, and harassment by a teacher because of their being Shia Muslims, a minority in Pakistan); *Korneenkov v. Holder*, 347 F. App'x 93 (5th Cir. 2009) (holding that the applicants' harassment in Russia due to their mental disabilities did not rise to the level of persecution when the applicants were physically and verbally abused by their teachers in school, the husband was harassed at his job, the husband was arrested by police officers and taken to a police station, and the wife was lured by men who attempted to rape her before she escaped); *Turangan v. Mukasey*, 307 F. App'x 11 (7th Cir. 2009) (holding that the incidents cited by the applicant amounted to mere harassment because they were not so severe that they constituted a threat to life or freedom, where the Indonesian applicant was attacked by two Muslim men at knife-point, his son and daughter were beat up by Muslim children, and his wife and mother were robbed on account of their Pentecostal Christian faith); *Ivanishvili v. Gonzales*, 433 F.3d 332, 340 (2d Cir. 2006); *Sahi v. Gonzales*, 416 F.3d 587, 589 (7th Cir. 2005); *Ahmed v. Ashcroft,* 341 F.3d 214, 217 (3d Cir. 2003); *Ciorba v. Ashcroft*, 323 F.3d 539, 545 (7th Cir. 2003) (finding that the questioning by police and searches of a house amounted to harassment, not persecution); *Najjar v. Ashcroft,* 257 F.3d 1262, 1291 (11th Cir. 2001); *Nelson v. INS*, 232 F.3d 258, 264 (1st Cir. 2000) (finding that three episodes of solitary confinement of less than 72 hours [each accompanied by physical abuse], periodic surveillance, threatening phone calls, occasional stops and searches, and visits to the applicant's place of work do not amount to past persecution); *Tamas-Mercea v. Reno*, 222 F.3d 417, 424 (7th Cir. 2000) (finding that tapping phone lines, opening mail, and questioning the applicant's wife does not rise to level of persecution); *Avetova-Elisseva v. INS*, 213 F.3d 1192 (9th Cir. 2000) (finding that discrimination against an Armenian living in Russia, including harassment and pushing by Russian officers because of her ethnicity and being denied a job because "there were no jobs for Armenians," did not rise to the level of persecution because incidents of hostility alone do not constitute persecution); *Singh v. INS*, 134 F.3d 962, 968–69 (9th Cir. 1998) (finding that rock throwing, damage to property, burglary of home, and stolen laundry, coconuts, and other items did not amount to persecution); *Mikhailevitch v. INS*, 146 F.3d 384, 390 (6th Cir. 1998); *Bradvica v. INS*, 128 F.3d 1009, 1012 (7th Cir. 1997) (finding that an arrest and detention following a pro-democracy rally is harassment, not persecution); *Faddoul v. INS,* 37 F.3d 185, 189 (5th Cir. 1994); *Baka v. INS*, 963 F.2d 1376, 1379 (10th Cir. 1992); *Balazoski v. INS*, 932 F.2d 638, 642 (7th Cir. 1991).

example, is generally not considered persecution.[186] However, the frequency and severity of the harassment or discrimination may enable that treatment to rise to the level of persecution. Violent conduct, for example, "generally goes beyond the mere annoyance and distress that characterize harassment."[187] Additionally, if the discrimination or harassment accumulates or "increases in severity to the extent that it leads to consequences of a substantially prejudicial nature," it may rise to the level of persecution.[188] Similarly, the context in which the harassment or discrimination occurs may be relevant to whether that treatment amounts to persecution.[189] For example, in the context of government sanctioned or supported ethnic cleansing, discrimination alone may rise to the level of persecution.[190] Accordingly, adjudicators must consider the context in which the harm occurs, as well as the totality of the instances of harm, in determining whether harassment or discrimination amounts to persecution.[191]

In determining whether harassment or discrimination rise to the level of persecution, adjudicators are encouraged to consider:

(1) how long the harassment or discrimination lasted;

---

[186] UNHCR Handbook, *supra* note 33, at ¶¶ 54–55. *See, e.g.*, *Mansour v. Ashcroft*, 390 F.3d 667 (9th Cir. 2004) (finding that discrimination against a Coptic Christian applicant in regard to his career as a medical doctor did not amount to persecution); *Ahmed v. Ashcroft*, 341 F.3d 214, 217 (3d Cir. 2003) (finding that discrimination against stateless Palestinians in Saudi Arabia did not amount to persecution); *Najjar v. Ashcroft*, 257 F.3d 1262, 1291 (11th Cir. 2011); *Mikhailevitch v. INS*, 146 F.3d 384, 390 (6th Cir. 1998) (finding that harassment by the KGB did not rise to the level of persecution); *Faddoul v. INS*, 37 F.3d 185, 189 (5th Cir. 1994); *Matter of V–F–D–*, 23 I&N Dec. at 859 (finding that discrimination and harassment on account of religion did not amount to persecution); *Matter of A–E–M–*, 21 I&N Dec. 1157, 1159 (BIA 1998) (finding that a single instance of a threat being painted on a house did not rise to the level of persecution).

[187] *Ivanishvili*, 433 F.3d at 340 (finding that the IJ failed to distinguish between harassment and persecution in the case of a Jehovah's Witness who was subjected to threats and attacks).

[188] AOBTC Workbook, pt. 1, *supra* note 34, at 26–27. *See Ivanishvili*, 433 F.3d at 342 (stating that "violent conduct generally goes beyond the mere annoyance and distress that characterize harassment"); *Krotova v. Gonzales,* 416 F.3d 1080 (9th Cir. 2005) (discussing case examples and holding that combination of sustained economic pressure, physical violence, and inability to practice religion amounted to persecution); *Sangha v. INS*, 103 F.3d 1482 (9th Cir. 1997) (finding that death threats and violence against the applicant's father amounted to persecution); *Matter of O–Z– & I–Z–*, 22 I&N Dec. 23 (BIA 1998) (finding that three physical attacks, a break-in and ransacking of the applicant's apartment, repeated anti-Semitic flyers, written threats, and extreme humiliation of the applicant's son cumulatively rose to the level of persecution).

[189] *See, e.g., Bescovik v. Gonzalez,* 467 F. 3d 223, 226 (2d Cir. 2006).

[190] *See, e.g., Ouda*, 324 F.3d at 454 (6th Cir. 2003) (requiring Palestinians to leave Kuwait because they were perceived enemies is sufficient alone to establish past persecution); *Duarte de Guinac v. INS*, 179 F.3d 1156 (9th Cir. 1999) (finding that an indigenous Quiche in Guatemala was not only discriminated against, but persecuted, after being conscripted into the Guatemalan military and then singled out for abuse); *Matter of Salama*, 11 I&N Dec. 536 (BIA 1966) (finding persecution where Jewish professionals were denied licenses to practice in their field due to a government campaign of discrimination).

[191] AOBTC Workbook, pt. 1, *supra* note 34, at 26–27.

(2) which human rights were affected;

(3) how the harassment or discrimination affected the particular applicant; and

(4) how much discrimination or harassment has been imposed on the applicant cumulatively.[192] The following examples may be significant enough to indicate discrimination or harassment amounting to persecution:

- Serious restrictions on the right to earn a livelihood;
- Serious restrictions on the access to normally available educational facilities;
- Arbitrary interference with privacy;
- Relegation to substandard dwellings;
- Enforced social or civil inactivity;
- Passport denial;
- Constant surveillance;
- Pressure to become an informer;
- Confiscation of property; and
- The accumulation and type of instances of discriminatory practices or harassment that have been imposed on the applicant.[193]

9. *Prosecution*

Whether the harm inflicted or feared is prosecution for an unlawful act, rather than persecution on account of one of the protected grounds in a common issue in asylum claims. This is because individuals fleeing prosecution are not generally able to meet the definition of "refugee" as defined in domestic and international law. As noted in UNHCR's Handbook, persecution is not the same as "punishment for a common law offense,"[194] and courts have rejected asylum and withholding claims of individuals who feared prosecution for the following offenses: an armed confrontation with the police,[195] assisting illegal immigrants from North Korea in China,[196] bribing a

---

[192] *See id.*, at 25–26.

[193] *Id.* at 26. *See, e.g., Matter of O–Z– & I–Z–*, 22 I&N Dec. 23, 26 (BIA 1998).

[194] UNHCR Handbook, *supra* note 33, ¶ 56.

[195] *Cruz-Samayoa v. Holder*, 607 F.3d 1145 (6th Cir. 2010) (holding that there is no evidence that the criminal prosecution the applicant faced in Guatemala because of his involvement in an armed confrontation with the Guatemalan police over the redistribution of land was a pretext for persecution on account of his political opinion).

[196] *Li.*, 633 F.3d at 136.

passport official,[197] evading conscription laws,[198] distributing Western films,[199] murder committed in the United States,[200] and violating currency laws.[201]

What may at first glance appear to be prosecution, however, may upon further examination amount to persecution. Prosecution under laws that are not in conformity with accepted human rights standards or those that are applied in a discriminatory manner may still constitute persecution.[202] Prosecution may become persecution under the following situations:

(1) where the prosecution is used as a pretext to persecute an individual on account of a protected ground;[203]

(2) where the punishment is unduly harsh given the nature of the offense;

(3) where the applicant receives harsher punishment than others who do not share a protected characteristic that he or she possesses or is perceived to possess;

(4) where the prosecution occurs to punish a protected characteristic;[204]

(5) where the prosecution is for a political crime;[205]

(6) where the prosecution is for violation of departure laws.[206] Thus, when evaluating whether prosecution could be considered persecution, careful consideration should be given to the type of punishment imposed or feared and the reasons for that punishment.

Criminal prosecution may amount to persecution where the type of punishment given is arbitrary, excessive, or disproportionately severe.[207] This includes situations

---

[197] *Janusiak v. INS*, 947 F.2d 46, 48 (3d Cir. 1991).

[198] *M.A. v. INS*, 899 F.2d 304, 312 (4th Cir. 1990).

[199] *Abedini v. INS*, 971 F.2d 188, 191 (9th Cir. 1992).

[200] *Saleh v. INS*, 962 F.2d 234 (2d Cir. 1992).

[201] *Matter of H–M–*, 20 I&N Dec. 683 (BIA 1993).

[202] UNHCR Handbook, *supra* note 33, ¶ 59.

[203] *Id.* ¶¶ 57–59. *See also Rodriguez-Roman v. INS*, 98 F.3d 416 (9th Cir. 1996); *Matter of A–G–*, 19 I&N Dec. 502 (BIA 1987).

[204] *See, e.g., Chang v. INS*, 119 F.3d 1055 (3d Cir. 1997); *Perkovic v. INS*, 33 F.3d 615 (6th Cir. 1994).

[205] *See, e.g., Matter of Izatula*, 20 I&N Dec. 149 (BIA 1990).

[206] *See, e.g., Chang*, 119 F.3d at 1055; *Nazaraghaie v. INS*, 102 F.3d 460 (10th Cir. 1996); *Rodriguez-Roman*, 98 F.3d at 416; *Matter of Sibrun*, 18 I&N Dec. 354 (BIA 1983).

[207] *See, e.g., Li v. Holder*, 559 F.3d at 1109 (criticizing the BIA for importing into Chinese law what would be a criminal act under U.S. law and ignoring the North Korean Human Rights Act of 2004); *Tagaga v. INS*, 228 F.3d 1030, 1034–35 (9th Cir. 2000) (finding that prosecution for treason for refusal to participate in persecution of Indo-Fijians constitutes persecution); *Bandari v. INS*, 227 F.3d 1160, 1168 (9th Cir. 2000) (finding that while the police's initial stop may have been for law enforcement, subsequent beatings were on account of religion); *Zahedi v. INS*, 222 F.3d 1157, 1165 (9th Cir. 2000) (prosecution by Iranian authorities for translating and copying the book *The Satanic Verses* is persecution on account of a political opinion, finding that the IJ failed to properly consider the documentary evidence submitted by the applicant); *Singh v. Ilchert*, 63 F.3d 1501, 1509 (9th Cir. 1995); *Matter of S–P–*, 21

Continued

in which the individual is deprived of basic due process rights or harmed while in detention. The BIA has provided guidance for identifying the persecutor's motive in this context, stating that adjudicators should look to:

(1) indications that the abuse was directed toward modifying or punishing opinion rather than conduct;

(2) treatment of other detainees who might be confronted by government agents in similar circumstances;

(3) conformity to procedures for criminal prosecution or military law;

(4) the extent to which anti-terrorism laws are defined and applied to suppress political opinion as well as illegal conduct; and

(5) the extent to which suspected political opponents are subjected to arbitrary arrest, detention, and abuse.[208] Arbitrary, excessive, or disproportionately severe harm, as well as deprivation of due process rights, such as lack of a fair trial or punishment imposed without the benefit of a judicial process,[209] may indicate that the prosecution was merely a pretext to persecute the individual on account of a protected ground.

Often, whether the prosecution of an applicant amounts to persecution is not a question of the type of punishment, but rather, a question of the alleged persecutor's motive for the prosecution. Prosecutions under laws that are "fairly administered"[210] and harm inflicted by police to extract information concerning criminal matters generally do not amount to persecution.[211] On the other hand, a malicious prosecution motivated by a protected ground may make an individual eligible for asylum.[212]

I&N Dec. 486 (BIA 1996); *Matter of Izatula*, 20 I&N Dec. 149, 157 (BIA 1990) (Vacca, concurring) ("Torture" and "conduct such as beating with bats and forcing one to drink one's own urine when thirsty ought not be mistaken for legitimate governmental investigations… ."); *Senathirajah v. INS*, 157 F.3d 210, 221 (3d Cir. 1998).

[208] *Matter of S–P–*, 21 I& Dec. 486 (BIA 1996).

[209] *Bellido v. Ashcroft*, 367 F.3d 840, 845 (8th Cir. 2004); *Behzadpour v. U.S.*, 946 F.2d 1351, 1353 (8th Cir. 1991).

[210] *Romeike v. Holder*, 718 F.3d 528 (6th Cir. 2013) (holding that Germany's enforcement of its general school attendance law against homeschoolers did not amount to persecution on account of a protected ground); *Ngure v. Ashcroft*, 367 F.3d 975, 991 (8th Cir. 2004); *Chang v. INS*, 119 F.3d at 1060; *see also Abedini v. INS*, 971 F.2d 188, 191 (9th Cir. 1992); *Behzadpour v. U.S.*, 946 F.2d 1351, 1353 (8th Cir. 1991).

[211] *See, e.g., Prasad v. INS*, 47 F.3d 336, 340 (9th Cir. 1995); *Ozdemir v. INS*, 46 F.3d 6, 8 (5th Cir. 1994); *Matter of T–*, 20 I&N Dec. 571 (BIA 1992).

[212] *See, e.g., Ralios Morente v. Holder*, 401 F. App'x 17 (6th Cir. 2010) (distinguishing between malicious prosecution and legitimate prosecution in the case of a Guatemalan applicant who feared prosecution by the Human Rights Commission for his innocent involvement in the local Civil Patrol); *Chen v. Holder*, 607 F.3d 511 (7th Cir. 2010) (holding that remand was required to determine whether the warrant for the applicant's arrest amounted to political persecution when the warrant was issued in response to her lawsuit against the local government in China for its failure to transfer new land or the

Continued

- **Practice Pointer**: Practitioners should present strong supporting evidence showing that the persecutor's motives for prosecuting the applicant were on account of a protected ground.
- **Practice Pointer**: A person who has been subjected to or fears harm inflicted by police to extract information, but who is ineligible for asylum or withholding of removal because the harm was not inflicted on account of one of the five enumerated grounds, may be eligible for protection under the Convention Against Torture, as there is no required "nexus" to a protected ground.[213]

The prosecution of certain types of conduct, such as political crimes or unlawful departures from a country, may be a pretext for persecution.[214] For example, if there is no legitimate means for changing a nondemocratic government, rebellion in an attempt to overthrow the government need not be considered criminal, and any actions taken by the government to punish such acts may amount to persecution.[215] Similarly, some countries impose severe penalties on nationals who depart unlawfully from the country or who remain abroad without authorization. An individual may be eligible for asylum if he or she would be subject to such penalties based on one of the five enumerated grounds.[216] Some courts have held that a country that severely punishes unlawful departure views persons who illegally leave as disloyal and subversive.[217] For example, courts have held that punishment of up to one year

---

money to build new homes, as promised in response to the razing of homes to construct a military building).

[213] See chapter 4 for more information regarding relief under the Convention Against Torture.

[214] *See Chang v. INS*, 119 F.3d at 1064 (3d Cir. 1997) (finding that the evidence of record suggested that China punished political dissidents under its State Security Law); *Perkovic v. INS*, 33 F.3d 615, 622 (6th Cir. 1994) (holding that punishment under laws against peaceful political expression is "on account of" political opinion); UNHCR Handbook, *supra* note 33, at ¶ 86 (stating that adjudicators should examine, inter alia, the nature of the act committed, the nature of the prosecution, and its motives in determining whether a political offender is a refugee). *But see Ngure v. Ashcroft*, 367 F.3d 975, 990 (8th Cir. 2004) (three prior arrests did not amount to persecution); *Kapcia v. INS*, 944 F.2d 702, 707–08 (10th Cir. 1991) (holding that punishment for the illegal distribution of political pamphlets is a legitimate government act and not persecution).

[215] *Matter of Izatula*, 20 I&N Dec. 149, 153–54 (BIA 1990) (citing *Dwomoh v. Sava*, 696 F. Supp. 970, 979 (S.D.N.Y. 1988)) (prosecution, beating, or torture of a coup participant may qualify as persecution). Such conduct, however, may result in a denial of asylum and withholding of removal under terrorism-related grounds. *See infra* pt. IV.5. for a detailed discussion of the terrorism-related grounds for barring an individual from asylum or withholding of removal eligibility.

[216] *See, e.g.*, *Chang v. INS*, 119 F.3d 1055, 1067 (3d Cir. 1997); *Matter of Exilus*, 18 I&N Dec. 276, 278 (BIA 1982) (applicant failed to demonstrate the harm feared for illegal departure from Haiti would be on account of one of the five enumerated grounds).

[217] *Chang*, 119 F.3d at 1064 (citing *Rodriguez-Roman*, 98 F.3d at 430–31, holding that the BIA erred in concluding that the severe punishment an individual would suffer upon return to Cuba following illegal departure would be merely criminal prosecution, rather than persecution on account of political opinion).

imprisonment for violation of state security laws in China constitutes persecution,[218] as does three years' imprisonment for violating the Cuban exit laws.[219]

Previous regulations promulgated by legacy INS and EOIR required that asylum officers and IJs give "due consideration" to evidence that the government of the applicant's country of nationality or last habitual residence persecutes its nationals or residents if they leave the country without authorization or seek asylum in another country. The final regulations implementing the Illegal Immigration Reform and Immigrant Responsibility Act of 1996 (IIRAIRA) removed these sections, previously found at 8 CFR §§208.13(b)(2)(ii) and 208.16(b)(4). Several commenters to the proposed regulations objected to the elimination of these sections. Legacy INS and EOIR responded that while the United States "continues to deplore and oppose certain countries' practice of severely punishing their citizens for illegal departure or for applying for asylum in another country," the regulations were "ambiguous" and did not clearly implement this policy.[220]

D. Past Persecution or Well-Founded Fear of Future Persecution

If the harm suffered or feared amounts to persecution, the applicant must then demonstrate either that the persecution already has occurred or that his or her fear of future persecution is "well-founded."[221]

> ➢ **Practice Pointer**: Each of these two kinds of persecution — past and future — can provide a separate and independent basis for protection. Practitioners should familiarize themselves with their clients' facts and argue all appropriate bases for protection.

1. Past Persecution

Past persecution is sufficient in and of itself to establish threshold eligibility for asylum.[222] To establish eligibility for asylum based on past persecution, an applicant must prove an incident or series of incidents that:

---

[218] *Id.* at 1067. *But see Chen v. Gonzales*, 434 F.3d 212, 221 (3d Cir. 2005) (finding that Chinese law barring illegal emigration is generally applicable to all illegal emigrants who return to China and nothing in the record supports the conclusion that the applicant would be singled out for persecution or torture).

[219] *Rodriguez-Roman*, 98 F.3d at 431. *But see Kozulin v. INS*, 218 F.3d 1112, 1117–18 (9th Cir. 2000) (finding that the applicant failed to demonstrate that he would be subjected to punishment by the Russian authorities for his illegal departure).

[220] *See* Inspection and Expedited Removal of Aliens; Detention and Removal of Aliens; Conduct of Removal Proceedings; Asylum Procedures; Final Rule 62 Fed. Reg. 10311, 10317 (Mar. 6, 1997) (to be codified at 8 CFR pt. 1, *et al.*).

[221] *See, e.g., Matter of Chen*, 20 I&N Dec. 16, 18 (BIA 1989).

[222] 8 CFR §208.13(b)(1) (2014). *See also Matter of A–T–*, 24 I&N Dec. 617 (AG 2008); *Matter of H–*, 21 I&N Dec. 337, 345–46 (BIA 1996) (finding that a Somali national whose father and brother were murdered and who was detained and tortured because of his clan membership suffered past persecution); *Matter of D–V–*, 21 I&N Dec. 77, 79–80 (BIA 1993) (finding that a Haitian woman gang-

Continued

(1) rises to the level of persecution;

(2) is on account of one of the five protected grounds;[223] and

(3) is committed by the government or by private actors the government is unable or unwilling to control.[224]

An adjudicator must make a specific finding regarding whether the applicant suffered past persecution, prior to determining whether there is a well-founded fear of future persecution.[225] If the IJ or BIA fails to provide a reasoned discussion of whether an individual was subjected to past persecution, the reviewing court is unable to provide meaningful review of the decision, and the case must be remanded for further consideration.[226]

The burden is on the applicant to show that he or she has suffered past persecution. If that burden is met, it is presumed that he or she also has a well-founded fear of future persecution.[227] The burden then shifts to the government to rebut that presumption. A presumption of well-founded fear may be rebutted if a preponderance of the evidence establishes that conditions in the country of persecution have fundamentally changed,[228] or the applicant could reasonably relocate safely to another part of the country.[229] If the government cannot show that country conditions have changed such that it is safe for the applicant to return or that

---

raped and beaten in her home suffered past persecution); *Matter of Chen*, 20 I&N Dec. at 18–19 (finding that the son of a Christian minister in China suffered severe past persecution that included denial of education, deprivation of food, denial of medical care, mistreatment of his father, ransacking of his home, and confiscation of papers and personal effects).

[223] *See infra* pt. II.E. for a detailed discussion of nexus and the protected grounds.

[224] *Knezevic v. Ashcroft*, 367 F.3d 1206, 1211 (9th Cir. 2004). *See infra* pt. II.F. for a detailed discussion of government and non-government persecutors.

[225] *See Matter of D–I–M–*, 24 I&N Dec. 448 (BIA 2008).

[226] *See, e.g.*, *Phommasoukha v. Gonzales*, 408 F.3d 1011, 1015 (8th Cir. 2005); *Hernandez-Barrera v. Ashcroft*, 373 F.3d 9, 13, 22 (1st Cir. 2004).

[227] 8 CFR §§208.13(b)(1), 1208.13(b)(1) (2014).

[228] 8 CFR §§208.13(b)(1)(i)(A), 1208.13(b)(1)(i)(A) (2014) (stating that the presumption may be rebutted if the adjudicator finds that "[t]here has been a fundamental change in *circumstances* such that the applicant no longer has a well-founded fear of persecution ... on account of race, religion, nationality, membership in a particular social group, or political opinion") (emphasis added). *See also Matter of H–*, Int. Dec. 3276 at 15, 24 (BIA 1995).

[229] 8 CFR §§208.13(b)(1)(i)(B), 1208.13(b)(1)(i)(B) (2014) (stating that the presumption may be rebutted if the adjudicator finds that "[t]he applicant could avoid future persecution by relocating to another part of the applicant's country ... and under all circumstances it would be *reasonable* to expect him to do so") (emphasis added). *See, e.g.*, *Balliu v. Gonzales*, 467 F.3d 609, 612 (7th Cir. 2006); *Un v. Gonzales*, 415 F.3d 205, 209 (1st Cir. 2005) (finding that the agency's failure to address past persecution precluded meaningful review of the applicant's entitlement to a presumption of fear of future persecution and was reversible error).

safe and reasonable internal relocation is possible, the presumption of a well-founded fear of future persecution stands.[230]

- **Practice Pointer**: In cases involving certain forms of past persecution, where the harm is "permanent and continuing," the presumption of well-founded fear of future persecution cannot be rebutted.[231] Examples of such "permanent and continuing" harm include forced sterilization[232] and, in some circuits, female genital mutilation.[233]

In order to retain the presumption of a well-founded fear after demonstrating past persecution, the applicant does not have to demonstrate that he or she will suffer identical harm, only that the fear of future harm is on account of the original basis for persecution.[234] However, if the future harm feared is unrelated to the past persecution claim[235] or is on account of a different statutory ground,[236] the burden remains on the applicant to demonstrate a well-founded fear of future persecution.[237] Current regulations mirror the BIA's decision in *Matter of N–M–A–*, which held that when the record reflects that the applicant no longer has a well-founded fear of persecution from his or her original persecutors, the applicant bears the burden of demonstrating a well-founded fear of persecution from a new source.[238]

---

[230] In an affirmative application, this analysis is done by the asylum officer adjudicating the claim, while in a defensive application, the DHS trial attorney is tasked with rebutting the presumption of a well-founded fear. *See* ch. 5 for a detailed discussion of burdens of proof. *See* chs. 7 and 8 for a detailed discussion of the affirmative and defensive asylum processes.

[231] *Matter of Y–T–L–*, 23 I&N Dec. 601 (BIA 2003).

[232] *Id. See also Hassan v. Gonzales,* 484 F.3d 513 (8th Cir. 2007); *Junshao Zhang v. Gonzales*, 434 F.3d 993, 1001 (7th Cir. 2006); *Qili Qu v. Gonzales*, 399 F.3d 1195, 1203 (9th Cir. 2005).

[233] *See Mohammed v. Gonzales*, 400 F.3d 785, 799–800 (9th Cir. 2005). *But see Matter of A–T–*, 24 I&N Dec. 617, 622–23 (AG 2008) *vacating in part Matter of A–T–*, 24 I&N Dec. 296, 299–301 (BIA 2007) and clarifying that the fact that a woman has been subjected to FGM in the past does not preclude a valid claim that she retains a well-founded fear of future persecution if it is established that she would be subject to additional FGM).

[234] *See, e.g., Bah v. Mukasey*, 529 F.3d 99, 103 (2d Cir. 2008) (stating that identical harm is not required; *Hassan v. Gonzales*, 484 F.3d 513 (8th Cir. 2007) (finding that the presumption of well-founded fear does not operate only as to the exact same harm experienced in the past).

[235] 8 CFR §§208.13(b)(1), (b)(1)(ii), 1208.13(b)(1), (b)(1)(ii) (2014). *See, e.g., Bace v. Ashcroft*, 352 F.3d 1133, 1137 (7th Cir. 2003).

[236] *See Matter of A–T–* 24 I&N Dec. at 622 (clarifying that "on the basis of the original claim" means that the future persecution feared is "on account of the same statutory ground" on which the applicant suffered past persecution).

[237] 8 CFR §§208.13(b)(1), 208.16(b)(1)(iii), 1208.13(b)(1), & 1208.16(b)(1)(iii) (2014).

[238] *Matter of N–M–A–*, 22 I&N Dec. 312, 318 (BIA 1998). *See* P. Schmidt, *The Presumption of Future Persecution Under the 2001 Asylum Regulations*, 21 Immigration Law Today 225 (Mar./Apr. 2002) (giving a comprehensive overview of these changes). The author of this article, Paul Schmidt, is a former member of the BIA.

> ➢ **Practice Pointer**: A similar presumption and allocation of the burden of proof applies in withholding of removal claims.[239]

i. Fundamental Change in Circumstances

The presumption of a well-founded fear of persecution may be rebutted if a "preponderance of the evidence establishes that since the time the persecution occurred conditions in the applicant's country of nationality have changed to such an extent that the applicant no longer has a well-founded fear of being persecuted if she were to return."[240] Simply demonstrating a change is not enough to rebut the presumption; the changed conditions must directly affect the risk of harm to the applicant based on one of the five protected grounds.[241]

There is some contradiction and tension between the application of this concept in the United States and internationally. According to legacy INS, a fundamental change in circumstances is intended to be broader than only changed country conditions, and could include other changes, including changes in "personal" circumstances, if "those changes are fundamental in nature and go to the basis of the fear of persecution."[242] In explaining this concept, legacy INS noted that it was designed to comply with the United States' international obligations under the 1967 Protocol Relating to the Status of Refugees.[243] However, guidance provided by UNHCR seems to directly contradict this assertion. The phrase "fundamental change in circumstances" is found in Article 1C(5) of the 1951 U.N. Convention Relating to the Status of Refugees, incorporated

---

239 8 CFR §§208.16(b)(1)(i)–(ii), 1208.16(b)(1)(i)–(ii) (2014). *See infra* pt. III. for a detailed discussion of withholding of removal. *See generally* ch. 4 for a detailed discussion of the shifting burdens of proof.

240 8 CFR §§208.13(b)(1)(i)(A), 1208.13(b)(1)(i)(A) (2014) (stating that the presumption may be rebutted if the adjudicator finds that "[t]here has been a fundamental change in *circumstances* such that the applicant no longer has a well-founded fear of persecution ... on account of race, religion, nationality, membership in a particular social group, or political opinion") (emphasis added). *See Matter of H–*, 21 I&N Dec. 337 (BIA 1996). *See also Tarubac v. INS*, 182 F.3d 1114, 1120 (9th Cir. 1999) (legacy INS failed to demonstrate that, in light of applicant's past persecution, the DOS profile provided sufficient evidence of changed country conditions to rebut the presumption of a well-founded fear); *Korablina v. INS*, 158 F.3d 1038, 1046 (9th Cir. 1998) (finding that the fact that members of the applicant's family were severely beaten soon after she left the Ukraine, with specific threats regarding her absence, indicates that the persecution would continue); *Fergiste v. INS*, 138 F.3d 14 (1st Cir. 1998) (the BIA erred as a matter of law in *not* applying the rebuttable presumption of future persecution to an individual who established that he suffered past persecution in Haiti).

241 *See Matter of N–M–A–,* 22 I&N Dec. at 312. *See also Bah v. Mukasey,* 529 F.3d 99 (2d Cir. 2008); *Mihaylov v. Ashcroft,* 379 F.3d 15, 23 (1st Cir. 2004); *Berishaj v. Ashcroft,* 378 F.3d 314, 327 (3d Cir. 2004); *Rios v. Ashcroft,* 287 F.3d 895, 901 (9th Cir. 2002) (stating that DHS "is obligated to introduce evidence that, on an individualized basis, rebuts a particular applicant's specific grounds for his well–founded fear of future persecution. Information about general changes in the country is not sufficient."); *Fergiste v. INS,* 138 F.3d 14, 19 (1st Cir. 1998).

242 *See* Asylum Procedures, 65 Fed. Reg. 76121, 76127 (Dec. 6, 2000) (supplementary information) (to be codified at 8 CFR pt. 208).

243 *Id.*

by reference into the 1967 Protocol.[244] Paragraph 135 of the UNHCR *Handbook* explains that:

> "Circumstances" refer to fundamental changes in the *country*, which can be assumed to remove the basis of the fear of persecution. A mere—possibly transitory—change in the facts surrounding the individual refugee's fear, which does not entail such major changes in circumstances, is not sufficient to make this clause applicable.[245]

At least one court has found a fundamental change in personal circumstances to rebut a presumption of well-founded fear where an applicant, who was abused as a child, became an adult.[246] The court noted that although it could find no case law to support its position, it relied on the broad language of the regulation and discussion of the regulation in the *Federal Register*.[247]

The BIA has interpreted this regulation in the context of coercive population measures.[248] It found that an asylum applicant whose wife was forcibly sterilized and who remained in China for seven years after the sterilization without additional harm occurring was nevertheless eligible for asylum.[249] The BIA reasoned that although the woman could not be sterilized again, and that could be interpreted as a change impacting well-founded fear of future persecution, the IJ had failed to take into account the continuing nature of the persecution inflicted on the applicant and his wife.[250] The BIA noted that the IJ's rationale could lead to the anomalous result that the very act of persecution itself would also constitute the change in circumstances and that it was "highly unlikely" Congress contemplated such an interpretation.[251] The BIA then took a contrary position in 2007 in *Matter of A–T–*[252] when it held that past FGM was a fundamental change in personal circumstances because FGM could not be practiced twice on one person.[253] That decision was later vacated by the AG, however.[254]

---

[244] *Id.*

[245] UNHCR Handbook, *supra* note 33, ¶ 135 (emphasis added).

[246] *Ixtlilco-Morales v. Keisler*, 507 F.3d 651, 654 (8th Cir. 2007).

[247] *Id.* at 655.

[248] *See Matter of Y–T–L–*, 23 I&N Dec. 601 (BIA 2003).

[249] *Id.* at 605.

[250] *Id.*

[251] *Id.*; *see also Hernandez-Barrera v. Ashcroft*, 373 F.3d 9, 23 (1st Cir. 2004) (noting the burden is not on the applicant to show his fear of persecution is not negated by changed circumstances; the burden is on the government).

[252] *Matter of A–T–*, 24 I&N Dec. 296 (BIA 2007), *vacated by Matter of A–T–*, 24 I&N Dec. 617 (AG 2008).

[253] *Id.*

[254] *Id.*

Most courts have focused on changed country conditions in determining whether there has been a fundamental change in circumstances to rebut the presumption of a well-founded fear of persecution. In a case involving the fall of the Taliban in Afghanistan, the U.S. Court of Appeals for the Eighth Circuit held that it was not enough for DHS to show a change in government, but it was required to show that the legal system had changed to such an extent that Christian converts would not be subjected to death for their religious beliefs under Afghanistan's current laws.[255] In the case of an Iraqi Assyrian, however, the Seventh Circuit did find it was proper for the IJ to take administrative notice that Saddam Hussein's regime ceased control of Iraq in April 2003 in finding changed circumstances.[256] Some other examples include the following:

- The U.S. Court of Appeals for the First Circuit found a fundamental change in circumstances in the case of a Cambodian supporter of the Sam Rainsy Party[257] and, more recently, a fundamental change in circumstances for Greeks in Albania;[258]
- The U.S. Court of Appeals for the Second Circuit found a fundamental change in circumstances in Montenegro when it became an independent state;[259]
- The U.S. Court of Appeals for the Fifth Circuit found a fundamental change in circumstances in Kosovo in the case of a Kosovar Muslim;[260]
- The Eighth Circuit found a fundamental change in circumstances in Kenya[261] and Liberia,[262] changed conditions in Sierra Leone,[263] and improved conditions in Mauritania;[264] and

---

[255] *Ahmadshah v. Ashcroft*, 396 F.3d 917, 921 (8th Cir. 2005) (finding that the government's evidence of changed conditions does not address the fear of persecution for apostasy).

[256] *Margos v. Gonzales*, 443 F.3d 593, 598 (7th Cir. 2006). *But see Hanna v. Keisler*, 506 F.3d 933, 939 (9th Cir. 2007) (holding that changed circumstances is not established merely by showing the Ba'ath party is no longer in power).

[257] *Ly v. Mukasey*, 524 F.3d 126, 133 (1st Cir. 2008).

[258] *Vasili v. Holder*, 732 F.3d 83, 90–92 (1st Cir. 2013); *Ruci v. Holder*, 720 F.3d 239, 243–44 (1st Cir. 2013).

[259] *Lecaj v. Holder*, 616 F.3d 111 (2d Cir. 2010) (finding that the 2006 Department of State report was sufficient evidence to show a fundamental change in circumstances).

[260] *Shehu v. Gonzales*, 443 F.3d 435, 439–40 (5th Cir. 2006).

[261] *Gitimu v. Holder*, 581 F.3d 769, 773–74 (8th Cir. 2009) (finding changed political conditions where the president of Kenya was from the applicant's political party, the country report indicated no politically motivated killings, and the applicant's family lived safely in Kenya).

[262] *Cooke v. Mukasey*, 538 F.3d 899, 908 (8th Cir. 2008).

[263] *Diallo v. Mukasey*, 508 F.3d 451, 455 (8th Cir. 2007).

[264] *Sow v. Mukasey*, 546 F.3d 953, 957 (8th Cir. 2008); *see also Ba v. Mukasey*, 539 F.3d 1265, 1269 (10th Cir. 2008) (finding improved conditions in Mauritania for Fulanis who suffered past persecution).

- The U.S. Court of Appeals for the Eleventh Circuit found a fundamental change in circumstances in Albania based on the contents of the Department of State reports.[265]

  ➢ **Practice Pointer**: Although some courts have held that personal changes in circumstances should be considered, it is possible to argue that a fundamental change in circumstances refers only to changed country conditions. The regulation itself does not include the word "personal," and international guidance clearly states that "circumstances" refer to fundamental changes in the country, not personal changes. A change in circumstances does, however, include personal changes in circumstances for purposes of the exception to the one-year filing deadline. See Part IV.A.2.i. for a detailed discussion of the changed circumstances exception to the one-year filing deadline.

ii. Internal Relocation

Under regulations that became effective January 5, 2001, an applicant may be denied asylum or withholding of removal if the applicant "could avoid future persecution by relocating to another part" of his or her home country.[266] If the applicant has established past persecution, the government may also rebut the presumption of a well-founded fear by demonstrating that the applicant could avoid persecution by relocating to another part of the country. Regarding the ability to avoid persecution, relevant considerations are whether the persecutor has the ability and willingness to target the applicant elsewhere in the applicant's country and whether the government has the ability and willingness to control the persecutor.[267]

An internal relocation alternative is only sufficient to rebut a presumption of a well-founded fear if, "under *all* the circumstances, it would be reasonable to expect the applicant to do so."[268] In determining the "reasonableness" of an internal relocation option, adjudicators should consider, among other things:

- Whether the applicant would face other serious harm in the place of suggested relocation;[269]

---

[265] *Mehmeti v. Att'y Gen.*, 572 F.3d 1196 (11th Cir. 2009) (relying solely on the Department of State country reports).

[266] 8 CFR §§208.13(b)(2)(ii), 1208.13(b)(2)(ii) (2014).

[267] *See, e.g., Arboleda v. Att'y Gen.* 434 F.3d 1220, 1226 (11th Cir. 2006) (finding that the applicant's personal experience and country conditions demonstrated that relocation was not a viable option because the persecutor, the FARC, operated countrywide and thus had the ability to persecute the applicant throughout the country); *Matter of C–A–L–*, 21 I&N Dec. 754 (BIA 1997).

[268] 8 CFR §§208.13(b)(1)(i)(B), (2)(ii), 208.16(b)(1)–(2), 1208.13(b)(1)(i)(B), (2)(ii), & 1208.16(b)(1)–(2) (2014) (emphasis added).

[269] Executive Office for Immigration Review; New Rules Regarding Procedures for Asylum and Withholding of Removal, 63 Fed. Reg. 31945, 31947 (June 11, 1998) (to be codified at 8 CFR pt. 208) (describing "other serious harm" as "harm that may not be inflicted on account of race, religion,

Continued

- Any ongoing civil strife within the country;[270]
- Administrative, economic, or judicial infrastructure;[271]
- Geographic limitations;
- Social, economic, and cultural constraints, such as age, gender, health, social, and familial ties; and[272]
- Any other factor specific to the case that would make it unreasonable to relocate,[273] such as the size of the country.[274]

The regulations also note that these factors "may or may not be relevant, depending on all the circumstances of the case, and are not necessarily determinative" of whether relocation is reasonable.[275]

There is no requirement that an applicant first attempt to relocate within the country of feared persecution prior to fleeing.[276] However, if the applicant did relocate and was able to live safely and openly for a significant period of time prior to fleeing, that may be evidence that he or she could reasonably relocate within the country of feared persecution, and thus, does not have a well-founded fear of future persecution.[277] Therefore, the circumstances under which the applicant lived after

---

nationality, membership in a particular social group, or political opinion, but is so serious that it equals the severity of persecution").

[270] *See, e.g., Awale v. Ashcroft,* 384 F.3d 527, 532 (8th Cir. 2004) (finding that evidence that members of Somali minority clans continue to be "subjected to harassment, intimidation, and abuse by armed gunmen of all affiliations" and that travel is difficult because rival groups control routes of transportation indicates that it would not be reasonable to require applicant to internally relocate).

[271] *See, e.g., Knezevic v. Ashcroft,* 367 F.3d 1206, 1214 (9th Cir. 2004) (finding that internal relocation would not be reasonable when there was evidence that Bosnian Serb applicants, ages 75 and 66, would have great difficulty finding employment while having no means of supporting themselves).

[272] 8 CFR §§208.13(b)(3), 208.16(b)(3), 1208.13(b)(3), & 1208.16(b)(3) (2014). *See, e.g., Knezevic v. Ashcroft,* 367 F.3d at 1214 (finding that internal relocation would not be reasonable when there was evidence that Bosnian Serb applicants, ages 75 and 66, would have great difficulty finding employment while having no means of supporting themselves).

[273] 8 CFR §§208.13(b)(3), 1208.13(b)(3) (2014). *See also* UNHCR *Handbook, supra* note 33, ¶ 91. The same factors are considered in determining whether a person's life or freedom would be threatened in a withholding of removal claim. 8 CFR §§208.16(b)(3), 1208.16(b)(3) (2014).

[274] *Matter of Kasinga,* 21 I&N Dec. 357 (BIA 1996) (finding countrywide persecution reasonable even when arising out of a local conflict due to Togo being a relatively small country).

[275] 8 CFR §§208.13(b)(3), 208.16(b)(3), 1208.13(b)(3), & 1208.16(b)(3) (2014).

[276] *Matter of C–A–L–,* 21 I&N Dec. 754 (BIA 1997). *See Kaiser v. Ashcroft,* 390 F.3d 653, 659–60 (9th Cir. 2004) (finding that the applicant could not avoid persecution through internal relocation when the applicant received threats while living in two distant areas of Pakistan).

[277] *See, e.g., Singh v. Holder,* 750 F.3d 84 (1st Cir. 2014) (holding that the applicant lacked a well-founded fear of persecution on account of his Sikh faith because he was able to relocate to Delhi and remain in India for several months without further harassment or arrest after his mistreatment at home and to obtain his travel visa without any undue restriction); *Moran-Quinteros v. Holder,* 352 F. App'x 974 (6th Cir. 2009) (finding that the applicant did not have a well-founded fear of persecution because

Continued

relocating are highly relevant.[278] For example, if the applicant did relocate, but was forced to live in hiding in order to protect him or herself, that may be evidence that the applicant's relocation was not reasonable under all of the circumstances.[279] Moreover, if the applicant did relocate but continued to be targeted and harmed by his or her persecutor, that may be strong evidence of his or her inability to safely and reasonably relocate, and thus, may strengthen his or her well-founded fear claim.[280]

- **Practice Pointer**: Whether an applicant could have avoided persecution by relocating is not relevant in determining whether he or she suffered past persecution on account of a protected ground. If the applicant suffered past persecution, whether he or she could safely relocate is relevant only in considering the applicant's ability to avoid future persecution for purposes of rebutting the presumption of a well-founded fear.[281]

The identity of the feared persecutor may be relevant to the reasonableness of an internal relocation option. If the feared persecutor is a government actor or is government-sponsored, there is a presumption that there is no reasonable internal relocation option and the burden is on DHS to overcome this presumption.[282] To overcome the presumption, DHS must demonstrate by a preponderance of the evidence that the applicant could relocate internally and that the relocation would be reasonable.

On the other hand, if the feared persecutor is a non-governmental actor, it is the applicant's burden to establish that he or she could not avoid persecution by

---

the applicant's family, including her father who had been threatened by guerillas in Guatemala, moved to another village in Guatemala and had lived there safely since 1990).

[278] *See, e.g., Gambashidzez v. Ashcroft,* 381 F.3d 187, 193 (3d Cir. 2004) (finding that the BIA erred in resting solely on the applicant's eight-month residence in another area of Georgia without a police encounter when denying applicant's claim, and stating that the BIA should have considered the circumstances in which the applicant lived during the period of relocation).

[279] 8 CFR §208.13(b)(2)(ii) (2014). *See, e.g., Essohou v. Gonzales*, 471 F.3d 518 (4th Cir. 2006).

[280] *See, e.g., Kaiser v. Ashcroft,* 390 F.3d at 659–60 (finding that threats received by the applicant while living in two distant areas of Pakistan compelled the conclusion that the applicant could not avoid persecution through internal relocation).

[281] 8 CFR §208.13(b)(1)(i)(B) (2014). *See, e.g., Hagi-Salad v. Ashcroft*, 359 F.3d 1044, 1048 (8th Cir. 2004). *See also infra* ch. 4 for a detailed discussion of the shifting burdens of proof.

[282] 8 CFR §§208.13(b)(3)(ii), 208.16(b)(3)(ii), 1208.13(b)(3)(ii), & 1208.16(b)(3)(ii) (2014). *See, e.g., Singh v. Ilchert*, 63 F.3d 1501 (9th Cir. 1995); *Singh v. Moschorak*, 53 F.3d 1031 (9th Cir. 1995) ("It has never been thought that there are safe places within a nation when it is the nation's government that has engaged in the acts of punishing opinion that have driven the victim to leave the country."); *see also Abdel-Masieh v. INS*, 73 F.3d 579, 587 (5th Cir. 1996) (holding that when a party seeking asylum demonstrates that a government is the "persecutor," the burden falls on DHS to show the government's persecutory actions are "truly limited to a clearly delineated and limited locality and situation"). *But see Matter of R–*, 20 I&N Dec. 621, 627 (BIA 1992) (denying asylum to a Sikh from the Punjab who had been subjected to brutal physical abuse by Indian police, because he failed to demonstrate he would face countrywide persecution).

relocating internally within his or her country or that such relocation would be unreasonable, unless the applicant already has suffered past persecution.[283] In those cases involving non-governmental persecutors, courts have considered whether an applicant has the ability to or can reasonably be expected to relocate to another area in his or her home country.[284] The BIA has also considered whether the applicant, if ordered removed, would have to pass through any unsafe part of his or her home country before arriving in a safe area.[285]

Courts have found that internal relocation would be unreasonable under the specific evidence presented for the following applicants:

- An individual who suffered past persecution at the hands of the FARC in Colombia;[286]
- A gay man suffering from AIDS in Mexico;[287]
- An individual in the Democratic Republic of Congo who was only safe due to efforts to hide;[288]
- An individual who fears the Taliban rebels in Afghanistan;[289]

---

[283] 8 CFR §208.13(b)(3)(i)–(ii) (2014).

[284] *See, e.g.*, *Lopez-Gomez v. Ashcroft*, 263 F.3d 442 (5th Cir. 2001) (finding applicant failed to show countrywide threat in Guatemala); *Etugh v. INS*, 921 F.2d 36, 39 (3d Cir. 1991); *Matter of A–E–M–*, 21 I&N 1157, 1177 (BIA 1998); *Matter of H–*, 21 I&N Dec. 337, 349 n.7 (BIA 1996); *Matter of [name not provided]*, A76 512 001 (IJ Oct. 18, 2000) (finding that applicant fleeing forced marriage in China could not be expected to relocate within the country), *reported in* 77 INTERPRETER RELEASES 1634–36 (Nov. 20, 2000).

[285] *Matter of H–*, 21 I&N Dec. 337, 349 n.7 (BIA 1996).

[286] *Arboleda v. Att'y Gen.*, 434 F.3d 1220, 1226 (11th Cir. 2006) (finding the record in this case compelled the conclusion that the FARC operates countrywide in Colombia and that relocation was not a viable option).

[287] *Boer-Sedano v. Gonzales*, 418 F.3d 1082, 1091 (9th Cir. 2005) (stating that "We hold, therefore, that after considering the cumulative evidence on the social and cultural constraints Boer-Sedano would face as a homosexual man in Mexico, his current health, and the likelihood that serious harm would come to him if forced to relocate to Mexico where he could not obtain his required medication, no reasonable fact-finder could conclude that the INS has carried its burden of showing that such relocation was reasonable.").

[288] *Essohou v. Gonzales*, 471 F.3d 518, (4th Cir. 2006) (vacating and remanding the BIA's denial of asylum based on the reasonableness of internal relocation where the court found that the facts on the record suggested that "[a]ny intermittent period in which Bockou Essohou was not specifically troubled by the Cobras was not due to a reasonable, internal relocation; rather, it was due to her efforts to hide in conjunction with the timing of the Cobras' forays").

[289] *Oryakhil v. Mukasey*, 528 F.3d 993, 1000 (7th Cir. 2008) (finding that to expect an applicant to revert to a soldier's lifestyle in a hostile, conflict-ridden region of Afghanistan and to place his family in jeopardy by doing so, does not "strike us as reasonable").

- An individual who fears the Chinese government;[290]
- A native of Afghanistan who repeatedly experienced anti-foreigner threats and violence while living in Germany;[291]
- A man persecuted in the past by the Shining Path revolutionary group in Peru;[292]
- Elderly Serbian individuals in Bosnia-Herzegovina who had lost their home and business, and who had no family members in the area;[293]
- A domestic violence and trafficking victim from China; and[294]
- Applicants from Pakistan.[295]
- On the other hand, courts have found that internal relocation would be reasonable under the specific evidence presented for the following applicants:
- Catholic and Christian applicants in Bangladesh;[296]
- Applicants who suffered past persecution in Guatemala on account of political opinion;[297]

---

[290] *Yang v. Gonzales*, 427 F.3d 1117 (8th Cir. 2005) (finding Chinese couple with two U.S. citizen children, who wished to have two more children, had a well-founded fear of persecution if they returned to China and could not reasonably relocate within China).

[291] *Mashiri v. Ashcroft*, 383 F.3d 1112, 1123 (9th Cir. 2004).

[292] *Cardenas v. INS*, 294 F.3d 1062 (9th Cir. 2002).

[293] *Knezevic v. Ashcroft*, 367 F.3d at 1214–15 (9th Cir. 2004). *See also Vladimirova v. Ashcroft*, 377 F.3d 690, 697 (7th Cir. 2004) (noting that the DOS report makes clear that individuals practicing unsanctioned religions face harassment throughout Bulgaria); *Hagi v. Ashcroft*, 359 F.3d 1044 (8th Cir. 2004) (remanding the case to the BIA because the BIA failed to properly consider the factors outlined in this regulation).

[294] *Gao v. Gonzales*, 440 F.3d 62, 71 (2d Cir. 2006) (vacating and remanding the BIA's determination that a Chinese asylum applicant fleeing domestic violence and human trafficking could reasonably relocate within the country. The court held that the BIA determination was contradicted by the record. The applicant testified that she had attempted unsuccessfully to relocate within China. The court further held that the BIA cannot solely determine whether the applicant could avoid persecution by relocating, but must also determine whether it would be *reasonable* to require relocation). *See also Tu Kai Yang v. Gonzales,* 427 F.3d 1117, 1122 (8th Cir. 2005) ("The IJ's suggestion that petitioners could potentially avoid persecution by relocating within China is incorrect.").

[295] *Kaiser v. Ashcroft*, 390 F.3d 653, 660 (9th Cir. 2004) ("Thus, the evidence compels the conclusion that petitioners could not relocate safely anywhere in Pakistan.").

[296] *Gomes v. Gonzales*, 429 F.3d 1264, 1267 (9th Cir. 2005) (finding that applicants, who claimed asylum based on being Catholics and Christians, failed to show by compelling evidence that they could not safely relocate within Bangladesh).

[297] *Pascual v. Mukasey*, 514 F.3d 483, 489 (6th Cir. 2007) (finding that the record indicated that the applicant could return to a "very quiet" mountainous region where his family has lived since 1991). *Lopez-Gomez v. Ashcroft*, 263 F.3d 442, 446 (5th Cir. 2001) (holding that the BIA's determination that the petitioners, who feared persecution based on political affiliation, could have relocated within Guatemala was supported by substantial evidence); *see also Mazariegos v. Office of the Att'y Gen.*, 241 F.3d 1320, 1328 (11th Cir. 2001) (finding substantial evidence supporting the BIA's determination that

Continued

- A Christian applicant in Indonesia;[298] and
- A Jewish applicant in Ukraine where there was a lack of evidence that anti-Semitism was sanctioned by the government.[299]

According to UNHCR's Handbook, "a person will not be excluded from refugee status merely because he could have sought refuge in another part of the country, if under all the circumstances it would not have been *reasonable* to expect him to do so."[300] UNHCR has noted that an internal flight alternative must be accessible in safety and durable in character.[301] Moreover, according to UNHCR, the possibility to find safety in other parts of the country must have existed at the time of flight and continue to be available when the refugee status determination is made.[302] In addition to physical safety, the applicant should have access to basic civil, political, and socioeconomic rights in the area of relocation.[303] According to one commentator, determinations of reasonableness should include consideration of the financial and logistical barriers to relocating internally and whether the refugee would be placed in an illusory or unpredictable situation.[304]

> ➢ **Practice Pointer**: Practitioners should be aware of the shifting burdens of proof regarding internal relocation. If an applicant has shown past persecution, or if the applicant has a well-founded fear of persecution by the government or a government-sponsored actor, internal relocation is presumed to be unreasonable and the burden of proof is on the government to show by a preponderance of the evidence that "it would be reasonable to expect the applicant to" relocate within the country of persecution.[305] The burden of establishing that internal relocation would

---

the petitioner, a soldier in the Guatemalan army who feared persecution at the hands of guerrillas, had a reasonable prospect of resettling safely within Guatemala).

298 *Setiadi v. Gonzales*, 437 F.3d 710, 714 n.3 (8th Cir. 2006) (finding that the record supported the BIA's determination that the applicant, who claimed asylum as a Christian fearing persecution, could relocate within Indonesia).

299 *Yakovenko v. Gonzales*, 477 F.3d 631, 637 (8th Cir. 2007) (upholding the BIA's determination that the petitioner, who claimed asylum because of past persecution based on her Jewish faith, failed to show that it would be unsafe or unreasonable to relocate in the Ukraine where the BIA and the IJ found a lack of evidence to corroborate that anti-Semitism was "sanctioned, supported, or tolerated by the Ukrainian government.").

300 UNHCR Handbook, *supra* note 33, ¶ 91 (emphasis added).

301 U.N. High Comm'r for Refugees, *An Overview of Protection Issues in Western Europe: Legislative Trends and Positions Taken by UNHCR*, 1 European Series no. 3, 32 (Sept. 1995), *available at* www.unhcr.org/46e65e1e2.pdf.

302 *Id.*

303 *Id.*; *see also* Guy S. Goodwin-Gill & Jane McAdams, THE REFUGEE IN INTERNATIONAL LAW 74 (2d ed. 1996). (noting that "for various reasons it may be unreasonable to expect the asylum seeker to move internally").

304 James Hathaway, THE LAW OF REFUGEE STATUS 134 (1st ed. 1991).

305 8 CFR §§208.13(b)(1)(B), 1208.13(b)(1)(B) (2014).

not be reasonable is only on the applicant if he or she does not establish past persecution and fears persecution at the hands of a non-government actor.[306] See chapter 4 for a detailed discussion of the shifting burdens of proof in asylum, withholding of removal, and CAT claims.

iii. Humanitarian Asylum

Even if a preponderance of the evidence demonstrates that there has been a fundamental change in country conditions or that internal relocation is an option for the applicant, the adjudicator may still grant asylum to the applicant if "the applicant has demonstrated compelling reasons for being unwilling or unable to return to the country arising out of the severity of the past persecution" or if "the applicant has established that there is a reasonable possibility that he or she may suffer other serious harm upon removal to that country."[307] In other words, a favorable exercise of the adjudicator's discretion may be warranted for humanitarian reasons, even if future persecution is unlikely.[308] A grant of asylum under these circumstances is often referred to as "humanitarian asylum."

a. Severity of Past Persecution

---

[306] 8 CFR §§208.13(b)(3)(i), 1208.13(b)(3)(i) (2014).

[307] 8 CFR §§208.13(b)(1)(iii), 1208.13(b)(1)(iii) (2014). *See Hanna v. Keisler*, 506 F.3d 933, 939 (9th Cir. 2007) (remanding claim for consideration of other serious harm Chaldean Catholic would face if returned to Iraq).

[308] *Matter of Chen*, 20 I&N Dec. 16, 19 (BIA 1989) (finding the applicant to be eligible for asylum based on past persecution alone, where the applicant suffered a long history of persecution beginning when he was eight years old, no longer had any family in China, and had a subjectively genuine fear of future persecution). *See also Lal v. INS*, 255 F.3d 998, 1003, *amended on reh'g,* 268 F.3d 1148 (9th Cir. 2001) (finding applicants were eligible for asylum based on the severity of their past persecution, which included repeated arbitrary detentions, painful and humiliating torture, sexual assault, threats, and severe intimidation); *Vongsakdy v. INS*, 171 F.3d 1203 (9th Cir. 1999) (finding that a Laotian national suffered egregious past persecution, including imprisonment in a labor camp, beatings, torture, inadequate food and water, denial of medical treatment, and a severed thumb); *Matter of S-A-K- and H-A-H-*, 24 I&N Dec. 464 (BIA 2008) (holding that discretion should be exercised to grant asylum to a mother and daughter who had been involuntarily subjected to FGM based on the severity of the persecution they suffered); *Matter of H–*, 21 I&N Dec. 337, 347–48 (BIA 1996) (holding that "[c]entral to a discretionary finding in past persecution cases should be careful attention to compelling, humanitarian considerations that would be involved if the refugee were to be forced to return to a country where he or she was persecuted in the past," and finding that humanitarian reasons may include the applicant's age, health, or family ties in the United States); *Matter of B–*, 21 I&N Dec. 66 (BIA 1995) (finding that an Afghani who had suffered persecution under the previous Communist regime was no longer at risk of persecution, but granting asylum based on the severity of the past persecution the applicant had suffered). *But see Reyes-Morales v. Gonzales,* 435 F.3d 937, 942 (8th Cir. 2006); *Ngarurih v. Ashcroft,* 371 F.3d 182 (4th Cir. 2004); *Francois v. INS*, 283 F.3d 926, 932 (8th Cir. 2002) (finding that applicant who was interrogated, threatened that her father would be killed, and denied an exit visa failed to demonstrate severe or long lasting harm sufficient to warrant humanitarian asylum); *Matter of N-M-A-*, 22 I&N Dec. 312 (BIA 1998) (noting that the harm was not of a great degree, suffered over a great period of time, and did not result in severe psychological trauma such that a grant in the absence of a well-founded fear was warranted).

The seminal case addressing eligibility for humanitarian asylum in the context of severe past persecution is *Matter of Chen*, where the BIA held that discretion should be exercised to grant the applicant asylum even though there was little likelihood of future persecution.[309] In that case, the applicant suffered a long history of persecution in China, including being held under house arrest when he was eight years old, deprived of the opportunity to go to school, abused by teachers and classmates, and physically abused, resulting in hearing loss, anxiety, and suicidal thoughts. The applicant no longer had any family in China and still had a subjectively genuine fear of future harm.[310] While *Matter of Chen* did not establish a clear measure for when past harm becomes severe enough to warrant a grant of asylum based on past persecution alone, the BIA stated that "*all* other factors, both *favorable* and adverse, should...be considered."[311] This means that while a comparable level of harm may warrant a favorable exercise of discretion, there is a range of past persecution that could qualify an applicant for humanitarian asylum.[312]

---

[309] *Matter of Chen*, 20 I&N Dec. 16 (BIA 1989). *See Lal v. INS*, 255 F.3d 998, 1003, *amended on reh'g*, 268 F.3d 1148 (9th Cir. 2001) (finding applicants were eligible for asylum based on the severity of their past persecution, which included repeated arbitrary detentions, painful and humiliating torture, sexual assault, threats, and severe intimidation); *Vongsakdy v. INS*, 171 F.3d 1203 (9th Cir. 1999) (finding that a Laotian national suffered egregious past persecution, including imprisonment in a labor camp, beatings, torture, inadequate food and water, denial of medical treatment, and a severed thumb); *Matter of H–*, 21 I&N Dec. 337, 347–48 (BIA 1996) (finding that humanitarian reasons may include the applicant's age, health, or family ties in the United States). *But see Francois v. INS*, 283 F.3d 926, 932 (8th Cir. 2002) (finding that applicant who was interrogated, threatened that her father would be killed, and denied an exit visa failed to demonstrate severe or long lasting harm sufficient to warrant humanitarian asylum).

[310] *Id.*

[311] *Id.* at 19. Advocates have submitted evidence regarding employment, certificates of achievement, school records, attendance at English classes, community involvement, and letters from the applicant's church, synagogue, or mosque attesting to membership, volunteer work, and attendance at services. *See, e.g., Tamara-Gomez v. Gonzales*, 447 F.3d 343, 348 n.4 (5th Cir. 2006) (noting that the applicants submitted letters from teachers, pastors, and friends confirming that the applicants were model members of the community).

[312] *Compare Matter of S–A–K– & H–A–H–*, 24 I&N Dec. 464 (BIA 2008) (holding that humanitarian asylum should be granted to a mother and daughter who had been involuntarily subjected to FGM, the daughter suffered the harm without anesthesia, the mother almost died from infection, both had to have follow-up procedures and the medical problems were ongoing, and the mother was beaten for opposing the procedure being performed on her daughters); *Matter of H–*, 21 I&N Dec. 337, 347 (BIA 1996) (remanding the case, noting that the Somali applicant was detained for five days and beaten and his father and brother were killed in clan warfare, and stating, "Central to a discretionary finding in past persecution cases should be careful attention to compelling, humanitarian considerations that would be involved if the refugee were to be forced to return to a country where he or she was persecuted in the past."); & *Matter of B–*, 21 I&N Dec. 66 (BIA 1995) (holding that discretion should be exercised to grant asylum to an Afghan applicant based on the severity of past persecution, where the applicant had been detained for 13 months during which time he was deprived of sleep, beaten, shocked, provided inadequate food and medical care, interrogated, and mentally tortured), *with Matter of N–M–A–*, 22 I&N Dec. 312 (BIA 1998) (finding that humanitarian asylum was not warranted where the applicant's father was kidnapped, his home was searched twice, and he was detained, beaten, and deprived of food

Continued

In *Matter of B–*, the BIA applied its *Matter of Chen* analysis and found that humanitarian asylum was appropriate where the applicant had been imprisoned for political reasons for 13 months under "deplorable" conditions.[313] Noting the routine use of various forms of physical torture and psychological abuse that had been used against the applicant, the BIA found that the applicant had compelling reasons for being unwilling or unable to return to Afghanistan arising out of the severity of the past persecution he had suffered.[314]

The BIA then clarified in *Matter of N–M–A–* that asylum is warranted for humanitarian reasons only if the applicant demonstrates "atrocious forms of persecution."[315] In that case, the Board declined to extend humanitarian asylum to an applicant who had been detained and beaten for one month, while knowing that his father who had disappeared was likely dead. The BIA looked to the degree of harm suffered, length of time the harm was inflicted, and lack of evidence of severe psychological trauma stemming from the harm.[316] More recently, the BIA granted humanitarian asylum to applicants from Somalia who had undergone female genital mutilation, noting that it was an "atrocious form of persecution that results in continuing physical pain and discomfort."[317]

Several circuit courts and the BIA have addressed whether past harm is severe enough to merit a grant of asylum when future persecution is unlikely.[318] Generally,

---

for three days). *Compare Lal v. INS*, 255 F.3d 998, 1003, *amended on reh'g,* 268 F.3d 1148 (9th Cir. 2001) (finding applicants were eligible for asylum based on the severity of their past persecution, which included repeated arbitrary detentions, painful and humiliating torture, sexual assault, threats, and severe intimidation); *& Vongsakdy v. INS*, 171 F.3d 1203 (9th Cir. 1999) (finding that a Laotian national suffered egregious past persecution, including imprisonment in a labor camp, beatings, torture, inadequate food and water, denial of medical treatment, and a severed thumb), *with Reyes-Morales v. Gonzales,* 435 F.3d 937, 942 (8th Cir. 2006) (finding that past persecution was not sufficiently serious to compel a discretionary grant in the absence of well-founded fear where the applicant was beaten to unconsciousness by the Salvadoran military, resulting in deformity and scars, and where the applicant's friend was killed); & *Ngarurih v. Ashcroft,* 371 F.3d 182 (4th Cir. 2004) (finding that past persecution was not sufficiently serious to compel a discretionary grant in the absence of well-founded fear where the applicant was detained at a local police station, threatened until he gave names of protest leaders, held in prison for several months, stripped of his clothing, held in a cell that was flooded with cold water that reached his chest during the first week, and held in a cell with no light, windows, or toilets).

313 *Matter of B–*, 21 I&N Dec. 66, 72 (BIA 1995).

314 *Id.*

315 *Matter of N–M–A–*, 22 I&N Dec. 312, 325 (BIA 1998).

316 *Id.* at 326.

317 *Matter of S–A–K– & H–A–H–*, 24 I&N Dec. 464, 465 (BIA 2008).

318 In *Lal v. INS*, the Ninth Circuit found that the applicants were eligible for asylum based on the severity of their past persecution, which included repeated arbitrary detentions, painful and humiliating torture, sexual assault, threats, and severe intimidation. *Lal v. INS*, 255 F.3d 998, 1003, *amended on reh'g*, 268 F.3d 1148 (9th Cir. 2001). Similarly, in *Vongsakdy v. INS,* the court found that a Laotian national who had been imprisoned in a labor camp and had suffered beatings, torture, inadequate food and water, denial of medical treatment, and a severed thumb had been subjected to egregious past persecution. *Vongsakdy v. INS*, 171 F.3d 1203 (9th Cir. 1999). The court also found the fact that the

Continued

in determining the severity of the past persecution, the following factors should be considered:

(1) duration of persecution;

(2) intensity of persecution;

(3) age at the time of persecution;

(4) persecution of family members;

(5) conditions under which the persecution was inflicted;

(6) whether it would be unduly frightening or painful for the applicant to return to the country of persecution; and

(7) whether there are continuing health or psychological problems or other negative repercussions stemming from the harm inflicted.[319] Although the severity of past harm can yield a grant of asylum even if there is no well-founded fear of future persecution, the applicant still must demonstrate that the severe harm was suffered on account of a protected characteristic.[320]

- **Practice Pointer**: Note that the regulations require that the compelling reasons for the applicant being unwilling or unable to return must arise out of the severity of the past persecution.[321]

---

applicant remained in Laos for a considerable period of time following his release from the labor camp was "irrelevant" to evaluating the "atrocity" of his past persecution. *Id.* at 1207; *see also Matter of Chen*, 20 I&N Dec. 16, 18–19 (BIA 1989) (finding that a favorable exercise of discretion may be warranted for humanitarian reasons despite changed country conditions), *codified by* 8 CFR §§208.13(b)(1)(iii), 1208.13(b)(1)(iii) (2014); *Matter of H–*, 21 I&N Dec. 337, 347–48 (BIA 1996) (finding that humanitarian reasons may include the applicant's age, health, or family ties in the United States); *Matter of B–F–O–*, A78 677 043 (BIA Nov. 6, 2001), *reported in* 21 Immigr. Law Today 135 (Mar. 2002) (in this unpublished decision, the BIA found that a Nicaraguan street child suffered atrocious forms of persecution, meriting a grant of asylum without regard to current country conditions). *But see Francois v. INS*, 283 F.3d 926, 932 (8th Cir. 2002) (finding that applicant, who was interrogated, threatened that her father would be killed, and denied an exit visa, failed to demonstrate severe or long-lasting harm sufficient to warrant humanitarian asylum); *Matter of N–M–A–*, 22 I&N Dec. 312, 326 (BIA 1998) (finding no compelling reasons where the applicant suffered a month-long detention, beatings, and the disappearance and likely death of his father, but where there was no evidence of severe psychological trauma). In *Sowe v. Mukasey*, the Ninth Circuit remanded a claim of humanitarian asylum by a Sierra Leonean applicant where the BIA failed to determine whether witnessing his parents' murder, the severing of his brother's hand, and the kidnapping of his sister provided compelling reasons for being unwilling to return to Sierra Leone. *Sowe v. Mukasey*, 538 F.3d 1281, 1287–88 (9th Cir. 2008). In *Niang v. Gonzales*, the Fourth Circuit stated that humanitarian asylum may be an option for women facing a "Sophie's choice" of either taking her U.S. citizen child to Senegal where the child will suffer FGM or leaving the child in the U.S. alone. *Niang v. Gonzales*, 492 F.3d 505, 514 n.13 (4th Cir. 2007). The BIA also granted humanitarian asylum in *Matter of S–A–K– and H–A–H–* to a mother and daughter based on the severity of the past FGM both had experienced. *Matter of S–A–K– and H–A–H–*, 24 I&N Dec. 464 (BIA 2008).

[319] *See* AOBTC Workbook, pt. I, *supra* note 34, at 49.

[320] *See, e.g., Lukwago v. Ashcroft*, 329 F.3d 157, 173–74 (3d Cir. 2003).

[321] 8 CFR §§208.13(b)(1)(iii), 1208.13(b)(1)(iii) (2014).

b. Other Serious Harm

The Board's approach to humanitarian asylum based on severity of past persecution is embodied at 8 CFR §1208.13(b)(1)(iii)(A). At that time, the second form of humanitarian asylum based on "other serious harm" had not yet been established. Eventually, however, the AG found the *Matter of Chen* approach to be too limited.[322] Thus, in 2001, the regulations were changed both to endorse the approach to humanitarian asylum based on severity of past persecution and to add a specific, additional, and separate basis for humanitarian asylum.[323] This alternative basis for humanitarian asylum states that an adjudicator may exercise his or her discretion to grant asylum in the absence of a well-founded fear of future persecution if "the applicant has established that there is a reasonable possibility that he or she may suffer other serious harm upon removal to that country."[324]

Prior to the BIA's decision in 2012 in *Matter of L–S–*, there had been little legal guidance interpreting the meaning of "other serious harm" under the regulation.[325] Although not part of the regulation itself, the Supplemental Information to the regulation clarified that "other serious harm" need not be inflicted on account of race, religion, nationality, membership in a particular social group, or political opinion.[326] However, such harm must itself be so serious that it equals the severity of persecution. Mere economic disadvantage or the inability to practice one's chosen profession would not qualify, whereas ongoing civil strife, such as that discussed in *Matter of B–*, may be an example of "other serious harm."[327] "Other serious harm" must be more than hardships that the applicant may experience upon removal after having spent a significant amount of time in the United States.[328]

---

[322] *See* 8 CFR §§208.13(b)(1)(iii)(B), 1208.13(b)(1)(iii)(B) (2014); Executive Office for Immigration Review; New Rules Regarding Procedures for Asylum and Withholding of Removal, 63 Fed. Reg. 31,945, 31,947 (proposed June 11, 1998) (to be codified at 8 CFR pt. 208) (Supplementary Information) (noting that "The Department recognizes, however, that the existing regulation may represent an overly restrictive approach to the exercise of discretion in cases involving past persecution, but no well-founded fear of future persecution. The Department believes it is appropriate to broaden the standards for the exercise of discretion in such cases.").

[323] *See* 8 CFR §§208.13(b)(1)(iii), 1208.13(b)(1)(iii) (2014); Executive Office for Immigration Review; New Rules Regarding Procedures for Asylum and Withholding of Removal, 63 Fed. Reg. 31,945, 31,947 (proposed June 11, 1998) (to be codified at 8 CFR pt. 208) (Supplementary Information).

[324] 8 CFR §§208.13(b)(1)(iii)(B), 1208.13(b)(1)(iii)(B) (2014). *See Matter of L–S–*, 25 I&N Dec. 705 (BIA 2012). *See also*, *Liti v. Gonzales*, 411 F.3d 631, 641–42 (6th Cir. 2005); *Belishta v. Ashcroft*, 378 F.3d 1078, 1081 (9th Cir. 2004).

[325] *See Matter of L–S–*, 25 I&N Dec. 705 (BIA 2012).

[326] Executive Office for Immigration Review; New Rules Regarding Procedures for Asylum and Withholding of Removal, 63 Fed. Reg. 31,945, 31,947 (proposed June 11, 1998) (to be codified at 8 CFR pt. 208) (Supplementary Information).

[327] *Id.*

[328] *See* Asylum Procedures, 65 Fed. Reg. 76121, 76127 (Dec. 6, 2000) (to be codified at 8 CFR pt. 208), *superseding Matter of H–,* 21 I&N Dec. 337, 347 (BIA 1996). *See infra* Part V for a detailed discussion of the exercise of discretion in asylum claims.

The "other serious harm" provision has not been applied or analyzed in case law to the extent of the severity of past persecution provision.[329] However, in the 2012 decision of *Matter of L–S–*, the BIA addressed this provision in detail. The Board noted that the "other serious harm" provision differs from the severity of past persecution provision in that "an applicant need not show that the harm suffered in the past was atrocious. Instead, the inquiry is forward-looking."[330] The BIA clarified that the focus of an "other serious harm" analysis should be on "current conditions and the potential for new physical or psychological harm that the applicant might suffer."[331] The BIA held that, while "other serious harm" must be so serious that it equals the severity of persecution,[332] it may be wholly unrelated to the applicant's

---

[329] *See, e.g., Precetaj v. Holder*, 649 F.3d 72, 75 (1st Cir. 2011) (noting the "other serious harm" provision as an alternative basis for humanitarian asylum, but citing law that predated it and discussing only relief based on the severity of past persecution); *Mehmeti v. Att'y Gen.*, 572 F.3d 1196, 1200–01 (11th Cir. 2009) (noting both provisions of the regulation but applying only the severity of past persecution provision); *Ngarurih v. Ashcroft*, 371 F.3d 182, 190 (4th Cir. 2004) (noting both the severity of past persecution and "other serious harm" avenues for humanitarian asylum, but focusing only on the former). *But see, e.g., Pllumi v. Att'y Gen.*, 642 F.3d 155, 162–63 (3d Cir. 2011) (cautioning, where the applicant claimed that medical treatment in Albania was insufficient to treat his severe injuries, that while countries' differing health care standards were not a basis for asylum," it is conceivable that, in extreme circumstances, harm resulting from the unavailability of necessary medical care could constitute 'other serious harm'"); *Kone v. Holder*, 596 F.3d 141, 152–53 (2d Cir. 2010) (stating that the Board may consider on remand "whether the mental anguish of a mother who was herself a victim of genital mutilation who faces the choice of seeing her daughter suffer the same fate, or avoiding that outcome by separation from her child, may qualify as such 'other serious harm'"); *Kholyavskiy v. Mukasey,* 540 F.3d 555, 577 (7th Cir. 2008) (remanding for consideration of "other serious harm" if the applicant's psychiatric medications, which he needed for functioning, might be unavailable in his country); *Mohammed v. Gonzales*, 400 F.3d 785, 801 (9th Cir. 2005) (remanding for consideration of possible "other serious harm" in light of Somalia's poverty; the decimation of the applicant's clan, which left female members like the applicant particularly vulnerable; and serious ongoing human rights abuses, including the killing of many civilian citizens in factional fighting); *Belishta v. Ashcroft*, 378 F.3d 1078 (9th Cir. 2004) (noting the applicant's possible eligibility for relief under 8 CFR §1208.13(b)(1)(iii)(B) (2004) where agents of the former Albanian regime—although motivated solely by money—reportedly tried to take the applicant's house, threatened and harassed both her and her family, shot out her windows, and left a bomb on her doorstep); *cf. Boer-Sedano v. Gonzales*, 418 F.3d 1082, 1090–91 (9th Cir. 2005) (finding that a gay man with Acquired Immune Deficiency Syndrome (AIDS), who faced unemployment, a lack of health insurance, and the unavailability of necessary medications in Mexico to treat his disease, showed a likelihood of "other serious harm" to make relocation within his country unreasonable when considered in the context of the "social and cultural constraints" placed upon his particular social group).

[330] *Matter of L–S–*, 25 I&N Dec. 705, 714 (BIA 2012).

[331] *Id.*

[332] *Id.* Circuit courts also have held that eligibility for asylum on the basis of a reasonable possibility of "other serious harm" is reserved for "the most atrocious abuse." *See, e.g., Naizgi v. Gonzales*, 455 F.3d 484, 488 (4th Cir. 2006). *But see Hanna v. Keisler*, 506 F.3d 933, 939 (9th Cir. 2007) (remanding claim for consideration of other serious harm Chaldean Catholic would face if returned to Iraq).

past harm and it need not be inflicted on account of the applicant's race, religion, nationality, membership in a particular social group, or political opinion.[333]

The BIA asserted that an applicant need only demonstrate a "reasonable possibility" of other serious harm.[334] In determining whether the applicant has established a "reasonable possibility" of "other serious harm," the BIA provided that adjudicators should focus on current conditions that could severely affect the applicant and "should pay particular attention to major problems that large segments of the population face or conditions that might not significantly harm others but that could severely affect the applicant."[335] Such conditions may include:

- Civil strife;
- Extreme economic deprivation beyond economic disadvantage;
- Situations where the applicant could experience severe mental or emotional harm or physical injury.[336]

The Board clarified that "other serious harm" determinations must be made on a case-by-case basis based on the totality of the circumstances.[337]

> ➢ **Practice Pointer**: Some contexts in which "other serious harm" claims may arise due to country conditions and other factors may include protection claims based on female genital mutilation, gang violence, mental illness, physical injury or illness, and generalized political and civil strife.[338]

2. *Well-Founded Fear of Future Persecution*

An applicant need not have suffered past persecution in order to qualify for asylum, as long as he or she is able to show a well-founded fear of future persecution.[339] The regulations provide that an applicant has a well-founded fear of persecution if:

(1) the applicant has a fear of persecution in his or her country of nationality or, if stateless, in his or her country of last habitual residence, on account of race, religion, nationality, membership in a particular social group, or political opinion;

(2) there is a reasonable possibility of suffering such persecution if he or she were to return to that country; and

---

333 *Matter of L–S–*, 25 I&N Dec. 705, 714 (BIA 2012).

334 *Id.*

335 *Id.*

336 *Id.*

337 *Id.* at 715.

338 *See* Sarah Sherman-Stokes, *Other Serious Harm: The Neglected Stepchild of Humanitarian-Asylum Law*, 17 BENDER'S IMMIGR. BULL. 1483 (2012).

339 INA §101(a)(42).

(3) he or she is unable or unwilling to return to, or avail him– or herself of the protection of, that country.[340] Thus, to demonstrate a well-founded fear, the applicant must show that there is a "reasonable possibility" of persecution.[341]

In *INS v. Cardoza-Fonseca,* the U.S. Supreme Court defined and quantified "reasonable possibility."[342] The Court stated, "One can certainly have a well-founded fear of an event happening when there is less than a 50% chance of the occurrence taking place," and suggested that even a 10 percent or 1-in-10 chance of persecution may amount to a "reasonable possibility" of persecution.[343] The Court, however, did not hold that a well-founded fear requires *at least* a 1-in-10 chance of persecution — only that there be a reasonable possibility of the feared persecution occurring.[344] It could, therefore, be argued that even a less than 1-in-10 chance is sufficient to meet the well-founded-fear standard. As the Second Circuit stated, a fear may be well-founded "even if there is only a slight, though discernible, chance of persecution."[345]

Overall, the applicant must demonstrate that "a reasonable person in the asylum applicant's circumstances would fear persecution if she were returned to her native country."[346] There are both subjective and objective components to demonstrating a well-founded fear of persecution, as described below.

i. Subjective and Objective Components

In order to be "well-founded," an asylum-seeker's fear must be both "subjectively genuine" and "objectively reasonable" given the conditions in his or her home country.[347] The subjective component requires a showing that the applicant has a fear — an apprehension or awareness of danger — and that the fear is genuine.[348] An

[340] 8 CFR §§208.13(b)(2)(i), 1208.13(b)(2)(i) (2014).

[341] 8 CFR §208.13(b)(2)(i)(B) (2014).

[342] *INS v. Cardoza-Fonseca*, 480 U.S. 421, 431 (1987).

[343] *Id.* at 440. *See also INS v. Stevic*, 467 U.S. 407, 104 S. Ct. 2489 (1984); *Diallo v. INS*, 232 F.3d 279, 284 (2d Cir. 2000) (finding that a fear may be well-founded "even if there is only a slight, though discernible, chance of persecution").

[344] *INS v. Cardoza-Fonseca*, 480 U.S. at 440.

[345] *Diallo v. INS*, 232 F.3d 279, 284 (2d Cir. 2000).

[346] *Matter of Mogharrabi*, 19 I&N Dec. 439, 445 (BIA 1987).

[347] *Id.*; 8 CFR §208.13(b)(2); UNHCR Handbook, *supra* note 33, ¶ 38. *See Kratchmarov v. Heston*, 172 F.3d 551, 553 (8th Cir. 1999); *Bhatt v. Reno*, 172 F.3d 978, 981 (7th Cir. 1999); *Mikhael v. INS*, 115 F.3d 299, 304 (5th Cir. 1997).

[348] UNHCR Handbook, *supra* note 33, ¶ 39; *Matter of Acosta,* 19 I&N Dec. 211 (BIA 1985). *See also Ravix v. Mukasey*, 552 F.3d 42, 46 (1st Cir. 2009) (noting that the applicants made several trips to Haiti from the United States and that their extended families remained in Haiti unharmed); *Samedov v. Gonzales*, 422 F.3d 704, 708 (8th Cir. 2005) (upholding IJ's finding that the applicant lacked a subjective fear because he entered and exited the United States several times before applying for asylum); *Knezevic v. Ashcroft*, 367 F.3d 1206, 1213 (9th Cir. 2004); *Bhatt v. Reno*, 172 F.3d 978, 981 (7th Cir. 1999).

applicant's "candid, credible and sincere testimony demonstrating a genuine fear of persecution satisfies the subjective component."[349]

> ➤ **Practice Pointer**: Practitioners should work closely with their clients to prepare thorough and detailed sworn affidavits setting forth their clients' genuine fear of persecution upon return to their native countries. As credibility is essential to demonstrating a subjectively genuine fear, it is essential to ensure that the applicant's testimony is detailed and specific, as well as consistent internally and with other evidence of record. See Chapter 4 for a detailed discussion of credibility.

An applicant's fear will not be found to be subjectively genuine if the fear is not honest or credible.[350] Thus, credibility is key to demonstrating a well-founded fear of persecution. If an applicant's testimony is found to be credible, however, it is rare that an asylum officer or IJ will find that an asylum applicant lacks a subjective fear. Most asylum applicants are genuinely afraid. They may, however, lack a fear of *persecution*. If the applicant's fear of return is based on general dissent or disagreement with the government, a desire for more personal freedom or improved economic circumstances, or a fear of natural disaster or famine, the applicant would not have a subjectively genuine fear of persecution for purposes of asylum eligibility.[351] An applicant also may be found to lack a subjective fear of return if he or she has voluntarily returned to the country of feared persecution without a compelling reason for doing so.[352]

A subjectively genuine fear must also be objectively reasonable in order to satisfy the requirements for asylum eligibility. This means that there must be a reasonable possibility that the applicant will actually suffer the feared persecution.[353] Thus, the

---

[349] *Berroteran-Melendez v. INS*, 955 F.2d 1251, 1256 (9th Cir. 1992) (citation omitted). *See also Matter of Acosta*, 19 I&N Dec. 211 (BIA 1985); UNHCR Handbook, *supra* note 33, ¶ 39.

[350] *See* ch. 4 for a detailed discussion of credibility determinations. Testimony alone may be sufficient to demonstrate an applicant's credibility and subjectively genuine fear. *See Matter of Mogharrabi*, 19 I&N Dec. 439 (BIA 1987). However, following the enactment of the REAL ID Act of 2005, Pub. L. 109–13, 119 Stat. 302, the INA provides that "[w]here a trier of fact determines that the applicant should provide evidence that corroborates otherwise credible testimony, such evidence *must* be provided unless the applicant does not have the evidence and cannot reasonably obtain the evidence." INA §208(b)(1)(B)(ii); 8 USC §1158(b)(1)(B)(ii) (2012) (emphasis added). *See infra* ch. 4 for a detailed discussion of corroborating evidence.

[351] UNHCR Handbook, *supra* note 33, ¶ 39; *Matter of Acosta*, 19 I&N Dec. 211 (BIA 1985) (noting that a genuine fear of persecution must be the applicant's primary motivation in seeking asylum, but need not be the only motivation).

[352] Of course, a voluntary return to one's home country does not always and inherently negate a well-founded fear of persecution. *De Santamaria v. Att'y Gen.*, 525 F.3d 999, 1011 (11th Cir. 2008). *See also Pavlova v. INS*, 441 F.3d 82, 89 n.5 (2d Cir. 2006) ("In light of strong attachments to their home countries, refugees may venture abroad in a state of uncertainty about the permanence of their departure, hoping the persecution will abate.")

[353] 8 CFR §208.13(b)(2)(i)(B) (2014).

objective component requires a showing that the fear is reasonable;[354] mere irrational apprehension is insufficient.[355] Meeting the objective component requires "credible, direct and specific evidence in the record, of facts that would support *reasonable* fear that the applicant faces persecution."[356] Accordingly, an asylum applicant may establish the objective basis of his or her fear by submitting evidence regarding the conditions in his or her home country. A number of BIA decisions have highlighted the increasing importance of such evidence.[357]

> ➢ **Practice Pointer**: An applicant may demonstrate that his or her fears are objectively reasonable by submitting country conditions reports and articles, expert affidavits applying the applicant's specific facts to the conditions in the country of feared persecution, affidavits of similarly situated individuals who have suffered similar persecution, and any other evidence of a pattern or practice of persecution against similarly situated individuals.

As long as an objective situation is established by the evidence, "it need not be shown that the situation will probably result in persecution, but it is enough that persecution is a reasonable possibility."[358]

> ➢ **Practice Pointer**: An applicant who suffered past persecution is not required to show that he or she has a subjective or objective fear of persecution, only that he or she was in fact persecuted.[359]

---

[354] *Samedov v. Gonzales*, 422 F.3d 704, 708 (8th Cir. 2005); *see also Francois v. INS*, 283 F.3d 926, 930 (8th Cir. 2002) ("The objective element requires a showing of credible, direct, specific evidence that a reasonable person would fear persecution … .").

[355] *Gonahasa v. INS*, 181 F.3d 538, 541 (4th Cir. 1999).

[356] *Berroteran-Melendez v. INS*, 955 F.2d 1251, 1256 (9th Cir. 1992) (emphasis in original). *See also Lolong v. Gonzales*, 484 F.3d 1173, 1178 (9th Cir. 2007) (en banc); *Zheng v. Gonzales*, 475 F.3d 30 (1st Cir. 2007) (finding that the applicant's fears were not objectively reasonable despite her opposition to China's coercive population control policies, because her circumstances were no different from other Chinese women of marriageable age and she intended to abstain from sex until marriage).

[357] *See, e.g.*, *Matter of S–M–J–*, 21 I&N Dec. 722, 724 (BIA 1997) (observing that the burden is on asylum applicants to provide evidence to buttress their claims); *Matter of Dass,* 20 I&N Dec. 120, 124–25 (BIA 1989) (highlighting the importance of background information in evaluating the applicant's testimony). *See also Banks v. Gonzales*, 453 F.3d 449, 453 (7th Cir. 2006) (stressing the need for "concrete, case-specific evidence" to demonstrate the risk faced by the applicant in the country from which he or she is seeking asylum); *Matter of Y–B–*, 21 I&N Dec. 1136, 1139 (BIA 1998) (noting that the weaker an applicant's testimony is, the greater the need for corroborating evidence).

[358] *INS v. Stevic*, 467 U.S. 407, 424–25 (1984). *See* 8 CFR §208.13(b)(2)(i)(B) (2014).

[359] *Torres v. Mukasey*, 551 F.3d 616, 629 (7th Cir. 2008) (finding that the IJ's analysis was incorrect because the IJ looked for facts to determine if the applicant had a subjective fear of persecution in the past).

ii. Matter of Mogharrabi Four-Part Test

The BIA in Matter of Mogharrabi set forth its test for determining whether an applicant for asylum has a well-founded fear of future persecution.[360] To establish a well-founded fear of persecution, the applicant must demonstrate:

(1) that he or she possesses a belief or characteristic that the persecutor seeks to overcome;

(2) that the persecutor is already aware, or there is a reasonable possibility the persecutor could become aware, that the applicant possesses this belief or characteristic;

(3) that the persecutor has the capability of punishing the applicant; and

(4) that the persecutor has the inclination to punish the applicant.[361]

In demonstrating prong one of this four-part test, the applicant must first identify the belief or characteristic that he or she believes would be targeted. The applicant must then provide evidence that he or she actually does possess that belief or characteristic. Such evidence may be his or her own testimony, the testimony of others who have personal knowledge of the applicant's belief or characteristic, or documentary evidence demonstrating that the applicant possesses that belief or characteristic.[362]

> ➢ **Practice Pointer**: A claim also may be based on a characteristic that the applicant does not actually possess but that the persecutor might impute to him or her. Each of the five protected grounds may be imputed to an applicant by the persecutor. For example, a persecutor may believe that the applicant is gay when he is not; a persecutor may believe the applicant is Coptic Christian when he is not; a persecutor may believe the applicant is a member of the Movement for Democratic Change when she is not. If such facts are present, practitioners should work with their clients to demonstrate a reasonable possibility that that persecutor might believe the applicant possesses the protected characteristic, even if the client does not actually possess it.

---

[360] *Matter of Mogharrabi*, 19 I&N Dec. 439, 446 (BIA 1987). *See also Matter of Acosta*, 19 I&N Dec. 211 (BIA 1985).

[361] *Matter of Mogharrabi*, 19 I&N Dec. at 446. *See also Matter of Acosta*, 19 I&N Dec. at 211. Note that although *Matter of Mogharrabi* states that the applicant must establish that the persecutor seeks to overcome the characteristic by means of "punishment," more recent case law holds that the persecutor need not intend to punish or have any malignant intent. *See Matter of Kasinga,* 21 I&N Dec. 357 (BIA 1996). *See also Pitcherskaia v. INS*, 118 F.3d 641 (9th Cir. 1997). Also note that *Matter of Acosta* required a finding that the persecutor could "easily" become aware that the applicant possessed the characteristic. *Matter of Mogharrabi* dropped the "easily" requirement in order to bring the analysis into compliance with the Supreme Court's decision in *INS v. Cardoza-Fonseca*, 480 U.S. 421 (1987).

[362] See ch. 4 for a detailed discussion of burdens of proof and evidence needed to meet those burdens.

In demonstrating the persecutor's awareness of the applicant's characteristic, it is enough to show a reasonable possibility that the persecutor will become aware that the applicant possesses the characteristic; however, mere speculation that the persecutor could become aware of the characteristic is not sufficient.[363]

In evaluating the capability of the persecutor to persecute the applicant, adjudicators will consider whether the persecutor is the government or a non-governmental actor. If a government actor, the extent of that actor's power and authority is relevant.[364] If a non-governmental actor, the extent to which the government is willing or able to control the non-governmental actor is relevant. Finally, an important consideration is the extent to which the government has the ability to enforce its will throughout the country.[365]

Finally, in evaluating the persecutor's inclination to persecute the applicant, adjudicators will consider any previous threats or harm from the persecutor, as well as the persecutor's treatment of individuals similarly situated to the applicant.[366] The applicant does not need to demonstrate that the persecutor is inclined to punish the applicant specifically or that the persecutor is motivated by malignant intent.[367]

iii. Other Important Considerations

In addition to the subjective and objective components, as well as the *Matter of Mogharrabi* test, certain factors may significantly impact the well-founded fear analysis. These include:

(1) whether the applicant could avoid persecution by relocating to another part of the country;[368]

---

[363] *Matter of Mogharrabi*, 19 I&N Dec. 439, 446 (BIA 1987).

[364] The regulations, however, provide that internal relocation is presumed to be unreasonable if the persecution feared is from a government or a government-sponsored persecutor. 8 CFR §208.13(b)(3)(ii) (2014).

[365] *See* U.S. Citizenship and Immigration Servs., RAIO Combined Training Course, Well-Founded Fear, at 15 (July 18, 2012) [hereinafter RAIO Training Course, Well-Founded Fear], *available at www.uscis.gov/sites/default/files/USCIS/About%20Us/Directorates%20and%20Program%20Offices/RAIO/Well%20Founded%20Fear%20LP%20(RAIO).pdf*. *See also* U.S. Citizenship & Immigration Servs., *Lesson: Asylum Eligibility Part II* at 7, in Asylum Officer Basic Training Course Participant Workbook (Mar. 13, 2009) [hereinafter AOBTC Workbook, pt. II], *available at www.uscis.gov/sites/default/files/USCIS/Humanitarian/Refugees%20%26%20Asylum/Asylum/AOBTC%20Lesson%20Plans/Well-Founded-Fear-31aug10.pdf*.

[366] *See* RAIO Training Course, Well-Founded Fear, *supra* note 365, at 16. *See also* AOBTC Workbook, pt. II, *supra* note 365, at 7.

[367] *See Matter of Kasinga,* 21 I&N Dec. at 357 (BIA 1996). *See also Pitcherskaia v. INS*, 118 F.3d 641 (9th Cir. 1997).

[368] 8 CFR §208.13(b)(2)(ii) (2014); *Matter of C–A–L–*, 21 I&N Dec. 754 (BIA 1997); *Matter of Acosta*, 19 I&N Dec. at 211; UNHCR Handbook, *supra* note 33, ¶ 91. *See supra* pt. II.D.1.ii. for a detailed discussion of internal relocation.

(2) whether there was a specific threat of harm made against the applicant;[369]

(3) the amount of time that the applicant spent in the country following threats or harm;[370]

(4) whether the applicant possessed a valid passport from the country of feared persecution;[371]

(5) whether the applicant ever returned to the country of feared persecution following the threats or harm suffered;[372]

(6) whether there is a pattern or practice of persecution[373] in that country and the applicant is similarly situated to others who have suffered persecution;[374]

(7) whether the applicant's family and friends have been targeted;[375] and

(8) whether the applicant is a refugee *sur place*.[376]

a. Specific Threat of Harm

The fact that the applicant was not harmed in the past is not determinative of whether his or her fear of future persecution is well-founded. A specific threat of harm to an asylum applicant on account of one of the five enumerated grounds may be sufficient to demonstrate a well-founded fear of persecution. Courts have asserted various thresholds that applicants must meet to show that threats of harm constitute *past* persecution,[377] but courts will also consider unfulfilled threats of harm, anonymous or otherwise, as part of a determination of whether there exists a well-founded fear of *future* persecution.[378] For example, although the Ninth Circuit found

---

[369] *See, e.g., Lim v. INS*, 224 F.3d 929, 936 (9th Cir. 2000).

[370] *Castillo v. INS*, 951 F.2d 1117 (9th Cir. 1991). *See also Li v. Ashcroft*, 396 F.3d 530 (3d Cir. 2005).

[371] UNHCR Handbook, *supra* note 33, ¶ 48.

[372] *Rodriguez v. INS*, 841 F.2d 865 (9th Cir. 1987). *See also Damaize-Job v. INS*, 787 F.2d 1332 (9th Cir. 1986).

[373] 8 CFR §208.13(b)(2)(iii) (2014).

[374] *Matter of Mogharrabi*, 19 I&N Dec. at 446. *See also Wiransane v. Ashcroft*, 366 F.3d 889, 894–95 (10th Cir. 2004) (an applicant is permitted to show that a person in his position, as opposed to himself specifically, could be subject to persecution).

[375] *See, e.g., Ventura v. INS*, 264 F.3d 1150, 1154 (9th Cir. 2001); *Mgoian v. INS*, 184 F.3d 1029, 1036–37 (9th Cir. 1999); *Rodriguez-Matamoros v. INS*, 86 F.3d 158 (9th Cir. 1996). *See also Li v. INS*, 92 F.3d 985, 987 (9th Cir. 1996); *Gebremichael v. INS*, 10 F.3d 28 (1st Cir. 1993); *Arriaga-Barrientos v. INS*, 937 F.2d 411, 414 (9th Cir. 1991); *Matter of Villalta*, 20 I&N Dec. 142 (BIA 1990).

[376] UNHCR Handbook, *supra* note 33, ¶¶ 94–96 (noting that an asylum applicant who was not a refugee when leaving his or her home country, but who becomes a refugee at a later date is called a refugee *sur place*).

[377] *See supra* pt. II.C. for a detailed discussion on threats and whether they rise to the level of persecution.

[378] *See Kaiser v. Ashcroft,* 390 F.3d 653, 658 (9th Cir. 2004); *Sotelo-Aquije v. Slattery,* 17 F.3d 33 (2nd Cir. 1994); *Cordero- Trejo v. INS,* 40 F.3d 482 (1st Cir. 1994) (stating that to infer that an applicant is unlikely to be persecuted because he was not killed during attempts to terrorize him leads to the absurd

Continued

that repeated death threats did not amount to *past* persecution where neither the applicant nor his family were ever "touched, robbed, imprisoned, forcibly recruited, detained, interrogated, trespassed upon, or even closely confronted" during a period of six years,[379] the court found instead that this threat of harm suggests that the applicant had a well-founded fear of future persecution.[380]

The circumstances and content of the threat must be evaluated in the context of the current conditions in the country of feared persecution.[381] In determining whether threats establish a well-founded fear of future persecution, the following factors should be considered:

(1) whether anyone received similar threats, and if so, what happened to them;

(2) the authority or power of the individual or group that made the threat;

(3) any activities that may have placed the applicant at risk; and

(4) the current conditions in the country of feared persecution.[382]

Overall, if the evidence demonstrates that a threat is serious and there is a reasonable possibility that it will be carried out, that threat may be sufficient to establish a well-founded fear of future persecution.

b. Remaining in the Country of Past or Feared Persecution

In determining whether an applicant has a well-founded fear of persecution, a relevant consideration may be the length of time an applicant remained in his or her home country after suffering persecution or becoming aware that he or she may become a target of persecution. A lapse in time between the incidents of harm and the applicant's flight from the country may indicate that the applicant does not possess a genuine fear of harm or that the persecutor does not have the ability or inclination to harm or further harm the applicant. Thus, an applicant who has remained in the country of persecution for a significant period of time following threats or acts of harm may not be able to establish a well-founded fear of future persecution.[383] For

---

result of denying asylum to those who were fortunate enough to survive); *Arteaga v. INS,* 836 F.2d 1227 (9th Cir. 1988); *Matter of Villalta,* 20 I&N Dec. at 142.

[379] *Lim v. INS*, 224 F.3d 929, 936 (9th Cir. 2000).

[380] *Id.* at 935.

[381] *See e.g., Canales-Vargas v. Gonzales,* 441 F.3d 739, 744–745 (9th Cir. 2006) (finding that the timing of threats – two or three weeks after the applicant publicly denounced the Shining Path guerrillas – was circumstantial evidence sufficient to establish the Shining Path as the source of the threats); *Kaiser v. Ashcroft,* 390 F.3d 653, 658 (9th Cir. 2004); *Gailius v. INS,* 147 F.3d 34 (1st Cir. 1998); *Cordero-Trejo v. INS,* 40 F.3d 482 (1st Cir. 1994); *Aguilera-Cota v. INS,* 914 F.2d 1375 (9th Cir.1990).

[382] *See* RAIO Training Course, Well-Founded Fear, *supra* note 364, at 20; AOBTC Workbook, pt. II, *supra* note 365, at 12.

[383] *See, e.g., Guang Zhao Zhang v. Holder*, 330 F. App'x 201 (1st Cir. 2009) (holding that the applicant did not have a well-founded fear of persecution based on his Protestant Christian religious beliefs because he did not show that he would be targeted personally and he lived with his uncle for three years and went to school for one semester without harm, while his parents, older brother, and older sister still live and work in China and have not been harmed); *Qinglin Cheng v. Holder*, 341 F. App'x 72 (5th Cir.

Continued

example, the U.S. Court of Appeals for the First Circuit upheld a finding that the applicant did not have a well-founded fear because he remained in Haiti two months after receiving a threat.[384]

> ➢ **Practice Pointer**: It is important to keep in mind that if past persecution has been established, the government and not the applicant would bear the burden of proving that there is no longer a well-founded fear of persecution.[385]

On the other hand, there may be valid reasons why the applicant could not flee earlier, as well as reasons why the persecutor was temporarily unable or disinclined to target the applicant. For example, in *Lim v. INS*, the applicant had remained in the Philippines for six years after receiving his first death threat.[386] The court found that his extended stay, although relevant, did not render his fear unreasonable, especially where the evidence suggested the threats he received became more menacing.[387]

Factors to consider in determining the impact of a lapse in time between the threats and/or harm and the applicant's flight include:

(1) the amount of time the applicant remained;

(2) the reason for the delay;

(3) the applicant's location during that time;

(4) the applicant's activities during that time; and

(5) the persecutor's activities during that time.[388]

2009) (finding that the evidence supported the denial of asylum because the applicant stayed in China for six years following his detention and attended underground churches over that time, and thus, did not have a well-founded fear of future persecution); *Li v. Ashcroft*, 396 F.3d at 530 (agreeing that the applicant did not establish a subjective fear of future when she had remained in Indonesia for two years after the robbery that formed the basis of her claim to asylum). *But see, e.g., Gonzalez v. INS*, 82 F.3d 903, 909 (9th Cir. 1996) (finding that the applicant's stay in Nicaragua for three years after the first threat did not undermine her well-founded fear because the threats were repeated, the applicant took steps to protect herself, and there was a pattern of violence against her family members).

[384] *Ravix v. Mukasey*, 552 F.3d 42, 46 (1st Cir. 2009)

[385] *See supra* pt. II.D.1. *See infra* chapter 4 for a detailed discussion of the shifting burdens of proof.

[386] *Lim v. INS*, 224 F.3d 929, 935 (9th Cir. 2000).

[387] *Id.*; *see also Reyes-Guerrero v. INS*, 192 F.3d 1241, 1243–44 (9th Cir. 1999) (granting asylum to an applicant who received death threats over seven years before fleeing); *Vongsakdy v. INS*, 171 F.3d 1203, 1207 (9th Cir. 1999) (finding the fact that the applicant's continued stay in Laos for a considerable period of time following his release from the labor camp was "irrelevant" to evaluating the "atrocity" of his past persecution). *But see Daneshvar v. Ashcroft*, 355 F.3d 615, 625 (6th Cir. 2004) (finding that applicant did not have a well-founded fear of future persecution because he "enjoyed as close to a normal life during his eight years in Iran after his release, as can be expected of a person living in a totalitarian Islamic state").

[388] *See* RAIO Training Course, Well-Founded Fear, *supra* note 365, at 21–22. *See also* AOBTC Workbook, pt. II, *supra* note 365, at 16.

- **Practice Pointer**: If a client has remained in the country of past or feared persecution after the relevant events, practitioners should explore with their clients the following questions: Did the client have the funds to depart? Did he or she need to arrange for the safety of his or her family members before leaving? Did the client hope that the situation would improve? Did the client want to continue promoting his or her cause? Was the client waiting for an opportunity to escape? Where was the client during that time — was he or she in hiding or living in the open as usual? Are there reasons why the persecutor was temporarily disinclined or unable to harm the client? Was there escalating harm or threats against the client during that time?

c. Possession of Valid Travel Documents

Asylum applicants may have left their home countries by obtaining a passport or other official travel document from their government. Courts have sometimes relied on the applicant's possession of a passport or official travel document as evidence that the government would not be inclined to harm the applicant, and therefore, he or she would not have a well-founded fear of persecution by his or her government.[389] In other cases, courts have recognized that the applicant's possession of a passport or official travel document does not necessarily mean that the applicant would not be in danger upon return to his or her home country.[390] With regard to this issue, UNHCR's Handbook provides:

> Possession of a passport cannot therefore always be considered as ... an indication of the absence of fear. A passport may even be issued to a person who is undesired in his country of origin, with the sole purpose of securing his departure, and there may also be cases where a passport has been obtained surreptitiously .... [T]he mere possession of a valid national passport is no bar to refugee status.[391]

In addition, the holder of a valid passport may not necessarily be a citizen of the country that issued the passport. Countries may issue "passports of convenience" to individuals in order to facilitate travel. Jordan, for example, has issued many passports to Palestinians. While passports may be evidence of citizenship, they are not conclusive. The existence of a passport and presumptions that stem from it, "'may be overcome by sufficient evidence that the holder of the passport is not a citizen' of the issuing country."[392] In this regard, UNHCR's Handbook also provides:

---

[389] *See, e.g.*, *Kratchmarov v. Heston*, 172 F.3d 551, 555 (8th Cir. 1999); *Huaman-Cornelio v. BIA*, 979 F.2d 995, 1000 (4th Cir. 1992); *Ravindran v. INS*, 976 F.2d 754, 760 (1st Cir. 1992).

[390] *See, e.g.*, *Damaize-Job v. INS*, 787 F.2d 1332, 1336 (9th Cir. 1986); *Matter of Pula*, 19 I&N Dec. 467, 472 (BIA 1987) (finding the applicant eligible for asylum even though the Yugoslav government issued him a passport).

[391] UNHCR Handbook, *supra* note 33, ¶ 48.

[392] *Palavra v. INS*, 287 F.3d 690, 692 (8th Cir. 2002) (vacating the BIA's finding that holders of Croatian passports were Croatian citizens, citing *Matter of Maccaud*, 14 I&N Dec. 429, 432 (BIA 1973)).

Possession of a passport creates a *prima facie* presumption that the holder is a national of the country of issue, unless the passport itself states otherwise. A person holding a passport showing him to be a national of the issuing country, but who claims that he does not possess that country's nationality, must substantiate his claim, for example, by showing that the passport is a so-called "passport of convenience" (an apparently regular national passport that is sometimes issued by a national authority to non-nationals).[393]

Adjudicators may consider the following factors in determining whether possession of a passport or official travel document undermines the applicant's well-founded fear of persecution:

(1) whether the passport-issuing or exit control agency is separate from the branch of government that seeks to harm the applicant and whether that agency is aware of the applicant's situation;

(2) whether the applicant obtained the documents surreptitiously through a bribe or through the help of a third party;[394]

(3) whether the government issued the documents so that the applicant would go into exile; and

(4) whether the applicant obtained the documents prior to the incidents that gave rise to his or her fear.[395]

d. Returning to the Country of Feared Persecution

An applicant's voluntary return to the country of feared persecution may raise questions regarding whether he or she has a well-founded fear of return to that country. Procedurally, the regulations provide that an applicant who returns to the country of feared persecution with a grant of advance parole is presumed to have abandoned his or her asylum claim.[396] This presumption of abandonment may be overcome by demonstrating compelling reasons for the return.[397] Additionally, the applicant may have experienced additional events while in the country of feared persecution that could be the basis of a new claim.

- **Practice Pointer**: Practitioners should advise their clients not to travel while their asylum applications are pending unless their clients first obtain advance parole travel documents. Even with advance parole, clients should be advised not to return to the country of past or feared

[393] UNHCR Handbook, *supra* note 33, ¶ 93.

[394] *See, e.g., Khup v. Ashcroft,* 376 F.3d at 905 (finding that the IJ erred in failing to consider the applicant's explanation that he obtained the passport through a broker to whom he paid a large sum of money).

[395] *See* RAIO Training Course, *supra* note 364, at 24; *See also* AOBTC Workbook, pt. II, *supra* note 365, at 19–20.

[396] 8 CFR §208.8(b) (2014).

[397] *Id.*

persecution. See Chapter 13 for a detailed discussion of advance parole for individuals with pending asylum applications.

Even if the asylum claim has not been abandoned procedurally, returning to the country of feared persecution may be detrimental to the applicant's case. Such a return may cast a negative light on the applicant's credibility or may negatively impact the well-founded fear analysis — the adjudicator may find the applicant's fear is not subjectively genuine and objectively reasonable.[398] For example, in *Loho v. Mukasey*, the Ninth Circuit held that an Indonesian's voluntary return to her home country on two occasions undermined her testimony that she experienced past suffering or that she feared returning home.[399] Other circuits, including the Seventh[400] and First,[401] have made similar findings. The Eleventh Circuit,[402] however, held that an IJ erred in determining that, despite the applicant's credible testimony that she feared persecution if returned to Colombia, her acts in previously returning to Colombia nullified her proof of subjective fear of future persecution. The court found that voluntary return to one's home country is a relevant consideration, but does not always and inherently negate a fear of future persecution.[403]

In evaluating the effect of an applicant's return to the country of feared persecution on his or her fear, the reasons why the applicant returned are relevant. If there were compelling reasons why he or she returned, the return may not affect his or her subjective fear.[404] Also relevant is what happened to the applicant, if anything, upon his or her return. Threats or harm experienced upon return may demonstrate that the applicant's fear remains objectively reasonable, whereas if the applicant was able to safely return without issue, that would undercut the reasonableness of his or her fear.[405]

---

398 *Ngarurih v. Ashcroft*, 371 F.3d 182, 188–89 (4th Cir. 2004); *Hakeem v. INS*, 273 F.3d 812, 816–17 (9th Cir. 2001).

399 *Loho v. Mukasey*, 531 F.3d 1016, 1018 (9th Cir. 2008).

400 *Tarraf v. Gonzales*, 495 F.3d 525, 530, 534 (7th Cir. 2007).

401 *Jean v. Gonzales*, 461 F.3d 87, 89, 91 (1st Cir. 2006).

402 *De Santamaria v. Att'y Gen.*, 525 F.3d 999, 1011 (11th Cir. 2008).

403 *Id. See also Cooke v. Mukasey*, 538 F.3d 899, 904 (8th Cir. 2008) (noting that first trip to the United States was to raise money to bring wife and children).

404 *See, e.g., Mukamusoni v. Ashcroft,* 390 F.3d 110 (1st Cir. 2004) (finding that the BIA erred when it focused only on the fact that the applicant returned to Rwanda on two occasions without considering the reasonable explanations for her return, and further finding that the circumstances surrounding the applicant's return were not sufficient to undermine her claim that she genuinely feared that she would be persecuted if returned to Rwanda). *See also Rodriguez v. INS,* 841 F.2d 865 (9th Cir. 1987); *Damaize-Job v. INS,* 787 F.2d 1332 (9th Cir. 1986) (finding that the applicant's return to the country of feared persecution because he wanted to help his uncle and sister who had been arrested was not inconsistent with a well-founded fear).

405 *See Ngarurih v. Ashcroft,* 371 F.3d 182 (4th Cir. 2004) (upholding a finding by the BIA that the applicant's experiences upon return to Kenya rebutted the presumption of well-founded fear created by his past persecution, and relying upon the fact that the applicant "undertook activities that placed him in

Continued

e. Pattern or Practice of Persecution

Ordinarily, asylum applicants must demonstrate their individualized fears of persecution based on their own experiences. However, an applicant need not show that he or she will be singled out individually for persecution if the applicant shows that:

(1) there is a pattern or practice of persecution on account of any of the protected grounds against a group or category of persons similarly situated to the applicant;[406] and

(2) the applicant belongs to or is identified with the persecuted group, so that a reasonable person in the applicant's position would fear persecution.[407] As provided in the regulations:

In evaluating whether the applicant has sustained his or her burden of proving that he or she has a well-founded fear of persecution, the asylum officer or immigration judge shall *not* require the applicant to provide evidence that he or she would be singled out individually for persecution if: (A) The applicant establishes that there is a pattern or practice in his or her country of nationality or last habitual residence of persecution of groups of persons similarly situated to the applicant on account of race, religion, nationality, membership in a particular social group, or political opinion; and (B) The applicant establishes his or her own inclusion in and identification with such group of persons such that his or her fear of persecution upon return is reasonable.[408]

Thus, a well-founded fear of future persecution may be based on harm against others who are similarly situated to the asylum applicant.[409] Where a number of similarly situated individuals face a similar type of harm, this strengthens rather than weakens an applicant's claim.[410]

- **Practice Pointer**: While proof of particularized persecution, *i.e.*, evidence that the applicant was singled out, may sometimes be needed to show a well-founded fear of future persecution, it is not required to establish past persecution.[411]

---

direct contact with government officials, seeking the protection of Kenya's laws" and did not suffer any mistreatment during his two months in Kenya).

[406] 8 CFR §208.13(b)(2)(iii)(A) (2014).

[407] 8 CFR §208.13(b)(2)(iii)(B) (2014).

[408] 8 CFR §§208.13(b)(2), 1208.13(b)(2)(iii) (2014) (emphasis added).

[409] *Matter of Mogharrabi*, 19 I&N Dec. 439, 446 (BIA 1987); *See also Wiransane v. Ashcroft*, 366 F.3d 889, 894–95 (10th Cir. 2004) (an applicant is permitted to show that a person in his position, as opposed to himself specifically, could be subject to persecution).

[410] *See, e.g., Bolanos-Hernandez v. INS*, 767 F.2d 1277, 1285 (9th Cir. 1984).

[411] *Id.* at 1211–12 (noting that the applicants' town was specifically targeted for bombing, invasion, occupation, and ethnic cleansing of Serbs by Croats).

"Pattern or practice" is determined on a case-by-case basis,[412] and the BIA has been reversed where it has failed to consider evidence concerning a pattern or practice of persecution of similarly situated persons.[413]

> ➤ **Practice Pointer**: A pattern or practice of persecution may be established by the Department of State's country report on human rights practices, and other such evidence of country conditions.[414] The BIA has held that Department of State reports are "highly probative" and are often given more weight than other forms of country conditions evidence.[415]

In demonstrating a "pattern or practice," there is no established rule regarding the type of group or number of people in the group, and the applicant is not required to show that "*every* individual in the vulnerable group must face [] serious persecution."[416] However, the members of the group or category must share some common characteristic that the persecutor seeks to overcome and that falls within one of the protected grounds in the refugee definition.[417]

---

[412] *See Feleke v. INS,* 118 F.3d 594 (8th Cir. 1997); *Makonnen v. INS,* 44 F.3d 1378, 1383 (8th Cir. 1995). *See also Li v. Ashcroft,* 396 F.3d at 530 (adopting the Eighth Circuit's definition of "pattern or practice" of persecution); *Matter of A–M–,* 23 I& N Dec. 737, 741 (BIA 2005) (applying the Eighth Circuit's standard in upholding the IJ's finding that the applicant failed to establish a pattern or practice of persecution in Indonesia against Chinese Christians). *See also Mitreva v. Gonzales,* 417 F.3d 761, 765 (7th Cir. 2005) (citing case examples, and noting that "courts have interpreted the regulation to apply only in rare circumstances"); *Meguenine v. INS,* 139 F.3d 25, 28 (1st Cir. 1998) (stating that to establish a pattern or practice of persecution the applicant must submit evidence of "systematic persecution" of a group).

[413] *See, e.g., Thavendran v. Gonzales*, 211 Fed. Appx. 74, 75 (2d Cir. 2007) (BIA erred in failing to consider whether there was a pattern or practice of persecution in Sri Lanka against individuals of Tamil ethnicity); *Cordero-Trejo v. INS*, 40 F.3d 482, 491–92 (1st Cir. 1994). *But see Gomes v. Gonzales*, 429 F.3d 1264, 1267 (9th Cir. 2005) (finding applicant failed to show that BIA's finding that there was no pattern or practice of persecution of Christians or Catholics was not supported by substantial evidence); *Capric v. Ashcroft*, 355 F.3d 1075, 1094 (7th Cir. 2004) (rejecting claim of applicant who relied on "State Department reports addressing [the former Federal Republic of Yugoslavia] generally and detailed ethnic cleansing campaigns in *other* regions") (emphasis in original).

[414] *Bromfield v. Mukasey*, 543 F.3d 1071, 1078 (9th Cir. 2008) (finding that the 2005 DOS country report compelled the conclusion that there exists in Jamaica a pattern or practice of persecution of gay men).

[415] *See Matter of H–L–H– & Z–Y–Z–*, 25 I&N Dec. 209 (BIA 2010).

[416] *Avetova-Elisseva v. INS*, 213 F.3d 1192, 1201 (9th Cir. 2000) (emphasis in original).

[417] *See, e.g., Meguenine v. INS,* 139 F.3d 25 (1st Cir. 1998) (finding that the applicant failed to establish well-founded fear based on pattern or practice of individuals similarly situated to him, because evidence indicated that those targeted were not persecuted because of the characteristic they shared with the applicant, but rather a characteristic the applicant did not possess – prominent opposition to Islamic fundamentalists).

Most courts have held that the pattern or practice must be systematic, pervasive, or organized.[418] The BIA has applied this standard, as have the First, Third, Seventh, and Eighth Circuits.[419] However, the Ninth Circuit has developed a lower "disfavored group" standard, holding that, even if the persecution is not systematic, persecution of some group members may support the applicant's fear of being singled out in the future if the applicant is similarly situated to those group members.[420] The Ninth Circuit explained:

> [I]f the applicant is a member of a "disfavored" group, but the group is not subject to systematic persecution, this court will look to (1) the risk level of membership in the group (i.e., the extent and the severity of persecution suffered by the group) and (2) the alien's individual risk level (i.e., whether the alien has a special role in the group or is more likely to come to the attention of the persecutors making him a more likely target for persecution).[421]

The Ninth Circuit maintains that "the more serious and widespread the threat of persecution to the group, the less individualized the threat of persecution needs to

---

[418] *Gunawan v. Att'y Gen.*, 305 F. App'x 908 (3d. Cir. 2009) (stating that to qualify as a "pattern or practice," the persecution must be "systemic, pervasive, or organized" and finding that the applicant's experiences on account of her Christian upbringing in Indonesia were not sufficiently severe to rise to the level of persecution); *Ashqar v. Holder*, 355 F. App'x 705 (4th Cir. 2009) (holding that the Palestinian applicant failed to demonstrate a well-founded fear of persecution in Israel on account of her husband's and her political beliefs because the applicant failed to show a documented pattern of the Israeli government persecuting the innocent wives of alleged or actual Hamas members who have not been directly implicated in terrorist attacks); *Mitreva*, 417 F.3d at 765; *Ngure v. Ashcroft*, 367 F.3d 975, 991 (8th Cir. 2004). *But see Sael v. Ashcroft,* 386 F.3d 922, 925 (9th Cir. 2004); *Mgoian v. INS,* 184 F.3d 1029, 1035 n. 4 (9th Cir. 1999) (citing *Kotasz v. INS,* 31 F.3d 847, 853 (9th Cir. 1994)), allowing a lower standard for a "disfavored group", *compared with Li v. Ashcroft,* 396 F.3d 530 (3d Cir. 2005) (finding that violence against Chinese Christians in Indonesia is not sufficiently widespread to constitute a "pattern or practice" of persecution); *Firmansjah v. Gonzales,* 424 F.3d 598, 607 n.6 (7th Cir. 2005) (noting that the court has not recognized a lower threshold of proof based on membership in a "disfavored group" where the evidence is insufficient to establish "pattern or practice"); *Kho v. Keisler,* 505 F.3d 50, 55 (1st Cir. 2007) (noting that the disfavored group analysis creates a threshold for relieving asylum applicants of the need to establish individualized persecution that is not found in the regulations), rejecting the Ninth Circuit's lower "disfavored group" standard.

[419] *See Kho*, 505 F.3d at 55 (rejecting the 9th Circuit's "disfavored group" analysis); *Li v. Ashcroft*, 396 F.3d at 530 (finding that violence against Chinese Christians in Indonesia is not sufficiently widespread to constitute a "pattern or practice" of persecution); *Mitreva*, 417 F.3d at 765; *Firmansjah*, 424 F.3d at 607 n.6 (rejecting the 9th Circuit's "disfavored group" analysis); *Meguenine v. INS*, 139 F.3d 25, 28 (1st Cir. 1998); *Feleke v. INS*, 118 F.3d 594 (8th Cir. 1997); *Makonnen v. INS*, 44 F.3d 1378, 1383 (8th Cir. 1995) (interpreting "pattern or practice" to mean "organized or systematic or pervasive persecution"); *Matter of A–M–*, 23 I&N Dec. 737, 741 (BIA 2005) (applying the Eighth Circuit's standard and upholding the finding that the applicant failed to establish a pattern or practice of persecution in Indonesia against Chinese Christians).

[420] *Mgoian v. INS*, 184 F.3d 1029, 1035 n.4 (9th Cir. 1999) (citing *Kotasz v. INS*, 31 F.3d 847, 853 (9th Cir. 1994)). *See also Sael v. Ashcroft*, 386 F.3d 922, 925 (9th Cir. 2004); *Singh*, 94 F.3d at 1353.

[421] *Mgoian*, 184 F.3d at 1035 n.4 (citing *Kotasz v. INS*, 31 F.3d 847, 853 (9th Cir. 1994)).

be."[422] The Ninth Circuit has held that the "disfavored" group analysis also applies to withholding of removal claims.[423] The First, Third, and Seventh Circuits, however, have rejected this lower "disfavored group" standard.[424]

In addition to demonstrating systematic, pervasive, or organized persecution, the applicant must show that the persecution is perpetrated or tolerated by state actors in order to meet the requirements to establish a pattern or practice of persecution.[425]

f. Persecution of Family and Friends

In addition to similarly situated individuals, adjudicators also have looked to the treatment of an applicant's family members and friends in assessing whether the applicant has a well-founded fear of persecution.[426] UNHCR's *Handbook* provides, "What .... happened to [the applicant's] friends and relatives and other members of the same racial or social group may well show that his fear that sooner or later he also will become a victim of persecution is well-founded."[427] Generally, the applicant must establish a connection between the persecution of the family member or friend and the harm that he or she fears.[428] For example, the family member or friend might

---

[422] *Id.* at 1035. *See also Kotasz*, 31 F.3d at 853–54; *Singh*, 94 F.3d at 1353. *See also Yong Hao Chen v. INS*, 195 F.3d 198, 204 (4th Cir. 1999) (noting the correlation between the seriousness of the threat of persecution to the "disfavored" group and the individualized nature of the threat).

[423] *See Wakkary v. Holder*, 558 F.3d 1049, 1062 (9th Cir. 2009) (noting that agency ignored large amount of evidence that Chinese Christians in Indonesia are widely disfavored, discriminated against and, in a substantial number of instances, persecuted).

[424] *See Kho*, 505 F.3d at 55 (rejecting the 9th Circuit's "disfavored group" analysis); *Li v. Ashcroft*, 396 F.3d at 530 (finding that violence against Chinese Christians in Indonesia is not sufficiently widespread to constitute a "pattern or practice" of persecution); *Firmansjah*, 424 F.3d at 607 n.6 (rejecting the 9th Circuit's "disfavored group" analysis).

[425] *Mitreva,* 417 F.3d at 765.

[426] *See, e.g., Ventura v. INS*, 264 F.3d 1150, 1154 (9th Cir. 2001) (past political persecution of family members provides evidence of imputed political opinion of the applicant), *rev'd on other grounds by INS v. Ventura*, 537 U.S. 12, 18 (2002); *Mgoian v. INS*, 184 F.3d 1029, 1036–37 (9th Cir. 1999) (evidence that all of the applicant's principal family members were subjected to forms of violence, persecution, and harassment gives rise to the inference that the family has become a target); *Rodriguez-Matamoros v. INS*, 86 F.3d 158 (9th Cir. 1996) (finding that the applicant had established a well-founded fear due in part to the threats to her family and the torture and killing of her sister). *See also Li v. INS*, 92 F.3d 985, 987 (9th Cir. 1996) (arrest of family member in church may provide basis for claim based on religious persecution); *Gebremichael v. INS*, 10 F.3d 28 (1st Cir. 1993) (finding a link between family membership and persecution); *Arriaga-Barrientos v. INS*, 937 F.2d 411, 414 (9th Cir. 1991) ("Acts of persecution against a petitioner's friends and family may establish a well-founded fear, notwithstanding an utter lack of persecution against the petitioner .... ."); *Matter of Villalta*, 20 I&N Dec. 142 (BIA 1990) (finding that the threats to the applicant's immediate family members and the murder of applicant's brother establish a well-founded fear of persecution).

[427] UNHCR Handbook, *supra* note 33, ¶ 43.

[428] *See, e.g., Matter of A–K–*, 24 I&N Dec. 275, 277–78 (BIA 2007) (finding that the applicant was not eligible for withholding of removal based on a fear that his daughters would be subjected to FGM because he did not establish a pattern or practice of persecution that was tied to him personally); *Matter*

Continued

share the applicant's religious beliefs or political opinion, or they might belong to the same ethnic or social group. On the other hand, where the mistreatment of the applicant's family is not linked to the applicant, courts have found that such mistreatment is not evidence that the applicant has a well-founded fear.[429]

For similar reasons, some courts have relied on the lack of harm or mistreatment of family members in finding that an applicant's claim is not well-founded.[430] For example, the continuing safety of a family member who shares the applicant's religious beliefs and actively practices the religion in the country of feared persecution may demonstrate that the applicant's fear is not well-founded.[431] Similarly, where the claimed social group is the family, a family member's continuing safety may be persuasive to an adjudicator in finding no well-founded fear.[432]

However, the lack of harm or mistreatment of family members may not be relevant in cases where the applicant has been singled out for mistreatment.[433] Similarly, if conditions in the country have changed substantially since the harm to the family members occurred, the applicant cannot rely on the past harm to establish a well-founded fear.[434]

---

of E–P–, 21 I&N Dec. 860 (BIA 1997) (finding that the applicant presented no evidence that the military was interested in her due to her relatives' political activities).

[429] *See, e.g.*, *Arriaga-Barrientos v. INS*, 937 F.2d 411 (9th Cir. 1991) (holding that the disappearance, for unknown reasons, of the applicant's two brothers who resided 800 kilometers away from the applicant did not demonstrate a well-founded fear); *Matter of E–P–*, 21 I&N Dec. at 862 (finding that the applicant failed to provide evidence linking the murder of her family members and the harm she fears upon return to her home country).

[430] *See, e.g.*, *El-Labaki v. Mukasey*, 544 F.3d 1, 6–7 (1st Cir. 2008) (finding that the applicant failed to prove the likelihood of future persecution, in part, because his family continued to reside in Lebanon as active and practicing Christians without being threatened or persecuted); *Agada v. Ashcroft*, 368 F.3d 867, 869 (8th Cir. 2004) (relying on evidence that the applicant's wife, sons, and siblings lived in Nigeria without harm); *Bhatt v. Reno*, 172 F.3d 978, 982 (7th Cir. 1999) (finding that the absence of evidence of harm to the applicant's family members undermines claim of well-founded fear); *Abedini v. INS*, 971 F.2d 188, 192 (9th Cir. 1992) (where the court relied on the applicant's testimony that none of his family members had been subject to persecution in finding that the applicant's fear was not well-founded); *Matter of A–E–M–*, 21 I&N Dec. 1157, 1160 (BIA 1998) (finding that applicant lacked a well-founded fear, in part, because his family members remained unharmed in Peru since his departure).

[431] *Budiono v. Mukasey*, 548 F.3d 44, 50 (1st Cir. 2008); *Santos-Lemus v. Mukasey*, 542 F.3d 738, 743 (9th Cir. 2008).

[432] *Id.*

[433] *See, e.g.*, *Nakibuka v. Gonzales*, 421 F.3d 473, 479 (7th Cir. 2005) (noting that there was no evidence that the applicant's relatives were politically active or closely associated with known opponents of the government); *Bellido v. Ashcroft*, 367 F.3d 840, 844 (8th Cir. 2004) (noting that the applicant should not suffer simply because his government has chosen to focus its efforts on persecuting only him); *Rios v. Ashcroft*, 287 F.3d 895, 902 (9th Cir. 2002).

[434] *Francois v. INS*, 283 F.3d 926, 931–32 (8th Cir. 2002).

> **Practice Pointer**: Practitioners should always explore with their clients whether family members and friends remain safe in their home countries. If they do, why are they safe? Do they not share the applicant's protected characteristics? Are they living in hiding or otherwise trying to hide their protected characteristic?

g. Refugee Sur Place

An asylum applicant may not meet the definition of refugee at the time the applicant leaves his or her home country. As noted in UNHCR's *Handbook*, "[t]he requirement that a person must be outside his country to be a refugee does not mean that he [or she] must necessarily have left that country … on account of well-founded fear."[435] An asylum applicant who was not a refugee when leaving his or her home country, but who becomes a refugee at a later date, is called a refugee "*sur place*."[436]

An individual becomes a refugee *sur place* because of circumstances arising in the individual's country of origin during his or her absence or as a result of his or her actions taken by the individual while abroad.[437] The *Handbook* notes that "[d]iplomats and other officials serving abroad, prisoners of war, students, migrant workers and others have applied for refugee status during their residence abroad and have been recognized as refugees."[438] USCIS also recognizes that changes occurring in an applicant's country, as well as activities by an applicant outside his or her country may make the applicant a refugee *sur place*.[439]

In *Azarshahy v. Ilchert*, the court found that the petitioner could establish his asylum claim as a refugee *sur place*, finding that "refugee status can be established based on facts arising after the applicant has left her country."[440] Similarly, the

---

[435] UNHCR Handbook, *supra* note 33, ¶ 94; *see also Wiransane v. Ashcroft*, 366 F.3d 889, 899 (10th Cir. 2004) ("[A]n applicant need not have fled his home country out of fear of persecution to qualify as a refugee.").

[436] UNHCR Handbook, *supra* note 33, ¶ 94.

[437] *Id.* ¶¶ 95, 96.

[438] *Id.* ¶ 95.

[439] *See* U.S. Citizenship & Immigration Servs., *Lesson: One-Year Filing Deadline* at 11, in Asylum Officer Basic Training Course Participant Workbook (Mar. 23, 2009) [hereinafter AOBTC Workbook, One-Year Filing Deadline], *available at www.uscis.gov/sites/default/files/USCIS/Humanitarian/Refugees%20%26%20Asylum/Asylum/AOBTC%20Lesson%20Plans/One-Year-Filing-Deadline-31aug10.pdf*. *See also* 8 CFR §208.4(a)(4)(i)(A) (2014); UNHCR Handbook, *supra* note 33, ¶ 94–95; *Matter of Mogharrabi*, 19 I&N Dec. 439 (BIA1987). *See generally* AOBTC Workbook, pt. II, *supra* note 365.

[440] *Azarshahy v. Ilchert*, 1994 WL 446040, at *5 (N.D. Cal., Aug. 10, 1994). *See also Lukwago v. Ashcroft*, 329 F.3d 157, 180 (3d Cir. 2003) (in remanding claim, court instructed the BIA to determine what effect the widespread publicity of the applicant's case has on his fear of future persecution); *Matter of G–A–*, 23 I&N Dec. 366 (BIA 2002) (en banc) (finding anti-regime activities abroad were relevant in a Convention Against Torture claim by an Iranian national); *Matter of Ngum*, A27 709 543 (BIA Dec. 13, 1999) (finding that adjudicators may consider political activities engaged in after entry into the United States that jeopardize an applicant's life or freedom in the applicant's native country, citing *Makonnen v. INS*, 44 F.3d 1378, 1384 (8th Cir. 1995)), & *reported in* David Cleveland,

Continued

Second Circuit remanded a claim to the BIA that was based solely on an applicant's activities in the United States, namely his membership in and political activities on behalf of the Chinese Democratic Party.[441] UNHCR's *Handbook* advises that "[r]egard should be had in particular to whether such actions may come to the notice of the authorities of the person's country of origin and how they are likely to be viewed by those authorities." Thus, claims by refugees *sur place* still must meet the *Matter of Mogharrabi* four-part test for establishing a well-founded fear of future persecution.[442]

> ➢ **Practice Pointer**: Practitioners should prepare and submit evidence demonstrating a reasonable possibility that the persecutor could become aware of the applicant's protected characteristic or might attribute to the applicant a characteristic that the persecutor seeks to overcome, as this is one of the most common reasons why claims based on refugee *sur place* are denied.

In determining whether an individual is a refugee *sur place*, the relevant factors to consider may include:

(1) whether the applicant was well-known or otherwise known to the persecutor in the country of feared persecution prior to his or her departure;

(2) whether the applicant holds a particularly visible position outside the country of feared persecution;

(3) the visibility level of the applicant's activities outside the country of feared persecution;

(4) the extent of the feared persecutor's network and/or systems for monitoring activities outside the country of feared persecution; and

(5) the persecutor's opinion of those who have resided in other countries.[443]

Protesting in the U.S. Can Establish a Well-Founded Fear of Future Persecution, Immigr. Daily, *available at www.ilw.com/articles/2005,0208-cleveland.shtm* (last visited Jan. 1, 2015); *Matter of Mogharrabi*, 19 I&N Dec. at 439 (an Iranian student who visited the Iranian interests section of the Algerian embassy in the United States and was threatened by an official there was found to be eligible for asylum).

[441] *Hongsheng Leng v. Mukasey*, 528 F.3d 135, 143 (2d Cir. 2008) (finding that the IJ failed to make appropriate findings about whether the Chinese government was aware or was likely to become aware of applicant's political activities in the United States). *See also Tun v. INS*, 445 F.3d 554 (2d Cir. 2006) (finding error where the IJ failed to consider whether the applicant's political activities in the United States established a well-founded fear of persecution).

[442] *Matter of Mogharrabi*, 19 I&N Dec. at 439 (finding that a reasonable person in the applicant's circumstances would fear persecution on account of political opinion, because the applicant's opposition to the authorities became known to an Iranian official at the Iranian Interests Section of the Algerian Embassy in the United States during an altercation, and it is known that the Iranian regime persecutes its opponents).

[443] *See* AOBTC Workbook, pt. II, *supra* note 365, at 20–21.

E. Nexus and the Five Protected Grounds

In addition to establishing past persecution or a well-founded fear of persecution, the applicant must show that the persecution suffered or feared is "on account of" his or her race, religion, nationality, membership in a particular social group, or political opinion.[444] In meeting this requirement, the applicant must first identify his or her characteristic that would lead to his or her persecution. The characteristic must be one of the five protected grounds enumerated in the statutory definition of refugee.[445] Second, the applicant must demonstrate that he or she actually embodies that protected characteristic or that the characteristic could be imputed to him or her. Third, the applicant must establish a connection or "nexus," either direct or circumstantial, between the protected characteristic and the persecution he or she suffered or fears.

What matters most when analyzing nexus is whether the persecutor's motivation to harm the applicant is based on a protected characteristic, and whether the protected characteristic is "at least one central reason" for the harm.[446] While an asylum applicant is not required to prove the exact motivation of his or her persecutor, he or she must "provide *some* evidence of it, direct or circumstantial."[447] This requires an examination of the persecutor's views of the applicant and any evidence of those views.[448] However, ultimately, it is not the persecutor's subjective intent that is relevant, but rather, the objective persecution.[449] There is no requirement that the persecutor be initially motivated to harm the applicant because of his or her protected characteristic.[450] There is also no requirement that the persecutor have punitive or

---

[444] INA §101(a)(42)(A); *INS v. Elias-Zacarias*, 502 U.S. 478, 482 (1992).

[445] *See* INA §101(a)(42)(A).

[446] INA §208(b)(1)(B)(i), as amended by §101(a) of the REAL ID Act, P.L. 109-13, 119 Stat. 302 (2005).

[447] *Id.* at 483 (emphasis in original). *See also Matter of J–B–N– & S–M–*, 24 I&N Dec. 208, 214 (BIA 2007) (finding that the burden of proof for the persecutor's motive may be met by testimonial evidence). *But see* Guy S. Goodwin-Gill & Jane McAdams, THE REFUGEE IN INTERNATIONAL LAW 50 (2d ed. 1996) (stating that "Nowhere in the drafting history of the 1951 Convention is it suggested that the motive or intent of the persecutor was ever to be considered as a controlling factor in either the definition or the determination of refugee status."); *see also* James Hathaway, *The Michigan Guidelines on Nexus to a Convention Ground*, 23 MICH. J. INT'L L. 210 (2002), *available at www.refugeecaselaw.org/nexus.asp*.

[448] *INS v. Elias-Zacarias*, 502 U.S. at 478.

[449] *Pitcherskaia v. INS*, 118 F.3d 641 (9th Cir. 1997).

[450] *Martinez-Buendia v. Holder*, 616 F.3d 711 (7th Cir. 2010) (finding that a woman from Colombia who had refused recruitment by FARC suffered persecution on account of her political opinion because the FARC interpreted her refusal as "anti-FARC" and targeted her with increasingly violent retribution post-refusal); *Tarubac v. INS*, 182 F.3d 1114 (9th Cir. 1999) (finding that even though the NPA had attempted to take money from the applicant and recruit her for reasons unrelated to a protected ground, the threat to kill her was triggered at least in part by the political and religious opinions that she articulated when she refused them).

malignant intent in targeting the applicant.[451] The persecutor may be attempting to overcome the applicant's protected characteristic out of a belief that he or she is "helping" the applicant.[452]

The BIA has held that, in meeting the nexus requirement, an asylum applicant must establish facts upon which a reasonable person would believe that the danger arises on account of one of the five protected grounds.[453] Federal courts have recognized, however, the difficulty in proving a persecutor's motive.[454] At least one circuit has held that if persecution is by the government and there is no legitimate prosecutorial purpose for the harm inflicted, there is a presumption that the government's motive is political.[455] Adjudicators may not base their "on account of" determinations on a "'non-evidence-based assumption[]' regarding conduct in another culture."[456] For example, use of ethnic slurs by interrogators does not necessarily prove a nexus to a protected ground.[457]

---

[451] *Matter of Kasinga*, 21 I&N Dec. at 357 (fining that the required persecutory motive was established even though the FGM may have been practiced by the applicant's tribe with "subjectively benign intent").

[452] *Id. See also Pitcherskaia v. INS*, 118 F.3d at 641 (stating that "The fact that a persecutor believes the harm he is inflicting is 'good for' his victim does not make it any less painful to the victim, or, indeed, remove the conduct from the statutory definition of persecution.").

[453] *Matter of Fuentes*, 19 I&N Dec. 658, 662 (BIA 1988).

[454] *See Guo v. Ashcroft*, 361 F.3d 1194, 1203 (9th Cir. 2004) (holding that resistance to discriminatory government action that results in persecution is persecution on account of a protected ground); *Baballah v. Ashcroft*, 367 F.3d 1067, 1077 n.10 (9th Cir. 2004) (noting that the use of the derogatory term "goy" by the Israeli marines demonstrated they were motivated by the applicant's ethnicity); *Bace v. Ashcroft*, 352 F.3d 1133, 1138 (7th Cir. 2003) (statements made by assailants suggesting that attacks were politically motivated were sufficient to meet "on account of" requirement); *Gailius v. INS*, 147 F.3d 34, 45 (1st Cir. 1998) (noting that "Persecutors have not been given adequate notice that our government expects them to sign their names and reveal their identities when they deliver threatening messages."); *Gonzales-Neyra v. INS*, 122 F.3d 1293, 1296 (9th Cir. 1997), *amended at* 133 F.3d 726 (9th Cir. 1998) (finding that threats to an applicant's life and business made after applicant expressed his political opinion were on account of this opinion and were not motivated solely by economic reasons); *Bolanos-Hernandez v. INS*, 767 F.2d 1277, 1285 (9th Cir. 1984) (finding that because authentic refugees are rarely able to offer direct corroboration of specific threats, the applicant's own credible testimony is sufficient).

[455] *Navas v. INS*, 217 F.3d 646, 658 (9th Cir. 2000).

[456] *Popova v. INS*, 273 F.3d 1251, 1258 (9th Cir. 2001) (rejecting the BIA's reliance on facts that applicant was able to pursue her medical education, travel outside of Bulgaria, and work in government-run medical facilities in finding that she was not persecuted "on account of" a protected ground).

[457] *Michailovna v. Mukasey*, 555 F.3d 734, 742 (9th Cir. 2009) (finding that utterance of an ethnic slur, standing alone, does not compel the conclusion that ethnicity was the central motivating reason); *Mitreva,* 417 F.3d at 764. *But see Azhgirevich v. Gonzales*, 185 Fed. Appx. 72, 74–75 (2d Cir. 2006) (finding sufficient nexus between an assault of a Russian woman and a protected ground of persecution where the attacker allegedly called the victim a "Russian whore" and said, "You should satisfy not only … one Muslim … [but] all the Muslims") (alteration in original).

If an asylum applicant is unable to provide sufficient proof that the persecutor's motivation is one of the five enumerated grounds, the claim will be denied.[458] For example, personal disputes are not included in the five enumerated grounds and the courts have rejected claims based on such disputes.[459] Similarly, courts and the BIA

---

[458] *See, e.g.*, *Vasili v. Holder*, 732 F.3d 83 (1st Cir. 2013) (finding that the applicant failed to demonstrate a nexus between the harm and his political activities because sheer speculation and supposition is not sufficient, and stating "it is no more than a guess that a nexus existed between the [incident] and a statutorily protected ground"); *Pheng v. Holder*, 640 F.3d 43 (1st Cir. 2011) (holding that the applicant did not establish nexus to her political opinion because she did not provide any testimony or evidence of what the rapist said or did that would support an inference that he was motivated by her political activities); *Kante v. Holder*, 634 F.3d 321 (6th Cir. 2011) (finding that the attack the applicant suffered at the hands of Guinea government forces was motivated by financial gain, rather than retribution for her father's political activity with the RPG); *Bueso-Avila v. Holder*, 663 F.3d 934 (7th Cir. 2011) (holding that the applicant failed to establish nexus to his religion because the fact that some of the threats at the hands of the MS-13 happened after church group meetings does not mean that the gang members were reacting to his religious beliefs); *Espinosa-Cortez v. Att'y Gen.*, 607 F.3d 101 (3d Cir. 2010) (finding no evidence to support a finding that threats were motivated by imputed political opinion where the entirety of to record showed the husband's close affiliation with the government); *Dallakoti v. Holder*, 619 F.3d 1264 (10th Cir. 2010) (holding that the applicant failed to establish nexus because "the Maoists' threats were motivated by the ability of petitioner to supply needed financial resources"); *Nosals v. Holder*, 320 F. App'x 469 (7th Cir. 2009) (finding that there was no evidence that the applicant's arrest and subsequent short imprisonment after a counter-demonstration in Latvia was in any way related to his Ukrainian ethnicity); *Nou v. Mukasey*, 542 F.3d 272, 274 (1st Cir. 2008) (court found that harm suffered was for enforcing ban on illegal fishing, not because of the applicant's political party affiliation); *Tamara-Gomez v. Gonzales*, 447 F.3d 343, 349–350 (5th Cir. 2006) (finding that the applicant failed to establish a nexus between the persecution and one of the five grounds and that claims based on dangers by policemen are not on account of a protected ground); *Oliva-Muralles v. Ashcroft*, 328 F.3d 25, 27 (1st Cir. 2003) (Guatemalan applicant could not tie the crimes that were committed against her or her neighbors to one of the five protected grounds); *Ontunez-Tursios v. Ashcroft*, 303 F.3d 341, 350–53 (5th Cir. 2002) (upholding BIA's determination that feared persecution over a land dispute was not on account of political opinion or membership in a particular social group); *Debab v. INS*, 163 F.3d 21, 27 (1st Cir. 1998) (holding that the applicant failed to establish a nexus between the threats he received and clandestine anti-government organizations); *Matter of C–A–L–*, 21 I&N Dec. 754, 756–57 (BIA 1997) (finding that a former Guatemalan soldier was not targeted on account of one of the five grounds where guerrillas sought to obtain information from him and attempted to recruit him due to his expertise as an artillery specialist); *Matter of R–*, 20 I&N Dec. 621, 624 (BIA 1992) (finding that the purpose of the mistreatment by police was to extract information regarding Sikh militants and not because of the applicant's political opinion or because the applicant was a Sikh); *Matter of T–*, 20 I&N Dec. 571, 575 (BIA 1992) (finding that an ethnic Tamil was not persecuted on account of his ethnicity or political views).

[459] *See, e.g.*, *Moura v. Holder*, 759 F.3d 1 (1st Cir. 2014); *Shehu v. Holder*, 531 F. App'x 1 (1st Cir. 2013) (holding that the applicant failed to establish a well-founded fear of future persecution because the harm he suffered in Albania was not on account of his political opinions, but rather, it was due to personal animosity between him and a particular individual); *Demiraj v. Holder*, 631 F.3d 194 (5th Cir. 2011); *Zoarab v. Mukasey*, 524 F.3d 777, 781 (6th Cir. 2008); *Wang v. Gonzales,* 445 F.3d 993, 998 (7th Cir. 2006); *Kozulin v. INS*, 218 F.3d 1112 (9th Cir. 2000); *Silva v. Ashcroft*, 394 F.3d 1, 6 (1st Cir. 2005); *Marquez v. INS*, 105 F.3d 374, 380 (7th Cir. 1997) (finding that "A personal dispute, no matter how nasty, cannot support an alien's claim of asylum."); *Iliev v. INS*, 127 F.3d 638, 642 (7th Cir. 1997); *Matter of Y–G–*, 20 I&N Dec. 794, 799 (BIA 1994).

have found that extortion, recruitment, and other harm may not be on account of a protected ground, but rather, on account of greed, economic grounds, generalized violence, or general criminal activity.[460] The adjudicator, however, may not ignore testimony, which establishes that a persecutor's motivation was more than just criminal in nature.[461]

> ➢ **Practice Pointer**: Nexus has been a hotly contested issue before the BIA and the federal courts in the context of gang-based asylum

---

[460] *See, e.g., Matter of M–E–V–G–*, 26 I&N Dec. 227, 235 (BIA 2014). *See also, Demiraj v. Holder*, 631 F.3d 194 (5th Cir. 2011) (holding that the applicant was not targeted because of her membership in her husband's family, but rather because of the suspect's attempt to seek personal revenge against the witness); *Magua v. Att'y Gen.*, 386 F. App'x 958 (11th Cir. 2010) (finding that the applicant did not show a nexus between the robbery of his store in South Africa because the perpetrators of the robbery robbed both the white store owner applicant and black store customers, indicating that the applicant was targeted for money, not because of his white race); *Amouri v. Holder*, 572 F.3d 29 (1st Cir. 2009) (holding that substantial evidence supported the determination that the attempted extortion and subsequent threats that the applicant suffered in Algeria was not on account of his political opinion, but rather, on account of unmitigated greed); *Sugiarto v. Holder*, 586 F.3d 90 (1st Cir. 2009) (finding no nexus to the applicant's religion because the only basis for such a conclusion was the applicant's belief that Christians "wouldn't have done such a thing"); *Quinteros-Mendoza v. Holder*, 556 F.3d 159 (4th Cir. 2009) (holding that religion was not the motive of the persecutor, but rather, money and personal animosity motivated the assaults); *Monsalve v. Holder*, 332 F. App'x 194 (5th Cir. 2009) (holding that the applicant failed to establish past persecution in Colombia on account of her political opinion or membership in a particular social group because there was no indication that the disgruntled vendors took out their frustrations on government employees for political reasons; rather, the evidence suggested that their motivation was purely economic); *Korneenkov v. Holder*, 347 F. App'x 93 (5th Cir. 2009) (finding that there was no evidence that the Russian police detained the husband on account of his mental disability and there was no evidence that the attempted rape of his wife was anything more than a random criminal act); *Velasquez-Garcia v. Holder*, 336 F. App'x 517 (6th Cir. 2009) (relying on *INS v. Elias-Zacarias*, 502 U.S. 478 (1992) in holding that the applicant did not suffer past persecution in Guatemala because there was no evidence that the guerillas' threats were based on anything more than an effort to recruit him away from the civil patrol and into their ranks); *Mballo v. Holder*, 340 F. App'x 317 (6th Cir. 2009) (holding that the applicant failed to establish past persecution in Guinea on account of an imputed or actual political opinion because the applicant consistently stated that the soldiers attacked him because he went to his father's defense and struck one of them, not because the soldiers imputed an opinion to him); *Diallo v. Holder*, 335 F. App'x 556 (6th Cir. 2009) (holding that the applicant failed to establish past persecution by rebel forces in Sierra Leone, because when he was kidnapped, robbed, and beaten by the rebels, that harm was motivated by economic reasons, not on account of any protected ground); *Cuevas v. INS*, 43 F.3d 1167 (7th Cir. 1995). *But see Escobar v. Holder*, 657 F.3d 537 (7th Cir. 2011) (finding that the applicant had been persecuted by FARC on account of his political opinion because, in addition to suffering economic mistreatment, FARC members hijacked the applicant's truck on three separate occasions, kidnapped him, ordered him to do their bidding at gunpoint, threatened to kill him and his family, threatened to destroy his trucks, and made good on their threat when the applicant hid by destroying his trucks and branding their call-sign on the wrecks); *Osorio v. INS*, 18 F.3d 1017, 1028 (2d Cir. 1994) ("The conclusion that a cause of persecution is economic does not necessarily imply that there cannot exist other causes of persecution.")

[461] *Aliyev v. Mukasey*, 549 F.3d 111, 118 (2d Cir. 2008) (noting that the BIA erred by failing to consider that attack and beating were motivated because the applicant was a Uyghur).

claims.[462] Thus, practitioners should fully explore all potential motives of gang members in targeting their clients and establishing evidentiary records of nexus. Expert testimony of gang mentality, fact witness testimony about observations, and what the gang members said and did should all be documented to avoid assumptions that such gang activities were merely criminal and not motivated by a protected ground. See Chapter 5 for a detailed discussion of gang-based asylum claims.

1. Mixed Motive

Courts have recognized that a persecutor may be motivated by several reasons, one or more of which may be protected grounds enumerated in the refugee definition.[463] It is not required that all of the persecutor's motives be related to a protected ground.[464] The presence of motives unrelated to a protected ground is not evidence of the absence of a motive related to a protected ground.[465] Additionally, the initial reason why the persecutor targeted the applicant is not determinative.

As UNHCR's *Handbook* notes:

It is evident that the reasons for persecution under these various headings will frequently overlap. Usually there will be more than one element combined in one person, *e.g.*, a political opponent who belongs to a religious or national group, or

---

[462] *See* chapter 5 for a full discussion of gang-based asylum claims.

[463] *Matter of Fuentes*, 19 I&N Dec. 658, 662 (BIA 1988).

[464] *Matter of J–B–N– & S–M–*, 24 I&N Dec. 208, 213 (BIA 2007). *See also Castro v. Holder*, 597 F.3d 93 (2d Cir. 2010) (holding that the IJ did not properly evaluate motive because even if recruitment was one reason for the applicant's persecution, the applicant need only show that his political opinion was "one central reason" for his persecution, not the sole reason for it); *Bi Xia Qu v. Holder*, 618 F.3d 602 (6th Cir. 2010) (stating that the applicant's was a mixed motive case and noting that the applicant was targeted both to secure the repayment of a loan from the applicant's father and because she was a woman whom the persecutor could force into a marriage in a place where forced marriages were accepted); *Ndayshimiye v. Att'y Gen.*, 557 F.3d 124 (3d Cir. 2009) (accepting the BIA's interpretation of "one central reason" except for its contention that the motive cannot be subordinate to another, and stating that the "plain language [of the statute] indicates that a persecutor may have more than one central motivation for his or her actions; whether one of those central reasons is more or less important than another is irrelevant."); *Parussimova v. Mukasey*, 533 F.3d 1128 (9th Cir. 2008) as amended and superseded by *Parussimova v. Mukasey*, 555 F.3d 734 (9th Cir. 2009) (finding that the applicant failed to establish ethnicity as a central reason for the persecution); *Girma v. INS*, 283 F.3d 664 (5th Cir. 2002); *Matter of S–P–*, 21 I&N Dec. 486 (BIA 1996); *Matter of Fuentes*, 19 I&N Dec. 658, 662 (BIA 1988). *See also* H. Conf. Rep. No. 109–72, at 288 (2005) (indicating that the persecutor need not be solely motivated to target the applicant because of the protected characteristic).

[465] *See, e.g., Menghesha v. Gonzales*, 450 F.3d 142 (4th Cir. 2006) (holding that the applicant was not required to prove that his political opinion was the Ethiopian government's sole motive for persecuting him, stating that an IJ may not "treat[] the presence of a nonpolitical motive as evidence of the absence of a political motive").

both, and the combination of such reasons in his person may be relevant in evaluating his well-founded fear.[466]

Some motives might be tied to the protected grounds and others might not.[467] The persecutor need not be motivated solely because of a protected ground. However, a protected ground must be "at least one central reason" for the persecutor's actions.[468]

Prior to the passage of the REAL ID Act in 2005, the applicant had to produce evidence from which it was reasonable to believe that the harm was motivated, at least in part, by an actual or imputed protected ground.[469] Under that standard, in *Matter of S–P–*, the Board of Immigration Appeals listed five factors to consider in determining the motive of the persecutor:

(1) indications that the abuse was directed toward modifying a perceived political view or punishing a criminal act;

(2) treatment of others in similar circumstances;

(3) conformity to procedures for criminal prosecutions or military law;

(4) the extent to which anti-terrorism laws are defined and apply to suppress political opinion as well as illegal conduct; and

---

[466] UNHCR Handbook, *supra* note 33, ¶ 67; *see, e.g., Matter of D–V–*, 21 I&N Dec. 77, 79–80 (BIA 1993) (finding that the applicant, an activist in a pro-Aristide church group, had a well-founded fear of persecution based on her political opinion and religion); *see also Osorio v. INS*, 18 F.3d 1017, 1028 (2d Cir. 1994) (finding that "persecution on account of the victim's political opinion" does not mean persecution solely on account of the victim's political opinion).

[467] *See Matter of S–P–*, 21 I&N Dec. 486, 489 (BIA 1996).

[468] INA §208(b)(1)(B)(i).

[469] *Matter of Fuentes*, 19 I&N 658 (BIA 1988); *see also Uwais v. Gonzales*, 478 F.3d 513, 517–18 (2d Cir. 2007) (finding that the BIA erred in finding that officer's motives were not motivated, even in part, by a protected ground); *Mohideen v. Gonzales*, 416 F.3d 567, 570 (7th Cir. 2005) (persecution on account of a protected ground does not mean persecution "solely" on account of one of those grounds); *Jahed v. INS*, 356 F.3d 991, 998 (9th Cir. 2004) (extortion coupled with the threat of political exposure satisfies the "on account of" requirement); *Girma v. INS*, 283 F.3d 664, 668 (5th Cir. 2002) (finding that despite being questioned by armed abductors about her political activities, substantial evidence supported the BIA's finding that the applicant had not established that persecution was "on account of" a protected ground where motivation could have been economic); *Bandari v. INS*, 227 F.3d 1160, 1168–69 (9th Cir. 2000) (finding that accusations made by Iranian police demonstrate their beatings were based on applicant's religion, not enforcement of a neutral law); *Agbuya v. INS*, 219 F.3d 962, 965–66 (9th Cir. 2000), *amended at* 241 F.3d 1224 (9th Cir. 2001) (holding that "persecutory conduct may have more than one motive, and so long as one motive is one of the statutory grounds, the requirements have been met") (citations omitted); *Briones v. INS*, 175 F.3d 727, 729 (9th Cir. 1999) (en banc) (finding that the asylum applicant's "activity as a confidential informer who sided with the Philippine military in a conflict that was political at its core certainly would be perceived as a political act by the group informed upon"); *Tarubac v. INS*, 182 F.3d 1114, 1119 (9th Cir. 1999) (finding that the applicant's expression of opposition to communism led to the most extreme persecution that she suffered and that the persecution was, therefore, not solely for economic or recruitment reasons).

(5) the extent to which suspected political opponents are subjected to arbitrary arrest, detention, and abuse.[470]

Now, however, in mixed motive cases, the applicant must "establish that race, religion, nationality, membership in a particular social group, or political opinion was or will be *at least one central reason* for persecuting the applicant."[471] This standard was enacted as part of the REAL ID Act of 2005 and applies to all asylum applications filed on or after May 11, 2005.[472]

In *Matter of J–B–N– & S–M–*, the BIA provided clarification of the "one central reason" standard, holding that Congress "purposely did not require that the protected ground be *the* central reason for the actions of the persecutors," but rather, that there be a nexus between the persecutor's motives and one of the enumerated grounds.[473] The BIA stated that the REAL ID Act did not radically alter the standard in mixed motive cases, because the protected ground must still be a central reason for persecution and the burden of proof may still be met by testimonial evidence.[474] The BIA confirmed, however, that in order to be a "central reason" for the persecutor's actions, the protected ground cannot be tangential or incidental to the persecutor's motivation.[475] A tangential motivation is one that is only "superficially relevant," while an incidental motivation is one that is "minor, casual, or subordinate to another" motive.[476]

To provide an example, in *Matter of J–B–N– & S–M–*, the BIA rejected the applicant's claim that his imputed Burundi nationality was "at least one central reason" for threats from his extended family, where the threats did not begin until after the applicant had won a valuable parcel of land from his aunt in a land dispute in Rwanda.[477] The BIA found that the imputed nationality motive was tangential to the persecution, as the dispute was, fundamentally, a personal one.[478]

Courts that have grappled with the "at least one central reason" language have held that previous mixed-motive case law has been superseded by the REAL ID Act.[479] The Ninth Circuit, for example, has held that an asylum applicant need not

---

[470] *Matter of S–P–*, 21 I&N Dec. 486, 494 (BIA 1996).

[471] INA §208(b)(1)(B)(i); 8 USC §1158(b)(1)(B)(i) (2012) (emphasis added).

[472] REAL ID Act of 2005, Pub. L. No. 109-13, 119 Stat. 302 (2005).

[473] *Matter of J–B–N– & S–M–*, 24 I&N Dec. 208, 212–13 (BIA 2007).

[474] *Id.* at 214.

[475] *Matter of J–B–N– & S–M–*, 24 I&N Dec. at 212–13.

[476] *Id.* (holding that the protected ground cannot be either superficially relevant to the reason for harm or subordinate to another reason for harm).

[477] *Id.* at 216.

[478] *Id.*

[479] *Shaikh v. Holder*, 702 F.3d 897, 902 (7th Cir. 2012) (recognizing that the "at least one central reason" may be a secondary or tertiary reason for the persecution, but finding no error in the case); *Michailovna v. Mukasey*, 555 F.3d 734, 740 (9th Cir. 2009); *Parussimova v. Mukasey*, 555 F.3d 734

Continued

show that the reason was the only reason or the most important reason, but has acknowledged that the new language places a more onerous burden on the applicant.[480] Overall, the protected ground cannot be "incidental, tangential, superficial, or subordinate to another reason for harm."[481] However, in *Nadayshimiye v. Att'y Gen.*, the Third Circuit found that the BIA erred in holding that an applicant must show that a protected ground for the persecution was not subordinate to any unprotected ground.[482]

2. *Establishing Motive*

In order to establish motive, there must be evidence that the applicant possesses a protected characteristic and that the persecutor either perceived that characteristic of the applicant or imputed that characteristic to the applicant (or will do so in the future).[483]

The applicant "does not bear the unreasonable burden of establishing the exact motivation of a 'persecutor' where different reasons for actions are possible."[484] However, the applicant must establish "facts on which a reasonable person would fear that the danger arises on account of" one of the five protected grounds.[485]

- **Practice Pointer**: Some common nexus pitfalls are situations involving personal disputes, extortion or attempts to increase wealth, generalized crime, or widespread civil strife.[486] In cases involving these issues, it is essential to provide evidence that the persecutor was also motivated by one of the five protected grounds and that the protected ground is at least one central reason for the persecution. Moreover, what may have begun as a personal dispute or attempt to increase wealth may evolve into a valid asylum claim. The fact that the initial threat or harm arose from an unprotected ground does not render the claim invalid. Be

---

(9th Cir. 2009) (stating that although the reason must be one principal motivation, it need not be 51% of the motivation, and holding that the applicant's Russian ethnicity was not at least one central reason for the alleged attack on her while she was in Kazakhstan, and therefore, she did not meet the requirements of the REAL ID Act); *Singh v. Mukasey*, 543 F.3d 1, 4–5 (1st Cir. 2008) (finding that neither political opinion, nor family membership, was one central reason for the attack the applicant suffered in India).

[480] *Id*.

[481] *Matter of J–B–N– & S–M–*, 24 I&N Dec. 208, 214 (BIA 2007), *modified by Ndayshimiye v. Att'y Gen.*, 557 F.3d 124 (3d Cir. 2009).

[482] *Ndayshimiye v. Att'y Gen.*, 557 F.3d 124 (3d Cir. 2009).

[483] *INS v. Elias-Zacarias*, 502 U.S. 478 (1992).

[484] *Matter of J–B–N– & S–M–*, 24 I&N Dec. 208, 211 (BIA 2007); *Matter of S–P–*, 21 I&N Dec. 486 (BIA 1996); *Matter of Fuentes*, 19 I&N Dec. 658, 662 (BIA 1988).

[485] *Matter of J–B–N– & S–M–*, 24 I&N Dec. at 211; *Matter of S–P–*, 21 I&N Dec. 486 (BIA 1996); *Matter of Fuentes*, 19 I&N Dec. 658, 662 (BIA 1988).

[486] *See infra* ch. 6 for a more in-depth discussion of these nexus problems as they arise in gang-based asylum claims.

prepared to address these counter-arguments about the persecutor's motive.

The persecutor's motive can be established by "direct or circumstantial evidence."[487] No one particular type of evidence is required. An example of direct evidence would be the persecutor's threat to the applicant that if he or she did not discontinue his or her political activities with the opposition party, he or she would be arrested. However, more often than not, there is no such direct evidence of the persecutor's motive, because persecutors do not always announce their motives or explain their actions.[488] In these situations, a persecutor's motive may be established by circumstantial evidence. Circumstantial evidence may include:

(1) country conditions reports and articles establishing the persecutor's views of individuals who are similarly situated to the applicant, for example, evidence that the persecutor views those individuals as opponents;

(2) evidence that the persecutor targets other individuals who share the applicant's protected characteristic, although such evidence is not *required*;[489]

(3) close proximity of the time of an arrest to the applicant's participation in a particular political meeting or religious ceremony; and

(4) the persecutor's statements and other circumstances surrounding the harmful acts.[490]

3. *Protected Grounds*

In addition to providing evidence of the persecutor's motive, the applicant must define which enumerated ground or grounds — race, religion, nationality, membership in a particular social group, or political opinion — apply to his or her claim. Then, the applicant must establish that he or she possesses that protected characteristic. Again, it is important to remember that the applicant may actually possess the protected ground or the persecutor may impute it to him or her. Although political opinion is the most common ground to be imputed to an applicant, USCIS takes the position that *any* of the five protected grounds may be imputed to an asylum applicant by a persecutor. When the persecution inflicted on the asylum applicant is because of an imputed characteristic related to any one of the five protected grounds,

---

[487] *INS v. Elias-Zacarias*, 502 U.S. 478 (1992); *Matter of J–B–N– & S–M–*, 24 I&N Dec. at 214.

[488] *INS v. Elias-Zacarias*, 502 U.S. 478 (1992).

[489] Dep't of Homeland Security Br. in *Matter of R–A–*, at 34–35 (stating that "As an evidentiary matter, it is certainly reasonable to expect that a person who is motivated to harm a victim because of a characteristic the victim shares with others would often be prone also to harm others who share the targeted characteristic. But evidence on this point should not be required in all cases in order for the applicant to satisfy the 'on account of' requirement.").

[490] *Boer-Sedano v. Gonzales*, 418 F.3d 1082, 1089 (9th Cir. 2005) (finding persecution on account of sexual orientation where the police officer arrested the asylum applicant only after asking him if he was gay and only after seeing him with a friend whom the officer believed to be the applicant's partner).

the persecution is still "on account of" that characteristic, regardless whether the applicant actually possesses it.[491]

i. Race

The first protected ground enumerated in the INA, race, is interpreted in its widest sense to include "all kinds of ethnic groups that are referred to as 'races' in common usage."[492] According to UNHCR, "Discrimination for reasons of race has found world-wide condemnation as one of the most striking violations of human rights" and "will frequently amount to persecution in the sense of the 1951 Convention."[493] Legacy INS in its *Basic Law Manual* cited apartheid in South Africa, the Holocaust, and slavery as examples of persecution on the basis of race.[494]

Race includes ethnicity and often overlaps with nationality.[495] For example, in finding that a Guatemalan member of the indigenous Quiche ethnic group suffered past persecution on account of race, the Ninth Circuit noted that the applicant was persecuted because of his "'ethnicity,' a category which falls somewhere between … 'race' and 'nationality.'"[496] In referring to this example, USCIS notes that race-based persecution often overlaps with several other protected grounds, stating:

---

[491] U.S. Citizenship & Immigration Servs., *Lesson: Asylum Eligibility Part III* at 15–16, in Asylum Officer Basic Training Course Participant Workbook (Mar. 12, 2009) [hereinafter AOBTC Workbook, pt. III], *available at www.uscis.gov/sites/default/files/USCIS/Humanitarian/Refugees%20%26%20 Asylum/Asylum/AOBTC%20Lesson%20Plans/Nexus-the-Five-Protected-Characteristics-31aug10.pdf. See, e.g., Ndayshimiye v. Att'y Gen.*, 557 F.3d 124 (3d Cir. 2009) (finding that race may be imputed to the applicant by the persecutor and that imputed race is a protected ground for asylum); *Amanfi v. Ashcroft*, 328 F.3d 719, 730 (3d Cir. 2003) (finding that the BIA erred in concluding that the applicant could not establish persecution on account of imputed membership in the social group of homosexuals when the applicant had testified that he was not homosexual).

[492] UNHCR Handbook, *supra* note 33, ¶ 68; AOBTC Workbook, pt. III, *supra* note 491, at 16. *See, e.g., Stserba v. Holder*, 646 F.3d 964 (6th Cir. 2011) (finding that a person of Russian "ethnicity" who suffered harm in Estonia suffered harm on account of race and may be eligible for relief); *Haile v. Holder*, 591 F.3d 572 (7th Cir. 2010) (finding that an ethnic Eritrean living in Ethiopia who was stripped of Ethiopian citizenship because of his ethnicity may have suffered past persecution on account of race).

[493] *Id.* ¶ 68–69.

[494] Immigration and Naturalization Serv., Basic Law Manual, U.S. Law and INS Refugee/Asylum Adjudications 37 (1994) (AILA 1995).

[495] UNHCR Handbook, *supra* note 33, ¶ 68.

[496] *Duarte de Guinac v. INS*, 179 F.3d 1156, 1159 n.5 (9th Cir. 1999); *See also Karapetyan v. Mukasey*, 543 F.3d 1118, 1127 (9th Cir. 2008) (court noted that use of ethnic slurs amply established the connection between the acts of persecution and the applicant's ethnicity); *Knezevic v. Ashcroft*, 367 F.3d 1206, 1210 (9th Cir. 2004) (persecution was based on applicants' Serbian ethnicity); *Baballah v. Ashcroft*, 367 F.3d 1067, 1075 n.10 (9th Cir. 2004) (in case of an Israeli applicant who was the child of a Muslim father and Jewish mother, the court noted that "ethnicity" falls between race and nationality); *Gafoor v. INS*, 231 F.3d 645, 653–54 (9th Cir. 2000) (granting asylum to Fijian of Indian descent); *Shoafera v. INS*, 228 F.3d 1070, 1074 n.2 (9th Cir. 2000) (where persecution was based on Amhara ethnicity); *Andriasian v. INS*, 180 F.3d 1033, 1042 n.15 (9th Cir. 1999) (where persecution based on Armenian ethnic origin was treated as on account of race); *Singh v. INS*, 94 F.3d 1353 (9th Cir. 1996)

Continued

The characteristic of being Quiche may be perceived by the persecutor or feared persecutor as a racial characteristic, an ethnic characteristic (nationality), an immutable characteristic shared with other members of a distinct group (particular social group), a religious characteristic (some communities still practice indigenous religions), or a political characteristic (indigenous communities were often linked with guerilla organizations). The important inquiry is whether the persecutor is motivated to harm the applicant on account of his or her being Quiche; if so, any one of the protected characteristics would likely apply.[497]

However, membership in a racial group does not automatically provide the basis for asylum unless the applicant can demonstrate individualized persecution or a pattern or practice of persecution against members of the specific racial group.[498]

> ➢ **Practice Pointer**: Courts have noted that widespread harassment and discrimination on account of race or ethnicity may strengthen the severity of individualized harm suffered by the applicant.[499] Thus, practitioners should document any pattern or practice of widespread targeting of individuals of the same race or ethnicity.

> ➢ **Practice Pointer**: UNHCR notes that "some gangs are motivated by racist or nationalist ideologies" and that gangs may fuel xenophobia and engage in hate crimes against ethnic and national minorities.[500] Practitioners should be sure to evaluate the facts of any gang-based asylum claim to determine if other protected grounds, besides particular social group, may have motived the gangs to harm their clients. See chapter 5 for a detailed discussion of gang-based asylum claims.

Racial discrimination or harassment usually is not sufficient to establish persecution because discrimination alone does not rise to the level of persecution

---

(where the claim of Indo-Fijian analyzed as on account of race). *But see, e.g., Magua v. Att'y Gen.*, 386 F. App'x 958 (11th Cir. 2010) (finding that the applicant did not show a nexus between the robbery of his store in South Africa and his race because the perpetrators of the robbery robbed both the white store owner applicant and black store customers, indicating that the applicant was targeted for money, not because of his white race); *Lopez-Castro v. Holder*, 577 F.3d 49 (1st Cir. 2009) (holding that the applicant, a Guatemalan national of indigenous Mayan Quiche ancestry, failed to establish a sufficient nexus between the past and future harm alleged and his ethnicity).

[497] AOBTC Workbook, pt. III, *supra* note 491, at 17.

[498] UNHCR Handbook, *supra* note 33, ¶ 70.

[499] *See, e.g., Sinha v. Holder*, 564 F.3d 1015 (9th Cir. 2009) (finding that the IJ applied an erroneous legal standard when he suggested that the fact that Indo-Fijians were frequently victims of harassment undercut the severity of the individualized harm suffered by the applicant, where the applicant was attacked by ethnic Fijians five times and the incidents occurred during periods of high racial tension and the attackers used ethnic slurs).

[500] U.N. High Comm'r for Refugees, *Guidance Note on Refugee Claims Relating to Victims of Organized Gangs*, p. 11 Div. of Int'l Prot. (Mar. 31, 2010), *available at* www.refworld.org/docid/4bb21fa02.html. *See generally* U.S. Dep't of Justice, EOIR Immigration Judge Benchbook, *available at www.justice.gov/eoir/vll/benchbook/* (last visited July 18, 2014).

unless it is particularly severe or an accumulation of discriminatory acts.[501] According to the UNHCR, where "a person's human dignity is affected to such an extent as to be incompatible with the most elementary and inalienable human rights, or where the disregard of racial barriers is subject to serious consequences," racial discrimination may amount to persecution.[502]

ii. Religion

The Universal Declaration of Human Rights and the International Covenant on Civil and Political Rights proclaim the right to freedom of thought, conscience, and religion. In those instruments, freedom of religion is recognized as a universal human right encompassing the right to have or adopt a religion; the freedom to observe, practice or teach a religion in public or private; and the right not to be coerced in a way that would impair the freedom to have or adopt a religion or belief.[503]

In 1998, Congress passed the International Religious Freedom Act (IRFA) to address concerns about religious freedom around the world.[504] The IRFA created within the U.S. Department of State (DOS) the Office of International Religious Freedom, which is responsible for assisting the Secretary of State in preparing an annual report for Congress on international religious freedom on September 1 of each year. The report describes the nature and extent of violations of religious freedom committed or tolerated by foreign governments.[505] The IRFA also called for the creation of the U.S. Commission on International Religious Freedom (USCIRF), an independent federal government agency, for the purpose of ensuring that the president and Congress receive independent recommendations and, where necessary, criticism of American policy that does not promote international religious freedom. USCIRF is independent of the executive branch and is not part of DOS. It compiles an annual report of its policy recommendations, including critiques on religious freedom abuses committed in numerous countries.[506]

---

[501] *See supra* pt. II.C.8. for a detailed discussion of what discrimination may rise to the level of persecution.

[502] UNHCR Handbook, *supra* note 33, ¶ 69.

[503] Universal Declaration of Human Rights, art. 18, G.A. Res. 217 (III) A, U.N. Doc.. A/RES/217(III) (Dec. 10, 1948) [hereinafter Declaration of Human Rights], *available at www.ohchr.org/EN/UDHR/Documents/UDHR_Translations/eng.pdf*; U.N. GAOR, International Covenant on Civil and Political Rights, art. 18, *done* Dec. 19, 1966, 172 U.N.T.S. 14668 [hereinafter Convention of Civil and Political Rights], *available at https://treaties.un.org/doc/Publication/UNTS/Volume%20999/volume-999-I-14668-English.pdf. See also* UNHCR Handbook, *supra* note 33, ¶ 71.

[504] International Religious Freedom Act (IRFA) of 1998, Pub. L. No. 105-292, 112 Stat. 2787, §102(b).

[505] *See* U.S. State Dep't, *International Religious Freedom Report for 2013 available at www.state.gov/j/drl/rls/irf/religiousfreedom/index.htm#wrapper* (last visited Oct. 31, 2014) (where the Department's annual reports are available).

[506] U.S. Comm'n on Int'l Religious Freedom (USCIRF), Annual Report, *available at www.uscirf.gov/reports-briefs/annual-report* (last visited Jan. 4, 2015) (where the Commission's annual reports are available, and where countries of particular concern listed in the 2009 report include Burma,

Continued

According to UNHCR, religion encompasses "freedom of thought, conscience or belief."[507] Protection from religious-based persecution, therefore, not only covers an individual's freedom to practice his or her own religion, but also covers acts of failing or refusing to observe a religion or to hold any particular religious belief.[508] In 2004 UNHCR issued *Guidelines on International Protection: Religion-Based Refugee Claims Under Article 1A(2) of the 1951 Convention and/or 1967 Protocol Relating to the Status of Refugees*[509] to complement the *Handbook*. These *Guidelines* offer guidance on defining "religion," defining religion-based "persecution," and assessing credibility based on knowledge of the religion.[510] The guidelines categorize religion-based asylum claims based on:

(1) religion as a belief;

(2) religion as an identity; and

(3) religion as a way of life.[511]

In this context, "belief" can be interpreted to include "theistic, non-theistic, and atheistic beliefs and may take the form of convictions or values about the divine."[512] "Identity" does not necessarily correlate to theological beliefs, "but can refer to one's membership in a community that observes or is bound together by common beliefs, rituals, traditions, ethnicity, nationality, or ancestry."[513] The guidelines note that "[i]n some cases, persecutors target religious groups not for their religious differences per se, but because they perceive others' religious identity as part of a threat to their own identity or legitimacy."[514] Finally, religion as a "way of life" can be "perceived in clothing or observance of particular practices."[515]

➢ **Practice Pointer**: Establishing the sincerity of belief, identity, or way of life is not required in every case to establish religious persecution. A persecutor can impute or attribute religion, faith, or practice to an individual or group, and an individual may be persecuted on the basis of

---

China, Eritrea, Iran, Iraq, Nigeria, Pakistan, Saudi Arabia, Sudan, Turkmenistan, Uzbekistan, and Vietnam).

[507] UNHCR Guidelines in Religion-Based Refugee Claims, *supra* note 117; UNHCR Handbook, *supra* note 33, ¶ 71.

[508] UNHCR Guidelines in Religion-Based Refugee Claims, *supra* note 117.

[509] *Id.*

[510] *See also* T.J. Gunn, *The Complexity of Religion and the Definition of 'Religion' in International Law*, 16 Harv. Hum. Rts. J. 189 (2003).

[511] UNHCR Guidelines in Religion-Based Refugee Claims, *supra* note 117.

[512] *Id.* ¶ 6.

[513] *Id.* ¶ 7.

[514] *Id.*

[515] *Id.* ¶ 8.

religion even if he or she adamantly denies the particular belief, identity, or way of life.[516]

As with the other protected grounds, the applicant must first establish that he or she possesses that protected characteristic. In assessing credibility of religious-based claims, asylum adjudicators at times rely on tests or quizzes regarding the religion in question. Adjudicators often believe there is only one correct answer to a question and that an adherent of the religion would know the answer. The advocacy community,[517] as well as the federal courts, has criticized this practice.[518] They reason that asylum-seekers who do not have a high level of schooling in their religion may only know basic information and often lack knowledge of more complex, formal, or obscure religious practices or beliefs.[519] Additionally, practices of the same religion may vary among different countries.[520] USCIS advises its asylum officers to recognize that a person can hold sincere religious beliefs without knowing everything about that religion and to refrain from judging credibility based on the individual's lack of knowledge of religious tenets, to recognize that religious practices vary between countries, and to recognize that suppression or fear of harm on account of religion may force the individual to practice their faith in secret or not at all.[521]

Moreover, adjudicators are encouraged to refrain from allowing their own biases about particular religions affect their questioning and the outcome of the case. At least one court has vacated a negative outcome in a religious persecution case based on clear bias on the part of the immigration judge, who referred to the applicants as

---

[516] *Id.* ¶ 9.

[517] *See, e.g.*, Lawyers Comm. for Human Rights, *Testing the Faithful: Religion and Asylum* (Nov. 2002), *available at* www.humanrightsfirst.org/refugees/reports/religion_surv_1102.pdf.

[518] *See Yan v. Gonzales*, 438 F.3d 1249, 1256 (10th Cir. 2006) (finding that "notwithstanding his stumbling over a few points of Christian doctrine, [the applicant] presented a coherent, personal testimony of his conversion to faith in Jesus Christ"); *Mezvrishvili v. Att'y Gen.*, 467 F.3d 1292, 1296–97 (11th Cir. 2006) (finding that the IJ assumed facts not in the record when he held the applicant to a level of religious devotion that the applicant did not assert); *Rizal v. Gonzales*, 442 F.3d 84, 90 (2d Cir. 2006) (rejecting the approach that a certain degree of doctrinal knowledge is necessary to establish eligibility for asylum on grounds of religious persecution); *Ahmadshah v. Ashcroft*, 396 F.3d 917, 920 n.2 (8th Cir. 2005) (finding that "[W]e are not convinced that a detailed knowledge of Christian doctrine is relevant to the sincerity of an applicant's belief; a recent convert may well lack detailed knowledge of religious custom.").

[519] *See* Lawyers Comm. for Human Rights, *supra* note 517, at 3. *See also, e.g., Lei Li v. Holder*, 629 F.3d 1154, 1159–60 (9th Cir. 2011) (finding that an adverse credibility determination was not supported where the Christian applicant thought Thanksgiving was a Christian holiday and did not know sufficient differences between the old and new testament).

[520] *See* Lawyers Comm. for Human Rights, *supra* note 517, at 4.

[521] U.S. Citizenship and Immigration Servs., RAIO Combined Training Course, International Religious Freedom Act and Religious Persecution Training Module, at 18–20 (Mar. 29, 2013) [hereinafter RAIO Training Course, IRFA Training], *available at www.uscis.gov/sites/default/files/USCIS/About%20Us/Directorates%20and%20Program%20Offices/RAIO/ifra-internatl-religious%20free-act-religious-persecution.pdf.*

"religious zealots."[522] The court found that the IJ departed from his judicial rule and his conduct amounted to a denial of due process.[523]

- ➢ **Practice Pointer**: Practitioners should prepare asylum applicants to explain in detail the personal significance of their religion to them, the practices they have engaged in, and specific facts relating to their persecution or feared persecution. These facts should be emphasized in closing arguments along with citations to corroborating documentation. See Chapters 7 and 8 for a detailed discussion of the procedures for seeking asylum before the asylum offices and immigration courts.

- ➢ **Practice Pointer**: Depending on the circumstances, it may also be appropriate for a practitioner to request that an adjudicator use narrative questioning, including open-ended questions, rather than the quiz-style questioning frequently used.

Mere membership in a particular religious community, however, will not normally be enough to establish an asylum claim.[524] Rather, an applicant must also demonstrate that he or she has been or will be persecuted on account of his or her religion. In meeting this burden, applicants do not necessarily need to show that they would be singled out for persecution if there is evidence indicating a pattern and practice of persecution against members of the applicants' religion.[525]

Persecution on account of religion may assume various forms, including the prohibition of membership in a religious community, of worship or observance in private or in public, of religious instruction, of religious conversion, or serious measures of discrimination imposed on persons because they practice their religion or belong to a particular religious community.[526] Some courts have held that forbidding one from practicing his or her religion amounts to persecution.[527] Others have held

---

[522] *Floroiu v. Gonzales*, 481 F.3d 970, 976 (7th Cir. 2007) (court vacated and remanded claim of Seventh Day Adventists from Romania, encouraged the BIA to send the case to a different IJ, and instructed the court clerk to send a copy of the decision to the AG).

[523] *Id.*

[524] *Ahmad v. INS*, 163 F.3d 457, 463 (7th Cir. 1999); *Refahiyat v. INS*, 29 F.3d 553, 557 (10th Cir. 1994) (holding that the mere assertion that one is aligned with a minority religion is not sufficient to establish a prima facie case of religious persecution); *See also* UNHCR Handbook, *supra* note 33, ¶ 73. *But see Qiu v. Holder*, 611 F.3d 403, 407–09 (7th Cir. 2010) (reversing the denial of asylum to an applicant who had practiced Falun Gong for only three months because the Department of State report indicated that any member of the religious organization, no matter how long he or she has been a member, will be punished in China if he or she continues to practice his or her religion).

[525] *See, e.g., Eduard v. Ashcroft*, 379 F.3d 182, 192 (5th Cir. 2004) (finding that the IJ erred in requiring Indonesian Christians to prove that they were singled out when the evidence indicated a pattern and practice of persecution of Christians).

[526] UNHCR Handbook, *supra* note 33, ¶ 71–72.

[527] *See, e.g., Shi v. Att'y Gen.*., 707 F.3d 1231 (11th Cir. 2013) (finding persecution on account of religion where church services were broken up, the family's bible was confiscated, and the applicant

Continued

that punishment for conversion from one religion to another may constitute persecution.[528] Even if the applicant was harmed for practicing the same religion in a different way then the persecutor may constitute persecution on account of religion. For example, a Moroccan woman with liberal Muslim beliefs was granted asylum after being harmed by her father, who held more orthodox Muslim views.[529]

Some countries have laws or legal systems based on religious principles. Such laws can mandate particular dress codes for women, criminalize conduct, reinforce certain gender roles, place restrictions on freedom of movement, codify requirements for frequency and timing of prayer, and others. However, laws or punishments related to an applicant's religion do not always amount to persecution on account of the applicant's religion. USCIS notes that the following issues should be considered:

(1) whether the law is neutral in intent;

(2) whether the law is neutrally or unequally enforced;

(3) how the persecutor views those who violate the law; and

(4) how compliance with the law affects the applicant's own religious beliefs.[530]

For example, if a law is neutral in intent, the fact that it might adversely affect a religious group does not necessarily mean that the harm the law caused is "on account of" an applicant's religion. USCIS provides the example of a curfew imposed during a period of civil unrest. Such a curfew might prevent individuals from attending evening religious services. However, if the law was not intended to target individuals because of their religious beliefs, but rather, to protect public safety, the requisite nexus to religion is not established.[531] On the other hand, if that same curfew law were only enforced against one particular religion, such selective enforcement would be evidence of the persecutor's motive to target members of a particular religion.

How the persecutor views violations of these laws also is relevant to establishing whether the requisite nexus exists. For example, if the persecutor views the applicant simply as a "law-breaker," that may not establish nexus to religion. However, if the persecutor views the applicant as breaking the law because of "improper" religious values, the requisite nexus may be established.

Finally, how compliance with certain religious laws affects the applicant's own religious beliefs is relevant to whether enforcement of those laws amounts to

---

was detained for several days, slapped, thrown to the floor, and handcuffed to an iron bar overnight outside in the rain); *Bucur v. INS*, 109 F.3d 399, 405 (7th Cir. 1997).

[528] *See, e.g., Shu Han Liu v. Holder*, 718 F.3d 706 (7th Cir. 2013) (reversing the denial of a motion to reopen based on changed conditions where the applicant had converted to Christianity and was facing return to China); *Bastanipour v. INS*, 980 F.2d 1129 (7th Cir. 1992) (finding that prosecution and punishment for renouncing Islam, which is punishable by death, is "on account of" religion).

[529] *Matter of S–A–*, 22 I&N Dec. 1328 (BIA 2000).

[530] AOBTC Workbook, pt. III, *supra* note 491, at 19.

[531] *Id.* at 20.

persecution on account of religion. For example, forced compliance with certain religious laws may be abhorrent to the applicant's own beliefs and may constitute persecution.[532] In *Fatin v. INS*, the Third Circuit considered religious laws in Iran requiring women to wear chadors or veils and stated that "the concept of persecution is broad enough to include governmental measures that compel an individual to engage in conduct that is not physically painful or harmful but is abhorrent to that individual's deepest beliefs."[533] The Third Circuit provided the example of requiring a person to renounce his or her religious beliefs or to desecrate an object of religious importance, stating that "[s]uch conduct might be regarded as a form of 'torture' and thus as falling within the Board's description of persecution."[534] Therefore, for applicants who actually possess the religious beliefs in question — in this case, an applicant who considers wearing chadors of veils to be so abhorrent to them that it would be tantamount to persecution — forced compliance with such religious laws may constitute persecution.[535] Similarly, courts have found that applicants of faith should not be required to hide their religion in order to escape or avoid persecution.[536]

iii. Nationality

Nationality, the third enumerated ground, refers to an individual's citizenship, but also to membership in an ethnic or linguistic group. As the UNHCR *Handbook* notes, "The co-existence within the boundaries of a State of two or more national (ethnic, linguistic) groups may create situations of conflict and also situations of persecution or danger of persecution."[537] Conflict due to the presence of two or more ethnic or linguistic groups within the same country has resulted in persecution of groups such as ethnic Albanians in former Yugoslavia, Kurds in Iraq, indigenous populations in Central America, Palestinians in the West Bank, ethnic groups in the former Soviet Union, and ethnic Eritreans in Ethiopia and ethnic Ethiopians in Eritrea.[538]

---

[532] *See, e.g., Fatin v. INS*, 12 F.3d 1233 (3d Cir. 1993) (finding that forced compliance with laws that are fundamentally abhorrent to a person's deeply held religious convictions may constitute persecution); *Matter of S–A–*, 22 I&N Dec. 1328 (BIA 2000) (finding that where a daughter's religious opinions were different than her father's concerning how she should dress and whom she should associate with, and the father attempted to impose his religious beliefs on his daughter through physical force, the serious harm suffered was "persecution on account of religion").

[533] *Fatin v. INS*, 12 F.3d at 1242 (citing *Matter of Acosta*, 19 I&N Dec. at 234 (BIA)).

[534] *Fatin v. INS*, 12 F.3d at 1242 (citing *Matter of Acosta*, 19 I&N Dec. at 222–23 (BIA)).

[535] *Id.* (clarifying that "[r]equiring an adherent of an entirely different religion or a non-believer to engage in the same conduct would not constitute persecution.").

[536] *See, e.g., Muhur v. Ashcroft*, 355 F.3d 958, 960–61 (7th Cir. 2004) (reversing the IJ's determination that the applicant, a Jehovah's Witness, was not entitled to asylum because she could avoid being noticed and escape persecution by hiding her religion).

[537] UNHCR Handbook, *supra* note 33, ¶ 75.

[538] *See, e.g.*, *Stserba v. Holder*, 646 F.3d 964 (6th Cir. 2011) (finding that Estonia's invalidation of the applicant's medical degree was economic persecution on account of his Russian ethnicity); *Mengstu v. Holder*, 560 F.3d 1055 (9th Cir. 2009) (finding that the applicant of Eritrean descent was expelled from Ethiopia on account of nationality, because the Ethiopian-Eritrean civil war was ethnically tinged and

Continued

Occasionally, nationality may overlap with the grounds of "race"[539] or even religion or political opinion.[540] As the UNHCR *Handbook* cautions:

It may not always be easy to distinguish between persecution for reasons of nationality and persecution for reasons of political opinion when a conflict between national groups is combined with political movements, particularly where a political movement is identified with a specific "nationality."[541]

Similarly, USCIS also notes that when conflicts among national, ethnic, or linguistic groups occur, persecution on account of nationality may overlap with persecution on account of political opinion, especially where a political movement is identified with a specific nationality.[542] In these situations, adjudicators should not assume that claims arising from the conflict are based solely on civil strife.[543] "Rather, the asylum officer must consider carefully the nature of the strife and determine whether the harm the applicant suffered or fears is connected to his or her nationality, or is harm that is incidental to armed conflict, irrespective of the applicant's nationality."[544]

The UNHCR *Handbook* provides that persecution for reasons of nationality may consist of adverse attitudes and measures directed against a national (ethnic, linguistic) minority.[545] Individuals who belong to a national minority often bring claims based on account of nationality.[546] However, there have been many cases where a person belonging to a majority group may fear persecution by a dominant minority.[547] For example, in Rwanda, the minority Tutsi group controlled the

---

the Ethiopian government solely targeted "Eritreans" for deportation and denationalization); *Al Yatim v. Mukasey*, 531 F.3d 584, 588 fn. 2 (8th Cir. 2008) (finding claim based on Palestinian ethnicity was claim based on nationality); *Knezevic v. Ashcroft*, 367 F.3d 1206, 1210 (9th Cir. 2004) (finding that persecution was based on applicant's Serbian ethnicity); *Baballah v. Ashcroft*, 367 F.3d 1067, 1077 n.10 (9th Cir. 2004) (persecution based on being child of mixed marriage between a Muslim and a Jew); *Shoafera v. INS*, 228 F.3d 1070, 1074 n.2 (9th Cir. 2000) (persecution based on Amhara ethnicity); *Perkovic v. INS*, 33 F.3d 615, 622–23 (6th Cir. 1994) (granting asylum to an ethnic Albanian from Yugoslavia); *Matter of O–Z– & I–Z–*, 22 I&N Dec. 23, 26 (BIA 1998) (finding anti-Semitic threats and beatings rise to level of persecution on account of Jewish "nationality").

[539] UNHCR Handbook, *supra* note 33, ¶ 74.

[540] *Id.* ¶ 75 (noting that "nationality" frequently intersects with persecution on account of "political opinion," especially when a particular nationality, ethnic, or linguistic group in a country shares the same political position).

[541] UNHCR Handbook, *supra* note 33, ¶ 75.

[542] AOBTC Workbook, pt. III, *supra* note 491, at 17.

[543] *Id.*

[544] *Id.*

[545] *Id.*

[546] *Id.* at 18; *See also* UNHCR Handbook, *supra* note 33, ¶ 76.

[547] *Id.; See also* UNHCR Handbook, *supra* note 33, ¶ 76.

government despite the existence of a majority tribal group, the Hutus. Both Tutsis and Hutus have presented valid claims for asylum.[548]

iv. Membership in a Particular Social Group

Perhaps the most complicated ground for asylum is the fourth ground, "membership in a particular social group."[549] According to UNHCR, "A 'particular social group' normally comprises persons of similar background, habits or social status."[550] Social group asylum claims typically involve persecution of a group because the government has no confidence in the group's loyalty to the regime, or the group is held to be an obstacle to the government's policies in some way.[551] In addition, claims based on an applicant's social group "may frequently overlap with a claim to fear of persecution on other grounds," such as race, religion, or political opinion.[552]

Demonstrating persecution based on membership in a particular social group generally involves a three-step process:

(1) Identify the group;

(2) Prove membership or perceived membership in that group; and

(3) Establish that the past or feared persecution is based on membership or perceived membership in that group (establish that the characteristics of that group motivated or would motivate the persecutor to target the applicant).[553]

Identifying and defining the particular social group is often the most difficult and the most critical step in establishing asylum eligibility based on this protected ground. "Particular social group" is not defined in the INA or the code of federal regulations. As the INA and the regulations do not provide guidance in this regard, whether or not a group is considered a "particular social group" for purposes of asylum eligibility is an issue that has yielded volumes of case law, both before the BIA and before the U.S. circuit courts of appeals.

---

[548] *See* AOBTC Workbook, pt. III, *supra* note 491, at 18.

[549] INA §101(a)(42)(A).

[550] UNHCR Handbook, *supra* note 33, ¶ 77.

[551] *Id.* ¶ 78 (noting that membership in a particular social group "may be at the root of persecution because there is no confidence in the group's loyalty to the Government or because the political outlook, antecedents or economic activity of its members, or the very existence of the social group as such, is held to be an obstacle to the Government's policies").

[552] *Id.* ¶ 77.

[553] *See, e.g., Lwin v. INS*, 144 F.3d 505, 510 (7th Cir. 1998); *Sanchez-Trujillo v. INS*, 801 F.2d 1571, 1574–75 (9th Cir. 1986) (adding a fourth requirement to show "special circumstances" that merit the recognition of a group-based claim and finding that the class of young, urban, working class males in El Salvador did not constitute a particular social group). The U.S. Court of Appeals for the Ninth Circuit further held that a social group "implies a collection of people closely affiliated with each other, who are actuated by some common impulse or interest." *Sanchez-Trujillo v. INS*, 801 F.2d at 1576.

Because of the confusion and uncertainty generated by this protected ground, UNHCR has issued guidelines that complement its *Handbook*, expounding further on this ground. Notably, these guidelines define "particular social group" as:

> [A] group of persons who share a common characteristic other than their risk of being persecuted, ***or*** who are perceived as a group by society. The characteristic will often be one which is innate, unchangeable, or which is otherwise fundamental to identity, conscience or the exercise of human rights.[554]

In addition, UNHCR highlights that the size of the particular social group is not relevant in determining whether a group exists, noting that a majority of the population could, under certain circumstances, constitute a particular social group, just as the majority of the population could hold certain religious beliefs or share the same race.[555]

In defining a particular social group, the group must exist independently of the persecution that has been suffered or that is feared; it cannot be defined by the harm itself. For example, for an applicant who was raped and battered by Salvadoran guerillas, the harm suffered was not on account of membership in the particular social group of "women who were raped and battered by Salvadoran guerillas."[556] However, it is possible that past harm — an immutable trait — may lead to an individual becoming a member of a group that is both perceived by society and that has defined boundaries. Thus, such an applicant may be able to establish eligibility for asylum based on a well-founded fear of future persecution on account of that defined social group.[557]

To satisfy the requirements of a particular social group, a voluntary association among the group members is not required.[558] Moreover, homogeneity of the group members is not required.[559] The size of the group does not need to be small to

---

[554] U.N. High Comm'r for Refugees, *Guidelines on International Protection: "Membership of a Particular Social Group" Within the Context of Article 1A(2) of the 1951 Convention and/or its 1967 Protocol Relating to the Status of Refugees*, ¶ 11 (May 7, 2002) [hereinafter UNHCR Guidelines on Membership of a Particular Social Group Protection] *available at www.unhcr.org/3d58de2da.html.*

[555] *Id.* ¶18.

[556] *Gomez v. INS*, 947 F.2d 660, 664 (2d Cir. 1991).

[557] *Lukwago v. Ashcroft*, 329 F.3d 157, 172 (3d Cir. 2003) (noting that the shared experience of enduring past harm may support defining a particular social group for purposes of establishing a well-founded fear of future persecution for an applicant who was abducted by rebel soldiers in Uganda and enslaved by the LRA).

[558] *Matter of C–A–,* 23 I&N Dec. 591, 956 (BIA 2006).

[559] *Id.* at 957. *See also Cece v. Holder*, 733 F.3d 662 (7th Cir. 2013) (rejecting that the breadth of the group is relevant, noting that it is the substance of the claim not the precise wording of the group that should drive the assessment); *Henriquez-Rivas v. Holder*, 707 F.3d 1081 (9th Cir. 2013) (clarifying that the particular social group need not be homogenous and overruling its precedent decisions that seemed to indicate otherwise). The AOBTC supports this notion that homogeneity of the group is not required. *See* AOBTC Workbook, pt. III, *supra* note 491, at 37. *But see Matter of W–G–R–*, 26 I&N Dec. 208

Continued

constitute a particular social group. However, the group should not be defined so broadly as to make it difficult to distinguish who is in the group and who is not in the group in the society in question, nor should it be defined so narrowly as to make it a group that is not recognized in the society.

Over time, the BIA has developed its own analysis for determining whether a group is considered a "particular social group" for purposes of asylum eligibility. In its seminal case of *Matter of Acosta* in 1985, the BIA defined particular social group to be "persons all of whom share a common, immutable characteristic," and clarified that particular social group is to be determined on a case-by-case basis.[560] The characteristic that defines the group "must be one that the members of the group either cannot change, or should not be required to change because it is fundamental to their individual identities or consciences."[561] The BIA reasoned that the other four protected grounds involve characteristics that people either could not change (race or nationality) or should not be required to change (religion or political opinion). The BIA further explained that the shared characteristic "might be innate, like sex, color, or kinship ties, or it might be a shared past experience such as former military leadership or land ownership."[562]

Some examples of accepted social groups defined by immutable or fundamental characteristics include: sexual orientation or sexual identity;[563] being an uncircumcised woman;[564] family;[565] clan membership;[566] land ownership and education;[567] and former status, occupation, or experience.[568] The *Acosta* approach

---

(BIA 2014) (finding the social group of former Mara 18 gang members was too diffuse and broad to meet the particularity requirement because "the group could include persons of any age, sex, or background"). Note that the BIA's recent social group decisions contradict its previous assertion that cohesiveness or homogeneity is not required to be a viable particular social group. *See Matter of C–A–*, 23 I&N Dec. 951, 957 (BIA 2006) ("Nor do we require an element of 'cohesiveness' or homogeneity among group members."). It is yet to be seen whether the circuit courts will defer to the BIA's new interpretation when it contradicts its own prior precedent.

[560] *Matter of Acosta*, 19 I&N Dec. 211, 233 (BIA 1985).

[561] *Id.*

[562] *Id.*

[563] *Matter of Toboso-Alfonso*, 20 I&N Dec. 819 (BIA 1990) (recognizing homosexuality as an immutable characteristic). *See also Karouni v. Gonzales*, 399 F.3d 1163 (9th Cir. 2005); *Amanfi v. Ashcroft*, 328 F.3d 719 (3d Cir. 2003); *Hernandez-Montiel v. INS*, 225 F.3d 1084 (9th Cir. 2000).

[564] *Matter of Kasinga*, 21 I&N Dec. 357, 366 (BIA 1996) (recognizing the status of being an uncircumcised woman as a characteristic one should not be required to change).

[565] *Lwin v. INS*, 144 F.3d 505 (7th Cir. 1998); *Gebremichael v. INS*, 10 F.3d 28 (1st Cir. 1993).

[566] *Matter of H–*, 21 I&N Dec. 337 (BIA 1996).

[567] *Tapiero de Orjuela v. Gonzales*, 423 F.3d 666 (7th Cir. 2005).

[568] *Benitez-Ramos v. Holder*, 589 F.3d 426 (7th Cir. 2009); *Sepulveda v. Gonzales*, 464 F.3d 770 (7th Cir. 2006); *Lukwago v. Ashcroft*, 329 F.3d 157 (3d Cir. 2003).

was endorsed by the First,[569] Second,[570] Third,[571] Sixth,[572] Seventh,[573] Eighth,[574] Ninth,[575] Tenth,[576] and Eleventh[577]Circuits—and the Fourth and Fifth Circuits have cited its language approvingly without explicitly endorsing the approach.[578]

Matter of Acosta remained the standard for particular social group claims until the BIA's decision in 2006, *Matter of C–A–*.[579] In *Matter of C–A–*, the BIA introduced two new factors — social visibility and particularity — without holding that these were requirements for all cognizable social groups. The BIA explained that an applicant must demonstrate that the social group is recognizable and distinct in the society in question. This analysis requires a close look at the shared trait asserted to define the group. It is not necessary for members of the group to identify themselves as a group in order to meet the social visibility and particularity requirements.[580] Rather, if the society in question is able to distinguish individuals who possess the relevant trait from individuals who do not, the group may be considered recognizable and distinct in the society.[581]

In *Matter of C–A–*, the BIA analyzed the group of former noncriminal drug informants working against the Cali drug cartel in Colombia. The BIA found that there was no common, immutable characteristic under *Acosta* because the decision to be an informant was not fundamental to the applicant's identity. Rather, it was the applicant's own decision to assume a calculated risk.[582] In analyzing the new factor

---

569 *Elien v. Ashcroft*, 364 F.3d 392, 396–97 (1st Cir. 2004); *Alvarez-Flores v. INS*, 909 F.2d 1, 7 (1st Cir. 1990).

570 *Koudriachova v. Gonzales*, 490 F.3d 255, 2007 U.S. App. LEXIS 15177, at *13–*15 (2d Cir. 2007).

571 *Fatin v. INS*, 12 F.3d 1233, 1239–40 (3d Cir. 1993).

572 *Castellano-Chacon v. INS*, 341 F.3d 533, 546–48 (6th Cir. 2003), *superseded by statute on other grounds as stated in Chen v. United States*, 434 F.3d 144, 151 (2d Cir. 2006).

573 *See, e.g.*, *Lwin v. INS*, 144 F.3d 505, 512 (7th Cir. 1998).

574 *Safaie v. INS*, 25 F.3d 636, 640 (8th Cir. 1994). Note that the Eighth Circuit's definition of a social group centers on *both* a "voluntary associational relationship" *and* a "common characteristic" that is "essentially beyond the petitioner's power to change or is so fundamental to the individual's identity or conscience that he or she ought not to be required to change." *Id.*

575 *Thomas v. Gonzales*, 409 F.3d 1177, 1184–87 (9th Cir. 2005) (en banc), *vacated on other grounds*, 547 U.S. 183 (2006).

576 *Niang v. Gonzales*, 422 F.3d 1187, 1199 (10th Cir. 2005).

577 *Castillo-Arias v. Att'y Gen.*, 446 F.3d 1190, 1196–97 (11th Cir. 2006), *cert. denied*, 127 S. Ct. 977 (Jan. 8, 2007).

578 *See Lopez-Soto v. Ashcroft*, 383 F.3d 228, 235 (4th Cir. 2004); *Ontunez-Tursios v. Ashcroft*, 303 F.3d 341, 352–53 (5th Cir. 2002).

579 *Matter of C–A–*, 23 I&N Dec. 951 (BIA 2006) (introducing two new factors — social visibility and particularity — for demonstrating that a group is viable as a particular social group for purposes of asylum eligibility).

580 *Id.* at 960–61.

581 *Id.*

582 *Id.* at 958.

of social visibility, the BIA found that the articulated group lacked social visibility because the group is hidden and confidential by nature.[583] This finding applied a literal visibility test instead of a more figurative visibility test when analyzing whether the group is perceived as such by society. The BIA also found that the articulated group lacked particularity because it was too loosely defined; it could include any person who passed along information to the government or to a competing cartel.[584]

Following *Matter of C–A–*, the BIA continued to apply the social visibility and particularity factors without holding that they were requirements for a social group to be viable. In *Matter of A–M–E– & J–G–U–*, the BIA considered a group of affluent Guatemalans and applied a three-prong analysis: common, immutable characteristic; social visibility; and particularity.[585] Although it did not state explicitly that these two additional factors were precedent for determining the viability of any particular social group moving forward, the BIA did refer to them as "factors" and "requirements" throughout its decision. In analyzing whether the group of affluent Guatemalans was a cognizable social group, the BIA stated that the shared characteristic must be "considered in the context of the country of concern and the persecution feared."[586]

The BIA confirmed that the group of affluent Guatemalans would meet the standards under *Matter of Acosta* because being affluent was a trait that individuals should not be required to change.[587] However, the BIA then went on to find that the social group was not viable because it did not meet the social visibility and particularity factors.[588] For social visibility, the BIA reasoned that the group did not share a common trait that was socially distinct in Guatemalan society because the country conditions evidence showed that criminality is pervasive against all Guatemalan socio-economic groups.[589] The BIA defined particularity as meaning "the proposed group can accurately be described in a manner sufficiently distinct that the group would be recognized in the society in question as a discreet class of persons."[590] It then stated that the group of affluent Guatemalans did not meet this factor because it was too amorphous and indeterminate; its membership could not be delimited because the concept of wealth could be subjectively defined to include a broad or narrow range of individuals.[591]

---

[583] *Id.* at 960.

[584] *Id.* at 957.

[585] *Matter of A–M–E– & J–G–U–*, 24 I&N Dec. 69 (BIA 2007) (referring to social visibility and particularity as "factors" and "requirements").

[586] *Id.* at 74.

[587] *Id.* at 73–74.

[588] *Id.* at 75.

[589] *Id.*

[590] *Id.* at 76.

[591] *Id.*

In 2008, the BIA made these two new factors of social visibility and particularity official requirements for demonstrating that a group was a "particular social group" for purposes of asylum eligibility.[592] In *Matter of S–E–G–* and *Matter of E–A–G–*, the BIA held that in addition to the group being based on a common, immutable characteristic, it must also be socially visible and particularly defined.[593] The BIA further explained that "social visibility" means that a group must be "recognizable by others in the community,"[594] while "particularity" means that a group must be defined in a manner sufficiently distinct to be recognized as a discrete, non-amorphous class of persons.[595] "[P]otentially large and diffuse segment[s] of society," will not meet the BIA's particularity requirement.[596]

Matter of S–E–G– involved the social groups of "Salvadoran youth who have been subjected to recruitment efforts by the MS–13 gang and who have rejected or resisted membership in the gang based on their own personal, moral, and religious opposition to the gang's values and activities" and those individuals' family members.[597] *Matter of E–A–G–* involved the groups of "persons resistant to gang membership" and "young persons who are perceived to be affiliated with gangs."[598] None of these groups were held to have met the BIA's new social visibility and particularity requirements.

Immigration advocates and the legal community harshly criticized these decisions as involving circular reasoning and conflated concepts. For example, throughout the decisions, the BIA often conflated its social visibility and particularity requirements with the nexus or "on account of" requirement, which is meant to be a separate question in determining asylum eligibility. Additionally, the BIA was unclear regarding whether "social visibility" meant literal visibility (ocular visibility) or figurative visibility. The BIA also was unclear regarding whether "particularity" required that the group be defined with clear, objective words, or whether it must also be narrow and homogenous. Finally, *Matter of S–E–G–* and *Matter of E–A–G–* left unclear whether previously accepted social groups, such as gay men from a certain country or women of a certain tribe who oppose female genital mutilation, still met the requirements for "particular social group."

---

592 *Matter of E–A–G–*, 24 I&N Dec. 591 (BIA 2008); *Matter of S–E–G–*, 24 I&N Dec. 579 (BIA 2008). The BIA had previously referenced social visibility and particularity; however, it was not until *Matter of E–A–G–* and *Matter of S–E–G–* that these were stated requirements for establishing a particular social group for purposes of asylum eligibility. *See Matter of A–M–E– & J–G–U–*, 24 I&N Dec. 69 (BIA 2007); *Matter of C–A–*, 23 I&N Dec. 951 (BIA 2006).

593 *Matter of E–A–G–*, 24 I&N Dec. at 591; *Matter of S–E–G–*, 24 I&N Dec. at 579.

594 *Matter of S–E–G–*, at 586.

595 *Id.* at 584.

596 *Id.* at 585.

597 *Id.* at 579.

598 *Matter of E–A–G–*, 24 I&N Dec. at 591.

Due to the confusing and unclear nature of the *Matter of S–E–G–* and *Matter of E–A–G–* decisions, the BIA's new "social visibility" and "particularity" requirements yielded a significant amount of case law from the U.S. circuit courts of appeals. Many courts adopted these new requirements.[599] However, other courts rejected one or both of these new requirements. The Third Circuit rejected both requirements entirely, stating that it was "hard-pressed to discern any difference between the requirement of 'particularity' and the discredited requirement of 'social visibility.' Indeed, they appear to be different articulations of the same concept and the government's attempt to distinguish the two oscillates between confusion and obfuscation, while at times both confusing and obfuscating."[600] The Seventh Circuit rejected the "social visibility" requirement, pointing out that members of many targeted groups "take pains to avoid being socially visible."[601] In that decision, Judge Posner queried whether an asylum seeker needed to have a sign on his back announcing his particular social group in order to demonstrate asylum eligibility.[602] The Seventh Circuit also issued an *en banc* decision stating that the breadth of the group was irrelevant to whether it constituted a particular social group, stating that it would be "antithetical to asylum law to deny refuge to a group of persecuted individuals who have valid claims merely because too many have valid claims."[603] Although the Ninth Circuit declined to reject the social visibility and particularity requirements, it held that a group does not need to be homogenous to be a "particular social group" for purposes of asylum eligibility.[604] The Ninth Circuit also agreed that the social visibility and particularity requirements had been conflated at times, and

---

[599] *Umana-Ramos v. Holder*, 724 F.3d 667, 671 (6th Cir. 2013); *Henriquez-Rivas v. Holder*, 707 F.3d 1081, 1089 (9th Cir. 2013); *Orellana-Monson v. Holder*, 685 F.3d 511, 521 (5th Cir. 2012); *Gaitan v. Holder*, 671 F.3d 678, 681 (8th Cir. 2012); *Rivera-Barrientos v. Holder*, 666 F.3d 641, 649–53 (10th Cir. 2012); *Mendez-Barrera v. Holder*, 602 F.3d 21, 26 (1st Cir. 2010); *Scatambuli v. Holder*, 558 F.3d 53 (1st Cir. 2009); *Al-Ghorbani v. Holder*, 585 F.3d 980, 991, 994 (6th Cir. 2009); *Ramos-Lopez v. Holder*, 563 F.3d 855, 858–62 (9th Cir. 2009); *Davila-Mejia v. Mukasey*, 531 F.3d 624, 629 (8th Cir. 2008); *Koudriachova v. Gonzales*, 490 F.3d 255 (2d Cir. 2007); *Ucelo-Gomez v. Mukasey*, 509 F.3d 70 (2d Cir. 2007); *Arteaga v. Mukasey*, 511 F.3d 940, 945 (9th Cir. 2007); *Castillo-Arias v. Att'y Gen.*, 446 F.3d 1190, 1197 (11th Cir. 2006). *But see Martinez v. Holder*, 740 F.3d 902, 910 (4th Cir. 2014) (declining to address social visibility); *Cece v. Holder*, 733 F.3d 662, 668 n.1 (7th Cir. 2013) (rejecting social visibility); *Valdiviezo-Galdamez v. Att'y Gen.*, 663 F.3d 582, 607 (3d Cir. 2011) (rejecting social visibility); *Lizama v. Holder*, 629 F.3d 440, 446–47 (4th Cir. 2011) (declining to address social visibility); *Crespin-Valladares v. Holder*, 632 F.3d 117, 126 (4th 2011) (declining to address social visibility); *Perdomo v. Holder*, 611 F.3d 662 (9th Cir. 2010) (describing social visibility and particularity as "factors to consider" rather than requirements); *Rojas-Perez v. Holder*, 699 F.3d 74 (1st Cir. 2010) (questioning the rationality of the BIA's application of social visibility); *Gatimi v. Holder*, 578 F.3d 611, 615–16 (7th Cir. 2009) (rejecting the social visibility requirement); *Benitez Ramos v. Holder*, 589 F.3d 426, 430 (7th Cir. 2009) (rejecting the social visibility requirement).

[600] *Valdiviezo-Galdamez v. Holder*, 663 F.3d 582, 608 (3d Cir. 2011).

[601] *Gatimi v. Holder*, 578 F.3d at 611; *Benitez-Ramos v. Holder*, 589 F.3d 426 (7th Cir. 2009).

[602] *See Gatimi v. Holder*, at 616 (7th Cir. 2009).

[603] *Cece v. Holder*, 733 F.3d 662, 674–75 (7th Cir. 2013).

[604] *Henriquez-Rivas v. Holder*, 707 F.3d 1081, 1093–94 (9th Cir. 2013).

stated that in determining social visibility, it was the perception of the persecutor that mattered most.[605]

After this clear circuit court split had developed, in 2014, the BIA issued two published decisions, *Matter of M–E–V–G–* and *Matter of W–G–R–*, which restated and clarified its "social visibility" and "particularity" requirements, while renaming social visibility as "social distinction."[606] Accordingly, the BIA now requires a three-prong test for determining whether a group is a "particular social group" for purposes of asylum eligibility:

(1) Determine whether the members of the group share a common, immutable characteristic;

(2) Determine whether the group is socially distinct in the context of the society in question; and

(3) Determine whether the group is sufficiently particular.[607]

In discussing and clarifying "social visibility," the BIA held that it does not mean literal or ocular visibility.[608] To avoid confusion, the BIA renamed this requirement "social distinction," and established that social distinction refers to whether a group is perceived and recognized as a distinct entity by society.[609] The BIA also asserted that social distinction is based on society's perception and not the persecutor's perception.

In discussing and clarifying "particularity," the BIA stood by its previous decisions establishing this requirement, confirming that particularity refers to the group being sufficiently distinct that it would constitute a discrete class of persons with definable boundaries.[610] Groups that are perceived as being too overbroad, too diffuse, too amorphous, or too subjective will be rejected as particular social

---

[605] *Id.* at 1089–91.

[606] *Matter of M–E–V–G–*, 26 I&N Dec. 227 (BIA 2014); *Matter of W–G–R–*, 26 I&N Dec. 208 (BIA 2014).

[607] *Matter of M–E–V–G–*, 26 I&N Dec. at 227; *Matter of W–G–R–*, 26 I&N Dec. at 208, *clarifying Matter of E–A–G–*, 24 I&N Dec. 591 (BIA 2008); *Matter of S–E–G–*, 24 I&N Dec. 579 (BIA 2008); *Matter of A–M–E– & J–G–U–*, 24 I&N Dec. 69 (BIA 2007); & *Matter of C–A–*, 23 I&N Dec. 951 (BIA 2006). Note that the "social distinction" requirement used to be called "social visibility." *See Matter of C–A–*, 23 I&N Dec. 951, 959–61 (BIA 2006) (noting that UNHCR's *Guidelines* confirm that "visibility" is an important element), *aff'd Castillo-Arias v. Att'y Gen.*, 446 F.3d 1190 (11th Cir. 2006), *cert. denied*, 127 S.Ct. 977 (Jan. 8, 2007). *See also Matter of E–A–G–*, 24 I&N Dec. 591, 594 (BIA 2007) and *Matter of S–E–G–*, 24 I&N Dec. 579, 586–88 (BIA 2007). The social group approach applied by the BIA in *Matter of E–A–G–* and *Matter of S–E–G–*, which required social visibility and particularity, was criticized by UNHCR in an amicus brief filed in the U.S. Court of Appeals for the Third Circuit in a gang-based persecution case. The brief is *available at www.unhcr.org/refworld/pdfid/49ef25102.pdf* (last visited June 7, 2014).

[608] *Matter of M–E–V–G–*, at 227; *Matter of W–G–R–*, at 208.

[609] *Matter of M–E–V–G–*, at 240–43; *Matter of W–G–R–*, at 215–18. *See also Matter of C–A–*, 23 I&N Dec. 951 (BIA 2006).

[610] *Matter of M–E–V–G–*, at 239–40; *Matter of W–G–R–*, at 213–15.

groups.[611] For example, in *Matter of W–G–R–*, the BIA found that "former members of the Mara 18 gang in El Salvador who have renounced their gang membership" was too diffuse, broad, and subjective, because "the group could include persons of any age, sex, or background."[612] Through this dicta, the BIA suggested that groups must be defined with more specificity, such as "the duration or strength of the members' active participation in the activity and the recency of their active participation."[613]

Both social distinction and particularity must be analyzed in the "context of the country of concern and the persecution feared."[614] These new requirements conflict with the BIA's previous decisions interpreting "particular social group" in parallel with race, religion, nationality, and political opinion, four grounds that do not require precise boundaries. They also seem to dramatically increase the evidentiary burden on asylum seekers, as it is likely impossible to demonstrate that a society recognizes a group as distinct without a country condition expert.[615] Moreover, these requirements will make it especially difficult for pro se applicants to formulate viable social groups to establish their eligibility for asylum.

For the several circuits that had adopted the BIA's previous social visibility (now social distinction) and particularity requirements,[616] *Matter of M–E–V–G–* and *Matter*

---

[611] *Matter of M–E–V–G–*, at 239–40; *Matter of W–G–R–*, at 213–15. *See also Matter of C–A–*, 23 I&N Dec. 951 (BIA 2006); *Matter of S–E–G–*, at 579 (BIA 2008); *Matter of A–M–E– & J–G–U–*, 24 I&N Dec. 69 (BIA 2007).

[612] *Matter of W–G–R–*, 26 I&N Dec. at 221.

[613] *Id.* at 222. *But see Matter of C–A–*, 23 I&N Dec. 951, 956–57 (BIA 2006) (stating that homogeneity was not a requirement for a group to be considered a particular social group). Note that such specificity in defining a social group risks causing the defined social group to fail the social distinction requirement. For example, most societies do not view "former gang members who are between 20 and 25 years old" any differently than "former gang members who are between 30 and 35 years old." These BIA decisions yield much confusion and establish a nearly impossible standard for defining a social group. Defining a group with enough specificity to meet the particularity requirement will cause the group to fail the social distinction prong of the test. On the other hand, defining the group in a way that shows it is a recognized group in society will cause the group to fail the particularity prong of the test. It is yet to be seen or established which social groups, if any, will be able to meet both of these new requirements in addition to the shared common, immutable characteristic requirement.

[614] *Matter of A–M–E– & J–G–U–*, 24 I&N Dec. at 69 (confirmed by *Matter of M–E–V–G–*, 26 I&N Dec. 227 (BIA 2014) & *Matter of W–G–R–*, at 208).

[615] *Matter of M–E–V–G–*, at 244 (stating that "Evidence such as country conditions reports, expert witness testimony, and press accounts of discriminatory laws and policies, historical animosities, and the like may establish that a group exists and is perceived as 'distinct' or 'other' in a particular society.").

[616] *Umana-Ramos v. Holder*, 724 F.3d 667, 671 (6th Cir. 2013); *Henriquez-Rivas v. Holder*, 707 F.3d 1081, 1089 (9th Cir. 2013); *Orellana-Monson v. Holder*, 685 F.3d 511, 521 (5th Cir. 2012); *Gaitan v. Holder*, 671 F.3d 678, 681 (8th Cir. 2012); *Rivera-Barrientos v. Holder*, 666 F.3d 641, 649–53 (10th Cir. 2012); *Mendez-Barrera v. Holder*, 602 F.3d 21, 26 (1st Cir. 2010); *Scatambuli v. Holder*, 558 F.3d 53 (1st Cir. 2009); *Al-Ghorbani v. Holder*, 585 F.3d 980, 991, 994 (6th Cir. 2009); *Ramos-Lopez v. Holder*, 563 F.3d 855, 858–62 (9th Cir. 2009); *Davila-Mejia v. Mukasey*, 531 F.3d 624, 629 (8th Cir. 2008); *Koudriachova v. Gonzales*, 490 F.3d 255 (2d Cir. 2007); *Ucelo-Gomez v. Mukasey*, 509 F.3d 70 (2d Cir. 2007); *Arteaga v. Mukasey*, 511 F.3d 940, 945 (9th Cir. 2007); *Castillo-Arias v. Att'y Gen.*,

Continued

of W–G–R– will likely have little impact. However, the BIA's dicta demanding such specificity to meet the particularity requirement, its seeming requirement of substantial evidence of sociological matters in the countries of feared persecution, and its clarification that it is society's perspective, not the persecutor's, that is relevant to the social distinction determination may conflict with even those circuits' precedent. Moreover, it is possible that the Third, Seventh, and Ninth Circuits, which had previously rejected, in whole or in part, social visibility and particularity,[617] may have to reconsider whether the BIA's interpretation of the statute is reasonable.[618] However, those courts may determine that the BIA's requirements do not merit deference because they are an impermissible and unreasonable interpretation of "particular social group."[619] Thus, now that the BIA has renamed social visibility as "social distinction" and reaffirmed this requirement, as well as its "particularity" requirement, the state of social group jurisprudence is most certainly in flux and unclear.

> ➢ **Practice Pointer**: Practitioners should be prepared to address social distinction and particularity in all jurisdictions and with all social groups, even those that have been long-established. It is more important than ever that practitioners formulate particular social groups carefully and with a clear understanding of their jurisdiction's current interpretation of "membership in a particular social group." Even very recent circuit court case law may no longer be useful to support a proposed social group.[620]

---

446 F.3d 1190, 1197 (11th Cir. 2006). *But see Martinez v. Holder*, 740 F.3d 902, 910 (4th Cir. 2014) (declining to address social visibility); *Cece v. Holder*, 733 F.3d 662, 668 n.1 (7th Cir. 2013) (rejecting social visibility); *Valdiviezo-Galdamez v. Att'y Gen.*., 663 F.3d 582, 607 (3d Cir. 2011) (rejecting social visibility); *Lizama v. Holder*, 629 F.3d 440, 446–47 (4th Cir. 2011) (declining to address social visibility); *Crespin-Valladares v. Holder*, 632 F.3d 117, 126 (4th 2011) (declining to address social visibility); *Perdomo v. Holder*, 611 F.3d 662 (9th Cir. 2010) (describing social visibility and particularity as "factors to consider" rather than requirements); *Rojas-Perez v. Holder*, 699 F.3d 74 (1st Cir. 2010) (questioning the rationality of the BIA's application of social visibility); *Gatimi v. Holder*, 578 F.3d 611, 615–16 (7th Cir. 2009) (rejecting the social visibility requirement); *Benitez Ramos v. Holder*, 589 F.3d 426, 430 (7th Cir. 2009) (rejecting the social visibility requirement).

[617] *Henriquez-Rivas v. Holder*, 707 F.3d 1081 (9th Cir. 2013); *Cece v. Holder*, 733 F.3d 662 (7th Cir. 2013); *Valdiviezo-Galdamez v. Holder*, 663 F.3d 582 (3d Cir. 2011); *Gatimi v. Holder*, 578 F.3d 611 (7th Cir. 2009).

[618] *See generally Nat'l Cable & Telecomms. Ass'n v. Brand X Internet Servs.*, 545 U.S. 967 (2005) (stating that the agency may invoke its authority to interpret a statute and decline to follow circuit precedent when the statute is ambiguous and has been interpreted differently among circuits). *See Matter of M–E–V–G–*, at 230 (noting that the BIA's reasonable interpretation of "membership in a particular social group" is entitled to deference).

[619] *See generally Nat'l Cable & Telecomms. Ass'n v. Brand X Internet Servs.*, 545 U.S. 967 (2005). See ch. 12 for a detailed discussion of federal court deference to agency interpretations.

[620] See ch. 5 for a detailed discussion of particular social group hot topics and several practice pointers for presenting gang and gender-based asylum claims.

Few circuit court cases addressing and applying the BIA's new three-prong test for determining the viability of a social group have been published following the BIA decisions in *Matter of M–E–V–G–* and *Matter of W–G–R–*. About one month after the BIA decisions, the Seventh Circuit considered the asylum claim of a Colombian woman whose family owned land in Colombia that the FARC wanted to tax and acquire.[621] The FARC targeted the applicant's uncle for extortion and then murdered him when he resisted. They then pressured the applicant's father to relinquish the title of his land to them and kidnapped him when he refused. While in FARC custody, the applicant's father said under duress that the title of the land belonged to the applicant and her sister. The FARC then turned their threats to the applicant and her sister, prompting them to flee. The applicant argued that she had suffered past persecution on account of her membership in a particular social group related to her status as a landowner and daughter of a landowner. After the IJ and BIA denied asylum, the Seventh Circuit found that the applicant had indeed suffered past persecution and could not safely and reasonably relocate.[622]

The court also found that the persecution N.L.A. suffered was on account of her membership in a valid particular social group based on her characteristic of being a Colombian landowner.[623] It focused its analysis on the particularity prong of the three-part test, stating that this group was particular. The court reiterated its findings in *Cece v. Holder* that it would be "antithetical to asylum law to deny refuge to a group of persecuted individuals who have valid asylum claims merely because too many have valid claims."[624] It also recognized that even if a large group is found valid for purposes of asylum eligibility, it does not mean that all members of that group would seek or receive asylum, as there are many elements that must be met in order for an individual to be granted asylum.[625] This decision confirms that the Seventh Circuit stands by its pre–*Matter of M–E–V–G–* and *Matter of W–G–R–* analysis for particular social group asylum claims.[626]

The Ninth Circuit also has addressed a particular social group asylum claim following the BIA decisions in *Matter of M–E–V–G–* and *Matter of W–G–R–*. In the case of a young Guatemalan man who had "tak[en] concrete steps to oppose gang membership and gang authority," the Ninth Circuit criticized the BIA for failing to properly apply its own new rule for determining the viability of a particular social

---

[621] *N.L.A. v. Holder*, 744 F.3d 425, 438–39 (7th Cir. 2014) (finding that Colombian land owners who refuse to cooperate with the FARC are a viable social group).

[622] *Id.*

[623] *Id.* (relying on *Cece v. Holder*, 733 F.3d 662 (7th Cir. 2013) (en banc) to dismiss the notion that a particular social group must be narrow in order to be valid).

[624] *Id.* at 438.

[625] *Id.*

[626] *See* National Immigrant Justice Center, *New BIA Decisions Undermine U.S. Obligations to Protect Asylum Seekers* (Feb. 18, 2014), *available at www.immigrantjustice.org/litigation/blog/new-bia-decisions-undermine-us-obligations-protect-asylum-seekers#.VJ7zip2rYAA*.

group.[627] In this case, the IJ granted asylum, but the BIA overturned the decision, finding that the particular social group that had been articulated was the same one that the BIA had rejected in *Matter of S–E–G–*. The BIA therefore had found that this group did not meet its social visibility and particularity requirements.[628] The Ninth Circuit remanded the case, finding that the BIA erred in applying its own new test. The court stated:

> To be consistent with its own precedent, the BIA may not reject a group solely because it had previously found a similar group in a different society to lack social distinction or particularity, especially where, as here, it is presented with evidence showing that the proposed group may in fact be recognized by the relevant society.[629]

The Ninth Circuit concluded that adjudicators must engage in a case-specific inquiry in applying the BIA's test for particular social group viability. Each particular social group analysis must be based on the evidence presented and must be specific to the society in question.[630] Ultimately, the Ninth Circuit declined to address the reasonableness of the new test for viability of a particular social group set forth in *Matter of M–E–V–G–* and *Matter of W–G–R–*, stating that the court wished to first allow the BIA the opportunity to properly apply its new test.[631]

Although the Ninth Circuit did not specifically address the reasonableness of the BIA's new test, it did state that its prior holding in *Henriquez-Rivas v. Holder* remained good law, but modified it based on the BIA's confirmation in *Matter of M–E–V–G–* and *Matter of W–G–R–* that social visibility depends on the perspective of society and not the persecutor.[632] The Ninth Circuit's previous analysis that the perspective of the persecutor may be sufficient to establish social visibility (now social distinction) has now been disavowed.[633]

- **Practice Pointer**: These post–*Matter of M–E–V–G–* and *Matter of W–G–R–* decisions highlight the importance of establishing a strong record at the asylum office and IJ levels of asylum claims. Although BIA precedent may present significant challenges in particular social group asylum claims, a strong record with evidence supporting each element of asylum eligibility and each potential counter-argument at the outset will yield more successful initial claims and will provide the BIA and circuit courts with support for finding in the applicants' favor on appeal.

---

[627] *Pirir-Boc v. Holder*, 750 F.3d 1077 (9th Cir. 2014).

[628] *Id.*

[629] *Id.* at 1084.

[630] *Id.*

[631] *Id.*

[632] *Id.* 1084–85.

[633] *Id.*

A strong record makes it easier for adjudicators to find in the applicant's favor.

Following the BIA's new three-prong test for determining the cognizability of a social group, even long-established social groups may no longer be viable. With that in mind, some examples of previously viable particular social groups under the facts and evidence presented have included:

- Families;[634]
- Persons with bipolar disorder who exhibit erratic behavior;[635]
- Honest former law-enforcement agents in Mexico;[636]
- Former members of the MS–13 gang in El Salvador;[637]
- Witnesses who testify against gang members;[638]

---

[634] *Crespin-Valladares v. Holder*, 632 F.3d 117 (4th Cir. 2011) (holding that "family members of those who actively oppose gangs in El Salvador by agreeing to be prosecutorial witnesses" was a particular social group); *Torres v. Mukasey*, 551 F.3d 616, 629 (7th Cir. 2008); *Vumi v. Gonzales*, 502 F.3d 150 (2d Cir. 2007); *Lopez-Soto v. Ashcroft*, 383 F.3d 228, 235 (4th Cir. 2004); *Jie Lin v. Ashcroft*, 377 F.3d 1014, 1028 (9th Cir. 2004); *Lwin v. INS*, 144 F.3d 505 (7th Cir. 1998); *Iliev v. INS*, 127 F.3d 638, 642 (7th Cir. 1997); *Gebremichael v. INS*, 10 F.3d 28 (1st Cir. 1993); *Matter of Acosta*, 19 I&N Dec. 211, 233 (BIA 1985) (noting kinship ties are a common, immutable characteristic), *overruled on other grounds by Matter of Mogharrabi*, 19 I&N Dec. 439 (BIA 1987). *But see Matter of S–E–G–*, 24 I&N Dec. 579, 585 (BIA 2008) (rejecting family members of Salvadoran youth who have been subjected to recruitment efforts by MS-13 and who have rejected or resisted membership in the gang as not a particular social group). Note that the question is not whether a specific family is well known or visible in the society. Rather, it is whether the society views the degree of relationship between the family members as so significant that the society distinguishes the group members from the rest of society based on that relationship. In other words, it is the perception of the family unit that matters, not the perception of the specific family in the relevant society. For example, in most societies, the nuclear family may qualify as a particular social group, but extended family groupings may not have enough social significance to meet the social distinction and particularity requirements. *See, e.g., Estrada-Posadas v. INS*, 924 F.2d 916, 919 (9th Cir. 1991) (finding that an extended family relationship of second cousins living far apart does not satisfy the requirements to demonstrate a particular social group).

[635] *Temu v. Holder*, 740 F.3d 887, 892–94 (4th Cir. 2014) (finding a viable social group meeting the then–social visibility, particularity, and immutable characteristic requirements even though bipolar disorder may be treated with medication). Note that although this Fourth Circuit decision was issued approximately one month before the BIA decisions in *Matter of M–E–V–G–* and *Matter of W–G–R–*, the case has since been granted by the IJ on remand.

[636] *R.R.D. v. Holder*, 746 F.3d 807 (7th Cir. 2014) (stating that the BIA failed to consider evidence that drug organizations have tried to locate and kill other officers who resigned from the police and left the country).

[637] *Martinez v. Holder*, 740 F.3d 902, 911 (4th Cir. 2014) (finding that former membership was an immutable characteristic); *Benitez-Ramos v. Holder*, 589 F.3d 426 (7th Cir. 2009) (noting that the applicant could not change his former membership in the Mara Salvatrucha).

[638] *Henriquez-Rivas v. Holder*, 707 F.3d 1081 (9th Cir. 2013) (stating that social visibility may be demonstrated by looking to the perceptions of the persecutors).

- Potential witnesses against a KLA leader;[639]
- The Lari ethnic group of the Kongo tribe;[640]
- Cameroonian widows;[641]
- Women who have escaped involuntary servitude after being abducted and confined by the Revolutionary Armed Forces of Colombia (FARC);[642]
- Women in China who have been subject to forced marriage and involuntary servitude;[643]
- Somali females,[644]
- Young, Albanian women living alone;[645]
- The educated, landowning class of Colombian cattle farmers;[646]
- Colombian land owners who refuse to cooperate with the FARC;[647]
- Wealthy landowners and business owners in Colombia;[648]
- Former U.S. embassy employees;[649]
- Former child soldiers;[650]
- Persons with disabilities;[651]

---

[639] *Gashi v. Holder*, 702 F.3d 130 (2d Cir. 2012).

[640] *Malonga v. Mukasey*, 546 F.3d 546, 554 (8th Cir. 2008) (finding that members of the tribe share a common dialect and accent, are identifiable by their surname and by their concentration in southern Congo's Pool region and that they are recognizable to others in Congo).

[641] *Ngengwe v. Mukasey*, 543 F.3d 1029, 1034 (8th Cir. 2008) (finding that widows in Cameroon have both gender and a shared past experience as immutable characteristics and that they are viewed by society as members of a particular social group).

[642] *Gomez-Zuluaga v. Att'y Gen.*, 527 F.3d 330, 348 (3d Cir. 2008).

[643] *Qu v. Holder,* 618 F.3d 602 (6th Cir. 2010).

[644] *Mohammed v. Gonzales*, 400 F.3d 785, 798 (9th Cir. 2005) (noting that applicant's nationality and gender were motivating characteristics for FGM because FGM "in Somalia is not clan specific, but rather is deeply imbedded in the culture throughout the nation and performed on approximately 98 percent of all females").

[645] *Cece v. Holder*, 733 F.3d 662, 673 (7th Cir. 2013).

[646] *Tapiero de Orjuela v. Gonzales*, 423 F.3d 666, 672 (7th Cir. 2005).

[647] *N.L.A. v. Holder*, 744 F.3d 425, 438–39 (7th Cir. 2014).

[648] *Cordoba v. Holder*, 726 F.3d 1106 (9th Cir. 2013).

[649] *Ang v. Gonzales*, 430 F.3d 50, 56 (1st Cir. 2005) (agreeing that applicant's work at the U.S. embassy and support for Americans could serve as basis for particular social group claim, but rejecting claim because no past persecution or well-founded fear).

[650] *Lukwago v. Ashcroft*, 329 F.3d 157, 178–79 (3d Cir. 2003).

[651] *Tchoukhrova v. Gonzales*, 404 F.3d 1181, 1189–90 (9th Cir. 2005) (finding "persons with disabilities are precisely the kind of individuals that our asylum law contemplates by the words 'particular social group'"), *rehearing en banc denied*, 430 F.3d 1222 (9th Cir. 2005) (dissent criticized court for creating a reverse derivative asylum claim by imputing harm suffered disabled child to

Continued

- Gay men with female sexual identities in Mexico;[652]
- A family that plays a prominent role in a minority group that is the object of widespread hostile treatment;[653]
- Parents of Burmese student dissidents;[654]
- Filipinos of Chinese ancestry;[655]
- Young women who are members of the Tchamba-Kunsuntu tribe who have not been subjected to female genital mutilation and who oppose the practice;[656]
- Women who oppose female genital mutilation;[657]
- Female members of a tribe;[658]
- Members of a Somali clan;[659]
- Mungiki defectors in Kenya;[660]
- Gay men in Cuba;[661]

---

parents). Although the U.S. Supreme Court vacated the Ninth Circuit's opinion in *Tchoukhrova* because the Ninth Circuit erred by reaching issues that the BIA had not ruled on in the first instance, *Gonzales v. Tchoukhrova*, 127 S. Ct. 57 (2006), the Ninth Circuit's opinion suggests that courts may be willing to view persons with disabilities as a particular social group.

[652] *Hernandez-Montiel v. INS*, 225 F.3d 1084 (9th Cir. 2000), *overruled on other grounds by Thomas v. Gonzales*, 409 F.3d 1177, 1187 (9th Cir. 2005) (en banc).

[653] *Mgoian v. INS*, 184 F.3d 1029, 1036 (9th Cir. 1999).

[654] *Lwin v. INS*, 144 F.3d 505, 512 (7th Cir. 1998).

[655] *Matter of V–T–S–*, 21 I&N Dec. 792, 798 (BIA 1997).

[656] *Matter of Kasinga*, 21 I&N Dec. 357, 365–66 (BIA 1996). Note that while some circuits have discussed gender as a basis for a particular social group, most have found that there must be some other characteristic tied to gender in order for the group to be a particular social group for purposes of asylum eligibility. Generally, persecutors are motivated not solely because of gender, but because of some other characteristic as well. *See, e.g., Safaie v. INS*, 25 F.3d 636, 640 (8th Cir. 1994); *Fatin v. INS*, 12 F.3d 1233, 1240 (3d Cir. 1993); *Gomez v. INS*, 947 F.2d 660, 664 (2d Cir. 1991). *But see, e.g., Niang v. Gonzales*, 422 F.3d 1187, 1199 (10th Cir. 2005) (acknowledging that gender alone could form a particular social group, but finding that being subject to FGM on account of the applicant's tribal membership constitutes persecution on account of membership in a particular social group)

[657] *Haoua v. Gonzales*, 472 F.3d 227, 232 (4th Cir. 2007).

[658] *Niang v. Gonzales*, 422 F.3d 1187, 1199 (10th Cir. 2005).

[659] *Matter of H–*, 21 I&N Dec. 337, 342–43 (BIA 1996). A clan is an extended family group whose members are linked by custom and culture. *See also Malonga v. Mukasey*, 546 F.3d 546 (8th Cir. 2008) (concluding that Lari ethnic group of the Kongo tribe is a particular social group because the members of the tribe share a common dialect and accent that is recognizable in society, the members are recognizable by their surnames, and the members are concentrated in southern Congo's Pool region).

[660] *Gathungu v. Holder*, 725 F.3d 900 (8th Cir. 2013) (stating that the group "Mungiki defectors" was socially visible in Kenya and that it was a shared past experience that was an immutable characteristic).

[661] *Matter of Toboso-Alfonso*, 20 I&N Dec. 819 (BIA 1990).

- Guatemalan street children;[662]
- Honduran street children;[663]
- Married women in India who have contracted HIV, who fear their families will disown them or force them to get a divorce, and who wish to or need to be employed;[664]
- Social outcasts in Colombia;[665]
- Unmarried Chinese women who have been subjected to arranged marriages according to feudal practices and who oppose such practices;[666]
- Women who have been subjected to or face being subjected to the practice of Trokosi, a system of indentured sexual servitude to fetish shrines;[667]
- Young, Westernized, educated, Muslim women who voice their political opinion;[668]
- Young, Westernized people who have defied traditional, Islamic values by marrying without parental permission;[669]
- Iranian women who find their country's gender-specific laws offensive and do not wish to comply with them;[670]
- Women in Jordan who have flouted repressive moral norms and face a high risk of honor killing;[671]
- Russian children with serious disabilities that are long-lasting or permanent in nature;[672]

---

[662] *Matter of A–M–L–, [number not provided]* (IJ Nov. 21, 2001) (Phoenix, AZ) (Richardson, IJ), *reported in* 79 *Interpreter Releases* 440 (Mar. 25, 2002).

[663] *Matter of Reyes-Diaz, [number not provided]* (IJ Aug. 2, 2001) (Los Angeles, CA) (Munoz, IJ).

[664] *Matter of [name not provided]*, (IJ Dec. 20, 2000) (Baltimore, MD) (Gossart, IJ), *reported in* 78 *Interpreter Releases* 233 (Jan. 15, 2001).

[665] *Matter of Faronda-Blandon*, A74 979 517 (IJ June 15, 2001) (York County Prison, PA) (Van Wyke, IJ), *reported in* 78 INTERPRETER RELEASES 1173 (July 16, 2001).

[666] *Matter of [name not provided]*, A76 512 001 (IJ Oct. 18, 2000) (Chicago, IL) (Zerbe, IJ), *reported in* 77 INTERPRETER RELEASES 1634 (Nov. 20, 2000); *see also Gao v. Gonzales*, 440 F.3d 62, 70–71 (2d Cir. 2006) (finding women who have been sold into marriage and who live in a part of China where forced marriages are considered valid and enforceable constitute a particular social group).

[667] *See* IJ Grants Asylum to Former 'Trokosi" Slave, 75 INTERPRETER RELEASES 165 (Feb. 2, 1998).

[668] *Matter of Sharmin*, A73 556 833 (IJ Sept. 27, 1996) (New York, NY) (IJ Bukszpan), *reported in* 74 *Interpreter Releases* 174 (Jan. 27, 1997).

[669] *Al-Ghorbani v. Holder*, 585 F.3d 980, 995 (6th Cir. 2009).

[670] *Fatin v. INS*, 12 F.3d 1233, 1241–42 (3d Cir. 1993).

[671] *Sarhan v. Holder*, 658 F.3d 649 (7th Cir. 2011).

[672] *Tchoukhrova v. Gonzales*, 404 F.3d 1181, 1189 (9th Cir. 2005)

- Persons who are HIV positive;[673]
- Students;[674]
- Members of a royal tribal family;[675]
- Members of a tribe;
- Mayan Quiché;[676]
- Professionals, business people, and highly educated individuals;[677]
- Former members of the national police;[678]
- Government employees;[679]
- Union members;[680] and
- Victims of trafficking or persons at risk of being trafficked.[681]

Of course, many of these groups may no longer be viable under the BIA's recently reaffirmed three-prong test.

Some examples of non-viable particular social groups under the facts and evidence presented have included:

- Jordanian men subject to honor killings;[682]
- Competing family business owners;[683]
- Friends of the Roma people;[684]
- Young Salvadoran men who resist gang recruitment;[685]

---

673 *Matter of [name not provided]*, A71 498 940 (IJ Oct. 31, 1995) (New York, NY), *reported in* 73 INTERPRETER RELEASES 901 (July 8, 1996).

674 *Matter of Villalta*, 20 I&N Dec. 142 (BIA 1990).

675 *Adebisi v. INS*, 952 F.2d 910, 913 (5th Cir. 1992).

676 *Ordonez-Quino v. Holder*, 760 F.3d 80 (1st Cir. 2014).

677 *Ananeh-Firempong v. INS*, 766 F.2d 621, 623 (1st Cir. 1985).

678 *Matter of Fuentes*, 19 I&N Dec. 658 (BIA 1988).

679 *Aguilera-Cota v. INS*, 914 F.2d 1375, 1380 n.3 (9th Cir. 1990).

680 *Bernal-Garcia v. INS*, 852 F.2d 144 (5th Cir. 1988).

681 *See generally* U.N. High Comm'r for Refugees, *Guidelines on International Protection: The Application of Article 1A(2) of the 1951 Convention and 1967 Protocol Relating to the Status of Refugees to Victims of Trafficking and Persons at Risk of Being Trafficked* (2006), *available at www.unhcr.org/publ/PUBL/443b626b2.pdf.*

682 *Khalili v. Holder*, 557 F.3d 429, 436 (6th Cir. 2009).

683 *Davila-Mejia v. Mukasey*, 531 F.3d 624, 629 (8th Cir. 2008).

684 *Donchev v. Mukasey*, 553 F.3d 1206, 1218 (9th Cir. 2009).

685 *Umana-Ramos v. Holder*, 724 F.3d 667, 672 (6th Cir. 2013); *Orellana-Monson v. Holder*, 685 F.3d 511 (5th Cir. 2012); *Gaitan v. Holder*, 671 F.3d 678 (8th Cir. 2012); *Santos-Lemus v. Mukasey*, 542 F.3d 738, 745 (9th Cir. 2008). *See also Constanza v. Holder*, 647 F.3d 749 (8th Cir. 2011).

- Salvadoran women between the ages of 12 and 25 who resisted gang recruitment;[686]
- Young women who resist gang recruitment;[687]
- Salvadoran youth who have been subjected to recruitment efforts by MS–13 and who have rejected or resisted membership in the gang based on their own personal, moral, and religious opposition to the gang's values and activities;[688]
- Young Guatemalan men who opposed the MS–13, were beaten and extorted by the gang, reported the gang to the police, and faced increased persecution as a result;[689]
- Former members of the Mara 18 gang in El Salvador who have renounced their gang membership;[690]
- Men in El Salvador who fear gang violence because of a former gang member who is also their family member;[691]
- Family members of local business owners;[692]
- Deportees from the United States;[693]
- Perceived wealthy Guatemalans returning from abroad;[694]
- Perceived wealthy Salvadorans returning from abroad;[695]
- Victims of gang threats and possible extortion;[696]

---

[686] *Rivera-Barrientos v. Holder*, 666 F.3d 641 (10th Cir. 2012) (stating that individuals who resist recruitment are "not in a substantially different situation from anyone who has crossed the gang, or who is perceived to be a threat to the gang's interests").

[687] *Mendez-Barrera v. Holder*, 602 F.3d 21 (1st Cir. 2010).

[688] *Matter of S–E–G–*, 24 I&N Dec. 479 (BIA 2008). *See also Umana-Ramos v. Holder*, 724 F.3d 667 (6th Cir. 2013).

[689] *Garcia v. Holder*, 746 F.3d 869 (8th Cir. 2014) (finding that the group lacked particularity and visibility required to be perceived by society as a cohesive group).

[690] *Matter of W–G–R–*, 26 I&N Dec. 208 (BIA 2014).

[691] *Fuentes v. Holder*, 764 F.3d 902 (8th Cir. 2014).

[692] *Quinteros v. Holder*, 707 F.3d 1006 (8th Cir. 2013).

[693] *Matter of W–G–R–*, 26 I&N Dec. 208 (BIA 2014). *See also Escobar v. Holder*, 698 F.3d 36 (1st Cir. 2012).

[694] *Sam v. Holder*, 752 F.3d 97 (1st Cir. 2014); *Ayala v. Holder*, 683 F.3d 15 (1st Cir. 2012); *Matul-Hernandez v. Holder*, 685 F.3d 703 (8th Cir. 2012).

[695] *Delcid-Zelaya v. Holder*, No. 12-9589 (10th Cir. 2013); *Garcia-Callejas v. Holder*, 666 F.3d 828 (1st Cir. 2012).

[696] *Tay-Chan v. Holder*, 699 F.3d 107 (1st Cir. 2012).

- Young, Americanized, well-off Salvadoran male deportees with criminal histories who opposed gangs;[697]
- Honduran youth who have been actively recruited by gangs but who have refused to join because they oppose the gangs;[698]
- Young Honduran males who refused to join gangs, notified the authorities of gang harassment tactics, and had an identifiable tormentor within the gang;[699]
- ICE informants;[700]
- Witnesses to a serious crime whom the government is unable or unwilling to protect;[701]
- Persons who face persecution by corrupt governmental and law enforcement authorities instigated by a politically connected spouse;[702]
- Young women who have been approached or threatened with kidnapping, forced prostitution, or killing by human traffickers;[703]
- Women subjected to rape as a method of government control;[704]
- Single women perceived to have substantial economic resources;[705]
- Former children of war;[706]
- Members of violent street gangs;[707]
- Affluent Guatemalans;[708]
- Criminal deportees;[709]

---

[697] *Lizama v. Holder*, 629 F.3d 440 (4th Cir. 2011) (stating that the defined group was not narrow or enduring enough to clearly delineate its membership or readily identify its members).

[698] *Matter of M–E–V–G–*, 26 I&N Dec. 227 (BIA 2014).

[699] *Zelaya v. Holder*, 668 F.3d 159 (4th Cir. 2012) (finding that the proposed group did not meet the particularity requirement).

[700] *Costa v. Holder*, 733 F.3d 13 (1st Cir. 2013).

[701] *de Carvalho-Frois v. Holder*, 667 F.3d 69 (1st Cir. 2012).

[702] *Ruiz-Cabrera v. Holder*, 748 F.3d 754 (7th Cir. 2014) (reasoning that marriage was the applicant's relationship to his alleged persecutor, not a characteristic shared by all members of the proposed group).

[703] *Kuci v. Att'y Gen.*, 299 Fed. Appx. 168 (3d Cir. 2008) (unpublished) (court rejected particular social group because it was a group defined by the harm).

[704] *Kante v. Holder*, 634 F.3d 321 (6th Cir. 2011).

[705] *Arevalo-Giron v. Holder*, 667 F.3d 79 (1st Cir. 2012).

[706] *Id.*

[707] *Cantarero v. Holder*, 734 F.3d 82 (1st Cir. 2013); *Arteaga v. Mukasey*, 511 F.3d 940, 945–46 (9th Cir. 2007).

[708] *Ucelo-Gomez v. Mukasey*, 509 F.3d 70, 74 (2d Cir. 2007); *Matter of A–M–E– & J–G–U–*, 24 I&N Dec. 69 (BIA 2007).

[709] *Toussaint v. Gonzales*, 455 F.3d 409, 417–18 (3d Cir. 2006); *Elien v. Ashcroft*, 364 F.3d 392, 397 (1st Cir. 2004).

- Drug traffickers;[710]
- Tattooed youth;[711]
- Honduran street children;[712]
- Abandoned Guatemalan children lacking protection;[713]
- Family business owners in Guatemala;[714]
- Small businesspeople indebted to private creditors;[715]
- Landowners in Honduras;[716]
- Noncriminal drug informants working against the Cali drug cartel;[717]
- Informants to the U.S. government regarding a drug smuggling ring;[718]
- Those willing to participate in the legal process, despite great personal risk, to ensure justice against criminal elements;[719]
- Young, attractive Albanian women forced into prostitution;[720]
- Young, unmarried Albanian women who are at risk of being kidnapped and forced into prostitution;[721]
- Young urban males;[722]
- Young, urban working class males of military age who have never served in the military or otherwise expressed support for the government;[723]
- Indigenous people comprising a large percentage of the population of a disputed area;[724]
- Mentally ill Jamaicans or mentally ill female Jamaicans;[725]

---

710 *Bastanipour v. INS*, 980 F.2d 1129, 1132 (7th Cir. 1992).

711 *Castellano-Chacon v. INS*, 341 F.3d 533 (6th Cir. 2003).

712 *Escobar v. Gonzales*, 417 F.3d 363, 367–68 (3d Cir. 2005).

713 *Guerra-Marchorro v. Holder*, 760 F.3d 126 (1st Cir. 2014).

714 *Davila-Mejia v. Mukasey*, 531 F.3d 624, 629 (8th Cir. 2008).

715 *Cruz-Funez v. Gonzales*, 406 F.3d 1187, 1191 (10th Cir. 2005).

716 *Urbina-Dore v. Holder*, 735 F.3d 952 (7th Cir. 2013).

717 *Matter of C–A–*, 23 I&N Dec. 951 (BIA 2006), *aff'd Castillo-Arias v. Att'y Gen.*, 446 F.3d 1190 (11th Cir. 2006), *cert. denied*, 127 S. Ct. 977 (Jan. 8, 2007).

718 *Scatambuli v. Holder*, 558 F.3d 53 (1st Cir. 2009) (stating that the group lacked social visibility).

719 *Bathula v. Holder*, 723 F.3d 889 (7th Cir. 2013).

720 *Rreshpja v. Gonzales*, 420 F.3d 551, 555–56 (6th Cir. 2005).

721 *Gjura v. Holder*, 695 F.3d 223 (2d Cir. 2012).

722 *Chavez v. INS*, 723 F.2d 1431, 1434 (9th Cir. 1984).

723 *Sanchez-Trujillo v. INS*, 801 F.2d 1571 (9th Cir. 1986).

724 *Pedro-Mateo v. INS*, 224 F.3d 1147, 1151 (9th Cir. 2000).

725 *Raffington v. INS*, 340 F.3d 720,723 (8th Cir. 2003).

- Disabled persons, insulin-dependent diabetics, or insulin-dependent diabetics who suffer from mental illness;[726]
- Former members of the military;[727]
- Males of military age who have sworn allegiance to neither faction;[728]
- Cooperative taxi drivers;[729]
- Pro-Aristide young students;[730]
- Tamil males between the ages of 15 and 45;[731]
- Salvadoran women previously raped and beaten by guerrillas;[732]
- Iranian women whose claims were based solely on gender and the harsh restrictions placed upon them as women;[733]
- Chinese citizens of low economic status;[734]
- Members of the criminal class;[735]
- Cheese makers who supplied guerrillas with food;[736] and
- Family members of military deserters.[737]

The question whether a social group is viable for purposes of asylum eligibility has generated a significant amount of case law in recent years. Two of the most debated are gender-based claims, involving victims of female genital mutilation, domestic violence, and forced marriage,[738] and claims based on gang violence

---

[726] *Mendoza-Alvarez v. Holder*, 714 F.3d 1161 (9th Cir. 2013).

[727] *Arriaga-Barrientos v. INS*, 937 F.2d 411, 414 (9th Cir. 1991).

[728] *Zapeda-Melendez v. INS*, 741 F.2d 285, 290 (9th Cir. 1986).

[729] *Matter of Acosta*, 19 I&N Dec. 211, 234 (BIA 1985), *modified on other grounds by Matter of Mogharrabi*, 19 I&N Dec. 439 (BIA 1987).

[730] *Civil v. INS*, 140 F.3d 52 (1st Cir. 1998).

[731] *Ravindran v. INS*, 976 F.2d 754, 761 n.5 (1st Cir. 1992).

[732] *Gomez v. INS*, 947 F.2d 660, 664 (2d Cir. 1991).

[733] *Safaie v. INS*, 25 F.3d 636, 640 (8th Cir. 1994).

[734] *Li v. INS*, 92 F.3d 985, 987 (9th Cir. 1996).

[735] *Bastanipour v. INS*, 980 F.2d 1129, 1132 (7th Cir. 1992).

[736] *Alvarez-Flores v. INS*, 909 F.2d 1, 7 (1st Cir 1990).

[737] *DeValle v. INS*, 901 F.2d 787, 792 (9th Cir. 1990).

[738] *Bah v. Gonzales*, 462 F.3d 637, 643 (6th Cir. 2006); *Abebe v. Gonzales*, 432 F.3d 1037, 1043 (9th Cir. 2005); *Mohammed v. Gonzales*, 400 F.3d 785, 795–96 (9th Cir. 2005); *Niang v. Gonzales*, 422 F.3d 1187, 1189 (10th Cir. 2005); *Abay v. Ashcroft*, 368 F.3d 634, 641–42 (6th Cir. 2004); *Kebede v. Ashcroft*, 366 F.3d 808, 811 (9th Cir. 2004); *Abankwah v. INS*, 185 F.3d 18, 23–24 (2d Cir. 1999); *Matter of A–K–*, 24 I&N Dec. 275 (BIA 2007); *Matter of A–T–*, 24 I&N Dec. 296, 299–301 (BIA 2007); *Matter of Kasinga*, 21 I&N Dec. 357, 365 (BIA 1996); *Matter of D–V–*, 21 I&N Dec. 77, 78–79 (BIA 1993). *See also Gao v. Gonzales*, 440 F.3d 62, 70–71 (2d Cir. 2006); *Yadegar-Sargis v. INS*, 297 F.3d 596 (7th Cir. 2002); *Fisher v. INS*, 79 F.3d 955 (9th Cir. 1996); *Sharif v. INS*, 87 F.3d 932 (7th

Continued

involving forced recruitment, extortion, threats, and physical violence targeted at prosecution witnesses, informants, family members, former gang members, women and girls labeled as gang property, and males of certain socio-economic classes.[739] These gender and gang-based claims are discussed in detail in Chapter 5.

- **Practice Pointer**: Remember that it is not enough simply to identify and define the particular social group at risk of persecution. Asylum applicants much also show that they are members of that particular social group and that the past or feared persecution is "on account" of that particular social group's common, immutable characteristics.[740]

v. Political opinion

Asylum is often referred to as "political asylum." Political opinion, of course, is just one of the five grounds enumerated in the definition of refugee. While a substantial number of asylum cases are political opinion claims, the four other grounds discussed above should not be overlooked.

Persecution on account of the fifth enumerated ground, political opinion, means "persecution on account of the *victim's* political opinion, not the persecutor's."[741] It may also mean persecution on account of a political opinion that the persecutor has attributed to the applicant. To meet his or her burden, an applicant must show,

---

Cir. 1996); *Safaie v. INS*, 25 F.3d 636, 640 (8th Cir. 1994); *Matter of R–A–*, 24 I&N Dec. 629 (AG 2008); *Matter of R–A–*, 22 I&N Dec. 906 (AG 2001); *Matter of S–A–*, 22 I&N Dec. 1328, 1335 (BIA 2000). The Center for Gender and Refugee Studies has legal expertise and many resources available to attorneys representing women fleeing gender-based violence. *See generally* the University of California Hastings' Center for Gender and Refugee Studies at *http://cgrs.uchastings.edu/* (last visited Jan. 4, 2015).

[739] *Matter of W–G–R–*, 26 I&N Dec. 208 (BIA 2014); *Matter of S–E–G–*, 24 I&N Dec. 579 (BIA 2008); *Matter of E–A–G–*, 24 I&N Dec. 591 (BIA 2008); *Matter of C–A–*, 23 I&N Dec. 951 (BIA 2006). *See also Martinez v. Holder*, 740 F.3d 902 (4th Cir. 2014); *Henriquez-Rivas v. Holder*, 2013 WL 518048 (9th Cir. 2013); *Gaitan v. Holder*, 671 F.3d 678 (8th Cir. 2012); *Orellana-Monson v. Holder*, 685 F.3d 511 (5th Cir. 2012); *Garcia-Callejas v. Holder*, 666 F.3d 828 (1st Cir. 2012); *Valdiviezo-Galdamez v. Att'y Gen.*, 663 F.3d 582 (3d Cir. 2011); *Lizama v. Holder*, 629 F.3d 440 (4th Cir. 2011); *Rivera Barrientos v. Holder*, 658 F.3d 1222 (10th Cir. 2011); *Escobar v. Holder*, 657 F.3d 537 (7th Cir. 2011); *Crespin v. Holder*, 632 F.3d 117 (4th Cir. 2011); *Martinez-Seren v. Holder*, 2010 WL 3452840, at *404 (9th Cir. 2010); *Bonilla-Morales v. Holder*, 607 F.3d 1132 (6th Cir. 2010); *Urbina-Mejia v. Holder*, 597 F.3d 360 (6th Cir. 2010); *Soriano v. Holder*, 569 F.3d 1162 (9th Cir. 2009); *Benitez Ramos v. Holder*, 589 F.3d 426 (7th Cir. 2009); *Gatimi v. Holder*, 578 F.3d 611 (7th Cir. 2009); *Scatambuli v. Holder*, 558 F.3d 53 (1st Cir. 2009); *Quinteros-Mendoza v. Holder*, 556 F.3d 159 (4th Cir. 2009); *Amilcar-Orellana v. Mukasey*, 551 F.3d 86 (1st Cir. 2008); *Arteaga v. Mukasey*, 511 F.3d 940 (9th Cir. 2007); *Shehu v. Att'y Gen.*, 482 F.3d 652 (3d Cir. 2007); *Ucelo-Gomez v. Mukasey*, 509 F.3d 70 (2d Cir. 2007).

[740] *Matter of Sanchez and Escobar*, 19 I&N Dec. 276, 285–86 (BIA 1985), *aff'd, Sanchez-Trujillo v. INS*, 801 F.2d 1571 (9th Cir. 1986); *see also Lukwago v. Ashcroft*, 329 F.3d 157, 170 (3d Cir. 2003).

[741] *INS v. Elias-Zacarias*, 502 U.S. 478, 482 (1992) (emphasis in original). *See, e.g., Liu v. Holder*, 692 F.3d 848 (7th Cir. 2012) (finding that the applicant's protest at a state-owned factory was economic, not political, activity and that any persecution he endured was not because of a protected ground).

through direct or circumstantial evidence, that there is a causal connection between the persecution suffered or feared and his or her actual or imputed political opinion.[742] It is not sufficient to demonstrate merely that the persecutor is motivated by political reasons.[743] If the persecutor was not aware or is unlikely to become aware of the applicant's political opinions or activities, nexus may not be established and the applicant's fear of future persecution may not be "well-founded."[744]

Political opinion has been interpreted to encompass a wide spectrum of views, not only views related to political parties or the political process. It includes, of course, any opinion regarding the government, its laws, or its policies. However, political opinion also encompasses more than just political ideology or action, as it requires adjudicators to consider the claim within the context of the country itself.[745] One commentator has noted that it should also include "any opinion on any matter in which the machinery of the state, government, and policy may be engaged."[746] According to UNHCR, political opinions are "opinions not tolerated by the authorities, which are critical of their policies or methods."[747]

---

[742] *See, e.g., Guerrero v. Holder*, 667 F.3d 74 (1st Cir. 2012) (finding that the applicant did not produce convincing evidence of a causal connection between his political beliefs and the harm he suffered at the hands of the FMLN guerillas in El Salvador); *Wanyama v. Holder*, 698 F.3d 1032 (8th Cir. 2012) (upholding the BIA's conclusion that the applicant did not show an objectively reasonable fear of future persecution because there was no evidence presented beyond mere speculation of the alleged political motivations behind the harm that the applicant's family members suffered in Kenya).

[743] *See, e.g., Leva-Montalvo v. INS*, 173 F.3d 749 (9th Cir. 1999) (finding that where all of the applicant's discussions with the "Recontras" centered on politics and ideology, there was no evidence indicating that their motives were purely criminal); *see also Vera-Valera v. INS*, 147 F.3d 1036 (9th Cir. 1998) (in establishing an imputed political opinion, court considers the political views the persecutor rightly or wrongly attributes to his or her victims).

[744] *See, e.g., Y.C. v. Holder*, 741 F.3d 324 (2d Cir. 2013) (concluding that there was insufficient evidence to suggest that the Chinese authorities would become aware of the applicants' pro-democracy activities while in the United States or that they would be targeted on that basis). *But see, e.g., Vincent v. Holder*, 632 F.3d 351 (6th Cir. 2011) (holding that the record established that the rebel forces in Sierra Leone knew that the applicant was a member in the Council of Churches, a group that actively voiced opposition to the use of child soldiers by the rebels, the rebels knew who he was, and the rebels were specifically targeting him when they burned his house).

[745] *Castro v. Holder*, 597 F.3d 93, 102–06 (2d Cir. 2010) (stating that the Immigration Judge failed to consider the claim of a Guatemalan police officer who reported drug corruption within the police within the "context" and "backdrop of Guatemala's volatile political history"); *Ahmed v. Keisler*, 504 F.3d 1183, 1193–98 (9th Cir. 2007).

[746] Guy S. Goodwin-Gill & Jane McAdams, *The Refugee in International Law* 69 (2d ed. 1996). *See generally* UNHCR Handbook, *supra* note 33.

[747] UNHCR Handbook, *supra* note 33, ¶ 80. The U.S. government recognized a specific situation of intolerance of individuals for their critique of a government's policies, by amending the definition of refugee in 1996 to provide protection to individuals who have suffered or who fear persecution because of their resistance to coercive population control measures in their home countries. These individuals are deemed to have been persecuted or to fear persecution on account of their political opinion. *See* INA §101(a)(42)(B). *See also Matter of G–C–L–*, 23 I&N Dec. 359, 361–62 (BIA 2002); *Matter of C–Y–Z–*, 21 I&N Dec. 915, 919–20 (BIA 1997); *Matter of X–P–T–*, 21 I&N Dec. 634, 638 (BIA 1996).

Continued

A person may express his or her political opinion or beliefs through actions as well as words.[748] For example, the Fourth Circuit stated that political opinion is prototypically exhibited by "evidence of verbal or openly expressive behavior by the applicant in furtherance of a particular cause," but that "less overtly symbolic acts may also reflect a political opinion."[749] The Court specified, however, that "whatever behavior an applicant seeks to advance as political, it must be motivated by an ideal or conviction of sorts before it will constitute grounds for asylum."[750] For example, in *Chang v. INS*,[751] the Third Circuit held that the asylum applicant had "manifested" his political opinion through his actions in defying the orders of the Chinese government. The court reasoned that "[s]imply because he did not call himself a dissident or couch his resistance in terms of a particular ideology renders his opposition no less political."[752]

Political opinion may also be expressed through the act of whistleblowing against corrupt government officials.[753] The Seventh Circuit's holdings in whistleblower cases have examined whether the applicant engaged in sufficient political agitation against state corruption.[754] Other circuits likewise have held that official retaliation against one who threatens to expose government corruption may, in certain circumstances, amount to political persecution.[755] Some circuits also have found that

---

China's one-child policy, forced sterilization, and forced abortion have all been found to be coercive population control measures.

[748] *Chang v. INS*, 119 F.3d 1055, 1063 (3d. Cir. 1997) (holding that the applicant had expressed his political opinion through his actions in defying the orders of the Chinese government). *See also Fedunyak v. Gonzales*, 477 F.3d 1126, 1129 (9th Cir. 2007). *But see Pavlyk v. Gonzales*, 469 F.3d 1082, 1089 (7th Cir. 2006).

[749] *Saldarriaga v. Gonzales*, 402 F.3d 461, 466 (4th Cir. 2005).

[750] *Id.*

[751] *Chang v. INS*, 119 F.3d 1055, 1063 (3d Cir. 1997).

[752] *Id.*; *see also Grava v. INS*, 205 F.3d 1177 (9th Cir. 2000) (whistleblowing found to be an expression of political opinion); *Tarubac v. INS*, 182 F.3d 1114, 1119 (9th Cir. 1999) (finding that the applicant's expression of opposition to communism led to the most extreme persecution that she suffered); *Osorio v. INS*, 18 F.3d 1017, 1029 (2d Cir. 1994) (holding that resistance is no less political simply because the asylum applicant did not state he belonged to a political party or which political philosophy he supported); *Montecino v. INS*, 915 F.2d 518, 520 (9th Cir. 1990) (holding that an ex-soldier's fear of reprisals by guerrillas was political persecution).

[753] *Fedunyak v. Gonzales*, 477 F.3d at 1129 (noting that to qualify as a whistleblower, the applicant need not expose government corruption to the public at large). *But see Pavlyk v. Gonzales*, 469 F.3d at 1089 (rejecting applicant claim based on whistleblowing because he did not take his evidence of corruption "to the public in quest of a political decision" and because as a public employee he would have limited First Amendment rights even within the United States).

[754] *Haxhiu v. Mukasey*, 519 F.3d 685, 690 (7th Cir. 2008); *Marquez v. INS*, 105 F.3d 374, 381 (7th Cir. 1997).

[755] *Yu v. Holder*, 693 F.3d 294 (2d Cir. 2012) (finding that where opposition to corruption transcends self-protection and represents a challenge to state-sanctioned modes of official behavior, an applicant may be eligible for asylum); *Perez-Ramirez v. Holder*, 648 F.3d 953 (9th Cir. 2011); *Antonyan v. Holder*, 642 F.3d 1250 (9th Cir. 2011); *Hayrapetyan v. Mukasey*, 534 F.3d 1330, 1338 (10th Cir. 2008);

Continued

informing the government about individuals involved in illegal activities, when doing so in a political context, may constitute persecution on account of political opinion.[756]

Unexpressed political opinions or beliefs may also be grounds for asylum if the persecutor could become aware of those opinions or beliefs.[757] UNHCR's *Handbook* provides:

There may, however, also be situations in which the applicant has not given any expression to his opinions. Due to the strength of his convictions, however, it may be reasonable to assume that his opinions will sooner or later find expression and that the applicant will, as a result, come into conflict with the authorities. Where this can reasonably be assumed, the applicant can be considered to have fear of persecution for reasons of political opinion.[758]

Similarly, the BIA has noted that an applicant's fear may be well-founded if the persecutor "could" become aware of the applicant's beliefs.[759]

Even neutrality may be a political opinion, particularly if it is shown that it was a conscious choice of the applicant and that the persecutor was motivated by that neutrality.[760] UNHCR and several federal courts have recognized that neutrality that is a conscious choice is a political opinion, especially in an "environment in which political neutrality is fraught with hazard."[761] For example, during conflict, often the persecutor's view is that there can be no neutrality — "you're either with us, or you're against us" — and the persecutor may impute an opposition political opinion to anyone who is neutral. For example, in *Rivera-Moreno*, the Ninth Circuit noted that it follows the doctrine of "hazardous neutrality," which recognizes that neutrality may constitute a political opinion in an environment fraught with hazard from government or antigovernment forces.[762] Similarly, in *Umanzor-Alvarado*, the First

---

Zhang v. Gonzales, 426 F.3d 540, 542 (2d Cir. 2005); *Hasan v. Ashcroft*, 380 F.3d 1114, 1120–21 (9th Cir. 2004); *Grava v. INS*, 205 F.3d 1177, 1181 (9th Cir. 2000).

756 *Saldarriaga v. Gonzales*, 402 F.3d 461, 467 (4th Cir. 2005).

757 *Matter of Mogharrabi*, 19 I&N Dec. 439, 446 (BIA 1987). *But see Sharif v. INS*, 87 F.3d 932, 935 (7th Cir. 1996).

758 UNHCR Handbook, *supra* note 33, ¶ 82.

759 *Matter of Mogharrabi*, 19 I&N Dec. at 446. *But see Sharif v. INS*, 87 F.3d at 935 (denying claim of a Westernized woman from Iran because "there [is no] evidence to suggest that she will voice her opposition to Iranian law when she returns to Iran").

760 *See, e.g., Rivera-Moreno v. INS*, 213 F.3d 481, 483–84 (9th Cir. 2000); *Sagarminaga v. INS*, 113 F.3d 1247 (10th Cir. 1997); *Lopez-Zeron v. U.S. Dep't of Justice*, 8 F.3d 636 (8th Cir. 1993); *Arriaga-Barrientos v. INS*, 937 F.2d 411 (9th Cir. 1991); *Umanzor-Alvarado v. INS*, 896 F.2d 14, 15–16 (1st Cir. 1990); *Arteaga v. INS*, 836 F.2d 1227, 1231–32 (9th Cir. 1988); *Matter of Vigil*, 19 I&N Dec. 572, 576–77 (BIA 1988).

761 *See generally* UNHCR Handbook, *supra* note 33. *See also, e.g., Rivera-Moreno v. INS*, 213 F.3d 481, 483–84 (9th Cir. 2000); *Umanzor-Alvarado v INS*, 896 F.2d 14, 15–16 (1st Cir. 1990); *Arteaga v. INS*, 836 F.2d 1227, 1231–32 (9th Cir. 1988).

762 *Rivera-Moreno*, 213 F.3d at 483 (finding, however, that the applicant had not established that the guerrillas sought to persecute her because of her neutrality).

Circuit held that neutrality may be considered a political opinion upon a showing that the applicant affirmatively chose to remain neutral, articulated this opinion, and had been or could reasonably be singled out for persecution on this basis.[763] An asylum applicant, however, must establish that the persecution he or she fears or suffered was because of his or her neutrality.[764]

Some examples of expressions of political opinions under the facts and evidence presented include:

- Active membership in opposing political parties;[765]
- Expression of feminist beliefs;[766]
- Exposure of government human rights abuses;[767]
- Whistleblowing or otherwise exposing government corruption;[768]
- Refusal to follow orders to commit human rights abuses;[769]
- Activities to protect or establish the right to association (such as union membership), workers' rights, or other civil liberties;[770]

---

763 *See Umanzor-Alvarado v. INS*, 896 F.2d at 15.

764 *See Sagarminaga v. INS*, 113 F.3d 1247 (10th Cir. 1997) (holding that the applicant failed to establish that the guerrillas would persecute her because of her decision to remain neutral); *Lopez-Zeron v. U.S. Department of Justice*, 8 F.3d 636 (8th Cir. 1993) (holding that Honduran asylum applicants failed to demonstrate they were targeted by the government because of their political neutrality); *Matter of Vigil*, 19 I&N Dec. 572, 576–77 (BIA 1988) (holding that applicant failed to show that he had articulated his neutrality previously and that he received some threat or could be "singled out" for persecution because of his neutrality).

765 *See, e.g., Sherpa v. Holder*, 469 F. App'x 54 (10th Cir. 2013).

766 *Fatin v. INS*, 12 F.3d 1233 (3d Cir. 1993).

767 *Cao v. Gonzales*, 407 F.3d 146, 153 (3d Cir. 2005).

768 *Ruqiang Yu v. Holder*, 693 F.3d 294, 298–300 (2d Cir. 2012) (where the applicant opposed corruption and wage theft at a state run enterprise); *Perez-Ramirez v. Holder*, 648 F.3d 953 (9th Cir. 2011) (holding that the applicant demonstrated nexus to political opinion as a whistleblower exposing government corruption in Mexico); *Antonyan v. Holder*, 642 F.3d 1250 (9th Cir. 2011); *Bu v. Gonzales*, 490 F.3d 424 (6th Cir. 2007) (where the applicant demonstrated against government corruption in China); *Sagaydak v. Gonzales*, 405 F.3d 1035, 1040–45 (9th Cir. 2005) (where the applicant, a government auditor, had exposed corruption in a private company in the context of political reforms and rooting out corruption in the Ukraine); *Grava v. INS*, 205 F.3d 1177 (9th Cir. 2000). *See also, Reyes-Guerrero v. INS*, 192 F.3d 1241, 1245 (9th Cir. 1999); *cf. Marquez v. INS*, 105 F.3d 374, 381 (7th Cir. 1997); *Hasan v. Ashcroft*, 380 F.3d 1114 (9th Cir. 2004). *See Zhang v. Gonzales*, 426 F.3d 540, 548 (2d Cir. 2005). *But cf. Musabelliu v. Gonzales*, 442 F.3d 991 (7th Cir. 2006) (finding that harm suffered was not on account of political opinion where the applicant's disclosure of public corruption to his military chain of command and a prosecutor was part of his duties as a brigadier general and not "a public political stand"); *Marku v. Ashcroft*, 380 F.3d 982 (6th Cir. 2004) (distinguishing *Grava v. INS* and *Reyes-Guerrero v. INS*, because Marku provided no evidence that her refusal to participate in public corruption was viewed as an expression of a political opinion).

769 *Barraza Rivera v. INS*, 913 F.2d 1443 (9th Cir. 1990).

770 *Osorio v. INS*, 18 F.3d 1017 (2d Cir. 1994); *Bernal-Garcia v. INS*, 852 F.2d 144 (5th Cir. 1988).

- Participation in certain student groups;[771]
- Participation in community improvement organizations or cooperatives, or participation in movements for land reform;[772]
- Hazardous neutrality, with neutrality established by pronouncement or actions;[773] and
- Perceived neutrality.[774]

a. Imputed Political Opinion

Political opinions, like the four other protected grounds, also can be "imputed" to an applicant,[775] and persecution based on a political opinion that the applicant is erroneously believed to hold can warrant a grant of asylum.[776] UNHCR also recognizes such claims. Its Handbook states that persecution based on political opinions may include situations in which "such opinions have come to the notice of the authorities or are *attributed* by them *to the applicant*."[777] One court has opined that imputed-opinion asylum applicants may have more difficulty proving their cases because they must prove their persecutors would make the same mistake again if they returned to their home countries.[778]

The context and political climate in the country of feared persecution also is relevant to the imputed political opinion and nexus analysis. For example, the Seventh Circuit in *Mustafa v. Holder* recently remanded an asylum case, holding that the BIA and IJ's conclusion that the applicant's attackers were motivated solely by a personal dispute and desire for personal revenge was not supported by substantial evidence. This was because the evidence of record showed that the applicant "assisted in the takedown of a high-ranking member of the PML-N immediately after

---

[771] *Osorio v. INS*, 18 F.3d 1017 (2d Cir. 1994).

[772] *Vera-Valera v. INS*, 147 F.3d 1036 (9th Cir. 1998); *Zamora-Morel v. INS*, 905 F.2d 833 (5th Cir. 1990).

[773] *See Rivera-Moreno v. INS*, 213 F.3d 481 (9th Cir. 2000); *Sangha v. INS*, 103 F.3d 1482, 1488 (9th Cir. 1997); *Ramos-Vazquez v. INS*, 57 F.3d 857, 863 (9th Cir. 1995); *Arriaga-Barrientos v. INS*, 937 F.2d 411, 413–14 (9th Cir. 1991).

[774] *See, e.g., Ramos-Vazquez v. INS*, 57 F.3d 857, 863 (9th Cir. 1995); *Arriaga-Barrientos v. INS*, 937 F.2d 411, 413–14 (9th Cir. 1991).

[775] *Uwais v. Att'y Gen.*, 478 F.3d 513, 517 (2d Cir. 2007); *Mulanga v. Ashcroft*, 349 F.3d 123, 133 n.7 (3d Cir. 2003); *Sangha v. INS*, 103 F.3d 1482, 1489 (9th Cir. 1997); *Singh v. Ilchert*, 69 F.3d 375, 379 (9th Cir. 1995); *Canas-Segovia v. INS*, 970 F.2d 599, 601–02 (9th Cir. 1992); *Matter of S–P–*, 21 I&N Dec. 486, 497 (BIA 1996).

[776] *INS v. Elias-Zacarias*, 502 U.S. 478 (1992); *Hamdan v. Mukasey*, 528 F.3d 986, 992–93 (7th Cir. 2008); *Ahmed v. Keisler*, 504 F.3d 1183, 1194–95 (9th Cir. 2007); *Pascual v. Mukasey*, 514 F.3d 483, 488 (6th Cir. 2007) (noting that imputed opinion persecution is premised on the persecutor's mistaken belief about the victim's views); *Singh v. Gonzales*, 406 F.3d 191, 196–97 (3d Cir. 2005). *See also Matter of S–P–*, 21 I&N Dec. 486, 497 (BIA 1996).

[777] UNHCR Handbook, *supra* note 33, ¶ 80 (emphasis added).

[778] *Pascual v. Mukasey*, 514 F.3d at 488.

the 1999 shift in power in Pakistan, and in the context of the facts . . . it would be unreasonable to conclude that his actions were viewed by his attackers as solely apolitical."[779] Thus, the actions of the persecutors were on account of the applicant's imputed political opinion.

Claims based on imputed political opinion have been accepted in cases in which the applicant was erroneously believed to support Falun Gong,[780] to be a member of a subversive group,[781] to be involved with the military,[782] to hold anti-guerrilla beliefs,[783] to be an opponent of communism,[784] to be a government supporter,[785] to be a dissident because he benefited from a U.S.-led airlift out of Iraq,[786] to have transported weapons for a rebel group,[787] and to have refused to cooperate with non-government forces or groups.[788] Claims that have been rejected include cases in which the applicant has failed to demonstrate that the persecutor had attributed a political opinion to him or her,[789] or that the persecution feared was not a "reasonable

---

[779] *Mustafa v. Holder*, 707 F.3d 743 (7th Cir. 2013) (noting that the attackers explicitly stated that they were carrying out the attack on behalf of a high-ranking member of the PML-N, there was evidence in the record of the highly polarized political context in which the attacks occurred, and the high-ranking member of the PML-N had emphasized his political power in delivering a threat against the applicant).

[780] *Gao v. Gonzales*, 424 F.3d 122 (2d Cir. 2005); *Lu v. Ashcroft*, 2004 U.S. App. LEXIS 3003 (9th Cir. 2004) (unpublished).

[781] *Maldonado-Cruz v. INS*, 883 F.2d 788 (9th Cir. 1990); *Matter of S–P–*, 21 I&N Dec. 486, 497 (BIA 1996).

[782] *Molina v. INS*, 170 F.3d 1247, 1249 (9th Cir. 1999).

[783] *Ventura v. INS*, 264 F.3d 1150, 1156 (9th Cir. 2001), *rev'd on other grounds*, 537 U.S. 12 (2002).

[784] *Agbuya v. INS*, 219 F.3d 962, 967 (9th Cir. 2000), *amended by* 241 F.3d 1224 (9th Cir. 2001).

[785] *Silaya v. Mukasey*, 524 F.3d 1066, 1072 (9th Cir. 2008) (finding political opinion imputed to daughter of World War II veteran in the Philippines believed to be a government supporter); *Aguilera-Cota v. INS*, 914 F.2d 1375 (9th Cir. 1990).

[786] *Al-Harbi v. INS*, 242 F.3d 882 (9th Cir. 2001).

[787] *Blanco-Lopez v. INS*, 858 F.2d 531 (9th Cir. 1988); *See also Briones v. INS*, 175 F.3d 727, 729 (9th Cir. 1999) (en banc) (finding that the asylum applicant's "activity as a confidential informer who sided with the Philippine military in a conflict that was political at its core certainly would be perceived as a political act by the group informed upon").

[788] *Jabr v. Holder*, 711 F.3d 835 (7th Cir. 2013) (stating that if political opposition is the reason an individual member of the Fatah party refused to cooperate with the Palestinian Islamic Jihad and that individual is persecuted for his refusal to cooperate, logic dictates that the persecution is on account of the individual's political opinion).

[789] *Ruiz-Cabrera v. Holder*, 748 F.3d 754 (7th Cir. 2014) (finding that substantial evidence supported the determination that the applicant failed to substantiate his claim that any political opinion would be imputed to him based on his wife's politics in Mexico, and stating that nothing in the record indicated that traffickers or politicians were likely to connect him to his wife's politics or to target him for those reasons); *Garcia-Milian v. Holder*, 755 F.3d 1026 (9th Cir. 2013); *Estrada-Escobar v. Ashcroft*, 376 F.3d 1042, 1047 (10th Cir. 2004); *Huaman Cornelio v. BIA*, 979 F.2d 995, 1000 (4th Cir. 1992); *Estrada-Posadas v. INS*, 924 F.2d 916, 919 (9th Cir. 1991), *overruled on other grounds by Thomas v. Gonzales*, 409 F.3d 1177, 1180 (9th Cir. 2005); *Arriaga-Barrientos v. INS*, 937 F.2d 411, 414 (9th Cir. 1991); *Matter of R–*, 20 I&N Dec. 621 (BIA 1992).

possibility."[790] The threshold question is how the persecutor views the applicant. Some factors to consider in determining if the persecutor has imputed a political opinion to an asylum seeker include: (1) whether the applicant has taken any actions that the persecutor would view as expressions of political opinion; (2) statements made by the persecutor that may provide evidence of the persecutor's view of the applicant or similarly situated individuals; (3) the persecutors' treatment of similarly situated individuals; (4) the overall political situation as evidenced by country condition reports; (5) the severity of any punishment the applicant has received; and (6) whether the persecutor has reasons unrelated to the applicant's political opinion to exert its authority against him or her.[791]

b. Coercive Population Control

Another type of political opinion-based asylum claim that has generated a substantial amount of case law is claims involving coercive population control programs. In 1996, the definition of refugee was amended to clarify that applicants who have suffered or who fear persecution for resistance to coercive population control measures in their home countries are deemed to have been persecuted or to have a well-founded fear of persecution on account of their political opinion. IIRIRA amended the term "refugee" to provide that:

> [A] person who has been forced to abort a pregnancy or to undergo involuntary sterilization, or who has been persecuted for failure or refusal to undergo such a procedure or for other resistance to a coercive population control program, shall be deemed to have been persecuted on account of political opinion, and a person who has a well-founded fear that he or she will be forced to undergo such a procedure or subject to persecution for such failure, refusal, or resistance shall be deemed to have a well-founded fear of persecution on account of political opinion.[792]

Thus, the expanded definition of refugee articulated four classes of refugees specific to the coercive population control context: (1) persons who have been forced to abort a pregnancy; (2) persons who have been forcibly sterilized; (3) persons who have been persecuted for failure or refusal to undergo such a procedure or for "other resistance" to a coercive population control program; and (4) persons who have a well-founded fear that they will be forced to undergo such a procedure or subject to persecution for such failure, refusal, or resistance.[793]

The amended definition of refugee applies retroactively.[794] The BIA announced in *G–C–L–*, however, that it would no longer grant untimely motions to reopen for

---

[790] *Aruta v. INS*, 80 F.3d 1389, 1395 (9th Cir. 1996).

[791] AOBTC Workbook, pt. III, *supra* note 491, at 78.

[792] INA §101(a)(42)(B); 8 USC §1101(a)(42)(B) (2012), as amended by §601 of IIRAIRA, *supra* note 97.

[793] INA §101(a)(42); *Matter of J–S–*, 24 I&N Dec. 520 (AG 2008).

[794] *Zhang v. Reno*, 27 F. Supp. 2d 476, 477 (S.D.N.Y. 1998).

asylum claims based on coercive population control policies because, at the time of the BIA's decision, more than five years had passed since the law changed under IIRIRA. [795] Untimely motions to reopen for asylum claims based on coercive population control measures, therefore, must be based on some other legal authority for untimely motions to reopen, such as changed circumstances,[796] joint motions to reopen,[797] or motions to reopen *sua sponte*.[798]

The BIA recognized the change in law in its decision *Matter of X–P–T–* in which it found that the applicant — who had violated China's one-child policy by having three children and as a result was forcibly sterilized — was statutorily eligible for asylum.[799] The BIA also found that the applicant was eligible for withholding of deportation.[800] Various circuits have agreed that forced abortions and sterilizations are per se persecution.[801]

Questions that have generated a substantial amount of case law in this area of asylum jurisprudence include whether harm or feared harm was or would be "forced," whether the involuntary insertion of an IUD rises to the same level of persecution as forced abortions or sterilizations, whether the victim's family members may be eligible for asylum based on harm suffered by the victim, what type of actions are considered to be "other resistance," and whether applicants who have not physically undergone a procedure may be eligible for asylum. These issues are addressed below.

1. What is "forced"?

If an applicant has been subjected to an abortion or sterilization procedure against his or her will, the applicant must establish that he or she was "forced" to undergo the procedure in order for it to constitute persecution on account of political opinion.[802]

---

[795] *Matter of G–C–L–*, 23 I&N Dec. 359, 361–62 (BIA 2002).

[796] *See, e.g., Xiu Ling Chen v. Holder*, 751 F.3d 876 (8th Cir. 2014) (declining to review the motion to reopen denial because the applicant did not provide previously unavailable documents and did not distinguish between women who have had children in China and those who return with children born abroad); *Zhu v. Att'y Gen.*, 744 F.3d 268 (3d Cir. 2014) (vacating the order denying the motion to reopen and finding that the BIA's opinion did not show meaningful consideration of much of the evidence the applicant submitted in support of her motion relating to forced sterilization in China, improperly relying on the fact that the documents had not been authenticated pursuant to 8 CFR §1287.6); *Zheng v. Holder*, 701 F.3d 237 (7th Cir. 2012) (holding that the applicant's claim based on two children born in the United States and feared enforcement of China's family planning policy was a change in personal circumstances, not a change in country conditions, and therefore, the case could not be reopened). *See infra* ch. 11 for a detailed discussion of Motions to Reopen.

[797] 8 CFR §§1003.2(c)(3)(ii), 1003.23(b)(1) (2014).

[798] *Id.* See ch. 11 for a detailed discussion of motions to reopen.

[799] *Matter of X–P–T–*, 21 I&N Dec. 634, 638 (BIA 1996).

[800] *Id.*

[801] *Wang v. Ashcroft*, 341 F.3d 1015, 1020 (9th Cir. 2003) (finding that forced abortions are per se persecution and trigger asylum eligibility).

[802] INA §101(a)(42).

An applicant seeking to demonstrate force "need not demonstrate that he was physically restrained during a 'forced' procedure. Rather, 'forced' is a much broader concept, which includes compelling, obliging, or constraining by mental, moral, or circumstantial means, in addition to physical restraint."[803]

The BIA has held that a procedure is "forced" by threats of harm within the meaning of the INA when: (1) a reasonable person would objectively view the threats for refusing the procedure to be genuine; and (2) the threatened harm, if carried out, would rise to the level of persecution.[804] Given the lack of a clear definition of what harm rises to the level of persecution, prong two is the more difficult part of the test for applicants to satisfy.

For example, the BIA rejected the Ninth Circuit's suggestion in *Lidan Ding v. Ashcroft* and *Wang v. Ashcroft* that economic harm that does not rise to the level of persecution could show that an abortion was "forced."[805] The BIA clarified that not all threats involving economic sanctions will rise to the level of persecution, and economic harm can only satisfy prong two of the "forced" test if that threatened economic harm would rise to the level of persecution itself.[806] According to the BIA's standards, economic sanctions that would satisfy prong two of the test, therefore, would involve "the deliberate imposition of severe economic disadvantage or the deprivation of liberty, food, housing, employment or other essentials of life."[807]

---

[803] *Lidan Ding v. Ashcroft*, 387 F.3d 1131, 1139 (9th Cir. 2004) (finding that a woman who was forced from her home into a van, taken to a hospital, pulled off the floor by two officials when she refused to get up, forced onto a hospital bed, and watched over by two officials had suffered a "forced" abortion even though she was not physically restrained during the procedure itself).

[804] *Matter of T–Z–*, 24 I&N Dec. 163, 168 (BIA 2007) (considering whether undergoing two abortions because of threatened job loss established that the procedures were forced).

[805] *Id.* at 169–70. *See Lidan Ding v. Ashcroft,* 387 F.3d 1131, 1139 (9th Cir. 2004); *Wang v. Ashcroft*, 341 F.3d 1015 (9th Cir. 2003).

[806] *Matter of T–Z–*, 24 I&N Dec. 163, 169–70 (BIA 2007).

[807] *Matter of Laipenieks*, 18 I&N Dec. 433, 456–57 (BIA 1983), *rev'd on other grounds*, 750 F.2d 1427 (9th Cir. 1985). *See also Matter of T–Z–*, 24 I&N Dec. 163 (BIA 2007) (finding that the deliberate imposition of severe economic disadvantage or the deprivation of liberty, food, housing, employment, or other essentials of life may amount to persecution); *Vicente-Elias v. Mukasey*, 532 F.3d 1086, 1091 (10th Cir. 2008) (upholding the IJ's determination that the poverty and discrimination suffered by the applicant because of his Mayan ancestry does not rise to the level of persecution); *Beck v. Mukasey,* 527 F.3d 737, 741 (8th Cir. 2008) (finding unfair prejudice and discrimination against Romani family in Hungary); *Kadri v. Mukasey*, 543 F.3d 16, 22 (1st Cir. 2008) (remanding applicant's claim that he could not earn a living as a medical doctor in Indonesia due to his sexual orientation); *Yun Jian Zhang v. Gonzales,* 495 F.3d 773 (7th Cir. 2007); *Li v. Gonzales*, 405 F.3d 171, 177 (4th Cir. 2005) (finding that deliberate imposition of severe economic disadvantage may rise to the level of persecution); *Zhen Hua Li v. Att'y Gen.,* 400 F.3d 157, 166 69 (3d Cir. 2005); *Baballah v. Ashcroft*, 367 F.3d 1067, 1075 (9th Cir. 2004) (noting that the IJ erred as a matter of law by requiring the applicant to show an absolute inability to support his family); *Gormley v. Ashcroft,* 364 F.3d 1172 (9th Cir. 2004); *Himri v. Ashcroft,* 378 F.3d 932, 937 (9th Cir. 2004) (finding that a Palestinian applicant's inability to avoid Kuwaiti state-sponsored economic discrimination, which may include denial of the rights to work, attend school, and to obtain drinking water, would amount to persecution), *as amended by* 2004 WL 1879255 (9th

Continued

The Second Circuit has upheld the BIA's standard, stating that an abortion is not forced unless the threatened harm for refusal would, if carried out, be sufficiently severe that it amounts to persecution.[808] For example, in *Xiu Fen Xia v. Mukasey*, the court held that the applicant's abortion was not forced within the meaning of the INA, because it did not meet the BIA's standard in *Matter of T–Z–*. In that case, the applicant had obtained an abortion from a private hospital before government authorities knew of her pregnancy, claiming that she feared sterilization, arrest of her and her family members, forced abortion, and a "really heavy fine."[809] The Second Circuit reasoned that because no government official was aware of the applicant's pregnancy, she had not sufficiently established a threatened harm, let alone a threatened harm so severe as to rise to the level of persecution.[810] Without evidence of pressure actually exerted, there is no "force."

The Fifth Circuit has also upheld the BIA's test for determining whether a coercive population control procedure was "forced" within the meaning of the INA. In *Yuqing Zhu v. Gonzales*, the Fifth Circuit found that a woman was subjected to a "forced" abortion within the meaning of *Matter of T–Z–* where she reasonably believed that she would be physically compelled to abort her pregnancy, she would lose her job, benefits, and housing, she would be imprisoned, she would be sterilized, Chinese authorities would not recognize her child, and her child would be denied services.[811] The court held that the threatened harm, in particular, the threat of a compelled abortion or forcible sterilization, would rise to the level of persecution if carried out.[812] Therefore, since the applicant reasonably believed the threats to be genuine and since the harm, if carried out, would rise to the level of persecution, the two-part test from *Matter of T–Z–* had been met and the abortion was "forced" within the meaning of the INA.

Overall, the BIA and most courts distinguish between pressure or persuasion to submit to a coercive population control procedure and being "forced" to undergo that

---

Cir. 2004); *Liao v. INS,* 293 F.3d 61, 69–70 (2d Cir. 2002); *Ambati v. Reno,* 233 F.3d 1054, 1060 (7th Cir. 2000); *Minwalla v. INS,* 706 F.2d 831, 835 (8th Cir. 1983); *Berdo v. INS*, 432 F.2d 824, 847 (6th Cir. 1970); *Kovac v. INS*, 407 F.2d 102, 107 (9th Cir. 1969); *Dunat v. Henry*, 297 F.2d 744, 746 (3d Cir. 1961); *Matter of Salama*, 11 I&N Dec. 536 (BIA 1966). *But see Damko v. INS*, 430 F.3d 626, 628 (2d Cir. 2005) (finding that economic restrictions must be so severe that they constitute a threat to life or freedom in order to amount to economic persecution); *Sharif v. INS*, 87 F.3d 932, 934–35 (7th Cir. 1996) (finding that inability to attend college and losing job but finding another does not amount to economic persecution); *see also Mirzoyan v. Gonzales*, 457 F.3d 217, 221–22 (2d Cir. 2006) (criticizing the BIA for not applying a consistent standard for economic persecution claims).

[808] *Xiu Fen Xia v. Mukasey*, 510 F.3d 162, 163 (2d Cir. 2007).

[809] *Id.*

[810] *Id.*

[811] *Zhu v. Gonzales*, 493 F.3d 588, 597–99 (5th Cir. 2007) (holding that the applicant's "abortion was indeed forced, as a reasonable person in Zhu's position 'would objectively view the threats for refusing the abortion to be genuine,' and that harm, 'if carried out, would rise to the level of persecution'").

[812] *Id.*

procedure. Threatened harm that would not rise to the level of persecution itself would constitute "pressure," but would not make the procedure "forced" within the meaning of the INA.

2. Involuntary Insertion of an IUD

Another line of coercive population control cases involves the question of whether the involuntary insertion of an intrauterine device (IUD) rises to the level of persecution under the INA. Courts have acknowledged that the involuntary insertion of an IUD is "a serious violation of personal privacy,"[813] but have taken an array of positions on this issue and frequently solicited BIA guidance.[814] The BIA attempted to provide this guidance in its precedent decision, *Matter of M–F–W– & L–G–*.[815] In that decision, the BIA rejected the argument that the insertion of an IUD equates to "involuntary sterilization" as the term is used in the INA definition of refugee, and found that the involuntary insertion of an IUD must be accompanied by aggravating circumstances in order to constitute persecution under the INA.[816] The BIA reasoned that unlike sterilization and abortion, the insertion of an IUD is not a permanent measure.[817]

Both before and after the BIA's precedent decision, the federal courts have taken a similar position, finding that a routine medical insertion of an IUD, absent allegations of force or physical abuse, does not constitute persecution.[818] However,

---

[813] *Qiao Hu a Li v. Gonzales*, 405 F.3d 171, 179 (4th Cir. 2005).

[814] *See Ying Zheng v. Gonzales*, 497 F.3d 201, 203 (2d Cir. 2007) (noting that the "BIA has not yet opined on this issue in a published, precedential opinion, thus depriving the bench, the bar and potential asylum applicants of guidance concerning whether and how they might approach the issue"). *See also Chao Qun Jiang v. USCIS*, 520 F.3d 132, 135 (2d Cir. 2008); *Li Fang Lin v. Mukasey*, 517 F.3d 685, 693–94 (4th Cir. 2008) (remanding where the BIA left unclear "how it factored the 'temporary' nature of IUD insertion and usage into its overall persecution calculus); *Feng Choi Yang v. Att'y Gen.*, 418 F.3d 1198, 1205 (11th Cir. 2005); *Yahong Zheng v. Gonzales*, 409 F.3d 804, 811–12 (7th Cir. 2005); *Meng Rong Fang v. Ashcroft*, 114 F. App'x 486, 488 (3d Cir. 2004) (unpublished).

[815] *Matter of M–F–W– & L–G–*, 24 I&N Dec. 633 (BIA 2008).

[816] *Id.* Previously, the BIA had taken the position that the forcible insertion of an insertion of an IUD was a "cognizable claim." *Zheng v. Gonzales*, 409 F.3d 804, 810 (7th Cir. 2005) (in overturning an adverse credibility determination, the court noted that the BIA took the position that the involuntary insertions of IUDs constituted a "cognizable claim" of persecution on account of political opinion under the amended refugee definition).

[817] *Matter of M–F–W– & L–G–*, 24 I&N Dec. 633, 636–40 (BIA 2008).

[818] *Li v. Gonzales*, 405 F.3d 171, 179 (4th Cir. 2005). *But see Li v. Ashcroft*, 356 F.3d 1153, 1158 (9th Cir. 2004) (a forced gynecological exam that the victim resisted by kicking and screaming constituted persecution). *But see Jiang v. BCIS*, 520 F.3d 132, 133 (2d Cir. 2008) (holding that because the BIA had not yet articulated in a precedent decision whether and under what conditions involuntary insertion of an IUD constitutes persecution, and because the BIA had taken inconsistent positions on the issue, a remand was necessary); *Li Fang Lin v. Mukasey*, 517 F.3d 685, (4th Cir. 2008) (holding that because the BIA had not provided a published, precedential opinion, it could not conduct a meaningful review). Both *Jiang* and *Li Fang Lin* were decided prior to BIA's decision in *Matter of M–F–W– & L–G–*, *supra* note 816.

recently, the same applicant from the BIA's precedent decision of *Matter of M–F–W– & L–G–* found her way back before the U.S. Court of Appeals for the Second Circuit, and the Court vacated the removal order against her.[819] Although the Second Circuit confirmed its agreement that involuntary IUD insertion does not equate to sterilization as the term is used under the Act,[820] it concluded that "the BIA did not sufficiently identify the standards it applied in determining that neither aggravating circumstances nor nexus were established in the case," and remanded for the BIA to rectify this omission.[821] Thus, the standard for determining whether "aggravating circumstances" exist remains unclear.

- **Practice Pointer**: Practitioners should do a detailed factual inquiry with their clients and discuss the totality of the circumstances involved in forcible insertions of IUDs in order to determine all of the potential aggravating factors that were present. All aggravating factors should be well-developed in the record.

3. Eligibility of Spouses

The BIA and the federal courts also have considered whether applicants may claim persecution based on their spouses being forced to undergo an abortion or sterilization procedure. In a now overruled decision, *Matter of C–Y–Z–*, the BIA held that an applicant whose spouse was forced to undergo an abortion or sterilization procedure can establish past persecution on account of political opinion and qualifies as a refugee under the INA, as amended by IIRAIRA.[822] Following *Matter of C–Y–Z–*, several courts also recognized claims by spouses of individuals forced to undergo population control procedures.[823] The BIA then went even further in *Matter of Y–T–L–* to clarify that forced sterilization of a spouse is grounds for asylum despite the fact that the spouse faces no future threat of that same harm.[824]

---

[819] *Wong v. Holder*, (2d Cir. 2011).

[820] *Id. See also Huang v. Holder*, 591 F.3d 124 (2d Cir. 2010) (foreclosing Wong's assertion that involuntary IUD insertion equates sterilization).

[821] *Wong v. Holder*, (2d Cir. 2011).

[822] *Matter of C–Y–Z–*, 21 I&N Dec. 915, 919–20 (BIA 1997), *vacated by Matter of J–S–*, 24 I&N Dec. 520 (AG 2008). *But see Lin v. U.S. DOJ*, 494 F.3d 296 (2d Cir. 2007) (holding that spouses of those subjected to or threatened with coercive birth control procedures are not *automatically* eligible for asylum, as suggested by *Matter of C–Y–Z–*; rather, applicants must demonstrate "other resistance to a coercive population control program" or "a well founded fear that he or she will be … subject to persecution for such … resistance… .").

[823] *See, e.g., Qiu v. Gonzales*, 399 F.3d 1195, 1203 (9th Cir. 2005); *Ge v. Ashcroft*, 367 F.3d 1121, 1127 (9th Cir. 2004); *Qui v. Ashcroft*, 329 F.3d 140, 144–45 (2d Cir. 2003); *Matter of G–C–L–*, 23 I&N Dec. 359 (BIA 2002) (finding that an applicant who violated the one-child policy by having two children and whose spouse was forced to undergo an abortion, as well as forced sterilization, was eligible for asylum).

[824] *Matter of Y–T–L–*, 23 I&N Dec. 601 (BIA 2003) (finding that forced sterilization of spouse is grounds for asylum despite the fact that applicant faces no future threat).

However, in *Matter of J–S–*, the AG vacated the BIA's decision in *Matter of C–Y–Z–*.[825] Although the AG acknowledged "that application of coercive population control procedures may constitute 'obtrusive government interference into a married couple's decisions regarding children and family' that may 'have a profound impact on both parties to the marriage,'" the AG held that an asylum applicant whose spouse was forced to undergo an abortion or sterilization procedure is not *per se* entitled to refugee status under INA §101(a)(42).[826] The AG based the decision on the plain text of the statute, reasoning that the text of the statute is limited to the person who was actually forced to "undergo" the involuntary procedure.[827]

The AG did confirm, however, that persons who have not physically undergone a forced abortion or sterilization procedure themselves may still be able to establish asylum eligibility on account of a well-founded fear of future persecution of being forced to undergo such a procedure.[828] Such an applicant may also be able to establish persecution or a well-founded fear of persecution "for failure or refusal to undergo such a procedure or for other resistance to a coercive population control program, or on other grounds enumerated in the Immigration and Nationality Act."[829] Finally, family members or other third parties may be able to demonstrate asylum eligibility based on forced coercive population control procedures imposed on others if the applicant can demonstrate that his or her personal harm suffered is serious enough to amount to persecution, or where the persecutor's motivation to harm the individual who underwent the procedure is to inflict emotional harm on the applicant.[830]

Matter of J–S– continues as precedent, and most circuits have followed the rule that an applicant's spouse's forced abortion or sterilization does not make the applicant automatically eligible for asylum. Rather, that applicant must establish his or her own persecution or well-founded fear of persecution. For example, in 2012 the First Circuit held that the spouse of a Chinese woman who was forced to undergo an abortion is not automatically "a person who has been forced to abort a pregnancy" under INA §101(a)(42)(B), and denied the applicant's asylum application.[831] Even

[825] *Matter of J–S–*, 24 I&N Dec. 520 (AG 2008) (vacating *Matter of C–Y–Z–*, 21 I&N Dec. 915 (BIA 1997) and *Matter of S–L–L–*, 24 I&N Dec. 1, 6 (BIA 2006)).

[826] *Matter of J–S–*, at 520 (AG 2008) (overruling the BIA's rule of *per se* spousal eligibility). *See also Shi Liang Lin v. U.S. Dep't of Justice*, 494 F.3d 296 (2d Cir. 2007) (en banc).

[827] *Matter of J–S–*, at 520 (AG 2008).

[828] *Id.*

[829] *Id.*.

[830] *See Matter of A–K–*, 24 I&N Dec. 275, 278 (BIA 2007) (recognizing asylum eligibility based on emotional persecution "where a person persecutes someone close to an applicant, such as a spouse, parent, child or other relative, with the intended purpose of causing emotional harm to the applicant, but does not directly harm the applicant himself").

[831] *Dong v. Holder*, 696 F. 3d 121 (1st Cir. 2012). *See also, e.g., Xin Nin He v. Holder*, 972 F. App'x 561 (9th Cir. 2014) (finding that, under *Matter of J–S–*, as a spouse of a victim of a forced abortion or sterilization, a reasonable fact finder would not be compelled to find that the applicant either resisted

Continued

before *Matter of J–S–*, at least one circuit had ruled that spouses should not *automatically* receive asylum.[832] Rather, applicants must demonstrate "other resistance to a coercive population control program" or "a well founded fear that he or she will be . . . subject to persecution for such . . . resistance."[833]

In those circuits that had automatically extended asylum to spouses of those forced to undergo sterilization or an abortion, it was not clear whether boyfriends, girlfriends, fiancées, and non-spouses could also claim such protection.[834] The BIA has rejected claims by unmarried partners,[835] and the circuits are divided on this issue.[836] The courts have also considered whether per se asylum eligibility extends to other family members. However, most courts have rejected these claims. The Second Circuit has held that parents and in-laws of persons persecuted under coercive family

---

China's one-child policy or had suffered persecution); *Yi Xian Chen v. Holder*, 705 F.3d 624 (7th Cir. 2013) (holding that the applicant had not suffered past persecution when he learned that his wife in China had been forcibly sterilized); *Jian Qiu Liu v. Holder*, 632 F.3d 820 (2d Cir. 2011) (finding that the harm inflicted on the applicant, who was punched repeatedly by family planning officials and detained for two days after his wife was taken away for an abortion, did not rise to the level of persecution).

[832] *Lin v. U.S. Dep't of Justice*, 494 F.3d 296 (2d Cir. 2007) (holding that spouses of those subjected to or threatened with coercive birth control procedures are not *automatically* eligible for asylum, as suggested by *Matter of C–Y–Z–*; rather, applicants must demonstrate "other resistance to a coercive population control program" or "a well founded fear that he or she will be … subject to persecution for such … resistance… .").

[833] *Id.*

[834] *See, e.g.*, *Pan v. Gonzales*, 449 F.3d 408, 415 (2d Cir. 2006) (noting the inadequacy of the reasoning by the BIA in *Matter of C–Y–Z–* and a circuit court split on the issue); *Wang v. Gonzales*, 152 Fed. Appx. 761, 769 (11th Cir. 2006) (finding that marriage to the spouse must have existed at the time of the spouse's forcible abortion to qualify for per se eligibility for asylum).

[835] *Matter of S–L–L–*, 24 I&N Dec. 1 (BIA 2006) (requiring that a spouse must have been opposed to the abortion or sterilization and legally married; but noting that unmarried applicants may qualify for asylum based on "other resistance" to coercive population control measures), *overruled in part by Lin v. U.S. DOJ*, 2007 WL 2032066 (2d Cir. 2007) (agreeing that unmarried partners do not automatically qualify for asylum but going further to state that *no relatives* of the individual who underwent the coercive population control procedure should automatically qualify for asylum).

[836] *See, e.g.*, *Lin v. Att'y Gen.*, 555 F.3d 1310, 1316 (11th Cir. 2009) (concluding that unmarried partners do not automatically qualify for protection under the forced abortion and forced sterilization provisions of the INA) ; *Zhang v. Gonzales*, 434 F.3d 993, 1001–02 (7th Cir. 2006) (granting asylum to husband of woman who was forced to have an abortion, even though the couple had divorced and the wife had subsequently remarried); *Ma v. Ashcroft*, 361 F.3d 553, 559 (9th Cir. 2004) (extending asylum to applicants whose common-law spouses suffered persecution). *But see Chen v. Gonzales*, 457 F.3d 670, 674 (7th Cir. 2006) (finding that refugee status does not extend to boyfriends of women forced to have abortions); *Wang v. Gonzales*, 152 Fed. Appx. 761, 769 (11th Cir. 2005) (finding that marriage to spouse must have existed at the time of the spouse's forcible abortion to qualify for per se eligibility for asylum); *Chen v. Ashcroft*, 381 F.3d 221, 235 (3d Cir. 2004) (refusing to grant asylum to unmarried applicant whose fiancée was forced by Chinese officials to have an abortion, even though the applicant and his fiancée were unable to marry due to China's inflated age requirements for marriage).

planning policies are not per se eligible for asylum.[837] That same court has found that the forced sterilization of the applicant's parent is not per se persecution of that child.[838] Both the Third and Ninth Circuits agreed that a coercive population control procedure against a parent is not per se persecution of the child.[839] In contrast, the Eighth Circuit has granted asylum to individuals whose siblings and siblings' spouses suffered forced sterilizations.[840] This area of asylum jurisprudence remains unsettled.

4. Other Resistance

A person who engages in "other resistance to a coercive population control program" is also eligible for asylum.[841] There are few precedential decisions defining what "other resistance" is. The BIA has stated that resistance can take many forms, including expressions of general opposition, attempts to interfere with enforcement of government policy, or other overt forms of resistance to the requirements of family planning laws.[842] For example, an applicant's removal of an IUD and refusal to have a second IUD inserted qualified as resistance to China's family planning policy.[843] Additional specific examples of "other resistance" include:

- Writing an article critical of population control practices and exposing the practice of infanticide;[844]
- A woman's vocal resistance to a marriage-age restriction and public announcement of her decision to marry even after the license was refused, which resulted in a forced gynecological examination that she physically resisted;[845]
- Physical altercation with birth control officials when they attempted to use coercive measures to enforce birth quotas;[846]
- Illegally removing a government-imposed IUD;[847] and

---

[837] *Ai Feng Yuan v. U.S. Dep't of Justice*, 416 F.3d 192, 197 (2d Cir. 2005).

[838] *Tao Jiang v. Gonzales*, 500 F.3d 137 (2d Cir. 2007); *Chen v. Gonzales*, 417 F.3d 303, 305 (2d Cir. 2005).

[839] *Wang v. Gonzales*, 405 F.3d 134 (3d Cir. 2005); *Xue Yun Zhang v. Gonzales*, 408 F.3d 1239 (9th Cir. 2005).

[840] *Yang v. Gonzales*, 427 F.3d 1117, 1118 (8th Cir. 2005).

[841] INA §101(a)(42); 8 USC §1101(a)(42) (2012).

[842] *Matter of S–L–L–*, 24 I&N Dec. 1, 11–12 (BIA 2006) (holding that merely impregnating a girlfriend or fiancée or seeking permission to marry or have children outside of the legal age limits does not constitute "resistance" under the meaning of the INA).

[843] *Matter of M–F–W– & L–G–*, 24 I&N Dec. 633, 638 (BIA 2008) ("[S]uch acts, while arguably not comprising active or forceful opposition to China's family planning policy, would certainly thwart the goals of the plan and be viewed with disfavor by Chinese officials implementing the plan.").

[844] *Cao v. Att'y Gen.*, 407 F.3d 146, 153 (3d Cir. 2005).

[845] *Xu Ming Li v. Ashcroft*, 356 F.3d 1153, 1160 (9th Cir. 2004) (en banc).

[846] *Li Bin Lin v. Gonzales*, 472 F.3d 1131 (9th Cir. 2007).

[847] *Feng Chai Yang*, 418 F.3d 1198, 1205 (11th Cir. 2005); *Lin v. Ashcroft*, 385 F.3d 748, 757 (7th Cir. 2004).

- Resisting forced injections and removing forced IUDs through private doctors.[848]

A claim based on "other resistance" does not require proof that the person resisting was resisting because of his or her opposition to coercive population control policies.[849] Rather, the applicant must show that the government was enforcing a coercive population program at the time of the events and that he or she resisted the program.[850]

In "other resistance" cases, beyond merely demonstrating resistance, the applicant must also demonstrate that the harm suffered or feared rises to the level of persecution and that the harm suffered or feared is on account of the resistance.[851] Harm that rises to the level of persecution may be physical,[852] psychological,[853] or other forms of cumulative harm, such as threats, economic harm,[854] and forced medical exams and procedures.[855] In determining whether psychological harm of a spouse or partner rises to the level of persecution in the coercive population control context, the BIA instructs a review of the following factors:

(1) whether the couple have other children together;

(2) the length of cohabitation;

(3) whether the couple holds itself out as a committed couple;

(4) whether the couple took any steps to have the relationship recognized in some fashion;

(5) whether the couple is financially interdependent; and

---

[848] *Yang v. Att'y Gen.*, 418 F.3d 1198, 1205 (11th Cir. 2005).

[849] *Li Bin Lin v. Gonzales*, 472 F.3d 1131, 1134 (9th Cir. 2007) (finding that an applicant must show: (1) the government was enforcing a coercive population program at the time of the events, and (2) the applicant resisted the program).

[850] *Id.*

[851] *Matter of M–F–W– & L–G–*, 24 I&N Dec. 633, 638 (BIA 2008) (finding that the applicant could not show harm rising to the level of persecution or that the harm was because of her resistance).

[852] *See, e.g., Yi Quing Yang v. Gonzales*, 494 F.3d 1311 (11th Cir. 2007) (Yang II) (per curiam) (finding that a brief physical altercation with family planning officials, a summons to a local security office, and an ongoing interest in the applicant by family planning authorities did not rise to the level of persecution), *superseding* 2007 WL 2000044 (July 12, 2007) (Yang I).

[853] *See, e.g., Matter of J–S–*, 24 I&N Dec. 520 (AG 2008) (recognizing that the application of coercive population control policies may have a profound impact on both parties to the marriage); *Matter of S–L–L–*, 24 I&N Dec. 1, 10–11 (BIA 2006).

[854] *See, e.g., Matter of T–Z–*, 24 I&N Dec. 163 (BIA 2007) (discussing economic persecution).

[855] *Xu Ming Li v. Ashcroft*, 356 F.3d 1153 (9th Cir. 2004) (en banc) (finding that a forced gynecological exam that lasted for half an hour and was followed by threats of being subjected to a similar procedure at any time was harm serious enough to rise to the level of persecution); *cf. Yun Yan Huang v. Att'y Gen.*, 429 F.3d 1002 (11th Cir. 2005) (holding that an intrusive state-ordered gynecological exam, which caused pain and discomfort, along with a 20-day detention following the applicant's refusal to undergo a second exam, did not rise to the level of persecution).

(6) whether there is objective evidence that the relationship continues while the applicant is in the United States.[856]

In addition to the harm rising to the level of persecution, the nexus requirement for the resistance must also be met; the applicant must show that the harm suffered or feared was on account of his or her resistance.[857] As the BIA explains, "The statute requires more than proof of an act of resistance and an unconnected imposition of harm that rises to the level of persecution. There must be a link between the harm and the 'other resistance.'"[858] That resistance must be directly related to the applicant's own opposition to a coercive family planning policy.[859] However, an individual who has not him or herself demonstrated resistance may be able to demonstrate through direct or circumstantial evidence that his or her partner's resistance has been or will be imputed to him or her.[860]

5. Applicants Who Have Not Physically Undergone a Procedure

Where there is no past persecution, adjudicators often reject claims as "speculative" and rely on Department of State reports showing that population controls are no longer strictly enforced.[861] An applicant who has not physically

---

[856] *Matter of S–L–L–*, 24 I&N Dec. 1, 10–11 (BIA 2006). *See supra* Part II.C. for a detailed discussion on the types of harm that rise to the level of persecution.

[857] *Matter of M–F–W– & L–G–*, 24 I&N Dec. 633, 638 (BIA 2008) (finding that the applicant could not show harm rising to the level of persecution or that the harm was because of her resistance).

[858] *Id.* (holding that the applicant could not show the required connection because the reinsertion of her IUD was part of a routine medical procedure, not for the purpose of targeting her for her opposition or resistance to the policy).

[859] *Shi Liang Lin v. U.S. Dep't of Justice*, 494 F.3d 296 (2d Cir. 2007) (en banc). *See also Ai Feng Yuan v. U.S. Dep't of Justice*, 416 F.3d 192 (2d Cir. 2005) (finding that parents-in-law failed to establish that they were opposed to the policy themselves, and therefore, they failed to establish persecution on account of a protected ground); *Xu Ming Li v. Ashcroft*, 356 F.3d 1153 (9th Cir. 2004) (en banc).

[860] *Shi Liang Lin v. U.S. Dep't of Justice*, 494 F.3d 296 (2d Cir. 2007) (en banc); *Zhang v. Gonzales*, 408 F.3d 1239 (9th Cir. 2005) (finding that the economic deprivation, lack of educational opportunities, and trauma from witnessing the applicant's father's forcible removal from the home were on account of the applicant's imputed political opinion based on her parents' resistance); *Lin v. Ashcroft*, 377 F.3d 1014, 1031 (9th Cir. 2004) (finding that the "discrimination or abusive treatment of children in families with more than one child may qualify them for refugee status" based on language in the INA that defines a refugee as someone who is persecuted for "other resistance" to a coercive population control program); *cf. Tao Jiang v. Gonzales*, 500 F.3d 137 (2d Cir. 2007) (finding that there was no evidence that resistance was imputed to the child of a woman who had undergone a forced sterilization procedure).

[861] *See, e.g., Yong Xiu Lin v. Holder*, 754 F.3d 9 (1st Cir. 2014) (finding that the applicant's evidence as to population control measures "in some areas of China" was insufficient to establish either a likelihood of persecution or materially changed circumstances); *Wanrong Lin v. Holder*, 771 F.3d 177 (4th Cir. 2014) (declining to review the asylum denial, noting that the Department of State report states that population controls are no longer strictly enforced in China); *Lin v. Holder*, 723 F.3d 300 (1st Cir. 2013) (upholding the BIA's determination that the applicant's fear of involuntary IUD insertion is too speculative to be considered well-founded); *Zheng v. Holder*, 666 F.3d 1064 (7th Cir. 2012) ("We need

Continued

undergone a forced abortion or sterilization procedure, must demonstrate his or her own asylum eligibility by establishing:

(1) he or she failed or refused to undergo an abortion or sterilization procedure, or resisted a coercive population control program;

(2) he or she suffered harm or has a well-founded fear of suffering harm rising to the level of persecution; and

(3) the persecution was inflicted, or he or she has a well-founded fear that it would be inflicted, for the resistance to the coercive population control program or for the failure or refusal to undergo the procedure.[862]

Asylum applications involving applicants who have not undergone coercive population control procedures, but who fear those procedures, have arisen in many contexts; however, two of the most common are changed personal circumstances — where another child has been born in or outside of the country of feared persecution, and changed country conditions — where coercive population control policies are applied differently than they were previously in the locality in question. In these cases, it is not enough to demonstrate a generalized or "speculative" fear of persecution.[863] Rather, the applicant must demonstrate that his or her fear is objectively reasonable by showing a personal risk of being singled out for persecution or that there is a pattern or practice of persecution of those similarly situated to him or her in the area where he or she resides.[864]

Similarly, for applicants seeking to reopen asylum proceedings based on "changed circumstances arising in the country of nationality," evidence of coercive population control policies may not be sufficient to meet the applicant's burden of proof if such

---

evidence-based law just as we need evidence-based medicine...Zheng has no feasible way of determining how likely it is that she'll be persecuted if she is returned to Fujian Province.").

[862] AOBTC Workbook, pt. I, *supra* note 34, at 38. *See Li v. Ashcroft*, 356 F.3d 1153 (9th Cir. 2004) (finding that a woman who opposes the Chinese government's population control policies and was subjected to a forced gynecological exam and threatened with future abortions and sterilization of her boyfriend is eligible for asylum); *Shan Liao v. U.S. Dep't. of Justice*, 293 F.3d 61 (2d Cir. 2002) (denying asylum to an applicant who failed to prove he would face economic persecution, that his 51-year-old wife was in danger of sterilization, or that he would be subjected to detention upon return); *Chen v. INS*, 266 F.3d 1094 (9th Cir. 2001) (granting withholding to an applicant who married and had a child without the permission of the Chinese government).

[863] *See, e.g., Yong Xiu Lin v. Holder*, 754 F.3d 9 (1st Cir. 2014) (finding that the applicant's evidence as to population control measures "in some areas of China" was insufficient to establish either a likelihood of persecution or materially changed circumstances); *Wanrong Lin v. Holder*, 771 F.3d 177 (4th Cir. 2014) (declining the review the asylum denial, noting that the Department of State report states that population controls are no longer strictly enforced in China); *Lin v. Holder*, 723 F.3d 300 (1st Cir. 2013) (upholding the BIA's determination that the applicant's fear of involuntary IUD insertion is too speculative to be considered well-founded); *Zheng v. Holder*, 666 F.3d 1064 (7th Cir. 2012) ("We need evidence-based law just as we need evidence-based medicine . . . Zheng has no feasible way of determining how likely it is that she'll be persecuted if she is returned to Fujian Province.").

[864] *See Matter of J–W–S–*, 24 I&N Dec. 185 (BIA 2007).

evidence does not specifically show any likelihood that the applicant or similarly situated nationals will be persecuted.[865] In some instances, courts have found a change in country conditions sufficient for purposes of a motion to reopen.[866] Courts have rejected motions to reopen, however, based on a change in personal circumstances,[867] upholding as reasonable the BIA's interpretation that a change in personal circumstances alone is insufficient for a motion to reopen.[868]

A contested issue in coercive population control cases is whether having more than one child, one or more of whom are born in the United States or elsewhere outside of China, establishes a claim for asylum.[869] Documents presented in *Shou*

[865] *See, e.g.*, *Matter of S–Y–G–*, 24 I&N Dec. 247 (BIA 2007) (rejecting applicant's motion to reopen asylum proceedings where applicant claimed that the birth of her second child in the United States would lead to persecution in her home province in China, which enforces general population control policies). *See also Chen v. Holder*, 751 F.3d 876 (8th Cir. 2014) (declining to review the motion to reopen denial finding that the applicant did not produce previously unavailable documents and that they did not distinguish between women who have had children in China and those who return with children born abroad); *Zheng v. Holder*, 701 F.3d 237 (7th Cir. 2012) (upholding the denial of the motion to reopen, finding that the birth of the applicant's two U.S. citizen children was a change in personal circumstances, not a change in country conditions); *Zheng v. Att'y Gen.*, 549 F.3d 260 (3d Cir. 2008) (remanding claims where the BIA erred by failing to consider that the applicants' motions to reopen were based on changed circumstances in China, not the birth of their children in the United States).

[866] *See, e.g.*, *Lin v. Mukasey*, 532 F.3d 596 (7th Cir. 2008) (finding that imposition of a fine that the applicant could not pay and would result in sterilization was a changed country condition). *See also, e.g.*, *Zhu v. Holder*, 744 F.3d 268 (3d Cir. 2014) (vacating the order denying the motion to reopen, finding that the BIA's opinion did not reflect meaningful consideration of much of the evidence the applicant submitted in support of the motion relating to forced sterilization in China).

[867] *Zheng v. Holder*, 701 F.3d 237 (7th Cir. 2012) (upholding the denial of the motion to reopen, finding that the birth of the applicant's two U.S. citizen children was a change in personal circumstances, not a change in country conditions); *Wei v. Mukasey*, 545 F.3d 1248, 1256 (10th Cir. 2008); *Zhang v. Mukasey*, 543 F.3d 851, 855–56 (6th Cir. 2008); *Yuen Jin v. Mukasey*, 538 F.3d 143, 147 (2d Cir. 2008); *Li Yun Lin*, 526 F.3d 1164, 1165–66 (8th Cir. 2008); *Qing Li Chen v. Mukasey*, 524 F.3d 1028, 1030 (9th Cir. 2008); *Cheng Chen v. Gonzales*, 498 F.3d 758, 760 (7th Cir. 2007); *Hai Fan Huang v. Att'y Gen.*, 249 F. App'x 293, 298 (3d Cir. 2007) (unpublished).

[868] *Matter of C–W–L–*, 24 I&N Dec. 346 (BIA 2007). See ch. 11 for a detailed discussion of motions to reopen.

[869] *See, e.g.*, *Matter of C–C–*, 23 I&N Dec. 899 (BIA 2006) (finding evidence submitted with motion to reopen did not indicate that Chinese national returning to that country with foreign born children have been subjected to forced sterilization). *See also, e.g.*, *Chen v. Holder*, 742 F.3d 171 (4th Cir. 2014) (remanding a forced sterilization claim because the BIA relied on the 2007 Department of State report for China and did not account for the contrary evidence that parents of two U.S.-born children could face persecution in China); *Chen v. Att'y Gen.*, 676 F.3d 112 (3d Cir. 2011) (finding that the applicants did not demonstrate a well-founded fear of persecution based on the birth of their two U.S. citizen children); *Yu v. Att'y Gen*, 513 F.3d 346, 349 (3d Cir. 2008) (holding the BIA's decision to credit the State Department reports over an expert affidavit was supported by substantial evidence); *Tian Ming Lin v. Gonzales*, 473 F.3d 48, 51 (2d Cir. 2007); *Shou Yung Guo v. Gonzales,* 463 F.3d 109 (2d Cir. 2006) (presenting documents undermining U.S. State Department reports and suggesting that there may be a policy of forced sterilization in the Fujian province); *Huang v. INS*, 421 F.3d 125, 129 (2d Cir. 2005) (rejecting claim of Chinese applicant with two U.S.-born children for failure to meet his burden of proof); *Yang v. Gonzales*, 427 F.3d 1117, 1118 (8th Cir. 2005) (finding that a Chinese couple with

Continued

Yung Guo v. Gonzales suggested that there may be an official policy of forced sterilization in the Fujian Province and that foreign-born children would be counted in determining violations of the one-child policy.[870] The Second Circuit found that those documents undermined the BIA's reliance on the U.S. State Department report stating that the Chinese government opposed forced sterilization, and remanded for consideration of changed circumstances and whether the applicant had a well-founded fear of persecution.[871] Similarly, the Eleventh Circuit has held that conditions in the Fujian province of China had materially changed with regard to forced sterilization of individuals with children born outside of China.[872] More recently, the Seventh Circuit has joined in casting doubt on the claim that Fujian authorities do not count children born outside of China for purposes of the one child policy, and has remanded cases for further consideration of changed country conditions.[873] In addition to children born outside the country of feared persecution, courts have grappled with whether having two children alone, both of whom were born in China, is sufficient grounds for a well-founded fear of persecution.[874] The BIA, however, has rejected both of these arguments.[875]

Coercive population control policies are applied differently in various localities, and often, they are applied differently than they were previously in the locality in

---

two U.S. citizen children, who wished to have two more children, had a well-founded fear of persecution if they returned to China); *Chen v. INS*, 195 F.3d 198 (4th Cir. 1999) (rejecting the claim of an applicant with three children where the record showed forced sterilizations were on decline in China, were limited to rural areas, and couples returning from abroad may be "excused" from paying penalties), *vacated on other grounds*, 537 U.S. 1016 (2002).

[870] *Shou Yung Guo v. Gonzales,* 463 F.3d 109 (2d Cir. 2006). *See also Yu v. Att'y Gen.*, 513 F.3d 346, 349 (3d Cir. 2008) (holding the BIA's decision to credit the State Department reports over an expert affidavit was supported by substantial evidence); *Tian Ming Lin v. Gonzales*, 473 F.3d 48, 51 (2d Cir. 2007).

[871] *Shou Yung Guo v. Gonzales,* 463 F.3d 109 (2d Cir. 2006).

[872] *Jiang v. Att'y Gen.*, 568 F.3d 1252, 1258 (11th Cir. 2009) (holding that, when a petitioner files a motion to reopen on the basis of changed country conditions, the petitioner's post-removal change in personal circumstances will not bar the motion).

[873] *Zheng v. Holder*, 722 F.3d 986 (7th Cir. 2013) (remanding the case in light of two recent decisions, *Ni v. Holder* and *Chen v. Holder*, that cast doubt on the claim that Fujian authorities do not count children born outside of China for purposes of the one-child policy); *Ni v. Holder*, 715 F.3d 620 (7th Cir. 2013) (holding that the BIA failed to meaningfully address documents bolstering the applicant's assertion that conditions in China have changed for the worse); *Qui Yun Chen v. Holder*, 715 F.3d 207 (7th Cir. 2013) (critiquing the BIA for its cursory treatment of the evidence and remanding the case to determine whether the applicant faces a substantial risk of compulsory sterilization if she is removed to China).

[874] *See, e.g.*, *Fang Huang v. Mukasey*, 523 F.3d 640 (6th Cir. 2008); *Jian Hui Shao v. BIA*, 465 F.3d 497, 503 (2d Cir. 2006).

[875] *Matter of J–H–S–*, 24 I&N Dec. 196 (BIA 2007); *Matter of J–W–S–*, 24 I&N Dec. 185 (BIA 2007) (finding that the evidence of record did not demonstrate that the Chinese government had a national policy of requiring forced sterilization of a parent who returns with a second child born outside of China).

question. Accordingly, the BIA developed a three-part test, which the Second Circuit upheld in *Shao v. Mukasey*, for an applicant to demonstrate his or her objective fear of persecution based on violation of coercive population control policies.[876] That test requires the applicant to:

(1) identify the details of the government policy in the local province, municipality, or other locally defined area that would be implicated;

(2) establish that the applicant is in violation of the policy and that the government would view the applicant to be in violation of the policy; and

(3) demonstrate that there is a reasonable possibility that the government would enforce the policy (that the violation would be punished in the local area in a way that would give rise to an objective fear of persecution).[877]

In evaluating prong one — identifying the government policy in the relevant location — adjudicators must consult country conditions reports for the local area where the applicant resides, and not just rely upon Department of State reports.[878] In evaluating prong two — whether there has been a violation of the policy — relevant considerations may include: the gender of the children, the spacing between the children's births, the parents' marital status, and whether or not the parents are government employees.[879] This three-prong test must be applied on a case-by-case

---

[876] *Matter of J–H–S–*, 24 I&N Dec. 196 (BIA 2007); *Shao v. Mukasey*, 546 F.3d 138 (2d Cir. 2008).

[877] *See Matter of J–H–S–*, 24 I&N Dec. 196 (BIA 2007) (finding that the evidence did not demonstrate that the birth of a second child would violate the family planning policy in the Fujian province). *See also Matter of J–W–S–*, 24 I&N Dec. 185 (BIA 2007) (finding that the evidence did not establish a national policy requiring forced sterilization upon the birth of a second child overseas and that the evidence was insufficient to show that any sanctions in the Fujian province would rise to the level of persecution); *Matter of C–C–*, 23 I&N Dec. 899 (BIA 2006) (finding that a violation of the policy was not established where the policy allows individuals to apply for the birth of a second child four years after the birth of the first child, and the applicant's second child was born six years after her firstborn). *See also Shao v. Mukasey*, 546 F.3d 138, 142–43 (2d Cir. 2008); *Huang v. INS*, 421 F.3d 125 (2d Cir. 2005).

[878] *Matter of J–W–S–*, 24 I&N Dec. 185 (BIA 2007) (finding that a well-founded fear was not established where country conditions evidence did not support the applicant's claim that he would be sterilized upon return to the Fujian province because of the birth of two children born in the U.S. and that the evidence was insufficient to show that any sanctions or penalties in the Fujian province would rise to the level of persecution); *Matter of C–C–*, 23 I&N Dec. 899 (BIA 2006) (finding that an affidavit submitted with motion to reopen was insufficient to show that Chinese nationals returning to that country with foreign born children have been subjected to forced sterilization, because the affidavit was generalized, not based on personal knowledge, did not specifically address situations of individuals similarly situated to the applicant, and contradicted the State Department report).

[879] *See Matter of S–Y–G–*, 24 I&N Dec. 247 (2007) (denying a motion to reopen proceedings based on the birth of a second child in the U.S. where the applicant's behavior would not be viewed as violating the family planning policies of the Fujian province because she was not a government employee and there was a seven-year interval between the birth of her two children).

basis and is meant to be applied in cases where a second or subsequent child has been born.[880]

- **Practice Pointer**: Practitioners should ensure that all evidence submitted is specific to the applicant and addresses the situations of individuals who are similarly situated to the applicant in the relevant location.

- **Practice Pointer**: In September 2001, the Resource Information Center, now part of USCIS, published a comprehensive report entitled *Chinese State Birth Planning in the 1990s and Beyond*, by Susan Greenhalgh, Ph.D. and Edwin Winckler, Ph.D., as part of its Perspective Series, designed to provide country condition information to asylum and immigration officers. UNHCR has shared its views on coercive population control as a basis for asylum in its August 2005 *Note on Refugee Claims Based on Coercive Family Planning Laws and Policies*.[881]

F. Government Actor or Groups the Government is Unable or Unwilling to Control

Once an asylum-seeker demonstrates past persecution or a well-founded fear of persecution on account of one of the enumerated statutory grounds, he or she must then show that the persecution suffered or feared is by the government or a group that the government is unable or unwilling to control.[882] Asylum claims are, in many cases, based on persecution by the government or authorities in the applicant's home country. Government actors may include national authorities, such as elected political leaders, members of the military, paramilitary units or other civilian forces controlled by the government,[883] and intelligence and security forces, or they may be local authorities, such as the police or other members of local law enforcement.[884] Where a government agent is the persecutor, it is not necessary to inquire whether the applicant ever sought protection from a government entity.[885]

Asylum claims may also be based on persecution at the hands of nongovernmental actors.[886] If the persecutor is not a government actor, the applicant must show that the

---

[880] *See Matter of J–H–S–*, 24 I&N Dec. 196, 202 (BIA 2007).

[881] *See* U.N. High Comm'r for Refugees, *UNHCR Note on Refugee Claims Based on Coercive Family Planning Laws or Policies , available at www.unhcr.org/cgi-bin/texis/vtx/refworld/rwmain/opendocpdf.pdf?docid=4301a9184* (last accessed Jan. 4, 2014).

[882] INA §208(b)(1). *See INS v. Elias-Zacarias*, 502 U.S. 478, 481–83 (1992).

[883] *See, e.g., Matter of Villalta*, 20 I&N Dec. 142, 147 (BIA 1990).

[884] *Zheng v. Mukasey*, 552 F.3d 277, 287 (2d Cir. 2009)

[885] *See Kantoni v. Gonzales,* 461 F.3d 894 (7th Cir. 2006); *Baballah v. Ashcroft,* 367 F.3d 1067, 1078 (9th Cir. 2004).

[886] *See, e.g., Nabulwala v. Gonzales,* 481 F.3d 1115, 1118 (8th Cir. 2007) (finding error where an IJ concluded that to qualify for asylum the applicant had to demonstrate government persecution);

Continued

government was unable or unwilling to control the persecutor, or that the government has not taken reasonable steps to provide meaningful protection to the applicant.[887] One court has interpreted "unable or unwilling" to mean that that the government has either condoned the private behavior or is completely helpless to protect the victim.[888] The UNHCR Handbook clarifies:

> Persecution is normally related to the action taken by the authorities of a country. It may also emanate from sections of the population that do not respect the standards established by the laws of the country concerned. A case in point may be religious intolerance, amounting to persecution, in a country otherwise secular, but where sizable fractions of the population do not respect the religious beliefs of their neighbors. Where serious discriminatory or other offensive acts are committed by the local populace, they can be considered as persecution if they are knowingly tolerated by the authorities, or if the authorities refuse, or prove unable, to provide effective protection.[889]

The BIA has recognized claims based on persecution by such nongovernmental actors as a rival clan in Somalia,[890] a Togolese tribe that practiced female genital mutilation,[891] and a spouse.[892] Similarly, federal decisions have granted petitions for

---

Menjivar v. Gonzales, 416 F.3d 918, 922–23 (8th Cir. 2005) (finding that the applicant's claim failed because the record did not compel the conclusion that the Salvadoran government was unable or unwilling to protect her from a gang member); *Castro-Perez v. Gonzales*, 409 F.3d 1069, 1072 (9th Cir. 2005) (finding that the applicant's claim failed because did not show the Honduran government was unable or unwilling to control or prosecute rape in the country); *Faruk v, Ashcroft,* 378 F.3d 940, 943 (9th Cir. 2004) (finding that the IJ erred in discounting persecution suffered by applicants at the hands of their family members when the applicants had established that the government was unable or unwilling to control their persecutors); *Avetova-Elisseva v. INS*, 213 F.3d 1192 (9th Cir. 2000) (finding that "it does not matter that financial considerations may account" for Russian government's inability to stop ethnic persecution, but that what matters is that the government "is unwilling or *unable*" to stop it) (emphasis in original); *Sotelo-Aquije v. Slattery*, 17 F.3d 33, 37 (2d Cir. 1994) (denying asylum for a man attacked by criminal thugs); *Matter of S–A–*, 22 I&N Dec. 1328 (BIA 2000) (finding that the applicant suffered persecution at the hands of her father and could not rely on the Moroccan authorities to protect her); *Matter of H–,* 21 I&N Dec. 337 (BIA 1996) (involving members of the opposition political party and clan); *Matter of Kasinga,* 21 I&N Dec. 357 (BIA 1996) (en banc) (finding persecution by family members); *Matter of Villalta*, 20 I&N Dec. 142, 147 (BIA 1990) (finding that the Salvadoran government appeared to be unable to control the paramilitary death squads). *See also* UNHCR Handbook, *supra* note 33, ¶ 65 ("Where serious discriminatory or other offensive acts are committed by the local populace, they can be considered as persecution if they are knowingly tolerated by the authorities, or if the authorities refuse, or prove unable, to offer effective protection.").

[887] *Aliyev v. Mukasey*, 549 F.3d 111, 118–19 (2d Cir. 2008); *Ngengwe v. Mukasey*, 543 F.3d 1029, 1035–36 (8th Cir. 2008); *Nabulwala v. Gonzales*, 481 F.3d 1115 (8th Cir. 2007).

[888] *Khilan v. Holder*, 557 F.3d 583, 585 (8th Cir. 2009) (noting that the police were willing to investigate the kidnapping and had arrested a number of suspects).

[889] UNHCR Handbook, *supra* note 33, ¶ 65.

[890] *Matter of H–*, 21 I&N Dec. 337 (BIA 1996).

[891] *Matter of Kasinga*, 21 I&N Dec. 357, 365 (BIA 1996).

[892] *Matter of A–R–C–G–*, 26 I&N Dec. 388 (BIA 2014).

review based on persecution by anti-Semitic gangs or skinheads,[893] FARC,[894] the New People's Army in the Philippines,[895] and the Communist Party Marxists (CPM) of India.[896] In addition, despite a group's demographics or diversity, courts have found that a person could suffer persecution "at the hands of his [or her] own people."[897] Generally, in these cases, the asylum applicant must show that it is not reasonable to seek protection elsewhere in his or her country.[898]

Generally, "unwilling" means situations where the government shares or does not wish to oppose the persecutor's opinion about the applicant's protected characteristic, or situations where the government is unwilling to intervene in what it perceives to be private disputes within a family or between tribes.[899] Evidence of unwillingness might be a refusal to investigate or make a report of acts of violence or harassment, direct statements to victims of harm expressing unwillingness to protect them, or country conditions evidence showing that similar reports of violence or harassment go uninvestigated.[900]

"Unable" means situations where the government is helpless to protect the victim, either because of civil war, inability to exercise authority over portions of the country, or lack of influence over certain groups.[901] Determining whether a

---

[893] *Krotova v. Gonzales*, 416 F.3d 1080, 1087 (9th Cir. 2005).

[894] *Arboleda v. Att'y Gen.*, 434 F.3d 1220, 1226 (11th Cir. 2006).

[895] *Agbuya v. INS*, 219 F.3d 962 (9th Cir. 2000), *amended by* 241 F.3d 1224 (9th Cir. 2001).

[896] *Maini v. INS*, 212 F.3d 1167, 1175 (9th Cir. 2000).

[897] *Id.* (stating that punishment for interfaith marriage is without question persecution on account of religion); *see also Matter of S–A–*, 22 I&N Dec. 1328 (BIA 2000) (granting asylum to a Moroccan woman with liberal Muslim beliefs who was persecuted by her father, who held more orthodox Muslim views).

[898] Note that if there has been past persecution at the hands of a non-governmental persecutor, internal relocation is presumed to be unreasonable and the burden shifts to DHS. 8 CFR §208.13(b)(3)(ii) (2014).

[899] UNHCR Handbook, *supra* note 33, ¶¶ 65, 98–99.

[900] *See, e.g., Gathungu v. Holder*, 725 F.3d 900, 908–09 (8th Cir. 2013) (finding that the Kenyan government was complicit in attacks on Mungiki defectors, despite contrary government statements); *Doe v. Holder*, 736 F.3d 871, 878 (9th Cir. 2013) (stating that the applicant need not show that the Russian government was against homosexuals, but only that it was unwilling to protect them); *Fiadjoe v. Att'y Gen.*, 411 F.3d 135, 160–63 (3d Cir. 2005) (reversing the denial of relief where a Ghanaian woman who was sexually and emotionally abused by her father who was a priest in Trokosi sect, where the Department of State report indicated that it would have been futile for her to go to the police); *Deloso v. Ashcroft*, 393 F.3d 907, 858, 866 n.5 (9th Cir. 2005) (finding that the government was unwilling or unable to stop persecution in rural Philippines where the applicant had to travel two hours to the nearest police station and persecution escalated after he reported the incidents); *Mashiri v. Ashcroft,* 383 F.3d 1112, 1121 (9th Cir. 2004).

[901] *See Madrigal v. Holder*, 716 F.3d 499, 506–07 (9th Cir. 2013) (finding that the Mexican government may be willing to control Los Zetas but that country conditions evidence indicates they are unable to do so); *Matter of H–,* 21 I&N Dec. 337, 345 (BIA 1996); *Matter of Villalta,* 20 I&N Dec. 142, 147 (BIA 1990).

government is unable to protect an applicant requires a careful evaluation of the applicant's own testimony in conjunction with country conditions evidence to investigate how similarly situated individuals are treated.[902]

The applicant is not required to show that the government was directly involved or complicit in the persecution.[903] However, the applicant must show more than general difficulty controlling or preventing private behavior.[904] Evidence that the government "condoned [the behavior] or at least demonstrated a complete helplessness to protect the victims" will strengthen an asylum claim based on persecution by a non-government actor.[905]

---

[902] *See Matter of H–*, 21 I&N Dec. 337, 345 (BIA 1996); *Matter of Villalta,* 20 I&N Dec. 142, 147 (BIA 1990).

[903] *See Nabulwala v. Gonzales*, 481 F.3d 1115, 1118 (8th Cir. 2007) (finding error where the IJ concluded that to qualify for asylum the applicant had to demonstrate government persecution; *Faruk v. Ashcroft*, 378 F.3d 940, 943 (9th Cir. 2004) (finding error where the IJ dismissed the persecution suffered by the applicants at the hands of their family members when the applicants had established that the government was unable or unwilling to control the family members).

[904] *See Salman v. Holder*, 687 F.3d 991 (8th Cir. 2012) (finding that the persecutor was a private actor and the Israeli government arrested, convicted, and sentenced the uncle's murderer); *Morgan v. Holder*, 634 F.3d 53 (1st Cir. 2011) (finding no connection to the Egyptian government whatsoever and no evidence of unwillingness or inability to protect the applicant by the government); *Guillen-Hernandez v. Holder*, 592 F.3d 883 (8th Cir. 2010) (finding that the government was willing to control the murderer where there was an extensive police investigation, trial, and conviction of the murderer); *Rahimzadeh v. Holder*, 613 F.3d 916 (9th Cir. 2010) (stating that the Dutch government had taken firm action against groups espousing violence in support of an Islamic extremist agenda and that the government sought to protect freedom of religion and did not tolerate its abuse); *Scatambuli v. Holder*, 558 F.3d 53 (1st Cir. 2009) (stating that the INA is not intended to protect aliens from violence based on personal animosity and that any link between the persecutors and the Brazilian police was highly uncertain); *Burbiene v. Holder*, 568 F.3d 251 (1st Cir. 2009) (finding that scattered incidences of violence or harassment are not enough to establish that a government is unwilling or unable to control violence and noting that the DOS country report indicates government efforts to combat organized crime rings in Lithuania); *Lopez Perez v. Holder*, 587 F.3d 456 (1st Cir. 2009) (finding that the applicant failed to show any connection between the sightings of dead bodies in Guatemala and any governmental action or inaction); *Khalili v. Holder*, 557 F.3d 429 (6th Cir. 2009) (finding that although there were loopholes in Jordan's penal code, Jordanian authorities prosecuted all honor crimes reported and police had placed potential victims in protective custody); *Khilan v. Holder*, 557 F.3d 583 (8th Cir. 2009) (finding no indication that the Indian government condoned persecution of individuals who opposed or were targeted by Kashmiri separatists and that the police had been willing to investigate the applicant's kidnapping, including arresting a number of suspects); *Ortiz-Araniba v. Keisler,* 505 F.3d 39, 42 (1st Cir. 2007) (upholding finding that Salvadoran government was able and willing to control the persecutor where he was prosecuted for his crimes against the applicant and served 4 years in prison; the court rejected claim that the government would be unable to protect her because she lived far from the nearest police station, and had no telephone); *Setiadi v. Gonzales,* 437 F.3d 710, 713–14 (8th Cir. 2006); *Menjivar v. Ashcroft,* 416 F.3d 918, 921 (8th Cir. 2005) (citing *Matter of McMullen,* 17 I&N Dec. 542, 546 (BIA 1980) & *Galina v. INS,* 213 F.3d 955, 958 (7th Cir. 2000)).

[905] *Menjivar v. Ashcroft,* 416 F.3d 918, 921 (8th Cir. 2005) (quoting *Galina v. INS,* 213 F.3d 955, 958 (7th Cir. 2000)). *See also Garcia v. Holder*, 756 F.3d 885 (5th Cir. 2014) (remanding to the BIA due to evidence that the applicant's encounters with the extortionists occurred shortly after the applicant gave information about himself and his location to government officials in El Salvador).

➤ **Practice Pointer**: Practitioners should emphasize any evidence that government actors committed or instigated the acts, condoned the acts, or was unable to prevent the acts by nongovernmental actors.[906]

Additionally, asylum-seekers are not required to show that the government's refusal to protect them was on account of one of the protected grounds, only that the government was unable or unwilling to prevent the persecution.[907] One court has held that it was error for an IJ to base an asylum denial on the applicant's failure to show that the police "refused" him, rather than that the government was unable or unwilling to protect him.[908]

Finally, an asylum applicant is not required to show that the government is unable or unwilling to control the private actors nationwide; it is enough to demonstrate the government's inability or unwillingness to control the private actors in a specific location.[909]

Another relevant inquiry in determining whether the government was unwilling or unable to protect the applicant is whether the applicant sought the protection of the government, and if not, whether he or she has a reasonable explanation as to why he or she did not seek government protection.[910] If seeking protection from or reporting persecution to government authorities would be futile or would result in further abuse, the applicant is not expected or required to report abuse to government authorities.[911] On the other hand, if the applicant does report persecution to

---

[906] *See Shehu v. Gonzales*, 443 F.3d 435, 437–38 (5th Cir. 2006); *Harutyunyan v. Gonzales*, 421 F.3d 64, 68 (1st Cir. 2005); *Roman v. INS*, 233 F.3d 1027, 1034 (7th Cir. 2000) (citing *Galina v. INS*, 213 F.3d 955, 958 (7th Cir. 2000)). *See also* AOBTC Workbook, pt. I, *supra* note 34, at 44.

[907] *See, e.g., Valdiviezo-Galdamez v. Att'y Gen.*., 502 F.3d 285, 288–89 (3d Cir. 2007).

[908] *Valdiviezo-Galdamez v. Att'y Gen.*, 502 F.3d 285, 288–89 (3d Cir. 2007).

[909] *See, e.g., Mashiri v. Ashcroft,* 383 F.3d 1112, 1122 (9th Cir. 2004). Note, however, that if the applicant could reasonably avoid persecution through internal relocation, the government would be able to rebut a presumption of well-founded fear. *See supra* Part II.D.1.ii for a detailed discussion of internal relocation.

[910] *See Ixtlilco-Morales v. Keisler,* 507 F.3d 651, 653 (8th Cir. 2007) (agreeing with a BIA finding that the applicant was too young to seek government protection); *Ornelas-Chavez v. Gonzales,* 458 F.3d 1052 (9th Cir. 2006) (holding that reporting not required if applicant can convincingly establish that doing so would have been futile or have subjected him or her to further abuse); *Castro-Perez v. Gonzales,* 409 F.3d 1069, 1072 (9th Cir. 2005) (applicant failed to show that government was unwilling or unable to control the harm); *Roman v. INS,* 233 F.3d 1027, 1035 (7th Cir. 2000) (finding that applicant's failure to show that he sought police protection supported conclusion that he did not suffer past persecution at the hands of coworkers); *Matter of S–A–,* 22 I&N Dec. 1328, 1335 (BIA 2000) (finding that testimony and country conditions indicated that it would be unproductive and possibly dangerous for a young female applicant to report her father's abuse to government).

[911] *Matter of S–A–*, 22 I&N Dec. 1327, 1333–35 (BIA 2000) (finding that testimony and country conditions indicated that it would be unproductive and possibly dangerous for a young female applicant to report her father's abuse to government). *See also, e.g.,* Lopez v. *Att'y Gen.*, 504 F.3d 1341, 1345 (11th Cir. 2007); *Ortiz-Araniba v. Keisler,* 505 F.3d 39 (1st Cir. 2007); *Ornelas-Chavez v. Gonzales,* 458 F.3d 1052, 1057 (9th Cir. 2006) (holding that reporting the harm to the government is not required

Continued

government authorities, and they provide a prompt response, it may be strong evidence that the government is, in fact, willing to protect the applicant.[912]

The following factors should be considered in determining whether the government was unable or unwilling to control the actor that harmed the applicant:

(1) whether there were reasonably sufficient governmental controls and restraints on the actions that harmed the applicant;

(2) whether the government had the ability and will to enforce those controls and restraints with respect to the entity that harmed the applicant;

(3) whether the applicant had access to those controls and constraints; and

(4) whether the applicant attempted to obtain protection from the government and the government's response, or failure to respond, to those attempts.[913]

USCIS advises that country conditions information should be consulted to supplement the applicant's own testimony regarding the government's inability or unwillingness to control the private actor persecutor.[914]

III. Withholding of Removal

An application for asylum is automatically considered to be an application for withholding of removal.[915] Withholding of removal under INA §241(b)(3) is a similar, but more limited, form of relief than asylum. It is based on Article 33 of the Refugee Protocol, which places a mandatory prohibition against returning an individual to a country where his or her "life or freedom would be threatened."[916] This is commonly referred to as the principle of *nonrefoulement* or non-return.

This principle of *nonrefoulement* under INA §241(b)(3)(A) states that the AG may not remove a person to a country where his or her life or freedom would be threatened because of his or her race, religion, nationality, membership in a particular

---

if the applicant can establish that doing so would have been futile or would have subjected him or her to further abuse); *Surita v. INS,* 95 F.3d 814, 819–20 (9th Cir. 1996).

[912] *See, e.g., Anacassus v. Holder*, 602 F.3d 14 (1st Cir. 2010) (noting that Haitian police intervened to protect the applicant at the demonstration which is evidence that the "authorities in Haiti are willing and able to protect" the applicant); *Ortiz-Araniba v. Keisler*, 505 F.3d 39, 42 (1st Cir. 2007).

[913] AOBTC Workbook, pt. I, *supra* note 34, at 44. *See also* UNHCR Handbook, *supra* note 33, ¶¶ 98–99; *Ortiz-Araniba v. Keisler*, 505 F.3d 39 (1st Cir. 2007); *Andriasian v. INS*, 180 F.3d 1033, 1042–43 (9th Cir. 1999) (emphasizing the widespread nature of the persecution of ethnic Armenians and the police officer's response when the applicant sought help in finding that the government of Azerbaijan was unable or unwilling to control Azeris); *Surita v. INS*, 95 F.3d 814, 819–20 (9th Cir. 1996).

[914] AOBTC Workbook, pt. I, *supra* note 34, at 44–47.

[915] 8 CFR §1208.3(b) (2014).

[916] Refugee Protocol, art. 33, *supra* note 32.

social group, or political opinion.[917] Under the Homeland Security Act of 2002, this prohibition against removal of an individual extends to the DHS secretary and other DHS officials.[918] Thus, like asylum, withholding of removal involves the elements of persecution, nexus, and the five protected grounds.

A. Legal Standards for Withholding of Removal

The burden is on the withholding of removal applicant to establish that his or her life or freedom would be threatened in the proposed country of removal on account of his or her race, religion, nationality, membership in a particular social group, or political opinion.[919] Unlike asylum, in meeting this burden, the withholding of removal applicant may rely on credible testimony alone, as such credible testimony may be sufficient to sustain the burden of proof without corroboration.[920]

- **Practice Pointer**: See chapter 4 for a detailed discussion of credibility and corroboration.

Like asylum, if an applicant demonstrates past persecution in the proposed country of removal on account of his or her race, religion, nationality, membership in a particular social group, or political opinion, that gives rise to a rebuttable presumption that the applicant's life or freedom would also be threatened in the future in the country of removal.[921] If an Immigration Judge refuses to make a finding regarding past persecution in a claim for withholding of removal, it may be reversible error.[922] The presumption of a well-founded fear may be rebutted if a preponderance of the evidence demonstrates either a fundamental change in circumstances such that the applicant's life or freedom would not be threatened on account of any of the five grounds upon removal to that country, or demonstrates that the applicant could avoid a future threat to his or her life or freedom by relocating to another part of the country of removal and, under all circumstances, it would be reasonable to expect the applicant to do so.[923] Upon a showing of past persecution, it is the government's

---

[917] INA §241(b)(3).

[918] *See* Homeland Security Act of 2002, Pub. L. No. 107-296, §§456, 1512, 1517, 116 Stat. 2135, 2200, 2310, 2311. Note, however, that the U.S. Citizenship and Immigration Services' asylum offices do not have jurisdiction to consider or adjudicate withholding of removal claims or claims for protection under the Convention Against Torture.

[919] 8 CFR §§208.16(b), 1208.16(b) (2014).

[920] *Id.*

[921] 8 CFR §§208.16(b)(1)(i), 1208.16(b)(1)(i) (2014) ("If the applicant is determined to have suffered past persecution…it shall be presumed that the applicant's life or freedom would be threatened in the future…"). *See, e.g., Ali v. Ashcroft*, 394 F.3d 780, 791 (9th Cir. 2005) (acknowledging a presumption that it is more likely than not the applicant would be persecuted where a Somali clan member was gang raped by another clan in the past); *Fergiste v. INS*, 138 F.3d 14, 20 (1st Cir. 1998).

[922] *See, e.g., Antipova v. Att'y Gen.*, 392 F.3d 1259, 1264–65 (11th Cir. 2004)

[923] 8 CFR §§208.16(b)(1)(i)(A)–(B), 1208.16(b)(1)(i)(A)–(B) (2014). *See, e.g., De Castro-Gutierrez v. Holder*, 713 F.3d 375, 381 (8th Cir. 2013) (finding that the applicant failed to demonstrate that moving to another part of the country would not avoid future threats).

burden to rebut the presumption that the applicant's life or freedom would be threatened in the future.[924]

Like asylum, this presumption for withholding of removal is only invoked if the future threat to the applicant's life or freedom would be on the basis of the original claim.[925] If the applicant's fear of a future threat to his or her life or freedom is unrelated to the past persecution, the applicant bears the burden of establishing that it is more likely than not that he or she would suffer such harm in the future.[926]

If the applicant could avoid a future threat to his or her life or freedom by relocating to another part of the country of removal and, under all circumstances, it would be reasonable to expect the applicant to do so, withholding of removal will not be granted.[927] If the actor feared is a government actor, it is presumed that the applicant could not reasonably relocate; however, if the actor is a non-government actor and there has not been past persecution, the applicant bears the burden of demonstrating that he or she cannot reasonably relocate.[928] The factors considered in determining the reasonableness of an internal relocation option are the same as those considered in the asylum context. These factors include, among others:

(1) whether the applicant would face other serious harm in the place of suggested relocation;

(2) any ongoing civil strife within the country;

(3) administrative, economic, or judicial infrastructure;

(4) geographical limitations; and

(5) social and cultural constraints, such as age, gender, health, social, and family ties.[929]

Like asylum, an applicant for withholding of removal need not provide evidence that he or she would be singled out individually in having his or her life or freedom threatened. If the applicant establishes that in the country of removal there is a pattern or practice of persecution of a group of persons similarly situated to the applicant on account of race, religion, nationality, membership in a particular social group, or political opinion, and if the applicant establishes his or her own inclusion in and identification with such group of persons such that it is more likely than not that his or her life or freedom would be threatened upon return to that country, the applicant may be granted withholding of removal.[930]

---

[924] 8 CFR §§208.16(b)(1)(ii), 1208.16(b)(1)(ii) (2014).

[925] *Id.*

[926] 8 CFR §§208.16(b)(1)(iii), 1208.16(b)(1)(iii) (2014).

[927] 8 CFR §§208.16(b)(2), 1208.16(b)(2) (2014).

[928] 8 CFR §§208.16(b)(3), 1208.16(b)(3) (2014).

[929] 8 CFR §§208.16(b)(3), 1208.16(b)(3) (2014).

[930] 8 CFR §§208.16(b)(2)(i)–(ii), 1208.16(b)(2)(i)–(ii) (2014).

Despite these similarities between asylum and withholding of removal, there are also significant differences. First, withholding of removal carries a higher legal standard of proof than asylum. If past persecution is not established, applicants for withholding of removal must demonstrate a "clear probability" of persecution, or in other words, that it is "more likely than not" that they would be persecuted if removed to their home countries.[931] This higher standard of proof is more difficult to satisfy than the well-founded fear standard for asylum, which requires only a showing of a "reasonable possibility" of persecution.[932]

- **Practice Pointer**: See chapter 4 for a detailed discussion and comparison of the various standards of proof.

Another important difference is that, while the granting of asylum is discretionary, if an applicant's life or freedom would be threatened in a country on account of one of the protected grounds, withholding that individual's removal to that particular country is mandatory.[933] Although it is a mandatory form of relief, the benefits of a grant of withholding of removal under INA §241(b)(3) differ significantly from the benefits of a grant of asylum.[934] Unlike asylum, withholding of removal is not derivative, meaning that an applicant granted withholding of removal cannot confer that status on his or her spouse and children.[935] Additionally, withholding of removal results in a removal order, and removal is only withheld with regard to the specific country or countries where the IJ has determined the applicant's life or freedom would be threatened.[936] Although an individual granted withholding of removal may

---

[931] 8 CFR §§208.16(b)(2), 1208.16(b)(2) (2014). *See INS v. Cardoza-Fonseca*, 480 U.S.421, 423 (1987); *INS v. Stevic*, 467 U.S. 407, 429–30 (1984). *See* ch. 4 for a detailed discussion and comparison of the various standards of proof.

[932] *Compare INS v. Cardoza-Fonseca*, 480 U.S.421, 431 (1987) (setting forth the asylum standard) *with INS v. Stevic*, 467 U.S. 407 (1984) (setting for the former INA §243(h) standard, which is now INA §241(b)(3)). *See* ch. 4 for a detailed discussion and comparison of the various standards of proof. *See also*, *Niang v. Gonzales*, 492 F.3d 505 (4th Cir. 2007) (observing that a petition for withholding of removal "cannot be based on a fear of psychological harm alone"); *Capric v. Ashcroft*, 355 F.3d 1075, 1095 (7th Cir. 2004) (noting that the "clear probability" standard is "a much more demanding burden"); *Lim v. INS*, 224 F.3d 929, 938 (9th Cir. 2000) (finding that although the applicant was eligible for asylum, because his risk of persecution was less than 50 percent, he did not qualify for withholding).

[933] *INS v. Cardoza-Fonseca*, 480 U.S.421, 429 (1987); *Gonzales-Neyra v. INS*, 122 F.3d 1293, 1297 (9th Cir. 1997), *amended by* 133 F.3d 726 (9th Cir. 1998). *But see Salazar v. Ashcroft*, 359 F.3d 45, 52 (1st Cir. 2004) (denying withholding of removal claim based on finding that Peruvian asylum applicant "may" be able to voluntarily depart to Venezuela).

[934] *See* ch. 13 for a detailed discussion of the benefits of asylum compared to the benefits of withholding of removal under INA §241(b)(3) and under the Convention Against Torture.

[935] *See* Cheri Attix, *Practice Pointer: Understanding Withholding of Removal*, AILA Asylum and Refugee Liaison Committee, AILA InfoNet Doc. No. 14021344 (Apr. 2, 2014), *available at www.aila.org/content/default.aspx?docid=47456*.

[936] *Id.*

remain in the United States and may be authorized to work, he or she cannot travel abroad and there is no pathway to permanent residence or citizenship.[937]

- **Practice Pointer**: For a detailed comparison of asylum and withholding of removal under INA §241(b)(3), see the AILA Asylum and Refugee Liaison Committee's Practice Pointer entitled "Understanding Withholding of Removal," available on AILA InfoNet at Doc. No. 14021344 and at *www.aila.org/content/default.aspx?docid=47456.*[938]

Finally, there are various statutory bars to asylum and withholding of removal relief. Some of these bars apply to both forms of relief, while others only apply to either asylum or to withholding of removal. These statutory bars and the important differences between the asylum and withholding of removal bars to relief are discussed below in Part IV.

IV. Grounds of Ineligibility and Statutory Bars to Asylum and Withholding of Removal

The 1951 Refugee Convention gave signatories the authority to deny protection to certain refugees who are "persons who are not considered to be deserving of international protection."[939] Specifically, the Convention notes that individuals who have committed certain crimes against peace, war crimes, crimes against humanity, or serious nonpolitical crimes outside the country of refuge, or who are guilty of acts contrary to the purposes and principles of the United Nations, are not deserving of international protection. Accordingly, under U.S. law, even if the asylum-seeker is able to demonstrate eligibility for asylum according to the legal standards discussed above, he or she may be barred from receiving and, in some cases, from applying for such relief.[940] A bar to asylum is not necessarily a bar to withholding of removal, and vice versa, although several of the bars apply to both forms of relief.[941]

- **Practice Pointer**: Individuals who are barred from both asylum and withholding of removal and who fear harm if they are returned to their home countries should consider applying for deferral of removal under the Convention Against Torture (CAT).[942] There are no bars to deferral of removal under CAT, although, like withholding of removal under INA §241(b)(3) and under the Convention Against Torture, deferral of removal under CAT is a more limited form of relief.

---

[937] *Id.*

[938] (last visited Dec. 28, 2014).

[939] Refugee Convention, *supra* note 50, at art. 1.F.; UNHCR Handbook, *supra* note 33, ¶¶ 140, 147–63.

[940] INA §§208(a)(2), (b)(2); 8 CFR §§208.13(c)(1), 1208.13(c)(1) (2014).

[941] See Part IV.B. for a detailed discussion of bars to asylum and withholding of removal eligibility.

[942] See ch. 3 for a detailed discussion of relief under the Convention Against Torture.

A. Grounds of Ineligibility for Asylum

There are three circumstances that render an asylum-seeker ineligible to apply for asylum on or after April 1, 1997:[943] (1) if there is a safe third country available to the asylum-seeker where his or her life or freedom would not be threatened and where he or she would have access to full and fair procedures for determining asylum eligibility;[944] (2) if the asylum-seeker did not file his or her application for asylum within one year of his or her arrival in the United States;[945] and (3) if the asylum-seeker previously applied for and was denied asylum.[946] There are exceptions to each of these three ineligibility grounds for asylum,[947] and these grounds do not apply at all to withholding of removal.[948]

1. Safe Third Country

An applicant is barred from applying for asylum if he or she may be removed to a "safe third country," unless the AG finds that it is in the public interest for the applicant to remain in the United States.[949] The removal must be "pursuant to a bilateral or multilateral agreement," and must be to a country other than the individual's home country or, in the case of a stateless person, other than the country of the individual's last habitual residence.[950] The "safe third country" must also be a country where the individual's "life or freedom would not be threatened on account of race, religion, nationality, membership in a particular social group, or political opinion," and where the individual would have "access to a full and fair procedure for determining a claim to asylum or equivalent temporary protection."[951] The AG may waive this bar upon finding that it is in the "public interest" for the individual to receive asylum in the United States.[952] Under the Homeland Security Act of 2002,

---

943 INA §208(a)(2); 8 CFR §208.4(a) (2014).

944 INA §208(a)(2)(A).

945 INA §§208(a)(2)(B), (d); 8 CFR §§208.4(a)(4)–(5) (2014).

946 INA §§208(a)(2)(C)–(D). This bar only applies if the applicant for asylum was issued a final order of removal. It does not apply if the previous application was denied only by the Asylum Office.

947 *See infra* pt. IV.A.2–3. for detailed discussions of the exceptions to the one-year filing deadline and the previous asylum denial ineligibility grounds.

948 *See* INA §241(b)(3); 8 CFR §§208.16, 1208.16 (2014).

949 INA §208(a)(2)(A); 8 USC §1158(a)(2)(A) (2012).

950 INA §208(a)(2)(A); 8 USC §1158(a)(2)(A) (2012).

951 INA §208(a)(2)(A); 8 USC §1158(a)(2)(A) (2012).

952 INA §208(a)(2)(A); 8 USC §1158(a)(2)(A) (2012).

this waiver authority would extend to the DHS secretary and other DHS officials.[953] This bar to asylum eligibility does not apply to unaccompanied children.[954]

Implementing this provision requires a treaty or agreement with each country to which the United States would attempt to remove persons who are not citizens of that country. For example, the United States signed a safe third country agreement with Canada on December 5, 2002.[955] Under the agreement, persons seeking refugee protection must make a claim in the first country they arrive in unless they qualify for an exception.[956] The agreement allows the United States to return "arriving aliens" to Canada, if that was their country of last presence, to seek protection under Canadian law, rather than under U.S. law. Similarly, the agreement allows Canada to return asylum-seekers to the United States, if the United States was their country of last presence.

Final U.S. regulations implementing this agreement were published on November 29, 2004,[957] and became effective on December 29, 2004.[958] Exceptions to the agreement include: citizens of Canada, asylum-seekers with close relatives in the United States, unaccompanied minors, holders of valid visas or admission documents to the United States, and persons for whom a determination has been made by the USCIS director that it is in the public interest to allow them to seek asylum, withholding of removal, or Convention Against Torture (CAT) relief in the United States.[959] The regulations subject asylum-seekers, as well as applicants for withholding of removal and CAT relief, to the safe-third-country bar if none of the exceptions applies.[960] The regulations also set forth procedures for stowaways and noncitizens subject to expedited removal.[961]

---

[953] *See* Homeland Security Act of 2002, Pub. L. No. 107-296, §§456, 1512, 1517, 116 Stat. 2135, 2200, 2310, 2311.

[954] INA §208(a)(2)(E); 8 USC §1158(a)(2)(E) (2012), as amended by the Trafficking Victims Protection Reauthorization Act of 2008, Pub. L. 110-457. See ch. 10 for a detailed discussion of the legal standards and procedures for unaccompanied children.

[955] Agreement Between the Government of the United States and the Government of Canada for Cooperation in the Examination of Refugee Status Claims from Nationals of Third Countries (Dec. 5, 2002), *available at www.refworld.org/docid/42d7b9944.html.*

[956] *Id.* Some exceptions include individuals with certain family relationships in Canada or the United States, unaccompanied minors, those holding particular documents, and if it would be in the public interest for the asylum-seeker to remain in that country to seek asylum. *See id.*

[957] Implementation of the Agreement Between the Government of the United States of America and the Government of Canada Regarding Asylum Claims Made in Transit and at Land Border Ports-of-Entry; Final Rule, 69 Fed. Reg. 69479 (Nov. 29, 2004) (to be codified at 8 CFR pt. 208, 212, & 235).

[958] *Id.*

[959] 8 CFR §208.30(e)(6)(iii) (2014).

[960] 8 CFR §1240.11(g)(4) (2014).

[961] 8 CFR §§208.30, 1208.30 (2014). See ch. 6 for a detailed discussion of expedited removal.

> **Practice Pointer**: Under the regulations, the safe third country provision does not apply at all to "unaccompanied alien children," as defined by 6 USC §279(g).[962] An unaccompanied alien child in the context of the safe third country provision is an unmarried child under the age of 18 who has no parent or legal guardian in the United States or Canada.[963] See chapter 10 for a detailed discussion of the legal standards and procedures for unaccompanied children.

Canadian regulations implementing the agreement were published in the *Canada Gazette*.[964] Some notable exceptions include unaccompanied minors, individuals subject to the death penalty in their home countries, and countries to which Canada has temporarily suspended removals (currently Afghanistan, Burundi, Democratic Republic of Congo, Haiti, Iraq, Liberia, Rwanda, and Zimbabwe).[965]

2. *One-Year Filing Deadline*

IIRAIRA imposed for the first time a timeline in which an applicant must file his or her asylum application.[966] All asylum applicants filing on or after April 1, 1998 must demonstrate that they filed for asylum within one year of the date of their last arrival in the United States, with limited exceptions.[967] Pursuant to amendments made by the 2008 Trafficking Victims Protection Reauthorization Act, this one-year filing deadline does not apply to unaccompanied children.[968] Thus, for an unaccompanied child who is not in valid immigration status, the one-year filing deadline analysis is foregone entirely. Significantly, this one-year filing deadline also does not apply to individuals seeking withholding of removal.

Some advocates have argued that the one-year filing deadline violates U.S. obligations under the 1967 U.N. Protocol Relating to the Status of Refugees, which the United States acceded to in 1968. These arguments, however, have been rejected

---

[962] 8 CFR §208.30(e)(6)(iii)(D) (2014).

[963] 6 USC §279(g)(2) (2012).

[964] Regulations Amending the Immigration and Refugee Protection Regulations, SOR/2004-217 (Can.), 138 C. Gaz. no. 22 (Nov. 3, 2004), *available at http://canadagazette.gc.ca/partII/2004/20041103/html/sor217-e.html*. For an overview of the exceptions that apply to asylum-seekers seeking entry into Canada, see the Canadian Council for Refugees website, at *www.ccrweb.ca/s3cFAQ.html*.

[965] SOR/2004-217, *supra* note 964.

[966] IIRAIRA, *supra* note 98, at §604(c), 110 Stat. 3009–694.

[967] 8 CFR §208.4(a) (2014). Note that although April 1, 1998, is the effective date of the one-year deadline, legacy INS extended an administrative 14-day grace period for applications filed with INS. Thus, applications with a filing date on or before April 15, 1998, were not subject to the one-year filing deadline as implemented by the Asylum Division.

[968] INA §208(a)(2)(E); 8 USC §1158(a)(2)(E) (2012), as amended by the Trafficking Victims Protection Reauthorization Act of 2008, Pub. L. 110-457, §235(d)(7)(A). Note that the TVPRA exempts only out-of-status unaccompanied children from the one-year filing deadline. Thus, the one-year filing deadline still must be analyzed for in-status unaccompanied children and accompanied minor principal applicants.

based on the "last in time" doctrine, which states that when domestic law clashes with U.S. international obligations, "[t]he duty of the courts is to construe and give effect to the latest expression of the sovereign will."[969] This rule is interpreted to indicate that conflicts between treaties and statutes are to be resolved based on their respective dates of enactment; whichever is later in time controls.[970]

> ➢ **Practice Pointer**: A comprehensive overview of the one-year deadline and concerns regarding its implementation can be found in "Center for Gender & Refugee Studies: The Implementation of the One-Year Bar to Asylum," 31 *Hastings Int'l & Comp. L. Rev.* 693 (Summer 2008) and in "Rejecting Refugees: Homeland Security's Administration of the One-Year Bar to Asylum," *William & Mary L. Rev.* Vol 52, 2010 (Sept. 29, 2010), available at *http://papers.ssrn.com/sol3/papers.cfm?abstract_id=1684231*. Other useful resources include a 2010 report by Human Rights First entitled, "The Asylum Filing Deadline: Denying Protection to the Persecuted and Undermining Governmental Efficiency," available at *www.humanrightsfirst.org/wp-content/uploads/pdf/afd.pdf*, as well as a 2010 report by the National Immigrant Justice Center, Human Rights First, and Penn State Law's Center for Immigrants' Rights entitled, "The One-Year Asylum Deadline and the BIA: No Protection, No Process," which examines how the one-year deadline has been applied by the BIA, available at *http://immigrantjustice.org/oneyeardeadline.*[971]

The one-year period is calculated from the date of the applicant's last arrival in the United States or from April 1, 1997, whichever is later. The term "last arrival" found in 8 CFR §1208.4(a)(2)(ii) refers to the asylum applicant's most recent arrival in the United States from a trip abroad.[972] Note, however, that the Second Circuit has held that the one-year period for filing an asylum application does not restart if the applicant's last arrival in the United States is the result of a brief trip abroad pursuant to advance parole.[973] Thus, for cases in the Second Circuit, it may not be the date of *last* arrival that governs. Although this remains good law in the Second Circuit as of the publication of this book, this rule specifically has been given negative treatment in the Third and Fifth Circuits.[974]

---

[969] *Whitney v. Robertson*, 12 U.S. 190, 195 (1888). *See, e.g.*, *Purwantono v. Gonzales*, 498 F.3d 822, 824 (8th Cir. 2007).

[970] *See generally* Emily S. Bremer, *The Dynamic Last-In-Time Rule*, 22.1 INDIANA INT'L & COMP. L. REV. 27-69 (2012), *available at https://journals.iupui.edu/index.php/iiclr/article/viewFile/17666/17821*.

[971] (all websites in this Practice Pointer last visited Dec. 27, 2014).

[972] *Matter of F–P–R–*, 24 I&N Dec. 681, 683 (BIA 2008).

[973] *See Joaquin-Porras v. Gonzales*, 435 F.3d 172 (2d Cir. 2006).

[974] *See Bouchikhi v. Holder*, 676 F.3d 173, 177 (5th Cir. 2012); *Daramy v. Att'y Gen.*, 365 F. App'x 351, 356 (3d Cir. 2010). As of the publication of this book, the Second Circuit's position has not been addressed positively or negatively in the other circuits.

An asylum application is considered filed on the date it is received by the USCIS Service Center or, under certain circumstances, the date it is mailed.[975] If the application is received by USCIS after the one-year period has elapsed, but clear and convincing documentary evidence demonstrates that the application was mailed within the statutory one-year period, the application may be considered timely.[976] The Fifth Circuit, in addressing the issue of the mailing date as the filing date, found that an IJ had no legal authority to reject an application that was mailed before the one-year filing deadline based on his interpretation that the regulation allowing this applied only to applications that the agency never received.[977]

For purposes of calculating the one-year period, the date of last arrival in the United States is counted as day zero. Thus, the first day in the calculation is the day after the last arrival in the United States.[978] For example, if an applicant last arrived on October 25, 2014, day one in calculating the one-year period would be October 26, 2014.

The one-year period usually ends on the same calendar day as the last arrival date on the following year. For example, an applicant who arrives on October 25, 2014 and files on October 25, 2015 will have timely filed.[979] An exception is when the last day for timely filing falls on a Saturday, Sunday, or legal holiday. In that case, filing on the next business day will be considered timely.[980]

The burden of proof is on the applicant to demonstrate that he or she filed an asylum application within one year of his or her last entry to the United States. The applicant is barred from applying for asylum if he or she fails to demonstrate "by clear and convincing evidence that the application has been filed within one year after the date of [his or her] arrival in the U.S."[981] The clear and convincing standard means that there is enough proof to produce a "firm belief or conviction as to the allegations sought to be established," and "where the truth of the facts asserted is

---

[975] *See* 8 CFR §§208.4(a)(2)(ii), 1208.4(a)(2)(ii) (2014); *Nakimbugwe v. Gonzales*, 475 F.3d 281 (5th Cir. 2007).

[976] *See* 8 CFR §§208.4(a)(2)(ii), 1208.4(a)(2)(ii) (2014).

[977] *Nakimbugwe v. Gonzales*, 475 F.3d 281, 285 (5th Cir. 2007).

[978] AOBTC Workbook, One-Year Filing Deadline, *supra* note 439, at 5. Note that the Asylum Division used to calculate the one-year period by counting the day of arrival as day one. However, following the Ninth Circuit's opinion in *Minasyan v. Mukasey*, 553 F.3d 1224 (9th Cir. 2009), the Asylum Division now calculates the day of arrival as day zero. In that opinion, the Ninth Circuit stated that the statute specifically provides that the one-year period commences after the date of arrival. The Asylum Division changed its calculation process in order to maintain a consistent national approach.

[979] AOBTC Workbook: One-Year Filing Deadline, *supra* note 439, at 5.

[980] 8 CFR §208.4(a)(2)(ii) (2014). *See Jorgji v. Mukasey*, 514 F.3d 53 (1st Cir. 2008) (finding that the applicant filed timely where she entered on Mar. 4, 2001, and provided documentary evidence that she filed on Monday, Mar. 4, 2002).

[981] INA §208(a)(2)(D); 8 USC §1158(a)(2)(D) (2012).

highly probable."[982] It falls somewhere between the preponderance of the evidence standard ("more likely than not" or greater than 50%) and the beyond a reasonable doubt standard used in criminal cases. Overall it is "the degree of evidence necessary to create a firm belief that the asserted fact is true."[983]

- **Practice Pointer**: See chapter 4 for a detailed discussion of the various standards of proof.

An asylum applicant is required to establish by "clear and convincing evidence" that he or she filed within one year, not that he or she entered on a particular date.[984] The applicant may provide either clear and convincing evidence that the date of last arrival was within the applicable one-year period or clear and convincing evidence that he or she was outside of the United States during the previous year immediately before the date of filing.[985]

In meeting the clear and convincing standard, an applicant may provide testimony, documentary evidence, or both. Testimony alone, when credible, may be sufficient to meet the clear and convincing standard.[986] Documentary evidence demonstrating timely filing may include passport entry stamps, I-94 cards or records, boarding passes or flight itineraries, leases, school or employment records from abroad within the past year, and witness affidavits from those with personal knowledge of the applicant's departure from abroad and those with personal knowledge of the applicant's arrival in the United States. An applicant's immigration documentation may also provide the requisite proof of a timely filing. According to at least one court, when an applicant's date of entry is "conceded," (*i.e.*, admitted and undisputed) at a master calendar hearing, the statute's requirement to present clear and convincing evidence does not apply.[987] Likewise, another court has held that the IJ's failure to consider the notice to appear which contained an entry date that could establish that the asylum application was filed within one year was a denial of due process.[988]

- **Practice Pointer**: Practitioners should assist their clients in avoiding the need to argue the exceptions to the one-year filing deadline. Compliance with the one-year filing deadline, rather than reliance on an exception, is

[982] *Matter of Patel*, 19 I&N Dec. 774 (BIA 1988).

[983] AOBTC Workbook: One-Year Filing Deadline, *supra* note 439, at 7.

[984] *Khunaverdiants v. Mukasey*, 548 F.3d 760, 765–66 (9th Cir. 2008) (finding that the BIA erred when it held that proof of the exact departure date was necessary to establish that the applicant filed within one year).

[985] AOBTC Workbook: One-Year Filing Deadline, *supra* note 439.

[986] 8 CFR §208.13(a) (2014); *Matter of S–M–J–*, 21 I&N Dec. 722 (BIA 1997). *See Singh v. Holder*, 649 F.3d 1161 (9th Cir. 2011) (stating that the corroboration requirements applied to the merits of the asylum claim rather than to the one-year filing deadline). *See also* AOBTC Workbook: One-Year Filing Deadline, *supra* note 439, at 7.

[987] *Hakopian v. Mukasey*, 551 F.3d 843, 845 (9th Cir. 2008).

[988] *Zheng v. Mukasey*, 552 F.3d 277, 286 (2d Cir. 2009).

the best and most practical way to avoid danger to clients' eligibility to apply for asylum.

All affirmative asylum applicants presenting applications before the asylum offices, even those who may not meet the requirements of the one-year filing deadline, are entitled to an asylum interview before an asylum officer and may not be denied a full asylum interview based solely on the one-year deadline.[989]

Even if an applicant did not file his or her application within one year of entry to the United States, he or she may still be able to demonstrate eligibility for asylum.[990] There are two exceptions to the one-year filing deadline: (1) if the applicant demonstrates "the existence of changed circumstances which materially affect the applicant's eligibility for asylum,"[991] and/or (2) if the applicant demonstrates "extraordinary circumstances relating to the delay in filing the application,"[992] the applicant may be excused for failing to timely file his or her application. In addition to demonstrating the presence of changed or extraordinary circumstances, the applicant must also show that he or she filed the application within a reasonable time of those circumstances.[993]

➢ **Practice Pointer**: Ignorance of the one-year filing deadline is not a valid excuse for failure to file an asylum application within one year of entry.

The standard of proof required to meet these exceptions is to the "satisfaction of the AG."[994] In other words, the applicant must demonstrate to the "satisfaction of the AG" that he or she qualifies for an exception to the one-year filing deadline.[995] The standard of "to the satisfaction of the [AG]," is a relatively low legal standard. The applicant is *not* required to establish that an exception applies beyond a reasonable

---

[989] AOBTC Workbook: One-Year Filing Deadline, *supra* note 439, at 4. *See infra* chapter 7 for a detailed discussion of the affirmative asylum procedures.

[990] INA §208(a)(2)(D); 8 CFR §208.4(a) (2014).

[991] *See* 8 CFR §§208.4(a)(4), 1208.4(a)(4) (2014).

[992] *See* 8 CFR §§208.4(a)(5), 1208.4(a)(5) (2014). An additional exception may exist for Salvadoran and Guatemalan ABC class members. *See* Settlement Provides Potential Relief for *ABC* Registrants Who Missed Asylum Filing Deadline, 79 INTERPRETER RELEASES 904 (June 10, 2002). Previously, in determining whether Guatemalan and Salvadoran nationals satisfied the registration requirement to receive ABC benefits under the settlement, USCIS required evidence of registration and the filing of an affirmative asylum application alone was not viewed as evidence satisfying the registration requirement. After the Ninth Circuit's findings in *Chaly-Garcia v. U.S.*, 508 F.3d 1201 (9th Cir. 2007), however, a Guatemalan or Salvadoran national who affirmatively filed an I-589 application on or after the date the court provisionally approved the settlement and prior to the conclusion of the designated registration period, is considered "registered;" *www.uscis.gov/sites/default/files/USCIS/Laws/Memoranda/Static_Files_Memoranda/Archives%201998-2008/2008/making_abc_registration_determinations_080508.pdf* (last visited Dec. 27, 2014).

[993] 8 CFR §§208.4(a)(4)–(5), 1208.4(a)(4)–(5) (2014).

[994] INA §208(a)(2)(B), (D); 8 CFR §208.4(a)(2)(i) (2014).

[995] 8 CFR §§208.4(a), 1208.4(a) (2014).

doubt, nor that an exception applies by clear and convincing evidence.[996] The applicant need only demonstrate that the exception applies through "credible evidence sufficiently persuasive to satisfy the Attorney General in the exercise of his reasonable judgment, considering the proof fairly and impartially."[997] The applicant need only demonstrate that "it is *reasonable* for the asylum officer to conclude that the exception applies under the circumstances."[998] The two exceptions to the one-year filing deadline are discussed below.

i. Changed Circumstances

One exception to the one-year filing deadline is where there are changed circumstances that materially affect an applicant's eligibility for asylum.[999] This exception embodies the principle of refugee *sur place*, meaning that some individuals become refugees after they have left their countries and been residing elsewhere.[1000] To show that the exception applies, there are three steps: (1) identify and show the existence of a changed circumstance; (2) demonstrate that the changed circumstance is material to the applicant's eligibility for asylum; and (3) establish that the application was filed within a reasonable period of time after the changed circumstance.[1001]

For step one, identifying the changed circumstance, the federal regulations list specific types of "changed circumstances" that may excuse a late filing of an asylum application.[1002] These may include, but are not limited to:

- Changes in conditions in the applicant's country of nationality or, if the applicant is stateless, country of last habitual residence;[1003]

---

[996] U.S. Citizenship & Immigration Servs., *Lesson: Asylum Eligibility Part IV: Burden of Proof, Standards of Proof, & Evidence* at 10, in Asylum Officer Basic Training Course Participant Workbook (Sept. 14, 2006) [hereinafter AOBTC Workbook, pt. IV], *available at www.uscis.gov/sites/default/files/USCIS/Humanitarian/Refugees%20%26%20Asylum/Asylum/AOBTC%20Lesson%20Plans/Burden-of-Proof-Standards-Proof-Evidence-31aug01.pdf.*

[997] *Matter of Bufalino*, 12 I&N Dec. 277, 282 (BIA 1967) (interpreting the "satisfaction of the Attorney General" standard).

[998] *Id.* (emphasis in original).

[999] INA §208(a)(2)(D).

[1000] UNHCR Handbook, *supra* note 33, ¶¶ 94–95. See *supra* pt. II.D.2.iii.g. for a detailed discussion of refugees *sur place*.

[1001] 8 CFR §§208.4(a), 1208.4(a) (2014).

[1002] *Id.*

[1003] *Vahora v. Holder*, 641 F.3d 1038 (9th Cir. 2011) (finding that the Gujarat riots in February 2002 were "India's worst religious violence in decades," leaving an estimated 2000 Muslims dead, and noting that the riots had directly impacted the applicant's family); *Fakhry v. Mukasey*, 524 F.3d 1057, 1063–64 (9th Cir. 2008) (finding relevant focus is on objective changes in country conditions, not on applicant's earlier intent or desire to seek asylum); *Mabasa v. Gonzales*, 455 F.3d 740 (7th Cir. 2006) (holding that the applicant did not show changed circumstances materially affecting his asylum eligibility because the political climate in Zimbabwe remained as oppressive as it was at the time of his

Continued

- Changes in applicable U.S. law;[1004]
- Changes in the applicant's personal circumstances while outside of the country of feared persecution that place the applicant at risk;[1005] or
- In the case of an applicant who had previously been included as a dependent in another applicant's pending asylum application, the loss of the spousal or parent-child relationship to the principal applicant through marriage, divorce, death, or attainment of age 21.[1006]

USCIS also addresses various types of changed circumstances,[1007] noting in its lesson plan that changed circumstances also may include:

- A change of government that is now hostile to the applicant's profession, such as journalism;
- The applicant's involvement in political organizing or other activities in the United States that are critical of the applicant's government;
- The applicant's conversion from one religion to another, or abandonment of religion altogether;
- Recent antagonism in the applicant's country toward the applicant's race or nationality; and
- Threats against the applicant's family members living abroad.[1008]

In 2007, the Ninth Circuit found that an Egyptian asylum applicant failed to establish changed personal circumstances after her arrival in the United States, finding that her past harassment in Egypt was on account of her political views, so her outspokenness in the United States was not actually a change in circumstances.[1009] Similarly, the Seventh Circuit found that an applicant from Zimbabwe failed to show changed circumstances, because the Mugabe government and oppressive climate in Zimbabwe were the same in 2006 as they were when the applicant arrived in the United States in 1999.[1010]

---

departure and the applicant's renewed political activities in the U.S. was the same activity that caused him to flee Zimbabwe in the first place).

[1004] 8 CFR §208.4(a)(4)(i)(B) (2014). *See, e.g., Zhu v. Gonzales*, 493 F.3d 588, 595 n.25 (5th Cir. 2007) (rejecting Zhu's argument that the change to the refugee definition in the United States to add individuals who have been forced to undergo coercive family planning procedures excused her delay in filing, because China's family planning laws existed as a basis for eligibility for asylum when Zhu arrived in the United States).

[1005] 8 CFR §208.4(a)(4)(i)(B) (2014).

[1006] 8 CFR §§208.4(a)(4)(i), 1208.4(a)(4)(i) (2014).

[1007] AOBTC Workbook, One-Year Filing Deadline, *supra* note 439, at 8–11.

[1008] *Id.* at 9–10.

[1009] *Ramadan v. Gonzales*, 479 F.3d 646, 657 (9th Cir. 2007) (en banc).

[1010] *Mabasa v. Gonzales*, 455 F.3d 740 (7th Cir. 2006).

In addition to establishing the fact that changed circumstances exist, the regulations also require that the applicant must demonstrate that the changes materially affect his or her eligibility for asylum. For example, in *Matter of A–M–*, the BIA found that the changes identified by the applicant — the bombing of a nightclub in Bali, Indonesia — were not material to his asylum eligibility because he was from a different island and of a different ethnicity and religion than the specific victims of the Bali bombing.[1011] The Ninth Circuit has provided a broad interpretation of what changed circumstances may be material to an asylum application, finding that the changed circumstances exception had been met for an Indian Muslim applicant after Gujarat riots destroying his home and farm and during which his brother disappeared.[1012]

Courts have held that an asylum applicant does not have to show that he or she was ineligible for asylum when he arrived in the United States before the changed circumstances exception may apply. For example, in *Mandebvu v. Holder*, the Sixth Circuit considered the applications of a husband and wife from Zimbabwe who actively criticized the Mugabe government and his ZANU-PF political party and entered the United States in 1999 and 2000 respectively after being threatened by ZANU-PF.[1013] The couple was served with Notices to Appear in August of 2007 and filed their applications for asylum in September of 2008, identifying the events surrounding the 2008 elections in Zimbabwe as changed circumstances materially affecting their eligibility for asylum.[1014] The IJ denied relief on the ground that the application was not timely, stating that an "incremental change" from poor country conditions to worse country conditions was insufficient to constitute changed circumstances because "it did not tip the scale such that respondents would suddenly be subject to persecution where they would not have been before."[1015] The BIA affirmed the IJ decision. However, the Sixth Circuit remanded the case, holding that applicants did not have to show that they were ineligible for asylum when they arrived in the United States; a changed condition that strengthened the applicants' already existing claim for asylum could be material and could be grounds for an exception to the one year filing deadline.[1016]

Similarly, in a 2004 decision by former Attorney General John Ashcroft in which he overturned a BIA summary affirmance of an IJ decision denying asylum to a Lebanese applicant, the AG relied on changed circumstances that had actually occurred a year or more after the applicant had applied for asylum.[1017] The applicant

---

1011 *Matter of A–M–*, 23 I&N Dec. 737 (BIA 2005).

1012 *Vahora v. Holder*, 641 F.3d 1038 (9th Cir. 2011).

1013 *Mandebvu v. Holder*, 755 F.3d 417 (6th Cir. 2014).

1014 *Id.* at 421–22.

1015 *Id.* at 424–26.

1016 *Id.*

1017 *See Matter of Marshi*, A26 980 386, at 7–8 (AG Feb. 13, 2004), *published on* AILA InfoNet at Doc. No. 04021390 (*posted* Feb. 13, 2004).

had entered the United States on a visitor's visa in 1986, but did not apply for asylum until 13 years later, in 1999. The changed circumstances were: (1) withdrawal of the Israeli Defense Forces from Lebanon in 2000; (2) the increased influence and autonomy of Hezbollah, and of the Syrian government and its proxies within Lebanon; and (3) the addition of Hezbollah, on Nov. 21, 2001, to the list of terrorist organizations covered by Executive Order No. 13224, which blocked access to its assets.[1018]

Prong three of the test for applying the changed circumstances exception to the one-year filing deadline is demonstrating that the applicant filed his or her application within a reasonable time of those material changed circumstances.[1019] For a full discussion of what is considered a "reasonable" amount of time, see Part iii below.

ii. Extraordinary Circumstances

The second exception to the one-year filing deadline is where extraordinary circumstances exist that directly relate to the applicant's delay in filing the application.[1020] The asylum regulations define "extraordinary circumstances" as "events or factors directly related to the failure to meet the one-year deadline."[1021] Such circumstances may excuse the failure to file within the one-year period as long as the applicant files the application "within a reasonable period given those circumstances."[1022] Therefore, like the changed circumstances exception, there are three steps to demonstrate that this exception applies: (1) identify and show that an extraordinary circumstance exists; (2) demonstrate that the extraordinary circumstance was directly related to the failure to timely file; and (3) establish that the application was filed within a reasonable period of time given the extraordinary circumstance.[1023]

The burden of proof is on the applicant to establish "to the satisfaction of the Attorney General" that the circumstances were "not intentionally created by the [applicant] through his or her own action or inaction, that those circumstances were directly related to the [applicant's] failure to file the application within the one-year period, and that the delay was reasonable under the circumstances."[1024] Under the regulations, "extraordinary circumstances" may include, but are not limited to:

[1018] *Id.*

[1019] 8 CFR §§208.4(a), 1208.4(a) (2014).

[1020] 8 CFR §§208.4(a)(5), 1208.4(a)(5) (2014).

[1021] 8 CFR §§208.4(a)(5), 1208.4(a)(5) (2014).

[1022] 8 CFR §§208.4(a)(5), 1208.4(a)(5) (2014).

[1023] 8 CFR §§208.4(a)(5), 1208.4(a)(5) (2014).

[1024] 8 CFR §§208.4(a)(5), 1208.4(a)(5) (2014).

- Serious illness or mental or physical disability, including any effects of persecution or violent harm suffered in the past, present, at least in part, during the one-year period after arrival;[1025]
- Legal disability (incapacity for the full enjoyment of ordinary legal rights, including minors and those mentally impaired) during the one-year period after arrival;[1026]
- Ineffective assistance of counsel (limited to attorneys or accredited representatives),[1027] provided that:
  - The applicant files a written affidavit setting forth in detail the agreement that was entered into with counsel with respect to the actions to be taken and what representations counsel did or did not make to the respondent in this regard;
  - The counsel whose integrity or competence is being impugned has been informed of the allegations leveled against him or her and given an opportunity to respond; and
  - The applicant indicates whether a complaint has been filed with appropriate disciplinary authorities with respect to any violation of counsel's ethical or legal responsibilities, and if not, why not;[1028]
- The applicant maintained Temporary Protected Status, lawful immigrant or nonimmigrant status, or was given parole, during at least part of the one-year period and until a reasonable period before the filing of the asylum application;[1029]
- The applicant filed an asylum application prior to the expiration of the one-year deadline, but that application was rejected by USCIS as not properly filed, was returned to the applicant for corrections, and was re-filed within a reasonable period thereafter;[1030] and
- The death or serious illness or incapacity of the applicant's legal representative or a member of the applicant's immediate family.[1031]

Unlike a changed circumstance, an extraordinary circumstance must occur during the period when it would have been timely for the applicant to file. This is because

[1025] 8 CFR §§208.4(a)(5)(i), 1208.4(a)(5)(i) (2014).

[1026] 8 CFR §§208.4(a)(5)(ii), 1208.4(a)(5)(ii) (2014).

[1027] *See, e.g., Viridiana v. Holder*, 646 F.3d 1230 (9th Cir. 2011).

[1028] 8 CFR §§208.4(a)(5)(iii), 1208.4(a)(5)(iii) (2014). *See Matter of Lozada*, 19 I&N Dec. 637 (BIA 1988).

[1029] 8 CFR §§208.4(a)(5)(iv), 1208.4(a)(5)(iv) (2014). *See Singh v. Holder*, 656 F.3d 1047 (9th Cir. 2011) (finding that applying for asylum less than three months after the applicant's last day of lawful nonimmigrant status was reasonable). *But see Al Ramahi v. Holder*, 725 F.3d 1133 (9th Cir. 2013) (finding that applying for asylum more than 15 months after the lapse of the applicants' lawful status was not reasonable).

[1030] 8 CFR §§208.4(a)(5)(v), 1208.4(a)(5)(v) (2014).

[1031] 8 CFR §§208.4(a)(5)(vi), 1208.4(a)(5)(vi) (2014).

the extraordinary circumstance must directly relate to the failure to timely file.[1032] If an extraordinary circumstance exists outside of the period of timely filing, that circumstance may still be considered when determining if the application was filed within a reasonable period of time of another changed or extraordinary circumstance.

In its precedent decision addressing "extraordinary circumstances," *Matter of Y–C–*, the BIA found that an applicant who entered the United States as an unaccompanied minor and who failed to file his application within one year of his arrival established that such failure was due to "extraordinary circumstances."[1033] The BIA set forth the following three-part test: the applicant (1) "must establish the existence or occurrence of the extraordinary circumstance;" (2) "must show that those circumstances directly relate to his failure to file the application within the 1-year period;" and (3) "must demonstrate that the delay in filing was reasonable under the circumstances."[1034] In finding that the applicant had met this test, the BIA noted that the applicant was 15 years old when he arrived in the United States as an unaccompanied minor, that he remained in the status of unaccompanied minor throughout the one-year period, that he was in legacy INS custody for one year, that five months after his release an IJ rejected his application for asylum, and that the application that was finally accepted by the IJ was filed within one year of his release from INS custody.[1035]

- **Practice Pointer**: Under the INA, as amended by the Trafficking Victims Protection Reauthorization Act of 2008 (TVPRA), the one-year filing deadline does not apply at all to "unaccompanied alien children," as defined by 6 USC §279(g).[1036] An unaccompanied alien child is a child under the age of 18 who has no parent or legal guardian in the United States who is able to provide care and physical custody.[1037] As of March 23, 2009, the effective date of the TVPRA, the one-year filing deadline analysis should be foregone for any unaccompanied alien child who is out of status, because it does not apply. The deadline is applicable to unaccompanied minors who are in lawful status because

---

[1032] *See, e.g., Vincent v. Holder*, 632 F.3d 351 (6th Cir. 2011) (stating that where the alien's marriage and his wife's death both occurred outside the one year, the extraordinary circumstances exception to the deadline could not be met); *Singh v. Holder*, 656 F.3d 1047, 1054–55 (9th Cir. 2011) (finding that the IJ confused the standard in requiring the applicant to demonstrate that the extraordinary circumstances were related to his reason for filing his asylum application, rather than related to his reason for his delay in filing the application).

[1033] *Matter of Y–C–*, 23 I&N Dec. 286 (BIA 2002).

[1034] *Id.* at 288.

[1035] *Id. See also El Himri v. Ashcroft*, 378 F.3d 932, 936 (9th Cir. 2004) (noting that the claim of a minor living with his parents was not time-barred). No unaccompanied minor would be subject to the one-year filing deadline today. *See* AOBTC Workbook, One-Year Filing Deadline, *supra* note 439, at 14; *see also* 8 CFR §208.4(a)(5)(ii) (2014).

[1036] INA §208(a)(2)(E); TVPRA, Pub. L. No. 110-457, §235(d)(7)(A).

[1037] 6 USC §279(g)(2) (2012).

the definition of "unaccompanied alien child" in the TVPRA includes the element of not having lawful status.[1038]

- **Practice Pointer**: Minors are generally dependent on adults for their care and cannot be expected to navigate legal systems in the same way as adults. A minor applicant is defined as someone under the age of 18 at the time of filing. The Asylum Division's policy is to find that all minors, whether accompanied or unaccompanied, have legal disability that constitutes an extraordinary circumstance.[1039] See chapter 10 for a detailed discussion of the legal standards and procedures for children.

For cases involving ineffective assistance of counsel, it is not the adjudicator's duty to evaluate whether the applicant received poor counsel, but rather, whether the regulatory elements have been fulfilled and whether the counsel's actions were directly related to the delay in filing.[1040]

The purpose of an exception for applicants who have maintained a lawful non-immigrant or immigrant status is to avoid forcing a premature application for asylum in cases where an individual believes that the circumstances in his or her country may improve.[1041] For example, an individual in the United States on an F-1 student visa may expect that the political situation in the country of feared persecution will change by the time he or she completes school. Such an individual may wish to avoid filing for asylum until it is absolutely necessary to do so.

- **Practice Pointer**: An individual may appear to have maintained a lawful immigration status, however, an admission on fraudulent documents or violation of a lawful status after entry may impact whether and when the extraordinary circumstance exception applies. For example, although an F-1 student may be admitted for "duration of status," the relevant date is the date he or she stopped attending school. The student must apply for asylum within a reasonable time of that date when he or she violated lawful status. However, knowledge of the violation of status is relevant. If the applicant did not know that he or she had violated status and believed he or she was maintaining a lawful status, that may extend the period of time before which he or she is expected to have filed an asylum application.

With regard to maintaining lawful immigrant or nonimmigrant status prior to filing the asylum application, legacy INS took the position that an individual should file an asylum application as soon as possible after the expiration of his or her valid status. It further maintained that waiting six months was "clearly" not reasonable and

[1038] INA §208(a)(2)(E); TVPRA, Pub. L. No. 110-457, §235(d)(7)(A).

[1039] AOBTC Workbook, One-Year Filing Deadline, *supra* note 439, at 15.

[1040] 8 CFR §292.3(a) (2014); *Matter of Lozada*, 19 I&N Dec. 637 (BIA 1988).

[1041] *See* 65 Fed. Reg. 76121, 76123, *supra* note 241.

that shorter periods of time should be considered on a case-by-case basis.[1042] The Ninth Circuit has held that the applicant's 364-day wait after his nonimmigrant status expired was not a reasonable period of time where there was no explanation for the delay.[1043] The Ninth Circuit, however, has criticized the BIA and IJ for not conducting the proper analysis in a case where an individual filed just over six months after his lawful status expired.[1044] The court noted that the reason given for the delay, gathering supporting documents for the claim, was not a *per se* invalid reason.[1045]

Mental health issues also have been recognized by the courts as an extraordinary circumstance directly related to the delay in filing. For example, the First Circuit affirmed the IJ's decision that a woman from Rwanda with post-traumatic stress disorder had an "extraordinary circumstance" for failing to file her asylum application in a timely fashion.[1046] Similarly, in an unpublished decision, the BIA found that a woman from the Gambia who had been subjected to female genital mutilation at 15 years of age and who suffered abuse at the hands of her spouse met the extraordinary circumstances exception due to her depression and post-traumatic stress disorder.[1047]

If an individual's initial attempt to file his or her application was timely and within the one-year period but there was a defect in the filing, that also may establish an extraordinary circumstance exception to the one-year filing deadline, as long as the defect was corrected and the application was re-filed within a reasonable period of time.[1048]

Other possible extraordinary circumstances are addressed in the USCIS's lesson plan for AOs on the one-year filing deadline, which notes that extraordinary circumstances may include "severe family or spousal opposition, extreme isolation within a refugee community, profound language barriers, or profound difficulties in cultural acclimatization."[1049]

[1042] *See id.*; *see also* AOBTC Workbook, One-Year Filing Deadline, *supra* note 439, at 18–20 (noting that delayed awareness, illness, and difficulty in obtaining legal assistance are factors in determining reasonableness).

[1043] *Husyev v. Mukasey*, 528 F.3d 1172, 1181 (9th Cir. 2008).

[1044] *Wakkary v. Holder*, 558 F.3d 1049, 1058–59 (9th Cir. 2009).

[1045] *Id.*

[1046] *Mukamusoni v. Ashcroft*, 390 F.3d 110, 117 (1st Cir. 2004)

[1047] *Matter of [name not provided]*, [*file no. redacted*] (BIA Aug. 8, 2007) (noting that applicant was currently undergoing treatment for depression and post-traumatic stress disorder), *available at http://bibdaily.com/pdfs/GambiaFGMexcep. circ. BIA8-8-06.pdf.*

[1048] 8 CFR §208.4(a)(6)(v) (2014).

[1049] AOBTC Workbook, One-Year Filing Deadline, *supra* note 439, at 7. *But see Culpatan v. Holder*, 612 F.3d 1088 (9th Cir. 2010) (finding that individually and in combination, it was not extraordinary circumstances where the applicant did not speak English, was detained for two months, and had his case transferred after he moved from Arizona to California); *Mutuku v. Holder*, 600 F.3d 1210, 1212

Continued

Like the changed circumstances exception, prong three of the test for applying the extraordinary circumstances exception to the one-year filing deadline is demonstrating that the applicant filed his or her application within a reasonable time of those extraordinary circumstances related to the delay in filing.[1050] For a full discussion of what is considered a "reasonable" amount of time, see Part iii below.

iii. Filing Within a Reasonable Period of Time

Once an applicant demonstrates the existence of a changed circumstance that materially affects his or her eligibility for asylum or an extraordinary circumstance directly related to his or her delay in filing the application, the applicant is then tasked with showing that he or she filed the application within a reasonable period of time of the changed or extraordinary circumstance.[1051] This analysis requires identifying the date of the changed or extraordinary circumstance and the amount of time that elapsed between that date and the date the applicant filed his or her application.[1052] What constitutes a reasonable period of time following changed or extraordinary circumstances is a fact-specific inquiry to be evaluated on a case-by-case basis. The BIA has strongly suggested that waiting six months or longer would not be reasonable.[1053]

Some factors that may impact what is reasonable may include: "[a]n applicant's education and level of sophistication, the amount of time it takes to obtain legal assistance, any effects of persecution and/or illness, when the applicant became aware of the … circumstance, and any other relevant factors."[1054] Additionally, if the applicant can establish that he or she did not become aware of the changed or extraordinary circumstances until after they occurred, such delayed awareness must be taken into account in determining what constitutes a "reasonable period."[1055]

(9th Cir. 2010) (finding that hoping conditions would change in Kenya did not constitute extraordinary circumstances). For an excellent overview of the one-year deadline provision, *see* Michele Pistone and Philip Schrag, *The New Asylum Rule: Improved but Still Unfair*, 16 GEO. IMMIGR. L.J. 1 (2001).

[1050] 8 CFR §§208.4(a), 1208.4(a) (2014).

[1051] 8 CFR §§208.4(a)(4)(ii), 1208.4(a)(4)(ii) (2014).

[1052] *See, e.g., Shi Jie Ge v. Holder*, 588 F.3d 90, 94–95 (2d Cir. 2009) (finding that the BIA erred in focusing on the date the applicant joined the political party instead of the date his activities were revealed to the Chinese government, which is what had prompted his asylum claim).

[1053] *Matter of T–M–H– & S–W–C–*, 25 I&N Dec. 193, 194 (BIA 2010); *Matter of A–T–*, 25 I&N Dec. 4, 6 (BIA 2009).

[1054] AOBTC Workbook, One-Year Filing Deadline, *supra* note 439, at 22. *See, e.g., Taslimi v. Holder*, 590 F.3d 981 (9th Cir. 2010) (finding that the applicant applied for asylum within a reasonable period of time following her religious conversation, because her conversion was a process that began on the date of her conversion ceremony, but took some time for her to incorporate into her life).

[1055] 8 CFR §§208.4(a)(4)(ii), 1208.4(a)(4)(ii) (2014); *see also Kanivets v. Riley*, 320 F. Supp. 2d 297, 300 (E.D. Pa. 2004) (remanding one-year deadline issue because IJ failed to consider arguments regarding changed circumstances and delayed awareness).

Moreover, circumstances that are not extraordinary circumstances related directly to the delay in filing since they did not occur within the one-year period may be considered in determining whether the application was filed within a reasonable time of changed or extraordinary circumstances.[1056] For example, if an applicant's mother was in the hospital after the one-year period had already passed, that circumstance would not be an extraordinary circumstance related to the delay in filing. However, it may be relevant to the determination whether the applicant filed her application within a reasonable period of time of another circumstance. The AOBTC encourages asylum officers to "give applicants the benefit of the doubt in evaluating what constitutes a reasonable time in which to file."[1057]

3. *Previous Asylum Denial*

An individual is not eligible to apply for asylum if he or she "has previously applied for asylum and had such application denied."[1058] This ineligibility ground does not apply to individuals seeking withholding of removal. For this ineligibility ground to apply in the asylum context, however, the previous asylum application must have been denied by an IJ or the BIA.[1059] A previous denial by an asylum officer is not a bar to applying for asylum.[1060] Moreover, an application may be considered, despite a previous denial by an IJ or the BIA, if the applicant "demonstrates to the satisfaction of the [AG] ... the existence of changed circumstances which materially affect the applicant's eligibility for asylum."[1061]

- **Practice Pointer**: If an asylum-seeker has an application that was previously denied by an IJ or the BIA and he or she wishes to file a new application based on the existence of changed circumstances, he or she would first need to file a motion to reopen before the IJ or BIA (whichever body made the final decision denying the initial asylum claim). The motion should explain: the changed circumstances, why those circumstances are material to the applicant's eligibility for relief, and why those new facts were not available and could not have been

---

[1056] *See, e.g.*, *Wakkary v. Holder*, 558 F.3d 1049 (9th Cir. 2009) (finding that taking time to gather identity documents and supporting documents the applicant considered vital to his claim is a valid reason for the delay in filing his application). *But see, e.g.*, *Al Ramahi v. Holder*, 725 F.3d 1133 (9th Cir., 2013) (holding that a 15-month delay was not reasonable where the alleged delay was due to ineffective assistance of counsel and the inability to file after issuance of the NTA).

[1057] *Id.*

[1058] INA §§208(a)(2)(C)–(D); 8 USC §1158(a)(2)(C)–(D) (2012).

[1059] 8 CFR §§208.4(a)(3), 1208.4(a)(3) (2014).

[1060] *See* Joseph E. Langlois, Memorandum to Asylum Office Directors, *Procedures for Implementing the One-Year Filing Deadline and Processing Cases Previously Denied by EOIR*, Washington, D.C. (Jan. 4, 2002).

[1061] INA §208(a)(2)(D); 8 USC §1158(a)(2)(D) (2012).

discovered or presented at an earlier stage in the proceedings.[1062] The motion should be accompanied by: (1) a copy of the IJ or BIA's decision; (2) the material evidence that could not have been discovered or presented before; (3) a complete copy of the new application for relief; and (4) any supporting documentation with table of contents.[1063] Once the applicant's proceedings are reopened, he or she may then apply for relief before the BIA or the Immigration Court based on those changed circumstances.[1064] See Chapter 11 for a detailed discussion of motions to reopen based on changed circumstances.

According to USCIS, in order to meet the "to the satisfaction of the [AG]" standard of proof, the applicant is *not* required to establish changed circumstances "beyond a reasonable doubt" or by "clear and convincing evidence."[1065] The applicant need only demonstrate that it is reasonable for the adjudicator to conclude that the exception applies under the circumstances by presenting "credible evidence sufficiently persuasive to satisfy the Attorney General in the exercise of his reasonable judgment, considering the proof fairly and impartially."[1066]

The asylum regulations provide that such changed circumstances may include, but are not limited to:

- Changes in conditions in the applicant's country of nationality or, if the applicant is stateless, country of last habitual residence;
- Changes in the applicant's circumstances that materially affect the applicant's eligibility for asylum, including changes in applicable U.S. law and activities the applicant becomes involved in outside of the country of feared persecution that place the applicant at risk; and
- In the case of an applicant who had previously been included as a dependent in another applicant's pending asylum application, the loss of the spousal or parent-child relationship to the principal applicant through marriage, divorce, death, or attainment of age 21.[1067]

[1062] 8 CFR §§1003.23(b)(3)–(4) (2014); U.S. Dep't of Justice, *Immigration Court Practice Manual* §§5.7(b)(ii), (e)(i) (hereinafter ICPM], *available at www.justice.gov/eoir/vll/OCIJPracManual/ocij_page1.htm*.

[1063] ICPM, *supra* note 1061, at §§3.3(c)(i)(D), 5.7(b)(ii).

[1064] *See* ch. 11 for a detailed discussion of motions to reopen.

[1065] AOBTC Workbook, pt. IV, *supra* note 996, at 14–15.

[1066] *Id.* (emphasis in original). See chapter 4 for a detailed discussion of the "to the satisfaction of the Attorney General" standard of proof.

[1067] 8 CFR §§208.4(a)(4)(i), 1208.4(a)(4)(i) (2014). Note, however, that if the applicant is initiating a new claim by filing a motion to reopen beyond the 90-day period for filing such motions, he or she must demonstrate "changed circumstances arising in the country of nationality or in the country to which deportation has been ordered, if such evidence is material and was not available and could not have been discovered or presented at the previous hearing." 8 CFR §1003.2(c)(3)(ii) (2014); *see also Matter of J–J–*, 21 I&N Dec. 976 (BIA 1997). The changed circumstances regulations for motions to

Continued

The regulations require that the applicant must file the new application for asylum within a "reasonable period" given those changed circumstances.[1068] If the applicant can establish that he or she did not become aware of the changed circumstances until after they occurred, such delayed awareness must be taken into account in determining what constitutes a "reasonable period."[1069]

B. Statutory Bars to Asylum and Withholding of Removal

In addition to these three ineligibility grounds for asylum, there are six statutory bars that prevent an applicant from being granted asylum, even if he or she may qualify as a "refugee" within the meaning of INA §101(a)(42)(A).[1070] These include: (1) if the applicant ordered, incited, assisted or otherwise participated in the persecution of others;[1071] (2) if the applicant has been convicted by a final judgment of a particularly serious crime in the United States, and thus constitutes a danger to the community;[1072] (3) if there are serious reasons for believing that the applicant has committed a serious nonpolitical crime outside of the United States prior to his or her arrival;[1073] (4) if there are reasonable grounds for regarding the alien as a danger to the security of the United States;[1074] (5) if the applicant meet the definition of a terrorist, has participated in terrorist activity, or has given material support to a terrorist organization;[1075] and (6) if the applicant was firmly resettled in another country prior to his or her arrival in the United States.[1076]

---

reopen do not recognize changes in the applicant's personal circumstances or changes in U.S. law. *See* 8 CFR §1003.2(c)(3)(ii) (2014). See also *infra* chapter 11 for a detailed discussion of motions to reopen.

[1068] 8 CFR §§208.4(a)(4)(ii), 1208.4(a)(4)(ii) (2014).

[1069] 8 CFR §§208.4(a)(4)(ii), 1208.4(a)(4)(ii) (2014).

[1070] INA §§208(b)(2)(A)–(B).

[1071] INA §§101(a)(42)(B), 208(b)(2)(A)(i).

[1072] INA §208(b)(2)(A)(ii). If a conviction is an aggravated felony for which there is an aggregate term of imprisonment for five years, it is a conviction for a particularly serious crime and automatically bars a grant of asylum. *See Matter of B–*, 20 I&N Dec. 427 (BIA 1991).

[1073] INA §208(b)(2)(A)(iii).

[1074] INA §208(b)(2)(A)(iv).

[1075] INA §§212(a)(3)(B)(i)(I)–(IV), (VI), 237(a)(4)(B). This bar is waivable by DHS under certain circumstances, including for persons who provided material support to terrorist organizations under duress. *See* INA §212(d)(3)(B)(i); *See generally* Michael Chertoff Memorandum on Exercise of Authority Under Sec. 212(d)(3)(B)(i) of the INA, Washington, DC [hereinafter Chertoff Memo. on Exercise of Authority Under INA §212(d)(3)(B)(i)] (Apr. 27, 2007), *available at www.uscis.gov/sites/default/files/USCIS/Laws/TRIG/2.26%20excersise%20of%20authority.pdf.*

[1076] 8 CFR §§208.13(c)(2)(i)(B), 208.15 (2014). An applicant is deemed firmly resettled if he or she entered the country with, or while in the country received, an offer of permanent resident status, citizenship, or other type of permanent status. *See* 8 CFR §§208.15, 1208.15 (2014). The government has the burden of proving firm resettlement, and the applicant may rebut firm resettlement by demonstrating an exception under 8 CFR §§208.15(a)–(b) (2014).

The first four of these bars — persecution of others, particularly serious crime, serious nonpolitical crime, and danger to the security of the United States — also bar an individual from being granted withholding of removal under INA §241(b)(3).[1077] However, the terrorist activity and firm resettlement bars to asylum do not apply to withholding of removal.

> ➢ **Practice Pointer**: Although the terrorist activity bar does not explicitly apply to withholding of removal, an individual described under INA §237(a)(4)(B) (individuals deportable for terrorist activities described in INA §§212(a)(3)(B) and 212(a)(3)(F)) "shall be considered an alien with respect to whom there are reasonable grounds for regarding as a danger to the security of the United States" and is barred from withholding of removal.[1078] Thus, applicants who are barred from asylum under the terrorist activity bar are likely also barred from withholding of removal.

Although the terrorist activity and firm resettlement bars do not apply to withholding of removal, there are two separate bars to withholding of removal that do not apply to asylum. These include: (1) if the applicant participated in Nazi persecution; and (2) if the applicant participated in genocide, torture, or extrajudicial killing.[1079]

> ➢ **Practice Pointer**: While these two bars apply only to withholding of removal, it is reasonable to conclude that such individuals also would be denied asylum as a matter of discretion or would be subject to other bars such as the serious nonpolitical crime bar.

This section discusses each of the statutory bars to asylum and withholding of removal, beginning with the four bars that apply to both asylum and withholding of removal.

1. *Persecution of Others*

An individual is barred from both asylum and withholding of removal if he or she "ordered, incited, assisted, or otherwise participated in the persecution of any person on account of race, religion, nationality, membership in a particular social group, or political opinion."[1080] For purposes of barring asylum and withholding of removal under the "persecutor bar," it must be demonstrated that the applicant's motivation

---

[1077] *See* INA §§241(b)(3)(B)(i)–(iv). *See also Matter of N–A–M–*, 24 I&N Dec. 336 (BIA 2007) (addressing the particularly serious crime bar to withholding of removal); *Matter of A–H–*, 23 I&N Dec. 774 (AG 2005) (addressing the persecution of others and danger to the security of the U.S. bars to withholding of removal); *Matter of McMullen*, 19 I&N Dec. 90 (BIA 1984) (addressing the serious nonpolitical crime bar to withholding of removal).

[1078] INA §241(b)(3)(B).

[1079] INA §241(b)(3)(B); 8 CFR §§208.16(d)(2), 1208.16(d)(2) (2014). *See* INA §212(a)(3)(E) (setting forth the standards for Nazi persecution, genocide, torture, and extrajudicial killing).

[1080] INA §§208(b)(2)(A)(i), 241(b)(3)(B)(i); 8 USC §§1158(b)(2)(A)(i), 1231(b)(3)(B)(i) (2012).

for the persecutory act was the victim's race, religion, nationality, membership in a particular social group, or political opinion.

The most obvious application of the persecutor bar is when the applicant has directly participated in a persecutory act on account of one of the protected grounds and admitted to those actions. For example, in *Nguyen v. Holder*, a member of the South Vietnamese Army admitted, "[I]t was our purpose and mission to hunt down the communists and interrogate them with methods that are considered to be torture."[1081] This applicant was denied asylum under the persecutor bar.

Most cases, however, do not involve such clear determinations that the persecutor bar applies. The AG has held that participation in persecution does not require "direct personal involvement in the acts of persecution."[1082] In fact, the AG found that "in certain circumstances statements of encouragement alone can suffice."[1083] For these reasons, the persecutor bar has generated a significant amount of case law by the BIA, the U.S. circuit courts of appeals, and the U.S. Supreme Court. These courts have considered what types of acts require exclusion from asylum eligibility under the persecutor bar beyond direct, knowing actions against victims on account of their race, religion, nationality, membership in a particular social group, or political opinion.

Specifically, courts have considered whether direct involvement under coercion or duress still merits being barred from asylum eligibility, whether individuals should be barred from asylum eligibility even if their involvement was peripheral to the persecution, and whether knowledge of the persecutory act alone without any actual participation is enough to bar asylum eligibility. In answering these questions, the courts have developed two general approaches — the objective effects approach and a more contextual, totality-of-the-circumstances approach. In general, there are three areas where courts continually find that the persecutor bar has been triggered: (1) when the applicant directly committed the persecutory acts, whether or not under duress; (2) when the applicant committed acts peripheral but necessary to the persecution; and (3) when the applicant has prior or contemporaneous knowledge that his or her actions will result in the persecution of others.[1084]

[1081] *Nguyen v. Holder*, 336 F. App'x 680 (9th Cir. 2009) Br. For Pet'r, at *11, 2005 WL 3526956 (C.A.9). *See also Ahmed v. Gonzales*, 221 F. Appx. 595, 596 (9th Cir. 2007) (finding that the applicant's "own account of his actions established that he assisted or otherwise participated in the persecution of persons on account of their political opinion").

[1082] *Matter of A–H–*, 23 I&N Dec. 774, 784–45 (AG 2005).

[1083] *Id.* (where the applicant was found to have participated in the persecution of others because he was instrumental in creating and sustaining ties between the armed group and the political movement, was aware of the armed group's actions, used his position of influence to encourage those atrocities, made statements condoning the persecution without disassociating himself from the acts, and appeared to have made statements that led to an increase in the persecution).

[1084] *See* Martin Forneret, *Pulling the Trigger: An Analysis of Circuit Court Review of the 'Persecutor Bar'*, 113 COLUM. L. REV. 1007–1050 (2013) (containing a great discussion of the persecutor bar and where courts should go after *Negusie v. Holder*, 555 U.S. 511 (2009)).

i. *Coercion or Duress*

Many asylum applicants have been barred from asylum eligibility for persecutory acts against others that were committed under direct threat of death or physical harm. For nearly 25 years, the BIA held that voluntariness and duress were extraneous to the analysis of whether an individual had engaged in the persecution of others, finding instead that the objective effect of the individual's actions was controlling.[1085] This is commonly referred to as the "*Fedorenko* Rule" or the "objective effect test." In so holding, the BIA relied on the U.S. Supreme Court's decision in *Fedorenko v. United States*, which addressed the persecutor bar in the context of the Displaced Persons Act and held that "whether an alien is compelled to assist in persecution is immaterial for persecutor-bar purposes."[1086]

Following the BIA's decision in *Matter of Laipenieks*, the immigration courts, the BIA, and several U.S. Circuit Courts of Appeals relied upon the BIA's reasoning to deny asylum and withholding of removal to individuals implicated in the persecution of others, even if their acts were not willful or voluntary.[1087] These courts have applied a purely textual analysis and reasoned that if Congress wanted courts to consider the applicant's intent or motivations, it could have provided that exception directly in the text of the statute.[1088]

The objective effect test has been called into question most, perhaps, when the applicant only assisted or participated in the persecution out of coercion or duress. Whether it is fair to bar an asylum applicant from protection when he or she was forced into persecutory acts by persecutors is disputable. Yet, courts have continued to stand by the objective effect test, maintaining that it is the actual resulting persecution that matters, not the intent of the applicant. For example, the Fifth Circuit in *Bah v. Ashcroft* found that even though the applicant was under threat of torture or death when the alleged persecutory acts were committed, his actions still triggered the persecutor bar.[1089] The applicant, a native and citizen of Sierra Leone, was forced to join the Revolutionary United Front (RUF) after witnessing the RUF kill his father and sister and being given an ultimatum — join the group or be killed. As a member of the RUF, Bah admitted that he had "murdered a female villager, and he had chopped off the limbs and heads of noncombatants."[1090] The Fifth Circuit rejected the

[1085] *Matter of Laipenieks*, 18 I&N Dec. 433 (1983) (interpreting former INA §212(a)(3)(E)(i) and stating that "an alien's motivation and intent are irrelevant to the issue of whether he 'assisted' in persecution . . . [I]t is the objective effect of an alien's actions which is controlling."). The BIA reiterated its approach to the persecutor bar in *Matter of Fedorenko*, 19 I&N Dec. 57 (BIA 1984) and *Matter of Rodriguez-Majano*, 19 I&N Dec. 811 (BIA 1988).

[1086] *Fedorenko v. United States,* 449 U.S. 490 (1981).

[1087] *Matter of Rodriguez-Majano*, 19 I&N Dec. 811 (BIA 1988); *Matter of Fedorenko*, 19 I&N Dec. 57 (BIA 1984).

[1088] *See, e.g., Bah v. Ashcroft*, 341 F.3d 348, 351 (5th Cir. 2003).

[1089] *Bah v. Ashcroft*, 341 F.3d 348, 349 (5th Cir. 2003).

[1090] *Id.* at 351.

applicant's argument that, given his forced recruitment, "he did not engage in political persecution because he did not share the RUF's intent of political persecution."[1091] Rather, he acted out of fear for his life. The Fifth Circuit reasoned that the applicant's "personal motivation is not relevant" because the INA did not explicitly provide a duress exception.[1092]

- **Practice Pointer**: Arguably, the Fifth Circuit erred in this analysis by misapplying the nexus test in the context of the persecutor bar. In determining whether the applicant was barred from asylum eligibility under the persecutor bar, the Fifth Circuit should have considered that he was not acting on account of his victims' political opinions, but rather, out of fear for his own life. Does it make sense for the court to use textual analysis to state that there is no duress exception in the text of the statute, but then ignore the nexus requirement that is in the plain text of the statute?

In articulating the opposing school of thought — the contextual approach — the Eighth Circuit in *Hernandez v. Reno* did consider the personal motivations and voluntariness of the applicant's actions as a forced member of the Organization for People in Arms (ORPA) in Guatemala. The Eighth Circuit stated that Courts "should engage in a particularized evaluation in order to determine whether an individual's behavior was culpable to such a degree that he could be fairly deemed to have assisted or participated in persecution."[1093] The court found that the BIA had erred in not evaluating all pertinent evidence to determine whether the applicant had engaged in the persecution of others when he participated in the killing of suspected government informants. According to the court, the BIA failed to consider the involuntariness of the applicant's involvement with the guerilla group, the death threats he received, the fact that he shared no persecutory motives with the guerrillas, that he expressed his disagreement to his commander, and that he fled at the first available opportunity.[1094] Although the case was remanded, the court concluded that, based on the record, the applicant "may be seen to have met his burden of proving that he did not assist or participate in the persecution of others."[1095] Rather than objectively considering the persecutory acts in a narrow textual analysis of the statute, the Eighth Circuit looked to the subjective level of culpability based on the

---

[1091] *Id.*

[1092] *Id. See also Fedorenko v. United States*, 449 U.S. 490, 512 (1981) ("Under traditional principles of statutory construction, the deliberate omission of the word 'voluntary' . . . compels the conclusion that the statute made *all* those who assisted in the persecution of civilians ineligible for visas.").

[1093] *Hernandez v. Reno*, 258 F.3d 806, 815 (8th Cir. 2001) (finding that the BIA "should have examined all aspects of Hernandez's testimony when determining whether his conduct constituted assistance in persecution" and distinguishing *Fedorenko).*

[1094] *Id.* at 814.

[1095] *Id.* at 815.

personal motivations and intent of the applicant in committing the acts.[1096] Essentially, the court interpreted the nexus requirement in the text of the persecutor bar as evidence of an implicit duress exception.[1097]

The Ninth Circuit also has found that "individual accountability must be established" in *Vukmirovic v. Ashcroft*, a case where a Bosnian Serb joined an anticommunist Serbian group formed to defend his town from invading Bosnian Croats. In this context, the applicant had physically harmed people with sticks and knives in clashes with Croats.[1098] The court stated that "holding that acts of true self-defense qualify as persecution would run afoul of the 'on account of' requirement in the provision. It would also be contrary to the purpose of the statute."[1099] Like the Eighth Circuit, the Ninth Circuit relied upon the textual "on account of language" in reading an implicit exception into the persecutor bar for those whose motives were not on account of one of the five protected grounds.

Later, the Ninth Circuit utilized a totality of the circumstances test in interpreting whether the persecutor bar applies.[1100] In *Miranda-Alvarado v. Gonzales*, the Ninth Circuit held that, in determining whether an applicant engaged in the persecution of others, an adjudicator must conduct a particularized evaluation of both personal involvement and purposeful assistance in order to assess culpability.[1101] The court upheld the denial of asylum and withholding of removal for a Peruvian interpreter who provided Quechua interpretation for the Peruvian military while the military tortured suspected members of the Shining Path. The court reasoned that the applicant's actions went beyond mere membership because he was a regular part of the interrogation teams, and without him, the interrogation could not proceed.[1102]

After this circuit split had developed, the United States Supreme Court considered whether there is a duress exception to the persecutor bar and specifically addressed the validity of the objective effect test. In 2009, in *Negusie v. Holder*, the U.S. Supreme Court addressed the persecutor bar in the context of the Immigration and Nationality Act and struck down the BIA's longstanding interpretation.[1103] The BIA,

---

[1096] *Id.*

[1097] *Id.*

[1098] *Vukmirovic v. Ashcroft*, 362 F.3d 1247, 1252 (9th Cir. 2004) (stating that the court "agree[s] with the Eighth Circuit, that 'courts should engage in a particularized evaluation' to determine culpability") (quoting *Hernandez v. Reno*, 258 F.3d 806, 813 (8th Cir. 2001)).

[1099] *Id.*

[1100] *See, e.g.*, *Mendoza-Lopez v. Gonzales*, 205 F. Appx. 630, 631 (9th Cir. 2006) (denying asylum under the persecutor bar to a man who had participated in the shooting of a civilian family and stood guard while civilians were tortured, even though the applicant initially joined the Guatemalan army out of duress, stating that the applicant had remained in the army beyond the required enlistment period, received a good salary, and was promoted).

[1101] *Miranda-Alvarado v. Gonzales*, 449 F.3d 915, 927 (9th Cir. 2006).

[1102] *Id.* at 928.

[1103] *Negusie v. Holder*, 555 U.S. 511 (2009).

like the Fifth Circuit, had relied on *Fedorenko* and the objective effect test in declaring that "[t]he fact that [Negusie] was compelled to participate as a camp guard, and may not have actively tortured or mistreated anyone, is immaterial."[1104] Negusie challenged this position, arguing that coercion and voluntariness do matter when applying the persecutor bar and that it was error by the BIA not to consider his motivation and intent.

The Supreme Court found that the BIA had erred in "adopting wholesale" the reasoning of *Fedorenko*, which addressed the Displaced Persons Act (DPA), rather than exercising its "interpretive authority" in considering the persecutor bar in the context of the INA, which was the statute at issue in *Negusie.*[1105] The Court noted important differences between the DPA and the INA in explaining why *Fedorenko* and its objective effect test does not dictate how the BIA ought to apply the persecutor bar in the context of the INA.[1106] Rather than assuming that the *Fedorenko* objective effect test, which addressed a different statute for a different purpose, was controlling, the BIA should have determined whether its conclusion that the persecutor bar admits no exception for involuntary or coerced conduct was reasonable in the context of the INA.[1107]

The Court ultimately found that the INA is ambiguous regarding whether coercion or duress is relevant in determining whether the persecutor bar applies, and thus, remanded the case so the BIA could "exercise[] its *Chevron* discretion to interpret the statute in question."[1108] To date, the BIA has not answered this question. On remand, it is possible that the BIA will again conclude that motive and intent are irrelevant to the application of the persecutor bar. However, it is also possible that the BIA will use a more contextual approach and interpret the persecutor bar as including an exception for coerced or involuntary acts. Such an interpretation by the BIA would clarify that many groups of people — child soldiers, individuals who held government positions during brutal regimes, and people forced to engage in violent acts during their country's civil wars, among others — may be eligible for asylum despite their alleged persecutory acts.

- **Practice Pointer**: Until the BIA decides *Negusie* on remand, practitioners should continue to argue that even though the term "duress" is absent from the statute, a duress exception is implicit in the textual "on account of" nexus text of the statute, which requires courts

[1104] *Id.* at 511.

[1105] *Id.* at 521.

[1106] *Id.* at 511–12. For an interesting discussion of the *Negusie* case, *see* Thomas Ragland, *Supreme Court Strikes Down Long-Standing BIA Interpretation of 'Persecutor Bar'*, ABA Immigr. Litigation, *available at http://apps.americanbar.org/litigation/committees/immigration/articles/0309_ragland.html* (last visited June 29, 2014).

[1107] *Negusie*, at 521.

[1108] *Id.* at 511. *See also Chevron U.S.A., Inc. v. Natural Resources Defense Council, Inc., supra* note 62.

to consider the motives of the applicant. The motives of the persecutor matter when considering the nexus requirement for asylum eligibility, so why shouldn't the motives of the applicant matter when considering the nexus requirement for the persecutor bar?

ii. Peripheral Involvement

The objective effect test of *Fedorenko* versus the contextual approach has continued to develop throughout another line of cases addressing asylum applicants who did not directly participate in persecutory acts, but had some kind of peripheral involvement in the persecution. In this line of cases, courts have addressed whether direct participation in the chain of events leading to persecution, witnessing and physical presence during the persecutory acts, and mere membership in a persecutory group are sufficient to trigger the persecutor bar.

a. Chain of Events

In "chain of events" cases, the majority of courts have found that in order for the applicant's action to trigger the persecutor bar, the action must have been a causal factor, even minimally, in the ultimate persecutory act. For example, a line of cases has developed in the Second Circuit addressing whether participating in chains of events leading to forced abortions in China triggers the persecutor bar.[1109] Beyond actually carrying out the procedure — which the Second Circuit has found to trigger the persecutor bar per se[1110] — other roles in the chain of events leading to the persecutory procedure may or may not trigger the persecutor bar.

- **Practice Pointer**: The forced abortion cases are unique in that forced abortion is a special category under the statute that is considered to be per se persecution on account of political opinion. Thus, even though the individuals who performed the forced abortions as part of their jobs may not have been motivated by victim's political opinions, the Second Circuit has imposed a strict liability approach on those who performed forced abortions. This line of cases may be distinguishable outside of the coercive population control context.

In *Xie v. INS*, the Second Circuit found that the applicant, a driver who transported women to forced abortions, assisted in the persecution of others because his actions contributed directly to the persecution.[1111] The Second Circuit also held that

---

[1109] *See Zhi Geng Li v. Holder*, 388 F. App'x 45 (2d Cir. 2010); *Yan Yan Lin v. Holder*, 584 F.3d 75 (2d Cir. 2009); *Weng v. Holder*, 562 F.3d 510 (2d Cir. 2009); *Guo Liang Lin v. Keisler*, 251 F. App'x 37 (2d Cir. 2007); *Xing Jie Guan v. USCIS*, 183 F. App'x 76 (2d Cir. 2006); *Guang Yan Lin v. INS*, 165 F. App'x 26 (2d Cir. 2006); *Zhang Jian Xie v. INS*, 434 F.3d 136 (2d Cir. 2006).

[1110] *See Zhi Geng Li v. Holder*, 388 F. App'x 45 (2d Cir. 2010); *Guang Yan Lin v. INS*, 165 F. App'x 26 (2d Cir. 2006) (finding that a doctor who participated in forced abortions was barred from asylum under the persecutor bar, without considering the fact that the doctor's motive was not the victim's political opinion).

[1111] *Xie v. INS*, 434 F.3d 136, 143 (2d Cir. 2006) (finding that "[w]here the conduct was active and had direct consequences for the victims" as opposed to conduct that was "tangential to the acts of

Continued

preparing women for the procedure and assisting afterward triggered the persecutor bar. The court stated that such actions, "even if relatively minor, aided in the process of enforcement of China's coercive family planning policy … [and] placed [the applicant] within the purview of the statutory bar."[1112]

Even serving as a guard where the persecutory acts occurred may constitute participating in the persecution of others. In *Chen v. Att'y Gen.*, the Eleventh Circuit found that a guard in a Chinese forced abortion facility assisted in the persecution of others.[1113] The court held that the asylum applicant's actions must be viewed in their entirety, stating, "Detention of an individual — when the act of detention itself is not the persecution at issue — is often an essential predicate to performing the act of persecution."[1114] Thus, even though the guard's own actions did not constitute persecution in and of themselves, they were neither "inconsequential" nor "peripheral" to the persecutory acts, and therefore, triggered the persecutor bar to asylum eligibility.[1115]

The Second, Seventh, and Ninth Circuits have also used the Eleventh Circuit's "essential predicate" analysis in determining whether various actions in chains of events triggered the persecutor bar. In *Boshtrakaj v. Holder*, the Second Circuit found that removing property from the homes of Albanians triggered the persecutor bar because those acts were early steps taken to cleanse the area of ethnic Albanians.[1116] The Seventh Circuit found that the act of taking individuals into custody to later face police abuse also triggered the persecutor bar because such acts were "genuine assistance in persecution" rather than an "inconsequential association with persecutors."[1117] Similarly, the Ninth Circuit held that escorting political prisoners and translating prisoners' statements, when the applicants knew that the prisoners

---

oppression and passive in nature," it was assistance in persecution and barred asylum under the persecutor bar).

[1112] *Xing Jie Guan v. USCIS*, 183 F. App'x 76, 78 (2d Cir. 2006). *But see Yan Yan Lin v. Holder,* 584 F.3d 75, 81 (2d Cir. 2009) (finding that the persecutor bar was not triggered when the assistance given by the applicant was provided to all pregnant women, whether in preparation for a forced abortion or not, and reasoning that the assistance did not "cause[] the abortions, nor [did they make it] more likely that they would occur.") (quoting *Weng v. Holder*, 562 F.3d 510, 515 (2d Cir. 2009)).

[1113] *Chen v. Att'y Gen.*, 513 F.3d 1255, 1259–60 (11th Cir. 2008). *See also Guo Liang Lin v. Keisler*, 251 F. App'x 37, 40 (2d Cir. 2007) (denying asylum under the persecutor bar where the applicant served as a guard to ensure that women did not escape a birth control facility). *But see Weng v. Holder*, 562 F.3d 510, 515 (2d Cir. 2009) (looking to the applicant's "behavior as a whole," concluding that her actions in providing postsurgical care were "at most, tangential, passive accommodation of the conduct of others," and overturning the IJ and BIA).

[1114] *Chen v. Att'y Gen.*, 513 F.3d 1255, 1259–60 (11th Cir. 2008).

[1115] *Id.* at 1258–59.

[1116] *Boshtrakaj v. Holder*, 324 F. App'x 99, 101 (2d Cir. 2009).

[1117] *Singh v. Gonzales*, 417 F.3d 736, 739–40 (7th Cir. 2005).

would later be beaten and tortured, was persecution and triggered the persecutor bar.[1118]

Yet, other courts have used the same "essential predicate" analysis to find that asylum applicants did not assist in the persecution of others. The Second Circuit held that the activities of an officer of the Cultural Management Bureau in China did not trigger the persecutor bar because there was no evidence that any act of persecution occurred in connection with his activities, nor evidence that the applicant had any knowledge of persecution.[1119] Similarly, the Sixth Circuit found that the immigration judge erred because he failed to consider whether the evidence of record established a causal relationship between the intelligence gathered by the asylum applicant and the persecution of individuals at the hands of the Peruvian military, or whether the applicant had any prior or contemporaneous knowledge of persecution by the military.[1120]

The BIA has also addressed the "chain of events" scenario. In *Matter of Rodriguez-Majano*,[1121] the BIA found that if an applicant's action or inaction furthers persecution in some way, he or she is ineligible for relief. However, if the harm or injury inflicted arose as the natural consequence of civil strife, for example, the harm resulting from such generalized civil strife is not persecution.[1122] What matters in chain of events cases is the causal relationship between the asylum applicant's action or inaction and the ultimate persecutory act that occurs.[1123]

b. Failure to Act

Courts also have considered whether the failure to act affirmatively in stopping persecution triggers the persecutor bar. For example, the Second Circuit held that the persecutor bar was not triggered when the asylum applicant, a Russian guard, was present at the time his fellow guards broke into a home and raped two girls, but did not participate in the persecution himself.[1124] The court reasoned that failing to prevent persecution was not the same as persecution.[1125] Similarly, in considering whether mere presence at an event may be considered participation in the persecution

---

[1118] *Ghazaryan v. Gonzales*, 449 F.3d 915, 929–30 (9th Cir. 2006); *Miranda Alvarado v. Gonzales*, 172 F. App'x 139, 140 (9th Cir. 2006).

[1119] *Xu Sheng Gao v. Att'y Gen.*, 500 F.3d 93, 98–102 (2d Cir. 2007).

[1120] *Diaz-Zanatta v. Holder*, 558 F.3d 450, 458–59 (6th Cir. 2009).

[1121] *Matter of Rodriguez-Majano*, 19 I&N Dec. 811 (BIA 1988).

[1122] *Id.* at 815 (finding that the applicant, who was forced to join the guerrillas and covered them with his weapon while they burned cars, was not a persecutor of others).

[1123] *See, e.g.*, *Kumar v. Holder*, 728 F.3d 993 (9th Cir. 2013); *Abdallahi v. Holder*, 690 F.3d 467 (6th Cir. 2012); *Castaneda-Castillo v. Holder*, 638 F.3d 354 (1st Cir. 2011); *Yan Yan Lin v. Holder*, 584 F.3d 75 (2d Cir. 2009); *Guo Qi Wang v. Holder*, 583 F.3d 86 (2d Cir. 2009); *Weng v. Holder*, 562 F.3d 510 (2d Cir. 2009); *Diaz-Zanatta v. Holder*, 558 F.3d 450 (6th Cir. 2009).

[1124] *Balachova v. Mukasey*, 547 F.3d 374, 386 (2d Cir. 2008).

[1125] *Id.* at 387 (noting that Balachova's inaction had no direct consequences for the victims).

of others, the Seventh Circuit found that the applicant, who was present at the murder of Jesuit priests and their cook in El Salvador, probably did not assist or participate in the persecution of others,[1126] but the court remanded the case for more fact-finding, noting that the BIA has used "assist" and "participate" interchangeably when interpreting the persecutor bar.[1127]

By contrast, the Ninth Circuit found that mere presence was enough to trigger the persecutor bar when a police officer was present at the time his fellow officers assaulted some Jehovah's witnesses. The court reasoned that the applicant police officer knew that these assaults would continue and that he would be expected to participate, yet he carried on in his position as a police officer.[1128]

➢ **Practice Pointer**: Practitioners should continue to fight mere presence cases, arguing that inaction does not rise to the level of persecution, which is required by the plain text of the statute. Moreover, adjudicators should look to the motives of the applicant; if there is no nexus to a protected ground in the applicant's inaction, it does not meet the requirements of the persecutor bar.

According to the BIA, "[m]ere membership in an organization, even one which engages in persecution, is not sufficient to bar one from relief."[1129] The asylum applicant is barred only if his or her action or inaction furthers that persecution in some way.[1130] The BIA clarified, "It is the objective effect of the [applicant's] actions which is controlling."[1131] However, being a member of a persecutory group may indeed lead to the applicant being barred from asylum under the persecutor bar. What matters is his or her inaction, not his or her mere membership.

For example, in *Ntamack v. Holder*, the Fourth Circuit held that a member of the Cameroonian gendarmerie forces was barred from asylum under the persecutor bar because of his failure to stop his unit's violent interrogation techniques.[1132] The court reasoned that the applicant's mere presence made a show of force and impeded the movements of the victims, which had the effect of "objectively further[ing] the persecution."[1133] Like the objective effect test described above, the court found the applicant's subjective intent to be irrelevant to his participation in the persecution.

[1126] *Doe v. Gonzales*, 484 F.3d 445, 449, 453 (7th Cir. 2007).

[1127] *Id.* at 450 (citing *Matter of Rodriguez-Majano*, 19 I&N Dec. 811, 814 (BIA 1988) & *Matter of A–H–*, 23 I&N Dec. 774, 784–85 (AG 2005)).

[1128] *Shirvanyan v. Gonzales*, 130 F. App'x 196, 197 (9th Cir. 2005).

[1129] *Matter of Rodriguez-Majano*, 19 I&N Dec. 811, 814–15 (BIA 1988).

[1130] *Id.*

[1131] *Id.*

[1132] *Ntamack v. Holder*, 372 F. App'x 407, 411 (4th Cir. 2010).

[1133] *Id.*

Most courts have confirmed that membership in a persecutory group, alone, is not sufficient to trigger the persecutor bar. For example, the Ninth Circuit has held that persecutory actions of a group as a whole should not be imputed automatically to the applicant member of that group.[1134] Rather, some action or inaction by the applicant must have furthered the persecution in some way.[1135]

iii. Knowledge of Persecutory Acts

Another line of cases addresses the issue whether the asylum applicant's knowledge that his or her actions or inactions would lead to the persecution of others alone is enough to trigger the persecutor bar. Courts have evaluated the applicant's purposeful involvement prior to the persecutory act, as well as the level of the applicant's scienter at the time he or she acted, to determine whether the persecutor bar applies.

For example, the Ninth Circuit, in *Miranda Alvarado v. Gonzales*, held that an interpreter in the Peruvian military, who had provided Quechua interpretation while the military interrogated and tortured suspected member of the Shining Path, was barred from asylum under the persecutor bar because he was a "necessary part of the interrogation."[1136] The court looked to the applicant's "individual accountability," finding that the determination whether the persecutor bar has been triggered requires a "particularized evaluation of both personal involvement and purposeful assistance in order to ascertain culpability."[1137] It reasoned, "Whether Miranda's assistance was material is measured by examining the degree of relation his acts had to the persecution itself."[1138] Since the applicant's actions were essential to the furtherance of the persecutory acts — the interrogation — the persecutor bar had been triggered and he was barred from asylum eligibility.[1139]

The Ninth Circuit elaborated on its scienter requirement further in *Gomez v. Gonzales*, finding that a Peruvian military intelligence officer was barred from asylum under the persecutor bar because he knew that the information he passed to his superiors would be used to persecute, torture, and murder people.[1140] Similarly, in *Ochoa v. Holder*, the Ninth Circuit found that a Guatemalan police officer who arrested members of guerilla groups, knowing that they would be tortured, assisted in

---

[1134] *Hasan v. Ashcroft*, 122 F. App'x 329, 330–31 (9th Cir. 2005). *See also Aroyan v. Gonzales*, 183 F. App'x 634, 635–36 (9th Cir. 2006)

[1135] *See, e.g., Ghazaryan v. Gonzales*, 172 F. App'x 139, 140 (9th Cir. 2006) (stating that when "acts were more than peripheral to the persecution . . . [and instead] performed a necessary role in facilitating persecution," an individual is not merely a member of the persecutory group and the persecutor bar is triggered).

[1136] *Miranda-Alvarado v. Gonzales*, 449 F.3d 915, 919 (9th Cir. 2006).

[1137] *Id.* at 927.

[1138] *Id.* at 928.

[1139] *Id.* at 928–30.

[1140] *Gomez v. Gonzales*, 182 F. App'x 634, 635 (9th Cir. 2006).

the persecution of others and was therefore barred from asylum under the persecutor bar.[1141] The court specified that the applicant's knowledge alone was sufficient to trigger the bar; neither the fact that he did not participate directly in the torture, nor the fact that he did not share the beliefs of the torturers mattered.[1142]

The Sixth Circuit has also addressed the scienter requirement, establishing a two-prong test to evaluate whether the persecutor bar applies to individuals based on their knowledge of the persecution.[1143] Prong number one addresses whether there was a direct connection between the applicant's actions and the persecutory acts so that the applicant actually assisted or participated in the persecution of others. If there is such a nexus, the evaluation moves on to prong number two, which states that the applicant must have acted with scienter, having some knowledge either prior to or contemporaneous with the persecutory acts.[1144] Like the Sixth Circuit, the First Circuit has held that "prior or contemporaneous knowledge" of the persecutory acts was necessary for an applicant to be barred from asylum eligibility under the persecutor bar.[1145]

This line of cases indicates that courts will not only look to the connection between the applicant's actions and the persecutory acts, but also will look to the applicant's prior or contemporaneous knowledge as a signal of intent or complicity in the persecution itself.[1146]

- **Practice Pointer**: If applicable, practitioners should highlight the applicant's ignorance of the effect of his or her actions as a sign that the applicant did not have the requisite scienter to assist or participate in the persecution.

1141 *Ochoa v. Holder*, 340 F. App'x 420, 422 (9th Cir. 2009).

1142 *Id.*

1143 *Diaz-Zanatta v. Holder*, 558 F.3d 450, 455 (6th Cir. 2009) (finding that a military intelligence officer in Peru who made reports that the military used to commit persecutory acts was not subject to the persecutor bar because she did not have knowledge of her role in these events, and upon learning of the persecutory acts, she began leaking information to the press).

1144 *Id. See also Parlak v. Holder*, 578 F.3d 457 (6th Cir. 2009) (clarifying its two-prong test from *Diaz-Zannatta v. Holder* and holding that the applicant was barred from asylum eligibility under the persecutor bar because he "voluntarily and knowingly" funded the PKK, a Turkish terrorist organization, and transported weapons for the group to use).

1145 *Castañeda-Castillo v. Gonzales*, 488 F.3d 17, 19–22 (1st Cir. 2007) (holding that the persecutor bar did not apply because the applicant had no prior or contemporaneous knowledge of a military attack on civilian villagers when he, as a member of the military unit, blocked an escape route outside a village where he was stationed).

1146 *See, e.g., Quitanilla v. Holder*, 758 F.3d 570 (4th Cir. 2014) (emphasizing that the applicant was a knowing participant in the acts of persecution committed by his military unit in El Salvador, as he was a sergeant who oversaw the investigation and capture of guerillas fighting in opposition to the El Salvadoran government); *Yan Yan Lin v. Holder*, 584 F.3d 75 (2d Cir. 2009); *Guo Qi Wang v. Holder*, 583 F.3d 86 (2d Cir. 2009); *Weng v. Holder*, 562 F.3d 510 (2d Cir. 2009); *Matter of D–R–*, 25 I&N Dec. 445 (BIA 2011).

Given the lack of a clear rule regarding what conduct, other than actually committing the persecutory act, constitutes assistance or participation in the persecution, this area of asylum law remains unsettled. Courts have considered the objective effect of the applicant's actions, how essential those actions were to the persecutory conduct, and whether there are any mitigating factors involved, such as duress or a lack of prior or contemporaneous knowledge. Although the objective effect of the individual's actions may still be controlling in some jurisdictions,[1147] it is yet to be seen how the law will evolve following the Supreme Court's ruling in *Negusie v. Holder*.[1148]

Generally, it seems that courts are leaning toward the contextual approach, rather than a strict objective effect test, with a majority of courts stating that the IJ and BIA must engage in a particularized evaluation in order to determine if the individual's behavior was culpable to such a degree that he or she could be deemed to have assisted or participated in the persecution of others.[1149] In the only published BIA case addressing the persecutor bar following *Negusie v. Holder*, the BIA seemed to take a more contextual approach as well, holding that the totality of the record supported the conclusion that the applicant assisted in the extrajudicial killing of 200 Bosnian Muslims that his unit was involved in capturing.[1150] The BIA referenced the applicant's command responsibility, his presence, his platoon's active participation, and the finding that he must have been aware that many other Bosnian Muslims who were similarly situated had been executed nearby several days earlier.[1151] This decision may indicate that the BIA is leaning toward a more contextual, totality of the circumstances approach.

> ➢ **Practice Pointer**: Overall, the persecutor bar requires a three-step analysis: (1) identify the persecutory act; (2) determine the applicant's relationship to the act; and (3) determine whether the applicant's participation was motivated by the victim's race, religion, nationality, membership in a particular social group, or political opinion. Both participation and nexus to a protected ground are required in order for

---

[1147] *Laipenieks v. INS*, 750 F.2d 1427, 1437 (9th Cir. 1985) (holding that the INS must show by clear and convincing evidence that the individuals harmed were persecuted solely because of their political opinion (or other enumerated ground)); *Matter of Fedorenko*, 19 I&N Dec. 57, 69–70 (BIA 1984). Both of these decisions have been called into question by the Supreme Court's decision in *Negusie v. Holder*, 129 S. Ct. 1159 (2009).

[1148] *Negusie v. Holder*, 555 U.S. 511 (2009).

[1149] *See, e.g.*, *Quitanilla v. Holder*, 758 F.3d 570 (4th Cir. 2014); *Pastor-Hernandez v. Holder*, 737 F.3d 902 (4th Cir. 2013); *Kumar v. Holder*, 728 F.3d 993 (9th Cir. 2013); *Abdallahi v. Holder*, 690 F.3d 467 (6th Cir. 2012); *Castaneda-Castillo v. Holder*, 638 F.3d 354 (1st Cir. 2011); *Yan Yan Lin v. Holder*, 584 F.3d 75 (2d Cir. 2009); *Weng v. Holder*, 562 F.3d 510 (2d Cir. 2009); *Diaz-Zanatta v. Holder*, 558 F.3d 450 (6th Cir. 2009); *Parlak v. Holder*, 578 F.3d 457 (6th Cir. 2009); *Vukmirovic v. Ashcroft*, 362 F.3d 1247, 1252 (9th Cir. 2004); *Hernandez v. Reno*, 258 F.3d 806, 813 (8th Cir. 2001).

[1150] *Matter of D–R–*, 25 I&N Dec. 445 (BIA 2011).

[1151] *Id.*

the persecutor bar to apply. In determining the applicant's relationship to that act, consider the following: Was the applicant directly involved? Coerced or forced into committing the act? An observer of the act? Someone with knowledge of the act? A member of a persecutory group? Also, were there any mitigating factors?

2. *Particularly Serious Crime*

Another statutory bar to both asylum and withholding of removal is if an individual "having been convicted by a final judgment of a particularly serious crime, constitutes a danger to the community of the United States."[1152] There are three basic elements to this bar to asylum: (1) whether the individual was convicted by a final judgment; (2) whether the crime is "particularly serious;" and (3) whether the applicant constitutes a danger to the community.

Pursuant to INA §101(a)(48)(A), a conviction exists for immigration purposes if: (1) a judge or jury has found the individual guilty or the individual has entered a plea of guilty or *nolo contendere* or has admitted sufficient facts to warrant a finding of guilt; and (2) the court has ordered some form of punishment, penalty, or restraint on the individual's liberty.[1153] The conviction is only final if direct appellate review has been waived or exhausted.[1154] Additionally, juvenile convictions do not constitute convictions for immigration purposes,[1155] nor convictions for particularly serious crimes if the applicant was under age 16 or was tried as a juvenile.[1156] Moreover, a conviction that occurred in a criminal proceeding that was demonstrably a "travesty of justice," can be questioned and the offense may not amount to a particularly serious crime.[1157]

If there is a conviction by final judgment, in analyzing whether the particularly serious crime bar applies, courts have focused on whether the crime is particularly serious and not whether the individual is a danger to the community. Previously, the BIA relied on the following criteria established in *Matter of Frentescu*[1158] to determine whether someone has been convicted of a particularly serious crime: (1) the nature of the conviction; (2) the circumstances and underlying facts of the conviction; (3) the type of sentence imposed; and (4) whether the type and

---

[1152] INA §§208(b)(2)(A)(ii), 241(b)(3)(B)(ii); 8 USC §§1158(b)(2)(A)(ii), 1231(b)(3)(B)(ii) (2012).

[1153] INA §101(a)(48)(A). *See Crespo v. Holder*, 631 F.3d 130 (4th Cir. 2011) (confirming that there must be both a finding or admission of guilt and some form or punishment or penalty in order to constitute a conviction for immigration purposes).

[1154] *Matter of Polanco*, 20 I&N Dec. 894 (BIA 1994).

[1155] *Matter of Devison*, 22 I&N Dec. 1362 (BIA 2000).

[1156] *Matter of Ramirez-Rivero*, 18 I&N Dec. 135 (BIA 1981).

[1157] *See Doe v. Gonzales*, 484 F.3d 445, 447, 451–52 (7th Cir. 2007) (finding that the applicant's murder conviction in El Salvador should not necessarily be a bar to asylum even though the IJ found he had committed a particularly serious crime).

[1158] *Matter of Frentescu*, 18 I&N Dec. 244, 247 (BIA 1982).

circumstances of the crime indicate that the applicant is a danger to the community.[1159] *Matter of Frentescu* now has been modified, however, by *Matter of N–A–M–.*[1160] Accordingly, the BIA no longer engages in a separate determination to address whether the applicant is a danger to the community. Instead, the BIA focuses on the "nature of the crime and not the likelihood of future serious misconduct."[1161] Therefore, the BIA's position is that if a crime is a particularly serious one, the applicant is automatically considered to be a danger to the community. The BIA also no longer focuses on the sentence imposed because it "is not the most accurate or salient factor to consider in determining the seriousness of an offense."[1162] Numerous federal courts, like the BIA, have rejected the argument that an adjudicator is required to make a separate determination regarding whether an individual is a danger to the community.[1163]

The particularly serious crime bar not only applies to the principal applicant, it also applies independently to a spouse or child who is included on an asylum application, but who has been convicted of a particularly serious crime. Such an individual is barred from being granted asylum as a derivative.[1164]

> ➢ **Practice Pointer**: Has an asylum applicant been "convicted of" or "arrested" for a crime? One way to find out is to submit a request for his or her rap sheet pursuant to 28 CFR §§16.32-16.33. The request must be sent to the Federal Bureau of Investigation's Criminal Justice Information Services Division, and must include a cover letter request, privacy waiver, completed form FD-258 fingerprint card, and certified check or money order for $18. See *www.fbi.gov/hq/cjisd/fprequest.htm* for complete details. Each state also has its own procedures for requesting criminal background check information.

[1159] *Id.* at 247.

[1160] *Matter of N–A–M–*, 24 I&N Dec. 336 (BIA 2007).

[1161] *Id.* at 342.

[1162] *Id.* at 343.

[1163] *Choeum v. INS*, 129 F.3d 29, 40–43 (1st Cir. 1997); *Hamama v. INS*, 78 F.3d 233, 240 (6th Cir. 1996); *Ahmetovic v. INS*, 62 F.3d 48, 52–53 (2d Cir. 1995); *Kofa v. INS*, 60 F.3d 1084, 1088–91 (4th Cir. 1995); *Feroz v. INS*, 22 F.3d 225, 227 (9th Cir. 1994); *Mosquera-Perez v. INS*, 3 F.3d 553, 558–59 (1st Cir. 1993); *Martins v. INS*, 972 F.2d 657, 660–61 (5th Cir. 1992); *Crespo-Gomez v. Richard*, 780 F.2d 932, 934–35 (11th Cir. 1986); *Matter of N–A–M–*, 24 I&N Dec. 336, 342 (BIA 2007) (modifying *Matter of Frentescu*, 18 I&N Dec. 244 (BIA 1982), stating that whether the applicant is a danger to the community is no longer a separate determination, and clarifying that the BIA focuses on the "nature of the crime and not the likelihood of future serious misconduct," nor the sentence imposed); *Matter of C*, 20 I&N Dec. 529, 533 (BIA 1992); *Matter of K–*, 20 I&N Dec. 418 (BIA 1991). *But see Matter of Q–T–M–T–*, 21 I&N Dec. 639 (BIA 1996) (Rosenberg, concurring and dissenting) (noting that legislative amendments highlighted a focus by U.S. Congress on "endangerment").

[1164] 8 CFR §208.21(a) (2014). See ch. 13 for a detailed discussion of derivative beneficiaries.

i. Aggravated Felonies

Under IIRAIRA, an individual convicted of an aggravated felony, as defined in INA §101(a)(43), is deemed to have been convicted of a particularly serious crime for purposes of asylum eligibility.[1165] IIRAIRA also expanded the definition of aggravated felony to include many minor, nonviolent offenses.[1166] For example, a theft offense for which the term of imprisonment imposed is one year or more, regardless of any suspension of sentence, is an aggravated felony.[1167]

- **Practice Pointer**: A term of imprisonment includes "the period of incarceration or confinement ordered by a court of law regardless of any suspension of the imposition or execution of that imprisonment or sentence in whole or in part."[1168] Thus, even deferred or suspended sentences may result in an individual's conviction falling within INA §101(a)(43) as an aggravated felony, thus barring him or her from asylum eligibility.

The list of crimes designated to be aggravated felonies under INA §101(a)(43) includes several specific crimes, as well as crimes that are only considered aggravated felonies if they carry a particular length of sentence or involve a certain amount of money.[1169] Thus, it is important to analyze the final disposition and sentence for any criminal charges against the applicant to determine if it actually is an aggravated felony that would trigger the particularly serious crime bar.

If an individual was convicted of an aggravated felony, he or she is automatically barred from asylum under the particularly serious crime bar.[1170] For purposes of withholding of removal, however, the bar is not automatic.[1171] Rather, if the applicant for withholding of removal has been convicted of an aggravated felony, it is the term of imprisonment that may trigger an automatic finding of a particularly serious crime, and thus, a bar to withholding of removal.[1172] If an individual has been convicted of an aggravated felony (or felonies) for which he or she was sentenced to an aggregate term of imprisonment of *at least five years*, he or she is considered to have committed a particularly serious crime and is barred from withholding of removal.[1173] In

---

[1165] INA §208(b)(2)(B)(i); 8 USC §1158(b)(2)(B)(i) (2012).

[1166] INA §101(a)(43).

[1167] *See* INA §101(a)(43)(G); 8 USC §1101(a)(43)(G) (2012).

[1168] INA §101(a)(48)(B).

[1169] INA §101(a)(43).

[1170] INA §208(b)(2)(B)(i) ("[A]n alien who has been convicted of an aggravated felony shall be considered to have been convicted of a particularly serious crime.").

[1171] INA §241(b)(3)(B) ("[A]n alien who has been convicted of an aggravated felony (or felonies) for which the alien has been sentenced to an aggregate term of imprisonment of at least five years shall be considered to have committed a particularly serious crime.").

[1172] *Id.*

[1173] *Id.*

calculating the aggregate term of imprisonment, concurrent sentences should not be added together, but instead, should be considered as being equal in length to the longest concurrent sentence.[1174] Even if an individual has been sentenced for less than five years in the aggregate, however, the adjudicator is not prohibited from finding that the individual has been convicted of a particularly serious crime.[1175] It is the nature of the crime that is most relevant to the inquiry of whether it constitutes a particularly serious crime.

Trafficking of controlled substances, as described in section 102 of the Controlled Substances Act and including a drug trafficking crime as defined under 18 USC §924(c), is an aggravated felony under INA §101(a)(43)(B).

> ➢ **Practice Pointer**: In determining whether a state drug offense should be considered a drug trafficking crime falling within the definition of "aggravated felony," the BIA has held that adjudicators must look to decisions from the federal circuit courts.[1176] Also, the specific drug must appear on the federal schedule of controlled substances at 21 USC §812 and 21 CFR §1308, and there must be an analogous federal law.

In 2002, the AG ruled that all aggravated felonies involving controlled substance trafficking, regardless of the sentence imposed, are presumptively particularly serious crimes, and therefore, will always bar asylum and withholding of removal.[1177] This presumption has been upheld by some federal courts, but cannot be applied retroactively.[1178]

The presumption may only be rebutted upon a demonstration of "extraordinary and compelling circumstances."[1179] In *Matter of Y–L–, A–G–, & R–S–R–*, the AG suggested six criteria that are required at a minimum to constitute "extraordinary and compelling circumstances." Each criterion must be present in order to rebut the presumption of a particularly serious crime for convictions of controlled substance trafficking aggravated felonies.[1180] These criteria include a showing that: (1) the crime involved a small quantity of a controlled substance; (2) the crime involved a modest amount of money paid in the transaction; (3) the applicant was only peripherally involved in the offense; (4) the crime involved an absence of violence

---

[1174] *Matter of Aldabesheh*, 22 I&N Dec. 983, 988–89 (BIA 1999).

[1175] INA §241(b)(3)(B). *See Matter of L–S–*, 22 I&N Dec. 645 (BIA 1999); *Matter of S–S–*, 22 I&N Dec. 458 (BIA 1999).

[1176] *Matter of Yanez-Garcia*, 23 I&N Dec. 390 (BIA 2002); *see, e.g.*, *Matter of Santos-Lopez*, 23 I&N Dec. 419 (BIA 2002) (finding that two misdemeanor offenses for marijuana possession under Texas law do *not* fall within the definition of "drug trafficking crime" under federal law).

[1177] *Matters of Y–L–, A–G–, R–S–R–*, 23 I&N Dec. 270 (AG 2002) (reversing *Matter of S–S–* as it relates to aggravated felony trafficking).

[1178] *Miguel-Miguel v. Gonzales*, 500 F.3d 941, 949–51 (9th Cir. 2007).

[1179] *Id.* at 274.

[1180] *Id.* at 276–77.

(actual or threatened, implicit or otherwise); (5) the crime involved an absence of organized crime and terrorist organization involvement (direct or indirect); and (6) the absence of harm to or adverse effects on juveniles.[1181] If the IJ fails to consider these factors, the claim must be remanded for additional findings.[1182]

For withholding cases not involving drug trafficking offenses for which the sentence (or aggregate sentences if more than one offense) is less than five years, an aggravated felony conviction is not automatically a bar to withholding of removal. Rather, the adjudicator must consider the nature of the conviction, the sentence imposed, and the circumstances and underlying facts of the crime.[1183] For both asylum and withholding of removal, it is the nature of the crime that is most relevant to the inquiry of whether a conviction constitutes a particularly serious crime.

- **Practice Pointer**: Whenever possible, because of the harsh consequences that result from a finding that an individual has committed an aggravated felony, an asylum applicant should argue that his or her offense does not constitute an aggravated felony. Particular attention should be paid to the effective dates of any amendments to the aggravated felony definition.[1184] An applicant convicted of an

---

[1181] *Id.*

[1182] *Lavira v. Att'y Gen.*, 478 F.3d 158, 166 (3d Cir. 2007).

[1183] *See Matter of L–S–*, 22 I&N Dec. 645 (BIA 1999) (conviction for bringing a noncitizen into the United States in violation of the law for which the individual received a three-and-one-half-month sentence is not a particularly serious crime).

[1184] Although ICE or legacy INS alleged that the individual in each of the following cases had been convicted of an aggravated felony, the courts found that the offense committed did not constitute an aggravated felony: *Lopez v. Gonzales*, 127 S. Ct. 625, 633 (2006) (finding that a drug offense that is a felony under state law but only a misdemeanor under federal law is not an aggravated felony); *Leocal v. Ashcroft*, 543 U.S. 1, 125 S. Ct. 377 (2004) (finding that DUIs under statutes requiring a mens rea of negligence or less are not crimes of violence and, therefore, not aggravated felonies); *Rashid v. Mukasey*, 531 F.3d 438, 447 (6th Cir. 2008) (finding two state misdemeanor drug convictions do not constitute an aggravated felony); *Arce-Vences v. Mukasey*, 512 F.3d 167, 171 (5th Cir. 2007) (possession of between 50 and 200 pounds of marijuana was found not to be an aggravated felony); *Smith v. Gonzales*, 468 F.3d 272, 278 (5th Cir. 2006) (two New York misdemeanor marijuana offenses are not aggravated felonies); *Lee v. Ashcroft*, 368 F.3d 218 (3d Cir. 2004) (filing a false tax return is not an aggravated felony); *Nugent v. Ashcroft*, 367 F.3d 162 (3d Cir. 2004) (theft by deception under Pennsylvania law is not a "theft offense" aggravated felony under the INA); *Jobson v. Ashcroft*, 326 F.3d 367 (2d Cir. 2003) (manslaughter in the second degree under New York law is not an aggravated felony); *Valansi v. Ashcroft*, 278 F.3d 203 (3d Cir. 2002) (embezzlement if no intent to defraud); *Dalton v. Ashcroft*, 257 F.3d 200, 208 (2d Cir. 2001) (a felony DUI under New York law is not an aggravated felony); *Xiong v. INS*, 173 F.3d 601 (7th Cir. 1999) (second-degree sexual assault of a child); *Matter of Sanudo*, 23 I&N Dec. 968 (BIA 2006) (domestic battery under the California Penal Code does not qualify as a crime of violence); *Matter of Gutierrez-Martinez*, A17 945 476, 2004 WL 880256, at *6 (BIA Mar. 9, 2004), *available at www.lexisnexis.com/practiceareas/immigration/pdfs/web487.pdf* (digital penetration is not rape); *Matter of Santos-Lopez*, 23 I&N Dec. 419 (BIA 2002) (two misdemeanor offenses for marijuana possession); *Matter of Ramos*, 23 I&N Dec. 336 (BIA 2002) (DWI under Massachusetts law); *Matter of Sweetser*, 22 I&N Dec. 709 (BIA 1999) (criminally negligent child abuse); *Matter of Alvarado-Alvino*, 22 I&N Dec. 718 (BIA 1999) (alien smuggling under INA §275(a));

Continued

aggravated felony should also consider seeking various forms of post-conviction relief available in criminal court.[1185] If, however, a court vacates a conviction for reasons solely related to rehabilitation or immigration hardship, rather than for a procedural or substantive defect in the underlying criminal proceeding, the conviction is not eliminated for immigration purposes.[1186]

- **Practice Pointer**: An excellent resource for information regarding the immigration consequences of criminal conduct or convictions is the National Immigration Project of the National Lawyers Guild.[1187] Another resource for immigration practitioners grappling with a criminal law question is the National Legal Aid and Defender Association's (NLADA) Defending Immigrants Partnership. NLADA's website[1188] contains state and federal law reference charts, key decisions, model pleadings, and practice tips.

ii. Non-Aggravated Felonies

Even if a crime is not an aggravated felony and even if the applicant has not been sentenced to an aggregate term of imprisonment of at least five years, a conviction can still be considered a particularly serious crime that bars an applicant from asylum and/or withholding of removal eligibility.[1189] Courts have rejected the argument that

---

Matter of [name not provided], A43 163 062 (IJ Oct. 3, 2000) (Florence, AZ) (Jeffries, IJ) (domestic violence-related misdemeanors not "crimes of violence"), *reported in* 77 INTERPRETER RELEASES 1633 (Nov. 20, 2000). *But see St. John v. Ashcroft*, 43 Fed. Appx. 281 (10th Cir. 2002) (use of false Social Security card is aggravated felony when loss to victims exceeds $10,000); *Matter of Small*, 23 I&N Dec. 448 (BIA 2002) (sexual abuse of a minor under New York law is an aggravated felony); *Matter of Martinez-Recinos*, 23 I&N Dec. 175 (BIA 2001) (perjury under California law is an aggravated felony).

1185 *See, e.g.*, Norton Tooby, *Evaluating the Chances for Post-Conviction Relief*, Nortontooby.com, *available at http://nortontooby.com/pdf/EvaluatingtheChancesofPCR.pdf* (last visited Jan. 3, 2015)..

1186 *Pickering v. Gonzales*, 454 F.3d 525, 526 (6th Cir. 2006) (finding that the "BIA correctly interpreted the law by holding that, if a court vacates an alien's conviction for reasons solely related to rehabilitation or to avoid adverse immigration hardships, rather than on the basis of a procedural or substantive defect in the underlying criminal proceedings, the conviction is not eliminated for immigration purposes").

1187 National Immigration Project of the National Lawyers Guild, 14 Beacon Street, Suite 506, Boston, MA 02108, (617) 227-9727, *www.nationalimmigrationproject.org*.

1188 *See* National Legal Aid & Defender Association's (NLADA) Defending Immigrants Partnership at *www.nlada.org/Defender/Defender_Immigrants*; *See also* Mary Kramer, *Immigration Consequences of Criminal Activity* (AILA 6th Ed. 2015), *available at http://agora.aila.org/product/detail/1148?sel=description*.

1189 *Matter of N–A–M–*, 24 I&N Dec. 336, 343 (BIA 2007). *See also Arbid v. Holder*, 700 F.3d 379 (9th Cir. 2012) (finding mail fraud that was not an aggravated felony to be a particularly serious crime); *Gao v. Holder*, 595 F.3d 549, 555–56 (4th Cir. 2010) (finding selling military technology that was not an aggravated felony to be a particularly serious crime); *Nethagani v. Mukasey*, 532 F.3d 150, 155–56 (2d Cir. 2008) (finding reckless endangerment for shooting a pistol into the air, a non-aggravated felony, to be a particularly serious crime); *Ali v. Achim*, 468 F.3d 462, 467–71 (7th Cir. 2006) (finding that

Continued

the crime must be an aggravated felony in order to be determined a particularly serious crime.[1190] The only exception to date is the Third Circuit, which has found that for purposes of withholding of removal, the crime must be an aggravated felony in order to bar relief.[1191]

For both asylum and withholding of removal, overall, it is the nature of the crime that matters most. UNHCR has suggested that the following elements be considered in determining the seriousness of an offense:

> [M]inority of the offender; parole; elapse of five years since the conviction or completion of sentence; general good character (for example, one offense only); offender was merely accomplice; other circumstances surrounding the offense (for example, provocation and self-defense).[1192]

Although UNHCR provided these suggestions in the context of whether crimes committed outside of the country of refuge constitute serious nonpolitical crimes, they are also useful in assessing whether a crime is a particularly serious crime.[1193] According to the Handbook, "[m]inor offenses punishable by moderate sentences are not grounds for exclusion . . . even if technically referred to as 'crimes' in the penal law of the country concerned."[1194] The Handbook recommends that the adjudicator balance the degree of persecution feared against the nature of the offense committed and take all relevant factors, including mitigating circumstances, into account.[1195] Mitigating factors, according to the Handbook, include the fact that the applicant has already served his or her sentence or has been granted an amnesty or pardon.[1196]

The balancing test to apply when making a determination of whether a conviction should be considered a "particularly serious crime" is found in *Matter of*

---

particularly serious crimes are not limited to aggravated felonies); *Matter of R–A–M–*, 25 I&N Dec. 657, 661–62 (BIA 2012) (finding possession of child pornography under the facts of the case to be a particularly serious crime). *But see Alaka v. Att'y Gen.*, 456 F.3d 88, 104–05 (3d Cir. 2006) (finding that only aggravated felonies can be particularly serious crimes), *but see Matter of M–H–*, 26 I&N Dec. 46 (BIA 2012) (applying *Matter of N–A–M–* in the Third Circuit notwithstanding *Alaka v. Att'y Gen.* based on *Brand X* deference).

[1190] *Delgado v. Holder*, 563 F.3d 863 (9th Cir. 2009); *Nethagani v. Mukasey*, 532 F.3d 150, 156 (2d Cir. 2008); *Ali v. Achim*, 468 F.3d 462, 468–69 (7th Cir. 2006) *Matter of N–A–M–*, 24 I&N Dec. 336, 337–41 (BIA 2007).

[1191] *Alaka v. Att'y Gen.*, 456 F.3d 88, 105 (3d Cir. 2006)

[1192] Guy S. Goodwin-Gill & Jane McAdams, THE REFUGEE IN INTERNATIONAL LAW 107 (2d ed. 1996).

[1193] *See, e.g.*, *Matter of Frentescu*, 18 I&N Dec. 244, 245 (BIA 1982) (holding that a particularly serious crime is more serious than a serious nonpolitical crime).

[1194] *Id.* at 245 (citing UNHCR Handbook, *supra* note 33, ¶ 155).

[1195] UNHCR Handbook, *supra* note 33, ¶¶ 156, 157.

[1196] UNHCR Handbook, *supra* note 33, ¶ 157. Note, however, that the U.S. Supreme Court has rejected this approach in the context of assessing whether an offense is a serious nonpolitical crime. *INS v. Aguirre-Aguirre*, 526 U.S. 415 (1999).

Frentescu.[1197] The adjudicator should consider such factors as the nature of the conviction, the circumstances and underlying facts of the conviction, the type of sentence imposed, and, most importantly, whether the type and circumstances of the crime indicate that the applicant will be a danger to the community.[1198] The BIA in *Frentescu* noted that a "particularly serious crime" is more serious than a "serious nonpolitical crime" and that UNHCR's Handbook defines a "serious" crime as "a capital crime or a very grave punishable act."[1199] However, more recently, in *Matter of N–A–M–*, the BIA has clarified that the focus on the inquiry should be on the "nature of the crime and not the likelihood of future serious misconduct," nor the sentenced imposed.[1200]

In *Matter of Jean*, the AG determined that asylum applicants who have committed violent or dangerous crimes should not be granted asylum, even if they are technically eligible, except in extraordinary circumstances.[1201] According to the AG, extraordinary circumstances in the case of violent or dangerous crimes would include those involving national security or foreign policy considerations, or cases in which the applicant clearly demonstrates exceptional or extremely unusual hardship.[1202] In *Matter of Jean*, the AG found that an asylum applicant convicted of second-degree manslaughter for killing a 19-month-old toddler in her care was ineligible for asylum. USCIS agrees, stating in its asylum officer training course that a crime of violence usually is a particularly serious crime.[1203]

Crimes found by courts to be "particularly serious crimes" given the specific facts and evidence presented include:

- Manslaughter;[1204]
- Aggravated battery;[1205]

[1197] *Matter of Frentescu*, 18 I&N Dec. at 244 (finding that an applicant sentenced to three months imprisonment and one year probation for a burglary offense was not convicted of a "particularly serious crime").

[1198] *Id.* at 245. *See also Yousefi v. INS*, 260 F.3d 318 (4th Cir. 2001); *Mahini v. INS*, 779 F.2d 1419, 1421 (9th Cir. 1986); *Matter of L–S–J–*, 21 I&N Dec. 973 (BIA 1997); *Matter of B–*, 20 I&N Dec. 427, 430 (BIA 1991).

[1199] *Id.*

[1200] *Matter of N–A–M–*, 24 I&N Dec. 336, 342–43 (BIA 2007).

[1201] *See Matter of Jean*, 23 I&N Dec. 373 (AG 2002).

[1202] *Id.* at 385.

[1203] U.S. Citizenship & Immigration Servs., *Lesson: Mandatory Bars to Asylum and Discretion* at 20, in Asylum Officer Basic Training Course Participant Workbook (Mar. 25, 2009) [hereinafter AOBTC Workbook, Mandatory Bars & Discretion], *available at www.uscis.gov/sites/default/files/USCIS/Humanitarian/Refugees%20%26%20Asylum/Asylum/Bars-to-Asylum-Discretion-31aug10.pdf.*

[1204] *Matter of Alcantar*, 20 I&N Dec. 801 (BIA 1994); *Matter of C–*, 20 I&N Dec. 529 (BIA 1992).

[1205] *Matter of D–*, 20 I&N Dec. 827 (BIA 1994); *Matter of B–*, 20 I&N Dec. 427 (BIA 1991).

- Assault and battery;[1206]
- Battery with a dangerous weapon;[1207]
- Assault with a dangerous weapon;[1208]
- Reckless endangerment;[1209]
- Armed robbery;[1210]
- Kidnapping and burglary;[1211]
- Aggravated kidnapping;[1212]
- Residential burglaries;[1213]
- Robbery;[1214]
- Drug trafficking;[1215]
- Possession of drugs with intent to distribute;[1216]
- Possession of child pornography;[1217]
- Mail fraud;[1218]

[1206] *Konou v. Holder*, 750 F.3d 1120 (9th Cir. 2014) (reasoning that the judge had enhanced the sentence with an additional three years of imprisonment for causing bodily injury and that the applicant had kicked his boyfriend twice after his boyfriend was already on the ground).

[1207] *Lapaix v. Att'y Gen.*, 605 F.3d 1138 (11th Cir. 2010) (agreeing that aggravated battery with a deadly weapon in Florida was a particularly serious crime); *Ali v. Achim*, 468 F.3d 462, 467–71 (7th Cir. 2006) (finding a particularly serious crime where a dangerous weapon was used in the battery).

[1208] *Matter of D–*, 20 I&N Dec. 827 (BIA 1994); *Matter of Juarez*, 19 I&N Dec. 664 (BIA 1988).

[1209] *Nethagani v. Mukasey*, 532 F.3d 150, 155 (2d Cir. 2008)

[1210] *Matter of L–S–J–*, 21 I&N Dec. 973 (BIA 1997); *Matter of D–*, 20 I&N Dec. 827 (BIA 1994); *Matter of Rodriguez-Coto*, 19 I&N Dec. 208, 210 (BIA 1985).

[1211] *Choeum v. INS*, 129 F.3d 29 (1st Cir. 1997).

[1212] *Groza v. INS*, 30 F.3d 814 (7th Cir. 1994).

[1213] *Lopez-Cardona v. Holder*, 662 F.3d 1110 (9th Cir. 2011); *Issaq v. Holder*, 617 F.3d 962 (7th Cir. 2010); *Nguyen v. INS*, 991 F.2d 621, 626 (10th Cir. 1993); *Matter of Garcia-Garrocho*, 19 I&N Dec. 423 (BIA 1986).

[1214] *Matter of Carballe*, 19 I&N Dec. 357 (BIA 1986).

[1215] *Perez-Palafox v. Holder*, 744 F.3d 1138 (9th Cir. 2014) (finding a particularly serious crime for the sale/transportation of a controlled substance); *Matter of Y–L–, A–G–, & R–S–R–*, 23 I&N Dec. 270 (A.G. 2002); *Matter of U–M–*, 20 I&N Dec. 327 (BIA 1991) (taking the position that all drug trafficking crimes, as defined under federal law, are particularly serious, no matter how small the amount).

[1216] *Crespo-Gomez v. Richard*, 780 F.2d 932 (11th Cir. 1986) (finding a particularly serious crime where the applicant was convicted of possession of cocaine for sale); *Mahini v. INS*, 779 F.2d 1419, 1421 (9th Cir. 1986) (finding a particularly serious crime where the applicant was convicted of possession of heroin with intent to distribute).

[1217] *Matter of R–A–M–*, 25 I&N Dec. 657, 661–62 (BIA 2012).

[1218] *Arbid v. Holder*, 674 F.3d 1138, 1143–44 (9th Cir. 2012).

- Evidence tampering;[1219]
- Export of military technology;[1220]
- Securities fraud amounting nearly $900,000;[1221]
- Non-aggravated felony money laundering;[1222]
- DUI with aggravating circumstances;[1223]
- Unauthorized access to a computer;[1224] and
- Felony menacing.[1225]

On the other hand, a single conviction of a misdemeanor is usually not a particularly serious crime.[1226] Crimes found *not* to be "particularly serious crimes" under the particular facts and evidence presented include:

- Burglary;[1227]
- Assault with a deadly weapon;[1228]
- Resisting arrest;[1229]
- Lewd and lascivious acts with a child under the age of 14;[1230]
- Three DUI convictions;[1231] and
- Possession of cocaine.[1232]

[1219] *Denis v. Att'y Gen.*, 633 F.3d 201, 213–17 (3d Cir. 2011) (finding a particularly serious crime for evidence tampering where the applicant violently dismembered and concealed his victim of second decree manslaughter).

[1220] *Gao v. Holder*, 595 F.3d 549, 557–58 (4th Cir. 2010).

[1221] *Kaplun v. Att'y Gen.*, 602 F.3d 260, 267–68 (3d Cir. 2010).

[1222] *Hakim v. Holder*, 628 F.3d 151 (5th Cir. 2010) (reasoning that the link to drug trafficking made the money laundering a particularly serious crime).

[1223] *Anaya-Ortiz v. Mukasey*, 594 F.3d 673, 678–80 (9th Cir. 2010) (finding a particularly serious crime where the driver crashed into a home and injured the person in the home).

[1224] *Tian v. Holder*, 576 F.3d 890, 896–98 (8th Cir. 2009).

[1225] *Matter of N–A–M–*, 24 I&N Dec. 336 (BIA 2007).

[1226] *Matter of Juarez*, 19 I&N Dec. 664 (BIA 1988).

[1227] *Matter of Frentescu*, 18 I&N Dec. at 244.

[1228] *Matter of Juarez*, 19 I&N Dec. 664, 665 (BIA 1988).

[1229] *Alphonsus v. Holder*, 705 F.3d 1031, 1043–49 (9th Cir. 2013) (remanding to the BIA for abuse of discretion regarding why resisting arrest under California Penal Code section 69 constitutes a particularly serious crime because the BIA's rationale that the crime was "against the orderly pursuit of justice" and that there was a "meaningful risk of harm" was contrary to prior decisions).

[1230] *Blandino-Medina v. Holder*, 712 F.3d 1338 (9th Cir. 2013) (stating that the offense wasn't per se a particularly serious crime and noting that DHS could not create additional categories of per se particularly serious crimes based solely on the elements of the offense).

[1231] *Delgado v. Holder*, 563 F.3d 863 (9th Cir. 2009).

[1232] *Matter of Toboso-Alfonso*, 20 I&N Dec. 819 (BIA 1990).

Once it is determined that the nature of the crime brings it within the "range" of a particularly serious crime, either party may present evidence to determine whether or not the crime should be treated as particularly serious.[1233] However, the inquiry does not involve "an examination of the respondent's family or community ties, the risk of persecution," or going "behind the record of conviction to redetermine the alien's innocence or guilt."[1234] If an applicant has been convicted of a particularly serious crime, he or she shall be considered a danger to the community under 8 CFR §§208.16(d)(2), 1208.16(d)(2).[1235]

In general, the question of law whether a conviction constitutes a particularly serious crime is subject to judicial review.[1236] However, some courts have found that there is no jurisdiction to review discretionary aspects of this determination, such as how the BIA or IJ weighed the *Frentescu* factors, whether an aggravated felony is particularly serious for purposes of withholding of removal, and others.[1237]

3. *Serious Nonpolitical Crimes*

A person is also ineligible for asylum and withholding of removal if there are serious reasons for considering that he or she has committed a serious nonpolitical crime outside of the United States prior to his or her arrival.[1238] The BIA has equated "serious reasons" to "probable cause."[1239] A serious nonpolitical crime must have been committed outside of the United States. Generally, a "serious nonpolitical crime" is less serious than a "particularly serious crime."[1240]

A crime can be considered a "serious nonpolitical crime" even if it did not result in a conviction. However, the adjudicator must find probable cause, or reasonable basis, to believe that the crime was committed before applying the bar for a crime that

---

[1233] *Matter of N–A–M–*, 24 I&N Dec. 336, 343–45 (BIA 2007).

[1234] *Matter of L–S–*, 22 I&N Dec. 645, 650–51 (BIA 1999).

[1235] *See Ahmetovic v. INS*, 62 F.3d 48, 53 (2d Cir. 1995); *Kofa v. INS*, 60 F.3d 1084 (4th Cir. 1995); *Matter of Q–T–M–T–*, 21 I&N Dec. 639, 655–56 (BIA 1996); *Matter of C–*, 20 I&N Dec. 529 (BIA 1992); *Matter of U–M–*, 20 I&N Dec. 327 (BIA 1991); *Matter of Carballe*, 19 I&N Dec. 357 (BIA 1986).

[1236] See ch. 12 for a detailed discussion of judicial review.

[1237] *Perez-Palafox v. Holder*, 744 F.3d 1138, 1144–45 (9th Cir. 2014); *Delgado v. Holder*, 648 F.3d 1095, 1099–1100 (9th Cir. 2011); *Nethagani v. Mukasey*, 532 F.3d 150, 153–55 (2d Cir. 2008); *Alaka v. Att'y Gen.*, 456 F.3d 88, 95–102 (3d Cir. 2006); *Afridi v. Gonzales*, 442 F.3d 1212, 1217–19 (9th Cir. 2006). *But see Pechenkov v. Holder*, 705 F.3d 444, 447–49 (9th Cir. 2012); *Tian v. Holder*, 576 F.3d 890, 896–98 (8th Cir. 2009); *Lovan v. Holder*, 574 F.3d 990, 997–98 (8th Cir. 2009); *Ali v. Achim*, 468 f.3d 462, 465–66, 470 (7th Cir. 2006).

[1238] INA §§208(b)(2)(A)(iii), 241(b)(3)(B)(iii); 8 USC §§1158(b)(2)(A)(iii), 1231(b)(3)(B)(iii) (2012).

[1239] *Matter of E–A–*, 26 I&N Dec. 1, 3 (BIA 2012). *See also Pronsivakulchai v. Gonzales*, 461 F.3d 903 (7th Cir. 2006); *Khouzam v. Ashcroft*, 361 F.3d 161, 165–66 (2d Cir. 2004).

[1240] *Matter of Frentescu*, 18 I&N Dec. 244, 247 (BIA 1982).

did not result in a conviction.[1241] Additionally, the applicant need not have personally carried out the act of harm; it is enough for the applicant to have been involved in the serious nonpolitical crime for him or her to be barred from asylum and withholding of removal eligibility.[1242]

Like the particularly serious crime bar, the serious nonpolitical crime bar applies independently to a spouse or child who is included on an asylum application if there are serious reasons to believe that he or she committed a serious nonpolitical crime. Such an individual is barred from being granted asylum as a derivative.[1243]

Whether a crime is political in nature is primarily a question of fact,[1244] and turns on whether "the political aspects of the offense outweigh its common-law character."[1245] If the common-law aspects of the offense outweigh the political nature of the crime, the crime will bar asylum and withholding of removal relief. If the crime is determined to have been political, then the adjudicator must consider the "atrocious nature" of the offense and also the "political necessity and success" of the methods used.[1246]

To determine whether a crime is political in nature, the BIA directs adjudicators to consider the following factors: (1) whether the act was directed at a governmental entity or political organization, versus a private or civilian entity; (2) whether the act was directed toward modification of the political organization of the State; and (3) whether there is a close and direct causal link between the crime and the political purpose.[1247] Therefore, a serious nonpolitical crime is a crime that: (1) was not committed out of genuine political motives; (2) was not directed toward the modification of the political organization or structure of the state; and (3) in which there is no direct, causal link between the crime committed and its alleged political purposes and object.[1248]

If the crime is found to be political in nature, the inquiry then shifts to whether it is "atrocious" in nature. If the offense is not of an atrocious nature, the IJ "must balance the seriousness of the criminal acts against the political aspect of the conduct to

[1241] *Khouzam v. Ashcroft*, 361 F.3d 161, 164 (2d Cir. 2004); *McMullen v. INS*, 788 F.2d 591, 599 (9th Cir. 1986); *Sindona v. Grant*, 619 F.2d 167, 174 (2d Cir. 1980).

[1242] *McMullen v. INS*, 788 F.2d 591, 599 (9th Cir. 1986).

[1243] 8 CFR §208.21(a) (2014). See ch. 13 for a detailed discussion of derivative beneficiaries.

[1244] *Id.* (citing *Ornelas v. Ruiz*, 161 U.S. 502 (1896)).

[1245] *Matter of McMullen*, 19 I&N Dec. 90, 97 (BIA 1984), *aff'd McMullen v. INS (II)*, 788 F.2d 591 (9th Cir. 1986) (finding that the applicant's participation in random acts of violence directed against civilians were acts of an atrocious nature out of proportion to the political goal of achieving a unified Ireland and were not within the political offense exception). *Matter of McMullen* was upheld by the Supreme Court in *INS v. Aguirre-Aguirre*, 526 U.S. 415, 426–31 (1999).

[1246] *INS v. Aguirre-Aguirre*, 526 U.S. 415, 429–32 (1999).

[1247] *Matter of E–A–*, 26 I&N Dec. 1, 3 (BIA 2012).

[1248] AOBTC Workbook, Mandatory Bars & Discretion, *supra* note 1203, at 23.

determine whether the criminal nature of the applicant's acts outweighs their political character."[1249] If "the crime is grossly out of proportion to the political objective or if it involves acts of an atrocious nature," then the balance will not be struck and the crime will likely bar asylum and withholding of removal relief.[1250]

UNHCR recommends that an adjudicator balance "the nature of the offense . . . committed by the applicant and the degree of persecution feared," noting that "[i]f a person has well-founded fear of very severe persecution, . . . a crime must be very grave in order to exclude him."[1251] The Supreme Court, however, has rejected this approach.[1252] Even if a crime was committed out of genuine political motives, it should be considered a serious nonpolitical crime if the act is disproportionate to the objective, or if it is atrocious or barbarous in nature.[1253]

Congress intended this bar to be consistent with article 1(F)(b) of the 1951 U.N. Convention Relating to the Status of Refugees.[1254] According to UNHCR's *Handbook*, the purpose of this bar "is to protect communities . . . from the danger of admitting a refugee who has committed a serious common crime."[1255] It also seeks "to render due justice to a refugee who has committed a common crime (or crimes) of a less serious nature or has committed a political offense."[1256] Non-serious offenses and political offenses are, therefore, exceptions to this bar to asylum and withholding of removal.

Acts that have constituted serious nonpolitical crimes given the facts and evidence presented include:

- Acts of violence against civilians;[1257]
- The recruitment or use of child soldiers;[1258]

[1249] *Id.* (citing *INS v. Aguirre-Aguirre*, 526 U.S. 415, 426–31 (1999)). In applying the balancing test, the BIA may consider whether the crime involves "self-defense." *Berhane v. Holder*, 606 F.3d 819 (6th Cir. 2010) (remanding to the BIA because it failed to account for self-defense and the nature and severity of "rock-throwing" weighed against the political objective).

[1250] *Matter of McMullen*, 19 I&N Dec. 90, 97–98 (BIA 1984).

[1251] *UNHCR Handbook*, *supra* note 33, at ¶156.

[1252] *INS v. Aguirre-Aguirre*, 526 U.S. 415 (1999).

[1253] *Id. See also Chay-Velasquez v. Ashcroft*, 367 F.3d 751 (8th Cir. 2004).

[1254] *McMullen v. INS*, 788 F.2d 591, 595 (9th Cir. 1986), *overruled in part on other grounds by Barapind v. Enomoto*, 400 F.3d 744, 751 (9th Cir. 2005).

[1255] UNHCR Handbook, *supra* note 33, ¶ 151.

[1256] *Id.*

[1257] *McMullen v. INS*, 788 F.2d 591, 595 (9th Cir. 1986).

[1258] Child Soldiers Accountability Act of 2008 (CSAA), Pub. L. No. 110-340 (Oct. 3, 2008), §2(d)(1). As mandated by Congress, an applicant who has been found deportable under INA §237(a)(4)(F) or inadmissible under INA §212(a)(3)(G) for recruitment of child soldiers "shall be considered an alien with respect to whom there are serious reasons to believe that the alien has committed a serious nonpolitical crime." *Id.* Therefore, under the Child Soldiers Accountability Act of 2008, any person who engaged in the recruitment or use of child soldiers is barred from asylum and withholding of

Continued

- Assault on a family planning official in China;[1259]
- Burning passenger buses and cars, throwing stones, pushing baskets of food off merchants' heads, and throwing merchandise off merchants' tables to disrupt the opposition party;[1260]
- Drug trafficking;[1261]
- Gang activities as a juvenile;[1262]
- Selling organs on the black market;[1263]
- Burning buses that served civilians, breaking windows, and fighting with police;[1264]
- A theft offense for which the sentence imposed was 15 years;[1265] and
- A robbery for which the sentence imposed was two years.[1266]

In contrast, acts that have been found *not* to constitute serious nonpolitical crimes given the facts and evidence presented include participation in resistance activities, supporting a coup against a military government,[1267] and throwing rocks at police during anti-government demonstrations.[1268] Where there is no opportunity for citizens

---

removal and is deemed to have committed a serious nonpolitical crime. *See* Child Soldiers Accountability Act of 2008, Pub. L. No. 110-340. *See also* U.S. Citizenship & Immigration Servs. Memorandum on Child Soldiers Accountability Act (Dec. 31, 2008), *published on* AILA InfoNet at Doc. No. 09012770 (last updated Jan. 27, 2009).

[1259] *Zheng v. Holder*, 698 F.3d 710, 712–14 (8th Cir. 2013) (finding a serious nonpolitical crime where the applicant had assaulted a family planning official in China for refusal to return the applicant's property).

[1260] *Matter of E–A–*, 26 I&N Dec. 1 (BIA 2012) (finding a serious nonpolitical crime for a member of a youth group of the Democratic Party of Cote d'Ivoire who did not harm anyone because the conduct posted an "inherent" risk of harm and therefore was disproportionate to its political character).

[1261] *Go v. Holder*, 640 F.3d 1047, 1052–53 (9th Cir. 2011).

[1262] *Urbina-Mejia v. Holder*, 597 F.3d 360, 369–70 (6th Cir. 2010).

[1263] *Guo Qi Wang v. Holder*, 583 F.3d 86 (2d Cir. 2009) (finding a serious nonpolitical crime where the applicant had schemed to deceive prisoners and their families to sell organs on the black market).

[1264] *Chay-Velasquez v. Ashcroft*, 367 F.3d 751, 755–56 (8th Cir. 2004).

[1265] *Matter of Ballester-Garcia*, 17 I&N Dec. 592 (BIA 1980), *modified in part by Matter of Gonzalez*, 19 I&N Dec. 682, 685 n.3 (BIA 1988) (modifying this precedent to the extent that it supports the practice of pretermitting asylum applications in cases involving applicants convicted of particularly serious crimes because the nature and gravity of the conviction "is not the only evidence that should be received and considered by an immigration judge or this Board in evaluating whether an otherwise eligible applicant warrants a grant of asylum as a matter of discretion").

[1266] *Matter of Rodriguez-Palma*, 17 I&N Dec. 465 (BIA 1980) *modified in part by Matter of Gonzalez*, 19 I&N Dec. 682, 685 n.3 (BIA 1988).

[1267] *Dwomoh v. Sava*, 696 F. Supp. 970, 979 (S.D.N.Y. 1988).

[1268] *Berhane v. Holder*, 606 F.3d 819 (6th Cir. 2010) (remanding to the BIA for further consideration and explanation of its position where the BIA had concluded that the criminal nature of the applicant's

Continued

to freely and peacefully change their laws, leaders, or form of government, participation in a *coup d'état* may be political in nature and may outweigh the common-law character of the offense, and therefore may not bar asylum and withholding of removal.[1269]

- **Practice Pointer**: Even though participation in a *coup d'état* may not constitute a serious nonpolitical crime, however, it may bar the applicant under other grounds, such as terrorism or providing material support to terrorists.[1270]

4. Danger to the Security of the United States

An applicant is barred from receiving asylum and withholding of removal if "there are reasonable grounds for regarding the [applicant] as a danger to the security of the United States."[1271] The withholding of removal section further provides that an applicant who has engaged in terrorist activity (as defined in INA §212(a)(3)(B)) is considered to be an individual with respect to whom there are reasonable grounds for regarding as a danger to the security of the United States.[1272]

These bars to asylum and withholding of removal mirror the bar found in Article 33(2) of the 1951 U.N. Convention Relating to the Status of Refugees, which provides that the protection of *nonrefoulement* may be denied to "a refugee whom there are reasonable grounds for regarding as a danger to the security of the country."[1273]

In interpreting the language, "reasonable grounds for regarding," the AG found that reasonable grounds means a standard "substantially less stringent than preponderance of the evidence" and compared it with "probable cause."[1274] "[I]f there is information that would permit a reasonable person to believe that the alien may pose a danger to national security," he or she may be barred from asylum and withholding of removal relief.[1275] The information relied upon "need not meet standards for admissibility of evidence in court proceedings."[1276] The AG has held

---

activities in Ethiopia of throwing rocks at police during demonstrations outweighed the actions' political components).

[1269] *Dwomoh v. Sava*, 696 F.Supp. 970 (S.D.N.Y. 1988).

[1270] *Matter of S–K–*, 23 I&N Dec. 936, 942 n.5 (BIA 2006). *See also Abdoulaye v. Holder*, 721 F.3d 485 (7th Cir. 2013) (disqualifying the applicant from asylum and withholding of removal because he gave material support to terrorists under INA §212(a)(3)(B)(iv)(VI) when they seized the governor in executing a planned coup in Niger).

[1271] INA §§208(b)(2)(A)(iv), 241(b)(3)(B)(iv); 8 USC §§1158(b)(2)(A)(iv), 1231(b)(3)(B)(iv) (2012).

[1272] INA §241(b)(3)(B); 8 USC §1231(b)(3)(B) (2012). *See Matter of S–K–*, 23 I&N Dec. 936, 942 n.5 (BIA 2006). *See also infra* pt. IV.B.5. for a detailed discussion of terrorist activity.

[1273] Refugee Convention, supra note 50, at art. 33(2).

[1274] *Matter of A–H–*, 23 I&N Dec. 774, 787–90 (AG 2005) (addressing former INA §243(h)(2)(D)).

[1275] *Matter of A–H–*, 23 I&N Dec. 774, at 789.

[1276] *Id.*

that this bar applies to "any nontrivial level of danger" or "any nontrivial degree of risk."[1277] Thus, the level of danger need not be serious, significant, or grave to trigger the provision, but generally must be a danger to the nation's defense, foreign relations, or economic interests.[1278] However, neither the mere existence of extradition proceedings nor an Interpol alert, nor guilt by association, may be the basis to deny asylum and withholding of removal under the danger to U.S. security bar.[1279]

Moreover, at least one court has disagreed with the AG's interpretation that "if there is information that would permit a reasonable person to believe that the alien may pose a danger to national security," he or she may be barred from asylum and withholding of removal relief.[1280] The Third Circuit held that the intent of U.S. Congress requires an inquiry into whether the individual "is" a danger, not whether the individual "may pose" a danger.[1281]

In *Yusupov v. Att'y Gen.*, the government of Uzbekistan had requested the extradition of the applicants, asserting that they participated with others in a movement seeking the "forced overthrow" of the Republic of Uzbekistan and the establishment on its territory of a "religious extremist Islamic fundamental state."[1282] The United States initiated an investigation and found video clips of Osama Bin Laden, an alleged Chechen militant attacking Russian troops and vehicles, a map of Pennsylvania State Police facilities, and an e-mail addressed to the applicants' former roommate that referenced "jihad" on the applicants' computer.[1283] The applicants explained that they had the clips to criticize the viewpoints advanced by the terrorist regimes and that the condemned the views in the video. They further explained that they used the word "jihad" in the meaning of an "inward spiritual struggle to attain perfect faith."[1284] On remand, the BIA determined that the applicants did, in fact, present an actual danger to national security. However, the Third Circuit held that neither the BIA nor the government had provided the court with substantial evidence that supported the assertion that the petitioners were a threat to the safety of the United States.[1285] Specifically, neither the BIA nor the government provided the name of any potential terrorist organization or extremist movement with which they claimed the applicants to be affiliated, nor did they provide a "coherent and reliable

---

[1277] *Matter of A–H–*, 23 I&N Dec. 774, at 788.

[1278] *See Yusupov v. Att'y Gen.*, 650 F.3d 968, 982–84 (3d Cir. 2011) [hereinafter *Yusupov* II]; *Matter of U–H–*, 23 I&N Dec. 355, 356 (BIA 2002).

[1279] *See Yusupov*, II at 982–84; *Matter of U–H–*, at 356.

[1280] *Matter of A–H–*, 23 I&N Dec. 774, 789 (AG 2005).

[1281] *Yusupov v. Att'y Gen.*, 518 F.3d 188, 190 (3d Cir. 2008) [hereinafter *Yusupov* I].

[1282] *Yusupov* II at 971.

[1283] *Yusupov* I at 188.

[1284] *Id.* at n. 7.

[1285] *Yusupov* II at 976.

narrative" connecting the applicants' seemingly innocuous actions and circumstances with any particular harm that the applicants posed to the United States.[1286]

Other cases, however, have barred applicants under this ground.[1287] In a highly publicized case, Sheik Abdel Rahman, whose followers were linked to the 1993 World Trade Center bombing, was found to be a danger to the security of the United States and ineligible for asylum and withholding of deportation.[1288] Other cases of individuals considered to be a danger to the security of the United States include a Palestine Liberation Organization member[1289] and an anti-Communist Cuban who had been convicted of placing explosives on vessels in Miami, firing on a Polish vessel, and threatening heads of state.[1290]

5. *Terrorism-Related Grounds*

An applicant who is described in INA §§212(a)(3)(B)(i)(I)–(IV) or (VI) or INA §237(a)(4)(B) is barred from being granted asylum.[1291] These individuals include those who:

- Have engaged in terrorist activity;[1292]
- There is reasonable ground to believe are engaged in or are likely to engage in terrorist activity;[1293]
- Have, under any circumstances indicating an intention to cause death or serious bodily harm, incited terrorist activity;[1294]
- Are representatives of a terrorist organization as defined in INA §212(a)(3)(B)(vi) or other group that endorses or espouses terrorist activity;[1295]

[1286] *Id.* at 981.

[1287] *See, e.g.*, *Malkandi v. Holder*, 576 F.3d 906 (9th Cir. 2008) (relying on the applicant's own admissions plus testimony and documentation from government officials, who alleged that the applicant served as a "travel facilitator" for a notorious al Qaeda operative whom the intelligence establishment believed was involved in several of al Qaeda's most infamous attacks against the U.S. interests overseas and was also connected to the alleged architect of the attacks of September 11, 2001).

[1288] *Ali v. Reno*, 829 F. Supp. 1415, 1434 (S.D.N.Y. 1993); *see also* "Sleuthing Shows Significant Slip-ups in Sheik Saga," 70 INTERPRETER RELEASES 1202 (Sept. 13, 1993).

[1289] *Azzouka v. Meese*, 820 F.2d 585 (2d Cir. 1987).

[1290] *Avila v. Rivkind*, 724 F. Supp. 945 (S.D. Fla. 1989). *But see Cheema v. Ashcroft*, 383 F.3d 848 (9th Cir. 2004) (finding that the BIA failed to apply both prongs of its own test of who constitutes a danger to the security of the United States).

[1291] INA §208(b)(2)(A)(v).

[1292] INA §§212(a)(3)(B)(i)(I). "Terrorist Activity" is defined at INA §212(a)(3)(B)(iii).

[1293] INA §§212(a)(3)(B)(i)(II).

[1294] INA §§212(a)(3)(B)(i)(III).

[1295] INA §§212(a)(3)(B)(i)(IV)(aa) and (bb).

- Are members of a terrorist organization defined under INA §§212(a)(3)(B)(vi)(I) or (II);[1296]
- Are members of a terrorist organization defined under INA §212(a)(3)(B)(vi)(III), unless there is clear and convincing evidence they did not know or should not reasonably have known the organization was a terrorist organization;[1297]
- Endorse or espouse terrorist activity or persuade others to endorse or espouse terrorist activity or support a terrorist organization;[1298]
- Have received military-type training from or on behalf of any organization that, at the time the training was received, was a terrorist organization;[1299]
- Are the spouses or children of individuals who are inadmissible under INA §212(a)(3)(B), if the activity causing the individuals to be found inadmissible occurred within the past five years, unless the spouses or children did not know or should not reasonably have known of the activity causing the individuals to be inadmissible, or there are reasonable grounds to believe the individuals have renounced the activity causing them to be found inadmissible;[1300] and
- Have been associated with a terrorist organization and intend while in the United States to engage solely, principally, or incidentally in activities that could endanger the welfare, safety, or security of the United States.[1301]

The only exception is if, in the case of an individual who is a representative of a terrorist organization or other group that endorses or espouses terrorist activity,[1302] the AG determines, in his or her discretion, that there are not reasonable grounds for regarding the applicant as a danger to the security of the United States.[1303]

> ➢ **Practice Pointer**: This exception was created to allow Palestine Liberation Organization representatives to attend meetings of the United Nations in New York. Therefore, in practice, this exception is not widely applicable.

The September 11, 2001, terrorism attacks on the Pentagon and the World Trade Center have made this bar to asylum a priority for DHS and EOIR. Soon after the attacks, Congress passed the USA PATRIOT Act of 2001, which expanded the already broad definition of terrorist activity and allowed for the mandatory detention of "suspected terrorists," even if they had been granted asylum or other relief from

[1296] INA §237(a)(4)(B) (referring to INA §212(a)(3)(B)(V)).

[1297] INA §§212(a)(3)(B)(i)(VI).

[1298] INA §237(a)(4)(B) (referring to INA §212(a)(3)(B)(i)(VII)).

[1299] INA §237(a)(4)(B) (referring to INA §212(a)(3)(B)(i)(VIII)).

[1300] INA §237(a)(4)(B) (referring to INA §§212(a)(3)(B)(i)(IX), 212(a)(3)(B)(ii)).

[1301] INA §237(a)(4)(B) (referring to INA §212(a)(3)(F)).

[1302] INA §212(a)(3)(B)(i)(IV).

[1303] INA §208(b)(2)(A)(v).

removal.[1304] The REAL ID Act then amended these provisions to broaden the categories of individuals who are inadmissible for terrorist-related activities even further.[1305] First, it broadened the INA definitions of "terrorist organization" and "engage in terrorist activity." Second, it expanded the bases for inadmissibility based on a person's support of terror-related activity. Finally, it made terror-related grounds for removability the same as those for inadmissibility.[1306]

Perhaps an unintended consequence of the INA's broad definition of terrorist organization, in particular the Tier III nondesignated category, in conjunction with its broadened definitions of "terrorist activity" and "engage in terrorist activity," has been the barring of numerous, otherwise-eligible refugees from asylum protection in the United States. "Terrorist organizations" under the INA's broad definition may include political parties and national liberation movements whose members, whether organized or not, may have used any weapon in furtherance of their cause or even in self-defense. Members of such groups or individuals who have provided material support to such groups may be found inadmissible as terrorists and thereby barred from asylum and withholding of removal. Many of these applicants' applications have been denied outright and numerous applications have been placed on indefinite "TRIG hold" before the Department of Homeland Security as the applicants await discretionary exemptions.

i. Terrorist Activity Defined

An applicant is barred from asylum and withholding of removal if he or she is found to have engaged in, to be likely to engage in, or to have incited terrorist activity.[1307] Terrorist activity means any activity that is unlawful under the laws of the place where it is committed and which involves any of the following:

- The highjacking or sabotage of any aircraft, vessel, or vehicle;
- The seizing or detaining, and threatening to kill, injure, or continue to detain, another individual in order to compel a third person (including a governmental organization) to do or abstain from doing any act as an explicit or implicit condition for the release of the individual seized or detained;
- A violent attack of an internationally protected person (as defined in 18 USC §1116(b)(4)) or the liberty of such person;
- An assassination;

1304 For a more in-depth analysis, *see* Regina Germain, *Rushing to Judgment: The Unintended Consequences of the USA PATRIOT Act for Bona Fide Refugees*, 16 GEO. IMMIGR. L.J. 505 (2002). *See also* Nancy Chang & Alan Kabat, *Summary of Recent Court Rulings on Terrorism-Related Matters Having Civil Liberty Implications*, Ctr. For Constitutional Rights (2004), *http://rci.rutgers.edu/~tripmcc/phil/ccr-summaryofcases.pdf.*

1305 *See* INA §212(a)(3)(B); 8 USC §1182(a)(3)(B) (2012).

1306 INA §§212(a)(3)(B)(i)(I), 237(a)(4)(B); 8 USC §§1182(a)(3)(B)(i)(I), 1227(a)(4)(B) (2012).

1307 INA §§208(b)(2)(A)(v), 241(b)(3)(B); 8 USC §§1158(b)(2)(A)(v), 1231(b)(3)(B) (2012).

- The use of any biological agent, chemical agent, or nuclear weapon;
- The use of any device, explosive, firearm, or other weapon or dangerous device (other than for mere personal monetary gain) with intent to endanger, directly or indirectly, the safety of one or more individuals or to cause substantial damage to property; and
- A threat, attempt, or conspiracy to do any of those acts.[1308]

Note that the broadest "terrorist activity" provision contained within the INA's definition is explicitly limited to those unlawful acts that involve the use of an explosive, firearm, or other weapon or dangerous device, *and* which are carried out "*other than* for mere personal monetary gain."[1309] Thus, although this provision within the definition of "terrorist activity" under the INA is "certainly broad" and "includes a great deal of conduct," the definition is not so broad as to include the sorts of common crimes that "no reasonable person would consider to be terrorist acts."[1310] As the Third Circuit explained:

First, the parenthetical phrase "other than for mere personal monetary gain" removes common crimes from the definition by requiring that the offending activity be conducted for reasons other than money. For that reason, offenses like robbery and burglary are not included in the definition. Second, the *mens rea* element of the provision requires the actor to have the specific intent to endanger the safety of individuals or to cause substantial damage to property.[1311]

> ➢ **Practice Pointer**: Significantly, the language "other than for mere personal monetary gain" could exclude many activities commonly alleged to be terrorist activities committed by Tier III terrorist organizations, such as acts of extortion.

The decisions of other circuits and the BIA support the Third Circuit's conclusion that common crimes are generally excluded from the definition of "terrorist activity." For example, in *Khan v. Holder*, the Ninth Circuit found that the Jammu and Kashmir Liberation Front met the definition of "terrorist organization" because of its activities in killing politicians, kidnapping the daughter of the Indian home Minister, and attacking Indian Army convoys, all of which constitute "terrorist activity."[1312] In *Matter of S–K–*, the BIA held that the Chin National Front in Burma met the definition of "terrorist organization" because "there was sufficient evidence in the record to conclude that the CNF uses firearms and/or explosives to engage in combat with the Burmese military."[1313] And in *Matter of A–H–*, the BIA concluded that

---

[1308] INA §212(a)(3)(B)(iii).

[1309] INA §212(a)(3)(B)(iii)(V)(b) (emphasis added).

[1310] *McAllister v. Att'y Gen.*, 444 F.3d 178, 185–86 (3d Cir. 2006).

[1311] *McAllister v. Att'y Gen.*, 444 F.3d 178, at 186.

[1312] *Khan v. Holder*, 584 F.3d 773, 785 (9th Cir. 2009).

[1313] *Matter of S–K–*, 23 I&N Dec. 936, 941 (BIA 2006).

armed insurgent groups in Algeria committed "terrorist acts" which included bombing of civilian targets, the assassination of political figures, the widespread murder of journalists and intellectuals, and the use of bombs and car bombs to attack property and people resulting in "hundreds of civilian deaths."[1314] These examples of "terrorist activity" stand in stark contrast to more common crimes perpetrated for "mere personal monetary gain."[1315]

ii. Engaging in Terrorist Activity

Individuals who engage in terrorist activity also are barred from asylum and withholding of removal.[1316] Although the withholding of removal statute does not specifically list engaging in terrorist activity as a bar to relief, an individual described under INA §237(a)(4)(B) (individuals deportable for terrorist activities described in INA §§212(a)(3)(B) and 212(a)(3)(F)) "shall be considered an alien with respect to whom there are reasonable grounds for regarding as a danger to the security of the United States" and thus is barred from withholding of removal.[1317] Consequently, applicants who are barred from asylum under the terrorist activity bar are likely also barred from withholding of removal.

"Engaging in terrorist activity" is defined under INA §212(a)(3)(B)(iv) and includes committing, inciting, preparing, and planning terrorist activities, as well as gathering information on potential targets of terrorist activity and soliciting funds, soliciting individuals, and providing material support to a "terrorist organization" or a terrorist activity.[1318]

The REAL ID Act broadened the definition of "engage in terrorist activity" to include direct participation or support of terrorist activity, as well as indirect support of terrorist activities or organizations.[1319] Perhaps most significantly, the REAL ID Act added that an applicant who provided material support or who acted as a solicitor for a person engaged in terrorist activity or a non-designated terrorist organization has engaged in terrorist activity himself.[1320] The only exception to this rule is if an applicant can demonstrate, by clear and convincing evidence, that he or she did not and should not have reasonably known that the material support or solicitation would

---

[1314] *Matter of A–H–*, 23 I&N Dec. 774, 775–76 (BIA 2005).

[1315] INA §212(a)(3)(B)(iii)(V)(b). *See also, McAllister v. Att'y Gen.*, 444 F.3d 178, 185–86 (3d Cir. 2006).

[1316] INA §§208(b)(2)(A)(v), 241(b)(3)(B).

[1317] INA §241(b)(3)(B).

[1318] INA §212(a)(3)(B)(iv).

[1319] INA §212(a)(3)(B)(iv).

[1320] *See, e.g., Barahona v. Holder*, 691 F.3d 349, 352 (4th Cir. 2012) (finding that a man has provided material support to the FMLN because members of the guerilla force had used his home and kitchen for their personal living needs and he did not refuse due to his fear of the forces); *Matter of S–K–*, 24 I&N Dec. 475 (BIA 2008) (reversing a previous denial based on material support because a new law provided that the Chin National Front must not be considered a terrorist organization).

further either a terrorist activity or organization.[1321] However, the AG or Secretary of State may choose, in their unreviewable discretion, not to apply the "material support bar."[1322]

Specifically, to engage in terrorist activity includes the following:

- To commit or incite to commit, under circumstances indicating an intention to cause death or serious bodily injury, a terrorist activity;
- To prepare or plan a terrorist activity;
- To gather information on potential targets for terrorist activity;
- To solicit funds or other things of value for a terrorist activity, a terrorist organization described in INA §212(a)(3)(B)(vi)(I) or (II);
- To solicit funds or other things of value for a terrorist activity, a terrorist organization described in INA §212(a)(3)(B)(vi)(III), unless the solicitor can demonstrate by clear and convincing evidence that he or she did not know, and should not reasonably have known, that the organization was a terrorist organization;
- To solicit any individual to engage in such conduct, for membership in a terrorist organization described in INA §212(a)(3)(B)(vi)(I) or (II), or for membership in a terrorist organization described in INA §212(a)(3)(B)(vi)(III), unless the solicitor can demonstrate by clear and convincing evidence that he or she did not know, and should not reasonably have known, that the organization was a terrorist organization;
- To commit an act that the actor knows or reasonably should know, affords material support, including a safe house, transportation, communications, funds, transfer of funds or other material benefit, false documentation or identification, weapons (including chemical, biological, or radiological weapons), explosives or training:
  - For the commission of a terrorist activity;
  - To any individual who the actor knows, or reasonably should know, has committed or plans to commit a terrorist activity;
  - To a terrorist organization described in INA §212(a)(3)(B)(vi)(I) or (II), or to any member of such an organization; and
  - To a terrorist organization described in INA §212(a)(3)(B)(vi)(III), or to any member of such an organization, unless the actor can demonstrate by clear and convincing evidence that he or she did not know, and should not reasonably have known, that the organization was a terrorist organization.[1323]

[1321] INA §§212(a)(3)(B)(iv)(IV)(cc), (V)(cc), (VI)(dd); 8 USC §§1182(a)(3)(B)(iv)(IV)(cc), (V)(cc), (VI)(dd) (2012).

[1322] INA §212(a)(3)(B)(iv).

[1323] INA §212(a)(3)(B)(iv).

In one of the few reported cases interpreting the "engage in terrorist activity" provision, the BIA found that there were "reasonable grounds to believe" that an Iranian national who was a supporter and member of the Mujahedin-e Khalq (MEK) was engaged in or was likely to engage in "terrorist activity."[1324] The Third Circuit denied asylum and withholding of removal to a former member of the Irish National Liberation Army who served as an armed lookout while other members shot at a Royal Ulster Constabulary (RUC) officer.[1325] The Eighth Circuit also denied asylum under this statutory bar to an applicant who had voluntarily participated in the activities of the Tamil Tigers.[1326] Similarly, the Ninth Circuit found that an Eritrean man had engaged in terrorist activities when he collected funds for the Eritrean Liberation Front (ELF), supplied it with provisions, and passed along street documents. The court found that these activities amounted to material support.[1327] The Ninth Circuit also found "reasonable grounds to believe" the individual would likely engage in terrorist activity after entering the United States when customs agents found "anti-American" materials on his computer, he had donated small amounts to Hamas social programs through a mosque, and his two cousins were Hamas members.[1328]

In contrast, in a pre-September 11th case, an IJ granted asylum to a convicted Irish Republican Army (IRA) bomber, finding that he had engaged in a "political offense" and not "terrorist activity."[1329] In reaching this conclusion, the IJ noted that no one had been injured in the bombing and that the applicant's acts were in furtherance of an ongoing conflict to rid Northern Ireland of British rule.[1330] In addition, the IJ found that because the RUC had engaged in "atrocious acts" against the Catholic population, the RUC was a "legitimate target" conforming to international law precepts of proportionality, necessity, and respect for the combatant/noncombatant distinction.[1331] The IJ reasoned that a "political offense" is "legitimate political violence," whereas terrorism that targets unarmed civilians is "illegitimate political violence."[1332] This is one of six Irish deportation cases that were terminated by the AG on December 11, 2000, in order to serve the interests of U.S. foreign policy.[1333]

[1324] *Matter of U–H–*, 23 I&N Dec. 355 (BIA 2002) (holding that the USA PATRIOT Act does not impose a new and higher standard of proof and that "reasonable grounds to believe" is akin to a "probable cause" standard).

[1325] *McAllister v. Att'y Gen.*, 444 F.3d 178, 191 (3d Cir. 2006) (finding the applicant removable for having engaged in terrorist activity).

[1326] *Perinpanathan v. INS*, 310 F.3d 594, 598–99 (8th Cir. 2002).

[1327] *Haile v. Holder*, 658 F.3d 1122 (9th Cir. 2011).

[1328] *Abufayad v. Holder*, 632 F.3d 623 (9th Cir. 2011).

[1329] *Matter of Pearson*, A72 472 870 (IJ Mar. 27, 1997) (New York, NY) (IJ, Williams), at 34.

[1330] *Matter of Pearson*, A72 472 870, at 33.

[1331] *Matter of Pearson*, A72 472 870, at 34 (citing *In re Doherty*, 599 F. Supp. 270 (S.D.N.Y. 1984)).

[1332] *Matter of Pearson*, A72 472 870, at 36. *See also Cheema v. Ashcroft*, 372 F.3d 1147, 1155 (9th Cir. 2004), *amended by* 383 F.3d 848 (9th Cir. 2004) (finding that wife's actions of sending money to

Continued

In 2001, a series of cases interpreting the "material support bar" drew criticism because the asylum officers found that victims of extortion by rebel groups in Colombia were ineligible for asylum because they had paid ransom for kidnapped family members. The asylum officers had determined that by paying ransom, these victims had provided "material support" to a terrorist organization.[1334] The U.S. Committee for Refugees, in a letter to former Attorney General John Ashcroft, stated that it was "ludicrous" to label the payment of ransom or other extortion fees "material support."[1335] DHS later reversed the decisions in these cases in the exercise of discretion.[1336]

iii. Terrorist Organization Defined

The REAL ID Act of 2005 also amended and expanded the definition of "terrorist organization."[1337] Before the REAL ID Act, a "terrorist organization" could be one designated by the Secretary of State or could be a group of two or more individuals, whether organized or not, which engages in terrorist activity (commonly referred to as a Tier III organization).[1338] Under the REAL ID Act, the Secretary of State may consult with both the Secretary of Homeland Security and the AG to designate a group as a terrorist organization, after finding that the organization "engages in terrorist activity."[1339] In addition, a group that solicits funds or membership for a terrorist activity or terrorist organization, or otherwise provides material support for a

---

widows and orphans does not constitute terrorist activity); *Humanitarian Law Project v. Gonzales*, 380 F. Supp. 2d 1134, 1138 (C.D. Cal 2005) (holding that the person must know of the organization's terrorist activities or classification).

[1333] *See* 78 INTERPRETER RELEASES 16 (Jan. 3, 2001).

[1334] *See* INS Statement, Colombian Asylum (Apr. 11, 2001).

[1335] *See* Germain, *supra* note 1304, at 512–13.

[1336] INA §212(a)(3)(B)(iv); 8 USC §1182(a)(3)(B)(iv) (2012).

[1337] INA §212(a)(3)(B)(vi); 8 USC §1182(a)(3)(B)(vi) (2012).

[1338] DHS has identified the following Tier III terrorist organizations in adjustment denials: "the Mujahidin" generally, the National Islamic Front of Afghanistan, and Jamiat-e-Islami (Afghanistan in the 1980s); Harakat-e-Islami (Afghanistan); "uprising against the Iraqi government" in southern Iraq in 1991; Kurdish Democratic Party (KDP)(Iraq); All-Burma Students Democratic Front (ABSDF) and God's Army (Burma); Unspecified "counter revolutionary group" in Cuba; Sudan People's Liberation Army (SPLA), National Democratic Alliance (NDA), Democratic Unionist Party (DUP)(Sudan); Eritrean People's Liberation Front (EPLF)(Eritrea in the 1970s and 1980s); Eritrean Liberation Front-RC (ELF-RC) and unnamed Eritrean opposition movements; Oromo Liberation Front (OLF); Ethiopian People's Revolutionary Party (EPRP); Coalition for Unity and Democracy (CUD); Alliance for Freedom and Democracy (AFD); Ogaden National Liberation Front (ONLF) (Ethiopia); "the Chechen Militia;" Federation Estudiantine et Scolaire de Cote d'Ivoire (FESCI)(Cote d'Ivoire); Akali Dal Mann (India); Awami League (Bangladesh), *as reported in* Melanie Nezer and Anwen Hughes, *Understanding the Terrorism Related Inadmissibility Grounds: A Practitioner's Guide*, AILA IMMIGR. & NATIONALITY LAW HANDBOOK, 579 fn. 17 (AILA 2009), *available at www.ailawebcle.org/resources/Resources%20for%208-16-11%20Seminar.pdf.*

[1339] INA §212(a)(3)(B)(vi)(II); 8 USC §1182(a)(3)(B)(vi)(II).

terrorist activity or organization, may also be considered a terrorist organization, even if not otherwise designated as such.[1340]

The INA defines "terrorist organization" as follows:

- Tier I — an organization designated under INA §219;
- Tier II — an organization otherwise designated, upon publication in the Federal Register, by the Secretary of State in consultation with or upon the request of the Attorney General or the Secretary of Homeland Security, as a terrorist organization, after finding that the organization engages in terrorist activity described in INA §212(a)(3)(B)(iv)(I)–(VI); or
- Tier III — an organization that is a group of two or more individuals, whether organized or not, which engages in, or has a subgroup which engages in, terrorist activity described in INA §212(a)(3)(B)(iv)(I)–(VI).

Tier I organizations are also referred to as Foreign Terrorist Organizations (FTO), and are organizations that embody three basic criteria: (1) it must be a foreign organization; (2) it must engage in terrorist activity or terrorism, or retain the capability and intent to engage in terrorist activity or terrorism; and (3) its activity or terrorism must threaten the security of U.S. nationals or the national security (national defense, foreign relations, or economic interests) of the United States.[1341] Tier I organizations are listed on the DOS website and include, among others: Hamas, Hizballah, Palestine Liberation Front, Revolutionary Armed Forces of Columbia (FARC), Shining Path (SL), al-Qa'ida (AQ), Real Irish Republican Army (RIRA), Communist Party of the Philippines/New People's Army, Ansar al-Islam, Islamic Jihad Union, Tehrik-e Taliban Pakistan, Indian Mujahedeen, and Boko Haram.[1342] Currently, there are 59 organizations designated as "foreign terrorist organizations" by the Secretary of State.[1343]

The Secretary of State designates organizations as "foreign terrorist organizations" pursuant to his or her authority under INA §219. A designation under §219 is effective for a period of two years and is subject to limited judicial review. Generally, due process rights do not apply to such organizations because they lack sufficient ties to the United States.[1344] In refusing to set aside the designations of the People's Mojahedin Organization of Iran and the LTTE, the D.C. Circuit held that such designations were political judgments, "decisions of a kind for which the Judiciary

---

[1340] INA §212(a)(3)(B)(iv)(IV)–(VI); 8 USC §1182(a)(3)(B)(iv)(IV)–(VI).

[1341] INA §219.

[1342] *See* U.S. Dep't of State, *Designated Foreign Terrorist Organizations*, *available at www.state.gov/j/ct/rls/other/des/123085.htm* (last visited Nov. 1, 2014).

[1343] *See* U.S. Dep't of State, Foreign Terrorist Organizations, *available at www.state.gov/j/ct/rls/other/des/123085.htm* (last visited Nov. 1, 2014).

[1344] *See, e.g.*, *32 County Sovereignty Comm. v. U.S. Dep't of State*, 292 F.3d 797 (D.C. Cir. 2002).

has neither aptitude, facilities nor responsibilities and have been long held to belong in the domain of political power not subject to judicial intrusion or inquiry."[1345]

Tier II organizations are designated by the Secretary of State after finding that the organization engages in terrorist activity as described in the INA. This authority is known as the Terrorist Exclusion List (TEL) authority, and a TEL designation will generally exclude individuals associated with entities on the TEL from entering the United States. Organizations on the TEL include, among others: Afghan Support Committee, Al-Hamati Sweets Bakeries, Al-Rashid Trust, Anarchist Faction for Overthrow, Army for the Liberation of Rwanda, Bank Al Taqwa Ltd., Continuity Irish Republican Arm, Dhamat Houmet Daawa Salafia, First of October Antifascist Resistance Group (GRAPO), Islamic Renewal and Reform Organization, Jamiat ul-Mujahideen, Japanese Red Army, Jerusalem Warriors, Libyan Islamic Fighting Group, Moroccan Islamic Combatant Group, New People's Army, People Against Gangsterism and Drugs (PAGAD), Revival of Islamic Heritage Society, Revolutionary United Front, The Islamic International Brigade, Tunisian Combat Group, Turkish Hizballah, and Ummah Tameer E-Nau.[1346]

Tier III organizations are also referred to as "undesignated terrorist organizations" because their activities are considered terrorist activities, but they have not undergone a formal designation process like Tier I and Tier II organizations. Instead, the determination of whether a group is a Tier III organization is made on a case-by-case basis in connection with the review of an application for an immigration benefit.[1347] Tier III organizations arise and change over time.

Despite the expansion of bars to asylum on terrorism grounds, being a member of a terrorist organization is not a per se bar to asylum or withholding of removal. Members of such organizations are, however, inadmissible to the United States and could be removed because of their membership.[1348] Even legacy INS conceded that members of terrorist organizations are eligible for asylum. In 1996, legacy INS issued a detailed memorandum on the terrorism provisions of AEDPA that stated that "members" of terrorist organizations may still be eligible for asylum, as long as they have not engaged in terrorist activities.[1349] Such membership, however, could be a

---

[1345] *People's Mojahedin Org. of Iran v. U.S. Dep't of State*, 182 F.3d 17 (D.C. Cir. 1999) (citation omitted).

[1346] *See* U.S. Dep't of State, *Terrorist Exclusion List (TEL), available at www.state.gov/j/ct/rls/other/des/123086.htm* (last visited Nov. 1, 2014).

[1347] *See* U.S. Citizenship & Immigration Servs., *Terrorism-Related Inadmissibility Grounds, available at www.uscis.gov/laws/terrorism-related-inadmissability-grounds/terrorism-related-inadmissibility-grounds-trig#Categories%20of%20Terrorist%20Organizations* (last visited Nov. 1, 2014).

[1348] INA §212(a)(3)(B)(i)(V); 8 USC §1182(a)(3)(B)(i)(V) (2012).

[1349] *See* INS Sends Instructions on Terrorist Exclusions, New Law Amends AEDPA, 73 INTERPRETER RELEASES 1439 (Oct. 11, 1996).

factor in determining whether the applicant merits asylum in the exercise of discretion.[1350]

The REAL ID Act made some other changes to the bars to asylum. While the mere membership exception to automatic disqualification for asylum is preserved for inadmissible applicants who are members of designated terrorist organizations, it is not available for removable applicants. INA §208(b)(2)(A)(v) makes applicants who are either inadmissible on specified terrorism grounds[1351] or are removable for terrorist activities (under INA §237(a)(4)(B)) ineligible for asylum. Inadmissibility on the grounds of membership in a designated terrorist organization[1352] is not among the grounds for denying asylum, nor is inadmissibility on the grounds of endorsement or espousal of terrorist activity.[1353] Therefore, the REAL ID Act makes some applicants who are inadmissible because of terror-related activities eligible for asylum relief, but applicants who are removable for terror-related activities are categorically ineligible for asylum.

Although members of designated terrorist organizations may be eligible for asylum, under the REAL ID Act, inadmissibility for mere membership in a *nondesignated* terrorist organization[1354] will bar an applicant from eligibility for asylum, unless the applicant can demonstrate by clear and convincing evidence that he or she did not know and should not reasonably have known that the organization was a terrorist organization.[1355]

iv. Exceptions and Waiver of Certain Grounds of Inadmissibility

The REAL ID Act gives certain designated officials waiver authority over some of the terrorism-related immigration provisions. Either the Secretary of State or Secretary of Homeland Security, in consultation with each other and the AG, may waive:

(1) inadmissibility of representatives of political, social, or other groups that endorse or espouse terrorist activity;

(2) inadmissibility of those who endorse or espouse terrorist activity, or persuade others to do so;

[1350] *See Kalubi v. Ashcroft*, 364 F.3d 1134, 1139 (9th Cir. 2004).

[1351] INA §208(b)(2)(A)(v); 8 USC §1158(b)(2)(A)(v) (2012), providing that an applicant may be denied asylum for terror-related grounds if he or she is inadmissible under INA §§212(a)(3)(B)(i)(I), (II), (III), (IV), or (VI). The asylum bar does not apply to inadmissible representatives of terrorist organizations or political or social groups that endorse terrorist activity (INA §212(a)(3)(B)(i)(IV)) if the AG determines, in his or her discretion, that there are not reasonable grounds for regarding the alien as a danger to the security of the United States. INA §208(b)(2)(A)(v); 8 USC §1158(b)(2)(A)(v) (2012).

[1352] INA §212(a)(3)(B)(i)(V); 8 USC §1182(a)(3)(B)(i)(V) (2012).

[1353] INA §212(a)(3)(B)(i)(VII); 8 USC §1182(a)(3)(B)(i)(VII) (2012).

[1354] INA §212(a)(3)(B)(vi)(III); 8 USC §1182(a)(3)(B)(vi)(III) (2012).

[1355] INA §§208(b)(2)(A)(v), 212(a)(3)(B)(i)(VI), (vi)(III); 8 USC §§1158(b)(2)(A)(v), 1182(a)(3)(B)(i)(VI), (vi)(III) (2012).

(3) the application of the definition of "terrorist organization" to groups who constitute one solely because a subgroup has engaged in terrorist activity; and

(4) the application of the material support bar.[1356] Additionally, the following individuals may be exempted from the terrorism-related bars to admission under INA §212(d)(3)(B):

- Persons who provided material support under duress to a Tier I, II, or III group;
- Persons who engaged in terrorist activity on behalf of a Tier I or II group, but did not do so knowingly or voluntarily;
- Members and representatives of Tier III groups;
- Persons who voluntarily engaged in terrorist activity as long as they did not do so on behalf of a Tier I or II group; and
- Spouses and children of persons inadmissible under INA §212(a)(3)(B) who are not covered by the statutory exceptions.[1357]

a. Exemptions from Terrorism-Related Inadmissibility Grounds

There is no statutory exception for the provision of "material support" under duress, nor does the INA allow an exception for the provision of even insignificant, *de minimus* support.[1358] As a practical matter, this has resulted in thousands of asylum denials and numerous affirmative asylum applications being placed on "TRIG hold." The only mitigation of the effects of these broad definitions, therefore, has been the exercise of discretionary authority by the Secretary of State or the Secretary of Homeland Security, in consultation with the AG, to promulgate an appropriate exemption.[1359] If no exemption exists, these cases could remain on hold

---

[1356] INA §212(d)(3)(B)(i); 8 USC §1182(d)(3)(B)(i) (2012), waiving the applicability of INA §§212(a)(3)
(B)(i)(IV)(bb), (VII), (iv)(VI), and (vi)(III) in certain circumstances.

[1357] *See* Melanie Nezer and Anwen Hughes, *Understanding the Terrorism Related Inadmissibility Grounds: A Practitioner's Guide*, AILA IMMIGR. & NATIONALITY LAW HANDBOOK, 579 fn. 17 (AILA 2009), *available at www.ailawebcle.org/resources/Resources%20for%208-16-11%20Seminar.pdf.*

[1358] *See, e.g., Ay v. Holder*, 743 F.3d 317 (2d Cir. 2014) (finding that the plain language of the material support bar was inconclusive as to whether a duress exception was implicit in its terms); *Annachamy v. Holder*, 733 F.3d 254 (9th Cir. 2013) (holding that the material support bar does not include an implied exception for legitimate political violence or support under duress, and deferring to the administrative waiver process supplied by Congress); *Alturo v. Att'y Gen.*, 716 F.3d 1310 (11th Cir. 2013) (holding that there is no implied exception to the material support bar for support provided to a terrorist organization involuntarily or under duress); *Baharona v. Holder*, 691 F.3d 349 (4th Cir. 2012); *Viegas v. Holder*, 699 f.3d 798 (4th Cir. 2012); *Singh-Kaur v. Ashcroft*, 385 F.3d 293 (3d Cir. 2004); *Matter of S–K–*, 23 I&N Dec. 936 (BIA 2006).

[1359] The authority to grant exemptions was expanded by the Consolidated Appropriations Act of 2008 to be exercised by the secretary of homeland security or the secretary of state. Consolidated Appropriations Act of 2008, Pub. L. No. 110-161, 121 Stat. 1844 (Dec. 26, 2007). *See also* U.S. Citizenship & Immigration Servs. Memorandum, *Discretionary Exemptions to Terrorist Activity Inadmissibility Grounds* (July 28, 2008), *published on* AILA InfoNet at Doc. No. 08081131 (*posted* Aug. 11, 2008).

indefinitely.[1360] Even if an exemption does exist, however, there is no formal procedure for seeking an exemption. Instead, USCIS identifies and adjudicates exemption-eligible cases on its own.

> ➢ **Practice Pointer**: Even though there is no formal process for seeking an exemption, practitioners should prepare and submit formal requests for consideration under the relevant exemption, along with supporting documentation. These requests should be made with the Asylum Office that had jurisdiction over the application, or with USCIS Asylum Division Headquarters, depending on the stage of the process.

When USCIS adjudicates an affirmative asylum case in which the applicant is inadmissible under one or more of the terrorism-related inadmissibility grounds (TRIG) set forth in INA §212(a)(3)(B), certain applications falling in this category will be placed on "TRIG hold" pending review and the possible future application of an exemption.[1361] The hold categories include:

(1) Applicants who are inadmissible under the terrorism-related provisions of the INA based on any activity or association that was not under duress relating to any Tier III undesignated terrorist organization, other than those for which an exception already exists;

(2) Applicants who are inadmissible under the terrorism-related provisions of the INA, other than material support, based on any activity or association related to a Tier I, II, or III terrorist organization where the activity or association was under duress;

(3) Applicants who voluntarily provided medical care to designated or undesignated terrorist organizations, to members of terrorist organizations, or to individuals who have engaged in terrorist activity; and

(4) Applicants who are inadmissible under INA §212(a)(3)(B)(i)(IX) as the spouses or children of individuals described above, whether or not the spouse or parent has applied for an immigration benefit.[1362]

The hold policy previously mandated that USCIS hold all cases in these categories, no matter the circumstances. This policy was revised in a November 20, 2011 memorandum, which clarified that categories 1 and 2 above could be denied if the adjudicator and subsequent reviewers determine that, in the totality of the

---

[1360] The indefinite hold period has been challenged in the federal courts, and they plaintiffs have survived government motions to dismiss. *See, e.g., Ahmed v. Mayorkas*, No. 08-1680 (N.D. Cal. filed Mar. 27, 2008); *Al-Karim v. Mukasey*, No. 08-671 (D. Colo. filed Apr. 2, 2008).

[1361] U.S. Citizenship & Immigration Servs., *Revised Guidance on the Adjudication of Cases Involving Terrorist-Related Inadmissibility Grounds and Amendment to the Hold Policy for Such Cases* (Feb. 13, 2009), *available at* AILA InfoNet Doc. 09052173 (last updated May 21, 2009).

[1362] *Id.*

circumstances, the applicant does not warrant a favorable exercise of discretion even if a discretionary exemption would be authorized at a future date.[1363]

In determining whether an asylum application should be placed on hold, an adjudicator will document the nature of the applicant's activities or association with the terrorist organization, the identity and nature of the organization, and the factors that warrant a denial of an exemption in the exercise of discretion.[1364] The adjudicator must complete the 212(a)(3)(B) Exemption Worksheet and, if denial in the exercise of discretion is recommended rather than placing the case "on hold," the case will be sent for Headquarters review.[1365]

> ➢ **Practice Pointer**: Given how difficult it can be to obtain adjudication and an exemption (even when the applicant is eligible), practitioners should always argue, based on the facts and evidence presented, that these particular bars do not apply and that, if they do, their client falls squarely within one of the exemptions. It is important to preserve these facts, evidence, and arguments on the record during the initial asylum application and interview.

There is no such "TRIG hold" or exemption process for cases that are being adjudicated before the immigration courts.[1366] Therefore, an asylum applicant whose application is adjudicated in removal proceedings and is found to be barred from relief under the terrorism-related inadmissibility grounds will be denied relief because there are no statutory exemptions to this bar. Once the applicant has a final order of removal, only then can the Secretaries of DHS and State and the AG consider the case for an exemption that has been approved.[1367] Even then, the terrorism-related inadmissibility ground must be the only impediment to granting asylum. If asylum was denied on any other basis, the applicant will not be considered for an exemption. If DHS is considering an individual for an exemption following a final order of removal, they will mail a "notice of referral" to non-detained individuals and personally serve detained individuals.[1368] Like for asylum cases before the asylum office, there is no process to affirmatively seek an exemption.

> ➢ **Practice Pointer**: Following a final order of removal, practitioners should notify the Immigration Judge or Board of Immigration Appeals,

---

[1363] *See* U.S. Citizenship & Immigration Servs., *Revised Guidance on the Adjudication of Cases Involving Terrorism-Related Inadmissibility Grounds and Further Amendment to the Hold Policy for Such Cases* (Nov. 20, 2011), *published on* AILA InfoNet Doc. 11112861 (*posted* Nov. 28, 2011).

[1364] *Id.*

[1365] *Id.*

[1366] *See* U.S. Citizenship & Immigration Servs. Fact Sheet, *Exemption Authority for Certain Terrorist-related Inadmissibility Grounds* (Oct. 23, 2008), *published on* AILA InfoNet at Doc. No. 08112066 (*posted* Nov. 20, 2008).

[1367] *See, id.*

[1368] *Id.*

as well as DHS counsel, that their clients are eligible for an exemption and discuss how to ensure that the exemption is considered. Practitioners also should assist their clients in seeking administrative stays of removal before U.S. Immigration and Customs Enforcement so their clients are not removed while the Secretary of Homeland Security and the Secretary of State consider their eligibility for an exemption.

> **Practice Pointer**: Asylum applicants denied asylum due to terrorism-related inadmissibility grounds before the immigration courts may be considered for an exemption under the authority of the Secretary of Homeland Security or the Secretary of State and, upon receipt of an exemption, must then move to reopen their asylum proceedings before the immigration court.[1369] For this reason, it is essential that the IJ or BIA decision contain language stating that "but for" the terrorism-related inadmissibility ground, relief would have been granted. Such language will assist with being considered for an exemption.

It exercising their discretionary authority under the INA, the Secretary of Homeland Security or the Secretary of State, in consultation with the AG, has periodically approved various exemptions, both situational and group-specific.[1370] In 2014, two new situational exemptions and six new group-specific exemptions have been approved.[1371]

All exemptions granted apply to those: (1) seeking any benefit or protection under the INA; (2) who have already been determined by USCIS to be otherwise eligible for the benefit; (3) who have undergone and passed all relevant background and security checks; and (4) who have fully disclosed in all applicable applications and/or interviews with U.S. government representatives and agents the nature and circumstances of any material support and any activity or association falling within INA 212(a)(3)(B) as well as all contact with a terrorist organization or its members.

The following situational exemptions have been issued:

- Material support under duress;
- Solicitation under duress;[1372]

[1369] *Id.*

[1370] *See* U.S. Citizenship & Immigration Servs., *Terrorism-Related Inadmissibility Grounds Exemptions*, *available at www.uscis.gov/laws/terrorism-related-inadmissability-grounds/terrorism-related-inadmissibility-grounds-exemptions* (last visited Nov. 1, 2014) (containing the full list of all exemptions granted to date).

[1371] The new situational exemptions were published in the *Federal Register* on February 5, 2014. *See* Exercise of Authority Under Section 212(d)(3)(B)(i) of The Immigration And Nationality Act, 79 Fed. Reg. 6914 (Feb. 5, 2014). They have not yet been posted to *uscis.gov*. The new group-specific exemptions have been posted to *uscis.gov* with their implementing memoranda.

[1372] *See* U.S. Citizenship & Immigration Servs. Memorandum on New TRIG Exemption for Solicitation (Feb. 23, 2011), *published on* AILA InfoNet Doc. 11022474 (*posted* Feb. 24, 2011).

- Receipt of military-type training under duress;[1373]
- Voluntary medical care;[1374]
- Certain aliens with existing immigration benefits;[1375]
- Insignificant material support to a Tier III organization;[1376] and
- Limited material support to a Tier III organization.[1377]

The following group-based exemptions have been issued:[1378]

- All Burma Students Democratic Front;[1379]
- All India Sikh Students Federation-Bittu Faction;[1380]
- Iraqi National Congress;[1381]
- Kurdish Democratic Party;[1382]
- Patriotic Union of Kurdistan;[1383]
- 10 named organizations in the Consolidated Appropriations Act of 2008, including: Karen National Union/Karen National Army, Chin National Front/Chin National Army, Chin National League for Democracy, Kayan New Land Party, Arakan Liberation Party, Tibetan Mustangs, Cuban Alzados, Karenni National

---

[1373] *See* U.S. Citizenship & Immigration Servs. Memorandum on New TRIG Exemption for Military-Type Training (Feb. 24, 2011), *published on* AILA InfoNet Doc. 11022470 (*posted* Feb. 24, 2011).

[1374] *See* U.S. Citizenship & Immigration Servs. Policy Memorandum on Material Support & The Provision of Medical Care (Nov. 28, 2011), *published on* AILA InfoNet Doc. 11112862 (*posted* Nov. 28, 2011).

[1375] *See* U.S. Citizenship & Immigration Servs., *Terrorism-Related Inadmissibility Grounds (TRIG) - Situational Exemptions* [hereinafter USCIS TRIG Situational Exemptions], *available at www.uscis.gov/unassigned/terrorism-related-inadmissibility-grounds-trig-situational-exemptions* (last visited Nov. 1, 2014). The two newest situational exemptions were published in the *Federal Register* on February 5, 2014. *See* 79 Fed. Reg. 6914, *supra* note 1371. They have not yet been posted to *uscis.gov*.

[1376] *See* 79 Fed. Reg. 6914, *supra* note 1371.

[1377] *See id.*

[1378] USCIS TRIG Situational Exemptions, *supra* note 1371.

[1379] *See* U.S. Citizenship & Immigration Servs. Memorandum on a New Discretionary Exemption for Activities and Associations Relating to the All Burma Students' Democratic Front (Dec. 29, 2010), *published on* AILA InfoNet Doc. 11010531 (*posted* Jan. 5, 2011).

[1380] *See* U.S. Citizenship & Immigration Servs. Memorandum on a New Discretionary Exemption for Material Support to the All India Sikh Students Federation-Bittu Faction (Dec. 29, 2010), *published on* AILA InfoNet Doc. 11010530 (*posted* Jan. 5, 2011).

[1381] *See* U.S. Citizenship & Immigration Servs. Memorandum on Discretionary Exemption for Activities Related to the INC, KDP, & PUK (Jan. 23, 2010), *published on* AILA InfoNet Doc. 11030133 (*posted* Mar. 1, 2011).

[1382] *Id.*

[1383] *Id.*

Progressive Party, "Appropriate groups affiliated with the Hmong," "Appropriate groups affiliated with the Montagnards," and African National Congress;

- Certain association or activities with the Kosovo Liberation Army;[1384]
- Iraqi Uprisings;[1385]
- Farabundo Marti para la Liberacion Nacional (FMLN);[1386]
- Nationalist Republican Alliance (ARENA);[1387]
- Ethiopia People's Revolutionary Party;[1388]
- Oromo Liberation Front;[1389]
- Tigray People's Liberation Front;[1390]
- Democratic Movement for the Liberation of Eritrean Kunama;[1391] and
- Eritrean Liberation Front.[1392]

Each group exemption has specific requirements and applicants must meet those specific requirements in order to be exempted from the bar to asylum eligibility.[1393]

[1384] *See* U.S. Citizenship & Immigration Servs. Policy Memorandum on Material Support Bar Exemptions for KLA Activities (July 13, 2012), *published on* AILA InfoNet Doc. 12071343 (*posted* July 13, 2012).

[1385] *See* U.S. Citizenship & Immigration Servs. Policy Memorandum on TRIG Exemption for Participation in Iraqi Uprising (Feb. 25, 2013), *published on* AILA InfoNet Doc. 13022544, (*posted* Feb. 25, 2013).

[1386] *See* U.S. Citizenship & Immigration Servs. Memorandum on TRIG Exemption for Farabundo Marti National Liberation Front & Nationalist Republican Alliance (Aug. 14, 2014), *published on* AILA InfoNet Doc. 14081461 (*posted* Aug. 14, 2014).

[1387] *Id.*

[1388] *See* U.S. Citizenship & Immigration Servs. Memorandum on TRIG Exemption for Ethiopian People's Revolutionary Party (Aug. 14, 2014), *published on* AILA InfoNet Doc. 14081465 (*posted* Aug. 14, 2014).

[1389] *See* U.S. Citizenship & Immigration Servs. Memorandum on TRIG Exemption for the Oromo Liberation Front (Aug. 14, 2014), *published on* AILA InfoNet Doc. 14081462 (*posted* Aug. 14, 2014).

[1390] *See* U.S. Citizenship & Immigration Servs. Policy Memorandum on TRIG Exemption for the Tigray People's Liberation Front (Aug. 14, 2014), *published on* AILA InfoNet Doc. 14081466 (*posted* Aug. 14, 2014).

[1391] *See* U.S. Citizenship & Immigration Servs. Policy Memorandum on TRIG Exemption for the Democratic Movement for the Liberation of Eritrean Kunama (Aug. 14, 2014), *published on* AILA InfoNet Doc. 14081463 (*posted* Aug. 14, 2014).

[1392] *See* U.S. Citizenship & Immigration Servs. Policy Memorandum on TRIG Exemption for the Eritrean Liberation Front (Aug. 14, 2014), *published on* AILA InfoNet Doc. 14081464 (*posted* Aug. 14, 2014).

[1393] *See* U.S. Citizenship & Immigration Servs., *Terrorism-Related Inadmissibility Grounds (TRIG) - Group-Based Exemptions*, *available at www.uscis.gov/unassigned/terrorism-related-inadmissibility-grounds-trig-group-based-exemptions* (last visited Nov. 1, 2014) (for the implementation memos for each group).

Often, group exemptions are limited to certain time periods, types of activities, and circumstances.

- **Practice Pointer**: Practitioners should analyze their clients' facts under the specific group requirements in order to determine if the applicants might fall within these group exemptions. USCIS lists each group and the requirements for each group exemption on its website at *www.uscis.gov/unassigned/terrorism-related-inadmissibility-grounds-trig-group-based-exemptions*. The implementation memoranda are also available for each group on USCIS's website.

- **Practice Pointer**: For a detailed discussion of the newest group exemptions (Democratic Movement for the Liberation of Eritrean Kunama, Eritrean Liberation Front, Ethiopian People's Revolutionary Party, Oromo Liberation Front, Tigray People's Liberation Front, and FLMN and ARENA), see the AILA Asylum and Refugee Committee's practice pointer entitled, "Making Sense of the New TRIG Exemptions."[1394]

b. Material Support Duress Exception

On April 27, 2007, the Secretary of Homeland Security exercised his waiver authority and decided that the material support bar would not apply to certain individuals who provided material support to certain terrorist organizations while under duress, if the waiver of the bar was warranted by the totality of the circumstances.[1395] The following factors should be considered in determining whether the individual provided material support under duress: (1) whether the applicant reasonably could have avoided, or took steps to avoid, providing material support; (2) the severity and type of harm inflicted or threatened; (3) to whom the harm was directed; and (4) in cases of threats alone, the perceived imminence of the harm threatened and the perceived likelihood that the harm would be inflicted.[1396]

In considering the totality of the circumstances, other factors to be considered in addition to these duress-related factors include:

(1) the amount, type, and frequency of material support provided;

[1394] Cheri Attix, "Making Sense of the New TRIG Exemptions" (Nov. 14, 2014), *published on* AILA InfoNet at Doc. No. 15032760 (*posted* 3/27/2015) Special thanks to Cheri Attix and the AILA Asylum and Refugee Liaison Committee.

[1395] *See* Michael Chertoff Memorandum on Exercise of Authority Under Sec. 212(d)(3)(B)(i) of the Immigration and Nationality Act, U.S. Dep't of Homeland Security (July 27, 2007) [hereinafter Chertoff Memorandum], *available at www.uscis.gov/sites/default/files/files/pressrelease/Duress_Waiver_27ap07.pdf*. *See also* U.S. Citizenship & Immigration Servs. Fact Sheet, *Concerning the Secretary's Exercise of Authority Under Sec. 212(d)(3)(B)(i)* (May 10, 2007), *published on* AILA InfoNet at Doc. No. 07051164 (*posted* May 11, 2007).

[1396] *See* Exercise of Authority Under Section 212(d)(3)(B)(i) of the Immigration and Nationality Act, 72 Fed. Reg. 26138 (May 8, 2007) (effective Apr. 27, 2007); *See also* Chertoff Memo., *supra* note 1395.

(2) the nature of the activities committed by the terrorist organization;

(3) the individual's awareness of those activities;

(4) the length of time since material support was provided;

(5) the individual's conduct since that time; and

(6) any other relevant factor.[1397]

USCIS has issued a memo that serves as guidance on obtaining asylum for applicants who are eligible but for the provision of material support to a terrorist organization.[1398] When an applicant who has provided material support to any terrorist organization is otherwise eligible for asylum, the adjudicating asylum officer must fill out the Material Support Exemption Worksheet,[1399] regardless of whether the terrorist organization is designated by the Secretary of Homeland Security as exempt. The USCIS Headquarters Asylum Division's Training, Research, and Quality (TRAQ) Branch will review all cases for possible applications of exemptions to the material support bar.[1400]

c. "Insignificant" and "Limited" Material Support to a Tier III Organization Exemptions

Among the most recent situational exemptions is the exemption for "insignificant" material support to a Tier III undesignated terrorist organization or person the applicant reasonably knows intends to engage in terrorist activity.[1401] It does not apply to support given to designated terrorist groups or their representatives. Furthermore, the support must not have been given with the "intent of furthering the terrorist or violent activities" of the individual or organization.[1402] What constitutes an "insignificant" amount of voluntary material support is not disclosed in the Federal Register notice and no examples are given.

> ➢ **Practice Pointer**: The more trivial the support, the more likely USCIS will be to apply this exemption. The "insignificant" determination likely will turn on the circumstances surrounding the support.

The other recent situational exemption is the exemption for "limited" material support to a Tier III undesignated terrorist organization or person the applicant

[1397] *See* Chertoff Memo., *supra* note 1395.

[1398] U.S. Citizenship & Immigration Servs., Memorandum on Processing Asylum Cases Involving Material Support (June 1, 2007), *published on* AILA InfoNet at Doc. No. 07070573 (*posted* Jul. 5, 2007).

[1399] *Id.*

[1400] *Id.*

[1401] *See* 79 Fed. Reg. 6914, *supra* note 1371.

[1402] *Id.*

reasonably knows intends to engage in terrorist activity.[1403] This exemption allows forgiveness for "limited" material support that involves:

(1) routine commercial transactions;

(2) routine social transactions (*i.e.*, which are executed in the satisfaction of certain well-established or verifiable family, social, or cultural obligations);

(3) humanitarian assistance; or

(4) substantial pressure that does not rise to the level of duress.[1404]

As with "insignificant," the term "limited" is not defined or explained and no examples are given in the *Federal Register* notice.[1405]

- ➢ **Practice Pointer**: The shorter in duration or smaller in number of instances of material support, as well as the more involuntary the material support was, the more likely USCIS will be to apply this exemption. For example, a single, one-time routine commercial transaction is likely to be found to be "limited."

- ➢ **Practice Pointer**: As no examples are given, and USCIS typically does not provide its analysis of individual applications of such exemptions, one can only speculate as to how these new exemptions will be applied.

The material support forgiven under the "limited" material support exemption must not have been provided "with any intent or desire to assist" any Tier III terrorist organization or activity.[1406] There is no such *mens rea* element for the "insignificant" material support exemption.

There are several requirements that are common to both new situational exemptions. The applicant must show:

(1) he or she did not know or should not reasonably have known that the material support given would be used to target non-combatants, U.S. citizens, or U.S. interests;

(2) the support did not include "military-type training" as defined by 18 USC §2339D;[1407]

[1403] *See id.*

[1404] *Id.*

[1405] *Id.*

[1406] *Id.*

[1407] 18 USC §2339D (2012) defines military-type training as "training in means or methods that can cause death or serious bodily injury, destroy or damage property, or disrupt services to critical infrastructure, or training on the use, storage, production, or assembly of any explosive, firearm, or other weapon, including any weapon of mass destruction pursuant to §2339D(c)(1)." It is not clear whether the statute refers to giving or receiving such training, but it is safe to assume that it refers to both.

(3) he or she has not engaged in any other terrorist activity including provision of material support to a designated terrorist organization;

(4) he or she poses no danger to the safety and security of the United States; and

(5) he or she warrants an exemption in the totality of the circumstances.[1408]

d. Limited General Discretionary Exemption

On August 10, 2012, the Secretary of Homeland Security, in consultation with the Secretary of State and the AG, exercised her discretionary authority not to apply INA §§212(a)(3)(B)(iv)(IV), (V), (VI), and (VIII) to certain qualified individuals with existing immigration benefits, other than a nonimmigrant visa, who are currently inadmissible due to prior associations with Tier III undesignated terrorist organizations.[1409] The new "limited general exemption" permits exemption of the following activities:

- Providing material support to;
- Soliciting funds or other things of value for;
- Soliciting individuals for membership in;
- Providing material support to; or
- Receiving military-type training from, or on behalf of, a qualified Tier III terrorist organization.[1410]

This exemption does not apply to Tier I or Tier II organizations, nor to individuals for whom there are reasonable grounds to believe that they are engaged in or likely to engage in terrorist activity.[1411]

The limited general exemption may be applied to immigration benefit applications under the INA, such as adjustment of status and asylee and refugee following-to-join petitions, for individuals who currently possess lawful status and are not in removal proceedings or subject to a final order of removal. It also applies to beneficiaries of an I-730 Refugee/Asylee Relative Petition filed by such an asylee or refugee.[1412] This exemption will only be considered if the individual and group criteria are met.[1413]

To be eligible for this exemption, the applicant must already have an existing immigration benefit on or before August 10, 2012. Such benefits may include:

- Admission as a refugee;

[1408] *See* 79 Fed. Reg. 6914, *supra* note 1371.

[1409] *See* U.S. Citizenship & Immigration Servs., Memorandum on Implementation of New 'Limited General' Discretionary Exemption Under INA §212(d)(3)(B)(i) for Qualified Applicants with Specified Associations and Activities with Qualified Undesignated or 'Tier III, Terrorist Organizations" (Sept. 26, 2012), *published on* AILA InfoNet Doc. No. 13022545 (*posted* Feb. 25, 2013).

[1410] *Id.*

[1411] *Id.*

[1412] *Id.*

[1413] *Id.*

- Grant of asylum;
- Grant of Temporary Protected Status;
- Grant of adjustment of status under NACARA or HRIFA;
- Grant of a similar immigration benefit other than a nonimmigrant visa; or
- Beneficiaries of an I-730 Refugee/Asylee Relative Petition filed at any time on or before August 10, 2012.[1414]

The individual's activities or associations must have been in relation to a Tier III organization only. The Tier III organization must not have at any time:

- Targeted U.S. interests or persons, including planned or attempted attacks;
- Engaged in a pattern or practice of torture, genocide, or the use of child soldiers;
- Been identified in the Specially Designated Nationals List or lists concerning Al-Qaida and the Taliban; or
- Been designated as a Tier I or Tier II terrorist organization.[1415]

In addition to the group qualifications, the individual must, to the satisfaction of the adjudicator:

- Establish that he or she is otherwise eligible for the immigration benefit or protection being sought;
- Undergo and pass all required background and security checks;
- Fully disclose, to the best of his or her knowledge, in all relevant applications and interviews with U.S. Government representatives and agents, the nature and circumstances of all activities or associations falling within the scope of INA section 212(a)(3)(B);
- Establish that he or she has not knowingly provided material support to any terrorist activities that targeted noncombatant persons or U.S. interests;
- Establish that he or she has not received training that itself poses a risk to the United States or U.S. interests (such as training on the production or use of a weapon of mass destruction, torture, or espionage);
- Establish that he or she is not in removal proceedings or subject to a final order of removal, unless the applicant is the beneficiary of an I-730 Refugee/Asylee Relative Petition;
- Have been associated with a qualified group as set forth in the Group Eligibility paragraph;
- Establish that he or she poses no danger to the safety and security of the United States; and

[1414] *Id.*

[1415] *Id.*

- Establish that he or she warrants an exemption in the totality of the circumstances.[1416]

Finally, the applicant must demonstrate that he or she warrants an exemption as a matter of discretion, given the totality of the circumstances. The factors to be considered are: (1) the length and nature of any TRIG-related activity; (2) the amount, type, and frequency of the applicant's activity; (3) the nature of the organization's terrorist activities and the individuals' awareness of those activities; (4) the individual's conduct since entering the United States; (5) the length of time that has elapsed since the individual engaged in the TRIG-related activity; and (6) any other relevant factors.[1417]

v. Alien Terrorist Removal Courts

Changes made to the INA in 1996 allow for special removal proceedings for noncitizen "terrorists" in which the U.S. government has the authority to use classified information.[1418] Under these procedures, applications for removal are submitted *ex parte* and *in camera*, and filed under seal with the removal court. Noncitizens have a right to be present at such a hearing and to be represented by counsel. Any noncitizen financially unable to obtain counsel is entitled to appointed counsel. The noncitizens are not permitted to have access to the classified information used against them, but are permitted to view unclassified summaries of the information. Noncitizens are not entitled to suppress evidence that they allege was unlawfully obtained, and the Federal Rules of Evidence do not apply in such hearings. Moreover, judges in these proceedings may not consider or grant asylum or withholding of removal claims. To date, the U.S. government has not used these special removal proceedings. ICE and legacy INS have, however, resorted to the use of secret, or classified, evidence in regular proceedings before immigration courts. The use of such evidence has been challenged in a small number of cases, sometimes successfully.[1419]

vi. Mandatory Detention of "Suspected Terrorists"

Under a controversial section of the USA PATRIOT Act, the AG or Deputy AG may certify a noncitizen as a "suspected terrorist" if he or she has "reasonable grounds to believe" the individual falls within one of seven security-related grounds of inadmissibility or deportability, or engages in any other activity that endangers the national security of the United States.[1420] This section allows for the detention of noncitizens who seek to overthrow the U.S. government by force or violence, and

---

[1416] *Id.*

[1417] *Id.*

[1418] *See* INA §501 *et seq.*; 8 USC §1531 (2012) *et seq.*

[1419] *See, e.g.*, *Jay v. Boyd*, 351 U.S. 345 (1956); *Kiareldeen v. Reno*, 71 F. Supp. 2d 402 (D.N.J. 1999); *Rafeedie v. INS*, 688 F.Supp. 729, 736 (D.D.C. 1988).

[1420] INA §236A(a)(3)(A); 8 USC §1226a(a)(3)(A) (2012).

those who have or are likely to engage in terrorist activity. It also permits the detention of noncitizens who are merely the spouse or child of a "suspected terrorist" or who are mere members of foreign terrorist organizations, without any allegations that they actually engaged in culpable conduct.[1421] The person may be detained even if "relief from removal [is] granted."[1422] A person granted asylum or withholding of removal who has been found not to be a threat to national security could, nevertheless, be detained as a "suspected terrorist."

> **Practice Pointer**: For a detailed discussion of the terrorism bars on asylum seekers and refugees in the United States, see Human Rights First's report "Denial and Delay" available at *www.humanrightsfirst.org/wp-content/uploads/pdf/RPP-DenialandDelay-FULL-111009-web.pdf.*

6. Firm Resettlement

An individual is barred from receiving asylum if it is determined that the he or she was "firmly resettled" in another country prior to arriving in the United States.[1423] Firm resettlement, however, is not a bar to withholding of removal. An applicant is considered "firmly resettled" if "prior to arrival in the United States, he [or she] entered into another country with, or while in that country received, an offer of permanent resident status, citizenship, or some other type of permanent resettlement."[1424] The key concept in a firm resettlement analysis is permanence. An offer of temporary residence does not compel a finding of firm resettlement.[1425]

> **Practice Pointer**: A good way to think of the firm resettlement bar is to consider that the United States aims to grant protection to those who genuinely need it. If a person has already found a place of safety where she may remain lawfully and indefinitely, then she has no need of asylum in the United States.

The length of time an applicant spent in a third country does not by itself establish firm resettlement.[1426] Moreover, an applicant cannot be firmly resettled in a country he or she never actually entered. On the other hand, an offer of permanent residence in another country may suffice to demonstrate firm resettlement even if the applicant

---

[1421] INA §236A(a)(3)(A); 8 USC §1226a(a)(3)(A) (2012).

[1422] INA §236A(a)(2); 8 USC §1226a(a)(2) (2012).

[1423] INA §208(b)(2)(A)(vi), 8 USC §1158(b)(2)(A)(vi) (2012).

[1424] 8 CFR §§208.15, 1208.15 (2014).

[1425] *Ali v. Ashcroft*, 394 F.3d 780, 790 (9th Cir. 2005) (citing *Camposeco-Montejo v. Ashcroft*, 384 F.3d 814, 819–20 (9th Cir. 2004) when finding that a Mexican FM-3 nonimmigrant visa does not amount to an offer of firm resettlement).

[1426] *Matter of Soleimani*, 20 I&N Dec. 99 (BIA 1989); *Matter of Portales*, 18 I&N Dec. 239 (BIA 1982).

never accepted the offer.[1427] If the applicant was firmly resettled but allowed that status to lapse after leaving, the firm resettlement bar will apply even if the applicant no longer has a right to return to the country of resettlement.[1428] If there was no offer of permanent resettlement, however, the applicant will not be considered firmly resettled and no further analysis is required.

Even if an asylum applicant is found to have received an offer of permanent resettlement in a third country before arriving in the United States, there are two exceptions to a finding of firm resettlement. An applicant will not be considered firmly resettled if it is established that his or her entry into that country was a necessary consequence of his or her flight from persecution, that he or she remained in that country only as long as was necessary to arrange onward travel, and that he or she did not establish significant ties in that country.[1429] The second exception is for situations in which the applicant can establish that the conditions of his or her residence in that country were so substantially and consciously restricted by the authority of the country that he or she was not in fact resettled.[1430] In making this last determination, the adjudicator must consider:

- The conditions under which other residents of the country live;
- The type of housing, whether permanent or temporary, made available to the applicant;
- The types and extent of employment available to the applicant;
- The extent to which the applicant received permission to hold property; and
- The extent to which the applicant enjoyed other rights and privileges, such as travel documentation that includes a right of entry and/or re-entry, education, public relief, or naturalization, ordinarily available to others resident in the country.[1431]

The BIA has laid out a framework for how a firm resettlement determination is to be made. It consists of an alternating burden of proof that begins with DHS having the initial burden to make a prima facie showing that the asylum applicant received an offer of some type of official status permitting the applicant to reside in a third country indefinitely.[1432] This showing may be made by direct or circumstantial

---

[1427] *Abdille v. Ashcroft*, 242 F.3d 477 (3d Cir. 2001) (finding that a "prime factor in the firm resettlement inquiry is the existence of an offer of permanent resident status, citizenship, or some other type of permanent resettlement," and rejecting a totality of the circumstances test).

[1428] *See, e.g., Abdalla v. INS*, 43 F.3d 1397, 1400 (10th Cir. 1994) (determining that the expiration of the applicant's UAE residence permit after entry in the U.S. did not affect the fact that he had firmly resettled in the UAE).

[1429] 8 CFR §§208.15(a), 1208.15(a) (2014).

[1430] 8 CFR §§208.15(b), 1208.15(b) (2014).

[1431] 8 CFR §§208.15(b), 1208.15(b) (2014).

[1432] *Matter of A–G–G–*, 25 I&N Dec. 486, 501 (BIA 2011).

evidence.[1433] Once DHS has produced some evidence, the burden shifts to the applicant to rebut that evidence by showing that such offer has not been made or that the applicant's circumstances would render him or her ineligible.[1434] If it is determined that the applicant was firmly resettled, he or she then has the burden to show that one of the two regulatory exceptions applies.[1435] A similar approach also has been used by the First,[1436] Third,[1437] Eighth,[1438] Ninth,[1439] and Tenth[1440] Circuits. These circuit courts accord primary importance to the existence of an offer of permanent resettlement; without such an offer, firm resettlement will not generally be found.

Other courts have adopted a totality of the circumstances approach.[1441] The totality of the circumstances approach allows a finding of firm resettlement even in the absence of an offer of permanent resettlement, based on the overall situation of the applicant in the third country. Even in courts that accord primary importance to an actual offer of resettlement, occasional exceptions have been made to find firm resettlement under the totality of the circumstances for applicants who seem to be forum shopping.[1442] Courts also refuse to allow applicants who have severed ties with countries that offered permanent status to bootstrap a claim for asylum on the rationale that they can no longer return to the country that offered them status.[1443]

An applicant who was accepted as a refugee by Denmark and who resided in the country for six months before coming to the United States was found to be ineligible for asylum.[1444] The court relied on the fact that Denmark issued her a passport and that her family members were residing in Denmark as refugees.[1445] In addition, the

---

[1433] *Id.*

[1434] *Id.* at 501–503.

[1435] *Id.* at 503.

[1436] *Bonilla v. Mukasey*, 539 F.3d 72, 78 (1st Cir. 2008); *Salazar v. Ashcroft*, 359 F.3d 45, 50–51 (1st Cir. 2004).

[1437] *Abdille v. Ashcroft*, 242 F.3d 477 (3d Cir. 2001).

[1438] *Rife v. Ashcroft*, 374 F.3d 606, 611 (8th Cir. 2004).

[1439] *Maharaj v. Gonzales*, 450 F.3d 961, 964 (9th Cir. 2006) (en banc).

[1440] *Elzour v. Ashcroft*, 378 F.3d 1143, 1151 (10th Cir. 2004).

[1441] *See, e.g.*, *Tchitchui v. Holder*, 657 F.3d 132 (2d Cir. 2011); *Sall v. Gonzales*, 437 F.3d 229, 232 (2d Cir. 2006).

[1442] *See, e.g.*, *Maharaj v. Gonzales*, 450 F.3d 961, 964 (9th Cir. 2006) (en banc). In *Maharaj*, the applicants had applied for refugee status in Canada and been given some benefits. They left before their claims were adjudicated and came to the United States in search of better job opportunities. Despite the fact that they had no offer of resettlement in Canada, the Court reserved the right to deem them firmly resettled under the totality of the circumstances.

[1443] *Firmansjah v. Gonzales*, 424 F.3d 598, 604 (7th Cir. 2005); *Abdalla v. INS*, 43 F.3d 1397, 1400 (10th Cir. 1994).

[1444] *Ali v. Reno*, 237 F.3d 591 (6th Cir. 2001).

[1445] *Ali v. Reno*, 237 F.3d 591, at 595.

court rejected her argument that she met the exception under 8 CFR §1208.15(a) that she did not establish "significant ties" in Denmark and only remained there "as long as was necessary to arrange onward travel."[1446] The court noted that when she was questioned regarding her reasons for leaving Denmark, she stated that she wanted to be with her husband, who was studying in the United States.[1447] The court also held that a declaration by the Danish authorities that they were no longer obligated to accept the applicant into their country did not undermine the firm resettlement determination.[1448] The court noted that the regulations look only to the applicant's status prior to his or her entry into the United States and thus preclude an applicant from "bootstrapping an asylum claim by unilaterally severing her existing ties with a third country after arriving in the U.S."[1449]

- **Practice Pointer**: Other reported cases finding an individual has been firmly resettled include: *Matter of D–X– and Y–Z–*,[1450] *Tchitchui v. Holder*,[1451] *Matter of K–R–Y– and K–C–S–*,[1452] *Sultani v. Gonzales*,[1453] *Nahrvani v. Gonzales*,[1454] *Mussie v. INS*,[1455] *Vang v. INS*,[1456] and *Abdalla v. INS*.[1457]

[1446] *Id.*

[1447] *Id.*

[1448] *Ali v. Reno*, 237 F.3d 591, at 596.

[1449] *Id.*; *see also Salazar v. Ashcroft*, 359 F.3d 45, 51 (1st Cir. 2004) (finding that the IJ's determination that the applicant was firmly resettled in Venezuela based on a residency stamp in his passport, residence there for one year, and several recent trips to Venezuela with that passport, as well as his marriage to a Venezuela citizen, was supported by substantial evidence); *Desta v. Ashcroft*, 329 F.3d 1179, 1187 (10th Cir. 2003) (petition for review denied where the asylum applicants lived for 18 months in Canada, received landed immigrant status there, and their son's birth there made him a Canadian citizen); *Abdille v. Ashcroft*, 242 F.3d 477, 480 (3d Cir. 2001) (holding that a prime element in firm resettlement inquiry is existence *vel non* of a government offer of permanent status; court rejected totality of circumstances approach and remanded to BIA for consideration of South African law). *See also, Diallo v. Ashcroft*, 381 F.3d 687 (7th Cir. 2004) (holding that the IJ erred in finding Mauritanian applicant had firmly resettled in Senegal because IJ failed to determine whether the applicant received an offer of permanent resettlement there).

[1450] *Matter of D–X– and Y–Z–*, 25 I&N Dec. 664 (BIA 2012) (applying *Matter of G–G–* and finding that a facially valid but fraudulently obtained permit for a Chinese citizen to reside in Belize is prima facie evidence of an offer of firm resettlement).

[1451] *Tchitchui v. Holder*, 657 F.3d 132, 136–37 (2d Cir. 2011) (finding firm resettlement where the applicant had significant ties to Guatemala prior to his persecution in Cameroon and finding that the significant ties to another country need not come post-persecution but may predate the persecution).

[1452] *Matter of K–R–Y– and K–C–S–*, 24 I&N Dec. 133 (BIA 2007) (finding applicants who became citizens of South Korea and had significant ties there were firmly resettled in South Korea).

[1453] *Sultani v. Gonzales*, 455 F.3d 878, 883 (8th Cir. 2006) (finding a family from Afghanistan granted refugee status in Australia was firmly resettled in Australia).

[1454] *Nahrvani v. Gonzales*, 399 F.3d 1148, 1150 (9th Cir. 2005) (finding that an Iranian national was firmly resettled in Germany where he was offered permanent residency, married a German citizen, and worked and traveled freely in Germany).

In contrast, the Ninth Circuit rejected a finding by an IJ that a Somali asylum applicant was firmly resettled in Ethiopia where the evidence credited by the IJ established that, although she remained in Ethiopia for five years, she had no right to remain there permanently.[1458] The court in that case found that in finding the applicant firmly resettled, the IJ misapplied Ninth Circuit law, specifically the case of *Cheo v. INS*. The IJ erred in interpreting *Cheo* to mean that "where an individual resides for a number of years in a third country without being bothered it is appropriate to presume firm resettlement."[1459] The court stated that this interpretation was incorrect and clarified that *Cheo* held that, "*in absence of evidence to the contrary*" the applicants' three-year residence in Malaysia triggered presumption of firm resettlement and shifted the burden to the applicant to show that they received no offer of permanent residence from Malaysia during that time.[1460] The Ninth Circuit continued stating that here, unlike in *Cheo*, the applicant offered evidence that she was not firmly resettled, which the IJ found credible. Therefore, the *Cheo* presumption did not apply.[1461] When the applicant presents evidence that she never had a right to remain permanently, the presumption of firm resettlement never arises.[1462] Similarly, the First Circuit held that the IJ erred in finding that a Colombian national was firmly resettled in Venezuela where there was no evidence in the record that he had the right to renew his residence stamp or that he ever lived in Venezuela.[1463]

In cases decided before firm resettlement was a mandatory bar to asylum, courts considered the issue of firm resettlement in determining whether an applicant merited asylum in the exercise of discretion. In *Matter of D–L– and A–M–*,[1464] the BIA denied asylum as a matter of discretion to Cuban nationals who had lived and worked

---

[1455] *Mussie v. INS*, 172 F.3d 329 (4th Cir. 1999) (finding firm resettlement despite incidents of racial taunting and threats, because applicant was granted asylum in Germany, resided there for six years, and received language schooling, transportation, rent assistance, travel documentation, and food from the German government).

[1456] *Vang v. INS*, 146 F.3d 1114 (9th Cir. 1998) (finding firm resettlement where the applicant lived in France for 12 years with refugee status).

[1457] *Abdalla v. INS*, 43 F.3d 1397 (10th Cir. 1994) (finding firm resettlement where the applicant lived in the United Arab Emirates for 20 years with a residence visa).

[1458] *Ali v. Ashcroft*, 394 F.3d 780, 782 (9th Cir. 2005).

[1459] *Id.* at 790 (citing *Cheo v. INS*, 162 F.3d 1227, 1229 (9th Cir. 1998)).

[1460] *Id.* (citing *Cheo v. INS*, 162 F.3d at 1229).

[1461] *Id.*; *see also Makadji v. Gonzales*, 470 F.3d 450, 452 (2d Cir. 2006) (finding IJ's determination that Mauritanian applicant was firmly resettled in Mali was not supported by substantial evidence and that IJ improperly placed burden of proof on the applicant to show he was not firmly resettled).

[1462] *Ali v. Ashcroft*, 394 F.3d 780, 782 (9th Cir. 2005).

[1463] *Bonilla v. Mukasey*, 539 F.3d 72, 78–83 (1st Cir. 2008).

[1464] *Matter of D–L– and A–M–*, 20 I&N Dec. 409 (BIA 1991).

in Spain for six years as lawful temporary residents with the option to become permanent residents of that country.[1465]

In contrast, the BIA found, in *Matter of Soleimani*,[1466] that an Iranian Jew who had resided in Israel for 10 months prior to her arrival in the United States was not firmly resettled in Israel. During her stay in Israel, she lived with her grandmother, studied Hebrew, and recuperated from an illness, but did not work or seek any benefits from the government. The BIA noted that the applicant had closer relatives in the United States and that her arrival in the United States was "reasonably proximate to her flight from Iran."[1467]

Overall, in determining whether an applicant was firmly resettled prior to entering the United States, the primary consideration is whether the applicant had an offer of permanent resident status, citizenship, or some other type of permanent resettlement was made.[1468] However, the totality of the circumstances may be considered in some circuits.[1469]

7. Bars to Withholding Only

There are two bars to eligibility for withholding of removal that do not apply to asylum: (1) if the applicant participated in Nazi persecution; and (2) if the applicant participated in genocide, torture, or extrajudicial killing.[1470]

> ➢ **Practice Pointer**: While these two bars apply only to withholding of removal, it is reasonable to conclude that such individuals also would be denied asylum as a matter of discretion or would be subject to other bars such as the serious nonpolitical crime bar.

An applicant is barred from withholding of removal if, under the direction of or in cooperation with the Nazi government of Germany, he or she ordered, incited, assisted, or otherwise participated in the persecution of any person because of race,

---

[1465] *See also Farbakhsh v. INS*, 20 F.3d 877 (8th Cir. 1994) (finding that an Iranian's four-year residence in Spain under a pending application for refugee status reasonably constituted firm resettlement even though he had no permission to work or study).

[1466] *Matter of Soleimani*, 20 I&N Dec. 99 (BIA 1989).

[1467] *Id.* at 107.

[1468] *See, e.g., Abdille v. Ashcroft*, 242 F.3d 477 (3d Cir. 2001) (rejecting a totality of the circumstances approach).

[1469] *See, e.g., Sall v. Gonzales*, 437 F.3d 229 (2d Cir. 2006) (holding that a determination of firm resettlement must be based on a totality of the circumstances); *Maharaj v. Gonzales*, 450 F.3d 961 (9th Cir. 2006); *Salazar v. Ashcroft*, 359 F.3d 45 (1st Cir. 2004) (stating that DHS bears the initial burden of showing firm resettlement, but that upon that showing, an applicant may rebut the presumption of firm resettlement or establish an exception to the bar).

[1470] INA §241(b)(3)(B); 8 CFR §§208.16(d)(2), 1208.16(d)(2) (2014). *See* INA §212(a)(3)(E) (setting forth the standards for Nazi persecution, genocide, torture, and extrajudicial killing).

religion, national origin, or political opinion, during the period beginning March 23, 1933, and ending on May 8, 1945.[1471]

An applicant also is barred from withholding if he or she has engaged in conduct that is defined as genocide for purposes of the International Convention on the Prevention and Punishment of Genocide.[1472] Genocide is defined in the convention as:

> [A]ny of the following acts committed with intent to destroy, in whole or in part, a national, ethnic, racial or religious group, such as: killing members of the group; causing serious bodily or mental harm to members of the group; deliberately inflicting on the group conditions of life calculated to bring about its physical destruction in whole or in part; imposing measures intending to prevent births within the group; forcibly transferring children from the group to another group.[1473]

In general, if there is evidence that one or more bars to withholding of removal apply, the burden shifts to the applicant to prove by a preponderance of the evidence that the bars do not apply.[1474] If the bars do apply, they are mandatory, and the nature of a person's criminal conduct or activity may not be balanced against the severity of the persecution.[1475]

- ➢ **Practice Pointer**: See chapter 4 for a detailed discussion of the burdens of proof in seeking asylum, withholding of removal, and protection under CAT.

V. Discretionary Form of Relief

Even if an asylum applicant establishes statutory eligibility for asylum — that he or she has a well-founded fear of persecution on account of one or more of the five enumerated grounds, and that no statutory bars apply — the applicant may be denied asylum as a matter of discretion.[1476] However, discretionary denials of asylum are rare and generally require "egregious negative activity by the applicant."[1477] In the

---

[1471] INA §241(b)(3)(B); 8 USC §1231(b)(3)(B) (referencing INA §237(a)(4)(D)).

[1472] INA §241(b)(3)(B); 8 USC §1231(b)(3)(B).

[1473] International Convention on the Prevention and Punishment of Genocide (done Dec. 9, 1948) 78 U.N.T.S. 277, art. II, (entered into force Jan. 12, 1951) [hereinafter Convention Against Genocide].

[1474] 8 CFR §§208.16(d)(2), 1208.16(d)(2) (2014).

[1475] *INS v. Aguirre-Aguirre*, 526 U.S. 415 (1999); *Crespo-Gomez v. Richard*, 780 F.2d 932 (11th Cir. 1986); *Matter of Rodriguez-Coto*, 19 I&N Dec. 208 (BIA 1985).

[1476] *See* INA §§208 (a), 208(b)(1); 8 CFR §§208.14(a)–(b), 1208.14(a)–(b) (2014). *See INS v. Cardoza-Fonseca*, 480 U.S. 421, 423 (1987) (noting that the AG is not required to grant asylum to everyone who meets the refugee definition); *Matter of A–H–*, 23 I&N Dec. 774, 780–83 (AG 2005); *Matter of Mogharrabi*, 19 I&N Dec. 439, 449 (BIA 1987).

[1477] *Zuh v. Mukasey*, 547 F.3d 504, 507–14 (4th Cir. 2008).

absence of any such adverse factors, asylum should be granted in the exercise of discretion.[1478] It is the applicant's burden to establish that a favorable exercise of discretion is warranted.[1479]

In making a discretionary determination, the asylum adjudicator must balance the positive and negative factors, consider both favorable and unfavorable factors, and evaluate the "totality of the circumstances."[1480] Where no single factor appears to support an IJ's discretionary denial, the case will be remanded for the IJ to consider the totality of the circumstances.[1481]

- **Practice Pointer**: For these reasons, it is essential to develop the record of an applicant's positive factors in corroborating documentation, testimony, and throughout the asylum proceedings.

Positive factors may include the applicant's legal entry to the United Sates; an application for asylum submitted while in legal status; severe past persecution;[1482] family, business, community, and employment ties to the United States; length of residence and property ownership in the United States; evidence of hardship to the applicant or his or her family if deported, particularly if it would yield a lack of family reunification; evidence of good moral character, value, or service to the community; rehabilitation if any criminal record is present; general humanitarian considerations, such as age and health;[1483] likelihood of future persecution;[1484] whether the applicant can meet the higher burden required for withholding of removal;[1485] and other relief granted.[1486]

Negative factors may include significant violations of the immigration laws; the applicant's journey to the United States and manner of entry or attempted entry;[1487] the existence of a criminal record and the severity and recency of the record,

---

[1478] *Matter of Pula*, 19 I&N Dec. 467, 474 (BIA 1987).

[1479] INA §208(b)(1); *Matter of Shirdel*, 19 I&N Dec. 33, 38 (BIA 1984).

[1480] *Zuh v. Mukasey*, 547 F.3d 504, 511 (4th Cir. 2008); *Kalubi v. Ashcroft*, 364 F.3d 1134, 1138 (9th Cir. 2004); *Matter of Pula*, 19 I&N Dec. at 473.

[1481] *Zuh v. Mukasey*, 547 F.3d at 513.

[1482] *Matter of Soleimani*, 20 I&N Dec. 99, 108 (BIA 1989); *Matter of Chen*, 20 I&N Dec. 16 (BIA 1989).

[1483] *Matter of H–*, 21 I&N Dec. 337, 347–48 (BIA 1996); *Matter of Pula*, 19 I&N Dec. 467 (BIA 1987).

[1484] *Id.*

[1485] *Id.*

[1486] *See generally Zuh v. Mukasey*, 547 F.3d 504, 513 (4th Cir. 2008).

[1487] *Matter of Pula,* 19 I&N Dec. 467, 473 (BIA 1987) (confirming that the totality of the circumstances and the actions of the applicant in traveling to and attempting to enter the U.S. should be examined in determining whether a favorable exercise of discretion is warranted).

including recidivism;[1488] lack of candor with immigration officials; failure to attend an asylum hearing in another country;[1489] and other bad character evidence or undesirability of the individual to be a resident.[1490]

> ➢ **Practice Pointer**: Because this is not an exhaustive list and it is the applicant's burden to establish that he or she merits a favorable exercise of discretion, an asylum applicant should present evidence on any relevant factors that support a favorable exercise of discretion.

In *Matter of Pula*, the BIA focused on factors related to the applicant's journey to and entry or attempted entry to the United States in making its discretionary determination.[1491] Among the factors that could be considered are: (1) whether the applicant passed through any other countries after leaving his or her home country; (2) whether orderly refugee procedures were available to the applicant in any of those countries; and (3) whether the applicant made any attempts to seek asylum before coming to the United States.[1492] In addition, the length of time the applicant remained in a third country and the applicant's living conditions, safety, and potential for long-term residency there are also relevant.[1493] Another factor mentioned by the BIA is whether the applicant has relatives legally residing in the United States or other personal ties to this country that motivated the applicant to seek asylum here rather than elsewhere.[1494] Also considered is whether the applicant engaged in fraud to circumvent orderly refugee procedures and the seriousness of the fraud.[1495] The BIA noted that the "use of fraudulent documents to escape the country of persecution itself is not a significant adverse factor."[1496] Most of these factors have now been included elsewhere in the asylum regulations, but may still remain part of the discretionary determination.

[1488] *Kouljinski v. Keisler*, 505 F.3d 534, (6th Cir. 2007) (court held IJ properly considered three driving under the influence (DUI) convictions in denying asylum as a matter of discretion); *Dhine v. Slattery*, 3 F.3d 613, 619–20 (2d Cir. 1993); *Matter of Jean*, 23 I&N Dec. 373 (AG 2002).

[1489] *Matter of Gharadaghi*, 19 I&N Dec. 311, 315 (BIA 1985). *But see Kalubi v. Ashcroft*, 364 F.3d 1134, 1138–39 (9th Cir. 2004) (stating that if an applicant's testimony on a particular issue is not found incredible for purposes of determining whether he is eligible for asylum, it cannot be found incredible for determining whether he merits a favorable exercise of discretion).

[1490] *See generally Zuh v. Mukasey*, 547 F.3d 504, 513 (4th Cir. 2008).

[1491] *Matter of Pula,* 19 I&N Dec. at 473.

[1492] *Id.* at 473–74.

[1493] *Id.* at 474.

[1494] *Id.*

[1495] *Id.*

[1496] *Id.*

There is no definitive list of factors that must be considered.[1497] However, all relevant favorable and adverse factors must be considered and weighed.[1498] In the absence of adverse factors, discretion should be exercised to grant asylum to eligible applicants.[1499] Overall, the BIA has held that "[t]he danger of persecution should generally outweigh all but the most egregious of adverse factors."[1500]

The following are examples of individuals denied asylum as a matter of discretion under the facts and evidence presented:

- An applicant with ties to an armed group that committed atrocities;[1501]
- An applicant who engaged in a sham marriage;[1502] and
- An applicant with three convictions for driving under the influence of alcohol.[1503]

If an applicant is denied asylum solely in the exercise of discretion and the applicant is subsequently granted withholding of removal, thereby precluding the applicant's spouse or minor children from following to join him or her, the denial of asylum must be reconsidered.[1504] Factors that should be considered include the reasons for the denial and reasonable alternatives available to the applicant, such as reunification with his or her spouse and minor children in a third country.[1505] A mere statement that this regulation was considered, without an explanation, is insufficient.[1506] The duty lies with the BIA, moreover, to reconsider the denial of asylum after a timely appeal by the applicant.[1507] In 2007, in *Matter of T–Z–*, the BIA instructed the IJ to reconsider the discretionary denial of asylum if, on remand, the IJ granted withholding of removal.[1508]

[1497] *Kalubi*, 364 F.3d at 1139.

[1498] *Id.*

[1499] *Id.*

[1500] *Matter of Pula*, 19 I&N Dec. 467, 474 (BIA 1987). *See also*, *e.g.*, *Matter of Kasinga*, 21 I&N Dec. 357 (BIA 1996) (finding that the applicant, who feared female genital mutilation, merited a favorable exercise of discretion despite her use of a false passport and her failure to seek asylum in Germany or Ghana); *Huang v. INS*, 436 F.3d 89, 97 (2d Cir. 2006) (finding that the following reasons given by the IJ for denying asylum as a matter of discretion were insufficient as a matter of law: (1) that the applicant embellished aspects of his testimony and (2) that he used a professional smuggler to flee his home country).

[1501] *Haddam v. Holder*, 2013 WL 6245782 (4th Cir. 2013).

[1502] *Aioub v. Mukasey*, 540 F.3d 609, 612 (7th Cir. 2008).

[1503] *Kouljinski v. Keisler*, 505 F.3d 534, 543 (6th Cir. 2007).

[1504] 8 CFR §§208.16(e), 1208.16(e) (2014); *See also Huang v. INS*, 436 F.3d 89, 92–93 (2d Cir. 2006).

[1505] 8 CFR §§208.16(e), 1208.16(e) (2014).

[1506] *See Kalubi*, 364 F.3d at 1141.

[1507] *Huang v. INS*, 436 F.3d 89, 93–94 (2d Cir. 2006).

[1508] *Matter of T–Z–*, 24 I&N Dec. 163, 176 (BIA 2007).

- **Practice Pointer**: If an individual's asylum or withholding of removal application is denied due to failure to meet the legal standards discussed in this chapter, due to one of the statutory bars, or due to a negative exercise of discretion in the asylum context, he or she may still be eligible for a similar form of relief, protection under the Convention Against Torture (CAT). The legal standards for CAT relief are discussed in chapter 3.

- **Practice Pointer**: The AILA Asylum and Refugee Committee developed a database of published asylum, withholding of removal, and CAT decisions of the Board of Immigration Appeals and U.S. circuit courts of appeals. As of the publication of this book, this database includes published cases from January 2009 to present, and additional case law is added each month. See the "Asylum Cases by Topic" pages on AILA InfoNet at *www.aila.org/infonet/curated-research/asylum-cases-by-topic*. The categories of case topics include credibility, deferral of removal under CAT, frivolous asylum applications, material support bar, miscellaneous, motions to reopen, one-year filing deadline, political opinion, religion, relocation, serious nonpolitical crime, social group, and standard of review.

VI. Conclusion

Demonstrating eligibility for asylum and withholding of removal relief can be difficult due to the numerous legal elements that must be met and the various interpretations of each legal element over time in each jurisdiction. The law is constantly developing, which makes the practice and application of U.S. asylum law incredibly complex. For these reasons, it is imperative for practitioners to thoroughly research the legal issues involved in every case so they may effectively and zealously advocate on behalf of their clients.

CHAPTER THREE

PROTECTION UNDER THE CONVENTION AGAINST TORTURE

Another related form of relief from removal is the protection of *nonrefoulement* (non-return) under the United Nations Convention Against Torture and Other Cruel, Inhuman, or Degrading Treatment or Punishment (CAT).[1] The CAT is a multilateral treaty that is intended not just to prevent torture, but also to establish measures to eliminate torture and to compensate victims of torture. The United States signed the CAT on April 18, 1988, under President Ronald Reagan. Although the Senate adopted its resolution of advice and consent on October 27, 1990, the CAT did not take effect in the United States until November 20, 1994, one month after President Bill Clinton deposited the ratification with the U.N. secretary general.[2] It was later enacted into U.S. law on October 21, 1998.[3]

On June 24, 2011, in marking the anniversary of the adoption of the CAT, President Barack Obama affirmed "the essential principle that under no circumstances is torture ever justified." President Obama continued:

> Torture and abusive treatment violate our most deeply held values, and they do not enhance our national security—they undermine it by serving as a recruiting tool for terrorists and further endangering the lives of American personnel. Furthermore, torture and other forms of cruel, inhuman or degrading treatment are ineffective at developing useful, accurate information. As President, I have therefore made it clear that the United States will prohibit torture without exception or equivocation, and I reaffirmed our commitment to the

---

* The author would like to thank Lisa R. Green of Lisa Green & Associates, P.C. for her invaluable input in reviewing this chapter.

[1] Convention Against Torture and Other Cruel, Inhuman or Degrading Treatment or Punishment (Convention or CAT), Dec. 10, 1984, 1465 U.N.T.S. 85 (entered into force June 26, 1987), *available at https://treaties.un.org/doc/Publication/UNTS/Volume%201465/v1465.pdf.*

[2] *See* U.N. Doc. 571 Leg/SER. E/13, IV.9 (1995). *See also Silva-Rengifo v. Att'y Gen.*, 473 F.3d 58, 64 (3d Cir. 2007), as amended (Mar. 6, 2007).

[3] Omnibus Consolidated and Emergency Supplemental Appropriations Act, Pub. L. No. 105-277, div. G, subdiv. B, tit. XXII §2242 (1999) of the Foreign Affairs Reform and Restructuring Act of 1998, 112 Stat. 2681-822, 105th Cong. 2d Sess. (1998); 144 Cong. Rec. No. H11265, Sec. 2242 (daily ed. Oct. 19, 1998), *available at www.gpo.gov/fdsys/pkg/CREC-1998-10-19/pdf/CREC-1998-10-19-pt1-PgH11044-3.pdf*; 136 Cong. Rec. S17486, 36198 (daily ed. Oct. 27, 1990); *Committee on Foreign Relations, Convention Against Torture and other Cruel, Inhuman or Degrading Treatment or Punishment*, S. Ex. Rept. 101-30, 101st Cong. 2d Sess. (Aug. 30, 1990).

> Convention's tenets and our domestic laws. As a nation that played a leading role in the effort to bring this treaty into force, the United States will remain a leader in the effort to end torture around the world and to address the needs of torture victims.[4]

The CAT has become a safety net for individuals who do not qualify for asylum or withholding of removal under Immigration and Nationality Act (INA) §241(b)(3). In many respects, the relief it provides and the limitations of that relief are similar to withholding of removal under INA §241(b)(3).[5] It prohibits the removal of an individual to a country where it is more likely than not that he or she would be tortured, but does not confer the possibility of adjustment of status to permanent residency, the ability to travel, nor the ability confer derivative status on a spouse or minor children.[6] Like withholding of removal under INA §241(b)(3), CAT relief also results in a removal order, and removal is only withheld with regard to the specific country or countries where the immigration judge (IJ) has determined the applicant is more likely than not to be tortured.[7]

CAT relief is, nevertheless, a valuable form of relief for individuals who may be barred from asylum or withholding under INA §241(b)(3) because of a criminal conviction or other statutory bar.[8] It is also valuable to individuals who are unable to establish that the persecution they fear is on account of their race, religion, nationality, membership in a particular social group, or political opinion, as CAT protection does not require a showing of nexus to a protected ground.[9]

This chapter provides an overview of the protection available under the CAT, the implementing legislation enacted in October 1998, the regulations that took effect in

---

[4] *See* White House Press Release, Office of the Press Secretary, Statement by the President on the International Day in Support of Victims of Torture (June 24, 2011), *available at www.whitehouse.gov/the-press-office/2011/06/24/statement-president-international-day-support-victims-torture*.

[5] *See supra* chapter 2 for a detailed discussion of withholding of removal under INA §241(B)(3) and its limitations; *infra* chapter 13 for a detailed discussion of the benefits of asylum compared to the benefits of withholding of removal under INA §241(b)(3) and under the CAT.

[6] U.S. Dep't of Justice, Executive Office for Immigration Review, *Factsheet: Asylum and Withholding of Removal Relief Convention Against Torture Protections* at 7–8 (Jan. 15, 2009), *available at www.justice.gov/eoir/press/09/AsylumWithholdingCATProtections.pdf*. *See infra* chapter 13 for a detailed discussion of the benefits of relief under CAT.

[7] *Id.*

[8] *See infra* pts. II.D. and III. for a detailed discussion of the bars to withholding of removal under the Convention Against Torture and the alternative form of CAT relief, deferral of removal, which has no statutory bars.

[9] *See* Appx. 10B (chart comparing asylum, withholding of removal under INA §241(b)(3), and Convention Against Torture relief); *see also Kalmalthas v. INS*, 251 F.3d 1279, 1283 (9th Cir. 2001) (noting that Convention Against Torture relief is "both broader and narrower" than a claim for asylum or withholding because on one hand, the petitioner does not have to meet the 'on account of' requirement of asylum and withholding, but on the other, must show it is 'more likely than not' — a higher probability standard — that they will be tortured if returned).

March 1999, and the policy memoranda issued by legacy Immigration and Naturalization Service (INS) General Counsel's Office, the U.S. Citizenship and Immigration Services (USCIS) Asylum Division, and the Executive Office for Immigration Review (EOIR).[10]

I. The Implementing Legislation

On October 21, 1998, Article 3 of the CAT was incorporated into U.S. domestic law when Congress passed and the president signed the Foreign Affairs Reform and Restructuring Act (FARRA).[11] Section 2242(a) of FARRA provides:

---

[10] For expert advice and assistance on Convention Against Torture Claims, contact World Organization for Human Rights USA, 1725 K Street, N.W., Suite 610, Washington, D.C. 20006; phone (202) 296-5702; fax (202) 296-5704; e-mail: *woatusa@woatusa.org*; website: *www.humanrightsusa.org*.

[11] Foreign Affairs Reform and Restructuring Act of 1998 (FARRA), Pub. L. No. 105-277, div. G, 112 Stat. 2681, 2681–761 to 2681–854 (codified in 8 U.S.C. §1231 (2012)).

Section 2242 of FARRA provides:

> 'United States Policy With Respect to the Involuntary Return of Persons in Danger of Subjection to Torture'
>
> (a) Policy—It shall be the policy of the United States not to expel, extradite, or otherwise effect the involuntary return of any person to a country in which there are substantial grounds for believing the person would be in danger of being subjected to torture, regardless of whether the person is physically present in the United States.
>
> (b) Regulations—Not later than 120 days after the date of enactment of this Act, the heads of the appropriate agencies shall prescribe regulations to implement the obligations of the United States under Article 3 of the United Nations Convention Against Torture and Other Forms of Cruel, Inhuman or Degrading Treatment Punishment, subject to any reservations, understandings, declarations, and provisos contained in the United States Senate resolution of ratification of the Convention.
>
> (c) Exclusion of Certain Aliens—To the maximum extent consistent with the obligations of the United States under the Convention, subject to any reservations, understandings, declarations and provisos contained in the United States Senate resolution of ratification of the Convention, the regulations described in subsection (b) shall exclude from the protection of such regulations aliens described in section 241(b)(3)(B) of the Immigration and Nationality Act (8 U.S.C. §1231(b)(3)(B) (2012)).
>
> (d) Review and Construction—Notwithstanding any other provision of law, and except as provided in the regulations described in subsection (b), no court shall have jurisdiction to review the regulations adopted to implement this section, and nothing in this section shall be construed as providing any court jurisdiction to consider or review claims raised under the Convention or this section, or any other determination made with respect to the application of the policy set forth in subsection (a), except as part of the review of a final order of removal pursuant to section 242 of the Immigration and Nationality Act (8 U.S.C. §1252 (2012)).
>
> (e) Authority to Detain—Nothing in this section shall be construed as limiting the authority of the Attorney General to detain any person under any provision of law, including, but not limited to, any provision of the Immigration and Nationality Act.
>
> (f) Definitions—

Continued

> It shall be the policy of the United States not to expel, extradite, or otherwise effect the involuntary return of any person to a country in which there are substantial grounds for believing the person would be in danger of being subjected to torture, regardless of whether the person is physically present in the United States.[12]

The implementing legislation required regulations to effectuate the CAT, and Congress barred challenges to these regulations, stating:

> Notwithstanding any other provision of law…no court shall have jurisdiction to review the regulations adopted to implement [CAT] or any other determination made with respect to the application of the policy [regarding expelling, extraditing, or otherwise involuntarily returning someone] except as part of the review of a final order of removal pursuant to [INA §242].[13]

Based on this directive from Congress in the Foreign Affairs Reform Restructuring Act, some courts have found that the CAT is not self-executing, and therefore, does not provide a source of independent enforceable rights.[14] However, even if the CAT is not self-executing, federal regulations are enforceable in court, and courts also have habeas jurisdiction.[15]

A. Regulations

FARRA required legacy INS, EOIR, and other government agencies to issue regulations implementing Article 3 of the CAT "[n]ot later than 120 days after the date of enactment" of FARRA.[16] The regulations, however, would be subject to "any reservations, understandings, declarations, and provisos contained in the United States Senate resolution of the ratification of the CAT."[17] The regulations, issued on February 19, 1999 and later amended on December 6, 2000, set forth the procedures

---

> (1) Convention Defined—In this section, the term 'Convention' means the U.N. Convention Against Torture and Other Forms of Cruel, Inhuman or Degrading Treatment or Punishment, done at New York on December 10, 1984.
>
> (2) Same Terms as in Convention—Except as otherwise provided, the terms used in this section have the meanings given those terms in the Convention, subject to any reservations, understandings, declarations, and provisos contained in the United States Senate resolution of ratification of the Convention.

[12] FARRA, *supra* note 11, §2242, 112 Stat. 268-822, ¶ 1.

[13] *See* FARRA, *supra* note 11, §2242(d). *See also* 8 CFR §§208.18(e), 1208.18(e) (2014).

[14] *See, e.g., Khouzam v. Att'y Gen.*, 549 F.3d 235, 241 n.4 (3d Cir. 2008); *Pierre v. Gonzales*, 502 F.3d 109, 114–15 (2d Cir. 2007); *Renkel v. United States*, 456 F.3d 640, 642, 644 (6th Cir. 2006).

[15] *See Auguste v. Ridge*, 395 F.3d 123, 137–38 & n.13 (3d Cir. 2005); *Habtemicael v. Ashcroft*, 370 F.3d 774, 782–89 (8th Cir. 2004); *Wang v. Ashcroft*, 320 F.3d 130, 140 (2d Cir. 2003); *Singh v. Ashcroft*, 351 F.3d 435, 440–42 (9th Cir. 2003); *Ogbudimkpa v. Ashcroft*, 342 F.3d 207, 212–22 (3d Cir. 2003); *Saint Fort v. Ashcroft*, 329 F.3d 191, 200–04 (1st Cir. 2003).

[16] *See* FARRA, *supra* note 11, §2242(b), 112 Stat. 2681–822.

[17] *Id.*

for applying for relief under CAT.[18] In most cases, IJs have jurisdiction in the first instance to decide CAT claims. The regulations also provided limitations on the time permitted to request reopening of a removal/deportation case for an individual to apply for CAT relief following the effectuation of CAT under U.S. law.

B. Possible Bars to Relief

FARRA mandated that "[t]o the maximum extent consistent with the obligations of the United States under the Convention" the regulations should exclude individuals barred from relief under the withholding of removal section of the Immigration and Nationality Act (INA).[19] Unlike the Refugee Convention and Protocol,[20] the CAT does not contain any exceptions to relief, nor are any exceptions contained in U.S. Senate reservations, understandings, declarations, or provisos. However, there are two forms of relief under the CAT—withholding of removal and deferral of removal.[21] While the same statutory bars to withholding of removal under INA §241(b)(3) apply to withholding of removal under CAT, there are no bars to deferral of removal, a more precarious form of CAT relief.[22]

C. Judicial Review

FARRA permits judicial review of a CAT claim, but only as part of a review of a final order of removal pursuant to §242 of the INA.[23] Arguably, this section of the legislation also permits a federal court to review the regulations implementing article 3.[24]

D. Detention

FARRA, moreover, in no way limits the attorney general's (AG) authority to detain individuals under the INA or any other provision of law. Individuals who have committed aggravated felonies or who are determined to be a threat to the security of the United States, therefore, may be subject to lengthy or indefinite detention despite being granted relief under the CAT.[25]

---

[18] *See* 8 CFR §§208.16–.18, 1208.16–.18 (2014).

[19] *See* FARRA, *supra* note 11, §2242(c), 112 Stat. 2681–822.

[20] Convention Relating to the Status of Refugees, *done* July 28, 1951, 189 U.N.T.S. 150 (entered into force Apr. 22, 1954) [hereinafter Refugee Convention]; Protocol Relating to the Status of Refugees, *done* Jan. 31, 1967, 606 U.N.T.S. 267 (entered into force Oct. 4, 1967) [hereinafter Refugee Protocol],

[21] *See infra* pt. III for a detailed discussion of the two forms of relief under the CAT.

[22] *See infra* pts. II.D. and III for a detailed discussion of the statutory bars to withholding of removal under CAT and the two forms of relief under CAT.

[23] *See* FARRA, *supra* note 11, §2242(d), 112 Stat. 2681–822.

[24] *See infra* chapter 12 for a detailed discussion of judicial review.

[25] *See* FARRA, *supra* note 11, §2242(e), 112 Stat. 2681–822. See chapter 9 for a detailed discussion of detention of individuals seeking protection in the United States.

E. Definitions

Finally, and perhaps most importantly, FARRA provides that the terms used in the implementing legislation have the same meanings as the terms used in the CAT, subject to any reservations, understandings, declarations, and provisos contained in the U.S. Senate resolution of ratification.[26] Thus, international law is an important source for interpreting the legislation and regulations.

F. Number of Cases Granted

Out of the 26,394 CAT cases filed in fiscal year 2014, the immigration courts granted only 536.[27] Nevertheless, it was a meaningful form of relief for the 536 individuals who might otherwise have been returned to their home countries.[28]

G. Prior Procedures for Relief Under the Convention Against Torture

Prior to the passage of FARRA, both legacy INS and EOIR had taken the position that article 3 of the CAT was not self-executing—meaning that, absent implementing legislation, the treaty does not provide a rule that courts must enforce.[29] The Board of Immigration Appeals (BIA), in *Matter of H–M–V–*,[30] held that it lacked jurisdiction to adjudicate CAT claims because there had been no legislation to implement article 3, no regulations had been promulgated with respect to article 3, and the U.S. Senate had declared that article 3 was not self-executing.[31]

Legacy INS, although taking the position that the CAT was not self-executing, had remarked that the executive, as one of the political branches, may "act to protect

---

[26] *See* FARRA, *supra* note 11, §2242(f), 112 Stat. 2681–822 to 2681–823.

[27] *See* U.S. Dep't of Justice, Executive Office for Immigration Review, Office of Planning, Analysis, & Technology, *FY 2014 Statistical Yearbook* (Mar. 2015), at M1 [hereinafter EOIR FY 2014 Statistical Yearbook], *available at www.justice.gov/eoir/statspub/fy14syb.pdf* (last visited Mar. 25, 2015).

[28] *Id. See also Immigration Relief Under CAT for Serious Criminals and Human Rights Violators: Hearing Before the House Subcomm. on the Judiciary*, 108th Cong., 1st Sess. 45, Ser. No. 34, at 11 (2003) (statement of C. Stewart Verdery, Asst. Secretary for Policy and Planning, Border and Transportation Security Directorate, U.S. Department of Homeland Security, estimating that 1,700 individuals had been granted CAT protection in the first four years after the implementing legislation was passed). A majority of the 536 applicants that were granted CAT relief were granted withholding of removal under CAT, EOIR FY 2014 Statistical Yearbook, *supra* note 27, at M1. Out of the 26,394 CAT cases presented, 10,602 were denied, 5,203 were withdrawn, and 715 were abandoned. *Id.* An additional 9,338 cases were listed as 'other' regarding outcome, perhaps meaning that for these claims another type of relief was granted. *See id.*

[29] *See, e.g., Foster v. Neilson*, 27 U.S. (2 Pet.) 253, 314 (1829), *overruled on other grounds by U.S. v. Percheman*, 32 U.S. 51 (1833). See chapter 1 for a detailed discussion of treaty law.

[30] *Matter of H–M–V–*, 22 I&N Dec. 256 (BIA 1998).

[31] For an in-depth analysis of why Article 3 of the CAT should be considered to be self-executing, see Kristen Rosati, United Nations Convention Against Torture: *A Self-Executing Treaty that Prevents the Removal of Persons Ineligible for Asylum and Withholding of Removal*, 26 DENV. J. INT'L L. & POL'Y 533–90 (1998).

rights a person may have under a treaty that is not self-executing."[32] As a result, legacy INS had established an informal process for presenting a claim under the CAT. That informal process ended on March 22, 1999, when the new regulations took effect.[33]

H. Decisions Pre-Dating the Implementing Regulations

The new regulations addressed procedures for individuals who fear torture upon return to their home country, but did not request CAT relief previously before an IJ, to request reopening of a removal/deportation case for the purpose of applying for CAT. However, the regulations limited the time period during which such individuals could file these motions to reopen. An individual whose order of removal became final before March 22, 1999 (the effective date of the implementing regulations) was permitted to file a motion to reopen within 90 days of the effective date of the regulations (or by June 21, 1999).[34]

On the other hand, an individual whose order of removal became final after March 22, 1999 should have had the opportunity to raise a CAT claim. The regulations, therefore, do not specifically address this category of cases. Nevertheless, an individual with a final order of removal issued after March 22, 1999 may be able to raise a claim under the CAT by filing a motion to reopen under the procedures and requirements set forth in 8 CFR §§1003.2 and 1003.3.[35] At least one court has held that individuals in removal proceedings on or after March 22, 1999, may file a motion to reopen without having to establish a prima facie claim for CAT relief.[36]

Individuals with requests for CAT relief pending with legacy INS on or before March 22, 1999, whose requests had not been finally decided yet, were provided written notice that after March 22, 1999, considerations for protection under CAT can only be obtained in accordance with the new regulations.[37] The notice also informed the individuals that they must file a motion to reopen with the immigration court or the BIA in order to seek relief under the CAT.[38] In addition, the notice was accompanied by a stay of removal effective for 30 days after the service of the notice

[32] *Immigration and Naturalization Serv., Basic Law Manual*, U.S. Law and INS Refugee/Asylum Adjudications at 11 (1994) (AILA 1995).

[33] 8 CFR §§208.18, 1208.18 (2014). *See also* 8 CFR §§208.16, 1208.16 (2014).

[34] 8 CFR §§208.18(b)(2), 1208.18(b)(2) (2014). *See Huang v. Ashcroft*, No. 03-16730, 2004 U.S. App. LEXIS 27903, at *2 (9th Cir. 2004) (holding that the time limit in 8 CFR §208.18(b)(2) [now also §1208.18(b)(2)] applies to all claims for protection under the CAT, without regard to the form of relief that might be granted).

[35] See chapter 11 for a detailed discussion of motions to reopen.

[36] *Qi Hang Guo v. U.S. Dep't of Justice*, 422 F.3d 61, 64 (2d Cir. 2005) (holding that the controlling regulation, 8 CFR §208.18(b)(1) (2014) [now also at §1208.18(b)(1) (2014)] allows for an applicant to file a motion to reopen without having to establish a prima facie claim for CAT relief).

[37] 8 CFR §§208.18(b)(3)(ii), 1208.18(b)(3)(ii) (2014).

[38] 8 CFR §§208.18(b)(3)(ii)(A), 1208.18(b)(3)(ii)(A) (2014).

on the individual.[39] A motion to reopen for an individual falling within this category was not subject to the normal requirements for reopening.[40] Moreover, the regulations specifically provide that "[s]uch a motion *shall* be granted if it is accompanied by a copy of the notice ... or by other convincing evidence that the alien had a request pending with [legacy INS] for protection under Article 3."[41]

If the individual's request was denied by legacy INS on or before March 22, 1999, the individual will be considered to have been "finally denied" withholding of removal and deferral of removal under the CAT.[42] Arguably, such an individual could file a motion to reopen if he or she met the normal requirements for such a motion under 8 CFR §§1003.2 and 1003.3.

> ➢ **Practice Pointer:** There are strict time and numerical limitations for filing motions to reopen before the immigration courts and the Board of Immigration Appeals. For a detailed discussion of these limitations, as well as options and strategies for seeking reopening of cases before the immigration courts or the Board of Immigration Appeals, see chapter 11 of this book.

If the individual's request was granted by legacy INS on or before March 22, 1999, the individual will be considered to have been granted withholding of removal under 8 CFR §§208.16(c), 1208.16(c), unless the individual is subject to a mandatory bar, in which case he or she will be considered to have been granted deferral of removal under 8 CFR §§208.17(a), 1208.17(a).[43]

II. Seeking Protection Under the Convention Against Torture in the United States

Even if an individual is not eligible for asylum under INA §208(a) or withholding of removal under INA §241(b)(3), he or she may be eligible for relief under the CAT.[44] For persons who fear being subjected to torture upon return to their home countries, the two most important provisions of the CAT are article 1, which defines

---

[39] 8 CFR §§208.18(b)(3)(ii)(A), 1208.18(b)(3)(ii)(A) (2014).

[40] 8 CFR §§208.18(b)(3)(ii)(A), 1208.18(b)(3)(ii)(A) (2014).

[41] 8 CFR §§208.18(b)(3)(ii)(A), 1208.18(b)(3)(ii)(A) (emphasis added) (2014).

[42] 8 CFR §§208.18(b)(4), 1208.18(b)(4) (2014).

[43] 8 CFR §§208.18(b)(4), 1208.18(b)(4) (2014).

[44] *Kporlor v. Holder*, 597 F.3d 222, 226–28 (4th Cir. 2010); *Li Fang Lin v. Mukasey*, 517 F.3d 685, 696–97 (4th Cir. 2008); *Paul v. Gonzales*, 444 F.3d 148, 156–57 (2d Cir. 2006); *Singh v. Ashcroft*, 398 F.3d 396, 404–06 (6th Cir. 2005); *Hamoui v. Ashcroft*, 389 F.3d 821, 827–28 (9th Cir. 2004); *Taha v. Ashcroft*, 389 F.3d 800, 802 (9th Cir. 2004); *Camara v. Ashcroft*, 378 F.3d 361, 371–72 (4th Cir. 2004); *Settenda v. Ashcroft*, 377 F.3d 89, 94–95 (1st Cir. 2004); *Sivakaran v. Ashcroft*, 368 F.3d 1028, 1029 (8th Cir. 2004); *Ramsameachire v. Ashcroft*, 357 F.3d 169, 184–86 (2d Cir. 2004); *Zubeda v. Ashcroft*, 333 F.3d 463, 476 (3d Cir. 2003); *Kamalthas v. INS*, 251 F.3d 1279 (9th Cir. 2001); *Mansour v. INS*, 230 F.3d 902 (7th Cir. 2000).

torture, and article 3, which sets forth the prohibition on returning an individual to torture.[45] The CAT also provides for the establishment of a Committee Against Torture (Committee) that is made up of ten experts and has the authority to hear claims between states that are parties to the CAT and claims by victims of a violation by a state party, but only if the state party recognizes the competence of the Committee to hear such claims.[46] The United States recognizes the competence of the Committee as follows:

> The United States declares, pursuant to article 21, paragraph 1, of the Convention, that it recognizes the competence of the Committee against Torture to receive and consider communications to the effect that a State Party claims that another State Party is not fulfilling its obligations under the Convention. It is the understanding of the United States that, pursuant to the above-mentioned article, such communications shall be accepted and processed only if they come from a State Party which has made a similar declaration.[47]

Nevertheless, the case law of the Committee is a useful tool for interpreting a state's obligation under article 3 and the definition of torture under article 1.[48]

- **Practice Pointer:** As a state party to the CAT, the United States is required to report to the Committee on its compliance with the CAT. On August 5, 2013, the U.S. Department of State (DOS) sent its third, fourth, and fifth reports to the U.N. Committee Against Torture, in which it reviewed U.S. efforts to comply with the CAT. The full text of the report is on the DOS website at *www.state.gov/documents/organization/213267.pdf*.

Other significant provisions of the CAT include: article 2(1), the requirement that countries that are parties to the CAT take effective legislative, judicial, or other measures to prevent acts of torture in their territories; articles 2(2) and 2(3), the principles that torture cannot be justified by any exceptional circumstances, such as war or public emergency, nor may torture be justified if committed by an individual acting under an order from a superior officer or a public authority; article 4, the obligation to criminalize torture under domestic law; article 10, the duty to educate and inform law enforcement personnel, public officials, and others regarding the

---

[45] CAT, *supra* note 1, art. 1 & 3.

[46] *See* CAT, *supra* note 1, arts. 17–24.

[47] *See* United Nations Treaty Collection, Ch. IV Human Rights, *Convention against Torture and Other Cruel, Inhuman and Degrading Treatment or Punishment*, available at *https://treaties.un.org/pages/viewdetails.aspx?src=treaty&mtdsg_no=IV-9&chapter=4&lang=en* (last visited Mar. 25, 2015).

[48] For Committee Against Torture decisions, *see* Office of the United Nations High Comm'r for Human Rights, Selected Decisions of the Committee Against Torture (November 1993 to May 2007), *available at www.ohchr.org/Documents/Publications/SDecisionsCATVolIen.pdf.*

prohibition against torture; and articles 13 and 14, the obligation to provide methods of redress for victims of torture, including the right to compensation.[49]

A. Definition of Torture

The CAT defines "torture" broadly as:

> [A]ny act by which severe pain or suffering, whether physical or mental, is intentionally inflicted on a person for such purposes as obtaining from him or a third person information or a confession, punishing him for an act he or a third person has committed or is suspected of having committed, or for any reason based on discrimination of any kind, when such pain or suffering is inflicted by or at the instigation of or with the consent or acquiescence of a public official or other person acting in an official capacity. It does not include pain or suffering arising only from, inherent in or incidental to lawful sanctions.[50]

Although the implementing legislation does not define torture, it specifically incorporates the CAT's definition, subject to any U.S. Senate understanding or reservations.[51] The CAT definition is also found in the regulations issued by legacy INS and EOIR on February 19, 1999, at 8 CFR §§208.18(a)(1), 1208.18(a)(1).

The BIA has defined torture as an act causing severe physical or mental pain or suffering that must be "an extreme form of cruel and inhuman treatment" and not lesser forms.[52] In interpreting the implementing regulations, the BIA explained that the act must be "specifically intended" to inflict severe physical or mental pain or suffering, and an act that results in unanticipated or unintended severity of pain or suffering does not constitute torture.[53] Additionally, the act must have an "illicit purpose" such as "obtaining information or a confession, punishment for a victim's or another's act, intimidating or coercing a victim or another, or any discriminatory purpose."[54] The act must be an intentional governmental act directed against a person in the offender's custody or control and "negligent acts or acts by private individuals not acting on behalf of the government" are not included within the definition of torture.[55] Finally, the act "does not include pain or suffering arising only from, inherent in, or incidental to lawful sanctions" such as a judicially imposed death penalty.[56] Note, however that although "lawful sanctions" cannot be torture, a

---

[49] CAT, *supra* note 1, arts. 2, 4, 10, 13, & 14.

[50] CAT, *supra* note 1, art. 1. *See also* 8 CFR §§208.18(a)(1), 1208.18(a)(1) (2014).

[51] *See* FARRA, *supra* note 11, §2242(f), 112 Stat. 2681–822 to 2681–823.

[52] *Matter of J–E–*, 23 I&N Dec. 291, 297–99 (BIA 2002).

[53] *Id.*

[54] *Id.*

[55] *Id.*

[56] *Id.*

government cannot exempt itself from its obligations under the CAT by defining acts that would constitute torture as lawful forms of punishment.[57]

In sum, torture does not include lesser forms of cruel and inhumane treatment, acts that result in unintended severity of pain and suffering, or lawful sanctions judicially imposed including the death penalty.[58] The six basic elements of torture include:

(1) the infliction of severe pain or suffering;

(2) an intentional act;

(3) an applicant under the custody or control of the offender;

(4) an act for one of many wrongful purposes, including obtaining information or a confession, punishment, intimidation, coercion, or discrimination;

(5) an act by or sanctioned by a public official; and

(6) an act not arising out of lawful sanctions.[59] These six elements of torture are discussed in detail below.

> ➤ **Practice Pointer**: Perhaps the most significant differences between asylum under INA §208(a) and withholding of removal under INA §241(b)(3) from protection under the CAT are that, for CAT relief, the torture *must be* by, at the instigation of, or with the acquiescence of a public official. However, it need not be on account of one of the five protected grounds; there is no nexus requirement.[60]

1. *Infliction of Severe Pain or Suffering*

First, there must be an infliction of pain or suffering, which must be severe and may be either physical or mental. Torture is an "extreme form of cruel and inhuman treatment and does not include lesser forms of cruel, inhuman or degrading treatment or punishment."[61]

Physical torture may include: beatings, burns, electrical shocks, exposure to excessive light or noise, sexual aggression, suspension, suffocation, and prolonged denial of sleep, food, hygiene, or medical assistance.[62] Rape is also increasingly

---

[57] 8 CFR §§208.18(a)(3), 1208.18(a)(3) (2014); *Ghebrehiwot v. Att'y Gen.*, 467 F.3d 344, 358–59 (3d Cir. 2006); *Nuru v. Gonzales*, 404 F.3d 1207, 1218–23 (9th Cir. 2005).

[58] 8 CFR §§208.18(a)(2), (3), & (5), 1208.18(a)(2), (3), & (5) (2014).

[59] 8 CFR §§208.18(a)(1), 1208.18(a)(1) (2014).

[60] 8 CFR §§208.18, 1208.18 (2014); *Matter of J–E–*, 23 I&N Dec. 291, 297–99 (BIA 2002).

[61] 8 CFR §§208.18(a)(2), 1208.18(a)(2) (2014).

[62] *See Torture and Other Cruel, Inhuman or Degrading Treatment or Punishment: Report of the Special Rapporteur*, U.N. ESCOR, Comm'n on Human Rights, 42nd Sess., ¶ 119, U.N. Doc. E/CN.4/1986/15 (1986); *see also Al-Saher v. INS*, 268 F.3d 1143, 1147 (9th Cir. 2001) (in reversing the BIA, court held that beatings and burns suffered by an Iraqi prisoner amounted to torture as defined by Convention and regulations).

recognized as a form of torture.[63] Some examples of physical pain and suffering found to be sufficiently severe to amount to torture under the facts and evidence presented include:

- Female genital mutilation / cutting;[64]
- Murder;[65]
- Rape;[66]
- Sustained and severe beatings;[67]
- Beatings, being forced to watch a rape, and threats that one's own wife will be raped;[68] and

---

[63] *See Report of the Special Rapporteur on Violence Against Women, Its Causes and Consequences*, U.N. Comm'n on Human Rights, 54th Sess., Provisional Agenda Item 9(a), ¶ 67, U.N. Doc. E/CN.4/1998/54 (1998); *see also Kioski v. Sweden*, Comm. No. 41/1996, *reported in Report of the Committee Against Torture*, U.N. GAOR, 51st Sess., Supp. No. 44, ¶ 9.6, U.N. Doc. A/51/44, at 86 (1996) (in which the Committee found substantial grounds for believing that a woman who had been the victim of past torture, including rape, would be subjected to torture if returned to Zaire). *See also Kaita v. Att'y Gen.*, 522 F.3d 288, 300 (3d Cir 2008) (finding that because of the severity of the pain inflicted, 'rape can be torture'). *But see Matter of J–E–*, 23 I&N Dec. 291 (BIA 2002) (indefinite detention, inhuman prison conditions, and police mistreatment of inmates in Haitian jails does not amount to torture).

[64] *Tunis v. Gonzales*, 447 F.3d 547, 550 (7th Cir. 2006); *Mohammed v. Gonzales*, 400 F.3d 785, 802 (9th Cir. 2005).

[65] *Madrigal v. Holder*, 716 F.3d 499 (9th Cir. 2013) (holding that if on remand the BIA determines that the individual is more likely than not to be murdered if returned to Mexico, that would constitute torture); *Cole v. Holder*, 659 F.3d 762, 771 (9th Cir. 2011) (''Acts constituting torture' under CAT 'are varied, and include beatings and killings.'' (quoting *Bromfield v. Mukasey*, 543 F.3d 1071, 1079 (9th Cir. 2008))); *Comollari v. Ashcroft*, 378 F.3d 694, 697 (7th Cir. 2004) (rejecting the argument that torture does not include assassination because a person could have a painless death).

[66] *Zubeda v. Ashcroft*, 333 F.3d 463, 472–73 (3d Cir. 2003) (and cases cited therein).

[67] *Kang v. Att'y Gen.*, 611 F.3d 157 (3d Cir. 2010) (holding that the BIA erred in determining that the interrogation techniques, which included beatings, pouring cold water, whippings, placing plastic bags over applicants heads to induce suffocation, hanging applicants in the air, shining bright lights in applicants' eyes, depriving the applicants of sleep, and shocking applicants with electrical currents, represented mere prison conditions and in ignoring the inherently tortuous nature of the treatment); *Zewdie v. Ashcroft*, 381 F.3d 804 (8th Cir. 2004) (holding that the individual, who was beaten repeatedly over a period of 26 days with wire whips and sticks by Ethiopian government officials, suffered torture); *Al-Saher v. INS*, 268 F.3d 1143, 1147 (9th Cir. 2001) (overturning Board of Immigration Appeals (BIA) holding that Iraqi prisoner had not been tortured, where he had suffered sustained and severe beatings for a one-month period and had been burned with cigarettes over an 8–10 day period). *But see Ireland v. United Kingdom*, 2 Eur. Ct. H.R. 25 (1978), *available at http://hudoc.echr.coe.int/sites/eng/pages/search.aspx?i=001-57506#{'itemid':['001-57506*']} (finding that suspected terrorists who were subjected to wall standing, hooding, and constant loud hissing noise, and who were deprived of sleep, food, and drink by the British Army were subjected to 'inhuman and degrading treatment, but *not* torture.' as cited with approval in *Matter of J–E–*, 23 I&N Dec. 291, 298 (BIA 2002)).

[68] *Namo v. Gonzales*, 401 F.3d 453, 455 (6th Cir. 2005) (case remanded due to changed circumstances in Iraq).

- Forced sterilization.[69]

On the other hand, more minor forms of harm that do not require medical attention may not constitute harm amounting to torture. Some examples of harm that does not rise to the level of torture under the facts and evidence presented include being:

- Punched and slapped;[70]
- Temporarily detained;[71]
- Sexually abused and humiliated;[72]
- Generally ostracized and abused;[73]
- Denied access to mental health care;[74]
- Detained indefinitely and treated inhumanely;[75]
- Imprisonment under severely substandard prison conditions;[76]
- Harassed and run off the road;[77] and
- Deprived of property.[78]

> ➢ **Practice Pointer**: Harm that is not severe physical or mental pain or suffering amounting to torture, however, may still rise to the level of persecution for purposes of asylum and withholding of removal. See

[69] *Bi Zhu Lin v. Ashcroft*, 183 F. Supp. 2d 551, 553 (D. Conn. 2002) (noting that the IJ found that forced sterilization was torture under the CAT). *But see Ni v. BIA*, 439 F.3d 177, 179–80 (2d Cir. 2006) (finding that whether forced sterilization constitutes torture is an open question, but that the IJ's failure to consider relief under CAT was reversible error); *Xiao v. Bd. of Immigration Appeals*, 165 F. App'x 911, 914 (2d Cir. 2006) ('[I]t remains an open question whether forcible sterilizations may be recognized as torture.').

[70] *Ay v. Holder*, 743 F.3d 317, 322 (2d Cir. 2014) (finding that a Turkish citizen who was punched and slapped after being arrested, without requiring medical attention, did not constitute severe pain or suffering to warrant CAT relief).

[71] *Cole v. Att'y Gen.*, 712 F.3d 517, 532–34 (11th Cir. 2013); *Prela v. Ashcroft*, 394 F.3d 515, 519 (7th Cir. 2005) (finding that the 24-hour detention, harassment for bribes, interrogation, threat, and hand injury of an ethnic Albanian in Kosovo was not harm amounting to torture).

[72] *Haider v. Holder*, 595 F.3d 276, 287–89 (6th Cir. 2010).

[73] *Mohammed v. Gonzales*, 477 F.3d 522, 527–28 (8th Cir. 2006).

[74] *Raffington v. Cangemi*, 399 F.3d 900, 904 (8th Cir. 2005).

[75] *Cadet v. Bulger*, 377 F.3d 1174, 1186–96 (11th Cir. 2004).

[76] *Gourdet v. Holder*, 587 F.3d 1 (1st Cir. 2009); *Settenda v. Ashcroft*, 377 F.3d 89 (1st Cir. 2004) (considering conditions of overpopulation, deprivation of food and water, and the spread of disease by unsanitary conditions and finding that it did not constitute torture).

[77] *Gui v. INS*, 280 F.3d 1217, 1230 (9th Cir. 2002).

[78] *Jo v. Gonzales*, 458 F.3d 104, 109 (2d Cir. 2006) (finding that the regulations make clear that in order to come within the definition of torture, the mental anguish must have its origin in the treatment, actual or threatened, of a person).

chapter 2 for a detailed discussion of the forms of harm that may rise to the level of persecution.

Mental torture, according to the Senate in its resolution of advice and consent, includes:

> [P]rolonged mental harm caused by or resulting from: (1) the intentional infliction or threatened infliction of severe physical pain or suffering; (2) the administration or application, or threatened administration or application, of mind altering substances or other procedures calculated to disrupt profoundly the senses or the personality; (3) the threat of imminent death; or (4) the threat that another person will imminently be subjected to death, severe physical pain or suffering, or the administration or application of mind altering substances or other procedures calculated to disrupt profoundly the sense or personality.[79]

Threatened harm against the applicant or others, as well as being forced to watch or listen to harm being inflicted on others may amount to severe mental pain and suffering, and thus, may constitute torture.[80] For example, torture of a U.S. citizen child, in the form of female genital mutilation (FGM), may be the basis of a CAT claim for the noncitizen mother based on the severe mental pain and suffering that it may cause her personally to know that her daughter is suffering such harm.[81] In dismissing an argument by DHS that assassination is not torture, the U.S. Court of Appeals for the Seventh Circuit provided another example of mental torture.[82] The court noted that "[e]ven if death itself is painless…the anticipation of it can be a source of acute mental anguish; if the threat of imminent albeit painless death were deliberately employed to cause such anguish, it would be a form of torture."[83]

2. *Intentional Act*

Second, the severe physical or mental pain or suffering must be intentionally inflicted to meet the definition of torture. As the regulations state, "In order to constitute torture, an act must be *specifically intended* to inflict severe physical or mental pain or suffering. An act that results in unanticipated or unintended severity of pain and suffering is not torture."[84] According to the BIA in *Matter of J–E–*, "specific

---

[79] 136 Cong. Rec. S17491–92 (daily ed. Oct. 27, 1990), *available at http://thomas.loc.gov/cgi-bin/query/F?r101:2:./temp/~r101SaW4Zq:e44928*: The regulations track verbatim the Senate understandings. *See* 8 CFR §§208.18(a)(4), 1208.18(a)(4) (2014).

[80] *See, e.g.*, *Habtemichael v. Ashcroft*, 370 F.3d 774 (8th Cir. 2004) (finding that threats of death sufficed to meet the threshold of severe pain provided that the intent requirement of CAT was met); *Zubeda v. Ashcroft*, 333 F.3d 463, 473 (3d Cir. 2003) (same).

[81] *Kone v. Holder*, 620 F.3d 760, 765–66 (7th Cir. 2010) (finding that where a child may be subject to FGM upon return to the home country, the parent may suffer direct psychological harm that may qualify him or her for relief under CAT); *Nwaokolo v. Ashcroft*, 314 F.3d 303 (7th Cir. 2002) (finding the BIA abused its discretion in denying motion to reopen).

[82] *Comollari v. Ashcroft*, 378 F.3d 694, 697 (7th Cir. 2004).

[83] *Id.*

[84] 8 CFR §§208.18(a)(5), 1208.18(a)(5) (emphasis added).

intent" is defined as "intent to accomplish the precise criminal act that one is later charged with."[85] Put another way, "the actor must intend the *actual consequences* of his conduct, as distinguished from the act that causes the consequences."[86] In contrast, "general intent" commonly "takes the form of recklessness ... or negligence."[87]

The act itself need not be an affirmative act, but could be an omission, especially if the perpetrator has an affirmative duty to act. However, as the BIA held in *Matter of J–E–*, if there is no specific intent by authorities to inflict severe physical or mental pain or suffering, the claim will be denied.[88] Whether an omitted act meets the definition of torture has been considered in a series of cases addressing the conditions in Haitian prisons. In these cases, the courts and the BIA considered whether the government and government officials had an affirmative duty to act and then omitted that duty to act in their treatment of detainees.

In *Matter of J–E–*, for example, a Haitian applicant claimed that he would be tortured upon his removal to Haiti because he would be detained as a criminal deportee for an indefinite amount of time.[89] His mother and grandfather had been killed in property disputes, but his family never had problems with the Haitian government.[90] In addition to his and his father's testimony, the applicant submitted DOS's human rights report on Haiti and five newspaper articles, all confirming the inhuman prison conditions in Haiti, including: "overcrowded and inadequate" facilities; deprivation of "food, water, medical care, sanitation, and exercise;" and malnourishment of prisoners.[91] The BIA held that "where there is no evidence that the authorities intentionally and deliberately detain deportees in order to inflict torture," when there is "no evidence that the authorities intentionally create and maintain [substandard prison] conditions in order to inflict torture," and when there is only evidence of "isolated instances of mistreatment that may rise to the level of torture" in Haitian prisons, such detention "does not constitute torture within the

---

[85] *Matter of J–E–*, 23 I&N Dec. 291, 301 (BIA 2002).

[86] *Villegas v. Mukasey*, 523 F.3d 984, 989 (9th Cir. 2008) (emphasis added).

[87] *Id.* (finding that there is no evidence that Haitian authorities are intentionally and deliberately creating and maintaining harsh prison conditions in order to inflict torture, which appear to be a result of the country's severe economic difficulties). *Accord Francois v. Gonzales*, 448 F.3d 645, 652 (3d Cir. 2006) (applicant failed to establish that prison conditions in Haiti constitute 'torture'; citing with approval *Auguste v. Ridge*, 395 F.3d 123, 137 (3d Cir. 2005), which affirmed a district court's holding 'that there must be some sort of underlying intentional direction of pain and suffering against a particular [applicant], more so than simply complaining of a general state of affairs'); *see also Al-Saher v. INS*, 268 F.3d 1143, 1147 (9th Cir. 2001) (noting beatings and burns inflicted by Iraqi officials were 'specifically intended to inflict severe pain').

[88] *See Matter of J–E–*, 23 I&N Dec. 291 (BIA 2002).

[89] *Id.* at 293.

[90] *Id.*

[91] *Id.*

meaning of 8 CFR §208.18(a)."[92] The BIA found that the general evidence of prison conditions alone, without evidence showing that the applicant would be specifically and intentionally targeted, was insufficient to establish that it is more likely than not that he would be tortured if returned to Haiti.[93]

However, the BIA distinguished *Matter of J–E–* in a Haitian prison conditions CAT claim involving a diabetic applicant who was dependent on insulin and who had also been diagnosed with serious and ongoing psychological disorders requiring three medications.[94] The BIA found an affirmative duty to act in providing essential medications to detainees and that it was unlikely that the applicant would receive medical or psychiatric treatment while imprisoned. As a result, the BIA concluded he would suffer *intentionally* severe abuse in prison.[95]

In addressing the intentional act element of torture in the context of prison conditions, the U.S. Circuit Court of Appeals for the Eleventh Circuit in *Jean-Pierre v. Att'y Gen.* held that the BIA erred in denying CAT relief to a gravely ill AIDS patient, because the IJ and BIA failed to consider the most important facts in support of his claim.[96] In denying CAT relief, the IJ had found that the applicant presented no evidence that "the Haitian government deliberately creates and maintains those conditions as a means of torturing inmates," referring to the substandard conditions in Haitian prisons.[97] Further, the IJ found that there was no evidence that the Haitian government specifically targets people with AIDS for torture in prison or that it intentionally provides substandard conditions in prisons in order to torture prisoners.[98] Thus, according to the IJ, the elements of the definition of torture were not met. The BIA agreed.

The Eleventh Circuit, however, found that the IJ and BIA had missed the point of the case. The court clarified that it was not just the substandard conditions in Haitian prisons that made it more likely than not that this applicant would be tortured upon removal, but rather the applicant's particular medical condition, which made it likely that he would attract retaliation from the guards while in prison for "acting out."[99] The court found sufficient evidence on the record that such retaliation would include

---

[92] *Id.* at 291.

[93] *Id.*

[94] *Matter of B–B–*, (BIA unpublished, Mar. 10, 2009). For more information, contact Yale Law School Prof. Michael Wishnie at *michael.wishnie@yale.edu*. Professor Wishnie oversees the Worker and Immigrants' Rights Clinic and handled this particular case.

[95] *Id.*

[96] *Jean-Pierre v. Att'y Gen.*, 500 F.3d 1315, 1326–27 (11th Cir. 2007); *see also Bosede v. Mukasey*, 512 F.3d 946, 952 (7th Cir. 2008) (holding that the immigration judge (IJ) cared little about the evidence in a CAT claim by an human immunodeficiency virus (HIV) positive Nigerian who feared torture in prison upon return).

[97] *Jean-Pierre v. Att'y Gen.*, at 1326–27.

[98] *Id.*

[99] *Id.*

physical assaults and mistreatment rising to the level of torture, including confined to a crawl-space, kalot marassa (a severe boxing of the ears), and beatings with metal rods, and that such treatment would be at the hands of government agents acting intentionally.[100]

Similarly, U.S. Circuit Court of Appeals for the Ninth Circuit reversed the denial of CAT relief where the evidence presented was not just of general prison conditions, but that the prison officials in Nigeria would single out the applicant, who suffered from AIDS.[101] In at least two unpublished decisions, HIV-positive applicants also have successfully argued that prison conditions in their home countries of Haiti and Cuba would amount to torture.[102]

Other courts, however, have upheld the BIA's decision in *Matter of J–E–*, finding that conditions in Haitian prisons do not amount to torture because there is no evidence that officials specifically intend to cause severe pain or suffering.[103] For example, in *Carry v. Holmes*, the district court held that:

> In assessing intent, the appropriate question is not whether Haiti subjects detainees to indefinite detention with the specific intent to torture them, but whether Haitian officials intentionally, *i.e.*, deliberately or purposefully (as opposed to accidentally or negligently), inflict severe pain and suffering upon the detainees for the purpose of, inter alia, punishing them or intimidating them.[104]

Overall, harsh prison conditions are not themselves a basis for relief without showing some sort of targeted intent to harm the individual.[105]

Every circuit court that has decided the issue has concluded that "torture" under CAT requires specific intent to inflict harm.[106] For example, in 2008, the U.S. Circuit

---

[100] *Id.*

[101] *Eneh v. Holder*, 601 F.3d 943, 948–49 (9th Cir. 2010).

[102] Karen Musalo & Meghann Boyle, *Lesbian, Gay, Bisexual Transgender, and HIV Asylum Law*, IMMIGRATION & NATIONALITY LAW HANDBOOK 371, 386 (AILA 2007–08 Ed.).

[103] *Pierre v. Gonzales*, 502 F.3d 109, 118–19 (2d Cir. 2007)

[104] *Carry v. Holmes*, 02-CV-0369Sr, 2003 U.S. Dist. LEXIS 26243, at *23 (W.D.N.Y. July 18, 2003) (citing 8 CFR §208.18(a)(1)).

[105] *Kang v. Att'y Gen.*, 611 F.3d 157, 165 n. 3 (3d Cir. 2010); *Gourdet v. Holder*, 587 F.3d 1 (1st Cir. 2009); *Pierre v. Gonzales*, 502 F.3d 109, 118 (2d Cir. 2007); *Jean-Pierre v. Att'y Gen.*, 500 F.3d 1315 (11th Cir. 2007); *Auguste v. Ridge*, 395 F.3d 123 (3d Cir. 2005); *Settenda v. Ashcroft*, 377 F.3d 89 (1st Cir. 2004).

[106] *See, e.g.*, *Fahmy v. Holder*, 576 Fed. Appx. 524 (6th Cir. 2014); *Escamilla v. Holder*, 459 Fed. Appx. __, No. 11-9520, 2012 U.S. App. LEXIS 4974, 2012 WL 760162 (10th Cir. Mar. 9, 2012); *Denis v. Att'y Gen.*, 633 F.3d 201, 217–19 (3d Cir. 2011); *Lopez-Amador v. Holder*, 649 F.3d 880 (8th Cir. 2011); *Cherichel v. Holder*, 591 F.3d 1002 (8th Cir. 2010); *Eneh v. Holder*, 601 F.3d 943 (9th Cir. 2010); *Gourdet v. Holder*, 587 F.3d 1, 4 (1st Cir. 2009); *Pierre v. Att'y Gen.*, 528 F.3d 180, 190–91 (3d Cir. 2008); *Villegas v. Mukasey*, 523 F.3d 984, 988 (9th Cir. 2008); *Pierre v. Gonzales*, 502 F.3d 109, 113–19 (2d Cir. 2007); *Jean-Pierre v. Att'y Gen.*, 500 F.3d 1315 (11th Cir. 2007); *Majd v. Gonzales*,

Continued

Court of Appeals for the Third Circuit reversed itself on the issue of whether willful blindness could be used to satisfy the specific intent requirement, concluding that specific intent to inflict severe pain or suffering is the standard.[107] In *Pierre v. Att'y Gen.*, the court stated that it was rejecting its discussion of willful blindness in *Lavira v. Att'y Gen.* as applied to the specific intent requirement.[108] The court also held that to the extent *Lavira* suggested that mere knowledge was sufficient to satisfy the specific intent requirement, it was overruling that suggestion, too.[109] Rather, it is the applicant's burden to establish that the torturer will have the goal, motive, or purpose of inflicting severe pain or suffering. The Third Circuit has since followed this decision in *Pierre* that willful blindness is not sufficient and that specific intent is required.[110]

3. *Under the Custody or Control of the Offender*

In addition to the requirements of severe pain and suffering that is intentionally inflicted, "to constitute torture an act must be directed against a person in the *offender's* custody or physical control."[111] In most cases, an individual would be in the physical custody of his or her torturer. Arguably, individuals who are victims of widespread acts of barbarity, such as germ warfare or bombing campaigns, also could contend that they were under the "control" of their torturers.[112] However, it is U.S. regulations, not the CAT itself, that require the victim to be under a public official's custody or physical control in order to meet the definition of torture.[113] Thus, the Ninth Circuit has reversed denials of CAT relief on this basis.[114] Other circuits, however, have not addressed this specific issue.

---

446 F.3d 590, 597 (5th Cir. 2006); *Auguste v. Ridge*, 395 F.3d 123, 148 (3d Cir. 2005); *Cadet v. Bulger*, 377 F.3d 1173, 1181, 1186–96 (11th Cir. 2004).

[107] *Pierre v. Att'y Gen.*, 528 F.3d 180, 190–191 (3d Cir. 2008).

[108] *Lavira v. Att'y Gen.*, 478 F.3d 158, 170 (3d Cir. 2007), *overruled by Pierre v. Att'y Gen.*, 528 F.3d 180 (3d Cir. 2008).

[109] *Pierre v. Att'y Gen.*, at 190.

[110] *Roy v. Att'y Gen.*, 693 F.3d 333 (3d Cir. 2012); *Denis v. Att'y Gen.*, 633 F.3d 201, 217–19 (3d Cir. 2011) (following *Pierre* in the context of an applicant who feared the infliction of pain if sent to Haitian prison with hyperthyroid condition and hypertension).

[111] 8 CFR §§208.18(a)(6), 1208.18(a)(6) (emphasis added). *See Azanor v. Ashcroft*, 364 F.3d 1013, 1019 (9th Cir. 2004) (to qualify for CAT relief, an applicant need not show that she would likely face torture while under the custody or control of a public official, rather she may qualify for CAT by showing that she is under the custody and control of 'private parties'); *Pascual-Garcia v. Ashcroft*, 73 F. App'x 232, 234 (9th Cir. 2003) (holding that CAT relief does not require that torture occur while the victim is in the custody or control of the public official).

[112] *See Comollari v. Ashcroft*, 378 F.3d at 697 (questioning in dicta whether the victim of a sniper or car bomber would be under the custody or control of the offender). *See also Pierre v. Att'y Gen.*, 528 F.3d 180 (3d Cir. 2008).

[113] *Compare* 8 CFR §§208.18(a)(6), 1208.18(a)(6) *with* Convention Against Torture, art. 1.

[114] *See Reyes-Reyes v. Ashcroft*, 384 F.3d 782, 788 (9th Cir. 2004); *Azanor v. Ashcroft*, 364 F.3d 1013, 1019–20 (9th Cir. 2004) (rejecting the custody or control language from *Matter of J–E–*).

4. *For a Broad Array of Wrongful Purposes*

Fourth, although there is no requirement of nexus to a protected ground for CAT relief, as there is for asylum under INA §208(a) or withholding of removal under INA §241(b)(3),[115] the CAT does require, that thc torture be inflicted for a wrongful purpose, such as obtaining information or a confession, punishment, intimidation, coercion, or discrimination.[116] This list is not exclusive, but indicates the type of motivation that typically underlies torture.[117] To provide an example, torture based on a person's religion, ethnicity, duration of stay in the United States, and drug-related convictions are sufficient reasons for granting CAT relief.[118] One commentator has suggested that the terms "intimidation" and "coercion" are such broad concepts that almost any reason for intentional torture would fall within these definitions.[119]

5. *By or Sanctioned By a Public Official*

Fifth, to constitute "torture," the harm must be "inflicted by or at the instigation of or with the consent or acquiescence of a public official or any person acting in an official capacity."[120] The applicant must establish that "current government officials acting in an official capacity would be responsible for such abuse."[121] One commentator has stated that this requirement "is perhaps the most significant limitation on CAT relief, particularly when private groups, such as organized private militias or "death squads," are engaged in torture as a political weapon."[122]

i. Public Official or Person Acting in Official Capacity

As noted by the Senate, "The Convention deals only with torture committed in the context of governmental authority, excluding torture that occurs as a wholly private act or, in terms more familiar in U.S. law, it applies to torture inflicted "under color

---

[115] *See, e.g., Matter of S–V–*, 22 I&N Dec. 1306, 1311 (BIA 2000).

[116] 8 CFR §§208.18(a)(1), 1208.18(a)(1).

[117] *See* S. Exec. Rep. No. 101-30, at 14 (1990), *available at http://detaineetaskforce.org/wp-content/uploads/2013/04/S.-Comm.-on-Foreign-Relations-Report-on-Convention-Against-Torture-and-Other-Cruel-Inhuman-or-Degrading-Treatment-or-Punishment-S.-Exec.-Rep.-No_.pdf.* (report of the Senate Foreign Relations Committee recommending ratification of the Convention)

[118] *Matter of G–A–*, 23 I&N Dec. 366, 372 (BIA 2002) (an applicant's 'criminal convictions in the United States, *however serious*, are not a bar to deferral of removal' under the Convention Against Torture) (emphasis added).

[119] *See* Kristen Rosati, *Finally! U.S. Law Implements Article 3 of the U.N. Convention Against Torture: An Analysis of the Legislation and Interim Regulations*, 2 IMMIGRATION & NATIONALITY LAW HANDBOOK 517, 526 (AILA 1999–2000 Ed.). *See also Camara v. Ashcroft*, 378 F.3d 361, 371 (4th Cir. 2004) (noting 'the applicant need not prove the reason for torture') (emphasis in original). *But see Matter of J–E–*, 23 I&N Dec. 291, 300 (BIA 2002) (finding no evidence that Haitian government's practice of detaining all criminal deportees is for a 'proscribed purpose').

[120] CAT, *supra* note 1, art. 1. *See* 8 CFR §§208.18(a)(1), 1208.18(a)(1) (2014).

[121] *Matter of Y–L–, A–G–, R–S–R–*, 23 I&N Dec. 270, 280 (AG 2002).

[122] *See* Rosati, *supra* note 119, at 522.

of law.'"[123] Thus, a viable CAT claim will only arise if it involves actions by a "public official" or a person "acting in an official capacity."[124] The AG has equated "acting in an official capacity" to acting "under color of law" as interpreted by courts considering cases under the Civil Rights Act.[125] However, courts have found that "acting in an official capacity" does not cover rogue actions by public officials.[126]

According to a decision by the Committee Against Torture, members of warring factions in Somalia, a country without a central government, "can fall within the phrase "public officials or other persons acting in an official capacity,'" because, "de facto, [they] exercise certain prerogatives that are comparable to those normally exercised by legitimate governments."[127] In an unpublished BIA decision, the BIA remanded a CAT claim from Mexico to the IJ to determine whether the public officials in Matamoros who would harm the applicant would be acting "under color of law," given "the high level penetration of corruption in Mexico, particularly along the border."[128] The Eighth Circuit has found that a public official "acts under color of law when he misuses power possessed by virtue of...law and made possible only because he was clothed with the authority of...law."[129] In contrast, wholly private actions will not support a CAT claim.[130]

---

[123] *See* S. Exec. Rep. No. 101–30, *supra* note 117, at 14. *See also Khouzam v. Ashcroft*, 361 F.3d 161, 170–71 (2d Cir. 2004) (Egyptian police officers who torture suspects to extract confessions do so with consent or willful blindness of higher level government officials; overruling *Matters of Y–L–, A–G–, R–S–R–*, 23 I&N Dec. 270, 285 (AG 2002)).

[124] 8 CFR §§208.18(a)(1), 1208.18(a)(1) (2014).

[125] *Matter of Y–L–*, 23 I&N Dec. 270, 285 (AG 2002). *See also Ramirez–Peyro v. Holder*, 574 F.3d 893, 899–901 (8th Cir. 2009).

[126] *See, e.g., Costa v. Holder*, 733 F.3d 13, 17–18 (1st Cir. 2013) (finding that two rogue police officers do not constitute government action); *Miah v. Mukasey*, 519 F.3d 784, 788 (8th Cir. 2008) (finding that an elected official was not acting in his official capacity in his rogue efforts to take control of others' property).

[127] *Elmi v. Australia*, Comm. No. 120/1998, Committee Against Torture, 22d Sess. CAT/C/22/D/120/1998 (25 May 1999), ¶6.5, at 10. *See Gomez-Beleno v. Holder*, 644 F.3d 139 (7th Cir. 2011) (finding that the BIA had 'failed to consider whether the term 'government' in the regulations implementing CAT applies to the FARC as the de facto government in parts of Colombia.'); *Saraj v. Gonzales*, 203 Fed. Appx. 99 (9th Cir. 2006). *But see Perinpanathan v. INS*, 310 F.3d 594, 599 (8th Cir. 2002) (torture by the LTTE, an illegal terrorist organization in Sri Lanka, cannot be considered torture by government officials).

[128] *Matter of X–*, (BIA unpublished decision Dec. 24, 2008), *available at http://bibdaily.com/pdfs/BIAu12-24-08MexicoCATremand.pdf.*

[129] *Ramirez-Peyro v. Holder*, 574 F.3d 893, 901 (8th Cir. 2009) (citations omitted) (finding that Mexican law enforcement officials would act under color of law in their future attempts to harm or torture him for being an informant for the U.S. government.).

[130] *Alhaj v. Holder*, 576 F.3d 533, 539, 2009 WL 2017934 (6th Cir. 2009) (finding that when there is a lack of instigation or acquiescence of harm by a public official, or a person acting in an official capacity, protection under CAT is unwarranted).

ii. Acquiescence

Even if the torture was not committed by a public official or person acting in an official capacity, if the applicant can show acquiescence of a public official, he or she may be granted CAT protection.[131] IJ and BIA decisions that fail to consider whether public officials acquiesced to torture will be remanded for legal error.[132] According to the Senate's understanding and to the federal regulations, to establish the acquiescence of a public official, the official must, "prior to the activity constituting torture, have awareness of such activity and thereafter breach his legal responsibility to intervene to prevent such activity."[133]

Thus, acquiescence must include two elements:

(1) awareness of the torture; and

(2) failure to intervene in breach of a legal responsibility to do so.[134]

"Awareness" includes "both actual knowledge and willful blindness."[135] Relying, in part, on the dictionary definition of "acquiescence," which is "silent or passive assent," the BIA held in *Matter of S–V–* that an applicant must do more than show that the government officials are aware of the activity but powerless to stop it.[136] Rather, the applicant must show that the government officials are "willfully accepting" of the torturous activities.[137] Thus, unlike asylum, according to the BIA,

---

[131] 8 CFR §§208.18(a)(7), 1208.18(a)(7) (2014).

[132] *Madrigal v. Holder*, 716 F.3d 499, 509–10 (9th Cir. 2013); *Cordoba v. Holder*, 726 F.3d 1106, 1117 (9th Cir. 2013); *Roye v. Att'y Gen.*, 693 F.3d 333, 343–44 (3d Cir. 2012); *Zelaya v. Holder*, 668 F.3d 159, 167–68 (4th Cir. 2012); *Cole v. Holder*, 659 F.3d 762, 773–74 (9th Cir. 2011); *Bromfield v. Mukasey*, 543 F.3d 1071, 1077–79 (9th Cir. 2008); *Mouawad v. Gonzales*, 485 F.3d 405, 413–14 (8th Cir. 2007) (finding IJ erred by failing to determine whether Hizballah commits acts of torture with consent of Lebanese government); *Habtemicael v. Ashcroft*, 370 F.3d 774, 780–83 (8th Cir. 2004).

[133] 136 Cong. Rec. S17491–92, *supra* note 79. *See also* 8 CFR §§208.18(a)(7), 1208.18(a)(7) (2014).

[134] 8 CFR §§208.18(a)(7), 1208.18(a)(7) (2014).

[135] *See* S. Exec. Rep. No. 101-30, *supra* note 117, at 9; *see also Bromfield v. Mukasey*, 543 F.3d 1071, 1079 (9th Cir. 2008); *Delgado v. Mukasey*, 508 F.3d 702, 708 (2d Cir. 2007); *Cruz-Funez v. Gonzales*, 406 F.3d 1187, 1192 (10th Cir. 2005) (finding that 'willful blindness' suffices to prove acquiescence); *Ontunez-Tursios v. Ashcroft*, 303 F.3d 341, 354 (5th Cir. 2002).

[136] *Matter of S–V–*, 22 I&N Dec. 1306, 1312 (BIA 2000) (denying motion to reopen to apply for Convention Against Torture relief by Colombian national who feared torture by guerrillas); *see also Mouawad v. Gonzales*, 479 F.3d 589, 596 (8th Cir. 2007) (holding that a government does not acquiesce to torture merely because it is aware of the torture but powerless to stop it, but finding IJ did not determine whether Hizballah commits acts of torture with consent of Lebanese government); *Chen v. Gonzales*, 470 F.3d 1131, 1142 (5th Cir. 2006) (finding the evidence did not compel the conclusion that Chinese officials will acquiesce to torture by snakeheads or money lenders).

[137] *Matter of S–V–, supra* note 136. *See Mojica-Sanchez v. Att'y Gen.*, 276 Fed. Appx. 882 (11th Cir. 2007) *But see Cruz-Funez v. Gonzales*, 406 F.3d 1187, 1192 (10th Cir. 2005) (finding that willful acceptance is not required for a government to acquiesce); *Zheng v. Ashcroft*, 332 F.3d 1186, 1193 (9th Cir. 2003).

CAT relief does not extend to persons fleeing groups the government is "unable to control."[138]

The BIA's interpretation of the term "acquiescence" in *Matter of S–V–* as requiring "willing acceptance" has been rejected by a growing number of U.S. circuit courts of appeals, including the Second, Third, Fourth, Fifth, Sixth, Ninth, and Tenth Circuits. These circuits have advanced a lower, "willful blindness" standard,[139] asserting that government acquiescence does not require actual knowledge of the tortuous conduct, only "willful blindness."[140] In these circuits, the "awareness"

---

[138] *Matter of S–V–*, 22 I&N Dec. at 1312 (citing *G.R.B. v. Sweden*, Comm. No. 83/1997, CAT/C/20/D/83/1997 (1997), a decision by the Committee Against Torture regarding fear of persecution by the Shining Path in Peru). *See also Menjivar v. Gonzales*, 416 F.3d 918, 923 (8th Cir. 2005) (upholding IJ's finding that the government did not acquiesce where police did not ignore threats and responding to the shooting by a gang within two hours); *Zeng v. Ashcroft*, 332 F.3d 1186, 1194–95 (9th Cir. 2003) (noting that correct inquiry is whether public officials would turn a blind eye to immigrant's torture by others); *Moshud v. Blackmun*, 68 F. App'x 328 (3d Cir. 2003) (denying motion to reopen because FGM is illegal in Ghana and public officials have condemned the practice); *Ontunez-Turcios v. Ashcroft*, 303 F.3d 341, 354–55 (5th Cir. 2002) (holding that 'willful blindness' is acquiescence under the CAT); *Matters of Y–L–, A–G–, R–S–R–*, 23 I&N Dec. 270, 280 (AG 2002) ('[V]iolence committed by individuals over whom the government has no reasonable control does not implicate the [Convention].'), *overruled in part on other grounds by Khouzam v. Ashcroft*, 361 F.3d 161, 170–71 (2d Cir. 2004) and *Zheng v. Ashcroft*, 332 F.3d 1186, 1196 (9th Cir. 2003). *But see Delgado v. Mukasey*, 508 F.3d 702, 709 (2d Cir. 2007)(remanding Colombian CAT claim based on fear of FARC where the BIA mischaracterized record and may have applied an inappropriately stringent standard.

[139] *Compare Matter of S–V–*, 22 I&N Dec. 1306 (BIA 2000) *with e.g., Afriyie v. Holder*, 613 F.3d 924, 937 (9th Cir. 2010); *Marroquin-Ochoma v. Holder*, 574 F.3d 574, 579–80 (8th Cir. 2009); *Amilcar-Orellana v. Mukasey*, 551 F.3d 86, 92 (1st Cir. 2008); *Reyes-Sanchez v. Att'y Gen.*, 369 F.3d 1239 (11th Cir. 2004).

[140] *See, e.g., Karki v. Holder*, 715 F.3d 792, 806–07 (10th Cir. 2013) (accepting the willful blindness standard and confirming that the willful blindness standard does not require the applicant to show that the government had actual knowledge of the specific threat); *Suarez-Valenzuela v. Holder*, 714 F.3d 241, 245–46 (4th Cir. 2013) (rejecting the willful acceptance standard of *Matter of S–V–* and accepting the willful blindness standard); *Pieschacon-Villegas v. Att'y Gen.*, 671 F.3d 303, 311 (3d Cir. 2011); *Hakim v. Holder*, 628 F.3d 151, 155–57 (5th Cir. 2010) (adopting the willful blindness standard and rejecting the willful acceptance standard of *Matter of S–V–*); *Aguilar-Ramos v. Holder*, 594 F.3d 701, 705–06 (9th Cir. 2010) (remanding where the BIA had used the willful acceptance standard instead of willful blindness); *Gomez-Zuluaga v. Att'y Gen.*, 527 F.3d 330, 349–51 (3d Cir. 2008); *Morales v. Gonzales*, 478 F.3d 972, 983–84 (9th Cir. 2007) (finding IJ error where the IJ addressed only direct government involvement while ignoring the willful blindness by the police of repeated sexual abuse); *Delgado v. Mukasey*, 508 F.3d 702, 708–09 (2d Cir. 2007); *Silva-Rengifo v. Att'y Gen.*, 473 F.3d 58, 65 (3d Cir. 2007) ('We cannot accept the Board's conclusion that the acquiescence that must be established under CAT requires actual knowledge of tortuous activity as required in *Matter of S–V–*'; an applicant need only show that the government was 'willfully blind'); *Rafiq v. Gonzales*, 468 F.3d 165, 166–67 (2d Cir. 2006); *Amir v. Gonzales*, 467 F.3d 921, 926 (6th Cir. 2006) (finding that *Matter of S–V–* directly conflicts with Congress's clear intent to include 'willful blindness' in the definition of 'acquiescence'); *Ornelas-Chavez v. Gonzales*, 458 F.3d 1052, 1060 (9th Cir. 2006) ('It is enough that public officials could have inferred the alleged torture was taking place, remained willfully blind to it, or simply stood by because of their inability or unwillingness to oppose it'; citing with approval *Zheng v. Ashcroft*, 332 F.3d 1186, 1194 (9th Cir. 2003)); *Ochoa v. Gonzales*, 406 F.3d 1166, 1172 (9th Cir.

Continued

element of acquiescence, therefore, includes "both actual knowledge and willful blindness."[141] It does not require "actual knowledge of the specific intent," or that the "public official approve of the torture even implicitly," or that "the entire foreign government would consent to or acquiesce in his torture."[142]

For example, in interpreting the term "acquiescence," the U.S. Court of Appeals for the Sixth Circuit considered the actions of Danish police officers, which included arresting assailants, incarcerating them, and offering to admonish them when the victim asked that they not be punished further.[143] Although the court found that these actions did not constitute acquiescence, in dicta, the court noted that under different circumstances, "such as where the authorities ignore or consent to severe domestic violence, the Convention [Against Torture] appears to compel protection for the victim."[144]

With regard to government acquiescence to torture by private or third parties, the U.S. Circuit Court of Appeals for the Eighth Circuit continues to hold that willful blindness is sufficient to establish that a government has acquiesced.[145] The U.S. Circuit Courts of Appeals for the Third and Ninth Circuits have also reached a similar conclusion.[146]

- **Practice Pointer**: Given the difficulty in defining a cognizable particular social group and establishing nexus to a protected ground in

---

2005) (finding that for relief under the CAT, an applicant 'need only prove the government is aware of a third party's tortuous activity and does nothing to prevent it'); *Lopez-Soto v. Ashcroft*, 383 F.3d 228, 240 (4th Cir. 2004) (finding that 'awareness includes both actual knowledge and willful blindness'); *Khouzam v. Ashcroft*, 361 F.3d 161, 171 (2d Cir. 2004) (finding that CAT relief does not require consent or approval to torturous conduct, only that government officials know of or remain willfully blind to an act and thereafter breach their legal responsibility to prevent it); *Zheng v. Ashcroft*, 332 F.3d 1186, 1194–96 (9th Cir. 2003) (stating that congressional intent only requires 'awareness' by government officials and not 'willful acceptance' of torture); *Ontunez-Tursios v. Ashcroft*, 303 F.3d 341 (5th Cir. 2002).

[141] *See* S. Exec. Rep. No. 101-30, *supra* note 117, at 9; *see also Bromfield v. Mukasey*, 543 F.3d 1071, 1079 (9th Cir. 2008); *Delgado v. Mukasey*, 508 F.3d 702, 708 (2d Cir. 2007); *Cruz-Funez v. Gonzales*, 406 F.3d 1187, 1192 (10th Cir. 2005) (finding that 'willful blindness' suffices to prove acquiescence); *Ontunez-Tursios v. Ashcroft*, 303 F.3d 341, 354 (5th Cir. 2002).

[142] *Madrigal v. Holder*, 716 F.3d 499, 509–10 (9th Cir. 2013) (remanding the case where there was evidence that the police and prison guards in Mexico were working with drug cartels that tortured former Mexican military members); *Cordoba v. Holder*, 726, F.3d 1106, 1117 (9th Cir. 2013) (finding that police officers may have acquiesced when they allowed Zetas with a kidnapped victim to go through a checkpoint).

[143] *Ali v. Reno*, 237 F.3d 591, 598 (6th Cir. 2001).

[144] *Id.* (citing with approval, inter alia, Barbara Alexander, Note, *Convention Against Torture: A Viable Legal Alternative Remedy for Domestic Violence Victims*, 15 AM. U. INT'L L. REV. 895 (2000)). *See* chapter 5 for a detailed discussion of domestic violence-based claims for protection.

[145] *Miah v. Mukasey*, 519 F.3d 784, 788 (8th Cir. 2008).

[146] *Zheng v. Ashcroft*, 332 F.3d 1186, 1194–97 (9th Cir. 2003); *Gomez-Zuluaga v. Att'y Gen.*, 527 F.3d 330 (3d Cir. 2008).

asylum and withholding of removal claims based on domestic or gang violence, practitioners always should make an alternative CAT claim on behalf of their clients. These cases have great potential for success, especially in circuits that rely upon a "willful blindness" standard for evaluating government acquiescence to torture.[147] See Chapter 5 of this book for a detailed discussion of protection claims based on domestic and gang violence.

Demonstrating government awareness is only the first step in meeting the government acquiescence requirement. In addition to awareness, the applicant must show that a government official had a legal duty to intervene with regard to the torture and that he or she breached that duty.[148] Courts have found that police officers' refusal to help victims[149] and the intentional denial of medical care[150] may meet this requirement for acquiescence.

In establishing a legal duty that was breached by a government official, it may be useful to look to the CAT itself, which includes numerous provisions directed at countries that are parties to the CAT to take effective legislative, judicial, or other measures to prevent acts of torture in their territories; to criminalize torture under domestic law; to educate and inform law enforcement personnel, public officials, and others regarding the prohibition against torture; and to review interrogation and custody procedures to prevent torture.[151] As one commentator has noted, "a violation of any of these international obligations, or a violation of any obligation found in domestic law, would arguably provide such a duty to intervene."[152] Thus, it may be argued that if a government is unable or unwilling to control private groups that engage in torture, it has breached its legal responsibility to protect individuals within its jurisdiction and may, therefore, be acquiescing to the torture carried out by these groups.[153]

In demonstrating that the acts of torture feared would be at the hands of a public official, either directly or via acquiescence, the applicant does not need to

---

[147] *See, e.g., Zalaya v. Holder*, 668 F.3d 159, 167–68 (4th Cir. 2012) (remanding to determine whether police refusal to help a victim who had been shot by the MS-13 gang constitutes acquiescence).

[148] 8 CFR §§208.18(a)(7), 1208.18(a)(7) (2014).

[149] *See, e.g., Zalaya*, 668 F.3d at 167–68 (remanding to determine whether police refusal to help a victim who had been shot by the MS-13 gang constitutes acquiescence).

[150] *See, e.g., Cole v. Holder*, 659 F.3d 762, 773–74 (9th Cir. 2011).

[151] *See* CAT, *supra* note 1, arts. 2(1), 4, 10, & 11.

[152] Rosati, *supra* note 119, at 521–22.

[153] *Id.* at 522. *But see Matter of S–V–*, 22 I&N Dec. 1306, 1312 (BIA 2000) (holding that 'acquiescence' does not include instances in which the government is unable to control the group that is feared, though the BIA's underlying definition of 'acquiescence' is no longer good law in many jurisdictions, as shown *supra*, though it may continue to have weight in others).

demonstrate that he or she reported the alleged torture to public officials.[154] A failure to report the acts of torture to the government does not necessarily indicate a lack of government acquiescence, as acquiescence may be shown through other facts. Similarly, efforts by somc government actors to prevent the acts of torture do not necessarily foreclose the possibility of acquiescence by other government actors.[155] A government may acquiesce in torture where some public officials seek to prevent torture, others are complicit, and the government is unable to prevent it.[156]

Under the facts and evidence presented, courts have found a lack of the requisite acquiescence in the following situations:

- Where police were ineffective or unresponsive;[157]
- Where a weak and inefficient judicial system led to the government's failure to investigate and punish individuals and criminal groups;[158]
- Where the government was unable to protect a witness from gang violence;[159]
- Where the government was unable to protect ex-gang members in prison;[160]
- Where the government had been unable to solve an existing human trafficking problem;[161]
- Where the government had taken action against or opposed the alleged torturers;[162]

[154] *See, e.g., Mayorga-Vidal v. Holder*, 675 F.3d 9, 19–20 (1st Cir. 2012); *Ornelas-Chavez v. Gonzales*, 458 F.3d 1052, 1059–61 (9th Cir. 2006).

[155] *See, e.g., De La Rosa v. Holder*, 598 F.3d 103, 109–11 (2d Cir. 2010) (remanding for the BIA to issue precedent addressing this issue).

[156] *Id.*

[157] *Garcia-Millan v. Holder*, 2014 WL 555138 (9th Cir. 2014); *Valdiviezo-Galdamez v. Att'y Gen.*, 663 F.3d 582, 609–12 (3d Cir. 2011) (finding a lack of acquiescence based on evidence that the government was opposed to gang violence, even though the applicant had made police reports on five occasions); *Marroquin-Ochoma v. Holder*, 574 F.3d 574, 579–80 (8th Cir. 2009); *Rreshpja v. Gonzales*, 420 F.3d 551, 557 (6th Cir. 2005) (finding a lack of acquiescence where the police did not ignore the complaint of a young Albanian woman's attempted kidnapping for prostitution, but could not solve the crime); *Reyes-Sanchez v. Att'y Gen.*, 369 F.3d 1239 (11th Cir. 2004) (finding a lack of acquiescence where the police investigated the terrorists' acts against the applicant).

[158] *Bartolo-Diego v. Gonzales*, 490 F.3d 1024, 1029 (8th Cir. 2007).

[159] *Green v. Att'y Gen.*, No. 11-3732 (3d Cir. Sept. 12, 2012); *Amilcar-Orellana v. Mukasey*, 551 F.3d 86, 92 (1st Cir. 2008) (finding a lack of acquiescence where the government was incapable of protecting witnesses against gangs)

[160] *Arteaga v. Mukasey*, 511 F.3d 940, 948–49 (9th Cir. 2007).

[161] *Rreshpja v. Gonzales*, 420 F.3d 551, 557 (6th Cir. 2005).

[162] *Valdiviezo-Galdamez v. Att'y Gen.*, (upholding denial of CAT where 'the record also indicates that the government seeks to combat the [gang] problem and protect its citizens'); *Purwantono v. Gonzales*, 498 F.3d 822, 855–56 (8th Cir. 2007) (finding a lack of acquiescence for a Muslim Indonesian who opposed recruitment by Laskar Jihad where the Indonesian government had taken action against Laskar Jihad); *Morales v. Att'y Gen.*, 488 F.3d 884, 891 (11th Cir. 2007) (denying CAT protection based on

Continued

- Where the government failed to apprehend the persons threatening the applicant and lacked the financial resources to eradicate the threat of torture;[163]
- Where there is no central government and the acting clans controlled Somalia through no official power;[164] and
- Where the respondent did not present evidence of consent or acquiescence by public officials.[165]

On the other hand, courts have found acquiescence of public officials in the following situations:

- Where government officials knew of private parties' abusive actions "and thereafter breach[ed] their legal responsibility to prevent [such actions]";[166]
- Where "private persecution of a particular sort is widespread and well-known but not controlled by the government";[167] and
- Where extortionists in El Salvador may have received information about the individual from government officials acting in their official capacities.[168]

  - **Practice Pointer**: As most country conditions reports do not specifically address government acquiescence, the detailed testimony of an expert witness can be a critical tool in demonstrating government acquiescence. Experts should not only discuss country conditions with regard to government officials' legal duties and trends in breaching those duties, but also should apply that information directly to the applicant's facts to explain the government's awareness of the torture under these specific circumstances. Experts should then explain how that conclusion fits consistently within the larger framework of government action or inaction in that country.

---

lack of acquiescence where the Colombian police provided protection and assistance in relocating the individual's dental business and investigated his claims); *Lukwago v. Ashcroft*, 329 F.3d 157, 182–83 (3d Cir. 2003) (finding a lack of acquiescence where the Ugandan government opposed guerrillas and did not initiate, condone, or acquiesce in child enslavement and conscription by the guerillas); *Ali v. Reno*, 237 F.3d 591, 596–98 (6th Cir. 2001) (finding a lack of acquiescence where the Danish police intervened to stop domestic violence, despite the fact that they were unable to do so).

[163] *Tamara-Gomez v. Gonzales*, 447 F.3d 343, 351 (5th Cir. 2006).

[164] *D-Muhumed v. Att'y Gen.*, 388 F.3d 814, 819–20 (11th Cir. 2004).

[165] *Guzman v. INS*, 327 F.3d 11, 16–17 (1st Cir. 2003); *Ontunez-Tursios v. Ashcroft*, 303 F.3d 341, 354–55 (5th Cir. 2002); *Cano-Merida v. INS*, 311 F.3d 960, 965–66 (9th Cir. 2002).

[166] *Khouzam v. Ashcroft*, 361 F.3d 161, 171 (2d Cir. 2004).

[167] *Castro-Martinez v. Holder*, 674 F.3d 1073, 1081 (9th Cir. 2011).

[168] *Garcia v. Holder*, 13-60381 (5th Cir. July 1, 2014).

6. *Not Arising Out of Lawful Sanctions*

Finally, the definition of torture does not include "pain or suffering arising only from, inherent in or incidental to lawful sanctions."[169] According to the Senate:

> [T]he United States understands that "sanctions" include judicially imposed sanctions and other enforcement actions authorized by United States law or by judicial interpretation of such law. Nonetheless, the United States understands that a State Party could not through its domestic sanctions defeat the object and purposes of the Convention to prohibit torture. The United States understands that international law does not prohibit the death penalty, and does not consider this Convention to restrict or prohibit the United States from applying the death penalty consistent with the Fifth, Eighth, and/or Fourteenth Amendments to the Constitution of the United States, including any constitutional period of confinement prior to the imposition of the death penalty.[170]

Thus, although "lawful sanctions" cannot be torture, a government cannot exempt itself from its obligations under the CAT by defining acts that would constitute torture as lawful forms of punishment.[171]

According to the regulations, "Lawful sanctions include judicially imposed sanctions and other enforcement actions authorized by law, including the death penalty, but do not include sanctions that defeat the object and purpose of the CAT to prohibit torture."[172] Notably, the regulation omits the requirement, found in the Senate understanding, that the lawful sanction be "authorized by *United States* law."[173]

In order to determine if a sanction is lawful, the IJ or BIA must first determine if the sanction is permitted under the law of the country in which it took place and whether the sanction is for a lawful purpose.[174] For example, lawful sanctions may include arrest and imprisonment for narcotics crimes in other countries.[175]

---

[169] CAT, *supra* note 1, art. 1(1); 8 CFR §§208.18(a)(3); 1208.18(a)(3) (2014).

[170] 136 Cong. Rec. S17491–92 & S36198–92 (daily ed. Oct. 27, 1990).

[171] 8 CFR §§208.18(a)(3), 1208.18(a)(3) (2014); *Ghebrehiwot v. Att'y Gen.*, 467 F.3d 344, 358–59 (3d Cir. 2006); *Nuru v. Gonzales*, 404 F.3d 1207, 1218–23 (9th Cir. 2005).

[172] 8 CFR §§208.18(a)(3), 1208.18(a)(3) (2014).

[173] *Compare* 136 Cong. Rec. S17491–92 & S36198–92 (daily ed. Oct. 27, 1990) *with* 8 CFR §§208.18(a)(3), 1208.18(a)(3) (2014).

[174] *See, e.g., Habtemicael v. Ashcroft*, 370 F.3d 774, 781 (8th Cir. 2004) (in remanding the CAT claim for further fact finding, the court noted that the IJ made no findings as to whether the rebel group [the EPLF] had the status of a recognized government when the applicant was forced into its service or whether it had the authority to impress an Ethiopian citizen into military service against the Ethiopian government); *Carry v. Holmes*, *supra* note 104, at 20–22 (in denying government's motion to dismiss, the court noted that 'there is nothing in the record to support the BIA's determination that indefinite detention of criminal deportees is permitted under Haitian law or that detention is being implemented for a lawful purpose'). *But see Cadet v. Bulger*, 377 F.3d 1173, 1193 (11th Cir. 2004) (finding that the

Continued

If the lawful sanctions exception is construed too broadly, it could be used to exclude brutal and torturous forms of punishment, such as stoning for adultery convictions.[176] To avoid the circular reasoning that the imposition of *any* lawful sanction would not defeat the object and purpose of the CAT because it is lawful and, therefore, outside of the definition of torture, it is necessary to determine whether the sanction would be authorized by U.S. law.[177] Because the regulations omit this requirement that the lawful sanction be authorized by U.S. law in order to fall outside the definition of torture – a requirement that is found in the Senate understanding – it could also be argued that the regulations are *ultra vires*.[178] For example, with regard to the death penalty:

> [I]f the method in which execution is conducted in another country is particularly barbarous or causes extreme pain and suffering, or if the imposition of death is not proportional to the crime committed, or if the death penalty is imposed without basic due process provided, advocates can argue that the imposition of the penalty in those circumstances constitutes torture.[179]

The few cases construing this term have held that, under the facts and evidence presented, lawful sanctions do not include:

- Being subject to terrible prison conditions in Niger as part of a lawful sanction for planning a coup d'état;[180]
- Imprisonment in a prison that is notorious for cruel and prolonged acts of torture against political opponents;[181]
- Intentionally barbaric prison conditions where the intent of the authorities is to discriminate, punish, coerce confessions, intimidate, or the like;[182]

---

district court did not err in concluding that indefinite detention of criminal deportees in Haiti is lawful government sanction and not CAT-prohibited torture).

[175] *McDaniel v. INS*, 142 F. Supp. 2d 219, 224 (D. Conn. 2001) (finding the prosecution under Decree 33 in Nigeria does not amount to torture).

[176] *See* Rosati, *supra* note 119, at 524.

[177] *Id.*

[178] *Compare* 136 Cong. Rec. S17491–92 & S36198–92 (daily ed. Oct. 27, 1990), *available at http://thomas.loc.gov/cgi-bin/query/F?r101:35:./temp/~r101XwRUtJ:e44928 with* 8 CFR §§208.18(a)(3), 1208.18(a)(3) (2014).

[179] Rosati, *supra* note 119, at 525.

[180] *Abdoulaye v. Holder*, 721 F.3d 485, 491–92 (7th Cir. 2013).

[181] *Hosseini v. Gonzales*, 471 F.3d 953, 960 (9th Cir. 2006) (finding that the U.S. Department of State (DOS) country reports make clear that Iran's treatment of political opponents, including the MEK, goes far beyond what could reasonably be regarded as 'lawful sanctions').

[182] *Pierre v. Gonzales*, 502 F.3d 109, 120–21 (2d Cir. 2007); *Auguste v. Ridge*, 395 F.3d 123 (3d Cir. 2005).

- Sanctioning a Falun Gong member for not reporting to the police after his arrest and violation of Chinese immigration laws;[183] and
- Sustained beatings for one month, and being burned with cigarettes over an eight– to 10-day period for misrepresenting religion and place of birth when applying for a job.[184]

On the other hand, under the facts and evidence presented, lawful sanctions may include the following:

- Detaining deportees for an indeterminate period, even where prisoners are beaten and deprived of adequate food, water, medical care, and sanitation;[185] and
- Substandard prison conditions.[186]

B. *Nonrefoulement* (Non-Return) Provision

The *nonrefoulement* (non-return) provision in the CAT prohibits, in absolute terms, the return of an individual to a country where he or she is in danger of being tortured. That provision states, "No State Party shall expel, return (*refouler*) or extradite a person to another State where there are substantial grounds for believing that he or she would be in danger of being subjected to torture."[187] In making this determination, the United States "shall take into account all relevant considerations including, where applicable, the existence in the State concerned of a consistent pattern of gross, flagrant, or mass violations of human rights."[188]

In order to invoke the *nonrefoulement* provision and obtain relief under the CAT, the applicant must demonstrate that it is "more likely than not" that he or she will be subject to torture upon removal.[189] The CAT protects against torture only, not lesser forms of harm. Moreover, the CAT protects against future torture only; the applicant must show that it is more likely than not that he or she will suffer torture in the future.[190] Ability to avoid future torture by relocating internally, as well as all other

---

[183] *Zhang v. Gonzales*, 432 F.3d 339, 345 (5th Cir. 2005).

[184] *Al-Saher v. INS*, 268 F.3d 1143, 1147 (9th Cir. 2001); *see also Khouzam v. Ashcroft*, 361 F.3d 161, 169 (2d Cir. 2004) (in overturning the BIA, the court noted that 'it would totally eviscerate the CAT to hold that once someone is accused of a crime it is a legal impossibility for any abuse inflicted on that person to constitute torture').

[185] *Matter of J–E–*, 23 I&N Dec. 291, 293, 300 (BIA 2002).

[186] *Alemu v. Gonzales*, 403 F.3d 572, 576 (8th Cir. 2005); *Cadet v. Bulger*, 377 F.3d 1173, 1193 (11th Cir. 2004).

[187] CAT, *supra* note 1, art. 3(1).

[188] CAT, *supra* note 1, art. 3(2).

[189] 8 CFR §§208.16(c)(2), 1208.16(c)(2) (2014); 136 Cong. Rec. S17492 (daily ed., Oct. 27, 1990); *Matter of M–B–A–*, 23 I&N Dec. 474 (BIA 2002); *Matter of J–E–*, 23 I&N Dec. 291, 303 (BIA 2002)

[190] *See, e.g., Niang v. Gonzales*, 422 F.3d 1187, 1202 (10th Cir. 2005); *El Himri v. Ashcroft*, 378 F.3d 932, 938 (9th Cir. 2004). However, past torture is probative evidence of the likelihood that an individual will be tortured again in the future. *See* 8 CFR §§208.16(c)(3)(i), 1208.16(c)(3)(i) (2014).

evidence relevant to the possibility of future torture may be considered in determining whether to invoke the *nonrefoulement* provision.[191]

> ➢ **Practice Pointer:** Even though an applicant for CAT relief must demonstrate that he or she will suffer future torture, past torture may be strong evidence that future torture is more likely than not to occur. See Part II.C. for a detailed discussion of the evidentiary requirements for CAT protection.

If an individual demonstrates all eligibility requirements for the invocation of the *nonrefoulement* provision under the CAT, there are two forms of CAT relief that may be granted — withholding of removal and, if any bars to withholding of removal apply, deferral of removal. There are no bars to deferral of removal protection.[192] Each of these concepts is discussed in detail below.

1. "More Likely Than Not" Standard

Both the CAT and implementing legislation require that there be "substantial grounds for believing [the applicant] would be in danger of being subjected to torture."[193] In interpreting this provision, the Senate, in its resolution of advice and consent, determined that "substantial grounds" means an individual must demonstrate it is "more likely than not that he [or she] would be tortured."[194] The regulations, similarly, place the burden of proof on the applicant "to establish that it is more likely than not that he or she would be tortured if removed to the proposed country of removal."[195] This is the same standard of proof applied in withholding of removal claims under INA §241(b)(3).[196]

---

[191] 8 CFR §§208.16(c)(3), 1208.16(c)(3) (2014). *See infra* pt II.C. of this chapter for a detailed discussion of the evidentiary requirements for demonstrating eligibility for CAT protection.

[192] *See infra* pt. III of this chapter for a detailed discussion of withholding of removal compared with deferral of removal under CAT. *See also infra* pt. II.D. of this chapter for a detailed discussion of the statutory bars to withholding of removal under CAT.

[193] *See id.*; FARRA, *supra* note 11, §2242(a), 112 Stat. 2681–822.

[194] 136 Cong. Rec. S17492 (daily ed., Oct. 27, 1990).

[195] *See* 8 CFR §§2 08.16(c)(2), 1208.16(c)(2) (2014). *See also Berishaj v. Ashcroft*, 378 F.3d 314, 332 (3d Cir. 2004) (in rejecting a CAT claim, court noted there was 'scant evidence' that it would be more likely than not that the applicant would be tortured upon return to Montenegro); *Cadet v. Bulger*, 377 F.3d 1173, 1180 (11th Cir. 2004); *Elien v. Ashcroft*, 364 F.3d 392, 398 (1st Cir. 2004); *Perinpanathan v. INS*, 310 F.3d 594, 599 (8th Cir. 2002) (burden of proof is on the applicant to establish it is more likely than not he or she would be tortured in proposed country of removal).

[196] *See Matter of M–B–A–*, 23 I&N Dec. 474 (BIA 2002) (evidence presented regarding the enforcement of Decree 33 in Nigeria was insufficient to establish that it was more likely than not the applicant would be tortured upon return); *Matter of J–E–*, 23 I&N Dec. 291, 303 (BIA 2002) (evidence of isolated acts of torture in Haitian prisons is insufficient to meet burden of proof). See also chapter 4 for a detailed discussion of the various standards of proof in protection claims, including claims under the CAT.

Where multiple entities or claims are involved, they should be aggregated in considering whether they meet the "more likely than not" to be tortured standard.[197] For example, in an unusual case in which an individual feared more than one entity in his home country, the Third Circuit held that the individual "is entitled to CAT protection if he is able to demonstrate that the cumulative probability of torture by the two entities exceeds 50%."[198]

The attorney general has held that the "more likely than not" standard cannot be met by merely stringing together a series of suppositions where the evidence does not show that each step in the hypothetical chain of events is more likely than not to happen.[199] Similarly, the Committee Against Torture has stated that the risk of torture "must be assessed on grounds that go beyond mere theory or suspicion," but clarified that "the risk does not have to meet the test of being highly probable."[200] Thus, the applicant has the burden of proving that every link in the chain leading to torture is more likely than not to occur.[201]

To determine whether future torture is more likely than not to occur, the adjudicator should apply a two-step test: (1) consider what is likely to happen to the applicant if removed; and (2) consider whether that amounts to the legal definition of torture.[202]

The BIA reviews de novo an IJ's prediction or finding regarding the likelihood that an individual will be tortured, because, like a conclusion relating to an individual's chance of persecution, it relates to whether the ultimate statutory requirement for establishing eligibility for relief has been met, and is therefore a mixed question of law and fact, or a question of judgment.[203]

---

[197] *Tran v. Gonzales*, 447 F.3d 937, 941–44 (6th Cir. 2006) (remanding where the BIA had disaggregated a Vietnamese applicant's claims, requiring a 51% chance of torture for each claim); *Kamara v. Att'y Gen.*, 420 F.3d 202, 213–15 (3d Cir. 2005) (finding that the BIA applied the wrong quantum of proof when it treated the likelihood of torture from different entities in Sierra Leone separately instead of aggregating them to reach a 51% chance of torture).

[198] *Kamara v. Att'y Gen.*, 420 F.3d 202, 213–14 (3d Cir. 2005).

[199] *Matter of J–F–F–*, 23 I&N Dec. 912, 917–18 (AG 2006) (overturning BIA's grant of deferral of removal under the CAT to a mentally ill man from the Dominican Republic convicted of rape where the IJ 'strung together a series of suppositions' by speculating what would happen to the applicant if he did not take his medication and was arrested and tortured by the police and by 'flip[ping] the burden [of proof] on its head' by finding facts based on the absence of evidence).

[200] U.N. Comm. Against Torture, *A.A. v. Switzerland*, Commc'n No. 268/2005, ¶ 8.3, U.N. Doc. No. CAT/C/38/D/268/2005 (May 11, 2007), *available at www.refworld.org/docid/47975afe21.html.*

[201] *Matter of J–F–F–*, 23 I&N Dec. 912 (AG 2006).

[202] *See Green v. Att'y Gen.*, 694 F.3d 503, 507–08 (3d Cir. 2012).

[203] *Matter of V–K–*, 24 I&N Dec. 500, 501–02 (BIA 2008) (holding that preponderance of the evidence did not show that it was more likely than not a Jew from the former Soviet Union would be tortured in the Ukraine). *See* chapters 11 and 12 for detailed discussions of administrative and judicial review.

2. *Torture Only*

The *nonrefoulement*, or non-return, provision of the Convention Against Torture protects individuals who are more likely than not to be subjected to "torture."[204] It does not apply in situations where individuals fear lesser forms of harm.[205]

- **Practice Pointer**: Individuals fearing lesser forms of harm may qualify for asylum or withholding of removal if the harm they fear rises to the level of persecution.[206]

3. *Objective Only*

Unlike asylum and withholding of removal under INA §241(b)(3), an applicant for relief under the CAT does not need to demonstrate a subjective element. Rather, the standard of proof is objective only.[207] However, general evidence of torture in a country is usually not sufficient; to meet his or her burden of proof, the applicant must provide specific evidence that he or she will be targeted and tortured.[208]

4. *Prospective Only*

Unlike asylum and withholding of removal under INA §241(b)(3), which provide protection for individuals who have suffered past persecution, the CAT only protects individuals who would suffer future torture upon their return.[209] Nevertheless, past torture is probative of whether an individual may be subjected to torture in the future. The regulations, therefore, specifically provide that "all evidence relevant to the

---

[204] *See* CAT, *supra* note 1, art. 3.

[205] *See supra* pt. II.A. for a detailed discussion of the type of harm that meets the definition of torture.

[206] See chapter 2 for a detailed discussion of the type of harm that rises to the level of persecution for purposes of asylum under INA §208(a) or withholding of removal under INA §241(b)(3).

[207] *See, e.g., Hosseini v. Gonzales*, 471 F.3d 953, 959–61 (9th Cir. 2006) (finding that the objective evidence from the Department of State reports indicated that the applicant was likely to be tortured, despite the fact that the applicant was found not credible); *Singh v. Ashcroft*, 398 F.3d 396, 404–06 (6th Cir. 2005); *Ramsameachire v. Ashcroft*, 357 F.3d 169, 184–86 (2d Cir. 2004); *Camara v. Ashcroft*, 378 F.3d 361, 371–72 (4th Cir. 2004). *But see Guo v. Gonzales*, 463 F.3d 109, 113–14 (2d Cir. 2006) (stating that *Ramsameachire v. Ashcroft* does not apply where the adverse credibility finding in regard to the asylum and withholding claims eliminated all factual basis for the CAT claim); *Gandziami-Mickhou v. Gonzales*, 445 F.3d 351 (4th Cir. 2006); *Ibrahim v. Gonzales*, 434 F.3d 1074, 1079–80 (8th Cir. 2006).

[208] *See, e.g., Mendez-Barrera v. Holder*, 602 F.3d 21, 27–28 (1st Cir. 2010); *Rashiah v. Ashcroft*, 388 F.3d 1126, 1133 (7th Cir. 2004); *Kamalthas v. INS*, 251 F.3d 1279 (9th Cir. 2001); *Mansour v. INS*, 230 F.3d 902 (7th Cir. 2000).

[209] *See* FARRA, *supra* note 11, §2242(a), 112 Stat. 2681–822; 8 CFR §§208.16(c)(2), 208.17(a), 1208.16(c)(2), & 1208.17(a) (2014). *See also, e.g., Niang v. Gonzales*, 422 F.3d 1187, 1202 (10th Cir. 2005) (finding that although past torture is a relevant consideration, it is only one factor in the assessment); *El Himri v. Ashcroft*, 378 F.3d 932, 938 (9th Cir. 2004) (in rejecting a CAT claim, the court noted that most of the violence against Palestinians in Kuwait ended when the constitutional government returned to Kuwait).

possibility of future torture shall be considered, including, but not limited to ... [e]vidence of past torture inflicted upon the applicant."[210]

5. No Internal Relocation Option

Despite the requirement that the torture feared must be by or at least sanctioned by a public official, an individual who fears torture must also address the issue of whether he or she could relocate to another part of his or her home country where he or she is not likely to be tortured.[211] The ability to internally relocate within the country of feared torture is relevant evidence that must be considered.[212] Thus, unlike asylum or withholding of removal under INA §241(b)(3), where past persecution shifts the burden to the government to prove that the applicant could relocate to avoid persecution, an applicant for CAT relief always must demonstrate that he or she will be tortured irrespective of where he or she relocates in the country of feared torture.[213]

The Committee Against Torture has considered the following factors in determining whether an individual has an internal relocation option:

(1) whether the individual had to leave his or her native area;

(2) whether a new location inside his or her country did not prove secure; and

---

[210] 8 CFR §§208.16(c)(3)(i), 1208.16(c)(3)(i) (2014). *See also Kioski v. Sweden*, Comm. No. 41/1996, *reported in Report of the Committee Against Torture*, U.N. GAOR, 51st Sess., Supp. No. 44, ¶ 9.3, U.N. Doc. A/51/44, at 86 (1996) (in which the Committee considered evidence of past detention and torture in finding that a woman from Zaire would be in danger of being subjected to torture upon return).

[211] *See* 8 CFR §§208.16(c)(2), 208.16(c)(3)(ii), 1208.16(c)(2), & 1208.16(c)(3)(ii) (2014); *see also Ramirez-Peyro v. Gonzales*, 477 F.3d 637, 641 (8th Cir. 2007) (finding the BIA could not engage in fact-finding where the IJ made no specific findings about the geographic reach of the Juarez Drug Cartel in Mexico).

[212] 8 CFR §§208.16(c)(3)(ii), 1208.16(c)(3)(ii) (2014).

[213] *See, e.g., Lemus-Galvan v. Mukasey*, 518 F.3d 1081, 1084 (9th Cir. 2008) (upholding the IJ's decision that the applicant had failed to establish that internal relocation in Mexico was impossible); *Hasan v. Ashcroft*, 380 F.3d 1114, 1122–23 (9th Cir. 2004). Notably, some courts have found that where the applicant has established a valid CAT claim, the burden is on the government to demonstrate that the applicant could relocate and that such relocation would make it unlikely he or she would suffer torture in his or her home country. *See, e.g., Perez-Ramirez v. Holder*, 648 F.3d 953, 958 (9th Cir. 2011) (finding that the BIA erred in failing to apply a presumption of a nationwide threat when it placed the burden on the applicant to show that he could not relocate within Mexico); *Yakovenko v. Gonzales*, 477 F.3d 631, 637 (8th Cir. 2007) (finding that the applicant did not establish that the harm inflicted by criminals was sufficient to establish that it would be unsafe or unreasonable to relocate within Ukraine). However, in the Ninth Circuit case of *Perez-Ramirez v. Holder*, for example, the court seems to have conflated its CAT analysis with its asylum analysis. Therefore, this conclusion may not have significant authority. *See Perez-Ramirez v. Holder*, 648 F.3d 953, 958 (9th Cir. 2011). See chapter 4 for a detailed discussion of the shifting burdens of proof.

(3) whether there are indications that the individual was being sought by police in his or her home country.[214]

C. Evidence to Support Claims for CAT Protection

The burden of proof is on the applicant "to establish that it is more likely than not he or she would be tortured if removed to the proposed country of removal."[215] As with claims for asylum under INA §208(a) and withholding of removal under INA §241(b)(3), the applicant's testimony alone, if credible, may be sufficient to sustain the burden of proof without corroboration.[216] All evidence shall be considered, and if the IJ or BIA fails to consider all evidence relevant to the possibility of future torture, the case will be remanded.[217]

1. Credibility

An individual's credibility is an increasingly contested part of asylum and withholding of removal claims and, not surprisingly, is also an issue in CAT claims. A negative credibility determination in an asylum or withholding of removal under INA §241(b)(3) claim, however, will not necessarily carry over into a CAT claim.[218]

---

[214] *Alan v. Switzerland*, Comm. No. 21/1995, Supp. No. 44, ¶11.4, U.N. Doc. A/51/44, at 74–75 (1996) (finding, based on the evidence, that it was not likely that a 'safe' area existed for the individual in Turkey).

[215] 8 CFR §§208.16(c)(2), 1208.16(c)(2) (2014).

[216] 8 CFR §§208.16(c)(2), 1208.16(c)(2) (2014). *See also Matter of J–E–*, 23 I&N Dec. 291, 302 (BIA 2002).

[217] *See Pieschacon-Villegas v. Att'y Gen.*, 671 F.3d 303, 312–13 (3d Cir. 2011) (remanding the case where the IJ and BIA had failed to consider all forms of evidence); *Aguilar-Ramos v. Holder*, 594 F.3d 701, 704–05 n.6 (9th Cir. 2010); *Mostafa v. Ashcroft*, 395 F.3d 622, 625–26 (6th Cir. 2005) (finding that the BIA failed to give adequate consideration to conditions in Iran and country condition reports submitted by the applicant); *Yi-Tu Lian v. Ashcroft*, 379 F.3d 457, 459 (7th Cir. 2004); *Zubeda v. Ashcroft*, 333 F.3d 463, 477–78 (3d Cir. 2003).

[218] *See Paul v. Gonzales*, 444 F.3d 148, 156–57 (2d Cir. 2006) (finding that an adverse credibility finding for asylum does not bar a motion to reopen on different grounds for CAT); *Singh v. Ashcroft*, 398 F.3d 396, 404–06 (6th Cir. 2005) (reversing the IJ after making a generalized negative credibility finding for failure to separately analyze credibility for CAT); *Hamoui v. Ashcroft*, 389 F.3d 821, 827–28 (9th Cir. 2004) (finding that the BIA abused its discretion in denying a motion to reopen for CAT based on asylum testimony); *Taha v. Ashcroft*, 389 F.3d 800, 802 (9th Cir. 2004) (reversing where the IJ and BIA used the adverse credibility finding for asylum to deny CAT); *Settenda v. Ashcroft*, 377 F.3d 89, 94–95 (1st Cir. 2004) (finding that a per se rule that an adverse credibility determination on an asylum claim automatically defeats a CAT claim would be erroneous); *Sivakaran v. Ashcroft*, 368 F.3d 1028, 1029 (8th Cir. 2004) (stating that a credibility finding used to deny asylum and withholding is not determinative of CAT); *Ramsameachire v. Ashcroft*, 357 F.3d 169, 184 (2d Cir. 2004); *Zubeda v. Ashcroft*, 333 F.3d 463, 476 (3d Cir. 2003) (noting that the 'taint of the earlier adverse credibility determination' should not be allowed to 'bleed through' to the CAT claim); *Camara v. Ashcroft*, 378 F.3d 361, 371–72 (4th Cir. 2004) (holding that the adverse credibility determination would not necessarily defeat the applicant's CAT claim where the applicant provided independent evidence that she would be tortured upon return); *Sivakaran v. Ashcroft*, 368 F.3d 1028, 1028 (8th Cir. 2004) (noting that the IJ's adverse credibility determination and adverse decisions on asylum and withholding are not determinative of the CAT claim); *Kalmalthas v. INS*, 251 F3d 1279, 1281 (9th Cir. 2001) (in vacating

Continued

Nevertheless, some courts have found that the negative credibility determination in asylum and withholding claims could be used to deny a CAT claim. Usually, such findings have occurred where the adverse credibility determination on the asylum and withholding claims eliminated all factual bases for the CAT claim or where the applicant relied on the same evidence to prove likelihood of torture as to prove likelihood of persecution.[219]

The REAL ID Act[220] changed how credibility determinations are made in claims for relief from removal, including CAT claims.[221] For cases filed on or after May 11, 2005, INA §240(c)(4)(C) allows the IJ to consider the totality of the circumstances in assessing a CAT applicant's credibility, including all relevant factors: demeanor, candor, responsiveness, plausibility, consistency of testimony, consistency of testimony and statements with other evidence of record, and any inaccuracies or falsehoods, without regard to whether an inconsistency, inaccuracy, or falsehood goes to the heart of the applicant's claim.[222]

> ➢ **Practice Pointer**: Although the credibility standards of the REAL ID Act may apply to CAT relief, however, the REAL ID Act standards for corroboration of evidence for asylum under INA §208(a) and withholding of removal under INA §241(b)(3) do not necessarily apply

---

the BIA's denial of a motion to reopen, the court found that 'country conditions alone can play a decisive role in granting relief under the Convention,' and the BIA failed to consider documentation of widespread torture against Tamil males in Sri Lanka); *Mansour v. INS*, 230 F.3d 902, 908 (7th Cir. 2000) (in vacating the BIA's denial of a motion to reopen by an Assyrian Christian from Iraq, the court noted, '[W]e are not comfortable with allowing a negative credibility determination in the asylum context to wash over the torture claim.'). *But see Perinpanathan v. INS*, 310 F.3d 594, 599 (8th Cir. 2002) (finding that the applicant's lack of credibility in conjunction with his failure to document the reasons why he believed he would be tortured eliminated his eligibility for CAT relief).

[219] *A.A. v. Switzerland*, *supra* note 200, ¶ 8.3. *See, e.g.*, *Fesehaye v. Holder*, 607 F.3d 523, 528 (8th Cir. 2010); *Manani v. Filip*, 552 F.3d 894, 903–04 (8th Cir. 2009); *Ismaiel v. Mukasey*, 516 F.3d 1198, 1206 (10th Cir. 2008) (finding that the BIA could reasonably refuse to believe claims of past torture based on negative credibility finding); *Lin-Jian v. Gonzales*, 489 F.3d 182, 192–93 (4th Cir. 2007); *Guo v. Gonzales*, 463 F.3d 109, 113–14 (2d Cir. 2006) (finding that *Ramsameachire* does not apply where the adverse credibility finding on asylum and withholding eliminates all factual bases for the CAT claim); *Ibrahim v. Gonzales*, 434 F.3d 1074, 1079–80 (8th Cir. 2006) (finding that the IJ did not err in failing to analyze credibility issues separately where the applicant relied on the same evidence to prove torture as to prove persecution); *Yang v. Dep't of Justice*, 426 F.3d 520, 522–23 (2d Cir. 2005) (distinguishing *Ramsameachire* and *Zubeda* because the factual findings leading to the lack of credibility were not analytically distinct from the CAT claim); *Aden v. Ashcroft*, 396 F.3d 966, 969 (8th Cir. 2005); *Niang v. Gonzales*, 422 F.3d 1187, 1202 (10th Cir. 2005) (holding that '[h]ere, our review of Ms. Niang's CAT claim is controlled by the permissible finding that she is untruthful'); *Efe v. Ashcroft*, 293 F.3d 899, 907–08 (5th Cir. 2002).

[220] REAL ID Act of 2005, Pub. L. No. 109-13, div. B, 119 Stat. 231, 302–23.

[221] *See* INA §240(c)(4)(C).

[222] *Id. See, e.g.*, *Owino v. Holder*, 575 F.3d 956 (9th Cir. 2009).

to CAT claims.[223] See chapter 4 for a detailed discussion of the credibility and corroboration requirements.

The CAT has addressed credibility in numerous decisions. The Committee has found, for example, that "complete accuracy is seldom to be expected by victims of torture" and that inconsistencies in the presentation of the facts that are not material do not raise doubts about the general veracity of the claim.[224] For example, with regard to claims of rape or sexual abuse, the Committee has found that it is reasonable for a victim to delay mentioning these grounds.[225] The Committee has stated, "It is well known that the loss of privacy and prospect of humiliation based on revelation alone of the acts concerned may cause both men and women to withhold the fact that they have been subjected to rape and/or other forms of sexual abuse until it appears absolutely necessary."[226] The Committee also has held that "it is not necessary that all the facts invoked by [the individual] should be proved; it is sufficient that the Committee should consider them to be sufficiently substantiated and reliable."[227]

- **Practice Pointer:** Torture survivors may be suffering from any number of trauma-related mental health disorders, and their symptoms may cause an individual to be reluctant, unwilling, or even unable to share their accounts and fear of torture. Additionally, the effects and symptoms of mental illnesses may yield inconsistent, contradictory, or confusing statements by the applicant.[228] Therefore, documenting any mental health disorder not only demonstrates some of the real and lasting effects of torture, but also, it may help to explain any inconsistent statements or testimony, contradictions, omissions, or

---

[223] *Compare* INA §208(b)(1)(B)(iii) & §241(b)(3)(C) *with* INA §240(c)(4)(C).

[224] *See, e.g.*, U.N. Comm. Against Torture, *Kisoki v. Sweden*, Commc'n No. 41/1996, ¶ 9.3, U.N. Doc. CAT/C/16/D/41/1996 (Feb. 12, 1996), *available at www1.umn.edu/humanrts/cat/decisions/CATVWS41.htm*; U.N. Comm. Against Torture, *Tala v. Sweden*, Commc'n No. 43/1996, ¶ 10.3, U.N. Doc. CAT/C/17/D/43/1996 (Mar. 7, 1996), *available at www1.umn.edu/humanrts/cat/decisions/CATVWS43.htm*; U.N. Comm. Against Torture, *Alan v. Switzerland*, Commc'n No. 21/1995, ¶ 11.3, U.N. Doc. CAT/C/16/D/21/1995 (1996), *available at www1.umn.edu/humanrts/cat/decisions/CATVWS21.htm.*

[225] U.N. Comm. Against Torture, *V.L. v. Switzerland*, Commc'n No. 262/2005, ¶ 8.8, U.N. Doc. CAT/C/37/D/262/2005 (Jan. 22, 2007), *available at www1.umn.edu/humanrts/cat/decisions/262-2005.html.*

[226] *Id.*

[227] U.N. Comm. Against Torture, *Aemei v. Switzerland*, Commc'n No. 34/1995, ¶ 9.6, U.N. Doc. CAT/C/18/D/34/1995 (1997), *available at www1.umn.edu/humanrts/cat/decisions/34-1995.html.*

[228] *See, e.g.*, *Fiadjoe v. Att'y Gen.*, 411 F.3d 135, 149–60 (3d Cir. 2005) (reversing the adverse credibility finding for a woman from Ghana who had been repeatedly physically and sexually abused by her father); *Nwaokole v. INS*, 314 F.3d 303, 309 (7th Cir. 2002).

implausibilities, thus avoiding a negative credibility finding.[229] Practitioners must take special precautions to establish an adequate record of an applicant's mental health disorder, including affidavits of the applicant and individuals who are aware of his or her mental health issues. The key evidence, however, is a detailed evaluation by a mental health professional who can explain the diagnosis, symptoms, treatment, and effects of the disorder on the applicant's ability to function normally.[230]

2. *All Relevant Evidence*

In determining whether torture is more likely than not, the CAT permits adjudicators to take into account "all relevant considerations including, where applicable, the existence in the State concerned of a consistent pattern of gross, flagrant or mass violations of human rights."[231]

The regulations contain a similar, though somewhat expanded provision that requires the adjudicator, in assessing whether it is more likely than not that an individual will be tortured, to consider "all evidence relevant to the possibility of future torture," including but not limited to:

(1) evidence of past torture inflicted upon the applicant;

(2) evidence whether the applicant could relocate to a part of the country of removal where he or she is not likely to be tortured;

(3) evidence of gross, flagrant, or mass violations of human rights within the country of removal; and

(4) other relevant information regarding conditions in the country of removal.[232]

Some courts have focused on particularized evidence specific to the applicant to find that the record compelled the conclusion that the applicant would more likely than not face torture if returned to his or her country.[233] Other courts have noted that

---

[229] The BIA has held that noncitizens in removal proceedings are presumed to be competent, and if there are no indicia of incompetency in a case, no further inquiry regarding competency is required. *Matter of M–A–M–*, 25 I&N Dec. 474 (BIA 2011). Moreover, if a mental health disorder was the cause for the applicant's delay in filing his or her asylum application, an adequate explanation on the record may enable him or her to fall within one of the exceptions to the one-year filing deadline. 8 CFR §§208.4(a)(5)(i), 1208.4(a)(5)(i) (2014).

[230] Vikram Badrinath, Dree K. Collopy, & Hans Christian Linnartz, *Evidentiary Issues in Asylum Cases*, AILA IMMIGRATION PRACTICE POINTERS (AILA 2013).

[231] CAT, *supra* note 1, art. 3(2).

[232] *See* 8 CFR §§208.16(c)(3)(i)–(iv), 1208.16(c)(3)(i)–(iv) (2014); *see also Jean-Pierre v. Att'y Gen.*, 500 F.3d 1315, 1326 (11th Cir. 2007) (holding that the BIA omitted from its analysis any review of the most important facts presented by the applicant, a gravely ill AIDS patient from Haiti); *Mapouya v. Gonzales*, 487 F.3d 396, 415 (finding the IJ erred by not addressing these four factors in assessing a CAT claim from Republic of Congo).

[233] *See, e.g., Ali v. Achim*, 468 F.3d 462, 472–73 (7th Cir. 2006) (finding that a CAT applicant from Somalia would more likely than not face torture upon return, but remanding to the BIA to determine

Continued

"country conditions alone can play a decisive role in granting relief under the Convention."[234] Generally, however, country conditions evidence must indicate that the individual would be personally at risk in order to be sufficient on its own to meet the more likely than not standard.[235] As noted by the Third Circuit, "Specific grounds must exist that indicate the individual would be personally at risk."[236]

> ➢ **Practice Pointer**: As most country conditions reports do not draw connections between the socio-political context in the applicant's native country and the applicant's own personal circumstances, the detailed testimony of an expert witness can be a critical tool in meeting the more likely than not standard. Experts should discuss current conditions in the country in question and explain in detail the personal and specific risk of torture that the applicant would face there.[237]

Although "evidence of gross, flagrant, or mass violations of human rights within the country of removal" may be helpful evidence for an applicant to present in meeting his or her burden of proof, notably, the absence of a pattern of gross, flagrant, or mass violations of human rights does not preclude an individual from CAT protection.[238] Overall, no matter what type of evidence is presented, the key to meeting the applicant's burden of proof is presenting evidence that demonstrates that the applicant is personally more likely than not to suffer torture upon return.[239]

The CAT assesses evidence of past torture and evidence of gross, flagrant, or mass human rights violations. In reaching its decisions, it has considered the following evidence:

- The position of the U.N. High Commissioner for Refugees (UNHCR);[240]
- The DOS Country Reports on Human Rights Practices;[241]

---

whether the torture would be at the instigation of or with the consent or acquiescence of a public official).

234 *Kalmalthas v. INS*, 251 F.3d 1279, 1281 (9th Cir. 2001) (holding that the BIA erred in denying motion to reopen based on previous asylum denial and negative credibility determination).

235 *See Pieschacon-Villegas v. Att'y Gen.*, 671 F.3d 303, 312–13 (3d Cir. 2011); *Mu Xiang Lin v. DOJ*, 432 F.3d 156, 160 (2d Cir. 2005).

236 *Sevoian v. Ashcroft*, 290 F.3d 166 (3d Cir. 2002); *Julmiste v. Ashcroft*, 212 F.Supp.2d 341, 346–49 (D.N.J. 2002).

237 *Cole v. Holder*, 659 F.3d 762, 771–73 (9th Cir. 2011).

238 *Matter of J–E–*, 23 I&N Dec. 291, 303 (BIA 2002).

239 *Mu Xiang Lin v. DOJ*, 432 F.3d 156, 160 (2d Cir. 2005).

240 *See Kisoki, supra* note 224, ¶ 9.5; U.N. Comm. Against Torture, *C.T. and K.M. v. Sweden*, Commc'n No. 279/2005, ¶¶ 5.3 & 7.7, CAT/C/37/D/279/2005 (Dec. 7, 2006), *available at www1.umn.edu/humanrts/cat/decisions/279-2005.html*.

241 *See* U.N. Comm. Against Torture, *Tapia Paez v. Sweden*, Commc'n No. 39/1996, ¶ 7.2, U.N. Doc. CAT/C/18/D/39/1996 (1997), *available at www.refworld.org/docid/3ae6b6de10.html*; U.N. Comm.

Continued

- Reports by the U.N. Commission on Human Rights;[242]
- Reports by Human Rights Watch;[243]
- Ratification of the CAT by the proposed country of return;[244]
- Acts committed outside the country of origin;[245]
- Medical evidence indicating the individual suffers from post-traumatic stress disorder (PTSD) and physical after-effects of past torture;[246] and
- Publicity surrounding a particular case that increases the likelihood of torture upon return.[247]

Similarly, in the United States, courts have relied on the following types of evidence to grant and deny CAT claims:

- Past treatment of the applicant;[248]
- Treatment of others in similar circumstances as the applicant;[249]

Against Torture, *Dar v. Norway*, Commc'n No. 249/2004, ¶ 2.5, U.N. Doc. CAT/C/38/D/249/2004 (May 16, 2007), *available at www1.umn.edu/humanrts/cat/decisions/249-2004.html.*

[242] *See Aemei, supra* note 227, ¶ 9.9.

[243] *See Tapia Paez, supra* note 241, ¶ 3.2.

[244] *See Alan, supra* note 214, ¶ 11.5 (finding that despite Turkey's ratification of the Convention Against Torture, the practice of torture is still systematic in Turkey).

[245] *See Aemei, supra* note 227, ¶ 9.5 (individual was active in an illegal and dissident political organization in Switzerland that was monitored by the Iranian secret police); U.N. Comm. Against Torture, *El Rgeig v. Switzerland*, Commc'n No. 280/2005, ¶¶ 5.3 & 7.4, U.N. Doc. CAT/C/37/D/280/2005 (Nov. 30, 2006), *available at www1.umn.edu/humanrts/cat/decisions/280-2005.html* (noting that the individual engaged in public demonstrations against Libya while in Switzerland).

[246] *See El Rgeig v. Switzerland, supra* note 245, ¶ 7.4.

[247] *See Elmi v. Australia*, Commc'n No. 120/1998, ¶ 6.8, U.N. Doc. CAT/C/22/D/120/1998 (May 25, 1998), *available at www1.umn.edu/humanrts/cat/decisions/120-1998.html.*

[248] *See, e.g., Abdoulaye v. Holder*, 712 F.3d 485, 491–92 (7th Cir. 2013) (finding that the applicant did not meet his burden of proof that he would be tortured in Niger where he was subject to prison for planning a coup); *Tchemkou v. Gonzales*, 495, F.3d 785, 794–95 (7th Cir. 2007) (finding that a Cameroonian woman would face torture if returned given her past treatment); *Zewdie v. Ashcroft*, 381 F.3d 804, 808–10 (8th Cir. 2004) (finding that although the Ethiopian applicant did not present medical evidence that his scars were from beatings, no reasonable fact finder under the *Elias-Zacarias* standard could fail to find him eligible for CAT relief); *Sackie v. Ashcroft*, 270 F.Supp.2d 596, 601–03 (E.D. Pa. 2003) (finding that the burden of proof was met where a child soldier in Liberia was threatened with death on numerous occasions, frequently given mid-altering substances, and cut on his back and arms); *Matter of W–G–R–*, 26 I&N Dec. 208, 224–25 (BIA 2014) (finding that the applicant did not meet his burden of proof where he was shot in the leg when members of his former gang, Mara 18, confronted him, but the events occurred more than 13 years after he left the gang).

[249] *Khup v. Ashcroft*, 376 F.3d 898, 904–06 (9th Cir. 2004) (relying in part on the torture of a fellow preacher by the military to find that there was at least a 51% chance that the applicant would be tortured in Burma); *Matter of J–E–*, 23 I&N Dec. 291, 302 (BIA 2002) (finding that the applicant did not meet the burden of proof in relying on isolated instances of torture of indefinite detainees in Haiti).

- DOS Country Reports on Human Rights Practices;[250]
- Human rights reports by nongovernmental organizations (NGOs);[251]
- DOS travel warnings;[252]
- DOS letter regarding whether failed asylum-seekers are subjected to torture;[253]
- Reports from Bureau for International Narcotics and Law Enforcement of DOS regarding police corruption and abuses;[254]
- The presence of international oversight or intervention by the International Committee for the Red Cross or UNHCR;[255]
- U.N. Committee Against Torture decisions, considered to bc advisory only;[256]
- Experts on judicial and penal system, as well as the use of torture in the applicant's home country;[257]

---

[250] *Mulyani v. Holder*, 771 F.3d 190 (4th Cir. 2014) (holding that it made sense for the BIA to rely on State Department reports because an inquiry into country conditions 'is directly within the expertise of the Department of State'); *Nadeem v. Holder*, 599 F.3d 869, 873–74 (8th Cir. 2010) (finding that evidence of general conditions in Pakistan was insufficient to meet the applicant's burden of proof); *Muradin v. Gonzales*, 494 F.3d 1208, 1210–11 (9th Cir. 2007) (finding that the applicant met his burden of proof, citing the DOS report on Armeia); *Hosseini v. Gonzales*, 471 F.3d 953, 960 (9th Cir. 2006) (relying on DOS reports for Iran); *Zewdie v. Ashcroft*, 381 F.3d 804, 806 (8th Cir. 2004); *Khup v. Ashcroft*, 376 F.3d 898, 904–06 (9th Cir. 2004) (relying in part on DOS country reports to find that there was at least a 51% chance that the applicant would be tortured in Burma); *Perinpanathan v. INS*, 310 F.2d 594, 599 (8th Cir. 2002); *Al-Saher v. INS*, 268 F.3d 1143, 1147 (9th Cir. 2001); *Mansour v. INS*, 230 F.3d 902, 907–08 (7th Cir. 2000); *Matter of G–A–*, 23 I&N Dec. 366, 369 (BIA 2002).

[251] *Khup v. Ashcroft*, 376 F.3d 898, 904–06 (9th Cir. 2004) (relying in part on an Amnesty International report to find that there was at least a 51% chance that the applicant would be tortured in Burma); *Matter of G–A–, supra* note 250, at 369 (relying on Iranian Christians International).

[252] *Id.* Travel warnings may be found at *www.travel.state.gov*.

[253] *Miah v. Mukasey*, 519 F.3d 784 (8th Cir. 2008); *Perinpanathan v. INS*, 310 F.3d 594, 599 (8th Cir. 2002) (the DOS letter concluded that several countries and UNHCR have monitored the return of thousands of Sri Lankans who had sought asylum, and that there was no evidence that the returnees have been tortured).

[254] *Matters of Y–L–, A–G–, R–S–R–*, 23 I&N Dec. 270, 282 (AG 2002), *overruled in part on other grounds by Khouzam v. Ashcroft*, 361 F.3d 161, 170–71 (2d Cir. 2004) and *Zheng v. Ashcroft*, 332 F.3d 1186, 1196 (9th Cir. 2003). The latest report may be found at *www.state.gov/g/inl/rls/nrcrpt/2001/c6085.htm*.

[255] *Matter of G–A–*, at 371; *Matter of J–E–*, 23 I&N Dec. 291, 301 (BIA 2002).

[256] *Matter of S–V–*, 22 I&N Dec. 1306, 1313 n.1 (BIA 2000).

[257] *Perez-Guerrero v. Att'y Gen.*, 717 F.3d 1224, 1231–33 (11th Cir. 2013) (finding that the applicant, a government informant regarding corruption in Mexico with drug cartels, did not meet his burden of proof, despite expert testimony that he would be killed); *Ali v. Achim*, 468 F.3d 462, 471–72 (7th Cir. 2006) (finding that the BIA ignored key evidence when it overlooked expert testimony and focused narrowly on general country conditions); *Khouzam v. Ashcroft*, 361 F.3d 161, 169 (2d Cir. 2004).

- The lack of harm or threats to applicant on voluntary visits to home country;[258]
- Opinions of other governments adjudicating torture claims;[259] and
- Personal knowledge by the applicant.[260]

> ➢ **Practice Pointer**: Often, courts are overly reliant upon the DOS country reports on human rights practices. Although these reports may be authoritative, courts also have recognized that they are not "Holy Writs immune to contradiction"[261] and that they "may be flawed."[262] Thus, if there is harmful information in the DOS reports, practitioners should arm themselves with this case law language recognizing the potential flaws.

D. No Bars to Protection Under the Convention Against Torture

Unlike asylum and withholding of removal, there are no bars to relief under the CAT. If an individual demonstrates that there are "substantial grounds for believing [he or she] would be in danger of being subjected to torture," in a particular country, the individual cannot be returned there.[263]

The implementing legislation, which was enacted on October 21, 1998, contains a provision requiring that the regulations implementing article 3 of the Convention Against Torture exclude individuals who fall within the bars to withholding of removal described in INA §241(b)(3)(B), but only "to the maximum extent consistent with the obligations of the United States under the Convention."[264] Since there are no bars under the CAT or under any U.S. reservations, understandings, declarations, or

---

[258] *Matters of Y–L–, A–G–, R–S–R–*, 23 I&N Dec. 270 (AG 2002), *overruled in part on other grounds by Khouzam v. Ashcroft*, 361 F.3d 161, 170–71 (2d Cir. 2004) and *Zheng v. Ashcroft*, 332 F.3d 1186, 1196 (9th Cir. 2003).

[259] *Matter of J–E–*, at 297 (noting while these opinions are not binding, they are instructive).

[260] *Wani Site v. Holder*, 656 F.3d 590 (7th Cir. 2011).

[261] *Ai Hua Chen v. Holder*, 742 F.3d 171, 179 (4th Cir. 2014); *Galina v. INS*, 213 F.3d 955, 959 (7th Cir. 2000).

[262] *Gonahasa v. INS*, 181 F.3d 538, 542 (4th Cir. 1999).

[263] CAT, *supra* note 1, art. 3(1). *See, e.g.*, U.N. Comm. Against Torture, *Tebourski v. France*, Commc'n No. 300/2006, ¶ 8.2, U.N. Doc. No. CAT/C/38/D/300/2006, (May 11, 2006), *available at www.refworld.org/docid/47975b0421.html* (individual convicted of terrorism charge in France should not have been deported to Tunisia, despite France's claim that he was a danger to domestic public order); *Tapia Paez*, *supra* note 241, ¶14.5 (despite the denial of asylum to this former member of the Shining Path in Peru, the Committee found that '[t]he nature of the activities in which the person concerned engaged cannot be a material consideration when making a determination under Article 3'); *Khouzam v. Ashcroft*, 361 F.3d 161, 164 (2d Cir. 2004) (noting evidence of a past crime is not a bar to deferral of removal); *Vukmirovic v. Ashcroft*, 362 F.3d 1247, 1253 (9th Cir. 2004) (noting that even if the applicant was found to be a persecutor, he would be eligible for deferral of removal under CAT); *Matter of G–A*, 23 I&N Dec. 366, 368 (BIA 2002) (an applicant's 'criminal convictions in the United States, *however serious*, are not a bar to deferral of removal' under the Convention Against Torture) (emphasis added).

[264] *See* FARRA, *supra* note 11, at §2242(c), 112 Stat. 2681–822.

provisos, advocates believed that this section would have no substantive effect. Nevertheless, legacy INS, in drafting the regulations, devised a process whereby individuals who would be subjected to torture are, in fact, barred from withholding of removal under the Convention Against Torture if they are barred from withholding of removal under INA §241(b)(3).[265] Such individuals are entitled to only the more precarious form of CAT relief known as deferral of removal.[266]

Moreover, in claims for protection under the CAT, DOS may obtain diplomatic assurances from the country of feared torture that it will not torture the applicant on his or her return. If the AG agrees, the application for CAT relief "shall not be considered further by an IJ, the BIA, or an asylum officer."[267] Thus, while rare, diplomatic assurances from the country of feared torture may bar an applicant from being granted protection under the CAT.[268]

III. Types of Relief Available Under the Convention Against Torture

Although there are no bars to relief under the CAT, legacy INS and EOIR have devised two separate forms of relief under CAT. The first, called withholding of removal under the CAT, is similar in many ways to withholding of removal under INA §241(b)(3), including the bars to relief. The second, called deferral of removal under the CAT, has no bars, but is a more precarious remedy that can be more easily terminated.

A. Withholding of Removal Under the Convention Against Torture

To be eligible for withholding of removal under the CAT, an applicant must establish that it is more likely than not he or she would be subjected to torture if removed to his or her home country or other proposed country of removal.[269] Mandatory bars to this type of withholding—identical to the bars to withholding under INA §241(b)(3)—are:

- Conviction by final judgment of a particularly serious crime;
- Commission of a serious, nonpolitical crime outside of the United States;

---

265 *See* 8 CFR §§208.16(d)(2), 1208.16(d)(2) (2014).

266 *See* 8 CFR §§208.17, 1208.17 (2014), and this chapter, at 4.3.2. *See also Matter of Jean*, 23 I&N Dec. 373, 376 n.7 (AG 2002) (finding that the applicant's criminal history was 'irrelevant in examining his or her entitlement to deferral of removal under the Convention'). *See infra* pt. III for a detailed discussion of the differences between withholding of removal and deferral of removal under CAT.

267 8 CFR §§208.18(c), 1208.18(c) (2014).

268 *See Hussain v. Mukasey*, 518 F.3d 534 (7th Cir. 2008) (mentioning the government's ability to obtain diplomatic assurances in CAT cases); *Khouzam v. Att'y Gen.*, 549 F.3d 235 (3d Cir. 2008).

269 *See generally* 8 CFR §§208.16(c), 1208.16(c) (2014). *See supra* pt. II.B.1. for a detailed discussion of the more likely than not standard.

- Participation in the persecution of others on account of race, religion, nationality, membership in a particular social group, or political opinion;
- Danger to the security of the United States;
- Engagement in terrorist activity, incitement of terrorist activity, or representation of a foreign terrorist organization;
- Assistance in Nazi persecution; and
- Engagement in genocide.[270]

In determining whether an individual merits withholding of removal under the CAT, first, the IJ must determine whether it is more likely than not that the individual would be tortured if removed to the proposed country of removal.[271] Next, the IJ must determine whether the individual is subject to mandatory denial under one of the bars contained in INA §241(b)(3).[272] If the individual has met his or her burden of proof and is not subject to a mandatory bar, the IJ must grant withholding of removal under the CAT.[273] Such a grant has the same benefits as a grant under INA §241(b)(3) – the individual may not be removed to a country in which it is more likely than not he or she would be subject to torture.[274]

If the individual has met his or her burden of proof, but is subject to a mandatory bar, the IJ must deny withholding of removal under the CAT and grant the individual deferral of removal instead.[275]

B. Deferral of Removal Under the Convention Against Torture

To be eligible for deferral of removal under the CAT, an applicant bears the same burden of establishing that it is more likely than not that he or she would be subjected to torture if removed to his or her home country or other proposed country of removal.[276] Unlike withholding of removal under INA §241(b)(3) or withholding of removal under the CAT, there are no bars to relief.[277]

---

[270] 8 CFR §§208.16(d)(2), 1208.16(d)(2) (2014). See chapter 2 for a more detailed discussion of these bars to withholding of removal relief.

[271] 8 CFR §§208.16(c)(4), 1208.16(c)(4) (2014). *See supra* pt. II.B.1. for a detailed discussion of the more likely than not standard.

[272] *See* 8 CFR §§208.16(c)(4), 1208.16(c)(4), 208.16(d)(2), & 1208.16(d)(2) (2014). See chapter 2 for a more detailed discussion of these bars to withholding of removal relief.

[273] *See* 8 CFR §§208.16(c)(4), 1208.16(c)(4) (2014).

[274] See chapter 13 for a detailed discussion of the benefits of CAT protection.

[275] *See* 8 CFR §§208.16(c)(4), 1208.16(c)(4), 208.17(a), and 1208.17(a) (2014).

[276] *See generally* 8 CFR §§208.17, 1208.17, and this chapter, at 4.2.

[277] *See, e.g.*, *Matter of G–A–*, 23 I&N Dec. 366, 368 (BIA 2002) (an applicant's 'criminal convictions in the United States, *however serious*, are not a bar to deferral of removal' under the Convention Against Torture) (emphasis added).

A grant of deferral, however, can be terminated more easily than withholding.[278] Moreover, a person who is granted deferral may be held in detention and is not entitled to employment authorization, though he or she may be released by U.S. Immigration and Customs Enforcement or issued employment authorization by USCIS.[279]

One commentator has suggested that the bars imposed for withholding of removal under the CAT, the termination process for deferral of removal, the barriers to initiating a CAT claim such as time and numerical limitations on motions to reopen, and the bar to relief if diplomatic assurances are received are all, arguably, invalid because they are beyond the scope of the implementing legislation.[280] However, these remain valid concepts under today's legal standards relating to protection under the CAT.

---

[278] *See* 8 CFR §§208.17(d), 1208.17(d) (2014). See chapter 14 for a detailed discussion of termination of deferral of removal under CAT.

[279] *See* 8 CFR §§208.17(c), 1208.17(c), and 241.3 to 241.5 (2014). See chapter 9 for a detailed discussion of detention of individuals seeking protection and chapter 13 for a detailed discussion of the benefits of CAT protection.

[280] Rosati, *supra* note 119.

CHAPTER FOUR

PROVING THE CASE: BURDENS, STANDARDS, AND EVIDENCE*

This chapter provides guidance on an asylum applicant's burden of proof, the Department of Homeland Security's (DHS) burden of proof, and the various standards of proof that adjudicators apply as they consider an applicant's eligibility for asylum, withholding of removal, and protection under the Convention Against Torture (CAT). This chapter also discusses the evidentiary standards under U.S. asylum law and how those standards are applied to both testimonial and documentary evidence. Finally, this chapter provides practice pointers for presenting and responding to evidence presented throughout the course of a claim for asylum, withholding of removal, or CAT relief.

I. Burden of Proof

"Burden of proof" is defined as "[t]he necessity or duty of affirmatively proving a fact or facts in dispute on an issue raised between the parties in a cause,"[1] and comprises both the "burden of production" and the "burden of persuasion."[2] In the context of U.S. asylum law, the "parties" are the asylum applicant and U.S. Department of Homeland Security (DHS), while the "dispute" is whether the applicant is eligible for asylum, withholding of removal, or CAT relief. The party who bears the burden of proof bears the burden to provide evidence and to persuade the adjudicator regarding the issue at hand.[3]

---

* The author would like to thank Vikram Badrinath of The Law Offices of Vikram Badrinath for his invaluable input in reviewing this chapter.

[1] BLACK'S LAW DICTIONARY (2d ed.), *available at http://thelawdictionary.org/burden-of-proof/* (last visited Jan. 15, 2015).

[2] Graham C. Lilly, AN INTRODUCTION TO THE LAW OF EVIDENCE §3.1 (3d ed. 1996). *See also Matter of S–S*, 21 I&N Dec. 121, 122 (BIA 1995) (citing *Matter of Acosta*, 19 I&N Dec. 211 (BIA 1985), *modified on other grounds by Matter of Mogharrabi*, 19 I&N Dec. 439 (BIA 1987)); U.S. Citizenship and Immigration Servs., RAIO Asylum Division, *Asylum Eligibility Part IV: Burden of Proof, Standards of Proof, and Evidence* at 4, in ASYLUM OFFICER BASIC TRAINING COURSE PARTICIPANT WORKBOOK (Sept. 14, 2006) [hereinafter AOBTC Workbook, pt. IV] *www.uscis.gov/sites/default/files/USCIS/Humanitarian/Refugees%20%26%20Asylum/Asylum/AOBTC%20Lesson%20Plans/Burden-of-Proof-Standards-Proof-Evidence-31aug01.pdf.*

[3] AOBTC Workbook, pt. IV, *supra* note 2.

A. Burden of Proof on the Applicant

The burden of proof is on the applicant for asylum, withholding of removal, or protection under CAT to establish that he or she is eligible for relief.[4] The asylum applicant may meet this burden by demonstrating that he or she: (1) is eligible to apply for asylum; (2) meets the definition of refugee under Immigration and Nationality Act (INA) §101(a)(42)(A); and (3) merits asylum as a matter of discretion.[5] If evidence indicates that a statutory bar to asylum may apply, the applicant also bears the burden of proving that the bar does not apply and that he or she is eligible to receive asylum.[6]

In meeting that burden, an asylum-seeker first must demonstrate that he or she is eligible to apply for asylum and that his application is not pretermitted by the one-year filing deadline,[7] a previous asylum denial,[8] or a safe third country available to the applicant.[9] These three circumstances may render the asylum-seeker ineligible to apply for asylum.[10] The applicant must establish by clear and convincing evidence that the application has been filed within one year of his or her most recent entry to the United States,[11] or in the alternative, to the satisfaction of the attorney general (AG), the existence of changed circumstances that materially affect eligibility for asylum or extraordinary circumstances that resulted in the delayed filing.[12] If the applicant has previously been denied asylum by an IJ or the BIA, he or she must demonstrate to the satisfaction of the attorney general the existence of changed circumstances that materially affect his or her eligibility for asylum.[13]

- **Practice Pointer**: These ineligibility grounds do not apply to withholding of removal under INA §241(b)(3) or protection under the CAT. See chapter 2 of this book for a detailed discussion of these ineligibility grounds and the available exceptions.

---

[4] INA §§208(a)(2), (b)(1)(B)(i), (b)(2)(A); 8 CFR §§208.13(a), 1208.13(a), 1240.8(d) (2014).

[5] INA §§208(A)(2), (b)(1)(B)(i), (b)(2)(A); 8 CFR §§208.13(a), 1208.13(a), 1240.8(d) (2014).

[6] INA §§208(A)(2), (b)(1)(B)(i), (b)(2)(A); 8 CFR §§208.13(a), 1208.13(a), 1240.8(d) (2014).

[7] INA §§208(a)(2)(B), (d); 8 CFR §§208.4(a)(4)–(5) (2014).

[8] INA §§208(a)(2)(C)–(D). This bar only applies if the applicant for asylum was issued a final order of removal. It does not apply if the previous application was denied only by the Asylum Office.

[9] INA §208(a)(2)(A).

[10] INA §208(a)(2); 8 CFR §208.4(a) (2014).

[11] INA §208(a)(2)(B); 8 CFR §208.4(a)(2)(i) (2014).

[12] INA §208(a)(2)(D); 8 CFR §208.4(a)(2)(i) (2014).

[13] INA §208(a)(2)(D); 8 CFR §208.4(a) (2014).

The applicant also must demonstrate that he or she has suffered past persecution[14] or has a well-founded fear of future persecution.[15] If the applicant has suffered past persecution, it is also his or her burden to establish the following: (1) in the case of a non-governmental actor, the government of the country of origin is unable or unwilling to control the persecution; and (2) if the government has established that the applicant no longer has a well-founded fear of future persecution, the applicant should be granted asylum in the exercise of discretion owing to compelling reasons for being unable or unwilling to return to the country arising out of the severity of past persecution or because there is a reasonable possibility that the applicant would suffer other serious harm upon removal to that country.[16]

If the applicant has not suffered past persecution, he or she must demonstrate a well-founded fear of future persecution.[17] In establishing a well-founded fear of persecution, the applicant must show there is a "reasonable possibility" of persecution, or in other words, that a reasonable person in the applicant's circumstances would fear persecution if returned to his or her home country.[18] The "reasonable possibility" standard of proof required to establish eligibility for asylum is lower than the "clear probability" standard of proof that is required to establish eligibility for withholding of removal or CAT relief.[19] Except where the feared persecution is by a government actor or is government-sponsored, this burden includes establishing that internal relocation within the country of feared persecution to avoid future persecution would not be reasonable.[20]

In addition to demonstrating past persecution or a well-founded fear of persecution, in meeting his or her burden of proof, the applicant must establish that race, religion, nationality, membership in a particular social group, or political opinion was or will be "at least one central reason" for persecuting the applicant.[21]

Finally, if there is evidence indicating that a mandatory bar to asylum might apply, then the applicant must establish by a preponderance of the evidence that the ground

---

[14] 8 CFR §§208.13(b)(1), 1208.13(b)(1) (2014); *Matter of Villalta*, 20 I&N Dec. 142, 147 (BIA 1990).

[15] 8 CFR §§208.13(b)(2), 1208.13(b)(2) (2014); *Matter of O–D–*, 21 I&N Dec. 1079, 1080 (BIA 1998), *modified on other grounds by Kourski v. Ashcroft*, 355 F.3d 1038 (7th Cir. 2004); *Hanaj v. Gonzales*, 446 F.3d 694 (7th Cir. 2006).

[16] 8 CFR §§208.13(b)(1)(iii), 1208.13(b)(1)(iii) (2014). Asylum granted on this basis is generally referred to as "humanitarian asylum." *Matter of Chen*, 20 I&N Dec. 16 (BIA 1989). *See* chapter 2 for a detailed discussion of humanitarian asylum.

[17] 8 CFR §§208.13(b)(2)(ii), 208.13(b)(3)(i) (2014).

[18] *See Matter of Mogharrabi*, 19 I&N Dec. 439, 445 (BIA 1987); *Matter of S–S–*, 21 I&N Dec. 121, 122 (BIA 1995). *See also Ahmed v. Gonzales*, 467 F.3d 669, 674 (7th Cir. 2006); *Tesfamichael v. Gonzales*, 469 F.3d 109, 113 (5th Cir. 2006); *Gao v. Ashcroft*, 299 F.3d 266, 272 (3d Cir. 2002); *Korablina v. INS*, 158 F.3d 1038, 1044 (9th Cir. 1998); *M.A. v. INS*, 899 F.2d 304, 311 (4th Cir. 1990).

[19] *See INS v. Cardoza-Fonseca*, 480 U.S. 421 (1987).

[20] 8 CFR §§208.13(b)(2)(ii), 208.13(b)(3)(i) (2014).

[21] INA §208(b)(1)(B)(i). See chapter 2 for a detailed discussion of nexus and the protected grounds.

for mandatory denial does not apply.[22] Such evidence may become part of the record by either the applicant or DHS's submission; however, once there is evidence that indicates a bar to asylum or withholding of removal might apply, it is the applicant's burden to persuade the trier of fact that the bar does not apply.

➢ **Practice Pointer**: The mandatory bars to asylum include: (1) if the applicant ordered, incited, assisted or otherwise participated in the persecution of others;[23] (2) if the applicant has been convicted by a final judgment of a particularly serious crime in the United States, and thus constitutes a danger to the community;[24] (3) if there are serious reasons for believing that the applicant has committed a serious nonpolitical crime outside of the United States prior to his or her arrival;[25] (4) if there are reasonable grounds for regarding the alien as a danger to the security of the United States;[26] (5) if the applicant meet the definition of a terrorist, has participated in terrorist activity, or has given material support to a terrorist organization;[27] and (6) if the applicant was firmly resettled in another country prior to his or her arrival in the United States. [28] The first four of these bars — persecution of others, particularly serious crime, serious nonpolitical crime, and danger to the security of the United States — also bar an individual from being granted withholding of removal under INA §241(b)(3) and under the CAT.[29] See chapter 2 of this book for a detailed discussion of these statutory bars and when they apply.

---

[22] 8 CFR §§208.13(c), 208.16(d)(2), 1208.16(d)(2), 1240.8(d) (2014). *See, e.g., Abdille v. Ashcroft*, 242 F.3d 477, 491 (3d Cir. 2001).

[23] INA §§101(a)(42)(B), 208(b)(2)(A)(i).

[24] INA §208(b)(2)(A)(ii). If a conviction is an aggravated felony for which there is an aggregate term of imprisonment for five years, it is a conviction for a particularly serious crime and automatically bars a grant of asylum. *See Matter of B–*, 20 I&N Dec. 427 (BIA 1991).

[25] INA §208(b)(2)(A)(iii).

[26] INA §208(b)(2)(A)(iv).

[27] INA §§212(a)(3)(B)(i)(I)–(IV), (VI), 237(a)(4)(B). This bar is waivable by DHS under certain circumstances, including for persons who provided material support to terrorist organizations under duress. *See* INA §212(d)(3)(B)(i); Michael Chertoff Memorandum on Exercise of Authority Under Sec. 212(d)(3)(B)(i) of the INA, Washington, DC [hereinafter Chertoff Mem. on Exercise of Authority Under INA §212(d)(3)(B)(i)] (Apr. 27, 2007), *available at www.uscis.gov/sites/default/files/USCIS/Laws/TRIG/2.26%20excersise%20of%20authority.pdf.*

[28] 8 CFR §§208.13(c)(2)(i)(B), 208.15 (2014). An applicant is deemed firmly resettled if he or she entered the country with, or while in the country received, an offer of permanent resident status, citizenship, or other type of permanent status. *See* 8 CFR §§208.15, 1208.15 (2014). The government has the burden of proving firm resettlement, and the applicant may rebut firm resettlement by demonstrating an exception under 8 CFR §§208.15(a)–(b) (2014).

[29] *See* INA §§241(b)(3)(B)(i)–(iv); 8 CFR §§208.16(d)(2), 1208.16(d)(2). *See also Matter of N-A-M–*, 24 I&N Dec. 336 (BIA 2007) (addressing the particularly serious crime bar to withholding of removal);

Continued

According to the Immigration and Nationality Act (INA), "[t]he testimony of the applicant may be sufficient to sustain the applicant's burden without corroboration, but only if the applicant satisfies the trier of fact that the applicant's testimony is credible, is persuasive, and refers to specific facts sufficient to demonstrate that the applicant is a refugee."[30] Thus, there is a three-step test that an applicant's testimony must pass in order to be sufficient to sustain his or her burden of proof without corroboration.

The testimony must: (1) be credible;[31] (2) be persuasive; and (3) refer to specific facts.[32] For a detailed discussion of credibility determinations for meeting prong one of this test, see Part III.A. of this chapter. "Specific facts" refers to fact and not opinion testimony, and statements of belief are generally insufficient to meet the third prong of this test.[33]

In determining whether the applicant has met his or her burden, the trier of fact may weigh credible testimony along with other evidence of record.[34] Thus, even if testimony is found to be credible, the applicant may nonetheless fail to meet his or her burden of proof that he or she is eligible for asylum and merits a favorable exercise of discretion.[35] For example, "other evidence of record," such as country

---

Matter of A–H–, 23 I&N Dec. 774 (AG 2005) (addressing the persecution of others and danger to the security of the U.S. bars to withholding of removal); *Matter of McMullen*, 19 I&N Dec. 90 (BIA 1984) (addressing the serious nonpolitical crime bar to withholding of removal).

[30] INA §208(b)(1)(B)(ii), as amended by §101(a)(3) of the REAL ID Act of 2005, Pub. L. 109-13, 119 Stat. 302, 303, div. B. The amendments apply to applications filed on or after the date of enactment, May 11, 2005.

[31] *See* INA §208(b)(1)(B)(iii) (addressing only the first prong of this test, "credibility"); *infra* pt. III.A. for a detailed discussion of credibility determinations.

[32] INA §208(b)(1)(B)(ii). *See also Cardoza-Fonseca v. INS*, 767 F.2d 1448, 1953 (9th Cir. 1985) (emphasis in original) (stating that "Accordingly, if documentary evidence is not available, the applicant's testimony will suffice if it is credible, persuasive, and refers to '*specific* facts that give rise to an inference that the applicant has been or has a good reason to fear that he or she will be singled out for persecution on one of the specified grounds' listed in section 208(a).") *aff'd* 480 U.S. 421, 426 (1987) (noting that the Ninth Circuit U.S. Court of Appeals agreed with the U.S. Court of Appeals for the Seventh Circuit's finding in *Carvajal-Munoz*, 743 F.2d 562, 574 (7th Cir. 1984) which required the applicant provide 'specific facts' through the introduction of "objective evidence" to prove eligibility for asylum).

[33] *See Carvajal-Munoz*, 743 F.2d 562 (7th Cir. 1984) (explaining that "[s]tatements of belief are insufficient" and citing *Pereira-Diaz v. INS*, 551 F.2d 1149, 1154 (9th Cir. 1977) which held that the petitioner's claims were "essentially undocumented statements of belief"); *Khalil v. Dist. Dir.*, 457 F.2d 1276 (9th Cir. 1972) (finding that petitioner's beliefs that she would be persecuted were based "solely on statements" made by herself and her witness, and noting that she offered "No factual support which might have demonstrated the reasonableness of this belief was offered").

[34] INA §208(b)(1)(B)(ii). *See Matter of Dass*, 20 I&N Dec. 120, 124 (BIA 1989) ("[W]here there are significant, meaningful evidentiary gaps, applications will ordinarily have to be denied for failure of proof.").

[35] *See* INA §208(b)(1)(B)(ii); *Matter of S–M–J–*, 21 I&N Dec. 722, 729 (BIA 1997) (finding that there may be situations where the adjudicator finds the applicant credible, but that the applicant did not meet

Continued

conditions reports, may establish that the applicant no longer has a well-founded fear of persecution because the conditions have changed or that the applicant can relocate internally to avoid persecution.

Where the trier of fact determines that the applicant should provide evidence that corroborates otherwise credible testimony, such evidence must be provided unless the applicant does not have the evidence and cannot reasonably obtain the evidence.[36] According to the Board of Immigration Appeals (BIA), "[b]ecause the burden of proof is on the alien, an applicant should provide supporting evidence, both of general country conditions and of the specific facts sought to be relied on by the applicant, where such evidence is available. If such evidence is unavailable, the applicant must explain its unavailability."[37] For a detailed discussion of the corroboration requirements, see Part III.B. of this chapter.

Despite this burden of proof, an applicant for asylum or withholding of removal should be given the "benefit of the doubt" where the applicant is unable to substantiate his or her statements, but where the testimony is generally credible and does not run counter to generally known facts.[38] Moreover, justice requires that an applicant for asylum or withholding of removal be afforded a meaningful opportunity to establish his or her claim.[39] For example, there should be no rule that prevents an asylum applicant from elaborating on the circumstances underlying an asylum claim when given the opportunity to take the witness stand.[40] Overall, the procedures for requesting relief should not be a search for a justification to deport an applicant.[41]

Although the burden of proof is on the applicant, the BIA has recognized a "cooperative approach" because the immigration judge (IJ), BIA, and DHS "all bear the responsibility of ensuring that refugee protection is provided where such

---

the required burden of proof); *Matter of Acosta*, 19 I&N Dec. 211, 214–15 (BIA 1985) (finding that an asylum applicant must persuade the adjudicator that the claimed facts are true and that he or she is eligible for asylum under the INA).

[36] INA §208(b)(1)(B)(ii). *See infra* pt. III. for a detailed discussion of the evidentiary requirements in asylum cases following the REAL ID Act of 2005, *supra* note 30, and pt. III.B. for a detailed discussion of the corroboration requirements.

[37] *Matter of S–M–J–*, 21 I&N Dec. 722, 724 (BIA 1997) (citing *Matter of Dass*, 20 I&N Dec. 120, 124 (BIA 1989)).

[38] *Id.* At 725. *See* this chapter at 2.6.4; *see also Matter of Pula*, 19 I&N Dec. 467, 476 (BIA 1987) (Heilman, concurring) (recognizing that asylum provisions are humanitarian in their essence and that the "normal" immigration laws cannot be applied in their usual manner to refugees), *superseded on other grounds by statute as recognized in Andriasian v. I.N.S.*, 180 F.3d 1033, 1043 (9th Cir. 1999).

[39] *See Matter of E–F–H–L–*, 26 I&N Dec. 319 (BIA 2014) (finding that an applicant for asylum or for withholding of removal is entitled to a hearing on the merits of those applications, including an opportunity to provide oral testimony and other evidence, without first having to establish prima facie eligibility for the requested relief); *Matter of Fefe*, 20 I&N Dec. 116 (BIA 1989). *See also Senathirajah v. INS*, 157 F.3d 210, 221 (3d Cir. 1998).

[40] *Senathirajah v. INS*, 157 F.3d at 221.

[41] *Id.*

protection is warranted by the circumstances of an asylum applicant's claim."[42] In this regard, the adjudicator has an affirmative duty to elicit sufficient information and to research country conditions to properly evaluate whether the applicant is eligible for protection.[43] Speculation or conjecture by the adjudicator, however, is impermissible.[44]

B. The Shifting Burdens of Proof

In preparing and presenting applications for asylum, withholding of removal, and CAT protection, it is essential that applicants understand when it is their burden of proof and when it is the government's burden of proof. Although the burden of proof is generally on the applicant to establish eligibility for relief, the burden of proof shifts to the government in two situations.[45] First, if the applicant establishes past persecution on account of one of the protected grounds, there is a presumption that the applicant also has a well-founded fear of future persecution and the burden shifts to DHS to rebut that presumption.[46] DHS may rebut the presumption of a well-founded fear of future persecution in two ways. The government must show by a preponderance of the evidence either (1) that there has been a fundamental change in circumstances since the applicant suffered persecution such that the applicant's fear of future persecution is no longer well-founded,[47] or (2) that the applicant could avoid future persecution by relocating to another part of the country of feared persecution

---

[42] *Matter of S–M–J–*, 21 I&N Dec. 722 (BIA 1997).

[43] 8 CFR §§208.9(b), 1208.9(b) (2014); *Matter of S–M–J–*, 21 I&N Dec. 722 (BIA 1997); U.N. High Comm'r for Refugees, *Handbook on Procedures and Criteria for Determining Refugee Status*, ¶¶ 196, 205(b)(i) HCR/1P/4/enG/Rev. 3 (2011) [hereinafter UNHCR Handbook] *available at www.refworld.org/docid/4f33c8d92.html.*

[44] *See, e.g., Jian He Zhang v. Holder*, 737 F.3d 501, 505–06 (8th Cir. 2013); *Xiu Ying Wu v. Att'y Gen.*, 712 F.3d 486 (11th Cir. 2013); *Yusupov v. Att'y Gen.*, 650 F.3d 968, 989–92 (3d Cir. 2011); *Tassi v. Holder*, 660 F.3d 710, 724 (4th Cir. 2011); *Chawla v. Holder*, 559 F.3d 998, 1007 (9th Cir. 2010); *Issiaka v. Att'y Gen.*, 569 F.3d 135, 138–41 (3d Cir. 2009); *Castilho de Oliveira v. Holder*, 564 F.3d 892, 896 (7th Cir. 2009); *Li v. Holder*, 559 F.3d 1096, 1102–07 (9th Cir. 2009); *Sok v. Mukasey*, 526 F.3d 48, 55–56 (1st Cir. 2008); *Torres v. Mukasey*, 551 F.3d 616, 631–32 (7th Cir. 2008); *Yan Xia Zhu v. Mukasey*, 537 F.3d 1034, 1038–40 (9th Cir. 2008); *Shahinaj v. Gonzales*, 481 F.3d 1027, 1029 (8th Cir. 2007); *Huang v. Gonzales*, 453 F.3d 142, 147–79 (2d Cir. 2006); *Mwembie v. Gonzales*, 443 F.3d 405, 409–14 (5th Cir. 2006); *Alexandrov v. Gonzales*, 442 F.3d 395, 407–09 (6th Cir. 2006); *Pramatarov v. Gonzales*, 454 F.3d 764, 765–66 (7th Cir. 2006); *Chaib v. Ashcroft*, 397 F.3d 1273, 1278–80 (10th Cir. 2005); *Secaida-Rosales v. INS*, 331 F.3d 297, 307–12 (2d Cir. 2003); *Dia v. Ashcroft*, 353 F.3d 228, 247–60 (3d Cir. 2003) (*en banc*); *Ezeaawima v. Ashcroft*, 325 F.3d 396, 403–08 (3d Cir. 2003); *Shah v. INS*, 220 F.3d 1062, 1069 (9th Cir. 2000); *Matter of Kasinga*, 21 I&N Dec. 357, 364–65 (BIA 1996); *Matter of Becerra-Miranda*, 12 I&N Dec. 358, 368 (BIA 1967).

[45] *Matter of S–M–J–*, 21 I&N Dec. 722, 730 n. 11 (BIA 1997) ("[T]he burden of proof is on the applicant to establish her asylum claim. We do not intend our analysis regarding the roles of the Service and the Immigration Judge to shift this burden. If the Service and the Immigration Judge do not carry out their roles, the applicant does not prevail by default.").

[46] 8 CFR §208.13(b)(1)(i) (2014).

[47] 8 CFR §208.13(b)(1)(i)(A) (2014). *See also Matter of H–*, 21 I&N Dec. 337, 346–49 (BIA 1996).

and that, under all circumstances, it would be reasonable to expect him or her to do so.[48] Thus, an applicant who has established past persecution on account of a protected characteristic does not bear the burden of establishing that it would be unsafe or unreasonable to relocate within the country of feared persecution to avoid future persecution. The applicant also does not bear the burden of establishing a well-founded fear of future persecution on the basis of the initial claim. However, if the basis of the claim is on account of a different protected ground than the ground that motivated the past persecution, the applicant maintains the burden of demonstrating a well-founded fear of persecution on account of the new protected ground.[49]

The second situation where the burden shifts to DHS is if the claimed persecutor is a government actor or is government-sponsored. In these circumstances, the burden shifts to DHS to establish by a preponderance of the evidence that the applicant could avoid future persecution by relocating within the country of feared persecution and, under all the circumstances, it would be reasonable for him or her to do so.[50] Regardless whether the persecutor is a government or non-government actor, DHS also bears the burden of proving a safe and reasonable internal relocation option if the applicant has established past persecution on account of a protected characteristic, as described above.

In these two situations, in the context of affirmative asylum applications filed before U.S. Citizenship and Immigration Services (USCIS), the asylum officer must both produce and evaluate the evidence. He or she may produce the evidence by eliciting testimony and conducting country conditions research. The asylum officer must then consider all available information and make a determination.[51] In defensive asylum applications, the DHS Immigration and Customs Enforcement's Assistant Chief Counsel shoulders the burden of production and persuasion before the immigration judge in these scenarios.[52]

If DHS meets its burden of rebutting the well-founded fear of future persecution, the burden then shifts back to the applicant to demonstrate either that he or she does have a well-founded fear of future persecution or that the adjudicator's discretion is warranted for humanitarian reasons, even if future persecution is unlikely. He or she may do so by showing that there are "compelling reasons for being unwilling or unable to return to the country arising out of the severity of the past persecution" or

[48] 8 CFR §208.13(b)(1)(i)(B) (2014). *See also Balliu v. Gonzales*, 467 F.3d 609, 612 (7th Cir. 2006); *Un v. Gonzales*, 415 F.3d 205, 209 (1st Cir. 2005).

[49] 8 CFR §208.13(b)(1) (2014) ("If the applicant's fear of future persecution is unrelated to the past persecution, the applicant bears the burden of establishing that the fear is well-founded").

[50] 8 CFR §208.13(b)(3)(ii) (2014).

[51] AOBTC Workbook, pt. IV, *supra* note 2, at 9.

[52] *See id.*

"that there is a reasonable possibility that he or she may suffer other serious harm upon removal to that country."[53]

II. Standards of Proof

The party who bears the burden of proof must produce a certain level of convincing or probative evidence and persuade the trier of fact of the existence of certain factual elements according to a specified "standard of proof" or degree of certainty.[54] There are several standards of proof relevant to asylum, withholding of removal, and CAT adjudications, including the following:

- Preponderance of the evidence;
- Reasonable possibility;
- More likely than not / clear probability;
- Clear and convincing evidence; and
- To the satisfaction of the AG.

Each of these standards of proof is discussed in detail below.

> ➤ **Practice Pointer**: It is critical for practitioners and adjudicators to distinguish among the different standards of proof and to know when each applies.

A. Preponderance of the Evidence

Facts must be established by a "preponderance of the evidence." This is the standard of proof used in most civil cases and is lower than the "beyond a reasonable doubt" standard that is used in criminal cases. This standard of proof means that it is more likely than not that the fact is true, or in other words, there is a more than a 50% chance that the fact is true. In determining whether this standard has been met, it is the quality of the evidence that governs, not the quantity of evidence.[55] This standard of proof is required in the following situations:

---

[53] 8 CFR §§208.13(b)(1)(iii), 1208.13(b)(1)(iii) (2014). *See Matter of L–S–*, 25 I&N Dec. 705 (BIA 2012) (noting that "other serious harm" may be wholly unrelated to the applicant's past harm and need not be inflicted on account of race, religion, nationality, membership in a particular social group, or political opinion, but the harm must be so serious that it equals the severity of persecution); *Matter of Chen*, 20 I&N Dec. 16 (BIA 1989). *See, e.g., Hanna v. Keisler*, 506 F.3d 933, 939 (9th Cir. 2007) (remanding claim for consideration of other serious harm Chaldean Catholic would face if returned to Iraq).

[54] Lilly, *supra* note 2; *see also* AOBTC Workbook, pt. IV, *supra* note 2, at 10.

[55] *See Matter of Y–B–,* 21 I&N Dec. 1136 (BIA 1998) ("When considering a quantum of proof, generalized information is insufficient. Specific, detailed, and credible testimony or a combination of detailed testimony and corroborative background evidence is necessary to prove a case for asylum. We recognize that a case may arise in which there is some ambiguity regarding an aspect of an alien's claim, at which time we might consider giving the alien the 'benefit of the doubt.'").

- For the applicant to establish he or she is eligible to apply for asylum;
- For the applicant to establish that he or she meets the definition of refugee under INA §101(a)(42)(A);
- For the applicant to establish that he or she merits asylum as a matter of discretion;
- If evidence indicates that a statutory bar to asylum may apply, for the applicant to prove that the bar does not apply and that he or she is eligible to receive asylum;
- If the applicant has demonstrated past persecution on account of a protected ground, for DHS to demonstrate a fundamental change in circumstances since the applicant suffered persecution such that the applicant's fear of future persecution is no longer well-founded;
- If the applicant has demonstrated past persecution on account of a protected ground, for DHS to demonstrate that the applicant could avoid future persecution by relocating to another part of the country of feared persecution and that, under all circumstances, it would be reasonable to expect him or her to do so; and
- If the claimed persecutor is a government actor or government-sponsored, for DHS to demonstrate that the applicant could avoid future persecution by relocating within the country of feared persecution and, under all the circumstances, it would be reasonable for him or her to do so.

B. Reasonable Possibility

The standard of proof used for demonstrating a well-founded fear of persecution for purposes of asylum eligibility is a "reasonable possibility" that the applicant would be persecuted. If a set of facts, substantiated by a preponderance of the evidence, demonstrates that there is a "reasonable possibility" that the applicant would be persecuted, he or she has met the required burden of proof.[56] This is the same standard applied when an adjudicator evaluates whether an applicant has established a reasonable fear of persecution or torture when conducting a reasonable fear screening interview to determine whether an applicant should be referred to an IJ to apply for withholding or deferral of removal.[57]

In considering and interpreting the required standard of proof for demonstrating a well-founded fear, the U.S. Supreme Court emphasized that "[o]ne can certainly have a well-founded fear of an event happening when there is less than a 50% chance of the occurrence taking place."[58] The Court went on to suggest that even a 1-in-10 chance might be sufficient to show a "reasonable possibility" of persecution.

Overall, in considering whether a "reasonable possibility" of persecution exists, adjudicators are to consider whether a reasonable person in the applicant's

---

[56] *See supra* pt. I.A.

[57] 8 CFR §208.31 (2014). See chapter 6 for a detailed discussion of reasonable fear interviews.

[58] *INS v. Cardoza-Fonseca*, 480 U.S. 421, 431, 440 (1987).

circumstances would fear persecution if returned to his or her home country.[59] Thus, the determination of whether a fear is well-founded does not rest on the statistical probability of persecution alone, but rather, on whether the fear is based on facts that would lead a reasonable person in similar circumstances to fear persecution.[60] In meeting this "reasonable possibility" standard and establishing that a fear is reasonable, the applicant must show by a preponderance of the evidence that certain events occurred or that certain conditions exist giving rise to the fear.[61]

The "reasonable possibility" standard of proof required to establish a well-founded fear of persecution for asylum eligibility is lower than the "clear probability" standard of proof that is required to establish a well-founded fear of persecution for withholding of removal eligibility, as discussed below.[62]

C. More Likely Than Not/Clear Probability

In considering and interpreting the required standard of proof for demonstrating a well-founded fear for purposes of withholding of removal under INA §241(b)(3) or protection under the CAT, the U.S. Supreme Court held that "would be persecuted" means the applicant must establish that it is "more likely than not" that he or she would be persecuted or tortured. "More likely than not" means a "clear probability" or a greater than 50 percent chance of persecution or torture.[63] This standard of proof is higher than the "reasonable possibility" standard of proof that is required to establish a well-founded fear of persecution for asylum eligibility.[64] Like for the reasonable possibility standard, however, demonstrating that it is "more likely than not" that the applicant would be persecuted or tortured requires a set of facts substantiated by a preponderance of the evidence in order to meet the applicant's burden of proof.[65]

---

[59] *Matter of Mogharrabi*, 19 I&N Dec. 439 (BIA 1987); *Matter of S–S–*, 21 I&N Dec. 121, 122 (BIA 1995). *See also Ahmed v. Gonzales*, 467 F.3d 669, 674 (7th Cir. 2006); *Tesfamichael v. Gonzales*, 469 F.3d 109, 113 (5th Cir. 2006); *Gao v. Ashcroft*, 299 F.3d 266, 272 (3d Cir. 2002); *Korablina v. INS*, 158 F.3d 1038, 1044 (9th Cir. 1998); *M.A. v. INS*, 899 F.2d 304, 311 (4th Cir. 1990).

[60] *Matter of Mogharrabi*, 19 I&N Dec. 439 (BIA 1987).

[61] *See* AOBTC Workbook, pt. IV, *supra* note 2, at 12.

[62] *See INS v. Cardoza-Fonseca*, 480 U.S. 421, 431, 440 (1987) ("Let us…presume that it is known that in the applicant's country of origin every tenth adult male person is either put to death or sent to some remote labor camp … . In such a case it would be only too apparent that anyone who has managed to escape from the country in question will have 'well-founded fear of being persecuted' upon his eventual return.").

[63] *INS v. Cardoza-Fonseca*, 480 U.S. 421 (1987); *INS v. Stevic*, 467 U.S. 407 (1984). *See* 8 CFR §§208.16(b)(1), 1208.16(b)(1) (2014).

[64] *See INS v. Cardoza-Fonseca*, 480 U.S. at 431, 440 ("Let us…presume that it is known that in the applicant's country of origin every tenth adult male person is either put to death or sent to some remote labor camp … . In such a case it would be only too apparent that anyone who has managed to escape from the country in question will have 'well-founded fear of being persecuted' upon his eventual return.").

[65] *See supra* pt. I.A.

D. Significant Possibility

The standard of proof used for demonstrating a credible fear of persecution or torture during a screening for asylum, withholding of removal under INA §241(b)(3), or relief under the CAT is a "significant possibility" that the applicant could establish eligibility for such relief in a full hearing before an IJ.[66]

This standard is not defined in the statute or regulations, nor has it been discussed in case law. However, the legislative history indicates that the standard "is intended to be a low screening standard for admission into the usual full asylum process."[67] It does not require that an applicant demonstrate that the chances of success are "more likely than not," only that there is a substantial and realistic possibility of success on the merits before an IJ.[68] On the other hand, this standard is not met when claims have "no possibility of success" or only a "minimal or mere possibility of success."[69] The legislative history therefore indicates that, since the credible fear process is intended to safeguard against sending refugees back to persecution or torture, the "significant possibility" standard must be lower than the "reasonable possibility" standard required in full asylum proceedings to determine eligibility for relief.

- ➢ **Practice Pointer**: In 2014, the USCIS Asylum Division revised its lesson plan that provides guidance to asylum officers for completing credible fear screening interviews.[70] According to legal scholars and advocates, the lesson plan was revised in a way that unlawfully heightened the standard of proof for demonstrating a credible fear of persecution and torture.[71] These scholars and advocates reason that, although the revised lesson plan still defines the standard as a "significant possibility" of persecution or torture, it deletes several references to the legislative history emphasizing the screening purpose

---

[66] INA §235(b)(1)(B)(v); 8 CFR §208.30 (2014). See chapter 6 for a detailed discussion of credible fear interviews.

[67] 142 Cong. Rec. S11491 (Sept. 27, 1996) (statement of Sen. Hatch), *available at www.gpo.gov/fdsys/pkg/CREC-1996-09-27/pdf/CREC-1996-09-27-pt1-PgS11491-2.pdf#page=1.*

[68] *See id.*; 142 Cong. Rec. H11071-02 (Sept. 25, 1996) (statement of Rep. Hyde), *available at http://thomas.loc.gov/cgi-bin/query/F?r104:16:./temp/~r104yr251f:e83463*: (noting that the "more likely than not" standard was redrafted from previously proposed legislation to accommodate a less restrictive credible fear determination).

[69] Statement of Sen. Hatch, *supra* note 67.

[70] *See* John Lafferty Memorandum on Release of Updated Asylum Division Officer Training Course Lesson Plan, *Credible Fear of Persecution and Torture Determinations*, Washington, DC [hereinafter Lafferty Mem. on Updated AOBTC Training for Credible Fear] (Feb. 28, 2014), *available at www.aila.org/content/default.aspx?docid=48256.*

[71] *Id. See, e.g.*, Bill Ong Hing Memorandum to John Lafferty, Chief, USCIS Asylum Division Concerning Lesson Plan, Credible Fear of Persecution and Torture Determinations [hereinafter Hing Response to Lafferty Mem. on Credible Fear] (Apr. 21, 2014), *available at http://static.squarespace.com/static/50b1609de4b054abacd5ab6c/t/53558353e4b02071f74ee3c4/1398113107754/Response%20to%20USCIS%20Credible%20Fear%20Memo,%20Bill%20Hing,%2004.21.2014.pdf.*

of credible fear interviews. Moreover, the structure, tone, and content of the lesson plan seem to require an asylum officer to complete a full assessment of the asylum seeker's potential asylum or CAT claim. The revisions also seem to conflate the credible fear standard with the full asylum and CAT standards, often without sufficient explanation and distinction. Unfortunately, the statistics seem to support these concerns, as the passage rate for credible fear interviews has dropped significantly since the implementation of the new lesson plan in February 2014.[72] The revised lesson plan is available on AILA InfoNet at Doc. No. 14041846.[73] Practitioners representing clients during credible fear interviews should be prepared to articulate the standard of proof required for demonstrating a credible fear of persecution or torture and to educate asylum officers on the proper legal standards in advocating for their clients.

To satisfy the credible fear of persecution standard, the applicant must demonstrate a "significant possibility" that he or she could establish in a full hearing before an IJ the following: (1) the applicant's testimony is credible; and (2) either he or she was persecuted in the past on account of a protected ground or there is a reasonable possibility that he or she will suffer the feared persecution on account of a protected ground.[74]

To satisfy the credible fear of torture standard, the applicant must demonstrate a "significant possibility" that he or she could establish in a full hearing before an IJ the following: (1) the applicant's testimony is credible; (2) he or she would be intentionally subjected to severe physical or mental harm in the country of feared torture; and (3) that the applicant fears a government official, a person acting in an official capacity, or someone acting at the instigation of or with the consent or acquiescence of a government official or person acting in an official capacity.[75]

E. Clear and Convincing Evidence

The "clear and convincing evidence" standard of proof applies to the one-year filing deadline for asylum applications. An applicant for asylum must demonstrate by "clear and convincing evidence" that he or she has filed his or her application within one year of the applicant's arrival in the United States, unless an exception applies.[76] "Clear and convincing" means a degree of proof that will produce "a firm belief or

---

[72] *See* U.S. Citizenship and Immigration Servs. Asylum Div., *Credible Fear Workload Report, Summary FY 09-14, published on* AILA InfoNet Doc. No. 14112500 (*posted* Nov. 25, 2014).

[73] *See www.aila.org/content/default.aspx?docid=48257* (last visited Dec. 24, 2014).

[74] *See* AOBTC Workbook, pt. IV, *supra* note 2, at 14.

[75] *See id.*

[76] INA §§208(a)(2)(B) and (D); 8 CFR §208.4(a)(2)(i) (2014). See also *infra* pt. II.F. for a discussion of the standard of proof for the exceptions to the one-year filing deadline.

conviction as to allegations sought to be established."[77] It falls between the preponderance of the evidence standard used in civil cases and the beyond a reasonable doubt standard used in criminal cases.[78]

F. To the Satisfaction of the Attorney General

The standard "to the satisfaction of the Attorney General" relates to the applicant's burden in demonstrating that, although he or she may be ineligible to apply for asylum for having a previous asylum denial or not filing the application within one year of entry, an exception applies. An asylum applicant cannot apply for asylum if he or she has previously applied for and been denied asylum by an IJ or the BIA, unless the applicant demonstrates "to the satisfaction of the Attorney General" that there are changed circumstances that materially affect his or her eligibility for asylum.[79] Similarly, an asylum applicant cannot apply for asylum more than one year after the date of his or her entry to the United States, unless the applicant demonstrates "to the satisfaction of the Attorney General" changed circumstances that materially affect his or her eligibility for asylum or extraordinary circumstances relating to the delay in filing his or her application.[80]

"To the satisfaction of the Attorney General" is one of the lower standards of proof applicable in the asylum context. It is lower than "beyond a reasonable doubt" and "clear and convincing evidence." The BIA has interpreted this standard as requiring "credible evidence sufficiently persuasive to satisfy the Attorney General in the exercise of his reasonable judgment, considering the proof fairly and impartially."[81] The BIA also has interpreted this standard in other immigration contexts to require a showing similar to the "preponderance of the evidence" standard.[82] The Asylum Division interprets this standard to mean that "it must be reasonable for the asylum officer to conclude that the exception applies."[83]

III. Evidentiary Standards

Applicants for asylum, withholding of removal, and CAT relief must provide evidence to establish the requisite facts according to the specified standard of proof

[77] *See* AOBTC Workbook, pt. IV, *supra* note 2, at 14.

[78] *See id.*

[79] INA §208(a)(2) 8 CFR §208.4(a) (2014).

[80] *Id.*

[81] *Matter of Bufalino*, 12 I&N Dec. 277, 282 (BIA 1967).

[82] *Matter of Barreiros*, 10 I&N Dec. 536, 538 (BIA 1964); *Matter of V–*, 7 I&N Dec. 460, 463 (BIA 1957).

[83] U.S. Citizenship & Immigration Servs., *Lesson: Mandatory Bars to Asylum and Discretion* at 20, in Asylum Officer Basic Training Course Participant Workbook (Mar. 25, 2009) [hereinafter AOBTC Workbook, Mandatory Bars & Discretion], *available at www.uscis.gov/sites/default/files/USCIS/Humanitarian/Refugees%20%26%20Asylum/Asylum/Bars-to-Asylum-Discretion-31aug10.pdf.*

and to corroborate those facts in ultimately meeting their burden of proof. Evidence may be in the form of testimony, written documents, or physical objects, and is evaluated by adjudicators to determine if the requisite evidentiary requirements have been met for: (1) accepting the evidence into the record; and (2) meeting the requisite burden of proof to establish eligibility for relief. These evidentiary standards, amended by the REAL ID Act of 2005 and codified at INA §208(b)(1)(B), are discussed below.[84]

A. Testimony and Credibility

An applicant for asylum cannot meet his or her burden of proof unless the applicant testifies under oath regarding the application for asylum.[85] He or she may present the testimony of witnesses to be considered and weighed along with the other evidence presented.[86]

- **Practice Pointer**: DHS has the authority to question any witness presented by the applicant.[87] This is an important consideration in selecting and presenting witness testimony in support of applicants' claims for relief.

- **Practice Pointer**: The testimony given by one asylum applicant in support of his or her own claim cannot be considered in evaluating another applicant's request for asylum without written consent because of the confidentiality requirements under 8 CFR §208.6. However, if an asylum applicant appears as a witness for another applicant, his or her testimony may be considered.

Overall, the applicant's right to present testimony cannot be nullified by a preliminary negative credibility determination by the IJ,[88] nor may it be supplanted by requiring the applicant to first show prima facie eligibility for the requested relief.[89] It is a due process right for an applicant to present testimony in support of his or her claim.[90]

---

[84] REAL ID Act of 2005, *supra* note 30, §§101(a)(3), 101(h)(2); INA §208(b)(1)(B); 8 CFR §208.13(a) (2014).

[85] *Matter of Fefe*, 20 I&N Dec. 116 (BIA 1989). *See also Matter of E–F–H–L–*, 26 I&N Dec. 319 (BIA 2014).

[86] 8 CFR §208.9 (2014).

[87] 8 CFR §208.9(g) (2014).

[88] *Kerciku v. INS*, 314 F.3d 913, 919 (7th Cir. 2003) (remanding case to the BIA where IJ did not allow applicant to present testimony in support of his claim after determining that the applicant's testimony regarding how he obtained documentary evidence was not credible).

[89] *See Matter of E–F–H–L–*, 26 I&N Dec. 319 (BIA 2014) (following *Matter of Fefe*, 20 I&N Dec. 116 (BIA 1989)).

[90] *See, e.g., Oshodi v. Holder*, 729 F.3d 882 (9th Cir. 2013).

In determining whether an applicant has met his or her burden of proof for asylum, withholding of removal, or CAT relief, the fact-finder may weigh credible testimony along with other evidence of record.[91] The applicant's testimony may be sufficient to sustain his or her burden of proof without corroboration, but only if the applicant satisfies the trier of fact that his or her testimony is: (1) credible; (2) persuasive; and (3) refers to specific facts sufficient to demonstrate that the applicant is a refugee.[92] Prongs two and three of this test cannot be met if the testimony presented is general, meager, or vague.[93] However, it has been found to be reversible error for an adjudicator to deny a claim based on insufficient testimonial detail if the fact-finder failed to elicit such testimony.[94]

Perhaps most importantly, prong one of this evidentiary standard cannot be met if the testimony is not credible. No matter how compelling the facts of a protection claim may be, if the applicant's testimony is found not credible, it can be fatal to his or her applications. Prior to the REAL ID Act of 2005, there was a presumption of credibility; however, post–REAL ID Act, there is no longer such a presumption.[95] Under the current legal standards established by the REAL ID Act of 2005, a trier of fact must base a credibility determination on the "totality of the circumstances and all relevant factors," including:

(1) demeanor, candor, or responsiveness of the applicant or witness;

(2) consistency between the applicant's or witness's written and oral statements;

(3) internal consistency of each such statement;

(4) consistency of such statements with other evidence of record;[96]

(5) any inaccuracies or falsehoods in such statements, without regard to whether an inconsistency, inaccuracy, or falsehood goes to the heart of the applicant's claim; and

(6) any other relevant factor.[97]

---

[91] INA §208(b)(1)(B)(ii).

[92] *Id.*; 8 CFR §§208.13(a), 1208.13(a) (2014) (stating that the testimony of an asylum applicant, "if credible in light of general conditions in the applicant's country of nationality or last habitual residence, *may* be sufficient to sustain the applicant's burden of proof without corroboration") (emphasis added). *See also Matter of Mogharrabi*, 19 I&N Dec. 439, 445 (BIA 1987) (finding that an applicant's own testimony may be sufficient, without corroborating evidence, to prove a well-founded fear of persecution where that testimony is believable, consistent, and sufficiently detailed to provide a plausible and coherent account of the basis for his or her fear).

[93] *Matter of Y–B–*, 21 I&N Dec. 1136 (BIA 1998) (finding that an applicant must demonstrate "specific, detailed facts supporting the reasonableness of his or her fear.").

[94] *Shunfu Li v. Mukasey*, 529 F.3d 121, 147–48 (2d Cir. 2008); *Qiu v. Ashcroft*, 329 F.3d 140, 152–53 (2d Cir. 2003).

[95] INA §§208(b)(1)(B)(iii), 240(c)(4)(C), 241(B)(1)(3)(C). Note, however, that there is a rebuttable presumption of credibility on appeal if no adverse credibility determination is explicitly made. *Id.*

[96] INA §208(b)(1)(B)(iii). A similar provision exists for withholding of removal claims. *See* INA §241(b)(3)(C). *See also* INA §240(c)(4)(C).

- **Practice Pointer**: The reference to "any other relevant factor" implies that if the trier of fact wishes to rely on any of the first five factors, they must be relevant to the adjudication of the asylum claim.

- **Practice Pointer**: These credibility provisions apply only to applications filed on or after May 11, 2005.[98]

Traditionally, an IJ has had significant and broad authority in determining whether an applicant or witness's testimony is credible.[99] Courts have concluded that, ordinarily, an IJ is in the best position to evaluate the accuracy, reliability, and demeanor of applicants and witnesses, as well as to consider contradictory evidence or an inherent improbability of a witness's testimony. Thus, an IJ's credibility determination is normally accorded substantial deference as a matter of practice and law.[100]

A credibility determination must be an independent analysis, separate and apart from the analysis of the sufficiency of the applicant's evidence.[101] Overall, each case must be evaluated on its own merits and adjudicators must conduct an individualized analysis and review of the claim.[102] Boilerplate or "cookie cutter" credibility findings are not tolerated.[103] Generally, in finding an applicant not credible, the adjudicator

---

[97] INA §208(b)(1)(B)(iii). *See, e.g., Matter of J–Y–C–*, 24 I&N Dec. 260, 263–66 (BIA 2007) (upholding an adverse credibility determination based on inconsistencies that did not go to the heart of the claim, inconsistencies between testimony and airport statements, demeanor, and lack of corroboration).

[98] *Matter of S–B–*, 24 I&N Dec. 42 (BIA 2006) (finding that where respondent initially filed with the Asylum Office and renewed his application in removal proceedings subsequent to May 11, 2005, the REAL ID Act provision was not applicable to credibility determinations made in his case).

[99] *Matter of O–D–*, 21 I&N Dec. 1079 (BIA 1998).

[100] *Matter of A–S–*, 21 I&N Dec. 1106 (BIA 1998); *Matter of Kulle*, 19 I&N Dec. 318, 331 (BIA 1985); *Matter of Boromand*, 17 I&N Dec. 450, 452 (BIA 1980). *See also Garcia v. INS*, 31 F.3d 441, 444–45 (7th Cir. 1994); *Artiga-Turcios v. INS*, 829 F.2d 720 (9th Cir. 1987); *Espinoza-Ojeda v. INS*, 419 F.2d 183 (9th Cir. 1969); *Matter of Magana*, 17 I&N Dec. 1, 14 (BIA 1979); *Matter of Teng*, 15 I&N Dec. 516 (BIA 1975).

[101] *See Torres v. Mukasey*, 551 F.3d 616, 629–30 (7th Cir. 2008); *Abdulai v. Ashcroft*, 239 F.3d 542, 551 n.6 (3d Cir. 2001). *But see Chen v. Gonzales*, 434 F.3d 212, 220–22 (3d Cir. 2005) (finding that post–REAL ID Act of 2005 even a credible applicant may be required to produce corroborating evidence, and thus, the denial would stand even though the IJ did not make a valid credibility assessment).

[102] *Paramasamy v. Ashcroft*, 295 F.3d 1047, 1050 (9th Cir. 2002); *Ghaly v. INS*, 58 F.3d 1425, 1431 (9th Cir. 1995); *Castillo v. INS*, 951 F.2d 1117, 1121 (9th Cir. 1991) (noting that a court will "not allow the [agency] to rely on 'boilerplate opinions' which set out general legal standards yet are devoid of statements that evidence an individualized review of the petitioner's circumstances").

[103] *Paramasamy v. Ashcroft*, 295 F.3d 1047, 1050 (9th Cir. 2002) (reversing negative credibility determination where IJ had made identical demeanor findings in two other cases); *Ghaly v. INS*, 58 F.3d 1425, 1431 (9th Cir. 1995); *Castillo v. INS*, 951 F.2d 1117, 1121 (9th Cir. 1991) (noting that a court will "not allow the [agency] to rely on 'boilerplate opinions' which set out general legal standards yet are devoid of statements that evidence an individualized review of the petitioner's circumstances").

must offer a specific, cogent reason for his or her finding.[104] An IJ's conclusions must be supported by substantial evidence, and courts will not defer to an IJ's credibility finding that is based on speculation or conjecture,[105] based on general and conclusory statements,[106] based on personal views or experiences,[107] or otherwise not supported by the record.[108]

---

[104] *Tewabe v. Gonzales*, 446 F.3d 533, 540 (4th Cir. 2006) (noting that the requirement that the IJ provide a specific and cogent reason for an adverse credibility determination "leaves ample room for the IJ to exercise common sense in rejecting [an applicant's] testimony"); *Wiransane v. Ashcroft*, 366 F.3d 889, 898 (10th Cir. 2004) (stating that the IJ "must have a legitimate articulable basis to question the petitioner's credibility, and must offer a specific, cogent reason for any stated disbelief."). *See also He v. Ashcroft*, 328 F.3d 593, 595 (9th Cir. 2003); *Mulanga v. Ashcroft*, 349 F.3d 123, 138 (3d Cir. 2003) (holding that IJ's mere "disbelief" of applicant's testimony regarding how she escaped from detention is unsound in light of testimony and country condition reports); *Secaida-Rosales v. INS*, 331 F.3d 297, 307 (2d Cir. 2003); *Paramasamy v. Ashcroft*, 295 F.3d 1047, 1054 (9th Cir. 2002) (finding that use of false documents for travel is not a proper basis for an adverse credibility finding); *Daiga v. INS*, 183 F.3d 797, 798 (8th Cir. 1999) (finding that the IJ articulated valid reasons for discrediting testimony, including that the applicant could not remember dates, her inconsistent testimony, and her submission of questionable documents); *DeLeon-Barrios v. INS*, 115 F.3d 392, 393 (9th Cir. 1997); *Matter of O–D–*, 21 I&N Dec. 1079, 1082 (BIA 1998) (finding that the applicant's submission of a counterfeit identity document generally discredits his testimony regarding asylum eligibility and specifically discredits his claim of identity), *distinguished by Kourski v. Ashcroft*, 355 F.3d 1038 (7th Cir. 2004) and *Hanaj v. Gonzales*, 446 F.3d 694 (7th Cir. 2006) (holding that if the applicant does not know that the documents are forged, it does not discredit the testimony) .

[105] *See, e.g., Jian He Zhang v. Holder*, 737 F.3d 501, 505–06 (8th Cir. 2013); *Xiu Ying Wu v. Att'y Gen.*, 712 F.3d 486 (11th Cir. 2013); *Yusupov v. Att'y Gen.*, 650 F.3d 968, 989–92 (3d Cir. 2011); *Tassi v. Holder*, 660 F.3d 710, 724 (4th Cir. 2011); *Chawla v. Holder*, 559 F.3d 998, 1007 (9th Cir. 2010); *Issiaka v. Att'y Gen.*, 569 F.3d 135, 138–41 (3d Cir. 2009); *Castilho de Oliveira v. Holder*, 564 F.3d 892, 896 (7th Cir. 2009); *Li v. Holder*, 559 F.3d 1096, 1102–07 (9th Cir. 2009); *Sok v. Mukasey*, 526 F.3d 48, 55–56 (1st Cir. 2008); *Torres v. Mukasey*, 551 F.3d 616, 631–32 (7th Cir. 2008); *Yan Xia Zhu v. Mukasey*, 537 F.3d 1034, 1038–40 (9th Cir. 2008); *Shahinaj v. Gonzales*, 481 F.3d 1027, 1029 (8th Cir. 2007); *Huang v. Gonzales*, 453 F.3d 142, 147–79 (2d Cir. 2006); *Mwembie v. Gonzales*, 443 F.3d 405, 409–14 (5th Cir. 2006); *Alexandrov v. Gonzales*, 442 F.3d 395, 407–09 (6th Cir. 2006); *Pramatarov v. Gonzales*, 454 F.3d 764, 765–66 (7th Cir. 2006); *Chaib v. Ashcroft*, 397 F.3d 1273, 1278–80 (10th Cir. 2005); *Secaida-Rosales v. INS*, 331 F.3d 297, 307–12 (2d Cir. 2003); *Dia v. Ashcroft*, 353 F.3d 228, 247–60 (3d Cir. 2003) (*en banc*); *Matter of Kasinga*, 21 I&N Dec. 357, 364–65 (BIA 1996); *Matter of Becerra-Miranda*, 12 I&N Dec. 358, 368 (BIA 1967).

[106] *See, e.g., Xiu Ying Wu v. Att'y Gen.*, 712 F.3d 486 (11th Cir. 2013) (finding that the IJ's "bald assertion" that the applicant's story is implausible could not support the adverse credibility determination and that the IJ relied too heavily on the country profile); *Butt v. Gonzales*, 429 F.3d 430, 436–37 (3d Cir. 2005) (dismissing the IJ's credibility finding based on the IJ's claim that the applicant's testimony was "thin" or "extremely vague" and documents were "equally flimsy").

[107] *Floroiu v. Gonzales*, 481 F.3d 970, 973–76 (7th Cir. 2007) (reversing the IJ's credibility finding where the IJ was biased and characterized the applicants as "religious zealots" who were "offensive to the majority"); *Huang v. Gonzales*, 403 F.3d 945, 948–51 (7th Cir. 2005) (reversing the IJ's credibility finding based on personal views about Catholicism).

[108] *Xiu Ying Wu v. Att'y Gen.,* 712 F.3d 486 (11th Cir. 2013); *Jabri v. Holder*, 675 F.3d 20, 24–26 (1st Cir. 2012); *Tang v. Att'y Gen.*, 578 F.3d 1270, 1275–81 (11th Cir. 2009); *Li v. Holder*, 559 F.3d 1096, 1102–07 (9th Cir. 2009); *Torres v. Mukasey*, 551 F.3d 616, 627 (7th Cir. 2008); *Niang v. Mukasey*, 511 F.3d 138, 145–47 (2d Cir. 2007); *Tewabe v. Gonzales*, 446 F.3d 533, 538–40 (4th Cir. 2006).

Although an adverse credibility finding is usually fatal to a claim for asylum, withholding of removal, or CAT relief, it is not always fatal. Even if portions of the applicant's testimony or claim may be found not credible, his or her eligibility for relief may survive. For example, a protection claim may survive an adverse credibility finding in the following situations:

- Where the applicant's past persecution claim is not credible, but his or her testimony regarding a well-founded fear of future persecution is credible (and vice versa);[109]
- Where the applicant's testimony is not credible, but there is independent objective evidence on the record to establish the facts at issue;[110]
- Where the applicant's testimony regarding one form of relief is not credible, but there are other facts and evidence that may establish eligibility for an alternative form of relief;[111] and
- Where the applicant's testimony on an issue is found credible for determining whether he or she is a refugee eligible for asylum, he or she cannot be found not credible on the same issue in determining whether he or she merits asylum as a matter of discretion.[112]

These situations are rare, however, as an asylum-seeker usually cannot conclusively prove every aspect of his or her case through external evidence alone.

---

[109] *See, e.g.*, *Boika v. Holder*, 727 F.3d 735 (7th Cir. 2013) (finding that the BIA abused its discretion when it did not consider the factually distinct claims of future persecution in Belarus and rejected these claims based solely on the past adverse credibility finding); *Lin-Jian v. Gonzales*, 489 F.3d 182, 191–93 (4th Cir. 2007); *Gebreeyesus v. Gonzales*, 482 F.3d 952, 955 (7th Cir. 2007); *Paul v. Gonzales*, 444 F.3d 148, 153–55 (2d Cir. 2006) (finding that the applicant presented a false affidavit concerning the claim of past persecution, but that the applicant could still present credible testimony regarding a well-founded fear of future persecution); *Niang v. Gonzales*, 422 F.3d 1187, 1198–2001 (10th Cir. 2005); *Guo v. Ashcroft*, 386 F.3d 556, 562–64 (3d Cir. 2004); *Al-Harbi v. INS*, 242 F.3d 882, 891–94 (9th Cir. 2001); *Matter of T–Z–*, 24 I&N Dec. 163, 165 (BIA 2007) (finding the applicant credible about forced abortions, but not credible about the applicant's activities in the United States); *Matter of J–H–S–*, 24 I&N Dec. 196 (BIA 2007).

[110] *See, e.g.*, *Lin v. Holder*, 736 F.3d 343, 354 (4th Cir. 2013); *Anim v. Mukasey*, 535 F.3d 243, 261 (4th Cir. 2008); *Adekpe v. Gonzales*, 480 F.3d 525, 530–33 (7th Cir. 2007); *Forgue v. Att'y Gen.*, 401 F.3d 1282, 1287 (11th Cir. 2005); *Camara v. Ashcroft*, 378 F.3d 361, 369–71 (4th Cir. 2004); *Al-Harbi v. INS*, 242 F.3d 882 (9th Cir. 2001).

[111] *See, e.g.*, *Singh v. Ashcroft*, 398 F.3d 396, 404–06 (6th Cir. 2005); *Ramsameachire v. Ashcroft*, 357 F.3d 169, 184–86 (2d Cir. 2004); *Camara v. Ashcroft*, 378 F.3d 361, 371–72 (4th Cir. 2004); *Sivakaran v. Ashcroft*, 368 F.3d 1028, 1029 (8th Cir. 2004); *Zubeda v. Ashcroft*, 333 F.3d 463, 476 (3d Cir. 2003). There must, however, remain a factual or evidentiary basis for the second claim for relief, notwithstanding the adverse credibility finding on the first claim that was denied for lack of credibility. *See, e.g.*, *Lin-Jian v. Gonzales*, 489 F.3d 182, 192–93 (4th Cir. 2007); *Guo v. Gonzales*, 463 F.3d 109 113–14 (2d Cir. 2006); *Ibrahim v. Gonzales*, 434 F.3d 1074, 1079–80 (8th Cir. 2006); *Aden v. Ashcroft*, 396 F.3d 966, 969 (8th Cir. 2005); *Efe v. Ashcroft*, 293 F.3d 899, 907–08 (5th Cir. 2002).

[112] *Kalubi v. Ashcroft*, 364 F.3d 1134, 1135 (9th Cir. 2004).

Moreover, negative credibility findings will be overturned when an asylum applicant's hearing is found to be fundamentally unfair[113] or when an adjudicator bases an adverse credibility determination on non-record testimony.[114] An adjudicator, however, is not required to ignore repeated and blatant inconsistencies throughout an applicant's hearing testimony, simply because when viewed individually, each consistency weakened his or her claim for relief.[115]

1. Demeanor

In particular, a credibility finding based on the applicant's demeanor will be accorded a high degree of deference by the reviewing court, especially in cases in which there are legitimate reasons for doubting the veracity of the applicant's testimony.[116] This is because an IJ generally is in the best position to evaluate an applicant or witness's demeanor. For example, not responding to an IJ's questions or responding after long pauses may indicate a lack of credibility that the transcript would not necessarily show.[117] However, at least one court has noted that the belief that demeanor alone can determine one's credibility has been tested and rejected by social scientists.[118] The Seventh Circuit U.S. Court of Appeals in *Mitondo v. Mukasey* advises that to determine whether someone is lying, the trier of fact should close his or her eyes and "pay attention to *what* is said, not *how* it is said or what the witness

---

[113] *Al Khouri v. Ashcroft*, 362 F.3d 461 (8th Cir. 2004) (finding that IJ prejudiced an unrepresented applicant's claim by not allowing him to testify regarding his whole asylum claim); *see also Kebede v. Ashcroft*, 366 F.3d 808, 811 (9th Cir. 2004) (acknowledging that a victim of sexual assault does not irredeemably compromise his or her credibility by failing to report the assault at the first opportunity); *Mulanga v. Ashcroft*, 349 F.3d 123, 137 (3d Cir. 2003) (holding that the IJ's reliance on airport statement of applicant to impeach her credibility was not supported by the record because the statement was not necessarily inconsistent with her asylum hearing testimony); *Wang v. Ashcroft*, 341 F.3d 1015, 1021 (9th Cir. 2003) (overturning an adverse credibility determination where the inconsistent statements were not material to whether the applicant was subjected to two forced abortions); *Hartooni v. INS*, 21 F.3d 336, 342 (9th Cir. 1994) (finding no credibility problem when a 14-year-old girl with poor English skills indicated on an application that neither she nor her family had been mistreated in Iran, but the applicant offered testimony regarding mistreatment); *Matter of S–A–*, 22 I&N Dec. 1328 (BIA 2000) (in overturning an IJ's negative credibility determination, the BIA noted that the IJ failed to identify any internal discrepancies in the applicant's testimony or between her testimony and the asylum application); *Matter of Kasinga*, 21 I&N Dec. 357 (BIA 1996) (holding that the IJ erred in finding the applicant not credible where she had adequately and reasonably explained several incidents where the IJ found such explanations to be irrational, unpersuasive, or inconsistent).

[114] *Gao v. Bd. of Immigration Appeals*, 482 F.3d 122, 134 (2d Cir. 2007) (finding that the IJ did not tether any of the inferences leading to his adverse credibility determination to anything in the record).

[115] *Kaur v. Gonzales*, 418 F.3d 1061, 1068 (9th Cir. 2005) (finding that IJ's credibility determination was supported by substantial evidence).

[116] *Matter of A–S–*, 21 I&N Dec. 1106, 1131 (BIA 1998). *See Ling Huang v. Holder*, 744 F.3d 1149 (9th Cir. 2014); *Jianli Chen v. Holder*, 703 F.3d 17, 24–26 (1st Cir. 2012). See chapter 12 for a detailed discussion of deference during judicial review.

[117] *Shrestha v. Holder*, 590 F.3d 1034, 1045 (9th Cir. 2010).

[118] *Mitondo v. Mukasey*, 523 F.3d 784, 788 (7th Cir. 2008).

looks like while saying it."[119] The Seventh Circuit has been highly critical of the BIA with regard to credibility determinations, asserting that deference is earned, not a birthright.[120] The court cited to repeated, egregious failures on the part of the immigration courts and the BIA to exercise the care commensurate with the stakes in an asylum case.[121]

Overall, an adjudicator's credibility finding that rests on demeanor, but is not supported by the record will not be credited. Moreover, boilerplate demeanor determinations or stereotyping may lead to reversal of an adverse credibility finding. Demeanor in combination with other evidence of an applicant's lack of credibility, however, may be persuasive to an adjudicator.

2. Inconsistencies and Omissions

Throughout the asylum process, applicants are tasked with recounting their tales of persecution, torture, or fears in returning to their home countries.[122] Often, these stories are difficult to articulate, the details may be unclear, or an applicant may be reluctant to provide the particulars of traumatic abuse or suffering.[123] However, inconsistent statements or discrepancies made almost anywhere in the asylum process can jeopardize an applicant's asylum claim.[124] An applicant's omissions may be just as important as what he or she states in the application for asylum or in his or her testimony.[125] In this regard, discrepancies, whether in the application itself or in the

---

[119] *Id.* (emphasis in original).

[120] *Kadia v. Gonzales*, 501 F.3d 817, 821 (7th Cir. 2007).

[121] *Id.*

[122] 8 CFR §235(b)(1)(B)(iii)(III), 8 CFR §1208.30(g)(2) (2014) (outlining credible fear procedures).

[123] *See, e.g., Fiadjoe v. Att'y Gen.*, 411 F.3d 125 (3d Cir. 2005) (recognizing that noncitizens who have been physically and sexually abused may be reluctant to explain details of their experience).

[124] *See, e.g., Ahmed v. Holder*, 765 F.3d 96 (1st Cir. 2014) (upholding the adverse credibility determination against a Somali petitioner who sought asylum while using various, inconsistent bases); *Lee v. Holder*, 765 F.3d 851 (8th Cir. 2014) (citing numerous inconsistencies in the applicant's asylum claim relating to harm allegedly suffered in the Burmese army and in Thailand); *Qing Hua Lin v. Holder*, 736 F.3d 343 (4th Cir. 2013) (upholding the BIA's finding of inconsistencies in the applicant's statements regarding her marital status and forced abortion); *Martinez v. Holder*, 734 F.3d 105 (1st Cir. 2013) (upholding the adverse credibility finding due the inconsistencies in the applicant's submissions and his testimony); *Fofana v. Holder*, 704 F.3d 554 (8th Cir. 2013) (upholding the IJ's adverse credibility determination based on "inconsistencies and implausibilities" in the Respondent's applications, testimony, and hearing exhibits); *Djadjou v. Holder*, 662 F.3d 265 (4th Cir. 2011) (upholding the adverse credibility determination based on an inconsistency arising from the applicant's eviction notice suggesting that she was not in hiding as she had claimed, and based on the omission in her application of her role in the SCNC).

[125] *See, e.g., Djadjou v. Holder*, 662 F.3d 265 (4th Cir. 2011) (upholding the adverse credibility determination based on an inconsistency arising from the applicant's eviction notice suggesting that she was not in hiding as she had claimed, and based on the omission in her application of her role in the SCNC); *Zamanov v. Holder*, 649 F.3d 969 (9th Cir. 2011) (holding that the inclusion of three additional incidents of arrest and mistreatment that were added to the applicant's claim in a supplemental declaration materially altered his claim in a way that casted doubt on his credibility).

testimony provided during the interview or hearing, may provide a basis for an asylum officer or IJ to make a negative credibility finding, which can be detrimental to the applicant's case.[126]

Prior to the REAL ID Act of 2005, minor discrepancies, inconsistencies, or omissions in an individual's asylum application or in his or her testimony that did not go to the heart of the asylum claim did not support an adverse credibility finding.[127] Similarly, minor discrepancies or typographical errors in official documents could not serve as a basis for a negative credibility finding.[128] Rather, discrepancies had to involve the heart of the asylum claim in order to support a negative credibility determination.[129] Moreover, prior to the REAL ID Act of 2005, previous inconsistent statements made by an applicant to immigration officials generally were not sufficient to support an adverse credibility finding when the record of the statement might not be reliable, the questions posed were not designed to elicit the "details" of any asylum claim, and an applicant who was abused by government officials in his or her home country might be reluctant to speak to U.S. government officials.[130]

---

[126] *Matter of A–S–*, 21 I&N Dec. 1106, 1109–1110 (BIA 1998).

[127] *See Tadesse v. Gonzales*, 492 F.3d 905, 910–11 (7th Cir. 2007); *Zhang v. DOJ*, 480 F.3d 104, 125–38 (2d Cir. 2007); *Sarr v. Gonzales*, 474 F.3d 783, 789–93 (10th Cir. 2007); *Kim v. Gonzales*, 458 F.3d 40, 44–45 (2d Cir. 2006); *Giday v. Gonzales*, 434 F.3d 543, 550–53 (7th Cir. 2006); *Butt v. Gonzales*, 429 F.3d 430, 437 N.10 (3d Cir. 2005); *Pergega v. Gonzales*, 417 F.3d 623, 628–29 (6th Cir. 2005); *Liu v. Ashcroft*, 372 F.3d 529, 534 (3d Cir. 2004); *Sylla v. INS*, 388 F.3d 924, 926–27 (6th Cir. 2004); *Bellido v. Ashcroft*, 367 F.3d 840, 843–44 (8th Cir. 2004); *Georgis v. Ashcroft*, 328 F.3d 962, 968 (7th Cir. 2003); *Bandari v. INS*, 227 F.3d 1160, 1165–67 (9th Cir. 2000); *Senathirajah v. INS*, 157 F.3d 210, 221 (3d Cir. 1998); *Osorio v. INS*, 99 F.3d 928, 931 (9th Cir. 1996); *Aguilera-Cota v. INS*, 914 F.2d 1375, 1382 (9th Cir. 1990); *Damaize-Job v. INS*, 787 F.2d 1332, 1337 (9th Cir. 1986); *Zavala-Bonilla v. INS*, 730 F.2d 562, 566 (9th Cir. 1984).

[128] *Shah v. INS*, 220 F.3d 1062, 1068 (9th Cir. 2000).

[129] *Krouchevski v. Ashcroft*, 344 F.3d 670, 673 (7th Cir. 2003) (although the applicant offered explanations for the inconsistencies, the reviewing court refused to overturn the negative credibility determination simply because an alternative finding could be supported by substantial evidence); *Disu v. Ashcroft*, 338 F.3d 13, 17–18 (1st Cir. 2003) (upholding a negative credibility determination where harm alleged was not mentioned in applicant's asylum application or at his initial interview); *Mendoza Manimbao v. Ashcroft*, 329 F.3d 655, 660 (9th Cir. 2003) ("Minor inconsistencies in the record that do not relate to the basis of an applicant's alleged fear of persecution, go to the heart of the asylum claim, or reveal anything about an asylum applicant's fear for his safety are insufficient to support an adverse credibility finding."); *De Leon-Barrios v. INS*, 116 F.2d 391, 393 (9th Cir. 1997) (upholding IJ and BIA finding that a Guatemalan asylum applicant was not credible where the applicant failed to present a satisfactory explanation for discrepancies in his two asylum applications); *see also Singh-Kaur v. INS*, 183 F.3d 1147 (9th Cir. 1999); *Hajiani-Niroumand v. INS*, 26 F.3d 832, 838 (8th Cir. 1994); *Khano v. INS*, 999 F.2d 1203, 1208 (7th Cir. 1993); *Ceballos-Castillo v. INS*, 904 F.2d 519, 520 (9th Cir. 1990).

[130] *Balasubramanrim v. INS*, 143 F.3d 157 (3d Cir. 1998) (reversing the BIA's negative credibility determination); *see also Ememe v. Ashcroft*, 358 F.3d 446, 453 (7th Cir. 2004) (testimonial inconsistencies alone do not support IJ's negative credibility determination where applicant was interviewed initially in Italian, and her native language was Amharic); *Singh v. INS*, 292 F.3d 1017, 1021 (9th Cir. 2002) (finding the applicant's airport interview lacked sufficient indicia of reliability and accuracy to support an adverse credibility determination); *Senathirajah v. INS*, 157 F.3d 210, 218 (3d

Continued

However, following the REAL ID Act, these standards changed and most circuits have found that the amendments abrogated their previous case law regarding credibility determinations.[131] Specifically, the amended INA now states that an inconsistency does not necessarily have to go to the "heart of the applicant's asylum claim" in order to yield an adverse credibility determination.[132] The Sixth Circuit U.S. Court of Appeals, however, has held that when applying this provision of the REAL ID Act, a credibility determination still must take into account the circumstances under which the statements were made.[133] The court also concluded that as long as statements in the application are not inconsistent with the oral testimony, mere lack of specificity in an application, compared with more detailed testimony at an evidentiary hearing, will not provide support for a finding that an applicant is not credible.[134]

Overall, the current approach to credibility determinations is for the adjudicator to look to the totality of the circumstances and the cumulative effect of any inconsistencies not directly material to an asylum claim.[135] An applicant's testimony

---

Cir. 1998) (finding that reliance on an airport interview for a credibility determination "seriously undermined the reliability of the administrative process"). Similarly, courts have noted that Asylum Office Assessments to Refer may lack indicia of reliability and therefore may not support a negative credibility finding. *See Koulibaly v. Mukasey*, 541 F.3d 613, 620 (6th Cir. 2008); *Singh v. Gonzales*, 403 F.3d 1081, 1087(finding a need for courts to ensure that there exist sufficient indicia of reliability before relying on an Asylum Office Assessment to Refer). *But see Yan Qin Xiao v. Mukasey*, 547 F.3d 712, 717 (7th Cir. 2008) (upholding negative credibility finding for applicant who failed to mention a past forced abortion during an airport interview and credible fear interview with an asylum officer).

[131] *See, e.g., Xiu Xia Lin v. Mukasey*, 534 F.3d 162, 167 (2d Cir. 2008) (concluding that previous holding that an IJ may not base an adverse credibility determination on inconsistencies and omissions that are collateral or ancillary to an applicant's claims has been abrogated by changes under the REAL ID Act). *See also Lin v. Mukasey*, 521 F.3d 22, 27–28 (1st Cir. 2008) (noting that the REAL ID Act overhauled the methodology to be used in making a credibility determination and eliminated the "heart of the claim" rule); *Chen v. Att'y Gen.*, 463 F.3d 1228, 1233 (11th Cir. 2006) (rejecting the applicant's argument that the inconsistencies and discrepancies relied on by the IJ were "trivial" and "irrelevant to the dispositive issues," citing to the new provision added by the REAL ID Act); *Jibril v. Gonzales*, 423 F.3d 1129, 1138 n.1 (9th Cir. 2005) (stating that the result it reached would have been different — the case would not have been remanded — if the REAL ID provision applied to the case).

[132] INA §208(b)(1)(B)(iii). *See, e.g., Slyusar v. Holder*, 740 F.3d 1068 (6th Cir. 2014); *Xia v. Att'y Gen.*, 608 F.3d 1233, 1240 (11th Cir. 2010); *Wang v. Holder*, 569 F.3d 531, 537–40 (5th Cir. 2009); *Rivas-Mira v. Holder*, 556 F.3d 1, 5–6 (1st Cir. 2009) (noting that the "heart of the matter rule is dead"); *Mitondo v. Mukasey*, 523 F.3d 784, 788–89 (7th Cir. 2008); *Chen v. Att'y Gen.*, 463 F.3d 1228, 1230–33 (11th Cir. 2006).

[133] *Kaba v. Mukasey*, 546 F.3d 741, 750 n.2 (6th Cir. 2008).

[134] *Id.*

[135] INA §208(b)(1)(B)(iii). *See, e.g., Carrizo v. Att'y Gen.*, 652 F.3d 1326 (11th Cir. 2011) (upholding the adverse credibility finding where the applicant claimed to be present at a rally where his mother was killed but presented no evidence that he was politically active, at the rally, or detained and beaten after); *Dehonzai v. Holder*, 650 F.3d 1 (1st Cir. 2011) (nothing that the applicant used nearly identical language to describe his mistreatment as that used in the Amnesty International report, and where his testimony was inconsistent and uncorroborated); *Lin v. Mukasey*, 534 F.3d 162, 165–68 (2d Cir. 2008)

Continued

will generally be found to be credible when it is plausible, detailed, internally consistent, consistent with the application, and unembellished.[136]

In order to support an adverse credibility determination, however, inconsistencies must actually be true inconsistencies.[137] Courts have found that the following circumstances do not necessarily indicate true inconsistencies for purposes of credibility:

- An application that is not as complete as the applicant's testimony;[138]
- Omission of events in a written application that are later testified to at an interview or hearing;[139]

(upholding an adverse credibility finding where the cumulative effect of collateral statements that were not directly material could have affected credibility); *Phal v. Mukasey*, 524 F.3d 85, 88–89 (1st Cir. 2008) (finding that the cumulative effect of minor inconsistencies coupled with larger inconsistencies and questions regarding documents was sufficient to uphold an adverse credibility finding); *Pan v. Gonzales*, 489 F.3d 80, 86–87 (1st Cir. 2007) (finding that the cumulative effect of minor inconsistencies between the trial and the interview were sufficient to uphold an adverse credibility finding); *Kadia v. Gonzales*, 501 F.3d 817, 821–22 (7th Cir. 2007) (reversing the IJ where he failed to distinguish between material lies and innocent mistakes, trivial inconsistencies, and harmless exaggerations).

[136] *Matter of B–*, 21 I&N Dec. 66, 70–72 (BIA 1995) (holding that IJ erred in finding that an Afghani asylum applicant was not truthful because he would not look at the IJ when he testified, failed to provide precise dates, and did not corroborate his testimony with the testimony of other witnesses). *See also Uwase v. Ashcroft*, 349 F.3d 1039 (7th Cir. 2003). On the other hand, an adjudicator may find an applicant not credible based on testimony that is inherently implausible. *See, e.g., Ismaiel v. Mukasey*, 516 F.3d 1198, 1205 (10th Cir. 2008) (finding that if the torture actually occurred, it would defy common sense for the applicant, who was assisted by counsel, to omit any mention of it on his asylum application); *Chen v. Mukasey*, 510 F.3d 797, 802 (8th Cir. 2007); *Yan v. Mukasey*, 509 F.3d 63, 68 (2d Cir. 2007); *Thiam v. Gonzales*, 496 F.3d 912, 914 (8th Cir. 2007).

[137] *See, e.g., Jabri v. Holder*, 675 F.3d 20 (1st Cir. 2012) (finding that the IJ relied on at least two perceived "inconsistencies" that were not direct inconsistencies); *Sea v. Holder*, 444 Fed. App'x 843 (6th Cir. 2011) (finding that a translation error in a medical document corroborating the applicant's injuries contributed significantly to the IJ's adverse credibility finding, and staying the appeal so that the applicant could present the error to the BIA); *Kueviakoe v. Att'y Gen.*, 567 F.3d 1301, 1304–06 (11th Cir. 2009) (reversing the adverse credibility determination where the inconsistencies between the testimony and written statements actually did not exist).

[138] *See, e.g., Suntharalinkam v. Gonzales*, 458 F.3d 1034, 1042–44 (9th Cir. 2006); *Smolniakova v. Gonzales*, 422 F.3d 1037, 1044–45 (9th Cir. 2005) (stating that "an applicant's testimony is not per se lacking in credibility simply because it includes details that are not set forth in the asylum application"); *Liti v. Gonzales*, 411 F.3d 631, 637–39 (6th Cir. 2005) (reversing adverse credibility, stating "we reject the BIA's underlying rationale that the [applicants] are required to provide an exhaustive, detailed list of their … activities in their asylum application"); *Vasha v. Gonzales*, 410 F.3d 863, 871 n.4 (6th Cir. 2005). In order to impact the adjudicator's credibility determination, there must be an actual connection between the omission and the applicant's credibility. The omission must also be material. *Lin v. Mukasey*, 534 F.3d 162, 165–68 (2d Cir. 2008); *Secaida-Rosales v. INS*, 331 F.3d 297, 306–13 (2d Cir. 2003); *Stoyanov v. INS*, 172 F.3d 731, 736 (9th Cir. 1999); *Osorio v. INS*, 99 F.3d 928, 932 (9th Cir. 1996).

[139] *See, e.g., Abulashvili v. U.S. Att'y Gen.*, 663 F.3d 197, 206 (3d Cir. 2011); *Torres v. Mukasey*, 551 F.3d 616, 631–34 (7th Cir. 2008); *Mousa v. Mukasey*, 530 F.3d 1026, 1027–29 (9th Cir. 2008); *Heng v.*

Continued

- Omission of certain details in testimony until cross-examination regarding those details;[140]
- Mistranslations;[141]
- Incompetent counsel;[142]
- Discrepancies where other evidence on the record corroborates the explanation for the discrepancy;[143] and
- Differences between statements made upon entry and during later, more formal proceedings.[144]

Gonzales, 493 F.3d 46, 49 (1st Cir. 2007); *Pavlova v. INS*, 441 F.3d 82, 90 (2d Cir. 2006); *Ssali v. Gonzales*, 424 F.3d 556, 562–64 (7th Cir. 2005).

[140] *See, e.g.*, *Lai v. Holder*, No. 10–73473, 2014 WL 5573318, at *3–4 (9th Cir. 2014) (finding the adverse credibility order flawed when it was based on the applicant's omission until cross-examination of details concerning third parties, which were not contradictory to his earlier testimony or application materials). *But see, e.g.*, *Lianhua Jiang v. Holder*, 754 F.3d 733 (9th Cir. 2014) (holding that the applicant's failure to testify until prompted about physical abuse that she had described in her declaration was sufficient to support the IJ's adverse credibility finding).

[141] *See, e.g.*, *Abulashvili v. Att'y Gen.*, 663 F.3d 197, 203 (3d Cir. 2011) (noting that it is "important to stress that the linguistic and cultural difficulties endemic in immigration hearings may frequently result in statements that appear to be inconsistent, but in reality arise from a lack of proficiency in English or cultural differences rather than attempts to deceive"); *Issiaka v. Att'y Gen.*, 569 F.3d 135, 141–43 (3d Cir. 2009); *Kueviakoe v. Att'y Gen.*, 567 F.3d 1301, 1305 (11th Cir. 2009); *Mapouya v. Gonzales*, 487 F.3d 396, 406–11 (6th Cir. 2007) (reversing adverse credibility determination where inconsistencies between the I-589 and testimony were immaterial and were due to translation errors).

[142] *See, e.g.*, *Yang v. Gonzales*, 478 F.3d 133, 142–44 (2d Cir. 2007).

[143] *See, e.g.*, *Zhi v. Holder*, 751 F.3d 1088 (9th Cir. 2014) (finding that the IJ's adverse credibility determination was not supported by substantial evidence because other evidence on the record corroborated the applicant's explanation for the alleged discrepancy in dates).

[144] *See, e.g.*, *Bassene v. Holder*, 737 F.3d 530, 537 (9th Cir. 2013) ("The differences in detail between statements made during less formal proceedings and later formal proceedings may not be used to undermine an applicant's credibility."). Courts have found interviews upon entry to lack indicia of reliability. *See, e.g.*, *Kartasheva v. Holder*, 582 F.3d 96, 104–07 (1st Cir. 2009); *Tang v. Att'y Gen.*, 578 F.3d 1270, 1279 (11th Cir. 2009); *Sing v. Mukasey*, 553 F.3d 207, 213–16 (2d Cir. 2009); *Koulibaly v. Mukasey*, 541 F.3d 613, 623–24 (6th Cir. 2008); *Yan Xia Zhu v. Mukasey*, 537 F.3d 1034, 1040–41 (9th Cir. 2008); *Moab v. Gonzales*, 500 F.3d 656, 660–62 (7th Cir. 2007); *Ucelo-Gomez v. Gonzales*, 464 F.3d 163, 167 (2d Cir. 2006); *Bao v. Gonzales*, 460 F.3d 426, 431–33 (2d Cir. 2006); *Latifi v. Gonzales*, 430 F.3d 103, 105 (2d Cir. 2005); *Rodriguez-Galicia v. Gonzales*, 422 F.3d 529, 536–38 (7th Cir. 2005); *Dong v. Gonzales*, 421 F.3d 573, 579 (7th Cir. 2005); *Fiadjoe v. Att'y Gen.*, 411 F.3d 136, 159 (3d Cir. 2005); *Singh v. Gonzales*, 403 F.3d 1081, 1086–90 (9th Cir. 2005); *Huang v. Gonzales*, 403 F.3d 945, 950 (7th Cir. 2005); *Wu v. Ashcroft*, 393 F.3d 418, 423–25 (3d Cir. 2005); *Kebede v. Ashcroft*, 366 F.3d 808, 811 (9th Cir. 2004). *But see, e.g.*, *Qing Hua Lin v. Holder*, 736 F.3d 343, 352 (4th Cir. 2013) (upholding adverse credibility finding based on inconsistencies between interview with CBP and later testimony and application materials, but noting "hesitation in relying on statements made" in the CBP interview setting); *Jianli Chen v. Holder*, 703 F.3d 17, 24–26 (1st Cir. 2012); *Djadjou v. Holder*, 662 F.3d 265, 274–75 (4th Cir. 2011); *Jiao Hua Huang v. Holder*, 620 F.3d 33, 37 (1st Cir. 2010) ("Inconsistencies between statements made during a credible fear interview and testimony during a hearing provide a legitimate basis for an adverse credibility determination.");

Continued

In order to affect an asylum or withholding of removal claim, inconsistencies also generally must be material. For example, in *Torres v. Mukasey*, the Seventh Circuit considered the asylum application of a man who claimed that he was persecuted while serving as a soldier in the Honduran army because of his membership in a particular social group — his family.[145] The applicant's family included four older brothers, three of whom were military deserters. The IJ rejected the applicant's claim based on lack of credibility. The Seventh Circuit found that the IJ erred in basing the adverse credibility determination on the applicant's reason for joining the military, because the applicant's motivation for joining the military was irrelevant to the claim for relief.[146] Therefore, the IJ's conclusion was not supported by substantial evidence.[147] Even though inconsistencies generally must be material, however, where immaterial inconsistencies are accompanied by other indications of dishonesty, adverse credibility still may be upheld.[148]

An applicant's testimony must be consistent, not only internally, but also with the other evidence of record. For this reason, consideration of the conditions in the applicant's country of origin is an important element in assessing the applicant's credibility.[149] In considering the conditions in the applicant's country of past or feared persecution, some adjudicators place great importance upon the DOS reports on human rights conditions,[150] and some courts have upheld adverse credibility determinations where objective background country information did not support an asylum applicant's claim.[151] However, adjudicators also have raised concerns that DOS "soft-pedals human rights violations by countries the United States wants to have good relations with."[152] One court has advised the BIA to treat the DOS reports with "a

---

Fesehaye v. Holder, 607 F.3d 523, 527 (8th Cir. 2010); *Villa-Londono v. Holder*, 600 F.3d 21, 24–25 (1st Cir. 2010); *Zhang v. Holder*, 585 F.3d 715, 721–26 (2d Cir. 2009); *Shkambi v. Att'y Gen.*, 584 F.3d 1041, 1050–51 (11th Cir. 2009); *Xiao v. Mukasey*, 547 F.3d 712, 717 (7th Cir. 2008); *Kanacevic v. INS*, 448 F.3d 129, 136–38 (2d Cir. 2006); *Guan v. Gonzales*, 432 F.3d 391, 398 (2d Cir. 2005); *Jalloh v. Gonzales*, 423 F.3d 894, 898–99 (8th Cir. 2005); *Li v. Ashcroft*, 378 F.3d 959, 962–64 (9th Cir. 2004).

[145] *Torres v. Mukasey*, 551 F.3d 616, 628 (7th Cir. 2008).

[146] *Id.*

[147] *Id.*

[148] *Lin v. Mukasey*, 534 F.3d 162, 165–68 (2d Cir. 2008); *Kaur v. Gonzales*, 418 F.3d 1061, 1066–67 (9th Cir. 2005); *Barreto-Claro v. Att'y Gen.*, 275 F.3d 1334, 1337–39 & n.8 (11th Cir. 2001); *Matter of A–H–*, 23 I&N Dec. 774, 786–67 (AG 2005).

[149] *See, e.g.*, *Cordero-Trejo v. INS*, 40 F.3d 482, 491 (1st Cir. 1994); UNHCR Handbook, *supra* note 43, ¶ 42.

[150] *See* U.S. Dep't of State, Human Rights Reports, *available at www.state.gov/j/drl/rls/hrrpt/* (last visited Dec. 24, 2014).

[151] *Khrystotodorov v. Mukasey*, 551 F.3d 775,783 (8th Cir. 2008) (holding that substantial evidence supported the IJ's credibility concerns due to significant variances between the applicant's testimony and the objective information in the background).

[152] *Gailius v. INS*, 147 F.3d 34, 46 (1st Cir. 1998) (citation omitted); *see also Shah v. INS*, 220 F.3d 1062, 1069–70 (9th Cir. 2000).

healthy skepticism" rather than as "Holy Writ."[153] Another court has urged adjudicators not to place undue weight on the DOS country reports because they cannot be expected to capture all details of every abuse in a given country, nor can anti-government groups be expected to monitor all abuses.[154]

An applicant should always be given the opportunity to respond to and explain any apparent inconsistencies, misrepresentations, or omissions.[155] A reasonable explanation that is not contradicted and that is supported by evidentiary material should be credited by an IJ.[156] If the BIA *sua sponte* raises concerns about an applicant's credibility, it must give the applicant an opportunity to offer an explanation of any perceived inconsistencies.[157] Failure to do so is a violation of due process.[158]

For example, in *Oshodi v. Holder*, the applicant was not given the opportunity to respond to alleged credibility problems.[159] In that case, an en banc court held that the IJ's refusal to hear the applicant's full testimony with respect to the abuses he suffered in Nigeria violated his due process rights because the denial of relief rested solely on an adverse credibility finding.[160] By precluding the applicant from testifying about critical events in his application, the IJ had "short-circuited his ability to judge accurately Oshodi's credibility."[161]

In general, the BIA instructs that an applicant may be given the "benefit of the doubt" if there is some ambiguity regarding an aspect of his or her asylum claim.[162]

---

[153] *Galina v. INS*, 213 F.3d 955, 959 (7th Cir. 2000); *see also Chen v. INS*, 359 F.3d 121, 130 (2d Cir. 2004) (noting that observations in State Department reports do not automatically discredit contrary evidence presented by the applicant and are not binding on the immigration court); *Niam v. Ashcroft*, 354 F.3d 652, 659 (7th Cir. 2004) (noting that the authors of the DOS reports are anonymous and cannot be cross-examined). *But see Gonahasa v. INS*, 181 F.3d 538 (4th Cir. 1999) ("If it is reasonable to suspect the State Department has a tendency to soft-pedal human rights violations, it may be just as reasonable to suspect that Amnesty International exaggerates them so they will not go without notice.").

[154] *Diallo v. U.S. Dep't of Justice*, 548 F.3d 232, 237(2d Cir. 2008).

[155] UNHCR Handbook, *supra* note 43, ¶ 199. *See, e.g., Soto-Olarte v. Holder*, 555 F.3d 1089, 1091–93 (9th Cir. 2009); *Kaita v. Att'y Gen.*, 522 F.3d 288, 299–300 (3d Cir. 2008) (reversing an adverse credibility determination where the IJ's complaints about the applicant's failure to explain were inconsistent with the IJ's constant interruptions); *Pang v. USCIS*, 448 F.3d 102, 109–11 (2d Cir. 2006); *Xue v. BIA*, 439 F.3d 111, 124–25 (2d Cir. 2006).

[156] *Dong v. Gonzales*, 421 F.3d 573 (7th Cir. 2005) (recognizing plausibility of claim over perceived inconsistencies).

[157] *Stoyanov v. INS*, 172 F.3d 731, 735 (9th Cir. 1999).

[158] *Id.*

[159] *Oshodi v. Holder*, 729 F.3d 883, 912 (9th Cir. 2013).

[160] *Id.*

[161] *Id.* ("The importance of an asylum and withholding applicant's testimony cannot be overstated, and the fact that Oshodi submitted a written declaration outlining the facts of his persecution is no response to the IJ's refusal to hear his testimony.").

[162] *Matter of Y–B–*, 21 I&N Dec. 1136, 1139 (BIA 1998).

In some cases, the applicant may be found credible even if he or she has trouble remembering specific facts.[163] However, omission of key events or numerous inconsistencies generally will lead to a finding that the applicant is not credible.[164]

- **Practice Pointer**: Given that even minor inconsistencies can lead to negative credibility determinations, an IJ's negative credibility determination is typically given great deference, and a negative credibility determination can result in the applicant's return to persecution or torture, it is critical for practitioners to properly prepare applicants and witnesses before the taking of any testimony. Proper preparation means knowing the facts and documentary evidence inside and out, educating the applicant or witness on what he or she can expect to happen, and predicting what questions an asylum officer, IJ, or DHS counsel might pose.[165]

- **Practice Pointer**: When adequately explained on the record, courts have recognized that an applicant's reluctance to discuss traumatic or painful experiences, or to report it in an asylum interview or application, may not be fatal to a credibility determination.[166] Therefore, practitioners should work with their clients to understand the reasons why certain omissions may have been made and to ensure that those reasons are fully explained and documented on the record.

3. *False Documents and Misrepresentations*

Many individuals fleeing persecution or torture travel to the United States through the use of false documents and some present those documents at the border to gain entry to the United States. Prior to the REAL ID Act, an adverse credibility finding because the applicant submitted a fraudulent document could not be upheld if there was no evidence that the applicant knew or suspected that the document was fraudulent.[167] Similarly, documents could not be rejected on the basis that the applicant's testimony was vague or inconsistent.[168] If U.S. authorities wished to dispute the authenticity of documents submitted by the applicant, they had to do so in

---

[163] *Matter of B–*, 21 I&N Dec. 66, 70–71 (BIA 1995).

[164] *Matter of A–S–*, 21 I&N Dec. 1106, 1109–1110 (BIA 1998).

[165] Vikram Badrinath, Dree K. Collopy, & Hans Christian Linnartz, *Evidentiary Issues in Asylum Cases*, AILA IMMIGRATION PRACTICE POINTERS (AILA 2013).

[166] *Paramasamy v. Ashcroft*, 295 F.3d 1047, 1053 (9th Cir. 2002) (finding that a failure to report a sexual assault in an asylum interview does not support an adverse credibility finding).

[167] *Gjerzai v. Gonzales*, 435 F.3d 800, 810–11 (7th Cir. 2006); *Kourski v. Ashcroft*, 355 F.3d 1038, 1039–40 (7th Cir. 2004); *Yeimane-Berhe v. Ashcroft*, 393 F.3d 907, 911–13 (9th Cir. 2004).

[168] *Zahedi v. INS*, 222 F.3d 1157, 1165 (9th Cir. 2000) (finding that the IJ failed to properly consider the documentary evidence submitted by the applicant).

a manner that did not violate due process.[169] Following the REAL ID Act, both the BIA and the federal courts agree that the use of fraudulent documents while fleeing persecution cannot alone form the basis of an adverse credibility finding.[170]

Other courts have addressed the presentation of false documents in support of applications for relief. These courts have looked to whether the applicant was aware of the documents' falsity in determining whether the false documents could impact the applicant's credibility. For example, in considering the application of a Macedonian man and his family, the IJ expressed concern that the certificate of dismissal from the man's former employer, which stated that he was dismissed from employment due to his political activities, as well as the "court decision" indicating that the applicant had been sentenced to prison "due to enemy activity," were fraudulent.[171] In response, the government submitted two consular reports concluding that the two documents were indeed fraudulent, the applicant submitted rebuttal evidence, and the government responded with a forensics report and testimony by the author of the report regarding his findings and methodology.[172] The applicant then testified that he never knowingly submitted any fraudulent documents, but the IJ made a negative credibility finding based on the fraudulent documents.[173]

On review, the Second Circuit U.S. Court of Appeals found that the submission of the fraudulent documents standing alone was insufficient to support a negative credibility finding where there is no indication or finding that the applicant knew or had reason to know that the documents were fraudulent.[174] The court concluded that "when an applicant contests that he knowingly submitted a fraudulent document, the IJ must make an explicit finding that the applicant knew the document to be fraudulent before the IJ can use the fraudulent document as the basis for an adverse credibility determination."[175] The court remanded the case, directing the adjudicator to determine whether the applicant had reason to know that the documents were fraudulent. In a similar case before the Tenth Circuit U.S. Court of Appeals, the court

---

169 *See, e.g., Kumar v. Gonzales*, 444 F.3d 1043, 1050–51 (9th Cir. 2006) (finding that the IJ erred in finding adverse credibility based on the uniformed conclusion that a document was fraudulent without submitting it to a handwriting expert or forensic lab).

170 *Singh v. Holder*, 638 F.3d 1264, 1271 (9th Cir. 2011); *Gulla v. Gonzales*, 498 F.3d 911, 917 (9th Cir. 2007); *Edimo-Doualla v. Gonzales*, 464 F.3d 276, 288–89 (2d Cir. 2006); *Zhang v. Gonzales*, 434 F.3d 993, 997 (7th Cir. 2006); *Dong v. Gonzales*, 421 F.3d 573, 577 (7th Cir. 2005); *Kaur v. Ashcroft*, 379 F.3d 876, 889 (9th Cir. 2004); *Paramasamy v. Ashcroft*, 295 F.3d 1047, 1054 (9th Cir. 2002); *Akinmade v. INS*, 196 F.3d 951, 955–56 (9th Cir. 1999); *Matter of O–D–*, 21 I&N Dec. 1079, 1081 (BIA 1998); *Matter of Pula*, 19 I&N Dec. 467, 474 (BIA 1987).

171 *Corovic v. Mukasey*, 519 F.3d 90, 98 (2d Cir. 2008).

172 *Id.*

173 *Id.*

174 *Id.*

175 *Id.*

stated, "Needless to say, if [the applicant] was unaware that the documents were not authentic, their forged status cannot impugn his credibility."[176]

Similarly, in some situations, asylum applicants have given false or limited information during their asylum interview or during their inspection upon arrival at an airport, yet have eventually been determined to be credible.[177] What matters most is the particular circumstances under which the false statements were made.[178] For example, false statements to an immigration officer where the individual fears being removed to his or her home country "can be entirely *consistent* with a fear of persecution" and may not be determinative of his or her credibility.[179] Furthermore, "A person who, because of his experiences, was in fear of the authorities in his own country may still feel apprehensive vis-à-vis any authority. He may therefore be afraid to speak freely and give a full and accurate account of his case" to authoritative figures in the United States, like immigration officers.[180] UNHCR agrees with this concept, stating in its Handbook that "[u]ntrue statements by themselves are not a reason for refusal of refugee status and it is the examiner's responsibility to evaluate such statements in the light of all the circumstances of the case."[181]

- **Practice Pointer**: It is imperative that practitioners work with their clients to make sure that the circumstances surrounding any false statements and any explanations related to fear of persecution or authority figures are adequately explained in the record.

An applicant's statements do not have to be clearly false, nor do they need to be deceitful for an adjudicator to make an adverse credibility finding, as long as the adjudicator's finding is supported by specific, cogent reasons.[182] However, even

---

[176] *Kabba v. Mukasey*, 530 F.3d 1239, 1246 (10th Cir. 2008).

[177] *Rodriguez-Galicia v. Gonzales*, 422 F.3d 529 (7th Cir. 2005) (reversing the Board of Immigration Appeals and finding the applicant credible notwithstanding a failure to recount claim at initial interview due to a fear of return to persecution and ignorance of the U.S. asylum process); *Ramsameachire v. Ashcroft*, 357 F.3d 169 (2d Cir. 2004); *Latifi v. Gonzales*, 430 F.3d 103 (2d Cir. 2005).

[178] *Singh v. Mukasey*, 553 F.3d 207, 212–14 (2d Cir. 2009). *See also Singh v. Holder*, 638 F.3d 1264, 1271 (9th Cir. 2011) (holding that a deception unrelated to escaping immediate danger or gaining entry into the United States can form the basis for an adverse credibility determination, even if it turns out to be irrelevant to the claim).

[179] *Rodriguez Galicia v. Gonzales*, 422 F.3d 529, 536–38 (7th Cir. 2005). *See also Kaur v. Ashcroft*, 379 F.3d 876, 889 (9th Cir. 2004) (finding that lies to border officials and presentation of a false passport do not reflect on credibility because they "are entirely consistent with her asylum claim"); *Yongo v. INS*, 355 F3d 27, 33 (1st Cir. 2004); *Balasubramanrim v. INS*, 143 F.3d 157, 164 (3d Cir. 1998).

[180] UNHCR Handbook, *supra* note 43, ¶ 198.

[181] UNHCR Handbook, *supra* note 43, ¶ 199. *See also Garrovillas v. INS*, 156 F.3d 1010, 1073 (9th Cir. 1998).

[182] *See, e.g., Liu v. Holder*, 714 F.3d 56 (1st Cir. 2013) (upholding the IJ's finding that Liu lacked credibility, noting that the applicant made several amendments to his asylum application only after a change in law that would have affected his claim); *Seng v. Holder*, 584 F.3d 13, 19 (1st Cir. 2009)

Continued

where an applicant lies in one part of the claim, the adjudicator may give weight to parts of the testimony found to be credible and approve the claim based on those parts.

4. *Other Relevant Factors — Mental Health of the Applicant*

Many individuals who are seeking asylum, withholding of removal, and CAT relief in the United States have faced physical harm, extreme mental suffering or cruelty, acts of torture, and other forms of severe persecution, such as rape and forced abortion. Many others have been witnesses to such acts. As such, many applicants may suffer from Post-Traumatic Stress Disorder (PTSD) or other trauma-related disorders, and may exhibit signs and symptoms of the same.

PTSD and other mental health issues, such as depression and anxiety, may cause an individual to be reluctant, unwilling, or even unable to share their accounts of persecution. Additionally, the effects and symptoms of mental illnesses may yield inconsistent, contradictory, or confusing statements by the applicant. Moreover, individuals who are suffering from mental health disorders, particularly those triggered by traumatic events, are generally focused on their own survival, rather than their legal status or the need to prepare and file an asylum application. Thus, asylum applicants who are suffering from mental health disorders may be found to lack credibility or their applications may be time-barred.[183]

Courts have reversed adverse credibility findings where the adjudicator failed to recognize the effects of mental health disorders, like PTSD.[184] Therefore, documenting any mental health disorder not only demonstrates some of the real and lasting effects of persecution or torture, but also, it may help to explain any inconsistent statements or testimony, contradictions, omissions, or implausibilities, thus avoiding a negative credibility finding.[185]

- **Practice Pointer**: Practitioners must take special precautions to establish an adequate record of an applicant's mental health disorder. First, have a thorough conversation with the applicant about their mental

(noting that a statement may be untrue due to "lack of knowledge, faulty memory, garbled expression or other reasons notwithstanding the declarants intent to speak the truth"); *Onsongo v. Gonzales*, 457 F.3d 849, 854 (8th Cir. 2006) (finding that the adverse credibility finding was supported by substantial evidence even though the IJ did not determine the applicant's statements to be "clearly false").

[183] *Nwaokole v. INS*, 314 F.3d 303, 309 (7th Cir. 2002).

[184] *See, e.g., Fiadjoe v. Att'y Gen.*, 411 F.3d 135, 149–60 (3d Cir. 2005) (reversing the adverse credibility finding for a woman from Ghana who had been repeatedly physically and sexually abused by her father).

[185] The BIA has held that noncitizens in removal proceedings are presumed to be competent, and if there are no indicia of incompetency in a case, no further inquiry regarding competency is required. *Matter of M–A–M–*, 25 I&N Dec. 474 (BIA 2011). Moreover, if a mental health disorder was the cause for the applicant's delay in filing his or her asylum application, an adequate explanation on the record may enable him or her to fall within one of the exceptions to the one-year filing deadline. 8 CFR §§208.4(a)(5)(i), 1208.4(a)(5)(i) (2014).

state at the time they gave prior testimony, as well as how they are feeling currently. While practitioners may not be qualified to diagnose an individual with a mental health issue, such conversations may raise awareness of an applicant's need to see a mental health professional. Second, prepare affidavits of the applicant and any individuals who are aware of his or her mental health issues to verify the existence of a mental health issue and to explain what symptoms have been observed, when the symptoms began, and the effects that those symptoms have had on the applicant's ability to function normally. Third, have the applicant undergo a detailed evaluation by a mental health professional who is qualified to diagnose mental health issues, such as PTSD or other trauma-related disorders. Fourth, obtain an affidavit from that professional to explain the diagnosis, symptoms, treatment, and effects of the disorder on the applicant's ability to function normally. Fifth, if the mental health professional is available to provide in-court testimony, prepare him or her for giving effective testimony before an IJ. If they are not able to provide testimony in court, ask them if they are able to provide telephonic testimony, and then file a Motion for Telephonic Testimony. Finally, practitioners should do their own research of the mental health disorder with which the applicant has been diagnosed. Submit objective information about the disorder that can help explain any inconsistent testimony or other potential credibility issues.[186]

5. *Other Relevant Factors — Cultural Differences*

Just as mental health professionals can be helpful in explaining the reasons for an applicant's inconsistent or vague testimony, other experts also can be extremely effective in addressing potential credibility issues. Besides educating an adjudicator on current social, economic, or political conditions in a particular country,[187] witnesses who are experts on the conditions in the asylum applicant's home country can be useful in assisting an adjudicator in understanding cultural differences, including differences in an applicant's demeanor when speaking, or an applicant's inability to recall dates, times, or specific events.[188] For example, in many cultures, calendars, schedules, dates, and times are not as important as they are in Western

---

[186] Vikram Badrinath, Dree K. Collopy, & Hans Christian Linnartz, *Evidentiary Issues in Asylum Cases*, AILA IMMIGRATION PRACTICE POINTERS (AILA 2013).

[187] *Hernandez-Montiel v. INS*, 225 F.3d 1084, 1089 (9th Cir. 2000) (giving significant weight to professor who testified that some homosexual men are subject to greater abuse in Mexican culture than others and helped establish a particular social group); *Lukwago v. Ashcroft*, 329 F.3d 157, 179 (3d Cir. 2003) (finding expert's testimony to be important and remanding to Board for consideration); *Castaneda-Hernandez v. INS*, 826 F.2d 1526, 1531 (6th Cir. 1987) (reversing Board and holding that expert testimony from three witnesses was more persuasive than State Department report); *Gailius v. INS*, 147 F.3d 34, 36 (1st Cir. 1998).

[188] *Fiadjoe v. Att'y Gen.*, 411 F.3d 135, 159–160 (3d Cir. 2005).

cultures.[189] An expert can assist and clarify to the court that an applicant's inability to remember such details is not based upon evasiveness or deception, but rather, on the unique cultural aspects of the applicant's country.

- **Practice Pointer**: Practitioners should thoroughly review and question applicants as to all statements made in the asylum process, including statements made upon arrival at an airport, sworn statements taken by immigration inspectors or asylum officers, and formal applications for asylum submitted directly to DHS. Doing so enables practitioners to engage in a more thorough preparation of the applicant before the taking of testimony and to more readily predict potential questions posed by immigration judges and DHS counsel. Practitioners should make note of and discuss each omission, vague testimony or lack of detail, inconsistent statement, or discrepancy in detail with applicants. They should also discuss ways in which these negative factors may be addressed and explained on the record.

- **Practice Pointer**: A Freedom of Information Act (FOIA) request to obtain all available records in connection with the applicant's asylum claim can be a very helpful tool for identifying potential credibility problems. In particular, if a practitioner did not attend an affirmative asylum interview, obtaining an asylum officer's notes recorded during the interview can be essential to identifying and preparing to address potential credibility issues upon referral of the case to an IJ. A recent settlement resulted in asylum officer notes no longer being exempt under the deliberative process privilege exemption of FOIA.[190] USCIS must now produce these notes upon request.

6. *Frivolous Applications*

At the time the applicant files for asylum (if on or after April 1, 1997), the AG is required to notify the applicant of the consequences of knowingly filing a frivolous application.[191] Under the Homeland Security Act of 2002, this responsibility to give notice extends to the DHS secretary and other DHS officials.[192] Several courts have held that the written warning contained in the I-589 Application for Asylum and for

---

[189] *Id.* at 158.

[190] *Martins v. USCIS*, No. C 13-00591 LB, 2013 WL 8284498 (N.D. Cal. July 3, 2013). *See also* David Cleveland, Dree Collopy, & Hilary Han, *Practice Pointer: Challenging the Admission of Asylum Officers' Notes and Assessments as Evidence in Immigration Court*, (July 24, 2013), AILA InfoNet at Doc. No. 13072449, available at *www.aila.org/content/default.aspx?docid=45179.*

[191] INA §208(d)(4)(A); 8 USC §1158(d)(4)(A); *see also* 8 CFR §§208.3(c)(5), 1208.3(c)(5), 1240.11(c)(1)(iii) (regarding DHS and IJ duty to notify).

[192] *See* Homeland Security Act of 2002, Pub. L. No. 107-296, §§456, 1512, 1517, 116 Stat. 2135, 2200, 2310, 2311; *see also* Appx. 2A, I-589 filing instructions (containing the following warning: "Applicants determined to have knowingly made a frivolous application for asylum will be permanently ineligible for any benefits under the [INA].").

Withholding of Removal is sufficient to comply with the statutory and regulatory notice requirements.[193]

An individual who knowingly makes a frivolous asylum application after receiving notice of the consequences of doing so is "permanently ineligible for any benefits under the [INA]."[194] The ineligibility for benefits under the INA is effective as of the date of the final determination on the application.[195] A finding that an applicant filed a frivolous application, however, is not a bar to withholding of removal relief, nor is it a bar to relief under the CAT.[196]

An applicant may be permanently barred from relief only if a final order by an IJ or the BIA specifically finds that the applicant knowingly filed a frivolous application.[197] Depending on the circuit, an application may be found to be frivolous even if it is found to be time-barred[198] and even it is withdrawn before issuance of a final decision.[199]

The regulations provide that an asylum application is "frivolous" if "any of its material elements is deliberately fabricated." A preponderance of the evidence must support the frivolousness finding, and the IJ must give specific and convincing reasons for determining that a preponderance of the evidence supports a frivolousness finding. Additionally, the IJ or the BIA must be "satisfied" that during the course of the proceedings the applicant "has had sufficient opportunity to account for any discrepancies or implausible aspects of the claim." An IJ may not base a frivolous determination on merely an adverse credibility assessment.

- **Practice Pointer**: The knowing placement of false information on an asylum application may also subject the applicant (or the person who placed the information on the application) to criminal and civil penalties.[200]

---

193 *Niang v. Holder*, No. 12-4156 (2d Cir. 2014) (finding that the written warning on the I-589 application was adequate notice of the consequences of filing a frivolous asylum application); *Ruga v. Att'y Gen.*, 757 F.3d 1193 (11th Cir. 2014) (same); *Pavlov v. Holder*, 697 F.3d 616 (7th Cir. 2012) (finding that the written advisals provided on the I-589 are sufficient notice); *Cheema v. Holder*, 693 F.3d 1045 (9th Cir. 2012) (same); *Ribas v. Mukasey*, 545 F.3d 922, 928 (10th Cir. 2008) (same).

194 INA §208(d)(6); 8 CFR §§208.3(c)(5), 1208.3(c)(5).

195 INA §208(d)(6); 8 USC §1158(d)(6).

196 8 CFR §§208.20, 1208.20.

197 8 CFR §§208.20, 1208.20.

198 *See Ghazali v. Holder*, 585 F.3d 289 (6th Cir. 2009) (finding time-barred application could be basis for frivolous finding); *Mingkid v. Att'y Gen.*, 468 F.3d 763, 768 (11th Cir. 2006) (same). *But see Luciana v. Att'y Gen.*, 502 F.3d 273, 280 (3d Cir. 2007) (finding that false statements in a time-barred application are not material and cannot form a basis for a frivolousness finding).

199 *Kulakchyan v. Holder*, 730 F.3d 993, 996 (9th Cir. 2013); *Zheng v. Holder*, 672 F.3d 178 (2d Cir. 2012); *Lazar v. Gonzales*, 500 F.3d 469, 476 (6th Cir. 2007); *Barreto-Claro v. Att'y Gen.*, 275 F.3d 1334, 1339 (11th Cir. 2001); *Matter of X–M–C–*, 25 I&N Dec. 322 (BIA 2010).

200 8 CFR §§208.3(c)(4), 1208.3(c)(4).

The distinction between frivolousness and adverse credibility determinations is a significant one that must be recognized and considered by adjudicators.[201] While adverse credibility may be based on "any inaccuracies or falsehoods … without regard to whether an inconsistency, inaccuracy, or falsehood goes to the heart of the applicant's claim,"[202] a "frivolous" application is one in which "any of its *material* elements is deliberately fabricated."[203] An adverse credibility finding alone cannot support a frivolous finding; rather, the adjudicator must make "specific findings" regarding what information was fabricated.[204] Additionally, the applicant must be given "sufficient opportunity to account for any discrepancies or implausible aspects of the claim."[205]

Therefore, in order the make a frivolous finding, an adjudicator must: (1) provide notice of the consequences of filing a frivolous application; (2) make a specific finding that the applicant knowingly filed a frivolous application; (3) find sufficient evidence in the record to support the finding that a material element of the application was deliberately fabricated; and (4) afford the applicant sufficient opportunity to account for discrepancies or implausible aspects of the claim.[206] Absent any of these requirements, the frivolous finding may not stand. Accordingly, an applicant may challenge a frivolous finding by arguing that:

- He or she did not receive proper notice of the consequences of filing a frivolous application;[207]
- The applicant did not knowingly make a frivolous application or deliberately fabricate an element of the application;[208]

---

[201] *See, e.g., Limbeya v. Holder*, 764 F.3d 894 (8th Cir. 2014) (reversing the finding of frivolousness where the applicant had admitted he misrepresented the name of the person who filled out his application, because the BIA had neglected to distinguish between an adverse credibility finding and a frivolous finding.); *Khadka v. Holder*, 618 F.3d 996 (9th Cir. 2010) (upholding the IJ's adverse credibility determination as supported by substantial evidence, but finding the frivolous determination to be procedurally unsound and not supported by a preponderance of the evidence).

[202] INA §208(b)(1)(B)(iii).

[203] 8 CFR §§208.20, 1208.20 (emphasis added).

[204] *Matter of B–Y–*, 25 I&N Dec. 236, 241 (BIA 2010); *Matter of Y–L–*, 24 I&N Dec. 151, 156 (BIA 2007).

[205] *Matter of B–Y–*, 25 I&N Dec. 236, 241 (BIA 2010). *See also Muhanna v. Gonzales*, 399 F.3d 582 (3d Cir. 2005); *Farah v. Ashcroft*, 348 F.3d 1153, 1158 (9th Cir. 2003).

[206] *Matter of Y–L–*, 24 I&N Dec. 151 (BIA 2007) (establishing the framework for frivolous findings).

[207] *See* INA §208(d)(6); 8 CFR §§208.3(c)(5), 1208.3(c)(5). *But see Niang v. Holder*, No. 12-4156 (2d Cir. 2014) (finding that the written warning on the I-589 application was adequate notice of the consequences of filing a frivolous asylum application); *Ruga v. Att'y Gen.*, 757 F.3d 1193 (11th Cir. 2014) (same); *Albu v. Holder*, No. 13-2864 (7th Cir. 2014) (finding adequate notice where the interpreter at the asylum interview adequately translated the warnings at the interview); *Pavlov v. Holder*, 697 F.3d 616 (7th Cir. 2012) (finding that the written advisals provided on the I-589 are sufficient notice); *Cheema v. Holder*, 693 F.3d 1045 (9th Cir. 2012) (same); *Ribas v. Mukasey*, 545 F.3d 922, 928 (10th Cir. 2008) (same).

- The allegedly fabricated facts or elements of the application are not material;[209] or
- The applicant did not have the opportunity to explain or address discrepancies or implausibilities.[210]

  > **Practice Pointer**: If an applicant wishes to challenge a frivolous finding, he or she may file a motion to reopen to seek reconsideration or review of the frivolous finding.[211] See chapter 11 for a detailed discussion of motions to reopen.

Frivolous findings are reviewed *de novo*.[212] Examples of cases where the courts have reversed or called into question the agency's frivolous finding include:

- Where the applicant timely retracted his false testimony;[213] and
- Where the applicant misrepresented the name of the person who filled out his application, but there was no specific explanation regarding how that misrepresented fact was material.[214]

On the other hand, examples of cases where the courts have upheld the agency's frivolous finding include:

- Where the applicant had multiple opportunities to retract his fraudulent applications and only did so on cross-examination; his attorney's advice that he should lie was not a valid defense to frivolousness;[215]
- Where the Iraqi applicant submitted her application under a false name under instructions from her husband;[216]

---

[208] *See* INA §208(d)(6); 8 CFR §§208.3(c)(5), 208.20, 1208.3(c)(5), 1208.20.

[209] *See* 8 CFR §§208.20, 1208.20.

[210] *See Matter of B–Y–*, 25 I&N Dec. 236, 241 (BIA 2010). *See also, Muhanna v. Gonzales*, 399 F.3d 582 (3d Cir. 2005); *Farah v. Ashcroft*, 348 F.3d 1153, 1158 (9th Cir. 2003).

[211] *See, e.g., Zhang v. Holder*, 617 F.3d 650, 665–69 (2d Cir. 2010); *Verano-Velasco v. Att'y Gen.*, 456 F.3d 1372, 1377 (11th Cir. 2006). *But see, e.g., Ribas v. Mukasey*, 545 F.3d 922, 931 (10th Cir. 2008); *Tchuinga v. Gonzales*, 454 F.3d 54, 60–61 (1st Cir. 2006).

[212] *See, e.g., Mingkid v. Att'y Gen.*, 468 F.3d 763, 769 (11th Cir. 2006).

[213] *See, e.g., Ruiz Del Cid v. Holder*, No. 13-3663 (6th Cir. 2014) (finding that even though the retraction of false testimony was four years after the asylum interview, the retraction was timely because it was the first opportunity that the applicant had to testify after the asylum interview and there was no evidence that his lie would have ever been exposed otherwise). *But see Matter of X–M–C–*, 25 I&N Dec. 322, 326 (BIA 2010) (finding that a frivolous finding was not mitigated by the applicant's subsequent recantation); *Barreto-Claro v. Att'y Gen.*, 275 F.3d 1334, 1337–39 & n.8 (11th Cir. 2001) (same).

[214] *See, e.g., Limbeya v. Holder*, 764 F.3d 894 (8th Cir. 2014) (reversing the finding of frivolousness where the applicant had admitted he misrepresented the name of the person who filled out his application, because the BIA had neglected to distinguish between an adverse credibility finding and a frivolous finding.).

[215] *Lazar v. Gonzales*, 500 F.3d 469 (6th Cir. 2007).

[216] *Aziz v. Gonzales*, 478 F.3d 854, 857–58 (8th Cir. 2007).

- Where the applicant shared details about being punished by Albanian authorities for the first time in his testimony and did not include that incident in his 1991 or 1997 applications;[217]
- Where an Ethiopian applicant filed a false application, swore to its truth, failed to modify it when given the opportunity, lied during her testimony, and then admitted to the falsity of her testimony and application;[218]
- Where the Cuban applicant materially misrepresented his status in a third country, despite the fact that he later recanted;[219] and
- Where fraudulent documents were submitted.[220]

B. Corroboration

The credible, persuasive, and specific testimony of an asylum applicant, standing alone, may be sufficient evidence to grant asylum.[221] This is because the nature of a refugee's circumstances may make it impossible for him or her to provide corroboration of his or her claim.[222] As Congress explained:

> Many aliens validly seeking asylum arrive in the United States with little or no evidence to corroborate their claims. This clause recognizes that a lack of extrinsic or corroborating evidence will not necessarily defeat an asylum claim where such evidence is not reasonably available to the applicant.[223]

However, even if an applicant's testimony is found credible by the adjudicator, such a finding is not necessarily dispositive.[224] Rather, for cases filed on or after May 11, 2005, the REAL ID Act allows an adjudicator to require corroborating evidence in support of an applicant's testimony in order to meet the applicant's burden of proof, "unless the applicant does not have the evidence and cannot reasonably obtain the evidence."[225] Supporting or corroborating evidence regarding an applicant's claim,

---

[217] *Ceraj v. Mukasey*, 511 F.3d 583, 588–91 (6th Cir. 2007).

[218] *Kifleyesus v. Gonzales*, 462 F.3d 937, 944–45 (8th Cir. 2006).

[219] *Barreto-Claro v. Att'y Gen.*, 275 F.3d 1334, 1337–39 & n.8 (11th Cir. 2001).

[220] *Sterkaj v. Gonzales*, 439 F.3d 273, 278–79 (6th Cir. 2006); *Selami v. Gonzales*, 423 F.3d 621, 624–26 (6th Cir. 2005); *Ignatova v. Gonzales*, 430 F.3d 1209, 1214–15 (8th Cir. 2005); *Fongwo v. Gonzales*, 430 F.3d 944, 947–49 (8th Cir. 2005).

[221] INA §208(b)(1)(B)(ii); 8 CFR §208.13(a), 1208.13(a) (2014). *See Matter of S–M–J–*, 21 I&N Dec. 722 (BIA 1997); *Matter of B–*, 21 I&N Dec. 66 (BIA 1995).

[222] *See Senathirajah v. INS*, 157 F.3d 210, 216 (3d Cir. 1998) ("Common sense establishes that it is escape and flight, not litigation and corroboration, that is foremost in the mind of an alien who comes to these shores fleeing detention, torture and persecution.").

[223] H.R. Rep. No. 109–72, at 165 (2005) (Conf. Rep.).

[224] *Matter of E–P–*, 21 I&N Dec. 860, 863 (BIA 1997) (finding that although the applicant's testimony was credible, the content of her testimony and the relevant evidence of record were not sufficient to meet her burden of proof).

[225] INA §208(b)(1)(B)(ii).

therefore, is an essential component of every asylum application. Some courts have even relied on lack of corroboration to make an adverse credibility finding.[226]

Corroborating evidence may be presented in the form of any or all of the following:[227]

- Identity documents and other official government documents;
- Privately-issued membership cards or other affiliation documents;[228]
- Affidavits from the applicant's family, friends, neighbors, or community members confirming his or her protected characteristic;
- Photographs of the applicant participating in various events;
- Letters from organizations of which the applicant is a member or affiliate;
- Objective, published descriptions of the characteristics or attributes, which designate members of the applicant's race, religion, nationality, political affiliation, or social group;
- Photographs of the applicant's injuries;
- Police reports recording the harm suffered or threatened;
- Arrest warrants or records, if the applicant was ever arrested due to his or her protected characteristic;[229]
- Affidavits from witnesses who were present during the act(s) of harm or mistreatment;
- Affidavits from individuals whom the applicant confided in about the incident(s), confirming any observed physical or psychological harm, such as markings on the applicant's body, torn clothes, injuries, crying, anxiety, or other unusual behaviors;

---

[226] *See supra* pt. III.A. for a detailed discussion of credibility findings. *See also, e.g., Carrizo v. Att'y Gen.*, 652 F.3d 1326 (11th Cir. 2011) (upholding the adverse credibility finding where the applicant claimed to be present at a rally where his mother was killed but presented no evidence that he was politically active, at the rally, or detained and beaten after); *Singh v. Holder*, 638 F.3d 1264, 1271 (9th Cir. 2011) (finding that where the IJ has reason in the record to doubt credibility, an absence of evidence may suffice to reject credibility where the need for the evidence is plain and the evidence is reasonably accessible).

[227] Vikram Badrinath, Dree K. Collopy, & Hans Christian Linnartz, *Evidentiary Issues in Asylum Cases*, AILA IMMIGRATION PRACTICE POINTERS (AILA 2013).

[228] *See, e.g., Camara v. Ashcroft*, 378 F.3d 361, 370–71 (4th Cir. 2004) (finding that the IJ erred by failing to consider independent evidence of persecution: *inter alia*, a notice of escape, a political party membership card, an arrest warrant, and DOS reports corroborating the applicant's claim).

[229] *See, e.g., Camara v. Ashcroft*, 378 F.3d 361, 370–71 (4th Cir. 2004) (finding that the IJ erred by failing to consider independent evidence of persecution: *inter alia*, a notice of escape, a political party membership card, an arrest warrant, and DOS reports corroborating the applicant's claim).

- Medical records, including evaluations of physical injuries and the likely cause of those injuries, letters from treating doctors, treatment reports, hospital admission records, or prescribed medications;
- Mental health records, including evaluations of mental health disorders and the likely trigger for those disorders, letters from treating mental health professionals, appointment records, or prescribed medications;
- Death certificates for the applicant's relatives, friends, neighbors, or community members who were targeted because of a qualifying characteristic;
- Newspaper or other media coverage, or coverage by human rights groups, of the incident(s) in which the applicant was involved;
- Evidence that the applicant attempted to supply certain corroborating documentation, but was unable to;
- I-94 card, visa, and stamped passport (even if false);
- Evidence of means of travel to the United States, including airline itineraries, bus tickets, or hotel receipts;
- Evidence of presence outside of the United States in the past year, including financial, medical, school, or work records;
- Affidavits from individuals who have personal knowledge of the applicant's arrival in the United States;
- Expert report regarding the conditions in the applicant's home country as they relate to the applicant's claims and assessing the applicant's risk of harm upon return;[230] and
- Country conditions reports and articles showing the conditions in the applicant's home country during the time of persecution and presently, including human rights reports from the U.S. Department of State, Amnesty International, Human Rights Watch, or other reputable organizations.[231]

Under the REAL ID Act of 2005, "[w]here the trier of fact determines that an applicant should provide evidence that corroborates otherwise credible testimony, such evidence must be provided unless the applicant does not have the evidence and

[230] *See, e.g.*, *Niam v. Ashcroft*, 354 F.3d 652, 658 (7th Cir. 2004) (noting that the scholar proffered by the applicant should have been considered an expert and that it was error for the IJ to refuse to allow her to testify telephonically from overseas).

[231] *See* 8 CFR §§208.12(a), 1208.12(a) (2014) (providing that adjudicators may rely on "other credible sources" for information on country conditions, such as international organizations, private voluntary agencies, news organizations, or academic institutions). *See, e.g.*, *Camara v. Ashcroft*, 378 F.3d 361, 370–71 (4th Cir. 2004) (finding that the IJ erred by failing to consider independent evidence of persecution: *inter alia*, a notice of escape, a political party membership card, an arrest warrant, and DOS reports corroborating the applicant's claim).

cannot reasonably obtain the evidence."[232] Thus, an applicant should provide "supporting evidence, both of general conditions and of the specific facts sought to be relied upon by the applicant, where such evidence is available," and where it is reasonable to expect such corroborating evidence.[233] In addition to documents related specifically to the asylum claim, an applicant is also expected to provide, if available, general corroborating evidence of persecution of similarly situated individuals.[234] Where such evidence is not available, the applicant must provide an explanation of why that evidence is unavailable.[235] An applicant is not, however, required to produce corroborating evidence that he or she could not reasonably obtain.[236]

In *Ren v. Holder*, the Ninth Circuit U.S. Court of Appeals described the criteria for requiring corroborating evidence under the REAL ID Act standards. The court set forth the following test:

(1) The IJ must determine whether an applicant's credible testimony alone meets his or her burden of proof;

(2) If it does, no corroborating evidence in necessary;

---

[232] INA §§208(b)(1)(B)(ii), 240(c)(4). A similar provision exists for withholding of removal claims. *See* INA §241(b)(3)(C). In addressing the REAL ID Act's amendment to the corroboration requirements for asylum, withholding, and CAT claims, the Seventh Circuit has stated in dicta that "[i]t is possible that the change is less than meets the eye, since now there is no dispute about the appropriateness of asking for corroboration in the common situation when the IJ has some doubt about an applicant's credibility." *Dawoud v. Gonzales*, 424 F.3d 608, 613 (7th Cir. 2005).

[233] *Matter of S–M–J–*, 21 I&N Dec. 722, 724–25 (BIA 1997).

[234] *Matter of S–M–J–*, at 726. An example provided by the BIA of corroboration regarding similarly situated individuals is that of a union vice-president who would be expected to provide documentation regarding the persecution of union members in her home country. *Id. But see Abankwah v. INS*, 185 F.3d 18 (2d Cir. 1999) (finding that the BIA was too exacting in the quantity and quality of evidence that it required); *Duarte de Guinac v. INS*, 179 F.3d 1156, 1162 (9th Cir. 1999) (criticizing the BIA for concluding that reports of widespread racial discrimination against Indians in Guatemala did not support the applicant's claim, where country condition reports could not corroborate specific acts of persecution). Similarly, the asylum applicant in *Singh v. Ilchert* presented documents regarding widespread and arbitrary arrest, detention, and abuse of persons suspected of affiliation with separatists and, thereby, demonstrated the reasonableness of his assertion that his persecution was on account of a political opinion imputed to him. *Singh v. Ilchert*, 63 F.3d 1501, 1511–12 (9th Cir. 1995). *See also Matter of S–P–*, 21 I&N Dec. 486 (BIA 1996) (relying on a DOS report regarding conditions in Sri Lanka in finding that the applicant was persecuted on account of imputed political opinion).

[235] *Matter of O–D–*, 21 I&N Dec. 1079, 1081 (BIA 1998), *vacated on other grounds by Hanaj v. Gonzales*, 446 F.3d 694, 700 (7th Cir. 2006); *Matter of S–M–J–*, 21 I&N Dec. 722, 724 (BIA 1997). *See also Salaam v. INS*, 229 F.3d 1234, 1239 (9th Cir. 2000) (finding that the applicant provided a reasonable explanation for the absence of documents, including his haste in fleeing the country and the danger in carrying documents critical of the Nigerian government).

[236] INA §§208(b)(1)(B)(ii), 240(c)(4), 241(b)(3)(C). *See also, Soeung v. Holder*, 677 F.3d 484, 488 (1st Cir. 2012); *Yan Juan Chen v. Holder*, 658 F.3d 246 (2d Cir. 2011) (finding that it was reasonable to expect the undocumented husband to testify in his wife's case, despite his fear of arrest); *San Kai Kwok v. Gonzales*, 455 F.3d 766, 771 (7th Cir. 2006).

(3) If the applicant's burden of proof has not yet been met, the IJ may require corroborating evidence; and

(4) If corroborating evidence is needed, the IJ must give the applicant notice that such evidence is required and an opportunity to produce the evidence or explain why it is not reasonably available.[237]

Although cases filed before May 11, 2005, were evaluated on a less demanding standard, the BIA had consistently held applicants to a duty of corroboration where corroborating evidence ought to be available.[238] Generally, the BIA maintained that in cases in which an applicant's claim is based primarily on personal experiences not reasonably subject to verification, corroborating documentary evidence of the applicant's particular experiences is not required.[239] Where, however, it is reasonable to expect corroborating evidence for certain alleged facts, such evidence should be provided.[240] According to the BIA, an applicant should be expected to provide easily obtainable documentary evidence such as evidence of his or her place of birth, media accounts of large demonstrations, evidence of publicly held office, or documentation of medical treatment.[241]

In its seminal case, *Matter of S–M–J–*, the BIA held that a Liberian asylum applicant had failed to meet her burden of proof where she did not provide any background information about country conditions in Liberia and did not explain whether such evidence was unavailable. As a result, there was no evidence of record to establish that the asylum applicant's tribe existed, or why anyone associated with an individual known as "Prince Anderson" would be targeted for persecution.[242]

Prior to the REAL ID Act of 2005, circuits had split over this corroboration requirement.[243] However, the REAL ID Act of 2005 seemed to codify the BIA's

---

[237] *Ren v. Holder*, 648 F.3d 1079, 1090–94 (9th Cir. 2011).

[238] *Matter of S–M–J–*, 21 I&N Dec. 722, 724 (BIA 1997).

[239] *Matter of S–M–J–*, 21 I&N Dec. 722, at 725.

[240] *Id.*; *see also Eta-Ndu v. Gonzales*, 411 F.3d 977, 984 (8th Cir. 2005) (finding that "the IJ and BIA may require corroborative evidence 'where it is reasonable to expect corroboration'") (internal quotation omitted).

[241] *Matter of S–M–J–*, at 725.

[242] *Matter of S–M–J–*, at 730. Note, however, that the BIA remanded the case to the IJ because the IJ relied on information not included in the record regarding conditions in Liberia and because the DOS report submitted as part of the record related to Zaire and not Liberia. *Id. See also Shan Liao v. U.S. Dep't. of Justice*, 293 F.3d 61 (2d Cir. 2002) (finding that the general background information in the case did not support the applicant's claim that he would be harmed upon return); *Matter of B–B–*, 22 I&N Dec. 309, 311 (BIA 1998) (in denying the respondent's motion to reopen to apply for asylum, the BIA found that previous counsel's insistence on corroborating evidence did not amount to egregious conduct or ineffective assistance of counsel); *Matter of V–T–S–*, 21 I&N Dec. 792, 797 (BIA 1997) (finding that an asylum applicant's failure to provide corroborating evidence, when such corroboration was available to him, weakened the persuasiveness of his testimony).

[243] *Compare El-Sheikh v. Ashcroft*, 388 F.3d 643, 647 (8th Cir. 2004), *Abdulai v. Ashcroft*, 239 F.3d 542 (3d Cir. 2001), *and Diallo v. INS*, 232 F.3d 279 (2d Cir. 2000) *with Zheng v. Gonzales*, 409 F.3d

Continued

position that although an asylum applicant's own testimony alone may be sufficient to sustain his or her burden of proof, an applicant should provide "supporting evidence, both of general conditions and of the specific facts sought to be relied on by the applicant, where such evidence is available."[244] If such evidence is unavailable, the applicant is required to provide an explanation of why it is unavailable.[245] The IJ must ensure that the applicant's explanation is included in the record.[246]

In *Matter of S–M–J–*, the BIA also acknowledged the roles of the IJ and trial attorneys in introducing country conditions evidence. The role of the trial attorney, according to the BIA, is to uphold international refugee law and to ensure that justice is done.[247] The BIA further stated that it expects the trial attorney "to introduce into evidence current country reports, advisory opinions, or other information readily available from the Resource Information Center."[248] With regard to IJs, the BIA held that they should state for the record how the testimony comports with background information and, if no such background information is part of the record, they must explain how the testimony was assessed without such information.[249] The BIA concluded that IJs have the authority to introduce evidence regarding country conditions and that both UNHCR's Handbook and the *Basic Law Manual* recommend the introduction of evidence by the adjudicator.[250]

The BIA has taken the position that these corroboration requirements are consistent with UNHCR's Handbook, which provides that an "applicant's statements cannot, however, be considered in the abstract, and must be viewed in the context of

---

804 (7th Cir. 2005), *Sidhu v. INS*, 220 F.3d 1085 (9th Cir. 2000), *and Ladha v. INS*, 215 F.3d 889 (9th Cir. 2000).

[244] *Matter of S–M–J–* at 724; *Matter of M–D–*, 21 I&N Dec. 1180, 1182–83 (BIA 1998), *reversed by Diallo v. INS*, 232 F.3d 279 (2d Cir. 2000) (holding BIA misapplied its corroboration standard by failing to rule on credibility of applicant's testimony); *Matter of S–P–*, 21 I&N Dec. 486 (BIA 1996); *Matter of Dass*, 20 I&N Dec. 120, 124 (BIA 1989). The BIA has held that the weaker an applicant's testimony, the greater the need for corroborative evidence. *Matter of Y–B–*, 21 I&N Dec. 1136, 1139 (BIA 1998).

[245] *Matter of O–D–*, 21 I&N Dec. 1079, 1081 (BIA 1998), *vacated on other grounds by Hanaj v. Gonzales*, 446 F.3d 694, 700 (7th Cir. 2006); *Matter of S–M–J–*, 21 I&N Dec., at 724; *see also Salaam v. INS*, 229 F.3d 1234, 1239 (9th Cir. 2000) (finding that the applicant provided a reasonable explanation for the absence of documents, including his haste in fleeing the country and the danger in carrying documents critical of the Nigerian government).

[246] *Matter of S–M–J–*, 21 I&N Dec., at 724.

[247] *Id.* at 727.

[248] *Id.* The Asylum Resource Information Center is a part of USCIS and posts country condition information on its website at *www.uscis.gov* ("Education and Resources" tab; then "Asylum Resources" hyperlink); *see also Matter of Fuentes*, 19 I&N Dec. 658, 662 (BIA 1988).

[249] *Matter of S–M–J–*, 21 I&N Dec., at 729–30.

[250] *Id.* at 729; *see also Secaida-Rosales v. INS*, 331 F.3d 297, 306 (2d Cir. 2003) (the IJ has an affirmative obligation to help establish and develop the record), *overruled on other grounds by Xiu Xia Lin v. Mukasey*, 534 F.3d 162 (2d Cir. 2008). *But see* INA §240(b); 8 USC §1229a(b) (2012), which no longer provides that IJs may "present" evidence.

the relevant background situation."[251] Courts, however, have continued to be critical of IJs and the BIA for placing unrealistic demands on asylum applicants, finding that in the circumstances of some cases it is unreasonable to expect an applicant to provide corroborating documentation.[252] Some courts have criticized IJs for the types of corroboration they have expected from applicants. For example, one court criticized an IJ's adverse credibility determination that was based on the fact that the applicant did not see a doctor after she was raped and, therefore, did not have a doctor's report.[253] The court noted that in many parts of the world, a young woman's report of rape is likely to bring shame and discredit upon her and her family.[254] In another case before the Second Circuit, the court found that the BIA erroneously required the applicant, who claimed he was a stateless Tibetan born in Nepal, to prove his nationality through documentary evidence alone.[255] In that case, the IJ had made an adverse credibility finding and the Second Circuit remanded with instructions for the BIA to review that finding.

The Third Circuit U.S. Court of Appeals established the following "three-part inquiry" to determine whether the IJ or BIA properly applied the rule in *S–M–J–*,[256] requiring corroborating evidence in certain circumstances following the amendments by the REAL ID Act. The Third Circuit asked whether the IJ or BIA made: (1) "an identification of facts for which it is reasonable to expect corroboration;" (2) an inquiry as to whether the applicant has provided information corroborating those facts; and if not, (3) an analysis of whether an applicant has adequately explained why he or she was unable to do so.[257] The Third Circuit has held that the REAL ID Act has not changed this required test.[258]

---

[251] *Matter of S–M–J–*, 21 I&N Dec., at 729 (citing UNHCR Handbook, ¶ 42); *see also Wiransane v. Ashcroft*, 366 F.3d 889, 898 (10th Cir. 2004) (finding that IJ erred by rejecting claim of Indonesian applicant because he failed to provide documentation that he was ethnically Chinese).

[252] *See, e.g., Hor v. Gonzales*, 421 F.3d 497, 501 (7th Cir. 2005) ("the notion that documentation is as regular, multicopied, and ubiquitous in disordered nations as in the United States … is unrealistic"); *Gjerazi v. Gonzales*, 435 F.3d 800, 809 (7th Cir. 2006) (finding that "it seems illogical to require a family fleeing a country to take precious time to search for and collect documents"); *Kabamba v. Gonzales*, 162 Fed. Appx. 337, 341 (5th Cir. 2006) (finding that given the country conditions in the Democratic Republic of Congo, it was unreasonable to require the applicant to provide further corroborating documents of her husband's political party affiliation).

[253] *Yan Xia Zhu v. Mukasey*, 537 F.3d 1034, 1039 (9th Cir. 2008).

[254] *Id.* at 1046 (Gould, J., concurring). *See also Maryenka v. Holder*, 592 F.3d 594, 601 (4th Cir. 2010) (noting that many victims do not report rape to the police or seek medical attention, and therefore, they may not have police or medical reports).

[255] *Urgen v. Holder*, 768 F.3d 269 (2d Cir. 2014).

[256] *Matter of S–M–J–*, 21 I&N Dec. 722, 725 (BIA 1997).

[257] *Toure v. Att'y Gen.*, 443 F.3d 310, 323 (3d Cir. 2006); *see also Mulanga v. Ashcroft*, 349 F.3d 123, 135–36 (3d Cir. 2003) (reversing the IJ's determination that the applicant failed to adequately corroborate her claim because the IJ failed to explain what corroborating evidence would be reasonably expected and failed to provide the applicant with an opportunity to explain its absence); *Bellido v.*

Continued

An IJ cannot deny a claim based on lack of adequate corroboration if he or she never provided notice of the deficiency to the applicant and an opportunity for the applicant to produce the evidence or explain why it is unavailable.[259] However, where an IJ made a finding that the applicant was not credible, there may not be a need to provide notice to the applicant that he or she should have submitted corroborating evidence.[260]

If an IJ determines that an applicant should have provided corroborating evidence, that ruling is a finding of fact. "No court shall reverse a determination made by a trier of fact with respect to the availability of corroborating evidence … unless the court finds … that a reasonable trier of fact is compelled to conclude that such corroborating evidence is unavailable."[261]

> ➢ **Practice Pointer**: These requirements make it imperative for applicants to seek out and present corroboration wherever possible and to document any difficulties in obtaining corroboration. If an applicant is unable to corroborate a claim, then this fact, in and of itself, should be properly documented, including what efforts, if any, the applicant has undertaken to obtain corroboration. If the need for corroborating evidence arises unexpectedly during a hearing, practitioners should move for adjournment or a continuance to allow for sufficient time to obtain the needed evidence.[262]

1. Evidence Specific to the Applicant

Evidence specific to the applicant may be in the form of documentation or testimony of witnesses. The BIA has outlined the standard for determining when corroborating evidence is required to support the specific facts of an applicant's claim, stating:

> [If] an applicant's claim relies primarily on personal experiences not reasonably subject to verification, corroborating documentary evidence of the asylum applicant's particular experience is not required. Unreasonable

---

Ashcroft, 367 F.3d 840, 844 (8th Cir. 2004) (noting the difficulty applicants have in obtaining documentation and holding "this should never serve to close the door on a grant of asylum").

[258] *Toure*, at 325 (interpreting INA §242(b)(4); 8 U.S.C. §1252(b)(4) (2012) , as amended by the REAL ID Act of 2005).

[259] *Oshodi v. Holder,* 729 F.3d 883, 912 (9th Cir. 2013); *Ren v. Holder*, 648 F.3d 1079, 1093 (9th Cir. 2011); *Qui v. Ashcroft*, 329 F.3d 140, 153–54 (2d Cir. 2003); *Paramasamy v. Ashcroft*, 295 F.3d 1047, 1054 (9th Cir. 2002).

[260] *Guta-Tolossa v. Holder*, 674 F.3d 57, 62–64 (1st Cir. 2012); *Abraham v. Holder,* 647 F.3d 624, 632–34 (7th Cir. 2011).

[261] INA §242(b)(4); 8 U.S.C. §1252(b)(4) (2012). *See infra* chapters 11 and 12 for detailed discussions of administrative and judicial review of IJ determinations regarding corroboration.

[262] *See Mulanga v. Ashcroft*, 349 F.3d 123, 135–36 (3rd Cir. 2003); *Poradisova v. Gonzales*, 420 F.3d 70, 79 (2nd Cir. 2005).

demands are not placed on an asylum applicant to present evidence to corroborate particular experiences (*e.g.*, corroboration from the persecutor). However, where it is reasonable to expect corroborating evidence for certain alleged facts pertaining to the specifics of an applicant's claim, such evidence should be provided.[263]

The BIA continued, stating, "If the applicant does not provide such information, an explanation should be given as to why such information was not presented … . The absence of such corroborating evidence can lead to a finding that an applicant has failed to meet [his or] her burden of proof."[264]

In determining whether an applicant should provide corroboration of otherwise credible testimony, the request must be reasonable.[265] The requested evidence "should provide documentary support for *material facts* which are central to [the applicant's] claim and easily subject to verification, such as evidence of his or her place of birth, media accounts of large demonstrations, evidence of publicly held office, or documentation of medical treatment."[266] Regarding specific documentary corroboration of an applicant's particular experiences, the BIA stated that such documentation is not required "unless the supporting documentation is of the type that would normally be created or available in the particular country and is accessible to the [applicant], such as through friends, relatives, or co-workers."[267]

If an adjudicator determines that corroborating evidence should be provided, he or she must: (1) identify the particular or type of document that should be submitted; (2) identify which aspects of the applicant's claim would have been reasonable to corroborate; and (3) explain how the request is reasonable in the particular case.[268] As the Second Circuit explained:

---

[263] *Matter of S–M–J–*, 21 I&N Dec. 722, 725 (BIA 1997). *See also* UNHCR Handbook, *supra* note 43, ¶ 205(a)(ii).

[264] *Matter of S–M–J–*, 21 I&N Dec. 722, 725 (BIA 1997). *See, e.g.*, *Salman v. Holder*, 687 F.3d 991 (8th Cir. 2012) (finding that the applicant failed to establish that the government condoned the harassment directed toward the applicant by private parties, or that it was helpless to protect against it); *Yan Juan Chen v. Holder*, 658 F.3d 246 (2d Cir. 2011) (holding that the applicant's undocumented husband was "available" to testify despite his fear of apprehension, noting that he would have been eligible for derivative asylum status and had every incentive to testify on his wife's behalf).

[265] *Dia v. Ashcroft*, 353 F.3d 228, 253 (3d Cir. 2003) (*en banc*) ("At most, an applicant must provide corroborating evidence only when it would be reasonably expected.").

[266] *Matter of S–M–J–*, 21 I&N Dec. 722, 725 (BIA 1997) (emphasis added). *See also Balogun v. Ashcroft*, 374 F.3d 492, 502–03 (7th Cir. 2004) (citing *Matter of S–M–J–* and emphasizing that corroboration should be required only as to "material facts" and only when the corroborative evidence is reasonably accessible).

[267] *Matter of S–M–J–*, 21 I&N Dec. 722, 726 (BIA 1997).

[268] *Hussain v. Gonzales*, 424 F.3d 622 (7th Cir. 2005); *Dorosh v. Gonzales*, 398 F.3d 379, 382–83 (6th Cir. 2004); *Gontcharova v. Ashcroft*, 384 F.3d 873 (7th Cir. 2004); *El-Sheik v. Ashcroft*, 388 F.3d 643, 647 (8th Cir. 2004); *Alvarado-Carillo v. INS*, 251 F.3d 44, 54 (2d Cir. 2001); *Abdulai v. Ashcroft*, 239 F.3d 542, 554 (3d Cir. 2001).

> What is "reasonably available" differs among societies and, given the widely varied and sometimes terrifying circumstances under which refugees flee their homelands, from one asylum seeker to the next… . [The] requirement that the [adjudicator] back [his or her] demands for corroborative evidence with a reasoned explanation – an explanation that responds to evidence of actual conditions in the asylum-seeker's former country of residence – constitutes one small, but crucial, defense against potentially mistaken, culturally based assumptions about the existence and availability of documents.[269]

Whether or not a request for corroboration is found to be reasonable depends on several factors, including: (1) the conditions in the country or society in question; (2) the circumstances under which the individual fled; (3) the individual characteristics of the applicant, such as age, level of education,[270] physical or mental health; (4) the type of evidence requested;[271] and (5) how much contact the applicant has with family or friends in the home country and those individuals' ability to provide the identified information.[272]

Once a reasonable request for corroboration has been made, the applicant must be provided with the opportunity to submit the requested corroborating evidence.[273] This is because an applicant may not be aware or may not understand which documents are relevant to his or her claim. However, an adjudicator should request additional documentation not already in the applicant's possession in the United States only if

---

[269] *Qiu v. Ashcroft*, 329 F.3d 140, 153–54 (2d Cir. 2003). *See also Balogun v. Ashcroft*, 374 F.3d 492, 502 (7th Cir. 2004).

[270] *Diallo v. INS*, 232 F.3d 279 (2d Cir. 2000) (finding the requested corroboration not to be reasonable, in part, because of the applicant's "functional illiteracy").

[271] *Durgac v. Gonzales*, 2005 WL 3275790 (7th Cir. 2005) (finding the IJ's request for corroboration of the applicant's detention and abuse from the same authorities responsible for the persecution to be unreasonable); *Smolniakova v. Gonzales*, 422 F.3d 1037, 1047 (9th Cir. 2004) (finding the IJ's request for a statement from an unidentified stranger who witnessed an ethnically motivated assault on the applicant not to be reasonable).

[272] *Liti v. Gonzales*, 411 F.3d 631, 640 (6th Cir. 2005) (finding a request for affidavits of family members in Albania and a brother in Greece to be reasonable, where the applicant was in frequent contact with them); *Hussain v. Gonzales*, 424 F.3d 622, 629–30 (7th Cir. 2005) (finding a request for affidavits from family and friends, documentation of involvement in a religious organization in Pakistan, reports to the police, and medical care for injuries sustained to be reasonable where the applicant was in regular contact with family and friends); *Dorosh v. Gonzales*, 398 F.3d 379, 383 (6th Cir. 2004) (finding a request for affidavits from the applicant's mother and friends in Ukraine to be reasonable, where the applicant was in contact with them); *Albathani v. INS*, 318 F.3d 365, 373 (1st Cir. 2003) (finding a request for statements regarding the applicant's claim that Hezbollah had visited his sister's house and threatened him to be reasonable, where the applicant had family members in the United States and elsewhere).

[273] *Poradisova v. Gonzales*, 420 F.3d 70, 79 (2d Cir. 2005); *Mulanga v. Ashcroft*, 349 F.3d 123, 135–36 (3d Cir. 2003) (finding that "the IJ erred by not alerting [the applicant] during the removal proceedings that the absence of corroboration of [her husband's political party] membership would lead to the denial of her application, thereby giving her an opportunity to explain her inability to corroborate"); *Matter of Y–B–*, 21 I&N Dec. 1136, 1139 (BIA 1998).

the adjudicator determines that the documentation is necessary to properly adjudicate the request for asylum.[274]

Before an adjudicator concludes that an applicant has failed to meet his or her burden of proof as a result of a failure to provide reasonably available corroborating evidence, the adjudicator must:

(1) give the applicant the opportunity to explain why the evidence was not submitted;

(2) ensure that the applicant's explanation is included in the record, and

(3) determine whether the explanation for failing to provide the documents is reasonable or not.[275]

Reasonable explanations for failure to provide corroborating documents may include the following:

(1) the documents were not accessible;[276]

(2) the request required obtaining documents from the persecutor;

(3) the documents were lost or destroyed;[277]

(4) inability to communicate with friends and family members;

(5) the applicant's personal circumstances such as poverty, lack of education, or lack of proficiency in English;[278] and

(6) current conditions in the country of feared persecution.[279]

- **Practice Pointer**: Applicants should always document their efforts to obtain corroborating evidence and keep careful records of those efforts in case it ever becomes necessary to provide an explanation to an adjudicator why certain corroborating evidence is unavailable.

2. *Country Conditions Reports and Articles*

An adjudicator is required to evaluate the applicant's claim in light of country conditions.[280] As the BIA stated:

---

[274] *See* INA §208(b)(1)(B)(ii); *Matter of Y–B–*, 21 I&N Dec. 1136 (BIA 1998); *Matter of S–M–J–*, 21 I&N Dec. 722 (BIA 1997).

[275] AOBTC Workbook, pt. IV, *supra* note 2, at 30.

[276] *Secaida-Rosales v. INS*, 331 F.3d 297, 311 (2d Cir. 2003) (finding the explanation reasonable where the documents were in the possession of the applicant's employer).

[277] *Diallo v. INS*, 232 F.3d 279, 289–90 (2d Cir. 2000).

[278] *Secaida-Rosales v. INS*, 331 F.3d 297, 311 (2d Cir. 2003) (finding the explanation reasonable where the applicant was living in a shelter and lacked proficiency in English).

[279] *Soumahoro v. Gonzales*, 415 F.3d 732 (7th Cir. 2005) (finding the explanation reasonable where an intervening civil war had broken out in the applicant's home country).

[280] AOBTC Workbook, pt. IV, *supra* note 2, at 17.

> [W]hen the basis of an asylum claim becomes less focused on specific events involving the [applicant] personally and instead is more directed to broad allegations regarding general conditions in the [applicant's] country of origin, corroborative background evidence that establishes a plausible context for the persecution claim (or an explanation for the absence of such evidence) may well be essential.[281]

In addition to information submitted by the applicant, an asylum officer may consider information from:

- The Department of State;
- USCIS Asylum Division Country of Origin Information researchers;
- The USCIS District Director for the district in which the applicant lives or seeks admission to the United States;
- International organizations;
- Private voluntary agencies;
- Academic institutions; and
- Any other credible source.[282]

In fact, given the context of a non-adversarial affirmative asylum adjudication, asylum officers are instructed to consider general country conditions information that corroborates aspects of the applicant's asylum claim, even if the applicant did not present that material.[283]

Perhaps the most relied-upon source for country conditions information is the Department of State (DOS). Its Bureau of Democracy, Human Rights, and Labor publishes a detailed annual report on human rights practices, as well as annual reports on religious freedom, in each country of the world.[284] Adjudicators also may request specific information from DOS. Adjudicators are not, however, bound by the information or opinions issued by DOS. Rather, they must consider the information along with credible testimony and other available evidence.[285] Moreover, the courts have raised concerns that DOS "soft-pedals human rights violations by countries the

---

[281] *Matter of S–M–J–*, 21 I&N Dec. 722, 724 (BIA 1997) (quoting *Matter of Dass*, 20 I&N Dec. 120, 124 (BIA 1989)).

[282] AOBTC Workbook, pt. IV, *supra* note 2, at 17–18. *See* 8 CFR §§208.12, 1208.12 (2012).

[283] *Yan Chen v. Gonzales*, 417 F.3d 268, 272 (2d Cir. 2005); *Mukamusoni v. Ashcroft*, 390 F.3d 110, 124–25 (1st Cir. 2004); *Zubeda v. Ashcroft*, 333 F.3d 463, 477–78 (3d Cir. 2003).

[284] 8 CFR §§208.11, 1208.11 (2014). *See generally* U.S. Dep't of State, Human Rights Reports, *available at www.state.gov/j/drl/rls/hrrpt/* (last visited Nov. 13, 2014); U.S. Dep't of State, International Religious Freedom Reports, *available at www.state.gov/j/drl/rls/irf/* (last visited Nov. 13, 2014).

[285] INA §208(b)(1)(B)(iii).

United States wants to have good relations with."[286] One court has advised the BIA to treat the DOS reports with "a healthy skepticism" rather than as "Holy Writ."[287] Another court has urged adjudicators not to place undue weight on the DOS country reports because they cannot be expected to capture all details of every abuse in a given country, nor can anti-government groups be expected to monitor all abuses.[288]

- **Practice Pointer**: Other useful sources for country conditions information are the country and topic or issue-specific reports by Human Rights Watch and Amnesty International. These are available at *www.hrw.org/publications* and *www.amnestyusa.org/research*. Newspaper and magazine articles may also be useful sources for corroborating specific events or issues prevalent in the applicants' native countries.

- **Practice Pointer**: Witnesses who are experts on the conditions in the applicant's home country also may be useful in educating an adjudicator on current socioeconomic or political conditions, the objective reasonableness of an applicant's claim, and the contours of a particular social group. Their testimony, in addition to assisting the court in understanding the applicant's fears, can provide important corroboration of events, government policies and practices, common human rights violations, and the inability or unwillingness of the government to control the actions of a particular social group. In particular, in cases involving countries where the systematic persecution of individuals with a certain characteristic is not well-documented, expert testimony can be essential in establishing nexus.[289] The Seventh Circuit has even suggested that the "immigration bureaucracy" needs its own expert, similar to the experts employed by the Social Security Administration.[290]

---

[286] *Gailius v. INS*, 147 F.3d 34, 46 (1st Cir. 1998) (citation omitted); *see also Shah v. INS*, 220 F.3d 1062, 1069–70 (9th Cir. 2000).

[287] *Galina v. INS*, 213 F.3d 955, 959 (7th Cir. 2000); *see also Chen v. INS*, 359 F.3d 121, 130 (2d Cir. 2004) (noting that observations in State Department reports do not automatically discredit contrary evidence presented by the applicant and are not binding on the immigration court); *Niam v. Ashcroft*, 354 F.3d 652, 659 (7th Cir. 2004) (noting that the authors of the DOS reports are anonymous and cannot be cross-examined). *But see Gonahasa v. INS*, 181 F.3d 538 (4th Cir. 1999) ("If it is reasonable to suspect the State Department has a tendency to soft-pedal human rights violations, it may be just as reasonable to suspect that Amnesty International exaggerates them so they will not go without notice.").

[288] *Diallo v. U.S. Dep't of Justice*, 548 F.3d 232, 237(2d Cir. 2008).

[289] *See* Vikram Badrinath, Dree K. Collopy, & Hans Christian Linnartz, *Evidentiary Issues in Asylum Cases*, AILA IMMIGRATION PRACTICE POINTERS (AILA 2013). This article also contains a useful checklist of tips for working with expert witnesses. *See id.*

[290] *See Banks v. Gonzales*, 453 F.3d 449, 454 (7th Cir. 2006).

3. *Benefit of the Doubt*

The circumstances that cause an individual to flee his **or** her home country often make it impossible for him or her to provide documentary evidence in support of an asylum application. The applicant may have been forced to flee without the opportunity to gather documents, or it may have been dangerous for the applicant to carry certain documents with him or her.[291] In recognition of the fact that bona fide refugees often are unable to provide documentation in support of their claims, UNHCR's Handbook provides:

> After the applicant has made a genuine effort to substantiate his story there may still be a lack of evidence for some of his statements … . [I]t is hardly possible for a refugee to "prove" every part of his case and, indeed, if this were a requirement the majority of refugees would not be recognized. It is therefore frequently necessary to give the applicant the benefit of the doubt.[292]

Where corroborating documents are not provided, the applicant should be given the benefit of the doubt where the testimony is generally credible and does not counter commonly known facts.[293] The benefit of the doubt should only be given, however, after "all available evidence has been obtained and checked and when the examiner is satisfied as to the applicant's general credibility."[294] In *Matter of S–M–J*, the BIA cited these paragraphs with approval.[295] In cases in which there is some ambiguity regarding an aspect of the applicant's claim, the BIA may give the applicant the benefit of the doubt.[296] The BIA will not do so, however, in cases in which the applicant has failed to meet his or her burden of proof.[297]

The Handbook also addresses the application of this principle in the case of minors as follows:

> If the will of the parents cannot be ascertained or if such will is in doubt or in conflict with the will of the child, then the examiner, in cooperation with the experts assisting him, will have to come to a decision as to the well-

[291] *See, e.g., Aguilera-Cota v. INS*, 914 F.2d 1375 (9th Cir. 1990) ("The last thing a victim may want to do is carry around a threatening note with him."). *See also* U.S. AOBTC Workbook, pt. IV, *supra* note 2, at 19.

[292] UNHCR Handbook, *supra* note 43, ¶ 203.

[293] *Matter of S–M–J–*, 21 I&N Dec. 722, 725 (BIA 1997).

[294] UNHCR Handbook, *supra* note 43, ¶ 204.

[295] *Matter of S–M–J–*, at 725 (BIA 1997); *see also Matter of Pula*, 19 I&N Dec. 467, 476 (BIA 1987) (Heilman, J., concurring) (recognizing that asylum provisions are humanitarian in their essence and that the "normal" immigration laws cannot be applied in their usual manner to refugees).

[296] *Matter of Y–B–*, 21 I&N Dec. 1136, 1139 (BIA 1998).

[297] *Id.*

foundedness of the minor's fear on the basis of all the known circumstances, which may call for a *liberal application* of the benefit of the doubt.[298]

The Sixth Circuit relied on this paragraph in finding that a minor girl who feared female genital mutilation if she returned to Ethiopia was eligible for asylum.[299] In the case of an unaccompanied minor, particular regard should be given to factors such as "the child's stage of development" and "his [or] her possibly limited knowledge of conditions in the country of origin."[300]

4. *Original Documents and Forensics Testing*

Many official and unofficial documents may be relevant in an asylum case, including: police reports or arrest warrants, records of fines paid, political membership cards, marriage certificates, birth certificates, divorce certificates, national registers, identity cards, passports, and foreign criminal conviction records. Generally, an asylum applicant will need to provide, whenever possible, the relevant original documents and to properly authenticate those documents and show proof of their chain of custody. For example, retaining and offering original mailing envelopes for affidavits sent from abroad can show chain of custody and bolster the document's provenance. However, inability to secure perfect authentication is not fatal to a document's admissibility.[301]

- **Practice Pointer**: Although the Federal Rules of Evidence (FRE) are not binding before the asylum office or in immigration court, they are guiding. Practitioners should garner a firm grasp of the concepts addressed in the FRE and seek to comport with those rules. See FRE 901–903 on authenticating documents, as well as FRE 1002 and 1003 on the admissibility of original and duplicate documents. The FRE are available online at *www.uscourts.gov/uscourts/RulesAndPolicies/rules/EV2009.pdf*.[302]

Authentication of foreign official records is governed by 8 CFR §§287.6, 1287.6. Documents from countries that signed the Convention Abolishing the Requirement of Legislation for Foreign Public Documents are authenticated by proper certification from the official having legal custody of the record. According to this convention, an

---

[298] UNHCR Handbook, *supra* note 43, ¶ 219 (emphasis added). See chapter 10 for a detailed discussion on the evidentiary standards for child asylum-seekers.

[299] *Abay v. Ashcroft*, 368 F.3d 634, 640 (6th Cir. 2004).

[300] U.N. High Comm'r for Refugees, *Guidelines on Policies and Procedures in Dealing with Unaccompanied Children Seeking Asylum*, ¶ 8.6 (Feb. 1997) [hereinafter UNHCR Guidelines on Unaccompanied Children Seeking Asylum], *available at www.unhcr.org/cgi-bin/texis/vtx/search?page=search&docid=3d4f91cf4&query=age%20assessment*. *See infra* chapter 10 for a detailed discussion of asylum standards and procedures for children.

[301] *Yan v. Gonzales*, 438 F.2d 1249, 1256 n. 7 (10th Cir. 2006); *Gui Cun Liu v. Ashcroft*, 372 F.3d 529 (3d Cir. 2004); *Matter of H–L–Z and Z–Y–Z*, 25 I&N Dec. 209, 214 n. 5 (BIA 2010).

[302] (last visited Mar. 25, 2015).

official designated by the signatory country must properly certify these documents. No certification by an American consular official is required of these documents. On the other hand, when the document is issued by a country that is not a signatory to the Convention, it must bear a "chain of certifications" back to the original document and ending with a certification by a U.S. consular officer authenticating the last foreign official's signature and authority. In sum, 8 CFR §§287.6, 1287.6 require the official having legal custody of an official record to attest to the copy. That copy must then be authenticated by a consular officer under 8 CFR §§287.6(b), 1287.6(b), unless the country is a signatory to the convention abolishing these requirements.

> ➢ **Practice Pointer**: Documents also may be authenticated pursuant to Federal Rule of Evidence 902(3), Federal Rule of Civil Procedure 44, or an expert with the requisite knowledge pursuant to Federal Rule of Evidence 901(a)-(b)(1).

Nonpublic documents may also be subject to some verification in the relevant country or in the United States. For example, many periodicals are received and recorded in the Library of Congress.

> ➢ **Practice Pointer**: Photoduplicates of particular issues and pages might be obtained through the Library of Congress's reading room at *www.loc.gov/rr/news/*.

Original foreign documents may be subjected to scrutiny by the government. Consular field investigations may call such documents into question, but these field investigations should be scrutinized and may well be found wanting. At a minimum, the applicant has the right to know the identity and background of the investigator, what sources were consulted in the investigation, and the content of their information.[303] Moreover, the applicant must be given the opportunity to rebut any adverse report.[304]

DHS also may subject a document to its own forensic examination. In such a case, an applicant should be given the opportunity to cross-examine the forensic examiner or supervisor of the lab.[305] An IJ has the power to subpoena such a witness,[306] and a judge's failure to subpoena a forensic examiner may be reversible error.[307] A foreign document may not be discounted based on speculation or conjecture.[308] Similarly, a forensic examiner's opinion must be based on actual knowledge and must be

---

[303] *Zhen Nan Lin v. DOJ*, 459 F.3d 255 (2d Cir. 2006).

[304] *Ezeagwuna v. Ashcroft*, 325 F.3d 396 (3d Cir. 2003); *Alexandrov v. Gonzales*, 442 F.3d 395, 404 (6th Cir. 2006).

[305] *See* INA §240(b)(4)(B).

[306] 8 CFR §§1003.35(b); 1287.4(a)(2)(ii) (2014).

[307] *Xue Tong Zou v. Att'y Gen.*, 367 Fed. App'x 36, 40 (11th Cir. 2010); *Olabanji v. INS*, 973 F.2d 1232 (5th Cir.1992).

[308] *Kourouma v. Holder*, 588 F.3d 234, 241 (4th Cir. 2009); *Nasir v. INS*, 122 F.3d 484, 488 (7th Cir.1997); *Daiga v. INS*, 183 F.3d 797, 798 (8th Cir.1999) (per curiam).

reasonable, or it should carry no weight.[309] Moreover, where a forensic examiner's conclusion is ambiguous, it should not be the basis for an adverse credibility finding.[310]

> **Practice Pointer**: The Department of Homeland Security has its own forensic document laboratory.[311]

Former BIA Member Lory Rosenberg, dissenting in *Matter of A–S–*, gave the following cautionary advice to asylum applicants concerning their documents:

> Before submitting this evidence, have the letters or certificates checked both by a forensics expert and an expert familiar with the circumstances in your country. Get a sworn and notarized statement concerning the paper on which the information is written, the credentials of the person making the statement or certificate, and a description of how, where, and when official documents are issued, who prepares them, how, where, and when you got them, and, if possible, provide an explanation for any variance from the normal condition of the document, in terms of the ink used on the document, the seals stamped on the document, the condition of the paper, and how the documents were either taken out of the country or delivered to you.[312]

Judge Rosenberg's thorough advice illustrates the importance and difficulty of the applicant's burden in asylum cases.

> **Practice Pointer**: If an applicant's resources allow it, it may be wise to hire a member of the American Board of Forensic Document Examiners to make an independent examination in challenging a forensic examination by DHS's chosen examiner.[313]

C. Evidence Presented by the Department of Homeland Security

In addition to preparing and presenting effective testimony and documentary evidence on behalf of the asylum applicant, practitioners should pay close attention to any evidence that is submitted by DHS. If the evidence presented by DHS is improper in any way, practitioners should not be afraid to make objections or move for the evidence to be excluded from the record. Challenging DHS evidence can have multiple benefits:

(1) It may lead to exclusion of the evidence;

---

[309] *Pasha v. Gonzales*, 433 F.3d 530 (7th Cir. 2005).

[310] *Zahedi v. INS*, 222 F.3d 1157, 1165 (9th Cir. 2000).

[311] U.S. Citizenship and Immigration Servs., Homeland Security Investigations (HSI) Forensic Laboratory, *available at www.ice.gov/hsi-fl* (last visited Jan. 17, 2015).

[312] *Matter of A–S–*, 21 I&N Dec. 1106, 1133 (BIA 1998) (Rosenberg, J., dissenting).

[313] A website listing members of the American Board of Forensic Document Examiners is available at *www.abfde.org*.

(2) DHS counsel may decide to negotiate or withdraw the contested evidence, rather than presenting embarrassing facts or a document or witness that it cannot actually produce;[314]

(3) Practitioners can increase their credibility with the court and send a signal to DHS that they will be a zealous advocate on behalf of their clients; and

(4) Objecting on the record maintains the issue and builds the record for any future appeals.

Although the immigration courts do not follow the Federal Rules of Evidence and the admissibility of evidence is generally favored, there is authority for making evidentiary objections in immigration court. First, the IJ and DHS counsel are not free to ignore the statute, regulations, and *Immigration Court Practice Manual*.[315] If DHS attempts to submit a document or testimony that is contrary to one of these rules, practitioners should object. Moreover, the substantive due process clause of the Fifth Amendment of the U.S. Constitution requires that the applicant be given a full and fair hearing on his or her claims.[316] If the admission and reliance upon any evidence would impact the fundamental fairness of the proceedings, practitioners should not be afraid to object and argue that it deprives the applicant of due process.[317] Challenging DHS evidence, whether testimonial or documentary, that interferes with the fundamental fairness of the applicant's case is fundamental to being a zealous advocate.

> ➢ ***Practice Pointer***: Practitioners may have several grounds to object to documents submitted by DHS or questions and answers sought by DHS counsel on cross-examination. For a useful list of objections commonly used in immigration court, see Appendix 5J of this book.

D. Administrative Notice

Administrative notice is the recognition of the existence and truth of certain facts, without the production of evidence.[318] It can only be taken regarding facts that are generally accepted as true or facts that reasonable people would not dispute, such as current events or the contents of official documents.[319] The purpose of allowing

---

[314] *See, e.g.*, *Hernandez-Guadarrama v. Ashcroft*, 394 F.3d 674 (9th Cir. 2005).

[315] *See* INA §240(b)(4); *Immigration Court Practice Manual*, available at *www.justice.gov/eoir/vll/OCIJPracManual/ocij_page1.htm* (last visited Mar. 25, 2015).

[316] *See Rusu v. INS*, 296 F.3d 316, 321–22 (4th Cir. 2002); *Matter of Toro*, 17 I&N Dec. 340 (BIA 1980); *Matter of Ramirez-Sanchez*, 17 I&N Dec. 504 (BIA 1980); *Matter of Lam*, 14 I&N Dec. 168 (BIA 1972).

[317] *Id.*

[318] 8 CFR §1003.1(d)(3)(iv) (2014); *Matter of R–R–*, 20 I&N Dec. 547, 555 (BIA 1992). *See also* FED. R. OF EVID. 201.

[319] *See* 8 CFR §1003.1(d)(3)(iv) (2014); AOBTC Workbook, pt. IV, *supra* note 2, at 20.

administrative notice is to enhance adjudicative efficiency without sacrificing adjudicative accuracy.[320]

> **Practice Pointer**: Administrative notice is not to be confused with personal opinions or views. Personal opinions or personal views are not to be considered by adjudicators and cannot form the basis for asylum decisions.[321]

Asylum officers generally do not take administrative notice; however, if they do, the decision to take administrative notice would require Headquarters approval.[322] On the other hand, an IJ may take administrative notice whenever he or she "knows of information that will be useful in making the decision."[323] In determining whether administrative notice of particular facts is appropriate, adjudicators will consider whether the facts are:

(1) narrow and specific or broad and general;

(2) central or peripheral;

(3) readily accepted or controversial;

(4) purely factual or mixed with judgment, policy, or political preference;

(5) readily provable or provable only with difficulty or not at all; or

(6) facts about the parties or unrelated to them.[324] An IJ's determination whether to take administrative notice is reviewed for abuse of discretion.[325]

Even if an IJ takes administrative notice of a fact, the opponent may still dispute that fact by submitting evidence.[326] Thus, if an IJ intends to take administrative notice of extra-record facts, due process requires that he or she provide notice and an opportunity to respond.[327] The majority of case law in this area concerns

---

[320] *See* Edward Cleary, McCormick on Evidence 1029, §359 (3d ed. 1988); U.S. Dep't of Justice, *EOIR Immigration Judge Benchbook, Administrative Notice* [hereinafter IJ Benchbook], *available at www.justice.gov/eoir/vll/benchbook/resources/sfoutline/administrative-notice.pdf* (last visited Nov. 13, 2014).

[321] *See Banks v. Gonzales*, 453 F.3d 449, 453–54 (7th Cir. 2006) (noting that IJs are not experts on country conditions and are prohibited from relying on their own views on how foreign regimes conduct themselves); *Kllokoqi v. Gonzales*, 439 F.3d 336, 344 (7th Cir. 2005) (same); AOBTC Workbook, pt. IV, *supra* note 2, at 20.

[322] *See* AOBTC Workbook, pt. IV, *supra* note 2, at 20.

[323] IJ Benchbook, *supra* note 320 (quoting *Castillo-Villagra v. INS,* 972 F.2d 1017, 1027 (9th Cir. 1992)) (internal citation omitted).

[324] *Id.*

[325] *Id.*

[326] *Id.*

[327] *Id.* (citing *Getachew v. INS,* 25 F.3d 841, 845 (9th Cir. 1994) ("Corollary to the right to a hearing before deportation is the right to a deportation decision based on the record created during and before the hearing. Therefore, due process requires the [immigration judge] to refrain from taking

Continued

administrative notice of "changed circumstances." [328] If the IJ plans to take administrative notice of events that occurred prior to the hearing, allowing the applicant an opportunity to rebut the facts at his or her removal hearing satisfies due process. If the events occurred after the hearing, however, the IJ must at least warn the applicant before taking notice of such events.[329]

- **Practice Pointer**: If an IJ attempts to take administrative notice of certain facts that may be harmful to the applicant's case, practitioners should request on the record, either orally or in writing, notice and an opportunity to respond.

IV. Conclusion

The effective preparation and presentation of an asylum application requires credible testimony, as well as strong corroborating evidence. In addition to the substance of the testimony and documentary evidence itself, how that evidence is presented to the adjudicator is also important; improper presentation of evidence can lead to its exclusion from the record, seriously impacting the strength of the applicant's claim. Proper preparation and presentation of evidence is fundamental to meeting an applicant's burden of proof, and thus, is fundamental to the success of any asylum, withholding of removal, or CAT application.

---

administrative notice of facts not in the record unless the procedures it follows are fair under the circumstances.")).

[328] *Id.*

[329] *Id.*

CHAPTER FIVE

HOT TOPICS: ASYLUM CLAIMS BASED ON GENDER AND GANG VIOLENCE*

In the spring and summer of 2014, a media frenzy covered the "surge" of unaccompanied children arriving from Central America at the United States/Mexico border, leading to the Obama administration's request for $3.7 billion to address the "border crisis."[1] Shortly thereafter, around July of 2014, the Obama administration returned to the widely discredited and costly practice of detaining families — Central American mothers and their children — who were crossing the border in an effort to deter more Central Americans from coming.[2] At the time, the press often raised and posed answers to the question, "Why are they coming?" While there may be no concrete or easy answer to this question, reviewing the conditions of the three countries sending the highest numbers of men, women, and children to the United States speaks volumes.

Today, Honduras, El Salvador, and Guatemala are listed in the top five countries having the highest murder rate per capita in the world, with Honduras ranking number one, El Salvador number four, and Guatemala number five.[3] These three

* The author would like to thank Clinical Professor Benjamin Casper of the University of Minnesota Law School's Center for New Americans for his invaluable input in reviewing this chapter.

[1] *See, e.g.*, Haeyoun Park, *Q and A: Children at the Border*, N.Y. TIMES (updated Oct. 21, 2014), *available at www.nytimes.com/interactive/2014/07/15/us/questions-about-the-border-kids.html?_r=0* (last visited Dec. 31, 2014); Laura Meckler & Colleen McCain Nelson, White House Seeks Emergency Funds to Counter Border Surge, Wall St. J. (updated July 8, 2014), available at *www.wsj.com/articles/white-house-seeks-emergency-funds-to-counter-border-surge-1404834485* (last visited Dec. 31, 2014); Dree Collopy, America's Leaders are Failing the Children, AILA Leadership Blog, (July 21, 2014), available at *http://ailaleadershipblog.org/2014/07/21/americas-leaders-are-failing-the-children/* (last visited Dec. 31, 2014).

[2] *See, e.g.*, Julia Preston, *Detention Center Presented as Deterrent to Border Crossings*, N.Y. TIMES (Dec. 15, 2014), *available at www.nytimes.com/2014/12/16/us/homeland-security-chief-opens-largest-immigration-detention-center-in-us.html* (last visited Dec. 31, 2014); Lutheran Immigration and Refugee Service & Women's Refugee Comm'n, Locking Up Family Values Again (Oct. 28, 2014), *available at http://womensrefugeecommission.org/resources/document/1085-locking-up-family-values-again* (last visited Dec. 31, 2014); Dree Collopy, *The Failings of Family Detention at Artesia, Immigration Impact* (Oct. 2, 2014), *available at http://immigrationimpact.com/2014/10/02/the-failings-of-family-detention-at-artesia/* (last visited Dec. 31, 2014).

[3] *See* U.N. Office on Drugs & Crime, *Global Study on Homicide* (2013), *available at www.unodc.org/documents/gsh/pdfs/2014_GLOBAL_HOMICIDE_BOOK_web.pdf* (last accessed Dec. 31, 2014). *See also* CNN, *Which Countries Have the World's Highest Murder Rates? Honduras Tops*

Continued

countries making up the Northern Triangle of Central America are widely thought of as failed states whose governments have lost control over their territory. In their place, third generation gangs have taken power as the de facto governments,[4] allowing violence to flourish both in the home and on the streets.[5] Sadly, much of this systematic and widespread violence has been targeted at women and children; yet, their governments are unable, and in many cases have refused, to protect these vulnerable populations, resulting in an exodus of women and children fleeing to the United States and seeking protection.

But are these women and children "refugees" under the Immigration and Nationality Act (INA)? Are they members of socially distinct and particular social groups? Is the violence motivated by a protected ground? Are the governments able or willing to control the private actors who carry out this violence in the home and on the streets? Can these women and children safely and reasonably relocate? These issues have been hotly contested in the courts, resulting in volumes of case law and varying interpretations of U.S. asylum law. This chapter will summarize these two complex areas of asylum law — claims based on gender and gang violence — and provide useful tools for analyzing, preparing, and presenting these claims.

---

the List, (updated Apr. 11, 2014), *available at www.cnn.com/2014/04/10/world/un-world-murder-rates/* (last visited Dec. 31, 2014).

[4] *See* Max G. Manwaring, *A Contemporary Challenge to State Sovereignty: Gangs and Other Illicit Transnational Criminal Organizations in Central America, El Salvador, Mexico, Jamaica, and Brazil* (December 2007), *available at www.strategicstudiesinstitute.army.mil/pdffiles/PUB837.pdf* (last visited Dec. 31, 2014).

[5] *See* Ctr. for Gender & Refugee Studies, *Central America: Femicides and Gender-Based Violence*, *available at http://cgrs.uchastings.edu/our-work/central-america-femicides-and-gender-based-violence* (last visited Dec. 31, 2014); Deborah Hastings, *In Central America, Women Killed 'With Impunity' Just Because They're Women*, N.Y. DAILY NEWS (Jan. 10, 2014), *available at www.nydailynews.com/news/world/femicide-rise-central-america-article-1.1552233* (last visited Dec. 31, 2014); Economist, *Violence Against Women in Latin America: Everyday Aggression* (Sept. 21, 2013), *available at www.economist.com/news/americas/21586575-laws-punish-domestic-violence-are-too-often-honoured-breach-everyday-aggression* (last visited Dec. 31, 2014); Pamela Constable, *Could Kids Fleeing Central America be Sent Back to Face More Gang Violence?*, Wash. Post (July 25, 2014), *available at www.washingtonpost.com/local/gang-member-deportations-in-90s-factor-in-border-crisis-some-contend/2014/07/25/10c5adda-0d1d-11e4-8341-b8072b1e7348_story.html* (last visited Dec. 31, 2014); Oscar Martinez, *Why the Children Fleeing Central America Will Not Stop Coming*, Nation (July 30, 2014), *available at www.thenation.com/article/180837/why-children-fleeing-central-america-will-not-stop-coming* (last visited Dec. 31, 2014); Frances Robles, *Fleeing Gangs, Children Head to U.S. Border*, N.Y. TIMES (July 9, 2014), *available at www.nytimes.com/2014/07/10/world/americas/fleeing-gangs-children-head-to-us-border.html* (last visited Dec. 31, 2014). *See also* U.S. Dep't of State, Country Human Rights Reports for 2013 on El Salvador, *available at www.state.gov/j/drl/rls/hrrpt/humanrightsreport/index.htm#wrapper*, Guatemala, *available at www.state.gov/j/drl/rls/hrrpt/humanrightsreport/index.htm#wrapper*, & Honduras, *available at www.state.gov/j/drl/rls/hrrpt/humanrightsreport/index.htm#wrapper* (last visited Dec. 31, 2014).

I. Asylum Claims Based on Gender

Thirty years ago, U.S. and international asylum law did not recognize gender-based violence as a form of persecution, mostly due to the relegation of gender-based violence to the private, rather than the public sphere.[6] Harm such as rape and domestic violence, for example, was considered to be driven by personal motivations, not by protected grounds under the INA and the U.N. Convention and Protocol Relating to the Status of Refugees (Refugee Convention and Protocol).[7] One commentator suggested that "the obstacles to women's eligibility for refugee status lie not in legal categories per se, but in the incomplete and gendered interpretation of refugee law — the failure of decision-makers 'to acknowledge and respond to the gendering of politics and women's relationship to the state.'"[8] However, for over two decades now, gender-related asylum claims have received increasing attention by advocates, the U.S. immigration authorities, and the federal courts.[9] In fact, advocates, through litigation and outreach, have driven greater attention by U.S. authorities and the courts, yielding important advances in the law.[10]

The tide began turning in May 1995, when legacy INS issued a memorandum to all asylum officers setting forth guidelines for adjudicating women's asylum claims.[11] In this memorandum, legacy INS acknowledged that women often experience gender-specific types of persecution. The memorandum reviewed the human rights context in which guidance on gender-related adjudications has evolved internationally, emphasized the importance of gender-sensitive interviewing techniques, and outlined how gender-related claims should be analyzed under U.S.

---

[6] Nancy Kelly, *Gender-Related Persecution: Assessing Asylum Claims of Women*, 26 CORNELL INT'L L. J., 625–74 (1993).

[7] *See* Immigration and Nationality Act of 1952 (INA), Pub. L. No. 82-414, 66 Stat. 163 (codified as amended at 8 U.S.C. §1101 *et seq.*) [hereinafter INA]; 1951 Convention Relating to the Status of Refugees, 19 U.S.T. 6259, 189 U.N.T.S. 150 (entered into force Apr. 22, 1954) [hereinafter Refugee Convention]; 1967 Protocol Relating to the Status of Refugees, 19 U.S.T. 6223, 606 U.N.T.S. 267 (entered into force Oct. 4, 1967) [hereinafter Protocol].

[8] Deborah Anker, *Legal Change from the Bottom Up: The Development of Gender Asylum Jurisprudence in the United States, in Gender to Refugee Law: From the Margins to the Center*, chapter 2 (quoting H. Crawley, Gender, Persecution and the Concept of Politics in the asylum Determination Process, 9 FORCED MIGRATION REVIEW 17–20 (2000)).

[9] For a concise overview of developments, *see* Misha Seay & Karen Musalo, *Gender-Based Asylum: Overview and Case Strategy*, AILA'S IMMIGRATION PRACTICE POINTERS (2014–15 ed.); Anker, *supra* note 8; Stephen Knight, *Seeking Asylum from Gender Persecution: Progress Amid Uncertainty*, 79 INTERPRETER RELEASES 689 (May 13, 2002).

[10] *See Matter of Kasinga*, 21 I&N Dec. 357 (BIA 1996); CGRS, *Matter of R–A–, available at http://cgrs.uchastings.edu/our-work/matter-r* (last visited Apr. 3, 2015); *Matter of A–R–C–G–*, 26 I&N Dec. 388 (BIA 2014). *See supra* for a detailed discussion of these, and other, landmark cases.

[11] *See* INS Memorandum from Phyllis Coven on Considerations for Asylum Officers Adjudicating Claims from Women (May 25, 1995), *published on* AILA InfoNet (*posted* May 31, 1995), *reproduced in* 72 INTERPRETER RELEASES 771 (June 5, 1995).

law. Courts, however, continued to admonish government attorneys for failing to adhere to the principles set forth in the 1995 legacy INS memorandum.[12] For example, the Ninth Circuit U.S. Court of Appeals criticized the Department of Justice (DOJ) for perpetuating the myth that "rape is just forceful sex by men who cannot control themselves."[13]

Legacy INS, in drafting its memorandum, relied in part on UNHCR's *Guidelines on the Protection of Refugee Women*,[14] in which UNHCR recommends gender-sensitive interviewing techniques and advises asylum adjudicators, in evaluating a gender-based claim, to be aware of the following factors in an applicant's country of origin: the position of women before the law, the political rights of women, the social and economic rights of women, the incidence of reported violence against women, and the consequences that may befall a woman on her return in light of the circumstances described in her claim.[15]

Then, in 2002, UNHCR issued its *Guidelines on International Protection: Gender-Related Persecution Within the Context of Article 1A(2) of the 1951 Convention and/or its 1967 Protocol Relating to the Status of Refugees*.[16] These Guidelines complement UNHCR's Handbook and give further guidance regarding how gender-based claims should be analyzed. The Guidelines note, for example, that trafficking women or minors for the purposes of forced prostitution or sexual exploitation is a form of persecution.[17] They also offer guidance on procedural issues such as interviewing techniques and evidentiary matters.[18] More recently, UNHCR

---

[12] *See, e.g.*, *Angoucheva v. INS*, 106 F.3d 781, 793 n.2 (7th Cir. 1997) (Rovner, J., concurring) ("I was taken aback by the argument that a sexual assault like this one could be attributed to sexual attraction alone."); *Matter of Sharmin*, A73 556 833 at 20 (IJ Sept. 27, 1996) (New York, NY) (IJ Bukszpan) (noting that legacy INS's closing argument, which referred to the domestic violence suffered by the applicant as a mere "family matter," is a position in direct contravention of its own gender guidelines).

[13] *Garcia-Martinez v. Ashcroft*, 371 F.3d 1066, 1076 (9th Cir. 2004) (citations omitted). *See also Klawitter v. INS*, 970 F.2d 149, 152 (6th Cir. 1992) (considering the asylum claim of a woman who had been sexually abused by a colonel in the Polish secret police and stating "it is clear that he was not 'persecuting her' … he simply was reacting to her repeated refusals to become intimate with him."); *Campos-Guardado v. INS*, 809 F.2d 285, 288 (5th Cir. 1987) (holding that the rape and trauma suffered by the Salvadoran applicant was of a personal nature, even though her attackers were shouting political slogans while murdering her uncle, who was the chairman of an agrarian cooperative).

[14] U.N. High Comm'r for Refugees, *Guidelines on the Protection of Refugee Women* (1991), *available at www.refworld.org/docid/3ae6b3310.html*.

[15] *Id.* ¶¶ 72–73.

[16] U.N. High Comm'r for Refugees, *Guidelines on International Protection No. 1: Gender-Related Persecution Within the Context of Article 1A(2) of the 1951 Convention and/or its 1967 Protocol Relating to the Status of Refugees*, HCR/GIP/02/01(May 7, 2002), available at *www.unhcr.org/publ/PUBL/3d58ddef4.pdf*.

[17] *Id.* ¶ 18. *See also* U.S. Dep't of State, Trafficking in Person Report (2009), *available at www.state.gov/g/tip/rls/tiprpt/2009/index.htm#*.

[18] *Id.* ¶¶ 35–37.

released guidance on refugee claims relating to female genital mutilation,[19] and on women and girls fleeing conflict.[20]

Over the past several years, progress has been made with respect to many gender-related asylum issues as advocates and adjudicators have become more educated about the contours of gender-based violence and women and girls' relationship to the state. As more and more gender-related asylum cases have been raised, immigration judges (IJs), the Board of Immigration Appeals (BIA), and federal courts have grappled with a variety of gender-related harm, including female genital mutilation/cutting, rape, honor killings, forced marriage, allegations of witchcraft, and domestic violence, among others. Typically, in gender-based asylum claims the persecutory acts are alleged to be motivated by the applicant's membership in a particular social group, though claims may be brought based on any of the five enumerated grounds, as well as a combination of multiple grounds. For example, a feared honor killing may be on account of a woman's gender, as well as religion, and feared FGM/C may be on account of a woman's gender, as well as her opposition to the practice.

- **Practice Pointer**: Given the increasing difficulty in convincing adjudicators that a particular social group is viable under BIA precedent, especially following the BIA's precedent decisions in *Matter of M–E–V–G–*[21] and *Matter of W–G–R–*,[22] practitioners should consider whether their clients may have been persecuted or may fear persecution on account of one of the four other protected grounds: race, religion, nationality, or political opinion.

The BIA's seminal case of *Matter of Acosta* laid the foundation for gender-based asylum claims, while also setting forth the BIA's initial legal standards for establishing persecution on account of membership in a particular social group.[23] The BIA stated:

> "Persecution on account of membership in a particular social group" mean[s] persecution that is directed toward an individual who is a member of a group of persons all of whom share a common, immutable characteristic. The shared characteristic might be an innate one *such as sex*, color, or kinship ties, or in some circumstances it might be a shared past experience such as former military leadership or land ownership. The particular kind of group

[19] U.N. High Comm'r for Refugees, *Guidance Note on Refugee Claims relating to Female Genital Mutilation* (May 2009), *available at www.unhcr.org/refworld/docid/4a0c28492.html* (last visited June 14, 2014).

[20] U.N. High Comm'r for Refugees, *Women and Girls Fleeing Conflict: Gender and the Interpretation and Application of the 1951 Refugee Convention* (Sept. 10, 2012), *available at www.unhcr.org/504dd7649.html* (last visited Mar. 27, 2015).

[21] *Matter of M–E–V–G–*, 26 I&N Dec. 227 (BIA 2014).

[22] *Matter of W–G–R–*, 26 I&N Dec. 208 (BIA 2014).

[23] *Matter of Acosta*, 19 I&N Dec. 211 (BIA 1985).

> characteristic that would qualify under this construction remains to be determined on a case-by-case basis. However, whatever the common characteristic that defines the group, it must be one that the members of the group either cannot change, or should not be required to change because it is fundamental to their individual identities or consciences.[24]

Following *Matter of Acosta*, in 1993, the Third Circuit U.S. Court of Appeals upheld the BIA's denial of relief to a woman who refused to wear a chador (an Islamic veil) and otherwise conform to the Iranian government's gender-specific laws, because the court found that the record below did not establish the applicant's contention that she was a member of the group of women whose opposition to the Iranian laws were so profound that she would choose to suffer the severe consequences of noncompliance.[25] However, despite denying the petition for review, the Third Circuit used language in its decision that opened the door to these types of gender-based claims — "that feminism could constitute a political opinion, that gender could define a [particular social group], and generally that women who were being subjected to serious abuse because of their gender deserve protection."[26] That same year, the BIA recognized rape as a form of political persecution, rather than general conditions of violence, and granted asylum to a Haitian woman and Aristide-supporter who had been gang-raped and beaten by members of the Haitian military.[27]

The BIA continued with its trend of recognizing gender as a motivating factor for persecution in issuing its ground-breaking decision of *Matter of Kasinga.*[28] In that case, the BIA granted asylum to a Togolese woman who had fled Togo in search of protection from FGM/C. The BIA found that "young women of the Tchamba-Kunsuntu Tribe who had not been subjected to FGM and who opposed the practice" was a viable particular social group, thereby laying the foundation for future particular social group claims based, at least in part, on gender.[29]

In 1999, however, the BIA's forward progress in recognizing gender-based violence as a form of persecution meriting protection was halted. An IJ had granted asylum to Rody Alvarado, a Guatemalan woman who fled years of brutal domestic violence, finding that "Guatemalan women who have been involved intimately with

---

[24] *Id.* at 233–34 (emphasis added).

[25] *Fatin v. INS*, 12 F.3d 1233 (3d Cir. 1993). Note that *Fatin v. INS* was authored by then–Third Circuit Judge Samuel Alito, now Associate Justice of the Supreme Court of the United States.

[26] Anker, *supra* note 8 (discussing the Third Circuit U.S. Court of Appeals' decision in *Fatin v. INS*, 12 F.3d 1233 (3d Cir. 1993)).

[27] *Matter of D–V–*, 21 I&N Dec. 77, 78–79 (BIA 1993). *But see Nelson v. INS*, 232 F.3d 258, 264 (1st Cir. 2000) (finding that a political activist and supporter of women's rights who suffered three episodes of solitary confinement of less than 72 hours (each accompanied by physical abuse), periodic surveillance, threatening phone calls, occasional stops and searches, and visits to her place of work was not subject to past persecution).

[28] *Matter of Kasinga*, 21 I&N Dec. 357, 365–66 (BIA 1996).

[29] *Id.*

Guatemalan male companions, who believe that women are to live under male domination" was a cognizable particular social group. However, on appeal by legacy INS, the BIA reversed the grant of asylum, finding that Ms. Alvarado had not demonstrated persecution on account of a protected ground.[30] The decision called into question whether domestic violence was a form of persecution and whether gender could define a particular social group. The BIA's decision sparked widespread outrage and criticism among advocates and nearly 15 years of unsettled law, yielding a series of executive actions, including interventions by three Attorneys General (AGs) and proposed regulations by the DOJ.[31]

Although an IJ eventually granted Ms. Alvarado asylum on remand in 2009, and another IJ granted a Mexican woman asylum on remand in 2010 in a similar domestic violence-based claim following submission of a DHS brief recommending a grant of asylum, neither of these decisions were precedential and the BIA remained silent regarding whether domestic violence was persecution on account of a protected ground and whether gender could define a particular social group.[32] Finally, in 2014, the BIA broke its silence and issued a precedent decision recognizing that domestic violence may be a form of persecution on account of a protected ground and that gender may form the basis of a particular social group.[33]

Despite these positive developments, asylum claims based on various forms of gender-based violence remain incredibly challenging, as such claims have generated both positive and negative outcomes before the BIA and the federal courts. As this area of asylum law continues to develop, it is essential for practitioners to learn lessons from the past and to continue to push the law forward for the future protection of victims of gender-based violence. The purpose of this section is to provide practitioners with the tools they need to convince adjudicators that their clients, as bona fide refugees, merit the protection envisioned by the U.N. Refugee Convention

---

[30] *Matter of R–A–*, 22 I&N Dec. 906 (BIA 1999).

[31] *See* Ctr. for Gender & Refugee Studies, *Matter of R–A–*, *available at http://cgrs.uchastings.edu/our-work/matter-r* (last visited Mar. 27, 2015); Karen Musalo, *A Short History of Gender Asylum in the United States: Resistance and Ambivalence May Very Slowly be Inching Towards Recognition of Women's Claims*, 29 Refugee Survey Quarterly No. 2 (2010), *available at* http://cgrs.uchastings.edu/publications; Asylum and Withholding Definitions, 65 Fed. Reg. 76588 (proposed Dec. 7, 2000).

[32] *See* Ctr. for Gender & Refugee Studies, *Matter of R–A–*, *supra* note 30; Ctr. for Gender & Refugee Studies, *Matter of L–R–*, *available at http://cgrs.uchastings.edu/our-work/matter-l-r* (last visited Mar. 27, 2015). DHS recommended a grant of asylum based on the particular social groups of "Mexican women in domestic relationships who are unable to leave" and "Mexican women who are viewed as property by virtue of their positions within a domestic relationship." *See Matter of L–R–*, DHS Supp. Br., 17–18 (Apr. 13, 2009), *available at http://cgrs.uchastings.edu/sites/default/files/Matter_of_LR_DHS_Brief_4_13_2009.pdf.* Copies of the briefs and decisions in these two cases are available on the Ctr. for Gender & Refugee Studies website at *http://cgrs.uchastings.edu/our-work/matter-r* and *http://cgrs.uchastings.edu/our-work/matter-l-r*.

[33] *Matter of A–R–C–G–*, 26 I&N Dec. 388 (BIA 2014). *See infra* pt. I.A.7. for a detailed discussion of domestic violence-based claims.

and Protocol. First, this section reviews the most common forms of persecution and torture against women, and how the courts have addressed asylum claims based on that harm. This section then provides detailed guidance and practice pointers for meeting the legal standards for particular social group, nexus, non-government persecutors/torturers, and internal relocation.

A. Common Forms of Gender-Based Persecution

The BIA and federal courts have addressed several forms of gender-based persecution in determining whether asylum-seekers were targeted and harmed on account of gender-related protected grounds. The types of persecution and torture generating the most case law have included:

(1) female genital mutilation/cutting;

(2) rape and sexual violence;

(3) honor killings;

(4) forced marriage;

(5) sex trafficking and forced prostitution;

(6) gender-specific laws and repressive social mores; and

(7) domestic violence.

Each of these is discussed below.

> **Practice Pointer**: Practitioners should note that the forms of persecution discussed below are not the only types of gender-based violence that may be grounds for an asylum claim. Unfortunately, gender, as well as the second-class status of women in many societies, is a motivating factor for various types of violence in countries around the world. For example, in some cultures, women, especially elderly women, are at risk for accusations that they are witches or engage in witchcraft. UNHCR has published a research paper on this topic entitled "Witchcraft allegations, refugee protection and human rights: a review of the evidence."[34] In other cultures, it is common for women to be targeted with acid attacks for dressing immodestly (*e.g.*, Iraq), status as a mistress or "second wife" (*e.g.*, Cambodia), refusal of love proposals or dowries (*e.g.*, Bangladesh), and other motives. These attacks typically involve acid being thrown in women's faces to severely disfigure them, and could certainly form valid bases for asylum protection.[35] Women also may suffer psychological harm and threats of harm rising to the

---

[34] U.N. High Comm'r for Refugees, *Witchcraft Allegations, Refugee Protection and Human Rights: A Review of the Evidence* (Jan. 2009), *available at www.unhcr.org/research/RESEARCH/4981ca712.pdf* (last visited June 14, 2014).

[35] *See* Acid Survivors Trust Int'l, *www.acidviolence.org/index.php/acid-violence/* (last visited Mar. 28, 2015).

level of persecution.[36] Even incidents that may not rise to the level of persecution on their own could amount to persecution when considered cumulatively, rather than as isolated incidents.[37] Adjudicators are required to consider the cumulative effects of harm in the aggregate.

1. Female Genital Mutilation/Cutting

In its 1996 ground-breaking decision, *Matter of Kasinga*, the BIA found that female genital mutilation (FGM), also known as female genital cutting (FGC), is a form of persecution and granted asylum to a Togolese woman who had fled Togo in search of protection from FGM/C.[38] The BIA relied in part on legacy INS's 1995 memorandum on considerations for adjudicating claims from women,[39] which acknowledged that FGM/C is a form of persecution.[40] After finding that FGM/C constitutes persecution, the BIA held that "young women of the Tchamba-Kunsuntu Tribe who had not been subjected to FGM and who opposed the practice" was a viable particular social group.[41]

Following *Matter of Kasinga*, the federal courts largely followed this precedent, finding that FGM/C was a form of persecution. However, the issue arose whether women who had already undergone the practice still had a well-founded fear of future persecution. The Ninth and Tenth Circuit U.S. Courts of Appeals found that past

---

[36] *See, e.g.*, *Mashiri v. Ashcroft*, 383 F.3d 1112, 1119 (9th Cir. 2004) (stating "threats may be compelling evidence of past persecution, particularly when they are specific and menacing and are accompanied by evidence of violent confrontations, near-confrontations and vandalism"); *Vatulev v. Ashcroft*, 354 F.3d 1207, 1210 (10th Cir. 2003) (recognizing that threats may constitute persecution). *See also* U.S. Citizenship & Immigration Servs., *Lesson: Female Asylum Applicants and Gender-Related Claims* at 22, in Asylum Officer Basic Training Course Participant Workbook (Mar. 12, 2009) [hereinafter AOBTC Workbook, Female Asylum Applicants], (Mar. 12, 2009), *www.uscis.gov/sites/default/files/USCIS/Humanitarian/Refugees%20%26%20Asylum/Asylum/AOBTC %20Lesson%20Plans/Female-Asylum-Applicants-Gender-Related-Claims-31aug10.pdf.*

[37] *See, e.g.*, *Ritonga v. Holder*, 633 F.3d 971, 975 (10th Cir. 2011) (stating that "cumulative effects of multiple incidents may constitute persecution"); *Shi-Chen v. Holder*, 604 F.3d 324 (7th Cir. 2010) (remanding due to the agency's failure to consider the cumulative effects of the harm); *Faruk v. Ashcroft*, 378 F.3d 940, 942 (9th Cir. 2004) (finding that the cumulative effects of beatings, attacks with rocks, verbal assaults threats, and denial of a marriage certificate rose to the level of persecution).

[38] *Matter of Kasinga*, 21 I&N Dec. at 365–66. Female genital mutilation, female genital cutting, and female circumcision are all terms used to refer to the practice of removing part of female genitalia for non-medical reasons. For an explanation and comparison of each, see Human Rights Watch's website at *www.hrw.org/news/2010/06/10/qa-female-genital-mutilation* (last visited Apr. 3, 2015). While FGM and FGM take into consideration the harm associated with the practice, female circumcision does not. It has been criticized as "misleading because it implicitly compares the practice with male circumcision, regardless of the fact that FGM is a considerably more invasive procedure and is not conducted for medical purposes." *Id.*

[39] *See* Phyllis Coven Mem. on Considerations for Asylum Officers Adjudicating Claims from Women, *supra* note 11.

[40] *Matter of Kasinga*, 21 I&N Dec. at 365–66..

[41] *Id.*

FGM/C a continuing form of harm that allows for a finding of a well-founded fear.[42] In *Matter of A–T–*, the BIA disagreed with such findings, holding that FGM/C was a one-time act that could not be repeated on the same woman; however, the AG vacated the BIA's decision in 2008.[43] In *Matter of A–T–*, the AG clarified the framework for analyzing social group cases involving FGM/C, stating that the best formulation may be "females [of the applicant's tribe or nationality] who have not yet undergone FGM as practiced in their culture."[44] The AG specified that the persecution is not only motivated by the applicant's gender, but also the fact that she has not already undergone FGM/C as practiced in her culture, and provided the example of "Somali females" as broader than the group that is actually targeted.[45] The AG clarified, however, that this would not preclude a claim by an applicant who has already undergone FGM/C, as long as the applicant is able to establish that she would be subject to additional FGM/C in her particular tribe or culture.[46] The AG relied on the Second Circuit U.S. Court of Appeals decision in *Bah v. Mukasey*, which held that FGM/C is not a one-time act, but one that is capable of repetition throughout a woman's life.[47]

The Eighth Circuit U.S. Court of Appeals went even further, finding that women who have undergone FGM/C also may be at risk of other forms of gender-based persecution in the future beyond.[48] In *Hassan v. Gonzales*, the court stated:

> [T]he government's argument erroneously assumes that FGM is the only form of persecution in Somalia and that having undergone the procedure, Hassan, as a Somali woman, is no longer at risk of other prevalent forms of persecution.

---

[42] *Mohammed v. Gonzales*, 400 F.3d 785, 795–96 (9th Cir. 2005); *Niang v. Gonzales*, 422 F.3d 1187, 1189 (10th Cir. 2005) (finding that opposition to FGM need not be proved to establish nexus and adopting the rationale in *Mohammed v. Gonzales*, 400 F.3d at 796 n.16). *See also Abay v. Ashcroft*, 368 F.3d 634, 641 (6th Cir. 2004) (dealing with a parent's fear for her children but finding that FMG "not only constitutes persecution for the asylum applicant to witness or experience the persecution of family members, but it serves to corroborate his or her own fear of persecution").

[43] *Matter of A–T–*, 24 I&N Dec. 296, 299–301 (BIA 2007) (finding that FGM does not qualify as "continuing persecution"), *vacated by Matter of A–T–*, 24 I&N Dec. 617 (AG 2008).

[44] *Matter of A–T–*, 24 I&N Dec. at 617.

[45] *Id.* (addressing *Mohammed v. Gonzales*, 400 F.3d 785, 796 (9th Cir. 2005)).

[46] *Id.*

[47] *See Bah v. Mukasey*, 529 F.3d 99, 114 (2d Cir. 2008) ("[F]emale genital mutilation is not necessarily a one-time event. . . . [R]ecord evidence reveals that genital mutilation, such as infibulation, is often repeated in Guinea."). *See also Kourouma v. Holder*, 588 F.3d 234 (4th Cir. 2009) (remanding the case of an asylum-seeker from Guinea whose husband had threatened to have her circumcised anew because she had only been partially circumcised before); *Hassan v. Gonzales*, 484 F.3d 513 (8th Cir. 2007) (remanding the case of an asylum-seeker from Somalia and stating, "the government's argument erroneously assumes that FGM is the only form of persecution in Somalia and that having undergone the procedure, Hassan, as a Somali woman, is no longer at risk of other prevalent forms of persecution. We have never held that a petitioner must fear the repetition of the exact harm that she has suffered in the past. Our definition of persecution is not that narrow.").

[48] *Hassan v. Gonzales*, 484 F.3d 513 (8th Cir. 2007).

> We have never held that a petitioner must fear the repetition of the exact harm that she has suffered in the past. Our definition of persecution is not that narrow.[49]

Even if there is no evidence on the record that FGM/C would be repeated upon the applicant's return to her home country and a preponderance of the evidence indicates that a fundamental change in conditions or internal relocation option would allow the applicant to be safe from future persecution, the BIA has held that FGM/C could be a basis for humanitarian asylum claims based on the severity of past harm[50] or, possibly, the risk of "other serious harm."[51]

- **Practice Pointer**: It is against the law in the United States to perform FGM/C on a person under 18 years of age. A parent who knowingly allows FGM/C to be performed on his or her child may also be subject to criminal penalties.[52] The Department of State (DOS) has identified the following 30 countries where FGM/C is prevalent: Benin, Burkina Faso, Cameroon, Central African Republic, Chad, Cote d'Ivoire, Democratic Republic of Congo, Djibouti, Egypt, Ethiopia, Eritrea, Gambia, Ghana, Guinea, Guinea-Bissau, Indonesia, Kenya, Liberia, Mali, Mauritania, Niger, Nigeria, Senegal, Sierra Leone, Somalia, Sudan, Tanzania, Togo, Uganda, and Yemen.[53]

The other issue with which the federal courts have grappled most in the FGM/C context is whether parents have valid asylum claims based on their fear that their

---

[49] *Id.* at 518.

[50] *Matter of S–A–K– and H–A–H–*, 24 I&N Dec. 464 (BIA 2008) (holding that discretion should be exercised to grant asylum to a mother and daughter who had been involuntarily subjected to FGM based on the severity of the persecution they suffered). *See also Benyamin v. Holder*, 579 F.3d 970 (9th Cir. 2009) (remanding for consideration of humanitarian asylum based on severity of past persecution due to FGM suffered in Indonesia).

[51] 8 CFR §§208.13(b)(1)(iii), 1208.13(b)(1)(iii) (2014). *See Matter of Chen*, 20 I&N Dec. 16, 19 (BIA 1989) (finding the applicant to be eligible for asylum based on past persecution alone, where the applicant suffered a long history of persecution beginning when he was eight years old, no longer had any family in China, and had a subjectively genuine fear of future persecution); *Matter of H–*, 21 I&N Dec. 337, 347–48 (BIA 1996) (holding that "[c]entral to a discretionary finding in past persecution cases should be careful attention to compelling, humanitarian considerations that would be involved if the refugee were to be forced to return to a country where he or she was persecuted in the past," and finding that humanitarian reasons may include the applicant's age, health, or family ties in the United States). *See supra* chapter 2 for a detailed discussion of the two grounds for humanitarian asylum – severity of past persecution and other serious harm.

[52] 18 USC §116 (2012).

[53] Notice of Implementation of the Illegal Immigration Reform and Immigrant Responsibility Act of 1996 Pertaining to Female Genital Mutilation (FGM), 63 Fed. Reg. 13433 (Mar. 19, 1998); *see also* U.S. Dep't of State, *Prevalence of the Practice of Female Genital Mutilation (FGM), Laws Prohibiting FGM and Their Enforcement, Recommendations on How to Best Work to Eliminate FGM* (2001) at 8–10, *available at http://2001-2009.state.gov/g/wi/rls/rep/crfgm/* (adding Indonesia and Yemen as countries where FGM is prevalent).

daughters will be subjected to FGM/C upon removal. Several federal courts have held that FGM/C performed on a daughter could amount to persecution of the parent.[54] In *Abay v. Ashcroft*, the Sixth Circuit U.S. Court of Appeals held that "where a parent and protector is faced with exposing her child to [FGM]" she could establish eligibility for asylum.[55] Other federal courts have held that a parent cannot base a withholding of removal claim based on fear of FGM/C to a U.S. citizen daughter.[56] Additionally, at least one federal court has refused to extend that protection to female children who remain in the home country and are at risk of FGM/C.[57]

Following this circuit court split,[58] the BIA clarified that an applicant cannot establish eligibility for asylum solely based on fear that his or her daughter would be subject to FGM/C if returned to the country of nationality.[59] Such facts alone do not establish the necessary nexus to a protected ground because the persecution the applicant fears must be on account of his or her own protected characteristic, not his or her child's protected characteristic.[60] If, however, the child was specifically

---

[54] *Abay v. Ashcroft*, 368 F.3d 634, 641–42 (6th Cir. 2004) (threat of FGM to daughter amounts to a well-founded fear for daughter *and* mother); *see also Abebe v. Gonzales*, 432 F.3d 1037, 1043 (9th Cir. 2005) (finding evidence indicated U.S. citizen daughter was at risk of FGM if she returned to Ethiopia with her parents); *Kebede v. Ashcroft*, 366 F.3d 808, 811 (9th Cir. 2004) (acknowledging that a victim of sexual assault does not irredeemably compromise his or her credibility by failing to report the assault at the first opportunity); *Abankwah v. INS*, 185 F.3d 18, 23–24 (2d Cir. 1999) (finding that Ghanaian woman of the Nkumssa tribe had a well-founded fear of FGM for engaging in premarital sex); *Matter of Quist*, A79 468 512 (BIA July 9, 2004), *available at www.lexisnexis.com/practiceareas/immigration/pdfs/web581%20Quist.pdf* (Gambian women married to Mandinka men who have not been subjected to FGM and who oppose the practice are a particular social group). *But see Matter of A–K–*, 24 I&N Dec. 275 (BIA 2007) (finding that an applicant may not establish eligibility for asylum based solely on the fear that his or her daughter will be subject to FGM upon return).

[55] *Abay v. Ashcroft*, *supra* note 54, at 641–42.

[56] *Niang v. Gonzales*, 492 F.3d 505, 513 (4th Cir. 2007); *Gumaneh v. Mukasey*, 535 F.3d 785, 789–90 (8th Cir. 2008); *Oforji v. Ashcroft*, 354 F.3d 609 (7th Cir. 2003).

[57] *Bah v. Gonzales*, 462 F.3d 637, 643 (6th Cir. 2006).

[58] For a detailed discussion of this circuit court split, see Dree Collopy, *Incorporating a Hardship Factor in Asylum Claims Based on Female Genital Mutilation: A Legislative Solution to Protect the Best Interests of Children*, 21 GEO. IMMIGR. L. J. 469 (Spring 2007).

[59] *Matter of A–K–*, 24 I&N Dec. 275 (BIA 2007).

[60] *Id. See Camara v. Holder*, 632 F.3d 1 (1st Cir. 2013) (finding that the fear that a child will be subjected to FGM is not a basis for relief to the parent); *Dieng v. Holder*, 698 F.3d 866 (6th Cir. 2012) (holding that DHS rebutted the presumption of future persecution in Senegal based on the applicant's own resistance to FGM); *Mariko v. Holder*, 632 F.3d 1 (1st Cir. 2011) (denying the individual's motion to remand, rejecting the attempt to base a claim for asylum on a fear that the couple's recently born U.S. citizen daughter would be subjected to FGM upon the family's removal to Guinea). *See also Hounmenou v. Holder*, 691 F.3d 967 (8th Cir. 2012) (finding that the applicant's daughter was unlikely to be subjected to FGM); *Diop v. Holder*, 586 F.3d 587 (8th Cir. 2009) (noting that FGM in Senegal is illegal and that the daughter was older than the typical age at which females in Senegal are subject to the most severe form of FGM, and finding that the applicant's fear, while subjectively genuine, was not objectively reasonable). *But see Gathungu v. Holder*, 725 F.3d 900 (8th Cir. 2013) (addressing the

Continued

targeted for FGM/C in order to harm the parent because of his or her opposition to FGM/C, it could be possible to establish a nexus to a protected characteristic of the parent.[61] Additionally, some courts have recognized that the practice of FGM/C on an applicant's daughter could constitute direct psychological persecution of the child's parents.[62] However, courts continue to demonstrate skepticism when considering these claims, holding that parents cannot be derivative beneficiaries of their children's asylum claims based on potential FGM/C.[63]

> ➢ **Practice Pointer**: Some invaluable resources for FGM/C-based asylum claims include: UNHCR's guidance note on claims relating to FGM/C[64] and Natalie Nanasi's article entitled "Lessons from *Matter of A–T–*: Guidance for Practitioners Litigating Asylum Cases Involving the Spectrum of Gender-Based Harms, from Female Genital Mutilation to Forced Marriage and Beyond."[65]

2. *Rape and Sexual Violence*

Twenty to thirty years ago, the federal courts had not yet recognized that rape was a form of gender-motivated persecution. For example, in 1987, the Fifth Circuit U.S. Court of Appeals upheld the denial of asylum to a Salvadoran woman whose uncle was the chairman of the local agrarian cooperative.[66] The woman had been raped and forced to watch as her attackers hacked her uncle to death while shouting political slogans. Yet, the Fifth Circuit found that the rape and trauma that she suffered was

---

social group of Munguki defectors fearing FGM on their daughters and holding that the group was socially visible in Kenya).

[61] *Matter of A–K–*, 24 I&N Dec. 275 (BIA 2007).

[62] *See, e.g., Kone v. Holder*, 620 F.3d 760 (7th Cir. 2010).

[63] *See Camara v. Holder*, 632 F.3d 1 (1st Cir. 2013) (finding that the fear that a child will be subjected to FGM is not a basis for relief to the parent); *Dieng v. Holder*, 698 F.3d 866 (6th Cir. 2012) (holding that DHS rebutted the presumption of future persecution in Senegal based on the applicant's own resistance to FGM); *Mariko v. Holder*, 632 F.3d 1 (1st Cir. 2011) (denying the individual's motion to remand, rejecting the attempt to base a claim for asylum on a fear that the couple's recently born U.S. citizen daughter would be subjected to FGM upon the family's removal to Guinea). *See also Hounmenou v. Holder*, 691 F.3d 967 (8th Cir. 2012) (finding that the applicant's daughter was unlikely to be subjected to FGM); *Diop v. Holder*, 586 F.3d 587 (8th Cir. 2009) (noting that FGM in Senegal is illegal and that the daughter was older than the typical age at which females in Senegal are subject to the most severe form of FGM, and finding that the applicant's fear, while subjectively genuine, was not objectively reasonable). *But see Gathungu v. Holder*, 725 F.3d 900 (8th Cir. 2013) (addressing the social group of Munguki defectors fearing FGM on their daughters and holding that the group was socially visible in Kenya).

[64] U.N. High Comm'r for Refugees, *Guidance Note on Refugee Claims relating to Female Genital Mutilation* (May 2009), *available at www.refworld.org/docid/4a0c28492.html* (last visited Jan. 2, 2015).

[65] Natalie Nanasi, *Lessons from Matter of A–T–: Guidance for Practitioners Litigating Asylum Cases Involving the Spectrum of Gender-Based Harms, from Female Genital Mutilation to Forced Marriage and Beyond*, 12-02 IMMIGR. BRIEFINGS 1 (Feb. 2012).

[66] *Campos-Guardado v. INS*, 809 F.2d 285, 288 (5th Cir. 1987).

personal in nature and not persecution on account of a protected ground.[67] Several years later, in 1992, the Sixth Circuit addressed the asylum claim of a woman who had been subjected to sexual violence by a colonel in the Polish secret police.[68] The court stated, "it is clear that he was not 'persecuting her' . . . he simply was reacting to her repeated refusals to become intimate with him."[69] Eventually, the courts began to recognize that rape could be a form of persecution.[70] For example, the Ninth Circuit U.S. Court of Appeals criticized the DOJ for perpetuating the myth that "rape is just forceful sex by men who cannot control themselves."[71]

The BIA also has recognized that rape may be a type of persecution motivated by an individual's gender. For example, the BIA granted asylum to a Haitian woman who had been gang-raped and beaten by members of the Haitian military, holding that she was not merely a victim of general conditions of violence, as the IJ had found.[72] Rather, she had been gang-raped and beaten because of her support for Aristide.[73]

Whether rape is motivated by membership in a particular social group, however, remains unsettled and largely depends on the social group and whether it meets the BIA's three-prong test for a viable social group. For example, in *Kante v. Holder*, the Sixth Circuit held that the IJ reasonably determined that "women subjected to rape as a method of government control" is not a particular social group because of its general, far-reaching, and circular nature.[74]

- **Practice Pointer**: Defining a legally cognizable particular social group is often the most difficult step in presenting gender-based asylum claims. See Part I.B. of this chapter for a detailed discussion of particular social groups in the context of gender-based claims, as well as

[67] *Id.*

[68] *Klawitter v. INS*, 970 F.2d 149, 152 (6th Cir. 1992).

[69] *Id.*

[70] *See, e.g., Hassan v. Gonzales*, 484 F.3d 513, 519 n.2 (8th Cir. 2007) (recognizing that rape and other violence against women may rise to the level of persecution); *Zubeda v. Ashcroft*, 333 F.3d 463 (3d Cir. 2003) (finding that rape can even rise to the level of torture); *Lopez-Galarza v. INS*, 99 F.3d 954, 960 (9th Cir. 1996) (stating that "rape and physical abuse at the hands of Sandinista military officers, coupled with her imprisonment, food deprivation, and forced labor satisfies the definition of 'persecution'").

[71] *Garcia-Martinez v. Ashcroft*, 371 F.3d 1066, 1076 (9th Cir. 2004) (citations omitted).

[72] *Matter of D–V–*, 21 I&N Dec. 77, 78–79 (BIA 1993). *But see Nelson v. INS*, 232 F.3d 258, 264 (1st Cir. 2000) (finding that a political activist and supporter of women's rights who suffered three episodes of solitary confinement of less than 72 hours (each accompanied by physical abuse), periodic surveillance, threatening phone calls, occasional stops and searches, and visits to her place of work was not subject to past persecution).

[73] *Matter of D–V–*, 21 I&N Dec. 77, 78–79 (BIA 1993).

[74] *Kante v. Holder*, 634 F.3d 321 (6th Cir. 2011).

chapter 2 of this book for a detailed discussion of social group jurisprudence and the current state of the law.

3. *Honor Killings*

An honor killing is a homicide of a family or community member due to the perpetrator's belief that the victim has brought shame or dishonor upon the family or community, usually due to the victim's disapproved romantic relationship, refusal to enter into an arranged marriage, being the victim of rape, sexual orientation, or dressing or acting in ways deemed inappropriate. Honor killings have been condemned by human rights organizations and have been established as a form of persecution meriting eligibility for asylum. For example, the Chicago Asylum Office granted asylum to a Jordanian man who feared he would be subjected to an "honor killing" for his intimate, non-marital relationship with a Bedouin woman.[75]

More recently, the Seventh Circuit U.S. Court of Appeals addressed honor killings in the context of an asylum claim by a woman from Jordan. The court recognized women in Jordan who have flouted repressive moral norms and face a high risk of honor killing as a viable social group.[76] Ms. Sarhan and her husband had entered the United States in the 1990s, and several years later, Mr. Sarhan's sister-in-law spread a rumor in Jordan that Ms. Sarhan had committed adultery. Ms. Sarhan's brother planned to kill Ms. Sarhan when she returned to Jordan to restore the family's honor, and she applied for asylum, withholding of removal, and Convention Against Torture (CAT) relief on that basis.[77] The IJ denied asylum based on the one-year filing deadline, but also denied withholding of removal, finding that Ms. Sarhan had not articulated a viable social group under the required legal standards, that she did not have a well-founded fear of persecution, and that the government of Jordan could protect her.[78] The BIA affirmed the IJ's decision.

On review, however, the Seventh Circuit held that it was more likely than not that, if Ms. Sarhan returned to Jordan, she would be severely harmed or murdered on account of her particular social group.[79] The BIA had concluded that the social group was not cognizable because it was defined based on the feared persecution. The Seventh Circuit, however, held that the group was defined by a shared experience since it was a function of a pre-existing moral code in Jordanian society.[80] In arguing that Ms. Sarhan did not have a well-founded fear of future persecution based on a protected ground, the government had asserted that Ms. Sarhan's brother would only be targeting Ms. Sarhan due to a personal dispute because he had not threatened any

---

[75] Letter Opinion by Robert Esbrook, A77 827 289 (Chicago Asylum Office, Feb. 25, 2002) *cited in* 79 INTERPRETER RELEASES 594 (Apr. 22, 2002).

[76] *Sarhan v. Holder*, 658 F.3d 649 (7th Cir. 2011).

[77] *Id.* at 651.

[78] *Id.* at 652–53.

[79] *Id.* at 650.

[80] *Id.* at 655.

other women who had committed adultery.[81] The Seventh Circuit rejected this argument, stating:

> There is no personal dispute between [Ms. Sarhan] and her brother. He has not vowed to kill her because of a quarrel about whether she or Besem should inherit a parcel of land, or because she did a bad job running his store, or because she broke Besem's favorite toy as a child. She faces death because of a widely-held social norm in Jordan—a norm that imposes behavioral obligations on her and permits Besem to enforce them in the most drastic way. The dispute between [Ms. Sarhan] and Besem is simply a piece of a complex cultural construct that entitles male members of families dishonored by perceived bad acts of female relatives to kill those women. The man who does the killing may have a personal motivation in the sense that he is angry that his sister has dishonored the family, or he may regret the need to take such an irrevocable step. Either way, he is killing her because society has deemed that this is a permissible—maybe in some eyes the only—correct course of action and the government has withdrawn its protection from the victims. The very fact that these are called "honor killings" demonstrates that they are killings with broader social significance.[82]

The court went on to compare honor killings to FGM/C, stating:

> In the same way, in a society that practices female genital mutilation, each family is responsible for carrying out the operation on its own girls. But the families are not taking this step to make a personal statement. They do it because their society tells them that they are harboring an outcast and their own social standing will suffer if they do nothing. . . . If Besem killed [Ms. Sarhan] it would be on account of her membership in the particular social group to which she has been assigned.[83]

Finally, the court held that the government of Jordan would be complicit in the harm that Ms. Sarhan would suffer, given the lenient sentences that perpetrators of honor killings receive, if any at all, the fact that the penal code provides a legal justification for honor crimes in Jordan, and the lack of protection provided to potential victims.[84] The Seventh Circuit granted the petition for review and remanded the case for further proceedings consistent with its decision. This case is a prime example of the main challenges in seeking asylum based on gender-based violence: articulating a cognizable particular social group,[85] demonstrating that the harm is on

---

[81] *Id.*

[82] *Id.* at 656.

[83] *Id.* at 657.

[84] *Id.* at 658.

[85] *See Ahmed v. Holder*, 611 F.3d 90 (1st Cir. 2010) (addressing the asylum claim of a Pakistani woman who feared abuse by her husband, being subjected to an honor killing, and forced conformance to cultural expectations about women; finding that the evidence indicates that honor killings are usually in response to specific "insults," but that the applicant had not established a record of any such incidents

Continued

account of a protected ground and not a personal dispute, and showing that the government is unable or unwilling to protect victims from private actors.

4. *Forced Marriage*

Forced marriage — a marriage that is enforced against the victim's wishes — has also been found to be a form of persecution.[86] According to the United Nations, fundamental human rights mandate that "no marriage shall be legally entered into without the full and free consent of both parties."[87] As USCIS notes in its training materials for gender-based asylum claims:

> Forced marriage takes place throughout the world and occurs for a variety of reasons stemming from issues such as poverty, gender discrimination, and lack of security. A family may sell or offer a daughter in marriage to alleviate the financial burden on the family, to settle a debt, to provide the daughter with a better life, or to afford additional wives for the male family members. In some contexts, forced marriage may provide a method to atone for criminal conduct or as punishment to the perpetrator of a gender-based crime such as rape. Forced marriage may serve the purpose of uniting two families or adhering to religious and cultural traditions. Also, families may wish to marry their daughters to protect them from rape or to keep their virginity intact.[88]

Forced marriage also violates numerous human rights, providing "an arena in which sexual abuse, sexual exploitation, domestic violence, forced labor, and slavery often go unnoticed. . . . A woman's attempt to refuse the forced marriage may result

---

that would trigger an honor killing; and holding that there was "too tenuous a nexus between this barbaric practice and [the applicant's] situation to support a claim of likely persecution"); *Faye v. Holder*, 580 F.3d 37 (1st Cir. 2009) (finding that Senegalese women who had a child out of wedlock, women who are considered adulterers because they gave birth to a child allegedly not their husbands, and women who have been abused by their husbands were not socially visible and particular social groups); *Al-Ghorbani v. Holder*, 585 F.3d 980 (6th Cir. 2009) (holding that the Yemeni applicants' family branch, as well as people who opposed Yemeni cultural and religious marriage customs, qualified as particular social groups).

[86] *See Matter of A–T–*, 24 I&N Dec. 296, 302–04 (BIA 2007); *Matter of [name not provided]*, A76 512 001 (IJ Oct. 18, 2000) (Chicago, IL) (Zerbe, IJ) (granting asylum to a 16-year-old girl who feared being subjected to a forced marriage in China), *reported in* 77 Interpreter Releases 1634 (Nov. 20, 2000).

[87] U.N. GAOR, Covenant on Consent to Marriage, Minimum Age for Marriage and Registration at Marriage, G.A. Res. 1763(A)(XVII) (Nov. 7, 1962) (Note the United States has not ratified this treaty); U.N. GAOR, Universal Declaration of Human Rights, G.A. Res. 217(a)(III) (Dec. 10, 1948).

[88] U.S. Citizenship & Immigration Servs., *Lesson: Female Asylum Applicants and Gender-Related Claims* at 14, in Asylum Officer Basic Training Course Participant Workbook (Mar. 12, 2009) [hereinafter AOBTC Workbook, Female Asylum Applicants], (Mar. 12, 2009), *www.uscis.gov/sites/default/files/USCIS/Humanitarian/Refugees%20%26%20Asylum/Asylum/AOBTC %20Lesson%20Plans/Female-Asylum-Applicants-Gender-Related-Claims-31aug10.pdf*.

in abusive and/or harmful treatment."[89] It poses particular human rights concerns for young girls, who often are subject to early marriage.[90]

However, forced marriage, a form of persecution, is distinguishable from arranged marriage, "an important tradition in many cultures," which is "often entered into willingly."[91] The BIA focused on this distinction in its decision in *Matter of A–T–*, stating "an arranged marriage between adults is not generally considered per se persecution."[92] In that case, the applicant feared that, upon return to Mali, her family would force her to enter into an arranged marriage with her first cousin.[93] The BIA noted that the record evidence showed that the applicant and her intended fiancé were of similar ages and backgrounds, and therefore, "it is not likely that she would be in a disadvantaged position in relation to her husband on account of her age or economic status."[94] The BIA noted that, while the applicant's preference to choose her own spouse is understandable, the BIA "[did] not see how the reluctant acceptance of family tradition over personal preference can form the basis for a withholding of removal claim."[95] Additionally, the BIA found that the applicant had presented insufficient evidence regarding the consequences she might face if she refuses to marry her intended fiancé, and that the applicant could reasonably relocate within Mali to avoid the marriage.[96]

In *Matter of A–T–*, the BIA also considered the proposed social group "young female members of the Bambara tribe who oppose arranged marriage," and found that the applicant failed to demonstrate a nexus between the harm and a protected ground.[97] The BIA questioned the viability of the social group, stating, "we are doubtful that young Bambara women who oppose arranged marriage have the kind of social visibility that would make them readily identifiable to those who would be inclined to persecute them … . Moreover, ... the respondent has expressed only a generalized fear of disobeying her authoritarian father."[98] The BIA concluded that the

[89] *Id.*

[90] *Id.* at 14–15.

[91] *Id.* at 15. *See* U.S. Dep't of State, 7 FAM 1459(b), *available at* http://foia.state.gov/masterdocs/07fam/07m1450.pdf; Ratna Kapur, *Travel Plans: Border Crossings and the Rights of Transnational Migrants*, 18 Harv. Hum. Rts. J. 01107, 124 (2005) (distinguishing forced and arranged marriages in analyzing British immigration policy).

[92] *Matter of A–T–*, 24 I&N Dec. 296, 302 (BIA 2007). *See also, Mansour v. Ashcroft,* 390 F.3d 667, 680 (9th Cir. 2004) (observing that arranged marriage, "while unfortunate and deplorable, may not constitute persecution if imposed on an adult").

[93] *Id.* at 298–99.

[94] *Id.* at 302.

[95] *Id.* at 302–03.

[96] *Id.* at 303.

[97] *Id.*

[98] *Id.* (citing *Matter of A–M–E– & J–G–U–,* 24 I&N Dec. 69, 74–75 (BIA 2007) and *Matter of C–A–,* 23 I&N Dec. 951, 959–61 (BIA 2006)).

applicant "has not met her burden of showing a clear probability either that she would be forced into an arranged marriage against her will or that she would be persecuted on account of her rejection of the marriage."[99]

Overall, "The key question in determining whether a forced marriage might constitute persecution is whether the victim experienced or would experience the marriage, or events surrounding the marriage, as serious harm."[100] Furthermore, *Matter of A–T–* teaches that a strong evidentiary record of the harm and the motives for that harm is the key to success in forced marriage — and any gender-based — protection claims.

- **Practice Pointer**: Some invaluable resources for asylum claims based on forced marriage include: Natalie Nanasi's article entitled "Lessons from *Matter of A–T–*: Guidance for Practitioners Litigating Asylum Cases Involving the Spectrum of Gender-Based Harms, from Female Genital Mutilation to Forced Marriage and Beyond"[101] and Danielle L.C. Beach's article entitled "Battlefield of Gendercide: Forced Marriages and Gender-Based Grounds for Asylum and Related Relief."[102]

5. *Sex Trafficking and Forced Prostitution*

The primary objective of trafficking in persons is to gain profit through the exploitation of human beings.[103] Women and girls in many countries are vulnerable to sex trafficking and forced prostitution, and unaccompanied or separated children may be especially vulnerable to these abuses. As UNHCR states in its *Guidelines on International Protection*, "Trafficking in the context of the sex trade is well documented and primarily affects women and children who are forced into prostitution and other forms of sexual exploitation."[104] It is a form of gender-related violence, which may constitute persecution.[105]

According to UNHCR, trafficking involves three essential and interlinked sets of elements:

(1) the act — recruitment transportation, transfer, harboring, or receipt of persons;

---

[99] *Id.* at 304.

[100] AOBTC Workbook, Female Asylum Applicants, *supra* note 36.

[101] Nanasi, *supra* note 65.

[102] Danielle L.C. Beach, Battlefield of Gendercide: Forced Marriages and Gender-Based Grounds for Asylum and Related Relief, 09-12 IMMIGR. BRIEFINGS 1 (Dec. 2009).

[103] U.N. High Comm'r for Refugees, *Guidelines on International Protection: The application of Article 1A(2) of the 1951 Convention and/or 1967 Protocol relating to the Status of Refugees to victims of trafficking and persons at risk of being trafficked*, HCR/GIP/06/07 (Apr. 7, 2006) ¶ 1, *available at www.unhcr.org/443b626b2.html*.

[104] *Id.* ¶ 3.

[105] *Id.* ¶¶ 19–20.

(2) the means — by threat or use of force or other forms of coercion, abduction, fraud, deception, abuse of power, abuse of position of vulnerability, or of giving or receiving of payments or benefits to achieve the consent of a person having control over the victim; and

(3) the purpose — exploitation of the victim through prostitution or other forms of sexual exploitation, forced labor or services, slavery or practices similar to slavery, servitude, or the removal of organs.[106]

Trafficking often involves severe harm, such as "abduction, incarceration, rape, sexual enslavement, enforced prostitution, forced labour, removal of organs, physical beatings, starvation, the deprivation of medical treatment."[107] According to UNCHR, "Such acts constitute serious violations of human rights which will generally amount to persecution."[108]

However, despite the egregious nature of the harm involved in cases of human trafficking, asylum claims based on sex trafficking and forced prostitution still face many challenges. Some questions contemplated by the courts include whether the act of trafficking was a one-time past experience that is unlikely to be repeated, whether the government was involved in the trafficking or was unable or unwilling to control the persecutors, and of course, whether a viable particular social group has been articulated.

With regard to the first question regarding whether the presumption of a well-founded fear of persecution due to past trafficking may be rebutted, UNHCR provides the following guidance:

- Particularly atrocious past experiences may result in the victim suffering "ongoing traumatic psychological effects which would render return to the country of origin intolerable;"[109]
- Following the actual experience of being trafficked, the victim "may face reprisals and/or possible re-trafficking should they be returned to the territory from which they have fled or from which they have been trafficked;"[110] and
- The victim also may fear "ostracism, discrimination or punishment by the family and/or the local community or, in some instances, by the authorities upon return. Such treatment is particularly relevant in the case of those trafficked into prostitution."[111]

---

[106] *Id.* ¶ 9.

[107] *Id.* ¶ 15.

[108] *Id.*

[109] *Id.* at ¶ 16.

[110] *Id.* at ¶ 17.

[111] *Id.* at ¶ 18.

According to UNHCR, "Trafficked women and children can be particularly susceptible to serious reprisals by traffickers after their escape and/or upon return, as well as to a real possibility of being re-trafficked or of being subjected to severe family or community ostracism and/or severe discrimination."[112] Although ostracism and discrimination may not normally rise to the level of persecution, it may rise to the level of persecution for a victim of trafficking as it may be aggravated by the trauma suffered during, and as a result of, the trafficking process.[113] As UNHCR notes, "Even if the ostracism from, or punishment by, family or community members does not rise to the level of persecution, such rejection by, and isolation from, social support networks may in fact heighten the risk of being re-trafficked or of being exposed to retaliation, which could give rise to a well-founded fear of persecution."[114] Thus, there are strong arguments to be made that women and girls who have suffered past persecution in the form of trafficking or forced prostitution also have a well-founded fear of future persecution.

Typically, situations of trafficking and forced prostitution involve private criminal actors, rather than governments. The courts, therefore, have contemplated whether asylum claims based on sex trafficking or forced prostitution involve government persecutors or groups that the government is unable or unwilling to control. For example, in the 2009 case of *Burbiene v. Holder*, the First Circuit U.S. Court of Appeals considered the asylum claim of a Lithuanian woman who feared that upon removal to Lithuania she or her daughter would be abducted and forced into prostitution.[115] In that case, Ms. Burbiene's friend had recently been kidnapped and almost sold into prostitution. After the kidnapping, her friend's parents had asked the Lithuanian police and the media for help, and Ms. Burbiene's friend was found five days later near the Polish border and returned to her family.[116] Ms. Burbiene's cousin had also previously been kidnapped and forced into prostitution after responding to an advertisement requesting childcare providers to work in Germany. The cousin was later arrested in a German prostitution raid and returned to Lithuania.[117] The IJ denied the applicant's asylum claim, finding that human trafficking in Lithuania is not the result of government action, government-supported action, or the government's unwillingness or inability to control private conduct. Therefore, the conduct did not amount to persecution under the INA.[118] The BIA affirmed the IJ's decision and dismissed the appeal.

---

[112] *Id.* ¶ 19.

[113] *Id.* ¶ 18.

[114] *Id.*

[115] *Burbiene v. Holder*, 568 F.3d 251 (1st Cir. 2009).

[116] *Id.* at 253.

[117] *Id.*

[118] *Id.* at n. 4.

In considering this case, the First Circuit held that substantial evidence supported the IJ and BIA's conclusion that Ms. Burbiene failed to establish a well-founded fear of persecution on account of a protected ground.[119] The court reasoned that trafficking in Lithuania is committed by a criminal element and that scattered incidences of violence or harassment are not enough to establish that a government is unwilling or unable to control violence; "[b]y definition, persecution has a systematic aspect."[120] In this case, the court found that the government of Lithuania is "making every effort to combat" human trafficking, "a difficult task not only for the government of Lithuania, but for any government in the world."[121] Thus, to overcome the challenge of showing that a government is unable or unwilling to control the persecutors, it is essential for asylum-seekers to build a strong record of systematic harm and the government's failure to provide meaningful protection to its citizens.

Burbiene v. Holder also involved the issue of defining a viable particular social group, another hurdle to making successful asylum claims based on sex trafficking and forced prostitution. In that case, the IJ held that "women and children in Lithuania who are under 40 years of age, and who fear being kidnapped by criminals" was not a cognizable social group for purposes of the INA as it had been interpreted by the BIA. The BIA agreed, citing *Rreshpja v. Gonzales*, a Sixth Circuit case that held that young, attractive Albanian women who fear being kidnapped and forced into prostitution do not constitute a viable particular social group for purposes of asylum eligibility.[122] The Sixth Circuit had reasoned that the social group could not circularly be defined by the fact that it suffers persecution, and the group must share a characteristic beyond their risk of being persecuted. The BIA agreed with that reasoning in considering Ms. Burbiene's claim.[123] The First Circuit did not reach this issue, as it rejected the petition for review based on Ms. Burbiene's failure to show that the persecutor was a government actor or group the government was unable or unwilling to control.[124]

In *Gjura v. Holder*, however, the Second Circuit U.S. Court of Appeals did reach the question of particular social group in the context of sex trafficking and forced prostitution. In that case, the Second Circuit considered the proposed social group of "young, unmarried Albanian women who are at risk of being kidnaped and forced into prostitution," and found that it does not constitute a viable social group for asylum purposes.[125] The BIA had found that group to be "too amorphous," noting the

[119] *Id.* at 252.

[120] *Id.* at 255.

[121] *Id.*

[122] *Id.* at 254 (citing *Rreshpja v. Gonzales*, 420 F.3d 551, 556 (6th Cir. 2005)).

[123] *Id.*

[124] *Id.* at 256.

[125] *Gjura v. Holder*, 695 F.3d 223 (2d Cir. 2012).

lack of evidence showing that young, unmarried Albanian women were targeted more than children and married Albanian women.[126] The Second Circuit agreed, citing the Sixth Circuit case of *Rreshpja v. Gonzales*, which held that a similar group was not cognizable for asylum purposes because "generalized, sweeping classifications" doe not establish social groups for asylum purposes.[127] The Second Circuit also agreed that "a social group may not be circularly defined by the fact it suffers persecution."[128] The court concluded, "When the harm visited upon members of a group is attributable to the incentives presented to ordinary criminals rather than to persecution, the scales are tipped away from considering those people a 'particular social group' within the meaning of the INA."[129]

The Seventh Circuit also has grappled with the particular social group question in the context of sex trafficking and forced prostitution of women from Albania. In *Cece v. Holder*, the Seventh Circuit considered the claim of a woman from Albania who feared being kidnapped and forced to join a prostitution ring.[130] The court found that "young Albanian women living alone" was a viable social group since it is a group united by a common, immutable characteristic, and the Seventh Circuit had already rejected the BIA's additional requirements of social visibility and particularity.[131] The BIA had rejected the proposed social group on the ground that it was defined in part by the persecution that Ms. Cece feared.[132] The Seventh Circuit disagreed, stating that a group can be defined in part by the persecution as long as that was not the only characteristic defining the group.[133] The court found that a viable social group may be defined by a combination of fundamental or immutable characteristics and others that are not protected characteristics; not all uniting characteristics need to be protected characteristics, as long as a protected characteristic is one reason for the persecution.[134] In addressing the proposed group of "young Albanian women who live alone," the court recognized that age, gender, nationality, and living status are all unchangeable and fundamental, and therefore, they meet the *Matter of Acosta* social group test.[135] The Seventh Circuit then remanded the case back to the BIA for reconsideration.

---

[126] *Id.* at 225.

[127] *Id.* at 226 (citing *Rreshpja v. Gonzales*, 420 F.3d 551, 555 (6th Cir. 2005)).

[128] *Id.* (quoting *Rreshpja v. Gonzales*, 420 F.3d 551, 556 (6th Cir. 2005)).

[129] *Id.* at 226–27.

[130] *Cece v. Holder*, 733 F.3d 662 (7th Cir. 2013).

[131] *Id.* at 673 (citing *Gatimi v. Holder*, 578 F.3d 611 (7th Cir. 2009) and declaring that the group could not be distinguished from other recognized groups based on immutable and fundamental traits).

[132] *Id.* at 671.

[133] *Id.*

[134] *Id.* at 672–73.

[135] *Id.* at 673.

In 2014 in *Paloka v. Holder*, the Second Circuit again considered the social group of "young Albanian women" and related groups in considering the asylum claim of an Albanian woman who had fled to the United States after several attempted kidnappings.[136] The IJ had denied the claim, stating that the articulated social groups were "too broad" and that the applicant was not targeted on account of a protected ground. Rather, she was a "good target for criminal opportunistic behavior."[137] The BIA agreed that the proposed groups were "not defined with sufficient particularity to be cognizable particular social groups," and agreed with the IJ's assessment that the harm lacked a nexus to a protected ground.[138]

In considering the case on review, the Second Circuit reviewed the BIA's social group jurisprudence, including its most recent precedential cases of *Matter of M–E–V–G–* and *Matter of W–G–R–* in which the BIA clarified its three-prong test for a cognizable social group.[139] The court also reviewed the related cases of *Rreshpja v. Gonzales, Cece v. Holder*, and its own *Gjura v. Holder*, as well as other gender-based social group claims before the circuit courts, noting that the BIA has now clarified the legal landscape for adjudicating particular social group claims.[140] The Second Circuit remanded the case, stating:

> [E]very consideration that classically supports the law's ordinary remand requirement does so here. The agency can bring its expertise to bear upon the matter; it can evaluate the evidence; it can make an initial determination; and, in doing so, it can, through informed discussion and analysis, help a court later determine whether its decision exceeds the leeway that the law provides.[141]

The Second Circuit went on to explain that the BIA's decisions in *Matter of M–E–V–G–* and *Matter of W–G–R–* are important for cases, like Ms. Paloka's, that "straddle the line between individuals threatened by state-sponsored or state-condoned criminality on account of their membership in a particular social group and individuals threatened only because they live in a country with pervasive criminality."[142]

Although the Second Circuit did not make a determination regarding the cognizability of the proposed social group in *Paloka v. Holder* and instead remanded the case for reconsideration in light of the BIA's decisions in *Matter of M–E–V–G–* and *Matter of W–G–R–*, the court did share its views in dicta. The court noted that, even though subjection to the same kind of harm does not in itself yield a cognizable particular social group, the "'shared trait of persecution does not disqualify an

---

[136] *Paloka v. Holder*, 762 F.3d 191, 193–95 (2d Cir. 2014).

[137] *Id.* at 194.

[138] *Id.*

[139] *Id.* at 195–97.

[140] *Id.* at 197.

[141] *Id.* at 197–98 (quoting *INS v. Ventura*, 537 U.S. 12, 17 (2002)).

[142] *Id.* at 198.

otherwise valid social group' and that persecution can be the 'catalyst' for societal recognition.'"[143] The court addressed the IJ's statement that it seemed that "the factors [Ms. Paloka] relied upon [as] constituting the elements of her particular social group are the elements which make her a good target for criminal opportunistic behavior."[144] The court noted that "being a victim of a crime or even being a likely target for criminal opportunistic behavior does not necessarily preclude the existence of a valid asylum claim . . . Indeed, those facing persecution may often be the most vulnerable to crimes, especially if the government condones or aids the perpetrators."[145]

The Second Circuit went on to suggest that the BIA might reconsider Ms. Paloka's proposed social group in light of "the Seventh Circuit's observation that both gender and youth are immutable characteristics that fit within the broad definition set out in *Acosta*."[146] It also noted that Ms. Paloka had refined her particular social group during the course of her appeal to include a specific age range of 15 to 25.[147] Based on these reasons, the court concluded that remand to the BIA was necessary for redetermination of whether Ms. Paloka has identified a cognizable social group in light of the BIA's recent clarifications.[148]

These cases illustrate that asylum claims based on sex trafficking and forced prostitution is an unsettled area of gender-based asylum jurisprudence that continues to develop. They also demonstrate the importance of precision in defining, supporting with evidence, and presenting proposed particular social groups, especially in light of the BIA's clarified legal standards.

> ➢ **Practice Pointer**: Outside the Third and Seventh Circuits, which have rejected the BIA's added requirements of social distinction and particularity, practitioners should be prepared to address social distinction and particularity in all jurisdictions and with all social groups, even those that have been long-established. However, practitioners also should continue to challenge these requirements as unreasonable restrictions on protection for bona fide refugees.[149] It is important to preserve these challenges for appeal. See Chapter 2 of this book for a detailed discussion of the history and development of the standard for particular social groups, as well as strategies for formulating a cognizable group.

---

[143] *Id.* (quoting *Matter of M–E–V–G–*, 26 I&N Dec. 227, 243 (BIA 2014)).

[144] *Id.*

[145] *Id.*

[146] *Id.* (citing *Cece v. Holder*, 733 F.3d 662, 671 (7th Cir. 2013)).

[147] *Id.* at 198–99.

[148] *Id.* at 199.

[149] See chapter 2 for a detailed discussion of the development of the BIA's particular social group standard and how the circuit courts have responded.

For the several circuits that had adopted the BIA's previous social visibility (now social distinction) and particularity requirements,[150] *Matter of M–E–V–G–* and *Matter of W–G–R–* will likely have little impact. However, the BIA's dicta demanding such specificity to meet the particularity requirement, its seeming requirement of substantial evidence of sociological matters in the countries of feared persecution, and its clarification that it is society's perspective, not the persecutor's, that is relevant to the social distinction determination may conflict with even those circuits' precedent. Moreover, it is possible that the Third, Seventh, and Ninth Circuits, which had previously rejected, in whole or in part, social visibility and particularity,[151] may have to reconsider whether the BIA's interpretation of the statute is reasonable.[152] However, those courts may determine that the BIA's requirements do not merit deference because they are an impermissible and unreasonable interpretation of "particular social group."[153] Thus, now that the BIA has renamed social visibility as "social distinction" and reaffirmed this requirement, as well as its "particularity" requirement, the state of social group jurisprudence is most certainly in flux and unclear.

---

[150] *Umana-Ramos v. Holder*, 724 F.3d 667, 671 (6th Cir. 2013); *Henriquez-Rivas v. Holder*, 707 F.3d 1081, 1089 (9th Cir. 2013); *Orellana-Monson v. Holder*, 685 F.3d 511, 521 (5th Cir. 2012); *Gaitan v. Holder*, 671 F.3d 678, 681 (8th Cir. 2012); *Rivera-Barrientos v. Holder*, 666 F.3d 641, 649–53 (10th Cir. 2012); *Mendez-Barrera v. Holder*, 602 F.3d 21, 26 (1st Cir. 2010); *Scatambuli v. Holder*, 558 F.3d 53 (1st Cir. 2009); *Al-Ghorbani v. Holder*, 585 F.3d 980, 991, 994 (6th Cir. 2009); *Ramos-Lopez v. Holder*, 563 F.3d 855, 858–62 (9th Cir. 2009); *Davila-Mejia v. Mukasey*, 531 F.3d 624, 629 (8th Cir. 2008); *Koudriachova v. Gonzales*, 490 F.3d 255 (2d Cir. 2007); *Ucelo-Gomez v. Mukasey*, 509 F.3d 70 (2d Cir. 2007); *Arteaga v. Mukasey*, 511 F.3d 940, 945 (9th Cir. 2007); *Castillo-Arias v. Att'y Gen.*, 446 F.3d 1190, 1197 (11th Cir. 2006). *But see Martinez v. Holder*, 740 F.3d 902, 910 (4th Cir. 2014) (declining to address social visibility); *Cece v. Holder*, 733 F.3d 662, 668 n.1 (7th Cir. 2013) (rejecting social visibility); *Valdiviezo-Galdamez v. Att'y Gen.*., 663 F.3d 582, 607 (3d Cir. 2011) (rejecting social visibility); *Lizama v. Holder*, 629 F.3d 440, 446–47 (4th Cir. 2011) (declining to address social visibility); *Crespin-Valladares v. Holder*, 632 F.3d 117, 126 (4th 2011) (declining to address social visibility); *Perdomo v. Holder*, 611 F.3d 662 (9th Cir. 2010) (describing social visibility and particularity as "factors to consider" rather than requirements); *Rojas-Perez v. Holder*, 699 F.3d 74 (1st Cir. 2010) (questioning the rationality of the BIA's application of social visibility); *Gatimi v. Holder*, 578 F.3d 611, 615–16 (7th Cir. 2009) (rejecting the social visibility requirement); *Benitez Ramos v. Holder*, 589 F.3d 426, 430 (7th Cir. 2009) (rejecting the social visibility requirement).

[151] *Henriquez-Rivas v. Holder*, 707 F.3d 1081 (9th Cir. 2013); *Cece v. Holder*, 733 F.3d 662 (7th Cir. 2013); *Valdiviezo-Galdamez v. Holder*, 663 F.3d 582 (3d Cir. 2011); *Gatimi v. Holder*, 578 F.3d 611 (7th Cir. 2009).

[152] *See generally Nat'l Cable & Telecomms. Ass'n v. Brand X Internet Servs.*, 545 U.S. 967 (2005) (stating that the agency may invoke its authority to interpret a statute and decline to follow circuit precedent when the statute is ambiguous and has been interpreted differently among circuits). *See Matter of M–E–V–G–*, at 230 (noting that the BIA's reasonable interpretation of "membership in a particular social group" is entitled to deference).

[153] *See generally, Nat'l Cable & Telecomms. Ass'n v. Brand X Internet Servs.*, 545 U.S. 967 (2005). See chapter 12 for a detailed discussion of federal court deference to agency interpretations.

6. Gender-Specific Laws and Repressive Social Mores

The first case that addressed whether a woman's refusal to conform to her government's gender-specific laws or to her country's repressive social mores was the Third Circuit U.S. Court of Appeals' 1993 decision in *Fatin v. INS.*[154] In that case, the Third Circuit, in an opinion written by now-Supreme Court Justice Samuel Alito, upheld the BIA's denial of relief to a woman who refused to wear a chador (an Islamic veil) and otherwise conform to the Iranian government's gender-specific laws. The court reasoned that the record below did not establish the applicant's contention that she was a member of the group of women whose opposition to the Iranian laws were so profound that she would choose to suffer the severe consequences of noncompliance.[155] However, despite denying the petition for review, the Third Circuit used language in its decision that opened the door to these types of gender-based claims — "that feminism could constitute a political opinion, that gender could define a [particular social group], and generally that women who were being subjected to serious abuse because of their gender deserve protection."[156]

Since *Fatin v. INS*, federal courts have found that women who refuse to conform to their government's gender-specific laws, such as noncompliance with gender-specific dress codes, may satisfy the definition of particular social group and that such noncompliance may rise to the level of persecution.[157] To establish harm rising to the level of persecution, such applicants would need to demonstrate that:

(1) they find the gender-specific laws offensive;

(2) they do not wish to comply with the laws; and

(3) compliance with the laws would be so abhorrent to the applicants that compliance would itself be tantamount to persecution.[158]

---

[154] *Fatin v. INS*, 12 F.3d 1233 (3d Cir. 1993).

[155] *Id.*

[156] Anker, *supra* note 8 (discussing the Third Circuit's decision in *Fatin v. INS*, 12 F.3d 1233 (3d Cir. 1993)).

[157] *See, e.g.*, *Safaie v. INS*, 25 F.3d 636, 640 (8th Cir. 1994) (stating that Iranian women who would refuse to conform to the country's gender-specific laws may constitute a particular social group); *Fatin v. INS*, 12 F.3d at 1241–42 (holding that an Iranian woman who finds gender-specific laws and repressive social norms objectionable or offensive may belong to a "particular social group" if her opposition is so profound that she would choose to suffer the severe consequences for noncompliance). Note, however, that *Safaie v. INS* has been criticized as incoherently measuring the cognizability of a social group by whether all group members would have a well-founded fear. *See* DHS Brief in *Matter of R–A–* (2004), *available at http://cgrs.uchastings.edu/sites/default/files/Matter%20of%20R-A-%20DHS%20brief.pdf* (last visited Apr. 3, 2015).

[158] *See Fatin v. INS*, 12 F.3d at 1241–42. *See also Yadegar-Sargis v. INS*, 297 F.3d 596, 604–05 (7th Cir. 2002) (finding that an Iranian woman's compliance with the dress code did not violate a tenet of her Christian faith and did not prevent her from attending church or practicing her faith, and therefore, the dress code was "not abhorrent to [the applicant's] deepest beliefs").

Additionally, women may be particularly vulnerable to persecution for refusal to follow repressive social norms imposed on them by society, and even their own families. For example, in *Matter of S–A–*, a Moroccan woman suffered severe abuse at the hands of her orthodox Muslim father because she believed in a liberal, egalitarian version of Islam. Her father targeted her with violence because her religious beliefs differed from her father's orthodox Muslim views concerning the proper role of women in Moroccan society.[159] The BIA granted her asylum, finding that she had suffered past persecution and has a well-founded fear of future persecution at the hands of her father on account of her liberal Muslim beliefs.[160]

Although these claims have been and may continue to be successful, however, they are not immune from challenge. For example, the Ninth Circuit, sitting en banc in *Fisher v. INS*,[161] reversed its previous decision, finding that the applicant, an Iranian woman, had failed to establish a well-founded fear of persecution on account of religion, political opinion, or membership in a particular social group. According to the Ninth Circuit, the harm suffered by the applicant did not amount to persecution because the applicant failed to establish that she would receive disproportionately severe punishment or that the laws were especially unconscionable.[162] Thus, like many other forms of gender-based violence, a woman's asylum claim based on gender-specific laws and/or repressive social mores merits requires a deep understanding of the case law in the relevant circuit, the prior treatment of gender-based claims, and the contours and complexities of demonstrating persecution on account of a gender-related protected ground.

7. *Domestic Violence*

Perhaps the form of gender-based violence that has been the most controversial and presented the highest hurdles to asylum-seekers as a basis for protection is domestic violence.[163] The seminal case of Ms. Rody Alvarado illustrates the

---

[159] *Matter of S–A–*, 22 I&N Dec. 1328 (BIA 2000).

[160] *Id.* at 1336–37.

[161] *Fisher v. INS*, 79 F.3d 955 (9th Cir. 1996).

[162] *Id.* at 961–62; *see also Yadegar-Sargis v. INS*, 297 F.3d 596 (7th Cir. 2002) (holding that an Iranian Christian woman who opposed wearing Islamic garb did not have a well-founded fear of persecution); *Sharif v. INS*, 87 F.3d 932 (7th Cir. 1996) (holding that an Iranian woman failed to establish past persecution or a well-founded fear of future persecution based on her status as a "Westernized woman").

[163] *See* Karen Musalo, "*A Tale of Two Women: The Claims for Asylum of Fauziya Kassindja, who Fled FGC, and Rody Alvarado, a Survivor of Partner (Domestic) Violence, in Arbel, Efrat*," Catherine Dauvergne, and Jenni Millbank, eds. GENDER IN REFUGEE LAW: FROM THE MARGINS TO THE CENTRE (New York: Routledge, 2014) At 73-97, available at *http://papers.ssrn.com/sol3/papers.cfm?abstract_id=2528337* (last visited Apr. 2, 2015). *See Matter of S–A–*, 22 I&N Dec. 1328, 1335 (BIA 2000) (granting asylum to a Muslim woman from Morocco who suffered domestic abuse at the hands of her father on account of her religious beliefs, which differed from her father's orthodox beliefs); *see also* U.N. High Comm'r for Refugees, Guidelines on International Protection No. 2: "Membership of a particular social group" within the context of *Article 1A(2) of the 1951 Convention*

Continued

complexities of this long-unsettled area of gender-based asylum law. In 1999, the BIA denied asylum to a Guatemalan woman named Rody Alvarado, who had fled Guatemala after 10 years of extreme physical, sexual, and psychological violence at the hands of her husband and ignored pleas for help from the police.[164] In denying asylum, the BIA left open the questions whether domestic violence constituted persecution and whether gender could be the basis, at least in part, for a viable particular social group. Attorney General Janet Reno vacated the BIA's controversial decision in 2001. The AG's reason for vacating the decision was to allow for the claim to be considered after final regulations regarding gender-based claims were issued.[165] Proposed regulations were issued in December 2000 for public comment.[166] These proposed regulations focused on what constitutes a particular social group, stating that the "crucial aspect" of the definition was immutability; the common trait should be "unchangeable or truly fundamental to an applicant's identity."[167] The proposed regulations also listed several factors that could be considered in addition to the *Matter of Acosta* test, including:

- Close affiliation actuated by common impulse or interest;[168]
- Voluntary associational relationship among members;[169]
- Societal recognition or understanding of the group as a segment of the population;
- Self-perception by group members of group status; and
- Whether distinctions are drawn within the society between those who have the characteristic at issue and those who do not.[170]

---

and/or its 1967 Protocol relating to the Status of Refugees, HCR/GIP/02/02 (May 7, 2002) ¶ 22, available at *www.unhcr.org/3d58de2da.html* (noting that in situations of domestic abuse, an applicant who cannot show that her persecutor is abusing her on a protected ground, may still qualify for refugee status upon a showing that her government is unwilling to extend protection based on one of the five grounds). Immigration judges (IJs) also have granted asylum to women who have been subjected to domestic violence in countries in which their governments were unable or unwilling to protect them. *See, e.g.*, *Matter of A–N–*, A73 603 840 (IJ Dec. 22, 2000) (IJ Grussendorf), *reported in* 78 INTERPRETER RELEASES 409 (Feb. 26, 2001) (granting asylum to a Jordanian woman); *Matter of Sharmin*, A73 556 833 (IJ Sept. 27, 1996) (New York, NY) (IJ Bukszpan), reported in 74 INTERPRETER RELEASES 174 (Jan. 27, 1997) (granting asylum to a Bangladeshi woman); *Matter of A– and Z–*, A72 190 893, A72 793 219 (IJ Dec. 20, 1994) (Arlington, VA) (IJ Nejelski), reported in 72 INTERPRETER RELEASES 521 (Apr. 17, 1995) (granting asylum to a Jordanian woman).

[164] *Matter of R–A–*, 22 I&N Dec. 906, 909 (BIA 1999).

[165] *Matter of R–A–*, 22 I&N Dec. 906 (AG 2001).

[166] *See* Asylum and Withholding Definitions, 65 Fed. Reg. 76588–98 (proposed Dec. 7, 2000) (to be codified at 8 CFR pt. 208).

[167] *Id.* at 76593.

[168] *Id.* at 76594 (drawing this consideration from the Ninth Circuit U.S. Court of Appeals' decision in *Sanchez-Trujillo v. INS*, 801 F.2d 1571 (9th Cir. 1986)).

[169] *Id.* (drawing this consideration from the Ninth Circuit's decision in *Sanchez-Trujillo v. INS*, 801 F.2d 1571 (9th Cir. 1986)).

[170] *Id.*

No final regulations were ever published, however. While the rule sat pending agreement of the newly created Department of Homeland Security (DHS) and the DOJ, AG John Ashcroft certified *Matter of R–A–* back to himself in 2003 and accepted new briefs by the parties in February 2004.

Astonishingly, DHS took the position in its brief that the applicant should be granted asylum and that the social group to which she belonged was "married women in Guatemala who are unable to leave the relationship."[171] DHS argued that this social group met the *Matter of Acosta* test because it was united by gender plus the applicant's marital status, which was immutable due to the context of the relevant culture.[172] DHS took the position that *Matter of Acosta* was the appropriate standard for determining the viability of a particular social group and urged the AG not to issue a precedential decision and instead await the final regulations.[173] Notably, relying on UNHCR guidance, DHS also argued that the size of the group is not relevant to whether the group is a cognizable social group for purposes of asylum eligibility.[174] DHS recommended a grant of relief to Ms. Alvarado.[175] After accepting briefs, instead of rendering a decision, Attorney General John Ashcroft remanded the case to the BIA in 2005 "for reconsideration following final publication of the proposed rule" on gender-based claims.[176]

- **Practice Pointer**: Practitioners making domestic violence-based asylum claims on behalf of their clients should read and use the DHS brief in preparing their arguments. The brief is available on the Center for Gender and Refugee Studies website.[177]

While *Matter of R–A–* was pending on remand to the BIA, the BIA's social group standards developed over a series of confusing cases including *Matter of C–A–*, *Matter of A–M–E– & J–G–U–*, *Matter of S–E–G–*, and *Matter of E–A–G–*.[178] These cases added two requirements to supplement the BIA's *Matter of Acosta* test for viability of a particular social group: social visibility (now social distinction) and particularity. During this time, it was unclear how these decisions might affect domestic violence-based claims like that of Ms. Alvarado. Following the 2008

[171] Br. of DHS at 26, *In re R–A–*, 22 I&N Dec. 906, 2001 WL 1744475 (BIA 2001), *available at http://cgrs.uchastings.edu/sites/default/files/Matter%20of%20R-A-%20DHS%20brief.pdf.*

[172] *Id.* at 20–25.

[173] *Id.* at 4–5, 19–25.

[174] *Id.* at 20–25.

[175] *Id.* at 19–42.

[176] *Matter of R–A–*, 23 I&N Dec. 694 (AG 2005).

[177] Brief of U.S. Dep't of Homeland Security on A 73 753 922's Eligibility for Relief, *available at http://cgrs.uchastings.edu/sites/default/files/Matter%20of%20R-A-%20DHS%20brief.pdf* (last accessed Apr. 1, 2015).

[178] See chapter 2 for a detailed discussion of the development of the BIA's particular social group test and the current legal standards for defining a viable social group and demonstrating persecution on account of that group.

decisions in *Matter of S–E–G–* and *Matter of E–A–G–* and the BIA's pronouncement that social visibility and particularity were requirements in addition to the *Matter of Acosta* test for demonstrating a viable social group, Attorney General Michael Mukasey again certified *Matter of R–A–* from the BIA, where it had been awaiting publication of the final regulations.[179] The AG then remanded the case with instructions that the BIA should proceed in light of the new social group test articulated in *Matter of S–E–G–*.[180]

In 2009, while *Matter of R–A–* remained pending on remand before the BIA, the BIA considered the asylum claim of a woman, Ms. L–R–, from Mexico who had fled an abusive domestic relationship in which she was regularly raped, held captive, beaten, and threatened with death.[181] The police had ignored her pleas.[182] The proposed social groups were "Mexican women in an abusive domestic relationship who are unable to leave" and "children of women in abusive relationships in Mexico who are unable to leave." However, in its brief, DHS rejected these groups as "impermissibly circular,"[183] instead proposing the two alternative groups of "Mexican women in domestic relationships who are unable to leave" and "Mexican women who are viewed as property by virtue of their positions within a domestic relationship."[184] DHS asserted that these proposed groups could satisfy immutability, social visibility, and particularity, depending on the facts and evidence presented.[185] DHS asked the BIA to remand the case to an IJ to provide Ms. L–R– with the opportunity to build an adequate record.[186]

DHS's brief was especially significant because it offered a framework for recognizing social groups based on domestic violence. In addressing the BIA's three-part test for viability of a social group, DHS again confirmed that gender and a woman's status in a relationship can be immutable.[187] It stated that social visibility could be demonstrated by evidence that a woman is viewed as property by her abuser and that society and the government understand and tolerate such abuse.[188] Finally, if the record showed that the group of persons in domestic relationships was sufficiently defined, the particularity prong of the test could be met. For example, if the laws of

---

[179] *Matter of R–A–*, 24 I&N Dec. 629 (BIA 2008).

[180] *Id.*

[181] *See* Ctr. for Gender & Refugee Studies, *Matter of L–R–*, *http://cgrs.uchastings.edu/our-work/matter-l-r* (last visited Jan. 2, 2014).

[182] *Id.*

[183] Br. of DHS, *In re L–R–*, at 6, *available at http://cgrs.uchastings.edu/sites/default/files/Matter_of_LR_DHS_Brief_4_13_2009.pdf* (last visited Jan. 2, 2014).

[184] *Id.* at 14.

[185] *Id.* at 17–20.

[186] *Id.* at 29.

[187] *Id.* at 16–17.

[188] *Id.* at 17–18.

the country in question recognize such a group, that group could be considered sufficiently particular.[189] In addressing nexus, DHS focused on the perspective of the persecutor, noting that where the government fails to provide meaningful protection and where women cannot escape abusive relationships, those factors may "play a central role in that persecutor's choice" of the applicant as his victim.[190]

DHS's position in *Matter of L–R–* led to the BIA's remand of both Ms. L–R–'s and Ms. Alvarado's cases to the IJs. Ms. Alvarado was finally granted asylum by the IJ in 2009 and Ms. L–R– was granted asylum in 2010.[191] Although these cases did not result in binding precedent or final regulations regarding particular social group, they paved the way for successful asylum claims based on domestic violence and provided guidance for analyzing such claims under the BIA's three-part social group test.[192]

> **Practice Pointer**: The Center for Gender and Refugee Studies at the University of California, Hastings College of Law provides legal expertise and resources to attorneys representing women asylum-seekers fleeing gender-related harm, and tracks decisions in these cases. The Center keeps a database of unpublished BIA and IJ decisions in gender-based asylum claims at *http://cgrs.uchastings.edu/search-cases*. Attorneys representing women fleeing persecution linked to their gender—such as honor killing, rape, gang violence, domestic violence, sexual trafficking, female genital mutilation—should fill out the "Assistance" form on the Center's website at *http://cgrs.uchastings.edu/assistance/request*.

After years of uncertainty regarding whether domestic violence victims could meet the legal requirements for asylum in the United States, the BIA broke its 15-year silence on the issue; on August 26, 2014, the BIA published a landmark decision ruling that women fleeing domestic violence can be members of a particular social group.[193] *Matter of A–R–C–G–* involved a mother of three from Guatemala who suffered "repugnant abuse" at the hands of her husband, including rapes, beatings, a broken nose, and burns with paint thinner that left her with scars.[194] The police in Guatemala had refused to interfere and her reports only resulted in death threats from her husband if she went to the police again. Her attempts to flee and stay with

---

[189] *Id.*

[190] *Id.* at 20–21.

[191] The history of both *Matter of R–A–* and *Matter of L–R–* are detailed on the Ctr. for Gender & Refugee Studies website, *available at http://cgrs.uchastings.edu/our-work/matter-r* and *http://cgrs.uchastings.edu/our-work/matter-l-r* (last visited Jan. 2, 2014).

[192] In fact, the BIA's decision in *Matter of R–A–* was vacated and has no precedential value at all. *Matter of R–A–*, Int. Dec. 3403 (BIA 1999), vacated (AG 2001).

[193] *Matter of A–R–C–G–*, 26 I&N Dec. 388 (BIA 2014).

[194] *Id.* at 389.

relatives also did not result in her protection, as her husband found her and threatened her if she did not return.[195] The BIA found that Ms. C–G– suffered harm rising to the level of persecution, and DHS agreed.

- **Practice Pointer**: A common argument by the government is that beatings may not rise to the level of persecution since they are not a threat to the individual's life or freedom. However, the courts have found that persecution encompasses more than threats to life or freedom and that non–life threatening violence and physical abuse may also rise to the level of persecution.[196] Practitioners should argue that beatings can rise to the level of persecution, as recognized by the BIA in *Matter of A–R–C–G–*.[197] Moreover, courts must consider the harm cumulatively, not as isolated incidents.[198] Finally, psychological harm and serious threats of harm also can rise to the level of persecution.[199] See chapter 2 of this book for a detailed discussion of the types of harm that may rise to the level of persecution.

In considering the proposed social group of "married women in Guatemala who are unable to leave their relationship," the Immigration Judge had denied Ms. C–G–'s asylum claim, finding that the violence she suffered was not on account of a gender-defined social group, but rather that it was the result of arbitrary criminality. On appeal, the BIA applied the facts of Ms. C–G–'s case to the BIA's recently clarified and re-affirmed three-part test for viability of social groups: immutability, social distinction, and particularity.[200] Based on the evidence presented, the BIA found that all three parts of this test were met, and remanded the case to the IJ to consider the remaining requirements for asylum.[201]

In addressing immutability, the BIA found that gender is an immutable characteristic and that marital status also can be immutable characteristic where the

---

[195] *Id.*

[196] *See, e.g., Tamas-Mercea v. Reno*, 222 F.3d 417, 424 (7th Cir. 2000); *Mitev v. INS*, 67 F.3d 1325, 1330 (7th Cir. 1995).

[197] *Matter of A–R–C–G–*, 26 I&N Dec. 388, 389 (BIA 2014).

[198] *See, e.g., Ritonga v. Holder*, 633 F.3d 971, 975 (10th Cir. 2011) (stating that "cumulative effects of multiple incidents may constitute persecution"); *Shi-Chen v. Holder*, 604 F.3d 324 (7th Cir. 2010) (remanding due to the agency's failure to consider the cumulative effects of the harm); *Faruk v. Ashcroft*, 378 F.3d 940, 942 (9th Cir. 2004) (finding that the cumulative effects of beatings, attacks with rocks, verbal assaults threats, and denial of a marriage certificate rose to the level of persecution).

[199] *See, e.g., Mashiri v. Ashcroft*, 383 F.3d 1112, 1119 (9th Cir. 2004) (stating "threats may be compelling evidence of past persecution, particularly when they are specific and menacing and are accompanied by evidence of violent confrontations, near-confrontations and vandalism"); *Vatulev v. Ashcroft*, 354 F.3d 1207, 1210 (10th Cir. 2003) (recognizing that threats may constitute persecution). *See also* AOBTC Workbook, Female Asylum Applicants, *supra* note 36, at 22.

[200] *See Matter of M–E–V–G–*, 26 I&N Dec. 227 (BIA 2014); *Matter of W–G–R–*, 26 I&N Dec. 208 (BIA 2014).

[201] *Matter of A–R–C–G–*, 26 I&N Dec. 388, 392–95 (BIA 2014).

individual is unable to leave the relationship.[202] The BIA advised that adjudicators must consider the applicant's own experiences, as well as objective evidence such as evidence of country conditions.[203] The BIA also found that "married women in Guatemala who are unable to leave their relationship" was sufficiently particular because the terms used to define the group — "married," "women," and "unable to leave the relationship" — have "commonly accepted definitions within Guatemalan society."[204] In making this determination, the BIA relied upon the facts of the case, as well as the applicant's experience with the police in which they refused to assist her because they would not interfere in a marital relationship.[205]

Finally, in considering whether the proposed group was socially distinct within the society in question, the BIA stated that it must "look to the evidence to determine whether a society … makes meaningful distinctions based on the common immutable characteristics of being a married woman in a domestic relationship that she cannot leave." The BIA noted that such evidence may include, among other sociopolitical factors, whether the society in question recognizes the need to offer protection to victims of domestic violence — specifically, whether the country has criminal laws designed to protect domestic violence victims and, if so, whether those laws are effectively enforced.[206] The BIA found that, despite the existence of laws in place to prosecute domestic violence claims, the record in Ms. C–G–'s case included evidence that Guatemala has a culture of "machismo and family violence," that "[s]exual offenses, including spousal rape, remain a serious problem," and that enforcement of the laws can be problematic because the police "often failed to respond to requests for assistance related to domestic violence."[207] The BIA emphasized that social distinction, like the other two prongs of its test for viability of a particular social group, is a case-by-case determination that depends on the facts and evidence presented in each individual case.[208]

This decision marks a critical turn in the BIA's interpretation of gender, and specifically, domestic violence-based asylum claims. It is especially valuable in that

---

[202] *Id.* at 392–93 (citing *Matter of Acosta* and *Matter of W–G–R–*).

[203] *Id.* at 393.

[204] *Id.*

[205] *Id.*

[206] *Id.* at 394.

[207] *Id.*

[208] *Id.* at 394–95. Arguably, this emphasis on the importance of a case-by-case determination – in particular, the way in which the BIA discussed this – only illuminates the BIA's incoherence in their departure from *Matter of Acosta*. In *Matter of A–R–C–G–*, the BIA stated, "We point out that cases arising in the context of domestic violence generally involve unique and discrete issues not present in other particular social group determinations, which extends to the matter of social distinction." *Id.* at 394. It seems that this qualification of extending social distinction to the domestic violence context as "unique and discrete" may be reflective of the BIA's inability to explain why the particular social group in *Matter of W–G–R–* is not cognizable, while the one in *Matter of A–R–C–G–* is.

it followed the BIA's 2014 clarification of its test for particular social group viability in *Matter of M–E–V–G–* and *Matter of W–G–R–* and analyzed a gender-based social group within that framework.[209]

- **Practice Pointer**: There are reports that DHS trial attorneys are sometimes arguing for a narrow reading of *Matter of A–R–C–G–*'s holding as not extending to non-marital relationships or being confined by nationality to Guatemala. However, the history of litigation leading to *Matter of A–R–C–G–*, especially DHS's own briefs in *Matter of R–A–* and *Matter of L–R–*, refute this. For example, the respondent in *Matter of L–R–* was a Mexican woman who was not married to her abuser. Additionally, *Matter of A–R–C–G–* was one of seven different domestic violence-based asylum cases spanning both married and unmarried women in domestic relationships from Guatemala, Honduras, and El Salvador in which the BIA made identical solicitation to AILA for amicus briefs.[210]
- **Practice Pointer**: For a terrific guide to preparing domestic violence-based asylum claims, see the Center for Gender & Refugee Studies' practice advisory, "Domestic Violence-Based Asylum Claims," available at *http://cgrs.uchastings.edu/sites/default/files/DV_Advisory_9-12-2014_FINAL_1.pdf* (last updated Sept. 12, 2014).

B. Particular Social Groups and Group Membership

In *Matter of Acosta*, the BIA recognized for the first time that gender alone may form the basis of a particular social group for asylum eligibility.[211] Then, in 1996 in *Matter of Kasinga*, the BIA specifically held that gender, in conjunction with other characteristics, may form the basis of a cognizable particular social group.[212] In that case, the applicant feared persecution on account of her membership in the particular social group of "young women of the Tchamba-Kunsuntu Tribe who have not had female genital mutilation, as practiced by that tribe, and who oppose the practice."[213] Few courts, however, have found that an individual may be eligible for asylum based on a particular social group defined solely by gender. This is because, generally, persecutors are motivated to harm the applicants because of their gender and some

---

[209] *Id.* at 392–95.

[210] B. Casper, *et al.*, "*Matter of M–E–V–G– and the BIA's Confounding Legal Standard for 'Membership in a Particular Social Group*,'" 14-06 IMMIGR. BRIEFINGS 1, n.363 (June 2014) (citing *Matter of M–E–V–G–*, 26 I&N Dec. 227, 250 (BIA 2014)); AILA Amicus Brief in *Matter of A–R–C–G–*, *available at www.aila.org/infonet/amicus-brief-mjv-rdcp-g-and-arc-g* (last visited Apr. 3, 2015).

[211] *Matter of Acosta*, 19 I&N Dec. 211 (BIA 1985).

[212] *Matter of Kasinga*, 21 I&N Dec. 357 (BIA 1996).

[213] *Id.*

other characteristic they possess, not their gender alone.[214] In addition to gender, some immutable characteristics commonly yielding women's need for protection include, but are not limited to:

- Clan or tribe;
- Religion;
- Nationality;
- Family membership;
- Sexual orientation;
- Status in a marriage or domestic relationship;
- Feminist beliefs or beliefs in women's rights;
- Opposition to gender-specific laws or repressive social norms; and
- Refusal to conform to gender-specific laws or repressive social norms.

Although few courts have found that an individual may be eligible for asylum based on a particular social group defined solely by gender, the Ninth Circuit relied on the *Matter of Acosta* immutable characteristic test in recognizing the particular social group of "Somali females" as cognizable.[215] In that case, the applicant had been subjected to FGM/C and the court found that the applicant's nationality and gender were the motivating characteristics because FGM/C "in Somalia is not clan specific, but rather is deeply imbedded in the culture throughout the nation and performed on approximately 98 percent of all females."[216] The Tenth Circuit U.S. Court of Appeals also relied on the *Matter of Acosta* test to find that both gender and tribal membership are immutable characteristics, and recognized the particular social

[214] *See Safaie v. INS*, 25 F.3d 636, 640 (8th Cir. 1994) (rejecting "Iranian women" as a viable social group because "no fact finder could reasonably conclude that all Iranian women had a well-founded fear of persecution based solely on their gender"); *Fatin v. INS*, 12 F.3d 1233, 1240 (3d Cir. 1993) (indicating that while the group "Iranian women" may satisfy the *Matter of Acosta* definition of social group because it includes individuals who share a common, immutable characteristic, the applicant had not established that she had a well-founded fear of persecution based solely on her gender); *Gomez v. INS*, 947 F.2d 660 (2d Cir. 1991) (finding that persecution on account of gender alone does not constitute persecution on account of membership in a particular social group).

[215] *Mohammed v. Gonzales*, 400 F.3d 785, 797 (9th Cir. 2005). *See also Hassan v. Gonzales*, 484 F.3d 513 (8th Cir. 2007) (remanding the case of an asylum-seeker from Somalia and stating, "the government's argument erroneously assumes that FGM is the only form of persecution in Somalia and that having undergone the procedure, Hassan, as a Somali woman, is no longer at risk of other prevalent forms of persecution. We have never held that a petitioner must fear the repetition of the exact harm that she has suffered in the past. Our definition of persecution is not that narrow.").

[216] *Id.* The court noted that such groups based on FGM could be more narrowly tailored depending on whether the applicant had undergone FGM in the way required by their culture. If they had not, the group could be defined as "Somali females who have not been subject to FGM as practiced in their society." *Id.*

group of "female members of the Tukulor Fulani tribe."[217] In responding to the concern that, if gender alone can form a particular social group, half of the population could be eligible for asylum, the court specified that the size of the particular social group is not relevant; the focus of the inquiry should be on whether there is a reasonable possibility that members of that group will be persecuted "on account of" their membership.[218]

- **Practice Pointer**: Although the approach of combining gender with some other characteristic is a common approach to defining gender-based particular social groups, there is no clear, principled basis for rejecting gender alone as a particular social group.[219] Arguably, the approach of combining gender with another characteristic merges the analysis of viability of the social group with nexus, and overlooks the "at least one central reason" standard for nexus.

Matter of Acosta's "common, immutable characteristic" test remains the starting point for defining any legally viable particular social group. However, as discussed in greater detail below in Part II, over time, the BIA has added two additional requirements to its *Acosta* test for defining a cognizable social group — social distinction and particularity.[220] These requirements have sparked harsh criticism and volumes of case law in the circuit courts, and they continue to be challenged. However, these requirements currently stand as precedent before the BIA and most circuits. Thus, for asylum-seekers articulating a gender-based social group, social distinction and particularity must be contended with in addition to *Matter of Acosta*'s common, immutable characteristic requirement.[221] Notably, in clarifying and

[217] *Niang v. Gonzales*, 422 F.3d 1189, 1199 (10th Cir. 2005) (acknowledging that gender alone can form the particular social group).

[218] *Id.*

[219] *See Matter of A–R–C–G–*, 26 I&N Dec. 388, 395 n.16 (BIA 2014); AILA Amicus Brief in *Matter of A–R–C–G–*, *available at www.aila.org/infonet/amicus-brief-mjv-rdcp-g-and-arc-g* (last visited Apr. 3, 2015). *See also Perdomo v. Holder*, 611 F.3d 662 (9th Cir. 2010).

[220] *See Matter of M–E–V–G–*, 26 I&N Dec. 227 (BIA 2014); *Matter of W–G–R–*, 26 I&N Dec. 208 (BIA 2014); *Matter of S–E–G–*, 24 I&N Dec. 579 (BIA 2008); *Matter of E–A–G–*, 24 I&N Dec. 591 (BIA 2008); *Matter of A–M–E– & J–G–U–*, 24 I&N Dec. 69 (BIA 2007); *Matter of C–A–*, 23 I&N Dec. 951 (BIA 2006). *See also supra* chapter 2 for a detailed discussion of particular social group jurisprudence and the status of this three-prong test in each circuit.

[221] *Matter of M–E–V–G–*, 26 I&N Dec. 227 (BIA 2014); *Matter of W–G–R–*, 26 I&N Dec. 208 (BIA 2014), *clarifying Matter of E–A–G–*, 24 I&N Dec. 591 (BIA 2008); *Matter of S–E–G–*, 24 I&N Dec. 579 (BIA 2008); *Matter of A–M–E– & J–G–U–*, 24 I&N Dec. 69 (BIA 2007); *Matter of C–A–*, 23 I&N Dec. 951 (BIA 2006). Note that the "social distinction" requirement used to be called "social visibility." *See Matter of C–A–*, 23 I&N Dec. 951, 959–61 (BIA 2006) (noting that UNHCR's *Guidelines* confirm that "visibility" is an important element), *aff'd Castillo-Arias v. U.S. Att'y Gen.*, 446 F.3d 1190 (11th Cir. 2006), *cert. denied*, 127 S.Ct. 977 (Jan. 8, 2007). *See also Matter of E–A–G–*, 24 I&N Dec. 591, 594 (BIA 2007) and *Matter of S–E–G–*, 24 I&N Dec. 579, 586–88 (BIA 2007). The social group approach applied by the BIA in *Matter of E–A–G–* and *Matter of S–E–G–*, which required social visibility and particularity, was criticized by UNHCR in an amicus brief filed in the U.S. Court of

Continued

reaffirming these two additional requirements, the BIA also reaffirmed its holdings in prior social group cases, asserting that the social groups in those cases meet the requirements of social distinction and particularity.[222] One case that the BIA reaffirmed is *Matter of Kasinga*, which significantly demonstrates that the BIA has recognized that gender-based social groups, depending on the facts and evidence presented, may meet its three-prong test for a cognizable social group.[223]

- **Practice Pointer**: Practitioners formulating particular social groups following the BIA's decisions in *Matter of M–E–V–G–* and *Matter of W–G–R–* should look to the BIA's analysis of *Matter of Kasinga* in those decisions for guidance on formulating a legally cognizable social group. Practitioners also should look to the BIA's analysis in *Matter of A–R–C–G–*, as that decision analyzed a gender-based social group under the BIA's three-prong test. Using similar language as the BIA did in addressing *Matter of Kasinga* in its *Matter of M–E–V–G–* and *Matter of W–G–R–* decisions and in *Matter of A–R–C–G–* to describe how a client's defined social group meets its three-part test, and citing to that language, will make it difficult for an IJ or the BIA to find that the group does not meet the BIA's new test.

The main challenge with meeting step one of the BIA's social group test — common, immutable characteristic — in demonstrating a viable social group based on gender is the fact that a social group must exist independently of the persecution. In other words, the group must not be defined solely by the fact that its members are being persecuted; that would be impermissibly circular.[224] "Victims of domestic violence," for example, generally would not be a viable particular social group. Such group formulations are tempting because a shared past experience has been found to be a common, immutable characteristic. However, such groups usually will fail the BIA's social group test.[225] On the other hand, as long as the defined group involves shared immutable characteristics apart from the persecution, including terms that reference the type of harm should not be fatal to the viability of the group. For example, as discussed above, young women who are members of the Tchamba-Kunsuntu tribe in Togo who have not been subjected to FGM/C and who oppose the practice, as well as young women living alone in Albania who are targeted for prostitution, have been held to be viable social groups.[226] Additionally, as UNHCR

Appeals for the Third Circuit in a gang-based persecution case. The brief is available at *www.unhcr.org/refworld/pdfid/49ef25102.pdf* (last visited June 7, 2014).

[222] *See Matter of M–E–V–G–*, 26 I&N Dec. at 237, 247; *Matter of W–G–R–*, 26 I&N Dec. at 218–19.

[223] *Matter of M–E–V–G–*, 26 I&N Dec. at 237, 247; *Matter of W–G–R–*, 26 I&N Dec. at 218–19.

[224] *See* DHS's Supp. Br., *Matter of L–R–* (BIA Apr. 13, 2009), *available at http://cgrs.uchastings.edu/our-work/matter-l-r*; *Matter of M–E–V–G–*, 26 I&N Dec. at 242; *Matter of A–M–E– & J–G–U–*, 24 I&N Dec. at 74.

[225] *See Matter of M–E–V–G–*, 26 I&N Dec. at 242; *Matter of A–M–E– & J–G–U–*, 24 I&N Dec. at 74.

[226] *Matter of Kasinga*, 21 I&N Dec. 357 (BIA 1996); *Cece v. Holder*, 733 F.3d 662 (7th Cir. 2013).

points out in its *Guidelines on International Protection*, a shared past experience of harm, such as being trafficked for example, may make a group particularly vulnerable and susceptible to subsequent violence or harm.[227] Thus, a shared past experience included in the group definition may be relevant to explaining the fear of future persecution.

> ➢ **Practice Pointer**: The government has argued in domestic violence-based asylum claims that a marital relationship is not immutable. However, the BIA in *Matter of A–R–C–G–* has recognized that marriage may be immutable if the woman is unable to leave the relationship. The BIA focuses on "whether dissolution of a marriage could be contrary to religious or other deeply held moral beliefs or if dissolution is possible when viewed in light of religious, cultural, or legal constraints."[228] In its brief in *Matter of L–R–*, DHS also noted that immutability of a domestic relationship can be established if the abuser would not recognize the separation or divorce as ending the relationship and his power and control over the victim.[229]

Defining a socially distinct group has emerged as a newer challenge for gender-based social group claims. "Social distinction" refers to whether a group is perceived and recognized as a distinct entity by society,[230] and it must be analyzed in the "context of the country of concern and the persecution feared."[231] It is the perception of society that matters, not the perception of the persecutor (which is relevant for establishing nexus).[232] In gender based claims, an important first step is to define the "society" involved in the social distinction inquiry. The society in question may not include the whole country, but rather, may be a more limited region or specific area of the country. For example, *Matter of Kasinga* addressed the perception of young women and the practice of FGM/C within a particular tribe.[233]

Once the society has been defined, the next step is to demonstrate through documentary and testimonial evidence that the society perceives the group as a

---

[227] U.N. High Comm'r for Refugees, Guidelines on International Protection: The application of Article 1A(2) of the 1951 Convention and/or 1967 Protocol relating to the Status of Refugees to Victims of Trafficking, *supra* note 103, ¶ 19.

[228] *Matter of A–R–C–G–*, 26 I&N Dec. 388, 392–93 (BIA 2014).

[229] DHS Supp. Br., *Matter of L–R–* (BIA Apr. 13, 2009), *available at http://cgrs.uchastings.edu/our-work/matter-l-r*.

[230] *Matter of M–E–V–G–*, 26 I&N Dec. at 240–43; *Matter of W–G–R–*, 26 I&N Dec. at 215–18. *See also*, *Matter of C–A–*, 23 I&N Dec. 951 (BIA 2006).

[231] *Matter of A–M–E– & J–G–U–*, 24 I&N Dec. 69 (BIA 2007) (confirmed by *Matter of M–E–V–G–*, 26 I&N Dec. 227 (BIA 2014) and *Matter of W–G–R–*, 26 I&N Dec. 208 (BIA 2014)).

[232] *Matter of W–G–R–*, 26 I&N Dec. at 218. *See supra* chapter 2 for a detailed discussion of social distinction and practice pointers for demonstrating that a social group is perceived as a distinct entity by society.

[233] *Matter of M–E–V–G–*, 26 I&N Dec. at 243.

distinct entity. According to the BIA, such evidence may include "country conditions reports, expert witness testimony, and press accounts of discriminatory laws and policies, historical animosities, and the like."[234] Any evidence that shows differential treatment of the group, higher rates of violence against the group, societal tolerance of violence against the group, and specific laws addressing the group, either for protection or discriminatory purposes, may be useful in demonstrating "that a group exists and is perceived as 'distinct' or 'other' in a particular society."[235] For example, in *Matter of A–R–C–G–*, the BIA found that the group "married Guatemalan women unable to leave the relationship" was socially distinct based on evidence that Guatemala has a culture of "machismo and family violence," the government "often failed to respond to requests for assistance related to domestic violence," and the Guatemalan police had refused to protect the applicant because they would not interfere in the marital relationship.[236]

> ➢ **Practice Pointer**: Practitioners should review country conditions reports for evidence of higher rates of violence against women in a society, as well as societal tolerance of violence against women. Reviewing the country's penal code and other laws also may help to identify laws that apply specifically to women, such as laws requiring women to wear particular clothing or prohibiting women from driving, for example. The use of an expert witness has become increasingly important in social group asylum claims, especially for demonstrating that the group is socially distinct. Practitioners should seek an expert witness who can speak to the historical treatment of certain groups of women in a society, as well as the current view and treatment of those groups of women.

Finally, the BIA has recognized that, under some circumstances, a group's persecution may be the factor that has made them socially distinct.[237] For example, in its *Guidelines for International Protection*, UNHCR discusses the treatment of trafficked women and children who have returned to their home countries after being trafficked, noting that these women and children stand out in society and are particularly susceptible to "severe family or community ostracism and/or severe

---

[234] *Matter of M–E–V–G–*, 26 I&N Dec. at 244.

[235] *Id. See Henriquez-Rivas v. Holder*, 707 F.3d 1081, 1092 (9th Cir. 2013) ("It is difficult to imagine better evidence that a society recognizes a particular class of individuals as uniquely vulnerable, because of their group perception by gang members, than that a special witness protection law has been tailored to its characteristics.").

[236] *Matter of A–R–C–G–*, 26 I&N Dec. 388, 393, 394 (BIA 2014).

[237] *Matter of M–E–V–G–*, 26 I&N Dec. at 242–43 (stating that some persons "may not be considered a group by themselves or by society unless and until [a persecutor] begins persecuting them. Upon their maltreatment, it is possible that these people would experience a sense of 'group,' and society would discern that this group of individuals, who share a common immutable characteristic, is distinct in some significant way.").

discrimination."[238] Evidence of such ostracism and severe discrimination by society may demonstrate that the gender-based group is, in fact, socially distinct.

"Particularity" also has become a challenge in defining a viable social group based on gender. According to the BIA, "particularity" refers to the group being sufficiently distinct that it would constitute a discrete class of persons with definable boundaries.[239] It should be possible to tell who is in the group and who is not. A group cannot be too overbroad, too diffuse, too amorphous, or too subjective, or it will be rejected as a viable social group.[240] Like for social distinction, particularity must be analyzed in the "context of the country of concern and the persecution feared."[241] In demonstrating particularity in the gender context, it is important for asylum-seekers to argue that the size of the group is not relevant — a group does not have to be small to merit protection under U.S. asylum law. Rather, the particular social group should be parallel to the other protected grounds of race, religion, nationality, and political opinion, none of which are limited in size.[242] Additionally, if there are "commonly accepted definitions in the society of which the group is a part," that may be evidence of the group's particularity.[243] For example, in the context of domestic violence-based asylum claims, many countries have definitions in their civil or criminal codes for "marriage," "common law marriage," or "domestic relationship."[244] If a group is defined by terms with a commonly understood meaning in society, that may demonstrate that there are defined boundaries to the group and that the group is particular.

---

[238] U.N. High Comm'r for Refugees, Guidelines on International Protection: The application of Article 1A(2) of the 1951 Convention and/or 1967 Protocol relating to the Status of Refugees to Victims of Trafficking, *supra* note 103, ¶ 18–19.

[239] *Matter of M–E–V–G–*, 26 I&N Dec. at 239–40; *Matter of W–G–R–*, 26 I&N Dec. at 213–15.

[240] *Matter of M–E–V–G–*, at 239-40; *Matter of W-G-R-*, at 213-15. *See also Matter of C–A–*, 23 I&N Dec. 951 (BIA 2006); *Matter of S-E-G-*, 24 I&N Dec. 579 (BIA 2008); *Matter of A-M-E- & J-G-U-*, 24 I&N Dec. 69 (BIA 2007).

[241] *Matter of A–M–E– & J–G–U–*, at 69 (confirmed by *Matter of M–E–V–G–*, at 227 and *Matter of W–G–R–*, at 208).

[242] *See, e.g., Cece v. Holder*, 733 F.3d 662, 673, 675 (7th Cir. 2013) (en banc) (confirming that a social group does not fail simply because it is "too broad and sweeping of a classification" because "[i]t would be antithetical to asylum law to deny refuge to a group of persecuted individuals who have valid claims merely because too many have valid claims"); *Perdomo v. Holder*, 611 F.3d 662, 669 (9th Cir. 2010) ("[W]e have rejected the notion that a persecuted group may simply represent too large a portion of a population to allow its members to qualify for asylum."); *Matter of H–*, 21 I&N Dec. 337, 343–44 (BIA 1996) (noting that size is an undue concern). *See also* Deborah Anker, *The Law of Asylum in the United States* at §5:41 (2014 Ed.) (articulating a "filtering" argument); AILA Amicus Brief in *Matter of A–R–C–G–, available at www.aila.org/infonet/amicus-brief-mjv-rdcp-g-and-arc-g* (last visited Apr. 3, 2015).

[243] *Matter of M–E–V–G–*, 26 I&N Dec. at 239.

[244] *See Matter of A–R–C–G–*, 26 I&N Dec. 388 (BIA 2014) (finding particularity based on the police's statements that they do not interfere with marriages, and the established terms of "married," "women," and "unable to leave the relationship" as commonly understood in society).

Some examples of viable gender-based particular social groups, under the facts and evidence presented, include:

- Cameroonian widows;[245]
- Females in the Tukulor Fulani tribe;[246]
- Somali females;[247]
- Young women who are members of the Tchamba-Kunsuntu tribe who have not been subjected to FGM/C and who oppose the practice;[248]
- Women who are opposed to and fear FGM/C;[249]
- Women who have been sold into marriage;[250]
- Young women living alone in Albania who are targeted for prostitution by traffickers;[251]
- Women who have been subjected to or face being subjected to the practice of Trokosi, a system of indentured sexual servitude to fetish shrines;[252] and
- Women in Jordan who have flouted repressive moral norms and face a high risk of honor killing;[253]
- Women who opposed the repressive and discriminatory Yemeni cultural and religious customs that prohibit mixed-class marriages and require paternal consent for marriage;[254]
- Christian women in Iran who do not wish to adhere to the Islamic female dress code;[255] and
- Married women in Guatemala who are unable to leave their relationship.[256]

---

[245] *Ngengwe v. Mukasey*, 543 F.3d 1029, 1034 (8th Cir. 2008) (finding that widows in Cameroon have both gender and a shared past experience as immutable characteristics and that they are viewed by society as members of a particular social group).

[246] *Niang v. Gonzales*, 422 F.3d 1189 (10th Cir. 2005).

[247] *Hassan v. Gonzales*, 484 F.3d 513 (8th Cir. 2007); *Mohammed v. Gonzales*, 400 F.3d 785, 795–96 (9th Cir. 2005); *Niang v. Gonzales*, 422 F.3d 1187, 1189 (10th Cir. 2005).

[248] *Matter of Kasinga*, 21 I&N Dec. 357, 365 (BIA 1996).

[249] *Agbor v. Gonzales*, 487 F.3d 499 (7th Cir. 2007).

[250] *Gao v. Gonzales*, 440 F.3d 62, 70–71 (2d Cir. 2006) (finding women who have been sold into marriage and who live in a part of China where forced marriages are considered valid and enforceable constitute a particular social group).

[251] *Cece v. Holder*, 733 F.3d 662 (7th Cir. 2013).

[252] *See IJ Grants Asylum to Former 'Trokosi' Slave*, 75 INTERPRETER RELEASES 165 (Feb. 2, 1998).

[253] *Sarhan v. Holder*, 658 F.3d 649 (7th Cir. 2011).

[254] *Al-Ghorbani v. Holder*, 585 F.3d 980 (6th Cir. 2009).

[255] *Yadegar-Sargis v. INS*, 297 F.3d 596 (7th Cir. 2002).

[256] *Matter of A–R–C–G–*, 26 I&N Dec. 388 (BIA 2014).

- Some examples of gender-based particular social groups that courts have found were not cognizable under the facts and evidence presented include:
- Salvadoran women previously raped and beaten by guerrillas;[257]
- Women subjected to rape as a method of government control;[258]
- Single women perceived to have substantial economic resources in Guatemala;[259]
- Young women who resist gang recruitment;[260]
- Salvadoran women between ages 12 and 25 who resisted gang recruitment;[261]
- Women who had a child out of wedlock/are considered adulterers because they gave birth to a child allegedly not their husband's/have been abused by their husbands;[262]
- Young, unmarried Albanian women who are at risk of being kidnapped and forced into prostitution;[263]
- Young (or those who appear to be young), attractive Albanian women who are forced into prostitution;[264]
- Iranian women whose claims were based solely on gender and the harsh restrictions placed upon them as women;[265] and
- Iranian women who have become "Westernized" while living in the United States.[266]

Of course, every proposed social group requires its own analysis based on the facts and the evidence presented; a finding that certain group is not a cognizable

---

[257] *Gomez v. INS*, 947 F.2d 660, 664 (2d Cir. 1991) (finding that they did not compose a particular social group because they lacked a "recognizable and discrete" attribute to enable their persecutors to distinguish them from other women). The Second Circuit U.S. Court of Appeals later clarified in that Gomez's claim was not rejected because the group was defined too broadly, but rather because she failed to show that she would be singled out for further harm on account of her past victimization. *Gao v. Gonzales*, 440 F.3d 62 (2d Cir. 2006).

[258] *Kante v. Holder*, 634 F.3d 321 (6th Cir. 2011).

[259] *Arevalo-Giron v. Holder*, 667 F.3d 79 (1st Cir. 2012).

[260] *Mendez-Barrera v. Holder*, 602 F.3d 21 (1st Cir. 2010).

[261] *Rivera-Barrientos v. Holder*, 666 F.3d 641 (10th Cir. 2012).

[262] *Faye v. Holder*, 580 F.3d 37 (1st Cir. 2009).

[263] *Gjura v. Holder*, 695 F.3d 223 (2d Cir. 2012).

[264] *Rreshpja v. Gonzales*, 420 F.3d 551 (6th Cir. 2005).

[265] *Safaie v. INS*, 25 F.3d 636, 640 (8th Cir. 1994); *see also* Deborah Anker, et al., *Defining 'Particular Social Group' in Terms of Gender: The Shah Decision and U.S. Law*, 76 INTERPRETER RELEASES 1005 (July 2, 1999). For a recent overview of how U.S. immigration laws have a negative impact on women asylum-seekers, see Lawyers Comm. for Human Rights, *Refugee Women at Risk: Unfair U.S. Laws Hurt Asylum Seekers* (2002), *available at www.humanrights first.org/refugees/reports/refugee_women.pdf*.

[266] *Sharif v. INS*, 87 F.3d 932 (7th Cir. 1996).

social group in the past does not mean that the same group cannot be found to be viable in a future case, and vice versa. In fact, many of the proposed social groups listed above were not considered in light of the BIA's three-prong test articulated in *Matter of M–E–V–G–* and *Matter of W–G–R–*, as there have been very few gender-based particular social groups that have been considered under this new restrictive test.[267] However, this body of case law still provides useful guidance for how a particular circuit or the BIA views gender-based social group claims, as well as what facts and evidence those bodies will find to be most persuasive.

- **Practice Pointer**: Practitioners should look to *Matter of Kasinga* and *Matter of A–R–C–G–*, as well as the BIA's analysis of *Matter of Kasinga* in its decisions in *Matter of M–E–V–G–* and *Matter of W–G–R–*, for guidance on how to formulate a cognizable social group under the BIA's three-part test. Using parallel language to define and describe a gender-based social group as the BIA itself has used in considering gender-based social groups under its own three-part test will yield strong legal arguments that will be difficult for an IJ or the BIA to dispute.

- **Practice Pointer**: Given the difficulty in meeting all three prongs of the BIA's test for a cognizable particular social group, practitioners should preserve challenges to the validity of the BIA's departure from the *Acosta* standard, especially while the circuits remain divided.[268] Practitioners also should advance all potential protected grounds that may apply. Many gender-based claims are not solely social group claims, as many involve elements of race or ethnicity, religion, nationality, or political opinion. For example, the daughter of a Muslim father, who believes in a liberal, egalitarian interpretation of Islam may be targeted on account of her religion, in addition to her social group.[269] Rape is often a weapon of war; in a war-torn country, a woman may be raped because she is a national of a particular country. Finally, gender-based claims often involve persecution on account of a woman's political opinion — her feminism, belief in equality and women's rights, opposition to male dominance, or belief in self-determination — especially if the woman has expressed her opposition or beliefs through her actions or words. Practitioners should work closely with their clients to talk about their beliefs and how they think they should be treated,

---

[267] *See, e.g., Matter of A–R–C–G–*, 26 I&N Dec. 388 (BIA 2014).

[268] For guidance on formulating these challenges to the BIA's social group standard, see *Matter of W–G–R–*, Case No. 14-70686 which is now on appeal before the Ninth Circuit. W–G–R–'s brief attacks both the social distinction and particularity standards themselves, as well as the BIA's application of those standards to the record.

[269] *Matter of S–A–*, 22 I&N Dec. 1328 (BIA 2000).

how they expressed those beliefs, and whether they suffered any consequences because of those expressions.

C. Nexus

Even if a social group is legally cognizable under the BIA's three-part test or the legal standards articulated by the relevant circuit, that is only one step in the analysis. As the Seventh Circuit noted in *Cece v. Holder*, even if an individual is a member of a particular social group, that does not necessarily mean that he or she will qualify for asylum; the requirement of nexus is "where the rubber meets the road" for social group claims.[270] This same concept holds true for gender-based claims under the other four protected grounds; in addition to demonstrating that the applicant embodies a protected characteristic — that he or she is a member of a certain race or ethnic group, holds certain religious beliefs, is a national of a certain country, or has certain political opinions — the applicant also must demonstrate through testimony and evidence that those characteristics did or would motivate the persecutor to harm him or her. The protected ground must be "at least one central reason" for the persecution; it need not be the dominant or most important reason.[271] While an asylum applicant is not required to prove the exact motivation of his or her persecutor, he or she must "provide *some* evidence of it, direct or circumstantial."[272] This requires an examination of the persecutor's views of the applicant and any evidence of those views.[273]

Nexus has been a hotly contested issue in gender-based asylum claims, as the persecutors are often private actors and are viewed as being motivated by personal reasons or random criminality, rather than a protected ground. In gender-based asylum claims, direct or circumstantial evidence of nexus may include:

- Direct references to the applicant's gender in the persecutor's statements or comments, whether said to the applicant or to others about the applicant (e.g., "I can do whatever I want to you because you're my wife" or "you're a woman, you are nothing");

---

[270] *Cece v. Holder*, 733 F.3d 662, 673, 675 (7th Cir. 2013) (en banc) (confirming that a social group does not fail simply because it is "too broad and sweeping of a classification" because "[i]t would be antithetical to asylum law to deny refuge to a group of persecuted individuals who have valid claims merely because too many have valid claims").

[271] INA §208(b)(1)(B)(i). See chapter 2 for a detailed discussion of nexus and the legal requirements for demonstrating the motives of the persecutor.

[272] *Id.* at 483 (emphasis in original). *See also Matter of J–B–N– & S–M–*, 24 I&N Dec. 208, 214 (BIA 2007) (finding that the burden of proof for the persecutor's motive may be met by testimonial evidence). *But see* Guy S. Goodwin-Gill & Jane McAdams, The Refugee in International Law 50 (2d ed. 1996) (stating that "Nowhere in the drafting history of the 1951 Convention is it suggested that the motive or intent of the persecutor was ever to be considered as a controlling factor in either the definition or the determination of refugee status."); *see also* James Hathaway, *The Michigan Guidelines on Nexus to a Convention Ground*, 23 MICH. J. INT'L L. 210 (2002), *available at www.refugeecaselaw.org/nexus.asp*.

[273] *INS v. Elias-Zacarias*, 502 U.S. at 478.

- Testimonial or documentary evidence of the specific circumstances in which the persecution took place — the location, the time of day, who was present, etc. (*e.g.*, a man following his wife to her friend's home and forcing her to return to his home may show that he views her as his property due to her status as a woman and his wife);
- Fact witness testimony of what the persecutor said and did;
- Circumstantial evidence of the context in the country in which the persecution took place (*e.g.*, country conditions reports and articles showing high rates of violence against women or showing a high tolerance in society of violence against women);[274]
- The legal and social norms that permit abuse against the applicant and similarly situated women in society (*e.g.*, references to women in the country's civil or criminal codes, common practices of permitting violently punishment of women for refusing or failing to follow strict gender roles, etc.);[275] and
- Expert testimony regarding how women similarly situated to the applicant are viewed in society, why they are viewed that way, and how they are treated by members of society and the state, as well as explaining the dynamics of the specific gender-based violence involved in the applicant's case.[276]

While direct evidence of the persecutor's motives often is the most obvious evidence of nexus, circumstantial evidence of a state and society's acceptance of violence against women can be persuasive in demonstrating a persecutor's motives. The proposed regulations, though never finalized, recognize the value of such circumstantial evidence in demonstrating nexus to a gender-related protected ground, stating:

> [E]vidence about patterns of violence in society against individuals similarly situated to the applicant may also be relevant to the "on account of" determination. [I]n the domestic violence context, an adjudicator would consider any evidence that the abuser uses violence to enforce power and control over the applicant because of the social status that a woman may acquire when she enters into a domestic relationship. This would include any

[274] *See Matter of Kasinga*, 21 I&N Dec. at 367–68 (noting that country conditions evidence shows that FGM is used to overcome the sexual characteristics of young women in the tribe).

[275] *See, e.g., Sarhan v. Holder*, 658 F.3d 649, 656 (7th Cir. 2011) (holding that nexus was established based on evidence of "a widely-held social norm in Jordan — a norm that imposes behavioral obligations [on the applicant and women in Jordan] and permits [her family] to enforce them in the most drastic way"). *See also* DHS's Supp. Br., *Matter of L–R–* (BIA Apr. 13, 2009) (recognizing that when a state and society accept violence against women, abusers are free to abuse), *available at http://cgrs.uchastings.edu/our-work/matter-l-r*.

[276] For example, the Ctr. for Gender & Refugee Studies has developed an affidavit with Nancy Lemon, a domestic violence expert, which explains that gender and intimate partner relationships are motivating factors for domestic violence. To request a copy of this affidavit and other helpful materials, contact CGRS at *http://cgrs.uchastings.edu/request-assistance-cgrs*.

direct evidence about the abuser's own actions, as well as any circumstantial evidence that such patters of violence are (1) supported by the legal system or social norms in the country in question, and (2) reflect a prevalent belief within society, or within relevant segments of society, that cannot be deduced simply by evidence of random acts within that society.[277]

Thus, establishing nexus in a gender-based asylum claim often comes down to building a strong evidentiary record of not only the persecutor's direct statements and actions, but also the high rates of violence and tolerance of violence against women in the society in question. Nexus to gender may also be inherent in the persecutory acts themselves. For example, in claims involving FGM/C, there is little question that genital mutilation occurs to a particular individual because she is female.[278] As the Ninth Circuit stated in *Mohammed v. Gonzales*:

> That is, possession of the immutable trait of being female is a motivating factor — if not a but-for cause — of the persecution. Indeed, the BIA has recognized that female genital mutilation is a form of gender-based persecution, explaining that female genital mutilation "is practiced, at least in some significant part, to overcome sexual characteristics of young women" and "to control women's sexuality."[279]

- **Practice Pointer**: Analogous arguments could be made to many forms of egregious sexual violence perpetuated by men upon women, such as gang rape. Such forms of persecution may, by their very nature, supply compelling direct or circumstantial evidence that gender was "at least one central reason" for the persecution.

D. Government Unable or Unwilling to Protect

Once an asylum-seeker demonstrates past persecution or a well-founded fear of persecution on account of one of the enumerated statutory grounds, he or she must then show that the persecution suffered or feared is by the government or a group that the government is unable or unwilling to control.[280] Many gender-based asylum claims involve non-government actors.[281]

---

[277] Asylum and Withholding Definitions, 65 Fed. Reg. 76588 (proposed Dec. 7, 2000).

[278] *Mohammed v. Gonzales*, 400 F.3d 785, 798 (9th Cir. 2005).

[279] *Id.*

[280] INA §208(b)(1). *See INS v. Elias-Zacarias*, 502 U.S. 478, 481–83 (1992).

[281] *See, e.g.*, *Menjivar v. Gonzales*, 416 F.3d 918, 922–23 (8th Cir. 2005) (finding that the applicant's claim failed because the record did not compel the conclusion that the Salvadoran government was unable or unwilling to protect her from a gang member); *Castro-Perez v. Gonzales*, 409 F.3d 1069, 1072 (9th Cir. 2005) (finding that the applicant's claim failed because did not show the Honduran government was unable or unwilling to control or prosecute rape in the country); *Matter of S–A–*, 22 I&N Dec. 1328 (BIA 2000) (finding that the applicant suffered persecution at the hands of her father and could not rely on the Moroccan authorities to protect her); *Matter of Kasinga,* 21 I&N Dec. 357 (BIA 1996) (en banc) (finding persecution by family members). *See also* U.N. High Comm'r for

Continued

If the persecutor is not a government actor, the applicant must show that the government was unable or unwilling to control the persecutor, or that the government has not taken reasonable steps to provide meaningful protection to the applicant.[282] One court has interpreted "unable or unwilling" to mean that that the government has either condoned the private behavior or is completely helpless to protect the victim.[283] The relevant test is whether the government has taken measures to reduce the risk of persecution to below the well-founded fear threshold (a 1 in 10 chance of persecution).[284] It is not necessary for the applicant to prove that she tried to seek government protection. However, if she did not, the applicant should be prepared to explain why doing so would have been futile or even dangerous.[285] The BIA has recognized gender-based asylum claims based on persecution by such nongovernmental actors as a Togolese tribe that practiced female genital mutilation,[286] a father,[287] and a spouse.[288]

In establishing the government's unwillingness or inability to protect the applicant, evidence demonstrating the following factors should be submitted:

- The government's complicity in the persecution;[289]
- A pattern and practice of government unresponsiveness to requests for protection or failure to prosecute or punish the actors;[290]
- If the applicant did not report the harm to the government or seek protection, that doing so would have been futile or potentially dangerous.[291]

Refugees, *Handbook on Procedures and Criteria for Determining Refugee Status*, ¶ 65 HCR/1P/4/enG/Rev. 3 (2011), [hereinafter UNHCR Handbook] *available at www.refworld.org/docid/4f33c8d92.html* ("Where serious discriminatory or other offensive acts are committed by the local populace, they can be considered as persecution if they are knowingly tolerated by the authorities, or if the authorities refuse, or prove unable, to offer effective protection.").

282 *Aliyev v. Mukasey*, 549 F.3d 111, 118–19 (2d Cir. 2008); *Ngengwe v. Mukasey*, 543 F.3d 1029, 1035–36 (8th Cir. 2008); *Nabulwala v. Gonzales*, 481 F.3d 1115 (8th Cir. 2007).

283 *Khilan v. Holder*, 557 F.3d 583, 585 (8th Cir. 2009) (noting that the police were willing to investigate the kidnapping and had arrested a number of suspects). The Center for Gender & Refugee Studies has challenged this standard as being inconsistent with and swallowing the well-founded fear standard. *See Matter of R–P–*, CGRS Amicus Brief, *available at http://cgrs.uchastings.edu/sites/default/files/R-P-_amicus_CGRS_4_20_2012.pdf* (last visited Apr. 3, 2015).

284 *See INS v. Cardoza-Fonseca*, 480 U.S. 421 (1987) (establishing the legal standard for well-founded fear).

285 *See, e.g., Sarhan v. Holder*, 658 F.3d 649, 650–51 (7th Cir. 2011); *Nabulwala v. Gonzales*, 481 F.3d 1115, 1116–18 (8th Cir. 2007); *Ali v. Ashcroft*, 394 F.3d 780, 785–87 (9th Cir. 2005).

286 *Matter of Kasinga*, 21 I&N Dec. 357, 365 (BIA 1996).

287 *Matter of S–A–*, 22 I&N Dec. 1328 (BIA 2000) (finding that the applicant suffered persecution at the hands of her father and could not rely on the Moroccan authorities to protect her).

288 *Matter of A–R–C–G–*, 26 I&N Dec. 388 (BIA 2014).

289 *See, e.g., Sarhan v. Holder*, 658 F.3d 549 (7th Cir. 2011) (focusing on country conditions evidence demonstrating that the government of Jordan tolerates and is indifferent to honor killings).

290 *See, e.g., Matter of A–R–C–G–*, 26 I&N Dec. 388 (BIA 2014).

Where countries have enacted laws recognizing the equal status of women or criminalizing certain behavior, such as rape, trafficking, or domestic violence, DHS frequently argues that such laws indicate the government's willingness to protect victims of gender-based persecution. However, many governments have enacted such laws but either refused or failed to enforce them effectively. In these situations, it can be essential to present evidence that, despite the existence of these laws, the government has failed to provide meaningful protection to these victims of violence. Where country reports and articles do not specifically address this issue, it can be critical to present expert testimony to educate the adjudicator on the failures of the country's protection system that is not documented in the country reports and articles.

E. Internal Relocation

An applicant may be denied asylum or withholding of removal if the applicant "could avoid future persecution by relocating to another part" of his or her home country.[292] If the applicant establishes past persecution on account of one of the protected grounds, or if the applicant establishes a well-founded fear of future persecution by a government or government-sponsored actor, internal relocation is presumed to be unreasonable and the burden of proof is on the government to show by a preponderance of the evidence that "it would be reasonable to expect the applicant to" relocate within the country of persecution.[293] However, the burden of establishing that internal relocation would not be reasonable is on the applicant if he or she does not establish past persecution and fears persecution at the hands of a non-government actor.[294]

Since many gender-based asylum claims involve private actors or groups that the government is unable and unwilling to control, whether the applicant could safely and reasonably relocate within the country of feared persecution is a common issue that arises in gender-based asylum claims. Asylum-applicants should be prepared to demonstrate to the adjudicator that they could not safely relocate within their country of feared persecution and, even if they could safely relocate, requiring the applicant to do so would not be reasonable. In demonstrating an inability to safely relocate, the applicant should provide evidence of the persecutor's ability and willingness to target her elsewhere in her country, as well as the government's inability and unwillingness

---

[291] *See, e.g., Ngengwe v. Mukasey*, 543 F.3d 1029, 1036 (8th Cir. 2009); *Lopez v. U.S. Att'y Gen.*, 504 F.3d 1341, 1345 (11th Cir. 2007); *Ornelas-Chavez v. Gonzales*, 458 F.3d 1052, 1058 (9th Cir. 2006); *Fiadjoe v. U.S. Att'y Gen.*, 411 F.3d 135, 161–62 (3d Cir. 2005); *Matter of S–A–*, 22 I&N Dec. 1328, 1335 (BIA 2000).

[292] 8 CFR §§208.13(b)(2)(ii), 1208.13(b)(2)(ii) (2014).

[293] 8 CFR §§208.13(b)(1)(B), 1208.13(b)(1)(B) (2014).

[294] 8 CFR §§208.13(b)(3)(i), 1208.13(b)(3)(i) (2014). See chapter 4 for a detailed discussion of the shifting burdens of proof in asylum, withholding of removal, and CAT claims.

to control the persecutor, as described above.[295] The geographic size of a country may also be relevant to whether the applicant may safely relocate.[296]

Even if the applicant can safely relocate, that relocation also must be reasonable under all the circumstances.[297] The applicant's gender may be relevant to the reasonableness of her relocation. Especially in countries where there are high rates of violence against women and that violence is tolerated by society and treated with impunity by the government, women may face significant obstacles in relocating. They may face other serious harm in the process of relocating or in the new location,[298] become the victims of ongoing civil strife within the country,[299] face a discriminatory infrastructure that could impact their ability to find a job and support themselves and their children,[300] and be ostracized or discriminated against by virtue of their status as a single woman without a family support network or an outsider who is new to the community.[301] Moreover, women who have already been victimized and who

---

[295] *See, e.g., Arboleda v. Att'y Gen.* 434 F.3d 1220, 1226 (11th Cir. 2006) (finding that the applicant's personal experience and country conditions demonstrated that relocation was not a viable option because the persecutor, the FARC, operated countrywide and thus had the ability to persecute the applicant throughout the country); *Matter of C–A–L–,* 21 I&N Dec. 754 (BIA 1997).

[296] *Matter of Kasinga,* 21 I&N Dec. 357 (BIA 1996) (finding countrywide persecution reasonable even when arising out of a local conflict due to Togo being a relatively small country).

[297] 8 CFR §§208.13(b)(1)(i)(B), (2)(ii), 208.16(b)(1)–(2), 1208.13(b)(1)(i)(B), (2)(ii), & 1208.16(b)(1)–(2) (2014) (emphasis added). *See Gao v. Gonzales*, 440 F.3d 62, 71 (2d Cir. 2006) (vacating and remanding the BIA's determination that a Chinese asylum applicant fleeing domestic violence and human trafficking could reasonably relocate within the country. The court held that the BIA determination was contradicted by the record. The applicant testified that she had attempted unsuccessfully to relocate within China. The court further held that the BIA cannot solely determine whether the applicant could avoid persecution by relocating, but must also determine whether it would be *reasonable* to require relocation). *See also Tu Kai Yang v. Gonzales,* 427 F.3d 1117, 1122 (8th Cir. 2005) ("The IJ's suggestion that petitioners could potentially avoid persecution by relocating within China is incorrect.").

[298] Executive Office for Immigration Review; New Rules Regarding Procedures for Asylum and Withholding of Removal, 63 Federal Register 31945, 31947 (June 11, 1998) (to be codified at 8 CFR pt. 208) (describing "other serious harm" as "harm that may not be inflicted on account of race, religion, nationality, membership in a particular social group, or political opinion, but is so serious that it equals the severity of persecution").

[299] *See, e.g., Awale v. Ashcroft,* 384 F.3d 527, 532 (8th Cir. 2004) (finding that evidence that members of Somali minority clans continue to be "subjected to harassment, intimidation, and abuse by armed gunmen of all affiliations" and that travel is difficult because rival groups control routes of transportation indicates that it would not be reasonable to require applicant to internally relocate).

[300] *See, e.g., Knezevic v. Ashcroft,* 367 F.3d 1206, 1214 (9th Cir. 2004) (finding that internal relocation would not be reasonable when there was evidence that Bosnian Serb applicants, ages 75 and 66, would have great difficulty finding employment while having no means of supporting themselves).

[301] 8 CFR §§208.13(b)(3), 208.16(b)(3), 1208.13(b)(3), & 1208.16(b)(3) (2014). *See also* UNHCR Handbook, *supra* note 281, ¶ 91. The same factors are considered in determining whether a person's life or freedom would be threatened in a withholding of removal claim. 8 CFR §§208.16(b)(3), 1208.16(b)(3) (2014).

are survivors of violence may be unable to reasonably relocate due to medical or mental health needs based on the physical harm and trauma they have suffered.

➢ **Practice Pointer**: If a client has suffered violence in the past, practitioners should advise her to seek a psychological evaluation. Such an evaluation may be significant in demonstrating past persecution, ongoing and continuing harm from the prior acts of violence, an applicant's difficulty in testifying about certain topics, the applicant's inability to safely and reasonably relocate within the country of feared persecution, and his or her eligibility for humanitarian asylum based on the severity of past persecution and risk of other serious harm. See chapter 2 of this book for a detailed discussion of each of these legal concepts and chapter 4 for a detailed discussion of the preparation and presentation of evidence in asylum claims.

There is no requirement that an applicant first attempt to relocate within the country of feared persecution prior to fleeing.[302] However, if the applicant did relocate and was able to live safely and openly for a significant period of time prior to fleeing, that may be evidence that she could reasonably relocate within the country of feared persecution, and thus, does not have a well-founded fear of future persecution.[303] Therefore, the circumstances under which the applicant lived after relocating are highly relevant.[304] For example, if the applicant did relocate, but was forced to live in hiding in order to protect herself, that may be evidence that the applicant's relocation was not reasonable under all of the circumstances.[305] Moreover, if the applicant did relocate but continued to be targeted and harmed by her persecutor, that may be strong evidence of her inability to safely and reasonably relocate, and thus, may strengthen her well-founded fear claim.[306]

---

[302] *Matter of C–A–L–*, 21 I&N Dec. 754 (BIA 1997). *See Kaiser v. Ashcroft*, 390 F.3d 653, 659–60 (9th Cir. 2004) (finding that the applicant could not avoid persecution through internal relocation when the applicant received threats while living in two distant areas of Pakistan).

[303] *See, e.g.*, *Singh v. Holder*, 750 F.3d 84 (1st Cir. 2014) (holding that the applicant lacked a well-founded fear of persecution on account of his Sikh faith because he was able to relocate to Delhi and remain in India for several months without further harassment or arrest after his mistreatment at home and to obtain his travel visa without any undue restriction); *Moran-Quinteros v. Holder*, 352 F. App'x 974 (6th Cir. 2009) (finding that the applicant did not have a well-founded fear of persecution because the applicant's family, including her father who had been threatened by guerillas in Guatemala, moved to another village in Guatemala and had lived there safely since 1990).

[304] *See, e.g., Gambashidzez v. Ashcroft,* 381 F.3d 187, 193 (3d Cir. 2004) (finding that the BIA erred in resting solely on the applicant's eight-month residence in another area of Georgia without a police encounter when denying applicant's claim, and stating that the BIA should have considered the circumstances in which the applicant lived during the period of relocation).

[305] 8 CFR §208.13(b)(2)(ii) (2014). *See, e.g.*, *Essohou v. Gonzales*, 471 F.3d 518 (4th Cir. 2006).

[306] *See, e.g., Kaiser v. Ashcroft,* 390 F.3d at 659–60 (finding that threats received by the applicant while living in two distant areas of Pakistan compelled the conclusion that the applicant could not avoid persecution through internal relocation); *Gao v. Gonzales*, 440 F.3d 62, 71 (2d Cir. 2006) (vacating and remanding the BIA's determination that a Chinese asylum applicant fleeing domestic violence and

Continued

➤ **Practice Pointer**: Even if a preponderance of the evidence demonstrates that internal relocation is an option for the applicant, the adjudicator may still grant asylum to the applicant if "the applicant has demonstrated compelling reasons for being unwilling or unable to return to the country arising out of the severity of the past persecution" or if "the applicant has established that there is a reasonable possibility that he or she may suffer other serious harm upon removal to that country."[307] In other words, a favorable exercise of the adjudicator's discretion may be warranted for humanitarian reasons, even if future persecution is unlikely.[308] A grant of asylum under these circumstances is often referred to as "humanitarian asylum." Practitioners should always plan to make an argument for humanitarian asylum for clients who suffered past persecution. Documenting the severity of the past

---

human trafficking could reasonably relocate within the country. The court held that the BIA determination was contradicted by the record. The applicant testified that she had attempted unsuccessfully to relocate within China. The court further held that the BIA cannot solely determine whether the applicant could avoid persecution by relocating, but must also determine whether it would be *reasonable* to require relocation). *See also Tu Kai Yang v. Gonzales,* 427 F.3d 1117, 1122 (8th Cir. 2005) ("The IJ's suggestion that petitioners could potentially avoid persecution by relocating within China is incorrect.").

[307] 8 CFR §§208.13(b)(1)(iii), 1208.13(b)(1)(iii) (2014). *See Hanna v. Keisler*, 506 F.3d 933, 939 (9th Cir. 2007) (remanding claim for consideration of other serious harm Chaldean Catholic would face if returned to Iraq).

[308] *Matter of Chen*, 20 I&N Dec. 16, 19 (BIA 1989) (finding the applicant to be eligible for asylum based on past persecution alone, where the applicant suffered a long history of persecution beginning when he was eight years old, no longer had any family in China, and had a subjectively genuine fear of future persecution). *See also Lal v. INS*, 255 F.3d 998, 1003, *amended on reh'g,* 268 F.3d 1148 (9th Cir. 2001) (finding applicants were eligible for asylum based on the severity of their past persecution, which included repeated arbitrary detentions, painful and humiliating torture, sexual assault, threats, and severe intimidation); *Vongsakdy v. INS*, 171 F.3d 1203 (9th Cir. 1999) (finding that a Laotian national suffered egregious past persecution, including imprisonment in a labor camp, beatings, torture, inadequate food and water, denial of medical treatment, and a severed thumb); *Matter of S–A–K– and H–A–H–*, 24 I&N Dec. 464 (BIA 2008) (holding that discretion should be exercised to grant asylum to a mother and daughter who had been involuntarily subjected to FGM based on the severity of the persecution they suffered); *Matter of H–*, 21 I&N Dec. 337, 347–48 (BIA 1996) (holding that "[c]entral to a discretionary finding in past persecution cases should be careful attention to compelling, humanitarian considerations that would be involved if the refugee were to be forced to return to a country where he or she was persecuted in the past," and finding that humanitarian reasons may include the applicant's age, health, or family ties in the United States); *Matter of B–*, 21 I&N Dec. 66 (BIA 1995) (finding that an Afghani who had suffered persecution under the previous Communist regime was no longer at risk of persecution, but granting asylum based on the severity of the past persecution the applicant had suffered). *But see Reyes-Morales v. Gonzales,* 435 F.3d 937, 942 (8th Cir. 2006); *Ngarurih v. Ashcroft,* 371 F.3d 182 (4th Cir. 2004); *Francois v. INS*, 283 F.3d 926, 932 (8th Cir. 2002) (finding that applicant who was interrogated, threatened that her father would be killed, and denied an exit visa failed to demonstrate severe or long lasting harm sufficient to warrant humanitarian asylum); *Matter of N–M–A–*, 22 I&N Dec. 312 (BIA 1998) (noting that the harm was not of a great degree, suffered over a great period of time, and did not result in severe psychological trauma such that a grant in the absence of a well-founded fear was warranted).

persecution, as well as the client's susceptibility to other serious harm is key to convincing an IJ that a client merits humanitarian asylum.

➢ **Practice Pointer**: Some invaluable resources for gender-based claims include: UNHCR's guidelines on gender-related persecution[309] and on trafficking victims;[310] UNHCR's *Handbook for the Protection of Women and Girls*;[311] U.S. Citizenship and Immigration Services' Asylum Officer Basic Training Course on Gender-Related Claims;[312] Fatma E. Marouf's article "The Emerging Importance of 'Social Visibility' in Defining a 'Particular Social Group' and its Potential Impact on Asylum Claims Related to Sexual Orientation and Gender;"[313] Deborah Anker's book, *The Law of Asylum in the United States* §§5:46, 53;[314] The National Immigrant Justice Center's asylum brief and resource bank for gender-based asylum claims;[315] and the Center for Gender and Refugee Studies' webpage on "Gender Asylum Guidelines"[316] and its practice advisory on "Domestic Violence-Based Asylum Claims."[317]

II. Asylum Claims Based on Gang Violence

Asylum claims based on gang violence have emerged as one of the most challenging types of claims to successfully present, mostly because of harmful precedent issued by the BIA and adopted by many circuit courts of appeals. However, despite negative precedent, recent events including the BIA's clarification and articulation of its test for viability of a particular social group and the ongoing

---

309 U.N. High Comm'r for Refugees, *Guidelines on International Protection No. 1: Gender-Related Persecution*, *supra* note 16.

310 U.N. High Comm'r for Refugees, *Guidelines on International Protection No. 7: The Application of Article 1A(2) of the 1951 Convention and/or its 1967 Protocol Relating to the Status of Refugees to Victims of Trafficking and Persons at Risk of Being Trafficked*, HCR/GIP/06/07 (Apr. 7, 2006), available at *www.unhcr.org/443b626b2.html* (last visited Jan. 2, 2014).

311 U.N. High Comm'r for Refugees, *Handbook for the Protection of Women and Girls* (Mar. 6, 2008), *available at www.unhcr.org/protect/PROTECTION/47cfae612.html* (last visited Jan. 1, 2015).

312 AOBTC Workbook, Female Asylum Applicants, *supra* note 36.

313 Fatma E. Marouf, *The Emerging Importance of "Social Visibility" in Defining a "Particular Social Group" and its Potential Impact on Asylum Claims Related to Sexual Orientation and Gender*, 27 YALE L. & POL'Y REV. 47 (Fall 2008).

314 Deborah Anker, THE LAW OF ASYLUM IN THE UNITED STATES §§5:46, 53 (14th ed. 2014).

315 Nat'l Immigrant Justice Ctr., *Gender-Based Asylum Claims*, *available at http://immigrantjustice.org/gender-based-asylum-brief-and-resource-bank* (last visited Jan. 1, 2015).

316 Ctr. for Gender & Refugee Studies, *Gender Asylum Guidelines*, *available at http://cgrs.uchastings.edu/search-materials/gender-asylum-guidelines* (last visited Jan. 2, 2015).

317 Ctr. for Gender & Refugee Studies, *Domestic Violence-Based Asylum Claims* (Sept. 12, 2014), *available at http://cgrs.uchastings.edu/sites/default/files/DV_Advisory_9-12-2014_FINAL_1.pdf* (last visited Mar. 29, 2015).

development of a "refugee crisis" due to the steady influx of migrants from Central America seeking protection in the United States, have provided an opportunity to review what we have learned to date and write on a blank slate in presenting these claims. This section addresses some of the challenges involved in presenting an asylum claim based on gang violence: whether a group constitutes a viable particular social group, whether opposition to a gang is a political opinion, whether religion is a trait that would motivate a gang to harm the applicant, whether there is evidence of nexus to a protected ground, whether the government is unable or unwilling to protect its citizens from gang violence, and whether the applicant can safely and reasonably relocate to escape gang violence.

A. Particular Social Groups and Membership

To demonstrate persecution based on membership in a particular social group, the applicant must:

(1) Identify a viable social group;

(2) Prove membership or perceived membership in that group; and

(3) Establish that the past or feared persecution is based on membership or perceived membership in that group (establish that the characteristics of that group motivated or would motivate the persecutor to target the applicant).[318]

Identifying and defining the particular social group is often the most difficult and the most critical step in establishing asylum eligibility based on this protected ground. Since "particular social group" is not defined in the INA or the Code of Federal Regulations, whether or not a group is considered a "particular social group" for purposes of asylum eligibility is an issue that has yielded volumes of case law, both before the BIA and before the U.S. circuit courts of appeals. Asylum claims based on gang violence have been at the heart of the development of the BIA's social group jurisprudence.[319]

In 2008, the BIA officially added two requirements to its "common, immutable characteristic" test for determining the viability of a social group for purposes of asylum eligibility — social visibility and particularity.[320] In *Matter of S–E–G–* and

---

[318] *See, e.g., Ndayshimiye v. Att'y Gen.*, 557 F.3d 124 (3d Cir. 2009) (accepting the BIA's interpretation of "one central reason" except for its contention that the motive cannot be subordinate to another, and stating that the "plain language [of the statute] indicates that a persecutor may have more than one central motivation for his or her actions; whether one of those central reasons is more or less important than another is irrelevant.").

[319] *See Matter of M–E–V–G–*, 26 I&N Dec. 227 (BIA 2014); *Matter of W–G–R–*, 26 I&N Dec. 208 (BIA 2014); *Matter of S–E–G–*, 24 I&N Dec. 579 (BIA 2008); *Matter of E–A–G–*, 24 I&N Dec. 591 (BIA 2008); *Matter of C–A–*, 23 I&N Dec. 951 (BIA 2006).

[320] *Matter of E–A–G–*, 24 I&N Dec. 591 (BIA 2008); *Matter of S–E–G–*, 24 I&N Dec. 579 (BIA 2008). The BIA had previously referenced social visibility and particularity; however, it was not until *Matter of E–A–G–* and *Matter of S–E–G–* that these were stated requirements for establishing a particular social group for purposes of asylum eligibility. *See Matter of A–M–E– & J–G–U–*, 24 I&N Dec. 69 (BIA 2007); *Matter of C–A–*, 23 I&N Dec. 951 (BIA 2006).

Matter of E–A–G–, the BIA explained that "social visibility" means that a group must be "recognizable by others in the community,"[321] while "particularity" means that a group must be defined in a manner sufficiently distinct to be recognized as a discrete, non-amorphous class of persons.[322] "[P]otentially large and diffuse segment[s] of society," will not meet the BIA's particularity requirement.[323]

Immigration advocates and the legal community harshly criticized these decisions as involving circular reasoning and conflated concepts. For example, throughout the decisions, the BIA often conflated its social visibility and particularity requirements with the nexus or "on account of" requirement, which is meant to be a separate question in determining asylum eligibility. Additionally, the BIA was unclear regarding whether "social visibility" meant literal visibility (ocular visibility) or figurative visibility. The BIA also was unclear regarding whether "particularity" required that the group be defined with clear, objective words, or whether it must also be narrow and homogenous.[324]

Following *Matter of S–E–G–* and *Matter of E–A–G–*, a clear circuit court split developed regarding whether these two new prongs of the social group test were reasonable interpretations of the law. Specifically, the Third and Seventh Circuits have refused to give deference to social visibility/distinction and particularity tests as unreasonable; the Eighth and Ninth Circuits have not yet determined whether the requirements are reasonable; the Fourth Circuit U.S. Court of Appeals has ruled that particularity is reasonable but has not yet ruled on social visibility/distinction; and all other circuits have found social visibility/distinction and particularity to be reasonable.[325] In 2014, the BIA responded with two published decisions, *Matter of*

---

[321] *Matter of S–E–G–*, 24 I&N Dec. 579, 586 (BIA 2008).

[322] *Id.* at 584.

[323] *Id.* at 585.

[324] *Matter of S–E–G–* and *Matter of E–A–G–* also left unclear whether previously accepted social groups, such as gay men from a certain country or women of a certain tribe who oppose female genital mutilation, still met the requirements for "particular social group."

[325] *Compare Valdiviezo-Galdamez v. Att'y Gen.*., 663 F.3d 582 (3d Cir. 2011), *Escobar v. Holder*, 657 F.3d 537 (7th Cir. 2011), *Benitez Ramos v. Holder*, 589 F.3d 426 (7th Cir. 2009), *Gatimi v. Holder*, 578 F.3d 611 (7th Cir. 2009) (refusing to give deference to the BIA's social distinction and particularity requirements), *with Henriquez-Rivas v. Holder*, 707 F.3d 1081 (9th Cir. 2013), *Gaitan v. Holder*, 671 F.3d 678 (8th Cir. 2012), *Martinez-Seren v. Holder*, 394 F. App'x 404 (9th Cir. 2010), *Soriano v. Holder*, 569 F.3d 1162 (9th Cir. 2009) (applying but not yet determining whether the requirements are reasonable), *and with Martinez v. Holder*, 740 F.3d 902 (4th Cir. 2014), *Lizama v. Holder*, 629 F.3d 440 (4th Cir. 2011), *Crespin v. Holder*, 632 F.3d 117 (4th Cir. 2011), *Quinteros-Mendoza v. Holder*, 556 F.3d 159 (4th Cir. 2009) (ruling that particularity is reasonable but not yet ruling on social visibility/distinction), *and with Orellana-Monson v. Holder*, 685 F.3d 511 (5th Cir. 2012), *Garcia-Callegas v. Holder*, 666 F.3d 828 (1st Cir. 2012), *Rivera Barrientos v. Holder*, 658 F.3d 1222 (10th Cir. 2011), *Bonilla-Morales v. Holder*, 607 F.3d 1132 (6th Cir. 2010), *Urbina-Mejia v. Holder*, 597 F.3d 360 (6th Cir. 2010), *Scatambuli v. Holder*, 558 F.3d 53 (1st Cir. 2009), *Amilcar-Orellana v. Mukasey*, 551 F.3d 86 (1st Cir. 2008) (ruling that both social visibility/distinction and particularity are reasonable).

M–E–V–G– and *Matter of W–G–R–*, which restated and clarified its "social visibility" and "particularity" requirements, while renaming social visibility as "social distinction." [326] Accordingly, the BIA now requires a three-step analysis for determining whether a group is a "particular social group" for purposes of asylum eligibility: (1) Determine whether the members of the group share a common, immutable characteristic; (2) Determine whether the group is socially distinct in the context of the society in question; and (3) Determine whether the group is sufficiently particular.[327]

In discussing and clarifying "social visibility," the BIA held that it does not mean literal or ocular visibility.[328] To avoid confusion, the BIA renamed this requirement "social distinction," and established that social distinction refers to whether a group is perceived and recognized as a distinct entity by society.[329] The BIA clarified that social distinction is based on society's perception and not the persecutor's perception.

In discussing and clarifying "particularity," the BIA stood by its previous decisions establishing this requirement, confirming that particularity refers to the group being sufficiently distinct that it would constitute a discrete class of persons with definable boundaries.[330] Groups that are perceived as being too overbroad, too diffuse, too amorphous, or too subjective will be rejected as particular social groups.[331] For example, in *Matter of W–G–R–*, the BIA found that "former members of the Mara 18 gang in El Salvador who have renounced their gang membership" was too diffuse, broad, and subjective, because "the group could include persons of any age, sex, or background."[332] Through this dicta, the BIA suggested that groups must

---

[326] *Matter of M–E–V–G–*, 26 I&N Dec. 227 (BIA 2014); *Matter of W–G–R–*, 26 I&N Dec. 208 (BIA 2014).

[327] *Matter of M–E–V–G–*, 26 I&N Dec. 227 (BIA 2014); *Matter of W–G–R–*, 26 I&N Dec. 208 (BIA 2014), *clarifying Matter of E–A–G–*, 24 I&N Dec. 591 (BIA 2008); *Matter of S–E–G–*, 24 I&N Dec. 579 (BIA 2008); *Matter of A–M–E– & J–G–U–*, 24 I&N Dec. 69 (BIA 2007); *and Matter of C–A–*, 23 I&N Dec. 951 (BIA 2006). Note that the "social distinction" requirement used to be called "social visibility." *See Matter of C–A–*, 23 I&N Dec. 951, 959–61 (BIA 2006) (noting that UNHCR's *Guidelines* confirm that "visibility" is an important element), *aff'd Castillo-Arias v. U.S. Att'y Gen.*, 446 F.3d 1190 (11th Cir. 2006), *cert. denied*, 127 S. Ct. 977 (Jan. 8, 2007). *See also Matter of E–A–G–*, 24 I&N Dec. 591, 594 (BIA 2007) and *Matter of S–E–G–*, 24 I&N Dec. 579, 586–88 (BIA 2007). The social group approach applied by the BIA in *Matter of E–A–G–* and *Matter of S–E–G–*, which required social visibility and particularity, was criticized by UNHCR in an amicus brief filed in the U.S. Court of Appeals for the Third Circuit in a gang-based persecution case. The brief is available at *www.unhcr.org/refworld/pdfid/49ef25102.pdf* (last visited June 7, 2014).

[328] *Matter of M–E–V–G–*, 26 I&N Dec. at 227; *Matter of W–G–R–*, 26 I&N Dec. at 208.

[329] *Matter of M–E–V–G–*, 26 I&N Dec. at 240–43; *Matter of W–G–R–*, 26 I&N Dec. at 215–18. *See also*, *Matter of C–A–*, 23 I&N Dec. 951 (BIA 2006).

[330] *Matter of M–E–V–G–*, at 239–40; *Matter of W–G–R–*, at 213–15.

[331] *Matter of M–E–V–G–*, at 239–40; *Matter of W–G–R–*, at 213–15. *See also Matter of C–A–*, 23 I&N Dec. 951 (BIA 2006); *Matter of S–E–G–*, 24 I&N Dec. 579 (BIA 2008); *Matter of A–M–E– & J–G–U*, 24 I&N Dec. 69 (BIA 2007).

[332] *Matter of W–G–R–*, 26 I&N Dec. at 221.

be defined with more specificity, such as "the duration or strength of the members' active participation in the activity and the recency of their active participation."[333] Both social distinction and particularity must be analyzed in the "context of the country of concern and the persecution feared."[334]

Several lines of cases have developed regarding particular social group claims in the context of gang violence,[335] including the following:

- Those who resist gang recruitment;[336]

---

[333] *Id.* at 222. *But see Matter of C–A–*, 23 I&N Dec. 951, 956–57 (BIA 2006) (stating that homogeneity was not a requirement for a group to be considered a particular social group). Note that such specificity in defining a social group risks causing the defined social group to fail the social distinction requirement. For example, most societies do not view "former gang members who are between 20 and 25 years old" any differently than "former gang members who are between 30 and 35 years old." These BIA decisions yield much confusion and establish a nearly impossible standard for defining a social group. Defining a group with enough specificity to meet the particularity requirement will cause the group to fail the social distinction prong of the test. On the other hand, defining the group in a way that shows it is a recognized group in society will cause the group to fail the particularity prong of the test. It is yet to be seen or established which social groups, if any, will be able to meet both of these new requirements in addition to the shared common, immutable characteristic requirement.

[334] *Matter of A–M–E– & J–G–U–*, at 69 (confirmed by *Matter of M–E–V–G–*, at 227 (BIA 2014) and *Matter of W–G–R–*, at 208).

[335] *Matter of M–E–V–G–*, 26 I&N Dec. 227 (BIA 2014); *Matter of W–G–R–*, 26 I&N Dec. 208 (BIA 2014); *Matter of S–E–G–*, 24 I&N Dec. 579 (BIA 2008); *Matter of E–A–G–*, 24 I&N Dec. 591 (BIA 2008); *Matter of C–A–*, 23 I&N Dec. 951 (BIA 2006). *See also Martinez v. Holder*, 740 F.3d 902 (4th Cir. 2014); *Henriquez–Rivas v. Holder*, 2013 WL 518048 (9th Cir. 2013); *Gaitan v. Holder*, 671 F.3d 678 (8th Cir. 2012); *Orellana-Monson v. Holder*, 685 F.3d 511 (5th Cir. 2012); *Garcia-Callegas v. Holder*, 666 F.3d 828 (1st Cir. 2012); *Valdiviezo-Galdamez v. Att'y Gen.*, 663 F.3d 582 (3d Cir. 2011); *Lizama v. Holder*, 629 F.3d 440 (4th Cir. 2011); *Rivera Barrientos v. Holder*, 658 F.3d 1222 (10th Cir. 2011); *Escobar v. Holder*, 657 F.3d 537 (7th Cir. 2011); *Crespin v. Holder*, 632 F.3d 117 (4th Cir. 2011); *Martinez-Seren v. Holder*, 394 F. App'x 404 (9th Cir. 2010); *Bonilla-Morales v. Holder*, 607 F.3d 1132 (6th Cir. 2010); *Urbina-Mejia v. Holder*, 597 F.3d 360 (6th Cir. 2010); *Soriano v. Holder*, 569 F.3d 1162 (9th Cir. 2009); *Benitez Ramos v. Holder*, 589 F.3d 426 (7th Cir. 2009); *Gatimi v. Holder*, 578 F.3d 611 (7th Cir. 2009); *Scatambuli v. Holder*, 558 F.3d 53 (1st Cir. 2009); *Quinteros-Mendoza v. Holder*, 556 F.3d 159 (4th Cir. 2009); *Amilcar-Orellana v. Mukasey*, 551 F.3d 86 (1st Cir. 2008); *Arteaga v. Mukasey*, 511 F.3d 940 (9th Cir. 2007); *Shehu v. Attn'y Gen.*, 482 F.3d 652 (3d Cir. 2007); *Ucelo-Gomez v. Mukasey*, 509 F.3d 70 (2d Cir. 2007).

[336] *Matter of S–E–G–*, 24 I&N Dec. 479 (BIA 2008) (rejecting "Salvadoran youth who have been subjected to recruitment efforts by MS-13 and who have rejected or resisted membership in the gang based on their own personal, moral, and religious opposition to the gang's values and activities" as a particular social group because it lacked "well-defined boundaries" that make a group particular and it also lacked social visibility). *See also Zalaya v. Holder*, 668 F.3d 159, 162, 166 (4th Cir. 2012) (rejecting the social group of "young Honduran males who (1) refuse to join the Mara Salvatrucha 13 gang (MS-13), (2) have notified the authorities of MS-13's harassment tactics, and (3) have an identifiable tormentor within MS-13"); *Orellana-Monson v. Holder*, 685 F.3d 511 (5th Cir. 2012) (finding that gang resisters in El Salvador lack social visibility and particularity); *Gaitan v. Holder*, 671 F.3d 678, 682 (8th Cir. 2012) (rejecting the social group of "young males from El Salvador who have been subjected to recruitment by MS-13 and who have rejected or resisted membership in the gang based on personal opposition to the gang"); *Constanza v. Holder*, 647 F.3d 749, 752 (8th Cir. 2011) (rejecting the social group of "persons resistant to gang membership"); *Larios v. Holder*, 608 F.3d 105

Continued

- Affluent or wealthy individuals;[337]
- Prosecutorial witnesses and informants;[338]
- Gang members or former gang members;[339]
- Tattooed youth or tattooed gang members;[340]
- Women and girls labeled as gang property;
- Males of certain socio-economic classes;
- Family members;[341] and

(1st Cir. 2010) (finding that gang resisters in Guatemala lack social visibility and particularity); *Mendez-Barrera v. Holder*, 602 F.3d 21 (1st Cir. 2010) (finding that gang resisters in El Salvador lack social visibility and particularity); *Ramos-Lopez v. Holder*, 563 F.3d 855 (9th Cir. 2009) (finding that gang resisters in Honduras lack social visibility and particularity); *Santos-Lemus v. Mukasey*, 542 F.3d 738 (9th Cir. 2008) (finding that "young men in El Salvador resisting gang membership" failed as a particular social group because the group lacked social distinction and particularity).

[337] *Lizama v. Holder*, 629 F.3d 440, 447–48 (4th Cir. 2011) (rejecting the social group of "young, Americanized, well-off Salvadoran male deportees with criminal histories who oppose gangs"); *Constanza v. Holder*, 647 F.3d 749, 752 (8th Cir. 2011) (rejecting the social group of "persons who have returned from the United States and are perceived as affluent").

[338] *Henriquez-Rivas v. Holder*, 707 F.3d 1082, 1090 (9th Cir. 2013) (en banc) (declining to decide whether "people who testified against gang members" was a legally cognizable social group, stating that social visibility did not mean literal visibility and that the perception of the persecutor is "highly relevant to, or even potentially dispositive of, the question of social visibility", and confirming that the group does not need to be homogenous to be sufficiently particular); *Zelaya v. Holder*, 668 F.3d 159 (4th Cir. 2012) (finding that the social group was not cognizable due to lack of particularity but agreeing that witnesses or informants might be a viable social group in the concurring opinion); *Garcia v. Att'y Gen.*, 665 F.3d 496 (3d Cir. 2011) (finding that a civilian witness who assisted law enforcement against violent gangs was a member of a viable social group because it is unified by the common, immutable characteristic of a shared past experience and therefore meets the *Matter of Acosta* test); *Velasco-Cervantes v. Holder*, 593 F.3d 975 (9th Cir. 2010) (finding that the social group was not cognizable due to lack of particularity); *Scatambuli v. Holder*, 558 F.3d 53 (1st Cir. 2009) (finding that the social group was not cognizable due to lack of social visibility); *Soriano v. Holder*, 569 F.3d 1162 (9th Cir. 2009) (finding that the social group was not cognizable due to lack of social visibility); *Matter of C–A–*, 23 I&N Dec. 951 (BIA 2006) (finding that the group of "non-criminal informants working against the Cali drug cartel" does not meet the social distinction requirement because such a group, by its very nature, seeks not to be recognized as a group by society while individual informants seek to keep their identities secret).

[339] *Arteaga v. Mukasey*, 511 F.3d 940, 945–46 (9th Cir. 2007) (finding that "gang members" and "former gang members" are not particular social groups, despite having the common trait of a shared past experience because the group's shared experience stems from criminal activity and any "voluntary association" is not the kind of association that is fundamental to human dignity).

[340] *Arteaga v. Mukasey*, at 940, 945 (finding that "tattooed gang members" is not a particular social group because it is not defined with particularity); *Castellano-Chacon v. INS*, 341 F.3d 533, 549 (6th Cir. 2003) (stating that "tattooed youth" does not constitute a particular social group because having a tattoo is not an innate characteristic and that tattooed youth are not closely affiliated with one another as a group).

[341] *Crespin-Valladares v. Holder*, 632 F.3d 117, 121, 125 (4th Cir. 2011) (finding that the social group of "family members of those who actively oppose the gangs in El Salvador by agreeing to be

Continued

- Individuals who actively oppose gangs.[342]

Several of these areas of social group jurisprudence are discussed in detail below.

> **Practice Pointer**: Despite the BIA's re-affirmed and clarified social group test, practitioners should continue to argue eligibility under *Matter of Acosta*. Practitioners also should continue to challenge the additional social distinction and particularity requirements as unreasonable requirements that are inconsistent with the BIA's own precedent (*Matter of Acosta*), divergent from prior domestic and international interpretations (especially from UNHCR guidance and Congressional intent), and incoherent (conflation of the particular social group test with nexus). The BIA's additional requirements effectively preclude pro se applicants and make the particular social group ground incongruent with the other four protected grounds. Therefore, it is an impermissible construction of the statute. Moreover, when Congress wanted to exclude individuals from asylum eligibility, it did so by enacting statutory bars to eligibility. Imposing these additional requirements, which essentially exclude large groups of individuals in need of protection from asylum eligibility, is against Congressional intent. Finally, the BIA has frequently conflated its social group analysis with its nexus analysis and has failed to explain how previously accepted social groups still qualify under its post-*Acosta* standard. Therefore, its new requirements seem arbitrary and unreasonable. On these bases, the additional requirements do not merit deference by the federal courts.[343]

> **Practice Pointer**: While continuing to challenge these standards, however, practitioners should be prepared to present social groups that are viable under the *Matter of M–E–V–G–* and *Matter of W–G–R–*

---

prosecutorial witnesses" was a viable social group because it was sufficiently particular); *Orellana-Monson v. Holder*, 685 F.3d 511, 521–22 (5th Cir. 2012) (finding that the social groups of "young Salvadoran males who are siblings of a member of the aforementioned social group" and "family members of Jose Orellana-Monson" were too broad and encompassed a diverse cross section of society; however, the court focused on the first articulated social group and did not address the more specific group of Jose's family); *Constanza v. Holder*, 647 F.3d 749, 752 (8th Cir. 2011) (rejecting the social group of "persons who fear harm to their families from gangs"); *Matter of S–E–G–*, 24 I&N Dec. 579, 585–86 (BIA 2008) (finding that family members of Salvadoran youth who have been subjected to recruitment efforts by the MS-13 gang and who have rejected or resisted membership was not a cognizable social group because it lacked particularity; family members was an amorphous, undefined category that could potentially include distant relatives).

[342] *Pirir-Boc v. Holder*, 750 F.3d 1077 (9th Cir. 2014); *Garcia v. Holder*, 746 F.3d 869, 872 (8th Cir. 2014) (rejecting the social group of "young Guatemalan men who have opposed the MS-13, have been beaten and extorted by that gang, [and] reported those gangs to the police").

[343] *See* B. Casper, *et al.*, *Matter of M–E–V–G– and the BIA's Confounding Legal Standard for 'Membership in a Particular Social Group*,' 14–06 IMMIGR. BRIEFINGS 1 (June 2014) (citing *Matter of M–E–V–G–*, 26 I&N Dec. 227, 250 (BIA 2014)).

standards. Moreover, it is essential for practitioners to understand their circuit's social group case law and its impact on their clients' cases. For cases in the Third, Seventh, and Ninth Circuits, where there has been some precedent rejecting all or calling into question all or parts of the BIA's social group test, practitioners should continue to argue that those decisions still govern following *Matter of M–E–V–G–* and *Matter of W–G–R–*.

1. Resisters of Gang Recruitment

Thanks to BIA precedent, threats and harm stemming from an applicant's resistance to gang members' recruitment efforts may represent the most challenging basis under which to claim asylum in the United States.[344] In the two BIA precedent cases establishing social visibility (now social distinction) and particularity as requirements for demonstrating a cognizable social group, the BIA addressed groups involving individuals who have resisted gang recruitment.[345] *Matter of S–E–G–* involved the social groups of "Salvadoran youth who have been subjected to recruitment efforts by the MS-13 gang and who have rejected or resisted membership in the gang based on their own personal, moral, and religious opposition to the gang's values and activities" and those individuals' family members.[346] Its companion case, *Matter of E–A–G–*, involved the groups of "persons resistant to gang membership" and "young persons who are perceived to be affiliated with gangs."[347] None of these groups were held to have met the BIA's social visibility and particularity requirements.

In *Matter of S–E–G–*, teenage twin brothers fled El Salvador after refusing the join the MS-13 gang, which retaliated by beating them, threatening them with death, and threatening to rape and kill their older sister. After the MS-13 killed another youth in their neighborhood who had resisted the gang's recruitment, the brothers and their sister fled.[348] The BIA rejected the proposed social group of "Salvadoran youth who have been subjected to recruitment efforts by the MS-13 gang and who have rejected or resisted membership in the gang based on their own personal, moral, and religious opposition to the gang's values and activities" as lacking social visibility because those who refuse recruitment are "not in a substantially different situation from anyone who has crossed the gang, or who is perceived to be a threat to the gang's

---

[344] *See, e.g.*, *Zelaya v. Holder*, 668 F.3d 159 (4th Cir. 2012) (stating that the proposed group was "materially indistinguishable" from the group in the BIA case *Matter of S–E–G–*, 24 I&N Dec. 579 (BIA 2008) without analyzing the specific facts involved in the case of a Honduran youth who had resisted gang recruitment and reported the retaliation he suffered to the police).

[345] *See Matter of S–E–G–*, 24 I&N Dec. 579 (BIA 2008); *Matter of E–A–G–*, 24 I&N Dec. 591 (BIA 2008).

[346] *Matter of S–E–G–*, at 579.

[347] *Matter of E–A–G–*, at 591.

[348] *Matter of S–E–G–*, at 579, 579–80.

interests."[349] The BIA also rejected the group as lacking the requisite particularity because the proposed group is united by characteristics that are "too amorphous" — lacking stable families and coming from middle to lower class families in areas controlled by gangs — such that "people's ideas of what those terms mean can vary."[350] The BIA concluded that the proposed group was made up of "a potentially large and diffuse segment of society," and therefore, lacked particularity.[351]

> ➢ **Practice Pointer**: The BIA asserted in *Matter of M–E–V–G–* that *Matter of S–E–G–* "should not be read as a blanket rejection of all factual scenarios involving gangs ... social group determinations are made on a case by case basis."[352]

Following *Matter of S–E–G–*, adjudicators have hesitated to grant asylum applications based on applicants' resistance to gang recruitment and the subsequent and often violent retaliation that they have suffered.[353] For example, in *Santos-Lemus v. Mukasey*, the Ninth Circuit held that young men from El Salvador who resist gang violence do not constitute a particular social group because the group lacks particularity and social visibility.[354]

In considering the social group of "young [Salvadoran] women recruited by gang members who resist such recruitment," the First Circuit accepted the BIA's social visibility and particularity requirements.[355] It stated that to be socially visible the group "must be generally recognized in the community as a cohesive group" and that to be particular the group must be defined in a way in which it is easy to identify who is a member of the group and who is not.[356] The court found that the articulated social

---

[349] *Id.* at 587.

[350] *Id.* at 585–86.

[351] *Id.* at 585.

[352] *Matter of M–E–V–G–*, 26 I&N Dec. 227, 251 (BIA 2014).

[353] *See Zalaya v. Holder*, 668 F.3d 159, 162, 166 (4th Cir. 2012) (rejecting the social group of "young Honduran males who (1) refuse to join the Mara Salvatrucha 13 gang (MS-13), (2) have notified the authorities of MS-13's harassment tactics, and (3) have an identifiable tormentor within MS-13"); *Orellana-Monson v. Holder*, 685 F.3d 511 (5th Cir. 2012) (finding that gang resisters in El Salvador lack social visibility and particularity); *Gaitan v. Holder*, 671 F.3d 678, 682 (8th Cir. 2012) (rejecting the social group of "young males from El Salvador who have been subjected to recruitment by MS-13 and who have rejected or resisted membership in the gang based on personal opposition to the gang"); *Constanza v. Holder*, 647 F.3d 749, 752 (8th Cir. 2011) (rejecting the social group of "persons resistant to gang membership"); *Larios v. Holder*, 608 F.3d 105 (1st Cir. 2010) (finding that gang resisters in Guatemala lack social visibility and particularity); *Mendez-Barrera v. Holder*, 602 F.3d 21 (1st Cir. 2010) (finding that gang resisters in El Salvador lack social visibility and particularity); *Ramos-Lopez v. Holder*, 563 F.3d 855 (9th Cir. 2009) (finding that gang resisters in Honduras lack social visibility and particularity); *Santos-Lemus v. Mukasey*, 542 F.3d 738 (9th Cir. 2008) (finding that "young men in El Salvador resisting gang membership" failed as a particular social group because the group lacked social distinction and particularity).

[354] *Santos-Lemus v. Mukasey*, 542 F.3d 738, 745 (9th Cir. 2008).

[355] *Mendez-Barrera v. Holder*, 602 F.3d 21, 26 (1st Cir. 2010).

[356] *Id.*

group failed both of these requirements, noting that the applicant failed to identify any characteristics that make the group visible in society and that the characteristics of the group — "young," "recruitment," and "resistance" — are too amorphous and subjective to establish a sufficient level of particularity.[357]

The Fifth, Sixth, and Tenth Circuits all rejected similar social groups as failing the social visibility and particularity prongs of the BIA's test. Specifically, the Fifth Circuit U.S. Court of Appeals considered the social group of "Salvadoran males between the ages of 8 and 15 who have been recruited by Mara 18 but have refused to join the gang because of their principal opposition to the gang and what they want."[358] The court, however, found that the articulated social group was "exceedingly broad and encompass[ing] a diverse cross section of society."[359] Therefore, the group failed both social visibility and particularity.

The Sixth Circuit considered and rejected the proposed social group of "young Salvadoran males who refused recruitment by 'Maras.'"[360] The court reasoned that the group could not "accurately be described in a manner sufficiently distinct that [it] would be recognized, in the society in question, as a discrete class of persons."[361] Similarly, the Tenth Circuit considered and rejected the proposed social group of "women in El Salvador between the ages of 12 and 25 who resisted gang recruitment."[362] Although the court found that the group was defined with sufficient particularity in that it was not vague or overbroad, it found that the group was not socially visible.[363] The court noted that to meet the social visibility prong of the test, the relevant trait must be "potentially identifiable by members of the community, either because it is evident or because the information defining the characteristic is publically accessible."[364]

In *Valdiviezo-Galdamez v. Att'y Gen.*, the Third Circuit twice considered the social group of "Honduran youth/young Honduran men who have been actively recruited by gangs but have refused to join because they oppose the gangs."[365] The Third Circuit repudiated the BIA's "social visibility" requirement as inconsistent with its own prior precedent in *Matter of Kasinga*, *Matter of Toboso-Alfonso*, and *Matter of Fuentes*, because the characteristics in those cases — opposition to the practice of FGM/C, sexual orientation, and former service as a policeman — were internal traits

---

[357] *Id.*

[358] *Orellana-Monson v. Holder*, 685 F.3d 511, 521 (5th Cir. 2012).

[359] *Id.* at 521–22.

[360] *Umana-Ramos v. Holder*, 724 F.3d 667, 670 (6th Cir. 2013).

[361] *Id.* at 674.

[362] *Rivera-Barrientos v. Holder*, 666 F.3d 641 (10th Cir. 2012).

[363] *Id.* at 650.

[364] *Id.* at 652.

[365] *Valdiviezo-Galdamez v. U.S. Att'y Gen.*, 663 F.3d 582 (3d Cir. 2011); *Valdiviezo-Galdamez v. U.S. Att'y Gen.*, 502 F.3d 285, 290 (3d Cir. 2007).

unknown to the public.[366] The court stated that limiting particular social groups to "characteristics that were highly visible and recognizable by others in the country in question," therefore, was inconsistent and an "insurmountable" hurdle for groups the BIA had already recognized.[367] The Third Circuit noted that the BIA provided no rationale for the social visibility requirement, and remanded the case for a second time to provide a "principled reason" for its adoption of this new requirement.[368] The Third Circuit also rejected the BIA's particularity requirement as an alternative articulation of social visibility. The court stated that "the government's attempt to distinguish the two oscillates between confusion and obfuscation, while at times both confusing and obfuscating."[369]

On remand from the Third Circuit, in *Matter of M–E–V–G–*, the BIA clarified its three-part test for determining the viability of a particular social group.[370] However, instead of considering for the third time the social group of "Honduran youth who have been actively recruited by gangs but who have refused to join because they oppose gangs," the BIA remanded the matter to the Immigration Judge to apply its clarified test for determining the viability of a particular social group.[371] There have only been two published cases considering a gang resistance-related social group following *Matter of M–E–V–G–* — one in the Eighth Circuit U.S. Court of Appeals and the other in the Tenth Circuit.[372] Most recently, in *Rodas-Orellana v. Holder*, the Tenth Circuit held that the proposed social group of "El Salvadoran males threatened and actively recruited by gangs, who resist joining because they oppose the gangs" failed to demonstrate social distinction.[373] The court concluded that *Matter of M–E–V–G–* and *Matter of W–G–R–* were consistent with their past interpretation of social visibility in *Rivera-Barrientos v. Holder*, and therefore, remand was not warranted.[374] Similarly, in *Garcia v. Holder*, the Eighth Circuit rejected the social group based on prior circuit precedent and *Matter of S–E–G–*.[375] This case did not, however, mention the BIA's clarified social group test or its 2014 precedential decisions.

Problematically, many adjudicators seem to be under the impression that *Matter of S–E–G–* precludes these claims, sometimes without analyzing the specific facts of the case.[376] In the Fourth Circuit case of *Zelaya v. Holder*, for example, the court stated

---

[366] *Valdiviezo-Galdamez*,, 663 F.3d at 582, 604.

[367] *Id.* at 604.

[368] *Id.*

[369] *Id.* at 608.

[370] *Matter of M–E–V–G–*, 26 I&N Dec. 227 (BIA 2014).

[371] *Id.*

[372] *See Rodas-Orellana v. Holder*, No. 14-9516, 2015 WL 859566, at *6 (10th Cir. Mar. 2, 2015); *Garcia v. Holder*, 746 F.3d 869 (8th Cir. 2014).

[373] *Rodas-Orellana v. Holder*, No. 14-9516, 2015 WL 859566, at *6 (10th Cir. Mar. 2, 2015);

[374] *Id.*

[375] *Garcia v. Holder*, 746 F.3d 869 (8th Cir. 2014).

[376] *See, e.g., Zelaya v. Holder*, 668 F.3d 159 (4th Cir. 2012).

that the proposed group of "young Honduran males who (1) refuse to join the Mara Salvatrucha 13 gang (MS-13); (2) have notified the authorities of MS-13's harassment tactics; and (3) have an identifiable tormentor within MS-13," was "materially indistinguishable" from *Matter of S–E–G–*.[377] The court did not analyze the specific facts of Mr. Zelaya's case, including the fact that he was presenting a claim from Honduras, not El Salvador, and the fact that he had reported the harm to the police.[378]

The circuit court decisions applying the BIA's three-part social group test in the context of resisters to gang recruitment also frequently conflate the analysis of the viability of a particular social group with the nexus analysis.[379] In *Orellana-Monson v. Holder*, for example, the Fifth Circuit found that the social group of "Salvadoran males, ages 8 to 15, who have been recruited by Mara 18 but have refused to join due to a principled opposition to gangs" lacked social visibility and particularity.[380] The court's reasoning was the "pervasive nature of Mara 18 [violence] against any non-gang member in El Salvadoran society" and its belief that individuals are targeted for reasons other than "particular political orientation, interests, lifestyle, or any other identifying factors."[381] In focusing on the reasons why the Mara 18 target certain individuals, the Fifth Circuit conflated the nexus analysis with its analysis regarding whether the proposed group was legally cognizable. According to the BIA, these are meant to be separate inquiries.[382]

- **Practice Pointer**: To avoid reflexive denials by adjudicators, practitioners should present alternative claims in addition to those based on resistance to recruitment, given the consistently negative precedent in this area. While it is not impossible to make a successful claim based on resistance to recruitment, presenting additional theories will provide the adjudicator with a less controversial basis on which to grant the claim.

2. *Affluent or Wealthy Individuals*

In *Matter of A–M–E– & J–G–U–*, the BIA considered a group of affluent Guatemalans and applied a three-prong analysis: common, immutable characteristic; social visibility; and particularity.[383] Although it did not state explicitly that these two additional factors were precedent for determining the viability of any particular social group moving forward, the BIA did refer to them as "factors" and "requirements"

---

[377] *Id.* at 166.

[378] *Id.* at 163–64.

[379] *See, e.g.*, *Orellana-Monson v. Holder*, 685 F.3d 511 (5th Cir. 2012).

[380] *Id.* at 516.

[381] *Id.* at 522.

[382] *See Matter of M–E–V–G–*, 26 I&N Dec. 227 (BIA 2014); *Matter of W–G–R–*, 26 I&N Dec. 208 (BIA 2014).

[383] *Matter of A–M–E– & J–G–U–*, 24 I&N Dec. 69 (BIA 2007) (referring to social visibility and particularity as "factors" and "requirements").

throughout its decision. In analyzing whether the group of affluent Guatemalans was a cognizable social group, the BIA stated that the shared characteristic must be "considered in the context of the country of concern and the persecution feared."[384]

The BIA confirmed that the group of affluent Guatemalans would meet the standards under *Matter of Acosta* because being affluent was a trait that individuals should not be required to change.[385] However, the BIA then went on to find that the social group was not viable because it did not meet the social visibility and particularity factors.[386] For social visibility, the BIA reasoned that the group did not share a common trait that was socially distinct in Guatemalan society because the country conditions evidence showed that criminality is pervasive against all Guatemalan socio-economic groups.[387] The BIA defined particularity as meaning "the proposed group can accurately be described in a manner sufficiently distinct that the group would be recognized in the society in question as a discreet class of persons."[388] It then stated that the group of affluent Guatemalans did not meet this factor because it was too amorphous and indeterminate; its membership could not be delimited because the concept of wealth could be subjectively defined to include a broad or narrow range of individuals.[389]

On appeal, the Second Circuit considered the group of "affluent Guatemalans" and confirmed that a viable social group must "possess some fundamental characteristic in common which serves to distinguish them in the eyes of a persecutor — or in the eyes of the outside world in general."[390] The court also recognized that a viable social group also must have well-defined boundaries, and:

> If 'wealth' defined the boundaries of a particular social group, a determination about whether any petitioner fit into the group (or might be perceived as a member of the group) would necessitate a sociological analysis as to how persons with various assets would have been viewed by others in their country.[391]

The court agreed with the BIA that the group "affluent Guatemalans" did not meet the BIA's social visibility and particularity requirements and denied the petition for review.

---

[384] *Id.* at 74.

[385] *Id.*

[386] *Id.*

[387] *Id.* at 75.

[388] *Id.* at 76.

[389] Id.

[390] *Ucelo-Gomez v. Mukasey*, 509 F.3d 70, 73 (2d Cir. 2007) (citing *Gomez v. INS*, 947 F.2d 660, 664 (2d Cir. 1991)).

[391] *Id.*

3. *Prosecutorial Witnesses and Informants*

Individuals who serve as witnesses and informants against gangs are extremely vulnerable to gang violence. Such asylum claims have yielded another line of particular social group cases in the BIA and federal courts. In *Matter of C–A–*, the BIA analyzed the group of "noncriminal drug informants working against the Cali drug cartel" in Colombia.[392] In that case, the applicant had access to information about the drug cartel through his personal relationship with the head of security for the cartel. The applicant passed along what he learned to a friend of his who worked for the government to investigate and prosecute narco-traffickers.[393] When the cartel discovered this, they brutally beat the applicant's son and promised to return.[394] The BIA found that there was no common, immutable characteristic under *Matter of Acosta* because the decision to be an informant was not fundamental to the applicant's identity. Rather, it was the applicant's own decision to assume a calculated risk.[395] Arguably, the shared past act of informing should have met the *Matter of Acosta* test as a common, immutable characteristic. However, the BIA drew a flawed analogy to its decision in *Matter of Fuentes*, which addressed the social group of former police officers, stating that serving as an informant was analogous to being a police officer in that both involved a decision to take a calculated risk.[396]

In analyzing the newly introduced factor of social visibility, the BIA found that the articulated group lacked social visibility because the group is hidden and confidential by nature.[397] This finding appeared to apply a literal visibility test instead of a more figurative visibility test when analyzing whether the group is perceived as such by society. The BIA also found that the articulated group lacked particularity because it was "too loosely defined;" it could include any person who passed along information to the government or to a competing cartel.[398] The BIA did confirm, however, that homogeneity of the group was not required.

On appeal, the Eleventh Circuit U.S. Court of Appeals considered the social group of "noncriminal drug informants working against the Cali drug cartel in Colombia" and agreed that social visibility was a reasonable requirement to determine whether the cartel's treatment of the group was distinct from the rest of the population.[399] The court also agreed with the BIA's concerns regarding the "numerosity and

---

[392] *Matter of C–A–*, 23 I&N Dec. 951 (BIA 2006).

[393] *Id.* at 952.

[394] *Id.* at 952–53.

[395] *Id.* at 958.

[396] *Id.* at 958–59. *See also Matter of Fuentes*, 19 I&N Dec. 658 (BIA 1988) (distinguishing between former police officers and current police officers and finding that former police officers meet the *Acosta* test due to their immutable shared past experience).

[397] *Id.* at 960–61.

[398] *Id.* at 957.

[399] *Castillo-Arias v. Att'y Gen.*, 446 F.3d 1190, 1198 (11th Cir. 2006).

inchoateness of noncriminal informants."[400] In deferring to the BIA's articulated standards and interpretations, the Eleventh Circuit denied the petition for review.[401]

Following the denial of asylum and the BIA's reasoning in *Matter of C–A–*, the First Circuit followed suit in *Scatambuli v. Holder*, finding that "informants to the U.S. government about a smuggling ring" was not a legally cognizable social group because it lacked social visibility.[402] Like the BIA in *Matter of C–A–*, the First Circuit seemed to apply a literal visibility test, rather than considering whether the group was perceived as a distinct entity by society.[403] Now that the BIA has clarified that social visibility does not mean literal or ocular visibility, cases involving confidential informants might no longer fail this test.

In addition to informants, there is a similar line of cases considering whether prosecutorial witnesses against gangs and cartels are members of viable social groups. In *Henriquez-Rivas v. Holder*, the Ninth Circuit considered the asylum claim of an applicant from El Salvador and his proposed social group of "witnesses who testify against gang members."[404] The court determined that this group may be a cognizable particular social group for purposes of asylum and ruled that "social visibility" does not mean literal or ocular visibility. Although the court did not determine whether social visibility was a valid requirement, it opined that "the perception of the persecutors may matter the most."[405] The Ninth Circuit confirmed that a group does not need to be homogenous in order to be particular.[406]

Significantly, in *Henriquez-Rivas v. Holder*, the Ninth Circuit overruled its prior particularity reasoning of *Velasco-Cervantes v. Holder* and *Soriano v. Holder*.[407] In *Velasco-Cervantes v. Holder*, the Ninth Circuit had considered the group of "former material witnesses for the government" and found that the group lacked particularity.[408] Despite the BIA's assertion in *Matter of C–A–* that groups do not need to be homogenous in order to be sufficiently particular, the Ninth Circuit had reasoned that any person of any origin could be involuntarily placed in the role of a material witness for the government in any type of legal proceeding.[409] Therefore, the

---

[400] *Id.*

[401] *Id.*

[402] *Scatambuli v. Holder*, 558 F.3d 53 (1st Cir. 2009). *See also Amilcar-Orellana v. Mukasey*, 551 F.3d 86, 91 (1st Cir. 2008) (rejecting the applicant's argument that he was a member of the particular social group of "non-confidential informants" and finding that the applicant's fear of persecution stemmed from a personal dispute, not any particular social group).

[403] *Id.* at 60.

[404] *Henriquez-Rivas v. Holder*, 707 F.3d 1081 (9th Cir. 2013).

[405] *Id.* at 1089.

[406] *Id.* at 1090.

[407] *See Velasco-Cervantes v. Holder*, 593 F.3d 975, 978 (9th Cir. 2010); *Soriano v. Holder*, 569 F.3d 1162, 1165–66 (9th Cir. 2009).

[408] *Velasco-Cervantes v. Holder*, 593 F.3d 975, 978 (9th Cir. 2010).

[409] *Id.*

group was not sufficiently particular. Previously, in *Soriano v. Holder*, the Ninth Circuit also had found that, like witnesses, "criminal government informants" lacked sufficient particularity to be a cognizable social group.[410] The court had stated that the group was too broad and was not cohesive enough under Ninth Circuit precedent.[411] However, the Ninth Circuit has now overruled this particularity reasoning.[412] In *Henriquez-Rivas v. Holder*, the Ninth Circuit stated:

> Our previous cases rejecting as a "particular social group" those acting as government informants are arguably in conflict with our holding today insofar as they required an additional element of shared birth, racial or ethnic origin, or some other innate aspect of homogeneity for the group to qualify as a "particular social group" . . . These cases reflect the confusion between the "particularity" and "social visibility" requirements. The diversity of "lifestyles" and "origin" to which these cases refer did not concern the "particularity" requirement per se, nor are they relevant to our analysis, as we explain above. Accordingly, the extent that *Soriano* and *Velasco-Cervantes* make considerations of diversity of lifestyle and origin the sine qua non of "particularity" analysis, they are overruled."[413]

Following *Henriquez-Rivas v. Holder*, the Ninth Circuit confirmed in *Cordoba v. Holder* that its decision in *Henriquez-Rivas v. Holder* abrogated its prior decisions seeming to require cohesiveness of a social group, including its decision in *Sanchez-Trujillo v. INS*.[414]

Other circuits, such as the Third and Fourth Circuits have grappled with the proposed social groups of witnesses and informants. For example, in *Zelaya v. Holder*, the Fourth Circuit found that the group "young Honduran males who (1) refuse to join the Mara Salvatrucha 13 gang (MS-13); (2) have notified the authorities of MS-13's harassment tactics; and (3) have an identifiable tormentor within MS-13," was too amorphous and not defined by a common, immutable characteristic.[415] However, in a concurrence, Judge Floyd considered the second characteristic of the social group. Although he agreed that individuals who have reported gang violence to the police may not satisfy the social visibility and particularity tests, Judge Floyd distinguished witnesses who testify against gangs, stating that such witnesses are both socially visible and particular.[416] Thus, testifying witnesses may be more likely than informants to be a viable social group, at least in the Fourth Circuit.

---

[410] *Soriano v. Holder*, 569 F.3d 1162, 1165–66 (9th Cir. 2009).

[411] *Id.* at 1166.

[412] *Henriquez-Rivas v. Holder*, 707 F.3d 1081 (9th Cir. 2013).

[413] *Id.* at 1093–94 (referring to and discussing its decisions in *Soriano v. Holder* and *Velasco-Cervantes v. Holder*).

[414] *Cordoba v. Holder*, 726 F.3d 1106, 1115–16 (9th Cir. 2013).

[415] *Zelaya v. Holder*, 668 F.3d 159, 166 (4th Cir. 2012).

[416] *Id.* at 169 (J. Floyd concurring).

In *Garcia v. Att'y Gen.*, the Third Circuit found that civilian witnesses who have the shared past experience of assisting law enforcement against violent gangs that threaten communities in Guatemala constitute a legally cognizable social group for purposes of asylum eligibility.[417] The court reasoned that the group is unified by a characteristic that members cannot change because it is based on their past actions that cannot be undone.[418] Moreover, even if members of this group could recant their testimony, they "should not be required to" do so.[419] Therefore, the group meets the *Matter of Acosta* test and is viable in the Third Circuit.

This case law indicates that witnesses and informants may be cognizable social groups for purposes of asylum eligibility, especially if a strong evidentiary record is built. In analyzing these groups under the BIA's three-part test for determining the viability of a social group, these groups should meet step one, immutability. Having informed or testified against gangs is unchangeable. Moreover, the belief that criminality is wrong and should be reported to law enforcement is a fundamental belief that individuals should not be required to abandon. For step two, the BIA's recent retreat from literal visibility in favor of social distinction in *Matter of M–E–V–G–* has opened the door to the ability to establish that these groups are perceived as distinct entities within the society in question. Step three, particularity, may remain the most difficult prong of the test to meet in these cases, especially due to the BIA's dicta in *Matter of W–G–R–* seeming to require homogeneity in order to meet the particularity requirement. However, Judge Floyd's concurrence in *Zelaya v. Holder* and the Ninth Circuit's *Henriquez-Rivas v. Holder* should support the argument that these groups, especially testifying witnesses, are sufficiently particular.

> ➢ **Practice Pointer**: Practitioners should continue to argue that groups do not need to be homogenous in order to meet the particularity test. First, such a requirement distinguishes the particular social group ground from the other four grounds (race, religion, nationality, and political opinion), none of which have size limitations and none of which require individuals sharing those traits to also share the same age, sex, and background. Requiring homogeneity is contrary to the principle of ejusdem generis ("of the same kind"), which directs that "particular social group" should be interpreted in parallel with the other four protected grounds.

4. Former Gang Members

Former gang members face a heightened risk of being targeted with violence at the hands of other gang members. The courts have considered whether such individuals merit protection under U.S. asylum law and have expressed concern about granting benefits to individuals who have been part of violent groups or who have engaged in

---

[417] *Garcia v. Att'y Gen.*, 665 F.3d 496, 504 (3d Cir. 2011).

[418] *Id.*

[419] *Id.*

violent criminal activities. Despite policy concerns, however, the Fourth, Sixth, and Seventh Circuits have recognized that former gang members should qualify as legally cognizable social groups under both the *Matter of Acosta* and *Matter of S–E–G–* standards.[420] Those courts ultimately agreed that the statutory bars enumerated in the Immigration and Nationality Act provided adequate safeguards against granting benefits to violent criminals.[421] Most importantly, these courts acknowledge that "former gang members" are united by "gang apostasy and opposition to violence."[422] It is this key element of conscience that characterizes the "former gang member" particular social group, not merely the temporal fact of no longer being in association with the gang.[423]

In *Benitez Ramos v. Holder*, the Seventh Circuit considered whether a former member of the Mara Salvatrucha was a member of a cognizable social group and distinguished former gang members from current gang members.[424] The court found that the group was characterized by a shared past experience that could not be changed.[425] The court rejected the BIA's social visibility requirement and noted that the social group of former gang members was neither unspecific nor amorphous and therefore was sufficiently particular to be a legally cognizable social group.[426] Finally, the court distinguished the Ninth Circuit's decision in *Arteaga v. Mukasey* as addressing current, rather than former gang members, and also found that there are mechanisms under the INA that permit denial of asylum to individuals undeserving of protection, namely the statutory bars and discretion.[427]

The Sixth and Fourth Circuits have joined the Seventh Circuit in finding that former gang membership is a shared past experience that is impossible to change. In *Urbina-Mejia v. Holder*, the Sixth Circuit explained that "once one has left the gang, one is forever a former member of that gang."[428] The court also noted that a former gang member is instantly identifiable by rival gangs and the former gang.[429] Although the court found that the proposed social group was legally cognizable, the claim was ultimately denied because the applicant had committed serious nonpolitical crimes outside of the U.S. and was therefore statutorily barred from asylum.[430]

---

420 *See Martinez v. Holder*, 740 F.3d 902, 913 (4th Cir. 2014); *Urbina-Mejia v. Holder*, 597 F.3d 360 (6th Cir. 2010); *Benitez Ramos v. Holder*, 589 F.3d 426 (7th Cir. 2009).

421 *See Martinez v. Holder*, at 913; *Urbina-Mejia v. Holder*, at 360; *Benitez Ramos v. Holder*, at 426.

422 *Martinez v. Holder*, at 912.

423 *See Martinez v. Holder*, 740 F.3d 902, 913 (4th Cir. 2014); *Urbina-Mejia v. Holder*, 597 F.3d 360 (6th Cir. 2010); *Benitez Ramos v. Holder*, 589 F.3d 426 (7th Cir. 2009).

424 *Benitez Ramos v. Holder*, 589 F.3d 426, 430–31 (7th Cir. 2009).

425 *Id.*

426 *Id.*

427 *Id.* at 431.

428 *Urbina-Mejia v. Holder*, 597 F.3d 360, 366 (6th Cir. 2010).

429 *Id.* at 366–67.

430 *Id.* at 369.

➢ **Practice Pointer**: Practitioners presenting former gang member claims should work closely with their clients to determine what, if any, criminal activity they participated in as a part of the gang. Any criminal activity should be discussed in detail and evaluated to determine if it might bar the applicant under the serious nonpolitical crime or persecutor bars to asylum and withholding of removal eligibility.[431] A strong evidentiary record should be built in support of arguments that these statutory bars do not apply.

In *Martinez v. Holder*, the Fourth Circuit joined the Sixth and Seventh Circuits in recognizing that a former gang member could establish viability as a social group based on the members' common, immutable characteristic based on their shared past experience.[432] The Fourth Circuit reasoned that the only way the applicant could remove himself from this social group of former gang members would be to rejoin the MS-13 gang in El Salvador.[433] Agreeing with the Seventh Circuit, the court stated that it would be perverse to interpret the INA to force individuals to rejoin gangs in order to avoid persecution.[434] The Fourth Circuit, like the Seventh, distinguished the Ninth Circuit's decision in *Arteaga v. Mukasey*, stating that the applicant in that case was still a gang member.[435] It also explicitly disagreed with the First Circuit's rejection of former gang members as a social group based on the notion that former gang members do not deserve refugee protection.[436] The Fourth Circuit reasoned that "associating with a criminal syndicate" is not included in the INA's list of actions that disqualify an applicant from withholding of removal relief, and that the First Circuit's prediction that holding in favor of a former gang member will "offer an incentive for aliens to join gangs here as a path to legal status" was doubtful at best.[437]

In *Martinez v. Holder*, the Fourth Circuit addressed the government's interpretation that a particular social group may not include members who engaged in past antisocial or criminal conduct and noted that, in focusing on the former status of membership in a gang, the government was "failing to recognize the distinct *current* status of membership in a group defined by gang apostasy and opposition to violence."[438] The Fourth Circuit joined the Sixth and Seventh Circuits in noting that the BIA had mischaracterized the Ninth Circuit's *Arteaga v. Mukasey* as a former

---

[431] INA §§208 (b)(2)(A)(i), 208 (b)(2)(A) (iii).

[432] *Martinez v. Holder*, 740 F.3d 902, 913 (4th Cir. 2014). *See also Urbina-Mejia v. Holder*, 597 F.3d 360 (6th Cir. 2010); *Benitez Ramos v. Holder*, 589 F.3d 426 (7th Cir. 2009).

[433] *Martinez v. Holder*, 740 F.3d 902, 905, 911 (4th Cir. 2014).

[434] *Id.* at 911 (referring to *Benitez Ramos v. Holder*, 589 F.3d 426 (7th Cir. 2009)).

[435] *Id.* at 912.

[436] *Id.* at 912, n. 3 (referring to *Cantarero v. Holder*, 734 F.3d 82 (1st Cir. 2013)).

[437] *Id.* (quoting *Cantarero v. Holder*, 734 F.3d 82, 86 (1st Cir. 2013)).

[438] *Id.* at 912.

gang member case.[439] The court noted that *Arteaga* is distinguishable, as it involved a respondent who was a current gang member, and was not a gang apostate or opponent of violence, like former gang members are.[440]

In *Arteaga v. Mukasey*, the Ninth Circuit rejected the social group of *current* gang members, specifically "American Salvadorian U.S. gang members of a Chicano-American street gang."[441] The applicant in that case was a current, but inactive member of the gang. The court expressed concern about the "voluntary" nature of the applicant's gang membership and stated that a shared criminal experience is not an innate characteristic because such traits are "materially at war with those [characteristics] we have concluded are innate for purposes of membership in a social group."[442] The court found that "participation in criminal activity is not fundamental to gang members' individual identities or consciences," and that to find otherwise would pervert the humanitarian purpose of refugee protection by giving "sanctuary to universal outlaws."[443] The Ninth Circuit held that current members of violent street gangs who assault people, traffic in drugs, and commit crimes are not a particular social group, but instead are best described as an "antisocial group."[444] The court also declined to offer protection to the applicant in the guise of being a former gang member, noting that disassociating from one group does not automatically put one in another group — of gang apostates or opponents of violence, for example.[445] Therefore, the courts have made clear that current gang members are distinguishable from former gang members, and former gang members who have made a conscious choice to defect, and thereby defy, the gang merit protection.

In contrast to the Fourth, Sixth, and Seventh Circuits, the First Circuit in *Cantarero v. Holder* agreed with the BIA that former gang membership is not distinct from current membership, stating that renunciation of gang membership did not change the fact that the shared past experiences included crimes and violence.[446] Therefore, the court rejected the notion that former gang members are deserving of refugee protection altogether.[447] It rejected the Sixth and Seventh Circuits' rationales stating, "[W]e disagree that Congress's decision not to expressly exclude former gang members [as a statutory bar to asylum] is probative of its intent as to whether they are

---

[439] *See Arteaga v. Mukasey*, 511 F.3d 940 (9th Cir. 2007).

[440] *Martinez v. Holder*, 740 F.3d 902, 905, 912 (4th Cir. 2014).

[441] *Arteaga v. Mukasey*, 511 F.3d 940 (9th Cir. 2007).

[442] *Id.* at 945–46.

[443] *Id.*

[444] *Arteaga v. Mukasey*, 511 F.3d 940, 945–46 (9th Cir. 2007).

[445] *Id.* at 946. U.S. Citizenship and Immigration Services agrees that a social group cannot be defined by terrorist, criminal, or persecutory activity or association, past or present. *See* Memorandum from Lynden D. Melmed, USCIS Chief Counsel, to Lori Scialabba, Associate Director, Refugee, Asylum and Int'l Operations, Guidance on *Matter of C–A–* (Washington, DC, January 12, 2007).

[446] *Cantarero v. Holder*, 734 F.3d 82, 87 (1st Cir. 2013).

[447] *Id.* at 86–87.

eligible for refugee status as a protected group."[448] Four months later, in 2014, the Fourth Circuit specifically addressed the First Circuit's findings in *Cantarero v. Holder* and forcefully rejected them.[449]

One month after the Fourth Circuit's decision and remand of *Martinez v. Holder*, in *Matter of W–G–R–*, the BIA reaffirmed that former members of Central American gangs (in this case the Mara 18 in El Salvador) who have renounced their gang membership do not present a cognizable particular social group.[450] *Matter of W–G–R–* is the companion case to *Matter of M–E–V–G–*, which the BIA issued in order to clarify its test for viability of a particular social group, and discusses it social group standards in nearly identical terms.[451] The BIA found that the social group of "former gang members who have renounced their gang membership" failed both the social distinction and particularity prongs of the BIA's three-part test.

According to the BIA, the group lacked social distinction because the record contained "scant evidence that Salvadoran society considers former gang members who have renounced their membership as a distinct social group."[452] The BIA stated that the group lacked particularity because it is too diffuse, broad, and subjective,[453] reasoning that the group could include persons of "any age, sex, or background," as well as any level of involvement in the gang.[454] The BIA explained that any group based on former membership may require additional definition with respect to "the duration or strength of the members' active participation . . . and the recency of their participation."[455] The BIA did not endeavor to distinguish or refute the Fourth Circuit's decision in *Martinez v. Holder* and also did not address its own precedents or the Ninth Circuit's *en banc* ruling in *Henriquez-Rivas v. Holder* that homogeneity is not required for a group to be a viable particular social group.[456]

Some gangs, such as the MS-13 and Mara 18 in Central America have a common practice of forcibly recruiting unwilling individuals. Where asylum-seekers have shown extenuating circumstances to explain their membership in a gang or explain the persecution that former members face, they have had more success, especially before IJs. For example, in one case, a young Guatemalan woman successfully argued that she had been forced to join a gang merely to survive, after being abandoned on the streets at age 10 and facing daily and increasingly more violent

---

[448] *Id.* at 86.

[449] *See Martinez v. Holder*, 740 F.3d 902 (4th Cir. 2014).

[450] *Matter of W–G–R–*, 26 I&N Dec. 208, 209 (BIA 2014) (considering the social group of "former members of the Mara 18 gang in El Salvador who have renounced their gang membership").

[451] *Id.* at 213, 216, 218.

[452] *Id.* at 222.

[453] *Id.*

[454] *Id.*

[455] *Id.* at 221–22.

[456] *See Matter of C–A–*, 23 I&N Dec. 951 (BIA 2006).

persecution at the hands of both street gangs and the police.[457] In another case, a Honduran male who had escaped from his gang was eligible for withholding of removal based on the fact that he had been forcibly tattooed and inducted into a gang, had not been involved in violence against others, and had a well-found fear of persecution by his former gang members as well as the police in his country.[458] In this case, the court found that the social group of former gang members constituted a protected social group.

➢ **Practice Pointer**: Practitioners should explore all potentially relevant facts with their gang member or former gang member clients, including the nature of their recruitment and induction into the gang, their activities while part of the gang, whether any violent or criminal activities were committed under duress, the circumstances surrounding the applicant's departure from the gang, what typically happens to members who leave the gang, and what harm or threats, if any, the applicant faced upon leaving or attempting to leave the gang.

5. *Tattooed Youth or Tattooed Gang Members*

The Sixth Circuit found that a young, tattooed male from Honduras who had belonged to MS-13 was not eligible for withholding of removal because members of the alleged social group did not share any common and immutable characteristics.[459] While the court found it possible to conceive of the members of MS-13 as a particular social group under the INA, sharing, for example, the common immutable characteristic of their past experiences together, their initiation rites, and their status as Spanish-speaking immigrants in the United States, it viewed the evidence presented as establishing, at best, that "tattooed youth" are targeted and prosecuted. The court declined to hold that "tattooed youth" constitute a particular social group.[460]

6. *Women and Girls Labeled as Gang Property*

In addition to the various gender-based asylum claims discussed previously in Part I of this chapter, an applicant's gender also may be a motivating trait for persecution at the hands of violent gangs. In many countries where gang violence has flourished, such as El Salvador, Guatemala, and Honduras, the societies have long histories of subjugation of women and their general exclusion from state protection. This combination, in addition to the patriarchal structure of gangs, has created a context

---

[457] *See Matter of E–S– and A–M–* [file no. redacted] (IJ Mar. 20, 2003) (Phoenix, AZ) (Richardson, IJ), *available at www.refugees.org/uploadedFiles/Participate/National_Center/Resource_Library/G.005.pdf*.

[458] *See Matter of Enamorado*, A77 530 541 (IJ Nov. 22, 1999) (Harlingen, TX) (Burkhart, IJ), *available at www.refugees.org/uploadedFiles/Participate/National_Center/Resource_Library/H.008.pdf*.

[459] *See Castellano-Chacon v. INS*, 341 F.3d 533, 546 (6th Cir. 2003), overruled in part on other grounds by *Almuhtaseb v. Gonzales*, 453 F.3d 743 (5th Cir. 2006).

[460] *See id.*

for gang violence motivated by gender. Although some gender-based asylum claims have been granted at the IJ level,[461] to date, few cases have been considered by the federal courts. The First and Tenth Circuits have addressed and rejected social group claims based on gender in the context of gang violence.[462] In the First Circuit's *Mendez-Barrera v. Holder* and the Tenth Circuit's *Rivera-Barrientos v. Holder*, the courts considered similar proposed social groups — "young women who resisted recruitment by gang members in El Salvador" and "women in El Salvador between the ages of 12 and 25 who resisted gang recruitment" — and found that the groups were not legally cognizable groups.[463]

Both circuits found these groups to lack social visibility. The First Circuit noted that the applicant failed to provide any evidence of social visibility or "to pinpoint any group characteristics that render members of the putative group socially visible in El Salvador," concluding that the proposed group "is simply too amorphous."[464] Likewise, the Tenth Circuit concluded that the applicant had presented no evidence demonstrating that society perceives young women who have resisted gang recruitment to be a distinct social group.[465]

The two circuits arrived at differing conclusions regarding particularity, however. The First Circuit found that the proposed social group of "young women who resisted recruitment by gang members in El Salvador" lacked sufficient particularity, stating, "Given her loose description of the group, it is virtually impossible to identify who is or is not a member."[466] The court reasoned that the group characteristics of "young," "recruitment," and "resistance," are "ambiguous" and "largely subjective."[467] The Tenth Circuit, on the other hand, found that the proposed social group of "women in El Salvador between the ages of 12 and 25 who resisted gang recruitment" satisfied the particularity requirement.[468]

---

[461] *See* U.S. Comm. for Refugees & Immigrants, *Gang-Related Asylum Resources: Immigration Judge Decisions/Briefs and Affidavits*, *available at www.refugees.org/resources/for-lawyers/asylum-research/gang-related-asylum-resources/immigration-judge.html* (last visited Jan. 3, 2015). For example, an IJ in Baltimore granted asylum to a woman based on her proposed social group of "Salvadoran women who are viewed as gang 'property' by virtue of the fact that [they were] successfully victimized by gang members once before." *See* Judge Williams' Mem. of Decision and Order in that case at *www.uscrirefugees.org/2010Website/5_Resources/5_4_For_Lawyers/5_4_1%20Asylum%20Research/5_4_1_2_Gang_Related_Asylum_Resources/5_4_1_2_3_Immigration_Judge_Decisions_Briefs_and_Affidavits/ES_018.pdf* (last visited Jan. 3, 2015).

[462] *See, e.g., Rivera-Barrientos v. Holder*, 658 F.3d 1222 (10th Cir. 2011); *Mendez-Barrera v. Holder*, 602 F.3d 21 (1st Cir. 2010); *Caal-Tiul v. Holder*, 582 F.3d 92 (1st Cir. 2009).

[463] *See, e.g., Rivera-Barrientos v. Holder*, at 1222; *Mendez-Barrera v. Holder*, at 21 (1st Cir. 2010).

[464] *Mendez-Barrera*, at 21, 26.

[465] *Rivera-Barrientos*, at 1222, 1231–35.

[466] *Mendez-Barrera v. Holder*, 602 F.3d 21, 27 (1st Cir. 2010).

[467] *Id.*

[468] *Rivera-Barrientos v. Holder*, 658 F.3d 1222, 1231 (10th Cir. 2011).

Few gender-based social groups have been considered by the federal courts in the context of gang violence beyond those related to resistance to recruitment. It is possible that gender-based social groups defined in a different way and supported with a strong evidentiary record will have greater success. However, in *Caal-Tiul v. Holder*, the First Circuit considered and rejected the social group of "indigenous women" in Guatemala. The court relied on *Matter of S–E–G–* in rejecting the social group, despite the fact that a completely different group had been advanced.[469] Thus, this case should not be authoritative regarding the treatment of gender-based social groups in the context of gang violence.

➢ **Practice Pointer**: Cases in which women have been taken as or are viewed as gang "girlfriends" or the gang's property have potential for success, especially following the BIA's decision in *Matter of A–R–C–G–*.[470] Practitioners should look to *Matter of A–R–C–G–* and consider structuring their gender-based social group argument regarding immutability, social distinction, and particularity in a parallel way.

7. Family Members

Scholars of the gang phenomenon in Central America have found that gang violence often generalizes to family members of the gangs' perceived enemies. Family membership, therefore, presents another social group that has been considered and analyzed by the BIA and the circuit courts. Family membership has long been a recognized social group, dating back to *Matter of Acosta*.[471] Following the BIA's addition of social distinction (then social visibility) and particularity to the requirement of demonstrating a common, immutable characteristic, however, the waters have been muddied. For example, even though the BIA found that family relationships could meet the social visibility requirement in *Matter of C–A–*,[472] it later found in *Matter of S–E–G–* that "family members of Salvadoran youth who have been subjected to recruitment efforts by MS-13 and who have rejected or resisted membership in the gang" was too amorphous to constitute a particular social group.[473] The BIA found that "family members" was an amorphous, undefined

---

[469] *Caal-Tiul v. Holder*, 582 F.3d 92, 95 (1st Cir. 2009).

[470] *Matter of A–R–C–G–*, 26 I&N Dec. 388 (BIA 2014) (finding that "married women in Guatemala who are unable to leave their relationship" can constitute a legally cognizable social group). For example, an IJ in Baltimore granted asylum to a woman based on her proposed social group of "Salvadoran women who are viewed as gang 'property' by virtue of the fact that [they were] successfully victimized by gang members once before." *See* Judge Williams' Mem. of Decision, *supra* note 461.

[471] *Matter of Acosta*, 19 I&N Dec. 211, 233 (BIA 1985) (specifically noting kinship ties as a common, immutable characteristic). *See also Matter of H–*, 21 I&N Dec. 37 (BIA 1996) (fining that members of a clan sharing kinship ties can constitute a viable social group for purposes of asylum eligibility).

[472] *Matter of C–A–*, 23 I7N Dec. 951, 959 (BIA 2006) ("family relationships are generally recognizable and understood by others to constitute social groups").

[473] *Matter of S–E–G–*, 24 I&N Dec. 579, 585–86 (BIA 2008).

category that could potentially include distant relatives.[474] Therefore, according to the BIA, the group lacked sufficient particularity.[475]

The Fifth Circuit made a similar finding in *Orellana-Monson v. Holder*, when it considered two proposed social groups: (1) "young Salvadoran males who are siblings" of "Salvadoran males, ages 8 to 15, who have been recruited by Mara 18 but have refused to join due to a principled opposition to gangs" and (2) "family members of Jose Orellana-Monson."[476] The court found that these groups were too broad because they encompassed a diverse cross section of society.[477] However, the court focused its analysis on the first articulated social group and did not directly address the second, more specific group of Jose's family.[478]

- **Practice Pointer**: It is possible that the BIA and Fifth Circuit would have made different findings if the social groups had been defined as a specific family instead of the broader groups "family members of Salvadoran youth" who have resisted gang recruitment and "young Salvadoran males who are siblings" of Salvadoran males, ages 8 to 15, who have resisted gang recruitment. Asylum claims specifying the social group as a particular family have been more successful.[479]

The Eighth Circuit also has rejected a family-based social group in the context of gang violence. In *Constanza v. Holder*, the court considered the social group of "a family that experienced gang violence."[480] In that case, the applicant's cousin had been robbed and murdered by the gang and the applicant's nephew had been kidnapped and held for ransom by the gang; however, the applicant's siblings and children remained in El Salvador and had not been targeted.[481] The court found that the family was "no different from any other Salvadoran family that has experienced gang violence," and therefore, the group lacked social visibility and particularity.[482]

- **Practice Pointer**: It could be argued that this case is not authoritative on this issue because the Eighth Circuit did not provide an explanation regarding why this proposed group was too broad and seemed to conflate its analysis regarding the viability of the proposed group with its well-founded fear analysis. These are meant to be two distinct legal issues requiring separate analyses.

---

[474] *Id.*

[475] *Id.*

[476] *Orellana-Monson v. Holder*, 685 F.3d 511, 521–22 (5th Cir. 2012).

[477] *Id.*

[478] *Id.*

[479] *See, e.g., Crespin-Valladares v. Holder*, 632 F.3d 177, 125–26 (4th Cir. 2011).

[480] *Constanza v. Holder*, 647 F.3d 749 (8th Cir. 2011).

[481] *Id.* at 752–53.

[482] *Id.* at 754.

Despite these BIA, Fifth Circuit, and Eighth Circuit decisions, however, several family-based asylum claims have been granted in the context of gang violence, especially before IJs.[483] In addition to several IJ decisions, the Fourth Circuit has recognized a social group based on membership in a specific family in a gang-based asylum claim.[484] In *Crespin-Valladares v. Holder*, the Fourth Circuit held that the social group of "family members of those who actively oppose the gangs in El Salvador by agreeing to be prosecutorial witnesses" was a viable social group because it was socially visible and sufficiently particular.[485] Citing the BIA decision in *Matter of C–A–*, the Fourth Circuit reasoned that family is a "readily identifiable" group and is "easily recognizable and understood by others to constitute a social group."[486] Therefore, it is socially visible. Moreover, the court stated that the boundaries of a family unit are "particular and well-defined;" it is clear who is in the group and who is not. Therefore, it is sufficiently particular.[487] The Fourth Circuit concluded, "[T]he family provides 'a prototypical example of a particular social group.' In fact, we can conceive of few groups more readily identifiable than the family."[488]

Interestingly, the Fourth Circuit later clarified that even though family members of a prosecutorial witness could form a cognizable social group, the person who actually agreed to be a witness was not part of a cognizable social group.[489] This clarification yields a seemingly illogical result that family-based claims may succeed even where claims based on the underlying reason for the persecution may not.

- **Practice Pointer**: Family-based claims seem to have more success when they involve specific family units, family ties to an individual who

[483] *See* U.S. Comm. for Refugees & Immigrants, *Gang-Related Asylum Resources: Immigration Judge Decisions/Briefs and Affidavits*, *available at* *www.refugees.org/resources/for-lawyers/asylum-research/gang-related-asylum-resources/immigration-judge.html* (last visited Jan. 3, 2015). For example, an IJ in Arlington granted asylum based on family as a social group to a woman whose husband was an undercover officer working against the gangs. The defined social group was "immediate relatives of Salvadoran police officers involved in anti-gang efforts." *See id.* An IJ in Baltimore granted asylum based on family as a social group to a Salvadoran boy whose brother had been killed as a consequence of his refusal to join the MS-13. The defined social group was "subset of nuclear . . . family at which MS 13 directed its persecution because of [the brother's] refusal to join MS 13." *See id.* An IJ in San Antonio granted asylum based on family as a social group to a teenage girl who was sexually harassed by gang members after her aunt and uncle testified against a gang member who had murdered their son. The defined social group was "family members who had challenged the authority of the gang." *See id.*

[484] *Crespin-Valladares v. Holder*, 632 F.3d 117, 121, 125 (4th Cir. 2011).

[485] *Id.*

[486] *Crespin-Valladares v. Holder*, 632 F.3d 177, 125–26 (4th Cir. 2011) (citing *Matter of C–A–*, 23 I7N Dec. 951, 959 (BIA 2006) ("family relationships are generally recognizable and understood by others to constitute social groups")).

[487] *Id.*

[488] *Id.* at 125–26 (citing and quoting *Sanchez-Trujillo v. INS*, 801 F.2d 1571, 1576 (9th Cir. 1986)).

[489] *Zelaya v. Holder*, 668 F.3d 159, 166 (4th Cir. 2012).

actively opposes a gang, and closer family ties, rather than distant relatives.[490] For example, ties to an immediate family member who is actively engaged in anti-gang efforts may present the strongest factual scenario for a particular social group claim based on family membership.

8. Individuals Who Actively Oppose Gangs

Shortly after the BIA's decisions in *Matter of M–E–V–G–* and *Matter of W–G–R–*, the Ninth Circuit considered a Guatemalan applicant's claim based on the proposed social group of "individuals taking concrete steps to oppose gang membership and gang authority."[491] The BIA had rejected this group as lacking social distinction (then social visibility) and particularity after noting that it was not meaningfully distinguishable from youth who resisted gang recruitment, a group that had consistently failed to be recognized by the BIA as a viable social group. The Ninth Circuit did not address whether this group was viable under the BIA's three-part test, but rather, found that the BIA "may not reject a group solely because it had previously found a similar group in a different society to lack social distinction or particularity."[492] The court stated that the BIA must make a case-by-case determination based on the facts and evidence presented. The Ninth Circuit then remanded the case for the BIA to consider the evidence in determining whether the group was cognizable under the circuit's standards set forth in *Henriquez-Rivas v. Holder*.[493]

- **Practice Pointer**: Presenting a successful asylum claim based on particular social group in the context of gang violence often requires the practitioner to educate and open the mind of the adjudicator through clear legal arguments, as well as a strong evidentiary record. To avoid reflexive denials, adjudicators may need to be reminded that the BIA asserted in *Matter of M–E–V–G–* that *Matter of S–E–G–* "should not be read as a blanket rejection of all factual scenarios involving gangs … social group determinations are made on a case by case basis."[494] Moreover, *Matter of E–F–H–L–* confirms that all applicants in removal proceedings shall have the opportunity to present oral testimony and other evidence without first having to establish prima facie eligibility for the requested relief.[495] Individualized facts and evidence must be

---

[490] *See* U.S. Comm. for Refugees & Immigrants, *Gang-Related Asylum Resources: Immigration Judge Decisions/Briefs and Affidavits, available at www.refugees.org/resources/for-lawyers/asylum-research/gang-related-asylum-resources/immigration-judge.html* (last visited Jan. 3, 2015).

[491] *Pirir-Boc v. Holder*, 750 F.3d 1077 (9th Cir. 2014).

[492] *Id.* at 1084.

[493] *See Henriquez-Rivas v. Holder*, 707 F.3d 1081 (9th Cir. 2013).

[494] *Matter of M–E–V–G–*, 26 I&N Dec. 227, 251 (BIA 2014).

[495] *Matter of E–F–H–L–*, 26 I&N Dec. 319 (BIA 2014) (considering the case of a Honduran family that was targeted due to their property ownership).

considered in lieu of importing the BIA's analysis from prior BIA decisions.

➢ **Practice Pointer**: Given the difficulty of establishing a cognizable social group in the context of gang-based violence, practitioners and applicants should always consider whether an asylum claim may be based on an alternative ground, such as race, religion, nationality, or political opinion. Presenting alternatives enables an adjudicator to choose the claim that he or she believes is least likely to be overturned on appeal. Political opinion and religion claims are discussed in detail below in sections I.B. and I.C.

B. Political Opinion

Persecution on account of political opinion or imputed political opinion, where a persecutor attributes, correctly or incorrectly, a hostile political opinion to a victim, has long been considered valid bases for asylum.[496] Political opinion has been interpreted to encompass a wide spectrum of views, not only views related to political parties or the political process. It includes, of course, any opinion regarding the government, its laws, or its policies, but also it encompasses more than just political ideology or action. According to UNHCR, political opinion is "understood in the broad sense, to incorporate any opinion on any matter in which the machinery of State, government, society, or policy may be engaged."[497] Overall, political opinions are "opinions not tolerated by the authorities, which are critical of their policies or methods."[498]

A person may express his or her political opinion or beliefs through actions as well as words.[499] Case law has recognized a broad range of actions and words as political, including: whistleblowing, refusal to conform to social norms, membership in certain organizations advocating for certain rights, membership in religious or spiritual organizations, refusal to join certain groups, belief in the rule of law, refusal

[496] *See INS v. Elias-Zacarias*, 504 U.S. 478 (1992); *Matter of S–P–*, 21 I&N Dec. 486 (BIA 1996).

[497] U.N. High Comm'r for Refugees, *Guidelines on International Protection No. 1: Gender-Related Persecution*, *supra* note 16, ¶ 32.

[498] UNHCR Handbook, *supra* note 281, ¶ 80. The U.S. government recognized a specific situation of intolerance of individuals for their critique of a government's policies, by amending the definition of refugee in 1996 to provide protection to individuals who have suffered or who fear persecution because of their resistance to coercive population control measures in their home countries. These individuals are deemed to have been persecuted or to fear persecution on account of their political opinion. *See* INA §101(a)(42)(B). *See also Matter of G–C–L–*, 23 I&N Dec. 359, 361–62 (BIA 2002); *Matter of C–Y–Z–*, 21 I&N Dec. 915, 919–20 (BIA 1997); *Matter of X–P–T–*, 21 I&N Dec. 634, 638 (BIA 1996). China's one-child policy, forced sterilization, and forced abortion have all been found to be coercive population control measures.

[499] *Chang v. INS*, 119 F.3d 1055, 1063 (3d. Cir. 1997) (holding that the applicant had expressed his political opinion through his actions in defying the orders of the Chinese government). *See also Fedunyak v. Gonzales*, 477 F.3d 1126, 1129 (9th Cir. 2007). *But see Pavlyk v. Gonzales*, 469 F.3d 1082, 1089 (7th Cir. 2006).

to be extorted, neutrality, and more.[500] Overall, adjudicators must consider the claim within the context of the country itself.[501]

Given that third generation gangs have essentially taken control of significant territory in Central America and other parts of the world, it may be argued that these gangs serve as de facto governments.[502] As UNHCR notes:

> [A]ctivities of gangs and certain State agents may be so closely intertwined that gangs exercise direct or indirect influence over a segment of the State or individual government officials. Where criminal activity implicates agents of the State, opposition to criminal acts may be analogous with opposition to State authorities.[503]

Moreover, understanding gang mentality is essential to understanding the context in which a gang may impute an opposing political opinion to a victim. As UNHCR states, central to gang mentality is:

> [T]he notion of respect and responses to perceived acts of disrespect. Because respect and reputation play such an important role in gang culture, members and entire gangs go to great lengths to establish and defend both. Refusals to succumb to a gang's demands and/or any actions that challenge or thwart the gang are perceived as acts of disrespect, and thus often trigger a violent and/or punitive response.[504]

Therefore, a decision to challenge gang authority may stem from a political opinion or may cause the gang to impute an opposing political opinion to the challenger, who may be perceived as a threat to the gang's power. USCIS has even

---

[500] See chapter 2, pt. II.E.v. for a detailed discussion of the different types of political opinions recognized by the BIA and federal courts.

[501] *Castro v. Holder*, 597 F.3d 93, 102–06 (2d Cir. 2010) (stating that the Immigration Judge failed to consider the claim of a Guatemalan police officer who reported drug corruption within the police within the "context" and "backdrop of Guatemala's volatile political history"); *Ahmed v. Keisler*, 504 F.3d 1183, 1193–98 (9th Cir. 2007); *Osorio v. INS*, 18 F.3d 1017, 1029–30 (2d Cir. 1994) (criticizing the BIA for "ignor[ing] the political context of the dispute").

[502] *See* Michael Boulton, *Living in a World of Violence: An Introduction to the Gang Phenomenon* (July 2011), *available at www.unhcr.org/4e3269629.pdf* (last visited Jan. 3, 2015); Max G. Manwaring, *A Contemporary Challenge to State Sovereignty: Gangs and Other Illicit Transnational Criminal Organizations (TCOs) in Central America, El Salvador, Mexico, Jamaica, and Brazil* (Dec. 2007), *available at www.strategicstudiesinstitute.army.mil/pubs/display.cfm?pubID=837* (last visited Jan. 3, 2015).

[503] U.N. High Comm'r for Refugees, *Guidance Note on Refugee Claims Relating to Victims of Organized Gangs*, ¶ 47 (Mar. 31, 2010), *available at www.unhcr.org/refworld/docid/4bb21fa02.html* (last visited Jan. 3, 2015).

[504] *Id.* ¶ 6.

recognized opposition to gangs as an example of a non-traditional political opinion.[505]

Applicants have made asylum claims based on political opinions expressed or imputed through their refusal to join the gang,[506] refusal to be extorted,[507] testifying as a witness or serving as an informant,[508] reporting gang violence to the police, and other such actions, including direct expressions of "anti-gang" opinions or belief in the rule of law. However, "anti-gang" or "rule of law" opinions have not been widely accepted as viable political opinions.

For example, in *Matter of S–E–G–* and *Matter of E–A–G–*, the BIA considered whether the applicants' refusal to join the recruiting gang in El Salvador was an

---

505 USCIS, *Nexus and the Protected Grounds*, at 29 (Apr. 30, 2013), *available at www.uscis.gov/sites/default/files/USCIS/About%20Us/Directorates%20and%20Program%20Offices/RAIO/nexus-protected-grounds.pdf* (last visited Apr. 3, 2015).

506 *See, e.g., Mayorga-Vidal v. Holder*, 675 F.3d 9, 18–19 (1st Cir. 2012) (finding that a young Salvadoran male's resistance to gang recruitment did not amount to a political opinion); *Rivera-Barrientos v. Holder*, 658 F.3d 1222 (10th Cir. 2011), *as corrected on denial of reh'g en banc*, 666 F.3d 641 (10th Cir. 2012) (finding that a young woman's resistance to gang recruitment did not amount to a political opinion); *Mendez-Barrera v. Holder*, 602 F.3d 21, 27 (1st Cir. 2010) (denying asylum because there was no evidence that the persecutors knew of the applicant's anti-gang political beliefs); *Martinez-Buendia v. Holder*, 616 F.3d 711, 716 (7th Cir. 2010) (finding that the FARC was motivated to harm to the applicant on account of her political opinion when she continued to refuse to cooperate with them); *Marroquin-Ochoma v. Holder*, 574 F.3d 574, 579 (8th Cir. 2009) (finding that the applicant's refusal to join the gang, without more, does not amount to persecution on account of an imputed political opinion); *Ramos-Lopez v. Holder*, 563 F.3d 855, 862 (9th Cir. 2009) (finding that a young Honduran man's refusal to join the gang did not qualify as a political opinion); *Barrios v. Holder*, 581 F.3d 849, 856 (9th Cir. 2009) (holding that a young Guatemalan man's refusal to join a gang did not amount to a political opinion); *Santos-Lemus v. Mukasey*, 542 F.3d 738, 747 (9th Cir. 2008) (finding that the applicant was not politically or ideologically opposed to the gangs and that the gang did not impute to him any particular political beliefs); *Matter of S–E–G–*, 24 I&N Dec. 579, 589 (BIA 2008); *Matter of E–A–G–*, 24 I&N Dec. 591, 597 (BIA 2008).

507 *See, e.g., Quinteros-Mendoza v. Holder*, 556 F.3d 159, 164–65 (4th Cir. 2009) (finding that the gang was motivated by money and personal animosity); *Marroquin-Ochoma v. Holder*, 574 F.3d 574, 578 (8th Cir. 2009) (stating that extortion could be on account of political opinion, but finding a lack of evidence of a political opinion in the case of a Guatemalan woman who worked in a bank at a large export company); *Ucelo-Gomez v. Mukasey*, 509 F.3d 70, 74 (2d Cir. 2007) (holding that the applicant was not persecuted on account of his political opinion because the gang was motivated by the desire for self-enrichment); *Shehu v. Att'y Gen.*, 482 F.3d 652, 657 (3d Cir. 2007) (holding that the Albanian gang was motivated by desire for money).

508 *See, e.g., Zelaya v. Holder*, 668 F.3d 159, 162 n.3 (4th Cir. 2012) (finding that the applicant did not "press his political opinions as a ground for asylum or withholding of removal under the INA in his petition for review of the BIA's final order"); *Velasco-Cervantes v. Holder*, 593 F.3d 975, 978 n.3 (9th Cir. 2010) (finding that the applicant failed to raise the political opinion argument on appeal); *Soriano v. Holder*, 569 F.3d 1162, 1164–65 (9th Cir. 2009) (finding that an applicant who had provided the police with information about other gang members who were subsequently arrested did not establish either an actual or imputed political opinion); *Castillo-Arias v. Att'y Gen.*, 446 F.3d 1190, 1193 (11th Cir. 2006) (finding that even though the applicant informed on the Cali drug cartel out of a sense of civic duty, the applicant was not persecuted on account of a political opinion).

expression of a valid political opinion for purposes of asylum eligibility.[509] The BIA stated that there was "no evidence respondents were politically active or made any anti-gang political statements . . . or what political opinion, if any, they held."[510] A line of cases that followed in the federal courts made similar findings that resistance to recruitment was not an expression of a political opinion, nor did such resistance cause the gang to impute a political opinion to the applicants.[511]

Even where there was direct evidence of the applicant's vocal opposition to the gang and the gang's recognition of that opposition, the Tenth Circuit found that the applicant was targeted "primarily" for recruitment purposes and not because of a political opinion.[512] In that case, the applicant had stated, "[N]o, I don't want to have anything to do with gangs. I do not believe in what you do."[513] The gang had responded to the applicant's opposition by stating, "If you don't want to join with us, if you don't participate with us, if you are against us, your family will pay."[514] The court ignored this critical evidence that the gang interpreted the applicant's resistance as being "against" them and deserving of punishment.

- **Practice Pointer**: Practitioners should clearly articulate their legal arguments and separate the analysis of whether an expression or action is a political opinion from whether the persecutors were motivated to harm the applicant because of that political opinion. In *Rivera-Barrientos v. Holder*, the Tenth Circuit seemed to conflate these legal

---

[509] *Matter of S–E–G–*, 24 I&N Dec. 579, 588 (BIA 2008); *Matter of E–A–G–*, 24 I&N Dec. 591, 596 (BIA 2008).

[510] *Matter of S–E–G–*, 24 I&N Dec. at 589; *Matter of E–A–G–*, 24 I&N Dec. at 591, 597.

[511] *See, e.g.*, *Mayorga-Vidal v. Holder*, 675 F.3d 9, 18–19 (1st Cir. 2012) (finding that a young Salvadoran male's resistance to gang recruitment did not amount to a political opinion); *Rivera-Barrientos v. Holder*, 658 F.3d 1222 (10th Cir. 2011), *as corrected on denial of reh'g en banc*, 666 F.3d 641 (10th Cir. 2012) (finding that a young woman's resistance to gang recruitment did not amount to a political opinion); *Mendez-Barrera v. Holder*, 602 F.3d 21, 27 (1st Cir. 2010) (denying asylum because there was no evidence that the persecutors knew of the applicant's anti-gang political beliefs); *Marroquin-Ochoma v. Holder*, 574 F.3d 574, 579 (8th Cir. 2009) (finding that the applicant's refusal to join the gang, without more, does not amount to persecution on account of an imputed political opinion); *Ramos-Lopez v. Holder*, 563 F.3d 855, 862 (9th Cir. 2009) (finding that a young Honduran man's refusal to join the gang did not qualify as a political opinion); *Barrios v. Holder*, 581 F.3d 849, 856 (9th Cir. 2009) (holding that a young Guatemalan man's refusal to join a gang did not amount to a political opinion); *Santos-Lemus v. Mukasey*, 542 F.3d 738, 747 (9th Cir. 2008) (finding that the applicant was not politically or ideologically opposed to the gangs and that the gang did not impute to him any particular political beliefs); *Matter of S–E–G–*, 24 I&N Dec. 579, 589 (BIA 2008); *Matter of E–A–G–*, 24 I&N Dec. 591, 597 (BIA 2008).

[512] *Rivera-Barrientos v. Holder*, 658 F.3d 1222 (10th Cir. 2011) (applying the wrong standard for nexus — according to the INA, a protected ground does not need to be the primary reason for the persecution, but rather "one central reason" for the persecution).

[513] *Id.* at 1225.

[514] *Id.*

arguments and did not properly evaluate the applicant's expressions in opposition to the gang.[515]

There are two cases currently pending before the Ninth Circuit that provide examples of this strategy: *Colocho v. Holder*[516] and *G–M– v. Holder*.[517] In *Colocho v. Holder*, a Salvadoran gang targeted a teenager with assaults and threats because of his participation in a youth group that was widely known to oppose the gang and its activities.[518] In *G–M– v. Holder*, a gang targeted a family of Salvadorans because of their proselytizing as Evangelical Christians recruiting youth into the church and discouraging gang membership.[519]

- **Practice Pointer**: In cases asserting a political opinion theory, it is essential to build a strong evidentiary record to demonstrate the applicants' activities, the gang members' knowledge of and reaction to those activities, and the gang's operation as the de facto government in the relevant country.

The First Circuit has noted that reporting criminal conduct of gang members to law enforcement does not compel the conclusion that it is an expression of a political opinion or that the gang would impute a political opinion to the applicant.[520]

Moreover, even if an expression or action is considered a political opinion, demonstrating that the persecutor targeted or would target the applicant on account of his or her political opinion has been a formidable challenge.[521]

C. Religion

Like political opinion, an individual's decision to resist a gang or to challenge a gang's authority also may stem from his or her moral religious beliefs. Persecution on account of religion has long been considered a valid basis for asylum. Freedom of religion is recognized as a universal human right encompassing the right to have or adopt a religion; the freedom to observe, practice or teach a religion in public or private; and the right not to be coerced in a way that would impair the freedom to have

---

[515] *See infra* pt. II.D. for a detailed discussion of nexus in gang-based asylum claims.

[516] *See* Brief of Amici Curiae, Harvard Immigration & Refugee Clinical Program and Other Immigration Rights Advocates in Support of Petitioner in *Colocho v. Holder*, Ninth Circuit No. 13-70470 (Nov. 19, 2013), *available at http://harvardimmigrationclinic.files.wordpress.com/2014/03/colocho-amicus-brief.pdf* (last visited Jan. 2, 2014).

[517] *See* Ctr. for Gender & Refugee Studies, *G–M– v. Holder*, *available at http://cgrs.uchastings.edu/our-work/g-m-v-holder* (last visited Jan. 2, 2014).

[518] *See* Brief of Amici Curiae, Harvard Immigration & Refugee Clinical Program and Other Immigration Rights Advocates in Support of Petitioner in *Colocho v. Holder*, *supra* note 516.

[519] *See* Ctr. for Gender & Refugee Studies, *G–M– v. Holder*, *supra* note 517. Note that while *G–M– v. Holder* could be categorized as a religion case, it also could be political opinion, given the family's proselytizing and recruiting youth to the church to discourage gang membership.

[520] *Amilcar-Orellana v. Mukasey*, 551 F.3d 86, 91 (1st Cir. 2008).

[521] *See infra* pt. II.D. for a detailed discussion of nexus in gang-based asylum claims.

or adopt a religion or belief.[522] According to UNHCR, religion encompasses "freedom of thought, conscience or belief."[523] Protection from religious-based persecution, therefore, not only covers an individual's freedom to practice his or her own religion, but also covers acts of failing or refusing to observe a religion or to hold any particular religious belief.[524]

UNHCR's guidelines categorize religion-based asylum claims based on:

(1) religion as a belief;

(2) religion as an identity; and

(3) religion as a way of life.[525]

In this context, "belief" can be interpreted to include "theistic, non-theistic, and atheistic beliefs and may take the form of convictions or values about the divine."[526] "Identity" does not necessarily correlate to theological beliefs, "but can refer to one's membership in a community that observes or is bound together by common beliefs, rituals, traditions, ethnicity, nationality, or ancestry."[527] The guidelines note that "[i]n some cases, persecutors target religious groups not for their religious differences per se, but because they perceive others' religious identity as part of a threat to their own identity or legitimacy."[528] Finally, religion as a "way of life" can be "perceived in clothing or observance of particular practices."[529]

In the context of gang violence, a person may be morally opposed to criminal activity and violence based on his or her religious beliefs. Therefore, forcing a person to join a gang may violate his or her religion and moral opposition to criminal activity and violence. Moreover, religious organizations' or groups' practices and activities may draw great animosity from the gangs. For example, preaching against gang membership and the gang's lifestyle, or proselytizing to encourage people to join a religious organization instead of a gang may be perceived as interference with the gangs' authority or direct threats to the gangs' power. As, UNHCR notes:

---

[522] Universal Declaration of Human Rights, Article 18; The International Covenant on Civil and Political Rights, Article 18. *See also* UNHCR Handbook, *supra* note 281, ¶ 71.

[523] U.N. High Comm'r for Refugees, Guidelines on International Protection No. 6: Religion-Based Refugee Claims under Article 1A(2) of the 1951 Convention and/or the 1967 Protocol relating to the Status of Refugees, HCR/GIP/04/06 (Apr. 28, 2004), available at *www.unhcr.org/40d8427a4.html*; UNHCR Handbook, *supra* note 281, ¶ 71.

[524] U.N. High Comm'r for Refugees, *Guidelines on International Protection No. 6: Religion-Based Refugee Claims*, *supra* note 523.

[525] U.N. High Comm'r for Refugees, *Guidelines on International Protection No. 6: Religion-Based Refugee Claims*, *supra* note 523, ¶ 5.

[526] *Id.* ¶ 6.

[527] *Id.* ¶ 7.

[528] *Id.*

[529] *Id.* ¶ 8. See chapter 2, pt. II.E.ii. for a detailed discussion of the various religious beliefs and forms of religious persecution recognized by the BIA and federal courts.

> The 1951 Convention ground of religion may be relevant for the analysis of a claim where the applicant's religious beliefs are incompatible with gang life style. It could, for example, be the case where the applicant refuses to join a gang because of his/her religious belief or conscience, or where a gang member who experiences religious conversion wants to exit the gang. An individual's religion or beliefs may also be a ground for persecution where intolerance and violence against people of other religions or beliefs in a particular society is promoted by gangs. In such contexts, it is important to consider whether the applicant's religious conviction has been or could be brought to the attention of gang members.[530]

Again, understanding gang mentality is essential to understanding the context in which a gang may perceive an individual as an opponent due to his or her religious beliefs or activities. As UNHCR states, central to gang mentality is:

> [T]he notion of respect and responses to perceived acts of disrespect. Because respect and reputation play such an important role in gang culture, members and entire gangs go to great lengths to establish and defend both. Refusals to succumb to a gang's demands and/or any actions that challenge or thwart the gang are perceived as acts of disrespect, and thus often trigger a violent and/or punitive response.[531]

Therefore, a decision to resist or challenge gang authority may stem from moral, religious beliefs and may be expressed through the individual's religious words or activities, causing the gang to perceive the individual as a threat to the gang's power.

As with the other protected grounds, the applicant must first establish that he or she possesses the protected characteristic — in this case a particular religion or set of moral, religious beliefs — and that the persecutor is aware of his or her beliefs or practices. Mere membership in a particular religious community, however, will not normally be enough to establish an asylum claim.[532] Rather, an applicant must also demonstrate that he or she has been or will be persecuted on account of his or her religion.[533]

---

[530] U.N. High Comm'r for Refugees, *Guidance Note on Refugee Claims Relating to Victims of Organized Gangs*, ¶ 32 (Mar. 31, 2010), *available at www.unhcr.org/refworld/docid/4bb21fa02.html* (last visited Jan. 3, 2015).

[531] *Id.* ¶ 6.

[532] *Ahmad v. INS*, 163 F.3d 457, 463 (7th Cir. 1999); *Refahiyat v. INS*, 29 F.3d 553, 557 (10th Cir. 1994) (holding that the mere assertion that one is aligned with a minority religion is not sufficient to establish a prima facie case of religious persecution); *see also* UNHCR Handbook, *supra* note 281, ¶ 73. *But see Qiu v. Holder*, 611 F.3d 403, 407–09 (7th Cir. 2010) (reversing the denial of asylum to an applicant who had practiced Falun Gong for only three months because the Department of State (DOS) report indicated that any member of the religious organization, no matter how long he or she has been a member, will be punished in China if he or she continues to practice his or her religion).

[533] *See infra* pt. II.D. for a detailed discussion of nexus in gang-based asylum claims.

➢ **Practice Pointer**: In cases asserting a religion theory, it is essential to build a strong evidentiary record to demonstrate the applicants' beliefs and activities, the gang members' knowledge of and reaction to those beliefs and activities, and gang mentality with regard to such beliefs and activities in the relevant country.

D. Nexus

Even if an applicant is able to establish a viable social group, political opinion, religion, or other protected ground in the context of gang violence,[534] these claims often fail to establish the requisite nexus to those protected grounds. To demonstrate eligibility for asylum, an applicant must establish by direct or circumstantial evidence that he or she was persecuted or fears persecution on account of one of the five protected grounds.[535] Asylum applicants often do not have direct evidence of gang members' motives for targeting them, and thus, most applicants must rely on circumstantial evidence.

➢ **Practice Pointer**: Practitioners should build a strong evidentiary record of the persecutors' motive. In addition to preparing evidence of the persecutors' motive, practitioners should draft a pre-interview or pre-hearing brief that clearly draws the connections for the adjudicator, especially when the evidence is circumstantial in nature. To date, the courts seem to be imposing unreasonable evidentiary standards and discounting both direct and circumstantial evidence in gang-based asylum claims. Directly explaining evidence of nexus in a brief and citing to the record will make it more difficult for the court to ignore and, if necessary, will maintain a clear issue for appeal.

Although a persecutor may have mixed motives for targeting the applicant,[536] a protected ground must be "at least one central reason" for the persecution.[537] According to the BIA, the protected ground cannot be tangential, incidental, superficial, or subordinate to another reason for harm.[538] However, a number of federal courts have rejected the BIA's requirement that a protected motive not be subordinate and have ruled that there can be more than one central reason for the persecution.[539] For example, in *Tapia Madrigal v. Holder*, the Ninth Circuit

[534] Note that third generation gangs have taken control over several indigenous parts of Central America. Thus, there may be potential race/ethnicity asylum claims in the context of gang violence as well.

[535] INA §208(b)(1)(B)(i) (amended by the REAL ID Act of 2005). *See INS v. Elias-Zacarias*, 502 U.S. 478 (1992) (stating that an applicant must establish by direct or circumstantial evidence that it is reasonable to believe that the harm was motivated in part by an actual or imputed protected ground).

[536] *Matter of J–B–N– & S–M–*, 24 I&N Dec. 208 (BIA 2007).

[537] INA §208(b)(1)(B)(i) (amended by the REAL ID Act of 2005).

[538] *Matter of J–B–N– & S–M–*, 24 I&N Dec. 208 (BIA 2007).

[539] *See, e.g., Ndayshimiye v. U.S. Att'y Gen.*, 557 F.3d 124, 129 (3d Cir. 2009) (concluding that the BIA's interpretation of the "one central reason" standard is in error to the extent that it would require an

Continued

emphasized that dual motives are not mutually exclusive; "if a retributory motive exists alongside a protected motive, an applicant need show only that a protected ground is 'one central reason' for his persecution."[540]

The BIA and some federal courts, however, continue misinterpreting this requirement in the context of gang-based asylum claims; they seem to require that the protected ground be *the* central reason for the persecution, rather than *one* central reason.[541] The nexus challenge in gang-based asylum claims, therefore, lies with demonstrating that gang members are motivated to harm the applicant, not to increase their size, wealth, and influence, and not because of general criminal intent or personal animosity, but rather to target a protected characteristic.

1. Nexus to a Political Opinion

As discussed above in part II.B., an individual's decision to challenge a gang — whether by resisting recruitment, refusing extortion efforts, testifying or informing against a gang, reporting gang violence to the police, directly expressing an anti-gang opinion or belief, or taking some other action viewed as against the gang's authority — may be driven by a political opinion or may result in the imputation of a political opinion by the gang.[542] However, demonstrating that the gang is motivated by a political opinion is a formidable challenge given the resistance by the courts to finding that gang violence is motivated by anything other than a desire to increase size, wealth, or power; general criminal intent; or personal animosity.

For example, in *Matter of S–E–G–* and *Matter of E–A–G–*, the BIA considered whether gangs in El Salvador targeted the applicants on account of their political opinion.[543] The BIA stated that there was no evidence "direct or circumstantial that [gangs] imputed, or would impute to them, an anti-gang political opinion," and concluded that the MS-13 gang members had no motive "other than increasing the size and influence of their gang."[544] The BIA relied on the Supreme Court case *INS v.*

---

asylum applicant to show that a protected ground for persecution was not "subordinate" to any unprotected motivation); *Marroquin–Ochoma v. Holder*, 574 F.3d 574, 577 (8th Cir. 2009); *Parussimova v. Mukasey*, 555 F.3d 734, 739–41 (9th Cir. 2009).

[540] *Tapia Madrigal v. Holder*, No. 10-73700 (9th Cir. May 13, 2013).

[541] *See, e.g., Matter of E–A–G–*, 24 I&N Dec. 591, 595 (BIA 2008) (holding that the Respondent had made no showing that he would be harmed on account of his affiliation with a gang. Rather, it was natural for violent gangs to recognize their rivals and seek to target one another); *Castellano-Chacon v. INS*, 341 F.3d 533, 550 (6th Cir. 2003) (finding that the Respondent could not establish that his gang membership constituted the basis for future persecution even though his tattoos made him physically distinguishable as a member of a gang); *Rivera-Barrientos v. Holder*, 658 F.3d 1222 (10th Cir. 2011) (holding that there may be other reasons for the prohibited persecution).

[542] U.N. High Comm'r for Refugees, *Guidance Note on Refugee Claims Relating to Victims of Organized Gangs*, ¶¶ 6, 47 (Mar. 31, 2010), *available at www.unhcr.org/refworld/docid/4bb21fa02.html* (last visited Jan. 3, 2015).

[543] *Matter of S–E–G–*, 24 I&N Dec. 579 (BIA 2008); *Matter of E–A–G–*, 24 I&N Dec. 591 (BIA 2008).

[544] *Matter of S–E–G–*, at 589; *Matter of E–A–G–*, at 597.

Elias-Zacarias, which held that forced recruitment by a guerilla group was not persecution on account of political opinion.[545]

Several courts have relied upon *Matter of S–E–G–* and *Matter of E–A–G–* to interpret *INS v. Elias-Zacarias* to mean that forced recruitment can never constitute persecution on account of political opinion.[546] These courts have found that resisters of gang recruitment are, instead, targeted because of economic and personal reasons. Even where there was direct evidence of the applicant's direct, vocal opposition to the gang; the gang's direct, vocal recognition of that opposition as "against" them; and a subsequent brutal attack of the applicant at the hands of the gang, who held her at knifepoint and gang raped her, the Tenth Circuit relied upon *INS v. Elias-Zacarias* to hold that the applicant was targeted "primarily" for recruitment purposes and not because of a political opinion.[547] In coming to this conclusion, the Tenth Circuit ignored direct evidence to the contrary, as well as the socio-political context in which the persecution occurred.

➢ **Practice Pointer**: Practitioners should clearly articulate their nexus argument by highlighting the direct and circumstantial evidence on the record in a legal brief, drawing connections to the evidence of record. Moreover, practitioners should emphasize to the adjudicator that a protected ground does not need to be the only reason for persecution, but rather "at least one central reason" for persecution.[548]

However, as the Seventh Circuit noted, the U.S. Supreme Court did not foreclose all of these claims.[549] Rather, what matters in determining whether refusing

---

[545] *INS v. Elias-Zacarias*, 502 U.S. 478, 482 (1992).

[546] *See, e.g., Mayorga-Vidal v. Holder*, 675 F.3d 9, 18–19 (1st Cir. 2012) (holding that a young Salvadoran male who resisted gang recruitment did not establish a well-founded fear of persecution on account of his political opinion); *Rivera-Barrientos v. Holder*, 658 F.3d 1222 (10th Cir. 2011), *as corrected on denial of reh'g en banc*, 666 F.3d 641 (10th Cir. 2012) (concluding that the gang targeted the applicant "primarily" for recruitment purposes, rather than her political opinion, despite direct evidence to the contrary); *Mendez-Barrera v. Holder*, 602 F.3d 21, 27 (1st Cir. 2010) (denying asylum because there was no evidence that the persecutors knew of the applicant's anti-gang political beliefs or targeted her for that reason); *Marroquin-Ochoma v. Holder*, 574 F.3d 574, 579 (8th Cir. 2009) (finding that the applicant's refusal to join the gang, without more, does not amount to persecution on account of an imputed political opinion); *Ramos-Lopez v. Holder*, 563 F.3d 855, 862 (9th Cir. 2009) (finding that the IJ's determination that a young Honduran man who refused to join the gang did not suffer persecution on account of political opinion was supported by substantial evidence); *Barrios v. Holder*, 581 F.3d 849, 856 (9th Cir. 2009) (holding that the gang targeted a young Guatemalan man who refused to join a gang for "economic and personal reasons," not because of his actual or imputed political opinion); *Santos-Lemus v. Mukasey*, 542 F.3d 738, 747 (9th Cir. 2008) (finding that the Salvadoran applicant was targeted for economic and personal reasons, not because of an actual or imputed political belief).

[547] *Rivera-Barrientos v. Holder*, 658 F.3d 1222 (10th Cir. 2011) (applying the wrong standard for nexus — according to the INA, a protected ground does not need to be the primary reason for the persecution, but rather "one central reason" for the persecution).

[548] *See Id.* at 1225.

[549] *See Martinez-Buendia v. Holder*, 616 F.3d 711, 716 (7th Cir. 2010).

recruitment constitutes persecution on account of a political opinion is the factual record of each case.[550] In considering the factual record in *Martinez-Buendia v. Holder*, the Seventh Circuit held that the applicant had demonstrated past persecution at the hands of the FARC on account of her actual and imputed political opinion.[551] The court based its decision on the applicant's testimony regarding the direct words of the FARC, as well as documentary evidence that the FARC viewed members of the Health Brigades, like the applicant, as political opponents.[552] The court found that the applicant's steadfast refusal to cooperate with the FARC stemmed from her political views and that the FARC's increasingly violent responses were motivated by those views.[553] The court distinguished the case from *INS v. Elias-Zacarias* because of the "post-refusal persecution" that the applicant had suffered, which the court interpreted as clear evidence of how the FARC interpreted her actions.[554]

> **Practice Pointer**: *Martinez-Buendia v. Holder* is an important tool for practitioners preparing and presenting political opinion-based asylum claims in the context of gang violence, because, as two scholars noted, "the court properly understood the limits of *Elias-Zacarias*, carefully considered circumstantial evidence, including the societal context in which the persecution occurred, and recognized that the FARC's view of Buendia as a political opponent would be solidified by her continued resistance despite the FARC's increasing violence."[555]

Forced recruitment cases in the gang context face similar nexus challenges as a previous line of cases addressing forced recruitment by guerilla forces.[556] Gangs, like guerilla forces, may recruit for reasons unrelated to any protected ground, such as the need to increase their ranks. Also, individuals may refuse to join or cooperate with gangs for a variety of reasons unrelated to any protected ground, such as the desire to continue going to school or the need to continue working on the family farm. Without facts and evidence beyond the recruitment effort and refusal, a connection between the persecution and a protected ground cannot be established.[557]

Similarly, an applicant's refusal of a gang's extortion attempts may stem from his or her political opinion or may cause the gang to impute a political opinion to the

---

[550] *Id.*

[551] *Id.* at 716–17.

[552] *Id.* at 717.

[553] *Id.*

[554] *Id.*

[555] Lisa Frydman & Neha Desai, *Beacon of Hope or Failure of Protection? U.S. Treatment of Asylum Claims Based on Persecution by Organized Gangs*, 12-10 IMMIGR. BRIEFINGS 1 (Oct. 2012).

[556] *See, e.g., INS v. Elias-Zacarias*, 502 U.S. 478 (1992); *Habtemicael v. Ashcroft*, 370 F.3d 774 (8th Cir. 2004); *Pedro Mateo v. INS*, 224 F.3d 1147 (9th Cir. 2000); *Chanchavac v. INS*, 207 F.3d 584 (9th Cir. 2000); *Miranda v. INS*, 139 F.3d 624 (8th Cir. 1998); *Matter of C–A–L–*, 21 I&N Dec. 754 (BIA 1997).

[557] *INS v. Elias-Zacarias*, 502 U.S. 478 (1992).

applicant. Thus, extortion combined with threats or harm may form the basis of a valid asylum claim, but only if there is some evidence connecting the threats or harm to one of the five protected grounds.[558] The courts that have considered these claims in the context of gang violence have generally found that the gang was motivated by the desire for self-enrichment, not a protected ground.[559]

For example, in *Marroquin-Ochoma v. Holder*, the Eighth Circuit acknowledged that extortion cases could be on account of political opinion; however in that case, the court found that the facts were insufficient to support such finding.[560] The applicant, a Guatemalan woman, worked at a bank at an export company. When the gang started recruiting and extorting her, she refused. She continued to refuse the gang's orders even though the gang's threats escalated. Eventually, the applicant fled Guatemala. The IJ found that "[i]nadequate evidence ha[d] been presented to indicate that the gangs actually operate in a political framework, and the problems the respondent had in no way were related to her expression of any political opinion. . . . Resistance to criminal activity is not a political opinion in this context."[561] The Eighth Circuit denied the petition for review, agreeing that insufficient evidence had been submitted to support a nexus to the applicant's actual or imputed political opinion. Importantly,

---

[558] *See, e.g.*, *Quinteros-Mendoza v. Holder*, 556 F.3d 159, 164–65 (4th Cir. 2009) (finding that the gang was motivated by money and personal animosity); *Marroquin-Ochoma v. Holder*, 574 F.3d 574, 578 (8th Cir. 2009) (stating that extortion could be on account of political opinion, but finding a lack of evidence of a political opinion in the case of a Guatemalan woman who worked in a bank at a large export company); *Ucelo-Gomez v. Mukasey*, 509 F.3d 70, 74 (2d Cir. 2007) (holding that the applicant was not persecuted on account of his political opinion because the gang was motivated by the desire for self-enrichment); *Shehu v. U.S. Att'y Gen.*, 482 F.3d 652, 657 (3d Cir. 2007) (holding that the Albanian gang was motivated by desire for money). *See also, e.g., INS v. Elias-Zacarias*, 502 U.S. 478 (1992); *Tapiero v. Orejuela*, 423 F.3d 666, 673 (7th Cir. 2005); *De Brenner v. Ashcroft*, 388 F.3d 629, 637 (8th Cir. 2004) (finding that the applicant was targeted on account of political opinion where the extortionist branded the applicant a political opponent, even though the extortionist also was interested in the applicant's wealth); *Yazitchian v. INS*, 207 F.3d 1164 (9th Cir. 2000) (finding persecution on account of political opinion where the extortion came at the instance of a government entity and the applicant belonged to an anti-government party); *Desir v. Ilchert*, 840 F.2d 723 (9th Cir. 1988) (finding government-sponsored extortion to be on account of the applicant's political opinion because people who resisted extortion were marked as subversives). *But see Gonzales-Neyra v. INS*, 122 F.3d 1293, 1296 (9th Cir. 1997) (holding that persecution of an applicant who refused to be extorted by the Shining Path in Peru was on account of his political opinion where the applicant told the Shining Path members that he would no longer pay to "support their 'armed struggle'" or "collaborate with a group that was trying to destroy [his] country").

[559] *See, e.g.*, *Quinteros-Mendoza v. Holder*, 556 F.3d at 164–65 (finding that the gang was motivated by money and personal animosity); *Marroquin-Ochoma v. Holder*, 574 F.3d at 578 (stating that extortion could be on account of political opinion, but finding a lack of evidence of a political opinion in the case of a Guatemalan woman who worked in a bank at a large export company); *Ucelo-Gomez v. Mukasey*, 509 F.3d at 74 (holding that the applicant was not persecuted on account of his political opinion because the gang was motivated by the desire for self-enrichment); *Shehu v. U.S. Att'y Gen.*, 482 F.3d at 657 (holding that the Albanian gang was motivated by desire for money).

[560] *Marroquin-Ochoma v. Holder*, 574 F.3d 574, 578 (8th Cir. 2009).

[561] *Id.*

however, the court did recognize that resistance to a gang "may have a political dimension" and that "evidence that a gang is politically minded could be considered evidence that the gang members would be somewhat more likely to attribute political opinions to resisters."[562]

> ➢ **Practice Pointer**: Although a gang may be initially motivated by economic interests or general criminal intent, persecution following expressions of resistance or refusal may be on account of the victim's political opinion.[563] Moreover, the motivations are not mutually exclusive; a persecutor may have mixed motives, and as long as a protected ground is "at least one central reason," the fact that the gang also is motivated by increasing its ranks or self-enrichment does not make the applicant ineligible for asylum.

Testifying witnesses and informants also have made political opinion asylum claims in the context of gang violence. While some of these claims were not addressed due to the applicant's failure to properly raise the issue on appeal, other claims have been unsuccessful in the federal courts due to a lack of the requisite nexus.[564] For example, in *Soriano v. Holder*, the Ninth Circuit considered the case of a Filipino man who had associated with gang members and participated in the gang's criminal activities.[565] After he was arrested, he served as an informant for the police and informed against the gang. The gang members were eventually arrested. Soriano fled and applied for asylum, claiming a well-founded fear of persecution on account of his political opinion.[566] The Ninth Circuit held that there was no evidence of the applicant's actual or imputed political opinion, nor was there any evidence of nexus.[567] The court reasoned that any future persecution would be motivated by

---

[562] *Id.*

[563] *See, e.g., Gonzales-Neyra v. INS*, 122 F.3d 1293, 1296 (9th Cir. 1997) (holding that persecution of an applicant who refused to be extorted by the Shining Path in Peru was on account of his political opinion where the applicant told the Shining Path members that he would no longer pay to "support their 'armed struggle'" or "collaborate with a group that was trying to destroy [his] country").

[564] *See, e.g., Zelaya v. Holder*, 668 F.3d 159, 162 n.3 (4th Cir. 2012) (finding that the applicant did not "press his political opinions as a ground for asylum or withholding of removal under the INA in his petition for review of the BIA's final order"); *Velasco-Cervantes v. Holder*, 593 F.3d 975, 978 n.3 (9th Cir. 2010) (finding that the applicant failed to raise the political opinion argument on appeal); *Soriano v. Holder*, 569 F.3d 1162, 1164–65 (9th Cir. 2009) (finding that an applicant who had provided the police with information about other gang members who were subsequently arrested did not establish either an actual or imputed political opinion, because the gang's motivation would be its desire to retaliate against the applicant); *Castillo-Arias v. Att'y Gen.*, 446 F.3d 1190, 1193 (11th Cir. 2006) (finding that even though the applicant informed on the Cali drug cartel out of a sense of civic duty, the applicant was not persecuted on account of a political opinion).

[565] *Soriano v. Holder*, 569 F.3d 1162, 1164–65 (9th Cir. 2009).

[566] *Id.*

[567] *Id.*

personal animosity and the gang's desire for retaliation, not Soriano's actual or imputed political opinion.[568] Therefore, there was no nexus to a protected ground.

Despite the difficulty of demonstrating nexus in political opinion cases, these arguments should continue to be made. First, there has been some success with these claims at the IJ level.[569] Additionally, the federal courts' decisions in these cases diverge from case law recognizing a broad range of opinions as political,[570] UNHCR guidance,[571] and a line of cases correctly considering the socio-political context in the country of persecution in determining whether an actual or imputed political opinion exists and whether persecution is on account of political opinion.[572]

> **Practice Pointer**: The adjudicator must consider the totality of the circumstances, so practitioners should present all relevant facts and evidence that may be relevant to the recruiter's or extorter's perception of the applicant's refusal to cooperate, including: the content of the gang members' statements or any threats made against the applicant; any statements made by the applicant when refusing to cooperate; any prior statements by the applicant against the gang; the applicant's activities in opposition to the gang; the family's opposition activities or association with any opposition groups; evidence of gang dynamics, code, or mentality; expert testimony showing how a gang views those who refuse to cooperate with them; and country conditions evidence establishing the socio-political context in the relevant country.

---

[568] *Id.*

[569] *See* U.S. Comm. for Refugees & Immigrants, *Gang-Related Asylum Resources: Immigration Judge Decisions/Briefs and Affidavits*, *available at www.refugees.org/resources/for-lawyers/asylum-research/gang-related-asylum-resources/immigration-judge.html* (last visited Jan. 3, 2015); Ctr. for Gender & Refugee Studies, *Search Asylum Case Outcomes*, *available at http://cgrs.uchastings.edu/search-cases* (last visited Jan. 4, 2015). For example, an IJ in New York held that "refusing to pay the taxes demanded by Mara-18, the Respondent engaged in an activity that was viewed by the gang as a politically charged rejection of its authority." Ctr. for Gender & Refugee Studies, *Case #8571*, *available at http://cgrs.uchastings.edu/search-cases* (last visited Jan. 4, 2015). An IJ in Baltimore found that "because gang members perceive all cooperation with the authorities in response to gang activity as an expression of political opposition to the gang's control, they interpreted the respondent's presence at the scene as such and imputed an anti-gang political opinion to her." Ctr. for Gender & Refugee Studies, *Case #6090*, *available at http://cgrs.uchastings.edu/search-cases* (last visited Jan. 4, 2015).

[570] *See supra* chapter 2, pt. II.E.v. for a detailed discussion of the different types of political opinions recognized by the BIA and federal courts.

[571] *See* U.N. High Comm'r for Refugees, *Guidance Note on Refugee Claims Relating to Victims of Organized Gangs*, ¶¶ 6, 47 (Mar. 31, 2010), *available at www.unhcr.org/refworld/docid/4bb21fa02.html* (last visited Jan. 3, 2015).

[572] *See, e.g.*, *Antonyan v. Holder*, 642 F.3d 1250 (9th Cir. 2011); *Martinez-Buendia v. Holder*, 616 F.3d 711, 716–17 (7th Cir. 2010); *Marroquin-Ochoma v. Holder*, 574 F.3d 574, 578 (8th Cir. 2009); *Gonzales-Neyra v. INS*, 122 F.3d 1293, 1296 (9th Cir. 1997).

2. *Nexus to Moral, Religious Beliefs*

Like a political opinion, a decision to resist a gang or challenge a gang's authority may stem from moral, religious beliefs.[573] Persecution on account of religion may assume various forms, including the prohibition of membership in a religious community, of worship or observance in private or in public, of religious instruction, of religious conversion, or serious measures of discrimination imposed on persons because they practice their religion or belong to a particular religious community.[574] However, demonstrating that the gang is motivated by an individual's religion or religious practices or activities is a formidable challenge given the resistance by the courts to finding that gang violence is motivated by anything other than a desire to increase size, wealth, or power; general criminal intent; or personal animosity.

Both the Fourth Circuit and the Seventh Circuit have considered whether persecution was on account of an applicant's religion in the context of gang violence, and both courts found a lack of evidence establishing the requisite nexus.[575] For example, in *Quintero-Mendoza v. Holder*, gang members attacked a Salvadoran applicant, a Seventh Day Adventist, several times outside of his church.[576] Gang members also directly threatened him, stating that he would suffer further harm if he continued to attend his church.[577] During these attacks, which also took place in other locations throughout the community, gang members demanded money from the applicant.[578] Eventually, the gang members were successful in suppressing the applicant's faith, as he stopped attending church in response to the attacks and threats being made against him. However, the attacks continued after the applicant stopped attending church.[579] The Fourth Circuit relied on these facts, in particular the gang members' demands for money, attacks at other locations besides outside his church, and continued attacks after he stopped attending church, to find that the requisite nexus to the applicant's religion had not been established.[580] Specifically, the court found that money and personal animosity, rather than the applicant's religion,

---

[573] *See supra* pt. II.C. for a detailed discussion of religious beliefs in the context of gang violence. *See also* U.N. High Comm'r for Refugees, *Guidance Note on Refugee Claims Relating to Victims of Organized Gangs*, ¶¶ 32 (Mar. 31, 2010), *available at www.unhcr.org/refworld/docid/4bb21fa02.html* (last visited Jan. 3, 2015).

[574] UNHCR Handbook, *supra* note 281, ¶ 71–72.

[575] *Bueso-Avila v. Holder*, 663 F.3d 934 (7th Cir. 2011) (finding that there was a lack of evidence that the gang was aware of the applicant's religious beliefs, as well as a lack of evidence that it was the gang's common practice to target individuals because of their religion); *Quintero-Mendoza v. Holder*, 556 F.3d 159 (4th Cir. 2009) (finding that the gang members were motivated by money and personal animosity, not religion).

[576] *Quintero-Mendoza v. Holder*, 556 F.3d 159, 160 (4th Cir. 2009) (finding that the gang members were motivated by money and personal animosity, not religion).

[577] *Id.*

[578] *Id.* at 164–65.

[579] *Id.*

[580] *Id.*

motivated the gang's attacks.[581] The Fourth Circuit stated that the applicant had provided "no evidence that his religion or political beliefs were more than incidental or tangential to any part of the persecution he suffered."[582]

Similarly, in the case of a Honduran Evangelical Christian who was attacked and harassed by gang members because he recruited youth to join his church youth group instead of the gangs, the Seventh Circuit agreed with the BIA that the applicant had not established the requisite nexus to a protected ground.[583] The court found that there was no direct evidence of nexus to the applicant's religion. Although the applicant testified that his and his church's activities and proselytizing posed a threat to the gang, that some attacks occurred following church meetings, and that other church members also had been targeted, the BIA held that the persecution "stemmed from the efforts of the gang members to forcibly recruit him."[584] The Seventh Circuit agreed, analogizing the case to *INS v. Elias-Zacarias*. The court stated, "[T]here is substantial evidence in the record to support the finding that the gang threatened Bueso-Avila simply because he was a youth who refused to join their street gang, regardless of his religious activities."[585] Notably, neither the BIA nor the Seventh Circuit carefully considered the country conditions evidence of gang violence in Honduras as providing important context for the persecution that the applicant suffered and the gang members' motives for harming the applicant.[586]

- ➢ **Practice Pointer**: Again it seems that the federal courts are applying the wrong standards in mixed motive cases arising in the context of gang violence, requiring that the protected ground is the only reason for the persecution, rather than "at least one central reason." It is essential for practitioners to clearly articulate the mixed motive standard, to build a strong evidentiary record showing that a protected ground is "at least one central reason" for the persecution, and to assist the adjudicator in applying the evidence to the correct legal standards. A written pre-interview or pre-hearing brief is often a necessity in these mixed motive cases.
- ➢ **Practice Pointer**: In building a strong evidentiary record in a religion-based claim, practitioners should include: any direct evidence of nexus, such as the content of gang members' and the applicant's statements; evidence that the gang members were aware of the applicant's religious beliefs and activities; evidence of how gang members perceive such beliefs or activities; evidence of the church or other religious

---

581 *Id.* at 164.

582 *Id.* at 165.

583 *Bueso-Avila v. Holder*, 663 F.3d 934, 935–36 (7th Cir. 2011).

584 *Id.* at 936.

585 *Id.* at 939.

586 *Id.* at 935–339.

> organization's influence in the community; evidence that the gang targets other individuals because of their religion or affiliation with religious groups; evidence of the circumstances surrounding any attacks or threats — where they took place, whether religious property was desecrated, etc.; evidence of any historical relationship between the religious organization and the gangs; and country conditions evidence establishing the socio-political context in the relevant country.[587]

Like political opinion claims, religion claims in the context of gang violence have had some success at the IJ level.[588] With articulate critique of and distinguishing from prior precedent, clear communication of the legal standards for demonstrating nexus, development of a strong evidentiary record, and precise application of the facts and evidence to the legal standards, asylum claims based on religion have potential for success.

3. *Nexus to Membership in a Particular Social Group*

Although the focus of social group asylum claims in the context of gang violence has centered on the viability of the proposed social groups, the nexus requirement must not be discounted in preparing these claims. To date, there is little guidance from the federal courts in analyzing nexus to membership in a particular social group. However, the First Circuit did address nexus in *Call-Tiul v. Holder*.[589] In that case, the First Circuit considered the proposed social group of indigenous Guatemalan women and concluded that the record lacked evidence that the gang threatened and harassed the applicant's daughter because of her status as an indigenous woman.[590] In concluding that "nothing in the record suggests anything more than a gang preying on a girl and reacting with threats to a parent who sought to interfere," the First Circuit disregarded significant circumstantial evidence on the record of high rates of violence against indigenous populations in Guatemala, that such violence was tolerated, and that indigenous populations were less likely to receive state protection than other populations in Guatemala.[591]

---

[587] *See id.* at 938.

[588] *See* U.S. Comm. for Refugees & Immigrants, *Gang-Related Asylum Resources: Immigration Judge Decisions/Briefs and Affidavits, available at www.refugees.org/resources/for-lawyers/asylum-research/gang-related-asylum-resources/immigration-judge.html* (last visited Jan. 3, 2015); Ctr. for Gender & Refugee Studies, *Case #6991 & Case #8989, available at http://cgrs.uchastings.edu/search-cases* (last visited Jan. 4, 2015) (search Asylum Case Outcomes).

[589] *Caal-Tiul v. Holder*, 582 F.3d 92 (1st Cir. 2009).

[590] *Id.* at 95.

[591] *Id. See also* AOBTC Workbook, Female Asylum Applicants, *supra* note 36, at 26 (stating that in analyzing nexus, DHS looks to direct and circumstantial evidence, including "patterns of violence in the society against individuals similarly situated to the applicant," as well as evidence that such violence "(1) [is] supported by the legal system or social norms in the country in question, and (2) reflect[s] a prevalent belief within society, or within relevant segments of society").

Thus, it appears that membership in a particular social group claims, if able to arrive at the nexus analysis at all, will face the same challenge as political opinion and religion claims — demonstrating that the gang was motivated by a protected ground in lieu of a desire to increase its ranks, wealth or power; random criminal activity; or personal animosity, or in situations of mixed motive, that a protected ground was "at least one central reason" for the persecution.[592]

4. *Demonstrating Nexus in Situations of Widespread Violence*

In addition to these motive problems, nexus is difficult to establish in the context of gang violence due to the widespread nature of gang violence; much of the population in countries where gangs have established a foothold of power is targeted for a variety of reasons. The challenge is demonstrating that, despite the widespread nature of the violence, each individual applicant was singled out for persecution because of his or her protected ground. As scholars have observed, the BIA has "characterized gangs as generating endemic civil strife and criminal violence that is both widespread and indiscriminate."[593] However, incidental harm is not sufficient to establish eligibility for asylum. Since widespread violence caused by civil strife or civil unrest between rival factions, such as the gangs and the government, does not by itself establish eligibility for asylum, it is essential for applicants to present strong evidence of nexus to a protected ground.[594] Important considerations include the nature of the civil strife and the degree to which it affects larger portions of the country, the context in which the applicant was harmed, and whether the applicant was singled out individually.

- **Practice Pointer**: Practitioners should educate adjudicators regarding the proper evidentiary standards and insist that the socio-political context of the country, as well as other circumstantial evidence of the persecutors' motives be carefully and thoroughly considered. Context is key in gang-based asylum claims.

---

[592] *But see Valdiviezo-Galdamez v. U.S. Att'y Gen.* 502 F.3d 285, 291 (3d Cir. 2007) ("No reasonable fact-finder could conclude that Galdamez was attacked for any reason other than his status as a young Honduran man who had been recruited to join the gang and refused to join."). Note, however, that after multiple remands to the BIA, the BIA found no nexus to a protected ground in *Matter of M–E–V–G–*, 26 I&N Dec. 227 (BIA 2014) and remanded the case to the Immigration Judge, where the case is currently pending.

[593] B. Casper, *et al.*, "*Matter of M–E–V–G– and the BIA's Confounding Legal Standard for 'Membership in a Particular Social Group*,'" 14-06 IMMIGR. BRIEFINGS 1 (June 2014) (citing *Matter of M–E–V–G–*, 26 I&N Dec. 227, 250 (BIA 2014)).

[594] *Eduard v. Ashcroft*, 379 F.3d 182, 190 (5th Cir. 2004); *Ali v. Ashcroft*, 366 F.3d 407 (6th Cir. 2004); *Meghani v. INS*, 236 F.3d 843, 847 (7th Cir. 2001) (citing *Mitev v. INS*, 67 F.3d 1325, 1330 (7th Cir. 1995)); *Rostomian v. INS*, 210 F.3d 1088 (9th Cir. 2000); *Matter of H–*, 21 I&N Dec. 337 (BIA 1996); *Matter of Villalta*, 20 I&N Dec. 142 (BIA 1990); *Matter of Fuentes*, 19 I&N Dec. 658 (BIA 1988); *Matter of Rodriguez-Majano*, 19 I&N Dec. 811 (BIA 1988). *See also* UNHCR Handbook, *supra* note 281, ¶ 164.

- **Practice Pointer**: Like for gender-based asylum claims, gang claims often face the challenges of demonstrating that the applicant is unable to safely and reasonably relocate within the country of feared persecution and establishing that the government is unable and unwilling to control the private actors who are targeting the applicant. However, most case law has not reached these hurdles, given that many stop at the analysis of viability of the social group or nexus. However, it is essential for practitioners to consider and prepare arguments to address these issues. For internal relocation, it can be useful to present evidence of the small size of the countries, as well as the pervasiveness of the gangs throughout the countries. Relocation must not only be safe, but also reasonable given all of the circumstances. For example, it may not be reasonable for an indigenous Mayan woman to try to relocate to another village where no one speaks her language or where she will be vulnerable as a single, unprotected woman. In regard to the government being unable or unwilling to control the gangs, practitioner should prepare to address any efforts by the governments in question to combat gang violence and whether those efforts have truly been effective in providing meaningful protection to its citizens. Expert witnesses can be essential to meeting applicants' burden of proof in regard to both of these legal elements of asylum eligibility.

E. Right to a Hearing on the Merits

Gang-based asylum claims illustrate the importance of articulating the protected ground and nexus very clearly and establishing a strong and thorough evidentiary record in support of the proposed theory. Unfortunately, due to an abundance of negative precedent, in addition to the challenges outlined above, such claims face the added challenge of convincing an adjudicator to even entertain the facts and evaluate the evidence with an open mind. In one case, for example, the IJ declined even to convene a merits hearing for an applicant who proposed a social group of "members of a family that is persecuted because of its property ownership in its hometown in Honduras."[595] Instead, after receiving evidence and legal briefs, the judge determined, as a matter of law, that the respondent was unable to demonstrate a viable social group.[596]

On appeal, however, the BIA confirmed that, in the course of removal proceedings, an applicant for asylum or withholding of removal is entitled to a hearing on the merits, including an opportunity to provide oral testimony and other evidence.[597] The applicant does not first have to establish prima facie eligibility for

[595] *See Matter of E–F–H–L–*, 26 I&N Dec. 319 (BIA 2014) (considering the IJ's decision on appeal).

[596] *Id.*

[597] *Id.*

the requested relief.[598] The BIA relied on its previous ruling in *Matter of Fefe* and the regulatory language at 8 CFR §1240.11(c)(3), which mandates that applications for asylum and withholding of removal will be decided "after an evidentiary hearing to resolve factual issues in dispute."[599] It also relied on INA §240(b)(4)(B), which states that an individual in removal proceedings "shall have a reasonable opportunity to examine the evidence against the alien, to present evidence on the alien's behalf, and to cross-examine witnesses presented by the Government."[600] This BIA decision provides an important weapon for practitioners in arguing that every asylum or withholding of removal applicant, even those whose claims are based on gang violence, must have the opportunity to present facts and evidence during an evidentiary hearing on the merits of his or her claim.

- **Practice Pointer**: In preparing an asylum claim based on gang violence, detailed fact-gathering should be completed prior to developing the legal strategy. Obtaining a complete picture of clients' stories and all potential issues is essential. Moreover, researching country conditions and consulting with an expert on the gang phenomenon and gang mentality should happen early in the process; placing clients' facts within the relevant socio-political context in presenting their claims is key to success. Finally, practitioners should recognize that their strategy might change over time. Submitting facts, evidence, and legal arguments too soon could be detrimental to the ultimate legal strategy and should be avoided.

- **Practice Pointer**: Given the difficulty of gang-based asylum claims, practitioners should set client expectations appropriately from the beginning of the representation and should litigate with an eye toward appeal. The best thing a practitioner can do for his or her client in preparing a gang-based asylum claim is presenting strong evidence with clear linkages to each legal element, in particular the existence of a viable social group and nexus. The cases that have had success on appeal are those that have built a strong evidentiary record below.

- **Practice Pointer**: Don't forget about the CAT! Given the willful blindness of the governments of Central America to the gang phenomenon, as well as the corruption and collusion of government officials in the violence, there has been some success at the IJ level with claims for protection under the CAT.[601] The CAT can be particularly

[598] *Id.*

[599] *Id.* (citing *Matter of Fefe*, 20 I&N Dec. 116 (BIA 1989) and 8 CFR §1240.11(c)(3)).

[600] *Id.* (quoting INA §240(b)(4)(B)).

[601] *See* U.S. Committee for Refugees and Immigrants, *Gang-Related Asylum Resources, available at www.refugees.org/resources/for-lawyers/asylum-research/gang-related-asylum-resources/immigration-judge.html* (last visited Apr. 3, 2015).

useful in cases involving social groups that may not be viable or cases where the persecutors were not motivated by a protected ground.

- **Practice Pointer**: Some invaluable resources for gang-related claims include: UNHCR's Guidance Note on Refugee Claims Relating to Victims of Organized Gangs;[602] Ben Casper, *et al.*, "*Matter of M–E–V–G– and the BIA's Confounding Legal Standard for 'Membership in a Particular Social Group*,'" 14-06 IMMIGR. BRIEFINGS 1 (June 2014); Lisa Frydman & Neha Desai, "Beacon of Hope or Failure of Protection? U.S. Treatment of Asylum Claims Based on Persecution by Organized Gangs," 12-20 IMMIGR. BRIEFINGS 1 (Oct. 2012); National Immigrant Justice Center's "Particular Social Group Practice Advisory: Applying for Asylum After *Matter of M–E–V–G–* and *Matter of W–G–R–*";[603] U.S. Committee for Refugees and Immigrants' *Gang Related Asylum Resources* webpage;[604] SEEKING ASYLUM FROM GANG-BASED VIOLENCE IN CENTRAL AMERICA: A RESOURCE MANUAL, published by the Capital Area Immigration Rights (CAIR) Coalition, which is available online.[605]

---

[602] U.N. High Comm'r for Refugees, *Guidance Note on Refugee Claims Relating to Victims of Organized Gangs*, (Mar. 2010), *available at www.refworld.org/pdfid/4bb21fa02.pdf* (last visited Jan. 1, 2015).

[603] Nat'l Immigrant Justice Ctr., *Particular Social Group Practice Advisory: Applying for Asylum After Matter of M–E–V–G– and Matter of W–G–R–, available at www.immigrantjustice.org/sites/immigrantjustice.org/files/NIJC%20PSG%20Practice%20Advisory_Final_3.4.14.pdf* (last visited Jan. 2, 2014).

[604] U.S. Comm. For Refugees & Immigrants, *Gang Related Asylum Resources*, *available at www.refugees.org/resources/for-lawyers/asylum-research/gang-related-asylum-resources/* (last visited Jan. 2, 2014).

[605] *See* CAIR Coalition, *Seeking Asylum from Gang-Based Violence in Central America: A Resource Manual* (2008), available at *www.ailf.org/lac/GangResourceManual.pdf*; *see also* Washington Office of Latin Am., Central American Gang-Related Asylum (May 2008), available at *www.wola.org/sites/default/files/downloadable/Central%20America/past/CA%20Gang-Related%20Asylum.pdf*.

CHAPTER SIX

SEEKING PROTECTION WHILE SUBJECT TO EXPEDITED REMOVAL AND REINSTATEMENT OF REMOVAL

The influx of people fleeing violence in Central America and seeking protection in the United States, coupled with increased enforcement and devotion of resources to the border, has significantly heightened the need for practitioners and government employees who are well-versed in the laws, regulations, and policies of expedited removal, as well as how those laws, regulations, and polices have been implemented and applied. This chapter discusses apprehensions at ports of entry and the border, the expedited removal and reinstatement of removal provisions, and the credible and reasonable fear standards and procedures.

The expedited removal provisions—the most controversial asylum changes included in the Illegal Immigration Reform and Immigrant Responsibility Act of 1996 (IIRAIRA), which took effect on April 1, 1997[1]—were the result of a perception by Congress that the asylum system was being abused by individuals arriving at ports of entry with false or no documents.[2] Many commentators have noted, however, that the abuses present in the early 1990s diminished significantly as a result of asylum reforms in 1995, and thus, expedited removal was not necessary.[3] Nevertheless, as a result of changes under IIRAIRA, the expedited removal process is currently applied at every land, air, and sea port of entry in the United States.

---

* The author would like to thank Mark R. Barr of Lichter Immigration for his invaluable input in reviewing this chapter.

[1] Illegal Immigration Reform and Immigrant Responsibility Act of 1996 (IIRAIRA), Pub. L. No. 104-208, div. C, 110 Stat. 3009, 3009–546 to 3009–724.

[2] *See, e.g.*, Bo Cooper, *Procedures for Expedited Removal and Asylum Screening Under [IIRAIRA]*, 29 CONN. L. REV. 1501, 1501–02 (1997).

[3] *See, e.g.*, U.S. Comm. for Immigration Reform, U.S. Refugee Policy: Taking Leadership, A Report to Congress 28–29 (June 1997), *available at www.utexas.edu/lbj/uscir/refugee/full-report.pdf*; Michele Pistone, Cato Institute, New Asylum Laws: Undermining an American Ideal 7–8, (Mar. 24, 1998), *available at www.cato.org/publications/policy-analysis/new-asylum-laws-undermining-american-ideal.*

In 2013, the Department of Homeland Security (DHS) made 662,483 apprehensions, with Mexico, Guatemala, Honduras, and El Salvador accounting for nearly 93 percent of all apprehensions.[4] The U.S. Customs and Border Protection (CBP) was responsible for 420,789 (64 percent) of those apprehensions, and 98 percent of CBP apprehensions occurred along the Southwest border.[5] Expedited removals represented 44 percent of all removals from the United States in 2013, and reinstatements represented 39 percent.[6] Nationals from Mexico, Guatemala, Honduras, and El Salvador accounted for 98 percent of all expedited removals and 99 percent of all reinstatements in 2013.[7]

These numbers have been increasing every year, with expedited removals and reinstatements representing a larger and larger percentage of all removals from the United States.[8] As asylum-seekers pass through this problem-plagued and often confusing process,[9] it is essential for practitioners and government officials to understand these provisions and to work together to ensure that individuals fleeing persecution and torture are not mistakenly returned to their persecutors and torturers in violation of U.S. international protection obligations.[10]

- **Practice Pointer**: In November of 2014, AILA filed a complaint with the DHS Office of Civil Rights and Civil Liberties, along with other organizations, reporting that CBP officers regularly fail to properly screen individuals to determine whether they have a fear of returning to their home country prior to removing them pursuant to the expedited removal provisions. These flawed screening practices block individuals fleeing persecution from access to the asylum system and return refugees back to their persecutors and torturers. The DHS Office of Civil Rights and Civil Liberties is currently investigating these CBP practices in response to the complaint. A copy of the complaint is

---

[4] *See* John Simanski, Annual Report on Immigration Enforcement Actions: 2013 at tbl. 1, p. 6, U.S. Dep't of Homeland Security (Sept. 2014), *available at www.dhs.gov/sites/default/files/publications/ois_enforcement_ar_2013.pdf* (showing that these countries contributed to 92.6 percent of apprehensions).

[5] *Id.*

[6] *Id.*

[7] *Id.*

[8] *See id.* at fig. 2, p. 6.

[9] *See* Daniel Martínez *et al.*, Am. Immigration Council, No Action Taken: Lack of CBP Accountability in Responding to Complaints of Abuse 2 (May 2014), *www.americanimmigrationcouncil.org/sites/default/files/No%20Action%20Taken_Final.pdf.*

[10] Under regulations issued in 1999, individuals arriving at ports of entry who are subject to expedited removal may also apply for relief under the Convention Against Torture and Other Cruel, Inhuman or Degrading Treatment or Punishment, Dec. 10, 1984, 1465 U.N.T.S. 85 (entered into force June 26, 1987) (Convention Against Torture, Convention, CAT). *See infra* note 252.

available on AILA InfoNet at Doc. No. 14111748 (last visited Jan. 9, 2015).[11]

I. Expedited Removal and Credible Fear

The expedited removal provisions of the Immigration and Nationality Act (INA) were added by section 302 of IIRAIRA and became effective on April 1, 1997.[12] These provisions allow DHS to order the immediate removal of an individual arriving at a port of entry or, in some cases, of an individual already physically present in the United States, without further hearing or review.[13] If, however, the individual expresses a fear of persecution or a desire to apply for asylum, DHS will detain the individual and must refer the individual for a "credible fear" interview with an asylum officer.[14] Similarly, an individual who expresses a fear of torture upon return will be interviewed to determine whether he or she has a credible fear of torture.[15] If the individual is found to have a credible fear of persecution or torture, he or she is placed in regular INA §240 removal proceedings for full consideration of his or her asylum claim or claim for protection under the Convention Against Torture (CAT).[16]

➢ **Practice Pointer**: For a detailed discussion of the legal standards for demonstrating a credible fear of persecution or torture, see Part II.F. of this chapter.

A. Who is subject to expedited removal under INA §235?

Expedited removal under INA §235 applies "[i]f an immigration officer determines" all of the following:

(1) that the subject is a foreign national (other than a Cuban who arrives by air at a port of entry);

(2) who is arriving in the United States or who entered without inspection or parole, is encountered by immigration within 100 air miles of a U.S. international land border, and has less than 14 days of continuous physical presence in the U.S.;[17]

---

[11] A copy of the complaint is also available on the National Immigrant Justice Center's website at *http://immigrantjustice.org/sites/immigrantjustice.org/files/images/Right%20to%20Asylum%20-%20CRCL%20Complaint%20Cover%20Letter%20-%2011.13.14%20FINAL%20PUBLIC.pdf.*

[12] Immigration and Nationality Act [hereinafter INA] INA §§235(a)(2), 235(b)(1).

[13] INA §235(b)(1)(A); 8 USC §1225(b)(1)(A) (2012).

[14] INA §235(b)(1)(A); 8 USC §1225(b)(1)(A) (2012).

[15] *See* 8 CFR §§208.30, 1208.30 (2014). See also chapter 4.

[16] Regulations Concerning the Convention Against Torture, Expedited Removal and the Credible Fear Process, 64 Fed. Reg. 8484 (Feb. 19, 1999) (to be codified at 8 CFR §208.30).

[17] Designating Aliens for Expedited Removal, 69 Fed. Reg. 48877 (Aug. 11, 2004). *See also* 8 CFR §235.3(b)(1)(i) (2014) (stating that "any absence" from the U.S. shall serve to break the period of continuous physical presence).

(3) is either inadmissible for seeking to procure or procuring a visa, other documentation, or admission by fraud or willfully misrepresenting a material fact or for not being in possession of a valid entry document; and

(4) does not indicate a fear of persecution or torture or an intention to apply for asylum.[18]

If all four elements apply, the officer shall order the individual's removal without further hearing.[19]

Specifically, the categories of individuals who are subject to expedited removal under INA §235 include the following:

- Noncitizens arriving at a port of entry with false or no documents who are inadmissible under INA §§212(a)(6)(C) or INA §212(a)(7);
- Noncitizens interdicted in international or U.S. waters and brought to the United States;
- Noncitizens who have not been "admitted" or "paroled" into the United States and who have not resided in the United States for two years or more; and
- Individuals paroled into the United States under INA §212(d)(5) (humanitarian parole) after April 1, 1997.[20]

Each of these categories is discussed in detail below.

1. Noncitizens Arriving at a Port of Entry with False or No Documents

Noncitizens are subject to expedited removal if the immigration officer at the port of entry determines that they are inadmissible under INA §§212(a)(6)(C) or (7) to the United States because they possess either false documents or no documents.[21] A false document may include a facially valid document that an individual obtained fraudulently or through willful misrepresentation of a material fact.[22] Expedited removal also applies to individuals seeking transit through the United States at a port of entry.[23]

---

[18] INA §235.

[19] *Id.*

[20] INA §235(b)(1); 8 CFR §§235.3(b)(1), 1235.3(b)(1) (2014). Although expedited removal under INA §235 applies to individuals who are arriving or who entered without inspection or parole, certain parolees (such as those paroled under INA §212(d)(5)) are treated as arriving aliens, and therefore, are subject to expedited removal.

[21] INA §235(b)(1)(A)(i); 8 CFR §§235.3(b)(1)(ii), 1235.3(b)(1)(ii) (2014).

[22] INA §212(a)(6)(C); 8 USC §1182(a)(6)(C) (2012).

[23] 8 CFR §§235.3(b)(1)(i), 1235.3(b)(1)(i) (2014). *See* 8 CFR §§1.1(q), 1001.1(q) (2014) for the definition of an "arriving alien." *See also* U.S. Citizenship and Immigration Servs., RAIO Asylum Division, *Lesson Plan on Credible Fear* at 7, in Asylum Officer Basic Training Course Participant Workbook (Apr. 14, 2006) [hereinafter AOBTC Workbook, Credible Fear], *available at www.uscis.gov/sites/default/files/USCIS/Humanitarian/Refugees%20%26%20Asylum/Asylum/AOBTC%20Lesson%20Plans/Credible-Fear-31aug10.pdf.*

➢ **Practice Pointer**: Noncitizens attempting to enter the United States at a land border port of entry from Canada must first establish that they are not ineligible for asylum and removable to Canada under the Safe Third Country Agreement,[24] through a threshold screening interview, in order to receive a credible fear interview.[25]

2. *Noncitizens Interdicted in International or U.S. Waters and Brought to the United States*

Noncitizens who are interdicted in international or U.S. waters and who are brought to the United States are also subject to expedited removal.[26]

3. *Noncitizens Who Have Not Been "Admitted" or "Paroled" into the U.S. and Who Have Not Resided in the U.S. for Two Years or More*

Expedited removal can be applied to individuals who entered the United States illegally—*i.e.*, who have not been admitted or paroled—and who have not resided in the United States for two or more years.[27] Although initially, the U.S. government did not apply expedited removal procedures to such individuals, it has increasingly done so.

In November 2002, the legacy Immigration and Naturalization Service (INS) announced that it would immediately begin to place all nonimmigrants who arrived in the United States illegally by sea in expedited removal proceedings.[28] The change was in response to what legacy INS perceived as a surge in illegal migration by sea, which it characterized as a threat to national security.[29]

In August 2004, DHS announced plans to expand the use of expedited removal to noncitizens who were in the United States less than 14 days and who were apprehended within 100 miles of the Mexican or Canadian border with the United States.[30] The announcement, however, limited implementation to the following CBP sectors: Laredo, McAllen, Del Rio, Marfa, El Paso, Tucson, Yuma, El Centro, San Diego, Blaine, Spokane, Havre, Grand Forks, Detroit, Buffalo, Swanton, and Houlton.[31] In 2006, DHS announced that it was expanding this program to the entire

---

[24] Agreement Between the Government of the United States and the Government of Canada for Cooperation in the Examination of Refugee Status Claims from Nationals of Third Countries (Dec. 5, 2002), *available at www.refworld.org/docid/42d7b9944.html*.

[25] 8 CFR §208.30(e)(6) (2014); *see also* the discussion of safe third countries in chapter 2.7.3.

[26] INA §§235(a)(1), (b)(1); AOBTC Workbook, Credible Fear, *supra* note 23, at 7.

[27] INA §235(b)(1)(A)(iii); 8 USC §1225(b)(1)(A)(iii) (2012).

[28] *See* Notice Designating Aliens Subject to Expedited Removal Under Section 235(b)(1)(A)(iii) of the Immigration and Nationality Act, 67 Fed. Reg. 68924 (Nov. 13, 2002).

[29] *Id.* at 68924. For an analysis and overview of how such provisions place asylum-seekers and refugees at risk, see Lory Rosenberg, *The Courts and Interception: The United States' Interdiction Experience and Its Impact on Refugees and Asylum Seekers*, 17 GEO. IMMIGR. L.J. 199, 215–18 (2003).

[30] *See* Designating Aliens for Expedited Removal, 69 Fed. Reg. 48877 (Aug. 11, 2004).

[31] *Id.* at 48880.

U.S. border, including all coastal areas adjacent to the United States' maritime borders.[32] If the noncitizen has been physically present in the United States for more than 14 days, he or she bears the burden of demonstrating this to the "satisfaction of the immigration officer" (usually a border patrol agent).[33]

- **Practice Pointer**: By regulation, the attorney general (AG) is not required to publish a notice in the *Federal Register* prior to applying expedited removal in the interior if the delay caused by publication would adversely affect the interests of the United States or the effective enforcement of the immigration laws.[34]

Lastly, to cover what it considered to be a "loophole" in the expedited removal process, DHS announced that it was expanding expedited removal to cover "illegal alien families."[35] To accommodate these families subject to expedited removal, DHS announced the May 15, 2006, opening of a 500-bed detention facility in Texas — the T. Don Hutto facility — that it claimed was specially equipped to meet family needs.[36] There were soon allegations of mistreatment and prison-like conditions in this facility.[37] On August 6, 2009, after years of controversy, media exposure, and a

---

[32] Press Release, U.S. Dep't of Homeland Security (DHS), Department of Homeland Security Streamlines Removal Process Along Entire U.S. Border (Jan. 30, 2006), *available at www.dhs.gov/xnews/releases/press_release_0845.shtm*.

[33] *See* Designating Aliens for Expedited Removal, 69 Fed. Reg. 48877, 48880 (Aug. 11, 2004).

[34] *See* 8 CFR §§235.3(b)(1)(ii), 1235.3(b)(1)(ii) (2014).

[35] Press Release, U.S. Dep't of Homeland Security & Immigration and Customs Enforcement (ICE), DHS Closes Loophole by Expanding Expedited Removal to Cover Illegal Alien Families (May 15, 2006), *available at www.immigration.com/newsletter1/iceilegalfaml.pdf*.

[36] *Id.*

[37] The American Civil Liberties Union brought 17 lawsuits against DHS Security Secretary Michael Chertoff, and six officials from ICE, on behalf of children detained at the T. Don Hutto (Hutto) detention facility in Taylor, TX. *See* Press Release, American Civil Liberties Union (ACLU), ACLU Challenges Illegal Detention of Immigrant Children Held in Prison-Like Conditions (Mar. 6, 2007), *available at* www.aclu.org/immigrants/detention/28865prs20070306.html; *see also* Women's Comm'n for Refugee Women & Children & Lutheran Immigration and Refugee Servs., *Locking Up Family Values: The Detention of Immigrant Families* (Feb. 2007), *available at www.womensrefugeecommission.org/hidden-reports/doc_download/150-locking-up-family-values-the-detention-of-immigrant-families*. These lawsuits contended that the Hutto facility violated the regulations arising out of *Flores v. Meese*, which ended in a 1997 court settlement that established minimum standards and conditions for the housing and release of all minors in federal immigration custody. *Flores v. Reno*, Stipulated Settlement Agreement, No. CV 85-4544-RJK (C.D. Cal. 1997). On August 27, 2007, a settlement was reached in the Hutto detention center litigation. *See* Press Release, ACLU, Landmark Settlement Announced in Federal Lawsuit Challenging Conditions at Immigrant Detention Center in Texas (Aug. 27, 2007), *available at www.aclu.org/immigrants-rights-prisoners-rights/landmark-settlement-announced-federal-lawsuit-challenging*.

lawsuit, DHS officials announced the closure of the T. Don Hutto family detention facility.[38]

However, in the summer of 2014, in response to an increase in mothers and children fleeing violence in Central America, the Obama administration resurrected and dramatically expanded its family detention practice in an effort to deter future border-crossers.[39] It hastily erected a facility in Artesia, New Mexico, with a capacity of over 600 women and children, which was closed down on December 15, 2014, following 14 grants of asylum out of 18 cases that went to the merits,[40] extensive media exposure, and a lawsuit regarding inhumane conditions and due process concerns.[41] However, the administration's conversion of an existing facility in Karnes City, TX, with a capacity of over 500 woman and children, and its opening of a new 2,400 bed facility in Dilley, TX, the administration has made clear its intentions to sustain its policy of detaining women and children in expedited removal proceedings.[42] Advocates continue to fight to end family detention.[43]

---

[38] See Press Release, ACLU, DHS Plan To Improve Immigration Detention And Close Hutto Facility A Good First Step (Aug. 6, 2009), *available at www.aclu.org/immigrants/detention/40612prs 20090806.html.*

[39] *See* Katharina Obser, *Locking Up Family Values Again: The Detention of Immigrant Families*, Women's Refugee Comm'n (Oct. 30, 2014), *available at http://womensrefugeecommission. org/blog/2176-locking-up-family-values-again-blog*; Dree Collopy, *The Failings of Family Detention at Artesia*, Am. Immigration Council (Oct. 2, 2014), *available at http://immigrationimpact.com/ 2014/10/02/the-failings-of-family-detention-at-artesia/*; Dree Collopy & Stephen Manning, *Why is Obama Still Locking Up So Many Innocent Women and Kids on U.S. Soil?*, The Guardian, *available at www.theguardian.com/commentisfree/2014/nov/04/obama-women-children-family-detention-centres*; Stephen Manning, *Let These Women Go*, AILA Leadership Blog, (Sept. 3 2014), *available at http://ailaleadershipblog.org/2014/09/03/let-these-women-go/* (last visited Jan. 19, 2015).

[40] *See* Am. Immigration Lawyers Assoc. (AILA), *Artesia Family Detention Asylum Case Examples*, AILA InfoNet. at Doc. No. 14102446 (Dec. 15, 2014), *available at www.aila.org/content/ default.aspx?bc=25667%7C50484.*

[41] *See M.S.P.C. v. Johnson* Compl. pending before the U.S. District Court for the District of Columbia, *available at http://americanimmigrationcouncil.org/sites/default/files/M.S.P.C.%20v.%20Johnson.pdf* (last visited Jan. 18, 2015). *See also* Press Release, Am. Immigration Council, Groups Sue U.S. Government Over Life-Threatening Deportation Process Against Mothers and Children (Aug. 22, 2014), *available at www.americanimmigrationcouncil.org/newsroom/release/groups-sue-us-government-over-life-threatening-deportation-process-against-mothers-.*

[42] *See* Press Release, Immigration and Customs Enforcement, ICE's New Family Detention Center in Dilley, TX, to Open in December (Nov. 18, 2014), *available at www.ice.gov/news/releases/ices-new-family-detention-center-dilley-texas-open-december* (last visited Jan. 17, 2015); Julia Preston, *Detention Center Presented as Deterrent to Border Crossings*, N.Y. TIMES, Dec. 16, 2014, at A18, *available at www.nytimes.com/2014/12/16/us/homeland-security-chief-opens-largest-immigration-detention-center-in-us.html?_r=0.*

[43] *See, e.g.*, Statement of the American Immigration Lawyers Association Submitted to the U.S. Commission on Civil Rights, *Briefing on State of Civil Rights at Immigration Detention Facilities* (Jan. 30, 2015), *available at* AILA InfoNet Doc. No. 15012045 *and at www.aila.org/advo-media/aila-correspondence/aila-mass-detention-of-asylum-seekers-is-a-humanit* (last visited Mar. 26, 2015).

4. *Individuals Paroled into the United States after April 1, 1997*

The definition of "arriving alien" includes an individual "paroled pursuant to §212(d)(5) of the Act."[44] Such individuals paroled after April 1, 1997, are subject to expedited removal upon the termination of parole.[45] Those parolees do not include individuals paroled pursuant to advance parole.[46]

> ➢ **Practice Pointer**: The attorney general also may initiate expedited proceedings to remove individuals convicted of an aggravated felony who are not permanent residents of the United States.[47] DHS may issue a final administrative removal order, and if the individual expresses a fear of return, DHS is required to refer him or her for a reasonable fear interview. This process is governed by INA §238 (rather than INA §235). See Part II. below for a detailed discussion of final administrative removal orders under INA §238.

B. Who is not subject to expedited removal?

The statute and regulations also exempt certain categories of individuals from the expedited removal process, including:

- Cuban citizens or nationals arriving at a port of entry or apprehended within 100 miles of the border;
- Pre–April 1, 1997 parolees;
- Unaccompanied minors;
- Stowaways;
- Crewmembers;
- Individuals seeking entry under the Visa Waiver Program;
- Noncitizens paroled into the U.S. with advance parole;
- Individuals with charges of inadmissibility other than INA §212(a)(6)(C) or 212(a)(7) for arriving at a port of entry with false or no documents; and
- LPRs, asylees, refugees, and others with additional protections.[48]

Each of these categories is discussed in detail below.

---

[44] 8 CFR §§1.1(q), 1001.1(q) (2014). *See* Memorandum from Immigration and Naturalization Serv., Policy Concerning Pre–April 1, 1997 Parolees (June 30, 1997), *reproduced in* 74 INTERPRETER RELEASES 1247 (Aug. 18, 1997).

[45] INA §212(d)(5); AOBTC Workbook, Credible Fear, *supra* note 23, at 7.

[46] AOBTC Workbook, Credible Fear, supra note 23, at 7. See also USCIS, ICE, CBP, Memorandum of Agreement, (Sept. 2008), available at *www.ice.gov/doclib/foia/reports/parole-authority-moa-9-08.pdf* (last visited Mar. 26, 2015).

[47] INA §238(b); 8 USC §1228(b) (2012).

[48] INA §235(b)(1); 8 CFR §§235.3(b)(1), 1235.3(b)(1) (2014).

- **Practice Pointer**: Asylum-seekers attempting to enter the United States at a land border port of entry with Canada must first establish eligibility for an exception to the Safe Third Country Agreement through a threshold screening interview in order to receive a credible fear interview.[49]

1. Cuban Citizens or Nationals Arriving at a Port of Entry or Apprehended Within 100 Miles of the Border

Expedited removal does not apply to a native or citizen of a country in the Western Hemisphere with whose government the United States does not have full diplomatic relations and who arrives by aircraft at a port of entry.[50] This provision currently applies only to Cuban citizens and nationals. Expedited removal is also not applicable to any native or citizen of Cuba arriving by sea,[51] at a land port of entry, or apprehended within 100 air miles of a U.S. border.[52] However, given a controversial agreement on December 17, 2014, by the United States and Cuba to restore diplomatic ties that were severed more than 50 years ago, it is possible that in the near future, the special provisions like these, which apply to Cuban citizens and nationals, will change or be applied differently.[53]

2. Pre-April 1, 1997 Parolees

Pursuant to INA §212(d)(5), DHS may parole any individual applying for admission — including those individuals who are inadmissible — to the United States on a case-by-case basis. Such parole may be granted in cases involving "urgent humanitarian reasons or significant public benefit,"[54] such as to obtain medical treatment in the United States, to visit a sick relative or attend a funeral in the United States, to prevent the inhumane separation of families, or to participate in or appear for civil litigation or criminal prosecution. An individual paroled into the United States under INA §212(d)(5) prior to April 1, 1997, is not subject to expedited

---

[49] 8 CFR §208.30(e)(6) (2014).

[50] INA §235(b)(1)(F), 8 USC §1225(b)(1)(F) (2012).

[51] Notice Designating Aliens Subject to Expedited Removal Under Section 235(b)(1)(A)(iii) of the Immigration and Nationality Act, 67 Fed. Reg. 68925 (Nov. 13, 2002).

[52] Designating Aliens for Expedited Removal, 69 Fed. Reg. 48877 (Aug. 11, 2004); *see* Memorandum from U.S. Customs and Border Protection (CBP) Comm'r, Jayson Ahern, Treatment of Cuban Asylum Seekers at Land Border Ports of Entry (June 10, 2005).

[53] *See* Daniel Trotta & Steve Holland, *U.S., Cuba Restore Ties After 50 Years*, Reuters (Dec. 17, 2014), *available at www.reuters.com/article/2014/12/17/us-cuba-usa-gross-idUSKBN0JV1H520141217*; Peter Baker, *U.S. to Restore Full Relations with Cuba, Erasing a Last Trace of Cold War Hostility*, N.Y. TIMES, Dec. 18, 2014, at A1, *available at www.nytimes.com/2014/12/18/world/americas/us-cuba-relations.html?_r=0.*

[54] INA §212(d)(5)(A).

removal.[55] This policy is reflected in the definition of "arriving alien" in 8 CFR §§1.1(q), 1001.1(q).[56]

3. *Unaccompanied Minors*

Unaccompanied minors, or "unaccompanied alien children," are children without lawful immigration status who have not reached the age of 18 and who have no parent or legal guardian in the United States available to provide care and physical custody.[57] Current law treats "unaccompanied alien children" differently than unauthorized adults or families with children who enter the United States. While adults and families with children may be subject to the expedited removal process, "unaccompanied alien children" (UACs) generally are exempt from expedited removal.[58]

When CBP or ICE apprehends a child, the agency must first determine whether the child meets the definition of UAC, and if so, whether that child is from a contiguous or non-contiguous country. Those determinations will establish the necessary protocol to be followed.[59] If CBP or ICE determines that the child meets the definition of UAC, that child will not be subject to the expedited removal proceedings under INA §235(b)(1), unless he or she has:

(1) engaged in criminal activity, in the presence of a DHS officer, that would qualify as an aggravated felony if committed by an adult;

(2) been convicted or adjudicated delinquent of an aggravated felony within the United States or another country, and the inspecting officer has confirmation of that order; or

---

[55] *See* Memorandum from Immigration and Naturalization Serv., *supra* note 44; *see also* AOBTC Workbook, Credible Fear, *supra* note 23, at 8.

[56] 8 CFR §§1.1(q), 1001.1(q) (2014) ("The term *arriving alien* means an applicant for admission coming or attempting to come into the United States at a port-of-entry, or an alien seeking transit through the United States at a port-of-entry, or an alien interdicted in international or United States waters and brought into the United States by any means, whether or not to a designated port-of-entry, and regardless of the means of transport. An arriving alien remains an arriving alien even if paroled pursuant to section 212(d)(5) of the Act, and even after any such parole is terminated or revoked. However, an arriving alien who was paroled into the United States before April 1, 1997, or who was paroled into the United States on or after April 1, 1997, pursuant to a grant of advance parole which the alien applied for and obtained in the United States prior to the alien's departure from and return to the United States, will not be treated, solely by reason of that grant of parole, as an arriving alien under section 235(b)(1)(A)(i) of the Act.").

[57] Trafficking Victims Protection Reauthorization Act of 2008 (TVPRA), Pub. L. No. 110-457 §235.

[58] *Id.*

[59] *See* 8 CFR §236.3; Office of the Inspector General, DHS, "CBP's Handling of Unaccompanied Alien Children," OIG 10-117 (2010), available at *www.oig.dhs.gov/assets/Mgmt/OIG_10-117_Sep10.pdf* (last visited Mar. 1, 2015); Office of Inspector General, DHS, "A Review of DHS' Responsibilities for Juvenile Aliens," OIG 05-45 (2005).

(3) previously been formally removed, excluded, or deported from the United States.[60]

If an unaccompanied minor is placed in expedited removal proceedings, the removal order must be reviewed and approved by the district director or deputy district director before the minor is removed from the United States.[61]

Most UACs, however, are not subject to expedited removal. Instead, for UACs from contiguous countries, CBP or ICE must screen the child within 48 hours of apprehension to determine whether:

(1) the child is a victim of trafficking or at risk of being trafficked;

(2) the child has a fear of returning to his or her country based on a credible fear of persecution; and

(3) the child can make an independent decision to withdraw his or her application for admission into the United States.[62]

If the child is not a victim of trafficking or at risk of being trafficked, does not have a fear of returning to his or her country based on a credible fear of persecution, and can make an independent decision to withdraw his or her application for admission, only then may CBP allow the child to voluntarily withdraw the application and immediately repatriate him or her without review by an IJ.[63] On the other hand, if all three of these conditions are not met, CBP must transfer the child to the custody of ORR and treat the child like a UAC from a non-contiguous country.

Children who are determined to be UACs from non-contiguous countries must be transferred, by law, to the custody of the Office of Refugee Resettlement (ORR) in the Department of Health and Human Services within 72 hours from the time that DHS assumed custody.[64] ORR will then complete a screening of the child to determine whether:

(1) the child has been a victim of trafficking;

(2) there is credible evidence that the child is at risk if returned; and

---

[60] INA §235(b)(1); 8 CFR §§235.3(b), 1235.3(b); INS, *Inspector's Field Manual,* chapter 17.15(f)(4) (Mar. 1998), available at *www.asylumlaw.org*, as added by INS Memorandum, P. Virtue, "Unaccompanied Minors Subject to Expedited Removal" (Aug. 21, 1997), *published on* AILA InfoNet at Doc. No. 97082191 (*posted* Aug. 21, 1997).

[61] INS, *Inspector's Field Manual,* chapter 17.15(f)(4) (Mar. 1998), available at *www.asylumlaw.org*, as added by INS Memorandum, P. Virtue, "Unaccompanied Minors Subject to Expedited Removal" (Aug. 21, 1997), *published on* AILA InfoNet at Doc. No. 97082191 (*posted* Aug. 21, 1997).

[62] TVPRA, *supra* note 57, at §235(a)(2).

[63] *Id.*

[64] *See Flores v. Reno*, Case No. CV 85-4544-RJK(Px) Settlement Agreement (C.D. Cal. 1997), at *https://cliniclegal.org/sites/default/files/attachments/flores_v._reno_settlement_agreement_1.pdf* (last visited Feb. 28, 2015); Office of Inspector General, DHS, "A Review of DHS's Responsibilities for Juvenile Aliens," OIG 05-45 (2005).

(3) the child has a possible claim to asylum.

If any of these factors exist, the child may seek relief while in INA §240 proceedings.[65] UACs who request asylum, will have their claims initially adjudicated by asylum officers even though they have been placed in removal proceedings.[66]

This exception to expedited removal recognizes that UACs require additional procedural safeguards and protections that are available to them in regular INA §240 removal proceedings, but that are not available in INA §235 expedited removal proceedings. UACs are, however, currently subject to reinstatement of removal proceedings.

> **Practice Pointer**: For a detailed discussion of the procedures for UACs and other child asylum-seekers, see Chapter 10.

4. *Stowaways*

Stowaways are not subject to the expedited removal program because stowaways arriving at a port of entry are not eligible to apply for admission or to be admitted to the United States.[67] They also are not considered applicants for admission and are not eligible for a full hearing in removal proceedings under INA §240.[68] If, however, they express a fear of persecution, a fear of torture, a fear of return to the country of proposed removal, or a desire or intention to apply for asylum, they will be given a credible fear interview by an asylum officer under INA §235(b)(1)(B).[69]

Even though a stowaway is not eligible for a regular hearing under INA §240, if the stowaway is found to have a credible fear of persecution or torture, the asylum officer will issue to him or her a Form I-863, Notice of Referral to Immigration Judge, and he or she will be referred to an immigration judge for a hearing conducted in accordance with the same rules as proceedings under INA §240.[70] Before the IJ, the stowaway may only apply for asylum, withholding of removal, or relief under the

---

[65] TVPRA, *supra* note 57, at §235(a)(5)(D).

[66] *See id.* at §§235(a)–(d). *See also* U.S. Citizenship and Immigration Servs. Memorandum from Joseph Langlois, Implementation of Statutory Change Providing USCIS with Initial Jurisdiction over Asylum Applications Filed by Unaccompanied Alien Children (Mar. 25, 2009), AILA InfoNet at Doc. No. 09042230 (*posted* Apr. 22, 2009), *available at www.uscis.gov/files/nativedocuments/UAC_filings_25mar09.pdf.*

[67] INA §235(a)(2).

[68] *Id.*

[69] *Id.*; *see also* 8 CFR §1235.1(d)(4). *See infra* pt. III.E. for a detailed discussion of the credible fear standards and procedures.

[70] *See* 8 CFR §§208.2(c)(1)(ii), 1208.2(c)(1)(ii); U.S. Citizenship and Immigration Servs., RAIO Asylum Division, Asylum Officer Basic Training Course, *Lesson Plan on Credible Fear* 8 (Feb. 28, 2014) [hereinafter USCIS Credible Fear Training], *available at http://cmsny.org/wp-content/uploads/credible-fear-of-persecution-and-torture.pdf.*

Convention Against Torture (CAT).[71] The parties are prohibited from raising any other issue, including issues of admissibility, removability, eligibility for waivers, and eligibility for forms of relief other than asylum or withholding.[72]

On the other hand, if the stowaway is found not to have a credible fear, the asylum officer will provide the stowaway with written notice of the decision and will inquire whether the stowaway wishes to have the decision reviewed by an IJ.[73] The negative decision is issued on Form I-869, Record of Negative Credible Fear Finding and Request for Review by Immigration Judge.[74] If the stowaway does not request a review by an IJ, the asylum officer refers the stowaway to the district director for completion of removal proceedings, in accordance with INA §235(a)(2).[75] It may be possible at this point, however, to arrange for a credible fear "re-interview."[76]

If the stowaway requests a review of the negative credible fear determination by an IJ, the asylum officer must arrange for the stowaway's detention and serve him or her with a Form I-863, Notice of Referral to Immigration Judge.[77] If the IJ concurs with the asylum officer's determination, the case will be returned to DHS for removal of the stowaway.[78] The IJ's decision is final and may not be appealed.[79] The asylum office, however, may reconsider a negative credible fear finding after providing notice to the IJ.[80] Applicants who would like their claim reconsidered should arrange for a credible fear "re-interview."[81] If the IJ finds that the stowaway has a credible fear, the stowaway will be permitted to file an asylum application before the IJ in accordance with 8 CFR §1208.4(b)(3)(iii).[82] The IJ will make a decision on the asylum application and that decision may be appealed by ICE or the stowaway to the BIA.[83] If the asylum application is ultimately denied, ICE will remove the stowaway in accordance with INA §235(a)(2).[84] If the asylum application is ultimately

---

[71] 8 CFR §§208.2(c)(1)–(2), 1208.2(c)(1)–(2). *See supra* chapter 2 for a detailed discussion of asylum and withholding of removal under INA §241(b)(3); chapter 3 for a detailed discussion of relief under the Convention Against Torture.

[72] *See* 8 CFR §§208.2(c)(1)(ii), 1208.2(c)(1)(ii); *see also* 8 CFR §§208.2(c)(3)(i), 1208.2(c)(3)(i), and 1235.1(d)(4).

[73] 8 CFR §§208.30(g), 1208.30(g).

[74] 8 CFR §§208.30(g), 1208.30(g).

[75] 8 CFR §§208.30(g), 1208.30(g).

[76] *See infra* Part III.E. for a detailed discussion of the credible fear standards and procedures.

[77] 8 CFR §§208.30(g)(1)(i), 1208.30(g)(1)(i).

[78] 8 CFR §1208.30(g)(2)(iv)(A).

[79] *Id.*

[80] *Id.*

[81] *See infra* Part III.E. for a detailed discussion of the credible fear standards and procedures.

[82] 8 CFR §1208.30(g)(2)(iv)(C).

[83] *Id.*

[84] *Id.*

approved, ICE must terminate removal proceedings in accordance with INA §235(a)(2).[85]

5. *Crewmembers*

Crewmembers who indicate a fear of persecution in their home countries, whether on or off their vessel or other conveyance, must be given an asylum application form to submit to the local DHS district director within 10 days.[86] The district director must, upon receiving the application, refer the individual to an immigration judge (IJ) for an asylum hearing.[87]

6. *Individuals Seeking Entry Under the Visa Waiver Program*

Under the Visa Waiver Program, nationals of certain designated countries are permitted to enter the United States without first obtaining a nonimmigrant visa.[88] Individuals applying for admission under the INA §217 Visa Waiver Program are not subject to expedited removal.[89] This exemption includes individuals entering with a passport from a Visa Waiver Program country, even if they are not actually nationals of that country.[90] If such individuals request asylum in the United States, they must be referred to an IJ for proceedings in immigration court.[91] The proceedings are limited to a determination of eligibility for asylum, withholding of removal, or CAT relief.[92]

7. *Noncitizens Paroled into the United States with Advance Parole*

Persons paroled into the United States pursuant to a grant of advance parole that was obtained prior to departure from the United States are not subject to expedited removal.[93]

8. *Individuals with Additional Charges of Inadmissibility*

Persons denied admission to the United States on charges other than having false or no documents under INA §§212(a)(6)(C) or 212(a)(7) also are not subject to expedited removal.[94]

---

[85] *Id.*

[86] 8 CFR §§208.5(b), 1208.5(b) (2014).

[87] 8 CFR §§208.5(b), 1208.5(b) (2014).

[88] INA §217; 8 USC §1187 (2012).

[89] 8 CFR §235.3(b)(10) (2014).

[90] *See Matter of Kanagasundram*, 22 I&N Dec. 963 (BIA 1999).

[91] 8 CFR §217.4(a)(1) (2014).

[92] 8 CFR §§208.2(c)(3)(i), 1208.2(c)(3)(i) (2014).

[93] USCIS Credible Fear Training, *supra* note 70, at 9.

[94] *See* 8 CFR §§235.3(b)(3), 1235.3(b)(3) (2014).

9. *LPRs, Refugees, Asylees, and Others with Additional Protections*

Finally, if an applicant for admission who is subject to expedited removal claims under oath to have been lawfully admitted for permanent residence (LPR), to have been previously admitted as a refugee, to have been previously granted asylum, or to be a U.S. citizen (USC), the immigration officer must attempt to verify the applicant's status.[95] If the status cannot be readily verified and the applicant claims under penalty of perjury that he or she is an LPR, an asylee, a refugee, or a USC, he or she is entitled to administrative review of a removal order[96] and his or her case will be referred to an IJ for review.[97] There is no appeal from the IJ's decision.[98]

Unlike asylum-seekers, such individuals are entitled to representation by counsel (at no expense to the government) at the IJ review.[99] Such individuals are also entitled to habeas corpus proceedings, but the court may only review whether the individual (1) is a noncitizen; (2) was ordered removed under INA §235(b)(1); or (3) is an LPR, refugee or asylee.[100] The court may not review whether the individual is actually inadmissible or entitled to any relief from removal.[101]

If the immigration officer verifies the LPR, refugee, or asylee status of the individual, but he or she appears to be inadmissible for other reasons, the officer may initiate regular removal proceedings against the individual under INA §240.[102] LPRs, refugees, and asylees are not subject to expedited removal.[103]

C. Withdrawal of Application for Admission

Rather than being subject to expedited removal, an applicant for admission may, in the discretion of the attorney general and at any time, be permitted to withdraw his

[95] 8 CFR §§235.3(b)(5)(i), 1235.3(b)(5)(i) (2014).

[96] INA §235(b)(1)(C); 8 USC §1225(b)(1)(C) (2012); 8 CFR §§235.3(b)(5)(i), 1235.3(b)(5)(i) (2014). *Matter of Lujan-Quitana*, 25 I&N Dec. 53 (BIA 2009) (finding that the Board of Immigration Appeals (BIA) lacked jurisdiction to review an appeal by DHS of an immigration judge's (IJ) decision to vacate an order of expedited removal after the IJ determined that the respondent was a U.S. citizen). *But see Diaz v. Reno*, 40 F. Supp. 2d 984 (N.D. Ill. 1999) (holding that a U.S. citizen erroneously removed to Mexico under the expedited removal process was barred, under the doctrine of sovereign immunity, from suing the attorney general (AG) and the legacy Immigration and Naturalization Service (INS) district director in their official capacity).

[97] 8 CFR §§235.3(b)(5)(iv), 1235.3(b)(5)(iv) (2014).

[98] 8 CFR §§235.3(b)(5)(iv), 1235.3(b)(5)(iv) (2014).

[99] *See* Exec. Office for Immigration Review Memorandum from Michael Creppy, Interim Operating Policy and Procedure Memorandum 97-3: Procedures for Credible Fear and Claimed Status Reviews (Mar. 25, 1997, as amended on Apr. 25, 1997) [hereinafter Creppy Mem. 97-3], *available at www.usdoj.gov/eoir/efoia/ocij/oppm97/97-3.pdf.*

[100] INA §242(e)(2); 8 USC §1252(e)(2) (2012).

[101] INA §242(e)(5); 8 USC §1252(e)(5) (2012).

[102] 8 CFR §§235.3(b)(5)(ii)–(iii), 1235.3(b)(5)(ii)–(iii) (2014).

[103] 8 CFR §§235.3(b)(5)(iii), 1235.3(b)(5)(iii) (2014).

or her application for admission and depart immediately from the United States in lieu of expedited removal under INA §235(b)(1).[104] The applicant's decision to withdraw his or her application for admission must be made voluntarily.[105] An applicant, however, does not have the "right" to withdraw his or her application for admission.[106] Permission to withdraw an application for admission should *not* normally be granted unless the applicant intends and is able to depart the United States immediately.[107] Moreover, an applicant permitted to withdraw his or her application for admission will normally remain in carrier or DHS custody pending departure, unless the district director determines that parole of the applicant is warranted under 8 CFR §212.5(b).[108] Individuals given permission to withdraw their applications for admission, because they have not been issued a removal order, are not subject to the five-year bar to readmission for having been removed pursuant to a removal order.[109]

DHS reported that 316,898 individuals were permitted to withdraw their applications for admission in fiscal year (FY) 2005.[110] Chapter 17.2 of the *Inspector's Field Manual* (IFM) provides that an applicant should be permitted to withdraw his or her application for admission if it is determined to be in "the best interest of justice that a removal order not be issued."[111] Factors that may be considered by an inspector in determining whether an applicant should be permitted to withdraw his or her application for admission include:

(1) the seriousness of the immigration violation;

(2) previous findings of inadmissibility against the applicant;

(3) intention on the part of the applicant to violate the law;

(4) ability to easily overcome the ground of inadmissibility;

(5) age or poor health of the applicant; and

(6) other humanitarian or public interest considerations.[112]

---

[104] INA §235(a)(4); 8 CFR §§235.4, 1235.4 (2014).

[105] 8 CFR §§235.4, 1235.4 (2014).

[106] 8 CFR §§235.4, 1235.4 (2014).

[107] 8 CFR §§235.4, 1235.4 (2014).

[108] 8 CFR §§235.4, 1235.4 (2014).

[109] *See* INA §212(a)(9)(A)(i).

[110] Mary Dougherty, Denise Wilson, & Amy WU, Annual Report on Immigration Enforcement Actions: 2005, U.S. Dep't of Homeland Security (Nov. 2005), *available at www.dhs.gov/xlibrary/assets/statistics/yearbook/2005/Enforcement_AR_05.pdf.*

[111] CBP, *Inspector's Field Manual* (IFM), at chapter 17.2 (Feb. 10, 2006), *available at* AILA InfoNet Doc. No. 11120959 *and at www.aila.org/infonet/cbp-inspectors-field-manual* (last visited Mar. 25, 2015).

[112] *Id.*

The IFM also acknowledges that detention space, workload, and resources may also affect whether applicants are permitted to withdraw their applications for admission.[113] Note, however, that in 2013, CBP announced that it would be discontinuing use of the IFM and that the manual would be replaced with the new "Officer's Reference Tool."[114] CBP has confirmed that the Officer's Reference Tool will not be made available to the public due to its designation as "Law Enforcement Sensitive."[115] Thus, the IFM serves only as a reference for potential CBP interpretations.

If an individual has claimed a fear of return or a desire to apply for asylum upon apprehension, he or she may dissolve his or her asylum claim at any time in the expedited removal process and seek to withdraw his or her application for admission. Making such a request, however, does not mean the individual will be allowed to withdraw and forego the issuance of an expedited removal order. In 2005, the U.S. Commission on International Religious Freedom expressed concern that in a few observed instances immigration officials improperly encouraged asylum-seekers to withdraw their applications for admission and concluded that "Customs and Border Protection (CBP) quality assurance mechanisms are inadequate to ensure that all officers comply with the policy that all withdrawals be 'strictly voluntary.'"[116] Similar complaints continue against CBP officers and their actions toward asylum-seekers, including efforts to coerce individuals to withdraw their claims for protection.[117]

---

[113] *Id.*

[114] *See* AILA Practice Alert, *CBP is Replacing Inspector's Field Manual with Officer's Reference Tool*, AILA InfoNet Doc. No. 14020749 (*posted* Feb. 7, 2014), *available at www.aila.org/content/default.aspx?docid=47401.*

[115] *Id.*

[116] U.S. Commission on International Religious Freedom, *Report on Asylum Seekers in Expedited Removal, Vol. I: Findings and Recommendations*, at 51 (Feb. 2005) [hereinafter USCIRF Report], *available at www.uscirf.gov/reports-briefs/special-reports/report-asylum-seekers-in-expedited-removal* (last visited Mar. 26, 2015).

[117] AILA Complaint to DHS Office of Civil Rights and Civil Liberties, Inadequate U.S. Customs and Border Protection (CBP) Screening Practices Block Individuals Fleeing Persecution from Access to the Asylum Process, (Nov. 13, 2014) [hereinafter AILA Complaint on Inadequate CBP Screening Practices], AILA InfoNet Doc. No. 14111748 (*posted* Nov. 17, 2014), available at *www.aila.org/content/default.aspx?docid=50710*; Human Rights First, How to Protect Refugees and Prevent Abuse at the Border (June 2014) [hereinafter Human Rights First on Preventing Abuse at the Border], available at *www.humanrightsfirst.org/sites/default/files/Asylum-on-the-Border-final.pdf*; Daniel Martínez, Am. Immigration Council, No Action Taken, supra note 9; Am. Immigration Council, Mexican and Central American Asylum and Credible Fear Claims, (May 2014) [hereinafter Am. Immigration Council on Mexican and Central American Asylum Claims], available at *http://immigrationpolicy.org/sites/default/files/docs/asylum_and_credible_fear_claims_final.pdf*. *See also www.HoldCBPAccountable.org.*

D. Challenges to the Expedited Removal Order

Depending on the individual's circumstances, he or she may have a number of available challenges to the expedited removal order. First, the individual may argue that the expedited removal procedures do not apply to him or her, either because all four of the elements listed above do not apply or because he or she falls within one of the categories of individuals who are exempt from the expedited removal process.[118] For example, if an individual arrives at the border of the United States and is charged with a ground of inadmissibility other than INA §212(a)(6)(C) or INA §212(a)(7) (for fraud or not having proper entry documents upon arrival), he or she must be placed in normal INA §240 removal proceedings, rather than expedited removal proceedings.[119]

- **Practice Pointer**: If the inspecting officer fails to follow the statute or the regulations in issuing an expedited removal order, practitioners should seek Customs and Border Protection review of the expedited removal order and also consider a habeas action, as discussed below in Part I.E.1.

Second, if an individual arrives at a port of entry and is being processed under the expedited removal provisions, he or she may challenge an expedited removal order by demonstrating that he or she is a U.S. citizen, lawful permanent resident, asylee, or refugee.[120] The inspecting officer should attempt to verify the claim. If the officer cannot verify the claim, the officer should issue the expedited removal order, but then refer the individual to an IJ for review of the order.[121] Unfortunately, in practice, especially along the southern border of the United States, inspecting officers frequently do not follow these procedures and remove the individual without referring him or her to an IJ.

- **Practice Pointer**: Practitioners should consider filing a habeas petition and seeking a temporary restraining order for a client who has status and a valid challenge to the expedited removal order before he or she is removed.[122]

E. Judicial Review of Expedited Removal

If an individual is subject to the expedited removal process and/or receives an expedited removal order, the INA severely limits judicial review of expedited

---

[118] *See supra* pts. I.A. and B. for a detailed discussion of who is subject to the expedited removal process.

[119] INA §235.

[120] *See* 8 CFR §235.3(b)(5) (2014).

[121] INA §2359b)(1)(C); 8 CFR §§235.3(b)(5)(iv), 235.6(a)(2)(ii) (2014).

[122] *See Jones v. Cunningham*, 371 U.S. 236, 240 (1963); *Smith v. U.S. Customs and Border Protection*, 741 F.3d 1016, 1020 n.3 (9th Cir. 2014).

removal orders and the expedited removal process.[123] In fact the INA expressly precludes jurisdiction in the courts of appeals over expedited removal orders. As the Seventh Circuit observed, the entire expedited removal process "can happen without any check on whether the person understood the proceedings, had an interpreter, or enjoyed any other safeguards … . [T]he procedure is fraught with risk of arbitrary, mistaken, or discriminatory behavior."[124]

> **Practice Pointer**: Given the limited challenges to an expedited removal order and the expedited removal process, before turning to litigation, practitioners should reach out directly to Customs and Border Protection to ensure that there was effective supervisory review. Practitioners should first contact the inspecting officer directly and then move up the chain of command. If these options fail, practitioners should request a formal review with the Director at the port of entry.

The limited options for judicial review are discussed below.[125]

1. Habeas Corpus Proceedings

The only route to judicial review that is authorized by the statute is found at INA §242(e)(2), which provides that an individual is entitled to habeas corpus proceedings, but the federal court may review only whether the individual: (1) is a nonimmigrant; (2) was ordered removed under INA §235(b)(1); or (3) is an LPR, asylee, or refugee.[126] In determining whether an individual has been ordered removed, the court's inquiry is limited to whether such an order was issued, and whether it relates to the individual.[127] The court may not review whether the individual is actually inadmissible or entitled to any relief from removal.[128]

It may be possible to challenge an expedited removal order in habeas corpus proceedings in district court under 28 USC §2241, which permits noncitizens to argue that their detention is unlawful or unconstitutional.[129] The individual must be "in custody" at the time of filing the habeas petition.[130] If the individual is removed after filing the habeas petition, however, that should not deprive the court of jurisdiction because the matter would not be moot.[131] A potential challenge to making such claims is the limited due process rights afforded to noncitizens who have not

---

[123] INA §§242(a)(2)(iii), (e); 8 USC §§1252(a)(2), (e) (2012).

[124] *Khan v. Holder*, 608 F.3d 325, 330 (7th Cir. 2010).

[125] See chapter 12 for a detailed discussion of judicial review.

[126] INA §242(e)(2); 8 USC §1252(e)(2) (2012).

[127] INA §242(e)(5); 8 USC §1252(e)(5) (2012).

[128] INA §242(e)(5); 8 USC §1252(e)(5) (2012).

[129] 28 USC §2241 (2012). *See also* U.S. Const. art. I §9 cl. 2; *INS v. St. Cyr,* 533 U.S. 289 (2001).

[130] 28 USC §2241 (2012).

[131] *See, e.g., Zegarra-Gomez v. INS*, 314 F.3d 112 (9th Cir. 2003); *Leitao v. Reno*, 311 F.3d 453 (1st Cir. 2002); *Steele v. Blackman, INS*, 236 F.3d 130, 134 n.4 (3d Cir. 2001).

effectuated an actual entry to the United States.[132] Thus, individuals apprehended at ports of entry would likely have more limited rights and a weaker claim than individuals apprehended within the United States.

2. *Limitations on Declaratory, Injunctive, and Equitable Relief*

Except for the limited authority to challenge the validity of the expedited removal system, noted below, no court (except the U.S. Supreme Court) may enter declaratory, injunctive, or other equitable relief in any action pertaining to an expedited removal order.[133]

3. *Prohibition on Certification of a Class Under Rule 23*

No court may certify a class under Rule 23 of the Federal Rules of Civil Procedure in any action for which judicial review of the expedited removal process is authorized.[134]

4. *Challenges to Validity of the System*

An action may be brought in the U.S. District Court for the District of Columbia to determine only whether the statute is constitutional and/or whether a regulation, written policy directive, written policy guideline, or written procedure is consistent with the statute and is not otherwise a violation of law.[135] The action must be filed no later than 60 days after the date the challenged section, regulation, directive, guideline, or procedure is first implemented.[136] A notice of appeal of an order issued by the district court may be filed not later than 30 days after the order is issued.[137] The district court, court of appeals, and Supreme Court are required to expedite to the greatest extent possible the disposition of these challenges.[138] In March and May 1997, three actions were brought challenging expedited removal on behalf of asylum-seekers and other applicants for admission to the United States. The challenges were unsuccessful and the consolidated lawsuits were subsequently dismissed.[139]

5. *Relief*

If the court determines that the individual was not ordered removed or that he or she is an LPR, was admitted as a refugee under INA §207, or was granted asylum

---

[132] *See United States ex rel. Knauff v. Shaughnessy*, 338 U.S. 537, 544 (1950); *Smith v. U.S. Customs and Border Protection*, 741 F.3d 1016, 1022 n.6 (9th Cir. 2014).

[133] INA §§242(e)(1)(A), (f); 8 USC §§1252(e)(1)(A), (f) (2012).

[134] INA §242(e)(1)(B); 8 USC §1252(e)(1)(B) (2012).

[135] INA §242(e)(3)(A); 8 USC §1252(e)(3)(A) (2012).

[136] INA §242(e)(3)(B); 8 USC §1252(e)(3)(B) (2012).

[137] INA §242(e)(3)(C); 8 USC §1252(e)(3)(C) (2012).

[138] INA §242(e)(3)(D); 8 USC §1252(e)(3)(D) (2012).

[139] *See American Immigration Lawyers Ass'n v. Reno*, 199 F.3d 1352 (D.C. Cir. Jan. 11, 2000), *aff'g* 18 F. Supp. 2d 38 (D.D.C. 1998). *See generally* Gerald Neuman, *Federal Court Issues in Immigration Law*, 78 TEX. L. REV. 1661, 1668–79 (June 2000) (section III on judicial review of expedited removal).

under INA §208, the court may not order a remedy or relief other than to require a hearing under INA §240.[140]

> **Practice Pointer**: Although judicial review of an expedited removal order is severely limited, another option may be to file a motion to reopen or reconsider directly with DHS if an individual believes that the expedited removal order was issued in error.[141]

F. Consequences of Expedited Removal

Pursuant to INA §212(a)(9)(A)(i), an arriving alien issued an order of removal under the expedited removal process or at the end of INA §240 proceedings initiated upon the individual's arrival is inadmissible to the United States for a period of five years of the date of the removal, unless the attorney general (AG) consents to his or her admission.[142] Under the Homeland Security Act of 2002, this authority extends to the DHS secretary and other DHS officials.[143] If the individual is ordered removed a second time or has been convicted of an aggravated felony, he or she is inadmissible for a period of 20 years, unless the AG consents to his or her admission.[144]

II. Administrative Removal Proceedings for Aggravated Felons

In addition to individuals subject to expedited removal proceedings under INA §235, certain individuals convicted of aggravated felonies as defined under INA §101(a)(48) may be subject to expedited proceedings and an administrative removal order pursuant to INA §238.[145] The AG may initiate these expedited proceedings to remove individuals convicted of an aggravated felony who are not permanent residents of the United States.[146] At least three courts have held this expedited process may apply to parolees.[147]

---

[140] INA §242(e)(4); 8 USC §1252(e)(4) (2012).

[141] *See* 8 CFR §103.5 (2014) (governing motions to reopen or reconsider DHS decisions, which should include expedited removal decisions).

[142] INA §§212(a)(9)(A)(i), (iii); 8 USC §§1182(a)(9)(i), (iii) (2012).

[143] *See* Homeland Security Act of 2002, Pub. L. No. 107-296, §§456, 1512, 1517, 116 Stat. 2135, 2200, 2310, 2311.

[144] INA §§212(a)(9)(A)(i), (iii); 8 USC §§1182(a)(9)(i), (iii) (2012).

[145] *See* INA §238(b); 8 CFR §238.1 (2014).

[146] INA §238(b); 8 USC §1228(b) (2012). Under the Homeland Security Act of 2002, this authority extends to the DHS secretary and other DHS officials. *See* Homeland Security Act of 2002, Pub. L. No. 107-296, §§456, 1512, 1517, 116 Stat. 2135, 2200, 2310, 2311.

[147] *Bamba v. Riley*, 366 F.3d 195 (3d Cir. 2004); *Bazan-Reyes v. INS*, 256 F.3d 600 (7th Cir. 2001); *see also United States v. Hernandez-Vermudez*, 356 F.3d 1011 (9th Cir. 2004) (finding that 8 USC §1228(b) (2012) applies to immigrants who are not admitted to the United States).

In determining whether INA §238 proceedings apply, DHS will question the individual and consider whether there is sufficient evidence to support a finding that he or she:

(1) is a noncitizen;

(2) has not been lawfully admitted for permanent residence or conditional permanent resident status under INA §216;

(3) has a final conviction of an aggravated felony as defined under INA §101(a)(48); and

(4) is deportable under INA §237(a)(2)(A)(iii) for conviction of an aggravated felony any time after admission.[148]

DHS must allege these elements in a Form I-851, Notice of Intent to Issue a Final Administrative Removal Order and serve it on the individual.[149] The I-851 is a charging document that includes allegations of fact and conclusions of law. The I-851 also must advise the individual of:

(1) the privilege of being represented by counsel;

(2) the right to request withholding of removal to a particular country if he or she fears persecution or torture in that country;

(3) the right to inspect evidence supporting the I-851; and

(4) the right to rebut the charges in the I-851 within 10 calendar days (or 13 calendar days, if the service of the I-851 was by mail).[150]

DHS must also provide the individual with a list of free legal services.[151]

A. Response to Form I-851, Notice of Intent to Issue a Final Administrative Deportation Order

The I-851 is served on the individual and his or her attorney. After service, the individual may rebut the charges within ten calendar days (or 13 days if the notice was sent in the mail).[152] In their responses, individuals may:

(1) designate their choice for country of removal;

(2) submit a written response rebutting the allegations supporting the charge in the I-851;

(3) request the opportunity to review DHS's evidence;

(4) submit a statement indicating an intention to request withholding of removal under 8 CFR §1208.16; and/or

---

[148] 8 CFR §§238.1(b)(1), 1238.1(b)(1) (2014).

[149] 8 CFR §§238.1(b)(2)(i), 1238.1(b)(2)(i) (2014).

[150] 8 CFR §§238.1(b)(2), 1238.1(b)(2) (2014).

[151] 8 CFR §§238.1(b)(2)(iv), 1238.1(b)(2)(iv) (2014).

[152] 8 CFR §§238.1(b)(2)(i), 1238.1(b)(2)(i) (2014).

(5) request in writing an extension of time for filing a response, stating the specific reasons why such an extension is necessary.[153]

If an individual does not submit a timely response or concedes deportability, DHS will issue a final administrative order of removal.[154]

B. Right to Request Withholding of Removal or Relief Under the Convention Against Torture

Individuals in this expedited process are not eligible for any discretionary relief from removal.[155] They may be eligible, however, to apply for withholding of removal under INA §241(b)(3), withholding of removal under the Convention Against Torture (CAT), or deferral of removal under the CAT.[156] The regulations require DHS to give notice of the right to request withholding of removal to a particular country, if the person ordered removed fears persecution or torture in that country.[157] If the individual requests withholding of removal, DHS will issue a final administrative order of removal and then immediately refer the individual to an asylum officer for a "reasonable fear" interview in accordance with 8 CFR §208.31.[158]

C. INA §240 Removal Proceedings

If the DHS trial attorney finds that the record raises an issue of material fact, he or she may issue a Notice to Appear to initiate removal proceedings under INA §240.[159] The officer may also initiate §240 proceedings if the officer finds the individual is "not amenable" to expedited proceedings under INA §238.[160]

If an individual is in §240 proceedings and meets the criteria for expedited proceedings for aggravated felons, the IJ, upon a motion by the DHS trial attorney, may terminate §240 proceedings to commence proceedings under INA §238.[161]

D. Judicial Review

Under the REAL ID Act, a petition for review filed with an appropriate court of appeals is the only means for judicial review of an order of removal.[162] This provision of the Act took effect immediately and applies to all removal order appeals,

---

[153] 8 CFR §§238.1(c)(1), 1238.1(c)(1) (2014).

[154] 8 CFR §§238.1(d)(1), 1238.1(d)(1) (2014).

[155] INA §238(b)(5); 8 USC §1228(b)(5) (2012).

[156] 8 CFR §§238.1(f)(3), 1238.1(f)(3) (2014). For more detailed information on the Convention Against Torture (CAT), see chapter 3.

[157] 8 CFR §238.1(b)(2)(i) (2014).

[158] 8 CFR §§208.31(a)–(b), 238.1(f)(3), 1208.31(a)–(b), 1238.1(f)(3) (2014). *See infra* pt. V. for a detailed discussion of the reasonable fear process.

[159] 8 CFR §§238.1(d)(2)(ii), 1238.1(d)(2)(ii) (2014).

[160] 8 CFR §§238.1(d)(2)(iii), 1238.1(d)(2)(iii) (2014).

[161] 8 CFR §§238.1(e), 1238.1(e) (2014).

[162] INA §242(a)(5); 8 USC §1252(a)(5) (2012).

regardless of when the removal order was issued.[163] An individual may seek judicial review under INA §242 of a final administrative removal order issued pursuant to INA §238.[164] The REAL ID Act clarifies that federal appellate review in accordance with procedures under INA §242 is the only method available for review of any removal order issued under any provision of the INA.[165]

If an individual would like to challenge a final administrative removal order, he or she must file a Petition for Review within 30 days of the order, even if he or she is in withholding-only proceedings.[166] The only circuit where an administrative removal order is not final until the conclusion of withholding-only proceedings is the Ninth Circuit.[167]

III. How Expedited Removal Works in Practice

The expedited removal process begins upon apprehension of an individual and their primary inspection, usually at a port of entry or near a U.S. border. Following primary inspection, certain individuals may be referred for secondary inspection, where a record of sworn statement is taken and a final order is given. If the individual falls within the categories of people who are not subject to expedited removal, those individuals are exempt and their cases proceed differently than those subject to expedited removal. If the individual is subject to expedited removal and expresses a fear of persecution or torture, he or she will be detained and scheduled for a "credible fear interview" with an asylum officer.

During the interview, the asylum-seeker must establish that there is a "significant possibility" of persecution or torture upon return to his or her home country. If the asylum officer concludes that there is such a significant possibility, the officer will refer the asylum-seeker to an IJ for INA §240 proceedings, during which he or she may make a claim for asylum, withholding, or CAT relief. On the other hand, if the asylum officer concludes that there is not a significant possibility of persecution or torture, the officer will make a negative credible fear finding.

The asylum-seeker may request review of the asylum officer's negative credible fear finding by an IJ. If the IJ agrees with the asylum officer, the asylum-seeker will be removed pursuant to the expedited removal order. If, however, the IJ does find that the asylum-seeker has a credible fear of persecution or torture, the IJ will overturn the asylum officer's finding and will place the asylum-seeker in INA §240 proceedings, during which the asylum-seeker may make his or her claim for asylum, withholding

---

[163] REAL ID Act of 2005, Pub. L. No. 109-13, div. B, §106(b), 119 Stat. 231, 311.

[164] *See* INA §§238(b)(3), 242(a)(1); 8 USC §§1228(b)(3), 1252(a)(1) (2012).

[165] REAL ID Act of 2005, Pub. L. No. 109-13, div. B, §106(d), 119 Stat. 231, 311.

[166] INA §242(a)(1)(5), (b)(1).

[167] *Ortiz-Alfaro v. Holder*, 694 F.3d 955, 958 (9th Cir. 2012). *See also Herrera-Molina v. Holder*, 597 F.3d 128, 132 (2d Cir. 2010) (raising this same issue, but not resolving it).

of removal, and/or CAT relief. These procedures and the legal standards involved during each step of the process are described in detail in this section.

A. Primary Inspection

When an individual arrives at a port of entry, an immigration officer inspects him or her at a primary inspection station. The primary inspector has only a few seconds to examine documents, run basic lookout queries, and ask pertinent questions.[168] Changes under the US-VISIT program added additional requirements for individuals to be fingerprinted and photographed. If the immigration officer completes this inspection and believes that the individual's documents are acceptable and that he or she is admissible to the United States, the individual is admitted. If, however, the primary inspector believes that there is a question about the individual's admissibility to the United States or that his or her documents are not acceptable, the inspector will refer the individual to secondary inspection.[169] During the primary inspection stage, an individual does not have the right to representation unless he or she has become the focus of a criminal investigation and has been taken into custody.[170] Approximately 362 million people passed through primary inspection in the United States in fiscal year 2013.[171]

B. Secondary Inspection

Millions of noncitizens are referred to secondary inspection each year, and over 35 million were referred in fiscal year 2013.[172] In order to determine whether an individual in secondary inspection is subject to the expedited removal process, the secondary inspector questions the individual regarding his or her documents.[173]

1. No Right to Representation

As in primary inspection, a noncitizen in secondary inspection does not have the right to representation unless he or she has become the focus of a criminal investigation and has been taken into custody.[174]

> ➢ **Practice Pointer**: Often, individuals in secondary inspection will make claims to valid immigration status and their admissibility to the United States. An inspecting officer may refer such individuals for a "deferred inspection," paroling them into the United States and requiring them to

[168] Inspection and Expedited Removal of Aliens; Detention and Removal of Aliens; Conduct of Removal Proceedings; Asylum Procedures, 62 Fed. Reg. 10318 (Mar. 6, 1997) (supplementary information).

[169] *Id.*

[170] 8 CFR §§292.5(b), 1292.5(b) (2014).

[171] *See* Lisa Seghetti, *Border Security: Immigration Inspections at Ports of Entry*, Cong. Research Serv. 13 (Oct. 31, 2014), *available at www.fas.org/sgp/crs/homesec/R43356.pdf.*

[172] *See id.*

[173] *Id.*

[174] 8 CFR §§292.5(b), 1292.5(b) (2014).

return to the port of entry with their documentation demonstrating their admissibility. It may be possible for practitioners to negotiate with CBP to secure the right to represent their clients during deferred inspections.[175] Practitioners should contact the CBP office at the relevant port of entry prior to the deferred inspection to discuss their client's case and to request the opportunity to appear at the deferred inspection with their client. Practitioners also should appear at the deferred inspection with their client, but should prepare their client well in case CBP does not allow the practitioner's presence during the inspection.

2. *Record of Sworn Statement — Form I-867 A and B*

During the secondary inspection interview, the inspector will seek to determine whether the noncitizen is in possession of a false document, invalid document, or no document.[176] If the inspector determines that the individual is subject to expedited removal, the inspector is required to take a sworn statement from the noncitizen on Forms I-867A and B, Record of Sworn Statement.[177] The inspector must read (or have read) to the noncitizen all information contained on the I-867A and create a record of the facts of the case along with the statement made by the noncitizen during the questioning on the I-867A. The officer then questions the individual regarding identity, alienage, and inadmissibility and records his or her responses on the I-867B.[178] During the questioning, the noncitizen must be given notice of the charges against him or her on Form I-860, Notice and Order of Expedited Removal, and must be given the opportunity to respond to those charges in his or her sworn statement.[179]

Following the questioning and recording of the noncitizen's statement, the inspector is required by regulation to read (or have read) to the noncitizen his or her statement.[180] The noncitizen must sign and initial each page of the statement and each correction.[181] After supervisory approval, the officer then serves the Form I-860 on the individual.[182] Interpretative assistance must be used if necessary to communicate with the noncitizen.[183]

---

[175] *See, e.g., Torres v. Ridge*, No. C04-525JCC, Stipulation to Dismiss Pl's. Mot. for a TRO (W.D. Wash. Apr. 13, 2004).

[176] 62 Fed. Reg. 10318, *supra* note 168.

[177] *See* 8 CFR §§235.3(b)(2)(i), 1235.3(b)(2)(i) (2014).

[178] 8 CFR §§235.3(b)(2)(i), 1235.3(b)(2)(i) (2014); IFM, *supra* note 111, at chapter 17.15(b)(2).

[179] 8 CFR §§235.3(b)(2)(i), 1235.3(b)(2)(i) (2014).

[180] 8 CFR §§235.3(b)(2)(i), 1235.3(b)(2)(i) (2014).

[181] 8 CFR §§235.3(b)(2)(i), 1235.3(b)(2)(i) (2014).

[182] 8 CFR §§235.3(b)(2)(i), 1235.3(b)(2)(i) (2014).

[183] 8 CFR §§235.3(b)(2)(i), 1235.3(b)(2)(i) (2014).

After consultation with nongovernmental organizations and the Office of the United Nations High Commissioner for Refugees (UNHCR), legacy INS included the following information on the I-867A, directed specifically to potential asylum-seekers:

> You do not appear to be admissible or to have the legal papers authorizing your admission to the United States. This may result in your being denied admission and immediately returned to your home country without a hearing. If a decision is made to refuse your admission into the United States, you may be immediately removed from this country, and if so, you may be barred from re-entry for a period of 5 years or longer.
>
> This may be your only opportunity to present information to me and the Immigration and Naturalization Service to make a decision. It is very important that you tell me the truth. If you lie or give misinformation, you may be subject to criminal or civil penalties, or barred from receiving immigration benefits or relief now or in the future.
>
> Except as I will explain to you, you are not entitled to a hearing or review.
>
> *U.S. law provides protection to certain persons who face persecution, harm or torture upon return to their home country. If you fear or have a concern about being removed from the United States or about being sent home, you should tell me so during this interview because you may not have another chance. You will have the opportunity to speak privately and confidentially to another officer about your fear or concern. That officer will determine if you should remain in the United States and not be removed because of that fear.*[184]

- **Practice Pointer**: Practitioners and organizations working with refugees and asylum-seekers across the country report that this information often is never read to the individual being screened. In other cases, it is not read to the individual in a language that he or she can understand. This is one of the many CBP screening problems that seem to be systemic in nature, preventing meritorious asylum claims from ever being heard.[185]

The I-867B requires the inspector to ask a series of questions regarding the noncitizen's fear of return to his or her home country. As noted above, interpretative assistance must be used if necessary to communicate with the noncitizen.[186] NGOs have expressed concern that, at some ports of entry, individuals are not afforded sufficient privacy to ensure confidentiality during the secondary inspection process. The questions that follow appear on the I-867B and were developed by legacy INS in consultation with nongovernmental organizations and UNHCR:

---

[184] Form I-867A (emphasis added). As noted above, this information must be read to *every* noncitizen subject to expedited removal.

[185] AILA Complaint on Inadequate CBP Screening Practices, *supra* note 117.

[186] 8 CFR §§235.3(b)(2)(i), 1235.3(b)(2)(i) (2014).

- Why did you leave your home country or country of last residence?
- Do you have any fear or concern about being returned to your home country or being removed from the United States?
- Would you be harmed if you are returned to your home country or country of last residence?
- Do you have any questions or is there anything else you would like to add?[187]

    - **Practice Pointer**: Practitioners and organizations working with refugees and asylum-seekers across the country also report that these questions often are never asked during the screening, or are not asked in a language that the individual can understand. Moreover, practitioners and organizations report anecdotal evidence that CBP officers often record incorrect answers that were never given by the individual, or coerce the individual into changing his or her answers. Unfortunately, these screening problems also seem to be systemic in nature, preventing meritorious asylum claims from ever being heard.[188]

If a fear or concern is expressed during questioning, immigration inspectors have been instructed to ask follow-up questions to ascertain the general nature of the fear or concern.[189] If the noncitizen indicates an intention to apply for asylum or a fear of persecution or torture, the inspecting officer shall not proceed further with removal and must refer the individual to an asylum officer for a credible fear interview.[190] The inspecting officer will not actually enter a removal order until the credible fear process is completed.

Inspectors have been instructed to consider both verbal and nonverbal cues given by the noncitizen.[191] Moreover, inspectors have been advised to "*not* go into detail on the nature of the [noncitizen's] fear of persecution or torture" and to "leave that for the asylum officer."[192] The IFM emphasizes the screening versus adjudicatory nature of the inspector's role in the expedited removal process. It states:

In determining whether to refer the alien, inspectors should not make eligibility determinations or weigh the strength of the claims, nor should they make credibility determinations concerning the alien's statements. The inspector should err on the side

---

[187] Form I-867B.

[188] AILA Complaint on Inadequate CBP Screening Practices, *supra* note 117; Human Rights First on Preventing Abuse at the Border, *supra* note 117; Am. Immigration Council on Inaction Over CBP Abuses, *supra* note 117; Am. Immigration Council on Mexican and Central American Asylum Claims, *supra* note 117.

[189] Memorandum from Immigration and Naturalization Serv., C. Sale, IIRAIRA Wire #25 at ¶7 (Mar. 31, 1997), *published on* AILA InfoNet Doc. No. 97033192 (*posted* Mar. 31, 1997).

[190] 8 CFR §§235.3(b)(2)(i), 235.3(b)(4), 1235.3(b)(2)(i), 1235.3(b)(4) (2014); IFM, *supra* note 111, at chapter 17.15(b)(2).

[191] *See* IFM, *supra* note 111, at chapter 17.15(d).

[192] *Id.* at chapter 17.15(b)(2) (emphasis added).

of caution and apply the criteria generously, referring to the asylum officer any questionable cases, including cases which might raise a question about whether the alien faces persecution. Do not make any evaluation as to the merits of such fear; that is the responsibility of the asylum officer. Immigration officers processing aliens for expedited removal may contact the asylum office point(s) of contact when necessary to obtain guidance on questionable cases involving an expression of fear or a potential asylum claim.[193]

Moreover, inspectors have been advised that individuals expressing a fear based on personal disputes, domestic violence, sexual and child abuse, child custody problems, coercive marriage or family planning practices, female genital mutilation, AIDS, land or money disputes, whistleblowing, and witnessing crimes may be eligible for asylum and should be referred to an asylum officer.[194] According to the field manual:

All officers should recognize that sometimes unusual cases have been found eligible for asylum that may not have initially appeared to relate to the five grounds contained in the definition of refugee … . Do not make judgment decisions concerning any fear of persecution, torture, or return. If in doubt, refer to an asylum officer for a determination. Any alien who by any means indicates a fear of persecution or return **may not** be removed from the United States until the alien has been interviewed by an asylum officer.[195]

Note, however, that in 2013, CBP announced that it would be discontinuing use of the IFM and that the manual would be replaced with the new "Officer's Reference Tool."[196] CBP has confirmed that the Officer's Reference Tool will not be made available to the public due to its designation as "Law Enforcement Sensitive."[197] Therefore, information from the IFM is no longer authoritative, but may serve as useful guidance for potential CBP interpretations.

- **Practice Pointer**: Frequent reports across the country indicate that CBP officers often inappropriately step into the role of asylum officer, analyzing the merit of the individual's claim and notifying individuals that the fears they have expressed are not grounds for asylum, rather than asking the questions and recording the answers to then refer the individual for an interview before an asylum officer.[198]

A copy of the I-867A and B is (or should be) given to each asylum-seeker referred for a credible fear interview.

---

[193] *Id.* at chapter 17.15(b)(2).

[194] *Id.* at chapter 17.15(d).

[195] *Id.* (emphasis in original).

[196] *See* AILA Practice Alert, *supra* note 114.

[197] *Id.*

[198] AILA Complaint on Inadequate CBP Screening Practices, *supra* note 117.

➤ **Practice Pointer**: It is important to obtain and review the I-867A and B forms with the asylum-seeker prior to a credible or reasonable fear interview, IJ review of the asylum officer's fear determination, or IJ hearing on the merits of the asylum, withholding, and/or CAT claim. Statements or responses contained on the I-867A and B have been used increasingly for impeachment purposes at asylum hearings.[199] Under the REAL ID Act of 2005, a trier of fact may base a credibility determination on any prior statements made by an applicant.[200] If the asylum-seeker does not have a copy of the I-867A and B, one may be obtained through a Freedom of Information Act request or an informal request from the asylum office or DHS office of chief counsel.

➤ **Practice Pointer**: The I-867A/B are almost always made part of the record of proceedings. Practitioners should object to their admission, especially if there is conflicting or otherwise damaging information contained in the forms. Practitioners may argue that these statements are inherently unreliable given the context in which they are recorded, as well as the widely recognized misconduct and violations by CBP officers in conducting these screenings and completing these statements. Practitioners also should review the regulations for the preparation of the I-867A/B and raise any regulatory violations as authority for keeping these documents out of the record as unreliable. Practitioners also may cite the respondent's inability to cross-examine the officer who produced the I-867A/B; therefore, its admission would violate INA §240(b)(4)(B). Though these documents typically are admitted, courts have made exceptions when circumstances indicate a lack of

---

[199] *See, e.g.*, *Xiao v. Mukasey*, 547 F.3d 712, 717 (7th Cir. 2008) (despite applicant's explanation that she felt shame about her forced abortion and therefore did not mention it at her airport or credible fear interviews, court upheld negative asylum decision based on this discrepancy); *Chatta v. Mukasey*, 523 F.3d 748, 752 (7th Cir. 2008) (upholding asylum denial by IJ based on discrepancy between minor's airport statements and testimony at hearing); *Simo v. Gonzales*, 445 F.3d 7, 12–13 (1st Cir. 2006) (upholding the BIA's adverse credibility finding based on inconsistencies between applicant's airport interview and hearing testimony); *Guan v. Gonzales*, 432 F.3d 391, 395–96 (2d Cir. 2005) (finding that the IJ and the BIA adverse credibility findings were based on substantial evidence insofar as they relied on inconsistencies between the applicant's airport interview and testimony before the IJ); *Zheng v. Gonzales*, 160 Fed. Appx. 501, 504 (7th Cir. 2005) (upholding IJ's adverse credibility determination, which relied on statements applicant made at the airport and during the credible fear interview, and which contradicted his testimony in immigration court); *Balogun v. Ashcroft*, 374 F.3d 492 (7th Cir. 2004) (upheld IJ's negative credibility determination based on discrepancies between airport statement and testimony); *Ramsameachire v. Ashcroft*, 357 F.3d 169 (2d Cir. 2004) (finding the BIA did not err in basing adverse credibility determination on inconsistencies between airport statement and testimony at removal hearing); *but see Mohamed v. Gonzales*, 312 Fed. Appx. 126, 128 (9th Cir. 2005) (finding IJ could not base an adverse credibility determination on false statements an applicant made during an airport interview regarding which countries he passed through to get to the United States because this inconsistency did not go to the heart of the asylum claim).

[200] INA §208(b)(1)(B); 8 USC §1158(b)(1)(B) (2012).

trustworthiness. As noted by *Matter of Barcenas*, 19 I&N Dec. 609 (BIA 1988), documentary evidence may only be admitted in immigration court if it is probative and if its use is fundamentally fair — admission and reliance upon the I-867A/B often is not.

Advocates and organizations have questioned the reliability of these sworn statements taken upon entry.[201] For example, the U.S. Commission on International Religious Freedom's Study on Asylum Seekers in Expedited Removal has documented the unreliability of the sworn statements taken during secondary inspection and on credible fear forms completed by asylum officers. The Study has produced a Fact Sheet[202] that it provided to Executive Office for Immigration Review (EOIR) and which was posted on EOIR's internal virtual law library.

- **Practice Pointer**: Practitioners should introduce the U.S. Commission on International Religious Freedom's fact sheet into evidence in cases in which the inspection statement and/or credible fear interview statement are at issue.[203]

Despite years of studies of the expedited removal process, these screening problems indicating unreliability of sworn statements upon inspection are ongoing. In 2014, the American Immigration Lawyers Association, along with other organizations who work with refugees and asylum-seekers, filed a formal complaint with the DHS Office of Civil Rights and Civil Liberties regarding unlawful screening actions by CBP officers, which result in the denial of access to the asylum system to bona fide refugees.[204]

The courts also have considered the reliability of statements made during secondary inspection.[205] The U.S. Court of Appeals for the Second Circuit, for example, has developed a four-part test to determine the reliability of an airport or other port of entry statement given by an asylum-seeker. The court noted that an adjudicator may take into account:

---

201 AILA Complaint on Inadequate CBP Screening Practices, *supra* note 117; Human Rights First on Preventing Abuse at the Border, *supra* note 117; Am. Immigration Council on Inaction Over CBP Abuses, *supra* note 117; Am. Immigration Council on Mexican and Central American Asylum Claims, *supra* note 117.

202 *See* U.S. Comm'n on Int'l Religious Freedom (USCIRF) Fact Sheet, *Findings concerning Forms I-867 and I-870 from USCIRF Study on Asylum Seekers in Expedited Removal* (Feb. 8, 2005) [hereinafter USCIRF Fact Sheet on Expedited Removal Forms], *available at www.uscirf.gov/index.php?option =comcontent&task=view&id=1892*.

203 *Id.*

204 AILA Complaint on Inadequate CBP Screening Practices, *supra* note 117.

205 *See Qing Hua Lin v. Holder*, 736 F.3d 343 (4th Cir. 2013); *Pouhova v. Holder*, 726 F.3d 1007 (7th Cir. 2013); *Ramsameachire v. Ashcroft*, 357 F.3d 169, 179–80 (2d Cir. 2004); *Balasubramanrim v. INS*, 143 F.3d 157, 164 (3d Cir. 1998); *see also Guan v. Gonzales*, 432 F.3d at 396 (finding that airport interview could be used to support adverse credibility finding where: (1) remarks were transcribed verbatim; (2) questions posed gave ample opportunity to describe persecution; (3) there was no indication of reluctance to reveal information; and (4) there was no evidence of translation problems).

(1) whether the record of the interview merely summarizes or paraphrases the applicant's statements rather than providing a verbatim account or transcript;

(2) whether the questions posed to the applicant seem designed to elicit details of an asylum claim;

(3) whether the applicant appears to have been reluctant to reveal information to immigration officials because of prior interrogation sessions or other coercive experiences in his or her home country; and

(4) whether the applicant's answers to the questions posed suggest that the applicant did not understand English or the translations provided by the interpreter.[206]

The Third, Fourth, and Seventh Circuits also have relied on similar factors in determining the reliability of sworn statements taken during CBP screening interviews.[207]

- **Practice Pointer**: Sometimes clients or their family members contact attorneys or representatives prior to crossing the border or arriving at a port of entry to seek asylum. Given all of the hurdles that asylum-seekers must jump with CBP to even get to the credible fear stage, practitioners should prepare an I-589 and G-28 in advance and provide those to the asylum-seekers before they seek entry to the United States. Practitioners should advise their clients to present these documents upon apprehension and to communicate their desire to seek asylum and fear of return. Otherwise, they may be improperly returned pursuant to expedited removal. Practitioners also should advise clients who are considering entry to seek asylum that they are likely to be detained, perhaps even for several months, given recent detention policies.

3. *Final Order*

If the noncitizen does not express a fear of return or a desire to apply for asylum, withholding of removal, or CAT relief, has not established that he or she has a valid entry document, and has not been permitted to withdraw his or her application for admission, the immigration officer will issue a final order of removal after it has been reviewed and approved by a supervisory immigration officer.[208] The individual is not entitled to a hearing before an IJ or to an appeal to the Board of Immigration Appeals (BIA).[209] Upon issuance of a final order, the noncitizen must be detained unless the attorney general determines that parole is necessary to meet a medical emergency or a legitimate law enforcement objective.[210]

---

206 *Ramsameachire v. Ashcroft*, 357 F.3d at 179–80; *see also Guan v. Gonzales*, 432 F.3d at 396.

207 *See Qing Hua Lin v. Holder*, 736 F.3d 343 (4th Cir. 2013); *Pouhova v. Holder*, 726 F.3d 1007 (7th Cir. 2013); *Balasubramanrim v. INS*, 143 F.3d 157, 164 (3d Cir. 1998).

208 8 CFR §§235.3(b)(7), 1235.3(b)(7) (2014).

209 8 CFR §§235.3(b)(2)(ii), 1235.3(b)(2)(ii) (2014).

210 8 CFR §§235.3(b)(2)(iii), 1235.3(b)(2)(iii) (2014).

➢ **Practice Pointer**: Practitioners should discuss the CBP screening process thoroughly with their clients and identify any abuses or screening errors. These abuses and errors should be reported to the AILA National Asylum and Refugee Liaison Committee, which is actively working with other organizations to advocate for solutions to these serious problems in the expedited removal system. Practitioners should fill out a case example form on AILA InfoNet[211] or e-mail *reports@aila.org* with the subject line, "Access to Credible Fear Interviews." Practitioners also should file individual complaints with the DHS Office of Civil Rights and Civil Liberties.[212]

C. Expression of Fear and Form M-444

If a noncitizen expresses a fear of persecution, a fear of torture, a fear of return to his or her home country, or a desire to apply for asylum, the immigration inspector should refer him or her for a credible fear interview with an asylum officer.[213] The immigration officer must provide the noncitizen with Form M-444, Information About Credible Fear Interview, in English or one of the 13 other languages into which the form has been translated.[214] The immigration officer must also explain Form M-444 to the noncitizen in a language he or she understands.[215] The form contains two signature lines, one for the interpreter (if one is used) and the other for the noncitizen to acknowledge receipt.[216]

The form contains information regarding the credible fear interview process, including notice that the asylum-seeker will have the opportunity to be interviewed by a specially trained asylum officer, that he or she may consult with family members, friends, or another representative, and that he or she may contact UNHCR. The form also contains a brief description of the credible fear legal standard, the right to an interpreter, the right to review by an IJ if the asylum officer determines that he or she does not have a credible fear, and the consequences of failing to establish a credible fear of persecution.[217] The asylum-seeker should also be provided with a list of pro bono or nonprofit organizations that provide assistance free of charge in the area where he or she is detained.

---

[211] AILA, *AILA Seeks Examples of CBP Denying Individuals Access to Credible Fear Interviews*, AILA InfoNet Doc. No. 14042941 (*posted* May 16, 2014), *available at www.aila.org/content/default.aspx?docid=48414* (last visited Jan. 9, 2015).

[212] Dep't of Homeland Security, *File a Civil Rights Complaint*, *available at www.dhs.gov/file-civil-rights-complaint* (last visited Jan. 9, 2015).

[213] 8 CFR §235.3(b)(4) (2014).

[214] 8 CFR §235.3(b)(4)(i) (2014). *See also* AILA, *Expedited Removal in a Nutshell*, 16 AILA MONTHLY MAILING 1021 (Dec. 1997).

[215] IFM, *supra* note 111, at chapter 17.15(d)(4).

[216] *Id.*

[217] 8 CFR §§235.3(b)(2)(i), 1235.3(b)(2)(i) (2014).

- **Practice Pointer**: Sometimes, rather than referring an apprehended asylum-seeker to an asylum officer for a credible fear interview, the inspecting officer will issue an expedited removal order and then parole the individual into the United States. Practitioners should contact the local CBP or ICE Enforcement and Removal Operations office to seek a credible fear interview on behalf of their client and/or rescission of the expedited removal order so their client may apply affirmatively for asylum. Usually, when these individuals are released, they are paroled under an Order of Supervision. Practitioners should communicate their client's desire for a credible fear interview to the Immigration and Customs Enforcement officer at the client's first reporting date under his or her Order of Supervision. Practitioners should concurrently contact the local asylum office to make this request.

- **Practice Pointer**: Individuals issued an expedited removal order and then paroled into the United States generally are not able to apply affirmatively for asylum. Under these circumstances, asylum offices will decline to entertain any affirmative asylum application. Instead, the asylum offices are instructed to determine the outcome and status of the credible fear adjudication and whether a charging document was issued but not filed with the Executive Office for Immigration Review.[218] Because such individuals are subject to the expedited removal/credible fear screening process, which has begun but was not completed, the asylum office will not take jurisdiction to hear an affirmative asylum claim. Instead, the asylum office will correct the error by preparing and filing the appropriate charging document with the immigration court.[219]

D. Detention

A noncitizen who is subject to expedited removal or who has been issued a removal order in expedited removal proceedings "shall be detained" pending determination and removal, except that parole is permitted only when DHS officials determine, in the exercise of discretion, that parole is required to meet a medical emergency or is necessary for a legitimate law enforcement objective.[220]

Initially, DHS applied a fairly generous standard for release to individuals subject to expedited removal who had been found by an asylum officer or IJ to have a "credible fear" of persecution. Releasing such individuals enables them to have access to legal counsel and interpreters, evidence, medical and mental health care, and other necessities in preparing and presenting an asylum claim. In the past,

---

[218] U.S. Citizenship and Immigration Servs., Affirmative Asylum Procedures Manual §III.B.3 at 39, *available at www.uscis.gov/sites/default/files/files/nativedocuments/Asylum_Procedures_Manual_2013 .pdf.*

[219] *Id.*

[220] INA §235(b)(1)(B)(ii), (iii)(IV); 8 CFR §§235.3(b)(2)(ii)-(iii), 1235.3(b)(2)(ii)-(iii) (2014).

individuals found to have a credible fear of persecution or torture were eligible for parole if they were able to establish: (1) their identity; (2) community ties; and (3) that they are not subject to any bars to asylum involving violence or misconduct.[221] Nevertheless, in some districts, asylum-seekers found to have a credible fear were denied any opportunity for release.[222]

On November 6, 2007, however, DHS issued a policy memorandum regarding the parole of asylum-seekers who have established a credible fear of persecution or torture.[223] The policy provided that parole decisions would be made on a case-by-case basis for urgent humanitarian reasons or significant public benefit.[224] Those found to have a credible fear would only be considered for parole if they fell within one of the categories set forth in 8 CFR §212.5(b).[225] Those categories included:

(1) individuals with serious medical conditions;

(2) pregnant women;

(3) juveniles;

(4) witnesses in judicial, administrative, or legislative proceedings; and

(5) individuals whose detention is not in the public interest.[226]

DHS would make a threshold assessment regarding whether the asylum-seeker, who had been found to have a credible fear, had established:

(1) his or her identity;

(2) that he or she does not pose a flight risk; and

---

[221] *See* Memorandum from Immigration and Naturalization Serv. Michael Pearson, Expedited Removal, Additional Policy Guidance (Dec. 30, 1997), *published on* AILA InfoNet Doc. No. 97123091 (*posted* Dec. 30, 1997).

[222] *See, e.g.*, U.S. Comm'n on Int'l Religious Freedom (USCIRF), *Expedited Removal Study Report Card: 2 Years Later*, at 5 (Feb. 8, 2007) [hereinafter USCIRF Expedited Removal Report Card], *available at www.uscirf.gov/reports/scorecard_FINAL.pdf* (noting the wide variation in release rates across the country for FY 2003, from 0.5 percent in New Orleans to 98 percent in Harlingen, and that the average detention period for an asylum-seeker found to have a credible fear is 60 days); Lawyers Comm. for Human Rights, *Refugees Behind Bars: The Imprisonment of Asylum Seekers in the Wake of the 1996 Immigration Act* (Aug. 1999), *available at www.humanrightsfirst.org/pubs/descriptions/behindbars.htm*; Lawyers Comm. for Human Rights, *Slamming the Golden Door: A Year of Expedited Removal* (Mar. 1998), *available at www.humanrightsfirst.org/pubs/descriptions/golden.htm*; AILA, *Credible Fear Screening for Individuals in Expedited Removal*, 16 AILA MONTHLY MAILING 1027 (Dec. 1997).

[223] *See* Memorandum from ICE, Parole of Arriving Aliens Found to Have a "Credible Fear" of Persecution or Torture (Nov. 6, 2007), *available at http://bibdaily.com*, and on the "Archive Search" box, type in "New ICE "Credible Fear" Parole Policy.

[224] *Id.* at 4.

[225] *Id.*

[226] 8 CFR §212.5(b) (2014).

(3) he or she is not a danger to the community.[227]

Then DHS would determine whether the individual fell within any of the categories set forth in 8 CFR §212.5(b).[228] With regard to the last category — individuals whose detention is not in the public interest — DHS acknowledged that "the term 'public interest' is not amenable to a single, standard definition" and, therefore, the decision to grant parole on this basis had to be documented by a well-reasoned justification.[229] Almost immediately, human rights and asylum advocates criticized this change in policy.[230]

DHS's 2007 policy has now been superseded by its 2009 policy directive addressing parole of arriving aliens found to have a credible fear of persecution or torture.[231] The current policy directive addresses the fifth regulatory category of individuals who may be considered for parole following a finding of credible fear — those whose detention is not in the public interest.[232] The policy directive states that "[p]arole remains an inherently discretionary determination entrusted to the agency; this directive serves to guide the exercise of that discretion."[233] It specifies the standard for release and procedures for considering parole eligibility. According to the 2009 policy directive, an individual found to have a credible fear of persecution or torture should be paroled if the Immigration and Customs Enforcement officer determines that:

(1) the individual's identity is sufficiently established;

(2) he or she does not pose a flight risk;

(3) he or she is not a danger to the community; and

(4) no additional factors weigh against his or her release.[234]

Under the current policy, as soon as practicable following a finding of credible fear, the Immigration and Customs Enforcement Field Office with custody of the individual shall provide him or her with the *Parole Advisal and Scheduling*

---

[227] ICE Memorandum, *supra* note 223, at 6.

[228] *Id.* at 6–7.

[229] *Id.* at 7–8.

[230] *See* Letter from Human Rights First to Julie Myers, ICE Assistant Secretary (Nov. 15, 2007), *available at www.humanrightsfirst.info/pdf/071120-asy-hrf-ltr-ice-parole-dir.pdf*; *see also* Letter from USCIRF to DHS Secretary Chertoff, USCIRF Expresses Concern to DHS Over New Policy Directive on Asylum Seekers (Nov. 15, 2007), *available at www.uscirf.gov/index.php?option=com_content&task=view&id=45&Itemid=47.*

[231] ICE Policy Directive, John Morton, Parole of Arriving Aliens Found to Have a Credible Fear of Persecution or Torture, (Dec. 8, 2009) [hereinafter Morton Policy Directive on Credible Fear], AILA InfoNet at Doc. No. 09121760 (*posted* Dec. 17, 2009), *available at www.ice.gov/doclib/dro/pdf/11002.1-hd-parole_of_arriving_aliens_found_credible_fear.pdf.*

[232] 8 CFR §212.5(b) (2014).

[233] Morton Policy Directive on Credible Fear, *supra* note 231, at 2.

[234] *Id.* at 6.

Notification and explain the contents to him or her, through an interpreter if necessary.[235] The officer will then complete the relevant portions of the notification, indicating the time when the individual will receive an initial interview on his or her eligibility for parole and the due date and instructions for submitting any documentary evidence the individual may wish the officer to consider.[236] No later than seven days following a finding that the individual has a credible fear, an Immigration and Customs Enforcement officer must conduct an interview with the individual to assess his or her eligibility for parole.[237] Within that same time period, the officer must complete the *Record of Determination/Parole Determination Worksheet* and submit it for supervisory review.[238]

The parole decision must be provided in writing to the individual within seven days of the parole interview. If the officer concludes that parole should be denied, the officer must draft a letter explaining the reasons for denying parole and notifying the individual that he or she may request redetermination of parole based on changed circumstances or additional evidence relevant to his or her identity, security risk, or risk of absconding.[239] The officer must provide that letter, along with the completed *Record of Determination/Parole Determination Worksheet* to the Field Office Director, Deputy Field Office Director, or Assistant Field Office Director for signature.[240] The written response is then provided to the individual or, if represented, his or her legal representative.[241] On the other hand, if the officer determines that parole should be granted, the individual will be provided with a date-stamped I-94 bearing the notation,

> "Paroled under 8 CFR §212.5(b). Employment authorization not to be provided on this basis."[242]

The individual may present a written request for redetermination of any decision denying parole and the ICE Field Office may consider such requests in its discretion.[243]

Since issuance of its 2009 policy directive, however, DHS increasingly has exercised its discretion not to release individuals found to have a credible fear of persecution and torture. For example, in the summer and fall of 2014, in an effort to deter future border-crossers, the Obama administration increased its detention of

[235] *Id.* at 5–6.

[236] *Id.* at 6.

[237] *Id.*

[238] *Id.*

[239] *Id.*

[240] *Id.*

[241] *Id.* at 9.

[242] *Id.*

[243] *Id.*

women and children asylum-seekers, refusing parole outright and opposing any release from detention, even after credible fear of persecution or torture had been demonstrated, arguing that they posed a national security risk under *Matter of D–J–*.[244] The administration even initiated the controversial building of a new family detention center to house up to 2,400 people in Dilley, TX, in anticipation of 2015 border-crossers.[245] This facility is now open and operating.[246]

> **Practice Pointer**: If a client is not paroled following a credible fear finding, practitioners should seek bond before the IJ in INA §240 proceedings.[247] For a detailed discussion of detention of asylum-seekers and strategies for seeking their release, see chapter 9 of this book.

E. Credible Fear Standards and Procedures

The purpose of the credible fear screening is to ensure access to a full hearing for all individuals who might qualify for asylum or protection under the CAT. Congress crafted the credible fear standard and process to prevent the removal of bona fide refugees to situations of persecution and torture during the expedited removal process and to ensure compliance with U.S. obligations under domestic and international law.[248] As one commentator noted, "Essentially, the asylum officer is applying a threshold screening standard to decide whether an asylum [or torture] claim holds enough promise that it should be heard through the regular, full process or whether, instead, the person's removal should be effected through the expedited process."[249]

---

[244] *See Matter of D–J–*, 23 I&N Dec. 572 (A.G. 2003).

[245] *See* ICE Press Release, *supra* note 42; Preston, *supra* note 42.

[246] AILA has joined forces with the Catholic Legal Immigration Network, the American Immigration Council, and RAICES to implement a pro bono project to represent the families detained in Dilley. For information on how to volunteer with this project, see AILA, *CARA Family Detention Pro Bono Project* (Mar. 18, 2015), *available at* AILA InfoNet Doc. No. 14100656 *and at www.aila.org/practice/pro-bono/find-your-opportunity/cara-family-detention-pro-bono-project.*

[247] *Matter of X–K–*, 23 I&N Dec. 731 (BIA 2005) (rejecting DHS's argument that an IJ could not conduct a bond hearing for an individual who entered without inspection, was placed in expedited removal, and was later referred for INA §240 proceedings).

[248] 142 Cong. Rec. S11491 (Sept. 27, 1996) (statement of Sen. Hatch), *available at www.gpo.gov/fdsys/pkg/CREC-1996-09-27/pdf/CREC-1996-09-27-pt1-PgS11491-2.pdf#page=1* ("The standard…is intended to be a low screening standard for admission into the usual full asylum process."). *See also* Inspection and Expedited Removal of Aliens; Detention and Removal of Aliens; Conduct of Removal Proceedings; Asylum Procedures, 62 Fed. Reg. 10312 (Mar. 6, 1997) (describing the nature of the credible fear standard as a screening mechanism that sets "a low threshold of proof of potential entitlement to asylum; many aliens who have passed the credible fear standard will not ultimately be granted asylum"); Regulations Concerning the Convention Against Torture, 64 Fed. Reg. 8479 (Feb. 19, 1999) (stating that the torture standard was designed to "ensure that no alien is removed from the United States under circumstances that would violate Article 3 [of the Convention Against Torture] without unduly disrupting the issuance and execution of removal orders consistent with Article 3").

[249] Bo Cooper, *Procedures for Expedited Removal and Asylum Screening under the Illegal Immigration Reform and Immigrant Responsibility Act of 1996*, 29 CONN. L. REV. 1501, 1503 (1997).

In order to qualify for a hearing before an IJ, an individual who has expressed a fear of persecution or a desire to apply for asylum must establish—in an interview conducted by an asylum officer—that he or she has a "credible fear of persecution."[250] Credible fear of persecution under the INA means that there is:

> [A] *significant possibility*, taking into account the credibility of the statements made by the [individual] in support of [his or her] claim and other such facts as are known to the officer, that the [individual] could establish eligibility for asylum under [INA §] 208.[251]

In other words, the applicant must demonstrate a significant possibility that he or she could establish a reasonable possibility of suffering persecution on account of a protected characteristic if returned to his or her home country.

An individual who indicates a fear of torture upon return to his or her home country will also be referred for a credible fear interview to determine whether he or she has a credible fear of torture.[252] To demonstrate a credible fear of torture, the applicant must show a significant possibility that he or she is eligible for withholding of removal or deferral of removal under the Convention Against Torture, pursuant to 8 CFR §208.16 or 8 CFR §208.17.[253] In other words, the applicant must show a significant possibility that he or she could establish that it is more likely than not he or she would be tortured upon removal to his or her home country.

Asylum officers have exclusive jurisdiction to make credible fear determinations and IJs have exclusive jurisdiction to review those determinations.[254] U.S. Citizenship and Immigration Services' Office of Refugee, Asylum and International Operations, which revised its Asylum Division Officer Training Course lesson plan on credible fear in February of 2014, instructs that "the credible fear 'significant possibility' standard of proof can be best understood as requiring that the applicant 'demonstrate a *substantial and realistic possibility* of succeeding,' but not requiring the applicant to show that he or she is more likely than not going to succeed before an immigration judge."[255] USCIS explains:

> A claim that has no possibility, or only a minimal or mere possibility, of success, would not meet the "significant possibility" standard. While a mere

---

[250] INA §235(b)(1)(B)(v); 8 USC §1225(b)(1)(B)(v) (2012) (emphasis added).

[251] INA §235(b)(1)(B)(v); 8 USC §1225(b)(1)(B)(v) (2012) (emphasis added).

[252] *See* 8 CFR §§208.30, 1208.30 (2014). For discussion of relief under the Convention Against Torture, see chapter 4.

[253] 8 CFR §208.30(e)(3) (2014).

[254] 8 CFR §§208.30(a), 1208.30(a) (2014).

[255] USCIS Credible Fear Training, *supra* note 70, at 15 (quoting Memorandum from Joseph E. Langlois, Asylum Division, Office of International Affairs on Increase of Quality Assurance Review for Positive Credible Fear Determinations and Release of Updated Asylum Officer Basic Training Course Lesson Plan, Credible Fear of Persecution and Torture Determinations (Apr. 17 2006)). The revised lesson plan is also available on AILA InfoNet at Doc. No. 14041846 (*posted* Apr. 18, 2014).

possibility of success is insufficient to meet the credible fear standard, the "significant possibility" standard does not require the applicant to demonstrate that the chances of success are more likely than not.[256]

In evaluating whether the applicant's claims meet the significant possibility standard for persecution claims, asylum officers are instructed to consider all elements of asylum eligibility,[257] including:

- Past persecution — there must be a significant possibility the applicant can establish that the harm he or she experienced was sufficiently severe to amount to persecution;
- Well-founded fear of persecution — if the applicant does not claim to have suffered any past harm, there must be a significant possibility the applicant can establish a well-founded fear of persecution that is both subjectively genuine and objectively reasonable;[258]
- Nexus and the motivations of the persecutor — there must be a significant possibility the applicant can establish that the persecutor was motivated to harm him or her on account of his or her race, religion, nationality, membership in a particular social group, or political opinion; and
- Persecutor — there must be a significant possibility the applicant can establish that the persecutor is either an agent of the government or an entity that the government is unable or unwilling to control.

If the applicant demonstrates a credible fear with respect to any country of proposed removal, regardless of citizenship or habitual residence and regardless whether he or she holds multiple citizenship or nationalities, the applicant must be referred to the IJ for a full hearing since he or she may be eligible for withholding of removal with respect to that country.[259]

---

[256] *Id.* at 14.

[257] *Id.* at 22–33.

[258] The applicant must show a significant possibility that he or she can meet the four-part *Matter of Mogharrabi* test, including possession of a protected characteristic, the persecutor's awareness that the applicant possesses a protected characteristic, the persecutor's capability to persecute the applicant, and the persecutor's inclination to persecute the applicant. *See Matter of Mogharrabi*, 19 I&N Dec. 439 (BIA 1987). Other factors relevant to the well-founded fear analysis include: any pattern or practice of persecution against persons similarly situated to the applicant; persecution of individuals closely related to the applicant, threats against the applicant, whether the applicant remained in the country after threats or harm, whether the applicant voluntarily returned to the country of feared persecution, and whether the applicant could safely and reasonably relocate internally within the country of feared persecution. *See supra* chapter 2 for a detailed discussion of the legal standards for establishing a well-founded fear of persecution.

[259] *See* USCIS Credible Fear Training, *supra* note 70, at 33–34.

In evaluating whether the applicant's claims meet the significant possibility standard for torture claims, asylum officers are instructed to consider all elements of the definition of torture and eligibility for CAT protection,[260] including:

- Intent — there must be a significant possibility the applicant can establish that the torture specifically intends to inflict severe physical or mental pain or suffering;
- Severe pain or suffering — there must be a significant possibility the applicant can establish that the harm constitutes severe pain or suffering;
- Government official — there must be a significant possibility the applicant can establish that the torturer is a public official or other person acting in an official capacity, or someone acting at the instigation of or with the consent or acquiescence of a public official or someone acting in official capacity;
- Custody or control — there must be a significant possibility the applicant can establish that he or she would be in the torturer's custody or physical control;
- Lawful sanctions — there must be a significant possibility the applicant can establish that the torture does not include pain or suffering arising only from, inherent in, or incidental to lawful sanctions;[261]
- Future harm — there must be a significant possibility the applicant can establish it is more likely than not he or she will be tortured in the future (past torture is strong evidence in support of a claim for protection based on future torture);[262] and
- Internal relocation — there must be a significant possibility the applicant can establish he or she could not safely and reasonably relocate to another part of his or her country.[263]

The statutory bars to asylum and withholding of removal do not apply and evidence that the applicant is or may be subject to a bar to asylum or withholding of removal has no impact on the asylum officer's credible fear finding.[264] Asylum officers, however, are instructed to "elicit and make note of all information relevant to whether or not a bar to asylum or withholding applies."[265] Officers should elicit information about whether the applicant:

- Participated in the persecution of others;
- Has been convicted by a final judgment of a particularly serious crime and constitutes a danger to the community;
- Is a danger to the security of the United States;

---

[260] *Id.* at 34–41.

[261] *See* 8 CFR §208.18 (2014) (defining torture).

[262] *See* 8 CFR §208.16 (2014) (establishing eligibility for CAT protection).

[263] *See id.*

[264] 8 CFR §208.30(e)(5) (2014).

[265] *See* USCIS Credible Fear Training, *supra* note 70, at 42.

- Is subject to the inadmissibility or deportability grounds relating to terrorist activity;
- Has committed a serious nonpolitical crime;
- Is a dual or multiple national who can avail himself or herself of the protection of a third state; and
- Was firmly resettled in another country prior to arriving in the United States.[266]

Ultimately, the IJ is responsible for determining whether one of the bars applies and the applicant is barred from receiving asylum or withholding of removal.[267]

The Office of Refugee, Asylum and International Operations announced in 2014 its release of the new lesson plan on credible fear for its Asylum Division Officer Training Course.[268] The lesson plan contains significant changes from the 2006 version and, as a result, USCIS Asylum Division Headquarters staff traveled to each asylum office to provide training on this revised lesson plan.[269] Legal scholars and advocates criticized these 2014 changes as unlawfully heightening the standard of proof for demonstrating a credible fear of persecution and torture.[270] These scholars and advocates reason that, although the revised lesson plan still defines the standard as a "significant possibility" of persecution or torture and includes much of the same language as the 2006 lesson plan, it deletes several references to the legislative history emphasizing the screening purpose of credible fear interviews.

For example, in explaining the function of the credible fear screening, the 2006 lesson plan provided that the "significant possibility" standard is intended to be "a

---

[266] *See* INA §§208(b)(2), 241(b)(3). Note that the safe third country and firm resettlement bars do not apply to withholding or deferral of removal. *See* INA §241(b)(3).

[267] *See supra* chapter 2 for a detailed discussion of the bars to asylum and withholding of removal.

[268] Memorandum from John Lafferty, Chief of Asylum Division, USCIS on Release of Updated Asylum Division Officer Training Course (ADOTC) Lesson Plan, *Credible Fear of Persecution and Torture Determinations* (Feb. 28, 2014) [Lafferty Mem. on Updated ADOTC Training], AILA InfoNet Doc. No. 14041845 (*posted* Apr. 18, 2014), *available at www.aila.org/content/default.aspx?docid=48256* (last visited Jan. 17. 2015).

[269] *Id.*

[270] *See, e.g.*, Sign-On Letter to John Lafferty, Chief of USCIS Asylum Division (June 16, 2014), posted on AILA InfoNet Jan. 13, 2015 at AILA Doc. No. 15011315, *available at www.aila.org/content/default.aspx?docid=51215*; Bill Ong Hing Memorandum to John Lafferty, Chief, USCIS Asylum Division Concerning Lesson Plan, Credible Fear of Persecution and Torture Determinations [hereinafter Hing Response to Lafferty Mem. on Credible Fear] (Apr. 21, 2014), *available at http://static.squarespace.com/static/50b1609de4b054abacd5ab6c/t/53558353e4b02071f74ee3c4/1398113107754/Response%20to%20USCIS%20Credible%20Fear%20Memo,%20Bill%20Hing,%2004.21.2014.pdfhttp:/static.squarespace.com/static/50b1609de4b054abacd5ab6c/t/53558353e4b02071f74ee3c4/1398113107754/Response%20to%20USCIS%20Credible%20Fear%20Memo,%20Bill%20Hing,%2004.21.2014*.pdf; Dree Collopy, *The Revised Credible Fear Lesson Plan: Enough is Enough!*, AILA Leadership Blog, (Apr. 25 ,2014), *available at http://ailaleadershipblog.org/2014/04/25/the-revised-credible-fear-lesson-plan-enough-is-enough/*.

low screening standard for admission into the usual full asylum process."[271] The 2006 lesson plan described the credible fear standard as "a net that will capture all potential refugees and individuals who would be subject to torture if returned to their country of feared persecution or harm. Such a protective net may also capture non-refugees and individuals who may not be subject to torture."[272] The 2006 lesson plan went on to instruct that any questions should be considered in light of the goal of catching all refugees who could qualify and that any reasonable doubt should be resolved in favor of the applicant.[273] The 2014 lesson plan removed all references to Congressional intent, the language describing the "significant possibility" standard as a low threshold standard, and the language describing the credible fear standard as a protective net.[274] The USCIS Asylum Division attributed its revisions to the significant increase in credible fear referrals and the increased allocation of resources it was having to devote to credible fear adjudications.[275] This reasoning, provided in the USCIS Asylum Division's memorandum announcing the release of the 2014 revised lesson plan, certainly seems to support the notion that the credible fear standard has been heightened.

Legal scholars and advocates also criticized the revised structure, tone, and content of the lesson plan as seeming to require an asylum officer to complete a full assessment of the asylum seeker's potential eligibility for asylum or CAT protection.[276] They further state that the revisions also conflate the credible fear standard with the full asylum and CAT standards, often without sufficient explanation and distinction.[277] For example, the 2014 lesson plan vastly expands the substantive explanations of the elements of asylum and CAT eligibility, seeming to require a full analysis of each legal element.[278] Unfortunately, the statistics seem to support these concerns, as the passage rate for credible fear interviews has dropped significantly since the implementation of the new lesson plan in February of 2014.[279]

- ➢ **Practice Pointer**: Practitioners representing clients during credible fear interviews should be prepared to articulate the standard of proof

---

[271] *See* AOBTC Workbook, Credible Fear, *supra* note 23, at 12 (citing a statement by Sen. Orrin Hatch).

[272] *Id.*

[273] *Id.*

[274] USCIS Credible Fear Training, *supra* note 70, at 11–12.

[275] Lafferty Mem. on Updated ADOTC Training, *supra* note 268.

[276] *See, e.g.,* Sign-On Letter to John Lafferty, *supra* note 270; Hing Response to Lafferty Mem. on Credible Fear, *supra* note 270; Collopy, AILA Leadership Blog, *supra* note 270.

[277] *Id.*

[278] USCIS Credible Fear Training, *supra* note 70, at 22–40.

[279] *See* U.S. Citizenship and Immigration Servs., *Credible Fear Workload Report, Summary FY 09-14*, AILA InfoNet Doc. No. 14112500, *available at www.aila.org/content/default.aspx?docid=50821* and *www.uscis.gov/sites/default/files/USCIS/Outreach/Notes%20from%20Previous%20Engagements/Asy-Credible-Reasonable-FearFY14-Q1.pdf* (last visited Dec. 24, 2014).

required for demonstrating a credible fear of persecution or torture and to educate asylum officers on the proper legal standards in advocating for their clients.

In addition to describing the significant possibility standard of proof, the 2014 lesson plan instructs asylum officers in interpreting and applying that standard. The lesson plan instructs that they should:

- Accord the benefit of the doubt to the applicant when there is reasonable doubt regarding the outcome of a credible fear determination;
- Consider whether the case presents novel or unique issues that merit consideration before an IJ;[280]
- Use legal interpretations most favorable to the applicant if there is disagreement among federal courts of appeals or if the claim raises an unresolved issue of law *and* if there is no DHS or Asylum Division policy or guidance on the issue.[281]

The applicant must establish his or her identity with a reasonable degree of certainty. He or she may do so with credible testimony alone if documentary proof of identity or nationality is not available.[282] The applicant also bears the burden of proof to establish a credible fear of persecution or torture. However, "there is a shared aspect of that burden in which asylum officers have an affirmative duty to elicit all information relevant to the legal determination."[283]

The applicant "must produce sufficiently convincing evidence that establishes the facts of the case, and . . . those facts must meet the relevant legal standard."[284] Most individuals subject to expedited removal do not have evidence or documentation corroborating their claimed fears. Given the nature of the credible fear screening process, an applicant may establish a credible fear with testimony alone. The Asylum Division now specifies that testimony alone is sufficient if the testimony is "credible, is persuasive, and refers to specific facts."[285]

---

[280] 8 CFR §208.30(e)(4) (2014).

[281] USCIS Credible Fear Training, *supra* note 70, at 16. In instructing that asylum officers should use legal interpretations most favorable to the applicant if there is disagreement among federal courts of appeals or if the claim raises an unresolved issue of law, the 2006 version of the lesson plan did not specify that this was only the case if there was no DHS or Asylum Division policy or guidance on the issue as the 2014 lesson plan does. Arguably, in making this change to the 2014 lesson plan, DHS is effectively giving itself authority to override circuit court splits and decide unresolved areas of law in the credible fear arena. This could become quite problematic, given the BIA's particular social group test, which has resulted in a circuit court split.

[282] USCIS Credible Fear Training, *supra* note 70, at 16–17.

[283] *Id.* at 12.

[284] *Id.* This evidentiary standard was added in the 2014 revisions to the lesson plan and did not exist in the 2006 lesson plan. Arguably, this implies that every fact must be established by convincing evidence, which is a much higher standard than the standard for a full asylum adjudication — a preponderance of the evidence.

[285] INA §208(b)(1)(B)(ii).

The Asylum Division now applies a three-prong test to determine whether the applicant's testimony is sufficient. It must be:

(1) credible;

(2) persuasive; and

(3) specific.[286]

"Specific facts" refers to actual facts as opposed to statements of belief or opinion. In addition to the applicant's testimony, the asylum officer must take account of "such other facts as are known to the officer," including relevant country conditions information.[287]

Asylum officers must "[take] into account the credibility of the statements made by the alien in support of the alien's claim and such other facts as are known to the officer."[288] In considering credibility, however, asylum officers do not make a final determination as to whether the applicant is credible. Rather, an asylum officer must determine whether the applicant has established that there is a significant possibility that the assertions underlying his or her claim could be found credible in a full asylum or withholding of removal hearing.[289] Asylum officers must consider the totality of the circumstances and all relevant factors, including demeanor, candor, responsiveness, consistency, plausibility, and falsehoods, as well as factors that may contribute to the appearance of a lack of credibility, including trauma the applicant has endured, passage of time since the events, vulnerability, cultural and communication differences, detention of the applicant, interpretation problems or differences in dialect or accent, and unfamiliarity with the phone system and use of an interpreter the applicant cannot see.[290] The Asylum Division states that "[t]he nature of expedited removal and the credible fear interview process — including detention, relatively brief and often telephonic interviews, etc. — further limits the reliability of and ability to evaluate [demeanor, candor, and responsiveness] in the credible fear context."[291]

Asylum officers are specifically instructed to probe inconsistencies between the applicant's statements during the credible fear interview and his or her statements taken by CBP upon apprehension and recorded in the I-867A and B.[292] However, asylum officers are cautioned to keep in mind the circumstances under which those

---

[286] USCIS Credible Fear Training, *supra* note 70, at 13. This three-prong test did not exist in the 2006 lesson plan. Arguably, it is the incorrect standard for credible fear since the test was taken from INA §208(b)(1)(B)(ii), which is the standard for asylum, not credible fear.

[287] INA §235(b)(1)(B)(v); 8 CFR §§208.16(c)(3)(iii)–(iv), 208.30(e)(2) (2014).

[288] INA§235(b)(1)(B)(v).

[289] USCIS Credible Fear Training, *supra* note 70, at 17–18.

[290] *Id.* at 18–20.

[291] *Id.* at 18.

[292] *Id.* at 20.

initial statements were made and to consider: (1) whether the questions posed at the port of entry or place of apprehension were designed to elicit the details of an asylum claim, and whether the immigration officer asked relevant follow-up questions; (2) whether the applicant was reluctant or afraid to reveal information during the first meeting with U.S. officials because of past abuse; and (3) whether the interview was conducted in a language other than the applicant's native language.[293]

While material inconsistencies may lead to denial, minor or trivial inconsistencies are irrelevant in the credible fear context. Moreover, applicants must be given the opportunity to address and explain any inconsistencies.[294] All reasonable explanations must be considered when assessing the applicant's credibility. If, however, the applicant fails to provide a reasonable explanation of the inconsistencies or if there is no significant possibility that he or she could successfully address the inconsistencies before an IJ, the asylum officer may make a negative credibility finding.[295] Asylum officers must specify in the written case analysis the basis for any negative credibility finding, noting any portions of the testimony found not credible, including the specific inconsistencies, lack of detail, or other factors, along with the applicant's explanation and the reason the explanation was deemed not reasonable.[296]

1. Rest Period

An individual who has expressed a fear of persecution or a desire to apply for asylum is allowed at least 48 hours to rest and prepare for the "credible fear" interview while he or she is detained at a DHS detention facility or local jail.[297] The individual may, however, request that the interview be conducted sooner, and the immigration inspector should convey that request to the asylum office.[298]

2. Location

- The "credible fear" interview is conducted at DHS detention facilities, local jails or, in some areas, at DHS district offices.[299]
- The regulations provide that the interview must be "separate and apart from the general public."[300]

---

[293] *Id.* at 21 (citing to *Balasubramanrim v. INS*, 143 F.3d 157 (3d Cir. 1998) and *Ramsameachire v. Ashcroft*, 357 F.3d 169, 179 (2d Cir. 2004)).

[294] *Id.* at 20.

[295] *Id.* at 21.

[296] *Id.* at 21–22.

[297] *See* IFM, *supra* note 111, at chapter 17.15(b)(13).

[298] IFM, *supra* note 111, at chapter 17.15(b)(13).

[299] *See* Inspection and Expedited Removal of Aliens; Detention and Removal of Aliens; Conduct of Removal Proceedings; Asylum Procedures, 62 Fed. Reg. 10319 (Mar. 6, 1997) (supplementary information).

[300] 8 CFR §208.30(d) (2014).

3. *Interviewers*

An asylum officer conducts the credible fear interview.[301] The INA defines an asylum officer as:

> [A]n immigration officer who (i) has had professional training in country conditions, asylum law, and interview techniques comparable to that provided to full time [asylum] adjudicators ... , and (ii) is supervised by an officer who ... has had substantial experience adjudicating asylum applications.[302]

All asylum officers undergo a basic, five-week training course.[303] In addition, all asylum officers conducting credible fear interviews receive specialized training in credible fear and expedited removal procedures.[304] The Asylum Division also conducts periodic quality assurance reviews of asylum officer (AO) decisions to ensure that any problems that arise are corrected.[305]

4. *Interview Procedures*

The AO must conduct the credible fear interview in a non-adversarial manner.[306] At the time of the interview, the AO will verify whether the asylum-seeker received Form M-444, Information About Credible Fear Interview,[307] and whether he or she understands the credible fear determination process.[308] The AO will conduct the interview using Form I-870, Record of Determination/Credible Fear Work Sheet, a five-page worksheet that the officer will complete during the interview. The I-870 requires the AO to read the following information to the asylum-seeker:

The purpose of this interview is to determine whether you may be eligible for asylum or protection from removal to a country where you fear persecution or torture. I am going to ask you questions about why you fear returning to your country or any other country you may be removed to. It is very important that you tell the truth during the interview and that you respond to all of my questions. This may be your only opportunity to give such information. Please feel comfortable telling me why you fear harm. U.S. law has strict rules to prevent the disclosure of what you tell me today about reasons why you fear harm. The information you tell me about the reasons for your fear will not be disclosed to your government, except in exceptional

---

[301] *Id.*

[302] INA §235(b)(1)(E); 8 USC §1225(b)(1)(E) (2012).

[303] U.S. Citizenship and Immigration Servs., Asylum Division Training Programs, *available at www.uscis.gov/humanitarian/refugees-asylum/asylum/asylum-division-training-programs* (last visited Jan. 17, 2015).

[304] *See INS Reports on First Three Months of Expedited Removal*, 74 INTERPRETER RELEASES 1101 (July 21, 1997).

[305] *Id.*

[306] 8 CFR §208.30(d) (2014).

[307] *See* this chapter, at 5.2.3.

[308] 8 CFR §208.30(d) (2014).

circumstances. The statements you make today may be used in deciding your claim and in any future immigration proceedings. It is important that we understand each other. If at any time I make a statement you do not understand, please stop me and tell me you do not understand so that I can explain it to you. If at any time you tell me something that I do not understand, I will ask you to explain.[309]

Throughout the interview, the AO is required to take notes in a question and answer format.[310] The question and answer notes from the credible fear interview "are not required to be a verbatim account of everything said at the interview," and the officer is not required to read the question and answer notes to the applicant as a sworn statement.[311] The officer is required, however, to create a summary of the material facts as stated by the applicant and to review the summary of material facts with the applicant at the end of the interview.[312] The applicant must be given the opportunity to correct any errors in the summary of material facts.[313] In addition to their statements during the interview, an asylum-seeker is permitted to present evidence during the interview, if available.[314]

Following the interview, AOs are required to create a written record of their determination, including the summary, any additional facts upon which they relied, and their determination of whether, in light of such facts, the asylum-seeker has established a credible fear of persecution.[315] Officers must prepare a brief written analysis of the case, including a short summary of the facts relevant to the credible fear determination, as well as a discussion of the reasons supporting the determination.[316] According to a 2008 policy memorandum, "This written analysis will allow the reviewer to determine that the decision was based on neutral, objective factors, and that the law was properly applied."[317]

In 2013, in response to the "surge" in credible-fear interviews and the Asylum Division's resource limitations, the Asylum Division reviewed this policy of requiring written assessments for all credible fear determinations and began a pilot

---

309 Form I-870 at 1.28.

310 *See* Memorandum from Joseph E. Langlois, Chief of Asylum Division on Revised Credible Fear Quality Assurance Review Categories and Procedures 4-5 (Dec. 23, 2008) [hereinafter Langlois Mem. on Revised Quality Assurance Review], available at *www.uscis.gov/sites/default/files/USCIS/Laws/Memoranda/Static_Files_Memoranda/Archives%201998-2008/2008/cf_qa_review_catproc_23dec08.pdf* (last visited Jan. 19, 2015).

311 *Id.* at 4.

312 8 CFR §208.30(d)(6) (2014); Langlois Mem. on Revised Quality Assurance Review, *supra* note 310, at 4–5.

313 8 CFR §208.30(d)(6) (2014).

314 8 CFR §208.30(d)(4) (2014).

315 8 CFR §208.30(e) (2014). *See* Langlois Mem. on Revised Quality Assurance Review, *supra* note 310, at 5.

316 *See* Langlois Mem. on Revised Quality Assurance Review, *supra* note 310, at 5.

317 *Id.*

program in the Houston Asylum Office to replace these written assessments with a credible fear determination checklist.[318] According to the Asylum Division:

> The credible fear determination checklist was designed to capture the same basic analysis currently contained in the brief written assessment, but in a format and manner that reduces the overall time required . . . to make a credible fear determination. Additionally, the credible fear determination checklist was designed to highlight the steps required in the credible fear analysis to allow for a more focused quality assurance review of cases.[319]

It is possible that this checklist eventually will be implemented into other asylum offices' credible fear procedures, depending on the success of the pilot program.

- **Practice Pointer**: A copy of the completed I-870 is available to asylum-seekers and their representatives or consultants. It is important to obtain a copy of the I-870, as well as the AO's written summary from the interview prior to an IJ review or hearing. Statements made by asylum-seekers at the credible fear interview may be and have been used for impeachment purposes.[320] The REAL ID Act of 2005 allows IJs to base credibility determinations on prior statements made by the applicant, whether oral or written, and whether or not they were under oath.[321]

- **Practice Pointer**: The U.S. Commission on International Religious Freedom's Study on Asylum-Seekers in Expedited Removal has documented the unreliability of the sworn statements taken during secondary inspection and credible fear forms completed by asylum officers. The Study has produced a Fact Sheet,[322] which was provided to EOIR and posted on EOIR's internal virtual law library. Practitioners

---

[318] *See* Memorandum from Ted H. Kim, Acting Chief of Asylum Division on Implementation of Credible Fear Determination Checklist Pilot, (Jan. 14, 2013), *available at www.uscis.gov/sites/default/files/USCIS/Outreach/Notes%20from%20Previous%20Engagements/2013/March%202013/Implementation-CF-DeterminationChecklist.pdf.*

[319] *Id.*

[320] *See, e.g.*, *Mohammed v. Att'y Gen.*, 547 F.3d 1340 (11th Cir. 2008) (upholding negative credibility determination based in part on applicant's failure to mention at his credible fear interview that he was held in "the 8" position); *Xiao v. Mukasey*, 547 F.3d 712, 717 (7th Cir. 2008) (despite applicant's explanation that she felt shame about her forced abortion and, therefore, did not mention it at her airport or credible fear interviews, court upheld negative asylum decision based on this discrepancy); *Simo v. Gonzales*, 445 F.3d 7, 12–13 (1st Cir. 2006) (upholding the BIA's adverse credibility finding based on inconsistencies between applicant's airport interview and hearing testimony); *Zheng v. Gonzales*, 160 Fed Appx. 501, 504 (7th Cir. 2005) (upholding IJ's adverse credibility determination that relied on statements applicant made at the airport and during the credible fear interview that contradicted his testimony in immigration court).

[321] INA §208(b)(1)(B); 8 USC §1158(b)(1)(B) (2012).

[322] *See* USCIRF Fact Sheet on Expedited Removal Forms, *supra* note 202.

should introduce the Fact Sheet into evidence in cases in which the credible fear interview statements are at issue.[323]

5. *Role of Attorney, Representative, or Consultant*

The asylum-seeker may consult with a person or persons of his or her choosing prior to the credible fear interview.[324] Such consultation must be at no expense to the government and may not unreasonably delay the process.[325] Any person or persons with whom the asylum-seeker chooses to consult may be present at the interview and may be permitted, in the discretion of the AO, to present a statement at the end of the interview.[326] The AO, in his or her discretion, may place reasonable limits on the number of people present at the interview and on the length of statement or statements made.[327] A consultant may be a relative, friend, clergy person, attorney, or representative.[328] Attorneys or representatives are not required to submit a Form G-28, Notice of Entry of Appearance as Attorney when acting as a consultant during the credible fear interview.[329]

In practice, AOs appear to conduct these interviews in much the same way they conduct affirmative asylum interviews, and allow for consultants to ask follow-up questions, provide documentation, and make closing statements. The Asylum Division encourages the use of consultants in the credible fear process and has noted that they generally facilitate the process and ensure that the asylum applicant's claim is fully elicited.[330]

6. *Interpretation*

If the asylum-seeker is unable to proceed effectively with the interview in English, and if the AO is unable to proceed competently in a language chosen by the asylum-seeker, the AO must arrange for the assistance of an interpreter in conducting the interview.[331] The interpreter may *not* be a representative or employee of the asylum-seeker's country of nationality or, if the asylum-seeker is stateless, his or her country of last habitual residence.[332] In at least one reported case, a federal court reversed a negative credibility determination based, in part, on statements given at a credible

---

[323] *Id.*

[324] INA §235(b)(1)(B)(iv), 8 USC §1225(b)(1)(B)(iv) (2012); 8 CFR §208.30(d)(4) (2014).

[325] INA §235(b)(1)(B)(iv), 8 USC §1225(b)(1)(B)(iv) (2012); 8 CFR §208.30(d)(4) (2014).

[326] 8 CFR §208.30(d)(4) (2014).

[327] *Id.*

[328] USCIS Credible Fear Training, *supra* note 70, at 43.

[329] *Id.*

[330] *See* Memorandum from Joseph Langlois on Role of Consultants in the Credible Fear Interview (Nov. 14, 1997), *available at http://americanimmigrationcouncil.org/sites/default/files/docs/lac/All%20of%20records%2015.pdf.*

[331] 8 CFR §208.30(d)(5) (2014).

[332] *Id.*

fear interview where the AO used an Italian interpreter because an Amharic interpreter was not available.[333] The court found that it was error for the IJ to make a negative credibility determination without first assessing the applicant's Italian language skills.[334]

AOs have also been instructed to accommodate an asylum-seeker's special request for a male or female interpreter and for interpreters who do (or do not) speak certain dialects or have certain accents.[335] Asylum-seekers may also request that the interpreter be physically present at the interview if they would have difficulty presenting their claim through a telephonic interpreter.[336]

The Asylum Division encourages consultants to monitor the quality of the interpretation asylum-seekers receive and permits co-consultants fluent in English and the asylum-seeker's language to attend the credible fear interview.[337] The consultant or co-consultant may interrupt the interview to point out problems with the interpretation.[338] If the interpreter is not competent or not neutral, the AO should ask whether the asylum-seeker or his or her consultant would like to change interpreters.[339] Asylum-seekers may provide their own interpreter, provided that an interpreter from a commercial telephonic service monitors the interpretation.[340]

- **Practice Pointer**: Some applicants may speak unusual languages or dialects, making it difficult for an asylum officer to find an adequate interpreter. Given the regulatory time constraints for credible fear interviews, the asylum officer may ask the applicant if he or she is competent and comfortable to complete the interview in his or her second language. In some cases, if an asylum officer cannot communicate with an applicant and cannot find an adequate interpreter, the officer may exercise his or her discretion to place the applicant in INA §240 proceedings without ever conducting a credible fear interview. The immigration court may have more time to find an adequate interpreter.

7. Dependents

A spouse or unmarried child under age 21 may be included in the credible fear determination of the principal applicant, if the spouse or child arrived in the United States with the principal applicant and if the spouse or child desires to be included in

---

[333] *Ememe v. Ashcroft*, 358 F.3d 446 (7th Cir. 2004).

[334] *Id.* at 453.

[335] *See* Memorandum from Joseph Langlois on Interpreters in the Credible Fear Process (Feb. 10, 1998).

[336] *Id.*

[337] *Id.*

[338] *Id.*

[339] *Id.*

[340] *Id.*

the principal applicant's determination.[341] Any accompanying spouse or child, however, has the right to have his or her credible fear determination made separately, and officers are instructed to question each member of the family to ensure that each family member's right to apply for asylum, withholding of removal, or CAT relief is preserved.[342]

> ➢ **Practice Pointer**: It is essential for practitioners representing families throughout the credible fear process to evaluate each individual for potential asylum eligibility. It is possible that a spouse may have a stronger claim or that a child may have his or her own asylum claim that is unrelated to the parent's. This is becoming more and more common due to the increase in families crossing the border and seeking asylum based on domestic violence. Violence may be experienced differently by each family member. Additionally, family members who were not subject to physical violence may have suffered their own psychological persecution. It is important to recall that parents cannot be included as derivative beneficiaries on a child's asylum claim. Thus, it is essential to explore their own potential claims, which may or may not be related to their child's

> ➢ **Practice Pointer**: Moreover, each individual should be evaluated for potential eligibility for other forms of immigration relief. For example, a spouse may, unknowingly, be a U.S. citizen, or a child may be eligible for Special Immigrant Juvenile Status. Although the credible fear process is related to asylum, withholding of removal, and CAT relief, practitioners' analyses should not be limited to those options.

8. Confidentiality

The same confidentiality requirements that apply in asylum adjudications also apply to credible fear and reasonable fear interviews.[343] Information contained in records pertaining to a credible fear determination "shall not be disclosed without the written consent of the applicant."[344] Additionally, the confidentiality of records indicating that the individual has received a credible fear interview before an asylum officer or credible fear review before an IJ "shall also be protected from disclosure."[345]

---

[341] *See* 8 CFR §§208.30(b), 1208.30(b) (2014); Memorandum from John Lafferty, Chief of Asylum Division on Guidance on Immediate Family Members in Credible Fear (June 27, 2014) [Lafferty Mem. on Immediate Family Members], AILA InfoNet Doc. No. 14100652 (*posted* Oct. 6, 2014), *available at www.uscis.gov/sites/default/files/USCIS/Outreach/Notes%20from%20Previous%20Engagements/2014/MEMO_Guidance_on_Immediate_Family_Members_in_Credible_Fear.pdf.*

[342] USCIS Credible Fear Training, *supra* note 70, at 43.

[343] *See* 8 CFR §§208.6, 1208.6 (2014).

[344] *Id.*

[345] *Id.*

9. Withdrawals

A person may dissolve his or her asylum claim at any time in the process and seek to withdraw his or her application for admission. If such a request is made, an asylum officer will interview the individual and complete a form entitled Request for Dissolution of the Credible Fear Process.[346] Making such a request, however, does not mean the individual will be allowed to withdraw and forego the issuance of an expedited removal order.[347]

10. Asylum Officer's Credible Fear Decision

The AO's decision does not become final until reviewed by a supervisory AO.[348] AOs have been instructed that an applicant who establishes a credible fear of torture, even if he or she does not have a credible fear of persecution (for asylum and withholding purposes), should be referred for a hearing before an IJ.[349]

If the AO determines that the asylum-seeker has a credible fear, the AO will inform the asylum-seeker and issue to him or her Form I-862, Notice to Appear, for full consideration of the asylum, withholding of removal, or CAT claim in proceedings under INA §240.[350] On the other hand, if the asylum-seeker is found *not* to have a credible fear of persecution or torture, the AO will inform the asylum-seeker and issue to him or her Form I-869, Record of Negative Credible Fear Finding, on which the asylum-seeker must indicate whether he or she desires review by an IJ.[351] In the case of a negative credible fear determination, the AO must also issue Form I-860, Notice and Order of Expedited Removal, unless the asylum-seeker is a stowaway.[352]

> ➢ **Practice Pointer**: In the case of a negative credible fear determination, practitioners should consider filing a request for review of the determination with the relevant asylum office, especially if the asylum officer applied the wrong legal or evidentiary standards or made other errors during the credible fear interview. Practitioners should make such requests in writing, setting forth the errors and explaining why the evidence in the record compels the opposite determination.

---

[346] *See* Memorandum from Joseph Langlois on Dissolution of Credible Fear Claims (July 26, 2000).

[347] *See supra* pt. I.C. for a detailed discussion of withdrawals of applications for admission.

[348] 8 CFR §208.30(e)(4) (2014).

[349] *See* Memorandum from Joseph Langlois on Implementation of Amendments to Asylum and Withholding of Removal Regulations, Effective March 22, 1999, at 4 (Mar. 18, 1999). For discussion of relief available to those who fear torture, see chapter 4.

[350] 8 CFR §208.30(f) (2014). See chapter 3.3 for information regarding §240 proceedings.

[351] 8 CFR §208.30(g)(1) (2014).

[352] *Id. See supra* Part I.B.4. for a detailed discussion of the asylum procedures for stowaways.

F. Credible Fear Review by an Immigration Judge

The INA allows for a prompt review of a negative credible fear determination by an IJ.[353] IJs have exclusive jurisdiction to review credible fear determinations.[354] The review must include the opportunity for the asylum-seeker to be heard and questioned by the IJ, either in person or by telephonic or video connection.[355] Credible fear reviews are closed to the public, unless the applicant sates for the record or submits a written statement that he or she is waiving that requirement.[356] The review must be conducted as expeditiously as possible, "to the maximum extent practicable within 24 hours, but in no case later than 7 days after" the negative credible fear determination.[357]

1. Standard of Review

The IJ review is a de novo review of the AO's negative credible fear determination.[358] The IJ must determine:

> [W]hether there is a significant possibility, taking into account the credibility of the statements made by the [asylum-seeker] in support of the [asylum-seeker's] claim and such other facts as are known to the [immigration judge], that the [asylum-seeker] could establish eligibility for asylum [under INA §208], withholding [under INA §241(b)(3)], or withholding under the Convention Against Torture.[359]

The IJ has no authority to review an asylum-seeker's custody status and make a bond or parole determination in the course of reviewing a negative credible fear determination.[360]

2. Procedures

If an asylum-seeker requests review of the AO's negative credible fear determination, the AO will serve the asylum-seeker with Form I-863, Notice of Referral to Immigration Judge.[361] The AO will then file the I-863 with the immigration court, and it is this action that commences the IJ's jurisdiction over the

---

353 INA §235(b)(1)(B)(iii)(III); 8 USC §1225(b)(1)(B)(iii)(III) (2012).

354 8 CFR §§208.30(a), 1208.30(a) (2014).

355 INA §235(b)(1)(B)(iii)(III); 8 USC §1225(b)(1)(B)(iii)(III) (2012).

356 8 CFR §§208.30(g)(2)(iii), 1208.30(g)(2)(iii) (2014).

357 INA §235(b)(1)(B)(iii)(III); 8 USC §1225(b)(1)(B)(iii)(III) (2012). *See* 8 CFR §1003.42(e) (2014); Exec. Office for Immigration Review Memorandum from Michael Creppy, Operating Policies and Procedures Memorandum No. 99-5: Implementation of Article 3 of the UN Convention Against Torture (May 14, 1999) [hereinafter Creppy Mem. 99-5], *available at www.usdoj.gov/eoir/efoia/ocij/oppm99/99_5.pdf.*

358 8 CFR §1003.42(d) (2014).

359 *Id.* For discussion of withholding of removal under the Convention Against Torture, see chapter 4.

360 8 CFR §1003.42(g) (2014).

361 8 CFR §208.30(g)(1)(i) (2014).

matter.[362] The AO also must provide the IJ with the written record of the determination, including copies of the I-863, the AO's notes, the summary of material facts, and other materials on which the negative credible fear determination was based.[363]

Negative credible fear reviews, unlike other IJ hearings, may be reviewed by telephone conference call "*without* the [asylum-seeker's] consent."[364] If the asylum-seeker is detained at the same location as the immigration court (such as a DHS or contract facility), the IJ review will be conducted in person.[365] The IJ may receive into evidence any oral or written statement that is material and relevant to any issue in the review.[366] According to the chief immigration judge, "credible fear review proceedings should *not* be as in-depth as a full asylum hearing."[367]

The IJ is required to record the review and make the recording a part of the record of proceedings.[368] The record of proceedings created by the immigration court, however, "shall *not* be merged with any later proceeding" under INA §240.[369] Once the review is completed, the record of proceeding is "retired."[370]

3. *Role of Attorney, Representative, or Consultant*

According to the expedited removal statute, asylum-seekers may *consult* with persons of their choosing *prior* to any review of the credible fear determination.[371] In a memorandum, the Office of the Chief Immigration Judge (OCIJ) has construed the statutory and regulatory provisions establishing that rule to mean that "[t]here is no right to *representation* prior to or *during* the review."[372] It is within the discretion of the IJ, according to the OCIJ, whether to permit persons with whom the asylum-seeker has consulted even to be "present" at the review.[373] The memorandum further notes that nothing in the statute, regulations, or the memorandum entitles an attorney to make an opening statement, call and question witnesses, cross-examine, object to written evidence, or make a closing argument.[374] For these reasons, according to the OCIJ, there is no need for the attorney or representative to file a Notice of Entry of

---

[362] 8 CFR §1003.42(a) (2014) .

[363] 8 CFR §§208.30(g)(2)(ii), 1208.30(g)(2)(ii), 1003.42(a) (2014).

[364] 8 CFR §1003.25(c) (2014) (emphasis added).

[365] *See* Creppy Mem. 99-5, *supra* note 357, at VI.

[366] 8 CFR §1003.42(c) (2014).

[367] *See* Creppy Mem. 99-5, *supra* note 357, at VI (emphasis added).

[368] *Id.*

[369] 8 CFR §1003.42(b) (2014).

[370] *See* Creppy Mem. 97-3, *supra* note 99, at IV.

[371] *See* INA §235(b)(1)(B)(iv); 8 USC §1225(b)(1)(B)(iv) (2012); *see also* 8 CFR §1003.42(c) (2014).

[372] *See* Creppy Mem. 99-5, *supra* note 357, at VI (emphasis in original).

[373] *Id.* at n.10.

[374] *Id.*

Appearance (Form EOIR-28).[375] As a result of this OCIJ memorandum, some IJs have not allowed attorneys and representatives to participate actively during a negative credible fear review.[376]

- **Practice Pointer**: Practitioners representing clients in expedited removal proceedings should file a motion to authorize counsel with the immigration court. There are three statutory provisions that provide for a client to be represented by counsel during a credible fear review in expedited removal proceedings. First, 5 USC §555(b) provides that any person "compelled to appear in person before an agency or representative thereof is entitled to be accompanied, represented, and advised by counsel, or if permitted by the agency, by other qualified representative." Second, INA §292 provides that "[i]n *any* removal proceedings before an immigration judge . . . the person concerned shall have the privilege of being represented (at no expense to the Government) by such counsel, authorized to practice in such proceedings, as he shall choose." Third, INA §235(b) contains no language limiting or repealing 5 USC §555(b) or INA §292. To the contrary, INA §235(b)'s explanation that "[s]uch review shall include an opportunity for the alien to be heard," arguably includes a right to be heard by counsel.

4. *Interpreters*

The immigration court is required to provide an interpreter if one is necessary.[377] If there is sufficient advance notice, the IJ should order a contract interpreter.[378] Given the expedited nature of the review, the Office of the Chief Immigration Judge anticipated that telephonic interpreters will be used extensively.[379]

5. *Decision*

If the IJ concurs with the AO's negative credible fear determination, the case will be returned to DHS for removal of the asylum-seeker.[380] On the other hand, if the IJ finds that the asylum-seeker possesses a credible fear of persecution, the IJ will vacate the order of the AO that was issued on Form I-860, and DHS may place the asylum-seeker in removal proceedings under INA §240, where the asylum-seeker may receive full consideration of his or her asylum claim.[381]

---

[375] *Id.*

[376] *See* INS Reports on First Three Months of Implementation of Expedited Removal, 74 INTERPRETER RELEASES 1101, 1103 (July 21, 1997).

[377] 8 CFR §1003.42(c) (2014).

[378] *See* Creppy Mem. 99-5, *supra* note 357, at VI.

[379] *Id.*

[380] 8 CFR §§208.30(f)(1), 1003.42(f) (2014).

[381] 8 CFR §1208.30(g)(2)(iv)(B) (2014). If the asylum-seeker is a stowaway, see chapter 3.4.

> **Practice Pointer**: The regulations state that USCIS "*may* commence removal proceedings under section 240" following an IJ's finding of a credible fear.[382] Thus, USCIS is not required to commence proceedings. Practitioners should consider alternatives that would allow clients to be released from custody and/or apply for other forms of relief for which they might be eligible. Practitioners should then negotiate directly with USCIS to advocate for those alternative options for their clients.

6. No Appeal

If an IJ determines that the applicant does not have a credible fear of persecution or torture and affirms the asylum officer's adverse credible fear determination, the IJ will remand the case for execution of the removal order pursuant to INA §235(b)(1)(B)(iii)(I). There is no appeal from an IJ's decision to affirm an adverse credible fear determination.[383] USCIS, however, may reconsider a negative credibility fear finding that has been concurred upon by an IJ after providing notice of its reconsideration to the IJ.[384]

> **Practice Pointer**: Practitioners should consider preparing and filing a motion to reconsider with the USCIS asylum office that entered the original adverse credible fear finding, even after an IJ has confirmed the asylum officer's negative credible fear determination.

G. Credible Fear Re-Interviews Prior to Departure

The Office of Refugee, Asylum, and International Operations may, at its discretion, offer a second credible fear interview to any asylum-seeker, even if he or she has failed to establish a credible fear of persecution before an AO or an IJ.[385] Re-interviews will occur if the asylum-seeker or his or her consultant makes a reasonable claim to the Office of Refugee, Asylum, and International Operations that compelling new information concerning the case exists and should be considered.[386] Immigration and Customs Enforcement is instructed to cooperate by continuing to detain the individual until the second adjudication, and potentially also a second review by an IJ, is completed.[387]

> **Practice Pointer**: If new facts or evidence is obtained that is material to the applicant's protection claim, practitioners should contact the asylum office that conducted the credible fear interview to request a re-

---

[382] 8 CFR §§208.30(g)(2)(iv)(B), 1208.30(g)(2)(iv)(B) (2014).

[383] 8 CFR §1003.42(f) (2014); *but see* this chapter, at 5.2.9.

[384] 8 CFR §§1003.42(d), 1208.30(g)(iv)(A) (2014).

[385] *See* Memorandum from M. Benson on Expedited Removal: Additional Policy Guidance (Dec. 30, 1997), AILA InfoNet at Doc. No. 98021090 (*posted* Feb. 10, 1998), *available at www.aila.org/content/default.aspx?docid=20278.*

[386] *Id.*; *see* appx. 6A for Office of Refugee, Asylum, and International Operations contact information.

[387] *Id.*

interview on behalf of their client. For information on how to contact each asylum office, as well as each office's preferred policies and procedures, see the "Asylum Office Guide — Best Practices," a guide that is regularly updated by the AILA Asylum and Refugee Liaison Committee. See Appendix 4E for a copy of the 2015 guide. It is also posted on AILA InfoNet at Doc. No. 12060844 and is available at *www.aila.org/content/default.aspx?bc=1016|6715|6721|8815|42869|40080* (last visited Jan. 19, 2015). Practitioners should prepare a formal request for a re-interview, detailing the new facts or evidence and its impact on the applicant's protection claim. Any documentary evidence should be attached to the request. Given the expedited nature of removals following adverse credible fear determinations, practitioners also should contact the asylum office and the local Immigration and Customs Enforcement office by phone, fax, and e-mail to ensure that the client is not removed before the request for re-interview is addressed by the asylum office.

IV. Oversight of the Expedited Removal Process

During the implementation of expedited removal, several governmental and nongovernmental groups have observed the expedited removal process in a variety of capacities, including as supervisors, as academics, or as consultants representing asylum-seekers during or after the process. It is, indisputably, a process that has drastically reduced the rights of noncitizens at ports of entry and dramatically increased the authority of immigration inspectors, AOs, and IJs. For these reasons, the legality and implementation of the expedited removal process is likely to be discussed and debated as long as the process is in existence. Some of the agencies and groups contributing to the ongoing discussion, along with their activities and reports, are summarized below.

A. Quality Assurance

In an effort to ensure that all districts implement expedited removal correctly, USCIS's Office of Refugee, Asylum and International Operations announced in 2006 that it would increase the number and categories of credible fear cases that are subject to mandatory quality review.[388] This policy was revised in late 2008.[389] Beginning December 23, 2008, only the following credible fear cases required a quality assurance review by Asylum Headquarters before a decision is issued:

- Cases involving a negative credible fear of persecution and torture;
- High-profile cases (*e.g.*, high-ranking foreign government officials or their family members, or any person whose case has been, or is likely to be, publicized);

[388] Langlois Mem. on Revised Quality Assurance Review, *supra* note 310, at 1.

[389] *Id.*

- Claims involving novel legal issues, or any case that a supervisory asylum prescreening officer believes should be reviewed by Asylum Headquarters; and
- Any case a supervisory AO, deputy director, or director believes should be reviewed.[390]

This policy was again revised in 2014 in response to the "surge" in credible-fear interviews and Asylum Division resource shortages.[391] Under the new policy, USCIS no longer reviews all cases involving a negative credible fear of persecution or torture determination. Rather, asylum offices must send a random sampling of credible fear and reasonable fear determinations — both positive and negative — to Headquarters for pre-decisional quality assurance review.[392] The Asylum Divisions continues to require quality assurance review for high-profile claims or novel legal issues, however, as well as for any case in which an asylum office director seeks such review.[393]

B. Government Accountability Office Reports

Section 302(b) of IIRAIRA required the Government Accountability Office (GAO) to report on the implementation of the expedited removal process. GAO issued a report in March of 1998 based on its review of legacy INS data and its observations from visits to five locations.[394] GAO reported that 79 percent of the individuals referred for a credible fear interview were found to have a credible fear by AOs.[395] The report, however, did not comment on the disparity in approval rates among asylum offices, ranging from a 93 percent approval rate in San Francisco to 59 percent in Houston and Miami.[396] GAO concluded that the immigration inspectors and supervisors documented that they followed certain legacy INS procedures 80 to 100 percent of the time.[397] Notably, GAO did not examine the quality or the correctness of the determinations made by inspectors, AOs, and IJs.

---

[390] *Id.*

[391] Memorandum from John Lafferty, Chief of Asylum Division, Changes to Credible Fear and Reasonable Fear Cases Requiring Quality Assurance Review (June 11, 2014), *published on* AILA InfoNet at Doc. No. 14081468 (*posted* Aug. 14, 2014), *available at* *www.aila.org/content/default.aspx?docid=49775.*

[392] *Id.*

[393] *Id.*

[394] U.S. Gov't Accountability Office, Report to Congressional Committees, *Illegal Aliens: Changes in the Process of Denying Aliens Entry into the United States* 4–5 (Mar. 1998) *available at* *www.gao.gov/products/GGD-98-81.*

[395] *Id.* at 7.

[396] *Id.* at 49.

[397] *Id.* at 4–5.

The International Religious Freedom Act of 1998 required a more in-depth study of the expedited removal process, particularly as it affected asylum-seekers.[398] The study, conducted by GAO with the opportunity for participation by experts, had to be completed by September 1, 2000.[399] Specifically, the GAO was required to examine whether immigration officers were engaging in any of the following conduct when dealing with individuals who may be eligible to be granted asylum:

- Improperly encouraging such [individuals] to withdraw their applications for admission;
- Incorrectly failing to refer such [individuals] for an interview by an asylum officer for a determination of whether they have a credible fear of persecution . . . ;
- Incorrectly removing such [individuals] to a country where they may be persecuted; and
- Detaining such [individuals] improperly or in inappropriate conditions.[400]

In September 2000, GAO published its finding in a report entitled *Illegal Aliens: Opportunities Exist to Improve the Expedited Removal Process*. In this report—which was sharply criticized by the refugee advocacy community—GAO summarized its mostly paper review of legacy INS files and found:

- INS generally followed its own procedures for documenting expedited removal cases;
- INS generally followed its own procedures for documenting the credible fear process; and
- Many asylum-seekers did not appear for their hearing after release.

As pointed out by the Expedited Removal Study in its critique of the GAO report, the questions posed by Congress in the International Religious Freedom Act of 1998 remain largely unanswered and the methodology employed by GAO was seriously flawed.[401] For example, the Expedited Removal Study's critique points out that in two percent of the randomly sampled 1,999 expedited removal files reviewed by GAO, legacy INS failed to refer individuals for a credible fear interview even though they had expressed a fear.[402] The study points out that this could mean that as many as 900 individuals may not have been referred despite expressing a fear.[403]

---

[398] *See* International Religious Freedom Act of 1998 (IRFA), Pub. L. No. 105-292, §605(a)(2), 112 Stat. 2787, 2814 (1998).

[399] *See* IRFA §§605(a)–(b), 112 Stat. at 2814–15.

[400] IRFA §605(a)(2), 112 Stat. at 2814.

[401] *See* The Expedited Removal Study, *Evaluation of the General Accounting Office's Second Report on Expedited Removal* (Oct. 2000), *available at http://w3.uchastings.edu/ers/reports/reports.htm*.

[402] *Id.* at 7.

[403] *Id.*

C. U.S. Commission on International Religious Freedom Report

The U.S. Commission on International Religious Freedom (USCIRF) was created by International Religious Freedom Act to monitor religious freedom in other countries and to advise Congress, the secretary of state, and the president on how best to promote religious freedom.[404] The International Religious Freedom Act also contained provisions authorizing USCIRF to designate experts in refugee and asylum law to conduct a study and submit a report—either with GAO or separately—on the expedited removal process.[405]

In 2003, USCIRF designated attorney Mark Hetfield, Professor Kate Jastram, attorneys Robert Divine[406] and Charles Kuck, Dr. Fritz Scheueren, Dr. Allen Keller, and Dr. Craig Haney as experts to conduct the study. USCIRF monitored seven ports of entry, interviewed almost 200 individuals in the expedited removal process, observed more than 400 secondary inspection interviews, reviewed over 400 credible fear files, and visited 16 detention centers. The study was completed in 2004. The authorizing legislation for both the GAO study and the study by USCIRF's designated experts included the grant of unrestricted access to all stages of the expedited removal process.[407]

The USCIRF report was submitted to Congress in February 2005, and is publicly available online.[408] USCIRF looked at the same four questions that GAO reported on, and made a series of findings and recommendations outlined in its report. Most notably, USCIRF found:

- At one port of entry, immigration officials were observed improperly encouraging asylum-seekers to withdraw their applications for admission;
- In 15 percent of observed cases, inspectors failed to refer individuals who expressed a fear of return for a credible fear interview;
- There was a very significant variation in asylum approval rates of individual IJs, and in 40 percent of the IJ denials, the judge cited that the applicant's testimony was inconsistent with the claim presented to the inspector or the AO at the credible fear interview;
- Only 2 percent of unrepresented applicants were granted asylum, while 25 percent of represented applicants were granted; and

---

[404] For more information about USCIRF and access to its country reports, see *www.uscirf.gov*.

[405] *See* IRFA §§605(a)(1), (b)(1) 112 Stat. at 2814.

[406] On July 1, 2004, Robert Divine left USCIRF when he was appointed USCIS chief counsel, at which time Chuck Kuck replaced him.

[407] *See* IRFA §605(c)(1), 112 Stat. at 2815.

[408] USCIRF Report, *supra* note 116.

- In fiscal year 2003, only 0.5 percent of asylum-seekers in New Orleans were released prior to a decision in their case, while in Harlingen, 98 percent were released.[409]

USCIRF also presented DHS and EOIR with a series of recommendations to improve the expedited removal process and ensure that bona fide refugees are not returned to persecution. Two years after presenting these recommendations, USCIRF issued a "report card" assessing how well the federal government agencies had implemented the recommendations.[410] Below is a summary of the grades[411] it gave:

CBP	F
ICE	D
USCIS (Asylum Office)	B
DHS (Agency-wide coordination)	D
DOJ/EOIR	C+
DHS and DOJ together	Grades from C to F

The federal courts have cited USCIRF's report in considering various procedures in the expedited removal process. For example, in its decision not to dissolve the *Orantes* injunction, which prohibits DHS from coercing or otherwise improperly encouraging Salvadorans detained by immigration authorities to waive their rights, the U.S. District Court for the Central District of California concluded that the "[d]ocumented levels of non-compliance with relevant standards indicate that the injunction is necessary to ensure that Salvadorans are able to exercise their right to apply for asylum freely and intelligently."[412]

On November 28, 2008, DHS issued a response to the USCIRF study in which DHS stated that it was in agreement with many of the USCIRF recommendations and stated that it was taking steps to implement the recommendations.[413] The letter also stated that DHS was implementing a quality assurance policy for asylum-seekers

---

[409] *See id.* at 50–62.

[410] *See* USCIRF Expedited Removal Report Card, *supra* note 222.

[411] A=Adopted and implemented; B=Largely adopted with progress in implementation; C=Largely adopted with little progress, or only partially adopted and implemented; D=Minimally addressed, but with little or no demonstration of ongoing commitment to address the objective of the recommendation; F=Rejected, or little evidence of meaningful action to address the objective of the recommendation. *Id.* at 13.

[412] *Orantes-Hernandez v. Gonzales*, 504 F. Supp. 2d 825 (C.D. Cal. 2007). For more on the *Orantes* case, *see* National Immigration Law Center, *The Orantes Injunction and Expedited Removal* (July 2006), *available at www.nilc.org/immlawpolicy/removpsds/orantes&expremoval_2006-07.pdf.*

[413] Dep't of Homeland Security letter to USCIRF (Nov. 28, 2008), *available at http://bibdaily.com/pdfs/11-28-08DHS BakerUSCIRF.pdf.*

subject to expedited removal.[414] On January 8, 2009, USCIRF then issued a response to DHS's response, stating that few of DHS's actions "accurately follow the recommendations or adequately address the problems identified in the USCIRF Report."[415] USCIRF asserted that "many of the same problems exist in the expedited removal and detention systems today as existed in 2005 when USCIRF issued its report," and emphasized its concern that "due to these systemic flaws, bona fide asylum seekers continue to be at great risk of being returned to countries where they face persecution."[416] USCIRF highlighted four recommendations to DHS:

- The Special Advisor for Refugees and Asylum Seekers requires greater authority so that he or she can effectively address and coordinate inter-bureau issues relating to asylum;
- Asylum seekers should not continue to be housed in jail-like facilities that create serious risks of psychological harm and significantly impede an asylum seeker's ability to access services and information necessary to present his or her case;
- New parole policies are necessary to ensure that asylum seekers who pose no risk of flight or danger are not subject to unnecessary detention; and
- Greater oversight is necessary to ensure qualified asylum seekers are not deported due to improper processing.[417]

Perhaps in response to USCIRF, DHS issued new parole guidelines in December of 2009, encouraging the release of individuals found to have a credible fear of persecution or torture if the Immigration and Customs Enforcement officer determines that: (1) the individual's identity is sufficiently established; (2) he or she does not pose a flight risk; (3) he or she is not a danger to the community; and (4) no additional factors weigh against his or her release.[418] USCIRF applauded this change in policy, stating that it was an important first step to fixing the flawed treatment of asylum seekers.[419]

However, four years later, in 2013, USCIRF published a new report, "Assessing the U.S. Government's Detention of Asylum Seekers: Further Action Needed to Fully Implement Reforms," finding that the U.S. government continues to detain asylum-

---

[414] *Id.*

[415] USCIRF letter to Dep't of Homeland Security (Jan. 8, 2009), *available at www.uscirf.gov/index2.php?option=com_content&do_pdf=1&id=2340.*

[416] *Id.*

[417] *Id.*

[418] Morton Policy Directive on Credible Fear, *supra* note 231, at 6.

[419] Press Release, USCIRF, ICE Parole Guideline is an Important First Step to Fix Flawed Treatment of Asylum Seekers (Dec. 23, 2009), available at *www.uscirf.gov/news-room/press-releases/ice-parole-guideline-important-first-step-fix-flawed-treatment-asylum.*

seekers under inappropriate conditions in jails and jail-like facilities.[420] USCIRF based its findings on its tours of ten detention facilities nationwide, as well as its meetings with officials and asylum-seekers.[421] USCIRF recommended that ICE codify into regulations its 2009 parole policy to release most asylum-seekers found to have a credible fear of persecution or torture, as well as further improvements to expand detainees' access to legal information, representation, and in-person hearings.[422] DHS continues to detain asylum-seekers, even after they are found to have a credible fear of persecution or torture.[423]

➢ **Practice Pointer**: Following monitoring and observation, USCIRF is currently working on another report analyzing the expedited removal process. The report is expected to be released to the public in 2015 in honor of the ten-year anniversary of USCIRF's 2005 report.[424]

D. Nongovernmental Organizations

Several nongovernmental organizations (NGOs), most notably the Expedited Removal Study, spent several years negotiating with legacy INS to obtain access to the expedited removal process, including secondary inspection. In January 2001, legacy INS finally granted NGOs access to the secondary-inspection phase of expedited removal, often referred to as the "black box."[425] These guidelines require that NGOs make requests to visit a port of entry in writing and at least two weeks before the requested visit. Access includes observing primary and secondary inspection and observing an individual secondary inspection interview if the interviewee consents.[426]

The Expedited Removal Study, a project of the Center for Human Rights and International Justice of the University of California, Hastings College of Law, was a three-year project, which released reports in May of 1998, 1999, and 2000. Its purpose was to conduct a comprehensive nationwide review of the expedited removal

---

[420] USCIRF Special Report, Assessing the U.S. Government's Detention of Asylum Seekers: Further Action Needed to Fully Implement Reforms (April 2013), available at *www.uscirf.gov/sites/default/files/resources/ERS-detention%20reforms%20report%20April%202013.pdf.*

[421] *Id.*

[422] *Id.*

[423] *See* ICE Press Release, *supra* note 42; Preston, *supra* note 42; AILA Artesia Examples, *supra* note 40; Collopy & Manning, *supra* note 39;Women's Comm'n for Refugee Women & Children, *supra* note 39; Collopy, *The Failings of Family Detention at Artesia*, *supra* note 39; Manning, *Let These Women Go*, *supra* note 39; *M.S.P.C. v. Johnson* Compl., *supra* note 41; Am. Immigration Council, Groups Sue U.S. Government Over Life-Threatening Deportation Process Against Mothers and Children *supra* note 41.

[424] Author phone meeting with representatives from USCIRF, Jan. 30, 2015.

[425] *See* Memorandum from M. Pearson on Secondary Inspection Access Guidelines for Visits by Non-Governmental Organizations (Jan. 22, 2001), AILA InfoNet Doc. No. 01051505 (*posted* May 15, 2001).

[426] *Id.* at 2.

process with a focus on how such procedures apply to asylum seekers. The Expedited Removal Study's second report, based primarily on anecdotal information from 736 cases, raised questions regarding the following:

- The accuracy of determinations made during the expedited removal process;
- The adequacy of expedited proceedings when complex legal or factual determinations, such as nexus and countrywide persecution, are required;
- Whether the quality of interpretation may impact credible fear determinations;
- The importance of IJ review;
- The breadth of secondary inspection;
- Parole;
- Conditions of detention;
- Notification of and access permitted to consular officers regarding asylum-seekers in detention; and
- The interrelation of expedited removal laws and refugee laws of other countries.[427]

A later report by the Expedited Removal Study raised concerns about access to the asylum process of individuals interdicted at sea, and legacy INS detention of Canada-bound asylum-seekers.[428] This report also analyzed data obtained from legacy INS and EOIR that showed:

- 91 percent of all persons subject to expedited removal were Mexican nationals;
- The San Ysidro (San Diego) port of entry had the highest number of people ordered removed under expedited removal (44 percent of all expedited removals in the country); and
- 88 percent of individuals given a credible fear interview were found to have a credible fear.[429]

The last report issued by the Expedited Removal Study was a critique of the GAO's Report on Expedited Removal.[430]

In addition, the Lawyers Committee for Human Rights (LCHR), now known as Human Rights First, issued a report that raised concerns regarding mistreatment of individuals at airports, inadequate translation, lack of access to counsel, and the detention of asylum-seekers found to have a credible fear of persecution.[431] LCHR

---

[427] *See* The Expedited Removal Study, *Report on the Second Year of Implementation of Expedited Removal* (May 1999), at 5, *available at http://w3.uchastings.edu/ers/reports/1999/toc&exec_sum.pdf.*

[428] *See* Thomas J. White Ctr. On Law & Gov't, *The Expedited Removal Study, Report on First Three Years of Implementation of Expedited Removal* (May 2000), 15 NOTRE DAME J.L. ETHICS & PUB. POL'Y 1 (Special Issue 2001).

[429] *Id.* at 5–6.

[430] *See* The Expedited Removal Study, *supra* note 427.

[431] *See Slamming the Golden Door: A Year of Expedited Removal*, *supra* note 222.

also issued a report on the continued detention of asylum-seekers who are held despite a finding that they possess a credible fear of persecution.[432] More recently, Human Rights First issued a 2011 report finding that, despite USCIRF's recommendations regarding the detention of asylum-seekers, DHS continues to detain asylum-seekers in jail-like facilities.[433] Human Rights First has also researched and examined the increase in families and protection requests at the U.S.-Mexico border. In 2014, it issued a report recommending strengthening U.S. asylum and immigration processing systems "based on a foundation of fair and timely, but not rushed, individualized assessments so that each person apprehended or detained on entry at the border is appropriately managed once inside the United States."[434] Human Rights First found that these steps were necessary to ensure that the U.S. is extending proper protections to those fleeing persecution.[435] Its comprehensive "blueprint" outlining the steps that the U.S. government should take to address the increase in requests for protection at the border highlights ongoing problems with the expedited removal process as it relates to asylum-seekers and those fleeing persecution and torture.[436]

Another NGO, the Catholic Legal Immigration Network (CLINIC), which has staff attorneys at many detention facilities, has reported that individuals in the expedited removal process have been subjected to extended interrogations in secondary inspection, denied a meaningful opportunity to make telephone calls from detention centers, and have not been provided with copies of the required forms.[437]

As the problems regarding expedited removal and processing of asylum-seekers continue to increase and remain unaddressed, several organizations in recent years have issued reports and recommendations, urging the U.S. government to make changes to protect bona fide refugees and to ensure U.S. compliance with domestic and international legal obligations. The following reports, complaints, lawsuits, and recommendations represent some examples of recent critiques of the expedited removal process:

---

[432] *See* Lawyers Comm. for Human Rights, *Refugees Behind Bars*, *supra* note 222.

[433] Human Rights First, *Jails and Jumpsuits: Transforming the US Immigration Detention System* (Oct. 5, 2011), *available at www.humanrightsfirst.org/resource/jails-jumpsuits-transforming-us-immigration-detention-system.*

[434] Human Rights First, *How to Manage the Increase in Families and Protection Requests at the Border* (June 25, 2014), *available at www.humanrightsfirst.org/resource/how-manage-increase-families-and-protection-requests-border.*

[435] *Id.*

[436] Human Rights First, *How to Protect Refugees and Prevent Abuse*, *supra* note 117.

[437] *See* AILA, *Credible Fear Screening, supra* note 222.

- American Civil Liberties Union, *et al.*: *M.S.P.C. v. Johnson* and *R.I.L.R. v. Johnson*;[438]
- American Immigration Council: "No Action Taken: Lack of CBP Accountability in Responding to Complaints of Abuse," (May 2014) and "Mexican and Central American Asylum and Credible Fear Claims," (May 2014);[439]
- American Immigration Lawyers Association, et al.: Complaint to DHS Office of Civil Rights and Civil Liberties, "Inadequate U.S. Customs and Border Protection (CBP) Screening Practices Block Individuals Fleeing Persecution from Access to the Asylum Process," (Nov. 13, 2014);[440]
- Human Rights Watch: "'You Don't Have Rights Here': U.S. Border Screening and Returns of Central Americans to Risk of Serious Harm," (October 2014);[441] and
- Women's Refugee Commission and Lutheran Immigration and Refugee Service: "Locking Up Family Values Again: The Detention of Immigrant Families," (October 2014).[442]

E. UNHCR

Over the past decade, since the implementation of expedited removal, the Washington, D.C. UNHCR office has conducted a number of ad hoc visits to ports of entry to observe the expedited removal process, and has provided written comments directly to legacy INS and DHS on its observations. UNHCR's access to expedited removal was formalized in a written agreement in February 2000, and is found in chapter 17.15(g) of the IFM.[443] Similar to the guidelines on NGO access referred to in the USCIRF Report,[444] UNHCR must make its requests in writing and may observe both primary and secondary inspection.[445]

UNHCR had commented on several occasions that it lacks resources, in personnel and finances, to monitor the process in a comprehensive manner and had stated that

---

[438] Am. Civil Liberties Union, *M.S.P.C. v. Johnson*, *available at www.aclu.org/immigrants-rights/mspc-v-johnson* (last visited Jan. 19, 2015); Am. Civil Liberties Union, *R.I.L.R. v. Johnson*, *available at www.aclu.org/immigrants-rights/rilr-v-johnson* (last visited Jan. 19, 2015).

[439] Daniel Martínez, Am. Immigration Council, *No Action Taken*, *supra* note 9; Am. Immigration Council on Mexican and Central American Asylum Claims, *supra* note 117.

[440] AILA Complaint on Inadequate CBP Screening Practices, *supra* note 117.

[441] Human Rights Watch, *'You Don't Have Rights Here': U.S. Border Screening and Returns of Central Americans to Risk of Serious Harm* (October 2014), *available at www.hrw.org/sites/default/files/reports/us1014_web_0.pdf.*

[442] Women's Comm'n for Refugee Women & Children & Lutheran Immigration and Refugee Servs., *Locking Up Family Values*, *supra* note 39.

[443] Note that the *Inspector's Field Manual* has now been replaced with the "Officer's Reference Tool," which **will not** be made available to the public. *See* AILA Practice Alert, *supra* note 114.

[444] *See* IFM, *supra* note 111, at chapter 17.15(g).

[445] *See* IFM, *supra* note 111, at chapter 17.15(g).

such monitoring might best be carried out by national organizations. In 2002, however, UNHCR initiated a more systematic approach for observing expedited removal procedures. From January through June of 2002, UNHCR—with funding from Harvard University's Carr Center for Human Rights at the Kennedy School of Government—conducted more in-depth field visits at Miami International Airport, John F. Kennedy Airport, Los Angeles International Airport, Newark Airport, and the San Ysidro land port of entry. UNHCR's report on its observations was given to DHS, but it was not shared with the public. However, findings from UNHCR's field visits were leaked to *The New York Times* and reported in an article on August 13, 2004. According to *The New York Times*, UNHCR expressed concern in its report about airport inspectors who improperly notified consulates about asylum-seekers' identities, who intimidated and discouraged some individuals from seeking asylum, and who, in 14 cases known to UNHCR, improperly concluded that the individuals were not eligible for asylum.[446]

UNHCR also issued an Information Bulletin in November 2003, in which it highlighted a number of continuing concerns about the expedited removal process, including inappropriate methods of questioning asylum-seekers, the poor quality of interpretation, the use of restraints at one port of entry, and the use of airport statements to impeach credibility.[447]

On February 8, 2007, UNHCR issued a press release welcoming the recommendations made by USCIRF in its 2005 report.[448] UNHCR stated that the changes recommended by USCIRF would "ensure that refugees are not removed by the United States without an opportunity to apply for asylum and meaningfully present their case."[449] UNHCR also expressed concern about detention of asylum-seekers subject to expedited removal because of the remote detention facilities in which they are held and their lack of access to legal assistance.[450] The press release further noted that in the previous six years, UNHCR had visited 48 detention centers in the United States, and had observed that "many asylum seekers lack the basic tools to present their cases such as access to legal materials, telephones and interpreters."[451]

---

[446] Rachel Swarns, *U.N. Report Cites Harassment of Immigrants Who Sought Asylum at American Airports*, N.Y. Times, Aug. 13, 2004, at A11, *available at www.nytimes.com/2004/08/13/world/threats-responses-immigration-un-report-cites-harassment-immigrants-who-sought.html.*

[447] The Information Bulletin is available from the Washington Office of UNHCR, and may be requested by calling (202) 296-5191 or by sending an e-mail to *usawa@unhcr.org*.

[448] Press Release, U.N. High Comm'r for Refugees, *United Nations Refugee Agency Welcomes Commission on International Religious Freedom's Expert Recommendations on Expedited Removal* (Feb. 8, 2007).

[449] *Id.*

[450] *Id.*

[451] *Id.*

In its 2010 Universal Periodic Review of the United States of America, UNHCR again examined the U.S. government's efforts to address USCIRF's 2005 recommendations regarding the expedited removal program and the commission's observation of significant gaps in safeguards to ensure that asylum-seekers are not removed without the opportunity to seek asylum.[452] UNHCR found that many of the commission's recommendations to address problems with the expedited removal program have not been implemented, and urged the United States to "re-examine the USCIRF recommendations and adopt further quality assurance mechanisms for those procedures affecting asylum-seekers who are apprehended at the border."[453] UNHCR also recommended that the United States fund another comprehensive border monitoring study and publish its findings.[454]

- **Practice Pointer**: In its role as an advisor to governments like that of the United States, UNHCR is currently in the process of conducting another study of the U.S. expedited removal process and how it affects asylum-seekers. Though its report will not be public, it expects to provide its confidential findings to the U.S. government sometime in 2015.[455]

V. Reinstatement of Removal and Reasonable Fear

Under INA §241(a)(5), the Secretary of Homeland Security may reinstate a prior order of removal, deportation, or exclusion against an individual who has illegally reentered the United States after having been removed or having departed voluntarily under that order.[456] The prior order of removal is reinstated from its original date and is not subject to being reopened or reviewed.[457] With few exceptions, the individual is not eligible and may not apply for relief, and he or she "shall be removed under the prior order at any time after reentry."[458] The reinstatement of removal provision was added by IIRAIRA and became effective April 1, 1997.[459] However, the provision also applies retroactively to individuals who illegally reentered the United States before that date, according to a 2006 Supreme Court case.[460]

---

[452] U.N. High Comm'r for Refugees, *Universal Periodic Review: United States of America* 3 (April 2010), *available at www.refworld.org/pdfid/4bcd741c2.pdf.*

[453] *Id.*

[454] *Id.*

[455] Author phone meeting with representatives from UNHCR, Jan. 30, 2015.

[456] INA §241(a)(5); 8 USC §1231(a)(5) (2012); 8 CFR §§241.8, 1241.8 (2014).

[457] INA §241(a)(5).

[458] *Id.*

[459] IIRAIRA, Pub. L. No. 104-208, div. C, §305, 110 Stat. 3009, 3009-599.

[460] *Fernandez-Vargas v. Gonzales*, 126 S. Ct. 2422, 2434 (2006) (finding that INA §241(a)(5) was not impermissibly retroactive). *See also Lattab v. Ashcroft*, 384 F.3d 8 (1st Cir. 2004) (holding that the

Continued

> **Practice Pointer**: Some individuals may be exempt from reinstatement of removal. See Part V.B. for a detailed discussion of the categories of individuals who are not subject to reinstatement of removal.

An exception to the general rule that an individual subject to reinstatement of removal is not eligible to apply for any relief exists if the individual expresses a fear of persecution or torture in the course of the administrative removal or reinstatement process. Such individuals may be eligible for withholding of removal under INA §241(b)(3) or protection under the CAT. They are not eligible for asylum, however.[461] Under such circumstances, DHS will detain the individual and must refer him or her for a "reasonable fear" interview with an asylum officer.[462] USCIS has exclusive jurisdiction to make reasonable fear determinations.[463] If the individual is found to have a reasonable fear of persecution or torture, he or she is placed in "withholding-only proceedings" for full consideration of his or her INA §241(b)(3) withholding of removal or CAT claim before an IJ.[464] EOIR has exclusive jurisdiction to review reasonable fear determinations.[465] The reasonable fear procedures went into effect on March 22, 1999. Any applicants subject to reinstatement prior to March 22, 1999, who were not served with a final decision, should have been given an opportunity to seek relief under the new process.[466]

> **Practice Pointer**: For a detailed discussion of the legal standards for demonstrating a reasonable fear of persecution or torture, see Part V.E. of this chapter.

Reinstatements accounted for 39 percent of all removals in 2013, and the number of removals based on reinstatement of final orders has increased every year from

---

reinstatement provision may be retroactively applied to individuals who illegally reentered before April 1, 1997 and did not qualify for any relief). *But see Valdez-Sanchez v. Gonzales*, 485 F.3d 1084, 1089–91 (10th Cir. 2007) (finding that DHS may not retroactively apply INA §241(a)(5) to an individual who illegally re-enters, marries a U.S. citizen and was granted adjustment of status all prior to IIRAIRA's effective date of April 1, 1997); *Faiz-Mohammed v. Ashcroft*, 395 F.3d 799, 810 (7th Cir. 2005) (finding that INA §241(a)(5) did not apply where the individual applied for adjustment prior to the enactment of IIRAIRA).

[461] 8 CFR §§208.31, 241.8(d) (2014).

[462] 8 CFR §§208.31(a), 1208.31(a) (2014).

[463] *Id.*

[464] 8 CFR §§208.31(e), 1208.31(e) (2014).

[465] 8 CFR §§208.31(a), 1208.31(a) (2014).

[466] *See* Memorandum from Immigration and Naturalization Serv. Joseph Langlois on Implementation of Amendments to Asylum and Withholding of Removal Regulations, Effective March 22, 1999 (Mar. 18, 1999) at 6.

2005 to 2013.[467] Individuals from Mexico, Guatemala, Honduras, and El Salvador accounted for 99 percent of all reinstatements in 2013.[468]

A. Who is Subject to Reinstatement of Removal?

Reinstatement of removal under INA §241(a)(5) applies to all noncitizens who reenter the United States illegally after having been removed or having departed voluntarily under a prior order of deportation, exclusion, or removal, unless an individual falls within one of the statutory or judicial exemptions discussed in Part V.B. of this chapter.[469]

> ➢ **Practice Pointer**: Practitioners should carefully review clients' entry documents, immigration histories, and current case law, as reinstatement of removal may not apply. For example, reinstatement may not apply to individuals who enter the United States with facially valid visas or other entry documents.[470] Moreover, individuals who file I-212 waivers prior to a reinstatement determination may be entitled to adjudication of that waiver.[471]

B. Who is Not Subject to Reinstatement?

The statute and, over time, the courts have exempted certain categories of individuals from reinstatement of removal under INA §241(a)(5). These categories of individuals include:

- Individuals applying for adjustment of status under INA §245A (legalization), who are covered under certain class action lawsuits, including *Catholic Social Services, Inc. v. Meese*, *League of United Latin American Citizens v. INS*, and *Zambrano v. INS*;[472]

---

467 John Simanski, Annual Report on Immigration Enforcement Actions: 2013 at 7, U.S. Dep't of Homeland Security (Sept. 2014), *available at www.dhs.gov/sites/default/files/publications/ois_enforcement_ar_2013.pdf*.

468 *Id.*

469 INA §241(a)(5); 8 CFR §§241.8, 1241.8 (2014). Note that even though the language of the statute only references prior orders of "removal," section 309(d)(2) of IIRAIRA specifies that any reference to an order of removal in the INA also refers to orders of deportation or exclusion.

470 *See Mora v. Smith*, No. C97-1758WD, slip op. (W.D. Wash., Dec. 17, 1997) (holding that reinstatement provision does not apply to individuals who entered with an I-688A employment authorization card).

471 *See Perez-Gonzalez v. Ashcroft*, 379 F.3d 783 (9th Cir. 2004).

472 *See* Legal Immigration Family Equality Act (LIFE Act), §1104(g), Pub. L. No. 106-554, 114 Stat. 2763 (Dec. 21, 2000). The relevant class action lawsuits include *Catholic Social Services Inc. v. Meese, vacated sub nom. Reno v. Catholic Social Services, Inc.*, 509 U.S. 43 (1993); *League of United Latin American Citizens v. INS, vacated sub nom. Reno v. Catholic Social Services, Inc.*, 509 U.S. 43 (1993); and *Zambrano v. INS, vacated sub nom. INS v. Zambrano*, 509 U.S. 918 (1993).

- Nicaraguan and Cuban applicants for adjustment of status under §202 of the Nicaraguan Adjustment and Central American Relief Act of 1997 (NACARA);[473]
- Eastern European, Guatemalan, and Salvadoran applicants for adjustment of status under NACARA §203;[474]
- Haitian applicants for adjustment of status under the Haitian Refugee Immigration Fairness Act of 1998 (HRIFA);[475] and
- Some individuals who reentered the United States *and* applied for immigration relief before April 1, 1997, the date that the reinstatement of removal provisions took effect — a potential judicial exemption in certain circuits.[476]

After the reinstatement of removal provisions took effect on April 1, 1997, a circuit court split developed regarding whether those provisions could apply retroactively to individuals who had reentered illegally prior to April 1, 1997.[477] Then, in 2006, in *Fernandez-Vargas v. Gonzales*, the U.S. Supreme Court held that reinstatement of removal under INA §241(a)(5) could apply retroactively to an individual who entered the United States before April 1, 1997, if that individual did

[473] LIFE Act §1505(a)(1) amending NACARA §202(a)(2); 8 CFR §§241.8(d), 1241.8(d) (2014).

[474] LIFE Act §1505(c).

[475] LIFE Act §1505(b)(1) amending HRIFA §902(a)(2); 8 CFR §§241.8(d), 1241.8(d) (2014).

[476] The First, Seventh, Ninth, and Eleventh Circuits have favorable retroactivity decisions. *See Chay Ixcot v. Holder*, 646 F.3d 1202, 1213 (9th Cir. 2011) (finding that INA §241(a)(5) was not retroactive in the case of an individual who reentered illegally and applied for asylum before April 1, 1997); *Faiz-Mohammed v. Ashcroft*, 395 F.3d 799, 810 (7th Cir. 2005) (finding that INA §241(a)(5) did not apply where the individual reentered and applied for adjustment of status prior to the enactment of IIRAIRA); *Sarmiento-Cisneros v. Ashcroft*, 381 F.3d 1277, 1278 (11th Cir. 2004); *Arevalo v. Ashcroft*, 344 F.3d 1, 4 (1st Cir. 2003). *See also Valdez-Sanchez v. Gonzales*, 485 F.3d 1084, 1089–91 (10th Cir. 2007) (stating that DHS may not retroactively apply INA §241(a)(5) to an individual who illegally re-enters, marries a U.S. citizen and was granted adjustment of status all prior to IIRAIRA's effective date of April 1, 1997). The First, Seventh, and Eleventh Circuits' decisions pre-date the Supreme Court's decision in *Fernandez-Vargas v. Gonzales*, which found that the reinstatement of removal provisions were not impermissibly retroactive for individuals who reentered prior to April 1, 1997 and did nothing to legalize their unlawful status prior to that date. *See Fernandez-Vargas v. Gonzales*, 548 U.S. 30 (2006). These decisions, however, should remain valid because the Supreme Court declined to address whether INA §241(a)(5) applied retroactively to an individual who illegally reentered but did affirmatively address his or her unlawful status prior to April 1, 1997. These decisions considered individuals who illegally reentered *and* took affirmative steps to legalize their status. *See Faiz-Mohammed v. Ashcroft*, 395 F.3d 799, 810 (7th Cir. 2005); *Sarmiento-Cisneros v. Ashcroft*, 381 F.3d 1277, 1278 (11th Cir. 2004); *Arevalo v. Ashcroft*, 344 F.3d 1, 4 (1st Cir. 2003). *See also Lattab v. Ashcroft*, 384 F.3d 8 (1st Cir. 2004) (holding that the reinstatement provision may be retroactively applied to individuals who illegally reentered before April 1, 1997 and did not qualify for any relief).

[477] Linton Joaquin, *Supreme Court Find That Reinstatement of Removal Applies to Pre-IIRIRA Entries*, 20 Immigrant's Rights Update 4 (Aug. 23, 2006), *available at www.nilc.org/removpsds153.html*; *Fernandez-Vargas v. Gonzales*, 548 U.S. 30, 36 (2006) (stating that "We granted certiorari to resolve a split among the Courts of Appeals over the application of §241(a)(5) to an alien who reentered illegally before IIRIRA's effective date.").

nothing to legalize his unlawful status prior to that date.[478] In that case, Fernandez-Vargas had been deported in 1981 and reentered illegally shortly thereafter. Even though his U.S. citizen son was born in 1989, prior to the effect of the reinstatement provisions, he did not attempt to legalize his status prior to that date. He filed an adjustment of status application and I-212 waiver application in March of 2001, after he had married his son's U.S. citizen mother.[479]

In holding that reinstatement of removal could apply retroactively to an individual who entered the United States before April 1, 1997, and did nothing to legalize his unlawful status prior to that date, the Supreme Court reasoned that INA §241(a)(5) does not penalize illegal reentry, but rather, establishes a process to "stop an indefinitely continuing [immigration] violation."[480] In concluding that Fernandez-Vargas had no retroactivity claim, the Supreme Court stated, "[I]t is the conduct of remaining in the country after entry that is the predicate action" triggering the application of INA §241(a)(5).[481] Since Fernandez-Vargas continued his unlawful presence after the reinstatement provisions took effect, his conduct was not completed prior to the change in law and INA §241(a)(5), therefore, applied to him.[482]

The Court declined to decide whether INA §241(a)(5) applies retroactively to individuals who illegally reentered *and* took affirmative steps to legalize their status prior to April 1, 1997.[483] This question, however, has been considered by the U.S. circuit courts of appeals.[484] The First, Seventh, Ninth, and Eleventh Circuits have

---

[478] *Fernandez-Vargas v. Gonzales*, 548 U.S. 30 (2006) (abrogating the Sixth and Ninth Circuit decisions in *Bejjani v. INS*, 271 F.3d 670 (6th Cir. 2001) and *Castro-Cortez v. INS*, 239 F.3d 1037 (9th Cir. 2001), which had held that INA §241(a)(5) did not apply retroactively to pre–April 1, 1997 entrants).

[479] *See id.* at 36; *see also Fernandez-Vargas v. Ashcroft*, 394 F.3d 881, 883 (10th Cir. 2005) aff'd sub nom. *Fernandez-Vargas v. Gonzales*, 548 U.S. 30 (2006).

[480] *Id.* at 44.

[481] *Id.*

[482] *Id.* at 45.

[483] *Id.* at 46.

[484] *See Chay Ixcot v. Holder*, 646 F.3d 1202, 1213 (9th Cir. 2011) (finding that INA §241(a)(5) was not retroactive in the case of an individual who reentered illegally and applied for asylum before April 1, 1997); *Herrera-Molina v. Holder*, 597 F.3d 128, 132, 137-38 (2d Cir. 2010) (upholding retroactivity of INA §241(a)(5) for an individual who reentered illegally and married a U.S. citizen prior to April 1, 1997, but who filed a family-based petition and adjustment of status application after April 1, 1997); *Molina Jerez v. Holder*, 625 F.3d 1058, 1070 (8th Cir. 2010) (upholding retroactivity of INA §241(a)(5) for an individual who reentered illegally and filed an asylum application before April 1, 1997); *Silva Rosa v. Gonzales*, 490 F.3d 403, 410 (5th Cir. 2007) (upholding retroactivity of INA §241(a)(5) for an individual who reentered illegally, married a U.S. citizen, and obtained approval of a visa petition pre-April 1, 1997, but whose adjustment of status application was filed after April 1, 1997); *Valdez-Sanchez v. Gonzales*, 485 F.3d 1084, 1091 (10th Cir. 2007) (considering an individual who reentered illegally and filed a petition to remove conditions on residence prior to April 1, 1997, and stating that DHS may not retroactively apply INA §241(a)(5) to an individual who illegally re-

Continued

found that INA §241(a)(5) does *not* apply retroactively to individuals who reentered illegally and took affirmative steps to legalize their status before April 1, 1997.[485] Thus, reinstatement of removal should not apply to individuals in these circuits, under these facts. Although the First, Seventh, and Eleventh Circuits' decisions predate *Fernandez-Vargas v. Gonzales*, these decisions should remain valid because the Supreme Court declined to address whether INA §241(a)(5) applied retroactively to an individual who illegally reentered and took affirmative steps to legalize their status prior to April 1, 1997.[486]

C. Determining Whether Reinstatement Applies

There are three statutory conditions, all of which must be met before INA §241(a)(5) is triggered. Thus, determining whether reinstatement of removal applies involves a three-part test:

(1) determine whether the individual has a prior deportation, exclusion, or removal order;

(2) determine whether the individual departed under the prior order, either pursuant to the order or voluntarily; and

(3) determine whether the individual reentered the United States illegally.[487]

DHS bears the burden of establishing the existence of the prior order, the individual's departure under that order, and the individual's illegal reentry.[488] Although there is no standard of proof expressly provided in the INA, DHS arguably must meet its burden by "clear, convincing and unequivocal evidence."[489]

For step two of the test, reinstatement of removal is not triggered if the individual has not departed the country following the removal, deportation, or exclusion

---

enters, marries a U.S. citizen, and is granted adjustment of status all prior to IIRAIRA's effective date of April 1, 1997). *Faiz-Mohammed v. Ashcroft*, 395 F.3d 799, 810 (7th Cir. 2005) (finding that INA §241(a)(5) did not apply where the individual reentered and applied for adjustment of status prior to the enactment of IIRAIRA); *Sarmiento-Cisneros v. Ashcroft*, 381 F.3d 1277, 1278 (11th Cir. 2004); *Arevalo v. Ashcroft*, 344 F.3d 1, 4 (1st Cir. 2003).

[485] *See Chay Ixcot v. Holder*, 646 F.3d 1202, 1213 (9th Cir. 2011) (finding that INA §241(a)(5) was not retroactive in the case of an individual who reentered illegally and applied for asylum before April 1, 1997); *Faiz-Mohammed v. Ashcroft*, 395 F.3d 799, 810 (7th Cir. 2005) (finding that INA §241(a)(5) did not apply where the individual reentered and applied for adjustment of status prior to the enactment of IIRAIRA); *Sarmiento-Cisneros v. Ashcroft*, 381 F.3d 1277, 1278 (11th Cir. 2004); *Arevalo v. Ashcroft*, 344 F.3d 1, 4 (1st Cir. 2003).

[486] *See Fernandez-Vargas v. Gonzales*, 548 U.S. 30, 46 (2006); *Faiz-Mohammed v. Ashcroft*, 395 F.3d 799, 810 (7th Cir. 2005); *Sarmiento-Cisneros v. Ashcroft*, 381 F.3d 1277, 1278 (11th Cir. 2004); *Arevalo v. Ashcroft*, 344 F.3d 1, 4 (1st Cir. 2003). *See also Lattab v. Ashcroft*, 384 F.3d 8 (1st Cir. 2004) (holding that the reinstatement provision may be retroactively applied to individuals who illegally reentered before April 1, 1997 and did not qualify for any relief).

[487] INA §241(a)(5).

[488] *See* 8 CFR §241.8(a) (2014).

[489] *Woodby v. INS*, 385 U.S. 276, 277 (1966).

order.[490] Note, however, that DHS could attempt to execute the outstanding order if the individual comes to DHS's attention.

> **Practice Pointer**: Often times, clients are unsure whether they have a prior order of removal, deportation, or exclusion. Practitioners may assist their clients in investigating this question by calling the Executive Office for Immigration Review's hotline at 1-800-898-7180 or filing a Freedom of Information Act request with DHS and EOIR. If a client does have a prior order of removal, deportation, or exclusion, practitioners should warn him or her that DHS could attempt to reinstate or execute the outstanding order at any time.

Step three of the test — determining whether an individual reentered illegally — can involve a complex legal analysis of entry, inspection, and admission issues. Arguably, because of the requirement of an illegal reentry, reinstatement does not apply to an individual with a prior removal order who approaches a port of entry and requests asylum. Such an individual has not effectuated any "entry" into the United States, let alone an illegal reentry.[491]

> **Practice Pointer**: Practitioners should argue that a client with a prior removal order who approached a port of entry and requested asylum is not subject to reinstatement and should advocate for the client to be scheduled for a credible fear interview with an asylum officer.

In analyzing step three, DHS may not have followed the reinstatement regulations pursuant to 8 CFR §241.8(a)(3), which require the officer to "consider all relevant evidence, including statements made by the [individual] and any evidence in the [individual's] possession" and "attempt to verify [the] claim, if any, that [the individual] was lawfully admitted, which shall include a check of Service data systems available to the officer."[492] A violation of these regulatory requirements might support a viable legal argument that step three of the statutory conditions has not been met and that reinstatement of removal should not apply to the individual.[493]

> **Practice Pointer**: The American Immigration Council's Legal Action Center has published an incredibly helpful practice advisory discussing reinstatement of removal in-depth and, on pages 22–23, specifically evaluating regulatory violations by DHS and whether those violations would be viable support for an argument that reinstatement of removal is not lawfully triggered under INA §241(a)(5). The practice advisory is

---

[490] INA §241(a)(5).

[491] *See, e.g., Matter of Patel*, 20 I&N Dec. 368, 371 (BIA 1991); *Matter of Ching and Chen*, 19 I&N Dec. 203, 205 (BIA 1984).

[492] 8 CFR §241.8(a)(3) (2014).

[493] *See* Am. Immigration Council and Nat'l Immigration Project, *Practice Advisory: Reinstatement of Removal* (Apr. 29, 2013), *available at www.legalactioncenter.org/sites/default/files/reinstatement_of_removal_4-29-13_fin.pdf.*

available on the American Immigration Council's website at *www.legalactioncenter.org/sites/default/files/reinstatement_of_removal_4-29-13_fin.pdf* (last visited Jan. 10, 2015).

Moreover, an individual may have reentered legally, but DHS may lack evidence of the legal reentry.[494] Thus, it is possible that the reinstatement of removal was issued in error and should be challenged, and the individual may need to supplement the administrative record with evidence of the legal entry.

- **Practice Pointer**: If a client entered legally and DHS reinstated a prior removal order due to a lack of evidence supporting a lawful entry, practitioners should assist their client in correcting or supplementing DHS's reinstatement record. Preparing and presenting evidence of a lawful entry to DHS and documentation in support of any legal or factual arguments that may be raised in a petition for review before a U.S. circuit court of appeals may convince DHS to reopen or reconsider its reinstatement order. It also will preserve any factual, legal, and due process challenges to the reinstatement order.[495] First, practitioners should correspond directly with the officer assigned to the case to supplement the administrative record and advocate for the reinstatement order to be rescinded. If direct correspondence with the officer does not solve the problem, practitioners should prepare and file with DHS a motion to reopen or reconsider the reinstatement order pursuant to 8 CFR §103.5.[496]

Finally, even if an individual does not have the required documents to make a substantively legal entry, if he or she presents him or herself at a port of entry and is inspected and admitted or "waved in" by an immigration officer after a prior order, it could be considered a procedurally regular, and therefore lawful, entry.[497] In such situations, it could be argued that the reinstatement provisions may not apply.

---

[494] *See* 8 CFR §241.8(a)(3) (2014).

[495] *See infra* pt. VI.B. for a detailed discussion on challenging reinstatement of removal orders. *See also Miller v. Mukasey*, 539 F.3d 159, 164 (2d Cir. 2008); INA §242(b)(4)(A) ("[T]he court of appeals shall decide the petition only on the administrative record on which the order of removal is based."). The reinstatement order and all related documentation makes up the administrative record for an appeal. *See* Federal Rule of Appellate Procedure 16. If the administrative record does not include the relevant evidence of a lawful entry, the individual may need to file a motion to supplement the administrative record pursuant to Federal Rule of Appellate Procedure 16(b).

[496] *See Ponta-Garca v. Ashcroft*, 386 F.3d 341, 343 n.1 (1st Cir. 2004) (suggesting that an individual may file a separate petition for review if DHS denies a motion to reopen or reconsider). *But see Tapia-Lemos v. Holder*, 696 F.3d 687, 690 (7th Cir. 2012) (dismissing a petition for review of a denial of a motion to reopen for lack of jurisdiction).

[497] *See* INA §101(a)(13)(A) (definitions of "admission" and "admitted"); *Matter of Quilantan*, 25 I&N Dec. 285 (BIA 2010); *Matter of Areguillin*, 17 I&N Dec. 308 (BIA 1980); *Matter of V-Q-*, 9 I&N Dec. 78 (BIA 1960); *Matter of G-*, 3 I&N Dec. 136 (BIA 1948). *See also Ponta-Garca v. Ashcroft*, 386 F.3d 341, 343 (1st Cir. 2004) (noting that in this situation "the reinstatement provision would appear to be

Continued

If all three conditions of the statute are met, and if the individual does not fall under one of the exemptions described above in Part V.B., he or she is subject to reinstatement of removal under INA §241(a)(5). DHS must provide written notice of the reinstatement determination to the individual.[498] If the individual has counsel who has filed a Form G-28, Notice of Entry of Appearance, DHS also is required to serve counsel with a copy of the reinstatement order.[499]

- **Practice Pointer**: Individuals who have reentered illegally after a prior removal, deportation, or exclusion order may be charged with criminal prosecution under INA §276, 8 USC §1326. In such situations, practitioners could contact the individual's federal defender to obtain copies of the reinstatement order and other immigration documentation, as well as information regarding the disposition of the criminal case.[500]

D. Judicial Review of Reinstatement

The courts of appeals may review challenges to the factual elements of a reinstatement order — whether DHS met its burden of proof to demonstrate the existence of a prior order, that the individual departed under that order, and that the individual reentered illegally. In completing its review, a court may only review the "administrative record on which the [reinstatement] order is based" and the court will treat DHS factual findings as "conclusive unless any reasonable adjudicator would be compelled to the contrary."[501]

Reinstatement proceedings also may involve any number of due process violations, including but not limited to lack of a full and fair hearing, lack of an impartial adjudicator, lack of a meaningful opportunity to prepare and present evidence, lack of a meaningful opportunity to rebut evidence or cross-examine witnesses, faulty or no service of the reinstatement order, lack of access to counsel, and lack of notice of the right to seek federal court review. These violations could occur at any stage of the process: issuance of the prior order of removal, deportation, or exclusion; the individual's departure from the United States; or following the individual's reentry. Although some courts have expressed concern about the reinstatement process,[502] courts generally have held that reinstatement of removal

---

inapplicable by its express terms"). *But see Tamayo-Tamayo v. Holder*, 709 F.3d 795 (9th Cir. 2013) (rejecting the argument that a procedurally regular entry is a legal entry); *Beekhan v. Holder*, 634 F.3d 723 (2d Cir. 2011) (same); *Anderson v. Napolitano*, 611 F.3d 275, 277-79 (5th Cir. 2010) (same); *Cordova-Soto v. Holder*, 659 F.3d 1029 (10th Cir. 2011).

[498] 8 CFR §241.8(b) (2014).

[499] 8 CFR §292.5(a) (2014).

[500] *See* Am. Immigration Council, *Practice Advisory: Reinstatement of Removal*, *supra* note 493.

[501] INA §§242(b)(4)(A), (B).

[502] *See, e.g., U.S. v. Charleswell*, 456 F.3d 347, 356–57 (3d Cir. 2006); *Lattab v. Ashcroft*, 384 F.3d 8, 21 n.6 (1st Cir. 2004); *Alvarez-Portillo v. Ashcroft*, 280 F.3d 858, 867 (8th Cir. 2002); *Bejjani v. INS*, 271 F.3d 670, 675–76 (6th Cir. 2001); *Castro-Cortez v. INS*, 239 F.3d 1037, 1047–50 (9th Cir. 2001).

proceedings provide sufficient due process to ensure that an individual is not wrongfully deported or removed.[503]

- **Practice Pointer**: In most cases where courts found adequate due process in reviewing challenges to the reinstatement process, the individuals had failed to demonstrate actual prejudice due to the alleged due process violations. Thus, practitioners who wish to raise due process violations on behalf of their clients in challenging reinstatement orders should endeavor to establish clear prejudice due to the alleged due process violations.

Other potential challenges to a reinstatement of removal order include:

- That the reinstatement provisions should not apply retroactively to individuals who reentered the United States prior to April 1, 1997, and attempted to regularize their status before that date;[504]

---

[503] *See, e.g., Ponta-Garcia v. Att'y Gen.*, 557 F.3d 158, 162–65 (3d Cir. 2009); *Avila v. Att'y Gen.*, 560 F.3d 1281, 1286 (11th Cir. 2009); *Garcia-Villeda v. Mukasey*, 531 F.3d 141, (2d Cir. 2008) (upholding the validity of the reinstatement regulation); *Lorenzo v. Mukasey*, 503 F.3d 1278, 1283–84 (10th Cir. 2007) (upholding the validity of the reinstatement regulation); *Morales-Izquierdo v. Gonzales*, 486 F.3d 484, 489–95 (9th Cir. 2007) (en banc) (upholding the validity of the reinstatement regulation); *De Sandoval v. Att'y Gen.*, 440 F.3d 1276, 1280–83 (11th Cir. 2006); *Ochoa-Carrillo v. Gonzales*, 437 F.3d 842, 846 (8th Cir. 2006); *Lattab v. Ashcroft*, 384 F.3d 8, 17–20 (1st Cir. 2004); *Briseno-Sanchez v. Heinauer*, 319 F.3d 324, 327–28 (8th Cir. 2003); *Duran-Hernandez v. Ashcroft*, 348 F.3d 1158, 1162-63 (10th Cir. 2003); *Warner v. Ashcroft*, 381 F.3d 534, 539 (6th Cir. 2004); *Ojeda-Terrazas v. Ashcroft*, 290 F.3d 292, 302 (5th Cir. 2002); *Gomez-Chavez v. INS*, 308 F.3d 796, 802 (7th Cir. 2002); *Alvarenga-Villalobos v. Ashcroft*, 271 F.3d 1169 (9th Cir. 2001); *see also Velasquez-Gabriel v. Crocetti*, 263 F.3d 102 (4th Cir. 2001) (holding that reinstatement does not operate in an impermissibly retroactive manner).

[504] *See Fernandez-Vargas v. Gonzales*, 548 U.S. 30, 46 (2006) (holding that INA §241(a)(5) did apply retroactively to an individual who reentered before April 1, 1997 but who did nothing to legalize his unlawful status prior to that date); *Chay Ixcot v. Holder*, 646 F.3d 1202, 1213 (9th Cir. 2011) (finding that INA §241(a)(5) was not retroactive in the case of an individual who reentered illegally and applied for asylum before April 1, 1997); *Herrera-Molina v. Holder*, 597 F.3d 128, 132, 137–38 (2d Cir. 2010) (upholding retroactivity of INA §241(a)(5) for an individual who reentered illegally and married a U.S. citizen prior to April 1, 1997, but who filed a family-based petition and adjustment of status application after April 1, 1997); *Molina Jerez v. Holder*, 625 F.3d 1058, 1070 (8th Cir. 2010) (upholding retroactivity of INA §241(a)(5) for an individual who reentered illegally and filed an asylum application before April 1, 1997); *Silva Rosa v. Gonzales*, 490 F.3d 403, 410 (5th Cir. 2007) (upholding retroactivity of INA §241(a)(5) for an individual who reentered illegally, married a U.S. citizen, and obtained approval of a visa petition pre–April 1, 1997, but whose adjustment of status application was filed after April 1, 1997); *Valdez-Sanchez v. Gonzales*, 485 F.3d 1084, 1091 (10th Cir. 2007) (considering an individual who reentered illegally and filed a petition to remove conditions on residence prior to April 1, 1997, and stating that DHS may not retroactively apply INA §241(a)(5) to an individual who illegally re-enters, marries a U.S. citizen, and is granted adjustment of status all prior to IIRAIRA's effective date of April 1, 1997). *Faiz-Mohammed v. Ashcroft*, 395 F.3d 799, 810 (7th Cir. 2005) (finding that INA §241(a)(5) did not apply where the individual reentered and applied for adjustment of status prior to the enactment of IIRAIRA); *Sarmiento-Cisneros v. Ashcroft*, 381 F.3d 1277, 1278 (11th Cir. 2004); *Arevalo v. Ashcroft*, 344 F.3d 1, 4 (1st Cir. 2003).

- That DHS failed to follow its own reinstatement regulations;[505]
- That DHS's arrest or evidence-gathering underlying the reinstatement order was in violation of the Fourth Amendment;[506]
- That the reinstatement of removal process is arbitrary and capricious, because it is left to the whim of the charging officer whether to initiate removal proceedings under INA §240 or to issue a reinstatement order;[507]
- That the individual is not the same individual alleged to have been removed previously;[508] and
- That the individual actually is a U.S. citizen.[509]

If an individual would like to challenge a reinstated removal order, he or she must file a Petition for Review within 30 days of the order, even if he or she is in withholding-only proceedings.[510] The only circuit where a reinstated removal order is not final until the conclusion of withholding-only proceedings is the Ninth Circuit.[511]

E. Consequences of Reinstatement

If an individual is subject to the reinstatement of removal provision, the prior order is reinstated from its original date and may not be reopened or reviewed by an

---

[505] *See U.S. ex rel. Accardi v. Shaughnessy*, 347 U.S. 260, 268 (1954) (stating that officers must follow agency regulations). Among other requirements, the regulations require that DHS officers determine whether the individual has a prior order, obtain the prior removal order, determine whether the individual is the same person as listed on the prior order, consider all relevant evidence in determining whether the individual reentered illegally, attempt to verify any claim of lawful entry, and ask the individual if he or she has a fear of return. 8 CFR §§241.8, 208.31 (2014).

[506] If there is evidence in the administrative record that the reinstatement order was based on evidence obtained during a raid, stop, search, or arrest that violated the Fourth Amendment, it may be argued that DHS cannot use that evidence to support its reinstatement decision. For more information on motions to suppress evidence and Fourth Amendment violations, see the Am. Immigration Council, *Practice Advisory on Motions to Suppress in Removal Proceedings: A General Overview* (Nov. 13, 2013), *www.legalactioncenter.org/sites/default/files/motions_to_suppress_in_removal_proceedings-_a_general_overview_11-12-13_fin.pdf*; as well as its supplemental *Practice Advisory on Motions to Suppress in Removal Proceedings: Fighting Back Against Unlawful Conduct by U.S. Customs and Border Protection* (Nov. 13, 2013), *available at www.legalactioncenter.org/sites/default/files/motions_to_suppress_in_removal_proceedings-_fighting_back_against_unlawful_cbp_conduct_11-13-13_fin.pdf* (last visited Jan. 16, 2015).

[507] *See Judulang v. Holder*, 132 S. Ct. 476 (2011) (criticizing an immigration system that turns on the "fortuity of an individual officer's decision").

[508] A situation of disputed identity may arise, and fingerprints may not be available or they may be unreliable.

[509] *See* INA §242(b)(5). *See, e.g., Batista v. Ashcroft*, 270 F.3d 8, 17 (1st Cir. 2001) (transferring a case to the district court to resolve a question of fact regarding whether the individual subject to a reinstatement order was actually a U.S. citizen).

[510] INA §242(a)(1)(5), (b)(1).

[511] *Ortiz-Alfaro v. Holder*, 694 F.3d 955, 958 (9th Cir. 2012). *See also Herrera-Molina v. Holder*, 597 F.3d 128, 132 (2d Cir. 2010) (raising this same issue, but not resolving it).

IJ.[512] Moreover, an individual subject to reinstatement of removal is not eligible for and may not apply for any relief under the INA and must be removed from the United States under the prior order of removal.[513] It may be possible, however, for an individual to seek judicial review before the federal courts.[514]

Even though the plain language of the statute says that, once DHS reinstates a prior order, "the [individual] is not eligible and may not apply for any relief under this Act,"[515] DHS is prohibited from returning the individual to a situation of persecution or torture.[516] If an individual expresses a fear during the reinstatement process, DHS must refer him or her to an asylum officer for a "reasonable fear" interview.[517] If the asylum officer determines that the individual has a "reasonable fear of persecution or torture," the individual may apply for withholding of removal or CAT protection before an IJ.[518]

> ➢ **Practice Pointer**: Practitioners also should consider whether their clients subject to reinstatement of removal might be eligible for the following forms of relief: adjustment of status under the Violence Against Women Act (VAWA);[519] T or U nonimmigrant status;[520] or

---

[512] INA §241(a)(5); 8 USC §1231(a)(5) (2012); 8 CFR §§241.8, 1241.8 (2014); *see also Morales-Izquierdo v. Gonzales*, 477 F.3d 691 (9th Cir. 2007) (finding that 8 CFR §241.8 (2014) comports with due process).

[513] INA §241(a)(5); 8 USC §1231(a)(5) (2012).

[514] *Chay Ixcot v. Holder*, 646 F.3d 1202, 1206 (9th Cir. 2011); *Garcia-Villeda v. Mukasey*, 531 F.3d 141, 144 (2d Cir. 2008); *Warner v. Ashcroft*, 381 F.3d 534, 536 (6th Cir. 2004); *Sarmiento-Cisneros v. Ashcroft*, 381 F.3d 1277, 1278 (11th Cir. 2004); *Arevalo v. Ashcroft*, 344 F.3d 1, 9 (1st Cir. 2003); *Avila-Macias v. Ashcroft*, 328 F.3d 108, 110 (3d Cir. 2003); *Briseno-Sanchez v. Heinauer*, 319 F.3d 324, 326 (8th Cir. 2003); *Duran-Hernandez v. Ashcroft*, 348 F.3d 1158, 1162 n.3 (10th Cir. 2003); *Ojeda-Terrazas v. Ashcroft*, 290 F.3d 292, 295 (5th Cir. 2002); *Gomez-Chavez v. ISN*, 308 F.3d 796, 800 (7th Cir. 2002); *Velasquez-Gabriel v. Crocetti*, 263 F.3d 102, 105 (4th Cir. 2001).

[515] INA §241(a)(5).

[516] *See* INA §241(b)(3); Convention Against Torture, art. 3; Regulations Concerning the Convention Against Torture, 64 Fed. Reg. 8478 (Feb. 19, 1999).

[517] 8 CFR §§208.31, 241.8(e) (2014).

[518] 8 CFR §§208.31(e), 1208.31(e), 241.8(e), 1241.8(e) (2014). *See also* 8 CFR §§208.2(c)(2), 1208.2(c)(2) (2014) (providing immigration judges with jurisdiction to consider claims for withholding of removal or CAT relief upon referral by an asylum officer). *See infra* pt. V. for a detailed discussion of reasonable fear interviews and proceedings.

[519] Practitioners may be able to argue that eligibility for a special VAWA waiver under INA §212(a)(9)(C)(iii) overcomes the INA §241(a)(5) bar to relief. Despite DHS's 2009 policy memo stating that INA §241(a)(5) applies to VAWA self-petitioners who qualify for a waiver under INA §212(a)(9)(C)(iii), Congressional intent supports the opposite conclusion. *See* Memorandum from Michael Aytes on Adjudicating Forms I-212 for Aliens Inadmissible Under Section 212(a)(9)(C) or Subject to Reinstatement Under Section 241(a)(5) of the Immigration and Nationality Act in light of *Gonzalez v. DHS*, 508 F.3d 1227 (9th Cir. 2007), at 6, n.5 (May 19, 2009). *But see* Violence Against Women and Dep't of Justice Reauthorization Act of 2005, Pub. L. No. 109-162, 1119 Stat. 2960 (Jan. 5, 2006), at §813(b) (stating, "It is the sense of Congress that the officials described in paragraph (1) should particularly consider exercising this authority [to consent to reapplication for admission after a

Continued

prosecutorial discretion.[521] For more creative relief options for individuals subject to reinstatement, see the American Immigration Council's detailed practice advisory on reinstatement of removal, available at *www.legalactioncenter.org/sites/default/files/reinstatement_of_removal_4-29-13_fin.pdf* (last visited Jan. 11, 2015).

Immigration consequences are not the only penalties applicable to individuals who have reentered the United States after deportation or removal. Reentering the United States without authorization after deportation or removal also is punishable by a fine or by imprisonment of not more than two years.[522] An individual convicted of an aggravated felony who subsequently illegally reenters may be sentenced to up to 20 years in prison.[523]

➢ **Practice Pointer**: Prior to advising an individual to apply affirmatively for asylum, practitioners should always determine whether the applicant may be subject to INA §241(a)(5). Determine whether he or she: (1) has been previously issued an order of removal, exclusion, or deportation; (2) was removed or departed voluntarily; and (3) illegally reentered the United States.[524]

---

previous order of removal, deportation, or exclusion] in cases under the Violence Against Women Act of 1994 …").

[520] Victims of trafficking or qualifying criminal activity who qualify for T or U nonimmigrant status may apply for waivers of most inadmissibility grounds. *See* INA §§212(d)(13), (14). Such individuals should seek to waive INA §212(a)(9)(A) for a prior order and INA §212(a)(9)(C)(i)(II) for illegal reentry after a prior order on the waiver application. If the waiver is approved, the prior order would be waived for purposes of INA §241(a)(5). Congressional intent supports this argument. *See* Violence Against Women and Dep't of Justice Reauthorization Act of 2005, Pub. L. No. 109-162, 1119 Stat. 2960 (Jan. 5, 2006), at §813(b) (stating, "It is the sense of Congress that the officials described in paragraph (1) should particularly consider exercising this authority [to consent to reapplication for admission after a previous order of removal, deportation, or exclusion] in cases … involving nonimmigrants described in subparagraph (T) or (U) of section 101(a)(15) of the [INA]…"). Additionally, the U visa regulations provide that DHS orders of removal, deportation, or exclusion will be "deemed canceled by operation of law as of the date of USCIS' approval of From I-918." 8 CFR §§214.14(c)(5)(i), (f)(6) (2014).

[521] DHS may exercise its discretion to place an individual in INA §240 removal proceedings before an immigration judge instead of subjecting him or her to reinstatement of removal. DHS also may exercise its discretion to cancel a reinstatement order or to defer the individual's removal. *See* Am. Immigration Council, *Practice Advisory: Prosecutorial Discretion: How to Advocate for Your Client* (June 24, 2011), *available at www.legalactioncenter.org/sites/default/files/ProsecutorialDiscretion-11-30-10.pdf.*

[522] INA §276(a); 8 USC §1326(a) (2012).

[523] INA §276(b); 8 USC §1326(b) (2012).

[524] For an excellent overview on current law regarding reinstatement and strategies for challenging the process, see AIC Legal Action Center Practice Advisory, *Reinstatement of Removal* (updated April 23, 2008), *available at www.legalactioncenter.org/sites/default/files/reinstatment.pdf.*

VI. How Reinstatement of Removal Works in Practice

The reinstatement of removal process begins upon apprehension of an individual, followed by the initiation of reinstatement proceedings under INA §241(a)(5). During reinstatement proceedings, DHS interrogates the individual and takes his or her sworn statement regarding whether the individual has a prior order of removal, deportation, or exclusion; whether he or she left pursuant to that order; and whether the individual unlawfully reentered. If the individual is exempt from reinstatement or if all three statutory conditions for reinstatement are not met, his or her case will proceed differently than those subject to reinstatement. If the individual is subject to reinstatement and expresses a fear of persecution or torture, he or she will be detained and scheduled for a "reasonable fear interview" with an asylum officer.

During the interview, the asylum-seeker must establish that there is a "reasonable possibility" of persecution or torture upon return to his or her home country. If the asylum officer concludes that there is such a reasonable possibility, the officer will refer the asylum-seeker to an IJ for withholding-only proceedings, during which he or she may make a claim for withholding of removal under INA §241(b)(3) or CAT relief. On the other hand, if the asylum officer concludes that there is not a reasonable possibility of persecution or torture, the officer will make a negative reasonable fear finding.

The individual may request review of the asylum officer's finding by an IJ. If the IJ agrees with the asylum officer, the individual's prior order will be reinstated and he or she will be removed pursuant to the prior order. If, however, the IJ does find that the individual has a reasonable fear of persecution or torture, the IJ will overturn the asylum officer's finding and will place the individual in withholding-only proceedings, during which the individual may make his or her claim for withholding of removal under INA §241(b)(3) and/or CAT relief. These procedures and the legal standards involved during each step of the process are described in detail in this section.

A. Reinstatement Proceedings Before DHS

Upon apprehension of an individual, DHS may initiate reinstatement proceedings. During those proceedings, a DHS officer interrogates the individual to determine whether all three statutory conditions for reinstatement are met: (1) the individual has been subject to a prior order of removal, deportation, or exclusion; (2) the individual left voluntarily or was removed pursuant to the order; and (3) the individual unlawfully reentered the United States.[525] Specifically, the officer must determine whether the individual has been subject to a prior order and "must obtain the prior order of exclusion, deportation, or removal relating to the [individual]."[526] The officer also must verify the identity of the individual to ensure that he or she actually is the

[525] INA §241(a)(5).

[526] 8 CFR §241.8(a)(1) (2014).

individual identified in the prior order.[527] If the identity of the individual is disputed, the officer will verify his or her identity by comparing his or her fingerprints with the fingerprints of the individual previously excluded, deported, or removed in Service records. In the absence of fingerprints in a disputed case, "the [individual] shall not be removed pursuant to this paragraph."[528] Finally, in determining whether the individual unlawfully reentered the United States, the officer "shall consider all relevant evidence, including statements made by the [individual] and any evidence in the [individual]'s possession."[529] If the individual claims that he or she was lawfully admitted, the officer "shall attempt to verify [his or her] claim," which "shall include a check of Service data systems available to the officer."[530] This interrogation takes place under oath and usually results in a written sworn statement.

In addition to verifying that reinstatement applies, DHS is required to ask the individual whether he or she has a fear of return.[531] If DHS determines that the individual is subject to reinstatement but the individual expresses such a fear, DHS must refer him or her to an asylum officer for a reasonable fear interview.[532]

- **Practice Pointer**: Even if an individual is subject to reinstatement, DHS may still place him or her in INA §240 proceedings. Once INA §240 proceedings have commenced, if DHS changes its strategy and wishes to reinstate removal, DHS must file a motion to terminate proceedings with the IJ. A decision to terminate is in the IJ's discretion.

At the end of the interrogation, the officer must complete the top part of Form I-871, Notice of Intent to Reinstate, which contains the factual allegations against the individual and notifies the individual that there is no right to a hearing before an IJ. DHS presents this form to the individual to sign and advises the individual that he or she may make a written or oral statement contesting the determination.[533] If the individual wishes to make a statement, "the officer shall allow [him or her] to do so and shall consider whether [his or her] statement warrants reconsideration of the determination."[534] If the officer does not need to reconsider the determination, his or her supervisor then signs the "Decision, Order and Officer's Certification" on the bottom of Form I-871. Once both the top and bottom portions of the form are completed, the order is immediately executable.

---

[527] 8 CFR §241.8(a)(2) (2014).

[528] *Id.*

[529] 8 CFR §241.8(a)(3) (2014).

[530] *Id.*

[531] 8 CFR §§208.31, 241.8(e) (2014).

[532] *See infra* pt. V.E. for a detailed discussion of reasonable fear standards and interview procedures.

[533] 8 CFR §241.8(b) (2014).

[534] *Id.*

B. Challenging DHS's Reinstatement Order

If an individual believes that a reinstatement order was applied erroneously, he or she may seek reopening or reconsideration directly with DHS.[535] The individual may also challenge the reinstatement order by filing a petition for review in federal court. Every circuit has held that it has jurisdiction over petitions for review of reinstatement orders.[536]

Before a petition for review of a reinstatement order is filed, however, it is essential to consider what impact, if any, a successful challenge will have on the individual's ability to remain in the United States. This is because even if a reinstatement order is vacated, DHS could still place the individual in removal proceedings under INA §240, and individuals subject to reinstatement are also subject to inadmissibility under INA §212(a)(9)(C)(i)(II) for having reentered illegally after a prior removal if they reentered after April 1, 1997. Thus, the individual's options for relief may be significantly limited, as a waiver of this ground is generally not available until ten years after the person's departure.[537]

- **Practice Pointer**: In assisting a client in determining whether to file a petition for review of a reinstatement order, practitioners should consider whether the individual meets the statutory requirements for relief, such as cancellation of removal, asylum, or voluntary departure. This is because if the court or DHS vacates the reinstatement order, the individual may then be in removal proceedings. Additionally, whether the individual is detained, granted a stay of removal, or has the ability to pay for representation could factor in to the individual's decision to challenge a reinstatement order.

- **Practice Pointer**: If a client wishes to file a petition for review of a reinstatement order, practitioners also should advise him or her to seek a stay of removal. This is because a petition for review does not automatically stay the individual's removal. A terrific practice advisory on seeking a stay of removal before a U.S. circuit courts of appeals is available on the National Immigration Project's website at *www.nationalimmigrationproject.org/legalresources/practice_advisorie*

---

535 *See* 8 CFR §103.5 (2014) (governing motions to reopen or reconsider DHS decisions, which should include reinstatement decisions).

536 *Chay Ixcot v. Holder*, 646 F.3d 1202, 1206 (9th Cir. 2011); *Garcia-Villeda v. Mukasey*, 531 F.3d 141, 144 (2d Cir. 2008); *Warner v. Ashcroft*, 381 F.3d 534, 536 (6th Cir. 2004); *Sarmiento-Cisneros v. Ashcroft*, 381 F.3d 1277, 1278 (11th Cir. 2004); *Arevalo v. Ashcroft*, 344 F.3d 1, 9 (1st Cir. 2003); *Avila-Macias v. Ashcroft*, 328 F.3d 108, 110 (3d Cir. 2003); *Briseno-Sanchez v. Heinauer*, 319 F.3d 324, 326 (8th Cir. 2003); *Duran-Hernandez v. Ashcroft*, 348 F.3d 1158, 1162 n.3 (10th Cir. 2003); *Ojeda-Terrazas v. Ashcroft*, 290 F.3d 292, 295 (5th Cir. 2002); *Gomez-Chavez v. ISN*, 308 F.3d 796, 800 (7th Cir. 2002); *Velasquez-Gabriel v. Crocetti*, 263 F.3d 102, 105 (4th Cir. 2001).

537 INA §212(a)(9)(C)(ii).

s/pa_Seeking_a_Judicial_Stay_of_Removal_May2012.pdf (last visited Jan. 15, 2015).

If the decision is made to file a petition for review of a reinstatement order, the petition for review must be filed within 30 days of the date of the reinstatement order.[538]

> **Practice Pointer**: The date of the reinstatement order can be found on the bottom part of From I-871, "Decision, Order and Officer's Certification." It is the date that DHS signed that portion of the form.

If an individual is in reasonable fear or withholding of removal proceedings, the 30-day petition for review clock may not start on the date of the reinstatement order. The Ninth Circuit has held that "where an alien pursues reasonable fear and withholding of removal proceedings following the reinstatement of a prior removal order, the reinstated removal order does not become final [for petition for review purposes] until the reasonable fear of persecution and withholding of removal proceedings are complete."[539] Outside the Ninth Circuit, however, it is advisable to file a petition for review within 30 days of the reinstatement order even if the individual is in reasonable fear or withholding-only proceedings. Doing so will safeguard the individual's right to judicial review.

If the individual misses the 30-day deadline to file a petition for review, he or she may file a motion to reopen or reconsider the reinstatement order with DHS.[540] If DHS denies the motion, the individual may file a petition or review of that denial. However, this option is not available in the Seventh Circuit.[541]

> **Practice Pointer**: The American Immigration Council has a helpful practice advisory on "How to File a Petition for Review," at *www.americanimmigrationcouncil.org/sites/default/files/how_to_file_a_petition_for_review_2011_update_4-23-13.pdf* (last visited Jan. 15, 2015). The American Immigration Council's practice advisory on "Reinstatement of Removal" also has a detailed section on challenging reinstatement orders by filing a petition for review. It addresses the following questions: What if DHS did not timely serve the reinstatement order?; What is the proper venue for a petition for review of a

---

[538] INA §242(b)(1); *Lemos v. Holder* , 636 F.3d 365, 366-67 (7th Cir. 2011); *Ponta-Garca v. Ashcroft*, 386 F.3d 341, 342-43 (1st Cir. 2004).

[539] *Ortiz-Alfaro v. Holder*, 694 F.3d 955, 958 (9th Cir. 2012). *See Herrera-Molina v. Holder*, 597 F.3d 128, 132 (2d Cir. 2010) (raising the issue but not resolving it).

[540] *See, e.g., Luna v. Holder*, 637 F.3d 85, 104-05 (2d Cir. 2011) (stating that a motion to reopen is the appropriate way to raise claims of ineffective assistance of counsel or government misconduct causing the individual to miss the petition for review deadline).

[541] *See Tapia-Lemos v. Holder*, 696 F.3d 687, 690 (7th Cir. 2012) (dismissing the petition for review of a denial of a motion to reopen a reinstatement order under 8 CFR §103.5 (2014) for lack of jurisdiction).

reinstatement order?; What if the person erroneously sought district court review of the reinstatement order?; Are there some reinstatement-related decisions that the circuit court will not review?; and If a petitioner has criminal convictions that would preclude the court of appeals from reviewing a petition for review, does the statutory bar also apply to reinstatement orders? This practice advisory is available on the American Immigration Council's website at *www.legalactioncenter.org/sites/default/files/reinstatement_of_removal_4-29-13_fin.pdf.*

In addition to challenging the reinstatement order itself, it may be possible for the individual to challenge the underlying prior order of removal, deportation, or exclusion. Whether collateral review of the prior order is available, however, depends on the circuit and whether the court will assume jurisdiction over that issue.[542] If an IJ or the BIA reopens the prior proceedings after DHS has issued a reinstatement order, however, the reinstatement order is no longer legally valid because the reopening of the prior proceedings vacates the underlying removal order.[543] Thus, the best option for challenging the prior order may be to file an administrative motion to reopen or reconsider before the IJ or BIA. If the BIA denies such a motion, the individual may file a petition for review before the U.S. circuit courts of appeals.[544] Such a petition would likely be consolidated with any pending petition for review of the reinstatement order.[545]

C. Expression of Fear

If, during the course of the reinstatement process or, in the case of certain aggravated felons, during the course of the administrative removal process, an individual expresses a fear of returning to his or her country of removal, he or she must be referred to an asylum officer for a reasonable fear determination.[546] In the absence of exceptional circumstances, asylum officers are required to conduct the reasonable fear interview and make the reasonable fear determination within 10 days of the referral.[547] If, however, the individual is serving a prison sentence, the asylum

---

[542] *See* INA §241(a)(5) (stating that a prior order is not subject to being reviewed), 242(a)(2)(D) (providing for review of legal and constitutional questions). *See also Torres-Tristan v. Holder*, 656 F.3d 653, 656 (7th Cir. 2011); *Villegas de la Paz v. Holder*, 614 F.3d 605, 610 (6th Cir. 2010); *Avila v. U.S. Att'y Gen.*, 560 F.3d 1281, 1284 (11th Cir. 2009); *Garcia-Villeda v. Mukasey*, 531 F.3d 141, 150 (2d Cir. 2008); *de Rincon v. Mukasey*, 539 F.3d 1133, 1138–39 (9th Cir. 2008); *Debeato v. AG*, 505 F.3d 231, 234-35, 237 (3d Cir. 2007); *Lorenzo v. Mukasey*, 508 F.3d 1278, 1281 (10th Cir. 2007); *Ramirez-Molina v. Ziglar*, 436 F.3d 508, 513–15 (5th Cir. 2006). For a detailed discussion of collateral review, see the American Immigration Council's practice advisory on reinstatement of removal. Am. Immigration Council, *Reinstatement of Removal* (Apr. 29, 2013), *available at www.legalactioncenter.org/sites/default/files/reinstatement_of_removal_4-29-13_fin.pdf* (last visited Jan. 16, 2015).

[543] *Nken v. Holder*, 129 S. Ct. 1749, 1759 (2009).

[544] *See* INA §242(a); *Kucana v. Holder*, 130 S. Ct. 827, 834, 838–39 (2010).

[545] *See* INA §242(b)(6).

[546] 8 CFR §§208.31(a), (b), 1208.31(a), (b) (2014).

[547] 8 CFR §§208.31(b), 1208.31(b) (2014).

officer will not conduct the reasonable fear interview until the individual's sentence is nearly completed or the individual is soon to be released to DHS custody.[548] The referring officer should give the applicant Form G-56, Notice of Reasonable Fear Interview and Form M-488, Information on Reasonable Fear Interview, and a list of legal services if the applicant is not represented.[549]

D. Detention

Asylum officers conduct reasonable-fear interviews for two categories of individuals: (1) those subject to reinstatement of removal because they illegally reentered the United States after having been removed or having departed voluntarily while under an order of removal, deportation, or exclusion;[550] and (2) those who are not lawful permanent residents, who are subject to an administrative removal order because they were convicted of one or more aggravated felonies after admission to the United States.[551] Thus, in most cases, individuals subject to reasonable fear interviews will be detained.

> ➢ **Practice Pointer**: If an individual is determined to have a reasonable fear of persecution or torture by an asylum officer or an IJ, it may be possible for him or her to argue that he or she is entitled to a bond hearing pursuant to INA §236(a). The Due Process Clause of the Fifth Amendment protects individuals from deprivation of their liberty interest without due process of law, including freedom from government detention.[552] There must be a justification for non-punitive detention that outweighs these significant liberty interests.[553] Additionally, the Supreme Court has stated that the authority to detain an individual cannot arise under a statute that does not affirmatively authorize such detention.[554] In the context of immigration detention, the applicable statutes are INA §§241(a), 235, and 236. INA §241(a)(5), the reinstatement statute, does not convey detention authority in any way. INA §241(a) conveys detention authority for individuals who have been ordered removed and have entered the removal period only. It may be argued that none of the specific situations that trigger the removal period set forth in the statute are present, and therefore, INA

---

[548] *Id.*

[549] *See* INS Memorandum, J. Weiss, "Guidelines for Children's Asylum Claims," at 8 (Dec. 10, 1998), *published on* AILA InfoNet (*posted* Jan. 25, 1999), *reproduced in* 76 INTERPRETER RELEASES 1 and Appendix I (Jan. 4, 1999), and *available at www.nlada.org/Training/Train_Civil/Equal_Justice/2007_Materials/109_2007_Kerwin_handout7*.

[550] *See* INA §241(a)(5); 8 CFR §241.8 (2014).

[551] *See* INA §238(b); 8 CFR §238.1 (2014).

[552] *Foucha v. Louisiana*, 504 U.S. 71, 80 (1992).

[553] *Zadvydas v. Davis*, 533 U.S. 678, 690 (2001).

[554] *Clark v. Martinez*, 543 U.S. 371, 385–86 (2005).

§241(a)(1)(B) is inapplicable. INA §235 refers to the detention of individuals upon arrival who have asserted a fear of return and whose credible fear proceedings are ongoing. That statute is not applicable in the reinstatement context. Thus, DHS's authority to detain an individual seeking protection from removal after having previously been removed must arise under INA §§236(a) or (c). If the individual is not subject to mandatory detention under INA §236(c), he or she could argue for release on bond pursuant to INA §236(a).[555]

- **Practice Pointer**: For a detailed discussion of detention of asylum-seekers and strategies for seeking their release, see chapter 9 of this book.

E. Reasonable Fear Standards and Interview Procedures

The purpose of the reasonable fear determination is to ensure compliance with U.S. treaty obligations not to return an individual to a situation of persecution or torture, while also adhering to laws directing certain categories of individuals to streamlined removal proceedings.[556] Similar to credible fear interviews in expedited removal proceedings, "reasonable fear determinations serve as a screening mechanism to identify potentially meritorious claims for further consideration by an immigration judge, and at the same time to prevent individuals subject to removal from delaying removal by filing clearly unmeritorious or frivolous claims."[557]

In order to qualify for a hearing before an IJ, an individual who has expressed a fear of persecution or torture must establish—in an interview conducted by an asylum officer—that he or she has a "reasonable fear" of persecution or torture.[558] The individual will be determined to have a "reasonable fear of persecution or torture" if he or she credibly "establishes a reasonable possibility that he or she would be persecuted on account of his or her race, religion, nationality, membership in a particular social group, or political opinion, or a reasonable possibility that he or she would be tortured in the country of removal," as torture is defined in the regulations.[559] The "reasonable possibility" standard used in reasonable fear determinations is higher than the "significant possibility" standard used in credible

[555] 8 CFR §1003.19 (2014); *Matter of Patel*, 15 I&N Dec. 666, 667 (BIA 1979).

[556] U.S. Citizenship and Immigration Servs., *Reasonable Fear of Persecution and Torture Determinations*, at 5, in Asylum Officer Basic Training Course Workbook (Aug. 6, 2008) [hereinafter AOBTC Workbook, Reasonable Fear and Torture Determinations], *available at www.uscis.gov/sites/default/files/USCIS/Humanitarian/Refugees%20%26%20Asylum/Asylum/AOBTC%20Lesson%20Plans/Reasonable-of-Persecution-Torture-Determinations-31aug10.pdf.*

[557] *Id.* at 5–6.

[558] 8 CFR §§208.31(c), 1208.31(c) (2014).

[559] 8 CFR §§208.31(c), 1208.31(c) (2014). Torture is defined in the regulations at 8 CFR §§208.18(a)(1) , 1208.18(a)(1) (2014). *See* chapter 2 for a detailed discussion of persecution on account of the five protected grounds; chapter 3 for a detailed discussion of the elements required to meet the definition of torture and the forms of protection under the Convention Against Torture.

fear determinations, but it is lower than the "more likely than not" standard required to establish eligibility for withholding of removal.[560] According to the USCIS Asylum Division, the "reasonable possibility" standard for reasonable fear determinations is the same legal standard used to establish a well-founded fear of persecution in the asylum context.[561]

> ➢ **Practice Pointer**: See chapter 4 of this book for a detailed discussion and comparison of the various standards of proof.

In considering whether the applicant has established a reasonable possibility of persecution upon his or her removal, the asylum officer will evaluate:

- Whether the harm the applicant fears is sufficiently severe to amount to persecution;
- Whether the feared harm would be on account of a protected characteristic (race, religion, nationality, membership in a particular social group, or political opinion);
- Whether the applicant suffered past persecution on account of a protected characteristic — if so, there is a presumption that the applicant also has a well-founded fear of future persecution on the same basis;
- Whether the applicant could safely and reasonably relocate within the country of feared persecution; and
- Whether the persecutor is either an agent of the government or an entity that the government is unable or unwilling to control.[562]

These determinations are no different than asylum officers' determinations in the affirmative asylum context.

In considering whether the applicant has established a reasonable possibility of torture upon his or her removal, the asylum officer will evaluate all elements of the definition of torture and eligibility for CAT protection,[563] including:

- Intent — there must be a reasonable possibility the feared harm would be specifically intended by the offender to inflict severe physical or mental pain or suffering;
- Severe pain or suffering — there must be a reasonable possibility the applicant will suffer severe physical or mental pain or suffering;

---

[560] *See* AOBTC Workbook, Reasonable Fear and Torture Determinations, *supra* note 556, at 8. *See also* EOIR Memorandum, Office of Chief Immigration Judge on Operating Policies and Procedures Memorandum No. 99-5: Implementation of Article 3 of the UN Convention Against Torture (May 14, 1999), AILA InfoNet (*posted* June 4, 1999), *available at www.usdoj.gov/eoir/efoia/ocij/oppm99/99_5.pdf*; *see also* chapter 5.

[561] *See* AOBTC Workbook, Reasonable Fear and Torture Determinations, *supra* note 556, at 8. *See* chapter 4 for a detailed discussion of the various legal standards used in asylum-related procedures.

[562] AOBTC Workbook, Reasonable Fear and Torture Determinations, *supra* note 556, at 10–12.

[563] *Id.* at 14–26.

- Government official — there must be a reasonable possibility the pain or suffering would be inflicted by or at the instigation of a public official or other person acting in an official capacity, or there must be a reasonable possibility the pain or suffering would be inflicted with the consent or acquiescence of a public official or other person acting in an official capacity;
- Custody or control — there must be a reasonable possibility the feared harm would be inflicted while the applicant is in the custody or physical control of the offender; and
- Lawful sanctions — there must be a reasonable possibility the feared harm would not arise only from, or be inherent in or incidental to lawful sanctions, unless there is a reasonable possibility those sanctions would defeat the object and purpose of the Convention Against Torture.[564]

Given the lower standard applied in the reasonable fear screening process, asylum officers are instructed not to consider whether the applicant could relocate to another part of his or her country.[565]

A finding of reasonable fear of persecution or torture cannot be based on past persecution or torture alone, because withholding of removal only provides protection from future persecution or future torture. Thus, the individual must demonstrate a reasonable possibility of future persecution or torture, regardless of the severity of the past persecution or torture.[566] Past persecution or torture, however, raises the presumption that the applicant's fear of future persecution or torture is reasonable.[567]

There are no bars to establishing a reasonable fear of persecution or torture.[568] Thus, when making a reasonable fear determination, the asylum officer is prohibited from considering whether the applicant is subject to any bars to withholding of removal.[569] Asylum officers are instructed, however, to elicit information related to possible bars and to flag cases with possible bars.[570] The IJ will make the ultimate decision regarding whether a mandatory bar to withholding of removal applies.[571]

Like in the credible fear process, the applicant bears the burden of proof in establishing a reasonable fear of persecution or torture. The testimony of the applicant, if credible, may be sufficient to meet his or her burden of proof without corroboration. Asylum officers are instructed to follow the Asylum Officer Basic Training Course guidance regarding credibility, burden of proof, and evidence from

---

[564] *See* 8 CFR §208.18 (2014) (defining torture).

[565] AOBTC Workbook, Reasonable Fear and Torture Determinations, *supra* note 556, at 26.

[566] AOBTC Workbook, Reasonable Fear and Torture Determinations, *supra* note 556, at 12.

[567] *Id.*

[568] 8 CFR §§208.31(c), 1208.31(c) (2014).

[569] 8 CFR §§208.31(c), 1208.31(c) (2014). See chapter 2.7.2 for a list of these mandatory bars.

[570] AOBTC Workbook, Reasonable Fear and Torture Determinations, *supra* note 556, at 26.

[571] 8 CFR §208.16(c)(4) (2014).

the affirmative asylum context in evaluating whether lack of corroboration affects the applicant's ability to establish a reasonable fear of persecution or torture.[572]

Unlike the credible fear process, an asylum officer in a reasonable fear interview must make an actual finding as to whether the applicant's claim is or is not credible.[573] He or she will consider the same factors as considered in evaluating credibility in the affirmative asylum context:

(1) demeanor, candor, or responsiveness;

(2) consistency between the applicant's written and oral statements;

(3) internal consistency of each such statement;

(4) consistency of such statements with other evidence of record;

(5) any inaccuracies or falsehoods in such statements; and

(6) any other relevant factor.[574]

Additionally, the asylum officer must take into account the effects of trauma, cultural factors, the use of an interpreter, and other factors that may impede clear communication or lead to misunderstandings.[575]

If parts of the applicant's testimony are found not credible, the asylum officer must evaluate whether those parts are relevant to the applicant's claim. If those portions of testimony are not relevant to the applicant's claim, they may not form the basis for an adverse credibility finding in the reasonable fear determination.[576] If there are any relevant inconsistencies or discrepancies, the asylum officer must provide the applicant the opportunity to address and explain them.[577] Asylum officers are instructed to review all prior testimony of the applicant and question him or her about any inconsistencies between that testimony and the testimony given during a reasonable fear interview.[578] An individual in the reasonable fear process may have previously requested asylum and withholding of removal. If an IJ has made a prior credibility determination, the asylum officer should accord deference to it, but is not strictly bound by the prior determination.[579] This is because the evidence presented or the nature of the claim may be different.

---

[572] AOBTC Workbook, Reasonable Fear and Torture Determinations, *supra* note 556, at 27.

[573] *Id.* at 9.

[574] INA §208(b)(1)(B)(iii). *See supra* chapter 4 for a detailed discussion of credibility standards and determinations.

[575] AOBTC Workbook, Reasonable Fear and Torture Determinations, *supra* note 556, at 9.

[576] *Id.*

[577] *Id.*

[578] *Id.* at 9–10.

[579] *Id.* at 10.

The asylum officer must conduct the interview in a non-adversarial manner, separate and apart from the general public.[580] In most cases, the applicant will be detained. At the beginning of the interview, the asylum officer should determine that the applicant has an understanding of the reasonable fear determination process and answer any questions that the applicant may have.[581] The asylum officer has the authority to administer oaths, verify the identity of the applicant, verify the identity of any interpreter, present and receive evidence, and question the applicant or any witnesses.[582] There is no need to submit a Form I-589 for the purposes of the reasonable fear screening process.[583]

- **Practice Pointer**: Practitioners should meet with their clients prior to a reasonable fear interview to review the client's procedural history, details of his or her protection claim, the purpose of the interview, the types of questions that could be asked, and the importance of providing truthful and detailed testimony.

1. *Orientation*

An asylum officer should first conduct an orientation with the applicant, which may be conducted by telephone.[584] The asylum officer should check whether the applicant has any medical problems and whether the applicant will have any special needs during the interview, such as an interpreter who speaks an unusual language.[585]

- **Practice Pointer**: If an applicant speaks an unusual language or dialect, the asylum officer will proceed in the applicant's next best language if necessary, but only if the applicant consents and demonstrates adequate competence in that language.

During the interview, the asylum officer should ensure that the applicant has received and understood the M-488, has a list of pro bono representatives if unrepresented, and if represented, the officer should obtain or confirm information on how to contact the representative.[586]

2. *Scheduling of the Interview*

In the absence of exceptional circumstances, the reasonable fear determination will be conducted within 10 days of the referral.[587] A case is not considered referred until the asylum office has received notice that a person requires a reasonable fear

---

580 8 CFR §§208.31(c), 1208.31(c) (2014).

581 8 CFR §§208.31(c), 1208.31(c) (2014).

582 8 CFR §§208.31(d), 1208.31(d) (2014).

583 *See* INS Memorandum, *supra* note 549, at 7.

584 *Id.* at 8.

585 *Id.*

586 *Id.*

587 8 CFR §§208.31(b), 1208.31(b) (2014).

screening and has also received the A-file.[588] In determining whether the interview or adjudication should be delayed, the asylum office is instructed to err on the side of ensuring that the applicant is able to present his or her full claim, so long as there is no evidence of intentional delay tactics or abuse of process.[589] The interview should normally be scheduled approximately 48 hours after the orientation, unless the applicant states that he or she is ready to proceed sooner.[590] Generally, if the applicant is represented, the asylum officer should schedule the interview for a date and time that the representative may be present, unless the representative requests an interview date that will prevent the asylum officer from making a reasonable fear determination within the requisite 10-day period *and* it appears the representative's request is based on a delay tactic or convenience, rather than to address legitimate conflicts with commitments that cannot be rescheduled.[591]

- **Practice Pointer**: Given the significant increase in individuals requiring reasonable fear interviews in recent years, the USCIS Asylum Division's resources are limited and reasonable fear interviews often do not occur within ten days of referral. Reasonable fear delays resulted in a class action lawsuit being filed by the American Civil Liberties Union, National Immigration Justice Center, and Reed Smith LLP on behalf of thousands of individuals fleeing persecution who have faced months of detention awaiting reasonable fear determinations.[592]

3. *Representation*

The applicant may be represented by counsel or an accredited representative at the interview, at no expense to the government.[593] The representative should submit a Form G-28, Notice of Entry of Appearance, signed by the attorney or representative and the applicant. The representative may present a statement at the end of the interview and, where appropriate, should be allowed to make clarifying statements.[594] The asylum officer, in his or her discretion, may limit the number of persons who may be present at the interview and the length of the representative's statement.[595] Representatives may participate in the interview by telephone if travel to a remote

---

[588] *See* INS Memorandum, *supra* note 549, at 7.

[589] *Id.* at 8.

[590] *Id.*

[591] *Id.* at 8–9.

[592] *See* Nat'l Immigrant Justice Ctr., *Detained Asylum Seekers Sue Obama Administration to End Long Waits for Initial Interviews* (Apr. 17, 2014), *available at www.immigrantjustice.org/sites/immigrantjustice.org/files/RFI%20brief%20FINAL%20filed.pdf*.

[593] 8 CFR §§208.31(c), 1208.31(c) (2014).

[594] 8 CFR §§208.31(c), 1208.31(c) (2014).

[595] 8 CFR §§208.31(c), 1208.31(c) (2014).

location is difficult on short notice, as long as their participation is at no expense to the government.[596]

- **Practice Pointer**: Practitioners should always exercise their right to be present during a reasonable fear interview and to ask clarifying questions at the end that will bring out important details relevant to the claim. Practitioners also should preserve arguments regarding asylum eligibility — not just withholding of removal eligibility — orally and in writing during the reasonable fear interview process.[597]

4. *Confidentiality*

The information regarding the applicant's fear of persecution or torture that he or she provided during the reasonable fear interview is confidential and cannot be disclosed without his or her written consent.[598] Asylum officers are instructed to explain the confidential nature of the interview to the applicant at the beginning of the interview.[599]

5. *Testimony and Evidence*

The applicant may present evidence, if available, relevant to the possibility of persecution or torture at the interview.[600] Country conditions information is integral to most reasonable fear determinations and asylum officers are instructed to take country conditions information into account in evaluating whether an individual has a reasonable fear of persecution or torture.[601]

The asylum officer is instructed to elicit the following information from the applicant during his or her reasonable fear interview:

- What the applicant fears would happen to him or her if returned to the particular country, including details regarding the specific type of harm the applicant fears;
- Whom the applicant fears;
- The relationship of the feared persecutor or torturer to the government or government officials;
- If a potential torturer is not a public official or someone acting in an official capacity, whether there is evidence that a public official or other person acting in

---

[596] *See* INS Memorandum, *supra* note 549, at 9.

[597] *See infra* pt. VI.F. for a detailed discussion of withholding-only proceedings and potential arguments regarding an individual's eligibility for asylum. *See also* AILA Amicus Br. submitted in *Perez-Guzman v. Holder* in the Ninth Circuit, posted Apr. 9, 2014 on AILA InfoNet at Doc. No. 14040940 and *available at www.aila.org/content/default.aspx?docid=48089.*

[598] 8 CFR §208.6 (2014).

[599] AOBTC Workbook, Reasonable Fear and Torture Determinations, *supra* note 556, at 29.

[600] 8 CFR §§208.31(c), 1208.31(c) (2014).

[601] AOBTC Workbook, Reasonable Fear and Torture Determinations, *supra* note 556, at 27–28.

an official capacity would have prior knowledge of the torture and would breach a legal duty to prevent the torture;

- The reasons someone would want to harm the applicant;
- Whether the applicant has been or would be in the feared offender's custody or control;
- Whether the harm the applicant fears may be pursuant to legitimate sanctions;
- Information about any individuals similarly situated to the applicant, including family members or others closely associated with the applicant, who have been threatened, persecuted, tortured, or otherwise harmed;
- Any groups or organizations the applicant is associated with that would place him or her at risk of persecution or torture, in light of country conditions information;
- Any actions the applicant has taken in the past (either in the country of feared persecution or another country, including the U.S.) that would place him or her at risk of persecution or torture, in light of country conditions information;
- Any experiences of persecution, torture, or other harm that the applicant has experienced in the past, including: a description of the type of harm, identification of who harmed the applicant, the reason the applicant was harmed, the relationship between the person who harmed the applicant and the government, whether the applicant was in that person's custody or control, and whether the harm was in accordance with legitimate sanctions.[602]

The applicant must also be given the opportunity to explain any relevant discrepancies in his or her testimony, including inconsistencies, inability to provide detail, and perceived implausibility.[603]

6. *Interpretation*

If the applicant is unable to proceed effectively in English, and if the asylum officer is unable to proceed competently in the language chosen by the applicant, the asylum officer must arrange for an interpreter in conducting the interview.[604] The interpreter may not be a representative or employee of the applicant's country, or if stateless, the applicant's country of last habitual residence.[605] Before or during the interview, the applicant's request for a male or female interpreter should be accommodated when possible.[606] If the applicant, the applicant's representative, or the asylum officer believes that the interpreter is either not competent or not neutral, the officer may terminate the interview and request a different interpreter.[607] The

[602] *Id.* at 30–31.

[603] *Id.* at 9–10.

[604] 8 CFR §§208.31(c), 1208.31(c) (2014).

[605] 8 CFR §§208.31(c), 1208.31(c) (2014).

[606] *See* INS Memorandum, *supra* note 549, at 12.

[607] *Id.*

applicant may provide his or her own interpreter.[608] If the applicant uses his or her own interpreter, the asylum officer is required to use a commercial interpreter to monitor the applicant's interpreter.[609]

> ➤ **Practice Pointer**: An asylum officer may conduct the interview in the applicant's language if the officer has been certified by the State Department (DOS) and if the local office permits asylum officers to conduct interviews in languages other than English.[610]

7. *Record*

Asylum officers must take notes in the question and answer format, recorded on a sworn statement.[611] At the end of the interview, the asylum officer must allow the applicant to read the sworn statement and make any corrections before signing it.[612] The asylum officer must create a summary of the material facts as stated by the applicant.[613] The asylum officer is required to place this information on Form I-899, Reasonable Fear Worksheet.[614] At the conclusion of the interview, the asylum officer must review the summary with the applicant and allow the applicant to correct any errors in the summary.[615]

8. *Withdrawals*

An applicant referred for a reasonable fear interview may seek to withdraw his or her request at any time during the reasonable fear process.[616] When such a request is made, the asylum officer must conduct an interview with the applicant to determine whether the decision to withdraw is entered into knowingly and willingly.[617] The officer must determine the following:

- The nature of the fear that the applicant originally expressed to the DHS officer;
- Why the applicant no longer wishes to seek protection and whether there are any particular facts that led the applicant to change his or her mind;
- Whether any coercion or pressure was brought to bear on the applicant in order to have him or her withdraw the request; and

---

[608] *Id.* at 10–11.

[609] *Id.*

[610] AOBTC Workbook, Reasonable Fear and Torture Determinations, *supra* note 556, at 29.

[611] *Id.* at 29–30.

[612] *Id.* at 30.

[613] 8 CFR §§208.31(c), 1208.31(c) (2014).

[614] *See* INS Memorandum, *supra* note 549, at 9.

[615] 8 CFR §§208.31(c), 1208.31(c) (2014).

[616] AOBTC Workbook, Reasonable Fear and Torture Determinations, *supra* note 556, at 32.

[617] *Id.*

- Whether the applicant clearly understands the consequences of withdrawal, including that he or she will be barred from any legal entry into the United States for a period that may run from five years to life.[618]

Information regarding whether the request to withdraw is knowing and voluntary is central to the officer's determination whether to process the withdrawal. As long as the request is knowing and voluntary, an asylum officer may process the withdrawal of the claim for protection, even if the applicant still fears harm.[619]

9. Decision

The asylum officer must create a written record of his or her determination, including a summary of the material facts as stated by the applicant, any additional facts relied on by the asylum officer, and the asylum officer's determination of whether, in light of such facts, the applicant has established a reasonable fear of persecution or torture.[620]

If the asylum officer determines that the applicant has not established a reasonable fear of persecution or torture, the asylum officer must inform the applicant in writing of the decision and must inquire whether the applicant wishes to have an IJ review the negative decision.[621] The asylum officer must use Form I-898, Record of Negative Reasonable Fear Interview Finding and Request for Review by Immigration Judge.[622] The applicant must indicate on Form I-898 whether he or she desires an IJ review.[623] An applicant who does not request an IJ review is subject to immediate removal from the United States.[624]

On the other hand, if the asylum officer determines that the applicant has a reasonable fear of persecution or torture, he or she must inform the applicant and issue a Form I-863, Notice of Referral to an Immigration Judge, for a full consideration of the request for withholding of removal only.[625]

> ➢ **Practice Pointer**: A terrific resource for navigating withholding-only proceedings is the "Withholding-Only Proceedings Toolkit" prepared by the Pennsylvania State University Dickinson School of Law's Center for Immigrants' Rights. The Toolkit is available online at *https://*

---

[618] *Id.*

[619] *Id.*

[620] 8 CFR §§208.31(c), 1208.31(c) (2014).

[621] 8 CFR §§208.31(f), 1208.31(f) (2014).

[622] 8 CFR §§208.31(f), 1208.31(f) (2014).

[623] 8 CFR §§208.31(f), 1208.31(f) (2014).

[624] *See* INS Memorandum, *supra* note 549, at 5. Re-interviews may be available for reasonable-fear applicants as well.

[625] 8 CFR §§208.31(e), 1208.31(e) (2014).

pennstatelaw.psu.edu/sites/default/files/documents/pdfs/Immigrants/Withholding-Only-Toolkit.pdf.[626]

F. Withholding-Only Proceedings Before an Immigration Judge

Once the Form I-863 is filed with the immigration court, the IJ has exclusive jurisdiction over the application for withholding of removal.[627] Withholding-only cases should be adjudicated within 10 days of the issuance of the I-863.[628] The Office of the Chief Immigration Judge, however, has instructed IJs that in scheduling and adjudicating withholding-only cases, IJs should balance the dictates of due process concerns and regulatory compliance concerns.[629] A hearing notice, entitled Notice of Withholding-Only Hearing, must be sent to the applicant in care of his or her custodial authority and to his or her attorney, if any, via an appropriate overnight courier.[630]

Withholding-only proceedings are more limited than removal proceedings under INA §240 and take place after an order of removal has already been issued by DHS. In withholding-only proceedings, an IJ is permitted to consider withholding of removal under INA §241(b)(3), withholding under the Convention Against Torture, and deferral of removal under the Convention Against Torture, and must adjudicate the case in accordance with 8 CFR §§208.16, 1208.16.[631]

DHS takes the position that the only relief that an individual may seek in these proceedings is withholding of removal under INA §241(b)(3) or withholding or deferral of removal under the CAT. However, there is a strong argument that such individuals remain eligible for asylum under INA §208, notwithstanding INA §241(a)(5)'s bar to relief. The plain language of the asylum statute states that "*Any alien* who is physically present in the United States or who arrives in the United States …, irrespective of such alien's status, may apply for asylum in accordance with this section … ."[632] Thus, in order to reconcile the asylum and reinstatement statutes, individuals must not be precluded from applying for asylum. Any

---

[626] (last visited Mar. 26, 2015).

[627] 8 CFR §§208.2(c)(2), 1208.2(c)(2) (2014).

[628] 8 CFR §§208.31(e), 1208.31(e) (2014).

[629] EOIR Memorandum, Office of Chief Immigration Judge, "Operating Policies and Procedures Memorandum No. 99-5: Implementation of Article 3 of the UN Convention Against Torture," at 661 (May 14, 1999), *published on* AILA InfoNet (*posted* June 4, 1999), and *available at* *www.usdoj.gov/eoir/efoia/ocij/oppm99/99_5.pdf.*

[630] *Id.*

[631] 8 CFR §§208.31(e), 1208.31(e) (2014). *See* 8 CFR §§208.16, 1208.16 (2014). See also chapter 2 for a detailed discussion of withholding of removal under INA §241(b)(3); chapter 3 for a detailed discussion of relief under the Convention Against Torture.

[632] INA §208(a)(1) (emphasis added). *See also Fernandez-Vargas v. Holder*, 548 U.S. 30, 35 n.4 (2006) (indicating that asylum remains available to individuals subject to reinstatement); *Herrera-Molina v. Holder*, 597 F.3d 128, 139 n.8 (2d Cir. 2010) (noting the Supreme Court's acknowledgement of the availability of asylum).

interpretation otherwise arguably conflicts with congressional intent and leads to arbitrary results, excluding bona fide refugees from seeking asylum. Additionally, INA §241(a)(5) does not actually state that an individual with a reinstated removal order is ineligible for asylum, only that the IJ has exclusive jurisdiction over any application for withholding of removal. Finally, the reinstatement regulations indicating that asylum is not available to individuals subject to reinstatement are arguably ultra vires to the statute and unlawful.[633]

- ➢ **Practice Pointer**: Practitioners should argue before the immigration courts that clients who pass the reasonable fear interview should not be limited to withholding of removal as a form of relief, but rather, should also be permitted to seek asylum under INA §208, notwithstanding INA §241(a)(5)'s bar to relief and the regulations governing reinstated removal proceedings.[634] Doing so preserves the issue in immigration court and before the Board of Immigration Appeals, even though the actual argument for asylum is unlikely to be addressed until the case reaches a court of appeals. Applicants have had some success with these arguments before the circuit courts. One woman, for example, had her expedited removal order rescinded and her case remanded for a new hearing during which she could seek asylum.[635]

- ➢ **Practice Pointer**: Practitioners also should consider negotiating with DHS to cancel the administrative removal order or reinstatement order and issue a Notice to Appear in INA §240 proceedings instead as a matter of prosecutorial discretion, especially in cases where clients were unlawfully prevented from access to a credible fear interview by improper or erroneous border screenings and where clients would be eligible for relief in INA §240 proceedings but not in INA §238(b) or 241(a)(5) proceedings.

1. Master Calendar Hearing

The initial appearance before an IJ in withholding-only proceedings is usually at a master calendar hearing. Since individuals in withholding-only proceedings do not receive traditional Notices to Appear (Form I-862), there are no formal charges to admit or deny. During that hearing, however, the IJ will advise the applicant of his or her rights, including the right to counsel at no expense to the government, the right to

---

[633] *Compare* INA §208(a) *with* 8 CFR §1208.31(e). *See* AILA Amicus Br. submitted in *Perez-Guzman v. Holder* in the Ninth Circuit, *published on* AILA InfoNet at Doc. No. 14040940 (*posted* Apr. 9, 2014).

[634] *See id.*

[635] *See, e.g.*, National Immigrant Justice Center, *Maldonado-Lopez v. Holder* (Feb. 4, 2014), *available at www.immigrantjustice.org/court_cases/maldonado-lopez-v-holder* (last visited Mar. 25, 2015).

present evidence, and the right to appeal to the BIA.[636] The IJ also will determine if the applicant will be seeking withholding of removal or protection under the CAT.[637] The applicant also will be given adequate time to prepare and file a Form I-589 withholding of removal application and will be scheduled for an individual hearing.[638] Once the IJ receives the I-589, a copy will be forwarded to DOS, and the IJ must schedule a merits hearing.[639]

- ➢ **Practice Pointer**: Practitioners should be prepared to file the applicant's I-589 application at the master calendar hearing. However, if necessary, practitioners may decide to file the I-589 at a later call-up date.
- ➢ **Practice Pointer**: Practitioners also should be prepared to raise any arguments regarding the unlawfulness of a reinstatement order or an administrative removal order, as well as asylum eligibility notwithstanding a reinstatement or administrative removal order. Doing so preserves these important issues for appeal and provides the IJ with the opportunity to request briefing and consider these issues.

2. *Individual Hearing*

During a withholding-only proceeding, the IJ will consider the applicant's eligibility for withholding of removal under INA §241(b)(3) or withholding or deferral of removal under the CAT. The applicant has the right to testify, call witnesses, present evidence, and cross-examine witnesses. DHS will cross-examine the applicant and any witnesses the applicant presents. The IJ also may question the applicant and any witnesses presented. The withholding-only proceeding may be conducted by videoconference or telephonically.[640] If an interpreter is needed, the immigration court must provide one.[641]

The applicant bears the burden of proof in establishing that he or she is eligible for withholding of removal under INA §241(b)(3) or CAT protection. If the applicant establishes that it is more likely than not that his or her life or freedom would be threatened in the country of removal on account of his or her race, religion, nationality, membership in a particular social group, or political opinion, he or she may be granted withholding of removal under INA §241(b)(3).[642] If the applicant

---

[636] INA §240(b)(4); 8 CFR §1240.10(a) (2014); *Immigration Court Practice Manual*, chapter 4.15(e), *available at www.justice.gov/eoir/vll/OCIJPracManual/Practice_Manual_review.pdf* (last visited Jan. 18. 2015).

[637] *Immigration Court Practice Manual*, chapter 7.4(h)(iii), *available at www.justice.gov/eoir/vll/OCIJPracManual/Practice_Manual_review.pdf* (last visited Jan. 18. 2015).

[638] *Immigration Court Practice Manual*, chapter 4.15(e), *available at www.justice.gov/eoir/vll/OCIJPracManual/Practice_Manual_review.pdf* (last visited Jan. 18. 2015).

[639] *Id.*

[640] *Id.*

[641] *Id.*

[642] *See also* chapter 2 for a detailed discussion of withholding of removal under INA §241(b)(3).

demonstrates that it is more likely than not that he or she would be tortured upon removal, he or she may be granted protection under the CAT.[643] If the IJ finds that it is more likely than not that the applicant will be persecuted or tortured upon his or her removal, the IJ will then consider whether the applicant is barred from a grant of withholding of removal.[644] If a bar applies, the only relief eligible to the applicant will be deferral of removal under the CAT.[645] If the applicant has established that it is more likely than not that he or she would be tortured in the country of removal, the IJ will grant deferral of removal.[646]

If the IJ grants withholding or deferral of removal, the applicant cannot be removed to the country where he or she fears persecution or torture, but may be removed to another country.[647] It is also possible that the applicant will continue to be detained following a positive IJ decision.[648] On the other hand, if the IJ does not grant withholding or deferral of removal, the applicant may appeal the IJ decision to the Board of Immigration Appeals.[649]

- **Practice Pointer**: Practitioners should be prepared to address any inconsistencies in the record, either from the applicant's sworn statement following his or her apprehension, the applicant's sworn statement during the reasonable fear interview, or prior statements that may be in his or her A-file.
- **Practice Pointer**: Practitioners also should be prepared to present testimony and evidence much like during INA §240 proceedings, including expert testimony, corroborating witnesses, medical documentation, and other evidence in support of the applicant's protection claim.

G. Reasonable Fear Review by an Immigration Judge

If the asylum officer determines that the person did not establish a reasonable fear of persecution, the person may seek review of that determination by an IJ.[650] The asylum officer must serve the applicant with Form I-863, Notice of Referral to the Immigration Judge.[651] The record of the determination, including copies of the I-863,

---

[643] *See also* chapter 3 for a detailed discussion of relief under the Convention Against Torture.

[644] *See* 8 CFR §208.16(d) (2014); INA §241(b)(3)(B).

[645] See chapter 2 for a detailed discussion of the bars to withholding of removal; chapter 3 for a detailed discussion of deferral of removal under CAT.

[646] *See* 8 CFR §208.17 (2014).

[647] See chapter 2 for a detailed discussion of withholding of removal under INA §241(b)(3); chapter 3 for a detailed discussion of relief under the Convention Against Torture.

[648] See chapter 9 for a detailed discussion of detention and strategies for seeking release.

[649] 8 CFR §§208.31(e), 1208.31(e) (2014).

[650] 8 CFR §§208.31(f), (g), 1208.31(f), (g) (2014).

[651] 8 CFR §§208.31(g), 1208.31(g) (2014).

the asylum officer's notes, the summary of material facts, and other materials on which the determination was based must be provided to the IJ with the negative determination.[652] It is likely that applicants who request a reasonable fear review will be detained at a DHS facility or in a federal, state, or local jail or prison. If the distance from the immigration court renders it impractical for the Asylum Office to file Form I-863 in person, the court administrator will allow the filing of Form I-863 by fax.[653] The IJ review shall be conducted within ten days of the filing of Form I-863. The hearing notice must be sent via an appropriate overnight courier to the applicant, in care of his or her custodial authority, and to the applicant's attorney, if any.[654]

The regulations do not describe how a reasonable fear review will be conducted. Because the proceedings resemble credible fear reviews, the chief immigration judge has instructed IJs that they should be modeled after credible fear review proceedings.[655] IJs are required to record reasonable fear review proceedings.[656] The proceedings may be conducted by videoconference or telephonically.[657] If an interpreter is necessary, the immigration court must provide one.[658] Since the regulations do not specify whether an applicant has the right to be represented by counsel during the reasonable fear review, the chief immigration judge has instructed IJs that it is within their discretion whether to permit an applicant to be represented by counsel during the reasonable fear review.[659]

The IJ must make a *de novo* determination of whether the applicant has established a reasonable fear of persecution or torture.[660] If the IJ agrees with the asylum officer's determination, the case will be returned to DHS for removal of the applicant, and the individual cannot appeal to the Board of Immigration Appeals.[661]

On the other hand, if the IJ disagrees with the asylum officer's determination and finds that the applicant has a reasonable fear of persecution or torture, the individual is placed in withholding-only proceedings and may apply for withholding of removal under INA §241(b)(3) or CAT relief on Form I-589.[662] The IJ may only consider the applicant's eligibility for withholding of removal under 8 CFR §§208.16, 1208.16,

---

[652] 8 CFR §§208.31(g), 1208.31(g) (2014).

[653] EOIR Memorandum, *supra* note 629, at 659.

[654] *Id.*

[655] *Id.*

[656] *Id.* at 660.

[657] *Id.*

[658] *Id.*

[659] *Id.*

[660] *Id.*

[661] 8 CFR §§208.31(g)(1), 1208.31(g)(1) (2014).

[662] 8 CFR §§208.31(g)(2), 1208.31(g)(2) (2014).

and must determine whether the applicant's removal must be withheld or deferred.[663] DHS or the applicant may appeal the IJ's decision to the BIA.[664] The BIA may only review the IJ's decision regarding the applicant's eligibility for withholding or deferral of removal under 8 CFR §§208.16, 1208.16.[665]

VII. Conclusion

As the United States pours more and more resources into border enforcement in response to the "surge" of border-crossers, many of whom are fleeing horrific violence and danger in Central America, it is increasingly crucial for advocates, officers, and adjudicators to have a firm grasp of the expedited removal, credible fear, reinstatement of removal, and reasonable fear standards and procedures. Advocates, officers, and adjudicators must work cooperatively to maintain the integrity of the U.S. asylum system, while ensuring that U.S. laws are implemented with accuracy and fairness.

---

[663] 8 CFR §§208.31(g)(2)(i), 1208.31(g)(2)(i) (2014).

[664] 8 CFR §§208.31(g)(2)(i), 1208.31(g)(2)(ii) (2014).

[665] 8 CFR §§208.31(g)(2)(i), 1208.31(g)(2)(ii) (2014); see also this chapter at 3.6.5 for more information on withholding-only proceedings.

CHAPTER SEVEN

AFFIRMATIVE ASYLUM PROCEDURES*

This chapter provides an overview of asylum procedures for applicants applying affirmatively before a U.S. Citizenship and Immigration Services (USCIS) Asylum Office. The process can be completed within a few months or may last for several years, depending on current processing times, agency policies, and individual applicants' circumstances. In some instances, the procedures may seem counterintuitive, cumbersome, or arbitrarily applied. It is necessary and, indeed, crucial to follow the regulations, instructions, and local rules throughout the process. This chapter is meant to serve as a helpful manual for those attempting to navigate the procedures for affirmative asylum applications.

➢ **Practice Pointer**: The number of applicants granted asylum affirmatively continues to drop from year to year. The most recent statistics available show a decrease from 17,389 affirmative asylum grants in 2012 to 15,266 grants in 2013, a 12 percent decrease.[1] As standards continue to be heightened and the asylum system becomes more and more stretched, it is increasingly important for practitioners to diligently and thoroughly prepare their clients' applications and to closely follow the relevant procedures in advocating for their clients.

---

* The author would like to thank Lisa R. Green of Lisa Green & Associates, P.C. for her invaluable input in reviewing this chapter.

[1] Daniel C. Martin & James E. Yankay, Annual Flow Report, *Refugees and Asylees: 2013*, U.S. Dep't of Homeland Security 5 (Aug. 2014), *available at www.dhs.gov/sites/default/files/publications/ois_rfa_fr_2013.pdf.*

- **Practice Pointer**: The USCIS Asylum Division's Affirmative Asylum Procedures Manual is the main procedural guide for processing affirmative asylum applications. It was last updated in November of 2013 and is available online at *www.uscis.gov/sites/default/files/files/nativedocuments/Asylum_Procedures_Manual_2013.pdf.*[2]

I. Who is Eligible to Apply for Asylum Affirmatively?

An applicant may file an affirmative application for asylum if he or she currently holds a valid immigration status (such as a visitor or student visa or Temporary Protected Status), his or her status has lapsed or expired (except for Visa Waiver Program entrants), or even if he or she holds no immigration status (for example, if he or she entered the country without inspection).

- **Practice Pointer**: Even applicants granted lawful permanent resident status may continue seeking asylum following the grant of permanent resident status. However, if an asylum applicant is granted permanent resident status, USCIS will provide written notice to the applicant that his or her asylum application will be presumed abandoned or dismissed without prejudice, unless the applicant submits a written request within 30 days of the notice that the asylum application be adjudicated.[3] If the applicant does not respond within 30 days of the written notice, USCIS may presume the asylum application abandoned and dismiss it without prejudice.[4]

Certain individuals, however, are ineligible to apply affirmatively for asylum. These include:

- Applicants who are in removal proceedings before the immigration court or Board of Immigration Appeals (BIA);
- Certain crewmen and stowaways;
- Visa Waiver Program entrants who are applicants for admission, or who overstayed or violated their status;
- Certain individuals ordered removed under INA §235(c) on security-related grounds;
- Certain nonimmigrants admitted under INA §101(a)(15)(S) as witnesses and informants;
- Individuals who are statutorily ineligible due to the one-year filing deadline, a previous asylum denial, or a safe third country; and

---

[2] (last visited Jan. 22, 2015).

[3] 8 CFR §208.14(g) (2014).

[4] *Id.*

- Certain dependents.

Each of these is discussed in detail below.

A. Applicants in Removal Proceedings

If an applicant is currently in removal, deportation, or exclusion proceedings or if he or she has previously been issued a removal, deportation, or exclusion order, the applicant may not file affirmatively for asylum before the USCIS Asylum Offices.

> ➢ **Practice Pointer**: If an applicant is an *American Baptist Churches v. Thornburgh* (*ABC*) class member,[5] he or she may be entitled to an affirmative asylum interview under the *ABC* Settlement, despite being in removal, deportation, or exclusion proceedings or being ordered removed, deported, or excluded previously.[6]

An applicant who has filed affirmatively, but has been issued a Notice to Appear (NTA) or other charging document that has been filed with an immigration court, is ineligible to proceed with the application pending before the USCIS.[7] On rare occasions, the Department of Homeland Security (DHS) may file a motion to dismiss on the grounds that, among other reasons, the NTA was improvidently issued or that circumstances have changed to such an extent that the continuation of the case is no longer in the best interest of the government.[8] The motion, however, must be adjudicated on the record like any other motion before the immigration judge or the Board of Immigration Appeals.[9] If the immigration court proceedings are dismissed, the applicant might be able to pursue an affirmative claim, if other bars do not apply. Similarly, if the immigration judge terminates immigration court proceedings — because the applicant is not removable, on joint motion by the parties, or otherwise — the applicant might then be able to pursue an affirmative asylum claim, as termination of proceedings means that he or she is no longer subject to the jurisdiction of the immigration court.[10]

> ➢ **Practice Pointer**: If a client is in removal proceedings but has never previously applied for asylum affirmatively before an Asylum Office, practitioners should consider negotiating with the DHS trial attorney

---

[5] *See infra* chapter 16 for a detailed discussion of the *ABC* Settlement and *ABC* class members.

[6] *See* Debbie Smith, *The ABC Settlement: A Guide for Class Members and Advocates*, 72 INTERPRETER RELEASES 1497 (Nov. 6, 1995); *see also* Am. Immigration Law Center, *The American Baptist Churches v. Thornburgh (ABC) Settlement Agreement*, *available at www.ailc.com/services/residency/abc-1.htm.*

[7] 8 CFR §§208.2(b), 1208.2(b). *See, e.g.*, *Matter of P–L–P–*, 21 I&N Dec. 887 (BIA 1997) (finding that an applicant who was issued a charging document on the day he filed his asylum application with the INS could not proceed with his affirmative application).

[8] 8 CFR §§239.2(a)(6), (7), (c), & 1239.2(c) (2014); *see also Matter of G–N–C–*, 22 I&N Dec. 281 (BIA 1998), *criticized on other grounds by Castro-Cortez v. INS,* 239 F.3d 1037, 1052 (9th Cir. 2001).

[9] *Matter of G–N–C–*, 22 I&N Dec. 281 (BIA 1998), criticized on other grounds by *Castro-Cortez v. INS*, 239 F.3d 1037, 1052 (9th Cir. 2001).

[10] 8 CFR §§208.2(b), 1003.13(b), 1003.14(a), 1208.2(b).

assigned to their client's case to seek the trial attorney's exercise of prosecutorial discretion in agreeing to a motion to terminate proceedings. Doing so could result in the termination of the client's removal proceedings and ensure "two bites at the asylum apple" — first, an affirmative application and second, if that application is denied, a defensive application.

➢ **Practice Pointer**: Given the ever-increasing limits on DHS resources due to the U.S. government's ongoing focus on immigration enforcement while failing to fix our broken immigration system, DHS increasingly issues Notices to Appear and serves the charging documents on the respondents, but then never files or significantly delays filing the NTAs with the immigration courts. If an NTA is not filed with the immigration court, the individual is not yet in removal proceedings.[11] Thus, practitioners should not automatically assume that a client's possession of an NTA signifies that the Asylum Office does not have jurisdiction over his or her asylum claim. Practitioners may call the Executive Office for Immigration Review's phone line at 1-800-898-7180 and enter their client's A number to determine whether his or her case is officially before the immigration courts. If the client's A number is not recognized in the system, it likely means that the NTA has not yet been filed with the court and he or she could apply affirmatively for asylum.

If the applicant has received a previous order of removal, deportation, or exclusion, he or she may still be able to apply for asylum before the immigration court. The applicant would need to prepare a motion to reopen his or her case, with the completed asylum application attached to the motion, and file the motion and application with the immigration judge (IJ) or the BIA, depending on where jurisdiction has vested.[12] If the applicant has been previously removed, deported, or excluded from the United States and illegally re-entered the United States, upon filing for asylum, he or she may be placed in reinstatement of removal proceedings and may only be eligible for withholding of removal.[13]

B. Other Individuals Ineligible for the Affirmative Asylum Process

Other categories of individuals ineligible for the affirmative asylum process are:

(1) certain alien crewmembers;

(2) certain stowaways;

---

[11] 8 CFR §1003.14(a)

[12] *See generally* 8 CFR §§208.4(b)(3)(ii), (4), 1208.4(b)(3)(ii), (4) (2014); *see also infra* chapter 8 for a detailed discussion of defensive asylum procedures; chapter 11 for a detailed discussion of motions to reopen.

[13] *See supra* chapter 6 for a detailed discussion of reinstatement of removal and withholding-only proceedings.

(3) Visa Waiver Program applicants for admission;

(4) Visa Waiver Program overstays and status violators;

(5) certain individuals ordered removed under INA §235(c) on security-related grounds; and

(6) certain nonimmigrants admitted under INA §101(a)(15)(S) (certain witnesses and informants).[14]

Individuals who fall within these categories and who file asylum applications with USCIS Service Centers will be served with From I-863, Notice of Referral to Immigration Judge when they appear at the USCIS Asylum Office. They will then be referred to immigration court for an asylum-only hearing, and the Asylum Office will forward the I-863 and asylum application to the appropriate immigration court.[15]

Crewmembers are not eligible to apply for asylum affirmatively before USCIS.[16] Rather, crewmembers who are in Immigration and Customs Enforcement (ICE) custody who express a desire to seek asylum or a fear of return will be given Form I-589, as well as information about the privilege of being represented by counsel and the consequences of knowingly filing a frivolous asylum application.[17] Such crewmembers will then have ten days to submit the completed Form I-589 to the ICE Field Office Director having jurisdiction over the port of entry at which their vessel arrived. The ten-day filing period may be extended for good cause.[18] Once the crewmember's application is filed, the ICE Field Office Director will serve him or her with Form I-863, Notice of Referral to Immigration Judge and forward the application to the appropriate immigration court for an asylum hearing.[19]

Like crewmembers, stowaways arriving at a port of entry are not eligible to apply for asylum affirmatively, nor are they eligible to apply for admission or to be admitted to the United States.[20] They also are not considered applicants for admission and are not eligible for a full hearing in removal proceedings under INA §240.[21] If, however, they express a fear of persecution, a fear of torture, a fear of return to the country of proposed removal, or a desire or intention to apply for asylum, they will be

---

[14] *See* 8 CFR §§208.2(c)(1), 1208.2(c)(1) (2014); *see also* U.S. Citizenship and Immigration Servs., *I-589, Application for Asylum and for Withholding of Removal, Instructions* 11 (Dec. 29, 2014) [hereinafter I-589 Instructions], *available at www.uscis.gov/sites/default/files/files/form/i-589instr.pdf*; U.S. Citizenship and Immigration Servs., *Affirmative Asylum Procedures Manual*, pt. III.L.3. (November 2013) [hereinafter *USCIS Affirmative Asylum Procedures Manual*], *available at www.uscis.gov/sites/default/files/files/nativedocuments/Asylum_Procedures_Manual_2013.pdf.*

[15] I-589 Instructions, *supra* note 14, at 11.

[16] 8 CFR §§208.2(c)(1), 1208.2(c)(1) (2014).

[17] 8 CFR §§208.5(b), 1208.5(b) (2014); I-589 Instructions, *supra* note 14, at 11.

[18] 8 CFR §§208.5(b), 1208.5(b) (2014); I-589 Instructions, *supra* note 14, at 11.

[19] 8 CFR §§208.5(b), 1208.5(b) (2014); I-589 Instructions, *supra* note 14, at 11.

[20] INA §235(a)(2); 8 CFR §§208.2(c)(1), 1208.2(c)(1) (2014).

[21] INA §235(a)(2).

given a credible fear interview by an asylum officer under INA §235(b)(1)(B).[22] If the stowaway is found to have a credible fear of persecution or torture, the asylum officer will issue to him or her a Form I-863, Notice of Referral to Immigration Judge, and he or she will be referred to an immigration judge for a hearing on his or her asylum, withholding of removal, or Convention Against Torture claim.[23]

Individuals who apply for admission under the Visa Waiver Program (VWP), or who are admitted under the VWP and later overstay or violate their status, are not eligible to apply for asylum affirmatively.[24] However, if an individual was admitted to the United States in VWP status and applies for asylum affirmatively, the Asylum Office should assume jurisdiction and adjudicate the application if the individual is maintaining valid VWP status and is not otherwise removable.[25]

C. Individuals Statutorily Ineligible to Apply for Asylum

In addition to these jurisdictional bars to affirmative asylum applications, certain categories of individuals are not eligible to apply for asylum.[26] These categories include:

- An individual who did not file his or her application for asylum within one year of his or her last arrival in the United States, unless the applicant establishes changed circumstances that materially affect his or her eligibility for asylum or extraordinary circumstances directly related to the delay in filing;
- An individual who previously has been denied asylum as a principal applicant by an immigration judge or the Board of Immigration Appeals, unless the applicant demonstrates the existence of changed circumstances that materially affect his or her eligibility for asylum or that he or she was a dependent on the prior application; and
- An individual who may be removed to a "safe third country" pursuant to a bilateral or multilateral agreement (for example, the U.S. and Canada have such an agreement).[27]

---

[22] *Id.*; *see also* 8 CFR §1235.1(d)(4). *See supra* chapter 6 for a detailed discussion of the credible fear standards and procedures.

[23] *See* 8 CFR §§208.2(c)(1)–(2), 1208.2(c)(1)–(2); U.S. Citizenship and Immigration Servs., RAIO Asylum Division, Asylum Officer Basic Training Course, *Lesson Plan on Credible Fear* 8 (Feb. 28, 2014) [hereinafter USCIS Credible Fear Training], *available at http://cmsny.org/wp-content/uploads/credible-fear-of-persecution-and-torture.pdf.*

[24] 8 CFR §§208.2(c)(1), 1208.2(c)(1) (2014).

[25] *See* 8 CFR §§208.2(c)(1), 208.4(b)(5), 217.4(b)(1), 1208.2(c)(1), & 1208.4(b)(5) (2014).

[26] INA §208(a)(2).

[27] INA §208(a)(2). *See* USCIS Affirmative Asylum Procedures Manual, *supra* note 14, at pt. III.P.1

These ineligibility grounds under INA §208(a)(2) are separate from the statutory bars under INA §208(b)(2),[28] making an individual ineligible to apply for asylum, versus barred from being granted asylum.

> ➢ **Practice Pointer**: The statutory bars to asylum also may apply and prevent an asylum officer from granting asylum. Thus, although they are distinct from the three ineligibility grounds listed above, the statutory bars have a similar effect during the affirmative asylum process — a denial of asylum or referral to the immigration court.[29] See chapter 2 of this book for a detailed discussion of these three ineligibility grounds, as well as each of the statutory bars to asylum.

Although individuals subject to these ineligibility grounds are not eligible to apply for asylum, only an asylum officer or immigration judge can make this determination after an interview or hearing has been conducted.[30] Thus, such individuals are not prevented from filing an affirmative asylum application, and they must be given an interview on their applications.[31] The asylum officer will determine during the affirmative asylum process whether the applicant is ineligible for asylum based on one or more of these ineligibility grounds.[32] If the officer is unable to grant asylum, he or she does not have authority to grant withholding of removal, and must refer the application to the immigration judge for consideration of other forms of relief such as withholding of removal under INA §241(b)(3) or protection under the Convention Against Torture (CAT).[33] The only exception is for claims adjudicated under the *ABC* settlement.[34]

1. One-Year Filing Deadline

First, an applicant is ineligible to apply for asylum if his or her application is time-barred. Most asylum applicants filing on or after April 1, 1998 must demonstrate that they filed for asylum within one year of the date of their last arrival in the United States, with limited exceptions.[35] The one-year period is calculated from the date of

---

[28] *See* INA §208(b)(2).

[29] *Compare* INA §208(a)(2), *with* INA §208(b)(2).

[30] *See* Memorandum from Joseph E. Langlois on Procedures for Implementing the One-Year Filing Deadline and Processing Cases Previously Denied by EOIR 14 (Jan. 4, 2002) [hereinafter Langlois Mem. on Procedures for One-Year Filing Deadline & Previous Denials]. *See also* 8 CFR §208.4 (2014); *USCIS Affirmative Asylum Procedures Manual*, *supra* note 14, at pt. III.P.

[31] *See* Langlois Mem. on Procedures for One-Year Filing Deadline & Previous Denials, *supra* note 30, at 14; *USCIS Affirmative Asylum Procedures Manual*, *supra* note 14, at pt. III.P.

[32] *See supra* chapter 2 for a detailed discussion of the ineligibility grounds and statutory bars to asylum and withholding of removal eligibility.

[33] 8 CFR §§208.16, 1208.16; *USCIS Affirmative Asylum Procedures Manual*, *supra* note 14, at pt. II.N.

[34] *See infra* chapter 16 for a detailed discussion of the *ABC* settlement and its class members.

[35] 8 CFR §208.4(a) (2014). Pursuant to amendments made by the 2008 Trafficking Victims Protection Reauthorization Act, this one-year filing deadline does not apply to unaccompanied children. INA §208(a)(2)(E); 8 USC §1158(a)(2)(E) (2012), as amended by the Trafficking Victims Protection

Continued

the applicant's "last arrival" in the United States, which refers to the asylum applicant's most recent arrival in the United States from a trip abroad.[36] An asylum application is considered filed on the date it is received by the USCIS Service Center or, under certain circumstances, the date it is mailed.[37] If the application is received by USCIS after the one-year period has elapsed, but clear and convincing documentary evidence demonstrates that the application was mailed within the statutory one-year period, the application may be considered timely.[38] For purposes of calculating the one-year period, the date of last arrival in the United States is counted as day zero. Thus, the first day in the calculation is the day after the last arrival in the United States.[39]

The burden of proof is on the applicant to demonstrate that he or she filed an asylum application within one year of his or her last entry to the United States. The applicant is barred from applying for asylum if he or she fails to demonstrate "by clear and convincing evidence that the application has been filed within one year after the date of [his or her] arrival in the U.S."[40] In meeting the clear and convincing standard, an applicant may provide testimony, documentary evidence, or both. Testimony alone, when credible, may be sufficient to meet the clear and convincing standard.[41]

Even if an applicant did not file his or her application within one year of entry to the United States, however, he or she may still be able to demonstrate eligibility for

---

Reauthorization Act of 2008, Pub. L. 110-457, §235(d)(7)(A). Note that the TVPRA exempts only out-of-status unaccompanied children from the one-year filing deadline. Thus, the one-year filing deadline still must be analyzed for in-status unaccompanied children and accompanied minor principal applicants.

[36] *Matter of F–P–R–*, 24 I&N Dec. 681, 683 (BIA 2008).

[37] *See* 8 CFR §§208.4(a)(2)(ii), 1208.4(a)(2)(ii) (2014); *Nakimbugwe v. Gonzales*, 475 F.3d 281 (5th Cir. 2007).

[38] *See* 8 CFR §§208.4(a)(2)(ii), 1208.4(a)(2)(ii) (2014).

[39] U.S. Citizenship & Immigration Servs., *Lesson: One-Year Filing Deadline*, at 5, in Asylum Officer Basic Training Course Participant Workbook (Mar. 23, 2009) [hereinafter AOBTC Workbook, One-Year Filing Deadline], *available at www.uscis.gov/sites/default/files/USCIS/Humanitarian/ Refugees%20%26%20Asylum/Asylum/AOBTC%20Lesson%20Plans/One-Year-Filing-Deadline-31aug10.pdf*. Note that the Asylum Division used to calculate the one-year period by counting the day of arrival as day one. However, following the Ninth Circuit's opinion in *Minasyan v. Mukasey*, 553 F.3d 1224 (9th Cir. 2009), the Asylum Division now calculates the day of arrival as day zero. In that opinion, the Ninth Circuit stated that the statute specifically provides that the one-year period commences after the date of arrival. The Asylum Division changed its calculation process in order to maintain a consistent national approach.

[40] INA §208(a)(2)(D); 8 USC §1158(a)(2)(D) (2012).

[41] 8 CFR §208.13(a) (2014); *Matter of S–M–J–*, 21 I&N Dec. 722 (BIA 1997). *See Singh v. Holder*, 649 F.3d 1161 (9th Cir. 2011) (stating that the corroboration requirements applied to the merits of the asylum claim rather than to the one-year filing deadline). *See also* AOBTC Workbook: One-Year Filing Deadline, *supra* note 39, at 7.

asylum.[42] There are two exceptions to the one-year filing deadline: (1) if the applicant demonstrates "the existence of changed circumstances which materially affect the applicant's eligibility for asylum," [43] and/or (2) if the applicant demonstrates "extraordinary circumstances relating to the delay in filing the application,"[44] the applicant may be excused for failing to timely file his or her application. In addition to demonstrating the presence of changed or extraordinary circumstances, the applicant must also show that he or she filed the application within a reasonable time of those circumstances.[45] The applicant must demonstrate to the "satisfaction of the Attorney General" that he or she qualifies for an exception to the one-year filing deadline.[46]

2. *Previous Asylum Denial*

Second, an applicant is ineligible to apply for asylum if he or she "has previously applied for asylum and had such application denied."[47] For this ineligibility ground to apply, however, the previous asylum application must have been denied by an IJ or the BIA.[48] A previous denial by an asylum officer does not make an individual ineligible to apply for asylum.[49] An applicant may apply for asylum affirmatively after a final denial or dismissal of a motion to reopen or reconsider by the Asylum Office, as long as he or she is not under the jurisdiction of the immigration court.[50] An applicant who withdrew a prior asylum application may also submit a new application, as long as the Asylum Office has jurisdiction to hear the claim.[51]

---

[42] INA §208(a)(2)(D); 8 CFR §208.4(a) (2014).

[43] *See* 8 CFR §§208.4(a)(4), 1208.4(a)(4) (2014).

[44] *See* 8 CFR §§208.4(a)(5), 1208.4(a)(5) (2014). An additional exception may exist for Salvadoran and Guatemalan ABC class members. *See* Settlement Provides Potential Relief for *ABC* Registrants Who Missed Asylum Filing Deadline, 79 INTERPRETER RELEASES 904 (June 10, 2002). Previously, in determining whether Guatemalan and Salvadoran nationals satisfied the registration requirement to receive ABC benefits under the settlement, USCIS required evidence of registration and the filing of an affirmative asylum application alone was not viewed as evidence satisfying the registration requirement. After the Ninth Circuit's findings in *Chaly-Garcia v. United States.,* 508 F.3d 1201 (9th Cir. 2007), however, a Guatemalan or Salvadoran national who affirmatively filed an I-589 application on or after the date the court provisionally approved the settlement and prior to the conclusion of the designated registration period, is considered "registered." *www.uscis.gov/sites/default/files/USCIS/Laws/Memoranda/Static_Files_Memoranda/Archives%201998-2008/2008/making_abc_registration_determinations_080508.pdf* (last visited Dec. 27, 2014).

[45] 8 CFR §§208.4(a)(4)-(5), 1208.4(a)(4)-(5) (2014).

[46] INA §208(a)(2)(B), (D); 8 CFR §§208.4(a)(2)(i), 1208.4(a)(2)(i) (2014).

[47] INA §§208(a)(2)(C)–(D); 8 USC §1158(a)(2)(C)–(D) (2012).

[48] 8 CFR §§208.4(a)(3), 1208.4(a)(3) (2014).

[49] *See* Joseph E. Langlois, Memorandum to Asylum Office Directors, *Procedures for Implementing the One-Year Filing Deadline and Processing Cases Previously Denied by EOIR*, Washington, DC (Jan. 4, 2002).

[50] *USCIS Affirmative Asylum Procedures Manual*, *supra* note 14, at pt. II.C.2.

[51] *Id.* A withdrawn asylum application, however, cannot be reopened, except in limited circumstances as provided in the ABC-NACARA Procedures Manual for rescission cases. *Id.*

Even if an application was previously denied by an IJ or the BIA, a new application may be considered if the applicant "demonstrates to the satisfaction of the [AG] ... the existence of changed circumstances which materially affect the applicant's eligibility for asylum."[52] Thus, the Asylum Office will interview the applicant to determine if there are changed circumstances after denial by the IJ or BIA that materially affect the applicant's eligibility for asylum.[53] If changed circumstances are established, the asylum officer will seek any additional information needed to make an asylum eligibility determination and will proceed with issuance of a decision on the new affirmative claim.[54]

The Asylum Office also may have jurisdiction to consider a new asylum claim after denial by the IJ or BIA, regardless of whether changed circumstances exist, if the applicant left the United States after the IJ or BIA denial and subsequently reentered legally.[55]

3. *Safe Third Country*

Third, an applicant is ineligible to apply for asylum if he or she may be removed to a "safe third country," unless the Attorney General finds that it is in the public interest for the applicant to remain in the United States.[56] The removal must be "pursuant to a bilateral or multilateral agreement," and must be to a country other than the individual's home country or, in the case of a stateless person, other than the country of the individual's last habitual residence.[57] The "safe third country" must also be a country where the individual's "life or freedom would not be threatened on account of race, religion, nationality, membership in a particular social group, or political opinion," and where the individual would have "access to a full and fair procedure for determining a claim to asylum or equivalent temporary protection."[58]

Implementing this provision requires a treaty or agreement with each country to which the United States would attempt to remove persons who are not citizens of that country. The United States has such an agreement with Canada.[59] Under the agreement, persons seeking refugee protection must make a claim in the first country

[52] INA §208(a)(2)(D); 8 USC §1158(a)(2)(D) (2012).

[53] *USCIS Affirmative Asylum Procedures Manual*, *supra* note 14, at pt. III.P.3.e.

[54] *Id.*

[55] *Id.* at pt. III.P.3.c.

[56] INA §208(a)(2)(A); 8 USC §1158(a)(2)(A) (2012). This bar to asylum eligibility does not apply to unaccompanied children, as defined by 6 USC §279(g). INA §208(a)(2)(E); 8 USC §1158(a)(2)(E) (2012), as amended by the Trafficking Victims Protection Reauthorization Act of 2008, Pub. L. 110-457; 8 CFR §208.30(e)(6)(iii)(D) (2014). *See infra* chapter 10 for a detailed discussion of the legal standards and procedures for unaccompanied children.

[57] INA §208(a)(2)(A); 8 USC §1158(a)(2)(A) (2012).

[58] INA §208(a)(2)(A); 8 USC §1158(a)(2)(A) (2012).

[59] Agreement Between the Government of the United States and the Government of Canada for Cooperation in the Examination of Refugee Status Claims from Nationals of Third Countries (Dec. 5, 2002), *available at http://www.refworld.org/docid/42d7b9944.html.*

they arrive in unless they qualify for an exception.[60] The agreement allows the United States to return "arriving aliens" to Canada, if that was their country of last presence, to seek protection under Canadian law, rather than under U.S. law. Similarly, the agreement allows Canada to return asylum-seekers to the United States, if the United States was their country of last presence. Final U.S. regulations implementing this agreement were published on November 29, 2004,[61] and became effective on December 29, 2004.[62] Canadian regulations implementing the agreement were published in the Canada Gazette.[63]

> ➢ **Practice Pointer**: Note that asylum-seekers who are subject to the U.S.-Canada safe third country agreement and who demonstrate an exception to the agreement will in most cases be subject to expedited removal and will not be permitted to apply affirmatively for asylum.[64]

D. Dependents

An asylum applicant may include his or her spouse and unmarried children under age 21 as dependents or derivative applicants on his or her application if they are physically present in the United States with the principal applicant.[65] A parent, however, may not be included as a dependent or derivative applicant on his or her child's asylum application.[66] Thus, where a child appears eligible for asylum based

---

[60] *Id.* Exceptions to the agreement include: citizens of Canada, asylum-seekers with close relatives in the United States, unaccompanied minors, holders of valid visas or admission documents to the United States, and persons for whom a determination has been made by the USCIS director that it is in the public interest to allow them to seek asylum, withholding of removal, or Convention Against Torture (CAT) relief in the United States. 8 CFR §208.30(e)(6)(iii) (2014).

[61] Implementation of the Agreement Between the Government of the United States of America and the Government of Canada Regarding Asylum Claims Made in Transit and at Land Border Ports-of-Entry; Final Rule, 69 Fed. Reg. 69479 (Nov. 29, 2004) (to be codified at 8 CFR pt. 208, 212, & 235).

[62] *Id.*

[63] Regulations Amending the Immigration and Refugee Protection Regulations, SOR/2004-217 (Can.), 138 C. Gaz. no. 22 (Nov. 3, 2004), *available at http://canadagazette.gc.ca/partII/2004/20041103/html/sor217-e.html*. For an overview of the exceptions that apply to asylum-seekers seeking entry into Canada, see the Canadian Council for Refugees website, at www.ccrweb.ca/s3cFAQ.html. Some notable exceptions include unaccompanied minors, individuals subject to the death penalty in their home countries, and countries to which Canada has temporarily suspended removals (currently Afghanistan, Burundi, Democratic Republic of Congo, Haiti, Iraq, Liberia, Rwanda, and Zimbabwe). Implementation of the Agreement Between the Government of the United States of America and the Government of Canada Regarding Asylum Claims Made in Transit and at Land Border Ports-of-Entry; Final Rule, 69 Fed. Reg. 69479 (Nov. 29, 2004) (to be codified at 8 CFR pt. 208, 212, & 235).

[64] *USCIS Affirmative Asylum Procedures Manual*, *supra* note 14, at pt. III.P.4. *See also supra* chapter 2 for a detailed discussion of the safe third country asylum ineligibility ground; chapter 6 for a detailed discussion of expedited removal procedures.

[65] INA §208(b)(3)(A). *See* Memorandum from Joseph E. Langlois on H.R. 1209 – Child Status Protection Act 2 (Aug. 7, 2002); Memorandum from William R. Yates on The Child Status Protection Act – Children of Asylees and Refugees 4 (Aug. 17, 2004).

[66] *See* INA §208(b)(3)(A).

on the persecution he or she suffered, it is essential to explore whether the parent has an asylum claim of his or her own.

> ➢ **Practice Pointer**: Practitioners representing families must evaluate each individual for their own independent asylum eligibility. It is possible that a spouse may have a stronger claim or that a child may have his or her own asylum claim that is unrelated to the parent's. Even when a family has suffered through the same acts of persecution, each family member may be experienced the harm differently. For example, a family member who was not subject to physical harm may have suffered psychological harm, either because of particular actions against him or her or against his or her loved ones.

As long as a child was unmarried and under 21 on the date his or her parent filed his or her asylum application, the Child Status Protection Act allows the child to continue to be classified as a child, even if he or she turns 21 during the parent's asylum application process. The child may still be granted asylum as a dependent or derivative applicant on the parent's application.[67] The "filing date" is the date that the application was received by USCIS.[68]

> ➢ **Practice Pointer**: Practitioners should determine the age of all of their client's children at the beginning of the representation. If a child is nearing age 21, it is important for practitioners to prioritize their client's case to file the asylum application before the child turns 21. Doing so will maintain his or her eligibility as a dependent applicant.

A derivative family member may lose his or her status as a derivative in the following situations:

- If the spouse or child withdraws his or her asylum claim;
- If the child marries;
- If the spouse divorces the principal applicant; or
- If the principal applicant dies.[69]

Derivative status may be lost at any time prior to issuance of the Asylum Office's final decision.[70] For example, even if a recommended approval has been issued, the decision is not yet final, and the recommended approval for a dependent who loses derivative status will be cancelled. When the Asylum Office becomes aware of the loss of the dependent's derivative status, the office will notify the principal applicant

---

[67] INA §208(b)(3)(B).

[68] 8 CFR §103.2(a)(7) (2014).

[69] *USCIS Affirmative Asylum Procedures Manual*, *supra* note 14, at pt. III.E.6.

[70] *Id.*

and the dependent in writing that the dependent cannot remain on the asylum application.[71]

- **Practice Pointer**: The loss of derivative status may qualify as a changed circumstance for purposes of determining whether the individual is subject to the one-year filing deadline in his or her own subsequent asylum claim as a principal applicant.[72] As long as he or she files the subsequent application within a reasonable time after becoming aware of the loss of derivative status, he or she should qualify for this exception to the one-year filing deadline.[73] See chapter 13 of this book for a detailed discussion of derivative beneficiaries.
- **Practice Pointer**: A dependent may lose derivative status after asylum approval, but before filing for adjustment of status to lawful permanent residency. Derivative status for purposes of adjustment of status may be lost in the situations described above, as well as if the principal asylee naturalizes to U.S. citizenship.[74] Under each of these circumstances, the dependent may not be included as a derivative applicant on the principal applicant's adjustment of status application.[75] Although the dependent will continue to have valid asylee status, if he or she wants to adjust status to lawful permanent resident, he or she must file a new I-589 application as a principal applicant and request asylum "nunc pro tunc."[76] See chapter 15 of this book for a detailed discussion of nunc pro tunc asylum applications for the purposes of adjustment of status.

II. Required Notices to Asylum and Withholding of Removal Applicants

The statute and regulations require that applicants for asylum and withholding of removal be notified of certain rights and warnings regarding the application process. These notices apply regardless whether the individual is applying affirmatively before the Asylum Office or defensively through the immigration court.[77] These include notice of the applicant's right to be represented, notice of the consequences of filing a

---

[71] *Id.* See chapter 13 for a detailed discussion of derivative beneficiaries.

[72] *See* 8 CFR §208.4(a)(4) (2014).

[73] *See id.* See also chapter 2 for a detailed discussion of the one-year filing deadline and the exceptions to this bar to asylum eligibility.

[74] See chapter 13 for a detailed discussion of derivative beneficiaries; chapter 15 for a detailed discussion of nunc pro tunc adjustment of status due to loss of derivative status.

[75] USCIS *Affirmative Asylum Procedures Manual*, *supra* note 14, at pt. III.E.7.

[76] *Id.*

[77] See chapter 7 for a detailed discussion of affirmative asylum procedures; see chapter 8 for a detailed discussion of defensive asylum procedures.

frivolous application, notice that information may be used to initiate removal proceedings or used by the government to satisfy its burden of proof, and notice of confidentiality.

A. Notice of Right to Be Represented

At the time the applicant files for asylum and withholding of removal, the U.S. attorney general is required to notify the applicant of the privilege of being represented by counsel and to provide the applicant with a list of pro bono representatives.[78] In proceedings before an asylum officer, an IJ, or the BIA, asylum and withholding of removal applicants may be represented by attorneys, law school students or graduates, reputable individuals of good moral character, accredited representatives, or accredited officials.[79]

B. Notice of Consequences of Filing a Frivolous Application

At the time the applicant files for asylum (if on or after April 1, 1997), the attorney general also is required to notify the applicant of the consequences of knowingly filing a frivolous application.[80] Several courts have held that the written warning contained in the I-589 Application for Asylum and for Withholding of Removal is sufficient to comply with the statutory and regulatory notice requirements.[81]

An individual who knowingly makes a frivolous asylum application after receiving notice of the consequences of doing so is "permanently ineligible for any

[78] INA §208(d)(4); 8 USC §1158(d)(4) (2012); 8 CFR §1240.11(c)(1)(iii) (2014) (regarding immigration judge (IJ)'s duty to notify); *see also* Appx. 2A, I-589 filing instructions, section IV: Right to Counsel (containing this notice and a toll-free number and website address to access for a list of attorneys and accredited representatives). Under the Homeland Security Act of 2002, this responsibility to give notice extends to the Secretary of the Department of Homeland Security and other DHS officials. *See* Homeland Security Act of 2002, Pub. L. No. 107-296, §§456, 1512, 1517, 116 Stat. 2135, 2200, 2310, 2311.

[79] *See generally* 8 CFR §§292.1, 1292.1 (2014).

[80] INA §208(d)(4)(A); 8 USC §1158(d)(4)(A) (2012); *see also* 8 CFR §§208.3(c)(5), 1208.3(c)(5), 1240.11(c)(1)(iii) (2014) (regarding DHS and IJ duty to notify). Under the Homeland Security Act of 2002, this responsibility to give notice extends to the DHS secretary and other DHS officials. *See* Homeland Security Act of 2002, Pub. L. No. 107-296, §§456, 1512, 1517, 116 Stat. 2135, 2200, 2310, 2311; *see also* Appx. 2A, I-589 filing instructions (containing the following warning: "Applicants determined to have knowingly made a frivolous application for asylum will be permanently ineligible for any benefits under the [INA].").

[81] *Niang v. Holder*, 762 F.3d 251 (2d Cir. 2014) (finding that the written warning on the I-589 application was adequate notice of the consequences of filing a frivolous asylum application); *Ruga v. U.S. Att'y Gen.*, 757 F.3d 1193 (11th Cir. 2014) (stating that "At least two other courts of appeals have concluded that delivery of this warning in the application itself, or at the time of the interview, suffices. *Ribas v. Mukasey,* 545 F.3d 922 (10th Cir.2008); *Cheema v. Holder,* 693 F.3d 1045 (9th Cir.2012). This court said the same thing in *Siddique v. Mukasey,* 547 F.3d 814 (7th Cir.2008). If it was not a holding then, it becomes a holding now."); *Pavlov v. Holder*, 697 F.3d 616 (7th Cir. 2012) (finding that the written advisals provided on the I-589 are sufficient notice); *Cheema v. Holder*, 693 F.3d 1045 (9th Cir. 2012) (same); *Ribas v. Mukasey*, 545 F.3d 922, 928 (10th Cir. 2008) (same).

benefits under the [INA]."[82] The ineligibility for benefits under the INA is effective as of the date of the final determination on the application.[83] A finding that an applicant filed a frivolous application, however, is not a bar to withholding of removal relief, nor is it a bar to relief under the Convention Against Torture.[84]

> ➢ **Practice Pointer**: The knowing placement of false information on an asylum application may also subject the applicant (or the person who placed the information on the application) to criminal and civil penalties.[85]

An applicant may be permanently barred from relief only if a final order by an IJ or the BIA specifically finds that the applicant knowingly filed a frivolous application.[86] The regulations provide that an asylum application is "frivolous" if "any of its material elements is deliberately fabricated."[87] A preponderance of the evidence must support the frivolousness finding,[88] and the IJ must give specific and convincing reasons for determining that a preponderance of the evidence supports a frivolousness finding.[89] Additionally, the IJ or the BIA must be "satisfied" that during the course of the proceedings the applicant "has had sufficient opportunity to account for any discrepancies or implausible aspects of the claim."[90] An IJ may not base a frivolous determination on merely an adverse credibility assessment.[91]

---

[82] INA §208(d)(6); 8 CFR §§208.3(c)(5), 1208.3(c)(5).

[83] INA §208(d)(6); 8 USC §1158(d)(6).

[84] 8 CFR §§208.20, 1208.20.

[85] 8 CFR §§208.3(c)(4), 1208.3(c)(4) (2014).

[86] 8 CFR §§208.20, 1208.20 (2014).

[87] 8 CFR §§208.20, 1208.20 (2014).

[88] *Matter of Y–L–*, 24 I&N Dec. 151, 157 (BIA 2007); *Ahir v. Mukasey*, 527 F.3d 912, 917 (9th Cir. 2008).

[89] *Matter of Y–L–*, 24 I&N Dec. 151 (BIA 2007).

[90] 8 CFR §§208.20, 1208.20 (2014); *see also Matter of Y–L–*, 24 I&N Dec. 151 (BIA 2007) (holding that an IJ must make a separate and specific finding regarding frivolousness and must give the applicant the opportunity to account for discrepancies); *Matter of [name not provided]*, A94 097 292 (BIA June 21, 2000), *reported in* 77 *Interpreter Releases* 1091–92 (July 31, 2000) (in this unpublished decision, the BIA overturned the IJ's "frivolous" finding based on a determination that the claim was "baseless" and exaggerated); *Aziz v. Gonzales*, 478 F.3d 854, 857 (8th Cir. 2007) (upholding IJ's finding that the applicant from Iraq filed a frivolous asylum application); *Sterkaj v. Gonzales*, 439 F.3d 273, 279 (6th Cir. 2006) (upholding frivolous finding where applicant submitted a fraudulent summons and "wanted" document); *Kifleyesus v. Gonzales*, 462 F.3d 937, 945 (8th Cir. 2006) (upholding IJ's frivolousness finding where the applicant filed a false application, failed to modify it, swore to the truth of the application, and was given sufficient opportunity to account for discrepancies); *Mingkid v. U.S. Att'y Gen.*, 468 F.3d 763, 770 (11th Cir. 2006) (finding that IJ failed to give the applicants a proper opportunity to explain any discrepancies); *Selami v. Gonzales*, 423 F.3d 621, 622 (6th Cir. 2005) (upholding the IJ's finding that the applicant submitted a frivolous application where the applicant submitted a fraudulent newspaper article and was given an opportunity to explain, but failed to articulate any explanation); *Farah v. Ashcroft*, 348 F.3d 1153 (9th Cir. 2003) (overturning frivolous determination where applicant was not given the opportunity to explain discrepancies); *Efe v. Ashcroft*,

Continued

➢ **Practice Pointer**: See chapter 4 for a detailed discussion of frivolous asylum applications and the legal standards that must be met for an adjudicator to make a finding of frivolousness.

C. Notice that Information May be Used to Initiate Removal Proceedings and Satisfy the Government's Burden of Proof

An asylum applicant also must be notified that the information provided in his or her asylum application, if filed on or after January 4, 1995, may be used as a basis for initiating removal proceedings and to satisfy DHS's burden of proof in exclusion, deportation, or removal proceedings.[92]

D. Notice of Confidentiality

Finally, an asylum applicant must be notified that his or her application will be kept confidential. The Form I-589, Application for Asylum and Withholding of Removal provides:

> [N]o information indicating that you have applied for asylum will be provided to any government or country from which you claim a fear of persecution. Regulations at 8 CFR §208.6 protect the confidentiality of asylum claims.[93]

Under 8 CFR §§208.6, 1208.6, DHS and EOIR shall not disclose any information contained in or pertaining to any asylum application, any records pertaining to any credible fear determination under 8 CFR §208.30, and any records pertaining to any reasonable fear determination under 8 CFR §208.31 without the written consent of the applicant.[94] DHS and EOIR also must keep confidential any records that indicate that an individual has applied for asylum, received a credible fear or reasonable fear interview, or received a credible fear or reasonable fear review.[95] If any records need to be transmitted to the Department of State in other countries, DHS and EOIR are required to coordinate with the Department of State to ensure that the confidentiality

---

293 F.3d 899 (5th Cir. 2002) (upholding frivolousness determination where applicant was given ample opportunity to clarify his testimony); *Barreto-Claro v. Att'y Gen.*, 275 F.3d 1334 (11th Cir. 2001) (upholding the finding of frivolousness).

[91] *Alexandrov v. Gonzales*, 442 F.3d 395, 407 (6th Cir. 2006) (finding that the IJ violated the applicant's due process rights by relying on two State Department reports in finding that the applicant's asylum application was frivolous); *Muhanna v. Gonzales*, 399 F.3d 582, 589 (3d Cir. 2005) (the court found that "by imposing a frivolousness finding based not on a thorough examination of the application but instead on her assessment of [the applicant's] credibility, and by consequently refusing to allow further testimony, the IJ ... deprived [the applicant] of due process.")

[92] 8 CFR §§208.3(c)(1), 1208.3(c)(1) (2014); *see also* Appx. 2A, I-589 filing instructions (containing the following warning: "Any information provided in completing this application may be used as a basis for the institution of, or as evidence in, removal proceedings, even if the application is later withdrawn").

[93] Appx. 2A, I-589 filing instructions, sec. III.

[94] 8 CFR §§208.6(a), 1208.6(a) (2014).

[95] 8 CFR §§208.6(b), 1208.6(b) (2014).

of those records is maintained.[96] Under the Homeland Security Act of 2002, this duty of confidentiality extends to the DHS secretary and other DHS officials.[97]

There are exceptions to this duty of confidentiality, however. The U.S. government may disclose information or records to other U.S. government officials or contractors who need to examine it for the purpose of adjudicating asylum applications, considering a request for a credible fear or reasonable fear interview or review, defending the U.S. government in any legal action related to an asylum application or credible fear or reasonable fear determination, or conducting any U.S. government investigation.[98] The otherwise confidential information or records may also be disclosed to any federal, state, or local court in the United States considering any legal action related to the adjudication of or proceedings for an asylum application or a credible fear or reasonable fear determination.[99] The broadest exception, found at 8 CFR §§208.6(a), 1208.6(a), allows for the disclosure of asylum information and records "*at the discretion of the Attorney General.*"[100]

III. What Are the Components of an Affirmative Asylum Application?

The first step in the affirmative asylum application process is to obtain and complete the Form I-589, Application for Asylum and for Withholding of Removal (I-589 or Form I-589) and prepare the asylum application package. At a minimum, an applicant must submit the completed, signed Form I-589 with any supplemental sheets or statements; two copies of the completed and signed I-589; and one passport-style photograph of the applicant.[101] If an applicant has a spouse or child in the United States who wants to be included as a dependent on the I-589, the applicant also must submit for each dependent one copy of the application, one passport-style photograph of the dependent, and evidence of the family relationship.[102]

An asylum application is incomplete if the I-589 does not include a response to each question, is unsigned, or is unaccompanied by the required supporting documents or copies.[103] Incomplete applications will be returned to the applicant within 30 days of receipt.[104] If USCIS does not return the application within 30 days, it will be deemed to be complete.[105] An incomplete application will not commence

[96] *Id.*

[97] *See* Homeland Security Act of 2002, Pub. L. No. 107-296, §§456, 1512, 1517, 116 Stat. 2135, 2200, 2310, 2311. For further discussion of confidentiality, see this chapter, at 3.3.5.

[98] 8 CFR §§208.6(c)(1), 1208.6(c)(1) (2014).

[99] 8 CFR §§208.6(c)(2), 1208.6(c)(2) (2014).

[100] 8 CFR §§208.6(a), 1208.6(a) (emphasis added) (2014).

[101] *USCIS Affirmative Asylum Procedures Manual*, *supra* note 14, at pt. II.A.3.

[102] *Id.*

[103] 8 CFR §§208.3(c)(3), 1208.3(c)(3) (2014).

[104] 8 CFR §§208.3(c)(3), 1208.3(c)(3) (2014).

[105] 8 CFR §§208.3(c)(3), 1208.3(c)(3) (2014).

the 150-day period after which the applicant may file an application for employment authorization.[106]

Although this is the minimum documentation required by USCIS, an affirmative asylum application filed with a USCIS Service Center or, as discussed below in Part IV, directly with an Asylum Office should include the following components:

- Cover letter listing and describing the enclosed documentation;
- Form G-28, Notice of Entry of Appearance as Attorney (if the applicant is represented);[107]
- Form I-589, Application for Asylum and for Withholding of Removal, signed and dated on page 9 by the applicant and including the applicant's printed name in his or her native language;[108]
- Supplement A, Form I-589 and Supplement B, Form I-589, signed and dated by the applicant and listing his or her name and A-number;
- One passport-sized photograph of the applicant attached to page 9 of the I-589;
- Sworn Statement by the applicant, detailing his or her claims;
- Identity documentation for the applicant;
- Evidence of the applicant's most recent entry to the United States;
- Identity documentation for any derivative applicants;
- Documentation establishing the derivative applicants' relationship to the principal applicant (birth certificates, or marriage certificate with divorce decree if the principal applicant or his or her spouse was previously married);
- Evidence that corroborates and supports the applicant's claims;[109]
- Country reports and articles describing the current conditions in the applicant's country of feared persecution or torture;
- Certified English translations for any documents that are not in English;
- Two copies of the complete application package; and
- One additional copy of the complete application package for each derivative applicant, with his or her passport-sized photograph attached to page 9 of the I-589.

---

[106] 8 CFR §§208.3(c)(3), 1208.3(c)(3) (2014). *See infra* pt. IX.B. for a detailed discussion of applying for work authorization while an affirmative asylum application is pending; *see also infra* chapter 13 for a detailed discussion of the benefits of asylum, including employment authorization.

[107] *See* U.S. Citizenship and Immigration Servs., *G-28, Notice of Entry of Appearance as Attorney or Accredited Representative*, *available at www.uscis.gov/g-28* (last visited Jan. 23, 2015).

[108] *See* Dree Collopy & Lisa Green, AILA Practice Pointer, *Completing the Form I-589* (July 14, 2014), AILA InfoNet Doc. No. 14071402 (*posted* July 14, 2014).

[109] See chapter 4 for a detailed discussion of the evidentiary requirements for establishing asylum eligibility, as well as a list of suggested forms of supporting evidence.

To date, there is no fee for filing an affirmative application for asylum,[110] nor is there a biometrics/fingerprinting fee.[111] The statute, however, permits the AG to impose a fee.[112]

> ➢ **Practice Pointer**: Often times, clients will retain their attorney shortly before the one-year filing deadline. Under these circumstances, practitioners should work with their clients to prepare the minimum documentation required for USCIS to accept the filing and should file the application as soon as possible.

The Form I-589, Application for Asylum and for Withholding of Removal, is revised approximately every two years. The current application form was revised on December 29, 2014. The I-589 requires biographic information about the applicant, his or her entry to the United States and prior U.S. immigration history, biographic information about the applicant's spouse and children, the applicant's last address abroad and his or her address history for the last five years, the applicant's education, the applicant's employment history for the last five years, the applicant's parents and siblings and their current locations, the protected grounds on which the applicant's claim is based, the harm suffered in the past and future harm feared, the applicant's journey to the United States, his or her legal status in any other countries, and any bars to relief that may apply.[113] This application form requires significant detail and precise information that is consistent with all other documentation presented, including the applicant's own sworn statement. It is essential that every single question on the I-589 has a response, even if the response is "N/A — Not Applicable" or "None." Otherwise, the application will be rejected by USCIS.[114]

> ➢ **Practice Pointer**: It is important for practitioners to use the current I-589 when preparing their clients' asylum applications, as using an outdated form could result in the rejection of the application by the USCIS Service Center. Practitioners should check the USCIS website for the most recent version of the I-589 form and to determine what previous versions, if any, are still accepted.[115]

---

[110] 8 CFR §1103.7 (2014).

[111] *Id.*

[112] INA §208(d)(3); 8 USC §1158(d)(3) (2014). Under the Homeland Security Act of 2002, this authority would extend to the DHS secretary. *See* Homeland Security Act of 2002, Pub. L. No. 107-296, §§456, 1512, 1517, 116 Stat. 2135, 2200, 2310, 2311.

[113] *See* U.S. Citizenship and Immigration Servs., *I-589, Application for Asylum and for Withholding of Removal* [hereinafter I-589 Application], *available at www.uscis.gov/sites/default/files/files/form/i-589.pdf* (last visited Jan. 23, 2015).

[114] I-589 Instructions, *supra* note 14, at 9; Collopy & Green, AILA Practice Pointer, *supra* note 108.

[115] *See* I-589 Application, *supra* note 113 (both the Form I-589 and the instruction are available at *www.uscis.gov/i-589*).

- **Practice Pointer**: For specific practice pointers and question-by-question guidance on completing the Form I-589, see AILA's "Practice Pointer: Completing the Form I-589," posted on July 14, 2014, on AILA InfoNet at Doc. No. 14071402 (last visited Jan. 23, 2015). This Practice Pointer is also available in this book at Appx. 2C.

The applicant must sign and date the I-589 in Part D, write his or her name in his or her native language, and sign any supplement forms. By signing the application, the applicant is indicating his or her awareness of the contents of the application and declaring under penalty of perjury that all statements in response to the questions are true and correct.[116] If the applicant fails to sign the I-589 in Part D., it will be returned to him or her as incomplete.[117] The applicant's signature at Part F. is not to be completed until the affirmative asylum interview, however.[118] Likewise, the applicant's signature at Part G. is not to be completed unless he or she is placed in removal proceedings and must sign before the immigration judge.[119]

Although the Form I-589 has large answer spaces for descriptions of harm and the applicant's fears, it is important for an applicant to prepare and submit a sworn personal statement in support of his or her application. A well-drafted, well-organized, and compelling sworn statement is essential to any asylum claim. The purpose of the applicant's sworn statement is to tell the applicant's story with detail and a focus on the facts that demonstrate each legal element for the relief he or she is seeking. It also provides an opportunity in advance of in-person testimony for the applicant to connect with the adjudicator on a human level, while also addressing any difficult issues or negative discretionary factors. Given the impact that any inconsistency, no matter how minor, may have on the applicant's credibility, it is essential for his or her sworn statement to be entirely consistent with the Form I-589, as well as all other documentation submitted in support of his or her application.

- **Practice Pointer**: There are competing schools of thought regarding how much detail should be included in clients' sworn statements. Some practitioners prefer to present a general description of the applicant's story and to allow the applicant to provide detail during in-person testimony. They argue that doing so avoids potential inconsistencies between the applicant's written and oral testimony. While it is important to make this decision on a case-by-case basis, this author generally supports the other school of thought and suggests preparing sworn statements that are thorough and detailed. First, a thorough and detailed sworn statement gets all of the important facts on the record. Additionally, getting all of the details and writing them down enables

---

[116] I-589 Instructions, *supra* note 14, at 6.

[117] *Id.*

[118] *Id.* at 7.

[119] *Id.*

practitioners to spot issues that may need further exploration and explanation. Making those explanations a part of the sworn statement is a way to address any concerns the adjudicator may have before even setting foot in the interview or courtroom. Working on preparing a detailed declaration also forces the applicant to think through a sequential timeline of what happened first, next, last, and helps the applicant to avoid mixing up events and perceived inconsistencies. Moreover, learning a client's whole story takes gaining the client's trust, as well as hours and hours of time spent with the client. No asylum officer or immigration judge has that luxury. Finally, a detailed and thorough sworn statement can be a useful tool in assisting the applicant in preparing for his or her interview or hearing.

➢ **Practice Pointer**: Sworn statements do not need to be notarized, but should include the declaration, "I swear under penalty of perjury, under the laws of the United States, that the statements I have provided herein are true and correct to the best of my knowledge and belief," followed by the applicant's dated signature. Any sworn statement that is not written in English must be accompanied by a certified English translation.

➢ **Practice Pointer**: For helpful guidance on preparing and presenting powerful narratives on behalf of clients, practitioners should read the article "Beyond Saints and Sinners: Discretion and the Need for New Narratives in the U.S. Immigration System" by Elizabeth Keyes[120] and the practice pointer "Storytelling & Immigration Law: A Practical Guide" by Erich Straub.[121]

In addition to the Form I-589 and sworn statement, supporting or corroborating evidence regarding an applicant's claim is an essential component of every asylum application. Under the REAL ID Act of 2005, "[w]here the trier of fact determines that an applicant should provide evidence that corroborates otherwise credible testimony, such evidence must be provided unless the applicant does not have the evidence and cannot reasonably obtain the evidence."[122] Thus, an applicant should provide "supporting evidence, both of general conditions and of the specific facts

---

[120] Elizabeth Keyes, Beyond Saints and Sinners: *Discretion and the Need for New Narratives in the U.S. Immigration System*, 26 GEO. IMMIGR. L. J. 207 (Winter 2012).

[121] Erich Straub, *Storytelling & Immigration Law: A Practical Guide* 59-65, AILA'S IMMIGRATION PRACTICE POINTERS (2014–15 Ed.) (available for download on AILA Agora).

[122] INA §§208(b)(1)(B)(ii), 240(c)(4). A similar provision exists for withholding of removal claims. *See* INA §241(b)(3)(C). In addressing the REAL ID Act's amendment to the corroboration requirements for asylum, withholding, and CAT claims, the Seventh Circuit has stated in dicta that "[i]t is possible that the change is less than meets the eye, since now there is no dispute about the appropriateness of asking for corroboration in the common situation when the IJ has some doubt about an applicant's credibility." *Dawoud v. Gonzales*, 424 F.3d 608, 613 (7th Cir. 2005).

sought to be relied upon by the applicant, where such evidence is available," and where it is reasonable to expect such corroborating evidence.[123] In addition to documents related specifically to the asylum claim, an applicant is also expected to provide, if available, general corroborating evidence of persecution of similarly situated individuals.[124] Where such evidence is not available, the applicant must provide an explanation of why that evidence is unavailable.[125] An applicant is not, however, required to produce corroborating evidence that he or she could not reasonably obtain.[126] Corroborating evidence may be presented in the form of any or all of the following:[127]

- Identity documents and other official government documents;
- Privately-issued membership cards or other affiliation documents;[128]
- Affidavits from the applicant's family, friends, neighbors, or community members confirming his or her protected characteristic;
- Photographs of the applicant participating in various events;
- Letters from organizations of which the applicant is a member or affiliate;

---

[123] *Matter of S–M–J–*, 21 I&N Dec. 722, 724-25 (BIA 1997).

[124] *Id.* at 726. An example provided by the BIA of corroboration regarding similarly situated individuals is that of a union vice-president who would be expected to provide documentation regarding the persecution of union members in her home country. *Id. But see Abankwah v. INS*, 185 F.3d 18 (2d Cir. 1999) (finding that the BIA was too exacting in the quantity and quality of evidence that it required); *Duarte de Guinac v. INS*, 179 F.3d 1156, 1162 (9th Cir. 1999) (criticizing the BIA for concluding that reports of widespread racial discrimination against Indians in Guatemala did not support the applicant's claim, where country condition reports could not corroborate specific acts of persecution). Similarly, the asylum applicant in *Singh v. Ilchert* presented documents regarding widespread and arbitrary arrest, detention, and abuse of persons suspected of affiliation with separatists and, thereby, demonstrated the reasonableness of his assertion that his persecution was on account of a political opinion imputed to him. *Singh v. Ilchert*, 63 F.3d 1501, 1511–12 (9th Cir. 1995). *See also Matter of S–P–*, 21 I&N Dec. 486 (BIA 1996) (relying on a DOS report regarding conditions in Sri Lanka in finding that the applicant was persecuted on account of imputed political opinion).

[125] *Matter of O–D–*, 21 I&N Dec. 1079, 1081 (BIA 1998), *vacated on other grounds by Hanaj v. Gonzales*, 446 F.3d 694, 700 (7th Cir. 2006); *Matter of S–M–J–*, 21 I&N Dec. 722, 724 (BIA 1997). *See also Salaam v. INS*, 229 F.3d 1234, 1239 (9th Cir. 2000) (finding that the applicant provided a reasonable explanation for the absence of documents, including his haste in fleeing the country and the danger in carrying documents critical of the Nigerian government).

[126] INA §§208(b)(1)(B)(ii), 240(c)(4), 241(b)(3)(C). *See also, Soeung v. Holder*, 677 F.3d 484, 488 (1st Cir. 2012); *Yan Juan Chen v. Holder*, 658 F.3d 246 (2d Cir. 2011) (finding that it was reasonable to expect the undocumented husband to testify in his wife's case, despite his fear of arrest); *San Kai Kwok v. Gonzales*, 455 F.3d 766, 771 (7th Cir. 2006).

[127] Vikram Badrinath, Dree K. Collopy, & Hans Christian Linnartz, *Evidentiary Issues in Asylum Cases*, AILA's Immigration Practice Pointers (2013-14 Ed.) (available for download on AILA Agora).

[128] *See, e.g.*, *Camara v. Ashcroft*, 378 F.3d 361, 370–71 (4th Cir. 2004) (finding that the IJ erred by failing to consider independent evidence of persecution: *inter alia*, a notice of escape, a political party membership card, an arrest warrant, and DOS reports corroborating the applicant's claim).

- Objective, published descriptions of the characteristics or attributes, which designate members of the applicant's race, religion, nationality, political affiliation, or social group;
- Photographs of the applicant's injuries;
- Police reports recording the harm suffered or threatened;
- Arrest warrants or records, if the applicant was ever arrested due to his or her protected characteristic;[129]
- Affidavits from witnesses who were present during the act(s) of harm or mistreatment;
- Affidavits from individuals whom the applicant confided in about the incident(s), confirming any observed physical or psychological harm, such as markings on the applicant's body, torn clothes, injuries, crying, anxiety, or other unusual behaviors;
- Medical records, including evaluations of physical injuries and the likely cause of those injuries, letters from treating doctors, treatment reports, hospital admission records, or prescribed medications;
- Mental health records, including evaluations of mental health disorders and the likely trigger for those disorders, letters from treating mental health professionals, appointment records, or prescribed medications;
- Death certificates for the applicant's relatives, friends, neighbors, or community members who were targeted because of a qualifying characteristic;
- Newspaper or other media coverage, or coverage by human rights groups, of the incident(s) in which the applicant was involved;
- Evidence that the applicant attempted to supply certain corroborating documentation, but was unable to;
- I-94 card, visa, and stamped passport (even if false);
- Evidence of means of travel to the United States, including airline itineraries, bus tickets, or hotel receipts;
- Evidence of presence outside of the United States in the past year, including financial, medical, school, or work records;
- Affidavits from individuals who have personal knowledge of the applicant's arrival in the United States;

[129] *See, e.g.*, *Camara v. Ashcroft*, 378 F.3d 361, 370–71 (4th Cir. 2004) (finding that the IJ erred by failing to consider independent evidence of persecution: *inter alia*, a notice of escape, a political party membership card, an arrest warrant, and DOS reports corroborating the applicant's claim).

- Expert report regarding the conditions in the applicant's home country as they relate to the applicant's claims and assessing the applicant's risk of harm upon return;[130] and
- Country conditions reports and articles showing the conditions in the applicant's home country during the time of persecution and presently, including human rights reports from the U.S. Department of State, Amnesty International, Human Rights Watch, or other reputable organizations.[131]

When the principal applicant is including derivative applicants, such as a spouse or unmarried child under the age of 21, on his or her application, the applicant must submit an additional copy of the complete asylum application with the derivative applicant's passport-sized photograph attached at page 9 of the copy of the Form I-589. The applicant also must submit evidence of the family relationship with the derivative applicant.[132] If the derivative applicant is a child, the relevant documentation is the child's birth certificate listing the principal applicant as the child's parent. If the derivative applicant is a spouse, the relevant documentation is the marriage certificate. If the applicant or derivative spouse was previously married, the divorce decree also must be submitted.[133] If the applicant does not have this primary evidence of relationship, he or she may submit secondary evidence, which may include, but is not limited to, medical records, school records, religious documents, or affidavits.[134] Relatives or others may provide affidavits, and the affiant need not be a U.S. citizen or lawful permanent resident.[135] Each affidavit should fully describe the event in question and explain how the affiant has personal knowledge of that event. The affidavit should be sworn and/or notarized, and should list the affiant's full name, address, date and place of birth, and relationship to the principal applicant.[136] The affiant also should provide a copy of his or her photo identification.

An asylum application will be considered incomplete and rejected upon receipt in each of the following situations:

---

[130] *See, e.g.*, *Niam v. Ashcroft*, 354 F.3d 652, 658 (7th Cir. 2004) (noting that the scholar proffered by the applicant should have been considered an expert and that it was error for the IJ to refuse to allow her to testify telephonically from overseas).

[131] *See* 8 CFR §§208.12(a), 1208.12(a) (2014) (providing that adjudicators may rely on "other credible sources" for information on country conditions, such as international organizations, private voluntary agencies, news organizations, or academic institutions). *See, e.g.*, *Camara v. Ashcroft*, 378 F.3d 361, 370–71 (4th Cir. 2004) (finding that the IJ erred by failing to consider independent evidence of persecution: *inter alia*, a notice of escape, a political party membership card, an arrest warrant, and DOS reports corroborating the applicant's claim). *See supra* chapter 4 for a detailed discussion of the evidentiary requirements for establishing asylum eligibility, as well as a list of suggested forms of supporting evidence.

[132] *USCIS Affirmative Asylum Procedures Manual*, *supra* note 14, at pt. II.A.3.

[133] *Id.*

[134] *Id. See also* 8 CFR §204.2(d)(2)(v) (2014).

[135] *USCIS Affirmative Asylum Procedures Manual*, *supra* note 14, at pt. II.A.3.

[136] *Id.*

- The application does not include a response to each of the questions contained in Form I-589;
- The application is unsigned;
- The application is submitted without the required photograph;
- The application is sent without the appropriate number of copies for any supporting materials submitted; and
- The applicant indicated in Part D that someone prepared the application other than his or herself or an immediate family member, and the preparer failed to complete Part E of the asylum application.[137]

Thus, applicants should carefully review their applications to ensure that all of these components are complete before filing the application.

IV. Where Should an Affirmative Asylum Application be Filed?

Affirmative asylum applications should be filed in accordance with the instructions on the Form I-589, Application for Asylum and for Withholding of Removal.[138] The instructions state that the application must be filed with the appropriate USCIS regional service center by mail.[139] A list of the regional service centers and the geographic areas they cover is found in the filing instructions of the I-589 in section "XII. Where to File?"[140]

The instructions also state that an applicant may submit his or her application directly with the Asylum Office having jurisdiction over the case in two situations: (1) if the Asylum Office Director or the Director of the Asylum Division gave express consent, and (2) if the applicant previously was included in a spouse's or parent's pending application but the applicant is no longer eligible to be included as a derivative applicant.[141] In the second situation, the applicant must include a cover letter referencing the previous application and explaining that he or she is now independently filing for asylum.[142] A Director normally will give consent to file in the local office if expeditious processing is required or if the applicant previously was denied or withdrew his or her asylum application but was not placed into deportation, exclusion, or removal proceedings.[143]

> **Practice Pointer**: Which Asylum Office has jurisdiction over an application depends on where the applicant resides. There are only eight

---

[137] I-589 Instructions, *supra* note 14, at 9.

[138] 8 CFR §§208.4(b), 1208.4(b) (2014).

[139] 8 CFR §§208.4(b)(1), 1208.4(b)(1) (2014).

[140] *See* I-589 Instructions, *supra* note 14, at 10.

[141] *Id.*

[142] *Id.*

[143] *USCIS Affirmative Asylum Procedures Manual*, *supra* note 14, at pt. II.B.2.

Asylum Offices in the United States: Arlington, Chicago, Houston, Los Angeles, Miami, Newark, New York, and San Francisco. Thus, each office has jurisdiction over a large geographic area. To determine which office has jurisdiction over a particular applicant, go to the USCIS website's "Asylum Office Locator" and type in the applicant's zip code at *https://egov.uscis.gov/crisgwi/go?action=offices.type&OfficeLocator.office_type=ZSY.*

- **Practice Pointer**: It is strongly recommended that applications be sent by certified mail, return receipt requested or some other method of delivery that can be tracked. It is important to have proof of where and when the application was filed.

If an applicant changes his or her address at any time after the I-589 application has been filed, he or she must file a Form AR-11, Alien Change of Address with the USCIS Service Center, and must also file a copy of the AR-11 directly with the local Asylum Office having jurisdiction over the applicant's case within ten days of the address change.[144] If the applicant does not file a change of address, the USCIS Service Center may send his or her application to an Asylum Office that does not have jurisdiction to decide the case, which could cause delays in the processing of the application. Moreover, the applicant may not receive important notices, such as the Receipt Notice, ASC Fingerprint Notification, or Interview Notice.

- **Practice Pointer**: Sending the AR-11 to the local Asylum Office will change the applicant's address for purposes of ensuring proper service of notices moving forward. However, an applicant also should file his or her AR-11 with USCIS. The AR-11 may be filed by mail or electronically. If an applicant files a paper Form AR-11, this will legally change the applicant's address but will not automatically update the applicant's address on other pending applications and petitions filed with USCIS.[145] Therefore, if an applicant chooses to file a paper copy of Form AR-11, the applicant will also need to call customer service at (800) 375-5283 to update his or her address on pending applications and petitions.[146] If an applicant changes his or her address online at *https://egov.uscis.gov/coa/displayCOAForm.do*, the applicant does not

---

[144] *Id.* at pt. III.A.1. *See* I-589 Instructions, *supra* note 14, at 11; *see also* USCIS Change of Address Information, *supra* note 145 (stating under *Penalties for Failure to Comply* that failure to give written notice to USCIS within 10 days of a change of address is a misdemeanor crime). If a person is in removal proceedings before an IJ or the BIA, an additional change of address form must be filed with the court. For cases pending in immigration court, *see www.usdoj.gov/eoir/eoirforms/eoir33/ICadr33.htm*, and for cases pending at the BIA *see www.usdoj.gov/eoir/eoirforms/eoir33bia.pdf*.

[145] Filing a paper copy of the AR-11 form will delay the process of notifying USCIS of the change of address significantly. *See* U.S. Citizenship and Immigration Servs., Change of Address Information, *How Do I Report My Change of Address*, *available at www.uscis.gov/addresschange*.

[146] Calling this customer service line by itself does not meet the legal requirement of completing an AR-11. *Id.*

also need to call the customer service number.[147] By using the online tool, an applicant is able to change his or her address for both legal purposes and for pending applications and petitions.[148] Even if the applicant changes his or her address online, however, the applicant must still file an AR-11 directly with the local Asylum Office, as described above.

V. What Happens After the Application is Filed?

After the affirmative application is filed, USCIS will initiate processing of the application, either at the USCIS Service Center or the local Asylum Office, depending on which office received the applicant's filing.

A. Initial Processing of Cases Filed with the USCIS Service Center

If the USCIS Service Center received the application, the Service Center will verify that the minimum components of the application were included and that USCIS has jurisdiction over the case by checking available databases for duplicate filings and multiple A-numbers or for evidence that the applicant has been in proceedings.[149] If there are missing components or if USCIS does not have jurisdiction over the application, the Service Center will reject the application and return it to the applicant, along with a rejection notice. On the other hand, if the minimum components were all included and the Service Center confirms jurisdiction over the application, it will issue an I-589 Receipt Notice.[150]

- **Practice Pointer**: Usually the applicant will receive the I-589 Receipt Notice within about two or three weeks of filing the application. If a Receipt Notice has not arrived within approximately three weeks of sending the application, practitioners should contact USCIS at 1-800-375-5283 to verify that the application was received and that it is being processed.

The Service Center will then match the I-589 application with any pre-existing A-files for the applicant. If there are no pre-existing A-files, the Service Center will create a new A-file.[151] The Service Center will then enter the I-589 in the Refugee Asylum and Parole System (RAPS), a computer database that tracks the processing of affirmative asylum applications, and forward the file to the appropriate Asylum Office.[152] Which Asylum Office has jurisdiction over the application moving forward

[147] *Id.*; see also U.S. Citizenship and Immigration Servs., Online Change of Address, available at *https://egov.uscis.gov/coa/displayCOAForm.do*.

[148] *See* USCIS Online Change of Address, *supra* note 148.

[149] *Id.* at pt. II.C.1.

[150] *Id.*

[151] *Id.*

[152] *Id.*

depends on the applicant's residence.[153] The Service Center must forward the file to the Asylum Office within 21 days of receipt of the complete I-589. Upon receipt of the A-file from the Service Center, the Asylum Office will verify that the A-file has been sent to the correct Asylum Office and confirm receipt of the file in RAPS.[154]

B. Initial Processing of Cases Filed Directly with the Asylum Office

An asylum application may be filed directly with the Asylum Office if the applicant has received the express consent of the Asylum Office Director or the Director of the Asylum Division, or if the applicant was previously included in a spouse or parent's pending application but he or she is no longer eligible to be included as a derivative applicant.[155] When an affirmative asylum application is filed directly with the Asylum Office, on the day of receipt, Asylum Office personnel will stamp the I-589 with the date of receipt and bring it to the attention of the Supervisory Asylum Officer, who determines whether direct filing with the Asylum Office is permitted. The officer will also review the I-589 to ensure that it meets the minimum requirements for completeness.[156]

If the affirmative asylum application was erroneously filed with the Asylum Office, it will be returned to the applicant with written instructions for how to correct the error and properly file the application.[157] On the other hand, if the application is complete and was properly filed with the Asylum Office, the I-589 will be entered into RAPS within one business day of receipt.[158] If previous A-files already exist, the Asylum Office will order the A-file and create a temporary file. If there are no previous A-files for the applicant, the Asylum Office will create an A-file and assign the applicant an A-number.[159]

If the Asylum Office receives and accepts jurisdiction over a new affirmatively filed application after a prior denial or withdrawal of a previous application, the Asylum Office will locate the A-file that contains the previous application and enter the new filing date in RAPS. A newly-filed I-589 will receive a new asylum interview and adjudication by an asylum officer; however the asylum officer may consider the interview notes and assessment from the previous application to develop lines of inquiry.[160] Similarly, if the Asylum Office receives and accepts jurisdiction over a principal applicant's application, who previously filed as a dependent on another asylum application, the Asylum Office will convert the former dependent into

---

[153] 8 CFR §100.4(f) (2014).

[154] *Id.* at pt. II.F.1.

[155] I-589 Instructions, *supra* note 14, at 10.

[156] *USCIS Affirmative Asylum Procedures Manual*, *supra* note 14, at pt. II.C.2.

[157] *Id.*

[158] *Id.*

[159] *Id.*

[160] *Id.*

a principal record in RAPS and conduct an interview based on the prior dependent's new application.[161]

C. Identity, Background, and Security Checks

According to the INA, "asylum cannot be granted until the identity of the applicant has been checked against all appropriate records or databases … to determine any grounds on which the [applicant] may be inadmissible to or deportable from the United States, or ineligible to apply for or be granted asylum."[162] The entry of the applicant into RAPS initiates automated records checks of the applicant in the Deportable Alien Control System, a computer database that tracks information about individuals in detention and in deportation, exclusion, or removal processes. It also initiates automated checks of the FBI name database and schedules applicants for fingerprinting and biometrics appointments at USCIS Application Support Centers (ASC).[163]

Once the fingerprinting and biometrics appointment is scheduled, the applicant will receive a Form I-797C, Notice of Action, "Fingerprint Notification" in the mail. The notice will notify the applicant that he or she has been scheduled to appear at an ASC to be fingerprinted and photographed for biometrics collection, and that completion of background identity and security checks is required in order to process the I-589 application. The notice will list the address of the ASC and its hours of operation, as well as a 14-day period during which the applicant may appear at the ASC to complete the biometrics collection. Finally, the notice will warn the applicant that failure to appear may result in dismissal of his or her asylum application, as well as referral to an immigration judge.

- **Practice Pointer**: Recently, ASC Fingerprint Notifications have been arriving along with the Receipt Notice for the I-589 or shortly thereafter. If practitioners' clients do not receive their ASC notices within approximately 30 days of the receipt of their applications, practitioners should make an inquiry with the USCIS Service Center.

The applicant must then appear at the ASC within the specified time period for his or her biometrics collection. Applicants are instructed to bring the original ASC Fingerprint Notification and photo identification with them to their ASC appointments. If the applicant does not have a photo-ID, the ASC will still collect his or her biometrics; however, there may be a delay during the appointment as a USCIS officer may interview the applicant regarding his or her identity.

- **Practice Pointer**: Practitioners should request a copy of their client's stamped ASC Fingerprint Notification following his or her attendance at the ASC appointment, as the applicant may need to provide proof of

---

[161] *Id.*

[162] INA §208(d)(5)(A)(i).

[163] *USCIS Affirmative Asylum Procedures Manual*, *supra* note 14, at pt. II.D.3.

attendance at his or her appointment later in the affirmative asylum process.

If the applicant fails to appear for his or her ASC appointment, his or her asylum application may be dismissed.[164] The applicant's failure to appear may be excused if he or she can show good cause for failure to attend by presenting evidence that there was not a single day during the two-week period that he or she could not reasonable attend.[165] A failure to comply with identity check procedures *must* be excused if the applicant demonstrates that his or her failure was a result of exceptional circumstances or improper notice (*i.e.*, the notice was not mailed to his or her current address and the address had been provided to the Asylum Division prior to the date the notice was mailed).[166]

D. Scheduling of the Asylum Interview

The Asylum Office's entry of the applicant into RAPS also initiates scheduling of the applicant's asylum interview in the Asylum Office's interview calendar.[167] In the absence of exceptional circumstances, the initial interview or hearing on the asylum application "shall commence not later than 45 days after the date the application is filed."[168] Usually, cases are automatically scheduled for an interview in the database. Approximately 22 days before a particular interview day, RAPS fills that day's open interview slots with cases previously entered into RAPS.[169] The Asylum Office also may manually schedule interviews if a particular case needs an expedited interview or needs rescheduling.[170]

> **Practice Pointer**: As of the publication of this book, there is a large backlog of tens of thousands of affirmative asylum cases that have not yet been scheduled for an interview.[171] This is attributable, in large part, to the influx of individuals, unaccompanied minors, and families fleeing Central America and Mexico and seeking protection at the U.S. southern border. This influx has necessitated a shift in the Asylum Division's resources toward completing credible and reasonable fear interviews, rather than affirmative asylum interviews.[172] Many of these cases have

---

[164] *Id.* at pt. III.K.1.

[165] *Id.* at pt. III.K.1.a.

[166] 8 CFR §208.10 (2014). *See* INA §240(e)(1) for examples of "exceptional circumstances."

[167] *Id.* at pt. II.G.

[168] INA §208(d)(5)(A)(ii).

[169] *USCIS Affirmative Asylum Procedures Manual*, *supra* note 14, at pt. II.G.2.

[170] *Id.*

[171] *See* U.S. Citizenship and Immigration Servs., *Asylum Office Statistics*, AILA InfoNet Doc. No. 14021957 (posted Feb. 19, 2014), *available at www.aila.org/content/default.aspx?docid=47513.*

[172] *See* Cheri Attix, *The Affirmative Asylum Backlog Explained*, AILA (Apr. 2, 2014), AILA InfoNet Doc. No. 14040248, *available at www.immigrantjustice.org/sites/immigrantjustice.org/files/AILA_Explanation%20of%20the%20Affirmative%20Asylum%20Backlog_4.2.14.pdf.*

been awaiting interview scheduling for significantly longer than the statutory period of 45 days — sometimes even one to two years. This is problematic for a number of reasons. First, many applicants still have spouses and children in their home countries who remain in danger of persecution and torture. Second, these applicants are kept in a state of limbo, without status and unable to fully integrate into American society. Finally, given the length of the delay — in some cases multiple years — the applicant's asylum claim may become stale and he or she may no longer be eligible for asylum by the time the applicant is scheduled for an interview. Practitioners, whose clients are stuck in the backlog, should consider filing an expedite request directly with the Asylum Office, especially if there are compelling reasons for the request, such as a family member in danger in the home country. AILA's "Asylum Office Guide — Best Practices" includes detailed information on how to directly contact each Asylum Office with such inquiries and requests. [173] If the Asylum Office is unresponsive, practitioners should file a request for case assistance with the CIS Ombudsman's office on the DHS-7001 form. This form is available on the Ombudsman's website and may be submitted online or by mail.[174]

➢ **Practice Pointer**: On December 26, 2014, the USCIS Asylum Division began prioritizing asylum applications for interview scheduling as follows: Priority 1 — applications that were scheduled for an interview, but the applicant requested a new interview date; Priority 2 — applications filed by children; and Priority 3 — all other pending affirmative asylum applications will be scheduled for interviews in the order they were received, with oldest cases scheduled first. *See USCIS Processing of Asylum Cases* at *www.uscis.gov/sites/default/files/USCIS/Humanitarian/Refugees%20%26%20Asylum/Asylum/USCIS_Reponds_to_Humanitarian_Caseload.pdf*. Given this new three-tiered system for interview scheduling, as well as the large backlog of cases that have already been awaiting interview scheduling for many months (some even years), it is likely that newly-filed affirmative asylum applications will be waiting one to two years on average before an interview is scheduled. Practitioners should advise their clients of the likely long waiting period and should diligently ensure that their clients do not take any actions that would stop the employment authorization clock from accruing time. Otherwise, the client may be waiting for one to two years

[173] *See* AILA, *Asylum Office Guide – Best Practices* (Mar. 17, 2015), AILA InfoNet Doc. No. 12060844, *available at www.aila.org/content/default.aspx?docid=40080*. The "Asylum Office Guide – Best Practices" is also available at Appx. 4E of this book.

[174] *See* Citizenship and Immigration Servs., *Ombudsman – Case Assistance*, *available at www.dhs.gov/case-assistance#*.

for their asylum interview without authorization to work in the meantime.

When RAPS fills an interview slot with a case, the system automatically generates an Interview Notice, as well as an identical Interview Notice for the applicant's representative if that representative is recorded in RAPS.[175] Asylum Office personnel must mail the notices to the applicant and his or her representative within three days of the notices being printed by RAPS and no less than 18 days before the scheduled interview date.[176] The Interview Notice informs the applicant of his or her interview date, time, and location. It also notifies the applicant that he or she must bring to the interview the applicant's identification, three copies of evidence of the applicant's family relationship to any derivative applicants listed on the application, any other evidence not previously-submitted, and an interpreter if he or she cannot speak English. The interpreter cannot be the applicant's attorney, representative, or witness. Finally, the notice informs the applicant that failure to appear for the interview or to provide a competent interpreter may result in referral of his or her application to an immigration judge.

If the applicant receives the Interview Notice and he or she or the applicant's representative cannot attend the interview on the date scheduled, a prompt reschedule request must be made in writing and submitted to the Asylum Office having jurisdiction over the application.[177] Such requests may be submitted by mail, email, or fax, depending on the local Asylum Office's preferred procedures for accepting reschedule requests.[178] The Asylum Office generally honors first-time reschedule requests made prior to the interview and up to 45 days after the interview date; however, if good cause is not shown, an Asylum Office may issue a Denial of Interview Reschedule Request.[179]

- **Practice Pointer**: Each Asylum Office has its own local procedures for reschedule requests. Most offices have a designated email address or fax number for submission of such requests in writing. Some suggest calling the office's phone number in addition to submitting the request in writing. Practitioners should consult AILA's "Asylum Office Guide — Best Practices," which is updated each year, for the local rules in their jurisdiction regarding reschedule requests.[180] See Appx. 4E of this book for a copy of this guide.

---

[175] *USCIS Affirmative Asylum Procedures Manual*, *supra* note 14, at pt. II.G.3.

[176] *Id.*

[177] *Id.* at pt. III.T.

[178] *Id.*

[179] *Id.*

[180] *See* AILA, Asylum Office Guide – Best Practices, *supra* note 173.

E. Collection of A-Files

After the interview notice is sent to the applicant, the Asylum Office will pull his or her A-file from the file room and assign the case to a responsible party.[181] If the A-file cannot be located and the asylum applicant appears for his or her interview, the interview may not be completed without the A-file, unless the applicant has a copy of the I-589.[182]

> ➢ **Practice Pointer**: In order to avoid delay due to a missing file, practitioners should bring an extra copy of the completed I-589to provide to the officer conducting the interview if needed.

Prior to the interview, the asylum officer assigned to the case will again confirm that the applicant is not under the jurisdiction of the Executive Office for Immigration Review.[183]

VI. What Happens When the Applicant Arrives for the Asylum Interview?

When an asylum applicant arrives at the Asylum Office (or the designated USCIS location for circuit rides[184]) on the day of his or her interview, he or she must pass through a security screening to enter the office. These screenings similar to a security screening at an airport; the applicant will walk through a metal detector and place any bags through an x-ray machine.

> ➢ **Practice Pointer**: Each Asylum Office has its own security screening procedures. Thus, practitioners who are visiting an Asylum Office for the first time should reach out to local asylum practitioners to inquire about these procedures in order to properly prepare their clients for what they should expect on the day of their asylum interview.

A. Check-In Procedures

After the applicant passes through security, he or she will check in with Asylum Officer personnel. Typically, this process begins with submitting the Interview Notice to the relevant Asylum Office personnel, who will note the time of the applicant's arrival by date and time-stamping the Interview Notice.[185] Asylum Office

---

[181] *USCIS Affirmative Asylum Procedures Manual*, *supra* note 14, at pt. II.H.

[182] *Id.*

[183] *Id.*

[184] Since there are only eight Asylum Offices in the United States, each covering a large geographic area, USCIS Asylum Officers periodically travel to other cities to conduct asylum interviews of applicants who live far away from the Asylum Office. *See* USCIS, *Asylum Division Overview* (Mar. 4, 2011), *available at www.uscis.gov/sites/default/files/USCIS/Resources/Resources%20for%20Congress/Congressional%20Reports/2011%20National%20Immigration%20%26%20Consular%20Conference%20Presentations/Asylum%20Division%20Overview.pdf* (last visited Mar. 26, 2015).

[185] *Id.* at pt. II.I.3.

personnel also will notify the officer assigned to the case regarding the applicant's arrival. Most Asylum Offices pre-assign cases, but some assign cases when applicants appear for their interviews. Regardless, case assignment is done at random.[186] One exception to this rule is if the applicant previously was denied asylum, but not placed in removal proceedings. Under these circumstances, Asylum Offices attempt to assign the case to the same officer who made the original decision or to a new officer supervised by a Supervisory Asylum Officer who reviewed the original decision.[187] Additionally, if a case is randomly assigned to an asylum officer who has a prior personal or professional relationship with the applicant, interpreter, or representative of the case, the officer must notify his or her Supervisory Asylum Officer. If there is a conflict of interest, the case will be reassigned.[188]

- **Practice Pointer**: If an applicant has a preference regarding the gender of his or her interviewing officer, the applicant should make that request to the Asylum Office prior to his or her interview. Asylum Offices generally attempt to honor these requests. For example, if an applicant suffered sexual violence at the hands of a man in her home country, she may feel more comfortable being interviewed by a female officer. AILA's "Asylum Office Guide — Best Practices" includes detailed information on how to directly contact each Asylum Office with such requests.[189]

B. Identity Checks

At the time of the interview, the applicant must provide complete information regarding his or her identity, including name, date and place of birth, and nationality.[190] Asylum cannot be granted until the identity of the applicant has been checked against all appropriate records or databases maintained by the attorney general or secretary of state, including the Automated Visa Lookout System.[191] These records and databases are checked to determine if the applicant is inadmissible to or deportable from the United States, or ineligible for asylum.[192] The U.S. Court of Appeals for the Ninth Circuit has held that this identity check requirement, added to the INA in 1996, does not impose any new burden of proof on the asylum applicant; instead, it imposes new duties on the attorney general and secretary of state.[193] While procedures vary from office to office, it is usually at the time of check in when

[186] *Id.* at pt. II.I.4.

[187] *Id.*

[188] *Id.*

[189] *See* AILA, *Asylum Office Guide – Best Practices* (Mar. 17, 2015), at AILA InfoNet Doc. No. 12060844. The "Asylum Office Guide – Best Practices" is also available at Appx. 4E of this book.

[190] 8 CFR §§208.9(b), 1208.9(b) (2014).

[191] INA §208(d)(5)(A)(i); 8 USC §1158(d)(5)(a)(i) (2012).

[192] INA §208(d)(5)(A)(i); 8 USC §1158(d)(5)(a)(i) (2012).

[193] *Kalouma v. Gonzales*, 512 F.3d 1073 (9th Cir. 2008).

Asylum Office personnel will again collect the applicant's biometrics, including a photograph of the applicant and his or her index fingerprints on each hand. A photograph and fingerprints of all dependent applicants 14 years old and older will also be collected. The biometrics will then be used to locate the applicant and all dependents 14 years old and older in the US-VISIT system, which verifies the subjects' identities and compares their biometric identifying information to information contained in the various databases.[194]

- **Practice Pointer**: If an applicant is appearing at a USCIS circuit ride location, rather than the Asylum Office, these check-in procedures may not apply and may vary. Practitioners should reach out to local asylum practitioners to gain an understanding of the local procedures at the various USCIS circuit ride locations.

C. Collection of Supplemental Evidence

Usually, upon check-in, Asylum Office personnel also will collect any other evidence or documentation that the applicant has brought with him or her that was not previously submitted. Note, however, that most Asylum Offices discourage submission of evidence on the day of the asylum interview. Some even prohibit and refuse to accept additional evidence on the day of the interview.

- **Practice Pointer**: Practitioners should plan to hand-deliver any supplemental supporting documentation to the Asylum Office *at least* one week in advance of the interview. Submitting supplemental documents closer to the interview date could result in rescheduling of the asylum interview and/or the evidence not being considered by the asylum officer. Most Asylum Offices, with the exception of New York, strongly discourage day-of evidence submissions. In fact, the Houston and Miami Asylum Offices encourage applicants to file all evidence together with the initial filing at the Service Center. Asylum Offices also encourage hand-delivery of supplemental application materials, advising that mailing supplemental documentation does not guarantee that it will be added to the A-file in time for the interview. It is a good practice to bring proof of the filing date, proof of delivery, and an extra copy of all supplemental evidence to the applicant's interview in case USCIS has not matched the supplemental evidence filing to the file prior to the interview. For the specific procedures for each Asylum Office, see AILA's "Asylum Office Guide — Best Practices," which is updated every year and posted on AILA InfoNet. The current version of the guide was posted on AILA InfoNet on March 17, 2015, at Doc. No.12060844. It is also available at Appx. 4E of this book.

---

[194] *USCIS Affirmative Asylum Procedures Manual*, *supra* note 14, at pt. II.I.1.

D. Verification of Fulfillment of Fingerprint Requirements

Prior to or at the time the applicant appears at the Asylum Office for his or her asylum interview, Asylum Office personnel will verify whether the applicant and any dependents 14 years of age or older who require fingerprinting have complied with the requirement of having their fingerprints taken at the ASC.[195] If the fingerprints have been completed, the interview will proceed.

It is possible that the databases will indicate that the applicant or his or her dependents have not, however, complied with the fingerprinting requirements. In that case, Asylum Office personnel must query the applicant when he or she appears for the interview as to whether he or she received the ASC appointment notice and appeared for the appointment.[196] If the applicant states that he or she did comply with the appointment, Asylum Office personnel will request proof of compliance in the form of the stamped ASC appointment notice. If the applicant has that proof, the interview may proceed and the officer will place a copy of the document in the applicant's A-file.[197]

> ➤ **Practice Pointer**: Practitioners should encourage their clients to bring their stamped ASC Fingerprint Notification forms with them to their asylum interviews. This simple step could help with preventing significant delays in the processing of their applications.

If the officer determines that the applicant did not appear for his or her appointment, however, the officer will then determine whether the failure to appear was the first or second time the applicant failed to appear.[198] If it was the first failure to appear for the ASC appointment, the applicant's interview will be rescheduled for a later date after the applicant is able to appear for biometrics collection. The officer will provide him or her with a Notice of Scheduling of Fingerprint Appointment, which explains the consequences for failure to appear at the new fingerprint appointment, and schedule the applicant for a new fingerprinting appointment.[199] The asylum interview also will be rescheduled and the asylum officer will document in the A-file that the applicant was scheduled for another fingerprinting appointment.[200]

On the other hand, if it was the applicant's failure to attend an ASC fingerprinting appointment for the second time, the failure is not excused and his or her application will be referred (if the applicant is not in valid status) or dismissed (if the applicant is

---

[195] *Id.* at pt. II.I.

[196] *Id.*

[197] *Id.*

[198] *Id.*

[199] *Id.*

[200] *Id.*

in valid status or if there is insufficient evidence to support issuance of an NTA).[201] If the principal applicant attended his or her ASC fingerprinting appointment, but his or her dependent failed to do so after receiving a second ASC appointment notice, the failure is not excused. Only the dependent's application will be dismissed or referred on this basis, however.[202] Asylum Office personnel are encouraged to process the dismissal or referral while the applicant is still present in the Asylum Office so the paperwork can be served on him or her (or the dependent) in person.[203]

➢ **Practice Pointer**: An asylum applicant may be granted employment authorization, but only after his or her application has been pending for 180 days.[204] When an application is received by USCIS, days begin to accrue on the "employment authorization clock." Various delays caused by the applicant throughout the asylum application process may stop the clock from accruing days, thereby preventing the applicant from reaching the 180 days for employment authorization purposes. If an applicant fails to attend his or her fingerprinting appointment at the ASC, that may be an event that stops the employment authorization clock, depending on the circumstances.[205] For example, if the failure to attend the ASC appointment was caused by the applicant and he or she cannot show good cause for failure to attend the appointment, the employment authorization clock will stop. However, if good cause is shown, or if the failure to attend was caused by USCIS, the employment authorization clock will not stop.[206] See Part IX.B. of this chapter and see chapter 13 of this book for a more detailed discussion of the eligibility requirements and procedures for applying for employment authorization while an asylum application is pending, as well as strategies to avoid stopping the clock.

It is also possible that an applicant did comply with the ASC fingerprint requirements, but his or her fingerprint results have expired or been rejected. In these situations, case processing should continue as normal and the applicant should be interviewed.[207] If the officer determines that the applicant otherwise appears to be eligible for asylum, the officer will schedule the applicant for another fingerprinting appointment. If, however, the applicant does not appear to be eligible for asylum for

---

[201] *Id.* at pt. II.I.2.b.ii. *See also* Memorandum from Joseph Langlois on Securing Compliance with Fingerprinting Requirements Prior to Asylum Interview and Amending Procedures for Issuance of Recommended Approvals (Sept. 12, 2006), AILA InfoNet Doc. No. 06091360 (*posted* Sept. 13, 2006).

[202] *USCIS Affirmative Asylum Procedures Manual*, *supra* note 14, at pt. II.I.2.b.ii.

[203] *Id.*

[204] INA §208(d)(2).

[205] *USCIS Affirmative Asylum Procedures Manual*, *supra* note 14, at pt. II.I.

[206] *Id.* at pt. II.I.2.b.i.

[207] *Id.*

reasons unrelated to fingerprint compliance, the officer will deny or refer the application to the immigration court.[208]

Sometimes, dependents have not yet complied with the fingerprinting requirements at the ASC because they were added to the asylum application after it was filed but before the asylum interview. In this situation, asylum officers must provide the dependent with a Notice of Scheduling of Fingerprinting Appointment and schedule him or her for a fingerprinting appointment. The asylum interview also will be rescheduled.[209]

- **Practice Pointer**: In the case of an added dependent who needs to be fingerprinted, the Asylum Office considers this to be a delay caused by the applicant. Therefore the employment authorization clock will stop.[210]
- **Practice Pointer**: It is possible that the identity background and security checks will reveal that an applicant has returned to the United States illegally after a prior removal or departure under a removal order. Such individuals may be subject to reinstatement of removal under INA §241(a)(5). If an asylum officer becomes aware that an applicant may be subject to reinstatement, the processing of the asylum application will stop and the asylum officer will contact the ICE Special Agent in Charge having jurisdiction over the applicant's place of residence to determine if the order has or will be reinstated.[211] Once a prior order is reinstated, the applicant is not permitted to apply for asylum, and the Asylum Office will administratively close the asylum application.[212] If ICE later refers the applicant for a reasonable fear interview, the asylum officer will interview the applicant and adjudicate the claim pursuant to reasonable fear procedures.[213] See chapter 6 of this book for a detailed discussion of reinstatement of removal and the reasonable fear standards and procedures.

E. Awaiting the Interview

After the applicant has completed the check-in process, Asylum Office personnel will then provide the applicant with the Record of Applicant and Interpreter Oaths form to review and will ask the applicant to complete the top portion of the form while waiting for his or her interview in the waiting room. The top portion of this

---

[208] *Id.*

[209] *Id.*

[210] *Id.*

[211] *Id.* at pt. III.S.1.

[212] *Id.* at pt. III.S.3.

[213] *See supra* chapter 6 for a detailed discussion of reinstatement of removal and reasonable fear procedures.

form requires the applicant to list his or her name, A-number, whether an interpreter will be used, what languages the interpreter speaks, and the interpreter's address. The form also includes a number of notices and warnings to the applicant regarding the oath that he or she must tell the truth, as well as notices and warnings to the interpreter that he or she must interpret truly and correctly to the best of his or her abilities, throughout the interview. The applicant and interpreter must review these notices and warnings prior to the interview, but must wait to sign the declarations in front of the asylum officer.

Asylum officers are encouraged to begin interviewing the applicant as expeditiously as possible and to explain any lengthy anticipated delays to the applicant.[214] When the officer is ready to begin the interview, he or she will call the applicant from the waiting room by number, rather than name, to preserve the applicant's confidentiality. Usually, the applicant is given a number upon check-in or the Asylum Office uses the last three digits of his or her A-number.[215] After the applicant's number is called, the asylum officer greets the principal applicant in the waiting room and accounts for any dependents and representative of record before escorting the relevant individuals back to the asylum officer's office.[216]

VII. What Happens During the Affirmative Asylum Interview?

Affirmative asylum interviews are conducted by asylum officers, and, unlike hearings for defensive claims, are (or should be) conducted in a non-adversarial manner.[217] The setting for the interview reflects its non-adversarial nature, as the interview takes place in the asylum officer's office — usually a room with a desk and computer. The asylum officer will sit on one side of the desk and the applicant, interpreter, and representative will sit on the other side of the desk. The purpose of the interview, according to the regulations, is "to elicit all relevant and useful information bearing on the applicant's eligibility for asylum."[218] The applicant may present witnesses and may submit affidavits of witnesses or other evidence.[219] Asylum officers are given special training in non-adversarial interview techniques.[220]

---

[214] *USCIS Affirmative Asylum Procedures Manual*, *supra* note 14, at pt. II.I.6.

[215] *Id.* at pt. II.I.7.

[216] *Id.* at pt. II.I.8.

[217] 8 CFR §§208.9(b), 1208.9(b) (2014).

[218] 8 CFR §§208.9(b), 1208.9(b) (2014).

[219] 8 CFR §§208.9(b), 1208.9(b) (2014).

[220] 8 CFR §§208.1(b), 1208.1(b) (2014); *see also* U.S. Citizenship and Immigration Servs., *Interviewing Part I: Overview of Nonadversarial Asylum Interview*, in Asylum Officer Basic Training Course Participant Workbook (Sept. 14, 2006), *available at www.uscis.gov/sites/default/files/USCIS/Humanitarian/Refugees%20%26%20Asylum/Asylum/AOBTC%20Lesson%20Plans/Interview%20Part-Overview-Nonadversarial-Asylum-Interview-31aug10.pdf.*

- **Practice Pointer**: There are special procedures and interviewing techniques for children's asylum claims. On December 10, 1998, legacy Immigration and Naturalization Service (INS) issued guidelines for children's asylum claims, which provide additional procedural protections for children in the affirmative asylum process.[221] A more recent resource is the Asylum Officer Basic Training Course Lesson Plan: Guidelines for Children's Asylum Claims (updated September 1, 2009).[222] See chapter 10 of this book for a detailed discussion of asylum standards and procedures for children.

A. Confidentiality

Under 8 CFR §§208.6, 1208.6, USCIS shall not disclose any information contained in or pertaining to any asylum application without the written consent of the applicant.[223] USCIS also must keep confidential any records that indicate that an individual has applied for asylum.[224] If any records need to be transmitted to the Department of State in other countries, USCIS is required to coordinate with the Department of State to ensure that the confidentiality of those records is maintained.[225] Thus, at the beginning of the asylum interview, the asylum officer will notify the applicant that everything he or she says during the interview will not be shared with third parties, in particular, the applicant's government or people in his or her country of feared persecution.

B. Interview Under Oath

Upon arrival in the asylum officer's office to begin the asylum interview, the officer will first request the applicant's, interpreter's, and representative's identity documents.

- **Practice Pointer**: Practitioners should bring their photo-ID and bar card (if a licensed attorney) with them to their client's asylum interview. Many offices require these documents to verify a representative's identity and ability to represent the client.

The officer also will ask the applicant and interpreter if they have had the opportunity to review the Record of Applicant and Interpreter Oaths form that was given to them upon check-in. The officer will answer any questions that the applicant or interpreter have about the form and declarations they must make as part of their oaths. The asylum officer will then place the applicant, interpreter, and any

---

[221] See this chapter at 3.5.

[222] *See* U.S. Citizenship and Immigration Servs., *Guidelines for Children's Asylum Claims*, in Asylum Officer Basic Training Course Participant Workbook (Sept. 1, 2009), *available at www.uscis.gov/files/article/AOBTC_Lesson_29_Guidelines_for_Childrens_Asylum_Claims.pdf.*

[223] 8 CFR §§208.6(a), 1208.6(a) (2014).

[224] 8 CFR §§208.6(b), 1208.6(b) (2014).

[225] *Id.*

dependents under oath.[226] The applicant and interpreter will both sign the Record of Applicant and Interpreter Oaths, which will be placed in the A-file.[227] The asylum officer also signs the Record of Applicant and Interpreter Oaths as a witness.[228]

At this time, the asylum officer also will verify that the Asylum Office has jurisdiction over the applicant's asylum application by confirming the applicant's address. If the applicant has moved outside of the Asylum Office's jurisdiction, the officer will not continue with the interview due to lack of jurisdiction.[229]

C. Interview of Dependents

The asylum officer must personally meet each dependent included as a derivative on the applicant's I-589; however, at the asylum officer's discretion, the dependents may be dismissed from the interview to wait in the waiting room.[230] Either before or after the asylum interview, the asylum officer must verify the dependent's identity, his or her relationship to the principal applicant, and ascertain the dependent's date, place, and manner of entry. The asylum officer also must ensure that the dependent is not under the jurisdiction of the immigration court and determine whether any mandatory bars apply.[231]

> ➢ **Practice Pointer**: If a dependent is subject to a mandatory bar, he or she may not be granted asylum as a derivative applicant along with the principal applicant. Rather, in this scenario, the Asylum Officer will either deny or refer the dependent's application, depending on his or her current immigration status.[232] See chapter 13 of this book for a detailed discussion of the policies and procedures for derivative asylum-seekers.

D. Interpreters

If the applicant is unable to proceed with the interview in English, the applicant must provide, at no expense to DHS, a competent interpreter.[233] The interpreter must be fluent in English and the applicant's native language or any other language in which the applicant is fluent.[234] The interpreter must be at least 18 years of age and may not be the applicant's attorney or representative, a witness testifying on the applicant's behalf, or a representative or employee of the applicant's country of nationality (or, if the applicant is stateless, the applicant's country of last habitual

---

[226] *USCIS Affirmative Asylum Procedures Manual*, *supra* note 14, at pt. II.J.2.

[227] *Id.*

[228] *Id.* at pt. II.J.4.a.

[229] *Id.* at pt. III.L.2.a.

[230] *Id.* at pt. II.J.3.

[231] *Id.*

[232] *Id.* at pt. III.E.9. *See also infra* pt. VIII.E. for a detailed discussion of the potential decisions an asylum officer may make at the conclusion of the affirmative asylum process.

[233] 8 CFR §§208.9(g), 1208.9(g) (2014).

[234] 8 CFR §§208.9(g), 1208.9(g) (2014).

residence).[235] The applicant's failure to provide an interpreter at the time of the interview, if without "good cause," may be considered by the Asylum Office to be a failure to appear.[236]

- **Practice Pointer**: Hearing-impaired applicants will be provided with a sign language interpreter by the Asylum Office. To obtain this service, the applicant should contact the Asylum Office with jurisdiction over his or her case as soon as notice of the interview date is received, so accommodations may be made in advance.[237]

USCIS has contemplated issuing regulations to provide government-funded interpreter services for affirmative asylum interviews.[238] However, to date, no such regulations have been promulgated. Instead, following a pilot program, USCIS now contracts with providers of interpretation services who monitor affirmative asylum interviews by telephone.[239]

- **Practice Pointer**: Some clients may prefer to proceed with their interview in English, as they may be fluent in English or proficient enough to effectively communicate in English. Moreover, providing testimony through an interpreter opens the door to miscommunications and the filtering of information and important details. Practitioners should have a detailed discussion with their clients regarding the pros and cons of using an interpreter, and explain the importance of every word and every detail given the severe negative impact that seeming inconsistencies, vagaries, or omissions may have on the applicant's credibility and eligibility for asylum. Whether a client provides testimony in his or her native language or in English is, ultimately, the client's decision. However, it is practitioners' duty to ensure that their clients are able to make an informed decision in this regard.

At the beginning of the asylum interview, the asylum officer will place the interpreter under oath, as described above. The officer also will verify the identity of the interpreter. The interpreter, like the applicant, however, is not required to present identity documents in order to interpret for the asylum applicant.[240] If the asylum officer believes that the issue of the individual's identity is material to his or her ability to interpret, the officer will consult with his or her supervisor. Only the

---

[235] 8 CFR §§208.9(g), 1208.9(g) (2014).

[236] 8 CFR §§208.9(g), 1208.9(g) (2014); see also infra this section.

[237] *USCIS Affirmative Asylum Procedures Manual*, *supra* note 14, at pt. II.J.4.b.; I-589 Instructions, *supra* note 14, at 12.

[238] *See* 72 Fed. Reg. 22601 (Apr. 30, 2007) (DHS's semiannual regulatory agenda).

[239] *USCIS Affirmative Asylum Procedures Manual*, *supra* note 14, at pt. II.J.4.b.

[240] *Id.* at pt. II.J.4.a.iii.

Asylum Office Director or his or her designee has the authority to dismiss or bar an individual from interpreting during an asylum interview.[241]

After administering the oath and verifying the interpreter's identity, the asylum officer will determine the language of interpretation. He or she will then explain to the applicant, through his or her interpreter, that a contract interpreter will be monitoring the interview to ensure the accuracy of interpretation by the applicant's interpreter.[242] The officer will then connect to a telephonic interpreter monitor, remind the monitor of the confidentiality requirements of the interview, and administer an oath to the contract interpreter monitor.[243] The monitor must affirm that: (1) he or she will truthfully, literally, and fully report to the asylum officer any mistranslation observed during the course of the interview; (2) he or she will immediately notify the officer if the monitor becomes aware of his or her inability to monitor in a neutral manner; and (3) he or she understands that all matters discussed during the interview are confidential and the monitor will not share what he or she hears with any person.[244]

The role of the interpreter monitor is limited to monitoring the interpretation by the interpreter provided by the applicant. The monitor may not serve as the primary interpreter if it is determined during the course of the interview that the applicant's interpreter is incompetent or otherwise insufficient.[245] If the applicant's interpreter requires assistance, he or she may occasionally ask the interpreter monitor for help in translating a word or phrase. The Affirmative Asylum Procedures Manual states, "As a general rule, the interpreter may be called upon to translate a word or two, but not a sentence or more."[246] Contract interpreter monitors may occasionally interject if the applicant's interpreter fails to provide adequate, accurate, or neutral interpretation. However, the interpreter monitor should not be allowed to interject excessively or inappropriately.[247] If there is a dispute between the monitor and the applicant's interpreter, the asylum officer is required to take note of both interpretations, but rely upon the monitor's interpretation in making his or her decision.[248] If the asylum officer experiences problems with the interpreter monitor, such as frequent or inappropriate interjections, unavailability, absence, or unresponsiveness when prompted, the asylum officer may request another monitor and should notify his or her supervisor of the issue.[249]

---

[241] *Id.*

[242] *Id.* at pt. II.J.4.b.v.

[243] *Id.* at pts. II.J.4.b.ii. & v.

[244] *Id.* at pt. II.J.4.b.v.

[245] *Id.* at pt. II.J.4.b.iv.

[246] *Id.*

[247] *Id.*

[248] *Id.*

[249] *Id.* at pt. II.J.4.b.v.

- **Practice Pointer**: Practitioners should prepare their clients and their clients' interpreters for the use of an interpreter monitor. Moreover, practitioners should be prepared to request that the asylum officer remind the interpreter monitor of his or her role as a monitor if he or she is excessively or inappropriately interjecting. For example, the interpreter monitor should not call attention to minor mistranslations, such as an adjective that might not be the monitor's choice but that accurately conveys the meaning of the applicant's statement.[250]

If the asylum officer believes that an applicant's interpreter is abusing his or her role as an interpreter by willfully changing, creating, omitting, or otherwise misrepresenting oral testimony of the applicant; exhibiting incompetent or insufficient language skills; using abusive or intimidating language; or otherwise disrupting the interview process, the officer will inform the interpreter of the problem and ask the interpreter to correct the behavior.[251] If the behavior continues, the officer will notify his or her supervisor and, with his or her approval, will terminate or cancel the interview. The officer will explain to all parties the reason why the interview is being terminated or cancelled and that the interview will be rescheduled. The applicant is expected to return with a different interpreter who has not been found to have abused the interpreter role.[252]

At the end of the interview, the asylum officer will ask the interpreter monitor if he or she has any final concerns about the interpretation provided by the applicant's interpreter. If not, the call will be disconnected.[253]

Each Asylum Office has a local policy on whether it permits an asylum officer to conduct an asylum interview in a language other than English. This is only allowed if the asylum officer is certified by the Department of State.[254] A certified officer may conduct the interview in the applicant's language if he or she agrees, or use the applicant's interpreter.[255] If the interview is conducted in a language other than English, it must be clearly noted in the asylum officer's interview notes.[256]

- **Practice Pointer**: If an asylum officer suggests proceeding in the applicant's native language, practitioners should confirm that the officer has been properly certified. They also should not agree to the interview moving forward in the applicant's native language if the practitioner him- or herself is not fluent in that language. It is essential for practitioners to understand every word that is communicated so they

---

[250] *Id.* at pt. II.J.4.b.iv.

[251] *Id.* at pt. II.J.4.a.v.

[252] *Id.*

[253] *Id.* at pt. II.J.4.b.v.

[254] *Id.* at pt. II.J.11.

[255] *Id.*

[256] *Id.*

may competently and zealously represent their client during the interview.

E. Applicants Unable to Testify on Their Own Behalf

If an applicant is mentally incompetent or if he or she has a physical disability, the applicant may be unable to testify on his or her own behalf.[257] It is possible that this may not be brought to the attention of the asylum officer until the interview itself. When an asylum officer becomes concerned that an applicant is not competent to testify, the officer must notify the supervisor of his or her concern.[258] If the supervisor believes there are reasonable grounds to question the competence of the applicant to provide testimony, Asylum Office personnel will speak with the representative, family member, or guardian accompanying the applicant to the Asylum Office, or with the applicant him or herself if practicable.[259]

It may be possible for another individual to testify on behalf of the applicant, if that individual has personal knowledge of the applicant's asylum claim. The individual cannot be the applicant's representative.[260] If there is no one available who has personal knowledge of the applicant's asylum claim, the asylum officer must contact Headquarters for guidance on how to proceed.[261] However, this is only an option in the case of an applicant whose condition is so severe that the possibility of him or her testifying at any time in the near future is ruled out.[262] The applicant also must be under the care of a physician, psychiatrist, or psychologist who certifies in a letter that the applicant is mentally or physically incompetent to be interviewed about his or her asylum application in the near professional's treatment, explain the applicant's condition and treatment or medications required, and confirm the long term prognosis of the applicant's mental or physical condition.[263]

- **Practice Pointer**: Even if the applicant is not incompetent or unable to testify on his or her own behalf, it still may be advisable for the applicant to be evaluated by a mental health professional. Many asylum-seekers have suffered violence and trauma that may have a significant impact on their ability to remember details, communicate clearly, and provide details about particular events. A mental health evaluation and diagnosis may assist in explaining these symptoms and avoiding a negative credibility determination. See chapter 4 of this book for a

---

[257] *Id.* at pt. II.J.12.

[258] *Id.*

[259] *Id.*

[260] *Id.* at pt. II.J.12.b.

[261] *Id.*

[262] *Id.* at pt. II.J.12.a.

[263] *Id.*

detailed discussion of psychological evaluations and working with mental health professionals.

F. Role of Attorney or Representative

The applicant has the privilege of being represented during the affirmative asylum process.[264] He or she may be represented by an attorney in good standing of the bar, a BIA accredited representative, a law student or law graduate not yet admitted to the bar (with certain restrictions described at 8 CFR §292.1(a)(2)), or a reputable person who fits certain criteria (as described under 8 CFR §292.1(a)(3)).[265] One study has shown that asylum applicants in removal proceedings who are represented by counsel are four to six times more likely to be granted asylum than applicants who are not represented.[266] Having an attorney may make the difference between an applicant being granted asylum or being placed in removal proceedings.

The counsel or representative must file a Form G-28, Notice of Entry of Appearance at the time the application is filed, or prior to or at the asylum interview.[267] If a G-28 was filed with the applicant's I-589 application, but the representative does not appear at the interview, the asylum officer will ask the applicant whether he or she is still represented by the individual listed on the G-28.[268] If the applicant states that he or she is no longer represented by that individual, the asylum officer will have the applicant sign a statement that he or she wishes to withdraw the individual on the G-28 from the asylum claim and will proceed with the interview.[269] On the other hand, if the applicant continues to be represented by the individual on the G-28, the asylum officer will explain that he or she may proceed without the representative but is not required to do so.[270] If the applicant wishes to proceed, he or she must sign a Waiver of Presence of Representative During an Asylum Interview. If the applicant does not wish to proceed, the asylum officer will reschedule the interview.[271]

The applicant's counsel or representative may be present during the interview, and upon the completion of the interview may make a statement or comment on the evidence presented.[272] The asylum officer has the discretion to limit the length of

---

[264] INA §208(d)(4); 8 USC §1158(d)(4) (2012).

[265] USCIS Affirmative Asylum Procedures Manual, *supra* note 14, at pt. II.J.5.a.

[266] *See* Andrew Schoenholtz & Jonathan Jacobs, *The State of Representation: Ideas for Change*, 16 GEO. IMMIGR. L.J. 739 (Summer 2002). U.S. immigration laws have been called "second only to the Internal Revenue Code in complexity." *U.S. v. Ahumada-Aguilar*, 295 F.3d 943, 950 (9th Cir. 2002) (citations omitted).

[267] 8 CFR §§292.4, 1292.4 (2014). The Form G-28 is available at *www.uscis.gov/files/form/g-28.pdf*.

[268] *USCIS Affirmative Asylum Procedures Manual*, *supra* note 14, at pt. II.J.5.d.

[269] *Id.*

[270] *Id.*

[271] *Id.*

[272] 8 CFR §§208.9(b), (d), 1208.9(b), (d) (2014).

such a statement or comment and may require the counsel or representative to submit the statement or comment in writing.[273] Although practices vary among and even within Asylum Offices, some asylum officers also permit the attorney or representative to ask the applicant follow-up questions at the end of the interview. The asylum officer may also grant a brief extension of time following an interview for the applicant or the applicant's counsel to submit additional evidence.[274] If the representative abuses his or her role during the interview and continues to do so despite repeated warnings, with approval of a supervisor, the asylum officer may ask the representative to leave the interview.[275] If the representative is asked to leave, the asylum officer will suspend the interview or continue at the applicant's request.[276]

G. Witnesses and Submission of Documents

An asylum applicant may present witnesses to testify on his or her behalf. There are no restrictions on the number of witnesses, age, immigration status, or relationship to the applicant. The only restriction is that an interpreter or representative may not act as a witness.[277] An asylum officer may, however, place a reasonable limit on the length and subject matter of a witness's statement, and may request the statement in writing.[278]

- **Practice Pointer**: If practitioners anticipate presenting witnesses in support of their client's application, they should notify the Asylum Office in advance of the interview and should remind the asylum officer of this request at the start of the interview. Practitioners should be prepared to provide a concise description of each witness's testimony, its purpose, and how it will assist in the decision-making process. See Appx. 4E for guidance on how to contact each local Asylum Office to provide advance notice of any witnesses.

An asylum applicant also may present documents in support of his or her application during the interview.[279] The documents must be submitted in duplicate and must be accompanied by certified English translations if they are not in English. Original documents are given more weight than copies and will be photocopied by the asylum officer. There are no restrictions on the amount or nature of documentation an applicant may submit.[280] However, as discussed above, most

---

[273] 8 CFR §§208.9(d), 1208.9(d) (2014); *see also* Appx. 4D, Sample Closing Statement.

[274] 8 CFR §§208.9(e), 1208.9(e) (2014).

[275] *USCIS Affirmative Asylum Procedures Manual*, *supra* note 14, at pt. II.J.5.e.

[276] *Id.*

[277] *Id.* at pt. II.J.6.

[278] *Id.*; 8 CFR §208.9 (2014).

[279] *USCIS Affirmative Asylum Procedures Manual*, *supra* note 14, at pt. II.J.7.

[280] *Id.*

Asylum Offices discourage and do not accept supplemental evidence unless it has been submitted in advance of the interview in accordance with the local rules.[281]

According to USCIS, an asylum officer may receive an original document as evidence in an asylum claim and retain it to determine its authenticity. Once the document is determined to be authentic it must promptly return the document to the asylum applicant.[282] On the other hand, if an asylum officer receives a document from an asylum applicant and determines that the document is fraudulent or was fraudulently obtained, the asylum officer may retain the document without the applicant's permission.[283] If the Asylum Office retains a document, it must send the applicant a Retention of Original Documents letter informing him that USCIS is retaining the document.[284] The submission of fraudulent documents may affect an applicant's eligibility for asylum.[285]

During the interview, the applicant may request additional time to submit evidence or certified English translations after the asylum interview, and the asylum officer, in consultation with the Supervisory Asylum Officer, may grant a brief extension of time at his or her discretion.[286] If an extension of time is granted, the asylum officer will notify the applicant that the extension will stop the employment authorization clock from accruing time, and will issue a Form I-72, listing the documents the applicant may submit.[287] If the applicant fails to submit the documents following the extension, the asylum officer will move forward with processing the application and issuing a decision.[288] An asylum officer also may request that the applicant submit additional documentation following the asylum interview. Such a request will not stop the employment authorization clock.[289]

H. Structure and Content of Questioning

Affirmative asylum interviews are conducted in a non-adversarial manner,[290] and asylum officers have been trained on non-adversarial interview techniques.[291] The

---

[281] *See* AILA, *Asylum Office Guide – Best Practices*, *supra* note 173.

[282] U.S. Citizenship and Immigration Servs. Memorandum on Authority of Asylum Officers to Retain Fraudulent Documents or Documents Fraudulently Obtained (Nov. 30, 2007), *published on* AILA InfoNet Doc. No. 07122065 (*posted* Dec. 20, 2007).

[283] *Id.*

[284] *USCIS Affirmative Asylum Procedures Manual*, *supra* note 14, at pt. II.J.8.

[285] *Id. See supra* chapter 4 for a detailed discussion of fraudulent documents and how they might affect an applicant's credibility for purposes of asylum eligibility.

[286] *USCIS Affirmative Asylum Procedures Manual*, *supra* note 14, at pt. III.H.1.

[287] *Id.*

[288] *Id.*

[289] *Id.* at pt. III.H.2.

[290] 8 CFR §§208.9(b), 1208.9(b) (2014).

[291] 8 CFR §§208.1(b), 1208.1(b) (2014); see also U.S. Citizenship and Immigration Servs., Interviewing Part I: Overview of Nonadversarial Asylum Interview, in Asylum Officer Basic Training Course

Continued

purpose of the interview, according to the regulations, is "to elicit all relevant and useful information bearing on the applicant's eligibility for asylum."[292] Thus, asylum officers usually will focus their questioning on the applicant's credibility, additional detail needed following review of the application and supporting documentation, and any legal issues that have been left unresolved based on the evidence submitted.

Typically, asylum officers begin their questioning by reviewing the information contained in pages one through four of the I-589, including the applicant's biographic information, entry to the United States and prior U.S. immigration history, address history, education and employment, family background, and the applicant's spouse and children's biographic information.[293] This process ensures the accuracy of the information and provides the applicant with an opportunity to amend or update the I-589. The asylum officer will make any necessary changes or updates by hand on the application throughout this process.

After the asylum officer has reviewed the I-589 with the applicant, the asylum officer usually will ask more substantive questions about the applicant's asylum claim. The following is a list of topics commonly asked about during the substantive portion of an asylum interview:

- Why are you afraid to return to your home country?
- What happened to you in your home country?
- Who did that to you? Was it the government? If not, could or would the government protect you? If not, why not?
- Why did they do that to you?
- When did these events take place?
- How often did this harm occur?
- Where were you when this happened?
- What do you think would happen to you if you go back to your home country now?
- What makes you think that would happen to you?
- Who do you fear?
- Why would they want to harm you?
- What are your religious beliefs/political opinions? What is your race/nationality? What is your social group?

Participant Workbook (Sept. 14, 2006), available at *www.uscis.gov/sites/default/files/USCIS/Humanitarian/Refugees%20%26%20Asylum/Asylum/AOBTC%20Lesson%20Plans/Interview%20Part-Overview-Nonadversarial-Asylum-Interview-31aug10.pdf*.

[292] 8 CFR §§208.9(b), 1208.9(b) (2014).

[293] *See* I-589 Application, *supra* note 113.

- How would the persecutors know or become aware of your race, religion, nationality, political opinion, or social group?
- How would they know you had returned?
- Do you have family and friends in your home country? Are they safe? If so, why?
- Could or would your government protect you? If not, why not? How do you know?
- When did you last enter the United States?
- How did you travel to the United States? What countries did you travel through? Did you have legal status in any of those countries?
- What is your current immigration status in the United States?
- Why did you apply for asylum when you did? Why didn't you apply sooner?
- Is there anywhere in your home country where you can be safe? If not, why not?
- Do you have a right to live in any other countries around the world? If so, where? What legal status do you have in those countries?

This list is not meant to be a comprehensive, but rather, a useful guide for understanding the topics that are usually covered during affirmative asylum interviews.

Following the substantive portion of the interview, the asylum officer usually will ask a series of questions to determine whether the applicant is subject to any ineligibility grounds or bars to asylum, including:

(1) if there is a safe third country available to the asylum-seeker where his or her life or freedom would not be threatened and where he or she would have access to full and fair procedures for determining asylum eligibility;[294]

(2) if the asylum-seeker did not file his or her application for asylum within one year of his or her arrival in the United States;[295]

(3) if the asylum-seeker previously applied for and was denied asylum;[296]

(4) if the applicant ordered, incited, assisted or otherwise participated in the persecution of others;[297]

(5) if the applicant has been convicted by a final judgment of a particularly serious crime in the United States, and thus constitutes a danger to the community;[298]

---

[294] INA §208(a)(2)(A).

[295] INA §§208(a)(2)(B), (d); 8 CFR §§208.4(a)(4)–(5) (2014).

[296] INA §§208(a)(2)(C)–(D). This bar only applies if the applicant for asylum was issued a final order of removal. It does not apply if the previous application was denied only by the Asylum Office.

[297] INA §§101(a)(42)(B), 208(b)(2)(A)(i).

[298] INA §208(b)(2)(A)(ii). If a conviction is an aggravated felony for which there is an aggregate term of imprisonment for five years, it is a conviction for a particularly serious crime and automatically bars a grant of asylum. *See Matter of B–*, 20 I&N Dec. 427 (BIA 1991).

(6) if there are serious reasons for believing that the applicant has committed a serious nonpolitical crime outside of the United States prior to his or her arrival;[299]

(7) if there are reasonable grounds for regarding the alien as a danger to the security of the United States;[300]

(8) if the applicant meet the definition of a terrorist, has participated in terrorist activity, or has given material support to a terrorist organization;[301] and

(9) if the applicant was firmly resettled in another country prior to his or her arrival in the United States.[302]

At the end of the asylum officer's questioning, the applicant's counsel or representative may make a statement or comment on the testimony and evidence presented.[303] Although practices vary among and even within Asylum Offices, some asylum officers also permit the attorney or representative to ask the applicant follow-up questions or identify topics that were not but should have been covered at the end of the interview.

> ➢ **Practice Pointer**: Applicants should be confronted with inconsistencies during the interview and given an opportunity to explain. According to the Asylum Officer Basic Training Course, asylum officers "must provide the applicant any opportunity during the interview to explain any discrepancy or inconsistency that is discovered."[304] If it becomes clear throughout the course of the interview that the asylum officer is concerned about the applicant's credibility, but the officer has not identified areas of concern or provided the applicant with an opportunity to explain inconsistencies, practitioners should request that the officer provide the applicant with this opportunity or ask the client follow-up

[299] INA §208(b)(2)(A)(iii).

[300] INA §208(b)(2)(A)(iv).

[301] INA §§212(a)(3)(B)(i)(I)–(IV), (VI), 237(a)(4)(B). This bar is waivable by DHS under certain circumstances, including for persons who provided material support to terrorist organizations under duress. *See* INA §212(d)(3)(B)(i); *See generally* Michael Chertoff Memorandum on Exercise of Authority Under Sec. 212(d)(3)(B)(i) of the INA, Washington, DC [hereinafter Chertoff Memo. on Exercise of Authority Under INA §212(d)(3)(B)(i)] (Apr. 27, 2007), *available at www.uscis.gov/sites/default/files/USCIS/Laws/TRIG/2.26%20excersise%20of%20authority.pdf*.

[302] 8 CFR §§208.13(c)(2)(i)(B), 208.15 (2014). An applicant is deemed firmly resettled if he or she entered the country with, or while in the country received, an offer of permanent resident status, citizenship, or other type of permanent status. *See* 8 CFR §§208.15, 1208.15 (2014). The government has the burden of proving firm resettlement, and the applicant may rebut firm resettlement by demonstrating an exception under 8 CFR §§208.15(a)–(b) (2014).

[303] 8 CFR §§208.9(b), (d), 1208.9(b), (d) (2014).

[304] *See* Asylum Officer Basic Training Course, *Interview Part 1: Overview of Nonadversarial Asylum Interview*, at 9 (Sept. 14, 2006), *available at www.uscis.gov/sites/default/files/USCIS/Humanitarian/Refugees%20%26%20Asylum/Asylum/AOBTC%20Lesson%20Plans/Interview%20Part-Overview-Nonadversarial-Asylum-Interview-31aug10.pdf* (last visited Mar. 27, 2015).

questions about the topics of concern to the officer to elicit an explanation from the applicant. If an asylum officer refuses this opportunity to explain, practitioners should consider asking to speak with a Supervisory Asylum Officer.

➢ **Practice Pointer**: In preparing clients for affirmative asylum interviews, practitioners should explain to their client that this may be the only chance he or she has to tell his or her story and to convince the officer that the applicant cannot safely return. Practitioners also should stress the importance of: (1) always telling the truth; (2) being consistent written testimony and evidence; (3) providing detailed answers; (4) notifying the officer if the applicant does not understand a question or needs a question to be repeated; and (5) saying "I don't know" or "I don't remember" instead of guessing an answer the applicant does not know or remember.

I. Note-Taking by the Asylum Officer

Asylum officers usually take notes throughout the asylum interview. These notes become part of the administrative record and are meant to be an informal transcript of what is said during the course of the asylum interview.[305] Under certain circumstances, asylum officers are instructed to switch to a more formal sworn statement format of note-taking. These circumstances include: (1) if the applicant admits, or there are serious reasons to believe, he or she is associated with an organization on one of the terrorist watch lists; (2) if the applicant admits, or there are serious reasons to believe, he or she is involved in terrorist activities; (3) if the applicant admits, or there are serious reasons to believe, he or she assisted or otherwise participated in the persecution of others; (4) if there are serious reasons for considering the applicant a threat to national security; (5) if the applicant admits, or there are serious reasons to believe, that he or she committed or was convicted of a serious crime outside of the U.S.; and (6) if the applicant admits, or there are serious reasons to believe, he or she committed human rights abuses.[306] This is because these circumstances relate to the mandatory bars to asylum and may be used to as a basis to institute removal proceedings against the applicant. The sworn statement format is a question and answer format. Although it is not verbatim, it is meant to provide a full and accurate record to the specific questions asked of the applicant and the applicant's specific answers.[307] The asylum officer must review the sworn statement

[305] *See* U.S. Citizenship and Immigration Servs. *Interviewing Part II: Note-Taking*, in Asylum Officer Basic Training Course (Aug. 10, 2009), *available at www.uscis.gov/sites/default/files/USCIS/Humanitarian/Refugees%20%26%20Asylum/Asylum/AOBTC%20Lesson%20Plans/Interview-Part-2-Notetaking-31aug10.pdf.*

[306] *USCIS Affirmative Asylum Procedures Manual*, *supra* note 14, at pt. II.J.9.

[307] *Id.*

with the applicant at the end of the interview and allow him or her to make any changes. The applicant must initial each page and sign the end of the statement.[308]

J. Conclusion of the Asylum Interview

At the end of the asylum interview, the asylum officer will review and explain to the applicant any corrections, additions, or changes made to his or her I-589 and will inform the applicant that by signing the I-589, he or she is affirming that the information on the application is true and correct.[309] The applicant and asylum officer will then sign Part F. on page 10 of his or her I-589 application form.[310]

At the end of the interview, the officer does not inform the applicant of the decision or give any indication of what the decision will be.[311] Rather, after the I-589 has been signed, the asylum officer will inform the applicant about the next steps in the process.[312] Depending on local office policies, the officer will either inform the applicant of a date and time to return to the Asylum Office to pick up his or her decision, or will inform the applicant that he or she will be served by mail.[313]

If the decision is to be picked up in person, the asylum officer will give the applicant a Pick-Up Notice. The notice will list the applicant's, as well as all dependents,' A-numbers, and will list the date and time that the applicant must return to pick up the decision.[314] Typically, the pick-up date is approximately two weeks after the asylum interview. The asylum officer will have the applicant sign the notice on behalf of him or herself and all dependents.[315] The applicant and all dependents age 14 and over must then appear in person on the date of the specified appointment to pick up the decision.[316] It is suggested, though not required, that the applicant also bring an interpreter with him or her to pick up the decision.

On the other hand, if the decision is to be served by mail, the asylum officer will give the applicant a Mail-Out Notice listing the applicant's and all dependents' A-numbers. The notice informs the applicant that he or she is not required to return to the office to receive a decision.[317] The applicant must sign the A-file copy of the notice to show that he or she was notified of how the decision will be processed.[318]

---

[308] *Id.*

[309] *Id.* at pt. II.K.1.

[310] *See* I-589 Application, *supra* note 113.

[311] *USCIS Affirmative Asylum Procedures Manual*, *supra* note 14, at pt. II.K.2.

[312] 8 CFR §§208.9(d), 1208.9(d) (2014).

[313] *Id.*

[314] *Id.* at pt. II.K.2.a.

[315] *Id.*

[316] *Id.*

[317] *Id.* at pt. II.K.2.b.

[318] *Id.*

Once the asylum officer is satisfied that the applicant understands the next step in the process, the officer will conclude the interview and escort the applicant back to the waiting room or exit.[319]

VIII. What if the Applicant Fails to Appear at the Interview?

An applicant's failure to appear for a scheduled interview without prior authorization may result in a dismissal of the asylum application or the waiver of the right to an interview.[320] As stated in the INA, "[I]n the case of an applicant for asylum who fails without prior authorization or in the absence of exceptional circumstances to appear for an interview . . . the application may be dismissed or the applicant may be otherwise sanctioned for such failure."[321] A dismissal may also result if the applicant fails to comply with fingerprint processing requirements and appointments, as described above.[322]

If the applicant or the applicant's counsel is unable to attend a scheduled interview or appointment, the applicant must exercise due diligence to contact the local Asylum Office to seek authorization not to appear for that interview and to request rescheduling.

- **Practice Pointer**: Each Asylum Office has its own local procedures for reschedule requests. Most offices have a designated email address or fax number for submission of such requests in writing. Some suggest calling the office's phone number in addition to submitting the request in writing. Practitioners should consult AILA's "Asylum Office Guide — Best Practices," which is updated each year, for the local rules in their jurisdiction regarding reschedule requests.[323] See the most recent guide at Appx. 4E of this book.
- **Practice Pointer**: Interview reschedule requests by the applicant or his or her representative will stop the employment authorization clock from accruing time toward the requisite 180 days needed to become eligible to be granted employment authorization.[324]

Given the severe consequences of failure to appear for the asylum interview or fingerprinting appointment, it is essential for applicants to properly update their addresses with USCIS upon any changes. This is not only required by law, but it also

---

[319] *Id.* at pt. II.K.2.c.

[320] 8 CFR §§208.10, 1208.10 (2014).

[321] INA §208(d)(5)(A)(v).

[322] 8 CFR §§208.10, 1208.10 (2014).

[323] *See* AILA, *Asylum Office Guide – Best Practices*, *supra* note 173.

[324] *See generally, USCIS Affirmative Asylum Procedures Manual*, *supra* note 14, at

ensures that the applicant has done his or her due diligence to receive USCIS notices.[325]

The Asylum Office will not issue a decision or referral until 45 days have passed after the missed interview.[326] Instead, the Asylum Office will mail a Failure to Appear Warning to the applicant and his or her representative.[327] This letter describes the consequences of failure to appear, lists procedural steps the applicant must take within 45 days of the missed interview to establish good cause for failing to appear for the interview, and explains the effect of failing to respond to the warning letter within the 45-day period.[328]

If the applicant responds within the 45-day period with an explanation for why he or she failed to appear, the Asylum Office will treat it as a reschedule request and determine whether there is good cause for the request.[329] Before determining whether good cause exists, the Asylum Office will consider whether the applicant's failure to appear was caused by lack of proper notice of the interview.[330] For example, if the notice of the interview or fingerprint appointment was not mailed to the applicant's current address and the address was provided to Office of Refugee, Asylum, and International Operations prior to the date the notice was mailed, that would excuse the applicant's failure to appear and the Asylum Office will reschedule the interview.[331] Notice is also improper in the following situations:

- If the file does not contain a copy of the Interview Notice;
- If the file contains a properly executed G-28, but RAPS is not updated to include the representative's correct information;
- USCIS received notification of a change of address prior to issuance of the Interview Notice, but failed to update RAPS before the notice was issued;
- The address in RAPS is not correct; and
- The Interview Notice is unreadable.[332]

However, if the applicant received "reasonable notice" of the interview or fingerprint appointment and still did not appear, the failure to appear will not be excused unless the applicant can show good cause.[333]

---

[325] *See supra* pt. IV. for a detailed discussion of the change of address requirements and guidance for notifying USCIS of an address change while an affirmative asylum application remains pending.

[326] *USCIS Affirmative Asylum Procedures Manual*, *supra* note 14, at pt. III.I.2.

[327] *Id.* at pt. III.I.

[328] *Id.*

[329] *Id.* at pt. III.I.2.a.

[330] *Id.*

[331] *Id.*

[332] *Id.*

[333] 8 CFR §§208.10, 1208.10 (2014).

Good cause means a "reasonable excuse for being unable to appear for an asylum interview."[334] Applicants' excuses for failure to appear and requests for rescheduling must be considered on a case-by-case basis before determining whether the request will be honored.[335] If the applicant establishes good cause and the Asylum Office honors the request to reschedule, the Asylum Office will generate an Interview Reschedule Notice. On the other hand, if the applicant does not establish good cause, the Asylum Office will issue a Denial of Interview Reschedule Request prior to issuing a Referral Notice for Failure to Appear or Dismissal of Asylum Application — Failure to Appear on day 46.[336]

If the applicant does not respond to the Failure to Appear Warning letter within the 45-day period, the Asylum Office will move forward with referring or dismissing the application and issuing the appropriate notice to the applicant and his or her representative.[337] If the applicant later files a response, on or after day 46, the Asylum Office will review the response and evaluate whether the applicant's failure to appear was caused by lack of proper notice or as a result of "exceptional circumstances."[338] If the failure to appear was caused by lack of proper notice, the Asylum Office will excuse the failure to appear and proceed with steps to continue with the case as described below.[339]

An applicant's failure to appear also may be excused after the 45-day period if the failure was the result of exceptional circumstances.[340] Exceptional circumstances is defined under INA §240(3)(1) as "circumstances (such as battery or extreme cruelty to the alien or any child or parent of the alien, serious illness of the alien, or serious illness or death of the spouse, child, or parent of the alien, but not including less compelling circumstances) beyond the control of the alien."[341] Exceptional circumstances in the context of considering a failure to appear for an asylum interview, however, is not limited to the express examples provided in the statute.[342] Asylum officers will consider the totality of the circumstances.

If an applicant wishes to establish exceptional circumstances for failure to appear, he or she must notify the Asylum Office in writing as soon as possible after receiving the referral or dismissal notice for failure to appear.[343] He or she should submit a written explanation describing in detail the exceptional circumstances that caused his

---

334 *USCIS Affirmative Asylum Procedures Manual*, *supra* note 14, at pt. III.I.2.a.

335 *Id.*

336 *Id.*

337 *Id.*

338 *Id.* at pt. III.I.2.b.

339 *Id.*

340 8 CFR §§208.10, 1208.10 (2014).

341 INA §240(e)(1).

342 *USCIS Affirmative Asylum Procedures Manual*, *supra* note 14, at pt. III.I.2.b.

343 *Id.*

or her failure to appear for the interview and include supporting documentary evidence, if available.[344] The Asylum Office will examine the written explanation and supporting documentation to determine if the applicant has established exceptional circumstances for failure to appear at the asylum interview.[345] He or she may request additional documentation or require the applicant to appear at the Asylum Office in person with his or her representative, if necessary.[346]

The Asylum Office must make a determination on the exceptional circumstances within ten business days of receiving the written explanation, unless additional documentation or an in-person appearance is requested.[347] Following review of the explanation and documentation, the asylum officer will complete the Determination of Exceptional Circumstances Worksheet and submit it to the Supervisory Asylum Officer to review and sign.[348] He or she will then issue a Determination of Failure to Demonstrate "Exceptional Circumstances" or a Determination Demonstrating "Exceptional Circumstances" to the applicant and his or her representative.[349]

If an applicant's failure to appear is excused by the Asylum Office after the application has been administratively closed and a dismissal letter has been issued, the Asylum Office will reopen the asylum application.[350] The Asylum Office will then reschedule the applicant for an asylum interview.[351]

In cases where the Asylum Office already referred the applicant for removal proceedings, but the applicant's failure to appear is later excused, the Asylum Office will coordinate with the ICE Office of Chief Counsel so that a DHS request for dismissal of proceedings may be submitted ot the immigration court.[352] A decision to move to dismiss proceedings is at the discretion of ICE, and an Asylum Office cannot guarantee that its request to ICE will result in a motion to dismiss.[353] If the immigration court dismisses the proceedings, the Asylum Office may then take jurisdiction over the case anew and reopen the asylum application after an immigration judge grants a request to dismiss proceedings.[354] If the immigration court denies the motion to dismiss, jurisdiction over the asylum application remains with the immigration court.[355]

---

[344] *Id.*

[345] *Id.*

[346] *Id.*

[347] *Id.*

[348] *Id.*

[349] *Id.*

[350] *Id.* at pt. III.I.2.c.

[351] *Id.*

[352] *Id.* at pt. III.I.2.b.

[353] *Id.*

[354] *Id.*

[355] *Id.*

- **Practice Pointer**: Upon receipt of a Determination Demonstrating "Exceptional Circumstances," the applicant may also contact the ICE Office of Chief Counsel to provide them with a copy and to request their joining in motion to dismiss removal proceedings. If ICE refuses to join in the motion, the applicant may submit his or her own motion with the immigration court for consideration by the immigration judge. The applicant should attach a copy of the Determination Demonstrating "Exceptional Circumstances" to his or her motion.
- **Practice Pointer**: Upon dismissal of proceedings by the immigration judge, an applicant can expedite the rescheduling of his or her asylum interview with the Asylum Office by mailing, emailing, or faxing a copy of the immigration judge's decision order dismissing the proceedings to the Asylum Office.

IX. What Happens Post-Interview?

After the asylum interview, the asylum officer will complete any background or security checks and conduct any additional research that he or she needs to complete in order to make a determination on the case. The officer will then prepare his or her decision and have it reviewed by the Supervisory Asylum Officer. The decision is then served on the applicant in person or by mail.

A. Asylum Officer Research

Following the asylum interview, the asylum officer may conduct additional research in considering the claims of the applicant. In reaching a decision on the asylum application, the asylum officer may rely on material provided by the Department of State, the Office of Refugee, Asylum, and International Operations, other DHS offices, or other credible sources, such as international organizations, private voluntary agencies, news organizations, or academic institutions.[356]

For example, the asylum officer may log in and review documentation in the Asylum Virtual Library, an online collection of documents produced and collected by Asylum Division Headquarters and Asylum Field Offices. Such documentation includes case law, country conditions information, decision writing templates, forms, policies and procedures, statistics, and training materials.[357] Asylum officers also have access to the RAIO Research Unit, whose mission is "to provide RAIO officers with credible and objective information on human rights and country conditions in order that applicants' claims may be adjudicated in a timely manner."[358]

---

[356] 8 CFR §§208.12(a), 1208.12(a) (2014).

[357] *Id.* at pt. II.M.1.

[358] *Id.* at pt. II.M.2.

Additionally, USCIS may, but is no longer required to, forward to the Department of State (DOS) a copy of the affirmative asylum application.[359] DOS has the option of providing detailed country condition information, an assessment of the accuracy of the applicant's assertions regarding conditions in the applicant's home country, information about whether individuals similarly situated to the applicant are persecuted in his or her home country, and any other information DOS believes to be relevant.[360] All such comments must be made part of the record.[361] The applicant must be given an opportunity to review and respond to the comments, unless they are classified.[362] In addition, an asylum officer may request specific comments regarding individual cases or types of claims, or other information the asylum officer deems appropriate.[363] The advice of DOS, however, is not binding on the Asylum Division or the courts.[364] If an asylum officer discloses information in an asylum application to DOS, he or she must inform the DOS employee of the confidentiality requirements of 8 CFR §208.6.[365]

In researching case law, including immigration judge, BIA, and federal court decisions, asylum officers are advised to be conscious of each type of decision's precedential value, if any. For example, IJ decisions are not precedent decisions and have no binding authority on asylum officers in deciding cases involving similar issues.[366] On the other hand, asylum officers must follow BIA precedent decisions when adjudicating cases involving similar issues, except to the extent that the decisions have been modified or overruled by subsequent BIA decisions or the Attorney General.[367] Additionally, if there is a conflicting precedent decision on the issue by a federal circuit court of appeals in the circuit in which the asylum decision is being made or by the Supreme Court, the asylum officer must follow the circuit court or Supreme Court decision.[368] In other words, BIA decisions apply nationwide, except in federal circuits with conflicting law.

There is one exception to this rule noted in the USCIS training course for asylum officers. When the BIA issues a precedent decision which interprets an ambiguous statutory issue and that new BIA decision conflicts with previously-issued circuit

---

[359] 8 CFR §§208.11(a), 1208.11(a) (2014); *see* Forwarding of Affirmative Asylum Applications to the Department of State, Final Rule, 74 Fed. Reg. 15367 (Apr. 6, 2009).

[360] 8 CFR §§208.11(b), 1208.11(b) (2014).

[361] 8 CFR §§208.11(d), 1208.11(d) (2014).

[362] 8 CFR §§208.11(c), 1208.11(c) (2014).

[363] 8 CFR §§208.11(a), 1208.11(a) (2014).

[364] *See* chapter 2.6.3. *But see* INA §208(b)(1)(B)(iii); 8 USC §1158(b)(1)(B)(iii) (2012), added by the REAL ID Act of 2005, Pub. L. No. 109-13, div. B, 119 Stat. 231, 302–23, specifically allowing adjudicators to rely on DOS reports when assessing credibility.

[365] *USCIS Affirmative Asylum Procedures Manual*, *supra* note 14, at pt. II.M.3.b.

[366] 8 CFR §§1003.1(g), 1003.38 (2014).

[367] 8 CFR §1003.1(g) (2014).

[368] *Id.*

court decisions, the BIA's ruling must be followed by Asylum Offices nationwide, unless the prior judicial precedent held that the court's construction was the only permissible reading of the statute. In other words, a circuit court's prior interpretation of a statute will overrule a subsequent BIA interpretation only if the relevant circuit court's decision held the statute to be unambiguous. If a circuit court revisits the issue in light of the BIA's new ruling, asylum officers must follow the circuit court's new ruling.[369]

B. Discovery of Adverse Information After an Asylum Interview

It is possible that an asylum officer may discover adverse information after an asylum interview has been completed. If such information is discovered before or during the interview, the asylum officer must provide the applicant with the opportunity to explain or respond to that information. However, if the officer discovers the adverse information after the interview, he or she may notify the applicant of the information in a Notice of Intent to Deny (if the applicant is maintaining a valid status or if his or her parole is valid) or in a Referral Notice (if the applicant is deportable or removable).[370] In compelling cases where the testimony was otherwise solid and convincing, the Asylum Office Director has the discretion to re-interview an applicant; however, this only takes place in "extremely exceptional circumstances."[371]

C. Preparation and Review of the Decision

Following the interview and the completion of any additional research, the asylum officer will prepare the decision. He or she may approve, deny, or refer the application, depending on the specific circumstances of the case. The asylum officer will write an Assessment of the case, explaining his or her decision and reasoning. Asylum Office personnel will then prepare the decision letter and other accompanying documents, such as a Notice to Appear (NTA) or I-94 card.

If the applicant qualifies as a refugee under INA §101(a)(42) and is not barred from relief under INA §§208(a)(2) or 208(b)(2), the officer will either prepare a Recommended Approval letter or an Asylum Approval letter, depending on the status of the applicant's identity and security checks.[372] Approval is recommended, but not final, in the following situations:

---

[369] U.S. Citizenship and Immigration Servs., *Sources of Authority*, in Asylum Officer Basic Training Course Participant Workbook (Oct. 31, 2007), *available at www.uscis.gov/sites/default/files/USCIS/Humanitarian/Refugees%20%26%20Asylum/Asylum/AOBTC%20Lesson%20Plans%20and%20Training%20Programs/Sources-of-Authority-31aug10.pdf.*

[370] *USCIS Affirmative Asylum Procedures Manual*, *supra* note 14, at pt. II.J.14.

[371] *Id. See also* Memorandum from Joseph E. Langlois to Asylum Directors, Supervisory Asylum Officers, & Asylum Officers on Discovery of Fraudulent Documents After the Asylum Interview (May 27, 1998).

[372] 8 CFR §208.14(b); *USCIS Affirmative Asylum Procedures Manual*, *supra* note 14, at pt. II.N.1.

- All background security checks have been completed for the principal applicant and all dependents, but an FBI name check response is pending for one or more of the family members;
- All background security checks have been completed for the principal applicant and all dependents, but the Asylum Officer does not have the A-file and there are no reasonable grounds for believing information in the A-file would materially impact the decision; and
- All background security checks have been completed for the principal applicant and all dependents, but a dependent appears to be subject to reinstatement of a final order and the Special Agent in Charge has not yet determined whether to reinstate the final order.[373]

A final approval may be prepared when results of all required identity and security checks for the principal applicant and all dependents are current and complete and allow for approval.[374]

By contrast, if the applicant is ineligible for asylum, the asylum office will prepare either a Notice of Intent to Deny (NOID) or a Referral Notice.[375] If the applicant is ineligible for asylum, but is maintaining valid immigrant, nonimmigrant, or Temporary Protected Status at the time the decision is mailed or personally served on the applicant, the Asylum Office will prepare and issue a NOID.[376] The NOID will provide the applicant ten days, plus six days for mailing (a total of 16 days) to rebut the reasons for the intended denial.[377] Due to regulatory requirements, if the basis for the NOID is, in part, based on Department of State comments, the NOID must cite to the use of the Department of State comment letter and note the specific information applied in reaching the adverse determination.[378] A copy of the Department of State comment letter should be attached for the applicant's reference.[379] The applicant's rebuttal response to the NOID must be considered before the asylum officer makes a final decision — grant or denial — on the case.[380] If the applicant is not maintaining valid status, however, and is inadmissible or deportable at the time the decision is mailed or personally served, the Asylum Office must refer the individual to the immigration court for adjudication of the application in removal proceedings.[381]

---

[373] *USCIS Affirmative Asylum Procedures Manual*, *supra* note 14, at pt. II.N.1.a.

[374] *Id.* at pt. II.N.1.b.

[375] *Id.* at pt. II.N.2.

[376] *Id.* at pt. II.N.2.c.

[377] *Id.*

[378] *Id. See* 8 CFR §208.11(c) (2014).

[379] *USCIS Affirmative Asylum Procedures Manual*, *supra* note 14, at pt. II.N.2.c.

[380] *Id.*

[381] *Id.* at pt. II.N.2.b.

Before a decision letter is served, the Supervisory Asylum Officer assigned to the case will review the case for procedural and substantive correctness and completeness.[382] This includes the following checklist:

- The applicant and the asylum officer signed the I-589, and corrections have been made accurately and clearly;
- The asylum officer's assessment is clear, concise, complete, and correct;
- The asylum officer's notes contain the proper elements as required in the training materials;
- The decision letter is correctly addressed to the applicant and any representative of record, accurately reflects the status of the case, and lists all dependents;
- The address on the documents matches the address in RAPS;
- Information and dates are correct and consistent throughout all documents (NTA, I-213, Assessment, I-589, I-94);
- The asylum officer signed the Form I-213, if required;
- The allegations, charges, and location of the immigration court listed on the NTA, if required, are correct;
- Any Record of Oath is properly executed;
- The Background Identity and Security Checklist is present and completed in accordance with the decision being issued;
- Each A-file is in neat, record order, with no loose papers or unconsolidated folders attached;
- RAPS is properly updated; and
- Copies of the relevant documents are in the dependent's A-file.[383]

After the Supervisory Asylum Officer reviews the case according to the checklist, he or she will sign or initial the Assessment, sign the decision, sign and date the NTA if required, sign the Form I-213 if required, and sign and date the Background Identity and Security Checklist.[384] The asylum officer will then prepare the case for service of the decision on the applicant and will place copies of the documents to be served in the applicant's A-file.[385]

It is not the role of the Supervisory Asylum Officer to ensure that the asylum officer decided the case as he or she would have decided it; asylum officers are given substantial deference once it has been established that their analysis is legally sufficient.[386] If a Supervisory Asylum Officer disagrees with the asylum officer's

---

[382] *Id.* at pt. II.O.1.

[383] *Id.* at pt. II.O.2.

[384] *Id.*

[385] *Id.* at pt. II.P.

[386] *Id.* at pt. II.O.3.

decision, he or she will discuss the case with the asylum officer. If their differences cannot be resolved, the Supervisory Asylum Officer will elevate the case to the Deputy Director or Director of the Asylum Office.[387]

D. Quality Assurance Procedures

Under the Asylum Division's Quality Assurance Program, the following cases must be referred to headquarters for review:[388]

- *Gender cases* (grants, referrals, and NOIDs of domestic violence cases where gender forms the basis of a particular social group, the applicant is found credible, and mandatory bars do not apply);
- *Contiguous territory and visa waiver grants* (grants of Mexican or Canadian asylum-seekers, and grants from VWP participating countries under 8 CFR §217.2(a));
- *National security-related* (grants of cases involving national security concerns where the concern was *not* resolved through vetting);
- *National security-related—Possible 212(d) Exemption (*e.g.*, material support)* (grants, referrals and NOIDs in which the applicant is eligible for asylum but for a terrorist ground of inadmissibility for which an exemption under §212(d)(3)(B)(i) is or may be available);
- *Persecutor-related issues* (grants of cases where evidence indicates that the applicant may have been involved in participating in persecution or human rights violations, and the individual meets the burden of proof to demonstrate that he or she should not be barred as a persecutor; referrals and NOIDs of cases involving an individual barred as a persecutor where the case may be publicized nationally or who may pose a threat to others);
- *Discretionary denials and referrals* (referrals and NOIDS of an applicant who meets the definition of a refugee and is otherwise eligible for asylum, but is denied or referred because of acts that are not a bar to asylum);
- *Those that have been or are likely to be publicized* (grants, referrals, and NOIDS of cases likely to have national exposure, not just local interest; such as where the applicant has publicized that he or she has filed or intends to file for asylum; cases involving notable individuals; or cases involving areas of law perceived in the media to be novel; could involve cases with resolved national security concerns);
- *Diplomats* (grants, referrals, and NOIDS of cases of sitting diplomats to the United States or United Nations, or other high-level government or military officials and/or their family members; high-ranking diplomats to other countries);

---

[387] *Id.*

[388] U.S. Citizenship and Immigration Servs. Asylum Div., Quality Assurance Referral Sheet (revised Feb. 10, 2011), AILA InfoNet Doc. No. 13110842 (*posted* Nov. 8, 2013).

- *Reasonable fear of persecution or torture* (a random sampling of reasonable fear of persecution and torture determinations; all reasonable fear determinations in which the individual is subject to a Final Administrative Removal Order; any case that a supervisor, deputy director, or director believes should be reviewed);[389]
- *Credible fear of persecution or torture cases* (a random sampling of credible fear of persecution or torture decisions; high-profile cases; claims involving novel legal issues; any case that a supervisor, deputy director, or director believes should be reviewed);[390]
- *NACARA*[391] (grants of cases where evidence indicates that the applicant may have been involved in participating in persecution or human rights violations, and individual meets burden of proof to demonstrate that he or she should not be barred as a persecutor; referrals of cases involving an individual barred as a persecutor where the case may be publicized nationally or who may pose a threat to others; all decisions in which the applicant is otherwise eligible for relief but for a terrorist ground of inadmissibility for which an exemption under §212(d)(3)(B)(i) is or may be available; referral or approval involving an unusual legal issue);
- *Cases with a prior denial by EOIR* (grants, referrals, and NOIDs);
- *Juvenile cases* (grants, referrals, and NOIDs of all cases in which the principal applicant is less than 18 years old at the time of filing); and
- *Asylum Office requests* (any case in which the Asylum Office Director requests review).

The circumstances requiring quality assurance review for credible and reasonable fear determinations changed in June of 2014.[392] Under the new policy, USCIS no longer reviews all cases involving a negative credible fear of persecution or torture determination. Rather, Asylum Offices must send a random sampling of credible fear and reasonable fear determinations — both positive and negative — to Headquarters

---

[389] USCIS used to require that all negative reasonable fear of persecution and torture determinations be referred to Headquarters for review. However, this policy was revised in 2014. *See* Memorandum from John Lafferty, Chief of Asylum Division, on Changes to Credible Fear and Reasonable Fear Cases Requiring Quality Assurance Review (June 11, 2014), AILA InfoNet Doc. No. 14081468 (*posted* Aug. 14, 2014).

[390] USCIS used to require that all negative credible fear of persecution and torture determinations be referred to Headquarters for review. However, this policy was revised in 2014. *See* Memorandum from John Lafferty, Chief of Asylum Division, on Changes to Credible Fear and Reasonable Fear Cases Requiring Quality Assurance Review (June 11, 2014), AILA InfoNet Doc. No. 14081468 (*posted* Aug. 14, 2014).

[391] See chapter 16 for a detailed discussion of NACARA relief.

[392] Memorandum from John Lafferty, Chief of Asylum Division on Changes to Credible Fear and Reasonable Fear Cases Requiring Quality Assurance Review (June 11, 2014), AILA InfoNet Doc. No. 14081468 (*posted* Aug. 14, 2014).

for pre-decisional quality assurance review.[393] The Asylum Division continues to require quality assurance review for high-profile claims or novel legal issues, however, as well as for any case in which an Asylum Office Director seeks such review.[394]

- **Practice Pointer**: See chapter 6 of this book for a detailed discussion of credible and reasonable fear determinations.

E. Service of the Decision

The INA states that "in the absence of exceptional circumstances, final administrative adjudication of the asylum application, not including administrative appeal, shall be completed within 180 days after the date an application is filed."[395] Thus, the service of the asylum officer's decision should occur within 180 days of the date on the applicant's I-589 Receipt Notice. However, as discussed above, there is currently a large backlog of tens of thousands of affirmative asylum cases that have not yet been scheduled for an interview, let alone issued a final administrative decision.[396] Many of these cases have been awaiting a decision for significantly longer than the statutory period of 180 days — some even one to two years.

- **Practice Pointer**: Practitioners, whose clients are stuck in the backlog, should consider filing an expedite request directly with the Asylum Office, especially if there are compelling reasons for the request, such as a family member in danger in the home country. AILA's "Asylum Office Guide — Best Practices" includes detailed information on how to directly contact each Asylum Office with such inquiries and requests.[397] If the Asylum Office is unresponsive, practitioners should file a request for case assistance with the CIS Ombudsman's office on the DHS-7001 form. This form is available on the Ombudsman's website and may be submitted online or by mail.[398]

- **Practice Pointer**: Some applications have been pending in the backlog for multiple years. In cases involving such unreasonable delays, practitioners should consider filing a complaint for writ of mandamus in federal district court. The Mandamus Act under 28 USC §1361

---

[393] *Id.*

[394] *Id.*

[395] INA §208(d)(5)(A)(iii).

[396] *See* U.S. Citizenship and Immigration Servs., Asylum Office Statistics, AILA InfoNet Doc. No. 14021957 (*posted* Feb. 19, 2014), *available at www.aila.org/content/default.aspx?docid=47513*; Cheri Attix, *The Affirmative Asylum Backlog Explained* (AILA Apr. 2, 2014), AILA InfoNet Doc. No. 14040248, *available at www.immigrantjustice.org/sites/immigrantjustice.org/files/AILA_Explanation%20of%20the%20Affirmative%20Asylum%20Backlog_4.2.14.pdf.*

[397] *See* AILA, *Asylum Office Guide – Best Practices*, *supra* note 173. The "Asylum Office Guide – Best Practices" is also available at Appx. 4E of this book.

[398] *See* CIS *Ombudsman – Case Assistance*, *supra* note 174.

authorizes the court to order a remedy and may be used to compel administrative agencies to act. In the lawsuit, the applicant would need to demonstrate that:

- (1) he or she has a clear right to the relief requested;
- (2) the agency has a clear duty to perform the act in question; and
- (3) no other adequate remedy is available.

Subject-matter jurisdiction for such a lawsuit lies under both the mandamus statute and the federal question statute at 28 USC §1331. In addition to the mandamus cause of action, practitioners also should simultaneously allege a cause of action under the Administrative Procedures Act §§555(b) and 706(1), as those sections provide a basis for a lawsuit when a government agency unreasonably delays or fails to act. Given that the INA has a clear statutory time frame for final administrative action on an asylum application, it may be argued that the agency has a clear duty to act and that it has unreasonably failed to do so. Prior to filing such a lawsuit, practitioners should take the steps suggested above (an expedite request and Ombudsman request for case assistance). Doing so will demonstrate in a future lawsuit that the applicant has exhausted all of his or her administrative remedies and that there is no other available remedy other than a mandamus suit. For a detailed discussion of and guidance for filing complaints for writ of mandamus, see the American Immigration Council's practice advisory, "Mandamus Actions: Avoiding Dismissal and Proving the Case," available on the Council's website.[399] Another helpful resource is Robert Pauw's book, *Litigating Immigration Cases in Federal Court*, available for purchase on AILA Agora.[400]

The decision of the asylum officer to approve, deny, or refer an asylum application must be communicated in writing to the applicant.[401] An applicant must appear in person to receive and acknowledge receipt of the decision.[402] In the asylum officer's discretion, the decision may be served by mail if appropriate, but generally decisions will be served on the applicant in person.[403] For all in-person service of decisions, most Asylum Offices will verify the identity of the applicant and all dependents 14 years old and older. Asylum Office personnel will call the applicant by number and

[399] Am. Immigration Council, *Mandamus Actions: Avoiding Dismissal and Proving the Case* (Aug. 6, 2009), *available at www.legalactioncenter.org/sites/default/files/lac_pa_081505.pdf.*

[400] *See* Robert Pauw, *Litigating Immigration Cases in Federal Court* (3d ed. 2013), *available at http://agora.aila.org/product/detail/1240* (last visited Jan. 24, 2015).

[401] 8 CFR §§208.19, 1208.19 (2014).

[402] 8 CFR §§208.19, 1208.19 (2014).

[403] 8 CFR §§208.19, 1208.19 (2014).

the principal applicant receives service on behalf of the family.[404] If NTAs are part of the decision package served, NTAs must be personally served on any dependents 14 years of age or older.[405] Before the decision is served, Asylum Office personnel will date stamp the decision letter (either at the time of pick-up or the day of mailing the decision).[406] If the applicant has a representative, a copy of the decision will be served on the representative, including by mail if he or she does not appear for the decision pick-up.[407]

1. Approval

The asylum officer has the authority to grant asylum in the exercise of discretion to an applicant who qualifies as a refugee under INA §101(a)(42), unless the applicant is prohibited from receiving asylum under INA §208(a)(2) or INA §208(b)(2).[408] The grant of asylum is effective for an indefinite period, subject to termination under certain conditions.[409] An applicant who is granted asylum is authorized to work and, after one year, is eligible for adjustment of status.[410] The asylee may confer derivative asylee status on his or her spouse and unmarried children under 21 years of age.[411]

> ➢ **Practice Pointer**: For a detailed description of the various benefits that accompany a grant of asylum in the United States, see chapter 13 of this book.

If the officer has recommended approval for one of the reasons described above in Part VIII.C., the decision package will include the Recommended Approval letter and Form AR-11, Alien Change of Address.[412] If the decision is served in person, Asylum Office personnel will inform the applicant that a final approval of the application may not be issued until the office receives results of the mandatory confidential background check.[413] The applicant will also be informed that he or she is required to notify USCIS of any change in address on the Form AR-11 by sending one copy to the address on the AR-11 and one copy to the Asylum Office.[414] The applicant will also sign the Asylum Office's file copy of the decision as proof of service.[415]

---

[404] *USCIS Affirmative Asylum Procedures Manual*, *supra* note 14, at pt. II.Q.

[405] *Id.*

[406] *Id.*

[407] *Id.*

[408] 8 CFR §§208.14(b), 1208.14(b) (2014). *See* chapter 2.7.

[409] 8 CFR §§208.14(e), 1208.14(e) (2014); *see also* this chapter, at 3.16.

[410] *See infra* pt. 3.9 and 3.13.

[411] INA §208(b)(3); 8 USC §1158(b)(3) (2012).

[412] *USCIS Affirmative Asylum Procedures Manual*, *supra* note 14, at pt. II.Q.1.

[413] *Id.*

[414] *Id.*

[415] *Id.*

If the officer was able to issue a final approval, the decision package will include the original Asylum Approval letter, a translation of the letter in the applicant's native or proficient language (if the applicant speaks one of the languages into which the letter has been translated), an original I-94 card for the principal applicant and each dependent that is endorsed with the asylum approval stamp, and Form AR-11, Alien Change of Address.[416] If the decision is served in person, Asylum Office personnel will inform the applicant of his or her duty to file the AR-11 within 10 days of any address change and will ask the principal applicant to sign the A-file copy of the decision as proof of service.[417]

If a dependent is subject to a mandatory bar or if he or she failed to follow the requirements for the identity and security checks, he or she may not be granted asylum as a derivative applicant along with the principal applicant. Rather, in this scenario, the Asylum Officer will either deny or refer the dependent's application, depending on his or her current immigration status.[418] An asylum officer has prosecutorial discretion regarding whether the place a dependent in removal proceedings before the immigration court if the dependent is inadmissible or deportable. Among the factors considered are:

(1) the likelihood the immigration court that would have jurisdiction over the dependent would accept the charging documents as sufficient to institute proceedings;

(2) the age of the dependent;

(3) whether the dependent has an application upon which he or she would be able to seek relief in front of an immigration judge;

(4) whether the dependent has a criminal record; and

(5) office resources.[419]

- **Practice Pointer**: See chapter 13 for a detailed discussion of the legal standards and procedures for derivative beneficiaries.
- **Practice Pointer**: There may be instances when an Asylum Office learns that an applicant was either under the jurisdiction of the immigration court or BIA or outside of the United States at the time of the asylum approval. However, lack of jurisdiction over an asylum application is not grounds for termination of asylum under 8 CFR §208.24. Thus, when the Asylum Office learns that it did not have jurisdiction over a claim when it approved the application, the Asylum Office must move to reconsider the asylum approval pursuant to 8 CFR §103.5(a)(5)(ii) in order to pursue rescission of asylum status.[420] The

[416] *Id.* at pt. II.Q.2.

[417] *Id.*

[418] *Id.* at pt. III.E.9.

[419] *Id.* at pt. III.E.9.a.

[420] *Id.* at pt. III.U.

Asylum Office will send the Motion to Reconsider letter to the asylee and will attach any unclassified documents that were relied upon in making the determination that the office lacked jurisdiction.[421] The asylee has 45 days to respond to the motion. If he or she does not respond within the 45 days, the Asylum Office will then issue a Notice of Rescission of Asylum Grant.[422] Upon receipt of a response from the asylee, the Asylum Office will review the response and make a determination whether the grounds for rescission were overcome. If an approval is rescinded, what happens next depends on a number of factors, including the applicant's prior status and whether he or she needs to file a new I-589.[423]

2. Denial

An asylum officer may issue a denial to an applicant who is maintaining valid nonimmigrant status at the time the application is decided.[424] Prior to issuing the denial, however, the asylum officer will issue a NOID to allow the applicant an opportunity to rebut the reasons for the denial. A NOID, like a denial, may only be issued to an individual maintaining valid nonimmigrant status. One exception to this general rule is that an *ABC* class member must be issued a NOID before a referral may be made to an IJ.[425] In the case of a NOID, the decision package will include the NOID letter.[426] If the NOID is served in person, Asylum Office personnel will inform the applicant of his or her duty to file the AR-11 within ten days of any address change and will ask the principal applicant to sign the A-file copy of the NOID as proof of service.[427]

After a NOID has been issued, the applicant will have the opportunity — usually a 16-day period — to respond with a rebuttal.[428] The actual time allotted is ten days to prepare the rebuttal, plus three days on either end for the mail to be delivered.[429] The rebuttal is considered timely if received on the next business day after the 16th day, if the last day of the rebuttal period is a weekend or holiday.[430] The asylum officer has discretion to grant a reasonable extension of time, generally no more than 30 days, to

[421] *Id.* at pt. III.U.1.

[422] *Id.* at pt. III.U.2.

[423] *Id.* at pt. III.U.3.

[424] 8 CFR §§208.14(c)(1), 1208.14(c)(1) (2014).

[425] See chapter 16 for more information on *ABC* class members & the *ABC Settlement*; *see also* Smith, *supra* note 6; Am. Immigration Law Ctr., *supra* note 6.

[426] *USCIS Affirmative Asylum Procedures Manual*, *supra* note 14, at pt. II.Q.4.

[427] *Id.*

[428] *Id.* at pt. II.N.2.c.

[429] *Id.* at pt. II.Q.4.

[430] *See* 8 CFR §1.2 (2014).

an applicant who requests an extension to prepare his or her rebuttal.[431] An applicant found eligible for asylum after the rebuttal period is processed for approval.[432] An applicant found ineligible for asylum, despite the rebuttal response, is processed for denial if the applicant is still in valid status or valid parole, or for referral if he or she is not.[433]

An asylum officer's decision denying an application must state the basis for the denial.[434] The denial must also contain an assessment of the applicant's credibility, unless the denial is due to the applicant's conviction of an aggravated felony. In the case of a denial, the decision package will include the Final Denial letter and a translation of the letter in the applicant's native or proficient language (if the applicant speaks one of the languages into which the letter has been translated), and a Form AR-11, Alien Change of Address.[435] If the decision is served in person, Asylum Office personnel will inform the applicant of his or her duty to file the AR-11 within ten days of any address change and will ask the principal applicant to sign the A-file copy of the decision as proof of service.[436]

The denial of an application filed by the principal applicant will result in the denial of asylum status to any dependents of the principal applicant who are included in the same application.[437] Such a denial, however, will not preclude a grant of asylum for a dependent who has filed a separate application, nor will such a denial bar the dependent from seeking asylum on the basis of having been previously denied asylum.[438]

- **Practice Pointer**: If a dependent is not in valid immigration status, he or she is not eligible to receive a final denial along with the principal applicant.[439] Rather, the asylum officer will determine whether the dependent is inadmissible or deportable and will exercise his or her discretion regarding whether to refer the dependent to the immigration court, as described below.

3. *Referral*

If the case is not granted and the applicant appears to be inadmissible or deportable, the asylum officer must refer the application to an IJ for adjudication in

---

[431] *USCIS Affirmative Asylum Procedures Manual*, *supra* note 14, at pt. III.H.3.

[432] *Id.* at pt. II.R.4.b. *See* 8 CFR §208.14(c) (2014).

[433] *USCIS Affirmative Asylum Procedures Manual*, *supra* note 14, at pt. II.R.4.a. *See* 8 CFR §208.14(c) (2014).

[434] 8 CFR §§208.14(c)(1), 1208.14(c)(1) (2014).

[435] *USCIS Affirmative Asylum Procedures Manual*, *supra* note 14, at pt. II.Q.5.

[436] *Id.*

[437] 8 CFR §§208.14(f), 1208.14(f) (2014).

[438] 8 CFR §§208.14(f), 1208.14(f) (2014).

[439] *USCIS Affirmative Asylum Procedures Manual*, *supra* note 14, at pt. III.E.9.c.

removal proceedings and issue the appropriate charging document.[440] Even if the applicant has filed an application to extend his or her period of nonimmigrant stay and that application remains pending, if his or her initial period of nonimmigrant stay has expired and the extension has not yet been approved, the Asylum Office must refer him or her to the immigration court.[441] If a charging document cannot be issued, the asylum officer will dismiss the application.[442] The referral may be made after an interview has been conducted or if the applicant, by failing to appear or provide an interpreter, is deemed to have waived his or her right to an interview.[443] If a case is referred for removal proceedings, the applicant is served with the NTA charging document, and the applicant may make his or her asylum claim anew before an immigration judge.

If the officer referred the case, the decision package will include the Referral Notice containing a checklist of the reasons for the referral, a translation of the Referral Notice in the applicant's native or proficient language (if the applicant speaks one of the languages into which the Referral Notice has been translated), an NTA charging document listing the factual allegations and charges of inadmissibility or deportability, a list of legal services, EOIR-33 Change of Address Form, and Form AR-11, Alien Change of Address.[444] Each individual 14 years of age or older must receive an individual NTA, legal services list, and EOIR-33 Change of Address Form.[445] If the decision is served in person, Asylum Office personnel will ask each individual 14 years of age or older to sign his or her NTA, ask the principal applicant to sign the NTA for any dependent under 14 years old, place the date of service on the Referral Notice, and complete the certificate of service section on the NTA.[446] Asylum Office personnel also will inform the applicant of the date and location of the hearing before the immigration court, that failure to appear can result in an in absentia removal order, and that the applicant is required to notify USCIS and the immigration of any change of address on Forms AR-11 and EOIR-33.[447]

The Asylum Office will file the referral packet with the immigration court, and once it is filed with the court, the Asylum Office no longer has jurisdiction over the asylum claim.[448] The referral packet contains a photocopy of the I-589 reflecting any changes made during the interview, copies of all documents in support of the I-589 application, the Notice to Appear with the original signature of the USCIS officer

---

[440] 8 CFR §§208.14(c), 1208.14(c) (2014).

[441] *Id. See also USCIS Affirmative Asylum Procedures Manual, supra* note 14, at pt. III.G.

[442] *Id.*

[443] 8 CFR §§208.14(c), 1208.14(c) (2014).

[444] *USCIS Affirmative Asylum Procedures Manual, supra* note 14, at pt. II.Q.3.

[445] *Id.*

[446] *Id.*

[447] *Id.*

[448] 8 CFR §208.2(b) (2014).

who signed and dated the document on page 1, a printout of the removal screen from the computer database showing the hearing date, time, and location, and a printout of the employment authorization clock screen.[449] The Asylum Office also will prepare the file for the ICE Office of the Principal Legal Advisor by ensuring that it contains a copy of the NTA, Referral Notice, and marked-up I-589. The file will be transferred to ICE, which represents the government in the immigration court hearing.[450]

- **Practice Pointer**: If a dependent is in valid immigration status, he or she is not inadmissible or deportable and will not be referred to the immigration court along with the principal applicant.[451] His or her A-number will not be included on the principal applicant's documentation.
- **Practice Pointer**: The asylum offices do not always send the full record to the immigration court. Thus, practitioners always should make an appointment or otherwise follow the immigration court's local rules for reviewing the applicant's court file. Reviewing the file will verify what documentation has been transferred and inform the practitioner of what documentation needs to be re-submitted to the court.
- **Practice Pointer**: The Asylum Division has established special affirmative asylum procedures for certain types of cases and has detailed those procedures in its *Affirmative Asylum Procedures Manual* at Part III.B. There are special procedures for children filing as principal asylum applicants, credible fear-screened affirmative asylum applicants, deceased applicants, applicants with physical and mental disabilities, applicants who may trigger national security matters, applicants designated as "special groups" due to legislation or litigation, LGBT applicants, and trafficking victims, among others.[452] Practitioners should consult the *Affirmative Asylum Procedures Manual* for details regarding these special procedures.

X. What If An Asylum Applicant Wants to Add a Dependent, Work, Travel, or Withdraw the Application During the Application Process?

Given the significant backlogs in the current affirmative asylum process, many applicants' family situations might change, they may need to work to support themselves, or they may need to travel abroad. However, asylum applicants are only authorized to work after their applications have been pending for 180 days. Additionally, departing the United States before a final decision on the applicant's

---

[449] *USCIS Affirmative Asylum Procedures Manual*, *supra* note 14, at pt. II.R.3.a.

[450] *Id.* at pt. II.R.3.b.

[451] *Id.* at pt. III.E.9.b.

[452] *Id.* at pt. III.B.

asylum application could place his or her eligibility in jeopardy or could result in the abandonment of the application altogether. It is important for applicants to understand and follow the procedures for adding dependents, obtaining work authorization, and securing a travel document while their I-589 applications remain pending with USCIS.

A. Adding a Dependent After the Initial Filing

A principal applicant may add to his or her asylum applicant a dependent spouse or child under age 21 who is in the United States at any time prior to issuance of a final denial, referral, or approval.[453] Even if the dependent previously filed for asylum as a separate principal applicant and even if the dependent was issued a NOID or final denial on his or her own application, the dependent may be added to the principal's application prior to its final adjudication.[454] Similarly, if the principal has been issued a NOID or a Recommended Approval letter, the application does not have a final decision and the dependent may still be added.[455]

To add a dependent prior to the asylum interview, the applicant should send to the USCIS service center one copy of the asylum application that includes the dependent's information, one passport-sized photograph of the dependent, one copy of the evidence of family relationship, and a cover letter stating that the applicant wishes to add a dependent to his or her asylum claim.[456] The service center will add the dependent in RAPS and forward the packet to the Asylum Office.[457]

To add a dependent at the time of the asylum interview, the dependent must accompany the principal applicant to the interview. The principal applicant must submit to the asylum officer the same packet described above. Asylum Office personnel will add the dependent in RAPS and will meet and interview the dependent.[458] If the dependent does not appear with the principal applicant at the time of the interview, the asylum officer will proceed with the interview of the principal applicant, will give the applicant an appointment to bring the dependent to the Asylum Office prior to the decision pick-up date, and will place the principal applicant's case on hold. If the dependent does not appear for the appointment, the asylum officer will proceed with adjudicating the case without the dependent.[459]

Finally, to add a dependent after the interview, but prior to the final decision, the principal applicant must send the same dependent packet described above to either

---

[453] *USCIS Affirmative Asylum Procedures Manual*, *supra* note 14, at pt. III.E.1.

[454] *Id.*

[455] *Id.*

[456] *Id.*

[457] *Id.*

[458] *Id.*

[459] *Id.*

the service center or the Asylum Office.[460] If it is sent to the service center, the service center will forward the packet to the Asylum Office for further processing. If it is sent to the Asylum Office, the office will place the principal applicant's case on hold and schedule the principal applicant and dependent for an appointment to come to the Asylum Office.[461] If the dependent appears, the Asylum Office will be able to include the dependent on the applicant's final decision. If not, the Asylum Office will proceed with adjudicating the case without the dependent.[462]

> ➢ **Practice Pointer**: It is essential for practitioners to notify the local Asylum Office as soon as possible that their client wishes to add a dependent. The notice should be sent in writing and evidence of the family relationship (a marriage or birth certificate) should be attached. Upon notification, the Asylum Office will add the dependent in RAPS and initiate the scheduling of a fingerprint appointment for the dependent, as well as other security checks. Asylum Office personnel also will conduct US-VISIT checks for any dependents added after the principal applicant's initial filing.[463]

There is no requirement that a family must pursue an asylum claim as a family.[464] For example, a husband and wife may both submit separate asylum applications as principal applicants. The Asylum Office will attempt to schedule them for their interviews on the same day and with the same asylum officer.[465]

Additionally, it is possible for an individual to be a principal applicant and a dependent simultaneously.[466] If the Asylum Office is aware of the cases in time, the family members will be scheduled for interviews on the same date and with the same asylum officer.[467] Asylum office personnel will locate and obtain all A-files, and the asylum officer will confirm with all applicants that they wish to proceed as principals and that one or all wish to proceed as dependents as well.[468] If the Asylum Office does not become aware of the simultaneous filing as principal and dependent until the interview of the first family member, the asylum officer will schedule the other family member for an interview as soon as possible and will not render a decision in the first applicant's case until all principal applicants have been interviewed.[469]

---

460 *Id.*

461 *Id.*

462 *Id.*

463 *Id.*

464 *Id.* at pt. III.E.2.

465 *Id.*

466 *Id.* at pt. III.E.3.

467 *Id.*

468 *Id.*

469 *Id.*

If the decisions for both family members' cases are the same, the asylum officer will proceed in rendering the decision, as described above. However, if the asylum officer determines that one applicant is eligible for approval as the principal, but the other applicant is not, the asylum officer will inform the prospective dependent that he or she is ineligible for an asylum approval as a principal applicant and determine whether he or she wishes to be processed as a dependent on the other claim.[470] If so, the dependent must so indicate in writing. If the dependent does not indicate this in writing, he or she will be processed under his or her claim as a principal.[471] If the individual is not eligible to be processed as a dependent — for example, a parent cannot be added as a dependent on a child's asylum claim — his or her case will be processed as a principal applicant.[472]

> **Practice Pointer**: For detailed guidance on the legal standards and procedures for derivative beneficiaries, see chapter 13 of this book.

B. Employment Authorization for Affirmative Asylum Applicants

An asylum applicant may not apply for employment authorization until his or her application has been pending for at least 150 days or he or she has received a recommended or final approval of asylum.[473] USCIS has 30 days from receipt to adjudicate an I-765, Application for Employment Authorization and cannot issue an employment authorization document until the asylum application has been pending for 180 days or more.[474] This 180-day period is referred to as the employment authorization "clock." USCIS's receipt of the asylum application starts the clock and the clock remains running unless the applicant's actions cause an interruption or delay in the processing of the application.[475] The following are examples of applicants' actions, which may stop the clock from accruing time:

- Interview reschedule requests by the applicant (clock stops until the applicant appears for the rescheduled interview);
- Failure to appear for an interview, unless the applicant can show lack of proper notice by USCIS (clock stops until the applicant appears for the interview);
- Failure of a representative to appear at the asylum interview, causing rescheduling of the interview (clock stops until the applicant appears for the rescheduled interview);
- Failure of a dependent to appear at the interview (clock stops until the applicant presents the requested dependent);

---

[470] *Id.*

[471] *Id.*

[472] *Id.*

[473] INA §208(d)(2); *USCIS Affirmative Asylum Procedures Manual*, *supra* note 14, at pt. III.F.2.

[474] INA §208(d)(2).

[475] *USCIS Affirmative Asylum Procedures Manual*, *supra* note 14, at pt. III.F.3.

- Failure to provide a competent interpreter causing rescheduling of the interview (clock stops until the applicant appears for the rescheduled interview);
- Rescheduling of the interview due to a representative abusing his or her role (clock stops until the applicant appears for the rescheduled interview);
- Putting the case on hold so the asylum officer can await a report on the analysis of a document believed to be fraudulent (clock stops until the officer receives the analysis);
- Requests by the applicant for the opportunity to submit additional documentation following conclusion of the interview (clock stops until the documents are submitted);
- If an asylum officer requires evidence of the applicant's residence to confirm jurisdiction and must put the case on hold for the applicant to provide that evidence (clock stops until the evidence is submitted);
- Requests to reschedule a pick-up appointment (clock stops until the applicant appears for the appointment, unless there is a final denial decision served);
- Failure to appear for a decision pick-up appointment[476] (clock stops until the applicant appears for the appointment, unless there is a final denial decision served);
- Requests for an extension of time to file a rebuttal to a NOID (clock stops until the rebuttal is filed); and
- Final denial of the asylum application (not a referral).[477]

  > **Practice Pointer**: See chapter 13 of this book for detailed guidance on how to seek employment authorization based on a pending asylum application, a discussion of recent policy changes regarding employment authorization for asylum-seekers, and practice tips to avoid stopping the employment authorization clock.

C. Departing the U.S. Before a Final Affirmative Asylum Decision

Certain departures from the United States while an affirmative asylum applicant's I-589 is pending may cause the agency to presume that the applicant has abandoned his or her application. These include: (1) if the applicant departs the U.S. without first obtaining advance parole; and (2) if the applicant departs the U.S. pursuant to a grant of advance parole and returns to this or her country of feared persecution.[478] In both instances, an applicant may overcome the presumption of abandonment; however any

[476] Note that if an applicant fails to appear for a decision pick-up appointment, the decision letter and any other documentation will be mailed to the applicant. *See generally,* USCIS Affirmative Asylum Procedures Manual, *supra* note 14, at pt. III.I.4. (November 2013), *available at www.uscis.gov/sites/default/files/files/nativedocuments/Asylum_Procedures_Manual_2013.pdf.*

[477] *See generally, USCIS Affirmative Asylum Procedures Manual, supra* note 14.

[478] *USCIS Affirmative Asylum Procedures Manual, supra* note 14, at pt. III.D.

return to the applicant's country of feared persecution may have a bearing on his or her ability to establish a well-founded fear.[479] Relevant factors may include the reasons for the departure, length and purpose of the departure, whether the applicant returned to the country of feared persecution, whether there were compelling reasons for doing so, what happened while the applicant was in his or her country of feared persecution, the circumstances for the applicant while in the country of feared persecution, and whether the applicant has returned to the U.S. and appeared for his or her asylum interview.[480] Thus, in order to avoid abandoning the application, an asylum applicant should apply for advance parole prior to his or her departure from the United States. Most importantly, he or she must not return to the country of feared persecution.

An asylum applicant may apply for advance parole on Form I-131, which is available on USCIS's website.[481] Asylum applicants must receive advance parole before leaving the United States. It is important to note, however, that advance parole does not guarantee that the applicant will be paroled into the United States. Rather, the asylum applicant must still undergo inspection by a U.S. Customs and Border Protection officer.[482]

➢ **Practice Pointer**: The Form I-131 does not contain specific instructions for asylum applicants applying for advance parole. At the USCIS Asylum Division Stakeholder meeting on October 23, 2013, AILA raised this issue and the Asylum Division advised that applicants should follow the instructions for "all others." The Asylum Division indicated that they would be raising the lack of specific instruction for asylum applicants at the next Service Center Operations meeting to hopefully improve the I-131 instructions and the information provided on the USCIS website.[483] For a detailed discussion of and procedural guidance for seeking advance parole while an asylum application is pending, see chapter 13 of this book.

---

479 *See supra* chapter 2 for a detailed discussion of returning to the country of feared persecution and what effect that could have on the applicant's eligibility for asylum.

480 *See supra* chapter 2 for a detailed discussion of returning to the country of feared persecution and what effect that could have on the applicant's eligibility for asylum. *See also USCIS Affirmative Asylum Procedures Manual*, *supra* note 14, at pt. III.D.

481 U.S. Citizenship and Immigration Servs., Form I-131 Application for Travel Document, *available at www.uscis.gov/i-131* (last visited Jan. 24, 2015).

482 *See* U.S. Citizenship and Immigration Servs. Fact Sheet, *Traveling Outside the United States as an Asylum Applicant*, *an Asylee, or a Lawful Permanent Resident Who Obtained Such Status Based on Asylum Status* (Jan. 4, 2007), *available at www.aila.org/content/default.aspx?docid=21301*.

483 *See* U.S. Citizenship and Immigration Servs. Asylum Division, *Stakeholder Meeting Agenda and Unofficial Notes*, AILA InfoNet Doc. No. 13110860, *available at www.aila.org/content/default.aspx?docid=46408*.

D. Withdrawal Requests

An applicant may withdraw his or her affirmative asylum application at any time prior to the issuance of a final decision, and the Asylum Office does not have authority to deny such a request.[484] All withdrawal requests must be made in writing. Thus, if the request is made orally in person during the asylum interview, the asylum officer will give the applicant a Declaration of Intent to Withdraw Asylum Application.[485] Upon receipt of the request to withdraw, the asylum officer will administratively close the case and generate an Administrative Termination letter, which the Asylum Office will mail to the applicant.[486]

The Asylum Office also will determine whether to initiate removal proceedings after considering whether there is sufficient information in the file to establish the applicant's alienage and inadmissibility or deportability, as well as considering whether the applicant may be eligible for an adjustment of status in the near future, among other factors.[487] If a charging document is to be issued, the Asylum Office will administratively close the case, prepare an NTA or I-863 as appropriate, and serve the documents on the applicant.[488]

XI. What if the Applicant Wants to Challenge the Asylum Office Decision?

An asylum applicant who is not granted asylum and is referred to an immigration judge may renew his or her request for asylum before the immigration judge. An asylum applicant who is maintaining a valid nonimmigrant status but has been denied asylum may file a new I-589 application with the Asylum Division.

> ➢ **Practice Pointer**: Typically, unless there are changed circumstances or new facts or evidence in support of the asylum claim, the Asylum Office will not change its first decision. Thus, any subsequent application should highlight what has changed since the Asylum Office considered the first I-589 application.

There is no appeal of an asylum officer's decision. Thus, any challenges to that decision must be raised directly with the Asylum Office where the case was adjudicated. One option is for applicants to informally contact the local Asylum Office to seek the opportunity to discuss the decision with the Supervisory Asylum Officer who reviewed the case. If the Supervisory Asylum Officer is unable to assist,

[484] 8 CFR §103.2(b)(6) (2014); *USCIS Affirmative Asylum Procedures Manual*, *supra* note 14, at pt. III.W.

[485] *USCIS Affirmative Asylum Procedures Manual*, *supra* note 14, at pt. III.W.1.

[486] *Id.* at pt. III.W.2.

[487] *Id.*

[488] *Id.*

the applicant may go up the chain and request review of the decision by the Asylum Office Director.

> ➢ **Practice Pointer**: For detailed information on how to contact the local Asylum Offices, see AILA's "Asylum Office Guide — Best Practices," which is updated each year and available on AILA InfoNet.[489] The guide contains the names and contact information for the Asylum Office Directors, as well as local procedures for filing inquiries and requests. A copy of the guide is available at Appx. 4E of this book.

A more formal option would be for the applicant to file a motion to reopen or reconsider the decision directly with the local Asylum Office that denied or referred the application.[490] Such motions may be filed on Form I-290B, Notice of Appeal or Motion;[491] however, it is not required that the motion be filed on that form and submitted with a filing fee.[492] Any motion to reopen or reconsider must be filed within 30 days of issuance of the Asylum Office's decision.[493] A motion to reopen is used to seek a new decision in light of new facts or documentary evidence that were not previously considered by the asylum officer and that may impact applicant's eligibility for asylum. The new facts and evidence should be submitted along with the I-290B.[494] A motion to reconsider, on the other hand, is used to seek reconsideration of a decision in light of factual or legal errors made by the adjudicator. A motion to reconsider should cite to the statute, regulations, or precedent decisions that support the applicant's argument that the asylum officer incorrectly applied the law, or should specify the facts or evidence that the officer misunderstood or failed to consider.[495]

> ➢ **Practice Pointer**: If the error in the case was particular egregious, it may be helpful to send a copy of the motion to the USCIS Asylum Division Headquarters office in Washington, D.C.

If the Asylum Office Director denies or dismisses the motion, the Asylum Office will prepare and issue to the applicant and any representative of record a written notice of denial or dismissal.[496] If the Asylum Office Director grants the motion,

---

[489] AILA, *Asylum Office Guide – Best Practices*, *supra* note 173.

[490] Procedures for filing a motion to reopen and reconsider can be found in USCIS's *Affirmative Asylum Procedures Manual* 118–20 (Feb. 2003), *available at www.uscis.gov/files/nativedocuments/Affrm AsyManFNL.pdf.*

[491] *See* Form I-290B, Notice of Appeal or Motion, *available at www.uscis.gov/i-290b* (last visited Jan. 24, 2015).

[492] *USCIS Affirmative Asylum Procedures Manual*, *supra* note 14, at pt. III.M.2.

[493] *See* INA §208(d)(5)(A)(iv); *USCIS Affirmative Asylum Procedures Manual*, *supra* note 14, at pt. III.M.1.

[494] *See* Form I-290B Instructions, *available at www.uscis.gov/sites/default/files/files/form/i-290binstr.pdf* (last visited Jan. 24, 2015).

[495] *Id.*

[496] *USCIS Affirmative Asylum Procedures Manual*, *supra* note 14, at pt. III.M.3.

Asylum Office personnel will notify the applicant and his or her representative in writing and determine whether re-interview is necessary.[497]

In cases where the Asylum Office referred the applicant to the immigration court, the applicant may already be in removal proceedings by the time the request for informal review is concluded or the formal motion to reopen or reconsider is decided. This means that jurisdiction over the application lies with the immigration court, not the Asylum Office. In such cases, if the Asylum Office has decided to change, reopen, or reconsider its decision, the Asylum Office may coordinate with the local ICE Office of Chief Counsel to either terminate the NTA or move to terminate removal proceedings so that the Asylum Office may re-open and re-adjudicate the asylum claim.[498] Once the NTA or proceedings have been terminated, the Asylum Office may grant the applicant's motion and re-adjudicate the claim.

---

[497] *Id.* at pt. III.M.4.

[498] *Id.* at pt. III.M.

CHAPTER EIGHT

DEFENSIVE CLAIMS FOR PROTECTION*

As the asylum standards have been heightened and the evidentiary burden on applicants has increased, the number of applicants granted asylum defensively has decreased.[1] From 11,978 defensive asylum grants in 2012 to 9,933 in 2013, statistics show a 17 percent decrease.[2] As standards continue to be heightened and the immigration court system becomes more and more stretched, it is increasingly important for practitioners to diligently and thoroughly prepare their clients' applications and to closely follow the relevant procedures in advocating for their clients.

➢ **Practice Pointer**: For detailed statistics and comparative charts regarding asylum cases received and completed before the U.S. immigration courts from fiscal year 2010 through fiscal year 2014, see the Executive Office for Immigration Review (EOIR) Office of Planning, Analysis, and Technology's "FY 2014 Statistics Yearbook"

* The author would like to thank Andres C. Benach of Benach Ragland LLP for his invaluable input in reviewing this chapter.

[1] *See, e.g.*, REAL ID Act of 2005; *Matter of M–E–V–G–*, 26 I&N Dec. 227 (BIA 2014); *Matter of W–G–R–*, 26 I&N Dec. 208 (BIA 2014).

[2] U.S. Dep't of Homeland Sec., *Yearbook of Immigration Statistics: 2013*, at tbl. 16 — Individuals Granted Asylum Affirmatively or Defensively: Fiscal Years 1990 to 2013 (Sept. 16, 2014), *available at www.dhs.gov/yearbook-immigration-statistics-2013-refugees-and-asylees*.

(March 2015).[3] Also see the EOIR "Asylum Statistics FY 2010 – 2014" (March 2015).[4]

This chapter provides an overview of asylum, withholding of removal, and deferral of removal procedures for applicants applying defensively before an immigration judge. The process can be completed within a few months or — in most cases of non-detained individuals — may last for several years. In some instances, the procedures may seem counterintuitive, cumbersome, or arbitrarily applied. It is necessary and, indeed, crucial to follow the statute, regulations, instructions, and local rules throughout the process. This chapter is meant to serve as a helpful manual for those navigating the procedures for defensive applications for protection.

- **Practice Pointer**: The EOIR's *Immigration Court Practice Manual* (ICPM) and *Board of Immigration Appeals Practice Manual* (*BIA Practice Manual*) are the main procedural guides for presenting defensive applications for protection. The ICPM was last updated in October of 2013 and is available online at *www.justice.gov/eoir/vll/OCIJPracManual/ocij_page1.htm.*[5] The *BIA Practice Manual* was last updated in August of 2014 and is available online at *www.justice.gov/eoir/vll/qapracmanual/apptmtn4.htm.*[6]

I. Where Do Defensive Proceedings Take Place?

An application for asylum, withholding of removal under INA §241(b)(3), and/or protection under the Convention Against Torture (CAT) in removal proceedings is referred to as defensive because these forms of relief are a defense to the Department of Homeland Security's efforts to remove an individual from the United States.

- **Practice Pointer**: Under the CAT regulations issued in February 1999, individuals physically present in the United States who are subject to various types of removal procedures are permitted to apply for relief under the CAT if they fear they will be subjected to torture upon return.[7] Unlike asylum, an individual cannot apply affirmatively for relief under the CAT.[8] Only immigration judges (IJs), the BIA, or federal courts can

---

[3] Available on AILA InfoNet Doc. No. 15031603 and online at *www.justice.gov/eoir/statspub/fy14syb.pdf* (last visited Mar. 31, 2015).

[4] Available on AILA InfoNet Doc. No. 15031604 and online at *www.ilw.com/immigrationdaily/news/2015,0316-EOIR.pdf* (last visited Mar. 31, 2015).

[5] (last visited Jan. 25, 2015).

[6] (last visited Jan. 25, 2015).

[7] See this chapter at 4.2.1 and 4.2.2 for an overview of the definition of torture and criteria for establishing relief under the CAT.

[8] *See* INS Memorandum, J. Langlois, "Implementation of Amendments to Asylum and Withholding of Removal Regulations, Effective March 22, 1999" (Mar. 18, 1999), at 6.

grant relief under the CAT. Individuals subject to expedited removal, reinstatement of removal, or administrative removal for aggravated felonies also are permitted to apply for relief under the CAT. Their claims are initially screened by an asylum officer.[9]

The proceedings take place before the U.S. immigration courts, which are part of the EOIR within the U.S. Department of Justice.[10] There are more than 50 immigration courts in the United States.[11] Immigration court proceedings are also conducted in Department of Homeland Security (DHS) detention centers nationwide, as well as many federal, state, and local correctional facilities.[12] In addition, hearings before IJs are sometimes conducted by video or telephone conference[13]

- **Practice Pointer**: For a complete list of immigration courts and judges, see EOIR's "Immigration Court Listing" at *www.justice.gov/eoir/sibpages/ICadr.htm.*[14]

A. Hearings by Video

A respondent need not be physically present before the IJ during his or her hearing. The Illegal Immigration Reform and Immigrant Responsibility Act of 1996 (IIRAIRA) specifically authorizes hearings by videoconference.[15] These video hearings are increasingly used for detained respondents, who are often many miles away from the court and the IJ.[16] To supplement its other immigration courts across the country, on July 19, 2004, EOIR established the Headquarters Court (HQIC), based in Arlington, VA. At present, HQIC has four IJs who hear cases and conduct both master calendar and individual hearings via videoconferencing on a regular basis. The purpose of the HQIC is to address short-term resource needs as they arise in the immigration courts nationwide.[17] For example, in the summer and fall of 2014, the IJs at the HQIC heard the cases of women and children detained at the Federal Law Enforcement Training Center in Artesia, New Mexico following the spring and summer's "surge" of border-crossers seeking protection in the United States.

---

[9] *See* this chapter, at 4.3.7.

[10] 8 CFR §1003.0(a) (2014).

[11] *Immigration Court Practice Manual* (hereinafter ICPM), chapter 1.6(a)(ii).

[12] *Id.*

[13] *See* ICPM, chapter 4.7.

[14] (last visited Jan. 25, 2015).

[15] Illegal Immigration Reform and Immigrant Responsibility Act of 1996 (IIRAIRA), Pub. L. No. 104-208, div. C, 110 Stat. 3009, 3009–546 to 3009–724. INA §240(b)(2)(A)(iii).

[16] *See* J.T. Hong, Practice Advisory, *Video Removal Hearings: A Violation of Due Process*? 20 IMMIGRATION LAW TODAY 545 (Nov. 2001) (providing a helpful list of objections to make on the record to a video hearing).

[17] For more information, see U.S. Dep't of Justice, Exec. Office of Immigration Review (EOIR) Fact Sheet, *EOIR Headquarters Immigration Court* (July 21, 2004), *available at www.usdoj.gov/eoir/press/04/HQICFactSheet.htm*.

- **Practice Pointer**: The chief IJ has given guidance to IJs on how they should conduct video hearings in a memorandum issued in August 2004.[18]

Conducting removal hearings by video raises a number of due process concerns, including interference with the following:

- The respondent's ability to effectively testify and his or her statutory right to present evidence on his or her own behalf;[19]
- Adequacy of the translation due to sound issues and the inability of the respondent and interpreter to see and hear each other;
- Access to counsel due to the inability of the respondent and his or her attorney to communicate directly and privately; and
- The respondent's ability to examine physical evidence presented by DHS or to cross-examine witnesses.[20]

However, most courts have held that video hearings do not violate due process.[21]

One court noted that video hearings do have the potential of violating due process by depriving an individual of a full and fair hearing.[22] For instance, where the use of videoconferencing interferes with a respondent's statutory right to be represented by his or her chosen attorney, to present evidence, or to examine evidence or cross-examine witnesses, and results in prejudice to the respondent, the hearing is not full and fair or consistent with due process.[23] Specifically, video hearings may interfere with an attorney's ability to fully represent the respondent and put the respondent's attorney in "a 'Catch-22' situation" where the attorney must choose between being with his or her client in the detention facility or being at the immigration court with

---

[18] *See* EOIR Memorandum from Michael J. Creppy on Interim Operating Policies and Procedures Memorandum No. 04-06: Hearings Conducted Through Telephone and Video Conference (Aug. 18, 2004), *available at www.usdoj.gov/eoir/efoia/ocij/oppm04/04-06.pdf.*

[19] INA §240(b)(4)(B).

[20] INA §240(b)(4) (setting forth the respondent's rights to be represented by counsel of his or her choosing, present evidence on his or her own behalf, examine evidence presented against him or her, and cross-examine witnesses).

[21] *See, e.g., Vilchez v. Holder*, 682 F.3d 1195, 1197 (9th Cir. 2012) (holding that the use of a video-conference hearing in removal proceedings did not violate an alien's due process rights and that the BIA had ruled consistent with 8 USC §1229a(b)(2)(iii) which expressly permits the use of video hearings); *Aslam v. Mukasey*, 537 F.3d 110, 115 (2d Cir. 2008) (stating that even though video conference hearings are permissible, they must comport with constitutional due process requirements); *But see Lacsina Pangilinan v. Holder*, 568 F.3d 708, 709 (9th Cir. 2009) (holding that a due process violation occurs when "(1) the proceeding was so fundamentally unfair that the alien was prevented from reasonably presenting his case, and (2) the alien demonstrates prejudice, which means that the outcome of the proceeding may have been affected by the alleged violation" thus, supporting the proposition that due process violations must be adjudicated on a case-by-case basis).

[22] *See Rusu v. INS*, 296 F.3d 316 (4th Cir. 2002).

[23] *Id.* at 321 n.7.

the IJ and DHS attorney.[24] As the Fourth Circuit noted, "under either scenario, the effectiveness of the lawyer is diminished; he simply must choose the least damaging option."[25] Additionally, video hearings "may render it difficult for a fact finder in an adjudicative proceeding to make credibility determinations and to gauge demeanor."[26] Although the Fourth Circuit recognized these potential problems with video hearings, it held that, under the specific facts involved in *Rusu v. INS*, the individual did not show prejudice and therefore, due process had not been violated.[27] Another court held that a hearing by videoconference violated due process when it prevented the applicant from reviewing key evidence.[28]

- **Practice Pointer**: Prior to a hearing by video, practitioners should file a motion seeking an in-person hearing on behalf of their client and highlighting the reasons why a video hearing is not appropriate for that particular case. Making this motion on the record preserves any arguments regarding due process violations for appeal. If the IJ denies the motion, practitioners should again make an oral objection to the use of videoconferencing at the beginning of the hearing. Practitioners also should make various objections to due process issues that arise throughout the hearing as a result of the hearing being conducted by video, and move the IJ to stop the proceedings and reschedule the case for an in-person hearing. If relief is denied practitioners should file an appeal to the BIA, noting any due process issues due to the videoconferencing and demonstrating how those problems prejudiced the respondent. Upon receipt of the transcript, practitioners should use the transcript to highlight those due process issues. For more strategies for objecting to video hearings that fail to comport with due process principles, see the American Immigration Council Legal Action Center's Practice Advisory, "Objecting to Video Merits Hearings" (Dec. 12, 2003), available at *www.legalactioncenter.org/sites/default/files/docs/lac/lac_pa_121203.*[29]

Appleseed, a nonpartisan, nonprofit network of public interest justice centers in the United States and Mexico, has studied and criticized the use of video hearings in immigration proceedings, urging EOIR to return to in-person merits hearings only and pointing out the lack of attorney-client confidential communications and lack of real-time document transmissions.[30] In 2009, Appleseed identified these problems

[24] *Id.* at 323.

[25] *Id.* at 322.

[26] *Id.*

[27] *Id.*

[28] *Rapheal v. Mukasey*, 533 F.3d 521, 532–33 (7th Cir. 2008).

[29] (last visited Feb. 14, 2015).

[30] Betsy Cavendish & Steven Shulman, *Reimagining the Immigration Court Assembly Line: Transformative Change for the Immigration Justice System*, Appleseed (May 2012), *available at*

Continued

and made various recommendations to EOIR.[31] Appleseed revisited the issue of video hearings in its 2012 report, and gave EOIR an "F" grade for its failure to make improvements.[32]Despite these potential due process violations, however, EOIR has continued its use of video hearings and asserted that they do not violate due process.

B. Immigration Judges

The Office of the Chief Immigration Judge (OCIJ) oversees the administration of the immigration courts nationwide and exercises administrative supervision over immigration judges, who are administrative law judges appointed by the Attorney General (AG) to preside over the proceedings.[33] There are more than 200 IJs in the United States.[34]

IJs are responsible for deciding cases in a timely and impartial manner, consistent with the Immigration and Nationality Act (INA), federal regulations, and precedent decisions of the BIA and federal appellate courts.[35] They have the power to make determinations of removability, deportability, and excludability; adjudicate applications for relief; review credible and reasonable fear determinations made by the DHS; conduct claimed status review proceedings; conduct custody hearings and bond redetermination proceedings; make determinations in rescission of adjustment of status and departure control cases; and take any other action consistent with applicable laws and regulations.[36] During these proceedings, IJs have the power to administer oaths, receive evidence, and interrogate, examine, and cross-examine individuals in proceedings, as well as witnesses.[37] IJs also may issue administrative subpoenas for the attendance of witnesses and the presentation of evidence.[38] Their decisions are subject to review by the BIA, pursuant to 8 CFR §1003.1.[39]

C. Jurisdiction

Jurisdiction vests, and proceedings before an IJ commence, when a charging document listing the factual allegations and charges of removability against the

---

www.appleseednetwork.org/wp-content/uploads/2012/03/Reimagining-the-Immigration-Court-Assembly-Line.pdf.

[31] Betsy Cavendish & Malcolm Rich, *Assembly Line Injustice: Blueprint to Reform America's Immigration Courts*, Appleseed (May 2009), *available at http://appleseednetwork.org/wp-content/uploads/2012/05/Assembly-Line-Injustice-Blueprint-to-Reform-Americas-Immigration-Courts1.pdf.*

[32] Cavendish & Shulman, *Reimagining the Immigration Court Assembly Line*, *supra* note 30, at 8.

[33] ICPM, chapter 2.1(a).

[34] ICPM, chapter 1.6(a)(ii).

[35] 8 CFR §1003.10(b) (2014).

[36] ICPM, chapter 1.5(a).

[37] 8 CFR §1003.10(b) (2014).

[38] *Id.*

[39] 8 CFR §1003.10(c) (2014).

respondent is filed with the immigration court by DHS.[40] However, sometimes removal proceedings may take place in a location different from where the charging document is filed.[41] IJs conducting telephonic or video hearings are instructed to make it clear on the record regarding where the hearing is taking place. According to the OCIJ, the hearing location is the location where the case is docketed for a hearing.[42] The IJs must also note the locations of the applicant, the applicant's representative, if any, and the DHS trial attorney.[43] The law that is to be applied by the IJs is the law of the hearing location (which may be different from the law where the IJ is sitting).[44]

> ➢ **Practice Pointer**: Where a notice to appear (NTA) has been issued and served on the respondent, but not filed with the immigration court, the immigration court does not have jurisdiction over the case. If the respondent is detained, however, he or she may file a motion for a bond redetermination hearing even if the NTA has not been filed with the court.[45] In these situations where the NTA has been served on the respondent but not filed with the immigration court, applicants may file their application for asylum affirmatively before U.S. Citizenship and Immigration Services (USCIS). The exception to this rule is for individuals who were issued NTAs after being placed in expedited removal proceedings. According to the *Affirmative Asylum Procedures Manual*, the asylum office is unlikely to assume jurisdiction over these individuals' applications. See chapter 7 for a detailed discussion of the legal standards and procedures for applying for asylum affirmatively before a USCIS Asylum Office.

D. Backlogs

Immigration court dockets have grown at a tremendous rate over the past decade, with the number of pending matters before the immigration courts increasing every year. At the end of fiscal year 2014, for example, there were 408,037 cases pending before the immigration courts, while the prior fiscal year ended with 344,230 pending matters.[46] This growing backlog of cases has resulted in a significant increase in wait

---

[40] 8 CFR §1003.14 (2014).

[41] 8 CFR §1003.11 (2014).

[42] *See* Creppy Memorandum on Hearings Conducted Through Telephone and Video Conference, *supra* note 18.

[43] *Id.*

[44] *Id.*; *see also Ramos v. Ashcroft*, 371 F.3d 948 (7th Cir. 2004) (denying DOJ's motion to transfer case to Eighth Circuit, where IJ was sitting in Chicago and conducting hearing via teleconference with respondent in Iowa; holding location of hearing was Chicago).

[45] ICPM, chapter 5.2(a)(i).

[46] TRAC Immigration, *Backlog of Pending Cases in Immigration Courts*, *available at http://trac.syr.edu/phptools/immigration/court_backlog/apprep_backlog.php* (last visited Feb. 14, 2015).

time for a hearing. In fiscal year 2014, for example, a respondent in removal proceedings had to wait an average of 567 days for his or her hearing.[47]

- **Practice Pointer**: For more immigration court statistics, *see* TRAC Immigration, available at *http://trac.syr.edu/immigration/*.[48] TRAC has also documented extensive disparities in asylum decisions by IJs. To see the asylum grant and denial rate for a particular IJ go to *http://trac.syr.edu/immigration/reports/judgereports/*.[49]
- **Practice Pointer**: Appleseed has published critical assessments of the immigration court system. Its key findings include a lack of fairness, impartiality, and professionalism in the immigration court process, and a lack of access to pro bono assistance by immigrants.[50]

EOIR has responded that it has moved forward with measures to improve adjudications, including a system to evaluate the performance of IJs and BIA members, a training plan for IJs and BIA members, a revised *IJ Benchbook*,[51] a pilot program to deploy supervisors to the field, a draft code of conduct for IJs and BIA members, and more.[52] TRAC Immigration evaluated EOIR's improvement measures and found that many of them had not yet been effectively implemented.[53]

II. How Do Defensive Proceedings Begin?

Removal proceedings begin when DHS files an NTA or other charging document[54] with the immigration court after the document has been served on the individual.[55] The NTA is a written notice to the individual that includes the following information:[56]

---

[47] TRAC Immigration, *Immigration Court Backlog Tool*, *available at http://trac.syr.edu/phptools/immigration/court_backlog/* (last visited Feb. 14, 2015).

[48] (last visited Feb. 14, 2015).

[49] (last visited Feb. 14, 2015).

[50] Cavendish & Shulman, Reimagining the Immigration Court Assembly Line, *supra* note 30; Cavendish & Rich, Assembly Line Injustice, *supra* note 31.

[51] EOIR, *Immigration Judge Benchbook*, *available at www.justice.gov/eoir/vll/benchbook/* (last visited Feb. 14, 2015).

[52] *See* Fact Sheet: EOIR's Improvement Measures—Update (June 5, 2009), *available at www.usdoj.gov/eoir/press/09/EOIRs22ImprovementsProgress060509FINAL.pdf.*

[53] TRAC Immigration, *Supporting Details: Implementation of the 22 Improvement Measures*, *available at* http://trac.syr.edu/immigration/reports/194/details.html (last visited Feb. 14, 2015).

[54] The NTA replaced the old Form I-221 Order to Show Cause, which was the charging document used to commence deportation proceedings, and the old Form I-122, Notice to Applicant for Admission Detained for Hearing before an Immigration Judge, which was the charging document used to commence exclusion proceedings. *See* 8 CFR §1003.13 (2014).

[55] 8 CFR §§1003.13, 1003.14 (2014); ICPM, chapter 4.2(a).

[56] 8 CFR §1003.15 (2014).

- The nature of the proceedings;
- The legal authority under which the proceedings are conducted;
- The acts or conduct alleged to be in violation of the law;
- The charge(s) against the individual and the statutory provision(s) alleged to have been violated;
- Notice of the opportunity to be represented by counsel at no expense to the government;[57]
- The requirement that the individual immediately provide the Attorney General with a written record of an address and telephone number and written notice of any future change of address or telephone number;[58]
- The time and place of the proceedings;[59] and
- The consequences of failing to appear at scheduled hearings, including a warning that a removal order will be entered *in absentia* if the Respondent fails to appear, unless there are exceptional circumstances.[60]

If the NTA filed with the immigration court does not contain all of this specific information, it does not meet the requirements for the initiation of removal proceedings under INA §239(a)(1).

The NTA also must be served on the respondent in a particular manner.[61] The INA and regulations require that the NTA be served on the respondent in person, or if personal service is not practicable, by mail to the respondent *or* the respondent's counsel of record.[62] Thus, if the respondent did not receive the NTA in person or by mail, and if the respondent's attorney did not receive the NTA by mail, service was

[57] After 10 days, the Attorney General may proceed. INA §239(b).

[58] INA §239(a)(1)(F)(ii). *See* 8 CFR §1003.15(d)(2) (2014) (stating that the notice of change of address should be provided to the immigration court on Form EOIR-33).

[59] *But see* INA §239(a)(2)(A) (noting that the time and place of the proceedings may be postponed or may change, and stating that written notice must be given to the Respondent in person or, if personal service is not practicable, by mail to the Respondent or the Respondent's counsel). Failure to note the date and time of the hearing on the NTA does not render the NTA ineffective, as long as a subsequent notice of the hearing was sent to the Respondent. *Popa v. Holder*, 571 F.3d 890 (9th Cir. 2009); *Dababneh v. Gonzales*, 471 F.3d 806 (7th Cir. 2006); *Guamanrrigra v. Holder*, 670 F.3d 404 (2d Cir. 2012); *Haider v. Gonzales*, 438 F.3d 902, 906–08 (8th Cir. 2006). The subsequent notice must state the new time and place for the hearing and the consequences of failing to appear. INA §239(a)(2)(A)(ii). Notice is not required at all, however, if the Respondent failed to provide a change of address. INA §239(a)(2)(B).

[60] INA §239(a)(1)(G)(ii).

[61] INA §239(a)(1); 8 CFR §1003.13 (2014).

[62] INA §239(a)(1); 8 CFR §1003.13 (2014). Note that, for cases commenced prior to April 1, 1997, the Form I-221, Order to Show Cause, initiated proceedings before the immigration court. The regulations require that an Order to Show Cause be served "in person to the alien, or by *certified mail* to the alien or the alien's attorney." 8 CFR §1003.13 (2014) (emphasis added). However, certified mail is no longer required for service of a Notice to Appear. *See id.*

improper. If service was improper and the respondent never received the NTA, the respondent was never notified of the initiation of removal proceedings, and an immigration judge may not order the respondent removed *in absentia* for failure to appear.[63]

Once the NTA has been filed with the immigration court, a court staff member will enter the case information in the EOIR database, which automatically schedules the matter for a master calendar hearing.

> ➢ **Practice Pointer**: Practitioners may determine a client's next hearing date by calling the EOIR hotline at 1-800-898-7180 and entering the client's A-number. The hotline also includes information regarding case processing, decisions, appeals, and filings.

The parties to immigration court proceedings include the "Respondent" — the individual who has been charged with removability by DHS — and the Department of Homeland Security itself.[64] DHS enforces the immigration and nationality laws and attorneys who work for DHS's component, U.S. Immigration and Customs Enforcement (ICE), represent the U.S. government's interests in immigration proceedings.[65] The DHS representative is often referred to as the "Assistant Chief Counsel" or government attorney.[66] The respondent may appear in proceedings with or without representation.[67] Upon request of the respondent or his or her representative, the IJ has the authority to waive the appearance of the respondent or his or her representative at specific hearings in removal proceedings.[68]

An IJ may conduct immigration court hearings in person, by videoconference, or by telephone conference.[69] Evidentiary hearings on the merits, however, may only be held by telephone if the respondent consents after being notified of the right to proceed in person or by videoconference.[70]

For hearings conducted by video or telephone conference, it is not required that the IJ, respondent, DHS attorney, and witnesses are present together in the same location.[71] For hearings conducted by video or telephone conference, documents must be filed with the immigration court having administrative control over the Record of

---

[63] *Matter of G–Y–R–*, 23 I&N Dec. 181 (BIA 2001).

[64] ICPM, chapter 4.3.

[65] ICPM, chapter 1.5(e).

[66] ICPM, chapter 4.3.

[67] ICPM, chapter 4.4. *See* 8 CFR §1292.1 (2014). *See also infra* pt. VII.D for a detailed discussion of representation in proceedings before the immigration court.

[68] 8 CFR §1003.25(a) (2014); ICPM, chs. 4.6, 4.15(m).

[69] ICPM, chapter 4.6.

[70] INA §240(b)(2); 8 CFR §1003.25(c) (2014); ICPM, chs. 4.6, 4.7(a).

[71] ICPM, chapter 4.7(b).

Proceedings. IJs often will allow documents to be faxed between the parties and the IJ during the hearings.[72]

Immigration court hearings proceed promptly on the date and time that the hearing is scheduled. If the Respondent is late to appear at a master calendar or individual hearing, the hearing may be held *in absentia* and he or she may be ordered removed.[73]

Hearings in immigration court are generally open to the public. However, applicants may request that evidentiary hearings involving applications for asylum, withholding of removal under INA §241(b)(3), or protection under the Convention Against Torture be closed, and an IJ must inquire whether the respondent requests such closure.[74] Additionally, hearings involving an abused child or spouse are closed to the public.[75] A party to the proceedings may make an oral or written motion asking the IJ to close a hearing, and IJs are authorized to close hearings that normally would be open to the public.[76]

Immigration court hearings are recorded electronically by the IJ.[77] On occasion, the IJ may authorize an off-the-record discussion; however, such discussions must then be summarized by the IJ on the record. The IJ asks the parties if the summary is accurate and complete and the parties are given the opportunity to add to or amend the summary.[78]

> ➢ **Practice Pointer**: If the IJ does not offer a summary of the off-the-record discussion after going back on the record, practitioners should request such a summary by the IJ.[79]

If an IJ's decision is appealed to the BIA, the recording of the proceedings is used to create a transcript to be sent to both parties.[80]

The official file containing the documents relating to the respondent and his or her proceedings is called the "Record of Proceedings," and is created and controlled by the immigration court.[81] The contents of the Record of Proceedings varies from case to case; however, at the conclusion of immigration court proceedings, the Record of Proceedings generally contains the following:

- The Form I-862, Notice to Appear or other charging document;

---

[72] ICPM, chapter 4.7(d).

[73] 8 CFR §1003.26 (2014); ICPM, chapter 4.8, 4.15, 4.16, 4.17.

[74] ICPM, chapter 4.9(a)(i).

[75] *Id.*; 8 CFR §§1003.27, 1003.31(d), 1003.46, 1208.6, 1240.10(b), 1240.11(c)(3)(i) (2014).

[76] 8 CFR §1003.27(b) (2014); ICPM, chapter 4.9(a)(iii).

[77] 8 CFR §1240.9 (2014); ICPM, 4.10(a)

[78] ICPM, 4.10(a).

[79] *Id.*

[80] ICPM, 4.10(b).

[81] 8 CFR §1003.36 (2014).

- Hearing notices;
- The Form EOIR-28, Notice of Entry of Appearance for any attorney or representative;
- Any Forms EOIR-33/IC Change of Address;
- The respondent's applications for relief;
- Any exhibits, motions, witness lists, or briefs;
- Recordings of the hearings; and
- All written orders and decisions of the IJ.[82]

> ➢ **Practice Pointer**: Practitioners should always keep in mind that all filings and submissions to the immigration court, as well as all testimony and oral arguments and requests made throughout the course of the proceedings, make up the Record of Proceedings. It is this record that the BIA will rely upon in making any determination on appeal. Thus, it is essential that practitioners litigate with an eye toward appeal and make sure that all significant facts, legal arguments, and objections are on the record in case an appeal eventually becomes necessary.

III. Who is Eligible to Apply for Defensive Protections?

An individual who is physically present in the United States and served with a Form I-862, Notice to Appear or other charging document that has been filed with the immigration court may apply defensively for asylum, withholding of removal, and protection under CAT before an IJ.[83] The information provided by an applicant in an asylum application filed on or after January 4, 1995, may be used as a basis for initiating removal proceedings and to satisfy ICE's burden of proof in exclusion, deportation, or removal proceedings.[84] Thus, even if the applicant filed affirmatively, he or she must proceed before an IJ if the charging document has been filed with the immigration court.[85] On rare occasions, ICE may file a motion to dismiss on the grounds that, among other reasons, the NTA was improvidently issued or that circumstances have changed to such an extent that the continuation of the case is no longer in the best interest of the government.[86] The motion, however, must be

---

[82] ICPM, chapter 4.10(c).

[83] 8 CFR §§208.2(b), 1208.2(b), 1240.1(a) (2014).

[84] 8 CFR §§208.3(c)(1), 1208.3(c)(1) (2014).

[85] 8 CFR §§208.2(b), 1208.2(b) (2014); *see also, e.g., Matter of P–L–P–*, 21 I&N Dec. 887 (BIA 1997) (finding that an applicant who was issued a charging document on the day he filed his asylum application with legacy INS could not proceed with his affirmative application).

[86] 8 CFR §§239.2(a)(6), (a)(7), (c), and 1239.2(c) (2014); *see also Matter of G–N–C–*, 22 I&N Dec. 281 (BIA 1998), *criticized on other grounds by Castro-Cortez v. INS*, 239 F.3d 1037, 1052 (9th Cir. 2001).

adjudicated on the record like any other motion before the IJ or the BIA.[87] If the immigration court proceedings are dismissed, the applicant may be able to pursue an affirmative claim, if other bars do not apply.

If the applicant had applied affirmatively, the NTA filed with the immigration court will contain a copy of the asylum application, along with any supporting documentation.[88] Under no circumstances, however, should any document containing references to the asylum officer's credibility findings be filed with the immigration court.[89] The BIA in a June 14, 2005, asylum appeal remanded the case for a new hearing because the IJ had admitted into evidence an asylum officer's completed assessment that included numerous credibility findings.[90] The BIA found that a revised operating policy and procedures memorandum issued in 2000 precluded this admission.[91]

> ➢ **Practice Pointer**: Some asylum applicants, such as individuals refused admission at a port of entry under the Visa Waiver Program, are permitted "asylum only" hearings before an IJ.[92] See chapter 6 for a detailed discussion on proceedings for Visa Waiver Program applicants for admission, overstays, and status violators.

By regulation, any application for asylum is deemed to be an application for withholding of removal.[93] Unlike asylum, an individual cannot apply affirmatively for withholding of removal under INA §241(b)(3) or relief under the CAT.[94] Only IJs may grant withholding of removal or CAT[95] protection to an individual who qualifies for such relief. The IJ will also determine whether an applicant is barred from asylum

---

[87] *Matter of G–N–C–*, 22 I&N Dec. 281 (BIA 1998), *criticized on other grounds by Castro-Cortez v. INS*, 239 F.3d 1037, 1052 (9th Cir. 2001).

[88] *See* EOIR Memorandum from Michael J. Creppy on Revised Operating Policy and Procedures Memorandum No. 00-01, Asylum Request Processing at 14 (Aug. 4, 2000), *available at www.usdoj.gov/eoir/efoia/ocij/ oppm00/OPPM00-01Revised.pdf.*

[89] *Id.*

[90] This BIA case is available at *www.lexisnexis.com/practiceareas/immigration/pdfs/web846.pdf.*

[91] Creppy Memorandum on Asylum Request Processing, *supra* note 88.

[92] *See* 8 CFR §§208.2(b), (c)(1)(iii), 1208.2(b), (c)(1)(iii) (2014); *see also Matter of Kanagasundram*, 22 I&N Dec. 963 (BIA 1999) (finding that legacy INS had improperly placed an asylum applicant from Sri Lanka in expedited removal proceedings and that applicant was entitled to an immediate referral to an IJ for an asylum hearing, despite the fact that he sought entry on a passport from the Netherlands under the Visa Waiver Pilot Program).

[93] 8 CFR §§208.3(b), 1208.3(b) (2014).

[94] 8 CFR §208.16(a) (2014). *See* INS Memorandum from Joseph Langlois, Implementation of Amendments to Asylum and Withholding of Removal Regulations, Effective March 22, 1999, at 6 (Mar. 18, 1999).

[95] Convention Against Torture and Other Cruel, Inhuman or Degrading Treatment or Punishment, Dec. 10, 1984, 1465 U.N.T.S. 85 (entered into force June 26, 1987).

or withholding of removal based on one or more of the grounds of ineligibility or statutory bars.[96]

- **Practice Pointer**: Individuals subject to expedited removal, reinstatement of removal, or administrative removal for aggravated felonies are also permitted to apply for withholding of removal under INA §241(b)(3) and/or relief under the CAT. Their claims are initially screened by an asylum officer. See chapter 6 for a detailed discussion of expedited removal and reinstatement of removal.

Individuals who are not physically present are ineligible for asylum and withholding of removal under INA §241(b)(3).[97] According to the implementing legislation for the CAT, however:

> [It is] the policy of the United States not to expel, extradite, or otherwise effect the involuntary return of any person to a country in which there are substantial grounds for believing the person would be in danger of being subjected to torture, *regardless of whether the person is physically present in the United States*.[98]

The regulations issued by legacy INS and EOIR after the passage of FARRA only address procedures for individuals physically present in the United States. According to legacy INS, FARRA required the implementation of only article 3 of the Convention, which the agency reasoned, like article 33 of the Refugee Convention, does not extend to individuals outside of the United States. As justification for this position, legacy INS cited *Sale v. Haitian Centers Council, Inc.*[99] Legacy INS stated, however, that individuals interdicted in international waters will be screened for CAT claims and will not be returned if they would be subjected to torture upon return. In addition, it appears that at least some individuals released from the Guantanamo prison facility who fear they will be tortured in their home countries have been sent to third countries by the United States.[100]

---

[96] *See supra* chapter 2 for a detailed discussion of the statutory bars to asylum and withholding of removal.

[97] INA §§208(a)(1), 241(b)(3).

[98] Foreign Affairs Reform and Restructuring Act of 1998, §2242(a), 112 Stat. 2681–822 (emphasis added).

[99] *Sale v. Haitian Centers Council, Inc.*, 509 U.S. 155 (1993).

[100] Tim Golden, *Chinese Leave Guantanamo for Albanian Limbo*, N.Y. Times June 10, 2007, at A1 (five Muslim men from the Uighur ethnic minority in Western China were found to pose no threat to the United States and released from Guantanamo prison in Cuba. They have been sent to Albania and are currently living in a refugee center there).

IV. Required Notices to Asylum and Withholding of Removal Applicants

The statute and regulations require that applicants for asylum and withholding of removal be notified of certain rights and warnings regarding the application process. These notices apply regardless whether the individual is applying affirmatively before the asylum office or defensively through the immigration court.[101] These include notice of the applicant's right to be represented, notice of the consequences of filing a frivolous application, notice that information may be used to initiate removal proceedings or used by the government to satisfy its burden of proof, and notice of confidentiality.

A. Notice of Right to Be Represented

At the time the applicant files for asylum and withholding of removal, the U.S. AG is required to notify the applicant of the privilege of being represented by counsel and to provide the applicant with a list of pro bono representatives.[102] Under the Homeland Security Act of 2002, this responsibility to give notice extends to the Secretary of the Department of Homeland Security and other DHS officials.[103] In proceedings before an asylum officer, an immigration judge, or the Board of Immigration Appeals, asylum and withholding of removal applicants may be represented by attorneys, law school students or graduates, reputable individuals of good moral character, accredited representatives, or accredited officials.[104]

B. Notice of Consequences of Filing a Frivolous Application

At the time the applicant files for asylum (if on or after April 1, 1997), the attorney general also is required to notify the applicant of the consequences of knowingly filing a frivolous application.[105] Several courts have held that the written warning contained in the I-589 Application for Asylum and for Withholding of

---

[101] *See supra* chapter 7 for a detailed discussion of affirmative asylum procedures.

[102] INA §208(d)(4); 8 USC §1158(d)(4) (2012); 8 CFR §1240.11(c)(1)(iii) (2014) (regarding the immigration judge's (IJ) duty to notify); *see also* app'x 9A, I-589 filing instructions, section IV: Right to Counsel (containing this notice and a toll-free number and website address to access for a list of attorneys and accredited representatives).

[103] *See* Homeland Security Act of 2002, Pub. L. No. 107-296, §§456, 1512, 1517, 116 Stat. 2135, 2200, 2310, 2311.

[104] *See generally* 8 CFR §§292.1, 1292.1 (2014).

[105] INA §208(d)(4)(A); 8 USC §1158(d)(4)(A) (2012); *see also* 8 CFR §§208.3(c)(5), 1208.3(c)(5), 1240.11(c)(1)(iii) (2014) (regarding DHS and IJ duty to notify). Under the Homeland Security Act of 2002, this responsibility to give notice extends to the DHS secretary and other DHS officials. *See* Homeland Security Act of 2002, Pub. L. No. 107-296, §§456, 1512, 1517, 116 Stat. 2135, 2200, 2310, 2311; *see also* Appx. 2A, I-589 filing instructions (containing the following warning: "Applicants determined to have knowingly made a frivolous application for asylum will be permanently ineligible for any benefits under the [INA].").

Removal is sufficient to comply with the statutory and regulatory notice requirements.[106]

An individual who knowingly makes a frivolous asylum application after receiving notice of the consequences of doing so is "permanently ineligible for any benefits under the [INA]."[107] The ineligibility for benefits under the INA is effective as of the date of the final determination on the application.[108] A finding that an applicant filed a frivolous application, however, is not a bar to withholding of removal relief, nor is it a bar to relief under the CAT.[109]

- ➢ **Practice Pointer**: The knowing placement of false information on an asylum application may also subject the applicant (or the person who placed the information on the application) to criminal and civil penalties.[110]

An applicant may be permanently barred from relief only if a final order by an IJ or the BIA specifically finds that the applicant knowingly filed a frivolous application.[111] The regulations provide that an asylum application is "frivolous" if "any of its material elements is deliberately fabricated."[112] A preponderance of the evidence must support the frivolousness finding,[113] and the IJ must give specific and convincing reasons for determining that a preponderance of the evidence supports a frivolousness finding.[114] Additionally, the IJ or the BIA must be "satisfied" that during the course of the proceedings the applicant "has had sufficient opportunity to account for any discrepancies or implausible aspects of the claim."[115] An IJ may not base a frivolous determination on merely an adverse credibility assessment.[116]

---

[106] *Niang v. Holder*, 762 F.3d 251 (2d Cir. 2014) (finding that the written warning on the I-589 application was adequate notice of the consequences of filing a frivolous asylum application); *Ruga v. U.S. Att'y Gen.*, 757 F.3d 1193 (11th Cir. 2014) (stating that "At least two other courts of appeals have concluded that delivery of this warning in the application itself, or at the time of the interview, suffices. *Ribas v. Mukasey,* 545 F.3d 922 (10th Cir.2008); *Cheema v. Holder,* 693 F.3d 1045 (9th Cir.2012). This court said the same thing in *Siddique v. Mukasey,* 547 F.3d 814 (7th Cir.2008). If it was not a holding then, it becomes a holding now."); *Pavlov v. Holder*, 697 F.3d 616 (7th Cir. 2012) (finding that the written advisals provided on the I-589 are sufficient notice); *Cheema v. Holder*, 693 F.3d 1045 (9th Cir. 2012) (same); *Ribas v. Mukasey*, 545 F.3d 922, 928 (10th Cir. 2008) (same).

[107] INA §208(d)(6); 8 CFR §§208.3(c)(5), 1208.3(c)(5).

[108] INA §208(d)(6); 8 USC §1158(d)(6).

[109] 8 CFR §§208.20, 1208.20.

[110] 8 CFR §§208.3(c)(4), 1208.3(c)(4) (2014).

[111] 8 CFR §§208.20, 1208.20 (2014).

[112] 8 CFR §§208.20, 1208.20 (2014).

[113] *Matter of Y–L–*, 24 I&N Dec. 151, 157 (BIA 2007); *Ahir v. Mukasey*, 527 F.3d 912, 917 (9th Cir. 2008).

[114] *Matter of Y–L–*, 24 I&N Dec. 151 (BIA 2007).

[115] 8 CFR §§208.20, 1208.20 (2014)*; see also Matter of Y–L–*, 24 I&N Dec. 151 (BIA 2007) (holding that an IJ must make a separate and specific finding regarding frivolousness and must give the applicant the opportunity to account for discrepancies); *Matter of [name not provided]*, A94 097 292 (BIA June

Continued

> ➢ **Practice Pointer**: See chapter 4 for a detailed discussion of frivolous asylum applications and the legal standards that must be met for an adjudicator to make a finding of frivolousness.

C. Notice that Information May be Used to Initiate Removal Proceedings and Satisfy the Government's Burden of Proof

The information provided by an applicant in an asylum application filed on or after January 4, 1995, may be used as a basis for initiating removal proceedings and to satisfy DHS's burden of proof in exclusion, deportation, or removal proceedings.[117]

D. Notice of Confidentiality

The Form I-589, Application for Asylum and Withholding of Removal provides:

> [N]o information indicating that you have applied for asylum will be provided to any government or country from which you claim a fear of persecution. Regulations at 8 CFR §208.6 protect the confidentiality of asylum claims.[118]

Under 8 CFR §§208.6, 1208.6, DHS and EOIR shall not disclose any information contained in or pertaining to any asylum application, any records pertaining to any

---

21, 2000), *reported in* 77 INTERPRETER RELEASES 1091–92 (July 31, 2000) (in this unpublished decision, the BIA overturned the IJ's "frivolous" finding based on a determination that the claim was "baseless" and exaggerated); *Aziz v. Gonzales*, 478 F.3d 854, 857 (8th Cir. 2007) (upholding IJ's finding that the applicant from Iraq filed a frivolous asylum application); *Sterkaj v. Gonzales*, 439 F.3d 273, 279 (6th Cir. 2006) (upholding frivolous finding where applicant submitted a fraudulent summons and "wanted" document); *Kifleyesus v. Gonzales*, 462 F.3d 937, 945 (8th Cir. 2006) (upholding IJ's frivolousness finding where the applicant filed a false application, failed to modify it, swore to the truth of the application, and was given sufficient opportunity to account for discrepancies); *Mingkid v. U.S. Att'y Gen.*, 468 F.3d 763, 770 (11th Cir. 2006) (finding that IJ failed to give the applicants a proper opportunity to explain any discrepancies); *Selami v. Gonzales*, 423 F.3d 621, 622 (6th Cir. 2005) (upholding the IJ's finding that the applicant submitted a frivolous application where the applicant submitted a fraudulent newspaper article and was given an opportunity to explain, but failed to articulate any explanation); *Farah v. Ashcroft*, 348 F.3d 1153 (9th Cir. 2003) (overturning frivolous determination where applicant was not given the opportunity to explain discrepancies); *Efe v. Ashcroft*, 293 F.3d 899 (5th Cir. 2002) (upholding frivolousness determination where applicant was given ample opportunity to clarify his testimony); *Barreto-Claro v. Att'y Gen.*, 275 F.3d 1334 (11th Cir. 2001) (upholding the finding of frivolousness).

[116] *Alexandrov v. Gonzales*, 442 F.3d 395, 407 (6th Cir. 2006) (finding that the IJ violated the applicant's due process rights by relying on two State Department reports in finding that the applicant's asylum application was frivolous); *Muhanna v. Gonzales*, 399 F.3d 582, 589 (3d Cir. 2005) (the court found that "by imposing a frivolousness finding based not on a thorough examination of the application but instead on her assessment of [the applicant's] credibility, and by consequently refusing to allow further testimony, the IJ ... deprived [the applicant] of due process.")

[117] 8 CFR §§208.3(c)(1), 1208.3(c)(1) (2014); *see also* Appx. 2A, I-589 filing instructions (containing the following warning: "Any information provided in completing this application may be used as a basis for the institution of, or as evidence in, removal proceedings, even if the application is later withdrawn").

[118] Appx 2A, I-589 filing instructions, section III.

credible fear determination under 8 CFR §208.30, and any records pertaining to any reasonable fear determination under 8 CFR §208.31 without the written consent of the applicant.[119] DHS and EOIR also must keep confidential any records that indicate that an individual has applied for asylum, received a credible fear or reasonable fear interview, or received a credible fear or reasonable fear review.[120] If any records need to be transmitted to the Department of State in other countries, DHS and EOIR are required to coordinate with the Department of State to ensure that the confidentiality of those records is maintained.[121] Under the Homeland Security Act of 2002, this duty of confidentiality extends to the DHS secretary and other DHS officials.[122]

There are exceptions to this duty of confidentiality, however, including for the disclosure of information or records to U.S. government officials or contractors who need to examine it in connection with the adjudication of asylum applications, the consideration of a request for a credible fear or reasonable fear interview or review, the defense of any legal action related to an asylum application or credible fear or reasonable fear determination, or any U.S. government investigation.[123] The otherwise confidential information or records may also be disclosed to any federal, state, or local court in the United States considering any legal action related to the adjudication of or proceedings for an asylum application or a credible fear or reasonable fear determination.[124] The broadest exception, found at 8 CFR §§208.6(a), 1208.6(a), allows for the disclosure of asylum information and records "*at the discretion of the Attorney General.*"[125]

V. What Are the Components of a Defensive Application for Protection?

As with an affirmative asylum application, a defensive application for asylum, withholding of removal, or protection under CAT begins with the completion of the Form I-589, Application for Asylum and for Withholding of Removal (I-589 or Form I-589). An asylum application is incomplete if the I-589 does not include a response to each question, is unsigned, or is unaccompanied by the required supporting documents or copies.[126]

---

[119] 8 CFR §§208.6(a), 1208.6(a) (2014).

[120] 8 CFR §§208.6(b), 1208.6(b) (2014).

[121] *Id.*

[122] *See* Homeland Security Act of 2002, Pub. L. No. 107-296, §§456, 1512, 1517, 116 Stat. 2135, 2200, 2310, 2311. For further discussion of confidentiality, see this chapter, at 3.3.5.

[123] 8 CFR §§208.6(c)(1), 1208.6(c)(1) (2014).

[124] 8 CFR §§208.6(c)(2), 1208.6(c)(2) (2014).

[125] 8 CFR §§208.6(a), 1208.6(a) (emphasis added) (2014).

[126] 8 CFR §§208.3(c)(3), 1208.3(c)(3) (2014).

- **Practice Pointer**: Rather than leaving blank answer spaces on the I-589, practitioners should write "Not Applicable," "None," or "Unknown." Blank answers may result in the application not being properly filed.[127]

If an affirmative asylum application has been referred to the IJ for consideration, the asylum office will file the referral packet with the immigration court, and once it is filed with the court, the asylum office no longer has jurisdiction over the asylum claim.[128] The referral packet contains a photocopy of the I-589 reflecting any changes made during the affirmative asylum interview, copies of all documents in support of the I-589 application, the Notice to Appear with the original signature of the USCIS officer who signed and dated the document on page 1, a printout of the removal screen from the computer database showing the hearing date, time, and location, and a printout of the employment authorization clock screen.[129] The asylum office also will prepare the file for the ICE Office of the Principal Legal Advisor by ensuring that it contains a copy of the NTA, Referral Notice, and marked-up I-589. The file will be transferred to ICE, which represents the government in the immigration court hearing.[130]

- **Practice Pointer**: Usually, the application and supporting documentation that is referred to the immigration court is not in the same order in which it was submitted to the asylum office. Thus, IJs sometimes will request that the applicant resubmit his or her application materials in accordance with the ICPM (*i.e.*, with a cover page, index of exhibits, lettered side tabs for exhibits, page numbers, and proof of service and two-hole punched at the top and bound). Practitioners should always make an appointment at the immigration court to review the court's file. If practitioners represented the client before the asylum office, reviewing the file allows the practitioner to confirm that all supporting documentation was, in fact, forwarded to the court from the asylum office and that it has become a part of the Record of Proceeding. On the other hand, if practitioners did not represent the client before the asylum office, reviewing the file enables the practitioner to learn what documentation has already been filed in support of the claim. Most immigration courts have specific procedures for file review that can be found on the courts' websites. These procedures change frequently, so practitioners should always research current practices in the relevant court prior to appearing to request file review.

---

[127] U.S. Citizenship and Immigration Servs., I-589 Instructions, at 4, *available at www.uscis.gov/sites/default/files/files/form/i-589instr.pdf* (last visited Jan. 30, 2015).

[128] 8 CFR §208.2(b) (2014).

[129] USCIS, *Affirmative Asylum Procedures Manual*, Part II.R.3.a. (Nov. 2013), *available at www.uscis.gov/sites/default/files/files/nativedocuments/Asylum_Procedures_Manual_2013.pdf* (last visited Jan. 22, 2015).

[130] *Id.* at II.R.3.b.

However, individuals also apply for asylum for the first time before the immigration court. A defensive asylum application filed directly with a U.S. immigration court should include the following components:

- Form EOIR-28, Notice of Entry of Appearance;[131]
- Cover page for court filings;[132]
- Form I-589, Application for Asylum and for Withholding of Removal, signed and dated on page 9 by the applicant;[133]
- One passport-sized photograph of the applicant attached to page 9 of the I-589;
- Index of Exhibits or Table of Contents listing the components of the filing;[134]
- Sworn Statement by the applicant, detailing his or her claims;
- Identity documentation for the applicant;
- Evidence of the applicant's most recent entry to the United States;
- Identity documentation for any derivative applicants;
- Documentation establishing the derivative applicants' relationship to the principal applicant (birth certificates, or marriage certificate with divorce decree if the principal applicant or his or her spouse was previously married);
- Evidence that corroborates and supports the applicant's claims;[135]
- Country reports and articles describing the current conditions in the applicant's country of feared persecution or torture;
- Certified English translations for any documents that are not in English;[136]
- Proof of Service.[137]

To date, there is no fee for filing a defensive application for asylum, nor is there a biometrics/fingerprinting fee.[138] The statute, however, permits the AG to impose a

---

[131] *See* ICPM, chapters 2.1(b), 2.3(c), 3.3(c)(i)(A).

[132] *See* ICPM, app'x F.

[133] *See* Dree Collopy & Lisa Green, AILA Practice Pointer, Completing the Form I-589 (July 14, 2014), AILA InfoNet Doc. No. 14071402 (posted on July 14, 2014).

[134] *See* ICPM, chapter 3.3(c)(i)(A) and app'x P.

[135] *See supra* chapter 4 for a detailed discussion of the evidentiary requirements for establishing asylum eligibility, as well as a list of suggested forms of supporting evidence.

[136] 8 CFR §1003.33 (2014) ("Any foreign language document offered by a party in a proceeding shall be accompanied by an English language translation and a certification signed by the translator that must be printed legibly or typed. Such certification must include a statement that the translator is competent to translate the document, and that the translation is true and accurate to the best of the translator's abilities."). *See also* ICPM, chapter 3.3(a) and app'x. H.

[137] *See* ICPM, chapter 3.3(c)(i)(A) and app'x. G.

[138] 8 CFR §1103.7(b)(4) (2014).

fee.[139] Similarly, there is no fee for withholding of removal under INA §241(b)(3) or protection under the CAT.

> ➤ **Practice Pointer**: Practitioners who prepare and file defensive I-589 applications for asylum, withholding of removal, or CAT protection on behalf of their clients must prepare and file a Form EOIR-28, Notice of Entry of Appearance, available at *www.justice.gov/eoir/eoirforms/eoir28.pdf*,[140] and the ICPM recommends that it be printed on **green** paper.[141] A copy of the form must be served on DHS.

The Form I-589, Application for Asylum and for Withholding of Removal (I-589) is revised approximately every two years. The current application form was revised on December 29, 2014. The I-589 requires biographic information about the applicant, his or her entry to the United States and prior U.S. immigration history, biographic information about the applicant's spouse and children, the applicant's last address abroad and his or her address history for the last five years, the applicant's education, the applicant's employment history for the last five years, the applicant's parents and siblings and their current locations, the protected grounds on which the applicant's claim is based, the harm suffered in the past and future harm feared, the applicant's journey to the United States, his or her legal status in any other countries, and any bars to relief that may apply.[142]

> ➤ **Practice Pointer**: An applicant may include his or her spouse and/or unmarried children under age 21 on his or her I-589 application. However, if the application is considered in removal proceedings before the immigration court, the judge may not have the authority to grant asylum to any spouse or child included in the application who is not also in proceedings.[143]

The I-589 application form requires significant detail and precise information that is consistent with all other documentation presented, including the applicant's own sworn statement. It is essential that every single question on the I-589 has a response, even if the response is "N/A — Not Applicable" or "None." Otherwise, the application may be rejected.[144]

---

[139] INA §208(d)(3); 8 USC §1158(d)(3) (2012). Under the Homeland Security Act of 2002, this authority would extend to the DHS secretary. *See* Homeland Security Act of 2002, Pub. L. No. 107-296, §§456, 1512, 1517, 116 Stat. 2135, 2200, 2310, 2311.

[140] (last visited Feb. 3, 2015).

[141] ICPM, chapter 11.2(f).

[142] *See* U.S. Customs and Immigration Servs., I-589, Application for Asylum and for Withholding of Removal, *available at www.uscis.gov/sites/default/files/files/form/i-589.pdf* (last visited Jan. 23, 2015).

[143] *See* U.S. Customs and Immigration Servs., I-589 Instructions, at 5 (Dec. 29, 2014) [hereinafter I-589 Instructions], *available at www.uscis.gov/sites/default/files/files/form/i-589instr.pdf*.

[144] I-589 Instructions, *supra* note 143, at 9; Collopy & Green, Practice Pointer: Completing the Form I-589, *supra* note 133.

- ➢ **Practice Pointer**: It is important for practitioners to use the current I-589 when preparing their clients' asylum applications, as using an outdated form could result in the rejection of the application. Practitioners should check the USCIS website for the most recent version of the I-589 form and to determine what previous versions, if any, are still accepted.[145]
- ➢ **Practice Pointer**: For specific practice pointers and question-by-question guidance on completing the Form I-589, see AILA's "Practice Pointer: Completing the Form I-589," posted on July 14, 2014, on AILA InfoNet at Doc. No. 14071402.[146] This practice pointer is also available in this book at Appx. 2C.

The applicant must sign and date the I-589 in Part D. By signing the application, the applicant is indicating his or her awareness of the contents of the application and declaring under penalty of perjury that all statements in response to the questions are true and correct.[147] The applicant's signature at Part G. is not to be completed until he or she is placed in removal proceedings and it must be signed before the immigration judge.[148]

An I-589 application for protection will be considered incomplete and rejected upon receipt in each of the following situations:

- The application does not include a response to each of the questions contained in Form I-589;
- The application is unsigned;
- The application is submitted without the required photograph; and
- The applicant indicated in Part D that someone prepared the application other than his or herself or an immediate family member, and the preparer failed to complete Part E of the asylum application.[149]

Although the Form I-589 has large answer spaces on pages five through eight for descriptions of harm and the applicant's fears, it is important for an applicant to prepare and submit a sworn personal statement in support of his or her application. It is also important that the applicant provide complete answers to these questions on the Form I-589 itself, as many IJs reject asylum application filings that do not contain substantive responses to the questions on the form.[150]

---

[145] *See* Form I-589, *supra* note 142. Both the Form I-589 and the instructions are available at this website.

[146] (last visited Jan. 23, 2015).

[147] I-589 Instructions, *supra* note 143, at 6.

[148] *Id.*

[149] I-589 Instructions, *supra* note 143, at 9.

[150] *See* Collopy & Green, Practice Pointer: Completing the Form I-589, *supra* note 133.

A well-drafted, well-organized, and compelling sworn statement is essential to any asylum claim. The purpose of the applicant's sworn statement is to tell the applicant's story with detail and a focus on the facts that demonstrate each legal element for the relief he or she is seeking. It also provides an opportunity in advance of in-person testimony for the applicant to connect with the adjudicator on a human level, while also addressing any difficult issues or negative discretionary factors. Given the impact that any inconsistency, no matter how minor, may have on the applicant's credibility, it is essential for his or her sworn statement to be entirely consistent with the Form I-589, as well as all other documentation submitted in support of his or her application.

➢ **Practice Pointer**: There are competing schools of thought regarding how much detail should be included in clients' sworn statements. Some practitioners prefer to present a general description of the applicant's story and to allow the applicant to provide detail during in-person testimony. They argue that doing so avoids potential inconsistencies between the applicant's written and oral testimony. While it is important to make this decision on a case-by-case basis, this author generally supports the other school of thought and suggests preparing sworn statements that are thorough and detailed. First, a thorough and detailed sworn statement gets all of the important facts on the record. Additionally, getting all of the details and writing them down enables practitioners to spot issues that may need further exploration and explanation. Making those explanations a part of the sworn statement is a way to address any concerns by the adjudicator before even setting foot in the interview or courtroom. Working on preparing a detailed declaration also forces the applicant to think through a sequential timeline of what happened first, next, last, and helps the applicant to avoid mixing up events and perceived inconsistencies. Moreover, learning a client's whole story takes gaining the client's trust, as well as hours and hours of time spent with the client. No asylum officer or immigration judge has that luxury. Finally, a detailed and thorough sworn statement can be a useful tool in assisting the applicant in preparing for his or her interview or hearing.

➢ **Practice Pointer**: Sworn statements do not need to be notarized, but should include the declaration, "I swear under penalty of perjury, under the laws of the United States, that the statements I have provided herein are true and correct to the best of my knowledge and belief," followed by the applicant's dated signature. Any sworn statement that is not written in English must be accompanied by a certified English translation.

➢ **Practice Pointer**: For helpful guidance on preparing and presenting powerful narratives on behalf of clients, practitioners should read the article "Beyond Saints and Sinners: Discretion and the Need for New

Narratives in the U.S. Immigration System" by Elizabeth Keyes[151] and the practice pointer "Storytelling & Immigration Law: A Practical Guide," by Erich Straub.[152]

In addition to the Form I-589 and sworn statement, supporting or corroborating evidence regarding an applicant's claim is an essential component of every asylum application. Under the REAL ID Act of 2005, "[w]here the trier of fact determines that an applicant should provide evidence that corroborates otherwise credible testimony, such evidence must be provided unless the applicant does not have the evidence and cannot reasonably obtain the evidence."[153] Thus, an applicant should provide "supporting evidence, both of general conditions and of the specific facts sought to be relied upon by the applicant, where such evidence is available," and where it is reasonable to expect such corroborating evidence.[154] In addition to documents related specifically to the asylum claim, an applicant is also expected to provide, if available, general corroborating evidence of persecution of similarly situated individuals.[155] Where such evidence is not available, the applicant must provide an explanation of why that evidence is unavailable.[156] An applicant is not, however, required to produce corroborating evidence that he or she could not

---

[151] Elizabeth Keyes, *Beyond Saints and Sinners: Discretion and the Need for New Narratives in the U.S. Immigration System*, 26 GEO. IMMIGR. L. J. 207 (Winter 2012).

[152] Erich Straub, *Storytelling & Immigration Law: A Practical Guide*, at 59–65, AILA'S IMMIGRATION PRACTICE POINTERS (2014–15 Ed.), available for download on AILA Agora.

[153] INA §§208(b)(1)(B)(ii), 240(c)(4). A similar provision exists for withholding of removal claims. *See* INA §241(b)(3)(C). In addressing the REAL ID Act's amendment to the corroboration requirements for asylum, withholding, and CAT claims, the Seventh Circuit has stated in dicta that "[i]t is possible that the change is less than meets the eye, since now there is no dispute about the appropriateness of asking for corroboration in the common situation when the IJ has some doubt about an applicant's credibility." *Dawoud v. Gonzales*, 424 F.3d 608, 613 (7th Cir. 2005).

[154] *Matter of S–M–J–*, 21 I&N Dec. 722, 724–25 (BIA 1997).

[155] *Id.* at 726. An example provided by the BIA of corroboration regarding similarly situated individuals is that of a union vice-president who would be expected to provide documentation regarding the persecution of union members in her home country. *Id. But see Abankwah v. INS*, 185 F.3d 18 (2d Cir. 1999) (finding that the BIA was too exacting in the quantity and quality of evidence that it required); *Duarte de Guinac v. INS*, 179 F.3d 1156, 1162 (9th Cir. 1999) (criticizing the BIA for concluding that reports of widespread racial discrimination against Indians in Guatemala did not support the applicant's claim, where country condition reports could not corroborate specific acts of persecution). Similarly, the asylum applicant in *Singh v. Ilchert* presented documents regarding widespread and arbitrary arrest, detention, and abuse of persons suspected of affiliation with separatists and, thereby, demonstrated the reasonableness of his assertion that his persecution was on account of a political opinion imputed to him. *Singh v. Ilchert*, 63 F.3d 1501, 1511–12 (9th Cir. 1995). *See also Matter of S–P–*, 21 I&N Dec. 486 (BIA 1996) (relying on a DOS report regarding conditions in Sri Lanka in finding that the applicant was persecuted on account of imputed political opinion).

[156] *Matter of O–D–*, 21 I&N Dec. 1079, 1081 (BIA 1998), *vacated on other grounds by Hanaj v. Gonzales*, 446 F.3d 694, 700 (7th Cir. 2006); *Matter of S–M–J–*, 21 I&N Dec. 722, 724 (BIA 1997). *See also Salaam v. INS*, 229 F.3d 1234, 1239 (9th Cir. 2000) (finding that the applicant provided a reasonable explanation for the absence of documents, including his haste in fleeing the country and the danger in carrying documents critical of the Nigerian government).

reasonably obtain.[157] Corroborating evidence may be presented in the form of any or all of the following:[158]

- Identity documents and other official government documents;
- Privately issued membership cards or other affiliation documents;[159]
- Affidavits from the applicant's family, friends, neighbors, or community members confirming his or her protected characteristic;
- Photographs of the applicant participating in various events;
- Letters from organizations of which the applicant is a member or affiliate;
- Objective, published descriptions of the characteristics or attributes, which designate members of the applicant's race, religion, nationality, political affiliation, or social group;
- Photographs of the applicant's injuries;
- Police reports recording the harm suffered or threatened;
- Arrest warrants or records, if the applicant was ever arrested due to his or her protected characteristic;[160]
- Affidavits from witnesses who were present during the act(s) of harm or mistreatment;
- Affidavits from individuals whom the applicant confided in about the incident(s), confirming any observed physical or psychological harm, such as markings on the applicant's body, torn clothes, injuries, crying, anxiety, or other unusual behaviors;
- Medical records, including evaluations of physical injuries and the likely cause of those injuries, letters from treating doctors, treatment reports, hospital admission records, or prescribed medications;
- Mental health records, including evaluations of mental health disorders and the likely trigger for those disorders, letters from treating mental health professionals, appointment records, or prescribed medications;

---

[157] INA §§208(b)(1)(B)(ii), 240(c)(4), 241(b)(3)(C). *See also, Soeung v. Holder*, 677 F.3d 484, 488 (1st Cir. 2012); *Yan Juan Chen v. Holder*, 658 F.3d 246 (2d Cir. 2011) (finding that it was reasonable to expect the undocumented husband to testify in his wife's case, despite his fear of arrest); *San Kai Kwok v. Gonzales*, 455 F.3d 766, 771 (7th Cir. 2006).

[158] Vikram Badrinath, Dree K. Collopy, & Hans Christian Linnartz, *Evidentiary Issues in Asylum Cases*, 2013 AILA'S IMMIGRATION PRACTICE POINTERS, (AILA 2013).

[159] *See, e.g., Camara v. Ashcroft*, 378 F.3d 361, 370–71 (4th Cir. 2004) (finding that the IJ erred by failing to consider independent evidence of persecution: *inter alia*, a notice of escape, a political party membership card, an arrest warrant, and DOS reports corroborating the applicant's claim).

[160] *See, e.g., Camara v. Ashcroft*, 378 F.3d 361, 370–71 (4th Cir. 2004) (finding that the IJ erred by failing to consider independent evidence of persecution: *inter alia*, a notice of escape, a political party membership card, an arrest warrant, and DOS reports corroborating the applicant's claim).

- Death certificates for the applicant's relatives, friends, neighbors, or community members who were targeted because of a qualifying characteristic;
- Newspaper or other media coverage, or coverage by human rights groups, of the incident(s) in which the applicant was involved;
- Evidence that the applicant attempted to supply certain corroborating documentation, but was unable to;
- I-94 card, visa, and stamped passport (even if false);
- Evidence of means of travel to the United States, including airline itineraries, bus tickets, or hotel receipts;
- Evidence of presence outside of the United States in the past year, including financial, medical, school, or work records;
- Affidavits from individuals who have personal knowledge of the applicant's arrival in the United States;
- Expert report regarding the conditions in the applicant's home country as they relate to the applicant's claims and assessing the applicant's risk of harm upon return;[161] and
- Country conditions reports and articles showing the conditions in the applicant's home country during the time of persecution and presently, including human rights reports from the U.S. Department of State, Amnesty International, Human Rights Watch, or other reputable organizations.[162]

Any foreign language document must be accompanied by an English language translation and a certification signed by the translator.[163] Such certification must include a statement that the translator is "competent to translate the document, and that the translation is true and accurate to the best of the translator's abilities."[164] If this exact regulatory language is not used, it is possible that the document will not be admitted as evidence in support of the applicant's claim for protection.

> ➢ **Practice Pointer**: The Immigration Court Practice Manual has a number of Appendices, which include samples of regularly filed

---

[161] *See, e.g.*, *Niam v. Ashcroft*, 354 F.3d 652, 658 (7th Cir. 2004) (noting that the scholar proffered by the applicant should have been considered an expert and that it was error for the IJ to refuse to allow her to testify telephonically from overseas).

[162] *See* 8 CFR §§208.12(a), 1208.12(a) (2014) (providing that adjudicators may rely on "other credible sources" for information on country conditions, such as international organizations, private voluntary agencies, news organizations, or academic institutions). *See*, *e.g.*, *Camara v. Ashcroft*, 378 F.3d 361, 370–71 (4th Cir. 2004) (finding that the IJ erred by failing to consider independent evidence of persecution: *inter alia*, a notice of escape, a political party membership card, an arrest warrant, and DOS reports corroborating the applicant's claim). *See supra* chapter 4 for a detailed discussion of the evidentiary requirements for establishing asylum eligibility, as well as a list of suggested forms of supporting evidence.

[163] 8 CFR §1003.33 (2014).

[164] *Id.*

documents in immigration court, such as a cover page, table of contents, certificate of translation, or proof of service.[165] These are very helpful tools for preparing documents that meet the regulatory and practice manual requirements.

When the principal applicant is including derivative applicants, such as a spouse or unmarried child under age 21, on his or her application, the applicant must submit evidence of the family relationship with any derivative applicant.[166] If the derivative applicant is a child, the relevant documentation is the child's birth certificate listing the principal applicant as the child's parent. If the derivative applicant is a spouse, the relevant documentation is the marriage certificate. If the applicant or derivative spouse was previously married, the divorce decree also must be submitted.[167] If the applicant does not have this primary evidence of relationship, he or she may submit secondary evidence, which may include, but is not limited to, medical records, school records, religious documents, or affidavits.[168] Relatives or others may provide affidavits, and the affiant need not be a U.S. citizen or lawful permanent resident.[169] Each affidavit should fully describe the event in question and explain how the affiant has personal knowledge of that event. The affidavit should be sworn and should list the affiant's full name, address, date and place of birth, and relationship to the principal applicant.[170]

Every application for protection filed with the immigration court must be accompanied by a proof of service.[171] A proof of service must include the following information: (1) the name or title of the party served; (2) the precise and complete address of the party served; (3) the date of service; (4) the means of service (e.g., hand delivery, regular mail, overnight mail, commercial courier, etc.); (5) a description of the document or documents being served; and (6) the name and signature of the person serving the document.[172]

The filing will be considered defective and will be rejected by the immigration court in the following situations:

- If it does not include a proof of service on the opposing party;
- If it does not comply with the language requirements;
- If it does not include the necessary signatures;

---

[165] *See* ICPM, at A-1 — Q-2, *available at www.justice.gov/eoir/vll/OCIJPracManual/Practice_Manual_review.pdf#page=25* (last visited Feb. 5, 2015).

[166] I-589 Instructions, *supra* note 143, at 5.

[167] *Id.*

[168] *Id. See also* 8 CFR §204.2(d)(2)(v) (2014).

[169] I-589 Instructions, *supra* note 143, at 5.

[170] *Id.*

[171] ICPM, chapter 3.2(e) and app'x. G; 8 CFR §1003.32(a) (2014).

[172] ICPM chapter 3.2(e)(i) and app'x. G.

- If it is not formatted correctly, as required by chapter 3 of the *Immigration Court Practice Manual*; and
- If it is illegible.[173]

The term "rejected" means that the filing is returned to the filing party because it is defective and therefore will not be considered by the immigration judge.[174] If a filing is rejected, the applicants should exercise due diligence to correct the error and refile promptly.[175]

As an incomplete, defective, or untimely filing could result in the individual's application for protection being rejected or denied, it is essential for applicants and their representatives to carefully review applications for protection prior to filing.

VI. What Are the Procedures for Filing a Defensive Application for Protection?

An IJ has exclusive jurisdiction over applications for protection filed by applicants who have been served with an NTA or other charging document, after the charging document has been filed with the immigration court.[176] Jurisdiction vests, and proceedings before the IJ commence, when the charging document is filed with the immigration court by DHS.[177]

If the applicant already filed an initial application with an asylum office, any information provided by the applicant in the application filed on or after January 4, 1995, may be used as a basis for initiating removal proceedings and to satisfy DHS's burden of proof in proceedings.[178] There is no need to file a new application if the claim is referred to an IJ.[179] As noted above, the asylum office will submit the previously filed application reflecting any changes made during the affirmative asylum interview, copies of all documents in support of the I-589 application, the NTA with the original signature of the USCIS officer who signed and dated the document, a printout of the removal screen from the computer database showing the hearing date, time, and location, and a printout of the employment authorization clock screen.[180] If there are errors in the previously filed application, or the applicant would

---

[173] ICPM, chapter 3.1(d)

[174] *Id.* at chapter 3.1(d)(i).

[175] *Id.* at chapter 3.1(d)(i).

[176] 8 CFR §§208.2(b), 1208.2(b), 1003.13(b) (2014).

[177] 8 CFR §1003.14(a) (2014).

[178] 8 CFR §§208.3(c)(1), 1208.3(c)(1) (2014).

[179] 8 CFR §1208.4 (2014).

[180] USCIS, *Affirmative Asylum Procedures Manual*, pt. II.R.3.a. (Nov. 2013), *available at www.uscis.gov/sites/default/files/files/nativedocuments/Asylum_Procedures_Manual_2013.pdf* (last visited Jan. 22, 2015).

like to provide additional details, the applicant may amend his or her application before the IJ.[181]

➢ **Practice Pointer**: Amendments to an I-589 may be made orally in court or may be submitted in writing. The applicant may submit amended pages, with the changes clearly reflected, by filing them with the immigration court in accordance with the court's filing deadlines and formatting requirements as set forth in the ICPM. Specifically, the amended pages should be accompanied by a cover page with the caption, "Amendment to Previously Filed Asylum Application."[182]

If the applicant is applying for asylum or other forms of protection for the first time in removal proceedings, his or her application is referred to as a defensive application.[183] The procedures for filing a defensive application for protection differ significantly from the procedures for filing an affirmative asylum application. A defensive application for asylum, withholding of removal, or protection under the CAT should be filed directly with the immigration court that has jurisdiction over the applicant's case.[184] However, the application may not be filed at the court's filing window or by mail or courier delivery. Rather, an applicant for asylum, withholding of removal, or protection under CAT must present his or her application in person in open court during a master calendar hearing before the IJ.[185]

The requirement to file an application in open court creates complications due to the one-year filing deadline for asylum eligibility; all applications for asylum must be filed within one year of the applicant's entry to the United States (with limited exceptions).[186] Since applicants and their representatives have little to no control over how the courts schedule their cases, whether or not the one-year filing deadline is met for asylum purposes is often out of the applicants' hands. It is essential for applicants to exercise due diligence to alert the court that they would like to timely file their applications and to seek the opportunity to do so.

➢ **Practice Pointer**: Practitioners whose clients are still within the one-year time period for filing applications for asylum, but who have been served with an NTA that has been filed with the immigration court, may take several steps to exercise due diligence in attempting to timely file their clients' applications. First, practitioners should file a Motion to Advance in writing, requesting that the court move the applicant's

---

[181] 8 CFR §1208.4(c) (2014); ICPM, chapter 3.1(b)(iii)(B).

[182] ICPM, chapter 3.1(b)(iii)(B).

[183] ICPM, chapter 3.1(b)(iii)(A).

[184] 8 CFR §§208.4(b)(3) (2014), 1208.4(b)(3).

[185] ICPM, chapter 3.1(b)(iii)(A); Creppy Memorandum on Asylum Request Processing, *supra* note 88, at 15.

[186] INA §208(a)(2)(B); 8 CFR §1208.4(a)(2) (2014). See chapter 2 for a detailed discussion of the one-year filing deadline and its limited exceptions.

master calendar hearing to an earlier date.[187] Such a motion should articulate the reasons for the request and the adverse consequences if the hearing date is not advanced. It should also specify the date of the applicant's one-year filing deadline so the court may attempt to reschedule the hearing prior to that date. The motion should be prepared and filed in accordance with Chapter 3 (filings) and Chapter 5 (motions) of the ICPM. Second, practitioners should follow the "Instructions for Submitting Certain Applications in Immigration Court and for Providing Biometric and Biographic Information to U.S. Citizenship and Immigration Services," and file the first three pages of the applicant's I-589, a copy of a completed G-28, and a copy of the instructions with USCIS. These instructions are available online at *www.uscis.gov/sites/default/files/files/article/PreOrderInstr.pdf*.[188] Upon receipt of these materials, USCIS will issue a receipt notice, followed by an appointment notice for biometrics collection. Although the application is not considered to be officially filed until it is presented in open court to an IJ, having a USCIS receipt notice will help demonstrate to the IJ that the applicant did everything in his or her power to timely file his or her application. Third, practitioners should "lodge" the application with the immigration court. Although lodging an application for asylum is for purposes of starting the clock for the applicant's employment authorization and *not* for the purposes of *filing* the application, lodging can demonstrate to the IJ that the applicant was ready to file the application within the one-year filing deadline and would have done so, but for the need to file in open court.[189]

According to these requirements, applicants filing defensively for protection usually will file their applications in open court at the first master calendar hearing, or the IJ will give the applicants a date for a subsequent master calendar hearing for purposes of filing their applications.[190]

➢ **Practice Pointer**: The same form, the I-589, is used to apply for all three forms of protection: asylum, withholding of removal under INA §241(b)(3), or protection under CAT. An applicant may initiate a claim for CAT relief by either requesting such relief before an IJ or presenting evidence and testimony indicating that he or she is more likely than not to be tortured upon removal to the country of feared torture.[191] If an

---

[187] *See* ICPM. chapters 1.7(h), 5.10(b).

[188] (last visited Feb. 6, 2015).

[189] *See* ICPM, chapter 4.15(l). See chapter 13 for a detailed discussion of lodging I-589 applications for purposes of employment authorization.

[190] *See infra* pt. IX. for a detailed discussion of master calendar hearings.

[191] 8 CFR §§208.13(c)(1), 1208.13(c)(1) (2014). *See* Creppy Memorandum on Asylum Request Processing, *supra* note 88, at 16–17; *see also* Form I-589, *supra* note 142.

applicant wants to seek CAT protection, practitioners should be sure to check the Convention Against Torture box at the top of page 1 of the I-589 and should provide a detailed answer to question 4 on page 6, "Are you afraid of being subjected to torture in your home country or any other country to which you may be returned?"[192] The answer should address all of the legal elements of the torture definition and show why it is more likely than not the applicant will be tortured upon his or her return.[193] See chapter 3 for a detailed discussion of the definition of torture and protection under the CAT.

The immigration court operates an asylum adjudications clock which measures the length of time an asylum application has been pending for each asylum applicant in removal proceedings. It tracks the number of days elapsed since the application was filed, not including any delays requested or caused by the applicant, and ending with the final administrative adjudication of the application.[194] Certain asylum applicants are eligible to receive employment authorization from DHS after the application has been pending for 180 days. Thus, EOIR provides DHS with access to its asylum adjudications clock for cases pending before EOIR.[195] The filing of the application starts accrual of time on the clock.

In some situations where the application has not yet been filed and the applicant is awaiting his or her opportunity to file the application in open court at a master calendar hearing, the applicant may wish to "lodge" his or her application with the court prior to filing it at the master calendar hearing.[196] Lodging the application does not mean that the application has been filed. However, it does start the clock from accruing time for purposes of employment authorization.[197] The applicant may lodge his or her application by mail or courier or by hand at the immigration court's filing window. The immigration court will place a date stamp and a "lodged not filed" stamp on the application and then return the application to the applicant.[198] The court does not retain a copy of the lodged application, and it is not placed in the Record of Proceedings; however, the date that the application was lodged with the court is electronically transmitted to DHS for purposes of tracking employment authorization eligibility.[199]

---

[192] *See* Form I-589, *supra* note 142.

[193] *See supra* chapter 3 for a detailed discussion of the definition of torture and protection under the Convention Against Torture.

[194] ICPM, chapter 4.15(l).

[195] INA §§208(d)(2), 208(d)(5)(A)(iii); 8 CFR §1208.7 (2014); ICPM, chapter 4.15(l).

[196] ICPM, chs. 3.1(b)(iii)(A), 4.15(l)(i).

[197] ICPM, chapter 4.15(l)(i).

[198] *Id.*

[199] *Id.*

> ➢ **Practice Pointer**: If a respondent lodges an asylum application by mail or courier, he or she must include a self-addressed, stamped envelope or other return packaging with the application so the court may return the stamped application to the respondent. The cover page must prominently state that the application is being submitted for the purpose of lodging. No proof of service is required to lodge the application.[200] See chapter 13 for a detailed discussion of seeking employment authorization while an asylum application is pending, as well as strategies to avoid stopping the employment authorization clock.

Only a respondent who plans to file a defensive asylum application, but has not yet done so, may lodge an asylum application.[201] A respondent whose application was initially filed with DHS and then referred to the court may not lodge his or her asylum application.[202]

VII. What Rights Does a Noncitizen Have in Immigration Court?

Individuals subject to removal proceedings have certain constitutional and statutory rights. Among these rights are:

- Rights under the Fourth Amendment;
- The right to due process — a full and fair hearing;
- The right not to incriminate oneself;
- The right to be represented in proceedings;
- The right to be provided a competent interpreter;
- The right to present, examine, and object to evidence;
- The right to cross-examine witnesses presented by DHS;
- The right to appeal; and
- The right to confidentiality.

Each of these rights is discussed in detail below.

A. Fourth Amendment Rights

Evidence obtained as a result of an egregious Fourth Amendment violation may be excluded in an immigration court proceeding.[203] Similarly, a violation of a regulatory

---

[200] ICPM, chapter 4.15(l)(i)(A).

[201] *Id.*

[202] *Id.*

[203] *See Pinto-Montoya v. Mukasey,* 540 F.3d 126, 131 (2d Cir. 2008) (holding that evidence ought to be suppressed only when it established that either an egregious violation that was fundamentally unfair had occurred or the violation undermined the reliability of the evidence); *Lopez-Rodriguez v. Mukasey*, 536 F.3d 1012 (9th Cir. 2008), *reh'g en banc denied sub nom. Lopez-Rodriguez v. Holder*, 560 F.3d 1098 (9th Cir. 2009) (finding that the exclusionary rule does apply in immigration proceedings to the extent

Continued

requirement by a DHS officer can result in evidence being excluded or proceedings invalidated where the regulation at issue benefits the noncitizen and the violation prejudiced his or her interests that were protected by the regulation.[204]

The following requirements should be met when filing a motion to suppress in immigration court proceedings. The motion should be in writing and should be accompanied by a detailed affidavit that explains the reasons why the evidence should be suppressed.[205] The individual seeking to suppress evidence initially bears the burden of proof and must establish a prima facie case that the evidence should be suppressed.[206] To establish a prima facie case, the individuals who seek suppression must supply specific, detailed statements based on personal knowledge.[207] The statements must not be general or conclusory, or be based on counsel.[208] A detailed affidavit must be supported by testimony.[209]

> ➢ **Practice Pointer**: For a detailed discussion of motions to suppress evidence in immigration court proceedings, see the American Immigration Council's practice advisories, "Motions to Suppress in Removal Proceedings: A General Overview," available at *www.legalactioncenter.org/sites/default/files/motions_to_suppress_in_r*

---

of requiring exclusion of any evidence obtained as a result of a deliberate violation of the Fourth Amendment, or the result of conduct that a reasonable officer should have known is in violation of the Constitution); *Orhorhaghe v. INS*, 38 F.3d 488 (9th Cir. 1994); *see also Gonzalez-Rivera v. INS*, 22 F.3d 1441 (9th Cir. 1994); *INS v. Lopez-Mendoza*, 468 U.S. 1032 (1984) (holding that the exclusionary rule does not apply in civil deportation proceedings to non-egregious violations of the Fourth Amendment); *U.S. v. Arvizu*, 122 S. Ct. 744 (2002) (although Fourth Amendment protections extend to brief investigatory stops, there is no violation if law enforcement officers have a "reasonable suspicion" of criminal activity); *Perez-Quiroz v. Gonzales,* 221 Fed. Appx. 676, 2007 U.S. App. LEXIS 4515, at *2–3 (9th Cir. 2007). For more detailed information, see Rebecca Chiao, *Fourth Amendment Limits on Immigration Law Enforcement*, 93-02 *Immigration Briefings* (Feb. 1993); *see also* Judy Wong, *Egregious Fourth Amendment Violations and the Use of the Exclusionary Rule in Deportation Hearings: The Need for Substantive Equal Protection Rights for Undocumented Immigrants*, 28 Colum. Hum. Rts. L. Rev.. 431, 442 (1997).

[204] *Singh v. Mukasey*, 553 F.3d 207, 214–16 (2d Cir. 2009) (finding applicant's statement should have been suppressed because it was unreliable due to the conditions of the interrogation and violations of federal regulations by the officers); *Matter of Garcia-Flores*, 17 I&N Dec. 325 (BIA 1980), *disapproved by Montilla v. INS,* 926 F.2d 162, 169 (2d Cir. 1991) (stating that "[A]n alien claiming the INS has failed to adhere to its own regulations regarding the right to counsel in a deportation hearing is not required to make a showing of prejudice before he is entitled to relief. All that needs to be shown is that the subject of the regulations were for the alien's benefit and that the INS failed to adhere to them.").

[205] *Matter of Wong*, 13 I&N Dec. 820, 822 (BIA 1971).

[206] *Matter of Tang*, 13 I&N Dec. 691, 692 (BIA 1971); *see also Matter of Barcenas*, 19 I&N Dec. 609 (BIA 1988).

[207] *Tang*, 13 I&N Dec. at 692.

[208] *Id.*

[209] *Barcenas*, 19 I&N Dec. at 611.

emoval_proceedings-_a_general_overview_1-26-15_fin.pdf,[210] "Motions to Suppress in Removal Proceedings: Fighting Back Against Unlawful Conduct by U.S. Customs and Border Protection," available at *www.legalactioncenter.org/sites/default/files/motions_to_suppress_in_removal_proceedings_fighting_back_against_unlawful_cbp_conduct_11-13-13_fin.pdf*,[211] and "Motions to Suppress in Removal Proceedings: Cracking Down on Fourth Amendment Violations By State and Local Law Enforcement Officers," available at *www.legalactioncenter.org/sites/default/files/motions_to_suppress_in_removal_proceedings_cracking_down_on_fourth_amendment_violations.pdf*.[212]

B. Right to Due Process

Due process protections under the Fifth Amendment extend to noncitizens who have entered the United States, whether lawfully or unlawfully.[213] Such protections do not extend to noncitizens seeking entry or admission to the United States.[214] One exception to this general rule is that returning lawful permanent residents (LPRs) are entitled to due process protection.[215]

The Fifth Amendment's due process clause requires that removal hearings be fundamentally fair.[216] Courts have found due process violations in removal hearings, under the facts and the evidence presented, in the following circumstances:

- Where the IJ failed to inform the applicant of the availability of free legal services, in violation of immigration regulations;[217]
- Where the BIA failed to give the applicant advance notice of its intention to consider an extra-record fact and in depriving the applicant of the opportunity to rebut that fact;[218]
- Where the IJ refused to continue the hearing;[219]

---

[210] (last visited Feb. 14, 2015).

[211] (last visited Feb. 14, 2015).

[212] (last visited Feb. 14, 2015).

[213] *See, e.g., Accardi v. Shaughnessy*, 347 U.S. 260 (1954), *superseded on other grounds by La Guerre v. Reno,* 164 F.3d 1035, 1038 (7th Cir. 1998).

[214] *See Shaughnessy v. Mezei*, 345 U.S. 206 (1953) (holding that "whatever the procedure authorized by Congress is, it is due process as far as an alien denied entry is concerned"); *see also Knauff v. Shaughnessy*, 338 U.S. 537, 543 (1950).

[215] *Landon v. Plasencia*, 459 U.S. 21 (1982).

[216] *See, e.g., Reno v. Flores*, 507 U.S. 292, 306 (1993); *see also Al Khouri v. Ashcroft*, 362 F.3d 461, 464 (8th Cir. 2004).

[217] *Leslie v. U.S. Att'y Gen.*, 611 F.3d 171 (3d Cir. 2010).

[218] *Burger v. Gonzales*, 498 F.3d 131, 135 (2d Cir. 2007).

[219] *Gjeci v. Gonzales*, 451 F.3d 416, 424 (7th Cir. 2006); *Subhan v. Ashcroft*, 383 F.3d 591, 595 (7th Cir. 2004).

- Where the IJ refused to hear testimony from the applicant's domestic violence experts;[220]
- Where the IJ cut off the applicant's testimony on the events of his alleged past persecution in Nigeria that were the foundation of his withholding of removal and CAT claims;[221]
- Where the IJ took administrative notice without giving the applicant the opportunity to rebut;[222]
- Where ineffective assistance of counsel prevented the respondent from reasonably presenting his case;[223]
- Where the IJ excluded substantial amounts of the asylum applicants' testimony;[224]
- Where a last-minute designation of Armenia as the country of deportation deprived the applicant of the opportunity to prepare and present relevant arguments and evidence regarding the harm he would suffer in Armenia;[225]
- Where a stowaway was denied the opportunity to have his asylum claim heard before an impartial immigration judge;[226]and
- Where the issue of the applicant's credibility was raised sua sponte without affording the applicant the opportunity to offer an explanation of any supposed inconsistencies.[227]

A neutral judge is one of the most basic due process protections.[228] The Ninth Circuit U.S. Court of Appeals has reopened an asylum case where it was apparent from the record that the IJ had pressured the *pro se* applicant, off the record, to withdraw his asylum application before taking any testimony in the case.[229] The court held that the IJ had not behaved as a neutral fact-finder interested in hearing the

---

[220] *Lopez-Umanzor v. Gonzales*, 405 F.3d 1049 (9th Cir. 2005).

[221] *Oshodi v. Holder*, 729 F.3d 883 (9th Cir. 2013).

[222] *Circu v. Gonzales*, 450 F.3d 990, 995 (9th Cir. 2006).

[223] *Lin v. Ashcroft*, 377 F.3d 1014, 1034 (9th Cir. 2004), *overruled on other grounds by Thomas v. Gonzales,* 409 F.3d 1177, 1187 (9th Cir. 2005). *But see Rafiyev v. Mukasey*, 536 F.3d 853, 861 (8th Cir. 2008); *Afanwi v. Mukasey*, 526 F.3d 788, 798 (4th Cir. 2008); *Magala v. Gonzales*, 434 F.3d 523, 525 (7th Cir. 2005).

[224] *Kerciku v. Ashcroft*, 314 F.3d 913, 918 (7th Cir. 2003).

[225] *Andriasian v. INS*, 180 F.3d 1033, 1041 (9th Cir. 1999).

[226] *Selgeka v. INS*, 184 F.3d 337 (4th Cir. 1999).

[227] *Stoyanov v. INS*, 172 F.3d 731, 735 (9th Cir. 1999) (finding that by raising the issue of the applicant's credibility sua sponte without affording the applicant an opportunity to offer an explanation of any supposed inconsistencies, the BIA violated the applicant's right to due process).

[228] *Abulashvili v. Att'y Gen.*, 663 F.3d 197 (3d Cir. 2011) (stating that an IJ has a responsibility to function as a neutral, impartial arbiter, and must refrain from taking on the role of advocate for either party); *Castilho de Oliveira v. Holder*, 564 F.3d 892 (7th Cir. 2009); *Reyes-Melendez v. INS*, 342 F.3d 1001 (9th Cir. 2003); *Cano-Merida v. INS*, 311 F.3d 960 (9th Cir. 2002).

[229] *Cano-Merida v. INS*, 311 F.3d 960 (9th Cir. 2002).

applicant's evidence because he indicated that he had already judged the asylum claim.[230] Similarly, the Sixth Circuit U.S. Court of Appeals found that an IJ abandoned her role as an impartial arbiter and became a zealous advocate by uncovering a witness that DHS did not reveal or present.[231] A neutral arbiter is, at a minimum, one who has not pre-decided the case and is not predisposed to disregard a witness's testimony based on that witness's participation in an advocacy group.[232]

Other U.S. courts of appeals that have been critical of the behavior and/or bias exhibited by IJs include: the Second Circuit,[233] the Third Circuit,[234] the Sixth Circuit,[235] the Seventh,[236] the Eighth Circuit,[237] and Ninth Circuit.[238] In response to this growing chorus of criticism, the attorney general issued a memorandum to IJs expressing concern about their conduct and the quality of their work.[239] The AG then proposed measures to improve the immigration courts and the Board of Immigration

---

[230] *Id.* at 964–65 (citations omitted); *see also U.S. v. Aguirre-Tello*, 353 F.3d 1199 (10th Cir. 2003) (finding that the IJ adequately advised the respondent of his rights and eligibility for relief).

[231] *Vasha v. Gonzales*, 410 F.3d 863, 873–75 (6th Cir. 2005) (finding applicant's due process rights were violated by the IJ's off-the-record discussions with the court clerk and the inclusion of evidence regarding the applicant's relationship with a prominent member of the local Albanian community).

[232] *Tun v. Gonzales*, 485 F.3d 1014, 1017, 1026 (8th Cir. 2007) (finding IJ erred in excluding testimony of witness from Physicians for Human Rights).

[233] *Ali v. Mukasey*, 529 F.3d 478 (2d Cir. 2008) (holding that the IJ's comments reflected disrespect for the applicant and impermissible reliance on preconceived assumptions about homosexuals, resulting in appearance of bias or hostility that precluded meaningful review by the Court of Appeals); *Huang v. Gonzales*, 453 F.3d 142, 143 (2d Cir. 2006) (finding IJ Chase appeared biased and hostile to Chinese asylum applicant and requesting a remand to a different immigration judge).

[234] *Cham v. Gonzales*, 445 F.3d 683, 686, 691 (3d Cir. 2006) (finding that the applicant "under the bullying nature" of the IJ was "ground to bits" and requesting the presence of the deputy attorney general at oral argument to answer what procedures are in place to address the IJ's repeated poor conduct).

[235] *Mapouya v. Gonzales*, 487 F.3d 396 (6th Cir. 2007) (finding IJ failed to properly consider the evidence or the legal standards and requesting that the case be remanded to a different IJ).

[236] *Torres v. Mukasey*, 551 F.3d 616, 626–27 (7th Cir. 2008) (although the court did not find a due process violation, the court found that the IJ's overactive role during the hearings, his demonstrated impatience, his improper lines of questioning, and his reliance on personal knowledge beyond the facts in the record tainted his credibility findings); *Floroiu v. Gonzales*, 481 F.3d 970, 971–73 (7th Cir. 2006) (criticizing the IJ for departing from his judicial role and manifesting a clear bias that constituted a denial of due process).

[237] *Shahinaj v. Gonzales*, 481 F.3d 1027, 1029 (8th Cir. 2007) (remanding case to the BIA, which failed to explain how IJ's findings and credibility determination as a whole were not tainted by the IJ's bias, and recommending that the case be assigned to a different IJ).

[238] *Recinos de Leon v. Gonzales*, 400 F.3d 1185, 1187 (9th Cir. 2005) (criticizing IJ for "incomprehensible" and "incoherent" opinion).

[239] Memorandum from Attorney General Alberto Gonzales to Immigration Judges (Jan. 9, 2006), *published on* AILA InfoNet at Doc. No. 06011064 (*posted* Jan. 10, 2006).

Appeals.[240] One change has been the development of a code of conduct for IJs and members of the BIA that, inter alia, requires IJs to be "patient, dignified and courteous."[241] The National Association of Immigration Judges also has released an Ethics and Professionalism Guide for Immigration Judges.[242]

> **Practice Pointer**: When is it appropriate to request that an IJ recuse himself or herself? According to the Office of the Chief Immigration Judge, "a judge should recuse him or herself when it would appear to a reasonable person, knowing all the relevant facts, that a judge's impartiality might reasonably be questioned."[243] For helpful guidance, see Nancy Peterson, Anthony Drago, and Suzannah Maclay's article in *AILA's Immigration Practice Pointers* (2014–15 Ed.) entitled, "Dealing with Difficult Judges and Trial Attorneys."

As noted above, the DHS attorney is authorized by regulation to call witnesses and present evidence, including classified information.[244] If classified information is received, the IJ must inform the applicant.[245] DHS or the agency providing the classified information may provide an unclassified summary for release to the applicant, but they are not required to do so.[246] At least one court has held that the use of classified or secret evidence violates due process.[247]

> **Practice Pointer**: The Office of the Chief Immigration Judge has advised IJs that they must maintain and preserve a thorough and complete record of proceedings. If IJs do go off the record during

[240] U.S. Dep't of Justice Announcement, *Measures to Improve the Immigration Courts and the Board of Immigration Appeals*" (Aug. 9, 2006), *published on* AILA InfoNet at Doc. No. 06080968 (*posted* Aug. 9, 2006).

[241] Codes of Conduct for the Immigration Judges and Board Members, 72 Fed. Reg. 35510 (June 20, 2007).

[242] Ethics and Professionalism Guide for Immigration Judges (Jan. 31, 2011), available at *www.justice.gov/eoir/sibpages/IJConduct/EthicsandProfessionalismGuideforIJs.pdf* (last visited Mar. 28, 2015). *See also* American Bar Association Commission on Immigration Report (including recommendations for IJs that emphasize cultural sensitivity and awareness and reform in the disciplinary process), available at *www.americanbar.org/content/dam/aba/migrated/leadership/2010/midyear/daily_journal/114B.authcheckdam.pdf* (last visited Mar. 28, 2015).

[243] EOIR Memorandum 05-02 from Office of Chief Immigration Judge on Procedures for Issuing Recusal Orders in Immigration Proceedings (Mar. 21, 2005) at 2, *available at www.usdoj.gov/eoir/efoia/ocij/oppm05/05-02.pdf.*

[244] 8 CFR §1240.11(c)(3)(iv) (2014).

[245] *Id.*

[246] *Id.*

[247] *See Kiareldeen v. Reno*, 71 F. Supp. 2d 402 (D.N.J. 1999), *rev'd on other grounds by Kiareldeen v. Ashcroft*, 273 F.3d 542 (3d Cir. 2001) (use of secret evidence to support continued detention violates due process).

proceedings, they must summarize what was discussed on the record.[248] If IJs do not complete this summary on their own, practitioners should request that they do so in order to ensure that there is a complete record of proceedings should an appeal become necessary.

C. Right Not to Incriminate Oneself

An individual in removal proceedings has the right to assert the Fifth Amendment privilege against self-incrimination.[249] If the individual is not an "arriving alien," DHS must establish the individual's alienage. The individual's refusal to testify, in the absence of any other evidence of record, is insufficient to constitute prima facie evidence of the individual's alienage and, therefore, insufficient to establish his or her deportability by clear, unequivocal, and convincing evidence.[250] The right not to incriminate oneself also applies during custodial interrogations.[251] An individual who, at a port of entry, was taken into an interrogation room, stripped of her passport and visa, and shackled at the ankles was found to be in the custody of legacy INS; her right against self-incrimination was thus violated by legacy INS questioning that was reasonably likely to inculpate her.[252]

- **Practice Pointer**: Asserting the Fifth Amendment privilege against self-incrimination is a strategic decision that must be made on a case-by-case basis, as such an assertion will likely lead to negative inferences about the individual. Practitioners must weigh whether more damage will be done by making such an assertion or more will be done by providing the relevant testimony.

D. Right to Representation

Although the government is not obligated to provide legal counsel to individuals in proceedings, such individuals do have the right to be represented by an attorney or other representative of his or her choice, at no expense to the government.[253] Noncitizens do not have a Sixth Amendment right to be represented in removal

---

[248] *See* EOIR Memorandum No. 03-06 from Office of the Chief Immigration Judge on Revised Operating Policy and Procedures for Going Off-Record During Proceedings (Oct. 10, 2003), *available at www.usdoj.gov/eoir/efoia/ocij/oppm03/03-06.pdf.*

[249] *Kastigar v. United States*, 406 U.S. 441, 444 (1972) (right against self-incrimination applies in civil and administrative proceedings); *Bilokumsky v. Tod*, 263 U.S. 149, 154–55 (1923), *overruled in part by INS v. Lopez-Mendoza*, 468 U.S. 1032 (1984); *Rios-Berrios v. INS*, 776 F.2d 859 (9th Cir. 1985).

[250] *Matter of Guevara*, 20 I&N Dec. 238 (BIA 1991).

[251] *Miranda v. Arizona*, 384 U.S. 436, 444 (1966).

[252] *United States v. Gonzalez-DeLeon*, 32 F. Supp. 2d 925 (W.D. Tex. 1998); *see also Hernandez-Montiel v. INS*, 225 F.3d 1084, 1098–99 (9th Cir. 2000), *overruled on other grounds by Thomas v. Gonzales,* 409 F.3d 1177 (9th Cir. 2005) (finding that BIA drew improper negative inference regarding persecution claim from applicant's failure to respond to questions about his arrests in the United States).

[253] 8 CFR §1003.16(b) (2014); ICPM, chapter 2.3(a).

proceedings.[254] The right to counsel in removal proceedings is, however, grounded in the Fifth Amendment's guarantee of due process.[255] In certain circumstances, depriving a noncitizen of the right to counsel may rise to the level of a due process violation.[256] The right to counsel is also a statutory right.[257] The INA provides for the right to representation in immigration court proceedings, but at no expense to the government.[258]

> ➢ **Practice Pointer**: EOIR announced that it is committed to promoting pro bono representation in immigration courts through a number of initiatives including: best practices and guidance to IJs and court staff, designating local pro bono liaison judges, encouraging pre-trial conferences, examining ways to meet the special needs of children, and increasing the availability of self-help material.[259] The Office of Legal Access Programs focuses on four main initiatives — the Legal Orientation Program, the Legal Orientation Program for Custodians of Unaccompanied Alien Children, the BIA Pro Bono Project, and the Model Hearing Program. For more information about these initiatives, see EOIR's website at *www.justice.gov/eoir/probono/probono.htm*.[260]

The regulations specify who is eligible to provide representation in removal proceedings.[261] An individual may be represented by:[262]

- An attorney eligible to practice law, who is a member in good standing of the bar of the highest court of any state;[263]

---

[254] *See Ponce-Leiva v. Ashcroft*, 331 F.3d 369, 374 (3d Cir. 2003); *see also Castro-O'Ryan v. INS*, 847 F.2d 1307, 1312 (9th Cir. 1988).

[255] *Prichard-Ciriza v. INS*, 978 F.2d 219, 222 (5th Cir. 1992).

[256] *Tawadrus v. Ashcroft*, 364 F.3d 1099, 1103 (9th Cir. 2004) (holding there must be a knowing and voluntary waiver of the right to counsel); *Al Khouri v. Ashcroft*, 362 F.3d 461, 464 (8th Cir. 2004) (finding no due process violation where applicant waived his right to counsel).

[257] *Ponce-Leiva*, 331 F.3d at 374–75.

[258] INA §§240(b)(4), 292; 8 USC §§1229a(b)(4), 1362 (2012); *see also* 8 CFR §§1240.3, 1292.1 (2014). *But see Machado v. Ashcroft*, No. Cs-02-0066-FVS, Preliminary Injunction Order (E.D. Wash., Mar. 5, 2002) (legacy INS ordered to hire a lawyer for a child in its custody at government expense or release him from detention). For more information regarding this class action suit seeking appointed counsel for children in immigration detention, see *Advocates File Class Action Suite to Compel INS to Provide Counsel for Detained Minors*, 79 INTERPRETER RELEASES 622 (Apr. 29, 2002).

[259] *See* Press Release, *EOIR to Expand and Improve Pro Bono Programs* (Nov. 15, 2007), *available at www.usdoj.gov/eoir/press/07/ProBonoEOIRExpandsImprove.pdf*.

[260] (last visited Feb. 14, 2015). *See also* Press Release, *EOIR Adds 12 New Legal Orientation Program Sites* (Oct. 15, 2008), *available at www.usdoj.gov/eoir/press/08/LegalOrientationProgramExpands101508.htm*.

[261] 8 CFR §§292.1, 1292.1 (2014).

[262] 8 CFR §1292.1 (2014); ICPM, chapter 2.1(a).

[263] 8 CFR §§1001.1(f), 1292.1(a)(1) (2014); ICPM, chapter 2.3.

- Law students and law graduates not yet admitted to the bar, provided they are under the direct supervision of a licensed attorney or accredited representative;[264]
- Reputable individuals of good moral character, who have a pre-existing relationship or connection with the noncitizen;[265]
- Accredited representatives who represent a nonprofit or charitable organization and who have been accredited by the BIA;[266] and
- Accredited officials of the noncitizen's government, who are present in the United States.[267]

In the asylum context, the right to counsel has been characterized as "fundamental."[268] As one court has noted, "With only a small degree of hyperbole, the immigration laws have been termed, 'second only to the Internal Revenue Code in complexity.' A lawyer is often the only person who could thread the labyrinth."[269] The BIA has held that "since the right to counsel is ... often essential to the fundamental fairness of a hearing, meticulous care must be exercised to ensure that a waiver of this right is competently and understandably made."[270] One study has shown that asylum applicants in removal proceedings who are represented by counsel are four to six times more likely to be granted asylum than applicants who are not represented.[271] Another study found that unrepresented asylum-seekers had a much lower chance of being granted asylum (2 percent) than those with an attorney (25 percent).[272]

> ➢ **Practice Pointer**: For detailed data comparing the outcomes of immigration court cases involving unaccompanied children with attorneys to those without attorneys, as well as similar data for cases

---

[264] 8 CFR §1292.1(a)(2) (2014); ICPM, chapter 2.5.

[265] 8 CFR §1292.1(a)(3) (2014); ICPM, chs. 2.8, 2.9(a).

[266] 8 CFR §§1292.1(a)(4), 1292.2(d) (2014); ICPM, chapter 2.4.

[267] 8 CFR §1292.1(a)(5) (2014); ICPM, chapter 2.9(c). For more information on representatives in immigration court, see 8 CFR §§292.2, 1292.2 (2014); EOIR Fact Sheet, *Representation of Aliens in Immigration Proceedings* (revised Mar. 20, 2006), *published on* AILA InfoNet at Doc. No. 05072760 (*first posted* July 27, 2005), *available at www.usdoj.gov/eoir/press/06/AccreditationFactSheet March202006.htm.*

[268] *Orantes-Hernandez v. Thornburgh*, 919 F.2d 549, 554 (9th Cir. 1990).

[269] *U.S. v. Ahumada-Aguilar*, 295 F.3d 943, 950–51 (9th Cir. 2002).

[270] *Matter of Gutierrez*, 16 I&N Dec. 226, 228 (BIA 1977).

[271] *See* Andrew Schoenholtz and Jonathan Jacobs, *The State of Asylum Representation: Ideas for Change*, 16 GEO. IMMIGR. L.J. 739 (Summer 2002). For a listing of free or low cost legal counsel, call (800) 870-3676 or visit the EOIR website at *www.usdoj.gov/eoir/probono/states.htm.*

[272] United States Comm'n on Int'l Religious Freedom, *Asylum Seekers in Expedited Removal: A Study Authorized by Section 605 of the International Religious Freedom Act of 1998* (Feb. 2005), *available at www.uscirf.gov/countries/global/asylum_refugees/2005/february/execsum.pdf.*

involving women and children, see TRAC Immigration's reports on its website.[273]

The right to counsel may be infringed by violating other statutory or regulatory provisions, such as by denying a motion for change of venue or denying a continuance necessary to permit representation by counsel of one's choice.[274] In addition, to waive the right to counsel, an IJ must: (1) inquire whether the applicant wishes to proceed without a lawyer, and (2) receive a knowing, voluntary, affirmative response from the applicant.[275]

When an applicant is unrepresented, however, IJs have a duty to "fully develop the record."[276] This duty cannot be delegated to the DHS attorney.[277] Courts have found that noncitizens appearing *pro se* in removal proceedings often lack the legal knowledge to navigate "the morass of immigration law" and have found it critical for IJs to "scrupulously and conscientiously probe into, inquire of, and explore for all relevant facts.[278] Where the IJ failed to develop the record fully by curtailing the applicant's testimony, failed to instruct the applicant that he or she should provide detailed responses, and failed to give the unrepresented applicant adequate time to review a 200-page court submission, the applicant's hearing was found to be fundamentally unfair.[279]

Attorneys and accredited representatives must register with EOIR in order to practice before the immigration courts.[280]

---

[273] *http://trac.syr.edu/immigration/reports/371/* and *http://trac.syr.edu/immigration/reports/377/* (last visited Mar. 28, 2015).

[274] *See Garcia-Guzman v. Reno*, 65 F. Supp. 2d 1077 (N.D. Cal. 1999) (finding that requiring counsel to appear telephonically was "woefully inadequate" where counsel notified legacy INS prior to the commencement of proceedings of the special needs of his "mute" client); *see also Ahumada-Aguilar*, 295 F.3d at 950–52 (finding that lack of a knowing and intelligent waiver of the right to counsel is a violation of due process where prejudice is shown). *But see Siddique v. Mukasey*, 547 F.3d 814, 816 (7th Cir. 2008) (finding that it lacked jurisdiction to review denial of continuance); *Al Khouri v. Ashcroft*, 362 F.3d 461, 464 (8th Cir. 2004) (finding that the applicant was given ample opportunity to obtain new counsel and the IJ did not abuse his discretion in denying applicant's request for a continuance).

[275] *Hernandez-Gil v. Gonzales*, 476 F.3d 803, 804 (9th Cir. 2007) (finding that the applicant was denied his statutory right to counsel where he told the IJ he was not prepared to go forward, that he did not want to proceed without his lawyer, and that he wanted a continuance so that he could proceed with his attorney present).

[276] *Al Khouri*, *supra* note 274, at 464 (citing *Jacinto v. INS*, 208 F.3d 725, 733–34 (9th Cir. 2000)). *But see Kalaj v. Gonzales*, 201 F. App'x. 345, 349 (6th Cir. 2006) ("Even were this court to hold with the Ninth Circuit ... that an IJ in an adversarial hearing must 'develop the record' according to a rule developed for non-adversarial social security hearings, that rule would not seem to apply here since the applicant did not appear 'without counsel.'").

[277] *Pangilinan v. Holder,* 568 F.3d 708, 709–10 (9th Cir. 2009)

[278] *Al Khouri*, *supra* note 274, at 464–65 (citing *Key v. Heckler*, 754 F.2d 1545, 1551 (9th Cir. 1985)).

[279] *Id.* at 465.

[280] 8 CFR §1292.1(a)(1), (a)(4), (f) (2014); ICPM, chapters 2.1(a), 2.3(b)(i), 2.4.

> ➢ **Practice Pointer**: For information regarding EOIR's eRegistry Program, including the announcement of the policy and final rule in the Federal Register, instructions on how to register and verify one's identity, and frequently asked questions, see the EOIR website at *www.justice.gov/eoir/engage/eRegistration.htm.*[281]

The attorney or representative must enter his or her appearance by filing a Form EOIR-28, Notice of Entry of Appearance with the immigration court and serving a copy of the EOIR-28 on DHS.[282] Forms EOIR-28 may be filed electronically or on paper.[283] If a paper Form EOIR-28 is submitted with other documents, it should be submitted on the top of the package, not as an exhibit or part of an exhibit.[284]

> ➢ **Practice Pointer**: After an attorney or accredited representative has registered with the EOIR eRegistry, he or she may file an EOIR-28 form electronically on EOIR's website at *https://portale.eoir.justice.gov.*[285] When the attorney or accredited representative's appearance is entered electronically, he or she must print out a copy of the electronically filed form and serve it on DHS.[286] A fillable Form EOIR-28 also is available on EOIR-28's website at *www.justice.gov/eoir/eoirforms/eoir28.pdf.*[287] EOIR strongly encourages that EOIR-28 forms be printed on green paper.[288]

Once an attorney or accredited representative has entered his or her appearance, the noncitizen should submit all filings and communications to the immigration court through the attorney or accredited representative.[289] The attorney or representative has an obligation to continue representation until a motion to withdraw or substitute counsel has been granted by the immigration court.[290]

An individual in proceedings may represent him or herself before the immigration court, although the immigration courts prefer that qualified professionals represent individuals.[291] IJs cannot give advice regarding the selection of a representative;

---

281 (last visited Feb. 6, 2015).

282 8 CFR §§1003.17(a), 1003.23(b)(1)(ii) (2014); ICPM, chapter 2.1(b).

283 ICPM, chapter 2.1(b).

284 ICPM, chapters 2.3(c), 3.3(c).

285 (last visited Feb. 6, 2015). ICPM, chapter 2.1(b)(i).

286 ICPM, chapter 2.1(c).

287 (last visited Feb. 6, 2015).

288 ICPM, chapters 2.3(c)(i), 11.2(f).

289 8 CFR §1292.5(a) (2014); ICPM, chapter 2.1(d).

290 ICPM, chapters 2.3(d), (i).

291 ICPM, chapter 2.2(a)

however, individuals in proceedings are provided with a list of free or low cost legal service providers within the region where the immigration court is located.[292]

> ➢ **Practice Pointer**: All of the lists of free legal service providers nationwide are available on the EOIR website at *www.justice.gov/eoir/probono/states.htm*.[293]

E. Right to a Competent Interpreter

Individuals in proceedings before the immigration court also have the right to a competent interpreter provided at government expense.[294] If an individual in immigration court proceedings cannot speak English fluently, the presence of a competent interpreter is essential for his or her meaningful participation in the hearing and to ensure the fundamental fairness of the proceedings.[295] Even where there is no due process violation, faulty or unreliable translations can undermine the evidence.[296] For example, the Ninth Circuit reversed a adverse credibility determination based on faulty or unreliable translations, noting that "some portions of the transcript read like, 'Who's on First.'"[297]

The court-provided interpreter, however, is not required to translate the entire proceeding for the applicant.[298] Nor is the court required to provide an interpreter to assist the applicant in completing the asylum application.[299] For example, in an unpublished decision, the BIA held that it was improper for the IJ to terminate proceedings in the case of a detained individual who was unable to complete his asylum application in English.[300]

---

[292] 8 CFR §§1003.61(a), 1292.2(a) (2014); ICPM, chapter 2.2(b).

[293] (last visited Feb. 6. 2015).

[294] 8 CFR §1003.22 (2014); ICPM, chapter 4.11.

[295] *See Matter of Tomas*, 19 I&N Dec. 464 (BIA 1987) (asylum claim of a Kanjobal speaker from Guatemala remanded because applicant could not adequately present his claim through the Spanish interpreter provided by the court); *see also Tun v. Gonzales*, 485 F.3d 1014, 1030 (8th Cir. 2007) ("Common sense informs us that evidence of improper translation may include direct evidence of mistranslated words, evidence that a witness is unable to understand a translator, or unresponsive answers from a witness."); *Singh v. Ashcroft*, 367 F.3d 1139, 1143–44 (9th Cir. 2004) (noting that standard for remand in an incompetent translation claim is whether a better translation would have made a difference in the outcome); *Augustin v. Sava*, 735 F.2d 32, 37 (2d Cir. 1984) (holding that asylum-seekers have a due process right to a translator in their hearings).

[296] *See He v. Ashcroft*, 328 F.3d 593, 598 (9th Cir. 2003).

[297] *Id.* at 597.

[298] *El Rescate Legal Services, Inc. v. EOIR*, 959 F.2d 742 (9th Cir. 1992) (finding that this policy does not deny applicants a reasonable opportunity to be present, to examine unfavorable evidence, to present favorable evidence, or to cross-examine government witnesses). A recent report has criticized this practice by the immigration courts. *See* Cavendish & Rich, *Assembly Line Injustice*, *supra* note 31.

[299] *Matter of Singh*, A78 494 845 (BIA Nov. 23, 2001).

[300] *Id. But see Matter of Liao*, A44 197 294 (BIA Oct. 22, 1999) (BIA, in unpublished decision, upheld IJ's decision to terminate proceedings where applicant did not have access to an interpreter).

The immigration court endeavors to accommodate the language needs of all respondents and witnesses, and will arrange for interpreters during individual hearings and, if necessary, master calendar hearings.[301] The immigration court uses staff interpreters employed by the immigration court, contract interpreters, and telephonic interpretation services.[302] Any person acting as an interpreter in a hearing shall swear or affirm to interpret or translate accurately, unless the interpreter is an employee of the United States government, in which case, no such oath or affirmation shall be required.[303]

> ➢ **Practice Pointer**: If there are misinterpretations or if the respondent or witness has difficulty communicating with and understanding the interpreter, it is essential for practitioners to raise these objections during the course of proceedings. Doing so will allow the IJ to continue the case to find a more competent interpreter and will also preserve the issue on the record for any potential appeal.

If an individual in proceedings anticipates that an interpreter will be needed at the individual hearing, the individual should request an interpreter, either by oral motion at the master calendar hearing, by written motion, or in a written pleading.[304] EOIR strongly encourages that requests for interpreters be made at the master calendar hearing, rather than following the hearing.[305]

A request for an interpreter, whether made orally or in writing, should contain the following information: (1) the name of the language requested; (2) the specific dialect of the language, if applicable; (3) the geographical locations where such dialect is spoken; (4) the identification of any other languages in which the respondent or witness is fluent; and (5) any other appropriate information necessary for the selection of an interpreter.[306]

F. Right to Present and Examine Evidence and to Cross-Examine Witnesses

In removal proceedings, noncitizens are entitled to "a reasonable opportunity to examine the evidence against [him or her], to present evidence on [his or her] own behalf, and to cross-examine witnesses presented by the Government."[307]

First, applicants for asylum, withholding of removal, and CAT protection "shall be examined under oath," and "may present evidence and witnesses on his or her own

---

[301] 8 CFR §1003.22 (2014); ICPM, chapters 4.11, 4.15(o), 4.16(e).

[302] 8 CFR §1003.22 (2014); ICPM, chapter 4.11.

[303] 8 CFR §1003.22 (2014).

[304] ICPM, chs. 4.15(i)(i), (o)(i). *See infra* pt. VII. for a detailed discussion of pleadings during master calendar hearings.

[305] ICPM. chapter 4.15(o).

[306] *Id.*

[307] INA §240(b)(4)(B); 8 CFR §1240.11(c)(3)(iii) (2014).

behalf."[308] Refusal to hear evidence in an asylum claim, therefore, is a denial of the right to present evidence under the INA and regulations.[309] For example, it is a denial of due process for IJs to interrupt applicants and to refuse to hear testimony regarding particular elements of the claim.[310] Similarly, in *Matter of E–F–H–L–*, the BIA considered the respondent's appeal of the IJ's denial of his applications for asylum and withholding of removal under INA §§208, 241(b)(3).[311] In that case, the IJ had found that the respondent's written application and prehearing brief did not demonstrate his prima facie eligibility for relief and determined that he was therefore not entitled to a hearing on the merits of his applications.[312] The BIA found that the IJ's decision was legally erroneous, and held that an applicant for asylum or for withholding of removal is entitled to a hearing on the merits of those applications, including an opportunity to provide oral testimony and other evidence, without first having to establish prima facie eligibility for the requested relief.[313]

In addition to the right to present evidence, a respondent also has the right to examine evidence presented against him or her.[314] The regulations further provide that noncitizens are entitled to a reasonable opportunity to object to the evidence presented against them.[315] These rights, however, do not entitle the respondent to examine national security information that DHS may proffer in opposition to the respondent's application for relief.[316] If DHS presents classified evidence and the IJ

---

[308] 8 CFR §1240.11(c)(3)(iii) (2014).

[309] *Pronsivakulchai v. Gonzales*, 461 F.3d 903, 908 (7th Cir. 2006) (finding that the IJ's refusal to hear evidence in asylum case denied the applicant the opportunity to be heard and to present evidence on her behalf in violation of INA §249(b)(4)(B) and 8 CFR §1240.1(c) (2014)).

[310] *See Colmenar v. INS*, 210 F.3d 967, 971 (9th Cir. 2000) (finding IJ behaved as a "partisan adjudicator" who sought to intimidate the applicant and his counsel); *see also Podio v. INS*, 153 F.3d 506 (7th Cir. 1999) (finding IJ's frequent interruptions of the applicant's testimony and refusal to permit the testimony of the applicant's witnesses also violate an applicant's right to due process); *Zhu v. Ashcroft*, 382 F.3d 521, 526 n.2 (5th Cir. 2004) (in remanding case, court noted that the commentary on the applicant's case by the IJ was "highly inappropriate" and "facially sexist"). *But see Ciorba v. Ashcroft*, 323 F.3d 539 (7th Cir. 2003) (holding that when IJ cut off pre-1991 testimony, attorney for applicant should have made an offer of proof to court or show any prejudice that resulted); *Morales v. INS*, 208 F.3d 323, 327 (1st Cir. 2000) (finding that although the judge was somewhat impatient, applicant was not denied a full hearing on his asylum application). For additional cases, see the discussion of evidence *infra* this section.

[311] *Matter of E–F–H–L–*, 26 I&N Dec. 319 (BIA 2014).

[312] *Id.* at 319.

[313] *Id.* (following *Matter of FeFe*, 20 I&N Dec. 116 (BIA 1989)).

[314] INA §240(b)(4); 8 CFR §1240.11(c)(3)(iii) (2014).

[315] 8 CFR §1240.10(a)(4) (2014).

[316] INA §240(b)(4); 8 CFR §1240.11(c)(3)(iv) (2014). *But see Kaur v. Holder*, 561 F.3d 957, 959–60 (9th Cir. 2009) (finding that the BIA abused its discretion by using secret evidence without giving the applicant sufficient notice about the parameters of that evidence to allow her to defend against it); *Kiareldeen v. Reno*, 71 F. Supp. 2d 402 (D.N.J. 1999), *rev'd on other grounds by Kiareldeen v. Ashcroft*, 273 F.3d 542 (3d Cir. 2001) (use of secret evidence to support continued detention violates

Continued

determines that it is relevant to the hearing, the IJ must inform the respondent and DHS and the IJ "may provide an unclassified summary of the information for release to the [respondent]."[317] The summary should be as detailed as possible so the respondent may have an opportunity to offer opposing evidence.[318] If the IJ bases his or her decision in whole or in part on the classified information, the IJ must state whether that information is material to the decision.[319]

> ➢ **Practice Pointer**: While discovery is significantly limited in immigration court, there a regulations and court practice rules that may permit some forms of discovery, from DHS's voluntary production of documents to subpoenas. See Part X.F. for a detailed discussion of discovery in immigration court.

In addition to presenting evidence for the record, DHS also may call witnesses to testify,[320] and respondents in removal proceedings have the right to cross-examine DHS's witnesses.[321] DHS must also make a reasonable effort to afford the respondent a reasonable opportunity to confront the witnesses against him or her.[322]

> ➢ **Practice Pointer**: DHS often presents documentation prepared by immigration officers who had prior contact with the respondent as evidence (*e.g.*, a record of sworn statement taken at a port of entry or notes and assessments prepared in connection with an affirmative asylum application). If this documentation contains adverse information, practitioners should object to its admission, arguing that its admission would violate the respondent's right to cross-examine witnesses against him or her. If the evidence is admitted to the record despite the objection, practitioners should consider requesting the opportunity to cross-examine the immigration officer. An IJ is not required, however, to permit cross-examination of immigration agents who prepared such documents without evidence that the agent is an unfriendly witness or an inaccurate recorder.[323] IJs are more likely to permit cross-

---

due process); *Federal Court Rules against Government in Secret Evidence Case*, 76 No. 44 INTERPRETER RELEASES 1657 (Nov. 15, 1999).

[317] 8 CFR §1240.11(c)(3)(iv) (2014).

[318] *Id.*

[319] *Id.*

[320] *Id.*

[321] INA §240(b)(4); 8 USC §1229a(b)(4); *see also* 8 CFR §1240.10(a)(4) (2014).

[322] *Saidane v. INS*, 129 F.3d 1063, 1065–66 (9th Cir. 1997) (legacy INS's reliance on a damaging hearsay affidavit rendered the hearing fundamentally unfair); *see also Kiareldeen v. Reno*, 71 F. Supp. 2d 402 (D.N.J. 1999), *rev'd on other grounds by Kiareldeen v. Ashcroft*, 273 F.3d 542 (3d Cir. 2001) (finding that legacy INS's reliance on secret evidence and the denial of a meaningful opportunity to cross-examine even one witness violated the right to due process).

[323] *Cruz-Espinoza v. INS*, 45 F.3d 308, 311 (9th Cir. 1995).

examination if there is evidence of coercion or that the information contained in the document is incorrect.[324]

G. Right to Appeal

Noncitizens generally have the right to appeal an IJ decision to the BIA.[325] Two notable exceptions to this rule are (1) in absentia orders;[326] and (2) IJ reviews of negative credible-fear determinations.[327] If an applicant waives his or her right to appeal, the IJ's order becomes final.[328] However, the waiver of the right to appeal, if not "considered and intelligent," violates due process.[329] If the IJ does not explain that the acceptance of the order as "final" amounts to a waiver of the right to appeal, the waiver is not a valid waiver.[330]

While the removal proceedings are in progress, a respondent may wish to appeal an IJ's ruling on a motion or other ruling related to the proceedings before the proceedings themselves have been resolved. Although the BIA does not ordinarily entertain such interlocutory appeals, it will rule on the merits of such appeals where it is necessary to address important jurisdictional questions regarding the administration of the immigration laws or to correct recurring problems in the handling of cases before IJs.[331]

Asylum-seekers in removal proceedings may appeal a negative BIA decision to a federal appeals court, unless they are barred because of a criminal conviction.[332] If, however, the appeal concerns whether a particular offense is a bar to review, federal courts have permitted review.[333]

H. Right to Confidentiality

Is there a right to confidentiality in asylum adjudications? According to the regulation on confidentiality, "Information contained in or pertaining to any asylum application … shall not be disclosed without the written consent of the

---

[324] *Id.* at 310.

[325] 8 CFR §1240.15 (2014); see also this chapter, at 3.10.

[326] *See infra* this section.

[327] See chapter 5.

[328] *See Matter of L–V–K–*, 22 I&N Dec. 976 (BIA 1999), *rev'd on other grounds by Konstantinova v. INS,* 195 F.3d 528 (9th Cir. 1999).

[329] *See U.S. v. Zarate-Martinez*, 133 F.3d 1194, 1097–98 (9th Cir. 1998) *questioned on other grounds by United States v. Balleteros-Ruiz,* 319 F.3d 1101, 1104 (9th Cir. 2003) (holding that an IJ's request that an individual raise his or her hand if he or she wishes to appeal violates due process).

[330] *Matter of Rodriguez-Diaz*, 22 I&N Dec. 1320, 1322–23 (BIA 2000). *See also Ali v. Mukasey*, 525 F.3d 171, (2d Cir. 2008) (finding that accepting the IJ decision as "final" can serve as an effective waiver of appeal when the record indicates the alien or his counsel understood the nature of the waiver).

[331] *See, e.g., Matter of Morales*, 21 I&N Dec. 130 (BIA 1995) (finding that the immigration court did not have jurisdiction to proceed with the case of an *ABC* class member).

[332] See chapter 12 for a detailed discussion of federal court review.

[333] *See, e.g., Coronado-Durazo v. INS*, 123 F.3d 1323 (9th Cir. 1997).

applicant…"[334] Moreover, the Form I-589 instructions provide, "[N]o information indicating that you have applied for asylum will be provided to any government or country from which you claim a fear of persecution. Regulations at 8 CFR sections 208.6 and 1208.6 protect the confidentiality of asylum claims."[335]

Remarkably, no exceptions are listed on the application form. There are exceptions, however, most of which are outlined in 8 CFR §§208.6(c), 1208.6(c). The broadest exception is found at 8 CFR §§208.6(a), 1208.6(a) and allows for the disclosure of asylum information and records "at the discretion of the Attorney General."[336] Under the Homeland Security Act of 2002, this discretion would extend to the DHS secretary.[337] In *Matter of Jean*, the AG invoked the discretion to disclose in publishing the asylum applicant's name in his precedent decision.[338] Normally, the BIA and AG precedent decisions list only the asylum applicants' initials.

A breach of confidentiality can have serious and dangerous effects for asylum-seekers, especially if an asylum-seeker's government learns that he or she has sought asylum. The unlawful disclosure of an application for asylum may even generate a new basis for seeking asylum. For example, in 2013, the BIA issued an unpublished decision in which it reopened asylum proceedings based on a breach of confidentiality.[339] The BIA stated:

> The respondent's motion alleges that a United States official advised her that in obtaining the respondent's travel documents, for the purpose of removal, he communicated by e-mail with the Chinese Consulate in such a way as to breach the confidentiality requirements at 8 CFR §1208.6. According to the respondent, she asked the official for copies of the emails, and he advised her that he deleted them. The respondent has proffered evidence of her attempts to obtain copies of the emails as well as other evidence concerning information supplied to the Chinese Consulate. The respondent asserts that circumstances in China have changed based in part on the government's awareness that the respondent is a failed asylum seeker. While the DHS has filed a statement of opposition to the motion, the DHS does not dispute the respondent's claims that confidentiality requirements may have been breached. We find it

---

[334] 8 CFR §§208.6(a), 1208.6(a) (2014). In *Lewis v. U.S. Dep't of Justice*, 2002 WL 982364, at *774 (Fed Cir. 2002), the Merits Systems Protection Board concluded that a breach of the confidentiality provision found at 8 CFR §208.6 (2014) was a firing offense, irrespective of whether the breach was harmless.

[335] Form I-589, *supra* note 142, at 4.

[336] 8 CFR §§208.6(a), 1208.6(a) (2014) (emphasis added).

[337] *See* Homeland Security Act of 2002, Pub. L. No. 107-296, §§456, 1512, 1517, 116 Stat. 2135, 2200, 2310, 2311.

[338] *Matter of Jean*, 23 I&N Dec. 373, 373 n.1 (AG 2002).

[339] *Matter of X–* (Feb. 26, 2013), *available at www.lexisnexis.com/legalnewsroom/immigration/b/insidenews/archive/2013/03/01/unpub-bia-asylum-victory-china-breach-of-confidentiality.aspx* (last visited Feb. 14, 2015).

> appropriate to reopen pursuant to 8 CFR §1003.2(a) and remand the record to the Immigration Judge for proceedings on whether the respondent is eligible for withholding of removal under the Act or protection under the Convention Against Torture in light of the new evidence in this matter.[340]

Like the asylum-seeker in the unpublished BIA decision, a confidentiality breach may occur when DHS employees request travel documents from an individual's home country.[341] Overseas investigations of asylum claims also risk a breach of confidentiality. At the request of DHS and legacy INS, overseas investigators (often nationals of the home country) have been sent out to verify the authenticity of arrest warrants, political party documents, and medical records. Asylum advocates have reported a marked increase in the number of these overseas investigations of asylum claims.

Whether overseas investigations cross the line and violate confidentiality is an issue that has been addressed by the U.S. circuit courts of appeals.[342] The Second Circuit has held that the U.S. government breached the confidentiality owed to an asylum applicant when it provided the Chinese government with an unredacted copy of the applicant's prison release certificate.[343] The court found that this breach potentially exposed the applicant and his family to a new risk and ordered the BIA to consider this new risk on remand.[344]

Similarly, the court held that the U.S. government breached the confidentiality of a Macedonian asylum applicant when it revealed to his home government that he was in contact with U.S. authorities and had previously been imprisoned for political activism in his home country.[345] The court in that case remanded the matter for a determination of whether the risk of persecution to the applicant based on the breach.[346] The Fourth Circuit held that confidentiality was breached when the government disclosed her unredacted police convocations to a Cameroonian official in a way that would allow him to infer that she had applied for asylum.[347]

On the other hand, the Eighth Circuit has held that a breach of confidentiality claim fails where the record does not reveal that any information contained in or

---

[340] *Id.*

[341] *See, e.g.,* Lisa Rab, *America's Promise to Protect Asylum-Seekers Gets Lost in the Paperwork*, Westword (Oct. 8, 2008) *available at www.westword.com/2008-10-09/news/america-s-promise-to-protect-asylum-seekers-gets-lost-in-the-paperwork/#Comments*.

[342] *Owino v. Holder*, 771 F.3d 527 (9th Cir. 2014); *La v. Holder*, 701 F.3d 566 (8th Cir. 2012); *Lyashchynska v. U.S. Att'y Gen.*, 676 F.3d 962 (11th Cir. 2012); *Corovic v. Mukasey*, 519 F.3d 90 (2d Cir. 2008); *Averianova v. Mukasey*, 509 F.3d 890 (8th Cir. 2007).

[343] *Zhen Nan Lin v. U.S. Dep't of Justice*, 459 F.3d 255, 262 (2d Cir. 2006) (rejecting the BIA's finding that a breach occurs only when sensitive information is revealed).

[344] *Id.* at 268.

[345] *Corovic v. Mukasey*, 519 F.3d 90, 95–96 (2d Cir. 2008).

[346] *Id.*

[347] *Anim v. Mukasey*, 535 F.3d 243, 255–56 (4th Cir. 2008)

pertaining to the asylum application was disclosed to an applicant's home government when investigating the authenticity of birth certificates.[348] Similarly, the Ninth Circuit held in an unpublished decision that an applicant for CAT relief did not have his right to confidentiality violated when an immigration official informed the Salvadoran Interpol office that the applicant was in immigration proceedings, because the information provided revealed nothing about the nature of the application for relief.[349]

In June of 2005, the director of the Asylum Division issued a fact sheet on confidentiality to all Asylum Office directors and deputy directors.[350] The fact sheet notes that if information is disclosed publicly regarding an asylum applicant, it could subject the applicant to retaliatory measures by government authorities or non-state actors. It further states that confidentiality is breached when "information contained in or pertaining to an asylum application is disclosed to a third party ... ."[351]

The only exceptions are: (1) consent by the applicant; (2) authorization by the secretary of DHS; or (3) disclosure to U.S. government officials on a need-to-know basis.[352] Similarly, a memorandum from former legacy Immigration and Naturalization Service (INS) General Counsel Bo Cooper, states that 8 CFR §208.6 "prohibits INS [now DHS] personnel from commenting to any third party on the nature or even the existence of individual applications for asylum."[353] Although there is an exception for disclosures "at the Attorney General's discretion," this does not extend, the memorandum noted, to legacy INS [now DHS] personnel.[354]

The memorandum contains nine guidelines for conducting overseas investigations. The following are three of those guidelines:

- If an investigation cannot be accomplished without compromising the confidentiality of the application, the investigation should be abandoned and the investigator should inform the requestor of the investigation of this fact.
- Generally, confidentiality of an asylum application is breached when information contained therein or pertaining thereto is disclosed to a third party, and the disclosure is of a nature that allows the third party to link the identity of the applicant to: (1) the fact the applicant has applied for asylum; (2) specific facts or

---

[348] *Averianova v. Mukasey*, 509 F.3d 890, 898 (8th Cir. 2007).

[349] *Velasco v. INS*, 87 Fed. App'x 35, 2004 WL 78208 (9th Cir. 2004). See chapter 4 for more information on Convention Against Torture relief.

[350] USCIS Asylum Division Fact Sheet, *Federal Regulations Protecting the Confidentiality of Asylum Applicants* (June 3, 2005), *published on* AILA InfoNet at Doc. No. 05062440 (*posted* Jun. 24, 2005), *available at www.uscis.gov/files/pressrelease/FctSheetConf061505.pdf.*

[351] *Id.* at 2.

[352] *Id.*

[353] *See* INS Memorandum from Bo Cooper on Confidentiality of Asylum Applications and Overseas Verification of Documents and Application Information (June 21, 2001), at 2.

[354] *Id.*

allegations pertaining to the individual asylum claim contained in the asylum application; or (3) facts or allegations that are sufficient to give rise to a reasonable inference that the applicant has applied for asylum. If one or the other part of this link is missing, then no breach has occurred.

- The content of the investigative report … must contain at a minimum: (1) the name and title of the investigator; (2) a statement that the investigator is fluent in the relevant language(s); (3) any other statements of the competency of the investigator; (4) the specific objective of the investigation; (5) the location(s) of any conversation or other searches conducted; (6) the name(s) and title(s) of the people spoken to in the course of the investigation; (7) the method used to verify the information; (8) the circumstances, content and results of each relevant conversation or searches; and (9) a statement that the Service investigator is aware of the confidentiality provisions found in 8 CFR §208.6.[355]

In 2012, the USCIS Asylum Division issued an updated fact sheet addressing the federal regulation protecting the confidentiality of asylum applicants.[356] The new fact sheet reiterates these same principles and provides a detailed question and answer section addressing complex issues related to confidentiality of asylum applications.[357]

The United Nations High Commissioner for Refugees (UNHCR) imposes a more bright-line rule on confidentiality. In an October 29, 1998, advisory opinion, UNHCR advised that governments "not share any information relating to individual cases with the country of origin."[358] One reason for this is that sharing such information "could increase the likelihood of retaliatory or punitive measures by the national authorities in the event the individuals are repatriated."[359] Another reason is that "sharing information with the countries of origin may endanger the security of any family members who may be residing in those countries."[360] As a general rule, according to UNHCR, dialogue with countries of origin on individual cases is *absolutely excluded.*[361] The only exception to the duty of confidentiality, according to UNHCR, is in the case of voluntary repatriation, when, with the consent of the individual, UNHCR shares information with the country of origin.[362]

---

[355] *Id.* at 3–7.

[356] USCIS Asylum Division Fact Sheet, *Federal Regulations Protecting the Confidentiality of Asylum Applicants* (Oct. 18, 2012), *available at www.uscis.gov/sites/default/files/USCIS/Outreach/Notes%20from%20Previous%20Engagements/2012/December%202012/Asylum-ConfidentialityFactSheet.pdf* (last visited Mar. 28, 2015).

[357] *Id.*

[358] United Nations High Commissioner for Refugees (UNHCR) Advisory Opinion (Oct. 29, 1998), at 1. For a copy of this advisory opinion, contact UNHCR at: 1775 K Street, NW, Suite 300, Washington, D.C. 20006; (202) 295-5191; *usawa@unhcr.ch.*

[359] *Id.*

[360] *Id.*

[361] *Id.* (emphasis added).

[362] *Id.* at 2.

VIII. What Special Protections Are Available in Immigration Court?

In addition to the rights that are available to all respondents in proceedings, certain groups of respondents — children and those suffering from mental health disorders — have diminished capacity, and thus, the law requires that they be granted special protections in removal proceedings in order for the proceedings to be deemed fundamentally fair.

A. Children

Children receive special protections and require unique considerations when they are in removal proceedings. The Trafficking Victims Protection Reauthorization Act of 2008 mandates that unaccompanied children in removal proceedings who wish to apply for asylum are permitted an initial nonadversarial proceeding before USCIS.[363] If USCIS does not grant asylum, the case may be referred to an immigration judge.

EOIR has adopted separate guidelines for proceedings involving unaccompanied minors and has encouraged immigration judges to conduct hearings in a way that is sensitive to the "best interests of the child."[364] These guidelines contain special rules for the return of unaccompanied minors to their home countries and will not permit their return or their placement in removal proceedings if they have been victims of a severe form of trafficking or are at risk of being trafficked.[365]

Additionally, although unaccompanied minors may otherwise be placed in removal proceedings, the U.S. Department of Health and Human Services must make efforts to provide them with pro bono counsel, including appointing child advocates in child-trafficking cases. EOIR regulations strongly discourage the appearance of an individual under 18 years of age in court without a guardian to speak on the minor's behalf.[366] However, neither the regulations nor the INA require the appointment of a

---

[363] Trafficking Victims Protection Reauthorization Act of 2008, Pub. L. No. 110-457, 122 Stat. 5044. For more information, see U.S. Citizenship and Immigration Servs., *Questions and Answers: USCIS Initiates Procedures for Unaccompanied Children Seeking Asylum* (Mar. 25, 2009), *available at* www.uscis.gov/files/article/tvpra_ qa_25mar2009.pdf. *See also* USCIS Memorandum from Joseph Langlois on Implementation of Statutory Change Providing USCIS with Initial Jurisdiction over Asylum Applications Filed by Unaccompanied Children (Mar. 25, 2009), *published on* AILA InfoNet at Doc. No. 09042230 (*posted* Apr. 22, 2009).

[364] Memorandum No. OPPM 07-01, from Chief Immigration Judge David Neal on Guidelines for Immigration Court Cases Involving Unaccompanied Alien Children (May 22, 2007), *available at www.justice.gov/eoir/efoia/ocij/oppm07/07-01.pdf.*

[365] *See* William Wilburforce Trafficking Victims Protection Reauthorization Act of 2008, Pub. L. No. 110-457, §235(a), 122 Stat. 5044; *see also* 8 USC §1232 (2012)..

[366] *See* 8 CFR §1240.10(c) (2014) ("The immigration judge shall require the respondent to plead to the notice to appear by stating whether he or she admits or denies the factual allegations and his or her removability under the charges contained therein. . . . The immigration judge shall not accept an admission of removability from an unrepresented respondent who is incompetent or under the age of 18 and is not accompanied by an attorney or legal representative, a near relative, legal guardian, or friend; nor from an officer of an institution in which a respondent is an inmate or patient.").

guardian ad litem in immigration court. At least one court has found that it was not an error for the IJ and BIA to refuse to appoint a guardian ad litem for a 16-year-old minor when he was represented by counsel and in the custody of legacy INS.[367]

Although neither the regulations nor the INA require the appointment of a guardian ad litem in immigration court, other safeguards are available to protect the interests of minors in removal proceedings. For example, when a minor is placed in the custody of a responsible adult pursuant to the regulations, notice must be served upon the adult and the minor even if the minor is over 14 years of age.[368] The minor is not expected to understand the notice and follow its orders on his or her own. In the case of a minor under 14 years of age, DHS must personally serve the NTA on the person with whom the minor resides.[369] Whenever possible, DHS should also personally serve the near relative, guardian, committee, or friend.[370]

The parent or guardian of a child who is representing that child in the proceedings must establish his or her own identity, as well as the identity of the child, and must also establish his or her parentage or provide a court order establishing guardianship.[371]

Since minors are considered to be legally incompetent, an IJ also is not permitted to accept admissions of removability from an unrepresented minor who is not accompanied by an attorney or legal representative, guardian, friend, or near relative.[372] This regulation does not preclude the IJ from accepting a minor's admissions to factual allegations, which may properly form the basis of a finding that the minor is removable.[373]

---

[367] *Chitay-Pirir v. INS*, 169 F.3d 1079, 1081 (7th Cir. 1999); *see also* chapter 10 for a detailed discussion of children's asylum claims.

[368] *See* 8 CFR §236.3 (2014); *Flores-Chavez v. Ashcroft*, 362 F.3d 1150 (9th Cir. 2004) (reversing an in absentia order against a 15 year old who was served with an order to show cause under 8 CFR §103.5a, but no service was provided to the adult custodian, and concluding that reading the statute to permit service solely on the minor violated DHS's own regulations and raised serious constitutional questions). *See also Llanos-Fernandez v. Mukasey*, 535 F.3d 79 (2d Cir. 2008).

[369] 8 CFR §103.5a(c)(2)(ii) (2014).

[370] *Id.*; *see also Mejia-Andino*, 23 I&N Dec. 533 (BIA 2002) (proceedings against a minor were properly terminated because service of the Notice to Appear was made on the minor's uncle, not her parents). *But see Flores-Chavez v. Ashcroft*, 362 F.3d 1150 (9th Cir. 2004) (finding DHS erred in not serving notice of hearing and charging document on the adult to whom the child was released from DHS custody).

[371] 8 CFR §103.21(c) (2014).

[372] 8 CFR §1240.10(c) (2014); *Immigration Judge Benchbook* at pt. II.B. (addressing incompetency and representation); *Flores-Chavez v. Ashcroft,* 262 F.3d 1150, 1156 (9th Cir. 2004) (stating that "juveniles are presumed unable to appear at immigration proceedings without the assistance of an adult"); *Davila-Bardales v. INS*, 27 F.3d 1 (1st Cir. 1994); *Matter of Mejia-Andino*, 23 I&N Dec. 533 (BIA 2002). *See also* 8 CFR §240.48(b) (2014) ("The immigration judge shall not accept an admission of deportability for an unrepresented respondent who is incompetent or under age 16 and is not accompanied by a guardian, relative, or friend; nor from an officer of an institution in which a respondent is an inmate or patient.").

[373] *Matter of Amaya-Castro*, 21 I&N Dec. 583 (BIA 1996).

The BIA specifically addressed the treatment of unaccompanied minors in removal proceedings, taking into consideration the unique procedural problems posed when respondents are minors.[374] In *Matter of Amaya-Castro*, the BIA considered the answers of a minor on a Form I-213, Record of Deportable Alien, and determined that the information contained in the Form I-213 was not in itself sufficient to establish the respondent's deportability.[375] The Board held that an IJ "must exercise particular care in determining [a minor's] deportability" and that the IJ must make a "comprehensive and independent inquiry" into a minor's deportability, particularly when the accuracy and reliability of the government's evidence may be questioned.[376] The BIA stated:

> The minor's age and pro se and unaccompanied status must be taken into consideration. The Immigration Judge must consider the reliability of the testimony given by such a minor in response to the factual allegations made against him in determining, after a comprehensive and independent inquiry, whether there is clear, unequivocal, and convincing evidence of the minor's deportability as charged … . If the Immigration Judge is assured that the respondent is both capable of understanding, and in fact understands, any facts that are admitted, and that those facts establish deportability, they may form the sole bases of a finding that the minor is deportable.[377]

The Board cited the Supreme Court in specifically recognizing that minors lack the maturity of adults as well as the experience, perspective, and judgment to recognize and avoid choices that could be detrimental to them.[378] It is principles such as these, relating to the potential vulnerability and limited capacity of minor respondents, which the immigration courts are required to consider in hearings involving minors.

Moreover, removal hearings for minors are to be scheduled on a separate juvenile docket where the IJ is encouraged not to wear his or her robe, employ child-sensitive questioning, and make appropriate credibility assessments given the child's age.[379]

---

[374] *See generally Matter of Amaya-Castro*, 21 I&N Dec. 583 (BIA 1996).

[375] *Id.* at 588 n.4.

[376] *Id.* at 586. *But see Matter of Ponce-Hernandez*, 21 I&N Dec. 784 (BIA 1999) (in the case of a 15-year-old minor who failed to appear for his deportation hearing, the BIA found that legacy INS met its burden of proof in establishing deportability on the basis of a Record of Deportable Alien (Form I-213), which documented the minor's identity and alienage).

[377] *Matter of Amaya-Castro*, 21 I&N Dec. 583, 587 (BIA 1996).

[378] *See Eddings v. Oklahoma*, 455 U.S. 104, 116 (1982) (stating that "Even the normal 16 year old customarily lacks the maturity of an adult."); *Bellotti v. Baird*, 443 U.S. 622, 635 (1979) (stating that "minors often lack the experience, perspective, and judgment to recognize and avoid choices that could be detrimental to them").

[379] *See* Memorandum No. OPPM 07-01 from Chief Immigration Judge David Neal on Guidelines for Immigration Court Cases Involving Unaccompanied Alien Children (May 22, 2007) [hereinafter Neal Mem. on Unaccompanied Alien Children], *available at www.justice.gov/eoir/efoia/ocij/oppm07/07-01.pdf*.

EOIR has recognized that a minor's testimony "may be limited not only by his or her ability to understand what happened, but also by his or her skill in describing the event in a way that is intelligible to adults."[380]

- **Practice Pointer**: Unaccompanied minors may have special forms of relief from removal available to them, such as Special Immigrant Juvenile Status. Additionally, minors may have been targeted, at least in part, on account of their heightened vulnerability as children. Thus, there may be a viable particular social group related to a child's status as a minor. See chapter 2 for a detailed discussion of the legal standards for particular social group asylum claims, and see chapter 10 for a detailed discussion of the special legal arguments and procedures for children asylum-seekers.
- **Practice Pointer**: On December 10, 1998, legacy INS issued guidelines for children's asylum claims, which provide additional procedural protections for children in the affirmative asylum process.[381] The Asylum Division also has a separate lesson plan for training asylum officers who hear children's asylum claims.[382] On May 22, 2007, the OCIJ issued an operating policies and procedures memorandum (OPPM) on policies and procedures for immigration court cases involving children.[383] While the IJs are not bound by legacy INS's guidelines, this OPPM incorporates by reference some of the child-questioning techniques referred to in the guidelines. For a detailed discussion of special asylum procedures and standards for children, see chapter 10 of this book.

B. Mental Incompetence

The AG is required to "prescribe safeguards to protect the rights and privileges" of mentally incompetent noncitizens in removal proceedings.[384] The safeguards required under the INA vary from case to case because competency issues may be caused by both physical and psychological conditions and may also involve a wide range of needs.

---

[380] *See id.*

[381] *See* this chapter, at 3.5.

[382] *See* U.S. Citizenship and Immigration Servs., *Guidelines for Children's Asylum Claims*, in Asylum Officer Basic Training Course Participant Workbook (Sept. 1, 2009) [hereinafter AOBTC Lesson Plan on Children's Asylum Claims], *available at www.uscis.gov/files/article/AOBTC_Lesson_29_Guidelines_for_Childrens_Asylum_Claims.pdf.*

[383] *See* Neal Mem. on Unaccompanied Alien Children, *supra* note 379.

[384] INA §240(b)(3); 8 USC §1229a(b)(3) (2012). Under the Homeland Security Act of 2002, this authority would extend to the DHS secretary and other DHS officials. *See* Homeland Security Act of 2002, Pub. L. No. 107-296, §§456, 1512, 1517, 116 Stat. 2135, 2200, 2310, 2311.

The regulations address some safeguards, including the requirements for service of a Notice to Appear on a mentally incompetent respondent.[385] If a person confined to a penal or mental institution is competent to understand the nature of the proceedings initiated against him or her, DHS must personally serve both the individual confined and the person in charge of the institution or hospital.[386] If the person confined is not competent to understand the nature of the proceedings, DHS must serve only the person in charge of the hospital or institution.[387] Whether or not the mentally incompetent person is confined, DHS must also personally serve the person with whom the incompetent individual resides.[388] Whenever possible, DHS should also serve the near relative, guardian, committee, or friend of the incompetent individual.[389]

Additionally, the regulations provide that an attorney or legal representative, legal guardian, near relative, or friend may "appear on behalf of" a respondent whose mental incompetency makes it "impracticable" for him or her to "be present" at a hearing.[390] If such a person cannot be found, the custodian of the individual will be requested to appear on his or her behalf.[391] Under such circumstances, an IJ may waive the presence of the mentally incompetent respondent.[392] If a mentally incompetent respondent does not have someone to represent him or her, the IJ may be required to appoint one on his or her behalf.[393]

Another safeguard is that an IJ may not accept an admission of removability from a mentally incompetent respondent who is not represented by an attorney or legal representative, a near relative, legal guardian, or friend.[394] In such cases, the IJ is required to hold a hearing on the issue of removability.[395]

Although the statute and regulations provide that safeguards must be established for mentally incompetent respondents, they provide little guidance regarding the definition of "incompetent" and how an IJ is to determine competency. Without proper guidance about determining the competency of a respondent and what safeguards are necessary to ensure a full and fair immigration court hearing for mentally incompetent respondents, many respondents were ordered deported without

---

[385] *See* 8 CFR §103.5a(c)(2)(ii) (2014).

[386] 8 CFR §103.5a(c)(2)(i) (2014).

[387] *Id.*

[388] 8 CFR §103.5a(c)(2)(ii) (2014).

[389] *Id.*

[390] 8 CFR §1240.4 (2014).

[391] *Id.*

[392] 8 CFR §1003.25(a) (2014).

[393] *See Matter of M–V– [number withheld]* (BIA Feb. 19, 2002), *reported in* 21 IMMIGRATION LAW TODAY 229 (Apr. 2002).

[394] 8 CFR §1240.10(c) (2014).

[395] *Id.*

any assessment of their competency and others languished in detention without access to counsel, only compounding their conditions. In May of 2011, however, the BIA issued a precedent decision, *Matter of M–A–M–*, which established a framework for IJs to follow in approaching removal proceedings for respondents with mental competency issues.[396]

Matter of M–A–M– clarified that respondents in immigration proceedings are presumed to be competent and, if there is no indicia of incompetency in a case, no further inquiry regarding competency is required.[397] In determining whether a respondent is competent to participate in immigration proceedings, IJs must determine whether he or she "has a rational and factual understanding of the nature and object of the proceedings, can consult with the attorney or representative if there is one, and has a reasonable opportunity to examine and present evidence and cross-examine witnesses."[398]

Because an individual's level of mental competence differs depending on his or her specific circumstances and may vary over time, the BIA instructed IJs to look to "indicia of incompetency" throughout the duration of the proceedings.[399] Indicia of incompetency may stem from observations of the respondent's functioning and behavior, testimonial evidence, or documentation submitted as part of the record.[400] As the American Immigration Council notes:

Potential indicators of serious mental disorders, which may give rise to competency issues, include difficulty communicating thoughts completely or coherently, perseveration, overly simplistic or concrete thinking, words or actions that do not make sense or suggest that the person is experiencing hallucinations or an altered version of reality, memory impairment, disorientation, an altered level of consciousness or wakefulness, or a high level of distraction, inattention or confusion.[401]

If there are indicia of incompetency, the IJ must make further inquiry to determine whether the respondent is sufficiently competent to proceed without safeguards.[402]

The measures an IJ takes to assess competency vary from case to case based on the specific circumstances involved.[403] For instance, an IJ may pose questions to the respondent about where the hearing is taking place, the nature of the proceedings, and

---

[396] *See Matter of M–A–M–*, 25 I&N Dec. 474 (BIA 2011).

[397] *Id.*

[398] *Id.* at 479. *See also* INA §240(b)(4)(B); 8 CFR §1240.10(a)(4) (2014).

[399] *Matter of M–A–M–*, 25 I&N Dec. 474, 480 (BIA 2011).

[400] *Id.* at 479.

[401] Am. Immigration Council, Legal Action Center, *Representing Clients with Mental Competency Issues Under Matter of M–A–M–*, at 3 (Nov. 30, 2011), *available at http://legalactioncenter.org/sites/default/files/docs/lac/Mental-Competency-Issues.pdf.*

[402] *Matter of M–A–M–*, 25 I&N Dec. 474, 477, 479 (BIA 2011).

[403] *Id.* at 480.

the respondent's state of mind.[404] An IJ also might ask the respondent "whether he or she currently takes or has taken medication to treat a mental illness and what the purpose and effects of that medication are."[405] In addition to asking questions of the respondent, an IJ may continue the proceedings to allow the respondent to find counsel, seek treatment, or gather and submit evidence regarding competency. Such evidence may include medical treatment reports, documentation from criminal proceedings, or letters and testimony from third party sources that bear on the respondent's mental health.[406] An IJ also may solicit testimony from family and friends or order a mental competency evaluation of the respondent.[407]

IJs may look to federal circuit court and prior BIA decisions for guidance in determining the respondent's level of competency. The Sixth Circuit has held that the only time a competency hearing is required is when an "*unrepresented* alien shows sufficient evidence of incompetency to require an attorney or guardian to represent the alien's interests ...."[408] The standard of competency in federal *criminal* trials is whether the accused: (1) has sufficient present ability to consult with counsel with a reasonable degree of rational understanding; and (2) has a rational as well as a factual understanding of the proceedings.[409]

In an unpublished decision, the BIA remanded a case to the IJ to determine whether an individual was "mentally competent to *meaningfully participate* in her own hearing."[410] If the IJ determined that he or she could not so participate, the IJ must appoint a guardian or representative for the individual and hold a new hearing to determine if he or she is eligible for relief from removal.[411] Overall, if an individual is unable to participate in his or her own defense, proceeding with a removal hearing may violate an individual's right to due process. Due process requires a meaningful opportunity to be heard,[412] but may not protect a mentally incompetent respondent

---

[404] *Id.*

[405] *Id.* at 481.

[406] *Id.*

[407] *Id.* (citing *Matter of J–F–F–*, 23 I&N Dec. 912, 915 (AG 2006) (where "at an IJ's request, DHS arranged for a psychiatric evaluation of a detained respondent, which led the psychiatrist to conclude that the respondent understood the proceedings and wanted to proceed with the hearing")).

[408] *Jadaan v. Gonzales,* 211 F. App'x 422, 431 (6th Cir. 2006) (emphasis in original).

[409] *Dusky v United States*, 362 U.S. 402, 403 (1960).

[410] *See Matter of M–V–, supra* note 393 (emphasis added).

[411] *Id. But see Nelson v. INS*, 232 F.3d 258, 261–62 (1st Cir. 2000) (finding applicant's statements that she has a "bad memory," that she "forget[s] things," and that she "get[s] pain" were "limited" symptoms that would *not* require IJ to request a custodian or other party to appear on her behalf); *Nee Hao Wong v. INS*, 550 F.2d 521, 523 (9th Cir. 1977) (holding due process does not require that proceedings be postponed until an incompetent individual is able to participate intelligently in the proceedings where he was accompanied by a state-appointed conservator who testified fully on his behalf).

[412] *See, e.g., Mathews v. Eldridge*, 424 U.S. 319, 348 (1976); *Kaczmarczyk v. INS*, 933 F.2d 588, 595 (7th Cir. 1991).

from deportation.[413] When the IJ's assessment of competency has been completed, the IJ must articulate his or her decision regarding the respondent's competency, as well as the reasoning supporting the decision, on the record.[414]

If the respondent lacks sufficient competency to proceed, the IJ must then evaluate appropriate safeguards based on the particular circumstances of the case before him or her.[415] As discussed above, the regulations provide some guidance regarding required safeguards.[416] Case law also provides guidance to IJs for determining how to fairly proceed when a respondent lacks competency. In *Matter of H–*, the BIA held that a respondent's due process rights were not violated where he was represented by an attorney who was able to introduce evidence and cross-examine witnesses, a doctor testified regarding his medical condition, and the respondent appeared to testify intelligently and rationally.[417]

Several federal circuit courts have also considered the fairness of proceedings involving respondents with indicia of mental incompetency. The Ninth Circuit has stressed the importance of protecting a mentally incompetent respondent's rights through necessary and proper safeguards.[418] In *Nee Hao Wong v. INS*, however, the Ninth Circuit held that the respondent's due process rights were not violated because there were appropriate safeguards in place: the respondent was represented by counsel and was accompanied by a state court-appointed conservator who testified fully on his behalf.[419] Similarly, where a respondent was represented and was able to answer questions to pose his version of the facts, the Tenth Circuit found that sufficient procedural safeguards were in place and the respondent had a meaningful opportunity to be heard.[420] In *Mohamed v. Gonzales*, the Eighth Circuit considered the case of a respondent who had answered the charges against him, testified in support of his claim, arranged for two witnesses to appear on his behalf, was aware of the nature and object of the proceedings, and vigorously resisted removal.[421] The court held that, under those circumstances, an IJ was not required to determine

[413] *See Nee Hao Wong v. INS,* 232 F.3d 521, 523 (9th Cir. 1977) (stating that deportation is "not a criminal proceeding, and the full trappings of procedural protections that are accorded criminal defendants are not necessarily constitutionally required for deportation proceedings"); *see also United States v. Mandycz,* 199 F. Supp. 2d 671, 675 (D. Mich. 2002) (finding that because due process does not protect incompetent defendants from deportation, a fortiori, it does not protect incompetent defendants from denaturalization).

[414] *Id.*

[415] *Id.* at 481–83.

[416] *See* 8 CFR §§1240.4, 1240.10(c), 1240.43 (2014).

[417] *Matter of H–*, 6 I&N Dec. 358 (BIA 1954). *See also Matter of J–F–F–*, 23 I&N Dec. 912, 922 (AG 2006) (stating that "It is appropriate for Immigration Judges to aid in the development of the record, and directly question witnesses.").

[418] *Nee Hao Wong v. INS,* 550 F.2d 521, 523 (9th Cir. 1977).

[419] *Id.*

[420] *Brue v. Gonzales*, 464 F.3d 1227, 1232–34 (10th Cir. 2006).

[421] *Mohamed v. Gonzales*, 477 F.3d 522, 526–27 (8th Cir. 2007).

competency.[422] Similarly, where a respondent was represented, his attorney did not request an evaluation, and the record did not contain evidence of incompetency, the First Circuit found that a respondent's due process rights were not violated.[423]

Drawing on guidance from the regulations and case law, the BIA found that examples of appropriate safeguards may include:

- Legal representation;
- Refusal to accept an admission of removability from an unrepresented respondent;
- Identification and appearance of a family member or close friend who can assist the respondent and provide the court with information;
- Docketing or managing the case to facilitate the respondent's ability to obtain legal representation and/or medical treatment in an effort to restore competency;
- Participation of a guardian in the proceedings;
- Continuance of the case for good cause shown;
- Closing the hearing to the public;
- Waiving the respondent's appearance;
- Actively aiding in the development of the record, including the examination and cross-examination of witnesses;
- Reserving appeal rights for the respondent; and
- Where no procedural safeguards would ensure a fair hearing, administrative closure while options are explored, such as seeking treatment for the respondent.[424]

If the severity of the respondent's mental competency issues precludes a fair hearing under any circumstances, termination of proceedings may be appropriate.[425] The BIA instructs, "The Immigration Judge will consider the facts and circumstances of [a respondent's] case to decide which of these or other relevant safeguards to utilize."[426] For any decision regarding competency issues, the IJ must articulate the rationale for his or her decision.[427] The IJ must then apply the appropriate safeguards he or she has identified.[428]

---

[422] *Id.*

[423] *Munoz-Monsalve v. Mukasey*, 551 F.3d 1, 6–8 (1st Cir. 2008).

[424] *Matter of M–A–M–*, 25 I&N Dec. 474, 483 (BIA 2011).

[425] *Immigration Judge Benchbook*, at 120 (suggesting that IJs consider "terminating cases where respondents are unable to proceed in light of mental health issues and a corresponding inability to secure adequate safeguards").

[426] *Id.*

[427] *Id.*

[428] *Id.* at 484.

- **Practice Pointer**: Practitioners representing mentally incompetent respondents should complete the following steps in securing their clients' due process rights:[429] (1) gather documentary evidence of the respondent's condition, and request a continuance if there is not enough time to collect this evidence before the next hearing; (2) present a written request to DHS, with a copy to the court, for documents bearing on the respondent's competence;[430] (3) file a Track III FOIA request for the respondent's A-file and medical documentation; (4) if DHS does not produce the documentation, file a Motion for Subpoena;[431] (5) arrange for a competency evaluation by a qualified expert;[432] (6) move for a competency hearing;[433] (7) move for various safeguards to secure the respondent's due process rights; (8) advocate for the respondent's release from detention or transfer to a facility closer to his or her support networks;[434] and (9) consider whether advocating for DHS to exercise prosecutorial discretion in closing or terminating the case may be the respondent's best option for relief.[435] Overall, it is essential for practitioners to create a record of their client's mental incompetency issues and to not rely solely on the IJ to recognize indicia of incompetence and identify and impose the necessary safeguards.

- **Practice Pointer**: Practitioners should carefully consider their ethical obligations when representing mentally incompetent individuals. A mentally incompetent individual may not be able to properly consent to representation. Practitioners should ask: Do you want to stay in the United States? Do you want me to help you do that? Can I help you in the courtroom?[436] If the individual lacks competence to consent to representation, practitioners should find out whether a family member or legal guardian has been appointed to manage the individual's affairs. If the individual does have a legal guardian, practitioners must obtain his or her consent before representing the individual.[437] A mentally incompetent individual also may be unable to effectively communicate with his or her attorney or actively participate in his or her defense.

[429] Am. Immigration Council, Legal Action Center, *Representing Clients with Mental Competency Issues Under Matter of M–A–M–*, at 6–10 (Nov. 30, 2011), *available at http://legalactioncenter.org/sites/default/files/docs/lac/Mental-Competency-Issues.pdf.*

[430] *See Matter of M–A–M–*, 25 I&N Dec. 474, 480 (BIA 2011).

[431] *See* INA §240(b)(1); 8 CFR §§1003.35(b), 1287.4 (2014).

[432] *See Matter of M–A–M–*, 25 I&N Dec. 474, 481 (BIA 2011).

[433] *See* Am. Immigration Council, *supra* note 429, at 9–10.

[434] *Id.* at 14–16.

[435] *Id.* at 21–22.

[436] *Id.* at 10.

[437] *Id.* at 11.

Termination or securing a guardian ad litem may be appropriate under such circumstances.[438]

- **Practice Pointer**: The Capital Area Immigrants' Rights (CAIR) Coalition has published a comprehensive manual to assist practitioners representing individuals who are mentally ill before the immigration courts. The manual also sets forth strategies for making claims for asylum, withholding of removal, and CAT claims. In 2013, CAIR published the second edition of the manual, entitled *Practice Manual for Pro Bono Attorneys Representing Detainees with Mental Disabilities in the Immigration Detention and Removal System*. The manual is available on CAIR's website at *www.caircoalition.org/2013/01/24/cair-coalition-releases-second-edition-of-mental-health-practice-manual/*.[439] Another useful resource is the Texas Appleseed report published in March of 2010, "Justice for Immigration's Hidden Population: Protecting the Rights of Persons with Mental Disabilities in the Immigration Court and Detention System," and available at *www.texasappleseed.net/index.php?option=com_docman&task=doc_download&gid=313&Itemid=*.[440]

- **Practice Pointer**: Mental illness may also be a protected characteristic for purposes of asylum.[441] Asylum-seekers have also claimed that they would be tortured, within the meaning of the CAT, due to inadequate access to necessary mental health care. While several of these claims have been denied, courts appear to implicitly recognize that such a claim, if supported by adequate evidence, would be viable.[442] In certain

---

[438] *Id.* at 12.

[439] (last visited Feb. 14, 2015).

[440] (last visited Feb. 14, 2015).

[441] *See, e.g., Temu v. Holder*, 740 F.3d 887 (4th Cir. 2014) (finding that "individuals with bipolar disorder who exhibit erratic behavior" qualifies as a cognizable particular social group). *Matter of J–M, [number not provided]* (BIA May 31, 2007) (finding that he had at least 10 percent likelihood that his bipolar disorder would cause him to be persecuted in a state psychiatric hospital, where he would be forced to undergo electric shock therapy without anesthesia), available at *http://bibdaily.com/pdfs/BIAu5-31-07JobeJ-M-.pdf*. The panel also held that "Peruvian psychiatric patients with serious and chronic mental illness" constituted a social group, which may be entitled to protection. *Id. But see Baptiste v. Att'y Gen. of the U.S.*, 229 Fed.Appx. 66, 2007 U.S. App. LEXIS 9400, at *3–*4 (3rd Cir. Apr. 25, 2007) (holding that petitioner, a Haitian citizen, failed both to show that disabled Haitians constituted a particular social group and that he was a member of such a group, given that his conditions, a limp and depression, were exceedingly minor); *Akhtar v. Att'y Gen.*, 138 Fed. Appx. 481, 483 (3rd Cir. 2005) (finding that an applicant pointed to no evidence showing that the treatment of disabled individuals in Pakistan rose to the level of persecution).

[442] *See, e.g., Lin v. Gonzales*, 2007 U.S. App. LEXIS 3041, at *4–*5 (2d Cir. 2007) (affirming BIA's decision to deny petitioner's motion to reopen, and finding that the evidence in the record did not support petitioner's contention that mental health patients in China were subject to abuse); *Raffington v. Cangemi*, 399 F.3d 900, 904 (8th Cir. 2005) (holding that while petitioner may not have access to the

Continued

cultures individuals suffering from mental illness or disabilities have been accused of being witches or engaging in witchcraft. UNHCR has published a research paper on this topic, entitled "Witchcraft allegations, refugee protection and human rights: a review of the evidence," (Jan. 2009) available at *www.unhcr.org/research/RESEARCH/4981ca712.pdf*. See chapter 2 for a detailed discussion of the protected grounds for asylum.

IX. What Happens at the Master Calendar Hearing?

Removal proceedings begin when DHS serves a Form I-862, Notice to Appear (NTA) on the respondent and files that NTA with the immigration court.[443] The NTA usually lists the date, time, and place of the initial master calendar hearing in the proceedings. If the NTA does not list the date, time, and location of the hearing, the immigration court usually will send a Notice of Hearing to the applicant.[444] To allow the respondent an opportunity to obtain counsel and to prepare to respond, at least ten days must pass between the service of the NTA on the respondent and the initial master calendar hearing.[445] The respondent may sign the Request for Prompt Hearing on the NTA to waive this 10-day requirement.[446]

By statute, the initial master calendar hearing must commence "not later than 45 days" for asylum applications initially filed with the IJ, unless there are exceptional circumstances.[447] Asylum applications filed on or after January 4, 1995, are placed on

---

same level of public and private mental health care in Jamaica as in the United States, that does not constitute torture within the meaning of the Convention Against Torture); *Matter of J–F–F–*, 23 I&N Dec. 912, 918 (BIA 2006) (holding that respondent's uninformed guess that he could not procure his medication in the Dominican Republic and a single sentence about the general shortage of mental health resources is not sufficient to demonstrate that he would be tortured if returned to the Dominican Republic under the Convention Against Torture). *But see Lavira v. Att'y Gen.*, 478 F.3d 158, 166–72 (3d Cir. 2007) (finding Haitian government's placement of an HIV-positive, above-the-knee amputee in a prison with "wholly inadequate" medical care constituted persecution because the government was "placing an individual in such conditions with the intent to inflict severe pain and suffering on that individual") (internal quotation marks and citation omitted); *Gomez-De Leon v. INS*, 2002 U.S. Dist. LEXIS 13606, at *14–*15 (D. Conn. 2002) (holding that under the Convention Against Torture, a person claiming that he or she would be tortured because of inadequate mental health care would have to show that the alleged torture would be inflicted by public officials or that it would be for the purpose of obtaining information, punishing or intimidating the person, or for a discriminatory reason); *Matter of Andy Taylor*, 24 *Immigr. Rptr.* B1-184 (BIA 2002) (holding that under the Convention Against Torture, the torture must be inflicted by public officials and there was no evidence that the Nicaraguan government either inflicts or acquiesces in torturous acts against persons who are vulnerable because of emotional problems).

[443] 8 CFR §§1003.13, 1003.14 (2014); ICPM, chapter 4.2(a).

[444] ICPM, chapter 4.15(c).

[445] INA §239(b)(1); ICPM, chapter 4.15(b).

[446] ICPM, chapter 4.15(b).

[447] INA §208(d)(5); 8 USC §1158(d)(5) (2012).

an expedited docket and should be completed, in the absence of exceptional circumstances, within 180 days after the application is filed with the court.[448] IJs have been instructed to allow for a minimum of 14 days between the master calendar and the individual calendar hearing, unless a two-week delay would prevent the court from completing the case in 180 days or the applicant requests an earlier date.[449] Currently, courts rarely adhere to these time periods because of their ever-expanding dockets. If the court causes a delay in processing the case, the individual will continue to accumulate time on his or her asylum "clock." The 180-day period is tied to the 180-day period during which an asylum applicant is ineligible for employment authorization.[450]

Unlike asylum claims, withholding of removal and deferral of removal claims under the CAT are not subject to the 180-day "clock" (or period during which asylum claims must be decided).[451] A CAT claim, however, will be adjudicated with all other claims for relief in removal proceedings.[452] Since there is no separate hearing for a CAT claim, an individual who is applying for asylum, as well as CAT relief may be subject to the 180-day expedited docket.[453] At least one court has held that an IJ abused his discretion in failing to give a CAT applicant adequate time to complete his application due to the deficiencies with his legal representation.[454]

Master calendar hearings are held for pleadings, scheduling, and other similar preliminary matters.[455] The purpose of the master calendar hearing is to:

- Advise the respondent of the right to an attorney or other representative at no expense to the government;
- Advise the respondent of the availability of free and low-cost legal service providers and provide the respondent with a list of such providers in the area where the hearing is being conducted;
- Advise the respondent of the right to present evidence;
- Advise the respondent of the right to examine and object to evidence and to cross-examine any witnesses presented by DHS;

---

[448] INA §208(d)(5)(a)(iii); 8 USC §1158(d)(5)(a)(iii) (2012); *see also* EOIR Memorandum, *supra* note 88, at 8.

[449] INA §208(d)(5)(a)(iii); 8 USC §1158(d)(5)(a)(iii) (2012).

[450] *See infra* pt. IX.B. and chapter 13 for a detailed discussion of the employment authorization clock and strategies for avoiding stopping the accrual of the 180 day period.

[451] *See* EOIR, OCIJ OPPM 11-02: The Asylum Clock (Nov. 15, 2011), available at *www.justice.gov/eoir/efoia/ocij/oppm11/11-02.pdf.*

[452] *Id.*

[453] For more information on the 180-day time period, *see* chapter 3.3.5.

[454] *Louis-Martin v. Ridge*, 322 F. Supp. 2d 556, 561–62 (M.D. Pa. 2004).

[455] INA §240(b); 8 CFR §1240.10 (2014); ICPM, chapter 4.15(a).

- Explain the charges and factual allegations contained in the NTA in non-technical language;
- Take pleadings;
- Identify and narrow the factual and legal issues;
- Set deadlines for filing applications for relief, briefs, motions, pre-hearing statements, exhibits, witness lists, and other documents;
- Provide certain warnings related to background and security investigations;
- Schedule hearings to adjudicate contested matters and applications for relief;
- Advise the respondent of the consequences of failing to appear at subsequent hearings; and
- Advise the respondent of the right to appeal to the Board of Immigration Appeals.[456]

These concepts are discussed in detail below.

A. Before the Master Calendar Hearing

Prior to the master calendar hearing, attorneys and representatives should be ready to file an EOIR-28, Notice of Entry of Appearance and any EOIR-33/IC, Change of Address for the respondent.[457] They also should be ready to file the I-589 application and any supporting documentation, especially if there is a potential one-year filing deadline issue. Filing the I-589 at the initial master calendar hearing also starts the accrual of days on the asylum "clock" for purposes of employment authorization eligibility (if the application is being filed for the first time and was not previously filed with the asylum office).

Attorneys and representatives also should meet with their clients prior to the master calendar hearing to do the following:

- Explain the nature and purpose of the immigration court proceedings;
- Discuss what will happen during the master calendar hearing, as well as the attorney or representative's role;
- Determine whether service of the NTA on the applicant was proper and whether the content of the Notice to Appear is deficient or inaccurate;
- Review the NTA together and discuss the factual allegations and charges against the respondent to make sure that he or she understands them;
- Advise the respondent of his or her legal rights in immigration court proceedings, including: the right to an attorney or other representative at no expense to the

---

[456] INA §§240(b)(4), 240(b)(5); 8 CFR §§1240.10, 1240.15 (2014); ICPM, chapter 4.15(e).

[457] These forms are available online on the EOIR website, available at *www.justice.gov/eoir/formslist.htm* (last visited Feb. 8, 2015).

government, the right to present evidence, the right to examine and object to evidence, and the right to cross-examine any witnesses presented by DHS;

- Explain the consequences of failing to appear for immigration court hearings;
- Explain the consequences under INA §208(d)(6) of knowingly making a frivolous asylum application;
- Discuss how the respondent will plead to the factual allegations and charges in the NTA;
- Discuss whether the respondent will challenge removability or concede removability and seek relief from removal;
- If the respondent is seeking relief, discuss the form(s) of relief from removal to ensure that the respondent understands the legal requirements;
- Notify the respondent that if applications for relief are not timely submitted or if the respondent does not appear as requested for the collection of biometrics, his or her application(s) may be deemed waived and abandoned;
- Discuss whether the respondent will use an interpreter in his or her individual hearing, and if so, what language and dialect the interpreter should speak, as well as any specific location of that particular dialect; and
- Discuss whether the respondent will designate a particular country of removal.[458]

  - ➢ **Practice Pointer**: For helpful guidance on developing a game plan for handling removal cases, see Andres Benach's article, "A Solid Game Plan for Handling Removal Cases," in AILA *VOICE* (December 2014), available at *www.aila.org/File/Related/14121141.pdf.*[459]

The facts alleged in the NTA may not be accurate. When DHS alleges that certain acts or conduct by the Respondent were in violation of the law and charges the Respondent with alleged violations of the INA,[460] these are allegations and not evidence and DHS's conclusions concerning inadmissibility or deportability based on those allegations are not always correct. In fact, it is not uncommon for DHS to allege a fact that is not accurate or to overreach in its charges against the Respondent. Thus, attorneys should never automatically accept those allegations and conclusions in an effort to focus on any relief from removal that might be available to the Respondent. Rather, attorneys should meet with the Respondent and discuss each factual allegation as it has been presented in the NTA. If there are any inaccuracies, these should be raised on the record of proceedings before the immigration court during the master calendar hearing.[461]

---

[458] INA §§240(b)(4), 240(b)(5); 8 CFR §§1240.10, 1240.15 (2014); ICPM, chapter 4.15(e).

[459] (last visited Mar. 30, 2015).

[460] *See* INA §239(a)(1)(D).

[461] Dree Collopy, Melissa Crow, & Rebecca Sharpless, *Challenges and Strategies Beyond Relief*, IMMIGRATION PRACTICE POINTERS (AILA 2014–15 ed.).

Additionally, attorneys must carefully analyze the charges of inadmissibility or deportability in light of the respondent's facts to determine if he or she was properly charged. A respondent in removal proceedings must be charged as either inadmissible under INA §212(a) or deportable under INA §237(a). The first step in this analysis is to determine whether the Respondent has already been admitted to the United States or is an arriving alien. Where the Respondent was improperly charged as deportable when he or she was actually inadmissible, or vice versa, the court should terminate the proceedings.[462]

If the Respondent was properly charged under INA §212(a) or INA §237(a), the next step in the analysis is to determine whether the specific charges against the Respondent are accurate.[463] Attorneys should review each charge and analyze it in light of the Respondent's specific facts. Any challenges to removability must be raised on the record of proceedings before the immigration court. It is possible that DHS has not established inadmissibility or deportability in the NTA, which also may lead to termination of the proceedings.[464]

- **Practice Pointer**: Beyond inaccuracy of the charges as discussed above, the following is a list of potential grounds for challenging the NTA: (1) Due process violations;[465] (2) Res judicata or collateral estoppel, where the issue or charge has already been considered and addressed or litigated;[466] (3) Notice of the proceedings or charge(s) against the Respondent was insufficient;[467] (4) The NTA was improvidently issued;[468] (5) The NTA was not issued by the proper authorities;[469] (6) The Respondent is a U.S. citizen or national, whether by birth, naturalization, automatic acquisition, or derivation from a relative;[470] (7) The Respondent was a citizen at the time he or she was convicted of the

---

[462] *Matter of R–D–*, 24 I&N Dec. 221 (BIA 2007).

[463] *See* INA §§212(a), 237(a) (listing the various inadmissibility and deportability grounds).

[464] *See Bilokumsky v. Tod*, 263 U.S. 149 (1923).

[465] These are discussed below in the sections on Motions to Suppress and Due Process Challenges.

[466] *See U.S. v. Utah Constr. & Mining Co.*, 384 U.S. 394, 422 (1966); *Oyeniran v. Holder*, 672 F.3d 800, 806–07 (9th Cir. 2012); *Al Mutarreb v. Holder*, 561 F.3d 1023, 1031 (9th Cir. 2009); *Bravo-Pedroza v. Gonzales*, 475 F.3d 1358 (9th Cir. 2007); *Guevara v. Gonzales*, 450 F3d 173 (5th Cir. 2006); *Duvall v. U.S. Att'y Gen.*, 436 F.3d 382 (3d Cir. 2006); *Medina v. INS*, 993 F.2d 499 (5th Cir. 1993); *Ramon-Sepulveda v. INS*, 824 F.2d 749 (9th Cir. 1987).

[467] *Matter of Lopez-Barrios*, 20 I&N Dec. 203 (BIA 1990); *Chowdhury v. INS*, 249 F.3d 970 (9th Cir. 2001); *Xiong v. INS*, 173 F.3d 601, 607–08 (7th Cir. 1999).

[468] *Matter of Vizcarra-Delgadillo*, 13 I&N Dec. 51 (BIA 1968). If the NTA was improvidently issued, DHS may cancel it. 8 CFR §§239.2(a), 1239.2(a) (2014). However, once the NTA has been filed with the immigration court, DHS cannot unilaterally terminate proceedings. DHS must instead move the immigration judge to terminate the proceedings. *See Matter of G–N–C–*, 22 I&N Dec. 281 (BIA 1998).

[469] 8 CFR §§239.1(a)(1)–(41) (2014).

[470] 8 CFR §§239.2(a)(1)–(2) (2014); *Matter of Cruz*, 15 I&N Dec. 236 (BIA1974). *See also* INA §§301–309, 316–320.

charges forming the basis of the removability ground;[471] (8) The Respondent is deceased or is not in the United States;[472] and (9) The Respondent has refugee or asylee status and that status has not been revoked.

If the statutory and regulatory requirements of service and content are not met, or if the factual allegations and charges of inadmissibility or deportability against the respondent are deficient, inaccurate, or unconstitutional, it is essential for attorneys to raise these issues and challenge the NTA on the record. Not only does this secure the respondent's rights under the law and preserve these important issues for appeal, but it also may lead to termination of the removal proceedings altogether.[473] Of course, it may be the case that the respondent does not want proceedings to be terminated. Thus, this is a strategic consideration that must be determined on a case-by-case basis.

Moreover, challenging the NTA is important because inaccurate or overreaching factual allegations and charges may affect the respondent's eligibility for relief, as well as his or her eligibility for release from detention.[474] They may also affect who has the burden of proof during that stage of the proceedings.[475] If the respondent is present in the United States without having been admitted or paroled, it is DHS's burden of proof to establish the respondent's alienage.[476] If DHS is able to demonstrate alienage, the burden then shifts to the respondent to demonstrate that he or she is lawfully present or not inadmissible as charged.[477] On the other hand, if the respondent was lawfully admitted, but is now deportable, the burden is on DHS to prove that the respondent is removable as charged by "clear and convincing evidence."[478] If DHS meets this burden, the burden then shifts to the respondent to demonstrate eligibility for relief from removal. Challenging allegations of alienage, inadmissibility, or deportability as set forth in the NTA shifts the burden of proof to DHS and may force DHS to meet its burden in an evidentiary hearing before the immigration court. This is essential to protect the respondent's rights and to preserve important issues for appeal. Furthermore, if DHS cannot meet its burden, proceedings against the respondent must be terminated.

- **Practice Pointer**: For a useful summary of the shifting burdens of proof in immigration court proceedings, see Nicholas Chavez, Michelle Mendez, and Philip Smith's article, "Whose Turn Is It?: Allocation of

---

[471] *Costello v. INS*, 376 U.S. 120 (1964).

[472] 8 CFR §239.2(a)(3)–(4) (2014).

[473] *Matter of G–N–C–*, 22 I&N Dec. 281 (BIA 1998).

[474] *See* INA §236(c).

[475] 8 CFR §1240.8 (2014).

[476] *Id.*

[477] 8 CFR §1240.8(c) (2014).

[478] INA §240(c)(3)(A); 8 CFR §1240.8(a) (2014).

Burdens of Proof in Removal Proceedings," in *AILA's Immigration Practice Pointers* (2014–15 ed.).

➢ **Practice Pointer**: For a helpful practice advisory on how to challenge the NTA and approach the factual allegations and charges strategically, see the American Immigration Council's advisory entitled, "Notices to Appear: Legal Challenges and Strategies," available at *www.legalactioncenter.org/sites/default/files/NTA%20PA%20FIN%206-27-14.pdf*.[479]

B. At the Master Calendar Hearing

If the Respondent is late to appear at a master calendar hearing, the hearing may be held *in absentia* and he or she may be ordered removed.[480] In any removal proceeding before an IJ in which the respondent fails to appear, the IJ shall order the respondent removed if: (1) DHS establishes by clear, unequivocal, and convincing evidence that the respondent is removable; and (2) DHS establishes by clear, unequivocal, and convincing evidence that written notice of the time and place of proceedings and written notice of the consequences of failure to appear were provided to the respondent or to his or her counsel of record.[481]

Written notice is considered sufficient if it was provided at the most recent address provided by the respondent. If the respondent fails to provide his or her address as required by 8 CFR §1003.15(d), no written notice is required for an IJ to proceed with an *in absentia* hearing.[482]

In *Matter of S–A–*, the BIA considered the appeal of an *in absentia* exclusion order of a respondent who arrived late for his hearing due to heavy traffic between Ft. Myer, FL and Miami, FL, where the hearing was held.[483] The respondent appeared approximately 30 minutes late and was ordered removed *in absentia* by the IJ.[484] The BIA held that "an applicant's general assertion that he was prevented from reaching his hearing on time by heavy traffic does not constitute reasonable cause that would warrant reopening of his in absentia exclusion proceedings."[485] Given the serious consequences of a late appearance, the respondent and counsel should arrive well before the scheduled time set for the master calendar hearing to allow enough time to

---

479 (last visited Feb. 16, 2015).

480 8 CFR §1003.26 (2014); ICPM, chapter 4.8, 4.15, 4.16, 4.17. *See, e.g., Matter of S–A–*, 21 I&N 1050 (BIA 1997) (holding that an applicant's general assertion that he was prevented from reaching his hearing on time by heavy traffic does not constitute reasonable cause that would warrant reopening of his in absentia exclusion proceedings).

481 8 CFR §1003.26(c) (2014).

482 8 CFR §1003.26(d) (2014).

483 *Matter of S–A–*, 21 I&N 1050 (BIA 1997).

484 *Id.* at 1050.

485 *Id.*

pass through mandatory security screening, find the proper court room, and sign in (if that judge uses a sign-in system for attorneys and representatives).[486]

> **Practice Pointer**: Most individuals who enter an immigration court must pass through a mandatory security screening, and often, there are long waiting lines to pass through security.[487] Regardless of such delays, all individuals must pass through security and be present in the courtroom on time and prepared for their hearings.

When it is time for the respondent's hearing, the IJ or court staff will call the applicant's name or A-number. At that time, the respondent and his or her attorney or representative make their way to the respondent's table and prepare to respond to the IJ's questions. The IJ starts the recording equipment at the beginning of the hearing and identifies on the record the type of proceeding being conducted; the respondent's name and A-number; the date, time, and place of the proceeding; and the presence of the parties.[488] The IJ also verifies the respondent's name, address, and telephone number. If his or her address or telephone number have changed, he or she must submit the Form EOIR-33/IC, Change of Address at that time.[489]

During the master calendar hearing, the IJ must advise the applicant of his or her right to representation; the availability of free legal services; and his or her rights to examine, object to, and present evidence, as well as to cross-examine witnesses.[490] If the applicant has not previously filed an application for asylum or withholding of removal with DHS and expresses a fear of returning to his or her home country, the IJ must also:

(1) advise the applicant that he or she may apply for asylum and withholding of removal;

(2) make the appropriate forms available;

(3) provide the applicant with a list of persons who provide pro bono representation; and

(4) advise the applicant of the consequences of knowingly filing a frivolous application for asylum.[491]

An IJ is not required to advise an individual of the right to apply for asylum if there is no plausible basis for such an application.[492]

---

[486] ICPM, chapter 4.15(d).

[487] ICPM, chapter 4.14.

[488] ICPM, chapter 4.15(f).

[489] *Id.*

[490] 8 CFR §1240.10(a) (2014).

[491] 8 CFR §1240.11(c)(1) (2014).

[492] *Valencia v. Mukasey*, 548 F.3d 1261, 1262 (9th Cir. 2008)

If the respondent is unrepresented or appearing "pro se," the IJ advises the respondent of his or her rights and obligations in immigration court hearings, including the right to be represented at no expense to the government. In addition, the IJ ensures that the respondent has received a list of free or low-cost legal service providers in the area.[493] The IJ is required to ask the applicant whether he or she desires representation,[494] and failure to do so may be grounds for the BIA to remand the claim to the IJ.[495] The respondent may waive the right to be represented and choose to proceed pro se. Alternatively, he or she may request a continuance of the proceedings so the respondent has the opportunity to obtain counsel or representation.[496]

If the respondent is represented, the attorney or representative should enter his or her appearance on behalf of the respondent by filing the Form EOIR-28, Notice of Entry of Appearance and serving a copy of the form on DHS.[497]

- **Practice Pointer**: Attorneys and representatives may appear telephonically at master calendar and bond redetermination hearings with the permission of the IJ. Requests to appear telephonically must be filed by submitting a motion with the immigration court in accordance with the time and filing requirements of the *Immigration Court Practice Manual* (ICPM).[498]

The respondent or the respondent's attorney or representative will then proceed with the respondent's pleadings.[499] Each IJ has his or her own preferences regarding how to take pleadings; however, many IJs use the pleading format that is set forth in the ICPM at Appendix M and EOIR strongly encourages use of this pleading format.[500]

---

[493] ICPM, chapter 4.15(g).

[494] 8 CFR §1240.10(a)(1) (2014).

[495] *See Matter of Michel*, 21 I&N Dec. 1101 (BIA 1998).

[496] 8 CFR §1240.6 (2014); ICPM, chapter 4.15(g).

[497] 8 CFR §1003.17 (2014); ICPM, chapter 4.15(h). The Form EOIR-28 is available at *www.justice.gov/eoir/eoirforms/eoir28.pdf* (last visited Feb. 8, 2015).

[498] *See* EOIR Memorandum No. 08-04 from David Neal on Guidelines for Telephonic Appearances by Attorneys and Representatives at Master Calendar and Bond Redetermination Hearings (July 30, 2008), AILA InfoNet Doc. No. 08080760 (*posted* Aug. 7, 2008), *available at www.usdoj.gov/eoir/efoia/ocij/oppm08/08-04.pdf. See also* chapter 4 of the new *Immigration Court Practice Manual, available at www.usdoj.gov/eoir/vll/OCIJPracManual/ocij_page1.htm*.

[499] Because asylum applications must be filed in open court, pleadings usually are completed orally during a master calendar hearing. However, under certain circumstances, pleadings may be completed in writing. ICPM, chapter 4.15(j). The IJ may permit written pleadings if the respondent concedes proper service of the NTA and signs the written pleading. *Id.* The ICPM lists the specific language that must be included in a written pleading and also contains a sample written pleading at Appendix L. *See* chapter 4.15(j), App'x L.

[500] ICPM, chapter 4.15(i)(i), App'x M.

> **Practice Pointer**: Prior to the master calendar hearing, practitioners should consult with advocates who have experience practicing before that particular IJ to determine how he or she conducts master calendar hearings and which format he or she prefers for pleadings. If the IJ prefers to use the sample oral pleading in the ICPM at Appendix M, practitioners should prepare his or her responses within that format prior to the master calendar hearing.[501]

During the pleading, the respondent or his or her attorney or representative should be prepared to do the following:

- Concede or deny service of the NTA;
- Request or waive a formal reading of the NTA;
- Request or waive an explanation of the respondent's rights and obligations in removal proceedings;
- Admit or deny the charges and factual allegations in the NTA;[502]
- Designate or decline to designate a country of removal;[503]
- State what application(s) for relief from removal, if any, the respondent intends to file;
- Identify and narrow the legal and factual issues;
- Estimate (in hours) the amount of time needed to present the case that the individual hearing;
- Request a date on which to file the application(s) for relief, if any, with the immigration court; and
- Request an interpreter for the respondent and witnesses, if needed.[504]

According to the ICPM, the DHS attorney should be prepared to:

- State DHS's position on all legal and factual issues, including eligibility for relief;
- Designate a country of removal;
- File with the immigration court and serve on the opposing party all documents that support the charges and factual allegations in the NTA; and
- Serve on the respondent the DHS biometrics instructions, if appropriate.[505]

---

[501] *See* ICPM, App'x M, *available at www.justice.gov/eoir/vll/OCIJPracManual/Practice_Manual_review.pdf#page=25.*

[502] 8 CFR §1240.10(c) (2014).

[503] Usually, for an asylum, withholding of removal, or CAT claim, respondents should decline to designate a country of removal since they fear removal to their native countries or countries of last habitual residence.

[504] ICPM, chapters 4.15(i)(i), 4.15(o)(i).

[505] ICPM, chapter 4.15(i)(ii).

If service of the NTA is improper, if the content is deficient or inaccurate, if there are grounds to contest the Respondent's removability, or if the evidence has been unconstitutionally obtained, it is important for respondents and their representatives to object to and otherwise challenge the NTA on the record during the proceedings. Doing so can:

(1) hold DHS to its burden of proof and/or shift the burden of proof to DHS;[506]

(2) preserve the respondent's rights on appeal;[507]

(3) lead to the termination of removal proceedings against the respondent;[508]

(4) preserve the respondent's eligibility for relief from removal; and

(5) assist the respondent in contesting mandatory detention under INA §236(c).

> ➢ **Practice Pointer**: For a detailed discussion on why and how to challenge the Notice to Appear, see Dree Collopy, Melissa Crow, and Rebecca Sharpless's article, "Challenges and Strategies Beyond Relief," available in AILA's *Immigration Practice Pointers* (2014–15 ed.)[509]

Most applicants seeking asylum, withholding of removal, or CAT relief decline to designate a country of removal in the event that removal is ordered. If the applicant declines, the IJ is required to designate a country for the applicant.[510] If the IJ designates a country other than the country of claimed persecution, the IJ must advise the applicant that he or she has the right to seek asylum and introduce evidence to contest removal to the country designated by the IJ.[511] An IJ may designate a country even if the applicant is not a citizen or national of the country[512] and regardless of whether the receiving country has made a commitment to accept the applicant.[513]

---

[506] 8 CFR §1240.8 (2014).

[507] *See Chambers v. Mukasey*, 520 F.3d 445 (5th Cir. 2008); *Matter of Velasquez*, 19 I&N Dec. 377, 380 (BIA 1986).

[508] *See Matter of Lopez-Barrios*, 20 I&N Dec. 203 (BIA 1990).

[509] Collopy, Crow, & Sharpless, *supra* note 461.

[510] 8 CFR §1240.10(f) (2014).

[511] *See, e.g.*, *Gebrekidan v. Clark*, 2006 U.S. Dist. LEXIS 83687, at *4–5 (W.D. Wash. 2006) (granting stay of removal to applicant who sought asylum from Eritrea after ICE attempted to remove him to Ethiopia); *see also Kossov v. INS*, 132 F.3d 405, 408 (7th Cir. 1998) (finding that the lack of such advice was a fundamental failure of due process). *But see Desta v. Ashcroft*, 329 F.3d 1179 (10th Cir. 2003) (finding that the BIA has the authority to designate an alternate country of deportation).

[512] INA §§241(b)(2)(E)(i)–(vii); 8 USC §§1231(b)(2)(E)(i)–(vii); *see also Pavlovich v. Gonzales*, 476 F.3d 613, 616 (8th Cir. 2007) (noting that INA §§241(b)(2)(E)(i)–(vii) allow the AG to remove an applicant to any country that falls within one of seven categories if the applicant cannot be removed to his or her country of citizenship or nationality, *citing Jama v. Imm. & Customs Enforcement*, 543 U.S. 335, 342 (2005)).

[513] 8 CFR §§241.15(d), 1240.10(f) (2014); *see also Zahren v. Gonzales*, 487 F.3d 1039, 2007 U.S. App. LEXIS 11542, at *9–10 (7th Cir. 2007).

The U.S. Supreme Court has established a four-stage inquiry for designation of countries of removal: (1) the country of the applicant's choice; (2) otherwise, the country of the applicant's citizenship; (3) otherwise, a country to which the applicant has a lesser connection; and (4) if these are impracticable, inadvisable, or impossible, the applicant will be removed to any country willing to accept the applicant.[514]

IJs should inform asylum applicants and other noncitizens in removal proceedings that they can be removed to another country under INA §241(b) in the discretion of the DHS secretary.[515]

If the attorney or representative is not ready to proceed with the respondent's pleading at the first master calendar hearing, the IJ may grant a continuance for good cause shown.[516] Any delay caused by the applicant, however, will stop the asylum "clock" from accruing time and could impact the applicant's eligibility to apply for employment authorization.[517]

> **Practice Pointer**: An applicant is eligible to apply for employment authorization when the "asylum clock" reaches 150 days and is eligible to be granted employment authorization when the clock reaches 180 days. For a more in-depth look at this issue, see the American Immigration Council, Legal Action Center's Practice Advisory, "Employment Authorization and Asylum: Strategies to Avoid Stopping the Asylum EAD Clock" (Feb. 5, 2014), available at *www.legalactioncenter.org/sites/default/files/employment_authorization_and_asylum_fin_2-5-14_0.pdf.*[518] See chapter 13 of this book for a detailed discussion of seeking employment authorization while an asylum application is pending, as well as strategies to avoid stopping the clock.

---

514 *Jama*, 543 U.S. at 341. *See Hadera v. Gonzales*, 494 F.3d 1154, 1157–58 (9th Cir. 2007) (finding the IJ erred by failing to designate the applicant's country of nationality after the applicant declined to designate a country of removal).

515 8 CFR §1240.10(f) (2014).

516 8 CFR §1240.6 (2014); *see also Gjeci v. Gonzales*, 451 F.3d 416, 424 (7th Cir. 2006) (refusal to continue hearing resulted in a denial of due process). *But see Alsamhouri v. Gonzales*, 484 F.3d 117, 123 (1st Cir. 2007) (finding that the denial of a continuance did not result in a fundamentally unfair hearing where the applicant had 16 months to obtain counsel and file his applications); *Berri v. Gonzales*, 468 F.3d 390, 395 (6th Cir. 2006) (finding applicants failed to show good cause where they had two years to prepare for their merits hearing); *Al Khouri v. Ashcroft*, 362 F.3d 461, 464 (8th Cir. 2004) (noting that IJs have wide discretion in managing their dockets and finding no abuse of discretion where the applicant was given ample opportunity to find another attorney).

517 *See* EOIR Memorandum No. OPPM 05-07 from the Office of the Chief Immigration Judge on Definitions and Use of Adjournment, Call-up, and Case Identification Codes (June 16, 2005), AILA InfoNet at Doc. No. 05070660 (*posted* July 6, 2005), *available at www.usdoj.gov/eoir/efoia/ocij/oppm05/05-07.pdf* (codes marked with an asterisk will stop the asylum clock until the next hearing).

518 (last visited Feb. 8, 2015).

Immigration court proceedings are bifurcated proceedings, separated into the removability and relief phases. The proceedings advance to the relief phase only if the IJ determines that the applicant is deportable or inadmissible.

DHS must establish that the applicant, if other than an "arriving alien," is deportable by clear and convincing evidence.[519] If the applicant has not been admitted or paroled into the United States, DHS must prove the applicant's alienage.[520] Usually this is done through the applicant's own admission at the hearing, but it may also be done by the submission of prior statements made by the applicant to legacy INS, DHS, or other government agencies.[521] If the applicant was searched, apprehended, or questioned in an unlawful manner prior to the applicant's hearing, it may be possible to have the evidence or prior statements excluded from consideration.[522]

If the applicant is an "arriving alien," the applicant must establish that he or she is clearly and beyond a doubt entitled to be admitted to the United States and is not inadmissible as charged.[523] An "arriving alien" is defined as a noncitizen "who seeks admission to or transit through the [United States] ... or who is interdicted in international or [U.S.] waters ... [or who is] paroled [into the United States] pursuant to [INA] §212(d)."[524]

Based on the admissions made by the applicant or the applicant's representative during the pleading, the IJ may determine that removability has been established by the admissions.[525] In order to do so, the IJ must be satisfied that no questions of law or fact remain.[526] If removability is not established by the admissions of the applicant, the IJ may schedule a separate hearing to determine any unresolved issues.[527] However, if removability has been established by the admissions of the respondent, the respondent should be prepared to state what application(s) for relief from removal, if any, he or she intends to file. If these application(s) are ready to be submitted at the time of pleadings, the IJ will accept the respondent's application(s) for relief. If not, the IJ will set a date for those applications to be submitted. If the

---

[519] INA §240(c)(3)(A); 8 USC §1229a(c)(3)(A); 8 CFR §1240.8 (2014). *But see Woodby v. INS*, 385 U.S. 276 (1966) (holding that legacy INS must establish deportability by evidence which is clear, *unequivocal*, and convincing).

[520] 8 CFR §1240.8(c) (2014).

[521] *See, e.g.*, 8 CFR §1240.7(a) (2014); *see also Matter of Ponce-Hernandez*, 21 I&N Dec. 784 (BIA 1999) (finding that the INS met its burden of proof in establishing a minor's deportability on the basis of a Record of Deportable Alien (Form I-213) that documented his identity and alienage).

[522] *See infra* this section.

[523] 8 CFR §1240.8(b) (2014).

[524] 8 CFR §§1.1(q), 1001.1(q) (2014).

[525] 8 CFR §1240.10(c) (2014).

[526] *Matter of Masri*, 22 I&N Dec. 1145 (BIA 1999).

[527] 8 CFR §1240.10(d) (2014).

requested relief is asylum, the IJ will schedule a second master calendar hearing for the respondent to submit his or her application in open court.

DHS is required to complete background and security investigations for certain applications for relief from removal, including asylum, withholding of removal, and protection under CAT.[528] Once the pleading has been taken at the master calendar hearing, the IJ will instruct the DHS attorney to provide the respondent with the DHS biometrics instructions. The respondent is expected to comply promptly with the instructions and abide by any deadlines set by the IJ. Failure to comply timely with the biometrics instructions will result in the application for relief being deemed abandoned and denied unless the respondent demonstrates that there was good cause for his or her failure to comply with the instructions.[529] If the respondent is detained, however, DHS is responsible for timely fingerprinting the respondent and obtaining all necessary information.[530]

In addition to the any change of address, the IJ's advisals to the respondent, the attorney or representative's entry of appearance, the taking of pleadings, the submission of any applications for relief from removal, and the transmittal of biometrics instructions to the respondent, an IJ also may entertain one or more motions during the preliminary hearing stage, such as motions to change venue, to terminate proceedings, or to suppress evidence.[531] The regulations suggest that all motions should be in writing and must state the grounds for the motion, the relief sought, and the jurisdiction of the court,[532] and a motion must be deemed unopposed unless a timely response is filed.[533]

- **Practice Pointer**: In practice, motions may be made orally and often are, without ever being in writing. However, given the language of the regulations, it is advisable that practitioners prepare and submit a written motion for the court and bring a copy to serve on DHS, even if making the motion in person during a hearing. If practitioners would like the IJ to rule on a motion during a hearing, the *Immigration Court Practice Manual* advises that the motion should be filed at least 15 days in advance of the hearing.[534]

The decision of whether to grant a change of venue motion rests solely in the discretion of the IJ.[535] In determining whether good cause exists, an IJ may consider a number of factors, including administrative convenience, location of witnesses, the

---

[528] 8 CFR §1003.47 (2014); ICPM, chapter 4.15(k).

[529] 8 CFR §1003.47(d) (2014); ICPM, chapter 4.15(k)(i).

[530] 8 CFR §1003.47(d) (2014); ICPM, chapter 4.15(k)(ii).

[531] *See* ICPM, chapter 5 for a detailed discussion of motions in immigration court.

[532] 8 CFR §1003.23(a) (2014).

[533] *Id.* For a sample motion, see Appx. 5F.

[534] ICPM, chapter 5.2(c).

[535] *Matter of Rivera*, 19 I&N Dec. 688, 690 (BIA 1988).

applicant's place of residence, and DHS's interests.[536] The OCIJ has issued a policy memorandum on motions to change venue that noted that the large number filed has created problems in caseload management. The memorandum urges IJs to "make an effort to ensure good cause has been shown."[537]

At the conclusion of the master calendar hearing, the IJ will provide the respondent with written notice of the date and time of the next hearing — either another master calendar hearing to submit the I-589 application or address any unresolved issues, or an individual evidentiary hearing on removability or the merits of the respondent's application(s) for relief.

- **Practice Pointer**: If a respondent is detained, the IJ may schedule him or her for a bond redetermination hearing during which the IJ will consider DHS's custody determination and any challenge to that determination by the respondent. For a detailed discussion of detention and bond, see chapter 9 of this book.

- **Practice Pointer**: Currently, most proceedings before the immigration courts are "removal proceedings." However, cases that were initiated long ago may be exclusion or deportation proceedings. For regulations regarding exclusion proceedings initiated before April 1, 1997, see 8 CFR §§1240.30–.38. For regulations regarding deportation proceedings initiated before April 1, 1997, see 8 CFR §§1240.40–.53.

X. What Happens After the Application is Filed?

After removability has been established and the I-589 application has been filed in open court, the IJ will schedule the respondent for his or her individual hearing on the merits of his or her application(s) for relief. Currently, if the respondent is not detained, there is an average waiting period of 594 days for the individual hearing date due to the overburdened dockets of the immigration courts.[538] Thus, a lot can happen between the master calendar hearing and the individual hearing. The court may seek comments from the Department of State regarding the respondent's application, the respondent must complete initial processing and a biometrics

---

[536] *Id.*; *see also Baires v. INS*, 856 F.2d 89 (9th Cir. 1988) (IJ's denial of a change of venue motion may violate an applicant's statutory and regulatory procedural rights to present evidence in support of the asylum claim by, among other things, depriving the applicant of the testimony of an expert and other witnesses); *Garcia-Guzman v. Reno*, 65 F. Supp. 2d 1077 (N.D. Cal. 1999) (finding that allowing counsel to appear telephonically was "woefully inadequate" where counsel notified legacy INS prior to the commencement of proceedings of the special needs of his mute client).

[537] *See* EOIR Memorandum No. 01-02 from the Office of the Chief Immigration Judge on Changes of Venue (Oct. 9, 2001) at 1–2, *reprinted in* 79 *Interpreter Releases* 66, 84–85 (Jan. 14, 2002), *available at www.usdoj.gov/eoir/efoia/ocij/oppm01/OPPM01-02.pdf.*

[538] TRAC Immigration, *Immigration Court Backlog Tool*, *available at http://trac.syr.edu/phptools/immigration/court_backlog/* (last visited Feb. 12, 2015).

appointment with DHS, the respondent may move and need to change his or her address with the immigration court, the respondent may need to file various motions with the immigration court, the respondent will file additional and updated documentation and evidence in support of his or her application(s) for protection as the individual hearing date draws near, the respondent may seek an informal or formal pre-hearing conference with DHS prior to the individual hearing, and the respondent will need to prepare for his or her testimony, as well as the testimony of any witnesses who will appear at the individual hearing on the respondent's behalf.

A. Department of State Comments

After the respondent has filed his or her asylum application with the immigration court, the court may, but is no longer required to, forward a copy of the application to the Department of State ("DOS") pursuant to 8 CFR §1208.11 and must then calendar the case for a merits hearing.[539] The reply from DOS, if any, must be given to both the applicant and DHS, unless the reply is classified.[540] The advice of DOS, however, is not binding on DHS or the courts.[541]

- **Practice Pointer**: Currently, it is rare that DOS will provide a reply or opinion in regard to a pending asylum claim before the immigration courts.

B. Initial Processing of the Application with USCIS

Individuals who apply for asylum, withholding of removal, and protection under the CAT are subject to identity, law enforcement, and security investigations or examinations related to their applications.[542] Failure to file the necessary documentation and comply with the requirements to provide biometrics and other biographical information in conformity with the applicable regulations, instructions for the applications, and the time allowed by the IJ's order constitutes abandonment of the application and the IJ may enter an order dismissing the application unless the applicant demonstrates that such failure was the result of good cause.[543] Thus, following the master calendar hearing and submission of the application for asylum, withholding of removal under INA §241(b)(3), or protection under the Convention Against Torture, the applicant must comply with the DHS instructions for submitting those applications and for providing biometric and biographic information to USCIS.[544]

---

[539] 8 CFR §1240.11(c)(2) (2014).

[540] *Id.*

[541] *Gailius v. INS*, 147 F.3d 34, 46 (1st Cir. 1998) (citations omitted) (noting concern that the DOS soft-pedals human rights violations by countries with which the United States wants to have good relations).

[542] 8 CFR §1003.47(b) (2014).

[543] 8 CFR §1003.47(c) (2014).

[544] *See* U.S. Citizenship and Immigration Servs., *Instructions for Submitting Certain Applications in Immigration Court and for Providing Biometric and Biographic Information to U.S. Citizenship and*

Continued

The respondent must send the following items to USCIS: (1) a clear copy of the first three pages of the completed I-589 that the respondent will be filing or has filed with the immigration court, which must include his or her full name, current mailing address, and A-number; (2) a copy of Form G-28, Notice of Entry of Appearance, if the respondent is represented; and (3) a copy of the DHS instructions.[545]

Current USCIS procedure requires that this documentation to be sent to USCIS Nebraska Service Center, Defensive Asylum Application with Immigration Court, P.O. Box 87589, Lincoln, NE 68501-7589.[546] After those three items are received at the USCIS Nebraska Service Center, the respondent will receive a USCIS receipt notice in the mail notifying him or her that USCIS has received the application.[547] This receipt notice usually arrives within about two or three weeks or submission of the USCIS filing.

> ➢ **Practice Pointer**: USCIS's biometrics procedures change periodically. It is important for practitioners to always research the current procedures prior to advising their clients on completing this important step in the process of seeking protection.

Completion of the steps on the instructions form first generates a receipt notice and then generates a biometrics appointment notice for the applicant and any dependent applicants. Failure to comply with processing requirements for biometrics will result in dismissal of the application unless the applicant demonstrates that such failure was the result of good cause.[548] Moreover, the IJ cannot grant asylum unless the applicant is in compliance with biometrics requirements under 8 CFR §1003.47.[549] If an IJ fails to provide the required instructions and warning, a dismissal of an application may be reversed.[550]

C. Biometrics Collection

Shortly after receipt of the USCIS receipt notice, the respondent and any dependent applicants included on his or her application will receive a notice for an appointment at an Application Support Center (ASC) indicating the individual's

---

Immigration Services [hereinafter USCIS Instructions for Applications and Biometrics], *available at www.uscis.gov/sites/default/files/files/article/PreOrderInstr.pdf* (last visited Feb. 8, 2015).

[545] *Id.*

[546] *Id.*

[547] *Id.*

[548] 8 CFR §§208.10, 1208.10 (2014).

[549] 8 CFR §§208.14, 1208.14 (2014). For more information, see U.S. Dep't of Homeland Security Fact Sheet, *USCIS and ICE Procedures Implementing EOIR Regulations on Background and Security Checks on Individuals Seeking Relief or Protection from Removal in Immigration Court or Before the BIA* (Aug. 8, 2006), *published on* AILA InfoNet Doc. No. 06081767 (*posted* Aug. 17, 2006), *available at www.uscis.gov/files/article/ JointFactsheet080806.pdf.*

[550] *See, e.g., Cui v. Mukasey*, 538 F.3d 1289, 1292 (9th Cir. 2008) (finding IJ abused his discretion by failing to grant a continuance so that the applicant could resubmit her fingerprints).

unique receipt number and instructing each person to appear for an appointment at a nearby ASC for collection of biometrics (a photograph, fingerprints, and signature).[551] The notice will notify the applicant that he or she has been scheduled to appear at an ASC to be fingerprinted and photographed for biometrics collection, and that completion of background identity and security checks is required in order to process the I-589 application. The notice will list the address of the ASC and its hours of operation, as well as a 14-day period during which the applicant may appear at the ASC to complete the biometrics collection. Finally, the notice will warn the applicant that failure to appear may result in dismissal of his or her asylum application.

The respondent and any dependents must then attend the biometrics appointment at the ASC and bring their photo identification and ASC appointment notices. If the applicant does not have a photo ID, the ASC will still collect his or her biometrics, however, there may be a delay during the appointment as a USCIS officer may interview the applicant regarding his or her identity. At the appointment, USCIS will collect their biometrics and provide a biometrics confirmation document — usually the stamped and signed ASC appointment notice.[552] This stamped notice should be provided to the immigration court prior to future hearings to demonstrate that the respondent and the dependents have complied with the biometrics requirements.[553]

If the respondent is not detained, it is the respondent's burden to ensure that his or her biometrics has been collected and remain current at the time of the individual hearing.[554] Thus, it is important that he or she follow the instructions provided by DHS and complete each of those steps. If the applicant fails to appear for his or her ASC appointment, the IJ cannot adjudicate his or her application(s) for protection.[555]

- **Practice Pointer**: Given the significant amount of time that most non-detained applicants must wait for their individual hearings, as well as the fact that it is the respondent's burden to provide his or her biometrics, it is essential for practitioners to call the ICE Office of Chief Counsel prior to an individual hearing to verify that the biometrics are, in fact, current. Typically, the duty attorney or court clerk is able to assist with confirming biometrics.
- **Practice Pointer**: If an applicant is detained, DHS is responsible for timely fingerprinting the respondent and obtaining all necessary information.[556]

---

[551] *Id.*

[552] USCIS Instructions for Applications and Biometrics, *supra* note 544.

[553] *Id.*

[554] 8 CFR §§103.16(a), 103.2(b)(9), 103.2(b)(13)(ii), 1003.47(d) (2014).

[555] INA §208(d)(5)(A)(i); 8 CFR §1003.47(g) (2014).

[556] 8 CFR §1003.47(d) (2014); ICPM, chapter 4.15(k)(ii).

After the respondent's biometrics have been collected, DHS initiates all relevant identity, law enforcement, or security investigations or examinations and completes those investigations or examinations as promptly as practicable.[557] DHS then advises the immigration judge of the results, on or before the date of the scheduled hearing on the applications for relief.[558] If DHS has not reported on the completion and results of the identity, law enforcement, and security checks by the date of the hearing, the IJ may continue proceedings for the purpose of completing those investigations or examinations, or may hear the case on the merits.[559] An IJ, however, may not grant an application for protection that is subject to the identity, law enforcement, or security investigations or examinations until after DHS has confirmed that the relevant checks have been completed and are current and the results have been reported to the IJ.[560]

According to the INA, "asylum cannot be granted until the identity of the applicant has been checked against all appropriate records or databases … to determine any grounds on which the [applicant] may be inadmissible to or deportable from the United States, or ineligible to apply for or be granted asylum."[561]

Once collected, biometrics are only valid for 15 months, after which they expire. Currently, most non-detained respondents need to wait a significant amount of time between their master calendar hearing and individual hearing — often well over 15 months — due to the immigration courts' overburdened dockets. Thus, it may be possible that the respondent and his or her dependents will need to have their biometrics collected again prior to the individual hearing. Failure to present up-to-date biometrics to an IJ may result in denial of his or her applications for relief.[562]

- **Practice Pointer**: Given the potential consequences of failing to provide unexpired biometrics to the immigration court, practitioners must ensure that their clients' biometrics are current prior to any individual hearing. To verify whether biometrics are current, practitioners should call the DHS Office of Chief Counsel that is party to the proceedings before the immigration court, provide the A-number of their client, and inquire whether his or her biometrics are current. If the biometrics are no longer current, practitioners must make arrangements for biometrics collection of their clients by completing the steps listed in the DHS "Instructions for Submitting Certain Applications in Immigration Court and for Providing Biometric and Biographic Information to U.S. Citizenship and Immigration Services" once again. These instructions are available at *www.uscis.gov/sites/*

---

[557] 8 CFR §1003.47(e) (2014).

[558] *Id.*

[559] 8 CFR §1003.47(f) (2014).

[560] 8 CFR §1003.47(g) (2014).

[561] INA §208(d)(5)(A)(i).

[562] 8 CFR §1003.47(d) (2014).

default/files/files/article/PreOrderInstr.pdf. Completing these steps will generate a new receipt notice and a new ASC appointment notice. The respondent and his or her dependents must then attend the new appointment at the ASC. If the respondent and his or her dependents do not receive a new biometrics notice after completing these steps, practitioners should fax the new receipt notice with a request for scheduling of fingerprints to SNAP at 214-489-4357.

D. Change of Address

While awaiting his or her individual hearing date, a respondent may be released from custody or may move to a new address. Once an NTA has been served, whether represented or not, respondents must notify the court within five days of any change of address or telephone number.[563] This notice must be provided in writing on Form EOIR-33/IC, Alien's Change of Address Form/Immigration Court, and a copy must be served on DHS.[564] It is essential for any respondent in removal proceedings to timely file a change of address form. Failure to do so may result in the immigration court sending hearing notices and other important correspondence to the wrong address, and a hearing may be held in the respondent's absence. In such situations, the respondent may be ordered removed *in absentia*.[565]

- **Practice Pointer**: Form EOIR-33/IC is available at *www.justice.gov/eoir/eoirforms/eoir33/ICadr33.htm*.[566] Practitioners should ensure that they are preparing and filing the most current version of the EOIR-33/IC form on behalf of their clients.[567]
- **Practice Pointer**: Respondents in removal proceedings also should file an AR-11 Change of Address with DHS. This process may be completed online at *https://egov.uscis.gov/coa/displayCOAForm.do*.[568] Notification to DHS of a change of address, however, does not constitute notification to the immigration court.[569]

The address obligations are slightly different for respondents who are detained. For detained respondents, DHS is obligated to report the location of the respondent's detention to the immigration court and to report when he or she is moved between detention locations or when he or she is released from custody.[570] If the respondent is released from custody, he or she also should file an EOIR-33/IC with the immigration

[563] 8 CFR §1003.15(d)(2) (2014); ICPM, chapter 2.2(c).

[564] 8 CFR §1003.15(d)(2) (2014); ICPM, chapter 2.2(c)(i).

[565] ICPM, chapter 2.2(c).

[566] (last visited Feb. 12, 2015).

[567] ICPM. chapter 2.2(c)(ii).

[568] (last visited Feb. 12, 2015).

[569] ICPM, chapter 2.2(c).

[570] 8 CFR §1003.19(g) (2014); ICPM, chapter 2.2(d).

court within 5 days of release from detention to ensure that immigration court records are current.[571]

If a respondent changes addresses or is released from custody, he or she also may need to file a Motion to Change Venue with the immigration court if he or she moves to a residence outside of the immigration court's jurisdiction.[572]

E. Motions and Inquiries

While awaiting his or her individual hearing, a respondent also may need to make various inquiries or requests with the immigration court. The means and format for doing so depends on the substance of the inquiry or request. All formal requests of the immigration court must be made by written motion containing the required content and supported by any relevant documentary evidence.[573] For example, the respondent may need to make any of the following motions while he or she awaits the individual hearing date:[574]

- Motion to Continue — if the respondent wishes for his or her hearing to be scheduled for a later date;[575]
- Motion to Advance — if the respondent wishes for his or her hearing to be scheduled for an earlier date;[576]
- Motion to Change Venue — if the respondent has changed addresses and moved outside of the immigration court's jurisdiction;[577]

---

[571] ICPM, chapter 2.2(d)(ii).

[572] 8 CFR §1003.20(b) (2014).

[573] *See generally,* ICPM, chapter 5.

[574] ICPM, chapter 5.10.

[575] ICPM, chapter 5.10(a). A Motion to Continue should set forth in detain the reasons for the request and, if appropriate, should be supported by evidence. It should also include the date and time of the hearing, as well as preferred dates that the party is available to re-schedule the hearing. *Id.* The filing of a Motion to Continue does not excuse the appearance of the respondent or his or her representative at any scheduled hearing. Therefore, until the motion is granted, the respondent and his or her representative must plan to appear at all hearings as originally scheduled. *Id.* An IJ may grant a motion to continue for good cause shown. 8 CFR §§1003.29, 1240.6 (2014).

[576] ICPM, chapter 5.10(b). Motions to Advance are generally discouraged. However, they may be appropriate if advancement of the hearing is necessary to preserve eligibility for relief or if there is a health crisis necessitating immediate action by the IJ. *Id.* The motion should completely articulate the reasons for the request and the adverse consequences if the hearing date is not advanced. *Id.*

[577] 8 CFR §1003.20 (2014); ICPM, chapter 5.10(c); *Matter of Rahman*, 20 I&N Dec. 480 (BIA 1992). Venue lies with the immigration court where jurisdiction vests pursuant to 8 CFR §1003.14 (2014) (where the charging document has been filed). 8 CFR §1003.20(a) (2014). An IJ may, for good cause, change venue upon motion by one of the parties, after the other party has been given notice and an opportunity to respond to the motion. 8 CFR §1003.20(b) (2014). In any Motion to Change Venue, the moving party must identify a fixed street address, city, state, and zip code where the respondent may be reached for further hearing notification. 8 CFR §1003.20(c) (2014). The Motion to Change Venue should contain the following information: (1) the date and time of the next scheduled hearing; (2) an admission or denial of the factual allegations and charges in the Notice to Appear (if the factual

Continued

- Motion for Substitution of Counsel — if a representative has already entered his or her appearance on behalf of the respondent and the respondent wishes to change representatives;[578]
- Motion to Withdraw as Counsel of Record — if a representative wishes to no longer be counsel of record for the respondent or if the respondent no longer wishes to be represented by his or her current representative;[579]
- Motion for Extension of Filing Deadline — if the respondent needs more time to gather evidence or prepare filings;[580]

---

allegations and charges have not yet been addressed); (3) a designation or refusal to designate a country of removal (if a country has not already been designated); (4) if the respondent will be requesting relief from removal, a description of the basis for eligibility (if the relief has not already been requested); (5) the address and telephone number of the location at which the respondent will be residing if the motion is granted; and (6) a detailed explanation of the reasons for the request. ICPM, chapter 5.10(c). If the respondent's address has changed, he or she must also file a Form EOIR-33/IC with the immigration court. *Id.* The filing of a Motion to Change venue does not excuse the respondent or his or her representative's appearance at any scheduled hearing. Therefore, until the motion has been granted, parties must appear for any hearings as originally scheduled. *Id.*

[578] 8 CFR §1003.17(b) (2014); ICPM, Chs. 2.3(i)(i), 5.10(d). Any Motion to Substitute Counsel must be accompanied by a paper Form EOIR-28, Notice of Entry of Appearance by the new attorney or representative. 8 CFR §1003.17(b) (2014); ICPM, chapter 2.3(i)(i). The motion should contain the following information: (1) the reasons for the substitution of counsel, in conformance with applicable state bar and other ethical rules; (2) evidence that prior counsel has been notified about the motion for substitution of counsel; (3) evidence of the respondent's consent to the substitution of counsel. ICPM, chapter 2.3(i)(i). The motion and EOIR-28 for new counsel should be served on DHS and prior counsel and must be accompanied by a proof of service. *Id.* In adjudicating a Motion for Substitution of Counsel, the time remaining before the next hearing and the reasons given for the substitution will be taken into consideration. *Id.* If the motion is granted, prior counsel does not need to file a Motion to Withdraw. However, until the Motion for Substitution of Counsel is granted, the original counsel remains the attorney of record and must appear at all scheduled hearings. *Id.*

[579] 8 CFR §1003.17(b) (2014); ICPM, chs. 2.3(i)(ii), 5.10(e). A Motion to Withdraw should contain the following information: (1) the reasons for the withdrawal of counsel, in conformance with applicable state bar or other ethical rules; (2) the last known address of the respondent; (3) a statement that the representative has notified the respondent of the request to withdraw as counsel or, if the respondent could not be notified, an explanation of the efforts made to notify him or her of the request; (4) evidence of the respondent's consent to withdraw or a statement of why evidence of consent is unobtainable; (5) evidence that the representative notified or attempted to notify the respondent of pending deadlines, the date, time, and place of the next scheduled hearing, the necessity of meeting deadlines and appearing at scheduled hearings, and the consequences of failing to meet deadlines or appear at scheduled hearings. ICPM, chapter 2.3(i)(ii). In adjudicating a Motion to Withdraw, the time remaining before the next hearing and the reasons given for the withdrawal will be taken into consideration. *Id.* Until the Motion to Withdraw is granted, the representative remains the attorney of record and must appear at all scheduled hearings. *Id.*

[580] ICPM, chs. 3.1(c)(iv), 5.10(f). A Motion for Extension should only be filed if absolutely necessary, as such motions are discouraged and parties are encouraged to meet all deadlines and avoid delay. ICPM, chapter 3.1(c)(iv)(A). Such a motion should clearly state: (1) when the filing is due; (2) the reasons for requesting an extension; (3) that the party has exercised due diligence to meet the current filing deadline; (4) that the party will meet a revised deadline; and (5) if the parties have communicated, whether the other party consents to the extension. ICPM, chapter 3.1(c)(iv)(C). The mere filing of a

Continued

- Motion to Accept an Untimely Filing — if the respondent would like an IJ to consider a filing despite its untimeliness;[581]
- Motion to Waive Representative's or Respondent's Appearance (for master calendar hearings) — if the respondent or his or her representative wishes not to appear in person at a master calendar hearing;[582]
- Motion to Permit Telephonic Appearance of Representative or Respondent — if the respondent or his or her representative wishes to appear for a master calendar hearing by telephone;[583]
- Motion to Request an Interpreter — if the respondent or his or her witnesses cannot testify in English and need the court to supply an interpreter;[584]

Motion for Extension does not excuse the respondent's failure to meet a deadline. Rather, a deadline is only extended upon the granting of the motion. ICPM, chapter 3.1(c)(iv).

[581] ICPM, chs. 3.1(d)(iii), 5.10(g). A Motion to Accept an Untimely Filing must explain the reasons for the late filing and show good cause for acceptance of the filing. Such motions should be supported with documentary evidence. ICPM, chapter 3.1(d)(iii). The consequences of untimely filing may be severe. ICPM, chapter 3.1(d)(ii). For example: (1) if an application for relief is untimely, the respondent's interest in that relief may be deemed waived or abandoned; (2) if a motion is untimely, it may be denied; (3) if a response to a motion is untimely, the motion may be deemed unopposed; (4) if a brief or pre-trial statement is untimely, the issues in question may be deemed waived or conceded; (5) if an exhibit is untimely, it may not be entered into evidence or it may be given less weight; (6) if a witness list is untimely, the witnesses on the list may be barred from testifying. *Id.*

[582] 8 CFR §1003.25(a) (2014); ICPM, Chs. 4.15(m), 5.10(i), 5.10(j). Respondents and representatives must appear at all master calendar hearings unless the IJ has granted a waiver of appearance for that particular hearing. ICPM, chapter 4.15(m). A Motion to Waive Representative's Appearance must be accompanied by written pleadings, must state the date and time of the master calendar hearing, and must explain the reasons for the request. ICPM, chapter 4.15(m)(i). A Motion to Waive Respondent's Appearance must state the date and time of the master calendar hearing and must explain the reasons for the request. ICPM, chapter 4.15(m)(ii). The representative or respondent's appearance is not waived until the motion has been granted, and if the motion is granted, it is specific to that hearing and does not apply to future hearings. ICPM, chapter 4.15(m)(iii).

[583] ICPM, chs. 4.15(n), 5.10(k). A Motion to Permit Telephonic Appearance should state the date and time of the master calendar hearing and explain the reasons for the request. ICPM, chapter 4.15(n). It also should state the telephone number of the respondent or representative, and unless expressly permitted by the IJ, cellular telephones should not be used for telephonic appearances. ICPM, chapter 4.15(n)(iii). The mere filing of a motion does not permit a telephonic appearance. Thus, the respondent or representative must plan to appear in person until the motion is granted. ICPM, chapter 4.15(n)(iv). If the motion is granted, it is specific to that hearing and does not apply to future hearings. ICPM, chapter 4.15(n)(v).

[584] ICPM, chs. 4.15(o)(i), 5.10(l). Parties are encouraged to request interpreters at the master calendar hearing. However, an interpreter may also be requested by written motion. ICPM, chapter 4.15(o)(i). A Motion to Request an Interpreter should contain the following information: (1) the name of the language requested, including any variations in spelling; (2) the specific dialect of the language; (3) the geographical locations where such dialect is spoken; (4) the identification of any other languages in which the respondent or witness is fluent; and (5) any other appropriate information necessary for the selection of an interpreter. *Id.*

- Motion to Present Video or Telephonic Testimony — if a witness cannot appear in person, but is available to provide testimony by video or telephone;[585] and
- Motion for Consolidation or for Severance — if the respondent has family members who are also in removal proceedings and the respondent wishes to join or separate the adjudication of their cases.[586]

This list of motions is not exclusive.[587] Rather, this list describes the most common types of motions filed in proceedings involving applications for relief in the forms of asylum, withholding of removal, and protection under CAT. The respondent, a representative, or DHS may make any request of the court in motion format.[588]

> ➢ **Practice Pointer**: For helpful guidance on making motions in immigration court, see the article, "Motion Practices Before the Immigration Court," by Cynthia Aziz, Andres Benach, and Manuel Rios in *AILA's Immigration Practice Pointers* (2013–14 ed.).

Although there is no official format for motions, all motions must include the following:[589]

- A cover page accurately describing the request;[590]
- The signed motion;

---

[585] ICPM, chs. 4.15(o)(ii)–(iii), 5.10(m)–(n). At the IJ's discretion, witnesses may testify by video or telephone. A Motion to Present Video Testimony must include an explanation of why the witness cannot appear in person, and parties wishing to present video testimony must comply with the requirements for witness lists at ICPM chapter 3.3(g). ICPM, chapter 4.15(o)(ii). If video testimony is permitted, the IJ will specify the time and manner under which the testimony may be taken. *Id.* A Motion to Present Telephonic Testimony at an individual hearing should contain the following information: (1) an explanation of why the witness cannot appear in person; and (2) the witness's telephone number and the location from which the witness will testify. ICPM, chapter 4.15(o)(iii)(A). Cellular telephones should not be used unless permitted by the IJ. ICPM, chapter 4.15(o)(iii)(C). If the witness is located abroad and international telephonic testimony is permitted, the requesting party should bring a pre-paid telephone card to the immigration court to pay for the call. ICPM, chapter 4.15(o)(iii)(D).

[586] ICPM Chs. 4.21, 5.10(p)–(q). Consolidation of cases is the administrative joining of separate cases into a single adjudication for all of the parties involved. ICPM, chapter 4.21(a) Consolidation is generally limited to cases involving immediate family members. *Id.* An IJ may consolidate cases at his or her discretion or upon motion of one or both of the parties, where appropriate. *Id.* A copy of the Motion for Consolidation should be filed in each case included in the request for consolidation. *Id.* Severance of cases is the division of a consolidated case into separate cases, relative to each individual. ICPM, chapter 4.21(b). An IJ may sever cases at his or her discretion or upon request of one or both of the parties. *Id.* A copy of the Motion for Severance should be filed for each case included in the request. *Id.*

[587] *See infra* chapter 11 for a detailed discussion of motions to reopen and motions to reconsider.

[588] *See generally,* ICPM chapter 5.

[589] *See* ICPM, chs. 3.3(c)(i), 5.2(b).

[590] ICPM, chs. 3.3(c)(vi), 5.2(b).

- Supporting documentation with table of contents (if any);[591]
- A proposed order for the IJ's signature;[592] and
- A proof of service.

All motions must state the grounds on which the motion is based, identify the relief or remedy sought, and comply with the ICPM's format and filing requirements.[593] If filing a motion, the respondent should make a good faith effort to ascertain DHS's position on the motion and should state DHS's position in the motion.[594] If the respondent is unable to ascertain DHS's position, he or she should describe in the motion the efforts made to contact DHS.[595] The IJ may issue his or her decision on the motion in writing or orally at a hearing.[596] If a respondent would like the IJ to make a decision on a particular motion at the upcoming hearing, he or she must file the motion at least 15 days prior to the hearing date.[597]

> ➤ **Practice Pointer**: Often, due to the overburdened dockets of the immigration courts, IJs are not be able to review a motion until slightly before or during the next hearing. Thus, if the request in the motion requires prompt attention or adjudication prior to the next hearing, practitioners should be diligent in calling the court to check on the status of the motion and work cooperatively with immigration court staff to ensure that the motion is brought to the IJ's attention in a timely manner.

More informal requests, such as status inquiries, may be made by calling the EOIR hotline or the immigration court having jurisdiction over the respondent's case. EOIR has an Automated Status Query system (ASQ), which provides information about the status of cases pending before the immigration courts or the BIA.[598] ASQ has a telephone menu in English and Spanish, and contains information on the following:

- The next hearing date, time, and location;
- The immigration judge who will hear the case;
- In asylum cases, the status and amount of time that has elapsed on the asylum clock;
- Immigration judge decisions;

---

[591] ICPM, chapter 5.2(e).

[592] ICPM, App'x Q.

[593] ICPM, chapter 5.2(b). *See generally*, ICPM chapter 3.

[594] ICPM, chapter 5.2(i).

[595] *Id.*

[596] ICPM, chapter 5.11.

[597] ICPM, chapter 3.1.(b)(i)(A).

[598] ICPM, chapter 1.7(c).

- Case appeal information; and
- Filing information.[599]

ASQ does not, however, contain information on bond proceedings or motions, other than post-order motions.[600] A respondent or his or her representative may access the respondent's case information by typing in the respondent's A-number.[601]

> ➢ **Practice Pointer**: The ASQ is accessible by calling 1-800-898-7180. If the respondent has a nine-digit A-number, practitioners should enter all nine digits. If the respondent has an eight-digit A-number, practitioners should enter a "0" before the A-number.

Informal status inquiries that cannot be answered by ASQ may be directed to the immigration court in which the proceedings are pending.[602] Immigration court staff may receive and answer inquiries, such as the status of a pending motion or bond proceeding information.[603] If immigration court staff cannot answer a telephone inquiry, the caller may be advised to submit the inquiry in writing, with a copy served on the opposing party.[604]

F. Discovery

DHS may have documents that are critical to the respondent's case that the respondent needs to review prior to his or her individual hearing. Gaining access to these documents may assist the respondent in meeting his or her burden of proof and in preparing counter-arguments and rebuttals for DHS's positions.

In general, there is no formal discovery in immigration court proceedings. However, the BIA has held that, notwithstanding allocation of the burden of proof, the party with more ready access to evidence substantiating a party's burden should come forward with it.[605] In addition, the BIA has recognized that the trial attorney's role in an asylum hearing is to produce any relevant evidence that would further adjudication of the individual's asylum claim.[606]

Although the Federal Rules of Civil Procedure do not apply in administrative proceedings, the following are measures that may be taken to obtain documents or testimony from DHS:

---

599 *Id.*

600 *Id.*

601 *Id.*

602 *Id.*

603 ICPM, chapter 1.7(d).

604 *Id.*

605 *Matter of Vivas*, 16 I&N Dec. 68 (BIA 1977).

606 *See Matter of S–M–J–*, 21 I&N Dec. 722 at 7–8 (BIA 1997).

(1) *Always* file a Freedom of Information Act (FOIA) request (Form G-639) with the USCIS National Records Center to obtain a copy of the respondent's complete A-file;[607]

(2) Ask the trial attorney for a copy of pertinent documents in the applicant's case;[608]

(3) Ask the IJ to order pre-hearing statements pursuant to 8 CFR §1003.21, including copies of exhibits;

(4) Ask the IJ to issue a subpoena for DHS to produce one or more specific documents or witnesses pursuant to 8 CFR §1287.4; and

(5) Ask the IJ to order the taking of a deposition pursuant to 8 CFR §1240.7(c).

First, under FOIA, agencies are obligated to disclose requested information, with various exceptions.[609] This statute, however, "demarcates the agency's obligation to disclose; it does not foreclose disclosure."[610] As the Supreme Court explained in *Chrysler Corp. v. Brown*, the purpose of the FOIA statute is to disclose information and is not to be used as a mechanism for shielding information from the public. Therefore, if regulations or case law direct an agency to produce documents, the agency cannot rely on FOIA and its exemptions to block disclosure of documents. Thus, respondents and their representatives should resist efforts by the IJ or DHS to restrict document production requests to FOIA requests.

- **Practice Pointer**: If a respondent first applied for asylum affirmatively before the USCIS Asylum Office, it is essential for practitioners to know what happened during the asylum interview. If a practitioner was retained after the applicant already completed the interview and was referred to the court, this can be difficult. However, a recent settlement

---

[607] President Barack Obama issued a Freedom of Information Act (FOIA) Memorandum on Jan. 21, 2009, to the heads of agencies in which he stated that FOIA should be administered with a presumption of openness and that all agencies should adopt a presumption in favor of disclosure. *See* White House Memorandum for Heads of Executive Departments and Agencies: Freedom of Information Act, *available at www.whitehouse.gov/the_press_office/Freedom_of_Information_Act/* (last accessed Feb. 28, 2015). Similarly, Attorney Eric General Holder issued a FOIA Memorandum to Heads of Executive Departments and Agencies on Mar. 19, 2009, echoing President Obama's directive and instructing agencies not to withhold information simply because it could legally do so. *See* Attorney General Memorandum for Heads of Executive Departments and Agencies: Freedom of Information Act, *available at www.usdoj.gov/ag/foia-memo-march2009.pdf* (last accessed Feb. 28, 2015). Individuals in removal proceedings are eligible for expedited processing of their FOIA request under the "Notice to Appear" track, effective March 30, 2007. For complete instructions, see USCIS Form G-639 and USCIS Fact Sheet, *Freedom of Information Act* (Feb. 28, 2007), *published on* AILA InfoNet at Doc. No. 07030165 (*posted* Mar. 1, 2007). For information on making a FOIA to U.S. Customs and Border Protection, *see www.cbp.gov/xp/cgov/admin/fl/foia/reference_guide.xml*. For information about making a FOIA request to EOIR, *see www.usdoj.gov/eoir/efoia/foiafact.htm*.

[608] *See* 8 CFR §103.2(b)(16) (2014).

[609] 5 USC §552(b) (2012).

[610] *Chrysler Corp. v. Brown*, 441 U.S. 281, 292 (1979).

has made it possible for practitioners to obtain the asylum officer's notes from the interview, which are like an informal Q&A transcript. Reviewing these notes prior to a hearing can be essential because DHS often uses the notes to argue a lack of credibility. Under *Martins v. USCIS*,[611] USCIS is required to provide asylum officer notes in response to FOIA requests, rather than withholding these notes under the deliberative process exemption. This settlement applies nationwide. Practitioners also may gain access to asylum officer notes by reviewing the immigration court's file (sometimes they are in there!) or by asking the DHS attorney for a copy. A Motion to Compel the Production of Documents also may be a useful way to gain access to asylum officer notes. Of course, it is always a strategic consideration whether to alert DHS of your desire to review these notes — doing so could bring potentially harmful information to the attention of DHS and the IJ.

Second, 8 CFR §103.2(b)(16) imposes a positive obligation on DHS to provide the respondent with an opportunity to inspect evidence.[612] The regulation requires DHS to inform the respondent about derogatory information, even if the respondent does not know about the derogatory information. Additionally, it requires that DHS provide the respondent with an opportunity to rebut that information. The regulation also requires that the information and documentation DHS uses be in the record of proceedings.

- **Practice Pointer**: DHS often refuses to provide documentation upon request and instead tells respondents to file a FOIA request. Although a FOIA request should always be filed, practitioners should not automatically accept DHS's refusal to provide documentation and should instead remind DHS of its regulatory duty to produce information.

Case law also has addressed DHS's duty to disclose documents.[613] In *Dent v. Holder*, the Ninth Circuit found that INA §240(c)(2)(B) and due process require the government to produce relevant documents and ruled that the government must provide Mr. Dent with the documentation he requested from his A-file.[614] The court

---

[611] *See Martins v. USCIS*, No. 13-00591 (N.D. Cal. July 3, 2013).

[612] 8 CFR §103.2(b)(16) (2014).

[613] *See, e.g.*, *Matter of Tahsir*, 16 I&N Dec. 56 (BIA 1976) (requiring that the petitioner be given evidence relied upon by legacy INS and confirming that if the government relies on classified information, it must provide the petitioner with a description of the information and opportunity to respond); *Matter of Mata*, 15 I&N Dec. 524 (BIA 1975) (overturning the revocation of a visa petition because the petitioner did not have access to relevant materials, did not have the opportunity to inspect the record, and therefore, did not have a reasonable opportunity to respond); *Matter of Holmes*, 14 I&N Dec. 647 (BIA 1974) (addressing the importance of disclosing evidence to an adverse party in the context of an I-130 petition).

[614] *Dent v. Holder*, 627 F.3d 365 (9th Cir. 2010).

stated that a respondent's review of evidence is often necessary because "injustice may be done if the government successfully shields its documents from a person who ought to have access to them, particularly when the documents might change the result of the proceedings."[615]

> ➢ **Practice Pointer**: If DHS refuses to provide documentation, arguing that it is protected or classified, practitioners should consider the following options (in addition to filing a FOIA request and a motion for subpoena): (1) ask the IJ to compel the government to produce the documents under a protective order; (2) ask the court to compel production under seal; (3) ask the court to make a factual finding about whether hidden documents should be presumed to be relevant; and (4) ask the court to compel the government to prove that hidden documents are not relevant.[616]

Third, pursuant to 8 CFR §1003.21(b), the IJ may order any part to file a pre-hearing statement of position that may include, but is not limited to:

- A statement of facts to which both parties have stipulated, together with a statement that the parties have communicated in good faith to stipulate to the fullest extent possible;
- A list of proposed witnesses and what they will establish;
- A list of exhibits, copies of exhibits to be introduced, and a statement of the reason for their introduction;
- The estimated time required to present the case; and
- A statement of unresolved issues involved in the proceedings.[617]

Moving the IJ to order a pre-hearing statement, whether in writing or orally during a hearing, may result in the production of documentation that will be helpful to the respondent in preparing his or her evidence and rebuttals to DHS's positions.

Fourth, if a witness is not reasonably available at the place of the hearing and his or her testimony is essential, the IJ may order the taking of a deposition either at his or her own instance or upon request by one of the parties.[618] The IJ's order must designate the official by whom the deposition shall be taken, may prescribe and limit

---

[615] *Id.* at 371.

[616] For these practice tips and more, see Rex Chen and Adam Rosen's article, "Document Production and Inspecting Evidence After *Dent v. Holder*: Hark – Hark – From Out the Thickest Fog," AILA'S IMMIGRATION PRACTICE POINTERS (2012–13 ed.). The American Immigration Council also has a useful practice advisory entitled, "*Dent v. Holder* and Strategies for Obtaining Documents from the Government During Removal Proceedings," *available at www.legalactioncenter.org/sites/default/files/dent_practice_advisory_6-8-12.pdf*, (last visited Mar. 31, 2015).

[617] 8 CFR §1003.21(b) (2014).

[618] 8 CFR §1003.35(a) (2014).

the content, scope, or manner of taking the deposition, and may direct the production of documentary evidence.[619]

Finally, an IJ also has exclusive jurisdiction to issues subpoenas requiring the attendance of witnesses or the production of documentary evidence, or both.[620] The IJ may issue a subpoena upon his or her own volition or upon request by DHS or the respondent.[621] If the respondent requests issuance of a subpoena, he or she must state what he or she expects to prove by the requested witnesses or documentary evidence and show that he or she has made diligent effort to produce the witness or documentary evidence.[622] The subpoena must state the title of the proceeding and command the person to whom it is directed to attend and to give testimony at a specific time and place. It also may command the person to produce the documents specified in the subpoena.[623] If the witness does not appear or produce the documents as requested, the IJ must request the United States Attorney for the district in which the subpoena was issued to report such neglect or refusal to the U.S. District Court and to issue an requiring the witness to appear or produce the documents.[624]

Overall, a failure by DHS to produce documents or by the IJ to compel document production may deny respondents in removal proceedings an opportunity to fully and fairly litigate their cases in violation of due process, as well as the statutory and regulatory requirements. Thus, respondents and their representatives should not limit their discovery to Track III FOIA requests. Instead, they should make requests directly to DHS and the IJ as described in this section and ensure that such requests are on the record of proceedings should an appeal become necessary.

G. Evidentiary Filings and Witness Lists

Asylum applicants have the right to a reasonable opportunity to present evidence on their own behalf.[625] Prior to an individual hearing, the respondent must ensure that all applications, exhibits, motions, witness lists, and criminal history charts (if required) have been prepared pursuant to the ICPM requirements and timely filed with the immigration court.[626]

- **Practice Pointer**: Records of Proceedings in removal proceedings are kept separate from Records of Proceedings in bond redetermination

[619] *Id.*

[620] 8 CFR §1003.35(b)(1) (2014).

[621] *Id.*

[622] 8 CFR §1003.35(b)(2) (2014).

[623] 8 CFR §1003.35(b)(3) (2014).

[624] 8 CFR §1003.35(b)(6) (2014).

[625] INA §240(b)(4); 8 USC §1229a(b)(4) (2012).

[626] ICPM, chapter 4.16(b).

proceedings. Thus, documents already filed in bond redetermination proceedings must be re-filed for removal proceedings.[627]

The Federal Rules of Evidence are not controlling in immigration court proceedings.[628] However, they are guiding and should always be kept in mind when preparing and presenting evidentiary filings and choosing witnesses. The test for the admissibility of evidence in immigration court proceedings is whether the evidence is probative and whether its use is fundamentally fair so as not to deprive the respondent of due process of law. [629] According to the Second Circuit, "fairness is closely related to the reliability and trustworthiness of the evidence."[630]

1. Supplemental Evidence Filings

As discussed above, respondents must file their I-589 application in open court at a master calendar hearing. Thus, most respondents have already filed their signed I-589, passport-sized photograph, initial supporting documentation, and documentation for his or her derivative applicants prior to the individual hearing. However, given the lengthy periods of time between the master calendar and individual hearings, most respondents will compile and file additional corroborating evidence in support of their applications for relief. Such evidence may include:[631]

- Identity documents and other official government documents;
- Privately issued membership cards or other affiliation documents;[632]
- Affidavits from the applicant's family, friends, neighbors, or community members confirming his or her protected characteristic;
- Photographs of the applicant participating in various events;
- Letters from organizations of which the applicant is a member or affiliate;
- Objective, published descriptions of the characteristics or attributes, which designate members of the applicant's race, religion, nationality, political affiliation, or social group;

---

[627] *Id.*

[628] *Matter of D–*, 20 I&N Dec. 827, 831 (BIA 1994).

[629] *Immigration Judge Benchbook* (Oct. 2001), chapter1, at I.A.2., *available at www.usdoj.gov/eoir/statspub/benchbook.pdf; see also Doumbia v. Gonzales*, 472 F.3d 957, 962 (7th Cir. 2007); *Ezeagwuna v. Ashcroft*, 301 F.3d 116, 127 (3d Cir. 2002), *rev'd on other grounds by Ezeagwuna v. Ashcroft,* 325 F.3d 396 (3d Cir. 2003); *Espinoza v. INS*, 45 F.3d 308, 310 (9th Cir. 1995); *Bustos-Torres v. INS*, 898 F.2d 1053, 1055 (5th Cir. 1990); *Matter of Ponce-Hernandez*, 21 I&N Dec. 784 (BIA 1999).

[630] *Felzcerek v. INS*, 75 F.3d 112, 115 (2d Cir. 1996).

[631] Vikram Badrinath, Dree K. Collopy, & Hans Christian Linnartz, *Evidentiary Issues in Asylum Cases*, in AILA Immigration Practice Pointers, (AILA 2013).

[632] *See, e.g.*, *Camara v. Ashcroft*, 378 F.3d 361, 370–71 (4th Cir. 2004) (finding that the IJ erred by failing to consider independent evidence of persecution: *inter alia*, a notice of escape, a political party membership card, an arrest warrant, and DOS reports corroborating the applicant's claim).

- Photographs of the applicant's injuries;
- Police reports recording the harm suffered or threatened;
- Arrest warrants or records, if the applicant was ever arrested due to his or her protected characteristic;[633]
- Affidavits from witnesses who were present during the act(s) of harm or mistreatment;
- Affidavits from individuals whom the applicant confided in about the incident(s), confirming any observed physical or psychological harm, such as markings on the applicant's body, torn clothes, injuries, crying, anxiety, or other unusual behaviors;
- Medical records, including evaluations of physical injuries and the likely cause of those injuries, letters from treating doctors, treatment reports, hospital admission records, or prescribed medications;
- Mental health records, including evaluations of mental health disorders and the likely trigger for those disorders, letters from treating mental health professionals, appointment records, or prescribed medications;
- Death certificates for the applicant's relatives, friends, neighbors, or community members who were targeted because of a qualifying characteristic;
- Newspaper or other media coverage, or coverage by human rights groups, of the incident(s) in which the applicant was involved;
- Evidence that the applicant attempted to supply certain corroborating documentation, but was unable to;
- I-94 card, visa, and stamped passport (even if false);
- Evidence of means of travel to the United States, including airline itineraries, bus tickets, or hotel receipts;
- Evidence of presence outside of the United States in the past year, including financial, medical, school, or work records;
- Affidavits from individuals who have personal knowledge of the applicant's arrival in the United States;
- Expert report regarding the conditions in the applicant's home country as they relate to the applicant's claims and assessing the applicant's risk of harm upon return;[634] and

---

[633] *See, e.g.*, *Camara v. Ashcroft*, 378 F.3d 361, 370–71 (4th Cir. 2004) (finding that the IJ erred by failing to consider independent evidence of persecution: *inter alia*, a notice of escape, a political party membership card, an arrest warrant, and DOS reports corroborating the applicant's claim).

[634] *See, e.g.*, *Niam v. Ashcroft*, 354 F.3d 652, 658 (7th Cir. 2004) (noting that the scholar proffered by the applicant should have been considered an expert and that it was error for the IJ to refuse to allow her to testify telephonically from overseas).

- Country conditions reports and articles showing the conditions in the applicant's home country during the time of persecution and presently, including human rights reports from the U.S. Department of State, Amnesty International, Human Rights Watch, or other reputable organizations.[635]

All evidentiary filings in immigration court must comply with the ICPM's detailed filing requirements discussed in Chapter 3. First, the filing location is usually the hearing location.[636] Second, a filing is not deemed "filed" until the immigration court has received it; the immigration courts do not recognize the "mailbox rule," and do not excuse untimeliness due to postal or delivery delays.[637] Third, immigration courts do not accept electronically filed documents (except for the EOIR-28). Thus, all filings must be filed by mail, courier, or hand-delivery.

> ➢ **Practice Pointer**: For a list of all immigration courts and their addresses, see EOIR's website at *www.justice.gov/eoir/sibpages/ICadr.htm*.[638]

> ➢ **Practice Pointer**: Practitioners should always use mailing or delivery services that allow delivery tracking. Doing so will avoid parcels being lost in the mail and also provides practitioners with a record of the date of the immigration court's receipt of the filing.

All evidentiary filings must include the following components in the following order:

- Form EOIR-28, Notice of Entry of Appearance (if one has not yet been filed);[639]
- Cover page;[640]
- Index of Exhibits or Table of Contents listing the components of the filing;[641]
- Tabbed and page-numbered exhibits;[642]

---

[635] *See* 8 CFR §§208.12(a), 1208.12(a) (2014) (providing that adjudicators may rely on "other credible sources" for information on country conditions, such as international organizations, private voluntary agencies, news organizations, or academic institutions). *See, e.g.*, *Camara v. Ashcroft*, 378 F.3d 361, 370–71 (4th Cir. 2004) (finding that the IJ erred by failing to consider independent evidence of persecution: *inter alia*, a notice of escape, a political party membership card, an arrest warrant, and DOS reports corroborating the applicant's claim). *See supra* chapter 4 for a detailed discussion of the evidentiary requirements for establishing asylum eligibility, as well as a list of suggested forms of supporting evidence.

[636] *See* 8 CFR §§1003.13, 1003.31 (2014); ICPM, chapter 3.1(a).

[637] ICPM, chs. 3.1(a)(iii), 3.1(c)(iii).

[638] (last visited Feb. 15, 2015).

[639] *See* ICPM, chapters 2.1(b), 2.3(c), 3.3(c)(i)(A).

[640] *See* ICPM, App'x F.

[641] *See* ICPM, chapter 3.3(c)(i)(A) and App'x P.

[642] ICPM, chapter 3.3(c)(iii)–(iv).

- Certified English translations for any documents that are not in English;[643]
- Required signature(s);[644] and
- Proof of Service.[645]

All filings must include a cover page, which must list include a caption and contain the following information:

(1) the name of the filing party;

(2) the address of the filing party;

(3) the title of the filing;

(4) the full name of each respondent covered by the filing;

(5) the A-number of each respondent;

(6) the type of proceeding involved (such as removal, deportation, exclusion, or bond);

(7) the date and time of the hearing; and

(8) any special circumstances in the top right corner and highlighted (*e.g.*, detained, joint motion, emergency motion, etc.).[646]

All documents that are not in English must be accompanied by a certified English translation.[647] The certificate of translation must be typed, signed by the translator, and attached to the foreign-language document. It must include the following:

(1) a statement that the translator is competent to translate the language of the document and that the translation is true and accurate to the best of the translator's abilities;

(2) a description of the document or documents that were translated; and

(3) the translator's address and telephone number.[648]

To be properly filed with the immigration court, all filings must include the original signature of the respondent or the respondent's representative, accompanied by his or her typed or printed name.[649] A signature represents a certification by the signer that: "he or she has read the document; to the best of his or her knowledge,

---

[643] 8 CFR §1003.33 (2014) ("Any foreign language document offered by a party in a proceeding shall be accompanied by an English language translation and a certification signed by the translator that must be printed legibly or typed. Such certification must include a statement that the translator is competent to translate the document, and that the translation is true and accurate to the best of the translator's abilities."). *See also* ICPM, chapter 3.3(a) and App'x H.

[644] ICPM, chapter 3.3(b).

[645] *See* ICPM, chapter 3.3(c)(i)(A) and App'x G.

[646] ICPM, chapter 3.3(c)(vi) and App'x F.

[647] 8 CFR §§1003.33, 1003.23(b)(1)(i) (2014); ICPM, chapter 3.3(a).

[648] ICPM, chapter 3.3(a) and App'x H.

[649] ICPM, chapter 3.3(b).

information, and belief formed after reasonable inquiry, the document is grounded in fact; the document is submitted in good faith; and the document has not been filed for any improper purpose."[650]

For all filings in immigration court, a party must serve an identical copy on the opposing party (or his or her representative) and must declare in writing that a copy has been served.[651] The written declaration is called a "Proof of Service," and must contain the following information:

(1) the name or title of the party served;

(2) the precise and complete address of the party served;

(3) the date of service;

(4) the means of service (*e.g.*, hand delivery, regular mail, overnight mail, commercial courier, etc.);

(5) the document or documents being served; and

(6) the name and signature of the person serving the document.[652]

A respondent must serve all filings on the designated DHS Office of Chief Counsel.[653] Service may be accomplished by hand-delivery, U.S. Postal Service, or commercial courier.[654] Service is complete by hand-delivery when the filing is hand-delivered to the responsible person at the relevant DHS office. If mailed or sent by commercial courier, service is complete when the filing is deposited with the U.S. Postal Service or commercial courier.[655]

> ➢ **Practice Pointer**: For a listing of all DHS Offices of Chief Counsel addresses, see Immigration and Customs Enforcement's webpage listing its "Principal Legal Advisor Offices" at *www.ice.gov/contact/legal.*[656]

These components must be properly formatted in accordance with the ICPM. Filings that are properly formatted are:

- Typed (the court prefers typed filings, but will accept legible handwritten filings);[657]
- Bear original signatures of the filing party;[658]

---

[650] *Id.*; 8 CFR §1003.102(j)(1) (2014).

[651] 8 CFR §§1003.17(a), 1003.23(b)(1)(ii), 1003.32(a) (2014); ICPM, chapter 3.2(a) and App'x G. Note that filings that are served during hearings and jointly filed motions do not need to be accompanied by a proof of service. ICPM, chapter 3.2(a).

[652] ICPM, chapter 3.2(e)(i).

[653] ICPM, chapter 3.2(b).

[654] ICPM, chapter 3.2(c).

[655] *Id.*

[656] (last visited Feb. 15, 2015).

[657] ICPM, chapter 3.3(c).

[658] *Id.*

- Assembled in the proper order (EOIR-28, cover page, index of exhibits or table of contents, exhibits, proof of service);[659]
- Original (the original filing must be provided to the immigration court and a copy to the opposing party);[660]
- Paginated by consecutive numbers placed at the bottom center or bottom right hand corner of each page (the page numbers should be listed on the index of exhibits or table of contents);[661]
- Tabbed with alphabetic tabs affixed to the right side of the pages;[662]
- Submitted on standard, white, single-sided, 8½″ x 11″ paper (smaller documents should be affixed to an 8½″ x 11″ sheet of paper, larger documents should be reduced in size by photocopying or other means);[663]
- Written in a font and type-size that is easily readable (Times New Roman 12-point font is preferred);[664]
- Written in text that is double-spaced (single-spaced footnotes are preferred);[665]
- Two-hole punched at the top (centered and 2¾″ inches apart);[666] and
- Stapled in the top left corner, or if stabling is impracticable, bound with removable binder clips (paper clips and ACCO-type fasteners are discouraged).[667]

Photocopies of supporting documents (*e.g.*, identity documents, photographs, newspaper articles, etc.), rather than originals, should be filed with the immigration court and served on DHS.[668] The originals, however, must be made available to DHS or the IJ for inspection during hearings.[669]

i. Defective Filings

Failure to include each of these components or to use the required format listed in the ICPM will result in a defective filing that may be rejected by the immigration court.[670] The filing will be considered defective and will be rejected by the immigration court in the following situations:

---

[659] ICPM, chapter 3.3(c)(i)(B).

[660] ICPM, chapter 3.3(c)(ii).

[661] ICPM, chapter 3.3(c)(iii).

[662] ICPM, chapter 3.3(c)(iv).

[663] ICPM, chapter 3.3(c)(v).

[664] ICPM, chapter 3.3(c)(vii).

[665] *Id.*

[666] ICPM, chapter 3.3(c)(viii).

[667] *Id.*

[668] ICPM, chapter 3.3(d)(iii).

[669] *Id.*

[670] ICPM, chapter 3.1(d)(i).

- If it does not include a proof of service on the opposing party;
- If it does not comply with the language requirements;
- If it does not include the necessary signatures;
- If it is not formatted correctly, as required by Chapter 3 of the ICPM; and
- If it is illegible.[671]

The term "rejected" means that the filing is returned to the filing party because it is defective and therefore will not be considered by the immigration judge.[672] If a filing is rejected, the applicants should exercise due diligence to correct the error and re-file promptly.[673]

As defective filing could result in the IJ's exclusion of the evidence from the record and the denial of the applications for protection, it is essential for applicants and their representatives to carefully review filings before filing them with the immigration court and serving them on DHS.

ii. Authentication of Documents

Section 287.6 of 8 CFR appears to require that official records and public documents from foreign countries be "certified," in the form of an official publication or a copy attested to by an authorized foreign officer, in order to be admissible. Limited case law on this issue suggests that it is *not* an absolute requirement, especially in asylum cases. An asylum applicant may be afraid to ask officials from his or her home country to certify an arrest warrant or conviction. The type of certification that may be required under this section varies depending on whether the country is a signatory to the 1961 Hague Convention Abolishing the Requirement of Legalisation for Foreign Public Documents.[674] Certification may be needed for "official records" from countries that are signatories to the Hague Convention. If the country at issue is not a signatory to the Convention, then certification may be needed for any "public documents" sought to be introduced. In determining whether 8 CFR §287.6 applies in a particular case, the IJ should first determine whether the document at issue is an "official record" or public document.[675] Official records include foreign vital statistics records, military records, census records, and judicial records. Public documents are defined in 8 CFR §287.6(c)(3) and include, inter alia, administrative documents and notarial acts.

Even if a document is found to be an official record or public document, courts have held that 8 CFR §287.6 is not the *sole* means of authentication available to an

---

[671] ICPM, chapter 3.1(d)

[672] *Id.* at chapter 3.1(d)(i).

[673] *Id.* at chapter 3.1(d)(i).

[674] For a list of countries that are signatories to this Convention, *see www.hcch.net/index_en.php?act =states.listing.*

[675] *Georgis v. Ashcroft*, 328 F.3d 962, 969 (7th Cir. 2003).

asylum applicant.[676] Rather, any recognized procedure for the authentication of documents should be permitted in immigration court.[677] Alternative means may include:

- Authenticating the document through the applicant's own testimony if it is consistent with Federal Rule of Evidence 901;[678]
- Allowing the opposing party to inspect the document, as provided under Federal Rule of Evidence 902(3) or Federal Rule of Civil Procedure 44;
- Providing information concerning how the document was obtained, identifying the source of the information contained in the document, and showing that there are consistencies between the information contained in the otherwise unauthenticated document and authenticated documents;[679] or
- Providing reasonable opportunity to the opposing party to investigate the authenticity and accuracy of the document, in which case the IJ may, for "good cause" shown, order that documents be treated as presumptively authentic.[680]

It is error for an IJ to reject a document solely because it was not authenticated in strict conformity with the regulation.[681] Moreover, courts have found that it is error for IJs to exclude documents based on lack of authentication when basing the denial of asylum on a lack of corroborating documents.[682]

At least one IJ has also found the authentication provisions under 8 CFR §287.6 to be permissive rather than mandatory in the asylum context. In *Matter of Long*

---

[676] *Id.* at 969; *see also Gui Cun Liu v. Ashcroft*, 372 F.3d 529, 533 (3d Cir. 2004) (finding that 8 CFR §287.6 is not an absolute rule of exclusion and is not the exclusive means of authenticating records before the IJ); *Khan v. INS*, 237 F.3d 1143, 1144 (9th Cir. 2001) ("[D]ocuments may be authenticated in immigration proceedings through any recognized procedure, such as those required by INS regulation or by the Federal Rules of Civil Procedure.").

[677] *See Vatyan v. Mukasey*, 508 F.3d 1179 (9th Cir. 2007). *See also Padilla-Martinez v. Holder*, 770 F.3d 825 (9th Cir. 2014).

[678] *Vatyan v. Mukasey*, 508 F.3d 1179, 1184–85 (9th Cir. 2007) (noting that Federal Rule of Evidence 901(b)(1) allows authentication through the testimony of a witness with knowledge). *See also Yongo v. INS*, 355 F.3d 27, 31 (1st Cir. 2004) (holding that INS officer could authenticate German immigration records through his testimony regarding their source and appearance).

[679] *Zhu v. Att'y Gen.*, 744 F.3d 268, 274 (3d Cir. 2014).

[680] *See* 31 C. Wright & C. Gold, *Federal Practice and Procedure* §7137, as cited in Virgil Wiebe & Serena Parker, *Asking for a Note from Your Torturer: Corroboration and Authentication Requirements in Asylum, Withholding and Torture Convention Claims*, 1 IMMIGRATION & NATIONALITY LAW HANDBOOK 428 (AILA 2001–02 ed.).

[681] *Vatyan*, 508 F.3d at 1184–85; *Jiang v. Gonzales*, 474 F.3d 25, 29 (1st Cir. 2007). *See also Qiu Yun Chen v. Holder*, 715 F.3d 207 (7th Cir. 2013) (finding that a document posted on a government website is presumptively authentic if government sponsorship can be verified by visiting the website itself).

[682] *Georgis v. Ashcroft*, 328 F.3d 962 (7th Cir. 2003); *Khan v. INS*, 237 F.3d 1143 (9th Cir. 2001). For an in-depth discussion of this issue, *see* V. Wiebe and S. Parker, *supra* note 680, at 414.

Sheng,[683] the IJ applied a two-part test in the claim of an asylum applicant from China. The IJ held that "where the applicant's testimony if (1) credible and consistent concerning the circumstances of his or her past persecution and/or well-founded fear of future persecution and (2) the applicant satisfactorily explains the failure to properly certify foreign documents offered to the court as evidence, the foreign documents should be admitted." This approach is a reasonable one and is similar to the approach in *Matter of S–M–J–*[684] that allows for an applicant to provide an explanation of why corroborating evidence is not available.[685]

2. *Witness Lists*

Most respondents also will identify various witnesses who may testify in support of their applications at their individual hearings. These witnesses may be fact witnesses who can confirm the respondent's protected characteristic(s), who were present during acts of harm or mistreatment, who have personal knowledge of the psychological or physical harm suffered by the respondent, who can confirm the respondent's date of entry to the United States, and who have personal knowledge, whether from their own experiences or otherwise, of the current conditions in the respondent's home country. Witnesses also may be medical or mental health professionals who have evaluated the respondent's physical or psychological harm, or country condition experts who can speak to the current conditions in the respondent's home country and assess the respondent's risk of harm upon return.

Increasingly, asylum applicants are relying on the testimony of expert and other witnesses to establish their eligibility for asylum. The testimony of experts and other witnesses must be under oath or affirmation administered by the IJ.[686] It is error for an IJ to refuse to allow testimony if it would have had a potential effect on the outcome of the hearing.[687]

The AG has noted that experts in immigration court proceedings do not need to be formally "qualified" as experts.[688] Nor is there a requirement that an academic, to be

---

[683] *Matter of Long Sheng*, A71 800 016 (IJ Baltimore, June 23, 1993), as cited in V. Wiebe and S. Parker, *supra* note 680, at 425.

[684] *Matter of S–M–J–*, 21 I&N Dec. 722 (BIA 1997).

[685] V. Wiebe and S. Parker, *supra* note 680, at 425–26.

[686] 8 CFR §1240.7(b) (2014).

[687] *See, e.g.*, *Morgan v. Mukasey*,529 F.3d 1202, 1210–11(9th Cir. 2008)(finding applicants were denied due process when IJ excluded two witnesses from testifying); *Tun v. Gonzales*, 485 F.3d 1014, 1017, 1026 (8th Cir. 2007) (finding the IJ erred in excluding a medical doctor's testimony because she had not been to Burma, she did not specialize in trauma or psychiatry, and her organization, Physicians for Human Rights, was an "advocacy group"); *Koval v. Gonzales*, 418 F.3d 798, 808 (7th Cir. 2005); *Boyanivskyy v. Gonzales*, 450 F.3d 286, 293 (7th Cir. 2006) (finding the IJ erred by excluding the testimony of corroboration witnesses); *Kerciku v. INS*, 314 F.3d 913, 918 (7th Cir. 2003). *But see Myslymi v. Gonzales*, 216 Fed. Appx. 571, 576 (7th Cir. 2007) (finding IJ properly disregarded expert whose testimony was "speculative and provided no insight into any specific threat [the applicants] might face ....").

[688] *See Matter of Marshi*, A26 980 386 (AG Feb. 13, 2004), at 5 (finding IJ erred in disallowing testimony from a U.S. Marine colonel who had extensive and impressive experience and qualifications,

Continued

qualified as an expert, have published academic books or articles on the precise subject matter of his or her testimony.[689]Courts have also held that it is not necessary for an expert to have traveled recently to the country in question.[690] Nor is there an absolute requirement that experts be present to be cross-examined in immigration court proceedings.[691]

However, some degree of competency is necessary. Judge Richard A. Posner in the Seventh Circuit criticized the use of a document expert by DHS who did not speak or read Albanian, but testified as an expert at the hearing that the applicant's Albanian documents were probably fakes.[692] He based this conclusion in part on the lack of accent marks and the type of technology used to make them.[693] Judge Posner noted that the "spirit of *Daubert*" [694] is applicable in proceedings before administrative agencies and "junk science" has no place. The court concluded that the expert, not knowing Albanian, should not have been allowed to testify that Albanian is always written with diacritical marks, nor should he have been allowed to testify about the printing technology when he stated that he did not know what printing resources the Albanian government had.[695] Similarly, the Eighth Circuit has held that an IJ's reliance on a Department of State forensic evaluation violated due process because it failed to identify the investigator, including the extent of the investigation and the methods used.[696]

It is important to provide information to the court on the witness's qualifications and expertise on the matter. If at all possible, it also is preferable and a best practice to have the expert and witnesses physically or telephonically present for cross-examination purposes. IJs have been criticized by federal courts for disregarding expert testimony and relying instead on non-record evidence, in most cases

---

where his testimony would have been material and supportive of the applicant's asylum claim), *published on* AILA InfoNet at Doc. No. 04021390 (*posted* Feb. 13, 2004).

[689] *Niam v. Ashcroft*, 354 F.3d 652, 660 (7th Cir. 2004). *See also Morgan*, 529 F.3d 1201, 1211(9th Cir. 2008) (holding that it was an error of law for the BIA's failure to consider the psychological report).

[690] *See, e.g.*, *Tun*, 484 F.3d at 1026 (8th Cir. 2007) (finding the IJ erred in excluding a medical doctor's testimony, in part, because she had not been to Burma); *see also Koval v. Gonzales*, 418 F.3d 798, 803 (7th Cir. 2005) (finding that although the expert had not been to Ukraine in 12 years, the IJ erred in refusing to admit his testimony).

[691] *Tun*, 484 F.3d at 1025–26 (finding that fairness rather than the rules of evidence govern admissibility and that the use of a report from a qualified witness, in the absence of any specific objections, is generally fair); *Yang v. Gonzales*, 427 F.3d 1117, 1121–22 (8th Cir. 2005) (finding error where IJ and BIA failed to accord weight to an affidavit from a non-testifying, facially qualified country condition expert).

[692] *Pasha v. Gonzales*, 433 F.3d 530, 532 (7th Cir. 2005).

[693] *Id.* at 531–32.

[694] *Id.* at 535; *see also Daubert v. Merrell Dow Pharmaceuticals*, 509 U.S. 579 (1993) (allowing for the exclusion of expert testimony of one who lacks expertise or uses questionable methods).

[695] *Pasha*, *supra* note 692, at 535.

[696] *Banat v. Holder*, 557 F.3d 886, 892–93 (8th Cir. 2009).

speculation and conjecture, when adjudicating cases.[697] The Seventh Circuit, in response, has called for administrative country experts to be appointed by the immigration courts, similar to vocational experts in Social Security (SS) cases.[698] Courts have also criticized the IJs' reliance on Department of State reports because the authors of the reports are anonymous and decision makers do not know the credentials of the individuals who assemble the reports or the trustworthiness of the evidence they have relied on.[699]

A respondent must notify the court in advance of the individual hearing whether he or she plans to present witness testimony in support of his or her application(s) for protection. If the respondent plans to present witness testimony, he or she must prepare and file a Proposed Witness List with the immigration court and serve a copy of the witness list on DHS.

A witness list should include the following information for each witness: (1) the name of the witness; (2) if applicable, the witness's A-number; (3) a written summary of the witness's testimony; (4) the estimated length of the testimony; (5) the language in which the witness will testify; and (6) a curriculum vitae or resume, if the witness is called as an expert.[700]

- **Practice Pointer**: Many IJs require that a written declaration or sworn statement of a witness be submitted in advance of the individual hearing if that witness is to be permitted to testify. It is essential for practitioners to research the preferences of the specific IJ before whom the respondent is to appear to ensure that all witnesses are able to present their testimony.
- **Practice Pointer**: Practitioners also should ensure that witnesses' written statements are sworn and/or notarized and that copies of their identification documents submitted as attachments to their statements.

A witness list package should contain: (1) a Form EOIR-28 (if not previously filed); (2) a cover page; (3) the witness list (incompliance with the requirements for witness lists); and (4) a proof of service.[701]

Some immigration judges prefer to have personal statements from witnesses in the form of an "affidavit," *i.e.*, a sworn statement signed before a notary. This may be a difficult or even deadly requirement for witnesses in foreign countries. According to

---

[697] *See Banks v. Gonzales*, 453 F.3d 449, 454 (7th Cir. 2006) (finding that the IJ played the role of country specialist, "a role for which an overworked lawyer who spends his life in the Midwest is so poorly suited").

[698] *Id.* at 453.

[699] *See Koval v. Gonzales*, 418 F.3d 798, 807 (7th Cir. 2005) (noting that the reports are prepared in general terms and offer more of a statement on the relationship of the U.S. government to that country than an account of individual circumstances).

[700] ICPM, chapter 3.3(g).

[701] ICPM, chapter 3.3(c)(i)(C).

28 USC §1746, the substitute for an affidavit is an unsworn declaration under penalty of perjury. The statute provides:

> Whenever, under any law of the United States or under any rule, regulation, order, or requirement made pursuant to any law, any matter is *required* or permitted to be supported, evidenced, established, or proved by the sworn declaration, verification, certificate, statement, oath or affidavit ... such matter may with like force and effect, be supported, evidenced, established, or proved by the unsworn declaration, certificate, verification, or statement, in writing of such person, which is subscribed by him, as true under penalty of perjury and dated, in substantially the following form: "If executed without the United States: I declare (or certify, verify, or state) under penalty of perjury under the laws of the United States of America that the foregoing is true and correct. Executed on (date). (Signature)."[702]

If a witness cannot testify in person at the hearing, the respondent must prepare and file a motion for telephonic testimony, as described above, and note the desire to present telephonic testimony on the witness list. An unopposed affidavit, however, may be given the same weight as in-person testimony.

3. *Filing Deadlines*

According to the ICPM, unless otherwise specified by the IJ, all filings in non-detained asylum cases are due 15 days before the individual hearing.[703] This deadline does not apply to exhibits or witnesses offered solely to rebut and/or impeach.[704] DHS must file its response within 10 days after the original filing with the immigration court.[705] For individual hearings involving detained respondents, filing deadlines are as specified by the immigration court.[706] All filing deadlines are calculated in calendar days (not business days), unless otherwise indicated.[707] Deadlines may be set on a specific date, (*e.g.*, a brief due on June 5, 2014),[708] or may be a specified period of time prior to or following a hearing (*e.g.*, 15 days prior to the individual hearing).[709]

- **Practice Pointer**: When calculating the pre-individual hearing filing deadline, the ICPM instructs that the day of the hearing is day "0," and the day before the hearing is day "1."[710] The days should be counted backwards from the hearing date and should include all calendar days

[702] 28 USC §1746 (2012).

[703] ICPM, chapter 3.1(b)(ii)(A).

[704] *Id.*

[705] *Id.*

[706] ICPM, chapter 3.1(b)(ii)(B).

[707] ICPM, chapter 3.1(c)(i).

[708] ICPM, chapter 3.1(c)(ii)(A).

[709] ICPM, chapter 3.1(c)(ii)(B).

[710] ICPM, chapter 3.1(c)(ii)(B).

> (including Saturdays, Sundays, and legal holidays), until day 15 is reached. If, however, day 15 falls on a Saturday, Sunday, or legal holiday, the deadline is construed to fall on the next business day.[711] A similar calculation is used for determining post-hearing deadlines.[712] For responses to filings (e.g., a response to a motion due within 10 days of the motion being filed with the immigration court), the day the original filing is received by the immigration court counts as day "0" and the following day counts as day "1."[713] For any deadline that falls on a Saturday, Sunday, or legal holiday, the deadline is construed to fall on the next business day.[714]

If a respondent cannot meet the relevant deadline, he or she must file a motion to request extension of the filing deadline.[715] A Motion for Extension should only be filed if absolutely necessary, as such motions are discouraged and parties are encouraged to meet all deadlines and avoid delay.[716]

Such a motion should clearly state: (1) when the filing is due; (2) the reasons for requesting an extension; (3) that the party has exercised due diligence to meet the current filing deadline; (4) that the party will meet a revised deadline; and (5) if the parties have communicated, whether the other party consents to the extension.[717]

The mere filing of a Motion for Extension does not excuse the respondent's failure to meet a deadline. Rather, a deadline is only extended upon the IJ's granting of the motion.[718]

The untimely submission of a filing could have serious consequences for a respondent in removal proceedings.[719] If an application for relief is untimely, the respondent's interest in the relief may be deemed waived or abandoned; if a motion is untimely, it may be denied; if a brief or pre-trial statement is untimely, the issues in question may be deemed waived or conceded; if an exhibit is untimely, it may not be entered into evidence or may be given less weight; if a witness list is untimely, the witnesses on the list may be barred from testifying; if a response to a motion is untimely, the motion may be deemed unopposed.[720] Thus, it is critically important for

---

[711] *Id.*

[712] ICPM, chapter 3.1(c)(ii)(C).

[713] ICPM, chapter 3.1(c)(ii)(E).

[714] ICPM, chapter 3.1(c)(ii).

[715] ICPM, chapter 3.1(C)(iv).

[716] ICPM, chapter 3.1(c)(iv)(A).

[717] ICPM, chapter 3.1(c)(iv)(C).

[718] ICPM, chapter 3.1(c)(iv).

[719] ICPM, chapter 3.1(d)(ii).

[720] *Id.*

a respondent in removal proceedings to ensure that all filings are submitted to the immigration court in a timely manner.[721]

4. *DHS Evidentiary Filings*

DHS may file evidence in support of the government's position on the respondent's case, and asylum applicants have the right to a reasonable opportunity to examine the evidence against them.[722] The only exception is that they are not entitled to examine national security information if such information is used to deny them admission to the United States or in determining their eligibility for discretionary relief.[723]

The DHS trial attorney may present classified evidence in an asylum hearing to either the IJ or BIA.[724] The IJ or BIA, before admitting the evidence, must determine that the classified evidence is relevant to the hearing.[725] The asylum applicant must be notified that classified evidence has been given to the IJ.[726] The agency that provides the classified evidence to the IJ or BIA may provide an unclassified summary to the applicant.[727] At least one IJ has requested that the agency also provide any exculpatory evidence, and when it failed to do so, found that the classified evidence would be viewed with "respectful skepticism."[728]

H. Pre-Hearing Conferences and Statements

Often it may be valuable to the respondent to speak with DHS prior to his or her individual hearing in order to discuss the evidence submitted, the proposed witnesses, and any potential agreements by the parties. Doing so may narrow the issues that need to be addressed at the individual hearing, which may benefit the respondent, but also the immigration court and DHS, given their limited resources. An IJ has the authority to schedule pre-hearing conferences or to require pre-hearing statements that may assist in narrowing the issues, obtaining stipulations between parties, exchanging information voluntarily, and otherwise simplifying and organizing the proceedings.[729] An IJ also has the authority to order any party to file a pre-hearing statement of position that may include, but is not limited to:

- A statement of facts to which both parties may have stipulated, together with a statement that the parties have communicated in good faith to stipulate to the fullest extent possible;

---

[721] ICPM, chapter 3.1(d)(iii).

[722] INA §240(b)(4); 8 USC §1229a(b)(4) (2012).

[723] *Id.*

[724] 8 CFR §1240.33(c)(4) (2014).

[725] *Id.*

[726] *Id.*

[727] *Id.*

[728] *Cheema v. Ashcroft*, 383 F.3d 848, 852 (9th Cir. 2004).

[729] 8 CFR §1003.21(a) (2014).

- A list of proposed witnesses and what they will establish;
- A list of exhibits, copies of exhibits to be introduced, and a statement of the reason for their introduction;
- The estimated time required to present the case; and
- A statement of unresolved issues involved in the proceedings.[730]

Even where pre-hearing conferences and statements are not ordered by an IJ, it is usually in the respondent's best interest to seek such pre-hearing actions by calling the DHS Office of Chief Counsel. First, all respondents should file a pre-hearing statement or brief in support of their claims for asylum, withholding of removal, and protection under CAT, even if such a statement or brief is not ordered by the court. Such briefs should contain the following components: (1) a cover page; (2) the brief; (3) a signature page signed by the respondent or respondent's representative; and (4) A proof of service.

Second, respondents should attempt to discuss with DHS the issues involved in the case prior to the individual hearing. Specifically, pre-hearing negotiations take place for the purpose of narrowing the issues; obtaining stipulations between the parties; exchanging information voluntarily; and otherwise simplifying and organizing the proceedings. Respondents or their representatives should call DHS counsel a week or two prior to the individual hearing to discuss the matter. Any agreements should be noted and raised with the IJ at the beginning of the individual hearing on the record.

> ➢ **Practice Pointer**: When calling DHS to initiate pre-hearing negotiations, practitioners should introduce themselves, explain what case they are calling about (client's name and A-number, hearing date, and type of relief), describe the desire to narrow the issues to simplify the proceedings, and explain to DHS what they want for their clients.

I. Preparing the Respondent's and Witnesses' Testimony

Prior to the individual hearing, a respondent and his or her witnesses also must prepare to provide their testimony in immigration court. A well-prepared respondent or witness is a respondent or witness who has been educated about the legal standards involved in the case, the procedures of the individual hearing, the purpose for those procedures, and the roles of all of the players involved in the hearing. Specifically, it is essential for the respondent and all witnesses to understand the following:

- The purpose and scope of their testimony;
- The relevant legal standards, including burden of proof and the legal elements the respondent needs to demonstrate in order to satisfy the judge;
- The documentary evidence that has been submitted and the importance of being consistent with that evidence during testimony;

---

[730] 8 CFR §1003.21(b) (2014).

- The roles and responsibilities of the representative, the DHS attorney, the judge, the interpreter, the witnesses, and any others who may take part in the hearing;
- The procedures of the individual hearing and what is going to happen, including the logistics of appearing in immigration court on the requested date and time;
- What to expect during direct examination — what questions the representative plans to ask and why;
- What to expect during DHS's cross-examination — what issues or potential problems may arise and how the respondent or witness should address those;
- The representative's role during cross-examination;
- The representative's ability to conduct a redirect examination to explain inconsistencies, address negative factors pointed out by DHS, repair wrong or misleading information, or address new matters brought out during cross-examination;
- The logistics of using an interpreter and tips for doing so;
- Tips for providing effective testimony; and
- The potential decisions of the IJ.

> ➤ **Practice Pointer**: Practitioners may wish to discuss the following tips for effective testimony with their clients and witnesses: (1) always tell the truth; (2) make eye contact with and direct answers to whoever asked the question (the respondent's representative, the DHS attorney, or the IJ); (3) listen very carefully to the question asked and answer that specific question in a clear and convincing way; (4) be polite and persistent in answering the DHS attorney's questions; (5) ask for questions to be repeated if necessary; (6) don't play the guessing game — if you don't know the answer or don't remember, say so; (7) understand the law; (8) know the evidence; (9) remember that testimony is just like a conversation; and (10) trust yourself and your attorney.

XI. What Happens at the Individual Hearing?

An individual hearing is an evidentiary hearing on contested matters, including removability and applications for relief.[731] In the context of individuals seeking protection in the form of asylum, withholding of removal, or CAT relief, an individual hearing is an evidentiary hearing on the merits of the respondent's application(s) for relief.

Evidentiary hearings on applications for asylum, withholding of removal, or protection under the CAT will be open to the public unless the respondent expressly

[731] ICPM, chapter 4.16(a).

requests the hearing to be closed.[732] The IJ must inquire whether the respondent requests such closure.[733] IJs may limit attendance or hold a closed hearing to protect witnesses, parties, or the public interest.[734] IJs also have the authority to place reasonable limitations on the number in attendance, with priority given to the press over the general public.[735]

The IJ has the authority to control the scope of any evidentiary hearing.[736] During the hearing, whether in person or via video, the applicant will be examined under oath on his or her application and may present evidence or witnesses on his or her own behalf.[737] The applicant has the burden of establishing that he or she merits relief in the form of asylum, withholding of removal, or protection under the CAT.[738] The DHS attorney also may call witnesses and present evidence for the record, including any relevant classified information.[739]

During an individual hearing, the parties should be prepared to make an opening statement, raise any objections to the other party's evidence, present witnesses and evidence on all issues, cross-examine opposing witnesses, object to testimony, and make a closing statement.[740] Over the course of the hearing, the IJ will mark all documentation and evidence on the record and hear any objections to the admission of that evidence; hear opening statements or more informal preliminary positions on relief; take the testimony of the respondent, his or her witnesses, and any witnesses presented by DHS; hear closing arguments; and, often, make and issue a decision on the application(s) for relief. Each of these parts of the individual hearing is discussed in detail below.

A. Preliminary Matters and the Marking of Evidence

At the beginning of an individual hearing, the IJ will enter the courtroom and turn on the recording equipment.[741] The individual hearing is recorded except for any off-the-record discussions.[742] On the record, the IJ will then identify the type of proceeding being conducted (*e.g.*, removal proceeding); the respondent's name and A-number; the date, time, and place of the proceedings; and the presence of the

---

[732] 8 CFR §1240.11(c)(3)(i) (2014).

[733] *Id.*

[734] 8 CFR §3.27(b) (2014).

[735] 8 CFR §3.27(a) (2014).

[736] 8 CFR §1230.11(c)(3)(ii) (2014).

[737] 8 CFR §1240.11(c)(3)(iii) (2014).

[738] *Id.*

[739] 8 CFR §1240.11(c)(3)(iv) (2014).

[740] ICPM, chapter 4.16(d).

[741] ICPM, chapter 4.16(c).

[742] *See* ICPM, chapter 4.10.

parties.[743] The IJ will then ask the parties to enter their appearance for the record, and will verify the respondent's name, address, and telephone number.[744]

- **Practice Pointer**: If the respondent's address or telephone number have changed, he or she should be prepared to submit a Form EOIR-33/IC, Alien's Change of Address.[745]

If the respondent or his or her witnesses' command of the English language is inadequate to fully understand and participate in removal proceedings, the court will provide one at government expense.[746] The IJ will administer an oath to the interpreter in the beginning of the individual hearing that the interpreter will interpret and translate accurately in court.[747]

The IJ will then proceed with preliminary matters. He or she will ask the parties if they have had the opportunity to discuss the case and whether there have been any agreements made to narrow the contested issues. At that time, the respondent or his or her representative and DHS will notify the court of any issues that they were able to agree to prior to the hearing.

- **Practice Pointer**: Practitioners should invest the time to prepare the strongest evidence, witness list, and pre-hearing brief possible, because the stronger the pre-hearing documentation, the more likely DHS is to agree to stipulate to particular issues. Additionally, strong evidence and persuasive legal arguments will assist in convincing the judge to side with practitioners' clients before taking any testimony.

The IJ will then address all of the documentation that was submitted prior to the individual hearing to mark it for the record of proceedings and to determine whether it may be admitted into the record of proceedings. IJs are instructed that "[t]he general rule with respect to evidence in immigration proceedings favors admissibility as long as the evidence is shown to be probative of relevant matters and its use is fundamentally fair so as not to deprive the alien of due process of law."[748] It is at this time that the respondent and his or her representative should object to any evidence submitted by DHS that may be contrary to the fundamental fairness of the

---

743 ICPM, chapter 4.16(c).

744 *Id.*

745 *Id.*

746 8 CFR §1003.22 (2014); ICPM, chapter 4.11.

747 8 CFR §1003.22 (2014); ICPM, chapter 4.11. The immigration court uses staff interpreters employed by the immigration court, as well as contract and telephonic interpreters. Staff interpreters take an oath to interpret and translate accurately at the time they are employed by the Department of Justice. Thus, the IJ will not need to administer an oath to a staff interpreter at the beginning of the individual hearing. ICPM, chapter 4.11.

748 *Immigration Judge Benchbook* (Oct. 2001), chapter1, at I.A.2., *available at www.usdoj.gov/eoir/statspub/benchbook.pdf*; *see also Doumbia v. Gonzales*, 472 F.3d 957, 962 (7th Cir. 2007); *Espinoza v. INS*, 45 F.3d 308, 310 (9th Cir. 1995).

proceedings. The respondent and his or her representative also should be prepared to respond to any objections to his or her own evidence by DHS.

The Federal Rules of Evidence are not controlling in immigration court proceedings.[749] However, they are guiding because they provide useful benchmarks for IJs regarding what evidence meets the standards of fundamental fairness for purposes of due process. Overall, the test for the admissibility of evidence in immigration court proceedings is whether the evidence is probative and whether its use is fundamentally fair.[750] As the Second Circuit noted, "[F]airness is closely related to the reliability and trustworthiness of the evidence."[751] Thus, it is essential for the respondent or his or her representative to make any objections to evidence at the earliest convenience, and at the very least, at the beginning of the individual hearing.[752]

The following is a list of common objections that the respondent and his or her representative may make to DHS's evidence:

- Relevance — if the evidence does not have probative value for the facts or issues in dispute;[753]
- Foundation — if DHS has not established the basis on which a document is supported;
- Authentication — if DHS has not submitted evidence the document is what it claims to be or did not show chain of custody;[754]
- Right to review and respond to evidence — if evidence is not reviewable, illegible, not translated, or submitted late by DHS;[755] and
- Right to cross-examine witnesses — if an affiant or creator of a document is not present for cross-examination.[756]

---

[749] *Matter of D–*, 20 I&N Dec. 827, 831 (BIA 1994).

[750] *See Ezeagwuna v. Ashcroft*, 301 F.3d 116, 127 (3d Cir. 2002), *rev'd on other grounds by Ezeagwuna v. Ashcroft,* 325 F.3d 396 (3d Cir. 2003); *see also Cotzojay v. Holder*, 725 F.3d 172 (2d Cir. 2013) (finding that evidence should be suppressed when it was obtained through egregious Fourth Amendment violations when ICE officers entered the Guatemalan individual's residence without consent in the middle of the night during a warrantless raid); *Oliva-Ramos v. U.S. Att'y Gen.*, 694 F.3d 259 (3d Cir. 2012) (finding that the exclusionary rule may apply in removal proceedings where an individual shows egregious violations of Fourth Amendment or other liberties that might transgress notions of fundamental fairness and undermine the probative value of the evidence obtained); *Ezeagwuna v. Ashcroft,* 325 F.3d 396 (3d Cir. 2003); *Bustos-Torres v. INS*, 898 F.2d 1053, 1055 (5th Cir. 1990); *Matter of Ponce-Hernandez*, 21 I&N Dec. 784 (BIA 1999).

[751] *Felzcerek v. INS*, 75 F.3d 112, 115 (2d Cir. 1996).

[752] ICPM, chapter 3.1(b)(ii).

[753] *See Matter of Ponce-Hernandez*, 22 I&N Dec. 784 (BIA 1999).

[754] *See* 8 CFR §§1287.6(a) (2014).

[755] INA §240(b)(4)(B); 8 CFR §1240.10(a)(4) (2014). *See also* ICPM, chapter 3.1(b)(ii)(A), 3.1(d)(ii), 4.16(a)(i) (regarding timeliness of court filings).

[756] INA §242(b)(3); 8 CFR §1240.10(a)(4) (2014).

Overall, the "golden rule" of evidence in immigration court is whether admission of the evidence would be fundamentally fair, because due process requires a full and fair hearing on claims.[757] If admission of the evidence would deprive the respondent of due process, it should not be admitted on the record of proceedings.[758] Just as a respondent or his or her representative must be prepared to object to DHS documentary evidence, he or she must also be prepared to respond to any objections by DHS to his or her own documentary evidence.

- **Practice Pointer**: If a respondent first applied for asylum affirmatively before the USCIS Asylum Office, DHS attorneys often seek to admit the Asylum Officer's notes and assessments into evidence before the immigration court or to rely upon the content of these documents to craft their cross-examination questions in an attempt to impeach a respondent or witness's testimony or to raise inconsistencies, omissions, vague testimony, or other problems that arose during the course of the asylum interview. In addition to reviewing these notes prior to the hearing by filing a FOIA request based on the nationwide settlement of *Martins v. USCIS*,[759] practitioners also should consider objecting to these documents as inadmissible or objecting to DHS attorneys' reliance upon the contents of these documents in crafting their cross-examination questions. Potential objections to the introduction or use of these documents include the following: (1) the respondent did not have the opportunity to examine and respond to the evidence;[760] (2) the respondent does not have the opportunity to cross-examine the asylum officer;[761] (3) DHS did not timely file these documents;[762] (4) the Office of the Chief Immigration Judge OPPM 00-01 and an unpublished BIA decision preclude the admission of these documents;[763] (5) the

---

[757] *See Rusu v. INS*, 296 F.3d 316, 321–22 (4th Cir. 2002).

[758] *Matter of Toro*, 17 I&N Dec. 340 (BIA 1980); *Matter of Ramirez-Sanchez*, 17 I&N Dec. 503 (BIA 1980); *Matter of Lam*, 14 I&N Dec. 168 (BIA 1972).

[759] *See Martins v. USCIS*, No. 13-00591 (N.D. Cal. July 3, 2013).

[760] *See* INA §240(b)(4)(B); 8 CFR §1240.10(a)(4) (2014); ICPM, chapter 3.1(d)(ii).

[761] *See* INA §240(b)(4)(B); 8 CFR §1240.10(a)(4) (2014); ICPM, chapter 3.1(d)(ii).

[762] *See* ICPM, chapter 3.1(b)(ii)(A), 4.16(a)(i). Note that DHS may accurately counter with the argument that these documents are offered solely to rebut and/or impeach, and thus, they are not subject to the ICPM's filing deadlines. *See id.*

[763] *See* Memorandum No. OPPM 00-01 from Michael J. Creppy, at 13–14 (Aug. 4, 2000), AILA Doc. No. 00080490, *available at* http://www.usdoj.gov/eoir/efoia/ocij/oppm00/OPPM00-01Revised.pdf (noting due process concerns with the admission and reliance upon asylum officer notes and assessments); *Matter of A097-103-163* (June 14, 2005), *available at www.lexisnexis.com/community/immigration-law/blogs/inside/archive/2006/06/29/bia-on-asylum-officer_2700_s-assessment-to-refer.aspx* (last visited July 18, 2013) (relying upon the Office of the Chief Immigration Judge's Mem. No. OPPM 00-01 in holding that asylum officer notes and assessments are not admissible). *See also Koulibaly v. Mukasey*, 541 F.3d 614, 620–21 (6th Cir. 2008) (holding that the Asylum Officer's Assessment, even with attached notes, lacked indicia of reliability, and finding as a result that the

Continued

information contained in the notes and assessments is inherently unreliable — documents not properly authenticated and/or no opportunity to cross-examine the officer who produced the documents;[764] (6) admission of the notes and assessments or permitting DHS to rely upon and reference the information contained therein violates the fundamental fairness of these proceedings.[765] If the IJ admits the documents into evidence over these objections, practitioners should consider whether to move for a continuance for time to examine and respond to evidence presented against the respondent or to request the right to cross-examine the asylum officer.[766] If DHS is unwilling to produce the asylum officer for cross-examination, practitioners should request that a subpoena be issued requiring the asylum officer's attendance at a hearing.[767] For a detailed discussion of how to access asylum officer notes and assessments and how to challenge their use in immigration court, see David Cleveland, Dree Collopy, and Hilary Han's article, "Challenging the Admission of Asylum Officers' Notes and Assessments as Evidence in Immigration Court," (July 24, 2013), available at AILA InfoNet Doc. No. 13072449.

B. Opening Statements

Following the marking of exhibits and entry of evidence on the record of proceedings, the IJ may continue with opening statements or more informal dialogue with the parties regarding their positions on the requested relief. Although most IJs do not entertain formal opening statements, such statements may be strategically useful or beneficial to the respondent in certain cases. An IJ may permit a more formal opening statement upon request. If the IJ permits one party to present an opening statement, he or she also will allow the opposing part to do the same. However, in most cases, rather than formal opening statements, IJs may simply ask the parties to articulate their theory of the case and positions on relief, or they may skip opening statements altogether and proceed to the taking of testimony.

Regardless whether a formal opening statement or more informal statement of position is given, these initial statements are the first opportunity the respondent has

---

adverse credibility determination was not based on substantial evidence); Agenda Items for EOIR/AILA Liaison Meeting 4/3/2008 at 16–17, *available at* AILA Doc. No. 08080461 ("Under no circumstances should any document containing reference to INS credibility findings be filed with the Court.").

[764] *See, e.g., Singh v. Gonzales*, 403 F.3d 1081 (9th Cir. 2005) (noting the inherent unreliability of the asylum interview process).

[765] *See Dent v. Holder*, 627 F.3d 365 (9th Cir. 2010); *Rusu v. INS*, 296 F.3d 316, 321–22 (4th Cir. 2002); *Matter of Toro*, 17 I&N Dec. 340 (BIA 1980); *Matter of Ramirez-Sanchez*, 17 I&N Dec. 504 (BIA 1980); *Matter of Lam*, 14 I&N Dec. 168 (BIA 1972).

[766] INA §240(b)(4)(B), 8 CFR §1240.10(a)(4) (2014); ICPM, chapter 3.1(d)(ii).

[767] 8 CFR §§1003.35, 1287.4(a)(2)(ii) (2014); ICPM, chapter 4.20.

to communicate to an open-minded IJ, present his or her legal theory, highlight his or her most important and persuasive facts, explain the applicable law, introduce a theme, and connect with the IJ through effective storytelling.[768] Thus, opening statements should personalize the respondent to the IJ, present concise information in a simple and logical way, and provide an overview of what the respondent expects to demonstrate through his or her testimony, the witnesses' testimony, and other evidence presented.

> ➢ **Practice Pointer**: Practitioners should not hesitate to request the opportunity to give a brief opening statement if it would be beneficial to the case. Whether or not a formal opening statement is prepared and presented, practitioners should always be prepared to offer a brief opening statement (five minutes or less) that covers the most compelling facts, the legal theory of the case, and the respondent's position on relief. Approaching even informal initial statements strategically will enable practitioners to capitalize on this opportunity to "hook" the IJ early.

C. Direct, Cross, and Re-Direct Examinations

Following the admission of evidence and any other preliminary matters, such as opening statements or initial discussions of the parties' positions on relief, the IJ will initiate the taking of testimony. Typically, this process begins with a discussion of the order of witnesses for the respondent and any witnesses DHS plans to present. Witnesses who are not testifying (other than the respondent) are usually sequestered and asked to sit in the court's waiting area until it is their turn to testify. Expert witnesses, however, do not have to be sequestered.

> ➢ **Practice Pointer**: IJs often wish to hear the testimony of the respondent first; however, there is no rule stating that this is a requirement. Practitioners should think strategically regarding the order of the testimony presented and what might be most persuasive to the IJ. For example, if country conditions are particularly complex, it may be effective to present the testimony of a country conditions expert prior to the respondent's testimony. Doing so might assist the judge in understanding the claim better and to place the applicant's fears into the proper context. Additionally, since the respondent cannot be sequestered during his or her own hearing, putting forth witnesses first allows the respondent to hear the witnesses' testimony prior to providing his or her own. This may allow the respondent to feel more relaxed during his or her own testimony and may assist the respondent with testifying consistently with the other witnesses.

---

[768] *See* Erich Straub, *Storytelling & Immigration Law: A Practical Guide*, IMMIGRATION PRACTICE POINTERS (AILA 2014–15 ed.).

The IJ will then call the respondent or first witness to the stand and will place him or her under oath. All witnesses, including the respondent, must be placed under oath by the IJ before testifying.[769] The respondent's representative will then proceed with his or her direct examination of the respondent or witness. The purpose of a direct examination is for the respondent or witness to tell his or her story and to demonstrate to the IJ that he or she can meet all legal requirements for being granted relief.

During the direct examination, DHS may object to any questions DHS believes to be improper. Although the Federal Rules of Evidence are not binding in immigration court, they are guiding. Objections to questioning and testimony, therefore, may be raised during the course of direct, cross, and re-direct examinations, and the IJ will determine whether the issue raised by the objecting party may impact the fundamental fairness of the proceedings.

Common objections during direct examinations of the respondent and witnesses include:

- Leading question — if the question itself suggests the answer;
- Lack of foundation — if facts necessary to answer the question asked have not yet been established on the record;
- Mischaracterization of testimony — if the questioner repeats a portion of what the respondent or witness said, but misquotes or mischaracterizes it;
- Asked and answered — if the questioner asks the same thing again after the respondent or witness has already provided an answer, even if the question is phrased differently;
- Calls for speculation — if the question poses a hypothetical or seeks information that is not based on the respondent or witness's first-hand knowledge;
- Calls for improper opinion — if the question asks for an opinion where the witness is not qualified as an expert on that subject or has no personal knowledge of that subject; and
- Witness not competent — if the witness is not qualified as an expert on that subject, lacks personal knowledge, or could not observe/remember/communicate the information.

> ➢ **Practice Pointer**: Practitioners should craft direct examination questions that avoid these and other objections. Objections can disrupt the flow of testimony or make the witness feel nervous or uncomfortable. Practitioners also should be prepared to respond to any objections by DHS. Often, DHS objections — leading, for example — are not accurate. Practitioners should not be hesitant to respond with an explanation why the question was proper.

---

[769] 8 CFR §1003.34 (2014); ICPM, chapter 4.16(e).

Also during the direct examination, the IJ may interject with his or her own questions for the respondent or witness. The IJ, as the fact-finder in the proceedings, may ask questions of respondents and all witnesses at any time during the hearing.[770]

- **Practice Pointer**: Most IJs will simply interject follow-up questions sporadically throughout a direct examination. Since this is permitted under the ICPM, practitioners should generally allow this and adjust their direct examinations accordingly. Practitioners also should take advantage of this opportunity to learn what issues with which the IJ remains concerned. Sometimes, however, an IJ will improperly take over questioning of the respondent. Although this can be sensitive, it may be necessary for respondent's counsel to raise an objection on the record to the IJ taking over the direct examination. Such actions by the IJ may interfere with the respondent's statutory right to present evidence and may violate the respondent's due process right to a full and fair hearing. Whether to make an objection to IJ questioning is a strategic question that should be made on a case-by-case basis.

Following the direct examination, DHS has the opportunity to cross-examine the respondent or witness. The scope of a cross-examination is generally limited to the issues raised on direct examination; however, DHS also may ask questions about any information contained in the application(s) for relief and supporting exhibits, even if not raised on direct. DHS usually focuses on a few basic, but important points, such as inconsistences and credibility concerns, reliability and authenticity of evidence, weak legal arguments, statutory bars to relief, and negative discretionary factors. DHS's goals are generally to poke holes in the respondent's legal theory, point out weaknesses or problems in arguing that the respondent is not eligible for the relief sought, and demonstrate that the IJ should not exercise discretion in favor of the respondent.

- **Practice Pointer**: DHS often uses the following techniques: (1) start and end crisply; (2) use leading questions (permitted on cross); (3) make a statement of fact and have the witness agree to it; (4) attempt to control the witness and prevent him or her from having the opportunity to explain answers; (5) use a confident, take-charge attitude; (6) use the witness to support DHS's legal theory; (7) discredit or limit the witness's testimony; (8) raise inconsistencies and credibility issues; and (9) focus on bad character. DHS also often focuses on dates and timelines. Practitioners should prepare their clients and witnesses very carefully with regard to chronologies.

- **Practice Pointer**: The most important thing a practitioner can do during cross-examination of his or her respondent or witness is to *listen*.

[770] INA §240(b)(1); ICPM, chapter 4.16(e).

> Practitioners must focus on protecting their client and the fundamental fairness of the proceedings and on making any necessary objections.

Just as DHS may object during direct examination, the respondent or his or her representative may object to any questions by DHS that may interfere with the fundamental fairness of the proceedings. The most common objections made in immigration court during cross-examinations of the respondent and witnesses include:

- Relevance — if the information sought has no probative value for the facts or issues in dispute;
- Lack of foundation — if facts necessary to answer the question asked have not yet been established on the record;
- Compound question — if two or more questions are asked within the framework of a single question so it is not clear which part of the question the respondent or witness is answering;
- Confusing, ambiguous, or misleading question — if a question is not posed in a clear and precise manner so that the respondent or witness knows with certainty what information is being sought;
- Overly broad — if the answer to the question will permit the introduction of just about anything into the hearing; if the question does not make clear what specific information is sought;
- Mischaracterization of testimony — if DHS changes a few words and then asks the witness to affirm the misstatement, or if DHS misquotes or mischaracterizes what a witness or exhibit says;
- Argumentative — if DHS states a conclusion and then asks the respondent or witness to argue with it, usually in an attempt to get the witness to change his or her mind;
- Asked and answered — if DHS asks the same thing again, even if rephrased, after the respondent or witness has already provided an answer, usually in an attempt to get the respondent or witness to change his or her answer;
- Privileged — if DHS seeks information that is subject to attorney/client privilege or the respondent or witness's 5th Amendment privilege against self-incrimination;
- Speculation — if the question asks the respondent or witness to guess or address a hypothetical, or if DHS seeks information that is not based on the respondent or witness's first-hand knowledge;
- Improper opinion — if the question asks for an opinion where the witness is not qualified as an expert on that subject or has no personal knowledge of that subject; and
- Witness not competent — if the witness is not qualified as an expert on that subject, lacks personal knowledge, or could not observe/remember/communicate the information.

- **Practice Pointer**: In addition to listening carefully in order to make any necessary objections, practitioners should listen carefully in order to note any issues that may need to be addressed on redirect examination. Practitioners should make a brief, bullet point list of the topics addressed by DHS on cross-examination, and make note of any problematic answers given by the respondent or witness that may require rebuttal, explanation, clarification, or rehabilitation.

Again, though not binding, the Federal Rules of Evidence are pertinent in determining whether the applicant was denied a fundamentally fair hearing as a result of evidence admitted or rejected by the IJ. Hearsay, for example, while generally admissible in immigration court proceedings, may constitute a due process violation under some circumstances if its admission would be fundamentally unfair.[771]

Following cross-examination, the respondent or his or her representative has the opportunity to conduct a redirect examination. The purpose of a redirect examination is not to repeat or re-hash what has already been covered during the direct examination. Rather, the purpose of a redirect examination is to rebut, explain, clarify, or further develop matters raised during cross-examination. The scope of a redirect examination should be limited to what was covered on cross. Redirect examinations should focus on explaining inconsistencies or negative factors pointed out by DHS, correcting wrong or misleading information, and developing new matters brought out on cross that were not covered during the initial direct examination.

- **Practice Pointer**: Whether to proceed with a redirect examination is a strategic consideration, because every redirect question implies that something was either forgotten or needs fixing. Practitioners should review the list of topics and problematic answers that they made during cross-examination and decide whether anything needs to be addressed or whether it can be ignored. If it's not broken, don't fix it. If you can't fix it, don't try!

- **Practice Pointer**: Focus on key points and make them quickly and forcefully. For rehabilitating a witness, ask the witness to explain why the inconsistency happened in order to lessen the impact of the

[771] *Matter of Grijalva*, 19 I&N Dec. 713 (BIA 1988); *see also Ezeagwuna v. Ashcroft*, 325 F.3d 396 (3d Cir. 2003) (remanding the case with instructions for to exclude a State Department letter concerning the results of an allegedly conducted "investigation" by an unknown individual into documents that the applicant had supposed in support of her application); *Cunanan v. INS*, 856 F.2d 1373 (9th Cir. 1988) (the test for hearsay is whether it is probative and whether its admission is fundamentally fair); *Saidane v. INS*, 129 F.3d 1063 (9th Cir. 1997) (reliance on a damaging hearsay affidavit rendered the hearing fundamentally unfair); *Kiareldeen v. Reno*, 71 F. Supp. 2d 402 (D.N.J. 1999), *rev'd on other grounds by Kiareldeen v. Ashcroft*, 273 F.3d 542 (3d Cir. 2001) (reliance on five reports by the FBI's Joint Terrorism Task Force in conjunction with the failure to produce any witness in support of the allegations in the reports violated due process).

inconsistency, or ask the witness to explain the negative factor to possibly mitigate it and to express remorse. For correcting the record, ask the witness to correct what was wrong or misleading. Always end on a high note and then immediately stop.

At the end of redirect examination, often the IJ, in his or her role as the fact-finder, will ask the respondent or witness any questions to seek any information that he or she needs in order to properly consider the testimony and the respondent's eligibility for relief from removal. This direct, cross, and redirect examination process will repeat with each witness.

D. Closing Arguments

After all witnesses have testified, the IJ will ask the respondent and DHS if any other testimony needs to be taken or if any other exhibits need to be submitted. If not, the IJ will close the evidentiary record and proceed with closing arguments.

Unlike opening statements, most IJs do wish to hear formal closing arguments from the parties. The respondent or his or her representative will proceed with a closing argument first, followed by DHS's closing argument. The respondent or his or her representative may request the opportunity to respond to DHS's closing argument; however, often, IJs do not allow such rebuttals, as doing so may lead to a lengthy back-and-forth exchange between the parties. Sometimes, rather than permitting a back-and-forth exchange between the parties, the IJ will question the parties about the legal issues in question.

E. Decision and Order

The decision whether to grant or deny asylum, withholding of removal, and/or CAT relief must be communicated to the respondent and to DHS.[772] Therefore, following closing arguments, the IJ will close the record and move forward with rendering a decision. The decision may be rendered orally or in writing.[773] Thus, the following scenarios are possible:

- The IJ may render an oral decision at the conclusion of the hearing;
- The IJ may render an oral decision during a future hearing; or
- The IJ may render a written decision on a later date.[774]

If the decision is rendered orally, it must be stated by the IJ in the presence of the parties and a signed memorandum summarizing the oral decision must be served on the parties.[775] If the IJ decides to issue his or her decision in writing, it must be served

---

[772] 8 CFR §1240.11(c)(4) (2014).

[773] 8 CFR §§1003.37(a), 1240.12(a) (2014).

[774] ICPM, chapter 4.16(g). *See* ICPM, chapter 1.5(c).

[775] 8 CFR §1003.37(a) (2014); ICPM, chapter 4.16(g).

on the parties by first class mail to the most recent address contained in the Record of Proceeding or by personal service.[776]

The IJ's decision must include a finding as to admissibility or deportability.[777] It must also contain reasons for granting or denying the request.[778] A decision that lacks sufficient factual findings and legal analysis will be remanded by the BIA to the IJ to correct the deficiencies.[779] The decision must conclude with an order of removal, termination, or other disposition in the case.[780] If the IJ grants withholding of removal, without a grant of asylum, the decision must include an explicit order of removal.[781] An IJ may issue a summary decision in lieu of an oral or written decision, but only if the applicant has admitted the charges of removability and is clearly ineligible for relief or chooses not to apply for relief.[782] Both parties have the right to appeal the IJ's decision,[783] and both parties have the right to waive appeal.[784] An appeal must be filed within 30 days of the IJ's decision.[785]

If relief is granted, the respondent is provided with DHS's post-order instructions.[786] These instructions describe the steps the respondent should follow to obtain documentation of his or her immigration status from USCIS.[787] If DHS has waived appeal and the IJ's order is final, an individual granted asylum should schedule an InfoPass appointment with USCIS to obtain documentation of his or her asylee status and employment authorization.[788] If DHS did not waive appeal and the IJ's order is not yet final, the individual must wait for the 30-day appeal period to pass and the order to become final before seeking documentation of his or her asylee status[789].

---

[776] 8 CFR §1003.37(a) (2014). A written copy of the decision will not be sent to a respondent who has failed to provide a written record of his or her address. 8 CFR §1003.37(b) (2014).

[777] 8 CFR §1240.12(a) (2014).

[778] *Id.*

[779] *Matter of S–H–*, 23 I&N Dec. 462 (BIA 2002).

[780] 8 CFR §§1240.12(a), (c) (2014).

[781] *Matter of I–S– & C–S–*, 24 I&N Dec. 432 (BIA 2008).

[782] *See* 8 CFR §1240.12(b) (2014); *Matter of A–P–*, 21 I&N Dec. 468 (BIA 1999) (finding the IJ properly issued a summary decision in the case an individual from Laos who was ineligible for asylum and withholding of removal because of a conviction for a particularly serious crime).

[783] 8 CFR §1240.15 (2014).

[784] ICPM, chs. 1.5(c), 4.16(h).

[785] *See infra* chapter 11 for a detailed discussion of the legal standards and procedures for appeals to the Board of Immigration Appeals.

[786] ICPM, chapter 4.16(i).

[787] *Id.*

[788] U.S. Dep't of Homeland Sec., *Post Order Instructions for Individuals Granted Relief or Protection from Removal by Immigration Court* (Apr. 1, 2005), *available at www.uscis.gov/sites/default/files/files/article/PostOrderInstr.pdf.*

[789] *Id.*

- **Practice Pointer**: DHS's post-order instructions are available online at *www.uscis.gov/sites/default/files/files/article/PostOrderInstr.pdf.*[790]
- **Practice Pointer**: An individual granted asylum may schedule an InfoPass appointment with USCIS online at *https://infopass.uscis.gov.*[791] He or she should not make an appointment earlier than three business days after the date of the IJ's order. The individual should bring a copy of the IJ's final order granting asylum with him or her to the InfoPass appointment, as well as passport-sized photographs and a photo ID (if he or she has one). USCIS will provide the individual with an I-94 card, noting his or her admission as an asylee and will initiate production of the individual's Employment Authorization Document.[792]
- **Practice Pointer**: Individuals granted relief, especially asylum, may be eligible for various benefits — immigration and otherwise — by virtue of their status. For a detailed discussion of asylee benefits and the benefits of withholding or deferral of removal status, see chapter 13 of this book.

If the IJ decides that the applicant is removable and orders the respondent removed, the IJ must advise the applicant of the decision and the consequences of the failure to depart the United States.[793] The IJ also must specify the country, or countries in the alternate, to which the applicant's removal may be directed.[794] If the applicant does not waive appeal, the IJ must give the applicant the Form EOIR-26, Notice of Appeal and advise the applicant of the right to appeal to the BIA.[795]

The IJ's decision is final unless a party timely appeals the decision to the BIA within 30 days or the case is certified to the BIA.[796] Certifying a case to the BIA means that the IJ has asked the BIA to review his or her decision.[797] This is a separate process from any appeal.[798] At the conclusion of immigration court proceedings, the IJ informs the parties of the deadline for filing an appeal with the BIA, unless the right to appeal has been waived.[799]

---

[790] (last visited Feb. 16, 2015).

[791] (last visited Feb. 16, 2015).

[792] *See* chapter 13 for a detailed discussion of the various benefits available to those individuals granted relief.

[793] 8 CFR §1240.13(d) (2014).

[794] 8 CFR §1240.12(c) (2014).

[795] 8 CFR §1240.13(d) (2014).

[796] 8 CFR §1003.39; ICPM, chapter 1.5(c). *See also* ICPM, chapter 6.

[797] ICPM, chapters 4.16(h), 6.5.

[798] *Id.*

[799] ICPM, chapters 4.16(h), 6.4

If the opportunity to appeal is knowingly and voluntarily waived, the IJ's decision becomes final.[800] A party may notify the IJ orally at the conclusion of proceedings that the party waives appeal.[801] That party generally may not file an appeal thereafter,[802] nor may the party retract, withdraw, or otherwise undo that waiver, except by a granted motion by the IJ or appeal to the BIA regarding the waiver.[803]

XII. What Happens if an Applicant is Detained but Granted Relief?

ICE must release an individual who is granted asylum from immigration detention. However, if an individual is detained when he or she is granted withholding of removal under INA §241(b)(3) or withholding or deferral of removal under the Convention Against Torture, ICE may choose to continue to detain the individual while seeking to remove him or her to another country (a country other than the country to which removal has been withheld by the IJ). If there is no significant likelihood of removal in the reasonably foreseeable future, however, the individual should be released.[804] While making this determination, ICE may continue to detain the individual. In general, however, ICE cannot continue to detain an individual indefinitely following a final order of removal. The U.S. Supreme Court in *Zadvydas v. Davis* held that it is illegal for ICE to continue to detain individuals where they cannot be removed in the reasonably foreseeable future.[805] The maximum period of time that an individual may be kept in detention following a final order of removal is six months.[806] The six-month period begins when the IJ's order of removal becomes final.[807]

ICE will consider the following factors in determining whether to release an individual:

- The history of the individual's efforts to comply with the order of removal;
- The history of DHS's efforts to remove individuals to the country in question or to third countries, including the ongoing nature of DHS's efforts to remove the individual and his or her assistance with those efforts;
- The reasonably foreseeable results of those efforts; and

---

[800] 8 CFR §1003.39 (2014); ICPM, chapter 6.4(a).

[801] ICPM, chapter 6.4(a).

[802] *See* 8 CFR §§1003.3(a)(1), 1003.1(d)(2)(i)(G) (2014); ICPM, chapter 6.4(a); *Matter of Shih*, 20 I&N Dec. 697 (BIA 1993).

[803] ICPM chapter 6.4(b); *Matter of Patino*, 23 I&N Dec. 74 (BIA 2001).

[804] 8 CFR §241.13(b) (2014).

[805] *Zadvydas v. Davis*, 533 U.S. 678 (2001). *See* 8 CFR §241.13(b)(2) (2014).

[806] 8 CFR §241.13(b)(2)(ii) (2014); *Zadvydas*, 533 U.S. at 678.

[807] 8 CFR §§241.13(b)(2)(ii), 1241.1 (2014).

- The views of the Department of State regarding the prospects for removal of individuals to the country or countries in question.[808]

In most cases, continued detention is improper and contrary to ICE's own policy favoring release of individuals granted relief by an IJ, absent exceptional concerns such as national security issues or danger to the community and absent any requirement under law to detain.[809] ICE must issue a written decision based on the administrative record, including any documentation provided by the individual, regarding the likelihood of removal and whether there is a significant likelihood that the individual will be removed in the reasonably foreseeable future under the circumstances.[810]

> ➢ **Practice Pointer**: Practitioners should assist their clients in preparing and sending to ICE a written request for release asserting why there is no significant likelihood that the client will be removed in the reasonably foreseeable future.[811] Any supporting documentation should be attached. ICE must respond in writing within 10 business days of receiving the request to acknowledge receipt of the request and explain the procedures that will be used to evaluate the request.[812] For detailed guidance on what such a request should look like and what supporting documentation should be included, see the PAIR Project's manual, "Getting Out of Detention After an Order of Deportation: Post-Order Custody Reviews and Habeas Corpus," available at *www.pairproject.org/images/Habeas.pdf*.[813]

If ICE determines that there is no significant likelihood that the individual will be removed in the reasonably foreseeable future, ICE must advise the individual.[814] Unless there are special circumstances justifying continued detention, ICE must promptly make arrangements for the individual's release.[815] ICE may establish appropriate conditions for release.[816] For example, ICE may decide to release an individual granted withholding or deferral of removal under an "Order of

---

808 8 CFR §241.13(f) (2014).

809 8 CFR §241.13(e) (2014). *See* Immigration and Customs Enforcement Field Guidance (Mar. 6, 2012) (citing Bo Cooper Mem. on Detention and Release during the Removal Period of Aliens Granted Withholding or Deferral of Removal (Apr. 21, 2000) and Michael Garcia Mem. on Detention Policy Where an Immigration Judge Has Granted Asylum and ICE Has Appealed (Feb. 9, 2004)), *available at http://immigrantjustice.org/sites/immigrantjustice.org/files/March%206,%202012%20ERO%20Field%20Guidance%20Reminder.pdf*.

810 8 CFR §241.13(g) (2014).

811 8 CFR §241.13(d)(1) (2014).

812 8 CFR §241.13(e)(1) (2014).

813 (last visited Feb. 16, 2015).

814 8 CFR §241.13(g)(1) (2014).

815 *Id.*

816 *Id.*

Supervision" that requires him or her to report regularly with ICE either in person or by phone, as well as a number of other requirements.[817] The purpose of these orders is to protect public safety and to promote the ability of ICE to effect the individual's removal should circumstances change in the future.[818] Violation of an Order of Supervision could have very serious consequences, including a withdrawal of the release approval and detention anew.[819] ICE may revoke its decision to release the individual at any time in order to remove him or her (for example, if circumstances change and there is a significant likelihood that the individual may be removed in the reasonably foreseeable future).[820]

On the other hand, ICE may determine that there is a significant likelihood that the individual will be removed in the reasonably foreseeable future. Under these circumstances, ICE will deny any requests for release and advise the individual that his or her detention will continue.[821] If an individual remains in ICE custody beyond six months after the IJ's order became final, however, he or she may seek release through a petition for a writ of habeas corpus under 28 USC §2241 — the mechanism for challenging his or her detention in federal court. This is because detention beyond six months is unlawful.[822]

> **Practice Pointer**: See chapter 9 of this book for a detailed discussion of the legal standards and procedures for the detention of individuals seeking protection in the United States.

XIII. How Can An Applicant Challenge an IJ's Decision?

If the applicant is denied relief, he or she has the right to file an appeal with the Board of Immigration Appeals.[823] The BIA has nationwide jurisdiction to review IJ decisions.[824] An appeal of an IJ decision is filed on a Form EOIR-26, Notice of Appeal.[825]

> **Practice Pointer**: Appeals of IJ decisions are distinct from motions to reopen or motions to reconsider, which are filed with the immigration court following a decision ending the proceedings.[826] See Chapter 11 of

---

[817] 8 CFR §§241.4, 241.13(b), 241.13(h)(1) (2014).

[818] 8 CFR §241.13(h)(1) (2014).

[819] 8 CFR §§241.13(h)(2), 241.13(i) (2014).

[820] 8 CFR §241.13(i)(2) (2014).

[821] 8 CFR §241.13(g)(2) (2014).

[822] 8 CFR §241.13(b)(2)(ii) (2014); *Zadvydas v. Davis*, 533 U.S. 678 (2001).

[823] 8 CFR §1003.38(a) (2014); ICPM, chapters 4.16(h), 6.1.

[824] 8 CFR §1003.1 (2014); ICPM chapters 1.2(c), 6.1.

[825] ICPM, chapter 6.2(b).

[826] ICPM, chapter 6.1. *See also* ICPM, chapter 5.

this book for a detailed discussion of motions to reopen and motions to reconsider.

The Notice of Appeal (Form EOIR-26) must be filed directly with the BIA, and must be *received* within 30 calendar days of the IJ's decision.[827] The appeal deadline is calculated from the date the IJ renders an oral decision or mails a written decision.[828]

➢ **Practice Pointer**: The date the IJ renders an oral decision or mails a written decision counts as day "0" and all calendar days are counted.[829] Day "30" is the appeal deadline, unless day "30" falls on a Saturday, Sunday, or legal holiday, in which case the deadline is construed to fall on the next business day.[830]

➢ **Practice Pointer**: Like the immigration courts, the BIA does not recognize the "mailbox rule" for filings. Instead, a Notice of Appeal is not considered filed until it has been *received* by the BIA.[831]

The Notice of Appeal must be accompanied by the appropriate fee or by a Form EOIR-26A, Appeal Fee Waiver Request.[832] Otherwise, the Notice of Appeal will not be deemed properly filed, the appeal will be rejected, and the decision of the IJ will be final if the 30-day appeal period has lapsed.[833] Additionally, if the respondent is represented, his or her representative must file an EOIR-27, Notice of Entry of Appearance of Attorney or Representative before the Board of Immigration Appeals along with the Notice of Appeal.[834]

After the Notice of Appeal has been filed with the BIA, jurisdiction over the case shifts from the immigration court to the BIA.[835] Upon receipt of the Notice of Appeal, the BIA will produce a transcript of the immigration court proceedings and send it to the parties, along with a briefing schedule setting forth the deadlines for the parties to file their written briefs with the BIA. The BIA will then consider the arguments on appeal, along with the Record of Proceedings, and issue its decision.

➢ **Practice Pointer**: For more information on BIA appeal procedures, see Chapter 11 of the book, as well as the BIA Practice Manual, which is

---

[827] 8 CFR §§1003.38(b)–(c), 1003.23 (2014); ICPM, chapter 6.2(b).

[828] 8 CFR §1003.38(b) (2014); ICPM, chapter 3.1(c)(ii)(D).

[829] *Id.*

[830] *Id.*

[831] 8 CFR §1003.38(c) (2014).

[832] 8 CFR §1003.38(d) (2014).

[833] *Id.*

[834] 8 CFR §1003.38(g) (2014).

[835] ICPM, chapter 6.3.

available online at *www.justice.gov/eoir/vll/qapracmanual/apptmtn4.htm*.[836]

An individual may also choose to challenge the IJ's decision by preparing and filing a written, signed Motion to Reopen or a Motion to Reconsider with the immigration court.[837] An IJ may upon his or her own motion at any time, or upon motion of DHS or the respondent, reopen or reconsider any case in which he or she has made a decision, unless jurisdiction is vested with the BIA.[838] A motion to reopen is a request for the court to reopen proceedings to consider new facts or documentation that are material to the relief requested but that were not previously available or discoverable.[839] A motion to reconsider is a request for the court to reconsider its decision due to alleged factual or legal error.[840]

Generally, a party may file only one motion to reconsider and one motion to reopen proceedings.[841] A motion to reconsider must be filed within 30 days of the date of entry of a final administrative order of removal.[842] A motion to reopen must be filed within 90 days of the date of entry of a final administrative order of removal.[843] There are various exceptions to these time and numerical limitations, including specific exceptions for asylum and withholding of removal applicants.[844]

- **Practice Pointer**: For more information on Motions to Reopen and Motions to Reconsider, see chapter 11 of the book, as well as chapter 5 of the ICPM, which is available online at *www.justice.gov/eoir/vll/OCIJPracManual/Practice_Manual_review.pdf#page=67*.[845]

XIV. What if the Respondent Fails to Appear for a Hearing?

A noncitizen who fails to attend immigration court proceedings after having been properly served with a NTA or whose counsel has been served pursuant to INA §239(a) will be ordered removed in absentia, *i.e.*, in his or her absence, if DHS establishes by clear, unequivocal, and convincing evidence that written notice was

---

[836] (*last visited Feb. 16, 2015*).

[837] 8 CFR §1003.23 (2014).

[838] 8 CFR §1003.23(b)(1) (2014).

[839] 8 CFR §1003.23(b)(3) (2014).

[840] 8 CFR §1003.23(b)(2) (2014).

[841] 8 CFR §1003.23(b)(1) (2014).

[842] *Id.*

[843] *Id.*

[844] 8 CFR §1003.23(b)(4)(i) (2014) (describing the changed circumstances exception for motions to reopen based on changed circumstances that materially affect an individual's eligibility for asylum and withholding of removal). See also infra chapter 11 for a detailed discussion of motions to reopen and motions to reconsider.

[845] (last visited Feb. 16, 2015).

provided and that the noncitizen is removable.[846] Written notice is not required if the noncitizen failed to provide the required address,[847] but only if he or she has received the appropriate warnings about the consequences of not providing the required address.[848]

A strong presumption applies that the applicant has received notice of the hearing if the notice is sent by certified mail. A weaker presumption of receipt applies when the notice is sent by regular mail.[849]

> **Practice Pointer**: Arriving 15 to 20 minutes late to court has been found to be a "brief and innocent" absence that is not a "failure to appear."[850] One court has held that arriving two hours late was not a failure to appear when the IJ was still in the courtroom.[851] However, this is not guaranteed. Thus, practitioners should always advise their clients to arrive at the immigration court well in advance of their hearings and that being late may result in their removal in absentia.

Such failure to appear after receiving the required notice of the consequences of failing to appear will bar an individual from the following forms of relief for a period of 10 years: cancellation of removal, voluntary departure, adjustment of status to lawful permanent residence, change of nonimmigrant status, and registry.[852]

An in absentia order may be rescinded upon the filing of a motion to reopen with the immigration court under the conditions outlined below.[853] The normal numerical

---

[846] INA §240(b)(5)(A); 8 USC §1229a(b)(5)(A) (2012).

[847] INA §240(b)(5)(B); 8 USC §1229a(b)(5)(B) (2012).

[848] *See Matter of G–Y–R–*, 23 I&N Dec. 181 (BIA 2001) (upholding an IJ's refusal to issue an in absentia order against an individual who was never advised of the consequences of her failure to provide legacy INS with a mailing address and who never received actual service of the NTA). *But see Matter of Ponce-Hernandez*, 21 I&N Dec. 784 (BIA 1999) (in the case of a minor who failed to appear for his deportation hearing, the BIA found that legacy INS met its burden of proof in establishing deportability on the basis of a Record of Deportable Alien (Form I-213), which documented the minor's identity and alienage); *Matter of Gomez-Gomez*, 23 I&N Dec. 522 (BIA 2002) (service on father by mail was proper service on minor).

[849] *Matter of M–R–A–*, 24 I&N Dec. 665 (BIA 2008); *Silva-Carvalho Lopes v. Mukasey*, 517 F.3d 156, 160 (2d Cir. 2008); *Santana-Gonzalez v. U.S. Att'y Gen.*, 506 F.3d 274, 278 (3d Cir. 2007); *Lopes v. Gonzales,* 468 F.3d 81, 85 (2d Cir. 2006); *Nibagwire v. Gonzales*, 450 F.3d 153, 156–57 (4th Cir. 2006); *Joshi v. Ashcroft,* 389 F.3d 732, 736–37 (7th Cir. 2004); *Ghounem v. Ashcroft,* 378 F.3d 740, 744–45 (8th Cir. 2004); *Salta v. INS,* 314 F.3d 1076, 1079 (9th Cir. 2002).

[850] *Abu-Hasirah v. U.S. Dep't of Homeland Sec.*, 478 F.3d 474, 475 (2d Cir. 2007) (holding that 15 minutes late was not a failure to appear); *Cabrera-Perez v. Gonzales*, 456 F.3d 109 (3d Cir. 2006) (holding that 15– to 20-minute delay not a failure to appear); *Alarcon-Chavez v. Gonzales*, 403 F.3d 343 (5th Cir. 2005) (holding that a 20 minute late arrival was not a failure to appear).

[851] *Perez v. Mukasey*, 516 F.3d 770, 774–75 (9th Cir. 2008).

[852] *See* INA §240(b)(7); 8 USC §1229a(b)(7) (2012).

[853] *See* Am. Immigration Ctr., Legal Action Center Practice Advisory, *Rescinding an In Absentia Order of Removal* (Sept. 21, 2004), *available at www.legalactioncenter.org/sites/default/files/lac_pa_092104.pdf*; *Matter of Guzman-Arguera*, 22 I&N Dec. 722 (BIA 1999).

and time limitations do not apply, however, when an individual seeks to reopen exclusion proceedings conducted in absentia.[854]

A. Motion to Reopen Within 180 Days of an In Absentia Order

Within this time period, the individual must demonstrate that the failure to appear was because of "exceptional circumstances." [855] Exceptional circumstances are defined as circumstances beyond the individual's control, "such as serious illness of the [individual] or serious illness or death of the spouse, child, or parent of the [individual], but *not* including less compelling circumstances."[856] When determining whether exceptional circumstances caused the applicant's failure to appear, the BIA may not rely on newly created evidentiary standards.[857]

Courts have found exceptional circumstances when failure to appear was due to:

- Erroneous advice by an attorney;[858]
- The applicant waiting for an interpreter to accompany her to her hearing;[859]
- Ineffective assistance of counsel;[860]
- Immigration consultant fraud;[861]
- Service of the hearing notice on the respondent but not on his or her counsel of record;[862] and
- An illness of the applicant's stepson that caused a 15-minute delay in appearing at the hearing.[863]

On the other hand, exceptional circumstances do not include:

- A car breaking down on the way to a hearing;[864]
- Traffic difficulties;[865]

---

[854] *See Matter of N–B–*, 22 I&N Dec. 590 (BIA 1999). *But see Matter of M–S–*, 22 I&N Dec. 349 (BIA 1998) (finding that an asylum applicant who did not receive oral notice in a language she understands need not file a motion to rescind the in absentia order, but may file a regular motion to reopen).

[855] INA §240(b)(5)(C)(i); 8 USC §1229a(b)(5)(C)(i) (2012).

[856] INA §240(e)(1); 8 USC §1229a(e)(1) (2012).

[857] *Singh v. INS*, 213 F.3d 1050, 1053 (9th Cir. 2000), *reversing Matter of B–A–S–*, 22 I&N Dec. 57 (BIA 1998) (denying motion to reopen that was not accompanied by medical evidence or affidavit of employer).

[858] *Galvez-Vergara v. Gonzales*, 484 F.3d 798, 801–02 (5th Cir. 2007).

[859] *Nazarova v. INS*, 171 F.3d 478, 484 (7th Cir. 1998).

[860] *Matter of Grijalva, 21 I&N Dec. 472* (BIA 1996).

[861] *Viridiana v. Holder*, 646 F.3d 1230 (9th Cir. 2011).

[862] *Hamazaspyan v. Holder*, 590 F.3d 744 (9th Cir. 2009).

[863] *Matter of Singh*, 21 I&N Dec. 998 (BIA 1997).

[864] *De Morales v. INS*, 116 F.3d 145, 149 (5th Cir. 1997).

[865] *Sharma v. INS*, 89 F.3d 545, 547 (9th Cir. 1996).

- The general assertion that the individual was prevented from reaching the hearing on time because of heavy traffic;[866]
- A long-standing minor illness;[867]
- Unsuccessful communications with an attorney regarding the next hearing date after a change of venue was granted, where the individual has failed to demonstrate ineffective assistance of counsel;[868]
- Failure to know about a post-remand removal hearing where the respondent had moved but not advised his new lawyer or the immigration court of his whereabouts;[869] or
- Pursuit of employment.[870]

B. Motion to Reopen Any Time After the In Absentia Order

Applicants must demonstrate that they did not receive notice in accordance with INA §239(a), or they were in federal or state custody and the failure to appear was through no fault of their own.[871] Courts have recently examined what proof is needed in cases where the applicant alleges he or she did not receive notice of the hearing.[872] The Eighth Circuit has held that where notice is sent by regular mail (*not*, as previously required, by certified mail), it was error for the IJ to require documentary evidence from the U.S. Postal Service or third-party affidavits demonstrating that service was improper.[873] The court reasoned that in cases where notice is sent by regular mail, the only proof of non-delivery is the applicant's statement that he did not receive delivery.[874] Similarly, in *Salta v. INS*,[875] the Ninth Circuit held that regular mail was not entitled to the same presumption of effective delivery. It further held that:

---

[866] *Matter of S–A–*, 21 I&N Dec. 1050 (BIA 1997).

[867] *Matter of Ali*, 21 I&N Dec. 1058 (BIA 1997) (interpreting the phrase "exceptional circumstances" as applied to the individual's failure to depart during the period of voluntary departure).

[868] *Matter of Rivera*, 21 I&N Dec. 599 (BIA 1996).

[869] *Vukmirovic v. Holder*, 640 F.3d 977 (9th Cir. 2011).

[870] *Matter of W–F–*, 21 I&N Dec. 503 (BIA 1996).

[871] INA §240(b)(5)(C)(ii); 8 USC §1229a(b)(5)(C)(ii) (2012).

[872] *See, e.g.*, *Matter of M–D–*, 23 I&N Dec. 540 (BIA 2002) (applicant can be charged with receipt of notice to appear and notice of hearing date where the notice is sent by certified mail to applicant's correct address, but is returned by U.S. Postal Service as unclaimed).

[873] *Ghounem v. INS*, 378 F.3d 740, 744–45 (8th Cir. 2004); *see also Nibagwire v. Gonzales*, 450 F.3d 153, 156 (4th Cir. 2006) (finding BIA abused its discretion in requiring applicant to rebut "string presumption" of delivery where NTA was sent by regular mail).

[874] *Ghounem,* 378 F.3d at 744.

[875] *Salta v. INS*, 314 F.3d 1076, 1079 (9th Cir. 2002). *See also Silva-Carvalho Lopes v. Mukasey*, 517 F.3d 156, 160 (2d Cir. 2008); *Santana-Gonzalez v. U.S. Att'y Gen*, 506 F.3d 274, 278 (3d Cir. 2007); *Nibagwire v. Gonzales,* 450 F.3d 153, 156–57 (4th Cir._2006); *Joshi v. Ashcroft,* 389 F.3d 732, 736–37 (7th Cir. 2004).

> Where a petitioner actually initiates a proceeding to obtain a benefit, appears at an earlier hearing, and has no motive to avoid the hearing, a sworn affidavit from [the petitioner] that neither she nor a responsible party residing at her address received the notice should ordinarily be sufficient to rebut the presumption of delivery and entitle [the petitioner] to an evidentiary hearing to consider the veracity of her allegations.[876]

The BIA has held in *Matter of M–R–A–* that when a NTA or Notice of Hearing is sent by regular mail there is a presumption of delivery, but it is weaker than the presumption that applies to documents sent by certified mail.[877] The Board instructed IJs to consider all relevant evidence including affidavits from the respondent, the exercise of due diligence in redressing the situation, any prior applications for relief that indicate incentive appear and prior appearances.[878] The BIA found that the asylum applicant in *Matter of M–R–A–* overcame the presumption of delivery of the Notice of Hearing because he submitted affidavits indicating he had not received it, had previously applied for asylum and appeared at his first removal hearing, and exercised due diligence in promptly obtaining counsel and requesting reopening.[879] At least one court has held that a sworn affidavit from the applicant is not required and that an unsworn typewritten letter along with other circumstantial evidence was sufficient to overcome the presumption of service.[880]

Another issue arising in cases regarding lack of notice is how soon the motion to reopen must be filed after the applicant learns of the in absentia order. By statute, a motion to reopen may be filed "at any time."[881] Courts have interpreted this to mean, literally, "at any time" and have reversed IJs who have denied motions to reopen if there has been a significant delay after the applicant learns of the in absentia order.[882]

A Motion to Reopen to Rescind an in Absentia Order will automatically stay the removal of an individual.[883] The BIA has no jurisdiction to review directly an in absentia order, except for a review of an IJ's denial of a motion to reopen.[884] Any

---

[876] *Id.* at 1079; *see also Matter of G–Y–R–*, 23 I&N Dec. 181 (BIA 2001) (upholding an IJ's refusal to issue an in absentia order against an individual who was never advised of the consequences of her failure to provide legacy INS with a mailing address and who never received actual service of the NTA); *Flores-Chavez v. Ashcroft*, 362 F.3d 1150 (9th Cir. 2004) (finding error where DHS failed to serve Notice of Hearing on adult to whom child was released).

[877] *Matter of M–R–A–*, 24 I&N Dec. 665 (BIA 2008).

[878] *Id.* at 675–76.

[879] *Id.*

[880] *Sembiring v. Gonzales*, 499 F.3d 981, 989–90 (9th Cir. 2007)

[881] INA §240(b)(5)(C)(ii); 8 USC §1 229a(b)(5)(C)(ii) (2012).

[882] *See Andia v. Ashcroft*, 359 F.3d 1181, 1184 (9th Cir. 2004) (finding error where IJ denied motion to reopen as a matter of discretion where the delay in filing was seven months); *see also Matter of A–A–*, 22 I&N Dec. 140, 144 n.4 (BIA 1998) (noting there is no statutory time limit where lack of notice is alleged and motion to reopen was filed 10 years after the in absentia order was issued).

[883] INA §240(b)(5)(C); 8 USC §1229a(b)(5)(C) (2012).

[884] *Matter of Gonzalez-Lopez*, 20 I&N Dec. 644 (BIA 1993).

petition for judicial review in federal court must be confined to the following issues: the validity of the notice, the reasons for failing to appear, and whether the individual is removable.[885] One exception to this rule is for individuals who claim to be nationals of the United States.[886]

➢ **Practice Pointer**: For a detailed discussion of motions to reopen, see chapter 11 of this book. For a detailed discussion of judicial review before the U.S. circuit courts of appeals, see chapter 12 of this book.

---

[885] INA §240(b)(5)(D); 8 USC §1229a(b)(5)(D) (2012).

[886] INA §242(b)(5); 8 USC §1252(b)(5) (2012).

CHAPTER NINE

DETENTION OF ASYLUM-SEEKERS*

Despite costing taxpayers nearly $2 billion annually and $5.46 million per day, Congress continues to mandate that the Department of Homeland Security (DHS) maintain 34,000 detention beds for undocumented individuals, and DHS continues to expand its use of detention, particularly for women and children apprehended upon arrival in the United States.[1] Thus, it is likely that an applicant for asylum, withholding of removal, or protection under the Convention Against Torture (CAT) may be detained during part or all of the adjudication process. Most asylum-seekers who are detained will be seeking asylum defensively before the immigration courts, and the procedures for seeking protection before the immigration court, though more difficult for a detained individual, are the same whether or not the individual is detained.[2]

Immigration and Customs Enforcement (ICE), one of the enforcement branches within DHS, detains well over 400,000 migrants annually and interprets appropriations report language to mandate a daily detention level of 34,000 migrants

---

* The author would like to thank Brittney Nystrom of the Lutheran Immigration and Refugee Service for her invaluable input in reviewing this chapter.

[1] Nat'l Immigration Forum, *Detention Costs Still Don't Add Up to Good Policy* (Sept. 24, 2014), *available at https://immigrationforum.org/blog/detention–costs–still–dont–add–up–to–good–policy/* (last visited Mar. 31, 2015); Nat'l Immigration Forum, *The Math of Immigration Detention: Runaway Costs for Immigration Detention Do Not Add Up to Sensible Policies* (Aug. 2013), *available at www.immigrationforum.org/images/uploads/mathofimmigrationdetention.pdf* (last visited Feb. 17, 2015). *See also* American Bar Association, Letter to Department of Homeland Security (DHS) Secretary Jeh Johnson, "ABA Concerns about Expansion of Immigration Detention, Including Detention of Women and Children Seeking Protection as Refugees" (Mar. 26, 2015), *available at www.americanbar.org/content/dam/aba/uncategorized/GAO/2015mar26_familydetention.authcheckdam.pdf* (last visited Mar. 31, 2015); Statement of the American Immigration Lawyers Association Submitted to the U.S. Commission on Civil Rights, Briefing on "State of Civil Rights at Immigration Detention Facilities" (Jan. 30, 2015), *posted on* AILA InfoNet Doc. No. 15012045 and *available at www.aila.org/advo–media/aila–correspondence/aila–mass–detention–of–asylum–seekers–is–a–humanit* (last visited Mar. 31, 2015).

[2] See chapter 8 for a detailed discussion of seeking asylum defensively before the immigration courts.

every day.[3] This number is referred to as the "detention bed quota" and has been a point of controversy in recent years.[4] As one organization notes, "No other law enforcement agency is subject to a statutory quota on the number of individuals it must detain."[5] Thousands of these detainees are asylum-seekers being held in jails or jail-like settings that compound the trauma from which they fled and pose serious barriers to the tools necessary for presenting an effective asylum claim, such as access to legal counsel,[6] witnesses and documentation, interpreters, medical and mental healthcare, and support networks. Moreover, detained individuals, including asylum-seekers, are rushed through proceedings on a faster immigration court docket[7] and most of them, being detained in remote locations far away from any immigration courts, have their cases heard by video, rather than in-person.[8] In short, the procedures for detained individuals, including asylum-seekers, are riddled with due process violations.[9]

> ➢ **Practice Pointer**: See *https://immigrationforum.org/policies/detention/*, the National Immigration Forum's website, for a compilation of reports on immigrant detention.[10]

---

[3] John F. Simanski, *Annual Report, Immigration Enforcement Actions: 2013*, U.S. Dep't of Homeland Sec., Office of Immigration Statistics (Sept. 2014), *available at www.dhs.gov/sites/default/files/publications/ois_enforcement_ar_2013.pdf* (last visited Feb. 17, 2015). *See also* Nat'l Immigrant Justice Ctr., I*mmigration Detention Bed Quota Timelin*e (Mar. 2014), *available at http://immigrantjustice.org/sites/immigrantjustice.org/files/Immigration_Detention_Bed_Quota_Timeline_2014_03.pdf* (last visited Feb. 17, 2015); Refugee Council USA, *Detention of Refugees, Asylum Seekers, and Other Vulnerable Persons in the United States*, *available at www.rcusa.org/uploads/pdfs/RCUSA_2013_Detention.pdf* (last visited Feb. 17, 2015).

[4] Nat'l Immigrant Justice Ctr., *Immigration Detention Bed Quota*, *supra* note 3.

[5] *Id.*

[6] U.S. Comm'n on Int'l Religious Freedom Special Report, *Assessing the U.S. Government's Detention of Asylum Seekers: Further Action Needed to Fully Implement Reforms*, *available at www.uscirf.gov/sites/default/files/resources/ERSdetention%20reforms%20report%20April%202013.pdf* (last visited Feb. 19, 2015); Human Rights First, *U.S. Detention of Asylum Seekers*, *supra* note 6 (stating that more than one–third of detained asylum seekers are not represented by counsel). *See also* Stephen Manning, *Ending Artesia*, *available at https://innovationlawlab.org/the–artesia–report/* (last visited Feb. 19, 2015) (discussing the significant reduction in deportations after the arrival of pro bono counsel for women and children detained at the Federal Law Enforcement Training Center in Artesia, New Mexico); TRAC Immigration, *Representation Key in Immigration Proceedings Involving Women with Children*, *available at http://trac.syr.edu/immigration/reports/377/* (last visited Feb. 19, 2015) (finding that even though they had been able to demonstrate "credible fear" of returning to their home country, deportation was ordered for 98.5 percent of women with children who were not represented by an attorney).

[7] ICPM, chapter 9.1(e).

[8] U.S. Comm'n on Int'l Religious Freedom Special Report, *Assessing the U.S. Government's Detention of Asylum Seekers*, *supra* note 6.

[9] All noncitizen detainees face these due process violations and humanitarian concerns. However, given the scope of this book, this chapter will refer to asylum–seekers and those seeking protection throughout.

[10] (last visited Mar. 31, 2015).

By law, all arriving asylum-seekers who are placed into expedited removal must be detained, and detention is mandatory pending credible and reasonable fear interviews.[11] For instance, over 3,000 asylum seekers were detained upon arrival in 2007 and over 3,000 more in 2008.[12] DHS expanded its detention practice to arriving families in 2006[13] and opened the 500-bed T. Don Hutto detention facility in Texas that it claimed was specially equipped to meet family needs.[14] Over 90 percent of the mothers detained in the Hutto facility expressed fear of return to their home countries.[15] There were soon allegations of mistreatment and prison-like conditions in this facility.[16] The detention of asylum-seekers and the negative impact that detention has on their ability to present their asylum claims was strongly criticized by human rights groups in the United States at that time, as it had been since long before the opening of the Hutto facility in 2006.[17]

---

[11] *See supra* chapter 6 for a detailed discussion of credible and reasonable fear procedures.

[12] Human Rights First, U.S. Detention of Asylum Seekers, *supra* note 6.

[13] U.S. Dep't of Homeland Sec., Immigration and Customs Enforcement News Release, *DHS Closes Loophole by Expanding Expedited Removal to Cover Illegal Alien Families* (May 15, 2006), *available at www.immigration.com/newsletter1/iceilegalfaml.pdf*.

[14] *Id.*

[15] *See* Women's Comm'n for Refugee Women & Children, & Lutheran Immigration and Refugee Serv., *Locking Up Family Values: The Detention of Immigrant Families* (Feb. 2007), *available at www.womenscommission.org/pdf/famdeten.pdf*; Women's Refugee Comm'n & Lutheran Immigration and Refugee Serv., *Locking Up Family Values Again: The Detention of Immigrant Families* (Oct. 2014), *available at http://womensrefugeecommission.org/blog/2176–locking–up–family–values–again–blog*.

[16] The American Civil Liberties Union (ACLU) brought 17 lawsuits against U.S. Department of Homeland Security (DHS) Secretary Michael Chertoff, and six officials from U.S. Immigration and Customs Enforcement (ICE), on behalf of children detained at the T. Don Hutto (Hutto) detention facility in Taylor, TX. *See* Am. Civil Liberties Union, *ACLU Challenges Illegal Detention of Immigrant Children Held in Prison–Like Conditions*, *available at www.aclu.org/immigrants/detention/28865prs20070306.html* (last visited Mar. 1, 2015); *see also* Women's Comm'n for Refugee Women & Children, & Lutheran Immigration and Refugee Serv., *Locking Up Family Values: The Detention of Immigrant Families* (Feb. 2007), *available at www.womenscommission.org/pdf/famdeten.pdf*. These lawsuits contended that the Hutto facility violated the regulations arising out of *Flores v. Meese*, which ended in a 1997 court settlement that established minimum standards and conditions for the housing and release of all minors in federal immigration custody. *Flores v. Reno*, Stipulated Settlement Agreement, No. CV 85–4544–RJK (C.D. Cal. 1997). On August 27, 2007, a settlement was reached in the Hutto detention center litigation. *See* Am. Civil Liberties Union, *ACLU Challenges Prison–Like Conditions at Hutto Detention Center*, *available at www.aclu.org/immigrants/detention/hutto.html* (last visited Mar. 1, 2015).

[17] Human Rights First, U.S. Detention of Asylum Seekers, *supra* note 6; Women's Comm'n for Refugee Women & Children, *et al.*, *Locking Up Family Values*, *supra* note 15. *See also* Nat'l Immigration Law Ctr., A Broken System: Confidential Reports Reveal Failures in U.S. Immigrant Detention Centers (June 2009), available at *www.nilc.org/immlawpolicy/arrestdet/A–Broken–System–2009–07.pdf*; Bill Frelick, U.S. Detention of Asylum Seekers and Human Rights, Amnesty Int'l (Mar. 2005) available at *www.migrationinformation.org/usfocus/display.cfm?ID=296*.

Following a change in administration when Barack Obama was elected President, in August 2009, ICE announced reforms that allegedly would address many of the complaints about immigration detention.[18] Specifically, ICE announced that within three to five years, it would: (1) design facilities located and operated solely for immigration detention purposes; (2) revise its immigration detention standards to reflect the conditions appropriate for various immigration detainee populations; (3) review its contracts with detention facilities to ensure that they comply with the new standards; and (4) devise a risk assessment and custody classification tool to place detainees in appropriate facilities.[19] As part of these 2009 reforms, ICE also announced — after years of controversy, media exposure, and a lawsuit — the shift of the T. Don Hutto family detention facility to holding only adult women.[20] In 2009, ICE also revised its policy of detaining all arriving asylum-seekers and issued new guidance, effective January 4, 2010, encouraging the release of asylum-seekers apprehended upon arrival once they have demonstrated a credible fear of persecution or torture.[21]

In 2013, however, the U.S. Commission on International Religious Freedom (USCIRF) published a special report on its study of ICE's progress toward implementing the reforms it had announced.[22] USCIRF concluded that "the U.S. continues to detain asylum seekers under inappropriate conditions in jails and jail-like facilities."[23] USCIRF continued:

> There is a need to codify into regulations the announced parole process and criteria, under which most asylum seekers found to have a credible fear of persecution are paroled rather than detained. More needs to be done to ensure that, when their detention is necessary, asylum seekers are housed only in civil facilities. In addition, USCIRF finds that further improvements are needed to expand detainees' access to legal information, representation, and in-person hearings.[24]

USCIRF discussed several legal process issues regarding the detention of asylum-seekers, including the location of detention centers in remote locations, which is a

---

[18] Immigration and Customs Enforcement (ICE) Fact Sheet, *2009 Immigration Detention Reforms* (Aug. 6, 2009), *published on* AILA InfoNet at Doc. No. 09080630 (*posted* Aug. 6, 2009).

[19] U.S. Comm'n on Int'l Religious Freedom Special Report, *Assessing the U.S. Government's Detention of Asylum Seekers*, *supra* note 6.

[20] *See* Am. Civil Liberties Union, DHS Plan To Improve Immigration Detention And Close Hutto Facility A Good First Step (Aug. 6, 2009), *available at www.aclu.org/immigrants/detention/40612prs20090806.html*.

[21] ICE, *Parole of Arriving Aliens Found to Have a Credible Fear of Persecution or Torture* (effective Jan. 4, 2010), *available at www.ice.gov/doclib/dro/pdf/11002.1–hd–parole_of_arriving_aliens_found_credible_fear.pdf* (last visited Feb. 17, 2015).

[22] *See generally*, *id*.

[23] *Id.* at 1.

[24] *Id.*

serious barrier to access to counsel; the use of video teleconferencing for merits hearings, rather than in-person hearings, which impacts attorney-client communications and immigration judges' credibility assessments; and the lack of effective "Know Your Rights" presentations.[25]

To date, DHS continues to detain asylum-seekers in its own facilities, as well as facilities it utilizes through contracts, such as county jails,[26] and criticisms against DHS for the conditions and practices in these facilities, as well as its detention policies, continue unabated.[27] Perhaps the ultimate criticism was in February of 2015 when the U.S. District Court for the District of Columbia enjoined DHS from using detention as a means of deterring future immigration to the United States and from considering deterrence of future immigration as a factor in custody determinations.[28] These DHS policies were established in the summer of 2014, in response to the increase in the number of mothers and children fleeing violence in Central America. This "surge" of refugees from Central America sparked the Obama Administration's resurrection and dramatic expansion of its family detention practice in an effort to deter future border-crossers.[29] It hastily erected a facility in Artesia, New Mexico,

---

[25] U.S. Comm'n on Int'l Religious Freedom Special Report, *Assessing the U.S. Government's Detention of Asylum Seekers*, *supra* note 6.

[26] *See* ICE, *Immigration Detention Overview and Recommendations* (Oct. 6, 2009), *available at www.ice.gov/doclib/about/offices/odpp/pdf/ice–detention–rpt.pdf* (last visited Mar. 31, 2015); ICE, *Detention Facility Locator*, *available at www.ice.gov/detention–facilities* (last visited Feb. 17, 2015).

[27] *See, e.g.*, Stephen Manning, *Ending Artesia*, *supra* note 6; Women's Refugee Comm'n & Lutheran Immigration and Refugee Serv., *Locking Up Family Values Again: The Detention of Immigrant Families* (Oct. 2014), *available at http://womensrefugeecommission.org/blog/2176–locking–up–family–values–again–blog*; *M.S.P.C. v. Johnson* compl. in the U.S. District Court for the District of Columbia, *available at http://americanimmigrationcouncil.org/sites/default/files/M.S.P.C.%20v.%20Johnson.pdf* (last visited Jan. 18, 2015); U.S. Comm'n on Int'l Religious Freedom Special Report, *Assessing the U.S. Government's Detention of Asylum Seekers*, *supra* note 6; Am. Civil Liberties Union, *ACLU Challenges Prison–Like Conditions at Hutto*, *supra* note 16; *see also* Women's Comm'n for Refugee Women & Children, *et al.*, *Locking Up Family Values*, *supra* note 15; Human Rights First, *In Liberty's Shadow: U.S. Detention of Asylum Seekers in the Era of Homeland Security* (Jan. 2004), *available at www.humanrightsfirst.org/asylum/libertys_shadow/Libertys_Shadow.pdf*; Human Rights Watch, *Presumption of Guilt: Human Rights Abuses of Post–September 11 Detainees* (Aug. 2002), *available at www.hrw.org/reports/2002/us911*; UNHCR Advisory Opinion (Apr. 15, 2002), *reproduced in* 79 INTERPRETER RELEASES 620 (Apr. 29, 2002); Human Rights Watch, *Locked Away: Immigration Detainees in Jails in the United States* (Sept. 1998), *available at www.hrw.org/reports98/us–immig*.

[28] *R.I. L–R–, et al., v. Jeh Charles Johnson, et al.*, 1:15–cv–00011–JEB (D.D.C. Feb. 20, 2015).

[29] *See* Women's Refugee Comm'n & Lutheran Immigrant and Refugee Serv., *Locking Up Family Values Again*, *supra* note 15; Manning, *Ending Artesia*, *supra* note 6; Dree Collopy, *The Failings of Family Detention at Artesia*, Immigration Impact (Oct. 2, 2014), *available at http://immigrationimpact.com/2014/10/02/the–failings–of–family–detention–at–artesia/* (last visited Jan. 18, 2015); Dree Collopy & Stephen Manning, *Why is Obama Still Locking Up So Many Innocent Women and Kids on U.S. Soil?*, The Guardian, *available at www.theguardian.com/commentisfree/2014/nov/04/obama–women–children–family–detention–centres* (last visited Jan. 18, 2015); Stephen Manning, *Let These Women Go*, AILA Leadership Blog (Sept. 3 2014), *available at http://ailaleadershipblog.org/2014/09/03/let–these–women–go/*.

with a capacity of over 600 women and children, which was closed down on December 15, 2014 following 14 grants of asylum out of 15 cases that went to the merits,[30] extensive media exposure,[31] and a lawsuit regarding inhumane conditions and due process concerns.[32] However, with the conversion of an existing facility in Karnes City, Texas, with a capacity of over 500 woman and children, and the opening of a new 2,400 bed facility in Dilley, Texas, the administration has made clear its intentions to sustain its policy of detaining women and children asylum-seekers.[33]

- **Practice Pointer**: Whether DHS's unlawful policy of detention-as-deterrent will endure is uncertain, however, given a recent preliminary injunction granted in a class action lawsuit, which prevents DHS from detaining class members for the purpose of deterring future immigration to the United States and from considering deterrence of future immigration as a factor in custody determinations.[34]
- **Practice Pointer**: Advocacy organizations continue the fight against family detention in the Dilley and Karnes facilities, and the American Immigration Lawyers Association, the Catholic Legal Immigration Network, the American Immigration Council, and the Refugee and Immigrant Center for Education and Legal Services have joined forces to continue the pro bono representation of the women and children detained in these facilities.[35]

---

[30] *See* Am. Immigration Lawyers Assoc., *Artesia Family Detention Asylum Case Examples*, AILA InfoNet. Doc. No. 14102446 (*posted* Feb. 13, 2015), *available at www.aila.org/infonet/family–detention–asylum–grant–examples*. Note that the "14 out of 15" number is the number of cases tried on the merits during the 21 weeks that the AILA pro bono project operated in Artesia. *See* Manning, *Ending Artesia, supra* note 6.

[31] *See, e.g.*, Wil S. Hylton, *The Shame of America's Family Detention Camps*, N.Y. Times Magazine (Feb. 4, 2015), *available at www.nytimes.com/2015/02/08/magazine/the–shame–of–americas–family–detention–camps.html?_r=0*; Collopy & Manning, *Why is Obama Still Locking Up So Many*, *supra* note 29.

[32] *See M.S.P.C. v. Johnson Compl.*, *supra* note 27; see also Am. Immigration Council, Groups Sue U.S. Government Over Life–Threatening Deportation Process Against Mothers and Children (Aug. 22, 2014), available at *www.americanimmigrationcouncil.org/newsroom/release/groups–sue–us–government–over–life–threatening–deportation–process–against–mothers–*.

[33] *See* ICE Press Release, *ICE's New Family Detention Center in Dilley, Texas to Open in December* (Nov. 18, 2014), *available at www.ice.gov/news/releases/ices–new–family–detention–center–dilley–texas–open–december*; N.Y. Times, *Detention Center Presented as Deterrent to Border Crossers* (Dec. 15, 2014), *available at www.nytimes.com/2014/12/16/us/homeland–security–chief–opens–largest–immigration–detention–center–in–us.html?_r=0*.

[34] R.*I. L–R–, et al., v. Jeh Charles Johnson, et al.*, 1:15–cv–00011–JEB (D.D.C. Feb. 20, 2015).

[35] *See* AILA, *CARA Family Detention Pro Bono Project*, *posted on* AILA InfoNet Doc. No. 14100656 and *available at www.aila.org/practice/pro–bono/find–your–opportunity/cara–family–detention–pro–bono–project* (last visited Apr. 1, 2015).

This chapter discusses current detention policies applicable to asylum-seekers and how asylum-seekers may seek release while they pursue their asylum claims before the U.S. immigration courts.

I. How Do Asylum-Seekers End Up in Detention?

In general, DHS bears the responsibility for the apprehension and detention of noncitizens in the United States.[36] ICE's Office of Enforcement and Removal Operations (ERO) manages and oversees federal immigration detention and detains individuals for the sole purpose of ensuring that they appear in court for immigration hearings and comply with removal orders. Individuals may be apprehended by Customs and Border Protection (CBP) upon apprehension at the border or port of entry, or by ICE after they have already entered the United States.[37] Following apprehension, individuals are transferred to the custody of ICE (if initially apprehended by CBP), and the ERO makes custody determinations, which may result in detention or release on bond, orders of supervision, or orders of recognizance.[38] An individual may be detained during the pendency of removal proceedings, and, if he or she is ordered removed, he or she may be detained for a certain period of time pending repatriation.[39] Individuals may be detained in DHS Processing Facilities, or in any public or private detention facility contracted by DHS to detain noncitizens.[40]

Many asylum-seekers are detained upon apprehension at the border and ports of entry, pursuant to the expedited removal provisions.[41] The expedited removal provisions of the Immigration and Nationality Act (INA) were added by section 302 of the Illegal Immigration Reform and Immigrant Responsibility Act (IIRAIRA) and became effective on April 1, 1997.[42] These provisions allow DHS to order the immediate removal of an individual arriving at a port of entry or, in some cases, of an individual already physically present in the United States, without further hearing or review.[43] If, however, the individual expresses a fear of persecution or a desire to apply for asylum, DHS will detain the individual and must refer the individual for a "credible fear" interview with an asylum officer.[44] Similarly, an individual who

---

[36] ICPM, chapter 9.1(a).

[37] *See* Simanski, *supra* note 3; Human Rights First, *'Ins' and 'Outs' of Immigration Detention*, *available at www.humanrightsfirst.org/wp–content/uploads/Detention–Infographic–2012.pdf* (last visited Feb. 17, 2015).

[38] Simanski, *supra* note 3.

[39] *Id.*

[40] 8 CFR §235.3(e); ICPM, Chapter 9.1(b).

[41] See chapter 6 for a detailed discussion of the expedited removal process.

[42] Illegal Immigration Reform and Immigrant Responsibility Act of 1996 (IIRAIRA), Pub. L. No. 104-208, div. C, 110 Stat. 3009, 3009–546 to 3009–724. INA §§235(a)(2), 235(b)(1).

[43] INA §235(b)(1)(A); 8 USC §1225(b)(1)(A) (2012).

[44] INA §235(b)(1)(A); 8 USC §1225(b)(1)(A) (2012).

expresses a fear of torture upon return will be interviewed to determine whether he or she has a credible fear of torture.[45]

A noncitizen who is subject to expedited removal or who has been issued a removal order in expedited removal proceedings "shall be detained" pending determination and removal. Parole is permitted only when DHS officials determine, in the exercise of discretion, that parole is required to meet a medical emergency or is necessary for a legitimate law enforcement objective.[46] Although the law requires that asylum-seekers subject to expedited removal remain in detention, even after an expression of fear, if the individual is found to have a credible fear of persecution or torture, he or she is placed in INA §240 proceedings for full consideration of his or her asylum claim or claim for protection under the Convention Against Torture (CAT).[47] He or she is also eligible for release at that time, either through parole at the discretion of ICE or through a bond redetermination hearing by an immigration judge (IJ).[48]

- **Practice Pointer**: If an asylum-seeker is subject to expedited removal, he or she does not have the opportunity to make an asylum claim before a USCIS asylum office. Rather, he or she is placed directly into a defensive posture and must seek relief in defense of removal from the United States. See chapter 6 for a detailed discussion of expedited removal and credible fear, as well as reinstatement of removal and reasonable fear.

Other individuals who were not apprehended and detained upon entry may wish to seek protection from persecution and/or torture following an interior apprehension and detention by ICE. Interior apprehensions may result from the following enforcement programs and actions: (1) priority enforcement program;[49] (2) fugitive

---

45 *See* 8 CFR §§208.30, 1208.30 (2014). *See also* chapter 4.

46 INA §235(b)(1)(B)(ii), (iii)(IV); 8 CFR §§235.3(b)(2)(ii)–(iii), 1235.3(b)(2)(ii)–(iii) (2014). *See* ICE, *Parole of Arriving Aliens Found to Have a Credible Fear of Persecution or Torture* (effective Jan. 4, 2010), *available at www.ice.gov/doclib/dro/pdf/11002.1–hd–parole_of_arriving_aliens_found_credible_fear.pdf* (last visited Feb. 17, 2015).

47 Regulations Concerning the Convention Against Torture, 64 Fed. Reg. 8484 (Feb. 19, 1999).

48 *See Matter of X–K–*, 23 I&N Dec. 731 (BIA 2005) (holding that a respondent initially screened in the expedited removal process, but who is subsequently placed in INA §240 proceedings following a positive credible fear determination, is eligible for a custody redetermination hearing before an IJ unless he or she is a member of any of the listed classes of respondents who are specifically excluded from an IJ's custody jurisdiction); *infra* pt. IV. for a detailed discussion of parole and bond.

49 DHS, Johnson Memorandum, *Policies for the Apprehension, Detention and Removal of Undocumented Immigrants* (Nov. 20, 2014), *available at www.dhs.gov/sites/default/files/publications/14_1120_memo_prosecutorial_discretion.pdf* (last visited Apr. 1, 2015); This Priority Enforcement Program replaced the Secure Communities program, which was discontinued on November 20, 2014. DHS, Johnson Memorandum, *Secure Communities* (Nov. 20, 2014), *available at www.dhs.gov/sites/default/files/publications/14_1120_memo_secure_communities.pdf* (last visited Apr. 1, 2015). *See also* ICE, *Secure Communities*, *available at www.ice.gov/secure–communities* (last visited Feb. 19, 2015).

operations;[50] (3) criminal alien program (in partnership with jails and prisons);[51] (4) 287(g) (in partnership with state and local police);[52] and (5) worksite enforcement.

> **Practice Pointer**: For more details on these, as well as other enforcement actions, see ICE's website at *www.ice.gov/ero*.[53]

Upon apprehension in the interior, ICE may arrest and detain the individual pending a decision on whether he or she is to be removed from the United States.[54] Such an individual may wish to seek asylum, withholding of removal under INA §241(b)(3), or protection under CAT in defense of his or her removal. Upon arrest of the individual, ICE will determine whether he or she is eligible for release or whether mandatory detention under INA §236(c) applies. Mandatory detention applies to individuals with certain criminal records who, when they are released, are:

- Inadmissible for committing an offense under INA §212(a)(2) (crimes involving moral turpitude and drug offenses);
- Deportable for committing an offense under INA §237(a)(2)(A)(ii)-(iii), (B), (C), or (D) (multiple crimes involving moral turpitude, aggravated felonies, drug offenses, firearms offenses, and crimes related to espionage);
- Deportable under INA §237(a)(2)(A)(i) (conviction for a crime involving moral turpitude committed within five years of admission) if the individual has been sentenced to a term of imprisonment of at least one year; or
- Inadmissible under INA §212(a)(3)(B) or deportable under INA §237(a)(4)(B) (involvement in terrorist activities).[55]

If mandatory detention applies, ICE usually will not release the individual until he or she has been granted relief by an IJ or deported. If mandatory detention does not apply, ICE may continue to detain the arrested individual or may release the individual on bond of at least $1,500 or on conditional parole.[56] ICE also may exercise the discretion to release the individual on his or her own recognizance or on alternatives to detention, such as ankle monitoring devices and orders of supervision. At any time, ICE may revoke a bond or parole, re-arrest the individual, and re-detain him or her.[57]

---

[50] ICE, *Fugitive Operations*, *available at www.ice.gov/fugitive–operations* (last visited Feb. 19, 2015).

[51] ICE, *Criminal Alien Program*, *available at www.ice.gov/criminal–alien–program* (last visited Feb. 19, 2015).

[52] ICE, *Delegation of Immigration Authority Section 287(g) Immigration and Nationality Act*, *available at www.ice.gov/287g* (last visited Feb. 19, 2015).

[53] (last visited Feb. 19, 2015).

[54] INA §236(a).

[55] INA §236(c)(1).

[56] INA §236(a)(1)–(2).

[57] INA §236(b).

➢ **Practice Pointer**: In 2003, to provide additional options for supervised release, Congress appropriated funds to pilot a five-year Intensive Supervision Appearance Program (ISAP) to operate in ten cities. The program ran from 2004-2009 and then Congress appropriated funds to extend the program nationwide. ISAP is now in its third iteration, ISAP III. [58] To Date, ISAP is the only alternative to detention program currently recognized by ICE.[59] ICE has, however, posted a request for proposals for a case management alternative to detention to be used for families. ISAP is operated by Behavioral Interventions Incorporated, which was acquired by the GEO Group, a major player in the private prison industry, in 2010. ISAP supervises participants with the use of electronic ankle monitors, installation of biometric voice recognition software, unannounced home visits, employer verification, and in-person reporting.[60]

Although most individuals fleeing protection will not want to contact their governments, every detained individual must be notified that he or she may communicate with the consular or diplomatic officers of the country of his or her nationality in the United States.[61] When contacting consular or diplomatic officials, DHS officers are not permitted to reveal the fact that any detained individual has applied for asylum or withholding of removal.[62]

➢ **Practice Pointer**: For a useful visual depiction of how individuals are apprehended and released, see Human Rights First's, "'Ins' and 'Outs' of Immigration Detention," available at *www.humanrightsfirst.org/wp-content/uploads/Detention-Infographic-2012.pdf.*[63]

II. Who is Eligible for Release?

Under current law, regulations, and DHS policies, the following applicants for asylum, withholding of removal under INA §241(b)(3), or relief under the Convention Against Torture are eligible for release from detention: (1) individuals found to have a credible fear; (2) non-criminals who have made a lawful or illegal

[58] *See* Lutheran Immigrant and Refugee Services Backgrounder, *Alternatives to Detention (ATD): History and Recommendations*, *available at http://lirs.org/wp–content/uploads/2013/04/LIRS–Backgrounder–on–Alternatives–to–Detention–3–12–13.pdf* (last visited Apr. 1, 2015).

[59] Office of Inspector General, *U.S. Immigration and Customs Enforcement's Alternatives to Detention* (Feb. 4, 2015), AILA InfoNet Doc. No. 15021866 (Feb. 18, 2015), *available at www.aila.org/infonet/dhs–oig–report–ice–alternatives–to–dentention?utm_source=Recent%20Postings%20Alert&utm_medium=Email&utm_campaign=RP%20Daily*.

[60] *Id.*

[61] 8 CFR §1236.1(e) (2014).

[62] *Id.*

[63] (last visited Feb. 17, 2015).

entry or who fall within the definition of "arriving alien;" (3) individuals who completed their criminal sentences prior to October 9, 1998; (4) individuals with final orders of removal who cannot be returned to their home countries; and (5) children.[64] Generally, it is ICE policy to favor the release of individuals who have been granted protection.[65]

A. Individuals Found to Have a Credible Fear

Individuals in the expedited removal process who have been determined to have a credible fear of persecution or torture may be eligible for release from detention.[66] This policy applies to individuals arriving at ports of entry; however, it does not necessarily apply to individuals apprehended between ports of entry.[67] A request for release under this policy must be made to the District Director for the ICE ERO office having jurisdiction over the place of detention.[68] The determination whether to release the asylum-seeker is entirely discretionary, and ICE's implementation of this policy has fluctuated in recent years.[69] For a detailed discussion of the release of asylum-seekers who have demonstrated a credible fear of persecution or torture, see Part IV. below.

---

[64] Children who are with their mothers, however, are being detained by ICE and may not be eligible for release. See American Bar Association, Letter to DHS Secretary Jeh Johnson, "ABA Concerns about Expansion of Immigration Detention, Including Detention of Women and Children Seeking Protection as Refugees" (Mar. 26, 2015), available at *www.americanbar.org/content/dam/aba/uncategorized/GAO/2015mar26_familydetention.authcheckdam.pdf* (last visited Mar. 31, 2015); Statement of the American Immigration Lawyers Association Submitted to the U.S. Commission on Civil Rights, Briefing on "State of Civil Rights at Immigration Detention Facilities" (Jan. 30, 2015), posted on AILA InfoNet Doc. No. 15012045 and available at *www.aila.org/advo–media/aila–correspondence/aila–mass–detention–of–asylum–seekers–is–a–humanit* (last visited Mar. 31, 2015).

[65] ICE, Garcia Memorandum, *Detention Policy Where an Immigration Judge has Granted Asylum and ICE has Appealed* (Feb. 9, 2004), *available at www.immigrationequality.org/wp–content/uploads/2011/12/Feb–9–2004–memo–on–release–after–asylum.pdf* (last visited Apr. 1, 2015).

[66] *See* ICE Policy Directive from John Morton on Parole of Arriving Aliens Found to Have a Credible Fear of Persecution or Torture (Dec. 8, 2009), AILA InfoNet Doc. No. 09121760 (*posted* Dec. 17, 2009), *available at www.ice.gov/doclib/dro/pdf/11002.1–hd–parole_of_arriving_aliens_found_credible_fear.pdf.*

[67] *See id.*

[68] *See id.;* ICE, *Parole of Arriving Aliens Found to Have a "Credible Fear" of Persecution or Torture* (Nov. 6, 2007), *available at www.rcusa.org/uploads/pdfs/ICEAsylum ParoleGuidance01–06–07.pdf.*

[69] ICE Policy Directive from John Morton on Parole of Arriving Aliens, *supra* note 66; ICE, *Parole of Arriving Aliens Found to Have a "Credible Fear" of Persecution or Torture* (Nov. 6, 2007), *available at www.rcusa.org/uploads/pdfs/ICEAsylumParoleGuidance01–06–07.pdf. But see* Women's Refugee Comm'n & Lutheran Immigration and Refugee Serv., *Locking Up Family Values Again*, *supra* note 15; Manning, *Ending Artesia*, *supra* note 6; ICE Press Release on Dilley, *supra* note 33; Julia Preston, *Detention Center Presented as Deterrent to Border Crossers*, N.Y. Times (Dec. 15, 2014), *available at www.nytimes.com/2014/12/16/us/homeland–security–chief–opens–largest–immigration–detention–center–in–us.html?_r=0* (last visited Jan. 17, 2015); Wil S. Hylton, *The Shame of America's Family Detention Camps*, N.Y. TIMES MAGAZINE (Feb. 4, 2015), *available at www.nytimes.com/2015/02/08/magazine/the–shame–of–americas–family–detention–camps.html?_r=0.*

B. Non-Criminals Who Have Made a Lawful or Illegal Entry or Who Fall Within the Definition of "Arriving Alien"

Individuals not subject to certain criminal grounds for detention, who lawfully or illegally entered the United States and who have not yet been ordered removed, deported, or excluded may seek release from detention before an IJ.[70] Individuals who fall within the definition of "arriving alien," *i.e.*, who seek admission or transit at a U.S. port of entry, if placed in removal (*not* expedited removal) proceedings, also may seek release from detention from ICE.[71]

C. Individuals Who Completed Their Criminal Sentences Prior to October 9, 1998

Individuals subject to removal based on certain criminal grounds[72] are subject to mandatory detention under INA §236(c) and may not seek release from detention while in removal proceedings.[73] However, if they completed the jail or prison sentence for the conviction and were released prior to October 9, 1998 (the date that mandatory detention went into effect),[74] they are eligible to seek release before ICE or an IJ.

D. Individuals with Final Orders of Removal Who Cannot Be Returned to Their Home Countries

An individual with a final order of removal, deportation, or exclusion is not eligible for release from detention unless the country designated for removal will not accept him or her, or the individual cannot be removed to that country due to a grant of withholding or deferral of removal. Generally, DHS must remove or release detained respondents within 90 days of a final order of removal.[75] During the removal period, DHS "shall detain" the individual.[76] However, DHS may continue to detain a respondent following the 90-day removal period as set forth in 8 CFR §241.14.[77]

---

[70] *See* 8 CFR §1003.19(h)(2)(i) (2014).

[71] 8 CFR §1003.19(h)(2)(ii) (2014).

[72] Criminal grounds, such as aggravated felonies, crimes involving moral turpitude (unless an exception applies), two or more crimes involving moral turpitude, multiple criminal convictions with an aggregate sentence of five years or more, controlled–substance offenses or trafficking, certain firearms offenses, prostitution and commercialized vice offenses, and engaging in terrorist activities, may subject an individual to mandatory detention under INA §236(c). *See* 8 CFR §1003.19(h)(2)(i) (2014). For a complete list, see INA §236(c)(1); 8 USC §1226(c)(1) (2012).

[73] INA §236(c)(1).

[74] *Matter of Garcia–Arreola*, 25 I&N Dec. 267 (BIA 2010); *Matter of Adeniji*, 22 I&N Dec. 1102 (BIA 1999) (finding that INA §236(c) does not apply to respondents whose most recent release from DHS custody occurred prior to October 9, 1998).

[75] INA §241(a)(1).

[76] INA §241(a)(2).

[77] 8 CFR §241.14(a) (2014).

For example, if an individual's release would pose a special danger to the public and his or her removal from the U.S. is not reasonably foreseeable, DHS may detain that individual beyond the 90-day removal period.[78] Such a decision may be reviewed by an IJ in continued detention review proceedings.

These proceedings are divided into two phases:

(1) reasonable cause hearings; and

(2) continued detention merits hearings.[79]

If an individual has been ordered removed but remains detained he or she may request that DHS determine whether there is a significant likelihood of removal in the reasonably foreseeable future.[80] If there is a significant likelihood of removal in the reasonably foreseeable future, DHS may continue to detain the individual. If not, however, the individual should be released unless DHS determines that continued detention is necessary because release would pose a special danger to the public.[81] Following such a determination, the matter is referred to an IJ for a reasonable cause hearing, during which the IJ will determine whether DHS has met its burden of showing a reasonable cause to go forward with a continued detention review merits hearing.[82] If there is a reasonable cause, the IJ will schedule the continued detention review merits hearing. If not, the individual is released.[83] At a continued detention review merits hearing, it is DHS's burden of proving by clear and convincing evidence that the individual should remain in custody because his or her release would pose a special danger to the public.[84] If DHS has met its burden, the IJ will order the continued detention of the individual. If not, the individual will be released.[85]

> ➢ **Practice Pointer**: For detailed descriptions of the procedures for reasonable cause hearings and continued detention merits hearings, see the ICPM at chapter 9.4.

DHS may continue to detain other individuals beyond the 90-day removal period as well. For example, individuals who have been granted withholding of removal under INA §241(b)(3) or withholding or deferral of removal under the Convention Against Torture have final orders of removal entered against them in conjunction with the granting of withholding or deferral relief. Thus, if an individual is detained when he or she is granted withholding of removal under INA §241(b)(3) or

---

[78] INA §241(a)(6); 8 CFR §1241.14(f) (2014).

[79] ICPM, chapter 9.4(a).

[80] 8 CFR §1241.13 (2014).

[81] *Id.*

[82] *See* 8 CFR §1241.13(f) (2014).

[83] 8 CFR §1241.13 (2014).

[84] 8 CFR §1241.14 (2014).

[85] *Id.*

withholding or deferral of removal under the Convention Against Torture, ICE may choose to continue to detain the individual while seeking to remove him or her to a third country (a country other than the country to which removal has been withheld by the IJ).[86] Generally, however, ICE policy is to release those granted protection.[87]

- **Practice Pointer**: The most controversial provision of the regulations implementing article 3 of the Convention Against Torture is the provision allowing the attorney general, deputy attorney general, or the "INS Commissioner" (as the regulation was written prior to the creation of the Department of Homeland Security (DHS)) to determine, in consultation with the secretary of state, whether assurances from the proposed country of removal are sufficiently reliable to allow an individual's removal to that country.[88] Thus, if the United States receives diplomatic assurances that a country not torture the individual upon repatriation, the United States may remove the individual, despite a grant of CAT protection.[89] The Third Circuit has held, however, that prior to removal on the basis of diplomatic assurances, the applicant: (1) must be afforded notice and an opportunity to test the reliability of those assurances in a hearing; (2) must have the opportunity to present evidence and arguments challenging the reliability of the diplomatic assurances, before a neutral decision-maker; and (3) must be afforded an individualized determination based on a record disclosed to the applicant.[90]

Following the expiration of the 90-day removal period, the individual may be released if he or she shows that his or her release will not pose a danger to the community or to the safety of other persons or property or a significant risk of flight

---

[86] 8 CFR §241.4(b)(3) (2014).

[87] Garcia Memorandum, *supra* note 65.

[88] *See* 8 CFR §§208.18(c), 1208.18(c). References to the legacy INS "Commissioner" after March 1, 2003, unless otherwise specified in the regulations, mean the director of U.S. Citizenship and Immigration Services (USCIS), the commissioner of U.S. Customs and Border Protection (CBP), and the assistant secretary for U.S. Immigration and Customs Enforcement (ICE). 8 CFR §1.1(d).

[89] *See* EOIR Memorandum, M. Creppy, "Operating Policies and Procedures Memorandum No. 99–5: Implementation of Article 3 of the UN Convention Against Torture" (May 14, 1999), *published on* AILA InfoNet (*posted* June 4, 1999), and *available at www.usdoj.gov/eoir/efoia/ocij/oppm99/99_5.pdf*. The first reported case in which diplomatic assurances were given was that of Hani Abdel Rahim Sayegh, a Saudi Arabia national who was suspected of involvement in the bombing of Khobar Towers, a U.S. military complex in Saudi Arabia. "Khobar Probe Figure Facing Deportation," *Washington Post*, Oct. 5, 1999, at p. A–10. The Saudi government provided assurances that Sayegh would not be tortured if returned to Saudi Arabia, though he did face trial there and execution by beheading if convicted. *Id.* As a result of these assurances, Sayegh was returned to Saudi Arabia. At least one court has held that a CAT applicant must be provided the opportunity to challenge the reliability of diplomatic assurances. See *Khouzam v. Hogan*, 497 F.Supp.2d 615 (M.D. Pa. 2007), *upheld by Khouzam v. Att'y. Gen. of the U.S.*, 549 F.3d 235 (3d Cir. 2008).

[90] *Khouzam v. Att'y. Gen.*, 549 F.3d 235 (3d Cir. 2008).

pending his or her removal from the United States.[91] The District Director of the ICE ERO office will make a custody determination.[92] He or she will conduct a records review, give notice to the individual so he or she may submit information in writing in support of release, and may exercise the discretion to interview the individual.[93] The District Director will consider the following factors:

- The nature and number of disciplinary infractions or incident reports received when incarcerated or while in DHS custody;
- The detainee's criminal conduct and convictions (nature and severity, sentences imposed, time served, probation and criminal parole history, evidence of recidivism, and other criminal history);
- Any psychiatric or psychological reports pertaining to the detainee's mental health;
- Evidence of rehabilitation;
- Favorable factors, such as ties to the United States;
- Prior immigration violations and history;
- The likelihood that the individual is a significant flight risk or may abscond to avoid removal (history of escapes, failures to appear for proceedings, absence without leave from any halfway house or sponsorship program, and other defaults); and
- Other information that is probative of whether the individual is likely to adjust to life in a community, engage in future acts of violence or criminal activity, pose a danger to the safety of him or herself or to other persons or property, or violate the conditions of release from immigration custody.[94]

After reviewing these factors, District Directors will consider whether the individual meets the criteria for release:

(1) travel documents are not available for the individual or removal is not practicable or in the public interest;

(2) the detainee is presently a non-violent person;

(3) the detainee is likely to remain nonviolent if released;

(4) the detainee is not likely to pose a threat to the community following release;

(5) the detainee is not likely to violate the conditions of release; and

(6) the detainee does not pose a significant flight risk if released.[95]

---

[91] 8 CFR §241.4(d)(1) (2014).

[92] 8 CFR §241.4(h)(1) (2014).

[93] 8 CFR §241.4(h)(1)–(2) (2014).

[94] 8 CFR §§241.4(h)(3), 241.4(f) (2014).

[95] 8 CFR §§241.4(h)(3), 241.4(e) (2014).

The District Director will then provide a decision in writing.[96]

Even though, following this custody determination, a district director may decide to continue to detain an individual beyond the 90-day removal period, the landmark Supreme Court case *Zadvydas v. Davis* prohibits the indefinite detention of noncitizens with final orders of removal where there is no significant likelihood of removal in the reasonably foreseeable future.[97] Overall, the maximum period of time that an individual may be kept in detention following a final order of removal is six months.[98] The six-month period begins when the IJ's order of removal becomes final.[99] Thus, if it is unlikely that ICE will be able to remove the individual in the reasonably foreseeable future, he or she is eligible for release from detention pursuant to *Zadvydas v. Davis* and the implementing regulations, which set forth the procedures for reviewing cases of individuals in detention with final orders of removal.[100]

Where the individual has provided good reason to believe or if DHS has determined that there is no significant likelihood of removal to a country to which he or she was ordered removed, or to a third country, in the reasonably foreseeable future, DHS's Headquarters Post-Order Detention Unit (HQPDU) will conduct a custody review pursuant to 8 CFR §241.13.[101] The individual may submit a written request for release, with supporting documentation (including evidence that he or she cooperated in obtaining necessary travel documents), to HQPDU asserting that there is no significant likelihood that he or she will be removed in the reasonably foreseeable future.[102] This request may be made at any time after the removal order becomes final. The individual does not need to wait for the 90-day removal period to expire first.[103] HQPDU must respond within 10 business days of receiving the individual's request to acknowledge receipt of the request and explain the procedures for evaluating the request.[104] First, HQPDU will consider whether the individual has cooperated fully in making reasonable efforts to comply with the removal order (for example, seeking a travel document).[105] Second, HQPDU may refer the request to the Department of State to seek information and assistance, and may exercise the

---

[96] 8 CFR §241.4(h)(4) (2014).

[97] *Zadvydas v. Davis*, 533 U.S. 678 (2001). *See* 8 CFR §241.13(b)(2) (2014).

[98] 8 CFR §241.13(b)(2)(ii) (2014); *Zadvydas v. Davis*, 533 U.S. 678 (2001).

[99] 8 CFR §§241.13(b)(2)(ii), 1241.1 (2014).

[100] *Zadvydas*, 533 U.S. at 678; 8 CFR §241.13(b) (2014).

[101] 8 CFR §241.13(a) (2014).

[102] 8 CFR §241.13(d)(1)–(2) (2014).

[103] 8 CFR §241.13(d)(3) (2014).

[104] 8 CFR §241.13(e)(1) (2014).

[105] 8 CFR §241.13(e)(2) (2014).

discretion to interview the individual.[106] Third, HQPDU must consider the following factors:

- The history of the individual's efforts to comply with the order of removal;
- The history of DHS's efforts to remove individuals to the country in question or to third countries, including the ongoing nature of DHS's efforts to remove this individual and his or her assistance with those efforts;
- The reasonably foreseeable results of those efforts; and
- The views of the Department of State regarding the prospects for removal of individuals to the country or countries in question.[107]

After its consideration of these factors, HQPDU must issue a written decision regarding whether there is a significant likelihood of removal in the reasonably foreseeable future.[108] If HQPDU finds that there is no significant likelihood of removal in the reasonably foreseeable future, DHS must promptly make arrangements for the release of the individual, unless there are special circumstances justifying continued detention.[109] On the other hand, if HQPDU finds that removal is likely in the reasonably foreseeable future, it will deny the request and notify the individual.[110] To seek release, such an individual would then be subject to the standards of 8 CFR §214.4 and would need to follow the procedures for release described above.[111]

E. Children

DHS apprehends thousands of children every year, many of whom are asylum-seekers or victims of trafficking, trauma, abuse, and abandonment. Although the number of children arriving in the U.S. had been steadily increasing over the past five years, in fiscal year 2014, an unprecedented number of unaccompanied children were apprehended at the southern border of the U.S.[112] Most of these children came from Honduras, Guatemala, and El Salvador, with a smaller number of children coming from Mexico.[113] Unaccompanied migrant children are generally detained and placed in removal proceedings; however, there are specific legal requirements for their care, custody, and release. First, when a child is apprehended by CBP, he or she must be

---

[106] 8 CFR §241.13(e)(3), (5) (2014).

[107] 8 CFR §241.13(f) (2014).

[108] 8 CFR §241.13(g) (2014).

[109] 8 CFR §241.13(g)(1) (2014).

[110] 8 CFR §241.13(g)(2) (2014).

[111] *Id.*

[112] U.S. Customs and Border Protection, *Southwest Border Unaccompanied Alien Children (FY 2014), available at www.cbp.gov/newsroom/stats/southwest–border–unaccompanied–children–2014* (last visited Feb. 17, 2015) (noting a 77% increase in arrivals at the southern border, from 38,759 unaccompanied children in fiscal year 2013 to 68,541 unaccompanied children in fiscal year 2014).

[113] *Id.*

given a Form I-770, Notice of Rights and Disposition.[114] If the child is under 14 years old or is unable to understand the notice, the notice shall be read and explained to him or her in a language the child understands.[115] The notice notifies the child of his or her right to request a hearing before an IJ.[116] If the child later decides to accept voluntary departure or to withdraw his or her application for admission, a new Form I-770 shall be given to and signed by the child.[117]

Second, the procedures to be followed after apprehension depend on whether or not the child is "unaccompanied" (under 18 and not in the care of a parent legal guardian at the time of apprehension); accompanied children remain in DHS custody, while unaccompanied children are required to be transferred to the Department of Health and Human Services' Office of Refugee Resettlement within 72 hours of apprehension.[118] These agencies are charged with compliance regarding the legal requirements for the care, custody, and prompt release of detained immigrant children.[119]

> ➢ **Practice Pointer**: For a detailed discussion of procedures for children seeking asylum, withholding of removal, and protection under CAT, see chapter 10 of this book.

Juveniles — individuals under the age of 18 — are eligible for release from DHS custody pursuant to 8 CFR §§236.3, 1236.3.[120] These regulations on the release of children codify provisions of the *Flores v. Reno* settlement regarding the apprehension and detention of children by INS, now DHS.[121] *Flores v. Reno* was a class action lawsuit filed against legacy INS to challenge its apprehension, detention, processing, and release of children in its custody. The lawsuit's 1997 settlement agreement set national policy regarding the treatment of children in INS custody and many of the agreement's terms were later codified in the federal regulations.[122] The settlement and regulations now apply to all children apprehended by DHS. However, DHS has taken the position that only unaccompanied children in its custody are

---

[114] 8 CFR §236.3(h), 1236.3(h) (2014).

[115] *Id.*

[116] *Id.*

[117] *Id.*

[118] 6 USC §279(g)(2) (2012).

[119] *See* 8 CFR §236.3, 1236.3 (2014); *Flores v. Reno*, 507 U.S. 292 (1993).

[120] 8 CFR §1236.4 (2014). *See also* 8 CFR §§212.5(b)(3), 1212.5(b)(3) (2014). Note that while the definition of "child" under the INA is an individual under age 21, a "juvenile" for purposes of custody under these regulations is an individual under age 18.

[121] *Flores v. Reno*, 507 U.S. 292 (1993); *see also* 75 INTERPRETER RELEASES 1020 (July 27, 1998). *See* Lutheran Immigrant and Refugee Services, Women's Refugee Commission, & Kids in Need of Defense, Flores Settlement Agreement & DHS Custody, available at *http://lirs.org/wp-content/uploads/2014/12/Flores-Family-Detention-Backgrounder-LIRS-WRC-KIND-FINAL1.pdf* (last visited Apr. 1, 2015).

[122] *See* 8 CFR §236.3, 1236.3 (2014).

covered. Recently, a lawsuit was filed to challenge this position and to enforce the *Flores* settlement in the family detention context.[123]

Under *Flores v. Reno,* children "must be held in the least restrictive setting appropriate to their age and special needs to ensure their protection and wellbeing."[124] The settlement also requires that children be released from custody without unnecessary delay to "a parent, legal guardian, adult relative, individual specifically designated by the parent, licensed program, or, alternatively, an adult who seeks custody who DHS deems appropriate."[125] When the child is released, DHS must serve both the adult to whom the child is released as well as the child with the Notice of Hearing and charging document.[126]

Specifically, the regulations require the timely release of children from detention, unless detention is required to secure his or her timely appearance before DHS or the immigration court or to ensure the child's or others' safety.[127] The child must be released to the following individuals, in order of preference:

- A parent;
- A legal guardian; or
- An adult relative (brother, sister, aunt, uncle, grandparent) who is not presently in DHS custody.[128]

If one of these individuals cannot be located and the child has identified a parent, legal guardian, or adult relative in DHS detention, "simultaneous release of the juvenile and the parent, legal guardian, or adult relative shall be evaluated on a discretionary case-by-case basis."[129] In the alternative, a parent or legal guardian who is detained or outside of the U.S. may designate, in a sworn affidavit executed in front of an immigration or consular officer, a person capable and willing to care for the child and to ensure the child's presence at all future proceedings before DHS and the immigration court.[130] In "unusual and compelling circumstances and in the discretion of the Director of the Office of Juvenile Affairs," a child also may be

---

[123] *See* American Immigration Council, Immigration Impact, Government Claims Children in Family Detention Centers Are Not Entitled to Protections (Mar. 18, 2015), available at *http://immigrationimpact.com/2015/03/18/government–claims–children–in–family–detention–centers–are–not–entitled–to–protections/* (last visited Apr. 1, 2015).

[124] Nat'l Immigrant Justice Ctr., *Fact Sheet: Children Detained by the Department of Homeland Security in Adult Detention Facilities* (May 2013), *available at www.immigrantjustice.org/sites/immigrantjustice.org/files/NIJC%20Fact%20Sheet%20Minors%20in%20ICE%20Custody%202013%2005%2030%20FINAL.pdf* (last visited Feb. 17, 2015).

[125] *Id.*

[126] *Flores–Chavez v. Ashcroft*, 362 F.3d 1150 (9th Cir. 2004).

[127] 8 CFR §§236.3(b)(1), 1236.3(b)(1) (2014).

[128] 8 CFR §§236.3(b)(1), 1236.3(b)(1) (2014).

[129] 8 CFR §§236.3(b)(2). 1236.3(b)(2) (2014).

[130] 8 CFR §§236.3(b)(3). 1236.3(b)(3) (2014).

released to an adult who executes an agreement to care for the child's well-being and to ensure the child's presence at all future proceedings.[131]

If detention is determined to be necessary, for such interim period of time as is required to locate suitable placement for the child, the child may be temporarily held by DHS authorities or placed in a DHS detention facility that has separate accommodations for children.[132] DHS and legacy INS have been criticized for violating the terms of the *Flores v. Reno* settlement, for detaining children longer than allowed under the law, and for the conditions under which children are held.[133]

> ➤ **Practice Pointer**: See Chapter 10 of this book for a detailed discussion of child asylum-seekers and the legal standards and procedures for keeping them in immigration detention custody and seeking their release.

III. Who is Not Eligible for Release?

The following individuals under current law and regulations are not eligible for release from detention: (1) individuals in expedited removal; (2) individuals subject to certain criminal grounds of deportation or inadmissibility; (3) terrorists; and (4) individuals with final orders of removal.

---

[131] 8 CFR §§236.3(b)(4). 1236.3(b)(4) (2014).

[132] 8 CFR §§236.3(d). 1236.3(d) (2014).

[133] *See, e.g.*, Women's Refugee Comm'n & Lutheran Immigration and Refugee Serv., *Locking Up Family Values Again*, *supra* note 15; Manning, *Ending Artesia*, *supra* note 6; Collopy, *The Failings of Family Detention at Artesia*, *supra* note 29; Collopy & Manning, *Why is Obama Still Locking Up So Many*, *supra* note 29; Manning, *Let These Women Go*, *supra* note 29; *M.S.P.C. v. Johnson* Compl., *supra* note 27; Am. Immigration Council, *Groups Sue U.S. Government*, *supra* note 32; Am. Immigration Council, *Children in Danger: A Guide to the Humanitarian Challenge at the Border* (July 2014), *available at www.immigrationpolicy.org/special–reports/children–danger–guide–humanitarian–challenge–border* (last visited Feb. 27, 2015); Human Rights Watch, *US: Surge in Detention of Child Migrants* (June 25, 2014), available at *www.hrw.org/news/2014/06/25/us–surge–detention–child–migrants* (last visited Feb. 17, 2015); Nat'l Immigrant Justice Ctr., *Fact Sheet: Children Detained by the Department of Homeland Security*, *supra* note 124; Women's Refugee Comm'n, *Halfway Home: Unaccompanied Children in Immigration Custody* (Feb. 2009), *available at http://womensrefugeecommission.org/programs/migrant–rights/55–programs/detention/808–immigration–custody–of–unaccompanied–children* (last visited Feb. 17, 2015); Am. Civil Liberties Union, *ACLU Challenges Prison–Like Conditions at Hutto*, *supra* note 16; *see also* Women's Refugee Comm'n & Lutheran Immigration and Refugee Serv., *Locking Up Family Values Again*, *supra* note 15; Physicians for Human Rights, *et al.*, *From Persecution to Prison: The Health Consequences of Detention for Asylum Seekers*, at 123, *available at www.survivorsoftorture.org/files/pdf/perstoprison2003.pdf* (criticizing DHS for detaining children and for its use of x–ray and dental examinations to determine age); Women's Comm'n for Refugee Women and Children, *Prison Guard or Parent?: INS Treatment of Unaccompanied Refugee Children* (May 2002), *available at www.womenscommissionorg /pdf/ins_det.pdf*; Human Rights Watch, *Detained and Deprived of Rights: Children in the Custody of the U.S. Immigration and Naturalization Service* (Dec. 1998), *available at www.hrw.org/reports98/ins2*.

A. Individuals in Expedited Removal

An individual in the expedited removal process is not eligible for release from detention unless he or she is found to have a credible fear of persecution or torture,[134] or he or she demonstrates that "parole is required to meet a medical emergency or is necessary for a legitimate law enforcement purpose."[135]

B. Individuals Subject to Criminal Grounds of Deportation or Inadmissibility

An individual who is detained and charged with being removable may be released on bond or parole as set forth in INA §236, as long as he or she is not subject to mandatory detention under INA §236(c). Individuals subject to removal based on one or more of the grounds listed below are subject to mandatory detention under INA §236(c) and may not seek release from detention while in removal proceedings, unless they completed the jail or prison sentence for the conviction and were released prior to October 9, 1998 (the date that mandatory detention went into effect).[136] The criminal grounds include:

- Aggravated felonies;
- Crimes involving moral turpitude (unless one of two exceptions applies);[137]
- Two or more crimes involving moral turpitude;
- Multiple criminal convictions if the aggregate sentence was five years or more;
- Controlled-substance offenses;
- Controlled-substance trafficking;
- Certain firearms offenses;
- Prostitution and commercialized vice offenses; and
- Engaging in terrorist activities.[138]

---

[134] *See Matter of X–K–*, 23 I&N Dec. 731 (BIA 2005) (holding that a respondent initially screened in the expedited removal process, but who is subsequently placed in INA §240 proceedings following a positive credible fear determination, is eligible for a custody redetermination hearing before an IJ unless he or she is a member of any of the listed classes of respondents who are specifically excluded from an IJ's custody jurisdiction). *See also supra* Part II.A. and Part IV. of this chapter for a detailed discussion of release upon a finding of a credible fear of persecution or torture.

[135] 8 CFR §§235.3(b)(2)(iii), 1235.3(b)(2)(iii) (non–stowaways), 208.5(b)(2), 1208.5(b)(2) (stowaways) (2014).

[136] *Matter of Garcia–Arreola*, 25 I&N Dec. 267 (BIA 2010); *Matter of Adeniji*, 22 I&N Dec. 1102 (BIA 1999) (finding that INA §236(c) does not apply to respondents whose most recent release from DHS custody occurred prior to October 9, 1998).

[137] *See* INA §212(a)(2)(A)(II) (petty offense exception). The other exception is for a single possession of 30 grams or less of marijuana.

[138] 8 CFR §1003.19(h)(2)(i) (2014). For a complete list, see INA §236(c)(1); 8 USC §1226(c)(1) (2012).

In order to be subject to mandatory detention, ICE must take a individual into custody when he or she is released from criminal custody.[139]

- **Practice Pointer**: The "when released" language in the statute has been a point of controversy, with the government taking the position that it can subject someone to mandatory detention even if ICE detains the person days, months, or even years after their release from criminal custody. The Board of Immigration Appeals agreed with the government's position in *Matter of Rojas*.[140] However, a growing number of federal district courts have held that "when released" requires that ICE detain the individual immediately at the time of his or her release from criminal custody.[141]
- **Practice Pointer**: Additional categories of individuals subject to mandatory detention are arriving aliens in removal proceedings and returning lawful permanent residents who are seeking admission.[142]

Such individuals are technically eligible for release under very restrictive criteria set forth in INA §236(c)(2), which allows the Attorney General to release such individuals if necessary to provide protection to a witness or person cooperating in the investigation of major criminal activity and the individual would not be a danger to the safety of persons or property.[143] Under the Homeland Security Act of 2002, this authority to release extends to the DHS secretary and DHS officials.[144] However, release under these criteria is unusual. Individuals who are subject to mandatory detention generally are not entitled to release on parole and are not entitled to a bond hearing. Rather, they must remain in detention while removal proceedings are pending against them.[145] If an individual is not subject to mandatory detention under INA §236(c), the provisions of INA §236(a) control.[146]

---

[139] INA §236(c) (stating that "the Attorney General shall take into custody any alien who" comes within these grounds "when the alien is released").

[140] *Matter of Rojas*, 23 I&N Dec. 117 (BIA 2001) (finding that a criminal respondent who is released from criminal custody after the expiration of the Transition Period Custody Rules is subject to mandatory detention under INA §236(c) even if the respondent is not immediately taken into custody by DHS authorities when released from incarceration).

[141] *See, e.g., Castaneda v. Souza,* 952 F.Supp.2d 307 (D. Mass. 2013); *Nimako v. Shanahan,* 2012 WL 4121102 (D.N.J. 2012); *Khoury v. Asher,* 2014 WL 954920 (W.D. Wash. 2014). *But see, e.g., Sylvain v. U.S. Att'y Gen.,* 714 F.3d 150 (3d Cir. 2013); *Hosh v. Lucero,* 680 F.3d 375 (4th Cir. 2012).

[142] *See* 8 CFR §§1001.1(q), 1003.19(h)(2)(i)(B).

[143] INA §236(c)(2).

[144] *See* Homeland Security Act of 2002, Pub. L. No. 107–296, §§456, 1512, 1517, 116 Stat. 2135, 2200, 2310, 2311.

[145] INA §236(c).

[146] *Matter of Adeniji*, 22 I&N Dec. 1102 (BIA 1999).

➢ **Practice Pointer**: Even lawful permanent residents can be detained without bond under INA §236(c) while their removal proceedings are pending.[147]

➢ **Practice Pointer**: Under BIA precedent, a respondent is not properly subject to mandatory detention under INA §236(c) if the government is "substantially unlikely to prevail" on the charge of deportability or inadmissibility that allegedly triggers mandatory detention.[148] Thus, if a client is not properly subject to mandatory detention, practitioners should request a "*Joseph* Hearing" in order to challenge their client's ongoing detention under INA §236(c).

➢ **Practice Pointer**: For other useful practice tips, see the ACLU Immigrants' Rights Project's "Challenging Mandatory and Prolonged Detention Pending a Final Decision of Removal," available at *www.aclu.org/files/assets/mandatory_detention_tips_-_june_2013_final.pdf.*[149]

C. Terrorists

Individuals subject to removal on terrorist grounds are not eligible for release from detention.[150] "Suspected terrorists" may also be detained under a controversial certification process contained in the USA PATRIOT Act.[151] Under this section of the USA PATRIOT Act, the Attorney General or his or her deputy may certify a noncitizen as a "suspected terrorist" if he or she has "reasonable grounds to believe"

---

[147] *Demore v. Kim*, 538 U.S. 510 (2003) (upholding mandatory detention of a noncitizen who conceded deportability and was not eligible for relief from removal apart from withholding). For practice tips on distinguishing the *Kim* decision, see Am. Immigration Council, Legal Action Center Practice Advisory, *Mandatory Detention after Demore v. Kim* (Aug. 29, 2003), AILA InfoNet Doc. No. 03082948 (*posted* Aug. 29, 2003).

[148] *Matter of Joseph*, 22 I&N Dec. 799 (BIA 1999).

[149] (last visited Feb. 17, 2015).

[150] INA §236(c)(1)(D); 8 USC §1226(c)(1)(D) (2012); 8 CFR §1003.19(h)(2)(i) (2014); *Matter of Khalifah*, 21 I&N Dec. 107 (BIA 1995) (finding that a respondent subject to criminal proceedings for alleged terrorist activities in the country to which DHS seeks to deport him is appropriately ordered detained without bond as a poor bail risk). *But see* INA §236(c)(2); 8 USC §1226(c)(2) (2012) (allowing the AG to release such individuals if necessary to provide protection to a witness or person cooperating in the investigation of major criminal activity and the individual would not be a danger to the safety of persons or property). This authority to release extends to the DHS secretary and DHS officials. *See* Homeland Security Act of 2002, Pub. L. No. 107–296, §§456, 1512, 1517, 116 Stat. 2135, 2200, 2310, 2311.

[151] *See* INA §236A; 8 USC §1226a (2012). For further discussion, see chapter 2.7.2; *see also* Office of the Inspector General, *The September 11 Detainees: A Review of the Treatment of Aliens Held on Immigration Charges in Connection with the Investigation of the September 11 Attacks* (June 2, 2003), *available at* www.usdoj.gov/oig/special/0306/index.htm; Am. Civil Liberties Union, *America's Disappeared: Seeking International Justice for Immigrants Detained After September 11* (Jan. 2004), *available at www.aclu.org/SafeandFree/SafeandFree.cfm?ID=14800&c=207*.

the individual falls within one of seven security-related grounds of inadmissibility or deportability, or engages in any other activity that endangers the national security of the United States.[152] This section allows for the detention of noncitizens who seek to overthrow the U.S. government by force or violence, and those who have or are likely to engage in terrorist activity. It also permits the detention of noncitizens who are merely the spouse or child of a "suspected terrorist" or who are mere members of foreign terrorist organizations, without any allegations that they actually engaged in culpable conduct.[153] The individual may be detained even if "relief from removal [is] granted."[154] A person granted asylum or withholding of removal who has been found not to be a threat to national security could, nevertheless, be detained as a "suspected terrorist." To date, no noncitizens have been subject to detention under this provision.[155]

D. Individuals with Final Orders of Removal

An individual with a final order of removal, deportation, or exclusion is not eligible for release from detention. However, even individuals with final orders may be released eventually. As discussed above, the Supreme Court in *Zadvydas v. Davis* held that noncitizens with final orders of removal could not be detained indefinitely.[156] If the country designated for removal or a third country will not accept him or her, and if there is no significant likelihood of removal in the reasonably foreseeable future, the individual should be released.[157]

➢ **Practice Pointer**: It may be possible to challenge an underlying final order if the individual is a United States citizen or if there were serious due process violations in arriving at the final order, including if the individual was never asked about fear. See chapters 11 and 12 of this book for a detailed discussion of administrative and judicial review of removal orders.

This is significant for asylum-seekers because individuals who have been granted withholding of removal under INA §241(b)(3) or withholding or deferral of removal under the CAT have a final order of removal entered against them in conjunction with the granting of withholding or deferral relief. Although ICE policy generally is to favor release of an individual who has been granted withholding of removal under INA §241(b)(3) or withholding or deferral of removal under the CAT,[158] ICE may choose to continue to detain the individual while seeking to remove him or her to

---

[152] INA §236A(a)(3)(A); 8 USC §1226a(a)(3)(A) (2012).

[153] INA §236A(a)(3)(A); 8 USC §1226a(a)(3)(A) (2012).

[154] INA §236A(a)(2); 8 USC §1226a(a)(2) (2012).

[155] *But see, e.g., Al–Siddiqi v. Achim*, 531 F.3d 490 (7th Cir. 2008).

[156] *Zadvydas v. Davis*, 533 U.S. 678 (2001).

[157] *Id.*; *see* 8 CFR §241.13(b)(2) (2014).

[158] Garcia Memorandum, *supra* note 65.

another country (a country other than the country to which removal has been withheld by the IJ). If there is no significant likelihood of removal in the reasonably foreseeable future, however, the individual should be released pursuant to *Zadvydas v. Davis* and the implementing regulations, which set forth the procedures for reviewing cases of individuals in detention with final orders of removal.[159] The maximum period of time that an individual may be kept in detention following a final order of removal is six months.[160] The six-month period begins when the IJ's order of removal becomes final.[161]

IV. Legal Standards and Procedures for Seeking Release

If the grounds of ineligibility for release do not apply, DHS should not detain an individual unless there is a risk that he or she will abscond, the individual poses a danger to persons or property, or the individual poses a risk to national security that cannot be mitigated by bond or other alternatives to detention.[162] This standard for custody and bond determinations was declared in *Matter of Patel*,[163] a case in which the BIA ordered the release of the respondent from detention on his own recognizance, after the IJ had reduced bond from $1,000 to $500. The *Matter of Patel* standard has been reaffirmed consistently and without modification.[164]

➢ **Practice Pointer**: In 2014, DHS issued a policy memorandum advising when detention should be used and when individuals should be released.[165] It states, "Absent extraordinary circumstances or the requirement of mandatory detention, field office directors should not expend detention resources on aliens who are known to be suffering from serious physical or mental illness, who are disabled, elderly, pregnant, or nursing, who demonstrate that they are primary caretakers of children or an infirm person, or whose detention is otherwise not in

---

159 *Zadvydas*, 533 U.S. at 678; 8 CFR §241.13(b) (2014).

160 8 CFR §241.13(b)(2)(ii) (2014); *Zadvydas*, 533 U.S. at 678.

161 8 CFR §§241.13(b)(2)(ii), 1241.1 (2014).

162 *Matter of Adeniji*, 22 I&N Dec. 1102, 1107–11 (BIA 1999); *Matter of Patel*, 15 I&N Dec. 666 (BIA 1976). *See also* 8 CFR §1003.19(h)(3) (2014) (stating that if an individual "is likely to appear for any scheduled proceeding or interview," release is favored).

163 *Matter of Patel*, 15 I&N Dec. 666 (BIA 1976).

164 *Matter of Adeniji*, 22 I&N Dec. at 1107–11; *Matter of Shaw*, 17 I&N Dec. 177, 178 (BIA 1979); *Matter of Andrade*, 19 I&N Dec. 488 (BIA 1987); *Matter of Vea*, 18 I&N Dec. 171, 174 (BIA 1981); *Matter of Spilionoulos*, 16 I&N Dec. 561, 563 (BIA 1978).

165 ICE, Johnson Memorandum, *Policies for the Apprehension, Detention and Removal of Undocumented Immigrants*, at 5 (Nov. 20, 2014), *available at www.dhs.gov/sites/default/files/publications/14_1120_memo_prosecutorial_discretion.pdf* (last visited Apr. 1, 2015).

the public interest."[166] Practitioners should rely on this language as a basis for arguing for their client's release.

An individual is more likely to meet his or her burden and merit a discretionary release if he or she demonstrates a stable address, work history, and family ties in the United States.[167] Additionally, "a strong likelihood that [an individual] will be granted relief from removal and thus [has] great incentive to appear for further hearings," favors release.[168] A bond may be set to provide assurance that a respondent will attend future hearings. An "appearance bond," however, is not required. As the BIA states in *Matter of Drysdale*, "Once it is determined that an alien does not present a danger to the community or any bail risk, then no bond should be required."[169]

There are two main avenues for seeking an individual's release from detention if he or she is eligible for release: (1) seeking parole or release from ICE; or (2) if ICE decides to maintain custody of the individual, seeking bond before an IJ in bond redetermination proceedings. Any request for release should discuss the following factors:

- Is the individual a flight risk?[170] Address likelihood of a grant of relief from removal,[171] whether the individual has a fixed address,[172] length of residence in the community,[173] the existence of family and community ties,[174] stable employment history,[175] whether the individual has ever tried to flee or escape the authorities,[176] and the individual's history of appearing upon request;[177]

---

[166] *Id.*

[167] *Matter of X–K–*, 23 I&N Dec. 731, 736 (BIA 2005).

[168] *Id.*

[169] *Matter of Drysdale*, 20 I&N Dec. 815, 817 (BIA 1994).

[170] *See Matter of Guerra*, 24 I&N Dec. 37, 40 (BIA 2006).

[171] *Matter of X–K–*, 23 I&N Dec. 731, 736 (BIA 2005).

[172] *Matter of Guerra*, 24 I&N Dec. at 37; *Matter of Patel*, 15 I&N Dec. 666 (BIA 1979).

[173] *Matter of Guerra*, 24 I&N Dec. at 37; *Matter of Andrade*, 19 I&N Dec. 488 (BIA 1987); *Matter of Shaw*, 17 I&N Dec. 177 (BIA 1979).

[174] *Matter of Guerra*, 24 I&N Dec. at 37; *Matter of Andrade*, 19 I&N Dec. at 488; *Matter of Shaw*, 17 I&N Dec. at 177; *Matter of Patel*, 15 I&N Dec. 666 (BIA 1979); *Matter of Sniliopoulos*, 16 I&N Dec. 561, 563 (BIA 1978) (holding that a $1,500 bond was appropriate for an Argentine respondent who had overstayed his B2 visa and had no family ties that entitled him to reside in the U.S. permanently in the future).

[175] *Matter of Guerra*, 24 I&N Dec. at 37; *Matter of Andrade*, 19 I&N Dec. at 488; *Matter of Shaw*, 17 I&N Dec. at 177; *Matter of Patel*, 15 I&N Dec. 666 (BIA 1979).

[176] *Matter of Guerra*, 24 I&N Dec. at 37; *Matter of Patel*, 15 I&N Dec. at 666; *Matter of San Martin*, 15 I&N Dec. 167 (BIA 1974).

[177] *Matter of Guerra*, 24 I&N Dec. at 37; *Matter of Andrade*, 19 I&N Dec. at 488; *Matter of Shaw*, 17 I&N Dec. at 177; *Matter of Patel*, 15 I&N Dec. at 666; *Matter of San Martin*, 15 I&N Dec. at 167.

- Is the individual a danger to persons or property? Address the existence of any criminal record,[178] any past immigration violations,[179] any past activities or affiliations with dangerous groups,[180] and the individual's reasons for entering the United States; and
- Is the individual a danger to national security? Address any past activities or affiliations with dangerous groups[181] and the individual's reasons for entering the United States.

  - **Practice Pointer**: Recently, in the context of refugees crossing the border and seeking protection after being subject to expedited removal procedures, DHS has asserted that asylum-seekers should not be released, even on bond, because release would implicate the national security interests of the United States. DHS argues that the detention of asylum-seekers is necessary to deter future asylum-seekers from crossing the southern border and to disrupt "active migration networks" in protecting national security. In making this argument, DHS asserts that *Matter of D–J–* applies.[182] Under *Matter of D–J–*, an IJ must review the custody redetermination of an individual in light of any Executive Branch statements that, because of a mass migration concerns, individual liberty interests weigh less.[183] Practitioners should argue that there is no declared national emergency that would trigger *Matter of D–J–* review, and distinguish the facts of that case from those of their

---

[178] *Matter of Guerra*, 24 I&N Dec. at 37 (finding that the IJ may consider evidence that the respondent was criminally charged in an alleged controlled substance trafficking scheme, even if the respondent was not convicted of a criminal offense); *Matter of Andrade*, 19 I&N Dec. at 488; *Matter of Shaw*, 17 I&N Dec. at 177 (finding that a $5,000 bond was appropriate in the case of a Jamaican respondent who awaited criminal charges for possession of firearms); *Matter of San Martin*, 15 I&N Dec. at 167 (finding that a high bond of $15,000 was appropriate where the respondent, a Colombian citizen, had been convicted of an illegal drug possession, was under pending charges for illegal cocaine possession, and failed to appear in criminal court).

[179] *Matter of Guerra*, 24 I&N Dec. at 37; *Matter of Andrade*, 19 I&N Dec. at 488 (noting that the respondent failed to appear at his scheduled deportation hearing); *Matter of Shaw*, 17 I&N Dec. at 177; *Matter of San Martin*, 15 I&N Dec. at 167 (finding that a high bond of $15,000 was appropriate where the respondent, a Colombian citizen, had previously been ordered deported and had illegally reentered the country); *Matter of Moise*, 12 I&N Dec. 102 (BIA 1967).

[180] *See, e.g., Matter of Khalifah*, 21 I&N Dec. 107 (BIA 1995) (finding that a respondent subject to criminal proceedings for alleged terrorist activities in the country to which DHS seeks to deport him is appropriately ordered detained without bond as a poor bail risk)

[181] *See, e.g., Matter of Khalifah*, 21 I&N Dec. 107 (BIA 1995) (finding that a respondent subject to criminal proceedings for alleged terrorist activities in the country to which DHS seeks to deport him is appropriately ordered detained without bond as a poor bail risk)

[182] *Matter of D–J–*, 23 I&N Dec. 572 (AG 2003).

[183] *Id.* at 582–83.

client's.[184] It is possible that DHS's "detain-to-deter" policy will soon end, however. In February of 2015, in response to a class action lawsuit, a judge for the U.S. District Court for the District of Columbia granted a preliminary injunction to prevent DHS from detaining class members for the purpose of deterring future immigration to the United States and from considering deterrence of future immigration as a factor in custody determinations.[185] For helpful guidance for understanding the impact of this injunction and how it is implemented, see the American Civil Liberties Union's Practice Advisory on *RILR v. Johnson*, available at *www.aclu.org/sites/default/files/assets/updated_rilr_advisory_03.03.15.pdf.*[186]

A. Requests for Release (or Parole) to ICE

Individuals who are considered under current law *not* to be eligible for a bond hearing before an IJ include: (1) individuals seeking admission to the United States at a port of entry, *i.e.*, "arriving aliens," as defined in 8 CFR §1001.1(q); (2) individuals subject to INA §236(c); and (3) individuals subject to deportation based on security-related grounds.[187] Rather than seeking bond before an IJ as described below in Part IV.B., these individuals must seek release or parole directly from ICE.

In general, parole requests should be made in writing to the District Director for the ICE Enforcement and Removal Office having jurisdiction over the individual's place of detention. The request should be in the form of a letter and should include the following information:

- The individual's name and A-number (as well as the name and A-numbers of any detained dependents);
- Reference to the applicable legal standard for release;
- The reasons why the individual meets the legal requirements for release;

---

[184] *See* 50 USC §1622(d) (2012); *Matter of D–J–*, 23 I&N Dec. at 580. In *Matter of D–J–*, the Attorney General stated that, where a National Emergency has been cleared, it may be appropriate to consider national security interests implicated by the encouragement of further unlawful mass migrations and the release of undocumented migrants into the U.S. without adequate screening. However, the Attorney General carefully tailored his opinion to apply when "[u]nder the circumstances of a declared National Emergency" a mass migration would strain DHS's ability to investigate the individual status of a noncitizen. *Id.* The National Emergency in *Matter of D–J–* concerned the use of Haiti as a staging ground for terrorist activity from Pakistan. *Id.; see* Declaration of National Emergency by Reason of Certain Terrorist Attacks, Proclamation 7463, 66 Fed. Reg. 48199 (Sept. 18, 2001).

[185] *R.I. L–R–, et al., v. Jeh Charles Johnson, et al.,* 1:15–cv–00011–JEB (D.D.C. Feb. 20, 2015).

[186] (last visited Apr. 1, 2015).

[187] 8 CFR §1003.19(h)(2)(i) (2014); *see Matter of Oseiwusu*, 22 I&N Dec. 19 (BIA 1998) (holding that an IJ has no authority over the custody of "arriving aliens," including an individual granted advance parole). These individuals may, however, request release from the district director, subject to the limitations discussed in this chapter at 3.8.2. and 3.8.4.

- An explanation why the individual is not a flight risk or a danger to the community;
- The full address where the individual will reside if parole is granted; and
- Any compelling humanitarian or positive discretionary factors.

Supporting documentation should be attached to this letter request. This documentation may include:

- A letter from the sponsor, relative, or friend with whom the individual will reside upon release (should be a U.S. citizen or lawful permanent resident who can support the individual financially during the course of removal proceedings and help him or her appear for all future proceedings before DHS or the immigration court);
- Proof of family ties in the United States (U.S. citizen or lawful permanent resident family members — evidence of their lawful immigration status and U.S. addresses);
- Evidence of ties to the community (involvement in a religious community, volunteer or charitable activities, school attendance, long-term residence in a particular neighborhood or community, etc.);
- Proof of property in the United States;
- Work history and evidence of stable employment in the United States;
- Proof of the individual's serious medical or mental health conditions (if applicable);
- Evidence of rehabilitation and good moral character (if the person has any criminal convictions);
- Evidence of the likelihood of relief in removal proceedings (strength of applications for relief, a committed attorney or representative, etc.); and
- Certified English translations for all non–English language documents.[188]

> ➢ **Practice Pointer**: Since DHS's determination to release or parole an individual is discretionary, its parole procedures change periodically as a result of changes in DHS policy, lawsuits filed on behalf of detainees, and instructions from the current administration. Thus, practitioners should research the current DHS procedures and guidelines prior to filing these requests. For a recent articulation of DHS's policy with regard to detention, see ICE's November 20, 2014 memorandum, "Policies for the Apprehension, Detention and Removal of

---

[188] For a more thorough explanation of the parole process, *see* Florence Immigrant and Refugee Rights Project, *How to Apply to the Department of Homeland Security for Release from Immigration Custody* (Mar. 2002), *available at www.lirs.org/InfoRes/PDFs/FlorenceProSe/Release–E.pdf.*

Undocumented Immigrants," available at *www.dhs.gov/sites/default/files/publications/14_1120_memo_prosecutorial_discretion.pdf.*[189]

- **Practice Pointer**: DHS often will agree to release an individual; however such release may be conditional or the individual may be subject to alternatives to detention, such as bond payments to secure future appearances, ankle monitors, or Orders of Supervision. For example, ICE's only official alternative to detention program is known as "ISAP," the Intensive Supervision Appearance Program. ISAP supervises participants with the use of electronic ankle monitors, installation of biometric voice recognition software, unannounced home visits, employer verification, and in-person reporting.[190] It is currently in its third iteration — "ISAP III."[191]

1. Requests for Release by Those Apprehended at the Border or a Port of Entry

An individual who is apprehended at a port of entry with false or no documents and is subject to expedited removal is not eligible for parole unless he or she demonstrates that "parole is required to meet a medical emergency or is necessary for a legitimate law enforcement purpose."[192] However, an individual subject to expedited removal who is found to have a credible fear of persecution or torture and referred to INA §240 removal proceedings before an IJ to apply for asylum or protection under the Convention Against Torture may be released upon demonstrating his or her true identity, that he or she has a sponsor (a person with legal status willing to provide food and shelter), and that he or she will report for all immigration appointments and hearings.[193] If the individual is subject to certain criminal or security-related bars, he or she is not likely to be paroled.[194]

---

[189] ICE, Johnson Memorandum, *Policies for the Apprehension, Detention and Removal of Undocumented Immigrants*, at 5 (Nov. 20, 2014), ("Absent extraordinary circumstances or the requirement of mandatory detention, field office directors should not expend detention resources on aliens who are known to be suffering from serious physical or mental illness, who are disabled, elderly , pregnant, or nursing, who demonstrate that they are primary caretakers of children or an infirm person, or whose detention is otherwise not in the public interest."), *available at www.dhs.gov/sites/default/files/publications/14_1120_memo_prosecutorial_discretion.pdf* (last visited Apr. 1, 2015).

[190] Office of Inspector General, *U.S. Immigration and Customs Enforcement's Alternatives to Detention* (Feb. 4, 2015), AILA InfoNet Doc. No. 15021866 (posted Feb. 18, 2015), *available at www.aila.org/infonet/dhs–oig–report–ice–alternatives–to–dentention?utm_source=Recent%20Postings%20Alert&utm_medium=Email&utm_campaign=RP%20Daily* (last visited Feb. 19, 2015).

[191] *See* Lutheran Immigrant and Refugee Services Backgrounder, *Alternatives to Detention (ATD): History and Recommendations*, *available at http://lirs.org/wp–content/uploads/2013/04/LIRS–Backgrounder–on–Alternatives–to–Detention–3–12–13.pdf* (last visited Apr. 1, 2015).

[192] 8 CFR §§235.3(b)(2)(iii), 1235.3(b)(2)(iii) (2014).

[193] *See Matter of X–K–*, 23 I&N Dec. 731 (BIA 2005) (holding that a respondent initially screened in the expedited removal process, but who is subsequently placed in INA §240 proceedings following a positive credible fear determination, is eligible for a custody redetermination hearing before an IJ unless

Continued

Initially, DHS applied a fairly generous standard for release to individuals subject to expedited removal who had been found by an asylum officer or IJ to have a "credible fear" of persecution.[195] Releasing such individuals enables them to have access to legal counsel and interpreters, evidence, medical and mental health care, and other necessities in preparing and presenting an asylum claim.

In the past, individuals found to have a credible fear of persecution or torture were eligible for parole if they were able to establish: (1) their identity; (2) community ties; and (3) that they are not subject to any bars to asylum involving violence or misconduct.[196] Nevertheless, in some districts, asylum-seekers found to have a credible fear were denied any opportunity for release.[197]

On November 6, 2007, however, the Bush administration's DHS issued a now-superseded policy memorandum regarding the parole of asylum-seekers who had established a credible fear of persecution or torture.[198] The policy provided that parole decisions would be made on a case-by-case basis for urgent humanitarian reasons or significant public benefit.[199] Those found to have a credible fear would only be considered for parole if they fell within one of the categories set forth in 8 CFR §212.5(b).[200]

Those categories included:

(1) individuals with serious medical conditions;

(2) pregnant women;

---

he or she is a member of any of the listed classes of respondents who are specifically excluded from an IJ's custody jurisdiction).

[194] *See* Memorandum from Michael Pearson on Expedited Removal: Additional Policy Guidance (Dec. 30, 1997), AILA InfoNet Doc. No. 97123091 (*posted* Dec. 30, 1997), *reprinted in* 75 *Interpreter Releases* 270 (Feb. 23, 1998).

[195] See chapter 6 for a detailed discussion of the credible and reasonable fear legal standards and procedures.

[196] *See* Pearson Mem. on Expedited Removal, *supra* note 194.

[197] *See, e.g.*, U.S. Comm'n on Int'l Religious Freedom, *Expedited Removal Study Report Card: 2 Years Later* (Feb. 8, 2007), at 5, *available at www.uscirf.gov/reports/scorecard_FINAL.pdf* (noting the wide variation in release rates across the country for FY 2003, from 0.5 percent in New Orleans to 98 percent in Harlingen, and that the average detention period for an asylum–seeker found to have a credible fear is 60 days); Lawyers Comm. for Human Rights, *Refugees Behind Bars: The Imprisonment of Asylum Seekers in the Wake of the 1996 Immigration Act* (Aug. 1999), *available at www.humanrightsfirst.org/pubs/descriptions/behindbars.htm*; Lawyers Comm. for Human Rights, *Slamming the Golden Door: A Year of Expedited Removal* (Mar. 1998), *available at www.humanrightsfirst.org/pubs/descriptions/golden.htm*; AILA, *Credible Fear Screening for Individuals in Expedited Removal*, 16 AILA MONTHLY MAILING 1027 (Dec. 1997).

[198] *See* ICE Memorandum on Parole of Arriving Aliens Found to Have a "Credible Fear" of Persecution or Torture (Nov. 6, 2007), *available at http://bibdaily.com*, and on the "Archive Search" box, type in "New ICE "Credible Fear" Parole Policy.

[199] *Id.* at 4.

[200] *Id.*

(3) juveniles;

(4) witnesses in judicial, administrative, or legislative proceedings; and

(5) individuals whose detention is not in the public interest.[201]

DHS would make a threshold assessment regarding whether the asylum-seeker, who had been found to have a credible fear, had established:

(1) his or her identity;

(2) that he or she did not pose a flight risk; and

(3) he or she was not a danger to the community.[202]

Then DHS would determine whether the individual fell within any of the categories set forth in 8 CFR §212.5(b).[203] With regard to the last category — individuals whose detention is not in the public interest — DHS acknowledged that "the term 'public interest' [was] not amenable to a single, standard definition" and, therefore, the decision to grant parole on this basis had to be documented by a well-reasoned justification.[204] Almost immediately, human rights and asylum advocates criticized this change in policy.[205]

DHS's 2007 policy has now been superseded by its 2009 policy directive addressing parole of arriving aliens found to have a credible fear of persecution or torture.[206] This current policy directive addresses the fifth regulatory category of individuals who may be considered for parole following a finding of credible fear – those whose detention is not in the public interest.[207] The policy directive states that "[p]arole remains an inherently discretionary determination entrusted to the agency; this directive serves to guide the exercise of that discretion."[208] It specifies the standard for release and procedures for considering parole eligibility. According to the 2009 policy directive, an individual found to have a credible fear of persecution or torture should be paroled if the Immigration and Customs Enforcement officer determines that:

(1) the individual's identity is sufficiently established;

(2) he or she does not pose a flight risk;

---

[201] 8 CFR §212.5(b) (2014).

[202] ICE Memorandum, *supra* note 198, at 6.

[203] *Id.* at 6–7.

[204] *Id.* at 7–8.

[205] *See* Human Rights First letter to Julie Myers, ICE Assistant Secretary (Nov. 15, 2007), *available at www.humanrightsfirst.info/pdf/071120–asy–hrf–ltr–ice–parole–dir.pdf*; *see also* USCIRF letter to DHS Security Secretary Chertoff (Nov. 15, 2007), *available at www.uscirf.gov/index.php?option=com_content&task=view&id=45&Itemid=47.*

[206] ICE Policy Directive from John Morton on Parole of Arriving Aliens, *supra* note 66.

[207] 8 CFR §212.5(b) (2014).

[208] ICE Policy Directive from John Morton on Parole of Arriving Aliens, *supra* note 66, at 2.

(3) he or she is not a danger to the community; and

(4) no additional factors weigh against his or her release.[209]

Under the current policy, as soon as practicable following a finding of credible fear, the ICE Field Office with custody of the individual shall provide him or her with the *Parole Advisal and Scheduling Notification* and explain the contents to him or her, through an interpreter if necessary.[210] The officer will then complete the relevant portions of the notification, indicating the time when the individual will receive an initial interview on his or her eligibility for parole and the due date and instructions for submitting any documentary evidence the individual may wish the officer to consider.[211] No later than seven days following a finding that the individual has a credible fear, an ICE officer must conduct an interview with the individual to assess his or her eligibility for parole.[212] Within that same time period, the officer must complete the *Record of Determination/Parole Determination Worksheet* and submit it for supervisory review.[213]

The parole decision must be provided in writing to the individual within seven days of the parole interview. If the officer concludes that parole should be denied, the officer must draft a letter explaining the reasons for denying parole and notifying the individual that he or she may request redetermination of parole based on changed circumstances or additional evidence relevant to his or her identity, security risk, or risk of absconding.[214] The office must provide that letter, along with the completed *Record of Determination/Parole Determination Worksheet* to the Field Office Director, Deputy Field Office Director, or Assistant Field Office Director for signature.[215] The written response is then provided to the individual or, if represented, his or her legal representative.[216] On the other hand, if the officer determines that parole should be granted, the individual will be provided with a date-stamped I-94 bearing the notation, "Paroled under 8 CFR §212.5(b). Employment authorization not to be provided on this basis."[217] The individual may present a written request for redetermination of any decision denying parole and the ICE Field Office may consider such requests in its discretion.[218]

---

[209] *Id.* at 6.

[210] *Id.* at 5–6.

[211] *Id.* at 6.

[212] *Id.*

[213] *Id.*

[214] *Id.*

[215] *Id.*

[216] *Id.* at 9.

[217] *Id.*

[218] *Id.*

The 2009 policy directive, however, only applies to individuals who arrive at ports of entry, not those apprehended between ports of entry.[219] For those individuals arriving at ports of entry, DHS increasingly has exercised its discretion not to release individuals found to have a credible fear of persecution and torture. For example, in the summer and fall of 2014, and continuing to this day, in an effort to deter future border-crossers, the Obama administration increased its detention of women and children asylum-seekers, refusing parole outright and opposing any release from detention, even after credible fear of persecution or torture had been demonstrated, arguing that they posed a national security risk under *Matter of D–J–*.[220] This policy has now been enjoined; however, the administration has built and opened a new family detention center to house up to 2,400 people in Dilley, Texas in anticipation of 2015 border-crossers.[221] Thus, it seems that family detention will continue, even if it is no longer under the auspices of *Matter of D–J–* and the need to deter future migration flows.

- **Practice Pointer**: If a client is not paroled following a credible fear finding, practitioners should seek bond before the IJ in INA §240 proceedings.[222] Bond procedures are described below in Part IV.B. of this chapter.

Some individuals apprehended upon arrival at the border or a port of entry, however, may not be subject to expedited removal. These individuals may be paroled upon demonstrating that there are "urgent humanitarian reasons" or that there would be a "significant public benefit" if he or she is released or paroled.[223] An individual may meet this burden by showing that he or she has a serious medical condition, is pregnant, or a juvenile (if an appropriate relative or nonrelative may take custody).[224]

An individual arriving at the border or a port of entry or who has had his or her parole status revoked and who is subject to the criminal grounds for detention under INA §236(c)(1) may only be released on parole upon a showing that it is necessary to provide protection to a witness or person cooperating in the investigation of major criminal activity and the individual would not be a danger to the safety of persons or property.[225]

---

[219] *Id.*

[220] *See Matter of D–J–*, 23 I&N Dec. 572 (A.G. 2003).

[221] *See* ICE Press Release on Dilley, *supra* note 33; Preston, *Detention Center Presented as Deterrent*, *supra* note 69; Hylton, *supra* note 31.

[222] *Matter of X–K–*, 23 I&N Dec. 731 (BIA 2005) (rejecting DHS's argument that an immigration judge (IJ) could not conduct a bond hearing for an individual who entered without inspection, was placed in expedited removal, and was later referred for INA §240 proceedings).

[223] INA §212(d)(5)(A); 8 USC §1182(d)(5)(A) (2012).

[224] 8 CFR §§212.5(b)(1)–(3) (2014).

[225] *See* INA §236(c)(2); 8 USC §1226(c)(2) (2012).

2. *Requests for Release by Those Granted Relief but Who Have Final Orders of Removal*

ICE must release an individual who is granted asylum from immigration detention. Although ICE policy generally is to favor release of an individual granted protection, if an individual is detained when he or she is granted withholding of removal under INA §241(b)(3) or withholding or deferral of removal under the CAT, ICE may choose to continue to detain the individual while seeking to remove him or her to another country (a country other than the country to which removal has been withheld by the IJ).[226] As discussed above, if there is no significant likelihood of removal in the reasonably foreseeable future, however, the individual should be released.[227] While making this determination, ICE may continue to detain the individual. In general, however, ICE cannot continue to detain an individual indefinitely following a final order of removal. The U.S. Supreme Court in *Zadvydas v. Davis* held that it is illegal for ICE to continue to detain individuals where they cannot be removed in the reasonably foreseeable future.[228] The maximum period of time that an individual may be kept in detention following a final order of removal is six months.[229] The six-month period begins when the IJ's order of removal becomes final.[230]

Procedurally, after the 90-day removal period expires, ICE must begin custody review procedures, and a detained individual may seek review of his or her custody status by ICE following expiration of the 90-day removal period.[231] The individual should prepare and send a written request for release asserting why there is no significant likelihood that he or she will be removed in the reasonably foreseeable future.[232] Any supporting documentation should be attached. ICE must respond in writing within 10 business days of receiving the request to acknowledge receipt of the request and explain the procedures that will be used to evaluate the request.[233]

In evaluating the request, ICE will consider the following factors in determining whether to release an individual:

- The history of the individual's efforts to comply with the order of removal;
- The history of DHS's efforts to remove individuals to the country in question or to third countries, including the ongoing nature of DHS's efforts to remove the individual and his or her assistance with those efforts;

---

[226] Garcia Memorandum, *supra* note 65.

[227] 8 CFR §241.13(b) (2014).

[228] *Zadvydas v. Davis*, 533 U.S. 678 (2001). *See* 8 CFR §241.13(b)(2) (2014).

[229] 8 CFR §241.13(b)(2)(ii); *Zadvydas*, 533 U.S. at 678.

[230] 8 CFR §§241.13(b)(2)(ii), 1241.1 (2014).

[231] 8 CFR §241.13(a) (2014).

[232] 8 CFR §241.13(d)(1) (2014).

[233] 8 CFR §241.13(e)(1) (2014).

- The reasonably foreseeable results of those efforts; and
- The views of the Department of State regarding the prospects for removal of individuals to the country or countries in question.[234]

In most cases, continued detention is improper and contrary to ICE's own policy favoring release of individuals granted relief by an IJ, absent exceptional concerns such as national security issues or danger to the community and absent any requirement under law to detain.[235] ICE must issue a written decision based on the administrative record, including any documentation provided by the individual, regarding the likelihood of removal and whether there is a significant likelihood that the individual will be removed in the reasonably foreseeable future under the circumstances.[236]

> ➢ **Practice Pointer**: Practitioners should assist their clients in preparing and sending to ICE the written request for release asserting why there is no significant likelihood that their client will be removed in the reasonably foreseeable future.[237] Any supporting documentation should be attached. For detailed guidance on what such a request should look like and what supporting documentation should be included, see the PAIR Project's manual, "Getting Out of Detention After an Order of Deportation: Post-Order Custody Reviews and Habeas Corpus," available at *www.pairproject.org/images/Habeas.pdf.*[238]

If ICE determines that there is no significant likelihood that the individual will be removed in the reasonably foreseeable future, ICE must advise the individual.[239] Unless there are special circumstances justifying continued detention, ICE must promptly make arrangements for the individual's release.[240] ICE may establish appropriate conditions for release.[241] For example, ICE may decide to release an individual granted withholding or deferral of removal under an "Order of Supervision" that requires him or her to report regularly with ICE either in person or

---

[234] 8 CFR §241.13(f) (2014).

[235] 8 CFR §241.13(e) (2014) *See* ICE Field Guidance from Gary Mead on Reminder on Detention Policy Where an Immigration Judge has Granted Asylum, Withholding of Removal or CAT (Mar. 6, 2012), *available at http://immigrantjustice.org/sites/immigrantjustice.org/files/March%206,%202012 %20ERO%20Field%20Guidance%20Reminder.pdf* (last visited Feb. 16, 2015) (citing Bo Cooper Memorandum on Detention and Release during the Removal Period of Aliens Granted Withholding or Deferral of Removal (Apr. 21, 2000) & Michael Garcia Memorandum on Detention Policy Where an Immigration Judge Has Granted Asylum and ICE Has Appealed (Feb. 9, 2004)).

[236] 8 CFR §241.13(g) (2014).

[237] 8 CFR §241.13(d)(1) (2014).

[238] (last visited Feb. 16, 2015).

[239] 8 CFR §241.13(g)(1) (2014).

[240] *Id.*

[241] *Id.*

by phone, as well as a number of other requirements.[242] The purpose of these orders is to protect public safety and to promote the ability of ICE to effect the individual's removal should circumstances change in the future.[243] Violation of an Order of Supervision could have very serious consequences, including a withdrawal of the release approval and detention anew.[244] ICE may revoke its decision to release the individual at any time in order to remove him or her (for example, if circumstances change and there is a significant likelihood that the individual may be removed in the reasonably foreseeable future).[245]

On the other hand, ICE may determine that there is a significant likelihood that the individual will be removed in the reasonably foreseeable future. Under these circumstances, ICE will deny any requests for release and advise the individual that his or her detention will continue.[246] If an individual remains in ICE custody beyond six months after the IJ's order became final, however, he or she may seek release through a petition for a writ of habeas corpus under 28 USC §2241 — the mechanism for challenging his or her detention in federal court. This is because detention beyond six months is unlawful.[247]

B. Bond

Individuals apprehended by DHS in the interior of the United States who are in removal proceedings and who are not subject to the criminal bars under INA §236(c)(1), who have physically entered the country (legally or illegally), and who do not have an administrative final order of removal, deportation, or exclusion, are generally eligible for a bond hearing before an IJ.[248] The BIA also has held that an individual initially screened for expedited removal, who was subsequently placed in removal proceedings under INA §240, is eligible for a custody redetermination hearing before an IJ.[249]

An IJ may not, however, redetermine the custody conditions imposed by DHS with respect to:

---

[242] 8 CFR §§241.4, 241.13(b), 241.13(h)(1) (2014).

[243] 8 CFR §241.13(h)(1) (2014).

[244] 8 CFR §§241.13(h)(2), 241.13(i) (2014).

[245] 8 CFR §241.13(i)(2) (2014).

[246] 8 CFR §241.13(g)(2) (2014).

[247] 8 CFR §241.13(b)(2)(ii) (2014); *Zadvydas v. Davis*, 533 U.S. 678 (2001).

[248] 8 CFR §1003.19(h)(2)(i) (2014). For a more in–depth overview of bond hearing law and procedures, see M. Linsky and L. Palumbo, "A Practitioner's Guide to Representing Aliens Seeking Release on Bond in Removal Proceedings," 1 IMMIGRATION & NATIONALITY LAW HANDBOOK 219–29 (AILA 2004–05 Ed.).

[249] *Matter of X–K–*, 23 I&N Dec. 731 (BIA 2005) (holding that a respondent initially screened in the expedited removal process, but who is subsequently placed in INA §240 proceedings following a positive credible fear determination, is eligible for a custody redetermination hearing before an IJ unless he or she is a member of any of the listed classes of respondents who are specifically excluded from an IJ's custody jurisdiction).

(1) individuals in exclusion proceedings;

(2) "arriving aliens" in removal proceedings, including individuals paroled after arrival pursuant to INA §212(d)(5);

(3) individuals described in INA §237(a)(4) (deportable for security-related grounds);

(4) individuals in removal proceedings who are subject to mandatory detention under INA §236(c)(1); and

(5) individuals in deportation proceedings subject to INA §242(a)(2) (as in effect prior to April 1, 1997).[250]

Although individuals who fall within these categories may not seek custody or bond redetermination before the IJ, nothing prohibits these individuals from seeking redetermination of custody conditions directly with DHS.[251] Moreover, nothing prohibits these individuals from seeking an IJ's review of whether they are properly included in those categories.[252] For example, the government takes the position that refugees who have failed to adjust status after one year in the United States revert after a year to "arriving alien" status, and therefore, IJs have no jurisdiction over an individual bond hearing for such refugees.[253] Individuals admitted under the Visa Waiver Program who have not been served with a Form I-862, Notice to Appear (NTA) also are not eligible for a bond hearing before an IJ.[254] For those individuals who are eligible to seek custody or bond redetermination before an IJ, however, the procedures are outlined below.

1. Initial Custody Determination

The initial custody determination is made by DHS under 8 CFR §1236.1. DHS may decide to keep the individual in custody with no bond, release the individual on bond (the amount determined by ICE), release the individual through an alternative to detention program like ISAP, or release the individual on his or her own recognizance. The individual may request reconsideration of ICE's custody determination or modification of the terms and conditions of release directly from ICE at any time.[255]

A request for custody redetermination or modification of the terms and conditions of release to ICE should be made in writing to the District Director for the Enforcement and Removal Office having jurisdiction over the individual's place of

[250] 8 CFR §1003.19(h)(2)(i) (2014).

[251] 8 CFR §1003.19(h)(2)(ii) (2014).

[252] *Id.*

[253] 8 CFR §1003.19(h)(2)(i)(B) (2014) (declaring that IJs have no jurisdiction over bond hearings for arriving aliens in removal proceedings).

[254] *Matter of Werner*, 25 I&N Dec. 45 (BIA 2009).

[255] 8 CFR §1236.1(d)(2) (2014).

detention. The request should be in the form of a letter and should include the following information:

(1) the individual's name and A-number;

(2) the reasons why the individual meets the relevant legal requirements for release;

(3) why continued detention, an ankle monitor, or high bond amount are not necessary to ensure that the individual will appear for his or her future proceedings before DHS and the immigration court;

(4) that the individual is not a flight risk or danger to the community;

(5) the full address where the individual will reside;

(6) who will support him or her financially and assist the individual with appearing as requested;

(7) likelihood of relief in removal proceedings; and

(8) any compelling humanitarian or positive discretionary factors (family ties, ties to the community, property, stable employment, medical or mental health conditions, and rehabilitation or good moral character).

Documentation demonstrating each of these factors should be attached to the request.

2. Review of ICE Custody and Bond Determinations

After an initial custody or bond determination by ICE, the individual may request review of ICE's custody or bond determination by an IJ.[256] Even if the respondent has been released from custody on bond by DHS, he or she may request redetermination of bond or the conditions of release with the IJ, as long as he or she makes this request with the IJ within seven days of his or her release.[257] After expiration of the seven-day period, the respondent may request review by the district director of the conditions of his or her release.[258] Otherwise, a request for redetermination of ICE's custody decision may be made before the IJ at any time before a final order of removal is issued under 8 CFR §1240.[259] Such a request may even be made before any charging document has been filed with the immigration court by DHS.[260]

In certain circumstances, IJs have jurisdiction over custody determinations.[261] By regulation, an IJ does not have jurisdiction to conduct a bond hearing involving:

- Respondents in exclusion proceedings;
- "Arriving aliens" in removal proceedings;

---

[256] 8 CFR §§1236.1(d)(1); 1003.19(a) (2014).

[257] 8 CFR §1236.1(d)(1) (2014); ICPM, chapter 9.3(b).

[258] 8 CFR §1236.1(d)(2) (2014).

[259] *Id.*

[260] ICPM, chapter 9.3(b).

[261] *See generally*, 8 CFR §1003.19 (2014); ICPM, chapters 9.1(a), 9.3.

- Respondents ineligible for release on security or related grounds; and
- Respondents ineligible for release on certain criminal grounds.[262]

An IJ also does not have jurisdiction to conduct a bond hearing when a bond becomes moot, such as when a respondent:

- Departs from the United States, whether voluntarily or involuntarily;
- Is granted relief from removal by the IJ and DHS does not appeal;
- Is granted relief from removal by the BIA;
- Is denied relief from removal by the IJ and the respondent does not appeal; and
- Is denied relief from removal by the BIA.[263]

Finally, IJs do not have bond jurisdiction in certain limited proceedings, such as credible fear, reasonable fear, claimed status review, asylum-only, and withholding-only proceedings.[264]

Pursuant to this jurisdiction, IJs have the authority to keep individuals detained in custody, release them, and determine the amount of bond, if any, under which individuals are to be released.[265] However, IJs have no jurisdiction over the location of detention and the conditions in the detention facility.[266]

3. *Bond Motions*

Upon a respondent's request, an IJ may conduct a bond hearing, during which the IJ has the authority to determine the amount of bond set by DHS.[267] A request for custody redetermination is usually made by an oral or written "Bond Motion" or "Motion for Bond Redetermination."[268] Such a motion may also be made, at the discretion of the IJ, by telephone.[269]

A request for custody or bond redetermination should contain the following information: (1) the full name and A-number of the respondent; (2) the bond amount set by DHS, if any; and (3) the location of the detention facility, if the respondent is detained.[270]

---

[262] 8 CFR §1003.19(h)(2)(i) (2014); ICPM, chapter 9.3(b)(i).

[263] ICPM, chapter 9.3(b)(ii).

[264] ICPM, chapter 9.3(b)(iii). *See also* ICPM, chapter 7.4.

[265] 8 CFR §1236.1(d)(1) (2014).

[266] ICPM, chapter 9.1(b).

[267] *Matter of P–C–M–*, 20 I&N Dec. 432 (BIA 1991) (finding that an IJ may not redetermine custody status on his or her own motion, only upon application by the respondent or the respondent's representative); ICPM, chapter 9.3(a).

[268] 8 CFR §1003.19(b); ICPM, chapter 9.3(c).

[269] 8 CFR §1003.19(b); ICPM, chapter 9.3(c).

[270] ICPM, chapter 9.3(c)(i).

There is no filing fee.[271] However, if available, a copy of the NTA should be provided with the request.[272] If the request for a bond hearing is made orally, the respondent should file evidence in support of his or her request in open court.[273] If the request for a bond hearing is made in writing, the respondent should file his or her supporting evidence together with the request.[274] Although the deadlines and requirements for filings in Chapter 3 of the ICPM do not apply in bond proceedings (unless otherwise directed by the IJ),[275] a request for a custody or bond redetermination hearing should include the following documents:

- Form EOIR-28, Notice of Entry of Appearance as Attorney or Representative, if the respondent is represented;
- Cover page;
- Signed motion for bond redetermination hearing, setting forth the respondent's legal arguments for release and referencing his or her supporting evidence;
- Table of contents or index of exhibits listing the supporting evidence;
- Tabbed and page-numbered exhibits; and
- Proof of service.[276]

The request should be made to one of the following offices, in this designated order: (1) the immigration court having jurisdiction over the respondent's place of detention, if he or she is detained; (2) the immigration court having administrative control over the case; or (3) the Office of the Chief Immigration Judge in Falls Church, VA, for designation of an appropriate immigration court.[277]

4. *Bond Redetermination Hearings*

An IJ will review ICE's custody or bond determination in bond proceedings.[278] The bond redetermination hearing is separate and apart from, and may not form any part of, the removal hearings or proceedings.[279] In fact, the records are kept completely separate; the IJ creates a bond record that is separate from the Record of Proceedings for the respondent's other immigration court proceedings.[280] All testimony, exhibits, motions, and legal arguments in support of custody or bond

---

[271] ICPM, chapter 9.3(c)(ii).

[272] ICPM, chapter 9.3(c).

[273] ICPM, chapter 9.3(e)(v).

[274] *Id.*

[275] *Id.*

[276] See chapter 8 for a detailed discussion of filings in immigration court.

[277] 8 CFR §1003.19(c)(1)–(3) (2014); ICPM, chapter 9.3(c)(iii).

[278] 8 CFR §1003.19(a) (2014).

[279] 8 CFR §§1003.19(d) (2014), 1236.1; ICPM, chapter 9.3(a); *Matter of Chirinos*, 16 I&N Dec. 276 (BIA 1977) (stating that a bond hearing is a hearing separate and apart from other proceedings).

[280] ICPM, chapter 9.3(e)(iv).

redetermination are not considered in removal proceedings and are not part of the record in removal proceedings, and vice versa.

➢ **Practice Pointer**: Practitioners may need to submit the same documentation twice, once in support of the respondent's request for bond redetermination and a second time in support of the respondents' application for relief in removal proceedings. If an exhibit is submitted in support of bond, but not submitted in removal proceedings, it will not be considered as support for the respondent's application for relief.

➢ **Practice Pointer**: Given the separate nature of bond proceedings, some IJs allow attorneys or representatives to enter a limited appearance for purposes of the bond hearing only. However, many IJs do not allow this practice. Practitioners should always be cognizant of the fact that until withdrawal of their appearance has been granted by an IJ, they are still responsible for representing the respondent.[281]

Upon receipt of the respondent's request for a bond hearing, the immigration court schedules the hearing for the earliest possible date and notifies the respondent and DHS.[282] An IJ may also rule on a bond redetermination request without holding a hearing; however, this is unusual.[283] If the respondent requests a bond hearing during another type of hearing (for example, during a master calendar hearing in removal proceedings), the IJ may: (1) stop the other hearing and conduct a bond hearing on that date; (2) complete the other hearing and conduct a bond hearing on that date; (3) complete the other hearing and schedule a bond hearing for a later date; or (4) stop the other hearing and schedule a bond hearing for a later date.[284]

During a bond hearing, the IJ determines whether the respondent is eligible for bond.[285] If so, the IJ then considers whether the respondent's release would pose a danger to property or persons, whether the respondent is likely to appear for future immigration proceedings, and whether the respondent is a threat to national security.[286]

Bond redetermination hearings are less formal than master calendar or individual hearings in removal proceedings, and are usually not recorded.[287] They are held at the immigration court where the request for bond redetermination is filed.[288] The

---

[281] ICPM, chapter 2.3(d), 2.3(i)(ii).

[282] ICPM, chapter 9.3(d).

[283] *Id.*

[284] *Id.*

[285] ICPM, chapter 9.3(e).

[286] *Id.*

[287] *Id.*; *Matter of Chirinos*, 16 I&N Dec. 276 (BIA 1977) (noting that bond hearings are informal and that there is no right to a transcript).

[288] ICPM, chapter 9.3(e)(i).

respondent may be represented at no expense to the government.[289] During the hearing, the DHS attorney states whether a bond has been set and, if so, the amount of the bond and DHS's justification for that amount.[290] The respondent or his or her representative then makes an oral offer of proof or "proffer" addressing whether the respondent's release would pose a danger to property or persons, whether the respondent is likely to appear for future immigration proceedings, and whether the respondent poses a danger to national security.[291] The parties are expected to submit relevant evidence, and the IJ, at his or her discretion, may place witnesses under oath and take testimony.[292] However, as noted in the ICPM, the "parties should be mindful that bond hearings are generally briefer and less formal than hearings in removal proceedings."[293]

- **Practice Pointer**: Despite the typically-informal nature of bond proceedings, practitioners should prepare their clients for any scenario, including providing detailed testimony during direct, cross, and re-direct examination. As DHS continues to increase its detention of asylum-seekers as a deterrent to future border-crossers, bond proceedings have become more formal and adversarial.[294] In the summer and fall of 2014, and continuing to date, DHS has been opposing the release of asylum-seekers who recently crossed the border, even after they have demonstrated a credible fear of persecution or torture. DHS has invoked *Matter of D–J–* in arguing that the alleged "surge" of refugees poses a national security risk and that these asylum-seekers must therefore remain in detention.[295] In February of 2015, however, in response to a class action lawsuit, a judge for the U.S. District Court for the District of Columbia granted a preliminary injunction to prevent DHS from detaining class members for the purpose of deterring future immigration to the United States and from considering deterrence of future immigration as a factor in custody determinations.[296]

The IJ's determination regarding custody status or bond may be based on any information available to the IJ or that is presented to the IJ by DHS or the individual.[297] Generally, an individual who is not subject to a criminal ground of

---

[289] ICPM, chapter 9.3(e)(ii).

[290] *Id.*

[291] *Id.*

[292] ICPM, chapter 9.3(e)(vi).

[293] *Id.*

[294] *See* ICE Press Release on Dilley, *supra* note 33; Preston, *Detention Center Presented as Deterrent*, *supra* note 69; Hylton, *supra* note 31.

[295] *See Matter of D–J–*, 23 I&N Dec. 572 (A.G. 2003).

[296] *R.I. L–R–, et al., v. Jeh Charles Johnson, et al.,* 1:15–cv–00011–JEB (D.D.C. Feb. 20, 2015).

[297] 8 CFR §1003.19(d) (2014); ICPM, chapter 9.3(e)(vii).

detention is eligible for a bond unless there is a finding that the individual is a threat to national security, likely to abscond, or a poor bail risk.[298] Factors that an IJ will consider in assessing an individual's eligibility for a bond may include:

- Family ties in the United States, particularly those who can confer immigration benefits on the respondent;[299]
- Length of residence in the community;[300]
- A fixed address in the United States;[301]
- Employment history in the United States, including length and stability;[302]
- Property in the United States;
- Ties to the community;
- Immigration records, including past immigration violations;[303]
- Attempts to escape from authorities or other flight to avoid prosecution;[304]
- Prior failures to appear for criminal or immigration court hearings;[305]
- Criminal record, including extensiveness and recency, as indicators of consistent disrespect for the law and ineligibility for relief from removal;[306]
- Any efforts toward rehabilitation, if a criminal record exists; and
- Likelihood of eligibility for relief from removal.[307]

Documentary proof of any or all of these factors noted above should be submitted to the IJ at the bond redetermination hearing. Any documents in a language other than

[298] *See Matter of Patel*, 15 I&N Dec. 666 (BIA 1976), superseded by statute as stated in *Matter of Valdez–Valdez*, 21 I&N Dec. 703 (BIA 1997). *But see Matter of D–J–*, 23 I&N Dec. 572 (BIA 2003) (finding that AG has broad discretion in bond proceedings and may consider national security interests implicated when noncitizens arrive by sea and where such arrivals may encourage future mass migrations).

[299] *Matter of Guerra*, 24 I&N Dec. 37 (BIA 2006); *Matter of Andrade*, 19 I&N Dec. 488 (BIA 1987); *Matter of Shaw*, 17 I&N Dec. 177 (BIA 1979); *Matter of Patel*, 15 I&N Dec. 666 (BIA 1979).

[300] *Matter of Guerra*, at 37; *Matter of Andrade*, at 488; *Matter of Shaw*, at 177.

[301] *Matter of Guerra*, at 37; *Matter of Patel*, at 666.

[302] *Matter of Guerra*, at 37; *Matter of Andrade*, at 488; *Matter of Shaw*, at 177; *Matter of Patel*, at 666.

[303] *Matter of Guerra*, at 37; *Matter of Andrade*, at 488; *Matter of Shaw*, at 177; *Matter of San Martin*, 15 I&N Dec. 167 (BIA 1974); *Matter of Moise*, 12 I&N Dec. 102 (BIA 1967).

[304] *Matter of Guerra*, at 37; *Matter of Patel*, at 666; *Matter of San Martin*, 15 I&N Dec. 167 (BIA 1974).

[305] *Matter of Guerra*, at 37; *Matter of Andrade*, at 488; *Matter of Shaw*, at 177; *Matter of Patel*, at 666; *Matter of San Martin*, at 167.

[306] *Matter of Guerra*, at 37; *Matter of Andrade*, at 488.

[307] *Matter of X–K–*, 23 I&N Dec. 731 (BIA 2005).

English should be translated into English and have a certificate of translation attached.[308]

The IJ will inform the parties orally or in writing of the decision and the reasons for the decision.[309] Usually, the decision is rendered orally, and because bond hearings are generally not recorded, the decision is not transcribed.[310]

5. *Appeal of the IJ's Bond Decision*

If DHS or the respondent wishes to challenge the IJ's decision following bond proceedings, the party may prepare and file an appeal with the Board of Immigration Appeals.[311] An appeal may be taken by DHS or the respondent to the BIA on Form EOIR-26 within 30 calendar days of the IJ's decision.[312] The appeal will not delay compliance with the order, nor will it stay the removal proceedings or removal.[313] If the respondent appeals, the IJ's bond decision remains in effect while the appeal is pending. If DHS appeals, the IJ's bond decision remains in effect while the appeal is pending, unless the BIA issues an emergency stay or the decision is automatically stayed by regulation.[314]

DHS may seek a discretionary stay of the IJ's custody or bond order when it appeals the IJ's decision on its own motion.[315] In some cases, DHS is entitled to an automatic stay of an IJ's custody or bond redetermination.[316] For example, if the ICE district director had previously denied the individual's request for release or set a bond at $10,000 or more, the IJ's order authorizing release (on bond or otherwise) must be stayed upon DHS's filing of a Form EOIR-43, Notice of Intent to Appeal the Custody Redetermination.[317] Whether to file the Form EOIR-43 is at the discretion of DHS.[318] If DHS decides to file this form, it must be filed with the immigration court

---

[308] For more information, see Am. Immigration Council, Legal Action Center Practice Advisory, *Arrest, Detention and Bond Procedures for Non–Citizens Without Criminal Convictions* (July 2008), *available at www.legalactioncenter.org/sites/default/files/lac_pa_011303.pdf*; Nat'l Lawyers Guild, Nat'l Immigration Project, *Bond Practice Manual* (1994); Florence Immigrant and Refugee Rights Project, *All About Bonds* (Mar. 2002), *available at www.lirs.org/ InfoRes/PDFs/FlorenceProSe/Bonds–E.pdf* (which contains a helpful bond worksheet).

[309] 8 CFR §1003.19(f) (2014).

[310] ICPM, chapter 9.3(e)(vii); *Matter of Chirinos*, 16 I&N Dec. 276 (BIA 1977) (noting that bond hearings are informal and that there is no right to a transcript).

[311] 8 CFR §§1003.38, 1236.1(d)(3)(i) (2014); ICPM, chapter 9.3(f).

[312] 8 CFR §§1003.38, 1003.19(f) (2014). *See also* this chapter, at 3.10.

[313] 8 CFR §1236.1(d)(4) (2014).

[314] 8 CFR §§1003.6(c), 1003.19(i) (2014); ICPM, chapter 9.3(f).

[315] 8 CFR §1003.19(i)(1) (2014).

[316] 8 CFR §1003.19(i)(2) (2014).

[317] *Id.*

[318] *Id.*

within one business day of the IJ's order, and the IJ's decision must remain in abeyance pending the BIA's decision on the appeal.[319]

Because bond hearings are generally not recorded, if the IJ issues an oral decision, it is not transcribed. Rather, if either party appeals, the IJ must prepare a written decision based on his or her notes from the bond hearing.[320] The record may contain any information in addition to the IJ's memorandum of decision and other Executive Office for Immigration Review (EOIR) forms.[321]

6. *Request for Subsequent Bond Redetermination*

After the initial bond redetermination by an IJ, a request for a subsequent bond redetermination may be made to the IJ.[322] Even if the initial bond redetermination is on appeal to the BIA, the IJ retains jurisdiction to address a subsequent bond redetermination request based on materially changed circumstances.[323]

The request must be made in writing and will be considered only if there is a showing that the individual's circumstances have "changed materially since the prior redetermination."[324] Like the initial bond redetermination request, a request for subsequent bond redetermination should contain the following information:

- The full name and A-number of the respondent;
- The bond amount set by DHS, if any; and
- The location of the detention facility, if the respondent is detained.[325]

There is no filing fee.[326] However, if available, a copy of the NTA should be provided with the request.[327]

> ➢ **Practice Pointer**: A psychological evaluation can be very persuasive evidence in demonstrating that the detained individual's circumstances have changed materially since the IJ's prior bond redetermination. Detention compounds the trauma that many asylum-seekers have

---

[319] *Id.*

[320] ICPM, chapter 9.3(e)(vii).

[321] *Matter of Chirinos*, 16 I&N Dec. 276 (BIA 1977) (noting that bond hearings are informal and that there is no right to a transcript).

[322] 8 CFR §1003.19(e) (2014); ICPM, chapter 9.3(c)(iv).

[323] *Matter of Valles*, 21 I&N Dec. 769 (BIA 1997).

[324] 8 CFR §1003.19(e) (2014); ICPM, chapter 9.3(c)(iv).

[325] ICPM, chapter 9.3(c)(iv). *See* ICPM, chapter 9.3(c)(i).

[326] ICPM, chapter 9.3(c)(ii).

[327] ICPM, chapter 9.3(c).

suffered and fled, and thus, a psychological evaluation can show the serious effects of detention on such victims.[328]

V. Removal Proceedings in Detention

Individuals who are not released by DHS or upon order of the IJ must complete their removal proceedings while in the DHS custody. Although the process of seeking asylum, withholding of removal under INA §241(b)(3), and CAT relief defensively before the immigration courts is the same,[329] detained respondents must overcome significant hurdles to effectively present their claims for relief. First, detention often compounds the trauma that victims of persecution and torture are already suffering upon their arrival to the United States.[330] Second, detention poses serious barriers to the tools necessary for presenting an effective asylum claim, such as access to legal counsel,[331] witnesses and documentation, interpreters, medical and mental healthcare, and support networks. Third, detained asylum-seekers, like all detainees, are rushed through proceedings on an expedited immigration court docket[332] and most of them, being detained in remote locations far away from any immigration courts, have their cases heard by video, rather than in-person. In short, the procedures for detained asylum-seekers, and detained individuals generally, are riddled with due process violations.

- **Practice Pointer**: Many detainees who fear persecution and torture in their home countries give up and risk their lives by returning because of the obstacles they face in detention and the trauma of being detained.

A. DHS's Responsibilities

DHS has various responsibilities related to detainees in removal proceedings. First, DHS is responsible for ensuring that detained respondents appear at all of their hearings.[333] Second, if a detained respondent is transferred between detention facilities, DHS must notify the immigration court upon moving the respondent.[334] DHS also must notify the respondent's attorney of record if the respondent is moved

[328] *See* Physicians for Human Rights & The Bellevue/NYU Program for Survivors of Torture, *From Persecution to Prison: The Health Consequences of Detention for Asylum–Seekers* (June 2003), *available at www.survivorsoftorture.org/files/pdf/perstoprison2003.pdf* (last visited Apr. 1, 2015).

[329] See chapter 8 for a detailed discussion of seeking asylum defensively before the immigration courts.

[330] *See* Physicians for Human Rights & The Bellevue/NYU Program for Survivors of Torture, *From Persecution to Prison: The Health Consequences of Detention for Asylum–Seekers* (June 2003), *available at www.survivorsoftorture.org/files/pdf/perstoprison2003.pdf* (last visited Apr. 1, 2015).

[331] U.S. Comm'n on Int'l Religious Freedom Special Report, Assessing the U.S. Government's Detention of Asylum Seekers, *supra* note 6; Human Rights First, U.S. Detention of Asylum Seekers, supra note 6.

[332] ICPM, chapter 9.1(e).

[333] ICPM, chapter 9.1(c).

[334] *See* 8 CFR §1003.19(g) (2014); ICPM, chapter 9.1(d)(i).

after the initial custody placement.[335] Similarly, if the respondent is released from DHS custody, DHS must notify the immigration court.[336] This notice must be provided in writing and must state the effective date of the change in custody location or status, as well as the respondent's current fixed address.[337]

> **Practice Pointer**: If a client is moved from one detention facility to another, or if he or she is released during the course of removal proceedings, practitioners should prepare and file a Form EOIR-33/IC with the immigration court on behalf of their client to ensure that the immigration court's records are up-to-date.[338] Generally, ICE policy advises that detainees should not be transferred away from immediate family, an attorney of record, pending or ongoing removal or bond proceedings.[339]

If a respondent is transferred to a different detention facility while proceedings are pending, the IJ with original jurisdiction over the case retains jurisdiction until that IJ grants a motion to change venue.[340] If the respondent appears before a new immigration court and a motion to change venue has not yet been granted, the new IJ does not have jurisdiction over the case, except for bond redeterminations.[341]

Finally, ICE may also have the responsibility to identify mental health concerns in respondents. In 2010, the American Civil Liberties Union filed a class action lawsuit on behalf of hundreds of immigration detainees in California, Arizona, and Washington who suffer from severe mental disabilities.[342] In the lawsuit, *Franco v. Holder*, the plaintiffs sued the U.S. government due to the administration's refusal to provide an attorney to such vulnerable individuals, even though they cannot understand the proceedings or defend themselves.[343] In October 2014, a federal judge ordered the U.S. government to implement a comprehensive system for identifying

---

[335] CE Policy 11022.1: Detainee Transfers, at 5.3, available at *www.ice.gov/doclib/detention–reform/pdf/hd–detainee–transfers.pdf* (last visited Apr. 1, 2015).

[336] *See* 8 CFR §1003.19(g) (2014); ICPM, chapter 9.1(d)(i).

[337] *Id.*

[338] ICPM, chapter 9.1(d)(i). *See* U.S. Dep't of Justice, Exec. Office of Immigration Review (EOIR), *Form EOIR–33, EOIR Immigration Court Listing*, *www.justice.gov/eoir/eoirforms/eoir33/ICadr33.htm* (last visited Feb. 18, 2015).

[339] ICE Policy 11022.1: Detainee Transfers, at 5.2, *available at www.ice.gov/doclib/detention–reform/pdf/hd–detainee–transfers.pdf* (last visited Apr. 1, 2015).

[340] ICPM, chapter 9.1(d)(ii).

[341] *Id.*

[342] ACLU, *Franco v. Holder* Case Developments, *available at www.aclusocal.org/franco/* (last visited Mar. 31, 2015).

[343] *Id.*

and protecting individuals with serious mental disorders in immigration detention centers in California, Arizona, and Washington.[344]

B. Legal Orientation Program

In some detention facilities, detained respondents are provided with a Legal Orientation Program (LOP) by local nonprofit organizations.[345] Since 2003, the EOIR has carried out LOPs for detained individuals in removal proceedings at certain detention facilities.[346] It was created "to provide detained [respondents] with essential and easy-to-understand information regarding the immigration court process, including their rights, responsibilities, and options for relief from removal."[347] The LOP is carried out through subcontracts with nonprofit legal organizations in cooperation with a number of local immigration courts and detention facilities.[348]

Through the LOP, representatives from nonprofit organizations provide information about immigration court procedures, as well as basic legal information, to large groups of detainees.[349] There are three components:

(1) the interactive group orientation, which is open to general questions;

(2) the individual orientation, where non-represented individuals can briefly discuss their cases with experienced counselors; and

(3) the referral/self-help component, where those with potential relief, or those who wish to voluntarily depart the country or request removal are referred to pro bono counsel, or given self-help legal materials and basic training through group workshops.[350]

According to EOIR, the LOP enables detained individuals to make wiser decisions, leads to a higher rate of detainees obtaining representation, allows non-profit organizations to reach a wider population, and facilitates a faster completion of cases resulting in fewer hearings and less time in detention.[351]

- ➢ **Practice Pointer**: A useful resource discussing the effectiveness of EOIR's LOP is the Vera Institute of Justice's "Legal Orientation Program Evaluation and Performance and Outcome Measurement Report, Phase II," available at *www.justice.gov/eoir/reports/*

---

[344] Order of the United States District Court for the Central District of California (Oct. 29, 2014), *www.aclusocal.org/wp–content/uploads/2014/10/ORD.DCT_.786–Order–Further–Implementing–PI.pdf* (last visited Mar. 31, 2015).

[345] *See* ICPM, chapter 1.4(c).

[346] EOIR, *Legal Orientation Program*, *www.justice.gov/eoir/probono/probono.htm#LOP* (last visited Feb. 18, 2015).

[347] ICPM, chapter 1.4(c).

[348] *Id.*

[349] EOIR Legal Orientation Program, *supra* note 346.

[350] *Id.*; ICPM, chapter 1.4(c).

[351] EOIR Legal Orientation Program, *supra* note 346.

LOPEvaluation-final.pdf.[352] This report notes that detained LOP participants have immigration court case processing times that are an average of 13 days shorter than non-program cases. This suggests that the LOP has important cost and resource-saving benefits for the immigration courts and the immigration detention system.

C. Hearings by Video or Telephone Conference

Proceedings for detained respondents are held either at the detention facility or at the immigration court, either by video or telephone conference.[353]

> ➢ **Practice Pointer**: Typically, there are security restrictions for entering detention facilities. Thus, for hearings held in the detention facilities, the parties and all witnesses must plan ahead and comply with the security requirements.[354]

A respondent need not be physically present before the IJ during his or her hearing. IIRAIRA specifically authorizes hearings by videoconference.[355] These video hearings are increasingly used for detained respondents, who are often many miles away from the court and the IJ.[356] To supplement its other immigration courts across the country, on July 19, 2004, EOIR established the Headquarters Court (HQIC), based in Arlington, VA. At present, HQIC has four IJs who hear cases and conduct both master calendar and individual hearings via videoconferencing on a regular basis. The purpose of the HQIC is to address short-term resource needs as they arise in the immigration courts nationwide.[357] For example, in the summer and fall of 2014, the IJs at the HQIC heard the cases of women and children detained at the Federal Law Enforcement Training Center in Artesia, NM, following the spring and summer's "surge" of border-crossers seeking protection in the United States.

Conducting removal hearings by video raises a number of due process concerns, including interference with the following:

- The respondent's ability to effectively testify and his or her statutory right to present evidence on his or her own behalf;[358]
- Adequacy of the translation due to sound issues and the inability of the respondent and interpreter to see and hear each other;

---

[352] (last visited Mar. 31, 2015).

[353] ICPM, chapter 9.1(e). *See* ICPM, chapter 4.7.

[354] *See* ICPM, chapter 4.14.

[355] INA §240(b)(2)(A)(iii).

[356] *See* J.T. Hong, Practice Advisory, *Video Removal Hearings: A Violation of Due Process?* 20 IMMIGRATION LAW TODAY 545 (Nov. 2001) (providing a helpful list of objections to make on the record to a video hearing).

[357] For more information, see EOIR Fact Sheet, *EOIR Headquarters Immigration Court* (July 21, 2004), *available at www.usdoj.gov/eoir/press/04/HQICFactSheet.htm.*

[358] INA §240(b)(4)(B).

- Access to counsel due to the inability of the respondent and his or her attorney to communicate directly and privately; and
- The respondent's ability to examine physical evidence presented by DHS or to cross-examine witnesses.[359]

However, most courts have held that video hearings do not violate due process.[360]

One court noted that video hearings do have the potential of violating due process by depriving an individual of a full and fair hearing.[361] For instance, where the use of videoconferencing interferes with a respondent's statutory right to be represented by his or her chosen attorney, to present evidence, or to examine evidence or cross-examine witnesses, and results in prejudice to the respondent, the hearing was not full and fair or consistent with due process.[362] Specifically, video hearings may interfere with an attorney's ability to fully represent the respondent and put the respondent's attorney in "a 'Catch-22' situation" where the attorney must choose between being with his or her client in the detention facility or being at the immigration court with the IJ and DHS attorney.[363] As the Fourth Circuit noted, "under either scenario, the effectiveness of the lawyer is diminished; he simply must choose the least damaging option."[364] Additionally, video hearings "may render it difficult for a fact finder in an adjudicative proceeding to make credibility determinations and to gauge demeanor."[365] A hearing by videoconference also may violate due process if it prevents the applicant from reviewing key evidence.[366]

Although the Fourth Circuit recognized these potential problems with video hearings, it held that, under the specific facts involved in *Rusu v. INS*, the individual did not show prejudice and therefore, due process had not been violated.[367] In that

---

[359] INA §240(b)(4) (setting forth the respondent's rights to be represented by counsel of his or her choosing, present evidence on his or her own behalf, examine evidence presented against him or her, and cross–examine witnesses).

[360] *See, e.g., Vilchez v. Holder*, 682 F.3d 1195, 1197 (9th Cir. 2012) (holding that the use of a video–conference hearing in removal proceedings did not violate an alien's due process rights and that the BIA had ruled consistent with 8 USC §1229a(b)(2)(iii) which expressly permits the use of video hearings); *Aslam v. Mukasey*, 537 F.3d 110, 115 (2d Cir. 2008) (stating that even though video conference hearings are permissible, they must comport with constitutional due process requirements); *But see Lacsina Pangilinan v. Holder*, 568 F.3d 708, 709 (9th Cir. 2009) (holding that a due process violation occurs when "(1) the proceeding was so fundamentally unfair that the alien was prevented from reasonably presenting his case, and (2) the alien demonstrates prejudice, which means that the outcome of the proceeding may have been affected by the alleged violation" thus, supporting the proposition that due process violations must be adjudicated on a case-by-case basis).

[361] *See Rusu v. INS*, 296 F.3d 316 (4th Cir. 2002).

[362] *Id.* at 321 n.7.

[363] *Id.* at 323.

[364] *Id.* at 322.

[365] *Id.*

[366] *Rapheal v. Mukasey*, 533 F.3d 521, 532–33 (7th Cir. 2008).

[367] *Rusu v. INS*, 296 F.3d 316 (4th Cir. 2002).

case, Rusu had fled his native Romania after being interrogated and tortured by the Romanian secret police, the "Securitate."[368] On one occasion, the Securitate held Rusu for three days, during which they tortured him by removing his teeth with pliers and a screwdriver. Upon escaping from Romania, Rusu made it to the United States, where he was detained in Farmville, Virginia.[369] During his hearing, Rusu was unable to speak clearly due to his damaged mouth and missing teeth; the IJ had to ask Rusu to repeat himself on numerous occasions; the transcript is marked "indiscernible" a total of 132 times; Rusu had difficulty understanding the questions of his counsel and the IJ, who were in a different location, hearing the case by video; and there were technological problems with the video conference equipment, at one point requiring the IJ to suspend the hearing to check the quality of the equipment and its ability to record Rusu's voice.[370] Yet, the Fourth Circuit held that Rusu failed to demonstrate prejudice, and therefore, due process had not been violated.[371] This case makes clear that, no matter how horrific the facts or how obvious the video conference problems may be, if the applicant does not show prejudice, due process violations will not be found.

- **Practice Pointer**: Prior to a hearing by video, practitioners should file a motion seeking an in-person hearing on behalf of their client and highlighting the reasons why a video hearing is not appropriate for that particular case. Making this motion on the record preserves any arguments regarding due process violations for appeal. In some courts, there is no accommodation for allowing detained individuals to appear in person. Therefore, all motions will be denied. However, that does not mean that the motions should not be made, as doing so preserves the issue for appeal. If the IJ denies the motion for in-person hearing, practitioners should again make an oral objection to the use of videoconferencing at the beginning of the hearing. Practitioners also should make various objections to due process issues that arise throughout the hearing as a result of the hearing being conducted by video, and move the IJ to stop the proceedings and reschedule the case for an in-person hearing. If relief is denied practitioners should file an appeal to the BIA, noting any due process issues due to the videoconferencing. Upon receipt of the transcript, practitioners should use the transcript to highlight those due process issues. For more strategies for objecting to video hearings that fail to comport with due process principles, see the American Immigration Council Legal Action Center's Practice Advisory, "Objecting to Video Merits Hearings" (Dec.

[368] *Id.*

[369] *Id.*

[370] *Id.*

[371] *Id.*

12, 2003), available at *www.legalactioncenter.org/sites/default/files/docs/lac/lac_pa_121203.*[372]

Appleseed, a nonpartisan, nonprofit network of public interest justice centers in the United States and Mexico, has studied and criticized the use of video hearings in immigration proceedings, urging EOIR to return to in-person merits hearings only and pointing out the lack of attorney-client confidential communications and lack of real-time document transmissions.[373] In 2009, Appleseed identified these problems and made various recommendations to EOIR.[374] Appleseed the revisited the issue of video hearings in its 2012 report, and gave EOIR an "F" grade for its failure to make improvements.[375]

Despite these potential due process violations, however, EOIR has continued its use of video hearings and asserted that they do not violate due process. The chief IJ has given guidance to IJs on how they should conduct video hearings in a memorandum issued in August 2004.[376]

D. Detention of Juveniles

In general, there are special procedures for juveniles under the age of 18 who are in federal custody, and these special procedures vary depending on whether the child is accompanied or unaccompanied.[377] DHS bears the initial responsibility for apprehension and detention of noncitizen children.[378] When DHS determines that a child is accompanied by a parent or legal guardian, DHS retains responsibility for the child's detention and removal.[379] However, when DHS determines that the child is unaccompanied (a child under 18 years old who does not have a parent or legal guardian in the United States to provide care and physical custody) and must be detained, DHS is required to transfer the child to the care of the Department of Health and Human Services' Office of Refugee Resettlement, which provides for the care and placement of the unaccompanied child.[380] Unaccompanied children who are released from custody are released to a parent, legal guardian, adult relative who is

---

[372] (last visited Feb. 14, 2015).

[373] Appleseed, *Reimagining the Immigration Court Assembly Line: Transformative Change for the Immigration Justice System* (2012), *available at www.appleseednetwork.org/wp–content/uploads/2012/03/Reimagining–the–Immigration–Court–Assembly–Line.pdf* (last visited Feb. 14, 2015).

[374] Appleseed, *Assembly Line Injustice: Blueprint to Reform America's Immigration Courts* (2009), *available at http://appleseednetwork.org/wp–content/uploads/2012/05/Assembly–Line–Injustice–Blueprint–to–Reform–Americas–Immigration–Courts1.pdf* (last visited Feb. 14, 2015).

[375] Appleseed, *Reimagining the Immigration Court Assembly Line*, *supra* note 373, at 8.

[376] *See* EOIR Memorandum No. 04–06 from Office of the Chief Immigration Judge on Interim Operating Policies and Procedures Memorandum: Hearings Conducted Through Telephone and Video Conference (Aug. 18, 2004), *available at www.usdoj.gov/eoir/efoia/ocij/oppm04/04–06.pdf.*

[377] 8 CFR §1236.3 (2014); ICPM, chapter 9.2(a).

[378] 8 CFR §1236.3 (2014); ICPM, chapter 9.2(b).

[379] 8 CFR §1236.3 (2014); ICPM, chapter 9.2(b).

[380] *See* 6 USC §279(a) (2012).

not in DHS detention, or, in limited circumstances, to an adult who is not a family member.[381]

- **Practice Pointer**: For a detailed discussion of procedures for unaccompanied and accompanied children seeking protection in the United States, as well as further information regarding their custody and release, see chapter 10 of this book.

VI. Conclusion

Given the current refugee crisis in Central America, the U.S. asylum system is increasingly overburdened, underfunded, and under attack by policymakers. However, despite costing taxpayers nearly $2 billion annually,[382] DHS's response, under directives from the current administration and Congress, is to continue to rely heavily on detention, often without individualized assessments, particularly for those individuals apprehended upon arrival in the United States.[383] Thus, it is more and more likely that an applicant for asylum, withholding of removal, or protection under the CAT may be detained during part or all of the process of seeking protection. It is essential for practitioners to be familiar with the legal standards and procedures for detention of asylum-seekers and to continue to push back against these Draconian, unjust, and inhumane policies.[384]

---

[381] 8 CFR §1236.3(b) (2014); ICPM, chapter 9.2(d).

[382] Nat'l Immigration Forum, *Detention Costs Still Don't Add Up to Good Policy* (Sept. 24, 2014), *available at https://immigrationforum.org/blog/detention–costs–still–dont–add–up–to–good–policy/* (last visited Mar. 31, 2015); Nat'l Immigration Forum, *The Math of Immigration Detention: Runaway Costs for Immigration Detention Do Not Add Up to Sensible Policies* (Aug. 2013), *available at www.immigrationforum.org/images/uploads/mathofimmigrationdetention.pdf* (last visited Feb. 17, 2015).

[383] *See* Women's Refugee Comm'n & Lutheran Immigration and Refugee Serv., *Locking Up Family Values Again*, *supra* note 15; Manning, *Ending Artesia*, *supra* note 6; Collopy, *The Failings of Family Detention at Artesia*, *supra* note 29; Collopy & Manning, *Why is Obama Still Locking Up So Many*, *supra* note 29; Manning, *Let These Women Go*, *supra* note 29.

[384] *See, e.g.*, Manning, *Ending Artesia*, *supra* note 6; Women's Refugee Comm'n & Lutheran Immigration and Refugee Serv., *Locking Up Family Values Again*, *supra* note 15; *M.S.P.C. v. Johnson* Compl., *supra* note 27; U.S. Comm'n on Int'l Religious Freedom Special Report, *Assessing the U.S. Government's Detention of Asylum Seekers*, *supra* note 6; Am. Civil Liberties Union, *ACLU Challenges Prison–Like Conditions at Hutto*, *supra* note 16; *see also* Women's Comm'n for Refugee Women & Children, *et al.*, *Locking Up Family Values*, *supra* note 15; Human Rights First, *In Liberty's Shadow*, *supra* note 27; Human Rights Watch, *Presumption of Guilt*, *supra* note 27; Human Rights Watch, *Locked Away*, *supra* note 27.

CHAPTER TEN

LEGAL STANDARDS AND PROCEDURES FOR CHILDREN*

The U.N. Convention on the Rights of the Child provides that "the 'best interests of the child' should be the primary consideration" in all actions involving children, and this principle has influenced laws and policies toward children in the United States and around the world.[1] In fact, special care and assistance for children is recognized as a universal human right.[2] Although children often are included as derivatives on their parents' or legal guardians' applications for asylum, withholding of removal under INA §241(b)(3), and Convention Against Torture (CAT) relief, regrettably, they often have their own independent protection needs as victims of persecution and torture. Children are subjected to abusive child labor practices; are recruited by regular or irregular armies, insurgent groups, and gangs; are sold into prostitution or indentured servitude; and are subjected to various other human rights abuses. As the United Nations High Commissioner for Refugees (UNHCR) notes:

> Almost half of the world's forcibly displaced people are children and many spend their entire childhood far from home. Whether they are refugees, internally displaced, asylum-seekers or stateless, children are at a greater risk of abuse, neglect, violence, exploitation, trafficking or forced military

---

* The author would like to thank Michelle N. Mendez of the Catholic Legal Immigration Network, Inc. for her invaluable input in reviewing this chapter.

[1] Convention on the Rights of the Child, G.A. Res. 44/25, U.N. Doc. A/RES/44/25, at art. 3(1) (Nov. 20, 1989) [hereinafter Convention on Rights of the Child], *available at www.un.org/documents/ga/res/44/a44r025.htm*. The United States has signed, but not ratified the Convention on the Rights of the Child. As a signatory, the United States may not engage in any acts that would defeat the object and purpose of the treaty. However, since the United States has not ratified the treaty, its provisions are only guiding, not binding.

[2] Convention on Rights of the Child, *supra* note 1, at arts. 3(1), 12(1); Universal Declaration of Human Rights, G.A. Res. 217A (III). U.N. Doc. A/810, at art. 25(2) [hereinafter Universal Declaration of Human Rights], *available at www1.umn.edu/humanrts/instree/b1udhr.htm*.

recruitment. They may also have witnessed or experienced violent acts and/or been separated from their families.[3]

In 2013, 50 percent of the world's refugee population was under 18 years old,[4] and the number of children fleeing to the United States has increased exponentially over the past five years, in large part due to the unfettered domestic and gang violence that has consumed the Northern Triangle of Central America (El Salvador, Guatemala, and Honduras).[5] According to U.S. Customs and Border Protection (CBP), 68,541 unaccompanied children were apprehended at the southwest border in fiscal year 2014, compared with 38,759 children in fiscal year 2013 — an increase of 77 percent.[6] As a result, children's asylum claims have received increasing attention by advocates, the Department of Homeland Security (DHS), the U.S. Citizenship and Immigration Services (USCIS) Asylum Division, and the immigration courts.

- **Practice Pointer**: Both UNHCR and the Women's Refugee Commission have written extensive reports on the push factors causing children to flee Central America. These reports are available for download on each of the organizations' websites:
  - *http://unhcrwashington.org/children* and
  - *https://womensrefugeecommission.org/forced-from-home-press-kit.*[7]

UNHCR and the United States have long recognized the particular vulnerability of refugee children — especially unaccompanied refugee children — and the need for special legal interpretations and procedural safeguards to address their unique needs as they seek asylum and other forms of protection.[8] This chapter discusses the special

---

[3] U.N. High Comm'r for Refugees (UNHCR), *Children: Protection and Building Resilience*, *available at www.unhcr.org/pages/49c3646c1e8.html* (last visited Feb. 20, 2015).

[4] UNHCR, *Facts and Figures about Refugees*, *available at www.unhcr.org.uk/about-us/key-facts-and-figures.html* (last visited Feb. 20, 2015).

[5] UNHCR, *Children on the Run*, *available at www.unhcrwashington.org/sites/default/files/1_UAC_Children%20on%20the%20Run_Full%20Report.pdf* (last visited Feb. 20, 2015); Women's Refugee Comm'n, *Forced From Home: The Lost Boys and Girls of Central America* (Oct. 2012), *available at https://womensrefugeecommission.org/forced-from-home-press-kit* (last visited Mar. 4, 2015). In fiscal year 2014, 27 percent of children apprehended along the southern border of the U.S. came from Honduras, 25 percent came from Guatemala, 24 percent came from El Salvador, and 23 percent came from Mexico. *See* U.S. Customs and Border Protection (CBP), *Southwest Border Unaccompanied Alien Children (FY 2014)*, *available at* http://www.cbp.gov/newsroom/stats/southwest-border-unaccompanied-children-2014 (last visited Feb. 20, 2015).

[6] CBP, *Southwest Border Unaccompanied Alien Children (FY 2014)*, *supra* note 5.

[7] (last visited Mar. 4, 2015).

[8] *See* UNHCR, *Guidelines on International Protection No. 8: Child Asylum Claims Under Articles 1(A)2 and 1(F) of the 1951 Convention and/or 1967 Protocol relating to the Status of Refugees* (Dec. 22, 2009), *available at www.refworld.org/docid/4b2f4f6d2.html* (last visited Feb. 20, 2015); UNHCR, *Policy on Refugee Children*, EC/SCP/82 (Aug. 6, 1993), *available at www.unhcr.org/3ae68ccc4.html* (noting that children's needs are different than adults' and stating that government actions relating to children must be "tailored to the different needs and potentials of refugee children"); UNHCR Exec.

Continued

legal interpretations and procedural safeguards available under U.S. asylum law in recognizing the unique needs of child refugees, and provides important guidance for advocates in representing children as they navigate the labyrinth of the U.S. asylum system.

I. Special Legal Standards

Whether accompanied by family members or unaccompanied, children experience persecution uniquely due to factors such as their age, level of maturity and development, and dependency on adults.[9] Moreover, a child's ability to recall events, knowledge of events giving rise to the claim, and knowledge of the asylum process in general may be significantly more limited than adults'.[10] Thus, a child-sensitive interpretation of U.S. asylum law is necessary to protect the best interests of the child as he or she seeks protection in the United States.

- **Practice Pointer**: Although the definition of "child" in U.S. immigration law is often a person under the age of 21, and this is how a child is defined for derivative asylum applicants, for purposes of asylum determinations for principal applicants, an individual is a child if he or she is under the age of 18.[11]

Although the definition of "refugee" contained in Article 1(A)2 of the 1951 Convention and 1967 Protocol and codified into U.S. law at INA §101(a)(42)(A) applies to all individuals regardless of their age, the refugee definition:

> [M]ust be interpreted in an age and gender-sensitive manner, taking into account the particular motives for, and forms and manifestations of, persecution experienced by children. Persecution of kin; under-age recruitment; trafficking of children for prostitution; and sexual exploitation or subjection to

---

Comm. Conclusion No. 47, U.N. Doc. No. 12A A/42/12/Add.1, *available at www.refworld.org/docid/3ae68c432c.html* (emphasizing that all actions taken on behalf of refugee children must be guided by the principle of the "best interests of the child"); UNHCR Exec. Comm. Conclusion No. 59, U.N. Doc. No. 12A A/44/12/Add.1, *available at www.refworld.org/docid/3ae68c4398.html* (drawing special attention to the needs of unaccompanied minors); UNHCR Executive Comm. Conclusion No. 107, U.N. Doc. No. A/AC.96/1048, *available at www.refworld.org/docid/471897232.html* (recognizing that children should be prioritized as one of the first recipients of refugee protection and assistance).

[9] *See* UNHCR, *Guidelines on International Protection No. 8*, *supra* note 8, at ¶ 2 (Dec. 22, 2009), available at *www.refworld.org/docid/4b2f4f6d2.html* (last visited Feb. 20, 2015).

[10] *See* U.S. Citizenship and Immigration Servs. (USCIS), *Guidelines for Children's Asylum Claims*, in Asylum Officer Basic Training Course Participant Workbook, at 36 (Sept. 1, 2009) [hereinafter AOBTC Lesson Plan on Children's Asylum Claims], *available at www.uscis.gov/files/article/AOBTC_Lesson_29_Guidelines_for_Childrens_Asylum_Claims.pdf.*

[11] *Compare* INA §101(b)-(c) *with* USCIS, Affirmative Asylum Procedures Manual, pt. III.B.1. (Nov. 2013), *available at www.uscis.gov/sites/default/files/files/nativedocuments/Asylum_Procedures_Manual_2013.pdf and* UNHCR, *Guidelines on International Protection No. 8*, *supra* note 8, at ¶ 7.

> female genital mutilation, are some of the child-specific forms and manifestations of persecution which may justify the granting of refugee status if such acts are related to one of the 1951 Refugee Convention grounds. States should, therefore, give utmost attention to such child-specific forms and manifestations of persecution as well as gender-based violence in national refugee status–determination procedures.[12]

U.S. courts generally have agreed with an age-appropriate interpretation of U.S. asylum law. For example, the Seventh Circuit U.S. Court of Appeals in *Liu v. Ashcroft* emphasized that "age can be a critical factor in the adjudication of asylum claims and may bear heavily on the question of whether an applicant was persecuted or whether she holds a well-founded fear of persecution."[13]

Alongside age, the following factors should be considered in appropriately applying the eligibility criteria for asylee status:

- The rights specific to children;
- The child's maturity and stage of development;
- Knowledge and/or memory of conditions in the country of origin;
- Vulnerability; and
- Ability to articulate certain views or opinions.[14]

In the case of an unaccompanied minor, particular regard should be given to factors such as "the child's stage of development" and "his [or] her possibly limited knowledge of conditions in the country of origin."[15]

UNHCR has noted that applications filed by minors seeking refugee status should be granted more liberal review than those submitted by adults.[16] Minors, similarly,

---

[12] U.N. Committee on the Rights of the Child (CRC), *General Comment No. 6 (2005): Treatment of Unaccompanied and Separated Children Outside Their Country of Origin,* U.N. Doc. No. CRC/GC/2005/6, at ¶ 74 (Sep. 2005) [hereafter CRC, General Comment No. 6], *available at www.unhcr.org/refworld/docid/42dd174b4.html.*

[13] *Liu v. Ashcroft*, 380 F.3d 307, 314 (7th Cir. 2004). *See also Jorge-Tzoc v. Gonzales*, 435 F.3d 146, 150 (2d Cir. 2006) (same).

[14] *See* UNHCR, *Guidelines on International Protection No. 8*, *supra* note 8, at ¶ 4.

[15] UNHCR, *Guidelines on Policies and Procedures in Dealing with Unaccompanied Children Seeking Asylum*, at ¶8.6, (Feb. 1997), *available at www.unhcr.org/publ/PUBL/3d4f91cf4.pdf.*

[16] U.N. High Comm'r for Refugees, *Handbook on Procedures and Criteria for Determining Refugee Status*, ¶¶ 214–17, U.N. Doc. No. HCR/1P/4/enG/Rev. 3 (2011) [hereinafter UNHCR Handbook], *available at www.refworld.org/docid/4f33c8d92.html* (observing that a minor's refugee status must be determined in the context of the minor's degree of mental development and maturity); *see also Matter of Devison*, 22 I&N Dec. 1362 (BIA 2000) (asserting that, in considering mandatory bars to asylum, courts do not treat a child's adjudication of delinquency as a conviction for immigration purposes). *But see Cruz-Diaz v. INS*, 86 F.3d 330, 331 (4th Cir. 1996) (stating that a 15-year-old asylum-seeker must show "a reasonable possibility of persecution or that a reasonable person in similar circumstances would fear persecution on account of his political beliefs or one of the other enumerated provisions of the statute" and finding no error in applying the same standard of proof to juveniles as is applied to adults because the standard necessarily includes consideration of age).

are entitled to a liberal application of the "benefit of the doubt" principle.[17] In recognition of the fact that bona fide refugees often are unable to provide documentation in support of their claims, UNHCR's Handbook provides:

> After the applicant has made a genuine effort to substantiate his story there may still be a lack of evidence for some of his statements … . [I]t is hardly possible for a refugee to "prove" every part of his case and, indeed, if this were a requirement the majority of refugees would not be recognized. It is therefore frequently necessary to give the applicant the benefit of the doubt.[18]

The Handbook also addresses the application of this principle in the case of minors as follows:

> If the will of the parents cannot be ascertained or if such will is in doubt or in conflict with the will of the child, then the examiner, in cooperation with the experts assisting him, will have to come to a decision as to the well-foundedness of the minor's fear on the basis of all the known circumstances, which may call for a *liberal application* of the benefit of the doubt.[19]

The Sixth Circuit U.S. Court of Appeals relied on this paragraph in finding that a minor girl who feared female genital mutilation if she returned to Ethiopia was eligible for asylum.[20]

The U.S. government also recognizes that, while the burden of proof remains on the child to establish his or her asylum claim, the effects of the child's "age, maturity, ability to recall events, potentially limited knowledge of events giving rise to the claim, and potentially limited knowledge of the asylum process" must be considered.[21] USCIS guidance encourages asylum officers to take an active role in gathering objective evidence to evaluate the child's claim and to work closely with the child's representative and support person in ensuring that the child's claim is fully explored.[22] USCIS also notes that, although the BIA has emphasized an applicant's burden to produce all accessible documents, credible testimony alone still can be sufficient, especially for a child, in meeting the applicant's burden of proof.[23]

---

[17] UNHCR Handbook, *supra* note 16, at ¶ 219, *cited with approval by Abay v. Ashcroft*, 368 F.3d 634, 640 (6th Cir. 2004). *See Hernandez-Ortiz v. Gonzales*, 496 F.3d 1042 (9th Cir. 2007); *Liu v. Ashcroft*, 380 F.3d 307, 314 (7th Cir. 2004); *Abay v. Ashcroft*, 368 F.3d 634, 639-40 (6th Cir. 2004); *Jorge-Tzoc v. Gonzales*, 435 F.3d 146 (2d Cir. 2006); *Matter of Chen*, 20 I&N Dec. 16, 1989 WL 331860 (BIA 1989).

[18] UNHCR Handbook, *supra* note 16, at ¶ 203.

[19] UNHCR Handbook, *supra* note 16, at ¶ 219 (emphasis added).

[20] *Abay v. Ashcroft*, 368 F.3d 634, 640 (6th Cir. 2004).

[21] AOBTC Lesson Plan on Children's Asylum Claims, *supra* note 10, at 36.

[22] *Id.*

[23] *Id.* at 43. *See Matter of S-M-J-*, 21 I&N Dec. 722 (BIA 1997); *Matter of Dass*, 20 I&N Dec. 120 (BIA 1989). *See also* INA §208(b)(1)(B)(ii); 8 CFR §208.13(a) (2014).

While these factors and more liberal application of these principles are to be applied throughout the asylum eligibility analysis for children, certain eligibility requirements are impacted more significantly by a child's age, maturity, and development, and therefore, require child-specific analyses.

These may include whether: (1) the harm rises to the level of persecution; (2) a child's fear is well-founded; (3) persecution was or would be motivated by a protected ground; (4) the government is unable or unwilling to control non-state actors; and (5) any ineligibility grounds or statutory bars to relief apply. The interpretation of these legal elements in children's asylum claims is discussed below.

- **Practice Pointer**: It is essential for practitioners to know their child clients and to be aware of the various factors that may affect his or her ability to participate in preparing and presenting an asylum claim. Some of these factors may include: a child's mental health and coping mechanisms; past experience; trauma suffered; re-traumatization triggers; extreme poverty or malnourishment; neglect, abuse, or violence suffered; age; intelligence and level of education; communication patterns; language barriers; family composition; social network and friends; cultural background; and context of his or her country of origin.

- **Practice Pointer**: Working with children, especially children who have survived violence, abuse, neglect, and trauma, requires sensitivity to a wide array of issues, as well as patience and commitment to building the trust necessary to effectively represent them. Practitioners should work to establish an atmosphere of support and a safe relationship, build trust, be informed about trauma, follow cues from body language, convey respect and empathy, use a friendly and relaxed approach, use age and developmentally appropriate language, take the child's social history into account, seek the assistance of mental health professionals when necessary, and employ other child-sensitive techniques "to create a nonjudgmental, supportive, and sympathetic environment that puts children at ease to the extent possible and that also facilitates self-expression by children."[24] When working with children to gather information about their claims, practitioners should: meet in a child-appropriate setting, explain the process to the child, explain the practitioner's role, meet several times for short periods, keep the meetings as casual and fun as possible, and use play and drawings while talking. Child-sensitive interviewing techniques include starting with neutral topics, using clear language, rephrasing questions, avoiding compound questions and legal jargon, using short and active words,

[24] Am. Bar Ass'n, *Standards for the Custody, Placement and Care, Legal Representation, and Adjudication of Unaccompanied Alien Children in the United States* (Aug. 2004), *available at www.americanbar.org/content/dam/aba/migrated/Immigration/PublicDocuments/Immigrant_Standards .authcheckdam.pdf.*

asking open-ended questions, showing empathy, reassuring the child, using the child's own words, taking breaks, and repeating and verifying information.

➢ **Practice Pointer**: There are many helpful resources available to assist practitioners in understanding best practices for working with child clients. For example, see "*Representing Unaccompanied Children: Training Manual for Pro Bono Attorneys*, Chapter 1: Representing Children in Immigration Matters," by Kids in Need of Defense, *www.supportkind.org/en/about-us/resources/manual/chapter-1*.[25]

A. Harm Rising to the Level of Persecution

First, the term "persecution" and what kinds of harm may rise to the level of persecution should be "assessed with regard to the age, opinions, feelings and psychological make-up of the applicant."[26] According to UNHCR, the best interests of the child principle requires that the harm be assessed from the child's perspective. Specifically, "This may include an analysis as to how the child's rights or interests are, or will be, affected by the harm. Ill-treatment which may not rise to the level of persecution in the case of an adult may do so in the case of a child."[27] USCIS echoes these guidelines, advising asylum officers that:

> The harm a child fears or has suffered may still qualify as persecution despite appearing to be relatively less than that necessary for an adult to establish persecution. This is because children, dependent on others for their care, are prone to be more severely and potentially permanently affected by trauma than adults, particularly when their caretaker is harmed.[28]

---

[25] (last visited Mar. 1, 2015).

[26] UNHCR, Guidelines on International Protection No. 8, *supra* note 8, at ¶ 10.

[27] UNHCR, Guidelines on International Protection No. 8, *supra* note 8, at ¶ 10.

[28] AOBTC Lesson Plan on Children's Asylum Claims, *supra* note 10, at 37. *See, e.g., Kholyavskiy v. Mukasey,* 540 F.3d 555, 571 (7th Cir. 2008) (holding that the adjudicator should have considered the "cumulative significance" of events to the applicant that occurred when he was between the ages of eight and thirteen, including discrimination and harassment, being mocked regularly and urinated on by other school children for being Jewish, being forced by his teachers to stand up and identify himself as a Jew on a quarterly basis, and being called slurs and being physically abused in his neighborhood); *Hernandez-Ortiz v. Gonzales*, 496 F.3d 1042 (9th Cir. 2007) ("[A] child's reaction to injuries to his family is different from an adult's. The child is part of the family, the wound to the family is personal, the trauma apt to be lasting…[I]njuries to a family must be considered in an asylum case where the events that form the basis of the past persecution claim were perceived when the petitioner was a child."); *Jorge-Tzoc v. Gonzales*, 435 F.3d 146, 150 (2d Cir. 2006) ("Jorge-Tzoc was a child at the time of the massacres and thus necessarily dependent on both his family and his community…This combination of circumstances [displacement — initially internal, resulting in economic hardship, and viewing the bullet-ridden body of his cousin] could well constitute persecution to a small child totally dependent on his family and community."); *Kahssai v. INS,* 16 F.3d 323, 329 (9th Cir. 1994) (Reinhardt, J., concurring opinion) ("The fact that she did not suffer physical harm is not determinative of her claim of persecution: there are other equally serious forms of injury that result from persecution.

Continued

While children may face similar types of harm as adults, they may experience that harm differently. Thus, harm suffered or feared by a child may be less than that experienced or feared by an adult but still qualify as persecution.[29] This is because the harm must be assessed from the perspective of the child. As UNHCR explains in its guidelines for child asylum claims:

> Immaturity, vulnerability, undeveloped coping mechanisms and dependency as well as the differing stages of development and hindered capacities may be directly related to how a child experiences or fears harm. Particularly in claims where the harm suffered or feared is more severe than mere harassment but less severe than a threat to life or freedom, the individual circumstances of the child, including his/her age, may be important factors in deciding whether the harm amounts to persecution. To assess accurately the severity of the acts and their impact on a child, it is necessary to examine the details of each case and to adapt the threshold for persecution to that particular child.[30]

Psychologically, children are "more likely to be distressed by hostile situations, to believe improbable threats, or to be emotionally affected by unfamiliar circumstances. Memories of traumatic events may linger in a child and put him/her at heightened risk of future harm."[31] Children are also more sensitive to acts that target close relatives.[32]

- **Practice Pointer**: Practitioners should consider whether harm inflicted against the child's family members might support a well-founded fear in the child, even if the child him or herself was not targeted directly.

There are certain child-specific rights due to children's age and dependency that are fundamental to their protection. Violation of these rights, which are set forth in

---

For example, when a young girl loses her father, mother and brother—sees her family effectively destroyed—she plainly suffers severe emotional and developmental injury.").

[29] *See* INS Memorandum from J. Weiss on Guidelines for Children's Asylum Claims (Dec. 10, 1998), *published on* AILA InfoNet at Doc. No. 99012590 (*posted* Jan. 25, 1999), *reproduced in* 76 *Interpreter Releases* 1, appx. I (Jan. 4, 1999), *available at www.abanet.org/publicserv/immigration/ins_guidelines_for_children.pdf*; *Hernandez-Ortiz v. Gonzales*, 496 F.3d 1042 (9th Cir. 2007) (finding that IJ should have considered applicant's case from perspective of a small child); *Jorge-Tzoc v. Gonzales*, 435 F.3d 146, 147–48 (2d Cir. 2006) (considering the harm suffered by the applicant from the perspective of a small child); *Liu v. Ashcroft*, 380 F.3d 307, 314 (7th Cir. 2004) (finding that age can be a critical factor in the adjudication of asylum claims and may bear heavily on whether the applicant was persecuted or has a well-founded fear); *Abay v. Ashcroft*, 368 F.3d 634, 640 (6th Cir. 2004) (overturning, on the basis of age, the IJ's finding that 9-year-old had not adequately expressed a fear of persecution).

[30] UNHCR, Guidelines on International Protection No. 8, *supra* note 8, at ¶ 15.

[31] *Id.* at ¶ 16.

[32] UNHCR, Guidelines on International Protection No. 8, *supra* note 8, at ¶ 17; AOBTC Lesson Plan on Children's Asylum Claims, *supra* note 10, at 36–39.

the U.N. Convention on the Rights of the child, may rise to the level of persecution.[33] These rights include, but are not limited to the following:

- The right not to be separated from parents;[34]
- Protection from all forms of physical and mental violence, abuse, neglect, and exploitation;[35]
- Protection from traditional practices prejudicial to the health of children;[36]
- A standard of living adequate for the child's development;[37]
- The right not to be detained or imprisoned unless as a measure of last resort;[38] and
- Protection from under-age recruitment.[39]

Additionally, there are several specific types of harm that are targeted at children due to their age, lack of maturity, or vulnerability.[40] UNHCR's Executive Committee has recognized the following forms of persecution that may be child-specific:

- Under-age recruitment;[41]
- Child trafficking;[42]
- Female genital mutilation;[43]
- Family and domestic violence;[44]
- Forced or underage marriage;
- Bonded or hazardous child labor;[45]
- Forced labor;[46]
- Forced prostitution;

---

[33] *See* Convention on Rights of the Child, *supra* note 1; AOBTC Lesson Plan on Children's Asylum Claims, *supra* note 10, at 39–40.

[34] Convention on Rights of the Child, *supra* note 1, at art. 9.

[35] *Id.* at art. 19.

[36] Convention on Rights of the Child, *supra* note 1, at art. 24.

[37] *Id.* at 27.

[38] *Id.* at 37.

[39] *Id.* at 38.

[40] AOBTC Lesson Plan on Children's Asylum Claims, *supra* note 10, at 39–40.

[41] *See* UNHCR, Guidelines on International Protection No. 8, *supra* note 8, at ¶ 19–23.

[42] *See Id.* at ¶ 24–28.

[43] *See Id.* at ¶ 31. *See also Abay v. Ashcroft*, 368 F.3d 634, 640 (6th Cir. 2004) (relying on UNHCR's guidelines in finding that a minor girl who feared female genital mutilation if she returned to Ethiopia was eligible for asylum).

[44] *See* UNHCR, Guidelines on International Protection No. 8, *supra* note 8, at ¶ 32–33.

[45] *See Id.* at ¶ 29–30.

[46] *Id.*

- Child pornography;
- Violations of survival and development rights;[47]
- Severe discrimination of children born outside strict family-planning laws;[48] and
- Statelessness due to loss of nationality and attendant rights.

These specific types of harm may befall children more frequently than adults due to their particular vulnerabilities.

B. Well-Founded Fear of Future Persecution

Second, an accurate assessment of whether a child has a well-founded fear of persecution requires a child-specific analysis of the whether the child's fear is subjectively genuine and objectively reasonable. The balance between subjective and objective elements may be more difficult for an adjudicator to assess, given that children may be unable to express their fear. For example, in *Abay v. Ashcroft*, the Sixth Circuit overturned the IJ's finding that a nine-year-old girl expressed only a "general ambiguous fear," noting that children may be incapable of articulating their fears in the same way as adults.[49] On the other hand, children may exaggerate their fear or have no objective basis for their fear.[50]

Moreover, children may not be able to understand and articulate the conditions in their home countries that make their fears reasonable. Thus, in some circumstances, the adjudicator may need to "make an objective assessment of the risk that the child would face, regardless of that child's fear."[51] Adjudicators also must consider child-specific circumstances in the child's country of origin, including the existence of child protection services, as these circumstances may be relevant to the reasonableness of the child's fear.[52] According to UNHCR, "When the parent or caregiver of a child has a well-founded fear of persecution for their child, it may be assumed that the child has such a fear, even if s/he does not express or feel that fear."[53]

The child's individual circumstances may also provide valuable insight into whether his or her fear is well-founded. For example, if the child has family members who are similarly situated to him or her and who have been harmed in the home country, such mistreatment of family members may support the child's well-founded fear.[54] Similarly, the child's circumstances of arrival in the United States may speak

---

[47] *See Id.* at ¶ 34–36.

[48] *See Id.* at ¶ 36.

[49] *Abay v. Ashcroft*, 368 F.3d 634, 640 (6th Cir. 2004).

[50] *See, e.g., Cruz-Diaz v. INS*, 86 F.3d 330, 331 (4th Cir. 1996).

[51] See UNHCR, Guidelines on International Protection No. 8, *supra* note 8, at ¶ 11.

[52] *See id.*

[53] *Id.*

[54] *Ananeh-Firempong v. INS*, 766 F.2d 621, 626 (1st Cir. 1985); *Matter of A–E–M–*, 21 I&N Dec. 1157 (BIA 1998).

to his or her well-founded fear; if the child's parents wish for him or her to be outside the country of origin due to fear for his or her safety, that may suggest that the child's fear is well-founded.[55] Additionally, if the child arrived in the United States with other asylum-seekers who have been found to have a well-founded fear of persecution, that may help to establish that the child's fear is well-founded.[56]

A child's age, maturity, development, and coping capacity also may influence whether the child has any safe and reasonable relocation options in the country of origin. Again, the best interests of the child principle should govern this determination.[57] A relocation that may be safe or reasonable for an adult may not be safe or reasonable in the case of a child.[58] For example, if an unaccompanied child does not have any relatives living in the country of origin willing to support or care for him or her, relocation would not be appropriate, as it could violate the right to life, survival and development, the best interests of the child, and the right not to be subjected to inhuman treatment.[59] Generally, it is not reasonable to expect a child to internally relocate by him or herself.[60]

C. Nexus to a Protected Ground

Third, children are not automatically eligible for asylum upon demonstrating past persecution or a well-founded fear of persecution. That persecution, like for adult claims, must be on account of a protected ground: race, religion, nationality, membership in a particular social group, or political opinion.[61]

Examples of persecution against children on account of their race, nationality, or ethnicity may include:

- Policies that deny children of a particular race or ethnicity the right to a nationality or to be registered at birth;
- Policies that deny children from particular ethnic groups their right to education or to health services;

---

[55] UNHCR Handbook, *supra* note 16, at ¶ 218.

[56] *See* 8 CFR §208.13(b)(2) (2014); UNHCR Handbook, *supra* note 16, at ¶ 217.

[57] See UNHCR, Guidelines on International Protection No. 8, supra note 8, at ¶ 53.

[58] *See id.* at ¶ 54–55.

[59] *See id.* at ¶ 56.

[60] AOBTC Lesson Plan on Children's Asylum Claims, *supra* note 10, at 42.

[61] *See* UNHCR, *Guidelines on International Protection No. 8*, *supra* note 8, at ¶ 40; AOBTC Lesson Plan on Children's Asylum Claims, *supra* note 10, at 42. *See e.g.*, *Lusingo v. Gonzalez*, 420 F.3d 193, 200 (3d Cir. 2005) (explaining that applicant's argument of well-founded fear of persecution was not based on the Tanzanian government's persecution of children, but instead on an imputed political opinion and fear of retaliation against him for causing embarrassment to the Tanzanian government); *Baballah v. Ashcroft*, 335 F.3d 981, 990–91 (9th Cir. 2003) (persecution of Israeli-Arab child of an intermarriage due to his mixed parentage is on account of either ethnicity or religion as a protected ground).

- Polices that aim to remove children from their parents on the basis of particular racial, ethnic, or indigenous backgrounds;
- Systematic targeting of girls belonging to ethnic minorities for rape or trafficking;[62] and
- Systematic targeting of children belonging to ethnic minorities for recruitment into armed forces or groups.[63]

Examples of persecution against children on account of their religion may include:

- Targeting of children because they are assumed to hold the same religious beliefs as their parents;[64]
- Targeting of a child's parents on account of their religion, resulting in severe traumatization of the child;[65]
- Extreme bullying, discrimination, and physical harm at the hands of fellow students, teachers, and school officials, and the police's refusal to provide protection;[66]
- Punishment of children for not fulfilling his or her assigned role or refusing to abide by the religious code;[67] and
- Harm because of a child's refusal to adhere to gender roles prescribed by a particular religion.[68]

Examples of persecution against children on account of their political opinions may include:

- Targeting of children engaging in student movements; and

---

[62] *See, e.g.*, *Paloka v. Holder*, 762 F.3d 191 (2d Cir. 2014); *Cece v. Holder,* 733 F.3d 662 (7th Cir. 2013).

[63] *See* UNHCR, Guidelines on International Protection No. 8, *supra* note 8, at ¶ 41.

[64] *See id.* at ¶ 42.

[65] *Rusak v. Holder*, 734 F.3d 894 (9th Cir. 2013) (holding that the applicant was entitled to a presumption of well-founded fear of future persecution where her mother had been arrested, beaten, and raped by police on account of the mother's church membership, the father had been severely beaten by police due to his religious affiliation and died of a heart attack thereafter, the applicant was severely traumatized by the abuse suffered by her parents, and there was not showing that conditions in Belarus had changed significantly since the time of the abuse).

[66] *Kholyavskiy v. Mukasey*, 540 F.3d 555 (7th Cir. 2008) (holding that substantial evidence did not support the IJ's determination that the individual was not subject to past persecution where he credibly testified that as a school child, he was forced into a school bathroom, his fellow students pulled down his pants and laughed at his circumcision; a girl had her dog attack and bite him so that he would not forget he was a Jew, and the police refused to help him locate the dog, forcing him to undergo a series of 40 rabies shots; his teachers required him to stand up and identify himself as a Jew each quarter; his school mates regularly mocked and urinated on him; and school officials did nothing to stop the discrimination).

[67] *See* UNHCR, *Guidelines on International Protection No. 8*, *supra* note 8, at ¶ 43.

[68] *See id.* at ¶¶ 44, 47.

- Targeting of children activists for distributing pamphlets, participating in demonstrations, acting as couriers, or engaging in subversive activities.[69]

Whether a child is capable of holding religious beliefs or political opinions is a question of fact and may depend on the child's maturity and development, level of education, and ability to articulate those beliefs or views. Moreover, a child may be unable to articulate his or her religion or political opinions.[70] The age and maturity of the child must be taken into account when considering his or her religious beliefs and political opinions, as well as his or her ability to articulate those beliefs and opinions.

However, as USCIS warns its officers in the context of political opinion claims, "Because the level of children's political activity varies widely among countries . . . asylum officers should not assume that age alone prevents a child from holding political opinions for which he or she may have been or will be persecuted."[71] In fact, the circuit courts have criticized IJs and the BIA for just that. In *Civil v. INS*, a case that considered the political opinion claim of a pro-Aristide Haitian youth, the First Circuit U.S. Court of Appeals criticized the IJ's conclusion that "it is almost inconceivable to believe that the Ton Ton Macoutes could be fearful of the conversations of 15-year-old children."[72] Similarly, the Ninth Circuit U.S. Court of Appeals overturned an adverse credibility determination by the BIA based on the BIA's conclusion that it was implausible that an 18-year-old had been vice present of a branch of the opposition movement.[73]

A persecutor also may impute religious beliefs or political opinions to a child based on his or her parents' or family members' beliefs or opinions.[74] Additionally, the fact that a child holds different religious beliefs or political opinions than his or her parents may itself lead to his or her persecution.

> **Practice Pointer**: Practitioners should carefully review their child client's family history and explore the child's understanding of his or her family's activities and beliefs. A thorough understanding of these factors may assist practitioners with identifying imputed religion or political opinion grounds for seeking asylum on behalf of their clients.

> **Practice Pointer**: If a child was targeted on account of an imputed religion or political opinion due to his or her parents' religious beliefs or political opinions, practitioners also should explore whether there may be a viable alternative asylum claim based membership in the particular social group of the family.

---

[69] *See* UNHCR, Guidelines on International Protection No. 8, *supra* note 8, at ¶ 45.

[70] AOBTC Lesson Plan on Children's Asylum Claims, *supra* note 10, at 44.

[71] *Id.*

[72] *Civil v. INS*, 140 F.3d 52 (1st Cir. 1998).

[73] *Salaam v. INS*, 229 F.3d 1234 (9th Cir. 2000).

[74] See UNHCR, Guidelines on International Protection No. 8, *supra* note 8, at ¶ 46.

> **Practice Pointer**: Practitioners also should consider whether the child's traits might cause a persecutor to impute a political opinion to him or her. As with adults, a child who refutes becoming associated with an armed force or group may be perceived as holding a political opinion that the force or group desires to eradicate.

Many children also bring claims based on their membership in various social groups. Although their young age is generally insufficient to meet the requirements for a viable social group, "other identity-based, economic and social characteristics of the child, such as family background, class, caste, health, education and income level, may increase the risk of harm, influence the type of persecutory conduct inflicted on the child and exacerbate the effect of the harm on the child."[75] UNHCR provides the following examples:

- Children who are homeless, abandoned, or otherwise without parental care may be at increased risk of sexual abuse and exploitation or of being recruited or used by an armed force, group, or criminal gang;
- Children with disabilities may be denied specialist or routine medical treatment or be ostracized by their family or community;
- Children born out of wedlock, in violation of coercive family planning polices, or through rape may face abuse and severe discrimination; and
- Pregnant girls may be rejected by their families and subject to harassment, violence, forced prostitution, or other demeaning work.[76]

A growing body of case law recognizes that children are eligible for asylum based on membership in a "particular social group." In an opinion vacated by the U.S. Supreme Court because the Ninth Circuit erred by reaching issues that the BIA had not ruled on in the first instance,[77] the Ninth Circuit held that seriously disabled Russian children and parents who provide their care constitute "a particular social group" due to their well-documented mistreatment by the state and society in general.[78] Similarly, in *Lukwago v. Ashcroft*, the Third Circuit U.S. Court of Appeals held that membership in a group of former child soldiers who have escaped captivity by rebels in Northern Uganda "fits precisely within the BIA's recognition that a shared past experience may be enough to link members of a 'particular social group.'"[79] Notably, the court specifically stated that this group is "*not* dependent on a

---

[75] UNHCR, Guidelines on International Protection No. 8, *supra* note 8, at ¶ 12.

[76] *Id.*

[77] *Gonzales v. Tchoukhrova*, 127 S. Ct. 57 (2006).

[78] *Tchoukhrova v. Gonzales*, 404 F.3d 1181, 1189–90 (9th Cir. 2005) ("[J]ust as their children's disabilities are 'immutable,' so is a parent's relationship to a disabled child. Because the parents and their disabled child incur harm as a unit, it is appropriate to combine family members into a single social group for purposes of asylum and withholding."), *vacated by Gonzales v. Tchoukhrova*, 549 U.S. 801 (2006).

[79] *Lukwago v. Ashcroft*, 329 F.3d 157, 179 (3d Cir. 2003).

member's current age, but rather the shared experience of abduction, persecution and escape at a time when he was a child."[80] In the same case, the court upheld the BIA's determination that the applicant was abducted by the rebels due to their need for labor, and that the applicant failed to demonstrate that the rebels targeted him because he was a child.[81] In a subsequent Third Circuit case, a juvenile applicant relied on *Lukwago* to argue that juvenile informants against international alien smuggling rings are similarly members of a "particular social group" based on a shared past experience.[82] Finding that the BIA had failed to provide a principled reason for denying the applicant's claim, the court of appeals remanded the case, noting that "once 'shared personal experience' is recognized as a legitimate immutable characteristic for defining 'a particular social group,' [that principle] is not easy to limit."[83]

Other courts have held that children are not considered to be a "particular social group" for purposes of establishing eligibility for asylum.[84] One court explained that children do not qualify as a "particular social group" because "unlike innate characteristics, such as sex or color, age changes over time, possibly lessening its role in personal identity."[85] For example, many jurisdictions have held that groups of young urban males do not constitute a "particular social group" within the meaning of the INA.[86] Youth asylum-seekers similarly have been unsuccessful in arguing membership in a social group of street children and fear of persecution based on pervasive violence against the group by government officials and street gangs.[87]

---

[80] *Id.* (emphasis added).

[81] *Id.* at 173.

[82] *Hong v. Att'y Gen.*, 165 F. App'x 995 (3d Cir. 2006).

[83] *Id.* at 1002.

[84] *Gomez v. INS*, 947 F.2d 660, 664 (2d Cir. 1991) ("Possession of broadly-based characteristics such as youth and gender will not by itself endow individuals with membership in a particular group.").

[85] *Lukwago*, *supra* note 79, at 179.

[86] *See, e.g.*, *Matter of Vigil*, 19 I&N Dec. 572, 575 (1988) (finding that a group of young, male, urban, unenlisted Salvadorans does not constitute a particular social group because "the factors that identify the respondent's group in the instant case (age, living environment, military status) are not factors that are 'fundamental to individual identity or conscience.'"); *Sanchez-Trujillo v. INS*, 801 F.2d 1571, 1576–77 (9th Cir. 1986) ("The class of young, working class, urban males of military age does not exemplify the type of 'social group' for which the immigration laws provide protection from persecution. Individuals falling within the parameters of this sweeping demographic division naturally manifest a plethora of different lifestyles, varying interests, diverse cultures, and contrary political leanings."); *Chavez v. INS*, 723 F.2d 1431, 1434 (9th Cir. 1984).

[87] *See e.g.*, *Guerra-Marchorro v. Holder*, 760 F.3d 126 (1st Cir. 2014) (holding that abandoned Guatemalan children lacking protection did not meet the standards for a cognizable social group); *Escobar v. Gonzales*, 417 F.3d 363 (3d Cir. 2005) ("Poverty, homelessness, and youth are far too vague and all-encompassing to be characteristics that set the perimeters for a protected group within the scope of the INA."); *Flores-Portillo v. Ashcroft*, 103 F. App'x 852, 853 (5th Cir. 2004) (finding that Honduran street children was "so broad that it was questionable whether it was a cognizable social group with a characteristic innate or fundamental to the group's identity."). Such cases have enjoyed some success, however, before the BIA and the immigration courts. *See, e.g.*, *Matter of B–F–O–* (BIA

Continued

Tattooed youth and young resisters of gang recruitment also have been unsuccessful social group claims for children and young adults.[88] In another line of cases, children of those directly victimized by coercive family planning policies are not per se eligible for immigration relief in their own right on the basis of their parent's persecution.[89]

> ➢ **Practice Pointer**: Many children in Central America are being targeted by the "third generation gangs" that rule large portions of El Salvador, Guatemala, and Honduras. It is essential for practitioners to continue bringing these valid asylum claims, despite the BIA's generally negative receipt of these claims. As the world changes and protection needs evolve along with the various types of violent conflict, U.S. asylum law needs to evolve as well. It is up to practitioners to continue making well-reasoned legal arguments supported by strong evidentiary records to demonstrate that these children merit protection under U.S. asylum law. See chapter 5 for a detailed discussion of gang-based asylum claims.

Now that the Board of Immigration Appeals (BIA) has set forth and re-affirmed its three-part test for viability of a social group, all social group claims have become markedly more challenging. The BIA now requires a three-step analysis for determining whether a group is a cognizable "particular social group" for purposes of asylum eligibility: (1) Determine whether the members of the group share a common,

---

2001) (unpublished) (finding that "abandoned street children in Nicaragua" met the requirements of a viable particular social group, where the boy had seen his parents killed by guerillas and been left on the streets where he was continuously vulnerable to violence and abuse), *posted on* AILA InfoNet Doc. No. 01120731 *and available at www.aila.org/infonet/bia-matter-of-b-f-o-11-06-01* (last visited Apr. 1, 2015); *Matter of A–M–L–, [number not provided]* (IJ Nov. 21, 2001) (Phoenix, AZ) (Richardson, IJ), *reported in* 79 INTERPRETER RELEASES 440 (Mar. 25, 2002); *Matter of Reyes-Diaz, [number not provided]* (IJ Aug. 2, 2001) (Los Angeles, CA) (Munoz, IJ).

[88] *Garcia v. Holder*, 746 F.3d 869 (8th Cir. 2014) (finding that the group lacked particularity and visibility required to be perceived by society as a cohesive group); *Umana-Ramos v. Holder*, 724 F.3d 667, 672 (6th Cir. 2013); *Zelaya v. Holder*, 668 F.3d 159 (4th Cir. 2012) (finding that the proposed group did not meet the particularity requirement); *Orellana-Monson v. Holder*, 685 F.3d 511 (5th Cir. 2012); *Gaitan v. Holder*, 671 F.3d 678 (8th Cir. 2012); *Rivera-Barrientos v. Holder*, 666 F.3d 641 (10th Cir. 2012) (stating that individuals who resist recruitment are "not in a substantially different situation from anyone who has crossed the gang, or who is perceived to be a threat to the gang's interests"); *Lizama v. Holder*, 629 F.3d 440 (4th Cir. 2011) (stating that the defined group was not narrow or enduring enough to clearly delineate its membership or readily identify its members); *Constanza v. Holder*, 647 F.3d 749 (8th Cir. 2011); *Mendez-Barrera v. Holder*, 602 F.3d 21 (2d Cir. 2010); *Santos-Lemus v. Mukasey*, 542 F.3d 738, 745 (9th Cir. 2008); *Castellano-Chacon v. INS*, 341 F.3d 533 (6th Cir. 2003); *Matter of M–E–V–G–*, 26 I&N Dec. 227 (BIA 2014); *Matter of S–E–G–*, 24 I&N Dec. 479 (BIA 2008).

[89] *See, e.g.*, *Chen v. Gonzalez*, 417 F.3d 303, 305 (2d Cir. 2005) (holding that the applicant, a native and citizen of the People's Republic of China, could not establish eligibility for refugee status on the basis of his mother's alleged forced sterilization); *Wang v. Gonzalez*, 405 F.3d 134, 144 (3d Cir. 2005) (stating that in a case where the applicant's parents were subject to government persecution after violating China's one-child-per-family policy, the child-applicant could not obtain relief because he did not show that the persecution threatened his own "life or freedom").

immutable characteristic; (2) Determine whether the group is socially distinct in the context of the society in question; and (3) Determine whether the group is sufficiently particular.[90]

Although age is "neither innate nor permanent as it changes continuously," being a child is a common, immutable characteristic at any given point in time.[91] A child cannot change his or her age in order to avoid the persecution feared. As UNHCR states, "The fact that the child eventually will grow older is irrelevant to the identification of a particular social group."[92] Being a child also is socially distinct; society views children as a group. Many government policies are age-driven, and most societies set children apart from adults because they require special attention or care.

Finally, being a child has distinct boundaries; one is either a child or he or she is not. Whether this meets the BIA's particularity prong, however, is questionable, given the Board's dicta in *Matter of W-G-R-*, which requires a group to be sufficiently distinct that it would constitute a discrete class of persons with definable boundaries.[93] "Children" may be perceived as being too overbroad, too diffuse, too amorphous, or too subjective because "the group could include persons of any age, sex, or background."[94] Thus, most viable social groups based on "children" may need to be accompanied by other characteristics defining the group more specifically. UNHCR suggests the following potentially viable social groups:

- Abandoned children;[95]
- Children with disabilities;[96]
- Orphans;[97]

---

[90] *Matter of M–E–V–G–*, 26 I&N Dec. 227 (BIA 2014); *Matter of W–G–R–*, 26 I&N Dec. 208 (BIA 2014), *clarifying Matter of E–A–G–*, 24 I&N Dec. 591 (BIA 2008); *Matter of S–E–G–*, 24 I&N Dec. 579 (BIA 2008); *Matter of A–M–E– & J–G–U–*, 24 I&N Dec. 69 (BIA 2007); *and Matter of C–A–*, 23 I&N Dec. 951, 959–61 (BIA 2006) (noting that UNHCR's *Guidelines* confirm that "visibility" is an important element), *aff'd Castillo-Arias v. Att'y Gen.*, 446 F.3d 1190 (11th Cir. 2006), *cert. denied*, 127 S.Ct. 977 (Jan. 8, 2007). Note that the "social distinction" requirement used to be called "social visibility." *See also Matter of E–A–G–*, 24 I&N Dec. 591, 594 (BIA 2007) and *Matter of S–E–G–*, 24 I&N Dec. 579, 586–88 (BIA 2007). The social group approach applied by the BIA in *Matter of E–A–G–* and *Matter of S–E–G–*, which required social visibility and particularity, was criticized by UNHCR in an amicus brief filed in the U.S. Court of Appeals for the Third Circuit in a gang-based persecution case. The brief is available at *www.unhcr.org/refworld/pdfid/49ef25102.pdf* (last visited June 7, 2014).

[91] UNHCR, Guidelines on International Protection No. 8, *supra* note 8, at ¶ 49.

[92] *Id.*

[93] *Matter of M–E–V–G–*, 26 I&N Dec. at 239–40; *Matter of W–G–R–*, 26 I&N Dec. at 213–15.

[94] *Matter of W–G–R–*, 26 I&N Dec. at 221.

[95] UNHCR, Guidelines on International Protection No. 8, *supra* note 8, at ¶ 50.

[96] *Id.* at ¶ 50.

[97] *Id.*

- Children born outside coercive family planning policies or of unauthorized marriages;[98]
- Street children;[99]
- Former child soldiers;[100]
- Children affected by HIV/AIDS;[101] and
- Children who are singled out as a target group for recruitment or use by an armed force or group.[102]

Like for gender-based claims, where it is the individual's gender combined with other gender-related characteristics that make up a viable social group (*e.g.*, "married women in Guatemala who are unable to leave their relationship"[103]), the individual's status as a child likely must be combined with other child-specific traits to constitute a cognizable group under BIA precedent.[104]

> ➢ **Practice Pointer**: Practitioners should consider whether the child's family might constitute a relevant social group. Family has been a long-recognized social group for purposes of asylum eligibility. Family units also are usually recognized as distinct within societies and have definable boundaries.[105]

> ➢ **Practice Pointer**: It also may be possible that harm to a child may constitute persecution of the child's parent, as children are too-often used as tools of harm against their parents.[106]

---

[98] *Id.*

[99] *Id.* at ¶ 51–52.

[100] *Id.* at ¶ 52.

[101] UNHCR, Guidelines on International Protection No. 8, *supra* note 8, at ¶ 52.

[102] UNHCR, Guidelines on International Protection No. 8, *supra* note 8, at ¶ 52.

[103] *Matter of A–R–C–G–*, 26 I&N Dec. 388 (BIA 2014).

[104] See chapters 2 and 5 for detailed discussions of the legal standards for formulating a viable particular social group under current law.

[105] *Crespin-Valladares v. Holder*, 632 F.3d 117 (4th Cir. 2011) (holding that "family members of those who actively oppose gangs in El Salvador by agreeing to be prosecutorial witnesses" was a particular social group); *Torres v. Mukasey*, 551 F.3d 616, 629 (7th Cir. 2008); *Vumi v. Gonzales*, 502 F.3d 150 (2d Cir. 2007); *Lopez-Soto v. Ashcroft*, 383 F.3d 228, 235 (4th Cir. 2004); *Jie Lin v. Ashcroft*, 377 F.3d 1014, 1028 (9th Cir. 2004); *Lwin v. INS*, 144 F.3d 505 (7th Cir. 1998); *Iliev v. INS*, 127 F.3d 638, 642 (7th Cir. 1997); *Gebremichael v. INS*, 10 F.3d 28 (1st Cir. 1993); *Matter of C–A–*, 23 I&N Dec. 951 (BIA 2006); *Matter of Acosta*, 19 I&N Dec. 211, 233 (BIA 1985) (noting kinship ties are a common, immutable characteristic), *overruled on other grounds by Matter of Mogharrabi*, 19 I&N Dec. 439 (BIA 1987).

[106] *See, e.g., Sumolang v. Holder*, 732 F.3d 1080 (9th Cir. 2013) (holding that an Indonesian hospital's alleged delay in treating an applicant's daughter was relevant to whether the applicant suffered past persecution, where the staff of the public hospital deliberately delayed administering medical treatment to the applicant's 3-month-old daughter on account of the applicant's race and religion in order to send a message to the child's parents).

In adjudicating children's asylum claims and considering nexus to one of the protected grounds, USCIS instructs its asylum officers to acknowledge that children may be unable to articulate a nexus to a protected characteristic because children may not understand the persecutor's intent.[107] USCIS states, "[A] nexus can still be found if the objective circumstances support the child's claim that at least one central reason for the past or future persecution is a protected ground."[108]

D. Government Actor or Groups the Government is Unable or Unwilling to Control

In asylum claims based on youth or childhood, more often than not, the persecutor is a non-State actor, such as "militarized groups, criminal gangs, parents and other caregivers, community and religious leaders."[109] Thus, part of the analysis of these claims usually must include consideration of whether the government is unable or unwilling to protect the child.[110] If it can be shown that the government has not taken sufficient action to provide meaningful protection to the child, this part of the eligibility analysis may be met. This assessment depends on whether the government's legal system criminalizes and provides sanctions for the persecutory conduct and whether the authorities actually investigate and punish according to those laws to protect children.[111] Additionally, this assessment must take into account the perspective of the child. As UNHCR states:

> [D]ue to their young age, children may not be able to approach law enforcement officials or articulate their fear or complaint in the same way as adults. Children may be more easily dismissed or not taken seriously by the officials concerned, and the officials themselves may lack the skills necessary to interview and listen to children.[112]

E. Grounds of Ineligibility and Bars to Relief

Several acts may render applicants undeserving of protection. Grounds of ineligibility and bars to asylum that apply to adults, however, may not apply to children at all, or may be applied differently in considering children's unique vulnerabilities and diminished emotional, mental, and intellectual maturity and development. Whether an ineligibility ground or bar to asylum applies must be an individualized analysis thoroughly considering all circumstances.

---

[107] AOBTC Lesson Plan on Children's Asylum Claims, *supra* note 10, at 43.

[108] *Id.* (citing INA §208(b)(1)(B)(i); *Matter of J–B–N– & S–M–*, 24 I&N Dec. 208 (BIA 2007); *Matter of S–P–*, 21 I&N Dec. 486 (BIA 1996).

[109] UNHCR, *Guidelines on International Protection No. 8*, *supra* note 8, at ¶ 37.

[110] *See* AOBTC Lesson Plan on Children's Asylum Claims, *supra* note 10, at 40. *See also Matter of V–T–S–,* 21 I&N Dec. 792 (BIA 1997); *Matter of Kasinga,* 21 I&N Dec. 357 (BIA 1996); *Matter of Villalta,* 20 I&N Dec. 142 (BIA 1990).

[111] UNHCR, *Guidelines on International Protection No. 8*, *supra* note 8, at ¶ 38.

[112] *Id.* at ¶ 39.

➢ **Practice Pointer**: See chapter 2 of this book for a detailed discussion of these grounds of ineligibility and statutory bars to relief.

1. Ineligibility Grounds

There are three circumstances that render an asylum-seeker ineligible to apply for asylum on or after April 1, 1997:[113] (1) if there is a safe third country available to the asylum-seeker where his or her life or freedom would not be threatened and where he or she would have access to full and fair procedures for determining asylum eligibility;[114] (2) if the asylum-seeker did not file his or her application for asylum within one year of his or her arrival in the United States;[115] and (3) if the asylum-seeker previously applied for and was denied asylum.[116] There are exceptions to each of these three ineligibility grounds for asylum,[117] and these grounds do not apply at all to withholding of removal.[118]

i. Safe Third Country

First, an applicant is barred from applying for asylum if he or she may be removed to a "safe third country."[119] The removal must be "pursuant to a bilateral or multilateral agreement," and must be to a country other than the individual's home country or, in the case of a stateless person, other than the country of the individual's last habitual residence.[120] The "safe third country" must also be a country where the individual's "life or freedom would not be threatened on account of race, religion, nationality, membership in a particular social group, or political opinion," and where the individual would have "access to a full and fair procedure for determining a claim to asylum or equivalent temporary protection."[121] This provision does not apply at all to unaccompanied children.[122]

---

[113] INA §208(a)(2); 8 CFR §208.4(a) (2014).

[114] INA §208(a)(2)(A).

[115] INA §§208(a)(2)(B), (d); 8 CFR §§208.4(a)(4)–(5) (2014).

[116] INA §§208(a)(2)(C)–(D). This bar only applies if the applicant for asylum was issued a final order of removal. It does not apply if the previous application was denied only by the Asylum Office.

[117] *See infra* Parts IV.A.2–3. for detailed discussions of the exceptions to the one-year filing deadline and the previous asylum denial ineligibility grounds.

[118] *See* INA §241(b)(3); 8 CFR §§208.16, 1208.16 (2014).

[119] INA §208(a)(2)(A); 8 USC §1158(a)(2)(A) (2012).

[120] INA §208(a)(2)(A); 8 USC §1158(a)(2)(A) (2012).

[121] INA §208(a)(2)(A); 8 USC §1158(a)(2)(A) (2012). The AG may waive this bar upon finding that it is in the "public interest" for the individual to receive asylum in the United States. INA §208(a)(2)(A); 8 USC §1158(a)(2)(A) (2012). Under the Homeland Security Act of 2002, this waiver authority would extend to the DHS secretary and other DHS officials. *See* Homeland Security Act of 2002, Pub. L. No. 107-296, §§456, 1512, 1517, 116 Stat. 2135, 2200, 2310, 2311.

[122] INA §208(a)(2)(E); 8 USC §1158(a)(2)(E) (2012), as amended by the Trafficking Victims Protection Reauthorization Act of 2008.

The United States currently has a safe-third country agreement with Canada.[123] Final U.S. regulations implementing this agreement were published on November 29, 2004,[124] and became effective on December 29, 2004.[125] "Unaccompanied minors" is a specified exception to the agreement under both U.S. and Canadian regulations implementing the agreement.[126] Under the regulations, the safe third country provision does not apply at all to "unaccompanied alien children," as defined by 6 USC §279(g).[127] An unaccompanied alien child in the context of the safe third country provision is an unmarried child under the age of 18 who has no parent or legal guardian in the United States or Canada.[128]

ii. One-Year Filing Deadline

Second, on or after April 1, 1998, and with limited exceptions, an individual is barred from applying for asylum if he or she fails to demonstrate "by clear and convincing evidence that the application has been filed within one year after the date of [his or her] arrival in the U.S."[129] Pursuant to amendments made by the 2008 Trafficking Victims Protection Reauthorization Act (TVPRA), this one-year filing deadline does not apply at all to "unaccompanied alien children," as defined by 6 USC §279(g).[130] An "unaccompanied alien child" is a child under the age of 18 who has no parent or legal guardian in the United States who is able to provide care and physical custody.[131] The definition of "unaccompanied alien child" in the TVPRA also includes the element of not having lawful status.[132] Thus, for an unaccompanied child who is not in valid immigration status, as of March 23, 2009, the effective date of the TVPRA, the one-year filing deadline analysis should be foregone entirely.

Since this amendment applies only to children who meet the definition of "unaccompanied alien child" in the TVPRA, certain children are still subject to the one-year filing deadline.[133] However, although the deadline applies and must be analyzed in considering many children's asylum claims, it is likely that the child falls

---

[123] Canada-U.S. Safe Third Country Agreement, available at *www.cic.gc.ca/english/department/laws-policy/menu-safethird.asp* (last visited Oct. 31, 2014).

[124] 69 Fed. Reg. 69479 (Nov. 29, 2004).

[125] *Id.*

[126] 8 CFR §208.30(e)(6)(iii) (2014).

[127] 8 CFR §208.30(e)(6)(iii)(D) (2014).

[128] 6 USC §279(g)(2) (2012).

[129] INA §208(a)(2)(D); 8 USC §1158(a)(2)(D) (2012).

[130] INA §208(a)(2)(E); 8 USC §1158(a)(2)(E) (2012), as amended by the Trafficking Victims Protection Reauthorization Act of 2008, P.L. No. 110-457, §235(d)(7)(A). Note that the TVPRA exempts only out-of-status unaccompanied children from the one-year filing deadline. Thus, the one-year filing deadline still must be analyzed for in-status unaccompanied children and accompanied minor principal applicants.

[131] 6 USC §279(g)(2) (2012).

[132] INA §208(a)(2)(E); TVPRA, P.L. 110-457, §235(d)(7)(A).

[133] *See* AOBTC Lesson Plan on Children's Asylum Claims, *supra* note 10, at 45–46.

squarely within one or both of the exceptions to the one-year filing deadline — changed circumstances and extraordinary circumstances.

One exception to the one-year filing deadline is where there are changed circumstances that materially affect an applicant's eligibility for asylum.[134] To show that the exception applies, there are three steps: (1) identify and show the existence of a changed circumstance; (2) demonstrate that the changed circumstance is material to the applicant's eligibility for asylum; and (3) establish that the application was filed within a reasonable period of time after the changed circumstance.[135] For step one, identifying the changed circumstance, the federal regulations list specific types of "changed circumstances" that may excuse a late filing of an asylum application.[136] In the case of a child who had previously been included as a dependent in another applicant's pending asylum application, the loss of the parent-child relationship to the principal applicant through the attainment of age 21, for example, is a "changed circumstance" that may excuse a late filing of an asylum application.[137]

The other exception to the one-year filing deadline is where extraordinary circumstances exist that directly relate to the applicant's delay in filing the application.[138] Like the changed circumstances exception, there are three steps to demonstrate that this exception applies: (1) identify and show that an extraordinary circumstance exists; (2) demonstrate that the extraordinary circumstance was directly related to the failure to timely file; and (3) establish that the application was filed within a reasonable period of time given the extraordinary circumstance.[139] Under the regulations, "extraordinary circumstances" may include, legal disability during the one-year period after arrival (i.e. incapacity for the full enjoyment of ordinary legal rights, including unaccompanied minors and those suffering from mental impairment).[140] Although the regulations provide "unaccompanied minor" as an example of legal disability during the one-year period, an "accompanied" minor may also meet the "extraordinary circumstances" exception, since the examples given in the regulations are not an exhaustive list.[141] As USCIS notes in its guidelines, "The same logic underlying the legal disability ground listed in the regulations is also relevant to accompanied minors: minors, whether accompanied or not, are generally dependent on adults for their care and cannot be expected to navigate adjudicator systems in the same manner as adults."[142] USCIS instructs its asylum officers, "As

[134] INA §208(a)(2)(D).

[135] 8 CFR §§208.4(a), 1208.4(a) (2014).

[136] *Id.*

[137] 8 CFR §§208.4(a)(4)(i), 1208.4(a)(4)(i) (2014).

[138] 8 CFR §§208.4(a)(5), 1208.4(a)(5) (2014).

[139] 8 CFR §§208.4(a)(5), 1208.4(a)(5) (2014).

[140] 8 CFR §§208.4(a)(5)(ii), 1208.4(a)(5)(ii) (2014).

[141] 8 CFR §§208.4(a)(5), 1208.4(a)(5) (2014); *see also El Himri v. Ashcroft*, 378 F.3d 932, 936 (9th Cir. 2004) (noting that the claim of a minor living with his parents was not time-barred).

[142] AOBTC Lesson Plan on Children's Asylum Claims, *supra* note 10, at 46.

long as an accompanied minor applicant applies for asylum while still a minor (while the legal disability is in effect), the applicant should be found to have filed within a reasonable period of time."[143]

In its precedent decision addressing "extraordinary circumstances," *Matter of Y–C–*, the BIA found that an applicant who entered the United States as an unaccompanied minor and who failed to file his application within one year of his arrival established that such failure was due to "extraordinary circumstances."[144] In finding that the applicant had met the three-part test for the exception, the BIA noted that the applicant was 15 years old when he arrived in the United States as an unaccompanied minor, that he remained in the status of unaccompanied minor throughout the one-year period, that he was in legacy INS custody for one year, that five months after his release an IJ rejected his application for asylum, and that the application that was finally accepted by the IJ was filed within one year of his release from INS custody.[145]

As minors are generally dependent on adults for their care and cannot be expected to navigate legal systems in the same way as adults, all minors, whether accompanied or unaccompanied, likely have legal disability that constitutes an extraordinary circumstance.[146]

iii. Previous Asylum Denial

Third, an individual is not eligible to apply for asylum if he or she "has previously applied for asylum and had such application denied" by an immigration judge (IJ) or the BIA.[147] An application may be considered, despite a previous denial by an IJ or the BIA, if the applicant "demonstrates to the satisfaction of the [AG] ... the existence of changed circumstances which materially affect the applicant's eligibility for asylum."[148] The asylum regulations provide that such changed circumstances may include, in the case of a child who had previously been included as a dependent in another applicant's pending asylum application, the loss of the parent-child relationship to the principal applicant through the attainment of age 21.[149] The

---

[143] *Id.*

[144] *Matter of Y–C–*, 23 I&N Dec. 286 (BIA 2002).

[145] *Id. See also El Himri v. Ashcroft*, 378 F.3d 932, 936 (9th Cir. 2004) (noting that the claim of a minor living with his parents was not time-barred).

[146] AOBTC Lesson Plan on Children's Asylum Claims, *supra* note 10, at 15.

[147] INA §§208(a)(2)(C)–(D); 8 CFR §§208.4(a)(3), 1208.4(a)(3) (2014).

[148] INA §208(a)(2)(D); 8 USC §1158(a)(2)(D) (2012).

[149] 8 CFR §§208.4(a)(4)(i), 1208.4(a)(4)(i) (2014). Note, however, that if the applicant is initiating a new claim by filing a motion to reopen beyond the 90-day period for filing such motions, he or she must demonstrate "changed circumstances arising in the country of nationality or in the country to which deportation has been ordered, if such evidence is material and was not available and could not have been discovered or presented at the previous hearing." 8 CFR §1003.2(c)(3)(ii) (2014); *see also Matter of J–J–*, 21 I&N Dec. 976 (BIA 1997). The changed circumstances regulations for motions to reopen do not recognize changes in the applicant's personal circumstances or changes in U.S. law. *See*

Continued

regulations require that the applicant must file the new application for asylum within a "reasonable period" given those changed circumstances.[150] If the applicant can establish that he or she did not become aware of the changed circumstances until after they occurred, such delayed awareness must be taken into account in determining what constitutes a "reasonable period."[151]

2. *Statutory Bars to Asylum*

In addition to these three ineligibility grounds for asylum, there are six statutory bars that prevent an applicant from being granted asylum, even if he or she may qualify as a "refugee" within the meaning of INA §101(a)(42)(A).[152] These include: (1) if the applicant ordered, incited, assisted or otherwise participated in the persecution of others;[153] (2) if the applicant has been convicted by a final judgment of a particularly serious crime in the United States, and thus constitutes a danger to the community;[154] (3) if there are serious reasons for believing that the applicant has committed a serious nonpolitical crime outside of the United States prior to his or her arrival;[155] (4) if there are reasonable grounds for regarding the alien as a danger to the security of the United States;[156] (5) if the applicant meet the definition of a terrorist, has participated in terrorist activity, or has given material support to a terrorist organization;[157] and (6) if the applicant was firmly resettled in another country prior to his or her arrival in the United States.[158]

---

8 CFR §1003.2(c)(3)(ii) (2014). *See also infra* chapter 11 for a detailed discussion of motions to reopen.

[150] 8 CFR §§208.4(a)(4)(ii), 1208.4(a)(4)(ii) (2014).

[151] 8 CFR §§208.4(a)(4)(ii), 1208.4(a)(4)(ii).

[152] INA §§208(b)(2)(A)–(B).

[153] INA §§101(a)(42)(B), 208(b)(2)(A)(i).

[154] INA §208(b)(2)(A)(ii). If a conviction is an aggravated felony for which there is an aggregate term of imprisonment for five years, it is a conviction for a particularly serious crime and automatically bars a grant of asylum. *See Matter of B–*, 20 I&N Dec. 427 (BIA 1991).

[155] INA §208(b)(2)(A)(iii).

[156] INA §208(b)(2)(A)(iv).

[157] INA §§212(a)(3)(B)(i)(I)–(IV), (VI), 237(a)(4)(B). This bar is waivable by DHS under certain circumstances, including for persons who provided material support to terrorist organizations under duress. *See* INA §212(d)(3)(B)(i); Memo, Chertoff, Secy. of DHS, Exercise of Authority Under Sec. 212(d)(3)(B)(i) (Apr. 27, 2007).

[158] 8 CFR §§208.13(c)(2)(i)(B), 208.15. An applicant is deemed firmly resettled if he or she entered the country with, or while in the country received, an offer of permanent resident status, citizenship, or other type of permanent status. *See* 8 CFR §§208.15, 1208.15. The government has the burden of proving firm resettlement, and the applicant may rebut firm resettlement by demonstrating an exception under 8 CFR §§208.15(a)–(b).

The first four of these bars — persecution of others, particularly serious crime, serious nonpolitical crime, and danger to the security of the United States — also bar an individual from being granted withholding of removal under INA §241(b)(3).[159]

These bars apply and must be analyzed both for children who are principle applicants and children who are derivative applicants on their parents' applications. For example, the particularly serious crime and serious nonpolitical crime bars not only apply to the principal applicant, but also apply independently to a child who is included on an asylum application, but who has been convicted of a particularly serious crime or for whom there are serious reasons to believe that he or she committed a serious nonpolitical crime. Such children may be barred from being granted asylum as a derivative.[160]

- **Practice Pointer**: See Part VI below for a detailed discussion of children as derivative applicants on their parents' asylum applications.

Although participation in the persecution of others, criminal or terrorist activity, and firmly resettling in another country before entering the United States may render certain applicants undeserving of protection, these bars to asylum must be applied differently to children's asylum applications, as children's unique vulnerabilities and diminished emotional, mental, and intellectual maturity and development must be considered. The younger the child, the greater the likelihood that he or she lacked the requisite mental capacity to be held responsible for particular acts that would normally bar an adult from protection. Therefore, whether an ineligibility ground or bar to asylum applies must be an individualized analysis thoroughly considering all circumstances.

For example, a child soldier's own rights may have been violated and he or she may be a victim, not only a perpetrator, of offenses against international law. The child may not be able to "understand and consent to acts that they are requested or ordered to undertake."[161] UNHCR provides guidance regarding what factors must be considered in applying ineligibility grounds and bars to asylum because of acts committed by children:

- Whether the child had the requisite intent and knowledge to be held individually responsible for the relevant act — Was the child sufficiently mature to understand the nature and consequences of his or her conduct? Was the child suffering from a mental disability, involuntarily intoxicated, or lacking maturity?

---

[159] *See* INA §§241(b)(3)(B)(i)–(iv). *See also Matter of N–A–M–*, 24 I&N Dec. 336 (BIA 2007) (addressing the particularly serious crime bar to withholding of removal); *Matter of A–H–*, 23 I&N Dec. 774 (AG 2005) (addressing the persecution of others and danger to the security of the U.S. bars to withholding of removal); *Matter of McMullen*, 19 I&N Dec. 90 (BIA 1984) (addressing the serious nonpolitical crime bar to withholding of removal).

[160] 8 CFR §208.21(a) (2014).

[161] UNHCR, Guidelines on International Protection No. 8, *supra* note 8, at ¶ 63.

- Whether the child acted under duress, coercion, or in defense of self or others — How old was the child? Why did the child become involved? How long was the child involved in those acts? Were there consequences for refusal to be involved? Was the child forced to use drugs, alcohol or medication? What was the child's level of education and understanding of the events in question? Was the child a victim of trauma, abuse, or ill treatment?;
- Whether the consequences of applying the ineligibility ground or bar to relief are proportional to the seriousness of the act committed — Were there mitigating or aggravating factors? What was the child's age, maturity, and vulnerability? What consequences and treatment would the child face upon return?[162]

In interpreting whether a child firmly resettled elsewhere prior to entering the United States, asylum officers are advised to consider that "a child's status in a third country will generally be the same as his or her parent's."[163] The BIA has long held that a parent's status is imputed to his or her children.[164]

A child-sensitive interpretation of U.S. asylum laws does not mean that child asylum-seekers are automatically entitled to relief. However, such an interpretation, along with accompanying procedural safeguards, is necessary to protect the best interests of the child as he or she proceeds through the labyrinth of the U.S. asylum system in seeking protection.

> **Practice Pointer**: In addition to asylum, children may be eligible for other child-specific forms of relief, such as Special Immigrant Juvenile Status (SIJS). Under INA §101(a)(27)(J), a "special immigrant" is an immigrant who is present in the United States: (1) who has been declared dependent in a juvenile court or whom the court has placed under the custody of an appointed guardian; (2) who is unable to be reunified with one or both parents due to abuse, neglect, or abandonment; (3) for whom it has been determined in juvenile proceedings that it would not be in the child's bet interest to be returned to his or her country of origin or last habitual residence; and (4) who merits a favorable exercise of DHS's discretion. Many children who are eligible for asylum may also be eligible for SIJS. Thus, practitioners should consider this option and pursue it concurrently if the child may

---

[162] *Id.* at ¶ 64.

[163] *See* AOBTC Lesson Plan on Children's Asylum Claims, *supra* note 10, at 47. *See also* 8 CFR §208.15 (2014).

[164] *Matter of Ng,* 12 I&N Dec. 411 (BIA 1967) (holding that a minor was firmly resettled in Hong Kong because he was part of a family that resettled in Hong Kong); *Matter of Hung,* 12 I&N Dec. 178 (BIA 1967) (holding that because parents were not firmly resettled in Hong Kong, the minor child also was not firmly resettled there). *See also Vang v. INS,* 146 F.3d 1114, 1116 (9th Cir. 1998) (holding that the parents' status is attributed to the minor when determining whether the minor has firmly resettled in another country).

be eligible. See chapter 16 of this book for a detailed discussion of related forms of relief, including SIJS.

➢ **Practice Pointer**: Children also may be eligible for T visas as victims of trafficking or U visas as victims of criminal activity. T visas are available to individuals who have been victims of severe forms of trafficking in persons, who are present in the U.S. as a result of such trafficking, who "would suffer extreme hardship involving unusual and severe harm upon removal," and who comply with government requests for assistance in investigating or prosecuting the acts of trafficking.[165] U visas are available to individuals who have "suffered substantial physical or mental abuse as a result of having been a victim" of qualifying criminal activity, which violated U.S. laws or occurred in the U.S., who possess information related to that criminal activity, and who aid in the investigation or prosecution of that criminal activity.[166] T and U visa holders may be eligible to adjust status after being in T or U status for three years. See chapter 16 of this book for a detailed discussion of related forms of relief, including T and U visas.

II. Application Procedures for Children

Children's brain make-up is different than adults' because their brains are still developing. This can affect their ability to comprehend their rights and the consequences of their actions.[167] The physiological differences in children's brains help explain why:

> [T]hey have not learned to coordinate emotion, intellect, behavior, and ability while considering long term-goals and consequences; they have a different sense of time, being much more focused on the immediate; they are much more impulsive with little consideration of or regard to long-term consequences; they evaluate risk differently, resulting in increased risk taking; and they are more susceptible to peer pressure and other outside influences.[168]

---

[165] INA §101(a)(15)(T)(i).

[166] INA §101(a)(15)(U)(i).

[167] *See* Kenneth J. King, *Waiving Childhood Goodbye: How Juvenile Courts Fail to Protect Children from Unknowing, Unintelligent, and Involuntary Waivers of Miranda Rights*, 2006 Wis. L. Rev. 431, 434–45 (2006); Sally T. Green, *The Admissibility of Expert Witness Testimony Based on Adolescent Brain Imaging Technology in the Prosecution of Juveniles: How Fairness and Neuroscience Overcome the Evidentiary Obstacles to Allow for Application of a Modified Common Law Infancy Defense*, 12 N.C.J.L. & TECH. 1 (Fall 2010).

[168] Dree K. Collopy, *No Minor Issue: The Diminished Capacity of Minors in Our Immigration System*, 12-04 IMMIGR. BRIEFINGS 1 (April 2012) (citing Laurence Steinberg & Elizabeth Scott, *Less Guilty by Reason of Adolescence: Developmental Immaturity, Diminished Responsibility, and the Juvenile Death Penalty*, 58 Am. Psychologist 1009, 1012–13 (2003)).

These important differences between children's and adults' brains, perceptions of experiences, analysis of situations, and capacity to process and reason with information has led to the recognition that children should be treated differently than adults in our legal system.[169]

In general, children have diminished capacity to exercise mature judgment and to understand the laws, the legal system, and the consequences of their actions. Given these particular vulnerabilities, children merit special protections and different treatment in many legal contexts, including in the application of U.S. asylum law. The Convention on the Rights of the Child recognizes the right of refugee children and children seeking refugee status to appropriate safeguards and humanitarian assistance in seeking such protections.[170] As UNHCR states, "Children may not be able to articulate their claims to refugee status in the same way as adults, and therefore, may require special assistance to do so."[171] Due to their "young age, dependency and relative immaturity, children should enjoy specific procedural and evidentiary safeguards to ensure that fair refugee status determination decisions are reached with respect to their claims."[172] Thus, special procedures exist for children to apply for asylum both affirmatively and defensively in the United States.

The first determination to be made in processing a child's claim for asylum, withholding of removal under INA §241(b)(3), or protection under the Convention Against Torture is whether the child meets the definition of "unaccompanied alien child" under 6 USC §279(g)(2). This is because child asylum-seekers who are unaccompanied are subject to different procedures than accompanied children.

- **Practice Pointer**: See Part III below for a detailed discussion of the asylum procedures for unaccompanied alien children.

In certain circumstances, a child's age might be in doubt and may require completion of an age assessment that takes into account both the physical appearance and the psychological maturity of the individual.[173] DNA testing usually will not be used unless authorized by law and with the consent of the individuals being tested.[174]

---

[169] *See* Steinberg & Scott, *Less Guilty by Reason of Adolescence*, *supra* note 168; Laurence Steinberg, *Cognitive and Affective Development in Adolescence*, 9 TRENDS IN COGNITIVE SCI. 69, 70 (2005) ("[A]t the core of adolescent cognitive development is the attainment of a more fully conscious, self-directed and self-regulating mind. This is achieved principally through the assembly of an advanced 'executive suite' of capabilities, rather than through specific advancement in any one of the constituent elements.").

[170] *See* Convention on Rights of the Child, *supra* note 1, at art. 22.

[171] UNHCR, *Guidelines on International Protection No. 8*, *supra* note 8, at ¶ 2.

[172] *Id.* at ¶ 65.

[173] UNHCR, *Guidelines on International Protection No. 8*, *supra* note 8, at ¶ 75.

[174] *Id.* at ¶ 76.

A. Priority Processing

UNHCR recommends that child applicants, whether they are accompanied or not, should normally be processed on a priority basis due to children's special protection and assistance needs.[175] Juvenile immigration cases must be heard in a timely manner, and at least one court has found that the right to a speedy juvenile proceeding is recognized under the fundamental fairness guarantees of due process.[176] Although UNHCR recommends reduced waiting periods for children at each stage of the asylum process, however, UNHCR also notes that "children require sufficient time in which to prepare for and reflect on rendering the account of their experiences. They will need time to build trusting relationships with their guardian and other professional staff and to feel safe and secure."[177]

In recent years, a "surge" of children has crossed the southern border of the United States to seek protection from the unfettered violence that has consumed the Northern Triangle of Central America (El Salvador, Guatemala, and Honduras).[178] According to CBP, 68,541 unaccompanied children were apprehended at the southwest border in fiscal year 2014, compared with 38,759 children in fiscal year 2013 — an increase of 77 percent.[179] As a result, the Obama Administration has termed the influx of children along the border "an urgent humanitarian situation" requiring coordination among federal government agencies.[180] Part of the response has been to prioritize the processing of children's asylum claims, both before the asylum offices and the immigration courts.

In December of 2014, the USCIS Asylum Division adjusted its scheduler to prioritize children's asylum claims over adult asylum claims.[181] This means that children's asylum interviews will be scheduled before those of adults and their asylum applications will be processed faster. Similarly, the Department of Justice has issued a directive to the immigration courts to "fast-track" the cases of recent arrivals across the southwest border of the United States, including unaccompanied

---

[175] UNHCR, Guidelines on International Protection No. 8, *supra* note 8, at ¶ 66.

[176] *In re Thomas J.*, 811 A.2d 310 (Md. 2002).

[177] UNHCR, Guidelines on International Protection No. 8, *supra* note 8, at ¶ 66.

[178] UNHCR, Children on the Run, *supra* note 5; Women's Refugee Comm'n, Forced From Home, *supra* note 5. In fiscal year 2014, 27 percent of children apprehended along the southern border of the U.S. came from Honduras, 25 percent came from Guatemala, 24 percent came from El Salvador, and 23 percent came from Mexico. See CBP, Southwest Border Unaccompanied Alien Children (FY 2014), *supra* note 5.

[179] CBP, Southwest Border Unaccompanied Alien Children (FY 2014), *supra* note 5.

[180] White House Press Release, *Presidential Memorandum, Response to the Influx of Unaccompanied Alien Children Across the Southwest Border*, (June 2, 2014), *available at www.whitehouse.gov/the-press-office/2014/06/02/presidential-memorandum-response-influx-unaccompanied-alien-children-acr.*

[181] USCIS, Processing of Asylum Cases, *available at www.uscis.gov/sites/default/files/USCIS /Humanitarian/Refugees%20%26%20Asylum/Asylum/USCIS_Reponds_to_Humanitarian_Caseload.pd f* (last visited Feb. 28, 2015).

alien children and families.[182] These have become known as "rocket dockets," and advocates have raised concerns about the due process violations that have resulted from such prioritizing of children's cases.[183] Not only do these rocket dockets delay other cases that were pending long before these children even entered the United States, but also, fast-tracking children's cases denies them an opportunity to recover and feel safe again so they can effectively make and participate in their asylum claims. The rocket dockets also create serious barriers to children's access to counsel, impairing their ability to find and retain attorneys and their attorneys' ability to establish the trust necessary to prepare strong applications for protection in the complex U.S. asylum system. Thus, as UNHCR notes, while it is important to process children's asylum claims on a priority basis due to their special needs, it is a fine line between reduced waiting periods and violation of children's due process rights.[184]

On August 6, 2014, the Vice President of the United States met with interested groups to discuss the southwest border situation, and specifically, the influx of unaccompanied children.[185] EOIR also met with interested groups on August 18, 2014 to hear their concerns related to the following issues for unaccompanied children in proceedings before the immigration courts: continuances to obtain representation; adjournments for other reasons; and appearances by custodians.[186] EOIR confirmed that unaccompanied children are being scheduled for a first master calendar hearing within 21 days of the immigration court's receipt of the charging document, and adults with children who have been released on alternatives to detention are being scheduled for a first master calendar hearing iwthin28 days of the immigration court's receipt of the charging document.[187] EOIR asserted that "[t]hereafter, any postponement, including a continuance to obtain representation, is at the discretion of the judge" and that nothing in the priority scheduling of these

---

[182] *See* Rory Carroll, *Migrant Courts' Quick Fix for Recently Arrived Children Brings New Problems*, The Guardian (Aug. 8, 2014), *available at www.theguardian.com/world/2014/aug/08/migrant-courts-quick-fix-recently-arrived-children-new-problems?wpisrc=nl-wonkbk&wpmm=1* (last visited Feb. 28, 2014); Kirk Semple, *Advocates in New York Scramble as Child Deportation Cases are Accelerated*, N.Y. Times (Aug. 4, 2014), *available at www.nytimes.com/2014/08/05/nyregion/advocates-scramble-as-new-york-accelerates-child-deportation-cases.html?_r=2.*

[183] *See, e.g.,* Nat'l Immigrant Justice Ctr., *Rocket Dockets Leave Due Process in the Dust* (Aug. 11, 2014), *www.immigrantjustice.org/staff/blog/rocket-dockets-leave-due-process-dust#.VPHdjEtSzwI*; AILA, *National Sign-On Letter Regarding Children Ordered Removed In Absentia Without Notice* (Feb. 9, 2015), *posted on* AILA InfoNet Doc. No. 15030961 *and available at www.aila.org/advo-media/aila-correspondence/sign-on-letter-children-removed-in-abstentia* (last visited Apr. 1, 2015).

[184] UNHCR, *Guidelines on International Protection No. 8*, *supra* note 8, at ¶ 66.

[185] EOIR, O'Leary Memorandum, *Docketing Practices Relating to Unaccompanied Children Cases and Adults with Children Released on Alternatives to Detention Cases in Light of the New Priorities* (Mar. 24, 2015), *posted on* AILA Doc. No. 15032702 *and available at www.aila.org/infonet/eoir-releases-memo-on-uac-fam-docketing-practices* (last visited Apr. 1, 2015).

[186] *Id.*

[187] *Id.*

cases "should inhibit a judge's discretion to reset the case to obtain representation."[188] EOIR also acknowledged that "several continuances might be warranted" in these cases.[189]

> ➢ **Practice Pointer**: Practitioners representing children in prioritized asylum claims before the asylum offices and immigration courts should seek interview rescheduling and continuances when necessary to provide enough time to prepare strong claims for protection on behalf of children. See chapter 8 for a detailed discussion of the procedures for seeking continuances before the immigration courts.

B. Capacity of a Child to Participate in the Application Process

While there is no age-based restriction for who may apply for asylum, whether the child's parents or legal guardians are aware of and consent to his or her application for asylum is a relevant consideration. In general, if the parents are not aware of or do not consent to the child's application, USCIS requires that its asylum officers determine whether the applicant has the requisite capacity to apply for asylum.[190] USCIS provides that it need not "process…applications if they reflect that the purported applicants are so young that they necessarily lack the capacity to understand what they are applying for or, failing that, that the applications do not present an objective basis for ignoring the parents' wishes."[191]

In one of the most famous children's asylum cases, legacy INS refused to consider the asylum application of 6-year-old Elian Gonzalez from Cuba because it considered his application to be legally void, the boy was not at risk of persecution or torture, and the boy's father in Cuba did not have conflicts of interest that would prevent him from pursuing the child's best interests. In upholding this determination, the Eleventh Circuit U.S. Court of Appeals deferred to the following INS discretionary policy choices: (1) 6-year-old children lack the capacity to sign and to submit personally an application for asylum; (2) 6-year-old children must be represented by an adult in immigration matters; (3) absent special circumstances, the proper adult is the child's parent, even when the parent is not in the country; and (4) the fact that the parent lives in a totalitarian state in and of itself does not constitute a special circumstance

---

[188] *Id.* (citing EOIR's OPPM 13-01 on continuances and administrative closure).

[189] *Id.*

[190] AOBTC Lesson Plan on Children's Asylum Claims, *supra* note 10, at 18–19. *See Gonzales v. Reno*, 212 F.3d 1338 (11th Cir. 2000) (holding that a 6-year-old child lacked the capacity to apply for asylum when his only living parent objects to the child's applying for asylum and the evidence indicates that the child will not be persecuted upon return to his country); *Polovchak v. Meese*, 774 F.2d 731, 736–37 (7th Cir. 1985) (stating that "[t]he minor's rights grow more compelling with age…" and holding that a 12-year-old was entitled to apply for asylum against his parents' wishes).

[191] Memorandum from Bo Cooper, INS General Counsel on Elian Gonzalez (Jan. 3, 2000), *available at www.uscis.gov/sites/default/files/USCIS/Laws/Memoranda/Archive%201998-2008/2000/ins_counsel_elian_gonzalez.pdf.*

requiring the selection of a nonparent representative.[192] The court was troubled, however, by the degree of obedience legacy INS paid to the wishes of the parent and by the fact that the child was from a Communist-totalitarian state that violated human rights and fundamental freedoms, but concluded that the policy choices were not unreasonable.[193]

In a case with the opposite result, the Seventh Circuit U.S. Court of Appeals in *Polovchak v. Meese* granted asylum to a 12-year-old boy against his parents' wishes to return to Russia.[194] The court evaluated the boy's capacity to assert his individual rights, stating:

> At the age of twelve, Walter was presumably near the lower end of an age range in which a minor may be mature enough to assert certain individual rights that equal or override those of his parents; at age seventeen (indeed, on the eve of his eighteenth birthday), Walter is certainly at the high end of such a scale, and the question whether he should have to subordinate his own political commitments to his parents' wishes looks very different. The minor's rights grown more compelling with age, particularly in the factual context of this case.[195]

USCIS warns asylum officers that they may need to determine who has the legal authority to speak for the child.[196] Where a child lacks capacity and a parent or legal guardian has the authority to speak for the child, notification of the parent or legal guardian that the child is applying for asylum will not violate the asylum confidentiality provisions.[197] USCIS also instructs that the Asylum Office Director should contact Headquarters for guidance in the following situations for principal applicant children under the age of 18: (1) if the child's parent or guardian has not given express consent for him or her to apply for asylum in the United States; (2) if the child's capacity to assert his or her own asylum claim is in question; (3) if there is a conflict between the child's and parents' interests concerning the asylum application; and (4) if the child is in a situation that endangers his or her health or welfare.[198] At that point, Headquarters will consult with the USCIS Office of Chief Counsel for guidance, as appropriate and as needed.[199]

---

[192] *See Gonzalez v. Reno*, 212 F.3d 1338 (11th Cir. 2000).

[193] *Id.* at 1352–53.

[194] *Polovchak v. Meese*, 774 F.2d 731, 736–37 (7th Cir. 1985). *See also* 8 CFR §103.2(a)(2) (2014) (providing that a parent or legal guardian may sign an application or petition of a person under the age of fourteen); 8 CFR §236.3(f) (2014) (providing for notice to parent of juvenile's application for relief).

[195] *Polovchak v. Meese*, 774 F.2d 731, 736–37 (7th Cir. 1985).

[196] AOBTC Lesson Plan on Children's Asylum Claims, *supra* note 10, at 18–19.

[197] 8 CFR §208.6 (2014).

[198] AOBTC Lesson Plan on Children's Asylum Claims, *supra* note 10, at 19; USCIS, *Affirmative Asylum Procedures Manual*, pt. III.B.1. (Nov. 2013), *available at www.uscis.gov/sites/default/files/files/nativedocuments/Asylum_Procedures_Manual_2013.pdf* (last visited Feb. 27, 2015).

[199] USCIS, *Affirmative Asylum Procedures Manual*, *supra* note 198 at pt. III.B.1. (Nov. 2013).

UNHCR recognizes the importance of an independent, qualified guardian to assist unaccompanied or separated children, as well as a legal representative who can support the child throughout the procedures of applying.[200] However, UNHCR also confirms that children have the right to express their views and to participate in a meaningful way. UNHCR states:

> A child's own account of his/her experience is often essential for the identification of his/her individual protection requirements and, in many cases, the child will be the only source of this information. Ensuring that the child has the opportunity to express these views and needs requires the development and integration of safe and child-appropriate procedures and environments that generate trust at all stages of the asylum process. It is important that children be provided with all necessary information in a language and manner they understand . . . This includes information about their right to privacy and confidentiality enabling them to express their views without coercion, constraint or fear of retribution.[201]

USCIS also recognizes the limitations regarding a child's ability to participate in the asylum application process, noting a number of developmental and circumstantial factors that impact that ability, including:

- Chronological age;
- Physical and emotional health;
- Physical, psychological, and emotional development;
- Societal status and cultural background;
- Cognitive processes;
- Educational experience;
- Language ability;
- Experiential and historical background;
- Chaotic social conditions;
- Experience with forms of violence;
- Lack of protection and caring by significant adults;
- Nutritional deficits;
- Physical disabilities; and
- Mental disabilities.[202]

In addition to these factors, USCIS notes that children bring to the asylum application process "a unique set of preconceived notions that could hinder the

---

[200] UNHCR, *Guidelines on International Protection No. 8*, *supra* note 8, at ¶ 68–69.

[201] *Id.* at ¶ 70.

[202] AOBTC Lesson Plan on Children's Asylum Claims, *supra* note 10, at 13–14.

officer's attempts to elicit information."[203] Such preconceptions may include the ideas that:

- All governments are corrupt;
- Others still at home will be harmed;
- He or she should feel guilty for fleeing; and
- Others will be privy to the testimony.[204]

Each of these preconceptions may cause a child not to trust the asylum officer and to refuse to communicate with the officer about the facts necessary to establish for asylum eligibility. The AOBTC encourages asylum officers to "earn the trust of the child applicant in order to dispel these preconceptions and put the applicant at ease."[205]

> ➢ **Practice Pointer**: Pursuant to 8 CFR §103.2(a)(2), parents can sign immigration forms for a child if the child is under 14 years old. Parents also can be given notice on behalf of their child under 8 CFR §236.3(f).

C. Affirmative Asylum Procedures for Children

In 1998, the Office of International Affairs (now the Office of Refugee, Asylum, and International Operations) issued a memorandum to all asylum officers setting forth guidelines for adjudicating children's asylum claims.[206] The guidelines established various procedural safeguards, such as child-sensitive interviewing techniques and the presence of a trusted adult during the interview, to ensure that children's claims are properly and fairly adjudicated.[207] The guidelines also acknowledge that the harm a child fears or suffered may be relatively less than an adult and still qualify as persecution.[208] The guidelines also outline how children's claims should be analyzed under U.S. law.[209] In drafting these guidelines, the Office of International Affairs considered UNHCR's *Guidelines on Policies and Procedures in Dealing with Unaccompanied Children Seeking Asylum* (1997); *Refugee Children: Guidelines on Protection and Care* (1994); and *Policy on Refugee Children* (1993). It also looked to the Canadian Immigration and Refugee Board's *Child Refugee Claimants: Procedural and Evidentiary Issues*, which addresses such issues as the

---

[203] *Id.* at 14.

[204] *Id.* at 14–15.

[205] *Id.* at 15.

[206] *See* INS Memorandum from Jeff Weiss on Guidelines for Children's Asylum Claims (Dec. 10, 1998), AILA InfoNet (*posted* Jan. 25, 1999), *reproduced in* 76 *Interpreter Releases* 1 and Appendix I (Jan. 4, 1999), a*vailable at www.uscis.gov/sites/default/files/USCIS/Laws%20and%20Regulations/Memoranda/Ancient%20History/ChildrensGuidelines121098.pdf.*

[207] *Id.* at 5–15.

[208] *Id.* at 19.

[209] *Id.* at 16–27.

criteria for appointing a representative and the type of proceedings and manner of questioning in such cases.

Today's guidance is set forth in the Asylum Officer's Basic Training Course (AOBTC) lesson plan on *Guidelines for Children's Asylum Claims*.[210] These guidelines provide a summary of international guidance for children's asylum claims, information on child development and preconceptions, procedural considerations for processing children's asylum cases, child-sensitive interviewing techniques, child-specific analyses of the legal standards for asylum, and guidance for derivative claims of children.[211] The guidelines apply to children under the age of 18 who apply for asylum independently by submitting a Form I-589 in their own name. However, the guidelines, in particular the procedural sections, apply to all derivative applicants under the age of 21.[212] The guidelines state:

Although young people between the ages of eighteen and twenty-one will be interviewed much in the same manner as adults, asylum officers should bear in mind that an applicant whose claim is based on events that occurred while under the age of eighteen may exhibit a minor's recollection of the past experiences and events.[213]

These guidelines for the U.S. Asylum Offices' adjudication of child asylum claims also apply to unaccompanied children in removal proceedings, because, pursuant to amendments made by the TVPRA of 2008, such children are allowed to apply for asylum initially in a non-adversarial proceeding before USCIS.[214] The Asylum Office only has jurisdiction over the claim, however, if the child meets the definition of "unaccompanied alien child" at the time of filing.[215]

➢ **Practice Pointer**: For a detailed discussion of asylum procedures for unaccompanied alien children, see Part III below.

1. *Asylum Interviews*

Although the components of a child's application for asylum and the process of submitting that application are largely the same as for adults, there are significant

---

[210] AOBTC Lesson Plan on Children's Asylum Claims, *supra* note 10.

[211] *See id.*

[212] *Id.* at 15.

[213] *Id.*

[214] Trafficking Victims Protection Reauthorization Act of 2008, Pub. L. No. 110-457, 122 Stat. 5044. For more information, see USCIS, *Questions and Answers: USCIS Initiates Procedures for Unaccompanied Children Seeking Asylum* (March 25, 2009), *available at* www.uscis.gov/files/article/tvpra_qa _25mar2009.pdf. *See also* USCIS Memorandum from Joseph Langlois on Implementation of Statutory Change Providing USCIS with Initial Jurisdiction over Asylum Applications Filed by Unaccompanied Children (Mar. 25, 2009), *published on* AILA InfoNet at Doc. No. 09042230 (*posted* Apr. 22, 2009).

[215] *See* Memorandum from Joseph E. Langlois, USCIS Asylum Division, on Implementation of Statutory Change Providing USCIS with Initial Jurisdiction over Asylum Applications Filed by Unaccompanied Alien Children (Mar. 25, 2009).

differences regarding how children are treated during asylum interviews before USCIS asylum officers. USCIS follows special guidelines for adjudicating asylum claims filed by principal applicant children under the age of 18,[216] as well as the guidance provided in the USCIS lesson plans on adjudicating child asylum claims.[217] These guidelines and procedures were developed in recognition of the fact that "[c]hild asylum applicants may be less forthcoming than adults and may hesitate to talk about past experiences in order not to relive their trauma," and with the goal of helping asylum officers interact more meaningfully with children during asylum interviews.[218]

First, USCIS advises that it is usually appropriate, though not required, for a trusted adult to be present with the child at the interview.[219] The presence of a trusted adult may help the child feel more trusting of the asylum officer and comfortable presenting their claim.[220] The role of the trusted adult should be to serve as a "support person," not to coach the child during the interview, answer questions for the child, or serve as a substitute for an attorney or representative.[221] Given concerns regarding the trafficking of children, asylum officers are advised to pay careful attention to the relationship between the child and the adult and whether the child seems uncomfortable or afraid. Asylum officers also should provide the child an opportunity to add any testimony in private.[222] Asylum officers may interview the adult in order to confirm the following:

- The adult's relationship or guardianship arrangement with the child;
- The adult's legal authority to speak on the child's behalf;
- Any information about the child's parents' knowledge of and consent to the asylum application; and
- Any information on the child's claim where the child's age at the time of harm or interview prevents him or her from fully detailing events.[223]

Second, if a child appears at the asylum interview without a parent or guardian, asylum officers are advised to ask certain questions about guardianship and parental knowledge and consent, including the location of the child's parents, whether the child has a guardian, whether the parents are aware of the child's whereabouts, and

---

[216] *See* Memorandum from Jeff Weiss on Guidelines for Children's Asylum Claims, *supra* note 206; USCIS, *Affirmative Asylum Procedures Manual*, pt. III.B.1. (Nov. 2013), *available at www.uscis.gov/sites/default/files/files/nativedocuments/Asylum_Procedures_Manual_2013.pdf* (last visited Feb. 27, 2015).

[217] AOBTC Lesson Plan on Children's Asylum Claims, *supra* note 10.

[218] *Id.* at 19.

[219] *Id.* at 19–20.

[220] *Id.* at 19.

[221] *Id.*

[222] *Id.* at 20.

[223] *Id.* at 20.

whether the parents are aware that the child has applied for asylum.[224] Specifically, asylum officers must ask the following questions:[225]

- With whom is the child living in the U.S.?
- Did anyone accompany the child to the interview?
- Is there a guardianship arrangement?
- If there is an adult caregiver but not a legal guardian, what arrangements has the adult made to provide for the child?
- Is there one or more living parent?
- Do the parents know that the child is applying for asylum in the U.S.?

If the answers to these questions raise any concerns regarding parental notification and confidentiality or the child's welfare and safety, asylum officers are advised to contact Headquarters for guidance.[226]

Third, asylum officers are advised to take the following concepts into consideration in conducting asylum interviews for children:

- Non-adversarial interviewing — Although all asylum interviews are nonadversarial pursuant to 8 CFR §208.9(b), a non-adversarial tone is crucial for children to testify fully and comfortably;[227]
- Interviewing with female asylum officers — Many girls and young women may feel more comfortable discussing their experiences, particularly those involving rape, sexual abuse, prostitution, or female genital mutilation, with female asylum officers;[228]
- Ensuring effective communication through an interpreter — Asylum officers must ensuring that the child understands the role of the interpreter and is able to understand the interpreter. They also must confirm the identity of any private interpreters and pay close attention to whether the child is comfortable or afraid of the interpreter (which may indicate that the interpreter is part of a child trafficking ring);[229]
- Building rapport through discussions of interests, family, hobbies, pets, sports, etc. — Many children are reluctant to talk to strangers about past trauma, so asylum officers may need to make an effort to build a friendly and supportive rapport with the child to enable the child to recount his or her fears or past experiences;[230]

---

[224] *Id.*

[225] *Id.* at 21.

[226] *Id.*

[227] *Id.* at 20.

[228] *Id.* at 21–22.

[229] *Id.* at 22.

[230] *Id.*

- Making an opening statement so the child knows what to expect — Asylum officers are advised to explain in simple terms what will happen during the asylum interview, the roles the asylum officer, applicant, interpreter, and attorney will play, the importance of telling the officer when the child does not understand a question, and that the events will not be shared with others;[231]
- Reading the applicant — Asylum officers are advised to watch for non-verbal cues such as puzzled looks, knitted eyebrows, downcast eyes, long pauses, and irrelevant responses, to determine whether the child understands the process and the questions;[232]
- Explaining how to respond to questions — It may be necessary for asylum officers to explain and provide examples to children regarding how to provide an "I don't know" response to a question;[233]
- Reassuring the applicant — Asylum officers are advised to offer verbal reassurances if the child begins to feel uncomfortable or embarrassed, or to shift the focus of the questioning to a non-threatening subject until the child regains his or her confidence;[234]
- Monitoring the child's needs and taking breaks — Children often cope with frustration or emotion by shutting down emotionally, falling into silence, or responding to a series of questions with "I don't know" or "I don't remember." Asylum officers are encouraged to suggest a brief recess when necessary;[235] and
- Concluding the interview — At the end of the interview, asylum officers are advised to return to a discussion of the neutral topics from the beginning of the interview to restore the child's sense of security, to ask if the child has any final questions, and to inform the child of the next steps in the process.[236]

Fourth, asylum officers are advised to use child-sensitive questioning and listening techniques tailored to the child's specific cognitive and conceptual skills.[237] A child's age, stage of language development, background, level of sophistication, and maturity are all important considerations in determining how to communicate effectively with a child asylum applicant.[238] USCIS advises its asylum officers to use the following techniques to elicit thorough information from child asylum-seekers:

- Use short, clear, age-appropriate questions;
- Avoid using long or compound questions;

---

[231] *Id.* at 23.

[232] *Id.*

[233] *Id.* at 24.

[234] *Id.*

[235] *Id.* at 25.

[236] *Id.*

[237] *Id.* at 25–31.

[238] *Id.* at 25.

- Use one or two syllable words in questions and avoid using three or four syllable words;
- Avoid complex verb constructions;
- Ask the child to define or explain a term or phrase in the question posed in order to check the child's understanding;
- Ask the child to define or explain the terms or phrases that he or she uses in answers, then use those terms;
- Use easy words over complex ones;
- Tolerate pauses, even if long;
- Ask the child to describe the concrete and observable, not the hypothetical or abstract;
- Use visualizable, instead of categorical terms
- Avoid the use of legalistic terms in questions, such as "persecution;"
- Avoid using idioms;
- Use the active voice, instead of passive, when asking a question;
- Avoid front-loading questions;
- Keep each question simple and separate;
- Avoid leading questions;
- Use open-ended questions to encourage narrative responses;
- Explain any repetition of questions;
- Never coerce a child into answering a question during the interview; and
- Accept that many children will not be immediately forthcoming about events that have caused great pain;
- Recognize that children may not know specific details and cannot be expected to present testimony with the same degree of precision as adults;
- Acknowledge that children may try to answer questions regarding measurements of distance or time without the experience to do so with any degree of accuracy;
- Follow-up questions are generally advisable in response to "I don't know" responses.[239]

UNHCR similarly advises that appropriate communication methods need to be selected based on the child's age, gender, cultural background, and maturity, as well as the circumstances of the flight and mode of arrival.[240] Additionally, non-verbal communication methods, such as "playing, drawing, writing, role-playing, story-

---

[239] *Id.* at 26–31.

[240] UNHCR, Guidelines on International Protection No. 8, *supra* note 8, at ¶ 71.

telling, and singing," may be necessary to facilitate a child's expression of his or her views.[241]

> **Practice Pointer**: Practitioners who are representing children also should use child-sensitive questioning and listening techniques in gathering information from children about their past experiences and fears. These USCIS and UNHCR guidelines provide a useful reference for practitioners in effectively and zealously representing children.

Fifth, USCIS also recognizes that credibility determinations for children require special considerations regarding demeanor, the effects of trauma, age and development, lapses in time between the events and the recounting of those events, special mental or emotional needs, limited knowledge of circumstances surrounding events, and the role of others in preparing children for their interviews.[242] For example, children often exhibit different body language than adults.[243] Additionally symptoms and signs of trauma, such as depression, indecisiveness, indifference, poor concentration, avoidance, disassociation, emotional passivity, memory loss or distortion, inappropriate laughter, or long pauses before providing answers may have a significant impact on a child's ability to present testimony and may be mistaken as indicators of fabrication or insincerity.[244] Moreover, a child's age and development at the time of events and at the time of retelling the events, as well as the amount of time that has passed between events and the retelling of those events, may affect his or her ability to recall and communicate those events.[245] Finally, some children may have been coached by adults to tell a particular story and may repeat that story at the interview in order not to anger or be punished by the adult. Asylum officers are advised to "undertake a careful and probing examination of the underlying merits of the child's case," and to recognize that a child may not have intended to deceive.[246]

Sixth, asylum officers are advised to take into account the child's ability to express his or her recollections and fears, and to recognize that children cannot testify with the same precision as adults.[247] As UNHCR notes:

Children cannot be expected to provide adult-like accounts of their experiences. They may have difficulty articulating their fear for a range of reasons, including trauma, parental instructions, lack of education, fear of State authorities or persons in positions of power, use of ready-made testimony by smugglers, or fear of reprisals. They may be too young or immature to be able to evaluate what information is important or to interpret what they have witnessed or experienced in a manner that is

---

[241] *Id.*

[242] *Id.* at 31–34.

[243] *Id.* at 31–32.

[244] *Id.* at 32.

[245] *Id.* at 34.

[246] *Id.* at 33–34.

[247] *Id.* at 34.

easily understandable to an adult. Some children may omit or distort vital information or be unable to differentiate the imagined from reality. They also may experience difficulty relating to abstract notions, such as time or distance. Thus, what might constitute a lie in the case of an adult might not necessarily be a lie in the case of a child. It is, therefore, essential that examiners have the necessary training and skills to be able to evaluate accurately the reliability and significance of the child's account.[248]

Additionally, for child asylum applications, the asylum officer may need to assume a greater burden of proof than the shared burden of proof between the asylum officer and adult applicant. For example, children may have only limited knowledge of country conditions or may be unable to explain the reasons why they were persecuted.[249] In such situations, asylum officers should "make special efforts to gather relevant country of origin information and other supporting evidence."[250] UNHCR and USCIS also advise that if the facts of the case cannot be ascertained or if the child is incapable of fully articulating his or her claim, the asylum officer may need to liberally apply the benefit of the doubt principle when evaluating the child's fear of persecution and credibility.[251] However, reasonable corroborating documentation may still be required for children. In addition to the child's own testimony, he or she should submit:

- Testimony or affidavits from family members or members of the child's community;
- Evidence from medical personnel, teachers, social workers, community workers, child psychologists, and others who have dealt with the child; and
- Documentary evidence of persons similarly situated to the child, physical evidence, and general country conditions information.[252]

> ➢ **Practice Pointer**: Practitioners should have their child clients evaluated by a mental health professional who has the necessary qualifications to evaluate children. Such evaluations may confirm the trauma the child suffered, his or her post-traumatic stress disorder or other manifestations of trauma, and his or her mental and emotional ability to communicate effectively.

2. Affirmative Asylum Decisions

According to the Affirmative Asylum Procedures Manual, a USCIS Asylum Office may not issue a final decision in any principal applicant child's case until

---

248 UNHCR, Guidelines on International Protection No. 8, *supra* note 8, at ¶ 72.

249 UNHCR, Guidelines on International Protection No. 8, *supra* note 8, at ¶ 74.

250 *Id.*

251 *Id.* at ¶ 73; AOBTC Lesson Plan on Children's Asylum Claims, *supra* note 10, at 34.

252 AOBTC Lesson Plan on Children's Asylum Claims, *supra* note 10, at 35.

Headquarters has issued a written concurrence.[253] Once the decision is made, it must be communicated to a child in a language and manner that he or she can understand. UNHCR advises that "[c]hildren need to be informed of the decision in person, in the presence of their guardian, legal representative, and/or other support person, in a supportive and non-threatening environment."[254] If the decision is negative, the message should be delivered to the child in a manner that avoids or reduces psychological stress or harm.[255]

D. Defensive Asylum Procedures for Children

As of June 30, 2014, 11 percent of cases pending before the immigration courts were juvenile cases.[256] While IJs are not bound by USCIS's guidelines for interviewing and adjudicating children's asylum applications, the Office of the Chief Immigration Judge has issued an operating policies and procedures memorandum (OPPM) on the topic.[257] This OPPM incorporates by reference some of the child-questioning techniques referred to in the guidelines. In addition, the OPPM gives guidance to judges on a broad array of issues impacting children in immigration court proceedings, including basic legal principles, an appropriate courtroom setting, appropriate court procedures, motions, the use of interpreters, and credibility assessments.[258] Although this OPPM was written specifically for cases involving UACs, many of its provisions apply to other cases where children are accompanied by a parent or guardian or where children testify as witnesses.[259] The topics that must be considered whenever a child is present as a respondent or witness include:

- The effect of age and development on a child's ability to participate in the proceedings;
- Gender;
- Mental health (including possible post-traumatic stress syndrome);
- General cultural sensitivity issues; and
- Appropriate questioning and listening techniques for child witnesses.[260]

---

[253] USCIS, Affirmative Asylum Procedures Manual, pt. III.B.1.a.x. (Nov. 2013), *available at www.uscis.gov/sites/default/files/files/nativedocuments/Asylum_Procedures_Manual_2013.pdf.*

[254] UNHCR, *Guidelines on International Protection No. 8*, *supra* note 8, at ¶ 77.

[255] *Id.*

[256] TRAC Immigration, *New Data on Unaccompanied Children in Immigration Court*, *available at http://trac.syr.edu/immigration/reports/359/* (last visited Mar. 1, 2015).

[257] *See* EOIR Memorandum No. 07-01 from David Neal on Guidelines for Immigration Court Cases Involving Unaccompanied Alien Children" (May 22, 2007), AILA InfoNet Doc. No. 07052360 (*posted* May 23, 2007), *available at www.justice.gov/eoir/efoia/ocij/oppm07/07-01.pdf* (last visited Feb. 28, 2015).

[258] *See id.*

[259] *See id.*

[260] *See* EOIR Memorandum No. 07-01, *supra* note 257, at 4.

The OPPM discusses basic principles that are central to the guidelines for IJs in considering children's asylum claims before the immigration courts.[261] First, every IJ is expected to employ child sensitive procedures whenever a child respondent or witness is present in the courtroom. What procedures are appropriate may depend on the age of the child and are to be determined by the IJ on a case-by-case basis.[262] Second, although questions of admissibility and eligibility for relief are governed by the INA and regulations, IJs should exercise their discretion in taking steps to ensure that a "child-appropriate" hearing environment is established, allowing a child to discuss freely the elements and details of his or her claim.[263] Third, although neither the INA nor the regulations permit IJs to appoint a legal representative or guardian ad litem, IJs should encourage the use of appropriate pro bono resources whenever a child respondent is not represented and whenever a child respondent needs assistance with understanding the proceedings and communicating with his or her legal representative.[264] Finally, all IJs must be trained and able to handle children's cases, even though certain courts may require specialized dockets for children's cases and responsibility for such dockets may be assigned to certain judges.[265]

EOIR has also issued a fact sheet, "Unaccompanied Alien Children in Immigration Proceedings," dated April 22, 2008, which provides information on legal representation, child-friendly courtroom environments, juvenile dockets, and other guidance for IJs when dealing with "this especially vulnerable population."[266] Although this fact sheet was written specifically with regard to UACs, its principles provide guidance for the treatment of all children appearing in immigration court as respondents or witnesses. The fact sheet alerts IJs to several fundamental questions that arise when a child is subject to proceedings before the immigration courts: (1) Does the child understand the nature of the proceeding? (2) Can the child effectively present evidence about his or her case? (3) Is there anyone who can properly advocate for the child's legal interests?[267]

1. Appropriate Courtroom Setting

The immigration courts are an adversarial setting by nature. However, EOIR advises IJs that cases involving children may require modifications to the ordinary

---

[261] *See id.* at 3–4.

[262] *See id.*

[263] *See id.* at 4.

[264] *See id. See also Chitay-Pirir v. INS*, 169 F.3d 1079, 1081 (7th Cir. 1999) (finding that it was not an error for the IJ and BIA to refuse to appoint a guardian ad litem for a minor aged 16 when he was represented by counsel and in the custody of legacy INS).

[265] *See* EOIR Memorandum No. 07-01, *supra* note 257, at 4.

[266] U.S. Dep't of Justice, Exec. Office for Immigration Review (EOIR), Unaccompanied Alien Children in Immigration Proceedings (Apr. 22, 2008), *available at www.justice.gov/eoir/press/08/UnaccompaniedAlienChildrenApr08.htm*.

[267] *Id.*

courtroom operations and configuration.[268] IJs are encouraged to foster a "child-friendly environment" in the immigration courtroom, including establishing special dockets for children to keep them separate from the general population, allowing child-friendly courtroom modifications, providing courtroom orientations to familiarize the children with the court, explaining the proceedings at the outset, preparing the child to testify, and employing child-sensitive questioning.[269]

First, since the courtroom is usually an unfamiliar place for children, children should be permitted to orient themselves to the courtroom and practice answering simple questions in the courtroom setting prior to their hearings.[270] Children are encouraged, under the supervision of court personnel, "to explore an empty courtroom, sit in all locations, and practice answering simple questions before the hearing."[271] For UACs, ORR provides orientations to explain immigration court proceedings in the children's native languages.[272]

Second, children's cases should be placed on a separate docket or scheduled separately from adult cases to facilitate the assistance of custodians or legal guardians, as well as legal service providers.[273] EOIR has established juvenile dockets to "facilitate consistency, encourage child-friendly courtroom practices, and promote pro bono representation."[274]

Third, IJs are encouraged to make "[s]imple, common sense adjustments" to the courtroom to accommodate children and enable them to participate more fully in the proceedings.[275] Some examples may include allowing the use of pillows or booster seats, permitting adult companions at counsel's table, allowing the child to bring a toy or other personal item into the courtroom, and permitting the child to testify while seated next to his or her trusted companion rather than from the witness stand.[276]

Fourth, IJs are advised to make use of video conferencing and telephonic appearances where appropriate.[277]

Finally, for in-person appearances, IJs are encouraged and permitted to remove their robe, as robes "may be disconcerting for younger respondents."[278] If dispensing

---

[268] *See* EOIR Memorandum No. 07-01, *supra* note 257, at 5.

[269] EOIR, *Unaccompanied Alien Children in Immigration Proceedings*, *supra* note 266.

[270] *See* EOIR Memorandum No. 07-01, *supra* note 257.

[271] *Immigration Court Practice Manual* (ICPM), chapter 4.22(c).

[272] *Id.*

[273] *Id.*; ICMP, chapter 4.22(a).

[274] EOIR, Unaccompanied Alien Children in Immigration Proceedings, *supra* note 266.

[275] See EOIR Memorandum No. 07-01, *supra* note 257.

[276] *Id.*; ICPM, chapter 4.22(d).

[277] *See* EOIR Memorandum No. 07-01, *supra* note 257, at 5–6.

[278] *Id.* at 6.

with the robe would enable the child to more effectively participate in the proceedings, the IJ is encouraged to do so.[279]

2. *Appropriate Courtroom Procedures*

In addition to establishing an appropriate courtroom setting, IJs are encouraged to employ courtroom procedures that take full account of the best interests of children in immigration court.[280] In cases where children are respondents, IJs are advised to make a brief opening statement at the outset of the proceedings to explain the nature and purpose of the proceedings, introduce the parties and discuss each person's role, and explain operational matters, such as the recording of the proceedings, note-taking, and telephonic or video conference appearances.[281]

IJs also are advised to allow time for the interpreter and the child to establish some rapport before testimony is taken, to watch closely for any indication that the child and interpreter are having difficulty communicating, and to use and encourage the use of age-appropriate language.[282]

EOIR observes that "stress and fatigue can adversely impact the ability of [children] to participate in [their] removal proceedings."[283] Thus, IJs should balance the requirement of giving the parties a full opportunity to present and challenge evidence with the need to limit the number of times that children must be brought to court. In balancing these factors, IJs should attempt to avoid any undue delays, require the parties to narrow issues through pre-trial conferences and stipulations, seek to limit the amount of time the child is on the witness stand, and recognize that children may require more frequent breaks than adults.[284]

In taking the testimony of children, IJs also should be confident that the child is competent to understand the oath and testify in the proceedings.[285] IJs should prepare the child to testify by explaining the oath in language the child can understand, notifying the child that it is all right for them to say "I don't know" or to request that a question be asked in another way, and explaining that if there is an objection to a question, the child should not feel at fault.[286]

IJs also should employ child-sensitive questioning and listening techniques and encourage the use of age-appropriate language and tone throughout the

---

[279] *Id.*

[280] *Id.*

[281] *Id.*

[282] *Id.* at 7.

[283] *Id.*

[284] *Id.*

[285] *Id.*

[286] *Id.*

proceedings.[287] The EOIR guidance incorporates USCIS's guidance for language and tone in eliciting information from children:

- Use short, clear, age-appropriate questions;
- Avoid using long or compound questions;
- Use one or two syllable words in questions and avoid using three or four syllable words;
- Avoid complex verb constructions;
- Ask the child to define or explain a term or phrase in the question posed in order to check the child's understanding;
- Ask the child to define or explain the terms or phrases that he or she uses in answers, then use those terms;
- Use easy words over complex ones;
- Tolerate pauses, even if long;
- Ask the child to describe the concrete and observable, not the hypothetical or abstract;
- Use visualizable, instead of categorical terms
- Avoid the use of legalistic terms in questions, such as "persecution;"
- Avoid using idioms;
- Use the active voice, instead of passive, when asking a question;
- Avoid front-loading questions;
- Keep each question simple and separate;
- Avoid leading questions;
- Use open-ended questions to encourage narrative responses;
- Explain any repetition of questions;
- Never coerce a child into answering a question during the interview; and
- Accept that many children will not be immediately forthcoming about events that have caused great pain;
- Recognize that children may not know specific details and cannot be expected to present testimony with the same degree of precision as adults;
- Acknowledge that children may try to answer questions regarding measurements of distance or time without the experience to do so with any degree of accuracy;
- Follow-up questions are generally advisable in response to "I don't know" responses.[288]

---

[287] *Id.*

[288] AOBTC Lesson Plan on Children's Asylum Claims, *supra* note 10, at 26–31; *See* EOIR Memorandum No. 07-01, *supra* note 257, at 7.

In considering children's testimony, IJs, like asylum officers, are advised to recognize that children usually will not be able to testify with the same degree of precision as adults.[289] Additionally, IJs are advised not to assume that inconsistencies are proof of dishonesty and should recognize that children's ability to understand what happened and to describe the events may be limited.[290] Moreover, IJs "should be mindful that children are highly suggestible and their testimony could be influenced by their desire to please judges or other adults."[291]

Finally, EOIR advises IJs that it is best to have as few people in the courtroom as possible because children's reluctance to testify about painful or embarrassing incidents may increase with the number of spectators or other respondents.[292] Therefore, IJs should control access to the courtroom.[293]

3. *Facilitation of Representation*

It is well-established that represented individuals have higher rates of success in immigration court. UNHCR, in its *Guidelines on Policies and Procedures in Dealing with Unaccompanied Children Seeking Asylum*,[294] recommends that an unaccompanied child be represented by an adult who would protect his or her interests and that the child have access to a qualified legal representative.[295] Yet, there is no obligation under the INA or the regulations for the U.S. government to provide legal counsel to indigent respondents in immigration court proceedings — even for children.[296] At least one court, however, has held that counsel must be appointed at government expense for a detained child.[297]

Unfortunately, the number of attorneys and clinics available to provide pro bono legal assistance to children is insufficient to meet the need. One study found that children were not represented about half of the time (48%) they appeared in immigration court, and less than a third (31%) of children in cases pending as of June

---

[289] *See* EOIR Memorandum No. 07-01, *supra* note 257, at 7.

[290] *Id.*

[291] *Id.*

[292] *Id.* at 8.

[293] *Id.*

[294] UNHCR, Guidelines on Policies and Procedures in Dealing with Unaccompanied Children, *supra* note 15.

[295] *Id.* at ¶ 8.3.

[296] ICPM, chapter 4.22(b) ("An Immigration Judge cannot appoint a legal representative or a guardian ad litem for unaccompanied juveniles.").

[297] *See Machado v. Ashcroft*, No. Cs-02-0066-FVS, Prelim. Inj. Order (E.D. Wash., Mar. 5, 2002) (legacy INS ordered to hire a lawyer for a child in its custody at government expense or release him from detention). For further discussion on the right to counsel for children in deportation proceedings, see J. Bhabha, *David and Goliath? Detained Alien Children and the Right to Counsel*, 7 *Bender's Immigr. Bull.* 582, 585 (May 15, 2002).

2014 had been able to secure an attorney.[298] The data also showed that the outcomes in children's cases "are all too often determined by whether an attorney was present to assist the child in presenting his or her case."[299] Where the child was represented, the IJ allowed the child to remain in the United States in 47% of the cases. Where the child appeared alone without representation, however, only one in ten (10%) were allowed to remain in the country.[300]

Recognizing the importance of the assistance of an attorney or representative in immigration court, EOIR encourages IJs to "use appropriate pro bono resources" and "facilitate pro bono representation" whenever a child is not represented.[301] EOIR also recognizes the dearth of pro bono resources for children and suggests that IJs regularly participate in pro bono attorney training programs "to help increase the available pool of legal representatives."[302]

- **Practice Pointer**: EOIR announced that it is committed to promoting pro bono representation in immigration courts through a number of initiatives including: best practices and guidance to IJs and court staff, designating local pro bono liaison judges, encouraging pre-trial conferences, examining ways to meet the special needs of children, and increasing the availability of self-help material.[303]

4. *Other Regulatory Protections*

Children also receive special protections under the regulations governing proceedings before the U.S. immigration courts. For example, in the case of a minor under 14 years old, DHS must personally serve the Notice to Appear on the person with whom the child resides.[304] Whenever possible, DHS should also personally serve the near relative, guardian, committee, or friend.[305] The parent or guardian of a child must establish his or her own identity, as well as the identity of the child, and must also establish his or her parentage or provide a court order establishing

---

[298] TRAC Immigration, *New Data on Unaccompanied Children in Immigration Court*, *available at* http://trac.syr.edu/immigration/reports/359/ (last visited Mar. 1, 2015).

[299] *Id.*

[300] *Id. See also* TRAC Immigration, *Representation for Unaccompanied Children in Immigration Court*, *available at* http://trac.syr.edu/immigration/reports/371/ (last visited Mar. 1, 2015).

[301] EOIR, Unaccompanied Alien Children in Immigration Proceedings, supra note 266; ICPM, chapter 4.22(b).

[302] *Id.*

[303] *See* U.S. Dep't of Justice News Release, *EOIR to Expand and Improve Pro Bono Programs* (Nov. 15, 2007), *available at* www.usdoj.gov/eoir/press/07/ProBonoEOIRExpandsImprove.pdf.

[304] 8 CFR §103.5a(c)(2)(ii) (2014).

[305] *Id.*; *see also Mejia-Andino*, 23 I&N Dec. 533 (BIA 2002) (proceedings against a minor were properly terminated because service of the Notice to Appear was made on the minor's uncle, not her parents). *But see Flores-Chavez v. Ashcroft*, 362 F.3d 1150 (9th Cir. 2004) (finding DHS erred in not serving notice of hearing and charging document on the adult to whom the child was released from DHS custody).

guardianship.[306] The Notice to Appear in immigration court must be served on the child's custodian or responsible adult, even if the child is over 14 years old.[307] In general, children are not expected to understand and follow the notice's orders on their own.

The regulations also strongly discourage the appearance of children under 18 years old in court without guardians to speak on their behalf. Specifically:

> The immigration judge shall not accept an admission of removability from an unrepresented respondent who is . . . under the age of 18 and is not accompanied by an attorney or legal representative, a near relative, legal guardian, or friend . . . When, pursuant to this paragraph, the immigration judge does not accept an admission of removability, he or she shall direct a hearing on the issues.[308]

Thus, an IJ is not permitted to accept admissions of removability from an unrepresented child who is not accompanied by a legal representative, near relative, legal guardian, or friend.[309]

This regulation, however, does not preclude the IJ from accepting a minor's admissions to factual allegations, which may properly form the basis of a finding that the minor is removable.[310] The BIA has cautioned that an IJ must exercise "particular care" in determining a minor's removability and must take into account the minor's age and unaccompanied status.[311] In *Matter of Amaya-Castro*, the BIA considered a child's answers on Form I-213, Record of Deportable Alien in considering whether the child was deportable from the United States.[312] The BIA found that the

---

[306] 8 CFR §103.21(c) (2014).

[307] 8 CFR §236.3; *Flores-Chavez v. Ashcroft*, 362 F.3d 1150 (9th Cir. 2004) (reversing an in absentia order against a 15 year old who was served with an order to show cause under 8 CFR §103.5a, but no service was provided to the adult custodian, and concluding that reading the statute to permit service solely on the minor violated DHS' own regulations and raised serious constitutional questions). *See also Llanos-Fernandez v. Mukasey*, 535 F.3d 79 (2d Cir. 2008).

[308] 8 CFR §1240.10(c) (2014).

[309] 8 CFR §1240.10(c); (2014) Immigration Judge Benchbook at pt. II.B. (addressing incompetency and representation); *Flores-Chavez v. Ashcroft,* 262 F.3d 1150, 1156 (9th Cir. 2004) (stating that "juveniles are presumed unable to appear at immigration proceedings without the assistance of an adult"); *Davila-Bardales v. I.N.S.*, 27 F.3d 1 (1st Cir. 1994); *Matter of Mejia-Andino*, 23 I&N Dec. 533, 2002 WL 31733182 (BIA 2002). *See also* 8 CFR §240.48(b) (2014) ("The immigration judge shall not accept an admission of deportability for an unrepresented respondent who is incompetent or under age 16 and is not accompanied by a guardian, relative, or friend; nor from an officer of an institution in which a respondent is an inmate or patient.").

[310] *Matter of Amaya-Castro*, 21 I&N Dec. 583 (BIA 1996).

[311] *Id.* at 6. *But see Matter of Ponce-Hernandez*, 21 I&N Dec. 784 (BIA 1999) (in the case of a 15-year-old minor who failed to appear for his deportation hearing, the BIA found that legacy INS met its burden of proof in establishing deportability on the basis of a Record of Deportable Alien (Form I-213), which documented the minor's identity and alienage).

[312] *Matter of Amaya-Castro*, 21 I&N Dec. 583 (BIA 1996).

information contained in the I-213 was not in itself sufficient to establish the child's deportability, and held that an IJ "must exercise particular care in determining [a child's] deportability" and must make a "comprehensive and independent inquiry" into the child's deportability, particularly when the accuracy and reliability of the government's evidence may be questioned.[313] The BIA stated:

> The minor's age and pro se and unaccompanied status must be taken into consideration. The IJ must consider the reliability of the testimony given by such a minor in response to the factual allegations made against him in determining, after a comprehensive and independent inquiry, whether there is clear, unequivocal, and convincing evidence of the minor's deportability as charged . . . . If the Immigration Judge is assured that the respondent is both capable of understanding, and in fact understands, any facts that are admitted, and that those facts establish deportability, they may form the sole bases of a finding that the minor is deportable.[314]

The Board cited the Supreme Court in specifically acknowledging that children lack the maturity of adults as well as the experience, perspective, and judgment to recognize and avoid choices that could be detrimental to them.[315] It is principles such as these, relating to the potential vulnerability and limited capacity of child respondents, which the immigration courts are required to consider in children's proceedings.

- **Practice Pointer**: In preparing children for proceedings in immigration court, practitioners should make sure the child understands each person's role in the courtroom, including the IJ, the DHS attorney, the interpreter, the representative, and the child. Sometimes it is helpful to draw a picture of the courtroom so the child can visualize what the setting will look like as he or she is prepared for testimony. Practitioners also should make sure the child understands his or her claim and employ child-friendly communication and listening techniques like those described in the USCIS and EOIR guidance.

III. Unaccompanied Alien Children Applying for Asylum

How a child's protection claim is processed depends largely on whether he or she meets the definition of "unaccompanied alien child" (UAC), a term of art established by the Homeland Security Act of 2002. A UAC is a child who: (1) has no lawful immigration status in the United States; (2) has not attained 18 years of age; and (3)

---

[313] *Id.* at 586.

[314] *Id.* at 587.

[315] *See Eddings v. Oklahoma*, 455 U.S. 104, 116 (1982) ("Even the normal 16 year old customarily lacks the maturity of an adult."); *Bellotti v. Baird*, 443 U.S. 622, 635 (1979) (stating that "minors often lack the experience, perspective, and judgment to recognize and avoid choices that could be detrimental to them").

does not have a parent or legal guardian in the United States or does not have a parent or legal guardian in the United States who is available to provide care and physical custody.[316] Currently, most UACs arrive in the United States from El Salvador, Guatemala, and Honduras, three countries that have become consumed by unfettered violence that has been met with impunity by these countries' governments.[317] Both boys and girls have been fleeing their homes and embarking on the dangerous journey to the United States to seek protection.[318] According to CBP, 68,541 unaccompanied children were apprehended at the southwest border in fiscal year 2014, compared with 38,759 children in fiscal year 2013 — an increase of 77 percent.[319] In fiscal year 2013, 27 percent of these children came from Honduras, followed by 25 percent from Guatemala, 24 percent from El Salvador, and 23 percent from Mexico.[320]

When these children enter the United States — most of whom enter by crossing the southwest border from Mexico — many are either apprehended by CBP near the border or arrested by ICE within the United States. How unaccompanied children are processed upon apprehension and the procedures for presenting an application for asylum or other protections depends on whether they are from a contiguous or non-contiguous country. These procedures, as well as the history of UAC policies, are discussed in detail below.

- **Practice Pointer**: For a useful chart depicting the flow of unaccompanied children through the U.S. immigration system, see Figure 2 in the VERA Institute for Justice's report entitled, "The Flow of Unaccompanied Children Through the Immigration System: A Resources for Practitioners, Policy Makers, and Researchers," *www.vera.org/sites/default/files/resources/downloads/the-flow-of-unaccompanied-children-through-the-immigration-system.pdf.*[321] This report also includes detailed discussions of the apprehension of unaccompanied children by DHS; the process of referral to ORR; intake, placement, and care in ORR custody; reunifying with a sponsor in the United States; immigration proceedings and legal services for unaccompanied children; and outcomes.[322]

---

[316] 6 USC §279(g)(2).

[317] UNHCR, *Children on the Run*, *supra* note 5. In fiscal year 2014, 27 percent of children apprehended along the southern border of the U.S. came from Honduras, 25 percent came from Guatemala, 24 percent came from El Salvador, and 23 percent came from Mexico. *See* CBP, *Southwest Border Unaccompanied Alien Children (FY 2014)*, *supra* note 5.

[318] Women's Refugee Comm'n, *Forced From Home*, *supra* note 5.

[319] CBP, *Southwest Border Unaccompanied Alien Children (FY 2014)*, *supra* note 5.

[320] *Id.*

[321] (last visited Mar. 4, 2015).

[322] VERA Institute of Justice, *The Flow of Unaccompanied Children Through the Immigration System: A Resource for Practitioners, Policy Makers, and Researchers* (March 2012), *available at*

Continued

A. The *Flores* Settlement

Prior to 1997, children seeking protection in the U.S. immigration system were treated largely the same as adults, from apprehension through proceedings through decisions on relief. However, immigrant rights and child welfare advocacy groups challenged the policies of treating children the same as adults under the INA in a class action lawsuit against INS, *Flores v. Reno*.[323] In 1997, the *Flores* Settlement established new nationwide policies for the way children were processed upon apprehension, detention, and release.[324] It required that all children apprehended by DHS be held in the "least restrictive setting appropriate to their age and special needs to ensure their protection and wellbeing."[325] Additionally, it mandated that children not be detained with an unrelated adult for more than 24 hours.[326] Finally, the settlement required that children be released from custody as soon as possible to a parent, legal guardian, adult relative, designated individual, or an adult who seeks custody and who is deemed appropriate by DHS.[327]

B. Homeland Security Act of 2002

In 2003, the Homeland Security Act took effect, which created DHS and further modified the procedures for the care and custody of children apprehended by DHS. It also defined "unaccompanied alien child" and developed procedures specific to children who fall within that definition.[328] Specifically, the Homeland Security Act gave jurisdiction over the care and custody of UACs to the Office of Refugee Resettlement (ORR), an agency within the Department of Health and Human Services that has experience functioning pursuant to child welfare principles.[329] If a child meets the definition of UAC, he or she must be transferred to ORR custody within 72 hours of apprehension. If he or she does not meet the definition of UAC, the child remains in DHS's custody.

---

www.vera.org/sites/default/files/resources/downloads/the-flow-of-unaccompanied-children-through-the-immigration-system.pdf (last visited Mar. 31, 2015).

323 *Reno v. Flores*, 507 U.S. 292 (1993).

324 *Flores v. Reno*, Case No. CV 85-4544-RJK(Px) Settlement Agreement (C.D. Cal. 1997) [hereinafter *Flores* Settlement Agreement], *available at https://cliniclegal.org/sites/default/files/attachments/flores_v._reno_settlement_agreement_1.pdf* (last visited Feb. 28, 2015). *See* INS Memorandum from Paul Virtue, Acting Executive Associate Commissioner, on Unaccompanied Minors Subject to Expedited Removal (Aug. 21, 1997). *See also* 8 CFR §§236.3, 1236.3 (2014).

325 Nat'l Immigrant Justice Ctr., *Fact Sheet: Children Detained by the Department of Homeland Security in Adult Detention Facilities* (May 2013), *available at www.immigrantjustice.org/sites/immigrantjustice.org/files/NIJC%20Fact%20Sheet%20Minors%20in%20ICE%20Custody%202013%2005%2030%20FINAL.pdf*; *See Flores* Settlement Agreement, *supra* note 324.

326 *See Flores* Settlement Agreement, *supra* note 324.

327 *See id.*

328 *See* 6 USC §279(g)(2).

329 Nat'l Immigrant Justice Ctr., Fact Sheet: Children Detained by DHS in Adult Detention Facilities, *supra* note 325.

C. The Trafficking Victims Protection Reauthorization Act of 2008

The Trafficking Victims Protection Act of 2000 and its reauthorization acts in 2005 and 2008 established child welfare values and procedures for UACs. Perhaps the most important piece of legislation for child asylum-seekers has been the William Wilberforce Trafficking Victims Protection Reauthorization Act of 2008 (TVPRA), which acknowledged the significant disadvantages that UACs face in seeking asylum in the United States and made specific changes to the processing of UACs' asylum applications.[330]

Specifically, Congress enacted various safeguards to protect UACs' rights as they seek asylum and related protections. These safeguards include:

- The right to apply for asylum before USCIS, even if the UAC is in removal proceedings;
- The elimination of the one-year filing deadline for UACs; and
- The elimination of the safe third country agreement for UACs.[331]

The TVPRA also established the procedures for processing UACs upon apprehension by CBP or ICE, as described below.

D. Processing of UACs Upon Apprehension by CBP or ICE

Although a UAC asylum-seeker is sometimes encountered for the first time by USCIS, it is most common for UACs to come into contact with USCIS after they have already been apprehended by CBP or ICE and been determined to meet the definition of UAC.[332] When CBP or ICE apprehends a child, the agency must first determine whether the child meets the definition of UAC, and if so, whether that child is from a contiguous or non-contiguous country. Those determinations will establish the necessary protocol to be followed.[333] Therefore, the arresting officer will

---

[330] *See* Trafficking Victims Protection Reauthorization Act of 2008, *supra* note 214, at §§235(a)–(d) (effective March 23, 2009).

[331] Memorandum from Joseph E. Langlois on Implementation of Statutory Change Providing USCIS with Initial Jurisdiction Over Asylum Applications Filed by Unaccompanied Alien Children, HQRAIO 120/12a (Mar. 25, 2009), *available at www.uscis.gov/sites/default/files/USCIS/Laws/Memoranda/Static_Files_Memoranda/2009/uac_filings_5f25mar09.pdf* (last visited Mar. 1, 2015).

[332] USCIS, Affirmative Asylum Procedures Manual, *supra* note 198 at 35; Memorandum from Ted Kim, Acting Chief, USCIS Asylum Division on Updated Procedures for Determination of Initial Jurisdiction over Asylum Applications Filed by Unaccompanied Alien Children (2013), *available* at AILA InfoNet at Doc. No. 13080847.

[333] *See* 8 CFR §236.3; U.S. Dep't of Homeland Security (DHS), Office of the Inspector Gen., *CBP's Handling of Unaccompanied Alien Children*, OIG 10-117 (2010), *available at www.oig.dhs.gov/assets/Mgmt/OIG_10-117_Sep10.pdf* (last visited Mar. 1, 2015); U.S. Dep't of Homeland Security, Office of the Inspector Gen., *A Review of DHS' Responsibilities for Juvenile Aliens*, OIG 05-45 (2005).

interview the child to obtain biographical information and will complete the Form I-213 Record of Deportable Alien.[334]

UACs also must be advised of their rights upon apprehension.[335] In *Perez Funez v. INS District Director*, the plaintiffs argued that minors are frequently coerced into choosing voluntary departure in lieu of pursuing relief that may be available to them.[336] As a result, DHS is now required to provide written advice to children of their rights.[337] For children from the contiguous countries of Mexico or Canada, who are apprehended near the border, DHS must inform them that they may make a telephone call to a parent, close relative, friend, or organization on the free legal services list before DHS presents the voluntary departure form and before the child is allowed to withdraw his or her application for admission.[338] For children from non-contiguous countries who are apprehended near the border, DHS must provide access to a telephone and the child must communicate with a parent, adult relative, friend, or organization on the free legal services list before DHS presents the voluntary departure form.[339]

1. Not Subject to Expedited Removal

First, if CBP or ICE determines that the child meets the definition of UAC, that child will not be subject to expedited removal proceedings. Under INA §235(b)(1), certain noncitizens may be removed from the United States without a removal hearing, including persons deemed inadmissible at the border due to material misrepresentations or a lack of a valid visa or entry document, persons who have not been admitted or paroled to the United States who cannot prove that they have been continuously present for two or more years, persons who have not been admitted or paroled to the United States who are encountered within 100 miles of the border and who cannot establish physical presence for the preceding 14 days, and certain persons arriving in the United States by sea.[340] However, a UAC is not subject to expedited removal proceedings unless he or she has: (1) engaged in criminal activity, in the presence of a DHS officer, that would qualify as an aggravated felony if committed by an adult; (2) been convicted or adjudicated delinquent of an aggravated felony within the United States or another country, and the inspecting officer has confirmation of that order; or (3) previously been formally removed, excluded, or

---

[334] DHS Office of the Inspector Gen., *CBP's Handling of Unaccompanied Alien Children*, *supra* note 333; DHS Detention and Removal Officers' Field Manual App'x 11-4: 2.1.1, 2.1.3 (Nov. 2003); DHS Detention and Removal Field Office Manual, Juvenile Protocol Manual, App'x 11-4 (Nov. 2003), *available at www.ice.gov/doclib/foia/dro_policy_memos/juvenileprotocolmanual2006.pdf.*

[335] *Perez-Funez v. District Director, INS,* 619 F. Supp. 656 (C.D. Cal. 1985).

[336] *Id.*

[337] *Id.*

[338] 8 CFR §§236.3(g), 1236.3(g) (2014).

[339] *Id.*

[340] INA §235(b)(1); 8 CFR §§235.3(b), 1235.3(b) (2014).

deported from the United States.[341] If an unaccompanied minor is placed in expedited removal proceedings, the removal order must be reviewed and approved by the District Director (DD) or deputy DD before the minor is removed from the United States.[342]

This exception to expedited removal recognizes that UACs require additional procedural safeguards and protections that are available to them in INA §240 removal proceedings but not in expedited removal proceedings. UACs are, however, currently subject to reinstatement of removal proceedings.

> ➢ **Practice Pointer**: For a detailed discussion of expedited removal and reinstatement of removal, see chapter 6 of this book.

2. *Contiguous vs. Non-Contiguous Countries*

The TVPRA established two sets of standards for UACs: one for UACs who come from "contiguous countries" (those that share a border with the United States) and another for UACs who come from "non-contiguous countries."[343] UACs from Mexico or Canada are considered to be from "contiguous countries," and are protected under less rigorous standards than children from "non-contiguous countries." Upon apprehension, all children are screened by the arresting agency to determine if they meet the definition of UAC and to determine if they are nationals of contiguous or non-contiguous countries.[344]

For UACs from contiguous countries, CBP or ICE must screen the child within 48 hours of apprehension to determine whether: (1) the child is a victim of trafficking or at risk of being trafficked; (2) the child has a fear of returning to his or her country based on a credible fear of persecution; and (3) the child can make an independent decision to withdraw his or her application for admission into the United States.[345] CBP uses the UAC Screening Form 93 and Form I-770 Notice of Rights and Request for Disposition during this process. If the child is not a victim of trafficking or at risk of being trafficked, does not have a fear of returning to his or her country based on a credible fear of persecution, and can make an independent decision to withdraw his or her application for admission, only then may CBP allow the child to voluntarily withdraw the applicant and immediately repatriate him or her without review by an IJ.[346] On the other hand, if all three of these conditions are not met, CBP must transfer the child to the custody of ORR and treat the child like a UAC from a non-contiguous country, as described below.

---

[341] INS, *Inspector's Field Manual,* chapter 17.15(f)(4) (Mar. 1998), *available at www.asylumlaw.org*, as added by INS Mem. from Paul Virtue, *supra* note 324.

[342] *Id.*

[343] Trafficking Victims Protection Reauthorization Act of 2008, *supra* note 214 at §235.

[344] *Id.*

[345] Trafficking Victims Protection Reauthorization Act of 2008, *supra* note 214 at §235(a)(2).

[346] *Id.*

> ➢ **Practice Pointer**: A 2011 report by Appleseed, a nonpartisan, non-profit network of public interest justice centers in the United States and Mexico, found that "no meaningful screening is being conducted" by CBP as required by the TVPRA.[347]

On the other hand, UACs from non-contiguous countries must be transferred, by law, to the custody of the Office of Refugee Resettlement in the Department of Health and Human Services. For these children, after completing the initial interview and I-213, the arresting officer will place the child in removal proceedings before an IJ pursuant to INA §240, serve on the child a Form I-862, Notice to Appear, and take him or her to a temporary holding area.[348] The temporary holding area must make the following services available to the child: toilets and sinks, drinking water and food, medical services if needed, temperature control and ventilation, adequate supervision, and contact with family members who were arrested with the child.[349]

Pursuant to the Homeland Security Act of 2002, the UAC must be transferred to ORR custody within 72 hours from the time that DHS assumed custody.[350] A maximum of five days is permitted if the UAC was apprehended in an area where there is no available ORR bed space.[351] Recently, however, the lack of adequate resources combined with the significant increase of UACs crossing the southern border in search for protection has created "several bottlenecks leading to children staying in CBP custody for more than the legal 72 hours."[352] The Federal Emergency Management Agency (FEMA) was even selected to coordinate and lead the U.S. government's response to the humanitarian crisis at the southern border. Many advocacy and child welfare organizations have called for a more appropriate response to the influx of children seeking protection, particularly in light of predictions that this "surge" of children will only continue.[353]

---

[347] Appleseed Foundation, *Children at the Border: The Screening, Protection, and Repatriation of Unaccompanied Mexican Minors* (2011), *available at http://appleseednetwork.org/wp-content/uploads/2012/05/Children-At-The-Border1.pdf* (last visited Mar. 4, 2015).

[348] DHS Detention and Removal Field Office Manual, Juvenile Protocol Manual, App'x 11-4 (Nov. 2003) [hereinafter DHS Juvenile Protocol Manual], *available at www.ice.gov/doclib/foia/dro_policy_memos/juvenileprotocolmanual2006.pdf.*

[349] U.S. Dep't of Homeland Security (DHS), Office of the Inspector Gen., *CBP's Handling of Unaccompanied Alien Children*, *supra* note 333.

[350] *See Flores* Settlement Agreement, *supra* note 324; U.S. Dep't of Homeland Security (DHS), Office of the Inspector Gen., *A Review of DHS' Responsibilities for Juvenile Aliens*, *supra* note 333.

[351] U.S. Dep't of Homeland Security (DHS), Office of the Inspector Gen., *A Review of DHS' Responsibilities for Juvenile Aliens*, *supra* note 333 at n. 20; DHS Juvenile Protocol Manual, *supra* note 334, at 14.

[352] Women's Refugee Comm'n, *What Happens When Unaccompanied Children Arrive at the U.S. Border?* (June 2014), *www.womensrefugeecommission.org/component/content/article/155-new-program-pages/migrant-rights-and-justice/2065-what-happens-when-unaccompanied-children-arrive-at-the-u-s-border* (last visited Mar. 4, 2015).

[353] *Id.*

➢ **Practice Pointer**: For a helpful comparison of the processing of UACs from contiguous versus non-contiguous countries, see AILA's "Recommendations on Legal Standards and Protections for Unaccompanied Children," posted on AILA InfoNet Doc. No. 14070847 and available at *www.aila.org/infonet/recommendations-legal-standards-protections-uacs*.[354]

3. ORR Custody

Once in ORR custody, ORR will screen the UAC to identify any medical or other immediate needs and must place the child in the least restrictive setting that is in the best interest of the child.[355] ORR uses a network of state licensed care providers, including foster care, group homes, shelters, and residential treatment centers.[356] The majority of care providers are located in Arizona, California, Florida, Illinois, New Jersey, New York, Oregon, Texas, Virginia, and Washington.[357] Each care provider must be licensed and must meet the high quality of care required by ORR.[358] Specifically, care providers must provide UACs with classroom education and vocational training, health care and mental health services, socialization and recreation, family reunification, and access to legal services and case management.[359]

ORR also will complete a screening of the child to determine whether: (1) the child has been a victim of trafficking; (2) there is credible evidence that the child is at risk if returned; and (3) the child has a possible claim to asylum. If any of these factors exist, the child is placed in removal proceedings before an immigration judge pursuant to INA §240 so he or she may seek relief.[360] While proceedings are pending, ORR assists with reunification of the child with family members or other sponsors, and will conduct home studies prior to release.[361] If the child cannot be released to the custody of a family member or sponsor, ORR will find an adequate

---

[354] (last visited Apr. 1, 2015).

[355] Trafficking Victims Protection Reauthorization Act of 2008, *supra* note 214, at §235(c)(2); U.S. Dep't of Health and Human Servs., Office of Refugee Resettlement (ORR), *Fact Sheet on Unaccompanied Children's Services* (2014), *available at www.acf.hhs.gov/sites/default/files/orr/unaccompanied_childrens_services_fact_sheet.pdf* (last visited Feb. 28, 2015); ORR, *About Unaccompanied Children's Services*, *available at www.acf.hhs.gov/programs/orr/programs/ucs/about* (last visited Feb. 28, 2015).

[356] ORR, *Fact Sheet on Unaccompanied Children's Services*, *supra* note 355; Federal Business Opportunities, Office of Refugee Resettlement Case Coordination Program (2010), *available at www.fpo.gov/?s=opportunitiy&mode=form&tab=core&id=c50c4ad575df879b25fb0826bccebb65&_c view=1* (last visited Feb. 28, 2015).

[357] Federal Business Opportunities, *supra* note 356.

[358] *See* ORR, *Division of Children's Services, Sponsor Care Agreement*, ORR-UAC FRP 4 (Rev. Sept. 15, 2014).

[359] ORR, *Fact Sheet on Unaccompanied Children's Services*, *supra* note 355.

[360] Trafficking Victims Protection Reauthorization Act of 2008, *supra* note 214, at §235(a)(5)(D).

[361] ORR, *Fact Sheet on Unaccompanied Children's Services*, *supra* note 355; ORR, *About Unaccompanied Children's Services*, *supra* note 355.

ORR shelter or foster home, as discussed below. ORR also funds follow-up services for at-risk children after release from ORR custody,[362] and is required to make every effort to provide legal counsel to UACs and legal orientation programs to their custodians.[363]

4. *Reunification with Family Members or Sponsors*

After placement with an ORR care provider, a case worker is assigned to the UAC, and that case worker will contact the UAC's family members or friends in the United States who may be able and willing to provide care and custody of the UAC.[364] If the family member or friend wishes to become the UAC's sponsor or custodian, he or she must submit an application for that designation.[365] Upon approval of the application, the custodian must sign a custodial agreement with the Department of Health and Human Services to assume responsibility for the UAC, and the UAC is then transferred to his or her custody.[366] The federal regulations require that UACs be released in the following order of preference: (1) a parent; (2) a legal guardian; or (3) an adult relative.[367]

Sponsors are provided with a family reunification packet, which contains the following documents:

- Authorization for Release of Information;
- Digital Fingerprint Instructions for Sponsors;
- Family Reunification Application;
- Family Reunification Checklist for Sponsors;
- Family Reunification Packet Cover Letter;
- Sponsor Care Agreement;
- Sponsor Handbook; and
- Letter of Designation for Care of a Minor.[368]

ORR, *Fact Sheet on Unaccompanied Children's Services*, *supra* note 340; ORR, *About Unaccompanied Children's Services*, *supra* note 355.

[363] Trafficking Victims Protection Reauthorization Act of 2008, *supra* note 214, at §§235(c)(4)–(5).

[364] ORR, *About Unaccompanied Children's Services*, *supra* note 355.

[365] Olga Byrne & Elise Miller, *The Flow of Unaccompanied Children Through the Immigration System: A Resource for Practitioners, Policy-Makers, and Researchers*, Vera Institute for Justice at 17–18 (Mar. 2012), *available at www.vera.org/sites/default/files/resources/downloads/the-flow-of-unaccompanied-children-through-the-immigration-system.pdf.*

[366] *Id.*

[367] 8 CFR §236.3 (2014). *See* Byrne & Miller, *supra* note 365, at 17–18.

[368] ORR, Unaccompanied Children's Services, *available at www.acf.hhs.gov/programs/orr/resource/unaccompanied-childrens-services* (last visited Mar. 1, 2015).

These documents set forth the sponsor's responsibilities and confirm that serving as a sponsor or custodian of a UAC is not a legal adoption, nor does it confer any immigration status on the UAC.[369]

➢ **Practice Pointer**: Each of these documents is available at *www.acf.hhs.gov/programs/orr/resource/unaccompanied-childrens-services*.[370] Practitioners representing UACs should assist sponsors with understanding their responsibilities and serving as effective custodians for UACs.

Sponsors also should attend the Legal Orientation Program for Custodians of Unaccompanied Alien Children (LOPC), a program that was created by the TVPRA and is administered by EOIR.[371] LOPC is a presentation that discusses the sponsor's responsibilities, including the obligation to ensure that the UAC appears at all future immigration court hearings; the process of immigration court proceedings; potential remedies before the immigration court; and the UAC's rights, including the right to attend school.[372]

➢ **Practice Pointer**: Given the valuable information provided at the LOPC, practitioners should inquire with the UAC's sponsor whether he or she has attended an LOPC. If not, practitioners should encourage such attendance, as sponsors are able to attend LOPCs even after they have assumed custody of the UAC. To schedule an LOPC for a sponsor, call the LOPC call center at 1-888-996-3848.

Upon release, ORR provides the UAC with a Verification of Release Form that contains the UAC's photo and biographic information.[373] This form may serve as the UAC's form of identification following release from ORR custody. Once the UAC is reunified with his or her sponsor, he or she is expected to reside with that sponsor.[374]

---

[369] *Id.*

[370] (last visited Mar. 1, 2015).

[371] *See* EOIR, *Legal Orientation Programs for Custodians of Unaccompanied Alien Children*, *available at www.justice.gov/eoir/probono/probono.htm#LOPC* (last visited Mar. 1, 2015); EOIR Memorandum on Legal Orientation Program for Custodians Program Guidance — Protecting Unaccompanied Alien Children from Mistreatment, Exploitation, and Trafficking (2012).

[372] EOIR Memorandum on Legal Orientation Program for Custodians Program Guidance, *supra* note 371. *See also Plyer v. Doe*, 457 U.S. 202 (1982).

[373] *See* Olga Byrne and Elise Miller, *The Flow of Unaccompanied Children Through the Immigration System: A Resource for Practitioners, Policy-Makers, and Researchers*, Vera Institute for Justice (Mar. 2012), *available at www.vera.org/sites/default/files/resources/downloads/the-flow-of-unaccompanied-children-through-the-immigration-system.pdf* (last visited Mar. 1, 2015).

[374] ORR, *Sponsor Care Agreement*, *available at www.acf.hhs.gov/programs/orr/resource/unaccompanied-childrens-services* (last visited Mar. 1, 2015).

5. *Appearances Before the Immigration Courts*

The UAC's sponsor is not required to attend the UAC's hearings before the immigration court; however, he or she must ensure that the UAC appears at all of his or her scheduled hearings.[375] During the hearing, the IJ usually asks questions about the sponsor's whereabouts, where the UAC is living, the identity of and relationship to any adult that is present with the UAC during the hearing, and the UAC's school attendance.[376]

- ➢ **Practice Pointer**: Practitioners should ensure that their UAC client is attending school and that he or she is attending the public school that corresponds with his or her address on file with the court. If there is a discrepancy between the UAC's school records and his or her address, the IJ may inquire whether the UAC actually is living at the listed address and/or whether the UAC is committing school enrollment fraud.[377]

Like any respondent in removal proceedings, UACs must first answer to the factual allegations and charges against him or her during the course of a Master Calendar Hearing. First, UACs may seek termination of proceedings if the Notice to Appear was improperly served.[378] The regulations require that if the UAC is under 14 years old, "service shall be made upon the person with whom the minor resides; whenever possible, service shall also be made on the near relative, guardian, committee, or friend."[379] Second, UACs also may seek termination of proceedings if the DHS attorney is unable to substantiate the factual allegations and establish the charges on the Notice to Appear.[380] Third, UACs also may seek to suppress the admission of the Form I-213 as evidence of their removability. Although I-213s are usually admissible, if the information contained therein is inaccurate or unreliable because it was obtained through coercion or duress, it is possible that the I-213 may

---

[375] *Id.*

[376] *See* Brian M. O'Leary, *Docketing Practices Relating to Unaccompanied Children Cases in Light of the New Priorities*, at 2–3 (Sept. 10, 2014), *available at www.justice.gov/eoir/statspub/Docketing-Practices-Related-to-UACs-Sept2014.pdf* (last visited Mar. 1, 2015); EOIR Memorandum on Legal Orientation Program for Custodians Program Guidance, *supra* note 371.

[377] Jennifer Bibby-Gerth, Michelle N. Mendez, & Christina Wilkes, *Operation: Preparation, Precision, and Bedside Manner in Unaccompanied Minors' Cases*, at 5, *available at http://ailadc.org/downloads/2014_Conference_Panel_4/4_16practiceadvisoryoperation.pdf* (last visited Mar. 1, 2015).

[378] *See, e.g., Matter of Mejia-Andino*, 23 I&N Dec. 533 (BIA 2002) (upholding termination of proceedings because the minor respondent's parents had not been served with the NTA).

[379] 8 CFR §§103.5a(c)(2)(ii), 236.2(a), 1003.13, 1003.14 (2014).

[380] *See* Lauren Hartley & James Gilbert, Am. Immigration Council, Penn State Dickinson School of Law, Notices to Appear: Legal Challenges and Strategies, ABA Commission on Immigration (June 2014), *available at www.legalactioncenter.org/sites/default/files/notices_to_appear_fin_6-30-14.pdf* (providing a detailed overview of options and considerations for challenging NTAs in immigration court) (last visited Mar. 1, 2015).

be suppressed and proceedings terminated due to DHS's failure to meet its burden of proof in establishing alienage and removability.[381]

> **Practice Pointer**: For detailed guidance on strategies for seeking termination of proceedings or suppression of evidence, or denying the charges on the Notice to Appear on behalf of UACs in immigration court, see the Practice Advisory by Jennifer Bibby-Gerth, Michelle N. Mendez, and Christina Wilkes, "Operation: Preparation, Precision, and Bedside Manner in Unaccompanied Minors' Cases," available at *http://ailadc.org/downloads/2014_Conference_Panel_4/4_16practiceadvisoryoperation.pdf*.[382]

If removability is established, the UAC may then seek various forms of relief from removal before the IJ. The most common forms of relief from removal for UACs are: asylum, withholding of removal under INA §241(b)(3), protection under the Convention Against Torture, Special Immigrant Juvenile Status, I-130 Petitions for Alien Relative filed by U.S. citizen or lawful permanent resident parents or step-parents, U visas, T visas, and Violence Against Women Act (VAWA) protection. This section focuses on asylum, withholding of removal under INA §241(b)(3), and protection under the Convention Against Torture, as the other forms of relief are outside the scope of this book.

> **Practice Pointer**: In determining whether a child is eligible for relief from removal, it is important for practitioners to conduct a detailed screening interview of the child, as well as his or her parents. This is because the child may be eligible for some forms of relief as a derivative on a parent's application (for example, U visas, T visas, and VAWA petitions).[383] See chapter 16 for a detailed discussion of related forms of relief.

6. Asylum Applications by UACs

UAC asylum applicants have the same burden of proof as adults and must establish that they meet the same definition of a refugee contained in the INA.[384] As UNHCR states in its *Handbook*, "The same definition of a refugee applies to all individuals, regardless of their age."[385] Although the substantive legal requirements

---

[381] *See id.; Matter of Gomez-Gomez*, 23 I&N Dec. 522, 524 (BIA 2002) ("We emphasize that while generally considered to be reliable and sufficient to establish alienage, not every Form I-213 that alleges alienage must be ultimately so found."); *Matter of Amaya-Castro*, 21 I&N Dec. 583, 586–87 & n.4 (BIA 1996) (holding that a 13-year-old child's factual admissions in court could establish his alienage, but the I-213 itself could not); *Matter of Barcenas*, 19 I&N Dec. 609 (BIA 1988) (finding that the I-213 was admissible where the information relates to the respondent and there is no evidence that the information is inaccurate or was obtained by coercion or duress).

[382] (last visited Mar. 1, 2015).

[383] *See* Bibby-Gerth, Mendez, & Wilkes, *supra* note 377.

[384] AOBTC Lesson Plan on Children's Asylum Claims, *supra* note 10, at 36.

[385] UNHCR Handbook, *supra* note 16, at ¶ 213.

for demonstrating eligibility for asylum are largely the same, however, the best interests of the child principle requires that adjudicators consider harm and fears through a child's perspective.[386] It also requires special safeguards and procedural considerations for children seeking asylum. Many of these procedural safeguards are discussed above in regard to child asylum-seekers generally. However, given the heightened vulnerability of UACs, special procedures and considerations have been legislated and implemented for UACs seeking asylum. These are discussed below.

i. Initial Jurisdiction of USCIS

Typically, the immigration courts have jurisdiction over asylum claims pursued in defense of deportation. However, in recognizing that an informal, non-adversarial setting is more appropriate for children than the intimidating, adversarial setting of removal proceedings before an immigration judge, Congress conferred the right to apply for asylum before a USCIS asylum officer, even for UACs in removal proceedings.[387] USCIS Asylum Offices, therefore, have initial jurisdiction over all asylum applications filed by UACs after March 23, 2009, whether they are filed affirmatively or defensively.[388] This means that UACs may file for asylum before USCIS even if they have been issued a Notice to Appear in immigration court, are in proceedings pending before the immigration court, or have cases on appeal to the BIA or on petition for review in federal court as of December 23, 2008.[389] In sum, the Asylum Office may address asylum applications for UACs in the following procedural postures:

- A UAC who has never been in removal proceedings, but who has filed his or her application affirmatively under standard affirmative asylum procedures; and
- A UAC in removal proceedings, who may apply for asylum with USCIS under the TVPRA's initial jurisdiction provision.

The asylum office may not, however, address the asylum application of a UAC whose case was referred to the immigration court after already being adjudicated by USCIS through the regular affirmative asylum procedures.[390] In that situation, the UAC may not re-file with USCIS, because USCIS has already exercised initial

---

[386] *See supra* pt. I for a detailed discussion of how the legal requirements for establishing asylum eligibility are applied differently to children.

[387] Memorandum from Joseph E. Langlois on Implementation of Statutory Change Providing USCIS with Initial Jurisdiction Over Asylum Applications Filed by Unaccompanied Alien Children, HQRAIO 120/12a (Mar. 25, 2009), *available at www.uscis.gov/sites/default/files/USCIS/Laws/Memoranda/Static_Files_Memoranda/2009/uac_filings_5f25mar09.pdf* (last visited Mar. 1, 2015). *See* Trafficking Victims Protection Reauthorization Act of 2008, *supra* note 214.

[388] *See* Trafficking Victims Protection Reauthorization Act of 2008, *supra* note 214, at §235(d)(7)(B); 6 USC §279(g)(2).

[389] USCIS, *Affirmative Asylum Procedures Manual*, *supra* note 198 at pt. III.B.1.a.

[390] *Id.*

jurisdiction in the case.[391] The procedural posture of the case is what determines the protocol to be followed by the asylum office in processing the application.

ii. Defensive Filings by UACs

Upon apprehension by CBP or ICE, UACs are usually issued a Notice to Appear before an immigration judge for removal proceedings under INA §240. During removal proceedings, if a UAC requests asylum, the DHS attorney will provide him or her with specific instructions for submitting a defensive Form I-589 asylum application to USCIS.[392] The IJ will then continue the case to provide time for the UAC to file his or her I-589 application with USCIS and have his or her claim adjudicated.

Following the grant of a continuance, the UAC must then follow DHS's instructions by sending the following items to the USCIS Nebraska Service Center address listed on the instructions sheet: (1) the completed, signed original and two copies of the Form I-589; (2) a completed Form G-28, Notice of Entry of Appearance as Attorney or Representative, if the child is represented; (3) any documentation demonstrating that he or she meets the definition of a UAC; and (4) a copy of the UAC instruction sheet.[393] The outer envelope should be addressed with the heading "UAC I-589."[394]

> ➤ **Practice Pointer**: Often times, defensive filings by UACs will get misprocessed at the Nebraska Service Center as a regular defensive asylum filing. Practitioners should write in bold, highlighted font on the cover letter: "TVPRA Filing (PRL). Forward to ZAR" (or to any other asylum office code). "PRL" is how USCIS codes UAC cases in their database to ensure that it is processed correctly under the TVPRA. Thus, this code highlighted on a cover letter should assist the Service Center with properly processing the application.

iii. Affirmative Filings by UACs

Although most asylum applications by UACs are filed with USCIS after the UAC was apprehended by CBP or ICE and placed in removal proceedings, some UACs may file affirmatively with USCIS. Like adults, UACs must prepare and file with USCIS an original, signed Form I-589, two copies of the signed I-589, one passport-

---

[391] *Id.*

[392] *See* DHS, *Instruction Sheet for an Unaccompanied Alien Child in Immigration Court to Submit an I-589 Asylum Application to U.S. Citizenship and Immigration Services (USCIS), available at http://immigrantjustice.org/sites/immigrantjustice.org/files/Appendix%20Q%20%20-%20ICE%20Instruction%20Sheet%20for%20UAC%20Asylum%20Applicants.pdf* (last visited Feb. 27, 2015).

[393] *Id.*

[394] USCIS, *Affirmative Asylum Procedures Manual*, *supra* note 198 at pt. III.B.1.a.i.

style photograph, and any supporting documentation.[395] In addition to the usual required and recommended documentation in support of an I-589, UACs should include a copy of the UAC Instruction Sheet and, if they were previously determined to be a UAC by CBP or ICE, evidence of that determination. This evidence may include the UAC Initial Placement Referral Form or the ORR Verification of Release Form.[396] If the child was not previously determined to be a UAC, he or she should submit documentation demonstrating that he or she is a UAC, along with his or her asylum application. The outer envelope should be addressed to the USCIS Nebraska Service Center with the heading "UAC I-589."[397]

- **Practice Pointer**: For both defensive and affirmative filings, if expedited processing is required due to extenuating circumstances, practitioners may seek permission from the local Asylum Office Director on behalf of their UAC clients to file the Form I-589 directly with the asylum office.[398] If the UAC continues to be in ORR custody, that may be a relevant factor meriting expeditious processing.[399]

iv. Initial Processing by USCIS

Upon receipt of the filing, the USCIS Nebraska Service Center will verify whether the UAC is in removal proceedings and enter the application into the database with the relevant code to indicate that special arrangements for an interview may be necessary.[400] If the UAC is in removal proceedings, the Nebraska Service Center will create a temporary file (T-file) containing the asylum application. This is because an A-file will already exist for a UAC who is currently in removal proceedings.[401]

After properly coding the application in the database, the Nebraska Service Center will issue a Receipt Notice confirming the agency's receipt of the application and send it to the UAC applicant. USCIS also will issue an Application Support Center (ASC) notice scheduling the UAC for an appointment for biometrics collection.[402]

---

[395] See chapter 7 for a detailed discussion of documentation that should be filed with an affirmative I-589 application.

[396] Memorandum from Ted Kim, Acting Chief, Asylum Division, USCIS on Updated Service Center Operations Procedures for Accepting Forms I-589 Filed by Unaccompanied Alien Children (June 4, 2013), *www.uscis.gov/sites/default/files/USCIS/Humanitarian/Refugees%20%26%20Asylum/Asylum/Minor%20Children%20Applying%20for%20Asylum%20By%20Themselves/service-ctr-ops-proced-accepting-form-i589-unaccompanied-alien-children.pdf* (last visited Feb. 28, 2015); Memorandum from Joseph E. Langlois on Statutory Change Affecting Service Center Operations' Procedures for Accepting Forms I-589 Filed by Unaccompanied Alien Children (Apr. 9, 2009).

[397] USCIS, *Affirmative Asylum Procedures Manual*, *supra* note 198 at pt. III.B.1.a.i.

[398] *Id.*

[399] *Id.*

[400] *Id.* at pt. III.B.1.a.ii.; Memorandum from Joseph E. Langlois on Special Group Code for Unaccompanied Alien Child Defensive Asylum Filings Changed to 'PRL,' (Apr. 2, 2009).

[401] USCIS, Affirmative Asylum Procedures Manual, *supra* note 198 at pt. III.B.1.a.iv.

[402] *See* DHS, *Instruction Sheet for an Unaccompanied Alien Child*, *supra* note 392.

The UAC must bring his or her receipt notice and ASC notice with him or her to the appointment at the ASC.[403] Following issuance of the receipt and ASC appointment notices, the Nebraska Service Center will forward the UAC's application to the local asylum office for adjudication.

> **Practice Pointer**: If the UAC is in removal proceedings and his or her application remains pending before USCIS at his or her next hearing before the immigration court the UAC should provide a copy of his or her USCIS receipt notice to the IJ and to the DHS attorney. The IJ may again continue the case to allow USCIS to adjudicate the UAC's asylum application.[404]

v. UAC Determination by the Asylum Office

A UAC is a child who (1) has no lawful immigration status in the United States; (2) has not attained 18 years of age; and (3) with respect to whom there is no parent or legal guardian in the United States who is available to provide care and physical custody.[405] Upon receipt of the application and files, the first step for the asylum officer is to determine whether the applicant is a UAC. For this reason, UACs should always file with their applications a copy of the UAC Instruction Sheet and, if they were previously determined to be a UAC by CBP or ICE, evidence of that determination, such as the UAC Initial Placement Referral Form or the ORR Verification of Release Form.[406] If they were not previously determined to be a UAC, they should file evidence of their UAC status.

Although a UAC asylum-seeker is sometimes encountered for the first time by USCIS, it is most common for UACs to come into contact with USCIS after they have already been apprehended by CBP or ICE and been determined to meet the definition of UAC, as described above.[407] In June 2013, USCIS issued a series of memoranda providing guidance for the initial jurisdiction of the asylum offices over UACs' applications. These memoranda identify certain groups of applicants who will be afforded all of the procedural and adjudicative benefits of a UAC:

---

[403] *Id.*

[404] *See* DHS, *Instruction Sheet for an Unaccompanied Alien Child*, *supra* note 392.

[405] *Id.*

[406] Memorandum from Ted Kim, Acting Chief, Asylum Division, USCIS on Updated Service Center Operations Procedures for Accepting Forms I-589 Filed by Unaccompanied Alien Children (June 4, 2013), *www.uscis.gov/sites/default/files/USCIS/Humanitarian/Refugees%20%26%20Asylum/Asylum/Minor%20Children%20Applying%20for%20Asylum%20By%20Themselves/service-ctr-ops-proced-accepting-form-i589-unaccompanied-alien-children.pdf* (last visited Feb. 28, 2015); Memorandum from Joseph E. Langlois on Statutory Change Affecting Service Center Operations' Procedures for Accepting Forms I-589 Filed by Unaccompanied Alien Children (Apr. 9, 2009).

[407] USCIS, *Affirmative Asylum Procedures Manual*, *supra* note 198 at; Memorandum from Ted Kim, Acting Chief, USCIS Asylum Division, Memorandum on Updated Procedures for Determination of Initial Jurisdiction over Asylum Applications Filed by Unaccompanied Alien Children (2013), *available on* AILA InfoNet at Doc. No. 13080847.

- Children who have already been determined by CBP or ICE to be a UAC;[408] and
- Applicants over 18 years old who were at one point designated as a UAC by DHS or the Department of Health and Human Services.[409]

Accordingly, if CBP or ICE has already determined that a child is a UAC and that status determination remained in place on the date the UAC filed his or her asylum application with USCIS, the asylum office will automatically adopt that previously-made determination without a separate factual inquiry or analysis regarding whether the applicant meets the definition of UAC.[410] The asylum offices also will accept applications from individuals over 18 years old and afford them all of the procedural and adjudicative benefits of a UAC, as long as the individual was at one point designated as a UAC and submits certain supporting documentation with his or her application.[411] Finally, children who CBP or ICE determined not to be UACs and children who never encountered CBP or ICE may seek to establish before USCIS that they are UACs, and receive all of the benefits that come with that designation.[412]

> ➢ **Practice Pointer**: For a helpful summary of these procedures, see the Practice Advisory by Jennifer Bibby-Gerth, Michelle N. Mendez, and Christina Wilkes, "Operation: Preparation, Precision, and Bedside Manner in Unaccompanied Minors' Cases," available at *http://ailadc.org/downloads/2014_Conference_Panel_4/4_16practiceadvisoryoperation.pdf*.[413]

Procedurally, the asylum officer will look for the following evidence of a previous UAC determination:

- Form I-213, Record of Deportable Alien;
- Form 93 (the CBP UAC screening form);
- ORR Initial Placement Form;

---

[408] USCIS, *Questions and Answers: Updated Procedures for Determination of Initial Jurisdiction over Asylum Applications Filed by Unaccompanied Alien Children* (June 10, 2013), *available at www.uscis.gov/sites/default/files/USCIS/Refugee,%20Asylum,%20and%20Int'l%20Ops/Asylum/ra-qanda-determine-jurisdiction-uac.pdf*.

[409] Memorandum from Ted Kim, Acting Chief, Asylum Division, USCIS, on Updated Service Center Operations Procedures for Accepting Forms I-589 Filed by Unaccompanied Alien Children (June 4, 2013), *available at www.uscis.gov/sites/default/files/USCIS/Humanitarian/Refugees%20%26%20Asylum/Asylum/Minor%20Children%20Applying%20for%20Asylum%20By%20Themselves/service-ctr-ops-proced-accepting-form-i589-unaccompanied-alien-children.pdf*.

[410] USCIS, *Questions and Answers on Initial Jurisdiction*, *supra* note 408; Memorandum from Ted Kim, Acting Chief, USCIS Asylum Division, on Updated Procedures for Determination of Initial Jurisdiction over Asylum Applications Filed by Unaccompanied Alien Children (2013), *available on* AILA InfoNet at Doc. No. 13080847; USCIS, Affirmative Asylum Procedures Manual, *supra* note 198.

[411] Kim Mem. on Updated Service Center Operations, *supra* note 409; Kim Mem. on Updated Procedures for Determination of Initial Jurisdiction, *supra* note 410.

[412] Kim Mem. on Updated Service Center Operations, *supra* note 409.

[413] (last visited Mar. 1, 2015).

- ORR Verification of Release Form; and
- The encounters tab in the ENFORCE Alien Removal Module database.[414]

If CBP or ICE determined that the applicant was a UAC and the child's UAC status determination remained in place at the time of filing with USCIS, the asylum officer will not question the applicant regarding his or her age or whether he or she is accompanied by a parent or legal guardian.[415] No USCIS determination of UAC status is required, even if there is evidence that the child may have turned 18 or may have reunited with a parent or legal guardian since the CBP or ICE determination.[416] Under these circumstances, the asylum officer will only conduct his or her own inquiry regarding the child's status as a UAC if there was an affirmative act terminating the previous UAC status determination before the I-589 was filed with USCIS. An example of such an act may include ICE taking the individual out of ORR custody and placing him or her in ICE custody as an adult detainee, either because the individual turned 18 years old or because the original UAC determination was not correct.[417]

On the other hand, if a determination of UAC status has not already been made, a USCIS determination in this regard is necessary. The asylum officer will review the application and evidence submitted and determine whether: (1) the applicant does not have a lawful immigration status in the United States; (2) the applicant was under 18 years old at the time of filing the Form I-589; and (3) the applicant was unaccompanied (i.e., had no parent or legal guardian in the United States who was able to provide care and physical custody) at the time of filing the Form I-589.[418]

USCIS is tasked with making the UAC determination most frequently when the applicant appears to be a UAC, is not in removal proceedings, and applies for asylum affirmatively with USCIS. Under these circumstances, the purpose of the determination is two-fold: (1) to determine whether the applicant is subject to the one-year filing deadline; and (2) to determine whether the asylum office must notify the Department of Health and Human Services that it has discovered a UAC.[419]

If, however, the potential UAC is in removal proceedings and CBP or ICE has not yet made a determination regarding UAC status, USCIS must make this determination in order to verify whether USCIS has jurisdiction over the case.[420] If

---

[414] USCIS, Affirmative Asylum Procedures Manual, *supra* note 198 at pt. III.B.1.a.iii.1.

[415] *Id.*

[416] *Id.*; Kim Mem. on Updated Procedures for Determination of Initial Jurisdiction, *supra* note 410.

[417] USCIS, *Affirmative Asylum Procedures Manual*, *supra* note 198 at n.9.

[418] *Id.* at pt. III.B.1.a.iii.2.a.; Kim Mem. on Updated Procedures for Determination of Initial Jurisdiction, *supra* note 410.

[419] USCIS, *Affirmative Asylum Procedures Manual*, *supra* note 198 at pt. III.B.1.a.iii.2.b.; Kim Mem. on Updated Procedures for Determination of Initial Jurisdiction, *supra* note 410.

[420] USCIS, *Affirmative Asylum Procedures Manual*, *supra* note 198 at pt. III.B.1.a.iii.2.c.; Kim Mem. on Updated Procedures for Determination of Initial Jurisdiction, *supra* note 410.

the child was a UAC at the time of filing the Form I-589, USCIS has jurisdiction.[421] If the child remains a UAC at the time of the asylum interview, USCIS should notify the Department of Health and Human Services that it has discovered a UAC.[422] If the asylum officer finds that USCIS does not have jurisdiction over the case, the officer must draft a memorandum explaining why the applicant was not a UAC at the time of filing and the case will be transferred back to the immigration court after Headquarters review.[423] The application will be administratively closed before USCIS and the applicant will then receive a Notice of Lack of Jurisdiction.[424] If, however, the asylum officer finds that USCIS does have jurisdiction over the case, the asylum office will move forward with interview scheduling.

> **Practice Pointer**: For updated USCIS guidance regarding the determination of initial jurisdiction over asylum applications filed by UACs in various custody circumstances and procedural postures, see USCIS's June 10, 2013 Questions and Answers, available at http://www.uscis.gov/sites/default/files/USCIS/Refugee,%20Asylum,%20and%20Int'l%20Ops/Asylum/ra-qanda-determine-jurisdiction-uac.pdf.[425]

vi. Notifying the Department of Health and Human Services of the UAC

As noted above, if USCIS determines that the applicant is a UAC and that determination has not previously been made by CBP or ICE, USCIS is tasked with notifying the Department of Health and Human Services of the discovery of a UAC.[426] This notification is required by the TVPRA and must be completed within 48 hours of discovery of the UAC.[427] Each asylum office has a designated point of contact for UAC issues. Thus, upon discovery of the UAC, the asylum officer will notify the office's UAC point of contact, who will then send an email to ORR at the email address designated for such notifications.[428]

> **Practice Pointer**: If an asylum officer encounters an applicant under 18 years old who may be a victim of a severe form of trafficking in persons, the officer must notify the office's UAC point of contact because the TVPRA also requires notification to the Department of Health and Human Services within 24 hours in these circumstances. The

---

421 USCIS, *Affirmative Asylum Procedures Manual*, *supra* note 198 at pt. III.B.1.a.iii.2.c.

422 *Id.*

423 *Id.*

424 *Id.* at pt. III.B.1.a.xi.

425 (last visited Mar. 4, 2015).

426 USCIS, Affirmative Asylum Procedures Manual, *supra* note 198 at pt. III.B.1.a.ix.

427 Trafficking Victims Protection Reauthorization Act of 2008, *supra* note 214, at §235(b)(2)(A).

428 USCIS, Affirmative Asylum Procedures Manual, *supra* note 198 at pt. III.B.1.a.ix.

UAC point of contact will then notify ORR via the designated email address.[429]

vii. USCIS Asylum Office Interview

Interviews for UACs must be scheduled manually, given the special processing and necessary procedural safeguards involved in the adjudication process. For example, if the UAC is in ORR custody, the Asylum Office will issue a G-56 appointment notice instead of a regular interview notice to inform the UAC of the interview location.[430] This is because UACs in ORR custody may need to be interviewed outside of the asylum office.[431] Additionally, interview scheduling "should be done as expeditiously as possible for UACs, particularly for those who are in ORR custody at the time of filing."[432] For UACs in removal proceedings, the asylum office "should attempt to schedule the asylum interview to occur prior to the next scheduled hearing date in Immigration Court."[433]

For UACs in ORR custody, the asylum office also will arrange for an interpreter for the UAC since he or she usually is unable to fulfill the general requirement under 8 CFR §208.9(g) to provide his or her own interpreter for the interview.[434] These interpreters are usually telephonic contract interpreters.[435]

If a represented UAC fails to appear for his or her asylum interview, the asylum officer will follow the regular guidance for adults who fail to appear for their asylum interviews.[436] If the UAC is unrepresented and fails to appear for his or her asylum interview, the asylum officer will reschedule the interview once. If the UAC fails to appear a second time without providing a reasonable excuse, the asylum officer will issue a UAC Notice for Failure to Appear and transfer the file to the ICE Office of Chief Counsel.[437]

Upon the UAC's appearance for his or her asylum interview, the asylum officer will conduct the interview according to the USCIS *Guidelines for Children's Asylum Claims* and the special considerations and safeguards necessary for determining asylum eligibility in light of the best interests of the child principle.[438] For a detailed discussion of these interviewing procedures and techniques, please see Part II.C.1. above. Following the asylum interview, the asylum office will provide the child with

---

[429] *Id.*

[430] *Id.* at pt. III.B.1.a.v.

[431] *Id.* at pt. III.B.1.a.vi.

[432] *Id.* at pt. III.B.1.a.v.

[433] *Id.*

[434] *Id.* at pt. III.B.1.a.viii.

[435] *See id.*

[436] *See id.* at pt. III.I. (discussing failure to appear for asylum interviews).

[437] *Id.* at pt. III.B.1.a.vii.

[438] *See* AOBTC Lesson Plan on Children's Asylum Claims, *supra* note 10, at 19–35.

a decision pick-up notice or a decision mail-out notice, containing instructions for how the child is to receive the decision on his or her case.

> ➢ **Practice Pointer**: Asylum officers will check the relevant databases prior to UAC asylum interviews to determine if the UAC has filed any other applications or petitions with USCIS. Often UACs will concurrently file I-360 petitions for Special Immigration Juvenile Status, or petitions for U or T nonimmigrant status. See the Affirmative Asylum Procedures Manual Appendix 76 for asylum officer instructions on how to handle concurrent filings by UACs.[439]

viii. USCIS Asylum Decision

If the asylum officer determines that the UAC is not eligible for asylum and a supervisor confirms that determination, the case must be forwarded to Headquarters for review and confirmed by Headquarters before it is served on the child asylum applicant.[440] Positive determinations, however, do not require Headquarters review and may be served on the child applicant.[441]

If a UAC is granted asylum, he or she is entitled to all benefits available to asylees.[442] On the other hand, if a UAC is not granted asylum by the asylum office, the next steps depend on whether the UAC is already in removal proceedings. If the UAC is not yet in removal proceedings, the asylum office will issue a Notice to Appear and refer him or her to the immigration court, where he or she may pursue an asylum claim before an immigration judge without filing a new I-589 application.[443] If the UAC was already in removal proceedings, the asylum office's next steps depend on the procedural posture of the case before the immigration court:

- If the proceedings have been continued for USCIS adjudication of the I-589, an active Notice to Appear already exists and the asylum office will issue a referral notice only;
- Similarly, if the proceedings have been administratively closed pending USCIS adjudication of the I-589, the asylum office will issue a referral notice, but does not need to issue a Notice to Appear; and

---

[439] USCIS, *Affirmative Asylum Procedures Manual*, *supra* note 198 at pt. III.B.1.a.xiii.

[440] USCIS Memorandum from John Lafferty, Chief of USCIS Asylum Division on Changes to Case Categories Requiring Asylum Headquarters Review (2014), *available at* AILA InfoNet Doc. No. 14013044.

[441] *Id.* Note that the Lafferty Memo changed the quality assurance procedures for UACs. Although all UAC cases used to require quality assurance review, as set forth in the Affirmative Asylum Procedures Manual, that requirement was modified by the Lafferty Memo. *See* USCIS, *Affirmative Asylum Procedures Manual*, *supra* note 198 at pt. III.B.1.a.x.

[442] USCIS, *Benefits and Responsibilities of Asylees* (Apr. 1, 2011), *available at* *www.uscis.gov/humanitarian/refugees-asylum/asylum/benefits-and-responsibilities-asylees* (last visited Mar. 3, 2015). See also chapter 13 for a detailed discussion of asylee benefits.

[443] USCIS, *Affirmative Asylum Procedures Manual*, *supra* note 198 at pt. III.B.1.a.xi.

- If the proceedings have been terminated without prejudice pending USCIS adjudication of the I-589, the asylum office will follow standard referral procedures, including issuance of a Notice to Appear.[444]

For continued or administratively closed cases, the asylum office does not need to serve the usual court packet on the immigration court. Rather, they will prepare the court packet and A-file and transfer the A-file to the immigration court. ICE will then serve the court packet on the immigration court.[445]

Upon referral from the asylum office after USCIS, the IJ will then move forward with hearing the UAC's asylum claim. The UAC may not re-file with USCIS, because USCIS has already exercised initial jurisdiction in the case.[446] If the IJ denies the UAC's application, the UAC may then file an appeal before the BIA by following the same procedures as adult applicants.[447]

> ➢ **Practice Pointer**: For a detailed guide filled with practice tips for practitioners representing unaccompanied minors, see the CAIR Coalition's January 2014 "Practice Manual for Pro Bono Attorneys Representing Unaccompanied Immigrant Children," available at *www.caircoalition.org/wp-content/files_mf/1391555303CAIRCoalitionPracticeManualforRepresentingUnaccompaniedImmigrantChildrenJan312014.pdf*.[448]

IV. Detention of Children

Children seeking asylum defensively may be in DHS custody through part or all of their asylum proceedings. In 1997, the *Flores v. Reno* settlement established nationwide policies for the way children must be processed upon apprehension, detention, and release.[449] It required that all children apprehended by DHS be held in the "least restrictive setting appropriate to their age and special needs to ensure their protection and wellbeing."[450] Additionally, it mandated that children not be detained with an unrelated adult for more than 24 hours.[451] Finally, the settlement also required that children be released from custody as soon as possible to a parent, legal guardian, adult relative, designated individual, or an adult who seeks custody and

---

[444] *Id.*

[445] *Id.*

[446] *Id.* at pt. III.B.1.a.

[447] See chapter 11 for a detailed discussion of appeals to the BIA.

[448] (last visited Mar. 4, 2015).

[449] *Flores* Settlement Agreement, *supra* note 324; *See Flores v. Reno,* 507 U.S. 292 (1993); *Flores v. Meese,* No. 85-cv-4544 (C.D. Cal. Sept. 1996). *See also* Mem. from Paul Virtue, *supra* note 324.

[450] Nat'l Immigrant Justice Ctr., Fact Sheet: Children Detained by DHS in Adult Detention Facilities, supra note 325; *see* Flores Settlement Agreement, *supra* note 324.

[451] *See Flores* Settlement Agreement, *supra* note 324.

who is deemed appropriate by DHS.[452] Many provisions of the *Flores v. Reno* settlement regarding the detention and release of children were later codified in the regulations at 8 CFR §§236.3, 1236.3.

On numerous occasions, DHS and legacy INS have been criticized for violating the terms of the *Flores v. Reno* settlement agreement and for the jail-like conditions under which children are held.[453] For example, in 2006, DHS expanded its detention practice to arriving families[454] and opened the 500-bed T. Don Hutto detention

---

[452] *See id.*

[453] The American Civil Liberties Union brought 17 lawsuits against U.S. Department of Homeland Security (DHS) Secretary Michael Chertoff, and six officials from U.S. Immigration and Customs Enforcement (ICE), on behalf of children detained at the T. Don Hutto (Hutto) detention facility in Taylor, TX. *See* Am. Civil Liberties Union (ACLU), *ACLU Challenges Illegal Detention of Immigrant Children Held in Prison-Like Conditions* (Mar. 6, 2007), *available at www.aclu.org/immigrants/detention/28865prs20070306.html*; *see also* Women's Comm'n for Refugee Women & Children and Lutheran Immigration and Refugee Serv., *Locking Up Family Values: The Detention of Immigrant Families* (Feb. 2007), *available at www.womenscommission.org/pdf/famdeten.pdf.* These lawsuits contended that the Hutto facility violated the regulations arising out of *Flores v. Meese*, which ended in a 1997 court settlement that established minimum standards and conditions for the housing and release of all minors in federal immigration custody. *Flores v. Reno*, Stipulated Settlement Agreement, No. CV 85-4544-RJK (C.D. Cal. 1997). On August 27, 2007, a settlement was reached in the Hutto detention center litigation. *See* Am. Civil Liberties Union (ACLU), ACLU Challenges Prison-Like Conditions at Hutto Detention Center (Mar. 6, 2007), *available at www.aclu.org/immigrants/detention/hutto.html. See also, e.g.,* Stephen Manning, *Ending Artesia, available at https://innovationlawlab.org/the-artesia-report/* (last visited Feb. 17, 2015); Women's Refugee Comm'n, *Locking Up Family Values Again: The Detention of Immigrant Families* (October 2014), *available at http://womensrefugeecommission.org/blog/2176-locking-up-family-values-again-blog* (last visited Jan. 18, 2015); *M.S.P.C. v. Johnson* Compl. in the U.S. District Court for the District of Columbia, *http://americanimmigrationcouncil.org/sites/default/files/M.S.P.C.%20v.%20Johnson.pdf* (last visited Jan. 18, 2015); U.S. Comm'n on Int'l Religious Freedom, *Assessing the U.S. Government's Detention of Asylum Seekers: Further Action Needed to Fully Implement Reforms* (Apr. 2013), *available at www.rcusa.org/uploads/pdfs/ERS-detention%20reforms%20report%20April%202013.pdf* (last visited Feb. 17, 2015); Human Rights First, *U.S. Detention of Asylum Seekers: Seeking Protection, Finding Prison* 1 (April 2009) *available at www.humanrightsfirst.org/pdf/090429-RP-hrf-asylum-detention-report.pdf*; Lutheran Immigration and Refugee Serv. and Women's Refugee Comm'n, *Locking Up Family Values: The Detention of Immigrant Families, available at www.refworld.org/docid/49ae507a2.html* (last visited Feb. 19, 2015); Physicians for Human Rights, *From Persecution to Prison: The Health Consequences of Detention for Asylum Seekers* (June 2003) at 123, *available at http://physiciansforhumanrights.org/library/documents/reports/report-perstoprison-2003.pdf*; Amnesty Int'l USA, *'Why Am I Here?' Children in Immigration Detention, available at* www.amnestyusa.org/refugee/ usa_children_summary.html (stating that approximately one third of children are detained in "harsh conditions in secure, jail-like facilities ..."); Women's Comm'n for Refugee Women and Children, *Prison Guard or Parent?: INS Treatment of Unaccompanied Refugee Children* (May 2002), *available at www.womenscommissionorg /pdf/ins_det.pdf*; Human Rights Watch, *Detained and Deprived of Rights: Children in the Custody of the U.S. Immigration and Naturalization Service* (Dec. 1998), *available at www.hrw.org/reports98/ins2.*

[454] DHS, Immigration and Customs Enforcement News Release, *DHS Closes Loophole by Expanding Expedited Removal to Cover Illegal Alien Families* (May 15, 2006), *available at www.immigration.com/newsletter1/iceilegalfaml.pdf.*

facility in Texas that it claimed was specially equipped to meet family needs.[455] There were soon allegations of mistreatment and prison-like conditions in this facility.[456] The detention of asylum-seekers — particularly children — and the negative impact that detention has on their ability to present their asylum claims was strongly criticized by human rights groups in the United States at that time.[457] The American Civil Liberties Union brought 17 lawsuits against Michael Chertoff, the Secretary of DHS, and six officials from ICE, on behalf of children detained at the T. Don Hutto detention facility in Taylor, TX.[458] These lawsuits contended that the Hutto facility violated the regulations arising out of *Flores v. Meese*, which ended in a 1997 court settlement that established minimum standards and conditions for the housing and release of all minors in federal immigration custody.[459] On August 27, 2007, a settlement was reached in the Hutto detention center litigation.[460] It was hoped that this settlement would improve the conditions for immigration children and their families.

In response, in August 2009, ICE announced reforms that allegedly would address many of the complaints about immigration detention.[461] As part of these 2009 reforms, ICE also announced — after years of controversy, media exposure, and a lawsuit — the shifting of the T. Don Hutto family detention facility to a facility for

---

[455] *Id.*

[456] *See* Am. Civil Liberties Union (ACLU), *ACLU Challenges Illegal Detention of Immigrant Children*, *supra* note 453; *see also* Women's Comm'n for Refugee Women, *Locking Up Family Values*, *supra* note 453. These lawsuits contended that the Hutto facility violated the regulations arising out of *Flores v. Meese*, which ended in a 1997 court settlement that established minimum standards and conditions for the housing and release of all minors in federal immigration custody. *Flores v. Reno*, Stipulated Settlement Agreement, No. CV 85-4544-RJK (C.D. Cal. 1997). On August 27, 2007, a settlement was reached in the Hutto detention center litigation. *See* Am. Civil Liberties Union (ACLU), *ACLU Challenges Prison-Like Conditions at Hutto*, *supra* note 453.

[457] Human Rights First, *U.S. Detention of Asylum Seekers: Seeking Protection, supra* note 453; Women's Comm'n for Refugee Women, *Locking Up Family Values*, *supra* note 453453. *See also* Nat'l Immigration Law Ctr., *A Broken System: Confidential Reports Reveal Failures in U.S. Immigrant Detention Centers* (June 2009), *available at www.nilc.org/immlawpolicy/arrestdet/A-Broken-System-2009-07.pdf*; Bill Frelick, *U.S. Detention of Asylum Seekers and Human Rights*, Amnesty International (Mar. 2005), *www.migrationinformation.org/usfocus/display.cfm?ID=296*.

[458] For information on the Hutto facility, see Women's Comm'n for Refugee Women, *Locking Up Family Values*, *supra* note 453.

[459] *Flores v. Reno*, Stipulated Settlement Agreement, No. CV 85-4544-RJK (C.D. Cal. 1997).

[460] Am. Civil Liberties Union (ACLU), *ACLU Challenges Prison-Like Conditions at Hutto*, *supra* note 453.

[461] ICE Fact Sheet, *2009 Immigration Detention Reforms* (Aug. 6, 2009), *published on* AILA InfoNet at Doc. No. 09080630 (*posted* Aug. 6, 2009).

adult women.[462] On August 6, 2009, the Obama Administration announced it would no longer send families to the Hutto facility.

- **Practice Pointer**: A 2009 documentary film, *The Least of These* captures the hardships and mental anguish of children in immigration detention. It was filmed at the T. Don Hutto facility. For more about the film and to view it online, go to *http://theleastofthese-film.com*.

However, most recently, in the summer of 2014, in response to the increase in the number of mothers and children fleeing violence in Central America, the Obama Administration resurrected and dramatically expanded its family detention practice in an effort to deter future border-crossers.[463] It hastily erected a facility in Artesia, New Mexico, with a capacity of over 600 women and children, which was closed down on December 15, 2014, following 14 grants of asylum out of 15 cases that went to the merits,[464] extensive media exposure,[465] and a lawsuit regarding inhumane conditions and due process concerns.[466] However, with the conversion of an existing facility in Karnes City, TX, with a capacity of over 500 woman and children, and the

---

[462] *See* Am. Civil Liberties Union (ACLU), *DHS Plan To Improve Immigration Detention And Close Hutto Facility A Good First Step* (Aug. 6, 2009), *available at www.aclu.org/immigrants/detention/40612prs20090806.html*.

[463] *See* Women's Comm'n for Refugee Women, *Locking Up Family Values*, *supra* note 453; Manning, *Ending Artesia*, *supra* note 453; Dree Collopy, *The Failings of Family Detention at Artesia*, Immigration Impact (Oct. 2, 2014), *available at http://immigrationimpact.com/2014/10/02/the-failings-of-family-detention-at-artesia/* (last visited Jan. 18, 2015); Dree Collopy & Stephen Manning, *Why is Obama Still Locking Up So Many Innocent Women and Kids on U.S. Soil?*, The Guardian, *available at www.theguardian.com/commentisfree/2014/nov/04/obama-women-children-family-detention-centres* (last visited Jan. 18, 2015); Stephen Manning, *Let These Women Go*, AILA Leadership Blog (Sept. 3 2014), *available at http://ailaleadershipblog.org/2014/09/03/let-these-women-go/* (last visited Jan. 19, 2015).

[464] *See* Am. Immigration Lawyers Assoc., *Artesia Family Detention Asylum Case Examples*, AILA InfoNet. Doc. No. 14102446 (*posted* Feb. 13, 2015), *available at www.aila.org/infonet/family-detention-asylum-grant-examples*. Note that the "14 out of 15" number is the number of cases tried on the merits during the 21 weeks that the AILA pro bono project operated in Artesia. *See* Stephen Manning, *Ending Artesia, available at https://innovationlawlab.org/the-artesia-report/* (last visited Feb. 19, 2015) (discussing the significant reduction in deportations after the arrival of pro bono counsel for women and children detained at the Federal Law Enforcement Training Center in Artesia, New Mexico).

[465] *See, e.g.*, N.Y. TIMES MAGAZINE, *The Shame of America's Family Detention Camps* (Feb. 4, 2015), *www.nytimes.com/2015/02/08/magazine/the-shame-of-americas-family-detention-camps.html?_r=0* (last visited Feb. 19, 2015); Collopy & Manning, *Why is Obama Still Locking Up So Many*, *supra* note 453.

[466] *See M.S.P.C. v. Johnson* Compl. in the U.S. District Court for the District of Columbia, *available at http://americanimmigrationcouncil.org/sites/default/files/M.S.P.C.%20v.%20Johnson.pdf* (last visited Jan. 18, 2015). *See also* Am. Immigration Council, *Groups Sue U.S. Government Over Life-Threatening Deportation Process Against Mothers and Children* (Aug. 22, 2014), *available at www.americanimmigrationcouncil.org/newsroom/release/groups-sue-us-government-over-life-threatening-deportation-process-against-mothers-* (last visited Jan. 18, 2015).

opening of a new 2,400 bed facility in Dilley, TX, the administration has made clear its intentions to sustain its policy of detaining women and children asylum-seekers.[467]

> ➢ **Practice Pointer**: Whether DHS's unlawful policy of detention-as-deterrent will endure is uncertain, however, given a recent preliminary injunction granted in a class action lawsuit, which prevents DHS from detaining class members for the purpose of deterring future immigration to the United States and from considering deterrence of future immigration as a factor in custody determinations.[468]

Criticisms against DHS for the conditions and practices in these facilities, as well as its treatment of children in DHS custody, continue unabated.[469] As the Lutheran Immigration and Refugee Service states, "Detention has been documented as psychologically damaging and completely inappropriate for toddlers and children. Holding vulnerable individuals, such as women and children, in jails or jail-like settings poses a serious threat to psychological health and risks re-traumatizing victims of abuse, torture and human trafficking."[470] Human Rights Watch notes that international human rights standards "provide for detention only as a last resort and for very short periods … . children should never be detained for immigration reasons

---

[467] *See* Immigration and Customs Enforcement, *ICE's New Family Detention Center in Dilley, Texas to Open in December* (Nov. 18, 2014), *available at www.ice.gov/news/releases/ices-new-family-detention-center-dilley-texas-open-december* (last visited Jan. 17, 2015); Julia Preston, *Detention Center Presented as Deterrent to Border Crossers*, N.Y. Times (Dec. 15, 2014), *available at www.nytimes.com/2014/12/16/us/homeland-security-chief-opens-largest-immigration-detention-center-in-us.html?_r=0* (last visited Jan. 17, 2015).

[468] *R.I. L–R–, et al., v. Jeh Charles Johnson, et al.,* 1:15-cv-00011-JEB (D.D.C. Feb. 20, 2015).

[469] *See, e.g.*, Stephen Manning, *Ending Artesia*, *available at https://innovationlawlab.org/the-artesia-report/* (last visited Feb. 17, 2015); Women's Comm'n for Refugee Women, *Locking Up Family Values*, *supra* note 453; *M.S.P.C. v. Johnson* Compl. in the U.S. District Court for the District of Columbia, *http://americanimmigrationcouncil.org/sites/default/files/M.S.P.C.%20v.%20Johnson.pdf* (last visited Jan. 18, 2015); Lutheran Immigration and Refugee Serv., *From Persecution to Prison: Child and Family Detention* (Aug. 2014), *available at http://lirs.org/wp-content/uploads/2014/08/LIRS-Family-Detention-Backgrounder-140807.pdf* (last visited Mar. 4, 2015); Human Rights Watch, *US: Surge in Detention of Child Migrants* (June 25, 2014), *available at www.hrw.org/print/news/2014/06/25/us-surge-detention-child-migrants* (last visited Feb. 19, 2015); U.S. Comm'n on Int'l Religious Freedom, *Assessing the U.S. Government's Detention of Asylum Seekers: Further Action Needed to Fully Implement Reforms* (Apr. 2013), *available at www.rcusa.org/uploads/pdfs/ERS-detention%20reforms%20report%20April%202013.pdf* (last visited Feb. 17, 2015); Am. Civil Liberties Union (ACLU), *ACLU Challenges Prison-Like Conditions at Hutto*, *supra* note 453; Human Rights First, *In Liberty's Shadow: U.S. Detention of Asylum Seekers in the Era of Homeland Security* (Jan. 2004), *available at www.humanrightsfirst.org/asylum/libertys_shadow/Libertys_Shadow.pdf*; Human Rights Watch, *Presumption of Guilt: Human Rights Abuses of Post-September 11 Detainees* (Aug. 2002), *available at www.hrw.org/reports/2002/us911*; Human Rights Watch, *Locked Away: Immigration Detainees in Jails in the United States* (Sept. 1998), *available at www.hrw.org/reports98/us-immig*.

[470] Lutheran Immigration and Refugee Serv., *From Persecution to Prison*, *supra* note 469.

. . . immigration detention can never be considered in a child's 'best interests.'"[471] Human Rights Watch specifies that current U.S. policies, especially those that apply to border-crossers, "fall short of international standards" and "is likely to result in the US conducting unlawful returns that will put these children at grave risk."[472]

In addition to these organizations' criticisms, a class-action lawsuit has been filed against the U.S. government for its failure to abide by the *Flores v. Reno* settlement in the context of family detention.[473] Although the settlement and regulations apply to all children apprehended by DHS, DHS has taken the position that only unaccompanied children in its custody are covered.[474]

> ➢ **Practice Pointer**: See chapter 9 of this book for a detailed discussion of the legal standards and procedures for detention and release of individuals seeking protection in the United States.

A. Apprehension

DHS apprehends thousands of children every year, many of whom are asylum-seekers or victims of trafficking, trauma, abuse, and abandonment. Although the number of children arriving in the U.S. had been steadily increasing over the past five years, in fiscal year 2014, an unprecedented number of unaccompanied children were apprehended at the southern border of the U.S.[475] Most of these children came from Honduras, Guatemala, El Salvador, and Mexico.[476] Undocumented migrant children are generally detained and placed in removal proceedings; however, there are specific legal requirements for their care, custody, and release.

First, when a child is apprehended, he or she must be given a Form I-770, Notice of Rights and Disposition.[477] If the child is under 14 years old or is unable to understand the notice, the notice shall be read and explained to him or her in a language the child understands.[478] The notice notifies the child of his or her right to request a hearing before an immigration judge.[479] If the child later decides to accept

---

[471] Human Rights Watch, *US: Surge in Detention of Child Migrants* (June 25, 2014), *available at www.hrw.org/print/news/2014/06/25/us-surge-detention-child-migrants* (last visited Feb. 19, 2015).

[472] *Id.*

[473] *See* American Immigration Council, Immigration Impact, *Government Claims Children in Family Detention Centers Are Not Entitled to Protections* (Mar. 18, 2015), *available at http://immigrationimpact.com/2015/03/18/government-claims-children-in-family-detention-centers-are-not-entitled-to-protections/* (last visited Apr. 1, 2015).

[474] *See* 8 CFR §236.3, 1236.3 (2014).

[475] CBP, *Southwest Border Unaccompanied Alien Children (FY 2014)*, *supra* note 5 (noting a 77% increase in arrivals at the southern border, from 38,759 unaccompanied children in fiscal year 2013 to 68,541 unaccompanied children in fiscal year 2014).

[476] *Id.*

[477] 8 CFR §§236.3(h), 1236.3(h) (2014).

[478] *Id.*

[479] *Id.*

voluntary departure or to withdraw his or her application for admission, a new Form I-770 shall be given to and signed by the child.[480]

B. Accompanied vs. Unaccompanied Children

DHS bears the initial responsibility for the apprehension and detention of children,[481] and there are special procedures for children in DHS custody, whether accompanied or unaccompanied.[482] The procedures to be followed after apprehension depend on whether or not the child is "unaccompanied" (under 18 and not in the care of a parent legal guardian at the time of apprehension). If DHS determines that a child is accompanied by a parent or legal guardian, DHS remains responsible for that child's detention and removal. ICE has established separate family detention standards, including standards for children in detention, which, according to ICE, attempt to recognize their vulnerability and special needs.[483] Unaccompanied children, on the other hand, are transferred to ORR within the Department of Health and Human Services within 72 hours of apprehension.[484] ORR then provides for the care and placement, where possible, of the UAC.[485] The only exceptions to this 72 hour rule are if: (1) the child is charged or convicted of a criminal offense other than entering without inspection; (2) the child is adjudicated a delinquent or subject to pending delinquency proceedings; (3) the child engaged in violent or extremely disruptive conduct; (4) the child escaped from another facility; or (5) there are other extraordinary or compelling reasons.[486] DHS and the Department of Health and Human Services, therefore, are charged with compliance regarding the legal requirements for the care, custody, and prompt release of detained immigrant children.[487]

C. Release from DHS Custody

The regulations confer on DHS the authority to continue holding an individual in custody or to grant parole in the exercise of discretion, and children are a group that DHS is required to give special consideration in this regard.[488] The parole and release of children to the care of a relative or responsible adult is encouraged for

---

[480] *Id.*

[481] ICPM, chapter 9.2(b).

[482] *See generally*, 8 CFR §§236.3, 1236.3 (2014).

[483] *See* Immigration and Customs Enforcement (ICE), *Family Residential Standards*, *available at www.ice.gov/detention-standards/family-residential* (last visited Mar. 3, 2015).

[484] 6 USC §279(g)(2) (2012).

[485] *See* 6 USC §279; ICPM chapter 9.2(b).

[486] *See* Memorandum from INS Commissioner Gene McNary, 69 No. 6 Interpreter Releases 189, App'x. I; Congressional Research Service Report, *Unaccompanied Alien Children: An Overview* (Sept. 8, 2014), *available at http://fas.org/spg/crs/homesec/R43599.pdf* (last visited Apr. 1, 2015).

[487] *See* 8 CFR §236.3, 1236.3 (2014); *Flores v. Reno*, 507 U.S. 292 (1993).

[488] 8 CFR §§212.5(b)(3), 236.3, 1236.3 (2014).

humanitarian reasons, even in certain situations where the release of an adult relative from detention would also be required.[489]

If it is determined that continued detention of a child is necessary to secure his or her timely appearance before DHS or the immigration court, or to ensure the child's safety or that of others, the case must be referred to the Juvenile Coordinator, who is responsible for finding suitable placement of the child in a facility designated for the occupancy of juveniles.[490] These may include juvenile facilities contracted by DHS, state or local juvenile facilities, or "other appropriate agencies authorized to accommodate juveniles by the laws of the state or locality."[491] Until a suitable placement can be found, the child may be temporarily held by DHS authorities or placed in any DHS detention facility having separate accommodations for juveniles.[492]

On the other hand, juveniles — individuals under the age of 18 — are eligible for release from DHS custody pursuant to 8 CFR §§236.3, 1236.3.[493] Under *Flores v. Reno,* children "must be held in the least restrictive setting appropriate to their age and special needs to ensure their protection and wellbeing."[494] The settlement also requires that children be released from custody without unnecessary delay to "a parent, legal guardian, adult relative, individual specifically designated by the parent, licensed program, or, alternatively, an adult who seeks custody who DHS deems appropriate."[495] Specifically, the regulations required that the child must be released to the following individuals, in order of preference:

- A parent;
- A legal guardian; or
- An adult relative (brother, sister, aunt, uncle, grandparent) who is not presently in DHS custody.[496]

If one of these individuals cannot be located and the child has identified a parent, legal guardian, or adult relative who is in DHS detention, "simultaneous release of the juvenile and the parent, legal guardian, or adult relative shall be evaluated on a discretionary case-by-case basis."[497] In the alternative, a parent or legal guardian who

---

[489] 8 CFR §212.5(a), (b) (2014).

[490] 8 CFR §§236.3(b)-(c), 1236.3(b)-(c) (2014).

[491] 8 CFR §§236.3(c), 1236.3(c) (2014).

[492] 8 CFR §§236.3(d), 1236.3(d) (2014).

[493] 8 CFR §1236.4 (2014). *See also* 8 CFR §§212.5(b)(3), 1212.5(b)(3) (2014). Note that while the definition of "child" under the INA is an individual under age 21, a "juvenile" for purposes of custody under these regulations is an individual under age 18.

[494] Nat'l Immigrant Justice Ctr., *Fact Sheet: Children Detained by DHS in Adult Detention Facilities, supra* note 325.

[495] *Id.*

[496] 8 CFR §§236.3(b)(1), 1236.3(b)(1) (2014); ICPM, chapter 9.2(d).

[497] 8 CFR §§236.3(b)(2). 1236.3(b)(2) (2014).

is detained or outside of the U.S. may designate, in a sworn affidavit executed in front of an immigration or consular officer, a person capable and willing to care for the child and to ensure the child's presence at all future proceedings before DHS and the immigration court.[498] In "unusual and compelling circumstances and in the discretion of the Director of the Office of Juvenile Affairs," a child also may be released to an adult who is not a parent, legal guardian, or adult relative, if that adult executes an agreement to care for the child's well-being and to ensure the child's presence at all future proceedings.[499] While many individuals must pay a bond in order to secure their release from immigration detention, a bond is not required to release a UAC to a qualified sponsor.[500]

If detention is determined to be necessary, for such interim period of time as is required to locate suitable placement for the child, the child may be temporarily held by DHS authorities or placed in a DHS detention facility that has separate accommodations for children.[501] DHS and legacy INS have been criticized for violating the terms of the *Flores v. Reno* settlement, for detaining children longer than allowed under the law, and for the conditions under which children are held.[502]

---

[498] 8 CFR §§236.3(b)(3). 1236.3(b)(3) (2014).

[499] 8 CFR §§236.3(b)(4). 1236.3(b)(4) (2014).

[500] 6 USC §279(b)(4) (2012); Trafficking Victims Protection Reauthorization Act of 2008, *supra* note 214, at §235(f)(2)(B).

[501] 8 CFR §§236.3(d). 1236.3(d) (2014).

[502] *See, e.g.*, Women's Comm'n for Refugee Women, *Locking Up Family Values*, *supra* note 453; Manning, *Ending Artesia*, *supra* note 453; Collopy, *The Failings of Family Detention*, *supra* note 453; Collopy & Manning, *Why is Obama Still Locking Up So Many, supra* note 453; Manning, *Let These Women Go, supra* note 453; *M.S.P.C. v. Johnson* Compl. in the U.S. District Court for the District of Columbia, *http://americanimmigrationcouncil.org/sites/default/files/M.S.P.C.%20v.%20Johnson.pdf* (last visited Jan. 18, 2015); Am. Immigration Council, *Groups Sue U.S. Government Over Life-Threatening Deportation Process Against Mothers and Children* (Aug. 22, 2014), *available at www.americanimmigrationcouncil.org/newsroom/release/groups-sue-us-government-over-life-threatening-deportation-process-against-mothers-* (last visited Jan. 18, 2015); Am. Immigration Council, *Children in Danger: A Guide to the Humanitarian Challenge at the Border* (July 2014), *available at www.immigrationpolicy.org/special-reports/children-danger-guide-humanitarian-challenge-border* (last visited Feb. 27, 2015); Human Rights Watch, *US: Surge in Detention of Child Migrants* (June 25, 2014), *available at www.hrw.org/news/2014/06/25/us-surge-detention-child-migrants* (last visited Feb. 17, 2015); Nat'l Immigrant Justice Ctr., *Fact Sheet: Children Detained by DHS in Adult Detention Facilities*, *supra* note 325; Women's Refugee Comm'n, *Halfway Home: Unaccompanied Children in Immigration Custody* (Feb. 2009), *available at http://womensrefugeecommission.org/programs/migrant-rights/55-programs/detention/808-immigration-custody-of-unaccompanied-children* (last visited Feb. 17, 2015); Am. Civil Liberties Union (ACLU), *ACLU Challenges Prison-Like Conditions at Hutto*, *supra* note 453; *see also* Women's Comm'n for Refugee Women, *Locking Up Family Values*, *supra* note 453; Physicians for Human Rights, *From Persecution to Prison*, *supra* note 453, at 123 (criticizing DHS for detaining children and for its use of x-ray and dental examinations to determine age); Women's Comm'n for Refugee Women and Children, *Prison Guard or Parent?*, *supra* note 453; Human Rights Watch, *Detained and Deprived of Rights: Children in the Custody of the U.S. Immigration and Naturalization Service* (Dec. 1998), *available at www.hrw.org/reports98/ins2*.

If a parent is located and is otherwise suitable to receive custody of the child, but the child indicates a refusal to be released to his or her parent, DHS must notify the parent of the child's refusal to be released to the parent, and the parent may then have the "opportunity to present his or her views to the district director, chief patrol agent, Director of the Office of Juvenile Affairs or immigration judge before a custody determination is made."[503]

If a child seeks release from detention, voluntary departure, parole, or any form of relief from removal that could effectively terminate some interest inherent in the parent-child relationship, or if the child's rights and interests are adverse to those of the parent, DHS must give any parent residing in the United States notice.[504] The parent must be afforded an opportunity to present his or her views and assert his or her interest.[505] This notice and opportunity must be provided before a determination is made as to the merits of the child's request.[506]

Upon release from custody, DHS should serve both the adult to whom the child is released as well as the child with the Notice of Hearing and charging document.[507]

V. In-Country Refugee Processing for Children

In its Presidential Memorandum dated September 30, 2014, which announced refugee admissions for fiscal year 2015, the Obama administration also indicated that individuals from Honduras, Guatemala, and El Salvador might be considered refugees within their countries of nationality or habitual residence.[508] The Department of State then announced an in-country refugee/parole program for minors in these three countries who have parents lawfully present in the United States.[509] The program will allow lawfully present parents in the United States to request access to the U.S. Refugee Admissions Program for their children who are still in Honduras, Guatemala, and El Salvador.[510] Children admitted as a refugee will be included in the Latin America/Caribbean regional allocation of the U.S. Refugee Admissions

---

503 8 CFR §§236.3(e), 1236.3(e) (2014).

504 8 CFR §§236.3(f), 1236.3(f) (2014).

505 *Id.*

506 *Id.*

507 *Flores-Chavez v. Ashcroft*, 362 F.3d 1150 (9th Cir. 2004).

508 *See* Memorandum for the Secretary of State on Presidential Determination on Refugee Admissions for Fiscal Year 2015 (Sept. 30, 2014), AILA InfoNet Doc. No. 14100142 (posted Oct. 1, 2015), *available at www.aila.org/content/default.aspx?docid=50258* (last visited Jan. 22, 2015).

509 *See* U.S. Dep't of State, Bureau of Population, Refugees, & Migration Fact Sheet, *In-Country Refugee/Parole Program for Minors in El Salvador, Guatemala, and Honduras with Parents Lawfully Present in the United States* (Nov. 14, 2014), *available at www.state.gov/j/prm/releases/factsheets/2014/234067.htm* (last visited Jan. 12, 2015).

510 *Id.*

Program, which is 4,000 for fiscal year 2015.[511] Children who are ineligible for refugee admission but still at risk of harm may be considered for parole on a case-by-case basis.[512]

To be eligible, the qualifying child in El Salvador, Guatemala, or Honduras must be: (1) the biological, step, or legally adopted child of the qualifying parent; (2) unmarried and under the age of 21; (3) a national of El Salvador, Guatemala, or Honduras; and (4) residing in his or her country of nationality.[513] The qualifying parent is any individual who is at least 18 years old and lawfully present in the United States in one of the following seven categories: permanent resident, Temporary Protected Status, parolee, deferred action, deferred enforced departure, or withholding of removal.[514] He or she can be included in the child's application under certain circumstances as well.[515] To apply, the qualifying parent must file Form DS-7699. This form can only be accessed and completed with the assistance of a designated Resettlement Agency.[516]

- **Practice Pointer**: For more information on this in-country refugee and parole processing program for children in Honduras, El Salvador, and Guatemala, see the Office of Refugee Resettlement's website at *www.acf.hhs.gov/programs/orr/resource/in-country-refugee-parole-processing-for-minors-in-honduras-el-salvador-and-guatemala-central-american-minors.cam*[517] as well as the ORR State Letter 15-01, available at *www.acf.hhs.gov/programs/orr/resource/state-letter-15-01*.[518]

This program launched in December 2014. Given the small number allocated and the requirement for children to have parents lawfully present in the United States, however, this program is unlikely to provide meaningful protection to the vast majority of children who need protection in these three countries and will not solve the problem of unaccompanied children making the dangerous trek through Mexico to cross into the United States via the southern border.

- **Practice Pointer**: In-country refugee processing has been criticized as an ineffective method for providing refugees with the protection they

---

[511] *Id.*

[512] *Id.*

[513] U.S. Dep't of Health and Human Serv., ORR, *In-Country Refugee/Parole Processing for Minors in Honduras, El Salvador, and Guatemala (Central American Minors — CAM), available at www.acf.hhs.gov/programs/orr/resource/in-country-refugee-parole-processing-for-minors-in-honduras-el-salvador-and-guatemala-central-american-minors.cam* (last visited Mar. 4, 2015).

[514] *Id.*

[515] *Id.*

[516] *Id.*

[517] (last visited Mar. 4, 2015).

[518] (last visited Mar. 4, 2015).

> need, because individuals seeking protection often need to attend appointments with U.S. officials, making them vulnerable to detection and attack. Moreover, the process has been criticized as lacking confidentiality protections, which is particularly dangerous in environments riddled with spies and informants, including gangs and corrupt law enforcement officers. Overall, "the delays in resettlement processing mean that those who seek protection through in-country processing remain at risk while they wait — sometimes for months, sometimes for much longer."[519]

Once a refugee has been legally designated as such and accepted for resettlement in the United States, he or she will be admitted to the United States as a refugee under section 207 of the INA. The refugee will then be assigned to a refugee assistance agency under the auspices of the U.S. Department of Health and Human Services' Office of Refugee Resettlement for guidance and help in the resettlement process.

VI. Children as Derivatives

An individual who has been granted asylum — an asylee — may confer derivative asylee status on their spouses and children who are either inside the United States and applying as dependent applicants, or who are outside of the United States and seeking asylee status as a derivative beneficiary.[520] Therefore, children may gain asylee status through successful asylum applications filed by their parents or legal guardians.[521]

A. Definition of "Child"

For purposes of obtaining asylee status as a dependent applicant or derivative beneficiary, "child" is defined as it is under section 101(b)(1) of the Immigration and Nationality Act.[522] To be considered a "child," the individual must be unmarried and under 21 years old.[523] Additionally, he or she must be one of the following:

- A child born in wedlock;
- A stepchild, provided that the marriage creating the stepchild-parent relationship occurred before the stepchild turned 18 years old;

---

[519] Human Rights First, *In-Country Refugee Processing for At-Risk Children in Central America: Potential Benefits and Risks* (Oct. 3, 2014), *available at www.humanrightsfirst.org/blog/country-refugee-processing-risk-children-central-america-potential-benefits-and-risks* (last visited Apr. 1, 2015).

[520] INA §208(b)(3); 8 CFR §§208.21(a)–(f), 1208.21(a)–(f) (2014). See chapter 13 for a detailed discussion of I-730 petitions for relatives of asylees.

[521] Joyce K. Dalrymple, *Seeking Asylum Alone: Using the Best Interests of the Child Principle to Protect Unaccompanied Minors*, 26 B.C. THIRD WORLD L.J., 131, 133–35 (2006).

[522] INA §208(b)(3)(A).

[523] INA §101(b)(1).

- A child legitimated under the law of the child's residence or domicile, or under the law of the father's residence or domicile, if such legitimation took place before the child turned 18 years old and the child was in the legal custody of the legitimating parent or parents at the time of legitimation;
- A child born out of wedlock, by, through whom, or on whose behalf a status, privilege, or benefit is sought by virtue of the relationship of the child to his or her natural mother, or to his or her father if the father has or had a bona fide parent-child relationship with the person;
- A child adopted while under age 16 if the child has been in the legal custody of, and has resided with, the adopting parent or parents for at least two years; or
- A child who is the natural sibling of an adopted child (as described above), who was adopted by the same parent or parents, and who was adopted while under age 18.[524]

Thus, under certain circumstances, stepchildren and adopted children may also gain asylee status as a dependent or derivative on a principal applicant parent or legal guardian's asylum application, as long as the parent-child relationship existed prior to the grant of asylum. A child who was *in utero* on the date of the asylum grant or refugee admission also is eligible for derivative status.[525]

> ➢ **Practice Pointer**: It may be possible for a principal asylum applicant who receives a recommended approval to marry prior to receipt of a final approval and, thereby, make his or her child or step-child eligible for asylum as a derivative beneficiary.

B. Accompanying Versus Following to Join

Children of asylum applicants may be granted asylum if accompanying or following to join the principal applicant.[526] If a child is physically present in the United States, he or she is accompanying the principal applicant, and may be included on the principal applicant's I-589 application. Such a child may be granted asylum concurrently as a dependent on the principal's application.[527] If the child is outside of the United States, however, the child would be following to join the principal applicant. Under these circumstances, the principal applicant, after being granted asylum, may file an I-730 Refugee/Asylee Relative Petition on the child's

---

[524] *Id.*

[525] 8 CFR §§207.7(c), 208.21(b), 1208.21(b) (2014).

[526] INA §208(b)(3)(A).

[527] INA §208(b)(3)(A). *See* Memorandum from Joseph E. Langlois on H.R. 1209 — Child Status Protection Act, at 2 (Aug. 7, 2002) [hereinafter Langlois Mem. on CSPA; Memorandum from William R. Yates on The Child Status Protection Act — Children of Asylees and Refugees, at 4 (Aug. 17, 2004) [hereinafter Yates Mem. on CSPA — Children of Asylees].

behalf in order to confer derivative asylee status and bring the child to the United States.[528]

- **Practice Pointer**: The I-730 Refugee/Asylee Petition and instructions are available on USCIS's website at *www.uscis.gov/i-730.*[529] For a detailed discussion on I-730 Refugee/Asylee Relative Petitions, please see chapter 13 of this book.

- **Practice Pointer**: Although an unmarried child under age 21 may be included as a dependent on a parent's I-589 asylum application or may be granted derivative asylum status through an I-730 Refugee/Asylee Relative Petition, a parent may not be included as a dependent applicant or derivative beneficiary based on his or her child's asylum application.[530] Thus, it is important for practitioners to complete a full analysis of asylum eligibility for each family member, including the parents of children who have suffered persecution or torture.

C. Existence of Parent-Child Relationship

The parent-child relationship must have existed prior to the grant of asylum to the principal applicant, and if the child is following to join the principal applicant, the parent-child relationship must continue to exist at the time the I-730 Refugee/Asylee Relative Petition was filed.[531]

It is essential that all children be listed on the principal applicant's Form I-589 application. Although there is no requirement that the child be included at the time of filing the I-589, the child must be included before the adjudication of the application in order to be granted asylum as a dependent applicant. Failure to include a child on the I-589 could complicate matters later: a dependent applicant may not be granted asylum concurrently with the principal applicant, an I-730 may not be approved for that child to gain derivative status, and a dependent applicant may not be issued a Notice to Appear along with the principal applicant for purposes of a future concurrent grant of asylum before the IJ if the case is referred to the immigration court.[532]

- **Practice Pointer**: Practitioners should make sure that *all* of their client's children — whether biological, step, or adopted — are included on the I-589 application at the time of filing. If additional children are born or if the principal applicant establishes a parent-child relationship with any other children before a decision is issued on his or her

---

[528] *See generally* 8 CFR §§207.7, 208.21, & 1208.21 (2014); *see* also Form I-730.

[529] (last visited Mar. 3, 2015).

[530] *See* INA §208(b)(3)(A); *Matter of A–K–*, 24 I&N Dec. 275 (BIA 2007).

[531] 8 CFR §§207.7(c), 208.21(b), & 1208.21(b) (2014).

[532] *See* Dree K. Collopy & Lisa Green, *Practice Pointer: Completing the Form I-589*, at 8 (July 14, 2014), *available at* AILA InfoNet Doc. No. 14071402.

application, practitioners should file an amended I-589 with the local asylum office where the application is pending to alert USCIS of the additional child(ren) as soon as possible.

D. Aged-Out Children

Prior to August 6, 2002, the date of enactment of the Child Status Protection Act of 2002 (CSPA), children could "age out" of eligibility as a dependent applicant or derivative beneficiary. However, the CSPA amended the INA to protect the "child" status of unmarried children of a principal applicant. Under the CSPA, unmarried children who are under age 21 when their parent or legal guardian filed for asylum, but who turn 21 before asylum is granted, are still considered "children" and are eligible to be granted asylum as a dependent applicant or derivative beneficiary.[533] The "filing date" is the date that the application was received by USCIS.[534] If the child turned 21 prior to August 6, 2002, however, he or she is not protected by the CSPA and would not be able to obtain asylee status through a parent or legal guardian's asylum application.[535]

Children who are beneficiaries of derivative asylum sometimes turn 21 before the I-730 Refugee/Asylee Relative Petition is adjudicated on their behalf or before their adjustment of status application is adjudicated. Unfortunately, the CSPA does not address these situations; however a USCIS policy memorandum does.[536] For asylum applications filed on or after August 2, 2002, a child who was under 21 at the time his or her parent filed for asylum continues to be eligible to have an I-730 filed on his or her behalf despite turning 21 before the I-730 is filed or approved.[537]

After being in valid asylee status and physically present in the United States for one year, the asylee may seek adjustment of status to lawful permanent residence before USCIS.[538] In the past, when the child was granted asylum as a derivative, but turned 21 years of age before an application for adjustment of status was filed, a *nunc*

---

[533] INA §208(b)(3) as amended by the Child Status Protection Act of 2002, Pub. L. No. 107-208 116 Stat. 927, *available at http://thomas.loc.gov/cgi-bin/query/D?c107:5:./temp/~c107jA5CH4::. See also* Langlois Mem. on CSPA, *supra* note 527.

[534] 8 CFR §103.2(a)(7) (2014).

[535] Yates Mem. on CSPA — Children of Asylees, *supra* note 527; Memorandum from Michael Petrucelli, Bureau of Citizenship and Immigration Servs. on Processing Derivative Refugees and Asylees under the Child Status Protection Act (July 23, 2003), *available at www.uscis.gov/sites/default/files/USCIS/Laws/Memoranda/Static_Files_Memoranda/Archives%201998-2008/2003/refcspa072303.pdf.*

[536] *See* Yates Mem. on CSPA — Children of Asylees, *supra* note 527; *see also The Child Status Protection Act: Breaking Down the Complicated 'Aging Out' Formula*, 23 Immigration Law Today 32 (May/June 2004); *see also* Am. Immigration Council Legal Action Center Practice Advisory, *The Child Status Protection Act* (Sept. 9, 2009), *available at www.legalactioncenter.org/sites/default/files/pa-cspa_0.pdf.*

[537] *See* Yates Mem. on CSPA — Children of Asylees, *supra* note 527.

[538] INA §209(b).

pro tunc (retroactive approval) procedure was permitted.[539] This procedure required an aged-out derivative to file an I-589 asylum application of his or her own.[540] Provided that the aged-out derivative remained unmarried, the asylum application was approved, *nunc pro tunc*, to the date of receipt of the original derivative asylee status.[541] The aged-out derivative did not have to individually meet the refugee definition, but he or she was interviewed by an asylum officer to verify and to ensure that no mandatory bars or other disqualifications applied.[542] A fingerprint check had to be completed if the fingerprint check was more than 15 months old.[543] In light of the CSPA, however, USCIS policy now provides that if the I-589 was filed by the principal when his or her child was under age 21, the child remains eligible for adjustment of status, unless the child turned 21 prior to August 2, 2002 and an adjustment application was not pending at the time the child turned 21.[544]

- **Practice Pointer**: Practitioners should determine the age of all of their client's children at the beginning of the representation. If a child is nearing age 21, it is important for practitioners to prioritize their client's case to file the asylum application before the child turns 21. Doing so will maintain his or her eligibility as a dependent applicant.
- **Practice Pointer**: For more details on asylee adjustment of status and nunc pro tunc applications, see chapter 15 of this book.

E. Loss of Derivative Status

A dependent or derivative family member may lose his or her status as a derivative in the following situations:

- If the spouse or child withdraws his or her asylum claim;
- If the child marries;
- If the spouse divorces the principal applicant; or
- If the principal applicant dies.[545]

Derivative status may be lost at any time prior to issuance of the Asylum Office's final decision.[546] For example, even if a recommended approval has been issued, the

---

[539] *See* INS Memorandum, J. Weiss, "Guidelines for Children's Asylum Claims," at 28 (Dec. 10, 1998), *published on* AILA InfoNet (*posted* Jan. 25, 1999), *reproduced in* 76 INTERPRETER RELEASES 1 and Appendix I (Jan. 4, 1999), *www.nlada.org/Training/Train_Civil/Equal_Justice/2007_Materials/109_2007_Kerwin_handout7*.

[540] *Id.*

[541] *Id.*

[542] *Id.*

[543] *Id.*

[544] *See* Yates Mem. on CSPA — Children of Asylees, *supra* note 527.

[545] USCIS, *Affirmative Asylum Procedures Manual*, *supra* note 198 at pt. III.E.6.

[546] *Id.*

decision is not yet final, and the recommended approval may be cancelled for a dependent who marries, and therefore, loses derivative status. When the Asylum Office becomes aware of the loss of the dependent's derivative status, the office will notify the principal applicant and the dependent in writing that the dependent cannot remain on the asylum application.[547]

- **Practice Pointer**: The loss of derivative status may qualify as a changed circumstance for purposes of determining whether the individual is barred by the one-year filing deadline in his or her own subsequent asylum claim as a principal applicant.[548] As long as he or she files the subsequent application within a reasonable time after becoming aware of the loss of derivative status, he or she should qualify for this exception to the one-year filing deadline.[549]
- **Practice Pointer**: A dependent may lose derivative status after asylum approval, but before the principal applicant and his or her dependents file for adjustment of status to lawful permanent residency. Under these circumstances, the dependent may not be included as a derivative applicant on the principal applicant's adjustment of status application.[550] Although the dependent will continue to have valid asylee status, if he or she wants to adjust status to lawful permanent resident, he or she must file a new I-589 application as a principal applicant and request asylum "nunc pro tunc."[551] See chapter 15 of this book for a detailed discussion of nunc pro tunc asylum applications for the purposes of adjustment of status.
- **Practice Pointer**: Under certain circumstances, a derivative may lose his or her status through no fault of his or her own. If a principal asylee's status is terminated due to commission of a crime, for example, his or her derivatives' status also would be terminated. See chapter 14 for a detailed discussion of termination of asylee status.

VII. Conclusion

As the violence continues unabated in Central America and around the world, and as the most vulnerable populations, including children, continue to fall victim to widespread and systematic violence, the significant number of children making the

---

[547] *Id.*

[548] *See* 8 CFR §208.4(a)(4) (2014).

[549] *See id.* See also chapter 2 for a detailed discussion of the one-year filing deadline and the exceptions to this bar to asylum eligibility.

[550] USCIS, *Affirmative Asylum Procedures Manual*, *supra* note 198 at pt. III.E.7.

[551] *Id.*

treacherous journey to the United States will only continue.[552] Thus, it is becoming more and more important for officers, advocates, and adjudicators in the U.S. asylum system to understand the particular vulnerabilities of children and to ensure that the safeguards enacted under U.S. law to protect the best interests of child asylum-seekers are recognized and properly applied.

---

552 *See* CBP, *Southwest Border Unaccompanied Alien Children (FY 2014)*, *supra* note 5; Women's Refugee Comm'n, *Forced From Home*, *supra* note 5.

CHAPTER ELEVEN

ADMINISTRATIVE REVIEW

Given the complexity of the U.S. asylum system and the high burden of proof and legal standards required to demonstrate eligibility for asylum, withholding of removal, and protection under the Convention Against Torture (CAT), applicants may receive final orders of deportation, exclusion, or removal at various stages in the process of seeking protection. If applicants wish to challenge these orders, whether entered long ago or recently, and whether entered by an Immigration Judge (IJ) or the Board of Immigration Appeals (BIA), applicants may seek various forms of administrative review. From appeals to the BIA, to motions to reopen and motions to reconsider, various remedies may exist for asylum-seekers who do not want to give up in their search for protection. [1] This chapter discusses these options for administrative review.

I. Appeals to the Board of Immigration Appeals

The BIA is the highest administrative body for interpreting and applying U.S. immigration and nationality laws uniformly throughout the United States. [2] It functions as an appellate body and is charged with the review of certain administrative decisions and adjudications under the Immigration and Nationality Act (INA). [3] The regulations require that the BIA "resolve the questions before it in a manner that is timely, impartial, and consistent with the Act and regulations." [4] Additionally, through its issuance of precedent decisions, the BIA provides "clear and uniform guidance" to agencies and adjudicators throughout the U.S. immigration system, as well as the general public, on the proper interpretation and administration of the INA and its implementing regulations.[5] The BIA is also responsible for "the

---

* The author would like to thank Ben Winograd of the Immigrant & Refugee Appellate Center, LLC for his invaluable input in reviewing this chapter.

[1] *Board of Immigration Appeals Practice Manual* [hereinafter *BIA Practice Manual*], chapter 4.2(a), *available at www.justice.gov/eoir/vll/qapracmanual/apptmtn4.htm* (last accessed Mar. 21, 2015).

[2] 8 CFR §1003.1(d)(1) (2014); *BIA Practice Manual*, chapter 1.2(a).

[3] 8 CFR §1003.1(d)(1) (2014). *See infra* pt. I.A. below for a detailed discussion of the jurisdiction of the BIA.

[4] 8 CFR §1003.1(d)(1) (2014).

[5] *Id.*; *BIA Practice Manual*, chapter 1.2(a).

recognition of organizations and the accreditation of representatives wishing to practice before the immigration courts, Department of Homeland Security (DHS), and the BIA,"[6] as well as the discipline of attorneys, representatives, and others who appear in a representative capacity before the BIA, DHS, or any IJ.[7]

The BIA is part of the Executive Office for Immigration Review (EOIR), which is located within the U.S. Department of Justice and which operates under the supervision of the Director of EOIR.[8] There are 15 Board Members, who are attorneys appointed by the Attorney General (AG).[9] Temporary Board Members, who have the same authority as Board Members to adjudicate assigned cases (but not to vote on *en banc* decisions of the BIA), may be designated for terms not to exceed six months.[10] Out of the 15 permanent Board Members, the AG designates one sitting Board Member to serve as the Chairman to direct, supervise, and establish internal operating procedures and policies of the BIA.[11] The AG also may designate up to two sitting Board Members to serve as Vice Chairmen to assist the Chairman in the performance of his or her duties and to serve in his or her absence.[12]

- **Practice Pointer**: The current Chairman of the BIA is David L. Neal, and the Vice Chairman is Charles Adkins-Blanch. The other Board Members are Patricia A. Cole, Michael J. Creppy, Edward R. Grant, Ann J. Greer, John W. Guendelsberger, David B. Holmes, Garry D. Malphrus, Ana Landazabal Mann, Neil P. Miller, Hugh G. Mullane, Roger A. Pauley, Linda S. Wendtland, and other Temporary Board Members as designated pursuant to 8 CFR §1003(a)(4). For a listing of Board Members, go to EOIR's website at *www.justice.gov/eoir/fs/biabios.htm#Temporary_Board_Members*.[13]

The BIA has a number of staff attorneys and other employees assisting Board Members in the execution of their duties, as directed by the Deputy AG.[14] The BIA Clerk's Office manages appellate records and information, processes adjudicated cases and serves decisions on parties, and provides management and administrative support to all BIA operations.[15] The BIA also maintains the Law Library and

---

[6] 8 CFR §1003.1(d)(5) (2014); *BIA Practice Manual*, chapters 1.2(a), 2.4.

[7] 8 CFR §1003.1(d)(5) (2014).

[8] 8 CFR §§1003.0(a), 1003.1(a)(1) (2014); *BIA Practice Manual*, chapter 1.2(b).

[9] 8 CFR §1003.1(a)(1) (2014); *BIA Practice Manual*, chapter 1.3(a). Currently, there are only 14 Board Members, as one of the 15 positions has been unfilled for several years.

[10] 8 CFR §1003.1(a)(4) (2014); *BIA Practice Manual*, chapter 1.3(c). Currently, there are several temporary Board Members who have been serving for several years, being re-appointed for six month terms. Arguably, this may be in violation of the regulations.

[11] 8 CFR §1003.1(a)(2)(i) (2014); *BIA Practice Manual*, chapter 1.3(b).

[12] 8 CFR §1003.1(a)(2) (2014); *BIA Practice Manual*, chapters 1.3(a), (b).

[13] (last visited Mar. 5, 2015).

[14] 8 CFR §1003.1(a)(6) (2014); *BIA Practice Manual*, chapter 1.3(d).

[15] *BIA Practice Manual*, chapter 1.3(e).

Immigration Research Center within the headquarters complex of EOIR, as well as a Virtual Law Library accessible on EOIR's website. The Virtual Law Library "serves as a comprehensive repository of immigration-related law and information for use by attorneys and the general public."[16]

> ➢ **Practice Pointer**: The Virtual Law Library is available at *www.justice.gov/eoir/vll/libindex.html*.[17]

A. Jurisdiction

The BIA has been given nationwide jurisdiction to review IJ decisions and orders, as well as certain decisions made by the DHS.[18] It provides guidance to IJs and DHS through published decisions[19] and its decisions are binding on IJs unless modified or overruled by the AG or a federal court.[20]

> ➢ **Practice Pointer**: Although the BIA's unpublished decisions are not binding on IJs as precedential, they may be guiding authority. The Immigrant & Refugee Appellate Center, LLC publishes an index of unpublished BIA decisions that is available for purchase from its website at *www.irac.net/unpublished/index/*.[21] The index is updated on a monthly basis with newly issued unpublished BIA decisions, and is a fantastic resource for decisions that may be persuasive to adjudicators in support of a client's applications for relief.

With regard to current claims for asylum, withholding of removal, or protection under the CAT, the BIA has appellate jurisdiction over:

- Decisions of IJs in removal proceedings, except that there is no appeal of the length of a period of voluntary departure granted by an IJ;
- Determinations relating to bond, parole or detention;
- Decisions of IJs in asylum proceedings (except for decisions of IJs during credible or reasonable fear review hearings); and
- Decisions of IJs regarding custody of individuals subject to a final order of removal made pursuant to 8 CFR §§241.14, 1241.14.[22]

Specifically, the BIA has appellate jurisdiction over IJ decisions in exclusion, deportation, and removal proceedings.[23] Therefore, an individual with a claim for

---

[16] *BIA Practice Manual*, chapter 1.3(f).

[17] (last visited Mar. 4, 2015).

[18] 8 CFR §1003.1 (2014); *BIA Practice Manual*, chapter 1.2(a); *Immigration Court Practice Manual* (ICPM), chapter 6.1.

[19] *BIA Practice Manual*, chapter 1.2(a).

[20] *Id.* at chapters 1.2(c), 1.4(a), 1.4(d).

[21] (last visited Mar. 31, 2015).

[22] 8 CFR §1003.1(b)(1)–(14) (2014); *BIA Practice Manual*, chapter 1.4(a).

[23] 8 CFR §1003.1(b) (2014).

asylum, withholding of removal, or protection under the CAT may appeal the IJ's decision to the BIA.[24] DHS also may appeal an IJ decision to the BIA, and IJs may certify their own decisions to the BIA for review.[25]

The BIA may review decisions of IJs regarding asylum applications filed by individuals who are not entitled to removal proceedings under INA §240.[26] Such individuals include crewmembers, stowaways, persons who have applied for admission or were admitted to the United States under the Visa Waiver Program, persons who have been ordered removed from the United States under INA §235(c) on security and related grounds, and individuals who are applicants for admission or who have been admitted under INA §101(a)(15)(S) as an informant.[27] The BIA does not, however, have jurisdiction to review negative credible fear determinations by IJs under the expedited removal process, nor does the BIA have jurisdiction to review negative reasonable fear determinations under reinstatement of removal or administrative removal proceedings.[28]

- **Practice Pointer**: The BIA may not review an order of removal entered in absentia. An individual who received an in absentia removal order must file a motion to reopen with the IJ.[29] If the individual did not receive oral warnings of the consequences of failing to appear, the individual may file a motion to reopen under the regulatory requirements found at 8 CFR §§1003.2(c) and 1003.23(b)(3).[30] See Part II of this chapter for a detailed discussion of motions to reopen.

- **Practice Pointer**: Appeals of IJ decisions are distinct from motions to reopen and motions to reconsider. These motions are filed with the immigration court, following a decision ending immigration court proceedings.[31] For a detailed discussion of motions to reopen and motions to reconsider, see Part II of this chapter.

---

[24] 8 CFR §1003.1(b) (2014); EOIR Memorandum from Michael J. Creppy on Operating Policies and Procedures Mem. No. 99-5: Implementation of Article 3 of the UN Convention Against Torture (May 14, 1999), *available at www.justice.gov/eoir/efoia/ocij/oppm99/99_5.pdf.*

[25] 8 CFR §1003.7 (2014).

[26] 8 CFR §§1003.1(b)(9), 208.2(b), 1208.2(b) (2014).

[27] 8 CFR §§208.2(b), 1208.2(b) (2014). For a comprehensive overview of practice before the BIA, see the *BIA Practice Manual*, *supra* note 1. *See* chapter 6 for a detailed discussion of the procedures for these individuals who are not entitled to INA §240 proceedings, as well as a detailed discussion of the credible and reasonable fear procedures.

[28] *See* chapter 6 for a detailed discussion of credible and reasonable fear determinations and ways to challenge negative decisions.

[29] *See Matter of Guzman-Arguera*, 22 I&N Dec. 722 (BIA 1999) and this chapter at 3.3.5.

[30] *See Matter of M–S–*, 22 I&N Dec. 349 (BIA 1998) and this chapter at 3.11.

[31] *See* ICPM, chapters 6.1, 5.

After an IJ renders his or her decision, a party may either file an appeal with the Board of Immigration Appeals, or file a motion with the IJ.[32] Once a party files an appeal with the BIA, jurisdiction is vested with the BIA and the IJ is divested of jurisdiction over the case.[33]

- **Practice Pointer**: If a party first files a motion to reopen or reconsider with the IJ and then files an appeal with the BIA, the IJ will lose jurisdiction over the motion, and the record of proceedings will be transferred to the BIA for consideration of the appeal.[34] Thus, it is a strategic consideration whether to file an appeal with the BIA or a motion to reopen or reconsider with the IJ. Of course, if the IJ denies a motion to reopen or reconsider, the respondent may then appeal that denial to the BIA.

B. Who Can File an Appeal?

An IJ's decision may be appealed only by the respondent subject to the proceedings, the respondent's legal representative, or the Department of Homeland Security.[35]

A Notice of Appeal may *not* be filed by an applicant who has knowingly and voluntarily waived appeal under 8 CFR §1003.39.[36] Prior to accepting the applicant's waiver of appeal, however, the IJ must also advise the applicant that he or she has the right to seek relief from removal.[37] Otherwise the applicant cannot make a considered and intelligent decision about whether to appeal.[38] The waiver of appeal generally cannot be retracted, withdrawn, or undone.[39] However, if a party wishes to challenge the validity of the waiver of appeal, the party may: (1) file a motion with the IJ explaining why the appeal waiver was not valid; or (2) file an appeal directly with the BIA that explains why the appeal was not valid.[40]

An individual's departure from the United States also may impact his or her eligibility to file an appeal. The departure of a person who is the subject of deportation proceedings *prior* to appealing a decision in his or her case will constitute

---

[32] *BIA Practice Manual*, chapter 4.2(a)(ii).

[33] *Id.*

[34] *Id.*

[35] 8 CFR §1003.3 (2014); ICPM, chapter 6.2(a); *BIA Practice Manual*, chapter 4.3(a).

[36] 8 CFR §1003.3(a)(1) (2014); *Matter of Shih*, 20 I&N Dec. 697 (BIA 1993); *BIA Practice Manual*, chapter 4.3(b)(i). *See also* 8 CFR §1003.1(d)(2)(i)(G) (2014).

[37] *United States v. Arrieta*, 224 F.3d 1076, 1079 (9th Cir. 2000).

[38] *Id. Narine v. Holder*, 559 F.3d 246, 249–51 (4th Cir. 2009) (holding that the term "final decision" is a term of art and that the applicant's waivers was not knowing or intelligent).

[39] *BIA Practice Manual*, chapter 4.3(b)(ii).

[40] *Matter of Patino*, 23 I&N Dec. 74 (BIA 2001); ICPM, chapter 6.4(b); *BIA Practice Manual*, chapter 4.3(b)(ii).

a waiver of his or her right to appeal.[41] The departure of a person who is the subject of deportation or removal proceedings, except for "arriving aliens" under 8 CFR §1001.1(q), while his or her appeal is *pending* will constitute a withdrawal of the appeal and the initial decision in the case will be final, as if no appeal had been taken.[42] One court has held that failure to give notice of the severe consequences of departing from the United States while an appeal is pending is a violation of due process.[43] One exception is when an applicant departs the United States while under an outstanding order of removal issued in absentia based on lack of notice. The BIA recently entertained an appeal on this issue and remanded the case to the IJ for further proceedings.[44]

It is possible that an individual will depart due to a removal by DHS, rather than departing voluntarily. The BIA has held that it does not lose jurisdiction if an individual is unlawfully removed while a BIA appeal is pending.[45]

IJs also may certify their own decisions to the BIA for review.[46] When a case is certified, the immigration court must serve a notice of certification on the parties. A briefing schedule is then served on the parties following certification.[47] However, even if an IJ certifies his or her own decision to the BIA, the BIA is not required to review it.[48] Certification of a case to the BIA is separate from any appeal. Therefore, a party wishing to appeal the IJ's decision must file an appeal with the BIA even if the IJ certified the case to the BIA.[49]

- **Practice Pointer**: The BIA is allowed to certify cases to itself as well.[50] It occasionally does this to resolve any issues regarding whether an appeal was timely filed.

C. Scope and Standard of Review

In August 2002, AG Ashcroft issued regulations that drastically changed the BIA appeals process. Perhaps one of the most sweeping changes was the elimination of the BIA's *de novo* review of an IJ's factual findings and credibility determinations. Under the new regulations, the BIA will not engage in *de novo* review of findings of

---

[41] 8 CFR §1003.3(e) (2014).

[42] 8 CFR §1003.4 (2014).

[43] *Martinez-de Bojorquez v. Ashcroft*, 365 F.3d 800 (9th Cir. 2004). *But cf. Villalvaso-Lugo v. Ashcroft*, 110 F. App'x 754, 755 (9th Cir. 2004) (rejecting application of the holding in *Martinez-de Bojorquez* where the petitioner failed to raise a constitutional challenge on appeal, and did not "contend that he was never warned about the severe effect of even a brief departure from the United States.").

[44] *Matter of Bulnes-Nolasco*, 25 I&N Dec. 57 (BIA 2009).

[45] *Matter of Diaz-Garcia*, 25 I&N Dec. 794 (BIA 2012).

[46] 8 CFR §§1003.1(c), 1003.7 (2014); ICPM, chapter 6.5; *BIA Practice Manual*, chapter 4.18.

[47] ICPM, chapter 6.5.

[48] 8 CFR §1003.7 (2014).

[49] *Id. See* 8 CFR §1003.3(d) (2014).

[50] 8 CFR §1003.7 (2014).

fact by the IJ, nor findings as to the credibility of testimony.[51] These facts and credibility findings are only to be reviewed to determine whether the IJ's findings are clearly erroneous.[52] Accordingly, the BIA will defer to the factual and credibility findings of the IJ unless they are clearly erroneous.[53]

The BIA, however, will review questions of law, discretion, judgment and all other issues in appeals from decisions of IJs *de novo*.[54] This includes *de novo* review of mixed questions of law and fact, such as whether it is likely that an applicant will be tortured,[55] whether the facts support a determination that harm rises to the level of persecution,[56] whether the facts support a determination that a fear of future persecution is well-founded,[57] and whether the facts support a determination that an asylum applicant was firmly resettled.[58] Any finding that relates to whether the ultimate statutory requirement for establishing eligibility for the relief sought has been met is a mixed question of law and fact.

- **Practice Pointer**: There has been debate between the BIA and the federal courts regarding the standard of review for mixed questions of law and fact. Whereas the BIA reviews the entire issue *de novo*, the federal courts have held that such inquiries must be broken down into their respective factual and legal parts and reviewed accordingly.[59] For a helpful discussion of this issue, as well as other standard of review issues before the BIA, see B. Winograd, "The Error of Their Ways: The Standards of Review Used by the BIA of Immigration Appeals," available at *http://ailadc.org/downloads/2014_Conference/11_1_bia_standards_of_review.docx*.[60] See chapter 12 of this book for a detailed discussion of the standards of review before the U.S. circuit courts of appeals.

Since the BIA generally defers to IJs' findings of fact unless they are clearly erroneous, the BIA will not engage in fact-finding in the course of deciding appeals.[61]

---

[51] 8 CFR §1003.1(d)(3)(i) (2014).

[52] 8 CFR §1003.1(d)(3)(i) (2014).

[53] *BIA Practice Manual*, chapter 1.4(c)(i)(A); *Matter of A–S–B–*, 24 I&N Dec. 493 (BIA 2008).

[54] 8 CFR §1003.1(d)(3)(ii) (2014); *BIA Practice Manual*, chapter 1.4(c)(i)(B).

[55] *See Matter of V–K–*, 24 I&N Dec. 500 (BIA 2008).

[56] *See Matter of A–S–B–*, 24 I&N Dec. 493, 497 (BIA 2008).

[57] *See Matter of H–L–H– & Z–Y–Z–*, 25 I&N Dec. 209, 212 (BIA 2010).

[58] *See Matter of A–G–G–*, 25 I&N Dec. 486, 488 (BIA 2011).

[59] *See, e.g., Kaplan v. Att'y Gen.*, 602 F.3d 260, 271 (3d Cir. 2010) (stating that "[g]lueing the two questions together … does not entitle the BIA to review the first question, the factual one, *de novo*," and that instead, the Board "must break down the inquiry into its parts and apply the correct standard of review to the respective components"). *See also Turkson v. Holder*, 667 F.3d 523 (4th Cir. 2012).

[60] (last visited Apr. 1, 2015).

[61] 8 CFR §1003.1(d)(3)(iv) (2014).

The only exception to this rule is that the BIA may take administrative notice of commonly known facts such as current events or the contents of official documents.[62] For example, the BIA has taken administrative notice of the content of state laws,[63] reports by the U.S. Department of State,[64] currency conversions,[65] reports of the Immigration and Refugee Board of Canada,[66] and official conviction records.[67] If a party believes that the BIA cannot properly resolve an appeal without further fact-finding, the party must file a motion for remand.[68] If the BIA concludes that further fact-finding is needed in a particular case, the BIA may remand the proceedings to the IJ.[69]

D. Automatic Stay of Removal

A stay of removal prevents DHS from executing an order of removal, deportation, or exclusion. Stays are automatic in some instances and discretionary in others.[70] A stay is automatic and the decision of the IJ may *not* be executed: (1) during the time allowed for the filing of an appeal, unless a waiver of the right to appeal is filed; (2) while an appeal is pending before the BIA; or (3) while a case is before the BIA by way of certification.[71] Exceptions to this rule are: (1) an appeal from an IJ decision denying the applicant's motion to reopen or reconsider or to stay deportation, unless the BIA expressly grants a stay or the appeal is from a motion to reopen in an in absentia case under 8 CFR §§1003.6(b) and 1003.23(b)(1)(v); and (2) an appeal of a bond redetermination under 8 CFR §§1003.19(i) and 1236.1. Automatic stays are valid and do not expire until the BIA renders a final decision on the case.[72]

- **Practice Pointer**: For detailed guidance for requesting a discretionary stay of removal, see chapters 6.3 and 6.4 of the *BIA Practice Manual*, available at *www.justice.gov/eoir/vll/qapracmanual/BIAPracticeManual .pdf#page=1*.[73]

---

[62] *Id.*

[63] *See, e.g., Matter of Cuellar-Gomez*, 25 I&N Dec. 850, 865 n. 15 (BIA 2012).

[64] *See, e.g., Matter of S–E–G–*, 24 I&N Dec. 579, 587 n.4 (BIA 2008).

[65] *See, e.g., Matter of S–K–*, 23 I&N Dec. 936, 945 n.13 (BIA 2006).

[66] *See, e.g., Matter of C–C–*, 23 I&N Dec. 899, 902 (BIA 2006).

[67] *See* Ben Winograd, *Index of Unpublished Decisions of the Board of Immigration Appeals* (2015 Ed.), *available at www.irac.net/unpublished/index/.*

[68] 8 CFR §1003.1(d)(3)(iv) (2014).

[69] *Id.*

[70] INA §240(b)(5); 8 CFR §§1003.2(f), 1003.6, 1003.23(b)(1)(v), 1003.23(b)(4)(ii), 1003.23(b)(4)(iii)(C) (2014); *BIA Practice Manual*, Chs. 6.1, 7.3(a)(iv).

[71] 8 CFR §1003.6 (2014); *BIA Practice Manual*, chapter 6.2(a).

[72] *BIA Practice Manual*, chapter 6.2(c).

[73] (last visited Mar. 6, 2015).

E. Procedures for Appeal of an IJ Order

Upon issuance of the IJ's decision and order, the applicant must first be provided with notice of his or her right to appeal. The applicant must then prepare and file his or her EOIR-26, Notice of Appeal, with the BIA within 30 days of the IJ's order. Upon receipt, the BIA will issue a receipt notice to notify the appellant and appellee that a Notice of Appeal has been received. If the appellant has indicated that he or she plans to file a written statement or appeal brief, the BIA will then issue a briefing schedule for the parties, along with the transcript of the proceedings before the IJ. Upon receipt of both briefs, the BIA will review both arguments and determine whether the case will be assigned to a single Board Member or a three-member panel, or considered en banc. Following review of the briefs and administrative record, the BIA will prepare and issue its decision. These procedures are described in detail below.

- **Practice Pointer**: In August 2002, AG Ashcroft issued regulations that drastically changed the BIA appeals process. The regulations eliminated the BIA's de novo review of an IJ's factual findings and credibility determinations,[74] increased the issuance of summary decisions, required simultaneous briefing by the parties if the noncitizen is in custody, and eliminated eight positions of the 23-member board.[75] The regulations should be read and re-read carefully before filing any appeal with the BIA.[76]

- **Practice Pointer**: For detailed guidance on the BIA of Immigration Appeals' procedures and rules, practitioners should consult and strictly follow the *BIA Practice Manual*, which is available on EOIR's website at *www.justice.gov/eoir/vll/qapracmanual/BIAPracticeManual.pdf#page =1.*[77]

1. Notice of Right to Appeal

Applicants who are entitled to appeal to the BIA must be given notice of their right to appeal by the IJ.[78] Upon finding that an applicant is removable and ordering

---

[74] The BIA must defer to the factual findings of the IJ unless they are clearly erroneous. *Matter of A–S–B–*, 24 I&N Dec. 493 (BIA 2008). The BIA, however, reviews de novo the IJ's prediction or finding regarding the likelihood that an applicant will be tortured because it relates to whether the ultimate statutory requirement for establishing eligibility for relief has been met and, therefore, is a mixed question of law and fact. *Matter of V–K–*, 24 I&N Dec. 500 (BIA 2008).

[75] *See* 67 Fed. Reg. 54878 (Aug. 26, 2002).

[76] *See also* AIC Legal Action Center Practice Advisory, "Practicing Before the BIA under the New "Procedural Reforms" Rule" (Jan. 10, 2003), *available at www.legalactioncenter.org/sites/default/files/lac_pa_091102.pdf*; *see also* "BIA Procedural Reform Regulation: A Topical Summary," 79 *Interpreter Releases* 1457 (Sept. 30, 2002).

[77] (last visited Mar. 5, 2015).

[78] 8 CFR §1003.3(a)(1) (2014).

the applicant removed, the IJ must furnish the applicant with a Form EOIR-26, Notice of Appeal and advise him or her of the right to appeal to the BIA within 30 days.[79]

If an applicant knowingly and voluntarily waives his or her right to appeal, the IJ's order becomes final.[80] Prior to accepting the applicant's waiver of appeal, however, the IJ must also advise the applicant that he or she has the right to seek relief from removal.[81] Otherwise, the applicant cannot make a considered and intelligent decision about whether to appeal.[82] A party's waiver of appeal at the conclusion of proceedings before the IJ will generally make him or her ineligible to file an appeal thereafter.[83] The waiver of appeal generally cannot be retracted, withdrawn, or undone.[84] However, if a party wishes to challenge the validity of the waiver of appeal, the party may: (1) file a motion with the IJ explaining why the appeal waiver was not valid; or (2) file an appeal directly with the BIA that explains why the appeal was not valid.[85]

2. *Timing of Appeal*

The properly completed and signed Form EOIR-26, Notice of Appeal must be received by the BIA within 30 calendar days after the IJ rendered his or her oral decision or mailed his or her written decision.[86] An appeal is not deemed "filed" until the BIA has actually *received* it; the BIA does not recognize the "mailbox rule."[87] The appeal deadline is calculated from the date the IJ renders an oral decision or mails a written decision.[88] That day counts as day "0" and all calendar days are counted.[89] Day "30" is the appeal deadline, unless day "30" falls on a Saturday, Sunday, or legal holiday, in which case the deadline is construed to fall on the next

---

[79] 8 CFR §§1240.13(d), 1240.15 (2014).

[80] 8 CFR §1003.39 (2014); ICPM, chapter 6.4(a). *See Matter of L–V–K–*, 22 I&N Dec. 976 (BIA 1999).

[81] *U.S. v. Arrieta*, 224 F.3d 1076, 1079 (9th Cir. 2000).

[82] *Id. See also Narine v. Holder*, 559 F.3d 246, 249–50 (4th Cir. 2009) (holding that the term "final decision" is a term of art and that the applicant's waivers were not knowing or intelligent).

[83] 8 CFR §§1003.3(a)(1) (2014); *Matter of Shih*, 20 I&N Dec. 697 (BIA 1993); ICPM, chapter 6.4(a). *See also* 8 CFR §1003.1(d)(2)(i)(G) (2014).

[84] *BIA Practice Manual*, chapter 4.3(b)(ii).

[85] *Matter of Patino*, 23 I&N Dec. 74 (BIA 2001); ICPM, chapter 6.4(b); *BIA Practice Manual*, chapter 4.3(b)(ii).

[86] 8 CFR §§1003.3(a)(1), 1003.38(b) (2014); ICPM, chapter 6.2(b); *BIA Practice Manual*, chapter 4.5. *See also Matter of Liadov*, 23 I&N Dec. 990 (BIA 2006) (The BIA does not have the authority to extend the 30-day time limit for filing an appeal to the BIA. Although the BIA may certify a case to itself under 8 CFR §1003.1(c) (2006), where exceptional circumstances are present, a short delay by an overnight delivery service is not a rare or extraordinary event that would warrant consideration of an untimely appeal on certification).

[87] 8 CFR §§1003.3(a)(1), 1003.38(b)(c) (2014); *BIA Practice Manual*, chapters 3.1(a)(i), 4.5(a).

[88] 8 CFR §1003.38(b) (2014); ICPM, chapter 3.1(c)(ii)(D); *BIA Practice Manual*, chapter 3.1(b)(ii).

[89] 8 CFR §1003.38(b) (2014); *BIA Practice Manual*, chapters 3.1(b)(i)–(ii).

business day.[90] The BIA does not excuse untimeliness due to postal or delivery delays, even if the error is caused by an overnight delivery service.[91] Moreover, the BIA does not have the authority to extend the time in which to file a Notice to Appeal.[92] Thus, it is essential for the 30-day appeal deadline to be met.

➢ **Practice Pointer**: In practice, the BIA will accept an appeal as timely-filed if the BIA was closed due to inclement weather on the day of the deadline.[93]

3. *Where to File the Appeal*

The BIA does not accept electronically filed documents, except for the Form EOIR-27, Notice of Entry of Appearance as Attorney or Representative Before the BIA of Immigration Appeals, which may be filed electronically by registered attorneys and fully accredited representatives.[94] Thus, all filings must be filed by mail, courier, or hand-delivery.

➢ **Practice Pointer**: After an attorney or accredited representative has registered with the EOIR eRegistry, he or she may file an EOIR-27 form electronically on EOIR's website at *https://portale.eoir.justice.gov*.[95] When the attorney or accredited representative's appearance is entered electronically, he or she must print out a copy of the electronically-filed form and serve it on DHS.[96] A fillable Form EOIR-27 also is available on EOIR's website at *www.justice.gov/eoir/eoirforms/eoir27.pdf*.[97] EOIR strongly encourages that EOIR-27 forms be printed on yellow paper.[98]

The Notice of Appeal and all attachments must be sent to the Board of Immigration Appeals, Office of the Chief Clerk, 5107 Leesburg Pike, Suite 2000, Falls Church, VA 20530.[99] The telephone number for the BIA's Office of the Chief Clerk is (703) 605-1007, and the office's public window hours are 8:00 am to 4:30 pm, Monday through Friday.

---

[90] 8 CFR §1003.38(b) (2014); *BIA Practice Manual*, chapter 3.1(b)(ii).

[91] *BIA Practice Manual*, chapter 3.1(a)(ii); *Matter of Liadov*, 23 I&N Dec. 990 (BIA 2006). *But see Sun v. U.S. Dep't of Justice*, 421 F.3d 105 (2d Cir. 2005); *Oh v. Gonzales*, 406 F.3d 611 (9th Cir. 2005).

[92] 8 CFR §1003.38(b) (2014); *BIA Practice Manual*, chapter 4.5(b). *See Matter of Liadov*, 23 I&N Dec. 990 (BIA 2006). *But see Irogoyen-Briones v. Holder*, 644 F.3d 943 (9th Cir. 2011) (holding that the 30-day appeal period is not jurisdictional); *Khan v. Dept. of Justice*, 494 F.3d 255 (2d Cir. 2007) (same); *Huerta v. Gonzales*, 443 F.3d 753 (10th Cir. 2006) (same).

[93] *See, e.g., Rufino Marquez-Rocha*, A201 073 660 (BIA Jan. 29, 2013), *available at www.scribd.com/doc/127013010/Rufino-Marquez-Rocha-A201-073-660-BIA-Jan-29-2013.*

[94] *BIA Practice Manual*, chapter 1.6(e)(iii). *See* 8 CFR §1292.1(f) (2014).

[95] (last visited Feb. 6, 2015). *See BIA Practice Manual*, chapter 2.1(b)(ii).

[96] *BIA Practice Manual*, chapter 2.1(c).

[97] (last visited Mar. 6, 2015).

[98] *BIA Practice Manual*, chapter 12.2(e).

[99] *BIA Practice Manual*, chapter 3.1(a)(iii).

- **Practice Pointer**: Practitioners should always use mailing or delivery services that allow delivery tracking. Doing so will avoid parcels being lost in the mail and also provides practitioners with a record of the date of the BIA's receipt of the filing.[100]

- **Practice Pointer**: If practitioners are struggling to meet a filing deadline, they may wish to use the services of the Immigrant & Refugee Appellate Center, LLC (IRAC). IRAC is located directly across the street from the BIA, and offers same-day filing service to assist individuals with pending appeals and their legal representatives. For pricing and additional information on IRAC's filing services, see *www.irac.net/bia-same-day-filing/*.[101]

4. Preparing the Appeal and Avoiding Summary Dismissal

When filing a notice of appeal with the BIA, the applicant should file a package containing the following components in the following order:[102]

- A check or money order for the appeal filing fee of $110, made payable to "United States Department of Justice," or, if the applicant is unable to pay the filing fee, a Form EOIR-26A, Appeal Fee Waiver Request;[103]
- Form EOIR-26, Notice of Appeal, completed in English, listing the A-number(s) of the appellant(s), signed at item #9, and containing a completed Proof of Service;[104]
- Form EOIR-27, Notice of Entry of Appearance as Attorney or Representative before the BIA if the applicant is represented on appeal;[105]
- A copy of the memorandum order of the oral decision or the written decision being appealed (not required, but encouraged);[106]
- Any supporting documentation, with certified English translations of any documents that are not in English;[107] and

---

[100] *See BIA Practice Manual*, chapters 3.1(a)(iii), 3.1(b)(iv).

[101] (last visited Mar. 5, 2015).

[102] *BIA Practice Manual*, chapter 3.3(c)(i)(A).

[103] 8 CFR §1003.3(a)(1) (2014); Form EOIR-26, *General Instructions* 1-2, (June 2014), *available at www.justice.gov/eoir/eoirforms/eoir26.pdf*; *BIA Practice Manual*, chapter 3.4.

[104] 8 CFR §1003.3(b) (2014); Form EOIR-26, *General instructions*, *supra* note 103, at 2; *BIA Practice Manual*, chapter 4.4(b)(iv).

[105] 8 CFR §§1003.2(g)(1), 1003.3(a)(3) (2014); Form EOIR-26, *General instructions*, *supra* note 103, at 2; *BIA Practice Manual*, chapters 2.1(b), 2.3(d), 2.4(c).

[106] *BIA Practice Manual*, chapter 4.4(f).

[107] 8 CFR §§1003.3(a)(3), 1003.2(g)(1), 1003.33 (2014); *BIA Practice Manual*, chapter 3.3(a) and App'x H (Sample Certificate of Translation). Note, however, that the BIA will not accept new evidence on appeal. Rather, the BIA considers only that evidence that was submitted during the proceedings below. *BIA Practice Manual*, chapter 4.8.

- Proof of Service, certifying that a copy of the complete filing was sent or delivered to opposing counsel at the relevant DHS Office of Chief Counsel.[108]

Each of these components is discussed in more detail below.

> ➤ **Practice Pointer**: For rules and guidance on how filings to the BIA must be formatted, see *BIA Practice Manual* chapter 3, available at *www.justice.gov/eoir/vll/qapracmanual/BIAPracticeManual.pdf#page=1.*[109] Generally, filings must begin with a cover page, be paginated, be on size 8 ½" x 11" paper, be tabbed with alphabetic tabs, use Times New Roman 12 point font, use double-spaced text and single-spaced footnotes, be two-hole punched at the top, and be bound by a staple in the upper left corner.[110]

i. Filing Fee

The current filing fee for an appeal to the BIA is $110 and that fee must be filed with the EOIR-26, Notice of Appeal.[111] The fee must be paid by check or money order, made payable to "United States Department of Justice,"[112] and must be stapled to the Form EOIR-26.[113] Applicants who cannot pay the filing fee should file a Form EOIR-26A, Fee Waiver Request with their Notice of Appeal.[114] If no fee is filed or if the Fee Waiver Request does not establish the inability to pay the required fee, the appeal will not be deemed properly filed and the IJ decision will become final.[115]

ii. EOIR-26, Notice of Appeal

The Form EOIR-26, Notice of Appeal must be completed in full and must contain all of the requested data.[116] When completing the EOIR-26, Notice of Appeal, it is essential that the form contains sufficient detail and lists the specific findings of fact or conclusions of law that are being challenged on appeal, with citation to supporting authority.[117] Otherwise, the BIA may summarily dismiss the appeal, as described below in Part I.E.5.[118] If the appellant requests review by a three-member panel, the appellant must state in the Notice of Appeal the factual or legal basis for such a

---

[108] 8 CFR §§1003.2(g)(1), 1003.3(a)(1), 1003.3(c) (2014); *BIA Practice Manual*, chapters 3.2(a), 3.2(d).

[109] (last visited Mar. 6, 2015).

[110] *BIA Practice Manual*, chapter 3.3(c) and App'x F (Sample Cover Page).

[111] 8 CFR §1003.3(a)(1) (2014); Form EOIR-26, *General Instructions*, supra note 103; *BIA Practice Manual*, chs. 3.4(d), 4.4(d).

[112] *BIA Practice Manual*, chapter 3.4(f)

[113] *BIA Practice Manual*, chapter 3.4(h).

[114] 8 CFR §§1003.3(a)(1), 1003.8(c) (2014); *BIA Practice Manual*, chapters. 3.4(c), 4.4(d).

[115] 8 CFR §§1003.8(c), 1003.38(d) (2014); *BIA Practice Manual*, chapter 3.4(g).

[116] *BIA Practice Manual*, chapter 4.4(b)(iv)(A)–(B).

[117] 8 CFR §1003.3(b) (2014); Form EOIR-26, *General Instructions*, *supra* note 103, at 2.

[118] 8 CFR §1003.1(d)(2) (2014); *BIA Practice Manual*, chapter 4.4(b)(iv)(D)–(E).

request under the standards set forth in 8 Code of Federal Regulations (CFR) §1003.1(e)(6).

If the appellant plans to file a brief or written statement in support of the appeal, he or she must so indicate in item #8 on the Form EOIR-26, Notice of Appeal.[119] Even if the appellant plans to submit a brief or written statement at a later date, the reasons for the appeal on the Form EOIR-26 must still be completed with sufficient detail. Otherwise, the appeal could be summarily dismissed. Similarly, the BIA may summarily dismiss an appeal if the appellant indicated on the Form EOIR-26 that he or she would file a written brief or statement, but then does not timely submit the brief or statement after receiving the briefing schedule from the BIA.[120]

If the appellant requests oral argument by checking "yes" in item #7 on the EOIR-26, he or she should explain why oral argument is warranted in item #6.[121] Oral argument before the BIA is rarely granted, and the BIA ordinarily will not grant oral argument unless a brief is also submitted.[122]

iii. Entry of Appearance

Even if the attorney or representative already has filed an EOIR-28 to appear on behalf of the respondent in immigration court, he or she must enter his or her appearance separately before the BIA by filing a Form EOIR-27, Notice of Entry of Appearance as Attorney or Representative Before the Board of Immigration Appeals and serving a copy of the EOIR-27 on DHS.[123] Forms EOIR-27 may be filed electronically, as described above, or on yellow paper.[124] As required for practicing before the immigration courts, attorneys and accredited representatives must register with EOIR in order to practice before the BIA.[125] In general, the BIA recognizes four categories of people who may present cases to the BIA:[126] unrepresented respondents,[127] attorneys,[128] accredited representatives,[129] and individuals expressly recognized by the BIA.[130]

---

[119] Form EOIR-26, at 2 (June 2014), *available at www.justice.gov/eoir/eoirforms/eoir26.pdf* (last visited Mar. 6, 2015); *BIA Practice Manual*, chapter 4.4(b)(iv)(C).

[120] Form EOIR-26, *supra* note 103, at 2; *BIA Practice Manual*, chapter 4.4(b)(iv)(C).

[121] Form EOIR-26, *General Instructions*, *supra* note 103, at 2–3.

[122] *Id.*; Form EOIR-26, *supra* note 119, at 2.

[123] 8 CFR §§1003.2(g)(1), 1003.3(a)(3) (2014); *BIA Practice Manual*, chapters 2.3(d), 2.4(c), 4.4(e).

[124] *BIA Practice Manual*, chapters 2.3(d)(i), 2.4(c). Although the Board welcomes and encourages EOIR-27 forms to be filed on yellow paper, colored paper is not required. *Id.* at chapter 2.2(e).

[125] 8 CFR §1292.1(f) (2014); *BIA Practice Manual*, chapter 2.1(c).

[126] 8 CFR §1292.1 (2014).

[127] *See BIA Practice Manual*, chapter 2.2.

[128] *See id.* at chapter 2.3.

[129] *See id.* at chapter 2.4.

[130] *See BIA Practice Manual*, chapters 2.5, 2.9.

➢ **Practice Pointer**: For information regarding EOIR's eRegistry Program, including the announcement of the policy and final rule in the *Federal Register*, instructions on how to register and verify one's identity, and frequently asked questions, see the EOIR website at *www.justice.gov/eoir/engage/eRegistration.htm.*[131]

iv. Service on DHS

Finally, the applicant must serve DHS with a copy of the Notice of Appeal and all attachments, and then declare in writing to the BIA that a copy has been so served.[132] Service may be accomplished by hand delivery or by mail,[133] and the Proof of Service must bear the actual date of transmission.[134] If the Proof of Service is not included in the filing with the BIA, the BIA will reject the submission.[135] A Proof of Service must contain the following information: (1) the name and title of the party being served; (2) the precise and complete address of the party being served; (3) the date of service; (4) the means of service; (5) the document or documents being served; (6) the name of the person serving the document; and (7) the signature of the person serving the document.[136]

➢ **Practice Pointer**: A sample Proof of Service is provided in the *BIA Practice Manual* at Appendix G, available on EOIR's website at *www.justice.gov/eoir/vll/qapracmanual/BIAPracticeManual.pdf#page=1.*[137]

v. Form EOIR-33/BIA, Change of Address

If the appellant moves to a new address while the appeal is pending, he or she must file a Form EOIR-33/BIA within five working days of the move.[138] This notice must be provided in writing on Form EOIR-33/BIA, Alien's Change of Address Form/BIA, and a copy must be served on DHS.[139] It is essential for any appellant to timely file a change of address form. Failure to do so may result in the BIA sending notices and important correspondence to the wrong address.

➢ **Practice Pointer**: Form EOIR-33/BIA is available on EOIR's website at *www.justice.gov/eoir/eoirforms/eoir33bia.pdf.*[140] Practitioners should

---

[131] (last visited Feb. 6, 2015).

[132] 8 CFR §§1003.2(g)(1), 1003.3(a)(1), 1003.3(c) (2014); *BIA Practice Manual*, chapter 3.2(a).

[133] *BIA Practice Manual*, chapter 3.2(b).

[134] *BIA Practice Manual*, chapter 3.2(c).

[135] *Id.* at chs. 3.1(c)(ii), 3.2(d).

[136] *Id.* at chapter 3.1(d).

[137] (last visited Mar. 6, 2015).

[138] Form EOIR-26, *General Instructions*, *supra* note 103, at 3.

[139] *Id. See* Form EOIR-33/BIA, *available at www.justice.gov/eoir/eoirforms/eoir33bia.pdf* (last visited Mar. 6, 2015).

[140] (last visited Mar. 6, 2015).

ensure that they are preparing and filing the most current version of the EOIR-33/BIA form on behalf of their clients.

- **Practice Pointer**: Respondents also should file an AR-11 Change of Address with DHS. This process may be completed online at *https://egov.uscis.gov/coa/displayCOAForm.do*.[141] Notification to DHS of a change of address, however, does not constitute notification to the BIA.

The address obligations are slightly different for respondents who are detained. For detained respondents, DHS is obligated to report the location of the respondent's detention to the immigration court and to report when he or she is moved between detention locations or when he or she is released from custody. If the respondent is released from custody, he or she also should file an EOIR-33/BIA with the BIA within five days of release from detention to ensure that the BIA's records are current.

- **Practice Pointer**: In addition to filing an EOIR-33, practitioners should file a specific request to have the case transferred from the detained docket to the non-detained docket. Otherwise, the Clerk's office might change the address but keep the case on the detained docket.

Attorneys or representatives must also notify the BIA if they change addresses or phone numbers by filing a new Form EOIR-27.[142]

5. *Initial BIA Processing of the Appeal*

Upon receipt of an appeal, the BIA will place a date stamp on the filing.[143] If the appeal is not properly filed, the Clerk's Office will reject the filing and return it to the party with an explanation for the rejection.[144] If an appeal is untimely, it will be dismissed.[145] If the appeal is not rejected or dismissed for being untimely, the Clerk's Office will issue a receipt notice to the parties, which is usually received within one to two weeks of filing.[146] The BIA will then obtain the record of proceedings from the immigration court.[147]

The BIA will then screen the case for summary dismissal.[148] The BIA may summarily dismiss an appeal or portion of an appeal in any case which:

---

[141] (last visited Feb. 12, 2015).

[142] Form EOIR-26, *General Instructions*, *supra* note 103, at 3.

[143] *BIA Practice Manual*, chapter 3.1(b).

[144] *Id.* at chapter 3.1(c)(ii). The most common reasons for rejection are failure to pay the filing fee and failure to submit a proof of service on the opposing party. *Id.*

[145] 8 CFR §§1003.1(d)(2)(i)(G), 1003.38(b) (2014); *BIA Practice Manual*, chapter 3.1(c)(iii).

[146] *BIA Practice Manual*, chapters 1.6(b)(iii), 3.1(d)(i), 4.2(d).

[147] *BIA Practice Manual*, chapter 4.2(d).

[148] 8 CFR §1003.1(e)(1) (2014).

- The party fails to specify the reasons for the appeal on the Notice of Appeal;
- The only reason for the appeal specified by the party involves a finding of fact or conclusion of law that was conceded by that party at a prior proceeding;
- The appeal is from an order that granted the party the relief that had been requested;
- The BIA is satisfied, from a review of the record, that the appeal is filed for an improper purpose, such as to cause unnecessary delay, or that the appeal lacks an arguable basis in factor or law;
- The party indicates on the Notice of Appeal that he or she will file a brief or statement in support of the appeal and, thereafter, does not file the brief or statement or reasonably explain his or her failure to do so;
- The appeal does not fall within the BIA's jurisdiction, or lies with the IJ rather than the BIA;
- The appeal is untimely, or barred by the party's waiver of the right of appeal that is clear on the record; and
- The appeal fails to meet essential statutory or regulatory requirements or is expressly excluded by statute or regulation.[149]

A summary dismissal constitutes the final decision of the BIA.[150]

During this initial screening, a Board Member also may grant an unopposed motion or a motion to withdraw an appeal, as well as a motion by DHS to remand any appeal from DHS.[151] A single Board Member also may adjudicate a case where remand is necessary due to procedural or ministerial defects.[152]

The BIA must promptly enter orders of summary dismissal or other miscellaneous dispositions described above.[153] In any case that has not been summarily dismissed or otherwise addressed during initial screening, the BIA will arrange for prompt completion of the record of proceedings and transcript, as well as issuance of a briefing schedule.[154] The BIA will send the briefing schedule and transcript to both parties.[155]

---

[149] 8 CFR §1003.1(d)(2)(i) (2014); *BIA Practice Manual*, chapter 4.16.

[150] 8 CFR §1003.1(d)(2)(ii) (2014).

[151] 8 CFR §1003.1(e)(2) (2014).

[152] *Id.*

[153] 8 CFR §1003.1(e)(8) (2014).

[154] 8 CFR §1003.1(e)(3) (2014); *BIA Practice Manual*, chapter 4.2(d).

[155] *BIA Practice Manual*, chapter 4.2(e)–(f).

6. *Submission of Appeal Briefs*

If the applicant indicates that he or she will be filing a separate written statement or brief on the Notice of Appeal, the BIA will send the parties a briefing schedule along with, in most cases, a transcript of the IJ proceedings.[156]

> ➤ **Practice Pointer**: What do you do when your transcript is filled with *[indiscernible]*s or is just plain wrong? When you find numerous *[indiscernible]*s in the transcript or mistakes, obviously the transcriber could not hear everything that was said at the hearing. Sometimes vital testimony is missing for the appeal. By statute, the government is required to keep "a complete record ... of all testimony and evidence produced at the proceeding." [157] Courts have long recognized the problem of inaccurate or incomplete transcripts in immigration court proceedings.[158] Regulations allow for supplementation of the transcript under 8 CFR §1003.1(d)(3)(iv), (e)(2), and the *BIA Practice Manual* gives instructions on what to do if a transcript is inaccurate or incomplete. [159] An applicant must file a Request for Correction of Transcript with the BIA Clerk's Office and the BIA recommends that the applicant file a sworn, detailed statement along with the BIA appeal brief which identifies the defects.

Briefs in support of or opposition to the appeal must be filed directly with the BIA in accordance with the filing requirements set forth in chapter 3 of the *BIA Practice Manual*.[160] An appeal brief advises the BIA of the party's position and arguments. It

---

[156] 8 CFR §1003.3(c)(1) (2014).

[157] INA §240(b)(4)(C); 8 USC §1229a(b)(4)(C) (2012).

[158] *Semenov v. Att'y Gen.*, 346 F3d.Appx. 783 (3d Cir. 2009); *Witjaksono v. Holder*, 573 F.3d 968 (10th Cir. 2009); *Garza-Moreno v. Gonzales*, 489 F.3d 239, 241 (6th Cir. 2007); *Kheireddine v. Gonzales*, 427 F.3d 80, 85 (1st Cir. 2005); *Ortiz-Salas v. INS*, 992 F.2d 105, 106–07 (7th Cir. 1993). *But see, e.g., Shewchun v. Holder*, 658 F.3d 557 (6th Cir. 2011) (holding that the IJ's failure to furnish a corrected transcript of her decision in a timely manner, absent a showing of prejudice, does not constitute a per se deprivation of due process).

[159] Chapter 4.2(f) of the *BIA Practice Manual* provides:

> (iii) *Defects in the transcript.*—Obvious defects in the transcript (e.g., photocopying errors, large gaps in the recorded record) should be brought to the immediate attention of the Clerk's Office. Such requests should be filed separately under a cover page titled "REQUEST FOR CORRECTION OF TRANSCRIPT." See Appendix B (Directory), Appendix F (Sample Cover Page). The Board, in its discretion, may remedy the defect where appropriate and feasible.
>
> Defects do not excuse the parties from existing briefing deadlines. Those deadlines remain in effect until the parties are notified otherwise. See Chapter 4.7(c) (Extensions).
>
> Where the Board does not or cannot remedy the purported defect in the transcript, and the party believes that defect to be significant to the party's argument or the adjudication of the appeal, the party should identify the defect and argue its significance with specificity in the appeal brief. The Board recommends that the brief be supported by a sworn, detailed statement. The Board will consider any allegations of transcript error in the course of adjudicating the appeal.

[160] 8 CFR §1003.3(c)(1) (2014); *BIA Practice Manual*, chapter 4.6(a)(i).

should be clear, concise, well-organized, and should cite to the record and legal authorities fully, fairly, and accurately.[161] The brief should focus on the facts and legal arguments in dispute and should not belabor facts or laws that are not in dispute.[162] According to the BIA, "A well-written brief is in the party's best interest and is therefore of great importance to the Board."[163]

First, the brief must be timely filed.[164] If the applicant is *not* in custody, the appellant usually will be provided 21 days in which to file a brief or written statement, unless a shorter period is given by the BIA in the briefing schedule.[165] The appellee is given the same period of time following the appellant's brief deadline.[166] If the applicant is detained, both appellant and appellee are given 21 days to file simultaneous briefs, unless a shorter period of time is specified by the BIA.[167] If a brief is not timely filed, the BIA may reject it at any time prior to the final adjudication of the appeal.[168] In its discretion, the BIA may consider a brief filed out of time or may summarily dismiss the case for failure to file a brief.[169]

- ➢ **Practice Pointer**: If an untimely brief is submitted, practitioners should include a Motion to Accept Late-Filed Brief setting forth in detail the reasons for the untimeliness and supported by affidavits and other evidence.[170]
- ➢ **Practice Pointer**: If a party indicates on the EOIR-26, Notice of Appeal, that he or she will file a written brief or statement, and then later decides not to file a brief or statement, practitioners should notify

---

[161] *BIA Practice Manual*, chapter 4.6(b).

[162] *Id.*

[163] *Id.*

[164] *Id.* at chapters 4.6(a), 4.7.

[165] 8 CFR §1003.3(c)(1) (2014).

[166] *Id.*

[167] *Id.*

[168] *BIA Practice Manual*, chapter 4.7(b).

[169] 8 CFR §§1003.1(d)(2)(i)(E), 1003.3(c)(1) (2014); *BIA Practice Manual*, chapters 4.7(f), 4.16. *See Kokar v. Gonzales*, 478 F.3d 803 (7th Cir. 2007) (finding summary dismissal was proper because no brief was filed); *Esponda v. Att'y Gen.*, 453 F.3d 1319 (11th Cir. 2006) (finding BIA abused its discretion in summarily dismissing appeal for failure to file a brief where Notice of Appeal set forth basis for appeal); *Singh v. Ashcroft*, 362 F.3d 1164 (9th Cir. 2003) (finding due process violation where BIA would not permit the late filing of a brief despite applicant demonstrating that briefing schedule was sent to the wrong address); *Garcia-Cortez v. Ashcroft*, 366 F.3d 749 (9th Cir. 2004) (finding that it was not appropriate for BIA to summarily dismiss case for failure to file a brief where the notice to appeal adequately set forth detailed reasons in support of the appeal). *But see Rioja v. Ashcroft*, 317 F.3d 514 (5th Cir. 2003) (upholding summary dismissal of the appeal where applicant indicated he would file a separate statement or brief and did not file one).

[170] *BIA Practice Manual*, chapter 4.7(d).

the BIA of this decision before the due date for the brief by filing a "Briefing Waiver."[171]

➢ **Practice Pointer**: The BIA does not issue receipt notices for briefs.[172] Thus, practitioners should submit briefs to the BIA in a manner that provides a record of delivery. Practitioners may confirm receipt of a brief by calling the ASQ line or the Clerk's Office.[173]

The BIA, upon written motion, may grant an extension of time to file an appeal brief for up to 90 days for good cause shown.[174] The filing of an extension request does not automatically extend the filing deadline for the brief; rather, the deadline stands until the BIA has affirmatively granted the extension request.[175] It is the BIA's policy to grant one briefing extension per party, if requested in a timely fashion.[176] Usually, the BIA will grant an additional 21 days, added to the original filing deadline.[177] Second extension requests are rarely granted.[178] Extension requests must be received by the BIA by the brief's original due date. Those received after the due date will not be granted.[179] Extension requests should comply with the BIA filing requirements in chapter 3 of the *BIA Practice Manual*, and should contain the following: (1) a cover page and caption labeled "Briefing Extension Request"; (2) when the brief is due; (3) the reason for the request; (4) a representation that the party making the request has exercised due diligence to meet the current deadline; (5) that the party will meet a revised deadline; and (6) a Proof of Service on the opposing party.[180]

Second, the appeal brief must be properly formatted.[181] It must have a cover page,[182] and the briefing notice from the BIA should be stapled on top of the cover page or otherwise attached to the brief in accordance with the instructions on the briefing notice.[183] In addition to a cover page, the brief must contain a caption.[184] The individual's A-number should be listed on the cover page, in the caption, and on the

---

[171] *Id.* at chapter 4.7(e).

[172] *Id.* at chapter 4.7(b).

[173] *Id.*

[174] 8 CFR §1003.3(c)(1) (2014); *BIA Practice Manual*, chapter 4.7(c).

[175] *BIA Practice Manual*, chapter 4.7(c).

[176] *Id.* at chapter 4.7(c)(i).

[177] *Id.*

[178] *Id.*

[179] *BIA Practice Manual*, chapter 4.7(c)(ii).

[180] *Id.* at chapter 4.7(c)(iv).

[181] *Id.* at chapters 3.3, 4.6(c).

[182] *Id.* at chapter 4.6(a) and Appendix F (Sample Cover Page).

[183] *Id.* at chapter 4.6(a).

[184] *Id.* at chapters 3.3(c)(vi), 4.6(c)(iii).

bottom right corner of each page of the brief.[185] The BIA requires briefs to be paginated and encourages parties to limit briefs to 25 pages or less.[186] Excessive use of footnotes is discouraged; however, the BIA does recommend the use of headings and topic sentences.[187] All briefs must be signed by the person who prepared the brief, as the signature represents to the BIA that has read the document, attested to its truth, and submitted it in good faith.[188] If prepared by an attorney or accredited representative, the brief also should list that individual's EOIR ID number, along with his or her signature.[189]

> ➢ **Practice Pointer**: If the respondent has multiple representatives, any representative with an EOIR-27 on file may sign the brief.[190]

Third, the BIA recommends that an appeal brief contain the following items:

- A concise statement of facts and procedural history of the case;
- A statement of issues presented for review;
- The standard of review;
- A summary of the argument;
- The argument; and
- A short conclusion stating the precise relief or remedy sought.[191]

Parties are expected to provide complete and clear citations to all authorities that comply with the BIA's Citation Guidelines.[192] Additionally, the BIA requests that the noncitizen be referred to as "respondent," the IJ be referred to as "the Immigration Judge," and the government be referred to as "DHS" or "the Department of Homeland Security."[193]

Finally, all briefs also must be served on the opposing party and must contain a Proof of Service.[194]

7. *BIA Review*

The record on appeal varies from case to case, but generally includes charging documents, hearing notices, notices of appearance, applications for relief and any

---

[185] *Id.* at chapter 4.6(c)(ii).

[186] *Id.* at chapter 4.6(b).

[187] *BIA Practice Manual*, chapter 4.6(c)(vii)–(viii).

[188] 8 CFR §1003.102(j)(1) (2014); *BIA Practice Manual*, chs. 3.3(b), 4.6(c)(i).

[189] *BIA Practice Manual*, chapter 4.6(c)(i).

[190] *Id.* at chapter 2.3(f).

[191] *Id.* at chapter 4.6(c)(iv).

[192] *Id.* at chapter 4.6(d) and Appendix J (Citation Guidelines).

[193] *Id.* at chapter 4.6(c)(v).

[194] 8 CFR §1003.3(c)(1) (2014); *BIA Practice Manual*, chapters 3.2(a), 3.2(d), 4.6(a) and App'x G (Sample Proof of Service).

accompanying documents, court-filed papers and exhibits, transcript of proceedings and oral decision of the IJ, written memorandum order or decision of the IJ, Notice of Appeal, briefing schedules, briefs, motions, correspondence, and any prior decisions by the BIA.[195] After completion of the record on appeal, including any briefs, motions, or other submissions on appeal, the BIA member or panel must review and issue a decision on the merits as soon as practicable.[196] Cases of detained respondents are prioritized.[197] The BIA uses a case management system to screen all cases and manage its caseload.[198] Under this system, for any case that has not been summarily dismissed as described above, the BIA adjudicates cases in one of three ways: (1) individual; (2) panel; or (3) en banc.[199]

i. Affirmances Without Opinion

Final regulations that permit a streamlined review process by the BIA were issued on October 18, 1999, and are found at 8 CFR §§1003.1 and 1003.2. Additional amendments to this process were issued on August 26, 2002.[200] The process was adopted to address the marked increase in the number of appeals filed with the BIA, which as of April 2002 had grown to a backlog of approximately 56,000 cases. The streamlined process allows for a single permanent Board Member to review the record on appeal and affirm the decision below without issuing an opinion in the case. Such an "affirmance without opinion" (AWO) is only issued if the result below was correct, any errors in the decision below were harmless or immaterial, and either the issues in the case are controlled by precedent or the factual or legal issues raised are so insubstantial that a three-member panel review is not warranted.[201] Since these streamlined procedures were issued in 2002, the backlog has been reduced to 22,940 as of the end of fiscal year 2013.[202] EOIR decreased the issuance of AWOs from 30 percent in FY2004, to less than 10 percent in FY2008, to approximately 4 percent in the beginning of FY2009,[203] to only 2 percent in 2011.[204] The BIA continues to phase out its use of AWOs.

---

[195] *BIA Practice Manual*, chapter 4.2(h).

[196] 8 CFR §1003.1(e)(8) (2014).

[197] *Id.*

[198] 8 CFR §1003.1(e) (2014).

[199] 8 CFR §1003.1(e)(3) (2014); *BIA Practice Manual*, chapter 1.3(a)(i)–(iii).

[200] *See* Board of Immigration Appeals: Procedural Reforms To Improve Case Management, 67 Fed. Reg. 54878 (Aug. 26, 2002).

[201] *See* 8 CFR §§1003.1(a)(7), 1003.1(e)(4)(i) (2014); *BIA Practice Manual*, chapter 4.15.

[202] *See* U.S. Dep't of Justice, EOIR, Office of Planning, Analysis, and Technology, *FY 2013 Statistics Yearbook* at W3 (Apr. 2014), *available at www.justice.gov/eoir/statspub/fy13syb.pdf.*

[203] *See* Fact Sheet: EOIR Improvement Measures – Update (June 5, 2009), *available at www.usdoj.gov/eoir/ press/09/EOIRs22ImprovementsProgress060509FINAL.pdf.*

[204] *See* Statement of Juan P. Osuna before the Committee on the Judiciary, United States Senate, "Improving Efficiency and Ensuring Justice in the Immigration Court System" (May 18, 2011), available at *www.justice.gov/eoir/press/2011/EOIRtestimony05182011.pdf* (last visited Apr. 1, 2015).

To date, all federal circuits courts of appeals (except the D.C. Circuit U.S. Court of Appeals, which does not review decisions of the BIA) have upheld the AWO process and found it to be constitutional.[205] Whether the BIA's refusal to refer a case to a three-judge panel is reviewable by a federal court, however, is an issue that has resulted in a circuit split. The First, Third, Fourth, and Ninth Circuit U.S. Courts of Appeals have held that a single member's refusal to refer the case to a three-judge panel is subject to review by a federal court and may be reversed in at least some situations.[206] In contrast, the Second, Eighth, and Tenth Circuit U.S. Courts of Appeals have found these decisions to be discretionary and not subject to judicial review.[207] In the Sixth Circuit U.S. Court of Appeals, the question remains unanswered.[208]

In order to avoid AWOs and other forms of summary dismissal, the Notice of Appeal should be as specific as possible. It should include a detailed description of the relevant facts, as well as a statement that the appeal is not appropriate for affirmance without opinion under 8 CFR §1003.1(a)(7), citing any of the following reasons:

- This appeal raises substantial legal issues [Identify legal issues or challenges to current precedent];

---

[205] *Albathani v. INS*, 318 F.3d 365, 377 (1st Cir. 2003); *Zhang v. U.S. Dep't of Justice*, 362 F.3d 155, 157–59 (2d Cir. 2004); *Dia v. Ashcroft*, 353 F.3d 228, 244 (3d Cir. 2003); *Khattak v. Ashcroft*, 332 F.3d 250, 253 (4th Cir. 2003); *Soadjede v. Ashcroft*, 324 F.3d 830, 832–33 (5th Cir. 2003); *Denko v. INS*, 351 F.3d 717, 730 (6th Cir. 2003); *Duarte v. Ashcroft*, 83 Fed. App'x 119, 122 (7th Cir. 2003) (not selected for publication in the *Federal Reporter*); *Ngure v. Ashcroft*, 367 F.3d 975, 981 (8th Cir. 2004), *reh'd denied*, 2004 U.S. App. LEXIS 18608 (8th Cir. 2004); *Falcon Carriche v. Ashcroft*, 350 F.3d 845, 852 (9th Cir. 2003); *Yuk v. Ashcroft*, 355 F.3d 1222, 1232 (10th Cir. 2004); *Mendoza v. U.S. Att'y Gen.*, 327 F.3d 1283, 1289 (11th Cir. 2003); For guidance on challenging AWO decisions, see Mary Kenney, *BIA Affirmance Without Opinion": What Federal Court Challenges Remain?*, Am. Immigration Ctr. Legal Action Center Practice Advisories, (Apr. 27, 2005), *available at www.legalactioncenter.org/sites/default/files/lac_pa_042705.pdf*; Mary Kenney, *How to Challenge an Affirmance without Opinion by a BIA Member*, Am. Immigration Ctr. Legal Action Center Practice Advisories (Sept. 27, 2002), *available at www.legalactioncenter.org/sites/default/files/lac_pa_100102.pdf*.

[206] *See, e.g., Quinteros-Mendoza v. Holder*, 556 F.3d 159, 161–64 (4th Cir. 2009); *Montez-Lopez v. Gonzales*, 486 F.3d 1163 (9th Cir. 2007); *Haoud v. Ashcroft*, 350 F.3d 201, 206–08 (1st Cir. 2003); *Purveegiin v. Gonzales*, 448 F.3d 684, 692 (3d Cir. 2006); *Cuellar Lopez v. Gonzales*, 427 F.3d 492, 495–99 (7th Cir. 2005); *Zhu v. Ashcroft*, 382 F.3d 521, 526–27 (5th Cir. 2004); *Chong Shin Chen v. Ashcroft*, 378 F.3d 1081, 1086–88 (9th Cir. 2004) (finding the decision reviewable where the underlying issue was not controlled by existing BIA or court precedent, and the factual and legal questions raised on appeal were not insubstantial).

[207] *See, e.g., Ibragimov v. Gonzales*, 476 F.3d 125, 138–39 (2d Cir. 2007); *Kambolli v. Gonzales*, 449 F.3d 454, 463 (2d Cir. 2006); *Hamdan v. Gonzales*, 425 F.3d 1051, 1057–58 (7th Cir. 2005); *Bropleh v. Gonzales*, 428 F.3d 772, 779 (8th Cir. 2005); *Mekhoukh v. Ashcroft*, 358 F.3d 118, 130 (1st Cir. 2004); *Ngure v. Ashcroft*, 367 F.3d 975, 980–88 (8th Cir. 2004); *Batalova v. Ashcroft*, 355 F.3d 1246, 1253 (10th Cir. 2004); *Tsegay v. Ashcroft*, 386 F.3d 1347, 1353–58 (10th Cir. 2004).

[208] *See, e.g., Hassan v. Gonzales*, 403 F.3d 429, 437 (6th Cir. 2005).

- This appeal raises novel factual issues [Describe issues];
- The underlying facts are in dispute [List facts in dispute];
- The decision of the IJ was incorrect as a matter of law [Describe error and cite case law, statute, or regulations];
- The respondent meets the eligibility criteria for relief from removal (deportation) [List form of relief and how respondent has met criteria];
- Errors by the IJ (or DHS trial attorney) were significant and material [Describe errors];
- The proceedings deprived the respondent of his or her rights under the INA, the Due Process Clause of the Fifth Amendment, etc. [List reasons why as specifically as possible]; and/or
- Summary affirmance would deprive the respondent of his or her rights under the INA, the Due Process Clause of the Fifth Amendment, etc. [List reasons why as specifically as possible].[209]

If the Board Member determines that the IJ's decision should be affirmed without opinion, the BIA will issue an order that reads as follows: "The Board affirms, without opinion, the result of the decision below. The decision below is, therefore, the final agency determination. *See* 8 CFR §3.1(e)(4)."[210] An AWO approves the result reached in the decision below, but does not necessarily imply approval of all the reasoning of that decision.[211] It does, however, signify the BIA's conclusion that "any errors in the decision of the immigration judge ... were harmless or nonmaterial."[212]

ii. Single Member Decisions

BIA cases are adjudicated by individual Board Members, unless the case falls within one of the six categories requiring a three-member panel.[213] These categories include:

- The need to settle inconsistencies among the rulings of different IJs;
- The need to establish precedent construing the meaning of laws, regulations, or procedures;

---

[209] The above examples were set forth in N. Wettstein, *How to Prevent Summary Dismissal of Your Appeal Before the BIA*, 21 IMMIGRATION LAW TODAY 284 (May 2002). If you are challenging the BIA's summary treatment of your appeal, you may wish to visit the AIC website at *www.americanimmigrationcouncil.org*, for additional guidance. *See* Mary Kenney, *How to Challenge a BIA 'Affirmance without Opinion,'* 21 IMMIGRATION LAW TODAY 629 (Oct. 2002); *Vargas-Garcia v. INS*, 287 F.3d 882 (9th Cir. 2002) (one of a series of Ninth Circuit decisions that criticizes the BIA for failure to give adequate notice of the specificity required on the Notice of Appeal form (EOIR-26) to individuals who seek review).

[210] 8 CFR §1003.1(e)(4)(ii) (2014).

[211] *Id.*

[212] *Id.*

[213] 8 CFR §1003.1(e) (2014).

- The need to review a decision by an IJ or DHS that is not in conformity with the law or with applicable precedents;
- The need to resolve a case or controversy of major national import;
- The need to review a clearly erroneous factual determination by an IJ;
- The need to reverse the decision of the IJ or DHS in a final order, other than nondiscretionary dispositions.[214]

For cases that do not fall within one of these six categories, single Board Members may summarily affirm an IJ's decision without issuing an opinion, as described above, if the result reached by the IJ was correct, any errors were harmless or immaterial, and the issues on appeal either are squarely controlled by precedent and do not involve a novel factual situation or are not so substantial that a written opinion is warranted.[215] Despite constitutional challenges to summary affirmances, virtually all circuits have upheld these procedures.[216]

The single Board Member also may issue a brief order affirming, modifying, or remanding the decision under review, unless he or she designates the case for decision by a three-member panel as described below.[217] A single Board Member also may reverse the IJ's decision if such reversal is plainly consistent with and required by intervening BIA or judicial precedent, an intervening act of Congress, or an intervening final regulation.[218]

According to the regulations, the BIA "shall dispose of all appeals assigned to a single Board member within 90 days of completion of the record on appeal."[219] The Chairman may, at his or her discretion, grant an extension of up to 60 days.[220] Under certain circumstances, the Chairman also may temporarily suspend the suggested time limits.[221]

---

[214] *Id.* at chapter 1.3(a)(i).

[215] 8 CFR §1003.1(e)(4) (2014).

[216] *See Martinez v. Mukasey*, 508 F.3d 255, 260 (5th Cir. 2007); *Zhang v. DOJ*, 362 F.3d 155 (2d Cir. 2004); *Blanco De Belbruno v. Ashcroft*, 362 F.3d 272 (4th Cir. 2004); *Yuk v. Ashcroft*, 355 F.3d 1222, 1228–32 (10th Cir. 2004); *Albathani v. INS*, 318 F.3d 365, 375–77 (1st Cir. 2003); *Dia v. Ashcroft*, 353, F.3d 228, 234–45 (3d Cir. 2003); *Garcia-Melendez v. Ashcroft*, 351 F.3d 657, 662–63 (5th Cir. 2003); *Denko v. INS*, 351 F.3d 717, 725–32 (6th Cir. 2003); *Georgis v. Ashcroft*, 328 F.3d 962, 966–67 & n.4 (7th Cir. 2003); *Loulou v. Ashcroft*, 354 F.3d 706, 708–09 (8th Cir. 2003); *Falcon Carriche v. Ashcroft*, 350 F.3d 845 (9th Cir. 2003); *Lonyem v. Att'y Gen.*, 352 F.3d 1338, 1342 (11th Cir. 2003).

[217] 8 CFR §1003.1(e)(5) (2014).

[218] *Id.*

[219] 8 CFR §1003.1(e)(8)(i) (2014).

[220] 8 CFR §1003.1(e)(8)(ii) (2014).

[221] 8 CFR §1003.1(e)(8)(iii) (2014).

iii. Three-Member Panel Decisions

Cases that fall within one of the following six categories or that are otherwise unsuitable for a single Board Member are adjudicated by a panel of three Board Members:

- Cases involving the need to settle inconsistencies among the rulings of different IJs;
- Cases involving the need to establish precedent construing the meaning of laws, regulations, or procedures;
- Cases involving the need to review a decision by an IJ or DHS that is not in conformity with the law or with applicable precedents;
- Cases involving the need to resolve a case or controversy of major national import;
- Cases involving the need to review a clearly erroneous factual determination by an IJ;
- Cases involving the need to reverse the decision of the IJ or DHS in a final order, other than nondiscretionary dispositions.[222]

It is the Chairman's duty to divide the BIA into three-member panels empowered to decide cases by majority vote.[223] The Chairman also may assign Board Members to serve on screening panels to implement the case management process.[224]

According to the regulations, the BIA shall dispose of all appeals assigned to a three-member panel within 180 days after an appeal is assigned to the panel.[225] The Chairman may, at his or her discretion, grant an extension of up to 60 days.[226] Under certain circumstances, the Chairman also may temporarily suspend the suggested time limits.[227]

iv. En Banc Decisions

Finally, the BIA also may, on its own motion by a majority vote of permanent Board Members, or by direction of the Chairman, consider or reconsider any case en banc.[228] En banc proceedings are usually ordered only where necessary to address an issue of particular importance or to maintain consistency of BIA decisions.[229]

---

[222] 8 CFR §1003.1(e)(6) (2014); *BIA Practice Manual* at chapter 1.3(a)(i)–(ii).

[223] 8 CFR §1003.1(a)(3) (2014); *BIA Practice Manual*, chapter 1.3(a)(ii).

[224] 8 CFR §1003.1(a)(3) (2014).

[225] 8 CFR §1003.1(e)(8)(i) (2014).

[226] 8 CFR §1003.1(e)(8)(ii) (2014).

[227] 8 CFR §1003.1(e)(8)(iii) (2014).

[228] 8 CFR §1003.1(a)(5) (2014); *BIA Practice Manual*, chapter 1.3(a)(iii).

[229] 8 CFR §1003.1(a)(5) (2014).

➢ **Practice Pointer**: Practitioners filing appeals regarding novel legal issues or issues that have resulted in circuit court splits should consider seeking *amicus curiae* support for their appeals from experts on the particular legal issues or organizations that may have a particular interest in how the appeal is resolved. The BIA may grant permission for *amicus curiae* to appear on a case-by-case basis, if the public interest would be served thereby,[230] but generally limits *amicus curiae* appearances to the filing of briefs.[231] AILA participates as *amicus curiae* in "matters that advance the interests of the Association and its members, or that generally promote the orderly and beneficial development of the law."[232] Practitioners who wish to obtain AILA Amicus assistance should contact any member of the AILA Amicus Committee, submit a request to *amicus@aila.org*, or complete the online form for submitting amicus requests.[233] For more information on requesting AILA Amicus assistance, see the guidelines available on AILA InfoNet at Doc. No. 09042436.[234]

8. *Oral Argument*

If oral argument before the BIA is desired, a request should be included in the Notice of Appeal.[235] Oral argument is heard at the BIA's discretion and is not often granted.[236] A three-member panel or the BIA en banc may hear oral argument, as a matter of discretion, at the BIA's offices and on such date and time as the BIA establishes.[237]

Cases may be selected for oral argument if they meet the following criteria: (1) the resolution of an issue of first impression; (2) alteration, modification, or clarification of an existing rule of law; (3) reaffirmation of an existing rule of law; (4) the resolution of a conflict of authority; and (5) discussion of an issue of significant public interest.[238] If a case is selected for oral argument, the BIA will notify the parties by sending a notice of selection after the briefing schedule has concluded.[239] The notice will specify the time and place selected for the arguments, as well as the

---

[230] 8 CFR §1292.1(d) (2014).

[231] *BIA Practice Manual*, chapters 2.10, 4.6(i), 8.7(d)(viii).

[232] AILA Amicus Committee, *Guidelines for Obtaining AILA Amicus Assistance* (Feb. 5, 2015), AILA InfoNet Doc. No. 09042436, *available at www.aila.org/membership/communities/sections/federal-court/aila-amicus-committee/aila-amicus-committee-guidelines-and-priorities*.

[233] *Id.*

[234] *Id.*

[235] 8 CFR §1003.1(e)(7) (2014); *BIA Practice Manual*, chapter 8.2(a).

[236] *BIA Practice Manual*, chapter 8.2(a).

[237] 8 CFR §1003.1(e)(7) (2014); *BIA Practice Manual*, chapters 4.2(g), 8.2(a).

[238] *BIA Practice Manual*, chapter 8.2(d).

[239] *Id.* at chapter 8.3(a).

issues that the parties must address.[240] The requesting party must confirm his or her interest in oral argument, and following confirmation, the BIA will fix the argument calendar.[241] If the party does not confirm an interest in oral argument, the party's request is deemed waived and the BIA will decide the case on the existing record.[242]

Only the parties, their representatives, and amicus curiae invited by the BIA may participate in oral argument.[243] Parties are limited to one representative of record.[244] If a representative of record wishes to share oral argument with another person, or wishes another person to argue in his or her place, he or she must submit a written request to the Oral Argument Coordinator at least 15 days in advance of the scheduled oral argument.[245] That person must submit an EOIR-27 to enter their appearance for oral argument only.[246] The parties are generally allotted 30 minutes per side to present their arguments with a portion of time reserved for rebuttal, if desired.[247] Board Members may ask questions at any time during oral argument, and the parties must answer the questions as directly as possible.[248]

> **Practice Pointer**: If practitioners are granted oral argument, they must follow the Rules of Oral Argument contained in Chapter 8.7 of the *BIA Practice Manual*, available at *www.justice.gov/eoir/vll/qapracmanual/BIAPracticeManual.pdf#page=1*.[249]

After the arguments, the BIA prepares a transcript of the arguments and serves the transcript on both parties.[250] The BIA's decision will be served on the parties in the same way as for appeals that do not involve oral argument.[251]

9. Withdrawal of Appeal

At any time, a party may voluntarily withdraw his or her own appeal.[252] The withdrawal must be in writing, and must be filed with the BIA and served on the

---

[240] *Id.*

[241] *Id.*

[242] *Id.*

[243] *BIA Practice Manual*, chapter 8.6(a).

[244] *Id.* at chapter 8.6(b).

[245] *Id.*

[246] *Id.*

[247] *BIA Practice Manual*, chapter 8.7(e)(viii).

[248] *Id.* at chapter 8.7(e)(x).

[249] (last visited Mar. 6, 2015).

[250] *BIA Practice Manual*, chapter 8.8(c).

[251] *Id.* at chapter 8.8(a).

[252] *BIA Practice Manual*, chapter 4.11(a).

opposing party.[253] When an appeal is withdrawn, the decision of the IJ becomes final and binding immediately, as if no appeal had ever been filed.[254]

10. Status Inquiries with the BIA

Informal requests, such as status inquiries, may be made by calling the EOIR hotline or the BIA Clerk's Office. EOIR has an Automated Status Query system (ASQ), which provides information about the status of cases pending before the immigration courts or the Board of Immigration Appeals.[255] ASQ has a telephone menu in English and Spanish, and contains following information related to cases pending before the BIA:

- Appeals of IJ decisions;
- Briefing deadlines; and
- Filing information.[256]

> ➢ **Practice Pointer**: Although ASQ also includes the number of days that have lapsed on the asylum clock (the number of days between the date the asylum application was filed with U.S. Citizenship and Immigration Services (USCIS) or at a hearing before an IJ and the date the IJ first issued a decision),[257] this number does not include: (1) the time accrued on the employment authorization document clock (EAD clock) following lodging at the immigration court window prior to filing the applicant in open court with the IJ; (2) delays requested or caused by the applicant, when the EAD clock is stopped; or (3) the time that USCIS may credit to an applicant's EAD clock upon remand by the BIA.[258] Thus, the number of days on the hotline does not reflect the true number of days on the EAD clock, unless the applicant did not lodge the application before filing it in open court, did not cause any delays, and the case was not remanded by the BIA.[259] For a detailed discussion of the EAD clock, see Chapter 13 of this book.

ASQ does not contain information on bond proceedings, motions, appeals of motions to reopen or reconsider, or remands from the federal courts to the BIA.[260] A

---

[253] *Id.*

[254] 8 CFR §1003.4 (2014); *BIA Practice Manual*, chapter 4.11(c).

[255] *BIA Practice Manual*, chapter 1.6(b)(i)(A).

[256] *Id.*

[257] EOIR and USCIS, "The 180-Day Asylum EAD Clock Notice," available at *www.uscis.gov/sites/default/files/USCIS/Humanitarian/Refugees%20%26%20Asylum/Asylum/Asylum_Clock_Joint_Notice.pdf* (last visited Mar. 12, 2015).

[258] *Id.*

[259] *Id.*

[260] *Id.*

respondent or his or her representative may access the respondent's case information in ASQ by typing in the respondent's A-number.[261]

> **Practice Pointer**: The ASQ is accessible by calling 1-800-898-7180. If the respondent has a 9-digit A-number, practitioners should enter all nine digits. If the respondent has an 8-digit A-number, practitioners should enter a "0" before the A-number.

Informal status inquiries that cannot be answered by ASQ may be directed to the BIA Clerk's Office.[262]

11. Motions Before the BIA

During the pendency of an appeal, the parties may need to make various requests with the BIA. All formal requests must be made by written motion containing the required content and supported by any relevant documentary evidence.[263] For example, the parties may need to make any of the following motions while an appeal is pending before the BIA:

- Motion to Remand – if the party wishes for the BIA to return jurisdiction to the IJ;[264]
- Motion to Expedite – if an expedited adjudication of the appeal is necessary to avoid impending and irreparable harm;[265]
- Motion to Withdraw Appeal – if the party no longer wishes to appeal and wishes for the IJ's decision to become final;[266]
- Motion to Withdraw as Counsel of Record – if a representative wishes to no longer be counsel of record for the respondent or if the respondent no longer wishes to be represented by his or her current representative;[267]
- Motion to Stay Removal – if the respondent wishes to prevent DHS from executing an IJ's removal order;[268]
- Motion to Consolidate or Join – if the party wishes to join separate appeals into a single adjudication for all of the parties involved;[269]

---

[261] *Id.*

[262] *Id.*

[263] *See generally, BIA Practice Manual*, chapter 5.

[264] *BIA Practice Manual*, chapter 5.8.

[265] *Id.* at chapters 5.9(a), 6.5.

[266] *Id.* at chapters 4.11, 5.9(b).

[267] *Id.* at chapters 2.3(j), 5.9(c).

[268] *Id.* at chapters 5.9(d), 6.3, 6.4.

[269] *Id.* at chapters 4.10(a), 5.9(e), 5.9(g).

- Motion to Sever – if the party wishes to divide a consolidated appeal into separate appeals;[270]
- Motion to Recalendar – if the party wishes to continue with proceedings that have been administratively closed or continued indefinitely;[271]
- Motion to Hold in Abeyance – if the party wishes for the BIA to put an appeal on hold while other matters are pending;[272]
- Motion to Amend – if the party wishes to amend a previous filing;[273]
- Motion for Substitution of Counsel – if a representative has already entered his or her appearance on behalf of the respondent and the respondent wishes to change representatives;[274]
- Motion for Extension of Filing Deadline – if the party wishes to request more time to file a brief or other documentation;[275] and
- Motion to Accept Late-Filed Brief – if the party would like the BIA to consider a brief despite its untimeliness.[276]

This list of motions is not exclusive. Rather, this list describes the most common types of motions filed during the pendency of an appeal before the BIA. The respondent, a representative, or DHS may make any request of the court in motion format.[277]

> ➢ **Practice Pointer**: For a detailed discussion of motions to reopen and motions to reconsider, see Part II below.

Although there is no official format for motions, all motions must be in writing, must be signed, and must be served on all parties.[278] Motions must state with particularity the grounds on which they are based and must identify the relief or remedy sought by the moving party.[279] Motions should contain the following documents in the following order:[280]

- Filing fee, stapled to the cover page of the motion, or Form EOIR-26A, Fee Waiver Request (if applicable);

---

[270] *BIA Practice Manual*, chapters 4.10(c), 5.9(f). *See Matter of Taerghodsi*, 16 I&N Dec. 260 (BIA 1977).

[271] *BIA Practice Manual*, chapter 5.9(h).

[272] *Id.* at chapter 5.9(i).

[273] *Id.* at chapter 5.9(k).

[274] *Id.* at chapter 2.3(j)(i).

[275] *Id.* at chapter 4.7(c).

[276] *Id.* at chapter 4.7(d).

[277] *See generally, BIA Practice Manual*, chapter 5.

[278] *Id.* at chapter 5.2(b).

[279] *Id.*

[280] *See BIA Practice Manual*, chapters 3.3(c)(i)(B), 5.2(b).

- A cover page accurately describing the request;[281]
- The signed motion;
- Supporting documentation with table of contents (if any);[282]
- EOIR-27, Notice of Appearance (if not already submitted);
- EOIR-33/BIA (if the individual's address has changed); and
- Proof of Service.[283]

All motions must comply with the Board's format and filing requirements.[284]

A motion will be deemed unopposed unless the opposing party responds within 13 days of the date of service of the motion.[285] However, non-opposition will not necessarily result in a grant of the motion.[286] Upon entry of a decision, the BIA will serve the decision on all parties by regular mail.[287]

12. Identity, Law Enforcement, or Security Investigations or Examinations

The BIA may not issue a decision affirming or granting immigration status, relief, protection from removal, or any other immigration benefit to a respondent if that benefit requires completion of identity, law enforcement, or security investigations if such investigations or examinations have never been completed, if the results are no longer current, or they have uncovered new information bearing on the merits of the application for relief.[288] If the investigations or examinations were never completed or if the results are no longer current, the BIA will either issue an order remanding the case to the IJ with instructions for DHS to complete the investigations or examinations, or provide notice to both parties that in order to complete adjudication of the appeal the case is being placed on hold until the investigations or examinations can be completed or updated and the results have been reported to the BIA.[289]

13. Issuance of the BIA Decision

The BIA's decision shall be in writing and copies of the decision must be served on both parties by mail.[290] Under 8 CFR §1003.13, the BIA is required to serve its decision on the applicant or his or her attorney of record by either "physically presenting or mailing [the] document."[291] The BIA announced that beginning March

---

[281] *Id.* at chapters 3.3(c)(i)(B), 3.3(c)(vi), 5.2(b).

[282] *Id.* at chapters 3.3(c)(i)(B), 5.2(b), 5.2(f).

[283] *Id.* at chapters 3.2(d), 3.3(c)(i)(B), 5.2(b) and Appendix G (Sample Proof of Service)

[284] *See generally*, *BIA Practice Manual*, chapter 3.

[285] 8 CFR §1003.2(g)(3) (2014); *BIA Practice Manual*, chapter 5.11.

[286] *BIA Practice Manual*, chapter 5.11.

[287] *Id.* at chapter 5.10.

[288] 8 CFR §1003.1(d)(6)(i) (2014).

[289] 8 CFR §1003.1(d)(6)(ii) (2014).

[290] 8 CFR §1003.1(f) (2014); *BIA Practice Manual*, chapter 4.2(i).

[291] 8 CFR §1003.13 (2014).

1, 2009, it would begin mailing a copy of the decision to both the applicant and the attorney of record.[292] If there is evidence, in the form of an affidavit, by the applicant or the attorney that the decision was not received, an applicant may request the BIA to reissue its decision in order to preserve the right to appeal to the circuit court or for purposes of filing a motion to reopen. Several courts have reviewed whether the BIA should reissue a decision that was not received.[293]

> ➤ **Practice Pointer**: Some courts have held that the BIA may not enter an order of removal in the first instance in cases in which the IJ did not find the applicant removable.[294]

The BIA's decision is final, except in cases that are reviewed by the AG.[295] The BIA must refer as case to the AG in the following situations:

- If the AG directs the BIA to refer the case to him or her;
- If the Chairman or a majority of the Board Members believe that a case should be referred to the Attorney General; and
- If the Secretary of Homeland Security, or designated DHS officials, refer the case to the AG for review.[296]

In any case the AG decides, he or she must state the decision in writing.[297]

Decisions of the BIA and decisions of the AG are binding on DHS and IJs in the administration of the U.S. immigration laws.[298] By majority vote of the permanent Board Members, selected three-member panel or en banc decisions by the BIA may be designated to serve as precedent for all future proceedings involving the same issues.[299] Decisions of the BIA are reviewable in federal court, depending on the nature of the appeal.

> ➤ **Practice Pointer**: For a detailed discussion of judicial review of BIA decisions, see chapter 12 of this book.

---

[292] *See* U.S. Dep't of Justice, News Release: Board to Begin Providing Copy of Decision to Aliens Who Are Represented by Counsel (Dec. 19, 2008), *available at www.usdoj.gov/eoir/press/08/BIAProvidesCourtesyCopy121908.pdf.*

[293] *See, e.g.*, *Hernandez-Velasquez v. Holder*, 611 F.3d 1073 (9th Cir. 2010) (*Jahjaga v. Att'y Gen.*, 512 F.3d 80, 82–83 (3d Cir. 2008); *Ping Chen v. Att'y Gen.*, 502 F.3d 73, 76–77 (2d Cir. 2007); *Singh v. Gonzales*, 494 F.3d 1170, 1172–73 (9th Cir. 2007).

[294] *Rhodes-Bradford v. Keisler*, 507 F.3d 77, 81 (2d Cir. 2007); *James v. Gonzales,* 464 F.3d 505 (5th Cir. 2006); *Noriega-Lopez v. Ashcroft,* 335 F.3d 874, 883 (9th Cir. 2003);

[295] 8 CFR §1003.1(d)(7) (2014); *BIA Practice Manual*, chapter 1.4(d).

[296] 8 CFR §1003.1(h)(1) (2014).

[297] 8 CFR §1003.1(h)(2) (2014).

[298] 8 CFR §1003.1(g) (2014).

[299] *Id.*; *BIA Practice Manual*, chapter 1.4(d)(i).

F. Interlocutory Appeals

The BIA may also consider interlocutory appeals made during the course of removal proceedings if a party seeks review of an IJ's ruling before the final decision is issued.[300] Although the BIA does not ordinarily entertain interlocutory appeals, it will rule on the merits of such appeals where it is necessary to address important jurisdictional questions regarding the administration of the immigration laws or to correct recurring problems in the handling of cases before IJs.[301]

Interlocutory appeals are filed on Form EOIR-26, Notice of Appeal.[302] In the answer space for "What decision are you appealing?" the appealing party must write the words "Interlocutory Appeal."[303] The party should not check any of the three options in box 5, but should indicate the date of the IJ's decision, the precise nature and disposition of that decision, and the precise issue being appealed.[304] If the appealing party wishes to submit a brief in support of the interlocutory appeal, it should be submitted either with or as soon as possible after the Notice of Appeal is filed.[305]

G. Bond Appeals

If DHS or the respondent wishes to challenge the IJ's decision following bond proceedings, the party may prepare and file an appeal with the BIA of Immigration Appeals.[306] An appeal may be taken by DHS or the respondent to the BIA on Form EOIR-26 within 30 calendar days of the IJ's decision.[307] The appeal will not delay compliance with the order, nor will it stay the removal proceedings or removal.[308] If the respondent appeals, the IJ's bond decision remains in effect while the appeal is pending. If DHS appeals, the IJ's bond decision remains in effect while the appeal is pending, unless the BIA issues an emergency stay or the decision is automatically stayed by regulation.[309]

DHS may seek a discretionary stay of the IJ's custody or bond order when it appeals the IJ's decision on its own motion.[310] In some cases, DHS is entitled to an

---

300 *See BIA Practice Manual*, chapter 4.14(a).

301 *BIA Practice Manual*, chapter 4.14(c). *See, e.g.*, *Matter of Morales*, 21 I&N Dec. 130 (BIA 1995–96) (finding that the immigration court did not have jurisdiction to proceed with the case of an *ABC* class member); *Matter of K–*, 20 I&N Dec. 418 (BIA 1991).

302 *BIA Practice Manual*, chapter 4.14(d).

303 *Id.*

304 *Id.*

305 *Id.* at chapter 4.14(e).

306 8 CFR §§1003.38, 1236.1(d)(3)(i) (2014); ICPM, chapter 9.3(f); *BIA Practice Manual*, chapter 7.

307 8 CFR §§1003.38, 1003.19(f) (2014); *BIA Practice Manual*, chapter 7.3(a)(ii).

308 8 CFR §1236.1(d)(4) (2014).

309 8 CFR §§1003.6(c), 1003.19(i) (2014); ICPM, chapter 9.3(f); *BIA Practice Manual*, chapter 7.3(a)(iv)(B).

310 8 CFR §1003.19(i)(1) (2014).

automatic stay of an IJ's custody or bond redetermination.[311] For example, if the ICE District Director had previously denied the individual's request for release or set a bond at $10,000 or more, the IJ's order authorizing release (on bond or otherwise) must be stayed upon DHS's filing of a Form EOIR-43, Notice of Intent to Appeal the Custody Redetermination.[312] Whether to file the Form EOIR-43 is at the discretion of DHS.[313] If DHS decides to file this form, it must be filed with the immigration court within one business day of the IJ's order, and the IJ's decision must remain in abeyance pending the BIA's decision on the appeal.[314]

Because bond hearings are generally not recorded, if the IJ issues an oral decision, it is not transcribed. Rather, if either party appeals, the IJ must prepare a written decision based on his or her notes from the bond hearing.[315] The record may contain any information in addition to the IJ's memorandum of decision and other EOIR forms.[316]

> ➢ **Practice Pointer**: For detailed guidance on preparing and filing a bond appeal, see chapter 7 of the *BIA Practice Manual*, available at *www.justice.gov/eoir/vll/qapracmanual/BIAPracticeManual.pdf#page=1*.[317]

II. Motions to Reopen and Reconsider

If an individual has received an administratively final deportation, exclusion, or removal order, he or she may file a motion to reopen or reconsider with the IJ or BIA.[318] Unlike an appeal, motions to reopen or reconsider seek review of a decision by the same body that had previously reviewed the case. Motions to reopen seek further review of a case based on new facts or documentary evidence that were previously unavailable, whereas motions to reconsider seek a second review of a case based on errors of fact or law made by the adjudicator. Regulations regarding motions to reopen and reconsider impose strict time limitations, restrict the number of motions that may be filed, and allow for only a few narrow exceptions to these limitations.[319]

---

311 8 CFR §1003.19(i)(2) (2014).

312 *Id.*

313 *Id.*

314 *Id.*

315 ICPM, chapter 9.3(e)(vii).

316 *Matter of Chirinos*, 16 I&N Dec. 276 (BIA 1977) (noting that bond hearings are informal and that there is no right to a transcript).

317 (last visited Mar. 6, 2015).

318 8 CFR §§1003.2, 1003.23 (2014).

319 *See* 8 CFR §§1003.2, 1003.23 (2014).

- **Practice Pointer**: When proceedings have been administratively closed, the proper motion is a motion to recalendar, not a motion to reopen.[320]

A. Motions to Reopen

A motion to reopen seeks a second review of a case based on new or previously unavailable evidence.[321] It asks the Immigration Court or BIA to reopen proceedings after the decision has been rendered so that the IJ or BIA can consider new facts and evidence in the case.[322] The motion must "state the new facts that will be proven at a hearing to be held if the motion is granted, and shall be supported by affidavits or other evidentiary material."[323] The respondent must demonstrate to the IJ or BIA that the new facts or evidence: (1) are material; (2) were unavailable during the original hearing; and (3) could not have been discovered or presented at the original hearing.[324] In general, a motion to reopen must be filed within 90 days of the final order,[325] and only one motion to reopen may be filed.[326] The BIA has noted that motions to reopen are "disfavored" and that it has broad discretion to deny such motions.[327]

- **Practice Pointer**: There are exceptions to the time and numerical limitations for filing motions to reopen, including if there are changed country conditions in the country of feared persecution. See Part II.H. below for a detailed description of these exceptions.

B. Motions to Reconsider

In contrast, a motion to reconsider "questions the [adjudicator's] decision for alleged errors in appraising the facts and law" and seeks a re-examination of the decision "in light of additional legal arguments, a change in law, or perhaps an argument or aspect of the case which was overlooked."[328] The motion must state with

---

[320] ICPM, chapters 5.7(i), 5.10(t); *BIA Practice Manual*, chapters 5.6(h), 5.9(h).

[321] *Matter of J–J–*, 21 I&N Dec. 976 at *4 n.1 (BIA 1997).

[322] ICPM, chapter 5.7(a); *BIA Practice Manual*, chapter 5.6(a).

[323] INA §240(c)(7)(B).

[324] 8 CFR §1003.2(c)(1) (2014). *See, e.g., Perez v. Holder*, 740 F.3d 57, 62–63 (1st Cir. 2014) (finding that the new evidence did not provide additional evidence of nexus to a protected ground in gang persecution of Guatemalan teachers, and therefore, the evidence was not material); *Victor v. Holder*, 616 F.3d 705, 710 (7th Cir. 2010) (finding that the new affidavit presented was not unobtainable prior to the original hearing); *Kaur v. BIA*, 413 F.3d 232, 234 (2d Cir. 2005) (finding that the new evidence was not material because the IJ's denial was based on adverse credibility and the new evidence did not address credibility); *Gebremaria v. Ashcroft*, 378 F.3d 734, 737–39 (8th Cir. 2004) (finding that the respondent's HIV status was known at the time of the original hearing, so it was not grounds for a motion to reopen).

[325] INA §240(c)(7)(C)(i); 8 CFR §1003.2(c)(2), 1003.23(b)(1), 1208.4(b)(3)(ii) (2014).

[326] 8 CFR §§1003.2(c)(2), 1003.23(b)(1) (2014).

[327] *Matter of Gutierrez-Lopez*, 21 I&N Dec. 479 at *10 (BIA 1996).

[328] *Matter of J–J–*, 21 I&N Dec. 976 at *4, n.1 (citations omitted). *See* ICPM, chapter 5.8(a); *BIA Practice Manual*, chapter 5.7(a).

particularity the errors of fact or law in the IJ or BIA's prior decision, with appropriate citation to authority and the record. If the motion is based on changes to the law, the motion should identify the charges and, where appropriate, provide copies of the law.[329] A motion to reconsider must be filed "within 30 days of the date of entry of a final administrative order of removal,"[330] and only one motion to reconsider may be filed.[331] Although an individual may file a motion to reconsider the denial of a motion to reopen, he or she may not file a motion to reconsider the denial of a motion to reconsider.[332]

A motion to reconsider an IJ decision that is pending when an appeal is filed or that is filed subsequent to the filing of an appeal with the BIA may be deemed a motion to remand the decision for further proceedings before the IJ.[333] Such a motion may be consolidated with and considered by the BIA in connection with the appeal.[334]

C. Who May Make a Motion to Reopen or Reconsider?

A motion to reopen or reconsider may be made by the BIA on its own motion, an IJ on his or her own motion, upon motion of DHS, or upon motion of the individual who has been ordered removed, deported, or excluded.[335] According to the regulations and the BIA, a motion to reopen or reconsider may not be filed by an individual who has departed the United States subject to a deportation, exclusion, or removal order.[336] The BIA and at least one court has held, however, that an IJ retains jurisdiction to reopen and rescind an *in absentia* order to address whether the applicant received proper notice of the hearing, even after the applicant had been removed.[337] Almost all circuit courts have struck down the departure bar regulations as impermissible agency action in conflict with the plain language of the motion to reopen or reconsider statutes.[338]

---

[329] ICPM, chapter 5.8(f) and App'x J (Citation Guidelines); *BIA Practice Manual*, chapter 5.7(g).

[330] INA §240(c)(6)(B); 8 CFR §§1003.2(b)(2), 1003.23(b)(1) (2014).

[331] 8 CFR §§1003.2(b)(2), 1003.23(b)(1) (2014).

[332] 8 CFR §§1003.2(b)(2), 1003.23(b)(1) (2014); ICPM, chapter 5.8(d); *BIA Practice Manual*, chapter 5.7(d).

[333] 8 CFR §1003.2(b)(1), 1003.2(c)(4) (2014).

[334] 8 CFR §1003.2(b)(1), 1003.2(c)(4) (2014).

[335] 8 CFR §§1003.2(a), 1003.23(b)(1) (2014).

[336] 8 CFR §§1003.2(d), 1003.23(b)(1) (2014); *Matter of Armendarez*, 24 I&N Dec. 646 (BIA 2008); *Matter of Yih-Hsiung Wang*, 17 I&N Dec. 565 (BIA 1980); *Matter of G–Y–B–*, 6 I&N Dec. 159 (BIA 1954).

[337] *Contreras-Rodriguez v. Att'y Gen.*, 462 F.3d 1314 (11th Cir. 2006); *Matter of Bulnes-Nolasco*, 25 I&N Dec. 57 (BIA 2009).

[338] *Santana v. Holder*, 731 F.3d 50 (1st Cir. 2013); *Bolieiro v. Holder*, 731 F.3d 32 (1st Cir. 2013); *Garcia-Carias v. Holder*, 697 F.3d 257 (5th Cir. 2012); *Lari v. Holder*, 697 F.3d 273 (5th Cir. 2012); *Contreras-Bocanegra v. Holder*, 678 F.3d 811 (10th Cir. 2012); *Jian Le Lin v. Att'y Gen.*, 681 F.3d 1236 (11th Cir. 2012); *Prestol Espinal v. Att'y Gen.*, 653 F.3d 213 (3d Cir. 2011); *Reyes-Torres v.*

Continued

D. Jurisdiction

A motion to reopen or reconsider a decision of an IJ should be filed with the immigration court having administrative control over the record of proceeding.[339] An IJ has jurisdiction in cases in which he or she has made a decision, unless jurisdiction has vested with the BIA.[340] If jurisdiction has vested with the BIA, the motion should be filed directly with the BIA.[341] The BIA has jurisdiction over cases in which it has rendered a decision,[342] as well as cases for which an appeal has already been filed with the BIA.[343] In these situations, any motion to reopen or reconsider filed with the IJ will be denied for lack of jurisdiction.

A motion to reopen or reconsider that is filed with the BIA while an appeal is before the BIA will be treated as a motion to remand and may be consolidated with the appeal.[344] Where the BIA dismisses an appeal solely for lack of jurisdiction, without adjudication on the merits, the IJ retains jurisdiction over any subsequent motion to reopen or reconsider.[345] The BIA, however, retains jurisdiction over a motion to reconsider its dismissal of an untimely appeal to the extent that the motion challenges the finding of untimeliness or requests consideration of the reasons for untimeliness.[346]

E. Standard of Review and Burden of Proof

The decision to grant or deny a motion to reopen or reconsider is within the discretion of the BIA or IJ, and the motion may be denied even if the moving party has made out a prima facie case for relief.[347] A motion to reopen will not be granted unless it appears to the BIA or the IJ that the evidence sought to be offered is material and was not available and could not have been discovered or presented at a prior hearing.[348] A motion to reopen also will not be granted for the purpose of allowing an

---

Holder, 645 F.3d 1073, 1075–77 (9th Cir. 2011); *Coyt v. Holder*, 593 F.3d 902, 905–08 (9th Cir. 2010); *William v. Gonzales*, 499 F.3d 329 (4th Cir. 2007).

[339] 8 CFR §1003.23(b)(1)(ii) (2014).

[340] 8 CFR §1003.23(b)(1) (2014).

[341] 8 CFR §1003.2(g)(2) (2014).

[342] 8 CFR §1003.2(a) (2014).

[343] 8 CFR §1003.23(b)(1) (2014). *See, e.g., Ilic-Lee v. Mukasey*, 507 F.3d 1044, 1049 (6th Cir. 2007) (finding that the IJ did not have jurisdiction over the motion to reopen after the notice of appeal had already been filed with the BIA and dismissing the appeal of the IJ's decision on the motion to reopen); *Marrero v. INS*, 990 F.2d 772, 777–78 (3d Cir. 1993).

[344] 8 CFR §§1003.2(b)(1), 1003.2(c)(4) (2014).

[345] *Matter of Lopez*, 22 I&N Dec. 16 (BIA 1998), *modifying Matter of Mladineo*, 14 I&N Dec. 591 (BIA 1974).

[346] *Id.*

[347] 8 CFR §§1003.2(a), 1003.23(b)(1)(iv) (2014); *see also Matter of Gutierrez-Lopez*, 21 I&N Dec. 479 at *10–11 (BIA 1996) (noting that the BIA may deny a motion to reopen even if the individual has made out a prima facie case if the relief would not be granted in the exercise of discretion).

[348] 8 CFR §§1003.2(c)(1), 1003.23(b)(3) (2014).

applicant the opportunity to apply for discretionary relief if the applicant's right to apply for such relief was fully explained to him or her and an opportunity to apply was afforded to the applicant at a previous hearing, unless the relief is sought on the basis of circumstances that arose after the hearing.[349]

Additionally, if the applicant is filing a motion to reopen in order to apply for asylum, withholding of removal, or CAT relief, the motion must be accompanied by a completed application and all supporting documents.[350] The motion also must reasonably explain the failure to request asylum prior to the completion of proceedings.[351] An applicant demonstrates prima facie eligibility for relief where the evidence reveals a reasonable likelihood that the statutory requirements have been satisfied.[352] The showing need not be conclusive.[353] Courts have overturned denials of motions to reopen upon finding that the BIA abused its discretion.[354]

F. Numerical Limitations

A party may file only one motion to reconsider and one motion to reopen, unless one of the exceptions listed below in Part H applies.[355] Additionally, motions filed before September 30, 1996 do not count toward the one motion limit.[356]

G. Time Limitations

A motion to reopen must be filed with the IJ or the BIA within 90 days of the date of entry of a final administrative order of removal, deportation, or exclusion.[357]

> ➢ **Practice Pointer**: A motion to reopen a decision of the BIA following judicial review in federal court is untimely if it is filed more than 90 days after the date of the decision of the BIA, even if it is filed within 90

---

[349] 8 CFR §§1003.2(c)(1), 1003.23(b)(3) (2014); *see also Hailemichael v. Gonzales*, 454 F.3d 878, 883–84 (8th Cir. 2006) (finding that the IJ abused her discretion in granting DHS's motion to reopen because she failed to explain whether the documents submitted were material and unavailable at the time of the hearing).

[350] 8 CFR §1003.23(b)(3) (2014).

[351] 8 CFR §§208.4(b)(3)(ii), 1208.4(b)(3)(ii) (2014); *see also Matter of R–R–*, 20 I&N Dec. 547 (BIA 1992) (finding that an asylum applicant must make a prima facie showing of his eligibility for asylum, as well as reasonably explain the failure to request asylum prior to the completion of deportation or exclusion proceedings).

[352] *Matter of S–V–*, 22 I&N Dec. 1306, 1308 (BIA 2000).

[353] *Id.*

[354] *See, e.g.*, *Yang v. Gonzales*, 478 F.3d 133, 143 (2d Cir. 2007) (finding BIA erred in failing to consider the disbarment of the applicant's attorney in considering his motion to reopen); *Mejia v. Ashcroft*, 298 F.3d 873, 880 (9th Cir. 2002) (finding BIA abused its discretion by failing, contrary to settled law, to hold that an applicant was prima facie eligible for relief and for failing to address newly submitted evidence). For additional discussion of the BIA's standards for review, see chapter 2.8.1.

[355] INA §§240(c)(6)(A), 240(c)(7)(A); 8 CFR §§1003.2(b)(2), 1003.2(c)(2), 1003.23(b)(1) (2014).

[356] ICPM, chapter 5.7(e)(v); *BIA Practice Manual*, chapter 5.6(e)(v).

[357] 8 CFR §§1003.2(c)(2), 1003.23(b)(1) (2014).

days of the order of the reviewing court.[358] See chapter 12 of this book for a detailed discussion of judicial review before the federal courts.

A motion to reconsider must be filed with the IJ within 30 days of the date of entry of a final administrative order of removal, deportation, or exclusion.[359] A motion to reconsider before the BIA must be filed with the BIA within 30 days after the mailing of the BIA decision.[360]

H. Exceptions to the Time and Numerical Limitations

There are six exceptions to the time and numerical limitations on filing motions to reopen. These include: (1) where the proceedings are reopened *sua sponte*;[361] (2) where the parties agree to reopening;[362] (3) where there are changed circumstances materially affecting eligibility for asylum, withholding of removal, and protection under CAT;[363] (4) where the order was entered *in absentia* and there are exceptional circumstances or there was no notice;[364] (5) where DHS asks for reopening due to fraud in the original proceedings or a crime supports termination of asylum;[365] and (6) where a case merits equitable tolling due to ineffective assistance of counsel.[366] Each of these exceptions is discussed in detail below. There are also special rules for certain motions to reopen filed by battered spouses, children, and parents.[367]

---

358 *Matter of Susma*, 22 I&N Dec. 947 (BIA 1999).

359 8 CFR §1003.23(b)(1) (2014).

360 8 CFR §1003.2(b)(2) (2014).

361 8 CFR §1003.2(a) (2014). *See, e.g., Matter of G–D–*, 22 I&N Dec. 1132 (BIA 1999); *Matter of X–G–W–*, 22 I&N Dec. 71 (BIA 1998); *Matter of Yewondwosen*, 21 I&N Dec. 1027 (BIA 1997).

362 8 CFR §1003.2(c)(3)(iii) (2014).

363 INA §240(c)(7)(C)(ii); 8 CFR §§1003.2(c)(3)(ii), 1003.23(b)(4)(i) (2014).

364 8 CFR §1003.2(c)(3)(i) (2014).

365 8 CFR §1003.2(c)(3)(iv) (2014). *See, e.g., Hailemichael v. Gonzales*, 454 F.3d 878 (8th Cir. 2006); *Efe v. Ashcroft*, 293 F.3d 899, 904 (5th Cir. 2002).

366 *Kuusk v. Holder*, 732 F.3d 202, 305 (4th Cir. 2013) (holding that equitable tolling is only appropriate where the individual was prevented from asserting a claim or extraordinary circumstances beyond the individual's control made it impossible to file on time); *Bead v. Holder*, 703 F.3d 591 (1st Cir. 2012) (finding that a person must demonstrate due diligence during the entire period of time he or she wishes to toll, including the time when the ineffective assistance should have been discovered and the time following the discovery and preceding the motion to reopen); *El-Gazawy v. Holder*, 690 F.3d 852, 859–60 (7th Cir. 2012) (finding that the individual must demonstrate that he or she "could not reasonably have been expected to file earlier"); *Avagyan v. Holder*, 646 F.3d 672, 679–70 (9th Cir. 2011) (maintaining a three-part test for due diligence and equitable tolling); *Mezo v. Holder*, 615 F.3d 616 (6th Cir. 2010) (citing its five-part test for equitable tolling); *Rashid v. Mukasey*, 553 F.3d 127 (2d Cir. 2008) (finding that a person must demonstrate due diligence during the entire period of time he or she wishes to toll, including the time when the ineffective assistance should have been discovered and the time following the discovery and preceding the motion to reopen); *Riley v. INS*, 310 F.3d 1253 (10th Cir. 2002) (adopting the Second Circuit's approach).

367 *See* INA §240(c)(7)(C)(iv).

1. Motion to Reopen Sua Sponte

Both the BIA and the IJ (if jurisdiction has not rested with the BIA) may reopen proceedings *sua sponte.*[368] *Sua sponte* reopening, however, is generally reserved for exceptional circumstances.[369] It is not meant to cure filing defects or to circumvent the regulations.[370] The burden is on the moving party to demonstrate exceptional circumstances.[371]

2. Joint Motion to Reopen

The time and numerical limitations do not apply to a motion to reopen or reconsider if all parties agree to the motion and the motion is jointly filed.[372] The procedure for requesting DHS's consent is to contact the U.S. Immigration and Customs Enforcement (ICE) Office of Chief Counsel's location that had jurisdiction over the case during the individual's immigration proceedings.[373] The request should be supported by affidavits or other evidence, including a complete copy of the application for relief.[374] The request should also include the proposed joint motion in a format that includes a signature block for the DHS attorney.[375]

DHS's consent will be given only in exceptional and compelling circumstances, according to a general counsel's office memorandum.[376] Factors DHS will consider are: (1) whether the new evidence is material; (2) whether the individual is statutorily eligible for relief; (3) whether the individual merits a favorable exercise of discretion; (4) the hardship to the individual and his or her U.S. citizen or lawful permanent resident (LPR) family members; (5) the individual's criminal history, if any; (6) the number and severity of the individual's immigration violations; (7) whether the individual has cooperated with, or his or her continued presence in the United States is desired for, a criminal or civil investigation or prosecution; and (8) whether the individual's removal is consistent with DHS objectives.[377]

---

[368] 8 CFR §§1003.2(a), 1003.23(b)(1) (2014).

[369] *Matter of Yauri*, 25 I&N Dec. 103, 110–12 (BIA 2009); *Matter of G–L–C–*, 23 I&N Dec. 359 (BIA 2002); *Matter of G–D–*, 22 I&N Dec. 1132 (BIA 1999); *Matter of L–V–K–*, 22 I&N Dec. 976 (BIA 1999); *Matter of J–J–*, 21 I&N Dec. 976 (BIA 1997).

[370] *Matter of J–J–*, 21 I&N Dec. 976 (BIA 1997).

[371] *Matter of Beckford*, 22 I&N Dec. 1216 (BIA 2000).

[372] 8 CFR §§1003.2(c)(3)(iii), 1003.23(b)(4)(iv) (2014).

[373] *See Office of the INS General Counsel, Revised Motions to Reopen Policy* (Dec. 23, 1997), *reprinted in* 75 INTERPRETER RELEASES 275 (Feb. 23, 1998). For a list of DHS district counsel offices, see App'x. 6D.

[374] *INS Revised Motions to Reopen Policy*, *supra* note 373.

[375] *Id.*

[376] *Id.*

[377] *Id.*

3. *Motion to Reopen Based on Changed Country Conditions*

The BIA or IJ may reopen a case to allow an applicant to apply or reapply for asylum, withholding of removal, or relief under the CAT based on changed circumstances arising in the country of nationality or in the country to which deportation has been ordered, if the evidence presented is material and was not available and could not have been discovered or presented at the previous hearing.[378] Although changed personal circumstances or extraordinary circumstances may excuse an applicant's failure to file his or her asylum application within one year of entry, those circumstances will not excuse filing a motion to reopen outside of the 90-day time period.[379] Motions to reopen cannot be based on changed personal circumstances, but must show a change in country conditions.[380]

Much of the jurisprudence addressing this rule has arisen from protection claims based on China's coercive population control policies. Most courts, including the

---

[378] INA §240(c)(7)(C)(ii); 8 CFR §§1003.2(c)(3)(ii), 1003.23(b)(4)(i) (2014). *See Haizem Liu v. Holder*, 727 F.3d 53, 57–58 (1st Cir. 2013) (finding that the mistreatment of Christians had not materially worsened since 2003); *Japarkylova v. Holder*, 615 F.3d 696, 702 (6th Cir. 2010) (advising that the applicant should file a motion to reopen based on changes in Kyrgyz Republic); *Malty v. Ashcroft*, 381 F.3d 942, 945–47 (9th Cir. 2004) (finding BIA abused its discretion in denying motion to reopen based on changed circumstances). *See also Mengistu v. Ashcroft*, 355 F.3d 1044, 1047 (7th Cir. 2004) (finding that the BIA's reliance on documents suggesting that Ethiopia had begun to withdraw its troops from Eritrea and that the United Nations had dispatched a peacekeeping mission was a "non sequitur" and did not address whether the applicant would face harm upon return); *Matter of J–G–*, 26 I&N Dec. 161 (BIA 2013) (finding that the applicant does not need to first rescind an in absentia order to file a motion to reopen based on changed circumstances); *Matter of A–N– and R–M–N–*, 22 I&N Dec. 953 (BIA 1999) (finding that asylum applicants from Afghanistan who were ordered deported in absentia need not demonstrate the cause of their failure to appear where their motion to reopen was based on changed country conditions); *Matter of J–J–*, 21 I&N Dec. 976 (BIA 1997).

[379] *Matter of C–W–L–*, 24 I&N Dec. 346 (BIA 2007) (denying an untimely motion to reopen where changed personal circumstances, not changed country conditions, were alleged). *See also, Matter of S–Y–G–*, 24 I&N Dec. 247 (BIA 2007) (articulating the BIA's standard for motions to reopen based on changed country conditions); *Matter of J–J–*, 21 I&N Dec. 976 (BIA 1997) (reiterating changed country conditions requirement for motions to reopen).

[380] *See, e.g., Almarez v. Holder*, 608 F.3d 638, 639–40 (9th Cir. 2010) (finding that HIV is a changed personal circumstance, not a changed country condition); *Averianova v. Holder*, 592 F.3d 931, 937 (8th Cir. 2010) (finding that limiting the exception to the time limitations for motions to reopen to changed country conditions is not a violation of equal protection); *Larngar v. Holder*, 562 F.3d 71, 76 (1st Cir. 2009) (a change typically will be categorized as a change in personal circumstances, as opposed to a change in country circumstances, if the change is self-induced); *Liu v. Att'y Gen.*, 555 F.3d 145, 151 (3d Cir. 2009); *Hui Zheng v. Holder*, 562 f.3d 647 (4th Cir. 2009) (following *Matter of C–W–L–* in finding that a motion to reopen beyond the 90-day period must be based on changed country conditions, not changed personal circumstances); *Chen v. Att'y Gen.*, 565 F.3d 805 (11th Cir. 2009); *Yuen Jin v. Mukasey*, 538 F.3d 143 (2d Cir. 2008); *Zhang v. Mukasey*, 543 F.3d 851, 857–58 (6th Cir. 2008); *Chen v. Mukasey*, 524 F.3d 1029 (9th Cir. 2008); *Wei v. Mukasey*, 545 f.3d 1248, 1255–57 (10th Cir. 2008); *Chen v. Gonzales*, 498 F.3d 758 (7th Cir. 2007); *Mekhael v. Mukasey*, 509 F.3d 326, 327(7th Cir. 2007) (finding full-scale war in Lebanon was not merely cumulative evidence); *Zheng v. Mukasey*, 509 F.3d 869 (8th Cir. 2007); *Wei Guang Wang v. BIA*, 437 F.3d 270, 273–74 (2d Cir. 2006); *Haddad v. Gonzales*, 437 F.3d 515, 517–18 (6th Cir. 2006); *Li Yong Zheng v. U.S. DOJ*, 416 F.3d 129, 130–31 (2d Cir. 2005).

BIA, have relied on the plain language of the regulations in holding that a change in personal circumstances alone, such as the birth of additional children, are not sufficient for a motion to reopen.[381] In fact, in *Matter of G–C–L–*, the BIA announced a withdrawal from its policy of automatically granting untimely motions to reopen for applicants fearing coercive population control methods.[382] The BIA reasoned that it had been five years since the law had changed to grant asylum on this basis and that the interest in finality of immigration proceedings took precedence.[383] Accordingly, individuals wishing to reopen their cases based on coercive population control methods — like any other individual seeking reopening based on changed circumstances — will have to show changed country conditions or that they meet one of the other exceptions to the 90-day time limit.

More recent events have had a similar impact on the law related to motions to reopen asylum claims. For example, any citizen or national of Iraq who applied for asylum or withholding of removal and whose claim was denied on or after March 1, 2003, based solely or in part on changed country conditions, was eligible to file a motion to reopen, notwithstanding any other provision of law, within six months of January 28, 2008, the date of enactment of the law.[384] The applicant was only eligible if she or he remained in the United States after the denial of the asylum or withholding claim original claim.[385]

Finally, courts have addressed whether individuals with previous asylum claims found to be frivolous or not credible were eligible to seek reopening based on changed circumstances in their home countries. The regulations state that if the applicant was previously denied asylum based on a finding that the application was frivolous, the applicant is ineligible to file a motion to reopen or reconsider, or for a stay of removal.[386] A negative credibility finding, however, will not make an individual ineligible for reopening based on changed circumstances.[387]

When a motion to reopen is based on a request for asylum, withholding of removal, or protection under CAT, and it is premised on new circumstances, the motion must contain a complete description of the new facts and articulate how those

---

[381] *See, e.g., Matter of C–W–L–*, 24 I&N Dec. 346 (BIA 2007) (barring a motion to reopen to file a successive asylum claim based on a change in personal circumstances); *Matter of S–Y–G–*, 24 I&N Dec. 247 (BIA 2007). *See also, e.g., Wei v. Mukasey*, 545 F.3d 1248, 1256 (10th Cir. 2008); *Yuen Jin v. Mukasey*, 538 F.3d 143 (2d Cir. 2007); *Zheng v. Att'y Gen.*, 549 F.3d 260, 267(3d Cir. 2007); *Cheng Chen v. Gonzales*, 498 F.3d 758, 760 (7th Cir. 2007).

[382] *Matter of G–C–L–*, 23 I&N Dec. 359 (BIA 2002).

[383] *Id.* at 362.

[384] National Defense Authorization Act of 2008, Pub. L. No., 110–181, §1247, *available at www.gpo.gov/fdsys/pkg/PLAW-110publ181/html/PLAW-110publ181.htm.*

[385] *Id.*

[386] 8 CFR §1003.23(b)(4)(i) (2014).

[387] *Boika v. Holder*, 727 F.3d 735, 742–44 (7th Cir. 2013).

circumstances affect the party's eligibility for relief.[388] The motion also must be accompanied by evidence of the alleged changed circumstances.[389]

4. *Motion to Reopen In Absentia Order Based on Lack of Notice*

A person who fails to appear at a removal hearing after proper notice shall be ordered removed *in absentia* if DHS has established "by clear, unequivocal, and convincing evidence" that written notice was provided and the individual is removable.[390] An *in absentia* removal order may not be appealed to the BIA.[391] Rather, an individual ordered removed *in absentia* must file a motion to reopen with the IJ, explaining why he or she missed the hearing. The standards for motions to reopen to rescind *in absentia* orders in deportation and exclusion proceedings differ from the standards in removal proceedings. If an individual was ordered deported or excluded *in absentia*, the time and numerical limitations do not apply to his or her motion to reopen.[392] If, however, the individual was ordered removed *in absentia*, the time limitations may *not* apply, but the numerical limitations do.[393]

A motion to reopen requesting that an *in absentia* order be rescinded asks the IJ to consider the reasons why the individual did not appear at his or her scheduled hearing.[394] An *in absentia* removal order may only be rescinded upon a motion to reopen filed beyond 90 days following the order in the following situations:

- If the motion to reopen is filed within 180 days after the date of the removal order if the individual demonstrates that the failure to appear was because of exceptional circumstances;[395] or
- If the motion to reopen is filed at any time after the date of the removal order if the individual did not receive proper notice in accordance with INA §239(a), or if the individual was in state or federal custody and the failure to appear was through no fault of his or her own.[396]

The filing of a motion to reopen under these circumstances must be filed with the IJ and not the BIA,[397] and will stay the removal of the individual pending disposition of the motion.[398]

---

[388] 8 CFR §1003.23(b)(4)(i) (2014); ICPM, chapter 5.7(e)(i); *BIA Practice Manual*, chapter 5.6(e)(i).

[389] 8 CFR §1003.23(b)(3) (2014); ICPM, chapter 5.7(e)(i); *BIA Practice Manual*, chapter 5.6(e)(i).

[390] INA §240(b)(5)(A).

[391] *Matter of Guzman*, 22 I&N Dec. 822 (BIA 1999).

[392] 8 CFR §§1003.2(c)(3)(i), 1003.23(b)(4)(iii) (2014); *Matter of N–B–*, 22 I&N Dec. 590 (BIA 1999); *Matter of Cruz-Garcia*, 22 I&N Dec. 1155 (BIA 1999).

[393] 8 CFR §§1003.2(c)(3), 1003.23(b)(4)(ii) (2014).

[394] ICPM, chapter 5.9(a). *See* ICPM, chapter 4.17.

[395] INA §240(b)(5)(C)(i); 8 CFR §§1003.2(c)(3)(i), 1003.23(b)(4)(ii) (2014).

[396] INA §240(b)(5)(C)(ii); 8 CFR §§1003.2(c)(3)(i), 1003.23(b)(4)(ii) (2014).

[397] *See, e.g., Singh v. Gonzales*, 436 F.3d 484 (5th Cir. 2006).

[398] INA §240(b)(5)(C).

The INA defines exceptional circumstances as circumstances "beyond the control of the alien," such as battery or extreme cruelty, serious illness or death of a spouse, parent, or child, "but not including less compelling circumstances."[399] The BIA employs a totality of the circumstances test in determining what is "exceptional" for purposes of considering a motion to reopen an *in absentia* order.[400] The totality of the circumstances may include: (1) supporting documentary evidence; (2) the respondent's efforts to contact the immigration court; (3) the respondent's promptness in filing the motion to reopen; (4) the strength of the respondent's underlying claim; (5) the harm the respondent would suffer if the motion to reopen is denied; and (6) any inconvenience to the government.[401] Some examples of exceptional circumstances that have merited a grant of a motion to reopen include:

- Where the respondent had confused the dates or times of the hearing;[402]
- Where the IJ had denied a continuance to respondent's counsel who was required to appear before a federal magistrate at the same time he was required to appear before the IJ;[403]
- Where there was ineffective assistance of counsel;[404] and
- Where the respondent was ordered removed *in absentia*, when he or she was present, but tardy.[405]

Individuals who are able to demonstrate exceptional circumstances such as these may file their motions to reopen an *in absentia* removal order within 180 days of the order, rather than within 90 days.

If the motion is based on the respondent not receiving proper notice of the hearing, there is no time limit for filing the motion to reopen.[406] Notice is sufficient if it is given at the most recent address provided by the respondent.[407] If the respondent changed addresses and did not notify the IJ of his or her change of address, "no

---

[399] INA §240(e).

[400] *Matter of W–F–*, 21 I&N Dec. 503, 509 (BIA 1996).

[401] *Kaweesa v. Gonzales*, 450 F.3d 62, 68–69 (1st Cir. 2006).

[402] *Id.*; *Singh v. INS*, 295 F.3d 1037 (9th Cir. 2002).

[403] *Herbert v. Ashcroft*, 325 F.3d 68 (1st Cir. 2003).

[404] *Aris v. Mukasey*, 517 F.3d 595 (2d Cir. 2008); *Montano Cisneros v. Att'y Gen.*, 514 F.3d 1224 (11th Cir. 2008); *Galvez-Vergara v. Gonzales*, 484 F.3d 798 (5th Cir. 2007); *Borges v. Gonzales*, 402 F.3d 398 (3d Cir. 2005); *Scorteanu v. INS*, 339 F.3d 407, 413–14 (6th Cir. 2003); *Lo v. Ashcroft*, 341 F.3d 934 (9th Cir. 2003); *Saakian v. INS*, 252 F.3d 21, 25 (1st Cir. 2001); *Matter of Grijalva*, 21 I&N Dec. 472 (BIA 1996).

[405] *See Camaj v. Holder*, 625 F.3d 988, 992, 93 (7th Cir. 2010); *Nazarova v. INS*, 171 F.3d 478 (7th Cir. 1999); *Jerezano v. INS*, 169 F.3d 613 (9th Cir. 1999).

[406] INA §240(b)(5)(C). *See Matter of G–Y–R–*, 23 I&N Dec. 181 (BIA 2001) (upholding an IJ's refusal to issue an in absentia order against an individual who was never advised of the consequences of her failure to provide legacy INS with a mailing address and who never received actual service of the NTA). *See also Matter of M–S–*, 22 I&N Dec. 349 (BIA 1998).

[407] INA §240(b)(5)(A).

written notice shall be required."[408] Previously, when notice of hearing was required by certified mail, there was a "strong presumption of effective service," and the respondent was required to present "substantial and probative evidence from the Postal Service, third party affidavits, or other similar evidence …" along with his or her motion to reopen.[409] However, now that notice is allowed by regular mail, the presumption of delivery is weaker, and the BIA has stated that "all relevant evidence ... must be considered."[410] In *Matter of M–R–A–*, The BIA held that the IJ may consider, among other evidence: (1) the respondent's affidavit; (2) affidavits from family members or other individuals who have personal knowledge of the facts; (3) the respondent's actions upon learning of the *in absentia* order and whether he or she exercised due diligence in seeking reopening; (4) evidence of prior applications or prima facie eligibility for relief, which would indicate an incentive to appear; (5) the respondent's previous attendance of hearings before the immigration court; and (6) whether the respondent properly changed his or her address with the court.[411]

> **Practice Pointer**: The BIA has held that an individual who is subject to an *in absentia* order does not have to first rescind that order before seeking to reopen proceedings based on changed country conditions, and further ruled that the one-motion numerical limitation is not applicable in this context.[412]

Other than exceptional circumstances or lack of notice, even motions to reopen *in absentia* orders are bound by the 90-day time limit.[413] The time and numerical limitations for motions to reopen *in absentia* orders may be subject to equitable tolling, as discussed below.[414]

5. *DHS Motions to Reopen*

If a motion to reopen or reconsider is filed by DHS in exclusion or deportation proceedings and the basis of the motion is fraud in the original proceeding or a crime that would support termination of asylum, the time and numerical limitations do not

---

[408] INA §240(b)(5)(B).

[409] *Matter of Grijalva*, 21 I&N Dec. 27, 37 (BIA 1995). *See, e.g., Mejia-Hernandez v. Holder*, 633 F.3d 818, 822–23 (9th Cir. 2011); *Sanchez v. Holder*, 627 F.3d 226, 232–34 (6th Cir. 2010); *Rodriguez-Cuate v. Gonzales*, 444 F.3d 1015, 1017–19 (8th Cir. 2006).

[410] *Matter of M–R–A–*, 24 I&N Dec. 665, 673–75 (BIA 2008).

[411] *Id.*

[412] *Matter of J–G–*, 26 I&N Dec. 161 (BIA 2013).

[413] *Matter of Monges*, 25 I&N Dec. 246 (BIA 2010).

[414] *See, e.g., Ruiz-Turcios v. Att'y Gen.*, 717 F.3d 847 (11th Cir. 2013); *Avila-Santoyo v. Att'y Gen.*, 713 F.3d 1357, 1362 n.4 (11th Cir. 2013); *Zhao v. INS*, 452 F.3d 154 (2d Cir. 2006); *Ray v. Gonzales*, 439 F.3d 582, 588–92 (9th Cir. 2006); *Borges v. Gonzales*, 402 F.3d 398 (3d Cir. 2005); *Pervaiz v. Gonzales*, 405 F.3d 488, 490 (7th Cir. 2005); *Joshi v. Ashcroft*, 389 F.3d 732, 734–35 (7th Cir. 2004); *Fajardo v. INS*, 300 F.3d 1018 (9th Cir. 2002); *Rodriguez-Lariz v. INS*, 282 F.3d 1218, 1223–26 (9th Cir. 2002).

apply.[415] The time and numerical limitations do not apply at all to DHS motions to reopen and motions to reconsider for cases in removal proceedings.[416]

6. *Ineffective Assistance of Counsel and Equitable Tolling*

Individuals in removal proceedings have a right to a reasonable opportunity to examine evidence presented against them, to present their own evidence, and to cross-examine witnesses.[417] However, ineffective assistance of counsel (IAC) may deprive individuals of this opportunity. The BIA has recognized the need for a remedy for IAC and has established a framework to evaluate whether IAC has occurred.[418] Under *Matter of Lozada,*[419] a motion to reopen or reconsider based on a claim of IAC requires: (1) that the motion be supported by an affidavit of the allegedly aggrieved respondent setting forth in detail the agreement that was entered into with counsel with respect to the actions to be taken and what representations counsel did or did not make to the respondent in this regard; (2) that counsel whose integrity or competence is being impugned be informed of the allegations leveled against him and be given an opportunity to respond; and (3) that the motion reflect whether a complaint has been filed with appropriate disciplinary authorities with respect to any violation of counsel's ethical or legal responsibilities, and if not, why not. The motion must show prejudice resulting from the counsel's ineffectiveness. At least one court has held that ineffective assistance can also be given by a paralegal, speaking on behalf of an attorney.[420]

- **Practice Pointer**: Motions to reopen based on ineffective assistance of counsel are considered under the standards set forth in *Matter of Lozada*[421] and *Matter of Assaad*[422] pending the outcome of any future rulemaking process.[423]

---

[415] 8 CFR §§1003.2(c)(3)(iv), 1003.23(b)(1) (2014).

[416] 8 CFR §§1003.2(c)(2)–(3), 1003.23(b)(1) (2014).

[417] INA §240(b)(4)(B).

[418] *See Matter of Lozada*, 19 I&N Dec. 637 (BIA 1988). Note that this framework was changed in *Matter of Compean I*, 24 I&N Dec. 710 (AG 2009). However, upon the urging of various advocacy organizations, the Attorney General (AG) reconsidered the case and issued a second *Matter of Compean* vacating the prior decision and returning to the *Matter of Lozada* framework. *Matter of Compean II*, 25 I&N Dec. 1 (AG 2009). The AG directed EOIR to initiate a rulemaking to address ineffective assistance of counsel and the *Lozada* framework; however, to date, no proposed rules have been published by EOIR.

[419] *Matter of Lozada*, 19 I&N Dec. 637 (BIA 1988).

[420] *Aris v. Mukasey*, 517 F.3d 595, 600–01 (2d Cir. 2008).

[421] *Matter of Lozada*, 19 I&N Dec. 637 (BIA 1988).

[422] *Matter of Assaad*, 23 I&N Dec. 553 (BIA 2003).

[423] *See Matter of Compean, Bangaly and J-E-C-*, 25 I&N Dec. 1 (AG 2009). *But see Afanwi v. Mukasey*, 526 F.3d 788, 799 (4th Cir. 2008) (holding that ineffective assistance of counsel is not a violation of due process). Note that *Afanwi v. Mukasey* was granted certiorari by the Supreme Court, which then remanded the case to the Fourth Circuit, where it has not yet been heard on remand.

A motion to reopen based on ineffective assistance of counsel may, under certain circumstances, excuse untimely filing of the motion.[424] If the individual filing the motion to reopen can demonstrate prejudice resulting from his or her counsel's ineffectiveness and that he or she exercised due diligence to seek reopening upon discovery of that ineffectiveness, the time may be "tolled" beyond the 90-day period for motions to reopen (or 180-day period for motions to reopen *in absentia* orders based on exceptional circumstances). At least two courts also have held that the numerical limitations on motions to reopen may be waived (or tolled) in cases in which an applicant has been defrauded by individuals purporting to provide legal representation.[425]

Each circuit has its own test for determining whether equitable tolling is applicable.[426] However, generally, questions of equitable tolling require at least a two-step analysis: (1) whether and when the ineffective assistance was or should have been discovered by a reasonable person; and (2) whether the individual exercised due diligence in filing a motion to reopen after discovering the ineffective assistance of counsel. According to the Supreme Court, an individual seeking equitable tolling bears the burden to establish, "that he has been pursuing his rights diligently" and "that some extraordinary circumstance stood in his way."[427]

---

[424] *Siong v. INS*, 376 F.3d 1030, 1036 (9th Cir. 2004).

[425] *See Rodriguez-Lariz v. INS*, 282 F.3d 1218, 1224 (9th Cir. 2002) (attorneys and non-attorney who failed to file a suspension application on time provided ineffective assistance of counsel and court remanded for BIA to grant second motion to reopen); *Lavorski v. INS*, 232 F.3d 124, 134–35 (2d Cir. 2000) (holding that ineffective assistance of counsel claim may be sufficient to justify equitable tolling, but applicant failed to exercise due diligence during period he sought to toll); *see also Fajardo v. INS*, 300 F.3d 1018, 1022 (9th Cir. 2002); *Socop-Gonzales v. INS*, 272 F.3d 1176, 1195 (9th Cir. 2001) (discussing generally the application of equitable tolling in circumstances where parties have failed to timely file a motion to reopen); *Varela v. INS*, 204 F.3d 1237, 1240 (9th Cir. 2000).

[426] *Kuusk v. Holder*, 732 F.3d 202, 305 (4th Cir. 2013) (holding that equitable tolling is only appropriate where the individual was prevented from asserting a claim or extraordinary circumstances beyond the individual's control made it impossible to file on time); *Bead v. Holder*, 703 F.3d 591 (1st Cir. 2012) (finding that a person must demonstrate due diligence during the entire period of time he or she wishes to toll, including the time when the ineffective assistance should have been discovered and the time following the discovery and preceding the motion to reopen); *El-Gazawy v. Holder*, 690 F.3d 852, 859–60 (7th Cir. 2012) (finding that the individual must demonstrate that he or she "could not reasonably have been expected to file earlier"); *Avagyan v. Holder*, 646 F.3d 672, 679–70 (9th Cir. 2011) (maintaining a three-part test for due diligence and equitable tolling); *Mezo v. Holder*, 615 F.3d 616 (6th Cir. 2010) (citing its five-part test for equitable tolling); *Rashid v. Mukasey*, 553 F.3d 127 (2d Cir. 2008) (finding that a person must demonstrate due diligence during the entire period of time he or she wishes to toll, including the time when the ineffective assistance should have been discovered and the time following the discovery and preceding the motion to reopen); *Riley v. INS*, 310 F.3d 1253 (10th Cir. 2002) (adopting the Second Circuit's approach).

[427] *Pace v. DiGuglielmo*, 544 U.S. 408, 418 (2005).

- **Practice Pointer**: For a detailed discussion of equitable tolling, see David Zhou's article, "Making Up for Lost Time: A Bright-Line Rule for Equitable Tolling in Immigration Cases."[428]

I. Contents of a Motion to Reopen or Reconsider

The federal regulations, as well as the immigration court and *BIA Practice Manual*, govern the content that must be included in a motion to reopen or reconsider.[429] All motions to reopen and motions to reconsider must be in writing and signed by the party or his or her representative.[430] They must be in English or accompanied by a certified English translation.[431] Both motions to reopen and motions to reconsider must state whether the validity of the exclusion, deportation, or removal order has been or is the subject of any judicial proceedings and, if so, the nature and date of the proceedings, the court in which the proceedings took place or is pending, and the result or status of the proceeding.[432] If the exclusion, deportation, or removal order is in effect, the motion to reopen must include a statement by or on behalf of the individual subject to the order regarding whether he or she is the subject of any pending criminal proceedings and, if so, the current status of those proceedings.[433] If the motion seeks discretionary relief, the motion must also include a statement by or on behalf of the moving party declaring whether he or she is the subject of any pending criminal prosecution and, if so, the nature and current status of the prosecution.[434] If oral argument is desired, a request should be made in the motion.[435]

A motion to reopen must state the new facts that will be proved at the hearing to be held if the motion is granted and must be supported by affidavits or other evidentiary material.[436] A motion to reopen proceedings for the purpose of submitting an application for relief must be accompanied by the application and all supporting documentation.[437] A motion to reopen will not be granted unless it appears to the BIA

---

[428] David Zhou, *Making Up for Lost Time: A Bright-Line Rule for Equitable Tolling in Immigration Cases*, 118 YALE L.J. 1245, 1246 (2009).

[429] 8 CFR §1003.2(e), 1003.23(b)(1)(i) (2014).

[430] 8 CFR §1003.23(b)(1)(i) (2014).

[431] 8 CFR §§1003.2(g)(1), 1003.23(b)(1) (2014).

[432] 8 CFR §§1003.2(e), 1003.23(b)(1)(i) (2014).

[433] 8 CFR §§1003.2(e), 1003.23(b)(1)(i) (2014).

[434] 8 CFR §§1003.2(e), 1003.23(b)(1)(i) (2014).

[435] 8 CFR §1003.2(h) (2014).

[436] 8 CFR §§1003.2(c)(1), 1003.23(b)(3), 103.5(a)(2) (2014); ICPM, chapter 5.7(b)(ii); *BIA Practice Manual*, chapter 5.6(a)(ii).

[437] 8 CFR §§1003.2(c)(1), 1003.23(b)(3) (2014). *See, e.g., Gen Lin v. Att'y Gen.*, 700 F.3d 683, 685–87 (3d Cor. 2012) (upholding the refusal to reopen an asylum case because the applicant failed to file a new asylum application with the motion to reopen); *Waggoner v. Gonzales*, 488 F.3d 632, 638–39 (5th Cir. 2007) (agreeing that a motion to reopen was properly denied where the respondent from Fiji argued changed circumstances but did not submit an application for asylum and withholding of removal with

Continued

or the IJ that the evidence sought to be offered is material and was not available and could not have been discovered or presented at a former hearing.[438]

A motion to reconsider must state the reasons for the motion by specifying the errors of fact or law in the prior IJ or BIA decision, and must be supported by pertinent legal authority.[439] If the motion is based on changes to the law, the motion should identify the charges and, where appropriate, provide copies of the law.[440] A party may not seek reconsideration of a decision denying a previous motion to reconsider.[441]

Motions to reopen and motions to reconsider must include the following documents:

- Form EOIR-27 (BIA) or EOIR-28 (IJ), Notice of Entry of Appearance if the moving party is represented by counsel;[442]
- A check or money order for $110 or fee waiver request (BIA),[443] or a fee receipt (IJ), if a fee is required;[444]
- A cover page labeled "Motion to Reopen" or "Motion to Reconsider";[445]
- A signed motion brief;[446]
- Documents and evidence in support of the motion;[447]
- If the motion is based on eligibility for relief, a copy of the application for that relief and all supporting documentation;[448]
- Proof of service on the opposing party;[449] and
- Form EOIR-33/IC or Form EOIR-33/BIA.[450]

If the motion to reopen is for an application that does not have a fee, no fee is required for the motion to reopen. For example, the $110 filing fee is not required for

---

the motion). *But see Matter of Yewondwosen*, 21 I&N Dec. 1025 (BIA 1997) (holding that the BIA or IJ may grant a motion to reopen where the individual fails to submit the application for relief in cases in which legacy INS/DHS joins in the motion).

438 8 CFR §§1003.2(c)(1), 1003.23(b)(3) (2014).

439 8 CFR §§1003.2(b)(1), 1003.23(b)(2) (2014).

440 ICPM, chapter 5.8(f) and App'x. J (Citation Guidelines); *BIA Practice Manual*, chapter 5.7(g).

441 8 CFR §§1003.2(b)(1), 1003.23(b)(2) (2014).

442 8 CFR §§1003.2(g)(1), 1003.23(b)(1)(ii) (2014); ICPM, chapters 5.7(b)(i), 5.9(b).

443 8 CFR §1003.2(g)(2)(i) (2014); *BIA Practice Manual*, chapters 3.4, 5.2, 5.6(b).

444 8 CFR §1003.23(b)(1)(ii) (2014); ICPM, chapters 3.4, 5.7(b)(i), 5.9(b)

445 ICPM, chapters 5.7(b)(i), 5.9(b) and App'x. F (Sample Cover Page).

446 8 CFR §1003.2(g)(3).

447 ICPM, chapters 5.2(e), 5.7(f); *BIA Practice Manual*, chs. 5.2(f), 5.6(f).

448 ICPM, chapters 5.2(g), 5.7(b)(i).

449 8 CFR §§1003.2(g)(1), 1003.23(b)(1)(ii) (2014).

450 ICPM, chapters 5.7(b)(i), 5.9(b).

motions to reopen or motions to reconsider based exclusively on a claim for asylum.[451]

If the opposing party is DHS, the motion should be served on the Office of Chief Counsel for the district in which the case was completed before the IJ.[452]

> ➢ **Practice Pointer**: For detailed guidance for preparing and filing motions to reopen and motions to reconsider with the immigration court, see the *Immigration Court Practice Manual*, chapters 5.7, 5.8, and 5.9, at *www.justice.gov/eoir/vll/OCIJPracManual/Practice_Manual_review.pdf#page=99*.[453] For detailed guidance for preparing and filing motions to reopen and motions to reconsider with the BIA, see chapters 5.6 and 5.7 of the *BIA Practice Manual*, available at *www.justice.gov/eoir/vll/qapracmanual/BIAPracticeManual.pdf#page=1*.[454]

J. Stays of Removal

The filing of a motion to reopen or a motion to reconsider does *not* stay the execution of any decision made in the case, except in the case of a motion to reopen an order entered *in absentia*.[455] A stay should be requested when the motion to reopen or reconsider is filed. Execution of the order will proceed unless a stay of execution is granted by the BIA, IJ, or DHS.[456]

> ➢ **Practice Pointer**: When removal is imminent, practitioners should file a motion for stay by hand or using a same-day delivery service. Practitioners also should call the BIA emergency stay line at 703-306-0093 to alert the BIA that an emergency stay has been filed. Otherwise, the motion for stay could get stuck in the mailroom and not reach an adjudicator until it is too late.

K. Replies to Motions

For motions filed with the BIA, the opposing party has 13 days from the date of service of the motion to file a brief in opposition to the motion directly with the BIA.[457] The BIA may extend the time within which a brief is to be submitted.[458] A

---

[451] *BIA Practice Manual*, chapter 3.4(b).

[452] 8 CFR §§1003.2(g)(1), 1003.23(b)(1)(ii) (2014).

[453] (last visited Mar. 7, 2015).

[454] (last visited Mar. 7, 2015).

[455] 8 CFR §§1003.2(f), 103.5(a)(1)(iv), 1003.23(b)(1)(v) (2014). *But see* INA §240(b)(5)(C) (stating that filing a motion to reopen based on failure to receive notice where an *in absentia* order was entered stays deportation); 8 CFR §1003.23(b)(4)(ii) (2014).

[456] 8 CFR §§1003.2(f), 1003.23(b)(1)(v) (2014).

[457] 8 CFR §1003.2(g)(3) (2014).

[458] *Id.*

motion is deemed unopposed unless a timely response is made.[459] However, the BIA may in its discretion consider a brief filed out of time.[460]

For motions filed with the IJ, the IJ may set and extend time limits for motions to reopen or reconsider.[461] Responses to motions to reopen and motions to reconsider are due within 15 days after the motion was received by the immigration court, unless otherwise specified by the IJ.[462] The IJ will deem the motion unopposed unless a timely response is made.[463]

L. Departure from the United States

A moving party's departure from the United States while a motion to reopen or reconsider is pending constitutes a withdrawal of the motion.[464] Moreover, according to the regulations and the BIA, a motion to reopen or reconsider may not be filed on behalf of an individual who has departed the United States subject to a deportation, exclusion, or removal order.[465] The BIA has held,[466] along with at least one court, that an IJ retains jurisdiction to reopen an *in absentia* case to address whether the applicant received notice of the hearing, even after the applicant had been removed.[467]

Several circuit courts have struck down the departure bar regulations as impermissible agency action in conflict with the plain language of the motion to reopen or reconsider statutes.[468] Although the Fourth Circuit agrees that individuals outside of the U.S. have a right to file a motion to reopen, the court has found that it was not an abuse of discretion to deny such a motion to reopen to seek asylum, because INA §208(a)(1) requires that the applicant be present in the United States in order to be eligible for asylum.[469]

---

[459] *Id.*; 8 CFR §1003.23(b)(1)(iv) (2014).

[460] 8 CFR §1003.2(g)(3) (2014).

[461] 8 CFR §1003.23(b)(1)(iv) (2014).

[462] ICPM, chapters 5.7(c), 5.9(c).

[463] 8 CFR §1003.23(b)(1)(iv) (2014).

[464] 8 CFR §§1003.2(d), 1003.23(b)(1) (2014).

[465] 8 CFR §§1003.2(d), 1003.23(b)(1) (2014); *Matter of Armendarez*, 24 I&N Dec. 646 (BIA 2008); *Matter of Yih-Hsiung Wang*, 17 I&N Dec. 565 (BIA 1980); *Matter of G–Y–B–*, 6 I&N Dec. 159 (BIA 1954).

[466] *Matter of Bulnes-Nolasco*, 25 I&N Dec. 57 (BIA 2009).

[467] *Contreras-Rodriguez v. Att'y Gen.*, 462 F.3d 1314 (11th Cir. 2006).

[468] *Santana v. Holder*, 731 F.3d 50 (1st Cir. 2013); *Bolieiro v. Holder*, 731 F.3d 32 (1st Cir. 2013); *Garcia-Carias v. Holder*, 697 F.3d 257 (5th Cir. 2012); *Lari v. Holder*, 697 F.3d 273 (5th Cir. 2012); *Contreras-Bocanegra v. Holder*, 678 F.3d 811 (10th Cir. 2012); *Jian Le Lin v. Att'y Gen.*, 681 F.3d 1236 (11th Cir. 2012); *Prestol Espinal v. Att'y Gen.*, 653 F.3d 213 (3d Cir. 2011); *Reyes-Torres v. Holder*, 645 F.3d 1073, 1075–77 (9th Cir. 2011); *Coyt v. Holder*, 593 F.3d 902, 905–08 (9th Cir. 2010); *William v. Gonzales*, 499 F.3d 329 (4th Cir. 2007); *Lin v. Gonzales*, 473 F.3d 979, 982 (9th Cir. 2007).

[469] *See Sadhvani v. Holder*, 596 F.3d 180 (4th Cir. 2009).

M. Effect of Motions to Reopen or Reconsider on Appeals

The filing of a motion to reopen or reconsider does not stay or extend the deadline for filing an appeal with the BIA.[470] Once an appeal has been filed with the BIA, the IJ no longer has jurisdiction over the case. Thus, motions may not be filed with the IJ after an appeal has been filed with the BIA.[471] A motion to reconsider that is filed with the BIA during the pendency of an appeal is generally treated as a motion to remand for further proceedings before the IJ.[472]

N. Rulings on Motions

The decision to grant or deny a motion to reopen or motion to reconsider is within the discretion of the IJ or BIA.[473] Rulings upon motions to reopen or reconsider must be made by written order.[474] A grant of a motion to reopen vacates the previous order and reinstates the removal proceedings. A grant of a motion to reconsider usually is accompanied by a new decision on the merits of the case. The IJ and BIA must clearly and fully explain any reasons for denial.[475]

Other than failure to comply with the numerical and timing limitations for a motion to reopen, an IJ or the BIA may deny a motion to reopen for: (1) failure to establish *prima facie* case for the underlying asylum, withholding of removal, or CAT relief; (2) failure to reasonably explain why the facts, evidence, or relief was not available sooner; and (3) as a matter of discretion.[476] A prima facie showing means "the evidence reveals a reasonable likelihood that the statutory requirements for relief have been satisfied."[477] It does not require a showing that the relief would be granted because a reopening it is not yet a ruling on the merits of the relief sought.[478]

A motion to reopen is not granted unless it appears to the IJ or BIA that the evidence offered is material and was not available and could not have been discovered or presented at an earlier stage in the proceedings.[479] A motion to reopen

---

[470] ICPM, chapters 5.7(g), 5.8(g); *BIA Practice Manual*, chapters 4.2(a)(ii), 5.7(h).

[471] ICPM, chapters 5.2(a), 5.7(h), 5.8(h); *BIA Practice Manual*, chapters 4.2(a)(ii), 5.6(g), 5.7(h).

[472] 8 CFR §1003.2(b)(1) (2014); *BIA Practice Manual*, chapter 5.7(h). *See BIA Practice Manual*, chapter 5.8.

[473] 8 CFR §§1003.2(a), 1003.23(b)(1)(iv) (2014).

[474] 8 CFR §1003.2(i) (2014).

[475] *Matter of M–P–*, 20 I&N Dec. 786 (BIA 1994). *See, e.g., Ruiz-Turcios v. Att'y Gen.*, 717 F.3d 847, 849 n.2 (11th Cir. 2013); *Smith v. Holder*, 627 F.3d 427, 634–39 (1st Cir. 2010); *Franco-Rosendo v. Gonzales*, 454 F.3d 965 (9th Cir. 2006); *Zhao v. Gonzales*, 404 F.3d 295, 304–06 (5th Cir. 2005); *Bhasin v. Gonzales*, 423 F.3d 977, 986 (9th Cir. 2005).

[476] *INS v. Rios-Pineda*, 471 U.S. 444 (1985). *See, e.g., Allabani v. Gonzales*, 402 F.3d 668, 675–78 (6th Cir. 2005); *Selimi v. Ashcroft*, 360 F.3d 736 (7th Cir. 2004); *Fesseha v. Ashcroft*, 333 F.3d 13, 20–21 (1st Cir. 2003); *Matter of Leon-Orosco and Rodrigues-Colas*, 19 I&N Dec. 136 (AG 1984).

[477] *Matter of S–V–*, 22 I&N Dec. 1306, 1308 (BIA 2000). *See Matter of C–C–*, 23 I&N Dec. 899 (BIA 2006); *Matter of Rodriguez-Vera*, 17 I&N Dec. 105 (BIA 1979).

[478] *Matter of L–O–G–*, 21 I&N Dec. 413 (BIA 1996).

[479] 8 CFR §§1003.2(c)(1), 1003.23(b)(3) (2014).

based on an application for relief will not be granted if it appears the individual's right to apply for that relief was fully explained and the individual had an opportunity to apply for that relief at an earlier stage in the proceedings, unless the relief is sought on the basis of circumstances that have arisen subsequent to that stage of the proceedings.[480]

The U.S. Supreme Court has given the AG great deference in exercising discretion in considering motions to reopen immigration court proceedings. In *INS v. Rios-Pineda*, the Court stated, "Even assuming the respondent's motion to reopen made out a *prima facie* case of eligibility ... the Attorney General had discretion to deny the motion."[481] The regulations also recognize the discretion to deny a motion to reopen even if the moving party has established a *prima facie* case for relief.[482]

The BIA may review an IJ's denial of a motion to reopen or motion to reconsider. In doing so, the BIA is not limited to the issues raised in the motion, but may review laws that were not addressed in the motion, as well as issues that the IJ did not address in his or her order that were not appealed.[483]

III. Conclusion

An unfavorable decision by the BIA is not necessarily the final word on an individual's case, as he or she may be able to seek review before the federal courts.[484] The U.S. circuit courts of appeals have exclusive jurisdiction to review final orders of removal, except for expedited removal orders under INA §235(b)(1).[485] Accordingly, the U.S. circuit courts of appeals may review:

- BIA decisions to issue a final order of removal, including findings of removability and denials of applications for relief;
- BIA decisions to deny a motion to reopen or a motion to reconsider; BIA decisions to deny asylum in asylum-only proceedings;
- Orders of removal issued by ICE under INA §241(a)(5) — reinstatement of removal; and

---

[480] *Id.*

[481] *INS v. Rios-Pineda*, 471 U.S. 444 (1985). *See also INS v. Abudu*, 485 U.S. 94 (1988) (extending substantial deference to EOIR in their decisions on motions to reopen in the asylum context); *INS v. Doherty*, 502 U.S. 314 (1992) (extending substantial deference to EOIR in their decisions on motions to reopen in the withholding context).

[482] 8 CFR §1003.2(a) (2014).

[483] *Sosa-Valenzuela v. Holder*, 692 F.3d 1103, 1109–12 (10th Cir. 2012).

[484] See chapter 12 for a detailed discussion of seeking judicial review before the federal courts.

[485] INA §242(a)(1). *See* chapter 4 for a detailed discussion of expedited removal and seeking protection from persecution and torture while subject to the expedited removal provisions. See chapter 12 for a detailed discussion of judicial review.

- Orders of removal issued by ICE under INA §238(b) — administrative removal.[486]

[486] *See* American Immigration Council, Legal Action Center Practice Advisory, "How to File a Petition for Review," at 3, available at *www.legalactioncenter.org/sites/default/files/how_to_file_a_petition_for_review_2011_update_4-23-13.pdf* (last visited Mar. 7, 2015).

Chapter Twelve
Judicial Review

The Immigration and Nationality Act (INA), allows judicial review of final orders of removal.[1] Therefore, decisions by the Board of Immigration Appeals (BIA) denying asylum, withholding of removal under INA §241(b)(3), and protection under the Convention Against Torture (CAT) may be reviewed by the U.S. circuit courts of appeals.[2] Section 242 of the INA as enacted by the Illegal Immigration Reform and Immigrant Responsibility Act of 1996 (IIRAIRA)[3] and as amended by the REAL ID Act of 2005,[4] sets forth the jurisdictional basis for petitions for review, as well as the rules and procedures that govern them.[5] The Federal Rules of Appellate Procedure (FRAP), as well as the local rules for the relevant U.S. circuit courts of appeals, are binding on individuals who wish to file petitions for review of the denial of asylum, withholding of removal, and CAT claims.

- ➢ **Practice Pointer**: The FRAP are available on the U.S. Courts website at *www.uscourts.gov/uscourts/rules/appellate-procedure.pdf*,[6] and each circuit's own local rules are listed on their websites.[7]

---

* The author would like to thank Thomas K. Ragland of Benach Ragland LLP for his invaluable input in reviewing this chapter.

[1] *See generally*, INA §242.

[2] *See id.*; Foreign Affairs Reform and Restructuring Act of 1998 (FARRA), Pub. L. No. 105-277, div. G, 112 Stat. 2681–822, §2242(d). *See also* 8 CFR §§208.18(e)(1), 1208.18(e)(1) (2014).

[3] Illegal Immigration Reform and Immigrant Responsibility Act of 1996 (IIRAIRA), Div. C of the Omnibus Appropriations Act of 1996 (H.R. 3610), Pub. L. No. 104-208, 110 Stat. 3009.

[4] REAL ID Act, Pub. L. No. 109-13, 119 Stat. 231 (May 11, 2005).

[5] INA §242(a).

[6] (last visited Mar. 7, 2015).

[7] *See, e.g.*, United States Court of Appeals for the Fourth Circuit, Fed. & Local Rules of Appellate Procedure, available at *www.ca4.uscourts.gov/rules-and-procedures/federal-local-rules-of-appellate-procedure* (last visited Mar. 7, 2015).

The most common avenue of review for individuals denied asylum, withholding of removal, or CAT relief in INA §240 proceedings is by filing a petition for review.[8] In very limited circumstances, a petition for review also may be filed to seek review of a removal order issued by the U.S. Department of Homeland Security (DHS). Arguably, because the REAL ID Act does not address habeas corpus review of detention, review may also be sought under a federal district court's general habeas corpus jurisdiction for individuals in DHS custody or subject to a final order of removal.[9] This chapter does not address current law and procedures for filing a habeas petition.[10] Rather, this chapter focuses on current law and procedures for filing petitions for review before the U.S. circuit courts of appeals.

- **Practice Pointer**: For further information regarding habeas petitions, see the American Immigration Council Legal Action Center's Practice Advisory, "Introduction to Habeas Corpus" (June 2008), available on the Legal Action Center's website at *www.legalactioncenter.org/sites/default/files/lac_pa0406.pdf.*[11]

I. Jurisdiction Over Petitions for Review

The Department of Justice's Office of Immigration Litigation (OIL) is the federal agency charged with writing motions and briefs and arguing cases on behalf of the U.S. government before the U.S. circuit courts of appeals.[12] Typically, the first issue this office evaluates upon being served with a new petition for review is whether the circuit court has jurisdiction to review the matter. Jurisdictional questions can be very complex in the immigration context, given the significant discretion afforded to federal agencies and the amendments to the INA made by IIRAIRA and the REAL ID Act of 2005, which include a number of restrictions on judicial review.[13] Thus, the proper filing of a petition for review of the denial of an asylum, withholding of removal, or CAT claim begins with a full understanding of when the circuit courts have jurisdiction over a petition for review and when they do not.

---

[8] INA §242; 8 USC §1252 (2012).

[9] *See generally* 28 USC §§2241, 1651 (2012); U.S. Const. art. I, §9, cl. 2; *see also* Gerald Seipp, *Federal Court Jurisdiction to Review Immigration Decisions: A Tug of War between the Three Branches*, 07-04 IMMIGRATION BRIEFINGS (West) 3 (Apr. 2007); Lucas Guttentag, *The 1996 Immigration Act: Federal Court Jurisdiction—Statutory Restrictions and Constitutional Rights*, 74 INTERPRETER RELEASES 245 (Feb. 10, 1997).

[10] For further information regarding habeas petitions, see Am. Immigration Council Legal Action Ctr. Practice Advisory, *Introduction to Habeas Corpus* (June 2008), *available at www.legalactioncenter.org/sites/default/files/lac_pa_0406.pdf* (last visited Mar. 7, 2015).

[11] (last visited Mar. 7, 2015).

[12] *See* U.S. Dep't of Justice, Civil Div., Office of Immigration Litigation (OIL), *Appellate Section*, *available at www.justice.gov/civil/appellate-section* (last visited Mar. 7, 2015).

[13] *See Chevron U.S.A. Inc. v. Natural Res. Def. Council*, 467 U.S. 837 (1978); INA §242(a)(2)(B).

Overall, the U.S. circuit courts of appeals have exclusive jurisdiction to review final orders of removal, except for expedited removal orders under INA §235(b)(1).[14] An order is final when a determination has been made by the BIA or when the period for seeking BIA review has expired.[15] Accordingly, the U.S. circuit courts of appeals may review the following:

- BIA decisions to issue a final order of removal, including findings of removability and denials of applications for relief;
- BIA decisions to deny a motion to reopen or a motion to reconsider;
- BIA decisions to deny asylum in asylum-only proceedings;
- Orders of removal issued by U.S. Immigration and Customs Enforcement (ICE) under INA §241(a)(5) — reinstatement of removal; and
- Orders of removal issued by ICE under INA §238(b) — administrative removal.[16]

Petitions for review may challenge: (1) erroneous applications or interpretations of the INA and its implementing regulations; (2) violations of constitutional rights; (3) erroneous findings of fact; and (4) abuse of discretion by the agency that issued the final order of removal. However, the circuit court's jurisdiction to review these challenges depends on whether a bar to judicial review under INA §242 applies to the decision, the nature of the claim, or the individual challenging the decision. If a bar to judicial review applies, the circuit court may only review questions of law or constitutional claims. Thus, it is essential for government employees, advocates, and practitioners to understand how the relevant circuit has interpreted the various bars to judicial review.

A. Bars to Judicial Review

Except as provided under the REAL ID Act,[17] a federal court is barred from reviewing a final order of removal in the following types of cases:

- Negative credible fear determinations;
- Noncitizens convicted of certain crimes; and
- Reinstated orders of removal.

Each of these is discussed below in greater detail.

---

[14] INA §242(a)(1). See chapter 4 for a detailed discussion of expedited removal and seeking protection from persecution and torture while subject to the expedited removal provisions.

[15] INA §101(a)(47)(B); 8 CFR §1241.1 (2014).

[16] *See* Am. Immigration Council Legal Action Ctr. Practice Advisory, *How to File a Petition for Review*, at 3, *available at www.legalactioncenter.org/sites/default/files/how_to_file_a_petition_for_review_2011_update_4-23-13.pdf* (last visited Mar. 7, 2015).

[17] INA §242(a)(2)(D); 8 USC §1252(a)(2)(D) (2012).

1. Negative Credible Fear Determinations

A determination by an immigration judge (IJ) that an individual failed to establish a credible fear of persecution in expedited removal proceedings is not reviewable in federal court (or by the BIA).[18]

2. Noncitizens Convicted of Certain Crimes

A federal court may *not* review a final order of removal of any individual who has been convicted of:

- An aggravated felony;
- A crime involving moral turpitude (unless such crime falls within a narrow exception);
- Two crimes involving moral turpitude;
- Two crimes for which the aggregate sentences to confinement are five years or more;
- Controlled substances offenses;
- Controlled substance trafficking offenses;
- Prostitution and prostitution-related offenses;
- Commercialized vice offenses;
- Certain firearms offenses; and
- Miscellaneous treason, sedition, and sabotage offenses; or
- If the individual is a drug abuser or a drug addict.[19]

If, however, the individual was placed in proceedings prior to April 1, 1997, the case may be a so-called "transitional" case in which judicial review is still available. A federal court may review whether a crime or offense constitutes an aggravated felony or other bar to review.

3. Reinstated Orders of Removal

An order of removal that is reinstated after an individual illegally re-enters the United States is "not subject to being reopened or reviewed."[20]

B. Restrictions on Judicial Review

The following determinations made during the adjudication of an asylum or withholding claim generally are *not* reviewable:

- Safe third country;

---

[18] INA §§235(b)(1)(B)(iii)(III), (C). See chapter 4 for a detailed discussion of credible fear determinations and ways to challenge negative credible fear findings.

[19] INA §242(a)(2)(C); 8 USC §1252(a)(2)(C) (2012).

[20] INA §241(a)(5); 8 USC §1251(a)(5) (2012). See chapter 4 for a detailed discussion of reinstatement of removal.

- One-year filing deadline;
- Previous denial of asylum;
- Terrorism-related bars to eligibility;
- Expedited removal determinations; and
- Discretionary determinations by the IJ or BIA.

Each of these restrictions on judicial review is discussed below in more detail.

1. *Safe Third Country*

A determination that the individual may not apply for asylum because he or she may be removed to a safe third country is not reviewable in federal court.[21]

2. *One-Year Filing Deadline*

According to the INA, "No court shall have jurisdiction to review any determination by the Attorney General" under the provisions listing exceptions to eligibility for asylum, including the safe third country, one-year filing deadline, and previous asylum denial grounds of ineligibility, as well as the "changed conditions" exception to the one-year filing deadline and previous asylum denial grounds.[22] Thus, a determination that an individual is not eligible for asylum because his or her application is time-barred and the applicant did not demonstrate that he or she falls within the extraordinary or changed circumstances exceptions, may not be reviewable by a circuit court.[23]

However, following the REAL ID Act's amendments to the INA, which restored direct judicial review of constitutional claims and questions of law,[24] some circuits have found that they do have jurisdiction to review the BIA's denial of asylum based on failure to meet the one-year filing deadline, as long as the one-year filing deadline issue constitutes a question of law or a constitutional claim.[25] Not all circuits have concluded that they may review issues related to the one-year filing deadline because

---

[21] INA §208(a)(3); 8 USC §1158(a)(3) (2012).

[22] INA §208(a)(3).

[23] *See* INA §208(a)(3); 8 USC §1158(a)(3) (2012).

[24] *See* INA §242(a)(2)(D).

[25] *See Lumataw v. Holder*, 582 F.3d 78, 83–85 (1st Cir. 2009) (holding that the Respondent had raised a "colorable, non-frivolous legal defect" underlying the IJ and BIA timeliness determinations, and that pursuant to 8 USC §1252(a)(2)(D), it properly fell within their jurisdiction to review); *Zheng v. Mukasey*, 552 F.3d 277, 286 (2d Cir. 2009); *Hakopian v. Mukasey*, 551 F.3d 843, 845 (9th Cir. 2008); *Khunaverdiants v. Mukasey*, 548 F.3d 760, 764–65 (9th Cir. 2008); *Lin v. Gonzales*, 190 F. App'x 301 (4th Cir. 2006); *Krisman v. Gonzales*, 199 F. App'x 299 (4th Cir. 2006). *See also Spina v. DHS*, 70 F.3d 116, 123 (2d Cir. 2006); *Iasu v. Chertoff*, 426 F. Supp. 2d 1124 (D. Cal. 2006); *Walters v. Ashcroft*, 198 F. App'x 78 (2d Cir. 2006); *Restrepo v. Winfrey*, 162 Fed. App'x 311 (5th Cir. 2006); *Tilley v. Chertoff*, 144 Fed. App'x 536 (6th Cir. 2005). *See also Moreno-Bravo v. Gonzales*, 463 F.3d 253 (2d Cir. 2006) (holding that any habeas petitions pending before an appellate court on the effective date of the REAL ID Act are properly converted to petitions for review and retained by that appellate court).

the courts have varying interpretations of what constitutes a "question of law." While most courts agree that a question of law includes the application of statutes and regulations to undisputed facts, only the Second and Ninth Circuit U.S. Courts of Appeals have held that questions of law also include mixed questions of law and fact.[26] Therefore, in the Second and Ninth Circuits, a determination regarding changed or extraordinary circumstances for purposes of the one-year filing deadline exceptions is considered a mixed question of law and fact, which the court has jurisdiction to review.[27]

- **Practice Pointer**: At least one court found that a determination regarding the one-year filing deadline is reviewable in habeas corpus proceedings in a federal district court.[28]

3. *Previous Asylum Denial*

A determination that an individual is ineligible for asylum because he or she was previously denied asylum and has failed to establish changed circumstances is *not* reviewable in federal court.[29]

4. *Terrorism-Related Bars to Eligibility for Relief*

A court may *not* review a determination that an individual is barred from asylum because he or she is inadmissible for: (1) having engaged in terrorist activity; (2) being likely to engage in such activity; (3) having incited such activity; (4) being a representative of a terrorist organization (as designated by the Secretary of State); (5) being a representative of a group that endorses terrorist activity; or (6) using his or her position of prominence to endorse or espouse terrorist activity.[30]

---

[26] *See Viridiana v. Holder*, 646 F.3d 1230, 1234 (9th Cir. 2011) (finding jurisdiction to review the mixed question of law and fact regarding whether immigration consultant fraud excuses the one-year filing deadline); *Taslimi v. Holder*, 590 F.3d 981, 985 (9th Cir. 2010); *Husyev v. Mukasey*, 528 F.3d 1172, 1178 (9th Cir. 2008); *Ramadan v. Gonzales*, 479 F.3d 646, 650 (9th Cir. 2007); *Chen v. DOJ*, 471 F.3d 315, 322 (2d Cir. 2006).

[27] *See Taslimi v. Holder*, 590 F.3d at 985; *Husyev v. Mukasey*, 528 F.3d at 1178; *Ramadan v. Gonzales*, 479 F.3d at 650; *Chen v. DOJ*, 471 F.3d 315, 322 (2d Cir. 2006). *But see .Khunaverdiants v. Mukasey*, 548 F.3d 760, 765 (9th Cir. 2008) (finding that facts must be undisputed to create a mixed question of law and fact); *Zhu v. Gonzales*, 493 F.3d 588, 596, n. 31 (5th Cir. 2007) (rejecting the Ninth Circuit's reasoning for their jurisdiction over mixed questions of law and fact under the REAL ID Act); *Nakimbugwe v. Gonzales*, 475 F.3d 281, 284 (5th Cir. 2007) (noting that "Many determinations of timeliness are based on an IJ's assessment of facts and circumstances that affected the applicant's filing, and even after the passage of the REAL ID Act, such rulings are clearly unreviewable by this Court).

[28] *See Kanivets v. Riley*, 320 F. Supp. 2d 297, 300–01 (E.D. Pa. 2004) (holding that the IJ erred in finding that the asylum application was time barred).

[29] INA §208(a)(3); 8 USC §1158(a)(3) (2012).

[30] INA §208(b)(2)(D); 8 USC §1158(b)(2)(D) (2012).

5. *Expedited Removal Determinations*

Individuals who are apprehended upon arrival with no documents or purportedly false documents have limited judicial review available through habeas corpus proceedings.[31] Such review is limited to issues of whether the individual is an alien, whether the individual was ordered removed in expedited proceedings, and whether the individual is a lawful permanent resident (LPR) or was previously granted asylum or admitted as a refugee.[32]

6. *Discretionary Determinations by the IJ or BIA*

The INA generally prohibits judicial review of discretionary decisions or actions specified by the INA to be within the discretion of the agencies.[33] In *Kucana v. Holder*, however, the U.S. Supreme Court specified that the restriction against review of discretionary determinations only applies to determinations that are made discretionary by statute, not to determinations that the Attorney General (AG) has declared to be discretionary through regulation.[34] Thus, judicial review is precluded if the decision is specified under the INA to be discretionary and if the decision is in fact discretionary.

The INA specifies that this rule applies to any discretionary determination "other than the granting of relief under section 208(a)" of the INA — asylum.[35] Moreover, withholding of removal under INA §241(b)(3) and protection under the CAT are not discretionary forms of relief. Thus, despite the jurisdiction-stripping provisions of INA §242(a)(2)(B), the circuit courts retain jurisdiction over most issues related to these forms of protection from persecution and torture, other than the specific asylum-related issues discussed above (*e.g.*, safe third country, one-year filing deadline, and previous asylum denial).

In the context of asylum, withholding of removal, and CAT claims, however, some circuit courts have found that they lack jurisdiction over the following discretionary determinations:

- The denial of a continuance;[36]
- The BIA's refusal to reopen a case *sua sponte*;[37] and

---

[31] INA §242(e)(2); 8 USC §1252(e)(2) (2012).

[32] INA §242(e)(2); 8 USC §1252(e)(2) (2012). *See also* chapter 4 for a detailed discussion of expedited removal and the types of determinations that may be reviewed by the federal courts.

[33] INA §242(a)(2)(B).

[34] *Kucana v. Holder*, 558 U.S. 233 (2010).

[35] INA §242(a)(2)(B)(ii); 8 USC §1252(a)(2)(B)(ii) (2012).

[36] *Malik v. Mukasey*, 546 F.3d 890 (7th Cir. 2008); *Yerkovich v. Ashcroft*, 381 F.3d 990 (10th Cir. 2004); *Onyinkwa v. Ashcroft*, 376 F.3d 797 (8th Cir. 2004).

[37] *Briones v. Att'y Gen.*, 443 Fed. Appx. 534 (11th Cir. 2011); *Gor v. Holder*, 607 F.3d 180 (6th Cir. 2010); *Luis v. INS*, 196 F.3d 36, 40 (1st Cir. 1999); *Ali v. Gonzales*, 448 F.3d 515, 518 (2d Cir. 2006) (per curiam); *Calle-Vujiles v. Ashcroft*, 320 F.3d 472, 474–75 (3d Cir. 2003); *Doh v. Gonzales*, 193 Fed. App'x 245, 246 (4th Cir. 2006) (per curiam) (unpublished); *Enriquez-Alvarado v. Ashcroft*, 371

Continued

- Any cause or claim regarding the AG's decision or action to commence proceedings, adjudicate cases, or execute removal orders. [38]

On the other hand, some courts have found that they do have jurisdiction over the following determinations:

- The denial of a continuance; [39] and
- Asylum claims by visa waiver program entrants, even though the BIA order does not expressly order removal.[40]

C. Questions of Law and Constitutional Claims

The courts generally will assume jurisdiction over non-discretionary determinations within the context of a discretionary benefit and, following the REAL ID Act's amendments to the INA, any questions of law or constitutional claims.[41] Questions of law may include whether an applicant is statutorily eligible for a particular form of relief (including discretionary forms of relief), as well as the application of statutes, regulations, and other legal concepts to undisputed facts.

Constitutional claims may challenge the violation of an individual's right to fundamentally fair proceedings and resulting interference with his or her Fifth Amendment liberty interest. Whether an individual's due process rights have been violated depends on the facts and circumstances of the case.

In general, courts will rely on the *Mathews v. Eldridge* test in balancing: (1) the individual's private interest affected; (2) the risk of erroneous deprivation of a private interest through the procedures used and the probative value of additional procedural safeguards; and (3) the government's interest.[42] A number of procedural safeguards also have been established by the statute and regulations, and violations of those safeguards may be grounds for constitutional due process claims before the circuit courts. For example, a respondent must be given a reasonable opportunity to present,

---

F.3d 246, 248–50 (5th Cir. 2004); *Harchenko v. INS,* 379 F.3d 405, 410–11 (6th Cir. 2004); *Pilch v. Ashcroft,* 353 F.3d 585, 586 (7th Cir.2003); *Tamenut v. Mukasey,* 521 F.3d 1000, 1005 (8th Cir. 2008) (*en banc*) (per curiam); *Ekimian v. INS,* 303 F.3d 1153, 1159 (9th Cir. 2002); *Belay-Gebru v. INS,* 327 F.3d 998, 1000–01 (10th Cir. 2003); *Lenis v. Att'y Gen.*, 525 F.3d 1291, 1292–93 (11th Cir. 2008).

[38] INA §242(g); 8 USC §1252(g) (2012); *see also Reno v. American-Arab Anti-Discrimination Comm.*, 525 U.S. 471 (1999); *Rodriguez v. Att'y Gen.*, 414 Fed. Appx. 484, 488 (3d Cir. 2011); *Adegbuji v. Fifteen ICE Agents*, 169 Fed. Appx. 733, 735 (3d Cir. 2006). *But see Chehazeh v. Att'y Gen.*, 666 F.3d 118 (3d Cir. 2012).

[39] *Sandoval-Luna v. Mukasey*, 526 F.3d 1243 (9th Cir. 2008); *Lendo v. Gonzales*, 493 F.3d 439 (4th Cir. 2007); *Alsamhouri v. Gonzales*, 484 F.3d 117 (1st Cir. 2007); *Zafar v. Att'y Gen.*, 461 F.3d 1357, 1360 (11th Cir. 2006); *Khan v. Att'y Gen.*, 448 F.3d 226 (3d Cir. 2006); *Ahmed v. Gonzales*, 447 F.3d 433 (5th Cir. 2006); *Sanusi v. Gonzales*, 445 F.3d 193 (2d Cir. 2006); *Abu-Khaliel v. Gonzales*, 436 F.3d 627 (6th Cir. 2006); *Subhan v. Ashcroft*, 383 F.3d 591 (7th Cir. 2004).

[40] *Shehu v. Att'y Gen.*, 482 F.3d 652, 656 (3d Cir. 2007); *Kanacevic v. INS*, 448 F.3d 129, 134–35 (2d Cir. 2006); *Nreka v. Att'y Gen.*, 408 F.3d 1361, 1367 (11th Cir. 2005).

[41] INA §242(a)(2)(D).

[42] *Mathews v. Eldridge*, 424 U.S. 319 (1976).

review, and respond to evidence and to cross-examine witnesses.[43] He or she also has the right to be represented at no expense to the government.[44] Denial of a motion to continue or motion to change venue, failure to allow witnesses to testify, inadequate translations, and an IJ's lack of neutrality are all circumstances that may interfere with an individual's due process rights in removal proceedings.

Finally, circuit courts also may review an exercise of discretion to ensure that it is a lawful exercise of discretion: (1) the adjudicator must give specific and cogent reasons for the decision, and (2) the reasons must be consistent with controlling law. Finally, courts retain jurisdiction to determine whether they have jurisdiction over a petition for review.

- **Practice Pointer**: Although the REAL ID Act restored the jurisdiction of the courts of appeals to review all constitutional issues and questions of law related to a final order of removal, it also eliminated habeas corpus jurisdiction over all final orders of deportation, exclusion, and removal.[45] Instead, it provides that a petition for review filed with an appropriate court of appeals is the sole and exclusive means for judicial review of such orders.[46] Any pending habeas corpus petition is automatically converted to a petition for review before the appropriate court of appeals.[47] Thus, outside of challenges to detention, few immigration issues remain reviewable under habeas corpus.[48] It is therefore essential for practitioners to assist their clients in filing timely petitions for review to preserve their right to seek judicial review.

---

[43] INA §240(b)(4)(B).

[44] INA §240(b)(4)(A).

[45] *See, e.g., Bakhtriger v. Elwood*, 360 F.3d 414 (3d Cir. 2004) (determining that the court lacked jurisdiction over a case involving an asylum applicant who sought habeas corpus review of a discretionary denial of asylum because his or her criminal convictions barred the filing of a petition for review).

[46] *See Spina v. DHS*, 70 F.3d 116, 123 (2d Cir. 2006); *Lasu v. Chertoff*, 426 F. Supp. 2d 1124 (D. Cal. 2006); *Walters v. Ashcroft*, 198 Fed. App'x 78 (2d Cir. 2006); *Restrepo v. Winfrey*, 162 Fed. App'x 311 (5th Cir. 2006); *Tilley v. Chertoff*, 144 Fed. App'x 536 (6th Cir. 2005); *see also INS v. St. Cyr*, 533 U.S. 289 (2001); *Kanivets v. Riley*, 320 F. Supp. 2d 297, 300 (E.D. Pa. 2004) (holding that the IJ erred in finding that the asylum application was time barred); Am. Immigration Council Practice Advisory, *Judicial Review Provisions of the REAL ID Act* (June 7, 2005), *available at www.legalactioncenter.org/sites/default/files/realid6705.pdf*.

[47] REAL ID Act of 2005, Pub. L. No. 109-13, div. B, §106, 119 Stat. 231, 310–11.

[48] For an excellent overview of these changes and of habeas corpus review, see the Am. Immigration Council Legal Action Ctr.'s Practice Advisory, *Judicial Review Provisions of the REAL ID Act* (June 7, 2005), available at *www.legalactioncenter.org/sites/default/files/realid6705.pdf* (last visited Mar. 7, 2015), Am. Immigration Council Legal Action Ctr.'s Practice Advisory, *Introduction to Habeas Corpus* (June 2008), *available at www.legalactioncenter.org/sites/default/files/lac_pa_0406.pdf* (last visited Mar. 7, 2015).

1. **Chevron *Deference***

Generally speaking, Congress intended the courts, not the agencies, to interpret statutes.[49] However, in some cases, Congress has delegated to the agency the authority to resolve ambiguities and fill gaps left by some statutes.[50] Where Congress delegates authority to an administrative agency to promulgate rules to implement a statute, that agency's interpretation of the statute usually is entitled to deferential review.[51] Under certain circumstances, therefore, the courts will defer to the agency's interpretation of the INA.

In *Chevron U.S.A., Inc. v. NRDC*, the Supreme Court developed a two-step analysis for determining the level of deference a court should give to the agency's interpretation of a statute it has been entrusted to administer. Step one requires the court to review the statute and determine "whether Congress has directly spoken to the precise question at issue."[52] If congressional intent is clear from the plain terms of the statute, the context, the legislative history, and traditional canons of statutory construction, which is the end of the analysis, "for the court, as well as the agency, must give effect to the unambiguously expressed intent of Congress."[53] If the statute is ambiguous or silent regarding the question at issue, the analysis moves on to step two of *Chevron.*[54]

Step two requires a court to review the statute and the agency's interpretation to determine "whether the agency's answer is based on a permissible construction of the statute."[55] If the statutory language constitutes "an express delegation to the agency to elucidate a specific provision of the statute by regulation," agency interpretations are given controlling weight unless they are "arbitrary, capricious, or manifestly contrary to the statute."[56] Even if delegation to the agency is more implicit, agency interpretations are afforded deference and are permissible as long as the agency's construction is reasonable.[57] In *National Cable & Telecommunications Association v. Brand X Internet Services* (hereinafter *Brand X*), the U.S. Supreme Court again considered what is considered a "permissible construction of the statute," specifically whether it was permissible for an agency to interpret the same statute differently than it had previously.[58] The Court found that *Chevron* deference to the agency is due

---

[49] *See generally*, Administrative Procedures Act, Pub. L. No. 79-404, 60 Stat. 237 (1946) (codified as amended at 5 USC §§500-596 (2012)).

[50] *See Chevron U.S.A., Inc. v. Natural Res. Defense Council*, 467 U.S. 837 (1984).

[51] *United States v. Mead Corp.*, 533 U.S. 218, 226–27 (2001).

[52] *Chevron U.S.A. Inc.*, at 842.

[53] *Id.* at 842–43.

[54] *Id.* at 843.

[55] *Id.*

[56] *Id.* at 844.

[57] *Id.* at 844–45.

[58] *Nat'l Cable & Telecomm. Ass'n v. Brand X Internet Servs.*, 545 U.S. 967, 980 (2005).

irrespective of inconsistent prior practices, as long as the policy change is adequately explained by the agency.[59]

However, not all agency interpretations of a statute will qualify for *Chevron* deference. As the Supreme Court clarified in *U.S. v. Mead Corp.*, only "when it appears that Congress delegated authority to the agency generally to make rules carrying the force of law, and that the agency interpretation claiming deference was promulgated in the exercise of that authority," does *Chevron* deference apply.[60] For example, agency interpretations entitled to *Chevron* deference might include notice-and-comment rulemaking or formal adjudications.[61] Other agency interpretations, such as those contained in "policy statements, agency manuals, and enforcement guidelines," do not merit *Chevron* deference.[62] The amount of weight accorded such an agency interpretation "depend[s] upon the thoroughness evident in its consideration, the validity of its reasoning, its consistency with earlier and later pronouncements, and all those factors which give it power to persuade, if lacking power to control."[63] This lesser deference is often referred to as "*Skidmore* deference."

2. **Brand X *Deference***

In certain circumstances, a circuit court must defer to an agency's interpretation of a statute even if that interpretation conflicts with the circuit court's contrary prior precedent.[64] For example, prior to the issuance of the BIA's decisions in *Matter of M–E–V–G–* and *Matter of W–G–R–*,[65] which clarified the BIA's additional requirements for demonstrating a viable social group for asylum purposes (social distinction and particularity), both the U.S. Courts of Appeals for the Third and Seventh Circuits had rejected the social visibility (now distinction) test and the Third Circuit had rejected particularity as a requirement.[66] According to *Brand X*, however, if a statute is ambiguous, the BIA may invoke its authority to interpret the statute

---

[59] *Id.* at 981.

[60] *United States v. Mead Corp.*, 533 U.S. 218, 226–27 (2001).

[61] *Id.* at 230.

[62] *Id.* at 235.

[63] *Skidmore v. Swift & Co.*, 323 U.S. 134, 140 (1944).

[64] *Nat'l Cable & Telecomms. Ass'n v. Brand X Internet Servs.*, 545 U.S. 967, 982 (2005). *See also Hernandez-Carrera v. Carlson*, 547 F.3d 1237, 1246–47 (10th Cir. 2008) (holding that *Brand X* applies to prior Supreme Court decisions as well, not just lower court decisions); *Gonzales v. Dep't of Homeland Security,* 508 F.3d 1227 (9th Cir. 2007); *Fernandez v. Keisler,* 502 F.3d 337 (4th Cir. 2007). For more information on *Brand X*, see Am. Immigration Council Legal Action Ctr., *Brand X in Immigration Cases*, *available at www.legalactioncenter.org/clearinghouse/litigation-issue-pages/brand-x-immigration-cases*.

[65] *Matter of M–E–V–G–*, 26 I&N Dec. 227 (BIA 2014); *Matter of W–G–R–*, 26 I&N Dec. 20 (BIA 2014).

[66] *See Cece v. Holder,* 733 F.3d 662 (7th Cir. 2013); *Valdiviezo-Galdamez v. Holder,* 663 F.3d 582 (3d Cir. 2011); *Gatimi v. Holder,* 578 F.3d 611, 616 (7th Cir. 2009).

instead of following circuit precedent, even in cases arising within that circuit.[67] Thus, for particular social group claims that arise in the Third and Seventh Circuits today, it remains to be seen whether the circuit courts will consider anew whether the BIA's interpretation of the INA is reasonable with respect to viability of particular social groups and potentially defer to the agency's interpretation, or whether the courts will stand by their previous determinations.

This example illustrates the concept that, where a statute is ambiguous, the circuit court is not bound by its prior precedent; rather, it might move to step two of the *Chevron* analysis and defer to the agency's interpretation. The circuit court may do so as long as the agency's interpretation is a permissible construction of the statute.[68] A circuit court's "prior judicial construction of a statute trumps an agency construction otherwise entitled to *Chevron* deference only if the prior court decision holds that its construction follows from the unambiguous terms of the statute and thus leaves no room for agency discretion."[69] On the other hand, if prior circuit precedent found that the statute unambiguously foreclosed the agency's interpretation under step one of *Chevron*, that precedent will continue to trump the agency's interpretation.[70]

3. *Application of* **Chevron** *and* **Brand X** *in the Immigration Context*

The circuit courts generally will defer to the BIA's interpretation of the INA in adjudicative decisions, because the BIA is charged with administration of that statute.[71] The Supreme Court has recognized that the BIA should be granted *Chevron* deference because "it gives ambiguous statutory terms concrete meaning through a process of case-by-case adjudication."[72] Whereas precedential BIA decisions merit *Chevron* deference, unpublished BIA decisions issued by a single member of the BIA are accorded no *Chevron* deference.[73] In addition, when the BIA is not charged with administration of a law, its interpretation of that law is reviewed *de novo*.[74] An important illustration of this rule occurs when a BIA decision interprets federal or

---

[67] *See Nat'l Cable & Telecomms. Ass'n v. Brand X Internet Servs.*, 545 U.S. 967 (2005).

[68] *Nat'l Cable & Telecomms. Ass'n v. Brand X Internet Servs.*, 545 U.S. 967, 984–86 (2005).

[69] *Id.* at 969.

[70] *Id.* at 982–83.

[71] *See* INA §103(a)(1) (providing that the "determination and ruling by the Attorney General with respect to all questions of law shall be controlling"); 8 CFR §1003.1(d)(1) (vesting the BIA with the authority to provide, through precedent decisions, "clear and uniform guidance to the Service, the immigration judges, and the general public on the proper interpretation and administration of the Act and its implementing regulations"). *See also Blake v. Gonzales,* 481 F.3d 152, 156 (2d Cir. 2007); *Miguel-Miguel v. Gonzales,* 500 F.3d 941, 947–48 (9th Cir. 2007); *Mejia v. Gonzales,* 499 F.3d 991, 996 (9th Cir. 2007).

[72] *INS v. Aguirre-Aguirre*, 526 U.S. 415, 426 (1999) (quoting *INS v. Cardoza-Fonseca,* 480 U.S. 421, 448–49 (1987)).

[73] *Rotimi v. Gonzales*, 473 F.3d 55, 57 (2d Cir. 2007) (per curiam); *Garcia-Quintero v. Gonzales*, 455 F.3d 1006, 1012–14 (9th Cir. 2006); *Miranda-Alvarado v. Gonzales,* 449 F.3d 915, 920–24 (9th Cir. 2006) (as amended).

[74] *Vargas-Sarmiento v. U.S. Dep't of Justice*, 448 F.3d 159, 165 (2d Cir. 2006).

state criminal laws, in which case the courts review such decisions *de novo*.[75] Finally, if the BIA never actually exercised its interpretive authority with respect to the statute it was charged with interpreting — the INA — but instead adopted another interpretation of the same concept from a different statute, that interpretation would not merit *Chevron* deference.[76]

Overall, the courts and agencies have shared power to interpret ambiguous statutes; however, the agency interpretation will trump the judicial decision if the agency has properly exercised its rulemaking authority. *Chevron* and *Brand X* deference apply only if: (1) the statute is ambiguous; (2) Congress has delegated authority to the agency to interpret the statutory provision at issue; (3) the agency has properly exercised its authority to make new law; and (4) the agency interpretation of the statute is permissibly within the bounds of what Congress intended.

II. Scope and Standard of Review

A circuit court may review a final order of removal only if the individual or DHS has exhausted all administrative remedies available and another court has not yet decided the validity of the removal order.[77] Thus, the party must first file an appeal with the BIA and await its adjudication before pursuing a petition for review before the U.S. circuit courts of appeals. All issues on appeal must first be presented to the BIA. Otherwise, the administrative remedies with regard to those issues will not be exhausted, and those issues will not be preserved for appeal to the circuit courts.

The circuit courts limit their review to the issues addressed and grounds relied upon by the BIA, unless the BIA has issued an Affirmance Without Opinion (AWO) decision or a decision incorporating the IJ's decision in its entirety. Under those circumstances, the circuit court may review the IJ's decision in the same way it reviews a final order of removal issued by the BIA; it will limit review to the issues addressed and grounds relied upon by the IJ.[78] If the BIA or IJ does not provide a reasoned explanation for its decision, including the rationale and factual basis for the decision, the decision may be reversed.

---

[75] *Michel v. INS*, 206 F.3d 253, 252 (2d Cir. 2000); *Amibola v. Ashcroft*, 378 F.3d 173, 176 (2d Cir. 2004).

[76] *Negusie v. Holder*, 129 S. Ct. 1159, 1167–68 (2009) (finding that the BIA had not exercised its own interpretive authority with regard to the INA in interpreting the persecutor bar to asylum eligibility, but rather, had erroneously adopted wholesale the *Federenko* rule, which interprets the persecutor bar in the context of a different statute). See chapter 2 for a detailed discussion of the persecutor bar and *Negusie v. Holder*.

[77] INA §242(d). If the reviewing court finds that the petition for review presents a ground that could not have been presented in the prior judicial proceeding or that the remedy provided by the prior proceeding was inadequate or ineffective to test the validity of the order, however, the circuit court may review the final order anew. INA §242(d)(2).

[78] *See* INA §242.

Moreover, the circuit courts must limit their review to the administrative record upon which the order of removal is based.[79] Whereas constitutional claims, issues of law, and the application of law to undisputed facts are all reviewed *de novo*, administrative findings of fact are conclusive unless "any reasonable adjudicator would be compelled to conclude to the contrary."[80] This includes findings of fact with respect to the availability of corroborating evidence as described in INA §§208(b)(1)(B), 240(c)(4)(B), or 241(b)(3)(C), unless the court finds that "a reasonable trier of fact is compelled to conclude that such corroborating evidence is unavailable."[81] Similarly, the AG's discretionary judgment on whether to grant asylum is conclusive unless "manifestly contrary to law and an abuse of discretion."[82] Decisions regarding withholding of removal and protection under CAT are not discretionary and, therefore, would not be subject to this limitation on review of the AG's exercise of discretion.[83] If judicial review of a discretionary determination is not precluded, discretionary determinations are reviewed for abuse of discretion. For example, if a determination is arbitrary, irrational, or contrary to law, it may be an abuse of discretion.

- **Practice Pointer**: Since the circuit courts must limit their review to the administrative record and the issues that have been raised before the BIA on appeal, it is essential for practitioners to litigate with an eye toward appeal. This requires ensuring that all testimony, evidence, objections, and legal arguments are on the record of proceedings before the immigration judge and that all arguments are raised on appeal to the BIA. New facts, issues, or arguments cannot be raised on appeal to the BIA, nor may they be raised in a petition for review before the circuit courts.

III. Procedures for Filing a Petition for Review

The INA, Federal Rules of Appellate Procedure (FRAP), and the local rules of the relevant circuit court govern the procedures for filing a petition for review before a U.S. circuit courts of appeals. The following is an overview of the procedures for filing a petition for review.

A. When to File

The petition for review must be filed not later than 30 days after the date of the final order of removal.[84] The time period begins running from the date of the BIA's

---

[79] INA §242(b)(4)(A), 8 USC §1252(b)(4)(A) (2012).

[80] INA §242(b)(4)(B); 8 USC §1252(b)(4)(B) (2012).

[81] INA §242(b)(4)(D).

[82] INA §242(b)(4)(D); 8 USC §1252(b)(4)(D) (2012).

[83] *See, e.g.*, *INS v. Cardoza-Fonseca*, 480 U.S. 421, 429 (1987).

[84] INA §242(b)(1); 8 USC §252(b)(1) (2012).

decision, and if the last day falls on a Saturday, Sunday, or legal holiday, the deadline is extended to the next day after the Saturday, Sunday, or legal holiday.[85] The petition for review must be *received* by the court clerk's office on or before the 30th.

This 30-day petition for review deadline is "mandatory and jurisdictional" and it is "not subject to equitable tolling."[86] Owing to the jurisdictional nature of the deadline, circuit courts are prohibited from considering late-filed petitions for review. At least three courts have held that they are expressly prohibited from extending the time limit, even for good cause, because the rule for review of agency proceedings is strictly jurisdictional.[87]

Moreover, the 30-day deadline is not extended by the filing of a motion to reopen or motion to reconsider, nor is it extended by a grant or extension of voluntary departure. Thus, even if an individual plans to file a motion to reconsider before the BIA, he or she also must file a petition for review within 30 days of the final order of removal in order to seek review of the BIA's underlying order. If the motion to reconsider, too, is denied by the BIA, a separate petition for review would need to be filed with the circuit court to seek review of that denial. Any circuit court review of a motion to reopen or reconsider must be consolidated with the court's review of the final order of removal.[88]

If the 30-day filing deadline is missed, there are few options for obtaining review of the final administrative order. One option may be for the individual to file a motion to reopen with the BIA. However, motions to reopen must be filed within 90 days of the final order,[89] and only one motion to reopen may be filed.[90] Given these time and numerical limitations, the motion may need to be based on one of the exceptions to these limitations.

Such motions may include: (1) motions to reopen *sua sponte*;[91] (2) joint motions to reopen;[92] (3) motions to reopen based on changed circumstances materially affecting eligibility for asylum, withholding of removal, and protection under the CAT;[93] (4) motions to reopen where exceptional circumstances or lack of notice led

---

[85] Fed. R. App. P. 26(a). Unless otherwise specified by the court, legal holidays include: New Year's Day, Martin Luther King Jr.'s Birthday, Washington's Birthday, Memorial Day, Independence Day, Labor Day, Columbus Day, Veterans' Day, Thanksgiving Day, and Christmas Day.

[86] *Stone v. INS*, 514 U.S. 386, 405 (1995).

[87] *Martinez-Serrano v. INS*, 94 F.3d 1256, 1258 (9th Cir. 1996); *Malvoisin v. INS*, 268 F.3d 74, 76 (2d Cir. 2001); *Prekaj v. INS*, 384 F.3d 265 (6th Cir. 2004); *Ruiz-Martinez v. Mukasey*, 516 F.3d 102 (2d Cir. 2006).

[88] INA §242(b)(6); 8 USC §1252(b)(6) (2012).

[89] INA §240(c)(7)(C)(i); 8 CFR §1003.2(c)(2), 1003.23(b)(1), 1208.4(b)(3)(ii) (2014).

[90] 8 CFR §§1003.2(c)(2), 1003.23(b)(1) (2014).

[91] 8 CFR §1003.2(a) (2014). *See, e.g., Matter of G–D–*, 22 I&N Dec. 1132 (BIA 1999); *Matter of X–G–W–*, 22 I&N Dec. 71 (BIA 1998); *Matter of Yewondwosen*, 21 I&N Dec. 1027 (BIA 1997).

[92] 8 CFR §1003.2(c)(3)(iii) (2014).

[93] INA §240(c)(7)(C)(ii); 8 CFR §§1003.2(c)(3)(ii), 1003.23(b)(4)(i) (2014).

to an order entered *in absentia*;[94] (5) motions to reopen by DHS;[95] and (6) motions to reopen based on ineffective assistance of counsel.[96]

> ➢ **Practice Pointer**: See chapter 11 of this book for a detailed discussion of motions to reopen before the BIA and strategies for overcoming the time and numerical limitations.

Another option to recover the right to judicial review upon missing the 30-day filing deadline may be to request that the BIA rescind and re-issue its decision in order to preserve the right to appeal to the circuit court or for purposes of filing a motion to reopen.[97] Several courts have reviewed whether the BIA should reissue a decision that was never received.[98] Decisions of the BIA are reviewable in federal court, including BIA decisions to deny a motion to reopen or reconsider.[99]

> ➢ **Practice Pointer**: For additional options to remedy a missed petition for review deadline, see the American Immigration Council Legal Action Center's Practice Advisory, "Suggested Strategies for Remedying Missed Petition for Review Deadlines or Filings in the Wrong Court," *www.legalactioncenter.org/sites/default/files/lac_pa_042005.pdf.*[100]

---

[94] 8 CFR §1003.2(c)(3)(i) (2014).

[95] 8 CFR §1003.2(c)(3)(iv) (2014). *See, e.g., Hailemichael v. Gonzales*, 454 F.3d 878 (8th Cir. 2006); *Efe v. Ashcroft*, 293 F.3d 899, 904 (5th Cir. 2002).

[96] *Kuusk v. Holder*, 732 F.3d 202, 305 (4th Cir. 2013) (holding that equitable tolling is only appropriate where the individual was prevented from asserting a claim or extraordinary circumstances beyond the individual's control made it impossible to file on time); *Bead v. Holder*, 703 F.3d 591 (1st Cir. 2012) (finding that a person must demonstrate due diligence during the entire period of time he or she wishes to toll, including the time when the ineffective assistance should have been discovered and the time following the discovery and preceding the motion to reopen); *El-Gazawy v. Holder*, 690 F.3d 852, 859-60 (7th Cir. 2012) (finding that the individual must demonstrate that he or she "could not reasonably have been expected to file earlier"); *Avagyan v. Holder*, 646 F.3d 672, 679–70 (9th Cir. 2011) (maintaining a three-part test for due diligence and equitable tolling); *Mezo v. Holder*, 615 F.3d 616 (6th Cir. 2010) (citing its five-part test for equitable tolling); *Rashid v. Mukasey*, 553 F.3d 127 (2d Cir. 2008) (finding that a person must demonstrate due diligence during the entire period of time he or she wishes to toll, including the time when the ineffective assistance should have been discovered and the time following the discovery and preceding the motion to reopen); *Riley v. INS*, 310 F.3d 1253 (10th Cir. 2002) (adopting the Second Circuit's approach).

[97] *See* 8 CFR §1003.1(c) (2014).

[98] *See, e.g., Jahjaga v. Att'y Gen..*,512 F.3d 80, 82–83 (3d Cir. 2008); *Ping Chen v. Att'y Gen.*, 502 F.3d 73, 76–77 (2d Cir. 2007); *Singh v. Gonzales*, 494 F.3d 1170, 1172–73 (9th Cir. 2007).

[99] *See generally* INA §242; Am. Immigration Council Legal Action Ctr. Practice Advisory, *How to File a Petition for Review*, at 3, *www.legalactioncenter.org/sites/default/files/how_to_file_a_petition_for_review_2011_update_4-23-13.pdf* (last visited Mar. 7, 2015).

[100] (last visited Mar. 8, 2015).

B. Where to File

The petition for review should be filed with the court of appeals for the judicial circuit in which the IJ completed the proceedings.[101] It is essential to identify the venue where the petition for review must be filed early on, as each circuit court has its own local rules, in addition to the FRAP, that govern what must be filed and how that documentation must be filed. Most paper filings must be sent to the circuit court clerk's office.[102] Although many circuits now use electronic filing systems for later pleadings, most circuits continue to require that the initial petition for review be filed and served on the respondents in hard copy.[103]

C. What to File

A petition for review of an order of removal "shall attach a copy of such order" and "shall state whether a court has upheld the validity of the order, and, if so, shall state the name of the court, the date of the court's ruling, and the kind of proceeding."[104] Although these are the only requirements stated in the INA, the local rules of the relevant circuit court may mandate additional requirements for the filing. Thus, before preparing and filing a petition for review, it is important to review the FRAP and the local circuit court's rules. Doing so will ensure compliance with all requirements, as well as a timely filing that will not be rejected.

Generally, petitions for review should include the following documents:

- A petition for review (see local rules for specific requirements);
- A copy of the BIA decision;
- The filing fee of $500[105] or an application for fee waiver demonstrating the individuals inability to pay the filing fee because of indigence;
- A certificate of service listing the names and addresses of the respondents served (usually the U.S. Attorney General, ICE Field Office Director, and Office of Immigration Litigation), as well as the date and manner of service;[106]
- A motion to stay removal; and

---

[101] INA §242(b)(2); 8 USC §1252(b)(2) (2012).

[102] Fed. R. App. P. 25(a)(1).

[103] Fed. R. App. P. 25(a)(2). *See also* local rules of the relevant circuit court.

[104] INA §242(c).

[105] Note that this is the current filing fee as of the date of this book. However, filing fees frequently change. It is advisable to check the local circuit court's rules for filing petitions for review to determine what current filing fees may be.

[106] *See* INA §242(b)(3)(A) ("The respondent is the Attorney General. The petition shall be served on the Attorney General and on the officer or employee of the Service in charge of the Service district in which the final order of removal under section 240 was entered."); Fed. R. App. P. 15(c), 25(d).

- The number of required copies (depends on the number of Respondents, FRAP 25, and local circuit court rules).[107]

  - ➢ **Practice Pointer**: An indigent petitioner also may move the court to appoint counsel to pursue the petition for review. The circuit courts appoint counsel in very few cases, and usually only where the individual has shown compelling legal and humanitarian reasons why the appointment of counsel is necessary.

Pursuant to the INA and FRAP 15, the petition for review itself should state the following:

- Whether a court has upheld the validity of the order, and, if so, the name of the court, the date of the court's ruling, and the type of proceeding;[108]
- The full name of each individual seeking review, as well as each individual's A-number;[109]
- The name of the agency as the respondent; and
- The order or part thereof to be reviewed.[110]

Although the content required for petitions for review is set forth in each circuit court's local rules, most circuit courts require the following content in addition to that listed above:

- Caption;
- Decision being reviewed;
- Jurisdiction and venue;
- Detention status (only required by some circuits);
- Pending applications (only required by some circuits);
- Prior court review;
- Grounds for relief; and
- Signature.

  - ➢ **Practice Pointer**: See Appendix 8C for a sample petition for review.
  - ➢ **Practice Pointer**: A petitioner may not be entitled to review under the "Fugitive Disentitlement Doctrine," which applies to individuals who

---

[107] Fed. R. App. P. 15(c) (stating that the petitioner must give "the clerk enough copies of the petition … to serve each respondent"). *See also* Fed. R. App. P. 25 and corresponding local rules.

[108] INA §242(c).

[109] Fed. R. App. P. 15(a)(2)(A). Even though the BIA decision usually lists the lead respondent's name only, followed by "et al.," every individual's full name must be listed on the petition for review, along with every A-number.

[110] INA §242(c).

have been issued final orders of removal and have failed to depart from the United States.[111]

D. Whom to Sue and Whom to Serve

The "Respondent" for a petition for review is the "Attorney General of the United States."[112] Thus, the Attorney General (AG), as well as "the officer or employee of the Service in charge of the Service district in which the final order of removal under section 240 was entered," should be served with the petition to review.[113] Generally, this means that, in addition to the AG, the petitioner should serve the "DHS ICE Field Office Director for Enforcement and Removal Operations" having jurisdiction over the district where the final administrative order was issued. Finally, it is also advisable for the petitioner to serve the "Department of Justice, Civil Division, Office of Immigration Litigation," which is the agency that represents the government before the U.S. circuit courts of appeals. The Office of Immigration Litigation (OIL) attorney assigned to the case will then enter his or her appearance before the court and notify the petitioner's counsel.

➢ **Practice Pointer**: Initial petition for review filings usually must be filed and served upon the respondents in hard copy.[114]

E. Attorney Admission and Entry of Appearance

An attorney may not file a petition for review before a circuit court unless he or she has already be admitted to practice before that circuit court or, in some circuits, files the application for admission simultaneously with or within a certain period of time of filing the petition for review. Some circuit courts also allow attorneys who have not been admitted to practice before them to appear *pro hac vice*. Attorney admissions and appearances are governed by FRAP 46 and the local circuit court's corresponding rules.

➢ **Practice Pointer**: For entry of appearance forms and instructions on admission to practice before a particular circuit court, see that circuit court's website or call the court clerk's office.

---

[111] *See, e.g.*, *Giri v. Keisler*, 507 F.3d 833, 835–36 (5th Cir. 2007); Gao *v. Gonzales*, 481 F.3d 173, 176 (2d Cir. 2007); *Garcia-Flores v. Gonzales*, 477 F.3d 439, 441 (6th Cir. 2007); *Sapoundjiev v. Ashcroft*, 376 F.3d 727, 728–29 (7th Cir. 2004); *Antonio-Martinez v. INS*, 317 F.3d 1089, 1093 (9th Cir. 2003); *Arana v. INS*, 673 F.2d 75, 77 (3d Cir. 1982). *But see Gutierrez-Almazan v. Gonzales*, 453 F.3d 956, 957 (7th Cir. 2006) (finding that the fugitive disentitlement doctrine did not apply where an alien voluntarily surrendered to authorities). See also Am. Immigration Council Legal Action Ctr. Practice Advisory, *The Fugitive Disentitlement Doctrine: FOIA and Petitions for Review* (May 29, 2008), *available at www.legalactioncenter.org/sites/default/files/lac_pa_fugdis.pdf.*

[112] INA §242(b)(3)(A).

[113] *Id.*

[114] Fed. R. App. P. 25(a)(2), (b).

- **Practice Pointer**: Practitioners should plan ahead and seek admission to the circuit courts having jurisdiction over the immigration courts where they practice most frequently. If there is not enough time to seek admission before a client's petition for review deadline, practitioners should seek assistance from AILA members who are reputable and experienced in filing petitions for review. Substitution of counsel may occur at a later date, following the practitioner's admission.

IV. Stays of Removal

Filing the petition for review and serving it on ICE does not automatically stay the removal of a petitioner "unless the court orders otherwise."[115] In fact, ICE may deport an individual upon issuance of the BIA's final order of removal; ICE is not even required to wait until the 30-day period for filing a petition for review has expired. Thus, an individual should seek a stay of removal when filing the petition for review. If a stay of removal is ordered by the circuit court, ICE must abide by that stay for as long as it remains in place. Until a stay is granted, in most circuits, ICE may remove the individual. The filing of a stay motion only temporarily stays the individual's removal in the U.S. Courts of Appeals for the Ninth and Second Circuits.[116]

- **Practice Pointer**: Practitioners should also consider seeking an administrative stay of removal before ICE and may decide to do so in lieu of or concurrently with a motion for stay of removal before the circuit court.[117] To seek an administrative stay of removal before ICE, practitioners should prepare and file a Form I-246, "Application for a Stay of Deportation or Removal" with the ICE Enforcement and Removal Operations Field Office having jurisdiction over their client. The Form I-246 is available at *www.ice.gov/sites/default/files/documents/Document/2014/ice_form_i_246.pdf*.[118]
  - Although instructions are provided on the I-246, the ICE field offices often have various local requirements. For example, even though the I-246 lists three acceptable forms of payment, many ICE offices only accept one form over another. Practitioners should reach out to other

[115] INA §242(b)(3)(B).

[116] *Deleon v. INS*, 115 F.3d 643, 644 (9th Cir. 1997) (stating that the filing of a stay motion automatically stays removal temporarily); *In the Matter of Immigration Petitions for Review Pending in the United States Court of Appeals for the Second Circuit*, Docket No. 12-4096 (Oct. 16, 2012) (acknowledging the Second Circuit's informal agreement with DHS that upon notification that a stay motion has been filed with the Second Circuit, DHS will not remove the individual until the court rules on the stay motion).

[117] *See* Fed. R. App. P. 18(a)(1).

[118] (last visited Mar. 10, 2015).

practitioners familiar with the practices of the specific ICE office's practices.

A stay motion must be filed with the circuit court that has jurisdiction over the petition for review.[119] It may be filed concurrently with the petition for review, or after the petition for review already has been filed.[120] There is no filing fee and stay motions must comply with FRAP 27 and the corresponding local rules of the circuit court.

> ➢ **Practice Pointer**: For more detailed guidance for preparing and filing stay motions, see the Practice Advisory, "Seeking a Judicial Stay of Removal in the Court of Appeals," available at *www.legalactioncenter.org/sites/default/files/seeking_a_judicial_stay_of_removal_fin_1-21-14.pdf*.[121] A sample stay motion, sample stay declaration, and guidelines for letters in support of stay requests also are available at *www.americanimmigrationcouncil.org/practice-advisories/seeking-judicial-stay-removal-court-appeals*.[122]

Previously, the circuit courts of appeals disagreed over what standard should be met in a motion for a stay of removal filed in conjunction with a petition for review. Some courts applied the clear and convincing standard under INA §242(f)(2),[123] whereas most others held that the clear and convincing standard under INA §242(f)(2) did not apply to temporary stays for petitions for review.[124] The U.S. Supreme Court has now spoken on the issue, finding that the traditional standard for stays — *not* the more demanding standard under INA §242(f)(2), governs a court of appeals' authority to stay the removal of a noncitizen pending judicial review.[125]

---

[119] INA §242(b)(2).

[120] *See* Am. Immigration Council Legal Action Ctr. Practice Advisory, *How to File a Petition for Review* (Feb. 28, 2011), *available at www.legalactioncenter.org/sites/default/files/how_to_file_a_petition_for_review_2011_update_4-23-13.pdf* (last visited Mar. 8, 2015).

[121] (last visited Apr. 2, 2015).

[122] (last visited Apr. 2, 2015).

[123] *See Weng v. Att'y Gen.*, 287 F.3d 1335 (11th Cir. 2002); *see also Ngarurih v. Ashcroft*, 371 F.3d 182, 195 n.13 (4th Cir. 2004) (citing with approval the clear and convincing standard in considering a petition for stay of removal).

[124] *See Hor v. Gonzales*, 400 F.3d 482, 485 (7th Cir. 2005); *Tesfamichael v. Gonzales*, 411 F.3d 169, 176 (5th Cir. 2005); *Faruqi v. DHS*, 360 F.3d 985, 988–89 (9th Cir. 2004); *Douglas v. Ashcroft*, 374 F.3d 230, 233–34 (3d Cir. 2004); *Bejjani v. INS*, 271 F.3d 670, 687–89 (6th Cir. 2001), *overruled on other grounds by Fernandez-Vargas v. Gonzales*, 126 S. Ct. 2422, 2427 (2006); *Arevalo v. Ashcroft*, 344 F.3d 1, 6–9 (1st Cir. 2003); *Mohammed v. Reno*, 309 F.3d 95, 98–100 (2d Cir. 2002); *see also Singh v. Ashcroft*, 375 F.3d 1007 (10th Cir. 2004) (motion must contain argument on likelihood of success on appeal, threat of irreparable harm, absence of harm to opposing party, and any risk of harm to public interest); *Rife v. Ashcroft*, 374 F.3d 606, 615 n.3 (8th Cir. 2004) (opting not to address the issue).

[125] *Nken v. Holder*, 129 S. Ct. 1749 (2009).

Thus, courts will consider the following factors in deciding whether a stay of removal should be granted: (1) likelihood of success on the merits; (2) potential for irreparable injury if a stay is not granted; (3) whether issuance of the stay will substantially injure the other parties interested in the proceeding; and (4) where the public interest lies.[126]

Each of these factors should be addressed in detail in the motion for stay of removal filed with the circuit court. Thus, unlike the petition for review, which is a relatively simple document, a motion for stay "requires a detailed analysis of the facts of petitioner's case, the legal issues raised in the case, the BIA's errors of law, and the hardships that would ensue if the petitioner were forced to return to his or her native country pending review of the petition."[127]

- **Practice Pointer**: Because the administrative record is filed with the circuit court within 40 days of service of the petition for review, most practitioners must prepare and file stay requests without access to the administrative record. This can be challenging, especially when a practitioner did not represent the individual before the BIA or IJ.[128] Practitioners should carefully review the BIA decision, seek documentation from the individual's prior counsel, and have detailed discussions with the individual regarding the facts and procedural history of the case in order to gather sufficient information for a motion for stay of removal.
- **Practice Pointer**: If an individual is removed from the United States following the final administrative removal order, and later prevails on a petition for review, it may be possible for that individual to return to the United States. See the American Immigration Council Legal Action Center's Practice Advisory, "Return to the United States After Prevailing on a Petition for Review or Motion to Reopen or Reconsider," available on the Legal Action Center's website at *www.legalactioncenter.org/sites/default/files/return_to_the_united_states_after_prevailing_on_a_petition_for_review_or_motion_to_reopen_or_reconsider.pdf*.[129]

---

[126] *Id.* (citing *Hilton* v. *Braunskill*, 481 U. S. 770, 776 (1987)).

[127] Am. Immigration Council Legal Action Ctr. Practice Advisory, *How to File a Petition for Review*, at 8 (Feb. 28, 2011), *available at www.legalactioncenter.org/sites/default/files/how_to_file_a_petition_for_review_2011_update_4-23-13.pdf* (last visited Mar. 8, 2015).

[128] *See id.*

[129] (last visited Mar. 9, 2015).

V. Termination of Voluntary Departure

Pursuant to the regulations, a grant of voluntary departure will terminate automatically upon the filing of a petition for review or other judicial challenge, and the alternate order of removal will take effect.[130] However, if a person then departs within 30 days of filing the petition for review and provides DHS with proof of departure and evidence that he or she remains outside of the United States, the departure will not be deemed a removal.[131]

All circuit courts except the U.S. Court of Appeals for the Fourth Circuit have held that the circuit courts may grant a stay of the voluntary departure period pending judicial review, as long as the request is filed prior to the expiration of the voluntary departure period.[132] In determining whether to stay the voluntary departure period, the courts apply the same four factors as they apply to stay of removal requests: (1) likelihood of success on the merits; (2) potential for irreparable injury if a stay is not granted; (3) whether issuance of the stay will substantially injure the other parties interested in the proceeding; and (4) where the public interest lies.[133]

---

[130] 8 CFR §1240.26(i). For more information, see Am. Immigration Council Legal Action Ctr. Practice Advisory, *Voluntary Departure Rule Q&A* (Dec. 22, 2008), *available at www.legalactioncenter.org/sites/default/files/VoluntaryDeparture_QandA_12_22_2008.pdf.*

[131] *Id.*

[132] *Dada v. Mukasey*, 554 U.S. 1, 3–4 (2008) (finding that an individual has the option to either abide by the terms of voluntary departure and receive the agreed-upon benefits, or alternatively, to forgo those benefits and remain in the United States to pursue an administrative motion) (stating that "The alien may be removed by the DHS within 90 days, even if the motion to reopen has yet to be adjudicated. But the alien may request a stay of the removal order, and, though the BIA has discretion to deny a motion for a stay based on the merits of the motion to reopen, it may constitute an abuse of discretion for the BIA to deny a motion for stay where the motion states non-frivolous grounds for reopening"); *Ngarurih v. Ashcroft,* 371 F.3d 182, 194 (4th Cir.2004) (concluding that the court could not grant injunctive relief because "8 USC §1252(a)(2)(B) precludes judicial review of the BIA's order granting voluntary departure.") *Nwakanma v. Ashcroft*, 352 F.3d 325, 327 (6th Cir. 2003) (noting that the court will apply injunctive relief factors when considering whether to grant the motion); *But see Garfias-Rodriguez v. Holder*, 649 F.3d 942, 950–51 (9th Cir. 2011) *adhered to on reh'g en banc*, 702 F.3d 504 (9th Cir. 2012) (stating that the majority of circuits agreed with the holding that Courts had "equitable authority to stay a petitioner's voluntary departure period" but that "each of these decisions was reached before the Attorney General promulgated 8 CFR §1240.26(i)" which "resolved the question of whether courts have authority to stay the voluntary departure period pending review, since it provides for the automatic termination of that period.")

[133] *Ngarurih v. Ashcroft,* 371 F.3d 182, 194 (4th Cir.2004) (concluding that the court could not grant injunctive relief because "8 USC §1252(a)(2)(B) precludes judicial review of the BIA's order granting voluntary departure."); *Desta v. Ashcroft*, 365 F.3d 741 (9th Cir. 2004) (holding that if the standard to stay removal of the individual is satisfied, the standard to stay voluntary departure is necessarily satisfied, as the same substantive standards govern both); *Nwakanma v. Ashcroft*, 352 F.3d 325, 327 (6th Cir. 2003) (noting that the court will apply injunctive relief factors when considering whether to grant the motion).

VI. Post-Filing Procedures

The procedures that follow the filing of a petition for review have been established by the INA, the FRAP, and each circuit court's local rules. This section addresses the most common procedures that follow the preparation and filing of a petition for review. However, practitioners *must* consult the FRAP and local rules in order to gain a complete and detailed understanding of what to expect and what is required in each circuit for each step of this process.

A. Service of the Petition

Upon receipt of the petition for review, the circuit court clerk's office will serve a copy of the petition for review (usually the one that has been provided by the petitioner) on each respondent.[134]

B. Issuance of Administrative Record and Briefing Schedule

Upon receipt of a petition for review, the circuit court usually issues a schedule for the parties to file the Certified Record of Proceedings (hereinafter, Administrative Record), Petitioner's Opening Brief, Respondent's Answering Brief, and Petitioner's Reply Brief.

C. Mediation

Pursuant to FRAP 33, most circuits allow immigration petitions for review to be accepted into the court's mediation programs. Usually, mediation must be requested before the parties have briefed the issues on appeal. The purpose of a mediation conference is to bring the parties together for the possibility of settlement in order to more efficiently dispose of cases pending before the circuit courts. Mediation is not very common in addressing petitions for review of denials of asylum, withholding of removal, and CAT relief.

D. Preparation and Filing of the Administrative Record

The agency is required to file the Administrative Record within 40 days of service of the petition for review.[135] The court may shorten or extend this deadline.[136] The Administrative Record typically consists of the order being challenged, any findings or reports on which the order is based, and the pleadings, evidence, and other parts of the proceedings before the agency, including transcripts of any hearings.[137] For a petition for review of a BIA decision, the EOIR usually prepares the Administrative Record and OIL files it with the circuit court. Upon receipt of the Administrative

---

[134] Fed. R. App. P. 15(c).

[135] Fed. R. App. P. 17(a).

[136] Fed. R. App. P. 17(a).

[137] Fed. R. App. P. 16(a).

Record, the clerk's office notifies all parties of the date on which the record was filed.[138]

E. Briefs

The parties must prepare and file briefs setting forth their arguments on appeal. These briefs must be timely filed in accordance with the deadlines set by the INA and the circuit court in its briefing schedule. The court may extend these deadlines, but only if good cause is shown.[139]

Specifically, the petitioner's opening brief must be filed not later than 40 days after the administrative record is made available.[140] If the petitioner fails to file a brief within the time provided, the court must dismiss the appeal unless doing so would result in manifest injustice.[141] The petitioner's opening brief must contain the following sections with appropriate headings (as well as any other content required by the circuit court's local rules):

- Corporate Disclosure Statement (only if one is required by FRAP 26.1);
- Table of Contents, with page references;
- Table of Authorities, with cases (alphabetically arranged), statutes, and other authorities and references to the pages in the brief where they are cited;
- Jurisdictional Statement, including the basis for subject-matter jurisdiction (with citations to applicable statutory provisions and stating relevant facts), the basis for the court of appeals' jurisdiction (with citations to applicable statutory provisions and stating relevant facts), the filing dates establishing the timeliness of the petition for review, and an assertion that the appeal is from a final order or judgment;
- Issues Presented for review;
- Statement of the Case, concisely setting out the relevant facts, describing relevant procedural history, and identifying the rulings presented for review (with references to the record);
- Summary of the Argument, concisely, clearly, and accurately stating the arguments made in the body of the brief;
- Argument, which must contain the petitioner's contentions and reasons for them, with citations to authorities and the record as well as statements of the standard of review for each issue (either within the argument or in its own section before the argument);
- Conclusion, stating the precise relief sought; and

---

[138] Fed. R. App. P. 17(a).

[139] INA §242(b)(3)(C); 8 USC §1252(b)(3)(C) (2012).

[140] INA §242(b)(3)(C); 8 USC §1252(b)(3)(C) (2012); Fed. R. App. P. 31(a)(1).

[141] INA §242(b)(3)(C); 8 USC §1252(b)(3)(C) (2012).

- Certificate of Compliance (if required by FRAP 32(a)(7)).[142]

Many circuits also require that opening briefs contain any request for oral argument, as well as a Certificate of Service.

The AG must then file the government's response brief in accordance with the briefing schedule set by the circuit court. Typically, the government must file its response brief within 30 days of service of the petitioner's opening brief.[143] The government's response brief should contain all of the same sections as those listed above.[144]

> ➢ **Practice Pointer**: The circuit court may not rely on arguments in an agency's brief that are different from the grounds stated or discernible in the agency's decision itself.[145]

Following the submission of the government's response brief, the petitioner may opt to file a brief in reply to the government's response brief.[146] The reply brief must be filed not later than 14 days after the brief of the AG.[147] It must contain a table of contents (with page references) and a table of authorities (citing alphabetically-arranged cases, statutes, and other authorities and referencing the pages on which those authorities are cited).[148] Typically the reply brief will also contain the arguments and a Certificate of Compliance and Certificate of Service. Generally, the reply brief should respond specifically to arguments raised in the government's response brief. A reply brief should not repeat arguments previously presented to the court in the petitioner's opening brief.

If pertinent and significant authorities come to a party's attention after the party's brief has been filed (or after oral argument but before decision), the party must promptly advise the circuit court by letter and copy all parties.[149] Such letters are often referred to as "28(j) Letters," named after the rule number in the FRAP. 28(j) Letters must set forth citations to the relevant authorities, state the reasons for the supplemental citations, and refer either to the relevant pages of the brief or the points argued orally.[150] Such letters must not exceed 350 words, and any response must be made promptly.[151]

---

[142] Fed. R. App. P. 28(a).

[143] Fed. R. App. P. 31(a)(1).

[144] Fed. R. App. P. 28(b) (noting that the jurisdictional statement, statement of the issues, statement of the case, and standard of review are not required for the response brief).

[145] *See Mengistu v. Ashcroft*, 355 F.3d 1044, 1047–48 (7th Cir. 2004) (citing *Bowman Transp., Inc. v. Arkansas-Best Freight Sys., Inc.*, 419 U.S. 281, 285–86 (1974)).

[146] Fed. R. App. P. 28(c).

[147] INA §242(b)(3)(C); 8 USC §1252(b)(3)(C) (2012); Fed. R. App. P. 31(a)(1).

[148] Fed. R. App. P. 28(c).

[149] Fed. R. App. P. 28(j).

[150] *Id.*

[151] *Id.*

The FRAP and the circuit court's local rules specify how briefs are to be formatted.[152] There are precise rules for type of paper used; photographs, illustrations, and tables; color and content of the brief's cover (blue for petitioner's opening brief, red for government's response brief, gray for any reply brief); how the brief is to be bound; paper size; line spacing; margins; typeface; type style; page limitations (30 pages for petitioner's opening brief and 15 pages for petitioner's reply brief); type-volume limitations; certificates of compliance; form of required appendices; and signatures.[153] The FRAP and local rules also specify how the parties are to be referenced, how the authorities and record are to be cited, and how supplemental authorities are to be brought to the court's attention.[154]

Upon receipt of both briefs, the circuit court will review the arguments and the administrative record and then determine if and when to hear oral argument on the issues presented for review.

F. Oral Argument

Any party may file and any court may require by local rule that a party present a statement explaining why oral argument should, or need not, be permitted.[155] Oral argument is not granted in every case. If a panel of three judges who have examined the briefs and record unanimously agrees that oral argument is unnecessary, oral argument will not be scheduled and the decision will be made on the briefs.[156] Oral argument is unnecessary if: (1) an appeal is frivolous; (2) the issues have been authoritatively decided; or (3) the facts and legal arguments are adequately presented in the briefs and record, and the decisional process would not be significantly aided by oral argument.[157]

If the circuit court determines that oral argument is necessary, the clerk's office will notify the parties of the date, time, and place of the oral argument, as well as the time allotted for argument.[158] The parties may agree to submit a case for decision on the briefs, but the court may still direct that the case be argued.[159] During oral argument, the petitioner usually opens and concludes the argument.[160]

---

[152] *See* Fed. R. App. P. 28, 32; local circuit court rules.

[153] *See* Fed. R. App. P. 32; local circuit court rules.

[154] *See* Fed. R. App. P. 28.

[155] Fed. R. App. P. 34.

[156] Fed. R. App. P. 34(a)(2).

[157] *Id.*

[158] Fed. R. App. P. 34(b).

[159] Fed. R. App. P. 34(f)

[160] Fed. R. App. P. 34(c).

G. Judgment and Final Mandate

Once the court has entered its opinion on the matter, the clerk must prepare, sign, and enter the judgment.[161] On the date that the judgment is entered, the clerk will serve all parties with a copy of the court's opinion of judgment, if judgment was entered without opinion.[162] Any petition for rehearing or petition for rehearing en banc must be filed within 45 days of entry of judgment.[163] The court's final mandate — when its judgment takes effect — is automatically issued seven calendar days after the time to file a petition for rehearing expires.[164]

- **Practice Pointer**: For detailed guidance on filing petitions for rehearing or petitions for rehearing en banc, see the American Immigration Council Legal Action Center's Practice Advisory, "How to File a Petition for Rehearing, Rehearing *En Banc* and Hearing *En Banc* in an Immigration Case," available at *www.legalactioncenter.org/sites/default/files/lac_pa_082704.pdf*.[165]

- **Practice Pointer**: Practitioners who are successful before the circuit court may be eligible to recover costs and fees under the Equal Access to Justice Act (EAJA), 28 USC §2412(d) and 5 USC §504 *et seq*.[166] The EAJA helps individuals vindicate their rights by challenging unfair and unjustified government action. It encourages individuals to challenge government action notwithstanding the cost in attorneys' fees, compensates parties for the cost of defending against unreasonable government action, and deters the government from prosecuting or defending cases in which its position is not substantially justified. Any motion for EAJA fees should include a declaration showing that the petitioner meets the net worth requirements of EAJA, an explanation of the fact that the petitioner is a prevailing party, an allegation that the position of the government was not substantially justified, an explanation of how the fee request is calculated, a declaration and attached attorney time log and list of costs incurred, and if enhanced fees are sought, declarations establishing that an enhanced fee is warranted and documentation establishing the prevailing market rate. For more information on the EAJA, see the American Immigration Council Legal Action Center's Practice Advisory, "Requesting Attorneys' Fees Under the Equal Access to Justice Act," available at

[161] Fed. R. App. P. 36(a).

[162] Fed. R. App. P. 36(b).

[163] Fed. R. App. P. 35, 40.

[164] Fed. R. App. P. 41.

[165] (last visited Mar. 11, 2015).

[166] *See, e.g.*, *Cohen v. Swacina*, 2009 WL 799430 (S.D. Fla. 2009); *Hua Fang v. Gonzales*, No. 03-71352, Filed order (Appellate Comm'r) (9th Cir. Oct. 30, 2006).

www.legalactioncenter.org/sites/default/files/requesting_attorneys_fees_under_the_equal_access_to_justice_act_6-7-14_fin.pdf.[167]

[167] (last visited Mar. 11, 2015).

CHAPTER THIRTEEN

BENEFITS FOR ASYLUM-SEEKERS AND ASYLEES*

Asylum-seekers are among some of the most vulnerable immigrants who arrive in the United States. Unlike resettled refugees, who have been selected for resettlement in the United States and who enjoy the support of the Office of Refugee Resettlement (ORR) of the Department of Health and Human Services and the Department of State (DOS) upon arrival, asylum-seekers have fled persecution and torture in their home countries, often in a state of urgency and with no advance planning.[1] Upon arrival in the United States, asylum-seekers have few resources and little support as they seek protection. While the number of benefits available to individuals certainly increases upon a grant of asylum, withholding of removal, or Convention Against Torture (CAT)[2] relief, obtaining these benefits can be a confusing and complex process, especially for unrepresented individuals. This chapter provides a detailed guide for seeking and obtaining the various benefits available to asylum-seekers, as well as individuals granted protection in the United States.

I. Benefits While the Application is Pending

Applicants for asylum, withholding of removal under Immigration and Nationality Act (INA) §241(b)(3), and protection under the CAT may be eligible for certain benefits while their I-589, Application for Asylum and for Withholding of Removal, remains pending. These may include employment authorization, Social Security numbers, federal tax ID numbers, and advance permission to travel abroad and re-

* The author would like to thank Lindsay M. Harris of the Center for Applied Legal Studies at Georgetown University Law Center for her invaluable input in reviewing this chapter.

[1] *See* Lindsay M. Harris, *From Surviving to Thriving? An Investigation of Asylee Integration into the United States*, New York University Review of Law and Social Change, Vol. 40.2 (forthcoming) (comparing the benefits available to refugees versus asylees). A draft of this forthcoming article is available at *http://papers.ssrn.com/sol3/papers.cfm?abstract_id=2585209*.

[2] Convention Against Torture and Other Cruel, Inhuman or Degrading Treatment or Punishment, Dec. 10, 1984, art. 3, 1465 U.N.T.S. 85 [hereinafter CAT] (entered into force June 26, 1987).

enter the United States while the application remains pending. Each of these potential benefits is discussed in detail below.

A. Employment Authorization

Unlike many applications for immigration benefits, asylum applicants are not automatically granted employment authorization, nor are they immediately eligible to apply for employment authorization based on having a pending asylum application.[3] An asylum applicant may be provided with employment authorization, but is not entitled to such authorization.[4] In fact, an asylum applicant cannot even request employment authorization until his or her I-589 has been filed or lodged and has been pending for at least 150 days. Although an applicant may request employment authorization after 150 days, however, employment authorization may not be granted until the I-589 has been pending for 180 days.[5]

Eligible applicants whose asylum applications have been pending for 150 days may prepare their application for employment authorization on Form I-765 and file it with U.S. Citizenship and Immigration Services (USCIS).[6] Upon receipt, by regulation, USCIS must process the application within 90 days of receipt.[7] If the application is approved, USCIS will issue an I-765 Approval Notice and an Employment Authorization Document (EAD) and send them to the applicant as evidence of his or her authorization to work in the United States while awaiting adjudication of his or her I-589 application.

- **Practice Pointer**: The procedures listed below are for individuals who applied for asylum on or after January 4, 1995.[8] Individuals who applied for asylum before January 4, 1995, are subject to different rules.

1. *Who is Eligible for an EAD?*

An asylum applicant who has not been convicted of an aggravated felony is eligible to apply for employment authorization in accordance with 8 CFR §§274a.12(c)(8), 1274a.12(c)(8), 274a.13(a)(2), 1274a.13(a)(2), as long as his or her asylum application has been pending for at least 180 days.[9] However, an applicant whose asylum application has been denied by an asylum officer (not referred) or denied by an immigration judge (IJ) within 150 days of filing the application is ineligible for employment authorization.[10] Similarly, an applicant who fails to appear

[3] *See* 8 CFR §§274a.12(a)(5), 274a.12(c)(8) (2014).

[4] INA §208(d)(2); 8 USC §1158(d)(2).

[5] INA §208(d)(2); 8 CFR §208.7(a)(1) (2014).

[6] *See* USCIS, *I-765, Application for Employment Authorization*, *available at www.uscis.gov/i-765* (last visited Mar. 12, 2015).

[7] 8 CFR §274a.13(d) (2014).

[8] *See* 8 CFR §§208.7(a)(3), 1208.7(a)(3) (2014).

[9] 8 CFR §§208.7(a)(1), 1208.7(a)(1) (2014).

[10] 8 CFR §§208.7(a)(1), 1208.7(a)(1). *See* 8 CFR §§208.14(c)(1), 1208.14(c)(1) (2014).

for an asylum interview or a hearing before an IJ is ineligible for employment authorization, unless the applicant demonstrates that the failure to appear was due to exceptional circumstances.[11]

- **Practice Pointer**: Since a referral to an IJ is not a final decision in the case, it does not constitute a denial of the asylum application for purposes of employment authorization eligibility.[12] Generally, in cases that are referred from the asylum office to the IJ, the time continues to accrue toward the 180 days following the referral.[13]
- **Practice Pointer**: Family members who are included on the principal applicant's I-589 application also may be eligible for employment authorization after the application has been pending 180 days, as they too are considered "asylum applicants" under title 8 §208.7 of the Code of Federal Regulations (CFR). Derivative applicants use the same (C)(8) code as the principal applicant and should provide evidence that they have been included in the principal's I-589 application (a copy of the I-589 or the family member's biometrics notice).

2. *When Can the EAD Application be Submitted?*

The Form I-765, Application for Employment Authorization (I-765) may be submitted to USCIS "no earlier" than 150 days after the date the completed asylum application was filed.[14] Even though the EAD application can be submitted after the I-589 has been pending for 150 days, in order for the EAD application to be granted, the asylum application must have been pending for at least 180 days without a decision.[15] This 180-day time period is commonly referred to as the "EAD clock." Thus, enough time must have accrued on the EAD clock before an asylum applicant may present an application for employment authorization and before that application for employment authorization may be approved.[16]

There are three exceptions to this rule: (1) individuals who filed an asylum application prior to January 4, 1995; (2) individuals who filed an asylum application based on the *American Baptist Churches v. Thornburgh*, 760 F. Supp. 796 (N.D. Cal. 1991) settlement agreement;[17] and (3) individuals whose asylum applications have

---

[11] 8 CFR §§208.7(a)(4), 1208.7(a)(4) (2014).

[12] 8 CFR §§208.14(c), 1208.14(c) (2014).

[13] 8 CFR §§208.7(a)(1), 1208.7(a)(1) (2014).

[14] 8 CFR §§208.7(a)(1), 1208.7(a)(1) (2014).

[15] 8 CFR §§208.7(a)(1), 1208.7(a)(1) (2014).

[16] 8 CFR §§208.7(a)(1), 1208.7(a)(1) (2014).

[17] *See* Exec. Office of Immigration Review (EOIR), Operating Policies and Procedures Memorandum (OPPM) 13-02: The Asylum Clock, at 4 (Dec. 2, 2013) [hereinafter OPPM 13-02: *The Asylum Clock*], *available at www.justice.gov/eoir/efoia/ocij/oppm13/13-02.pdf*

been recommended for approval.[18] These individuals do not need to wait 180 days to become eligible for employment authorization.

- **Practice Pointer**: There are two 180-day time periods that are measured throughout the processing of asylum applications. The 180-day adjudication period, pursuant to INA §208(d)(5)(A)(iii) refers to the time in which an IJ must decide an asylum case. The 180-day "EAD clock," pursuant to INA §208(d)(2), refers to the waiting period before an asylum applicant may become eligible for an EAD. Various actions throughout the asylum application process may stop one or both "clocks" from accruing time and other actions may re-start one or both "clocks." Thus, at any given time, there may be a different amount of time accrued on the adjudications clock, versus the EAD clock. Generally, practitioners and their clients are most concerned with the EAD clock, as that directly impacts the clients' eligibility for employment authorization.

The EAD clock does not start until the individual's "complete asylum application" has been received and accepted as filed by USCIS or the immigration court or lodged with the immigration court.[19] A "complete asylum application" is one that has all of the questions answered, is signed by the application, and includes the required additional supporting documentation.[20] Of course, it is not required that all supporting documentation be submitted at the time of filing the application in order for the application to be accepted as "complete." Since the EAD clock starts upon filing or lodging the complete I-589 application,[21] the date listed on the USCIS I-589 Receipt Notice, the date the I-589 is stamped as "lodged not filed" by the immigration court, or the date the I-589 is filed in open court is usually the date when time began to accrue toward the 180-day period for employment authorization.

- **Practice Pointer**: See chapter 7 of this book for a detailed discussion of affirmative asylum procedures and practice pointers for preparing, filing, and avoiding rejection of the I-589 by USCIS upon filing. See chapter 8 of this book for a detailed discussion of defensive asylum procedures and practice pointers for lodging the I-589 application with the court in order to start the EAD clock, as well as filing the I-589 application in open court.

---

[18] 8 CFR §§208.7(a)(1), 1208.7(a)(1); *see* 8 CFR §§274a.12(c)(8), 1274a.12(c)(8) (2014).

[19] 8 CFR §§208.7(a)(1), 1208.7(a)(1) (2014); EOIR OPPM 13-03: *Guidelines for Implementation of the A.B.T. Settlement Agreement*, at 3-5 (Dec. 2, 2013) [hereinafter OPPM 13-03: *A.B.T. Settlement*], *available at www.justice.gov/eoir/efoia/ocij/oppm13/13-03.pdf.*

[20] 8 CFR §§208.3, 1208.3 (2014). See chs. 7 and 8 for detailed descriptions of what documents are required for a complete asylum application to be filed.

[21] 8 CFR §§208.7(a)(1), 1208.7(a)(1) (2014).

Getting the EAD clock started is only the first challenge for asylum-seekers in becoming eligible to seek employment authorization. This is because any number of actions — usually any kind of delay caused by the applicant — may cause the EAD clock to stop accruing time.[22] The clock will only re-start once the delay has been resolved.

> ➢ **Practice Pointer**: Historically, there have been many problems with implementation and interpretation of the EAD clock statute and regulations, which negatively impacted asylum-seekers' eligibility for employment authorization. In 2011, however, the American Immigration Council's Legal Action Center filed a nationwide class action lawsuit, *A.B.T. v. USCIS*,[23] which resulted in a settlement agreement in which USCIS and the Executive Office for Immigration Review (EOIR) agreed to implement significant changes to their policies regarding the EAD clock.[24] The settlement agreement went into effect in December of 2013.[25] For detailed information about the settlement agreement and its impact, see "Frequently Asked Questions about the Asylum Clock Class Action Settlement" (updated Feb. 4, 2014), available at *http://legalactioncenter.org/sites/default/files/FAQ%202-5-14%20FIN.pdf.*[26]

The following actions may cause the EAD clock to stop accruing time during the pendency of an asylum application before USCIS:

- A request to transfer a case to a new asylum office or interview location, including when the transfer is based on a new address;[27]

---

[22] 8 CFR §§208.7(a)(2), 1208.7(a)(2) (2014).

[23] *A.B.T. et al. v. USCIS*, No. 11-02108 (W.D. Wash. *Filed* December 15, 2011). For more information about the lawsuit, including the pleadings, see the Legal Action Center's website at *www.legalactioncenter.org/litigation/asylum-clock.*

[24] *A.B.T. et al. v. USCIS*, Settlement Agreement (Dec. 3, 2013), *http://legalactioncenter.org/sites/default/files/KLOK-Revised%20Settlement%20Agreement.pdf* (last visited Mar. 12, 2015).

[25] *See* OPPM 13-02: *The Asylum Clock*, *supra* note 17; OPPM 13-03: *A.B.T. Settlement*, *supra* note 19; USCIS Memorandum on Issuance of Revised Procedures Regarding Failure to Appear and Reschedule Requests (Oct. 17, 2013), *available at www.uscis.gov/sites/default/files/USCIS/Outreach/Notes%20from%20Previous%20Engagements/2013/Asylum-Issuance-Revised-Procedures-Failure-toAppear-RescheduleReq.pdf* (last visited Mar. 12, 2015); USCIS Memorandum on Application of the 'Exceptional Circumstances' Standard in Cases Where an Applicant has Failed to Appear for an Asylum Interview (Oct. 17, 2013), *available at www.uscis.gov/sites/default/files/USCIS/Outreach/Notes%20from%20Previous%20Engagements/2013/Asylum-Application-Exceptional-Circumstances.pdf* (last visited Mar. 12, 2015).

[26] (last visited Mar. 12, 2015).

[27] EOIR and USCIS, *The 180-Day Asylum EAD Clock Notice*, *available at www.uscis.gov/sites/default/files/USCIS/Humanitarian/Refugees%20%26%20Asylum/Asylum/Asylum_Clock_Joint_Notice.pdf* (last visited Mar. 12, 2015).

- Failure to appear for a fingerprint appointment;[28]
- Interview reschedule requests by the applicant (clock stops until the applicant appears for the rescheduled interview);
- Failure to appear for an interview, unless the applicant can show lack of proper notice by USCIS (clock stops and does not re-start unless the applicant makes a written request to the asylum office to reschedule the interview within 45 days and shows "good cause" for missing the interview, and then appears for the rescheduled interview[29]);
- Failure of a representative to appear at the asylum interview, causing rescheduling of the interview (clock stops until the applicant appears for the rescheduled interview);
- Failure of a dependent to appear at the interview (clock stops until the applicant presents the requested dependent);
- Failure to provide a competent interpreter causing rescheduling of the interview (clock stops until the applicant appears for the rescheduled interview);
- Rescheduling of the interview due to a representative abusing his or her role (clock stops until the applicant appears for the rescheduled interview);
- Putting the case on hold so the asylum officer can await a report on the analysis of a document believed to be fraudulent (clock stops until the officer receives the analysis);
- Requests by the applicant for the opportunity to submit additional documentation following conclusion of the interview (clock stops until the documents are submitted);
- If an asylum officer requires evidence of the applicant's residence to confirm jurisdiction and must put the case on hold for the applicant to provide that evidence (clock stops until the evidence is submitted);
- Requests to reschedule a pick-up appointment (clock stops until the applicant appears for the appointment, unless there is a final denial decision served);
- Failure to appear for a decision pick-up appointment[30] (clock stops until the applicant appears for the appointment, unless there is a final denial decision served; if referred, clock does not re-start until first master calendar hearing before the IJ[31]);

---

[28] *Id.*

[29] *Id.* For reschedule requests made after 45 days, the applicant must show "exceptional circumstances" to have the interview rescheduled. He or she may not be able to re-start the EAD clock. *See id.*

[30] Note that if an applicant fails to appear for a decision pick-up appointment, the decision letter and any other documentation will be mailed to the applicant. *See generally* USCIS, *Affirmative Asylum Procedures Manual*, pt. III.I.4. (Nov. 2013), *available at www.uscis.gov/sites/default/files/files/nativedocuments/Asylum_Procedures_Manual_2013.pdf* (last visited Jan. 22, 2015).

[31] USCIS & EOIR, The 180-Day Asylum EAD Clock Notice, *supra* note 27.

- Requests for an extension of time to file a rebuttal to a Notice of Intent to Deny (NOID) (clock stops until the rebuttal is filed); and
- Final denial of the asylum application (not a referral).[32]

For asylum cases pending before the immigration court, at the conclusion of each hearing, the IJ will assess the reason for the adjournment. If the adjournment is requested or caused by the applicant, the EAD clock will stop until the next hearing. The following actions may cause the EAD clock to stop accruing time during the pendency of an asylum application before the immigration courts:

- Requests for a continuance to find an attorney;
- Requests by an applicant or his or her representative for additional time to prepare the case;
- The applicant's or representative's declining of an expedited asylum hearing date;[33]
- Requests for a continuance to file an application;
- Requests for a continuance due to U.S. Department of Homeland Security (DHS) adjudications of petitions (*e.g.*, I-130, I-730);
- Motions between hearings that delay the case, such as a motion to continue or a motion to change venue, that are granted;
- Failure of the applicant, attorney or representative, or witness to appear at the hearing;
- Failure of the applicant, without good cause, to follow the biometrics requirements;[34]
- Requests for an in-person hearing;
- Illness of the applicant, attorney or representative, or witness;
- Requests for forensic analysis;
- Joint requests by the parties for adjournment;
- Contested charges;
- Administrative closure of the proceedings;[35] and

---

[32] *See generally,* U.S. Immigration and Citizenship Services (USCIS), *Affirmative Asylum Procedures Manual*, *supra* note 30.

[33] The *A.B.T. et al. v. USCIS* Settlement Agreement requires that immigration judges (IJs) set individual hearings no earlier than 45 days after a master calendar hearing, which lessens the need for asylum applicants to decline the first hearing date that is offered by the IJ. *See A.B.T. et al. v. USCIS*, Settlement Agreement, *supra* note 24.

[34] 8 CFR §§208.7(a)(2), 1208.7(a)(2) (2014).

[3535] At this time, Department of Homeland Security (DHS) takes the position that administrative closure stops the employment authorization document (EAD) clock from accruing time. However, if 180 days has already accrued prior to administrative closure, the applicant should be able to continue to be eligible for an EAD and renew his or her previously-issued EAD. *See* Application for Employment

Continued

- Issuance of a decision by the IJ.[36]

If the IJ denies the asylum application before 180 days have elapsed, the applicant will not be eligible for employment authorization, even if an appeal is filed with the BIA.[37] However, if the applicant appeals the decision to the Board of Immigration Appeals (BIA) and the BIA remands the case back to the IJ (including remands following an appeal to the U.S. circuit courts of appeals), the EAD clock will be credited with the total number of days between the IJ's decision and the date of the BIA's remand order.[38] The applicant will continue to accrue time on the EAD clock when the asylum claim is pending on remand, unless the applicant causes or requests a delay, as described above.[39]

> **Practice Pointer**: For all applicant-caused delays before the immigration court, EOIR requires that the clock remain stopped until the next hearing, even if the applicant cures the delay before the next hearing.[40]

Asylum applicants whose cases are pending before USCIS may determine how many days have elapsed on the EAD clock, or may raise errors or problems regarding the EAD clock calculation, by contacting the relevant "point of contact" at the asylum office that has jurisdiction over the case.[41]

> **Practice Pointer**: The assigned points of contact at the asylum offices will change and may change before USCIS updates its contacts list. Thus, practitioners may reach the correct person at the asylum office by asking for the "EAD POC" or "Clock POC." If the asylum office is unable to resolve the problem within a reasonable time period, practitioners may contact *asylumhq.eadclock@dhs.gov*.[42]

Asylum applicants whose cases are pending before the immigration court or BIA may determine the number of days elapsed on the EAD clock by calling the EOIR's

---

Authorization (Form I-765) pursuant to 8 CFR §274a.12(c)(8) from the Administrative Appeals Office (DHS Sept. 6, 2013) (non-precedent decision), available at *www.aila.org/content/default.aspx?bc =9418|10567|45915*. Even applicants whose cases are administratively closed, however, should argue that the time on the EAD clock continues to accrue. If administrative closure is merely a "docket management tool that has no jurisdictional effect" and the case otherwise remains pending and undecided, the EAD clock should continue to run following administrative closure. *See id.* at 4.

[36] USCIS & EOIR, *The 180-Day Asylum EAD Clock Notice*, *supra* note 27, at 2; OPPM 13-02: The Asylum Clock, *supra* note 17.

[37] USCIS & EOIR, *The 180-Day Asylum EAD Clock Notice*, *supra* note 27.

[38] *Id.*

[39] *Id.*

[40] *See* OPPM 13-02: *The Asylum Clock*, *supra* note 17, at 7, 11.

[41] *Id.*; USCIS, *Employment Authorization Asylum Clock Contacts*, (Apr. 30, 2014), *available at www.uscis.gov/sites/default/files/files/nativedocuments/EAD_and_KLOK_POCs_4_30_14.pdf.*

[42] *Id.*

hotline at 1-800-898-7180.[43] The hotline reports the number of days between the date the asylum application was filed with USCIS or at a hearing before an IJ and the date the IJ first issued a decision.[44] However, this number does not include:

- The time accrued on the EAD clock following lodging at the immigration court window prior to filing the applicant in open court with the IJ;
- Delays requested or caused by the applicant, when the EAD clock is stopped; or
- The time that USCIS may credit to an applicant's EAD clock upon remand by the BIA.[45]

Thus, the number of days on the hotline does not reflect the true number of days on the EAD clock, unless the applicant did not lodge the application before filing it in open court, did not cause any delays, and the case was not remanded by the BIA.[46] If an applicant did lodge his or her application at the immigration court window, he or she may determine the time accrued on the EAD clock by adding the number of days between the date of lodging the application and the date the application was filed in open court with the IJ (or the current date if the applicant has not yet had a hearing to file the application).[47] If an applicant's case was remanded by the BIA, he or she may determine the time accrued on the EAD clock by adding the number of days between the IJ's decision and the date of the BIA's remand order (or the current date since time continues to accrue while the case is on remand unless there are delays requested or caused by the applicant on remand).[48]

For cases pending before the immigration court, applicants who have questions or who wish to raise errors in the EAD clock calculation should do so with the IJ during the hearing, or with the court administrator in writing.[49] If the issue has not been correctly resolved at the immigration court level, he or she may contact the Assistant Chief Immigration Judge for the appropriate immigration court in writing, or if the case is on appeal, the EOIR Office of General Counsel.[50]

> **Practice Pointer**: The IJ will not address motions related to the EAD clock. This is not the appropriate manner to address errors in the time calculation.

> **Practice Pointer**: For a detailed discussion of how the EAD clock functions, common asylum clock problems and possible resolutions, how to address asylum EAD clock problems, and strategies for arguing that the clock should not be stopped in particular situations, see the

[43] USCIS & EOIR, The 180-Day Asylum EAD Clock Notice, *supra* note 27.

[44] *Id.*

[45] *Id.*

[46] *Id.*

[47] *Id.*

[48] *Id.*

[49] *Id.*

[50] *Id. See* OPPM 13-02: The Asylum Clock, *supra* note 17.

American Immigration Council Legal Action Center's Practice Advisory, "Employment Authorization and Asylum: Strategies to Avoid Stopping the Asylum EAD Clock," available at *www.legalactioncenter.org/sites/default/files/employment_authorization_and_asylum_fin_2-5-14_0.pdf*.[51]

3. *What Should be Filed?*

To apply for employment authorization, the applicant should file a completed and signed Form I-765, Application for Employment Authorization, along with the necessary supporting documentation.[52] Such supporting documentation should include:

- Two passport-sized photographs of the applicant (with the applicant's name and A# printed on the back of each), attached to the completed and signed Form I-765;
- Filing fee check or money order in the amount of $380, made payable to "U.S. Department of Homeland Security," if a fee is required;
- Form G-28, Notice of Entry of Appearance (if represented);
- A copy of the front and back of any previous employment authorization document(s);
- Evidence that the applicant has a pending asylum application;
- A copy of the biographic page of the applicant's passport (if available);
- A copy of the applicant's photo identification (if available); and
- A copy of the front and back of the applicant's most recent I-94 card (if available).[53]

> ➢ **Practice Pointer**: Practitioners should compile the above-listed documentation with a cover letter listing the documentation. The cover letter should include an explanation of the time elapsed on the EAD clock. Including this information may assist in clearing up any questions that the service center staff may have when the staff is processing the I-765 and may avoid improper rejection of the I-765.

In completing the I-765, item number 16 requires the applicant to list which category under which he or she is applying for employment authorization. Applicants who are applying based on having a pending Form I-589, Application for Asylum, as well as their family members who are physically present in the United States and

---

[51] (*last visited Mar. 12, 2015*).

[52] *See* USCIS, I-765, *Application for Employment Authorization*, *supra* note 6.

[53] *See* USCIS, *Instructions for I-765, Application for Employment Authorization*, *available at* *www.uscis.gov/sites/default/files/files/form/i-765instr.pdf* (last visited Mar. 12, 2015).

included as dependents on the I-589 application, should enter category "(C)(8)" in item 16 when preparing the Form I-765.[54]

> **Practice Pointer**: Along with their Form I-765 and the supporting documentation listed above, derivative applicants should provide evidence that they have been included in the principal's I-589 application, such as a copy of the I-589 or the family member's own biometrics notice.

There is no filing fee for an initial I-765 application based on a pending asylum application.[55] A fee is required for a renewal, however, unless the applicant is eligible for a fee waiver under 8 CFR §§103.7(c), 1103.7(c).[56] The fee may be waived if the applicant is able to substantiate that he or she is unable to pay the application fee. Applicants must file an affidavit or unsworn declaration asking for the waiver, stating their belief that they are deserving of employment authorization, and the reasons for their inability to pay the fee.[57] USCIS also recommends completing and filing Form I-912, Request for Fee Waiver, along with the I-765 application.

> **Practice Pointer**: For detailed instructions on preparing and filing an I-912 fee waiver request, see USCIS's website at *www.uscis.gov/i-912*.[58] Applicants for a fee waiver generally must show: (1) they are below 150 percent of the federal poverty line; (2) they are a recipient (or household member of a recipient) of a means-tested federal or state benefit; and (3) financial hardship, which is usually shown through an affidavit.

> **Practice Pointer**: If no fee is required, practitioners should state this in the cover letter that is filed with the I-765 application and cite to the relevant law. Practitioners also may consider highlighting this statement in yellow to bring it to the attention of the service center staff. I-765s are often wrongly rejected by the service center due to the fact that there is no filing fee included, even when no filing fee is required. Attempts to preempt this can avoid delay for clients.

Regarding proof that the applicant has a pending I-589 application, this may include a USCIS receipt notice if the I-589 remains pending before USCIS, a USCIS receipt notice noting that an I-589 application has been filed defensively, the Form I-589 stamped "received" by the immigration court, a copy of the next hearing notice before the immigration court, a copy of the BIA filing receipt for an appeal, or other evidence that the application remains under administrative or judicial review.[59]

---

[54] *Id.* at 1.

[55] 8 CFR §§274a.13(a)(1), 1274a.13(a)(1) (2014).

[56] 8 CFR §§274a.13(a)(2), 1274a.13(a)(2) (2014).

[57] 8 CFR §§103.7(c), 1103.7(c) (2014).

[58] (last visited Apr. 1, 2015).

[59] *See* USCIS, Instructions for I-765, Application, *supra* note 53.

- **Practice Pointer**: For cases pending before the immigration court, practitioners should have the immigration judge's legal assistant stamp the I-589 "received" at the time of filing the I-589 in open court. Practitioners should request the I-589 itself be stamped, rather than a cover page or other document in the filing. Sometimes, USCIS will not accept other stamped documents as evidence that the I-589 itself has been filed.

- **Practice Pointer**: It is usually best to send as much proof of a pending I-589 as possible to avoid improper rejection of the I-765 by the service center. For example, if an I-589 is pending before the immigration court, the applicant should submit the USCIS receipt notice noting the defensive filing, the Form I-589 stamped as received, and a copy of the next hearing notice.

- **Practice Pointer**: Asylum-seekers and asylees also may file their EAD applications online. This process may be faster and does not require the applicant to sign the form, which can be helpful when a client lives far away from his or her attorney or representative. Additionally, no photos are required if the EAD application is filed online. The process involves completing the form online, printing the cover sheet that is automatically generated, and filing any supporting documents, such as those listed above. See USCIS's website at *www.uscis.gov/e-filing-i-765*[60] for additional information on completing and filing the EAD application online.

4. *Where Should the EAD Application be Filed?*

The application should be filed with the USCIS service center that has jurisdiction over the residence of the applicant.[61] Currently, applications for employment authorization based on pending asylum applications, as well as those based on granted asylum status, are filed with either the Phoenix or Dallas Lockbox, depending on where the applicant lives.[62] Applications for employment authorization based on granted withholding of removal status under INA §241(b)(3) or CAT are filed with the Chicago Lockbox.[63]

- **Practice Pointer**: Before filing an application for employment authorization, practitioners should always check USCIS's website and the up-to-date instructions on the Form I-765 to determine the relevant filing location, as the filing locations frequently change.

[60] (last visited Apr. 2, 2015).

[61] *See* 8 CFR §§274a.13(a)(2), 1274a.13(a)(2) (2014).

[62] *See* USCIS, Direct Filing Addresses for Form I-765, Application for Employment Authorization, available at *www.uscis.gov/i-765-addresses* (last visited Mar. 12, 2015).

[63] *Id.*

5. *How is an EAD Application Processed?*

Upon receipt of the Form I-765 and supporting documentation, USCIS will initiate processing of the application. Any Form I-765 that is not signed or submitted with the correct fee will be rejected with a notice that Form I-765 is deficient. The deficiency may be corrected and the I-765 filing may be resubmitted.[64]

Once Form I-765 has been accepted, USCIS will issue a receipt notice and mail it to the applicant and his or her representative. The form and supporting documentation also will be checked for completeness. If the form is not completely filled out or if it is not filed with the required initial evidence, it may be denied.[65] USCIS may issue a request for additional evidence, and may even request that the individual appear at a USCIS office for an interview, although interviews for I-765 applications are rare.[66]

USCIS also may require the applicant to appear at a USCIS Application Support Center (ASC) to provide biometrics before the application is adjudicated and the EAD card is produced. If necessary, USCIS will issue an ASC appointment notice scheduling the applicant for an appointment at a local ASC. If the applicant does not attend the ASC appointment, his or her application may be denied.[67]

If the I-765 application is approved, USCIS usually mails an I-765 approval notice and the EAD card directly to the applicant. If the application is denied, USCIS will send a written notice explaining its basis for the denial.[68] If the applicant has an attorney or representative who has filed a G-28, that individual will be copied on all USCIS correspondence.

For initial applications for employment authorization based on asylum, USCIS has 30 days from the date the I-765 is filed to grant or deny the application.[69] No employment authorization may be issued, however, prior to the expiration of the 180-day period following the filing of an application for asylum that was filed on or after April 1, 1997.[70] Thus, if the asylum applicant files the I-765 application after 150 days have lapsed on the EAD clock, USCIS will not issue an EAD within 30 days. Rather, USCIS would have to wait until day 180 to issue the EAD.[71]

For all other EAD applications and for EAD renewal applications, USCIS must adjudicate the application within 90 days of receipt.[72] Failure to complete the adjudication within 90 days should result in the grant of an interim EAD for a period

---

[64] *See* USCIS, Instructions for I-765, *supra* note 53, at 9.

[65] *Id.*

[66] *Id.*

[67] *Id.*

[68] *Id.* at 10.

[69] 8 CFR §§208.7(a)(1), 1208.7(a)(1) (2014).

[70] 8 CFR §§208.7(a)(1), 1208.7(a)(1) (2014).

[71] *See supra* Part I.A.2.

[72] 8 CFR §§274a.13(d), 1274a.13(d) (2014).

not to exceed 240 days.[73] The interim EAD will automatically terminate if the application for employment authorization is denied.[74]

> **Practice Pointer**: To request an interim EAD after the I-765 has been pending for 90 days (or 30 days for an initial I-765 based on asylum, unless the EAD clock has not accrued 180 days yet), applicants should call the USCIS National Customer Service Center or make an InfoPass appointment at a local USCIS office.[75] The local USCIS offices used to be able to produce interim EADs on-site. However, as of August of 2006, they no longer produce EADs on-site.[76] Thus, it is recommended that applicants call the National Customer Service Center (NCSC) at 1-800-375-5283 to request an interim EAD. The NCSC has a service request category specific to EAD-related inquiries: "Outside Regulatory Processing Time." These requests are forwarded to the appropriate service center or National Benefits Center. USCIS should either adjudicate the I-765 or issue an interim EAD Card within 10 days of receiving the request.[77] Currently, there are widespread processing delays for EAD applications of asylum-seekers, perhaps due to the large backlogs across the country of long-pending asylum applications. However, USCIS has not been issuing interim EADs in a timely manner, if at all, despite the regulatory requirement to do so. Advocacy organizations are currently working to raise and address this widespread problem.

6. *What if the EAD Expires Before the I-589 is Adjudicated?*

If an EAD is granted and issued based on a pending asylum application, given the current backlogs in processing I-589 applications before USCIS and the immigration courts, it is possible that the I-589 may still be pending as the expiration date of the initial EAD is approaching. Employment authorization is renewable during the period of time necessary for the asylum officer or IJ to decide the asylum application and, if necessary, for the completion of any administrative or judicial review.[78]

To file a renewal application, the applicant must file a completed and signed Form I-765, the required fee (unless waived under 8 CFR §§103.7(c), 1103.7(c)) and proof

---

[73] *Id.*

[74] *Id.*

[75] *See* USCIS, Instructions for I-765, *supra* note 53, at 10.

[76] *See* USCIS Public Notice, *USCIS Reminds Customers of Filing Change for Employments Authorization Documents [EAD]* (revised Aug. 9, 2006), *available at www.uscis.gov/files/pressrelease/EADFilingCh072806PN.pdf.*

[77] *See* USCIS Memorandum from Michael Aytes on Response to Recommendation 35, Recommendations on USCIS Processing Delays for Employment Authorization Documents, *available at www.dhs.gov/xlibrary/assets/uscis_response_to_cisomb_recommendation35_01_02_09.*pdf (last visited Mar. 12, 2015).

[78] 8 CFR §§208.7(b), 1208.7(b) (2014).

that the applicant is continuing to pursue his or her asylum application.[79] Depending on the stage of the applicant's immigration proceedings, he or she must submit either a copy of: (1) the asylum denial, referral notice, or charging document for IJ proceedings; (2) a BIA receipt of timely appeal for applications pending at the BIA; or (3) the petition for review date stamped by the appropriate court for claims pending in federal court.[80]

> **Practice Pointer**: The EAD renewal process also may be completed online, as described above. The instructions are on USCIS's website at *www.uscis.gov/e-filing-i-765.*[81]

In order for the employment authorization to be renewed before its expiration date, the I-765 must be filed 100 days before the expiration of the previously issued employment authorization.[82] Applications for EAD renewals will be accepted up to 120 days before the expiration of the employment authorization documents.[83]

> **Practice Pointer**: Practitioners should check current processing times for I-765 applications on the USCIS website and prepare to file the renewal application at least that many months prior to the expiration date on the EAD. Typically, USCIS will not reject the renewal application, but usually will not grant and issue the new EAD until the current EAD expires.

7. *Is an EAD Still Valid After an I-589 is Denied?*

If an applicant's I-765 application is pending when his or her I-589 application for asylum is denied, the I-765 also will be denied.[84] If an applicant is granted employment authorization and obtains an EAD after he or she accrued 180 days on the EAD clock, how long the EAD remains valid depends on the procedural posture of the case. If the applicant received the EAD while his or her case was pending before USCIS and the asylum office denies (not refers) the I-589, the EAD will remain valid until the expiration of the EAD or 60 days after the asylum office denial, whichever is later.[85] If the applicant received the EAD while his or her case was

[79] 8 CFR §§208.7(c), 1208.7(c) (2014).

[80] 8 CFR §§208.7(c), 1208.7(c) (2014).

[81] (last visited Apr. 2, 2015).

[82] Although 8 CFR §§208.7(d), 1208.7(d) state that the application must be filed 90 days before the expiration of the EAD, a USCIS Public Notice states that the application must be filed 100 days before, effective August 1, 2006. *See* USCIS Public Notice, "USCIS Reminds Customers of Filing Change for Employments Authorization Documents [EAD]," at 2 (revised Aug. 9, 2006), *available at www.uscis.gov/files/pressrelease/EADFilingCh072806PN.pdf.*

[83] USCIS, *Employment Authorization Document*, *available at www.uscis.gov/green-card/green-card-processes-and-procedures/employment-authorization-document* (last visited Mar. 29, 2015) (stating "you cannot file for a renewal EAD more than 120 days before your original EAD expires").

[84] 8 CFR §§208.7(a)(1), 1208.7(a)(1) (2014).

[85] 8 CFR §§208.7(b)(1), 1208.7(b)(1) (2014).

pending before USCIS and the asylum office refers the I-589 to the immigration court, the EAD will remain valid and the applicant may seek renewal of the EAD while the case remains pending before the immigration court.[86] If the applicant received the EAD while his or her case was pending before the immigration court, and the IJ denies the asylum application, the applicant may continue to renew his or her EAD throughout administrative and judicial review.[87] If he or she does not appeal, or if the application is ultimately denied after all appeals have been exhausted, employment authorization terminates on the expiration date listed on the EAD.[88]

B. Social Security Cards

In addition to an EAD, asylum applicants often need Social Security numbers to open bank accounts, file taxes, or provide another form of documentation to employers while completing their Form I-9. Asylum applicants are eligible for social security cards upon receipt of their EAD. Their cards, however, will bear the notation, "Valid for Work Only with DHS Authorization."

There is often a significant delay from the date employment authorization is granted until the immigration authorities notify the Social Security Administration (SSA) that the applicant is authorized to work. There is a further delay of up to six weeks before an application for a Social Security number is processed. The lack of a Social Security number during this interim period should not result in a denial of employment or delay in beginning employment. Under Internal Revenue Service (IRS) regulations,[89] an employer that has an employee who has not been issued a Social Security number can accept the following documentation for employment and payroll: (1) a receipt for the application for a Social Security number, along with the employee's name and address as shown on the receipt and the expiration date of the receipt; or (2) a copy of the application for a Social Security card (Form SS-5) until the card is issued.[90]

Additionally, asylum-seekers often experience difficulty in applying for social security numbers even after issuance of an EAD under category (C)(8) (pending asylum application) because the local SSA offices often require a second form of government-issued photo identification, such as a passport. Many asylum-seekers arrive in the United States without passports or other forms of photo identification, and some have no access to such documents due to the lack of a functioning government or because they are fleeing their governments. The SSA's refusal to issue social security numbers to these asylum applicants often prevents them from working

---

[86] *See* 8 CFR §208.14(c).

[87] 8 CFR §§208.7(b), 1208.7(b).

[88] 8 CFR §§208.7(b)(2), 1208.7(b)(2).

[89] 26 CFR §31.6011(b)–2(c)(2).

[90] These procedures are explained more fully in Internal Revenue Serv. (IRS) Publication Circular E and Circular E Supp., *available at www.irs.gov/publications/p15/index.html*.

or being issued state identity documents and driver's licenses. The AILA Asylum and Refugee Liaison Committee has raised this issue with the SSA. However, it continues to be a problem in certain SSA offices.

- **Practice Pointer**: AILA members whose clients are experiencing this document problem at the SSA office should advise their clients to first try going to a different SSA office. They also should contact their local AILA SSA liaison to raise the issue and request that it be addressed with the local SSA office. AILA members also should send the following information to *reports@aila.org* with the subject line "Asylum Applicant SSNs": (1) the approximate date the SSA refused to issue the social security number; (2) which SSA office the asylum applicant went to; and (3) which country the asylum applicant is from.[91]

- **Practice Pointer**: What are the implications of using or having used a false SSN? For a thorough discussion of this issue, see C. Wheeler, "Immigration Consequences of Using a False Social Security Number," 8 *Bender's Immigr. Bull.* 952 (June 1, 2003).

C. Federal Individual Tax ID Numbers

Both asylees and asylum applicants may need to apply to the IRS for an Individual Taxpayer Identification Number (ITIN).[92] Any individual who has a federal tax reporting or filing requirement and does not qualify for a social security number needs an ITIN.[93] An individual who lacks a social security number but wants to open a bank account also needs an ITIN, since banks are required to report any interest earned on their accounts.[94]

In order to obtain an ITIN, an individual must fill out a revised IRS Form W-7 and attach a federal income tax return (unless the individual qualified for an exception).[95] The individual must also provide proof of identity.[96] The IRS website lists the 13

---

[91] *See* AILA, *Call for Examples: Asylum Applicants Lacking a Secondary ID*, AILA InfoNet Doc. No. 14102144 (*posted* Oct. 21, 2014), *available at www.aila.org/advo-media/agency-liaison/case-examples/asylum-applicants-lacking-a-secondary-id* (last visited Mar. 12, 2015).

[92] *See generally* IRS, *Individual Taxpayer Identification Number (ITIN), available at www.irs.gov/individuals/article/0,,id=96287,00.html.*

[93] *Id.*

[94] *See, e.g.*, Nat'l Assoc. of Foreign Student Advisors (NAFSA), *Opening a Student Bank Account, available at www.nafsa.org/Find_Resources/_Sidebars/Opening_a_Student_Bank_Account/.*

[95] IRS, *Individual Taxpayer Identification Number (ITIN), supra* note 92; Form W-7 is available at *www.irs.gov/pub/irs-pdf/fw7.pdf.* The applicant's Form W-7, tax return, and proof of identity should be mailed to: Internal Revenue Service, Austin Service Center, ITIN Operation, P.O. Box 149342, Austin, TX, 78714-9342.

[96] IRS, *Individual Taxpayer Identification Number (ITIN), supra* note 92.

types of documents that are acceptable for proving identity.[97] ITINs are not a valid form of identification outside the tax system.[98]

D. Advance Parole to Travel for Affirmative Applicants

Given the significant backlogs in processing I-589 applications before USCIS, some asylum applicants may desire to travel abroad during the pendency of their I-589 applications. Departing the United States before a final decision on the applicant's asylum application, however, could place his or her eligibility in jeopardy or could result in the abandonment of the application altogether. It is important for applicants to understand and follow the procedures for securing a travel document while their I-589 application remains pending before USCIS.

- **Practice Pointer**: In general, practitioners should advise their asylum-applicant clients *against* traveling abroad during the pendency of their I-589 application. Traveling abroad is very risky and there is no guarantee that the applicant will be readmitted to the United States or that his or her asylum application will not be adversely affected.

- **Practice Pointer**: Asylum applicants in removal proceedings before the immigration courts must never leave the United States. If they leave the United States while they are in removal proceedings, they will have "self-deported," and will not be able to reenter the United States.

Certain departures from the United States while an affirmative asylum applicant's I-589 is pending may cause the agency to presume that the applicant has abandoned his or her application. These include: (1) if the applicant departs the United States without first obtaining advance parole; and (2) if the applicant departs the United States pursuant to a grant of advance parole and returns to this or her country of feared persecution.[99] In both instances, an applicant may overcome the presumption of abandonment; however, any return to the applicant's country of feared persecution will have a bearing on his or her ability to establish a well-founded fear.[100] Relevant factors may include the reasons for the departure, length and purpose of the departure, whether the applicant returned to the country of feared persecution, whether there were compelling reasons for doing so, what happened while the applicant was in his or her country of feared persecution, the circumstances for the applicant while in the country of feared persecution, and whether the applicant has returned to the United States and appeared for his or her asylum interview.[101] Thus, in

---

[97] *Id.*

[98] *Id.*

[99] USCIS, *Affirmative Asylum Procedures Manual*, *supra* note 30, at pt. III.D.

[100] *See* ch. 2 for a detailed discussion of returning to the country of feared persecution and what effect that could have on the applicant's eligibility for asylum.

[101] *See* ch. 2 for a detailed discussion of returning to the country of feared persecution and what effect that could have on the applicant's eligibility for asylum. *See also* USCIS, *Affirmative Asylum Procedures Manual*, *supra* note 30, at pt. III.D.

order to avoid abandoning the application, an asylum applicant should apply for advance parole prior to his or her departure from the United States.[102] Most importantly, he or she must not return to the country of feared persecution.

Advance parole is permission to reenter the United States after traveling abroad. By law, certain individuals, such as asylum applicants, must apply for advance parole and have an approved advance parole travel document in hand before leaving the United States.[103] Attempts to reenter the United States following travel abroad without prior authorization may have very severe consequences, especially for asylum applicants, as explained above. Even departures pursuant to advance parole could have very severe consequences. In fact, USCIS provides an extensive warning in this regard on its Form I-131 instructions for advance parole applications.[104]

---

[102] USCIS, *USCIS Reminds Applicants for Travel Documents to Apply Early* (Oct. 19, 2009), *www.aila.org/File/Related/102209%20USCIS%20AdvanceParole%20Update%20and%20Fact Sheet.pdf* (last visited Mar. 12, 2015); USCIS, *USCIS Reminds Applicants for Adjustment of Status, Asylum, Legalization, and TPS Beneficiaries to Obtain Advance Parole Before Traveling Abroad* (May 29, 2009), *available at www.aila.org/infonet/uscis-obtain-parole-before-traveling-abroad* (last visited Mar. 12, 2015); USCIS Fact Sheet, *Traveling Outside the United States as an Asylum Applicant, an Asylee, or a Lawful Permanent Resident Who Obtained Such Status Based on Asylum Status* (Jan. 4, 2007), *available at www.aila.org/content/default.aspx?docid=21301* (last visited Jan. 24, 2015).

[103] USCIS, *USCIS Reminds Applicants for Travel Documents to Apply Early*, *supra* note 102; USCIS, *USCIS Reminds Applicants for Adjustment of Status, Asylum, Legalization, and TPS Beneficiaries to Obtain Advance Parole*, *supra* note 106; USCIS Fact Sheet, *Traveling Outside the United States as an Asylum Applicant, an Asylee, or a Lawful Permanent Resident*, *supra* note 106.

[104] As stated in the I-131 Instructions:

"For any kind of Advance Parole Document provided to you while you are in the United States:

(1) Leaving the United States, even with an Advance Parole Document, may impact your ability to return to the United States.

(2) If you use an Advance Parole Document to leave and return to a port-of-entry in the United States, you will, upon your return, be an "applicant for admission."

(3) As an applicant for admission, you will be subject to inspection at a port-of-entry, and you may not be admitted if you are found to be inadmissible under any applicable provision of INA sections 212(a), 235, or any other provision of U.S. law regarding denial of admission to the United States. If DHS determines that you are inadmissible, you may be subject to expedited removal proceedings or to removal proceedings before an immigration judge, as authorized by law and regulations.

(4) As noted above, issuance of an Advance Parole Document does *not* entitle you to parole and does *not* guarantee that DHS will parole you into the United States upon your return.

(5) As noted above, DHS will make a separate discretionary decision whether to parole you each time you use an Advance Parole Document to return to the United States.

(6) If, upon your return, you are paroled into the United States, you will remain an applicant for admission.

(7) As noted above, DHS may revoke or terminate your Advance Parole Document at any time, including while you are outside the United States. Even if you have already been paroled, upon your return to the United States DHS may also revoke or terminate your parole in accordance with 8 CFR 212.5.

Continued

> **Practice Pointer**: All practitioners should discuss these travel warnings in detail with their clients before agreeing to move forward with seeking an advance parole travel document on their clients' behalf.

If, despite the warnings against travel, an asylum applicant still needs to travel abroad while his or her I-589 remains pending, the applicant may apply for advance parole on Form I-131, which is available on USCIS's website.[105] He or she must plan ahead, as it takes approximately 90 days for USCIS to adjudicate I-131 applications and grant advance parole travel documents.[106] Along with the completed and signed Form I-131, applicants should submit the following documentation:

- Two passport-sized photographs of the applicant (with the applicant's name and A# printed on the back of each), attached to the completed and signed Form I-131;
- Filing fee check or money order in the amount of $360, made payable to "U.S. Department of Homeland Security," if a fee is required;
- Form G-28, Notice of Entry of Appearance (if represented);
- Evidence that the applicant has a pending asylum application;

If you are outside the United States, revocation or termination of your Advance Parole Document may preclude you from returning to the United States unless you have a valid visa or other document that permits you to travel to the United States and seek admission.

(8) If you are in the United States when DHS revokes or terminates your parole, you will be an unparoled applicant for admission, and may be subject to removal as an applicant for admission who is inadmissible under INA section 212, rather than as an admitted alien who is deportable under INA section 237. In addition to the above, if you received deferred action under DACA, you should also be aware of the following:

(a) Even after USCIS or ICE has deferred action in your case under DACA, you should not travel outside the United States unless USCIS has approved your application for an Advance Parole Document. Deferred action will terminate automatically if you travel outside the United States without obtaining an Advance Parole Document from USCIS.

(b) If you obtain an Advance Parole Document in connection with a decision to defer removal in your case under DACA and if, upon your return, you are paroled into the United States, your case will generally continue to be deferred. The deferral will continue until the date specified by USCIS or ICE in the deferral notice given to you or until the decision to defer removal action in your case has been terminated, whichever is earlier.

(c) If you have been ordered excluded, deported, or removed, departing from the United States without having had your exclusion, deportation, or removal proceedings reopened and administratively closed or terminated will result in your being considered excluded, deported, or removed, even if USCIS or ICE has deferred action in your case under DACA and you have been granted advance parole."

USCIS, *Form I-131 Instructions*, at 5-6, *available at www.uscis.gov/sites/default/files/files/form/i-131instr.pdf* (last visited Mar. 12, 2015).

[105] USCIS, *Form I-131 Application for Travel Document*, *available at www.uscis.gov/i-131* (last visited Jan. 24, 2015).

[106] USCIS, *USCIS Reminds Applicants for Travel Documents to Apply Early*, *supra* note 102; USCIS, *USCIS Reminds Applicants for Adjustment of Status, Asylum, Legalization, and TPS Beneficiaries to Obtain Advance Parole*, *supra* note 106; USCIS Fact Sheet, *Traveling Outside the United States as an Asylum Applicant, an Asylee, or a Lawful Permanent Resident*, *supra* note 106.

- An explanation or evidence demonstrating the applicant's need to travel;
- A copy of the biographic page of the applicant's passport (if available);
- A copy of the applicant's photo identification (if available); and
- A copy of the front and back of the applicant's most recent I-94 card (if available).[107]

When preparing the Form I-131, there is no specific guidance given for asylum applicants applying for advance parole. At the USCIS Asylum Division Stakeholder meeting on October 23, 2013, AILA raised this issue and the Asylum Division advised that applicants should follow the instructions for "all others."[108] The Asylum Division indicated that it would raise the lack of specific instructions for asylum applicants at the next Service Center Operations meeting to hopefully improve the I-131 instructions and the information provided on the USCIS website.[109]

Asylum applicants must receive their advance parole document before departing the United States. It is important to note, however, that advance parole does not guarantee that the applicant will be paroled into the United States. Rather, the asylum applicant must still undergo inspection by an immigration inspector from U.S. Customs and Border Protection.[110]

II. Immigration Benefits for Those Granted Protection

What benefits are available to an individual who has been granted protection from persecution or torture in the United States depends on the form of relief he or she was granted. Individuals granted asylum in the United States (asylees) have a variety of immigration-related and public benefits that those granted withholding of removal under INA §241(b)(3) or protection under the CAT do not enjoy. The following chart depicts these critical differences, which are discussed in detail throughout this section:

---

[107] *See* USCIS, *Form I-131 Instructions*, *supra* note 104, at 7–11.

[108] *See* USCIS Asylum Division Stakeholder Meeting Agenda and Unofficial Notes, AILA InfoNet at Doc. No. 13110860, *available at www.aila.org/content/default.aspx?docid=46408* (last visited Jan. 24, 2015).

[109] *See id.*

[110] *See* USCIS Fact Sheet, *Traveling Outside the United States as an Asylum Applicant, an Asylee, or a Lawful Permanent Resident*, *supra* note 106.

BENEFITS COMPARISON CHART	Asylum	Withholding of Removal under INA §241(b)(3)	CAT Protection
Right to Remain in the U.S.	Confers permission to remain in the U.S.	Prohibits removal to the country of feared persecution, but does not prohibit removal to other countries	Prohibits removal to the country of feared torture, but does not prohibit removal to other countries
Documentation of Status	Asylum Approval letter or IJ Order granting asylum; I-94 card showing admission as asylee	IJ Order showing order of removal, but noting removal withheld to the country of feared persecution	IJ Order showing order of removal, but noting removal withheld to the country of feared torture
EAD	Confers automatic employment authorization upon grant	Confers eligibility to apply for employment authorization under category (A)(10)	Confers eligibility to apply for employment authorization for those granted withholding, but not necessarily for those granted deferral of removal
Travel	Confers eligibility to file an application for a refugee travel document to travel outside the U.S.	No ability to travel outside of the U.S. and then re-enter	No ability to travel outside of the U.S. and then re-enter
Family	Spouses and children in the U.S. may be granted asylum as derivatives; confers eligibility to petition for spouses and children to follow to join the asylee in the U.S.	No ability to include spouses and children as dependent applicants or to petition for spouses and children	No ability to include spouses and children as dependent applicants or to petition for spouses and children
Lawful Permanent Residency (LPR) and Citizenship	Confers eligibility to apply for LPR status after one year physically present in the U.S. as an asylee	No pathway to permanent residence or citizenship	No pathway to permanent residence or citizenship
Public Benefits	Confers potential eligibility for federal means-tested public benefits, means-tested refugee cash and medical assistance, refugee social services, matching grant, and a medical screening	No eligibility for public benefits	No eligibility for public benefits

➢ **Practice Pointer**: For a comprehensive overview of the differences between asylum and withholding of removal benefits, see Cheri Attix's practice pointer, "Understanding Withholding of Removal," available on AILA InfoNet at Doc. No. 14021344 (*posted* Feb. 13, 2014) and at *www.aila.org/infonet/uscis-understanding-withholding-of-removal*.[111]

A. Right to Remain in the United States

Perhaps the most obvious benefit for an individual granted asylum, withholding of removal under INA §241(b)(3), or protection under the CAT is the right to remain in the United States, where the individual may be safe from the persecution or torture from which he or she fled. However, while asylees are granted permission to remain in the United States, individuals granted withholding of removal or CAT relief are actually ordered removed. Despite their removal orders, however, the U.S. government is prohibited from removing them to the country where it is more likely than not that his or her life or freedom would be threated or where it is more likely than not that he or she would be tortured.[112] Therefore, their removal is withheld, but only from the specific country or countries of feared persecution or torture.[113]

B. Evidence of Status

The second benefit for individuals granted protection in the United States is documentation of their status and permission to be in the United States. Again, however, the benefits for asylees in this regard are far superior to those for individuals granted withholding of removal or CAT relief.

An individual granted asylum before the USCIS asylum office will automatically receive the following documents upon being granted asylum: (1) Asylum Approval letter, confirming approval of the application and describing the various benefits that accompany a grant of asylum in the United States; (2) I-94 card, endorsed with the asylum approval stamp that bears the date of asylum approval, signature, asylum office code, and office ID number of the adjudicating officer; and (3) EAD card with the asylee's photo and biographic information, noting that he or she is authorized to work pursuant to a grant of asylum (category (A)(5)), which is valid for two years.[114]

The asylee will receive the Asylum Approval letter and I-94 card on the day that he or she picks up the decision. The EAD card usually follows in the mail approximately two weeks later.

An individual granted asylum by an IJ, however, will receive only the IJ's decision and order granting him or her asylum. He or she must then take certain steps

---

[111] (last visited Mar. 11, 2015).

[112] INA §241(b)(3); 8 CFR §§208.16, 1208.16 (2014).

[113] INA §§241(b)(1)-(3); 8 CFR §§208.16(d)(1), 208.16(f), 1208.16(d)(1), 1208.16(f) (2014); *Matter of I-S- & C-S-*, 24 I&N Dec. 432 (BIA 2008). *See* Cheri Attix, AILA Asylum and Refugee Liaison Comm., *Practice Pointer: Understanding Withholding of Removal*, *published on* AILA InfoNet Doc. No. 14021344 (*posted* Feb. 13, 2014) (last visited Dec. 28, 2014).

[114] USCIS, Affirmative Asylum Procedures Manual, *supra* note 30, at pts. II.Q.2. & III.F.4. Note that, while asylees are granted initial EADs valid for two years, which are automatically generated, withholding of removal grantees must prepare and file applications for EADs and, upon being granted an EAD, it is only valid for one year.

in order to obtain his or her I-94 card and EAD card once the IJ's order becomes final — upon waiver of appeal by DHS or after the 30-day appeal period has passed with no appeal filed. These asylees must make an InfoPass appointment with USCIS online at *https://infopass.uscis.gov*.[115] The appointment should be made at least three days after the IJ's order to allow USCIS sufficient time to receive the individual's data from the immigration court.[116] The asylee should bring the following documents with him or her to the InfoPass appointment:

- InfoPass appointment confirmation form;
- Photo identification;
- Two passport-size photographs of each asylee; and
- The IJ's final order granting asylum.[117]

USCIS will provide an I-94 card as evidence of the individual's admission to the United States as an asylee. USCIS also will initiate the production of the asylee's EAD at that time. The EAD card will then be sent to the asylee by mail to his or her address on file with USCIS.[118]

> **Practice Pointer**: Asylees granted asylum in immigration court will only be able to attend an InfoPass appointment with USCIS to obtain an I-94 and initiate production of their EAD after the IJ's order is final. If DHS has waived appeal or if the 30 day appeal period has passed since the date of the IJ's order, the IJ's order is final. Practitioners may check whether DHS has filed an appeal by calling the EOIR's hotline at 1-800-898-7180 and typing in their clients' A-numbers. If DHS does file an appeal, the individual may still be eligible for employment authorization based on having an application for asylum pending beyond 180 days. If the BIA then affirms the IJ's order granting asylum, the order is final and the individual may move forward with making an InfoPass appointment to obtain an EAD.[119]

> **Practice Pointer**: Often, InfoPass appointments are not available for several weeks. Practitioners should consider making an InfoPass appointment for their client in advance of the individual hearing so he or she has an appointment scheduled as close as possible to the hearing. After the hearing, if the IJ has not issued a decision, if the decision is

---

[115] USCIS, *Post-Order Instructions for Individuals Granted Relief or Protection from Removal by Immigration Court*, *available at www.uscis.gov/sites/default/files/files/article/PostOrderInstr.pdf* (last visited Mar. 11, 2015).

[116] *Id.*

[117] *Id.*

[118] *See* Catholic Legal Immigration Network, Inc., *Asylee Eligibility for Resettlement Assistance*, at 7, *available at https://cliniclegal.org/sites/default/files/234843_clinic_asylee_final_1-30-12.pdf* (last visited Apr. 2, 2015).

[119] *Id.*

not favorable, or if DHS reserves appeal, practitioners may always cancel the InfoPass appointment and schedule a new one once a favorable, final decision has been issued.

An individual granted withholding of removal or protection under CAT, however, will not receive any evidence of his or her status other than the IJ's order granting withholding of removal under INA §241(b)(3) or withholding or deferral of removal under the CAT. This can be problematic because the IJ's order first notes a removal order entered against the individual, and then notes that removal has been withheld or deferred under INA §241(b)(3) or CAT. When these individuals show the IJ's order as evidence of their status to a landlord, an employer, a school, a social security office, a bank, or other body as proof of their immigration status, the IJ's order often is met with confusion and a demand for better documentation. Fortunately, individuals who have been granted withholding of removal, as well as some individuals granted deferral of removal, are eligible to apply for an EAD card, which is a much more accepted form of identification and evidence of status.[120]

- **Practice Pointer**: Practitioners should provide their clients with a letter explaining what withholding of removal or deferral of removal is and why the IJ's order is valid evidence of their right to be present in the United States. Often, it helps to include a warning that discrimination on the basis of immigration status is prohibited and punishable by federal law.[121]

C. Employment Authorization

The third, and often most desired, benefit upon being granted protection in the United States is the ability to work legally. Given how complicated it can be for applicants to apply for and receive an EAD while their I-589 applications are pending, many individuals are not able to obtain work authorization until after they have been granted relief. Individuals who have received a final grant of asylum by USCIS, IJ, or BIA are automatically authorized for employment by virtue of their status as "asylees."[122] Individuals who have received a final grant of withholding of removal under INA §241(b)(3) or CAT also are eligible for employment authorization, but must apply for that authorization first.[123] Those granted deferral of removal under CAT, are not necessarily eligible for employment authorization, but often are able to apply and receive employment authorization as an individual with a

[120] *See infra* pt. II.C. for a detailed discussion of EADs for those granted withholding or deferral of removal.

[121] *See* Attix, *Practice Pointer: Understanding Withholding of Removal*, *supra* note 113.

[122] 8 CFR §§274a.12(a)(5), 1274a.12(a)(5) (2014). *See also* D. Cleveland, *Employment Authorization for Asylees*, IMMIGRATION & NATIONALITY LAW HANDBOOK 85 (AILA 2009–10 ed.), *available on* AILALink.

[123] 8 CFR §§274a.12(a)(10), 1274a.12(a)(10) (2014).

final order of removal who is released on an order of supervision.[124] This is a discretionary determination by DHS. The procedures for obtaining EADs for those granted each of these forms of relief are discussed below.

1. EADs for Asylees

Asylees are immediately authorized for employment upon being granted asylum, whether or not they have an EAD.[125] An EAD is not required for asylees to be able to work. Typically, however, it is beneficial for asylees to obtain an EAD. Not only does this serve as a form of photo identification that many asylees do not otherwise have, but also, many employers do not understand that asylees are eligible to work by virtue of their status. Although employers should recognize that asylees do not need an EAD to be employment authorized, it is beneficial for asylees to obtain EADs to avoid any questions about authorization to work, the answers to which may be difficult for a new asylee to explain.

> **Practice Pointer**: Practitioners may need to assist their clients following a grant of asylum with explaining to various employers their clients' eligibility to work by virtue of their asylee status. Usually, a simple letter citing the law and inviting the employer to contact you with any questions will suffice. It may also be useful to include the number for the Office of Special Counsel for Immigration-Related Unfair Employment Practices hotline for employers in the letter (1-800-255-8155), and to attach a copy of the "Refugees and Asylees Have the Right to Work" flyer available online at *www.justice.gov/crt/about/osc/pdf/refugee_asyleeflyer32510.pdf.*[126] For large companies, it may be useful to copy the company's general counsel or legal department or to suggest that the employer forward the relevant information to their legal department. If employers still are not convinced of the asylee's authorization to work, practitioners may suggest that their client call the Office of Special Counsel for Immigration-Related Unfair Employment Practices hotline at 1-800-255-7688.

In the past, asylees had to prepare and file a Form I-765, Application for Employment Authorization, along with supporting documentation — a process similar to that described above for asylum applicants applying for EADs. Changes to the law under the Enhanced Border Security and Visa Entry Reform Act of 2002,[127] however, required legacy Immigration and Naturalization Service (INS), now DHS, to provide immediate employment authorization to asylees. Under these changes, the I-589, which already includes the applicant's photographs and fingerprints, is

---

[124] 8 CFR §§274a.12(c)(18), 1274a.12(c)(18) (2014).

[125] 8 CFR §§274a.12(a)(5), 1274a.12(a)(5) (2014).

[126] (last visited Mar. 11, 2015).

[127] *See generally* Enhanced Border Security and Visa Entry Reform Act of 2002, Pub. L. No. 107-173, 116 Stat. 543.

substituted for the I-765.[128] In implementing these changes, a policy effective on October 1, 2006, allows for the issuance of a two-year EAD on form I-766 to individuals and their dependents granted asylum by USCIS's Asylum Division through the affirmative asylum process. Information on obtaining these EADs will be provided to individuals with notice of their asylum grant.[129]

Thus, asylees who are granted asylum affirmatively by a USCIS asylum office usually receive their EADs automatically upon being granted asylum (category (A)(5)).[130] Once USCIS issues the Asylum Approval letter, it initiates production of the asylee's EAD, which is mailed to the asylee's home address listed in the USCIS database. EADs usually arrive approximately two weeks following a grant of asylum from the asylum office.

> ➢ **Practice Pointer**: If an asylee does not receive his or her EAD from USCIS following a grant of asylum from the asylum office, he or she should contact the asylum office that granted the case to inquire regarding the EAD. For details on how to contact the local asylum office, see the AILA "Asylum Office Guide — Best Practices," which is posted on AILA InfoNet at Doc. No. 12060844.[131] A copy of the guide is available at Appendix 4E of this book.

Asylees who are granted asylum defensively in immigration court, however, need to take certain steps in order to initiate production of their EADs. These asylees must make an InfoPass appointment with USCIS online at *https://infopass.uscis.gov*.[132] The appointment should be made at least three days after the IJ's order to allow USCIS sufficient time to receive the individual's data from the immigration court.[133] The asylee should bring the following documents with him or her to the InfoPass appointment:

- InfoPass appointment confirmation form;
- Photo identification;

---

[128] For more details, see Agency Information Collection Activities; Proposed Collection; Comment Request, 67 Fed. Reg. 64911 (Oct. 22, 2002).

[129] *See* USCIS Public Notice, *New Process for Issuing Employment Authorization Documents to Asylees* (Sept. 14, 2006), AILA InfoNet Doc. No. 06091560 (*posted* Sept. 15, 2006), *available at www.uscis.gov/files/pressrelease/AsyleeEAD.pdf*. Similarly, in July 2008, USCIS announced that refugees will also be issued a two-year EAD. *See* USCIS Update, *USCIS Extends Validity Period of Employment Authorization Documents (EAD) for Refugees* (July 11, 2008), *published on* AILA InfoNet Doc. No. 08071167 (*posted* July 11, 2008), *available at www.uscis.gov/files/article/EAD_Validity_11Jul08.pdf*.

[130] USCIS, *Affirmative Asylum Procedures Manual*, *supra* note 30, at pt. III.F.4.

[131] (last visited Mar. 11, 2015).

[132] USCIS, *Post-Order Instructions for Individuals Granted Relief or Protection from Removal by Immigration Court*, *available at www.uscis.gov/sites/default/files/files/article/PostOrderInstr.pdf* (last visited Mar. 11, 2015).

[133] *Id.*

- Two passport-size photographs of each asylee; and
- The IJ's final order granting asylum.[134]

At the InfoPass appointment, USCIS will provide an I-94 card as evidence of the individual's admission to the United States as an asylee. USCIS also will initiate the production of the asylee's EAD at that time. The EAD card will then be sent to the asylee by mail to his or her address on file with USCIS, and usually arrives approximately two weeks after the InfoPass appointment.[135] In some cases, USCIS might direct the asylee to submit his or her fingerprints at an Application Support Center before the EAD card may be produced.[136] In other cases, USCIS might notify the asylee that he or she must prepare and file an I-765 application with supporting documentation in order to obtain his or her EAD card.[137] However, asylees always should request at the InfoPass appointment that the card be automatically produced and sent to them pursuant to the provisions of the Enhanced Border Security and Visa Reform Act of 2002, which took effect on November 14, 2002.[138]

> ➢ **Practice Pointer**: Asylees granted asylum in immigration court should only make their InfoPass appointment with USCIS after the IJ's order is final. If DHS has waived appeal or if the 30-day appeal period has passed since the date of the IJ's order, the IJ's order is final. Practitioners may check whether DHS has filed an appeal by calling the EOIR's hotline at 1-800-898-7180 and typing in their client's A-number. If DHS does file an appeal, the individual may still be eligible for employment authorization based on having an application for asylum pending beyond 180 days. If the BIA then affirms the IJ's order granting asylum, the order is final and the individual may move forward with making an InfoPass appointment to obtain an EAD.[139]

> ➢ **Practice Pointer**: Often, InfoPass appointments are not available for several weeks. Practitioners should consider making an InfoPass appointment for their client in advance of the individual hearing so he or she has an appointment scheduled as close as possible to the hearing. After the hearing, if the IJ has not issued a decision, if the decision is not favorable, or if DHS reserves appeal, practitioners may always

---

[134] *Id.*

[135] *See* Catholic Legal Immigration Network, Inc., *Asylee Eligibility for Resettlement Assistance*, at 7, *available at https://cliniclegal.org/sites/default/files/234843_clinic_asylee_final_1-30-12.pdf* (last visited Apr. 2, 2015).

[136] *Id.*

[137] *See supra* Parts I.A.3–5.

[138] U.S. Enhanced Border Security and Visa Entry Reform Act, PL 107-173, 116 Stat. 543 (May 14, 2002) §309. *See also* INA §208(c)(1)(B); 8 CFR §§208.7, 274a.12(a)(5), (10), 1208.7.

[139] USCIS, *Post-Order Instructions for Individuals Granted Relief or Protection from Removal by Immigration Court*, *available at www.uscis.gov/sites/default/files/files/article/PostOrderInstr.pdf* (last visited Mar. 11, 2015).

cancel the InfoPass appointment and schedule a new one once a favorable, final decision has been issued.

An asylee may apply to renew his or her EAD after two years, when the validity date on his or her current card is nearing expiration. The process for requesting renewal of the EAD is very similar to the process described above in Parts I.A.3-5. However, the renewal process also may not be necessary, as asylees are authorized to work by virtue of their status of asylees and do not require an EAD to work.[140] Moreover, many asylees become eligible to seek permanent resident status after one year of physical presence as an asylee in the United States, and therefore, are permanent residents by the time their category (A)(5) EADs expire.[141]

- **Practice Pointer**: Whereas EADs for asylees are automatically generated and are valid for two years, withholding of removal grantees must apply for EADs and their EADs are valid for one year only.
- **Practice Pointer**: If the asylee does not apply for permanent resident status and wishes to renew his or her EAD, he or she must pay the $380 filing fee for the I-765[142] or demonstrate eligibility for a fee waiver, usually by filing a Form I-912 with the required supporting documentation.[143]

2. *EADs for Those Granted Withholding of Removal*

Individuals who have received a final grant of withholding of removal under INA §241(b)(3) or CAT are eligible for employment authorization, but must apply for employment authorization on Form I-765 to receive their EAD (category (A)(10)).[144] To apply for employment authorization, the applicant should file a completed and signed Form I-765, Application for Employment Authorization, along with the necessary supporting documentation.[145] Such supporting documentation should include:

- Two passport-sized photographs of the applicant (with the applicant's name and A# printed on the back of each), attached to the completed and signed Form I-765;
- Form G-28, Notice of Entry of Appearance (if represented);
- A copy of the front and back of any previous employment authorization document(s);

---

[140] 8 CFR §§274a.12(a)(5), 1274a.12(a)(5) (2014).

[141] *See infra* pt. II.G. and ch. 15 of this book for detailed discussions of seeking lawful permanent resident status as an asylee.

[142] USCIS, Instructions for I-765, *supra* note 53, at 8–9.

[143] *See* USCIS, I-912, *Request for Fee Waiver*, *available at www.uscis.gov/i-912* (last visited Apr. 2, 2015).

[144] 8 CFR §§274a.12(a)(10), 1274a.12(a)(10) (2014).

[145] *See* USCIS, I-765, *Application for Employment Authorization*, *supra* note 6.

- Evidence that the applicant has been granted withholding of removal (usually the IJ decision and order granting withholding of removal);
- A copy of the biographic page of the applicant's passport (if available);
- A copy of the applicant's photo identification (if available); and
- A copy of the front and back of the applicant's most recent I-94 card (if available).[146]

In completing the Form I-765, item number 16 on the form requires the applicant to list which category under which he or she is applying for employment authorization. Applicants who are applying based on a grant of withholding of removal should enter category "(A)(10)" in item 16 when preparing the Form I-765.[147] There is no filing fee for an initial I-765 application based on a grant of withholding of removal, nor is there a filing fee for a renewal application based on withholding of removal status.[148]

> ➤ **Practice Pointer**: Practitioners should note in the cover letter for the I-765 filing that no fee is required for withholding of removal grantees and cite to the relevant law and the I-765 instructions. Practitioners may also consider highlighting this statement in yellow to bring it to the attention of the service center staff. I-765s are often wrongly rejected by the service center due to the fact that there is no filing fee included, even when no filing fee is required. Attempts to preempt this can avoid delay for clients.

The application should be filed with the USCIS service center that has jurisdiction over the residence of the applicant.[149] Currently, applications for employment authorization based on a grant of withholding of removal status under INA §241(b)(3) or CAT are filed with the Chicago Lockbox.[150]

> ➤ **Practice Pointer**: Before filing an application for employment authorization, practitioners should always check USCIS's website and the up-to-date instructions for Form I-765 to determine the relevant filing location, as the filing locations frequently change.

I-765 applications for those granted withholding of removal are processed in the same way as those for pending asylum applicants, as described in Part I.A.5. above. First, if the application is complete, USCIS will initiate processing and issue a receipt notice.[151] The receipt notice usually arrives approximately two weeks after

---

[146] *See* USCIS, *Instructions for I-765 Application*, *supra* note 53.

[147] *Id.* at 4.

[148] *Id.* at 8.

[149] *See* 8 CFR §§274a.13(a)(2), 1274a.13(a)(2) (2014).

[150] *See* USCIS, *Direct Filing Addresses for Form I-765*, *supra* note 62.

[151] *See* USCIS, Instructions for I-765, *supra* note 53, at 9.

submission of the application. USCIS will then process the application. Often, USCIS will require the applicant to appear at an ASC to provide biometrics before the application is adjudicated and the EAD card is produced.[152] If necessary, USCIS will issue an ASC appointment notice scheduling the applicant for an appointment at a local ASC. If the applicant does not attend the ASC appointment, his or her application may be denied.[153] If the I-765 application is approved, USCIS will mail an I-765 approval notice and the EAD card directly to the applicant. If the application is denied, USCIS will send a written notice explaining its basis for the denial.[154]

USCIS must adjudicate the application within 90 days of receipt.[155] Failure to complete the adjudication within 90 days will result in the grant of an interim EAD for a period not to exceed 240 days.[156] The interim EAD will automatically terminate if the application for employment authorization is denied.[157]

> ➢ **Practice Pointer**: To request an interim EAD after the I-765 has been pending for 90 days, applicants should call the USCIS National Customer Service Center or make an InfoPass appointment at a local USCIS office.[158] The local USCIS offices used to be able to produce interim EADs on-site. However, as of August of 2006, they are no longer producing EADs on-site.[159] Thus, it is recommended that applicants call the National Customer Service Center (NCSC) at 1-800-375-5283 to request an interim EAD. The NCSC has a service request category specific to EAD-related inquiries: "Outside Regulatory Processing Time." These requests are forwarded to the appropriate service center or National Benefits Center. USCIS should either adjudicate the I-765 or issue an interim EAD card within 10 days of receiving the request.[160]

3. Deferral of Removal under the CAT

Although individuals granted withholding of removal under the CAT are eligible for employment authorization as described above, those granted deferral of removal under the CAT, are not necessarily eligible for employment authorization. There is no employment authorization category specified for individuals granted deferral of

---

[152] *Id.*

[153] *Id.*

[154] *Id.* at 10.

[155] 8 CFR §§274a.13(d), 1274a.13(d) (2014).

[156] *Id.*

[157] *Id.*

[158] *See* USCIS, Instructions for I-765, *supra* note 53, at 10.

[159] *See* USCIS Public Notice, *USCIS Reminds Customers of Filing Change for Employments Authorization Documents [EAD]* (revised Aug. 9, 2006), *available at www.uscis.gov/files/pressrelease/EADFilingCh072806PN.pdf.*

[160] *See* Aytes Memo. on Response to Recommendation 35, *supra* note 77.

removal under the CAT pursuant to 8 CFR §§208.17, 1208.17. Rather, individuals granted deferral of removal often apply for employment authorization under the (C)(18) category for individuals with a final order of removal who have been released on an order of supervision.[161]

These individuals must demonstrate: (1) they are under a final order of removal; (2) they have been released from detention under an order of supervision; (3) they cannot be removed due to the refusal of all potential countries of removal or because the removal of the individual is otherwise impracticable or contrary to the public interest; and (4) they merit a favorable exercise of discretion by DHS.[162] DHS may also consider the existence of other factors, such as the individual's economic necessity to be employed, a dependent spouse or children in the United States who rely on the individual for support, and the anticipated length of time before the individual can be removed.[163]

Individuals who have received a final grant of deferral of removal under the CAT must apply for employment authorization on Form I-765 to request issuance of an EAD at the discretion of DHS (category (C)(18)).[164] To apply for employment authorization, the applicant should file a completed and signed Form I-765, Application for Employment Authorization, along with the necessary supporting documentation.[165] Such supporting documentation should include:

- Two passport-sized photographs of the applicant (with the applicant's name and A# printed on the back of each), attached to the completed and signed Form I-765;
- Filing fee check or money order in the amount of $380, made payable to "U.S. Department of Homeland Security";
- Form G-28, Notice of Entry of Appearance (if represented);
- A copy of the front and back of any previous employment authorization document(s);
- Evidence that the applicant has been ordered removed, but granted deferral of removal (usually the IJ decision and order granting deferral of removal);
- Evidence that the applicant is on an Order of Supervision with U.S. Immigration and Customs Enforcement (ICE);
- Evidence that it is not in the public interest to remove the individual and that he or she merits a favorable exercise of discretion (evidence of good moral character, contributions to U.S. society, and all ties to the United States);
- Evidence of economic necessity to be employed;

---

161 8 CFR §§274a.12(c)(18), 1274a.12(c)(18) (2014).

162 *Id.*

163 *Id.*

164 8 CFR §§274a.12(c)(18), 1274a.12(c)(18) (2014).

165 *See* USCIS, I-765, *supra* note 6.

- Evidence of any dependent family members in the United States;
- A copy of the biographic page of the applicant's passport (if available);
- A copy of the applicant's photo identification (if available); and
- A copy of the front and back of the applicant's most recent I-94 card (if available).[166]

In completing the Form I-765, item number 16 on the form requires the applicant to list which category under which he or she is applying for employment authorization. Applicants who are applying based on a grant of deferral of removal should enter category "(C)(18)" in item 16 when preparing the Form I-765.[167]

The application should be filed with the USCIS service center that has jurisdiction over the residence of the applicant.[168] Currently, applications for employment authorization based on a grant of deferral of removal under the CAT — the (C)(18) category — are filed with the Chicago Lockbox.[169]

> ➢ **Practice Pointer**: Before filing an application for employment authorization, practitioners should always check USCIS's website and the up-to-date instructions for Form I-765 to determine the relevant filing location, as the filing locations frequently change.

I-765 applications for those granted deferral of removal are processed in the same way as those for pending asylum applicants, as described in Parts I.A.5. and II.C.2. above. First, if the application is complete, USCIS will initiate processing and issue a receipt notice.[170] The receipt notice usually arrives approximately two weeks after submission of the application. USCIS will then process the application. Often, USCIS will require the applicant to appear at an ASC to provide biometrics before the application is adjudicated and the EAD card is produced.[171] If necessary, USCIS will issue an ASC appointment notice scheduling the applicant for an appointment at a local ASC. If the applicant does not attend the ASC appointment, his or her application may be denied.[172] If the I-765 application is approved, USCIS will mail an I-765 approval notice and the EAD card directly to the applicant. If the application is denied, USCIS will send a written notice explaining its basis for the denial.[173]

USCIS must adjudicate the application within 90 days of receipt.[174] Failure to complete the adjudication within 90 days will result in the grant of an interim EAD

---

[166] *See* 8 CFR §§274a.12(c)(18), 1274a.12(c)(18) (2014); USCIS, Instructions for I-765, *supra* note 53.

[167] *See* USCIS, Instructions for I-765, *supra* note 53, at 5.

[168] *See* 8 CFR §§274a.13(a)(2), 1274a.13(a)(2) (2014).

[169] See USCIS, Direct Filing Addresses for Form I-765, *supra* note 62.

[170] *See* USCIS, Instructions for I-765, *supra* note 53, at 9.

[171] *Id.*

[172] *Id.*

[173] *Id.* at 10.

[174] 8 CFR §§274a.13(d), 1274a.13(d) (2014).

for a period not to exceed 240 days.[175] The interim EAD will automatically terminate if the application for employment authorization is denied.[176]

> **Practice Pointer**: To request an interim EAD after the I-765 has been pending for 90 days, applicants should call the USCIS National Customer Service Center or make an InfoPass appointment at a local USCIS office.[177] The local USCIS offices produced interim EADs on-site; however, as of August of 2006, they no longer produce EADs on-site.[178] Thus, it is recommended that applicants call the National Customer Service Center (NCSC) at 1-800-375-5283 to request an interim EAD. The NCSC has a service request category specific to EAD-related inquiries: "Outside Regulatory Processing Time." These requests are forwarded to the appropriate service center or National Benefits Center. USCIS should either adjudicate the I-765 or issue an interim EAD card within 10 days of receiving the request.[179]

D. Social Security Card

Fourth, asylees are eligible for "unrestricted" Social Security cards (cards that do not bear the notation "Valid for Work Only with DHS Authorization") immediately upon being granted asylum. Asylees also do not need employment authorization to apply for a Social Security card. They may apply immediately upon being granted asylum by USCIS, the immigration court (provided DHS has not appealed the decision), or the BIA. To apply for a Social Security card, asylees must go to the local SSA office, and must bring documentation of their asylum status. They may show any of the following documents:

- I-94 card (with an "asylum granted" stamp);
- EAD card (showing a grant under the (A)(5) category); or
- The original IJ order granting asylum (either with a waiver of appeal by DHS or, if 30 days have passed, confirmation that DHS has not appealed by calling the EOIR hotline at 1-800-898-7180).[180]

If asylees have a photo identification document, they also should bring that document to the SSA office to apply for a social security card.

---

175 *Id.*

176 *Id.*

177 *See* USCIS, Instructions for I-765, *supra* note 53, at 10.

178 *See* USCIS Public Notice, *USCIS Reminds Customers of Filing Change for Employments Authorization Documents [EAD]* (revised Aug. 9, 2006), *available at www.uscis.gov/files/pressrelease/EADFilingCh072806PN.pdf.*

179 *See* Aytes Mem. on Response to Recommendation 35, *supra* note 77.

180 *See generally* Soc. Sec. Admin. Information on Processing SSN Card Requests from Asylees, *available at www.socialsecurity.gov/people/immigrants/* (last visited Mar. 29, 2015).

There is often a significant delay from the date employment authorization is granted until the immigration authorities notify the SSA that the applicant is authorized to work. There is a further delay of up to six weeks before an application for a social security number is processed. The lack of a Social Security number during this interim period should not result in a denial of employment or delay in beginning employment. Although an employer will eventually need to record a Social Security number for wage reporting purposes, once an employee has satisfied the I-9 documentation requirements, the employer must allow him or her to work regardless of whether he or she has been issued a Social Security number.[181]

Under IRS regulations,[182] an employer that has an employee who has not been issued an Social Security number can accept the following documentation for employment and payroll: (1) a receipt for the application for a Social Security number, along with the employee's name and address as shown on the receipt and the expiration date of the receipt; or (2) copy of the application for a Social Security number (Form SS-5) until the card is issued.[183] Employers using E-Verify should delay running an E-Verify query until the worker is issued a Social Security number.[184] It is unlawful for an employer to refuse to hire an asylee or to prevent him or her from starting work because the asylee does not possess a Social Security number.[185]

- **Practice Pointer**: The Form SS-5 application can be found online on the SSA's website at *www.ssa.gov*. Individuals may apply for a Social Security card in person or by mail. Individuals also may call the SSA's toll-free number at 1-800-772-1213 or visit the local SSA office for more information.
- **Practice Pointer**: Practitioners may need to assist their clients following a grant of asylum with explaining to various employers their clients' eligibility to work even before a Social Security number has been issued, even if the employer uses E-Verify. Usually, a simple letter citing the law and inviting the employer to contact you with any questions will suffice. It may also be useful to include the number for the Office of Special Counsel for Immigration-Related Unfair Employment Practices hotline for employers in the letter (1-800-255-8155), and to attach a copy of the "Refugees and Asylees Have the Right to Work" flyer available online at *www.justice.gov/crt/*

---

[181] Office of Special Counsel for Immigration-Related Unfair Emp't Practices, *Refugees and Asylees Have the Right to Work*, *available at www.justice.gov/crt/about/osc/pdf/refugee_asyleeflyer32510.pdf* (last visited Mar. 13, 2015).

[182] 26 CFR §31.6011(b)–2(c)(2).

[183] These procedures are explained more fully in Internal Revenue Serv. Publication Circular E and Circular E Supp., *available at www.irs.gov/publications/p15/index.html.*

[184] Office of Special Counsel for Immigration-Related Unfair Emp't Practices, *supra* note 181.

[185] *Id.*

about/osc/pdf/refugee_asyleeflyer32510.pdf.[186] For large companies, it may be useful to copy the company's general counsel or legal department or to suggest that the employer forward the relevant information to their legal department. If employers still are not convinced of the asylee's authorization to work, practitioners may suggest that their client call the Office of Special Counsel for Immigration-Related Unfair Employment Practices hotline at 1-800-255-7688.

E. Refugee Travel Document

Fifth, asylees may travel outside of the United States if they follow special rules governing their travel. Individuals granted withholding of removal or CAT relief, however, cannot travel abroad and re-enter the United States, as they have final orders of removal and any departure from the United States would execute their removal orders.

Asylees are subject to special rules for traveling outside of the United States. Most importantly, asylees must never travel back to the country of feared persecution. Travel to the country of claimed persecution may result in the loss of asylee or lawful permanent resident (LPR) status.[187] USCIS has issued a fact sheet that warns of the consequences that may result if an asylee or LPR returns to the country of claimed persecution.[188] Asylum may be terminated based on a fundamental change in circumstances, fraud, lack of a genuine fear of persecution, or because the asylee or LPR voluntarily availed himself or herself of the home country's protection.[189] The underlying asylum status may be terminated even if the individual has already become a lawful permanent resident.[190]

> ➢ **Practice Pointer**: All practitioners should discuss these travel warnings in detail with their clients before and after they are granted asylum, as well as before their clients apply for Refugee Travel Documents and travel abroad.
>
> ➢ **Practice Pointer**: Any time outside of the United States after being granted asylum also will delay the asylee's eligibility date to apply for LPR status, as he or she must be physically present in the United States in valid asylee status for a total of one year prior to seeking adjustment of status to permanent residence.[191] Practitioners should ensure that their

---

[186] (last visited Mar. 11, 2015).

[187] INA §208(c)(2)(D).

[188] USCIS Fact Sheet, *Traveling Outside the United States as an Asylum Applicant, an Asylee, or a Lawful Permanent Resident*, *supra* note 106.

[189] *Id.*; INA §208(c)(2).

[190] *Id.*

[191] INA §209(b).

> clients are aware that their travel abroad may delay their eligibility to seek LPR status. The amount of time spent outside of the United States after the date asylum is granted is the amount of time that the applicant's eligibility to apply for LPR status will be delayed.

Additionally, asylees must receive advance permission to travel by applying for and obtaining a Refugee Travel Document (RTD) prior to his or her departure.[192] The applicant for an RTD must hold valid refugee status under INA §207, valid asylee status under INA §208, or must be a permanent resident as a direct result of his or her refugee or asylee status.[193]

An application for an RTD may be made by filing Form I-131 with DHS.[194] Form I-131 is available on USCIS's website,[195] and is the same form required for advance parole (described above in Part I.D.) and a re-entry permit. Asylees seeking RTDs should plan ahead, as it usually takes up to 90 days for USCIS to adjudicate I-131 applications. Along with the completed and signed Form I-131, applicants should submit the following documentation:

- Two passport-sized photographs of the applicant (with the applicant's name and A# printed on the back of each), attached to the completed and signed Form I-131;
- Filing fee check or money order in the amount of $135 (for applicants age 16 and older) or $105 (for applicants under age 16), made payable to "U.S. Department of Homeland Security";
- Biometrics fee check or money order in the amount of $85[196] (for applicants ages 14-79), made payable to "U.S. Department of Homeland Security";
- Form G-28, Notice of Entry of Appearance (if represented);
- Evidence that the applicant has been granted asylum (Asylum Approval letter, I-94 card annotated granted asylum, and/or EAD listing category (A)(5));
- A copy of the applicant's photo identification (if available); and
- A copy of the front and back of the applicant's most recent I-94 card.[197]

Note that there is a fee for filing Form I-131.[198] Filing fees periodically change, so it is important to check the regulations and form instructions prior to filing Form I-131. If the individual has an RTD that remains valid, USCIS will not issue a new

---

[192] 8 CFR §223.1(b) (2014). *See* USCIS, Form I-131 Instructions, *supra* note 104, at 3.

[193] 8 CFR §223.2(b)(2) (2014). *See* USCIS, Form I-131 Instructions, *supra* note 104, at 1.

[194] 8 CFR §223.2(a) (2014).

[195] USCIS, Form I-131 Application for Travel Document, *supra* note 105.

[196] This biometrics fee may be combined with the filing fee in a single payment of $220, made payable to "U.S. Department of Homeland Security."

[197] *See* USCIS, Form I-131 Instructions, *supra* note 104, at 7–11.

[198] 8 CFR §§103.7(b)(1), 1103.7(b)(1) (2014).

document unless the individual returns the original valid document along with the I-131 application materials or demonstrates that the document was lost.[199]

➢ **Practice Pointer**: Practitioners should always check USCIS's website at *www.uscis.gov/i-131-addresses* for the most recent filing address listed for Refugee Travel Documents, as filing locations frequently change.

In limited circumstances, a refugee or asylee *may* be granted an RTD *after* his or her departure from the United States.[200] The USCIS Overseas District Director with jurisdiction over the asylee's location makes this decision in his or her discretion.[201] The refugee or asylee must demonstrate that he or she: (1) did not intend to abandon his or her residence; (2) did not engage in activities inconsistent with his or her refugee or asylee status; and (3) has been outside of the United States for less than one year.[202] Thus, the application must be made within one year of the refugee or asylee's last departure from the United States, and should explain why he or she failed to apply for an RTD before departing from the United States.[203] Such circumstances are narrow and, therefore, as a general rule a refugee or asylee should always obtain a travel document *prior* to departure. For individuals outside the United States for more than one year, humanitarian parole under INA §212(d)(5) may be available.[204]

Upon receipt of the I-131, USCIS will ensure completeness and issue a receipt notice.[205] Then USCIS will begin processing the application and inform the applicant by written notice to go to a local ASC for a biometrics appointment.[206] The applicant must appear for his or her biometrics appointment, or the application may be denied.[207] If granted, the RTD is valid for one year and may not be extended.[208]

➢ **Practice Pointer**: If the asylee needs to travel abroad before receiving the RTD, he or she may do so, as long as the asylee completes his ASC appointment before departing.[209] An RTD may be sent to a U.S.

---

[199] USCIS, Form I-131 Instructions, *supra* note 104, at 3.

[200] *Id.*; 8 CFR §223.2(b)(2)(ii) (2014); *see also* INS Memorandum from Bo Cooper on Readmission of Asylees and Refugees Without Travel Documents (Nov. 23, 1999), *published on* AILA InfoNet Doc. No. 01050405 (*posted* May 4, 2001).

[201] USCIS, Form I-131 Instructions, *supra* note 104, at 3.

[202] 8 CFR §223.2(b)(2)(ii) (2014); *see also* Cooper Mem. on Readmission of Asylees and Refugees Without Travel Documents, *supra* note 200.

[203] USCIS, Form I-131 Instructions, *supra* note 104, at 3.

[204] INS Memorandum, B. Cooper, "Readmission of Asylees and Refugees Without Travel Documents" (Nov. 23, 1999), *published on* AILA InfoNet at Doc. No. 01050405 (*posted* May 4, 2001).

[205] USCIS, Form I-131 Instructions, *supra* note 104, at 7.

[206] *Id.*

[207] USCIS, Form I-131 Instructions, *supra* note 104, at 3.

[208] *Id.*

[209] 8 CFR §223.2(b)(2) (2014); USCIS, Form I-131 Instructions, *supra* note 104, at 3.

embassy, consulate, or DHS office abroad for the asylee to pick up, if he or she so requests upon filing the I-131 application.[210]

- **Practice Pointer**: An RTD is only valid for one year, and generally, an asylee should have six months of validity on the document in order to travel. In fact, many countries will not grant visas unless there is at least six months of validity on the RTD. Asylees who have adjusted to permanent resident status may apply for a re-entry permit rather than an RTD. Although a re-entry permit has a higher filing fee, it is valid for two years, and thus, may be preferable for certain asylees who have been granted permanent resident status.

F. Derivative Asylum Status for Family Members

Sixth, an asylee's spouse and unmarried children under age 21 may be granted asylum as derivatives if accompanying or following to join the asylee.[211] There are different procedures for conferring asylum status on derivatives depending on whether the spouse and children are physically present in the United States and included as dependents on the I-589, or are outside of the United States and need to follow to join the asylee.[212] Although spouses and children may be granted derivative asylum status, however, spouses and children may not be granted withholding of removal under INA §241(b)(3) or protection under the CAT as derivatives.[213]

- **Practice Pointer**: In order to prevent a client's family from being ordered removed without him or her, practitioners should file separate I-589 applications for each family member in removal proceedings, especially if there are any difficult issues or uncertainties regarding the principal applicant's eligibility for asylum.

- **Practice Pointer**: Practitioners should consider whether a principal applicant's family members should file their own I-589 applications independently and include the principal applicant as a dependent on their applications as well. Although family members may have suffered the same experiences together in their home countries, and one family member seems to have suffered the most serious harm, the family members may have experienced the harm differently and may have their own independent claims. For example, if a wife was abducted and raped, her husband may have suffered psychologically as a witness to that harm. Filing an independent claim for each family member may

---

[210] USCIS, Form I-131 Instructions, *supra* note 104, at 3.

[211] INA §208(b)(3)(A).

[212] 8 CFR §§208.21(c)–(d), 1208.21(c)–(d) (2014).

[213] *Saval v. Holder*, 623 F.3d 664, 671 (9th Cir. 2010); *Cendrawasih v. Holder*, 571 F.3d 128, 131 (1st Cir. 2009); *Arif v. Mukasey*, 509 F.3d 677, 680–82 (5th Cir. 2007); *Delgado v. Att'y Gen.*, 487 F.3d 855, 862 (11th Cir. 2007).

provide the family as a whole with more opportunities for a positive outcome.

1. *Who May Qualify as a Derivative?*

An asylee's spouse who is accompanying or following to join him or her may be granted asylum upon a grant of asylum to the principal applicant.[214] According to the INA, and individual is not a "spouse" unless both parties were "physically present in the presence of each other" at the marriage ceremony, "unless the marriage shall have been consummated."[215]

An asylee's child also may be granted asylum if accompanying or following to join the principal applicant who was granted asylum.[216] Under the INA, a "child" includes an unmarried person under 21 years of age who is:

- A child born in wedlock;
- A stepchild, whether or not born out of wedlock, if the child was under age 18 at the time the marriage creating the stepchild relationship occurred;
- A child legitimated under the law of the child's residence or domicile, or under the law of the father's residence or domicile, whether in or outside of the United States, if such legitimation took place while the child was under age 18 and the child was in the legal custody of the legitimating parent(s) at the time of legitimation;
- A child born out of wedlock, by, through whom, or on whose behalf a status, privilege, or benefit is sought by virtue of the relationship of the child to its natural mother or to its natural father if the father has or had a bona fide parent-child relationship with the person; and
- A child adopted while under age 16, if the child has been in the legal custody of and has resided with the adopting parent(s) for at least two years (and his or her sibling adopted while under age 18 by the same parent(s)).[217]

A spouse or child may not, however, be eligible for asylum as a derivative if he or she is ineligible for asylum for the following reasons: (1) he or she ordered, incited, assisted, or otherwise participated in the persecution of others; (2) he or she, having been convicted by a final judgment of a particularly serious crime, constitutes a danger to the community of the United States; (3) there are serious reasons for believing that he or she has committed a serious nonpolitical crime outside the United States prior to his or her arrival; (4) there are reasonable grounds for regarding him or her as a danger to the security of the United States; and (5) he or she is described under INA §§212(a)(3)(B)(i) or 237(a)(4)(B) (relating to terrorist activity), unless he

---

[214] INA §208(b)(3)(A); 8 CFR §§208.21(a), 1208.21(a) (2014).

[215] INA §101(a)(35).

[216] INA §208(b)(3)(A); 8 CFR §§208.21(a), 1208.21(a) (2014).

[217] INA §101(b)(1). Note that there are other situations where an individual may be considered a "child" under the INA; however, these are less relevant to the issues surrounding derivative asylees. *See id.*

or she is a representative of a group or organization and there are not reasonable grounds for regarding him or her as a danger to the security of the United States.[218]

➢ **Practice Pointer**: A parent may not be included as a dependent applicant on his or her child's asylum application, nor may a child asylee petition for a parent to follow to join him or her in asylum status.[219] Thus, if the principal applicant is a child, practitioners should determine whether there are grounds to file an independent I-589 application for the child's parent or parents.

In order to gain derivative asylum status, the spousal or parent-child relationship must have existed at the time that asylum was granted and must continue to exist at the time of filing for accompanying or following-to-join benefits (Form I-730) and at the time of the spouse or child's subsequent admission to the United States.[220]

➢ **Practice Pointer**: Since the familial relationship must exist at the time the applicant was granted asylum in order for the applicant's family members to gain derivative asylum status, practitioners should advise their clients to take the steps necessary to ensure that all relevant relationships exist prior to the completion of the asylum application process. For example, an applicant may wish to marry his or her spouse prior to issuance of a final approval in order to secure the spouse's eligibility for derivative asylum benefits.

There are limited exceptions to this rule. One exception is if a child was born after asylum was granted, but was *in utero* on the date of the asylum grant. Such a child may still be eligible to accompany or follow-to-join the asylee.[221] Another exception was created by the Child Status Protection Act (CSPA),[222] which allows a child to continue to be classified as a child, even if he or she turns 21 during the processing of the parent's asylum application. As long as the child was unmarried and under 21 on the date his or her parent filed the asylum application, he or she will continue to be considered a child and may still be granted asylum as a derivative.[223] The "filing date" is the date that the application was received by USCIS.[224]

---

[218] 8 CFR §§207.7(b), 208.21(a), 1208.21(a). *See* ch. 2 for a detailed discussion of these grounds of ineligibility for asylum.

[219] *See* INA §208(b)(3)(A); U.S. Citizenship & Immigration Servs., *Lesson: Guidelines for Children's Asylum Claims* at 13, in Asylum Officer Basic Training Course Participant Workbook (Sept. 1, 2009) [hereinafter AOBTC Workbook, Children's Asylum Claims], *available at www.uscis.gov/sites/default/files/USCIS/Humanitarian/Refugees%20%26%20Asylum/Asylum/AOBTC%20Lesson%20Plans/Guidelines-for-Childrens-Asylum-Claims-31aug10.pdf.*

[220] 8 CFR §§207.7(c), 208.21(b), 1208.21(b).

[221] 8 CFR §§207.7(c), 208.21(b), 1208.21(b).

[222] To learn more about the Child Status Protection Act, see C. Wheeler, *AILA's Focus on the Child Status Protection Act* (2nd Ed. 2014).

[223] INA §208(b)(3)(B); Child Status Protection Act (CSPA), Pub. L. No. 107-208, 116 Stat. 927 (2002). *See* AOBTC Workbook, Children's Asylum Claims, *supra* note 219; *see also* INS Memorandum from

Continued

➢ **Practice Pointer**: If an individual turned 21 prior to August 6, 2002, he or she is not eligible for continued classification as a child unless the asylum application was pending on August 6, 2002.[225]

The CSPA protects children in the United States who are included on principal applicants' I-589 applications and who age out while those I-589 applications are being processed.[226] Unfortunately, the CSPA does not specifically address other situations where children may age out of derivative asylum status. A USCIS memorandum, however, addresses the treatment of child beneficiaries who turn 21 while awaiting adjudication of I-730, Refugee/Asylee Relative Petitions filed on their behalf, as well as child derivatives who turn 21 before they are able to adjust status to lawful permanent residence based on their asylum status.[227] For asylum applications filed on or after August 2, 2002, a child who was under 21 at the time his or her parent filed for asylum continues to be eligible to have an I-730 filed on his or her behalf despite turning 21 before the I-730 is filed or approved.[228]

➢ **Practice Pointer**: For a detailed discussion of child asylees who age out before adjustment of status, see chapter 15 of this book.

➢ **Practice Pointer**: Practitioners should determine the age of all of their client's children at the beginning of the representation. If a child is nearing age 21, it is important for practitioners to prioritize their client's case to file the asylum application before the child turns 21. Doing so will maintain his or her eligibility as a dependent applicant.

A derivative family member may lose his or her status as a derivative in the following situations:

- If the spouse or child withdraws his or her asylum claim;
- If the child marries;
- If the spouse divorces the principal applicant; or

Joseph Langlois on H.R. 1209—Child Status Protection Act (Aug. 7, 2002), *published on* AILA InfoNet Doc. No. 02090531 (*posted* Sep. 5, 2002); USCIS Interoffice Memorandum from William Yates on The Child Status Protection Act—Children of Asylees and Refugees (Aug. 17, 2004), *published on* AILA InfoNet Doc. No. 04091561 (*posted* Sept. 15, 2004); *The Child Status Protection Act: Breaking Down the Complicated 'Aging Out' Formula*, 23 IMMIGRATION LAW TODAY 32 (May/June 2004); Am. Immigration Council, Legal Action Ctr. Practice Advisory, *The Child Status Protection Act* (Sept. 9, 2009), *available at www.legalactioncenter.org/sites/default/files/pa-cspa_0.pdf.*

[224] 8 CFR §103.2(a)(7) (2014).

[225] AOBTC Workbook, Children's Asylum Claims, *supra* note 219, at 48-49.

[226] INA §208(b)(3)(B); Child Status Protection Act (CSPA), Pub. L. No. 107-208, 116 Stat. 927 (2002). *See* AOBTC Workbook, Children's Asylum Claims, *supra* note 219.

[227] *See* Yates Mem. on The Child Status Protection Act, *supra* note 223; *see also The Child Status Protection Act: Breaking Down the Complicated 'Aging Out' Formula*, *supra* note 223; *see also* Am. Immigration Council, The Child Status Protection Act, *supra* note 223.

[228] *See id.* For more information on filing I-730s, see this chapter at 3.15.

- If the principal applicant dies.[229]

Derivative status may be lost at any time prior to the spouse or child's admission to the U.S. as an asylee.[230]

> **Practice Pointer**: An individual may lose derivative status as well if the principal applicant naturalizes to U.S. citizenship before the derivative has entered on an approved I-730, as well as if the principal applicant naturalizes before the derivative has adjusted status to LPR status. Given the significant delays for derivatives to enter on I-730 petitions and the complications that a loss of derivative status can cause a derivative seeking to adjust status, practitioners should advise their principal asylee clients not to naturalize until their derivative relatives are on U.S. soil and have become permanent residents of the United States. See chapter 15 of this book for a detailed discussion of adjustment of status for derivative asylees.

> **Practice Pointer**: The loss of derivative status qualifies as a changed circumstance for purposes of determining whether the individual is subject to the one-year filing deadline in his or her own subsequent asylum claim as a principal applicant.[231] As long as he or she files the subsequent application within a reasonable time after becoming aware of the loss of derivative status, he or she should qualify for this exception to the one-year filing deadline.[232] For a detailed discussion and guidance for filing an affirmative asylum application for an individual who was once a derivative applicant, see chapter 7 of this book.

> **Practice Pointer**: A dependent may lose derivative status after asylum approval, but before the principal applicant and his or her dependents file for adjustment of status to lawful permanent residency. Under these circumstances, the dependent may not be included as a derivative applicant on the principal applicant's adjustment of status application.[233] Although the dependent will continue to have valid asylee status, if he or she wants to adjust status to lawful permanent resident, he or she must file a new I-589 application as a principal applicant and request asylum "*nunc pro tunc*."[234] See chapter 15 of this book for a detailed

[229] USCIS, *Affirmative Asylum Procedures Manual*, *supra* note 30, at pt. III.E.6.

[230] *Id.*

[231] *See* 8 CFR §208.4(a)(4) (2014).

[232] *See id. See also* ch. 2 for a detailed discussion of the one-year filing deadline and the exceptions to this bar to asylum eligibility.

[233] USCIS, *Affirmative Asylum Procedures Manual*, *supra* note 30, at pt. III.E.7.

[234] *Id.*

discussion of *nunc pro tunc* asylum applications for the purposes of adjustment of status.

2. Accompanying Spouses and Children

If an asylee's spouse and unmarried children under age 21 are physically present in the United States and were included as dependents on the asylee's application, they will automatically derive asylum status through the principal applicant when he or she is granted asylum.[235] For affirmative applications, the spouse and children must be included on the I-589 and must appear for the principal applicant's asylum interview at the USCIS asylum office. For defensive applications, however, a spouse and children may only be included as dependents on the principal applicant's I-589 if the spouse and children themselves also are in removal proceedings before the immigration court. Otherwise, the IJ does not have jurisdiction to grant them asylum along with the principal applicant. These spouses and children, who were not in removal proceedings with the principal asylee, would need to follow-to-join the principal asylee through the process described below in Part II.F.3.

Upon approval of an affirmative asylum application by USCIS, each dependent family member who is physically present and included on the I-589 will receive his or her own Asylum Approval letter and I-94 card on the same day as the principal asylee. Upon approval of a defensive asylum application by an immigration judge, each dependent family member whose removal case had been consolidated with the principal applicant's will receive a copy of the IJ Order granting asylum and will be able to request an I-94 card, as described above in Part II.B. In either situation, the family member is considered an asylee upon the grant of asylum to the principal applicant, and may receive most of the same benefits as the principal asylee, including an EAD, as discussed above in Part II.C.

- **Practice Pointer**: Although derivative asylees may receive most of the same benefits as principal asylees, they may not file I-730 petitions to bring their relatives to the United States. Rather, I-730 petitions may only be filed by the principal asylee in regard to his or her spouse or children under age 21.[236]

To include a spouse or child as a dependent on the I-589, the applicant must list each family member on Part A.II. and indicate "yes" in response to the questions, "Is this person in the U.S.?" and "If in the U.S., is your spouse/child to be included in this application?"[237] The principal applicant must submit for each dependent one

---

[235] INA §208(b)(3)(A). *See* Langlois Mem. on H.R. 1209 — Child Status Protection Act, *supra* note 223, at 2; Yates Mem. on The Child Status Protection Act, *supra* note 223, at 4.

[236] USCIS, *Instructions for I-730, Refugee/Asylee Relative Petition*, at 1, *available at www.uscis.gov/sites/default/files/files/form/i-730instr.pdf* (last visited Mar. 13, 2015).

[237] USCIS, *I-589, Application for Asylum and for Withholding of Removal*, at 2–3, *available at www.uscis.gov/sites/default/files/files/form/i-589.pdf* (last visited Mar. 13, 2015).

copy of the application, one passport-style photograph of the dependent attached to page 9 of his or her copy of the I-589, and evidence of the family relationship.[238]

If the derivative applicant is a child, the relevant supporting documentation is the child's birth certificate listing the principal applicant as the child's parent. If the derivative applicant is a spouse, the relevant documentation is the marriage certificate. If the applicant or derivative spouse was previously married, the divorce decree for each prior marriage also must be submitted.[239] If the applicant does not have this primary evidence of relationship, he or she may submit secondary evidence, which may include, but is not limited to, medical records, school records, religious documents, or affidavits.[240] Relatives or others may provide affidavits, and the affiant need not be a U.S. citizen or lawful permanent resident.[241] Each affidavit should fully describe the event in question and explain how the affiant has personal knowledge of that event. The affidavit should be sworn and should list the affiant's full name, address, date and place of birth, and relationship to the principal applicant.[242]

Although a principal applicant cannot add his or her spouse and children to an I-589 if the principal is in removal proceedings and the spouse and children are not, a principal applicant may add dependents who are inside the United States to his or her affirmative asylum application pending before USCIS at any time prior to issuance of a final denial, referral, or approval.[243] Even if the dependent previously filed for asylum as a separate principal applicant and even if the dependent was issued a NOID or final denial on his or her own application, the dependent may be added to the principal's application prior to its final adjudication.[244] Similarly, if the principal has been issued a NOID or a Recommended Approval letter, the application does not have a final decision and the dependent may still be added.[245]

To add a dependent to an affirmative asylum application prior to the asylum interview, the applicant should send to the USCIS service center one copy of the asylum application that includes the dependent's information, one passport-sized photograph of the dependent, one copy of the evidence of family relationship, and a cover letter stating that the applicant wishes to add a dependent to his or her asylum claim.[246] The service center will add the dependent in the Refugee, Asylum and

---

[238] USCIS, *Affirmative Asylum Procedures Manual*, *supra* note 30, at pt. II.A.3.; USCIS, *Instructions for I-589, Application for Asylum and for Withholding of Removal*, at 5, *available at www.uscis.gov/sites/default/files/files/form/i-589instr.pdf* (last visited Mar. 13, 2015).

[239] USCIS, *Affirmative Asylum Procedures Manual*, *supra* note 30, at pt. II.A.3.

[240] *Id. See also* 8 CFR §204.2(d)(2)(v).

[241] USCIS, *Affirmative Asylum Procedures Manual*, *supra* note 30, at pt. II.A.3.

[242] *Id.*

[243] USCIS, *Affirmative Asylum Procedures Manual*, *supra* note 30, at pt. III.E.1.

[244] *Id.*

[245] *Id.*

[246] *Id.*

Parole System (RAPS), the automated records system for managing and tracking asylum and refugee applications, and forward the packet to the Asylum Office.[247]

To add a dependent at the time of the affirmative asylum interview, the dependent must accompany the principal applicant to the interview. The principal applicant must submit to the asylum officer the same packet described above. Asylum Office personnel will add the dependent in RAPS and will meet and interview the dependent.[248] If the dependent does not appear with the principal applicant at the time of the interview, the asylum officer will proceed with the interview of the principal applicant, will give the applicant an appointment to bring the dependent to the Asylum Office prior to the decision pick-up date, and will place the principal applicant's case on hold. If the dependent does not appear for the appointment, the asylum officer will proceed with adjudicating the case without the dependent.[249]

Finally, to add a dependent after the affirmative asylum interview, but prior to the final decision, the principal applicant must send the same dependent packet described above to either the service center or the Asylum Office.[250] If it is sent to the service center, the service center will forward the packet to the Asylum Office for further processing. If it is sent to the Asylum Office, the office will place the principal applicant's case on hold and schedule the principal applicant and dependent for an appointment to come to the Asylum Office.[251] If the dependent appears, the Asylum Office will be able to include the dependent on the applicant's final decision. If not, the Asylum Office will proceed with adjudicating the case without the dependent.[252]

- ➢ **Practice Pointer**: It is essential for practitioners to notify the local Asylum Office as soon as possible that their client wishes to add a dependent. The notice should be sent in writing and evidence of the family relationship (a marriage or birth certificate) should be attached. Upon notification, the Asylum Office will add the dependent in RAPS and initiate the scheduling of a fingerprint appointment for the dependent, as well as other security checks. Asylum Office personnel also will conduct US-VISIT checks for any dependents added after the principal applicant's initial filing.[253]

- ➢ **Practice Pointer**: There is no requirement that a family must pursue an asylum claim together as a family. For example, a husband and wife may both submit separate asylum applications as principal applicants before USCIS or before the immigration court, if both are in removal

[247] *Id.*

[248] *Id.*

[249] *Id.*

[250] *Id.*

[251] *Id.*

[252] *Id.*

[253] *Id.*

proceedings. Additionally, it is possible for an individual to be a principal applicant and a dependent simultaneously.[254] For detailed processing information for affirmative asylum applications in these scenarios, see chapter 7 of this book.

3. Following-to-Join Spouses and Children

An asylee's spouse and children may not be granted asylum as derivatives automatically, like those spouses and children described above. First, the spouse and children may have been physically present in the United States at the time the asylee's application was granted by an immigration judge, but may not have been in removal proceedings along with the principal applicant.[255] Second, the spouse and children may not have been included on the I-589 at the time it was granted. Third, the spouse and children may not have been physically present in the United States with the asylee. In each of these situations, the asylee must request accompanying or following-to-join benefits for the spouse and children.[256] The asylee may request these benefits for his or her spouse or unmarried child under age 21 who is inside the United States, regardless of the spouse or child's status in the U.S. The asylee also may request these benefits for his or her spouse or unmarried child under age 21 who is outside of the United States.[257]

To request these benefits, the asylee must file a Form I-730, Refugee/Asylee Relative Petition, along with supporting evidence, for each family member who may derive asylum status.[258] A separate request must be filed for each qualifying family member, and each request must be filed *within two years of the date in which the asylee was granted asylum status*, unless it is determined by USCIS that the two-year period should be extended for humanitarian reasons.[259] The I-730 may only be filed by the principal refugee or asylee.[260] Family members who derived their refugee or asylee status from the principal refugee or asylee are not eligible to file an I-730 on behalf of their spouses and children.[261]

- **Practice Pointer**: Relatives other than spouses and unmarried children under age 21 may be eligible for resettlement to the United States

---

[254] *Id.* at pt. III.E.3.

[255] *See* USCIS, Instructions for I-589, *supra* note 238, at 5.

[256] 8 CFR §§208.21(c)-(d), 1208.21(c)(d) (2014). *See* 8 CFR §207.7 (2014).

[257] Note that unmarried children who have reached age 21 may continue to be considered children, as long as they were under the age of 21 at the time the principal applicant filed his or her application for asylum. INA §208(b)(3); Child Status Protection Act (CSPA), Pub. L. No. 107-208, 116 Stat. 927 (2002). *See* Yates Mem. on The Child Status Protection Act, *supra* note 223; *see also The Child Status Protection Act: Breaking Down the Complicated 'Aging Out' Formula*, *supra* note 223; *see also* Am. Immigration Council, The Child Status Protection Act, *supra* note 223.

[258] 8 CFR §§208.21(c)–(d), 1208.21(c)(d) (2014).

[259] 8 CFR §§207.7(d), 208.21(c)–(d), 1208.21(c)–(d) (2014) (emphasis added).

[260] 8 CFR §207.7(d) (2014); *see* 8 CFR §§208.21(c)–(d), 1208.21(c)–(d) (2014).

[261] 8 CFR §207.7(d) (2014).

> through the U.S. Refugee Resettlement Program. For more information, see J. Guilfoyle, "The Refugee Resettlement Program: How It Might Help the Relatives of Your Asylee Clients," 23 *Immigration Law Today* 48 (Sept./Oct. 2004). Priority Three family reunification applications were abruptly halted in 2008 after a pilot DNA testing project suggested there may be fraud in the Priority Three processing of affidavits of relationships from certain countries in Africa.[262] Advocacy groups called on the Department of State to resume the program,[263] and it was resumed in October of 2012 with a new Affidavit of Relationship form and requirement for DNA evidence of certain claimed biological parent-child relationships.[264] The first arrivals in the United States under the revamped Priority Three program are expected in fiscal year 2015.[265]

Form I-730 is available on USCIS's website.[266] Along with the completed and signed Form I-730, applicants should submit the following documentation:

- One passport-sized photograph of the applicant (with the applicant's name and A# printed on the back of each), attached to the completed and signed Form I-730;[267]
- Form G-28, Notice of Entry of Appearance (if represented);
- Evidence that the petitioner has been granted asylum (Asylum Approval letter or IJ order granting asylum, I-94 card annotated granted asylum, and/or EAD listing category (A)(5));
- For a spouse — marriage certificate and divorce decrees or death certificates demonstrating lawful termination of any prior marriages of the petitioner or beneficiary, with certified English translations if necessary;
- For a child — birth certificate showing the petitioner is the parent, as well as any other documentation required to demonstrate that the child meets the INA definition of "child" described above (*e.g.*, marriage certificate showing the petitioner's marriage to the child's parent, adoption decree and evidence of residence with the petitioner, evidence of legitimation, etc.);

---

[262] U.S. Dep't of State, Bureau of Population, Refugees and Migration, *Fraud in the Refugee Family Reunification (Priority Three) Program Fact Sheet*, *available at www.state.gov/g/prm/rls/115891.htm.*

[263] *See, e.g.*, AILA Letter to Bureau of Population, Refugees and Migration (July 7, 2009) urging reinstatement of program; *AILA Comments on Refugee Admissions Program for Fiscal Year 2010* (July 7, 2009), *published on* AILA InfoNet Doc. No. 09071070 (*posted* July 10, 2009).

[264] *See* Congressional Research Service, *Refugee Admissions and Resettlement Policy* (Feb. 18, 2015), *available at http://fas.org/sgp/crs/misc/RL31269.pdf* (last visited Apr. 2, 2015).

[265] *See id.*

[266] USCIS, Instructions for I-730, Refugee/Asylee Relative Petition, *supra* note 236.

[267] 8 CFR §§207.7(e), 208.21(c)–(d), 1208.21(c)–(d) (2014).

- Secondary evidence of relationship, if the primary evidence listed above is not available (*e.g.*, religious institution records, school records, census records, or affidavits);[268]
- Birth certificate of the beneficiary, with certified English translation if necessary;
- A copy of the beneficiary's photo identification (if available); and
- A copy of the front and back of the beneficiary's most recent I-94 card, if he or she is in the United States (if available).[269]

Note that there is no filing fee for Form I-730.[270] The burden of proof is on the asylee to establish by a preponderance of the evidence that the beneficiary of each I-730 petition is an eligible spouse or unmarried child under 21.[271] Thus, it is essential that the supporting documentation listed above be complete and thorough, especially documentation of the qualifying relationship.

> ➢ **Practice Pointer**: In the absence of a birth certificate, baptismal certificate, school or church records, it may be possible to establish parentage through voluntary DNA testing.[272] The test must be conducted by a parentage testing laboratory that is accredited by the American Association of Blood Banks (AABB).[273] See *www.aabb.org* for a list of accredited laboratories. DNA testing can be expensive and is conducted at the expense of the petitioner. It is the petitioner's burden of proof to establish the required relationship.

Currently, an asylee must file the I-730 and supporting documentation with either the USCIS Nebraska Service Center or Texas Service Center, depending on where

---

[268] Sometimes an asylee will not have a marriage certificate or a birth certificate to prove the relationship. The instructions to the I-730, *available at www.uscis.gov/files/form/I-730instr.pdf,* provide that an applicant may submit secondary evidence of the relationship. *See also Matter of Kodwo*, 24 I&N Dec. 479 (BIA 2008) (which notes other types of evidence that may be used to establish the dissolution of a marriage).

[269] 8 CFR §§204.2(a)(1)(i)(B), (a)(1)(iii)(B), (a)(2), (d)(2), & (d)(5) (2014). *See* USCIS, Form I-730 Instructions, at 3-4, *available at http://www.uscis.gov/sites/default/files/files/form/i-730instr.pdf* (last visited Mar. 14, 2015).

[270] 8 CFR §207.7(d) (2014).

[271] 8 CFR §§207.7(e), 208.21(f), 1208.21(f) (2014).

[272] *See INS Issues Guidance on Blood and DNA Testing for Establishing Parentage*, 77 INTERPRETER RELEASES 1096 (July 2000). For more information on DNA testing, see *www.unhcrwashington.org/family-reunification*, *www.uscis.gov/humanitarian/refugees-asylum/refugees/united-states-refugee-admissions-program-usrap-consultation-worldwide-processing-priorities*, and *www.uscis.gov/sites/default/files/USCIS/Outreach/Upcoming%20National%20Engagements/Upcoming%20National%20Engagement%20Pages/2013%20Events/August%202013/I-730-USCIS-Presentation.pdf.*

[273] USCIS, *Refugee/Asylee Relative Petition (Form I-730)*, at 22-24, *available at www.uscis.gov/sites/default/files/USCIS/Outreach/Upcoming%20National%20Engagements/Upcoming%20National%20Engagement%20Pages/2013%20Events/August%202013/I-730-USCIS-Presentation.pdf* (last visited Apr. 2, 2015).

the asylee lives.[274] Upon receipt of a completed and signed I-730 that includes all of the required supporting documentation, USCIS will issue a receipt notice and send that notice to the asylee petitioner.

> **Practice Pointer**: Practitioners should always check USCIS's website at *www.uscis.gov/i-730* for the most recent filing address listed for I-730, Refugee/Asylee Relative Petitions, as filing locations frequently change.

After the I-730 has been received and is being processed, USCIS may require the beneficiary to provide biometrics for identity, background, and security checks. If the beneficiary is 14 years old or over, he or she must be fingerprinted and photographed.[275] If the relative is in the United States and is subject to biometrics collection, he or she will be notified in writing of the appointment time at the local ASC.[276] If the relative is outside of the United States, however, he or she will be provided biometrics collection instructions by DHS, the Department of State, or Overseas Processing Entities (*i.e.*, organizations who assist the U.S. government).[277] If the beneficiary fails to appear for a scheduled biometrics appointment or otherwise fails to provide required biometrics, the I-730 may be denied.[278]

Following biometrics collection, USCIS may request that a beneficiary who is inside the United States appear for an interview.[279] If such a request is made, the beneficiary will receive a written notice of the date, time, and place of the scheduled interview. The petitioner also may be asked to appear for the interview.[280] The interview is conducted by a USCIS officer under oath. If the beneficiary is not fluent in English, he or she must bring a competent interpreter who is fluent in both English and the beneficiary's language.[281] Failure to provide a competent interpreter could result in denial of the petition.[282] The officer may provide his or her decision on the day of the interview or at a later date.

> **Practice Pointer**: Beneficiaries scheduled for interviews before USCIS should bring a copy of the I-730 filing, some form of identification (passport, travel or ID documents, or Form I-94), and any additional evidence not already submitted. All additional evidence must be submitted in triplicate. Beneficiaries also may wish to bring witnesses to testify on their behalf, as well as their legal representative, if applicable.

---

[274] USCIS, Instructions for I-730, Refugee/Asylee Relative Petition, *supra* note 236.

[275] *See* USCIS, Form I-730 Instructions, *supra* note 236, at 4.

[276] *Id.*

[277] *Id.*

[278] *Id.*

[279] *Id.*

[280] *See* 8 CFR §103.2(a)(9) (2014).

[281] *See* 8 CFR §208.9(g) (2014).

[282] *See* USCIS, Form I-730 Instructions, *supra* note 236, at 5.

On the other hand, if the relative is outside of the United States, he or she will be interviewed by a DHS or the DOS officer in accordance with the set procedures for refugee and asylee derivative interviews in the specific country. The relative will be notified of the date, time, and place of the interview and will receive instructions in that regard.[283]

> **Practice Pointer**: Currently, USCIS conducts interviews and collects biometrics of beneficiaries living abroad *after* approval of the I-730 petition in the United States. However, in March of 2014, USCIS implemented a process that will be phased in over time, in which USCIS will no longer approve Form I-730 before interviewing and collecting biometrics from beneficiaries abroad.[284] These changes are currently in phase one, and I-730 cases for beneficiaries residing in China are being transferred from USCIS service centers to USCIS international field offices in China for completion of the interview and final case adjudication.[285]

If the spouse or child is found to be ineligible for derivative asylee status, the I-730 will be denied, and USCIS will send written notice stating the basis for the denial to the principal asylee.[286] There is no appeal available for a denied I-730.[287] The denial, however, is without prejudice to the consideration of a new petition or motion to reopen the refugee or asylee relative petition proceeding.[288]

If the I-730 is approved, however, USCIS will notify the asylee of the approval.[289] For derivative spouses and children who are inside the United States, USCIS will issue documentation reflecting the derivatives' current status as asylees.[290] Derivatives, like principal asylees, are authorized to work incident to their status and do not need an EAD to work. However, derivatives may apply for an EAD to obtain documentation of their employment authorization, as described above.[291]

For derivative spouses and children who are outside the United States, USCIS will send the approved I-730 petition to DOS for transmission to the U.S. embassy or consulate having jurisdiction over the area where the asylee's spouse and children are located.[292] It is at that time, that the spouse and children are usually provided

---

[283] *Id.*

[284] *See* USCIS, I-730, Refugee/Asylee Relative Petition, available at *www.uscis.gov/i-730* (last visited Apr. 2, 2015).

[285] *See id.*

[286] 8 CFR §§208.21(e), 1208.21(e).

[287] 8 CFR §§207.7(g), 208.21(e), 1208.21(e).

[288] 8 CFR §§207.7(g), 208.21(e), 1208.21(e).

[289] 8 CFR §§208.21(c)-(d), 1208.21(c)(d).

[290] 8 CFR §§208.21(c), 1208.21(c).

[291] *Id.*

[292] 8 CFR §§208.21(d), 1208.21(d).

instructions for biometrics collection, medical examination, and interview. Following the interview, the spouse and children may be granted permission to enter the United States as derivative asylees. Upon their entry to the United States, they will be considered asylees and will be issued an I-94 card indicating their admission in valid asylum status. These derivatives also are employment authorized incident to their status.

As long as the principal asylee's status is not revoked, the approved I-730 petition will remain valid for the duration of the derivative's relationship to the asylee and, in the case of a child, while the child is under age 21 and unmarried.[293] After the I-730 has been used by the beneficiary for admission to the United States as a derivative asylee, however, the I-730 will not confer future immigration benefits.[294] Following admission as an asylee, a derivative spouse or child shall be granted asylum for an indefinite period unless the principal's status is revoked.[295]

- **Practice Pointer**: If a principal asylee's status is revoked, all derivatives' status also will be revoked automatically, even if the reasons for revocation are unrelated to the derivatives. See chapter 14 of this book for a detailed discussion of termination of status.

G. Lawful Permanent Resident Status

Asylum also provides more permanent protection. An asylee — not a withholding or deferral of removal grantee — may adjust to lawful permanent resident status after one year in asylee status in the United States,[296] and may eventually become a U.S. citizen. To request lawful permanent resident status, the asylee must apply for adjustment of status by filing Form I-485, Application to Adjust Status, along with all of the required supporting documentation.[297]

To qualify, the asylee must: (1) have been physically present in the United States for at least one year after being granted asylum; (2) continue to meet the definition of refugee under INA §101(a)(42)(A); (3) not be firmly resettled in any foreign country; and (4) be admissible as an immigrant under INA §212(a), except that the grounds of inadmissibility relating to lack of a proper travel document, labor certification, or likelihood of becoming a public charge do not apply. Moreover, the attorney general may waive any other ground of inadmissibility for humanitarian purposes, to ensure family unity, or when it is in the public interest, except for drug trafficking and security-related grounds.[298]

---

[293] 8 CFR §§208.21(c)–(d), 1208.21(c)–(d).

[294] *Id.*

[295] 8 CFR §§208.21(g), 1208.21(g).

[296] *See generally* INA §209; 8 CFR §§209.1, 209.2, 1209.1, 1209.2.

[297] USCIS, *I-485, Application to Register Permanent Residence or Adjust Status*, *available at www.uscis.gov/i-485* (last visited Mar. 14, 2015).

[298] INA §209(b), (c); 8 CFR §§209.2(a), 1209.2(a).

➢ **Practice Pointer**: See chapter 15 of this book for a detailed discussion of adjustment of status for asylees, refugees, and their derivative family members.

III. Responsibilities of Those Granted Protection

With the benefits of a grant of asylum, withholding of removal under INA §241(b)(3), or protection under the CAT come responsibilities that grantees must follow. In general, all individuals granted protection in the United States must pay taxes on income earned in the United States, and may be subject to severe consequences upon commission of any crimes, even seemingly insignificant charges and charges that are later expunged. All grantees also are obligated to keep their address updated with USCIS, and certain male grantees between the ages of 18 and 26 must register for the Selective Service.

A. Change of Address

There are no restrictions regarding where an asylee may live in the United States. However, asylees are required to notify USCIS of any future changes of address within 10 days of moving. There may be immigration and criminal consequences for failure to timely notify USCIS of a change of address. Under INA §§265, 266(b), willfully failing to notify USCIS of a new address is a misdemeanor that can be punished by a fine of up to $200 and 30 days in jail.[299] Additionally, an individual may be deportable for failure to timely notify USCIS of a new address.[300] Thus, it is important for individuals granted relief to take this responsibility seriously.

A change of address may be completed with USCIS online by using the "Online Change of Address" tool,[301] calling the USCIS National Customer Service Center at 1-800-375-5283, or filing a Form AR-11, Alien's Change of Address Card, which is available on USCIS's website.[302]

➢ **Practice Pointer**: Practitioners should advise their clients upon a grant of relief of his or her obligation to timely notify USCIS of his or her change of address, and to print a confirmation of his or her change of address in case proof of timely submission of a change of address becomes necessary in the future.

B. Selective Service Registration

All male asylees between the ages of 18 and 26 must register for the Selective Service, a federal government agency whose mission is "to be prepared to provide

---

[299] INA §§265, 266(b).

[300] INA §237(a)(3)(A).

[301] USCIS, Change of Address, *available at https://egov.uscis.gov/coa/displayCOAForm.do* (last visited Mar. 11, 2015).

[302] USCIS, AR-11, Change of Address, *available at www.uscis.gov/ar-11* (last visited Mar. 11, 2015).

trained and untrained personnel to the [Department of Defense] in the event of a national emergency and to be prepared to implement an Alternative Service Program for registrants classified as conscientious objectors."[303]

Failure to register for the Selective Service may negatively impact the asylee's ability to become a U.S. citizen or to obtain other benefits in the United States, such as federal student aid, most federal jobs, and federal job training.[304] Asylees often are registered automatically upon grant of status. If they are not registered, however, male asylees between the ages of 18 and 26 must register with the Selective Service System.

> ➢ **Practice Pointer**: Asylees may verify whether they already have been registered by going to the Selective Service System's website and entering their last name, Social Security number, and date of birth.[305] If they are not found in the system, they should register online by going to *www.sss.gov/RegVer/wfRegistration.aspx* or by completing the registration form at *www.sss.gov/PDFs/Regform_copyINT.pdf* and mailing it to the Selective Service System, P.O. Box 94739, Palatine, IL 60094-4739.

IV. Public Benefits

Following approval of their asylum applications, asylees may be eligible to receive a variety of public benefits, either through a local organization funded by the Department of Health and Human Services, Office of Refugee Resettlement (ORR), or through the state in which they reside. These may include federal means-tested public benefits, means-tested refugee cash and medical assistance, refugee social services, Matching Grants, and a medical screening. The following is a list of many of the potential public benefits for asylees:[306]

- Supplemental Security Income — a monthly cash payment to low-income people with few resources who are age 65 or older, blind, or disabled (available for seven

[303] Selective Serv. Sys., About the Agency, *available at www.sss.gov/ABOUT.HTM* (last visited Mar. 11, 2015).

[304] *See* Selective Serv. Sys., *Selective Service System Online Registration*, *available at www.sss.gov/RegVer/wfRegistration.aspx* (last visited Mar. 11, 2015).

[305] Selective Serv. Sys., *Selective Service Online Registration Verification*, *available at www.sss.gov/RegVer/wfVerification.aspx* (last visited Mar. 11, 2015).

[306] Catholic Legal Immigration Network, Inc., *Asylee Eligibility for Resettlement Assistance*, at 4-5, *available at https://cliniclegal.org/sites/default/files/234843_clinic_asylee_final_1-30-12.pdf* (last visited Mar. 14, 2015). This list is not all-inclusive. See Appendix 9D for a full list of the public benefits available to individuals granted relief.

years after status is granted and up to nine years if the individual has applied for citizenship);[307]

- State Nutritional Assistance Program (formerly "Food Stamps") — a debit card that can be used at grocery stores to allow low-income people to buy food necessary for good health;[308]
- Temporary Assistance for Needy Families (TANF) — a monthly cash payment to low-income parents or relatives caring for children under age 18 in the same household (available for the first seven years after status is granted, but individuals cannot receive assistance for more than five years total);[309]
- Medicaid — reimburses doctor and hospital costs for certain low-income people, primarily pregnant women, families with children, the elderly, and the disabled (available for the first seven years after status is granted);[310]
- Refugee Cash Assistance and Refugee Medical Assistance (RCA and RMA) — a federally funded program available to needy asylees who are not eligible for other cash or medical assistance programs such as TANF, SSI, or Medicaid (available for up to eight months from the date status is granted);[311]
- Refugee Social Services — designed to smooth adjustment and facilitate early self-sufficiency, including job preparation and placement and English language classes (services vary by state);[312]
- Matching Grant — an early employment program administered by private resettlement agencies as an alternative to public cash assistance, which provides job counseling and placement, case management, transitional cash, and living assistance (limited slots available and only good candidates for early employment

---

[307] *See* Social Sec'y Admin., *Supplemental Security Income (SSI) Benefits*, *available at www.ssa.gov/disabilityssi/ssi.html* (last visited Mar. 14, 2015).

[308] *See* U.S. Dep't of Agriculture, *Supplemental Nutrition Assistance Program (SNAP) Eligibility*, *available at www.fns.usda.gov/snap/eligibility* (last visited Mar. 14, 2015).

[309] *See* U.S. Dep't of Health & Human Servs., Office of Family Assistance, *About TANF*, *available at www.acf.hhs.gov/programs/ofa/programs/tanf/about* (last visited Mar. 14, 2015).

[310] *See* Ctrs. for Medicare & Medicaid Servs., *Eligibility for Non-Citizens in Medicaid and CHIP*, *www.medicaid.gov/medicaid-chip-program-information/by-topics/outreach-and-enrollment/downloads/overview-of-eligibility-for-non-citizens-in-medicaid-and-chip.pdf* (last visited Mar. 14, 2015).

[311] *See* U.S. Dep't of Health & Human Servs., Office of Refugee Resettlement, *About Cash & Medical Assistance*, *available at www.acf.hhs.gov/programs/orr/programs/cma/about* (last visited Mar. 14, 2015).

[312] *See* U.S. Dep't of Health & Human Servs., Office of Refugee Resettlement, *About Refugee Social Services*, *available at www.acf.hhs.gov/programs/orr/programs/matching-grants/about* (last visited Mar. 14, 2015).

are chosen; individuals must enroll within 31 days from the date status is granted);[313]

- Medical Screening — a preventative medical screening and assessment provided by the state's Department of Public Health for early diagnosis and treatment of any illness (screening for TB, parasites, hepatitis, as well as school vaccinations for children); and
- Torture Treatment Centers — a program funded by ORR for victims of torture to provide rehabilitation, including treatment of the physical and psychological effects of torture, social and legal services, research, and training for health care providers.[314]

Which of these benefits are available to an asylee or individual granted withholding of removal depends on the eligibility standards for each program, as well as the timing and location in which they are sought.[315] It is essential for asylees and withholding of removal grantees to seek these benefits immediately upon being granted relief, as many of them are only available for a certain amount of time, which begins running on the date of the grant of relief.[316]

> **Practice Pointer**: Asylees also may be eligible to use employment services from One-Stop Career Centers, including job search assistance, career counseling, and occupational skills training. For more information on employment services from One-Stop Career Centers, call 1-877-872-5627 or go to *www.careeronestop.org*.[317]

> **Practice Pointer**: For more information on public benefits for asylees, visit the Office of Refugee Resettlement's website at *www.acf.hhs.gov/programs/orr*. [318] ORR used to fund a National Asylee Information & Referral Line at 1-800-354-0365, which was operated by Catholic Charities of the Archdiocese of New York. The goal of the referral line was to link asylees with local refugee service providers and benefits for which they are statutorily eligible, including job placement, English classes, cash assistance, and medical assistance. However, after

---

313 *See* U.S. Dep't of Health & Human Servs., Office of Refugee Resettlement, *About the Volunteer Agencies Matching Grant Program*, *available at www.acf.hhs.gov/programs/orr/programs/matching-grants/about* (last visited Mar. 14, 2015).

314 *See* Nat'l Consortium of Torture Treatment Programs, *NCTTP Member Centers*, *available at www.ncttp.org/members.html* (last visited Mar. 14, 2015).

315 *See* Catholic Legal Immigration Network, Inc., *Asylee Eligibility for Resettlement Assistance*, at 4-5, *available at https://cliniclegal.org/sites/default/files/234843_clinic_asylee_final_1-30-12.pdf* (last visited Mar. 14, 2015). See also Appendix 9D for a detailed description of the public benefits available to individuals granted relief.

316 See Appendix 9D for a detailed description of the public benefits available to individuals granted relief.

317 (last visited Mar. 14, 2015).

318 (last visited Mar. 11, 2015).

11 years in operation, this referral line no longer exists, as it was defunded in September of 2012.[319]

➤ **Practice Pointer**: For a comprehensive study of the benefits available to asylees, as well as a useful guide for understanding these benefits to better serve asylee clients, see Lindsay M. Harris's article, "From Surviving to Thriving? An Investigation of Asylee Integration in the United States."[320] Also see Appendix 9D for a detailed description of the public benefits available to those granted relief.

Many of these benefits programs are available for a limited period of eight months that starts running from the date of the grant of asylum.[321] Thus, it is essential for asylees to seek these benefits right away upon a grant of asylum in order to maximize the benefits available to them.

➤ **Practice Pointer**: Practitioners should notify their asylee clients of these public benefits right away upon being granted asylum and assist them in locating a local ORR-funded organization or the state office that processes benefits. Because some of these benefits are time-limited, practitioners should encourage their clients to contact these organizations as soon as possible so they may receive assistance in applying for and seeking these benefits.

➤ **Practice Pointer**: Currently, four USCIS asylum offices — Arlington, Los Angeles, New York, and San Francisco — host periodic comprehensive "Asylee Benefits Orientations" at their offices. These orientations are sponsored by various nonprofit organizations, such as the International Rescue Committee, which conduct presentations to educate recent asylum grantees about the immigration and public benefits available to them and to answer questions that new asylees may have.[322] The AILA Asylum and Refugee Liaison Committee is collaborating with USCIS and ORR to initiate the implementation of

---

[319] CLINIC, *Asylee Information*, *available at https://cliniclegal.org/resources/toolkits/asylee-information* (last visited Apr. 2, 2015).

[320] Lindsay M. Harris, *From Surviving to Thriving? An Investigation of Asylee Integration into the United States*, NEW YORK UNIVERSITY REVIEW OF LAW AND SOCIAL CHANGE, Vol. 40.2 (forthcoming) (comparing the benefits available to refugees versus asylees). A draft of this forthcoming article is available at *http://papers.ssrn.com/sol3/papers.cfm?abstract_id=2585209.*

[321] *See, e.g.*, U.S. Dep't of Health & Human Servs., Office of Refugee Resettlement, *About Cash & Medical Assistance*, *available at www.acf.hhs.gov/programs/orr/programs/cma/about* (last visited Mar. 14, 2015).

[322] *See* USCIS Handouts, *Asylee Benefits Orientations*, *available at www.uscis.gov/sites/default/files/USCIS/Outreach/Notes%20from%20Previous%20Engagements/Asy-AdditionalHandouts-12814.pdf* (last visited Mar. 14, 2015); USCIS, *Questions and Answers: USCIS Asylum Division Quarterly Stakeholder Meeting*, at 4–5 (Mar. 19, 2013) *available at www.uscis.gov/sites/default/files/USCIS/Outreach/Notes%20from%20Previous%20Engagements/2013/March%202013/QuestionsAnswers-Mar192013.pdf* (last visited Mar. 14, 2015).

these programs at the other four asylum offices (Chicago, Houston, Miami, and Newark). Practitioners whose clients, granted affirmatively or defensively, reside in the Arlington, Los Angeles, New York, and San Francisco jurisdictions should inform their clients of these orientations, assist them in learning the date and time of the next scheduled orientation, and encourage them to attend.[323]

V. Conclusion

For victims of persecution and torture, gaining protection in the United States is often only the first step along the path to true survival. It is essential for practitioners working with these vulnerable populations to have a full understanding of the immigration and public benefits and responsibilities that accompany a grant of protection in the United States, and to impart that knowledge on their clients so they can truly thrive.[324]

---

[323] *See* Lindsay M. Harris, *From Surviving to Thriving? An Investigation of Asylee Integration into the United States*, NEW YORK UNIVERSITY REVIEW OF LAW AND SOCIAL CHANGE, Vol. 40.2 (forthcoming) (comparing the benefits available to refugees versus asylees). A draft of this forthcoming article is available at *http://papers.ssrn.com/sol3/papers.cfm?abstract_id=2585209*.

[324] Lindsay M. Harris, *From Surviving to Thriving? An Investigation of Asylee Integration into the United States*, NEW YORK UNIVERSITY REVIEW OF LAW AND SOCIAL CHANGE, Vol. 40.2 (forthcoming) (comparing the benefits available to refugees versus asylees). A draft of this forthcoming article is available at *http://papers.ssrn.com/sol3/papers.cfm?abstract_id=2585209*.

Chapter Fourteen

Termination of Status*

Although a grant of asylum, withholding of removal under section 241(b)(3) of the Immigration and Nationality Act (INA), or protection under the Convention Against Torture (CAT) may permit an individual to remain safely in the United States, these forms of relief do not convey a right to remain permanently. In fact, all three forms of relief may be terminated, some more easily than others. This chapter examines the legal standards and procedures for termination of asylum, withholding of removal under INA §241(b)(3), and protection under CAT. It also reviews the legal standards and procedures for termination of refugee status.

I. Termination of Asylum and Withholding of Removal

Asylum does not convey a right to remain permanently in the United States and may be terminated by the Attorney General (AG),[1] even after an asylee becomes a lawful permanent resident (LPR).[2] Withholding of removal under INA §241(b)(3) also may be terminated.[3] Asylees and withholding of removal grantees may not be deported or removed from the United States unless their asylum status or withholding order has been terminated first.[4] There are legal grounds that must be met and specific procedures that must be followed before asylum or withholding of removal

* The author would like to thank Sandra Grossman of Grossman Law, LLC for her invaluable input in reviewing this chapter.

[1] Immigration and Nationality Act (INA) §208(c)(2); 8 CFR §§208.24(a), 1208.24(a).

[2] USCIS Fact Sheet, *Traveling Outside the United States as an Asylum Applicant, an Asylee, or a Lawful Permanent Resident Who Obtained Such Status Based on Asylum* (revised Jan. 4. 2007), AILA InfoNet Doc. No. 06122875 (*posted* Dec. 28, 2006), *available at www.uscis.gov/files/pressrelease/AsylumTravel122706FS.pdf. But see Robleto-Pastora v. Holder*, 567 F.3d 437, 444–45 (9th Cir. 2009) (holding that asylum termination provisions do not apply to a lawful permanent resident (LPR) subject to removal proceedings, even though the lawful permanent residency was obtained based on asylee status).

[3] 8 Code of Federal Regulations (CFR) §§208.24(b), 1208.24(b) (2014).

[4] 8 CFR §§208.22, 1208.22 (2014).

may be terminated. The grounds and procedures for termination listed below are for applications that were granted after April 1, 1997.

A. Grounds for Terminating Asylum

A grant of asylum may be terminated by an asylum officer if asylum was granted by U.S. Citizenship and Immigration Services (USCIS), by an immigration judge (IJ) or the Board of Immigration Appeals (BIA) pursuant to a motion to reopen, or in INA §240 proceedings if it is determined that the individual:

- was not eligible for asylum at the time it was granted and there is a showing of fraud in the application;
- no longer meets the definition of refugee, owing to a fundamental change in circumstances;
- engaged in the persecution of others;
- having been convicted by final judgment of a particularly serious crime, constitutes a danger to the community of the United States;
- has committed a serious nonpolitical crime outside of the United States;
- is a danger to the security of the United States;
- has engaged in terrorist activity;
- may be removed to a safe third country, pursuant to a bilateral or multilateral agreement;
- has voluntarily availed him- or herself of the protection of his or her home country or, if stateless, the country of last habitual residence by returning to the country with permanent resident status or the reasonable possibility of obtaining such status in that country; or
- has acquired a new nationality and enjoys the protection of the country of his or her new nationality.[5]

Thus, any fraud, changes in the country of feared persecution, criminal acts or convictions, terrorist or other unlawful activities, return to the country of feared persecution, or lawful immigration status in another country may lead the U.S. Department of Homeland Security (DHS) to argue that an asylee's status should be terminated and to take steps toward that goal.

> ➢ **Practice Pointer:** Upon a grant of asylum, practitioners should warn their clients in writing of all of the actions that could jeopardize their status as asylees. Practitioners also should advise their clients to notify their attorneys or representatives immediately upon any actions — whether an arrest, travel outside the United States, or grant of status in another country — that could affect his or her maintenance of status.

---

[5] *See* 8 CFR §§208.24(a)–(f), 1208.24(a)–(f) (2014); INA §208(c)(2).

B. Grounds for Rescinding a Grant of Asylum

Although a distinct process from termination of asylum, there also may be grounds for the USCIS Asylum Office to rescind the asylee's asylum status.[6] If the Asylum Office did not have jurisdiction over the asylum application that it granted, it must move to reconsider the asylum approval pursuant to 8 Code of Federal Regulations (CFR) §103.5(a)(5)(ii) in order to pursue rescission of asylum status.[7] Lack of jurisdiction, however, is not grounds for termination under 8 CFR §208.24, as described above in Part I.A.[8] The Asylum Office must pursue rescission of asylum status in two situations: (1) if the applicant was under the jurisdiction of the Executive Office for Immigration Review (EOIR) at the time of the asylum approval; or (2) if the applicant was outside of the United States at the time of the asylum approval.[9]

C. Grounds for Terminating Withholding of Removal

A grant of withholding of removal under INA §241(b)(3) also may be terminated by an asylum officer if withholding was granted under the jurisdiction of USCIS, or by an IJ or the BIA pursuant to a motion to reopen if it is determined that the individual:

- was not eligible for withholding at the time it was granted and there is a showing of fraud in the application;
- is no longer entitled to withholding due to a fundamental change in circumstances in the country to which removal was withheld;
- engaged in the persecution of others;
- having been convicted by final judgment of a particularly serious crime, constitutes a danger to the community of the United States;
- has committed a serious nonpolitical crime outside of the United States; or
- is a danger to the security of the United States.[10]

Thus, any fraud, changes in the country of feared persecution, criminal charges or convictions, terrorist or other unlawful activities may lead the Department of Homeland Security (DHS) to argue that an order of withholding of removal should be terminated and to take steps toward that goal.

> ➢ **Practice Pointer:** Upon a grant of withholding of removal, practitioners should warn their clients in writing of all of the actions that could

---

[6] *See* USCIS, *Affirmative Asylum Procedures Manual*, pt. III.U. (Nov. 2013), *available at www.uscis.gov/sites/default/files/files/nativedocuments/Asylum_Procedures_Manual_2013.pdf* (last visited Apr. 2, 2015). *See also* 8 CFR §103.5(a)(5)(ii).

[7] USCIS, *Affirmative Asylum Procedures Manual*, *supra* note 6, at pt. III.U.

[8] *Id.*

[9] *Id.*

[10] *See* 8 CFR §§208.24(b)–(e), 1208.24(b)–(e) (2014).

jeopardize their grant of protection. Practitioners also should advise their clients to notify their attorneys or representatives immediately upon any actions, such as an arrest, that could affect his or her order of withholding protection.

- **Practice Pointer:** DHS may, in some instances, require a withholding of removal grantee to write letters to third countries requesting safe haven. These letters may be drafted in a way that fully explains why withholding of removal was granted, any criminal convictions, any dependency on state assistance, and other such factors that may influence a state to be unlikely to offer safe haven to the individual.

D. Procedures for Termination by USCIS

In cases in which the individual was granted asylum under the jurisdiction of USCIS, USCIS may elect to initiate and conduct termination proceedings at the Asylum Office, or to issue a Notice to Appear (NTA) concurrently with a Notice of Intent to Terminate Asylum Status (NOIT) by EOIR to vest the immigration court with jurisdiction over the termination proceedings.[11] Generally, if an asylum approval was issued by the Asylum Office, the Asylum Office will conduct the termination proceedings rather than vesting the immigration court with jurisdiction.[12] This is because the majority of asylees whose termination proceedings occur before EOIR are those who will be or already have been placed into proceedings by another branch of DHS, or are being detained based on a criminal conviction.[13] The Asylum Office that has jurisdiction over the asylee's place of residence is the office that handles any termination proceedings for that individual.[14] USCIS does not have jurisdiction to terminate asylum that was granted by EOIR.[15]

In order to terminate asylum status at the Asylum Office, it is USCIS's burden to establish one or more of the termination grounds listed in 8 CFR §208.24 (and listed above in Part I.A.) by a preponderance of the evidence.[16] However, before asylum status may be terminated, the Asylum Office must first issue to the asylee a NOIT listing the grounds for the intended termination and containing a summary of the unclassified evidence supporting those grounds.[17] In order to issue a NOIT, the Asylum Office must have information that, on its face, indicates that asylum

[11] 8 CFR §208.24(f); USCIS *Affirmative Asylum Procedures Manual*, *supra* note 6, at pt. III.V.1.c.

[12] USCIS *Affirmative Asylum Procedures Manual*, *supra* note 6, at pts. III.V.3.a.

[13] *Id.*

[14] *Id.* at pt. III.V.1.c.

[15] *Id.*

[16] *Id.* at pt. III.V.1.b.

[17] 8 CFR §§208.24(c), 1208.24(c) (2014); USCIS *Affirmative Asylum Procedures Manual*, *supra* note 6, at pts. III.V.1.b., III.V.3.

termination may be appropriate.[18] In other words, there must be a prima facie case supporting termination.[19]

> ➢ **Practice Pointer:** Sometimes, USCIS may have information that does not establish a prima facie case in support of termination, but that raises questions about the viability of the asylee's status. Under these circumstances, the Asylum Office may request a voluntary interview with the asylee.[20] If the asylee does not cooperate, the Asylum Office may coordinate with the Office of Fraud Detection and National Security or ICE Investigations to develop additional information.[21]

The asylee must be given an interview with an asylum officer during which he or she will have the opportunity to present evidence showing that he or she is still eligible for asylum.[22] The NOIT must be served on the individual at least 30 days before the termination interview date.[23] It must be served personally and properly pursuant to the requirements of 8 CFR §103.5a.[24] Specifically, the NOIT must be: (1) delivered to the asylee personally; (2) delivered to his or her home by leaving it with someone of suitable age and discretion; (3) delivered to the office of an attorney or other person by leaving it with "a person in charge;" or (4) mailed by certified or registered mail, return receipt requested, addressed to the asylee at his or her last known address.[25]

Upon receipt of the NOIT, the asylee may waive the 30-day period and request an earlier interview, or may waive the interview entirely and admit the allegations in the NOIT in writing.[26] The asylee also may prepare and file a written rebuttal to the NOIT.[27]

> ➢ **Practice Pointer:** The filing of a Freedom of Information Act (FOIA) request will delay termination proceedings until the asylee has received a response and his or her file has been returned to the Asylum Office.[28] Thus, practitioners should consider filing a FOIA request; not only does a FOIA request assist the asylee with knowing what adverse information

---

[18] USCIS *Affirmative Asylum Procedures Manual*, *supra* note 6, at pt. III.V.1.b.

[19] *Id.*

[20] *Id.*

[21] *Id.*

[22] 8 CFR §§208.24(a), (c), 1208.24(a), (c).

[23] 8 CFR §§208.24(c), 1208.24(c); USCIS *Affirmative Asylum Procedures Manual*, *supra* note 6, at pts. III.V.1.b., III.V.3.

[24] USCIS *Affirmative Asylum Procedures Manual*, *supra* note 6, at pts. III.V.3.

[25] 8 CFR §103.5a(a)(2).

[26] USCIS *Affirmative Asylum Procedures Manual*, *supra* note 6, at pts. III.V.3.

[27] *Id.*

[28] *Id.* at pt. III.V.6.

may be in his or her file, but also, it buys the asylee more time to gather rebuttal evidence and prepare for the termination interview.

At the termination interview, the asylum officer will place the asylee, any dependent family members, and any interpreter under oath. The nature of the interview is non-adversarial and is conducted in a similar manner as an affirmative asylum interview; however, the termination interview need only explore issues relevant to termination of asylum.[29]

If, following the interview, the Asylum Office finds that there is insufficient evidence to meet the preponderance of the evidence standard to terminate asylee status, the individual will receive a Notice of Continuation of Asylum Status and will remain in valid asylee status.[30] If, on the other hand, the asylum officer determines that the individual is no longer eligible for asylum or withholding of removal, the individual must be given written notice that his or her asylum status or withholding of removal, and any employment authorization issued pursuant thereto, have been terminated.[31] Specifically, the individual will receive a NOIT, a Form I-213, Record of Deportable Alien (if required), and an NTA.[32] Regardless whether the individual is an LPR or an asylee, after asylum status is terminated, the Asylum Office must place the individual before the immigration court.[33] The individual's employment authorization issued as a result of his or her asylum status is automatically terminated upon termination of asylum status.[34]

Termination of status applies to the principal, as well as his or her derivatives, whether they were granted derivative asylum status as dependents on the I-589 Application for Asylum or through an I-730 Refugee/Asylee Relative Petition.[35] However, if the termination grounds apply only to a dependent, only the asylee status of the dependent is terminated.[36]

E. Procedures for Rescission by USCIS

The Asylum Office must pursue rescission of asylum status — a different process than termination — in two situations: (1) if the applicant was under the jurisdiction of the EOIR at the time of the asylum approval; or (2) if the applicant was outside of the United States at the time of the asylum approval.[37] If the Asylum Office did not have

---

[29] *Id.* at pt. III.V.4.

[30] *Id.* at pts. III.V.1.b., III.V.5.f.

[31] 8 CFR §§208.24(c), 1208.24(c) (2014).

[32] USCIS *Affirmative Asylum Procedures Manual*, *supra* note 6, at pts. III.V.5.d.

[33] *Id.*

[34] *Id.* at pt. III.V.5.e.

[35] 8 CFR §§208.24(d), 208.21(g); USCIS *Affirmative Asylum Procedures Manual*, *supra* note 6, at pts. III.V.5.d.

[36] USCIS *Affirmative Asylum Procedures Manual*, *supra* note 6, at pts. III.V.5.d.

[37] *Id.* at pt. III.U.

jurisdiction over the asylum application that it granted, it must move to reconsider the asylum approval pursuant to 8 CFR §103.5(a)(5)(ii) in order to pursue rescission of asylum status.[38] The Asylum Office will send a Motion to Reconsider to the asylee, indicating one of the two reasons for rescission, with any unclassified documents supporting the determination of lack of jurisdiction at the time of approval.[39] This motion will be sent to the derivative beneficiary if the Asylum Office had jurisdiction over the principal applicant at the time of granting asylum, but did not have jurisdiction over the derivative.[40]

An asylee is given 45 days from the date of the motion to respond.[41] Upon receipt of any timely response, the Asylum Office will review the documentation to determine whether it rebuts the reasons provided for the proposed rescission.[42] If the reasons for rescission are successfully rebutted, the Asylum Office will send the asylee an Affirmation of Asylum Grant After Motion to Reconsider affirming the asylum grant.[43]

On the other hand, if the Asylum Office rescinds the asylum grant based on EOIR jurisdiction, it will send the former asylee a Notice of Rescission of Asylum Grant, administratively close the asylum application, and transfer the file to ICE.[44] If it is determined that the applicant was not in the United States at the time of the asylum approval, the actions for rescission will depend on whether the applicant received advance parole or not, whether he or she traveled back to the country of feared persecution, and whether his or her absence from the United States affects the applicant's substantive claim.[45] These cases are rare. If a case is rescinded under these grounds, the former asylee is provided with a Notice of Rescission of Asylum Grant.[46]

Any derivative asylees' status also must be rescinded along with the principal applicants.[47] However if the derivative asylee's status is rescinded under these grounds, only the asylee status of the dependent is rescinded, not the principal.[48]

---

[38] *Id.*

[39] *Id.* at pt. III.U.1.

[40] *Id.*

[41] *Id.* at pt. III.U.2.

[42] *Id.*

[43] *Id.*

[44] *Id.* at pt. III.U.2.a.

[45] *Id.* at pt. III.U.2.b.

[46] *Id.*

[47] *Id.* at pt. III.U.2.

[48] *Id.* at pt. III.U.2.c.

F. Procedures for Termination by an IJ or the BIA

There are three situations in which the IJ or BIA may terminate a grant of asylum or withholding of removal or deportation. First, an IJ may terminate a grant of asylum or withholding of removal or deportation made under the jurisdiction of USCIS at any time after the individual has been served with the notice to terminate by USCIS.[49] Second, termination by an IJ or the BIA may occur in conjunction with a later exclusion, deportation, or removal proceeding.[50] Third, an IJ or the BIA may reopen a case, pursuant to 8 CFR §§1003.2, 1003.23, for the purpose of terminating a grant of asylum or withholding of removal or deportation made under the jurisdiction of the EOIR.

With regard to the second situation — termination by an IJ or the BIA in conjunction with later removal proceedings — the BIA has held that a grant of asylum is not an "admission" to the United States under INA §101(a)(13)(A).[51] Therefore, an asylee is properly charged under INA §212 as inadmissible when issued an NTA before the immigration court. Moreover, since a grant of asylum is not an "admission," when termination of an individual's asylum status occurs in conjunction with removal proceedings pursuant to 8 CFR §1208.24, the IJ must first make a threshold determination regarding the termination of asylum status prior to resolving issues of removability and eligibility for relief from removal.[52]

In seeking a reopening before the IJ or BIA for the purpose of terminating a grant of asylum or withholding of removal, DHS must file the motion to reopen, which is subject to the numerical and time limitations set forth in the regulations.[53]

Only a few narrow exceptions to these numerical and time limitations are available to DHS: (1) changed circumstances material to the individual's eligibility for relief, the evidence of which was previously unavailable;[54] (2) fraud in the

---

[49] 8 CFR §§208.24(f), 1208.24(f) (2014).

[50] 8 CFR §§208.24(f), 1208.24(f) (2014).

[51] *Matter of V–X–*, 26 I&N Dec. 147 (BIA 2013).

[52] *Id.*

[53] *See* 8 CFR §§208.24(f), 1208.24(f) (2014). *See* ch. 11 for a detailed discussion of motions to reopen, the numerical and time limitations, and the narrow exceptions to those limitations.

[54] INA §240(c)(7)(C)(ii); 8 CFR §§1003.2(c)(3)(ii), 1003.23(b)(4)(i) (2014); *see e.g.*, *Malty v. Ashcroft*, 381 F.3d 942, 945–46 (9th Cir. 2004) (holding that the BIA erred in denying a motion to reopen because the Respondent's new evidence of changed circumstances was qualitatively different than what he initially filed); *Bernabe v. Holder,* 581 Fed. App'x 647, 648 (9th Cir. 2014); *Fustaguio Do Nascimento v. Mukasey*, 549 F.3d 12, 16 (1st Cir. 2008); *Hailemichael v. Gonzales*, 454 F.3d 878, 883 (8th Cir. 2006) (holding that DHS failed to demonstrate that the applicant committed fraud in the original proceedings). *But see Najmabadi v. Holder*, 597 F.3d 983 (9th Cir. 2010) (holding that the evidence presented at motion to reopen was not qualitatively different and thus, not previously unavailable); *Larngar v. Holder*, 562 F.3d 71, 74 (1st Cir. 2009) (agreeing with the BIA determination that evidence of a material change in circumstances was previously unavailable but denying that the change related to country conditions and overcame an untimely motion to reopen. Rather, only the petitioner's personal circumstances had changed).

original proceedings;[55] or (3) a crime supporting termination of relief.[56] If the proceedings are reopened by the IJ or BIA, DHS has the burden of establishing, by a preponderance of the evidence, one or more of the grounds for termination discussed above.[57]

To establish fraud as a ground for termination, DHS must satisfy a two-step test by showing, by a preponderance of the evidence, that: (1) there was fraud in the individual's application for asylum; and (2) the fraud was such that the individual was not eligible for asylum at the time it was granted.[58] According to the BIA, proof that the individual knew of the fraud in the application is not required in order to satisfy the first criterion.[59] DHS, however, must separately prove that, under the true facts, the individual was not eligible for asylum at the time it was granted.[60]

Whether knowledge of the fraud is necessary to establish grounds for termination of asylum is an issue that has been considered by the BIA and circuit courts. Recently, in 2014, the BIA clarified its position on this issue. In *Matter of P–S–H–*, the BIA reviewed the IJ's termination of asylum based on fraud in the individual's application. DHS had filed a motion to reopen the Indian national's proceedings after the respondent's attorney was found guilty of making false statements in asylum applications.[61] In support of termination, DHS submitted a report of its investigation and testimony of a Foreign Service National Investigator that the medical certificate in question was fraudulent, narratives in the respondent's asylum statement that were common to about 300 other applications, two affidavits that were worded identically, and an inconsistency between the testimony of the Foreign Service National Investigator and the sworn statement of the respondent's friend.[62] The respondent asserted that he had no knowledge of the fraud in his asylum application and argued that DHS must prove knowledge of fraud in order to terminate his grant of asylum.[63] The IJ disagreed and ordered termination, and the respondent appealed to the BIA.

[55] 8 CFR §1003.2(c)(3)(iv) (2014). *See, e.g., Urooj v. Holder*, 734 F.3d 1075 (9th Cir. 2013); *Diallo v. Gonzales*, 447 F.3d 1274, 1279–80 (10th Cir. 2008); *Ntangsi v. Gonzales*, 475 F.3d 1007 (8th Cir. 2007); *Hailemichael v. Gonzales*, 454 F.3d 878 (8th Cir. 2006); *Efe v. Ashcroft*, 293 F.3d 899, 904 (5th Cir. 2002).

[56] 8 CFR §1003.2(c)(3)(iv) (2014). *See, e.g., Hailemichael v. Gonzales*, *id.*, at 878; *Efe v. Ashcroft*, *id.*, at 904. *See also Gutierrez v. Holder*, 730 F.3d 900 (9th Cir. 2013); *Pechenkov v. Holder*, 705 F.3d 444 (9th Cir. 2012); *Hernandez-Vasquez v. Holder*, 430 Fed. App'x 448 (6th Cir. 2011).

[57] 8 CFR §§208.24(f), 1208.24(f) (2014). *See also Ntangsi v. Gonzales*, 475 F.3d 1007, 1012–13 (8th Cir. 2007) (reversing termination of asylum status where neither the IJ nor the BIA placed the burden of proving fraud on the government).

[58] *Matter of P–S–H–*, 26 I&N Dec. 329 (BIA 2014).

[59] *Id.* (clarifying *Matter of A–S–J–*, 25 I&N Dec. 893 (BIA 2012)).

[60] *Id.*

[61] *Id.* at 332.

[62] *Id.* at 332–33.

[63] *Id.* at 333.

The BIA held that the regulations do not require that DHS prove that the individual had knowledge of the fraud.[64] Rather, the inquiry is only whether there was fraud in the original proceeding.[65] In making this holding, the BIA addressed the Eighth Circuit U.S. Court of Appeals case law cited by the respondent, which relied upon adverse credibility case law and the traditional definition of fraud in holding that DHS must show that the applicant knew the statement or document was fraudulent at the time the applicant submitted it to the IJ in order to terminate asylum on the basis of fraud.[66] The BIA stated that the question whether an individual is credible or has made a fraudulent misrepresentation is distinguishable from the question of whether asylum should be terminated based on fraud.

The BIA relied on the plain language of the termination regulations, which simply require DHS to establish "fraud in the alien's application," but do not specify that the individual must have been personally involved in or aware of the fraud, to conclude that "the regulations do not require the DHS to establish, for purposes of showing that there was fraud in an alien's asylum application, that the alien knew of the fraud."[67] The BIA also considered Congress's intent, stating:

> The existence of fraud in an asylum application is a serious matter that undermines the integrity of the entire asylum process. We, therefore, doubt that Congress intended an asylum application containing fraud to be immune from termination if the alien would have been ineligible at the time it was granted, even if he or she was not complicit in the fraud.[68]

Thus, the BIA concluded that to terminate a grant of asylum based on fraud, the individual's knowledge of the fraud is not necessary. DHS need only prove, by a preponderance of the evidence, that: (1) there was fraud in the individual's asylum application; and (2) the fraud was such that the individual was not eligible for asylum at the time it was granted.[69]

- **Practice Pointer:** Practitioners should continue to argue, based on Eighth Circuit law, as well as analogies to other provisions in the INA where fraud must be "willful" (or knowing and voluntary), that an asylee cannot be held responsible for fraud that was not willfully committed.[70]

---

[64] *Id.*

[65] *Id.* at 334.

[66] *Id.* at 334–35 (BIA 2014) (addressing *Ntangsi v. Gonzales*, 475 F.3d 1007, 1012 (8th Cir. 2007); *Hailemichael v. Gonzales*, 454 F.3d 878, 885 (8th Cir. 2006)).

[67] *Matter of P–S–H–*, at 335–36.

[68] *Id.* at 335.

[69] *Id.* at 337–38.

[70] *See Ntangsi v. Gonzales*, 475 F.3d 1007, 1012 (8th Cir. 2007); *Hailemichael v. Gonzales*, 454 F.3d 878, 885 (8th Cir. 2006). *See also* INA §212(a)(6)(C)(i).

II. Termination of Derivative Asylum Status

The termination of asylum status for a person who was the principal applicant will automatically result in the termination of the asylum status of any spouse and children who received derivative status based on the asylum application of the principal.[71] Such a termination, however, does not preclude the spouse or child from separately asserting an asylum or withholding of removal claim.[72]

III. Termination of CAT Protection

Protection under the CAT, whether withholding or deferral of removal, also may be terminated. However, there are different standards and procedures depending on the type of relief. In general, deferral of removal may be terminated more easily thank withholding of removal.[73]

A. Termination of Withholding of Removal under CAT

The procedures for termination of a grant of withholding of removal under the CAT are the same procedures as for termination of a grant of withholding of removal under INA §241(b)(3). An IJ or the BIA may reopen a case, pursuant to 8 CFR §§1003.2, 1003.23, for the purpose of terminating withholding of removal under the CAT. DHS must file the motion to reopen with the IJ or the BIA, depending on where jurisdiction lies, and such motions to reopen are subject to the numerical and time limitations set forth in the regulations.[74] Only a few narrow exceptions are available to these numerical and time limitations, such as changed circumstances material to the individual's eligibility for relief, the evidence of which was previously unavailable,[75] fraud in the original proceedings,[76] or a crime supporting termination

---

[71] 8 CFR §§208.24(d), 1208.24(d) (2014); *see e.g.*, *Kurshumi v. Ashcroft*, 102 Fed. App'x 172, 176 n. 3 (1st Cir. 2004) (noting that an applicant who had himself been denied asylum might still be eligible as an asylee as a derivative of his wife's status, but such status would depend wholly on the validity of the wife's claim); *Singh v. Holder*, 488 Fed. App'x 476, 478 (2d Cir. 2012) (noting that in accordance with 8 CFR §208.24(d) when the principal loses asylee status, so do their derivatives).

[72] 8 CFR §§208.24(d), 1208.24(d) (2014).

[73] *See, e.g.*, *Khouzam v. Hogan*, 497 F. Supp. 2d 615, 619 (D. MD 2007) (Here, the decision to terminate Khouzam's deferral was apparently made on January 24, 2007, and he would have been eligible for removal on June 1, 2007. However, Khouzam was not informed of this decision until May 29, 2007, when he reported for a regular check-in with ICE. The district court stayed his removal, and at the time of press, Khouzam's fate was undetermined). *See also Ali v. Mukasey*, 529 F.3d 478 (2d Cir. 2008) (describing evidence used in motion to terminate deferral under CAT which included information from the U.S. Embassy in Guyana and information that the applicant was a danger to the community and DHS would not be permitted to detain him indefinitely).

[74] *See* 8 CFR §§208.24(f), 1208.24(f) (2014). *See* ch. 11 for a detailed discussion of motions to reopen, the numerical and time limitations, and the narrow exceptions to those limitations.

[75] INA §240(c)(7)(C)(ii); 8 CFR §§1003.2(c)(3)(ii), 1003.23(b)(4)(i) (2014).

[76] 8 CFR §1003.2(c)(3)(iv). *See, e.g., Hailemichael v. Gonzales*, 454 F.3d 878, at 878 (8th Cir. 2006)); *Efe v. Ashcroft*, 293 F.3d 899, 904 (5th Cir. 2002).

of relief.[77] In reopened proceedings, DHS has the burden of establishing, by a preponderance of the evidence, one or more of the grounds for termination.[78]

B. Termination of Deferral of Removal under CAT

The grant of deferral of removal is a more precarious status that may be more easily terminated than withholding of removal.[79] First, DHS must file a motion for hearing on termination. If the IJ grants that motion, the court will schedule a hearing on termination. Both parties will have the opportunity to present evidence to the court prior to the hearing. During the hearing, the respondent has the burden of proof to demonstrate eligibility anew for deferral of removal under CAT. If the respondent meets his or her burden of proof, the deferral of removal order will remain in place. Otherwise, the order will be terminated.

1. Motion for Hearing on Termination

To terminate a grant of deferral of removal, DHS must first file a motion for a hearing to consider termination with the immigration court that issued the order granting deferral of removal.[80] If the motion is filed with another court, it must be rejected for lack of proper venue.[81] The DHS motion is not subject to the ordinary motion to reopen requirements.[82]

DHS's motion must be granted if: (1) it is accompanied by evidence that is "relevant to the possibility" that the individual would be tortured in the country to which removal has been deferred; and (2) if that evidence was not presented at the previous hearing.[83] In *Matter of C–C–I–*, the BIA considered this standard and the evidentiary threshold for reopening proceedings to consider whether deferral of removal should be terminated.[84] The BIA focused on the plain language of the regulation and emphasized that evidence "relevant to the possibility" of torture is sufficient to schedule a hearing on termination.[85] The BIA noted that the purpose of

---

[77] 8 CFR §1003.2(c)(3)(iv). *See, e.g., Hailemichael*, at 878; *Efe*, 293 F.3d at 904.

[78] 8 CFR §§208.24(f), 1208.24(f) (2014). *See also Ntangsi v. Gonzales*, 475 F.3d 1007, 1012–13 (8th Cir. 2007) (reversing termination of asylum status where neither the IJ nor the BIA placed the burden of proving fraud on the government).

[79] *See, e.g., Khouzam v. Hogan*, 497 F. Supp. 2d 615, 619 (D. MD 2007). *See also Ali v. Mukasey*, 529 F.3d 478 (2d Cir. 2008) (describing evidence used in motion to terminate deferral under CAT which included information from the U.S. Embassy in Guyana and information that the applicant was a danger to the community and DHS would not be permitted to detain him indefinitely).

[80] 8 CFR §§208.17(d)(1), 1208.17(d)(1). *See also* EOIR Memorandum from Michael Creppy on Operating Policies and Procedures Mem. No. 99-5: Implementation of Article 3 of the UN Convention Against Torture, at 11 (May 14, 1999), *available at www.usdoj.gov/eoir/efoia/ocij/oppm99/99_5.pdf.*

[81] *See also* Creppy Mem., *supra* note 80.

[82] *Id.* at 10.

[83] *Id.*; *Matter of C–C–I–*, 26 I&N Dec. 375 (BIA 2014).

[84] *Matter of C–C–I–*, at 378–81.

[85] *Id.* at 378.

this provision is to "provide for a streamlined termination process for deferral of removal," "so that deferral can be terminated quickly and efficiently when appropriate."[86] The BIA also clarified that "[t]he evidence may have been previously available as long as it was not presented and considered at the hearing where deferral of removal was granted."[87]

In *Matter of C–C–I–*, DHS sought reopening of a Nigerian man's proceedings based on a report from the Consular Anti-Fraud Unity of the U.S. Embassy in Lagos, Nigeria, which contradicted the respondent's claim in stating that "the current democratically elected government has no interest in continuing the violent policies of the previous Abacha dictatorship towards the Ogoni people."[88] The consular report also found that the death certificate submitted in support of the respondent's application is fraudulent.[89] DHS also submitted a *New York Times* article that contradicted the respondent's claims regarding his uncle's execution and burial.[90] The BIA found that this evidence was "relevant to the possibility" that the respondent would be tortured in Nigeria and had not been previously presented.[91] Thus, the case merited reopening for a hearing on termination of deferral of removal.

> ➤ **Practice Pointer:** Given the low evidentiary threshold that DHS must meet to get proceedings reopened for consideration of termination of deferral of removal, practitioners should advise their clients who have been granted deferral of removal to routinely collect up-to-date information on the country to which his or her removal has been deferred. Doing so will help to ensure a fast response to any motion filed by DHS seeking a hearing on termination.

The regulations do not address whether the IJ's decision on the motion to schedule a hearing on termination is appealable,[92] however, the BIA has considered appeals on the very issue of whether the IJ erred in reopening a case for a hearing on termination of deferral of removal.[93] Thus, it is likely that this issue may be considered by the BIA on appeal.

---

86 *Id.* (quoting Regulations Concerning the Convention Against Torture, 64 Fed. Reg. 8478, 8481–82 (Feb. 19, 1999), the supplemental information accompanying the regulation).

87 *Id. See Khouzam v. Att'y Gen.*, 549 F.3d 235, 240 n.3 (3d Cir. 2008) (recognizing that the ordinary requirements for a motion to reopen do not apply to motions to reopen for a termination hearing on deferral of removal).

88 *Matter of C–C–I–*, 26 I&N Dec. 375, 379 (BIA 2014).

89 *Id.*

90 *Id.* at 380.

91 *Id.* at 380–81.

92 Creppy Memo., *supra* note 80.

93 *See, e.g., Matter of C–C–I–*, 26 I&N Dec. 375, 379 (BIA 2014).

2. *Notice of Termination Hearing*

If the IJ grants the motion for a hearing on termination, the immigration court must provide notice to the individual of the date, time, and place of the hearing.[94] The hearing should not be scheduled earlier than 10 days for removal proceedings (14 days for deportation proceedings) after service of the notice.[95] The notice must also inform the individual that he or she may supplement the information in his or her initial application for relief under the CAT.[96] If the individual chooses to submit supplemental information, he or she must submit it within 10 calendar days of service of the notice, or 13 calendar days if service of the notice is by mail.[97]

3. *Department of State Comments*

At the expiration of the 10– or 13-day period for supplementing the initial application, the immigration court will forward a copy of the original application, and any supplemental information that the individual or DHS has provided, to the Department of State (DOS), together with notice of the date, time, and place of the termination hearing.[98] DOS then has the option to provide comments on the case in accordance with 8 CFR §§208.11, 1208.11.[99] Specifically, DOS may provide detailed country condition information, an assessment of the accuracy of the applicant's assertions regarding conditions in the applicant's home country, and any other information it believes to be relevant.[100]

4. *Hearing on Termination*

If DHS's motion for a hearing on termination is granted, the IJ must conduct the hearing and make a *de novo* determination as to whether the individual previously granted deferral of removal is more likely than not to be subjected to torture upon his or her removal to the country of feared torture.[101] The determination must be based on the record of the proceeding, the initial application, and any new evidence submitted by DHS or the individual.[102] Moreover, the IJ is not collaterally estopped from comparing testimony given at the termination hearing to testimony given at the initial merits hearing.[103] The burden of proof is on the individual previously granted deferral to establish, under the legal standards set forth in 8 CFR §§208.16(c),

---

[94] 8 CFR §§208.17(d)(2), 1208.17(d)(2) (2014).

[95] Creppy Mem., *supra* note 80.

[96] 8 CFR §§208.17(d)(2), 1208.17(d)(2) (2014).

[97] 8 CFR §§208.17(d)(2), 1208.17(d)(2) (2014).

[98] 8 CFR §§208.17(d)(2), 1208.17(d)(2) (2014).

[99] 8 CFR §§208.17(d)(2), 1208.17(d)(2) (2014).

[100] 8 CFR §§208.11(a)–(b), 1208.11(a)–(b) (2014).

[101] 8 CFR §§208.17(d)(3), 1208.17(d)(3) (2014).

[102] 8 CFR §§208.17(d)(3), 1208.17(d)(3) (2014).

[103] *Matter of C–C–I–*, 26 I&N Dec. 375, 385–86 (BIA 2014). *See also Ali v. Mukasey*, 529 F.3d 478, 489 (2d Cir. 2008).

1208.16(c), that it is more likely than not that he or she would be tortured in the country to which removal has been deferred.[104]

If the IJ determines that it is more likely than not that the individual would be subjected to torture in the country to which removal has been deferred, the order of deferral must remain in place.[105] However, if the individual has not met his or her burden of proof, the deferral of removal order must be terminated and the individual may be removed to that country.[106] Appeal of the IJ's decision lies with the BIA.[107]

In *Matter of C–C–I–*, the BIA considered the appropriate scope of a hearing on the termination of deferral of removal. In particular, the BIA assessed the applicability of the doctrine of collateral estoppel to the grant of deferral of removal in the subsequent termination hearing under 8 CFR §§208.17(d)(3), 1208.17(d)(3).[108] In *Matter of C–C–I–*, the IJ had found during a termination hearing that the respondent did not establish that it is more likely than not that he will be tortured in Nigeria. The IJ based this finding on the respondent's lack of credibility and inability to meet his burden of proof with corroborative documentary evidence alone.[109] The BIA found no clear error regarding the IJ's credibility finding and agreed that the lack of credible testimony and corroborating evidence led to the correct conclusion that the respondent failed to establish that it is more likely than not that he will be tortured in Nigeria.[110]

The respondent argued that the IJ is collaterally estopped from comparing the testimony that he gave at the 2012 termination hearing with his previous testimony in 1999, arguing that any 1999 testimony and issues could not be re-litigated.[111] The BIA responded that "[t]he respondent's collateral estoppel argument would negate the purpose of [the regulation], which allows for termination of deferral of removal where evidence relevant to the possibility that the alien would be tortured in the country of removal was not considered at the previous hearing."[112] The Board

---

[104] 8 CFR §§208.17(d)(3), 1208.17(d)(3) (2014).

[105] 8 CFR §§208.17(d)(4), 1208.17(d)(4) (2014). *See e.g.*, *Matter of G–A–*, 23 I&N Dec. 366, 372 (BIA 2002) (agreeing with the IJ's determination that the respondent had satisfied his burden of showing that it was more likely than not that he would be tortured if returned to Iran); *Bromfield v. Mukasey*, 543 F.3d 1071 (9th Cir. 2008) (remanding where the IJ failed to consider the substantial evidence that the government of Jamaica acquiesced to the torture of gay men).

[106] 8 CFR §§208.17(d)(4), 1208.17(d)(4) (2014). *See e.g.*, *Oduche-Nwakaihe v. Att'y Gen.*, 363 Fed. App'x 898 (3d Cir. 2010); *In Re Y–L–*, 23 I&N Dec. 270, 271 (2002) (holding that respondents had not met their burden of showing that it was more likely than not that they would be tortured if returned to their countries of origin).

[107] 8 CFR §§208.17(d)(4), 1208.17(d)(4) (2014).

[108] *Matter of C–C–I–*, 26 I&N Dec. 375, 381–86 (BIA 2014).

[109] *Id.* at 381.

[110] *Id.* at 384.

[111] *Id.* at 385.

[112] *Id.*

highlighted the plain language of the regulation stating that the IJ "shall make a *de novo* determination, based on the record of proceeding and initial application in addition to any new evidence,"[113] and distinguished the Ninth Circuit U.S. Court of Appeals case of *Oyeniran v. Holder*, stating that no new evidence had been presented in that case.[114] Finally, the BIA emphasized the "temporary form of protection" that deferral of removal accords the recipient, stating that it "prevents the alien's *refoulement* only until removal is possible."[115]

5. *Termination at the Request of the Individual*

At any time while the grant of deferral of removal is in effect, the individual may make a written request to the immigration court to terminate the deferral order.[116] The immigration court must have administrative control of the case pursuant to 8 CFR §1003.11.[117] If the IJ is satisfied, based on the written record, that the individual's request is knowing and voluntary, the order of deferral will be terminated and the individual may be removed.[118] If the IJ determines that the individual's request is not knowing and voluntary, the individual's request may not serve as a basis for terminating the order of deferral.[119] If necessary, the IJ may calendar a hearing for the sole purpose of determining whether the individual's request is knowing and voluntary.[120] If the IJ determines at the hearing that the individual's request is knowing and voluntary, the deferral of removal order must be terminated.[121] If it is not knowing and voluntary, the IJ may not terminate the order based on the individual's request.[122]

6. *Diplomatic Assurances*

At any time while deferral of removal is in effect, the AG may determine whether deferral should be terminated based on diplomatic assurances forwarded by the Secretary of State pursuant to 8 CFR §§208.18(c), 1208.18(c).[123] The Secretary of

---

[113] *Id.*

[114] *Id.* at 385–86. *See Oyeniran v. Holder*, 672 F.3d 800 (9th Cir. 2012) (holding that DHS was "conclusively barred from re-litigating" the salient findings made in support of the initial grant of the alien's application for deferral of removal).

[115] *Matter of C–C–I–*, 26 I&N Dec. 375, 385 (BIA 2014). *See also Ali v. Mukasey*, 529 F.3d 478, 489 (2d Cir. 2008) (stating that "the merits of the alien's [CAT] claim may be revisited").

[116] 8 CFR §§208.17(e)(1), 1208.17(e)(1) (2014).

[117] 8 CFR §§208.17(e)(1), 1208.17(e)(1) (2014).

[118] 8 CFR §§208.17(e)(2), 1208.17(e)(2).

[119] *Id.*

[120] *Id.*

[121] *Id.*

[122] *Id.*

[123] 8 CFR §§208.17(f), 1208.17(f). *See, e.g., Khouzam v. Att'y Gen.*, 549 F.3d 235 (3d Cir. 2008) (finding that prior to removal on the basis of diplomatic assurances, due process requires that the individual be afforded notice and an opportunity to test the reliability of those assurances in a hearing that comports with *Abdulai* and its progeny, that the individual have an opportunity to present evidence

Continued

State may forward assurances that the Secretary of State has received from a specific country that the individual would not be tortured if he or she were removed to that country.[124] The AG or his or her delegates must determine, in consultation with the Secretary of State, whether the assurances are sufficiently reliable to allow the individual's removal to that country consistent with article 3 of the Convention Against Torture.[125] If it is determined that the assurances are sufficiently reliable, the individual's claim for protection under CAT shall not be considered further, and the individual may be removed.[126]

> ➤ **Practice Pointer**: It is noteworthy that the regulations do not empower the AG to terminate a grant of withholding under the CAT after receiving diplomatic assurances. This is one important distinction between withholding and deferral of removal under CAT.

IV. Termination of Refugee Status

The AG or DHS may terminate the refugee status of any individual (and of any spouse or child who has derivative refugee status) if the AG or DHS determines that the individual was not in fact a refugee within the meaning of INA §101(a)(42) at the time of his or her admission to the United States.[127] A refugee is, however, subject to removal even if his or her refugee status has not been terminated.[128]

---

and arguments challenging the reliability of diplomatic assurances before a neutral and impartial decision-maker, and that the individual be afforded an individualized determination of the matter based on a record disclosed to him or her).

[124] 8 CFR §§208.18(c)(1), 1208.18(c)(1).

[125] 8 CFR §§208.18(c)(2), 1208.18(c)(2). References to the legacy INS "Commissioner" after March 1, 2003, unless otherwise specified in the regulations, mean the director of USCIS, the commissioner of U.S. Customs and Border Protection, and the assistant secretary for U.S. Immigration Customs and Enforcement. 8 CFR §1.1(d) (2014).

[126] 8 CFR §§208.18(c)(3), 1208.18(c)(3) (2014); *see generally, Khouzam v. Att'y Gen.*, 549 F.3d 235 (3d Cir. 2008) (discussing deferral of removal under CAT and requiring that prior to removal, an alien must "be afforded notice and an opportunity to test the reliability of those assurances in a hearing ... have an opportunity to present, before a neutral and impartial decision-maker, evidence and arguments challenging the reliability of diplomatic assurances proffered by the Government, and the Government's compliance with the relevant regulations" as well as "be afforded an individualized determination of the matter based on a record disclosed to the alien."); *see also Masopust v. Fitzgerald*, No. 2:09-CV-1495-ARH, 2010 WL 324378, at *3 (W.D. Pa. Jan. 21, 2010) (distinguishing with regard to diplomatic assurances between deferral of removal under CAT and extradition).

[127] INA §207(c)(4); 8 USC §1157(c)(4) (2012).

[128] *See, e.g., Matter of Smriko*, 23 I&N Dec. 836, 840 (BIA 2005) (removal proceedings may be commenced against a refugee without prior termination of refugee status); *Romanishyn v. Gonzales*, 455 F.3d 175, 186 (3d Cir. 2006) (holding that refugee who adjusted status is subject to removal even though his refugee status was never terminated); *Kaganovich v. Gonzales*, 470 F.3d 894, 898 (9th Cir. 2006) (observing that "an alien who arrives in the United States as a refugee may be removed even if refugee status has never been terminated").

To seek termination of refugee status, the district director in the district where the individual is located must notify the individual in writing of DHS's intent to terminate the individual's refugee status. The individual has 30 days from the date the notice is served upon him or her, or delivered to his or her last known address, to present written or oral evidence to show why his or her refugee status should not be terminated.[129] Upon termination of refugee status, the individual will be placed in expedited removal proceedings pursuant to INA §§235, 240, and 241.[130] There is no appeal from the termination of refugee status by the district director.[131]

- **Practice Pointer:** The U.N. High Commissioner for Refugees takes the position that a person admitted to the United States as a refugee continues to maintain refugee status even after the person adjusts status and becomes an LPR. The implication of this opinion is that because the person continues to be a refugee, the person should not be subject to removal on criminal grounds, but only on the cessation grounds in the Refugee Convention and Protocol.[132]

V. Conclusion

The fact that asylum, withholding of removal under INA §241(b)(3), and protection under the CAT are not permanent forms of protection make it essential for practitioners to challenge any potential bars to asylum eligibility. Achievement of U.S. citizenship is the one true permanent protection for victims of persecution and torture, and asylum is the only relief that provides a legal pathway to LPR status, and eventually, U.S. citizenship.

---

[129] 8 CFR §207.9 (2014).

[130] *Id.*

[131] *Id.*

[132] *See Becoming LPR Does Not Terminate Refugee Status, UNHCR Says*, 80 INTERPRETER RELEASES 413 and App'x III (Mar. 17, 2003). *See also Smriko v. Ashcroft*, 387 F.3d 279, 281 (3d Cir. 2004) (in remanding case to BIA, court suggests applicant's argument that despite his adjustment to LPR status he still retains his refugee status is supported by INA and legislative history).

CHAPTER FIFTEEN

ADJUSTMENT OF STATUS[*]

An individual granted asylum or admitted as a refugee may adjust to lawful permanent resident (LPR) status under section 209 of the Immigration and Nationality Act (INA) and eventually may become a U.S. citizen.[1] Thus, asylum provides a more permanent form of protection than withholding of removal under INA §241(b)(3) or protection under the Convention Against Torture (CAT). This chapter discusses the legal standards for an asylee or refugee to adjust to LPR status, as well as the procedures for seeking LPR status.

I. Legal Standards for the Adjustment of Status of Asylees

Unlike refugees, asylees are not required to adjust to LPR status.[2] However, there are many benefits to obtaining LPR status, the most significant of which is that — as the name suggests — it is a more permanent form of relief. To qualify for adjustment of status, individuals granted asylum under INA §209 must:

- Have been physically present in the United States for at least one year after being granted asylum;
- Continue to meet the definition of refugee under INA §101(a)(42) or be the spouse or child of such a refugee;
- Not be "firmly resettled" in any foreign country;
- Apply for adjustment (using Form I-485); and

---

[*] The author would like to thank Jennifer D. Cook of Benach Ragland LLP for her invaluable input in reviewing this chapter.

[1] *See generally* Immigration and Nationality Act (INA) §209; 8 CFR §§209.1, 209.2, 1209.1, 1209.2 (2014).

[2] INA §209(b).

- Be admissible as an immigrant under INA §212(a), except that the grounds of inadmissibility relating to lack of a proper travel document, labor certification, or likelihood of becoming a public charge do not apply.[3]

Each of these legal requirements is discussed in more detail below.

> ➢ **Practice Pointer**: Prior to the passage of the REAL ID Act in 2005, only 10,000 asylees could adjust each year.[4] If a number was not available, the asylee was to be placed on a waiting list on a priority basis by the date the application was filed. The backlog of asylees awaiting adjustment grew significantly over the years. Before the REAL ID Act, it was estimated that a wait could be as long as 12 years. Fortunately, the REAL ID Act eliminated the wait by repealing the cap on adjustments for asylees.

A. Physical Presence

A principal asylee's physical presence starts accruing on the date the asylee is granted asylum, and only time spent in the United States counts toward the one-year physical presence requirement.[5] For derivative asylees (spouses and children), if the derivative asylee was physically present in the United States when U.S. Citizenship and Immigration Services (USCIS) approved his or her I-730 relative petition or the principal asylee's I-589 asylum application, the derivative asylee starts accruing physical presence on the approval date of the petition or application. If the derivative asylee is outside of the United States when USCIS approves the I-730 relative petition, however, his or her physical presence begins accruing on the date of his or her admission as an asylee.[6] If an asylee travels outside of the United States following admission as an asylee, that time outside of the United States will not count toward the one-year physical presence requirement. The asylee must wait to apply for adjustment of status until his or her cumulative physical presence equals one year in the United States following admission as an asylee.[7]

B. Definition of Refugee

Although an applicant must demonstrate that he or she continues to meet the definition of refugee under INA §101(a)(42) in order to adjust status as an asylee, USCIS officers generally will not re-adjudicate the underlying asylum claim at the time of adjustment.[8] If there is new evidence that the asylee may not have met the

---

[3] INA §209(b); 8 CFR §§209.2(a)(1), 1209.2(a)(1) (2014).

[4] INA §209(b).

[5] U.S. Citizenship & Immigration Servs., Policy Manual, Vol. 7 Adjustment of Status, pt. M Asylee Adjustment, *www.uscis.gov/policymanual/Print/PolicyManual-Volume7-PartM-Chapter2.html* (last visited Mar. 16, 2015).

[6] *Id.*

[7] *Id.*

[8] *Id.*

definition of refugee at the time of the asylum grant, however, the USCIS officer will refer the case for termination of status proceedings.[9]

C. Firm Resettlement

If an applicant has "firmly resettled" in another country, he or she is not eligible to obtain adjustment of status as an asylee in the United States. An applicant may be considered firmly resettled in another country if he or she has been offered resident status, citizenship, or some other type of permanent resettlement in another country.[10] The USCIS officer adjudicating the adjustment of status application generally will focus on any evidence of resettlement subsequent to the grant of asylum since prior firm resettlement will already have been considered during the asylum application process.[11]

D. Application for Adjustment of Status

The application, with the appropriate fee, should be filed with the USCIS office designated in the instructions to Form I-485, Application to Register Permanent Residence or Adjust Status (I-485).[12] Upon acceptance of the application, the applicant must submit to a medical examination to determine the mental and physical condition of the applicant.[13] An applicant may be interviewed by a USCIS officer, or the interview may be waived.[14] After the interview or waiver, the applicant will be notified of the decision in writing.[15] If the application is approved, USCIS will record the asylee's admission as an LPR, as of the date one year before the date of approval of the I-485 application.[16] If the applicant is denied, however, the asylee will be notified of the reasons for the denial and may renew the application in INA §240 removal proceedings before an immigration judge (IJ).[17]

In *Matter of K–A–*, the Board of Immigration Appeals (BIA) set forth the procedural framework for asylee adjustment where the applicant has been placed in removal proceedings.[18] First, the BIA clarified that, pursuant to 8 CFR §1209.2(c), once an asylee has been placed in removal proceedings, the IJ and BIA have original and exclusive jurisdiction to adjudicate his or her applications for adjustment of status and a waiver of inadmissibility under INA §209(c).[19] Second, the BIA held that

---

[9] *Id. See* ch. 14 for a detailed discussion of the legal standards and procedures for termination of status.

[10] *Id.*

[11] *Id.*

[12] 8 CFR §§209.2(c), 1209.2(c) (2014).

[13] 8 CFR §§209.2(d), 1209.2(d) (2014).

[14] 8 CFR §§209.2(e), 1209.2(e) (2014).

[15] 8 CFR §§209.2(f), 1209.2(f) (2014).

[16] 8 CFR §§209.2(f), 1209.2(f) (2014).

[17] 8 CFR §§209.2(f), 1209.2(f) (2014).

[18] *Matter of K–A–*, 23 I&N Dec. 661 (BIA 2004).

[19] *Id.* (distinguishing *Matter of H–N–*, 22 I&N Dec. 1039 (BIA 1999)).

an asylee may adjust status in removal proceedings as a form of relief without first having his or her asylum status terminated.[20] The BIA reasoned that, although the IJ had authority to terminate the respondent's asylee status on the basis of her aggravated felony conviction, the IJ did not commit reversible error when she deferred consideration of the U.S. Department of Homeland Security's (DHS) termination request pending adjudication of the respondent's applications for relief under INA §209.[21] Prior to *Matter of K–A–*, DHS took the position that the agency that granted asylum had to first terminate asylum status before the individual could seek adjustment of status in removal proceedings.

Even if an asylee's status has been terminated, he or she still may be eligible to apply for adjustment of status under INA §209(b) in removal proceedings.[22] In *Siwe v. Holder*, the Fifth Circuit U.S. Court of Appeals considered the case of a Cameroonian man who had been convicted of an aggravated felony.[23] Following his release from prison, DHS had issued a Notice to Appear (NTA) charging him with deportability for the aggravated felony. DHS also formally moved to terminate his asylum status.[24] The IJ terminated asylum due to the aggravated felony conviction, which was a particularly serious crime, and then pretermitted Siwe's request to adjust status, finding that the termination of Siwe's asylum status disqualified him from adjustment of status under INA §209(b).[25] On appeal before the BIA, a one-member panel dismissed the appeal, holding that the IJ correctly determined that Siwe was statutorily ineligible to adjust status under INA §209(b) because his asylum had been terminated.

Siwe filed a petition for review, asking the Fifth Circuit to consider whether the BIA erred as a matter of law in its conclusion that the termination of asylum status made Siwe ineligible to adjust status under INA §209(b). The Fifth Circuit examined the plain language of the statute, and noted that "[n]owhere in this section does Congress require that an alien's asylum, once granted, still must be in effect at the time he applies for adjustment of status."[26] The court said that even if the phrase "any alien granted asylum" is ambiguous, other portions of the statute confirm congressional intent. First, INA §209(a) — which applies only to refugees — explicitly mandates that admission as a refugee must "ha[ve] not been terminated" before the refugee's status may be adjusted. There is no such language in the asylee adjustment provision.[27] Second, INA §209(b) mandates only that an asylee seeking to

---

[20] *Id.*

[21] *Id.* at 667

[22] *See, Siwe v. Holder*, 742 F.3d 603 (5th Cir. 2014).

[23] *Id.*

[24] *Id.* at 605.

[25] *Id.* at 606.

[26] *Id.* at 608.

[27] *Id.*

adjust status "continue[] to be a refugee."[28] Finally, the Fifth Circuit stated that if the court read INA §209 — as the IJ and BIA did — to mean that any individual whose asylum has been terminated is barred *ipso facto* from applying for adjustment of status, such a construction would "obviate the need for the waiver mechanism" set forth in INA §209(c) and would effectively "abrogate Congress's careful balancing of interests, as codified in Section 209(c)."[29]

Thus, even if an asylee's status has been terminated, he or she still may be eligible to adjust status under INA §209(b) in removal proceedings.[30] However, an asylee who already has adjusted status to LPR, but who is later rendered removable for criminal conduct, is ineligible to "re-adjust" or acquire LPR status again under INA §209(b), even with a waiver.[31]

E. Admissibility

If the applicant is inadmissible for a ground other than lack of a proper travel document, labor certification, or likelihood of becoming a public charge, that inadmissibility ground may be waivable under INA §209(c),[32] which provides that the Attorney General (AG) may waive any other ground of inadmissibility for humanitarian purposes, to ensure family unity, or when it is otherwise in the public interest, except for drug trafficking and security-related grounds.[33] The application for a waiver may be requested along with the application to adjust status.[34]

> ➢ **Practice Pointer**: See Part V. below for a detailed discussion of the legal standards and procedures for INA §209(c) waivers.

II. Legal Standards for the Adjustment of Status of Refugees

Under INA §209(a), refugees admitted to the United States under INA §207 must be re-examined and re-inspected by USCIS for admission as an LPR after being physically present in the United States for one year.[35] A refugee qualifies for adjustment of status if:

- His or her admission has not been terminated by the AG or DHS;

---

[28] *Id.* at 609.

[29] *Id.*

[30] *See, Siwe v. Holder*, 742 F.3d 603 (5th Cir. 2014).

[31] *Matter of C–J–H–*, 26 I&N Dec. 284 (BIA 2014). *See also Robleto-Pastora v. Holder*, 591 F.3d 1051 (9th Cir. 2010).

[32] *See generally* INA §209(c); 8 CFR §§209.2(b), 1209.2(b) (2014).

[33] INA §209(b), (c); 8 CFR §§209.2(b), 1209.2(b) (2014). *See infra* pt. V. below for a detailed discussion of waivers Under INA §209(c), which are available for almost all grounds of inadmissibility for asylees and refugees who seek to adjust their status. The only two exceptions are drug trafficking and security-related grounds.

[34] 8 CFR §§209.2(b), 1209.2(b) (2014).

[35] INA §209(a).

- He or she has been physically present in the United States for at least one year; and
- He or she is admissible as an immigrant under INA §212(a), except that the grounds of inadmissibility relating to lack of a proper travel document, labor certification, or likelihood of becoming a public charge do not apply.[36]

The application, with the appropriate fee, should be filed with the USCIS office designated in the instructions to the Form I-485.[37] Upon acceptance of the application, the applicant must submit to biometrics collection.[38] Unless there were medical grounds of inadmissibility at the time of the refugee's entry, no repeat medical examination is required.[39] The refugee, however, must establish compliance with the vaccination requirements under the INA.[40] An applicant may be interviewed by a USCIS officer to determine his or her admissibility as an LPR, or the interview may be waived.[41]

After the interview or waiver, the applicant will be notified of the decision in writing.[42] If the refugee is found to be admissible, USCIS will approve the application, admit the individual for lawful permanent residence as of the date of his or her arrival in the United States, and issue proof of such status.[43] If the refugee is determined to be inadmissible, however, the refugee may request waiver of the grounds of inadmissibility under INA §209(c).[44] Similar to asylees, the AG or DHS also may waive any other ground of inadmissibility for humanitarian purposes, to ensure family unity, or when it is in the public interest, except for drug trafficking and security-related grounds.[45] The application for a waiver may be requested with the application to adjust status.[46]

Unlike asylees, refugees are *required* to appear before a DHS officer one year after their entry to determine their admissibility.[47] Upon a determination of

---

[36] INA §§209(a), (c); 8 CFR §§209.1, 1209.1 (2014). *See infra* pt. IV below for a detailed discussion of waivers Under INA §209(c), which is available for almost all grounds of inadmissibility for asylees and refugees who seek to adjust their status. The only two exceptions are drug trafficking and security-related grounds.

[37] 8 CFR §§209.1b), 1209.1(b) (2014).

[38] 8 CFR §§209.1b), 1209.1(b) (2014).

[39] 8 CFR §§209.1(c), 1209.1(c) (2014).

[40] 8 CFR §§209.1(c), 1209.1(c) (2014).

[41] 8 CFR §§209.1(d), 1209.1(d) (2014).

[42] 8 CFR §§209.1(e), 1209.1(e) (2014).

[43] 8 CFR §§209.1(e), 1209.1(e) (2014).

[44] INA §209(c); 8 CFR §§209.1(f), 1209.1(f) (2014).

[45] INA §209(c); 8 CFR §§209.1(f), 1209.1(f) (2014).

[46] 8 CFR §§209.1(f), 1209.1(f) (2014).

[47] 8 CFR §§209.1(a)(1), 1209.1(a)(1) (2014).

inadmissibility, DHS may detain the refugee and initiate removal proceedings.[48] If a refugee is found inadmissible, detained, and placed in removal proceedings, he or she should request a copy of the NTA, which will list the grounds on which the government is seeking removal, and renew the request for adjustment of status in proceedings before an IJ.[49]

In 2009, Immigration and Customs Enforcement (ICE) began to detain refugees who failed to apply for adjustment of status one year after their entry, even if they had no criminal record.[50] DHS took the position that unadjusted refugees revert after a year to "arriving alien" status, and thus, they could be detained and held without a bond redetermination hearing before an IJ while their proceedings were pending.[51] This position contradicted the reasoning of the AG in *Matter of Jean*.[52] In that decision, the AG relied on INA §235(b)(2)(A) in asserting the government's right to detain refugees who have stayed in the United States for more than a year but have been denied LPR status. The reliance on that provision, which governs the removal of aliens other than "arriving aliens," indicated that the AG did not consider refugees denied LPR status to revert to "arriving alien" status. This practice changed in 2012 when the BIA issued its decision in *Matter of D–K–*.[53]

In *Matter of D–K–*, the BIA clarified that refugees are conditionally admitted to the United States upon their arrival. Thus, even if they have not adjusted status to LPR, they are not "arriving aliens" and may not be held in detention, deprived of a right to a bond redetermination hearing before an IJ.[54] Although this decision decreased the unlawful detention of unadjusted refugees, it also impacted their right to have USCIS review their adjustment of status applications in the first instance.

---

[48] *See* INA §209(a) (stating that refugees who have been in the United States for one year and have not yet acquired permanent residence status "*shall* ... return or be returned to the custody of the Department of Homeland Security for inspection and examination") (emphasis added); *Matter of Jean*, 23 I&N Dec. 373, 381 (AG 2002) (reading INA §209(a) with INA §235(b)(2)(A); 8 USC §1225(b)(2)(A) in mind, and concluding that if a refugee who surrenders to DHS for inspection "'is not clearly and beyond a doubt entitled to be admitted,' he or she must be detained for a removal proceeding").

[49] *See* INA §235(b)(2)(A); 8 USC §1225(b)(2)(A) (2012) (ordering a proceeding under INA §240; 8 USC §1229a) (2012); 8 CFR §§209.1(e), 1209.1(e) (2014) (declaring that a refugee whose application for permanent residence has been denied must be notified in writing of the reasons for the denial and of the refugee's right to renew the request for permanent residence in removal proceedings under INA §240; 8 USC §1229a).

[50] *See, e.g.*, Emily Creighton, *DHS Interprets Law to Detain Refugees Across the Country*, Am. Immigration Council (Nov. 24, 2009), *available at http://immigrationimpact.com/2009/11/24/dhs-interprets-law-to-detain-refugees-across-the-country/*; USCIS National Stakeholders Meeting Questions and Answers, Question 4 (June 30, 2009), *available at www.uscis.gov/files/nativedocuments/june_2009_agenda_with_responses.pdf.*

[51] 8 CFR §1003.19(h)(2)(i)(B) (2014) (declaring that IJs have no jurisdiction over bond hearings for arriving aliens in removal hearings).

[52] *Matter of Jean*, 23 I&N Dec. 373 (AG 2002).

[53] *Matter of D–K–*, 25 I&N Dec. 761 (BIA 2012).

[54] *Matter of D–K–*, 25 I&N Dec. 761 (BIA 2012).

Prior to *Matter of D–K–*, USCIS maintained initial jurisdiction over all adjustment of status applications by refugees, even if a refugee was placed in removal proceedings.[55] Refugees in removal proceedings were required to present their applications for adjustment of status before USCIS, and if USCIS denied their applications, the proceedings before the IJ were reopened.[56] Refugees could then present their adjustment applications anew before the IJ. Following *Matter of D–K–*, however, refugees may be charged in the NTA under INA §237, rather than INA §212, and may be placed in removal proceedings without a prior determination by USCIS that they are inadmissible to the United States.[57] Therefore, IJs now may adjudicate an initial application for adjustment of status by an unadjusted refugee in removal proceedings.[58]

- **Practice Pointer**: Arguably, the BIA's reasoning in *Matter of D–K–* is at odds with its later 2013 decision in *Matter of V–X–*, which held that a grant of asylum (arguably analogous to admission as a refugee) is not an "admission" to the United States under INA §101(a)(13)(A).[59] See chapter 14 of this book for a detailed discussion of *Matter of V–X–*.

Prior to *Matter of D–K–*, the courts also considered whether termination of refugee status was a precondition to placing a refugee in removal proceedings. In *Matter of Smriko*, the BIA held that a refugee who had adjusted his status to LPR may be placed in removal proceedings even if his refugee status had not been terminated first.[60] Several courts agreed, affirming the BIA's holding in *Matter of Smriko* and finding that a refugee who had adjusted status to LPR may be placed in removal proceedings.[61] At least one court, however, has suggested that refugees do not lose their refugee status after they adjust to LPR status.[62] Such individuals are,

[55] *See Matter of H–N–*, 22 I&N Dec. 1039 (BIA 1999); *Matter of Garcia-Alzugaray*, 19 I&N Dec. 407 (BIA 1986); 8 CFR §1209.1 (2010) (2014).

[56] *See* 8 CFR §§209.1(e), 1209.1(e) (2014) (nothing that there is no appeal of a USCIS denial of adjustment of status for a refugee, but that the applicant could renew his or her application in removal proceedings).

[57] *Matter of D–K–*, 25 I&N Dec. 761 (BIA 2012) (distinguishing *Matter of Garcia-Alzugaray*, 19 I&N Dec. 407 (BIA 1986).

[58] *Matter of D–K–*, 25 I&N Dec. 761 (BIA 2012).

[59] *Matter of V–X–*, 26 I&N Dec. 147 (BIA 2013).

[60] *Matter of Smriko*, 23 I&N Dec. 836 (BIA 2005).

[61] *Romnishyn v. Att'y Gen..*, 455 F.3d 175 (3d Cir. 2006); *Gutnik v. Gonzales*, 469 F.3d 683 (7th Cir. 2006); *Kaganovich v. Gonzales*, 470 F.3d 894 (9th Cir. 2006); *Vong Xiong v. Att'y Gen.*, 484 F.3d 530 (8th Cir. 2007).

[62] *See Smriko v. Ashcroft*, 387 F.3d 279, 281 (3d Cir. 2004) (in remanding AWO case to BIA, court suggests that applicant's argument that despite his adjustment of status to LPR, he still retains his refugee status, is supported by the INA and legislative history). *But see Robleto-Pastora v. Holder*, 567 F.3d 437, 444–450 (9th Cir. 2009) (rejecting applicant's argument that he is eligible to re-adjust after being ordered removed because his asylee status remains intact); *Saintha v. Mukasey*, 516 F.3d 243, 252 (4th Cir. 2008) (holding that a refugee who already has adjusted status may not re-adjust status in removal proceedings).

however, subject to removal.[63] The United Nations High Commissioner for Refugees (UNHCR) takes the position that a person admitted to the United States as a refugee continues to maintain refugee status even after the person adjusts status and becomes an LPR. According to UNHCR, because the person continues to be a refugee, the person should not be subject to removal on criminal grounds, but only on the cessation grounds in the Refugee Convention and Protocol.[64]

The BIA also has considered whether refugees who previously acquired LPR status are prohibited from applying for adjustment of status and a waiver of inadmissibility anew in removal proceedings.[65] In *Matter of S–I–K–*, the BIA held that a refugee who already has acquired permanent resident status may not apply for adjustment of status and a waiver of inadmissibility under INA §209(c). The BIA based its decision on the plain language of INA §209(a)(1)(C), which specifies that adjustment of status of individuals admitted as refugees applies to those who have "not acquired permanent resident status."[66]

III. Adjustment of Status of Derivative Asylees

Derivative spouses and unmarried children under age 21 who have obtained asylum status based on their familial relationship to a principal asylee also are eligible for adjustment of status, as long as they meet the requirements of INA §209(b).[67] Pursuant to INA §209(b)(3), derivative asylees must continue to meet the definition of a spouse or child of a refugee. Derivatives must meet this definition both at the time of filing an application for adjustment of status and at the time of adjudication of that application.[68] A derivative asylee spouse fails to meet the eligibility requirement if the marital relationship has ended.[69] A derivative asylee

---

[63] *See Romanishyn v. Gonzales*, 455 F.3d 175, 186 (3d Cir. 2006) (holding that refugee who adjusted status is subject to removal even though his refugee status was never terminated); *accord Maiwand v. Gonzales*, 501 F.3d 101, 106–07 (2d Cir. 2007); *Kaganovich v. Gonzales*, 470 F.3d 894, 897–98 (9th Cir. 2006).

[64] *See Becoming LPR Does Not Terminate Refugee Status, UNHCR Says*, 80 INTERPRETER RELEASES 413 and App'x III (Mar. 17, 2003). *See also Smriko v. Ashcroft*, 387 F.3d 279, 281 (3d Cir. 2004) (in remanding case to BIA, court suggests applicant's argument that despite his adjustment to LPR status he still retains his refugee status is supported by INA and legislative history).

[65] *Matter of S–I–K–*, 24 I&N Dec. 324 (BIA 2007).

[66] *Id.* (finding that the Ukrainian refugee's eligibility for adjustment of status was foreclosed by the plain language of the statute, because he had already adjusted status to LPR previously). *See also Saintha v. Mukasey*, 516 F.3d 243 (4th Cir. 2008) (concluding that a refugee who had already acquired LPR status could not meet the requirement under the plain language of INA §209(a)(1)(C).

[67] INA §209(b); 8 CFR §§209.2(a), 1209.2(a) (2014).

[68] USCIS, *Policy Manual*, Vol. 7 Adjustment of Status, pt. M, *supra* note 5.

[69] INA §101(a)(35).

child fails to meet the eligibility requirement if he or she marries or otherwise no longer meets the INA definition of child.[70]

> ➤ **Practice Pointer**: A derivative asylee does not lose his or her asylum status when the required relationship to the principal asylee ends. Rather, he or she only loses the ability to adjust status as a derivative asylee.[71] It may be possible for such an individual to file for asylum *nunc pro tunc* in order to cure his or her ineligibility to adjust status, as described below.

Similarly, if the principal asylee no longer meets the definition of refugee under INA §101(a)(42) at the time the derivative seeks to adjust status, then the derivative asylee will no longer qualify.[72] In fact, if a principal asylee's asylum status is ever revoked, all derivatives' status will be revoked automatically, even if the reasons for revocation are unrelated to the derivatives' own actions.[73] Such derivatives would no longer be eligible to adjust status as asylees. Each of these circumstances is discussed in detail below.

A. Principal Asylee No Longer a Refugee Under INA §101(a)(42)

In order to adjust status pursuant to a grant of asylum, an individual must demonstrate that he or she continues to meet the definition of refugee under INA §101(a)(42), as described above.[74] Derivative applicants must demonstrate that they are the spouse or child of such a refugee.[75] Thus, if the principal asylee no longer meets the definition of refugee, his or her derivatives are not "a spouse or child of such a refugee" and are not eligible to adjust status as asylees.[76]

A principal asylee may no longer meet the definition of refugee under INA §101(a)(42) in various circumstances, including:

- If the principal asylee naturalizes and becomes a U.S. citizen; and
- If the principal asylee's asylum status is terminated or revoked pursuant to 8 CFR §208.21(g), 1208.21(g).

Upon naturalization of the principal asylee or termination of the principal asylee's status, the principal asylee's spouse and children no longer meet the definition of "a

---

[70] INA §101(b)(1).

[71] USCIS, *Policy Manual*, Vol. 7 Adjustment of Status, pt. M, *supra* note 5.

[72] INA §209(b)(3) (stating that the derivative must meet the definition of "spouse or child of such a refugee"). *See* USCIS, *Policy Manual*, Vol. 7 Adjustment of Status, pt. M, *supra* note 5.

[73] *See* 8 CFR §§208.21(g), 1208.21(g) (2014). *See* ch. 14 of this book for a detailed discussion of termination of status.

[74] INA §209(b)

[75] INA §209(b)(3).

[76] *Id.*

spouse or child of such refugee," and, therefore, are not eligible for adjustment of status.[77]

- **Practice Pointer**: Practitioners should advise their principal asylee clients not to naturalize until their derivative relatives have entered on I-730 Refugee/Asylee Relative Petitions and are on U.S. soil. Principal asylee clients also should not naturalize until their derivative relatives have become LPRs of the United States. See chapter 13 of this book for a detailed discussion of loss of derivative status.

- **Practice Pointer**: Under certain circumstances, the principal asylee's status will be terminated due to his or her actions — a criminal act, returning to the country of past or feared persecution as a resident, etc. Even if the derivative asylee him- or herself did not engage in such activities that would risk termination of status, the derivative will lose status along with the principal. There is no mechanism under the law to protect derivatives from losing their status along with the principal. See chapter 14 of this book for a detailed discussion of the legal standards and procedures for termination of status.

B. Death of Principal Asylee

Previously, the death of the principal asylee meant that his or her derivative spouse and children were no longer eligible to adjust status as asylees. However, §204(*l*) amended the INA to allow USCIS to approve the adjustment of status application for a derivative asylee spouse or child of a deceased principal asylee, as long as the derivative meets all requirements under INA §204(*l*).[78] Such derivatives must demonstrate: (1) they resided in the United States at the time of the death of the principal asylee; (2) they continue to reside in the United States; and (3) approval of the application would be in the public interest.[79]

- **Practice Pointer**: This provision applies to adjustment of status applications adjudicated on or after October 28, 2009, even if the principal asylee died before October 28, 2009.[80]

C. Derivative Asylees Ineligible for Adjustment of Status

Derivative spouses and children may become ineligible for adjustment of status due to loss of the derivative relationship at any time prior to adjudication of the

---

[77] *Id. See* USCIS, *Policy Manual*, Vol. 7 Adjustment of Status, pt. M, *supra* note 5.

[78] *See* INA §204(l). *See also* USCIS, *Basic Eligibility for Section 204(l) Relief for Surviving Relatives*, *available at www.uscis.gov/green-card/green-card-through-family/basic-eligibility-section-204l-relief-surviving-relatives* (last visited Mar. 16, 2015).

[79] INA §204(*l*).

[80] *See* INA §204(l); USCIS *Adjudicator's Field Manual*, ch. 10.21(C), *available at www.uscis.gov/iframe/ilink/docView/AFM/HTML/AFM/0-0-0-1.html* (last visited Apr. 2, 2015).

adjustment of status application. The following derivative asylees are ineligible for adjustment of status due to loss of the derivative relationship:

- Divorced spouses;
- Married children; and
- Children 21 years old or older who are not protected under the Child Status Protection Act (CSPA) (*i.e.*, children who turned 21 years old prior to August 6, 2002 who did not have an I-730, I-485, or parent's I-589 pending on August 6, 2002).

These individuals are no longer considered spouses and children of the principal asylee; therefore, they are no longer eligible to adjust status as derivative asylees.[81]

The CSPA amended INA §§207 and 208(b)(3) to permit continued classification as a child for certain derivatives who were under age 21 at the time the principal applicant applied for asylum or refugee status and who turned 21 on or after August 6, 2002. Although the CSPA did not specifically address children who turned 21 prior to adjustment of status, USCIS issued a policy memorandum stating as follows:

> In order to give full effect to the statutory provisions, CIS has determined that a derivative applicant eligible for continued classification as a child under the CSPA will be considered a child for all related eligibility determinations. Thus, for asylum applications under section 208 of the Act, adjustment applications under section 209 of the Act, admission to the United States as a refugee, and following to join applications, the amendments made by the CSPA to the Act benefit an alien who aged out on or after August 6, 2002.[82]

In all cases, including for adjustment of status, in order for a derivative to continue to be considered eligible for CSPA age-out protection, the derivative child must remain unmarried.[83]

Accordingly, in order for a child derivative to maintain eligibility to adjust status based on his or her derivative asylum status, the child must:

- Be under age 21 at the time the principal applicant requested asylum or refugee status (at the time the I-589 or I-590 was filed);
- Be listed on the Form I-589 prior to a final USCIS decision on an asylum application or the Form I-590 prior to adjudication of the application for refugee status;
- Turn 21 on or after August 6, 2002, unless an adjustment of status application already was pending for him or her at the time the child turned 21; and

---

[81] *See* INA §§101(a)(35), 101(b)(1); USCIS, *Policy Manual*, Vol. 7 Adjustment of Status, pt. M, *supra* note 5.

[82] *See* USCIS Interoffice Memorandum from William Yates on The Child Status Protection Act—Children of Asylees and Refugees, at 1 (Aug. 17, 2004), *published on* AILA InfoNet at Doc. No. 04091561 (*posted* Sept. 15, 2004).

[83] *See id.*

- Remain unmarried prior to adjustment of status.[84]

Children who do not maintain eligibility to adjust status as described above may still be eligible to adjust status following a *nunc pro tunc* asylum application, as described below.

> ➢ **Practice Pointer**: If a child marries after his or her grant of derivative asylum status, but then divorces and is unmarried at the time of filing for adjustment of status, he or she may qualify once again as a derivative asylee child, as long as he or she is still under age 21 or is protected under the CSPA.[85]

D. *Nunc Pro Tunc* Asylum Applications

Nunc pro tunc means "now for then," and *nunc pro tunc* asylum applications may be submitted and approved to "cure" a loss of derivative status by granting asylum to a prior derivative asylee as a principal asylee so that the applicant then may be eligible to adjust status as an asylee.[86] Under this process, a former derivative who is no longer able to meet the definition of "spouse" or "child" under the INA must file a new I-589 asylum application with USCIS as a principal *nunc pro tunc* applicant.[87] An individual may need to seek asylum *nunc pro tunc* prior to seeking adjustment of status in the following circumstances:

- The principal asylee naturalizes;
- The derivative spouse asylee divorces the principal applicant;
- The derivative child asylee marries; or
- The derivative child asylee turns 21 years old and is not protected by the CSPA (*i.e.*, children who turned 21 years old prior to August 6, 2002 who did not have an I-730, I-485, or parent's I-589 pending on August 6, 2002).

The procedures for seeking asylum *nunc pro tunc* are the same for all of these individuals. The application must be filed directly with the USCIS asylum office having jurisdiction over the applicant's place of residence.[88] If the individual's biometrics were last taken over 15 months ago, a new biometrics appointment will be scheduled and the applicant must complete biometrics collection or his or her application will not be approved.[89]

---

[84] *See id.*

[85] USCIS, *Policy Manual*, Vol. 7 Adjustment of Status, pt. M, *supra* note 5.

[86] *See* USCIS, Affirmative Asylum Procedures Manual, at pt. III.E.7. (Nov. 2013), *available at www.uscis.gov/sites/default/files/files/nativedocuments/Asylum_Procedures_Manual_2013.pdf* (last visited Mar. 16, 2015).

[87] *Id.*

[88] *Id.* at pt. III.E.7.a.

[89] *Id.* at pt. III.E.7.c.

Following biometrics collection, the asylum office will then schedule the individual for an interview with an asylum officer.[90] Because the former derivative need not independently establish his or her eligibility for asylum, the asylum officer generally will not review the underlying asylum claim at the time of the interview.[91] Rather, the asylum officer will verify: (1) the individual's identity; (2) the individual's physical presence in the United States; (3) the individual's asylee status; (4) that the individual is not under the jurisdiction of the immigration court; and (5) that no mandatory bars to asylum eligibility apply (*i.e.*, persecution of others; conviction of a particularly serious crime; commission of a serious nonpolitical crime outside the United States; reasonable grounds for regarding the individual a danger to the security of the United States; participation in terrorist activities or organizations; and firm resettlement in a third country).[92] Thus, the individual should provide the following documentation:

- Valid photo identification documents (employment authorization document (EAD), Refugee Travel Document (RTD), state driver's license or ID document);
- Evidence of asylee status (Asylum Approval letter or IJ order granting asylum, endorsed I-94 card, EAD under category (A)(5)); and
- Any evidence demonstrating that the mandatory bars to asylum do not apply and/or evidence of positive discretionary factors, if necessary.[93]

There is a presumption that the individual who lost derivative status is eligible for a grant of asylum on his or her own; however, the asylum officer has the discretion to interview an individual on the merits of the asylum claim if: (1) the individual is a national of a country different from the principal applicant and does not appear to have a fear of harm in that country; (2) the individual never lived with the principal applicant; (3) the principal applicant derived asylum through fraud but that principal applicant's asylum status has not been terminated; or (4) the officer otherwise believes the individual may not be entitled to a grant of asylum as a principal applicant.[94]

> ➢ **Practice Pointer**: Although *nunc pro tunc* asylum applicants generally do not have to establish independent eligibility for asylum, practitioners should ensure that their clients who apply for *nunc pro tunc* benefits have a general knowledge of the underlying asylum claim, as well as current country conditions in the country of past or feared persecution. Clients should be able to articulate why they still cannot return to that country and why they still are entitled to a grant of asylum.

---

[90] *Id.* at pt. III.E.7.a.

[91] *Id.*

[92] *Id.*

[93] *See id.*

[94] *Id.* at pt. III.E.7.b.

If the application is approved, the asylum office will grant asylum *nunc pro tunc* to a date in the past, depending on the date the individual was admitted as a derivative asylee. If the individual was granted asylum by USCIS or an IJ, the asylum office will grant asylum *nunc pro tunc* to the date of the principal applicant's asylum approval.[95] If the individual was granted asylum while physically present in the United States, pursuant to an approved I-730 Refugee/Asylee Relative Petition, the asylum office will grant asylum *nunc pro tunc* to the date of approval of the I-730.[96] If the individual was outside of the United States when the principal asylee's application was granted and then entered the United States pursuant to an I-730 petition, the asylum office will grant asylum *nunc pro tunc* to the date of the individual's entry into the United States.[97] The asylum office will provide the individual with an Asylum Approval – *Nunc Pro Tunc* letter and an accompanying I-94 card showing admission as an asylee, backdated to the relevant date.[98] A former derivative who applies for a grant of asylum as a principal *nunc pro tunc* may include any qualifying dependents in his or her application, and, if the application is granted, he or she may petition for qualifying relatives on an I-730, Refugee/Asylee Relative Petition.[99]

If the former derivative is ineligible for approval *nunc pro tunc* as a principal applicant due to a criminal record or mandatory bar to asylum, the asylum officer will issue a Notice of Intent to Deny (NOID).[100] If the evidence making the former derivative ineligible for a final approval constitutes a ground for termination under 8 Code of Federal Regulations (CFR) §208.24 and the prior asylum status had been granted by USCIS, the asylum officer also will initiate termination of the former derivative's asylee status and issue a Notice of Intent to Terminate (NOIT).[101] If the prior asylum status was granted by an IJ or the BIA, USCIS does not have jurisdiction to terminate the asylee status.[102] Instead, after completion of the former derivative's case before the asylum office, USCIS may exercise its discretion to coordinate with DHS to request and assist in preparing and filing a motion to reopen before the IJ for a hearing on termination.[103] The applicant will have the opportunity to prepare a rebuttal to any NOID and/or NOIT.[104] If he or she overcomes the reasons for the NOID and/or NOIT, the asylum office will issue the approval letter and I-94

---

[95] *Id.* at pt. III.E.7.c.

[96] *Id.*

[97] *Id.*

[98] *Id.*

[99] *Id.* at pt. III.E.7.e.

[100] *Id.* at pt. III.E.7.d.

[101] *Id.*

[102] *Id.*

[103] *Id. See* ch. 14 of this book for a detailed discussion of the legal standards and procedures for termination before USCIS or the IJ or BIA.

[104] *Id.* at pt. III.E.7.d.

card as described above.[105] If the grounds are not overcome, however, a denial letter will be issued either at that time or, if there is a current termination proceeding, at the end of the termination proceeding along with the termination notice.[106]

> **Practice Pointer**: See chapter 14 of this book for a detailed discussion of the legal standards and procedures for termination of status.

These *nunc pro tunc* procedures apply to all derivatives who are no longer eligible for derivative status regardless of whether the derivative was granted asylum status by an asylum office or IJ, or entered the United States as an asylee pursuant to an approved I-730 Refugee/Asylee Relative Petition.[107]

IV. Adjustment of Status Applications for Asylees and Refugees

In seeking adjustment of status, all principal refugees or asylees, as well as all derivatives, must file their own, independent application packages. To apply for adjustment of status as an asylee or refugee, the applicant must first prepare Form I-485.[108] The applicant should indicate in Part 2 that he or she is applying based on a grant of asylum (box "d.") or that he or she is applying based on admission as a refugee (box "h.").[109] Additionally, many questions on pages 3–5 of Form I-485 seek information regarding the applicant's admissibility for permanent residence, and it is essential that the applicant provide answers that are consistent with his or her asylum application.[110] For example, on page 3, question 1.b. asks whether the applicant has ever been arrested.[111] Many applicants for adjustment of status based on an underlying grant of asylee or refugee status have been arrested in their home countries in connection with the persecution they suffered. Such applicants should answer "yes" to this question and include an addendum to the I-485 explaining the nature of the arrest.

> **Practice Pointer**: For any "yes" answers, practitioners should prepare explanatory addenda to provide USCIS with the information to determine whether the applicant is admissible. As discussed above, certain grounds of inadmissibility — lack of a valid entry document, labor certification, or becoming a public charge — are automatically waived, while most others may be waived under INA §209(c) by filing

---

[105] *Id.*

[106] *Id.*

[107] *Id.* at pt. III.E.7.

[108] 8 Code of Federal Regulations (CFR) §§209.2(c), 1209.2(c) (2014). *See* USCIS, Form I-485, Application to Register Permanent Residence or Adjust Status, *available at www.uscis.gov/sites/default/files/files/form/i-485.pdf* (last visited Mar. 17, 2015).

[109] *See* USCIS, *Form I-485*, *supra* note 108, at 1.

[110] *Id.* at 3–5.

[111] *Id.* at 3.

Form I-602, as discussed below.[112] Drug trafficking and security-related grounds are not waivable, however, so practitioners should be extremely cautious and precise in assisting their clients with completing part 3.C. on page 3 of the I-485 application. The inadmissibility grounds under INA §212(a)(3)(B) are incredibly broad and are not waivable under INA §209(c) for purposes of adjustment of status eligibility.[113]

➢ **Practice Pointer**: While completing the information on the Form I-485, it is important for practitioners to ensure that all information is consistent with the applicant's underlying asylum claim. Although USCIS should not re-adjudicate the underlying asylum claim, USCIS may seek to verify that the underlying grant of asylum was lawful. Any indication of fraud in the underlying claim due to inconsistencies could lead to denial of the I-485, as well as termination of the underlying grant of asylum. If practitioners did not represent the asylee in seeking asylum, practitioners should ask their clients for copies of the I-589 and supporting documentation filed previously. If the client no longer has this documentation, practitioners should prepare and file request for the applicant's "A-file" under the Freedom of Information Act.

Form I-485 must be signed and the form with the original signature must be submitted to USCIS. Copies of signatures are not accepted.[114] In addition to submitting the completed and signed Form I-485, the applicant must compile and attach all of the necessary supporting documentation, including the following:[115]

- Form G-28, Notice of Entry of Appearance (if represented);
- Two passport-sized photographs of the applicant (with the applicant's name and A# printed on the back of each), attached to the completed and signed Form I-485;
- Filing fee check or money order in the amount of $985 made payable to "U.S. Department of Homeland Security," if the applicant is an asylee (not required for refugees), or in the alternative, a Form I-912 Request for Fee Waiver with supporting documentation;
- Biometrics fee check or money order in the amount of $85 made payable to "U.S. Department of Homeland Security," if the applicant is age 14 to 78 (required for both asylees and refugees);
- Completed Form G-325A, Biographic Information Sheet for applicants between 14 and 79 years of age;

---

[112] *See infra* pt. V. for a detailed discussion of waivers under INA §209(c).

[113] See ch. 2 for a detailed discussion of the terrorism-related grounds of inadmissibility.

[114] USCIS, Instructions for I-485, Application to Register Permanent Residence or Adjust Status, at 2, *available at www.uscis.gov/sites/default/files/files/form/i-485instr.pdf* (last visited Mar. 17, 2015).

[115] *See generally id.*

- Evidence that the applicant was granted refugee or asylee status (Asylum Approval letter of IJ order granting asylum, endorsed I-94 card, EAD indicating category (A)(5), and RTD biographic page);
- Evidence of physical presence in the United States for at least one year cumulatively since admission as a refugee or the grant of asylum status (*e.g.*, lease, mortgage, or deed showing home address; employer letter or pay stubs; school records; tax returns and W-2s; bank or credit card statements or other financial documentation; and affidavits);
- A copy of the applicant's birth certificate, with certified English translation if the birth certificate is not in English;
- A copy of the applicant's photo identification (if available);
- A copy of the applicant's most recent I-94 card;
- Completed Medical Examination, Form I-693, in the envelope sealed by the USCIS-approved civil surgeon;
- Certified final dispositions for any arrests, charges, or convictions;
- Documentation demonstrating the requisite family relationship for derivative spouses and children (marriage certificate, divorce decrees or death certificates of any prior spouses, birth certificate, adoption decree, etc.); and
- Certified English translations of any documents that are not English.

  ➢ **Practice Pointer**: Applicants for adjustment of status also may concurrently file an I-765, Application for Employment Authorization and an I-131, Application for Travel Document (in the case of a refugee or asylee, an RTD). These applications are included in the filing fee for the I-485 application. See the instructions for I-765 applications at *www.uscis.gov/sites/default/files/files/form/i-765instr.pdf* and for I-131 applications, *www.uscis.gov/sites/default/files/files/form/i-131instr.pdf.*[116] See chapter 13 for a detailed discussion of legal requirements and procedures for filing these applications.

All applicants for adjustment of status must complete a medical examination to determine the mental and physical condition of the applicant.[117] Refugees applying for adjustment of status one year after admission as refugees, however, need only submit the vaccination portion of the Form I-693 (pages 1, 4, and 6), not the entire medical report, unless a Class A was noted on their overseas medical exam.[118] In general, refugees are not required to comply with the vaccination requirements while overseas. Similarly, derivative asylees who completed a medical exam overseas during the I-730 process do not have to file a new completed medical exam with their I-485 applications, as long as the I-485 is filed within two years of entry to the United

[116] (last visited Mar. 17, 2015).

[117] 8 CFR §§209.2(d), 1209.2(d) (2014).

[118] USCIS, *Instructions for I-485*, *supra* note 108, at 4.

States. Like refugees, these derivatives are still required to submit evidence of their vaccinations, including parts 1–5 of the Form I-693.[119]

➢ **Practice Pointer**: The medical exam must be conducted by a USCIS-approved civil surgeon. To find an approved civil surgeon in the area, go to USCIS's website at *https://egov.uscis.gov/crisgwi/go?action=offices.type&OfficeLocator.office_type=CIV* and type in the applicant's zip code. Practitioners should assist their clients in locating a USCIS-approved civil surgeon who may complete the I-693 medical exam form.

The signed, completed Form I-485 and supporting documentation should be filed with the USCIS office designated in the instructions to the Form I-485.[120] Currently, I-485 applications based on asylee or refugee status are filed with either the USCIS Phoenix or Dallas Lockboxes, depending on where the applicant resides.[121]

➢ **Practice Pointer**: Before filing an application to adjust status based on asylee or refugee status, practitioners should always check USCIS's website and the up-to-date instructions for Form I-485 to determine the relevant filing location, as the filing locations frequently change.

Upon receipt of the application, USCIS will ensure that the I-485 is complete and that all required documentation has been submitted. If the form is not completely filled out or if the applicant fails to establish a basis of eligibility for adjustment of status, USCIS may deny the application without further processing.[122] If complete, USCIS will issue an I-485 receipt notice and send it to the applicant and his or her attorney or representative of record. The receipt notice usually arrives approximately two weeks after submission of the application.

USCIS will then process the application. Usually, USCIS will require the applicant to appear at an Application Support Center (ASC) to provide biometrics for purposes of identity, background, and security checks.[123] USCIS will issue an ASC appointment notice scheduling the applicant for an appointment at a local ASC. If the applicant does not appear for his or her ASC appointment, his or her application may be denied.[124]

USCIS may request additional evidence or schedule an interview appointment with the applicant. However, additional evidence and interviews are not necessary for

---

[119] USCIS, *Policy Manual*, Vol. 7 Adjustment of Status, pt. M, *supra* note 5, at ch. 4.a.

[120] 8 CFR §§209.2(c), 1209.2(c) (2014).

[121] *See* USCIS, *Direct Filing Addresses for Form I-485, Application to Register Permanent Residence or Adjust Status*, *available at www.uscis.gov/i-485-addresses* (last visited Mar. 17, 2015).

[122] USCIS, Instructions for I-485, *supra* note 108, at 6.

[123] *Id.* at 2, 6.

[124] *Id.* at 2.

all adjustment of status applications for refugees and asylees.[125] If an interview is scheduled, USCIS will send the applicant written notice of the date, time, and place of the interview. The applicant should bring his or her I-94 card, travel document, and any other original documents to the interview.[126] He or she also may bring an attorney or representative to the interview before USCIS. The interview will be conducted under oath.[127]

After the interview or if an interview is waived, the applicant will be notified of the decision in writing.[128] If the application is approved, USCIS will record the asylee's admission as an LPR, as of the date one year before the date of approval of the I-485 application.[129] USCIS will also issue an I-485 Welcome Notice and initiate production of the individual's Permanent Resident Card (green card). The card will be mailed directly to the applicant. If the application is denied, however, the asylee will be notified of the reasons for the denial in writing and may renew the application in INA §240 removal proceedings before an IJ.[130] If an asylee has been placed in removal proceedings, the IJ and BIA have exclusive jurisdiction over his or her adjustment of status and waiver applications.[131]

- **Practice Pointer**: See chapter 8 of this book for a detailed discussion of defensive applications before the U.S. immigration courts, as well as guidance for filing and presenting these applications.
    - **Practice Pointer**: USCIS does not always refer asylees for removal proceedings upon denying their I-485 applications. While these asylees may continue to reside in the United States in valid asylum status (unless their status is terminated following termination proceedings), it may be in their best interest for practitioners to negotiate with DHS to either place them in proceedings so they may renew their I-485 before an IJ or assist their clients in applying anew for adjustment of status. This must be a case-by-case determination depending on the reasons for denial of adjustment of status, as well as the applicant's personal circumstances.
    - **Practice Pointer**: For a comprehensive guide to refugee and asylee adjustment procedures, see the "Refugee and Asylee Adjustment Toolkit" (August 2014) prepared by The Pennsylvania State University Dickinson School of Law's Center for Immigrants' Rights and The Boston University School of Law's Immigrants' Rights Clinic. The

---

[125] *See* 8 CFR §§209.2(e), 1209.2(e) (2014); USCIS, *Instructions for I-485*, *supra* note 108, at 6.

[126] USCIS, *Instructions for I-485*, *supra* note 108, at 6.

[127] *Id.*

[128] 8 CFR §§209.2(f), 1209.2(f) (2014).

[129] 8 CFR §§209.2(f), 1209.2(f) (2014).

[130] 8 CFR §§209.2(f), 1209.2(f) (2014).

[131] 8 CFR §1209.2(c) (2014).

Toolkit can be found at *www.bu.edu/law/news/documents/Refugeeand AsyleeAdjustmentToolkit.pdf*.[132]

V. INA §209(c) Waivers for Asylees and Refugees

A person admitted as a refugee or granted asylum is eligible to adjust to LPR status one year after admission or after the grant of asylum.[133] Such individuals, however, must demonstrate that they are admissible to the United States as permanent residents.[134] As noted above, the INA specifies that the grounds of inadmissibility relating to lack of a proper travel document, labor certification, or likelihood of becoming a public charge do not apply to asylees and refugees seeking adjustment of status.[135] Even if the applicant is inadmissible for a different ground, that ground may be waivable under INA §209(c).[136] Pursuant to INA §209(c), the AG has the discretion to waive any other ground of inadmissibility for humanitarian purposes, to ensure family unity, or when it is otherwise in the public interest, except for controlled substance trafficking and certain security-related grounds.[137]

The 209(c) discretionary waiver may be requested concurrently along with the application to adjust status, or upon notification by a USCIS officer that such a waiver is necessary (often at the interview stage).[138] Additionally, a refugee or asylee who has not yet adjusted status and becomes deportable or inadmissible may be eligible for adjustment of status in removal proceedings,[139] provided the inadmissibility is not on grounds that would disqualify him or her for adjustment of status. If in removal proceedings, refugees or asylees should inform the IJ that they wish to apply for adjustment of status. To seek such relief, they should submit Form I-485, Application to Register Permanent Residence or Adjust Status, and Form I-602, Application by Refugee for Waiver of Grounds of Excludability.[140]

---

[132] (last visited Mar. 17, 2015).

[133] INA §209, 8 USC §1159 (2012).

[134] INA §§209(a)(2), (b)(5).

[135] INA §209(b); 8 CFR §§209.2(a)(1), 1209.2(a)(1) (2014).

[136] *See generally* INA §209(c); 8 CFR §§209.2(b), 1209.2(b) (2014).

[137] INA §209(c); 8 CFR §§209.1(f), 209.2(b), 1209.1(f), 1209.2(b) (2014).

[138] 8 CFR §§209.2(b), 1209.2(b) (2014); USCIS *Adjudicator's Field Manual*, *supra* note 80, at ch. 41.6(b). *See* USCIS Memorandum from Michael Aytes, on Waivers Under Section 209(c) of the Immigration and Nationality Act (AFM Update 05-33), at 1 (Oct. 31, 2005), *published on* AILA InfoNet at Doc. No. 05110962 (*posted* Nov. 9, 2005), *available at www.uscis.gov/sites/default/files/USCIS/Laws/Memoranda/Static_Files_Memoranda/Archives%201998-2008/2005/209cadjwvr103105.pdf* (last visited Mar. 17, 2015).

[139] *Matter of K–A–*, 23 I&N Dec. 661, 663-64 (BIA 2004); 8 CFR §§209.2(c), 1209.2(c) (2014).

[140] *See* 8 CFR §1240.11(a) (2014). *See also* ch. 8 for a detailed discussion of procedures for filing applications in immigration court.

- **Practice Pointer**: For a helpful how-to guide on INA §209(c) waivers, which includes sample waiver forms, see Julie C. Ferguson's book, *AILA's Focus on Waivers Under the Immigration and Nationality Act* (AILA 2008).[141]

If an applicant knows that he or she will need a waiver, the applicant should prepare and file Form I-602, along with supporting documentation, concurrently with the I-485 application.[142] Although this form was once required to seek waiver of certain grounds of inadmissibility under INA §209(c), USCIS determined that the form provided information already available in other records accessible to the adjudicator.[143] To improve efficiency of the 209(c) waiver process, therefore, USCIS revised the *Adjudicator's Field Manual* to provide adjudicators with the discretion to adjudicate and grant §209(c) waivers without Form I-602 to refugee and asylee adjustment applicants who are inadmissible on any ground that may be waived, except for INA §212(a)(1) (health-related grounds).[144]

USCIS may grant a waiver without requiring Form I-602 if: (1) the applicant is inadmissible under a ground of inadmissibility that may be waived, other than INA §212(a)(1) (health grounds); (2) USCIS records and other information available to the adjudicator contain sufficient information to assess eligibility for a waiver; and (3) there is no evidence to suggest that negative factors would adversely impact the exercise of discretion.[145] If these requirements are met, "it is in the public interest to grant the waiver without requiring submission of Form I-602. In addition, it is in the public interest to decrease the burden on both the applicant and USCIS with respect to processing paperwork that is already available to the adjudicator."[146] Otherwise, Form I-602 is required in order for the adjudicator to approve the waiver.[147]

In considering a §209(c) waiver, the adjudicator must determine whether a waiver is warranted on humanitarian, family unity, or other public interest grounds.[148] These grounds must be balanced against the seriousness of the offense that rendered the individual inadmissible to determine whether granting the waiver is in the best interest of the United States.[149]

---

[141] *See also The Waivers Book: Advanced Issues in Immigration Practice* (AILA 2011).

[142] USCIS *Adjudicator's Field Manual*, *supra* note 80, at ch. 41.6(b). *See* USCIS, *I-602, Application by Refugee for Waiver of Grounds of Excludability*, *available at www.uscis.gov/sites/default/files/files/form/i-602.pdf* (last visited Mar. 17, 2015); Aytes Mem. on Waivers Under Section 209(c) of the INA, *supra* note 138, at 2.

[143] Aytes Memo. on Waivers Under Section 209(c) of the INA, *supra* note 138, at 2.

[144] *Id.*

[145] USCIS *Adjudicator's Field Manual*, *supra* note 80, at ch. 41.6(b)(1). *See also* Aytes Mem. on Waivers Under Section 209(c) of the INA, *supra* note 138, at 4–5.

[146] Aytes Mem. on Waivers Under Section 209(c) of the INA, *supra* note 138, at 5..

[147] *Id.*; USCIS *Adjudicator's Field Manual*, *supra* note 80, at ch. 41.6(b)(2).

[148] USCIS *Adjudicator's Field Manual*, *supra* note 80, at ch. 41.6(b).

[149] *Matter of H–N–*, 22 I&N Dec. 1039 (BIA 1999).

Positive factors may include: (1) family ties in the United States; (2) a long period of residence in the United States; (3) hardship to the respondent and his or her family members of the respondent is removed; (4) value and service to the community; and (5) good moral character of the respondent.[150]

In setting forth these factors, the BIA in *Matter of H–N–* considered the case of a 37-year-old Cambodian woman who was convicted of second-degree robbery and was sentenced to three to six years in prison. She then applied for adjustment of status and was found inadmissible, so she applied for a waiver under INA §209(c).[151] In granting the waiver, the BIA relied on her four U.S. citizen children, husband who resided legally in the United States, and her 15-plus years of residence in the United States. The BIA concluded that the record "indicat[ed] that the respondent's conviction [was] not indicative of her overall character," and stated that she was "a person who would be an asset to our society."[152]

In general, unless there are significant negative factors that clearly outweigh the positive factors, a refugee or asylee's need for protection from persecution should be the strongest of discretionary factors, and the adjudicator should approve the §209(c) waiver application.[153] However, in a decision reversing the BIA's grant of a waiver under INA §209(c), the AG criticized the BIA's decision in *Matter of H–N–*, and ruled that individuals who commit violent or dangerous crimes resulting in inadmissibility under INA §212(a)(2) will not be granted this discretionary waiver except in extraordinary circumstances resulting in exceptional or extremely unusual hardship.[154] Thus, under *Matter of Jean*'s current precedent, a waiver for "violent or dangerous crimes" is unlikely to be granted absent extraordinary circumstances, "such as those involving national security or foreign policy considerations, or cases in which an alien clearly demonstrates that the denial of status adjustment would result in exceptional and extremely unusual hardship."[155]

Depending on the gravity of the underlying criminal offense, "such a showing of exceptional and extremely unusual hardship might still be insufficient."[156] The Fifth, Seventh, Ninth, and Eleventh Circuit Courts of Appeals have all affirmed that the AG did not exceed his statutory authority in establishing a heightened standard for §209(c) waivers for those convicted of violent or dangerous crimes.[157]

---

[150] *Id.*

[151] *Id.*

[152] *Id.*

[153] USCIS *Adjudicator's Field Manual*, *supra* note 80, at ch. 41.6(b).

[154] *Matter of Jean*, 23 I&N Dec. 373 (AG 2002) (finding refugee convicted of manslaughter for killing a 19-month-old toddler in her care was not eligible for a waiver under §209(c)).

[155] *Id.*

[156] *Id.*

[157] *See also Makir-Marwil v. Att'y Gen.*, 681 F.3d 1227 (11th Cir. 2012); *Rivas-Gomez v. Gonzales*, 441 F.3d 1072 (9th Cir. 2006); *Jean v. Gonzales*, 452 F.3d 392 (5th Cir. 2006); *Ali v. Achim*, 468 F.3d 462 (7th Cir. 2006).

- ➢ **Practice Pointer**: Practitioners seeking to establish "exceptional and extremely unusual hardship" for purposes of a §209(c) waiver for a client convicted of a violent or dangerous crime should look to *Matter of Recinas*, 23 I&N Dec. 467 (BIA 2002) and *Matter of Monreal*, 23 I&N Dec. 56 (BIA 2001) for instruction on demonstrating this heightened standard of hardship to the client and his or her family.

The BIA has since attempted to limit the application of this heightened standard. In *Matter of K–A–*, the BIA emphasized that the AG's heightened standard was limited to those convicted of "violent or dangerous crimes," not necessarily all aggravated felonies.[158] However, the BIA did note in dicta that "even nonviolent aggravated felonies will generally constitute significant negative factors militating strongly against a favorable exercise of discretion."[159] The BIA concluded that even in the cases of individuals convicted of aggravated felonies, if there are "truly compelling countervailing equities," such as a disabled child, the applicant should "become the beneficiary of the Attorney General's discretion under sections 209(b) and (c)."[160]

- ➢ **Practice Pointer**: Given the challenge of convincing the AG to exercise discretion in granting an INA §209(c) waiver in cases involving aggravated felonies or other serious crimes, practitioners should work with their clients to develop and present compelling documentary and testimonial of all potential positive discretionary factors. Such factors may include: (1) length of residence in the United States; (2) religious community and/or community involvement; (3) volunteer and charitable activities; (4) U.S. citizen or LPR family members and any medical, psychological, emotional, developmental, financial, or other hardships they may suffer without the applicant in the United States; (5) payment of taxes and other contributions to American society; (6) stable employment; and (7) any other evidence of rehabilitation or good moral character. For a detailed list of possible forms of evidence of these positive factors, see the "Refugee and Asylee Adjustment Toolkit" (August 2014) prepared by The Pennsylvania State University Dickinson School of Law's Center for Immigrants' Rights and The Boston University

---

[158] *Matter of K–A–*, 23 I&N Dec. 661 (BIA 2004) (upholding the grant of adjustment of status to an asylee convicted of possession of forged instrument who was the mother of two U.S. citizen children, one of whom was disabled). *See also Rivas-Gomez v. Gonzales*, 441 F.3d 1072 (9th Cir. 2006), superseded by 225 Fed. App'x 680 (9th Cir. 2007) (emphasizing that not all noncitizens with aggravated felony convictions were subject to the AG's heightened standard, only those who "engage in violent criminal acts").

[159] *Matter of K–A–*, 23 I&N Dec. 661, 666 (BIA 2004) (nevertheless, the Board of Immigration Appeals (BIA) upheld the grant of adjustment of status to an asylee convicted of possession of forged instrument who was the mother of two U.S. citizen children, one of whom was disabled).

[160] *Id.* at 666.

School of Law's Immigrants' Rights Clinic. The Toolkit is available online at *www.bu.edu/law/news/documents/RefugeeandAsyleeAdjustmentToolkit.pdf.*[161]

VI. Conclusion

Adjustment of status to LPR is a very important step for asylees and refugees in leaving behind their sense of "statelessness" as they search not only for protection, but for a sense of belonging and a true place to call home. It is essential for practitioners to fully understand the legal standards, potential pitfalls, and procedures for representing their clients along this important path to LPR status, and eventually, U.S. citizenship.

161 (last visited Mar. 17, 2015).

CHAPTER SIXTEEN

RELATED FORMS OF RELIEF[*]

In addition to asylum, withholding of removal, and protection under the Convention Against Torture (CAT), other forms of relief may be available to victims of violence and trauma. Persons fleeing persecution or torture should always explore all forms of relief, many of which are easier to obtain than asylum, withholding of removal, and CAT for qualified persons. While many forms of relief are beyond the scope of this book, this chapter reviews the related relief that is most relevant for victims of violence and trauma, as well as those who fear persecution and torture in their home countries. Specifically, this chapter provides brief overviews of the following relief: T and U visas for victims of trafficking and qualifying criminal activity; Special Immigrant Juvenile Status (SIJS) and other special immigrants; Temporary Protected Status (TPS); humanitarian parole; and relief under the *American Baptist Churches v. Thornburgh* Settlement (*ABC*), the Nicaraguan Adjustment and Central American Relief Act (NACARA), the Haitian Refugee Immigration Fairness Act (HRIFA), and the Cuban Adjustment Act (CAA).

➢ **Practice Pointer**: For more detailed analyses of various forms of relief beyond asylum, withholding, and CAT, see AILA's *Representing Clients in Immigration Court*, which addresses adjustment of status, waivers, cancellation of removal, voluntary departure, and much more. For a comprehensive guide to all forms of waivers, see AILA's *The Waivers Book*, which provides complete guidance on waivers of criminal, health-related, misrepresentation and fraud, and immigration violation grounds.

[*] The author would like to thank Michelle N. Mendez of the Catholic Legal Immigration Network, Inc. for her invaluable input in reviewing this chapter.

I. T and U Visas for Victims of Trafficking and Crimes

In October 2000, Congress passed the Victims of Trafficking and Violence Protection Act (VTVPA) in response to the approximately 700,000 persons trafficked worldwide each year who are primarily women and children.[1] Estimates are between 14,500 and 17,500 of these individuals are trafficked into the United States annually.[2] In order to protect these victims from future harm, the VTVPA provides for two types of nonimmigrant (or temporary) visas, the "T" and the "U" visas. An individual who obtains a T or U visa may, after three years, obtain permanent residency. The VTVPA is particularly relevant to asylum-seekers because often, in desperation, they fall prey to human traffickers and other criminals when fleeing their dire situations at home — or, once on U.S. soil, become crime victims. All asylum applicants should be screened for possible relief under the VTVPA. If the applicant is currently in removal proceedings in immigration court, it may be possible to have the case administratively closed, continued, or even terminated to allow the applicant to apply to U.S. Citizenship and Immigration Services (USCIS) for a T or a U visa.[3]

A. T Visas

To receive T-1 classification under the VTVPA and regulations, an individual must:

- Be a victim of a "severe form of trafficking of persons";
- Be physically present in the United States or at a U.S. port of entry on account of such trafficking;
- Have complied with "any reasonable request for assistance in the investigation or prosecution of acts of trafficking" or be under 15 years of age; and

---

[1] Victims of Trafficking and Violence Protection Act of 2000 (VTVPA), Pub. L. No. 106-386, §102(b)(1), 114 Stat. 1464, 1466. The VTVPA was amended and reauthorized by the Trafficking Victims Protection Reauthorization Act of 2003, Pub. L. No. 108-193, 117 Stat. 2875, and the Trafficking Victims Protection Reauthorization Act of 2005, Pub. L. No. 109-164, 119 Stat. 3558 (2006), and the Trafficking Victims Protection Reauthorization Act of 2008, Pub. L. No. 110-457, 122 Stat. 5044 (2008).

[2] VTVPA §102(b)(1), 114 Stat. 1466; *see also* U.S. Dep't of State (DOS), *Trafficking in Persons Report,* United States Country Narrative, at 397-98 (June 2014), *available at www.state.gov/documents/organization/226844.pdf*; Congressional Research Service, Trafficking in Persons: U.S. Policy and Issues for Congress (Feb. 19, 2013), *available at http://fas.org/sgp/crs/row/RL34317.pdf*.

[3] *See* INS Memorandum from Michael Cronin on Victims of Trafficking and Violence Protection Act of 2000 (VTVPA) Policy Mem. No. 2 on "T" and "U" Nonimmigrant Visas (Aug. 30, 2001), *reprinted in* 78 INTERPRETER RELEASES 1758, App'x II (Nov. 12, 2001), *available at www.asistahelp.org/documents/resources/Policy_Memo__Cronin__83001_DFC4BA7F5E85D.pdf*. For many other materials and documents useful when filing for a T or U visa, see the Nat'l Lawyers Guild's Nat'l Immigration Project, at *www.nationalimmigrationproject.org/domestic-violence/domvioindex.htm#ContentSections*.

- Show he or she would suffer "extreme hardship involving unusual or severe harm upon removal."[4]

Severe forms of trafficking include sex trafficking, involuntary servitude, debt bondage, peonage, and slavery.[5] Evidence that an individual is a victim of trafficking usually is provided by a law enforcement agency (LEA) endorsement, but such an endorsement is not an absolute requirement. A personal statement—one detailing the trafficking and good-faith attempts to secure the endorsement—may suffice.[6] Specifically, a T visa application should contain a statement by the applicant describing the facts of his or her victimization, including the nature and scope of any force, fraud, or coercion used against the victim.[7] The statement also should describe what the applicant has done to report the crime to an LEA and his or her good faith attempts to obtain the LEA endorsement. Secondary evidence of the applicant's victimization, as well as his or her participation in an investigation or prosecution, includes trial transcripts, court documents, police reports, news articles, and copies of reimbursement forms for travel to and from court.[8] Trafficking victims under age 15 are not required to show compliance with reasonable requests for assistance by LEAs.[9]

> **Practice Pointer**: A victim of a severe form of trafficking in persons should contact the LEA who he or she has assisted to request an endorsement. If there has not yet been contact with an LEA, the applicant should contact the nearest FBI field office or U.S. Attorney's Office to file a complaint, assist in the investigation or prosecution, and request the endorsement. Alternatively, the applicant may contact the Department of Justice, Civil Rights Division, Trafficking in Persons and Worker Exploitation Task Force complaint hotline at 1-888-428-7581 to file a complaint and be referred to an LEA.[10]

In addition to establishing that he or she was a victim of a severe form of trafficking in persons and that he or she assisted in the investigation or prosecution of those acts of trafficking, a T visa applicant also must show that he or she is physically

---

[4] *See* Immigration and Nationality Act (INA) §101(a)(15)(T); 8 USC §1101(a)(15)(T) (2012); 8 CFR §214.11 (2014). *See also* U.S. Citizenship & Immigration Servs., Interoffice Memorandum, William Yates, Trafficking Victims Protection Reauthorization Act of 2003" (Apr. 15, 2004), *published on* AILA InfoNet at Doc. No. 04060110 (*posted* June 1, 2004).

[5] VTVPA §103(8), 114 Stat. 1470; 22 USC §7102(8) (2012).

[6] 8 Code of Federal Regulations (CFR) §214.11(h) (2014).

[7] 8 CFR §214.11(f)(3) (2014).

[8] 8 CFR §§214.11(f)(3), 214.11(h) (2014).

[9] 8 CFR §§214.11(d)(2)(vi), 214.11(h)(3) (2014).

[10] 8 CFR §214.11(f)(4) (2014). *See also* U.S. Dep't of Justice, Trafficking in Persons and Worker Exploitation Task Force, *available at http://www.justice.gov/usao-ndia/human-trafficking-response-team/report-case.*

present in the United States on account of trafficking.[11] This requirement applies to an individual who is present because he or she is being subjected to a severe form of trafficking in persons, was recently liberated from a severe form of trafficking in persons, or was subject to severe form of trafficking in persons at some point in the past and whose continuing presence in the United States is directly related to the original trafficking in persons.[12] If the applicant has escaped from the trafficker, the applicant must show that he or she has not had the opportunity to depart the United States due to trauma, injury, lack of resources, lack of travel documents, or other such factors.[13]

In defining "extreme hardship," the regulations provide that such hardship cannot be based on mere economic detriment or the lack of social or economic opportunities.[14] Factors that may be considered include:

- age and personal circumstances of the applicant;
- serious mental or physical illness;
- the nature and extent of the physical and psychological consequences of severe forms of trafficking in persons;
- the impact of the loss of access to U.S. courts and the criminal justice system;
- whether the applicant would be penalized for having been a victim of trafficking upon return to his or her home country, and the likelihood of re-victimization and the need, ability, or willingness of foreign authorities to protect the applicant;
- the likelihood of severe harm from the trafficker in the home country; and
- the likelihood that the applicant's safety would be threatened by civil unrest or armed conflict in the home country.[15]

An individual is ineligible to receive T nonimmigrant status if there is substantial reason to believe that he or she has committed an act of a severe form of trafficking in persons.[16]

> ➢ **Practice Pointer**: Some excellent resources for guidance on T visa eligibility and procedures are: (1) *Identification and Legal Advocacy for Trafficking Survivors*, 3rd Edition (T-Visa Manual) by the New York Anti-Trafficking Network, available at *http://aaldef.org/docs/T-visa-manual-3rd-ed%281208%29.pdf*;[17] (2) "A Guide for Legal Advocates Providing Services to Victims of Trafficking" by Legal Aid Foundation

[11] 8 CFR §214.11(g) (2014).

[12] *Id.*

[13] 8 CFR §214.11(g)(2) (2014).

[14] 8 CFR §214.11(i)(1) (2014).

[15] *Id.*

[16] 8 CFR §214.11(c) (2014).

[17] (last visited Mar. 17, 2015).

of Los Angeles, available at *www.uscrirefugees.org/2010Website/5_Resources/5_4_For_Lawyers/5_4_3_Human_Trafficking_Resources/5_4_3_1_Human_Trafficking_Manuals/AGuidefor_LegalAdvocates.pdf*;[18] (3) *Meeting the Legal Needs of Human Trafficking Victims* (ABA 2009) by J. Bruggeman and E. Keyes, available at *www.americanbar.org/content/dam/aba/migrated/2011_build/domestic_violence/dv_trafficking.authcheckdam.pdf*;[19] and (4) Asista's webpage on T visas, available at *www.asistahelp.org/index.cfm?nodeID=23555&audienceID=1*.[20]

A T visa holder may confer derivative T status to a spouse, child, parent, and unmarried siblings under 18 years of age.[21] T visa holders also are eligible for employment authorization[22] and medical and social service benefits.[23] The annual cap on T visas is 5,000 per year.[24] A T visa is granted for four years.[25]

After three years of continuous physical presence in the United States in T-1 visa status, the T visa holder may seek adjustment of status to lawful permanent residence (LPR).[26] Note that even though all of the grounds of inadmissibility apply in considering eligibility for adjustment of status for T visa holders, there is a national interest waiver available that waives all but grounds related to national security, public charge, international child abduction, and renunciation of U.S. citizenship to avoid taxation.[27]

- ➢ **Practice Pointer**: For detailed descriptions of the procedures for filing an applicant for a T visa, see the regulations at 8 Code of Federal Regulations (CFR) §214.11(k)–(v). For detailed descriptions of T visa adjustment of status eligibility and procedures, see the regulations at 8 CFR §245.23.

---

[18] (last visited Mar. 17, 2015).

[19] (last visited Mar. 17, 2015).

[20] (last visited Mar. 17, 2015).

[21] INA §101(a)(15)(T); 8 USC §1101(a)(15)(T) (2012); *see also* 8 CFR §214.11(o)(1) (2014).

[22] INA §101(i)(2); 8 USC §1101(i)(2) (2012).

[23] VTVPA §§107(b)(1)(A)–(B), 114 Stat. 1475.

[24] INA §214(o)(2); 8 USC §1184(o)(2) (2012); 8 CFR §214.11(m) (2014).

[25] 8 CFR §§214.11(p)(1)–(2) (2014).

[26] 8 CFR §§214.11(p)(1)–(2), 245.23 (2014).

[27] *See* INA §212(d)(13)(B)(ii); 8 USC §1182(d)(13)(B)(ii) (2012); 8 CFR §§1212.16(b)(1), (c) (2014). Regulations regarding adjustment of status for T and U visa holders and their qualifying family members were issued in 2008. For more information, *see* U.S. Citizenship & Immigration Servs., Fact Sheet: U.S. Citizenship & Immigration Servs., Publishes New Rule for Nonimmigrant Victims of Human Trafficking and Specified Criminal Activity (Dec. 9, 2008), *available at www.uscis.org* (type in "Fact Sheet T U Visa" on the search box). For a more in-depth discussion of the T visa, see "INS Publishes Interim Rule Implementing 'T' Visa Requirements, Procedures for Trafficking Victims," 79 INTERPRETER RELEASES 173 (Feb. 4, 2002). A copy of Form I-914, Application for T Nonimmigrant Status, is *available at www.uscis.gov/files/form/i-914.pdf*.

➢ **Practice Pointer**: A trafficking victim also may meet the definition of refugee and qualify for asylum. See United Nations (U.N.) High Commissioner for Refugees (UNHCR), Guidelines on International Protection: The Application of Article 1A(2) of the 1951 Convention and/or 1967 Protocol Relating to the Status of Refugees to Victims of Trafficking and Persons at Risk of Being Trafficked (Apr. 2006).[28] See also UNHCR, Refugee Protection and Human Trafficking: Selected Legal Reference Materials (Dec. 2008); [29] UNHCR, Considerations on the Issue of Human Trafficking from the Perspective of International Refugee Law and UNHCR's Mandate (Mar. 2009);[30] and UNHCR, Human Trafficking and Refugee Protection: UNHCR's Perspective (Oct. 2009).[31]

B. U Visas

A "U" visa is a form of relief available to individuals who have been victims of qualifying criminal activity in violation of the laws of the United States.[32] Qualifying criminal activity may include rape, torture, trafficking, incest, domestic violence, sexual assault, abusive sexual contact, prostitution, sexual exploitation, stalking, female genital mutilation, being held hostage, peonage, involuntary servitude, slave trade, kidnapping, abduction, unlawful criminal restraint, false imprisonment, blackmail, extortion, manslaughter, murder, felonious assault, witness tampering, obstruction of justice, perjury, fraud in foreign labor contracting, and any attempt, conspiracy, other related crimes, or solicitation to commit any of these crimes.[33] The criminal activity must have violated the laws of the United States or occurred in the United States or U.S. territories.[34] In addition to the requirements for the type of criminal activity, individuals must demonstrate that they:

- Have been a victim of qualifying criminal activity;

---

[28] U.N. High Comm'r for Refugees, Guidelines on International Protection: The Application of Article 1A(2) of the 1951 Convention and/or 1967 Protocol Relating to the Status of Refugees to Victims of Trafficking and Persons at Risk of Being Trafficked (Apr. 2006), available at *www.unhcr.org/443b626b2.html.*

[29] *Id.*

[30] *Id.*

[31] *Id.*

[32] INA §101(a)(15)(U).

[33] INA §101(a)(15)(U)(iii). See U.S. Citizenship & Immigration Servs., Memorandum from Michael Aytes on Applications for U Nonimmigrant Status; Revisions to Adjudicator's Field Manual (AFM) Chapter 39 (AFM Update AD06-11) (Jan. 6, 2006), *published on* AILA InfoNet Doc. No. 06011763 (*posted* Jan. 17, 2006), available at *www.uscis.gov/sites/default/files/U.S. Citizenship & Immigration Servs.,/Laws/Memoranda/Static_Files_Memoranda/Archives%201998-2008/2006/unonimms010606.pdf.*

[34] INA §101(a)(15)(U)(i)(IV).

- Suffered substantial physical or mental abuse as a result of having been a victim of qualifying criminal activity;
- Possess information concerning the criminal activity; and
- Have been helpful, are helpful, or are likely to be helpful to law enforcement, prosecutors, or other authorities who investigate and prosecute criminal activity.[35]

In considering whether physical or mental abuse is "substantial," adjudicators will consider a number of factors including, but not limited to: the nature of the injury inflicted or suffered; the severity of the perpetrator's conduct, the severity of the harm suffered; the duration of the infliction of the harm, and the extent to which there is permanent or serious harm to the appearance, health, or physical or mental soundness of the victim, including aggravation of preexisting conditions.[36] If a single act alone does not rise to the level of substantial physical or mental abuse, a series of acts may be considered together.[37]

> ➢ **Practice Pointer**: The factor, "aggravation of preexisting conditions" is comparable to the "eggshell" doctrine in tort law that holds a defendant liable for the plaintiff's unforeseeable and uncommon reactions to or injuries from the defendant's tortious activity. Practitioners may be able to use the tort law in their states to develop analogous supporting arguments.

To possess credible and reliable information concerning the criminal activity, the applicant must have knowledge of details and specific facts regarding the criminal activity.[38] If the victim has not yet reached age 16, or is incapacitated or incompetent, however, a parent, guardian, or "next friend" may possess the information regarding the qualifying crime.[39]

Like the T visa, an applicant's primary evidence that he or she has been or is likely to be helpful to law enforcement or prosecutors is a certification from the certifying law enforcement agency that the applicant has been helpful, is being helpful, or is likely to be helpful in the investigation or prosecution of the qualifying criminal activity, and since the initiation of cooperation, has not refused or failed to provide information and assistance that is reasonably requested.[40] If the applicant is not yet 16 years old, or is incapacitated or incompetent, however, a parent, guardian, or "next friend" may provide the required assistance.[41]

---

[35] INA §101(a)(15)(U)(i)(I)-(III); 8 CFR §214.14(b) (2014).

[36] 8 CFR §214.14(b)(1) (2014).

[37] *Id.*

[38] 8 CFR §214.14(b)(2) (2014).

[39] *Id.*

[40] 8 CFR §214.14(b)(3) (2014).

[41] *Id.*

> **Practice Pointer**: For a comprehensive compilation of U visa resources and guidance for determining eligibility and understanding the procedures for seeking U nonimmigrant status, see Asista's webpage on U visas, *www.asistahelp.org/en/access_the_clearinghouse/u_visa/*.[42] A fantastic guide to U visa legal standards and procedures is the Immigrant Legal Resource Center's book, *The U Visa: Obtaining Status by Immigrant Victims of Crime*, *www.ilrc.org/publications/the-u-visa*.[43]

After many years of waiting,[44] the much anticipated U visa regulations were published on September 17, 2007, and went into effect on October 17, 2007.[45] A correction to these regulations was published on September 27, 2007, which provided that there is no filing fee for a U visa application.[46] Prior to issuance of the U visa regulations, "interim" U nonimmigrant relief was available to U visa applicants.[47]

To apply for U nonimmigrant status, an applicant must file the following forms and documentation with USCIS:[48]

- Form I-918, Petition for U Nonimmigrant Status;

---

[42] (last visited Mar. 17, 2015). *See also* U Visa Toolkit for Law Enforcement Agencies and Prosecutors, *http://iwp.legalmomentum.org/reference/additional-materials/immigration/u-visa/tools/police-prosecutors/U-visa_toolkit_August_2011.pdf* (last visited Apr. 3, 2015); Womenslaw.org, *www.womenslaw.org/laws_state_type.php?id=10271&state_code=US* (last visited Mar. 29, 2015); USCIS, *Victims of Criminal Activity: U Nonimmigrant Status*, *www.uscis.gov/humanitarian/victims-human-trafficking-other-crimes/victims-criminal-activity-u-nonimmigrant-status/victims-criminal-activity-u-nonimmigrant-status* (last visited Mar. 29, 2015).

[43] (last visited Apr. 2, 2015).

[44] Prior to the publication of the regulations, in response to the U.S. Department of Homeland Security's (DHS) failure to issue them for almost seven years, organizations assisting U visa applicants had filed a lawsuit seeking the issuance of regulations. *See* Compl., *Catholic Charities CYO v. Chertoff*, C07-01307-PJH (N.D. Cal. Mar. 6, 2007). A copy of the complaint is *available at http://vocesunidas.org/downloads/3-6-07UVisaComplaint-Updated.pdf*.

[45] New Classification for Victims of Criminal Activity; Eligibility for the U Nonimmigrant Status, 72 Fed. Reg. 53013 (Sept. 17, 2007).

[46] New Classification for Victims of Criminal Activity; Eligibility for ''U'' Nonimmigrant Status; Correction, 72 Fed. Reg. 54813 (Sept. 27, 2007).

[47] Those who received interim U relief were encouraged to apply for U nonimmigrant status within 180 days of the issuance of the regulations. The summary to the U visa regulations states: "Aliens who have been granted interim relief from U.S. Citizenship & Immigration Servs. are encouraged to file for U nonimmigrant status within 180 days of the effective date of this interim rule. U.S. Citizenship & Immigration Servs. will no longer issue interim relief upon the effective date of this rule; however, if the alien has properly filed a petition for U nonimmigrant status, but U.S. Citizenship & Immigration Servs. has not yet adjudicated that petition, interim relief will be extended until U.S. Citizenship & Immigration Servs. completes its adjudication of the petition." 72 Fed. Reg. 53013, 53014 (Sept. 17, 2007). *See* 8 CFR §214.14(c)(6) (2014).

[48] 8 CFR §214.14(c)(1) (2014) (stating that U.S. Citizenship & Immigration Servs. has sole jurisdiction over all petitions for U nonimmigrant status). U.S. Citizenship & Immigration Servs. accepts all U visa petition filings at its Vermont Service Center.

- Biometrics fee check or money order in the amount of $85, made payable to "U.S. Department of Homeland Security;"
- Form I-918, Supplement B, U Nonimmigrant Status Certification, signed by a designated certifying official within the six months immediately preceding submission of the U visa petition to USCIS;
- Any additional evidence regarding the qualifying crime, the physical or mental abuse suffered, the victim's helpfulness to the certifying agency, and the location of the crime;
- A statement by the victim regarding the facts of the victimization and addressing all eligibility requirements for U nonimmigrant status;
- Form I-192, Application for Advance Permission to Enter as Nonimmigrant in accordance with 8 CFR §212.17, if the applicant is inadmissible (a waiver exists under INA §212(d)(13) for all grounds of inadmissibility except for those related to Nazi persecution and genocide);[49]
- Form I-918, Supplement A, Petition for Qualifying Family Member of U-1 Recipient, if the U visa petitioner has qualifying family members;
- Evidence of the qualifying familial relationship; and
- Form I-192, Application for Advance Permission to Enter as Nonimmigrant in accordance with 8 CFR §212.17, if the qualifying family member is inadmissible.[50]

Since USCIS has sole jurisdiction over all U visa petitions, an individual who is in INA §240 removal proceedings still must file his or her petition and supporting documentation directly with USCIS.[51] Even an individual who already has been ordered removed following Immigration and Nationality Act (INA) §240 removal proceedings must file his or her U visa petition directly with USCIS.[52] Immigration judges (IJs) may, however, maintain jurisdiction over I-192 waiver applications.[53]

> ➢ **Practice Pointer**: Practitioners whose clients are in removal proceedings should assist their clients in seeking agreement by U.S. Immigration and Customs Enforcement (ICE) counsel to, as a matter of discretion, file a joint motion to terminate proceedings without prejudice or a motion for administrative closure while the U visa petition is being considered by USCIS. If a client has already been ordered removed, practitioners may want to consider seeking a stay of removal from ICE

---

[49] 8 CFR §§214.14(c)(1), (2)(i)–(iv) (2014).

[50] 8 CFR §214.14(f)(2)–(3) (2014) .

[51] 8 CFR §214.14(c)(1)(i) (2014).

[52] 8 CFR §214.14(c)(1)(ii) (2014).

[53] For example, in the case of an LPR in removal proceedings, a practitioner could submit an I-192 waiver before the IJ. If it is approved, the practitioner could seek termination of the proceedings and then file a U visa petition with USCIS.

so that the removal order is not executed as the client is awaiting adjudication of his or her U visa petition. Upon approval of the U visa petition, practitioners should assist their clients in filing motions to reopen and terminate their prior proceedings based on their valid U visa status. Given the time and numerical limitations for motions to reopen, practitioners should seek agreement by ICE to join in the motion to reopen.[54]

The visa is granted for up to four years in the aggregate.[55] After three years of continuous physical presence in U nonimmigrant status in the United States, the U visa holder may apply to adjust status to lawful permanent residence.[56] Only 10,000 U-1 visas may be issued per year.[57] Due to this annual cap, it could take years for a U visa to be adjudicated. However, while U visa petitions are pending, USCIS places U visa petitions on a waiting list and grants them deferred action or parole.[58] This enables these U visa petitioners to apply for work authorization while waiting for additional U visas to become available.[59]

U-1 visa holders may petition for their qualifying family members to receive derivative U nonimmigrant status – spouses, children, parents (if the U-1 visa holder is under 21), and unmarried siblings under age 18.[60] These family members may accompany or follow-to-join the U-1 visa holder if they meet the eligibility criteria set forth in the regulations at 8 CFR §214.14(f)(1).[61] U visa holders and their derivative family members are employment authorized incident to their U nonimmigrant status, and USCIS will automatically issue an employment authorization document (EAD) to U visa grantees who are physically present in the United States.[62] U visa derivatives who follow-to-join the principal U visa holder, however, must apply for an EAD after they have arrived in the United States.

- **Practice Pointer**: For detailed descriptions of the procedures for filing an application for a U visa and petitioning for qualifying family members, see the regulations at 8 CFR §§214.14(c), (f). For detailed

[54] 8 CFR §214.14(c)(5)(i) (2014).

[55] 8 CFR §214.14(g) (2014).

[56] 8 CFR §245.24(b) (2014).

[57] INA §214(o)(2); 8 CFR §214.14(d)(1) (2014). There is no cap for family members deriving status from the principal applicant, such as spouses, children, or other eligible family members.

[58] USCIS, *Victims of Criminal Activity: U Nonimmigrant Status*, *available at www.uscis.gov/humanitarian/victims-human-trafficking-other-crimes/victims-criminal-activity-u-nonimmigrant-status/victims-criminal-activity-u-nonimmigrant-status* (last visited Apr. 3, 2015).

[59] *Id.*

[60] INA §101(a)(15)(U)(ii); 8 CFR §214.14(f)(1) (2014).

[61] *See* 8 CFR §214.14(f)(2) (2014) for a detailed description of the filing procedures for family members.

[62] 8 CFR §§214.14(c)(7), (f)(7) (2014).

descriptions of U visa adjustment of status eligibility and procedures, see the regulations at 8 CFR §245.24.

II. Special Immigrants

A special immigrant is a person who qualifies for lawful permanent resident status under special programs. Individuals who meet the eligibility standards of the various special immigrant programs may seek special immigrant status by completing and signing Form I-360, and then submitting that form with the correct filing fee and supporting documentation to the relevant USCIS address listed on the I-360 instructions.[63] Upon approval of an I-360 petition, special immigrants may apply for adjustment of status under INA §245 and receive lawful permanent resident status if they are eligible. Below is a description of the special immigrant programs most relevant to victims of persecution and torture.

A. Special Immigrant Juvenile Status

A noncitizen juvenile may be eligible for lawful permanent residence pursuant to Special Immigrant Juvenile Status (SIJS) if he or she is present in the United States and meets the following requirements:

- He or she must be a dependent of the juvenile court or the court must have legally committed the child to, or placed him or her under the custody of, an agency or department of a state, or an individual or entity appointed by a state or juvenile court;[64]
- A state or juvenile judge must issue a court finding that the child's reunification with one or both parents is not viable due to abuse, neglect, or abandonment, or a similar basis under state law; and
- A state or juvenile judge has determined that it is not in the juvenile's best interest to be returned to the juvenile's or his or her parents' previous country of nationality or country of last habitual residence.[65]

  > **Practice Pointer**: For case law and guidance for interpreting the "one or both parents" language in the SIJS requirements, see Michelle Mendez and Martin Gauto's article, "SIJS and the 'One or Both' Parents Language," available at *https://cliniclegal.org/resources/articles-clinic/sijs-and-one-or-both-parents-language.*[66]

---

[63] *See* U.S. Citizenship & Immigration Servs., I-360, Petition for Amerasian, Widow(er), or Special Immigrant, *available at www.uscis.gov/i-360* (last visited Mar. 18, 2015).

[64] This includes children in dependency, guardianship/probate as well as delinquency proceedings.

[65] INA §101(a)(27(J), as amended by the Trafficking Victims Protection Reauthorization Act of 2008, Pub. L. 110-457. The statutory changes made by the TVPRA of 2008 supersede portions of the CFR relating to SIJS at 7 CFR 204.11.

[66] (last visited Apr. 3, 2015).

In order to file an I-360 petition for SIJS, an individual must first have a state court order that contains specific findings. The state court must decide: (1) to declare the individual a dependent of the court or to legally place the individual with a state agency, a private agency, or a private person; (2) it is not in the individual's best interest to return to his or her home country; and (3) he or she cannot be reunited with a parent because of abuse, abandonment, neglect, or similar reasons under state law.[67] The juvenile court order submitted with an I-360 petition for SIJS must use the new statutory language, "reunification with one or both parents is not viable," rather than the prior language.[68]

Upon receipt of a state court order, the individual may be eligible for SIJS if: (1) he or she is under 21 years old on the date of filing the I-360 petition; (2) the state court order is valid and in effect on the date of filing the I-360 petition and when USCIS makes a decision on the application, *unless the individual "aged out" of the state court's jurisdiction due to no fault of his or her own*; (3) the individual is unmarried (including a child whose marriage ended because of annulment, death, or divorce) at the time of filing the I-360 and at the time of adjudication by USCIS; and (4) the individual is inside the United States at the time of filing Form I-360.[69]

➢ **Practice Pointer**: With regard to the second requirement above, in 2014, certain USCIS offices began denying I-360 petitions for SIJS for children between the ages of 18 and 21. They reasoned that, at the time the I-360 was filed, the children were no longer under the jurisdiction of the state court that issued the predicate order. This is because in certain states where the age of majority is 18, the state court's jurisdiction will terminate automatically when a child turns 18 (Massachusetts, for example). The Center for Human Rights & Constitutional Law sued USCIS claiming that this practice was in violation of the nationwide *Perez-Olano* settlement agreement,[70] and USCIS rescinded its policy,

---

[67] *See* U.S. Citizenship & Immigration Servs., Eligibility Status for SIJ, *available at www.uscis.gov/green-card/special-immigrant-juveniles/eligibility-sij-status/eligibility-status-sij* (last visited Mar. 18, 2015).

[68] USCIS Memorandum, Donald Neufeld and Pearl Chang, "Trafficking Victims Protection Reauthorization Act of 2008: Special immigrant Juvenile Status Provisions" HQOPS 70, 8.5 p.2 (Mar. 24, 2009). Note that the previous language stated that the juvenile was "eligible for long-term foster care."

[69] *See* U.S. Citizenship & Immigration Servs., Eligibility Status for SIJ, *available at www.uscis.gov/green-card/special-immigrant-juveniles/eligibility-sij-status/eligibility-status-sij* (last visited Mar. 18, 2015).

[70] Center for Human Rights and Constitutional Law, *Perez-Olano Case*, *available at http://immigrantchildren.org/Perez_Olano_Case.html* (last visited Apr. 2, 2015). *See also Perez-Olano, et al. v. Holder, et al.*, Case No. CV 05-3604 (C.D. Cal.), Settlement Agreement, *available at www.uscis.gov/sites/default/files/USCIS/Laws/Legal%20Settlement%20Notices%20and%20Agreements/Perez-Olano%20v%20Holder/Signed_Settlement_Agreement.pdf* (last visited Apr. 2, 2015); USCIS, Settlement Agreement in *Perez-Olano, et al. v. Holder, et al., available at www.uscis.gov/laws/legal-*

Continued

confirming that USCIS may not deny I-360 petitions filed after a child ages out of state court jurisdiction.

➢ **Practice Pointer**: For detailed guidance on seeking Special Immigrant Juvenile Status (SIJS), see the Immigrant Legal Resource Center's issue page at *www.ilrc.org/resources/special-immigrant-juvenile-status-sijs*.[71] Other helpful resources are:

- (1) The SIJS Caseworker's Toolkit for Children in Federal Custody, available at *www.brycs.org/sijs-toolkit/*;[72]
- (2) the Immigrant Legal Resource Center's "Immigration Benchbook for Juvenile and Family Court Judges," *www.uscrirefugees.org/2010Website/5_Resources/5_4_For_Lawyers/5_4_2_Special_Immigrant_Juvenile_Status/5_4_2_1_Manuals/2010_sijs_benchbook.pdf*;[73]
- (3) U.S. Committee for Refugees and Immigrants' "Introduction and Overview to Special Immigrant Juvenile Status," available at *http://uscrirefugees.org/2010Website/5_Resources/5_4_For_Lawyers/5_4_2_Special_Immigrant_Juvenile_Status/5_4_2_1_Manuals/2010_sijs-chapter_03-sijs_overview.pdf*;[74] and
- (4) Catholic Legal Immigration Network, Inc.'s "Toolkit for Working with Unaccompanied Children," available at *https://cliniclegal.org/resources/unaccompanied-migrant-children-toolkit*.[75]

B. Special Immigrant Iraqi and Afghan Translators or U.S. Government Employees

Special immigrant status may be available to Afghan and Iraqi nationals, both outside and inside the United States, who worked directly for the U.S. military as translators or interpreters in Afghanistan and Iraq.[76] This program remains active.[77]

Previously, additional programs were available for Iraqi and Afghan nationals who have been employed by or on behalf of the U.S. government in Iraq and

---

settlement-notices/settlement-agreement-perez-olano-et-al-v-holder-et-al-case-no-cv-05-3604-us-district-court-central-district-california (last visited Apr. 2, 2015).

[71] (last visited Apr. 3, 2015).

[72] (last visited Mar. 18, 2015).

[73] (last visited Mar. 18, 2015).

[74] (last visited Mar. 18, 2015).

[75] (last visited Mar. 18, 2015).

[76] National Defense Authorization Act for Fiscal Year 2006, Pub. L. 109-163, 119 Stat. 3136, as amended by Pub. L. No. 110-36, 121 Stat. 227. *See* U.S. Citizenship & Immigration Servs., Fact Sheet, *Special Immigrant Status Now Available for Civilian Translators* (Aug. 3, 2006), *available at www.uscis.gov/files/pressrelease/TranslatorExpansionFS02Jul07.pdf*.

[77] *See* USCIS, Iraqi and Afghan SIV Programs, *available at http://travel.state.gov/content/visas/english/immigrate/types/iraqi-afghan-translator.html* (last visited Apr. 3, 2015).

Afghanistan for a period of at least one year. While the program for Afghan nationals has been extended and remains active, the program for Iraqi nationals has not been extended.[78] Iraqi nationals who worked for a period of at least one year must have applied for Chief of Mission approval by September 30, 2014.[79] Afghan nationals who worked for a period of at least one year must apply for Chief of Mission approval by December 31, 2015. The program will end when all 4,000 of the visas allocated have been issued or on March 31, 2017.[80]

Eligible individuals under these programs and their family members may gain admission to the United States and apply for permanent residency through the special immigrant petition process.[81] If such individuals' I-360 petitions are approved, USCIS will forward the approved petition to the Department of Statue for consular processing of the special immigrant visa. If the individual is already inside the United States, however, he or she may file an I-485, Application to Register Permanent Residence or Adjust Status upon approval of the I-360 petition.[82]

III. Temporary Protected Status

In 1990, the United States enacted a temporary protected status (TPS) provision of the INA, which permits the Attorney General (AG) to grant temporary safe haven in

[78] *See* USCIS, Iraqi and Afghan SIV Programs, *available at http://travel.state.gov/content/visas/english/immigrate/types/iraqi-afghan-translator.html* (last visited Apr. 3, 2015).

[79] National Defense Authorization Act for Fiscal Year 2008, Pub. L. 110-181, §1244, as amended by Pub. L. 110-242. *See* Memorandum from Donald Neufeld on Special Immigrant Visas for Certain Iraqis under Section 1244 of Public Law 110-181, the National Defense Authorization Act for Fiscal Year 2008, as amended, *available at www.uscis.gov/sites/default/files/U.S. Citizenship & Immigration Servs.,/Laws/Memoranda/Static_Files_Memoranda/Archives%201998-2008/2008/ad08-17.pdf* (last visited Mar. 18, 2015); U.S. Citizenship & Immigration Servs., Green Card for an Iraqi Who Assisted the U.S. Government, *available at www.uscis.gov/green-card/green-card-through-job/green-card-through-special-categories-jobs/green-card-iraqi-who-assisted-us-government* (last visited Mar. 18, 2015); USCIS, Special Immigrant Visas for Iraqis – Who Were Employed By/On Behalf of the U.S. Government, *available at http://travel.state.gov/content/visas/english/immigrate/types/iraqis-work-for-us.html* (last visited Apr. 3, 2015).

[80] *See* USCIS, Iraqi and Afghan SIV Programs, *available at http://travel.state.gov/content/visas/english/immigrate/types/iraqi-afghan-translator.html* (last visited Apr. 3, 2015); USCIS, Special Immigrant Visas for Afghans – Who Were Employed By/On Behalf of the U.S. Government, available at *http://travel.state.gov/content/visas/english/immigrate/types/afghans-work-for-us.html* (last visited Apr. 3, 2015).

[81] *See* U.S. Citizenship & Immigration Servs., I-360, Petition for Amerasian, Widow(er), or Special Immigrant, *supra* note 63.

[82] U.S. Citizenship & Immigration Servs., Green Card for an Afghan or Iraqi Translator, *available at www.uscis.gov/green-card/green-card-through-job/green-card-through-special-categories-jobs/green-card-afghan-or-iraqi-translator* (last visited Mar. 18, 2015); U.S. Citizenship & Immigration Servs., Green Card for an Iraqi Who Assisted the U.S. Government, available at *www.uscis.gov/green-card/green-card-through-job/green-card-through-special-categories-jobs/green-card-iraqi-who-assisted-us-government* (last visited Mar. 18, 2015).

the United States to foreign nationals.[83] The AG may designate TPS for nationals of any country that is experiencing: (1) an ongoing armed conflict posing serious threat to personal safety; (2) an environmental disaster resulting in a substantial, but temporary, disruption of living conditions; or (3) extraordinary and temporary conditions that prevent nationals from returning in safety.[84] The current countries designated for TPS include El Salvador, Guinea, Haiti, Honduras, Liberia, Nicaragua, Sierra Leone, Somalia, Sudan, South Sudan, and Syria.[85]

TPS is only granted to individuals who are already physically present in the United States on the date the designation is made by the AG. It is generally not available to individuals who arrive after the date of initial designation. Exceptions to this general rule over time have been re-designations of Burundi, Haiti, Liberia, Kosovo, Sierra Leone, and Sudan, which allowed individuals arriving after the initial designation date to apply for TPS.[86]

Although the specific requirements vary depending on the designated country, an individual may be granted TPS if he or she:

- Is a national of a country designated by the AG;
- Has been continuously physically present in the United States since the effective date of the most recent designation;
- Has been continuously residing in the United States since a date set by the AG;
- Is admissible as an immigrant, except as provided for under 8 CFR §§244.3, 1244.3;
- Has not been convicted of a felony or two or more misdemeanors in the United States and does not fall within one of the mandatory bars to withholding of removal; and
- Timely registers for TPS or, if in valid status during the registration period, registers within 60 days from the expiration of such status.[87]

  ➢ **Practice Pointer**: Warning! A parent's continuous physical presence and continuous residence in the United States cannot be imputed to a child for purposes of establishing the child's eligibility for TPS.[88]

---

[83] INA §244; 8 USC §1254a (2012).

[84] INA §244(b)(1); 8 USC §1254a(b)(1) (2012).

[85] *See* U.S. Citizenship & Immigration Servs., *Countries Currently Designated for TPS*, *available at* *www.uscis.gov/humanitarian/temporary-protected-status-deferred-enforced-departure/temporary-protected-status#Countries%20Currently%20Designated%20for%20TPS* (last visited Mar. 18, 2015).

[86] *See, e.g.*, USCIS, *TPS Designated Country: Haiti*, *available at www.uscis.gov/humanitarian/temporary-protected-status-deferred-enforced-departure/tps-designated-country-haiti* (last visited Apr. 3, 2015).

[87] *See* 8 CFR §§244.2, 1244.2 (2014).

[88] *Matter of Duarte-Luna & Luna*, 26 I&N Dec. 324 (BIA 2014).

To apply for TPS, qualified individuals should complete a Form I-821, Application for Temporary Protected Status, together with a Form I-765, Application for Employment Authorization. Applicants should attach the following evidence: (1) identity and nationality evidence to show they are a national of a country designated for TPS (passport, birth certificate, national ID card with photograph of the applicant, etc.); (2) date of entry evidence to show when they entered the United States (passport, I-94 card, entry stamp, etc.); (3) evidence of continuous residence in the United States since the date specified for the relevant country (evidence of home addresses, employment records, school records, utility and other monthly bills, hospital or medical records, affidavits, etc.); and (4) certified English translations for any documents that are not in English.[89] Whether filing and/or biometrics fees are required depends on the specific circumstances of the applicant, as well as whether the application is the initial filing or subsequent re-filing. Applicants should carefully follow the instructions on the Form I-821 while completing the I-821, compiling the forms and documentation, determining the filing and biometrics fees, and mailing the application to USCIS.[90] The forms, any filing and/or biometrics fees, and supporting documentation should be filed with the USCIS address listed on the I-821's instructions.[91]

- **Practice Pointer**: For a detailed description of how USCIS processes applications for TPS, see USCIS's website at *www.uscis.gov/humanitarian/temporary-protected-status-deferred-enforced-departure/temporary-protected-status#Application%20Process%20When%20Filing%20for%20TPS%20for%20the%20First%20Time*.[92]
- **Practice Pointer**: If an individual is in removal proceedings and is eligible for TPS, Practitioners should notify DHS that their client is *prima facie* eligible for TPS and ask DHS to agree to administratively close or terminate proceedings.[93] It may also be possible to file a TPS application before the IJ for late initial registration.[94]

---

[89] *See* U.S. Citizenship & Immigration Servs., What to File, *available at www.uscis.gov/humanitarian/temporary-protected-status-deferred-enforced-departure/temporary-protected-status#What%20to%20File* (last visited Mar. 18, 2015).

[90] *See* U.S. Citizenship & Immigration Servs., Instructions for Application for Temporary Protected Status, *available at www.uscis.gov/sites/default/files/files/form/i-821instr.pdf* (last visited Mar. 18, 2015).

[91] *Id.*

[92] (last visited Mar. 18, 2015).

[93] *See* INS Memorandum from Deputy General Counsel Carpenter on Administrative Closure When Alien is Prima Facie Eligible for TPS or DED (Feb. 7, 2002), AILA InfoNet Doc. No. 02040338 (*posted* Apr. 3, 2002); *Matter of Barrientos*, 24 I&N Dec. 100 (BIA 2007).

[94] *See Matter of Echevarria*, 25 I&N Dec. 512 (BIA 2011).

If USCIS approves the TPS application, USCIS will issue I-821 and I-765 approval notices, as well as an EAD, if requested.[95] On the other hand, if USCIS denies the TPS application, USCIS will issue a written notice, explaining the reasons for the denial.[96] The applicant may appeal the denial to the USCIS Administrative Appeals Office by preparing and filing a Form I-290B.[97] An applicant for TPS also may seek *de novo* review by an IJ in removal proceedings, regardless of whether all appeal rights before USCIS have been exhausted.[98] Usually, this occurs when "notarios" or other individuals unauthorized to practice law have been involved and the application has been deemed abandoned. When a TPS application is deemed abandoned, USCIS will issue a Notice to Appear.[99]

Individuals granted TPS are permitted to remain in the United States and to obtain employment authorization during the period designated by the AG and any extensions of that period.[100] They also may enjoy the privilege to travel abroad with prior consent by applying for and obtaining an advance parole travel document pursuant to 8 CFR §244.15.[101] For purposes of adjustment of status under INA §245, individuals in valid TPS status are considered as being in, and maintaining, lawful status as a nonimmigrant.[102] Therefore, depending on the individual TPS holder's specific circumstances, he or she eventually may become eligible to adjust status to lawful permanent resident.[103]

- **Practice Pointer**: In 2012, the BIA held that an individual who leaves the United States temporarily pursuant to a grant of advance parole does not make a "departure … from the United States" within the meaning of INA §§212(a)(9)(B)(i)(II), and therefore, would not trigger the three and ten-year unlawful presence bars by leaving.[104] Thus, TPS holders who initially entered without inspection who are married to U.S. citizens may be able to adjust status to lawful permanent residence following a grant

---

[95] *See* U.S. Citizenship & Immigration Servs., *Application Process, available at www.uscis.gov/humanitarian/temporary-protected-status-deferred-enforced-departure/temporary-protected-status#Application%20Process%20When%20Filing%20for%20TPS%20for%20the%20First%20Time* (last visited Mar. 18, 2015).

[96] *Id.*

[97] *See* U.S. Citizenship & Immigration Servs., *Appealing a Denial, available at www.uscis.gov/humanitarian/temporary-protected-status-deferred-enforced-departure/temporary-protected-status#How%20to%20Appeal* (last visited Mar. 18, 2015); U.S. Citizenship & Immigration Servs., I-290B, Notice of Appeal or Motion, *available at www.uscis.gov/i-290b* (last visited Mar. 18, 2015).

[98] *Matter of Lopez-Aldana*, 25 I&N Dec. 49 (BIA 2009).

[99] *See, e.g., Matter of Henriquez Rivera*, 25 I&N Dec. 575 (BIA 2011).

[100] 8 CFR §244.10(f)(2)(i)-(ii) (2014).

[101] 8 CFR §244.10(f)(2)(iii) (2014).

[102] 8 CFR §244.10(f)(2)(iv) (2014).

[103] *See* INA §245(a).

[104] *Matter of Arrabally & Yerrabelly*, 25 I&N Dec. 771 (BIA 2012).

of advance parole and subsequent re-entry to the United States on that document. Of course, practitioners would need to fully analyze the individual's eligibility for adjustment of status and other potential inadmissibility grounds prior to advising this as a course of action for their clients.

Even if an individual does not have grounds to adjust status to lawful permanent residence, it has been said by some that there is nothing more permanent than TPS. Liberians, for example, who were first granted TPS in 1991,[105] previously had Deferred Enforced Departure through September 30, 2016,[106] and recently received a TPS extension due to an outbreak of the Ebola virus.[107]

- **Practice Pointer**: Recipients of TPS may affirmatively apply for asylum while maintaining their TPS status.[108] TPS recipients may also apply for asylum after their TPS status terminates or expires. If, however, a TPS recipient has been in the United States for more than one year, he or she should file for asylum within a "reasonable period" after his or her TPS status terminates or expires and argue that the termination or expiration of TPS is an extraordinary circumstance directly relating to the delay in filing the asylum application, and therefore, the application is not barred by the one-year filing deadline.[109]

IV. Humanitarian Parole

When an otherwise inadmissible individual needs temporary admission to the United States for urgent humanitarian reasons or for significant public benefit, the DHS secretary may provide that individual with temporary "humanitarian" parole.[110] Decisions to grant humanitarian parole are completely discretionary and are made by

---

[105] *See* White House Memorandum for The Secretary of Homeland Security Re: Deferred Enforced Departure for Liberians (Mar. 23, 2009), *available at www.whitehouse.gov/the_press_office/Presidential-Memorandum-Regarding-Deferred-Enforced-Departure-for-Liberians*.

[106] *See* U.S. Citizenship & Immigration Servs., DED Granted Country – Liberia, *available at www.uscis.gov/humanitarian/temporary-protected-status-deferred-enforced-departure/ded-granted-country-liberia/ded-granted-country-liberia* (last visited Mar. 18, 2015).

[107] *See* USCIS, DHS Announces Temporary Protected Status Designations for Liberia, Guinea, and Sierra Leone, available at *www.uscis.gov/news/dhs-announces-temporary-protected-status-designations-liberia-guinea-and-sierra-leone* (last visited Apr. 3, 2015).

[108] *See* ch. 3.2.

[109] *See* 8 CFR §§208.4(a)(5)(iv), 1208.4(a)(5)(iv) (2014) (providing that an "extraordinary circumstance" may include maintaining TPS status "until a reasonable period before the filing of the asylum application").

[110] INA §212(d)(5)(A); 8 USC §1182(d)(5)(A) (2012); *see e.g., Pllumi v. Att'y Gen.*, 642 F.3d 155, 162 (3d Cir. 2011).

the secretary on a case-by-case basis.[111] The grant of parole lasts only as long as the emergency situation and may not exceed one year.[112] Humanitarian parole is most frequently granted for critical medical treatment, attendance at funerals, family reunification, and comparable emergency situations.[113] Humanitarian parole may also be granted to refugees or asylees who travel outside of the United States and whose refugee travel documents expire.

> **Practice Pointer**: The Government Accountability Office (GAO) issued a report in February 2008 on the humanitarian parole process and offered recommendations for improving the process. See GAO, "Internal Controls for Adjudicating Humanitarian Parole Cases are Generally Effective, but Can Be Strengthened (Feb. 2008)," available at *www.gao.gov/new.items/d08282.pdf.* A chart of the adjudication process is found on page 10 of the report.

Humanitarian parole may only be requested for persons located outside the United States, and may be filed by the prospective parolee, a sponsoring relative, an attorney, or any other interested individual or organization.[114] Applicants for humanitarian parole must submit a Form I-131, Application for Travel Document, and a Form I-134, Affidavit of Support.[115] In addition, the applicant should include supporting evidence, including:

- Evidence that the applicant has sufficient resources or financial support so that he or she will not become a public charge while in the United States, including a statement of how and by whom medical care, housing, transportation, and other subsistence needs will be met for the applicant;

---

[111] INA §212(d)(5)(A); 8 USC §1182(d)(5)(A) (2012); *see also* Nina Bernstein, *A Contest of Suffering, With the U.S. as a Prize*, N.Y. TIMES, Oct. 14, 2005, at B1, *available at www.nytimes.com/2005/10/14/nyregion/14orphan.html?pagewanted=all&_r=0* (reporting that only 20 percent of the 6,718 applications for humanitarian parole were approved by DHS between 2000–05); *see e.g., Pllumi v. Att'y Gen.*, 642 F.3d 155, 162 (3d Cir. 2011) (recognizing that the unavailability and unwillingness of resources in his home country to treat his severe mental illness may create grounds for the BIA to grant humanitarian parole on remand); *Aguilar-Mejia v. Holder*, 616 F.3d 699, 705 (7th Cir. 2010) (noting that petitioner would not be treated for AIDs/HIV if he were returned and encouraging the Attorney General, "if asked by Aguilar–Mejia," to consider… "'humanitarian parole,' or any other discretionary remedy that may be granted on humanitarian grounds.").

[112] For more information in Humanitarian Parole, access the U.S. Citizenship & Immigration Servs. website at *www.uscis.gov/humanitarian/humanitarian-parole.*

[113] *See* USCIS, Humanitarian Parole Program, *available at www.uscis.gov/sites/default/files/USCIS/Resources/Resources%20for%20Congress/Humanitarian%20Parole%20Program.pdf* (last visited Apr. 3, 2015).

[114] *See* U.S. Citizenship & Immigration Servs., Humanitarian Parole, *available at www.uscis.gov/humanitarian/humanitarian-parole* (last visited Mar. 18, 2015).

[115] *Id. See* U.S. Citizenship & Immigration Servs., I-131, Application for Travel Document, *available at www.uscis.gov/i-131* (last visited Mar. 18, 2015); U.S. Citizenship & Immigration Servs., I-134, Affidavit of Support, *available at www.uscis.gov/i-134* (last visited Mar. 18, 2015).

- Evidence of the claimed circumstances that led the applicant to seek humanitarian parole and the length of time for which parole is requested (not to exceed one year);
- A statement of why a U.S. visa cannot be obtained in lieu of humanitarian parole, including evidence of previous attempts to obtain visas;
- Evidence of the relationship between the applicant and the sponsor; and
- Information about the sponsor, including his or her name, date, place of birth, address, citizenship or immigration status, occupation, and financial resources.[116]

If an attorney is filing the application for humanitarian parole on behalf of the parolee, a G-28, Notice of Entry of Appearance must be included with the application materials.[117] Additionally, there is a filing fee of $360 for seeking humanitarian parole pursuant to Form I-131.[118] A biometrics fee is not required; however, if a biometrics collection is necessary, the individual will be notified in writing by USCIS.[119] Currently, all requests for humanitarian parole must be submitted to the USCIS Dallas Lockbox.[120] Such requests are generally addressed within 120 days of receipt by USCIS.[121]

> ➢ **Practice Pointer**: It is essential for practitioners and applicants to review and follow the current I-131 instructions and check the USCIS website for up-to-date filing fee, filing address, and processing time information, as these frequently change.[122]

If parole is granted, the individual may enter the United States for the amount of time specified in the parole approval. On the other hand, if the request is denied, there is no appeal, as decisions regarding humanitarian parole are left solely to the discretion of the secretary of DHS.[123] However, if the applicant's circumstances change, a new application may be submitted as a new case for consideration. This requires another submission of the required forms, filing fee, and evidence.[124]

---

[116] *See* U.S. Citizenship & Immigration Servs., *Humanitarian Parole*, *supra* note 114.

[117] *Id. See* U.S. Citizenship & Immigration Servs., G-28, Notice of Entry of Appearance as Attorney or Accredited Representative, *available at www.uscis.gov/g-28* (last visited Mar. 18, 2015).

[118] U.S. Citizenship & Immigration Servs., Instructions for Application for Travel Document, at 10, *available at www.uscis.gov/sites/default/files/files/form/i-131instr.pdf* (last visited Mar. 18, 2015).

[119] *Id.* at 9–10.

[120] *See* U.S. Citizenship & Immigration Servs., *Humanitarian Parole*, *supra* note 114.

[121] *Id.*

[122] *See id.*; U.S. Citizenship & Immigration Servs., Instructions for Application for Travel Document, *available at www.uscis.gov/sites/default/files/files/form/i-131instr.pdf* (last visited Mar. 18, 2015).

[123] INA §212(d)(5)(A); U.S. Citizenship & Immigration Servs., *Humanitarian Parole*, *supra* note 114.

[124] U.S. Citizenship & Immigration Servs., *Humanitarian Parole*, *supra* note 114.

V. *ABC* Settlement

Salvadoran and Guatemalan nationals who registered for relief under the *American Baptist Churches v. Thornburgh*[125] (*ABC*) settlement agreement are provided with certain benefits and procedural protections during the processing of their asylum applications. The settlement agreement is the result of a suit filed in the U.S. District Court for the Northern District of California in 1985 against legacy Immigration and Naturalization Service (INS), the Executive Office for Immigration Review (EOIR), and the U.S. Department of State (DOS). The plaintiffs, a certified class of Guatemalan and Salvadoran nationals, alleged that legacy INS, EOIR, and DOS had discriminated against Salvadoran and Guatemalan asylum applicants. In 1990, the parties to the lawsuit reached a settlement, known as the *ABC* Settlement Agreement, which was approved by the court in 1991.

Under the terms of the settlement agreement, class members are entitled to a stay of deportation; administrative closure of pending immigration proceedings; an initial or *de novo* interview and adjudication by specially trained asylum officers; an adjudication pursuant to the asylum regulations published July 1, 1990; and employment authorization. Additionally, *ABC* class members may not be detained by DHS or removed from the United States while their claims are pending except under the limited circumstances noted below. *ABC* class members, however, may waive these rights.[126]

In 2007, the U.S. Court of Appeals for the Ninth Circuit considered what evidence is sufficient to demonstrate membership in the *ABC* class. The court found that a Guatemalan national who applied for asylum on the date the *ABC* settlement agreement was approved, who orally informed an immigration officer that he intended to apply for the new asylum program for Guatemalans, and who received work authorization six times in which he designated his eligibility as "Special Group: ABC" was sufficient evidence to show he was an *ABC* class member.[127]

> ➢ **Practice Pointer**: *ABC* class members were granted additional benefits under the Nicaraguan Adjustment and Central American Relief Act, which was signed into law on November 19, 1997. One of these benefits is not being subject to reinstatement of removal.[128]

---

[125] *Am. Baptist Churches (ABC) v. Thornburgh*, 760 F. Supp. 796 (N.D. Cal. 1991).

[126] *See, e.g.*, *Matter of Gutierrez-Lopez*, 21 I&N Dec. 479 (BIA 1996) (holding that class member may waive *ABC* benefits to reopen case to apply for adjustment of status).

[127] *Chaly-Garcia v. United States*, 508 F.3d 1201 (9th Cir. 2007). U.S. Citizenship & Immigration Servs., established a new policy after this case. *See* U.S. Citizenship & Immigration Servs., New Policy for *ABC* Registration Determinations after *Chaly-Garcia*, *available at www.uscis.gov* (at the search box, type in "ABC Registration Determinations After *Chaly-Garcia*").

[128] *See* INS Memorandum, Implementation of Amendment to the Legal Immigration Family Equity Act (LIFE) regarding applicability of INA section 241(a)(5) (reinstatement) to NACARA 203 beneficiaries (Feb. 22, 2001), *available at www.uscis.gov/sites/default/files/files/pressrelease/ncra_lfe.pdf* (last visited Apr. 3, 2015).

Salvadoran nationals who meet the following requirements are eligible for *ABC* class member benefits:

- Physical presence in the United States on or before September 19, 1990, (there is no continuous physical presence requirement);
- Submission of an *ABC* registration form or a TPS registration form (regardless of whether TPS was granted) to legacy INS between January 1 and October 30, 1991; and
- Submission of an application for asylum on or before January 31, 1996 (or, because of a two-week grace period granted by legacy INS, before February 16, 1996), *or* submission of an application after the cut-off date but within 90 days of receiving Notice 5, a specific notice form under the *ABC* Settlement Agreement.

Guatemalan nationals who meet the following requirements are eligible for *ABC* class member benefits:[129]

- Physical presence in the United States on or before October 1, 1990 (there is no requirement of continuous physical presence);
- Submission of an *ABC* registration form to legacy INS on or before December 31, 1991; and
- Submission of an application for asylum on or before January 3, 1995.

  - **Practice Pointer**: To verify if an individual is a member of the *ABC* class, send a fax to (703) 807-2438. While this fax is still in operation, it is unclear how often it is checked.

  - **Practice Pointer**: Currently, all *ABC* class members must use Form AR-11 to notify USCIS of any change of address. *ABC* class members also must notify the asylum office with jurisdiction over their asylum applications of any changes of address. USCIS closed the *ABC* Project post office box that it previously used for the approximately 240,000 class members to submit changes of address.[130]

ABC class members who would otherwise be eligible for benefits are excluded if they have been convicted of an aggravated felony, or if they were apprehended at the time of entry into the United States after December 19, 1990. A determination of

---

[129] *See* U.S. Citizenship & Immigration Servs. Fact Sheet, Guatemalan Asylum applicants in the Context of the *ABC* Settlement Agreement and Section 203 of the Nicaraguan Adjustment and Central American Relief Act (NACARA) (Feb. 28, 2007), *available at www.uscis.gov/files/pressrelease/GuatemalanAsylum022807.pdf.*

[130] *See* Important Announcement for Class Members of *American Baptist Churches v. Thornburgh* (*ABC*) Regarding Change of Address Notifications, Discontinuance of Form I–855, ABC Change of Address Form, and Permanent Closure of the ABC Project Post Office Box, 70 Fed. Reg. 45410 (Aug. 5, 2005); *see also* U.S. Citizenship & Immigration Servs., Press Release, Follow-Up Message: USCIS Announces New Address Change Procedures for *ABC* Class Members (Nov. 30, 2005), *published on* AILA InfoNet at Doc. No. 05120165 (*posted* Dec. 1, 2005).

whether an individual was apprehended at the time of entry may only be made by an asylum officer, and not by an IJ or the BIA.[131]

An *ABC* class member may only be detained if he or she:

- Has been convicted of a crime involving moral turpitude for which the sentence actually imposed exceeded a term of imprisonment of six months;
- Poses a national security risk; or
- Poses a threat to public safety.[132]

VI. Nicaraguan Adjustment and Central American Relief Act

On November 19, 1997, the Nicaraguan Adjustment and Central American Relief Act (NACARA)[133] was signed into law. NACARA provides relief from the harsh provisions of the Illegal Immigration Reform and Immigrant Responsibility Act (IIRAIRA)[134] for Central Americans from Nicaragua, El Salvador, and Guatemala, as well as for individuals from several other countries. Cuban and Nicaraguan nationals receive the most generous treatment under NACARA in the form of lawful permanent residency status for those who qualify.

Salvadoran and Guatemalan nationals, as well as nationals from the former Soviet Union, the former Yugoslavia, and other Eastern European countries, receive the benefit of having their claims for suspension of deportation adjudicated under former INA §244(a).[135] Section 244(a) had more generous provisions for calculating continuous physical presence and for establishing hardship. In addition, individuals who are eligible to apply for relief under NACARA are not subject to the annual cap of 4,000.[136] Such individuals are, however, barred from seeking judicial review of the determination by the AG of whether they meet the requirements set forth below.[137]

The AG has authorized asylum officers to make initial eligibility determinations regarding NACARA suspension claims for NACARA-eligible asylum-seekers and *ABC* class members with asylum applications pending before the Asylum Division. NACARA/*ABC* interviews are currently being conducted by asylum officers. If an asylum officer determines that a NACARA case should be referred to the

[131] *See Matter of Morales*, 21 I&N Dec. 130 (BIA 1995) (finding that the IJ and BIA lack jurisdiction to determine whether an *ABC* class member was apprehended at the time of entry for purposes of determining eligibility under the *ABC* Settlement Agreement).

[132] *Am. Baptist Churches v. Thornburgh*, 760 F. Supp. 796, 804 (N.D. Cal. 1991).

[133] Nicaraguan Adjustment and Central American Relief Act (NACARA), Pub. L. No. 105-100, 111 Stat. 2160, 2193–201 (1997).

[134] Illegal Immigration Reform and Immigrant Responsibility Act of 1996 (IIRAIRA), Pub. L. No. 104-208, div. C, 110 Stat. 3009, 3009–546 to 3009–724.

[135] NACARA §203(a)(1), 111 Stat. 2196–98.

[136] *See* this chapter at 6.9.2.

[137] NACARA §§202(f), 203(a)(1), 111 Stat. 2196–98.

immigration court, the case must first be referred to USCIS Asylum Headquarters for review in the following situations: (1) grants where the applicant may have engaged in persecution or human rights violations, but meets the burden of proof that he or she should not be barred as a persecutor;[138] (2) referrals involving individuals barred as a persecutor where the case may be publicized nationally or who may pose a threat to others; (3) all decisions where the applicant is otherwise eligible for relief but for a terrorist ground of inadmissibility for which an exemption is or may be available; and (4) a referral or approval involving an unusual legal issue.[139] Persons covered by NACARA who are in removal proceedings may apply to an immigration judge for adjustment of status or suspension of deportation.

- **Practice Pointer**: Final regulations implementing the adjustment of status provisions for Nicaraguan and Cuban nationals were issued in March 2000.[140] Interim regulations implementing the suspension of deportation and special rule cancellation of removal provisions for nationals of Guatemala, El Salvador, and former Soviet Bloc countries were issued in May 1999.[141]

Cuban nationals who entered the United States prior to December 1, 1995, were eligible for lawful permanent residence provided they applied for adjustment of status before April 1, 2000.[142] Spouses, minor children, or unmarried adult sons and daughters of Cuban nationals who adjusted status under this provision were also eligible for adjustment of status, regardless of their entry date, if they applied before April 1, 2000.[143]

Nicaraguan nationals who entered the United States prior to December 1, 1995, were eligible for lawful permanent residence provided they applied for adjustment of status before April 1, 2000.[144] Spouses, minor children, or unmarried adult sons and daughters of Nicaraguan nationals who adjusted under this provision were also

---

[138] *See Jose Santos Luna-Canales*, A094 142 206 (BIA Apr. 28, 2011) (unpublished) (finding that the respondent was not subject to the NACARA persecutor bar because he avoided combat while serving as a member of the DM-3 unit in the Salvadoran Army and because of his youth and lack of sophistication at the time), *available at www.scribd.com/doc/198853617/Jose-Santos-Luna-Canales-A094-142-206-BIA-April-28-2011.*

[139] U.S. Citizenship & Immigration Servs., Asylum Division, *Quality Assurance Referral Sheet* (revised Jan. 23, 2009), *published on* AILA InfoNet at Doc. No. 09012378 (*posted* Jan. 23, 2009).

[140] *See* Adjustment of Status for Certain Nationals of Nicaragua and Cuba, 65 Fed. Reg. 15846 (Mar. 24, 2000).

[141] *See* Suspension of Deportation and Special Rule Cancellation of Removal for Certain Nationals of Guatemala, El Salvador, and Former Soviet Bloc Countries, 64 Fed. Reg. 27856–81 (May 21, 1999).

[142] 8 CFR §§245.13(a), 1245.13(a) (2014); NACARA §§202(a)(1), (b)(1), 111 Stat. 2193–94.

[143] 8 CFR §§245.13(b), 1245.13(b) (2014); NACARA §§202(d), 111 Stat. 2195.

[144] 8 CFR §§245.13(a), 1245.13(a) (2014); NACARA §§202(a)(1), (b)(1), 111 Stat. 2193–94.

eligible for adjustment of status, regardless of their entry date, if they applied before April 1, 2000.[145]

Salvadoran nationals are eligible to seek suspension of deportation under the provisions of law that existed prior to the passage of IIRAIRA if they:

- Entered the United States on or before September 19, 1990 and registered for benefits under the *ABC* Settlement Agreement,[146] or applied for TPS on or before October 31, 1991, (which automatically registered Salvadorans as *ABC* class members); *or*
- Applied for asylum on or before April 1, 1990.[147]

The spouses, minor children, or unmarried adult sons and daughters of Salvadorans eligible for such relief may also have their cases adjudicated under pre-IIRAIRA rules.[148] In the cases of adult sons or daughters, they must demonstrate that they entered the United States on or before October 1, 1990.[149] Any grants of suspension are not subject to the annual cap of 4,000.[150] The regulations, which took effect on June 21, 1999, afford the principal applicants a rebuttable presumption that they would meet the extreme hardship requirement for suspension of deportation.[151]

Guatemalan nationals[152] are eligible to seek suspension of deportation under the provisions of law that existed prior to the passage of IIRAIRA if they:

- Entered the United States on or before October 1, 1990 and registered for benefits under the *ABC* Settlement Agreement[153] on or before December 31, 1991; *or*
- Applied for asylum on or before April 1, 1990.[154]

The spouses, minor children, or unmarried adult sons and daughters of Guatemalans eligible for such relief may also have their cases adjudicated under pre-IIRAIRA rules.[155] In the cases of adult sons or daughters, they must demonstrate that

---

[145] 8 CFR §§245.13(b), 1245.13(b) (2014); NACARA §§202(d), 111 Stat. 2195.

[146] *See* this chapter at 6.3.

[147] NACARA §203(a)(1), 111 Stat. 2196–98.

[148] *Id.*

[149] *Id.*

[150] *Id. See also* 8 CFR §§240.60 *et seq.*, 1240.60 *et seq.* (2014).

[151] 8 CFR §§240.64(d)(1), 1240.64(d)(1) (2014). For detailed instructions on analyzing and preparing a NACARA claim, *see* Mark Silverman and Linton Joaquin, *NACARA for Guatemalans, Salvadorans, and Former Soviet Bloc Nationals*, 1 IMMIGRATION & NATIONALITY LAW HANDBOOK 251 (AILA 2004–05 Ed.).

[152] *See* U.S. Citizenship & Immigration Servs., Fact Sheet, *Guatemalan Asylum applicants in the Context of the ABC Settlement Agreement and Section 203 of the Nicaraguan Adjustment and Central American Relief Act (NACARA)* (Feb. 28, 2007), *available at www.uscis.gov/files/pressrelease/GuatemalanAsylum022807.pdf.*

[153] *See* this chapter at 6.3.

[154] NACARA §203(a)(1), 111 Stat. 2196–98.

[155] *Id.*

they entered the United States on or before October 1, 1990.[156] Any grants of suspension are not subject to the annual cap of 4,000.[157] The regulations, which took effect on June 21, 1999, afford the principal applicants a rebuttable presumption that they would meet the extreme hardship requirement for suspension of deportation.[158]

Nationals of former Soviet Union and Warsaw Pact countries are eligible to have their suspension of deportation claims considered under pre-IIRAIRA rules if they:

- Entered the United States on or before December 31, 1990;
- Filed an application for asylum on or before December 31, 1991; *and*
- At the time of filing, were nationals of the Soviet Union, Russia, any republic of the former Soviet Union, Latvia, Estonia, Lithuania, Poland, Czechoslovakia, Romania, Hungary, Bulgaria, Albania, East Germany, Yugoslavia, or any state of the former Yugoslavia.[159]

Unlike nationals from El Salvador and Guatemala, nationals of former Soviet Bloc countries have not been afforded the rebuttable presumption of extreme hardship in the determination of whether they qualify for suspension of deportation.

> ➢ **Practice Pointer**: For an analysis of NACARA eligibility and a detailed discussion of the analytical framework for NACARA cases, see Mark Silverman and Linton Joaquin's article, "NACARA for Guatemalans, Salvadorans, and Former Soviet Bloc Nationals," which makes up Chapter 1 of the Immigrant Legal Resource Center's *Winning NACARA Suspension Cases* manual. The manual is available online at *www.ilrc.org/files/documents/ilrc-nacara_manual.pdf.*[160] Silverman and Linton suggest the following steps in analyzing a NACARA case: (1) analyze the client's NACARA and then suspension/cancellation eligibility; and (2) determine where, when, and how to bring the case.

VII. Haitian Refugee Immigration Fairness Act

The Haitian Refugee Immigration Fairness Act[161] (HRIFA) was signed into law on October 21, 1998. HRIFA permitted certain categories of Haitian nationals to apply for adjustment of status to permanent residency. The final regulations, effective on their date of issuance, were released in March 2000.[162] Principal beneficiaries

---

[156] *Id.*

[157] *Id. See also* 8 CFR §§240.60 *et seq.*, 1240.60 *et seq.* (2014).

[158] 8 CFR §§240.64(d)(1), 1240.64(d)(1) (2014).

[159] NACARA §203(a)(1), 111 Stat. 2196–98.

[160] (last visited Apr. 3, 2015).

[161] Haitian Refugee Immigration Fairness Act (HRIFA), Pub. L. No. 105-277, div. A, §101(h), tit. IX (secs. 901–04), 112 Stat. 2681, 2681–538 to 2681–542.

[162] *See* Adjustment of Status for Certain Nationals of Haiti, 65 Fed. Reg. 15835 (Mar. 24, 2000); 8 CFR §§245.15, 1245.15 (2014).

must have filed their applications on or before March 31, 2000.[163] There is no application deadline for dependents.

To be eligible for benefits as a principal beneficiary, a Haitian national:

- Must have been physically present in the United States on December 31, 1995;[164]
- Must have remained continuously physically present in the United States since December 31, 1995;[165]
- Must not be inadmissible to the United States under any grounds of inadmissibility for which HRIFA does not specify an exception;[166] and
- Must belong to one of five classes set forth in §902(b)(1) of HRIFA.

The classes include any Haitian national who: (1) filed for asylum before December 31, 1995; (2) was paroled into the United States before December 31, 1995, after having been identified as having a credible fear of persecution, or paroled for emergency reasons or reasons deemed strictly in the public interest; (3) was an unmarried child under age 21 at the time of his or her arrival and on December 31, 1995, and arrived without parents and has remained in the United States without parents; (4) was an unmarried child under age 21 at the time of his or her arrival and on December 31, 1995, and became orphaned after arriving in the United States; or (5) was an unmarried child under age 21 at the time of his or her arrival and on December 31, 1995, and was abandoned by his or her parents or guardians prior to April 1, 1998, and has remained abandoned.[167]

The following grounds of inadmissibility under the INA do not apply to HRIFA applicants:

- §212(a)(4)—a noncitizen likely to become a public charge;
- §212(a)(5)—a noncitizen without a labor certification or proper qualifications for certain occupations;
- §212(a)(6)(a)—a noncitizen present without admission or parole;
- §212(a)(7)(a)—a noncitizen not in possession of a valid visa; and
- §212(a)(9)(B)—a noncitizen unlawfully present in the United States.[168]
- To be eligible for benefits as a dependent beneficiary, an individual must be:
- A national of Haiti;
- The spouse, child, or unmarried son or daughter of a principal HRIFA beneficiary at the time the principal was granted adjustment of status;

---

[163] *See* 8 CFR §§245.15(c)(2)(i), 1245.15(c)(2)(i) (2014); HRIFA §902(a)(1)(A), 112 Stat. 2681–538.

[164] 8 CFR §§245.15(c)(1), 1245.15(c)(1) (2014).

[165] 8 CFR §§245.15(c)(4), 1245.15(c)(4) (2014).

[166] 8 CFR §§245.15(c)(3), 1245.15(c)(3) (2014).

[167] 8 CFR §§245.15(b)(1), 1245.15(b)(1) (2014); HRIFA §902(b)(1), 112 Stat. 2681–538 to 2681–539.

[168] 8 CFR §§245.15(e)(1), 1245.15(e)(1) (2014); HRIFA §902(a)(1)(B), 112 Stat. 2681–538.

- Physically present in the United States; and
- Not inadmissible to the United States under any grounds not excepted by HRIFA.[169]

VIII. Cuban Adjustment Act

The Cuban Adjustment Act of 1966 (CAA)[170] provides an avenue for Cuban citizens or natives to become lawful permanent residents of the United States. Congress provided the AG with the discretion to provide LPR status to Cuban citizens or natives who have been admitted or paroled into the United States and have been present in the United States for at least one year following admission or parole.[171] In 2008 and 2009, USCIS issued a memorandum and amended guidance to its field leadership on the processing of initial parole requests and renewal parole requests by natives and citizens of Cuba.[172] The CAA also makes the applicant's spouse and children eligible to receive LPR status.[173] The adjustment of status is purely discretionary, and an applicant may be granted adjustment of status even if he or she does not meet the ordinary requirements for adjustment under INA §245.[174]

Applicants seeking adjustment of status under the CAA may file with USCIS.[175] Immigration judges have no jurisdiction to adjudicate a Cuban Adjustment Act application filed by an "arriving alien," except in cases in which the individual has been placed in removal proceedings after returning to the United States after a grant of advance parole.[176]

---

[169] 8 CFR §§245.15(d), 1245.15(d) (2014); HRIFA §902(d), 112 Stat. 2681–539 to 2681–540.

[170] Cuban Adjustment Act of 1966, Pub. L. No. 89-732, 80 Stat. 1161 (8 USC §1255 note).

[171] 8 CFR §§245.2(a)(2)(ii), 1245.2(a)(2)(ii) (2014).

[172] U.S. Citizenship & Immigration Servs., Interoffice Memorandum from Chief of Field Operations: Processing of Initial Parole or renewal Parole Requests Presented by Natives or Citizens of Cuba to USCIS Field Offices (March 4, 2008), *available at www.uscis.gov/files/pressrelease/CubanParole_4Mar08.pdf*; *see also* U.S. Citizenship & Immigration Servs., Interoffice Memorandum from Chief of Field Operations on Amended guidance regarding Processing of Initial Parole and Renewal Parole Requests Presented by Natives or Citizens of Cuba to USCIS Field Offices (Feb. 3, 2009), available at *www.uscis.gov/files/nativedocuments/CPmemoAmend-2-3-09.pdf.*

[173] For more information access the USCIS website at *www.uscis.gov* (search for "Cuban Natives or Citizens Seeking Lawful Permanent Resident Status").

[174] *Id.*

[175] *See id.* (providing documentation requirements, applicable U.S. Citizenship & Immigration Servs., forms, and information on where and when to file).

[176] *Borges v. Att'y Gen.*, 383 Fed. App'x 891, 893–94 (11th Cir. 2010) (citing, with approval, the BIA holding in *Matter of Martinez–Montalvo*, that 8 CFR §§245.2(a)(1) and 1245.2(a)(1) effectively divest the IJ of jurisdiction over arriving aliens' applications for adjustment of status unless they can meet the conditions of 8 CFR §1245.2(a)(1)(ii)."); *Matter of Martinez-Montalvo*, 24 I&N Dec. 778 (BIA 2009). *But see Matter of Artigas*, 23 I&N Dec. 99, 106 (BIA 2001) (finding that "an Immigration Judge has jurisdiction to consider an application for adjustment of status under the Cuban Adjustment Act made by a respondent charged in removal proceedings as an arriving alien without a valid visa.").

Individuals born outside Cuba whose Cuban citizenship is not documented with a Cuban passport, may establish Cuban citizenship for the purposes of adjustment under the Cuban Adjustment Act through the submission of a Cuban birth certificate issued by the Civil Registry of Cuba in Havana, Cuba, or a Cuban consular certificate documenting their birth to at least one Cuban parent within the consular district served by the consulate.[177]

- **Practice Pointer**: Many individuals who seek adjustment under the Cuban Adjustment Act have actually entered the United States as citizens of a third country. *See* "U.S. Offers Refuge to Cubans, Even if They're Not From Cuba," *Wall Street Journal*, April 7, 2009, A12. In fiscal year 2008, nationals of the following countries received permanent residency under the Cuban Adjustment Act: Venezuela (129), Mexico (40), Colombia (26), Peru (11), Spain (10), Ukraine (9), Argentina (7), Canada (7), Chile (7), Ecuador (7).[178]

---

[177] *Matter of Vazquez*, (AAO 2007) *available at www.uscis.gov/files/pressrelease/Vazquez073107.pdf.*

[178] *See id.*

APPENDICES

APPENDIX 1A
INTERVIEWING TECHNIQUES

A crucial and time-consuming part of representing or assisting an individual who is applying for asylum is gathering information about the claim from the applicant. It is often necessary to meet with the applicant on several occasions before beginning the task of completing the asylum application form. The interviewing process may be hampered because the applicant is often traumatized by his or her past experiences. Also, the applicant may initially lack the trust or confidence needed to share information about his or her past or the reasons for the harm he or she suffered. There may also be cultural or language barriers to overcome. Here are a few tips for getting over some of the hurdles you may encounter.

EXPLAIN YOUR ROLE AS AN ATTORNEY

Applicants for asylum come from a wide variety of backgrounds. Many may never have had contact with an attorney in their home countries. It is important to explain to the applicant that you represent him or her and that you do not work for the U.S. authorities. You should also note that you have a duty of confidentiality and may not reveal information to anyone without the applicant's permission. Explaining your role several times during the course of the representation is a useful way to reassure the client and build trust in the attorney-client relationship.

DESCRIBE THE ASYLUM PROCESS

As Kafka's *The Trial* so aptly demonstrates, not knowing what to expect during a trial or hearing process can be frustrating, if not terrifying. Walk the applicant through the maze of the asylum process at the first interview and summarize the process at later interviews. It may be comforting for an applicant who is applying in removal proceedings to know that if he or she is not granted asylum by the immigration judge, there is an opportunity to appeal the decision to the Board of Immigration Appeals and, possibly, to a federal appeals court. In contrast, an applicant who seeks asylum in expedited removal proceedings should be informed of the need to fully present his or her claim at the "credible fear" interview, due to the swift and limited review of negative determinations.

EXPLAIN ASYLUM IN NONLEGAL TERMS

An applicant who understands the concept of asylum will be able to provide more relevant information to you during your interview sessions. Some applicants mistakenly believe that they must demonstrate that they will be persecuted for political reasons and are unaware of the other grounds for seeking asylum. It is also important to explain that the term persecution is broadly defined under U.S. law. Moreover, informing the applicant of the requirement that the persecution must be "on account of" one of the five enumerated grounds will prepare the applicant for your questions focusing on the reasons why the persecutor harmed or intends to harm him or her.

SCHEDULE SEVERAL MEETINGS WITH THE APPLICANT

An applicant who has met with you on several occasions will develop confidence in you and will most likely divulge more information about his or her asylum claim at each meeting. Some applicants may have been coached by smugglers or individuals from their home countries on the "story" they should tell U.S. authorities. Other applicants may conceal information that they believe may be harmful to their claims. It is important to impart to the asylum applicant the need to know the truth and all of the details regarding the applicant's fear of returning. At times, information that the applicant believes to be detrimental to his or her claim is actually helpful and may ultimately be the reason why he or she is granted asylum. Be prepared for your client's story to change as you discuss his or her claim over a period of time. It may, for example, take time for an applicant to reveal to you that he or she was sexually assaulted or took part in activities considered to be subversive in his or her home country.

OBTAIN A COMPETENT INTERPRETER

If you and the applicant do not speak the same language, it is essential to obtain a competent interpreter for your interviews with the applicant. Before an interview, the interpreter should be instructed to provide an exact interpretation of your questions and comments and of the applicant's responses. Be aware that applicants may not be able to relate certain aspects of their claims in the presence of a person of the opposite sex, or, in some cases, of the same sex. Ask the applicant if he or she would feel more comfortable with a male or female interpreter. Also, applicants may be reluctant to speak openly in front of spouses, children, siblings, or other family members.

LEARN ABOUT THE APPLICANT'S COUNTRY

In addition to human rights reports and current country condition reports, read as much as you can about the history of the applicant's country, its cultures, customs, religions, and traditions. There may even be movies or documentaries about the applicant's home country available at your local library, online, or through a movie rental service. The applicant's story will become clearer to you as you gain an understanding of his or her background.

LET THE APPLICANT PLAY AN ACTIVE ROLE IN DEVELOPING THE CLAIM

No one likes to feel helpless or powerless, including the applicant. Give the applicant assignments that will assist both you and the applicant in preparing his or her claim. Ask the applicant to write out his or her reasons for seeking asylum in a narrative form for your next interview. (If the applicant is unable to read and write, ask whether a family member or friend could assist or have the applicant tape record a narrative.) Ask the applicant to gather documents and letters in support of the claim, including identity documents, proof of membership in organizations or religious communities, or proof of military service. If he or she has access to a library or the Internet, the applicant may even be able to compile country condition reports for you. The applicant may also be able to identify family and friends who can corroborate parts of his or her claim. As an attorney, most likely a pro bono one, you need all of the help you can get, so don't overlook the applicant.

For additional interviewing techniques, you may wish to review:

- UNHCR Training Module RLD 4, Interviewing Applicants for Refugee Status (1995), available at *www.unhcr.org/publ/PUBL/3ae6bd670.pdf;* or
- S. Yale-Loehr and K. Ozmun, "Initial Interviews," *Navigating the Fundamentals of Immigration Law: Guidance and Tips for Successful Practice* (AILA 2013–14 Ed.).

APPENDIX 1B

SAMPLE INTAKE FORM

(This intake form may be used at an initial interview to obtain a general overview of the applicant's claim and to determine whether any bars to asylum may apply and whether any other forms of relief may be available to the applicant.)

<u>Personal/Family Information</u>

Applicant's Name ____

Address ____

Telephone No. ______________________________ Fax No. ________________

Any other names used ____

A# ____________________ Date of Birth ___________ Sex _____ Marital Status ______

Place of Birth (POB) __________________ Country of Citizenship ________________
(if the country where applicant was born no longer exists, the applicant may be stateless)

POB of Mother ______________, Father ______________, Grandparents _____________
(if a parent or grandparent was born in the U.S., the applicant may be a derivative U.S. citizen)

Is Spouse, Parent, Sibling, or Child a U.S. Citizen or Lawful Permanent Resident? ______
(If yes, applicant may be able to immigrant to the United States through a family member)

Languages Spoken by Applicant ____________________________________

Other Countries of Residence ______________________________________

Type of Residency Permit, if any ___________________________________
(Applicant is not eligible for asylum if he or she was "firmly resettled" in a third country)

Religion __________________________ Ethnic Group ___________________________

Profession/Work __________________________ Education ______________________
(An applicant who has a specialized skill or profession may qualify for an employment-based visa)

Present Employer, if any ____

Previous Employers ____

____

Trafficking or Crime Victim ____
(Was the applicant a victim of a severe form of trafficking in persons or a victim of a serious crime? He or she may be eligible for a "T" or "U" visa, which eventually could lead to permanent residency. See ch. 6.)

Immigration Information

Date of Last Entry______________ Place of Last Entry ______________________

Manner of Last Entry (*e.g.*, with visa, without inspection, with false document, by claiming to be U.S. citizen) ____

Type of travel document (or passport) used, if any ______________________

Type of visa, if any ________________ Date of expiration ____________________

Passport: Country ______________ Date issued _________ Expiration Date _________
(In most cases, but not all, an applicant is a citizen of the country that issued his or her passport)

Present immigration status ____

Previous entries to the U.S., if any (including date/length of stay/manner of entry) _______

____

Have any U.S. immigration petitions been filed on behalf of the applicant? ___________

If so, what type and when? ____

Has the applicant previously applied for asylum in the U.S.? ____ When? ___________
(If yes, it is important to obtain any previously filed applications and note that the applicant may be ineligible for asylum unless he or she demonstrates changed country conditions)

Has the applicant previously obtained asylum, permanent residency or other immigration status in the U.S.? ________ If so, what type? ____________________ When? ________

Has the applicant ever appeared before an Immigration Judge? _______ When? ________
(If yes, it's important to question the applicant to determine if he or she has been previously deported from the United States, received voluntary departure, or whether the case was administratively closed)

If in removal proceedings, how did applicant come to the attention of the DHS? ________

Did the applicant make any statements to DHS? _______ When? ______ Where? ______
(If so, it's important to obtain all records from the DHS)

> *Make copies of any immigration documents and travel documents the applicant may have for his or her file. Also, file a Freedom of Information Act (FOIA) request form (Form G-639) as soon as possible to obtain a copy of the applicant's DHS file.*

Asylum Information

Reasons for fleeing home country ___________________________________

Actual physical or emotional harm (or torture) suffered by the applicant ______________

(If the applicant has suffered physical or emotional harm or has been subjected to torture, a physician or mental health professional may examine the applicant and submit a professional assessment of the applicant's physical and/or mental condition)

Reasons for fear of future harm (including any past harm to individuals similarly situated to the applicant, such as family members or friends) ___________________________

Who or what entities does the applicant fear? Is it the government or a government figure, the police, the military, a rival clan or ethnic group, members of a political party, death squads, or a rebel group? ___________________________________

If it is a nongovernmental entity, could the applicant seek protection from the government?

If not, why not? ___________________________________

Why is the person or groups the applicant fears seeking to harm him or her? ___________

What would happen to the applicant if he or she was returned to his or her home country?

Would it be reasonable for the applicant to relocate to another part of the country? Why not?

APPENDIX 1C

CHECKLIST FOR BARS TO ASYLUM AND WITHHOLDING OF DEPORTATION

Bars to Asylum Only

- ☐ **Previous Denial**. If an asylum application was previously denied by an immigration judge or the Board of Immigration Appeals, the applicant is ineligible unless he or she demonstrates changed country conditions.

- ☐ **One-Year Deadline**. The applicant must file for asylum within one year after the date of his or her arrival in the United States, unless he or she demonstrates changed country conditions or extraordinary circumstances to excuse the delay.

- ☐ **Firm Resettlement**. Applicants are ineligible if they received an offer of permanent residency, citizenship, or other permanent status in a third country prior to coming to the United States, unless they demonstrate that their rights were restricted in that country or that they passed through that country in their flight from persecution, only remained as long as was necessary to arrange onward travel, and did not establish significant ties to the country.

- ☐ **Safe Third Country**. If the applicant can be sent to a safe third country pursuant to a bilateral or multilateral agreement, he or she is ineligible to apply for asylum. To date, one such agreement exists, between the United States and Canada.

- ☐ **Aggravated Felony**. An applicant convicted of an aggravated felony is barred from asylum.

Bars to Withholding of Removal and Asylum

- ☐ **Particularly Serious Crime**. An applicant convicted of an aggravated felony is deemed to have been convicted of a particularly serious crime for purposes of asylum. If he or she received an aggregate sentence of five years or more for an aggravated felony or felonies, the crime is deemed to be particularly serious for purposes of withholding of removal. Other crimes that are not aggravated felonies will be considered on a case-by-case basis to determine whether they are particularly serious.

- ☐ **Serious Nonpolitical Crime**. An applicant is ineligible for asylum and withholding if he or she committed a serious nonpolitical crime outside of the United States.

- ❑ **Persecutor of Others**. An applicant is ineligible for asylum or withholding if he or she engaged in the persecution of others on account of race, religion, nationality, membership in a particular social group, or political opinion.

- ❑ **Danger to the Security of the United States**. An applicant is ineligible for asylum or withholding if he or she is found to be a danger to the security of the United States. An applicant who is found to have engaged in terrorist activity is deemed to be a danger to the security of the United States for purposes of withholding.

- ❑ **Terrorism**. An applicant is ineligible for asylum and withholding of deportation if he or she is found to have engaged in terrorist activity, which may include providing minimal support to a terrorist organization, even if the support was provided under duress. A waiver for individuals who provided material support "under duress" is available. An applicant is barred from asylum for inciting terrorist activity or for being a representative of a terrorist organization. Mere membership, however, is not a bar to asylum or withholding.

Bars to Withholding Only

- ❑ **Participation in Nazi Persecution**. An applicant is ineligible for withholding if he or she, under the direction of the Nazi government of Germany, persecuted others on account of race, religion, national origin, or political opinion between March 23, 1933, and May 8, 1945.

- ❑ **Participation in Genocide**. An applicant is ineligible for withholding of removal if he or she engaged in genocide.

> *Note that even if a bar mentioned above applies to the applicant, he or she may still be eligible for relief from deportation under the U.N. Convention Against Torture if he or she is likely to be subjected to torture by the government (or because of the government's acquiescence) if he or she is returned to his or her home country. See Chapter 3.*

APPENDIX 1D

SAMPLE QUESTIONS/TOPICS FOR APPLICANT INTERVIEWS

Applying for asylum, withholding of removal, and protection under the Convention Against Torture requires that the practitioner gain his or her client's trust in order to gather all of the important details of the client's story and to effectively present the facts in a persuasive manner. This process takes time and patience, often requiring several lengthy meetings with the client before there is even enough information to draft the client's declaration. The following topics and questions may serve as a helpful starting point for practitioners when setting out to clearly present their clients' stories with significant detail. This list, however, is not meant to be a substitute for individualized questions and important follow-up questions that may elicit more detail from the client.

PAST PERSECUTION

1. Have you, your family, or close friends or colleagues ever experienced harm, mistreatment, or threats in the past by anyone? If yes, what happened?

2. When did this happen?

3. Who caused the harm/mistreatment/threats?

4. Why do you believe that you were harmed? Why did they target you specifically?

5. Please provide a complete timeline of events, from the initial act of persecution (if you suffered past persecution) or from the initial moment that you felt afraid to be in your home country, through your entry to the United States.

FEAR OF PERSECUTION

6. What are your protected characteristic(s)?

7. Why does your protected characteristic make you afraid? Would you be targeted because of that?

8. Who would target you?

9. What would they do to you?

10. Why would they target you specifically?

11. How would the persecutors become aware of your protected characteristic?

12. How do you know that this would happen to you? What makes you believe this?

13. Is it possible to/are you willing to change your protected characteristic in order to protect yourself?

14. Do you have any other family members, friends, neighbors, colleagues still in your home country who share your protected characteristic? If so, who specifically and how often are you in contact with them?

15. If so, are they safe? If they are safe, why are they safe while you would be in danger? What distinguishes them from you?

16. If they are not safe, what has happened or what will likely happen to them?

FEAR OF TORTURE

17. Are you afraid of being subjected to torture in your home country or any other country to which you may be returned? If so, why?

18. Who would torture you?

19. Please describe the torture you fear.

20. Why would they torture you specifically?

21. How do you know that this would happen to you? What makes you believe this?

GENERAL QUESTIONS

22. Is there anywhere in your home country where you could live safely? Why or why not?

23. After leaving your home country, did you or your family members travel through or reside in any other country before entering the United States? If so, what country, how long were you there, what was your status there?

24. Have you or your family members ever applied for or received any lawful status in any country other than your home country?

25. If so, what country, what was your status, how long were in you that status, why did you leave, and are you entitled to return?

26. Did you apply for refugee status or asylum while you were there? If yes, what was the outcome of that application? If not, why not?

27. Have you, your parents, or your siblings ever applied for refugee status, asylum, or withholding of removal in the United States? If so, on what grounds, when, and what was the outcome?

28. Have you or your family members ever belonged to or associated with any organizations or groups in your home country (political parties, student groups, religious organizations, military or paramilitary groups, ethnic groups, human rights groups, the press or media, etc.)? If yes, please explain the group, your position in the group, your level of participation in the group, the length of time you were involved in the group, and whether you still participate in this group.

29. Have you or any of your family members ever ordered, assisted, or otherwise participated in causing harm or suffering to any other person because of their race, religion, nationality, social group, or political opinion? If yes, please explain.

30. After you left your home country, did you ever return there? If so, when, for how long, why, and did anything happen while you were there? When was the last time you were in your home country?

31. Have you or your family members ever committed any crime and/or been arrested, charged, convicted, or sentenced for any crimes in the United States? If so, what happened, when, where, what were the formal charges, and what was your sentence?

32. Have you or your family members ever committed any crime and/or been arrested, charged, convicted, or sentenced for any crimes outside the United States? If so, what happened, when, where, what were the formal charges, and what was your sentence?

SUPPORTING EVIDENCE

33. What supporting documentation can you provide to corroborate your claims? See Appendix 3A for more specific topics on supporting documentation that a practitioner may discuss with his or her client.

34. What family members, friends, neighbors, colleagues might be able to verify what happened to you as witnesses?

35. What family members, friends, neighbors, colleagues might be able to verify that your fears are reasonable given the conditions in your home country (either because of their own similar experiences or because of their personal knowledge of the conditions there)?

APPENDIX 2A

FORM I-589, APPLICATION FOR ASYLUM AND FOR WITHHOLDING OF REMOVAL AND INSTRUCTIONS

Department of Homeland Security
U.S. Citizenship and Immigration Services

U.S. Department of Justice
Executive Office for Immigration Review

OMB No. 1615-0067; Expires 12/31/2016

I-589, Application for Asylum and for Withholding of Removal

START HERE - Type or print in black ink. See the instructions for information about eligibility and how to complete and file this application. There is NO filing fee for this application.

NOTE: Check this box if you also want to apply for withholding of removal under the Convention Against Torture. ☐

Part A.I. Information About You

1. Alien Registration Number(s) (A-Number) *(if any)*
2. U.S. Social Security Number *(if any)*
3. Complete Last Name
4. First Name
5. Middle Name
6. What other names have you used *(include maiden name and aliases)?*
7. Residence in the U.S. *(where you physically reside)*

Street Number and Name | Apt. Number

City | State | Zip Code | Telephone Number ( )

8. Mailing Address in the U.S. *(if different than the address in Item Number 7)*

In Care Of *(if applicable)*: | Telephone Number ( )

Street Number and Name | Apt. Number

City | State | Zip Code

9. Gender: ☐ Male ☐ Female
10. Marital Status: ☐ Single ☐ Married ☐ Divorced ☐ Widowed
11. Date of Birth *(mm/dd/yyyy)*
12. City and Country of Birth
13. Present Nationality *(Citizenship)*
14. Nationality at Birth
15. Race, Ethnic, or Tribal Group
16. Religion
17. *Check the box, a through c, that applies:* **a.** ☐ I have never been in Immigration Court proceedings.
b. ☐ I am now in Immigration Court proceedings. **c.** ☐ I am **not** now in Immigration Court proceedings, but I have been in the past.
18. *Complete 18 a through c.*
a. When did you last leave your country? *(mmm/dd/yyyy)* ______ **b.** What is your current I-94 Number, if any? ______
c. List each entry into the U.S. beginning with your most recent entry. *List date (mm/dd/yyyy), place, and your status for each entry. (Attach additional sheets as needed.)*

Date ______ Place ______ Status ______ Date Status Expires ______

Date ______ Place ______ Status ______

Date ______ Place ______ Status ______

19. What country issued your last passport or travel document?
20. Passport Number
Travel Document Number
21. Expiration Date *(mm/dd/yyyy)*
22. What is your native language *(include dialect, if applicable)?*
23. Are you fluent in English? ☐ Yes ☐ No
24. What other languages do you speak fluently?

For EOIR use only.

For USCIS use only.
Action:
Interview Date: ______
Asylum Officer ID#: ______

Decision:
Approval Date: ______
Denial Date: ______
Referral Date: ______

Form I-589 (Rev. 12/29/14) Y

Part A.II. Information About Your Spouse and Children

Your spouse ☐ I am not married. (Skip to **Your Children** below.)

1. Alien Registration Number (A-Number) *(if any)*	2. Passport/ID Card Number *(if any)*	3. Date of Birth *(mm/dd/yyyy)*	4. U.S. Social Security Number *(if any)*
5. Complete Last Name	6. First Name	7. Middle Name	8. Maiden Name
9. Date of Marriage *(mm/dd/yyyy)*	10. Place of Marriage	11. City and Country of Birth	
12. Nationality *(Citizenship)*	13. Race, Ethnic, or Tribal Group	14. Gender ☐ Male ☐ Female	
15. Is this person in the U.S.? ☐ Yes *(Complete Blocks 16 to 24.)* ☐ No *(Specify location):*			
16. Place of last entry into the U.S.	17. Date of last entry into the U.S. *(mm/dd/yyyy)*	18. I-94 Number *(if any)*	19. Status when last admitted *(Visa type, if any)*
20. What is your spouse's current status?	21. What is the expiration date of his/her authorized stay, if any? *(mm/dd/yyyy)*	22. Is your spouse in Immigration Court proceedings? ☐ Yes ☐ No	23. If previously in the U.S., date of previous arrival *(mm/dd/yyyy)*
24. If in the U.S., is your spouse to be included in this application? *(Check the appropriate box.)* ☐ Yes *(Attach one photograph of your spouse in the upper right corner of Page 9 on the extra copy of the application submitted for this person.)* ☐ No			

Your Children. List **all** of your children, regardless of age, location, or marital status.

☐ I do not have any children. *(Skip to Part A.III., **Information about your background.**)*

☐ I have children. Total number of children: ______________.

(NOTE: *Use Form I-589 Supplement A or attach additional sheets of paper and documentation if you have more than four children.)*

1. Alien Registration Number (A-Number) *(if any)*	2. Passport/ID Card Number *(if any)*	3. Marital Status *(Married, Single, Divorced, Widowed)*	4. U.S. Social Security Number *(if any)*
5. Complete Last Name	6. First Name	7. Middle Name	8. Date of Birth *(mm/dd/yyyy)*
9. City and Country of Birth	10. Nationality *(Citizenship)*	11. Race, Ethnic, or Tribal Group	12. Gender ☐ Male ☐ Female
13. Is this child in the U.S. ? ☐ Yes *(Complete Blocks 14 to 21.)* ☐ No *(Specify location):*			
14. Place of last entry into the U.S.	15. Date of last entry into the U.S. *(mm/dd/yyyy)*	16. I-94 Number *(If any)*	17. Status when last admitted *(Visa type, if any)*
18. What is your child's current status?	19. What is the expiration date of his/her authorized stay, if any? *(mm/dd/yyyy)*	20. Is your child in Immigration Court proceedings? ☐ Yes ☐ No	
21. If in the U.S., is this child to be included in this application? *(Check the appropriate box.)* ☐ Yes *(Attach one photograph of your spouse in the upper right corner of Page 9 on the extra copy of the application submitted for this person.)* ☐ No			

Part A.II. Information About Your Spouse and Children (Continued)

1. Alien Registration Number (A-Number) *(if any)*	**2.** Passport/ID Card Number *(if any)*	**3.** Marital Status *(Married, Single, Divorced, Widowed)*	**4.** U.S. Social Security Number *(if any)*
5. Complete Last Name	**6.** First Name	**7.** Middle Name	**8.** Date of Birth *(mm/dd/yyyy)*
9. City and Country of Birth	**10.** Nationality *(Citizenship)*	**11.** Race, Ethnic, or Tribal Group	**12.** Gender ☐ Male ☐ Female
13. Is this child in the U.S. ? ☐ Yes *(Complete Blocks 14 to 21.)* ☐ No *(Specify location):*			
14. Place of last entry into the U.S.	**15.** Date of last entry into the U.S. *(mm/dd/yyyy)*	**16.** I-94 Number *(If any)*	**17.** Status when last admitted *(Visa type, if any)*
18. What is your child's current status?	**19.** What is the expiration date of his/her authorized stay, if any? *(mm/dd/yyyy)*	**20.** Is your child in Immigration Court proceedings? ☐ Yes ☐ No	
21. If in the U.S., is this child to be included in this application? *(Check the appropriate box.)* ☐ Yes *(Attach one photograph of your spouse in the upper right corner of Page 9 on the extra copy of the application submitted for this person.)* ☐ No			
1. Alien Registration Number (A-Number) *(if any)*	**2.** Passport/ID Card Number *(if any)*	**3.** Marital Status *(Married, Single, Divorced, Widowed)*	**4.** U.S. Social Security Number *(if any)*
5. Complete Last Name	**6.** First Name	**7.** Middle Name	**8.** Date of Birth *(mm/dd/yyyy)*
9. City and Country of Birth	**10.** Nationality *(Citizenship)*	**11.** Race, Ethnic, or Tribal Group	**12.** Gender ☐ Male ☐ Female
13. Is this child in the U.S. ? ☐ Yes *(Complete Blocks 14 to 21.)* ☐ No *(Specify location):*			
14. Place of last entry into the U.S.	**15.** Date of last entry into the U.S. *(mm/dd/yyyy)*	**16.** I-94 Number *(If any)*	**17.** Status when last admitted *(Visa type, if any)*
18. What is your child's current status?	**19.** What is the expiration date of his/her authorized stay, if any? *(mm/dd/yyyy)*	**20.** Is your child in Immigration Court proceedings? ☐ Yes ☐ No	
21. If in the U.S., is this child to be included in this application? *(Check the appropriate box.)* ☐ Yes *(Attach one photograph of your spouse in the upper right corner of Page 9 on the extra copy of the application submitted for this person.)* ☐ No			
1. Alien Registration Number (A-Number) *(if any)*	**2.** Passport/ID Card Number *(if any)*	**3.** Marital Status *(Married, Single, Divorced, Widowed)*	**4.** U.S. Social Security Number *(if any)*
5. Complete Last Name	**6.** First Name	**7.** Middle Name	**8.** Date of Birth *(mm/dd/yyyy)*
9. City and Country of Birth	**10.** Nationality *(Citizenship)*	**11.** Race, Ethnic, or Tribal Group	**12.** Gender ☐ Male ☐ Female
13. Is this child in the U.S. ? ☐ Yes *(Complete Blocks 14 to 21.)* ☐ No *(Specify location):*			
14. Place of last entry into the U.S.	**15.** Date of last entry into the U.S. *(mm/dd/yyyy)*	**16.** I-94 Number *(If any)*	**17.** Status when last admitted *(Visa type, if any)*
18. What is your child's current status?	**19.** What is the expiration date of his/her authorized stay, if any? *(mm/dd/yyyy)*	**20.** Is your child in Immigration Court proceedings? ☐ Yes ☐ No	
21. If in the U.S., is this child to be included in this application? *(Check the appropriate box.)* ☐ Yes *(Attach one photograph of your spouse in the upper right corner of Page 9 on the extra copy of the application submitted for this person.)* ☐ No			

Form I-589 (Rev. 12/29/14) Y Page 3

Part A.III. Information About Your Background

1. List your last address where you lived before coming to the United States. If this is not the country where you fear persecution, also list the last address in the country where you fear persecution. *(List Address, City/Town, Department, Province, or State and Country.)*
(NOTE: Use Form I-589 Supplement B, or additional sheets of paper, if necessary.)

Number and Street *(Provide if available)*	City/Town	Department, Province, or State	Country	Dates From *(Mo/Yr)*	To *(Mo/Yr)*

2. Provide the following information about your residences during the past 5 years. List your present address first.
(NOTE: Use Form I-589 Supplement B, or additional sheets of paper, if necessary.)

Number and Street	City/Town	Department, Province, or State	Country	Dates From *(Mo/Yr)*	To *(Mo/Yr)*

3. Provide the following information about your education, beginning with the most recent.
(NOTE: Use Form I-589 Supplement B, or additional sheets of paper, if necessary.)

Name of School	Type of School	Location *(Address)*	Attended From *(Mo/Yr)*	To *(Mo/Yr)*

4. Provide the following information about your employment during the past 5 years. List your present employment first.
(NOTE: Use Form I-589 Supplement B, or additional sheets of paper, if necessary.)

Name and Address of Employer	Your Occupation	Dates From *(Mo/Yr)*	To *(Mo/Yr)*

5. Provide the following information about your parents and siblings (brothers and sisters). Check the box if the person is deceased.
(NOTE: Use Form I-589 Supplement B, or additional sheets of paper, if necessary.)

Full Name	City/Town and Country of Birth	Current Location
Mother		☐ Deceased
Father		☐ Deceased
Sibling		☐ Deceased
Sibling		☐ Deceased
Sibling		☐ Deceased
Sibling		☐ Deceased

Part B. Information About Your Application

(NOTE: Use Form I-589 Supplement B, or attach additional sheets of paper as needed to complete your responses to the questions contained in Part B.)

When answering the following questions about your asylum or other protection claim (withholding of removal under 241(b)(3) of the INA or withholding of removal under the Convention Against Torture), you must provide a detailed and specific account of the basis of your claim to asylum or other protection. To the best of your ability, provide specific dates, places, and descriptions about each event or action described. You must attach documents evidencing the general conditions in the country from which you are seeking asylum or other protection and the specific facts on which you are relying to support your claim. If this documentation is unavailable or you are not providing this documentation with your application, explain why in your responses to the following questions.

Refer to Instructions, Part 1: Filing Instructions, Section II, "Basis of Eligibility," Parts A - D, Section V, "Completing the Form," Part B, and Section VII, "Additional Evidence That You Should Submit," for more information on completing this section of the form.

1. Why are you applying for asylum or withholding of removal under section 241(b)(3) of the INA, or for withholding of removal under the Convention Against Torture? Check the appropriate box(es) below and then provide detailed answers to questions A and B below.

I am seeking asylum or withholding of removal based on:

☐ Race ☐ Political opinion

☐ Religion ☐ Membership in a particular social group

☐ Nationality ☐ Torture Convention

A. Have you, your family, or close friends or colleagues ever experienced harm or mistreatment or threats in the past by anyone?

☐ No ☐ Yes

If "Yes," explain in detail:
1. **What happened;**
2. **When the harm or mistreatment or threats occurred;**
3. **Who caused the harm or mistreatment or threats; and**
4. **Why you believe the harm or mistreatment or threats occurred.**

B. Do you fear harm or mistreatment if you return to your home country?

☐ No ☐ Yes

If "Yes," explain in detail:
1. **What harm or mistreatment you fear;**
2. **Who you believe would harm or mistreat you; and**
3. **Why you believe you would or could be harmed or mistreated.**

Part B. Information About Your Application (Continued)

2. Have you or your family members ever been accused, charged, arrested, detained, interrogated, convicted and sentenced, or imprisoned in any country other than the United States?

☐ No ☐ Yes

If "Yes," explain the circumstances and reasons for the action.

3.A. Have you or your family members ever belonged to or been associated with any organizations or groups in your home country, such as, but not limited to, a political party, student group, labor union, religious organization, military or paramilitary group, civil patrol, guerrilla organization, ethnic group, human rights group, or the press or media?

☐ No ☐ Yes

If "Yes," describe for each person the level of participation, any leadership or other positions held, and the length of time you or your family members were involved in each organization or activity.

3.B. Do you or your family members continue to participate in any way in these organizations or groups?

☐ No ☐ Yes

If "Yes," describe for each person your or your family members' current level of participation, any leadership or other positions currently held, and the length of time you or your family members have been involved in each organization or group.

4. Are you afraid of being subjected to torture in your home country or any other country to which you may be returned?

☐ No ☐ Yes

If "Yes," explain why you are afraid and describe the nature of torture you fear, by whom, and why it would be inflicted.

Form I-589 (Rev. 12/29/14) Y Page 6

Part C. Additional Information About Your Application

(NOTE: *Use Form I-589 Supplement B, or attach additional sheets of paper as needed to complete your responses to the questions contained in Part C.*)

1. Have you, your spouse, your child(ren), your parents or your siblings ever applied to the U.S. Government for refugee status, asylum, or withholding of removal?

☐ No ☐ Yes

If "Yes," explain the decision and what happened to any status you, your spouse, your child(ren), your parents, or your siblings received as a result of that decision. Indicate whether or not you were included in a parent or spouse's application. If so, include your parent or spouse's A-number in your response. If you have been denied asylum by an immigration judge or the Board of Immigration Appeals, describe any change(s) in conditions in your country or your own personal circumstances since the date of the denial that may affect your eligibility for asylum.

2.A. After leaving the country from which you are claiming asylum, did you or your spouse or child(ren) who are now in the United States travel through or reside in any other country before entering the United States?

☐ No ☐ Yes

2.B. Have you, your spouse, your child(ren), or other family members, such as your parents or siblings, ever applied for or received any lawful status in any country other than the one from which you are now claiming asylum?

☐ No ☐ Yes

If "Yes" to either or both questions (2A and/or 2B), provide for each person the following: the name of each country and the length of stay, the person's status while there, the reasons for leaving, whether or not the person is entitled to return for lawful residence purposes, and whether the person applied for refugee status or for asylum while there, and if not, why he or she did not do so.

3. Have you, your spouse or your child(ren) ever ordered, incited, assisted or otherwise participated in causing harm or suffering to any person because of his or her race, religion, nationality, membership in a particular social group or belief in a particular political opinion?

☐ No ☐ Yes

If "Yes," describe in detail each such incident and your own, your spouse's, or your child(ren)'s involvement.

Part C. Additional Information About Your Application (Continued)

4. After you left the country where you were harmed or fear harm, did you return to that country?

☐ No ☐ Yes

If "Yes," describe in detail the circumstances of your visit(s) (for example, the date(s) of the trip(s), the purpose(s) of the trip(s), and the length of time you remained in that country for the visit(s).)

5. Are you filing this application more than 1 year after your last arrival in the United States?

☐ No ☐ Yes

If "Yes," explain why you did not file within the first year after you arrived. You must be prepared to explain at your interview or hearing why you did not file your asylum application within the first year after you arrived. For guidance in answering this question, see Instructions, Part 1: Filing Instructions, Section V. "Completing the Form," Part C.

6. Have you or any member of your family included in the application ever committed any crime and/or been arrested, charged, convicted, or sentenced for any crimes in the United States?

☐ No ☐ Yes

If "Yes," for each instance, specify in your response: what occurred and the circumstances, dates, length of sentence received, location, the duration of the detention or imprisonment, reason(s) for the detention or conviction, any formal charges that were lodged against you or your relatives included in your application, and the reason(s) for release. Attach documents referring to these incidents, if they are available, or an explanation of why documents are not available.

Part D. Your Signature

I certify, under penalty of perjury under the laws of the United States of America, that this application and the evidence submitted with it are all true and correct. Title 18, United States Code, Section 1546(a), provides in part: Whoever knowingly makes under oath, or as permitted under penalty of perjury under Section 1746 of Title 28, United States Code, knowingly subscribes as true, any false statement with respect to a material fact in any application, affidavit, or other document required by the immigration laws or regulations prescribed thereunder, or knowingly presents any such application, affidavit, or other document containing any such false statement or which fails to contain any reasonable basis in law or fact - shall be fined in accordance with this title or imprisoned for up to 25 years. I authorize the release of any information from my immigration record that U.S. Citizenship and Immigration Services (USCIS) needs to determine eligibility for the benefit I am seeking.

Staple your photograph here or the photograph of the family member to be included on the extra copy of the application submitted for that person.

***WARNING:* Applicants who are in the United States illegally are subject to removal if their asylum or withholding claims are not granted by an asylum officer or an immigration judge. Any information provided in completing this application may be used as a basis for the institution of, or as evidence in, removal proceedings even if the application is later withdrawn. Applicants determined to have knowingly made a frivolous application for asylum will be permanently ineligible for any benefits under the Immigration and Nationality Act. You may not avoid a frivolous finding simply because someone advised you to provide false information in your asylum application. If filing with USCIS, unexcused failure to appear for an appointment to provide biometrics (such as fingerprints) and your biographical information within the time allowed may result in an asylum officer dismissing your asylum application or referring it to an immigration judge. Failure without good cause to provide DHS with biometrics or other biographical information while in removal proceedings may result in your application being found abandoned by the immigration judge. See sections 208(d)(5)(A) and 208(d)(6) of the INA and 8 CFR sections 208.10, 1208.10, 208.20, 1003.47(d) and 1208.20.**

Print your complete name.	Write your name in your native alphabet.

Did your spouse, parent, or child(ren) assist you in completing this application? ☐ No ☐ Yes *(If "Yes," list the name and relationship.)*

(Name)	*(Relationship)*	*(Name)*	*(Relationship)*

Did someone other than your spouse, parent, or child(ren) prepare this application? ☐ No ☐ Yes *(If "Yes," complete Part E.)*

Asylum applicants may be represented by counsel. Have you been provided with a list of persons who may be available to assist you, at little or no cost, with your asylum claim? ☐ No ☐ Yes

Signature of Applicant *(The person in Part A.I.)*

[ ]

Sign your name so it all appears within the brackets

Date *(mm/dd/yyyy)*

Part E. Declaration of Person Preparing Form, if Other Than Applicant, Spouse, Parent, or Child

I declare that I have prepared this application at the request of the person named in Part D, that the responses provided are based on all information of which I have knowledge, or which was provided to me by the applicant, and that the completed application was read to the applicant in his or her native language or a language he or she understands for verification before he or she signed the application in my presence. I am aware that the knowing placement of false information on the Form I-589 may also subject me to civil penalties under 8 U.S.C. 1324c and/or criminal penalties under 18 U.S.C. 1546(a).

Signature of Preparer	Print Complete Name of Preparer		
Daytime Telephone Number ( )	Address of Preparer: Street Number and Name		
Apt. Number	City	State	Zip Code

Part F. To Be Completed at Asylum Interview, if Applicable

NOTE: *You will be asked to complete this part when you appear for examination before an asylum officer of the Department of Homeland Security, U.S. Citizenship and Immigration Services (USCIS).*

I swear (affirm) that I know the contents of this application that I am signing, including the attached documents and supplements, that they are ☐ all true or ☐ not all true to the best of my knowledge and that correction(s) numbered ____ to ____ were made by me or at my request. Furthermore, I am aware that if I am determined to have knowingly made a frivolous application for asylum I will be permanently ineligible for any benefits under the Immigration and Nationality Act, and that I may not avoid a frivolous finding simply because someone advised me to provide false information in my asylum application.

Signed and sworn to before me by the above named applicant on:

Signature of Applicant	Date *(mm/dd/yyyy)*
Write Your Name in Your Native Alphabet	Signature of Asylum Officer

Part G. To Be Completed at Removal Hearing, if Applicable

NOTE: *You will be asked to complete this Part when you appear before an immigration judge of the U.S. Department of Justice, Executive Office for Immigration Review (EOIR), for a hearing.*

I swear (affirm) that I know the contents of this application that I am signing, including the attached documents and supplements, that they are ☐ all true or ☐ not all true to the best of my knowledge and that correction(s) numbered ____ to ____ were made by me or at my request. Furthermore, I am aware that if I am determined to have knowingly made a frivolous application for asylum I will be permanently ineligible for any benefits under the Immigration and Nationality Act, and that I may not avoid a frivolous finding simply because someone advised me to provide false information in my asylum application.

Signed and sworn to before me by the above named applicant on:

Signature of Applicant	Date *(mm/dd/yyyy)*
Write Your Name in Your Native Alphabet	Signature of Immigration Judge

Supplement A, Form I-589

A-Number *(If available)*	Date
Applicant's Name	Applicant's Signature

List All of Your Children, Regardless of Age or Marital Status

(NOTE: Use this form and attach additional pages and documentation as needed, if you have more than four children)

1. Alien Registration Number (A-Number) *(if any)*	2. Passport/ID Card Number *(if any)*	3. Marital Status *(Married, Single, Divorced, Widowed)*	4. U.S. Social Security Number *(if any)*
5. Complete Last Name	6. First Name	7. Middle Name	8. Date of Birth *(mm/dd/yyyy)*
9. City and Country of Birth	10. Nationality *(Citizenship)*	11. Race, Ethnic, or Tribal Group	12. Gender ☐ Male ☐ Female
13. Is this child in the U.S. ? ☐ Yes *(Complete Blocks 14 to 21.)* ☐ No *(Specify location):*			
14. Place of last entry into the U.S.	15. Date of last entry into the U.S. *(mm/dd/yyyy)*	16. I-94 Number *(If any)*	17. Status when last admitted *(Visa type, if any)*
18. What is your child's current status?	19. What is the expiration date of his/her authorized stay, if any? *(mm/dd/yyyy)*	20. Is your child in Immigration Court proceedings? ☐ Yes ☐ No	
21. If in the U.S., is this child to be included in this application? *(Check the appropriate box.)* ☐ Yes *(Attach one photograph of your spouse in the upper right corner of Page 9 on the extra copy of the application submitted for this person.)* ☐ No			

1. Alien Registration Number (A-Number) *(if any)*	2. Passport/ID Card Number *(if any)*	3. Marital Status *(Married, Single, Divorced, Widowed)*	4. U.S. Social Security Number *(if any)*
5. Complete Last Name	6. First Name	7. Middle Name	8. Date of Birth *(mm/dd/yyyy)*
9. City and Country of Birth	10. Nationality *(Citizenship)*	11. Race, Ethnic, or Tribal Group	12. Gender ☐ Male ☐ Female
13. Is this child in the U.S. ? ☐ Yes *(Complete Blocks 14 to 21.)* ☐ No *(Specify location):*			
14. Place of last entry into the U.S.	15. Date of last entry into the U.S. *(mm/dd/yyyy)*	16. I-94 Number *(If any)*	17. Status when last admitted *(Visa type, if any)*
18. What is your child's current status?	19. What is the expiration date of his/her authorized stay, if any? *(mm/dd/yyyy)*	20. Is your child in Immigration Court proceedings? ☐ Yes ☐ No	
21. If in the U.S., is this child to be included in this application? *(Check the appropriate box.)* ☐ Yes *(Attach one photograph of your spouse in the upper right corner of Page 9 on the extra copy of the application submitted for this person.)* ☐ No			

Supplement B, Form I-589

Additional Information About Your Claim to Asylum

A-Number *(if available)*	Date
Applicant's Name	Applicant's Signature

NOTE: *Use this as a continuation page for any additional information requested. Copy and complete as needed.*

Part ______________

Question ______________

Department of Homeland Security
U.S. Citizenship and Immigration Services
Department of Justice
U.S. Executive Office for Immigration Review

OMB No. 1615-0067; Expires 12/31/2016

I-589, Application for Asylum and for Withholding of Removal

Instructions

What Is the Purpose of This Form?

This form is used to apply for asylum in the United States and for withholding of removal (formerly called "withholding of deportation"). This application may also be used to apply for protection under the Convention Against Torture. You may file this application if you are physically present in the United States, and you are not a U.S. citizen.

NOTE: You **must** submit an application for asylum within 1 year of arriving in the United States, unless there are changed circumstances that materially affect your eligibility for asylum or extraordinary circumstances directly related to your failure to file within 1 year. (See **Part C, Additional Information about Your Application, in Section V on Part 1** of the instructions for further explanation.)

You may include in your application your spouse and unmarried children who are under 21 years of age and physically present in the United States. You **must** submit certain documents for your spouse and each child included as required by these instructions. Children 21 years of age or older and married children must file separate applications. If you are granted asylum and your spouse and/or any unmarried children under 21 years of age are outside the United States, you may file Form I-730, Refugee and Asylee Relative Petition, for them to gain similar benefits.

Instruction Sections: Filing Information and How Your Application Will Be Processed

The instructions are divided into two sections:

The first section has filing information. This section discusses basic eligibility criteria and guides you through filling out and filing the application.

The second section explains how your application will be processed. This section also describes potential interim benefits available while your application is pending.

Read these instructions carefully. The instructions will help you complete your application and understand how it will be processed. If you have questions about your eligibility, how to complete the form, or the asylum process, you may wish to consult an attorney or other qualified person to assist you. (See **Section IV, Right to Counsel, in Part I** of these instructions.)

***WARNING:* Applicants in the United States illegally are subject to removal if their asylum or withholding claims are not granted by an asylum officer or an immigration judge. Any information provided in completing this application may be used as a basis for the institution of, or as evidence in, removal proceedings, even if the application is later withdrawn.**

Applicants determined to have knowingly made a frivolous application for asylum will be permanently ineligible for any benefits under the Immigration and Nationality Act (INA). You may not avoid a frivolous finding simply because someone advised you to provide false information in your asylum application.

If filing with U.S. Citizenship and Immigration Services (USCIS), unexcused failure to appear for an appointment or to provide biometrics (such as fingerprints) and other biographical information within the time allowed may delay eligibility for employment authorization and result in an asylum officer dismissing your asylum application or referring it to an immigration judge. Applicants and eligible dependents in removal proceedings who fail without good cause to provide USCIS with their biometrics or their biographical information as required within the time allowed may have their applications found abandoned by the immigration judge. See sections 208(d)(5)(A) and 208(d)(6) of the INA and 8 Code of Federal Regulations (CFR) sections 208.10, 1208.10, 208.20, 1003.47(d), and 1208.20.

Table of Contents

Table of Contents *(Continued)*

Part 1. Filing Instructions

I. Who May Apply and Filing Deadlines

You may apply for asylum irrespective of your immigration status and even if you are in the United States unlawfully.

You MUST file this application within 1 year after you arrived in the United States, unless you can show that there are changed circumstances that affect your eligibility for asylum or extraordinary circumstances that prevented you from filing within 1 year. (See **Section IV, Right to Counsel, in Part I** of these instructions.)

If you have previously been denied asylum by an immigration judge or the Board of Immigration Appeals, you must show that there are changed circumstances that affect your eligibility for asylum.

The determination of whether you are permitted to apply for asylum will be made once you have had an asylum interview with an asylum officer or a hearing before an immigration judge. Even if you are not eligible to apply for asylum for the reasons stated above, you may still be eligible to apply for withholding of removal under section 241(b)(3) of the INA or under the Convention Against Torture before the Immigration Court.

II. Basis of Eligibility

A. Asylum

In order to qualify for asylum, you must establish that you are a refugee who is unable or unwilling to return to his or her country of nationality, or last habitual residence in the case of a person having no nationality, because of persecution or a well-founded fear of persecution on account of race, religion, nationality, membership in a particular social group, or political opinion. This means that you must establish that race, religion, nationality, membership in a particular social group, or political opinion was or will be at least one central reason for your persecution or why you fear persecution. (See section 208 of the INA; 8 CFR sections 208 and 1208, et seq.)

If you are granted asylum, you and any eligible spouse or child included in your application will be permitted to remain and work in the United States and may eventually adjust to lawful permanent resident status. **If you are not granted asylum, the Department of Homeland Security (DHS) may use the information you provide in this application to establish that you are removable from the United States.**

B. Withholding of Removal

Your asylum application is also considered to be an application for withholding of removal under section 241(b)(3) of the INA, as amended. It may also be considered an application for withholding of removal under the Convention Against Torture if you checked the box at the top of **Page 1** of the form, or if the evidence you present indicates that you may be tortured in the country of removal. (See 8 CFR sections 208.13(c)(1) and 1208.13(c)(1)). If asylum is not granted, you may still be eligible for withholding of removal.

Regardless of the basis for the withholding application, you will not be eligible for withholding if you:

1. Assisted in Nazi persecution or engaged in genocide;
2. Have persecuted another person;
3. Have been convicted by a final judgment of a particularly serious crime and therefore represent a danger to the community of the United States;
4. Are considered for serious reasons to have committed a serious non-political crime outside the United States; or

5. Represent a danger to the security of the United States. (see section 241(b)(3) of the INA; 8 CFR sections 208.16 and1208.16.)

Withholding of Removal Under Section 241(b)(3) of the INA

In order to qualify for withholding of removal under section 241(b)(3) of the INA, you must establish that it is more likely than not that your life or freedom would be threatened on account of race, religion, nationality, membership in a particular social group, or political opinion in the proposed country of removal.

If you obtain an order withholding your removal, you cannot be removed to the country where your life or freedom would be threatened. This means that you may be removed to a third country where your life or freedom would not be threatened. Withholding of removal does not adhere derivatively to any spouse or child included in the application. They would have to apply for such protection on their own.

If you are granted withholding of removal, this would not give you the right to bring your relatives to the United States. It also would not give you the right to become a lawful permanent resident of the United States.

Withholding of Removal Under the Convention Against Torture

The Convention Against Torture refers to the United Nations Convention Against Torture and Other Cruel, Inhuman, or Degrading Treatment or Punishment.

To be granted withholding of removal to a country under the Convention Against Torture, you must show that it is more likely than not that you would be tortured in that country.

"Torture" is defined in Article 1 of the Convention Against Torture and at 8 CFR sections 208.18(a) and 1208.18(a). For an act to be considered torture, it must be an extreme form of cruel and inhuman treatment, it must cause severe physical or mental pain and suffering, and it must be specifically intended to cause severe pain and suffering.

Torture is an act inflicted for such purposes as obtaining from the victim or a third person information or a confession, punishing the victim for an act he or she or a third person has committed or is suspected of having committed, intimidating or coercing the victim or a third person, or for any reason based on discrimination of any kind.

Torture must be inflicted by or at the instigation of, or with the consent or acquiescence of, a public official or other person acting in an official capacity. The victim must be in the custody or physical control of the torturer. Torture does not include pain or suffering that arises only from, is inherent in, or is incidental to lawful sanctions, although such actions may not defeat the objective and purpose of the Convention Against Torture.

Form I-589, will be considered an application for withholding of removal under the Convention Against Torture if you tell the immigration judge that you would like to be considered for withholding of removal under the Convention Against Torture, or if it is determined that evidence indicates that you may be tortured in the country of removal.

To apply for withholding of removal under the Convention Against Torture, you must check the box at the top of **Page 1** of the application and fully complete Form I-589.

You must include a detailed explanation of why you fear torture in response to Part B, Question 4 of the application. In your response, you must write about any mistreatment you experienced or any threats made against you by a government or somebody connected to a government.

Only immigration judges and the Board of Immigration Appeals may grant withholding of removal or deferral of removal under the Convention Against Torture. If you have applied for asylum, the immigration judge will first determine whether you are eligible for asylum under section 208 of the INA and for withholding of removal under section 241(b)(3) of the INA. If you are not eligible for either asylum under section 208 of the INA or withholding of removal under section 241(b)(3) of the INA, the immigration judge will determine whether the Convention Against Torture prohibits your removal to a country where you fear torture.

As implemented in U.S. law, Article 3 of the Convention Against Torture prohibits the United States from removing you to a country in which it is more likely than not that you would be subject to torture. The Convention Against Torture does not prohibit the United States from returning you to any other country where you would not be tortured. This means that you may be removed to a third country where you would not be tortured. Withholding of removal under the Convention Against Torture does not allow you to adjust to lawful permanent resident status or to petition to bring family members to come to, or remain in, the United States.

C. Deferral of Removal Under the Convention Against Torture

If it is more likely than not that you will be tortured in a country but you are ineligible for withholding of removal, your removal will be deferred under 8 CFR sections 208.17(a) and 1208.17(a). Deferral of removal does not confer any lawful or permanent immigration status in the United States and does not necessarily result in release from detention. Deferral of removal is effective only until it is terminated. Deferral of removal is subject to review and termination if it is determined that it is no longer more likely than not that you would be tortured in the country to which your removal is deferred or if you request that your deferral be terminated.

D. Legal Sources Relating to Eligibility

The documents listed below are some of the legal sources relating to asylum, withholding of removal under section 241(b)(3) of the INA, and withholding of removal or deferral of removal under the Convention Against Torture. These sources are provided for reference only. You do not need to refer to them in order to complete your application.

1. Section 101(a)(42) of the INA, 8 U.S.C. 1101(a)(42) (defining"refugee");
2. Section 208 of the INA, 8 U.S.C. 1158 (regarding eligibility for asylum);
3. Section 241(b)(3) of the INA, 8 U.S.C. 1231(b)(3) (regarding eligibility for withholding of removal);
4. Title 8 of the CFR sections 208 and 1208, et seq.;
5. Article 3 of the Convention Against Torture and Other Cruel, Inhuman or Degrading Treatment or Punishment as ratified by section 2242(b) or the Foreign Affairs Reform and Restructuring Act of 1998 and 8 CFR section 208, as amended by the Regulations Concerning the Convention Against Torture: Interim Rule, 64 FR 8478-8492 (February 19, 1999) (effective March 22, 1999); 64 FR 13881 (March 23, 1999);
6. The 1967 United Nations Protocol relating to the Status of Refugees;
7. The 1951 Convention relating to the Status of Refugees; and
8. The Office of the United Nations High Commissioner for Refugees, Handbook on Procedures and Criteria for determining Refugee Status (Geneva, 1992).

III. Confidentiality

The information collected will be used to make a determination on your application. It may also be provided to other government agencies (Federal, State, local, and/or foreign) for purposes of investigation or legal action on criminal and/or civil matters and for issues arising from the adjudication of benefits. However, no information indicating that you have applied for asylum will be provided to any government or country from which you claim a fear of persecution. Regulations at 8 CFR sections 208.6 and 1208.6 protect the confidentiality of asylum claims.

IV. Right to Counsel

Immigration law concerning asylum and withholding of removal or deferral or removal is complex. You have a right to provide your own legal representation at an asylum interview and during immigration proceedings before the Immigration Court at no cost to the U.S. Government.

If you need or would like help to complete this form and to prepare your written statements, assistance from pro bono (free) attorneys and/or voluntary agencies may be available. Voluntary agencies may help you for no fee or a reduced fee, and attorneys on the list referred to below may take your case for no fee. If you have not already received from USCIS or the Immigration Court a list of attorneys and accredited representatives, you may obtain a list by calling **1-800-870-3676** or visiting the U.S. Department of Justice (DOJ), Executive Office for Immigration Review (EOIR) Web site at www.usdoj.gov/eoir/probono/states.htm.

Representatives of the United Nations High Commissioner for Refugees (UNHCR) may be able to assist you in identifying persons to help you complete the application. RefWorld, available on UNHCR's Web site, provides useful country conditions information through a variety sources. Contact information for the UNHCR is :

United Nations High Commissioner for Refugees
1775 K Street NW Ste 300
Washington, DC 20006
Telephone: 202-296-5191
Web site: www.unhcr.org

Calls from Detention Centers and Jails. Asylum-seekers in detention centers and jails may call UNHCR collect at **202-296-5191** or toll-free at **1-888-272-1913** on Monday, Wednesday, and Friday, 2 p.m. - 5 p.m. (Eastern Standard Time).

V. Completing the Form

Type or print all of your answers in black ink on Form I-589. Your answers must be completed in English. Forms completed in a language other than English will be returned to you. Provide the specific information requested about you and your family. **Answer all the questions asked.**

If any question does not apply to you or you do not know the information requested, answer "none," "not applicable," or "unknown."

Provide detailed information and answer the questions as completely as possible. Applications filed with missing information may be returned to you as incomplete. If you need more space, attach Form I-589 Supplement A or B (included in the application package) and/or additional sheet(s) indicating the question number(s) you are answering.

You are strongly urged to attach additional written statements and documents that support your claim. Your written statements should include events, dates, and details of your experiences that relate to your claim for asylum.

NOTE: Put your Alien Registration Number (A-Number) (if any), name (exactly as it appears in Part A.I. of the form), signature, and date on each supplemental sheet and on the cover page of any supporting documents.

You will be permitted to amend or supplement your application at the time of your asylum interview before an asylum officer and at your hearing in Immigration Court by providing additional information and explanations about your asylum claim.

Part A.I. Information About You

This part asks for basic information about you. Alien Registration Number (A-Number) refers to your USCIS file number. If you do not already have an A-Number, USCIS will assign one to you.

You must provide your residential street address (the address where you physically live) in the United States in Part A.I., Question 7, of the asylum application. You may also provide a mailing address, if different from the address where you reside, in Question 8. If someone else is collecting your mail for you at your mailing address, you may enter that person's name in the "In Care Of" field in your response to Question 8. If your mailing address is a post office box, include that address in Question 8 **and** include a residential address where you physically live in Question 7.

In Question 12, use the current name of the country. Do not use historical, ethnic, provincial, or other local names.

If you entered the country with inspection, Form I-94 number referred to in Question 18b is the number on Form I-94, Arrival-Departure Record, given to you when you entered the United States. In Question 18c, enter the date and status as it appears on Form I-94. If you did not receive Form I-94, write "None." If you entered without being inspected by an immigration officer, write "No Inspection" in Question 18c in the current status or status section.

Part A.II. Spouse and Children

You must list your spouse and all of your children in this application, regardless of their age, marital status, whether they are in the United States, or whether or not they are included in this application or filing a separate asylum application.

You may ask to have included in your asylum application your spouse and/or any children who are under 21 years of age and unmarried, if they are in the United States. Children who are married and/or children who are 21years of age or older must file separately for asylum by submitting their own Form I-589.

If you apply for asylum while in proceedings before the Immigration Court, the immigration judge may not have authority to grant asylum to any spouse or child included in your application who is not also in proceedings.

When including family members in your asylum application, you **must** submit one additional copy of your completed asylum application and primary documentary evidence establishing your family relationship for each family member, as described below:

1. If you are including your spouse in your application, submit three copies of your marriage certificate and three copies of proof of termination of any prior marriages.
2. If you are including any unmarried children under 21years of age in your application, submit three copies of each child's birth certificate.

If you do not have and are unable to obtain these documents, you must submit secondary evidence. Secondary evidence includes but is not limited to medical records, religious records, and school records. You may also submit an affidavit from at least one person for each event you are trying to prove. Affidavits may be provided by relatives or others. Persons providing affidavits need not be U.S. citizens or lawful permanent residents.

Affidavits must:

1. Fully describe the circumstances or event(s) in question and fully explain how the person acquired knowledge of the event(s);
2. Be sworn to or affirmed by persons who were alive at the time of the event(s) and have personal knowledge of the event(s) (date and place of birth, marriage, etc.) that you are trying to prove; and
3. Show the full name, address, and date and place of birth of each person giving the affidavit and indicate any relationship between you and the person giving the affidavit.

If you submit secondary evidence or affidavits, you must explain why primary evidence (e.g., birth or marriage certificate) is unavailable. You may explain the reasons primary evidence is unavailable using Form I-589 Supplement B or additional sheets of paper. Attach this explanation to your secondary evidence or affidavits.

If you have more than four children, complete the Supplement A Form for each additional child or attach additional pages and documentation providing the same information asked in Part A.II. of Form I-589.

Part A.III. Information About Your Background

Answer Questions 1 through 5, providing details as requested for each question. Your responses to the questions concerning the places you have lived, your education, and your employment history must be in reverse chronological order starting with your current residence, education, and employment and working back in time.

Part B. Information About Your Application

This part asks specific questions relevant to eligibility for asylum, for withholding of removal under section 241(b)(3) of the Act, or for withholding of removal under the Convention Against Torture. At Question 1, check the box(es) next to the reason(s) that you are completing this application. For all other questions, check "Yes" or "No" in the box provided.

If you answer "Yes" to any question, explain in detail using Form I-589 Supplement B or additional sheets of paper, as needed.

You must clearly describe any of your experiences, or those of family members or others who have had similar experiences that may show that you are a refugee.

If you have experienced harm that is difficult for you to write down and express, you must be aware that these experiences may be very important to the decision-making process regarding your request to remain in the United States. At your interview with an asylum officer or hearing with an immigration judge, you will need to be prepared to discuss the harm you have suffered. If you are having trouble remembering or talking about past events, we suggest that you talk to a lawyer, an accredited representative, or a health professional who may be able to help you explain your experiences and current situation.

Part C. Additional Information About Your Application

Check "Yes" or "No" in the box provided for each question. If you answer "Yes" to any question, explain in detail using Form I-589 Supplement B or additional sheets of paper, as needed.

If you answer "Yes" to Question 5, you must explain why you did not apply for asylum within the first year after you arrived in the United States. The Government will accept as an explanation certain changes in the conditions in your country, certain changes in your own circumstances, and certain other events that may have prevented you from applying earlier.

For example, some of the events the Government might consider as valid explanations include but are not limited to the following:

1. You have learned that human rights conditions in your country have worsened since you left;
2. Because of your health, you were not able to submit this application within 1 year after you arrived;
3. You previously submitted an application, but it was returned to you because it was not complete, and you submitted a complete application within a reasonable amount of time.

Federal regulations specify some of the other types of events that may also qualify as valid explanations for why you filed late. These regulations are found at 8 CFR, sections 208.4 and 1208.4. The list in the regulations is not all-inclusive, and the Government recognizes that there are many other circumstances that might be acceptable reasons for filing more than 1 year after arrival.

If you are unable to explain why you did not apply for asylum within the first year after you arrived in the United States or your explanation is not accepted by the Government, you may not be eligible to apply for asylum, but you could still be eligible for withholding of removal.

Part D. Your Signature

You must sign your application in Part D and respond to the questions concerning any assistance you received to complete your application, providing the information requested. Sign after you have completed and reviewed the application.

If it is determined that you have knowingly made a frivolous application for asylum, you can be permanently ineligible for any benefits under the INA. (See section 208(d)(6) of the INA.)

According to regulations at 8 CFR sections 208.20 and 1208.20, an application is frivolous if any of its material elements is deliberately fabricated. (See Section IV, Right to Counsel, in Part 1 of these instructions if you have any questions.) Note that you may not avoid a frivolous finding simply because someone advised or told you to provide false information on your asylum application.

Part E. Signature of Person Preparing Form, If Other Than You

Any person, other than an immediate family member (your spouse, parent(s) or children), who helped prepare your application must sign the application in Part E and provide the information requested.

Penalty for Perjury

All statements in response to questions contained in this application are declared to be true and correct under penalty of perjury. You and anyone, other than an immediate family member, who assists you in preparing the application must sign the application under penalty of perjury. Your signature is evidence that you are aware of the contents of this application. Any person assisting you in preparing this form, other than an immediate family member, must include his or her name, address, and telephone number and sign the application where indicated in Part E.

Failure of the preparer to sign will result in the application being returned to you as an incomplete application.

If USCIS or EOIR later learns that you received assistance from someone other than an immediate family member and the person who assisted you willfully failed to sign the application, this may result in an adverse ruling against you.

Title 18, United States Code (U.S.C.), Section 1546(a), provides in part:

> Whoever knowingly makes under oath, or as permitted under penalty of perjury under Section 1746 of Title 28, knowingly subscribes as true, any false statement with respect to a material fact in any application, affidavit, or other document required by the immigration laws or regulations prescribed thereunder, or knowingly presents any such application, affidavit, or other document containing any such false statement shall be fined in accordance with this title or imprisoned not more than 10 years, or both.

If aggravating factors exist, the maximum term of imprisonment could reach 25 years.

If you knowingly provide false information on this application, you or the preparer of this application may be subject to criminal penalties under Title 18 of the U.S.C. and to civil penalties under section 274C of the INA, 8 U.S.C.324c.

Part F. To Be Completed at Asylum Interview, If Applicable

Do not sign your application in Part F before filing this form. You will be asked to sign your application in this space at the conclusion of the interview regarding your claim.

NOTE: You must, however, sign Part D of the application.

Part G. To Be Completed at Removal Hearing, If Applicable

Do not sign your application in Part G before filing this form. You will be asked to sign your application in this space at the hearing before the immigration judge.

NOTE: You must, however, sign Part D of the application.

You are again reminded that, if is determined that you have knowingly made a frivolous application for asylum, you can be permanently ineligible for any benefits under the INA. (See section 208(d)(6) of the INA.)

According to regulations at 8 CFR sections 208.20 and 1208.20, an application is frivolous if any of its material elements is deliberately fabricated. Again, note that you may not avoid a frivolous finding simply because someone advised or told you to provide false information on your asylum application.

VI. Required Documents and Required Number of Copies That You Must Submit With Your Application

You must submit the following documents to apply for asylum and withholding of removal:

1. **The completed, signed original and two copies of your completed application, Form I-589,** and the original and two copies of any supplementary sheets and supplementary statements. If you choose to submit additional supporting material, see **Section VII, Additional Evidence That You Should Submit, in Part 1** of these instructions. You **must** include three copies of each document. You should make and keep an additional copy of the completed application for your own records.

2. **An additional copy of your completed application, Form I-589,** with supplementary statements, for each family member listed in Part A.II. whom you want to have included in your application.

3. **Three copies of primary or secondary evidence** of relationship, such as birth or school records of your children, marriage certificate, or proof of termination of marriage, for each family member listed in Part A.II. whom you want to have included in your application.

   NOTE: If you submit an affidavit, you must submit the original and two copies. (For affidavit requirements, see **Part A.II in Part 1, Section V,** of these instructions.)

4. **One passport-style photograph** of yourself and of each family member listed in Part A. II. who is included in your application. The photos must have been taken no more than 30 days before you file your application. Using a pencil, print the person's complete name and A-Number (if any) on the back of his or her photo.

5. **Three copies of all passports or other travel documents** (cover to cover) in your possession and three copies of any U.S. immigration documents, such as a Form I-94, Arrival-Departure Record, for you and each family member included in your application, if you have such documents.

6. **If you have other identification documents** (e.g., birth certificate, military or national identification card, driver's license, etc.), we recommend that you submit three copies with your application and bring the original(s) with you to the interview.

Copies. *Documents filed with this application should be photocopies.* If you choose to send an original document, USCIS or the Immigration Court may keep that original document for its records.

Translations. Any document containing foreign language submitted to USCIS must be accompanied by a full English language translation that the translator has certified as complete and accurate, and by the translator's certification that he or she is competent to translate from the foreign language into English.

VII. Additional Evidence That You Must Submit

You must submit reasonably available corroborative evidence showing (1) the general conditions in the country from which you are seeking asylum, and (2) the specific facts on which you are relying to support your claim.

If evidence supporting your claim is not reasonably available or you are not providing such corroboration at this time, you must explain why, using Form I-589 Supplement B or additional sheets of paper.

Supporting evidence may include but is not limited to newspaper articles, affidavits of witnesses or experts, medical and/or psychological records, doctors' statements, periodicals, journals, books, photographs, official documents, or personal statements or live testimony from witnesses or experts.

If you have difficulty discussing harm you have suffered in the past, you may wish to submit a health professional's report explaining this difficulty.

VIII. Fee

There is no fee for filing this application.

XI. Biometrics, Including Fingerprints and Photographs

Applicants for asylum are subject to a biometrics check of all appropriate records and other information databases maintained by the U.S. Attorney General and U.S. Secretary of State.

You and your eligible spouse or children over 14 years of age listed on your asylum application must provide biometrics. You and your spouse and children will be given instructions on how to complete this requirement. You will be notified in writing of the time and location of the Application Support Center where you must go to be fingerprinted and photographed.

If filing with USCIS, unexcused failure to appear for a scheduled appointment or to provide your required biometrics, including fingerprints and photograph, or to provide other biographical information within the time allowed, may delay eligibility for employment authorization and/or result in an asylum officer dismissing your asylum application or referring it to an immigration judge. For applicants before an immigration judge, such failure without good cause may constitute an abandonment of your asylum application and result in the denial of employment authorization. (See 8 CFR section 1003.47(d)).

At the time you file your Form I-589, you **must** submit photographs as specified in **Section VI, Required Documents and Required Number of Copies That You Must Submit With Your Application, in Part 1** of these instructions.

X. Organizing Your Application

Put your application together in the following order, forming one complete package (if possible, secure with binder clips and rubber bands so that material may be easily separated):

1. Your original Form I-589, with all questions completed, and the application signed by you in Part D and signed by any preparer in Part E; and
2. One passport-style photograph of you stapled to the form at Part D.

Behind your original Form I-589, attach in the following order:

1. One Form G-28, Notice of Entry of Appearance as Attorney or Representative, signed by you and the attorney or representative, if you are represented by an attorney or representative;
2. The originals of all supplementary sheets and supplementary statements submitted with your application;
3. One copy of any additional supporting documentation;
4. One copy of the evidence of your relationship to your spouse and unmarried children under 21 years of age to be included in your application, if any; and
5. Two copies of the items listed above in your original package, except your photograph.

If you are including family members in your application, attach one additional package for each family member. Arrange each family member's package as follows:

1. One copy of your completed, signed Form I-589 and supplementary sheets submitted with the original application. In Part A.II., staple in the upper right corner one passport-style photo of the family member to be included; and
2. One copy of Form G-28, if any.

For example, if you include your spouse and two children, you should submit your original package, plus two duplicates for you, plus one package for your spouse and one package for each child, for a total of six packages. Be sure each has the appropriate documentation.

NOTE: Any additional pages submitted should include your printed name (exactly as it appears in Part A.I. of the form), A-Number (if any), signature and date.

XI. Incomplete Asylum Applications

An asylum application that is incomplete will be returned to you by mail within 30 days of receipt of the application by USCIS. An application that has not been returned to you within 30 days of having been received by USCIS will be considered complete, and you will receive written acknowledgement of receipt from USCIS.

The filing of a complete application starts the 150-day period you must wait before you may apply for employment authorization. If your application is not complete and is returned to you, the 150-day period will not begin until you resubmit a complete application. (See Section V, Employment Authorization, Part 2 of these instructions for further information regarding eligibility for employment authorization.)

An application will be considered incomplete in each of the following cases:

1. The application does not include a response to each of the questions contained in Form I-589;
2. The application is unsigned;
3. The application is submitted without the required photograph;
4. The application is sent without the appropriate number of copies for any supporting materials submitted; or
5. You indicated in Part D that someone prepared the application other than yourself or an immediate family member and the preparer failed to complete Part E of the asylum application.

XII. Where to File?

Although USCIS will confirm in writing its receipt of your application, you may wish to send the completed forms by registered mail (return receipt requested) for your own records.

If you are in proceedings in Immigration Court:

If you are currently in proceedings in Immigration Court (that is, if you have been served with Form I-221, Order to Show Cause and Notice of Hearing; Form I-122, Notice to Applicant for Admission Detained for Hearing Before an Immigration Judge; Form I-862, Notice to Appear; or Form I-863, Notice of Referral to Immigration Judge), you are required to file your Form I-589 with the Immigration Court having jurisdiction over your case.

At the master calendar hearing, counsel for DHS will provide you with a form entitled *Instructions For Submitting Certain Applications In Immigration Court and For Providing Biometric and Biographical Information to U.S. Citizenship and Immigration Services* (Pre-Filing Instructions) that you must follow. The Pre-Filing Instructions may also be obtained at www.uscis.gov. The following paragraphs describe the Pre-Filing Instructions that you will have to follow.

In addition to filing your Form I-589 with the immigration judge and serving a copy on the appropriate Immigration and Customs Enforcement (ICE) Office of Chief Counsel, you must also complete the following requirements before the immigration judge can grant relief or protection in your case.

Send the following three items to the USCIS Nebraska Service Center:

1. A clear copy of the first three pages of your completed Form I-589 that you will be filing or have filed with the Immigration Court, which must include **your full name, current residential address, current mailing address, and A-Number. Do not** submit any documents other than the first three pages of the completed Form I-589;
2. A copy of Form EOIR-28, Notice of Entry of Appearance as Attorney or Representative Before the Immigration Court, if you are represented; and
3. A copy of the Pre-Filing Instructions provided by counsel for DHS that you received at your first master calendar hearing in immigration removal proceedings.

USCIS Nebraska Service Center
Defensive Asylum Application with Immigration Court
P.O. Box 87589
Lincoln, NE 68501-7589

Note: There is no filing fee required for Form I-589 applications.

After the three items are received at the USCIS Nebraska Service Center, **you will receive**:

1. A USCIS receipt notice indicating that USCIS received your Form I-589; and
2. An Application Support Center (ASC) notice for you and any eligible spouse and children included in your Form I-589 who are also in removal proceedings. Each ASC notice will indicate the individual's unique receipt number and will provide instructions for each person to appear for an appointment at a nearby ASC for collection of biometrics (such as your photograph, fingerprints, and signature). If you do not receive the ASC notice in 3 weeks, call **1-800-375-5283** (1-800-767-1833, TDD for the hearing impaired).

NOTE: If you also mail applications for other forms of relief that you are applying for while in removal proceedings, as specified by the Pre-Filing Instructions (see side B) provided by counsel for DHS at your master calendar hearing, you will receive two notices with different receipt numbers. You must wait for and take both scheduling notices to your ASC appointment.

You (and your eligible spouse and children) must then:

1. **Attend** the biometrics appointment at the ASC and obtain a **biometrics confirmation** document before leaving the ASC; and
2. **Retain** your **ASC biometrics confirmation** as proof that your biometrics were taken and bring it to your future Immigration Court hearings.

NOTE: If the instructions above should change for submitting copies of the first three pages of your asylum application to the USCIS Nebraska Service Center for purposes of receiving the receipt notice and ASC scheduling appointment, you will be provided the changed instructions, either at the master calendar hearing or at another point in the Immigration Court proceedings. Follow the instructions you are provided, or else you may not receive the ASC biometrics scheduling notice in a timely manner.

1. After completion of exclusion, deportation, or removal proceedings, and in conjunction with a motion to reopen under 8 CFR part 3, with the Immigration Court having jurisdiction over the prior proceeding, any such motion must reasonably explain the failure to request asylum prior to the completion of the proceedings; or

2. In proceedings under 8 CFR 208.2(c) and 1208.2(c) and after Form I-863, Notice of Referral to Immigration Judge, has been served on you and filed with the Immigration Court, an immigration judge will have exclusive jurisdiction over your case.

If you are in proceedings before the Board of Immigration Appeals:

You may file your Form I-589 with the Board of Immigration Appeals in conjunction with a motion to remand or reopen under 8 CFR 1003.2 and 1003.8. You may file an initial Form I-589 with the Board of Immigration Appeals only if the Board of Immigration Appeals has jurisdiction over your case. Any such motion must reasonably explain the failure to request asylum and/or withholding of removal prior to the completion of the proceedings.

If you are not in proceedings in Immigration Court or before the Board of Immigration Appeals:

Mail your completed Form I-589 and any other additional information to the USCIS Service Center as indicated below.

If you previously applied for and were denied asylum by USCIS or if you were previously included in a spouse's or parent's pending application but you are no longer eligible to be included as a dependent, mail your completed I-589 to the Asylum Office having jurisdiction over your place of residence. (See www.uscis.gov/asylum for information on Asylum Office jurisdiction.) Include a letter with your application stating that you previously applied for asylum and were denied or that you are now filing independently for asylum. Reference in the letter the application on which you were a dependent.

If you live in:	**Mail your application to:**
Alabama, Arkansas, Colorado, District of Columbia, Florida, Georgia, Louisiana, Maryland, Mississippi, New Mexico, North Carolina, Oklahoma, Western Pennsylvania* (*in the jurisdiction of the Pittsburgh Sub-office*), Puerto Rico, South Carolina, Tennessee, Texas, U.S.Virgin Islands, Utah, Vermont, Virginia, West Virginia, or Wyoming	**USCIS Texas Service Center** Attn: Asylum P.O. Box 851892 Mesquite, TX 75185-1892

If you live in:	**Mail your application to:**
Alaska, Northern California*, Idaho, Illinois, Indiana, Iowa, Kansas, Kentucky, Michigan, Minnesota, Missouri, Montana, Nebraska, Northern Nevada* (*in the jurisdiction of the Reno Sub-office*), North Dakota, Oregon, Ohio, South Dakota, Washington, or Wisconsin	**USCIS Nebraska Service Center** P.O. Box 87589 Lincoln, NE 68501-7589
Arizona, Southern California*, Guam, Hawaii, or Northern Nevada* (*in the jurisdiction of the Las Vegas Sub-office*),	**USCIS California Service Center** P.O. Box 10881 Laguna Niguel, CA 92607-0881
Connecticut, Delaware, Maine, Massachusetts, New Hampshire, New Jersey, New York, Eastern Pennsylvania* (*in the jurisdiction of the Pittsburgh Sub-office*), Rhode Island, or Vermont	**USCIS Vermont Service Center** Attn: Asylum 75 Lower Welden Street St. Albans, VT 05479-0589

***NOTE:** Applicants living in California, Nevada, and Pennsylvania should call the USCIS National Customer Service Center or their local Asylum Office if they are unsure where to mail their applications.

National Customer Service Center: 1-800-375-5283

TDD for the Hearing Impaired: 1-800-767-1833

California and Nevada Residents

Los Angeles Asylum Office: 714-808-8000

San Francisco Asylum Office: 415-293-1234

Pennsylvania Residents

Arlington Asylum Office: 703-235-4100

Newark Asylum Office: 201-531-0555

Information concerning asylum offices and where to file asylum applications is also available on the USCIS Web site at www.uscis.gov.

You may file your completed Form I-589 directly with the Asylum Office having jurisdiction over your case only if:

1. You have received the express consent of the Asylum Office Director or the Director of the Asylum Division to do so; or

2. You were previously included in a spouse's or parent's pending application but you are no longer eligible to be included as a derivative applicant. In such cases, you must include a cover letter referencing the previous application and explaining that you are now independently filing for asylum.

The following categories of individuals are not entitled to an asylum interview at a USCIS Asylum Office:

1. Certain alien crewmembers;
2. Certain stowaways;
3. Visa Waiver Program applicants for admission;
4. Visa Waiver Program overstays and status violators;
5. Certain aliens ordered removed under section 235(c) of the INA on security-related grounds; and
6. Certain nonimmigrants admitted under section101(a)(15)(S) of the INA (e.g., witnesses and informants).

Individuals subject to these special categories who file asylum applications with USCIS Service Centers will be served with Form I-863, Notice of Referral to Immigration Judge, when they appear at the USCIS Asylum Office and will be referred to Immigration Court for an asylum-only hearing.

If you fall into one of the above categories and you have not yet been served with Form I-863, you may file your completed Form I-589 with USCIS Service Center having jurisdiction over your application. The Asylum Office Director may elect to serve you with Form I-863, in which case the Asylum Office Director will forward your asylum application to the appropriate Immigration Court.

If you are an alien crewmember in custody and you have been given Form I-589 as well as information about the privilege of being represented by counsel and the consequences of knowingly filing a frivolous asylum application, you have 10 days within which to submit your completed Form I-589 to the Immigration and Customs Enforcement (ICE) Field Office Director having jurisdiction over the port of entry at which your vessel arrived. The Field Office Director may extend the 10-day filing period for good cause. Once you file your application, the Field Office Director will serve you with Form I-863 and immediately forward your application to the appropriate Immigration Court.

Part 2. Information Regarding Post-Filing Requirements

I. Notification Requirements When Your Address Changes

If you change your address, you must inform USCIS in writing within 10 days of moving.

While your asylum application is pending with the Asylum Office, you must notify the Asylum Office on Form AR-11, Alien's Change of Address Card, or by a signed and dated letter notifying USCIS within 10 days after you change your address.

The address that you provide on the application, or the last change of address notification that you submitted, will be used by USCIS for mailing. Any notices mailed to that address will constitute adequate service, except that personal service may be required for the following: Form I-122, Notice to Alien Detained for Hearing by an Immigration Judge; Form I-221, Order to Show Cause; Form I-862, Notice to Appear; Form I-863, Notice of Referral to Immigration Judge; and Form I-860, Notice and Order of Expedited Removal.

If you are already in proceedings in Immigration Court, you must notify the Immigration Court on EOIR Form 33, Alien's Change of Address Card, of any changes of address within 5 days of the change in address. You must send the notification to the Immigration Court having jurisdiction over your case. You must also notify USCIS on Form AR-11, Alien's Change of Address Card, or by a signed and dated letter within 10 days after you change your address.

II. Asylum Interview Process

If you are not in proceedings in Immigration Court, you will be notified by the USCIS Asylum Office of the time, date, and place (address) of a scheduled interview.

USCIS suggests that you bring a copy of your Form I-589 with you when you have your asylum interview. An asylum officer will interview you under oath and make a determination concerning your claim. In most cases, you will not be notified of the decision in your case until a date after your interview.

You have the right to legal representation at your interview, at no cost to the U.S. Government. (See **Section IV, Right to Counsel.**) You also may bring witnesses with you to the interview to testify on your behalf.

If you are unable to proceed with the asylum interview in fluent English, you must provide, at no expense to USCIS, a competent interpreter fluent in both English and a language that you speak fluently.

Your interpreter must be at least 18 years of age. The following persons cannot serve as your interpreter: your attorney or representative of record, a witness testifying on your behalf at the interview, or a representative or employee of your country. Quality interpretation may be crucial to your claim. Such assistance must be obtained at your expense prior to the interview.

Failure without good cause to bring a competent interpreter to your interview may be considered an unexcused failure to appear for the interview. Any unexcused failure to appear for an interview may prevent you from receiving employment authorization, and your asylum application may be dismissed or referred directly to the Immigration Court.

If you are hearing-impaired and require the services of a sign language interpreter in your language, one will be provided for you. Contact the Asylum Office with jurisdiction over your case as soon as you receive a notice for your asylum interview to notify the office that you will need a sign language interpreter in your language so that accommodations can be made in advance.

If available, you must bring some form of identification to your interview, including any passport(s), other travel or identification documents, or Form I-94, Arrival-Departure Record. You may bring to the interview any additional available items documenting your claim that you have not already submitted with your application. All documents must be submitted in triplicate.

If members of your family are included in your application for asylum, they must also appear for the interview and bring any identity or travel documents they have in their possession.

III. Status While Your Application Is Pending

While your case is pending, you will be permitted to remain in the United States. After your asylum interview, if you have not been granted asylum and appear to be removable under section 237 of the INA, 8 U.S.C. 1227, or inadmissible under section 212 of the INA, 8 U.S.C. 1182, your application will be referred to the Immigration Court by the Asylum Office.

IV. Travel Outside the United States

If you leave the United States without first obtaining advance parole from USCIS using Form I-131, Application for a Travel Document, we will presume that you have abandoned your application. If you obtain advance parole and return to the country of claimed persecution, we will presume that you abandoned your application, unless you can show that there were compelling reasons for your return.

NOTE: The application process for advance parole varies depending on your personal circumstances. Use InfoPass on the USCIS Web site to check with your local USCIS District Office for application instructions. Additional information on obtaining advance parole is available from the USCIS Web site at www.uscis.gov.

V. Employment Authorization While Your Application Is Pending

You will be granted permission to work if your asylum application is granted.

Simply filing an application for asylum does not entitle you to employment authorization. You may request permission to work if your asylum application is pending and 150 days have lapsed since your application was accepted by USCIS or the Immigration Court. (See 8 CFR sections 208.7(a)(1) and 1208.7(a)(1).) Any delay in the processing of your asylum application that you request or cause will not be counted as part of the 150-day period.

If your asylum application has not been denied within 180 days from the date of filing a complete asylum application, you may be granted permission to work by filing Form I-765, Application for Employment Authorization, with USCIS. Follow the instructions on that application and submit it with a copy of evidence as specified in the instructions that you have a pending asylum application.

Each family member whom you have asked to be included in your application and who also wants permission to work must submit a separate Form I-765.

You may obtain copies of Form I-765 by calling the USCIS forms line at 1-800-870-3676 or from the USCIS Web site at www.uscis.gov.

USCIS Privacy Act Statement

AUTHORITIES: The information requested on this application, and the associated evidence, is collected pursuant to Sections 208 and 241(b)(3) of the Immigration and Nationality Act, as amended.

PURPOSE: The primary purpose for providing the requested information on this form is to determine eligibility for asylum in the United States, and for withholding of removal. The information may also be used to apply for deferral of removal under the Convention Against Torture.

DISCLOSURE: The information you provide is voluntary. However, failure to provide the requested information, and any requested evidence, may delay a final decision or result in the denial of your benefit request.

ROUTINE USES: The information you provide on this benefit application may be shared with other federal, state, local, and foreign government agencies and authorized organizations in accordance with approved routine uses, as described in the associated published system of records notices [**DHS-USCIS-010 - Asylum Information and Pre-Screening**, which can be found at www.dhs.gov/privacy]. The information may also be made available, as appropriate for law enforcement purposes or in the interest of national security.

USCIS Forms and Information

You can get USCIS forms and immigration-related information on the USCIS Web site at **www.uscis.gov**. You may order USCIS forms by calling the toll-free number at **1-800-870-3676**. You may also obtain forms and information by telephoning the USCIS National Customer Service Center at **1-800-375-5283** (1-800-767-1833, TDD for the hearing impaired).

Additional information concerning asylum and withholding of removal is available on the USCIS Web site at www.uscis.gov/asylum and the EOIR Web site at www.usdoj.gov/eoir.

Penalties

If you knowingly and willfully falsify or conceal a material fact or submit a false document with Form I-589, we will deny your Form I-589 and may deny any other immigration benefit.

In addition, you will face severe penalties provided by law and may be subject to criminal prosecution.

For specific information, see see **Part E in Part 1, Section V,** of these instructions.

Paperwork Reduction Act

An agency may not conduct or sponsor an information collection and a person is not required to respond to a collection of information unless it displays a currently valid OMB control number. The public reporting burden for this collection of information is estimated at 12 minutes per response, including the time for reviewing instructions, and completing and submitting the form. Send comments regarding this burden estimate or any other aspect of this collection of information, including suggestions for reducing this burden to: U.S. Citizenship and Immigration Services, Regulatory Coordination Division, Office of Policy & Strategy, 20 Massachusetts Ave NW, Washington, DC 20529-2140. OMB No. 1516-0067. **Do not mail your completed Form I-589 to this address.**

Supplements to Form I-589

Form I-589, Supplement A - For use to complete Part A.II.

Form I-589, Supplement B - For use to complete Parts B and C and to provide additional information for any other part of the application.

APPENDIX 2B

CHECKLIST FOR ASYLUM APPLICATION (FORM I-589)

CHECKLIST FOR FORM I-589

Now, more than ever, it is important for applicants to file complete and detailed applications for asylum. An incomplete or incorrectly filed application could delay the receipt of employment authorization and cause additional problems at the asylum interview or hearing before the immigration judge (IJ). An incomplete application may also cause the application to be filed beyond the one-year deadline, requiring additional proof that an earlier filing had been attempted.

> ➢ ***Note***: Read the I-589 filing instructions completely and carefully. This checklist is not a substitute for the instructions.

- ☐ **Complete every question**. An unanswered question may result in the application being returned as incomplete. If the question addresses information provided in the applicant's declaration, provide a summary response and the notation "see attached declaration for additional information."

- ☐ **Attach a declaration from the applicant**. An effective way of presenting the asylum claim is in a narrative form in chronological order. A declaration allows the applicant to present his or her claim in this manner. Always include a summary of the claim at the beginning of the declaration. *See* appx. 2C, Sample Declaration.

- ☐ **List the applicant's spouse and *all* children**. This information should be given whether or not the spouse and children are present in the United States and should include all children regardless of their age or marital status.

- ☐ **Make sure the applicant signs the form**. The applicant should only sign a completed form and only after he or she has thoroughly reviewed the contents of the application and the declaration. By signing the form, the applicant certifies under penalty of perjury that the information and evidence submitted are true and correct. If it is determined that the applicant knowingly submitted a frivolous application, he or she may be permanently barred from obtaining any immigration benefits under the Immigration and Nationality Act. An application is frivolous if the applicant knowingly makes a material misrepresentation.

- ☐ **The preparer must also sign the form**. The only exception is if the preparer is an immediate family member (spouse, parent, or child) of the applicant. If anyone assisted the preparer, he or she must also sign the form. The preparer's failure to sign will result in the application being returned as incomplete.

- ☐ **Send by certified mail to the correct service center**. If the applicant is filing affirmatively (*i.e.,* he or she is not in removal proceedings) the application must be filed with a U.S. Citizenship and Immigration Services service center. Always file the application by certified mail, return receipt requested. *See* Section XII, "Where to File" in the instructions to the application. *(If, however, the applicant is applying for the first time in removal proceedings, the applicant must file the I-589 with the immigration court at a master calendar hearing.)* If the applicant is filing in immigration court, the applicant must be present with his or her attorney and submit the application in a hearing in front of the IJ.

CHECKLIST FOR FILING THE I-589

> ➢ ***Note***: Read the I-589 filing instructions completely and carefully. This checklist is not a substitute for the instructions that are currently 13 pages in length.

- ☐ The original and two copies of the completed, signed form, including any supplementary sheets, affidavits, and statements.

- ☐ Three copies of supporting documentation, including passports, travel documents, and identity documents, marriage certificate (if spouse is included in the application), birth certificates (for children under 21 included in the application), and documentation of country conditions. The applicant should take all original documents to the asylum interview. If the documents are numerous, it may be useful to make an index of the supporting documents and to tab each document for easy reference.

- ☐ Three copies of any medical reports, evaluations, or assessments submitted in support of the applicant's claim.

- ☐ An additional copy of the complete application and all attached documentation for each family member present in the United States who is included in the application.

- ☐ One passport-style photograph for the applicant and each family member included in the application (taken no more than 30 days before submitting the application).

- ☐ Form G-28 (Notice of Entry of Appearance as Attorney or Representative) signed by the applicant and the attorney or accredited representative.

- ☐ **Translations**. Any documents in languages other than English must be accompanied by an English translation and a certificate of translation certifying that the translation is true and correct. See appx. 3D, Sample Certificate of Translation:

See also Section X, "Organizing Your Application," in the instructions to the application.

***Reminder**: Always keep a complete set of any documents submitted to the asylum office or immigration court!*

APPENDIX 2C

PRACTICE POINTER: QUESTION-BY-QUESTION GUIDANCE ON COMPLETING THE FORM I-589, APPLICATION FOR ASYLUM AND FOR WITHHOLDING OF REMOVAL

Practice Pointer: Completing the Form I-589

Question-By-Question Guidance on Completing the Form I-589, Application for Asylum and for Withholding of Removal

By Lisa Green and Dree K. Collopy, Asylum and Refugee Liaison Committee
July 14, 2014

The following practice pointer provides tips to help ensure proper completion of Form I-589, Application for Asylum and Withholding of Removal. While it offers an overview of each question on the Form I-589, it is not a substitute for conducting thorough research and fully investigating the facts of each individual case to determine how to best present the application.

GENERAL PRACTICE POINTERS

- The application should be typed (preferable) or handwritten in BLACK ink.
- What may appear to be a simple question could be critical to your client's eligibility for asylum. Do not assume that the answer to a question will be straight-forward; you should explore all possible answers with your clients. Due to language and cultural barriers, filling out the I-589 often can prove to be a long, tedious process. Please plan accordingly; the I-589 should never be rushed and often will not be completed in one sitting.
- Generally, you should provide answers to all of the questions in the application. If the answer to a question is not simple and/or requires explanation, or your client is unsure of the information, place an asterisk by the answer along with a comment, "See Supplement B" (handwritten is fine if you cannot type it in). You can then list explanations on the I-589 Supplement B form. It is usually advisable to include explanations, especially if there are unusual circumstances. See the discussion below for specific examples of where this issue might arise.
- Ensure that ALL the information in the form is consistent with ALL the supporting documentation submitted, including your client's affidavit, witness affidavits, and country conditions evidence. It is critical to ensure that each supporting document is internally consistent and consistent with all supporting documents. Review the credibility and corroboration requirements for establishing asylum eligibility, particularly following the enactment of the REAL ID Act. Credibility and corroboration are more essential than ever before . You may find it helpful to complete the longer answers on pages 5-8 of the I-589 after you and your client have completed a detailed declaration and the client has provided all supporting documentation; important details tend to emerge during the

preparation of the case. If there are any inconsistencies, they should be explained or fixed.

- Do not leave blank spaces, except in Part A. II. (Information About Spouse and Children) if you have checked the boxes "I am not married" or "I do not have any children." The service center may reject an I-589 if there are blank spaces. If the answer is none or does not apply, write "None" or "N/A."

PART A.I. INFORMATION ABOUT YOU (This is information about the APPLICANT)

- Submitting an I-589 is automatically an application for both withholding of removal under INA § 241(b)(3) ("withholding") and asylum under INA § 208(a). Thus, there is no need to check a separate box to request withholding. However, relief under the Convention Against Torture ("CAT") must be separately requested by checking the box found above PART A.I. on the form in order to apply. Additionally, the "Torture Convention" box on Page 5, Part B, Question 1 should also be checked. Please note that U.S. Citizenship and Immigration Services ("USCIS") Asylum Offices only have jurisdiction to adjudicate asylum. They cannot adjudicate applications for withholding or CAT. However, even if your client is applying affirmatively for asylum, it is important to check the two CAT boxes, if warranted, in order to preserve that remedy in court.

- Question 1 – Alien Registration Number:
    - The Alien Registration Number is also referred to as the "A" number. It is an 8 or 9 digit number preceded with an "A." If you are preparing an affirmative asylum application and your client has never had any contact with DHS, there is the possibility that s/he does not have an A number. If this is the case, enter "N/A." An A number will be generated upon filing the asylum application and will be noted on the receipt notice. The I-589 can then be amended at the interview to include the A number. If your client has had previous applications with DHS or is in removal proceedings, s/he should have an A number. You can find this number on most documentation from DHS.

- Question 2 – Social Security Number:
    - The question simply asks for a U.S. social security number. It does not ask for any social security number ever <u>used.</u> Ask your client if they have a valid social security number. If they do not, list "N/A."

- Questions 3-5 – Biographical Information:
    - Ensure that your client's name matches his/her identity documents unless your client entered under a false name. If your client entered under a false name, use your client's legal name.
    - In some cultures/countries, people do not have first, middle, and/or last names. If your client does not have a first, middle, or last name, leave that spot blank. Do not write in "N/A" or "None" on the application, as USCIS might issue documents with "N/A" or "None" as part of the name. For applicants who do not have a first name, USCIS will "rename" the person as "FNU" (first name

unknown). Your client either will have to prove that they do in fact have a first name or, if granted asylum and USCIS documents show the first name as "FNU," your client will have to complete a legal name change. Otherwise, they will be known as "FNU." There are many "FNUs" in the U.S.
  - In some countries or cultures, the order of names can be confusing. Talk to your client to ensure that you are listing the order of their names correctly. Keep in mind, however, that the name must match the identity documents.
  - Sometimes your client's true name does not match the name on their identity documents. List their true name, and then list the name that is on their documentation under Question 6. Put an asterisk after their true name and fully explain the circumstances. In this instance, your client should attempt to produce identity documents to corroborate the true and correct name.
  - If your client's legal name does not match DHS documents, specify this in Question 6.

- Question 6 – Other Names Used:
  - List any names that your client has ever used. Ask your client about this specifically and in many different ways, as they may initially be inclined to state that they have not used other names. For example:
    - If the applicant has two last names, s/he easily could have used one or the other at some time. S/he also could have reversed the order. Include all variations, including and excluding hyphens if necessary.
    - Ask about nicknames.
    - Ask about aliases.
    - If they entered on a false name, list that name here.
    - Ask about maiden names.

- Question 7 – Address in the U.S.:
  - "Address in the U.S." is where your client is physically residing and the telephone number associated with that residence. The mailing address is listed separately in Question 8.

- Questions 8 – Mailing Address:
  - If your client's mailing address/phone number is the same as their physical residence, write "Same as above" in the first line of the address and phone number questions. Do not leave these blank.
  - If your client's name is not on the mailbox, be sure to include the relevant individual's name in the "c/o" space for mailing purposes.

- Question 9 – Gender:
  - If your client's circumstances or asylum claim involves issues of gender identity, insert an asterisk in this space and note "See Supplement B." Add your explanation to the Supplement B form in the back of the I-589 application.

- Question 10 – Marital Status:

- Sometimes, the answer to Question 10 is not clear cut. Different cultures have different definitions of married, single, divorced, and widowed. For example, your client may consider him/herself married or divorced, even if there was never a legal ceremony or recording of a certificate. Under the laws of their home country (e.g. customary or common law), it still may be a viable marriage/divorce. In cases such as this, you will have to research to see what documentation is available to establish the marital status. The Foreign Affairs Manual ("FAM"), Country Reciprocity Schedule is a good starting place. Please note, though, that the FAM is not always up-to-date and should be used as a starting point only. If this issue is germane to the asylum claim, additional research will be necessary. If it is not germane to the case, you can always add an asterisk with an explanation on the Supplement B form.
- Your client may respond that s/he is single because s/he is not currently living with his/her spouse. In this situation, the correct answer may actually be "married" or "divorced," depending on the circumstances.
- Overall, be sure to engage in detailed fact-finding on the question of marital status, and keep in mind that cultural differences may lead to different definitions of these concepts.

- Question 11 – Date of Birth:
  - If your client has supplied you with identity documents, make sure that the date of birth you write on the form is the same as the date on these documents. If there is a discrepancy between what your client is telling you and the date on the documents, or if there is a discrepancy within the documents themselves, put an asterisk with an explanation on the Supplement B form.
  - In some cultures and during certain periods of countries' histories, birthdays are not recorded and/or are unknown. If your client states January 1 of some year, this is usually an indication that they do not really know the exact date of their birth. DHS is aware of this issue. Again, you can include the client's best guess or choose to write unknown and, in either scenario, put an asterisk and explain in the Supplement B form.

- Question 12 – City and Country of Birth:
  - Ensure that this answer comports with the client's biographical documents that you are filing. If there are inconsistencies between documents or what your client is reporting, be sure to note with an asterisk and provide an explanation in the Supplement B form.
  - Clients may state that they are from the closest or biggest city/town to their village, rather than the actual village. It is not uncommon for birth certificates to list the town where the birth was recorded as the place of birth, rather than the actual place of birth. Be sure to probe your client in detail about this to determine the actual place of birth if they were in fact born in a village. Again, if there are discrepancies between what your client tells you and his/her biographical documents, add an asterisk and explain in the Supplement B form.

- Question 13 – Present Nationality (Citizenship):

- The term "nationality" refers not only to citizenship or membership of an ethnic or linguistic group, but may occasionally overlap with the term "race." *See* UNHCR, *Handbook on Procedure and Criteria for determining Refugee Status under the 1951 Convention and the 1967 Protocol relating to the status of Refugees*, HCR/IP/4/Eng/Rev. 1, ¶ 74 (1979, rev. 1992).
- In most cases, this is an easy question to answer because nationality and citizenship are the same. However, in some cases, nationality and citizenship will be different, or the country in which your client was a national or citizen no longer exists. Additionally, your client may have a nationality, but be stateless. In these situations, be sure to add an asterisk and explain in the Supplement B form.

- **Question 14** – Nationality at Birth:
  - Question 14 is relatively straightforward, as the question asks for nationality only at the time of birth (as opposed to the nationality/citizenship query in Question 13). Note, however, that this may not be the same as the country of birth. Remember that some countries have changed their names or gained independence during your client's lifetime. For example, a client may have been born in the USSR, but since become a citizen of Belarus. In this situation, be sure to give the correct historical name of the country of nationality at birth. Clients may also consider their nationality to be different from their country of birth. For example, Jews from the former Soviet Union may consider their nationality as Jewish rather than USSR.

- **Question 15** – Race, Ethnic, or Tribal Group:
  - If the case is based on one of these characteristics, it is critical that the correct information be listed. For example, do not write "Black" if the case is based on a tribal group. It is important to list the specific tribe.

- **Question 16** – Religion:
  - If your client belongs to a specific denomination of a religion, be sure to list this. For example, if your client is an Evangelical Christian, do not simply list "Christian."

- **Question 17** – Procedural History:
  - It is critical that you understand the procedural posture of your case. Clients may be confused about this. The best practice is to ask this question in the simplest of terms and in a variety of ways. For example, you may want to ask the following: Have you ever been contacted by immigration?, Have you ever seen an immigration judge?, Have you ever been in jail?, Have you ever been fingerprinted?, etc.

- **Question 18** – Exit of Home Country/Entry to U.S.:
  - If your client entered legally, besure that the dates inthis question match up with his/her passport stamps and I-94 card, if your client has one. If your client entered without inspection ("EWI") and is unsure of the exact date of entry, write

his/her best guess, include an asterisk, and provide an explanation in the Supplement B form.

- Keep in mind that this question addresses the statutory one-year filing deadline. When completing this question, ask if your client has documents to prove the entry date or to prove that s/he was outside the U.S. within one year of filing his/her application.
- If some of the answers are not applicable – for example, the I-94 number or the date status expires for someone who entered EWI – list "N/A."
- If your client is in F-1 or J-1 status, and they were admitted for the duration of their status, list "D/S."

- Questions 19 - 21 – Passport/Travel Document Information:
  - If your client does not have a passport, place "N/A" in all of the answer spaces. If your client entered on a false passport and still has that passport, list "N/A" with an asterisk and explain the entry with the false passport in the Supplement B form.

- Question 22 – Native Language:
  - Native language refers to the language the applicant spoke in his or her home while growing up. If relevant, the tribal language should be included here. The language of education should be listed in Question 24 (see below). Remember to include specific dialect(s), if relevant.

- Question 23 – Fluent in English?
  - Unless your client's first language is English or their English is perfect, check the "NO" box. This preserves his/her ability to have an interpreter present at an affirmative asylum interview.
  - In cases where your client is not a native English speaker, it is advisable to bring an interpreter to the interview. Applicants get nervous at their interviews, which may affect their ability to communicate in English. Even seemingly fluent English speakers may find their ability compromised under the stressful circumstances of an asylum interview.
  - Please note that, unlike an individual hearing in immigration court, USCIS will NOT provide an interpreter for an affirmative asylum interview. Instead, the applicant must provide his/her own interpreter. USCIS will also provide an interpreter to monitor the interview and ensure that the interpretation is correct.
  - For defensive asylum applications in immigration court, request an interpreter for the individual hearing at the master calendar hearing. Be sure to request an interpreter in the client's best language, including the specific dialect. If possible, have a native speaker at the individual hearing to serve as a monitor to ensure that the court's interpreter is interpreting clearly and correctly.

- Question 24 – Other Languages Spoken:
  - List all other languages in which your client is fluent. See Question 23 above for a discussion of fluency.

AILA InfoNet Doc. No. 14071402. (Posted 7/14/14)

- If your client does not speak any languages other than the ones you have already listed, write "None" here. If this is left blank, the application will likely be rejected.

PART A. II INFORMATION ABOUT SPOUSE AND CHILDREN

SPOUSE:

- Please note that above Question 1, you must check the box "I am not married" if this is the case.
- As noted previously noted, ask your client detailed questions about their marital status. If there are any doubts, include an asterisk and an explanation in the Supplement B form. You will have to prove marital status in order for the spouse to be granted asylum as a derivative.

- If you are in doubt about whether a marriage is legal, err on the side of including the spouse here and consider providing an explanation in the Supplement B form. Failure to do so may exclude the spouse from eligibility as the beneficiary of an I-730 Refugee/Asylee Relative Petition.

- QUESTIONS 1- 23 – Spouse's Biographical Information:
  - If your client is NOT married and you already checked the "I am not married" box, it is not necessary to put "None" or "N/A" in any of the questions in this section. You can simply leave these questions blank.
  - Please see comments in Part A.II. regarding how to fill out the corresponding biographical information for your client's spouse.
  - If your client has more than one spouse, you must list information for all the spouses. However, be sure to inform you client that even if the multiple marriages are valid in the country where they were entered into, DHS will NOT recognize any marriages after the first marriage as viable for purposes of the I-730 Refugee/Asylee Relative Petition or for inclusion as a derivative applicant.

- Question 24 – Including Spouse in the Application:
  - If your client's spouse is not in the U.S., leave this blank. Your client will need to file an I-730 Refugee/Asylee Relative Petition for the spouse after the asylum application is approved if they want to come to the U.S.
  - If the spouse is already in the U.S. and wants to be eligible for derivative status, check the "YES" box; if your client is successful in obtaining affirmative asylum, the spouse will be considered a derivative (as long as you have proved the legal relationship) and will automatically be issued an I-94 card reflecting asylee status. If the principal applicant becomes eligible for work authorization while the case is pending, the spouse will also be eligible. Note, however, that the spouse must file a separate I-765 application.
  - If the principal is in removal proceedings, the court will only have jurisdiction to grant asylum to the spouse if the spouse has also been issued a Notice to Appear.

Otherwise, upon being granted asylum by the court, the applicant must file an I-730 Refugee/Asylee Relative Petition for the spouse.

- o There may be circumstances in which a spouse in the U.S. does not wish to risk being placed in removal proceedings. If this is the case, the applicant may check the "NO" box and include the spouse in the affirmative I-589. If asylum is ultimately granted to the principal applicant, an I-730 may be filed for the spouse.

<u>CHILDREN:</u>

- Please note that above Question 1, you must check the box "I do not have any children" or "I have children."

- If your client has adopted children, include them in the number of children listed. Note that if the children were customarily adopted, you will need to do research to determine if the adoption was legal under the laws of the country in which the adoption occurred. If you cannot make that assessment when filing the application, place an asterisk by the biographical information of the child who was customarily adopted and provide an explanation in the Supplement B form.

- You do not have to include deceased children or children who were legally adopted from the applicant into another family.

- Keep in mind that the purpose of this section is to ensure that children will be granted derivative asylum or an I-730 Refugee/Asylee Relative Petition if the applicant is granted asylum. If a child is NOT listed on this section, and your client later applies for the unnamed child, this may pose a serious challenge. It is therefore better to list <u>all</u> children, regardless of age or marital status, and provide explanations in the Supplement B form.

- If possible, review each child's birth certificate to confirm his/her date of birth. This will avoid future issues with the consulate during the I-730 process.

- In an affirmative asylum approval, a derivative child will be automatically approved and issued an I-94 card, provided that you have proven the legal relationship.

- In removal proceedings, the court will only have jurisdiction to grant asylum to the child if the child has been issued a Notice to Appear.

- Note that if there is not enough space to list all of the applicant's children on the I-589 form itself, the Supplement A form may be used to list any additional children.

- Question 21 – Include Children in the Application:
  - o Please see the comments above in the Spouse section, Question 24.

PART A.III INFORMATION ABOUT YOUR BACKGROUND

- This section requests a lot of addresses and dates, which are often difficult for applicants to remember. If your client responds with a simple, "I don't know" or "I don't remember," ask more specific questions to get as much information as you can. For example, you can create a written or pictorial timeline for them to fill out. If there are gaps or the dates don't match up, clarify these with your client. This can be a tedious process, but it is important.

- Be sure that all of the information is consistent with the supporting documentation and the client's declaration. For example, if your client states that she was involved at a political protest at her university in July of 2009, be sure that the information listed in this section shows that she was at that university during the period covering July of 2009.

- If your client simply cannot remember necessary information, list as much information as you can and provide any explanations in the Supplement B form. Remember that many asylum applicants are victims of trauma, and may have difficulty remembering certain things as a result. If this is the case, be sure to obtain a psychological evaluation explaining these issues.

- Question 1 – Address Prior to Coming to U.S.:
    - Include the client's last address in the country in which persecution occurred, in addition to the applicant's last address abroad if your client lived in a different country before entering the U.S.

- Question 2 – Residence for Past 5 Years:
    - The answer to this may be a repeat of the information in Question 1. Be sure that the addresses are listed in reverse chronological order and that there are no gaps in the dates.
    - Again, it is essential that all addresses are consistent with the applicant's affidavit and supporting documentation.

- Question 3 – Education:
    - In some countries, the "type of school" does not mirror the U.S. education system. List what your client tells you and then include an asterisk and an explanation in the Supplement B form.
    - You may want to do some preliminary research to ensure that the education system your client explains to you is consistent with stated country practices.
    - If your client has school records, be sure that the information in this section comports with those documents, as well as your client's affidavit. Note that all schools attended must be listed here, not just the last five years.

- Question 4 – Employment:
    - If your client disclosed unlawful employment to you, you must include it in this section.

- Remember, your client's credibility is one of the most important factors in the asylum adjudication. If the client hides something, such as unauthorized employment, and the officer/judge discovers it, this could negatively impact the officer's/judge's credibility determination. Generally, it is better to err on the side of disclosure.

- Question 5 – Parents and Siblings:
  - As discussed in Part A.I. Question 12, be sure that your client tells you the actual place of birth of his/her parents or siblings, not simply the closest city.
  - If your client does not have any siblings, write "N/A" or "None." USCIS may return the application as incomplete if you leave these spaces blank.
  - Include step-parents, as well as half- and step-siblings.

<u>PART B. INFORMATION ABOUT YOUR APPLICATION</u>

- Initially, this section requires that you submit general country conditions evidence to corroborate the specific facts of the applicant's claim. If you cannot provide this information, you must explain why. Generally, State Department reports are what asylum officers and immigration judges rely upon most for general country conditions. These can be located at http://www.state.gov/j/drl/rls/hrrpt/. However, keep in mind that State Department reports can be superficial and may not specifically address the issues involved in your client's case. Do not despair if the State Department report does not support your client's claim. You can also file reports from experts or non-governmental organizations, such as Amnesty International or Human Rights Watch, to support your client's application. However, be prepared to explain how these additional reports prove that the State Department report is incomplete or incorrect if that is the case. You should also research to see if there are news or journal articles about the relevant country and events. Discuss your research with your client and revise your client's affidavit as you become more informed about your client's home country.

- In addition to general country conditions evidence, it is critical to file as many specific supporting documents as possible. These should verify the facts of your client's case and corroborate his/her claims. Make sure that all facts in these supporting documents are internally consistent, as well as consistent with your client's affidavit and other supporting documents

- Question 1 – Why you are Applying:
  - As mentioned in the general comments above, check the "Torture Convention" box if your client wants to apply for CAT relief.
  - You can and should check more than one box if there are multiple possible claims.
  - If you are unsure if a ground applies to your case, it is better to check too many boxes than to leave one off. Be prepared at the interview or master calendar hearing to explain how each protected ground applies to your client's case.

- Questions from Part B.1.A. - Part C.6.:

- These questions address the basis of your client's asylum application. It is recommended that the answers to all of these questions be addressed in detail in your client's affidavit. Preparing a detailed written affidavit with your client is essential to the fact-gathering process, ensures that your client's claims are clear, allows your client to organize his/her story clearly in his/her own mind, provides the client with a tool to use to refresh his/her memory prior to an interview or hearing, and enables you to identify and address difficult issues.
- After you have completed the affidavit, provide short summary answers on the I-589 for each question followed by the statement, "Please see sworn affidavit for additional details."
- The answers to these questions on the I-589 form should be summaries of the most important points responsive to the questions asked. Be sure to respond to each of the numbered sub-questions asked under each lettered question in the space provided. Answering each of those sub-questions should provide the asylum officer or immigration judge with enough information to understand the basis of the case.
- Again, be sure that all information provided in these answers is completely consistent with your client's affidavit and with the supporting documentation.
- If your answer to a question here is "NO" and it does not require any explanation, write "N/A" in the answer space.

- Question 1.A. – Past Persecution:
  - The answer to this question must always be "YES" if you are relying on past persecution. As described above, provide summary answers for each of the four sub-questions listed, followed by "Please see sworn affidavit for additional details."
  - If your client (or family, friends, or colleagues) has not experienced past persecution and the case is based on future persecution, only then should you write "NO." Remember, however, that even if your case is based on a fear of future persecution, your client's fear is informed by what has happened to others, and any harm that has been inflicted on anyone who is similarly situated to your client should be mentioned here.

- Question 1.B – Future Persecution:
  - The answer to this question must always be "YES," unless your case is based on the exceptions of humanitarian asylum or the "other harm doctrine" under 8 CFR §208.13. If your client does not fear future persecution and you cannot meet the exceptions listed in the regulations, your client cannot be granted asylum, withholding, or CAT (must meet future torture as opposed to future persecution standard).
  - As described above, provide summary answers for each of the three sub-questions listed, followed by "Please see sworn affidavit for additional details."

- Question 2 – Past Treatment:
  - This question asks about the applicant and the applicant's family members.

AILA InfoNet Doc. No. 14071402. (Posted 7/14/14)

- This question will give USCIS information on whether your client or his/her family members were persecuted in the past. Additionally, it will garner information regarding the "serious nonpolitical crime" bar to asylum codified at INA §208(a)(2)(A)(iii).
- Clients may not understand the legal terms mentioned in this question. It is important to educate your client and clearly explain these terms. If your client has experienced any of these in his or her home country as a result of persecution, you must check "Yes."
- As described above, provide a summary answer addressing the relevant question, followed by "Please see sworn affidavit for additional details."

- Question 3.A – Membership in Groups:
  - In many cases, the answer to this question will be "YES." If your client's claim is based on membership in a certain group (religious organization, political party, etc.), be sure to include that group here, even if it is not a formally recognized group *(i.e.* social group). For example, for religious persecution, be sure to list the church the client belonged to. For political persecution, list the political party.
  - List all groups, even if they are not related to the claim of persecution.
  - Be sure to discuss each group with your client as this question also attempts to identify individuals who may be ineligible for asylum due to Terrorism-Related Inadmissibility Grounds (TRIG). For a general overview on TRIG, see the USCIS website. If your client has been in any type of army, militia, resistance, or guerrilla group, be sure to discuss these in great detail with your client so you can determine whether your client might be ineligible for asylum under INA §§212(a)(3)(B); 237(a)(4)(B).
  - As described above, provide summary answers for each piece of information requested, followed by "Please see sworn affidavit for additional details."

- Question 3.B – Current Participation:
  - If the basis of your client's claim is membership in a particular social group, answer "YES" and provide an explanation as to why the group is immutable or unchangeable.
  - If your client's claim is based on the group(s) discussed in Question 3.A., but he/she no longer participates in the group(s), provide an explanation as to why there is still a risk of future persecution based on that group membership. For example, if your client stopped all political activity since coming to the U.S., explain why there is still a risk of future persecution based on his/her political opinion or activities.
  - As described above, provide summary answers for each piece of information requested, followed by "Please see sworn affidavit for additional details."

- Question 4 – Torture:
  - This question addresses the issue of CAT eligibility. If your client is applying for CAT, the answer to this question must be "YES," or your client will be found ineligible for CAT.

AILA InfoNet Doc. No. 14071402. (Posted 7/14/14)

- Refer to the definition of torture found at 8 CFR §208.18 and in applicable case law. When responding to this question, the harm you describe must rise to the level of "torture" and must have been committed by, at the instigation of, or with the acquiescence of a government official. The harm must also have been inflicted for one of the specific purposes under the definition of "torture" (to punish, threaten, intimidate, etc.).
- A mentioned previously, aThough asylum offices lack jurisdiction to adjudicate CAT claims, these answers should be completed even if the applicant is applying affirmatively.
- As described above, provide summary answers for each piece of information requested, followed by "Please see sworn affidavit for additional details."

PART C. ADDITIONAL INFORMATION ABOUT YOUR APPLICATION

- Part C provides the adjudicator with information about any bars to asylum eligibility that may be applicable in your client's case. Thus, these should be answered very carefully and precisely, with any exceptions or explanations clearly articulated.

- Question 1 – Previous Applications:
  - Pursuant to 8 CFR §208.4(a)(3), an applicant can reapply for asylum as long as the previous application was not denied by an immigration judge (IJ) or the BIA.
  - An applicant can also reapply for asylum if there has been a change in circumstances that materially affect the applicant's eligibility for asylum, regardless of the procedural history of the case. *See* INA §208 (a)(2)(D). Beware, however, that if your client's previous application was adjudicated by an IJ, the BIA, or a federal court, jurisdiction for a new application may lie with that tribunal through a motion to reopen, and an affirmative application to USCIS may be denied for lack of jurisdiction.
  - If family members have applied for asylum or refugee status in the U.S., give their names, A-numbers, dates of application, and results. Consider filing FOIA requests to obtain family members' A-files prior to submitting your client's I-589 to ensure that there are no inconsistencies with or information that would be damaging to your client's claim.
  - As described above, provide summary answers for each piece of information requested, followed by "Please see sworn affidavit for additional details."

- Questions 2.A. and 2.B – Firm Resettlement:
  - These questions address the issue of firm resettlement. Your client must disclose all pertinent information, even if it raises a potential issue. *See* INA §208(a)(2)(A)(vi) and 8 CFR §208.15 and relevant BIA and circuit court case law for the definition and parameters of firm resettlement.
  - If your client had legal status in another country prior to coming to the U.S., it does not automatically mean that he or she was firmly resettled. Be sure to research the nature of the prior legal status (duration, rights accorded, etc.) and include that information as part of your evidence, along with any pertinent evidence of conditions in the country in which your client had status.

AILA InfoNet Doc. No. 14071402. (Posted 7/14/14)

- With regard to Question 2.A., asylum offices expect the client to disclose even transit stops in airports on the way to the U.S.
- As described above, provide summary answers for each piece of information requested, followed by "Please see sworn affidavit for additional details."

- Question 3 – Persecution of Others:
  - This question addresses the bar to asylum/withholding under INA §208(b)(2)(A)(i).
  - Review the statute, regulations, and relevant case law to assess the parameters of this bar, to determine whether this may pose an obstacle to your client being granted relief, and to inform your response to this question.
  - As described above, provide summary answers for each piece of information requested, followed by "Please see sworn affidavit for additional details."

- Question 4 – Return to Country of Persecution:
  - You must include ANY and ALL times your client returned to the country of persecution, no matter how short, whether the entry was legal or otherwise, and regardless of timing.
  - The answer to this question will be used in assessing your client's well-founded fear of returning to the country of claimed persecution. Frequent returns or lengthy returns to the country of persecution without any issues may result in the adjudicator deciding that your client no longer has a well-founded fear of persecution.
  - If your client returned to the country of persecution, it is important to discuss this in the affidavit and to provide an explanation of how it does not compromise his/her fear. For example, if your client returned, but had to remain in hiding in order to remain safe, or if your client traveled in/out of the country for a short duration before s/he was harmed, these facts may serve to mitigate the impact of the trip.
  - As described above, provide summary answers for each piece of information requested, followed by "Please see sworn affidavit for additional details."

- Question 5 – One-Year Filing Deadline:
  - This question addresses the one-year bar to asylum found at INA §208(a)(2)(B).
  - Your client must provide documentation to establish that his or her application was filed within one year of into the United States. An I-94 or entry stamp is the best evidence in this regard. However, if your client entered EWI, secondary evidence in the form of affidavits from the applicant and/or others or documents establishing that your client was outside the U.S. within the year preceding the filing of the application should be presented. The more evidence, the better. In removal proceedings, you may be able to rely on the I-94, date of the I-213, or date of the credible fear/reasonable fear interview to demonstrate timely filing.
  - If your client is filing outside the one-year deadline, you must clearly identify the exception to the one-year deadline that applies to your client's case and explain why it applies. The changed and extraordinary circumstances exceptions are found at 8 CFR §§ 208.4 (a)(4)-(5), 1208.4(a)(4)-(5).

- As described above, provide summary answers for each piece of information requested, followed by "Please see sworn affidavit for additional details."

- Question 6 – Crimes in the U.S.:
  - This question addresses the issue of the "particularly serious crime" bar codified at INA §208(b)(2)(ii). It also addresses the exercise of discretion.
  - Review the statute, regulations, and relevant case law to assess the parameters of this bar, to determine whether the bar might pose an obstacle to relief for your client, and to help inform your response to this question.
  - If your client has ever been arrested for a crime, provide certified final dispositions and explain why each arrest does not meet the definition of a "particularly serious crime."
  - As described above, provide summary answers for each piece of information requested, followed by "Please see sworn affidavit for additional details."

PART D. SIGNATURE AND CERTIFICATIONS

- The applicant must sign the application in both English and in his or her native language, if the Roman alphabet is not used in the native language. If the client's native language uses the same alphabet as English, but spells the name differently or uses diacritical marks, the native manner of spelling the name should be used. For example – Ahmed Ali Mohamed in Somali is Axmed Cali Moxamed; Ho Chi Minh in Vietnamese is Hồ Chí Minh.

- The applicant must include his/her signature and date.

- If the applicant's spouse, parent, or child(ren) helped to prepare the application, you must check "YES" and include their name and relationship.

- You must check "YES" in response to the question, "Did someone else besides your spouse, parent or child(ren) prepare this application?" because you, as the attorney, assisted in the preparation of the application.

- Sometimes clients have received a notice of low/pro bono attorneys from the court or other agencies. If so, check the "YES" box.

PART E. DECLARATION OF PERSON PREPARING FORM, IF OTHER THAN APPLICANT, SPOUSE, PARENT OR CHILD

- You, as the attorney, must fill out this section and include a signed and dated Form G-28, Notice of Entry of Appearance with the I-589 application.

PART F AND G TO BE COMPLETED AT INTERVIEW OR REMOVAL HEARING

- Do not have your client complete this section until you are in front of the asylum officer or immigration judge and your client is asked to do so.

AILA InfoNet Doc. No. 14071402. (Posted 7/14/14)

APPENDIX 2D
SAMPLE DECLARATION

SWORN DECLARATION OF [redacted], A# [redacted]

I, [redacted], swear under penalty of perjury, under the laws of the United States, that the following is true and correct to the best of my knowledge and belief:

Background

1. My name is [redacted] and I was born on April 27, 1991. I am an indigenous Mayan and I am from Todos Santos, Guatemala. I grew up speaking Mam, and I speak some Spanish. I am a devout Evangelical Christian. My older sister, [redacted], raised me and two other sisters because my parents died. Three brothers and another sister of mine also died when I was growing up.

2. Before my parents died, my family fled to Mexico to escape the civil war in Guatemala. My brothers were separated from the family on our journey to Mexico. After the rest of us arrived safe in Mexico, my father returned to Guatemala to look for my brothers, but he never returned because he was killed. We never heard from my brothers again and believe that they were also killed. My mother was very scared. She, me, and some of my siblings returned to Guatemala to find out more about my father and brothers. After my sisters and I were back in Guatemala, my mother traveled back to Mexico to get the sister who had stayed behind. Neither my sister nor my mother ever returned. I believe that both of them were killed. When my mother disappeared, my oldest sister [redacted] was about 15 years old. Since then, [redacted] had to raise me and my two other sisters alone in Guatemala.

3. In Todos Santos, I went to school for maybe three years. I wanted to continue going to school, but I couldn't because you have to pay if you want to go to school. Todos Santos is a very poor, Mayan area and it is far from things like the school and the police station. We were very poor and hardly had money to eat, so at age eight I had to go to work. [redacted] and I worked in a finca in Ixcan where we washed clothes and worked with corn and coffee plants. I worked there for about eight years before I met [redacted], my husband. I was about 16 or 17 years old when I met my husband.

4. I love [redacted] because he is a kind man. He is nice to everyone he meets and treats everyone with kindness. He smiles and greets everyone on the street and is a devout Christian. He puts others' needs before his own.

5. [redacted] and I moved back to live together in Todos Santos, and we married on April 6, 2009. Life with [redacted] was nice because we are in love and we share a deep connection

with our Christian faith. I was happy to have a stable family that I never had growing up. [REDACTED] was a deacon and I sang in the women's choir of our church. He preached about God and peace and spread the word of God in our community. He would carry his bible while preaching and talking to everyone in our community about peace.

The M-18 gang labeled [REDACTED] their enemy and attacked him. They followed, threatened, and beat him for about two years.

6. [REDACTED] was a strong preacher and a good preacher. He spread the word of God to many, even those who would not first hear the word. He preached to everyone in our community, even gang members, about peace and nonviolence. He preached that the lifestyle of the gangs is not the way of God and that we should do as God teaches and live a life of peace. He wanted everyone to see that peace was the right way to live. Unfortunately, [REDACTED]'s preaching got him into trouble with the M-18 gang, who wear red. They suspected him of disloyalty because they saw him preaching to members of the MS-13 and even accused him of being part of the MS-13. They wanted [REDACTED] to be loyal to them instead and asked him to join their gang as a sign of loyalty and respect. [REDACTED], strong in the word of God, refused. Instead, he told them that he was a Christian and did not believe in violence. He believed in peace.

7. After that first encounter, [REDACTED] continued to preach the word of God. The M-18 continued to harm him. They had labeled [REDACTED] their enemy. They followed him, punched him, hit him, and threatened to kill him. These attacks happened near our home, outside of our church, and even in the middle of the street, sometimes when I was with him. They would throw stones at [REDACTED] beat him with their fists, and they even threatened to kill him with knives and held him at knifepoint.

8. The M-18 often attacked [REDACTED] on his way home from preaching the word of God in our community. Once, I remember seeing [REDACTED] almost make it home safely when three men from M-18 came and began beating him. I could not go and help [REDACTED] because there were three of them, but I saw this happen through a window in our house. I was terrified and did not know what to do. I was so scared they were going to kill [REDACTED]. I could not move.

9. On several Sundays, the M-18 would be waiting outside of our church for [REDACTED] to come out. Several times, they attacked my husband right outside of our church when we were on our way home from church. The M-18 are people of violence who do not like anything that goes against their way of life, like messages of peace and spreading the word of God.

10. There was a period of time when I often saw [REDACTED] come home looking bruised, injured, and like he had been beaten up. This was in late 2008, when I was pregnant with our first son, [REDACTED]. I do not know of every time that the M-18 hurt my husband because if I did not see it happen, he would not tell me about it. [REDACTED] did not want to worry

me because I was pregnant with and we were both worried that the stress of these attacks would somehow harm the baby. But I knew that the M-18 continued to beat him regularly because I would often see him come home with bruises and injuries from the things they used to hit him.

11. When I was pregnant with our first son , the M-18 attacked in front of me when we left church together. They accused him of being disloyal and their rival. was strong in his faith even though he was scared. He said he was not in any gang and that he was a Christian man and believed in nonviolence. He said he did not believe in their criminal way of life. When he said these things, the gang members beat him and called him a liar. I remember I was so scared that they were going to kill him. I cried and cried and screamed at them to leave him alone. But one of the M-18 grabbed me so that I would not be able to help but could only watch him being beaten.

12. was born on June 16, 2009, but he died about five months later of pneumonia. I blame the M-18 for 's death. and I felt imprisoned in our own house. We were afraid to leave because of the M-18. We knew if they saw us leave, they would attack again and keep us from getting to the doctor, who lived far away from our house. We were afraid that they would hurt or kill . The day that passed away was October 31st. That is the day that our town has a big celebration for El Dia De Los Muertos. During this celebration, everyone from our town is in the streets celebrating. and I thought that day was our chance to get to the doctor. Since there were so many people outside, we hoped and prayed that we could walk into the crowd and get to a doctor without the M-18 seeing us. This seemed to be our only option, so we left our house with . I was carrying in my arms as we hurried and made it safely to the crowd. But sadly, after getting to the crowd and just when I felt hopeful that we could get to the doctor, I looked down at and he stopped breathing. and I were inconsolable.

13. This was a very difficult time for us because not only were we grieving our child, but we also had to deal with the M-18's continued death threats and constant beatings against my husband. The M-18 did not care that we just lost our son. They continued their attacks against .

My husband fled Guatemala in 2010, thinking that he could protect me and our unborn son. But instead, the gang turned their threats and violence against me and our unborn son, .

14. In 2010, I was pregnant again with our second son, . One Sunday, when and I were on our way home from church, the M-18 attacked and started beating him in front of me again. I saw these men beat my husband with their fists while I cried and yelled for them to let him go. The M-18 yelled at me not to interfere, grabbed my arms and made me watch, then threatened to rape me while they were beating .

They beat him so hard that day that both ████ and I thought the M-18 were going to kill him then and there.

15. After this incident, ████ and I worried that the stress of this event and my constant worrying about our unborn son would harm our baby. We kept thinking about ████ and were afraid that we would lose another child because of the M-18's violence against us. ████ thought that our lives and the life of our baby were in danger. ████ and I thought that if he left Guatemala, the M-18 would leave me and our unborn child alone. After all, it was ████ they wanted to hurt because of his preaching. This was the most difficult decision, because we did not want to live apart, but we had to protect our unborn child. We thought that we could protect our son by ████ fleeing. So we decided that ████ would leave in secret, in the middle of the night so that no one would see him. ████ fled to the United States, where he lives today. We just wanted a safe life for our baby and thought that if ████ left, I would be able to raise our child in safety.

16. Unfortunately, we were wrong. Right after ████ left, the M-18 turned their threats and violence against me. The M-18 already knew where to find me and they already knew that I was ████'s wife because they had seen us together so many times and knew where we lived together in our house. When the M-18 found out that ████ had left Todos Santos, three of them came to my house and asked me where my husband was. They said that he was in a rival gang and that they were looking for him to kill him as their enemy. I told them that I did not know where he was and repeated that ████ was not a part of any gang because we are Christians. That was when they tried to rape me. One of the men pushed me on to my bed and grabbed my hands so that I couldn't move while another took off his belt like he wanted to rape me. I tried to defend myself but I couldn't because there were three of them and they were grabbing my hands. I continued to cry and begged for them to stop. I begged for them not rape me.

17. One of the M-18 members was standing by the door and told the others that they shouldn't rape a pregnant woman. That was when they grabbed a knife, held it against my belly, and threatened to cut out my baby to make my husband return to Guatemala. I kept crying and praying that they would leave my baby alone. I was so scared that they would do something to my baby. While I was crying and begging for them to stop, they laughed and me and made fun of me. They kept ahold of my arms, put them behind my back, and hit me with their hands and fists on my face over and over again until my nose bled all over my face. Instead of cutting out my baby that day, they beat me. They hit me so much that I was afraid that I would lose the baby. They said that they were going to hurt me to make my husband return to Guatemala so that they could kill him. When they stopped beating my face, they told me that if I went to the police about this, they would find me and kill me. They threatened to kidnap my son when he was born to make my husband return to Guatemala.

18. Even though they threatened to kill me if I went to the police, I went anyway. I had to do something and needed someone to protect me since ████ was gone. When I went to the police, I was scared because of what had happened. I told them what had happened and asked them to protect me. I described the attack as best as I could and then the three men from M-18 who came to my house were arrested. They were arrested for one day and one night. I thought that they would be arrested for a long time, but they were released so soon. I was disappointed and even more scared for my life and the life of my unborn child because the M-18 were free after only one day and one night.

19. After the M-18 men were released, those same three men came to my house again. They stormed through the door into my house and told me that they knew that I went to the police. They said, "You did it, you did it, you went to the police." They pushed me hard against the wall and then they hit my face, on my nose again. They were so angry that I had gone to the police. I didn't know what to do but cry and beg them to leave me alone. I thought for sure that they were going to kill me for going to the police. They hit me until my nose was bleeding all over my face again. Then they repeated their threat to me that when my baby was born, they would kidnap him to make my husband come back. Then they threatened to kill me because I had reported them. They said that if I go to the police again, they will certainly kill me. Then they left.

20. After that, the M-18 members kept coming after me. For the next two years, I did not go to the police because I was afraid that they would actually kill me like they promised they would do. During these two years, they continued their threats against me, saying that they would keep hurting me until ████ returned so that they could kill him. Every time that they walked by my house they threw rocks onto my roof, they would call me by my first name, ████, or my middle name, ████. They know my face, they know who I am, and they know where I live. They would throw rocks at me and at my house every day. They were always threatening me. There were few days when the M-18 left me alone; those days were rare.

After my son ████ was born, the M-18's violence and threats continued. I felt helpless because no matter what I did, I did not feel like I could protect my son.

21. My son, ████ was born on July 20, 2010. After that, I tried to never leave my house, hoping that the M-18 would stop their vicious threats and attacks on me and hoping that by staying inside I could protect ████. I talked to ████ and he told me to stay in the house so that they couldn't hurt me or ████. But the M-18 continued to come after me and then started to come after my son. They would sit outside of my house for hours and yell my name, yell for me to come out, yell for my husband, and throw rocks at my house.

22. In 2012, the M-18 came into my house again. was about two years old at the time, and one of them grabbed him by his ears and his hair. Another grabbed me so that I couldn't help . They threatened to rape me. I was so afraid and thought that for sure they were going to rape and kill me, then kidnap my son. Then, the one grabbing pulled out a knife and held it near as if he was going to cut or stab . I felt so desperate, like I couldn't help or save my son. I have never been so afraid in my life. I could not let them kill my child, but I felt helpless, like there was nothing I could do to stop them. I was screaming and crying. I begged them to stop hurting us. But as I was screaming and crying, they hit me over and over again on my face and on my nose. My nose was bleeding all over my face while my child watched. They said "you may as well give up and surrender." Between their punches and hits, I kept begging them to leave alone. All I cared about was his safety. started to cry and one of them tried to cover his mouth, but was crying so loudly. They repeated their threats against us, saying that if isn't going to come home to them, they would kill me and . After that, they left. I was so relieved that they did not use the knife on . All I wanted was for to be safe.

23. After that happened, I went to the police again. I did not know what else to do. The M-18 had held a knife to my two-year-old son and made it clear that they were not going to stop doing this to us until returned so they could kill him. Even though I was really afraid to go to the police, I did not know what else to do. I thought that maybe this time, the police would help me since my son was in danger. I went to the police again, but this time the police did not do anything. I begged them to file a report and protect me and my son from those men so that they would leave me alone. I asked them for a document for some form of protection from the police. But the police did nothing. I was so upset that the police were not doing their job and would not keep me and safe. When they refused to help me, I was even more scared because of the threats the M-18 had made after I reported them the first time. I kept hearing their words in my head, telling me that they would kill me if I went to the police again. I hoped and prayed that they would not find out.

24. After the police refused to do anything, I bought a lock for my door to try to have more security and to try to keep the M-18 out of my house. I rarely left my house because I was too scared of the M-18 and their attacks. I was too afraid to leave my house to go anywhere except for church.

25. I lived in complete fear because I knew that the police would not protect me and the M-18 kept waiting for me outside of my house. They would be out there for hours, yelling at me to come out and threatening me. Whenever I left my house to go to church, I would take with me. The M-18 would wait for me and follow me on my way home from church. They would repeat their threats to me over and over again. They said that they would never leave me and alone until my husband came back.

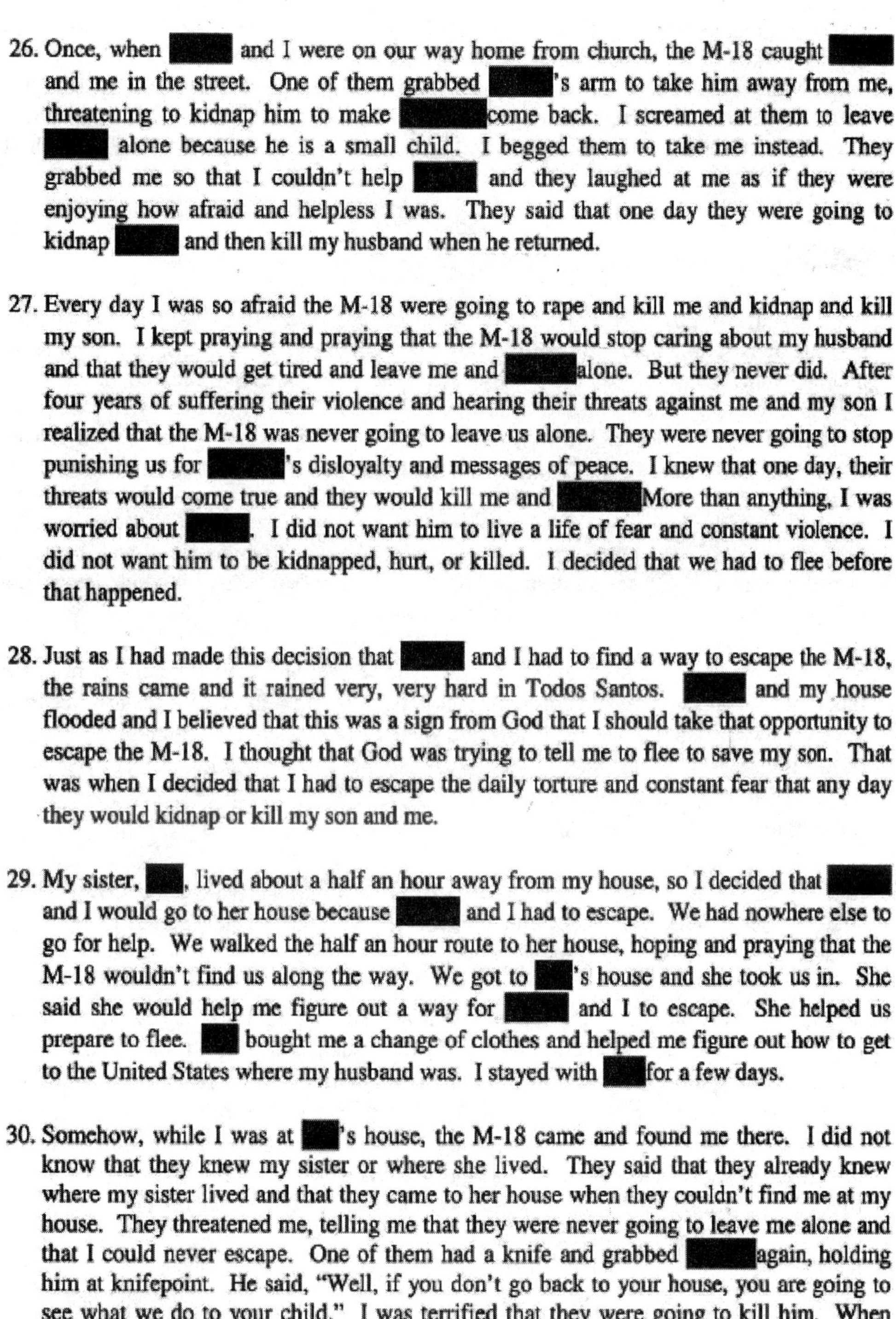

26. Once, when █████ and I were on our way home from church, the M-18 caught █████ and me in the street. One of them grabbed █████'s arm to take him away from me, threatening to kidnap him to make █████ come back. I screamed at them to leave █████ alone because he is a small child. I begged them to take me instead. They grabbed me so that I couldn't help █████ and they laughed at me as if they were enjoying how afraid and helpless I was. They said that one day they were going to kidnap █████ and then kill my husband when he returned.

27. Every day I was so afraid the M-18 were going to rape and kill me and kidnap and kill my son. I kept praying and praying that the M-18 would stop caring about my husband and that they would get tired and leave me and █████ alone. But they never did. After four years of suffering their violence and hearing their threats against me and my son I realized that the M-18 was never going to leave us alone. They were never going to stop punishing us for █████'s disloyalty and messages of peace. I knew that one day, their threats would come true and they would kill me and █████ More than anything, I was worried about █████. I did not want him to live a life of fear and constant violence. I did not want him to be kidnapped, hurt, or killed. I decided that we had to flee before that happened.

28. Just as I had made this decision that █████ and I had to find a way to escape the M-18, the rains came and it rained very, very hard in Todos Santos. █████ and my house flooded and I believed that this was a sign from God that I should take that opportunity to escape the M-18. I thought that God was trying to tell me to flee to save my son. That was when I decided that I had to escape the daily torture and constant fear that any day they would kidnap or kill my son and me.

29. My sister, ███, lived about a half an hour away from my house, so I decided that █████ and I would go to her house because █████ and I had to escape. We had nowhere else to go for help. We walked the half an hour route to her house, hoping and praying that the M-18 wouldn't find us along the way. We got to ███'s house and she took us in. She said she would help me figure out a way for █████ and I to escape. She helped us prepare to flee. ███ bought me a change of clothes and helped me figure out how to get to the United States where my husband was. I stayed with ███ for a few days.

30. Somehow, while I was at ███'s house, the M-18 came and found me there. I did not know that they knew my sister or where she lived. They said that they already knew where my sister lived and that they came to her house when they couldn't find me at my house. They threatened me, telling me that they were never going to leave me alone and that I could never escape. One of them had a knife and grabbed █████ again, holding him at knifepoint. He said, "Well, if you don't go back to your house, you are going to see what we do to your child." I was terrified that they were going to kill him. When they grabbed █████, my sister yelled at them saying that they had no right to be in her

7

house and that they had no right to go into my house. They were about to hit me when my sister lifted and waved a big stick at them as if she was going to hit them. She was angry and yelling at them and waving the stick at them. That was when they left. But before they left, they turned around and said, "You, too" to my sister, threatening her. I am not sure if they left her alone because I have not been able to speak with ██ much. I am very worried about her.

██ and I fled Guatemala around June 5, 2014.

31. Around June 5, 2014, ██ and I fled Guatemala. My sister ██ helped arrange passage by bus. She paid a coyote 18,000 Quetzals that she borrowed, using her house to guarantee that we would pay the money back. The bus took us into Mexico, but dropped ██ and me off at some place where we had to stay for one month. While we were there, we were not allowed to leave. I was scared and did not know what would happen next. All I wanted was to find safety. After a month, the coyote took us with some other woman I did not know to a man who would get us across the river. We got into the man's canoe with him to cross the big river into the United States. ██ was strapped to my back and I sat in the canoe. At one point, the other woman stood and the canoe turned over and ██ and I fell in the water. I was terrified because I do not know how to swim. The canoe man pulled me out of the water.

32. When we made it to the other side of the river, ██ and I were separated from the other woman and the canoe man. It was dark, cold, and ██ and I were still wet from the river. I decided that we needed to find shelter from the cold and found a bush for us to rest underneath. While ██ and I were resting, an immigration officer came up to us. I was so happy to see him because I thought he was going to help us get away from the cold and to help us find safety in the United States.

33. ██ and I went with the immigration officer to a building where we were held for several hours. We cooperated with him the whole time and never tried to run away because we thought he was going to help us.

34. The immigration officers asked me questions and kept telling me to sign a paper for my deportation. I did not understand what the papers said. I also could not understand the officers very well because they were not speaking in Mam. They also were not speaking in Spanish because the Spanish words they were using were mixed with some other language that I did not know or understand. The officer kept showing me papers and telling me to sign them, but I kept telling them over and over that I was not going to sign the papers. I kept telling them I could not return to Guatemala because I had been threatened and harmed. I refused to sign the papers because I did not want to be deported back to the M-18 in Guatemala. I had to save my son so I never signed the papers. The officers were very angry with me for not signing the papers. I did not really understand what was happening. I just knew that ██ and I could not go back to Guatemala.

35. A few hours later, immigration officers told me and ████ to get on a bus. I thought they were telling us that the bus would take us to an airplane to go back to Guatemala. I was terrified that we going right back to Guatemala. I asked a woman where they were taking us and the woman said she didn't know. We were on the bus for many hours and then came to a place that had airplanes. I asked another person where they were taking us and she told us we were in Texas. Then in Texas we got another bus and they brought us to this detention center.

████ and I have been detained for five months.

36. About a month after we arrived at the detention center, another immigration officer interviewed me. The interview was in Spanish and not my best language Mam, but I am competent in Spanish and wanted to give the interview because I wanted to tell the officer what had happened to me and my family in Guatemala. I told the officer in Spanish that my husband and I were Christians and did not believe in violence. I told the officer that the gang members saw ████ as their enemy and accused him of being their rival. I told the officer about the violence that followed and about what happened to me and my son ████ after ████ fled. I did my best to answer the officer's questions and to explain in Spanish what had happened – the violence, the threats, and the never-ending fear. I did my best to explain why my family and I can't go back to Guatemala because we will be returning to our deaths. I hope and pray that the United States will save our lives.

37. I have been in detention with my four-year-old son for five months and I am very worried about his health. During the time that we have been here, ████ has continued to lose weight. When we arrived in Artesia, ████'s cheeks were plump and he had a little belly. Now, he is only 35 pounds. He is skin and bones, and he is still losing weight. He continues to get nose bleeds, but the doctors here keep saying that he is fine. He continues to get sick because the other children in here are sick. Recently, ████ has been having problems with his eyes and he had to get medicine for that. I continue to have gastritis problems and even though I am taking the medicine that the doctors here give me, it is not working. I am suffering from bouts of nausea, but the doctors tell me that I am healthy. My lawyer and my husband have to pay money into my phone account just so that I can call my lawyer and so that my son can speak to his father, whom he has never met because ████ was forced to flee the constant threats and attacks of the M-18 before ████ was born. But even here, I am grateful because ████ and I are safe from the gang. I would rather be here than back in Guatemala, where we will most certainly be killed.

████ and I cannot go back to Guatemala or we will be killed by the M-18.

38. ████ and I cannot go back to Guatemala and we do not have the right to live anywhere else in the world. I am afraid that we will be threatened, beaten, kidnapped, tortured, and killed. The M-18 know who we are, know where we lived, and I know that they will find

us if we are forced to return. They already proved that they can find us when they showed up at my sister's house looking for us. There is nowhere else in Guatemala that we can live because we are Mayan and do not speak fluent Spanish. I do not have any family member to go to other than my sister █████, and the M-18 would easily find me there like they did before. Even if we did try to live somewhere else, I know they would find us. Guatemala is not very big and the M-18 is everywhere.

39. If █████ and I are forced to return to Guatemala, we will certainly die at the hands of the M-18. Todos Santos is a small community, and the M-18 already know who we are, so they will know that we are back the very same day we return. If █████ and I are forced to return, the M-18 will find us, kidnap us, rape me, and kill us with knives. They are capable of such violence and they will do it because we ran away from them like they warned us not to do. They threatened me before by saying that they would never leave me alone, and they will surely take out their anger on me for having tried to escape them. Once they kill me, it would be easy for them to kidnap and kill █████. They are vicious, violent people who the police cannot stop. Most of the police won't even try to help. I know this because the police would not protect me in the past. The police even told me that there was nothing they could do in 2012 when I reported the violence for the second time. I do not believe that █████ and I will be safe if we are forced to return to Todos Santos. If we are forced to return, we will certainly be returning to our deaths. I pray that we are able to stay here where we are safe.

40. I dream of living with my husband and my son and having the safe, happy life that we deserve but have never had because of the M-18. A life where I do not have to worry that my husband will be beaten with rocks and sticks, kicks and fists, and threatened with knives almost every day just because the M-18 say he is their enemy. I dream of seeing my son hug his father for the first time in a home where no one beats us, holds knifes against our bodies, or threatens us with rape, kidnapping, and death because they are after my family for preaching peace. I dream of a life where █████, █████, and I can go to church and walk home and live as a happy family without fear of being beaten and killed. This is a life that I hope to have with my son and my husband here in the United States.

Respectfully submitted,

__________________________ ____________________

█████ Date

10

APPENDIX 3A

CHECKLIST FOR SUPPORTING DOCUMENTATION

After passage of the REAL ID Act of 2005, supporting documentation is more important than ever in establishing eligibility for asylum and withholding of removal. *See* chapter 4.

Supporting documentation may be obtained from obvious and a few not-so-obvious sources. You may find yourself testing the limits of your creativity. Below is a checklist to help with your research. But don't be surprised if your best leads come from the applicant.

Try to obtain:

- ❑ **Documents that specifically mention the applicant**. These may include identity documents, media reports of the persecution suffered by the applicant, records that establish the applicant's ethnicity, religion, or nationality, and proof of the applicant's party or group memberships or affiliations. These may be documents that the applicant brought with him or her to the United States or, more likely, are documents obtained after the applicant arrived in the United States. Be creative! An affidavit from the applicant's rabbi in the United States may be submitted as proof of the applicant's religion. A picture of the applicant in his uniform may be submitted to demonstrate his service in the military. Statements from friends, neighbors, and relatives who witnessed an event or who may be able to substantiate the applicant's claim may also be submitted.

- ❑ **Medical reports and evaluations from health care professionals**. The harm the applicant suffered may be corroborated by the health care professionals who have examined or are treating the applicant. Submit reports, affidavits, X-rays, and photographs. See the National Consortium of Torture Treatment Programs at www.ncttp.org for a list of treatment centers and appendix 3C for a sample affidavit from a physician.

- ❑ **Expert Opinions**. Other sources of valuable information are experts from a variety of disciplines. Consider obtaining affidavits from academics who have studied the conditions in the applicant's country or a legal expert who can attest to the criminal penalties likely to be imposed on the applicant if returned. Another source is the Office of the United Nations High Commissioner for Refugees, which may verify the applicant's refugee status in a third country or offer an advisory opinion on a particular point of law. *See* appendix 3C.

- ❑ **Demonstrative evidence**. Consider the possibility of introducing, for example, a map of the applicant's escape route or a model or reproduction of the instrument or device used to harm or torture the applicant.

- ❑ **Country condition documentation**. This information is available from many sources, including Human Rights Watch, Amnesty International, the Department of State's *Country Reports on Human Rights Practices*, U.S. Citizenship and Immigration Services' Resource Information Center, and newspapers, both foreign and domestic. *See* appendix 12B for sources and websites.

- ❑ **Foreign Law**. If the applicant fears that he or she will be punished upon return to his or her home country for illegal exit, his or her sexual orientation, or other reasons that may be the basis of a claim, the law of the applicant's home country should be submitted. If nationality is at issue in the applicant's case, the nationality laws of the country of birth or last habitual residence should be submitted. The laws of many countries are available from the Library of Congress. *See* appendix 12B.
- ❑ **Proof of Attempts to Obtain Documents**. If the applicant has tried but failed to obtain documentation, those failed attempts could be submitted as evidence that the documentation is not available. The evidence may be in the form of a letter, a fax, or even phone bills (as proof of overseas calls). If attempts are made in-person, a non-party witness might be able to submit an affidavit attesting to the encounter.
- ❑ **Proof of Why It Would Be Dangerous to Attempt to Obtain Documents**. Often asylum applicants are from countries where communication by telephone, fax, mail, and even e-mail is closely monitored. In such circumstances it would be unreasonable to expect an asylum applicant to obtain documents from his or her home country. It is necessary, however, to show why it is dangerous to even attempt to obtain these documents. Such proof may be available from country conditions experts or reports.

More specifically, supporting documentation may include any or all of the following:

- ❑ One passport-style photograph of the applicant and each of his or her family members.
- ❑ Sworn Declaration of the applicant. *See* appendix 2D.
- ❑ Identity documents, such as the applicant's passport, driver's license, and government-issued identification card.
- ❑ Other official government documents, such as marriage, divorce, or death certificates.
- ❑ Privately-issued membership card or other affiliation documents.
- ❑ Sworn affidavits from the applicant's family, friends, neighbors, or community members, who can confirm his or her protected characteristic(s).
- ❑ Photographs that corroborate the various aspects of the applicant's case.
- ❑ Letters from organizations of which the applicant is a member or affiliate.
- ❑ Objective, published descriptions of the characteristics or attributes, which designate members of the applicant's race, religion, nationality, political affiliation, or social group.
- ❑ Photographs of the injuries and physical harm that the applicant suffered.

- ❑ Police reports recording the harm suffered or threatened.
- ❑ Arrest records, if the applicant was ever arrested because of his or her protected characteristic(s).
- ❑ Sworn affidavits for witnesses who were present during the act(s) of harm or mistreatment, confirming what happened. *See* appendix 3B.
- ❑ Sworn affidavits from anyone the applicant confided in about the incident(s), confirming any observed physical or psychological harm, such as markings on the applicant's body, torn clothes, injuries, crying, anxiety, or unusual behaviors. *See* appendix 3B.
- ❑ Medical records, including evaluations of physical injuries and the likely cause of those injuries, letters from treating doctors, treatment reports, hospital admission records, or prescribed medications.
- ❑ Mental health records, including evaluations of mental health disorders and the likely trigger for those disorders, letters from treating mental health professionals, appointment records, or prescribed medications. *See* appendix 3C.
- ❑ Sworn affidavits from individuals who have suffered similar persecution in the country of past or feared persecution. *See* appendix 3B.
- ❑ Death certificates or medical records for the applicant's relatives, friends, neighbors, or community members who were targeted because of their same or similar protected characteristic(s).
- ❑ Newspaper or other media coverage, or coverage by human rights groups, of the incident(s) in which the applicant was targeted or harmed.
- ❑ I-94 card, visa, and stamped passport (even if false).
- ❑ Evidence of the applicant's travel to the United States (airline itineraries, bus tickets, hotel receipts, etc.).
- ❑ Evidence of the applicant's presence outside of the United States in the past year, including financial, medical, school, or work records.
- ❑ Sworn affidavits from individuals who have personal knowledge of the applicant's date of arrival in the United States. *See* appendix 3B.
- ❑ Expert report regarding the conditions in the country of past or feared persecution, as they relate to the applicant's claims. *See* appendix 3C.
- ❑ Country conditions reports and articles showing the conditions in the applicant's home country during the time of persecution and presently.
- ❑ Certified English translations of all non-English documents. The certificates of translation must contain the following regulatory language, or the translations will

not be accepted: "I, [TRANSLATOR'S NAME], am competent to translate from [LANGUAGE] into English, and certify that the translation of this document is true and accurate to the best of my abilities." *See* appendix 3D.

- ☐ Evidence of good moral character and rehabilitation, if needed.

Note*: This list is not all-inclusive. Think outside the box and be creative. Brainstorm with your client – he is she is often your best resource for identifying supporting documentation.*

Note*: Documentation should be paginated, indexed, tabbed, and highlighted for easy reference.*

APPENDIX 3B

SAMPLE WITNESS AFFIDAVIT TEMPLATE

SWORN AFFIDAVIT OF [INSERT NAME OF WITNESS]

I, [insert name of witness], swear under penalty of perjury, under the laws of the United States, that the following statements are true and correct to the best of my knowledge and belief:

1. Insert paragraph explaining witness's full name and address, date and place of birth, country of citizenship, immigration status in the United States, what the witness does for a living, and any other biographic information, such as information about a spouse and/or children.

2. Insert paragraph explaining how the witness knows the applicant, whether the witness knew the applicant in the country of feared persecution, and how often the witness has contact with the applicant now.

3. Insert several paragraphs explaining (from the witness's perspective and in his or her own words) what happened to the applicant in the country of feared persecution. The paragraphs should provide answers to all of the following questions: What happened? When did these events occur? Who did this to the applicant? Why was the applicant targeted? How did the persecutors know about the applicant's protected characteristic(s)? Why were those characteristics offensive to the persecutors?

4. Insert paragraph explaining how the witness knows that this happened to the applicant and how the witness knows that the applicant was targeted because of his or her protected characteristic(s). What makes the witness believe that this is the reason why the applicant was targeted?

5. Insert several paragraphs explaining your own experiences in the applicant's country. The paragraphs should provide answers to all of the following questions: What happened to the witness? When did this happen? Who did this? Why was the witness targeted and harmed? What was the persecutor's motive? How does the witness know that this was the persecutors' motive? Is the witness safe anywhere in that country today? If not, why not?

6. Insert several paragraphs explaining what the witness believes would happen to the applicant if he or she is forced to return to the country of feared persecution. The paragraphs should provide answers to all of the following questions: When would this happen? Who would do this to the applicant? How does the witness know that this would happen? Why would the applicant be targeted? How would the persecutors know to target him or her? What makes the witness believe that this is what would happen to the applicant?

7. Insert several paragraphs discussing the current country conditions in the country of feared persecution. The paragraphs should provide answers to all of the following questions: Is the country a safe place for the applicant to go? Why not? Are other individuals in the applicant's circumstances safe there? If not, what happens to them? Who targets people like the applicant? Why are they targeted? How do you know this?

8. Insert a paragraph summarizing why the applicant needs to stay here. Please discuss his or her inability to return to the country of feared persecution, as well as any personal, discretionary circumstances.

9. Briefly explain what the witness wants the U.S. government to do for the applicant (e.g., provide protection, grant asylum, etc.).

Respectfully submitted,

____________________________________ ________________

[INSERT THE WITNESS'S NAME AND SIGN ABOVE] Date

Sworn to before me this _______ day of _______ in the year _______,

____

[NOTARY PUBLIC]

APPENDIX 3C
SAMPLE EXPERT AFFIDAVITS

SAMPLE EXPERT AFFIDAVIT—COUNTRY CONDITIONS

Affidavit

State of Illinois }
County of Cook }

I, Heather McClure, being duly sworn, state as follows:

1. I, Heather McClure, am Resource Director of the Midwest Human Rights Partnership for Sexual Orientation (MHRPSO) in Chicago, Illinois. MHRPSO is a human rights project of the Heartland Alliance for Human Needs & Human Rights (formerly Travelers & Immigrants Aid), also in Chicago, Illinois. MHRPSO investigates and documents human rights violations against gay men, lesbians, and people with HIV/AIDS in Guatemala, and other focus countries. On January 23, 1997, I testified in the court of _______________ to the authenticity of the documents I gathered in Guatemala City during a fact-finding trip from September 13–22, 1996. These documents were submitted to the court in January 1997, by _______________, lawyer for the _______________.

2. It has been brought to my attention that on the day of the aforementioned hearing, the court raised questions as to what constitutes or determines gay male identity. To help the court make its determination, I refer it to Attorney General Order No. 1895-94, dated June 19, 1994 (as reprinted in the "Task Force Update: Newsletter of the Lesbian and Gay Immigration Rights Task Force, Inc.," Fall 1996, Attachment A), and Stephen O. Murray's *Latin American Male Homosexualities* (University of New Mexico Press, 1995), a collection of anthropological essays that examine different homosexual practices throughout Latin America in relation to issues of family, society, culture, politics, economics, and ethnicity. Additional clarification is offered by (1) a mission statement describing the services of OASIS, a prominent HIV/AIDS prevention center in Guatemala City directed by Dr. Ruben Mayorga (Attachment B), and (2) a presentation of cases of patients with HIV/AIDS compiled by physicians affiliated with the Guatemalan Association for the Prevention and Control of AIDS (admitted into evidence by Judge __________ on January 23, 1997).

3. In Attorney General Order No. 1895-94, dated June 19, 1994, David A. Martin states legacy INS's position that "homosexuals do constitute a particular social group." Martin continues, "[a]ccordingly, our briefs should not pursue arguments that homosexuality fails to define a particular social group because it is not an immutable characteristic. Nor should the INS argue that homosexuals are too diverse and non-cohesive a group to qualify as a particular social group." As the documentation below illustrates, homosexuals in

Guatemala do not share many of the cultural ways of life that, in large part, distinguish U.S. homosexuals. Guatemalan homosexuals, nevertheless, still should be regarded as a particular social group with their own particular characteristics that have adapted in response to a history, and an economic and political system that are very different from those of the United States.

4. Both Dr. Murray's research and Dr. Mayorga's work in Guatemala City demonstrate that in Guatemala a homosexual man cannot be determined by the extent to which his sexual orientation is known to family, friends, and doctor; by his lack of membership in a gay organization; or by his involvement in heterosexual relationships (including marriage).

a. Dr. Stephen Murray's research in Guatemala City reveals that "one major difference between North American and Latin American men engaged in recurrent homosexual relations is that Latin Americans live with their family of origin until they marry. . . . In my 1980 sample of homosexually active men in Guatemala City, the only men who did not live with their parents lived with wives of their own."

b. Murray identifies reasons for the influence Latin American families exert over their children: "[B]esides greater centrality in socialization, the Latin American family retains economic functions … . In societies experienced by most as capricious and heartless, the family provides more than merely psychological shelter. If an individual is struck down by illness or injury and has no family to provide support, he or she will be reduced to begging in the streets. Examples of this horrific danger are readily visible." Continues Murray, "[B]ecause revelation of homosexuality is a basis for expulsion from the home, and because of the economic as well as psychological security provided by the family, homosexually active Latin Americans cultivate family relations to a greater extent than do those who can take them for granted."

c. Further, Dr. Murray links the strong influence of the family to the lack of gay and lesbian organizations in Guatemala City (to date, none exists). Murray writes that the centrality of family is a long-enduring obstacle to gay self-identification and gay community-building because "[men's] residence with families scattered throughout cities precludes the development of gay neighborhoods." Without gay neighborhoods, such as those "gay ghettos" established in the United States after World War II, there exists in Guatemala tremendous obstacles to the formation of gay consciousness, culture, and community as these have developed in Anglo North America.

d. As I testified on January 23, 1997, there are currently no gay or lesbian organizations in Guatemala. Though lesbians and gay men are involved in many prominent human rights and HIV/AIDS prevention and treatment organizations, they are not open about their sexual orientation, nor do they use their common sexual preferences as a basis for establishing gay and/or lesbian organizations. When I interviewed Guatemalans (gays, lesbians, and individuals of unidentified sexual orientation) as to why gays and lesbians were not more visible, I was told repeatedly that they are afraid they will be victims of violence, in addition to losing their jobs and the support of their families and friends.

e. The likelihood of violence against gays and lesbians is increased by a common misconception in Guatemalan society that lesbians and gay men are also "AIDS carriers." Conversely, people with HIV/AIDS are assumed to be gay or lesbian. AIDS-phobia and homophobia reinforce one another. Thus, there is a two-fold danger of being perceived, or exposed, as HIV-positive and/or homosexual—status in one group strongly implies membership within the other.

f. The presentation of cases of patients with HIV/AIDS compiled by physicians affiliated with the Guatemalan Association for the Prevention and Control of AIDS (admitted into evidence by Judge __________ on January 23, 1997) attests to additional risks that persons with HIV/AIDS take when they seek out medical care for HIV/AIDS in Guatemala. Case #7 (page 4) records that "there was no confidentiality of [the patient's] diagnosis within this hospital. Almost all of the doctors and nurses were made aware [of her HIV-positive status] and they asked her questions about her sexual conduct." On September 25, the patient was approached by "a journalist and a camera person" who wanted an interview. The patient "believes that it was one of the nurses of the hospital that contacted the press and television with her name and other confidential facts."

This case, like others documented by the Guatemalan Association for the Prevention and Control of AIDS, testifies to the lack of confidentiality afforded patients with HIV/AIDS (*see* Case #2). Given the tremendous social stigma associated with homosexuality (*see* documents admitted into evidence by Judge __________) and HIV/AIDS in Guatemala (*see* all patient cases), and the violence directed against gay men, lesbians, and persons with HIV/AIDS (*see* Cases #1 and #8, and other documents admitted into evidence by Judge __________), a gay man who seeks medical treatment for HIV/AIDS runs the risk of having his sexuality exposed to other doctors and nurses not responsible for his care, other patients, and society at large through the media. The consequences of such exposure could be the increased likelihood that he will be a target of violence, and will suffer other types of social rejection (including loss of job, family, and colleagues). If a gay man has no other alternative but to seek medical treatment for AIDS-related symptoms, it is highly probable that he will not divulge his sexuality for fear of possible exposure or retribution.

g. Additionally, Dr. Mayorga testifies in his affidavit dated September 19, 1996 (admitted into evidence on January 23, 1997), that "two gay men who have participated in OASIS' workshops were beaten upon leaving a gay bar (Metropolis) by a group of unknown men. They robbed them of a few personal items … and (the two men) suffered from bruises and cuts on their backs, necks and faces." Though it is not known whether the men's association with OASIS played a part in their perpetrators' motivations to attack them, it is evident that the general societal respect in the United States accorded gays and lesbians is not replicated in Guatemala. Instead, a gay Guatemalan man clearly endangers himself through his association with places deemed gay or lesbian (*e.g.*, bars), and may put himself at risk for affiliating himself with HIV/AIDS organizations perceived as sympathetic to gays and lesbians.

h. Thus, U.S. expectations that gay identity be defined through an individual's openness with his family about his sexual orientation, and membership in gay organizations, grows from the particular cultural and economic histories of Anglo-America. Similar criteria, when applied to Guatemalan gay men, obscures the very different family pressures, economic scarcity, and lack of a social safety net—as well as a dearth of institutions openly supportive of gay men, and risks of associating with those organizations—that help to define gay male identity in Guatemala.

i. Murray describes how gay men respond to severe homophobia and AIDS-phobia when he writes that gay men's association with like others is limited. He observes, "[F]or fear of having their reputation 'burned' (*quemada*) and their security thereby endangered, many persons involved in homosexual behavior avoid being seen with or being acknowledged by males who might be judged effeminate and also avoid places where homosexuals are known to congregate. The same pattern existed among homosexual Anglo Americans in the mid-1960s, although then and there it was fear of losing jobs more than Latin Americans' fear of the family learning of stigmatizing association." Dr. Mayorga's letter attests the very real fear of violence adds to men's concern that their families or employers will learn of their sexual orientation as a result of their involvement in organizations that might be perceived as places "where homosexuals are known to congregate."

j. Additional survival mechanisms gay men may adopt to avoid repercussions include living "double lives." As Dr. Murray explains, "Latinos [and others] can compartmentalize homosexuality—in space or time. According to Goode (1960), compartmentalization of roles is a common response to role strain; by no means is it unique to managing masculine self-presentation while engaged in homosexual behavior in Latin America. In Latin America, as in Anglo North America, there is 'a traditional difference between that which people know and that which they agree to admit that they know, that which they see and that which they speak of.'" (Henry James, quoted in Murray). One survival mechanism for gay men is marriage, or involvement in highly visible heterosexual relationships.

k. Both men's and women's social and professional standing in Guatemala is highly determined by their marital status. Consequently, the great majority of Guatemalans marry in their early– to mid-20s. A Guatemalan man who is unmarried by the age of approximately 30 is often suspected of being gay and may be victimized in the ways described above.

l. Though there are no exact statistics as to how many gay men marry, the AIDS epidemic in the last 10 years in Guatemala illustrates that a greater proportion of married men are involved in gay relationships than previously believed. Dr. Mayorga admits that "very little is know[n] about the spread of HIV among this population of men who have sexual relations with other men in developing countries and, in general, there are no prevention programs nor special attention designed with this population in mind. And [i]t is estimated that sexual activity among men is more frequent than previously thought. As an example, in the HIV/AIDS clinic of the St. John of God General Hospital in Guatemala, of the 397 men with HIV/AIDS, 187 have had sexual relations with other men" (from OASIS Introduction). This same phenomenon, of married men having extramarital sex with other men (including gay sex workers), is prevalent enough that OASIS cites it as causally related to the increased transmission of HIV from husbands to their wives and to their children in utero.

5. In conclusion, the above demonstrates that a Guatemalan gay man's involvement in a marriage or other form of heterosexual relationship is not necessarily an indicator of his sexual practices or even his sexual identity. Instead, a gay man may choose to be married for the same reason he may decide never to reveal to his family or doctor the true nature of his sexual orientation: to avoid social and familial censure and, consequently, the risk of more serious repercussions, including physical violence, for being recognized as a gay man. Similarly, the failure of a gay man to involve himself in an organization that is sympathetic to gays and lesbians does not belie his sexuality; instead, it attests to the potential danger of association with such organizations. Indeed, the gap between sexual identity and sexual practice in Guatemala is a testament to the intensity and prevalence of homophobia and AIDS-phobia in that country, which can erupt into violence against individuals who are, or are perceived to be, gay and/or HIV-positive.

6. Finally, though __________ is in the United States, it is very difficult to "shake off" deeply ingrained mechanisms that, in Guatemala, are necessary for a gay man's physical, emotional, and economic survival. It is even more likely that these mechanisms will continue to determine a gay man's life in the United States if he remains in contact with his family, and is dependent for emotional support on a Guatemalan immigrant community shaped by the same cultural values that oppressed the gay male when he lived in Guatemala.

7. The process of "coming out" for lesbians and gay men is a gradual one and can take many years, even decades. Many American lesbians and gay men never reveal their sexual orientation to their families, doctors, colleagues, or employers; do not belong to gay and lesbian organizations; and have been married or are currently choosing to end marriages due to their sexual orientation.

8. __________ has had to struggle against additional obstacles, including the very real threat of state-sanctioned physical violence against those who are gay or lesbian (see MINUGUA, Report No. 22, Team No. 5, admitted into evidence) in a society whose judicial and security institutions have been identified as highly responsible for extensive human rights violations (documented by the U.S. Department of State and Amnesty International) against "undesirables" and "subversives," including homosexuals. In addition, widespread and severely debilitating social stigmas against gays, lesbians, and people with HIV/AIDS in Guatemala are realities most Americans never have to face. These challenges may have made __________'s ability to live as an openly gay man that much more difficult to achieve. Though these forces cannot erase his sexual orientation, they can define to a large extent the choices he feels he has, as a gay Guatemalan man, for expressing himself both in Guatemala and in the United States.

I declare under penalty of perjury that the foregoing is true and correct. Executed on this 3rd day of February 1997, in the City of Chicago, County of Cook, State of Illinois.

Subscribed and sworn to before me this ____ day of _________, ____

_____________________________ _____________________________

Notary Public Heather McClure

SAMPLE EXPERT AFFIDAVIT—MEDICAL

OFFICE OF THE IMMIGRATION JUDGE
EXECUTIVE OFFICE FOR IMMIGRATION REVIEW

In the Matter of the Application for Asylum and Withholding of Removal of ____________________ a/k/a, ____________________	A # ______________ **AFFIDAVIT OF DOUGLAS SHENSON, MD, MPH**

STATE OF NEW YORK }
} ss.:
COUNTY OF THE BRONX }

DOUGLAS SHENSON, MD, MPH, being duly sworn, deposes and says:

1. I am an American physician licensed in the State of New York, currently working as an Assistant Professor in the Department of Epidemiology and Social Medicine, at Montefiore Medical Center/Albert Einstein College of Medicine. I am fully trained and board-eligible in the specialty of Internal Medicine.

2. I am a graduate of Tulane University School of Medicine and Tulane University School of Public Health and Tropical Medicine. In addition to holding medical and public health degrees, I have earned a bachelor's and a master's degree in Human Sciences from Oxford University in England. My clinical training was at the Residency Program in Social Internal Medicine at Montefiore Medical Center/Albert Einstein College of Medicine, where my last year I held the position of Chief Resident.

3. Since completing my clinical training, I have practiced in the Bronx. Because I speak French fluently, my colleagues have over the years referred to me a large number of West African and Haitian patients. I have been designated as an expert witness in the New York Eastern District court case of HIV-infected Haitian refugees seeking legal representation during their incarceration at Guantanamo U.S. Naval Base in Cuba.

4. I have a long-standing interest in medical human rights, and have published on the subject. I am on the Board of Directors of *Doctors of the World*, an American-based humanitarian and human rights group affiliated with the French organization, *Médecins du Monde*. I have received specialized postgraduate training in the use of medical skills for the documentation and treatment of human rights victims. Several human rights organizations have referred to me for evaluation individuals who have been subjected to torture or

physical maltreatment in their homeland. These organizations include Physicians for Human Rights, Church World Services, The Lawyers Committee for Human Rights, and PEN.

5. __________, Esq. requested that I conduct a physical examination of Mr. _____ in order to evaluate Mr. _____'s physical condition in light of his allegations that he was physically abused by government officials prior to this flight from __________ to this country.

6. I have had the opportunity to review the medical records that were provided to Mr. _____ through the Department of Homeland Security, by the Wackenhut Facility ("Wackenhut").

7. On January 19, 1993, I was able to visit Mr. _____ at Wackenhut, where he is currently being detained, and conducted a thorough clinical examination. During the course of that examination, Mr. _____ described the events surrounding his incarceration in __________. On February 81, 1992, four soldiers forcibly entered Mr. _____'s apartment and beat him severely. He was repeatedly hit in the face, on the head, and about the ears. He was kicked in the stomach when he fell to the ground. At one point, after getting up from the floor, he was pushed into a metal chair on which he gashed his right forearm. During the beating, one of the soldiers attacked him with a whip while another pinned his arms behind his back with a metal-buckled belt or cord. These beatings continued for approximately 15 minutes.

8. Mr. _____ was then bodily carried (with his arms still pinned back) and tossed into the back of a waiting van. He landed on his head and shoulders, apparently dislocating his right shoulder. He was then taken to _____________ prison where he was held for 165 days. During his incarceration he received inadequate medical attention for his multiple injuries. His right shoulder was placed in a primitive cast, but was otherwise left unattended. He described to me the great fear he experienced during that period, not knowing when he would be released or what his fate might be.

9. Mr. _____ also described a variety of changes in his health which began following his beatings in the _____________. He stated he now has great difficulty concentrating and is often forgetful. He suffers from frequent headaches, is unable to sleep at night and finds himself sleeping through much of the day. He is very sad and sometimes cries without any proximate cause. He is continuously anxious and has little appetite. He also states his hearing is impaired since his beatings.

10. On physical examination, Mr. _____ exhibits numerous scars. I asked him to point out how he sustained each one, and my findings are as follows: He has a 6 cm circular scar on the superior aspect of his right shoulder which follows the form of a crude buckle; he has a trailing 4 cm scar on the anterior aspect of his left shoulder consistent with a whipping; he has a 4 cm poorly joined scar on the medial surface of his left arm consistent with the "tearing" wound of a tightly bound rope; he has a well-joined 4 cm scar on his right forearm consistent with a cut from a sharp object such as a metal chair; he has a 3 cm trailing

scar on the anterior aspect of his left thigh, which is also consistent with a whipping wound; he has a 3 cm poorly healed scar on his right anterior shin, which he states resulted from an earlier sports accident.

11. Mr. _____ also has an asymmetrical hearing loss, with apparent sensorineural damage to his right ear (positive Weber Test). His tympanic membranes have been damaged, with probable perforation.

12. Based on my examination and experience in diagnosing other victims of physical maltreatment and torture, my assessment is that his multiple sights and symptoms are entirely consistent with the story he recounts. The fact that Mr. _____ attributes a rather dramatic scar to an unrelated sports accident persuades me further that he is telling the truth.

13. I would be willing to further explain my assessment, and answer any other questions relevant to this matter if requested to do so, whether in writing or orally.

Sworn to before me this
20th day of January 1993.

________________________ ___________________________________
Notary Public DOUGLAS SHENSON, MD, MPH

APPENDIX 3D

CERTIFICATE OF TRANSLATION

I, ______________________________, am competent to translate from
(name of translator)

____________________________________ into English, and certify that the translation of
(language)

____
(name of documents)

Is true and accurate to the best of my abilities.

____________________________________ ____________________________________
(signature of translator) (typed/printed name of translator)

____
(address of translator)

____
(address of translator)

____
(telephone number of translator)

APPENDIX 3E

CASE THEORY AND EVIDENCE MATRIX

This chart is a tool for solidifying your case theory and determining how to meet your client's burden of proof. It is meant to assist you in identifying the pieces that will make up the legally sufficient and compelling picture that you will paint for the adjudicator on behalf of your client. The chart below relates to seeking asylum under INA §208(a). However, such a chart may be prepared for withholding of removal under INA §241(b)(3) or protection under the Convention Against Torture.

Along the left side of the chart are the main legal elements for demonstrating asylum eligibility. Along the top of the chart are the authorities you will need to identify and meet in order to demonstrate your client's eligibility for asylum, as well as the facts and evidence you will need to identify, collect, prepare, and present in order to meet your client's burden of proof. For each legal elements listed along the left side of the chart, you should identify the applicable statute and regulations, case law, relevant facts, supporting documentation, and any procedural instructions or local rules specific to that legal element. You should then write that information in the relevant space in the chart. This exercise will help to build and solidify your case theory, recognize which legal elements require further development, and ensure that your client is able to meet his or her burden of proof.

ASYLUM UNDER INA § 208(a)

Legal Element:	Applicable Statute and Regulations:	Applicable Case Law:	Relevant Facts:	Supporting Documentation:	Any Procedural Instructions or Local Rules:
Physical Presence in the U.S.					
Outside Country of Nationality or Last Habitual Residence					
Unable/Unwilling to Return					
Unable/Unwilling to Avail Self of that Country's Protection					
Past Persecution Suffered					

Well-Founded Fear of Future Persecution *(Subjective and Objective Components, Matter of Mogharrabi 4-Part Test)*					
Identify Protected Characteristic(s) *(3-Part Test for PSG)*					
Applicant Embodies those Characteristic(s)					
Persecution Was/Would be on Account of Those Characteristic(s)					
Government Actor or Private Actor the Government is Unable/Unwilling to Control					
Any Changed Circumstances?					
Any Internal Relocation Options?					
Any Ineligibility Grounds or Statutory Bars?					
Merits a Favorable Exercise of Discretion					

APPENDIX 4A

SAMPLE COVER LETTER TO USCIS SERVICE CENTER

This sample letter is not a substitute for the filing instructions. Practitioners always must carefully review the Form I-589 filing instructions, as they frequently change. Additionally, if the applicant is in removal proceedings, the application must be field with the immigration court, not with USCIS.

[Letterhead or Return Address]

[Date]

Via Certified Mail [Number] – Return Receipt Requested

U.S. Citizenship and Immigration Services
[Texas, Nebraska, California, or Vermont] Service Center
Attn: ASYLUM
[Address]
[Address]

RE: I-589 Application for Asylum
Applicant: [Name, A#]

Dear Sir or Madam:

Enclosed please find a completed Form I-589, Application for Asylum, submitted by [Name], along with the following supporting documentation:

1. Original, signed **Form I-589, Application for Asylum** by [Name], with the required photograph attached thereto.
2. **Form G-28, Notice of Entry of Appearance.**
3. **Sworn Declaration of [Name],** stating, "[Quote from declaration summarizing claim]."
4. **Copy of [Name]'s passport, [visa, entry stamp, and I-94 card, if applicable],** as evidence of [his/her] identity, entry into the United States, and [type of status, if applicable].
5. [Other identity documents, if applicable].
6. [Certificates to establish familial relationships if there are dependent family members. These may include marriage and divorce certificates for spouses or birth certificates for children, along with certified English translations].

7. [Evidence showing the applicant possesses the protected characteristic(s) that place him/her in danger].
8. [Evidence showing the applicant suffered past persecution, including any expert medical or psychological evaluations].
9. [Sworn affidavits from individuals who have personal knowledge of what happened to the applicant in the country of feared persecution and/or who have personal knowledge of the current conditions there].
10. [Expert affidavit describing his/her qualifications, knowledge of the conditions in the country of feared persecution, and how those conditions would impact the applicant specifically].
11. **Country Reports and articles evidencing [Country]'s dire human rights record,** as well as the persecution and torture of those who [describe the applicant], including:
    - **U.S. Department of State Country Report on Human Rights Practices in [Country], [year of report],** reporting, "[Quote from report]."
    - [Other country conditions reports and articles].

In addition to the above-listed application and supporting documentation, **please find attached two copies of this complete application package.**

[Also attached is a copy of Form I-589 for [Name of relative], [description of relationship to applicant], along with [his/her] photograph attached to Part D, a signed Form G-28, and a complete copy of all supporting documentation listed above.

Prior to [Name]'s asylum interview, we will provide additional documentation in support of the application, including but not limited to [description of supporting documentation that is not being submitted with the initial filing].

Thank you for your kind consideration of this application. Please do not hesitate to contact our office should you have any questions.

Sincerely,

[Attorney for the Applicant]

APPENDIX 4B

CHECKLIST FOR PREPARING FOR THE ASYLUM INTERVIEW

❑ **Interpreter**. If the applicant is not fluent in English, he or she must bring an interpreter to the interview. A competent interpreter is essential for a successful interview. Always practice with the interpreter prior to the interview to ensure that the interpreter understands the applicant and is able to translate correctly the vocabulary used by you, the asylum officer, and the applicant. It is also important that the applicant feel comfortable with the interpreter and be able to discuss sensitive matters in the interpreter's presence. Note: The asylum officer will obtain a monitor to listen to the interpretation at the interview. The officer will telephone a language service and place the telephone on speaker mode to allow the monitor to hear the interpretation.

❑ **Original Documents**. The applicant should bring the original of all personal documents submitted with the asylum application, such as the passport, driver's license, political party identification card, etc. It is not uncommon for the officer to make new copies of the originals at the interview. Note: Asylum officers are authorized to confiscate documents that they believe are fake or fraudulent and may also submit them to a forensics lab for analysis.[1]

❑ **Additional Documents**. If you obtain additional documents in support of the applicant's claim, take the original and three copies to the interview. If the documents are numerous, make an index to assist the asylum officer. *See* appendix 4E, AILA's Asylum Office Guide—Best Practices for the Procedures for Filing Additional Documents before the Interview.

❑ **Prepare the Applicant**. Always give the applicant a copy of his or her asylum application and declaration. Ask him or her to read and re-read the application prior to the interview to refresh his or her memory regarding dates and events. If the applicant is illiterate, have the interpreter record the contents of the application and declaration so that the applicant can listen several times to it prior to the interview. Instruct the applicant to tell the truth, to listen carefully to the asylum officer's questions, and to answer the questions asked, if he or she is able. Tell the applicant that it is acceptable to respond that he or she does not know an answer to a question, and that the applicant should not guess when answering a question. If the applicant's spouse or children are included on the application, also prepare them in the manner

[1] *See* USCIS *Affirmative Asylum Procedures Manual* (Nov. 2013) at 16–17, *available at www.uscis.gov/sites/default/files/files/nativedocuments/Asylum_Procedures_Manual2013.pdf.*

noted above if they will be testifying. *See* appendix 4C, Interview Guidance for Applicants.

- ☐ **Note Any Corrections**. If any corrections need to be made to the application, submit a letter (and two copies) to the asylum officer noting the corrections on the day of the interview, prior to the start of the interview. Corrections also may be made orally at the start of the interview.

- ☐ **Mock Interviews**. If the applicant knows what to expect at the interview, he or she will be less nervous and better able to express him- or herself. Pretend you are the asylum officer and conduct an interview from beginning to end. Point out to the applicant instances in which he or she is not clearly expressing him– or herself.

- ☐ **Make a List of Key Points**. You will not be permitted to question the applicant at length during the interview, but most asylum officers will allow some follow-up questions by the attorney or representative. Make a list of key points that the applicant should make at the interview. As the applicant mentions these points during the interview, cross them off your list. If the applicant has not addressed a few of these points by the end of the interview, ask him or her questions to elicit responses regarding these points.

- ☐ **Take Detailed Notes at the Interview**. Asylum interviews are not videotaped or recorded. If you later want to change an asylum officer's findings, it is helpful to have detailed or verbatim notes from the interview.

- ☐ **Ask the Asylum Officer**. After asking the applicant any follow-up questions you may have, ask the asylum officer whether he or she sees any outstanding issues or problem areas, and offer to address them with additional evidence, if possible.

- ☐ **Prepare an Oral *and* Written Closing Statement**. Most asylum officers will allow attorneys to make a closing statement. You should take advantage of this opportunity and orally summarize why the applicant is eligible for and deserving of asylum at the conclusion of the interview. In addition, it is extremely helpful to submit, at the conclusion of your oral closing statement, a written closing statement that cites regulations, cases, and other authority regarding why the applicant should be granted asylum. *See* appendix 4D, Sample Closing Statement. The asylum officer must draft an assessment of the case for his or her supervisor. Your written closing may aid the officer in recalling the applicant's basis for asylum and in locating relevant case law that supports the claim.

APPENDIX 4C

INTERVIEW GUIDANCE FOR APPLICANTS

Below are some of the main concepts that practitioners should discuss in detail with their clients prior to their clients' interview.

- **Tell the truth**. While this might seem obvious, the truth is the most important ingredient for success. The facts of the case and the applicant's credible presentation of those facts are the most powerful evidence in support of eligibility for asylum. It is essential for the applicant to remember the importance of being truthful and credible during the asylum interview. Applicants should be reminded that lying on an asylum application or at an asylum interview not only can cause the application to be denied, but it also can bar the applicant from ever getting permanent resident status or other immigration benefits.

- **Know the evidence**. Applicants should be provided with a complete copy of all documentation filed with USCIS so the applicant can be completely familiar with the contents of his or her application. This is especially true of the applicant's sworn declaration in support of his or her asylum application, because the asylum officer will evaluate the applicant's credibility by comparing his or her in-person testimony with what he or she has said in the declaration. If there are any inaccuracies in the applicant's sworn declaration, the applicant should bring them to his or her representative's attention before the interview, so the declaration can be amended as necessary.

- **Be detailed**. Nothing enhances an asylum applicant's credibility more than details. The applicant should be advised to be specific, detailed, and thorough.

- **Answer the questions asked**. Applicants should be advised to listen carefully t each question the asylum officer asks and to answer the specific question asked. Asylum officers are looking for the information they need to clear up any uncertainties and add any necessary detail in order to grant asylum. Providing complete and honest answers to the question asked is essential. Applicants also should be advised that if they do not completely understand the question, they should ask that it be repeated. It is important that applicants are able to communicate with the examiner clearly and without confusion.

- **Understand the law**. Asylum is available to any individual in the United States who is unable or unwilling to return to his or her home country because he or she has suffered persecution or has a well-founded fear of future persecution on account of his or her race, religion, nationality, political opinion, or membership in a particular social group. Applicants must understand what this means and how it relates to his or her story. Thus, when reviewing the most important facts with the applicant, practitioners should explain the reasons why certain facts are legally significant. Understanding the law will assist the applicant in highlighting the most important facts and details during the interview process.

- **Understand the attorney's role**. Even though a representative may be present at the interview, ultimately, it is up to the applicant to be able to describe what happened to him or her and why he or she is afraid to return. The representative is there to: (1) make sure that the asylum officer behaves professionally and appropriately; (2) make sure that the applicant provides all the relevant information; (3) help clarify questions, ambiguities; (4) draw the examiner's attention to documentary evidence; and (5) give the applicant confidence. The representative cannot answer questions for the applicant; however, the applicant ma ask his or her representative questions if needed.

- **Bring a good interpreter**. If the applicant cannot communicate clearly in English, it is essential that he or she identify a strong English speaker to serve as an interpreter. A weak interpreter might undermine the applicant's testimony, confuse the officer, and cause the examiner to refer the case to the immigration judge. If the applicant does not know someone who is capable of translating well, he or she should hire a professional.

- **Trust yourself and your attorney**. Applicants should be reminded that this is their chance to tell their story, which is the most important aspect of their application. They should trust that detailed. Honest testimony will be the best possible evidence, especially when it fits in nicely with the evidence previously prepared and submitted.

APPENDIX 4D

SAMPLE WRITTEN CLOSING STATEMENT

Do not rely on your oral closing statements alone at the interview. Asylum officers conduct numerous interviews prior to reaching a decision in any particular case. They may not remember your eloquent and compelling closing statement. A written closing, with a well-organized argument for why your client meets the elements for an asylum grant, along with citations to relevant case law, regulations, statutes, and asylum officer memos and training materials may be the difference between a grant and referral. Keep it short, no more than five pages, unless it is a complex case. Remember, too, that the officer may not be a lawyer, so avoid legalese.

[Letterhead]

[Date]

Via Hand Delivery

Asylum Officer
_________________ Asylum Office
Department of Homeland Security
USCIS
[Address]
[Address]

CLOSING STATEMENT ON BEHALF OF __________; A# __________

Mr. __________, the principal asylum applicant in this case, and his wife through her derivative status, are eligible for and deserving of asylum under §208 of the Immigration and Nationality Act (INA). Mr. __________'s asylum claim is based on both the past persecution if they are required to return to __________. Mr. __________ and his family suffered persecution at the hands of the __________ military and police because of their political opinion (imputed and actual), religion, race, and membership in a particular social group. Moreover, they have a well-founded fear of persecution in the future if they are returned to __________, based on the above-mentioned grounds.

As demonstrated by Mr. __________'s application, declaration, supporting documentation, and interview today, Mr. __________ fears persecution because: (1) he has been accused by the __________ military of supplying sensitive, strategic information to a government at war with __________; (2) he deserted from the __________ military by not returning to complete his military services; (3) he and his family have been accused of engaging in antigovernment activities; and (4) he is a member of an ethnic and religious minority group that has been persecuted by the __________ government.

Below, I have addressed the following legal issues in Mr. __________'s asylum claim: (1) that his persecutors have imputed a political opinion to him; (2) that he has a well-founded fear of persecution based on his refusal to serve in the __________ military; (3) that he faces persecution upon return because of his religion; and (4) that he faces persecution because of his race or membership in a particular social group because he is a member of an ethnic minority.

I. Political Opinion

Mr. __________ has been accused by the __________ military of supplying military information to a government at war with the government of his home country. (Mr. __________'s Declaration at para. __, hereinafter (D. at __.") His brother, __________, was arrested, interrogated, and brutally tortured by the __________ military based on the military's belief that Mr. __________ and his family members are politically opposed to the __________ government. (D. at __.) Furthermore, Mr. __________'s desertion from the military, along with the desertion of numerous family members, has resulted in the government's belief that he and his family members are politically opposed to the __________ government. (D. at __.)

In the past, Mr. __________ has demonstrated his actual opposition to the government by refusing to join the __________ Party, the ruling party of __________ (D. at __.), by protesting the government's taking of his family's land, for which he was arrested (D. at __.), and his desertion from the military (D. at __.). Mr. __________'s asylum claim is, therefore, based on his actual and imputed political opinion.

Political opinions that give rise to asylum claims are defined as "opinions not tolerated by the authorities, which are critical of their policies or methods," and "such opinions [that] have come to the notice of the authorities or are attributed by them to the applicant." *United Nations Handbook on Procedures and Criteria for Determining Refugee Status*[1] (Geneva 1992) (hereinafter *UN Handbook*) at ¶80. An imputed political opinion, whether correctly or incorrectly attributed, is a basis for asylum within the meaning of INA § 208. *Ravindran v. INS,* 976 F.2d 754, 760 (1st Cir. 1992). The doctrine of imputed political opinion arose in recognition of the fact that "[i]f the persecutor thinks the person guilty of a political opinion, then that person is at risk," at as much risk, in fact, as a person who actually holds a political belief contrary to that of the persecutor. *Lazo-Majano v. INS,* 813 F.2d 1432, 1435 (9th Cir. 1987). This doctrine has been an integral part of the analyses in many asylum cases. *See, e.g., Aguilera-Cota v. INS,* 914 F.2d 1375, 1379 (9th Cir. 1990); *Beltran-Zavala v. INS,* 912 F.2d 1027, 1030 (9th Cir. 1990).

Under the imputed political opinion doctrine, the proper focus is not on the actual political beliefs of the victim, but rather on the "motivation of the persecutor." *Hernandez-Ortiz v. INS,* 777 F.2d 509, 516 (9th Cir. 1985). The BIA has concurred in the above-noted analysis for determining when persecution is on account of "political opinion." *See Matter of Maldonado-Cruz,* 19 I&N Dec. 509 (BIA 1988). In looking at the victim from the persecutor's perspective, one considers what particular conscious acts of the victim or

---

[1] It should be noted that the U.S. Supreme Court has held that the *UN Handbook* provides "significant guidance" in determining whether an asylum applicant meets the definition of "refugee." *INS v. Cardoza-Fonseca*, 480 U.S. 421, 438–39 & n.22 (1987).

other circumstances would cause the persecutor to attribute a political opinion to the victim. *Desir v. Ilchert,* 840 F.2d 723, 728 (9th Cir. 1988).

Mr. __________ has demonstrated through his testimony, his asylum application, and the letter from his brother, __________ (found at Tab __ of the Supporting Documentation), that the __________ military will harm, torture, or kill him because of his political opinions, imputed and real, if he is returned to __________. The accusations and threats made by the __________ military against Mr. __________ constitute direct evidence of his persecutors' motives. (D. at __.) Moreover, the documentary evidence establishes that other individuals similarly accused of spying or opposing the government have been tortured and killed by the __________ government. (*See* Tabs __, __, __, __, __, __, __, and __ of the Supporting Documentation.)

II. Refusal to Serve in the Military

Mr. __________'s fear of persecution is also based on his refusal to serve in and desertion from the __________ military. Mr. __________ opposes serving in the military based on his moral beliefs and opposition to the objectives of the military. In his past military service, he became aware of the human rights abuses committed by the __________ military in the __________ war (D. at __.) and does not want to participate in such abuses.

Mr. __________ qualifies for asylum based on his refusal to serve for two separate reasons. First, his refusal to serve is based on his moral convictions. Secondly, he qualifies based on the disproportionate treatment he is likely to suffer for his desertion based on his religion, nationality, membership in a particular social group, and political opinion.

The BIA recognized in *Matter of A.G.*, 19 I&N Dec. 502, 506 (BIA 1987), that a person may qualify for asylum based on his refusal to serve in the military "where the [person] would necessarily be required to engage in inhuman conduct as a result of the military service required by the government." Paragraph 170 of the *UN Handbook* further provides that "the necessity to perform military service may be the sole ground for a claim to refugee status . . . when a person can show that the performance of military service would have required participation in military action contrary to his genuine political, religious or moral convictions, or to valid reasons of conscience."

The documentary evidence submitted as Supporting Documentation at Tabs __, __, __, __, __, __, and __ overwhelmingly demonstrates that the __________ military engaged in systematic human rights abuses throughout the __________ war. Many innocent civilians were targeted and killed by __________. Mr. __________'s desertion from the military by refusing to return to complete his military service was based on both his refusal to participate in the political objectives of the __________ government and his moral convictions. (D. at __, __, and __.)

The *UN Handbook* at ¶169 also recognizes that a deserter may be considered a refugee if he "would suffer disproportionately severe punishment for the military offense based on his race, religion, nationality, membership of a particular social group or political opinion." The Supporting Documentation at Tabs __, __, __, __, and __, demonstrates that members of Mr. __________'s religious and ethnic group suffer disproportionate punishment at the hands of the __________ military and police. Mr. __________ is likely to be tortured and executed for his act of desertion. (D. at __.)

III. Religion

Mr. __________ and his family have suffered and are likely to suffer persecution in the future in __________ on account of their religious beliefs. Mr. __________ recounted in his declaration the widespread physical and verbal abuse, discrimination, and harassment that he and his family members suffered in __________ throughout their lives. (D. at __, __, __, and __.) These abuses continued through his higher education and military service. (D. at __, __, __, and __.)

The *UN Handbook* at ¶72 notes that "[p]ersecution for reasons of religion may assume various forms," including "serious measures of discrimination imposed on persons because they practise their religion or belong to a particular religious community."

In addition to Mr. __________'s declaration, the Supporting Documentation at Tabs __ and __ provides substantial evidence of the mistreatment and persecution of Mr. __________'s religious group in __________. The report, __________, lists numerous recent examples of the persecution of members of this religious group in __________. These individuals have been persecuted for refusing to join the ruling party, for having ties to the United States, because they are perceived to be opponents of the __________ government, and because they have deserted from the military. Mr. __________ falls into each of these categories and, therefore, has a well-founded fear of persecution because he is similarly situated to others who have been persecuted because of their religion. *See* 8 CFR §§208.13(b)(2), 1208.13(b)(2).

IV. Race; Membership in a Particular Social Group

Mr. __________ and his family also fear persecution because they are __________, an ethnic minority group in __________. This ethnic minority group could be characterized as either a race or particular social group according to the criteria set forth in the *UN Handbook* and the case law in the United States. The __________ people are a separate ethnic and linguistic group in __________, according to the Supporting Documentation at Tab __. Mr. __________'s declaration chronicles his own efforts on behalf of his ethnic group (D at __.) and that his ethnic heritage was an additional cause of mistreatment, harassment, and discrimination (D. at __, __, and __.).

The *UN Handbook* at ¶68 states that "[r]ace . . . has to be understood in its widest sense to include all kinds of ethnic groups. . . . Discrimination for reasons of race has found worldwide condemnations one of the most striking violations of human rights." The BIA has similarly defined "particular social group" as a group of individuals who "share a common, immutable characteristic . . . which members of the group either cannot change, or should not be required to change, because it is fundamental to their individual identities or consciences." *Matter of Acosta*, 19 I&N Dec. 211, 233 (BIA 1985).

The __________ population in __________ has been continually and systematically oppressed by the government. The reports from __________ on the persecution of this ethnic group have been numerous and graphic. __________'s brutal treatment of this ethnic group has been labelled "genocide" by international human rights groups. *See* Supporting Documentation at Tabs __, __, __, and __.

Whether Mr. __________'s ethnicity is characterized as a particular social group or race, the harm he is likely to suffer because of it is the same. Mr. __________ and his family fear that they will be subjected to "genocide" if they are returned because of their ethnicity.

Mr. __________ also belongs to the particular social group of a family that has been singled out and targeted as being subversives and opponents of the government. His brother was arrested, interrogated, and brutally tortured because of his family is believed to be disloyalty to government. (D. at __ and Supporting Documentation at Tabs __ and __.) As a member of a targeted "family," and Mr. __________ himself a target, he has a well-founded fear of persecution. Several of Mr. __________'s family members were interviewed and granted refugee status by the United States. *See* Supporting Documentation at Tabs __, __, __, and __. Mr. __________ also fears persecution because his family, as a group, has been sought out and targeted for persecution.

V. Conclusion

Based on the foregoing reasons, it is respectfully requested that Mr. __________ and his wife, __________, be granted asylum in the United States.

If you require any additional information regarding Mr. __________'s asylum claim, please do not hesitate to contact me at *[phone number]*.

Respectfully submitted,

____

Attorney for the Applicants

Appendix 4E

Asylum Office Guide – Best Practices

Updated March 2, 2015

Arlington, VA (ZAR)

This office is often referred to as "ZAR." It changes its rules and procedures frequently. Published rules are sometimes not followed. Nonetheless, ZAR in general is a friendly office.

Location and Contact Information

Street Address:
Arlington Asylum Office
1525 Wilson Blvd, #300; Arlington, VA 22209

Mail Address:
Arlington Asylum Office
1525 Wilson Blvd, Mailstop 2500; Arlington VA 20598-2500

Main: (703) 235-4100 / Fax: (703) 812-8455
Arlington.Asylum@uscis.dhs.gov

Director: Jedidah Hussey
Deputy Director: Antonio Donis

1. **Walk-in Time for Inquiries**: members of the public, without an appointment, may walk in on Wednesdays from 7:00 am–3:00 pm.

2. **Open to the Public**:
   Monday – Wednesday: 7:00 am–3:00 pm
   Thursday: 7:00 am–1:00 pm
   Friday: 7:00 am–3:00 pm
   People may walk in during these times and request an appointment, or make an inquiry, to be answered later.

3. **Rescheduling Requests**: send reschedule requests via fax, and then telephone ZAR

4. **Delivery of Documents**: ZAR will not accept deliveries from couriers such as Fed Ex and UPS. Mailstop 2500 is in the state of Maryland, perhaps resulting in a five-day delay. A lawyer, or paralegal who brings a letter from the lawyer verifying the paralegal's employment, may walk in and hand-deliver documents.

Additional evidence must be submitted one week in advance or your case will be rescheduled. While this has been their policy for some time, it began to be strictly enforced as of February 9, 2015. As a result, you should now bring in supplementary documents, in triplicate, one week before the interview. You need a table of contents, and tabs (either on the bottom or on the side).

Documents may be hand-delivered Monday, Tuesday, or Thursday between 7:00 am–11:00 am and Wednesday between 7:00 am–3:00 pm.

See two memorandum dated January 14, 2015, one from Jedidah Hussey on hours of operation and another on document submission for more details.

5. **Local AILA Liaison Chairs**:
   FOR AILA MEMBERS ONLY
   See *www.aila.org* for your local AILA liaison, *published on* AILA InfoNet at Doc. No. 12060844 (*posted* 03/19/15).

6. Service Area: This Asylum Office serves the following states: Alabama, Georgia, Maryland, North Carolina, South Carolina, Virginia, West Virginia, and the District of Columbia.
   This office also serves the following counties in the state of Pennsylvania: Allegheny, Armstrong, Beaver, Bedford, Blair, Bradford, Butler, Cambria, Clarion, Clearfield, Crawford, Elk, Erie, Fayette, Forest, Greene, Indiana, Jefferson, Lawrence, McKean, Mercer, Somerset, Venango, Warren, Washington, Westmoreland.

7. Additional Information: ZAR often answers questions by quoting from the *Affirmative Asylum Procedure Manual.*

Chicago, IL (ZCH)

Location and Contact Information

181 West Madison Street, Suite 3000; Chicago, IL 60602

Main: (312) 849-5200 / Fax: (312) 849-5201
chicago.asylum@uscis.dhs.gov

Asylum Office Director: Kenneth Madsen, ext. 5225
Asylum Office Deputy Director: Lisa Flanagan
Congressional Liaison: (312) 849-5200

Hours of Operation: 8:00 a.m. to 4:00 p.m.

1. **Waiting Period**: The Chicago Asylum Office is currently experiencing a significant backlog in the scheduling of cases for interviews and in issuing decisions. Although

some applicants are interviewed within 45 days, many applicants have not received an interview notice for one year or more after filing. The number of circuit rides decreased significantly in FY2014.

2. **Rescheduling Requests**: Rescheduling requests must be hand written and sent via mail, hand delivery, or fax to the attention of Supervisor Timothy Bondy or Kelly Burch. You may contact Timothy Bondy at 312-849-5211.

3. The request for a rescheduled interview must include the reason for the request and why the applicant or attorney cannot appear on the scheduled date.

4. You may also contact the Chicago Asylum Office by e-mail at *chicago.asylum@uscis.dhs.gov*. Asylum officers are bound by confidentiality restrictions and therefore may not be able to respond via e-mail, so please include your contact information in the e-mail.

5. **Filing Documentation**: The Chicago Asylum Office pre-assigns officers to cases a week before the interview. Attorneys may submit additional supplementary documents to the Chicago Asylum Office on Wednesday through Friday prior to the interview and it will make it to the file for review by the pre-assigned officer.

6. **Liaison Committee Chairs**:
   FOR AILA MEMBERS ONLY
   See *www.aila.org* for your local AILA liaison, *published on* AILA InfoNet at Doc. No. 12060844 (*posted* 03/19/15).

7. **Service Area**: The Chicago Asylum Office has jurisdiction over cases arising in Idaho, Illinois, Indiana, Iowa, Kansas, Kentucky, Michigan, Minnesota, Missouri, Montana, Nebraska, North Dakota, Ohio, South Dakota, and Wisconsin.

8. **Additional Information**:
   - If an attorney is representing several family members, including multiple principal applicants and multiple derivatives, send a letter to the Chicago Asylum Office after filing the asylum applications to request that the principal applicants in the family be scheduled for asylum interviews on the same day. The Chicago Asylum Office will not otherwise know that the principal applicants are related and relying on similar evidence.
   - Water is allowed in the Asylum Office. Food is not allowed.

Houston, TX (ZHN)

Location and Contact Information.

Street Address:
16630 Imperial Valley Drive, Suite 200; Houston, TX 77060

Mail Address:
P.O. Box 670626; Houston, TX 77267-0626

Main: (281) 931-2100 / Fax: (281) 931-1309 (please send all inquiries to the e-mail)
Houston.Asylum@uscis.dhs.gov (please send all inquiries to the e-mail)

Asylum Office Director: Marie Hummert, ext. 2174
Asylum Office Deputy Director: Jessica Walter, ext. 2172
AILA Liaison – Supervisory Asylum Officer (SAO): Will Bierman
Congressional Liaison: Mary Winkler: (714) 808-8203

Hours of Operation: 7:00 am–4:00 pm, Monday through Friday.

1. **Waiting Period**: Three to four weeks from filing to interview for cases interviewed at the Houston Office. The number and frequency of circuit rides (to Memphis, TN; Salt Lake City, UT; Denver, CO) was reduced in FY13. Accordingly, significant delays will likely accrue for those cases. Cases that would otherwise be interviewed in a circuit ride location will be interviewed in Houston at the request and expense of the applicant.

2. **Rescheduling Requests**: All requests to reschedule must be made by the applicant in writing by either mailing or faxing a letter to the Asylum Office, attention "Rescheduling". In addition to the mail/fax request, attorneys and representatives may also submit an e-mail to the e-mail address noted above for inquiries, advising of the request for reschedule and identifying the date on which the request was mailed/faxed. Documentation must be submitted supporting the reason for the reschedule.

3. **Filing Documentation**: The Houston Asylum Office prefers documentation be filed with the asylum application at the Texas Service Center. In the event that supplemental documentation needs to be filed, Houston requests that it be filed with their office (not the Texas Service Center) well in advance of the interview. Houston would like to avoid large filings on the day of the interview. Day-of submissions may delay a decision in the case or necessitate a follow-up interview at a later date. Post-interview, any additional documentation may be faxed to the attention of the officer who conducted the interview.

4. **Liaison Committee Chairs**:
   FOR AILA MEMBERS ONLY
   See *www.aila.org* for your local AILA liaison, *published on* AILA InfoNet at Doc. No. 12060844 (*posted* 03/19/15).

5. **Service Area and Circuit Rides**: The Houston Asylum Office serves the following states: Arkansas, Colorado, Louisiana, Mississippi, Oklahoma, New Mexico, Tennessee, Texas, Utah, and Wyoming.

The office does circuit rides to Denver, CO; Salt Lake City, UT; and Memphis, TN. Depending on the applicant's location, the scheduled interview will be either at the Houston Asylum Office or circuit ride location nearest the applicant's address. If an applicant does not want to wait for the upcoming circuit ride, he or she can request to schedule an interview at the Houston Asylum Office, though travel costs will be at their own expense.

6. **Additional Information**:
   - Photo identifications must be presented to be admitted to the office.
   - Cell phones must be turned off when entering the waiting area. (Since every cell phone now has a camera function, the guards usually just say that cell phones are prohibited to avoid having to explore the functions of each phone.)
   - Cameras (including camera phones) are not allowed in the waiting area and offices.
   - Applicants must provide their own interpreters.
   - If an applicant is attending an interview with children, it is requested that the applicant also bring someone (not the interpreter) who can monitor the children in the waiting area while the applicant's interview is conducted.
   - Decisions will be scheduled for pick-up at the office, unless the applicant lives greater than 200 miles from the office, in which case a decision can be mailed. All decisions for circuit ride locations are mailed.
   - If an applicant has special needs, it is recommended this be communicated to the asylum office once the applicant receives notice of the interview.
   - Applicants should bring all original documents (passports, certificates, letters, etc.) in their possession for which copies have been submitted as part of the application or supplemental materials.

Los Angeles, CA (ZLA):

Location and Contact Information:

Street Address:
1585 South Manchester Avenue; Anaheim, CA 92802
Mailing Address:
P.O. Box 65015; Anaheim, CA 92802

Main: 714-808-8000 / Fax: 714-635-8707
Admin Fax: 714-635-9136 / APSO Fax: 714-635-5611
losangeles.asylum@uscis.dhs.gov (general inquiries)

The main phone number is typically only answered in the morning. Calling in the afternoon and reaching someone is generally only possible if you have the direct dial number of the person you need to reach. For a list of contact information for supervisory personnel, see the Los Angeles Asylum Office Contact list, *published on* AILA InfoNet at Doc. No. 14072944 (7/29/14).

Asylum Office Director: David Radel, *David.M.Radel@uscis.dhs.gov*, (714) 808-8206
Acting Deputy Director: Marianne Hong, *Marianne.x.hong@uscis.dhs.gov*, (714) 808-8205.
Congressional Liaison: Mary Winkler, *Mary.L.Winkler@uscis.dhs.gov*, (714) 808-8203

Hours of Operation: Monday through Friday, 6:00 am to 6:00 pm daily

1. **Waiting Period**:
   From Filing to Interview: ZLA currently has a backlog of over 10,000 uninterviewed applications stretching back to FY2011. They are attempting to interview newly filed applications on a first-in, first-out basis in order to minimize the potential of people taking advantage of the backlog merely to obtain work authorization. However, the office continues to receive more new cases than it can schedule. As a result, if you file an application and you do not receive an interview notice within three–four weeks after filing, it is likely that your application has become part of the backlog. ZLA is unable to estimate how long a case that is part of the backlog will have to wait for interview.

   On the Day of the Interview: The office reported in July 2014, that it has been able to improve the wait times to 1 hour or less on the day of the interview. In the past, it has been common to wait two–three hours or longer past the scheduled interview time to be called in by an officer. Morning cases still waiting at noon were told to go to lunch and come back. If you have a morning case and you have not been told to go to lunch by noon, you may inquire at the check-in window to see if your case has been assigned and, if so, whether the officer will be able to begin the interview soon or whether you should go to lunch. No food or drink is allowed in the waiting room. There is a water fountain.

   To Pick-up the Decision: Out of status applicants return to the office two weeks after their interview to pick up the decision. Once there, ZLA reports that 80 percent of applicants wait 30 minutes or less to receive their decisions. Decisions that are mailed out, either because the applicant is in status or because processing (including background checks and headquarters review, if necessary) has not been completed, can take significantly longer.

2. **Scheduling and Rescheduling Requests**:
   Getting an Application Out of the Backlog: If you believe that extraordinary circumstances exist that warrant getting a case scheduled for interview earlier than it would otherwise, you can submit a written request for an expedited interview to Mary Winkler. Urgent requests can be sent to Marianne Hong or David Radel. Please include evidence of the extraordinary circumstance(s). Where possible given the office's limited ability to schedule and/or reschedule interviews, the office does attempt to prioritize scheduling requests in cases where the EAD clock has been stopped at less than 180 days.

Rescheduling Requests: All attorney inquiries and reschedule requests should be sent in writing to Mary Winkler via e-mail at *Mary.L.Winkler@uscis.dhs.gov* or via fax to 714-254-4203. Reschedule requests should be sent in as early as possible in advance of the interview date and, at the very latest, must be received within 45 days after the interview date.

If Mary Winkler is out of the office, you may send interview reschedule requests to Lead Supervisory USCIS Assistant Kristi Cottrell via e-mail at *Kristi.L.Cotrell@uscis.dhs.gov* or via fax at (714) 635-8707.

For urgent requests, you may contact Deputy Director Marianne Hong or Director David Radel via e-mail at *Marianne.x.hong@uscis.dhs.gov* or *David.M.Radel@uscis.dhs.gov* or via fax at (714) 635-9136.

Any inquiries about whether the request has been granted or not should be directed to Mary Winkler. In cases where there has been no reply, contact Director Radel or Deputy Director Hong directly at their numbers above.

Note that a request to reschedule stops the asylum processing KLOK until the applicant appears for the rescheduled interview. Due to the backlog, ZLA's ability to reschedule interviews is extremely limited. Thus, making a rescheduling request risks having the case go into the backlog with a stopped KLOK, making it impossible for the applicant to apply for work authorization no matter how long it takes to get the case rescheduled.

Stand-By List: Applicants in the backlog may request to be placed on a "stand-by" list to be called if a regularly scheduled case does not appear for interview. Standby calls require the applicant to arrive at the office within a short period of time, usually within an hour. If you would like your case to be included on the standby list, please contact Supervisory USCIS Assistant Carlos Mejia via e-mail at: *Carlos.E.Mejia@uscis.dhs.gov* or request at window 1 to have your client placed on the standby list.

3. **Filing Documentation**: Any supplementary documents must be received by the asylum office in triplicate at least one week prior to the date of interview. They must be sent to the attention of Kristi Cotrell by mail or fax (619) 635-9136, or delivered in person. If you are sending fewer than 5 pages, you can e-mail them to *losangelesasylum@uscis.dhs.gov*. Please label the documents with the applicant's name, A-number, and interview time and date (if applicable).

   Applicants who submit documentation on the day of the interview, either to the officer or at the window, risk having their interview rescheduled and their EAD clock stopped. Limited exceptions may be made on a case-by-case basis, but only with the approval of the duty officer. Applicants will need to show good cause for the untimely submission and that the same-day review of the documents will not significantly burden the interviewing officer. An exception to this is a case called from the stand-by list.

4. **Liaison Committee Chairs**:
   FOR AILA MEMBERS ONLY
   See *www.aila.org* for your local AILA liaison, *published on* AILA InfoNet at Doc. No. 12060844 (*posted* 03/19/15).

5. **Service Area and Circuit Rides**: The Los Angeles Asylum Office has jurisdiction over cases arising out of Arizona, Hawaii, the Territory of Guam, select California counties (Imperial, Los Angeles, Orange, Riverside, San Bernardino, San Diego, San Luis Obispo, Santa Barbara, and Ventura) and select Nevada counties (Clark, Esmerelda, Lincoln, and Nye).

   The Los Angeles Asylum Office does circuit rides in Arizona, Hawaii, and the Territory of Guam. It does not do circuit rides in Nevada; those cases are interviewed in the Los Angeles Asylum Office.

   An asylum officer is sent on a "circuit ride" detail to either Phoenix, Hawaii, or Guam on a periodic basis. The frequency and length of such details largely depends on the number of filings in a given area. The circuit rides take place at a USCIS facility.

   Under ordinary circumstances, Phoenix rides occur each quarter, and Hawaii and Guam circuit rides occur once or twice a year. No circuit rides to Guam or Hawaii were conducted in fiscal year 2013, but circuit rides resumed to Phoenix, Hawaii and Guam in FY2014 and are expected to continue through FY2015.

   An applicant who resides in a circuit ride location who can present proof of extraordinary circumstances can request to be interviewed at ZLA. However, due to the backlog, ZLA may not be able to honor the request. The procedure for making such a request is the same as for scheduling/ rescheduling above.

6. **Additional Information**:
   - Visitors to the Los Angeles Asylum Office are permitted to take cell phones, laptops, PDAs, and other electronic devices onto the premises. Audio and video recording devices must not be used on the premises. Attorneys are allowed to take notes on a laptop during interview.
   - Cell phones must be silenced (vibrate or low volume) while in the waiting area. Cell phones must be completely turned off during interviews.
   - Detailed information on other topics, including ABC/NACARA, reinstatement, credible and reasonable fear interviews, work authorization issues, as well as a list of contact information for supervisory personnel can be found in the AILA/ LACBA Liaison Meeting Notes from July 16, 2014, *published on* AILA In-

foNet at Doc. No. 14072942 (*posted* 7/29/14).

Miami, FL (ZMI)

Location and Contact Information:

99 Southeast 5th Street, 3rd Floor; Miami, FL 33131

Main: (305) 960-8600 / Fax: (305) 530-6071

Asylum Office Director: Varsenik Papazian
Asylum Office Deputy Director: Kimberly M. Aguilar

Hours of Operation: 7:30 am–4:00 pm, Monday through Thursday

1. **Waiting Period**: On the day of the interview, the waiting period is less than 1 hour.

2. **Rescheduling Requests**: If applicants or their attorneys need to reschedule an interview, they should send a fax. The first request is generally honored, as long as it states a reason for the reschedule and is signed by the applicant or the attorney/representative. A second request is generally granted as long as it states a good cause for inability to appear with supporting documentation. After two reschedules, the applicant may receive a "final reschedule" notice.

3. **Filing Documentation**: The Asylum Office would like to have all documents filed together at the same time. It is possible to supplement, but they prefer one complete filing including application and all supporting documentation.

4. **Liaison Committee Chairs**:
   FOR AILA MEMBERS ONLY
   See *www.aila.org* for your local AILA liaison, *published on* AILA InfoNet at Doc. No. 12060844 (*posted* 03/19/15).

5. **Circuit Rides**: The Miami Asylum Office does circuit rides in Jacksonville, Florida, the Commonwealth of Puerto Rico, and the United States Virgin Islands.

Newark, NJ (ZNK)

Location and Contact Information:

1200 Wall Street West, 4th Floor; Lyndhurst, NJ 07071

Main: (201) 508-6100 / Fax: (201) 531-1877

Asylum Office Director: Susan Raufer, *susan.raufer@uscis.dhs.gov*

Asylum Office Deputy Director: Lorie Heinrich, *lorie.heinrich@uscis.dhs.gov*
Congressional Liaison: Vacant

Hours of Operation: Monday through Thursday, 7:30 am–4:30 pm (appointment only)
Friday, 8:00 am–3:00 pm (walk-in hours)

The building has public parking. There is a cafeteria on the first floor of the building.

1. **Waiting Periods**: Asylum applicants are usually called in for a scheduled interview relatively promptly (within an hour of checking in with the front desk).

2. **Rescheduling Requests**: Rescheduling requests must be submitted by hand or faxed as soon as possible. They must include the applicant's name, alien number, Form G-28, date of scheduled interview, and reasons behind the rescheduling request. The requests should be directed to Acting Support Unit Supervisor, Estela Carr, for all interview locations.

   Rescheduling requests made by the applicant will be randomly rescheduled by a computer. On occasions where the asylum office is the reason for rescheduling, the office will manually set the date to accommodate the attorney's schedule.

   The new rescheduled date is generally between three weeks and a year, or longer, due to current backlogs.

   The first rescheduling request is honored without an explanation, but subsequent requests will be considered on a case-by-case basis.

   In the case of a no-show, please contact the office no more than two weeks after the scheduled date to request the interview be rescheduled, and be prepared to provide a reason for the no-show.

3. **Filing Supporting Documentation**: The Newark Asylum Office pre-assigns cases several days prior to the interview. Additional supplementary documents should be submitted to the office at least one week prior to the interview. Submitting supporting material on the date of the interview may cause the case to be rescheduled. Materials can be dropped off at the front desk or mailed directly to the Asylum Office, and should be tabbed and indexed.

   To make a specific request for a special accommodation (female interviewer, handicap accessibility, presence of student observers or witnesses, etc.), please contact the office ahead of time.

4. **Liaison Committee Chairs**:
   FOR AILA MEMBERS ONLY
   See *www.aila.org* for your local AILA liaison, *published on* AILA InfoNet at Doc.

No. 12060844 (*posted* 03/19/15).

5. **Service Area and Circuit Rides**: This Asylum Office serves the following states: Connecticut, Delaware, Maine, Massachusetts, New Hampshire, New Jersey, Rhode Island, and Vermont; as well as certain counties in New York and Pennsylvania.

   The Newark Asylum Office does circuit rides throughout Connecticut, Delaware, Maine, Massachusetts, New Hampshire, New Jersey, Rhode Island, and Vermont.

   Asylum Officers currently do circuit rides to Boston, MA, at irregular intervals of one to three months, to conduct interviews for one week, generally from Monday afternoon through Friday morning. The front desk will be setup on Monday morning for the week of interviews.

   In early 2015, the Newark Asylum Office is planning to establish a permanent sub-office in Boston, MA, that will have regular business hours and policies similar to the Newark Asylum Office. Additional details will become available once the sub-office is established.

   The interviews in Boston, MA, are currently conducted at:
   John F. Kennedy Federal Building, Room 605
   Government Center
   15 New Sudbury Street; Boston, MA 02203-0002
   Main: (617) 565-9030

   Asylum Officers travel to St. Albans, VT periodically.
   The interviews are conducted at:
   St. Albans Field Office
   64 Gricebrook Road; St. Albans, VT 05478

   Asylum Officers travel to Buffalo, NY periodically.
   The interviews are conducted at:
   Buffalo District Office
   130 Delaware Avenue; Buffalo, NY 14202

6. **Additional Information**: The deputy director and the director will respond to e-mails and will reply to letter or phone follow-ups as necessary. E-mails should contain contact and reply information, but should not contain any confidential information.

   A detailed list of asylum officers and supervisors and designated support staff is provided by the asylum office to local asylum office liaisons.

   There is an expedite procedure in place to obtain interviews at the Newark Asylum Office for cases which present exigent or humanitarian concerns. Please contact your local liaison for further details.

New York City (ZNY)

Location and Contact Information:

Street Address:
One Cross Island Plaza
133-33 Brookville Blvd, 3rd Floor; Rosedale, NY 11422
Mailing Address:
One Cross Island Plaza, 3rd Floor; Rosedale, NY 11422

Main: (718) 723-5954 / Fax: (718) 723-1121
NewYork.Asylum@uscis.dhs.gov

Asylum Office Director: Patricia Menges, ext. 1002, *patricia.menges@uscis.dhs.gov*
Asylum Office Deputy Director: Ashley Caudill-Mirillo, ext. 1004, *ashley.caudill.mirillo @uscis.dhs.gov*

Hours of Operation: 7:30 am–4:15 pm (walk-in hours)

Case inquiries and questions regarding agency/office policy and procedure can be submitted via mail, in-person, fax, telephone, or e-mail. Send correspondence to the attention of the Immigration Analysts.

Please direct complaints or concerns to the director or deputy director via mail or fax. In addition, if you submit a case inquiry or pose a question to the Immigration Analysts and do not receive a response within three weeks, please send a letter to the director or deputy director via mail or fax. The director and deputy director will not respond to phone calls or e-mails.

The building has no parking, but there is parking on the street nearby. There is a cafeteria on the first floor.

1. **Waiting Period**: Occasionally, you may experience waiting room delays. Interview times are staggered to minimize delays. To minimize the inconvenience to visitors, the office has adopted a pager system that allows applicants, interpreters, and attorneys to exit the secure waiting room while they are waiting, enabling them to use electronic devices and patronize the café downstairs. The office will send a signal to the pager approximately 15 minutes before the AO will call the case. This provides the applicant with plenty of time to return to the waiting room and pass through security. Pagers can be obtained from the front desk. The office also has a children's corner with books, toys, and games. There are also two computers with children's games located in the waiting room. This is to make the waiting room more family-friendly.

2. **Rescheduling Requests**: To reschedule, send in a written request via mail, hand-delivery, or fax, prior to the date of the interview. A first request is normally granted without explanation. Subsequent requests may require an explanation and will be determined on a case-by-case basis. Follow-ups on reschedule requests should be submitted if a response is not received within 30 days.

3. **Filing Documentation**: The New York Asylum Office does not pre-assign cases. Supporting materials can be submitted prior to the interview or with the front desk on the morning of the interview when the applicant checks in. You should not wait to give this documentation to the officer at the commencement of the interview.

4. **Liaison Committee Chairs**:
   FOR AILA MEMBERS ONLY
   See *www.aila.org* for your local AILA liaison, *published on* AILA InfoNet at Doc. No. 12060844 (*posted* 03/19/15).

5. **Additional Information**:
   - No water or food is allowed in the secure waiting area.
   - All electronic devices (including but not limited to cellular telephones, laptops, iPads, etc.) must be turned off while you are inside the secure waiting area.
   - The New York Asylum Office is very strict about time. Applicants, attorneys, and interpreters must check in no later than 30 minutes beyond the appointment time. Any cases that are not prepared to check in and move forward within 30 minutes of their appointment time will be rescheduled unless they can show emergent or extenuating circumstances.

San Francisco, CA (ZSF)

Location and Contact Information:

Street Address:
75 Hawthorne Street, 3rd Floor, Room 303 S; San Francisco, CA 94105
The reception area and waiting room are on the 1st floor. When the officer is ready to begin the interview, the applicant (and attorney and/or interpreter) will proceed to the 3rd floor.

Mailing Address:
P.O. Box 77530; San Francisco, CA 94107

Main: (415) 293-1234 / Fax: (415) 293-1269

Asylum Office Director: Emilia Bardini, *emilia.m.bardini@uscis.dhs.gov*
Asylum Office Deputy Director: Calton Yue, *Calton.Yue@uscis.dhs.gov*
Congressional Liaison: Michelle Henderson: *SanFranciscoAsylum@uscis.dhs.gov*

Hours of Operation: Monday through Friday, by appointment only. Public window open for inquiries Friday morning 8:00 am–12:00 pm. Documents may be dropped off on Mondays 12:00pm–2:00 pm.

1. **Waiting Period**: Interviews take place Mondays through Thursdays, at 8:30 am or 10:15 am. Officers have two interviews daily (back-to-back interviews). The 8:30 am interview usually begins around 9:00 am, and the 10:15 am interview usually starts around 11:00 am, sometimes later. Interviews take an average of two hours.

2. **Rescheduling Requests**: The asylum office will take reschedule requests before the interview or the day of the interview. Requests before the interview date must be in writing, via fax or mail. Special requests may be made directly to the director or deputy director in cases of medical urgency. The office also accepts "short notice requests;" if the attorney and client can come in for an interview on short notice, usually around two or three days before an open interview slot, they can sign up with the director.

   The scheduler generally cannot be contacted directly, and therefore it is recommended to include in the request any potential upcoming conflicts. Although confirmation of a reschedule request by mail or fax should be provided, attorneys should not expect anyone to contact him or her to confirm the new date. If the new interview is approved, attorneys or applicants should expect a new interview notice by mail. In UAC cases interview scheduling can be arranged with the scheduler working through Supervisor Vincent Ferri, *Vincent.Ferri@uscis.dhs.gov*. Given the current backlogs, an applicant should not expect a rescheduled interview for six months or more. Also, reschedule requests sometimes fall through the cracks. If you feel that this has happened, it is recommended to e-mail the director or deputy director.

3. **Filing Documentation**: The San Francisco Asylum Office accepts filings at the front window on Monday afternoon between 12:00 pm–2:00 pm. They also accept documentation by mail, however many attorneys have noted that mailed documents do not reach the file by the time of the interview, or are lost. If you mail documents, definitely get a tracking number. Hand-delivery of the documents to the front window is a common method to make sure the documents reach the file. The San Francisco Asylum Office considers timely submission of documents to be by Monday of the week before the interview.

   When an applicant arrives to an interview with additional documents, the front desk will take them and add them to the file. However, they will most likely reschedule the interview.

4. **Liaison Committee Chairs**:
   FOR AILA MEMBERS ONLY

See *www.aila.org* for your local AILA liaison, *published on* AILA InfoNet at Doc. No. 12060844 (*posted* 03/19/15).

5. **Service Area and Circuit Rides**: The San Francisco Asylum Office does circuit rides in Alaska, Oregon, and Washington.

   The San Francisco Asylum Office serves the following counties in the state of California: Alameda, Alpine, Amador, Butte, Calaveras, Colusa, Contra Costa, Del Norte, El Dorado, Fresno, Glenn, Humboldt, Inyo, Kern, Kings, Lake, Lassen, Madera, Marin, Mariposa, Mendocino, Merced, Modoc, Mono, Monterey, Napa, Nevada, Placer, Plumas, Sacramento, San Benito, San Francisco, San Joaquin, San Mateo, Santa Clara, Santa Cruz, Shasta, Siskiyou, Solano, Sonoma, Stanislaus, Sutter, Tehama, Trinity, Tulare, Tuolumne, Yolo, and Yuba.

   The San Francisco Asylum Office serves the following counties in the state of Nevada: Carson City, Churchill, Douglas, Elko, Eureka, Humboldt, Lander, Lyon, Mineral, Pershing, Storey, Wash, and White Pine.

6. **Additional Information**:
   - **The Interview Day**:
     a. Parking can be tricky, although there are several paid lots in the area. If taking BART, the office is a 10-minute walk from the Montgomery station. It is advisable to arrive at least 15 minutes before the appointment time. There are two metal detector stations that everyone must pass through before getting to the appointment window. The San Francisco Asylum Office also maintains the right to consider the applicant a "no-show" if he or she is more than 15 minutes late. Public transportation delays (which do happen) are generally not an excuse for late arrivals.
     b. At the conclusion of the interview, attorneys are allowed follow-up or the opportunity to make a closing statement. However, SF Asylum Officers are specifically trained not to provide any indication of how they will decide the case. So after the applicant finishes the interview portion, if attorneys ask questions of the officer, such as "do you have any concerns about the case that I can help you answer," asylum officers generally say something like, "I've heard all the facts and will be making my decision based on those." It is difficult to engage the officer in any kind of discussion, but with some officers it can be done.
     c. If there is a problem with an asylum officer during the interview, it is recommended to speak to his or her supervisor.
     d. Interviews take an average of two hours.
   - **Notice Pick-up**:

     Applicants are required to pick up their decision letters approximately 15 days after the interview. If at the time of the pick-up the letter is not ready, the person at the front desk advises that an applicant can return on a subsequent Friday to check on the status of the decision, or that it will be mailed to them.

- **After Final Denial of an In-status Applicant**:
  a. If someone was denied by the asylum office while in status and would like to re-apply for asylum, mail a copy of the I-589 and the decision letter directly to the SF asylum office and state in a cover letter that you are re-applying. However, do not expect to be rescheduled for a new interview until the director or assistant director has been contacted; the SF office deals with this so infrequently, they do not have a procedure for re-filed applications. Additionally, in the interview, the asylum officer may not understand what is going on, so the attorney may have to explain.
  b. If the client prefers to go to court after a final denial, then a request for an NTA should be mailed or faxed. In that correspondence, the client should also provide proof that the applicant is no longer in status (such as an expired I-94). The SF office cannot estimate when an NTA will be produced, but anecdotal evidence suggests it usually takes many months. If it takes months, contact the director or assistant director.

APPENDIX 5A

EOIR REMOVAL PROCEEDINGS PROCESS

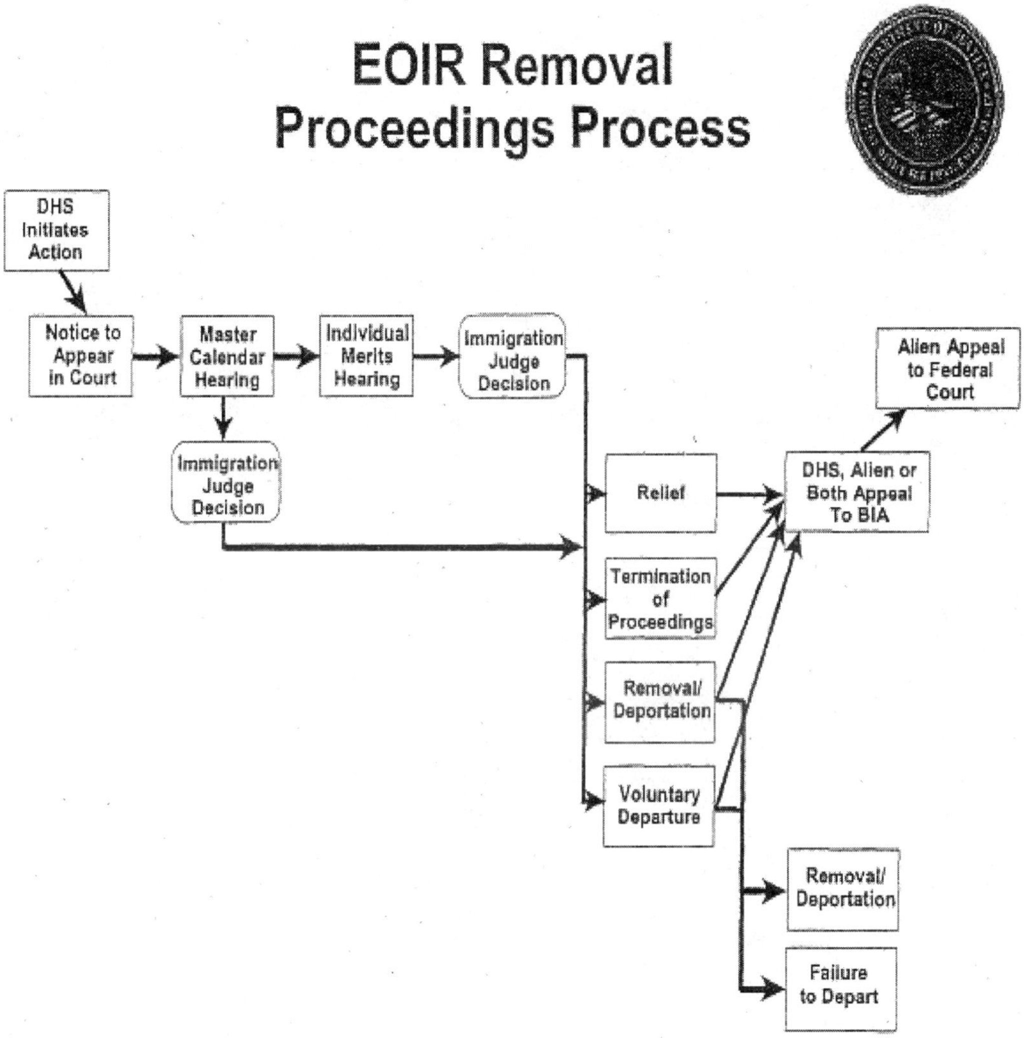

EOIR Removal Proceedings Process

DHS Initiates Action

Notice to Appear in Court

Master Calendar Hearing

Individual Merits Hearing

Immigration Judge Decision

Immigration Judge Decision

Relief

Termination of Proceedings

Removal/ Deportation

Voluntary Departure

DHS, Alien or Both Appeal To BIA

Alien Appeal to Federal Court

Removal/ Deportation

Failure to Depart

APPENDIX 5B

STEPS IN THE PREPARATION OF AN IMMIGRATION COURT CASE

Every case before the immigration courts is unique and requires its own individualized strategy and procedures.[1] Thus, this list is not meant to apply exactly as listed to every single case; any given case may require that these tasks be completed in a different order or that different steps be taken altogether. However, the list below is meant to provide practitioners with a general idea of the various steps involved—at one point or another—in most cases before the U.S. immigration courts.

1. Initial consultation with client to get the facts of the case.
2. Initial research to determine whether the client was properly charged with removability/inadmissibility under the INA.
3. Initial research to determine whether the client is eligible for relief from removal (asylum, withholding of removal, protection under the Convention Against Torture, cancellation of removal, adjustment of status, waivers, TPS, U visas, prosecutorial discretion, termination, voluntary departure, etc.).
4. Prepare detailed analysis letter explaining eligibility for relief and case strategy, as well as next steps.
5. Meet with client to discuss case strategy and next steps.
6. Prepare and file Freedom of Information Act Request to obtain copies of client's immigration file.
7. Thoroughly review immigration history and documents.
8. If the applicant is seeking asylum, withholding of removal, or CAT case, prepare Form I-589 and the initial supporting documentation to file in open court at the first Master Calendar Hearing.
9. Attend initial Master Calendar Hearing at the Immigration Court:
    - Plead to the allegations and charges in the Notice to Appear;
    - Notify the immigration judge what relief the client will be seeking;

[1] *See* ch. 8 for a detailed discussion of the procedures for seeking asylum, withholding of removal, and protection under the Convention Against Torture before the immigration courts. *See also Immigration Court Practice Manual, available at: www.justice.gov/eoir/office-chief-immigration-judge-0* (last visited Apr. 29, 2015).

- File applications for relief or obtain deadlines for applications for relief;
- Obtain Individual Hearing date; and
- **NOTE**: Often times, there are multiple Master Calendar Hearings. For instance, if an asylum application is to be filed, it must be filed in open court. Thus, after the initial Master Calendar Hearing, the judge will keep the case on the Master Calendar docket and will schedule a second Master Calendar Hearing for filing of the asylum application if it is not filed at the first hearing.

10. Identify and draft detailed list of documentary evidence needed to support the application for relief. In an asylum case, such evidence typically includes:

    - Identity documents and other official government documents;
    - Privately-issued membership cards or other affiliation documents;
    - Affidavits from the applicant's family, friends, neighbors, or community members confirming his or her protected characteristic;
    - Photographs of the applicant participating in political or religious events;
    - Letters from organizations of which the applicant is a member or affiliate;
    - Objective, published descriptions of the characteristics or attributes, which designate members of your client's race, religion, nationality, political affiliation, or social group;
    - Photographs of the applicant's injuries;
    - Police reports recording the harm suffered or threatened;
    - Arrest records, if your client was ever arrested due to his or her protected characteristic;
    - Affidavits from witnesses who were present during the act(s) of harm or mistreatment;
    - Affidavits from anyone whom the applicant confided in about the incident(s), confirming any observed physical or psychological harm, such as markings on the applicant's body, torn clothes, injuries, crying, anxiety, or unusual behaviors;
    - Medical records, including evaluations of physical injuries and the likely cause of those injuries, letters from treating doctors, treatment reports, hospital admission records, or prescribed medications;
    - Mental health records, including evaluations of mental health disorders and the likely trigger for those disorders, letters from treating mental health professionals, appointment records, or prescribed medications;

- Death certificates for the applicant's relatives, friends, neighbors, or community members who were targeted because of a qualifying characteristic;
- Newspaper or other media coverage, or coverage by human rights groups, of the incident in which the applicant was involved;
- Evidence that your client attempted to supply certain corroborating documentation, but was unable to;
- I-94 card, visa, and stamped passport (even if false);
- Evidence of means of travel to the United States (airline itineraries, bus tickets, hotel receipts, etc.);
- Evidence of presence outside of the United States in the past year, including financial, medical, school, or work records;
- Affidavits from individuals who have personal knowledge of the applicant's arrival in the United States;
- Expert report regarding the conditions in the applicant's home country, as they relate to the applicant's claims;
- Country conditions reports and articles showing the conditions in the applicant's home country during the time of persecution and presently;
- Certified English translations of any non-English documents; and
- Evidence of good moral character and rehabilitation if the applicant has any negative equities, such as an arrest.

11. Develop potential witness list. Witnesses may include:
    - Psychologists/therapists/doctors;
    - Witnesses of the events that occurred;
    - Witnesses of the harm suffered;
    - Witnesses who suffered similar persecution;
    - Witnesses who have personal knowledge of the trends and conditions in the home country; and
    - Character witnesses.
12. Legal research to support and develop case theory.
13. Country conditions research to find supporting evidence of the trends and conditions in the country of feared persecution or torture.
14. Research to find potential expert witnesses on the specific issues involved in the case.
15. Secure an expert witness and provide them with detailed guidance of what information you would like included in their report.
16. Review the expert's report and schedule a meeting with the expert to discuss.

17. Meet with the expert to discuss any potential issues with the report.
18. Develop list of interview questions to ask the applicant while preparing his or her sworn declaration.
19. Meet with the applicant to obtain information for his or her sworn declaration.
    - **NOTE**: Typically, it takes several meetings with the applicant in order to gain the applicant's trust, learn their "voice," and obtain all of the detailed information necessary for the sworn declaration.
20. Draft sworn declaration.
21. Meet with the applicant to review sworn declaration, obtain more details, and answer follow-up questions.
22. Finalize declaration, review it line by line with the applicant, and have the applicant sign the declaration.
23. Develop list of interview questions to ask each witness for preparation of their sworn declarations.
24. Meet with each witness to obtain information for his or her declaration.
25. Draft sworn declarations of each witness.
26. Meet with each witness to review sworn declaration, obtain more details, and answer follow-up questions.
27. Finalize each witness declaration, review them line by line with each witness, and have each witness sign their declaration.
28. Frequent follow up with witnesses to finalize declarations.
29. Frequent follow up with expert to finalize written report.
30. Frequent follow up with client to finalize declaration and to collect the documentary evidence needed.
31. Draft application form (if not completed earlier in the process).
32. Prepare cover letter and filing pursuant to the Instructions for Submitting Certain Applications in Immigration Court and for Providing Biometric and Biographic Information to U.S. Citizenship and Immigration Services. *See* appendix 5E.
33. Obtain receipt notice from USCIS and advise client.
34. Obtain biometrics notice from USCIS and advise client.

35. Prepare application for employment authorization for client and file with USCIS (once the client becomes eligible to apply).
    - Receipt notice, biometrics notice, approval notice → advise client each step
36. Get foreign language documents translated to English and prepare certificates of translation for each document.
37. Draft various motions throughout the course of the case, as needed.
    - **NOTE**: common motions in an asylum case are: Motion to Continue, Motion to Change Venue, Motion for Telephonic Testimony, Motion for Pre-Hearing Conference, Motion to Accept Additional Exhibits Out of Time, etc.
38. Complete additional legal research and country conditions research throughout the course of the case.
39. Draft brief to apply the client's facts to the law and demonstrate the client's eligibility for the relief sought.
40. Review, revise, and finalize brief (usually multiple drafts).
41. Compile the application and all supporting documentation.
42. Review all documentation to ensure complete accuracy and to make sure that there are no inconsistencies.
43. Prepare detailed Index of Exhibits, which describes each exhibit.
44. Page-number all evidence.
45. Insert letter tabs for each exhibit and compile/bind the filing.
46. Prepare proposed witnesses list, with descriptions of testimony.
47. File application, all evidence, witness list, any motions, and the brief at least 15 days prior to the Individual Hearing and serve copies on the ICE office of chief counsel.
48. Review and analyze any exhibits filed by the ICE office of chief counsel.
49. Prepare any objections to ICE's documentary evidence.
50. Prepare responses to potential objections from ICE regarding the client's evidence.
51. Schedule preparatory meetings with client and each witness.
52. Prepare direct examinations for client and each witness.
53. Identify potential cross-examination questions for client and each witness.

54. Meet with client and each witness to prepare them for their testimony.
    - Explain what to expect at the hearing;
    - Complete a thorough Q&A session; and
    - Role play.
55. Prepare list of preliminary issues to raise with the court (any amendments to application/exhibits, order of witnesses, etc.).
56. Prepare main "talking points" to reference during hearing.
57. Prepare list of potential objections.
58. Prepare closing argument.
59. Call ICE office of chief counsel to discuss the case, identify any issues that may be stipulated to, and otherwise streamline the proceedings.
60. Represent the client at the Individual Hearing.
    - Preliminary issues—amendments/corrections, order of witnesses, any stipulations, brief opening statements, etc.;
    - Admission of evidence into the record and any objections to documentary evidence;
    - Direct examination of the respondent;
    - ICE cross-examines the respondent, object to any improper questions;
    - Repeat with all witnesses;
    - Immigration judge will often ask his or her own questions of the witnesses and the attorneys throughout the hearing;
    - Closing arguments;
    - Immigration judge will issue an oral decision or will reserve for a written decision; and
    - **NOTE**: Depending on how many witnesses there are, the court is sometimes unable to get through all witnesses in one hearing. Thus, there may be multiple Individual Hearings.
61. Follow-up tasks, including:
    - Explaining the judge's decision to the client;
    - Advising the client in regard to next steps; and
    - If relief is granted, assisting the client in obtaining proof of status and related benefits.

APPENDIX 5C

SAMPLE I-213, RECORD OF DEPORTABLE/INADMISSIBLE ALIEN

U.S. Department of Homeland Security   Subject ID : 289284779   **Record of Deportable/Inadmissible Alien**

Family Name (CAPS) | First | Middle
Sex: M | Hair: BLK | Eyes: BRO | Complexion: MED

Country of Citizenship: EL SALVADOR | Passport Number and Country of Issue | File Number: Case No: A
Height: 68 | Weight: 170 | Occupation

U.S. Address | Scars and Marks

Date, Place, Time, and Manner of Last Entry: Unknown Date, Unknown Time | Passenger Boarded at
F.B.I. Number | ☒ Single ☐ Divorced ☐ Married ☐ Widower ☐ Separated

Number, Street, City, Province (State) and Country of Permanent Residence
Method of Location/Apprehension: NCA 518.3

Date of Birth: Age: 25 | Date of Action: 02/03/2011 | Location Code: WAS/WAS
At/Near: Sterling, VA | Date/Hour: 02/03/2011 0600

City, Province (State) and Country of Birth: SAN SALVADOR, SAN SALVADOR, EL SALVADOR | AR ☒ | Form: (Type and No.) Lifted ☐ Not Lifted ☐
By: DAVID BRICKLEY

NIV Issuing Post and NIV Number | Social Security Account Name | Status at Entry | Status When Found

Date Visa Issued | Social Security Number | Length of Time Illegally in U.S.

Immigration Record: NEGATIVE - See Narrative | Criminal Record: None Known

Name, Address, and Nationality of Spouse (Maiden Name, if Appropriate) | Number and Nationality of Minor Children

Father's Name, Nationality and Address, if Known: ...TIONALITY: EL SALVADOR | Mother's Present and Maiden Names, Nationality, and Address, if Known: ...ALITY: EL SALVADOR

Monies Due/Property in U.S. Not in Immediate Possession: None Claimed | Fingerprinted? ☒ Yes ☐ No | Systems Checks | Charge Code Word(s): I6A

Name and Address of (Last)(Current) U.S. Employer | Type of Employment | Salary | Hr | Employed from/to

Narrative (Outline particulars under which alien was located/apprehended. Include details not shown above regarding time, place and manner of last entry, attempted entry, or any other entry, and elements which establish administrative and/or criminal violation. Indicate means and route of travel to interior.)

FINS:

Left Index fingerprint   Right Index fingerprint

None

Record of Deportable/Excludable Alien:
SUBJECT:

SYNOPSIS:
(hereafter referred to as Subject) is a native and citizen...(CONTINUED ON I-831)

ANDREW M. ORTON
DEPORTATION OFFICER
(Signature and Title of Immigration Officer)

Alien has been advised of communication privileges AMD 2/3/11 (Date/Initials)

Distribution:

A-File

Stat

Stat

Received: (Subject and Documents) (Report of Interview)

Officer: ANDREW M. ORTON

on: February 3, 2011 at 1408 (time)

Disposition: Notice to Appear Detained (I-862)

Examining Officer: CRAIG MATHENY

Form I-213 (Rev. 08/01/07)

U.S. Department of Homeland Security Continuation ...ge for Form I213

Alien's Name	File Number	Date
[redacted]	A[redacted] Event No: [redacted]	02/03/2011

of El Salvador by virtue of birth in San Salvador, El Salvador on [redacted] On 02/03/2011, while participating in Fugitive Operations for the Washington Field Office, Subject was located and apprehended by ICE ERO. Subject entered the United States without inspection and is present without admission or parole. Subject is inadmissible under Section 212(a)(6)(A)(i) of the INA and was processed as Notice to Appear.

A# [redacted]
SSN NONE FOUND
FBI# [redacted]
FINS [redacted]

On 02/03/2011, at approximately 0530 hours, Fugitive Operations Officers conducted an address check in an effort to locate Subject, a known associate of fugitive alien [redacted] (A[redacted]). Officers targeted the last known residential address ([redacted]), where there was credible information that Subject was residing. At approximately 0545 hours, officers observed an individual (later identified as [redacted]) exiting the residence. Officers approached and identified themselves to Mr. [redacted] indicated that he resides at the above address. Mr. [redacted] invited officers into the apartment, thereby granting consent to enter. Officers entered the residence and identified Subject. Subject was found to be in possession of expired El Salvador passport #[redacted]. Subject was taken into custody without incident.

At the ICE Enforcement and Removal Operations (ERO) office in Lorton, VA, a rolled set of Subject?s fingerprints were submitted via IDENT/IAFIS (Integrated Automated Fingerprint Identification System). IDENT/IAFIS queries were negative (no hit found).

IMMIGRATION HISTORY:
Subject claims he entered United States (EWI) on 08/02/2005 at Phoenix, AZ.

CRIMINAL HISTORY:
Records checks revealed A MISDEMEANOR CONVICTION FOR DRIVING WITHOUT A LICENSE ON 02/24/2007 IN LOUDEN COUNTY, VIRGINIA.

GANG AFFILIATION:
Subject is known to be affiliated with MS-13. He is known by the moniker ?Nene? or ?El Nene.?

INTEL:
No intelligence information was provided by Subject.

MILITARY STATUS:
Subject claims never to have served in the US military.

HEALTH STATUS:
Subject appears healthy and claimed no other medical/health problems. Subject appears healthy. Subject indicated that he takes no prescription medication.

CONSULAR NOTIFICATION:
Subject declined to invoke his right to consular notification.

TELEPHONE CALLS:
Subject declined to make any phone calls.
...(CONTINUED ON NEXT PAGE)

Signature	Title
ANDREW M. ORTON	DEPORTATION OFFICER

2 of 3 Pages

Form I-831 Continuation Page (Rev. 08/01/07)

U.S. Department of Homeland Security

Continuation Page for Form I213

Alien's Name	File Number	Date
[redacted]	A[redacted] Event No: [redacted]	02/03/2011

CASE DISPOSITION:
The subject was processed as Notice to Appear and was placed in Removal Proceedings.
Subject will be detained without bond in ICE custody.

SUMMARY:
Subject was processed within IDENT and ENFORCE. Subject was informed that he will be scheduled for a hearing date before an Immigration Judge.

Signature	Title
ANDREW M. ORTON	DEPORTATION OFFICER

3 of 3 Pages

Form I-831 Continuation Page (Rev. 08/01/07)

APPENDIX 5D

SAMPLE I-862, NOTICE TO APPEAR

U. S. Department of Justice
Immigration and Naturalization Service

Notice to Appear

In removal proceedings under section 240 of the Immigration and Nationality Act:

File No: [redacted]

In the Matter of:

Respondent: [redacted] currently residing at:

[redacted] 000-000-0000

(Number, street, city, state and ZIP code) (Area code and phone number)

☐ 1. You are an arriving alien.

☒ 2. You are an alien present in the United States who has not been admitted or paroled.

☐ 3. You have been admitted to the United States, but are deportable for the reasons stated below.

The Service alleges that:

1) You are not a citizen or national of the United States.

2) You are a native of EL SALVADOR and a citizen of EL SALVADOR;

3) You entered the United States at or near UNKNOWN POE on or about UNKNOWN DOE;

4) You were not then admitted or paroled after inspection by an Immigration Officer.

On the basis of the foregoing, it is charged that you are subject to removal from the United States pursuant to the following provision(s) of law:

Section 212 (a) (6) (A)(i) of the Immigration and Nationality Act (Act), as amended, as an alien present in the United States without being admitted or paroled, or who has arrived in the United States at any time or place other than designated by the Attorney General.

☐ This notice is being issued after an asylum officer has found that the respondent has demonstrated a credible fear of persecution or torture.

☐ Section 235(b)(1) order was vacated pursuant to: ☐ 8 CFR 208.30(f)(2) ☐ 8 CFR 235.3(b)(5)(iv)

YOU ARE ORDERED to appear before an immigration judge of the United States Department of Justice at:

31 HOPKINS PLAZA, GEO. H. FALLON BLDG. #440, BALTIMORE, MD 21201-0000

(Complete Address of Immigration Court, including Room Number, if any)

on December 15, 2008 (Date) at 8:30 AM (Time) to show why you should not be removed from the United States based on the charge(s) set forth above.

W Logan, SM
(Signature and Title of Issuing Officer)

Date: OCT 2 2 2008 ARLINGTON, VA
(City and State)

See reverse for important information

Form I-862(Rev. 3/22/99)N

Notice to Respondent

Warning: Any statement you make may be used against you in removal proceedings.

Alien Registration: This copy of the Notice to Appear served upon you is evidence of your alien registration while you are under removal proceedings. You are required to carry it with you at all times.

Representation: If you so choose, you may be represented in this proceeding, at no expense to the Government, by an attorney or other individual authorized and qualified to represent persons before the Executive Office for Immigration Review, pursuant to 8 CFR 3.16. Unless you so request, no hearing will be scheduled earlier than ten days from the date of this notice, to allow you sufficient time to secure counsel. A list of qualified attorneys and organizations who may be available to represent you at no cost will provided with this Notice.

Conduct of the hearing: At the time of your hearing, you should bring with you any affidavits or other documents which you desire to have considered in connection with your case. If any document is in a foreign language, you must bring the original and a certified English translation of the document. If you wish to have the testimony of any witnesses considered, you should arrange to have such witnesses present at the hearing.

At your hearing you will be given the opportunity to admit or deny any or all of the allegations in the Notice to Appear and that you are inadmissible or deportable on the charges contained in the Notice to Appear. You will have an opportunity to present evidence on your own behalf, to examine any evidence presented by the Government, to object, on proper legal grounds, to the receipt of evidence and to cross examine any witnesses presented by the Government. At the conclusion of your hearing, you have a right to appeal an adverse decision by the immigration judge.

You will be advised by the immigration judge before whom you appear, of any relief from removal for which you may appear eligible including the privilege of departing voluntarily. You will be given a reasonable opportunity to make any such application to the immigration judge.

Failure to appear: You are required to provide the INS, in writing, with your full mailing address and telephone number. You must notify the Immigration Court immediately by using Form EOIR-33 whenever you change your address or telephone number during the course of this proceeding. You will be provided with a copy of this form. Notices of hearing will be mailed to this address. If you do not submit Form EOIR-33 and do not otherwise provide an address at which you may be reached during proceedings, then the Government shall not be required to provide you with written notice of your hearing. If you fail to attend the hearing at the time and place designated on this notice, or any date and time later directed by the Immigration Court, a removal order may be made by the immigration judge in your absence, and you may be arrested and detained by the INS.

Request for Prompt Hearing

To expedite a determination in my case, I request an immediate hearing. I waive my right to have a 10-day period prior to appearing before an immigration judge.

____
(Signature of Respondent)

Before:

________________________ Date: ________________
(Signature and Title of INS Officer)

Certificate of Service

This Notice To Appear was served on the respondent by me on OCT 2 2 2008 (Date), in the following manner and in compliance with section 239(a)(1)(F) of the Act:

☐ in person ☐ by certified mail, return receipt requested ☒ by regular mail

☐ Attached is a credible fear worksheet.

☒ Attached is a list of organizations and attorneys which provide free legal services.

The alien was provided oral notice in the ________ language of the time and place of his or her hearing and of the consequences of failure to appear as provided in section 240(b)(7) of the Act.

____
(Signature of Respondent if Personally Served)

[signature] CR
(Signature and Title of Officer)

Form I-862(Rev. 3/22/99)N

APPENDIX 5E

INSTRUCTIONS FOR SUBMITTING FORM I-589 IN IMMIGRATION COURT AND FOR PROVIDING BIOMETRIC AND BIOGRAPHIC INFORMATION TO USCIS, ALONG WITH SAMPLE COVER LETTER TO USCIS SERVICE CENTER

INSTRUCTIONS FOR SUBMITTING CERTAIN APPLICATIONS IN IMMIGRATION COURT AND FOR PROVIDING BIOMETRIC AND BIOGRAPHIC INFORMATION TO U. S. CITIZENSHIP AND IMMIGRATION SERVICES

A. Instructions for Form I-589 (Asylum and for Withholding of Removal)*

In addition to filing your application and supporting documents with the Immigration Court and serving a complete copy of your application on the appropriate Immigration and Customs Enforcement (ICE) Office of Chief Counsel, you must also complete the following requirements before the Immigration Judge can grant relief or protection in your case:

SEND these 3 items to the address below:

(1) A clear copy of the **first three pages** of your completed Form I-589 (Application for Asylum and for Withholding of Removal) that you will be filing or have filed with the Immigration Court, which must include your **full name, your current mailing address, and your alien number (A-number)**. (Do Not submit any documents other than the first three pages of the completed I-589),

(2) A copy of Form G–28 (Notice of Entry of Appearance as Attorney or Accredited Representative) if you are represented, and

(3) A copy of these instructions.

USCIS Nebraska Service Center
Defensive Asylum Application With Immigration Court
P.O. Box 87589
Lincoln, NE 68501-7589

Please note that there is **no filing fee required** for your asylum application.

After the 3 items are received at the USCIS Nebraska Service Center, **you will receive:**

- A **USCIS receipt notice** in the mail indicating that USCIS has received your asylum application, and
- An **ASC notice** for you, and separate Application Support Center (ASC) notices for each dependent included in your application. Each ASC notice will indicate the individual's unique receipt number and **will provide instructions for each person to appear for an appointment at a nearby ASC for collection of biometrics** (such as your photograph, fingerprints, and signature). If you do not receive this notice in 3 weeks, call (800) 375-5283. If you also mail applications under Instructions B, you will receive 2 notices with different receipt numbers. You must wait for and take both scheduling notices to your ASC appointment.

You (and your dependents) must then:

- **Attend** the biometrics appointment at the ASC, and obtain a **biometrics confirmation** document before leaving the ASC, and
- **Retain** your **ASC biometrics confirmation** as proof that your biometrics were taken, and bring it to your future Immigration Court hearings.

*** NOTE: IF YOU ARE FILING A FORM I-589 AND/OR ANOTHER APPLICATION, SEE THE REVERSE OF THIS FORM FOR ADDITIONAL INSTRUCTIONS.**

Important: Failure to complete these actions and to follow any additional instructions that the Immigration Judge has given you could result in delay in deciding your application or in your application being deemed abandoned and dismissed by the court. Revised 9/5/13

APPENDIX 5F

SAMPLE MOTION AND SAMPLE BRIEF

During the course of an asylum hearing in removal proceedings, it may become necessary to file one or more motions. You may wish to change venue if the applicant is released from detention or changes his or her address. Or you might want to reopen a case in which the applicant has been deported in absentia or in which his or her application for asylum has been previously denied. If the applicant is not removable from the United States and was erroneously placed in removal proceedings, you would, of course, file a motion to terminate proceedings. If the U.S. Department of Homeland Security (DHS) trial attorney agrees with your position on a particular request, it is helpful to file a joint motion with the court. See appendix 12A for a list of telephone numbers and addresses of DHS chief counsel offices.

Most, but not all motions, must be in writing. It is important to consult the *Immigration Court Practice Manual* for time and contents requirements before filing a motion in immigration court. The manual is available at *www.justice.gov/eoir/vll/OCIJPracManual/ocij_page1.htm*.

If the motion or brief involves an issue that is novel or has been contested in other cases, you may be able to obtain sample motions or briefs on the issue from immigrant advocacy groups, or in some cases, directly from the attorneys who have prepared them. Some websites that maintain brief banks include: National Immigration Project of the National Lawyers Guild (*www.nationalimmigrationproject.org*), Center for Gender and Refugee Studies (*http://cgrs.uchastings.edu*), The World Organization for Human Rights USA (*http://humanrightsusa.org*), and U.S. Committee for Refugees and Immigrants (*www.refugees.org/resources/for-lawyers/*).

The sample motion in this appendix is a Motion to Change Venue. Rules and local practice regarding changes of venue vary from court to court and sometimes from judge to judge. If you are filing a motion to change venue and are unsure of the requirements, call the immigration court, as well as a local immigration attorney or local nonprofit agency, for more information. You should also read the Executive Office for Immigration Review *Immigration Practice Manual* at §5.10(c) on motions to change venue, available at *www.justice.gov/eoir/vll/OCIJPracManual/Chap%205.pdf*.

Following the sample motion is a sample brief. The sample brief provided is the brief filed in *Matter of R–A–*, a gender-based, domestic violence asylum case. Sometimes immigration judges (IJs) will request briefs from both parties on a narrow issue of law, such as whether an individual has been convicted of a particularly serious crime. A general brief regarding an applicant's eligibility for asylum and withholding may be submitted to the immigration judge prior to the hearing and is particularly useful in cases involving a novel legal argument.

Reminder: all motions and briefs must be filed with a certificate of service and must meet deadlines set by *Immigration Court Practice Manual* or the IJ.

UNITED STATES DEPARTMENT OF JUSTICE
EXECUTIVE OFFICE FOR IMMIGRATION REVIEW
OFFICE OF THE IMMIGRATION JUDGE
HARLINGEN, TEXAS

In the Matter of:	)	
	)	File No. A__________
____________________	)	
	)	In Removal Proceedings
	)	
	)	
	)	

RESPONDENT'S MOTION REQUESTING CHANGE OF VENUE

Respondent, _____________, by and through her undersigned counsel, hereby requests this court to grant a change of venue of her removal hearing from Harlingen, Texas, to Houston, Texas, pursuant to 8 CFR §§1003.20 and 1240.1. Respondent requests a change of venue so that she may adequately prepare and present testimony in support of her request for asylum and withholding of removal. In support of this Motion, Respondent would show the following:

1. Respondent currently resides at ____________ St., Houston, TX _____, which is in the jurisdiction of the Houston Immigration Court.

2. Respondent is represented by _______________, an attorney who maintains her office at _______________, Houston, TX, also within the jurisdiction of the Houston Immigration Court.

3. Respondent has admitted the allegations of the Notice to Appear, conceded that she is removable, and has filed an application for asylum with this court.

4. Because the issue of whether Respondent is removable has been resolved, there is no prejudice to the Department of Homeland Security if venue is changed to the Houston Immigration Court.

5. In addition, Respondent's witnesses reside in the jurisdiction of the Houston Immigration Court. Moreover, Respondent is currently unemployed and is, therefore, unable to incur the cost of traveling to the Harlingen Immigration Court.

6. Pursuant to *Baires v. INS*, 856 F.2d 89 (9th Cir. 1988) and *Chlomos v. U.S. Dept. of Justice*, 516 F.2d 310 (3d Cir. 1975), it would be an abuse of discretion to deny a

change of venue in a case in which there would be little or no inconvenience to the government.

Based on the foregoing reasons, Respondent respectfully requests that venue in this case be changed to from Harlingen, Texas, to Houston, Texas.

Dated this ______ day of __________, 20___.

Respectfully submitted,

____
Attorney for Respondent

[address]
[phone]

CERTIFICATE OF SERVICE

I certify that a true and correct copy of the foregoing Motion was served this ______ day of __________, 20___ on the DHS trial attorney at _______________, Harlingen, TX by first-class U.S. mail, postage prepaid.

____

[Attach three copies of a Proposed Order—sample orders may be found at *www.justice.gov/eoir/vll/OCIJPracManual/appendix_Q.pdf*]

UNITED STATES COURT OF APPEALS
FOR THE _______ CIRCUIT

____________________________		
[name of Petitioner]	)	
	)	
Petitioner,	)	**File No.________________**
	)	
v.	)	
	)	**A# ____________________**
________________,	)	
Attorney General,	)	
	)	
Respondent	)	
____________________________	)	

PETITION FOR REVIEW

The above named petitioner hereby petitions for the review of a final order of [deportation] [removal] entered by the Board of Immigration Appeals on ______________ [date of BIA decision].

A copy of the BIA's decision is attached. To date, no court has upheld the validity of the order.

____
[signature of attorney or petitioner]

Dated: __________________

[(1) COMPLETE ALL BLANK SPACES EXCEPT "FILE NO.". THE COURT CLERK'S OFFICE WILL ASSIGN A NUMBER.
(2) ATTACH CERTIFICATE OF SERVICE AND THE BIA DECISIONS. CHECK LOCAL RULES FOR OTHER NECESSARY ATTACHMENTS.
(3) THIS DOCUMENT SHOULD BE SERVED ON THE ATTORNEY GENERAL, AND ON THE OFFICER OR EMPLOYEE OF DHS IN CHARGE OF THE DISTRICT IN WHICH THE FINAL ORDER OF REMOVAL WAS ENTERED. PETITIONER MAY ALSO WANT TO SERVE A COPY OF THE PETITION FOR REVIEW ON THE OFFICE OF IMMIGRATION LITIGATION, THE LOCAL DHS DISTRICT COUNSEL'S OFFICE, IF ANY, AND POSSIBLY THE LOCAL ICE REMOVAL OFFICERS.]

SAMPLE BRIEF

UNITED STATES DEPARTMENT OF JUSTICE
ATTORNEY GENERAL JOHN ASHCROFT

BRIEF ON BEHALF OF RODI ALVARADO PEÑA
TO THE ATTORNEY GENERAL OF THE UNITED STATES

Karen Musalo
Resident Scholar
University of California
Hastings College of Law
200 McAllister Street
San Francisco, CA 94102
(415) 565-4720

Attorney for Petitioner
Rodi Alvarado Peña

Table of Contents

Table of Authorities

Cases: Page

Statutes & Regulations:

Secondary Authority:

A) Legal Materials

I. Introduction and Procedural Background

Ms. Rodi Alvarado Peña [Ms. Alvarado or Respondent] was subjected to more than ten years of unspeakably brutal violence at the hands of her husband, Francisco Osorio. (Record (Rec.) at 4-6.)[1] The violence which Osorio inflicted upon her caused severe physical injury and extreme mental anguish. (Rec. at 693-705.) Ms. Alvarado could neither escape Osorio within Guatemala, nor secure any protection whatsoever from the official authorities. (Rec. at 241-43; 700-02.) None of these facts are in dispute.

On the basis of this record, on September 20, 1996, an Immigration Judge (IJ) granted Ms. Alvarado asylum in the United States. (Rec. at 197.) The IJ ruled that the harm she suffered constituted persecution, that the government of Guatemala was unwilling to protect her, and that the persecution was on account of two of the required statutory grounds social group membership and political opinion. (Rec. at 190-97.) The social group was defined by nationality, gender, and marital status (Guatemalan women, who have been involved intimately with Guatemalan male companions, who believe that women are to live under male domination) (Rec. at 193), and the political opinion was that of opposition to male domination. (Rec. at 196.)

The former Immigration and Naturalization Service (INS) appealed the decision. On June 11, 1999, in a sharply divided 10-5 vote, the BIA reversed the IJ s grant of asylum to Ms. Alvarado. (Rec. at 27.) The Board accepted that the husband s violent abuses rose to the level of persecution, and that Ms. Alvarado had been unable to obtain state protection. (Rec. at 11.) However, the BIA majority rejected the IJ s ruling that the persecution was on account of social

---

[1] Note that all citations to the record are to the Certified Administrative Record produced for the appeal from the June 1999 BIA decision to the Ninth Circuit Court of Appeals, which appeal was later stayed.

group membership and political opinion. (Rec. at 11-27.)

Counsel for Ms. Alvarado filed a timely Petition for Review with the Ninth Circuit Court of Appeals on July 9, 1999, and simultaneously sought certification of the decision by then Attorney General Janet Reno. The Ninth Circuit Court of Appeals stayed proceedings pending a decision by Attorney General Reno on the request for certification. In December 2000 and January 2001, the Department of Justice (DOJ) and Attorney General Reno took two separate but related actions related to Ms. Alvarado s case. On December 7, 2000, the DOJ issued a Proposed Rule[2] which directly addresses the issues raised in Ms. Alvarado s case, and on January 19, 2001, the Attorney General accepted certification, vacated the BIA s decision, and directed the Board to decide the case pursuant to this rule, when issued in final form.[3] The Commentary to the Proposed Rule explicitly states that it removes certain barriers that the *In re R-A-* decision seems to pose to claims that domestic violence, against which a government is either unwilling or unable to provide protection, rises to the level of persecution of a person on account of membership in a particular social group. [4] The Proposed Rule, which is now under the jurisdiction of the

---

[2] Department of Justice, Immigration and Naturalization Service, *Asylum and Withholding Definitions*, 65 Fed. Reg. 76588 (Dec. 7, 2000) [hereinafter Proposed Regulation or Proposed Rule].

[3] The order reads as follows:

> Pursuant to 8 C.F.R. § 3.1(h)(1)(iii), the Acting Commissioner of the Immigration and Naturalization Service has referred to the Attorney General for review the June 11, 1999, decision of the Board of Immigration Appeals (Board) that overturned the Immigration Judge s decision dated September 20, 1996. The June 11, 1999 decision of the Board is hereby vacated and the matter is remanded to the Board for reconsideration. I direct the Board to stay reconsideration of the decision until after the proposed rule published at 65 Fed. Red. 76588 (Dec. 7, 2000) is published in final form. The Board should then reconsider the decision in light of the final rule.

Attorney General s Order No. 2379-2001 (January 19, 2001).

[4] Supplementary Information to Proposed Regulation, *supra* note 2, at 76589 [hereinafter Commentary].

2

Department of Homeland Security (DHS), has not yet been published in final form; however, the government is on record as stating that the regulation represents its best interpretation of the refugee definition.[5]

On February 21, 2003, Attorney General John Ashcroft directed the Board of Immigration Appeals to certify to him the decision in *Matter of R-A-*. On March 24, 2003, Ms. Alvarado s counsel requested permission to brief the issues, and asked for clarification as to whether the Proposed Rule continued to represent the agency s best interpretation of the refugee definition. The request for clarification noted that meaningful briefing requires that counsel be put on notice of any departure from this position. [6] The request to brief was denied by the Attorney General on September 5, 2003, and on November 4, 2003, 62 members of the House of Representatives made an appeal to the Attorney General that he allow briefing; their request was representative of sustained Congressional interest in the case and the issues it raises regarding the protection of women victims of gender violence.[7] On December 8, 2003, Attorney General Ashcroft issued an

---

[5] Among the forums in which this position has been stated for the record include before the BIA during the June 21, 2001, en banc argument of the case, *INS v. Vallabhaneni*, A76-724-694 (Transcript of June 21, 2001, BIA hearing en banc, at 45-46).

[6] The letter stated:

> [C]larification is necessary regarding the status of the Proposed Rule. The DOJ has publicly taken the position that the Proposed Rule represents its interpretation of the refugee definition. Counsel requests clarification as to whether this continues to be the DOJ s position, and whether it is the position of the Department of Homeland Security (DHS). Meaningful briefing requires that counsel be put on notice of any departure from this position.

Letter from Karen Musalo to Attorney General John Ashcroft, dated March 24, 2003.

[7] In addition to the letters regarding the denial of briefing from members of Congress, *see* (1) Letter of May 2, 2003, to Attorney General John Ashcroft and Department of Homeland Security Secretary Thomas J. Ridge from 15 members of the Senate (in support of gender-based asylum and expressing concern about Rodi Alvarado's case); (2) Letter of February 27, 2003, to Attorney General Ashcroft from 49 members of the House of Representatives (in support of gender-based asylum and expressing concern about Rodi Alvarado's case); (3) Letter of September 29, 2000, to Attorney General Janet Reno from eight

order for both parties to submit briefs; this brief is submitted pursuant to that order. There have been no official statements by DOJ or DHS that the Proposed Rule no longer represents the government s position; thus it will be assumed that it continues to represent the government s best interpretation of the refugee definition.

II. Facts of the Case

The facts of Ms. Alvarado s claim for asylum are undisputed; both the immigration judge and the BIA found Ms. Alvarado to be credible in all respects. Ms. Alvarado was sixteen years of age when she married her husband Francisco Osorio, a former soldier in the Guatemalan military. From the inception of their marriage Osorio subjected her to violent physical and sexual abuse. He would hit or kick Ms. Alvarado whenever he felt like it, wherever [they] happened to be: in the house, on the street, on the bus. (Rec. at 694.) He would mistreat her when he was drunk and when he was sober. (Rec. at 328.) Her husband dislocated her jaw when her menstrual period was 15 days late (Rec. at 694); kicked her violently in the spine when she failed to heed his demand that she abort her three to four month old fetus (Rec. at 694); kicked her in her genital

---

members of the Senate (urging immediate action to reverse the Board s denial in *Matter of R-A-*); (4) Letter of September 18, 2000, to Attorney General Janet Reno from 54 members of the House of Representatives (in support of gender-based asylum and requesting a meeting to discuss the issue); (5) Letter of February 14, 2000, to Attorney General Reno from seven members of the Senate (asking the Attorney General to reverse the BIA's decision in an honor killing case, referring to *Matter of R- A-* and expressing concern that the BIA lacks sufficient understanding of current standards in both United States asylum law and policy and international human rights law.); (6) Letter of December 2, 1999, to Attorney General Reno from five members of the Senate, asking the Attorney General to clarify the gender guidelines for asylum and reinstate the grant in *Matter of R-A-*); (7) Letter of September 16, 1999, to Attorney General Reno from 53 members of the House of Representatives (expressing concern about the denial of asylum to Rodi Alvarado and asking the Attorney General to reinstate the grant in *Matter of R-A-*); (8) Letter of July 22, 1999, to Attorney General Janet Reno from the Congressional Hispanic Caucus (supporting Ms. Alvarado's asylum claim and requesting certification of *Matter of R-A-*).

4

area so violently that she suffered internal hemorrhaging (Rec. at 695); and brutally raped her time and time again, both vaginally and anally, beating her before and during the unwanted sex. (Rec. at 694-95.) Osorio, who had guns and knives at his ready disposal, pistol-whipped Ms. Alvarado, broke windows and mirrors with her head, punched, and slapped her, threatened her with his machete, and dragged her down the street by her hair. (Rec. at 697-700.)

Ms. Alvarado s efforts to escape her husband within Guatemala were futile. She sought refuge at her brother s and parents homes, but her husband was always able to track her down. (Rec. at 238.) On one occasion, in the hope of evading her husband, Ms. Alvarado took her older child out of school, and rented a room outside of the city. Although she told no one where she had gone, Osorio found her, and proceeded to beat and kick her into unconsciousness in front of their two children. (Rec. at 696-97.)

After more than ten years of this violent abuse, Ms. Alvarado decided that the only way to save her life was to flee Guatemala. (Rec. 702-03.) This was a very wrenching decision for her, because in leaving, she had to abandon the people she care[d] about most her family and her two year old son, and seven year old daughter. (Rec. at 705.) Although the pain of separation was, and continues to be, tremendous, Ms.Alvarado believes it is for the best, because if her husband had succeeded in his efforts to kill her, her children would have no mother at all. (Rec. at 706.)

Osorio repeatedly expressed his opinion that he had the right to treat Ms. Alvarado as he did, because of her gender and their relationship; the abuse was accompanied by statements such as You re my woman, you do what I say (Rec. at 696), You re my woman, and I can do whatever I want (Rec. at 695), You don t order me (Rec. at 694), and I can do it if I want to. (Rec. at 697.)

As this record makes abundantly clear, Osorio was correct in his assertions that because Ms. Alvarado was his woman he could do to her whatever he wanted with complete impunity. Neither the police nor the courts of Guatemala intervened once over the entire course of this decade-long brutal marital relationship. The police did not come when called by a desperate Ms. Alvarado on the telephone, and they never took any steps to arrest Osorio or require him to appear in response to written complaints which Ms. Alvarado filed. (Rec. at 700-02.) Osorio enjoyed the same impunity within the court system; when Ms. Alvarado went before a judge, he told her that he would not interfere in domestic matters or disputes. (Rec. at 243.) The police had communicated essentially the same thing, telling Ms. Alvarado that they would not provide her any assistance because she should take care of it at home. (Rec. at 700.)

Extensive record evidence on country conditions in Guatemala demonstrates that the absolute failure of protection to Ms. Alvarado by law enforcement and judicial personnel is not an aberration. To the contrary, such failure of protection is the norm, and reflects deeply entrenched attitudes regarding the subordinate status of women in Guatemalan society. Women suffer *de jure* as well as the *de facto* discrimination. The Guatemalan Civil Code accords legal primacy to the husband in the marital relationship;[8] such provisions have led international bodies to express

---

[8] Rec. at 739:

> Guatemalan women are even discriminated against legally. The Guatemalan civil code [sic] recognizes the male as a married couple s legal representative...A husband can legally forbid his wife to engage in activities outside the home. The husband also has the primary authority in disposing of joint property.

Jennifer Tisdale, Abuse of Women in Today s Guatemala, Guatemala Human Rights Commission/USA, *Guatemala Bulletin*, Fourth Quarter 1992.

concern over the discrimination institutionalized in law in Guatemala.[9] Beyond the Guatemalan Civil Code, many other norms in Guatemalan law are discriminatory and contradict the principle of equality guaranteed in the Constitution. (Rec. at 737.) These *de jure* denials of equality are compounded by discrimination in the administration of justice and application of the law. (Rec. at 737.)

Gross gender inequality in Guatemala is not a recent phenomena; women historically have been oppressed, (Rec. at 739) and cultural norms persist that conceive of women as subordinate to men[.] (Rec. at 737.) All of this has led to a situation wherein the conditions women live in are among the worst in Latin America. (Rec. at 739.) The education of women is considered unimportant because [a woman s] place is [in] the home. (Rec. at 742.) More than 80% of the illiterate persons in Guatemala are female (Rec. at 742), and the country has the highest rate of females without formal education in all of Latin America. (Rec. at 742.)

The *de jure* and *de facto* subordinate status of women is inextricably related to the broad acceptance of violence against them; this violence is tolerated...and legitimized by laws and customs (Rec. at 736) and what is culturally taught and learned about what a woman is and the role she must play are significant factors sustaining...violence toward women[.] (Rec. at 744.)

---

[9] Rec. at 398:

> Members of the UN Committee on the Elimination of Discrimination against Women reported in April that Guatemala s report and presentation to the Committee increased their concern at the discrimination institutionalized in law. They also expressed alarm that Guatemala s Constitutional Court had ruled that none of the country s Civil Code required change, despite Guatemala s ratification of the Convention on the Elimination of Discrimination against Women, which was automatically incorporated into domestic law and requires that states not discriminate on the basis of gender.

Lawyers Committee for Human Rights, *Critique: Review of the U.S. Department of State s Country Reports on Human Rights Practices for 1994* (July 1995).

Domestic violence has reached epidemic proportions in Guatemala; a 1990 survey of 1,000 women reported that 48% had been battered by their partners, who used [f]ists, feet, knives, razor blades, sledge hammers and pieces of wood to attack them. (Rec. at 423.) Out of every ten women murdered, four are killed by their husbands. (Rec. at 740.) Other statistics are equally grim: an officer of a Fire Fighters Corps responsible for women and children...determined that in a six hour shift, 90 per cent of women treated for physical injuries had been attacked by their partners (Rec. at 423), and a doctor reported that 75 per cent of women admitted to his hospital with injuries were victims of spousal abuse. (Rec. at 423.)

Although they are the victims of these brutal assaults, women are most often portrayed as the provocator[s] of the abuse (Rec. at 425), reinforcing the societal attitudes of discrimination and ignorance regarding the human rights of women[.] (Rec. at 425.) As was Ms. Alvarado s experience, women who turn to the police or the courts confront the attitude that domestic violence is not a real problem, or even a human rights violation. (Rec. at 429.) Both the police and the courts generally encourage women seeking their help to keep the problem to themselves. (Rec. at 429.) As of 1994, a year before Ms. Alvarado fled Guatemala, there were no shelters for battered women in the country. (Rec. at 431.)

III. Argument

1) Ms. Alvarado Has a Well-Founded Fear of Persecution on Account of her Social Group Membership and Political Opinion

In order to qualify for refugee status, an individual is required to show that she has suffered past persecution or has a well-founded fear of future persecution on account of race, religion, nationality, political opinion or membership in a particular social group. Immigration & Nationality Act (INA) § 101(a)(42)(A), 8 U.S.C. § 1101(a)(42)(A) (2003). The persecution must be by the government, or individuals that the government is unable or unwilling to control. *He v. Ashcroft*, 328 F.3d 593, 603 (9th Cir. 2003); *Navas v. INS*, 217 F.3d 646, 655-56 (9th Cir. 2000) . As the uncontroverted evidence in this case establishes, Ms. Alvarado meets the refugee definition because she has been persecuted, and reasonably fears future persecution, on account of her memberhip in a gender-defined particular social group, and on account of her political opinion of resistance to the brutal abuse meted out by her husband; this abuse occurred in a situation where the government of Guatemala failed to provide even the least measure of protection.

A. The Harm Ms. Alvarado Suffered Constitutes Persecution

Courts have long held that threats to life or freedom, or other egregious physical and psychological harms, inflicted by the government or by persons the government is unable or unwilling to control, constitute persecution. *See, e.g.*, *He v. Ashcroft, supra*; *Rios v. Ashcroft*, 287 F.3d 895, 900 (9th Cir. 2002); *Agbuya v. INS*, 241 F.3d 1224 (9th Cir. 2001), *Shoafera v. INS*, 228 F.3d 1070 (9th Cir. 2000), *Singh v. INS*, 94 F.3d 1353 (9th Cir. 1996), *Kovac v. INS*, 407 F.2d 102, 105-07 (9th Cir. 1969).

Because domestic abuse involves severe and repeated physical and psychological harm that poses an immediate threat to a woman s life and freedom, the Department of Justice has expressly recognized domestic violence as a type of mistreatment that constitutes persecution under U.S. asylum laws.[10] Indeed, because of its severe nature and intentional infliction by its perpetrator, the harm resulting from domestic violence has been found so abhorrent as to fit the definition of torture.[11]

Throughout the litigation of this case, neither the government (previously the INS) nor the BIA has contested that the harm Ms. Alvarado suffered was more than sufficient (Rec. at 11) to constitute persecution. Likewise, neither the government nor the BIA contested that Ms. Alvarado was unable to avail herself of any assistance from the government. And they could not have reasonably done so: the utter failure of the Guatemalan government to respond is established through Ms. Alvarado s account of her repeated but futile attempts to obtain assistance from the police and courts, coupled with the documentary evidence that government officials do not view domestic violence as a real problem, or even a human rights violation. (Rec. at 429.) Given the severity of the physical and psychological abuse she suffered, and the extreme degree, intensity, duration and frequency of that harm, there can be no question that Ms. Alvarado was persecuted within the meaning of the statute.

---

[10] *See* Phyllis Coven, Department of Justice, Immigration and Naturalization Service, Office of International Affairs, *Considerations for Asylum Officers Adjudicating Asylum Claims From Women* 4 (1995); Rec. at 649-52 [DOJ Gender Guidelines]; Department of Justice, Immigration and Naturalization Service, *U.S. Law and INS Refugee/Asylum Adjudications:* THE BASIC LAW MANUAL (1994).

[11] *See* U.N. Commission On Human Rights, 52nd Sess., Item 9 (a) of the Provisional Agenda, *1996 Report of the Special Rapporteur on Violence Against Women, its Causes and Consequences*, Resolution 1995/85, E/CN.4/1996/53 (1996), at 14, ¶ 50 (indicating that domestic violence should be understood and treated as a form of torture).

B. Ms. Alvarado was Persecuted on Account of her Membership in a Particular Social Group

The IJ who granted Ms. Alvarado protection ruled that the brutal domestic violence she suffered was causally linked to her membership in a social group defined by the characteristics of gender, marital status, and nationality. The judge s recognition of a gender-defined social group, and her finding of a nexus between the harm and the described group, is based on well-established precedent, and is fully supported by the record in this case. Furthermore, the recognition that claims of gender-persecution come within the protection of the refugee definition, is consistent with international trends,[12] and has been affirmed by the most recent guidance from the Office of the United Nations High Commissioner for Refugees.[13]

---

[12] Among the countries accepting gender claims are Australia, Austria, Canada, Germany, New Zealand, Spain, the United Kingdom, and the United States. *See infra* notes 16, 33; International Gender Asylum Decisions and Law, available at <http://www.uchastings.edu/cgrs/law/intl.html>. Countries with legislation specific to asylum claims based on gender-based persecution includes Ireland, Denmark and South Africa. *See, e.g.,* Refugee Act 1996 ¶ 1 (Ireland) (defining social group to include a group of persons whose defining characteristic is their belonging to the female or the male sex....); Refugees Act 1998, Act No. 130 ¶ 1(xxi) (South Africa) (defining social group to include a group of persons of particular gender....); *see also* International Gender Asylum Decisions and Law, *supra.* Gender guidelines for asylum claims have been issued by a wide range of countries, led by the United States and Canada. *See, e.g.,* DOJ Gender Guidelines, *supra* note 10; Immigration and Refugee Board of Canada, *Guideline 4: Women Refugee Claimants Fearing Gender-Related Persecution: Update* (Nov. 25, 1996); Immigration Appeal Authority, *Asylum Gender Guidelines* (November 2000) (United Kingdom), available at <http://www.iaa.gov.uk/32.htm>; Australian Department of Immigration and Multicultural Affairs, *Refugee and Humanitarian Visa Applicants: Guidelines on Gender Issues for Decision Makers* (July 1996), available at <http://www.uchastings.edu/cgrs/law/guidelines/aust.pdf>. Other countries with gender guidelines include the Netherlands, Norway, and Sweden. *See* Governmental Gender Guidelines for Asylum Adjudicators, available at <http://www.uchastings.edu/cgrs/law/guidelines.html>.

[13] UNHCR, Guidelines on International Protection: Gender-Related Persecution within the context of Article 1A(2) of the 1951 Convention and/or its 1967 Protocol relating to the Status of Refugees (HCR/GIP/02/01, 7 May 2002) (hereinafter UNHCR Gender Guidelines); UNHCR, Guidelines on International Protection: Membership in a Particular Social Group within the context of Article 1A(2) of the 1951 Convention and/or its 1967 Protocol relating to the Status of Refugees , ¶ 19 (HCR/GIP/02/02, 7 May 2002) (hereinafter UNHCR Social Group Guidelines).

1. Ms. Alvarado s Social Group is Cognizable under the Law

In its seminal *Acosta*[14] decision, the BIA ruled that for the particular social group ground to be interpreted consistently with the other statutory grounds, the defining characteristics of the group must be either immutable or fundamental. The immutable/fundamental criteria test is widely accepted by federal courts across the United States,[15] and has been frequently cited with approval by foreign tribunals.[16] It has recently been adopted by the Ninth Circuit,[17] as an alternative to its long-standing voluntary associational relationship [18] test, and it has been incorporated into the Proposed Rule.[19]

The social group recognized by the IJ in Ms. Alvarado s case is defined by gender, marital status, and nationality, each of which meet the *Acosta* criteria. First, the BIA in *Acosta* explicitly identified sex as the type of immutable or fundamental characteristic by which a social group

---

[14] *Matter of Acosta,* 19 I. & N. Dec. 211 (BIA 1985), *overruled on other grounds by Matter of Mogharrabi*, 19 I. & N. Dec. 439 (BIA 1987).

[15] *See, e.g., Lwin v. INS*, 144 F.3d 505, 511-112 (7th Cir. 1998) (applying *Acosta* to find that Burmese students share common immutable characteristics); *Fatin v. INS*, 12 F.3d 1233 (3rd Cir. 1993) (gender could define a social group pursuant to *Acosta*); *Ananeh-Firempong v. INS*, 766 F.2d 621 (1st Cir. 1985) (individuals of a specific ethnic group associated with the former government constitute a particular social group).

[16] *See, e.g., Islam (A.P.) v. Secretary of State for the Home Dept., and Regina v. Immigration Appeal Tribunal and Another Ex Parte Shah (A.P.)*, [1999] 2 W.L.R. 1015 (House of Lords) (United Kingdom) (relying on and quoting *Acosta* s influential, important and seminal reasoning) (Opinions of Lord Steyn, Lord Hoffman and Lord Hope); Refugee Appeal No. 71427/99, ¶97 (Refugee Status Appeals Authority 2000) (New Zealand) (relying on the good working rule from *Acosta*); *Canada (Attorney General) v. Ward*, [1993] 2 S.C.R. 689, 736-37 (discussing and quoting from *Acosta* at length).

[17] *Hernandez-Montiel v. INS*, 225 F.3d 1084, 1092-93 (9th Cir. 2000).

[18] *Sanchez-Trujillo v. INS*, 801 F.2d 1571 (9th Cir. 1986).

[19] Proposed Regulations, *supra* note 2, at 76598.

12

could be defined. In 1996 the BIA applied that principle in its landmark *Kasinga* ruling, where it held that a social group defined by gender in combination with other chacteristics is cognizable. *Matter of Kasinga,* 21 I. & N. Dec. 357 (BIA 1996). The social group in *Kasinga* was defined by gender, ethnicity, bodily integrity, and opposition to female genital mutilation ([y]oung women of the Tchamba-Kunsuntu Tribe who have not had FGM, as practiced by the tribe, and who oppose the practice. *Id.* at 365.

The federal courts have also recognized that gender could appropriately define a particular social group under U.S. asylum laws. *See Fatin v. INS*, 12 F.3d 1233, 1240-41 (3rd Cir. 1993); *Safaie v. INS*, 25 F.3d 636, 640 (8th Cir. 1994) (We agree with the Third Circuit that a group of women, who refuse to conform... may well satisfy the definition.). Notably, prior to the Board s decision in *Kasinga,* the DOJ itself observed that the *Acosta* social group formulation supported the cognizability of a social group based on gender, either alone or as part of a combination.[20] The Commentary to the Proposed Rule affirms the viability of gender-defined social groups, stating that to be immutable, the common trait must be unchangeable, or truly fundamental to an applicant s identity. Gender is clearly such an immutable trait. [21]

Second, although marital status is not inherently immutable, there are circumstances such as prevail in Ms. Alvarado s case where marital status constitutes an immutable trait.[22] Ms. Alvarado s brutal and domineering husband simply would not permit her to leave the

---

[20] DOJ Gender Guidelines, *supra* note 10, at 13-15; Rec. at 649-52.

[21] Commentary, *supra* note 4, at 76593.

[22] The Commentary to the Proposed Rule recognizes this principle, stating that there may be circumstances in which an applicant s marital status could be considered immutable. *Id.*

relationship, and there was no one in Guatemala who would intervene on her behalf. Osorio transformed what should have been a consensual relationship into one that was immutable, and he could do this because the authorities of Guatemala abdicated their responsibility to protect Ms. Alvarado. Osorio hunted her down every time she attempted to leave him, and told her on numerous occasions that she could neither escape him in life[23] or in death.[24] His threats continued even after she fled Guatemala; Ms. Alvarado s sister recounted in a letter that Osorio had said if she comes back, I will not let her live. (Rec. at 686.)

Osorio could both make and carry through on his threats with impunity because of the institutionalized discrimination against women in Guatemala, and the absolute failure of governmental protection. (Rec. at 429-30, 736-37, 739, 742, 744.) It is in this respect that nationality becomes a defining characteristic of the social group: it acts as a limiting and contextualizing factor to the characteristics of gender and marital status, an explicit recognition that social group cognizability is not determined in the abstract, but in the context of particular countries, societies and cultures.

---

[23] On one occasion Ms. Alvarado told Osorio she wanted to get far away from him so he could not find her. He replied:

> [Y]ou will suffer much worse than what I have done to you so far...If you ever try to leave, I will come find you. And when I find you, I could kill you, but I m not going to do that. I will break your legs. I will cripple you so that you will be in a wheelchair for the rest of your life. I will mark your face so it will be scarred forever, it will be twisted and deformed.

(Rec. at 704.)

On another occasion Osorio pulled out a machete in the middle of the night, and taunted her, saying:

> Just you wait, you can t hide, even if you are buried underground, you can t hide from me...you can t get away...I will cut off your legs so you can t get away any more.

(Rec. at 698.)

[24] Once when Ms. Alvarado was so desperate about her circumstances that she attempted to take her own life, through an overdose, Osorio said, If you want to die, go ahead. But from here, you are not going to leave. (Rec. at 699-700.)

The inclusion of nationality as a characteristic of Ms. Alvarado s social group is analogous to the inclusion of tribal affiliation (*e.g.*, women of the Tchamba-Kunsuntu Tribe) as a social group characteristic in the *Kasinga* decision. In each case the characteristic limits the social group from the potentially larger group; in *Kasinga,* the characteristic of tribal affiliation limited the social group from a larger group defined solely by gender, intact genitalia and opposition to female genital mutilation. In Ms. Alvarado s case, the characteristic of nationality limits the group from one defined exclusively by gender and marital status without reference to geographical limits. Characteristics that reference country or region can be found as a matter of routine in refugee cases involving the particular social group ground. *See, e.g., Lukwago v. Ashcroft*, 329 F.3d 157, 171 (3rd Cir. 2003) (social group of children *from Northern Uganda* who are abducted and enslaved ...) (emphasis added); *Lwin*, 144 F.3d at 512 (social group of parents of *Burmese* student dissidents) (emphasis added); *Fatin*, 12 F.3d at 1241 (social group of *Iranian* women who refuse to conform) (emphasis added).

The Proposed Rule explicitly adopts an approach which incorporates the evaluation of societal conditions, norms and attitudes into the determination of social group cognizability. Included in its list of factors that may be considered... in deciding whether a particular social group exists [25] are whether the group is recognized to be a societal faction or is otherwise a recognized segment of the population *in the country in question* or whether *the society in which the group exists* distinguishes members of the group for different treatment or status than is accorded to other members of the society. [26]

---

[25] Proposed Regulations, *supra* note 2, at 76594.

[26] *Id.* at 76598 (emphasis added).

These factors from the Proposed Rule lend further support to the cognizability of Ms. Alvarado s social group. The record in this case establishes that in Guatemala, women as a recognized segment of the population are singled out for different (*i.e.*, discriminatory) treatment. Women who are married are subject to discrimination on the basis of both their gender and their marital status. The bias is enshrined in the laws, where women have lesser rights than men. (Rec. at 739.) It is evidenced in the discrimination in the administration of justice and application of the law (Rec. at 737) which allow the police and the courts to respond dismissively to their serious complaints of maimings and death threats by their husbands. And it is evident in the pervasive and persistent attitudes that women [are] subordinate to men. (Rec. at 737.) The Commentary to the Proposed Rule specifically notes the relevance of evidence that the institutions of the society at hand offer fewer protections or benefits to members of the group than to other members of society. [27] This is certainly the case for women in Guatemala.

2. Ms. Alvarado was Persecuted on Account of her Social Group Membership

The statutory language on account of requires that there be a causal relationship, or nexus, between the persecution and one of the enumerated grounds. Nexus is established when the persecutor is motivated by a cognizable ground in inflicting the harm, or the harm is directed at the applicant because of the protected characteristic. *INS v. Elias-Zacarias,* 502 U.S. 478, 482-83 (1992); *Kasinga*, 21 I. & N. Dec. 357; *Matter of S-P-*, 21 I. & N. Dec. 486 (BIA 1996).

> [A]n applicant does not bear the unreasonable burden of establishing the exact motivation of a persecutor where different reasons for actions are possible. *Matter of Fuentes,* 19 I&N Dec. 658, 662 (BIA 1988). Rather, an asylum applicant bear[s] the burden of

[27] *Id.* at 76594.

> establishing facts on which a reasonable person would fear that the danger arises on account of his race, religion, nationality, membership in a particular social group, or political opinion.

Id. at 489-90. Further, it is well-established that nexus may be established by either direct or circumstantial evidence. *Elias-Zacarias*, 502 U.S. at 482-83; *Baballah v. Ashcroft*, 335 F.3d 981, 990 (9th Cir. 2003); *Rios v. Ashcroft*, 287 F.3d at 900. Significantly, in *Kasinga*, the Board ruled that societal and cultural factors are also to be taken into account in determining nexus. 21 I. & N. Dec. at 366-67. The Proposed Rule also adopts this approach.[28]

At issue in this case is whether Osorio tormented and abused Ms. Alvarado because she was his *wife*, a status which incorporates gender and marital status. Osorio s comments and actions throughout the course of the relationship leave no doubt on this point. Time and time again in the midst of the vicious abuse, and in response to Ms. Alvarado s protestations Osorio affirmed his right to do as he did because she was his wife: You re my woman, you do what I say (Rec. at 696); You re my woman, and I can do whatever I want (Rec. at 695); You don t order me (Rec. at 694), and I can do it if I want to. (Rec. at 697.) It was clear to Ms. Alvarado that her husband s animus was not personal to her as an *individual*, but directed towards her as his *wife*; when directly questioned on this point, she testified that her husband would batter any woman to whom he was married. (Rec. at 325.)

Persecutors are often not as vocal about their motives as was Osorio. *See, e.g., Bolanos-Hernandez v. INS*, 767 F.2d 1277, 1285 (9th Cir. 1984) (Persecutors are hardly likely to provide their victims with affidavits attesting to their acts of persecution.). However, even if he had remained silent, the record would have been more than sufficient to establish the nexus

---

[28] *Id.* at 76593.

between his brutal persecution of Ms. Alvarado and her status as his wife. The extensive body of literature on domestic violence directly address its purposes and motivations, and make quite clear the gender and marital status link. The following is but a small sample of excerpts from scholarly literature on the issue which was *admitted into the record* in this case:

> " Wife-beating is, therefore, not an individual, isolated or aberrant act,.... but a social license, a duty or sign of masculinity, deeply ingrained in culture, widely practiced, denied and completely or largely immune from sanction. *It is inflicted on women in the position of wives* for their actual or suspected failure to properly carry out their role, for their failure to produce, serve or be properly subservient[.] [29]

> " [V]iolence against *wives* is a function of the belief ...that men are superior and that *the women they live with* are their possessions or chattels that they can treat as they wish and as they consider appropriate. [30]

> " Domestic violence has been revealed [to be] gender specific....[O]f all spousal violence crimes, ninety-one percent were victimizations of *women by their husbands or ex-husbands.* [31]

> " Domestic violence is not gender-neutral...severe, repeated domestic violence is overwhelmingly initiated by *men and inflicted upon women.* [32]

Osorio s own words and actions, coupled with an understanding of domestic violence provides direct evidence that the persecution was motivated by gender and marital status. However, there is still more evidence on this point. The BIA held in *Kasinga* that the nexus

---

[29] Copelon, Rhonda, *Recognizing the Egregious in the Everyday: Domestic Violence as Torture,* 25 COLUM. HUM. RTS. L. REV. 291, 335 (1994); (Exhibit 2-J) (emphasis added).

[30] *Id* at 304; (Exhibit 2-J) (emphasis added).

[31] Thomas, Dorothy Q. and Michele E. Beasley, *Domestic Violence as a Human Rights Issue,* 58 ALBANY L. REV. 1119, 1128 (1995); (Exhibit 2-M) (emphasis added).

[32] Copelon, *supra* note 29 at 303 (Exhibit 2-J)(emphasis added).

determination includes an analysis of societal and cultural norms;[33] this approach is reiterated in the Commentary to the Proposed Rule:

> [E]vidence about patterns of violence in the society against individuals similarly situated to the applicant may also be relevant to the on account of determination. For example, in the domestic violence context, an adjudicator would consider any evidence that the abuser uses violence to enforce power and control over the applicant because of the social status that a woman may acquire when she enters into a domestic relationship. This would include any direct evidence about the abuser s own actions, as well as any circumstantial evidence that such patterns of violence are *(1) supported by the legal system or social norms in the country in question, and (2) reflect a prevalent belief within society, or within relevant segments of society....*[34] [Emphasis added.]

The evidence is clear on these points. The legal system in Guatemala supports the patterns of violence by abdicating its responsibility to intervene to protect victims of domestic battering. The prevalent beliefs within society, which support and perpetuate the violence, include the beliefs that women are subordinate to men (Rec. at 737), that domestic violence as a social problem is unimportant (Rec. at 429), and that the woman is to blame when familial violence takes place.

---

[33] The approach to determining nexus which considers the abuser s actions within the societal / country context has been widely accepted; it is commonly referred to as a bifurcated nexus analysis. *See, e.g., Minister for Immigration and Multicultural Affairs v. Khawar* [2002] HCA 14 (Australian High Court), available at <http://scaleplus.law.gov.au/html/highcourt/0/2002/0/2002041114.htm>; *Islam, supra* note 16; Refugee Appeal No. 71427/99, *supra* note 16, ¶106 (New Zealand); UNHCR Social Group Guidelines, *supra* note 13. The British House of Lords illustrated its rationale by reference to the persecution of Jews prior to the Second World War:

> Suppose oneself in Germany in 1935.... [S]uppose that the Nazi government in those early days did not actively organise violence against Jews, but pursued a policy of not giving any protection to Jews subjected to violence by neighbours. A Jewish shopkeeper is attacked by a gang organised by an Aryan competitor who smash his shop, beat him up and threaten to do it again if he remains in business. The competitor and his gang are motivated by business rivalry and a desire to settle old personal scores, but *they would not have done what they did unless they knew that the authorities would allow them to act with impunity.* And the ground upon which they enjoyed impunity was that the victim was a Jew.... An essential element in the persecution, the failure of the authorities to provide protection, is based upon race.

Islam, supra, ¶133 (Lord Hoffman) (emphasis added).

[34] Commentary, *supra* note 4, at 76593.

19

(Rec. at 425.) The social norms and beliefs include such a broad acceptance of domestic violence that a man can batter his wife in public or drag her by the hair down the street, as Osorio did to Ms. Alvarado and no one will lift a finger to stop the violence.

C. Ms. Alvarado was Persecuted on Account of Her Political Opinion

The IJ who granted Ms. Alvarado s claim for asylum made the finding that she had resisted her husband s brutal acts of domination. (Rec. at 196.) The IJ ruled that her resistance was the expression of a political opinion against male domination, and constituted a challenge to [Osorio s] opinion that women are to be subordinate to men. (Rec. at 196.) Osorio s violent behavior towards his wife was meant to punish her for the actual opinion she held, or the opinion he attributed to her that men have no right to treat women in the manner in which he treated her.

Asylum claims often involve overlapping grounds of persecution. *See, e.g., Baballah v. Ashcroft*, 335 F.3d 981 (ethnicity and religion); *Gafoor v. INS*, 231 F.3d 645 (9th Cir. 2000) (race and imputed political opinion); *Lal v. INS*, 255 F.3d 998, *as amended*, 268 F.3d 1148 (9th Cir. 2001) (religion and political opinion). The IJ s ruling that Osorio was motivated *both* by Ms. Alvarado s status as his wife and her political opinion of resistance is supported by the record as well as by scholarly literature regarding the phenomenon of domestic violence. Most experts recognize that domestic violence is a tool aimed at gaining power in order to control the intimate partner, [35] that it is part of a broad-scale system of domination of women,[36] and that it must be

[35] Karl Hempel, M.D., *Domestic Violence*, THE HEALTH GAZETTE (1998), available at <http://www.tfn.net/HealthGazette/domestic.html>.

[36] Kimberle Williams Crenshaw, *Mapping the Margins: Intersectionality, Identity Politics, and Violence Against Women of Color, in* THE PUBLIC NATURE OF PRIVATE VIOLENCE: THE DISCOVERY OF

understood in its social and cultural context as the extension of the domination and control of husbands over their wives. [37]

That men use spousal abuse as a means by which to perpetuate male domination and patriarchal social systems has likewise been recognized by many international organizations. For example, in a special report on the causes and consequences of violence against women, the United Nations Special Rapporteur on Violence Against Women concluded that [i]n intimate violence, male supremacy, ideology and conditions &confer upon men the sense of entitlement, if not the duty, to chastise their wives. [38]

This understanding of domestic violence explains why Osorio would escalate his abuse upon the least sign of resistance on Ms. Alvarado s part. Furthermore, because domestic violence is quintesssentially about issues of power and subordination in intimate relationships, domestic violence is necessarily motivated by status (*i.e.* social group) as well as by resistance (*i.e.* insubordination). Osorio s rage at Ms. Alvarado s resistance is consonant with an understanding of domestic violence as purposeful behavior intended to exert power, to eradicate resistance and to perpetuate subordination.

1. Ms. Alvarado s Resistance Constitutes a Political Opinion

Ms. Alvarado did not agree with the prevailing social and cultural norms of male domination and abuse. Her disagreement was expressed within the context of her relationship

---

DOMESTIC ABUSE 93, 93 (1994).

[37] R. Emerson Dobash and Russell Dobash, VIOLENCE AGAINST WIVES 15 (1979).

[38] *1996 Report of the Special Rapporteur, supra* note 11, at 7, ¶ 3.

with Osorio. Although she was terrorized by him, she demonstrated her resistance through both her words and her actions. On a number of occasions, when he was in the throes of tormenting her, she spoke up and directly challenged him, protesting his right to force sex on her (Rec. at 695); to rape her anally (Rec. at 696); and to use her head as a battering ram against furniture. (Rec. at 697.) On other occasions she expressed her resistance by her actions: she reported his abuse to the police (Rec. at 700); she attempted to use the judicial system (Rec. at 701); contrary to his demands that she not leave him, she fled to her parents and brother s home, and then to a rented room in an effort to resist his control. (Rec. at 696.) She went to seek medical treatment, even though she knew he would be enraged. (Rec. at 696.) And finally, when none of that was successful in vindicating her right to be free of abuse, she flouted his assertion of absolute authority over her by leaving his sphere of control, and fleeing to the United States. (Rec. at 702.)

Testimony by a psychotherapist who treated her in the United States affirms the depth of Ms. Alvarado s belief in her right not to be abused by her spouse. The psychotherapist, Dr. Linda Bersing, is an expert on women s issues and Latin America who has counseled women for more than two decades. She testified that Ms. Alvarado was quite different from other women with whom she had met over the years. (Rec. at 305) The difference, she testified, was that Ms. Alvarado had a will..to fight ; she believed she had the right to do something and she was really determined , and unlike other women who might end up believing that they deserve the abuse, she did not accept her situation. (Rec. at 306.)

Courts have long held that the term political opinion extends to a range of beliefs and philosophies, and is not limited to notions regarding political parties and ideologies. *See, e.g.*,

Chang v. INS, 119 F.3d 1055, 1063 (3rd Cir. 1997) (an asylum seeker need not call herself a dissident or articulate resistance in terms of a particular ideology); *Osorio v. INS*, 18 F.3d 1017, 1030 (2nd Cir. 1994) (holding that refugee law does not require that [the asylum seeker] be a politician and ruling that to require an individual to state which political party he belongs to, which political philosophy he espouses or which political leaders he supports...betrays an impoverished view of what political opinions are....); *Lazo-Majano v. INS*, 813 F.2d 1432, 1435 (9th Cir. 1987), *overruled on other grounds by Fisher v. INS*, 79 F.3d 955 (9th Cir. 1996) (*en banc*) (views of a poor domestic and washerwoman who does not participate in politics nonetheless political).

Feminism has been expressly recognized as a political opinion. *See, e.g., Fatin*, 12 F.3d at 1242 (In this case, if the petitioner s political opinion is defined simply as feminism, she would presumably satisfy the first element [establishing a political opinion], *for we have little doubt that feminism qualifies as a political opinion* within the meaning of the relevant statutes. (Emphasis added)). A woman s deeply held opinion that her husband does not have the right to violate her physical and psychological integrity is one of the most fundamental expressions of feminism, because freedom from domestic violence is a necessary condition for the attainment of all other societal equalities.[39] Ms. Alvarado believes in the right to this equality, and her words and actions

[39] The United Nations Declaration on the Elimination of Violence Against Women recognizes that violence against women is the essential and ultimate social mechanism by which women are forced into a subordinate position as compared to men. Declaration on the Elimination of Violence against Women, G.A. Res. 48/104, U.N. GAOR Supp. (No. 49), at 217, U.N. Doc. A/48/49 (1993).

throughout her relationship were an expression of this belief, and were not simply the articulation of the common human desire not to be harmed or abused [40]

2. Ms. Alvarado was Persecuted on Account of her Political Opinion

As discussed above, the extensive literature establishes that the fundamental purpose of domestic violence is to punish, humiliate, and exercise power over the victim on account of her gender (Rec. at 39) and to extinguish any actual or perceived dissent. Osorio was motivated to batter Ms. Alvarado because of her status as his wife, and he was motivated to batter her because she resisted and challenged his right to exert absolute power and control over her.

There was not a single time when Ms. Alvarado resisted Osorio that he did not respond by even more brutal treatment. Osorio vowed to kill her for leaving him. (Rec. at 704.) When she tried to escape by renting a room, he beat her unconscious. (Rec. at 696.) When she refused his command to go to the hospital to abort their child, he battered her and attempted to induce a miscarriage. (Rec. at 694.) He pulled a machete on her when she refused to go for a walk in the middle of the night. (Rec. at 698.)

The least hint of resistance, or questioning of his authority resulted in escalated abuse: Osorio became enraged when she asked him not to drink so much (Rec. at 694); he threatened to kill her when she tried to resist forced sex: Just do it, or I ll finish you off (Rec. at 695.) When Ms. Alvarado simply remarked that Osorio had arrived home late, he hit and punched her, saying that he didn t have to answer to her. (Rec. at 699.) Perhaps most telling of all are Osorio s

---

[40] The BIA made this characterization of Ms. Alvarado s opinions in its decision reversing the IJ. (Rec. at 13.)

threats to his wife as to what he would do should she ever leave him which would be the ultimate throwing off of his authority. He told her:

> [Y]ou will suffer much worse than what I have done to you so far...If you ever try to leave, I will come find you. And when I find you, I could kill you, but I m not going to do that. I will break your legs. I wil cripple you so that you will be in a wheelchair for the rest of your life. I will mark your face so it will be scarred forever, it will be twisted and deformed. (Rec. at 704.)

The fact that Osorio was motivated to punish Ms. Alvarado for her resistance is evident in the sequence of events the repeated cycles of resistance, followed by violence and threats of violence. The conclusion that the battering was, in part, politically-motivated, is reinforced by the scholarly literature on domestic violence, which as detailed above recognizes it as purposeful conduct, intended to extinguish resistance, and to dominate and control.[41]

D. Ms. Alvarado has Suffered Atrocious Past Persecution and has Established a Well-founded fear of Future Persecution

A well-founded fear of persecution may be presumed if an asylum applicant establishes past persecution. The regulations in force when Ms. Alvarado s case was adjudicated provided that the presumption could be rebutted only upon a showing by a preponderance of the evidence that country conditions had changed to such an extent that the fear of persecution was no longer well-founded. 8 C.F.R. § 208.13(b)(1)(i). Current regulations provide for rebuttal upon proof by a preponderance 1) of a fundamental change in circumstances such that the applicant no longer has a well-founded fear of persecution ; or 2) that the applicant could avoid persecution by

---

[41] *See* V. Michael McKenzie, DOMESTIC VIOLENCE IN AMERICA 8 (1995) ([s]pousal battery is a choice men exercise intentionally and purposefully to resolve conflict and achieve their goals of dominance, and coercive control of women).

internal relocation within the country of origin if, under all the circumstances, it would be reasonable to expect her to do so. 8 C.F.R. §§ 1208.13(b)(1)(i)(A) & (B).

Even in cases where the presumption of a well-founded fear has been rebutted, asylum may be granted in the exercise of discretion when the applicant has demonstrated compelling reasons for being unwilling or unable to return to the country arising out of the severity of the past persecution or there is the reasonable possibility that the applicant may suffer other serious harm upon removal to the home country. 8 C.F.R. §§ 1208.13(b)(1)(iii)(A) & (B).

It is undisputed that Ms. Alvarado has suffered past persecution, and there is no evidence in the record of changed country conditions, changed circumstances, or reasonable internal relocation, which could rebut the presumption in her favor of a well-founded fear. Even in the absence of the regulatory presumption, the record evidence establishes that a reasonable person in Ms. Alvarado s circumstances would fear persecution. *Matter of Mogharrabi*, 19 I. & N. Dec. 439 (BIA 1987). Moreover, given the duration and extreme severity of the abuse, and its ongoing physical and psychological effects, Ms. Alvarado qualifies for a grant of protection even in the absence of a well-founded fear of persecution.

1. Ms. Alvarado has Established a Well-Founded Fear of Persecution

The IJ ruled that Ms. Alvarado was entitled to the regulatory presumption of a well-founded fear on the basis of her past persecution, and that there was no evidence that conditions in Guatemala had changed to such an extent ... to obviate the Respondent s need for protection. (Rec. at 192.) There is no evidence to support a rebuttal even under the revised regulation s broader grounds; there have been no changed circumstances, and the record is clear on the futility of Ms. Alvarado s attempts to escape her husband through internal relocation. (Rec. at 235, 238-240.)

Ms. Alvarado can establish a well-founded fear of persecution even in the absence of the regulatory presumption. An applicant s fear is well-founded if it is subjectively genuine and objectively reasonable, or if a reasonable person in the circumstances would fear persecution. *INS v. Cardoza-Fonseca*, 480 U.S. 421, 430-43 (1987); *Mogharrabi*, 19 I. & N. Dec. at 445. The particular facts of this case, considered in the context of scholarly research on domestic violence, can only lead one to the conclusion that any reasonable person in Ms. Alvarado s circumstances would fear persecution.

Osorio asserted on numerous occasions that Ms. Alvarado could never escape him. (Rec. at 699-700.) He tracked her down on every occasion that she did attempt to leave, and among the many threats that he made was that he would make her suffer worse than ever before should she attempt to leave him. (Rec. at 704.) His threats against her did not cease with her departure from Guatemala; Ms. Alvarado s sister recounted that Osorio has her under a death threat (Rec. at 679), and that if she comes back he will not let her live. [42] (Rec. at 686.) The gravity of these threats is underscored by the literature on domestic violence, *see supra* at section B.2, and by observations made by the Violence Against Women Office (VAWO) of the Department of Justice, which were incorporated into the Commentary to the Proposed Regulation:

---

[42] Ms. Alvarado has more than met the well-founded fear burden for asylum; on these facts, she has also met the higher standard of clear probability required for restriction on removal. *INS v. Stevic*, 467 U.S. 407 (1984). A clear probability of persecution may be shown where a specific threat is made by a person with the will and ability to carry it out. *Bolanos-Hernandez*, 767 F.2d at 1285. As amply demonstrated by the record, Osorio has both the will and ability to carry out his threat that he will not let her live.

> [I]n relationships involving domestic violence, past behavior is a strong predictor of future behavior by the abuser. *See, e.g.*, United States Department of Justice, Understanding Domestic Violence: A Handbook for Victims and Profesionals. ... [D]omestically and internationally, domestic violence centers on power and control over the victim. Consequently, when victims attempt to flee the abusive relationship, or otherwise assert their independence, abusers often pursue them and escalate the violence to regain or reassert control. *See, e.g.*, United States Department of Justice, Stalking and Domestic Violence under the Violence Against Women Act (1998). *The risk to lethality to the victim is typically greatest when she attempts to escape the abuse, and in contrast to other persecution cases where the persecutor s desire to harm the victim may wane if the victim leaves, the victim s attempt to leave typically increases the abuser s motivation to locate and harm her.*[43]

The VAWO also commented that because of the abuser s intimate relationship with the victim, he is likely to possess important information about where the victim could go or to whom she would turn for assistance. [44]

Therefore, it is clear that Osorio s threats should be taken seriously, and that Ms. Alvarado may be assumed to be at higher risk now than she was at any point in her relationship with Osorio (*i.e.*, escape puts victim at the greatest risk to lethality). The VAWO s observations are also particularly relevant to the issue of internal relocation, as they recognize the ability intimate partners have to locate the victim. Osorio has demonstrated his ability through his past successes in tracking down Ms. Alvarado. The fact that they have children together is also a significant consideration; should Ms. Alvarado be forced to return to Guatemala, there is no doubt that she would want to see her children, who have been residing with Osorio s parents. (Rec. at 705.) This would certainly make it virtually a foregone conclusion that Osorio would be able to locate Ms. Alvarado.

---

[43] Commentary, *supra* note 4, at 76595 (emphasis added; some citations omitted).

[44] *Id.* at 76596.

2. Ms. Alvarado Qualifies for a Grant of Asylum Even in the Absence of a Well-founded Fear

An applicant may obtain asylum even if she has no well-founded fear in the future, provided that she has compelling reasons arising out of the severity of the past persecution for being unwilling to return. 8 C.F.R. § 1208.13(b)(1)(iii). *See also Lal*, 255 F.3d at 1002; *Lopez-Galarza v. INS*, 99 F.3d 954, 960-63 (9th Cir. 1996); *Matter of Chen*, 20 I & N. Dec. 16 (BIA 1989). Assuming *arguendo* that Ms. Alvarado could not establish a well-founded fear of persecution, she would still qualify for asylum because the harm which she suffered was exceptionally severe and atrocious.

Persecution is stamped on every page of this record. Although this observation was made by Ninth Circuit jurist John T. Noonan upon reading the record in the *Lazo-Majano* case, *see* 813 F.2d at 1434, it could just as well have been said about the record in the instant case. It is impossible to read the record in Ms. Alvarado s case without reaching the conclusion that her home had become a virtual torture chamber, where her husband was at liberty to rape, sodomize, whip, kick, and beat her. Bones were dislocated, internal hemorrhaging occurred, flesh was cut and bruised, and sexually transmitted diseases were passed on.

The physical harm was extreme and long-lasting; in her affidavit, Ms. Alvarado testified that she suffers from severe, recurring headaches from being hit and kicked in the head, dragged by the hair, or her head used as a battering ram. (Rec. at 705.) She still suffers from severe abdominal pains and irregular menstrual periods from the rapes and blows to her abdomen and genital area, and has recurring pains in her arm and chest from being pulled across the bed when her husband would force sex upon her. (Rec. at 696, 705.)

But it is not only the physical harms which have ongoing consequences for Ms. Alvarado; she continues to suffer from the psychological and emotional repercussions of this exceptionally brutal abuse. She regularly has nightmares that she is back in Guatemala, and the thought of this makes her so desperate and fearful that she cannot get back to sleep. (Rec. at 704-05.)

There can be no doubt that Ms. Alvarado s abuse rises to the severity of harm necessary for a grant of asylum even in the absence of a well-founded fear of persecution. The physical and psychological harm she endured are equivalent to that present in cases where asylum was granted on the basis of severe past persecution. *See, e.g., Lopez-Galarza*, 99 F.3d 954 (female applicant imprisoned for 15 days, repeatedly raped and subjected to other physical abuse); *Matter of B-*, Int. Dec. 3251 (BIA 1995) (Afghan interrogated, physically abused, detained for 15 months, and forced to serve in the Army because of assistance to the mujahideen); *Chen*, 20 I. & N. Dec. 16 (Chinese applicant and his family suffered brutal physical and psychological mistreatment over more than a decade during the Cultural Revolution). In addition, although it is not a requirement, Ms. Alvarado not only endured atrocious forms of persecution in the past, but she continues to suffers from ongoing physical and emotional consequences arising from the ten years of battering and torment. *See Lal*, 255 F.3d at 1006 (although existence of lasting physical or emotional disability may sometimes be a factor in determining the severity of an applicant's past persecution, it has not been a requirement.).

IV. Conclusion

1) Ms. Alvarado Should be Granted Asylum

A. Ms. Alvarado Should Be Granted Asylum on the Existing Record

30

Ms. Alvarado has suffered tremendously for the last twenty years of her life. From 1984, the date of her marriage, until 1995, when she fled Guatemala, she was the victim of her husband s unrestrained brutality. And from 1995 to 2004, she has suffered what is now almost a decade of separation from her children. When she left Guatemala, her son was a toddler; he is now nearly twelve years old; her daughter, who was a young girl, is in her late teens. Because they live with Osorio s parents, she has had only the most minimal contact with them over the years.

As detailed in Part I, *supra*, Ms. Alvarado s claim for asylum has been pending for almost *ten years* since 1995, when she first appeared before an immigration judge. Each delay has increased her anguish over her separation from her children, as well as her feeling of insecurity regarding her ultimate fate.

The record in Ms. Alvarado s case is extremely well-developed. Her declaration is detailed, her testimony was extensive, and the documentary evidence regarding relevant conditions in Guatemala is comprehensive. Extensive briefing, including that of *amicus curiae*, has occurred at each step of adjudication, and has included in-depth discussion of the scholarly literature on domestic violence. Furthermore, current briefing has addressed Ms. Alvarado s eligibility for protection not only under existing caselaw, but pursuant to the Proposed Regulations as well. Factors relevant under the Proposed Regulations are well-developed in the existing record, and a remand is not required to further develop the record for these purposes.

Ms. Alvarado s case is ripe for decision. Justice and fairness require an adjudication on the existing record, and on the basis of the arguments that have been submitted throughout the past decade in this case. To further delay a decision in this case is to deny Ms. Alvarado the opportunity to regain the peace of mind that comes with a resolution of her claim for protection, and more importantly the opportunity for family reunification at long last.

B. There are no Adverse Factors which Negatively Impact the Exercise of Discretion

Asylum is a discretionary remedy, and may be denied in the exercise of discretion by the Attorney General, or his delegates. However, where an individual has established a well-founded fear of persecution, asylum should only be denied in the exercise of discretion on the basis of genuine compelling factors factors important enough to warrant returning a *bona fide* refugee to a country where he may face a threat of imminent danger to his life or liberty. *Hernandez-Ortiz v. INS*, 777 F.2d 509, 519 (9th Cir. 1995). Not only are there no compelling factors which would justify a denial in this case there are simply no adverse factors *whatsoever*. Ms. Alvarado has established statutory eligibility, and in the total absence of negative factors, should be granted relief in the exercise of discretion.

Respectfully Submitted,

____

Karen Musalo, Resident Scholar
Stephen Knight, Research Fellow (on brief)
University of California
Hastings College of Law
200 McAllister Street
San Francisco, CA 94102
(415) 565-4720

DATED: February 18, 2004

DECLARATION OF SERVICE BY MAIL
Matter of Rodi Alvarado Peña

I, Stephen Knight, declare that I am at least 18 years of age, that I am not a party to the within cause, that my business address is Center for Gender & Refugee Studies, UC Hastings College of the Law, 200 McAllister Street, San Francisco, CA, 94102. On February 18, 2004, I served

BRIEF ON BEHALF OF RODI ALVARADO PEÑA TO THE ATTORNEY GENERAL OF THE UNITED STATES

on the person listed below by placing a true copy thereof in a prepaid sealed envelope with first-class postage thereon fully prepaid, in the United States mail at San Francisco, California, addressed as follows:

George R. Martin
Acting Chief Appellate Counsel
U.S. I.C.E.
U.S. D.H.S.
5113 Leesburg Pike, Suite 200
Falls Church, VA 22041

I declare under penalty of perjury under the laws of the State of California that the foregoing is true and correct. Executed on February 18, 2004, at San Francisco, California.

____

Stephen Knight

APPENDIX 5G

SAMPLE INDEX OF EXHIBITS FOR I-589 FILING

UNITED STATES DEPARTMENT OF JUSTICE
EXECUTIVE OFFICE FOR IMMIGRATION REVIEW
UNITED STATES IMMIGRATION COURT
DENVER, COLORADO

In the Matters of:	**DETAINED IN ARTESIA**
[redacted]	**File Nos.:** [redacted]
In Removal Proceedings	**Next Master Calendar Hearing** [redacted] **before Judge Trujillo**

INDEX OF EXHIBITS IN SUPPORT OF RESPONDENTS' APPLICATIONS FOR ASYLUM, WITHHOLDING OF REMOVAL, AND PROTECTION UNDER THE CONVENTION AGAINST TORTURE

The Respondents, [redacted] and [redacted], through undersigned counsel, submits the following exhibits A – G, along with Proof of Service, in support of their Applications for Asylum, Withholding of Removal, and Protection Under the Convention Against Torture.

TAB **PAGE**

A. **Form I-589,** Application for Asylum and for Withholding of Removal. **1-12**

B. **Birth Certificate of** [redacted], with certified English translation attached thereto, as evidence of parent-child relationship with the principal applicant, [redacted]. Please note that Ms. [redacted]'s Guatemalan ID card is in the possession of Immigration and Customs Enforcement. It will be submitted as evidence of her identity and Guatemalan citizenship prior to her Individual Hearing. **13-17**

C. **Letter of** [redacted], Ms. [redacted]'s sister, with certified English translation attached thereto. Eva personally witnessed acts of persecution by the gang in Guatemala against Ms. [redacted] and her four-year-old son. She verifies that the reason Ms. [redacted] fled Guatemala was to save her and her son's lives, and confirms that gang members "continue looking for her to kill her." **18-19**

D. **Photographs of Ms.** [redacted] **and her son** [redacted], which Ms. [redacted]'s husband and [redacted]'s father, [redacted], kept close while praying for their safety, after he was forced to flee Guatemala to save his own life. **20-21**

E. **Letter of Victoria Sanford, Ph.D.**, an expert on Maya communities in Guatemala, stating that "In the societies of Guatemala . . . communities see women and children targeted by gangs as a distinct group, as a direct result of their vulnerability, susceptibility to harm, and the steps taken to avoid harms. . . . Once targeted, women and children cannot escape the gangs or receive protection from their violence." **22-25**

F. **Letter of Elliot Young, Ph.D.**, an expert on cross-border smuggling, paramilitary groups on the border, and clandestine trafficking of migrants, verifying, "It is not an exaggeration to say that Guatemala is experiencing a war that reaches every level of society. Today the surge of unaccompanied minors and women fleeing Guatemala seeking protection can be linked directly to the social and political crisis taking place in country today." **26-31**

G. **Department of State, Guatemala 2013 Human Rights Report**, stating, "Considerable violence was attributed to gangs" and noting "corruption and inadequate investigation and prosecution of such crimes" by the government of Guatemala. The report also discusses the widespread violence against women and marginalization of indigenous communities, making them more vulnerable to such gang violence. **32-62**

Respectfully submitted,

________________________ ________________
Dree K. Collopy Date

BENACH RAGLAND LLP
1333 H Street NW, Suite 900 West
Washington, DC 20005
T: 202-644-8600
F: 202-644-8615
E: dcollopy@benachragland.com
EOIR ID: OG444350

AILA-Coordinated Pro Bono Attorney
ArtesiaLegalDefenseTeam@gmail.com

Counsel for Respondents

UNITED STATES DEPARTMENT OF JUSTICE
EXECUTIVE OFFICE FOR IMMIGRATION REVIEW
UNITED STATES IMMIGRATION COURT
DENVER, COLORADO

In the Matters of:	)	**DETAINED IN ARTESIA**
[redacted]	)	**File Nos.:** [redacted]
In Removal Proceedings	)	**Next Individual Hearing** [redacted] **before Judge Trujillo**

INDEX OF ADDITIONAL EXHIBITS IN SUPPORT OF RESPONDENTS' APPLICATIONS FOR ASYLUM, WITHHOLDING OF REMOVAL, AND PROTECTION UNDER THE CONVENTION AGAINST TORTURE

The Respondents, [redacted] and [redacted], through undersigned counsel, submits the following exhibits H – S , along with Proof of Service, in support of their Applications for Asylum, Withholding of Removal, and Protection Under the Convention Against Torture. Please note that the Respondents previously submitted exhibits A – G with their applications at their Master Calendar hearing on October 17, 2014.

TAB **PAGE**

H. **Ms. [redacted]'s Guatemalan Birth Certificate and Guatemalan ID Card,** with certified English translation attached. **63-75**

I. **Marriage Certificate,** as evidence of the familial relationship between Ms. [redacted] and her husband, Mr. [redacted], with certified English translation attached. **76-82**

J. **Sworn Statement of** [redacted], stating, "If [redacted] and I are forced to return to Guatemala, we will certainly die at the hands of the M-18. . . . If [redacted] and I are forced to return, the M-18 will find us, kidnap us, rape me, and kill us with knives. They are capable of such violence and they will do it because we ran away from them like they warned us not to do. . . . I dream of seeing my son hug his father for the first time in a home where no one beats us, holds knifes against our bodies, or threatens us with rape, kidnapping, and death because they are after my family for preaching peace. I dream of a life where [redacted], [redacted], and I can go to church and walk home and live as a happy family without fear of being beaten and killed." **83-94**

K. **Sworn Statement of** [redacted], where he details the daily death threats and constant beatings at the hands of the M-18, who wrongly believed him

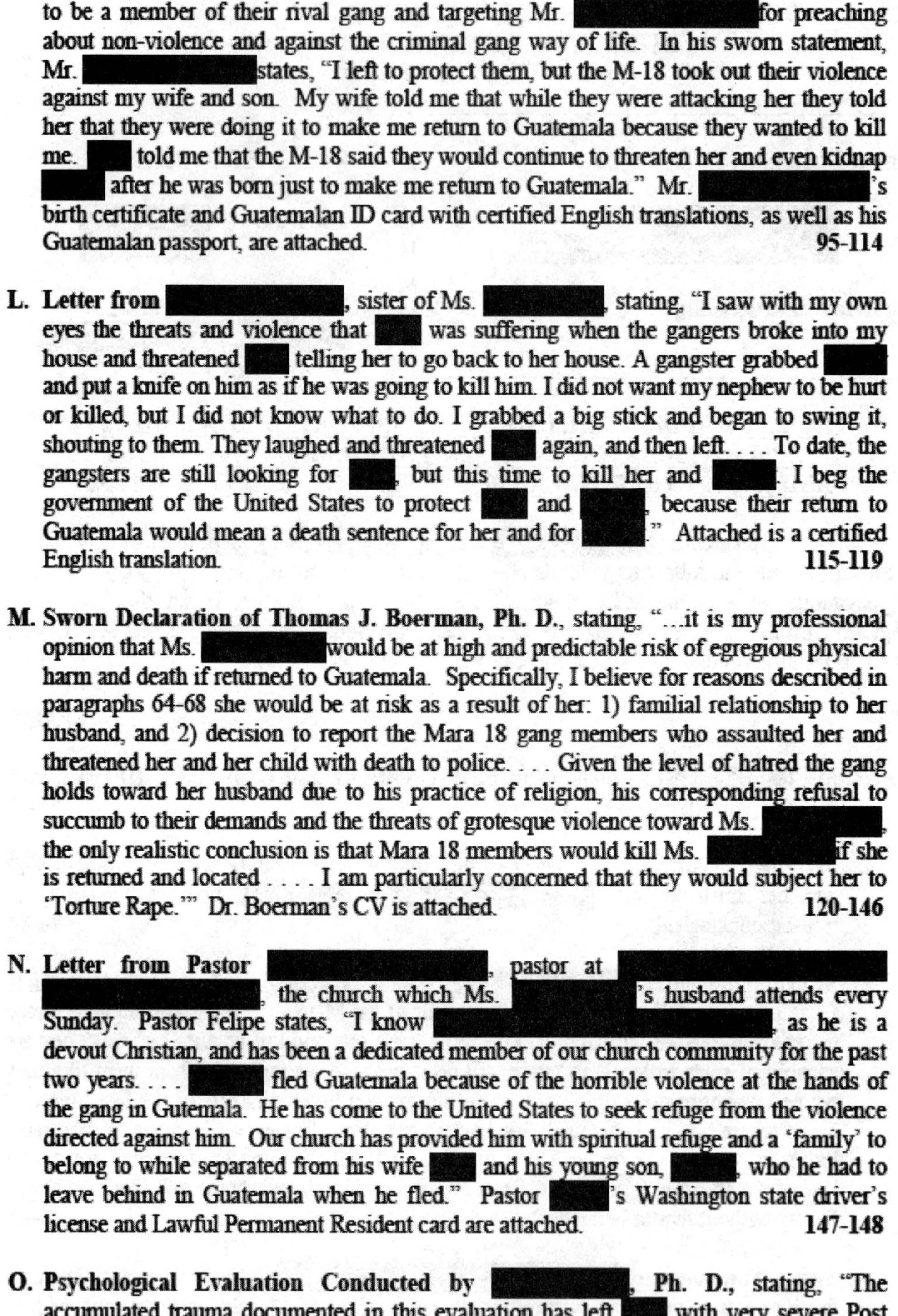

to be a member of their rival gang and targeting Mr. for preaching about non-violence and against the criminal gang way of life. In his sworn statement, Mr. states, "I left to protect them, but the M-18 took out their violence against my wife and son. My wife told me that while they were attacking her they told her that they were doing it to make me return to Guatemala because they wanted to kill me. told me that the M-18 said they would continue to threaten her and even kidnap after he was born just to make me return to Guatemala." Mr. 's birth certificate and Guatemalan ID card with certified English translations, as well as his Guatemalan passport, are attached. **95-114**

L. **Letter from** , sister of Ms. , stating, "I saw with my own eyes the threats and violence that was suffering when the gangers broke into my house and threatened telling her to go back to her house. A gangster grabbed and put a knife on him as if he was going to kill him. I did not want my nephew to be hurt or killed, but I did not know what to do. I grabbed a big stick and began to swing it, shouting to them. They laughed and threatened again, and then left. . . . To date, the gangsters are still looking for , but this time to kill her and . I beg the government of the United States to protect and , because their return to Guatemala would mean a death sentence for her and for ." Attached is a certified English translation. **115-119**

M. **Sworn Declaration of Thomas J. Boerman, Ph. D.**, stating, "...it is my professional opinion that Ms. would be at high and predictable risk of egregious physical harm and death if returned to Guatemala. Specifically, I believe for reasons described in paragraphs 64-68 she would be at risk as a result of her: 1) familial relationship to her husband, and 2) decision to report the Mara 18 gang members who assaulted her and threatened her and her child with death to police. . . . Given the level of hatred the gang holds toward her husband due to his practice of religion, his corresponding refusal to succumb to their demands and the threats of grotesque violence toward Ms. , the only realistic conclusion is that Mara 18 members would kill Ms. if she is returned and located . . . . I am particularly concerned that they would subject her to 'Torture Rape.'" Dr. Boerman's CV is attached. **120-146**

N. **Letter from Pastor** , pastor at , the church which Ms. 's husband attends every Sunday. Pastor Felipe states, "I know , as he is a devout Christian, and has been a dedicated member of our church community for the past two years. . . . fled Guatemala because of the horrible violence at the hands of the gang in Gutemala. He has come to the United States to seek refuge from the violence directed against him. Our church has provided him with spiritual refuge and a 'family' to belong to while separated from his wife and his young son, , who he had to leave behind in Guatemala when he fled." Pastor 's Washington state driver's license and Lawful Permanent Resident card are attached. **147-148**

O. **Psychological Evaluation Conducted by** , **Ph. D.**, stating, "The accumulated trauma documented in this evaluation has left with very severe Post

Traumatic Stress Disorder. . . . If she learns that she and her son are to be deported, the psychological stress is likely to be so overwhelming that she would be at risk for psychotic breakdown or for suicide. ████ is four years old and is suffering from severe anxiety and depression. His condition has worsened physically and emotionally in the nearly five months that he and his mother have been in detention." Dr. ████'s CV is attached. **149-167**

P. Additional Evidence of the Dire Human Rights Conditions in Guatemala, for those like Ms. ██████ and her family who have been labeled as enemies of the gangs.

- **Michael Boulton,** ***Living in a World of Violence: An Introduction to the Gang Phenomenon*****, UNHCR (July 2011),** http://www.unhcr.org/4e3269629.pdf, stating "It is common for *mara* gangs to make broad threats which also include the victim's family and threats of rape to female members of the resistor's family have been reported. A refusal to join the gang or 'clika' will result in actual violence directed towards the gang resistor and his/her family as the norm." **168-197**

- ***Guatemala Country Summary 2014*****, HUMAN RIGHTS WATCH (Jan. 2014),** http://www.hrw.org/sites/default/files/related_material/guatemala_5.pdf, stating, "Powerful criminal organizations engage in widespread acts of violence and extortion. The intimidation and corruption of the justice system officials, as well as the absence of an effective witness protection program, contribute to high levels of impunity." **198-203**

- **Hal Brands,** ***Crime Violence, and the Crisis in Guatemala: A Case Study in the Erosion of the State*****, STRATEGIC STUDIES INSTITUTE (May 2010)** http://www.strategicstudiesinstitute.army.mil/pdffiles/PUB986.pdf, stating, "From Petén in the north, to Huehuetenango in the west, to parts of Guatemala City itself, as much as 40 percent of Guatemalan territory is either subject to dispute or effectively beyond the control of the police and the central government." **204-238**

- ***U.N. Official Cites Ongoing Torture in Guatemala*****, LATIN AMERICAN HERALD TRIBUNE (2009)** http://www.laht.com/article.asp?CategoryId=23558&ArticleId=337946, stating, "The appearance of mutilated bodies and of women with signs of having had their hands tied or having been raped, burned or strangled is clear evidence that torture continues to happen in Guatemala. . . ." The article also states, "Guatemalan prosecutors and judges appear to have no interest in investigating instances of torture. . . ." **239**

- ***Guatemala: Violence Perpetrated by Criminal Gangs and Cases of Popular Justice; Protection Offered by the State (2008-March 2012)*****, IMMIGRATION AND REFUGEE BOARD OF CANADA (May 7, 2012),** http://www.refworld.org/docid/4fc4a9962.html, stating, "According to an investigator for the UN-sponsored International Commission Against Impunity in

Guatemala, gangs in the country 'have the power that terrorist groups have in other countries.'" The report also states, "According to Human Rights Watch, gangs use violence against 'those who defy their control and those who refuse to pay extortion money.'" **240-244**

- ***Fact Sheet: Gangs in Guatemala*, GUATEMALA HUMAN RIGHTS COMMISSION** http://www.ghrc-usa.org/Publications/GangFactSheet.pdf, stating "The two largest gangs in Guatemala are *Mara Salvatrucha* (MS-13) and the *Barrio 18* (18th Street gang). Together their members make up 95% of the total number of gang members in the country." **245-246**

- ***From Survivors to Defenders: Women Confronting Violence in Mexico, Honduras & Guatemala*, NOBEL WOMEN'S INITIATIVE (June 5 2012),** http://nobelwomensinitiative.org/2012/06/from-survivors-to-defenders-women-confronting-violence-in-mexico-honduras-and-guatemala/, stating, "Both governments and non-state actors are systematically committing crimes against women – and the perpetrators are rarely brought to justice. We found that the three governments sustain policies and practices that work against human rights in general, and deny the rights of women." **247-294**

- **Max G. Manwaring, *A Contemporary Challenge to State Sovereignty: Gangs and Other Illicit Transnational Criminal Organizations in Central America, El Salvador, Mexico, Jamaica, and Brazil*, STRATEGIC STUDIES INSTITUTE (Dec. 2007),** http://www.strategicstudiesinstitute.army.mil/pdffiles/PUB837.pdf, stating, "The cases of the *Mara Salvatrucha* (MS-13) and the Eighteenth Street (*Mara*-18 or MS-18) gangs . . . illustrate the real impact of second and third-generation gangs functioning as networks with extensive transnational linkages. . . . Thanks to the activities of disaffected street gangs, overall crime rates have increased dramatically throughout the Central American region. . . . Guatemala's murder rate has risen 40 percent from 2001 to 2004 and is now approximately 50 per 100,000." **295-339**

- **Hal Brands, *Third Generation Gangs and Criminal Insurgency in Latin America*, Small Wars Journal (July 4, 2009),** http://smallwarsjournal.com/jrnl/art/third-generation-gangs-and-criminal-insurgency-in-latin-america, stating, "MS-13 and M-18 are just as vicious; they leave decapitated bodies in the streets and have in several cases massacred busloads of innocent travelers. . . . In cities in Mexico, Guatemala, El Salvador, and Brazil, gang violence has become so intense that the authorities have simply retreated from these areas, surrendering them to the gangs. **340-348**

- **Max G. Manwaring, *Street Gangs: The New Urban Insurgency*, STRATEGIC STUDIES INSTITUTE (Mar. 2005)** http://www.strategicstudiesinstitute.army.mil/pdffiles/pub597.pdf, stating, "More specifically, 3,500 people, including more than 455 women, were murdered in Guatemala in 2004. A majority of those murders took place in public, in broad daylight, and many of the mutilated bodies were left as grisly reminders of the gangs' prowess. Clearly, the governments'' corruption and lack of control of national territory have allowed criminal gangs and other organized criminal organizations to operate with impunity within each country of Central American – and across borders." **349-375**

- **John P. Sullivan & Robert J. Bunker,** ***A Crucible of Conflict: Third Generation Gang Studies Revisited*****, 19 Journal of Gang Research 1, 1-20 (Summer 2012),** ***available at*** https://www.academia.edu/8459989/A_Crucible_of_Conflict_Third_Generation_Gang_Studies_Revisited, stating, "An example of the impact of gang brutality on the state ca be seen in Guatemala where maras dominate urban and rural areas alike, using beheadings and mass violence to ensure collection of street taxes from bus operators and merchants and inter-operating with cartels – including Los Zetas – to smuggle drugs and control territory in so-called 'zones of impunity.'" **376-395**

Q. **Political Constitution of the Republic of Guatemala.** **396-438**

R. **Unpublished Immigration Judge Decisions,** recognizing family as a cognizable social group in the context of individuals seeking protection from gang-based violence. **439-464**

S. **Receipt Notice of I-589 from USCIS,** as evidence that both Respondents have complied with instructions for filing I-589 applications before the Immigration Court. **465-466**

Respectfully submitted,

________________________ _______________

Dree K. Collopy Date

BENACH RAGLAND LLP
1333 H Street NW, Suite 900 West
Washington, DC 20005
T: 202-644-8600
F: 202-644-8615
E: dcollopy@benachragland.com
EOIR ID: OG444350

AILA-Coordinated Pro Bono Attorney
ArtesiaLegalDefenseTeam@gmail.com

Counsel for Respondents

APPENDIX 5H

PRACTICE POINTERS ON DIRECT AND CROSS-EXAMINATION OF THE ASYLUM APPLICANT

As you prepare for your asylum hearing, it is helpful to outline your direct examination and anticipated cross-examination. Review the questions over and over with the asylum applicant during your interviews and, later, in a mock hearing. The following are useful tips to employ when preparing your direct examination and in anticipating the U.S. Department of Homeland Security (DHS) attorney's cross-examination.

Starting

Begin your direct examination with simple questions that are easy for the applicant to answer and that will give the applicant time to become accustomed to testifying in court. It is highly beneficial and recommended that you make an opening statement to the immigration judge. If you do not, you may want to ask the applicant a question at the beginning of the hearing that allows the applicant to provide an overview of the case.

Concluding

End both your direct and re-direct with the strongest aspects of the applicant's claim.

Weak Points

Often it is helpful to address the weak points of the applicant's claim in your direct examination. If weak points are revealed only during cross-examination, the immigration judge may believe the applicant is evasive or dishonest.

Voluntary Departure

Ask voluntary departure questions at the beginning of the hearing, never at the end. Remember, it's better to end with the strongest points regarding the applicant's claim.

Cross-Examination

In asking the applicant anticipated cross-examination questions, always include questions that contain mistakes regarding the applicant's previous testimony. Advise the applicant of the importance of correcting such errors. Also, during the mock hearing, it is useful for the applicant to practice correcting these errors.

Emotional and Physical Harm

Ask questions not only about the events surrounding the applicant's claim, but also about the emotional and physical state of the applicant before, during, and after such events. It is important for the immigration judge to understand the trauma an individual may experience from witnessing such an event or its aftermath.

Positive and Negative Discretionary Factors

Asylum is a discretionary form of relief. An individual who meets the definition of refugee may be denied asylum at the discretion of the immigration judge. Generally, only the most egregious adverse factors should result in an asylum denial. It is imperative that positive discretionary factors, such as the presence of family members lawfully in the United States; letters from employers, co-workers, houses of worship, volunteer work, teachers, and neighbors; grades from school or classes the applicant and the applicant's children are attending.

Objections

Advise the applicant that the DHS attorney may ask questions that are improper or irrelevant. Instruct the applicant that if an objection is made, the applicant should not answer the question until the matter is resolved by the immigration judge. If the applicant does not speak English, explain prior to the hearing that there may be untranslated discussions regarding questions, documents, or witnesses, and that these discussions are a normal part of the hearing.

Organization

In most cases, the best way to organize questions is chronologically. There may be cases, however, where a different order is preferable, especially if applicant fears more than one persecutor. For example, if the applicant fears both the government and a nongovernmental actor, it may be best to organize questions chronologically, but separately, regarding each persecutor that the applicant fears.

Follow-Up Questions

An applicant may forget to mention a fact or detail of his or her claim while testifying. Make sure to ask non-leading follow-up questions during the direct and re-direct examination to elicit this information from the applicant. Practice this beforehand! It's hard not to be leading when your client has left out a small, but vital piece of information.

Comprehension

Applicants sometimes have difficulty understanding the immigration judge or DHS trial attorney because of their manner of speaking or the vocabulary they use. Advise the applicant that he or she should never answer a question that he or she does not understand. The applicant can ask that a question be repeated or rephrased. If an interpreter is being used, instruct the applicant to inform the immigration judge if he or she has difficulty understanding the interpreter.

DIRECT EXAMINATION OF THE APPLICANT

The Beginning—Simple Questions

Simple questions at the start of your direct examination will put the applicant at ease and allow him or her to become accustomed to answering questions in court. If an interpreter is used, these questions will allow the applicant to become accustomed to the accent and speech patterns of the interpreter, as well.

- Please state your full name.
- Where were you born?
- Are you a citizen of ______?

- How old are you?
- When were you born?
- Are you married?
- Where does your spouse live?
- How many children do you have?
- How old are they?
- Where do your children live?

Thorny Issues

Address the thornier issues in the case near the beginning of the direct examination, if possible. As noted above, it is better to save the stronger portions of the claim for later. Thorny issues that may arise in asylum claims include:

- Manner of entry into the United States (*e.g.*, use of false documents, the use of documents fraudulently obtained, or illegal entry);
- Eligibility for voluntary departure;
- Criminal convictions (in addition to questions regarding crimes and sentences, ask the applicant about his or her efforts toward rehabilitation and feelings of remorse for past actions);
- Reasons for remaining in or returning to the country of claimed persecution;
- Lack of corroborating evidence. Note: if the applicant lacks proof of his or her identity, membership in a political party, or other aspect of his or her claim, the applicant must explain why he or she has been unable to obtain such evidence or why it would be unreasonable to attempt to obtain it.

The Middle—The Heart of the Claim

To begin this part of the direct examination, ask the applicant, "Why did you come to the United States?" or "Why did you leave your home country?" The applicant should begin with a brief summary of his or her claim, such as: *I came to the United States because I feared that I would be killed by the government because I am a member of _________, a religious minority, and I was an outspoken opponent of the government.* Then the applicant should be asked questions that elicit a chronological account of the harm he or she suffered and/or why he or she has a well-founded fear of persecution.

- Details matter! Ask probing questions so that the applicant provides as much detail as possible. Make sure, however, that you also ask these questions prior to the hearing so that you are not surprised in court by the applicant's responses.
- Be creative! Applicants who have difficulty remembering dates could establish approximate dates by providing details regarding the season, political events, religious celebrations, or even the ages of their children.

- Listen! Make sure that you, the interpreter, the DHS attorney, or the immigration judge do not inadvertently cut off the applicant's testimony. Always ask whether the applicant has any further comments if an interruption takes place.

The End—The Lasting Impression

End your direct examination with a summary of the strongest points of the applicant's claim. Sometimes this may be done by asking questions such as:

- Why did you leave your home country?
- Who or what did you leave behind?
- Have you been affected physically and emotionally by what has happened to you in your home country?
- In what way?

Applicants who have experienced or witnessed traumatic events may continue to experience emotional, as well as physical effects. If so, such applicants should also be referred for treatment. *See* appendix 6H for a list of treatment centers. It is also important to ask the applicant at or near the end of the direct examination:

- What do you think will happen to you if you are returned to your home country?
- Why?

Humanize your client. Let the immigration judge know what a responsible, respectable, honorable person she is. Does she help out in her neighborhood, church, school, or community? Is she a good mother? What activities does she do with her children? Is she attending classes? What are her future plans if she remains here? The DHS attorney might object that such questions are not relevant, but they are. They are relevant to whether the applicant merits asylum as a matter of discretion and most judges not only allow them, but are very interested in and swayed by the responses.

CROSS-EXAMINATION OF THE APPLICANT

In an effort to determine whether the applicant is eligible for or deserving of asylum or withholding of removal, the DHS attorney may ask the applicant questions regarding:

Family Members Who Have Remained in the Applicant's Home Country

If the applicant has family members who live in his or her home country, the applicant should indicate how the applicant's situation is different than that of his or her family members (if this is so) or provide information regarding why his or her family members have remained and the problems or difficulties, if any, they are experiencing.

Failure to Report Crimes or Abuses to the Police or Other Governmental Authority

If the applicant suffered harm in his or her home country, but failed to report it to the police, he or she will need to explain why. Was the applicant afraid of the authorities or would such a report have been futile or dangerous? These are areas that need to be explored when questioning the applicant prior to the hearing and addressed during direct examination.

Economic Reasons for Coming to the United States

The applicant may have chosen the United States as a country of refuge for a variety of reasons. The applicant may have friends or family members in the United States, or a desire to further his or her education, or he or she may have chosen the United States because of the freedoms enjoyed by its residents. It is also well known that may immigrants come to the United States to work. The applicant may have chosen the United States for any one or all of these reasons. If the applicant also came here believing that he or she would be able to find a job, in addition to fleeing the harm he or she experienced, the applicant should be truthful and acknowledge this. In answering, however, the applicant should reiterate the primary motive for leaving his or her home country.

Lack of Political Activity

Even though the applicant may not have been politically active in his or her home country, the applicant may still be eligible for asylum based on a political opinion imputed to him or her, or because of his or her race, religion, nationality, or membership in a particular social group. When the applicant is questioned about a lack of political activity, he or she should reiterate the basis for the asylum claim.

Failure to Mention an Event or Detail on the Asylum Application

When completing the asylum application, it is often useful to provide as many details as possible regarding the applicant's claim. Nevertheless, at the hearing, the applicant may (and almost always does) mention a fact or detail not included in the application. In response to a question by the DHS attorney regarding why the applicant failed to mention it on his or her asylum application, the applicant should offer an explanation. Was the applicant previously uncomfortable in speaking about a particular aspect of his or her claim? Did the applicant tell you and you decided to leave it out of the application? Or did the applicant, in preparing for the hearing, begin to remember more aspects and details regarding a particular event?

Inconsistencies in the Applicant's Testimony or Between the Testimony and the Application

We all make mistakes, but such mistakes could be fatal (literally) if they involve a material fact in the applicant's claim. Under the REAL ID Act, even minor inconsistencies that do not go to the heart of the asylum applicant can be used to establish an applicant is not credible. Does the applicant have difficulty remembering? If so, the applicant should emphasize when answering questions that he or she has difficulty remembering and that the answers given are based on his or her recollection or are approximations. If the applicant makes a mistake when testifying on his or her application, the applicant should state this in his or her answer. Individuals who have experienced or witnessed traumatic events may have difficulty remembering. If applicant is experiencing memory problems, you may wish to refer him or her for treatment. *See* appendix 12B. Applicants should also be advised that if the DHS attorney misstates their previous testimony or their statement on the application, they should correct such mistakes in their response.

Country Conditions

The applicant should be made aware of the country condition information submitted in his or her case. He or she also usually has firsthand knowledge of conditions in his or her country. Sometimes, however, the DHS attorney will ask a question that the applicant is unable to answer. The applicant should be instructed not to guess, and, if he or she is asked to guess, an objection should be made.

Misstatements Made upon Entry

The applicant may have made misstatements to a U.S. Embassy official or an airport inspector or border patrol agent when he or she was apprehended. He or she may have made misrepresentations regarding his or her country of origin or reasons for coming to the United States. The applicant needs to explain why he or she made such statements. Occasionally, an applicant will claim that he or she did not make the misrepresentations that DHS claims were made. In such cases, it is important to request the opportunity to question the officer who reported that the applicant made such statements.

Failure to Apply for Asylum in Other Countries

Applicants may be questioned regarding whether they applied for asylum in any countries that they passed through en route to the United States. If the applicant did not apply in such countries, he or she will be asked why. Many applicants are unaware of asylum procedures in other countries or have fled their home countries with the intention of being reunited with friends and family members in the United States. The applicant should state his or her reasons for failing to apply in the countries he or she resided in or traveled through on the way to the United States.

Failure to Immediately Depart from the Country of Claimed Persecution

The applicant may have remained in his or her home country for several months or longer after he or she was harmed or threatened. It is important for the applicant to state when he or she decided to leave, the steps taken in arranging to leave, and the difficulties encountered in planning to leave.

Failure to Present Corroborating Evidence

The REAL ID Act imposes an even greater burden on the applicant to produce corroborating evidence in support of his or her claim. Often, it is unreasonable to expect the applicant to contact his or her home government, which has engaged in persecution, to corroborate the claim. Many times, individuals flee with little or nothing to prove their claim. The applicant should state any attempts made to locate corroborating evidence and, if no steps were taken, why it would be unreasonable to expect corroboration.

Manner of Entry

The applicant's manner of entry is almost always an issue in an asylum case. Did he or she enter legally on a valid passport? If so, DHS will argue either that the government is not really after the applicant because it would not have issued him or her a passport to leave the country or that the applicant committed fraud by telling a consular official overseas that he or she was coming to study or to visit as a tourist. Is the applicant better off in the eyes of DHS if he or she entered with a false passport and visa? Not really. DHS will argue that this is a person who lied to DHS inspectors at the airport to get into the United States and is probably lying now. What if the applicant resorted to using the services of a smuggler? DHS will ask detailed questions about the amount the applicant paid the smuggler and whether the smuggler informed him or her about what to say when seeking asylum. If the applicant is a victim of human traffickers, however, he or she may be eligible for a form of relief under the Victims of Trafficking and Violence Protection Act. *See* chapter 16.

APPENDIX 51

TESTIMONY TIPS FOR THE RESPONDENT AND WITNESSES

Proper preparation of the applicant and his or her witnesses is essential to the success of any asylum, withholding of removal, or Convention Against Torture claim before the immigration court. In addition to carefully crafting and reviewing direct examination questions and cross-examination topics with the applicant and witnesses, however, it is also important to discuss the below concepts with each individual.

1. **Always tell the truth.** While this might seem obvious, the truth is the most important ingredient for success. You are representing your client because you believe he or she is eligible for the relief sought. The facts of your client's case and your client's credible presentation are the most powerful evidence you have. It is essential that your client remember the importance of being truthful and credible during his or her hearing.

2. **Make eye contact with and direct answers to whoever is asking the questions**, whether it is you, the Judge, or the government attorney.

3. **Listen very carefully to the question asked and answer that exact question in a clear and convincing way.** Your client must provide complete and honest answers to the questions asked, while keeping his or her answers simple and clear. He or she should use persuasive language and say his or her answers with conviction. Your client should not ramble or provide information that is not relevant to the exact question asked.

4. **Be polite and persistent in answering the DHS attorney's questions.** The DHS attorney might ask your client questions in a manner that seems rude or aggressive. He or she may also seem as if he or she does not believe your client. Remember that no matter what, your client needs to answer the question asked in a truthful, polite, and courteous way. Even if the DHS attorney is not being respectful, your client needs to be respectful. Getting frustrated or defensive can only hurt your client's credibility and his or her case. The DHS attorney might also ask your client a question multiple times by using different wording in an attempt to get your client to say something that might hurt his or her case. Your client should not be afraid to stand his or her ground and give the same answer multiple times.

5. **Ask for questions to be repeated if necessary.** If your client does not understand a question or if he or she needs a question repeated, he or she should politely notify the court that he or she did not understand the question or politely request that the question be repeated.

6. **Don't play the guessing game.** If your client does not know the answer to a question, it is better for him or her to say "I don't know" or "I don't remember" than to try to guess or make something up.

7. **Understand the law.** Your client should keep in mind the main points of his or her testimony throughout all of his or her answers. Make sure your client understands the legal elements that need to be proved for him or her to be granted relief.

8. **Know the evidence.** Remind your client that you prepared a detailed packet of exhibits to support his or her application(s) for relief from removal. He or she should have been provided with a copy of those documents. It is essential that your client is familiar with all of the documents submitted on his or her behalf. This is especially true of his or her sworn declaration. The judge will evaluate his or her credibility by comparing his/her live testimony with what he or she has said in the statement. Thus your client must be thoroughly familiar with his or her statement. If there are any inaccuracies or discrepancies in the sworn declaration, you should ask your client to bring them to your attention BEFORE the hearing, so you can amend it as necessary.

9. **Remember that this is just a conversation.** Your client will be nervous, because it is natural to be nervous. Keep in mind that your client is there to provide the information asked, nothing more.

10. **Trust yourself and your attorney.** Remind your client about all the preparation you have done together and the documentary evidence you have submitted. Your client should trust that detailed testimony will be his or her best evidence, especially when it fits in nicely with the evidence previously submitted. Remind your client of your role in the proceedings: You cannot answer questions for your client, but you are there to: (1) make sure the most important facts are on the record; (2) help clarify questions or ambiguities; (3) draw the judge's attention to the documentary evidence; (4) protect your client's rights and object to anything improper by the DHS attorney; and (5) give your client confidence.

APPENDIX 5J

OBJECTIONS IN IMMIGRATION COURT

The following is a list of common objections used in immigration court and tips for using these objections throughout the course of an immigration court hearing. Making objections is an essential aspect of zealous advocacy; objecting on the record of proceedings protects clients' rights and maintains any violations of those rights as issues for appeal. Relevance and fundamental fairness are the principal evidentiary concerns in immigration court. Therefore, even though the Federal Rules of Evidence, which are based on these principles of relevance and fairness, are not binding in immigration court, they are guiding. If DHS seeks to admit evidence that has no probative value or asks questions that are not relevant to the issues in question, object! If the admission of DHS's evidence would deprive the respondent of due process or if DHS's form or manner of questioning is not consistent with a fundamental fairness, object! If DHS or the immigration judge moves for the respondent's documentary or testimonial evidence to be kept out of the record, object! *See* chapter 4.

TIPS FOR RESPONDING TO DHS OBJECTIONS TO RESPONDENT'S DOCUMENTARY OR TESTIMONIAL EVIDENCE

1. **Directly address the specific concern noted by DHS/the immigration judge.**
2. **Keeping the evidence out violates the Respondent's right to present evidence on his or her own behalf.**
   - INA §240(b)(4)(B); 8 CFR §1240.10(a)(4).
3. **The evidence is material to the Respondent's claim. Keeping it out violates fundamental fairness and deprives the Respondent of due process.**
   - Due process requires a full and fair hearing on claims and without this documentation or testimony on the record, this is not a full and fair hearing.
   - *See Matter of Toro*, 17 I&N Dec. 340 (BIA 1980); *Matter of Ramirez-Sanchez*, 17 I&N Dec. 503 (BIA 1980); *Matter of Lam*, 14 I&N Dec. 168 (BIA 1972).

TIPS FOR OBJECTING TO DHS EVIDENCE

1. **Object to the evidence and seek to keep it out of the record.**
   - Cite legal authority → the Immigration and Nationality Act, federal regulations, *Immigration Court Practice Manual*, and case law (see below).
   - When all else fails, argue that due process requires a full and fair hearing; the admission of the evidence would violate fundamental fairness.

2. **If the immigration judge admits the evidence.**
   - Request a continuance (if it is damaging and time is needed to prepare a response).
   - Request that the evidence be given less weight.

OBJECTIONS TO DHS EVIDENCE

FUNDAMENTAL FAIRNESS = THE GOLDEN RULE OF EVIDENCE IN IMMIGRATION COURT – if use of the evidence is not consistent with a fair hearing or would deprive the Respondent of due process

- *See Matter of Toro*, 17 I&N Dec. 340 (BIA 1980); *Matter of Ramirez-Sanchez*, 17 I&N Dec. 503 (BIA 1980); *Matter of Lam*, 14 I&N Dec. 168 (BIA 1972).
- Due process requires a full and fair hearing on claims. *See, e.g., Rusu v. INS*, 296 F.3d 316, 321-22 (4th Cir. 2002).

RELEVANCE – if the evidence does not have probative value for the facts/issues in dispute

- Along with fundamental fairness, this is the only other bar to admissibility of evidence in immigration court. *See Matter of Ponce-Hernandez*, 22 I&N Dec. 784 (BIA 1999).

FOUNDATION – if DHS has not established the basis on which a document is supported

AUTHENTICATION – if DHS has not submitted evidence the document is what it claims to be

- Copies of official records submitted? → Must have attestation by the officer who has legal custody of the original and must be accompanied by a certification that it is a true copy of the document. *See* 8 CFR §1287.6(a).
- Official records submitted? → Must establish chain of custody.
- Certain documents are self-authenticating (certified copies of public records, statutes printed by a public authority, etc.).

RIGHT TO REVIEW AND RESPOND TO EVIDENCE – if DHS evidence is not reviewable, is illegible, or is not translated, or if evidence submitted late by DHS

- Right to review and respond to evidence presented against him or her → INA §240(b)(4)(B); 8 CFR §1240.10(a)(4).
- Late filing? → Immigration Court Practice Manual requires timely filing (unless submitted for impeachment purposes only). *See* ICPM 3.1(b)(ii)(A), 4.16(a)(i). Also notes right to sufficient time to review and respond to evidence. *See* ICPM 3.1(d)(ii).

RIGHT TO CROSS EXAMINE WITNESSES – if the affiant or creator of the document in question is not present for cross examination

- Right to cross-examine witnesses → INA §242(b)(3); 8 CFR §1240.10(a)(14).

EVIDENCE OBTAINED UNLAWFULLY / IN VIOLATION OF THE CONSTITUTION – if the evidence was obtained in violation of applicable laws, including the Constitution, the Respondent may move to suppress that evidence

- 4th Amendment prohibition against unlawful search and seizure ("the exclusionary rule") → usually only if there is widespread abuse or egregious violations which transgress notions of fundamental fairness. *See INS v. Lopez-Mendoza*, 468 U.S. 1032 (1984).
- 5th Amendment due process clause → if evidence obtained by coercion or other activity that violates due process. *See Matter of Toro*, 17 I&N Dec. 340 (BIA 1980).
- Statutory or regulatory violations → if the actors violated the requirements of the INA and federal regulations in obtaining the evidence in question

OBJECTIONS TO DHS QUESTIONS/ANSWERS SOUGHT

RELEVANCE – if the information sought has no probative value for the facts/issues in dispute

FOUNDATION – if DHS asks about something they assume witness has personal knowledge of

COMPOUND – if DHS asks two or more questions within the framework of a single question, so it is not clear which part the witness is answering

CONFUSING, AMBIGUOUS, MISLEADING – if a question not posed in a clear and precise manner so that the witness knows with certainty what information is being sought

OVERLY BROAD – if the answer to DHS's question will permit the introduction of just about anything into the hearing; witness needs to know with certainty what information is sought

MISQUOTES A WITNESS OR EXHIBIT/MISCHARACTERIZES TESTIMONY – if DHS changes a few words and then asks the witness to affirm the misstatement; if DHS misquotes or mischaracterizes what a witness or exhibit says

ARGUMENTATIVE – if DHS states a conclusion and then asks the witness to argue with it, usually in an attempt to get the witness to change their mind

ASKED AND ANSWERED – if DHS asks the same thing again and again, even if rephrasing, in an attempt get the witness to answer differently

PRIVILEGED – if DHS seeks information that is subject to attorney/client privilege or the witness's 5th Amendment privilege against self-incrimination

SPECULATION – if DHS asks the witness to guess or address a hypothetical; if DHS asks for information that is not based on witness's first-hand knowledge

IMPROPER OPINION – if DHS asks for an opinion or answer to a hypothetical where the witness is not qualified as an expert on that subject

COMPETENCY OF WITNESS – if the witness isn't qualified as an expert on that subject; if the witness lacks personal knowledge about the subject; if the witness was not able to observe/remember/communicate that information

APPENDIX 5K

UNDERSTANDING WITHHOLDING OF REMOVAL

Practice Pointer: Understanding Withholding of Removal
By Cheri Attix, AILA Asylum and Refugee Liaison Committee
Updated April 2, 2014

Withholding of Removal under INA section 241(b)(3) is perhaps the most misunderstood form of relief that can be granted in immigration court. While it is an important form of protection for a client who fears persecution in his home country, it is not merely a lesser form of asylum and should not be approached as such. Offers by government counsel to stipulate to withholding in lieu of asylum seem to be more and more common. These should be considered very carefully, as should any decision not to appeal a denial of asylum when withholding has been granted. The information in this advisory should be thoroughly considered and explained to the client before any decision to "just take withholding" is made. Even when withholding is the only viable option, lack of a clear understanding of the differences between asylum and withholding of removal can place your client's life or his family members' lives in danger.

This advisory does not address the legal differences in eligibility or burden of proof between asylum and withholding of removal. These are easily found in the law and regulations. It focuses instead on the main conceptual and practical differences between the two forms of relief and how a grant of withholding will affect your client going forward.

What is Withholding of Removal?

Many practitioners think of withholding of removal as simply a more limited and difficult to obtain version of asylum. It is easy to see where one could get that impression since the regulations governing the burden of proof for both asylum and withholding of removal are found at 8 CFR § 208 *et seq*. It is a mistake, however, to think of withholding in this way. It is a very different form of relief.

We see how different it is when we look at the actual section of the law that provides for withholding of removal. This law is found at INA § 241(b)(3), in the section of the Act dealing with the "detention and removal of aliens ordered removed" from the United States. 8 U.S.C. § 1231(b)(3). As the title of the code section suggests, before granting withholding of removal, the immigration judge is required to issue an order of removal. Matter of I-S- & C-S-, 24 I & N Dec. 432 (BIA 2008). This order is then "withheld" pursuant to INA § 241(b)(3), which provides that, "the Attorney General may not remove an alien to a country if the Attorney General decides that the alien's life or freedom would be threatened in that country because of the alien's race, religion, nationality, membership in a social group or political opinion." Id.

The provision for withholding of removal is the codification of the requirement of *non-refoulement* under the United Nations Convention and Protocol Relating to the Status of

Refugees.[1] 189 U.N.T.S. 137, done on July 28, 1951 and entered into force April 22, 1954; 606 U.N.T.S. 267, 6 I.L.M. 78 (1967). *Non-refoulement* is a fancy (and shorter) way of saying "not returning someone to persecution." As a signatory to the Refugee Convention and Protocol, the United States has an international obligation to avoid *refoulement*, but we do not have an international obligation to do anything more.[2] An alien granted withholding of removal is merely granted protection from return to the country or countries where he has demonstrated that his life or freedom would be threatened. This alien is not resettled; he cannot sponsor a spouse or children; and is not given any lawful immigration status *per se*. Asylum, in contrast, is actual resettlement. We allow asylees to sponsor their spouses and children; and we give them a legal status that can eventually lead to U.S. citizenship.

For those aliens who are undesirable as immigrants—those who have committed disqualifying crimes or are otherwise undeserving of discretion[3]—withholding allows the United States to comply with its obligation of *non-refoulement*, but at the same time, to exercise some measure of control over whether or not it allows resettlement. Withholding of removal is, therefore, the minimum protection that the United States is obligated to offer bona fide refugees under the Refugee Convention and Protocol.

The differences in benefits between asylum and withholding are well known: unlike an asylee, a person granted withholding of removal cannot sponsor her spouse and children, cannot obtain a refugee travel document, and cannot apply for permanent residence. There are other differences, however, that not as well understood. Explaining those differences is the purpose of this advisory.

1. Withholding is not Derivative

This is a corollary of not being able to sponsor a spouse and children, but until relatively recently it was not widely recognized as an issue in immigration court. Several recent circuit court cases, however, have upheld removal orders against the spouses and children of aliens who had been granted withholding of removal in the same proceedings. Saval v. Holder, 623 F.3d 664, 671 (9th Cir. 2010); Cendrawasih v. Holder, 571 F.3d 128, 131 (1st Cir. 2009); Arif v. Mukasey, 509 F.3d 677, 680-82 (5th Cir. 2007); Delgado v. Att'y Gen. of the U.S., 487 F.3d 855, 862 (11th Cir. 2007). The courts have emphasized that spouses and children who are in removal proceedings cannot be granted withholding of removal as derivatives. In each of these cases, the attorney had

[1] In a slightly different form, withholding of removal (under former section 243(h) of the INA) actually pre-dates the U.N. Convention and Protocol. When Congress passed the Refugee Act in 1980, thereby implementing the U.N. Convention and Protocol, the language of section 243(h) was brought into conformity with the Article 33 of the Convention. See, INS v. Stevic, 467 U.S. 407 (1984). INA section 243(h) was later re-designated section 241(b)(3).

[2] Article 33, clause 1 of the Convention simply states: "No Contracting State shall expel or return ("refouler") a refugee in any manner whatsoever to the frontiers of territories where his life or freedom would be threatened on account of his race, religion, nationality, membership in a social group or political opinion."

[3] Since 1998, the one-year filing deadline has resulted in many asylum applicants being granted only withholding of removal, not because they were undeserving of asylum or undesirable as immigrants, but simply because they were tardy in filing their asylum applications.

failed to file a separate I-589 and request withholding of removal for each family member in proceedings.

<u>Practice Pointer:</u> In order to prevent your client's family from being ordered removed without her, it is necessary to file a separate I-589 for each family member in any case where the principal's eligibility for asylum is in question on any basis.[4] These I-589s should not be confused with the copies of the principal's I-589 that you would normally provide. They are separate applications requesting withholding of removal in each family member's name.

2. Other Countries of Removal

Withholding of removal is country specific. This means that the removal order is only withheld with regard to the specific country or countries where the immigration judge has determined that the alien's life or freedom would be threatened. If there is an alternative country to which the alien can be removed where her life or freedom would not be threatened, the removal order can be executed to that alternative country notwithstanding the order granting withholding of removal. In other words, a grant of withholding of removal only protects the alien from being removed to the country where she is in danger; it does not protect her from removal to any other country. For example, let's say that a citizen of Azerbaijan demonstrates that his life or freedom would be threatened if he were returned to Azerbaijan. The immigration judge must order that his removal to Azerbaijan be withheld. However, if this person was born in Russia, the immigration judge could order that he be removed to Russia in the alternative. He is thus protected from return to Azerbaijan, but he is also removed from the United States.

Unlike asylum, withholding can be granted with regard to *any* country that the alien might be removed to, not just the country of nationality (or, if stateless, the country of last residence). If the alien would face a threat to his or her life or freedom in an alternative country of removal that has been designated by the Immigration Judge, she can and must request and argue for withholding of removal to that country *as well as* to her country of nationality.

The list of countries to which aliens can be removed is found at INA sections 241(b)(1)&(2); 8 U.S.C. § 1231(b)(1)&(2). The list begins with the country of citizenship and continues to the country of birth, country of residence, and several countries to which the alien may have no ties at all, including the "country in which is located the foreign port from which the alien left for the United States." The subsection to be most concerned about is (b)(2)(E)(i)-(vi), which lists the countries that are least likely to accept a returned alien. While the other subsections require that the United States obtain the country's advance approval before removal goes forward, the Supreme Court has held that there is no requirement that the country of removal be notified or consent to accept the alien before removal to a country listed in 8 USC §1231(b)(2)(E)(i)-(vi) takes place. <u>Jama v. Immigration and Customs Enforcement</u>, 543 U.S. 335 (2005). <u>See</u>, 8 CFR § 241.15. The only protection an alien has from removal to those countries is a grant of

[4] The Asylum Office does not have jurisdiction to grant withholding of removal, so it is not necessary to file additional separate I-589s for family members when filing affirmatively. If the case is referred to the immigration court, the separate I-589s can be filed at the first master calendar.

withholding of removal or a determination by the immigration judge that removal would be "impracticable, inadvisable or impossible." 8 USC §1231(b)(2)(E)(vii).

Practice Pointer: If the alien does not have a viable argument for withholding of removal to an alternative country of removal that the immigration judge has designated, it is up to the practitioner to point out to the immigration judge why removal to an alternative country designated under 8 USC §1231(b)(2)(E)(i)-(vi) would be "impracticable, inadvisable or impossible." See, Jama, *supra*, at 342; Mendis v. Filip, 554 F.3d 335, 340 n. 5 (2nd Cir. 2009). Practitioners should be prepared to make these arguments on the record and/or brief and document the issue.

It is important to remember that an alternative order of removal to any country designated under 8 USC §1231(b)(2)(E)(i)-(vi) may result in your client being refused admission to the designated country and summarily deported by that country to the country where she faces persecution. Arguably, placing an alien in this situation is a violation of the obligation of *non-refoulement* because, although the United States itself does not remove the alien to the country where he or she would face a threat to her life or freedom, it puts her in the position of being *refouled* by a third country. If your client is removed to an alternative country and that country refuses to admit him when he gets there, the United States has no legal obligation to return him to the United States.

Practice Pointer: Beware of government counsel who suggest the designation of alternative countries for removal at the master calendar. If alternative countries are designated by the judge during pleadings, make sure that you address the issue of withholding of removal to these alternative countries (and if that argument is not strong, the issue of impracticality, inadvisability or impossibility) in your evidence, your brief to the court, and your client's testimony. Make a strong record and do not fail to appeal an alternative order of removal even if withholding is granted.

3. Removal Order

Assuming there is no alternative country for removal, the judge will still enter a removal order to your client's country of citizenship before withholding is granted. Although this order will not be executed, the mere existence of a removal order is a hugely complicating factor that affects your client's life in several important ways.

a. Documentation

When an applicant is granted withholding of removal by an immigration judge, he or she will have only the order issued by the immigration court. The local U.S. Citizenship and Immigration Service (USCIS) office will not issue any sort of documentation because withholding isn't considered an immigration status per se. The court's order will also, confusingly, state that the person is ordered removed to his home country in addition to the fact that withholding was granted. When your client shows the order to a social security office, a school, a landlord, a bank, or a potential employer as proof of his immigration status, he will typically be met with confusion and a demand that better documentation be provided before any further transaction can commence.

Practice Pointer: As a practitioner, you should be prepared to provide your client with a letter explaining what withholding is, and why no better documentation of status can be provided. A warning that discrimination on the basis of immigration status is prohibited and punishable by federal law may also be necessary.

Fortunately, those granted withholding of removal are eligible to apply for an Employment Authorization Document or EAD (also known as a work permit), which will at least give them an actual document. But, the EAD will not state that withholding of removal has been granted. It will only show category (a)(10). Having a card helps somewhat; but for laymen in the community who are not familiar with the EAD codes, the card does not typically clear up all the confusion. Additionally, the EAD must be obtained every year; and if it expires before the new card is issued, the client is left without any photo ID showing lawful presence in the interim.

b. Order of Supervision

Because those granted withholding of removal are first ordered removed, they may be placed on orders of supervision with Immigration and Customs Enforcement (ICE). Conceptually, an order of supervision is best thought of as "immigration probation." The client is required to check in with an ICE deportation officer on a regular basis, keep the officer apprised of any change in address or employment, and notify the deportation officer prior to leaving the state. Typically, the frequency of check-ins decreases over time for withholding grantees, but the order of supervision remains until, and unless, it is cancelled by ICE. This represents a significant restriction on your client's freedom of movement.

c. Inability to Travel Abroad

An applicant who has been granted withholding of removal is protected from removal by the United States government to the country where her life or freedom would be threatened, but she can self-execute the removal order if she leaves the United States on her own. The grant of withholding gives her no right to return to the United States if she leaves. And, once gone, the removal order means that before she could return on a non-immigrant or immigrant visa, she would either have to wait 5 to 10 years or seek permission to re-apply for admission by filing an I-212 waiver. INA 212(a)(9)(A). Additionally, if the applicant had more than six months of unlawful presence prior to filing her I-589[5], leaving the United States will trigger either the 3- or 10-year bar at INA 212(a)(9)(B).

[5] "No period of time in which an alien has a bona fide application for asylum pending under INA section 208 shall be taken into account in determining the period of unlawful presence in the United States unless the alien worked without authorization during that period." INA 212(a)(9)(B)(iii)(II).

d. Future Opportunities to Immigrate

Aliens who have been granted withholding of removal often come back to you years later after getting married to U.S. citizens. They want to adjust status, but you still have to deal with that removal order. If your client was not charged as an arriving alien,[6] she will have to reopen her immigration court case before she can proceed. If this occurs more than 90 days after the removal order, you will have to pursue a joint motion with your local Office of Chief Counsel to reopen the case. Depending on how cooperative your local Chief Counsel is, this may be easy or impossible. If Chief Counsel refuses to join a motion to reopen, your only remaining option is to file a motion asking the judge to reopen proceedings *sua sponte*.

If your client was never admitted or paroled into the United States prior to being granted withholding of removal, she will likely[7] not be eligible for adjustment of status, even if the case were reopened. Consular processing is the only option. Even if she was admitted or paroled, if a motion to reopen is unsuccessful, she will still have to leave the United States to consular process. This becomes extremely risky because once she leaves the United States, the removal order will be self-executed. The bar at INA 212(a)(9)(A) will have to be waived if she wants to immigrate without remaining abroad for 5 to 10 years.

Any other bars to admission will also have to be waived before your client can immigrate to the United States through consular processing. If there was unlawful presence, the 3- or 10-year bars at INA 212(a)(9)(B) will have to be waived. Your client may also be inadmissible for misrepresentation under INA 212(a)(6)(C)(i). Asylum applicants often use false documents to try to enter the United States. This is generally not a bar to the granting of asylum or withholding, but immigration through a spouse or other family member is a different matter. Clients who additionally require a waiver for misrepresentation run the risk of being found permanently inadmissible if the waiver is not granted. INA 212(a)(6)(C)(i). Those who may have misrepresented themselves as U.S. citizens, either at entry or otherwise, do not even have a waiver available. INA 212(a)(6)(C)(ii). They are permanently barred from immigrating to the United States. Id.

Practice Pointer: Before even considering consular processing for a client who was granted withholding, thoroughly review all potential grounds of inadmissibility and whether your client will be eligible for the appropriate waiver(s).

If the immigrant visa is denied at the consulate abroad, there is no way to re-enter the United States based on the former grant of withholding.

[6] The immigration court lacks jurisdiction over the adjustment of status of arriving aliens. 8 CFR § 1245.2(a)(ii). If your client was charged as an arriving alien, you can apply directly to USCIS for adjustment of status without having to reopen the removal proceedings. If your client is granted adjustment of status by USCIS, you can then move for termination of the removal order by the immigration court.

[7] There do not appear to be any published cases addressing the issue of whether a grant of withholding of removal is considered an admission. However, the BIA recently decided that a grant of *asylum* was not an admission to the United States under INA section 101(a)(13)(A). Matter of V-X-, 26 I&N Dec. 147 (BIA 2013).

AILA InfoNet Doc. No. 14021344. (Posted 4/2/14)

Conclusion

In many cases, withholding is a good result. It protects your client from return to the country where she fears persecution and allows her to remain in the United States indefinitely with the right to work and receive certain public benefits. It is not the easiest status to live with, however, so make sure that there truly is no better alternative before accepting an offer to stipulate to withholding or waiving an appeal when asylum has been denied. Beware also of alternative countries of removal and always make sure that every family member has his or her own I-589 if there is any question of the principal's asylum eligibility.

AILA InfoNet Doc. No. 14021344. (Posted 4/2/14)

APPENDIX 5L

FLOWCHART OF EXPEDITED REMOVAL/CREDIBLE FEAR PROCESS

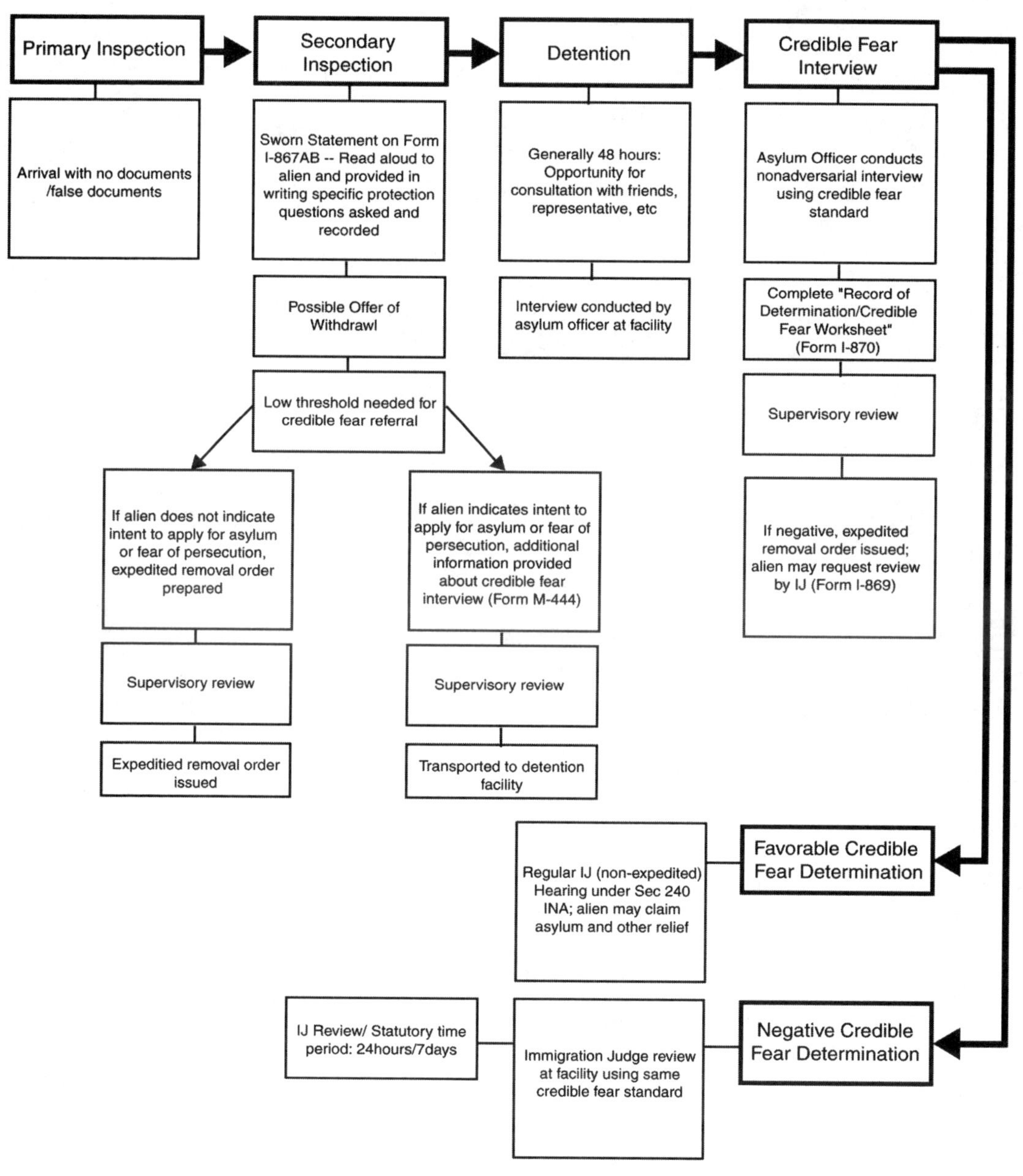

APPENDIX 6A

FLOWCHART OF IMMIGRATION DETENTION

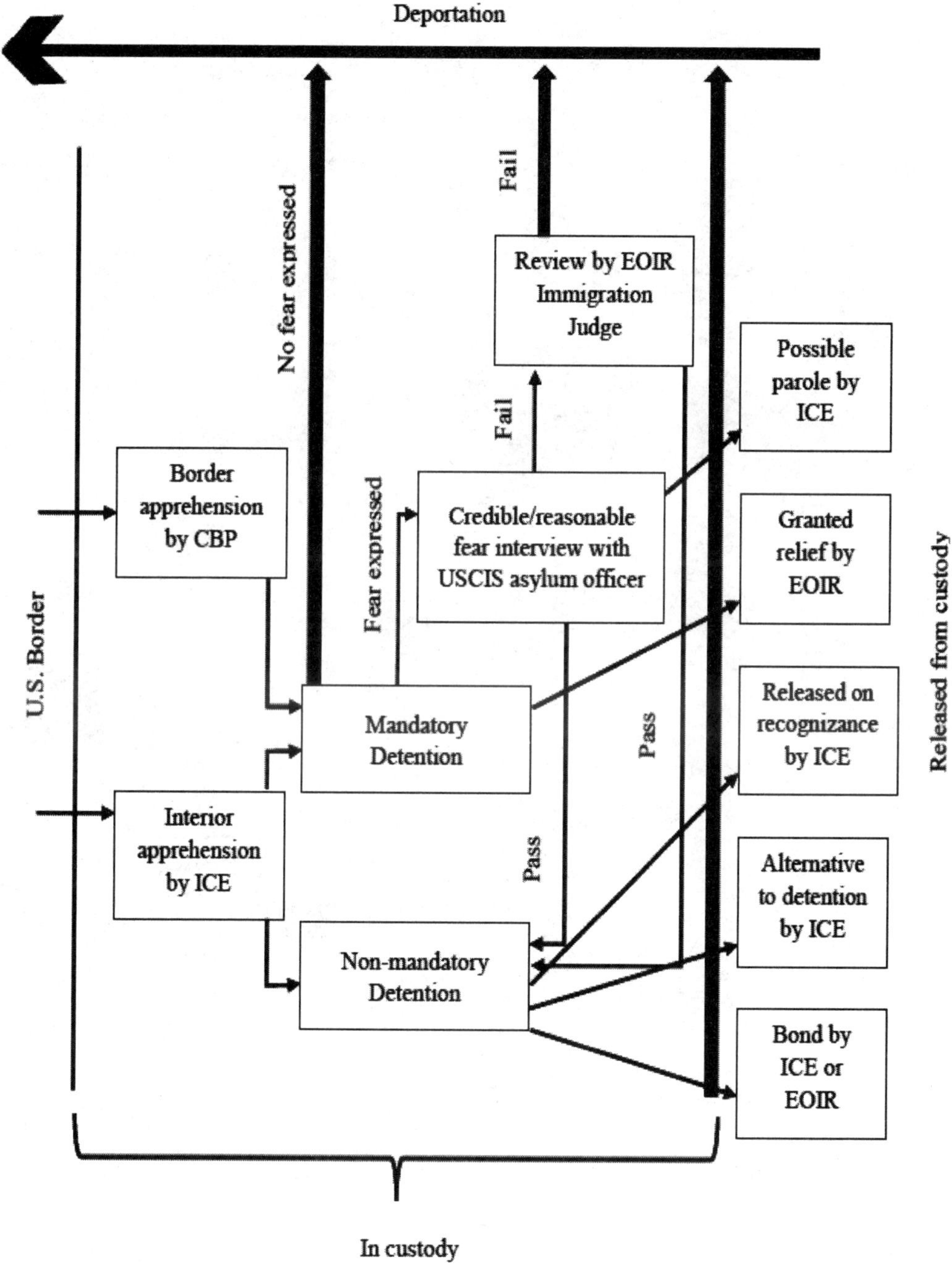

APPENDIX 6B

SAMPLE RELEASE REQUEST

Below is a sample release request to Immigration and Customs Enforcement (ICE) for those seeking protection who are not mandatory detainees. Rules and local practice regarding release requests vary from jurisdiction to jurisdiction and sometimes from ICE officer to ICE officer. If you are filing a release request and are unsure of the requirements, call the ICE officer assigned to your client's case, as well as a local immigration attorney or local nonprofit organization, for more information. Note that the context of the sample letter below is for an asylum-seeker who has passed her credible fear interview. There are other contexts outside of the border apprehension context in which an asylum-seeker may seek release from ICE. *See* appendix 6A.

[DATE]

VIA [METHOD OF DELIVERY]

Officer [Name]
Immigration and Customs Enforcement
[ICE Enforcement and Removal Operations Address]

RE: [Client Name, A Number]

Dear Officer [Name]:

We write to request the parole of [Client Name], who is currently in ICE custody at [Location]. Ms. [Client Name] passed her credible fear interview on [Date], and her case is currently being transferred to the [Location] Immigration Court. Thus, it has been found that there is a significant possibility that Ms. [Client Name] could establish eligibility for asylum under INA §208.

Ms. [Name] is 21-years-old and fled Guatemala in fear for her life after suffering violent abuse at the hands of her partner, who viewed her as his property and refused to permit her to leave the relationship. She attempted to escape to her sister's home, but her partner found her, forced her to return to her home, and continued to beat, rape, and abuse her. Ms. [Name]'s attempts to seek protection from the police were futile, as the police refused to involve themselves in what they perceived as a private, family matter and to otherwise protect her. In addition to the severe physical harm she suffered, Ms. [Name] has suffered profound psychological harm, and this psychological harm is only compounded by her ongoing detention in the United States. Ms. [Name] is currently suffering from depression and post-traumatic stress disorder, and it is Dr. [Name]'s recommendation that she be released immediately to prevent further psychological harm.

Ms. [Name] has family members here in the United States who are willing to receive, maintain, and support her. Her aunt and uncle, [Names], are lawful permanent residents who live at [Address]. They own their own business, [Name of Business], located in [Place], as well as their own home. Please find attached herein the following documentation in support of this release request:

1. Copy of Credible Fear Interview Results by USCIS Asylum Officer;
2. Copy of psychological evaluation of [Name];
3. Affirmation by [Sponsors] that they will care for and support Ms. [Name];
4. Copy of [Sponsor]'s permanent resident cards;
5. Copy of [Sponsor]'s most recent tax returns;
6. Proof of [Sponsor]'s employment; and
7. Proof of [Sponsor]'s home ownership.

Ms. [Name] is not a flight risk, as she came here for the sole purpose of seeking protection while in the care of her family members in [Location]. Moreover, she has no prior arrests or convictions and is not a danger to the community.

In addition, Ms. [Name] has a strong chance of succeeding on her asylum claim. The Asylum Officer found her credible and available country conditions evidence supports the reasonableness of her fear. It is entirely likely that Ms. [Name] will be granted asylum, and thus, she has every incentive to appear for her removal hearings.

Despite being transported from jail to jail and being detained for over a month before being permitted her credible fear interview, Ms. [Name] has been completely cooperative with DHS officials since her arrival. She will continue to cooperate fully throughout her attempt to procure protection from persecution in the United States. Thus, Ms. [Name] is the ideal candidate for release from removal or other alternatives to detention.

Also attached herein, please find our signed G-28, Notice of Entry of Appearance for your records. Please do not hesitate to contact us should you have any questions. We will follow up shortly with a phone call, and look forward to discussing this matter with you further.

Sincerely,

[Attorney Name with Signature Above]

APPENDIX 6C

SAMPLE BOND MOTION

Below is a sample bond motion, with sample cover page, index of exhibits, proposed order, and proof of service. Rules and local practice regarding bond vary from court to court and sometimes from judge to judge. If you are filing a bond motion and are unsure of the requirements, call the immigration court, as well as a local immigration attorney or local nonprofit organization, for more information. You should also read the Executive Office for Immigration Review *Immigration Court Practice Manual* at Chapters 5 (Motions before the Immigration Court) and 9 (Detention and Bond), *available at: www.justice.gov/eoir/office-chief-immigration-judge-0.*

DETAINED

UNITED STATES DEPARTMENT OF JUSTICE
EXECUTIVE OFFICE FOR IMMIGRATION REVIEW
UNITED STATES IMMIGRATION COURT
ARLINGTON, VIRGINIA

	)	
In the Matter of:	)	
	)	
	)	
[redacted]	)	**File No.: A**[redacted]
	)	
	)	
	)	
<u>In Removal Proceedings</u>	)	

No Hearing Calendared **NTA issued February 3, 2011**

RESPONDENT'S MOTION FOR BOND HEARING

UNITED STATES DEPARTMENT OF JUSTICE
EXECUTIVE OFFICE FOR IMMIGRATION REVIEW
UNITED STATES IMMIGRATION COURT
ARLINGTON, VIRGINIA

In the Matter of:	)	
	)	
	)	**DETAINED**
	)	
[redacted]	)	**A**[redacted]
	)	
	)	**No Hearing Calendared**
	)	**NTA issued February 3, 2011**
In Removal Proceedings	)	

RESPONDENT'S MOTION FOR BOND HEARING

Pursuant to 8 C.F.R. §1003.19, the respondent, Mr. [redacted] [redacted], through undersigned counsel, respectfully moves this court to set a bond hearing in his case at the earliest possible date. Mr. [redacted] is currently in the custody of the Department of Homeland Security (DHS) at the Rappahannock Regional Facility located at 1745 Jefferson Davis Highway, Stafford, VA 22554. *See* Exh. G. In support of this motion, Mr. [redacted], through undersigned counsel, states as follows:

1. Under 8 C.F.R. §1003.19(c), a request for a bond hearing may be filed in any of the following: (1) the Immigration Court having jurisdiction over her place of detention; (2) the Immigration Court having administrative control over her case; and (3) the Office of the Chief Immigration Judge

for assignment. *See* Exhs. F–G. Even if no charging document has been filed with the Court by ICE, the Immigration Court still has the authority to conduct a bond hearing. *See* 8 C.F.R. §1003.14(a); *see also* Exh. F. Mr. ██████████'s request for a bond hearing is not precluded under 8 C.F.R. §1003.19(h)(2)(i).

2. Pursuant to INA §236(a), DHS should not detain Mr. ██████████ unless there is a risk that he will abscond, pose a danger to persons or property, or pose a risk to national security. *Matter of D–J–*, 23 I&N Dec. 572 (BIA 2003); *Matter of Adeniji*, 22 I&N Dec. 1102, 1107–11 (BIA 1999); *Matter of Patel,* 15 I&N Dec. 666 (BIA 1976); 8 C.F.R. §1236.1(c)(8). He is more likely to meet his burden and merit a discretionary release on bond if he demonstrates a stable address, work history, and family ties in the United States. *Matter of X–K–*, 23 I&N Dec. 731, 736 (BIA 2005). His discretionary release is also favored if he demonstrates a likelihood that he will receive a grant of relief from removal, because he will then have great incentive to appear for hearings. *Id.*

3. Mr. ██████████ has not been convicted of any crimes against persons or property, nor has he been convicted of any violent crimes. Rather, he has a record of stable employment to support his U.S. citizen daughter and other family members, and is involved in his religious community. He

is well-regarded as a hard-working, contributing member of American society. He is not a threat to persons or property. *See* Exhs. A–D.

4. Mr. ██████ has no affiliation with any group that poses a threat to national security. In fact, Mr. ██████ is not affiliated with any groups other than his religious community, Christ the Redeemer Catholic Church. *See* Exh. C.

5. Mr. ██████ has received assurances of support from U.S. citizen and permanent resident family members who live in this area, as well as members of his community and his employer. *See* Exhs. B, D. Mr. ██████'s U.S. citizen and permanent resident family members have the means to provide him with a place to stay, all necessities, and legal representation. *See* Exhs. D, E. They have promised to ensure that he appears for all hearings. Their support indicates that Mr. ██████ will not become a flight risk.

6. Additionally, Mr. ██████ is the sole financial supporter for his two-month-old baby daughter, who is a U.S. citizen and who lives at ██████, Mr. ██████'s home address. *See* Exhs. A–B, D–E. He has every incentive to stay in one place, communicate regularly with his attorney, receive all notices of hearings, and appear for all hearings.

7. Further, Mr. [redacted] fears returning to El Salvador, and has a valid claim for relief from removal in the form of asylum, withholding of removal, and protection under the Convention Against Torture. Mr. [redacted] has secured an attorney to ensure that he presents his case properly and substantiates it adequately. As he is prima facie eligible for these forms of relief from removal, he has a strong incentive to appear for all hearings before the Immigration Court and to comply with any orders or requests by the U.S. government.

8. Mr. [redacted]'s strong family ties to this area, including his two-month-old U.S. citizen daughter; his stable home address; his stable employment history at [redacted], where he is considered a "great asset;" his lack of any violent criminal history against persons or property; his lack of association with any groups that pose a threat to national security; his contributions to his church community; his good moral character; and his opportunity to successfully defend himself from removal illustrate that Mr. [redacted] does not present a flight risk, nor does he pose a danger or risk to persons, property, or the national security. *See Adeniji*, 22 I&N Dec. 1102 (discussing *Patel,* 15 I&N Dec. 666).

9. In light of the above factors, Mr. [redacted] respectfully requests that he be granted a bond hearing so that he may demonstrate his eligibility for release from DHS custody. Further, Mr. [redacted] respectful-

ly requests that he be ordered released on his own recognizance, or in the alternative, released under reasonable bond.

Respectfully Submitted,

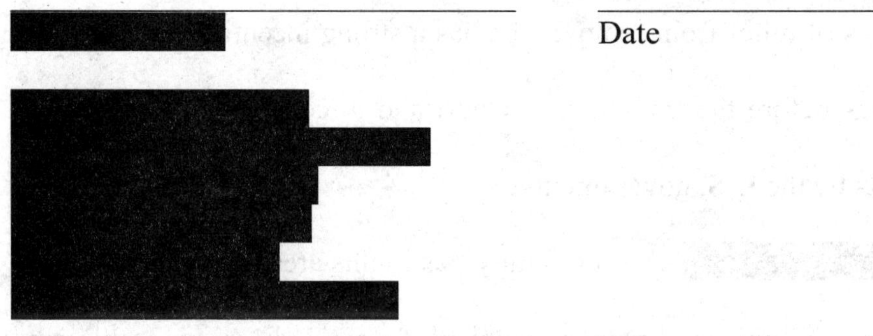

Date

Counsel for the Respondent

UNITED STATES DEPARTMENT OF JUSTICE
EXECUTIVE OFFICE FOR IMMIGRATION REVIEW
UNITED STATES IMMIGRATION COURT
ARLINGTON, VIRGINIA

In the Matter of:	)	
	)	
	)	**DETAINED**
	)	
[redacted]	)	**A**[redacted]
	)	
	)	**No Hearing Calendared**
	)	**NTA issued February 3, 2011**
In Removal Proceedings	)	

INDEX OF EXHIBITS IN SUPPORT OF RESPONDENT'S MOTION FOR BOND HEARING

The Respondent, Mr. [redacted], submits the following exhibits A-G, in support of his Motion for Bond Hearing.

TAB **PAGE**

A. **Birth Certificate of** [redacted], Mr. [redacted]'s U.S. citizen two-month-old baby daughter. 1

B. **Documentation of Employment with** [redacted], where Mr. [redacted] has been working since [redacted] and where he is considered a "great asset" who has "demonstrated a vast amount of knowledge and has a wonderful work ethic." 2–6

C. **Evidence of Contributions to Church Community**, in the form of a letter from Christ the Redeemer Catholic Church thanking Mr. [redacted] for his contributions. 7

D. **Letters of support**, attesting to Mr. [redacted]'s good moral character, including letters from:

- [redacted], U.S. citizen and sister-in-law of Mr. [redacted], stating that prior to being placed in ICE custody, Mr. [redacted] lived with her and will continue to live with her at [redacted] should he be released from custody. She further asserts her ongoing support of Mr. ████████, particularly with regard to ensuring that he appears for any immigration proceedings and follows any requirements imposed by the immigration authorities. A copy of Ms. ████'s U.S. passport is also attached herein **8–9**

- **Letter from** ████████, U.S. citizen, co-worker, and Godfather of Mr. ████████'s baby daughter, attesting to Mr. ████████'s good moral character. Evidence of Mr. ████'s U.S. citizenship status is also attached. **10–11**

- **Letter from** ████████, U.S. citizen and friend of Mr. ████████, stating that Mr. ████████ is the main financial support for his U.S. citizen daughter and other family members, and confirming that he has a fear of returning to El Salvador. Evidence of Ms. ████'s U.S. citizenship status is also attached. **12–13**

E. Evidence of Mr. ████████'s stable home address, in the form of his Sprint telephone bill. **14**

F. Copy of Notice to Appear, issued by DHS on February 3, 2011. **15–16**

G. Online Detainee Locator System, as evidence that Mr. ████████ is detained at a location that is within this Court's jurisdiction. **17**

Respectfully Submitted,

______________________ ______________________
████████ Date

████████

Counsel for the Respondent

UNITED STATES DEPARTMENT OF JUSTICE
EXECUTIVE OFFICE FOR IMMIGRATION REVIEW
UNITED STATES IMMIGRATION COURT
ARLINGTON, VIRGINIA

In the Matter of:	)
	)
	) **DETAINED**
	)
[redacted]	) **A**[redacted]
	)
	) **No Hearing Calendared**
	) **NTA issued February 3, 2011**
In Removal Proceedings	)

ORDER OF THE IMMIGRATION JUDGE

UPON CONSIDERATION of the Respondent's Motion for Bond Hearing, it is HEREBY ORDERED that said motion is ☐ **GRANTED** ☐ **DENIED** because:

- ☐ DHS does not oppose the motion.
- ☐ The respondent does not oppose the motion.
- ☐ A response to the motion has not been filed with the court.
- ☐ Good cause has been established for the motion.
- ☐ The court agrees with the reasons stated in the opposition to the motion.
- ☐ The motion is untimely per ____________________.
- ☐ Other:____.

Deadlines:

- ☐ The application(s) for relief must be filed by ______________________.
- ☐ The respondent must comply with DHS biometrics instructions by ________.

DONE AND ORDERED THIS _______ day of ______________, 2011.

____
Immigration Judge

Certificate of Service
This document was served by: [ ] Mail [ ] Personal Service
To: [ ] Alien [ ] Alien c/o Custodial Officer [ ] Alien's Atty/Rep [ ] DHS
Date: ______________________ By: Court Staff______________________

UNITED STATES DEPARTMENT OF JUSTICE
EXECUTIVE OFFICE FOR IMMIGRATION REVIEW
UNITED STATES IMMIGRATION COURT
ARLINGTON, VIRGINIA

In the Matter of:	)	
	)	
	)	**DETAINED**
	)	
	)	
[redacted]	)	**A**[redacted]
	)	
	)	**No Hearing Calendared**
	)	**NTA issued February 3, 2011**
In Removal Proceedings	)	

PROOF OF SERVICE

On the 3rd day of March, 2011, I, [redacted], caused to be served the foregoing Respondent's Motion for Bond Hearing, and all attached pages, including Exhibits A-G, on the U.S. Department of Homeland Security, ICE Office of Chief Counsel at 901 North Stuart Street, Suite 708, Arlington, Virginia 22203 via U.S. certified mail.

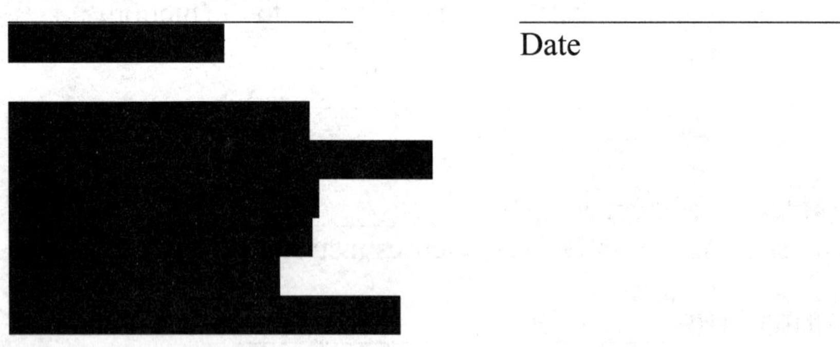
Date

Counsel for the Respondent

Appendix 7A

Flowchart of Unaccompanied Alien Children's Apprehension, Processing, and Custody

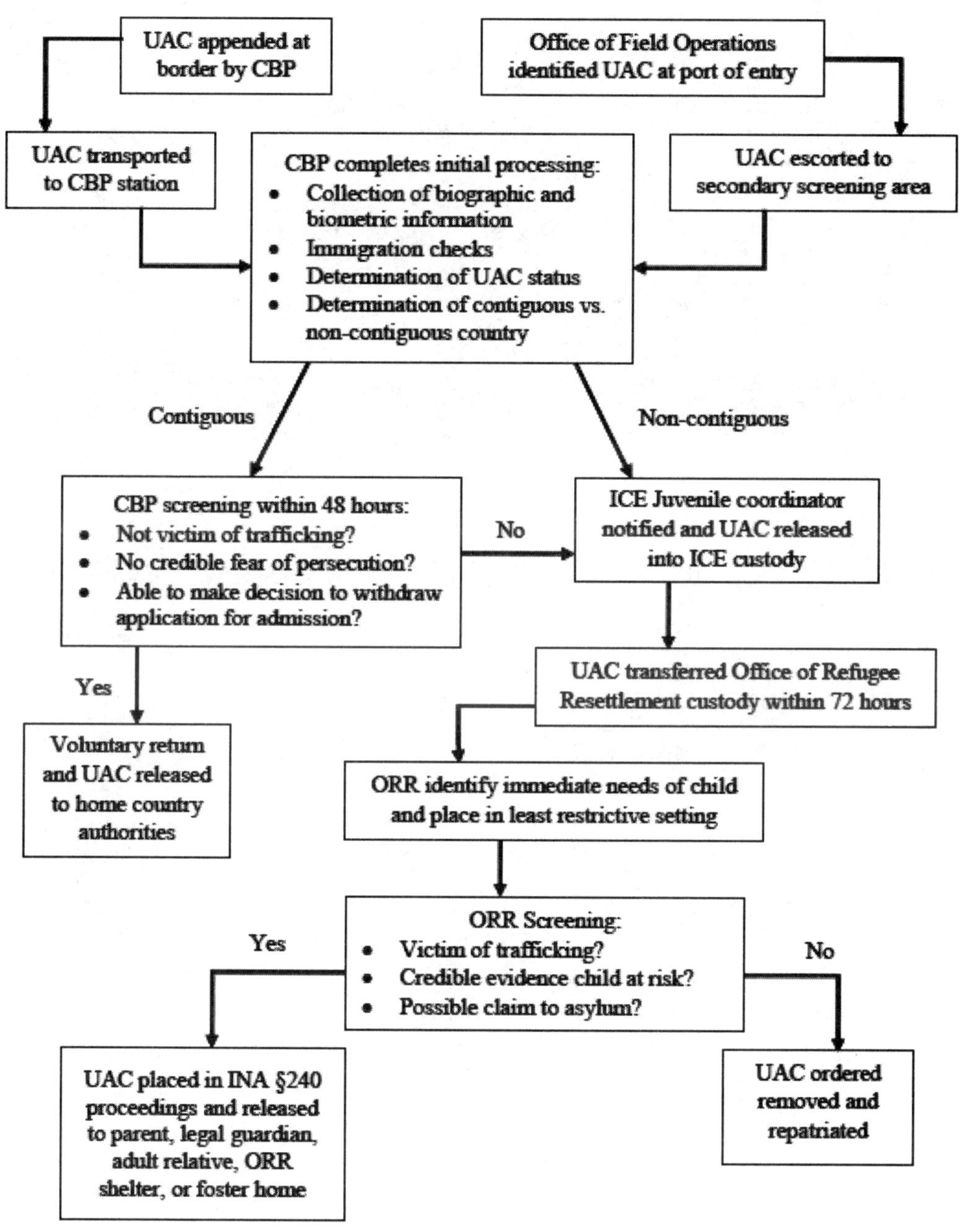

Appendix 7B

Child-Sensitive Interviewing Techniques

Asylum officers and immigration judges are advised to use specific techniques to elicit thorough information from child asylum-seekers. Attorneys and representatives should use these same techniques throughout the fact-gathering process when representing child asylum-seekers. For more information on child-sensitive interviewing techniques, see the USCIS Asylum Officer Basic Training Course, "Guidelines for Children's Asylum Claims," *available at www.uscis.gov/sites/default/files/USCIS/Humanitarian/Refugees%20%26%20Asylum/Asylum/AOBTC%20Lesson%20Plans/Guidelines-for-Childrens-Asylum-Claims-31aug10.pdf*, and see UNHCR's "Guidelines on International Protection No. 8" on child asylum claims, *available at www.refworld.org/docid/4b2f4f6d2.html.*

Do:	Do Not:
Explain your role, why you are meeting, and that you will not share the information with others	Talk about sensitive topics until the child knows who you are, understands why you are meeting, and feels comfortable
Conduct the interview in an environment that generates trust	Use a judgmental tone or choice of words
Start with neutral topics	Jump straight to the traumatic events
Use short, clear questions	Use long or compound questions
Use one or two-syllable words	Use three or four-syllable words
Ask the child to define or explain a term or phrase in the question posed to check the child's understanding	Use complex verb constructions
Ask the child to define or explain terms or phrases that he or she uses in answers, then use those same terms	Use legal terms, such as "persecution" or "particular social group"
Tolerate pauses, even if long	Coerce a child into answering a question
Ask the child to describe the concrete and observable	Ask the child to describe the hypothetical or abstract
Use visualizable terms	Use categorical terms
Explain any repetition of questions	Use idioms
Use the active voice	Use the passive voice
Keep questions simple and separate	Use front-loading questions

Use open-ended questions to encourage narrative responses	Use leading questions
Accept that many children will not be immediately forthcoming about events that have caused great pain	Be satisfied with "I don't know" responses – instead, ask follow up questions
Recognize that children may not know specific details	Expect children to present testimony with the same degree of precision as adults
Acknowledge that children may try to answer questions regarding measurements of distance or time without the experience to do so with any degree of accuracy	Expect children to be able to accurately measure distance and time
Take age, gender, cultural back-ground, and maturity into account in formulating questions	Use the same techniques, word choice, and question structure for all children
Use non-verbal communication methods, such as playing, drawing, writing, role-playing, story-telling, and singing	Use a formal, question-and-answer interview style
Use active and reflective listening	Use passive listening in which you are not a participant who is demonstrating an interest in understanding
Show empathy	Make the child feel like you cannot relate to him or her
Continually check-in with the child regarding how he or she is feeling	Ignore how the child may be feeling as the interview progresses
Hold shorter meetings and take breaks	Conduct long interview sessions without breaks

APPENDIX 8A

FORM EOIR-26 AND INSTRUCTIONS

U.S. Department of Justice
Executive Office for Immigration Review
Board of Immigration Appeals

OMB# 1125-0002
Notice of Appeal from a Decision of an Immigration Judge

GENERAL INSTRUCTIONS
(Please read carefully before completing and filing Form EOIR-26)

A. When to Appeal:

- Use this form (Form EOIR-26) only to appeal a decision by an **Immigration Judge**. If you wish to appeal a decision of the U.S. Citizenship and Immigration Services (USCIS), you must use a different form (Form EOIR-29).
- You must send the Notice of Appeal so that it is **received** by the Board within thirty (30) calendar days after the Immigration Judge's oral decision, or within thirty (30) calendar days after the date the Immigration Judge's written decision was mailed (if no oral decision was rendered).
- Simply mailing your Notice of Appeal in thirty (30) days or less is not enough. Your Notice of Appeal must **arrive** at the Board in thirty (30) days or less. If your Notice of Appeal arrives late, your appeal will be dismissed.

B. Where to Appeal:

Mail or deliver in person to this address:	Board of Immigration Appeals Clerk's Office 5107 Leesburg Pike, Suite 2000 Falls Church, VA 20530

C. How to Appeal:

- Read all of these instructions. **Note:** If you are the person in proceedings, you are the "Respondent" or "Applicant." You are also the "Appellant" if you are filing an appeal of a decision by an Immigration Judge.
- Fill out all three pages of the Notice of Appeal completely, answering items # 1 - 12 **in English only**.
- List in item # 1 the name(s) and Alien Number(s) ("A" numbers) of **all** Respondents/Applicants who are appealing the decision of the Immigration Judge.
- Sign item # 9.
- List the mailing address of the Respondent(s)/Applicant(s) in item # 10.
- Translate all documents that you attach to the Notice of Appeal into English. All translations must include the translator's statement stating that the translator is competent and that the translation is true and accurate.
- Write your name(s) and "A" Number(s) on all documents attached to the Notice of Appeal.
- Mail or give a copy of the completed Notice of Appeal and any attached documents to the opposing party. Complete and sign the "Proof of Service" to show you did this (item # 12). **Note:** If you are the Respondent or Applicant, the "Opposing Party" is the Assistant Chief Counsel of the U.S. Immigration and Customs Enforcement (ICE) of the Department of Homeland Security (DHS).
- Your appeal may be rejected or dismissed if you fail to properly complete the "Proof of Service" (item # 12).

D. Paying for the Appeal:

Attach a check or money order to the Notice of Appeal for exactly one hundred and ten dollars (U.S. $110) made payable to "United States Department of Justice." All checks must be drawn on a bank located in the United States. If there are not sufficient funds in your account, your appeal may be dismissed.

Form EOIR-26
Revised June 2014

. Write the name(s) and "A" Number(s) of all Respondent(s)/Applicant(s) on the check or money order.

- If you cannot pay for the appeal, complete a Fee Waiver Request (Form EOIR-26A) and attach it to the Notice of Appeal. The Board will review your request and decide whether to allow the appeal without payment of the fee.
- Your appeal may be rejected or dismissed if you fail to submit a fee or a properly completed Fee Waiver Request (Form EOIR-26A).

E. Lawyer or Representative Allowed:

- You may be represented by an attorney or representative who is authorized to appear before the EOIR. If you are represented by an attorney or authorized representative, he or she **must** file, **with** the Notice of Appeal, a Notice of Entry of Appearance as Attorney or Representative Before the Board of Immigration Appeals (Form EOIR-27).

F. Specify Reasons for the Appeal:

- Give specific details why you disagree with the Immigration Judge's decision.
- Most appeals are reviewed by a single Board Member. If you assert that your appeal warrants review by a three-Board Member panel, you may identify the specific factual or legal basis for your contention.

  Cases will be reviewed by a three-member panel only if the case presents one of these circumstances:
  - The need to settle inconsistencies among the rulings of different Immigration Judges;
  - The need to establish a precedent construing the meaning of laws, regulations, or procedures;
  - The need to review a decision by an Immigration Judge that is not in conformity with the law or with applicable precedents;
  - The need to resolve a case or controversy of major national import;
  - The need to review a clearly erroneous factual determination by an Immigration Judge; or
  - The need to reverse the decision of an Immigration Judge other than a reversal under 8 C.F.R. § 1003.1(e)(5) (i.e., permitting a single Board Member to reverse a decision that has been affected by changes in statutes, regulations or case law.)

- Specify the finding(s) of fact, the conclusion(s) of law, or both, that you are challenging. If a question of law is presented, cite supporting legal authority. If the dispute is over the findings of fact, identify the specific facts you are challenging.
- Where the appeal concerns discretionary relief, state whether the alleged error relates to statutory grounds of eligibility or to the exercise of discretion. Identify the specific factual and legal findings you are challenging.
- If you do not give specific reasons, with details, in item # 6, or in attachments to your Notice of Appeal, the Board may dismiss your appeal on that basis alone.

G. Briefs:

- Indicate in item # 8 whether you intend to file an additional written brief or statement at a later date. The Board will send you a briefing schedule and, when appropriate, a transcript of the testimony.
- Even if you intend to file an additional brief or statement at a later date, you still must give detailed reasons for your appeal on the Notice of Appeal in item # 6 and attachments.

H. Oral Argument:

- If you ask for oral argument in item # 7, the Board will notify you if your request is granted.
- Even if you ask for oral argument, you still must give detailed reasons for your appeal on the Notice of Appeal in item # 6 and attachments.

Form EOIR-26
Revised June 2014

- The Board ordinarily will not grant a request for oral argument unless you also file a brief.
- If you request oral argument, you should also state in item # 6 why you believe your case warrants review by a three-member panel.

I. Change of Address:

- If you move after sending your Notice of Appeal to the Board, you must give your new address **to the Board** within five (5) working days after you move. Use an alien's Change of Address Form (Form EOIR-33/BIA).
- Attorneys or representatives must also let the Board know if they change addresses or phone numbers, using Form EOIR-27. An attorney's or representative's change of address notification is only effective for the case in which it is submitted.

J. Further Information:

- For further guidance please see the Board of Immigration Appeals *Practice Manual,* which is available on the EOIR website at www.justice.gov/eoir.

K. Paperwork Reduction Act:

- Under the Paperwork Reduction Act, a person is not required to respond to a collection of information unless it displays a valid OMB control number. We try to create forms and instructions that are accurate, can be easily understood, and which impose the least possible burden on you to provide us with information. The estimated average time to complete this form is thirty (30) minutes. If you have comments regarding the accuracy of this estimate, or suggestions for making this form simpler, you can write to the Executive Office for Immigration Review, Office of the General Counsel, 5107 Leesburg Pike, Suite 2600, Falls Church, Virginia 20530.

L. Privacy Act Notice:

- The information on this form is authorized by 8 C.F.R. §§ 1003.3, 1003.38 in order to appeal a decision of an Immigration Judge to the Board of Immigration Appeals. The information you provide is required to appeal the decision and failure to provide the requested information may result in denial of your request. EOIR may share this information with others in accordance with approved routine uses described in EOIR systems of records notices.

Departure From the United States:

If you leave the United States after an Immigration Judge's decision in removal or deportation proceedings, but before you appeal the decision to the Board, you may have waived your right to appeal. If you leave the United States after filing an appeal with the Board, but before the Board decides your appeal, your appeal may be withdrawn and the Immigration Judge's decision put into effect as if you had never filed an appeal.

Summary Dismissal of Appeal:

The Board may summarily dismiss any appeal or portion of any appeal in which: (1) The appellant fails to specify the reasons for the appeal (see Part F); (2) The only reason specified by the appellant for his/her appeal involves a finding of fact or conclusion of law that was conceded by him/her at a prior proceeding; (3) The appeal is from an order that granted the appellant the relief that had been requested; (4) The appeal is filed for an improper purpose, such as unnecessary delay, or lacks an arguable basis in fact or law, unless the Board determines that it is supported by a good faith argument for extension, modification, or reversal of existing law; (5) The appellant indicates on Form EOIR-26 that he/she will file a separate brief or statement in support of the appeal and, thereafter, does not file such brief or statement, or reasonably explain his/her failure to do so, within the time set for filing (see Part G); (6) The appeal does not fall within the Board's jurisdiction or jurisdiction lies with the Immigration Judge rather than the Board; (7) The appeal is untimely or barred by an affirmative waiver of the right to appeal that is clear on the record; or (8) The appeal fails to meet essential statutory or regulatory requirements or is expressly excluded by statute or regulation.

WARNING! You must:

- Sign the Notice of Appeal (item # 9).
- Include the fee or Fee Waiver Request (Form EOIR-26A).
- Complete and sign the Proof of Service.
- Make sure your appeal is **received** at the Board on or before the filing due date.

U.S. Department of Justice
Executive Office for Immigration Review
Board of Immigration Appeals

OMB# 1125-0002
Notice of Appeal from a Decision of an Immigration Judge

Staple Check or Money Order Here. Include Name(s) and "A" Number(s) on the face of the check or money order.

1. List Name(s) and "A" Number(s) of all Respondent(s)/Applicant(s):

For Official Use Only

! **WARNING:** Names and "A" Numbers of everyone appealing the Immigration Judge's decision must be written in item #1. The names and "A" numbers listed will be the only ones considered to be the subjects of the appeal.

2. I am ☐ the Respondent/Applicant ☐ DHS-ICE *(Mark only one box.)*

3. I am ☐ DETAINED ☐ NOT DETAINED *(Mark only one box.)*

4. My last hearing was at ______________________ *(Location, City, State)*

5. **What decision are you appealing?**

Mark only one box below. If you want to appeal more than one decision, you must use more than one Notice of Appeal (Form EOIR-26).

☐ I am filing an appeal from the Immigration Judge's decision ***in merits proceedings*** (example: removal, deportation, exclusion, asylum, etc.) dated ______________________ .

☐ I am filing an appeal from the Immigration Judge's decision ***in bond proceedings*** dated ______________________. (For DHS use only: Did DHS invoke the automatic stay provision before the Immigration Court? ☐ Yes. ☐ No.)

☐ I am filing an appeal from the Immigration Judge's decision ***denying a motion to reopen or a motion to reconsider*** dated ______________________ .

(Please attach a copy of the Immigration Judge's decision that you are appealing.)

Form EOIR-26
Revised Oct. 2013

Page 1 of 3

6. **State in detail the reason(s) for this appeal. Please refer to the General Instructions at item F for further guidance. You are not limited to the space provided below; use more sheets of paper if necessary. Write your name(s) and "A" number(s) on every sheet.**

(Attach additional sheets if necessary)

! **WARNING:** You must clearly explain the specific facts and law on which you base your appeal of the Immigration Judge's decision. The Board may summarily dismiss your appeal if it cannot tell from this Notice of Appeal, or any statements attached to this Notice of Appeal, why you are appealing.

7. Do you desire oral argument before the Board of Immigration Appeals? ☐ Yes ☐ No

8. Do you intend to file a separate written brief or statement after filing this Notice of Appeal? ☐ Yes ☐ No

! **WARNING:** If you mark "Yes" in item #7, you should also include in your statement above why you believe your case warrants review by a three-member panel. The Board ordinarily will not grant a request for oral argument unless you also file a brief.

If you mark "Yes" in item #8, you will be expected to file a written brief or statement after you receive a briefing schedule from the Board. The Board may summarily dismiss your appeal if you do not file a brief or statement within the time set in the briefing schedule..

9. **SIGN HERE** X ______________________________ ______________

Signature of Person Appealing
(or attorney or representative)

Date

Form EOIR-26
Revised Oct 2013

Page 2 of 3

10. **Mailing Address of Respondent(s)/Applicant(s)**

(Name)

(Street Address)

(Apartment or Room Number)

(City, State, Zip Code)

(Telephone Number)

11. **Mailing Address of Attorney or Representative for the Respondent(s)/Applicant(s)**

(Name)

(Street Address)

(Suite or Room Number)

(City, State, Zip Code)

(Telephone Number)

NOTE: You must notify the Board within five (5) working days if you move to a new address or change your telephone number. You must use the Change of Address Form/Board of Immigration Appeals (Form EOIR-33/BIA).

NOTE: If an attorney or representative signs this appeal for you, he or she must file *with this appeal*, a Notice of Entry of Appearance as Attorney or Representative Before the Board of Immigration Appeals (Form EOIR-27).

12. **PROOF OF SERVICE (You Must Complete This)**

I ______________________ mailed or delivered a copy of this Notice of Appeal
(Name)

on ______________________ to ______________________
(Date) (Opposing Party)

at ______________________
(Number and Street, City, State, Zip Code)

SIGN HERE X ______________________
Signature

NOTE: If you are the Respondent or Applicant, the "Opposing Party" is the Assistant Chief Counsel of DHS - ICE.

WARNING: If you do not complete this section properly, your appeal will be rejected or dismissed.

WARNING: If you do not attach the fee or a completed Fee Waiver Request (Form EOIR-26A) to this appeal, your appeal may be rejected or dismissed.

HAVE YOU?

- ☐ Read all of the General Instructions
- ☐ Provided all of the requested information
- ☐ Completed this form in English
- ☐ Provided a certified English translation for all non-English attachments
- ☐ Signed the form
- ☐ Served a copy of this form and all attachments on the opposing party
- ☐ Completed and signed the Proof of Service
- ☐ Attached the required fee or Fee Waiver Request
- ☐ If represented by attorney or representative, attach a completed and signed EOIR-27

Page 3 of 3

Form EOIR-26
Revised Oct. 2013

APPENDIX 8B

SAMPLE BIA BRIEF

Below is a redacted sample brief to the Board of Immigration Appeals on appeal of the decision of the immigration judge. Practitioners should ensure that their briefs comply—both in substance and in format—with the *Board of Immigration Appeals Practice Manual, available at www.justice.gov/eoir/board-immigration-appeals-2.*

UNITED STATES DEPARTMENT OF JUSTICE
EXECUTIVE OFFICE FOR IMMIGRATION REVIEW
BOARD OF IMMIGRATION APPEALS
FALLS CHURCH, VIRGINIA

In The Matter of:	)	
[redacted]	)	**File Nos: A[redacted] (Lead)**
	)	**A[redacted]**
	)	**A[redacted]**
Respondents	)	
In Removal Proceedings	)	

RESPONDENTS' BRIEF ON APPEAL

The Respondents, [redacted], his wife [redacted], and their son [redacted], through undersigned counsel, respectfully submit this Brief on Appeal in support of their appeal of the decision of the Immigration Judge ("IJ") dated September 25, 2013 (hereinafter "IJ Dec."). The IJ erred in denying the Respondents' applications for asylum, withholding of removal, and protection under the Convention Against Torture. For the reasons set forth below, the Respondents' appeal should be granted, the IJ's decision should be reversed, and the Respondents should be granted asylum in the United States under section 208(a) of the Immigration and Nationality Act ("INA"). Alternatively, the Respondents should be granted protection under Article 3 of the Convention Against Torture.

I. INTRODUCTION

The IJ erred in denying Respondents' applications for asylum and, in the alternative, for withholding of removal under the Convention Against Torture. First, as set forth in detail below, the IJ erred in finding that [redacted] failed to articulate a viable particular social group under the INA. The IJ erroneously concluded that the social group to which [redacted] belongs – wealthy, educated, prominent and recognizable Honduran business leaders who have made business decisions adverse to the local population – lacks the qualities of immutability, particularity, and social visibility that are required under the precedent decisions of the Board of Immigration Appeals ("BIA" or "Board").

Second, the IJ erred in finding that [redacted] failed to demonstrate the requisite nexus between the harm he fears and his membership in the proposed social group. The IJ incorrectly decided that the threats [redacted] experienced and the persecution he fears arose from a mere personal dispute and not on account of a protected ground.

Third, the IJ erred in finding that [redacted] failed to demonstrate a likelihood that he would be tortured in Honduras with the consent or acquiescence of government authorities, and thus that he does not qualify for protection under the Convention Against Torture. The IJ acknowledged that the police in Honduras act with impunity, commit human rights violations, are inept when it comes to investigating crimes or prosecuting criminals, and that they bluntly refused [redacted] request for assistance and advised that they could not protect him. Notwithstanding these findings and controlling circuit precedent on what qualifies as "acquiescence," the IJ incorrectly concluded that the facts were insufficient to support a Convention Against Torture claim.

Accordingly, the IJ's decision should be reversed and the Respondents should be granted the requested relief from removal.

II. ISSUES PRESENTED

(1) Whether the IJ erred in concluding that [redacted] failed to demonstrate eligibility for asylum based on a well-founded fear of persecution in Honduras on account of his membership in a particular social group;

(2) Whether the IJ erred in concluding that the group articulated by [redacted] – wealthy, educated, prominent and recognizable Honduran business leaders who have made business decisions adverse to the local population – is not a viable social group under the INA, because it lacks immutability, particularity, and social visibility;

(3) Whether the IJ erred in concluding that [redacted] failed to demonstrate a nexus between the persecution he fears and his membership in a particular social group; and

(4) Whether the IJ erred in concluding that [redacted] failed to demonstrate eligibility for withholding of removal under the Convention Against Torture, because he failed to prove that it is more likely than not that he would face torture in Honduras with the consent or acquiescence of the Honduran government.

III. STANDARD OF REVIEW AND BURDENS OF PROOF

The BIA reviews factual determinations of the IJ, including findings as to the credibility of testimony, under the "clearly erroneous" standard. 8 C.F.R. §1003.1(d)(3)(i). The Board may review questions of law, discretion, and judgment and all other issues in appeals from IJ decisions de novo. 8 C.F.R. §1003.1(d)(3)(ii). Except for taking administrative notice of commonly known facts, the Board will not engage in fact-finding in the course of deciding appeals. 8 C.F.R. §1003.1(d)(3)(iv). If further fact-finding is needed in a particular case, the Board may remand to the IJ for further proceedings and the entry of a new decision. *Id.*; *Matter of S-H-*, 23 I&N Dec. 462 (BIA 2002).

A respondent applying for relief from removal bears the burden of establishing that he is eligible for any requested benefit and that it should be granted in the exercise of discretion. 8 C.F.R. §1240.8(d). An asylum applicant who claims persecution on account of membership in a particular social group must prove that his membership in the group "was or will be a central reason for his persecution." *Matter of W-G-R-*, 26 I&N Dec. 208, 224 (BIA 2014). A persecutor's actual motive is a matter of fact to be determined by the IJ and reviewed by the BIA for clear error. 8 C.F.R. §1003.1(d)(3)(i). *See Matter of N-M-*, 25 I&N Dec. 526, 532 (BIA 2011). Nonetheless, although the determination whether an individual has demonstrated eligibility for asylum on account of membership in a particular social group "is often a fact-specific inquiry, the ultimate determination whether a particular social group has been established is a question of law," which the Board reviews de novo. *Id.* at 209-10.

An applicant for protection under the Convention Against Torture bears the burden to demonstrate that it is more likely than not that he would be tortured if removed and that such torture would be with the consent or acquiescence of the government. 8 C.F.R. §1208.16(c)(2). A public official acquiesces to torture if, prior to the activity constituting torture, the official has awareness of such activity and thereafter breaches his or her legal responsibility to intervene to prevent such activity. 8 C.F.R. §1208.18(a)(7). The likelihood of torture is a question of fact that the BIA reviews for clear error. *W-G-R-*, 26 I&N Dec. at 224.

IV. BACKGROUND FACTS AND PROCEDURAL HISTORY

The Respondents, [redacted], his wife [redacted] [redacted], and their son [redacted]

[redacted], are natives and citizens of Honduras. They were admitted to the United States at Washington, D.C. on October 18, 2011, on valid B-2 nonimmigrant visas.

A. Proceedings before the Asylum Office

On March 12, 2012, less than six months after arriving in the U.S., [redacted] filed a Form I-589 Application for Asylum and Withholding of Removal, on which he included [redacted] and [redacted] as derivative beneficiaries. The Respondents attended an asylum interview on April 16, 2012 before the Arlington Asylum Office of U.S. Citizenship and Immigration Services ("USCIS"). The Respondents' period of authorized stay in B-2 status expired on April 17, 2012, and they did not apply to extend that status.

In support of his request for asylum, [redacted] submitted a detailed Form I-589 Application for Asylum along with extensive supporting evidence, including his own sworn affidavit and numerous corroborating documents. *See* **Exh. 2** (Application for Asylum and Supporting Exhibits 3-32 submitted to the Arlington Asylum Office). [redacted] asserted that he fears persecution in Honduras at the hands of individuals the government is unable or unwilling to control, on account of his membership in a particular social group made up of wealthy, educated, prominent, and recognizable Honduran business leaders whose business decisions have adversely affected the local population. **Exh. 2 Tab 3** (Statement of [redacted]).

[redacted] related that until he fled Honduras in October 2011, he was a senior Manager of the [redacted] Company, a timber producer that is one of the largest companies in the country and the second-largest timber producer in Honduras. The [redacted] factory in Yoro, which is a city approximately 250 kilometers from the capital Tegucigalpa, was the largest employer in the region, at one time employing more than 700 workers. **Exh. 2 Tabs 3, 19.** The position of Manager is the highest-ranking position at [redacted] and is correspondingly well-paid – 2491 lempiras (roughly $131) per day – and includes company-provided housing, domestic staff, security, meals and groceries, and vehicles. The position of Manager is prestigious and highly visible – ███ noted that he is well-known not only in Yoro and the surrounding area, but throughout Honduras and neighboring countries due to his commercial relations with vendors and with the transportation crews that ship ███'s timber products throughout Central America. In addition, ███ is closely associated with ███, because he worked for the company for 20 years prior to fleeing Honduras with his family.

███'s wife, ███, was a professor at the Technologic University of Honduras and the Private University of San Pedro Sula, both located in the city of San Pedro Sula, Honduras. **Exh. 2 Tab 23.** ███'s and ███'s 11-year-old son, ███, attended the Happy Days School and Freedom High School, which are among the most prestigious bilingual schools in Honduras. **Exh. 2 Tab 26.** ███ indicated that he and his family belong to a wealthy, educated, and prominent social class in Honduran society. By contrast, most of the unskilled laborers who work at the ███ factory in Yoro are uneducated or have very little education and are paid an average wage of only 144 lempiras (roughly $7.61) per day. The workers at ███ view ███, the senior Manager, as the person ultimately responsible for management decisions, including factory production goals, cost saving measures, and the reduction of the workforce and firing of employees. **Exh. 2 Tab 3.**

Due to a reduction in the international and national market for timber, caused by the global economic crisis, from 2007 through 2010 ███ was forced to lay off hundreds of unskilled laborers from the timber production section of the factory Yoro. And because ███ lacked the financial stability to pay the full pensions of employees who were laid off, delays in pension payments stretched up to three years in some cases. The laid off workers, who had lost their income and were not receiving promised pension payments, viewed ███ as being responsible for the company's management decisions. The workers also lost their housing when they were laid off, as these employees lived in company-provided housing while they were working for . *Id.*

As a result, began receiving violent threats from anonymous callers, either directly on his personal cellular phone or through his security personnel, challenging his wealth and prominence in contrast to the poverty and lack of opportunity now facing the workers who had been laid off. Mr. ("Mr. "), who was Chief of Production at the Yoro factory and second in command of the production department (after), also began receiving threats. Mr. was responsible for informing employees in his department that they had been terminated, under the cost-reduction plan being implemented by and the facility Manager, . *Id.*

related that on February 19, 2010, Mr. was shot and killed in Yoro by unknown assailants. **Exh. 2 Tabs 3, 10**. Thereafter, received increasing numbers of threatening phone calls from unknown persons. The callers warned that he too would be killed or tortured if the fired workers did not receive their pension payments. Despite the serious threats, remained in Yoro because he was committed to improving 's economic situation, although he increased his own protection by arranging to have bodyguards 24 hours a day. Mr. ("Mr. "), who was chief of security at the factory, was assigned to be 's primary personal security guard. **Exh. 2 Tab13.**

By late 2010, 's economic prospects had improved somewhat and financial projections indicated that pension debts might be completely paid by 2012. Nonetheless, Mr. received many anonymous phone calls demanding information about 's whereabouts, under threat of death. Mr. refused to answer the callers' demands.

On September 30, 2011, while on the way from his home to the factory in Yoro, Mr. was tortured and shot to death. **Exh. 2 Tabs 6, 7, 8, 9.** After the murder of his personal security guard, received many death threats on his own cellular phone. Just over a week after Mr. was killed, on October 8, 2011, received a call warning him not to return to the factory in Yoro. The caller stated that he knew the location and movements of 's wife and son, including the color and make of his wife's car, where she was employed, and the name of 's school. The caller made clear that 's entire family was at risk of being killed. **Exh. 2 Tab 3.**

Consequently, and his family quickly fled their home in San Pedro Sula and traveled to his sister's house in Tegucigalpa. While in the capital city, went with his sister, who is an attorney, to file reports with both the Secretary of Security, Department of Criminal Investigations, of the Republic of Honduras and the National Human Rights Commission of the Republic of Honduras. **Exh. 2 Tabs 4, 5.** continued to receive threatening calls, during which the callers stated that he had been located in Tegucigalpa and warned that he and his family would be found anywhere they went in Honduras. The family remained hidden in Tegucigalpa for about one week, then they secretly returned to their house in San Pedro Sula to pack their belongings. On October 18, 2011, and his wife and son fled Honduras, departing from the airport in San Pedro Sula and flying to Washington, D.C. **Exh. 2 Tab 3.** In addition to , was interviewed by the Asylum Officer.

On April 30, 2012, the Arlington Asylum Office declined to grant asylum and referred the Respondents' case to the Immigration Court.

B. Proceedings before the Immigration Judge

On April 30, 2012, the Department of Homeland Security ("DHS") issued Notices to Appear charging the Respondents with removability under INA §237(a)(1)(B), as visa overstays. **Exh. 1.** At a Master Calendar Hearing before the

IJ on May 21, 2012, the Respondents, through counsel, admitted the factual allegations in the Notices to Appear, conceded the charge of removability, and renewed their application for asylum, withholding of removal, and protection under the Convention Against Torture. Tr. 33-34. The Respondents submitted additional evidence in support of their claim, including the U.S. Department of State 2012 Country Report on Human Rights Practices in Honduras, sworn statements from 14 different individuals, media articles concerning violent attacks on Honduran executives, and evidence of police corruption in Honduras and the government's inability to protect executives from harm. **Exh. 3 Tabs D-K.**

At Individual Calendar Hearings on September 12, 2013 and September 25, 2013, the IJ heard testimony and accepted evidence in support of ████'s application for asylum and, in the alternative, for relief under the Convention Against Torture. Tr. 38-189. The following witnesses provided testimony, under oath, before the IJ: ████, ████, and Mr. Creelman. Tr. 35-141.

C. Decision of the Immigration Judge

At the conclusion of the hearing on September 25, 2013, the IJ issued an oral decision denying the Respondents' applications for asylum, withholding of removal, and protection under the Convention Against Torture. IJ Dec. at 1-26. At the outset, the IJ found that ████, ████, and Mr. ████ all provided credible testimony in support of the Respondents' persecution claim. *Id.* at 20. DHS did not challenge the IJ's positive credibility finding, nor did the government dispute the essential facts presented in ████'s asylum application and supporting documentary evidence. Tr. 29. However, the IJ concluded that ████ failed to sustain his legal burden of demonstrating either a well-founded fear of persecution in Honduras on account of a protected ground or a clear probability that he would face torture in Honduras with the consent or acquiescence of the Honduran government. IJ Dec. at 20-26.

First, the IJ held that ████ failed to articulate a viable particular social group under the law. *Id.* at 20. The IJ stated:

> The group that the respondent has identified is one that is lacking in the requisite quality of immutability. It is a circular group defined by the harm that the persecutor fears. There is no question that wealth is not an immutable characteristic. … The Court finds that wealth and prominent and business leadership and decision making are all characteristics, whether you consider them separately or whether you link them together, that are lacking in immutability because such acquired traits are not beyond the power of the applicant to change, and they are not so fundamental to his conscience that they ought not require to be changed.

Id. at 20-21.

Second, the IJ found that the group articulated by [redacted] lacked particularity. *Id.* at 21. According to the IJ, "the respondents' efforts to narrow the group by restricting it to the category of not only wealthy, educated and prominent Honduran business leaders, but those people who have made business decisions adverse to the local population does not make the identified group any more viable under the law because those are only additional characteristics that are too broad and amorphous to have any well-defined boundaries." *Id.* The IJ opined that some business decisions might be regarded as adverse by some in the local population but not adverse by others. *Id.* "And so, when you consider the group in its totality as a whole, it is not enduring enough to clearly delineate its membership or to readily identify its members." *Id.* at 22. Further, the IJ stated that the particular social group articulated by [redacted] "is clearly a contrived group, which is defined by the harm that the respondent fears." *Id.*

Third, the IJ held that [redacted] failed to demonstrate a nexus between the harm feared and the social group he defined. *Id.* The IJ stated:

> [I]t is notable that in this case the respondent did not have any difficulties in Honduras until he initiated the layoffs of the employees and failed to pay them. … These are people who wanted to get paid for the labor that they provided so that they could feed and clothe and house themselves and their families. … If the workers had received their pay,

> or if they were to receive their pay, nothing suggests that they would have any interest at all in targeting the respondent.

Id. at 23. According to the IJ, "[t]his is a personal dispute that lacks the requisite nexus between the harm that the respondent fears and any viable ground in the statute, including membership in a particular social group." *Id.* The would-be persecutors' only motivation, the IJ found, was a desire to be paid. *Id.* at 25. Ultimately, the IJ held that "[b]ecause the respondent cannot connect the harm that he fears to a protected ground, he does not qualify for asylum, and his inability to meet the lower standard for asylum means that he cannot meet the higher legal burden required to qualify for withholding under the Act." *Id.*

The IJ also denied the Respondents' request for protection under Article 3 of the Convention Against Torture, finding that ███████ "failed to demonstrate that the individuals who threatened to harm him have the approval or the acquiescence of the government of Honduras." *Id.* at 25. The IJ conceded that evidence submitted by ███████ reveals "a certain degree of ineptness and lack of training and corruption" among the police in Honduras. *Id.* But she rejected the argument that these facts show "that the individuals who threatened to harm [███ ████] have the approval or acquiescence of the government of Honduras." *Id.* The IJ explained her reasoning:

> [T]he police in Honduras have another problem. That is they are out committing human rights violations, acting with impunities, so when they do try to enforce the law, they do it with a certain vengeance that is unacceptable by international standards. But, unfortunately, that is an indication that people in Honduras, criminals, do not act with the consent or acquiescence of public officials[.]

Id. In addition, the IJ found that when ███████ reported the murder of his bodyguard and the threats he had received, the police "did what they could do. They took a report. They were honest with him, and they said, this is a problem. Other executives have had problems. Get yourself some protection." *Id.* at 26. According to the IJ, "that is not consent or acquiescence" and thus is not the basis for a viable request for protection under the Convention Against Torture. *Id.*

In sum, the IJ acknowledged that [redacted] and his family "are clearly people who are frightened [and] are clearly people who are at risk," but "not everyone who is afraid can be protected under U.S. asylum and withholding laws[.]" *Id.* Having denied all applications for relief, the IJ ordered the Respondents removed to Honduras as charged in the Notices to Appear under INA §237(a)(1)(B). *Id.*

D. Appeal to the Board of Immigration Appeals

On October 23, 2013, the Respondents timely filed a Notice of Appeal with the Board of Immigration Appeals ("BIA" or "Board"). This brief is timely filed in support of the Respondents' appeal.

V. APPLICABLE LAW

An applicant for asylum must demonstrate either past persecution or a well-founded fear of persecution on account of race, religion, nationality, political opinion, or membership in a particular social group. INA §§101(a)(42)(A), 208(a). The statute does not define "particular social group," but the BIA has defined the term as a group meeting three criteria: (1) its members share common, immutable characteristics; (2) the group is defined with sufficient particularity; and (3) the group is socially distinct within the society in question, a requirement previously referred to as "social visibility." *See Matter of M-E-V-G-*, 26 I&N Dec. 227, 237 (BIA 2014); *W-G-R-*, 26 I&N Dec. at 210-12.

An "immutable characteristic" is one "that the members of the group either cannot change, or should not be required to change because it is fundamental to their individual identities or consciences." *W-G-R-*, 26 I&N Dec. at 212 (quoting *Matter of Acosta*, 19 I&N Dec. 211, 233 (BIA 1985)). The defining characteristic can be an innate attribute or a shared past experience. *Id.* at 212-13.

"Particularity" refers to the definition of the group itself – it must "provide a clear benchmark for determining who falls within the group," use terms that "have commonly accepted definitions in the society in which the group is a part," and "not be amorphous, overbroad, diffuse, or subjective." *Id.* at 214. The particularity requirement puts outer limits on the definition of a particular social group, taking into account the social and cultural context of an asylum applicant's country of citizenship. *Id.*

The requirement of social distinction refers to a group's recognition in society. *Id.* at 216. The requirement – previously referred to as "social visibility" – was recently renamed to clarify that "ocular visibility" is not required, either of the group as a whole or of individuals in the group. *Id.*[1] For a group to be "socially distinct,"

> there must be evidence showing that society in general perceives, considers, or recognizes persons sharing the particular characteristic to be a group. Although the society in question need not be able to easily identify who is a member of the group, it must be commonly recognized that the shared characteristic is one that defines the group.

Id. at 217. And although persecutory conduct aimed at a group "cannot *alone* define the group," the views of the persecutor can "play a role in causing members of society to view a particular group as distinct." *Id.* at 215, 223 (emphasis added). The United States Court of Appeals for the Fourth Circuit, in whose jurisdiction this case arises, has endorsed the immutability and particularity criteria, but has explicitly declined to hold that the social visibility (now renamed social distinction) criterion is a reasonable interpretation of the INA. *Martinez v. Holder*, 2014 U.S. App. LEXIS 1250, at *16 (4th Cir. Jan. 23, 2014); *Zelaya v. Holder*, 668 F.3d 159, 165 n.4 (4th Cir. 2012).

An applicant for asylum must also demonstrate the required nexus between

---

[1] The Board's "social distinction" requirement, recently articulated in *Matter of W-G-R-*, 26 I&N Dec. 208 (BIA 2014), and *Matter of M-E-V-G-*, 26 I&N Dec. 227 (BIA 2014), was announced subsequent to the IJ's decision in this case. IJ Dec. at 18 (stating that "membership in a particular social group requires that the group … possess a recognized level of social visibility").

the harm he fears and his membership in a cognizable social group, such that the risk of persecution is shown to be on account of his membership in the specified group. *W-G-R-*, 26 I&N Dec. at 223. "Whether that nexus exists depends on the views and motives of the persecutor." *Id.* at 223-24 (citing *N-M-*, 25 I&N Dec. 526). Thus, the applicant bears the burden of showing that his belonging to a particular social group was, or will be, a central reason for the persecution feared. *Id.* at 224; *see also* INA §208(b)(1)(B)(i).

An applicant for protection under Article 3 of the Convention Against Torture bears the burden of demonstrating that it is more likely than not that he would be tortured if removed and that such torture would be with the consent or acquiescence of the government. 8 C.F.R. §1208.16(c)(2). *See also Turkson v. Holder*, 667 F.3d 523, 526 (4th Cir. 2012). Acquiescence of a public official requires that the public official, prior to the activity constituting torture, have awareness of such activity and thereafter breach his or her legal responsibility to intervene to prevent such activity. 8 C.F.R. §1208.18(a)(7).

VI. ARGUMENT

A. The IJ erred in finding that ██████ failed to articulate a viable particular social group under the INA

The IJ erred in concluding that the group identified by ██████ – wealthy, educated, prominent, and recognizable Honduran business leaders who have made business decisions adverse to the local population – lacks the requisite characteristics of immutability, particularity, and social visibility (social distinction) to qualify as a "particular social group" under the INA.

1. Immutability

First, the IJ erroneously concluded that the characteristics which define ██ ████'s particular social group "are lacking in immutability because such acquired traits are not beyond the power of the applicant to change, and they are not so fundamental to his conscience that they ought not require to be changed." IJ Dec. at 21. The IJ's ruling is contrary to controlling circuit precedent.

In *Martinez v. Holder*, the Fourth Circuit recently considered the issue of immutability in the context of an application based on claimed membership in the particular social group of former members of the violent Mara Salvatrucha gang ("MS-13") in El Salvador. 2014 U.S. App. LEXIS 1250, at *2. The IJ and the BIA had rejected Martinez's contention that former gang membership could qualify as an immutable characteristic, because it "'result[ed] from the voluntary association with a criminal gang.'" *Id.* at *3. On review, the court found, to the contrary, that Martinez's proposed social group meets the immutability requirement because "he cannot change his status as a former gang member except by rejoining MS-13." *Id.* at *18. In reaching this conclusion, the court relied on BIA decisions holding that the shared immutable characteristic "'might be an innate one such as sex, color, or kinship ties, or in some circumstances *it might be a shared past experience* such as former military leadership or land ownership.'" *Id.* at *7 (quoting *Acosta*, 19 I&N Dec. at 233); *see also W-G-R-*, 26 I&N Dec. at 213 ("The critical requirement is that the defining characteristic of the group must be something that either cannot be changed or that the group members should not be required to change in order to avoid persecution.").

Likewise in the Respondents' case. The characteristics that define ███ ██████'s social group – wealth, education, prominence, and recognition in Honduran society as a business leader coupled with the experience of having made business decisions adverse to the local population – are not characteristics that he has the power to change. ██████████ testified that if he were to return to Honduras, the people who threatened his life will "continue persecuting me" because they are determined to "kill the responsible – the person responsible of the problems that they have, the financial problems that they have." Tr. 77. He testified further that even if he were to leave his position at the ██████ company, he is a "well-known person in Honduras" and regardless of whether he left his employer and cut his ties "I'm still going to be recognized as the person, as the [redacted] executive who, who caused … this situation of poverty and that people are facing now." *Id.* at 77-78. According to [redacted], as "the head person in command," Tr. 38, he was perceived as *El Jefe*, The Boss, "and the person the employees perceived as the one responsible for each action made in favor or against their interests … [including] personnel reduction plans or terminations, and cost reductions." **Exh. 2 Tab 3**.

[redacted] testified that even if he returned to Honduras and did something completely different, like becoming a coffee farmer, "Regardless, I will be linked as the executive who caused all the problems of owing money to the employees." Tr. 78. [redacted]'s position as an executive at [redacted] may have been a voluntary association, and he may have carried out the company's layoff decisions purely as a responsibility of his position, but like the status of former gang membership in *Martinez*, such former voluntary acts or associations can nonetheless qualify as immutable characteristics that an individual is later powerless to change.

The IJ erred in concluding that [redacted]'s identified social group "is lacking in the requisite quality of immutability." IJ Dec. at 20. At the outset, the IJ accurately noted that wealth alone does not qualify as an immutable characteristic. IJ Dec. at 21; *see also Matter of A-M-E- & J-G-U-*, 24 I&N Dec. 69, 76 (BIA 2007); *Matter of S-V-*, 22 I&N Dec. 1306, 1310 (BIA 2000) (actions motivated by "perceived wealth" are insufficient to support a finding of persecution based on membership in a particular social group); *Matter of V-T-S-*, 21 I&N Dec. 792, 799 (BIA 1997) (wealth as common trait of kidnapping victims is insufficient where applicant did not demonstrate persecution on account of a protected ground). Some courts also have rejected social groups based solely on wealth or perceived wealth. *See, e.g., Sicaju-Diaz v. Holder*, 663 F.3d 1, 4 (1st Cir. 2011); *Bolshakov v. INS*, 133 F.3d 1279, 1281 (9th Cir. 1998). In addition, the BIA has found that wealthy individuals who are targeted for the sole purpose of "extorting money for [the assailants'] cause" failed to establish that the persecution suffered was on account of a protected ground. *Matter of T-M-B-*, 21 I&N Dec. 775, 778 (BIA 1997). In *T-M-B-*, the Board noted that the applicant's persecutors had "no interest" in her beyond her association with the family business and "the ability of the business to generate financial support." *Id.* at 779. Thus, asylum is not warranted where the "threats and infliction of harm directed at the respondent are appropriately characterized as extortion[.]" *Id.* at 780.

However, when the characteristic of "wealth" is more specifically defined, and is present in combination with other traits such as land ownership and education or former status or occupation, the courts have found this status to qualify as a protected social group. *See, e.g.*, *Tapiero de Orjuela v. Gonzales*, 423 F.3d 666 (7th Cir. 2005) (educated land-owning cattle farmers in Colombia); *Sepulveda v. Gonzales*, 464 F.3d 770 (7th Cir. 2006) (former employees in Attorney General's office in Colombia). In *Tapiero de Orjuela*, in particular, the court noted that a particular characteristic "such as education, manner of speech, or profession" may be more mutable than race, ethnicity, or religion, "but these traits are nevertheless distinguishing markers within a given society that are not easily changed or hidden." 423 F.3d at 672.[2] The court explained that wealth *combined with* ownership of a particular type of land (cattle ranches) and educational status met the "shared past experiences" basis for social group designation that was articulated in *Acosta*, in part because even if the applicant's family were to give up its land, cattle ranching, and educational opportunities, they still would not escape persecution; they would continue to be targeted based on past membership in the cattle farming, land-owning class. *Id.*

[2] *Tapiero de Orjuela* was cited with approval by the Fourth Circuit in *Temu*, 2014 U.S. App. LEXIS 868, at *22. The Fourth Circuit observed: "Time and again, case law from this Court, other circuits, and the BIA has accepted social groups that, as part of their def-

Likewise, in *Sepulveda v. Gonzales*, the court found that because the past cannot be changed and is therefore immutable, the "shared past experience" definition could be "easily satisfied by a group of former employees of a particular institution." 464 F.3d at 772; *see also Matter of Fuentes*, 19 I&N Dec. 658, 662 (BIA 1988) (holding that a group of similarly situated former national police officers could be considered a discrete group with defined boundaries). And in *Escobar v. Holder*, 757 F.3d 537 (7th Cir. 2011), the court considered the persecution claim of a locally prominent former trucker who had resisted the efforts of a revolutionary organization to co-opt his trucks. The applicant's trucking company possessed a "special skill" and it would be "impossible for him to change either this or the fact that he rebelled against" the organization's commands, and "[t]his would be so even if he were to return to Colombia as a coffee farmer or a teacher." *Escobar*, 757 F.3d at 546.

Most recently, the Seventh Circuit reaffirmed its analysis in *Tapiero de Orjuela* and ruled that Colombian land owners who refuse to cooperate with the Revolutionary Armed Forces of Colombia ("FARC") comprise a legitimate particular social group under the INA. *N.L.A. v. Holder*, 2014 U.S. App. LEXIS 3971 (7th Cir. 2014).[3] The victims of FARC violence in *N.L.A.* included individuals who – like [redacted] – refused to pay the money that was demanded of them and were then threatened or even killed as a result. *Id.* at *1-9. To avoid that fate, the petitioner in *N.L.A.* behaved just as the Respondents did:

> Because N.L.A. believed that her family was in imminent danger, the family immediately bought tickets, leaving their home vacant, their business in the hands of a partner, and most of their possessions behind. N.L.A. and her family entered the United States with valid tourist visas … and filed an application for asylum and withholding of re-

---

initions, contain components that might not meet the BIA's legal standards." *Id.*

[3] Although *N.L.A. v. Holder* arises in the Seventh Circuit, it is instructive for the Respondents' case, as the Fourth Circuit has recently cited approvingly to the Seventh Circuit's analysis of particular social group asylum claims. *See Martinez*, 2014 U.S. App. LEXIS 1250, at *19-28; *Temu*, 2014 U.S. App. LEXIS 686, at *22-25.

moval … within the one year application deadline.

Id. at *7-8. Despite finding N.L.A.'s testimony credible, the IJ denied her claim for failure to demonstrate persecution on account of membership in a legitimate particular social group. *Id.* at *4, *9. The BIA affirmed the IJ's decision, concluding – much like the IJ in ███'s case below – that the proposed social group "is not immutable, as one can change one's status by selling, losing, or abandoning one's property, as the respondent did here." *Id.* at *34. Similarly, the IJ rejected ███'s proposed group because the characteristics of "wealth and prominence and business leadership and decision making" are "acquired traits that are not beyond the power of the applicant to change[.]" IJ Dec. at 21.

On review, the Seventh Circuit found in *N.L.A.* that the Board had "misconstru[ed] the nature of the threat" faced by the petitioner and "fumbled the analysis" in denying her request for asylum, based partly on its conclusion that she failed to articulate a "cognizable social group." *Id.* at *13, *20, *27. The court stated:

> Our cases have made clear that sometimes an asylum applicant acquires membership in a group with a qualifying immutable characteristic because a shared past experience or status cannot be undone. For this reason, the educated, landowning class of cattle farmers targeted by the FARC constitutes a social group.

Id. at *28-29 (collecting cases); *see also Temu*, 2014 U.S. App. LEXIS 686, at *24 (rejecting BIA's finding that the proposed social group lacks immutability where "the BIA's opinion advances two factual findings that are impossible to reconcile without violating fundamental rules of logic[,]" because "Mr. Temu's membership in his proposed group is not something he has the power to change").

Unlike the social group considered in *Acosta* – taxi drivers in San Salvador who refused to participate in guerrilla-sponsored work stoppages – ███ cannot avoid persecution in Honduras by cutting ties with his former employer or taking up a different profession. *See Acosta*, 19 I&N Dec. at 234. As he credibly testified, even if [redacted] were to return and take up an entirely different profession, such as being a farmer, he would not escape persecution at the hands of those who repeatedly threatened his life and tortured and murdered his former bodyguard. *See* Tr. 78. By contrast, the BIA found that immutability was lacking in *Acosta* because "the members of the group could avoid the threats of the guerrillas either by changing jobs or by cooperating in work stoppages" and the "facts do not show that the persecution of taxi drivers continued even after they stopped working as drivers." 19 I&N Dec. at 232, 234. Here, the IJ's finding of no immutability is inconsistent with her conclusion that [redacted] offered credible testimony that he would be targeted and persecuted in Honduras even if he no longer worked as an executive and even if he cut all ties with his former employer [redacted]. *See* IJ Dec. at 26 ("These are clearly people who are at risk[.]"). As the Fourth Circuit admonished in *Temu*, a decision that rests on such "logical contradictions" cannot be sustained. 2014 U.S. App. LEXIS 868, at *7.

2. Particularity

Second, the IJ erred in finding that the social group to which [redacted] belongs is lacking in particularity, because the characteristics of the proposed group "are too broad and amorphous to have any well-defined boundaries." IJ Dec. at 21. The IJ's conclusion is both legally unsound and contradicted by the evidence of record.

The BIA discussed the particularity requirement in *W-G-R-*, finding that the proposed social group in that case – former members of the Mara 18 gang in El Salvador who have renounced their gang membership – failed the particularity test because "it is too diffuse, as well as being too broad and subjective." 26 I&N Dec. at 221. The Board held that for such a group to meet the requirement of particularity, it "will often need to be further defined." *Id.* at 222. However, as the Seventh Circuit recently cautioned, it is not appropriate to "determine the legitimacy of social groups by the narrowness of the category." *N.L.A.*, 2014 U.S. App. LEXIS

3971, at *32; *see also Cece v. Holder*, 733 F.3d 662, 674 (7th Cir. 2013) (en banc) (specifically rejecting "broadness" as a per se bar to protected status). As the same court has also observed:

> Many of the groups recognized by the Board and courts are indeed quite broad. These include: women in tribes that practice female genital mutilation; *Matter of Kasinga*, 21 I.&N. Dec. at 365, *Agbor* [*v. Gonzales*, 487 F.3d 499, 502 (7th Cir. 2007)]; persons who are opposed to involuntary sterilization, 8 U.S.C. § 1101(a)(42)(B); *Chen v. Holder*, 604 F.3d 324, 332 (7th Cir.2010); members of the Darood clan and Marehan subclan in Somalia, *In re H-*, 21 I.&N. Dec. at 340, 343 (1% of the population of Somalia are members of the Marehan subclan); homosexuals in Cuba, *In re Toboso–Al*fonso, 20 I. & N. Dec. 819, 822–23 (BIA 1990); Filipinos of Chinese ancestry living in the Philippines, *Matter of V–T–S–*, 21 I. & N. Dec. 792, 798 (BIA 1997) (approximately 1.5% of the Philippines population has an identifiable Chinese background); *Singh v. INS*, 94 F.3d 1353, 1359 (9th Cir.1996) (rejecting the notion that an applicant is ineligible for asylum merely because all members of a persecuted group might be eligible for asylum). The ethnic Tutsis of Rawanda numbered close to 700,000 before the genocide of 1994, and yet a Tutsi singled out for murder who managed to escape to the United States could surely qualify for asylum in this country. And undoubtedly any of the six million Jews ultimately killed in concentration camps in Nazi-controlled Europe could have made valid claims for asylum, if only they had had that opportunity. Many of our asylum laws originated out of a need to address just such refugees from World War II. It would be antithetical to asylum law to deny refuge to a group of persecuted individuals who have valid claims merely because too many have valid claims. *See Iao* [*v. Gonzales*, 400 F.3d 530, 533 (7th Cir. 2005)]; *Singh*, 94 F.3d at 1359.

Cece, 733 F.3d at 674; *see also N.L.A.*, 2014 U.S. App. LEXIS 3971, at *33 ("We have stated in no uncertain terms that denying legitimate asylum applications merely because the group of applicants might be too great is unreasoned and impermissible.").

The Fourth Circuit likewise has rejected the BIA's particularity analysis where an otherwise overly broad group is defined in a way that limits its membership to individuals with an identifiable trait. *See Temu*, 2014 U.S. App. LEXIS 868, at

*19-20. The Fourth Circuit recently explained:

> The BIA is correct that the label of mental illness can cover a broad range of severity. On its own, it is possible – though we do not decide – that the group of individuals with bipolar disorder lacks particularity because of its breadth, but that is not Mr. Temu's proposed group. Rather, Mr. Temu limits his group to those individuals with bipolar disorder who exhibit outwardly erratic behavior. It may well be that mental illness lacks particular boundaries, … [but] Mr. Temu's group does not suffer from the same shortcoming, because it is limited to a specific mental illness so severe that individuals are visibly, identifiably disturbed.

Id. Compare Crespin-Valladares v. Holder, 632 F.3d 117, 120-21, 125-26 (4th Cir. 2011) (finding that the "group consisting of family members of those who actively oppose gangs in El Salvador by agreeing to be prosecutorial witnesses" qualifies as a particular social group); *with Lizama v. Holder*, 629 F.3d 440, 447 (4th Cir. 2011) (holding that "wealth, Americanization, and opposition to gangs are all amorphous characteristics that neither provide an adequate benchmark for determining group membership nor embody concrete traits that would readily identify a person as possessing those characteristics") (internal citation omitted).

The particular social group to which ██████ belongs *is* defined narrowly to include only those individuals in Honduran society who are wealthy, educated, prominent, and recognizable business leaders *and* who have made business decisions adverse to the local population. The group is not overly broad, diffuse, or subjective, as it is limited to those who "would perceive themselves as part of a discrete group" that is "recognized within the society." *W-G-R-*, 26 I&N Dec. at 221. ██████ and ██████ both testified as to the characteristics that mark ██████ out in Honduran society, including his high-level professional position, his recognizability as the "face" of ████, and his wealth, level of education, and personal privileges as compared to the population in general and the workers whom he supervised in particular. *See* Tr. 68-79, 99-109. Moreover, the national police at the Secretary of Security of Honduras who took [REDACTED]'s report quickly recognized the societal group to which he belonged, and they just as quickly advised that they were unable to protect him. *See* Tr. 64. [REDACTED] credibly testified:

> Basically, I told them the entire situation since the very beginning when they started, and even the death of the people, what was happening, what was going on, they took my report, and, basically, what it is was advised to us it was for us to take our own personal measures because, because they could not protect us, they couldn't do anything. … They explained to us that *there were other business executives that were going through the same situation*, and that in case that they wanted to kill us, they couldn't do anything for us.

Tr. 64 (emphasis added); *see also* **Exh. 2 Tab 4** (Complaint to Republic of Honduras Secretary of Security, Department of Criminal Investigations); **Exh. 3 Tab F** at p.95 (Affidavit of Milgian Judith [REDACTED]).

Unlike the social group considered in *W-G-R-*, [REDACTED] has presented credible evidence that the class of individuals in Honduras who are like him – wealthy, educated, prominent, and recognizable business leaders who have made business decisions adverse to the local population – are "perceived, considered, [and] recognized" in Honduran society as a distinct group. 26 I&N Dec. at 222. Members of the group also are frequently targeted owing to their status, are threatened as [REDACTED] was, and, in a shocking number of cases, are either murdered or forced to flee for their lives – like [REDACTED] [REDACTED], and many others about whom the Respondents testified and provided evidence. *See* Tr. 72-74. *See also W-G-R-*, 26 I&N Dec. at 214 ("In assessing a claim, it may be necessary to take into account the social and cultural context of the alien's country of citizenship or nationality.").

The IJ also erred in rejecting [REDACTED]'s proposed social group by breaking the group up and then finding that each of its separate characteristics – wealth, business decisions, etc. – is "too broad and amorphous" to meet the particularity requirement. IJ Dec. at 21. As the Fourth Circuit recently cautioned, "While each component of [a] group might not satisfy the particularity requirement individually," a decision-maker "must consider [the group's] definition as a whole." *Temu*, 2014 U.S. App. LEXIS 868, at *20-22 ("Nothing in the statute requires that if a group is defined by a collection of traits, that each individual trait must meet all the criteria for a 'particular social group.'"). Although the IJ claims to have "consider[ed] the group in its totality as a whole," her analysis of the group's individual characteristics suggests that, as the BIA did in *Temu*, she "missed the forest for the trees." *Id.* at *20. ███████'s proposed group is defined by a group of characteristics that, taken together, describe a specific and recognizable group in Honduran society. The group also is sufficiently limited to those Honduran executives who have made decisions adverse to the local population, a characteristic – as the national police immediately recognized – that often has causes them to be singled out and targeted for persecution.

The Fourth Circuit has noted that "Time and again, case law from this Court, other circuits, and the BIA has accepted social groups that, as part of their definitions, contain components that might not meet the BIA's legal standards." *Id.* at *22 (collecting cases); *see also Crespin-Valladares*, 632 F.3d at 120-21, 125-26. Contrary to the IJ's conclusion, ███████'s group is sufficiently discrete and recognizable in Honduran society – including by national police officials at the Secretary of Security of the Republic of Honduras – to meet the particularity requirement.

3. Social distinction

Third, the IJ mistakenly failed to recognize that the group to which ███ ███████ belongs is socially visible in Honduran society. That ███████ belongs to a group which is socially distinct in Honduras was confirmed by the response he received from the officers at the Secretary of Security's Department of Criminal Investigations in Tegucigalpa. *See* **Exh. 2 Tab 4.** When he visited their offices to report the murder of his bodyguard and the death threats he was receiving, the national police told [redacted] that "there were other business executives that were going through the same situation, and that in case that they wanted to kill us, they couldn't do anything for us." Tr. 64. [redacted] reiterated, on cross-examination, that the police "asked me to take my own measurements because there were cases from executives just like me that they had not been resolved yet." Tr. 92.

Far from being a "contrived" social group, [redacted] belongs to a group that the country's national police recognized as soon as he registered his complaint, responding that "other business executives [] were going through the same situation" and that they were aware of other cases "from executives just like me." Tr. 64, 92. In *Temu*, the Fourth Circuit observed that "one highly relevant factor" in assessing social visibility (i.e., social distinction) "is if the applicant's group is singled out for greater persecution than the population as a whole." 2014 U.S. App. LEXIS 686, at *7; *see also Matter of C-A-*, 23 I&N Dec. 951, 960-61 (BIA 2006) (defining social visibility as whether a group is "understood by others to constitute" a social group). That is the case here, where the group sometimes is referred to by the shorthand term of "executives," and where certain members who have made decisions adverse to their workers or members of the local population are targeted for persecution. *Temu* explained further:

> A group cannot be defined solely by the fact of its persecution, *Gatimi v. Holder*, 578 F.3d 611, 616 (7th Cir. 2009), so evidence that members of a society have a label for a proposed group helps suggest that the group has a common thread outside of its victimhood[.]

2014 U.S. App. LEXIS 686, at *17.

The IJ erred further in characterizing [redacted]'s particular social group as being "defined by the harm the respondent fears." IJ Dec. at 22. It is undisputed that "persecutory conduct aimed at a social group cannot alone define the group, which must exist independently of the persecution." *W-G-R-*, 26 I&N Dec. at 215.

However, the fact that the group's members have been subjected to harm may be relevant for determining whether the group meets the social distinction requirement. *Matter of A-M-E- & J-G-U-*, 24 I&N Dec. 69, 74 (BIA 2007). The BIA recently provided an example of such a situation, which is particularly apposite to [redacted]'s case. In *Matter of M-E-V-G-*, the Board held that although former employees of a country's attorney general share an immutable characteristic, they would not normally be seen as a group by society. 26 I&N Dec. 227, 242 (BIA 2014). However, once the government begins to persecute these individuals, they may begin to share a sense of "group" and the society may also begin to see the members of that group as being distinct in some significant way. *Id.* at 242-43. The Board explained:

> The act of persecution … may be the catalyst that causes the society to distinguish the former employees in a meaningful way and consider them a distinct group, but the immutable characteristic of their shared past experience exists independent of the persecution.

Id. at 243.

Analogously, it is in part because wealthy, educated, prominent, and recognizable business leaders like [redacted] are targeted for persecution that Honduran society – including officers at the national Secretary of Security – views them as a discrete group. The group is not, however, entirely defined by the fact of persecution, as members of the group would share immutable characteristics even absent the persecution. A group member's trait of having made business decisions adverse to the local population is an immutable characteristic that he or she is powerless to change, and is a factor that may cause the individual to be targeted for threats and harm. *See W-G-R-*, 26 I&N Dec. at 212-13 ("The defining characteristic can be … a shared past experience."). But this does not amount to defining the group by the persecution alone. *See id.* at 215. Here, the particular social group is defined not solely by the fact that its members are persecuted, but the persecution is a factor that renders the group socially distinct within Honduran society.

See M-E-V-G-, 26 I&N Dec. at 242.

B. The IJ erred in finding that [redacted] failed to prove the required nexus between the persecution he fears and his membership in the specified particular social group

The IJ also erred in concluding that [redacted] "failed to demonstrate a nexus between the harm that he fears and the social group that he has defined." IJ Dec. at 22. According to the IJ,

> There is insufficient evidence to suggest that the people whom the respondent fears cared one iota about his education, about his prominence, or his wealth or any adverse decisions that he made unrelated to their pay. These are people who wanted to get paid for the labor that they provided so that they could feed and clothe and house themselves and their families. ... If the workers had received their pay, or if they were to receive their pay, nothing suggests that they would have any interest at all in targeting the respondent. And so, this is not about the respondent's membership in a made up particular social group.

Id. at 23. The IJ's decision misstates the evidence and incorrectly describes [redacted]'s situation as a mere "personal dispute that lacks the required nexus" for asylum purposes. *Id.*

The nexus requirement – in this case, whether [redacted] was persecuted on account of membership "in his proposed group" – is a factual question and [redacted] bears the burden of proving that his membership in the group was or will be a central reason for his persecution. *Temu*, 2014 U.S. App. LEXIS 686, at *7; *W-G-R-*, 26 I&N Dec. at 224.

Contrary to the IJ's assessment, the record contains undisputed evidence that the individuals who threatened [redacted]'s life *did* care about his prominence, his wealth, and his decisions as the executive in charge of the [redacted] facility in Yoro, Honduras, and that he *would* continue to face threats and harm in Honduras even if his antagonists eventually were paid or were rehired by the company. In a sworn statement in support of his asylum application, [redacted] attested:

> On February 19th, 2010 unknown individuals killed the Chief of Pro-

> duction of the ████ Company located in Yoro, Mr. ████ ████ who was the second person, after me, in command of the production department, the threats against me became stronger, and calls were made from different unknown cellular numbers, unknown males voices, the calls were made directly to my cellular phone and they were normally made between 6AM and 10PM.
>
> I think the calls were made from former employees, because they would use phrases like, "since you son of a bitch and you have your stomach full, you don't fucking care about the rest of us, pay us or else we are going to skin you alive", "If we do not see payments this week, someone else will die dog," "Your guards are not going to stop us, we can get to casas blancas to kill you."

Exh. 2 Tab 3. And in his supplemental affidavit to the Immigration Court, which was prepared nearly two years after his departure from Honduras, ████ ████ attested:

> In HONDURAS there is no response from the authorities in my case, and there are many other cases like mine, where administrators, managers, area heads, government area heads, persons who belong to a privileged class in Honduran society, are being murdered, at such a pace that the United Nations classifies Honduras as the most violent country in the world outside of war zones. …
>
> After October 18, 2011 and throughout 2012 and 2013 many people, former employees, current employees, and drivers of ████, have been looking for information in an attempt to locate me within Honduras. They have been seeking information on me and my family (my son and wife). Several times these individuals have approached current employees who have worked very closely with me at ████, such as ████, who is the Head of Production. … These men asked ████ ████, "When will that dog ████ ████ come back, because we're waiting for him, to settle scores." …
>
> Furthermore, a group of ex-employees … have asked ████, "When will that son of a bitch ████ ████ be back, because we're waiting for him." … They have asked ████ this question multiple times, especially in June and July 2013, when nearly two years have already passed since my departure from Honduras. … I know these people continue associating the debt ████ owes them, their problems, and their hatred for ████ with me, and I am very fearful for my life.

. . .

> I am very fearful for my life, because I know that they are looking for me, to kill me, and that my pursuers will not rest until they achieve their goal. I know that, in view of the position of manager of [redacted] that I held for many years, and the business decisions I had to make, my life and the lives of my wife and so are in grave danger in Honduras. … People like me, who have executive positions and belong to a privileged social class in Honduras, are being murdered and there is no response or protection by the authorities.

Exh. 3 Tab E.

Furthermore, in his sworn testimony to the Immigration Court, [redacted] reported that his former colleague Mr. [redacted] "had been approached, and they had asked him, when is the dog returning, returning back? We have to fix and adjust things with him." Tr. 75. He testified also that "the people that I had the problems with they continue persecuting me and … they're saying that after I come back, they're going to fix the problems with me personally." Tr. 77. Asked what he meant by this, [redacted] replied: "Basically that they're going to kill the responsible – the person responsible of the problems that they have, the financial problems that they have." *Id.*

[redacted]'s sworn statements and testimony, along with the corroborating evidence submitted, reveals that he was threatened not merely owing to a personal dispute, but allegedly because 'his stomach was full' and 'he didn't care about the workers' and he was regarded as being responsible for the company's failure to pay wages and pensions. As [redacted] explained, because he belonged to a privileged social class and held an executive position – and because he was the 'face of the company' who had made the business decisions that caused the workers' financial difficulties – he was targeted by ex-employees determined to "settle scores" with him. *See W-G-R-*, 26 I&N Dec. at 223-24 ("Whether that nexus exists depends on the views and motives of the persecutor."); *N-M-*, 25 I&N Dec. 526.Thus, the evidence demonstrates that [redacted]'s membership in the proposed social group was one central reason for the threats he received and his resulting well-founded fear of persecution. *See W-G-R-*, 26 I&N Dec. at 224.

The evidence further demonstrates that could not avoid being targeted and harmed in Honduras even by leaving , or even if the company were to pay the workers what they demanded. The IJ's contrary finding is belied by the witnesses' testimony and the documentary evidence submitted. As reported, nearly two years after he fled Honduras, those who sought to harm him continued to actively search for him and ask his whereabouts, in order to "fix" him personally and to kill the person they deemed responsible for their grievances. These facts distinguish 's case from the persecution claim addressed by the Board in *Matter of T-M-B-*, 21 I&N Dec. 775 (BIA 1997), which was relied upon by the IJ. *See* IJ Dec. at 19, 24, 26. In *T-M-B-*, the BIA found that the guerrillas who threated the respondent did so solely to extort money for their cause. 21 I&N Dec. at 778. Because they "had no interest in the alien beyond her ability to pay them," the respondent could not prove a nexus between the threats she received and a protected ground for asylum. *N-M-*, 25 I&N Dec. at 530 n.3. By contrast, has offered unchallenged testimony and evidence that his persecutors' motivation was *not* merely financial, but rested also on a perceived disparity in social status and privilege and on the workers' conviction that 's business decisions were the cause of their misfortune.

In addition, provided evidence and offered credible testimony about other executives who were targeted, threatened, attacked, and, in certain cases, killed after having made adverse business decisions that impacted their employees and families. *See* Tr. 72-79, 88-90, 108-109. *See also Martinez*, 2014 U.S. App. LEXIS 1250, at *6-7 (noting that respondent feared persecution for having repudiated the gang in part because two of his friends who attempted to leave the gang were killed). Among the victims similarly situated to were Mr. , who was 's immediate predecessor at (threatened and murdered); Mr. [redacted] the former chief of power production at [redacted] (threatened and murdered); Mr. [redacted], the former chief of production at [redacted] (attempted murder by arson); and Mr. [redacted], president of a transportation cooperative that provided services to [redacted] (murdered). *See* Tr. 72-74. As the BIA has previously recognized, a group of similarly situated former employees can qualify as a cognizable particular social group. *See Fuentes*, 19 I&N Dec. at 662.

In sum, contrary to the IJ's decision, [redacted] has met his burden of demonstrating that he belongs to a cognizable social group in Honduras and that his membership in the group is a central reason for both the threats he received and the harm he fears upon return. *See W-G-R-*, 26 I&N Dec. at 224. It is unclear how the IJ could simultaneously accept as credible the evidence and testimony presented, acknowledging that "[t]hese are clearly people who are frightened" and "clearly people who are at risk," IJ Dec. at 26, yet also conclude that [redacted] was not targeted and threatened because of his social status as an executive and owing to the business decisions he made, which inarguably sparked the wrath of his persecutors. *See Temu*, 2014 U.S. App. LEXIS 868, at *7-9.

C. The IJ erred in finding that [redacted] failed to establish eligibility for protection under Article 3 of the Convention Against Torture

Finally, the IJ erred in concluding that [redacted] failed to prove that it is more likely than not that he would be tortured in Honduras with the consent or acquiescence of Honduran authorities. According to the IJ, despite evidence that the police in Honduras are inept, corrupt, lack training, act with impunity, and commit human rights violations, "that is not consent or acquiescence, and it is not the basis for a viable claim for protection pursuant to Article 3 of the Convention Against Torture." IJ Dec. at 26.

The IJ's conclusion is inconsistent with the Fourth Circuit's recent decision in *Zelaya v. Holder*, 668 F.3d 159 (4th Cir. 2012), which also considered a Convention Against Torture claim from a Honduran respondent who alleged that police in Honduras consent or acquiesce to torture. The court stated:

> What is clear to us is that the BIA did not take issue with the IJ's grave concern that Zelaya would be killed by MS-13 if he is removed to Honduras. What is not clear to us, however, is why the police officer's ultimate refusal to help Zelaya in any way when he reported that he had just been threatened with a gunshot by a member of MS-13 for resisting MS-13's recruitment efforts does not satisfy Zelaya's burden of proving that it is more likely than not that if Zelaya is removed to Honduras, he would endure severe pain or suffering, whether physical or mental, intentionally inflicted on him for such purposes as punishing him for resisting MS-13 recruitment or coercing him to join MS-13, with the awareness of the local police that this would take place and the breach of the local police's legal responsibility to intervene to prevent it from happening.

Id. at 168. Likewise, the IJ did not dispute [redacted]'s genuine assertion of fear that he would be harmed or killed if he returned to Honduras. IJ Dec. at 26. What is unclear from the IJ's decision is why she determined that the refusal of Honduran officials to help [redacted] in any way when he reported the threats he received, as well as the torture and murder of his bodyguard, did not satisfy his burden of proving that it is more likely than not that if removed to Honduras, he too would face torture with the awareness of the police and the breach of their legal responsibility to intervene to protect him. The court's decision in *Zelaya*, which is binding on both the IJ and the BIA in this case, dictates a contrary conclusion and a grant of [redacted]'s Convention Against Torture claim.

The Fourth Circuit's decision in *Lizama v. Holder*, 629 F.3d 440 (4th Cir. 2011), upon which the IJ relied, is plainly distinguishable from the Respondents' case. *See* IJ Dec. at 25-26. In *Lizama*, the court rejected the petitioner's Convention Against Torture claim for failure to demonstrate acquiescence, because "[t]he Salvadoran government does not have a policy or practice of refusing assistance to persons who receive threats or are otherwise victims of gang violence" and "the Salvadoran government's 'strong-hand law enforcement policy' is having a 'noticeable effect,' at least in the short term, of curbing gang violence." 629 F.3d at 449-50; *see also Martinez*, 2014 U.S. App. LEXIS 1250, at *28 (noting that "country condition information reflects that government officials in El Salvador are taking some steps to address the difficult problem of gang violence there").

In marked contrast, officers at the Secretary of Security, Department of Criminal Investigations in Honduras candidly told that "they could not protect [him], they couldn't do anything" and they recommended that he "take [his] own personal measures." Tr. 64. By way of explanation, the officers indicated that "there were other business executives that were going through the same situation, and that in case they wanted to kill us, they couldn't do anything for us." *Id.* Unlike in *Lizama* (and *Martinez*), the evidence in the Respondents' case establishes that the Honduran government *does* have a policy or practice of refusing assistance to persons who receive threats or are otherwise victims of violence. The country's national police openly admitted as much to when he came to them in search of help and protection.

Moreover, the IJ acknowledged this fact, stating that the authorities "took a report. They were honest with him, and they said, this is a problem. Other executives have had problems. Get yourself some protection." IJ Dec. at 26. The IJ's factual finding simply cannot be squared with her legal conclusion that failed to prove that the Honduran government acquiesces, or is willfully blind to, torture carried out by groups or individuals that it is unable or unwilling to control.

As the Seventh Circuit has recently noted, even where a government is "engaged in more concerted and successful efforts" to combat acts of violence and torture by nongovernmental actors, this "does not necessarily mean that it cannot also remain willfully blind to the torturous acts" being committed. *N.L.A.*, 2014 U.S. App. LEXIS 3971, at *37. The court declared:

> Where a government contains officials that would be complicit in tor-

> ture, and that government, on the whole, is admittedly incapable of actually preventing that torture, the fact that some officials take action to prevent the torture would seem neither inconsistent with a finding of government acquiescence nor necessarily responsive to the question of whether torture would be inflicted by or at the instigation of or with the consent or acquiescence of a public official or other person acting in an official capacity.

Id. at *37-38. Other circuit courts have agreed. *See Pieschacon-Villegas v. Att'y Gen. of the U.S.*, 671 F.3d 303, 312 (3d Cir. 2011) ("The mere fact that the Colombian government is engaged in a protracted civil war with the FARC does not necessarily mean that it cannot remain willfully blind to the torturous acts of the FARC); *De La Rosa v. Holder*, 598 F.3d 103, 110 (2d Cir. 2010).

In the Respondents' case, the evidence does not indicate that *any* Honduran officials are actively trying to prevent the torture that [redacted] fears. The government's awareness that acts amounting to torture are occurring or will occur, and its breach thereafter to carry out its legal duty to intervene and prevent the torture, amounts to acquiescence. *See* 8 C.F.R. §1208.18(a)(7). Accordingly, the IJ erred in denying [redacted]'s request for withholding of removal under the Convention Against Torture.

VII. CONCLUSION

Based on the foregoing, the Respondents' appeal should be sustained, the decision of the Immigration Judge should be reversed, and the Respondents should be granted asylum in the United States under INA §208(a). In the alternative, the Respondents should be granted withholding of removal under the Convention Against Torture pursuant to 8 C.F.R. §1208.16(c).

Respectfully submitted,

______________________________ ______________________________

Thomas K. Ragland
BENACH RAGLAND LLP
1333 H Street NW, Suite 900 West
Washington, D.C. 20005
T: 202.644.8600 / F: 202.644.8615
tkragland@benachragland.com

Date

Counsel for Respondents

APPENDIX 8C

SAMPLE PETITION FOR REVIEW

UNITED STATES COURT OF APPEALS
FOR THE _______ CIRCUIT

________________________		
[name of Petitioner]	)	
	)	
Petitioner,	)	**File No.________________**
	)	
v.	)	
	)	**A# ____________________**
______________,	)	
Attorney General,	)	
	)	
Respondent	)	
________________________	)	

PETITION FOR REVIEW

The above named petitioner hereby petitions for the review of a final order of [deportation] [removal] entered by the Board of Immigration Appeals on _____________ [date of BIA decision].

A copy of the BIA's decision is attached. To date, no court has upheld the validity of the order.

____
[signature of attorney or petitioner]

Dated: _________________

[(1) COMPLETE ALL BLANK SPACES EXCEPT "FILE NO.". THE COURT CLERK'S OFFICE WILL ASSIGN A NUMBER.
(2) ATTACH CERTIFICATE OF SERVICE AND THE BIA DECISIONS. CHECK LOCAL RULES FOR OTHER NECESSARY ATTACHMENTS.
(3) THIS DOCUMENT SHOULD BE SERVED ON THE ATTORNEY GENERAL, AND ON THE OFFICER OR EMPLOYEE OF DHS IN CHARGE OF THE DISTRICT IN WHICH THE FINAL ORDER OF REMOVAL WAS ENTERED. PETITIONER MAY ALSO WANT TO SERVE A COPY OF THE PETITION FOR REVIEW ON THE OFFICE OF IMMIGRATION LITIGATION, THE LOCAL DHS DISTRICT COUNSEL'S OFFICE, IF ANY, AND POSSIBLY THE LOCAL ICE REMOVAL OFFICERS.]

APPENDIX 9A

FORM I-765 AND INSTRUCTIONS

OMB No. 1615-0040; Expires 02/28/2018

Department of Homeland Security
U.S. Citizenship and Immigration Services

I-765, Application For Employment Authorization

For USCIS Use Only	**Fee Stamp**	**Action Block**	**Initial Receipt**	**Resubmitted**
			Relocated	
			Received	**Sent**
			Completed	
☐ **Application Approved** ☐ **Authorization/Extension Valid From**____ ☐ **Authorization/Extension Valid To**____		☐ **Application Denied - Failed to establish:** ☐ **Eligibility under 8 CFR 274a.12 (a) or (c)** ☐ **Economic necessity under 8 CFR 274a.12(c)(14), (18) and 8 CFR 214.2(f)**	**Approved**	**Denied**
			A#	
Subject to the following conditions: ____		☐ **Applicant is filing under section 274a.12**____		

I am applying for: ☐ Permission to accept employment. ☐ Replacement (of lost employment authorization document).
☐ Renewal of my permission to accept employment (attach a copy of your previous employment authorization document).

1. Full Name
(Family Name) (First Name) (Middle Name)

2. Other Names Used (include Maiden Name)

3. U.S. Mailing Address
(Street Number and Name) (Apt. Number)
(Town or City) (State) (ZIP Code)

4. Country of Citizenship or Nationality

5. Place of Birth
(Town or City) (State/Province) (Country)

6. Date of Birth (mm/dd/yyyy)

7. Gender ☐ Male ☐ Female

8. Marital Status
☐ Married ☐ Single ☐ Divorced ☐ Widowed

9. Social Security Number (Include all numbers you have ever used, if any)

10. Alien Registration Number (A-Number) or **Form I-94 Number** (if any)

11. Have you ever before applied for employment authorization from USCIS?
☐ Yes (Complete the following questions.)
Which USCIS Office? Dates
Results (Granted or Denied - attach all documentation)
☐ No (Proceed to **Question 12.**)

12. Date of Last Entry into the U.S., on or about (mm/dd/yyyy)

13. Place of Last Entry into the U.S.

14. Status at Last Entry (B-2 Visitor, F-1 Student, No Lawful Status, etc.)

15. Current Immigration Status (Visitor, Student, etc.)

16. Eligibility Category. Go to the "**Who May File Form I-765?**" section of the Instructions. In the space below, place the letter and number of the eligibility category you selected from the instructions. For example, (a)(8), (c)(17)(iii), etc.
( ) ( ) ( )

17. (c)(3)(C) Eligibility Category. If you entered the eligibility category (c)(3)(C) in **Question 16** above, list your degree, your employer's name as listed in E-Verify, and your employer's E-Verify Company Identification Number or a valid E-Verify Client Company Identification Number in the space below.
Degree Employer's Name as listed in E-Verify
Employer's E-Verify Company Identification Number or a Valid E-Verify Client Company Identification Number

18. (c)(26) Eligibility Category. If you entered the eligibility category (c)(26) in **Question 16** above, please provide the receipt number of your H-1B principal spouse's most recent Form I-797 Notice of Approval for Form I-129.

Applicant's Signature

I certify, under penalty of perjury, that the foregoing is true and correct. Furthermore, I authorize the release of any information that U.S. Citizenship and Immigration Services needs to determine eligibility for the benefit I am seeking. I have read the "**Who May File Form I-765?**" section of the instructions and have identified the appropriate eligibility category in **Question 16**.

Signature ____
Date of Signature (mm/dd/yyyy) ____
Telephone Number ____

Signature of Person Preparing Form, If Other Than Applicant

I declare that this document was prepared by me at the request of the applicant and is based on all information of which I have any knowledge.

Signature ____
Date of Signature (mm/dd/yyyy) ____
Printed Name ____
Address ____

Form I-765 02/13/15 Y

OMB No. 1615-0040; Expires 02/28/2018

Instructions for I-765, Application for Employment Authorization

Department of Homeland Security
U.S. Citizenship and Immigration Services

What Is the Purpose of This Form?

Certain aliens who are temporarily in the United States may file Form I-765, Application for Employment Authorization, to request an Employment Authorization Document (EAD). Other aliens who are authorized to work in the United States without restrictions must also use this form to apply to USCIS for a document that shows such authorization. Review **Eligibility Categories** to determine whether you should use this form.

If you are a lawful permanent resident, a conditional resident, or a nonimmigrant authorized to be employed with a specific employer under 8 CFR 274a.12(b), do **not** use this form.

Definitions

Employment Authorization Document (EAD): Form I-688, Form I-688A, Form I-688B, Form I-766, or any successor document issued by USCIS as evidence that the holder is authorized to work in the United States.

Renewal EAD: An EAD issued to an eligible applicant upon the expiration of a previous EAD issued under the same category.

Replacement EAD: An EAD issued to an eligible applicant when the previously issued EAD has been lost, stolen, mutilated, or contains erroneous information, such as a misspelled name.

Interim EAD: An EAD issued to an eligible applicant when USCIS has failed to adjudicate an application within 90 days of a properly filed EAD application, or within 30 days of a properly filed initial EAD application based on an asylum application filed on or after January 4, 1995. The interim EAD will be granted for a period not to exceed 240 days and is subject to the conditions noted on the document. *The Interim EAD provisions apply to individuals filing Form I-765 based on Consideration of Deferred Action for Childhood Arrivals only after a determination on deferred action is reached.*

Who May File Form I-765?

USCIS adjudicates a request for employment authorization by determining whether an applicant has submitted the required information and documentation, and whether the applicant is eligible. In order to determine your eligibility, you must identify the category in which you are eligible and fill in that category in **Question 16** on Form I-765. Enter only **one** of the following category numbers on the application form. For example, if you are a refugee applying for an EAD, write **"(a)(3)"** at **Question 16.**

For easier reference, the categories are subdivided as follows:

1. **Asylee/Refugee Categories (and their Spouse and Children**

   A. **Refugee–(a)(3).** File Form I-765 with either a copy of your Form I-590, Registration for Classification as Refugee, approval letter, or a copy of a Form I-730, Refugee/Asylee Relative Petition, approval notice.

   B. **Paroled as a Refugee–(a)(4).** File Form I-765 with a copy of your Form I-94, Arrival-Departure Record.

   C. **Asylee (Granted Asylum)–(a)(5).** File Form I-765 with a copy of the USCIS letter, or judge's decision, granting you asylum. It is not necessary to apply for an EAD as an asylee until 90 days before the expiration of your current EAD.

   D. **Asylum Applicant (With a Pending Asylum Application) Who Filed for Asylum on or After January 4, 1995–(c)(8).** For specific instructions for applicants with pending asylum claims, see section entitled **"Special Filing Instructions for Those with Pending Asylum Applications ((c)(8))."**

2. **Nationality Categories**

   A. **Citizen of Micronesia, the Marshall Islands, or Palau–(a)(8).** File Form I-765 if you were admitted to the United States as a citizen of the Federated States of Micronesia (CFA/FSM), the Marshall Islands (CFA/MIS), or Palau under agreements between the United States and the former trust territories.

   B. **Deferred Enforced Departure (DED)/Extended Voluntary Departure–(a)(11).** File Form I-765 with evidence of your identity and nationality.

C. Temporary Protected Status (TPS)–(a)(12) and (c)(19). A category (a)(12) EAD is issued to an individual granted TPS under 8 CFR 244. A category (c)(19) EAD is a temporary treatment benefit under TPS pursuant to 8 CFR 244.5.

To request an EAD based on TPS, file Form I-765 with Form I-821, or with evidence that your initial Form I-821 was accepted or approved. Include evidence of nationality and identity as required by the Form I-821 instructions. If you are requesting extension of TPS status, also include a copy (front and back) of your last available TPS document: EAD, Form I-94, or approval notice.

To register for TPS, you must file a Form I-765 with From I-821, Application for Temporary Protected Status, for each applicant, regardless of age, even if you are not requesting employment authorization. No fee is required for Form I-765 filed as part of TPS registration. (Form I-821 has separate fee requirements.)

If you have been granted TPS by an immigration judge (IJ) or the Board of Immigration Appeals (BIA) and are requesting your first EAD, you must submit evidence of your IJ or BIA grant of TPS with your application for an EAD along with a copy of your I-821 application that the IJ or BIA approved. You must also follow the instructions for filing your application as described in the most recent TPS *Federal Register* notice regarding a TPS designation or extension for your country. As further instructed in those notices, once you receive your I-797 application receipt notice, you must also send an e-mail to **tpsijgrant.vsc@dhs.gov** with the following information: Your name; your A number; your date of birth; the receipt number for your application; and the date you were granted TPS.

D. NACARA Section 203 Applicants Who Are Eligible to Apply for NACARA Relief With USCIS–(c)(10). See the instructions to Form I-881, Application for Suspension of Deportation or Special Rule Cancellation of Removal, to determine if you are eligible to apply to USCIS for NACARA 203 relief.

If you are eligible, you may file a Form I-765 with the Form I-881. See Instructions to Form I-881 for filing location. If you file the Form I-765 separately from the Form I-881 see **"Where to File?"** instructions. Your response to **Question 16** on the Form I-765 must be "(c)(10)."

E. Dependent of TECRO E-1 Nonimmigrant–(c)(2). File Form I-765 with the required certification from the American Institute in Taiwan if you are the spouse or unmarried dependent son or daughter of an E-1 employee of the Taipei Economic and Cultural Representative Office.

3. Foreign Students

A. F-1 Student Seeking Optional Practical Training in an Occupation Directly Related to Studies: (c)(3)(A)–Pre-completion Optional Practical Training; (c)(3)(B)–Post-completion Optional Practical Training; (c)(3)(C)–17-month extension for STEM Students (Students With a degree in Science, Technology, Engineering, or Mathematics). File Form I-765 with a Certificate of Eligibility of Nonimmigrant (F-1) Student Status (Form I-20 A-B/I-20 ID) endorsed by a Designated School Official within the past 30 days. If you are a STEM student requesting a 17-month extension under the eligibility code (c)(3)(C), you must also submit a copy of your degree and the employer name as listed in E-Verify, along with the E-Verify Company Identification Number, or a valid E-Verify Client Company Identification Number for the employer with whom you are seeking the 17-month OPT extension. This information must be provided in **Question 17** of the form.

B. F-1 Student Offered Off-Campus Employment Under the Sponsorship of a Qualifying International Organization–(c)(3)(ii). File Form I-765 with the international organization's letter of certification that the proposed employment is within the scope of its sponsorship, and a Certificate of Eligibility of Nonimmigrant (F-1) Student Status – For Academic and Language Students (Form I-20 A-B/I-20 ID) endorsed by the Designated School Official within the past 30 days.

C. F-1 Student Seeking Off-Campus Employment Due to Severe Economic Hardship–(c)(3)(iii). File Form I-765 with Form I-20 A-B/I-20 ID, Certificate of Eligibility of Nonimmigrant (F-1) Student Status -- For Academic and Language Students, and any evidence you wish to submit, such as affidavits, that detail the unforeseen economic circumstances that cause your request, and evidence that you have tried to find off-campus employment with an employer who has filed a labor and wage attestation.

D. J-2 Spouse or Minor Child of an Exchange Visitor–(c)(5). File Form I-765 with a copy of your J-1 (principal alien's) Certificate of Eligibility for Exchange Visitor (J-1) Status (Form IAP-66). You must submit a written statement with any supporting evidence showing that your employment is not necessary to support the J-1 but is for other purposes.

E. **M-1 Student Seeking Practical Training After Completing Studies–(c)(6).** File Form I-765 with a completed Form I-539, Application to Change/ Extend Nonimmigrant Status, according to the filing instructions for Form I-539. You must also include Form I-20 M-N, Certificate of Eligibility for Nonimmigrant (M-1) Student Status – For Vocational Students endorsed by the Designated School Official within the past 30 days, with your application.

4. **Eligible Dependents of Employees of Diplomatic Missions, International Organizations, or NATO**

A. **Dependent of A-1 or A-2 Foreign Government Officials–(c)(1).** Submit Form I-765 with Form I-566, Interagency Record of Request-A, G, or NATO Dependent Employment Authorization or Change/Adjustment to/from A, G, or NATO Status, Dependent Employment Authorization, through your diplomatic mission to the Department of State (DOS). The DOS will forward all favorably endorsed applications directly to the Nebraska Service Center for adjudication.

B. **Dependent of G-1, G-3 or G-4 Nonimmigrant–(c)(4).** Submit Form I-765 with Form I-566, Interagency Record of Request-A, G, or NATO Dependent Employment Authorization or Change/ Adjustment to/from A, G, or NATO Status, Dependent Employment Authorization, through your international organization to the Department of State (DOS). (In New York City, the United Nations (UN) and UN missions should submit such applications to the United States Mission to the UN (USUN).) The DOS or USUN will forward all favorably endorsed applications directly to the Nebraska Service Center for adjudication.

C. **Dependent of NATO-1 Through NATO-6–(c)(7).** Submit Form I-765 with Form I-566, Interagency Record of Request-A, G, or NATO Dependent Employment Authorization or Change/Adjustment to/from A, G, or NATO Status, Dependent Employment Authorization, to NATO SACLANT, 7857 Blandy Road, C-027, Suite 100, Norfolk, VA 23551-2490. NATO/SACLANT will forward all favorably endorsed applications directly to the Nebraska Service Center for adjudication.

5. **Employment-Based Nonimmigrant Categories**

A. **B-1 Nonimmigrant Who Is the Personal or Domestic Servant of a Nonimmigrant Employer–(c)(17)(i).** File Form I-765 with:

1. Evidence from your employer that he or she is a B, E, F, H, I, J, L, M, O, P, R, or TN nonimmigrant and you were employed for at least 1 year by the employer before the employer entered the United States, or your employer regularly employs personal and domestic servants and has done so for a period of years before coming to the United States; and

2. Evidence that you have either worked for this employer as a personal or domestic servant for at least 1 year, or evidence that you have at least 1 year's experience as a personal or domestic servant; and

3. Evidence establishing that you have a residence abroad that you have no intention of abandoning.

B. **B-1 Nonimmigrant Domestic Servant of a U.S. Citizen–(c)(17)(ii).** File Form I-765 with:

1. Evidence from your employer that he or she is a U.S. citizen; and

2. Evidence that your employer has a permanent home abroad or is stationed outside the United States and is temporarily visiting the United States or the citizen's current assignment in the United States will not be longer than 4 years; and

3. Evidence that he or she has employed you as a domestic servant abroad for at least 6 months prior to your admission to the United States.

C. **B-1 Nonimmigrant Employed by a Foreign Airline– (c)(17)(iii).** File Form I-765 with a letter from the airline fully describing your duties and stating that your position would entitle you to E nonimmigrant status except for the fact that you are not a national of the same country as the airline or because there is no treaty of commerce and navigation in effect between the United States and that country.

D. **Spouse of an E-1/E-2 Treaty Trader or Investor–(a)(17) or Spouse of an E-3 Certain Specialty of Occupation Professional from Australia.** File Form I-765 with evidence of your lawful status and evidence you are a **spouse** of a principal E-1/E-2, such as your Form I-94, and a copy of the principal's visa, and your marriage certificate. (Other relatives or dependents of E-1/E-2 aliens who are in E status are not eligible for employment authorization and may not file under this category.)

E. **Spouse of an L-1 Intracompany Transferee–(a)(18).** File Form I-765 with evidence of your lawful status and evidence you are a **spouse** of a principal L-1, such as your Form I-94, and a copy of the principal's visa and your marriage certificate. (Other relatives or dependents of L-1 aliens who are in L status are not eligible for employment authorization and may not file under this category.)

F. Spouse of an E-2 CNMI Investor–(c)(12). File Form I-765 with evidence of your lawful status and evidence you are a **spouse** of a principal E-2 CNMI Investor, and a copy of the principal E-2 CNMI Investors long-term business certificate or Foreign Investment Certificate. (Please note that spouse of a principal E-2 CNMI Investor who obtained status on the basis of a Foreign Retiree Investment Certification is not eligible for employment authorization and may not file under this category.)

G. Spouse of an H-1B Nonimmigrant–(c)(26). File Form I-765 along with documentation of your current H-4 admission or extension of stay. You must also submit documentation establishing either that the H-1B principal has an approved Immigrant Petition for Alien Worker (Form I-140), or that your current H-4 admission or extension of stay was approved pursuant to the principal H-1B nonimmigrant's admission or extension of stay based on sections 106(a) and (b) of the American Competitiveness in the Twenty-First Century Act (AC21). For your convenience, you may file Form I-765 with Form I-539, Application to Extend/ Change Nonimmigrant Status. However, USCIS will not process Form I-765 (except filing fees), until **after** USCIS has adjudicated Form I-539. You may also file Form I-765 at the same time as Form I-539 **and** Form I-129, Petition for a Nonimmigrant Worker. The 90-day period for adjudicating Applications for Employment Authorization (Form I-765) filed together with Form I-539 does not begin until USCIS has determined whether you are eligible for the underlying H-4 nonimmigrant status, and that the principal is eligible for H-1B status. Please see the USCIS Web site at **www.uscis.gov/I-765** for the most current information on where the file this benefit request.

1. **Proof of Your Status.** Submit a copy of your current Form I-797 approval notice for Form I-539 or Form I-94 showing your admission as an H-4 nonimmigrant or your most recent approved extension of stay; and

2. **Proof of Relationship to the Principal H-1B.** Submit a copy of the marriage certificate for you and the principal H-1B nonimmigrant. If you cannot submit a copy of your current Form I-797, Form I-94, or marriage certificate, USCIS will consider secondary evidence.

3. **Basis for Work Authorization.** Acceptable documentation includes:

   a. **Approved Form I-140.** Submit evidence that the H-1B principal is the beneficiary of an *approved* Immigrant Petition for Alien Worker (Form I-140). You may show this by submitting a copy of the H-1B principal's Form I-797 approval notice for Form I-140; or

   b. **H-1B Principal Received AC21 106(a) and (b) Extension.** Submit evidence that the principal H-1B nonimmigrant has received an extension of stay under AC21 106(a) and (b). You may show this by submitting copies of the H-1B principal's passports, prior Forms I-94, and current and prior Forms I-797 for Form I-129. In addition, please submit evidence to establish one of the following bases for the H-1B extension of stay:

   Based on Filing of a Permanent Labor Certification Application. Submit evidence that the H-1B principal is the beneficiary of a Permanent Labor Certification Application that was filed at least 365 days prior to the expiration of the 6-year limitation of stay. You may show this by submitting a copy of a print out from the Department of Labor's (DOL's) Web site or other correspondence from DOL showing the status of the H-1B principal's Permanent Labor Certification Application. If DOL certified the Permanent Labor Certification, you must also submit a copy of Form I-797 Notice of Receipt for Form I-140 establishing that the Form I-140 was filed within 180 days of DOL certifying the Permanent Labor Certification; or

   Based on a Pending Form I-140. If the preference category sought for the principal H-1B spouse does not require a Permanent Labor Certification Application with DOL, submit evidence that the H-1B principal's Form I-140 was filed at least 365 days prior to the expiration of the 6-year limitation of stay and remains pending. You may show this by submitting a copy of the Form I-797 Notice of Receipt for Form I-140.

4. **Secondary Evidence.** If you do not have the evidence listed in 1, 2, or 3 above, you may ask USCIS to consider other evidence ("secondary evidence") in support of your application for employment authorization as an H-4 spouse. For example, in establishing the Basis for Employment Authorization as described in 3a and 3b, you may submit the receipt number of the H-1B principal's most current Form I-129 extension of stay or the receipt number of the H-1B principal's approved Form I-140 petition.

   Failure to provide the evidence listed above or secondary evidence may result in the delay or denial of your application for employment authorization. For additional information on secondary evidence, see **Evidence** in the **General Instructions** section.

6. **Family-Based Nonimmigrant Categories**

   A. **K-1 Nonimmigrant Fiance(e) of U.S. Citizen or K-2 Dependent–(a)(6).** File Form I-765 if you are filing within 90 days from the date of entry. This EAD cannot be renewed. Any EAD application other than for a replacement must be based on your pending application for adjustment under (c)(9).

   B. **K-3 Nonimmigrant Spouse of U.S. Citizen or K-4 Dependent–(a)(9).** File Form I-765 along with evidence of your admission such as copies of your Form I-94, passport, and K visa.

   C. **Family Unity Program–(a)(13).** If you are filing for initial or extension of Family Unity benefits, complete and submit Form I-817, Application for Family Unity Benefits, according to the filing instructions on Form I-817. An EAD will be issued if your Form I-817 is approved; you do not need to submit Form I-765.

   If your non-expired Family Unity EAD is lost or stolen, file Form I-765 with proper fee(s), along with a copy of your approval notice for Family Unity benefits, to request a replacement.

   D. **LIFE Family Unity–(a)(14).** If you are applying for initial employment authorization under Family Unity provisions of section 1504 of the LIFE Act Amendments, or an extension of such authorization, you should not use this form. Obtain and complete Form I-817, Application for Family Unity Benefits. If you are applying for a replacement EAD that was issued under LIFE Act Amendments Family Unity provisions, file Form I-765 with the required evidence listed in the **"Required Documentation"** section of these instructions.

   E. **V-1, V-2, or V-3 Nonimmigrant–(a)(15).** If you have been inspected and admitted to the United States with a valid V visa, file this application along with evidence of your admission, such as copies of your Form I-94, passport, and K visa. If you have been granted V status while in the United States, file this application along with evidence of your V status, such as an approval notice. If you are in the United States but you have not yet filed an application for V status, you may file this application at the same time as you file your application for V status. USCIS will adjudicate this application after adjudicating your application for V status.

7. **EAD Applicants Who Have Filed for Adjustment of Status**

   A. **Adjustment Applicant–(c)(9).** File Form I-765 with a copy of the receipt notice or other evidence that your Form I-485, Application for Permanent Residence or Adjust Status, is pending. You may file Form I-765 together with your Form I-485.

   B. **Adjustment Applicant Based on Continuous Residence Since January 1, 1972–(c)(16).** File Form I-765 with your Form I-485, Application to Register for Permanent Residence or Adjust Status; a copy of your receipt notice; or other evidence that the Form I-485 is pending.

   C. **Renewal EAD for National Interest Waiver Physicians:** If you are filing for a renewal EAD based on your pending adjustment status and an approved National Interest Waiver Physician petition, you must also include evidence of your meaningful progress toward completing the national interest waiver obligation. Such evidence includes documentation of employment in any period during the previous 12 months (e.g., copies of W-2 forms). If you did not work as a national interest waiver physician during any period of the previous 12 months, you must explain and provide a statement of future intent to work in the national interest waiver employment program.

8. **Other Categories**

   A. **N-8 or N-9 Nonimmigrant–(a)(7).** File Form I-765 with the required evidence listed in the **"Required Documentation"** section of these instructions.

   B. **Granted Withholding of Deportation or Removal (a)(10).** File Form I-765 with a copy of the Immigration Judge's order. It is not necessary to apply for a new EAD until 90 days before the expiration of your current EAD.

C. **Applicant for Suspension of Deportation--(c)(10).** File Form I-765 with evidence that your Form I-881, Application for Suspension of Deportation or Special Rule Cancellation of Removal (Pursuant to Section 203 of Public Law 105-100 (NACARA)), or Form EOIR-40, is pending.

D. **Paroled in the Public Interest--(c)(11).** File Form I-765 if you were paroled into the United States for emergent reasons or reasons strictly in the public interest.

E. **Deferred Action--(c)(14).** File Form I-765 with a copy of the order, notice, or document reflecting the exercise of deferred action. To determine your eligibility for work authorization, you must establish economic necessity. USCIS will consider whether you have an economic need to work by reviewing your current annual income, your current annual expenses, and the total current value of your assets. Provide this financial information on Form I-765WS, Form I-765 Worksheet. If you would like to provide an explanation, complete **Part 3. Explanation**, of the worksheet. It is not necessary to submit supporting documentation, though it will be accepted and reviewed if you choose to submit it.

F. **Consideration of Deferred Action for Childhood Arrivals--(c)(33).**

1. You must file Form I-765 with Form I-821D if you meet the guidelines described in the Form I-821D Filing Instructions. Enter (c)(33) in **Question 16** as the letter and number of the category for which you are applying.

   a. To determine your eligibility for work authorization, you must establish economic necessity. USCIS will consider whether you have an economic need to work by reviewing your current annual income, your current annual expenses, and the total current value of your assets. Provide this financial information on Form I-765WS, Form I-765 Worksheet. If you would like to provide an explanation, complete **Part 3. Explanation**, of the worksheet. It is not necessary to submit supporting documentation, though it will be accepted and reviewed if you choose to submit it. You do not need to include other household member's financial information to establish your own economic necessity.

   b. The 90-day period for adjudicating Form I-765 filed together with Form I-821D does not begin until DHS has decided whether to defer action in your case.

   c. The fee for Form I-765 filed based on the Consideration of Deferred Action for Childhood Arrivals category cannot be waived. Biometric collection and the biometric services fee for Form I-765 based on the Consideration of Deferred Action for Childhood Arrivals category is also required and cannot be waived.

2. If U.S. Immigration and Customs Enforcement (ICE) deferred action on your case, file a stand-alone Form I-765 with a copy of the order, notice, or document reflecting the exercise of deferred action. To determine your eligibility for work authorization, you must establish economic necessity. USCIS will consider whether you have an economic need to work by reviewing your current annual income, your current annual expenses, and the total current value of your assets. Provide this financial information on Form I-765WS, Form I-765 Worksheet. If you would like to provide an explanation, complete **Part 3. Explanation**, of the worksheet. It is not necessary to submit supporting documentation, though it will be accepted and reviewed if you choose to submit it. You do not need to include other household member's financial information to establish your own economic necessity.

   When completing the Form I-765:

   a. Enter "Unlawful Status: Deferred Action for Childhood Arrivals by ICE" for **Question 15**.

   b. Enter (c)(33) in **Question 16** as the letter and number of the category for which you are applying.

G. **Final Order of Deportation--(c)(18).** File Form I-765 with a copy of the order of supervision and a request for employment authorization that may be based on but not limited to the following:

1. Existence of a dependent spouse and/or children in the United States who rely on you for support;

2. Existence of economic necessity to be employed; and

3. Anticipated length of time before you can be removed from the United States.

H. **LIFE Legalization Applicant--(c)(24).** We encourage you to file File Form I-765 together with your Form I-485, Application to Register Permanent Residence or Adjust Status, to facilitate processing. However, you may file Form I-765 at a later date with evidence that you were a CSS, LULAC, or Zambrano class member applicant before October 1, 2000, and with a copy of the receipt notice or other evidence that your Form I-485 is pending.

I. T-1 Nonimmigrant–(a)(16). If you are applying for initial employment authorization as a T-1 nonimmigrant, file Form I-765 only if you did not request an employment authorization document when you applied for T nonimmigrant status. If you have been granted T nonimmigrant status and this is a request for a renewal or replacement of an employment authorization document, file Form I-765 along with evidence of your T nonimmigrant status, such as an approval notice.

J. T-2, T-3, or T-4 Nonimmigrant–(c)(25). File Form I-765 with a copy of your T-1 (principal alien's) approval notice and proof of your relationship to the T-1 principal.

K. U-1 Nonimmigrant–(a)(19). If you are applying for initial employment authorization as a U-1 nonimmigrant, file Form I-765 only if you did not request an employment authorization document when you applied for U nonimmigrant status. If you have been granted U nonimmigrant status and this is a request for a renewal or replacement of an employment authorization document, file Form I-765 along with evidence of your U nonimmigrant status, such as an approval notice.

L. U-2, U-3, U-4, or U-5–(a)(20). If you obtained U nonimmigrant status while in the United States, you must submit a copy of the approval notice for your U nonimmigrant status. If you were admitted to the United States as a U nonimmigrant, you must submit a copy of your passport with your U nonimmigrant visa.

M. VAWA Self-Petitioners–(c)(31). If you are the principal beneficiary or qualified child of an approved VAWA self-petition, you are eligible for work authorization. File Form I-765 with evidence of your status, such as a copy of Form I-360 approved notice. Additionally, you may file Form I-765 together with your initial VAWA self-petition.

General Instructions

Each application must be properly signed and filed. A photocopy of a signed application or a typewritten name in place of a signature is not acceptable.

Each application must be accompanied by the appropriate filing fee.

If you are under 14 years of age, your parent or legal guardian may sign the application on your behalf.

Evidence. You must submit all required initial evidence along with all the supporting documentation with your application at the time of filing.

If a required document does not exist or cannot be obtained, you must demonstrate this and submit secondary evidence pertinent to the facts at issue. If secondary evidence does not exist or is unavailable you must demonstrate this and submit two or more sworn affidavits by non-parties who have direct knowledge of the event and circumstances.

If you are electronically filing this application, you must follow the instructions provided on the USCIS Web site, **www.uscis.gov**.

Biometrics Services Appointment. After receiving your application and ensuring completeness, USCIS will inform you in writing when to go to your local USCIS Application Support Center (ASC) for your biometrics services appointment. Failure to attend the biometrics services appointment may result in denial of your application.

Copies. Unless specifically required that an original document be filed with an application or petition, a legible photocopy may be submitted. Original documents submitted when not required may remain a part of the record and will not be automatically returned to you.

Translations. Any document containing foreign language submitted to USCIS must be accompanied by a full English language translation which the translator has certified as complete and accurate, and by the translator's certification that he or she is competent to translate from the foreign language into English.

How To Fill Out Form I-765

1. Type or print legibly in black ink.
2. If extra space is needed to complete any item, attach a continuation sheet, write your name and Alien Registration Number (A-Number) (if any), at the top of each sheet of paper, indicate the Part and item number to which your answer refers, and date and sign each sheet.
3. Answer all questions fully and accurately. State that an item is not applicable with "N/A." If the answer is none, write "None."

Required Documentation

All applications must be filed with the documents required below in addition to the particular evidence required for the category listed in **"Who May File Form I-765?"** with fee, if required.

If you are required to show economic necessity for your category, submit a list of your assets, income, and expenses. Provide this financial information on Form I-765WS, Form I-765 Worksheet. If you would like to provide an explanation, complete Part 3, Explanation, of the worksheet.

Assemble the documents in the following order:

1. Your application with the filing fee. See **"What Is the Filing Fee?"** for details.

2. If you are mailing your application to USCIS, you must also submit:

   A. A copy of Form I-94, Arrival-Departure Record (front and back), if available. If you are filing Form I-765 under the (c)(9) category, Form I-94 is not required.

   B. A copy of your last EAD (front and back). If no prior EAD has been issued, you must submit a copy of a government-issued identity document, such as a passport showing your picture, name, and date of birth; a birth certificate with photo ID; a visa issued by a foreign consulate; or a national ID document with photo and/or fingerprint. The identity document photocopy must clearly show the facial features of the applicant and the biographical information. If you are filing under the (c)(33) category, additional documentation beyond what you submit under **"3. What Documents Do You Need to Provide to Prove Identity?"** of the filing instructions for Form I-821D, Consideration of Deferred Action for Childhood Arrivals, is not required.

   C. You **must** submit two identical color photographs of yourself taken within 30 days of filing your application. The photos must have a white to off-white background, be printed on thin paper with a glossy finish, and be unmounted and unretouched.

      The passport-style photos must be 2" by 2". The photos must be in color with full face, frontal view on a white to off-white background. Head height should measure 1" to 1 3/8" from top to bottom of chin, and eye height is between 1 1/8" to 1 3/8" from bottom of photo. Your head must be bare unless you are wearing headwear as required by a religious order of which you are a member. Using pencil or felt pen, lightly print your name and Alien Receipt Number on the back of the photo.

Special Filing Instructions for Those With Pending Asylum Applications ((c)(8))

Asylum Applicant (with a pending asylum application) who filed for asylum on or after January 4, 1995. You must wait at least 150 days following the filling of your asylum claim before you are eligible to apply for an EAD. Any delay in processing the asylum application that is caused by you, including unexcused failure to appear for fingerprinting and other biometrics capture, will not be counted as part of that 150 days. If you fail to appear for your asylum interview or for a hearing before an immigration judge, you will be ineligible for an EAD. If you have received a recommended approval for a grant of asylum, you do not need to wait the 150 days and may apply for an EAD immediately upon receipt of your recommended approval. If you file Form I-765 early, it will be denied. File Form I-765 with:

1. A copy of the USCIS acknowledgement mailer which was mailed to you;

2. Other evidence that your Form I-589 was filed with USCIS;

3. Evidence that your Form I-589 was filed with an Immigration Judge at the Executive Office for Immigration Review (EOIR); or

4. Evidence that your asylum application remains under administrative or judicial review.

Asylum applicant (with a pending asylum application) who filed for asylum and for withholding of deportation prior to January 4, 1995, and is *NOT* in exclusion or deportation proceedings.

You may file Form I-765 at any time; however, it will only be granted if USCIS finds that your asylum application is not frivolous. File Form I-765 with:

1. A complete copy of your previously filed Form I-589;

2. A copy of your USCIS receipt notice;

3. A copy of the USCIS acknowledgement mailer;

4. Evidence that your Form I-589 was filed with EOIR;

5. Evidence that your asylum application remains under administrative or judicial review; or

6. A copy of the USCIS acknowledgement mailer.

Asylum applicant (with a pending asylum application) who filed an initial request for asylum prior to January 4, 1995, and is IN exclusion or deportation proceedings. If you filed your Request for Asylum and Withholding of Deportation (Form I-589) prior to January 4, 1995, and you are IN exclusion or deportation proceedings, file your EAD application with:

1. A date-stamped copy of your previously filed Form I-589;

2. A copy of Form I-221, Order to Show Cause and Notice of Hearing, or Form I-122, Notice to Applicant for Admission Detained for Hearing Before Immigration Judge;

3. A copy of EOIR-26, Notice of Appeal, date stamped by the Office of the Immigration Judge;

4. A date-stamped copy of a petition for judicial review or for *habeas corpus* issued to the asylum applicant; or

5. Other evidence that you filed an asylum application with EOIR.

Asylum application under the ABC Settlement Agreement--(c)(8). If you are a Salvadoran or Guatemalan national eligible for benefits under the ABC settlement agreement, American Baptist Churches v. Thornburgh, 760 F. Supp. 976 (N.D. Cal. 1991), follow the instructions contained in this section when filing your Form I-765.

You must have an asylum application (Form I-589) on file either with USCIS or with an Immigration Judge in order to receive work authorization. Therefore, submit evidence that you have previously filed an asylum application when you submit Form I-765. You are not required to submit this evidence when you apply, but it will help USCIS process your request efficiently.

If you are renewing or replacing your EAD, you must pay the filing fee.

Mark your application as follows:

1. Write "ABC" in the top right corner of your EAD application. You must identify yourself as an ABC class member if you are applying for an EAD under the ABC settlement agreement.
2. Write "(c)(8)" in **Question 16** of the application.

You are entitled to an EAD without regard to the merits of your asylum claim. Your application for an EAD will be decided within 60 days if: (1) you pay the filing fee, (2) you have a complete pending asylum application on file, and (3) you write "ABC" in the top right corner of your EAD application. If you do not pay the filing fee for an initial EAD request, your request may be denied if USCIS finds that your asylum application is frivolous. However, if you cannot pay the filing fee for an EAD, you may qualify for a fee waiver under 8 CFR 103.7(c).

Special Filing Instructions for Spouses of E-2 CNMI Investors ((c)(12)).

Spouses of certain principal E-2 CNMI Investors (E-2C) are eligible to seek employment in the CNMI. An EAD issued under this category is only valid for employment in the Commonwealth of Northern Mariana Islands (the CNMI).

To determine if you are eligible for an EAD under this section, you must determine what type of investor certificate was issued by the CNMI to your spouse, the principal E-2 CNMI Investor. If your spouse was issued either a Long-Term Business Certificate or Foreign Investment Certificate, you may be eligible for an EAD under this category. If your spouse, the principal E-2 CNMI Investor, was issued a Foreign Retiree Investment Certification, you are not eligible to receive an EAD under this category.

File Form I-765 with:

1. Documentation, such as a marriage certificate establishing a legal marriage between you and the principal E-2C. Additionally, documentation such as divorce or death certificates establishing the termination of any prior marriages of you and your spouse.
2. Documentation establishing that you reside in the Commonwealth of the Northern Mariana Islands.
3. Documentation establishing that you have obtained E-2C status as a dependent.
4. Evidence that your spouse has obtained E-2C status.
5. A copy of your spouse's CNMI issued Long-Term Business Certificate or Foreign Investment Certificate.

What Is the Filing Fee?

The filing fee for Form I-765 is $380.

Exceptions:

Initial EAD. If this is your initial application and you are applying under one of the following categories, a filing fee is **not** required:

1. (a)(3) Refugee;
2. (a)(4) Paroled as Refugee;
3. (a)(5) Asylee;
4. (a)(7) N-8 or N-9 nonimmigrant;
5. (a)(8) Citizen of Micronesia, Marshall Islands, or Palau;
6. (a)(10) Granted Withholding of Deportation;
7. (a)(16) Victim of Severe Form of Trafficking (T-1);
8. (a)(19) U-1 Nonimmigrant;
9. (c)(1), (c)(4), or (c)(7) Dependent of certain foreign government, international organization, or NATO personnel;
10. (c)(8) Applicant for asylum (an applicant filing under the special ABC procedures must pay the fee); or
11. (c)(31) VAWA Self-Petitioner.

Special Instructions for Childhood Arrivals ((c)(33)). All requestors under this category must submit biometrics. The biometrics services fee of $85 is required for all requestors. ***The biometrics services fee and the filing fee for this form cannot be waived.***

Renewal EAD. If this is a renewal application and you are applying under one of the following categories, a filing fee is **not** required:

1. (a)(8) Citizen of Micronesia, Marshall Islands, or Palau;
2. (a)(10) Granted Withholding of Deportation;
3. (c)(1), (c)(4), or (c)(7) Dependent of certain foreign government, international organization, or NATO personnel;
4. (c)(9) or (c)(16) Adjustment applicant who applied after July 30, 2007.

Replacement EAD. If this is your replacement application, and you are applying under one of the following categories, a filing fee is **not** required:

1. (c)(1), (c)(4), or (c)(7) Dependent of certain foreign government, international organization, or NATO personnel.

   NOTE: If you are requesting a replacement EAD under the (c)(9) or (c)(16) Adjustment applicant who applied after July 30, 2007 category, then the full filing fee will be required; however, no biometrics fee is required.

Card Error:

1. If the card issued to you contains incorrect information that is not attributed to USCIS error, a new Form I-765 and filing fee are required. Form I-765 must be accompanied by the card containing the error.
2. If the card issued to you contains incorrect information that is attributed to a USCIS error, a new Form I-765 and filing fee are not required. Instead, you must submit a letter, accompanied by the card containing the error to the Service Center or National Benefit Center that approved your last employment authorization request.

You may be eligible for a fee waiver under 8 CFR 103.7(c) if you are filing for an EAD related to your application or grant of TPS.

Use the following guidelines when you prepare your check or money order for the Form I-765 fee:

1. The check or money order must be drawn on a bank or other financial institution located in the United States and must be payable in U.S. currency; and
2. Make the check or money order payable to **U.S. Department of Homeland Security**.

   NOTE: Spell out U.S. Department of Homeland Security; do not use the initials "USDHS" or "DHS."

NOTE: If you filed Form I-485, Application to Register Permanent Residence or Adjust Status, as of July 30, 2007, ***and you paid the Form I-485 filing fee***, no fee is required to also file a request for employment authorization on Form I-765. You may file the Form I-765 with your Form I-485, or you may submit the Form I-765 at a later date. If you file Form I-765 separately, you must also submit a copy of your Form I-797C, Notice of Action, receipt as evidence of the filing of Form I-485 as of July 30, 2007.

Notice to Those Making Payment by Check. If you send us a check, it will be converted into an electronic funds transfer (EFT). This means we will copy your check and use the account information on it to electronically debit your account for the amount of the check. The debit from your account will usually take 24 hours and will be shown on your regular account statement.

You will not receive your original check back. We will destroy your original check, but we will keep a copy of it. If the EFT cannot be processed for technical reasons, you authorize us to process the copy in place of your original check. If the EFT cannot be completed because of insufficient funds, we may try to make the transfer up to two times.

How to Check If the Fees Are Correct

The fee on this form is current as of the edition date appearing in the lower right corner of this page. However, because USCIS fees change periodically, you can verify if the fees are correct by following one of the steps below:

1. Visit our Web site at **www.uscis.gov**, select "Forms Filing Fees" and check the appropriate fee; **or**
2. Telephone our National Customer Service Center at **1-800-375-5283** and ask for the fee information. For TDD (hearing impaired) call: **1-800-767-1833**.

Where to File?

Please visit the USCIS Web site at **www.uscis.gov/I-765** or contact the USCIS National Customer Service Center at **1-800-375-5283** for the most current information about where to file this benefit request. For TDD (hearing impaired) call: **1-800-767-1833**.

Address Change

If you have changed your address, you must inform USCIS of your new address. For information on filing a change of address go to the USCIS Web site at **www.uscis.gov/addresschange** or contact the USCIS National Customer Service Center at **1-800-375-5283**. For TDD (hearing impaired) call: **1-800-767-1833**.

NOTE: Do not submit a change of address request to USCIS Lockbox facilities because USCIS Lockbox facilities do not process change of address requests.

Processing Information

Any Form I-765 that is not signed or accompanied by the correct fee will be rejected with a notice that Form I-765 is deficient. You may correct the deficiency and resubmit Form I-765. An application or petition is not considered properly filed until accepted by USCIS.

Initial processing. Once Form I-765 has been accepted, it will be checked for completeness, including submission of the required initial evidence. If you do not completely fill out the form, or file it without required initial evidence, you will not establish a basis for eligibility, and we may deny your Form I-765.

Biometric collection, interview, and requests for more information. We may request more information or evidence, or we may request that you appear at a USCIS office for an interview, which may include collection of biometrics (fingerprints, photograph, and signature). We may also request that you submit the originals of any copy. We will return these originals when they are no longer required.

You may be required to provide biometrics at a USCIS Application Support Center (ASC) in order for your EAD application to be adjudicated and your card to be produced. If necessary, USCIS will send you a notice scheduling you for an ASC appointment for the electronic collection of your biometrics. The ASC notice will inform you of the documents that you must bring with you to the appointment. If you fail to attend your ASC appointment, your EAD application may be denied.

Approval. If approved, your EAD will either be mailed to you or you may be required to visit your local USCIS office to pick it up.

Denial. If your application cannot be granted, you will receive a written notice explaining the basis of your denial.

Interim EAD. If you have not received a decision within 90 days of receipt by USCIS of a properly filed EAD application or within 30 days of a properly filed initial EAD application based on an asylum application filed on or after January 4, 1995, you may request interim work authorization by calling the USCIS National Customer Service Center at **1-800-375-5283** or by appearing in person at your local USCIS Field Office by making an **InfoPass** appointment. For TDD (hearing impaired) call: **1-800-767-1833**. For further processing at a USCIS Field Office, you must bring proof of identity and any notices that you have received from USCIS in connection with your application for employment authorization. *The Interim EAD provisions apply to individuals filing Form I-765 based on Consideration of Deferred Action for Childhood Arrivals only after a determination on deferred action is reached.*

USCIS Forms and Information

To ensure you are using the latest version of this form, visit the USCIS Web site at **www.uscis.gov** where you can get USCIS forms and immigration-related information. If you do not have internet access, you may order USCIS forms by calling our toll-free number at **1-800-870-3676**. You may also obtain forms and information by calling our USCIS National Customer Service Center at **1-800-375-5283**. For TDD (hearing impaired) call: **1-800-767-1833**.

As an alternative to waiting in line for assistance at your local USCIS office, you can now schedule an appointment through the USCIS Internet-based system, **InfoPass**. To access the system, visit the USCIS Web site. Use the **InfoPass** appointment scheduler and follow the screen prompts to set up your appointment. **InfoPass** generates an electronic appointment notice that appears on the screen.

Penalties

If you knowingly and willfully falsify or conceal a material fact or submit a false document with your Form I-765, we will deny your Form I-765 and may deny any other immigration benefit.

In addition, you will face severe penalties provided by law and may be subject to criminal prosecution.

USCIS Privacy Act Statement

AUTHORITIES: The information requested on this application, and the associated evidence, is collected pursuant to the Immigration and Nationality Act, 8 U.S.C. section 1324a, as amended.

PURPOSE: The primary purpose for providing the requested information on this form is to determine eligibility for certain aliens who are temporarily in the United States requesting an Employment Authorization Document (EAD).

DISCLOSURE: The information you provide is voluntary. However, failure to provide the requested information, and any requested evidence, may delay a final decision or result in the denial of your benefit request.

ROUTINE USES: The information you provide on this benefit application may be shared with other federal, state, local, and foreign government agencies and authorized organizations in accordance with approved routine uses, as described in the associated published system of records notices [**DHS-USCIS-001 - Alien File, Index, and National File Tracking System; DHS-USCIS-007 - Benefit Information System; and DHS/USCIS-010 - Asylum Information and Pre-Screening**, which can be found at **www.dhs.gov/privacy**]. The information may also be made available, as appropriate for law enforcement purposes or in the interest of national security.

Paperwork Reduction Act

An agency may not conduct or sponsor an information collection and a person is not required to respond to a collection of information unless it displays a currently valid OMB control number. The public reporting burden for this collection of information is estimated as follows: 3.42 hours for reviewing instructions and completing and submitting Form I-765; 1.17 hours associated with biometrics processing; .50 hours for reviewing instructions and completing Form I-765WS; and .50 hours associated with providing passport-style photographs. Send comments regarding this burden estimate or any other aspect of this collection of information, including suggestions for reducing this burden, to: U.S. Citizenship and Immigration Services, Regulatory Coordination Division, Office of Policy and Strategy, 20 Massachusetts Ave NW, Washington, DC 20529-2140. OMB No. 1615-0040. **Do not mail your completed Form I-765 to this address.**

APPENDIX 9B

FORM I-131 AND INSTRUCTIONS

Application for Travel Document
Department of Homeland Security
U.S. Citizenship and Immigration Services

USCIS
Form I-131
OMB No. 1615-0013
Expires 03/31/2016

For USCIS Use Only	Receipt	Action Block	To Be Completed by an *Attorney/ Representative*, if any. ☐ Fill in box if G-28 is attached to represent the applicant.
☐ **Document Hand Delivered** By: ____ Date: __/__/__			
Document Issued ☐ Re-entry Permit *(Update "Mail To" Section)* ☐ Refugee Travel Document *(Update "Mail To" Section)* ☐ Single Advance Parole ☐ Multiple Advance Parole *Valid Until:* __/__/__		**Mail To** *(Re-entry & Refugee Only)* ☐ Address in *Part 1* ☐ US Consulate at: ____ ☐ Intl DHS Ofc at: ____	Attorney State License Number: ____

► **Start Here.** Type or Print in Black Ink

Part 1. Information About You

1.a. Family Name *(Last Name)*

1.b. Given Name *(First Name)*

1.c. Middle Name

Physical Address

2.a. In Care of Name

2.b. Street Number and Name

2.c. Apt. ☐ Ste. ☐ Flr. ☐

2.d. City or Town

2.e. State **2.f.** Zip Code

2.g. Postal Code

2.h. Province

2.i. Country

Other Information

3. Alien Registration Number (A-Number)

► A-

4. Country of Birth

5. Country of Citizenship

6. Class of Admission

7. Gender ☐ Male ☐ Female

8. Date of Birth *(mm/dd/yyyy)* ►

9. U.S. Social Security Number *(if any)*

►

Form I-131 03/22/13 N

Page 1 of 5

Part 2. Application Type

1.a. ☐ I am a permanent resident or conditional resident of the United States, and I am applying for a reentry permit.

1.b. ☐ I now hold U.S. refugee or asylee status, and I am applying for a Refugee Travel Document.

1.c. ☐ I am a permanent resident as a direct result of refugee or asylee status, and I am applying for a Refugee Travel Document.

1.d. ☐ I am applying for an Advance Parole Document to allow me to return to the United States after temporary foreign travel.

1.e. ☐ I am outside the United States, and I am applying for an Advance Parole Document.

1.f. ☐ I am applying for an Advance Parole Document for a person who is outside the United States.

If you checked box "1.f." provide the following information about that person in 2.a. through 2.p.

2.a. Family Name *(Last Name)*

2.b. Given Name *(First Name)*

2.c. Middle Name

2.d. Date of Birth *(mm/dd/yyyy)* ►

2.e. Country of Birth

2.f. Country of Citizenship

2.g. Daytime Phone Number ( ) -

Physical Address (If you checked box 1.f.)

2.h. In Care of Name

2.i. Street Number and Name

2.j. Apt. ☐ Ste. ☐ Flr. ☐

2.k. City or Town

2.l. State **2.m.** Zip Code

2.n. Postal Code

2.o. Province

2.p. Country

Part 3. Processing Information

1. Date of Intended Departure *(mm/dd/yyyy)* ►

2. Expected Length of Trip *(in days)*

3.a. Are you, or any person included in this application, now in exclusion, deportation, removal, or rescission proceedings? ☐ Yes ☐ No

3.b. If "Yes", Name of DHS office:

4.a. Have you ever before been issued a reentry permit or Refugee Travel Document? *(If "Yes" give the following information for the last document issued to you):* ☐ Yes ☐ No

4.b. Date Issued *(mm/dd/yyyy)* ►

4.c. Disposition *(attached, lost, etc.)*:

If you are applying for a non-DACA related Advance Parole Document, skip to Part 7; ***DACA recipients must complete Part 4 before skipping to Part 7.***

Part 3. Processing Information *(continued)*

Where do you want this travel document sent? *(Check one)*

5. ☐ To the U.S. address shown in **Part 1 (2.a through 2.i.)** of this form.

6. ☐ To a U.S. Embassy or consulate at:

6.a. City or Town

6.b. Country

7. ☐ To a DHS office overseas at:

7.a. City or Town

7.b. Country

If you checked "6" or "7", where should the notice to pick up the travel document be sent?

8. ☐ To the address shown in **Part 2 (2.h. through 2.p.)** of this form.

9. ☐ To the address shown in **Part 3 (10.a. through 10.i.)** of this form.:

10.a. In Care of Name

10.b. Street Number and Name

10.c. Apt. ☐ Ste. ☐ Flr. ☐

10.d. City or Town

10.e. State **10.f.** Zip Code

10.g. Postal Code

10.h. Province

10.i. Country

10.j. Daytime Phone Number ( ) -

Part 4. Information About Your Proposed Travel

1.a. Purpose of trip. *(If you need more space, continue on a separate sheet of paper.)*

1.b. List the countries you intend to visit. *(If you need more space, continue on a separate sheet of paper.)*

Part 5. Complete Only If Applying for a Re-entry Permit

Since becoming a permanent resident of the United States (or during the past 5 years, whichever is less) how much total time have you spent outside the United States?

1.a. ☐ less than 6 months
1.b. ☐ 6 months to 1 year
1.c. ☐ 1 to 2 years
1.d. ☐ 2 to 3 years
1.e. ☐ 3 to 4 years
1.f. ☐ more than 4 years

2. Since you became a permanent resident of the United States, have you ever filed a Federal income tax return as a nonresident or failed to file a Federal income tax return because you considered yourself to be a nonresident? *(If "Yes" give details on a separate sheet of paper.)*

☐ Yes ☐ No

Part 6. Complete Only If Applying for a Refugee Travel Document

1. Country from which you are a refugee or asylee:

If you answer "Yes" to any of the following questions, you must explain on a separate sheet of paper. Include your Name and A-Number on the top of each sheet.

2. Do you plan to travel to the country named above? ☐ Yes ☐ No

Since you were accorded refugee/asylee status, have you ever:

3.a. Returned to the country named above? ☐ Yes ☐ No

3.b. Applied for and/or obtained a national passport, passport renewal, or entry permit of that country? ☐ Yes ☐ No

3.c. Applied for and/or received any benefit from such country (for example, health insurance benefits)? ☐ Yes ☐ No

Since you were accorded refugee/asylee status, have you, by any legal procedure or voluntary act:

4.a. Reacquired the nationality of the country named above? ☐ Yes ☐ No

4.b. Acquired a new nationality? ☐ Yes ☐ No

4.c. Been granted refugee or asylee status in any other country? ☐ Yes ☐ No

Part 7. Complete Only If Applying for Advance Parole

On a separate sheet of paper, explain how you qualify for an Advance Parole Document, and what circumstances warrant issuance of advance parole. Include copies of any documents you wish considered. *(See instructions.)*

1. How many trips do you intend to use this document? ☐ One Trip ☐ More than one trip

If the person intended to receive an Advance Parole Document is outside the United States, provide the location (City or Town and Country) of the U.S. Embassy or consulate or the DHS overseas office that you want us to notify.

2.a. City or Town

2.b. Country

If the travel document will be delivered to an overseas office, where should the notice to pick up the document be sent?:

3. ☐ To the address shown in **Part 2 (2.h. through 2.p.)** of this form.

4. ☐ To the address shown in **Part 7 (4.a. through 4.i.)** of this form.

4.a. In Care of Name

4.b. Street Number and Name

4.c. Apt. ☐ Ste. ☐ Flr. ☐

4.d. City or Town

4.e. State 4.f. Zip Code

4.g. Postal Code

4.h. Province

4.i. Country

4.j. Daytime Phone Number ( ) -

Part 8. Signature of Applicant *(Read the information on penalties in the Form instructions before completing this Part.)* If you are filing for a Re-entry Permit or Refugee Travel Document, you must be in the United States to file this application.

1.a. I certify, under penalty of perjury under the laws of the United States of America, that this application and the evidence submitted with it is all true and correct. I authorize the release of any information from my records that U.S. Citizenship and Immigration Services needs to determine eligibility for the benefit I am seeking.

Signature of Applicant

1.b. Date of Signature *(mm/dd/yyyy)* ►

2. Daytime Phone Number ( ) -

NOTE: If you do not completely fill out this form or fail to submit required documents listed in the instructions, your application may be denied.

Part 9. Information About Person Who Prepared This Application, If Other Than the Applicant

NOTE: If you are an attorney or representative, you must submit a completed Form G-28, Notice of Entry of Appearance as Attorney or Accredited Representative, along with this application.

Preparer's Full Name

Provide the following information concerning the preparer:

1.a. Preparer's Family Name *(Last Name)*

1.b. Preparer's Given Name *(First Name)*

2. Preparer's Business or Organization Name

Preparer's Mailing Address

3.a. Street Number and Name

3.b. Apt. ☐ Ste. ☐ Flr. ☐

3.c. City or Town

3.d. State **3.e.** Zip Code

3.f. Postal Code

3.g. Province

3.h. Country

Preparer's Contact Information

4. Preparer's Daytime Phone Number ( ) - Extension

5. Preparer's E-mail Address *(if any)*

Declaration

To be completed by all preparers, including attorneys and authorized representatives: I declare that I prepared this benefit request at the request of the applicant, that it is based on all the information of which I have knowledge, and that the information is true to the best of my knowledge.

6.a. Signature of Preparer

6.b. Date of Signature *(mm/dd/yyyy)* ►

NOTE: If you require more space to provide any additional information, use a separate sheet of paper. You must include your Name and A-Number on the top of each sheet.

Instructions for Application for Travel Document

Department of Homeland Security
U.S. Citizenship and Immigration Services

USCIS
Form I-131
OMB No. 1615-0013
Expires 03/31/2016

What Is the Purpose of This Form?

This form is for applying to U.S. Citizenship and Immigration Services (USCIS) for the following travel documents:

1. Reentry Permit

A Reentry Permit allows a permanent resident or conditional resident to apply for admission to the United States upon returning from abroad during the permit's validity without the need to obtain a returning resident visa from a U.S. Embassy or consulate.

2. Refugee Travel Document

A Refugee Travel Document is issued to a person in valid refugee or asylee status, or to a permanent resident who obtained such status as a refugee or asylee in the United States. Persons who hold asylee or refugee status and are not permanent residents must have a Refugee Travel Document to return to the United States after travel abroad, unless they possess an Advance Parole Document. A Department of Homeland Security (DHS) officer at the U.S. port-of-entry will determine your admissibility when you present your travel document.

3. Advance Parole Document

Parole allows an alien to physically enter into the United States for a specific purpose. A person who has been "paroled" has not been admitted to the United States and remains an "applicant for admission" even while paroled.

DHS, as a matter of discretion, may issue an Advance Parole Document to authorize an alien to appear at a port-of-entry to seek parole into the United States. The document may be accepted by a transportation company in lieu of a visa as an authorization for the holder to travel to the United States. An Advance Parole Document is not issued to serve in place of any required passport.

WARNING: The document does not entitle you to be paroled into the United States; a separate discretionary decision on a request for parole will be made when you arrive at a port-of-entry upon your return.

WARNING: DHS may revoke or terminate your Advance Parole Document at any time, including while you are outside the United States, in which event you may be unable to return to the United States unless you have a valid visa or other document that permits you to travel to the United States and seek admission.

NOTE: Generally, if you are in the United States and have applied for adjustment of status to that of a lawful permanent resident, your application will be deemed abandoned if you leave the United States without first obtaining an Advance Parole Document. Your application for adjustment of status generally will not be deemed abandoned, even if you do not apply for an Advance Parole Document before traveling abroad while an adjustment application is pending, if you currently are in one of the following nonimmigrant classifications, and remain eligible for and would be admissible in one of the following categories upon applying for admission at a port-of-entry:

a. An H-1 temporary worker, or H-4 spouse or child of an H-1;

b. An L-1 intracompany transferee, or L-2 spouse or child of an L-1;

c. A K-3 spouse, or K-4 child of a U.S. citizen; **or**

d. A V-1 spouse, or V-2/V-3 child of a lawful permanent resident.

NOTE: Upon returning to the United States, most individuals must present a valid H, L, K, or V nonimmigrant visa and must continue to be otherwise admissible. If you do not have a valid or unexpired H, L, K, or V nonimmigrant visa, then you generally need to obtain an H, L, K, or V nonimmigrant visa at a U.S. Department of State (DOS) visa issuing post. Individuals will need a valid nonimmigrant visa, advance parole, or other travel document to present for reentry.

4. Advance Parole for Individuals Outside the United States

The granting of an Advance Parole Document for individuals outside the United States is an extraordinary measure used sparingly to allow an otherwise inadmissible alien to the United States and to seek parole into the United States for a temporary period of time due to urgent humanitarian reasons or for significant public benefit (significant public benefit parole is typically limited to law enforcement or homeland security-related reasons). An Advance Parole Document cannot be used to circumvent normal visa-issuance procedures and is not a means to bypass delays in visa issuance.

Who May File Form I-131?

Each applicant must file a separate application for a travel document.

1. Reentry Permit

a. ***If you are in the United States*** as a permanent resident or conditional permanent resident, you may apply for a Reentry Permit. You must be physically present in the United States when you file the Reentry Permit application and complete the biometrics services requirement. After filing your application for a Reentry Permit, USCIS will inform you in writing when to go to your local Application Support Center (ASC) for your biometrics services appointment. See **General Requirements, Item Number 3., "Biometrics Services Requirement"**.

NOTE: A Reentry Permit may be sent to a U.S. Embassy or consulate or DHS office abroad for you to pick up, if you make such a request when you file your application.

With the exception of having to obtain a returning resident visa abroad, a Reentry Permit does not exempt you from compliance with any of the requirements of U.S. immigration laws. If you are in possession of a valid unexpired Reentry Permit, you will not be deemed to have abandoned your status as a permanent resident or conditional permanent resident based solely on the duration of your absence(s) from the United States while the permit is valid.

An absence from the United States for 1 year or more will generally break the continuity of your required continuous residence for the purpose of naturalization. If you intend to remain outside the United States for 1 year or more, you may be eligible to file Form N-470, Application to Preserve Residence for Naturalization Purposes. For further information, contact your local USCIS office.

b. Validity of Reentry Permit

(1) Generally, a Reentry Permit issued to a permanent resident is valid for 2 years from the date of issuance. See 8 CFR section 223.3(a)(1). However, if you have been outside the United States for more than 4 of the last 5 years since becoming a permanent resident the permit will be limited to 1 year, except that a permit with a validity of 2 years may be issued to the following:

(a) A permanent resident whose travel is on the order of the U.S. Government, other than an exclusion, deportation, removal, or rescission order;

(b) A permanent resident employed by a public international organization of which the United States is a member by treaty or statute; or

(c) A permanent resident who is a professional athlete and regularly competes in the United States and worldwide.

(2) A Reentry Permit issued to a conditional resident is valid for 2 years from the date of issuance, or to the date the conditional resident must apply for removal of the conditions on his or her status, whichever date comes first.

(3) A Reentry Permit may not be extended.

c. A Reentry Permit may not be issued to you if:

(1) You have already been issued such a document, and it is still valid, unless the prior document has been returned to USCIS or you can demonstrate that it was lost; **or**

(2) A notice was published in the *Federal Register* that precludes the issuance of such a document for travel to the area where you intend to go.

NOTICE to permanent or conditional permanent residents concerning possible abandonment of status: If you do not obtain a Reentry Permit, lengthy or frequent absences from the United States could be factors supporting a conclusion that you have abandoned your permanent resident status. If DHS determines, upon your return to the United States, that you have abandoned your permanent resident status, you may challenge that determination if you are placed in removal proceedings.

2. Refugee Travel Document

a. ***If you are in the United States*** in valid refugee or asylee status, or if you are a permanent resident as a direct result of your refugee or asylee status in the United States, you may apply for a Refugee Travel Document. You should apply for a Refugee Travel Document **BEFORE** you leave the United States. **If biometrics services are required and you fail to appear to have the biometrics collected, the application may be denied.**

After filing your application for a Refugee Travel Document, USCIS will inform you in writing when to go to your local USCIS ASC for your biometrics services appointment. Unless you have other appropriate documentation, such as a Permanent Resident Card and passport, you must have a Refugee Travel Document to return to the United States after temporary travel abroad. A Refugee Travel Document may be sent to a U.S. Embassy or consulate or DHS office abroad for you to pick up, if you request it when you file your application.

b. ***If you are outside of the United States*** and:

(1) Have valid refugee or asylee status; or

(2) You are a permanent resident as a direct result of your refugee or asylee status in the United States, you may be permitted to file Form I-131 and apply for a Refugee Travel Document. The USCIS Overseas District Director with jurisdiction over your location makes this decision in his or her discretion.

Your application must be filed within one year of your last departure from the United States and should include an explanation of why you failed to apply for a Refugee Travel Document before you departed from the United States.

Travel Warning Regarding Voluntary Re-availment

WARNING to asylees who travel to the country of claimed persecution: If you applied for asylum on or after April 1, 1997, your asylum status may be terminated if the U.S. Government determines that you have voluntarily availed yourself of the protection of your country of nationality or, if stateless, country of last habitual residence. See section 208(c)(2)(D) of the Immigration and Nationality Act (INA), 8 U.S.C. 1158(c)(2)(D).

c. Validity of Refugee Travel Document

(1) A Refugee Travel Document is valid for 1 year.

(2) A Refugee Travel Document may not be extended.

d. A Refugee Travel Document may not be issued to you if:

(1) You have already been issued such a document and it is still valid, unless the prior document has been returned to USCIS or you can demonstrate that it was lost; **or**

(2) A notice was published in the *Federal Register* that precludes the issuance of such a document for travel to the area where you intend to go.

NOTE: You should apply for a Refugee Travel Document before you leave the United States. However, a Refugee Travel Document may be sent to a U.S. Embassy or consulate or DHS office abroad for you to pick up, if you make such a request when you file your application. Departure from the United States before a decision is made on the application usually does not affect the application decision. However, if biometric collection is required and the applicant departs the United States before biometrics are collected, the application may be denied.

NOTICE to permanent residents who obtain permanent residence as a result of their refugee or asylee status: If you do not obtain a Reentry Permit (see Reentry Permit information in section 1. above) and remain outside the United States, lengthy or frequent absences from the United States, could be factors supporting a conclusion that you have abandoned your permanent resident status . With the exception of having to obtain a returning resident visa abroad, a Reentry Permit does not exempt you from compliance with any of the requirements of U.S. immigration laws. If you are in possession of a valid unexpired Reentry Permit, you will not be deemed to have abandoned your status as a permanent resident or conditional permanent resident based solely on the duration of your absence(s) from the United States while the permit is valid.

An absence from the United States for 1 year or more will generally break the continuity of your required continuous residence for purpose of naturalization. If you intend to remain outside the United States for 1 year or more, you may be eligible to file Form N-470, Application to Preserve Residence for Naturalization Purposes. For further information, contact your local USCIS office.

If DHS determines, upon your return to the United States, that you have abandoned your permanent resident status, you may challenge that determination if you are placed in removal proceedings, and seek a determination whether you may retain asylum status even if you cannot retain permanent resident status.

3. Advance Parole Document for Individuals in the United States

a. If you are in the United States and seek an Advance Parole Document, you may apply if:

(1) You have a pending application to adjust status, Form I-485, and you seek to travel abroad for "urgent humanitarian reasons" or in furtherance of a "significant public benefit," which may include a personal or family emergency or bona fide business reasons.

(2) You have a pending application for Temporary Protected Status (TPS) (Form I-821), have been granted TPS, or have been granted T or U nonimmigrant status. Whether you are permitted to retain TPS upon your return will depend on whether you continue to meet the requirements for TPS. If you have TPS and leave and reenter the United States during the validity period of your Advance Parole Document, you will not break the continuous physical presence requirement for maintaining your TPS.

Important: If you have a TPS or other application *pending* and you leave the United States on advance parole, you may miss important notices from USCIS regarding your application, including requests for additional evidence. If you do not respond timely to these notices, USCIS may deem your application abandoned and you will not receive the benefit you seek. It is very important that you make appropriate arrangements to ensure that you do not miss any such important notices.

(3) You have been granted parole pursuant to INA section 212(d)(5), **AND** you seek to travel outside the United States for urgent humanitarian reasons or a significant public benefit. Humanitarian reasons include travel to obtain medical treatment, attend funeral services for a family member, or visit an ailing relative.

Check **Item Number 1.d.** in **Part 2.** of the form.

(4) USCIS or U.S. Immigration and Customs Enforcement (ICE) has deferred action in your case as a childhood arrival based on the guidelines described in the Secretary of Homeland Security's memorandum issued on June 15, 2012 ("Deferred Action for Childhood Arrivals" (DACA)). USCIS may, in its discretion, grant advance parole if you are traveling outside the United States for educational purposes, employment purposes, or humanitarian purposes.

(a) Educational purposes include, but are not limited to, semester abroad programs or academic research;

(b) Employment purposes include, but are not limited to, overseas assignments, interviews, conferences, training, or meetings with clients; **and**

(c) Humanitarian purposes include, but are not limited to, travel to obtain medical treatment, attend funeral services for a family member, or visit an ailing relative.

Check **Item Number 1.d.** in **Part 2.** of the form.

Travel for vacation is not a valid purpose. *You must NOT file Form I-131 with your deferred action request or your package will be rejected and returned to you.*

(5) USCIS has granted you IMMACT 90 or LIFE Act Family Unity Program benefits, **AND** you seek to travel outside the U.S. temporarily for urgent humanitarian reasons or in furtherance of a significant public benefit, which may include a personal or family emergency or bona fide business reasons.

(6) You have a pending application for temporary resident status pursuant to INA section 245A, and you seek to travel abroad temporarily for urgent humanitarian reasons or in furtherance of a significant public benefit, which may include a personal or family emergency or bona fide business reasons.

(7) You have been granted V status in the United States, **AND** you seek to travel abroad for urgent humanitarian reasons or in furtherance of a significant public benefit, which may include a personal or family emergency or bona fide business reasons.

b. Travel Warning

Before you apply for an Advance Parole Document, read the following travel warning carefully.

For any kind of Advance Parole Document provided to you while you are in the United States:

(1) Leaving the United States, even with an Advance Parole Document, may impact your ability to return to the United States.

(2) If you use an Advance Parole Document to leave and return to a port-of-entry in the United States, you will, upon your return, be an "applicant for admission."

(3) As an applicant for admission, you will be subject to inspection at a port-of-entry, and you may not be admitted if you are found to be inadmissible under any applicable provision of INA sections 212(a), 235, or any other provision of U.S. law regarding denial of admission to the United States. If DHS determines that you are inadmissible, you may be subject to expedited removal proceedings or to removal proceedings before an immigration judge, as authorized by law and regulations.

(4) As noted above, issuance of an Advance Parole Document does *not* entitle you to parole and does *not* guarantee that DHS will parole you into the United States upon your return.

(5) As noted above, DHS will make a separate discretionary decision whether to parole you each time you use an Advance Parole Document to return to the United States.

(6) If, upon your return, you are paroled into the United States, you will remain an applicant for admission.

(7) As noted above, DHS may revoke or terminate your Advance Parole Document at any time, including while you are outside the United States. Even if you have already been paroled, upon your return to the United States DHS may also revoke or terminate your parole in accordance with 8 C.F.R. 212.5.

If you are outside the United States, revocation or termination of your Advance Parole Document may preclude you from returning to the United States unless you have a valid visa or other document that permits you to travel to the United States and seek admission.

(8) If you are in the United States when DHS revokes or terminates your parole, you will be an unparoled applicant for admission, and may be subject to removal as an applicant for admission who is inadmissible under INA section 212, rather than as an admitted alien who is deportable under INA section 237. In addition to the above, if you received deferred action under DACA, you should also be aware of the following:

(a) Even after USCIS or ICE has deferred action in your case under DACA, you should not travel outside the United States unless USCIS has approved your application for an Advance Parole Document. Deferred action will terminate automatically if you travel outside the United States without obtaining an Advance Parole Document from USCIS.

(b) If you obtain an Advance Parole Document in connection with a decision to defer removal in your case under DACA and if, upon your return, you are paroled into the United States, your case will generally continue to be deferred. The deferral will continue until the date specified by USCIS or ICE in the deferral notice given to you or until the decision to defer removal action in your case has been terminated, whichever is earlier.

(c) If you have been ordered excluded, deported, or removed, departing from the United States without having had your exclusion, deportation, or removal proceedings reopened and administratively closed or terminated will result in your being considered excluded, deported, or removed, even if USCIS or ICE has deferred action in your case under DACA and you have been granted advance parole.

c. If you are in the United States and seek an Advance Parole Document, a document may not be issued to you if:

(1) You hold a nonimmigrant status, such as J-1, that is subject to the 2-year foreign residence requirement as a result of that status. Exception: If you are someone who was subject to this requirement but are now eligible to apply for adjustment of status to lawful permanent resident, USCIS may consider your application for advance parole; **or**

(2) You are in exclusion, deportation, removal, or rescission proceedings, unless you have received deferred action under DACA. You may, however, request parole from ICE. See NOTE below.

d. If you depart from the United States before the Advance Parole Document is issued, your application will be considered abandoned.

NOTE: Do not use this form if you are seeking release from immigration custody and you want to remain in the United States as a parolee. You should contact your local ICE office about your request (**www.ice.gov/contact/ero**).

4. Advance Parole Document for Individuals Outside the United States

If you are outside the United States and need to visit the United States temporarily for an urgent humanitarian reason or for significant public benefit:

a. You may apply for an Advance Parole Document; however, your application must be based on the fact that you cannot obtain the necessary visa and any required waiver of inadmissibility. Under these conditions, an Advance Parole Document is granted on a case-by-case basis for temporary entry, according to conditions as prescribed.

b. A person in the United States may file this application on your behalf. This person must complete **Part 1.** of the form with information about him or herself.

c. If you entered the United States with an Advanced Parole Document and need to remain in the United States beyond the authorized parole period to accomplish the purpose for which parole was approved, you must re-file Form I-131 with all supporting documentation.

NOTE: Do not use this form if you are seeking release from immigration custody and you want to remain in the United States as a parolee. You should contact ICE about your request.

General Instructions

If you are completing this form on a computer, the data you enter will be captured using 2D barcode technology. This capture will ensure that the data you provide is accurately entered into USCIS systems. As you complete each field, the 2D barcode field at the bottom of each page will shift as data is captured. Upon receipt of your form, USCIS will use the 2D barcode to extract the data from the form. Please **do not damage the 2D barcode** (puncture, staple, spill on, write on, etc.) as this could affect the ability of USCIS to timely process your form.

USCIS provides most forms in PDF format free of charge through the USCIS Web site. In order to view, print, or fill out our forms, you should use the latest version of Abobe Reader, which can be downloaded for free at http://get.adobe.com/reader/.

Each application must be properly signed and accompanied by the appropriate fee. (See the section entitled "What is the Filing Fee?") A photocopy of a signed application or a typewritten name in place of a signature is not acceptable. If you are under 14 years of age, your parent or legal guardian may sign the application on your behalf.

Evidence. You must submit all required initial evidence along with all the supporting documentation with your application at the time of filing. If you are electronically filing this application, you must follow the instructions provided on the USCIS Web site, **www.uscis.gov**.

Biometrics Services Appointment. After receiving your application and ensuring completeness, USCIS will inform you in writing when to go to your local USCIS Application Support Center (ASC) for your biometrics services appointment. Failure to attend the biometrics services appointment may result in denial of your application.

Copies. Unless specifically required that an original document be filed with an application, a legible photocopy may be submitted. Original documents submitted when not required may remain a part of the record, and will not be automatically returned to you.

Translations. Any document containing foreign language submitted to USCIS must be accompanied by a full English language translation which the translator has certified as complete and accurate, and by the translator's certification that he or she is competent to translate from the foreign language into English.

How To Fill Out Form I-131

1. Type or print legibly in black ink.
2. If extra space is needed to complete any item, attach a continuation sheet, write your name and Alien Registration Number (A-Number) (if any), at the top of each sheet of paper; indicate the **Part** and **Item Numbers** to which your answer refers; and date and sign each sheet.
3. Answer all questions fully and accurately. If an item is not applicable or the answer is none, print or type N/A.

General Requirements

1. Initial Evidence

All applications must include a **copy of an official photo identity document showing your photo, name, and date of birth.** (Examples: Your current Employment Authorization Document, if available; a valid government-issued driver's license; passport identity page; Form I-551, Permanent Resident Card, or any other official identity document.) The copy must **clearly** show the photo and identity information. **Form I-94, Arrival-Departure Document, is not acceptable as a photo identity document.**

You must file your application with all required evidence. Not submitting required evidence will delay the issuance of the document you are requesting. We may request additional information or evidence, or we may request that you appear at a USCIS office for an interview or for fingerprinting (See this section "**Biometric Services Requirement**" of these instructions).

If you are applying for:

a. Reentry Permit

You **must** attach:

(1) A copy of the front and back of your Form I-551; or

(2) If you have not yet received your Form I-551, a copy of the biographic page(s) of your passport and a copy of the visa page showing your initial admission as a permanent resident, or other evidence that you are a permanent resident; or

(3) A copy of the Form I-797, Notice of Action, approval notice of an application for replacement of your Form I-551 or temporary evidence of permanent resident status.

b. Refugee Travel Document

You **must** attach a copy of the document issued to you by USCIS showing your refugee or asylee status and the expiration date of such status.

c. Advance Parole Document

If you are in the United States, you **must** attach:

(1) A copy of any document issued to you by USCIS showing your present status, if any, in the United States; and

(2) An explanation or other evidence showing the circumstances that warrant issuance of an Advance Parole Document; or

(3) If you are an applicant for adjustment of status, a copy of a USCIS receipt as evidence that you filed the adjustment application; or

(4) If you are traveling to Canada to apply for an immigrant visa, a copy of the U.S. consular appointment letter; or

(5) If USCIS has deferred action in your case under DACA, you must include a copy of the Form I-797, Notice of Action, showing that the decision on your Form I-821D was to defer action in your case. If ICE deferred action in your case under DACA, submit a copy of the approval order, notice or letter issued by ICE.

You must complete *Part 4.* of the form indicating how your intended travel fits within one of the three purposes below. You must also provide evidence of your reason for travel outside of the United States including the date(s) of travel and the expected duration outside the United States. If your Advance Parole application is approved, the validity date(s) of your Advance Parole Document will be for the duration of the documented need for travel. Below are examples of acceptable evidence:

Educational Purposes

(a) A letter from a school employee acting in an official capacity describing the purpose of the travel and explaining why travel is required or beneficial; or

(b) A document showing enrollment in an educational program requiring travel.

Employment Purposes

A letter from your employer or a conference host describing the need for the travel.

Humanitarian Purposes

(a) A letter from your physician explaining the nature of your medical condition, the specific medical treatment to be sought outside of the United States, and a brief explanation why travel outside the U.S. is medically necessary; or

(b) Documentation of a family member's serious illness or death.

d. Advance Parole Document for individuals outside the United States

***If you are applying for an Advance Parole Document for a person who is outside the United States*, you must attach:**

(1) A complete description of the urgent humanitarian or significant public benefit reason for which an Advance Parole Document is requested and include copies of any evidence you wish to be considered, which indicate the length of time for which the parole is requested;

(2) If an Advance Parole Document is requested for medical reasons, evidence from medical professionals that establishes the medical need, a statement of how and by whom medical care, transportation, housing, and other expenses and subsistence needs will be met;

(3) An Affidavit of Support (Form I-134), with evidence of the sponsor's occupation and ability to provide necessary support;

(4) A statement explaining why a U.S. visa cannot be obtained, including when and where attempts were made to obtain a visa, or an explanation of why a visa was not sought to enter the United States;

(5) A statement explaining why a waiver of inadmissibility cannot be obtained to allow issuance of a visa, including when and where attempts were made to obtain a waiver, and a copy of any DHS decision on your waiver request, or an explanation of why a waiver has not been sought; and

(6) A copy of any decision on an immigrant petition filed for the person seeking to enter the United States, and evidence regarding any pending immigrant petition.

2. Photographs

a. If you are outside the United States and filing for a Refugee Travel Document, or if you are in the United States and filing for an Advance Parole Document:

You **must** submit 2 identical color photographs of yourself taken within 30 days of the filing of this application. The photos must have a white to off-white background, be printed on thin paper with a glossy finish, and be unmounted and unretouched.

NOTE: Because of the current USCIS scanning process, if a digital photo is submitted, it needs to be produced from a high-resolution camera that has at least 3.5 mega pixels of resolution.

Passport-style photos must be 2" x 2." The photos must be in color with full face, frontal view on a white to off-white background. Head height should measure 1" to 1 3/8" from top of hair to bottom of chin, and eye height is between 1 1/8" to 1 3/8" from bottom of photo. Your head must be bare unless you are wearing headwear as required by a religious denomination of which you are a member. Using pencil or felt pen, lightly print your name and A-Number on the back of the photo.

b. If applying for an Advance Parole Document for individuals outside the United States:

(1) If you are applying for an Advance Parole Document, and you are outside the United States, submit photographs with your application.

(2) If you are filing an Advance Parole Document on behalf of another person who is outside the United States, submit the required photographs of the person to be paroled.

3. Biometrics Services Requirement

a. All applicants for a Refugee Travel Document or a Reentry Permit must complete biometrics at an ASC or if applying for a Refugee Travel Document while outside of the U.S. at an overseas USCIS facility. If you are between ages 14 through 79 and you are applying for a Refugee Travel Document or Reentry Permit, you must also be fingerprinted as part of USCIS biometrics services requirement. After you have filed this application, USCIS will notify you in writing of the time and location for your biometrics services appointment. Failure to appear to be fingerprinted or for other biometrics services may result in a denial of your application.

b. All applicants for Reentry Permits and/or Refugee Travel Documents between the ages of 14 through 79 are required to pay the additional **$85** biometrics services fee. (See the section entitled "**What Is the Filing Fee?**")

c. If you are outside the U.S. and are applying for an Advance Parole Document for humanitarian reasons or for significant public benefit, USCIS will notify you in writing whether biometric collection is required. If required, USCIS will advise you of the location for your biometrics services appointment.

4. Invalidation of Travel Document

Any travel document obtained by making a material false representation or concealment in this application will be invalid. A travel document will also be invalid if you are ordered removed or deported from the United States.

In addition, a Refugee Travel Document will be invalid if the United Nations Convention of July 28, 1951, shall cease to apply or shall not apply to you as provided in Articles 1C, D, E, or F of the Convention.

Expedite Request Instructions

To request expedited processing of an application for a Reentry Permit, Refugee Travel Document. or an Advance Parole Document for an individual outside the United States, write the word EXPEDITE in the top right corner of the application in black ink. We recommend providing e-mail addresses and a fax number with any expedite request for the Reentry Permit, Refugee Travel Document, or Advance Parole Document.

Include a written explanation of the reason for the request to expedite with an supporting evidence available. The burden is on the applicant to demonstrate that one or more of the expedite criteria have been met. The criteria are as follows:

1. Severe financial loss to company or individual;
2. Extreme emergent situation;
3. Humanitarian situation; or
4. Non-profit status of requesting organization in furtherance of the cultural and social interests of the United States Department of Defense or National Interest Situation. (Note: The request must come from an official United States Government entity and state that a delay will be detrimental to our Government.

What Is the Filing Fee?

Reentry Permit: The filing fee for a Reentry Permit is **$360**. A biometrics services fee of **$85** is required for applicants ages 14 through 79.

Refugee Travel Document: The filing fee for a Refugee Travel Document for an applicant **age 16 or older** is **$135**. The fee for a child **younger than 16** is **$105**. A biometrics services fee of **$85** is required for applicants ages 14 through 79.

Advance Parole Document (including individuals whose cases were deferred pursuant to DACA): The filing fee for Advance Parole is **$360**. The biometrics services fee is not required.

Advance Parole Document for Individuals Outside the united States: The filing fee for an Advance Parole Document for an individual who is outside the United States is **$360**. The biometrics services fee is not required. The filing fee may be waived based upon a demonstrated inability to pay. Applicants should file Form I-912, Fee Waiver Request when filing this form to ensure such requests are supported in accordance with 8 CFR 103.7(c).

NOTE: If you filed Form I-485 on or after July 30, 2007, and you paid the I-485 application fee required, then no fee is required to file a request for an Advance Parole Document or Refugee Travel Document on Form I-131 if your Form I-485 is still pending, if:

1. You now hold U.S. refugee or asylee status, and are applying for a Refugee Travel Document (see **Form I-131, Part 2., Application Type, Item Number 1.b.**); or
2. You are applying for an Advance Parole Document to allow you to return to the United States after temporary foreign travel (see **Form I-131, Part 2., Application Type, Item Number 1.d.**).

Under these circumstances, you may file Form I-131 together with your Form I-485, or you may submit Form I-131 at a later date. If you file Form I-131 separately, you must also submit a copy of your Form I-797, Notice of Action, receipt as evidence that you filed and paid the fee for Form I-485 required on or after July 30, 2007.

Replacement Travel Document: If you are filing to replace a travel document that was lost, stolen, mutilated, or contains erroneous information, such as a misspelled name, a filing fee is required.

NOTE: If you are requesting a replacement Advance Parole Document as an adjustment applicant filed under the fee structure implemented July 30, 2007, then the full filing fee will be required; however, no biometrics services fee is required.

Incorrect Card: No fee is required if you are filing to correct a USCIS error on your travel document. If USCIS did not cause the error, you must pay the application fees.

Use the following guidelines when you prepare your check or money order for the Form I-131 fees:

1. The check or money order must be drawn on a bank or other financial institution located in the United States and must be payable in U.S. currency; **and**
2. Make the check or money order payable to **U.S. Department of Homeland Security**.

   NOTE: Spell out U.S. Department of Homeland Security; do not use the initials "USDHS" or "DHS."
3. If you live outside the United States, contact the nearest U.S. Embassy or consulate for instructions on the method of payment.

Notice to Those Making Payment by Check

If you send us a check, it will be converted into an electronic funds transfer (EFT). This means we will copy your check and use the account information on it to electronically debit your account for the amount of the check. The debit from your account will usually take 24 hours and will be shown on your regular account statement.

You will not receive your original check back. We will destroy your original check, but we will keep a copy of it. If the EFT cannot be processed for technical reasons, you authorize us to process the copy in place of your original check. If the EFT cannot be completed because of insufficient funds, we may try to make the transfer up to two times.

How to Check if the Fees Are Correct

The filing and biometrics services fees on this form are current as of the edition date appearing in the lower left corner of this page. However, because USCIS fees change periodically, you can verify if the fees are correct by following one of the steps below:

1. Visit the USCIS Web site at **www.uscis.gov**, select "FORMS," and check the appropriate fee; or
2. Telephone the USCIS National Customer Service Center at **1-800-375-5283** and ask for the fee information. For TDD (hearing impaired) call: **1-800-767-1833**.

Where to File?

Please see our Web site at **www.uscis.gov/I-131** or call our USCIS National Customer Service Center at **1-800-375-5283** for the most current information about where to file this benefit request. For TDD (hearing impaired) call: **1-800-767-1833**.

Address Changes

If you have changed your address, you must inform USCIS of your new address. For information on filing a change of address go to the USCIS Web site at **www.uscis.gov/addresschange** or contact the USCIS National Customer Service Center at **1-800-375-5283**. For TDD (hearing impaired) call: **1-800-767-1833**.

NOTE: Do not submit a change of address to the **USCIS Lockbox** facilities because the **USCIS Lockbox** facilities do not process change of address requests.

Processing Information

Any Form I-131 that is not signed or accompanied by the correct fee(s) will be rejected with a notice that Form I-131 is deficient. You may correct the deficiency and resubmit Form I-131. An application or petition is not considered properly filed until accepted by USCIS.

Initial Processing

Once a Form I-131 has been accepted, it will be checked for completeness, including submission of the required initial evidence. If you do not completely fill out the form, or file it without required initial evidence, you will not establish a basis for eligibility, and we may deny your Form I-131.

Requests for More Information, Including Biometrics, or Interview

We may request more information or evidence, or we may request that you appear at a USCIS office for an interview. We may also request that you submit the originals of any copy. We will return these originals when they are no longer required.

At the time of any interview or other appearance at a USCIS office, USCIS may require you to provide biometrics information (e.g., photographs, fingerprints) to verify your identity and update your background information..

Decision

The decision on Form I-131 involves a determination of whether you have established eligibility for the requested document. You will be notified of the decision in writing.

What If You Claim Nonresident Alien Status on Your Federal Income Tax Return?

If you are an alien who has been admitted as an immigrant or adjusted status to that of an immigrant, and are considering the filing of a nonresident alien tax return or the non-filing of a tax return on the ground that you are a nonresident alien, you should carefully review the consequences of such actions under the INA.

If you file a nonresident alien tax return or do not file a tax return, you may be regarded as having abandoned residence in the United States and as having lost your permanent resident status under the INA. As a consequence, you may be ineligible for a visa or other document for which permanent resident aliens are eligible.

You may also be inadmissible to the United States if you seek admission as a returning resident, and you may become ineligible for adjustment of status as a permanent resident, or naturalization on the basis of your original entry.

USCIS Forms and Information

To ensure you are using the latest version of this form, visit the USCIS Web site at **www.uscis.gov** where you can obtain the latest USCIS forms and immigration-related information. If you do not have internet access, you may order USCIS forms by calling our toll-free number at **1-800-870-3676**. You may also obtain forms and information by telephoning our USCIS National Customer Service Center at **1-800-375-5283**. For TDD (hearing impaired) call: **1-800-767-1833**.

As an alternative to waiting in line for assistance at your local USCIS office, you can now schedule an appointment through the USCIS Internet-based system, **InfoPass**. To access **InfoPass**, please visit the USCIS Web site. Use the **InfoPass** appointment scheduler and follow the screen prompts to set up your appointment. **InfoPass** generates an electronic appointment notice that appears on the screen.

Penalties

If you knowingly and willfully falsify or conceal a material fact or submit a false document with this request, we will deny your Form I-131 and may deny any other immigration benefit.

In addition, you will face severe penalties provided by law and may be subject to criminal prosecution.

USCIS Privacy Act Statement

AUTHORITIES: The information requested on this form, and the associated evidence, is collected under the Immigration and Nationality Act, section 101, et seq.

PURPOSE: The primary purpose for providing the requested information on this form is to determine if you have established eligibility for the immigration benefit for which you are filing. The information you provide will be used to grant or deny the benefit sought.

DISCLOSURE: The information you provide is voluntary. However, failure to provide the requested information, and any requested evidence, may delay a final decision or result in denial of your form.

ROUTINE USES: The information you provide on this form may be shared with other Federal, State, local, and foreign government agencies and authorized organizations following approved routine uses described in the associated published system of records notices **[DHS-USCIS-007 - Benefits Information System and DHS-USCIS-001 - Alien File, Index, and National File Tracking System of Records,** which can be found at **www.dhs.gov/privacy]**. The information may also be made available, as appropriate, for law enforcement purposes or in the interest of national security.

Paperwork Reduction Act

An agency may not conduct or sponsor an information collection, and a person is not required to respond to a collection of information unless it displays a currently valid OMB control number. The public reporting burden for this collection of information is estimated at 3 hours and 34 minutes per response, including the time for reviewing instructions and completing and submitting the form. Send comments regarding this burden estimate or any other aspect of this collection of information, including suggestions for reducing this burden to: U.S. Citizenship and Immigration Services, Regulatory Coordination Division, Office of Policy and Strategy, 20 Massachusetts Ave NW, Washington, DC 20529-2140; OMB No .1615-0013. **Do not mail your completed Form I-131 to this address.**

APPENDIX 9C

FORM I-730 AND INSTRUCTIONS

Department of Homeland Security
U.S. Citizenship and Immigration Services

OMB No. 1615-0037; Expires 04/30/2017

I-730, Refugee/Asylee Relative Petition

DO NOT WRITE IN THIS BLOCK - FOR USCIS OFFICE ONLY

Section of Law	Action Stamp	Receipt
☐ 207 (c)(2) Spouse ☐ 207 (c)(2) Child ☐ 208 (b)(3) Spouse ☐ 208 (b)(3) Child		
Reserved		Remarks

☐ Beneficiary Not Previously Claimed
☐ Beneficiary Previously Claimed On: ____________ (e.g., Form I-590, Form I-589, etc.) CSPA Eligible: ☐ Yes ☐ No ☐ N/A

START HERE - Type or print legibly in black ink.

My Status: ☐ Refugee ☐ Lawful Permanent Resident based on previous Refugee status
☐ Asylee ☐ Lawful Permanent Resident based on previous Asylee status

The beneficiary is my: ☐ Spouse
☐ Unmarried child who is a (n): ☐ Biological Child ☐ Stepchild ☐ Adopted Child

Number of relatives for whom I am filing separate Form I-730s: ________ (________ of ____________)

Part 1. Information About You, the Petitioner

Family Name (Last name), Given Name (First name), Middle Name:

Address of Residence (Where you physically reside)

Street Number and Name: | Apt. Number

City: | State or Province:

Country: | Zip/Postal Code:

Mailing Address (If different from residence) - C/O:

Street Number and Name: | Apt. Number:

City: | State or Province:

Country: | Zip/Postal Code:

Telephone Number including Country and City/Area Code:

Your E-Mail Address, if available:

Gender: a. ☐ Male b. ☐ Female | Date of Birth (mm/dd/yyyy):

Country of Birth: | Country of Citizenship/Nationality:

U.S. Alien Registration Number: A- | U.S. Social Security Number (If applicable):

Part 2. Information About Your Alien Relative, the Beneficiary

Family Name (Last name), Given Name (First name), Middle Name:

Address of Residence (Where the beneficiary physically resides)

Street Number and Name: | Apt. Number

City: | State or Province:

Country: | Zip/Postal Code:

Mailing Address (If different from residence) - C/O:

Street Number and Name: | Apt. Number

City: | State or Province:

Country: | Zip/Postal Code:

Telephone Number including Country and City/Area Code:

The Beneficiary's E-Mail Address, if available:

Gender: a. ☐ Male b. ☐ Female | Date of Birth (mm/dd/yyyy):

Country of Birth: | Country of Citizenship/Nationality:

U.S. Alien Registration Number: A- | U.S. Social Security Number (If applicable):

Form I-730 (04/09/15) Y Page 1

Part 1. Information About You, the Petitioner (Continued)

Other Names Used (Including maiden name):

If married, Name of Spouse, Date (mm/dd/yyyy), and Place of Present Marriage:

If previously married, names of prior spouses:

Dates (mm/dd/yyyy) and Places Previous Marriages Ended: Please provide documentation indicating how marriages ended (e.g., death certificate, divorce certificate, etc.):

Date (mm/dd/yyyy) and Place Asylee Status was granted in the United States

OR

Date (mm/dd/yyyy) and Place you received your approval for Refugee Status while living abroad

If You Were Approved for Refugee Status, Date (mm/dd/yyyy) and Place Admitted to the United States as a Refugee:

Part 2. Information About Your Alien Relative, the Beneficiary (Continued)

Other Names Used (Including maiden name):

If married, Name of Spouse, Date (mm/dd/yyyy), and Place of Present Marriage:

If previously married, names of Prior Spouses:

Dates (mm/dd/yyyy) and Places Previous Marriages Ended: Please provide documentation indicating how marriages ended (e.g., death certificate, divorce certificate, etc.):

☐ Beneficiary is currently in the United States.
☐ Beneficiary is outside the United States and will apply for travel authorization at a USCIS Office or a U.S. Embassy or consulate in:

City and Country

To Be Completed By Attorney or Representative, if any.

☐ Fill in box if G-28 is attached to represent the petitioner.

Volag Number:

Attorney State License Number:

Part 2. Information About Your Alien Relative, the Beneficiary (Continued)

Name and mailing address of the beneficiary written in the language of the country where he or she now resides:

Family Name:	Given Name:	Middle Name:
Address - C/O:		
Street Number and Name:		Apt. Number:
City/State or Province:	Country:	Zip/Postal Code:

Check the box, a through d, that applies:

a. ☐ The beneficiary has never been in the United States

b. ☐ The beneficiary is now in immigration court proceedings in the United States Where?

c. ☐ The beneficiary has never been in immigration court proceedings in the United States

d. ☐ The beneficiary is not now in immigration court proceedings in the United States, but has been in the past. Where?

What is the beneficiary's native language?	Is the beneficiary fluent in English? ☐ No ☐ Yes	What other languages does the beneficiary speak fluently:

Form I-730 (04/09/15) Y Page 2

Part 2. Information About Your Alien Relative, the Beneficiary (Continued)

List each of the beneficiary's entries into the United States; if any, beginning with the most recent entry. Submit a copy of each I-94 and/or copy of the beneficiary's passport showing all the entry and exit stamps for each entry. Attach an additional sheet if the beneficiary has more than two entries into the United States:

Date of Arrival (mm/dd/yyyy):	Place (City and State):	Status:
I-94 Number:	Date Status Expires (mm/dd/yyyy):	Passport Number:
Travel Document Number:	Expiration Date for Passport or Travel Document:	Country of Issuance for Passport or Travel Document:

Date of Arrival (mm/dd/yyyy):	Place (City and State):	Status:
I-94 Number:	Date Status Expires (mm/dd/yyyy):	Passport Number:
Travel Document Number:	Expiration Date for Passport or Travel Document:	Country of Issuance for Passport or Travel Document:

Part 3. 2-Year Filing Deadline

Are you filing this application more than 2 years after the date you were admitted to the United States as a refugee or granted asylee status? ☐ No ☐ Yes

If you answered "Yes" to the previous question, explain the delay in filing and submit evidence to support your explanation (Attach additional sheets of paper if necessary):

Part 4. Warning

***WARNING:* Any beneficiary who is in the United States illegally is subject to removal if Form I-730 is not granted by USCIS. Any information provided in completing this petition may be used as a basis for the institution of, or as evidence in, removal proceedings, even if the petition is later withdrawn. Unexcused failure by the beneficiary to appear for an appointment to provide biometrics (such as fingerprints and photographs) and biographical information within the time allowed may result in denial of Form I-730. Information provided on this form and biometrics and biographical information provided by the beneficiary may also be used in producing an Employment Authorization Document if the beneficiary is granted derivative refugee or asylee status.**

Part 5. Signature of Petitioner	*Read the information on penalties in the instructions and the warning in **Part 4.** before completing this section and sign below. If someone other than the beneficiary helped you to prepare this petition, that person must complete **Part 7.***

I certify or, if outside the United States, I swear or affirm, under penalty of perjury under the laws of the United States of America, that this petition and the evidence submitted with it is all true and correct. I authorize the release of any information from my record that U.S. Citizenship and Immigration Services needs to determine eligibility for the benefit I am seeking.

Signature	Print Full Name	Date (mm/dd/yyyy)	Daytime Telephone Number

***NOTE:** If you do not completely fill out this form or if you fail to submit the required documents listed in the instructions, your relative may not be found eligible for the requested benefit and this petition may be denied.*

Part 6. Signature of Beneficiary, if in the United States	*Read the information on penalties in the instructions and the warning in **Part 4.** before completing this section and sign below. If someone other than the petitioner helped you to prepare this petition, that person must complete **Part 7.***

NOTE: If the beneficiary is not currently in the United States, this section should be left blank.

I certify under penalty of perjury under the laws of the United States of America, that this petition and the evidence submitted with it is all true and correct. I authorize the release of any information from my record that U.S. Citizenship and Immigration Services needs to determine eligibility for the benefit I am seeking.

Signature	Print Full Name	Date (mm/dd/yyyy)	Daytime Telephone Number

***NOTE:** If you do not completely fill out this form or if you fail to submit the required documents and biometrics listed in the instructions, you may not be found eligible for the requested benefit and this petition may be denied.*

Part 7. Signature of Person Preparing Form, If Other Than Petitioner or Beneficiary Above

I declare that I prepared this petition at the request of ______________ *(name of persons above), and it is based on all of the information of which I have knowledge.*

Signature	Print Full Name	Date (mm/dd/yyyy)	Daytime Telephone Number

Firm Name and Address	E-Mail Address (If any)

Part 8. To Be Completed at Interview of Beneficiary, If Applicable (14 years of age or older)

Beneficiaries in the United States will be interviewed by USCIS officers. Their petitioners may also be interviewed. Beneficiaries living overseas will be interviewed by a USCIS officer or a DOS consular officer.

I swear (affirm) that I know the contents of this petition that I am signing, including the attached documents and supplements, and that they are ☐ all true or ☐ not all true to the best of my knowledge and that corrections numbered ________ to ________ were made by me or at my request. With these corrections, the information on this form is now true.

Signed and sworn before me by the beneficiary named herein on:

Signature of Beneficiary

Date (mm/dd/yyyy)

Write your Name in your Native Alphabet

Signature of USCIS Officer or DOS Consular Officer

☐ Beneficiary Approved for Travel, Admission Code: ________

☐ Petition Returned to Service Center via NVC

CBP Action Block

Form I-730 (04/09/15) Y Page 4

Department of Homeland Security
U.S. Citizenship and Immigration Services

OMB No. 1615-0037; Expires 04/30/2017

Form I-730, Refugee/Asylee Relative Petition

Who May File Form I-730?

If you have been admitted to the United States as a refugee or if you have been granted status in the United States as an asylee, and you were the principal applicant for your family, you may file Form I-730, Refugee/Asylee Relative Petition **provided that** your refugee admission or asylum grant occurred within the past 2 years. Approval of Form I-730 for a relative abroad does not guarantee visa issuance. A separate Form I-730 must be filed for each qualifying family member for whom you are petitioning.

Who May Not File Form I-730?

You are not eligible to file this petition if:

1. You were granted status as an accompanying or following-to-join derivative refugee or asylee;
2. You were admitted to the United States as a refugee more than 2 years ago (see **NOTE 1**);
3. You were granted status in the United States as an asylee more than 2 years ago (see **NOTE 1**); or
4. You became a naturalized U.S. citizen prior to filing Form I-730, Petition for Alien Relative. If you are currently a U.S. citizen, you may also file Form I-130 to petition for your spouse or children at any time. (*Note:* If you previously filed Form I-730 for your relative when you were a principal refugee or principal asylee or a Lawful Permanent Resident (LPR) who acquired such status after being admitted to the United States as a principal refugee or being granted asylum as a principal asylee, and have since become a naturalized U.S. citizen, United States Citizenship and Immigration Services (USCIS) may continue to process your Form I-730 if it has not been adjudicated).

NOTE 1: The 2-year limitation may be waived by USCIS for humanitarian reasons. Explain in Part 3 of the form why you could not file within 2 years of being granted status. USCIS will make a decision based upon the explanation.

Who Is Eligible to Receive Accompanying or Following-to-Join Benefits?

Your spouse and/or your unmarried child(ren) under the age of 21, whether living inside or outside of the United States, are eligible for accompanying or following-to-join benefits **provided that** the family member(s) qualify under the conditions described below.

If you are a principal refugee

1. The relationship between you and your relative must have existed on the date you were admitted to the United States as a refugee and must continue to exist.
   - **a.** If the person you are filing for is a child who was conceived but not yet born on the date you were admitted to the United States, the relationship will be considered to exist as of the date you were admitted to the United States (See **NOTE 2**).
   - **b.** The mother of such child is not an eligible relative unless the mother was married to you, the principal refugee, when you were admitted to the United States.

NOTE 2: If your child was physically born in the United States, then the child is a U.S. citizen, and you do not need to file this form. You should obtain documentation of the child's citizenship, such as a birth certificate or passport.

If you are a principal asylee

1. The relationship between you and your relative must have existed on the date you were granted asylum in the United States and must continue to exist.
   - **a.** If the person you are filing for is a child who was conceived but not yet born on the date you were granted asylum in the United States, the relationship will be considered to exist as of the date you were granted asylum in the United States (See **NOTE 3**).
   - **b.** The mother of such child is not an eligible relative unless the mother was married to you, the principal asylee, when you were granted asylum in the United States.

NOTE 3: If your child was physically born in the United States, then the child is a U.S. citizen and you do not need to file this form. You should obtain documentation of the child's citizenship such as a birth certificate or passport.

Children who have reached 21 years of age

1. For asylees, a child who is under 21 years of age on the date the Form I-589, Application for Asylum and Withholding of Removal, is received by USCIS will continue to be classified as a child for purposes of determining asylum eligibility and related benefits. For refugees, a child who is under the age of 21 on the date the principal alien is first interviewed by USCIS will continue to be classified as a child for purposes of determining refugee eligibility and related benefits. In both cases, in order to be considered a derivative child, the principal alien must have listed the child on Form I-589, Registration for Classification as Refugee, as appropriate, prior to the derivative's 21st and prior to adjudication of the application. If your Form I-589 or Form I-590 was filed before August 6, 2002, **and your child turned 21 years of age prior to that date**, that application must still have been pending on August 6, 2002, in order for your child to continue to be classified as a child.

In all cases, your child must be unmarried on the date you filed this petition, and at the time it is decided by USCIS in order to receive derivative asylum or refugee status.

2. A spouse or child of a principal refugee must not have ordered, incited, assisted, or otherwise participated in the persecution of another (see INA Section 207(c)(2)(A)) and must be otherwise admissible as an immigrant. A spouse or child of a principal asylee must not be subject to the mandatory bars of 8 CFR Section 208.21. Note: if the spouse or child of a principal asylee is otherwise inadmissible as an immigrant, this fact may be considered in determining whether USCIS will exercise favorable discretion to grant accompanying or following-to-join asylee benefits to such spouse or child.

A petition may not be approved for the following persons

1. A spouse or child who has previously been granted refugee or asylee status;

2. An adopted child, if the adoption took place after the child became 16 years of age, or if the child has not been in legal custody and living with the adoptive parent(s) for at least 2 years;

3. A stepchild, if the marriage that created this relationship took place after the child became 18 years of age;

4. A husband or wife, if each was not physically present at the marriage ceremony, and the marriage was not consummated;

5. A husband or wife, if it is determined that such alien has attempted or conspired to enter into a marriage for the purpose of evading immigration laws; and

6. A parent, sister, brother, grandparent, grandchild, nephew, niece, uncle, aunt, cousin, or in-law.

***Warning:* If your alien relative is in the United States illegally, he or she is subject to removal if Form I-730 is not granted by USCIS. Any information provided in completing this petition may be used as a basis for initiating, or as evidence in, removal proceedings, even if the petition is later withdrawn. Unexcused failure of your alien relative to appear for an appointment to provide biometrics (such as fingerprints) and other biographical information within the time allowed may result in dismissal of the petition. See 8 CFR Section 103.2(b)(13).**

Penalty for Perjury. All statements in response to questions contained in this petition are declared to be true and correct under penalty of perjury. You and anyone who assists you in preparing the petition must sign the petition under penalty of perjury. Your signature is evidence that you are aware of the contents of this petition. Any person assisting you in preparing this form must include his or her name, address, telephone number, and sign the petition where indicated in Part 7. Failure of the preparer to sign will result in the petition being returned to you as an incomplete petition. If USCIS later learns that you received assistance from someone who **willfully** failed to sign the petition, this may result in an adverse ruling against you.

Title 18, United States Code (U.S.C.), Section 1546(a), provides in part:

> Whoever knowingly makes under oath, or permitted under penalty of perjury under Section 1746 of Title 28, United States Code, knowingly subscribes as true, any false statement with respect to a material fact in any application, affidavit, or other document required by the immigration laws or regulations prescribed thereunder, or knowingly presents any such application, affidavit, or other document containing any such false statement shall be fined in accordance with this title or imprisoned not more than 10 years, or both.

If aggravating factors exist, the maximum term of imprisonment for a conviction under 18 U.S.C. Section 1546(a) could reach 25 years.

If you knowingly provide false information on this petition, you or the preparer of this petition may be subject to criminal penalties under Title 18 of the U.S.C. and to civil penalties under section 274C of the INA, 8 U.S.C. 1324c.

General Instructions

Type or print legibly in blue or black ink.

If you need extra space to complete any item, attach a separate sheet of paper, indicate the item number, date, and sign each sheet of paper.

Answer all questions fully and accurately. Portions left unanswered may result in a Request for Evidence. If the previous marriages portion does not apply to you, state "None." For all other portions that do not apply to you, state "N/A."

In **Part 2**, on Page 1, supply the *current* residential and mailing addresses (include the mailing address if it is different from the residential address) of your alien relative and indicate whether your alien relative is living inside or outside of the United States. If your alien relative is outside of the United States, indicate at which USCIS Office or U.S. Embassy or consulate your alien relative will apply for travel authorization.

In **Part 2** on Page 2, supply the *current* mailing address of your alien relative *written in the language of the country where he or she now resides*, in order for him or her to receive an interview notice or other correspondence from USCIS.

Failure to provide your relative's mailing address in the language of the country where he or she resides may result insignificant delays in interviewing your relative and processing this petition.

If your alien relative is inside the United States, both you and your alien relative, if 14 years of age or older, must sign the petition at the time of filing.

Page 3, Part 2. Information About Your Alien Relative, the Beneficiary (continued). Complete all sections. Regarding the Admission/travel document. Provide the I-94 admission number which may have been received from U.S. Customs and Border Protection in connection with arrival and admission to the United States, or from U.S. Citizenship and Immigration Services if immigration status was granted within the United States. The I-94 number is on the Form I-94 Arrival-Departure Record, which may be noted as the Departure Number on some versions. If CBP did not provide a Form I-94 upon arrival/admission to the United States, a print out of the Form I-94 may be obtained according to the instructions provided by CBP. Also, provide the date of admission and the date that the authorized stay expired or will expire.

If a passport or other travel document was used at the last admission to the United States, enter the number in the space provided even if the document is now expired. Provide the country of issuance and expiration date as well.

If your alien relative is outside of the United States, only you are required to sign the petition at the time of filing.

Regardless of the location of your alien relative, he or she will be required at the time of the interview to review the information on this petition, verify that it is accurate, and sign it.

Submission of Documents. You must submit one readable photocopy of each required document to USCIS. Do not submit original documents unless you are asked to provide them. For example, USCIS may require that you provide the original document of any copy you submit.

Translation. Documents in a foreign language must be accompanied by a complete English translation. The translator must certify that the translation is accurate and that he or she is competent to translate.

What Documents Do You Need to Prove Eligibility and A Family Relationship?

Certain documents are required to be submitted with this petition to show that you are eligible to file Form I-730 and to show that a relationship exists between you and your relative. (If the documents described below are not available, see the sections of these instruction entitled "What If a Document Is Not Available?" and "What If Secondary Evidence Is Not Available?")

1. In all cases, submit **evidence of your status** as a refugee or asylee in the United States.

2. In all cases, submit a recently taken clear **photograph** of the family member for whom you are filing. The photograph must be a full frontal picture of your family member, and meet passport specifications. For more information on photographs, you may call the USCIS National Customer Service Center at **1-800-375-5283**. For TTY (deaf or hard of hearing) call: **1-800-767-1833**.

3. If you are petitioning for your **husband or wife,** submit your marriage certificate and the birth certificate of your spouse. If you or your spouse were previously married to other people, submit evidence of the legal termination of the previous marriages such as a divorce or death certificate. Evidence of any legal name change must also be submitted, if applicable.

4. If you are petitioning for your **child** and you are the **natural mother,** whether the child was born in or out of wedlock, submit the child's birth certificate showing both the child's name and your name. Evidence of any legal name change must also be submitted if the names on the birth certificate do not match the names on the petition.

5. If you are petitioning for your **child** and you are the **natural father,** submit the child's birth certificate showing both the child's name and your name. If you were married to the child's mother, submit your marriage certificate. If you or the child's mother were previously married to other people, submit evidence of the legal termination of the previous marriages.

   If you were married to the child's mother, submit evidence that the child was legitimated by civil authorities and submit evidence that a bona fide parent/child relationship exists or existed between you and the child. Evidence of a bona fide parent/child relationship should provide that you have emotional and financial ties to the child, and that you have shown genuine interest in the child's general welfare. Such evidence may include (but is not limited to) the following:

   a. Money order receipts;

   b. Canceled checks showing financial support of the child;

   c. Income tax returns in which you claim the child as a dependent and a member of your household;

   d. Medical or insurance records that include the child as a dependent;

   e. School records for the child;

   f. Correspondence between you and the child; or

   g. Notarized affidavits of reliable persons who are knowledgeable about the relationship. Evidence of any legal name change must also be submitted, if applicable.

6. If you are petitioning for your **stepchild,** submit the child's birth certificate and the marriage certificate between you and the child's natural parent. If you or the child's natural parent were ever previously married to other people, submit evidence of the legal termination of the previous marriage(s). Evidence of any legal name changes must also be submitted, if applicable.

7. If you are petitioning for your **adopted child,** submit a certified copy of the adoption decree and evidence that you resided together with the child for at least 2 years. If you were granted legal custody of the child prior to the adoption, submit a certified copy of the court order granting custody. Evidence of any legal name changes must also be submitted, if applicable.

What If A Document Is Not Available?

If the documents described above are not available from the civil authorities, you must submit the following, as secondary evidence, along with a statement from the appropriate civil authority certifying that the required document(s) is (are) not available.

1. ***Religious institution record:*** A certificate under the seal of the religious institution where the baptism, dedication, or comparable rite occurred within 2 months after birth, showing the date and place of the child's birth, the date of the religious ceremony, and the names of the child's parents.
2. ***School record:*** A letter from the authorities of the school(s) attended, showing the date of admission to the school, the child's date and place of birth, and the names of both parents, if shown on the school records.
3. ***Census record:*** State or Federal census record showing name, place of birth, and date of birth, or the age of the person(s) listed.

What If Secondary Evidence is Not Available?

If the secondary evidence described above is not available, you can submit affidavits. If you submit affidavits, they must overcome the absence of primary and secondary evidence.

Affidavits

Submit written statements sworn to or affirmed by 2 persons who were living at the time and who have personal knowledge of the event you are trying to prove: for example, the date and place of birth, marriage, divorce, or death. The persons making the affidavits do not have to be U.S. citizens.

Each affidavit should contain the following information regarding the person making the affidavit: his or her full name, address, date, and place of birth and his or her relationship to you, if any; full information concerning the event; and complete details concerning how the person acquired the knowledge of the event.

What Additional Documents Must You Submit?

If your alien relative is in the United States, please submit a copy of both sides of his or her Form I-94, Arrival-Departure Record, if any.

Biometrics (Fingerprints and Photographs)

Identity, background, and security checks are required on your alien relative before he or she may be granted derivative asylum or refugee status. For example, USCIS must check the records of the U.S. Federal Bureau of Investigation (FBI) and other information, including all relevant databases of the U.S. Government before derivative asylum or derivative refugee status may be granted to your relative. To facilitate these checks, USCIS may require your alien relative to provide biometrics. Where applicable, this means that if your relative is 14 years of age or over, he or she must be fingerprinted and photographed. Your alien relative will be given instructions on how to complete this requirement. If your alien relative is living in the United States and is subject to biometrics collection, he or she will be notified in writing of the appointment time and the location of the Application Support Center (ASC), or the designated Law Enforcement Agency where he or she must go to be fingerprinted and photographed. If your relative is living outside of the United States, he or she will be given instructions, if applicable, for fingerprinting and photographs by DHS, the Department of State (DOS), or Overseas Processing Entities (OPEs) (i.e., organizations who assist the U.S. government).

Your relative's unexcused failure to appear for a scheduled appointment or to provide biometrics where required, including fingerprints and photographs, or to provide other biographical information within the time allowed may result in the denial of your Form I-730.

Where to File?

Please see our Web site at www.uscis.gov/I-730 or call the USCIS National Customer Service Center at **1-800-375-5283** for the most current information about where to file this benefit request. For TTY (deaf or hard of hearing) call: **1-800-767-1833.**

Interview Process

If your alien relative is living in the United States, USCIS may request that he or she appear for an interview. A written notice of the date, time, and place (address) of the scheduled interview will be sent to your relative. (In addition to your alien relative, you, the petitioner, may be asked to appear for an interview.) See 8 C.F.R. Section 103.2(a)(9) ("[A] petitioner... [or] a beneficiary...may be required to appear...for an interview."). Your alien relative generally will be required to appear at an ASC for biometrics collection before the interview will take place (see Biometrics (Fingerprints and Photographs) section of the instructions).

USCIS suggests that your alien relative bring a copy of your Form I-730 to the interview. An immigration officer will interview your alien relative under oath and make a determination concerning your petition. Your alien relative may receive notification of the decision in the case on the day of the interview, or he or she will in some cases be notified of the decision on a date after the interview. Your alien relative has the right to legal representation at the interview, at no cost to the United States Government. Your alien relative also may bring witnesses to the interview to testify on his or her behalf.

If your alien relative, *who resides in the United States*, is unable to proceed with the interview in fluent English *and* you are applying for derivative *asylum* status for your relative, he or she must provide at no expense to USCIS a competent interpreter fluent in both English and a language that your alien relative speaks fluently. See 8 C.F.R. 208.9(g). (See **Note** 4 if you are applying for derivative refugee status for your relative). The interpreter must be at least 18 years of age. The following persons cannot serve as the interpreter: you or your alien relative's attorney or representative of record; a witness testifying on your alien relative's behalf at the interview; or a representative or employee of your country. Quality interpretation may be crucial to your petition. Assistance must be obtained at your expense prior to the interview.

Failure without good cause to bring a competent interpreter to the interview may be considered an unexcused failure to appear for the interview. Any unexcused failure to appear for an interview may result in dismissal of your petition (See NOTE 4).

If you are hearing-impaired and require the services of a sign-language interpreter in your language, one will be provided for you. Contact the asylum office with jurisdiction over your case as soon as you receive a notice for your interview to notify the office that you will need a sign-language interpreter in your language, so that accommodations can be made in advance.

NOTE 4: Although current regulations only require individuals seeking asylum to bring competent interpreters to the interview in the United States, USCIS strongly suggests that individuals seeking derivative refugee status bring an interpreter for the interview in accordance with these instructions.

If available, your alien relative must bring some form of identification to the interview, including any passport(s), other travel or identification documents, or Form I-94 (Arrival-Departure Record). Your alien relative may bring to the interview any additional available items in support of the petition that have not already been submitted with your petition. All documents must be submitted in triplicate.

If your alien relative is living outside of the United States, he or she will be interviewed by an appropriate U.S. Government official in accordance with DHS and DOS procedures for refugee and asylee derivative interviews in the specific country. Your relative will be notified of the date,time, and place for his or her interview.

What Are the Penalties for Committing Marriage Fraud?

1. Title 8, United States Code, Section 1325, states that any person who knowingly enters into a marriage contract for the purpose of evading any provision of the immigration laws shall be imprisoned for not more than 5 years, or fined not more than $250,000, or both.
2. Title 18, United States Code, Section 1001, states that whoever willfully and knowingly falsifies a material fact, makes a false statement, or makes use of a false document will be fined up to $10,000 or imprisoned up to 5 years, or both.

What Is Our Authority for Collecting This Information?

USCIS requests the information on Form I-730 to carry out the immigration laws contained in Title 8, United States Code, Sections 1157(c)(2) and 1158(b)(3). USCIS needs this information to determine whether a person is eligible for immigration benefits. The information you provide and the information provided by your relative beneficiary, including biometrics, may also be disclosed to other Federal, State, local, and foreign law enforcement and regulatory agencies during the course of the investigation by USCIS or for other lawful purposes, subject to applicable confidentiality provisions. You do not have to give this information. However, if you refuse to give some or all of it, your petition may be denied.

USCIS Forms and Information

To ensure you are using the latest version of this form, visit the USCIS Web site at **www.uscis.gov** where you can obtain the latest USCIS forms and immigration-related information. If you do not have internet access, you may order USCIS forms by calling our toll-free number at **1-800-870-3676**. You may also obtain forms and information by telephoning our USCIS National Customer Service Center at **1-800-375-5283**. For TTY (deaf or hard of hearing) call: **1-800-767-1833**.

As an alternative to waiting in line for assistance at your local USCIS office, you can now schedule an appointment through USCIS Internet-based system, **InfoPass**. To access the system, visit USCIS Web site. Use the **InfoPass** appointment scheduler and follow the screen prompts to set up your appointment. **InfoPass** generates an electronic appointment notice that appears on the screen.

NOTE: Asylum Offices do not use InfoPass. If you have a question regarding a petition in the jurisdiction of an Asylum Office, you should contact the National Customer Service Center at 1-800-375-5283 or visit our Internet Web site at www.uscis.gov. For TTY (deaf or hard of hearing) call: 1-800-767-1833.

USCIS Privacy Act Statement

AUTHORITIES: The information requested on this benefit petition, and the associated evidence, is collected pursuant to Sections 103 [8 U.S.C. 1103], 208(b)(3), 207(c), and 290 [8 U.S.C. §1360] of the Immigration and Nationality Act, as amended.

PURPOSE: The primary purpose for providing the requested information on this benefit petition is to determine if you have established eligibility for certain family members to obtain derivative refugee or asylee status. USCIS will use the information you provide to grant or deny the benefit sought on behalf of a relative.

DISCLOSURE: The information you provide is voluntary. However, failure to provide the requested information, and any requested evidence, may delay a final decision or result in denial of your benefit request.

ROUTINE USES: The information you provide on this benefit petition may be shared with other federal, state, local, and foreign government agencies and authorized organizations in accordance with approved routine uses, as described in the associated published system of records notices DHS/USCIS-007- Benefit Information System and DHS/USCIS/ICE/CBP-001 - Alien File, Index, and National File Tracking System of Records, which can be found at **www.dhs.gov/privacy**. The information may also be made available, as appropriate for law enforcement purposes or in the interest of national security.

USCIS Compliance Review and Monitoring

By signing this form, you have stated under penalty of perjury (28 U.S.C. 1746) that all information and documentation submitted with this form is true and correct. You have also authorized the release of any information from your records that USCIS may need to determine eligibility for the benefit you are seeking and consented to USCIS' verification of such information.

The Department of Homeland Security has the right to verify any information you submit to establish eligibility for the immigration benefit you are seeking at any time. USCIS' legal right to verify this information is in 8 U.S.C. 1103, 1155, 1184, and 8 CFR Parts 103, 204, 205, and 214. To ensure compliance with applicable laws and authorities, USCIS may verify information before or after your case has been decided. Agency verification methods may include, but are not limited to: review of public records and information; contact via written correspondence, the Internet, facsimile, or other electronic transmission, or telephone; unannounced physical site inspections of residences and locations of employment; and interviews. Information obtained through verification will be used to assess your compliance with the laws and to determine your eligibility for the benefit sought.

Subject to the restrictions under 8 CFR Part 103.2(b) (16), you will be provided an opportunity to address any adverse or derogatory information that may result from a USCIS compliance review, verification, or site visit after a formal decision is made on your case or after the agency has initiated an adverse action which may result in revocation or termination of an approval.

Paperwork Reduction Act

An agency may not conduct or sponsor an information collection and a person is not required to respond to a collection of information unless it displays a currently valid OMB control number. The public reporting burden for this collection of information is estimated at 40 minutes per response, including the time for reviewing instructions, and completing and submitting the form. Send comments regarding this burden estimate or any other aspect of this collection of information, including suggestions for reducing this burden, to: U.S. Citizenship and Immigration Services, Regulatory Coordination Division, Office of Policy and Strategy, 20 Massachusetts Avenue, N.W., Washington, DC 20529-2140. OMB No. 1615-0037. **Do not mail your completed Form I-730 to this address.**

Check List

- ☐ **1.** Did you answer each question on Form I-730 according to the instructions on the form?
- ☐ **2.** Did you sign and date Form I-730?
- ☐ **3.** Did you submit proof of your status as a refugee or asylee in the United States?
- ☐ **4.** Did you submit documented proof of relationship, including copies and translations?
- ☐ **5.** Did you submit the beneficiary's photo?
- ☐ **6.** Did you provide the beneficiary's address where he or she is residing now?
- ☐ **7.** Did you provide the beneficiary's name and address as written in the language of his or her country of residence?
- ☐ **8.** If your beneficiary is currently residing in the United States, did he or she review the information on this petition for accuracy?
- ☐ **9.** If your beneficiary is currently residing in the United States, did he or she read the certification statement, sign it, and date it?

APPENDIX 9D

BENEFITS AVAILABLE TO ASYLEES AND REFUGEES

Following a grant of asylee or refugee status, asylees and refugees may be eligible to receive a variety of public benefits, either through a local organization funded by the Department of Health and Human Services, Office of Refugee Resettlement, or through the state in which they reside. For a comprehensive study of the benefits available to asylees, as well as a useful guide for understanding these benefits to better serve asylee clients, see Lindsay M. Harris's article, "From Surviving the Thriving? An Investigation of Asylee Integration in the United States."[1] Appendix A from Ms. Harris's article, which lists all of the public benefits available to asylees and refugees, is reprinted below, with permission of the author and the publisher.

---

[1] Lindsay M. Harris, *From Surviving to Thriving? An Investigation of Asylee Integration into the United States*, New York University Review of Law and Social Change, Vol. 40.2 (forthcoming) (comparing the benefits available to refugees versus asylees). A draft of this forthcoming article is *available at http://papers.ssrn.com/sol3/papers.cfm?abstract_id=2585209.*

DRAFT ONLY

Forthcoming in the New York University Review of Law and Social Change, Vol. 40.2, 2016.

VII. APPENDICES

a. Appendix A: Benefits Available to Asylees and Refugees[336]

Asylees and refugees are eligible for a number of benefits. These are outlined below:

Federal (Non-ORR) Administered Benefits for which Refugees and Asylees may be eligible:

- **Temporary Assistance for Needy Families** (TANF) is available for families with children under age 18, but income and eligibility standards vary by state.[337] TANF is available for the first seven years after status is granted, but individuals cannot receive assistance for more than five years in a lifetime.
- **Supplemental Security Income** (SSI) is a means-tested federally administered program available for the aged (65 plus), blind, and disabled who meet income and resource requirements– for seven years after status is granted. Refugees and asylees can access SSI for up to nine years if they have applied for citizenship. States may choose to supplement SSI benefits.[338]
- **Medicaid** is available for seven years after status is granted. Medicaid is a joint federal-state program to provide health benefits to low-income children, parents, pregnant woman, elderly, and disabled individuals.
- **The State Children's Health Insurance Program** (SCHIP) provides for low to moderate-income children whose families had incomes just above Medicaid eligibility threshold for their states. Eligibility depends on the age of the child and the state they are living in and can range from 100 to 300% of the poverty line.

[336] Thank you to Thomas Pabst and Ronald Munia with the Office of Refugee Resettlement for reviewing this appendix and ensuring that the information is accurate.

[337] Eligibility criteria and the amount of assistance awarded depend on the individual state and their policies. This means that a refugee or asylees in one state may receive a higher or lower amount of financial assistance than a similarly situated individual in another state. One challenge to refugee integration is the federal/state system because having so many separate systems makes it difficult to "create one policy with the same benchmarks for the whole country." Dwyer, *supra* note 42 at 15; *see also* Columba Refugee Resettlement Report, supra note __ at iv, 13 ("Each state implements major assistance programs like [TANF, SNAP, and CHIP] through different mechanisms and at different levels of support."). States also do not consistently track total enrollment in benefits by immigration status. According to ORR Director of the Refugee Services Division, Ronald Munia, refugees and asylees represent a "miniscule" population for the states. The fact that refugees and asylees must first access state benefits for which they are eligible means that ORR is unable to track asylee or refugee enrollment in benefits. Interview with Ronald Munia, Director of Refugee Services Division, Office of Refugee Resettlement, Department of Health and Human Services, on November 19, 2013. The GAO 2012 Report also notes the inconsistencies between states for refugees accessing benefits; because cash assistance and benefits vary from state to state, a poor refugee family in one state may not be eligible for assistance, but would be in another state. *See* GAO July 2012 Report, *supra* note __ at X.

[338] UNHCR has expressed concern about "the yearly issue of loss of eligibility for [SSI] benefits by elderly and disabled refugees" and urged the US, in its 60th anniversary report, to engage in "comprehensive, interagency collaboration and adoption of any necessary legislation, including an interim extension of eligibility for those benefits." *See* UNHCR Proposed Pledges for the United States, supra note __.

DRAFT ONLY
Forthcoming in the New York University Review of Law and Social Change, Vol. 40.2, 2016.

- The **Supplemental Nutrition Assistance Program** (SNAP), formerly known as "the Food Stamp Program" is available to low-income families with income below 135% of the federal poverty line.[339]
- When a refugee has exhausted all sources of federal assistance, states may provide assistance through "**General Assistance (GA) Programs**," funded by the State, though few states actually provide GA. California and New York have some limited GA programs that asylees and refugees can access.
- **Medical Screening** - Conducted by State or local health departments or their proxies for the diagnosis, treatment and prevention of communicable diseases and other conditions of public health importance. This usually includes screening for tuberculosis (TB), parasites, and hepatitis B, as well as school vaccinations.
- **Women, Infants and Children (WIC)** - Provides supplemental food packages for nutritionally at-risk, low-income pregnant, breastfeeding, and postpartum women; infants; and children up to five years of age.
- **One-Stop Career Center System** - Department of Labor funded nationwide network of employment centers that provide information and assistance for people who are looking for jobs, or who need education and training to get a job. Services include training referrals, career counseling, job listings, and other employment services.
- **Job Corps** – Department of Labor funded centers to help eligible youth aged 16- 24 achieve employment, earn a high school diploma or GED and/or learn a vocational trade.

ORR Administered Benefits for which Refugees and Asylees may be eligible:

- If a refugee or asylee is not eligible for mainstream federal assistance (TANF or SSI), [340], then ORR-funded **Refugee Cash Assistance** (RCA) is provided for eight months from date of grant of status.[341] The RCA payment is based on the individual state's TANF assistance levels.
- If a refugee or asylee is not eligible for Medicaid or CHIP, then ORR-funded **Refugee Medical Assistance** (RMA) is available for up to eight months. The RMA benefits are based on the state's Medicaid program.
- **Matching Grant** – as an alternative to cash assistance through RCA, refugees and asylees can enroll in the Matching Grant program, which combines an initial grant of cash and health benefits with a work-oriented program emphasizing self-sufficiency within 120 or maximum 180 days through employment and ESL.[342] The program requires voluntary

[339] *See* http://www.fns.usda.gov/snap/supplemental-nutrition-assistance-program-snap (last visited April 14, 2014).
[340] Federal assistance includes Temporary Assistance for Needy Families (TANF) or Supplemental Security Income (SSI). Generally, these refugees are singles, childless couples, and two-parent families in certain states with restrictive TANF programs.
[341] The length of eligibility for RMA and RCA is determined by ORR appropriations. INA §412(e)(1) allows ORR to reimburse states for RCA and RMA for up to 36 months. Current funding allows for 8 months of cash and medical assistance, and this has been the funding level since October 1991. *See* CRS Refugee Resettlement Report, *supra* note

[342] http://www.acf.hhs.gov/programs/orr/programs/matching-grants/about; *see also* Legislative authority in the Refugee Act – The History of the Matching Grant Program, Office of Refugee Resettlement: http://www.acf.hhs.gov/programs/orr/resource/the-history-of-the-matching-grant-program (last visited August 26, 2013).

DRAFT ONLY
Forthcoming in the New York University Review of Law and Social Change, Vol. 40.2, 2016.

agencies, grantees of ORR, to provide case management and ensure that the client has access to housing and adequate food.[343] Voluntary agencies select the individuals they want to participate in the program, "based primarily, though not necessarily exclusively, on the refugee's readiness to work – including his or her level of motivation, English skills, education or previous work experience, and physical and mental health."[344]

- Refugees and asylees are eligible for **Refugee Social Assistance** for up to five years after their arrival or the asylum grant. This includes employment and employability services, job training and preparation, assistance with the job search, placement, and retention, English-language and vocational training, skills recertification, job related daycare, transportation, translation and interpreter services, and case management.[345] In reality, due to budgetary constraints, many resettlement agencies are unable to provide meaningful services beyond the first 8 months of benefits eligibility for RCA and RMA.

ORR reimburses the states for RCA and RMA costs for refugees and asylees who are ineligible for TANF. Unfortunately, the TANF program does not have a unique identifier for refugees or asylees enrolled in TANF, so there is no way to determine accurately the breakdown of refugees or asylees receiving each type of assistance. ORR's funding allocations to the states are made to the states based on the number of refugee arrivals in the 36 months prior to the fiscal year in question.[346] This does not take into account the number of asylees granted within a state, nor does it factor in secondary migration of refugees beyond the state of their original resettlement.[347]

In resettling refugees, the law provides that "local voluntary agency activities should be conducted in close cooperation and advance consultation with state and local governments."[348] No consultation system exists for asylees. Although the system and the actual consultation/cooperation between stakeholders for refugee resettlement may be less than ideal,[349] nothing comparable is even contemplated for asylees. Unlike refugees, who are initially resettled in a specific geographic location[350], often in a group, asylees settle more in a more random, haphazard fashion, presumably based on a host of individual factors.

---

[343] https://www.acf.hhs.gov/sites/default/files/orr/orr_fact_sheet_benefits_at_a_glance.pdf (last visited April 14, 2014)
[344] GAO Refugee Employment Report, *supra* note __ at 13, 17. According to the most recent ORR Report to Congress, for 2012: "In FY 2012, MG services were provided to 35,166 individuals, including refugees (71 percent), Cuban/Haitian entrants (15 percent), asylees (11 percent), SIV holders (three percent), certified victims of human trafficking and Amerasians...." ORR Report to Congress 2012, *supra* note __ at 22.
[345] https://www.acf.hhs.gov/sites/default/files/orr/orr_fact_sheet_benefits_at_a_glance.pdf (last visited April 14, 2014)
[346] *Id.* at §1522 (c)(1)(B)
[347] GAO July 2012 Report, *supra* note __ at 20-21 (explaining that the Office of Refugee Resettlement defines secondary resettlement as moving from one community to another after initial resettlement. "According to ORR, refugees relocate for a variety of reasons: better employment opportunities, the pull of an established ethnic community, more welfare benefits, better training opportunities, reunification with relatives, or a more congenial climate.").
[348] 8 U.S.C. §1522(a)(1)(B)(iii).
[349] *See* Columbia Refugee Resettlement Report, *supra* note __ at 12-13. Some states have tried to address inadequate cooperation/consultation on refugee resettlement numbers. For example, Tennessee passed the Refugee Absorptive Capacity Act – Tenn. Code. Ann. Sections 4-38-101 to 4-38-104. *See* GAO July 2012 Report, *supra* note __.
[350] Under 8 U.S.C. §1522(a)(2)(c)(iii) the ORR Director must consider numerous factors including (i) the "proportion of refugees and comparable entrants in the population in the area; (ii) the "availability of employment opportunities, affordable housing, and public and private resources (including educational, health care, and mental health services), for refugees in the area; (iii) the likelihood of self-sufficiency; and (iv) likely secondary migration of refugees to that area, when considering where to resettle refugees."

DRAFT ONLY
Forthcoming in the New York University Review of Law and Social Change, Vol. 40.2, 2016.

ORR also provides grants to support various programs and services for refugees and asylees nationwide:[351]

- **Targeted Assistance Grants**: "The targeted assistance program (TAG) funds employment and other services for refugees who reside in counties with unusually large refugee populations. The targeted assistance program provides such counties with supplementation of other available service resources to help the local refugee population obtain employment with less than one year's participation in the program. "In FY 2012, ORR obligated $28.1 million for targeted assistance activities for refugees and entrants. Of this amount, $25.3 million was awarded by formula to 29 states on behalf of the 59 counties eligible for targeted assistance grants."[352]
- **Discretionary Grants** – ORR awards grants on a competitive basis to support refugee communities with special needs. Refugees and asylees who have been in the U.S. more than five years may access the programs funded through these grants.[353] These grants cover many different programs, including the Services for Survivors of Torture Program, through which ORR provides funding, under the Torture Victims Relief Act of 1998, and technical assistance to institutions delivering direct services to torture survivors.[354] Other programs covered according to the 2011 ORR Report to Congress include the Preferred Communities Program and various programs to support refugee health, education, employment, efforts in microenterprise, starting a home child care business, and agriculture. A July 2012 Report discusses ORR "micro-enterprise assistance and individual development accounts" – designed to "facilitate integration by helping refugees start business in the communities where they live…"[355] These grants are not, however, available in all communities.
- Some of ORR's grants are awarded to **Mutual Assistance Associations**, community-based organizations usually created and run by former refugees, to help people from same region integrate into the U.S.[356]
- **Preferred Communities Program** – ORR awards grants to provide "intensive medical case management services to clients increasing the capacity of affiliate staff to critical health emergencies. Preferred Communities grants not only provide the basic requirements of resettlement but also specialized services that are intended to offer refugees greater opportunities for economic independence and integration."[357]

---

[351] The GAO has noted that these ORR funded programs that are focused on integration "may not be as widely available as cash and medical assistance." *See* GAO July 2012 Report, *supra* note __ at 32.
[352] ORR Report to Congress 2012, *supra* note __ at 22. In 2011, this amount was significantly higher -- $48.5 million. *See* ORR Report to Congress FY 2011 at 7-8.
[353] ORR Report to Congress 2012, *supra* note __ at 38.
[354] *See* http://www.acf.hhs.gov/programs/orr/programs/survivors-of-torture/about; *see also* ORR Report to Congress 2012, *supra* note __ at iii (reporting that ORR grants to non-profit organizations totaled $10.8 million to provide services to survivors of torture).
[355] GAO July 2012 Report, *supra* note __ at 34.
[356] *See* Dwyer, *supra* note 42.
[357] ORR Report to Congress 2012, *supra* note __ at 47-49 (In FY 2012, ORR awarded 20 continuation grants, totaling $4.2 million and nine new grants totaling $1.9 million to national voluntary agencies to support the resettlement of newly arriving refugees in communities where they will have the best opportunities for integration, and to provide support for populations that have special needs.").

APPENDIX 9E

ASYLEE ELIGIBILITY FOR RESETTLEMENT ASSISTANCE

CATHOLIC LEGAL IMMIGRATION NETWORK, INC.

Asylee Eligibility for Resettlement Assistance

The National Asylee Information & Referral Line

A joint project of Catholic Legal Immigration Network, Inc. and Catholic Charities, Archdiocese of New York. Funding provided through a grant awarded by the Office of Refugee Resettlement, Administration for Children and Families, U.S. Department of Health and Human Services.

A GUIDE BY **CATHOLIC LEGAL IMMIGRATION NETWORK, INC.**

Asylee Eligibility for Resettlement Assistance

What is an asylee?

An asylee is legally defined as a person who flees his or her country and is unable or unwilling to return due to persecution or a well-founded fear of persecution. The persecution may be on the basis of race, religion, nationality, political opinion, or membership in a social group. Procedurally, a prospective asylee enters the United States as an alien in some other immigration category, enters without inspection, is paroled into the United States for consideration of an asylum claim, or is placed in expedited removal proceedings at the port of entry. The person then applies for asylum and if successful, is granted.

About 47% of asylum grants are handled by the immigration courts, which are located in cities throughout the U.S. About 53% of asylum grants are handled by the U.S. Citizenship and Immigration Services or "USCIS," which has eight regional asylum offices throughout the U.S.

How is asylum status documented?

Asylees will usually have either an *Asylum Approval Letter from a USCIS Asylum Office OR an Order of an Immigration Judge Granting Asylum under § 208 of the INA*. An order from a judge is NOT final unless:

1. U.S. Immigration and Customs Enforcement (ICE) has waived the right to appeal the decision granting asylum; OR

2. if ICE has reserved the right to appeal the decision, 30 days have passed and ICE has *not* filed an appeal (call the EOIR Case Status Line at 1-800-898-7180 and enter the A-number of the applicant to find out if ICE has filed an appeal).

Proof of asylum status can also be found on other documents, such as the I-94 or the Employment Authorization Document (EAD). Additional information is provided in the Office of Refugee Resettlement (ORR) State Letter #00-17 on Status and Documentation Requirements for the Refugee Resettlement Program in Chart #3. This letter may be found on the ORR website at **http://www.acf.hhs.gov/programs/orr/policy/sl00-17.htm**.

A GUIDE BY **CATHOLIC LEGAL IMMIGRATION NETWORK, INC.** 1

Note: Asylum applicants (with the exception of Cuban and Haitian entrants) and individuals who have received a notice of recommended asylum approval are *not* eligible for federal refugee benefits and services.

Are asylees work authorized?

Yes. People who have been granted asylum are authorized to work in the U.S.

How can asylees document their work authorization?

Asylees must meet the same employment eligibility requirements as other U.S. workers. These are found on USCIS Form I-9 (Employment Eligibility Verification). The I-9 requires workers to submit either:

- one document that shows *both* identity and work authorization; OR
- one document that shows identity *and* one document that shows work authorization.

Asylees, like all other workers, can choose which documents listed on the I-9 to submit as proof of employment eligibility. By law, an employer CANNOT demand that a worker submit a particular document or refuse to hire a worker because the worker does not have a green card. Asylees who believe they may be victims of unlawful employment discrimination based on immigration status may call the Office of Special Counsel for Immigration Related Unfair Employment Practices (OSC) at 1-800-255-7688 or visit the OSC website at **http://www.usdoj.gov/crt/osc/**.

The following documents are most commonly used by asylees to show employment eligibility. Other, additional documents may be found on the I-9.

- **Employment Authorization Document (EAD) that contains a photograph (Form I-766):** An unexpired EAD shows *both* identity and work authorization. Therefore, an unexpired EAD is sufficient by itself and does not require any additional documentation. Once an EAD expires, an asylee may provide other documents to satisfy the I-9 requirements. The asylee is not required to keep renewing the EAD. However, it is advisable to maintain a valid EAD until the green card is received, as this will help to avoid any status documentation problems, especially with the Department of Motor Vehicles (DMV). (The expiration date on the EAD applies only to the EAD itself and not to the immigration status of asylee, which does not expire.)

- **Social Security Card:** Asylees are authorized to receive unrestricted social security cards. An unrestricted social security card is evidence of work authorization and, together with a state driver's license or state ID card which establishes identity, can be used to document employment eligibility. Asylees who obtained their social security cards prior to April 2001 may have restricted cards which say, "Valid for Work Only with INS Authorization." They are authorized to return to the Social Security Administration to receive a new, unrestricted card. For more information on this policy, see ORR State Letter #01-09 on the ORR website at **http://www.acf.hhs.gov/programs/orr/policy/sl01-09.htm**.
- **State Driver's License or ID Card:** A state driver's license or ID card establishes identity and can be used together with an unrestricted social security card, which establishes work authorization, to document employment eligibility.

Note: The I-9 requires all documents to be unexpired. Also, older versions of the EAD (Forms I-688, I-688A, and I-688B) are not acceptable. USCIS' *Handbook for Employers* (M-274), available on the USCIS website, has a helpful question and answer section on the I-9.

What if asylees have an error on their I-94 card or lose their I-94 card?

Asylees sometimes find that their I-94 contains an error, such as a misspelled name, incorrect date of birth, incorrect date of entry, or expiration date. Rather than applying by mail for a corrected I-94 (a process that can take several months), current USCIS policy allows asylees to obtain a corrected I-94 on a walk-in basis at the USCIS district office, but *only if the initial I-94 was issued by a USCIS office*, such as the asylum office or district office. If the I-94 was issued by U.S. Customs and Border Protection (CBP) at a port of entry and contains an error, the asylee should return to the nearest port of entry or CBP deferred inspection office to obtain a corrected I-94. For a list of CBP ports of entry, refer to **http://www.cbp.gov/xp/cgov/toolbox/ports/**. There is no fee for a corrected I-94 when the error was made by USCIS or CBP. Asylees who lose their I-94 may apply to USCIS for a replacement card using Form I-102 with the correct fee.

What kind of benefits and services[1] are asylees eligible for?

Type of Assistance	Description	Eligibility Period for Asylees (from date of asylum grant)
Federal Means-Tested Public Benefits		
1. Supplemental Security Income (SSI)	1. A monthly cash payment to low-income people with few resources who are age 65 or older, blind, or disabled.	1. 7 years (with exceptions)[2]
2. SNAP (formerly Food Stamps)	2. Debit card that can be used at grocery stores. Allow low-income people to buy food necessary for good health.	2. No time limit
3. Temporary Assistance for Needy Families (TANF)	3. A monthly cash payment to low-income parents or relatives caring for children under 18 in the same household.	3. Varies[3]
4. Medicaid	4. Reimburses doctor and hospital costs for certain low-income people, primarily pregnant women, families with children, the elderly, and the disabled.	4. Varies[4]
Means-Tested Refugee Cash and Medical Assistance (RCA & RMA)	A federally funded program available to needy asylees *who are not eligible for other cash or medical assistance programs* such as TANF, SSI, or Medicaid.	up to 8 months

1 Most, but not all, of these services are funded by ORR through grants to State governments or to private voluntary agencies. However, in the award of contracts for services, States will target resources to the communities of high concentration of refugees and asylees. Therefore, these services may not be available in all communities.

2 As this guide is going to print, legislation is pending in Congress that would extend the eligibility period from 7 years to 9 years. For updated information, refer to the National Immigration Law Center website at **http://nilc.org/immspbs/ssi/index.htm**.

3 The eligibility period is determined by the state. Some states (IN, MS, OH, SC, and TX) limit TANF for asylees who entered the U.S. on or after 8/22/96 to the first 5 years after obtaining asylum status.

4 AL, MS, ND, OH, TX, VA, and WY have time limits on Medicaid for asylees. These states limit Medicaid for asylees who entered the U.S. on or after 8/22/96 to the first 7 years after obtaining asylum status.

Type of Assistance	Description	Eligibility Period for Asylees (from date of asylum grant)
Refugee Social Services	Designed to smooth adjustment and facilitate early self-sufficiency. These include job preparation and placement and English language classes. The range of services varies by state.	5 years (however, some refugee social services provided pursuant to discretionary grants are not time-limited)
Matching Grant	An early employment program administered by private resettlement agencies as an alternative to public cash assistance. Provides job counseling and placement, case management, transitional cash, and living assistance. Selective: only those who are good candidates for early employment are chosen, and it is based on availability of slots.	180 days (but must be enrolled within 31 days of asylum grant date[5]
Medical Screening	A preventive medical screening and assessment provided by the State Dept. of Public Health to asylees for early diagnosis and treatment of any illness. Usually includes screening for TB, parasites, and hepatitis, as well as school vaccinations for asylee children. Not available in every location.	Varies. Where available, medical screening is strongly recommended and should be arranged within the first 90 days after asylum grant.
Torture Treatment Centers	Funded by ORR for victims of torture to provide rehabilitation, including the treatment of the physical and psychological effects of torture, social and legal services, research, and training for health care providers.	No time limit

5 An asylee may be enrolled within 31 days of *notification* of grant of asylum if an exception letter to the program guidelines is obtained from the ORR MG Team.

Are Cuban and Haitian asylum applicants eligible for benefits and services?

Yes. People from Cuba and Haiti who have applied for asylum are eligible for benefits and services if they have not received a final, non-appealable, legally enforceable order of removal, deportation, or exclusion and the application for asylum is still pending. Whether a person has an order of removal, deportation, or exclusion can be difficult to determine, so ORR recommends that eligibility workers request that each applicant sign a written declaration, under penalty of perjury, that the applicant is eligible and then contact USCIS or the Executive Office for Immigration Review to verify immigration status.

The eligibility period for benefits and services begins only once, on the date of the asylum application, and does not restart after asylum, should asylum be granted. The following documents may be used by Cuban and Haitian asylum applicants to show eligibility for benefits and services:

- USCIS receipt for filing Form I-589 (Application for Asylum)
- I-94 arrival/departure card stamped with "Form I-589 filed"
- Document stamped by an immigration judge showing an asylum application has been filed
- Employment Authorization Document with the code C08
- Employment Authorization Document (older version I-688B) with the provision of law 274a.12(c)(8)

For more information, refer to ORR State Letter #00-17 on Status and Documentation Requirements for the Refugee Resettlement Program at **http://www.acf.hhs.gov/programs/orr/policy/sl00–17.htm**.

How can asylees obtain an Employment Authorization Document (EAD)?

According to the Enhanced Border Security and Visa Reform Act of 2002, which took effect on 11/14/02, asylees are to receive an Employment Authorization Document (EAD) at no charge immediately upon being granted asylum. The initial EAD is mailed to the asylee within 7-10 days and is valid for two years. The EAD can be renewed for a fee, which can be waived if the asylee is unable to pay. The procedures for obtaining the initial EAD depend on how the asylee obtained asylum status.

Asylees granted asylum by an immigration judge, the Board of Immigration Appeals, or a federal court should schedule an InfoPass appointment at their local USCIS office at least three business days after the date on the order granting asylum to obtain both an EAD and an I-94. They need to bring their copy of the order granting asylum and some form of photo identification. The I-94 is given at the appointment, and the EAD is mailed to the asylee within 7-10 days after the appointment (card delivery can take up to 2 additional weeks). In some cases, the asylee may be directed to submit fingerprints at an Application Support Center before EAD card production can begin. In these cases, the EAD is mailed within 7-10 days after submitting fingerprints.

Asylees granted asylum by the USCIS Asylum Office receive the EAD in the mail within 2-4 weeks after receiving their asylum approval letter. The I-94 is issued together with the approval letter.

Derivative asylees (the spouse and children of an asylee) entering the U.S. through a Refugee and Asylee Relative Petition (Form I-730) will be processed for an EAD at the port of entry and receive the EAD in the mail 2-4 weeks later. The I-94 will still be issued at the port of entry.

Can asylees travel outside the United States?

Prior to their departure from the U.S., asylees are required to obtain USCIS permission to re-enter the U.S. after their trip abroad. Permission is obtained by filing Form I-131 to receive a Refugee Travel Document. Asylees should be especially cautious about travel to the country where they were persecuted. For more information, refer to the USCIS fact sheet on asylee travel at **http://www.uscis.gov/files/pressrelease/AsylumTravel122706FS.pdf**.

Are asylees required to report a change of address?

Yes. Asylees (like all aliens in the U.S.) are required to report a change of address to the Department of Homeland Security by filing Form AR-11 with USCIS. The Form AR-11 can be filed by mail or online. It can be found on the USCIS website at **http://www.uscis.gov**.

Are asylees eligible for a green card?

Yes. Asylees are eligible to apply for adjustment of status (a green card) after one year of physical presence in the U.S. (from the date of the asylum grant) using Form I-485. Professional assistance through an immigration attorney or a Board of Immigration Appeals recognized non-profit organization is recommended to ensure the application is completed correctly and includes all the required attachments. A list of recognized organizations is available on the U.S. Department of Justice website at **http://www.justice.gov/eoir/ra.html**.

The fee for the I-485 now includes the fees for an EAD and a Refugee Travel Document. Therefore, an asylee who pays the current I-485 fee is not required to pay an additional fee for the EAD or Refugee Travel Document, if needed while the I-485 is pending. Asylees who are unable to pay the I-485 fee may apply for a fee waiver. On 9/17/09, USCIS released a list of questions and answers about adjustment of status for asylees, available on its website, **http://www.uscis.gov**, under "News."

How long does it take for asylees to receive a green card?

Green card processing times are posted on the USCIS website, **http://www.uscis.gov**. As of the date this guide is being printed, asylee green card processing times are 4-8 months.

Can asylees bring their immediate family members to the United States?

Asylees can request derivative asylum status for their spouse and unmarried children under age 21 by filing Form I-730 (Refugee and Asylee Relative Petition). There is no filing fee for the I-730. The I-730 allows family members to join the asylee in the U.S. The I-730 *must* be filed within two years of receiving asylum status. Family members, as derivative asylees, are eligible for resettlement assistance from the date of their entry into the U.S., which is found on the I-94 card.

Can asylees get student loans?

Asylees are eligible for federal student financial aid, including grants, loans, and work study programs, from the U.S. Department of Education. For more information, contact the Federal Student Aid Information Center at 1-800-433-3243 or see *The Guide to Federal Student Aid* (available in English and Spanish) at **http://studentaid.ed.gov/students/publications/student_ guide/index.html**.

Where can I find more information?

Visit the CLINIC website at **http://cliniclegal.org/asylees**.

The National Asylee Information & Referral Line

1-800-354-0365 (for asylees only)

The National Asylee Information & Referral Line is funded by the Office of Refugee Resettlement (ORR) and administered by Catholic Legal Immigration Network, Inc. (CLINIC) in partnership with Catholic Charities of the Archdiocese of New York. The goal of the referral line is to link asylees with local refugee service providers and benefits for which they are statutorily eligible, including job placement, English classes, cash assistance, and medical assistance. The line provides information in 18 languages and is for asylees only. Service providers or others with questions about resettlement benefits and services for asylees should contact their State Refugee Coordinator (on the ORR website at **http://www.acf.hhs.gov/programs/orr/partners/state_coordina.htm**) or CLINIC.

CATHOLIC LEGAL IMMIGRATION NETWORK, INC.

Catholic Legal Immigration Network, Inc. (CLINIC)
415 Michigan Ave., NE, Suite 200
Washington, DC 20017
Tel. 202.635.5820 • Fax 202.635.2649
www.cliniclegal.org

January 2012

Photo credits for front cover (clockwise, left to right):
Human Issues Collaborative, Inc.; ©LAURA SIKES; ©LAURA SIKES; ©LAURA SIKES; Aliza Becker; David Bacon; Jeff Chenoweth.

APPENDIX 10A

AFFIRMATIVE AND DEFENSIVE ASYLUM PROCESS CHART

AFFIRMATIVE (*See* chapter 7 and appendix 4 for a more in-depth examination of each step in the affirmative process.)	DEFENSIVE (*See* chapter 8 and appendix 5 for a more in-depth examination of each step in the defensive process.)
Interview Potential Applicant During the initial interviews with the applicant, it is important to determine: (1) that the applicant has a basis for submitting a claim; (2) that the applicant is eligible to apply affirmatively; (3) that the applicant is not barred from seeking asylum; and (4) that the applicant is not subject to reinstatement of removal because he or she was previously removed or ordered deported and subsequently re-entered the United States illegally.	**Interview Potential Applicant** During the initial interviews with the applicant, it is important to determine whether he or she: (1) has a basis for submitting a claim; (2) is eligible for any *other* relief in removal proceedings (*see* chapter 16); (3) was referred by an asylum officer after an affirmative or credible fear interview; and (4) is subject to a bar to asylum or withholding of removal.
Prepare the Application In addition to answering all of the questions on Form I-589, Application for Asylum and Withholding of Removal, it is useful to prepare a declaration of the applicant that gives a detailed, chronological account of the basis for the applicant's fear of returning to his or her home country. *See* appendices 1 and 2B for practice pointers.	**Release from Detention** If the applicant is detained, release from detention may be sought at a bond hearing before an immigration judge (IJ) or through the parole process administered by ICE. *See* chapter 9.

AFFIRMATIVE (*See* chapter 7 and appendix 4 for a more in-depth examination of each step in the affirmative process.)	**DEFENSIVE** (*See* chapter 8 and appendix 5 for a more in-depth examination of each step in the defensive process.)
File the Application Carefully read and follow the instructions on the I-589 and file the application with the correct number of copies and the required documentation at the appropriate U.S. Citizenship and Immigration Services (USCIS) service center. USCIS will send an acknowledgment of receipt of the application or will return the application if it is not complete or has been incorrectly filed.	**Prepare the Application** In addition to answering all of the questions on Form I-589, Application for Asylum and Withholding of Removal, it is useful to prepare a declaration of the applicant that gives a detailed, chronological account of the basis for the applicant's fear of returning to his or her home country. See appendices 1 and 2D for practice pointers. *Note*: The information provided on the asylum application may be used to satisfy Department of Homeland Security's (DHS) burden of proof in removal proceedings. If the applicant previously filed for asylum affirmatively or defensively or has had a credible fear interview under the expedited removal process, it is imperative that copies of the previous applications, statements, and/or interview notes be obtained prior to preparing the applicant's I-589.
Fingerprint Notice The applicant will receive an appointment to be fingerprinted after a complete application is filed. **Notice of Interview** **An interview will normally be scheduled within 30 to 45 days after the application is filed. A notice will be sent to the applicant approximately two weeks before the interview informing the applicant of the date, time, and location of the interview.** *Note*: Always inform USCIS and the asylum office of any change of address to ensure that the interview notice and decision information is received.	**Master Calendar Hearings** At the applicant's master calendar, the following matters will be addressed: **Pleadings** The IJ will read the allegations and charges in the Notice to Appear and will ask the applicant or his or her attorney to respond to them. **Filing of the Application** Carefully read and follow the instructions on the I-589 and file the application with the correct number of copies and the required documentation at the immigration court. The application must be filed at a master calendar hearing (not at the court filing window). **Motions** The IJ will consider a variety of motions at this stage, including motions for a continuance, for change of venue, and for withdrawal or substitution of counsel.

AFFIRMATIVE (*See* chapter 7 and appendix 4 for a more in-depth examination of each step in the affirmative process.)	DEFENSIVE (*See* chapter 8 and appendix 5 for a more in-depth examination of each step in the defensive process.)
Asylum Interview The applicant will be interviewed by an asylum officer who has reviewed the application submitted by the applicant. If the applicant does not speak English fluently, he or she must bring an interpreter to the interview. The applicant may be represented by counsel at the interview and may bring witnesses and submit additional documentation. *See* appendix 3 for a checklist and practice pointers.	**Hearing on Deportability or Inadmissibility** If the charge or charges on the Notice to Appear are contested, the IJ may schedule a separate hearing on whether the applicant is subject to removal from the United States. If the IJ finds that the applicant is not subject to removal, applying for relief from removal is no longer necessary.
Employment Authorization The Application for Employment Authorization, Form I-765, may be submitted "no earlier" than 150 days after the date the completed asylum application is filed. An individual is ineligible for employment authorization if he or she has been convicted of an aggravated felony or if his or her application for asylum was denied by an asylum officer or IJ within 150 days after submitting his or her application. See chapter 13 for more information regarding employment authorization for asylum applicants.	

AFFIRMATIVE (*See* chapter 7 and appendix 4 for a more in-depth examination of each step in the affirmative process.)	**DEFENSIVE** (*See* chapter 8 and appendix 5 for a more in-depth examination of each step in the defensive process.)
Decision **The asylum officer may grant, deny, or refer an asylum claim. At the end of the asylum officer interview, the applicant will be informed where and when he or she must appear to acknowledge receipt of the asylum officer's written decision. If the interview is conducted on a circuit ride by the asylum officer, the decision may be mailed to the applicant.** **Grant** An applicant is eligible to apply for permanent residency one year after he or she has granted asylum. Prior to granting asylum, the asylum office must check the identity of the applicant against all appropriate records and databases maintained by the secretaries of DHS and State and the attorney general, including the Automated Visa Lookout System. **Denial** An applicant will only be issued a denial if he or she is in lawful status. Prior to issuing a denial, the asylum officer must provide the applicant with a Notice of Intent to Deny and allow the applicant to submit a rebuttal.	**Merits Hearing on Requested Relief (Individual Calendar Hearing)** If the applicant has been determined to be subject to removal, his or her application for asylum and withholding and any other form of relief sought will be considered by the IJ at an individual calendar hearing. A hearing on the merits is usually completed within 180 days after the application is filed with the IJ.
Referral If the asylum claim is not granted and the applicant appears to be deportable or inadmissible, he or she will be issued a Notice to Appear for removal proceedings. *See* DEFENSIVE side of the Asylum Process Chart.	**Appeal to BIA** The IJ's decision to grant or deny asylum or withholding of removal may be appealed by the applicant *or* DHS to the Board of Immigration Appeals (BIA) within 30 days after the date of the IJ's decision by filing a Notice of Appeal with the BIA.

AFFIRMATIVE (*See* chapter 7 and appendix 4 for a more in-depth examination of each step in the affirmative process.)	DEFENSIVE (*See* chapter 8 and appendix 5 for a more in-depth examination of each step in the defensive process.)
No Appeal/Motions to Reopen or Reconsider There is no appeal from an asylum officer's decision. An applicant who is referred for removal proceedings may renew his or her request for asylum before an IJ. Under some circumstances it may be possible to file a motion to reopen or reconsider with Asylum HQ or the asylum office that issued the decision. *See* chapter 7.	**Judicial Review** A negative decision by the BIA may be appealed to a federal court *unless* the contested issue involves one or more of the following determinations, which are not reviewable: (1) the availability of a safe third country; (2) the one-year filing deadline (if the issue does not involve a question of law or constitutional claim); (3) the previous denial bar; or (4) the terrorist bar. *See* chapter 12.

APPENDIX 10B

A COMPARISON OF THE FORMS OF PROTECTION AVAILABLE UNDER U.S. LAW

Protection under article 3 of the Convention Against Torture (CAT) is not the same as asylum or as withholding of removal. The following chart, adapted from legacy INS materials compares these forms of protection:

Asylum	Withholding of Removal	CAT
Not a treaty obligation	A treaty obligation (art. 33)	A treaty obligation
Discretionary	Mandatory	Mandatory
One-year filing deadline	No filing deadline	No filing deadline
Standard requires a *well-founded fear of persecution* on account of race, religion, nationality, membership in a particular social group, or political opinion in the country in question. Harm feared must be on account of a protected ground.	Standard requires that it is *more likely than not that the person would be persecuted* on account of race, religion, nationality, membership in a particular social group, or political opinion in the country in question. Harm feared must be on account of a protected ground.	Standard requires that the person is *more likely than not to be tortured* in the country in question. Harm feared need not be on account of a protected ground.
Persons ineligible for protection include certain criminals, terrorists, persecutors.	Persons ineligible for protection include certain criminals, terrorists, persecutors.	No bars to protection for deferral of removal applicants.
Basis for adjustment to legal permanent resident status.	Not basis for adjustment to legal permanent resident status.	Not basis for adjustment to legal permanent resident status.
Immediate family members may be granted same status derivatively.	Family members may not be granted derivative status.	Family members may not be granted derivative status.
Grant confers permission to remain in United States.	Grant prohibits only removal to country of risk; does not prohibit removal to nonrisk country.	Grant prohibits only removal to country of risk; does not prohibit removal to nonrisk country.

APPENDIX 10C

TEMPORARY PROTECTED STATUS

The Temporary Protected Status (TPS) statute and DHS regulations (INA §244 and 8 CFR §244) provide eligible noncitizens from designated countries a temporary stay of removal and employment authorization for the designated TPS period and for any extensions. For eligibility information, please see 8 CFR §244. TPS does not lead to permanent resident status. When a TPS designation ends, beneficiaries revert to the immigration status they had prior to TPS (unless that benefit has expired or been terminated) or to any other status they may have been granted while in TPS.

Countries Currently Designated for TPS	Most Recent	Current Expiration Date	Federal Register Cite (most recent)
El Salvador	03/09/2001	09/09/2016	73 FR 57128
Guinea	11/21/2014	05/21/2016	79 FR 69511
Haiti	07/23/2011	01/22/2016	79 FR 11808, 79 FR 25141
Honduras	01/05/1999	07/05/2010	73 FR 57133
Liberia	11/21/2014	05/21/2016	79 FR 69502
Nicaragua	01/05/1999	07/05/2010	73 FR 57138
Sierra Leone	11/21/2014	05/21/2016	79 FR 69506
Somalia	09/16/1991	03/17/2011	74 FR 37043
South Sudan	09/02/2014	05/02/2016	79 FR 52019
Sudan	11/04/1997	05/02/2010	73 FR 47606
Syria	01/05/2015	09/30/2016	80 FR 2454

APPENDIX 10D

BENEFITS COMPARISON CHART

Asylum, withholding of removal, or protection under the Convention Against Torture are forms of protection that yield varying benefits and responsibilities. These are compared in the chart below.

Benefits Comparison Chart	Asylum	Withholding of Removal under INA §241(b)(3)	CAT Protection
Right to Remain in the U.S.	Confers permission to remain in the U.S.	Prohibits removal to the country of feared persecution, but does not prohibit removal to other countries	Prohibits removal to the country of feared torture, but does not prohibit removal to other countries
Documentation of Status	Asylum Approval letter or IJ Order granting asylum; I-94 card showing admission as asylee	IJ Order showing order of removal, but noting removal withheld to the country of feared persecution	IJ Order showing order of removal, but noting removal withheld to the country of feared torture
EAD	Confers automatic employment authorization upon grant	Confers eligibility to apply for employment authorization under category (A)(10)	Confers eligibility to apply for employment authorization for those granted withholding, but not necessarily for those granted deferral of removal
Travel	Confers eligibility to file an application for a refugee travel document to travel outside the U.S.	No ability to travel outside of the U.S. and then re-enter	No ability to travel outside of the U.S. and then re-enter
Family	Spouses and children in the U.S. may be granted asylum as derivatives; confers eligibility to petition for spouses and children to follow to join the asylee in the U.S.	No ability to include spouses and children as dependent applicants or to petition for spouses and children	No ability to include spouses and children as dependent applicants or to petition for spouses and children
LPR and Citizenship	Confers eligibility to apply for LPR status after one year physically present in the U.S. as an asylee	No pathway to permanent residence or citizenship	No pathway to permanent residence or citizenship
Public Benefits	Confers potential eligibility for federal means-tested public benefits, means-tested refugee cash and medical assistance, refugee social services, matching grant, and a medical screening	No eligibility for public benefits	No eligibility for public benefits

APPENDIX 11A
ASYLUM OFFICES

Office of Refugee, Asylum, and International Operations

20 Massachusetts Avenue, NW, Suite 3300, Washington, DC 20591
(202) 272-1601 / (202) 272-1676 (fax)

Joseph E. Langlois, *Associate Director*

U.S. Citizenship and Immigration Services Asylum Division

20 Massachusetts Avenue, NW, Washington, DC 20591
(202) 272-1625 / (202) 272-1681 (fax)

John Lafferty, *Chief*

Arlington, VA (ZAR)

Jedidah Hussey, Director
1525 Wilson Blvd, Suite 300
Mailstop 2500
Arlington, VA 20598
(703) 235-4100
(703) 812-8455 (fax)

Jurisdiction: DC, western PA, MD, VA, WV, NC, GA (except Atlanta expedited removal and stowaways cases, which are handled by NY), AL, and SC

Chicago, IL (ZCH)

Kenneth Madsen, Director
181 West Madison Street, Suite 3000
Chicago, IL 60602
(312) 849-5200
(312) 849-5201 (fax)

Jurisdiction: IL, IN, MI, WI, MN, ND, SD, KS, MO, OH, IA, NE, MT, ID, and KY

Houston, TX (ZHN)

Marie Hummert, Director
16630 Imperial Valley Drive, Suite 200
Houston, TX 77060

Mailing Address:
P.O. Box 670626
Houston, TX 77267-0626
(281) 931-2100
(281) 931-1309 (fax)

Jurisdiction: LA, AR, MS, TN, TX, OK, NM, CO, UT, and WY

Los Angeles, CA (ZLA)

George Mihalko, Director
1585 S. Manchester Avenue
Anaheim, CA 92802

Mailing Address:
P.O. Box 65015
Anaheim, CA 92815-8515
(714) 808-8000
(714) 635-8707 (fax)

Jurisdiction: AZ, southern CA (within the jurisdiction of the Los Angeles and San Diego district offices), southern NV (within the jurisdiction of the Las Vegas Suboffice), HI, and Guam

Miami, FL (ZMI)

Varsenik Papazian, Director
99 SE 5th Street, 3rd Floor
Miami, FL 33131
(305) 960-8600
(305) 530-6071 (fax)

Jurisdiction: FL, Puerto Rico, and the U.S. Virgin Islands

Newark, NJ (ZNK)

Susan Raufer, Director
1200 Wall Street West, 4th Floor
Lyndhurst, NJ 07071
(201) 508-6100
(201) 531-1877 (fax)

Jurisdiction: NY (within the boroughs of Manhattan and the Bronx, the Buffalo District Office), PA (excluding the jurisdiction of the Pittsburgh Suboffice), CT, DE, ME, MA, NH, NJ, RI, and VT

Rosedale, NY (ZNY)

Patricia Menges, Director
One Cross Island Plaza
133-33 Brookville Blvd., 3rd Floor
Rosedale, NY 11422
(718) 723-5954
(718) 723-1121 (fax)

Jurisdiction: NY (excluding the jurisdiction of the Buffalo District Office and the boroughs of Manhattan and the Bronx)

San Francisco, CA (ZSF)

Emilia Bardini, Director
75 Hawthorne St., 3rd Fl., Room 303S
San Francisco, CA 94105
(415) 293-1234
(415) 293-1269 (fax)

Mailing Address:
P.O. Box 77530
San Francisco, CA 94107

Jurisdiction: northern CA (within the jurisdiction of the San Francisco District Office), northern NV (within the jurisdiction of the Reno Suboffice), OR, WA, and AK

EXECUTIVE OFFICE FOR IMMIGRATION REVIEW

Board of Immigration Appeals

Office of the Chief Clerk

5107 Leesburg Pike, Suite 2000; Falls Church, VA 20530
(703) 605-1007

Office of the Chief Immigration Judge

5107 Leesburg Pike, Suite 2500; Falls Church, VA 20530
(703) 305-1247

Brian M. O'Leary, *Chief Immigration Judge*

Michael C. McGoings, *Deputy Chief Immigration Judge*

Edward F. Kelly, *Deputy Chief Immigration Judge*

ASSISTANT CHIEF IMMIGRATION JUDGES

Rico J. Bartolomei
Area of responsibility: San Diego, East Mesa, Imperial, Eloy, Florence, Phoenix, Tucson
Back-up: Thomas Y. K. Fong

John W. Davis
Area of responsibility: Bloomington, Cleveland, Denver, Las Vegas, Kansas City, Omaha, Salt Lake City, El Paso, El Paso SPC
Back-up: Print Maggard

Jill H. Dufresne
Area of responsibility: Batavia, Boston, Buffalo, Chicago, Detroit, Hartford
Back-up: Deepali Nadkarni

Thomas Y. K. Fong
Area of responsibility: Adelanto, Honolulu, Los Angeles, Saipan
Back-up: Rico J. Bartolomei

MaryBeth Keller
Area of responsibility: Conduct and Professionalism; Labor Management Issues
Back-up: Christopher A. Santoro

Print Maggard
Area of responsibility: Portland, San Francisco, Seattle, Tacoma
Back-up: John W. Davis

Deepali (Dee) Nadkarni
Area of responsibility: Dallas, Houston, Houston SPC, San Antonio, Pearsall, Harlingen, Port Isabel
Back-up: Jill H. Dufresne

Christopher A. Santoro
Area of responsibility: Arlington, Baltimore, HQIC, Philadelphia, York, Charlotte, Memphis, New Orleans, Oakdale
Back-up: MaryBeth Keller

Elisa M. Sukkar
Area of responsibility: Atlanta, Krome, Lumpkin (Stewart), Miami, Orlando, San Juan
Back-up: Robert D. Weisel

Jack H. Weil
Area of responsibility: Vulnerable Populations
Back-up: Christopher A. Santoro

Robert D. Weisel
Area of responsibility: Elizabeth, Fishkill, Newark, New York, Ulster, Varick
Back-up: Elisa M. Sukkar

Immigration Courts and Judges

Arizona

Eloy
1705 E. Hanna Road,
Suite 366
Eloy, AZ 85131
(520) 466-3671

Immigration Judges
DeVitto, James
Feldman, Irene
Phelps, Richard
Spencer-Walters, Linda

Florence
3260 N. Pinal Parkway
Avenue
Florence, AZ 85132
(520) 868-3341

Immigration Judges
Arellano, Silvia R.
Coughlon, Robert
Taylor, Bruce A.

Phoenix
200 East Mitchell Drive,
Suite 200
Phoenix, AZ 85012
(602) 640-2747

Immigration Judges
Freerks, LaMonte S.
Hollis, Wendell
Richardson, John W.

Tucson
300 West Congress,
Suite 300
Tucson, AZ 85701
(520) 670-5212

Immigration Judges
Keenan, Sean H.
O'Leary, Thomas M.

California

Adelanto
Adelanto Detention Facility
10250 Rancho Road,
Suite 201A
Adelanto, CA 92301
(760) 246-5404

Immigration Judges
Everett, Timothy
Lee, Amy
McGrail, Elizabeth

East Mesa
East Mesa CCA
446 Alta Road, Suite 5400
San Diego, CA 92158
(619) 661-3327

Immigration Judges
De Paolo, Zsa Zsa
McSeveney, Robert B.C.

Imperial
2409 La Brucherie Road
Imperial, CA 92251
(760) 370-5200

Immigration Judges
Vacant

Los Angeles
606 S. Olive Street,
15th Floor
Los Angeles, CA 90014
(213) 894-2811

Immigration Judges
Bakke Varzandeh, Joyce
Bank, Ira E.
Bass, Lori
Bither, Christine A.
Burke, David
Costa, Philip
Dorfman, Arlene
Dunkel-Bradley, Dorothy
Fong, Thomas Y.K.
Ho, Anna
Hong, Jungyoun
Latimore, Jan D.
Laurent, Scott D.
Little, Monica
Munoz, Lorraine J.
Naselow-Nahas, Tara
Neumeister, William
O'Connor, Lee
Peters, Rose C.
Riley, Kevin W.
Rooyani, Rodin
Ruane, Rachel
Sitgraves, D.D.
Stancill, Christine E.
Tabaddor, A. Ashley
Travieso, Frank
Vahid-Tehrani, Gita

San Diego
401 West "A" Street,
Suite 800
San Diego, CA 92101
(619) 557-6052

Immigration Judges
Bartolomei, Jr., Richard J.
Clemente, Jesus
Fernandez, Ignacio P.
Ipema, Jr., Henry
Law, Philip S.
Renner, Renee L.

San Francisco
100 Montgomery Street,
Suite 800
San Francisco, CA 94104
(415) 705-4415

Immigration Judges
Daw, Alison
Geisse, Loreto
Griswold, Stephen
Hayward, Miriam R.
Hoogasian, Amy
King, Carol A.
Lyons, Joren
Maggard, Robert Print
Marks, Dana Leigh
Murry, Anthony S.
Ramirez, Laura L.
Webber, Polly A.
Yamaguchi, Michael J.

COLORADO
Denver
1961 Stout Street,
Suite 3101
Denver, CO 80294
(303) 844-5815

Immigration Judges
Davis, John W.
Livingston, Donn L.
Trujillo, Eileen R.
Tsankov, Mimi

CONNECTICUT
Hartford
AA Ribicoff Federal Bldg
& Courthouse
450 Main Street
Room 628
Hartford, CT 06103-3015
(860) 240-3881

Immigration Judges
Straus, Michael W.
Verrillo, Philip

FLORIDA
Miami
One Riverview Square
333 S. Miami Avenue,
Suite 700
Miami, FL 33130
(305) 789-4221

Immigration Judges
Alexander, Scott G.
Chapa, Teofilo
Dowell, J. Daniel
Horn, Michael C.
Lane, Denise A. Marks
Lopez-Enriquez, Maria
Mander, Stephen E.
Mart, H. Kevin
Martinez-Esquivel,
Lourdes
Mateo, Rene
Rodriquez de Jongh,
Lourdes
Sanders, Charles J.
Sukkar, Elisa M.
Torreh-Bayouth, Lilliana

Miami Krome (Detained)
Krome North Processing
Center
18201 SW 12th Street
Building #1, Suite C
Miami, FL 33194
(786) 422-8700
Mailing Address:
P.O. Box 940998
Miami, FL 33194

Immigration Judges
Ford, Rex J.
Opaciuch, Adam
Opaciuch, John

Orlando
3535 Lawton Road,
Suite 200
Orlando, FL 32803
(407) 722-8900

Immigration Judges
Chapman, Kevin
Ghartey, Victoria L.
Grim, James
Karden, Stuart F.
Lippman, Daniel
Ortiz-Segura, Rafael B.

GEORGIA
Atlanta
180 Spring Street, SW,
Suite 241
Atlanta, GA 30303
(404) 331-0907

Immigration Judges
Cassidy, William A.
Garcia, Madeline
Houser Jr., Wayne K.
Pelletier, J. Dan
Wilson, Earle

Stewart
146 CCA Road
P.O. Box 248
Lumpkin, GA 31815
(229) 838-1320

Immigration Judges
Arrington, Saundra
Chait, Barry S.
Trimble, Dan

HAWAII
Honolulu
PJKK Federal Building
300 Ala Moana Blvd.,
Rm. 8-112
Honolulu, HI 96850
(808) 541-1870

Immigration Judges
Beamer, Dayna
Wagner, Jr., Clarence M.

ILLINOIS

Chicago
525 West Van Buren Street, Suite 500
Chicago, IL 60607
(312) 697-5800

Immigration Judges
Cuevas, Carlos
DiMarzio, Philip
Fujimoto, James R.
Giambastiani, Jennie L.
McNulty, Sheila
Perez-Guzman, Virginia
Vinikoor, Robert D.

Chicago Detained
536 Clark Street,
Room B1330/1320
Chicago, IL 60605
(312) 697-5800

LOUISIANA

New Orleans
One Canal Place
365 Canal Street,
Suite 2450
New Orleans, LA 70130
(504) 589-3992

Immigration Judge
Mesa, Myrna A.

Oakdale
1900 E. Whatley Road
Oakdale, LA 71463
(318) 335-0365

Immigration Judges
Beatmann, Sr., Jerry
Duck, Jr., John A.
Reese, Agnelis L.

MARYLAND

Baltimore
George Fallon Federal Bldg
31 Hopkins Plaza, Rm. 440
Baltimore, MD 21201
(410) 962-3092

Immigration Judges
Crosland, David W.
Dornell, Lisa
Kessler, Elizabeth A.
Slavin, Denise N.
Williams, Phillip T.

MASSACHUSETTS

Boston
JFK Federal Building
15 New Sudbury Street
Room 320
Boston, MA 02203
(617) 565-3080

Immigration Judges
D'Angelo, Matthew J.
Day, Steven F.
Feder, Robin
Gagnon, Paul M.
O'Malley, Brenda
O'Sullivan, Maureen
Shapiro, Leonard I.

MICHIGAN

Detroit
P.V. McNamara Federal Bldg
477 Michigan Avenue,
Suite 440
Detroit, Michigan 48226
(313) 226-2603

Immigration Judges
Nettles, Marsha K.
Paruch, David H.

MINNESOTA

Bloomington
Bishop Henry Whipple Federal Bldg.
1 Federal Drive, Suite 1850
Fort Snelling, MN 55111
(612) 725-3765

Immigration Judges
Castro, Susan E.
Nickerson, Jr., William J.
Olmanson, Kristin W.

MISSOURI

Kansas City
2345 Grand Boulevard,
Suite 525
Kansas City, MO 64108
(816) 581-5000

Immigration Judge
Davis, Paula

NEBRASKA

Omaha
1717 Avenue H, Suite 100
Omaha, NE 68110
(402) 348-0310

Immigration Judges
Anderson, Jack L.
Morris, Daniel A.

NEVADA

Las Vegas
3365 Pepper Lane,
Suite 200
Las Vegas, NV 89120
(702) 458-0227

Immigration Judges
Alberdi, Yon K.
Romig, Jeffrey L.
Sharda, Munish

NEW JERSEY

Elizabeth
625 Evans Street
Room 148A

Elizabeth, NJ 07201
(908) 787-1355

Immigration Judges
Harbeck, Dorothy
Tadal, Mirlande

Newark
970 Broad Street,
Room 1200
Newark, NJ 07102
(973) 645-3524

Immigration Judges
Finston, Leo A.
Garcy, Annie S.
Khan, Amiena A.
Riefkohl, Alberto J.

NEW YORK
Batavia
4250 Federal Drive,
Room F108
Batavia, NY 14020
(585) 345-4300

Immigration Judges
Connelly, Steven
Reid, John B.

Buffalo
130 Delaware Avenue,
Suite 410
Buffalo, NY 14202
(716) 551-3442

Immigration Judge
Montante, Jr., Philip J.

Fishkill
Downstate Correctional
Facility
121 Red Schoolhouse
Road
Fishkill, NY 12524
(845) 838-5700

Immigration Judge
Sagerman, Roger

New York City
26 Federal Plaza,
12th Floor, Room 1237
New York, NY 10278
(917) 454-1040
Immigration Judges
Bain, Terry A.
Balasquide, Javier
Brennan, Noel A.
Bukszpan, Joanna M.
Cheng, Mary
Chew, George T.
Christensen, Jesse
Gordon-Uruakpa,
Vivienne
Hom, Sandy K.
Laforest, Brigitte
Lamb, Elizabeth A.
Leeds, Frederic G.
Loprest, Jr., Frank
McManus, Margaret
Morace, Philip L.
Mulligan, Thomas
Nelson, Barbara A.
Poczter, Aviva
Rohan, Patricia A.
Schoppert, Douglas B.
Segal, Alice
Sichel, Helen
Van Wyke, William P.
Vomacka, Alan A.
Weisel, Robert D.
Wright, Virna
Zagzoug, Randa

Ulster
Ulster Correctional Facility
Berme Road
P.O. Box 800
Napanoch, NY 12458
(845) 647-2223

Immigration Judge
Sagerman, Roger

Varick Street
201 Varick Street,
Room 1140
New York, NY 10014
(212) 620-6279

Immigration Judges
Page, Alan L.
Videla, Gabriel C.

NORTH CAROLINA
Charlotte
5701 Executive Center
Drive, Suite 400
Charlotte, NC 28212
(704) 817-6140

Immigration Judges
Couch, V. Stuart
Holmes-Simmons, Theresa
Pettinato, Barry

NORTHERN MARIANA ISLANDS
Saipan
Marina Heights II Building
Suite 301
Marina Heights Business
Park
Saipan, MP 96950
(670) 322-0601

Immigration Judge
Wagner, Jr., Clarence

OHIO
Cleveland
801 W. Superior Avenue
Suite 13 - 100
Cleveland, OH 44113
(216) 802-1100

Immigration Judges
Brown, Alison
Evans Jr., D. William
Janas, Thomas W.

OREGON
Portland
1220 SW 3rd Avenue,
Suite 500
Portland, OR 97204
(503) 326-6341

Immigration Judges
Bennett, Michael H.
Sloan, Andrea

PENNSYLVANIA
Philadelphia
Robert Nix Federal Bldg
& Courthouse
900 Market Street,
Suite 504
Philadelphia, PA 19107
(215) 656-7000

Immigration Judges
Honeyman, Charles M.
Malloy, Rosalind K.
Mills, Miriam
Morley, Steven

York
3400 Concord Road,
Suite #2
York, PA 17402
(717) 755-7555
Mailing Address:
P.O. Box 20370
York, PA 17402

Immigration Judge
Durling, Walter A.

PUERTO RICO
Guaynabo (San Juan)
San Patricio Office Center
#7 Tabonuco Street,
Room 401
Guaynabo, PR 00968-4605
(787) 749-4386

Immigration Judges
Guilloty, Crimilda
Lopez-Defillo, Irma

TENNESSEE
Memphis
Brinkley Plaza
80 Monroe Ave, Suite 501
Memphis, TN 38103
(901) 528-5883

Immigration Judges
Holt, Rebecca L.
Pazar, Charles E.

TEXAS
Dallas
1100 Commerce Street,
Suite 1060
Dallas, TX 75242
(214) 767-1814

Immigration Judges
Baird, Michael
Kimball, R. Wayne
Nugent, James A.
Ozmun, Richard R.
Sims, Deitrich H.

El Paso
700 E. San Antonio
Avenue, Suite 750
El Paso, TX 79901
(915) 534-6020

Immigration Judges
Hough, Robert
Roepke, Thomas

El Paso SPC
Service Processing Center
8915 Montana Avenue,
Suite 100
El Paso, TX 79925
(915) 771-1600

Immigration Judges
Abbott, William L.
Gonzalez, Guadalupe
Mahtabfar, Sunita
Ruhle, Stephen

Harlingen
2009 West Jefferson
Avenue, Suite 300
Harlingen, TX 78550
(956) 427-8580

Immigration Judges
Achtsam, Howard
Ayala, David

Houston
Continental Center II
600 Jefferson, Suite 900
Houston, TX 77002
(713) 718-3870

Immigration Judges
Brisack, Chris A.
Yam, Mimi S.
Yates, Clarease Rankin
Walton, Richard D.

Houston SPC
Houston Service Processing Center
5520 Greens Road
Houston, TX 77032
(281) 594-5600

Immigration Judges
Greenstein, Saul
Luis, Lisa

Pearsall
566 Veterans Drive
Pearsall, TX 78061
(210) 368-5700

Immigration Judges
Harlow, Craig
Santander, Daniel J.

Port Isabel
Port Isabel Processing Center
27991 Buena Vista Blvd.
Los Fresnos, TX 78566
(956) 547-1789

Mailing Address:
2009 West Jefferson Avenue, Suite 300
Harlingen, TX 78550

Immigration Judges
Hunsucker, Keith
Powell, Robert

San Antonio
800 Dolorosa Street, Suite 300
San Antonio, TX 78207
(210) 472-6637

Immigration Judges
Burkhart, Margaret D.
Crossan, Jr., Thomas G.
Burkholder, Gary D.
Martinez, Anibal D.
McPhaul, Glenn P.

UTAH

Salt Lake City
2975 South Decker Lake Drive, Suite 200
West Valley City, UT 84119
(801) 524-3000

Immigration Judges
Anderson, David C.
Baker, Glen R.

VIRGINIA

Arlington
1901 South Bell Street, Suite 200
Arlington, VA 22202
(703) 603-1300

Immigration Judges
Bryant, John M.
Burman, Lawrence O.
Schmidt, Paul W.
Snow, Thomas G.

Headquarters
1901 South Bell Street, Suite 200
Arlington, VA 22202
(703) 603-1350

Immigration Judges
Bain, Quynh Vu
Harris, Rodger C.
Hladylowycz, Roxanne C.
Owens, Robert P.

WASHINGTON

Seattle
1000 Second Avenue, Suite 2500
Seattle, WA 98104
(206) 553-5953

Immigration Judges
DeFonzo, Paul A.
Parchert, Brett M.
Walsh, John F.

Tacoma
1623 East "J" Street, Suite 3
Tacoma, WA 98421
(253) 779-6020

Immigration Judges
Fitting, Tammy
Odell, John C.
Scala, Theresa

ICE OFFICE OF THE PRINCIPAL LEGAL ADVISOR (FORMERLY OFFICES OF CHIEF COUNSEL)

ARIZONA
Patricia M. Vroom, Chief Counsel
Office of the Chief Counsel
P.O. Box 25158
Phoenix, AZ, 85002
(602) 744-2412
OPLA-PD-PHO-OCC@ice.dhs.gov

Florence Detention Center
Trial Attorney Unit
3250 N. Pinal Parkway Avenue
Florence, AZ, 85132

Tucson Sub-Office
Trial Attorney Unit
6431 S. Country Club Road
Tucson, AZ, 85706-5907

Eloy Detention Center
Trial Attorney Unit
1705 East Hanna Road
Eloy, AZ, 85131

CALIFORNIA
Leslie Ungerman, Chief Counsel
Office of the Chief Counsel
P.O. Box 26449
San Francisco, CA, 94126-6449
(415) 705-4604
OPLA-PD-SFR-OCC@ice.dhs.gov

Jason B. Aguilar, Chief Counsel
Office of the Chief Counsel
880 Front Street Room 2246
San Diego, CA
(619) 557-6343
OPLA-PD-SND-OCC@ice.dhs.gov

Sandra D. Anderson, Chief Counsel
Office of the Chief Counsel
606 South Olive Street 8th Floor
Los Angeles, CA, 90014
(213) 894-2805
OPLA-PD-LOS-OCC@ice.dhs.gov

East Mesa Detention Facility
Office of the Chief Counsel
880 Front Street Suite 2246
San Diego, CA, 92101

Adelanto Detention Facility
Adelanto West
10400 Rancho Road
Adelanto, CA, 92301

El Centro Detention Facility
1115 N. Imperial Avenue
El Centro, CA, 92243

COLORADO
Corina E. Almeida, Chief Counsel
Office of the Chief Counsel
12445 East Caley Avenue
Centennial, CO, 80111-6432
(303) 784-6560
OPLA-PD-DEN-OCC@ice.dhs.gov

CONNECTICUT
Hartford Sub-Office
Office of the Chief Counsel
Ribicoff Federal Building
450 Main Street, Room 483
Hartford, CT, 06103-3060
OPLA-PD-HAR-OCC@ice.dhs.gov

FLORIDA
Broward Transitional Center
3900 North Powerline Road
Pompano Beach, FL, 33072

Krome Service Processing Center
18201 SW 12th Street
Miami, FL, 33194-2700

Howard W. Marbury, Jr., Chief Counsel
Office of the Chief Counsel
333 S. Miami Avenue Suite 200
Miami, FL, 33130
(305) 400-6160
OPLA-PD-MIA-OCC@ice.dhs.gov

Ken Padilla, Chief Counsel
Office of the Chief Counsel
3535 Lawton Road Suite 100
Orlando, FL, 32803
(407) 812-3600
OPLA-PD-ORL-OCC@ice.dhs.gov

GEORGIA

Alfredia Owens, Chief Counsel - Office of the Chief Counsel
180 Spring Street SW Suite 332
Atlanta, GA, 30303
(404) 893-1400
OPLA-PD.ATL-OCC@ice.dhs.gov

Stewart County Detention Facility
146 CCA Road
Lumpkin, GA, 31815

HAWAII

Patricia Beattie, Chief Counsel
595 Ala Moana Boulevard
Honolulu, HI, 96813
(808) 532-2149
OPLA-PD-HHW-OCC@ice.dhs.gov

ILLINOIS

Karen E. Lundgren, Chief Counsel
Office of the Chief Counsel
525 W. Van Buren Suite 701
Chicago, IL, 60607
(312) 542-8200
OPLA-PD-CHI-OCC@ice.dhs.gov

LOUISIANA

Alice Miller, Chief Cousel
Office of the Chief Counsel
1250 Poydras Street Suite 2100
New Orleans, LA, 70113
(504) 599-7938
OPLA-PD-NOL-OCC@ice.dhs.gov

La Salle Detention Facility
830 Pinehill Road
Jena, LA, 71342

Oakdale Sub-Office
Office of the Chief Counsel
1010 E. Whateley Rd. Litigation Unit/OCC
Oakdale, LA, 71463-1128
(318) 335-7500
OPLA-PD-NOL-OCC@ice.dhs.gov

MASSACHUSETTS

Jo Ellen Ardinger, Chief Counsel - Office of the Chief Counsel
JFK Federal Building 15 New Sudbury Street, Room 425
Boston, MA, 02203
(617) 565-3140
OPLA-PD-BOS-OCC@ice.dhs.gov

MARYLAND

Melody A. Brukiewa, Chief Counsel
Office of the Chief Counsel
Fallon Federal Building 31 Hopkins Plaza, Room 1600
Baltimore, MD, 21201
(410) 637-4060
OPLA-PD-BAL-OCC@ice.dhs.gov

MICHIGAN

Catherine Pincheck, Chief Counsel
Office of the Chief Counsel
Federal Building
333 Mt. Elliott Street, 2nd Floor
Detroit, MI, 48207
(313) 568-6033
OPLA-PD-DET-OCC@ice.dhs.gov

MINNESOTA
Jim Stolley, Chief Counsel
Office of the Chief Counsel
1 Federal Drive Suite 1800
Ft. Snelling, MN, 55111
(952) 853-2970
OPLA-PD-SPM-BLM-OCC@ice.dhs.gov

MISSOURI
Kansas City Sub-Office
Office of the Chief Counsel
2345 Grand Boulevard Suite 500
Kansas City, MO, 64108
OPLA-PD-CHI-KAN-OCC@ice.dhs.gov

NORTH CAROLINA
Charlotte Sub-Office
Office of the Chief Counsel
5701 Executive Center Drive
Charlotte, NC, 28212
OPLA-PD-ATL_CLT-OCC@ice.dhs.gov

NEBRASKA
Omaha Sub-Office
Office of the Chief Counsel
1717 Avenue H Room 174
Omaha, NE, 68110
OPLA-PD-SPM-OMA-OCC@ice.dhs.gov

NEW JERSEY
Elizabeth Detention Facility
625 Evans Street Room 135
Elizabeth, NJ, 07201
OPLA-PD-NEW-ELZ-OCC@ice.dhs.gov

Jane Minichiello, Chief Counsel
Office of the Chief Counsel
970 Broad Street Room 1104B
Newark, NJ, 07102
(973) 776-5400
OPLA-PD-NEW-OCC@ice.dhs.gov

NEVADA
Las Vegas Sub-Office
Trial Attorney Unit
3373 Pepper Lane
Las Vegas, NV, 89120
(702) 433-7288
OPLA-PD-LOS-LVG-OCC@ice.dhs.gov

NEW YORK
Wen-Ting Cheng, Chief Counsel
Office of the Chief Counsel
P.O. Box 3507
New York, NY, 10008-3507
(212) 264-5916
OPLA-PD-NYC-OCC@ice.dhs.gov

Varick Street Service Processing Center
Litigation Unit
201 Varick Street, Room 1130
New York, NY, 10014

Carla J. Hengerer, Chief Counsel
Office of the Chief Counsel
130 Delaware Avenue Room 203
Buffalo, NY, 14202
(716) 855-7920
OPLA-PD-BUF-OCC@ice.dhs.gov

Castle Point (Institutional Removal Program at Ulster and Downstate Correctional Facilities)
Castle Point, NY, 12511
P.O. Box 606
Castle Point, NY 12511

Buffalo Federal Detention Facility
Office of the Chief Counsel
4250 Federal Drive
Batavia, NY, 14020
OPLA-PD-BUF-BTV-OCC@ice.dhs.gov

OHIO
Cleveland Sub-Office
Office of the Chief Counsel
Anthony J. Celebreeze Federal Building
1240 E. 9th Street, Room 585
Cleveland, OH, 44199
OPLA-PD-DET-CLE-OCC@ice.dhs.gov

OREGON
Portland Sub-Office
Office of the Chief Counsel
1220 SW 3rd Avenue Suite 300
Portland, OR, 97204

PENNSYLVANIA
York County Prison
3400 Concord Road
York, PA, 17402

Kent J. Frederick, Chief Counsel
Office of the Chief Counsel
900 Market Street Suite 346
Philadelphia, PA, 19107
(267) 479-3500
OPLA-PD-PHI-OCC@ice.dhs.gov

PUERTO RICO
Vivian Reyes-Lopez, Chief Counsel
Office of the Chief Counsel
San Patricio Office Center
7 Tabonuco Street, Suite 300
Guaynabo 00968
(787) 706-2352
OPLA-PD-SAJ-OCC@ice.dhs.gov

TENNESSEE
Memphis Sub-Office
Office of the Chief Counsel
80 Monroe Ave Suite 502
Memphis, TN, 38103
(901) 544-0630
OPLA-PD-NOL-OCC@ice.dhs.gov

TEXAS
Huntsville Sub-Office
Office of the Chief Counsel
Huntsville Office P.O. Box 237
Huntsville, TX, 77342-0237

Harlingen Sub-Office
Office of the Chief Counsel
1717 Zoy Street
Harlingen, TX, 78552
OPLA-PD-SNA-HLG-OCC@ice.dhs.gov

Livingston Sub-Office
Office of the Chief Counsel
P.O. Box 1139
Livingston, TX, 77351

Port Isabel Detention Center
27991 Buena Vista Blvd
Los Fresnos, TX, 78566

Elias Gastelo, Chief Counsel
Office of the Chief Counsel
1545 Hawkins Boulevard Suite 275
El Paso, TX, 79925
(915) 782-7900
OPLA-PD-ELP-OCC@ice.dhs.gov

Paul B. Hunker III, Chief Counsel
Office of the Chief Counsel
125 E. John Carpenter Fwy. Suite 500
Irving, TX, 75062
(972) 373-2300
OPLA-PD-DAL-OCC@ice.dhs.gov

Jo Ann McLane, Chief Counsel
Office of the Chief Counsel
8940 Fourwinds Drive Room 5045
San Antonio, TX, 78239
(210) 967-7050
OPLA-PD-SNA-OCC@ice.dhs.gov

Sarah Hartnett, Chief Counsel
Office of the Chief Counsel
126 Northpoint Drive Room 2020
Houston, TX, 77060
(281) 931-2046
PD-HOU-OCC.OPLA@ice.dhs.gov

Pearsall Detention Center
South Texas Detention Complex
566 Veterans Drive
Pearsall, TX, 78061

UTAH
Salt Lake City Sub-Office
Office of the Chief Counsel
2975 Decker Lake Drive Stop C

West Valley City, UT, 84119-6098
OPLA-PD-DEN-SLC-OCC@ice.dhs.gov

VIRGINIA
Raphael Choi, Chief Counsel
Office of the Chief Counsel
1901 Bell Street 9th Floor
Arlington, VA, 22202
(703) 235-2700
OPLA-PD-WAS-OCC@ice.dhs.gov

WASHINGTON
Raphael Sanchez, Chief Counsel - Office of the Chief Counsel
1000 Second Avenue Suite 2900
Seattle, WA, 98104
(206) 613-6500
OPLA-PD-SEA-OCC@ice.dhs.gov

Northwest Detention Center
Office of the Chief Counsel
1623 East J Street Suite 2
Tacoma, WA, 98421

Detention Facilities

For additional information or updates, see *www.ice.gov/detention-facilities.*

Federally Owned Facilities[1]

Arizona

Phoenix

Florence Service Processing Center
3250 N. Pinal Parkway
Florence, AZ, 85132
(520) 868-5862

Florence Correctional Center
1100 Bowling Rd.
Florence, AZ, 85132
(520) 868-9095

Office-in-Charge
Katrina S. Kane

Florida

Miami

Krome Service Processing Center
18201 SW 12th Street
Miami, FL, 33194
(305) 207-2100

Office-in-Charge
Marc J. Moore

Louisiana

New Orleans

Oakdale Federal Detention Center
2105 East Whatley Road
Oakdale, LA, 7146
(318) 335-4466

Office-in-Charge
Philip T. Miller

New York

Buffalo

Buffalo Federal Detention Facility
4250 Federal Drive
Batavia, NY, York
(585) 344-6500

Office-in-Charge
Michael T. Phillips

Texas

El Paso

El Paso Processing Center
8915 Montana Ave.
El Paso, TX, 79925
(915) 225-1901

Office-in-Charge
Adrian P. Macias

San Antonio

Port Isabel Service Processing Center
27991 Buena Vista Blvd.
Los Fresnos, TX, 78566
(956) 547-1700

Office-in-Charge
Enrique M. Lucero

Washington

Seattle

Tacoma Northwest Detention Center
1623 E J Street, Suite 2
Tacoma, WA, 98421-1615
(253) 779-6000

Office-in-Charge
Nathalie R. Asher

---

[1] All these facilities, except for Seattle, are U.S. Immigration and Customs Enforcement (ICE)–owned and –operated service processing centers (SPCs) or federal detention facilities (FDFs). The Seattle facility is federally owned, but contractor-operated.

Contractor-Owned and Operated Facilities

ARIZONA

Phoenix

[Corrections Corp. of America]
Eloy Detention Center
1705 E. Hanna Road
Eloy, AZ, 85131
(520) 466-4141

Office-in-Charge
Katrina S. Kane

CALIFORNIA

Los Angeles

Adelanto Detention Facility
10400 Rancho Road
Adelanto, CA, 92301
(760) 561-6100

Office-in-Charge
David A. Marin

San Diego

[Corrections Corp. of America]
Otay Detention Facility
446 Alta Road, Suite 5400
San Diego, CA, 92143
(619) 661-9119

Office-in-Charge
Gregory Archambeault

San Francisco

Contra Costa West County Detention Facility
5555 Giant Highway
Richmond, CA, 94806
(510) 262-4200

Office-in-Charge
Timothy S. Aitken

COLORADO

Denver

Denver Contract Detention Facility
3130 North Oakland Street
Aurora, CO, 80010
(303) 361-6612

Office-in-Charge
John P. Longshore

NEW JERSEY

Newark

[Corrections Corp. of America]
Elizabeth Contract Detention Facility
625 Evans Street
Elizabeth, NJ, 07201
(908) 352-3776

Delaney Hall Detention Facility
451 Doremus Avenue, NJ
(973) 274-0115

Office-in-Charge
John Tsoukaris

TEXAS

El Paso

West Texas Detention Facility
401 S. Vaquero Avenue
Sierra Blanca, TX, 79851
(915) 369-2272

Office-in-Charge
Adrian P. Macias

Houston

[Corrections Corp. of America]
Houston Contract Detention Facility
15850 Export Plaza Drive
Houston, TX, 77032
(281) 449-1481

Joe Corley Detention Facility
500 Hilbig Rd
Conroe, TX, 77301
(936) 521-4000

Office-in-Charge
Steven Paul Boll

San Antonio
[Corrections Corp. of America]
Laredo Contract Detention Facility
4702 East Saunders Street
Laredo, TX, 78401
(956) 727-4118

South Texas Detention Facility
566 Veteran's Drive
Pearsall, TX, 78061
(830) 334-2939

Office-in-Charge
Enrique M. Lucero

Juvenile Shelter Care Facilities

Juveniles apprehended by the U.S. Department of Homeland Security are held in juvenile detention centers or in shelter care facilities located throughout the United States.

Appendix 11B

Useful Websites

The following publications are additional sources of information regarding asylum and refugee law that may be useful as you prepare your case:

U.S. Government Websites:

(a) U.S. Citizenship and Immigration Services (USCIS)—www.uscis.gov

This site contains a great deal of useful information, including:

- Immigration and Nationality Act
- Title 8 of the Code of Federal Regulations
- *Federal Register* excerpts
- Forms (including G-28, I-589, I-131, I-730, I-765)
- *Affirmative Asylum Procedures Manual*
- Policy memoranda

(b) Asylum Resources Information Center—www.uscis.gov/tools/asylum-resources

(c) Executive Office for Immigration Review—www.usdoj.gov/eoir

This site contains:

- *Immigration Court Practice Manual*—www.justice.gov/eoir/office-chief-immigration-judge-0.
- *Immigration Judges' Benchbook*—www.justice.gov/eoir/immigration-judge-benchbook
- EOIR asylum statistics—www.justice.gov/eoir/statspub.htm
- BIA precedent decisions—www.justice.gov/eoir/ag-bia-decisions (including a headnote table—www.justice.gov/eoir/bia-precedent-chart)
- *BIA Practice Manual*—www.justice.gov/eoir/board-immigration-appeals-2
- Questions and answers
- Information on immigration courts, including local rules, addresses, and phone numbers

(d) U.S. Department of State—www.state.gov (includes the human rights reports—www.state.gov/g/drl/rls/hrrp, and Annual Report on Religious Freedom, www.state.gov/g/drl/rls/irf)

(e) Office of Personnel Management—www.opm.gov (includes a publication on citizenship laws of the world, www.opm.gov/extra/investigate/IS-01.pdf)

(f) Office of Refugee Resettlement (includes information on public benefits available asylees and refugees)—www.acf.hhs.gov/programs/orr

(g) U.S. Commission on International Religious Freedom—www.uscirf.gov

(h) Government Printing Office daily updates of CFR—www.ecfr.gov/cgi-bin/ECFR?page=browse

(i) Library of Congress, for U.S. laws and laws of other countries—www.loc.gov/law/help/guide.php

(j) Freedom of Information Act Reference Guide—www.archives.gov/foia

Canadian Government Website:

Immigration and Refugee Board of Canada—http://www.irb-cisr.gc.ca/eng

Nongovernmental Organizations (NGO) Websites:

The following sites are excellent sources of information on country conditions, immigrants rights, and resources for those who are representing asylum seekers:

(a) American Civil Liberties Union—www.aclu.org/issues/immigrants-rights

(b) Amnesty International—www.amnesty.org/en/

(c) Association for Women's Rights in Development—www.awid.org

(d) asylumlaw.org—www.asylumlaw.org

(e) Catholic Legal Immigration Network, Inc.—http://cliniclegal.org

(f) Center for Gender and Refugee Studies—http://cgrs.uchastings.edu

(g) Center for Victims of Torture—http://cvt.org

(h) Freedom House—www.freedomhouse.org

(i) HIAS—www.hias.org

(j) HRI (Human Rights Internet)—www.hri.ca

(k) Human Rights First—www.humanrightsfirst.org

(l) Human Rights Watch—www.hrw.org

(m) HuriSearch—www.hurisearch.org

(n) Immigration Equality—www.immigrationequality.org

(o) International Crisis Group—www.crisisgroup.org/home/index.cfm

(p) International Refugee Rights Initiative—www.refugeelegalaidinformation.org

(q) International Rehabilitation Council for Torture Victims—www.irct.org

(r) Kids in Need of Defense—http://supportkind.org

(s) Lawyers' Committee for Civil Rights—www.lccr.com

(t) Lutheran Immigration and Refugee Service—http://lirs.org

(u) National Consortium of Torture Treatments Programs—www.ncttp.org

(v) National Immigrant Justice Center—www.immigrantjustice.org

(w) National Immigration Law Center—www.nilc.org

(x) National Immigration Project of the National Lawyers Guild—www.nationalimmigrationproject.org

(y) Tahirih Justice Center—www.tahirih.org

(z) Torture Abolition and Survivors support Coalition—www.tassc.org

(aa) U.S. Committee for Refugees and Immigrants—www.refugees.org

(bb) University of Minnesota Human Rights Library—www1.umn.edu/humanrts/

United Nations Websites:

(a) United Nations High Commissioner for Refugees—www.unhcr.org

This website contains:

- country-specific information about refugees
- 1951 U.N. Convention Relating to the Status of Refugees
- 1967 Protocol Relating to the Status of Refugees
- UNHCR's Handbook on Procedures and Criteria for Determining Refugee Status
- International Protection Guidelines
- RefWorld—www.refworld.org

(b) United Nations Human Rights Council— www.ohchr.org/en/hrbodies/hrc/pages/hrcindex.aspx

This website contains:

- Committee Against Torture decisions—http://tbinternet.ohchr.org/_layouts/treatybodyexternal/TBSearch.aspx?Lang=en&TreatyID=1&DocTypeID=68
- United Nations human rights treaties
- United Nations documents, reports, and publications

Legal Websites:

(a) AILA InfoNet—www.aila.org; a member service of the American Immigration Lawyers Association, InfoNet provides news of recent legislation, regulatory activity, agency meetings, and more. The AILA Asylum and Refugee Committee also has compiled published federal court and BIA cases from 2009 to present and has categorized these cases by topic on AILA InfoNet—www.aila.org/infonet/curated-research/asylum-cases-by-topic.

(b) ASIL Guide to Electronic Resources for International Law—www.asil.org/resources/electronic-resource-guide-erg; includes a guide to researching international law on the Internet.

(c) University of Minnesota Human Rights Library asylum and refugee resources—www1.umn.edu/humanrts/center/asylum/refugee_index.html; includes refugee treatises and instruments, UNHCR country of origin information, selected U.S. cases, and other publications.

(d) University of Michigan refugee case law site—www.reflaw.org; this site collects, indexes, and publishes selected recent court decisions from federal and supreme court decisions from the United States, Great Britain, Canada, Australia, New Zealand, Austria, Germany, and Switzerland.

(e) American Immigration Council—www.americanimmigrationcouncil.org; AIC's Legal Action Center provides mentoring and practice materials to attorneys across the country on all issues relating to immigration, including asylum. Its practice advisories, available online at www.legalactioncenter.org, address cutting-edge issues in immigration law, including asylum and appeal issues.

(f) National Immigration Project of the National Lawyers Guild—http://nipnlg.org/publications.htm. NIP's practices advisories provide in-depth analysis for many complex legal issues, including those related to asylum and judicial review.

(g) Georgetown Law Library, Center for Applied Legal Research, Asylum Case Research Guide—www.law.georgetown.edu/library/research/guides/calsasylumlawresearchguide.cfm; this page describes some basic sources for research on behalf of individuals seeking asylum in the United States.

(h) Cornell University Law School, Legal Information Institute—www.law.cornell.edu; includes federal and state court decisions, U.S. Code, U.S. Constitution, Code of Federal Regulations, basic legal information, international law, United Nations materials, and laws of foreign countries.

(i) Refugee Law Reader—www.refugeelawreader.org; includes cases, documents, articles, and others materials regarding refugee law, with a particular focus on the European asylum system.

(j) Researching Refugee Law, by Marci Hoffman (UC Berkeley)— www.law.berkeley.edu/library/dynamic/guide.php?id=64

(k) National Legal Aid and Defenders Association, Defending Immigrants Partnership webpage—www.nlada.org/Defender/Defender_Immigrants; includes charts analyzing the immigration consequences of state convictions, recent cases and news stories.

(l) Bender's Immigration Bulletin— www.lexisnexis.com/legalnewsroom/immigration/default.aspx; includes cases from around the country, many unpublished and not available elsewhere. Archives also available for searches.

(m) TRAC Immigration reports—http://trac.syr.edu/immigration/reports; includes data from immigration courts relating to asylum.

(n) Association for the Prevention of Torture—www.apt.ch/en, includes a compilation of torture laws.

(o) Detention Watch Network—www.detentionwatchnetwork.org/nondiscrimination includes information on international human rights laws regarding detention.

(p) University of St. Thomas Interprofessional Center—USCIS Memos regarding Asylum, available at www.stthomas.edu/ipc/legal/ImmigLaw/USCISMemos.html.

(q) HealTorture.org Legal Training Page—www.healtorture.org/content/legal-training, includes links to country condition information, legal information, and webinars.

Websites for U.S. Courts of Appeal

First Circuit—www.ca1.uscourts.gov

Second Circuit—www.ca2.uscourts.gov

Third Circuit—www.ca3.uscourts.gov

Fourth Circuit—www.ca4.uscourts.gov

Fifth Circuit—www.ca5.uscourts.gov

Sixth Circuit—www.ca6.uscourts.gov

Seventh Circuit—www.ca7.uscourts.gov

Eighth Circuit—www.ca8.uscourts.gov

Ninth Circuit—www.ca9.uscourts.gov

Tenth Circuit—www.ca10.uscourts.gov

Eleventh Circuit—www.ca11.uscourts.gov

D.C. Circuit—www.cadc.uscourts.gov

Federal Circuit—www.cafc.uscourts.gov

Other Sources

AILA*Link* Online—www.ailalink.org, is a fully searchable, immigration law research website provided by AILA Publications.

APPENDIX 11C

RECOMMENDED SOURCES, TEXTS, AND TOOLS

The following publications are additional sources of information regarding asylum and refugee law that may be useful as you prepare your case:

Primary Sources:

- Immigration and Nationality Act (codified at Title 8 of the U.S. Code)—www.uscis.gov and through AILA Publications at www.agora.aila.org.
- Title 8 of the Code of Federal Regulations—www.uscis.gov and through AILA Publications at www.agora.aila.org.

UNHCR Publications:

- UNHCR Handbook and Guidelines on Procedures and Criteria for Determining Refugee Status under the 1951 Convention and the 1967 Protocol relating to the Status of Refugees—www.unhcr.org/3d58e13b4.html.
- UNHCR Guidelines on International Protection Numbers 1–10—www.unhcr.org/cgi-bin/texis/vtx/search?page=&comid=4a27bad46&cid=49aea93ae2&keywords=RSDguidelines.
- UNHCR Executive Committee Conclusions—www.unhcr.org/pages/49e6e6dd6.html.
- Other UNHCR Publications—www.unhcr.org/pages/49c3646c 4b8.html.

International Treaties, Foreign Law, and Customary International Law:

- Office of U.N. High Commissioner for Human Rights—www.ohchr.org. For documents and information related to the Convention Against Torture, go to www.ohchr.org/en/hrbodies/cat/pages/catindex.aspx.
- UNHCR—www.unhcr.org.
- UNHCR's RefWorld—www.refworld.org.
- www.refugeecaselaw.org—a website of the University of Michigan Law School, containing refugee and asylum cases from the highest courts of Australia, Austria, Canada, Germany, New Zealand, Switzerland, the United Kingdom, and the United States.
- The Office of Personnel Management's Citizenship Laws of the World—www.multiplecitizenship.com/documents/IS-01.pdf.
- Library of Congress Law Library—located at 101 Independence Avenue SE, Washington, DC 20540 and available at (202) 707-5079 and www.loc.gov/law/public/law.html. To seek guidance from the Library of Congress, go to www.loc.gov/rr/askalib/ask-law.html.

- UNHCR's Washington Office—usawa@unhcr.org provides assistance in determining refugee status or "firm resettlement" of asylum applicants in third countries.

BIA and Federal Court Decisions:

- AILA Asylum Cases by Topic—a compilation of published BIA and federal court asylum cases from 2009 to present, available at www.aila.org/infonet/curated-research/asylum-cases-by-topic.
- EOIR Virtual Law Library—www.justice.gov/eoir/virtual-law-library.
- Index of Unpublished Decisions of the Board of Immigration Appeals—available for purchase from the Immigrant and Refugee Appellate Center at www.irac.net/unpublished/index/.

Legacy INS, DHS, and EOIR Policy Directives, Memoranda, Statements, and Field Manuals:

- AILA Publications—www.agora.aila.org.
- AILA InfoNet—www.aila.org.
- USCIS website—www.uscis.gov.
- ICE website—www.ice.gov.
- EOIR website—www.usdoj.gov/eoir.

Government Manuals:

- *Affirmative Asylum Procedures Manual*—www.uscis.gov/sites/default/files/files/nativedocuments/Asylum_Procedures_Manual_2013.pdf.
- *Asylum Officer Basic Training Course Lesson Modules*—www.uscis.gov/humanitarian/refugees-asylum/asylum/asylum-division-training-programs.
- *Immigration Court Practice Manual*—www.justice.gov/eoir/office-chief-immigration-judge-0.
- *ICE Performance-Based National Detention Standards*—www.ice.gov/detention-standards/2011.
- *Board of Immigration Appeals Practice Manual*—www.justice.gov/eoir/board-immigration-appeals-2.

Federal Rules:

- Federal Rules of Evidence—available for download at www.uscourts.gov/file/rules-evidence.
- Federal Rules of Civil Procedure—available for download at www.uscourts.gov/file/rules-civil-procedure.
- Federal Rules of Appellate Procedure—available for download at www.uscourts.gov/file/rules-appellate-procedure.

Online Databases:

- AILALink Online—www.ailalink.org.
- UNHCR RefWorld—www.reworld.org.
- CALS Asylum Case Research Guide—a compilation of resources by the Georgetown Law Library, available at www.law.georgetown.edu/library/research/guides/CALSAsylumLawResearchGuide.cfm.

Practice Advisories and Case Assistance:

- American Immigration Council, Legal Action Center—www.legalactioncenter.org/practice-advisory-topics.
- Center for Gender and Refugee Studies—http://cgrs.uchastings.edu/request-assistance/requesting-assistance-cgrs.
- National Immigration Project of the National Lawyers Guild—http://nipnlg.org/publications.htm.

Books and Other Texts:

- I. Kurzban, *Kurzban's Immigration Law Sourcebook* (biennial editions)—www.agora.aila.org.
- AILA's *Navigating the Fundamentals of Immigration Law* (annual editions)—www.agora.aila.org.
- AILA's *Immigration Practice Pointers* (annual editions)—www.agora.aila.org.
- D. Anker, *Law of Asylum in the United States* (2015 ed.)
- D. Martin, *Asylum Case Law Sourcebook* (biennial editions)
- National Immigrant Justice Center, *Basic Procedural Manual for Asylum Representation Affirmatively and in Removal Proceedings* (Nov. 2014)—http://immigrantjustice.org/sites/immigrantjustice.org/files/NIJC%20Asylum%20Manual_11%202014%20final.pdf.

TABLE OF DECISIONS

Alphabetization is letter-by-letter (e.g., "Jiannong Jiang" precedes "Jian Qiu Liu").

A

B

C

D

E

F

G

H

I

J

K

L

M

N

O

P

Q

R

S

T

U

V

W

X

Y

Z

Subject-Matter Index

A

B

C

D

E

F

I

J

K

L

M

N

O

P

Q

R

S

T

U

V

W

Y

Z